## 11. Format for Bank Reconciliation:

| | | |
|---|---|---|
| Cash balance according to bank statement ...................... | | $xxx |
| Add: Additions by company not on bank statement ........................................... | $xx | |
| Bank errors ............................................. | xx | xx |
| | | $xxx |
| Deduct: Deductions by company not on bank statement ........................................... | $xx | |
| Bank errors ............................................. | xx | xx |
| Adjusted balance ........................................................ | | $xxx |
| | | |
| Cash balance according to company's records ............... | | $xxx |
| Add: Additions by bank not recorded by company .. | $xx | |
| Company errors .................................................... | xx | xx |
| | | $xxx |
| Deduct: Deductions by bank not recorded by company ......................................... | $xx | |
| Company errors .................................................... | xx | xx |
| Adjusted balance ........................................................ | | $xxx |

## 12. Inventory Costing Methods:

1. First-in, First-out (FIFO)
2. Last-in, First-out (LIFO)
3. Average Cost

## 13. Interest Computations:

$$\text{Interest} = \text{Face Amount (or Principal)} \times \text{Rate} \times \text{Time}$$

## 14. Methods of Determining Annual Depreciation:

STRAIGHT-LINE: $\dfrac{\text{Cost} - \text{Estimated Residual Value}}{\text{Estimated Life}}$

DOUBLE-DECLINING-BALANCE: Rate* × Book Value at Beginning of Period

*Rate is commonly twice the straight-line rate (1/Estimated Life).

## 15. Adjustments to Net Income (Loss) Using the Indirect Method

| | Increase (Decrease) |
|---|---|
| Net income (loss) | $ XXX |
| Adjustments to reconcile net income to net cash flow from operating activities: | |
| Depreciation of fixed assets | XXX |
| Amortization of intangible assets | XXX |
| Losses on disposal of assets | XXX |
| Gains on disposal of assets | (XXX) |
| Changes in current operating assets and liabilities: | |
| Increases in noncash current operating assets | (XXX) |
| Decreases in noncash current operating assets | XXX |
| Increases in current operating liabilities | XXX |
| Decreases in current operating liabilities | (XXX) |
| Net cash flow from operating activities | $ XXX |
| | or |
| | $(XXX) |

## 16. Contribution Margin Ratio $= \dfrac{\text{Sales} - \text{Variable Costs}}{\text{Sales}}$

## 17. Break-Even Sales (Units) $= \dfrac{\text{Fixed Costs}}{\text{Unit Contribution Margin}}$

## 18. Sales (Units) $= \dfrac{\text{Fixed Costs} + \text{Target Profit}}{\text{Unit Contribution Margin}}$

## 19. Margin of Safety $= \dfrac{\text{Sales} - \text{Sales at Break-Even Point}}{\text{Sales}}$

## 20. Operating Leverage $= \dfrac{\text{Contribution Margin}}{\text{Income from Operations}}$

## 21. Variances

$\dfrac{\text{Direct Materials}}{\text{Price Variance}} = \left(\begin{array}{c}\text{Actual Price} - \\ \text{Standard Price}\end{array}\right) \times \text{Actual Quantity}$

$\dfrac{\text{Direct Materials}}{\text{Quantity Variance}} = \left(\begin{array}{c}\text{Actual Quantity} - \\ \text{Standard Quantity}\end{array}\right) \times \dfrac{\text{Standard}}{\text{Price}}$

$\dfrac{\text{Direct Labor}}{\text{Rate Variance}} = \left(\begin{array}{c}\text{Actual Rate per Hour} - \\ \text{Standard Rate per Hour}\end{array}\right) \times \text{Actual Hours}$

$\dfrac{\text{Direct Labor}}{\text{Time Variance}} = \left(\begin{array}{c}\text{Actual Direct Labor Hours} - \\ \text{Standard Direct Labor Hours}\end{array}\right) \times \dfrac{\text{Standard Rate}}{\text{per Hour}}$

$\begin{array}{c}\text{Variable Factory} \\ \text{Overhead Controllable} \\ \text{Variance}\end{array} = \begin{array}{c}\text{Actual Variable} \\ \text{Factory} \\ \text{Overhead}\end{array} - \begin{array}{c}\text{Budgeted Variable} \\ \text{Factory Overhead}\end{array}$

$\begin{array}{c}\text{Fixed Factory} \\ \text{Overhead} \\ \text{Volume} \\ \text{Variance}\end{array} = \left(\begin{array}{c}\text{Standard Hours} \\ \text{for 100\% of} \\ \text{Normal} \\ \text{Capacity}\end{array} - \begin{array}{c}\text{Standard} \\ \text{Hours for} \\ \text{Actual Units} \\ \text{Produced}\end{array}\right) \times \begin{array}{c}\text{Fixed Factory} \\ \text{Overhead} \\ \text{Rate}\end{array}$

## 22. Rate of Return on Investment (ROI) $= \dfrac{\text{Income from Operations}}{\text{Invested Assets}}$

Alternative ROI Computation:

$$\text{ROI} = \dfrac{\text{Income from Operations}}{\text{Sales}} \times \dfrac{\text{Sales}}{\text{Invested Assets}}$$

## 23. Capital Investment Analysis Methods:

1. Methods That Ignore Present Values:
   A. Average Rate of Return Method
   B. Cash Payback Method
2. Methods That Use Present Values:
   A. Net Present Value Method
   B. Internal Rate of Return Method

## 24. Average Rate of Return $= \dfrac{\text{Estimated Average Annual Income}}{\text{Average Investment}}$

## 25. Present Value Index $= \dfrac{\text{Total Present Value of Net Cash Flow}}{\text{Amount to Be Invested}}$

## 26. Present Value Factor for an Annuity of $1 $= \dfrac{\text{Amount to Be Invested}}{\text{Equal Annual Net Cash Flows}}$

REEVE WARREN DUCHAC

# FINANCIAL & MANAGERIAL
# ACCOUNTING
# USING EXCEL FOR SUCCESS

**James M. Reeve**
Professor Emeritus of Accounting
University of Tennessee, Knoxville

**Carl S. Warren**
Professor Emeritus of Accounting
University of Georgia, Athens

**Jonathan E. Duchac**
Professor of Accounting
Wake Forest University

SOUTH-WESTERN
CENGAGE Learning

Australia • Brazil • Japan • Korea • Mexico • Singapore • Spain • United Kingdom • United States

**SOUTH-WESTERN**
CENGAGE Learning™

**Financial & Managerial Accounting, Using Excel for Success**

**James M. Reeve**
**Carl S. Warren**
**Jonathan E. Duchac**

**Vice President of Editorial, Business:** Jack W. Calhoun

**Editor-in-Chief:** Rob Dewey

**Executive Editor:** Sharon Oblinger

**Editorial Assistant:** Courtney Doyle

**Marketing Coordinator:** Nicki Parsons

**Sr. Marketing Manager:** Kristen Hurd

**Sr. Marketing Communications Manager:** Libby Shipp

**Sr. Content Project Manager:** Cliff Kallemeyn

**Sr. Media Editor:** Scott Fidler

**Media Editor:** Jessica Robbe

**Frontlist Buyer, Manufacturing:** Doug Wilke

**Sr. Art Director:** Stacy Shirley

**Sr. Rights Specialist:** Deanna Ettinger

**Rights Specialist:** Sam Marshall

For product information and technology assistance, contact us at **Cengage Learning** **Customer & Sales Support, 0-354-9706**

For permission to use material from this text or product, submit all requests oe at **www.cengage.com/pessions** Further permissions questions be emailed to **permissionrequest@cege.com**

Library of Congress Control Number: 2011924○

Student Edition ISBN-13: 978-1-111-53522-3
Student Edition ISBN-10: 1-111-53522-1

**South-Western Cengage Learning**
5191 Natorp Boulevard
Mason, OH 45040
USA

Cengage Learning products are represented in nada by Nelson Education, Ltd.

For your course and learning solutions, visit **ww.cengage.com**

Purchase any of our products at your local colleg store or at our preferred online store **www.cengagebrain.com**

Printed in China
4 5 15 14

# The Author Team

## James M. Reeve

Dr. James M. Reeve is Professor Emeritus of Accounting and Information Management at the University of Tennessee. Professor Reeve taught on the accounting faculty for 25 years, after graduating with his Ph.D. from Oklahoma State University. His teaching effort focused on undergraduate accounting principles and graduate education in the Master of Accountancy and Senior Executive MBA programs. Beyond this, Professor Reeve is also very active in the Supply Chain Certification program, which is a major executive education and research effort of the College. His research interests are varied and include work in managerial accounting, supply chain management, lean manufacturing, and information management. He has published over 40 articles in academic and professional journals, including the *Journal of Cost Management, Journal of Management Accounting Research, Accounting Review, Management Accounting Quarterly, Supply Chain Management Review,* and *Accounting Horizons.* He has consulted or provided training around the world for a wide variety of organizations, including Boeing, Procter & Gamble, Norfolk Southern, Hershey Foods, Coca-Cola, and Sony. When not writing books, Professor Reeve plays golf and is involved in faith-based activities.

## Carl S. Warren

Dr. Carl S. Warren is Professor Emeritus of Accounting at the University of Georgia, Athens. Dr. Warren has taught classes at the University of Georgia, University of Iowa, Michigan State University, and University of Chicago. Professor Warren focused his teaching efforts on principles of accounting and auditing. He received his Ph.D. from Michigan State University and his B.B.A. and M.A. from the University of Iowa. During his career, Dr. Warren published numerous articles in professional journals, including *The Accounting Review, Journal of Accounting Research, Journal of Accountancy, The CPA Journal,* and *Auditing: A Journal of Practice & Theory.* Dr. Warren has served on numerous committees of the American Accounting Association, the American Institute of Certified Public Accountants, and the Institute of Internal Auditors. He has also consulted with numerous companies and public accounting firms. Warren's outside interests include playing handball, golfing, skiing, backpacking, and fly-fishing.

## Jonathan Duchac

Dr. Jonathan Duchac is the Merrill Lynch and Co. Professor of Accounting and Director of the Program in Enterprise Risk Management at Wake Forest University. He earned his Ph.D. in accounting from the University of Georgia and currently teaches introductory and advanced courses in financial accounting. Dr. Duchac has received a number of awards during his career, including the Wake Forest University Outstanding Graduate Professor Award, the T.B. Rose Award for Instructional Innovation, and the University of Georgia Outstanding Teaching Assistant Award. In addition to his teaching responsibilities, Dr. Duchac has served as Accounting Advisor to Merrill Lynch Equity Research, where he worked with research analysts in reviewing and evaluating the financial reporting practices of public companies. He has testified before the U.S. House of Representatives, the Financial Accounting Standards Board, and the Securities and Exchange Commission; and has worked with a number of major public companies on financial reporting and accounting policy issues. In addition to his professional interests, Dr. Duchac is the Treasurer of The Special Children's School of Winston-Salem; a private, nonprofit developmental day school serving children with special needs. Dr. Duchac is an avid long-distance runner, mountain biker, and snow skier. His recent events include the Grandfather Mountain Marathon, the Black Mountain Marathon, the Shut-In Ridge Trail run, and NO MAAM (Nocturnal Overnight Mountain Bike Assault on Mount Mitchell).

# A History of Success

For nearly **85** years, *Accounting* and its adaptations have been used effectively to teach generations of businessmen and women. The text has been used by millions of business students. For many, this book provides the only exposure to accounting principles that they will ever receive. As the most successful business textbook of all time, it continues to introduce students to accounting through a variety of time-tested ways.

This new adaptation starts a new journey into learning more about the changing needs of accounting students through a variety of new and innovative research and development methods. Our Blue Sky Workshops brought accounting faculty from all over the country into our book development process in a very direct and creative way. Many of the features and themes present in this text are a result of the collaboration and countless conversations we have had with accounting instructors over the last several years. 11e continues to build on this philosophy and strives to be reflective of the suggestions and feedback we receive from instructors and students on an ongoing basis. We are very happy with the results, and think you will be pleased with the improvements we have made to the text.

The original author of *Accounting*, James McKinsey, could not have imagined the success and influence this text has enjoyed or that his original vision would continue to lead the market into the twenty-first century. As the current authors, we appreciate the responsibility of protecting and enhancing this vision, while continuing to refine it to meet the changing needs of students and instructors. Always in touch with a tradition of excellence but never satisfied with yesterday's success, this edition enthusiastically embraces a changing environment and continues to proudly lead the way. We sincerely thank our many colleagues who have helped to make it happen.

*Carl S. Warren*

*Jonathan Duchac*

"The teaching of accounting is no longer designed to train professional accountants only. With the growing complexity of business and the constantly increasing difficulty of the problems of management, it has become essential that everyone who aspires to a position of responsibility should have a knowledge of the fundamental principles of accounting."

**—James O. McKinsey, Author, first edition, 1929**

## Unique Excel Success Learning System:

### 6 Formulas + 4 Steps = Excel Success

In developing this learning system, instructors expressed:

- Excel is the most important software application students will use in business.
- Employers want graduates to know Excel.
- Many instructors *do not* use Excel because they believe they do not have the time to teach it in class.
- Many instructors *do* use Excel to learn and reinforce accounting concepts.

With the increased development of software applications, this textbook introduces students to a new learning approach. *Financial & Managerial Accounting Using Excel for Success* effectively uses Excel to teach accounting in an easy way.

### The Power of Six Simple Formulas

By learning just six simple Excel formulas, students can solve most accounting problems, from posting a basic journal entry to calculating the internal rate of return. Here are the six basic formulas that are covered in the text:

1. =SUM
2. =MIN
3. =VLOOKUP (one time)
4. =IF (one time)
5. =IRR (one time) and =PV (one time)
6. $A$5 (absolute and relative references)

### Four Easy Steps

The innovative four-step system encourages students to:

1. Read the accounting concept.
2. Follow along as the Excel Success Example steps through how to solve the accounting concept problem.
3. Practice using the "Try It" Tutorial.
4. Apply knowledge by completing the Excel Success Special Activity.

Here is a depiction of the four steps in the Excel Success Learning System:

### Step 1

**Step 1 is to Read and Learn the Accounting Concept**. You can introduce the concept in lecture, and your students will read the concept in the textbook. This example is Valuation at Lower of Cost or Market.

## Valuation at Lower of Cost or Market

See Appendix E for more information

If the cost of replacing inventory is lower than its recorded purchase cost, the **lower-of-cost-or-market (LCM) method** is used to value the inventory. *Market,* as used in *lower of cost or market,* is the cost to replace the inventory. The market value is based on normal quantities that would be purchased from suppliers.

The lower-of-cost-or-market method can be applied in one of three ways. The cost, market price, and any declines could be determined for the following:

1. Each item in the inventory.
2. Each major class or category of inventory.
3. Total inventory as a whole.

The amount of any price decline is included in the cost of merchandise sold. This, in turn, reduces gross profit and net income in the period in which the price declines occur. This matching of price declines to the period in which they occur is the primary advantage of using the lower-of-cost-or-market method.

To illustrate, assume the following data for 400 identical units of Item A in inventory on December 31, 2012:

| | |
|---|---|
| Unit purchased cost | $10.25 |
| Replacement cost on December 31, 2012 | 9.50 |

Since Item A could be replaced at $9.50 a unit, $9.50 is used under the lower-of-cost-or-market method.

Exhibit 8 illustrates applying the lower-of-cost-or-market method to each inventory item (A, B, C, and D). As applied on an item-by-item basis, the total lower-of-cost-or-market is $15,070, which is a market decline of $450 ($15,520 − $15,070). This market decline of $450 is included in the cost of merchandise sold.

In Exhibit 8, Items A, B, C, and D could be viewed as a class of inventory items. If the lower of cost or market is applied to the class, the inventory would be valued at $15,472, which is a market decline of $48 ($15,520 − $15,472). Likewise, if Items A, B, C, and D make up the total inventory, the lower of cost or market as applied to the total inventory would be the same amount, $15,472.

## Step 2

**Step 2 of Excel Success is to Reinforce the Accounting Concept Using the Excel Example:**

- The illustration is re-created using Excel.
- The *formulas* are displayed, not the resulting *values.*
- Students use easy steps to understand how to create a basic Excel formula.

**eXcel success**

The lower of cost or market inventory schedule from Exhibit 8 can be developed on a spreadsheet as follows:

| | A | B | C | D | E a. | F b. | G c. |
|---|---|---|---|---|---|---|---|
| 1 | | | | | | | |
| 2 | | | | | | Total | |
| 3 | Item | Inventory Quantity | Unit Cost Price | Unit Market Price | Cost | Market | Lower of C or M |
| 4 | A | 400 | $ 10.25 | $ 9.50 | =B4*C4 | =B4*D4 | =MIN(E4:F4) |
| 5 | B | 120 | 22.50 | 24.10 | =B5*C5 | =B5*D5 | =MIN(E5:F5) |
| 6 | C | 600 | 8.00 | 7.75 | =B6*C6 | =B6*D6 | =MIN(E6:F6) |
| 7 | D | 280 | 14.00 | 14.75 | =B7*C7 | =B7*D7 | =MIN(E7:F7) |
| 8 | Total | | | | =SUM(E4:E7) | =SUM(F4:F7) | =SUM(G4:G7) |
| 9 | | | | | | | |

d.

e.     f.

Develop the formulas by the following steps:
- **a.**     Enter in cell E4 the formula for the total cost, =B4*C4.
- **b.**     Enter in cell F4 the formula for the total market, =B4*D4.
- **c.**     Enter in cell G4 a =MIN function to calculate the lower of cost or market, as follows:

=MIN(E4:F4)

This function will return the minimum value within the range of cells from E4 to F4.

- **d.**     Copy E4:G4 to E5:G7.
- **e.**     Enter in E8 a formula to sum the column, =SUM(E4:E7)
- **f.**     Copy E8 to F8:G8

**TryIt**   Go to the hands-on **Excel Tutor** for this example!

## Step 3

**Step 3 is the Try It Tutorial.** This is a hands-on tutorial that walks the student through the in-chapter example. Students actively participate in the learning process using the Try It Tutorial. The Try It Tutorials are available to students 24/7. It's just that easy! Students receive an access code automatically with a new copy of the textbook that provides them access to the Try It Tutorials. The Tutorials are also built into CengageNOW, our premier online homework solution.

| | A | B | C | D | E | F | G | H | I |
|---|---|---|---|---|---|---|---|---|---|
| G3 | | | | | | Total | | | |
| 1 | | | | | | | | | |
| 2 | Item | Inventory Quantity | Unit Cost Price | Unit Market Price | Cost | Market | Lower of C or M | | |
| 3 | A | 400 $ | 10.25 $ | 9.50 | 4,100.00 | 3,800.00 | =MIN( | | |
| 4 | B | 120 | 22.50 | 24.10 | | | | | |
| 5 | C | 600 | 8.00 | 7.75 | | | | | |
| 6 | D | 280 | 14.00 | 14.75 | | | | | |
| 7 | Total | | | | | | | | |

Begin in cell **G3** (where the calculation result will display).

Start the formula with an equal sign (=) then type **MIN** and an open parenthesis (.

☞ **Note:** Remember that there are NEVER any spaces in an Excel formula.

Click in cell **E3**.

## Step 4

**Step 4 is the Excel Success End-of-Chapter Problem.** At this point, students have learned the accounting concept, reinforced it in Excel, and received **hands-on** experience in creating simple Excel formulas via the Try It Tutorial. Now it's time for them to complete their homework.

## Excel Success Special Activities

### SA 6-1  Lower of cost or market

All-Tech, Inc., has five inventory items with the following quantities, unit costs, and unit market values:

|    | A | B | C | D |
|----|------|--------------------|------------------------|--------------------------|
| 1 |  |  | **Unit** | **Unit** |
| 2 |  | **Inventory** | **Cost** | **Market** |
| 3 | **Item** | **Quantity** | **Price** | **Price** |
| 4 | A | 250 | $   4.50 | $   4.20 |
| 5 | B | 340 | 9.20 | 8.90 |
| 6 | C | 90 | 12.90 | 13.50 |
| 7 | D | 125 | 18.90 | 21.80 |
| 8 | E | 440 | 11.30 | 11.40 |
| 9 | Total |  |  |  |
| 10 |  |  |  |  |

a. Open the spreadsheet file name *SA6-1_1e*.
b. Complete the spreadsheet by determining the lower of cost or market valuation for inventory.
c. When you have completed the inventory table, perform a "save as," replacing the entire file name with the following:
   *SA6-1_1e[your first name initial]_[your last name]*

Here is what the problem looks like:

|    | A | B | C | D | E | F | G |
|----|------|-----------|---------|---------|------|--------|----------|
| 1 |  |  | All-Tech, Inc. |  |  |  |  |
| 2 |  |  |  |  |  | Total |  |
|  |  |  | Unit | Unit |  |  |  |
|  |  | Inventory | Cost | Market |  |  | Lower of |
| 3 | Item | Quantity | Price | Price | Cost | Market | C or M |
| 4 | A | 250 | $  4.50 | $  4.20 |  |  |  |
| 5 | B | 340 | 9.20 | 8.90 |  |  |  |
| 6 | C | 90 | 12.90 | 13.50 |  |  |  |
| 7 | D | 125 | 18.90 | 21.80 |  |  |  |
| 8 | E | 440 | 11.30 | 11.40 |  |  |  |
| 9 | Total |  |  |  |  |  |  |
| 10 |  |  |  |  |  |  |  |
| 11 |  |  |  |  |  |  |  |
| 12 | a. Enter in cell E4 the formula for the total cost. |  |  |  |  |  |  |
| 13 | b. Enter in cell F4 the formula for the total market. |  |  |  |  |  |  |
| 14 | c. Enter in cell G4 a formula to calculate the lower of cost or market. |  |  |  |  |  |  |
| 15 | d. Copy these cells to the remaining items. |  |  |  |  |  |  |
| 16 | e. Total the cost, market, and lower of cost or market columns. |  |  |  |  |  |  |
| 17 |  |  |  |  |  |  |  |

Students open an Excel file and develop the formulas, learning how to solve this accounting problem. At any time, students can refer to the Excel Success example within the chapter to help them successfully complete the problem.

The following specific content changes, implemented in *Financial & Managerial Accounting, 11e*, are continued in this text.

Textbooks continue to play an invaluable role in the teaching and learning environments. Continuing our focus from previous editions, we reached out to accounting instructors in an effort to improve the textbook presentation. Our research informed us of the need to remain current in the areas of emerging trends and to continue to look for ways to make the book more accessible to students. The results of this collaboration with hundreds of accounting instructors are reflected in the following major improvements made to this edition.

## International Financial Reporting Standards (IFRS)

IFRS is on the minds of many accounting educators of today. While the future is still unclear, our research indicates a growing need to provide more basic awareness of these standards within the text. We have incorporated some elements of IFRS throughout the text as appropriate to provide this level of awareness, being careful not to encroach upon the core GAAP principles that remain the hallmark focus of the book. These elements include icons that have been placed throughout the financial chapters which point to specific IFRS-related content, outlined with more detail in Appendix E. This table outlines the IFRS impact on the accounting concept. Additionally, within Appendix E, you will find homework questions to test students on their knowledge of IFRS.

## International Connection

*International Connection* features highlight IFRS topics from a real-world perspective and appear in Chapters 1, 4, 6, 9, 11, and 14.

# InternationalConnection

### IFRS FOR STATEMENT OF CASH FLOWS

The statement of cash flows is required under International Financial Reporting Standards (IFRS). The statement of cash flows under IFRS is similar to that reported under U.S. GAAP in that the statement has separate sections for operating, investing, and financing activities. Like U.S. GAAP, IFRS also allow the use of either the indirect or direct method of reporting cash flows from operating activities. IFRS differ from U.S. GAAP in some minor areas, including:

- Interest paid can be reported as either an operating or a financing activity, while interest received can be reported as either an operating or an investing activity. In contrast, U.S. GAAP reports interest paid or received as an operating activity.
- Dividends paid can be reported as either an operating or a financing activity, while dividends received can be reported as either an operating or an investing activity. In contrast, U.S. GAAP reports dividends paid as a financing activity and dividends received as an operating activity.
- Cash flows to pay taxes are reported as a separate line in the operating activities, in contrast to U.S. GAAP, which does not require a separate line disclosure.

*IFRS are further discussed and illustrated on pages 632–639 and in Appendix E.

## Mornin' Joe International

Our authors have prepared statements for Mornin' Joe under IFRS guidelines as a basis for comparison with U.S.-prepared statements. This allows students to see how financial reporting differs under IFRS.

See pages 630-634

### IFRS Reporting

The statement of financial position (balance sheet) presentation for cash for Mornin' Joe International under IFRS is as follows:

| Mornin' Joe International<br>Statement of Financial Position<br>December 31, 2012 | |
|---|---:|
| **Current assets** | |
| Prepaid insurance ..................................................... | € 24,000 |
| Merchandise inventory—at lower of cost | |
|    (first in, first out) or realizable value.................................... | 120,000 |
| Accounts receivable (net of allowance for doubtful accounts)............. | 292,700 |
| Financial assets at fair value through profit or loss ........................ | 465,000 |
| **Cash and cash equivalents** ............................................. | 235,000 |
|    Total current assets ................................................. | €1,136,700 |

IFRS provides flexibility in the order in which the balance sheet accounts are presented. However, assets are normally presented from the least liquid to the most liquid. Liquidity is the ability to turn an asset into cash; thus, cash is the most liquid asset, and is presented last. Presenting current assets from least liquid to most liquid is intended to emphasize the going concern concept, which assumes that the company will remain in business. In contrast, U.S. GAAP presents current assets in order of their liquidity beginning with cash.

## IFRS Training Video and IFRS PowerPoint Presentation

A training video with the voice of our distinguished author, Jim Reeve, will walk an instructor through the nuances of this complex topic. A PowerPoint deck, based on the training video, will allow instructors to customize the presentation for delivery to their students.

## The Accounting Equation

A new format has been implemented in Chapter 2 for analyzing transactions. This new format includes the following elements: (1) transaction description, (2) analysis, (3) journal entry, and (4) accounting equation impact. This will help

students understand that a transaction ultimately affects the accounting equation—
*Assets = Liabilities + Stockholders' Equity.*

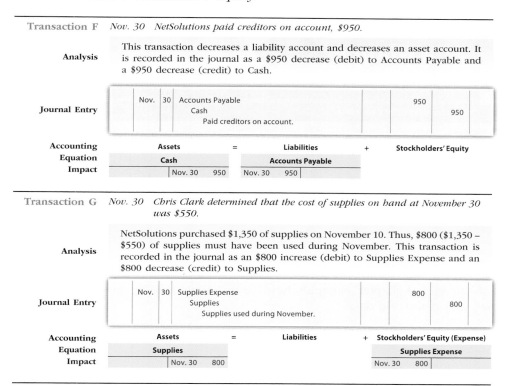

**Transaction F**   *Nov. 30   NetSolutions paid creditors on account, $950.*

**Analysis**   This transaction decreases a liability account and decreases an asset account. It is recorded in the journal as a $950 decrease (debit) to Accounts Payable and a $950 decrease (credit) to Cash.

**Journal Entry**

| Nov. | 30 | Accounts Payable | | 950 | |
| | | Cash | | | 950 |
| | | Paid creditors on account. | | | |

**Accounting Equation Impact**

| Assets | = | Liabilities | + | Stockholders' Equity |
|---|---|---|---|---|
| Cash | | Accounts Payable | | |
| Nov. 30   950 | | Nov. 30   950 | | |

**Transaction G**   *Nov. 30   Chris Clark determined that the cost of supplies on hand at November 30 was $550.*

**Analysis**   NetSolutions purchased $1,350 of supplies on November 10. Thus, $800 ($1,350 − $550) of supplies must have been used during November. This transaction is recorded in the journal as an $800 increase (debit) to Supplies Expense and an $800 decrease (credit) to Supplies.

**Journal Entry**

| Nov. | 30 | Supplies Expense | | 800 | |
| | | Supplies | | | 800 |
| | | Supplies used during November. | | | |

**Accounting Equation Impact**

| Assets | = | Liabilities | + | Stockholders' Equity (Expense) |
|---|---|---|---|---|
| Supplies | | | | Supplies Expense |
| Nov. 30   800 | | | | Nov. 30   800 |

# Differential Analysis

A new uniform method for performing differential analysis is employed for all the differential analysis illustrations and end-of-chapter materials. This approach provides the student a consistent solution grid for solving differential analyses.

# Product Costing

We have simplified the discussion on cost markups for product pricing by moving the total cost and variable cost concepts to an appendix. We retained the product cost concept in the chapter body as a primary example of cost markups.

# Financial Analysis and Interpretation

New Financial Analysis and Interpretation learning objectives have been added to the financial chapters and where appropriate, linked to real-world situations. FAI encourages students to go deeper into the material to analyze accounting information and improve critical thinking skills.

# Updated At a Glance

Students prepare for homework and tests by referring to our end-of-chapter grid which outlines learning objectives, linking concept coverage to specific examples. Through our updated At a Glance, students can review the chapter's learning objectives and key learning outcomes. In addition, all the *Example Exercises* and *Practice Exercises* have been indexed so that each learning objective and key outcomes can be viewed.

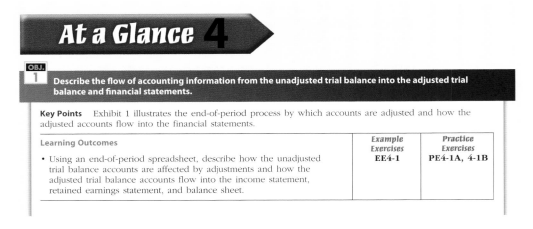

**At a Glance 4**

**OBJ. 1** Describe the flow of accounting information from the unadjusted trial balance into the adjusted trial balance and financial statements.

**Key Points**  Exhibit 1 illustrates the end-of-period process by which accounts are adjusted and how the adjusted accounts flow into the financial statements.

| Learning Outcomes | Example Exercises | Practice Exercises |
|---|---|---|
| • Using an end-of-period spreadsheet, describe how the unadjusted trial balance accounts are affected by adjustments and how the adjusted trial balance accounts flow into the income statement, retained earnings statement, and balance sheet. | EE4-1 | PE4-1A, 4-1B |

## End-of-Chapter Exercises and Problems

All of our end-of-chapter materials have been updated, using new data, company names, and real-world data.

## Test Bank

With the assistance of over fifteen distinguished professors, we completely revamped our test bank. We created more multiple choice, matching, and problem type questions.

## Excel Templates

Our Excel templates have been enhanced to allow professors to turn off the "instant feedback" asterisks. Based on the file provided to them, students can complete the spreadsheet and email the file to their instructor. The instructor can then input a code that will automatically grade the student's work. These Excel templates complement end-of-chapter problems. They are located on the companion website (www.cengagebrain .com) and also within CengageNOW. At the CengageBrain.com home page, search for the ISBN of this title (from the back cover of the book) using the search box at the top of the page. This will take you to the product page where these resources can be found.

Instructors can visit http://login.cengage.com to access resources.

# Chapter-by-Chapter Enhancements

## Chapter 1: Introduction to Accounting and Business

- *Google* replaces *Starbucks* in the chapter opening example.
- Proprietorships, partnerships, corporations, and limited liability companies (LLC) are now discussed with the business entity concept.
- Added an International Connection feature to introduce students to IFRS.
- New Financial Analysis and Interpretation (FAI): **Ratio of Liabilities to Stockholders' Equity** using real-world companies *McDonald's* and *Google*.
- Added new Example Exercise, Practice Exercise, and end-of-chapter exercises to correspond with the new FAI.

## Chapter 2: Analyzing Transactions

- A new format has been implemented in Chapter 2 to help students better understand how to analyze and record transactions.
- A table summarizing common transaction terminology has also been added. This table includes common transaction terms and the related accounts that would be debited and credited in a journal entry.
- New Financial Analysis and Interpretation: **Horizontal Analysis** using a fictitious company, *J. Holmes, Attorney at Law, P.C.* and a real-world company, *Apple Inc.*
- Added new Example Exercise, Practice Exercise, and end-of-chapter exercises to correspond with the new FAI.

## Chapter 3: The Adjusting Process

- The *Accounting Equation Impact* feature described in Chapter 2 is also used in Chapter 3 to describe and illustrate adjusting entries.
- New chapter opener features *Rhapsody*, an Internet-based music service.
- New Financial Analysis and Interpretation: **Vertical Analysis** continuing with fictitious company, *J. Holmes, Attorney at Law, P.C.* and adding a real-world company, *RealNetworks, Inc.*

## Chapter 4: Completing the Accounting Cycle

- The Flow of Accounting Information exhibit at the beginning of the chapter has been revised to show the flow of accounting data from the adjusted trial balance directly into the income statement, retained earnings statement, and balance sheet.
- New Financial Analysis and Interpretation: **Working Capital and Current Ratio** using *Electronic Arts, Inc.* and *Take-Two Interactive Software, Inc.*
- Added new Example Exercise, Practice Exercise, and end-of-chapter exercises to correspond with the new FAI.

## Chapter 5: Accounting for Merchandising Businesses

- The computation of cost of merchandise sold (under the periodic inventory system) has been moved from the beginning of the chapter to an end-of-chapter appendix.
- A new section has been added that summarizes the effects of merchandise transactions on the merchandise inventory account. This is illustrated using a T account for merchandise inventory.

# Chapter-by-Chapter Enhancements

- Moved coverage of "Accounting Systems for Merchandisers" to our online site (www .cengage.com/accounting/reeve).
- New Financial Analysis and Interpretation: **Ratio of Net Sales to Assets** using real-world company *Dollar Tree, Inc.*
- Added new Example Exercise and Practice Exercise to correspond with the new FAI.

## Chapter 6: Inventories

- New Financial Analysis and Interpretation: **Inventory Turnover and Number of Days, Sales in Inventory** using real-world companies *Best Buy* and *Zales*.
- Added new Example Exercise and Practice Exercise to correspond with the new FAI.

## Chapter 7: Sarbanes-Oxley, Internal Control, and Cash

- Updated chapter graphic for better clarity and snapshot comprehension.
- New Financial Analysis and Interpretation: **Ratio of Cash to Monthly Cash Expenses** using real-world company *Evergreen Solar, Inc.*
- Added new Example Exercise and Practice Exercise to correspond with the new FAI.

## Chapter 8: Receivables

- New Financial Analysis and Interpretation: **Accounts Receivable Turnover and Number of Days' Sales in Receivables** using real-world company *FedEx*.
- Added new Example Exercise and Practice Exercise to correspond with the new FAI.

## Chapter 9: Fixed Assets and Intangible Assets

- Updated many chapter graphics for better clarity and snapshot comprehension.
- New Financial Analysis and Interpretation: **Fixed Asset Turnover Ratio** using real-world company *Starbucks Corporation*.
- Added new Example Exercise and Practice Exercise to correspond with the new FAI.

## Chapter 10: Current Liabilities and Payroll

- The example of *Starbucks Corporation* on long-term debt has been replaced by *P.F. Chang's*.
- Updated Wage Bracket Withholding table, based on data from the *2010 Publication 15*.
- Removed discussion of social security cap on withholding (above $100,000).
- Updated Business Connection feature to cover *General Motors* and its pension problems.
- New Financial Analysis and Interpretation: **Quick Ratio** using real-world company *TechSolutions, Inc.*
- Added new Example Exercise and Practice Exercise to correspond with the new FAI.

## Chapter 11: Corporations: Organization, Stock Transactions, and Dividends

- New Financial Analysis and Interpretation: **Earnings per Share** using *Hasbro, Bank of America Corporation*, and *JPMorgan Chase & Co.*
- Added new Example Exercise and Practice Exercise to correspond with the new FAI.

## Chapter 12: Long-Term Liabilities: Bonds and Notes

* Updated Business Connection feature on U.S. government debt.
* Updated Business Connection feature to cover *General Motors* bonds.
* Added an Integrity, Objectivity, and Ethics feature to discuss "Liar's Loans."
* New Financial Analysis and Interpretation: **Number of Times Interest Charges Are Earned** using *Under Armour, Inc.*
* Added new Example Exercise and Practice Exercise to correspond with the new FAI.

## Chapter 13: Investments and Fair Value Accounting

* Added an Integrity, Objectivity, and Ethics box titled *"Loan Loss Woes"* on mortgage loans called "sub-prime" and "Alt-A" loans.
* Updated Business Connection feature to "Apple's Entrance to Streaming Music."
* Revised "Value and Reporting Investments" to simplify the reading process.
* New Financial Analysis and Interpretation: **Dividend Yield** using *News Corporation*.
* Added new Example Exercise and Practice Exercise to correspond with the new FAI.
* Moved "Accounting for Held-to-Maturity Investments" appendix to www.cengagebrain.com. Students, using the ISBN on the back of this book, can navigate to the companion site. Instructors can visit http://login.cengage.com to access resources.

## Mornin' Joe

* To expand students' understanding of financial statement preparation outside the United States, the authors took our unique company example, *Mornin' Joe,* and show how it goes international. They prepared a set of financial statements following IFRS guidelines. To aid in learning, callout features pinpoint the differences between U.S. GAAP and IFRS.

## Chapter 14: Statement of Cash Flows

* Updated Business Connection feature to "Cash Crunch!" featuring *Chrysler Group LLC.*
* New Financial Analysis and Interpretation: **Free Cash Flow** using *Research in Motion, Inc.,* maker of BlackBerry® smartphones.
* Added new Example Exercise and Practice Exercise to correspond with the new FAI.

## Chapter 15: Financial Statement Analysis

* Real-world financial statement analysis problem uses data from the *Nike, Inc.* 2010 10-K. A portion of Nike's 10-K is located in Appendix D.
* Updated Integrity, Objectivity, and Ethics feature discusses "Chief Financial Officer Bonuses."
* Updated Integrity, Objectivity, and Ethics feature to "Buy Low, Sell High."

## Chapter 16: Managerial Accounting Concepts and Principles

* The chapter opener has been modified to feature Paul Stanley of *KISS*. He has a custom guitar built by *Washburn Guitars*.
* Updated Business Connection feature to "Build-to-Order" about *Dell Inc.*

# Chapter-by-Chapter Enhancements

## Chapter 17: Job Order Costing

- Updated Business Connection feature to discuss "BMW's Factory Labor Experiment."

## Chapter 18: Process Cost Systems

- Updated Business Connection feature entitled "Fridge Pack" to discuss *Alcoa Inc.*

## Chapter 19: Cost Behavior and Cost-Volume-Profit Analysis

- Updated Business Connection feature entitled "Breaking Even in the Airline Industry" to discuss the airline industry.
- Added a new Business Connection feature to highlight franchising using real-world companies such as *McDonald's, Wendy's, Dunkin' Donuts,* and *Fatburger.*

## Chapter 20: Variable Costing for Management Analysis

- Updated Business Connection feature to Contribution Margin by Store for Chipotle Mexican Grill.

## Chapter 21: Budgeting

- Updated Business Connection feature called the "U.S. Federal Budget Deficit."
- Simplified the writing of definitions and other content explanations.

## Chapter 22: Performance Evaluation Using Variances from Standard Costs

- Added a new Business Connection feature to highlight *Brinker International*, the operator of popular chains such as *Chili's* and *On the Border.*

## Chapter 23: Performance Evaluation for Decentralized Operations

- Chapter opener replaces *K2 Sports* with *E.W. Scripps Company*, a conglomerate of media companies.
- Added a new Business Connection feature entitled "Centralized vs. Decentralized Research and Development."

## Chapter 24: Differential Analysis and Product Pricing

- Chapter opener replaces *RealNetworks, Inc.* with *Facebook.*

## Chapter 25: Capital Investment Analysis

- Updated chapter opener with a cleaner writing style.
- Added a new Business Connection feature called "*Avatar:* The Most Expensive Movie Ever Made (and the Most Successful)."

## Chapter 26: Cost Allocation and Activity-Based Costing

- Updated Integrity, Objectivity, and Ethics in Business feature to highlight a new fraud case under False Claims Act.
- Simplified terminology regarding activity rate calculation.

## Chapter 27: Cost Management for Just-in-Time Environments

- New Business Connections box with contemporary illustrations of just-in-time practices and results.

*Financial & Managerial Accounting, Using Excel for Success,* is unparalleled in pedagogical innovation. Our constant dialogue with accounting faculty continues to affect how we refine and improve the text to meet the needs of today's students. Our goal is to provide a logical framework and pedagogical system that caters to how students of today study and learn.

**Clear Objectives and Key Learning Outcomes**    To guide students, the authors provide clear chapter objectives and important learning outcomes. All the chapter materials relate back to these key points and outcomes, which keeps students focused on the most important topics and concepts in order to succeed in the course.

**Example Exercises**    Example Exercises reinforce concepts and procedures in a bold, new way. Like a teacher in the classroom, students follow the authors' example to see how to complete accounting applications as they are presented in the text. This feature also provides a list of Practice Exercises that parallel the Example Exercises so students get the practice they need. In addition, the Practice Exercises include references to the chapter Example Exercises so that students can easily cross-reference when completing homework.

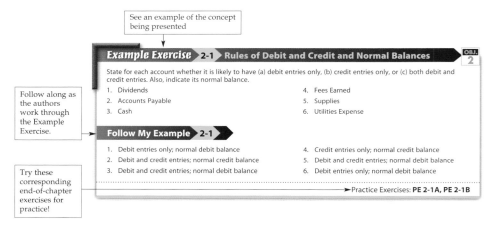

**"At a Glance" Chapter Summary**    At the end of each chapter, the "At a Glance" summary grid ties everything together and helps students stay on track.

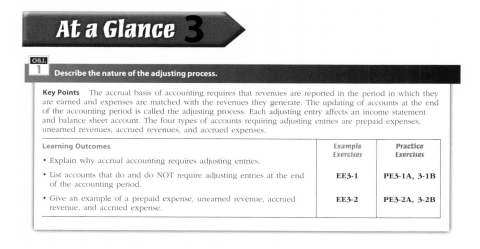

**Real-World Chapter Openers**   Building on the strengths of past editions, these openers continue to relate the accounting and business concepts in the chapter to students' lives. These openers employ examples of real companies and provide invaluable insight into real practice. Several of the openers created especially for this edition focus on interesting companies such as Rhapsody, Razor, E.W. Scripps Company, a diverse media concern, and Facebook.

**Continuing Case Study**   Students follow a fictitious company, NetSolutions, throughout Chapters 1–5, which demonstrates a variety of transactions. The continuity of using the same company facilitates student learning especially for Chapters 1–4, which cover the accounting cycle. Also, using the same company allows students to follow the transition of the company from a service business in Chapters 1–4 to a merchandising business in Chapter 5.

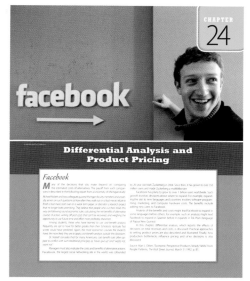

**Illustrative Problem and Solution**   A solved problem models one or more of the chapter's assignment problems so that students can apply the modeled procedures to end-of-chapter materials.

**Integrity, Objectivity, and Ethics in Business**   In each chapter, these cases help students develop their ethical compass. Often coupled with related end-of-chapter activities, these cases can be discussed in class or students can consider the cases as they read the chapter. Both the section and related end-of-chapter materials are indicated with a unique icon for a consistent presentation.

## Integrity, Objectivity, and Ethics in Business

### CHIEF FINANCIAL OFFICER BONUSES

A recent study by compensation experts at Temple University found that chief financial officer salaries are correlated with the complexity of a company's operations, but chief financial officer bonuses are correlated with the company's ability to meet analysts' earnings forecasts. These results suggest that financial bonuses may provide chief financial officers with an incentive to use questionable accounting practices to improve earnings. While the study doesn't conclude that bonuses lead to accounting fraud, it does suggest that bonuses give chief financial officers a reason to find ways to use accounting to increase apparent earnings.

Source: E. Jelesiewicz, "Today's CFO: More Challenge but Higher Compensation," *News Communications* (Temple University, August 2009).

# Hallmark Features

**Business Connection and Comprehensive Real-World Notes**   Students get a close-up look at how accounting operates in the marketplace through a variety of *Business Connection* boxed features.

## Business Connection

### *AVATAR*: THE MOST EXPENSIVE MOVIE EVER MADE (AND THE MOST SUCCESSFUL)

Prior to the release of the blockbuster *Avatar* in December 2009, many were skeptical if the movie's huge $500 million investment would pay off. After all, just to break even the movie would have to perform as one of the top 50 movies of all time. To provide a return that was double the investment, the movie would have to crack the top ten. Many thought this was a tall order, even though James Cameron, the force behind this movie, already had the number one grossing movie of all time: *Titanic*, at $1.8 billion in worldwide box office revenues. Could he do it again? That was the question.

So, how did the film do? Only eight weeks after its release, Avatar had become the number one grossing film of all time, with over $2.2 billion in worldwide box office revenue. Executives at Fox anticipated that the profit might double after the film was released on DVD in the summer of 2010. Needless to say, James Cameron, 20th Century Fox, and other investors are very pleased with their return on this investment.

Sources: Michael Cieply, "A Movie's Budget Pops from the Screen," *New York Times*, November 8, 2009; "Bulk of Avatar Profit Still to Come," *The Age*, February 3, 2010.

**Market Leading End-of-Chapter Material**   Students need to practice accounting so that they can understand and use it. To give students the greatest possible advantage in the real world, *Financial and Managerial Accounting Using Excel for Success,* goes beyond presenting theory and procedure with comprehensive, time-tested, end-of-chapter material.

# Online Solutions

South-Western, a division of Cengage Learning, offers a vast array of online solutions to suit your course needs. Choose the product that best meets your classroom needs and course goals. Please check with your Cengage representative for more details or for ordering information.

## CengageNow

**CengageNOW** is a powerful course management and online homework tool that provides robust instructor control and customization to optimize the student learning experience and meet desired outcomes. CengageNOW offers:

- Auto-graded homework (static and algorithmic varieties), test bank, Personalized Study Plan, and eBook are all in one resource.
- Easy-to-use course management options offer flexibility and continuity from one semester to another.
- Different levels of feedback and engaging student resources guide students through material and solidify learning.
- The most robust and flexible assignment options in the industry.
- "Smart Entry" helps eliminate common data entry errors and prevents students from guessing their way through the homework.
- The ability to analyze student work from the gradebook and generate reports on learning outcomes. Each problem is tagged in the Solutions Manual and CengageNOW to AICPA, IMA, AACSB, and ACBSP outcomes so you can measure student performance.

## CengageNOW Upgrades:

- Our General Ledger Software is now being offered in a new online format. Your students can solve selected end-of-chapter assignments in a format that emulates commercial general ledger software.
- For a complete list of CengageNOW upgrades, refer to page 6 in the brochure in front of the Instructor Edition.
- New Design: CengageNOW has been redesigned to enhance your experience.

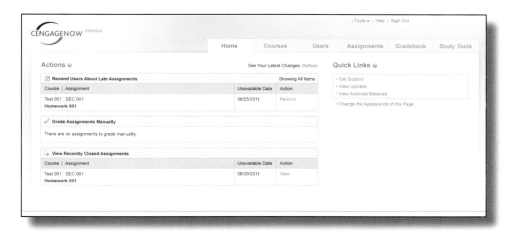

**For a CengageNOW demo, visit:** www.cengage.com/community/warren

To access additional course materials and companion resources, please visit www.cengagebrain.com.

## Aplia

**Aplia** is a premier online homework product that successfully engages students and maximizes the amount of effort they put forth, creating more efficient learners. Aplia's advantages are:

- In addition to static and algorithmic end-of-chapter homework, Aplia offers an **extra problem set** to give you more options!
- Students can receive **unique**, **detailed feedback** and the full solution after each attempt on homework.
- "**Grade It Now**" maximizes student effort on each attempt and ensures students do their own work. Students have three attempts. Each attempt produces an algorithmic variety. The final score is an average of the three attempts.
- "**Smart Entry**" helps eliminate common data entry errors and prevents students from guessing their way through the homework.

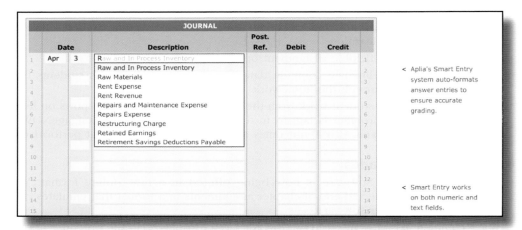

### Aplia Upgrades:

- Increased Instructor Control: Instructors now have more options in how they assign materials from the question banks.
- ApliaText: Interactive ApliaText allows students to use eBooks in a new way. This unique flip-book also includes a Chapter Recap that helps students craft their own personal study guide.

**For an Aplia demo, visit:** www.aplia.com/accounting

## WebTutor™

**WebTutor™ on Blackboard® and WebCT®**—Improve student grades with online review and test preparation tools in an easy-to-use course cartridge.

Visit www.cengage.com/webtutor for more information.

# For the Instructor

When it comes to supporting instructors, South-Western is unsurpassed. *Financial & Managerial Accounting, Using Excel for Success,* continues the tradition with powerful print and digital ancillaries aimed at facilitating greater course successes.

**Instructor's Manual**   The Instructor's Manual includes: Brief Synopsis, List of Objectives, Key Terms, Ideas for Class Discussion, Lecture Aids, Demonstration Problems, Group Learning Activities, Exercises and Problems for Reinforcement, and Internet Activities. Suggested Approaches incorporate many modern teaching initiatives, including active learning, collaborative learning, critical thinking, and writing across the curriculum.

**Solutions Manual**   The Solutions Manual contains answers to all exercises, problems, and activities in the text. The solutions are author-written and verified multiple times for numerical accuracy and consistency.

**Test Bank**   The Test Bank includes more than 3,500 True/False questions, Multiple-Choice questions, and Problems, each marked with a difficulty level, chapter objective, and AASCB/AICPA/ACBSP tagging.

**ExamView® Pro Testing Software**   This intuitive software allows you to easily customize exams, practice tests, and tutorials and deliver them over a network, on the Internet, or in printed form. In addition, ExamView comes with searching capabilities that make sorting the wealth of questions from the printed test bank easy. The software and files are found on the IRCD.

**PowerPoint®**   Each presentation, which is included on the IRCD and on the product support site, enhances lectures and simplifies class preparation. Each chapter contains objectives followed by a thorough outline of the chapter that easily provides an entire lecture model. Also, exhibits from the chapter, such as the new Example Exercises, have been recreated as colorful PowerPoint slides to create a powerful, customizable tool.

**Instructor Excel® Templates**   These templates provide the solutions for the Enhanced Excel® templates created for students. These templates have been enhanced to afford you the ability to turn off the "just in time" feedback asterisks. You can provide students with files that do not automatically grade, instead grading once returned to you completed.

**Instructor's Resource CD**   The Instructor's Resource CD includes the PowerPoint® Presentations, Instructor's Manual, Solutions Manual, Test Bank, ExamView®, General Ledger Inspector, and Excel® Template Solutions.

# For the Student

Students come to accounting with a variety of learning needs. *Financial & Managerial Accounting, Using Excel for Success,* offers a broad range of supplements in both printed form and easy-to-use technology. We continue to refine our entire supplement package around the comments instructors have provided about their courses and teaching needs.

**Study Guide** This author-written guide provides students Quiz and Test Hints, Matching questions, Fill-in-the-Blank questions (Parts A & B), Multiple-Choice questions, True/False questions, Exercises, and Problems for each chapter.

**Working Papers for Exercises and Problems** The traditional working papers include problem-specific forms for preparing solutions for Exercises, A & B Problems, the Continuing Problem, and the Comprehensive Problems from the textbook. These forms, with preprinted headings, provide a structure for the problems, which helps students get started and saves them time.

**Blank Working Papers** These Working Papers are available for completing exercises and problems either from the text or prepared by the instructor. They have no preprinted headings. A guide at the front of the Working Papers tells students which form they will need for each problem and are available online in a .pdf, printable format.

**Enhanced Excel® Templates** These templates are provided for selected long or complicated end-of-chapter problems and provide assistance to the student as they set up and work the problem. Certain cells are coded to display a red asterisk when an incorrect answer is entered, which helps students stay on track. Selected problems that can be solved using these templates are designated by an icon.

 **General Ledger Software** The GL software is now being offered in a new online format. Students can solve selected end-of-chapter assignments in a format that emulates commercial general ledger software. Students make entries into the general journal or special journals, track the posting of the entries to the general ledger, and create financial statements or reports. This gives students important exposure to commercial accounting software, yet in a manner that is more forgiving of student errors. Assignments are automatically graded online.

**Product Support Web Site www.cengagebrain.com/** At the CengageBrain home page, students can search for the ISBN of this textbook. This will take them to the product support page which contains resources such as quizzes, enhanced Excel templates, and other supplemental material. Instructors can use login.cengage.com to access resources.

# Acknowledgments

Many of the enhancements made to *Financial & Managerial Accounting, Using Excel for Success,* are a direct result of countless conversations we've had with principles of accounting professors and students over the past several years. We want to take this opportunity to thank them for their perspectives and feedback on textbook use.

The following instructors are members of our Blue Sky editorial board, whose helpful comments and feedback continue to have a profound impact on the presentation and core themes of this text:

Rick Andrews
*Sinclair Community College*

Mia Breen
*De Anza Community College*

Anne M. Cardozo
*Broward College*

James Cieslak
*Cuyahoga Community College*

Rebecca A. Foote
*Middle Tennessee State University*

Gloria Grayless
*Sam Houston State University*

Robert Gronstal
*Metropolitan Community College*

Curtis Gustafson
*South Dakota State University*

Lynn P. Hedge
*NHTI—Concord's Community College*

Audrey Hunter
*Broward College*

Phillip Imel
*Northern Virginia Community College— Annandale Campus*

Christopher Kwak
*De Anza College*

Bruce W. McClain
*Cleveland State University*

Jenny Resnick
*Santa Monica College*

Lawrence A. Roman
*Cuyahoga Community College*

Robert Smolin
*Citrus College*

Robert C. Urell
*Irvine Valley College*

The following students attended our Blue Sky session, providing insights into the life of an accounting student:

Stacy Appleton
*Northern Kentucky University*

Danny Bradford
*Xavier University*

Steve Busey
*Xavier University*

Brandon Butcher
*Xavier University*

Suzanne Buzek
*Xavier University*

Jenny Daugherty
*Northern Kentucky University*

Richard Farmer
*Sinclair Community College*

Bobby Freking
*Xavier University*

Steve Latos
*Xavier University*

Cristi Liska
*Northern Kentucky University*

Mallory Malinoski
*Xavier University*

Clare McGrath
*Xavier University*

Hecia Mpanga
*Xavier University*

Jessica Nichols
*Northern Kentucky University*

Oscar Ochieng
*Northern Kentucky University*

Rick Riva
*Sinclair Community College*

Max Roberts
*Sinclair Community College*

Anthony Saxon
*Xavier University*

The following individuals took the time to participate in surveys, online sessions, content reviews, and test bank revisions:

Bridget Anakwe
*Delaware State University*

Julia L. Angel
*North Arkansas College*

Leah Arrington
*Northwest Mississippi Community College*

Donna T. Ascenzi
*Bryant and Stratton College—Syracuse Campus*

Ed Bagley
*Darton College*

James Baker
*Harford Community College*

Lisa Cooley Banks
*University of Michigan*

LuAnn Bean
*Florida Institute of Technology*

Judy Beebe
*Western Oregon University*

Brenda J. Bindschatel
*Green River Community College*

Eric D. Bostwick
*The University of West Florida*

Bryan C. Bouchard
*Southern New Hampshire University*

Mike Bowyer
*Montgomery Community College*

Thomas M. Branton
*Alvin Community College*

Keven Breaux
*Nicholls State University*

Eddy Burks
*Troy University*

Hoa Burrows
*Miami-Dade College*

Gene Buyan
*Bryan College*

Celestino Caicoya
*Miami Dade College*

John Callister
*Cornell University*

Fonda Carter
*Columbus State University*

# Acknowledgments

Deborah Chabaud
*Louisiana Technical College*

Ring Chen
*Northeastern Illinois University*

James Cieslak
*Cuyahoga Community College*

Marilyn G. Ciolino
*Delgado Community College*

Earl Clay
*Cape Cod Community College*

Lisa M. Cole
*Johnson County Community College*

Ellen Cook
*University of Louisiana at Lafayette*

Sue Cook
*Tulsa Community College*

Cori Oliver Crews
*Waycross College*

Julie Daigle
*Ft. Range Community College*

Julie Dailey
*Central Virginia Community College*

Bobbie Daniels
*Jackson State University*

John M. Daugherty
*Pitt Community College*

Becky Davis
*East Mississippi Community College*

Vaun Day
*Central Arizona College*

Stan Deal
*Azusa Pacific Universit*

Ginger Dennis
*West Georgia Technical College*

Alireza Dorestani
*Northeastern Illinois University*

Terry Elliott
*Morehead State University*

Scott A. Elza
*Wisconsin Indianhead Technical College*

Patricia Feller
*Nashville State Community College*

Mike Foland
*Southwestern Illinois College—Belleville*

Brenda S. Fowler
*Alamance Community College*

Ann Gabriel
*Ohio University*

Kenneth Gaines
*East-West University*

Susan Galbreath
*Lipscomb University*

Jeanne Gerard
*Franklin Pierce University*

Christopher Gilbert
*East Los Angeles College, Montery Park, CA*

Mark S. Gleason
*Metropolitan State University, St. Paul, Minnesota*

Marina Grau
*Houston Community College*

Judith Grenkowicz
*Kirtland Community College*

Vicki Greshik
*Jamestown College*

Lillian S. Grose
*Our Lady of Holy Cross College*

Denise T. Guest
*Germanna Community College*

Bruce J. Gunning
*Kent State University at East Liverpool*

Amu Haas
*Kingsborough C.C.*

Rosie Hale
*Southwest Tennessee Community College*

Sara Harris
*Arapahoe Community College*

Matthew P. Helinski
*Northeast Lakeview College*

Siriyama Kanthi Herath
*Clark Atlanta University*

Patricia Holmes
*Des Moines Area Community College*

Wanda Hudson
*Alabama Southern Community College*

Yousef Jahmani
*Savannah State University*

Todd A. Jensen
*Sierra College*

Paul T. Johnson
*Mississippi Gulf Coast Community College*

Janice Kerber
*Durham Technical Community College*

Darenda Kersey
*Black River Technical College*

Mary Kline
*Black Hawk College*

Jan Kraft
*Northwest College*

Ray Kreiner
*Piedmont College*

David W. Krug
*Johnson County Community College*

Cathy Xanthaky Larson
*Middlesex Community College*

Brenda G. Lauer
*Northeastern Junior College*

David Layne
*Taft College*

Stacy LeJeune
*Nicholls State University*

Ted Lewis
*Marshalltown Community College*

Marion Loiola
*SUNY—Orange County Community College*

Ming Lu
*Santa Monica College*

Don Lucy
*Indian River State College*

Debbie Luna
*El Paso Community College*

Anna L. Lusher
*Slippery Rock University*

Kirk Lynch
*Sandhills Community College*

Annette Maddox
*Georgia Highlands College*

Cynthia McCall
*Des Moines Area Community College*

Bridgette Mahan
*Harold Washington College*

Robert Mahan
*Milligan College*

Irene Meares
*Western New Mexico University*

James B. Meir
*Cleveland State Community College*

John L. Miller
*Metropolitan Community College*

Peter Moloney
*Cerritos College*

Kathy Moreno
*Abraham Baldwin Agricultural College*

Janet Morrow
*East Central Community College*

Pamela G. Needham
*Northeast Mississippi Community College*

Jeannie M. Neil
*Orange Coast College, Costa Mesa, CA*

Carolyn Nelson
*Coffeyville Community College*

Joseph Malino Nicassio
*Westmoreland County Community College*

Robert L. Osborne
*Ohio Dominican University*

Scott Paxton
*North Idaho College*

Ronald Pearson
*Bay College*

Rachel Pernia
*Essex County College*

Erick Pifer
*Lake Michigan College*

Marianne G. Pindar
*Lackawanna College*

Kenneth J. Plucinski
*State University of New York at Fredonia*

Debbie Porter
*Tidewater Community College*

Shirley J. Powell
*Arkansas State University—Beebe*

Eric M. Primuth
*Cuyahoga Community College*

Michael Prindle
*Grand View University*

Rita Pritchett
*Brevard Community College*

Judy Ramsay
*San Jacinto College—North*

Patrick Reihing
*Nassau Community College*

Richard Rickel
*South Mountain Community College*

Sharon Robertson
*Tri-County Community College*

Pat Rogan
*Cosumnes River College*

Patricia G. Roshto
*University of Louisiana—Monroe*

Martin Sabo
*Community College of Denver*

R. Schaa
*Black River Technical College*

John Schafer
*Hannibal-Lagrange College*

Tracy M. Schmeltzer
*Wayne Community College*

Debbie Schmidt
*Cerritos College*

Jennifer Schneider
*Gainesville State College*

Dennis C. Shea
*Southern New Hampshire University*

Esmond Skeete
*Morris Brown College*

Robert W. Smith (retired)
*formerly of Briarcliffe College—Patchogue, NY Campus*

Kimberly D. Smith
*County College of Morris*

Richard Snapp
*Olympic College—Bremerton*

Teresa Speck
*Saint Mary'S University of Minnesota*

John L. Stancil
*Florida Southern College*

Barry Stephens
*Bemidji State University*

Jeff Strawser
*Sam Houston State University*

Stacie A. Surowiec
*Harford Community College*

Eric H. Sussman
*UCLA Anderson Graduate School of Management*

Bill Talbot
*Montgomery College*

Kenneth J. Tax
*Farmingdale State College (SUNY)*

Ronald Tidd
*Central Washington University*

Erol C. Tucker, Jr.
*The Victoria College*

Henry Velarde
*Malcolm X College*

Angela Waits
*Gadsden State Community College*

Dale Walker
*Arkansas State University*

Shunda Ware
*Atlanta Technical College*

Dale Westfall
*Midland College*

Cheryl C. Willingham
*Wisconsin Indianhead Technical College*

Bob Willis
*Rogers State University*

Patrick B. Wilson
*Tennessee Board of Regents*

Emily Wright
*Macmurray College*

Jay E. Wright
*New River Community College*

Benny Zachry
*Nicholls State University*

The following instructors created content for the supplements that accompany the text:

LuAnn Bean
*Florida Institute of Technology*

Gary Bower
*Community College of Rhode Island*

Doug Cloud
*Pepperdine University*

Ana Cruz & Blanca Ortega
*Miami Dade College*

Kurt Fredricks
*Valencia Community College*

Lori Grady
*Bucks County Community College*

Jose Luis Hortensi
*Miami Dade College*

Christine Jonick
*Gainesville State College*

Patti Lopez
*Valencia Community College*

Don Lucy
*Indian River State College*

Tracie Nobles
*Austin Community College*

Craig Pence
*Highland Community College*

Alice Sineath
*Forsyth Technical Community College*

Janice Stoudemire
*Midlands Technical College*

# Brief Contents

# Contents

## Chapter 5  Accounting for Merchandising Businesses  217

## Chapter 6  Inventories  275

**Practice Set: Art by Design**
This set is a service and merchandising business operated as a corporation. It includes narrative for six months of transactions, which are to be recorded in a general journal. The set can be solved manually or with the General Ledger software.

excel
SUCCESS
excel
SUCCESS

© AP Photo/Paul Sakuma

# Introduction to Accounting and Business

## *Google™*

**W**hen two teams pair up for a game of football, there is often a lot of noise. The band plays, the fans cheer, and fireworks light up the scoreboard. Obviously, the fans are committed and care about the outcome of the game. Just like fans at a football game, the owners of a business want their business to "win" against their competitors in the marketplace. While having your football team win can be a source of pride, winning in the marketplace goes beyond pride and has many tangible benefits. Companies that are winners are better able to serve customers, provide good jobs for employees, and make money for their owners.

One such successful company is **Google**, one of the most visible companies on the Internet. Many of us cannot visit the Web without using Google to power a search. As one writer said, "Google is the closest thing the Web has to an ultimate answer machine." And yet, Google is a free tool—no one asks for your credit card when you use Google's search tools.

Do you think Google has been a successful company? Does it make money? How would you know? Accounting helps to answer these questions. Google's accounting information tells us that Google is a successful company that makes a lot of money, but not from you and me. Google makes its money from advertisers.

This textbook introduces you to accounting, the language of business. Chapter 1 begins by discussing what a business is, how it operates, and the role that accounting plays.

# Nature of Business and Accounting

**OBJ. 1** Describe the nature of a business, the role of accounting, and ethics in business.

A **business**[1] is an organization in which basic resources (inputs), such as materials and labor, are assembled and processed to provide goods or services (outputs) to customers. Businesses come in all sizes, from a local coffee house to Starbucks, which sells over $10 billion of coffee and related products each year.

The objective of most businesses is to earn a **profit**. Profit is the difference between the amounts received from customers for goods or services and the amounts paid for the inputs used to provide the goods or services. This text focuses on businesses operating to earn a profit. However, many of the same concepts and principles also apply to not-for-profit organizations such as hospitals, churches, and government agencies.

## Types of Businesses

Three types of businesses operated for profit include service, merchandising, and manufacturing businesses.

Each type of business and some examples are described below.

**Service businesses** provide services rather than products to customers.

    Delta Air Lines (transportation services)
    The Walt Disney Company (entertainment services)

**Merchandising businesses** sell products they purchase from other businesses to customers.

    Wal-Mart (general merchandise)
    Amazon.com (Internet books, music, videos)

**Manufacturing businesses** change basic inputs into products that are sold to customers.

    Ford Motor Co. (cars, trucks, vans)
    Dell Inc. (personal computers)

1 A complete glossary of terms appears at the end of the text.

# The Role of Accounting in Business

The role of accounting in business is to provide information for managers to use in operating the business. In addition, accounting provides information to other users in assessing the economic performance and condition of the business.

Thus, **accounting** can be defined as an information system that provides reports to users about the economic activities and condition of a business. You may think of accounting as the "language of business." This is because accounting is the means by which businesses' financial information is communicated to users.

The process by which accounting provides information to users is as follows:

1. Identify users.
2. Assess users' information needs.
3. Design the accounting information system to meet users' needs.
4. Record economic data about business activities and events.
5. Prepare accounting reports for users.

As illustrated in Exhibit 1, users of accounting information can be divided into two groups: internal users and external users.

**Note:**
Accounting is an information system that provides reports to users about the economic activities and condition of a business.

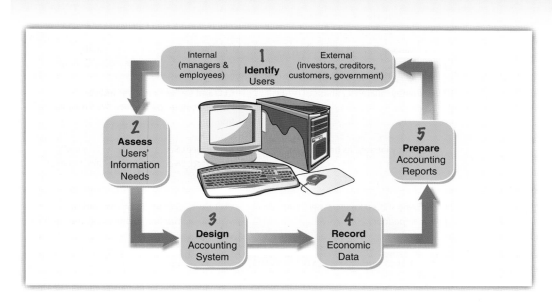

**EXHIBIT 1**

**Accounting as an Information System**

Internal users of accounting information include managers and employees. These users are directly involved in managing and operating the business. The area of accounting that provides internal users with information is called **managerial accounting** or **management accounting**.

The objective of managerial accounting is to provide relevant and timely information for managers' and employees' decision-making needs. Oftentimes, such information is sensitive and is not distributed outside the business. Examples of sensitive information might include information about customers, prices, and plans to expand the business. Managerial accountants employed by a business are employed in **private accounting**.

External users of accounting information include investors, creditors, customers, and the government. These users are not directly involved in managing and operating the business. The area of accounting that provides external users with information is called **financial accounting**.

The objective of financial accounting is to provide relevant and timely information for the decision-making needs of users outside of the business. For example, financial reports on the operations and condition of the business are useful for banks and other creditors in deciding whether to lend money to the business. **General-purpose financial statements** are one type of financial accounting report that is distributed to external users. The term *general-purpose* refers to the wide range of decision-making needs that these reports are designed to serve. Later in this chapter, general-purpose financial statements are described and illustrated.

## Role of Ethics in Accounting and Business

The objective of accounting is to provide relevant, timely information for user decision making. Accountants must behave in an ethical manner so that the information they provide users will be trustworthy and, thus, useful for decision making. Managers and employees must also behave in an ethical manner in managing and operating a business. Otherwise, no one will be willing to invest in or loan money to the business.

**Ethics** are moral principles that guide the conduct of individuals. Unfortunately, business managers and accountants sometimes behave in an unethical manner. A number of managers of the companies listed in Exhibit 2 engaged in accounting or

**EXHIBIT 2**   **Accounting and Business Frauds**

| Company | Nature of Accounting or Business Fraud | Result |
|---|---|---|
| American International Group, Inc. (AIG) | Used sham accounting transactions to inflate performance. | CEO resigned. Executives criminally convicted. AIG paid $126 million in fines. |
| Computer Associates International, Inc. | Fraudulently inflated its financial results. | CEO and senior executives indicted. Five executives pled guilty. $225 million fine. |
| Enron | Fraudulently inflated its financial results. | Bankrupcty. Senior executives criminally convicted. Over $60 billion in stock market losses. |
| Fannie Mae | Improperly shifted financial performance between periods. | CEO and CFO fired. Company made a $9 billion correction to previously reported earnings. |
| HealthSouth | Overstated performance by $4 billion in false entries. | Senior executives criminally convicted. |
| Qwest Communications International, Inc. | Improperly recognized $3 billion in false receipts. | CEO and six other executives criminally convicted of "massive financial fraud." $250 million SEC fine. |
| Satyam Computer Services | Significantly inflated assets and earnings. | Chairman and founder is in jail; investors lost billions. |
| Terex | Recorded profit prematurely and inflated profits. | Company paid $8 million to Securities and Exchange Commission in settlement. |
| Tyco International, Ltd. | Failed to disclose secret loans to executives that were subsequently forgiven. | CEO forced to resign and subjected to frozen asset order and criminally convicted. |
| United Rental | Inflated profits to meet earnings forecasts and analysts expectations. | Vice chairman and chief financial officer indicted for conspiracy, securities fraud, and insider trading. |
| Xerox Corporation | Recognized $3 billion in revenue prior to when it should have been. | $10 million fine to SEC. Six executives forced to pay $22 million. |

business fraud. These ethical violations led to fines, firings, and lawsuits. In some cases, managers were criminally prosecuted, convicted, and sent to prison.

What went wrong for the managers and companies listed in Exhibit 2? The answer normally involved one or both of the following two factors:

**Failure of Individual Character.** An ethical manager and accountant is honest and fair. However, managers and accountants often face pressures from supervisors to meet company and investor expectations. In many of the cases in Exhibit 2, managers and accountants justified small ethical violations to avoid such pressures. However, these small violations became big violations as the company's financial problems became worse.

**Culture of Greed and Ethical Indifference.** By their behavior and attitude, senior managers set the company culture. In most of the companies listed in Exhibit 2, the senior managers created a culture of greed and indifference to the truth.

As a result of the accounting and business frauds shown in Exhibit 2, Congress passed new laws to monitor the behavior of accounting and business. For example, the Sarbanes-Oxley Act of 2002 (SOX) was enacted. SOX established a new oversight body for the accounting profession, called the Public Company Accounting Oversight Board (PCAOB). In addition, SOX established standards for independence, corporate responsibility, and disclosure.

How does one behave ethically when faced with financial or other types of pressure? Guidelines for behaving ethically are shown in Exhibit 3.[2]

---

1. Identify an ethical decision by using your personal ethical standards of honesty and fairness.
2. Identify the consequences of the decision and its effect on others.
3. Consider your obligations and responsibilities to those that will be affected by your decision.
4. Make a decision that is ethical and fair to those affected by it.

**EXHIBIT 3**

**Guidelines for Ethical Conduct**

---

## Integrity, Objectivity, and Ethics in Business

**BERNIE MADOFF**

In June 2009, Bernard L. "Bernie" Madoff was sentenced to 150 years in prison for defrauding thousands of investors in one of the biggest frauds in American history. Madoff's fraud started several decades earlier when he began a "Ponzi scheme" in his investment management firm, Bernard L. Madoff Securities LLC.

In a Ponzi scheme, the investment manager uses funds received from new investors to pay a return to existing investors, rather than basing investment returns on the fund's actual performance. As long as the investment manager is able to attract new investors, he or she will have new funds to pay existing investors and continue the fraud. While most Ponzi schemes collapse quickly when the investment manager runs out of new investors, Madoff's reputation, popularity, and personal contacts provided a steady stream of investors which allowed the fraud to survive for decades.

## Opportunities for Accountants

Numerous career opportunities are available for students majoring in accounting. Currently, the demand for accountants exceeds the number of new graduates entering the job market. This is partly due to the increased regulation of business caused by the accounting and business frauds shown in Exhibit 2. Also, more and

---

2 Many companies have ethical standards of conduct for managers and employees. In addition, the Institute of Management Accountants and the American Institute of Certified Public Accountants have professional codes of conduct.

more businesses have come to recognize the importance and value of accounting information.

As indicated earlier, accountants employed by a business are employed in private accounting. Private accountants have a variety of possible career options within a company. Some of these career options are shown in Exhibit 4 along with their starting salaries. Accountants who provide audit services, called auditors, verify the accuracy of financial records, accounts, and systems. As shown in Exhibit 4, several private accounting careers have certification options.

**EXHIBIT 4**    **Accounting Career Paths and Salaries**

| Accounting Career Track | Description | Career Options | Annual Starting Salaries* | Certification |
|---|---|---|---|---|
| Private Accounting | Accountants employed by companies, government, and not-for-profit entities. | Bookkeeper | $36,125 | |
| | | Payroll clerk | $34,875 | Certified Payroll Professional (CPP) |
| | | General accountant | $42,000 | |
| | | Budget analyst | $44,375 | |
| | | Cost accountant | $43,750 | Certified Management Accountant (CMA) |
| | | Internal auditor | $48,250 | Certified Internal Auditor (CIA) |
| | | Information technology auditor | $56,500 | Certified Information Systems Auditor (CISA) |
| Public Accounting | Accountants employed individually or within a public accounting firm in tax or audit services. | Local firms | $45,063 | Certified Public Accountant (CPA) |
| | | National firms | $54,250 | Certified Public Accountant (CPA) |

Source: Robert Half 2010 Salary Guide (Finance and Accounting), Robert Half International, Inc.
*Mean salaries of a reported range. Private accounting salaries are reported for large companies. Salaries may vary by region.

Accountants and their staff who provide services on a fee basis are said to be employed in **public accounting**. In public accounting, an accountant may practice as an individual or as a member of a public accounting firm. Public accountants who have met a state's education, experience, and examination requirements may become **Certified Public Accountants (CPAs)**. CPAs generally perform general accounting, audit, or tax services. As can be seen in Exhibit 4, CPAs have slightly better starting salaries than private accountants. Career statistics indicate, however, that these salary differences tend to disappear over time.

Because all functions within a business use accounting information, experience in private or public accounting provides a solid foundation for a career. Many positions in industry and in government agencies are held by individuals with accounting backgrounds.

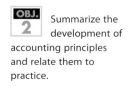
**OBJ. 2** Summarize the development of accounting principles and relate them to practice.

# Generally Accepted Accounting Principles

If a company's management could record and report financial data as it saw fit, comparisons among companies would be difficult, if not impossible. Thus, financial accountants follow **generally accepted accounting principles (GAAP)** in preparing reports. These reports allow investors and other users to compare one company to another.

Accounting principles and concepts develop from research, accepted accounting practices, and pronouncements of regulators. Within the United States, the **Financial Accounting Standards Board (FASB)** has the primary responsibility for developing accounting principles. The FASB publishes *Statements of Financial Accounting Standards* as well as *Interpretations* of these Standards. In addition, the **Securities and Exchange Commission (SEC),** an agency of the U.S. government, has authority over the accounting and financial disclosures for companies whose shares of ownership (stock) are traded and sold to the public. The SEC normally accepts the accounting principles set forth by the FASB. However, the SEC may issue *Staff Accounting Bulletins* on accounting matters that may not have been addressed by the FASB.

Many countries outside the United States use generally accepted accounting principles adopted by the **International Accounting Standards Board (IASB)**. The IASB issues *International Financial Reporting Standards (IFRSs)*. Significant differences currently exist between FASB and IASB accounting principles. However, the FASB and IASB are working together to reduce and eliminate these differences into a single set of accounting principles. Such a set of worldwide accounting principles would help facilitate investment and business in an increasingly global economy.

See Appendix E for more information

In this chapter and text, accounting principles and concepts are emphasized. It is by this emphasis on the "why" as well as the "how" that you will gain an understanding of accounting.

# InternationalConnection

## INTERNATIONAL FINANCIAL REPORTING STANDARDS (IFRS)

IFRS are considered to be more "principles-based" than U.S. GAAP, which is considered to be more "rules-based." For example, U.S. GAAP consists of approximately 17,000 pages, which includes numerous industry-specific accounting rules. In contrast, IFRS allow more judgment in deciding how business transactions are recorded. Many believe that the strong regulatory and litigation environment in the United States is the cause for the more rules-based GAAP approach. Regardless, IFRS and GAAP share more in common than differences.*

*Differences between U.S. GAAP and IFRS are further discussed and illustrated in Appendix E.

## Business Entity Concept

The **business entity concept** limits the economic data in an accounting system to data related directly to the activities of the business. In other words, the business is viewed as an entity separate from its owners, creditors, or other businesses. For example, the accountant for a business with one owner would record the activities of the business only and would not record the personal activities, property, or debts of the owner.

A business entity may take the form of a proprietorship, partnership, corporation, or limited liability company (LLC). Each of these forms and their major characteristics are listed below.

**Note:**
Under the business entity concept, the activities of a business are recorded separately from the activities of its owners, creditors, or other businesses.

| Form of Business Entity | Characteristics |
|---|---|
| **Proprietorship** is owned by one individual. | • 70% of business entities in the United States. <br> • Easy and cheap to organize. <br> • Resources are limited to those of the owner. <br> • Used by small businesses. |
| **Partnership** is owned by two or more individuals. | • 10% of business organizations in the United States (combined with limited liability companies). <br> • Combines the skills and resources of more than one person. |

*(continued)*

| Form of Business Entity | Characteristics |
|---|---|
| **Corporation** is organized under state or federal statutes as a separate legal taxable entity. | • Generates 90% of business revenues.<br>• 20% of the business organizations in the United States.<br>• Ownership is divided into shares called stock.<br>• Can obtain large amounts of resources by issuing stock.<br>• Used by large businesses. |
| **Limited liability company (LLC)** combines the attributes of a partnership and a corporation. | • 10% of business organizations in the United States (combined with partnerships).<br>• Often used as an alternative to a partnership.<br>• Has tax and legal liability advantages for owners. |

The three types of businesses discussed earlier—service, merchandising, and manufacturing—may be organized as proprietorships, partnerships, corporations, or limited liability companies. Because of the large amount of resources required to operate a manufacturing business, most manufacturing businesses such as Ford Motor Company are corporations. Most large retailers such as Wal-Mart and Home Depot are also corporations.

## The Cost Concept

Under the **cost concept**, amounts are initially recorded in the accounting records at their cost or purchase price. To illustrate, assume that Aaron Publishers purchased the following building on February 20, 2010, for $150,000:

| | |
|---|---|
| Price listed by seller on January 1, 2010 | $160,000 |
| Aaron Publishers' initial offer to buy on January 31, 2010 | 140,000 |
| Purchase price on February 20, 2010 | 150,000 |
| Estimated selling price on December 31, 2012 | 220,000 |
| Assessed value for property taxes, December 31, 2012 | 190,000 |

Under the cost concept, Aaron Publishers records the purchase of the building on February 20, 2010, at the purchase price of $150,000. The other amounts listed above have no effect on the accounting records.

The fact that the building has an estimated selling price of $220,000 on December 31, 2012, indicates that the building has increased in value. However, to use the $220,000 in the accounting records would be to record an illusory or unrealized profit. If Aaron Publishers sells the building on January 9, 2014, for $240,000, a profit of $90,000 ($240,000 − $150,000) is then realized and recorded. The new owner would record $240,000 as its cost of the building.

The cost concept also involves the objectivity and unit of measure concepts. The **objectivity concept** requires that the amounts recorded in the accounting records be based on objective evidence. In exchanges between a buyer and a seller, both try to get the best price. Only the final agreed-upon amount is objective enough to be recorded in the accounting records. If amounts in the accounting records were constantly being revised upward or downward based on offers, appraisals, and opinions, accounting reports could become unstable and unreliable.

The **unit of measure concept** requires that economic data be recorded in dollars. Money is a common unit of measurement for reporting financial data and reports.

**Example Exercise** **1-1** **Cost Concept** **OBJ. 2**

On August 25, Gallatin Repair Service extended an offer of $125,000 for land that had been priced for sale at $150,000. On September 3, Gallatin Repair Service accepted the seller's counteroffer of $137,000. On October 20, the land was assessed at a value of $98,000 for property tax purposes. On December 4, Gallatin Repair Service was offered $160,000 for the land by a national retail chain. At what value should the land be recorded in Gallatin Repair Service's records?

**Follow My Example** **1-1**

$137,000. Under the cost concept, the land should be recorded at the cost to Gallatin Repair Service.

Practice Exercises: **PE 1-1A, PE 1-1B**

# The Accounting Equation

**OBJ. 3** State the accounting equation and define each element of the equation.

The resources owned by a business are its **assets**. Examples of assets include cash, land, buildings, and equipment. The rights or claims to the assets are divided into two types: (1) the rights of creditors and (2) the rights of owners. The rights of creditors are the debts of the business and are called **liabilities**. The rights of the owners are called **owner's equity**. The following equation shows the relationship among assets, liabilities, and owner's equity:

**Assets = Liabilities + Owner's Equity**

This equation is called the **accounting equation**. Liabilities usually are shown before owner's equity in the accounting equation because creditors have first rights to the assets.

Given any two amounts, the accounting equation may be solved for the third unknown amount. To illustrate, if the assets owned by a business amount to $100,000 and the liabilities amount to $30,000, the owner's equity is equal to $70,000, as shown below.

**Assets – Liabilities = Owner's Equity**
$$\$100{,}000 - \$30{,}000 = \$70{,}000$$

**Example Exercise** ▶ **1-2** ▶ Accounting Equation **OBJ. 3**

John Joos is the owner and operator of You're A Star, a motivational consulting business. At the end of its accounting period, December 31, 2011, You're A Star has assets of $800,000 and liabilities of $350,000. Using the accounting equation, determine the following amounts:

a. Owner's equity, as of December 31, 2011.
b. Owner's equity, as of December 31, 2012, assuming that assets increased by $130,000 and liabilities decreased by $25,000 during 2012.

**Follow My Example** ▶ **1-2** ▶

a.     Assets = Liabilities + Owner's Equity
   $800,000 = $350,000 + Owner's Equity
Owner's Equity = $450,000
b. First, determine the change in Owner's Equity during 2012 as follows:
     Assets = Liabilities + Owner's Equity
   $130,000 = –$25,000 + Owner's Equity
Owner's Equity = $155,000

Next, add the change in Owner's Equity on December 31, 2011, to arrive at Owner's Equity on December 31, 2012, as shown below.
Owner's Equity on December 31, 2012 = $605,000 = $450,000 + $155,000

Practice Exercises: **PE 1-2A, PE 1-2B**

# Business Transactions and the Accounting Equation

**OBJ. 4** Describe and illustrate how business transactions can be recorded in terms of the resulting change in the elements of the accounting equation.

Paying a monthly telephone bill of $168 affects a business's financial condition because it now has less cash on hand. Such an economic event or condition that directly changes an entity's financial condition or its results of operations is a **business transaction**. For example, purchasing land for $50,000 is a business transaction. In contrast, a change in a business's credit rating does not directly affect cash or any other asset, liability, or owner's equity amount.

# BusinessConnection

## THE ACCOUNTING EQUATION

The accounting equation serves as the basic foundation for the accounting systems of all companies. From the smallest business, such as the local convenience store, to the largest business, such as Ford Motor Company, companies use the accounting equation. Some examples taken from recent financial reports of well-known companies are shown below.

| Company | Assets* | = | Liabilities | + | Owner's Equity |
|---|---|---|---|---|---|
| The Coca-Cola Company | $ 40,519 | = | $20,047 | + | $20,472 |
| Dell, Inc. | 26,500 | = | 22,229 | + | 4,271 |
| eBay, Inc. | 15,593 | = | 4,509 | + | 11,084 |
| Google | 31,768 | = | 3,529 | + | 28,239 |
| McDonald's | 28,462 | = | 15,079 | + | 13,383 |
| Microsoft Corporation | 77,888 | = | 38,330 | + | 39,558 |
| Southwest Airlines Co. | 14,308 | = | 9,355 | + | 4,953 |
| Wal-Mart | 163,429 | = | 98,144 | + | 65,285 |

*Amounts are shown in millions of dollars.

**Note:**
**All business transactions can be stated in terms of changes in the elements of the accounting equation.**

All business transactions can be stated in terms of changes in the elements of the accounting equation. How business transactions affect the accounting equation can be illustrated by using some typical transactions. As a basis for illustration, a business organized by Chris Clark is used.

Assume that on November 1, 2011, Chris Clark organizes a corporation that will be known as NetSolutions. The first phase of Chris's business plan is to operate NetSolutions as a service business assisting individuals and small businesses in developing Web pages and installing computer software. Chris expects this initial phase of the business to last one to two years. During this period, Chris plans on gathering information on the software and hardware needs of customers. During the second phase of the business plan, Chris plans to expand NetSolutions into a personalized retailer of software and hardware for individuals and small businesses.

Each transaction during NetSolutions' first month of operations is described in the following paragraphs. The effect of each transaction on the accounting equation is then shown.

**Transaction A**  *Nov. 1, 2011  Chris Clark deposited $25,000 in a bank account in the name of NetSolutions in return for shares of stock in the corporation.*

Stock issued to owners (stockholders), such as Chris Clark, is referred to as **capital stock.** The owner's equity in a corporation is called **stockholders' equity.**

This transaction increases the asset (cash) on the left side of the equation by $25,000. To balance the equation, the stockholders' equity (capital stock) on the right side of the equation increases by the same amount.

The effect of this transaction on NetSolutions' accounting equation is shown below.

| **Assets** | = | **Stockholders' Equity** |
|---|---|---|
| Cash | = | Capital Stock |
| a. 25,000 | | 25,000 |

The accounting equation shown above is only for the business, NetSolutions. Under the business entity concept, Chris Clark's personal assets, such as a home or personal bank account, and personal liabilities are excluded from the equation.

**Transaction B**  *Nov. 5, 2011  NetSolutions paid $20,000 for the purchase of land as a future building site.*

The land is located in a business park with access to transportation facilities. Chris Clark plans to rent office space and equipment during the first phase of the business plan. During the second phase, Chris plans to build an office and a warehouse on the land.

The purchase of the land changes the makeup of the assets, but it does not change the total assets. The items in the equation prior to this transaction and the effect of the transaction are shown below. The new amounts are called *balances*.

| | Assets | | = | Stockholders' Equity |
|---|---|---|---|---|
| | Cash | + Land | = | Capital Stock |
| Bal. | 25,000 | | | 25,000 |
| b. | −20,000 | +20,000 | | |
| Bal. | 5,000 | 20,000 | | 25,000 |

**Nov. 10, 2011**   *NetSolutions purchased supplies for $1,350 and agreed to pay the supplier in the near future.*   **Transaction C**

You have probably used a credit card to buy clothing or other merchandise. In this type of transaction, you received clothing for a promise to pay your credit card bill in the future. That is, you received an asset and incurred a liability to pay a future bill. NetSolutions entered into a similar transaction by purchasing supplies for $1,350 and agreeing to pay the supplier in the near future. This type of transaction is called a purchase *on account* and is often described as follows: *Purchased supplies on account, $1,350.*

The liability created by a purchase on account is called an **account payable**. Items such as supplies that will be used in the business in the future are called **prepaid expenses**, which are assets. Thus, the effect of this transaction is to increase assets (Supplies) and liabilities (Accounts Payable) by $1,350, as follows:

| | Assets | | | = | Liabilities + Stockholders' Equity | |
|---|---|---|---|---|---|---|
| | Cash | + Supplies | + Land | = | Accounts Payable + | Capital Stock |
| Bal. | 5,000 | | 20,000 | | | 25,000 |
| c. | | +1,350 | | | +1,350 | |
| Bal. | 5,000 | 1,350 | 20,000 | | 1,350 | 25,000 |

**Nov. 18, 2011**   *NetSolutions received cash of $7,500 for providing services to customers.*   **Transaction D**

You may have earned money by painting houses or mowing lawns. If so, you received money for rendering services to a customer. Likewise, a business earns money by selling goods or services to its customers. This amount is called **revenue**.

During its first month of operations, NetSolutions received cash of $7,500 for providing services to customers. The receipt of cash increases NetSolutions' assets and also increases the stockholders' equity in the business. The revenues of $7,500 are recorded in a Fees Earned column to the right of Capital Stock. The effect of this transaction is to increase Cash and Fees Earned by $7,500, as shown below.

| | Assets | | | = | Liabilities + | Stockholders' Equity | |
|---|---|---|---|---|---|---|---|
| | Cash | + Supplies + | Land | = | Accounts Payable + | Capital Stock + | Fees Earned |
| Bal. | 5,000 | 1,350 | 20,000 | | 1,350 | 25,000 | |
| d. | +7,500 | | | | | | +7,500 |
| Bal. | 12,500 | 1,350 | 20,000 | | 1,350 | 25,000 | 7,500 |

Different terms are used for the various types of revenues. As illustrated above, revenue from providing services is recorded as **fees earned**. Revenue from the sale of merchandise is recorded as **sales**. Other examples of revenue include rent, which is recorded as **rent revenue**, and interest, which is recorded as **interest revenue**.

Instead of receiving cash at the time services are provided or goods are sold, a business may accept payment at a later date. Such revenues are described as *fees earned on account* or *sales on account*. For example, if NetSolutions had provided services on account instead of for cash, transaction (d) would have been described as follows: *Fees earned on account, $7,500.*

In such cases, the firm has an **account receivable**, which is a claim against the customer. An account receivable is an asset, and the revenue is earned and recorded as if cash had been received. When customers pay their accounts, Cash increases and Accounts Receivable decreases.

**Transaction E**  *Nov. 30, 2011*  *NetSolutions paid the following expenses during the month: wages, $2,125; rent, $800; utilities, $450; and miscellaneous, $275.*

During the month, NetSolutions spent cash or used up other assets in earning revenue. Assets used in this process of earning revenue are called **expenses**. Expenses include supplies used and payments for employee wages, utilities, and other services.

NetSolutions paid the following expenses during the month: wages, $2,125; rent, $800; utilities, $450; and miscellaneous, $275. Miscellaneous expenses include small amounts paid for such items as postage, coffee, and newspapers. The effect of expenses is the opposite of revenues in that expenses reduce assets and stockholders' equity. Like fees earned, the expenses are recorded in columns to the right of Capital Stock. However, since expenses reduce stockholders' equity, the expenses are entered as negative amounts. The effect of this transaction is shown below.

| Assets | | | = | Liabilities + | | Stockholders' Equity | | | | |
|---|---|---|---|---|---|---|---|---|---|---|
| Cash | + Supplies + | Land | = | Accounts + Payable | Capital + Stock | Fees – Earned | Wages – Exp. | Rent – Exp. | Utilities – Exp. | Misc. Exp. |
| Bal. 12,500 | 1,350 | 20,000 | | 1,350 | 25,000 | 7,500 | | | | |
| e. –3,650 | | | | | | | –2,125 | –800 | –450 | –275 |
| Bal. 8,850 | 1,350 | 20,000 | | 1,350 | 25,000 | 7,500 | –2,125 | –800 | –450 | –275 |

Businesses usually record each revenue and expense transaction as it occurs. However, to simplify, NetSolutions' revenues and expenses are summarized for the month in transactions (d) and (e).

**Transaction F**  *Nov. 30, 2011*  *NetSolutions paid creditors on account, $950.*

When you pay your monthly credit card bill, you decrease the cash in your checking account and decrease the amount you owe to the credit card company. Likewise, when NetSolutions pays $950 to creditors during the month, it reduces assets and liabilities, as shown below.

| Assets | | | = | Liabilities + | | Stockholders' Equity | | | | |
|---|---|---|---|---|---|---|---|---|---|---|
| Cash | + Supplies + | Land | = | Accounts + Payable | Capital + Stock | Fees – Earned | Wages – Exp. | Rent – Exp. | Utilities – Exp. | Misc. Exp. |
| Bal. 8,850 | 1,350 | 20,000 | | 1,350 | 25,000 | 7,500 | –2,125 | –800 | –450 | –275 |
| f. –950 | | | | –950 | | | | | | |
| Bal. 7,900 | 1,350 | 20,000 | | 400 | 25,000 | 7,500 | –2,125 | –800 | –450 | –275 |

Paying an amount on account is different from paying an expense. The paying of an expense reduces stockholders' equity, as illustrated in transaction (e). Paying an amount on account reduces the amount owed on a liability.

**Transaction G**  *Nov. 30, 2011*  *Chris Clark determined that the cost of supplies on hand at the end of the month was $550.*

The cost of the supplies on hand (not yet used) at the end of the month is $550. Thus, $800 ($1,350 − $550) of supplies must have been used during the month. This decrease in supplies is recorded as an expense, as shown below.

|  | **Assets** | | | = | **Liabilities +** | | **Stockholders' Equity** | | | | | | |
|---|---|---|---|---|---|---|---|---|---|---|---|---|---|
|  | Cash | + Supplies + | Land | | Accounts Payable | + Capital Stock | + Fees Earned | − Wages Exp. | − Rent Exp. | − Supplies Exp. | − Utilities Exp. | − Misc. Exp. |
| Bal. | 7,900 | 1,350 | 20,000 | = | 400 | 25,000 | 7,500 | −2,125 | −800 | | −450 | −275 |
| g. | | −800 | | | | | | | | −800 | | |
| Bal. | 7,900 | 550 | 20,000 | | 400 | 25,000 | 7,500 | −2,125 | −800 | −800 | −450 | −275 |

*Nov. 30, 2011   NetSolutions paid $2,000 to stockholders (Chris Clark) as dividends.*   **Transaction H**

**Dividends** are distributions of earnings to stockholders. The payment of dividends decreases cash and stockholders' equity. Like expenses, dividends are recorded in a separate column to the right of Capital Stock as a negative amount. The effect of the payment of dividends of $2,000 is shown below.

|  | **Assets** | | | = | **Liabilities +** | | | **Stockholders' Equity** | | | | | |
|---|---|---|---|---|---|---|---|---|---|---|---|---|---|
|  | Cash | + Supp. + | Land | | Accounts Payable | + Capital Stock | − Dividends + | Fees Earned | − Wages Exp. | − Rent Exp. | − Supplies Exp. | − Utilities Exp. | − Misc. Exp. |
| Bal. | 7,900 | 550 | 20,000 | = | 400 | 25,000 | | 7,500 | −2,125 | −800 | −800 | −450 | −275 |
| h. | −2,000 | | | | | | −2,000 | | | | | | |
| Bal. | 5,900 | 550 | 20,000 | | 400 | 25,000 | −2,000 | 7,500 | −2,125 | −800 | −800 | −450 | −275 |

Dividends should not be confused with expenses. Dividends do not represent assets or services used in the process of earning revenues. Instead, dividends are considered a distribution of earnings to stockholders.

**Summary** The transactions of NetSolutions are summarized below. Each transaction is identified by letter, and the balance of each accounting equation element is shown after every transaction.

|  | **Assets** | | | = | **Liabilities +** | | | **Stockholders' Equity** | | | | | |
|---|---|---|---|---|---|---|---|---|---|---|---|---|---|
|  | Cash | + Supp. + | Land | = | Accounts Payable + | Capital Stock | − Dividends + | Fees Earned − | Wages Exp. − | Rent Exp. − | Supplies Exp. − | Utilities Exp. − | Misc. Exp. |
| a. | +25,000 | | | | | +25,000 | | | | | | | |
| b. | −20,000 | | +20,000 | | | | | | | | | | |
| Bal. | 5,000 | | 20,000 | | | 25,000 | | | | | | | |
| c. | | +1,350 | | | +1,350 | | | | | | | | |
| Bal. | 5,000 | +1,350 | 20,000 | | +1,350 | 25,000 | | | | | | | |
| d. | +7,500 | | | | | | | +7,500 | | | | | |
| Bal. | 12,500 | 1,350 | 20,000 | | 1,350 | 25,000 | | 7,500 | | | | | |
| e. | −3,650 | | | | | | | | −2,125 | −800 | | −450 | −275 |
| Bal. | 8,850 | 1,350 | 20,000 | | 1,350 | 25,000 | | 7,500 | −2,125 | −800 | | −450 | −275 |
| f. | −950 | | | | −950 | | | | | | | | |
| Bal. | 7,900 | 1,350 | 20,000 | | 400 | 25,000 | | 7,500 | −2,125 | −800 | | −450 | −275 |
| g. | | −800 | | | | | | | | | −800 | | |
| Bal. | 7,900 | 550 | 20,000 | | 400 | 25,000 | | 7,500 | −2,125 | −800 | −800 | −450 | −275 |
| h. | −2,000 | | | | | | −2,000 | | | | | | |
| Bal. | 5,900 | 550 | 20,000 | | 400 | 25,000 | −2,000 | 7,500 | −2,125 | −800 | −800 | −450 | −275 |

You should note the following:

1. The effect of every transaction *is an increase or a decrease in one or more of the accounting equation elements.*
2. The two sides of the accounting equation are *always equal.*
3. The stockholders' equity (owner's equity) is *increased by amounts invested by stockholders (capital stock).*

4. The stockholders' equity (owner's equity) is *increased by revenues and decreased by expenses*.
5. The stockholders' equity (owner's equity) is *decreased by dividends paid to stockholders*.

As discussed earlier, the owner's equity in a corporation is called stockholders' equity. Stockholders' equity is classified as:

1. Capital Stock
2. Retained Earnings.

Capital stock is shares of ownership distributed to investors in a corporation. It represents the portion of stockholders' equity contributed by investors. For NetSolutions, shares of capital stock of $25,000 were distributed to Chris Clark in return for investing in the business.

**Retained earnings** is the stockholders' equity created from business operations through revenue and expense transactions. For NetSolutions, retained earnings of $3,050 were created by its November operations (revenue and expense transactions), as shown below.

**NetSolutions**
**Retained Earnings**
**November Operations**
**(Revenue and Expense Transactions)**

|  | Fees Earned | − | Wages Exp. | − | Rent Exp. | − | Supplies Exp. | − | Utilities Exp. | − | Misc. Exp. |
|---|---|---|---|---|---|---|---|---|---|---|---|
| Trans, d. | +7,500 | | | | | | | | | | |
| Trans, e. | | | −2,125 | | −800 | | | | −450 | | −275 |
| Trans, g. | | | | | | | −800 | | | | |
| Balance, Nov. 30 | 7,500 | | −2,125 | | −800 | | −800 | | −450 | | −275 |

$3,050

Stockholders' equity created by investments by stockholders (capital stock) and by business operations (retained earnings) are reported separately. Since dividends are distributions of earnings to stockholders, dividends reduce retained earnings.

The effects of investments by stockholders, dividends, revenues, and expenses on stockholders' equity are illustrated in Exhibit 5.

**EXHIBIT 5**

**Types of Transactions Affecting Stockholders' Equity**

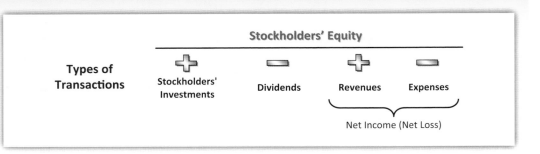

**Example Exercise** ▶ **1-3** ▶ **Transactions**    OBJ. 4

Salvo Delivery Service is owned and operated by Joel Salvo. The following selected transactions were completed by Salvo Delivery Service during February:

1. Received cash from owner as additional investment in exchange for capital stock, $35,000.
2. Paid creditors on account, $1,800.
3. Billed customers for delivery services on account, $11,250.

*(Continued)*

4. Received cash from customers on account, $6,740.
5. Paid dividends, $1,000.

Indicate the effect of each transaction on the accounting equation elements (Assets, Liabilities, Stockholders' Equity, Dividends, Revenue, and Expense). Also, indicate the specific item within the accounting equation element that is affected. To illustrate, the answer to (1) is shown below.

(1) Asset (Cash) increases by $35,000; Stockholders' Equity (Capital Stock) increases by $35,000.

**Follow My Example** ▷ **1-3** ▷

(2) Asset (Cash) decreases by $1,800; Liability (Accounts Payable) decreases by $1,800.
(3) Asset (Accounts Receivable) increases by $11,250; Revenue (Delivery Service Fees) increases by $11,250.
(4) Asset (Cash) increases by $6,740; Asset (Accounts Receivable) decreases by $6,740.
(5) Asset (Cash) decreases by $1,000; Dividends increases by $1,000.

Practice Exercises: **PE 1-3A, PE 1-3B**

# Financial Statements

**OBJ. 5** Describe the financial statements of a corporation and explain how they interrelate.

After transactions have been recorded and summarized, reports are prepared for users. The accounting reports providing this information are called **financial statements**. The primary financial statements of a corporation are the income statement, the retained earnings statement, the balance sheet, and the statement of cash flows. The order that the financial statements are prepared and the nature of each statement is described as follows.

| Order Prepared | Financial Statement | Description of Statement |
|---|---|---|
| 1. | **Income statement** | A summary of the revenue and expenses *for a specific period of time*, such as a month or a year. |
| 2. | **Retained earnings statement** | A summary of the changes in retained earnings that have occurred *during a specific period of time*, such as a month or a year. |
| 3. | **Balance sheet** | A list of the assets, liabilities, and stockholders' equity *as of a specific date*, usually at the close of the last day of a month or a year. |
| 4. | **Statement of cash flows** | A summary of the cash receipts and cash payments for a *specific period of time*, such as a month or a year. |

The four financial statements and their interrelationships are illustrated in Exhibit 6, on page 18. The data for the statements are taken from the summary of transactions of NetSolutions on page 13.

All financial statements are identified by the name of the business, the title of the statement, and the *date* or *period of time*. The data presented in the income statement, the retained earnings statement, and the statement of cash flows are for a period of time. The data presented in the balance sheet are for a specific date.

## Income Statement

The income statement reports the revenues and expenses for a period of time, based on the **matching concept**. This concept is applied by *matching* the expenses incurred during a period with the revenue that those expenses generated. The excess of the revenue over the expenses is called **net income**, net profit, or **earnings**. If the expenses exceed the revenue, the excess is a **net loss**.

The revenue and expenses for NetSolutions were shown in the equation as separate increases and decreases. Net income for a period increases the stockholders' equity (retained earnings) for the period. A net loss decreases the stockholders' equity (retained earnings) for the period.

**Note:**
When revenues exceed expenses, it is referred to as *net income, net profits,* or *earnings.* When expenses exceed revenues, it is referred to as *net loss.*

The revenue, expenses, and the net income of $3,050 for NetSolutions are reported in the income statement in Exhibit 6, on page 18. The order in which the expenses are listed in the income statement varies among businesses. Most businesses list expenses in order of size, beginning with the larger items. Miscellaneous expense is usually shown as the last item, regardless of the amount.

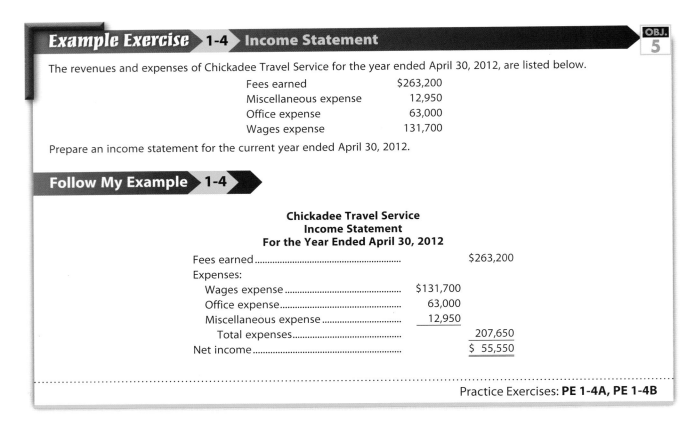

**Example Exercise** **1-4** **Income Statement**

OBJ. 5

The revenues and expenses of Chickadee Travel Service for the year ended April 30, 2012, are listed below.

| | |
|---|---|
| Fees earned | $263,200 |
| Miscellaneous expense | 12,950 |
| Office expense | 63,000 |
| Wages expense | 131,700 |

Prepare an income statement for the current year ended April 30, 2012.

**Follow My Example** **1-4**

**Chickadee Travel Service**
**Income Statement**
**For the Year Ended April 30, 2012**

| | | |
|---|---|---|
| Fees earned | | $263,200 |
| Expenses: | | |
| Wages expense | $131,700 | |
| Office expense | 63,000 | |
| Miscellaneous expense | 12,950 | |
| Total expenses | | 207,650 |
| Net income | | $ 55,550 |

Practice Exercises: **PE 1-4A, PE 1-4B**

## Retained Earnings Statement

The retained earnings statement reports the changes in the retained earnings for a period of time. It is prepared *after* the income statement because the net income or net loss for the period must be reported in this statement. Similarly, it is prepared *before* the balance sheet, since the amount of retained earnings at the end of the period must be reported on the balance sheet. Because of this, the retained earnings statement is often viewed as the connecting link between the income statement and balance sheet.

The following two types of transactions affected NetSolutions' retained earnings during November:

1. Revenues and expenses, which resulted in net income of $3,050.
2. Dividends of $2,000 paid to stockholders (Chris Clark).

These transactions are summarized in the retained earnings statement for NetSolutions shown in Exhibit 6.

Since NetSolutions has been in operation for only one month, it has no retained earnings at the beginning of November. For December, however, there is a beginning balance—the balance at the end of November. This balance of $1,050 is reported on the retained earnings statement.

To illustrate, assume that NetSolutions earned net income of $4,155 and paid dividends of $2,000 during December. The retained earnings statement for NetSolutions for December is shown at the top of the next page.

**NetSolutions**
**Retained Earnings Statement**
**For the Month Ended December 31, 2011**

| | | |
|---|---:|---:|
| Retained earnings, December 1, 2011 | | $1,050 |
| Net income for November | $4,155 | |
| Less dividends | 2,000 | |
| Increase in retained earnings | | 2,155 |
| Retained earnings, December 31, 2011 | | $3,205 |

---

## Example Exercise  1-5  Retained Earnings Statement    OBJ. 5

Using the income statement for Chickadee Travel Service shown in Example Exercise 1-4, prepare a retained earnings statement for the year ended April 30, 2012. Adam Cellini, the owner, invested an additional $50,000 in the business in exchange for capital stock, and dividends of $30,000 were paid during the year. Retained earnings were $30,000 on May 1, 2011, the beginning of the current year.

### Follow My Example  1-5

**Chickadee Travel Service**
**Retained Earnings Statement**
**For the Year Ended April 30, 2012**

| | | |
|---|---:|---:|
| Retained earnings, May 1, 2011 | | $30,000 |
| Net income for the year | $55,550 | |
| Less dividends | 30,000 | |
| Increase in retained earnings | | 25,550 |
| Retained earnings, April 30, 2012 | | $55,550 |

Practice Exercises: **PE 1-5A, PE 1-5B**

## Balance Sheet

The balance sheet in Exhibit 6 reports the amounts of NetSolutions' assets, liabilities, and stockholders' equity as of November 30, 2011. The asset and liability amounts are taken from the last line of the summary of transactions on page 13. Retained earnings as of November 30, 2011, is taken from the retained earnings statement. The form of balance sheet shown in Exhibit 6 is called the **account form**. This is because it resembles the basic format of the accounting equation, with assets on the left side and the liabilities and stockholders' equity sections on the right side.[3]

The assets section of the balance sheet presents assets in the order that they will be converted into cash or used in operations. Cash is presented first, followed by receivables, supplies, prepaid insurance, and other assets. The assets of a more permanent nature are shown next, such as land, buildings, and equipment.

In the liabilities section of the balance sheet in Exhibit 6, accounts payable is the only liability. When there are two or more liabilities, each should be listed and the total amount of liabilities presented as follows:

Bank loan officers use a business's financial statements in deciding whether to grant a loan to the business. Once the loan is granted, the borrower may be required to maintain a certain level of assets in excess of liabilities. The business's financial statements are used to monitor this level.

| **Liabilities** | | |
|---|---:|---:|
| Accounts payable | $12,900 | |
| Wages payable | 2,570 | |
| Total liabilities | | $15,470 |

---

3 An alternative form of balance sheet, called the *report form,* is illustrated in Chapter 5. It presents the liabilities and stockholders' equity sections below the assets section.

**EXHIBIT 6**

**Financial Statements for NetSolutions**

### NetSolutions
### Income Statement
### For the Month Ended November 30, 2011

| | | |
|---|---:|---:|
| Fees earned ..................................................... | | $7,500 |
| Expenses: | | |
| Wages expense..................................................... | $2,125 | |
| Rent expense ..................................................... | 800 | |
| Supplies expense..................................................... | 800 | |
| Utilities expense..................................................... | 450 | |
| Miscellaneous expense .......................................... | 275 | |
| Total expense ................................................. | | 4,450 |
| Net income..................................................... | | $3,050 |

### NetSolutions
### Retained Earnings Statement
### For the Month Ended November 30, 2011

| | | |
|---|---:|---:|
| Retained earnings, November 1, 2011 ............................ | | $ 0 |
| Net income for November ......................................... | $3,050 | |
| Less dividends..................................................... | 2,000 | |
| Increase in retained earnings ....................................... | | 1,050 |
| Retained earnings, November 30, 2011 ............................ | | $1,050 |

### NetSolutions
### Balance Sheet
### November 30, 2011

| **Assets** | | **Liabilities** | |
|---|---:|---|---:|
| Cash ................. | $ 5,900 | Accounts payable ..................... | $ 400 |
| Supplies.............. | 550 | **Stockholders' Equity** | |
| Land ................. | 20,000 | Capital stock.......................... | $25,000 |
| | | Retained earnings..................... | 1,050 |
| | | Total stockholders' equity .............. | $26,050 |
| | | Total liabilities and | |
| Total assets ........... | $ 26,450 | stockholders' equity ................. | $ 26,450 |

### NetSolutions
### Statement of Cash Flows
### For the Month Ended November 30, 2011

| | | |
|---|---:|---:|
| Cash flows from operating activities: | | |
| Cash received from customers.................................... | $ 7,500 | |
| Deduct cash payments for expenses and payments | | |
| to creditors ................................................. | 4,600 | |
| Net cash flow from operating activities......................... | | $ 2,900 |
| Cash flows from investing activities: | | |
| Cash payments for purchase of land ............................ | | (20,000) |
| Cash flows from financing activities: | | |
| Cash received from issuing stock .............................. | $ 25,000 | |
| Deduct cash dividends.......................................... | 2,000 | |
| Net cash flow from financing activities ......................... | | 23,000 |
| Net cash flow and November 30, 2011, cash balance................. | | $ 5,900 |

**Example Exercise** 1-6 **Balance Sheet**

OBJ.
5

Using the following data for Chickadee Travel Service as well as the retained earnings statement shown in Example Exercise 1-5, prepare a balance sheet as of April 30, 2012.

| | |
|---|---|
| Accounts receivable | $ 31,350 |
| Capital stock | 100,000 |
| Accounts payable | 12,200 |
| Cash | 53,050 |
| Land | 80,000 |
| Supplies | 3,350 |

**Follow My Example** 1-6

**Chickadee Travel Service**
**Balance Sheet**
**April 30, 2012**

| Assets | | Liabilities | | |
|---|---|---|---|---|
| Cash.......................... | $ 53,050 | Accounts payable.................... | | $ 12,200 |
| Accounts receivable ........... | 31,350 | **Stockholders' Equity** | | |
| Supplies ...................... | 3,350 | Capital stock........................ | $100,000 | |
| Land.......................... | 80,000 | Retained earnings ................... | 55,550 | |
| | | Total stockholders' equity............ | | 155,550 |
| Total assets.................... | $167,750 | Total liabilities and stockholders' equity.............. | | $167,750 |

Practice Exercises: **PE 1-6A, PE 1-6B**

## Statement of Cash Flows

The statement of cash flows consists of the following three sections, as shown in Exhibit 6:

1. operating activities,
2. investing activities, and
3. financing activities.

Each of these sections is briefly described below.

**Cash Flows from Operating Activities** This section reports a summary of cash receipts and cash payments from operations. The net cash flow from operating activities normally differs from the amount of net income for the period. In Exhibit 6, NetSolutions reported net cash flows from operating activities of $2,900 and net income of $3,050. This difference occurs because revenues and expenses may not be recorded at the same time that cash is received from customers or paid to creditors.

**Cash Flows from Investing Activities** This section reports the cash transactions for the acquisition and sale of relatively permanent assets. Exhibit 6 reports that NetSolutions paid $20,000 for the purchase of land during November.

**Cash Flows from Financing Activities** This section reports the cash transactions related to cash investments by the stockholders, borrowings, and cash dividends. Exhibit 6 shows that Chris Clark invested $25,000 in the business in exchange for capital stock and dividends of $2,000 were paid during November.

Preparing the statement of cash flows requires that each of the November cash transactions for NetSolutions be classified as an operating, investing, or financing activity. Using the summary of transactions shown on page 13, the November cash transactions for NetSolutions are classified as shown at the top of the next page.

| Transaction | Amount | Cash Flow Activity |
|---|---|---|
| a. | $ 25,000 | Financing (Issuance of capital stock) |
| b. | −20,000 | Investing (Purchase of land) |
| d. | 7,500 | Operating (Fees earned) |
| e. | −3,650 | Operating (Payment of expenses) |
| f. | −950 | Operating (Payment of account payable) |
| h. | −2,000 | Financing (Payment of cash dividends) |

Transactions (c) and (g) are not listed above since they did not involve a cash receipt or payment. In addition, the payment of accounts payable in transaction (f) is classified as an operating activity since the account payable arose from the purchase of supplies, which are used in operations. Using the preceding classifications of November cash transactions, the statement of cash flows is prepared as shown in Exhibit 6.[4]

The ending cash balance shown on the statement of cash flows is also reported on the balance sheet as of the end of the period. To illustrate, the ending cash of $5,900 reported on the November statement of cash flows in Exhibit 6 is also reported as the amount of cash on hand in the November 30, 2011, balance sheet.

## Example Exercise 1-7 Statement of Cash Flows

**OBJ. 3**

A summary of cash flows for Chickadee Travel Service for the year ended April 30, 2012, is shown below.

Cash receipts:
Cash received from customers .............................................. $251,000
Cash received from issuing capital stock................................... 50,000

Cash payments:
Cash paid for expenses ................................................. 210,000
Cash paid for land ..................................................... 80,000
Cash paid for dividends................................................. 30,000

The cash balance as of May 1, 2011, was $72,050. Prepare a statement of cash flows for Chickadee Travel Service for the year ended April 30, 2012.

## Follow My Example 1-7

**Chickadee Travel Service**
**Statement of Cash Flows**
**For the Year Ended April 30, 2012**

| | | |
|---|---|---|
| Cash flows from operating activities: | | |
| Cash received from customers ............................. | $251,000 | |
| Deduct cash payments for expenses ....................... | 210,000 | |
| Net cash flows from operating activities.................... | | $ 41,000 |
| Cash flows from investing activities: | | |
| Cash payments for purchase of land ....................... | | (80,000) |
| Cash flows from financing activities: | | |
| Cash received issuing capital stock........................ | $ 50,000 | |
| Deduct cash dividends..................................... | 30,000 | |
| Net cash flows from financing activities .................... | | 20,000 |
| Net decrease in cash during year ............................. | | $(19,000) |
| Cash as of May 1, 2011 ....................................... | | 72,050 |
| Cash as of April 30, 2012 ..................................... | | $ 53,050 |

Practice Exercises: **PE 1-7A, PE 1-7B**

4 This method of preparing the statement of cash flows is called the "direct method." This method and the indirect method are discussed further in Chapter 14.

Since November is NetSolutions' first period of operations, the net cash flow for November and the November 30, 2011, cash balance are the same amount, $5,900, as shown in Exhibit 6. In later periods, NetSolutions will report in its statement of cash flows a beginning cash balance, an increase or a decrease in cash for the period, and an ending cash balance. For example, assume that for December NetSolutions has a decrease in cash of $3,835. The last three lines of NetSolutions' statement of cash flows for December would be as follows:

| | |
|---|---|
| Decrease in cash | $3,835 |
| Cash as of December 1, 2011 | 5,900 |
| Cash as of December 31, 2011 | $2,065 |

## Interrelationships Among Financial Statements

Financial statements are prepared in the order of the income statement, retained earnings statement, balance sheet, and statement of cash flows. This order is important because the financial statements are interrelated. These interrelationships for NetSolutions are shown in Exhibit 6 and are described below.[5]

| Financial Statements | Interrelationship | NetSolutions Example (Exhibit 6) |
|---|---|---|
| Income Statement *and* Retained Earnings Statement | Net income or net loss reported on the income statement is also reported on the retained earnings statement as either an addition (net income) to or deduction (net loss) from the beginning retained earnings. | NetSolutions' net income of $3,050 for November is added to the beginning retained earnings on November 1, 2011, in the retained earnings statement. |
| Retained Earnings Statement *and* Balance Sheet | Retained earnings at the end of the period reported on the retained earnings statement is also reported on the balance sheet as retained earnings. | NetSolutions' retained earnings of $1,050 as of November 30, 2011, on the retained earnings statement also appears on the November 30, 2011, balance sheet as retained earnings. |
| Balance Sheet *and* Statement of Cash Flows | The cash reported on the balance sheet is also reported as the end-of-period cash on the statement of cash flows. | Cash of $5,900 reported on the balance sheet as of November 30, 2011, is also reported on the November statement of cash flows as the end-of-period cash. |

The preceding interrelationships are important in analyzing financial statements and the impact of transactions on a business. In addition, these interrelationships serve as a check on whether the financial statements are prepared correctly. For example, if the ending cash on the statement of cash flows doesn't agree with the balance sheet cash, then an error has occurred.

# Financial Analysis and Interpretation: Ratio of Liabilities to Stockholders' Equity

**OBJ. 6** Describe and illustrate the use of the ratio of liabilities to stockholders' equity in evaluating a company's financial condition.

The basic financial statements illustrated in this chapter are useful to bankers, creditors, owners, and others in analyzing and interpreting the financial performance and condition of a company. Throughout this text, various tools and techniques that are often used to analyze and interpret a company's financial performance and condition are described and illustrated. The first such tool that is discussed is useful in analyzing the ability of a company to pay its creditors.

5 Depending on the method of preparing the cash flows from operating activities section of the statement of cash flows, net income (or net loss) may also appear on the statement of cash flows. This interrelationship or method of preparing the statement of cash flows, called the "indirect method," is described and illustrated in Chapter 14.

The relationship between liabilities and owner's equity, expressed as a **ratio of liabilities to stockholders' equity**, is computed as follows:

$$\text{Ratio of Liabilities to Stockholders' Equity} = \frac{\text{Total Liabilities}}{\text{Total Stockholders' Equity}}$$

NetSolutions' ratio of liabilities to stockholders' equity at the end of November is 0.015, as computed below.

$$\text{Ratio of Liabilities to Stockholders' Equity} = \frac{\$400}{\$26,050} = 0.015$$

To illustrate, balance sheet data (in millions) for Google Inc. and McDonald's Corporation are shown below.

|  | Dec. 31, 2009 | Dec. 31, 2008 |
|---|---|---|
| **Google Inc.** |  |  |
| Total liabilities | $ 3,529 | $ 2,646 |
| Total stockholders' equity | 28,239 | 22,690 |
|  |  |  |
| **McDonald's Corporation** |  |  |
| Total liabilities | $15,079 | $14,112 |
| Total stockholders' equity | 13,383 | 15,280 |

The ratio of liabilities to stockholders' equity as of December 31, 2009 and 2008 for Google and McDonald's is computed below.

|  | Dec. 31, 2009 | Dec. 31, 2008 |
|---|---|---|
| **Google Inc.** |  |  |
| Total liabilities | $ 3,529 | $ 2,646 |
| Total stockholders' equity | 28,239 | 22,690 |
| Ratio of liabilities to stockholders' equity | 0.12 | 0.12 |
|  | ($3,529/$28,239) | ($2,646/$22,690) |
| **McDonald's Corporation** |  |  |
| Total liabilities | $15,079 | $14,112 |
| Total stockholders' equity | 13,383 | 15,280 |
| Ratio of liabilities to stockholders' equity | 1.13 | 0.92 |
|  | ($15,079/$13,383) | ($14,112/$15,280) |

The rights of creditors to a business's assets come before the rights of the owners or stockholders. Thus, the lower the ratio of liabilities to stockholders' equity, the better able the company is to withstand poor business conditions and pay its obligations to creditors.

Google is unusual in that it has a very low amount of liabilities; thus, its ratio of liabilities to stockholders' equity of 0.12 is small. In contrast, McDonald's has more liabilities; its ratio of liabilities to stockholders' equity is 1.13 and 0.92 on December 31, 2009 and 2008, respectively. Since McDonald's ratio of liabilities to stockholders' equity increased slightly from 2008 to 2009, its creditors are slightly more at risk on December 31, 2009, as compared to December 31, 2008. Also, McDonald's creditors are more at risk than are Google's creditors. The creditors of both companies are, however, well protected against the risk of nonpayment.

## Example Exercise 1-8 Ratio of Liabilities to Stockholders' Equity OBJ. 6

The following data were taken from Hawthorne Company's balance sheet:

|  | Dec. 31, 2012 | Dec. 31, 2011 |
| --- | --- | --- |
| Total liabilities | $120,000 | $105,000 |
| Total stockholders' equity | 80,000 | 75,000 |

a. Compute the ratio of liabilities to stockholders' equity.
b. Has the creditors' risk increased or decreased from December 31, 2011, to December 31, 2012?

### Follow My Example 1-8

a.

|  | Dec. 31, 2012 | Dec. 31, 2011 |
| --- | --- | --- |
| Total liabilities | $120,000 | $105,000 |
| Total stockholders' equity | 80,000 | 75,000 |
| Ratio of liabilities to stockholders' equity | 1.50 | 1.40 |
|  | ($120,000/$80,000) | ($105,000/$75,000) |

b. Increased

Practice Exercises: **PE 1-8A, PE 1-8B**

## At a Glance 1

### OBJ. 1 Describe the nature of a business, the role of accounting, and ethics in business.

**Key Points**   A business provides goods or services (outputs) to customers with the objective of earning a profit. Three types of businesses include service, merchandising, and manufacturing businesses.

Accounting is an information system that provides reports to users about the economic activities and condition of a business.

Ethics are moral principles that guide the conduct of individuals. Good ethical conduct depends on individual character and firm culture.

Accountants are engaged in private accounting or public accounting.

| Learning Outcomes | Example Exercises | Practice Exercises |
| --- | --- | --- |
| • Distinguish among service, merchandising, and manufacturing businesses. | | |
| • Describe the role of accounting in business and explain why accounting is called the "language of business." | | |
| • Define ethics and list the two factors affecting ethical conduct. | | |
| • Describe what private and public accounting means. | | |

**OBJ. 2**

## Summarize the development of accounting principles and relate them to practice.

**Key Points** Generally accepted accounting principles (GAAP) are used in preparing financial statements. Accounting principles and concepts develop from research, practice, and pronouncements of authoritative bodies.

The business entity concept views the business as an entity separate from its owners, creditors, or other businesses. Businesses may be organized as proprietorships, partnerships, corporations, and limited liability companies. The cost concept requires that purchases of a business be recorded in terms of actual cost. The objectivity concept requires that the accounting records and reports be based on objective evidence. The unit of measure concept requires that economic data be recorded in dollars.

| Learning Outcomes | Example Exercises | Practice Exercises |
|---|---|---|
| • Explain what is meant by generally accepted accounting principles. | | |
| • Describe how generally accepted accounting principles are developed. | | |
| • Describe and give an example of what is meant by the business entity concept. | | |
| • Describe the characteristics of a proprietorship, partnership, corporation, and limited liability company. | | |
| • Describe and give an example of what is meant by the cost concept. | EE1-1 | PE1-1A, 1-1B |
| • Describe and give an example of what is meant by the objectivity concept. | | |
| • Describe and give an example of what is meant by the unit of measure concept. | | |

**OBJ. 3**

## State the accounting equation and define each element of the equation.

**Key Points** The resources owned by a business and the rights or claims to these resources may be stated in the form of an equation, as follows:

Assets = Liabilities + Owner's Equity

| Learning Outcomes | Example Exercises | Practice Exercises |
|---|---|---|
| • State the accounting equation. | | |
| • Define assets, liabilities, and owner's equity. | | |
| • Given two elements of the accounting equation, solve for the third element. | EE1-2 | PE1-2A, 1-2B |

**OBJ. 4**

## Describe and illustrate how business transactions can be recorded in terms of the resulting change in the elements of the accounting equation.

**Key Points** All business transactions can be stated in terms of the change in one or more of the three elements of the accounting equation.

| Learning Outcomes | Example Exercises | Practice Exercises |
|---|---|---|
| • Define a business transaction. | | |
| • Using the accounting equation as a framework, record transactions. | EE1-3 | PE1-3A, 1-3B |

## 5 Describe the financial statements of a corporation and explain how they interrelate.

**Key Points**   The primary financial statements of a corporation are the income statement, the retained earnings statement, the balance sheet, and the statement of cash flows. The income statement reports a period's net income or net loss, which is also reported on the retained earnings statement. The ending retained earnings reported on the retained earnings statement is also reported on the balance sheet. The ending cash balance is reported on the balance sheet and the statement of cash flows.

| Learning Outcomes | Example Exercises | Practice Exercises |
|---|---|---|
| • List and describe the financial statements of a corporation. | | |
| • Prepare an income statement. | EE1-4 | PE1-4A, 1-4B |
| • Prepare a retained earnings statement. | EE1-5 | PE1-5A, 1-5B |
| • Prepare a balance sheet. | EE1-6 | PE1-6A, 1-6B |
| • Prepare a statement of cash flows. | EE1-7 | PE1-7A, 1-7B |
| • Explain how the financial statements of a corporation are interrelated. | | |

## 6 Describe and illustrate the use of the ratio of liabilities to stockholders' equity in evaluating a company's financial condition.

**Key Points**   A ratio useful in analyzing the ability of a business to pay its creditors is the ratio of liabilities to stockholders' equity. The lower the ratio of liabilities to stockholders' equity, the better able the company is to withstand poor business conditions and pay its obligations to creditors.

| Learning Outcomes | Example Exercises | Practice Exercises |
|---|---|---|
| • Describe the usefulness of the ratio of liabilities to stockholders' equity. | | |
| • Compute the ratio of liabilities to stockholders' equity. | EE1-8 | PE1-8A, 1-8B |

# Key Terms

account form (17)
account payable (11)
account receivable (12)
accounting (3)
accounting equation (9)
assets (9)
balance sheet (15)
business (2)
business entity concept (7)
business transaction (9)
capital stock (10)
Certified Public Accountant (CPA) (6)
corporation (8)

cost concept (8)
dividends (13)
earnings (15)
ethics (4)
expenses (12)
fees earned (11)
financial accounting (3)
Financial Accounting Standards Board (FASB) (7)
financial statements (15)
general-purpose financial statements (4)
generally accepted accounting principles (GAAP) (6)

income statement (15)
interest revenue (11)
International Accounting Standards Board (IASB) (7)
liabilities (9)
limited liability company (LLC) (8)
management (or managerial) accounting (3)
manufacturing business (2)
matching concept (15)
merchandising business (2)
net income (or net profit) (15)
net loss (15)

objectivity concept (8)

owner's equity (9)

partnership (7)

prepaid expenses (11)

private accounting (3)

profit (2)

proprietorship (7)

public accounting (6)

ratio of liabilities to
    stockholders' equity (22)

rent revenue (11)

retained earnings (14)

retained earnings statement (15)

revenue (11)

sales (11)

Securities and Exchange
    Commission (SEC) (7)

service business (2)

statement of cash flows (15)

stockholders' equity (10)

unit of measure concept (8)

## Illustrative Problem

Cecil Jameson, Attorney-at-Law, P.C. is organized as a professional corporation owned and operated by Cecil Jameson. On July 1, 2011, Cecil Jameson, Attorney-at-Law, has the following assets, liabilities, and capital stock: cash, $1,000; accounts receivable, $3,200; supplies, $850; land, $10,000; accounts payable, $1,530; capital stock, $10,000. Office space and office equipment are currently being rented, pending the construction of an office complex on land purchased last year. Business transactions during July are summarized as follows:

a. Received cash from clients for services, $3,928.

b. Paid creditors on account, $1,055.

c. Received cash from Cecil Jameson as an additional investment, in exchange for capital stock, $3,700.

d. Paid office rent for the month, $1,200.

e. Charged clients for legal services on account, $2,025.

f. Purchased supplies on account, $245.

g. Received cash from clients on account, $3,000.

h. Received invoice for paralegal services from Legal Aid Inc. for July (to be paid on August 10), $1,635.

i. Paid the following: wages expense, $850; answering service expense, $250; utilities expense, $325; and miscellaneous expense, $75.

j. Determined that the cost of supplies on hand was $980; therefore, the cost of supplies used during the month was $115.

k. Paid dividends, $1,000.

### Instructions

1. Determine the amount of retained earnings as of July 1, 2011.

2. State the assets, liabilities, and stockholders' equity as of July 1 in equation form similar to that shown in this chapter. In tabular form below the equation, indicate the increases and decreases resulting from each transaction and the new balances after each transaction.

3. Prepare an income statement for July, a retained earnings statement for July, and a balance sheet as of July 31, 2011.

4. (Optional). Prepare a statement of cash flows for July.

### Solution

1.

$$\text{Assets} - \text{Liabilities} = \text{Stockholders' Equity}$$
$$(\$1,000 + \$3,200 + \$850 + \$10,000) - \$1,530 = \text{Capital Stock} + \text{Retained Earnings}$$
$$\$15,050 - \$1,530 = \$10,000 + \text{Retained Earnings}$$
$$\$3,520 = \text{Retained Earnings}$$

**2.**

|  | **Assets** | | | | = **Liabilities +** | | **Stockholders' Equity** | | | | | | | | | |
|---|---|---|---|---|---|---|---|---|---|---|---|---|---|---|---|---|
|  | Cash + | Accts. Rec. + | Supp. + | Land = | Accts. Pay. + | Capital Stock + | Retained Earnings – | Dividends + | Fees Earned – | Paralegal Exp. – | Rent Exp. – | Wages Exp. – | Utilities Exp. – | Answering Service Exp. – | Supp. Exp. – | Misc. Exp. |
| Bal. | 1,000 | 3,200 | 850 | 10,000 | 1,530 | 10,000 | 3,520 | | | | | | | | | |
| a. | +3,928 | | | | | | | | 3,928 | | | | | | | |
| Bal. | 4,928 | 3,200 | 850 | 10,000 | 1,530 | 10,000 | | | 3,928 | | | | | | | |
| b. | –1,055 | | | | –1,055 | | | | | | | | | | | |
| Bal. | 3,873 | 3,200 | 850 | 10,000 | 475 | 10,000 | | | 3,928 | | | | | | | |
| c. | +3,700 | | | | | +3,700 | | | | | | | | | | |
| Bal. | 7,573 | 3,200 | 850 | 10,000 | 475 | 13,700 | | | 3,928 | | | | | | | |
| d. | –1,200 | | | | | | | | | | –1,200 | | | | | |
| Bal. | 6,373 | 3,200 | 850 | 10,000 | 475 | 13,700 | | | 3,928 | | –1,200 | | | | | |
| e. | | + 2,025 | | | | | | | + 2,025 | | | | | | | |
| Bal. | 6,373 | 5,225 | 850 | 10,000 | 475 | 13,700 | | | 5,953 | | –1,200 | | | | | |
| f. | | | +245 | | +245 | | | | | | | | | | | |
| Bal. | 6,373 | 5,225 | 1,095 | 10,000 | 720 | 13,700 | | | 5,953 | | –1,200 | | | | | |
| g. | +3,000 | –3,000 | | | | | | | | | | | | | | |
| Bal. | 9,373 | 2,225 | 1,095 | 10,000 | 720 | 13,700 | | | 5,953 | | –1,200 | | | | | |
| h. | | | | | +1,635 | | | | | –1,635 | | | | | | |
| Bal. | 9,373 | 2,225 | 1,095 | 10,000 | 2,355 | 13,700 | | | 5,953 | –1,635 | –1,200 | | | | | |
| i. | –1,500 | | | | | | | | | | | –850 | –325 | –250 | | –75 |
| Bal. | 7,873 | 2,225 | 1,095 | 10,000 | 2,355 | 13,700 | | | 5,953 | –1,635 | –1,200 | –850 | –325 | –250 | | –75 |
| j. | | | –115 | | | | | | | | | | | | –115 | |
| Bal. | 7,873 | 2,225 | 980 | 10,000 | 2,355 | 13,700 | | | 5,953 | –1,635 | –1,200 | –850 | –325 | –250 | –115 | –75 |
| k. | –1,000 | | | | | | | –1,000 | | | | | | | | |
| Bal. | 6,873 | 2,225 | 980 | 10,000 | 2,355 | 13,700 | 3,520 | –1,000 | 5,953 | –1,635 | –1,200 | –850 | –325 | –250 | –115 | –75 |

**3.**

### Cecil Jameson, Attorney-at-Law
### Income Statement
### For the Month Ended July 31, 2011

| | | |
|---|---|---|
| Fees earned............................................................ | | $5,953 |
| Expenses: | | |
| Paralegal expense............................................. | $1,635 | |
| Rent expense .................................................... | 1,200 | |
| Wages expense ................................................. | 850 | |
| Utilities expense .............................................. | 325 | |
| Answering service expense ............................. | 250 | |
| Supplies expense .............................................. | 115 | |
| Miscellaneous expense .................................... | 75 | |
| Total expenses............................................ | | 4,450 |
| Net income ........................................................... | | $1,503 |

### Cecil Jameson, Attorney-at-Law, P.C.
### Retained Earnings Statement
### For the Month Ended July 31, 2011

| | | |
|---|---|---|
| Retained earnings, July 1, 2011........................................ | | $3,520 |
| Net income for the month ........................................... | $1,503 | |
| Less dividends ................................................................ | 1,000 | |
| Increase in retained earnings......................................... | | 503 |
| Retained earnings, July 31, 2011..................................... | | $4,023 |

*(continued)*

**Cecil Jameson, Attorney-at-Law**
**Balance Sheet**
**July 31, 2011**

| Assets | | Liabilities | |
|---|---|---|---|
| Cash .............................. | $ 6,873 | Accounts payable .............. | $ 2,355 |
| Accounts receivable .............. | 2,225 | **Stockholders' Equity** | |
| Supplies......................... | 980 | Capital stock................... $13,700 | |
| Land ............................ | 10,000 | Retained earnings.............. 4,023 | |
| | | Total stockholders' equity....... | 17,723 |
| | | Total liabilities and | |
| Total assets ..................... | $20,078 | stockholders' equity......... | $20,078 |

4. Optional.

**Cecil Jameson, Attorney-at-Law**
**Statement of Cash Flows**
**For the Month Ended July 31, 2011**

| | | |
|---|---|---|
| Cash flows from operating activities: | | |
| Cash received from customers ...................................... | $6,928* | |
| Deduct cash payments for operating expenses...................... | 3,755** | |
| Net cash flows from operating activities ............................ | | $3,173 |
| Cash flows from investing activities................................. | | — |
| Cash flows from financing activities: | | |
| Cash received from issuing capital stock ........................... | $3,700 | |
| Deduct cash dividends ............................................ | 1,000 | |
| Net cash flows from financing activities............................ | | 2,700 |
| Net increase in cash during year.................................... | | $5,873 |
| Cash as of July 1, 2011 ............................................. | | 1,000 |
| Cash as of July 31, 2011............................................ | | $6,873 |

*$6,928 = $3,928 + $3,000
**$3,755 = $1,055 + $1,200 + $1,500

# Discussion Questions

1. Name some users of accounting information.

2. What is the role of accounting in business?

3. Why are most large companies like Microsoft, PepsiCo, Caterpillar, and AutoZone organized as corporations?

4. Murray Stoltz is the owner of Ontime Delivery Service. Recently, Murray paid interest of $3,200 on a personal loan of $60,000 that he used to begin the business. Should Ontime Delivery Service record the interest payment? Explain.

5. On October 3, A2Z Repair Service extended an offer of $75,000 for land that had been priced for sale at $90,000. On November 23, A2Z Repair Service accepted the seller's counteroffer of $82,000. Describe how A2Z Repair Service should record the land.

6. a. Land with an assessed value of $400,000 for property tax purposes is acquired by a business for $525,000. Ten years later, the plot of land has an assessed value of $700,000 and the business receives an offer of $1,000,000 for it. Should the monetary amount assigned to the land in the business records now be increased?

   b. Assuming that the land acquired in (a) was sold for $1,000,000, how would the various elements of the accounting equation be affected?

7. Describe the difference between an account receivable and an account payable.

8. A business had revenues of $430,000 and operating expenses of $615,000. Did the business (a) incur a net loss or (b) realize net income?

9. A business had revenues of $825,000 and operating expenses of $708,000. Did the business (a) incur a net loss or (b) realize net income?

10. What particular item of financial or operating data appears on both the income statement and the retained earnings statement? What item appears on both the balance sheet and the retained earnings statement? What item appears on both the balance sheet and the statement of cash flows?

# Practice Exercises

| Learning Objectives | Example Exercises | |
|---|---|---|
| **OBJ. 2** | **EE 1-1** *p. 8* | **PE 1-1A  Cost concept** |

On June 10, Easy Repair Service extended an offer of $95,000 for land that had been priced for sale at $118,500. On August 2, Easy Repair Service accepted the seller's counteroffer of $105,000. On August 27, the land was assessed at a value of $80,000 for property tax purposes. On April 1, Easy Repair Service was offered $125,000 for the land by a national retail chain. At what value should the land be recorded in Easy Repair Service's records?

**OBJ. 2**  **EE 1-1** *p. 8*  **PE 1-1B  Cost concept**

On February 7, AAA Repair Service extended an offer of $50,000 for land that had been priced for sale at $65,000. On February 21, AAA Repair Service accepted the seller's counteroffer of $57,500. On April 30, the land was assessed at a value of $40,000 for property tax purposes. On August 30, AAA Repair Service was offered $90,000 for the land by a national retail chain. At what value should the land be recorded in AAA Repair Service's records?

**OBJ. 3**  **EE 1-2** *p. 9*  **PE 1-2A  Accounting equation**

Shannon Cook is the owner and operator of Galaxy LLC, a motivational consulting business. At the end of its accounting period, December 31, 2011, Galaxy has assets of $800,000 and liabilities of $450,000. Using the accounting equation, determine the following amounts:

a. Owner's equity, as of December 31, 2011.

b. Owner's equity, as of December 31, 2012, assuming that assets increased by $175,000 and liabilities decreased by $60,000 during 2012.

**OBJ. 3**  **EE 1-2** *p. 9*  **PE 1-2B  Accounting equation**

Jan Petri is the owner and operator of You're the One, a motivational consulting business. At the end of its accounting period, December 31, 2011, You're the One has assets of $575,000 and liabilities of $125,000. Using the accounting equation, determine the following amounts:

a. Owner's equity, as of December 31, 2011.

b. Owner's equity, as of December 31, 2012, assuming that assets increased by $85,000 and liabilities increased by $30,000 during 2012.

**OBJ. 4**  **EE 1-3** *p. 14*  **PE 1-3A  Transactions**

Queens Delivery Service is owned and operated by Lisa Dewar. The following selected transactions were completed by Queens Delivery Service during June:

1. Received cash in exchange for capital stock, $18,000.

2. Paid creditors on account, $1,800.

3. Billed customers for delivery services on account, $12,500.

4. Received cash from customers on account, $6,900.

5. Paid cash dividends, $4,000.

Indicate the effect of each transaction on the accounting equation elements (Assets, Liabilities, Stockholders' Equity, Dividends, Revenue, and Expense). Also, indicate the specific item within the accounting equation element that is affected. To illustrate, the answer to (1) is shown below.

(1) Asset (Cash) increases by $18,000; Stockholders' Equity (Capital Stock) increases by $18,000.

| Learning Objectives | Example Exercises | |
|---|---|---|
| OBJ. 4 | EE 1-3 *p. 14* | **PE 1-3B  Transactions** |

Motorcross Delivery Service is owned and operated by Jim Smith. The following selected transactions were completed by Motorcross Delivery Service during February:

1. Received cash in exchange for capital stock, $30,000.

2. Paid advertising expense, $1,200.

3. Purchased supplies on account, $450.

4. Billed customers for delivery services on account, $7,500.

5. Received cash from customers on account, $4,900.

Indicate the effect of each transaction on the accounting equation elements (Assets, Liabilities, Stockholders' Equity, Dividends, Revenue, and Expense). Also, indicate the specific item within the accounting equation element that is affected. To illustrate, the answer to (1) is shown below.

(1) Asset (Cash) increases by $30,000; Stockholders' Equity (Capital Stock) increases by $30,000.

| OBJ. 5 | EE 1-4 *p. 16* | **PE 1-4A  Income statement** |
|---|---|---|

The revenues and expenses of Dynasty Travel Service for the year ended June 30, 2012, are listed below.

| | |
|---|---|
| Fees earned | $950,000 |
| Office expense | 222,000 |
| Miscellaneous expense | 16,000 |
| Wages expense | 478,000 |

Prepare an income statement for the current year ended June 30, 2012.

| OBJ. 5 | EE 1-4 *p. 16* | **PE 1-4B  Income statement** |
|---|---|---|

The revenues and expenses of Escape Travel Service for the year ended November 30, 2012, are listed below.

| | |
|---|---|
| Fees earned | $942,500 |
| Office expense | 391,625 |
| Miscellaneous expense | 15,875 |
| Wages expense | 562,500 |

Prepare an income statement for the current year ended November 30, 2012.

| OBJ. 5 | EE 1-5 *p. 17* | **PE 1-5A  Retained earnings statement** |
|---|---|---|

Using the income statement for Dynasty Travel Service shown in Practice Exercise 1-4A, prepare a retained earnings statement for the current year ended June 30, 2012. Nancy Coleman, the owner, invested an additional $60,000 in the business in exchange for capital stock during the year and cash dividends of $36,000 were paid during the year. Retained earnings as of July 1, 2011, was $175,000.

| OBJ. 5 | EE 1-5 *p. 17* | **PE 1-5B  Retained earnings statement** |
|---|---|---|

Using the income statement for Escape Travel Service shown in Practice Exercise 1-4B, prepare a retained earnings statement for the current year ended November 30, 2012. Brett Daniels, the owner, invested an additional $45,000 in the business in exchange for capital stock during the year and cash dividends of $25,000 were paid during the year. Retained earnings as of December 1, 2011, was $375,000.

| OBJ. 5 | EE 1-6 *p. 19* | **PE 1-6A  Balance sheet** |
|---|---|---|

Using the following data for Dynasty Travel Service as well as the retained earnings statement shown in Practice Exercise 1-5A, prepare a balance sheet as of June 30, 2012.

| | |
|---|---:|
| Accounts payable | $ 24,000 |
| Accounts receivable | 64,000 |
| Capital stock | 135,000 |
| Cash | 156,000 |
| Land | 300,000 |
| Supplies | 12,000 |

**OBJ. 5**  EE 1-6 *p. 19*

### PE 1-6B  Balance sheet

Using the following data for Escape Travel Service as well as the retained earnings statement shown in Practice Exercise 1-5B, prepare a balance sheet as of November 30, 2012.

| | |
|---|---:|
| Accounts payable | $ 52,500 |
| Accounts receivable | 94,375 |
| Capital stock | 145,000 |
| Cash | 56,750 |
| Land | 362,500 |
| Supplies | 6,375 |

**OBJ. 5**  EE 1-7 *p. 20*

### PE 1-7A  Statement of cash flows

A summary of cash flows for Dynasty Travel Service for the year ended June 30, 2012, is shown below.

| | |
|---|---:|
| Cash receipts: | |
| Cash received from customers | $920,000 |
| Cash received from issuing capital stock | 60,000 |
| Cash payments: | |
| Cash paid for operating expenses | 710,000 |
| Cash paid for land | 208,000 |
| Cash paid for dividends | 36,000 |

The cash balance as of July 1, 2011, was $130,000.

Prepare a statement of cash flows for Dynasty Travel Service for the year ended June 30, 2012.

**OBJ. 5**  EE 1-7 *p. 20*

### PE 1-7B  Statement of cash flows

A summary of cash flows for Escape Travel Service for the year ended November 30, 2012, is shown below.

| | |
|---|---:|
| Cash receipts: | |
| Cash received from customers | $875,000 |
| Cash received from issuing capital stock | 45,000 |
| Cash payments: | |
| Cash paid for operating expenses | 912,500 |
| Cash paid for land | 67,500 |
| Cash paid for dividends | 25,000 |

The cash balance as of December 1, 2011, was $141,750.

Prepare a statement of cash flows for Escape Travel Service for the year ended November 30, 2012.

**OBJ. 6**  EE 1-8 *p. 23*

**F·A·I**

### PE 1-8A  Ratio of liabilities to stockholders' equity

The following data were taken from White Company's balance sheet:

| | Dec. 31, 2012 | Dec. 31, 2011 |
|---|---:|---:|
| Total liabilities | $375,000 | $287,500 |
| Total stockholders' equity | 300,000 | 250,000 |

a. Compute the ratio of liabilities to stockholders' equity.

b. Has the creditor's risk increased or decreased from December 31, 2011 to December 31, 2012?

*Learning
Objectives*

*Example
Exercises*

**OBJ. 6**   **EE 1-8** *p. 23*

**PE 1-8B   Ratio of liabilities to stockholders' equity**

The following data were taken from Stone Company's balance sheet:

|  | Dec. 31, 2012 | Dec. 31, 2011 |
|---|---|---|
| Total liabilities | $340,000 | $300,000 |
| Total stockholders' equity | 500,000 | 400,000 |

a. Compute the ratio of liabilities to stockholders' equity.

b. Has the creditor's risk increased or decreased from December 31, 2011 to December 31, 2012?

## Exercises

**OBJ. 1**

**EX 1-1   Types of businesses**

The following is a list of well-known companies.

1. H&R Block
2. eBay Inc.
3. Wal-Mart Stores, Inc.
4. Ford Motor Company
5. Citigroup
6. Boeing
7. SunTrust
8. Alcoa Inc.
9. Procter & Gamble
10. FedEx
11. Gap Inc.
12. Hilton Hospitality, Inc.
13. CVS
14. Caterpillar
15. The Dow Chemical Company

a. Indicate whether each of these companies is primarily a service, merchandise, or manufacturing business. If you are unfamiliar with the company, use the Internet to locate the company's home page or use the finance Web site of **Yahoo** (http://finance. yahoo.com).

b. For which of the preceding companies is the accounting equation relevant?

**OBJ. 1**

**EX 1-2   Professional ethics**

A fertilizer manufacturing company wants to relocate to Jones County. A report from a fired researcher at the company indicates the company's product is releasing toxic by-products. The company suppressed that report. A later report commissioned by the company shows there is no problem with the fertilizer.

Should the company's chief executive officer reveal the content of the unfavorable report in discussions with Jones County representatives? Discuss.

**OBJ. 2**

**EX 1-3   Business entity concept**

Rocky Mountain Sports sells hunting and fishing equipment and provides guided hunting and fishing trips. Rocky Mountain Sports is owned and operated by Mike Weber, a well-known sports enthusiast and hunter. Mike's wife, Susan, owns and operates Madison Boutique, a women's clothing store. Mike and Susan have established a trust fund to finance their children's college education. The trust fund is maintained by National Bank in the name of the children, Kerri and Kyle.

a. For each of the following transactions, identify which of the entities listed should record the transaction in its records.

| Entities | |
|---|---|
| R | Rocky Mountain Sports |
| B | National Bank Trust Fund |
| M | Madison Boutique |
| X | None of the above |

1. Susan authorized the trust fund to purchase mutual fund shares.

2. Susan purchased two dozen spring dresses from a Chicago designer for a special spring sale.

3. Mike paid a breeder's fee for an English springer spaniel to be used as a hunting guide dog.

4. Susan deposited a $3,000 personal check in the trust fund at National Bank.

5. Mike paid a local doctor for his annual physical, which was required by the workmen's compensation insurance policy carried by Rocky Mountain Sports.

6. Mike received a cash advance from customers for a guided hunting trip.

7. Susan paid her dues to the YWCA.

8. Susan donated several dresses from inventory for a local charity auction for the benefit of a women's abuse shelter.

9. Mike paid for dinner and a movie to celebrate their fifteenth wedding anniversary.

10. Mike paid for an advertisement in a hunters' magazine.

b. What is a business transaction?

---

OBJ. 3

✔ Starbucks,
$3,046

### EX 1-4  Accounting equation

The total assets and total liabilities (in millions) of Peet's Coffee & Tea Inc. and Starbucks Corporation are shown below.

|  | Peet's Coffee & Tea | Starbucks |
| --- | --- | --- |
| Assets | $176 | $5,577 |
| Liabilities | 32 | 2,531 |

Determine the stockholders' (owners') equity of each company.

---

OBJ. 3

✔ Dollar Tree,
$1,253

### EX 1-5  Accounting equation

The total assets and total liabilities (in millions) of Dollar Tree Inc. and Target Corporation are shown below.

|  | Dollar Tree | Target Corporation |
| --- | --- | --- |
| Assets | $2,036 | $44,106 |
| Liabilities | 783 | 30,394 |

Determine the stockholders' (owners') equity of each company.

---

OBJ. 3

✔ a. 600,000

### EX 1-6  Accounting equation

Determine the missing amount for each of the following:

|  | Assets | = | Liabilities | + | Stockholders' (Owners') Equity |
| --- | --- | --- | --- | --- | --- |
| a. | × | = | $150,000 | + | $450,000 |
| b. | $275,000 | = | × | + | 50,000 |
| c. | 615,000 | = | 190,000 | + | × |

---

OBJ. 3, 4

✔ b. $530,000

### EX 1-7  Accounting equation

Todd Olson is the sole stockholder and operator of Alpha, a motivational consulting business. At the end of its accounting period, December 31, 2011, Alpha has assets of $800,000 and liabilities of $350,000. Using the accounting equation and considering each case independently, determine the following amounts:

a. Stockholders' equity as of December 31, 2011.

b. Stockholders' equity as of December 31, 2012, assuming that assets increased by $150,000 and liabilities increased by $70,000 during 2012.

c. Stockholders' equity as of December 31, 2012, assuming that assets decreased by $60,000 and liabilities increased by $20,000 during 2012.

d. Stockholders' equity as of December 31, 2012, assuming that assets increased by $100,000 and liabilities decreased by $40,000 during 2012.

e. Net income (or net loss) during 2012, assuming that as of December 31, 2012, assets were $975,000, liabilities were $400,000, and no additional capital stock was issued or dividends paid.

OBJ. 3

**EX 1-8   Asset, liability, stockholders' equity items**

Indicate whether each of the following is identified with (1) an asset, (2) a liability, or (3) stockholders' equity (retained earnings):

a. cash

b. wages expense

c. accounts payable

d. fees earned

e. supplies

f. land

OBJ. 4

**EX 1-9   Effect of transactions on accounting equation**

Describe how the following business transactions affect the three elements of the accounting equation.

a. Invested cash in business in exchange for capital stock.

b. Purchased supplies for cash.

c. Purchased supplies on account.

d. Received cash for services performed.

e. Paid for utilities used in the business.

OBJ. 4

✔ a. (1) increase $250,000

**EX 1-10   Effect of transactions on accounting equation**

a. A vacant lot acquired for $100,000 is sold for $350,000 in cash. What is the effect of the sale on the total amount of the seller's (1) assets, (2) liabilities, and (3) stockholders' equity (retained earnings)?

b. Assume that the seller owes $75,000 on a loan for the land. After receiving the $350,000 cash in (a), the seller pays the $75,000 owed. What is the effect of the payment on the total amount of the seller's (1) assets, (2) liabilities, and (3) stockholders' equity (retained earnings)?

c. Is it true that a transaction always affects at least two elements (Assets, Liabilities, or Stockholders' Equity) of the accounting equation? Explain.

OBJ. 4

**EX 1-11   Effect of transactions on stockholders' equity**

Indicate whether each of the following types of transactions will either (a) increase stockholders' equity or (b) decrease stockholders' equity:

1. issuing capital stock in exchange for cash

2. revenues

3. expenses

4. paying dividends

OBJ. 4

**EX 1-12   Transactions**

The following selected transactions were completed by Speedy Delivery Service during October:

1. Received cash in exchange for capital stock, $30,000.

2. Purchased supplies for cash, $1,500.

3. Paid rent for October, $4,000.

4. Paid advertising expense, $2,500.

5. Received cash for providing delivery services, $18,750.

6. Billed customers for delivery services on account, $41,500.

7. Paid creditors on account, $6,000.

8. Received cash from customers on account, $26,200.

9. Determined that the cost of supplies on hand was $250; therefore, $1,250 of supplies had been used during the month.

10. Paid cash dividends, $2,000.

Indicate the effect of each transaction on the accounting equation by listing the numbers identifying the transactions, (1) through (10), in a column, and inserting at the right of each number the appropriate letter from the following list:

a.  Increase in an asset, decrease in another asset.

b.  Increase in an asset, increase in a liability.

c.  Increase in an asset, increase in stockholders' equity.

d.  Decrease in an asset, decrease in a liability.

e.  Decrease in an asset, decrease in stockholders' equity.

**OBJ. 4**

✔ d. $13,200

### EX 1-13  Nature of transactions

Jeremy Zabel operates his own catering service. Summary financial data for February are presented in equation form as follows. Each line designated by a number indicates the effect of a transaction on the equation. Each increase and decrease in stockholders' equity, except transaction (5), affects net income.

| | Assets | | | = | Liabilities + | | | Stockholders' Equity | | | |
|---|---|---|---|---|---|---|---|---|---|---|---|
| | Cash | + Supplies + | Land | = | Accounts Payable + | Capital Stock + | Retained Earnings − | Dividends + | Fees Earned − | Expenses |
| Bal. | 25,000 | 2,000 | 75,000 | | 12,000 | 25,000 | 65,000 | | | |
| 1. | +29,000 | | | | | | | | 29,000 | |
| 2. | −20,000 | | +20,000 | | | | | | | |
| 3. | −14,000 | | | | | | | | | −14,000 |
| 4. | | +1,000 | | | +1,000 | | | | | |
| 5. | −2,000 | | | | | | | −2,000 | | |
| 6. | −7,000 | | | | −7,000 | | | | | |
| 7. | | −1,800 | | | | | | | | −1,800 |
| Bal. | 11,000 | 1,200 | 95,000 | | 6,000 | 25,000 | 65,000 | −2,000 | 29,000 | −15,800 |

a.  Describe each transaction.

b.  What is the amount of net decrease in cash during the month?

c.  What is the amount of net increase in stockholders' equity during the month?

d.  What is the amount of the net income for the month?

e.  How much of the net income for the month was retained in the business?

**OBJ. 5**

### EX 1-14  Net income and dividends

The income statement of a corporation for the month of December indicates a net income of $120,000. During the same period, $130,000 in cash dividends were paid.

▬▬▶ Would it be correct to say that the business incurred a net loss of $10,000 during the month? Discuss.

**OBJ. 5**

✔ Leo: Net income, $60,000

### EX 1-15  Net income and stockholders' equity for four businesses

Four different corporations, Aries, Gemini, Leo, and Pisces, show the same balance sheet data at the beginning and end of a year. These data, exclusive of the amount of stockholders' equity, are summarized as follows:

| | Total Assets | Total Liabilities |
|---|---|---|
| Beginning of the year | $400,000 | $100,000 |
| End of the year | 750,000 | 300,000 |

On the basis of the above data and the following additional information for the year, determine the net income (or loss) of each company for the year. (*Hint:* First determine the amount of increase or decrease in stockholders' equity during the year.)

Aries:    No additional capital stock was issued and no dividends were paid.

Gemini:  No additional capital stock was issued, but dividends of $40,000 were paid.

Leo:      Additional capital stock of $90,000 was issued, but no dividends were paid.

Pisces:   Additional capital stock of $90,000 was issued and dividends of $40,000 were paid.

**OBJ. 5**

### EX 1-16 Balance sheet items

From the following list of selected items taken from the records of Hoosier Appliance Service as of a specific date, identify those that would appear on the balance sheet:

1. Accounts Receivable
2. Capital Stock
3. Cash
4. Fees Earned
5. Land
6. Supplies
7. Supplies Expense
8. Utilities Expense
9. Wages Expense
10. Wages Payable

**OBJ. 5**

### EX 1-17 Income statement items

Based on the data presented in Exercise 1-16, identify those items that would appear on the income statement.

**OBJ. 5**

✔ Retained earnings, June 30, 2012: $482,000

### EX 1-18 Retained earnings statement

Financial information related to Lost Trail Company, a corporation, for the month ended June 30, 2012, is as follows:

| | |
|---|---|
| Net income for June | $125,000 |
| Dividends | 18,000 |
| Retained earnings, June 1, 2012 | 375,000 |

a. Prepare a retained earnings statement for the month ended June 30, 2012.

b. Why is the retained earnings statement prepared before the June 30, 2012, balance sheet?

**OBJ. 5**

✔ Net income: $449,000

### EX 1-19 Income statement

Universal Services was organized on October 1, 2012. A summary of the revenue and expense transactions for October follows:

| | |
|---|---|
| Fees earned | $800,000 |
| Wages expense | 270,000 |
| Rent expense | 60,000 |
| Supplies expense | 9,000 |
| Miscellaneous expense | 12,000 |

Prepare an income statement for the month ended October 31.

**OBJ. 5**

✔ (a) $45,000

### EX 1-20 Missing amounts from balance sheet and income statement data

One item is omitted in each of the following summaries of balance sheet and income statement data for the following four different corporations:

| | Aquarius | Libra | Scorpio | Taurus |
|---|---|---|---|---|
| Beginning of the year: | | | | |
| Assets | $300,000 | $500,000 | $100,000 | (d) |
| Liabilities | 120,000 | 260,000 | 76,000 | $120,000 |
| End of the year: | | | | |
| Assets | 420,000 | 700,000 | 90,000 | 248,000 |
| Liabilities | 110,000 | 220,000 | 80,000 | 136,000 |
| During the year: | | | | |
| Additional issuance of capital stock | (a) | 100,000 | 10,000 | 40,000 |
| Dividends | 25,000 | 32,000 | (c) | 60,000 |
| Revenue | 190,000 | (b) | 115,000 | 112,000 |
| Expenses | 80,000 | 128,000 | 122,500 | 128,000 |

Determine the missing amounts, identifying them by letter. (*Hint:* First determine the amount of increase or decrease in stockholders' equity during the year.)

**EX 1-21    Balance sheets, net income**

Financial information related to the corporation of Lady Interiors for July and August 2012 is as follows:

|  | July 31, 2012 | August 31, 2012 |
|---|---|---|
| Accounts payable | $ 90,000 | $100,000 |
| Accounts receivable | 200,000 | 240,000 |
| Capital stock | ? | ? |
| Cash | 80,000 | 95,000 |
| Retained earnings | 130,000 | 170,000 |
| Supplies | 20,000 | 15,000 |

a.  Prepare balance sheets for Lady Interiors as of July 31 and August 31, 2012.

b.  Determine the amount of net income for August, assuming that no additional capital stock was issued and no dividends were paid during the month.

c.  Determine the amount of net income for August, assuming that no additional capital stock was issued, but dividends of $35,000 were paid during the month.

**EX 1-22    Financial statements**

Each of the following items is shown in the financial statements of ExxonMobil Corporation.

1.  Accounts payable
2.  Cash equivalents
3.  Crude oil inventory
4.  Equipment
5.  Exploration expenses
6.  Income taxes payable
7.  Investments
8.  Long-term debt

9.  Marketable securities
10. Notes and loans payable
11. Notes receivable
12. Operating expenses
13. Prepaid taxes
14. Sales
15. Selling expenses

a.  Identify the financial statement (balance sheet or income statement) in which each item would appear.

b.  Can an item appear on more than one financial statement?

c.  Is the accounting equation relevant for ExxonMobil Corporation?

**EX 1-23    Statement of cash flows**

Indicate whether each of the following activities would be reported on the statement of cash flows as (a) an operating activity, (b) an investing activity, or (c) a financing activity:

1.  Cash received from fees earned.
2.  Cash paid for expenses.
3.  Cash paid for land.
4.  Cash received from issuing capital stock.

**EX 1-24    Statement of cash flows**

A summary of cash flows for Absolute Consulting Group for the year ended July 31, 2012, is shown below.

| | |
|---|---|
| Cash receipts: | |
| Cash received from customers | $187,500 |
| Cash received from issuing additional capital stock | 40,000 |
| Cash payments: | |
| Cash paid for operating expenses | 127,350 |
| Cash paid for land | 30,000 |
| Cash paid for dividends | 5,000 |

The cash balance as of August 1, 2011, was $27,100.

Prepare a statement of cash flows for Absolute Consulting Group for the year ended July 31, 2012.

**OBJ. 5**

✔ Correct amount of total assets is $88,200.

### EX 1-25 Financial statements

Empire Realty, organized May 1, 2012, is owned and operated by Bertram Mitchell. How many errors can you find in the following statements for Empire Realty, prepared after its first month of operations?

**Empire Realty**
**Income Statement**
**May 31, 2012**

| | | |
|---|---:|---:|
| Sales commissions ............................................. | | $233,550 |
| Expenses: | | |
| Office salaries expense......................................... | $145,800 | |
| Rent expense................................................. | 49,500 | |
| Automobile expense........................................... | 11,250 | |
| Miscellaneous expense......................................... | 3,600 | |
| Supplies expense ............................................. | 1,350 | |
| Total expenses ............................................. | | 211,500 |
| Net income ................................................. | | $ 67,050 |

**Bertram Mitchell**
**Retained Earnings Statement**
**May 31, 2011**

| | |
|---|---:|
| Retained earnings, May 1, 2012............................................. | $ 36,800 |
| Less dividends during May................................................. | 9,000 |
| | $ 27,800 |
| Additional issuance of capital stock during May ............................ | 11,250 |
| | $ 39,050 |
| Net income for May ....................................................... | 67,050 |
| Retained earnings, May 31, 2012 ........................................... | $106,100 |

**Balance Sheet**
**For the Month Ended May 31, 2012**

| Assets | | Liabilities | |
|---|---:|---|---:|
| Cash ............................ | $14,850 | Accounts receivable ..................... | $ 64,350 |
| Accounts payable ................ | 17,100 | Supplies ............................... | 9,000 |
| | | **Stockholders' Equity** | |
| | | Capital stock .................. $ 21,250 | |
| | | Retained earnings ............. 106,100 | |
| | | Total stockholders' equity....... | 137,350 |
| | | Total liabilities and | |
| Total assets ..................... | $31,950 | stockholders' equity ......... | $210,700 |

**OBJ. 6**

### EX 1-26 Ratio of liabilities to stockholders' equity

The Home Depot, Inc., is the world's largest home improvement retailer and one of the largest retailers in the United States based on net sales volume. The Home Depot operates over 2,000 Home Depot® stores that sell a wide assortment of building materials and home improvement and lawn and garden products.

The Home Depot reported the following balance sheet data (in millions):

| | Feb. 1, 2009 | Feb. 3, 2008 |
|---|---:|---:|
| Total assets | $41,164 | $44,324 |
| Total stockholders' equity | 17,777 | 17,714 |

a. Determine the total liabilities as of February 1, 2009, and February 3, 2008.

b. Determine the ratio of liabilities to stockholders' equity for 2009 and 2008. Round to two decimal places.

c. What conclusions regarding the margin of protection to the creditors can you draw from (b)?

**OBJ. 6**

### EX 1-27 Ratio of liabilities to stockholders' equity

Lowe's, a major competitor of The Home Depot in the home improvement business, operates over 1,600 stores. For the years ending January 30, 2009, and February 1, 2008, Lowe's reported the following balance sheet data (in millions):

|  | Jan. 30, 2009 | Feb. 1, 2008 |
|---|---|---|
| Total assets | $32,686 | $30,869 |
| Total liabilities | 14,631 | 14,771 |

a. Determine the total stockholders' equity as of January 30, 2009, and February 1, 2008.

b. Determine the ratio of liabilities to stockholders' equity for 2009 and 2008. Round to two decimal places.

c. What conclusions regarding the margin of protection to the creditors can you draw from (b)?

d. Using the balance sheet data for The Home Depot in Exercise 1-26, how does the ratio of liabilities to stockholders' equity of Lowe's compare to that of The Home Depot?

## Problems Series A

**OBJ. 4**

✔ Cash bal. at end of September: $37,700

### PR 1-1A   Transactions

On September 1 of the current year, Maria Edsall established a business to manage rental property. She completed the following transactions during September:

a. Opened a business bank account with a deposit of $40,000 in exchange for capital stock.

b. Purchased supplies (pens, file folders, and copy paper) on account, $2,200.

c. Received cash from fees earned for managing rental property, $6,000.

d. Paid rent on office and equipment for the month, $2,700.

e. Paid creditors on account, $1,000.

f. Billed customers for fees earned for managing rental property, $5,000.

g. Paid automobile expenses (including rental charges) for month, $600, and miscellaneous expenses, $300.

h. Paid office salaries, $1,900.

i. Determined that the cost of supplies on hand was $1,300; therefore, the cost of supplies used was $900.

j. Paid dividends, $1,800.

#### Instructions

1. Indicate the effect of each transaction and the balances after each transaction, using the following tabular headings:

| Assets | | | = Liabilities + | | | Stockholders' Equity | | | | | | |
|---|---|---|---|---|---|---|---|---|---|---|---|---|
| Cash + | Accounts Receivable + | Supplies = | Accounts Payable + | Capital Stock | − Dividends | + Fees Earned | − Rent Expense | − Salaries Expense | − Supplies Expense | − Auto Expense | − Misc. Expense |

2. ➤ Briefly explain why the stockholders' investments and revenues increased stockholders' equity, while dividends and expenses decreased stockholders' equity.

3. Determine the net income for September.

4. How much did September's transactions increase or decrease retained earnings?

**OBJ. 5**

✔ 1. Net income: $40,000

### PR 1-2A   Financial statements

Following are the amounts of the assets and liabilities of New World Travel Agency at December 31, 2012, the end of the current year, and its revenue and expenses for the year. The retained earnings was $105,000 on January 1, 2012, the beginning of the current year. During the current year, dividends of $10,000 were paid.

| | | | |
|---|---|---|---|
| Accounts payable | $ 25,000 | Rent expense | $45,000 |
| Accounts receivable | 60,000 | Supplies | 5,000 |
| Capital stock | 15,000 | Supplies expense | 3,000 |
| Cash | 110,000 | Utilities expense | 18,000 |
| Fees earned | 200,000 | Wages expense | 90,000 |
| Miscellaneous expense | 4,000 | | |

#### Instructions

1. Prepare an income statement for the current year ended December 31, 2012.

2. Prepare a retained earnings statement for the current year ended December 31, 2012.

3. Prepare a balance sheet as of December 31, 2012.

4. What item appears on both the retained earnings statement and the balance sheet?

**OBJ. 5**

✔ 1. Net income:
$26,400

### PR 1-3A  Financial statements

Heidi Fritz established Freedom Financial Services on March 1, 2012. Freedom Financial Services offers financial planning advice to its clients. The effect of each transaction and the balances after each transaction for March are shown below.

| | Assets | | | = Liabilities + | | Stockholders' Equity | | | | | | | |
|---|---|---|---|---|---|---|---|---|---|---|---|---|---|
| | Cash | + Accounts Receivable | + Supplies | = Accounts Payable | + Capital Stock | − Dividends | + Fees Earned | − Salaries Expense | − Rent Expense | − Auto Expense | − Supplies Expense | − Misc. Expense |
| a. | +45,000 | | | | +45,000 | | | | | | | |
| b. | | +6,540 | | +6,540 | | | | | | | | |
| Bal. | 45,000 | | 6,540 | 6,540 | 45,000 | | | | | | | |
| c. | −1,800 | | | −1,800 | | | | | | | | |
| Bal. | 43,200 | | 6,540 | 4,740 | 45,000 | | | | | | | |
| d. | +84,000 | | | | | | +84,000 | | | | | |
| Bal. | 127,200 | | 6,540 | 4,740 | 45,000 | | 84,000 | | | | | |
| e. | −22,500 | | | | | | | | −22,500 | | | |
| Bal. | 104,700 | | 6,540 | 4,740 | 45,000 | | 84,000 | | −22,500 | | | |
| f. | −17,100 | | | | | | | | | −13,500 | | −3,600 |
| Bal. | 87,600 | | 6,540 | 4,740 | 45,000 | | 84,000 | | −22,500 | −13,500 | | −3,600 |
| g. | −48,000 | | | | | | | −48,000 | | | | |
| Bal. | 39,600 | | 6,540 | 4,740 | 45,000 | | 84,000 | −48,000 | −22,500 | −13,500 | | −3,600 |
| h. | | | −4,500 | | | | | | | | −4,500 | |
| Bal. | 39,600 | | 2,040 | 4,740 | 45,000 | | 84,000 | −48,000 | −22,500 | −13,500 | −4,500 | −3,600 |
| i. | | +34,500 | | | | | +34,500 | | | | | |
| Bal. | 39,600 | 34,500 | 2,040 | 4,740 | 45,000 | | 118,500 | −48,000 | −22,500 | −13,500 | −4,500 | −3,600 |
| j. | −15,000 | | | | | −15,000 | | | | | | |
| Bal. | 24,600 | 34,500 | 2,040 | 4,740 | 45,000 | −15,000 | 118,500 | −48,000 | −22,500 | −13,500 | −4,500 | −3,600 |

### Instructions

1. Prepare an income statement for the month ended March 31, 2012.

2. Prepare a retained earnings statement for the month ended March 31, 2012.

3. Prepare a balance sheet as of March 31, 2012.

4. (Optional). Prepare a statement of cash flows for the month ending March 31, 2012.

**OBJ. 4, 5**

✔ 2. Net income:
$12,150

### PR 1-4A  Transactions; financial statements

On January 1, 2012, Carlton Myers established Vista Realty. Carlton completed the following transactions during the month of January:

a. Opened a business bank account with a deposit of $25,000 in exchange for capital stock.

b. Purchased supplies (pens, file folders, paper, etc.) on account, $2,500.

c. Paid creditor on account, $1,600.

d. Earned sales commissions, receiving cash, $25,500.

e. Paid rent on office and equipment for the month, $5,000.

f. Paid dividends, $8,000.

g. Paid automobile expenses (including rental charge) for month, $2,500, and miscellaneous expenses, $1,200.

h. Paid office salaries, $3,000.

i. Determined that the cost of supplies on hand was $850; therefore, the cost of supplies used was $1,650.

### Instructions

1. Indicate the effect of each transaction and the balances after each transaction, using the following tabular headings:

| Assets | = Liabilities + | | | | Stockholders' Equity | | | | | |
|---|---|---|---|---|---|---|---|---|---|---|
| | | | | | | Office | | | | |
| | Accounts | Capital | | Sales | Rent | Salaries | Auto | Supplies | Misc. | |
| Cash + Supplies = | Payable + | Stock | – Dividends + | Commissions | – Expense | – Expense | – Expense | – Expense | – Expense | |

2. Prepare an income statement for January, a retained earnings statement for January, and a balance sheet as of January 31.

### PR 1-5A  Transactions; financial statements

Kean Dry Cleaners is owned and operated by Wally Lowman. A building and equipment are currently being rented, pending expansion to new facilities. The actual work of dry cleaning is done by another company at wholesale rates. The assets, liabilities, and capital stock of the business on March 1, 2012, are as follows: Cash, $15,000; Accounts Receivable, $31,000; Supplies, $3,000; Land, $36,000; Accounts Payable, $13,000; Capital Stock, $25,000. Business transactions during March are summarized as follows:

a. Wally Lowman invested additional cash in the business with a deposit of $28,000 in exchange for capital stock.

b. Paid $14,000 for the purchase of land as a future building site.

c. Received cash from cash customers for dry cleaning revenue, $17,000.

d. Paid rent for the month, $5,000.

e. Purchased supplies on account, $2,500.

f. Paid creditors on account, $12,800.

g. Charged customers for dry cleaning revenue on account, $34,000.

h. Received monthly invoice for dry cleaning expense for March (to be paid on April 10), $13,500.

i. Paid the following: wages expense, $7,500; truck expense, $2,500; utilities expense, $1,300; miscellaneous expense, $2,700.

j. Received cash from customers on account, $28,000.

k. Determined that the cost of supplies on hand was $1,900; therefore, the cost of supplies used during the month was $3,600.

l. Paid dividends, $8,000.

**Instructions**

1. Determine the amount of retained earnings as of March 1 of the current year.

2. State the assets, liabilities, and stockholders' equity as of March 1 in equation form similar to that shown in this chapter. In tabular form below the equation, indicate increases and decreases resulting from each transaction and the new balances after each transaction.

3. Prepare an income statement for March, a retained earnings statement for March, and a balance sheet as of March 31.

4. (Optional). Prepare a statement of cash flows for March.

### PR 1-6A  Missing amounts from financial statements

The financial statements at the end of Alpine Realty's first month of operations are as follows:

**Alpine Realty**
**Income Statement**
**For the Month Ended June 30, 2012**

| | | |
|---|---:|---:|
| Fees earned.................................................... | $ | (a) |
| Expenses: | | |
| Wages expense.............................................. | $120,000 | |
| Rent expense................................................. | 40,000 | |
| Supplies expense ........................................... | (b) | |
| Utilities expense............................................. | 8,000 | |
| Miscellaneous expense..................................... | 10,000 | |
| Total expenses ......................................... | | 190,000 |
| Net income .................................................... | | $110,000 |

**Alpine Realty**
**Retained Earnings Statement**
**For the Month Ended June 30, 2012**

| | | |
|---|---|---|
| Retained earnings, June 1, 2012 ..................................... | | $      (c) |
| Net income for June ........................................ | $      (d) | |
| Less dividends ............................................. | 50,000 | |
| Increase in retained earnings....................................... | | (e) |
| Retained earnings, June 30, 2012 ................................... | | $      (f) |

**Alpine Realty**
**Balance Sheet**
**June 30, 2012**

| Assets | | Liabilities | |
|---|---|---|---|
| Cash ........................... | $ 185,000 | Accounts payable .......... | $40,000 |
| Supplies....................... | 5,000 | **Stockholders' Equity** | |
| Land .......................... | 60,000 | Capital stock............... $150,000 | |
| | | Retained earnings.......... (h) | |
| | | Total stockholders' equity ... | (i) |
| | | Total liabilities and | |
| Total assets .................... | $      (g) | stockholders' equity ..... | $      (j) |

**Alpine Realty**
**Statement of Cash Flows**
**For the Month Ended June 30, 2012**

| | | |
|---|---|---|
| Cash flows from operating activities: | | |
| Cash received from customers..................................... | $      (k) | |
| Deduct cash payments for expenses and payments to creditors..... | 155,000 | |
| Net cash flow from operating activities .......................... | | $      (l) |
| Cash flows from investing activities: | | |
| Cash payments for acquisition of land ........................... | | (m) |
| Cash flows from financing activities: | | |
| Cash received from issuing capital stock ......................... | $      (n) | |
| Deduct cash dividends ........................................... | (o) | |
| Net cash flow from financing activities........................... | | (p) |
| Net cash flow and June 30, 2012, cash balance .................... | | $      (q) |

**Instructions**

By analyzing the interrelationships among the four financial statements, determine the proper amounts for (a) through (q).

## Problems Series B

OBJ. 4

✔ Cash bal. at end of January: $73,500

**PR 1-1B   Transactions**

Cody Macedo established an insurance agency on January 1 of the current year and completed the following transactions during January:

a.  Opened a business bank account with a deposit of $75,000 in exchange for capital stock.

b.  Purchased supplies on account, $3,000.

c.  Paid creditors on account, $1,000.

d.  Received cash from fees earned on insurance commissions, $11,800.

e.  Paid rent on office and equipment for the month, $4,000.

f.  Paid automobile expenses for month, $600, and miscellaneous expenses, $200.

g.  Paid office salaries, $2,500.

h.  Determined that the cost of supplies on hand was $1,900; therefore, the cost of supplies used was $1,100.

i.  Billed insurance companies for sales commissions earned, $12,500.

j.  Paid dividends, $5,000.

**Instructions**

1.  Indicate the effect of each transaction and the balances after each transaction, using the following tabular headings:

| Assets | | | = Liabilities + | | Stockholders' Equity | | | | | | |
|---|---|---|---|---|---|---|---|---|---|---|---|
| | | | Accounts | Capital | | Fees | Rent | Salaries | Supplies | Auto | Misc. |
| Cash + | Receivable + | Supplies = | Payable + | Stock | – Dividends + | Earned – | Expense – | Expense – | Expense – | Expense – | Expense |

2. ━━━━▶ Briefly explain why the stockholders' investments and revenues increased stockholders' equity, while dividends and expenses decreased stockholders' equity.

3. Determine the net income for January.

4. How much did January's transactions increase or decrease retained earnings?

---

**OBJ. 5**

✔ 1. Net income: $80,000

**PR 1-2B  Financial statements**

The amounts of the assets and liabilities of St. Simon Travel Service at June 30, 2012, the end of the current year, and its revenue and expenses for the year are listed below. The retained earnings was $90,000 at July 1, 2011, the beginning of the current year, and dividends of $30,000 were paid during the current year.

| | | | |
|---|---|---|---|
| Accounts payable | $ 25,000 | Rent expense | $ 75,000 |
| Accounts receivable | 90,000 | Supplies | 12,000 |
| Capital stock | 60,000 | Supplies expense | 10,000 |
| Cash | 123,000 | Taxes expense | 8,000 |
| Fees earned | 500,000 | Utilities expense | 36,000 |
| Miscellaneous expense | 11,000 | Wages expense | 280,000 |

**Instructions**

1. Prepare an income statement for the current year ended June 30, 2012.

2. Prepare a retained earnings statement for the current year ended June 30, 2012.

3. Prepare a balance sheet as of June 30, 2012.

4. What item appears on both the income statement and retained earnings statement?

---

**OBJ. 5**

✔ 1. Net income: $91,900

**PR 1-3B  Financial statements**

Rory Kalur established Computers 4 Less on February 1, 2012. The effect of each transaction and the balances after each transaction for February are shown below.

| | Assets | | | = Liabilities + | | Stockholders' Equity | | | | | | |
|---|---|---|---|---|---|---|---|---|---|---|---|---|
| | Cash + | Accounts Receivable + | Supplies = | Accounts Payable + | Capital Stock | – Dividends + | Fees Earned – | Salaries Expense – | Rent Expense – | Auto Expense – | Supplies Expense – | Misc. Expense |
| a. | +120,000 | | | | +120,000 | | | | | | | |
| b. | | | +10,400 | +10,400 | | | | | | | | |
| Bal. | 120,000 | | 10,400 | 10,400 | 120,000 | | | | | | | |
| c. | +118,000 | | | | | | +118,000 | | | | | |
| Bal. | 238,000 | | 10,400 | 10,400 | 120,000 | | 118,000 | | | | | |
| d. | –32,000 | | | | | | | | –32,000 | | | |
| Bal. | 206,000 | | 10,400 | 10,400 | 120,000 | | 118,000 | | –32,000 | | | |
| e. | –5,000 | | | –5,000 | | | | | | | | |
| Bal. | 201,000 | | 10,400 | 5,400 | 120,000 | | 118,000 | | –32,000 | | | |
| f. | | +83,000 | | | | | +83,000 | | | | | |
| Bal. | 201,000 | 83,000 | 10,400 | 5,400 | 120,000 | | 201,000 | | –32,000 | | | |
| g. | –23,000 | | | | | | | | | –15,500 | | –7,500 |
| Bal. | 178,000 | 83,000 | 10,400 | 5,400 | 120,000 | | 201,000 | | –32,000 | –15,500 | | –7,500 |
| h. | –48,000 | | | | | | | –48,000 | | | | |
| Bal. | 130,000 | 83,000 | 10,400 | 5,400 | 120,000 | | 201,000 | –48,000 | –32,000 | –15,500 | | –7,500 |
| i. | | | –6,100 | | | | | | | | –6,100 | |
| Bal. | 130,000 | 83,000 | 4,300 | 5,400 | 120,000 | | 201,000 | –48,000 | –32,000 | –15,500 | –6,100 | –7,500 |
| j. | –30,000 | | | | | –30,000 | | | | | | |
| Bal. | 100,000 | 83,000 | 4,300 | 5,400 | 120,000 | –30,000 | 201,000 | –48,000 | –32,000 | –15,500 | –6,100 | –7,500 |

**Instructions**

1. Prepare an income statement for the month ended February 29, 2012.

2. Prepare a retained earnings statement for the month ended February 29, 2012.

3. Prepare a balance sheet as of February 29, 2012.

4. (Optional). Prepare a statement of cash flows for the month ending February 29, 2012.

**PR 1-4B  Transactions; financial statements**

On June 1, 2012, Lindsey Brown established Equity Realty. Lindsey completed the following transactions during the month of June:

a.  Opened a business bank account with a deposit of $15,000 in exchange for capital stock.

b.  Paid rent on office and equipment for the month, $4,000.

c.  Paid automobile expenses (including rental charge) for month, $1,200, and miscellaneous expenses, $800.

d.  Purchased supplies (pens, file folders, and copy paper) on account, $1,000.

e.  Earned sales commissions, receiving cash, $18,500.

f.  Paid creditor on account, $600.

g.  Paid office salaries, $2,500.

h.  Paid dividends, $5,000.

i.  Determined that the cost of supplies on hand was $300; therefore, the cost of supplies used was $700.

**Instructions**

1.  Indicate the effect of each transaction and the balances after each transaction, using the following tabular headings:

| Assets | = | Liabilities | + | | | | Stockholders' Equity | | | | |
|---|---|---|---|---|---|---|---|---|---|---|---|
| Cash + Supplies | = | Accounts Payable | + Capital Stock | – Dividends | + Sales Commissions | – Rent Expense | – Office Salaries Expense | – Auto Expense | – Supplies Expense | – Misc. Expense |

2.  Prepare an income statement for June, a retained earnings statement for June, and a balance sheet as of June 30.

**PR 1-5B  Transactions; financial statements**

Anny's Dry Cleaners is owned and operated by Anny Brum. A building and equipment are currently being rented, pending expansion to new facilities. The actual work of dry cleaning is done by another company at wholesale rates. The assets, liabilities, and capital stock of the business on June 1, 2012, are as follows: Cash, $25,000; Accounts Receivable, $30,000; Supplies, $5,000; Land, $50,000; Accounts Payable, $18,000; Capital Stock, $35,000. Business transactions during June are summarized as follows:

a.  Anny Brum invested additional cash in the business with a deposit of $15,000 in exchange for capital stock.

b.  Purchased land for use as a parking lot, paying cash of $20,000.

c.  Paid rent for the month, $3,000.

d.  Charged customers for dry cleaning revenue on account, $22,000.

e.  Paid creditors on account, $13,000.

f.  Purchased supplies on account, $1,000.

g.  Received cash from cash customers for dry cleaning revenue, $28,000.

h.  Received cash from customers on account, $27,000.

i.  Received monthly invoice for dry cleaning expense for June (to be paid on July 10), $21,500.

j.  Paid the following: wages expense, $14,000; truck expense, $2,100; utilities expense, $1,800; miscellaneous expense, $1,300.

k.  Determined that the cost of supplies on hand was $3,400; therefore, the cost of supplies used during the month was $2,600.

l.  Paid dividends, $1,000.

**Instructions**

1.  Determine the amount of retained earnings as of June 1.

2.  State the assets, liabilities, and stockholders' equity as of June 1 in equation form similar to that shown in this chapter. In tabular form below the equation, indicate increases and decreases resulting from each transaction and the new balances after each transaction.

*(continued)*

3. Prepare an income statement for June, a retained earnings statement for June, and a balance sheet as of June 30.

4. (Optional) Prepare a statement of cash flows for June.

**OBJ. 5**

✔ i. $130,000

### PR 1-6B Missing amounts from financial statements

The financial statements at the end of Cyber Realty's first month of operations are shown below.

**Cyber Realty**
**Income Statement**
**For the Month Ended October 31, 2012**

| | | |
|---|---|---|
| Fees earned.......................................................... | | $250,000 |
| Expenses: | | |
| Wages expense...................................................... | $ (a) | |
| Rent expense....................................................... | 30,000 | |
| Supplies expense.................................................... | 11,000 | |
| Utilities expense.................................................... | 9,000 | |
| Miscellaneous expense.............................................. | 3,000 | |
| Total expenses ................................................. | | 180,000 |
| Net income ........................................................ | | $ (b) |

**Cyber Realty**
**Retained Earnings Statement**
**For the Month Ended October 31, 2012**

| | | |
|---|---|---|
| Retained earnings, October 1, 2012...................................... | | $ (c) |
| Net income ......................................................... | $ (d) | |
| Less dividends ...................................................... | (e) | |
| Increase in retained earnings.......................................... | | (f) |
| Retained earnings, October 31, 2012..................................... | | $ (g) |

**Cyber Realty**
**Balance Sheet**
**October 31, 2012**

| Assets | | Liabilities | |
|---|---|---|---|
| Cash ................................ | $77,000 | Accounts payable ............... | $ 30,000 |
| Supplies............................ | 8,000 | **Stockholders' Equity** | |
| Land ............................... | (h) | Capital stock ................... | $ (j) |
| | | Retained earnings............... | (k) |
| | | Total stockholders' equity........ | (l) |
| | | Total liabilities and | |
| Total assets ........................ | $ (i) | stockholders' equity........... | $ (m) |

**Cyber Realty**
**Statement of Cash Flows**
**For the Month Ended October 31, 2012**

| | | |
|---|---|---|
| Cash flows from operating activities: | | |
| Cash received from customers ......................................... | $ (n) | |
| Deduct cash payments for expenses and payments to creditors .......... | 158,000 | |
| Net cash flow from operating activities................................. | | $ (o) |
| Cash flows from investing activities: | | |
| Cash payments for acquisition of land................................. | | (75,000) |
| Cash flows from financing activities: | | |
| Cash received from issuing capital stock............................... | $100,000 | |
| Deduct cash dividends................................................ | 40,000 | |
| Net cash flow from financing activities ................................ | | (p) |
| Net cash flow and October 31, 2012, cash balance ....................... | | $ (q) |

### Instructions

By analyzing the interrelationships among the four financial statements, determine the proper amounts for (a) through (q).

## Continuing Problem

✔ 2. Net income:
$1,980

Pat Sharpe enjoys listening to all types of music and owns countless CDs. Over the years, Pat has gained a local reputation for knowledge of music from classical to rap and the ability to put together sets of recordings that appeal to all ages.

During the last several months, Pat served as a guest disc jockey on a local radio station. In addition, Pat has entertained at several friends' parties as the host deejay.

On June 1, 2012, Pat established a corporation known as PS Music. Using an extensive collection of music MP3 files, Pat will serve as a disc jockey on a fee basis for weddings, college parties, and other events. During June, Pat entered into the following transactions:

June 1. Deposited $5,000 in a checking account in the name of PS Music in exchange for capital stock.

  2. Received $3,600 from a local radio station for serving as the guest disc jockey for June.

  2. Agreed to share office space with a local real estate agency, Downtown Realty. PS Music will pay one-fourth of the rent. In addition, PS Music agreed to pay a portion of the salary of the receptionist and to pay one-fourth of the utilities. Paid $750 for the rent of the office.

  4. Purchased supplies from City Office Supply Co. for $350. Agreed to pay $100 within 10 days and the remainder by July 5, 2012.

  6. Paid $450 to a local radio station to advertise the services of PS Music twice daily for two weeks.

  8. Paid $700 to a local electronics store for renting digital recording equipment.

  12. Paid $350 (music expense) to Cool Music for the use of its current music demos to make various music sets.

  13. Paid City Office Supply Co. $100 on account.

  16. Received $500 from a dentist for providing two music sets for the dentist to play for her patients.

  22. Served as disc jockey for a wedding party. The father of the bride agreed to pay $1,250 the 1st of July.

  25. Received $400 for serving as the disc jockey for a cancer charity ball hosted by the local hospital.

  29. Paid $240 (music expense) to Galaxy Music for the use of its library of music demos.

  30. Received $900 for serving as PS disc jockey for a local club's monthly dance.

  30. Paid Downtown Realty $400 for PS Music's share of the receptionist's salary for June.

  30. Paid Downtown Realty $300 for PS Music's share of the utilities for June.

  30. Determined that the cost of supplies on hand is $170. Therefore, the cost of supplies used during the month was $180.

  30. Paid for miscellaneous expenses, $300.

  30. Paid $1,000 royalties (music expense) to National Music Clearing for use of various artists' music during the month.

  30. Paid dividends of $500.

### Instructions

1. Indicate the effect of each transaction and the balances after each transaction, using the following tabular headings:

| Assets | | | = | Liabilities | + | | | | Stockholders' Equity | | | | | | |
|---|---|---|---|---|---|---|---|---|---|---|---|---|---|---|---|
| | | | | | | | | | | | Office | Equipment | | | |
| | Accts. | | | Accounts | Capital | | | Fees | Music | Rent | Rent | Advertising | Wages | Utilities | Supplies | Misc. |
| Cash + | Rec. + | Supplies = | Payable + | Stock | – Dividends + | Earned – | Exp. – | Exp. – | Exp. – | Exp. – | Exp. – | Exp. – | Exp. – | Exp. |

2. Prepare an income statement for PS Music for the month ended June 30, 2012.

3. Prepare a retained earnings statement for PS Music for the month ended June 30, 2012.

4. Prepare a balance sheet for PS Music as of June 30, 2012.

## Cases & Projects

You can access the Cases & Projects online at **www.cengage.com/accounting/reeve**

© AP Photo/Paul Sakuma

# Analyzing Transactions

## *Apple, Inc.* ™

**E**very day it seems like we get an incredible amount of incoming e-mail messages; you get them from your friends, relatives, subscribed e-mail lists, and even spammers! But how do you organize all of these messages? You might create folders to sort messages by sender, topic, or project. Perhaps you use keyword search utilities. You might even use filters/rules to automatically delete spam or send messages from your best friend to a special folder. In any case, you are organizing information so that it is simple to retrieve and allows you to understand, respond, or refer to the messages.

In the same way that you organize your e-mail, companies develop an organized method for processing, recording, and summarizing financial transactions. For example, **Apple, Inc.**, has a huge volume of financial transactions, resulting from sales of its innovative computers, digital media (iTunes),

iPods, iPhones, and iPads. When Apple sells an iPad, a customer has the option of paying with credit card, a debit or check card, an Apple gift card, a financing arrangement, or cash. In order to analyze only the information related to Apple's cash transactions, the company must record or summarize all these similar sales using a single category or "cash" account. Similarly, Apple will record credit card payments for iPads and sales from financing arrangements in different accounts (records).

While Chapter 1 uses the accounting equation (Assets = Liabilities + Owner's Equity) to analyze and record financial transactions, this chapter presents more practical and efficient recording methods that most companies use. In addition, this chapter discusses possible accounting errors that may occur, along with methods to detect and correct them.

**OBJ. 1** Describe the characteristics of an account and a chart of accounts.

# Using Accounts to Record Transactions

In Chapter 1, the November transactions for NetSolutions were recorded using the accounting equation format shown in Exhibit 1. However, this format is not efficient or practical for companies that have to record thousands or millions of transactions daily. As a result, accounting systems are designed to show the increases and decreases in each accounting equation element as a separate record. This record is called an **account**.

To illustrate, the Cash column of Exhibit 1 records the increases and decreases in cash. Likewise, the other columns in Exhibit 1 record the increases and decreases in the other accounting equation elements. Each of these columns can be organized into a separate account.

An account, in its simplest form, has three parts.

1. A title, which is the name of the accounting equation element recorded in the account.
2. A space for recording increases in the amount of the element.
3. A space for recording decreases in the amount of the element.

The account form presented below is called a **T account** because it resembles the letter T. The left side of the account is called the *debit* side, and the right side is called the *credit* side.[1]

| Title | |
|---|---|
| Left side | Right side |
| *debit* | *credit* |

1 The terms *debit* and *credit* are derived from the Latin *debere* and *credere*.

**EXHIBIT 1**   **NetSolutions November Transactions**

| | Assets | | | = | Liabilities + | | Stockholders' Equity | | | | | | | |
|---|---|---|---|---|---|---|---|---|---|---|---|---|---|---|
| | | | | | Accounts | Capital | | Fees | Wages | Rent | Supplies | Utilities | Misc. |
| | Cash | + Supp. + | Land | = | Payable + | Stock | − Dividends + | Earned − | Exp. − | Exp. − | Exp. − | Exp. − | Exp. |
| a. | +25,000 | | | | | +25,000 | | | | | | | |
| b. | −20,000 | | +20,000 | | | | | | | | | | |
| Bal. | 5,000 | | 20,000 | | | 25,000 | | | | | | | |
| c. | | +1,350 | | | +1,350 | | | | | | | | |
| Bal. | 5,000 | 1,350 | 20,000 | | 1,350 | 25,000 | | | | | | | |
| d. | +7,500 | | | | | | | +7,500 | | | | | |
| Bal. | 12,500 | 1,350 | 20,000 | | 1,350 | 25,000 | | 7,500 | | | | | |
| e. | −3,650 | | | | | | | | −2,125 | −800 | | −450 | −275 |
| Bal. | 8,850 | 1,350 | 20,000 | | 1,350 | 25,000 | | 7,500 | −2,125 | −800 | | −450 | −275 |
| f. | −950 | | | | −950 | | | | | | | | |
| Bal. | 7,900 | 1,350 | 20,000 | | 400 | 25,000 | | 7,500 | −2,125 | −800 | | −450 | −275 |
| g. | | −800 | | | | | | | | | −800 | | |
| Bal. | 7,900 | 550 | 20,000 | | 400 | 25,000 | | 7,500 | −2,125 | −800 | −800 | −450 | −275 |
| h. | −2,000 | | | | | | −2,000 | | | | | | |
| Bal. | 5,900 | 550 | 20,000 | | 400 | 25,000 | −2,000 | 7,500 | −2,125 | −800 | −800 | −450 | −275 |

The amounts shown in the Cash column of Exhibit 1 would be recorded in a cash account as follows:

**Note:** Amounts entered on the left side of an account are debits, and amounts entered on the right side of an account are credits.

**Cash**

| | | | | | |
|---|---|---|---|---|---|
| Debit Side of Account | (a) (d) | 25,000 7,500 | (b) (e) (f) (h) | 20,000 3,650 950 2,000 | Credit Side of Account |
| | Balance | 5,900 | | | |

Balance of account →

Recording transactions in accounts must follow certain rules. For example, increases in assets are recorded on the **debit** (left side) of an account. Likewise, decreases in assets are recorded on the **credit** (right side) of an account. The excess of the debits of an asset account over its credits is the **balance of the account**.

To illustrate, the receipt (increase in Cash) of $25,000 in transaction (a) is entered on the debit (left) side of the cash account shown above. The letter or date of the transaction is also entered into the account. This is done so if any questions later arise related to the entry, the entry can be traced back to the underlying transaction data. In contrast, the payment (decrease in Cash) of $20,000 to purchase land in transaction (b) is entered on the credit (right) side of the account.

The balance of the cash account of $5,900 is the excess of the debits over the credits as shown below.

| | |
|---|---|
| Debits ($25,000 + $7,500) . . . . . . . . . . . . . . . . . . . . . . . . . . . . . . . . . . . . . . . | $32,500 |
| Less credits ($20,000 + $3,650 + $950 + $2,000). . . . . . . . . . . . . . . . . . . . . . . . . . . . . . . . . | 26,600 |
| Balance of Cash as of November 30, 2011 . . . . . . . . . . . . . . . . . . . . . . . . . . . . . . . . . . . . | $ 5,900 |

The balance of the cash account is inserted in the account, in the Debit column. In this way, the balance is identified as a debit balance.[2] This balance represents NetSolutions' cash on hand as of November 30, 2011. This balance of $5,900 is reported on the November 30, 2011, balance sheet for NetSolutions as shown in Exhibit 6 of Chapter 1.

2 The totals of the debit and credit columns may be shown separately in an account. When this is done, these amounts should be identified in some way so that they are not mistaken for entries or the ending balance of the account.

In an actual accounting system, a more formal account form replaces the T account. Later in this chapter, a four-column account is illustrated. The T account, however, is a simple way to illustrate the effects of transactions on accounts and financial statements. For this reason, T accounts are often used in business to explain transactions.

Each of the columns in Exhibit 1 can be converted into an account form in a similar manner as was done for the Cash column of Exhibit 1. However, as mentioned earlier, recording increases and decreases in accounts must follow certain rules. These rules are discussed after the chart of accounts is described.

## Chart of Accounts

A group of accounts for a business entity is called a **ledger**. A list of the accounts in the ledger is called a **chart of accounts**. The accounts are normally listed in the order in which they appear in the financial statements. The balance sheet accounts are listed first, in the order of assets, liabilities, and stockholders' equity. The income statement accounts are then listed in the order of revenues and expenses.

**Assets** are resources owned by the business entity. These resources can be physical items, such as cash and supplies, or intangibles that have value. Examples of intangible assets include patent rights, copyrights, and trademarks. Assets also include accounts receivable, prepaid expenses (such as insurance), buildings, equipment, and land.

**Liabilities** are debts owed to outsiders (creditors). Liabilities are often identified on the balance sheet by titles that include *payable*. Examples of liabilities include accounts payable, notes payable, and wages payable. Cash received before services are delivered creates a liability to perform the services. These future service commitments are called *unearned revenues*. Examples of unearned revenues include magazine subscriptions received by a publisher and tuition received at the beginning of a term by a college.

**Stockholders' equity** is the stockholders' right to the assets of the business. Stockholders' equity is represented by the balance of the capital stock and retained earnings accounts. A **dividends** account represents distributions of earnings to stockholders.

**Revenues** are increases in stockholders' equity (retained earnings) as a result of selling services or products to customers. Examples of revenues include fees earned, fares earned, commissions revenue, and rent revenue.

## BusinessConnection

### THE HIJACKING RECEIVABLE

A company's chart of accounts should reflect the basic nature of its operations. Occasionally, however, transactions take place that give rise to unusual accounts. The following is a story of one such account.

Before strict airport security was implemented across the United States, several airlines experienced hijacking incidents. One such incident occurred when a Southern Airways DC-9 en route from Memphis to Miami was hijacked during a stopover in Birmingham, Alabama. The three hijackers boarded the plane in Birmingham armed with handguns and hand grenades. At gunpoint, the hijackers took the plane, the plane's crew, and the passengers to nine American cities, Toronto, and eventually to Havana, Cuba.

During the long flight, the hijackers demanded a ransom of $10 million. Southern Airways, however, was only able to come up with $2 million. Eventually, the pilot talked the hijackers into settling for the $2 million when the plane landed in Chattanooga for refueling.

Upon landing in Havana, the Cuban authorities arrested the hijackers and, after a brief delay, sent the plane, passengers, and crew back to the United States. The hijackers and $2 million stayed in Cuba.

How did Southern Airways account for and report the hijacking payment in its subsequent financial statements? As you might have analyzed, the initial entry credited Cash for $2 million. The debit was to an account entitled "Hijacking Payment." This account was reported as a type of receivable under "other assets" on Southern's balance sheet. The company maintained that it would be able to collect the cash from the Cuban government and that, therefore, a receivable existed. In fact, Southern Airways was repaid $2 million by the Cuban government, which was, at that time, attempting to improve relations with the United States.

**Expenses** result from using up assets or consuming services in the process of generating revenues. Examples of expenses include wages expense, rent expense, utilities expense, supplies expense, and miscellaneous expense.

A chart of accounts should meet the needs of a company's managers and other users of its financial statements. The accounts within the chart of accounts are numbered for use as references. A numbering system is normally used, so that new accounts can be added without affecting other account numbers.

Exhibit 2 is NetSolutions' chart of accounts that is used in this chapter. Additional accounts will be introduced in later chapters. In Exhibit 2, each account number has two digits. The first digit indicates the major account group of the ledger in which the account is located. Accounts beginning with 1 represent assets; 2, liabilities; 3, stockholders' equity; 4, revenue; and 5, expenses. The second digit indicates the location of the account within its group.

Procter & Gamble's account numbers have over 30 digits to reflect P&G's many different operations and regions.

| Balance Sheet Accounts | Income Statement Accounts |
|---|---|
| **1. Assets** | **4. Revenue** |
| 11  Cash | 41  Fees Earned |
| 12  Accounts Receivable | **5. Expenses** |
| 14  Supplies | 51  Wages Expense |
| 15  Prepaid Insurance | 52  Rent Expense |
| 17  Land | 54  Utilities Expense |
| 18  Office Equipment | 55  Supplies Expense |
| **2. Liabilities** | 59  Miscellaneous Expense |
| 21  Accounts Payable | |
| 23  Unearned Rent | |
| **3. Stockholders' Equity** | |
| 31  Capital Stock | |
| 32  Retained Earnings | |
| 33  Dividends | |

Each of the columns in Exhibit 1 has been assigned an account number in the chart of accounts shown in Exhibit 2. In addition, Accounts Receivable, Prepaid Insurance, Office Equipment, and Unearned Rent have been added. These accounts will be used in recording NetSolutions' December transactions.

# Double-Entry Accounting System

**OBJ. 2** Describe and illustrate journalizing transactions using the double-entry accounting system.

All businesses use what is called the **double-entry accounting system**. This system is based on the accounting equation and requires:

1. Every business transaction to be recorded in at least two accounts.
2. The total debits recorded for each transaction to be equal to the total credits recorded.

The double-entry accounting system also has specific **rules of debit and credit** for recording transactions in the accounts.

## Balance Sheet Accounts

The debit and credit rules for balance sheet accounts are as follows:

| Balance Sheet Accounts | | | | | |
|---|---|---|---|---|---|
| **ASSETS** Asset Accounts | | = **LIABILITIES** Liability Accounts | | + **STOCKHOLDERS' EQUITY** Stockholders' Equity Accounts | |
| Debit for increases (+) | Credit for decreases (−) | Debit for decreases (−) | Credit for increases (+) | Debit for decreases (−) | Credit for increases (+) |

# Income Statement Accounts

The debit and credit rules for income statement accounts are based on their relationship with stockholders' equity (retained earnings). As shown on page 53, stockholders' equity accounts are increased by credits. Since revenues increase stockholders' equity (retained earnings), revenue accounts are increased by credits and decreased by debits. Since stockholders' equity (retained earnings) accounts are decreased by debits, expense accounts are increased by debits and decreased by credits. Thus, the rules of debit and credit for revenue and expense accounts are as follows:

**Income Statement Accounts**

| Revenue Accounts | | Expense Accounts | |
|---|---|---|---|
| Debit for decreases (–) | Credit for increases (+) | Debit for increases (+) | Credit for decreases (–) |

# Dividends

The debit and credit rules for recording dividends are based on the effect of dividends on stockholders' equity (retained earnings). Since dividends decrease stockholders' equity (retained earnings), the dividends account is increased by debits. Likewise, the dividends account is decreased by credits. Thus, the rules of debit and credit for the dividends account are as follows:

**Dividends**

| Debit for increases (+) | Credit for decreases (–) |
|---|---|

# Normal Balances

The sum of the increases in an account is usually equal to or greater than the sum of the decreases in the account. Thus, the **normal balance of an account** is either a debit or credit depending on whether increases in the account are recorded as debits or credits. For example, since asset accounts are increased with debits, asset accounts normally have debit balances. Likewise, liability accounts normally have credit balances.

The rules of debit and credit and the normal balances of the various types of accounts are summarized in Exhibit 3. Debits and credits are sometimes abbreviated as Dr. for debit and Cr. for credit.

When an account normally having a debit balance has a credit balance, or vice versa, an error may have occurred or an unusual situation may exist. For example, a credit balance in the office equipment account could result only from an error, because a business cannot have more decreases than increases of office equipment. But a debit balance in an accounts payable account could result from an overpayment.

## Example Exercise 2-1   Rules of Debit and Credit and Normal Balances   OBJ. 2

State for each account whether it is likely to have (a) debit entries only, (b) credit entries only, or (c) both debit and credit entries. Also, indicate its normal balance.

1. Dividends
2. Accounts Payable
3. Cash
4. Fees Earned
5. Supplies
6. Utilities Expense

### Follow My Example 2-1

1. Debit entries only; normal debit balance
2. Debit and credit entries; normal credit balance
3. Debit and credit entries; normal debit balance
4. Credit entries only; normal credit balance
5. Debit and credit entries; normal debit balance
6. Debit entries only; normal debit balance

Practice Exercises: **PE 2-1A, PE 2-1B**

**EXHIBIT 3** **Rules of Debit and Credit, Normal Balances of Accounts**

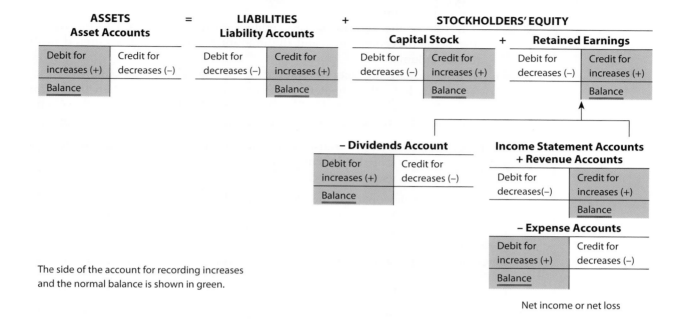

The side of the account for recording increases and the normal balance is shown in green.

Net income or net loss

## Journalizing

Using the rules of debit and credit, transactions are initially entered in a record called a **journal**. In this way, the journal serves as a record of when transactions occurred and were recorded. To illustrate, the November transactions of NetSolutions from Chapter 1 are used.

*Nov. 1   Chris Clark deposited $25,000 in a bank account in the name of NetSolutions in return for shares of stock in the corporation.*

**Transaction A**

This transaction increases an asset account and increases a stockholders' equity account. It is recorded in the journal as an increase (debit) to Cash and an increase (credit) to Capital Stock.

**Analysis**

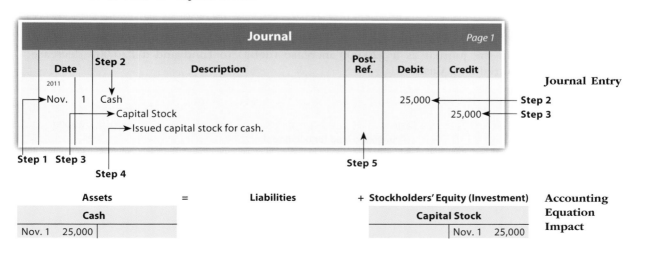

**Journal Entry**

**Accounting Equation Impact**

The transaction is recorded in the journal using the following steps:

A journal can be thought of as being similar to an individual's diary of significant day-to-day life events.

Step 1.  The date of the transaction is entered in the Date column.

Step 2.  The title of the account to be debited is recorded at the left-hand margin under the Description column, and the amount to be debited is entered in the Debit column.

Step 3.  The title of the account to be credited is listed below and to the right of the debited account title, and the amount to be credited is entered in the Credit column.

Step 4.  A brief description may be entered below the credited account.

Step 5.  The Post. Ref. (Posting Reference) column is left blank when the journal entry is initially recorded. This column is used later in this chapter when the journal entry amounts are transferred to the accounts in the ledger.

The process of recording a transaction in the journal is called **journalizing**. The entry in the journal is called a **journal entry**.

The following is a useful method for analyzing and journalizing transactions:

1. Carefully read the description of the transaction to determine whether an asset, a liability, a stockholders' equity, a revenue, an expense, or a dividends account is affected.
2. For each account affected by the transaction, determine whether the account increases or decreases.
3. Determine whether each increase or decrease should be recorded as a debit or a credit, following the rules of debit and credit shown in Exhibit 3.
4. Record the transaction using a journal entry.

The following table summarizes terminology that is often used in describing a transaction along with the related accounts that would be debited and credited.

| | Journal Entry Account | |
| Common transaction terminology | Debit | Credit |
| --- | --- | --- |
| Received cash for services provided | Cash | Fees Earned |
| Services provided on account | Accounts Receivable | Fees Earned |
| Received cash on account | Cash | Accounts Receivable |
| Purchased on account | Asset account | Accounts Payable |
| Paid on account | Accounts Payable | Cash |
| Paid cash | Asset or expense account | Cash |
| Issued capital stock | Cash and/or other assets | Capital Stock |
| Paid dividends | Dividends | Cash |

The remaining transactions of NetSolutions for November are analyzed and journalized next.

**Transaction B**  *Nov. 5   NetSolutions paid $20,000 for the purchase of land as a future building site.*

**Analysis**  This transaction increases one asset account and decreases another. It is recorded in the journal as a $20,000 increase (debit) to Land and a $20,000 decrease (credit) to Cash.

**Journal Entry**

| Nov. | 5 | Land | | 20,000 | |
| | | Cash | | | 20,000 |
| | | Purchased land for building site. | | | |

**Accounting Equation Impact**

| Assets | = | Liabilities | + | Stockholders' Equity |
| --- | --- | --- | --- | --- |

**Land**

| Nov. 5 | 20,000 | |

**Cash**

| | Nov. 5 | 20,000 |

*Nov. 10  NetSolutions purchased supplies on account for $1,350.*  **Transaction C**

This transaction increases an asset account and increases a liability account. It is recorded in the journal as a $1,350 increase (debit) to Supplies and a $1,350 increase (credit) to Accounts Payable.  **Analysis**

| Nov. | 10 | Supplies | | 1,350 | |
|---|---|---|---|---|---|
| | | Accounts Payable | | | 1,350 |
| | | Purchased supplies on account. | | | |

**Journal Entry**

| Assets | = | Liabilities | + | Stockholders' Equity |
|---|---|---|---|---|
| **Supplies** | | **Accounts Payable** | | |
| Nov. 10    1,350 | | Nov. 10    1,350 | | |

**Accounting Equation Impact**

---

*Nov. 18  NetSolutions received cash of $7,500 from customers for services provided.*  **Transaction D**

This transaction increases an asset account and increases a revenue account. It is recorded in the journal as a $7,500 increase (debit) to Cash and a $7,500 increase (credit) to Fees Earned.  **Analysis**

| Nov. | 18 | Cash | | 7,500 | |
|---|---|---|---|---|---|
| | | Fees Earned | | | 7,500 |
| | | Received fees from customers. | | | |

**Journal Entry**

| Assets | = | Liabilities | + | Stockholders' Equity (Revenue) |
|---|---|---|---|---|
| **Cash** | | | | **Fees Earned** |
| Nov. 18    7,500 | | | | Nov. 18    7,500 |

**Accounting Equation Impact**

---

*Nov. 30  NetSolutions incurred the following expenses: wages, $2,125; rent, $800; utilities, $450; and miscellaneous, $275.*  **Transaction E**

This transaction increases various expense accounts and decreases an asset (Cash) account. You should note that regardless of the number of accounts, *the sum of the debits is always equal to the sum of the credits in a journal entry*. It is recorded in the journal with increases (debits) to the expense accounts (Wages Expense, $2,125; Rent Expense, $800; Utilities Expense, $450; and Miscellaneous Expense, $275) and a decrease (credit) to Cash, $3,650.  **Analysis**

| Nov. | 30 | Wages Expense | | 2,125 | |
|---|---|---|---|---|---|
| | | Rent Expense | | 800 | |
| | | Utilities Expense | | 450 | |
| | | Miscellaneous Expense | | 275 | |
| | | Cash | | | 3,650 |
| | | Paid expenses. | | | |

**Journal Entry**

| Assets | = | Liabilities | + | Stockholders' Equity (Expense) |
|---|---|---|---|---|
| **Cash** | | | | **Wages Expense** |
| | Nov. 30    3,650 | | | Nov. 30    2,125 |

**Accounting Equation Impact**

| **Rent Expense** |
|---|
| Nov. 30    800 |

| **Utilities Expense** |
|---|
| Nov. 30    450 |

| **Miscellaneous Expense** |
|---|
| Nov. 30    275 |

**Transaction F** *Nov. 30 NetSolutions paid creditors on account, $950.*

**Analysis**

This transaction decreases a liability account and decreases an asset account. It is recorded in the journal as a $950 decrease (debit) to Accounts Payable and a $950 decrease (credit) to Cash.

**Journal Entry**

| Nov. | 30 | Accounts Payable | 950 | |
| | | Cash | | 950 |
| | | Paid creditors on account. | | |

**Accounting Equation Impact**

| Assets | = | Liabilities | + | Stockholders' Equity |
|---|---|---|---|---|
| **Cash** | | **Accounts Payable** | | |
| Nov. 30    950 | | Nov. 30    950 | | |

**Transaction G** *Nov. 30 Chris Clark determined that the cost of supplies on hand at November 30 was $550.*

**Analysis**

NetSolutions purchased $1,350 of supplies on November 10. Thus, $800 ($1,350 – $550) of supplies must have been used during November. This transaction is recorded in the journal as an $800 increase (debit) to Supplies Expense and an $800 decrease (credit) to Supplies.

**Journal Entry**

| Nov. | 30 | Supplies Expense | 800 | |
| | | Supplies | | 800 |
| | | Supplies used during November. | | |

**Accounting Equation Impact**

| Assets | = | Liabilities | + | Stockholders' Equity (Expense) |
|---|---|---|---|---|
| **Supplies** | | | | **Supplies Expense** |
| Nov. 30    800 | | | | Nov. 30    800 |

**Transaction H** *Nov. 30 NetSolutions paid $2,000 to stockholders (Chris Clark) as dividends.*

**Analysis**

This transaction decreases assets and stockholders' equity. This transaction is recorded in the journal as a $2,000 increase (debit) to Dividends and a $2,000 decrease (credit) to Cash.

**Journal Entry**

| | | Journal | | | Page 2 |
|---|---|---|---|---|---|
| **Date** | | **Description** | **Post. Ref.** | **Debit** | **Credit** |
| 2011 Nov. | 30 | Dividends | | 2,000 | |
| | | Cash | | | 2,000 |
| | | Paid dividends to stockholder. | | | |

**Accounting Equation Impact**

| Assets | = | Liabilities | + | Stockholders' Equity (Dividends) |
|---|---|---|---|---|
| **Cash** | | | | **Dividends** |
| Nov. 30  2,000 | | | | Nov. 30  2,000 |

## Integrity, Objectivity, and Ethics in Business

**WILL JOURNALIZING PREVENT FRAUD?**

While journalizing transactions reduces the possibility of fraud, it by no means eliminates it. For example, embezzlement can be hidden within the double-entry bookkeeping system by creating fictitious suppliers to whom checks are issued.

Excel can be used to input a journal entry as follows:

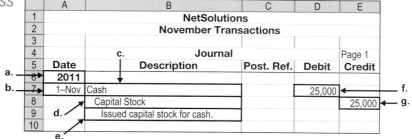

a. In cell A6, the journal year is entered (type 2011).

b. The month and day is then entered for each transaction. In cell A7, type "11-1".

c. The account to be **debited** is entered in cell B7 (type "Cash").

d. The account to be **credited** is entered and indented in cell B8 (type "Capital Stock"). Use the Excel indent format button to make the indention.

e. A description of the transaction is entered and indented, twice, in cell B9 (type "Issued capital stock for cash.").

f. The amount of the **debit** is entered in cell D7 (type 25000). Use the Excel comma format to insert commas.

g. The amount of the **credit** is entered in cell E8 (type 25000).

**Try**_It_    Go to the hands-on **Excel Tutor** for this example!

**Example Exercise** ▶ 2-2 ▶ **Journal Entry for Asset Purchase**    OBJ. 2

Prepare a journal entry for the purchase of a truck on June 3 for $42,500, paying $8,500 cash and the remainder on account.

**Follow My Example** ▶ 2-2 ▶

| | | Debit | Credit |
|---|---|---|---|
| June 3 | Truck............................................................................................... | 42,500 | |
| | Cash ........................................................................................... | | 8,500 |
| | Accounts Payable ....................................................................... | | 34,000 |

Practice Exercises: **PE 2-2A, PE 2-2B**

# Posting Journal Entries to Accounts

OBJ. **3** Describe and illustrate the journalizing and posting of transactions to accounts.

As illustrated, a transaction is first recorded in a journal. Periodically, the journal entries are transferred to the accounts in the ledger. The process of transferring the debits and credits from the journal entries to the accounts is called **posting**.

The December transactions of NetSolutions are used to illustrate posting from the journal to the ledger. By using the December transactions, an additional review of analyzing and journalizing transactions is provided.

**Dec. 1**    *NetSolutions paid a premium of $2,400 for an insurance policy for liability, theft, and fire. The policy covers a one-year period.*    **Transaction**

Advance payments of expenses, such as for insurance premiums, are called prepaid expenses. Prepaid expenses are assets. For NetSolutions, the asset purchased is insurance protection for 12 months. This transaction is recorded as a $2,400 increase (debit) to Prepaid Insurance and a $2,400 decrease (credit) to Cash.    **Analysis**

| Dec. | 1 | Prepaid Insurance | 15 | 2,400 | |
|---|---|---|---|---|---|
| | | Cash | 11 | | 2,400 |
| | | Paid premium on one-year policy. | | | |

**Journal Entry**

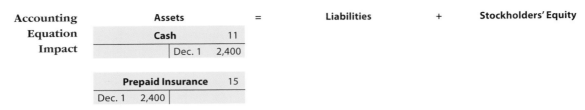

The posting of the preceding December 1 transaction is shown in Exhibit 4. Notice that the T account form is not used in Exhibit 4. In practice, the T account is usually replaced with a standard account form similar to that shown in Exhibit 4.

The debits and credits for each journal entry are posted to the accounts in the order in which they occur in the journal. To illustrate, the debit portion of the December 1 journal entry is posted to the prepaid account in Exhibit 4 using the following four steps:

Step 1. The date (Dec. 1) of the journal entry is entered in the Date column of Prepaid Insurance.

Step 2. The amount (2,400) is entered into the Debit column of Prepaid Insurance.

Step 3. The journal page number (2) is entered in the Posting Reference (Post. Ref.) column of Prepaid Insurance.

Step 4. The account number (15) is entered in the Posting Reference (Post. Ref.) column in the journal.

**EXHIBIT 4** **Diagram of the Recording and Posting of a Debit and a Credit**

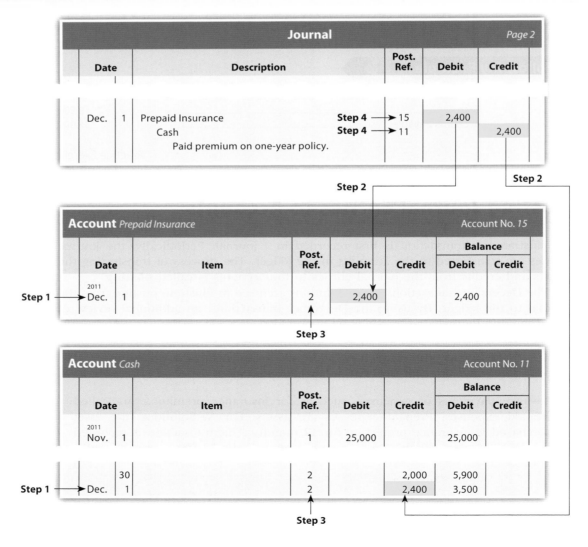

As shown in Exhibit 4, the credit portion of the December 1 journal entry is posted to the cash account in a similar manner.

The remaining December transactions for NetSolutions are analyzed and journalized in the following paragraphs. These transactions are posted to the ledger in Exhibit 5 on pages 68–69. To simplify, some of the December transactions are stated in summary form. For example, cash received for services is normally recorded on a daily basis. However, only summary totals are recorded at the middle and end of the month for NetSolutions.

The general ledger can be created in the <u>same</u> workbook on a separate worksheet. The general ledger (*GL*) worksheet references cells from the journal worksheet (*JE*) in order to post the journal entries into the ledger accounts.

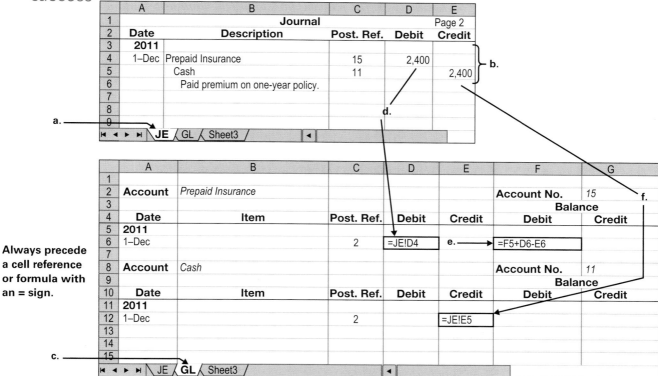

**Always precede a cell reference or formula with an = sign.**

**Build a formula by clicking on a referenced cell.**

a. Label a worksheet JE. This will be used as the spreadsheet journal.
b. Create the Dec. 1 *prepaid insurance* journal entry in the JE worksheet.
c. Label a new worksheet "GL" for general ledger.
d. In cell D6 of the GL worksheet, enter a cell reference to the **debit** of Prepaid insurance from the JE worksheet.
e. In cell F6, enter a formula to compute the new balance (previous balance plus debits minus credits, =F5+D6-E6.)
f. In cell E12 (of the GL worksheet), enter a cell reference for the **credit** to Cash from the JE worksheet.

**Try**It  Go to the hands-on **Excel Tutor** for this example!

---

Dec. 1  *NetSolutions paid rent for December, $800. The company from which*    **Transaction**
*NetSolutions is renting its store space now requires the payment of rent*
*on the first of each month, rather than at the end of the month.*

The advance payment of rent is an asset, much like the advance payment of the insurance premium in the preceding transaction. However, unlike the insurance premium, this prepaid rent will expire in one month. When an asset is purchased with the expectation that it will be used up in a short period of time, such as a month, it is normal to debit an expense account initially. This avoids having to transfer the balance from an asset account (Prepaid Rent) to an expense account (Rent Expense) at the end of the month. Thus, this transaction is recorded as an $800 increase (debit) to Rent Expense and an $800 decrease (credit) to Cash.

**Analysis**

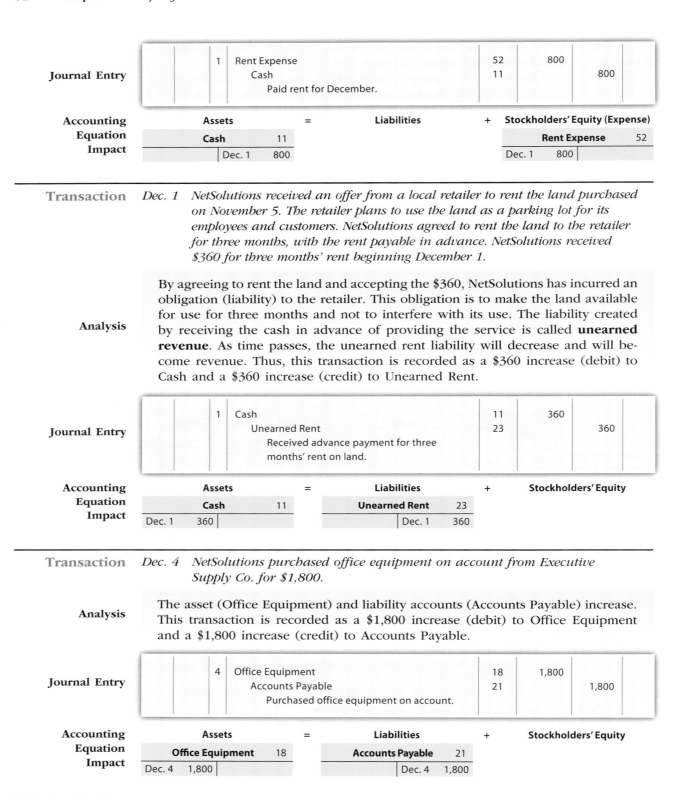

**Journal Entry**

| | | 1 | Rent Expense | 52 | 800 | |
| | | | Cash | 11 | | 800 |
| | | | Paid rent for December. | | | |

**Accounting Equation Impact**

| Assets | | = | Liabilities | + | Stockholders' Equity (Expense) | |
|---|---|---|---|---|---|---|
| **Cash** | 11 | | | | **Rent Expense** | 52 |
| Dec. 1 | 800 | | | | Dec. 1 | 800 |

---

**Transaction** *Dec. 1  NetSolutions received an offer from a local retailer to rent the land purchased on November 5. The retailer plans to use the land as a parking lot for its employees and customers. NetSolutions agreed to rent the land to the retailer for three months, with the rent payable in advance. NetSolutions received $360 for three months' rent beginning December 1.*

**Analysis**
By agreeing to rent the land and accepting the $360, NetSolutions has incurred an obligation (liability) to the retailer. This obligation is to make the land available for use for three months and not to interfere with its use. The liability created by receiving the cash in advance of providing the service is called **unearned revenue**. As time passes, the unearned rent liability will decrease and will become revenue. Thus, this transaction is recorded as a $360 increase (debit) to Cash and a $360 increase (credit) to Unearned Rent.

**Journal Entry**

| | | 1 | Cash | 11 | 360 | |
| | | | Unearned Rent | 23 | | 360 |
| | | | Received advance payment for three months' rent on land. | | | |

**Accounting Equation Impact**

| Assets | | = | Liabilities | | + | Stockholders' Equity |
|---|---|---|---|---|---|---|
| **Cash** | 11 | | **Unearned Rent** | 23 | | |
| Dec. 1 | 360 | | Dec. 1 | 360 | | |

---

**Transaction** *Dec. 4  NetSolutions purchased office equipment on account from Executive Supply Co. for $1,800.*

**Analysis**
The asset (Office Equipment) and liability accounts (Accounts Payable) increase. This transaction is recorded as a $1,800 increase (debit) to Office Equipment and a $1,800 increase (credit) to Accounts Payable.

**Journal Entry**

| | | 4 | Office Equipment | 18 | 1,800 | |
| | | | Accounts Payable | 21 | | 1,800 |
| | | | Purchased office equipment on account. | | | |

**Accounting Equation Impact**

| Assets | | = | Liabilities | | + | Stockholders' Equity |
|---|---|---|---|---|---|---|
| **Office Equipment** | 18 | | **Accounts Payable** | 21 | | |
| Dec. 4 | 1,800 | | Dec. 4 | 1,800 | | |

---

**Transaction** *Dec. 6  NetSolutions paid $180 for a newspaper advertisement.*

**Analysis**
An expense increases and an asset (Cash) decreases. Expense items that are expected to be minor in amount are normally included as part of the miscellaneous expense. This transaction is recorded as a $180 increase (debit) to Miscellaneous Expense and a $180 decrease (credit) to Cash.

| | 6 | Miscellaneous Expense | 59 | 180 | | Journal Entry |
| | | Cash | 11 | | 180 | |
| | | Paid for newspaper advertisement. | | | | |

| Assets | | = | Liabilities | + | Stockholders' Equity (Expense) | Accounting |
|---|---|---|---|---|---|---|
| **Cash** | 11 | | | | **Miscellaneous Exp.** 59 | Equation |
| Dec. 6 | 180 | | | | Dec. 6  180 | Impact |

---

**Dec. 11  NetSolutions paid creditors $400.** — Transaction

A liability (Accounts Payable) and an asset (Cash) decrease. This transaction is recorded as a $400 decrease (debit) to Accounts Payable and a $400 decrease (credit) to Cash. — Analysis

| | 11 | Accounts Payable | 21 | 400 | | Journal Entry |
| | | Cash | 11 | | 400 | |
| | | Paid creditors on account. | | | | |

| Assets | | = | Liabilities | | + | Stockholders' Equity | Accounting |
|---|---|---|---|---|---|---|---|
| **Cash** | 11 | | **Accounts Payable** | 21 | | | Equation |
| Dec. 11 | 400 | | Dec. 11  400 | | | | Impact |

---

**Dec. 13  NetSolutions paid a receptionist and a part-time assistant $950 for two weeks' wages.** — Transaction

This transaction is similar to the December 6 transaction, where an expense account is increased and Cash is decreased. This transaction is recorded as a $950 increase (debit) to Wages Expense and a $950 decrease (credit) to Cash. — Analysis

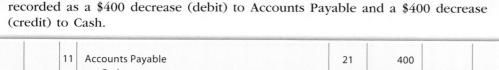

| Journal | | | | | Page 3 |
|---|---|---|---|---|---|
| Date | Description | Post. Ref. | Debit | Credit | |
| 2011 | | | | | |
| Dec. 13 | Wages Expense | 51 | 950 | | |
| | Cash | 11 | | 950 | |
| | Paid two weeks' wages. | | | | |

Journal Entry

| Assets | | = | Liabilities | + | Stockholders' Equity (Expense) | Accounting |
|---|---|---|---|---|---|---|
| **Cash** | 11 | | | | **Wages Expense** 51 | Equation |
| Dec. 13 | 950 | | | | Dec. 13  950 | Impact |

---

# BusinessConnection

## COMPUTERIZED ACCOUNTING SYSTEMS

Computerized accounting systems are widely used by even the smallest of companies. These systems simplify the record keeping process in that transactions are recorded in electronic forms. Forms used to bill customers for services provided are often completed using drop–down menus that list services that are normally provided to customers. An auto-complete entry feature may also be used to fill in customer names. For example, type "ca" to display customers with names beginning with "Ca" (Caban, Cahill, Carey, and Caswell). And, to simplify data entry, entries are automatically posted to the ledger accounts when the electronic form is completed.

One popular accounting software package used by small- to medium-sized businesses is QuickBooks®. Some examples of using QuickBooks to record accounting transactions are illustrated and discussed in Chapter 5.

| Transaction | Dec. 16   *NetSolutions received $3,100 from fees earned for the first half of December.* |
|---|---|
| **Analysis** | An asset account (Cash) and a revenue account (Fees Earned) increase. This transaction is recorded as a $3,100 increase (debit) to Cash and a $3,100 increase (credit) to Fees Earned. |

| | | | | | |
|---|---|---|---|---|---|
| | 16 | Cash | 11 | 3,100 | |
| **Journal Entry** | | Fees Earned | 41 | | 3,100 |
| | | Received fees from customers. | | | |

**Accounting Equation Impact**

| Assets | = | Liabilities | + | Stockholders' Equity (Revenue) |
|---|---|---|---|---|
| **Cash**                11 | | | | **Fees Earned**              41 |
| Dec. 16   3,100 | | | | Dec. 16   3,100 |

| Transaction | Dec. 16   *Fees earned on account totaled $1,750 for the first half of December.* |
|---|---|
| **Analysis** | When a business agrees that a customer may pay for services provided at a later date, an **account receivable** is created. An account receivable is a claim against the customer. An account receivable is an asset, and the revenue is earned even though no cash has been received. Thus, this transaction is recorded as a $1,750 increase (debit) to Accounts Receivable and a $1,750 increase (credit) to Fees Earned. |

| | | | | | |
|---|---|---|---|---|---|
| | 16 | Accounts Receivable | 12 | 1,750 | |
| **Journal Entry** | | Fees Earned | 41 | | 1,750 |
| | | Fees earned on account. | | | |

**Accounting Equation Impact**

| Assets | = | Liabilities | + | Stockholders' Equity (Revenue) |
|---|---|---|---|---|
| **Accounts Receivable**   12 | | | | **Fees Earned**              41 |
| Dec. 16   1,750 | | | | Dec. 16   1,750 |

| Transaction | Dec. 20   *NetSolutions paid $900 to Executive Supply Co. on the $1,800 debt owed from the December 4 transaction.* |
|---|---|
| **Analysis** | This is similar to the transaction of December 11. This transaction is recorded as a $900 decrease (debit) to Accounts Payable and a $900 decrease (credit) to Cash. |

| | | | | | |
|---|---|---|---|---|---|
| | 20 | Accounts Payable | 21 | 900 | |
| **Journal Entry** | | Cash | 11 | | 900 |
| | | Paid creditors on account. | | | |

**Accounting Equation Impact**

| Assets | = | Liabilities | + | Stockholders' Equity |
|---|---|---|---|---|
| **Cash**                11 | | **Accounts Payable**   21 | | |
| Dec. 20   900 | | Dec. 20   900 | | |

**Example Exercise   2-3   Journal Entry for Fees Earned**    OBJ. 3

Prepare a journal entry on August 7 for the fees earned on account, $115,000.

**Follow My Example   2-3**

| Aug. 7 | Accounts Receivable.......................................... | 115,000 | |
|---|---|---|---|
| | Fees Earned.......................................... | | 115,000 |

Practice Exercises: **PE 2-3A, PE 2-3B**

*Dec. 21   NetSolutions received $650 from customers in payment of their accounts.*

When customers pay amounts owed for services they have previously received, one asset increases and another asset decreases. This transaction is recorded as a $650 increase (debit) to Cash and a $650 decrease (credit) to Accounts Receivable.    Analysis

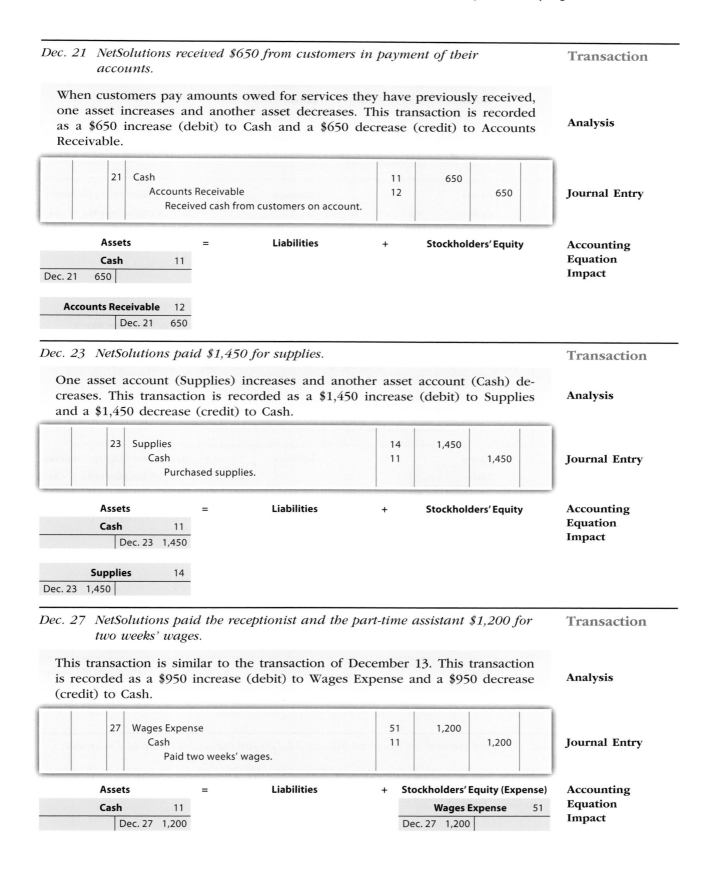

| | 21 | Cash | 11 | 650 | |
| | | Accounts Receivable | 12 | | 650 |
| | | Received cash from customers on account. | | | |

Journal Entry

**Assets** = **Liabilities** + **Stockholders' Equity**    Accounting Equation Impact

| **Cash** | 11 |
| Dec. 21 | 650 | |

| **Accounts Receivable** | 12 |
| | Dec. 21 | 650 |

*Dec. 23   NetSolutions paid $1,450 for supplies.*    Transaction

One asset account (Supplies) increases and another asset account (Cash) decreases. This transaction is recorded as a $1,450 increase (debit) to Supplies and a $1,450 decrease (credit) to Cash.    Analysis

| | 23 | Supplies | 14 | 1,450 | |
| | | Cash | 11 | | 1,450 |
| | | Purchased supplies. | | | |

Journal Entry

**Assets** = **Liabilities** + **Stockholders' Equity**    Accounting Equation Impact

| **Cash** | 11 |
| | Dec. 23 | 1,450 |

| **Supplies** | 14 |
| Dec. 23 | 1,450 | |

*Dec. 27   NetSolutions paid the receptionist and the part-time assistant $1,200 for two weeks' wages.*    Transaction

This transaction is similar to the transaction of December 13. This transaction is recorded as a $950 increase (debit) to Wages Expense and a $950 decrease (credit) to Cash.    Analysis

| | 27 | Wages Expense | 51 | 1,200 | |
| | | Cash | 11 | | 1,200 |
| | | Paid two weeks' wages. | | | |

Journal Entry

**Assets** = **Liabilities** + **Stockholders' Equity (Expense)**    Accounting Equation Impact

| **Cash** | 11 |
| | Dec. 27 | 1,200 |

| **Wages Expense** | 51 |
| Dec. 27 | 1,200 | |

| | | |
|---|---|---|
| **Transaction** | *Dec. 31   NetSolutions paid its $310 telephone bill for the month.* | |
| **Analysis** | This is similar to the transaction of December 6. This transaction is recorded as a $310 increase (debit) to Utilities Expense and a $310 decrease (credit) to Cash. | |

| | | | | | |
|---|---|---|---|---|---|
| | 31 | Utilities Expense | 54 | 310 | |
| **Journal Entry** | | Cash | 11 | | 310 |
| | | Paid telephone bill. | | | |

**Accounting Equation Impact**

| Assets | | = | Liabilities | + | Stockholders' Equity (Expense) | |
|---|---|---|---|---|---|---|
| **Cash** | 11 | | | | **Utilities Expense** | 54 |
| Dec. 31 | 310 | | | | Dec. 31   310 | |

---

| | |
|---|---|
| **Transaction** | *Dec. 31   NetSolutions paid its $225 electric bill for the month.* |
| **Analysis** | This is similar to the preceding transaction. This transaction is recorded as a $225 increase (debit) to Utilities Expense and a $225 decrease (credit) to Cash. |

**Journal Entry**

| | | | | Page 4 |
|---|---|---|---|---|
| **Journal** | | | | |

| Date | | Description | Post. Ref. | Debit | Credit |
|---|---|---|---|---|---|
| 2011 | | | | | |
| Dec. | 31 | Utilities Expense | 54 | 225 | |
| | | Cash | 11 | | 225 |
| | | Paid electric bill. | | | |

**Accounting Equation Impact**

| Assets | | = | Liabilities | + | Stockholders' Equity (Expense) | |
|---|---|---|---|---|---|---|
| **Cash** | 11 | | | | **Utilities Expense** | 54 |
| Dec. 31 | 225 | | | | Dec. 31   225 | |

---

| | |
|---|---|
| **Transaction** | *Dec. 31   NetSolutions received $2,870 from fees earned for the second half of December.* |
| **Analysis** | This is similar to the transaction of December 16. This transaction is recorded as a $2,870 increase (debit) to Cash and a $2,870 increase (credit) to Fees Earned. |

| | | | | | |
|---|---|---|---|---|---|
| | 31 | Cash | 11 | 2,870 | |
| **Journal Entry** | | Fees Earned | 41 | | 2,870 |
| | | Received fees from customers. | | | |

**Accounting Equation Impact**

| Assets | | = | Liabilities | + | Stockholders' Equity (Revenue) | |
|---|---|---|---|---|---|---|
| **Cash** | 11 | | | | **Fees Earned** | 41 |
| Dec. 31   2,870 | | | | | Dec. 31   2,870 | |

---

| | |
|---|---|
| **Transaction** | *Dec. 31   Fees earned on account totaled $1,120 for the second half of December.* |
| **Analysis** | This is similar to the transaction of December 16. This transaction is recorded as a $1,120 increase (debit) to Accounts Receivable and a $1,120 increase (credit) to Fees Earned. |

| | | | | | |
|---|---|---|---|---|---|
| | 31 | Accounts Receivable | 12 | 1,120 | |
| **Journal Entry** | | Fees Earned | 41 | | 1,120 |
| | | Fees earned on account. | | | |

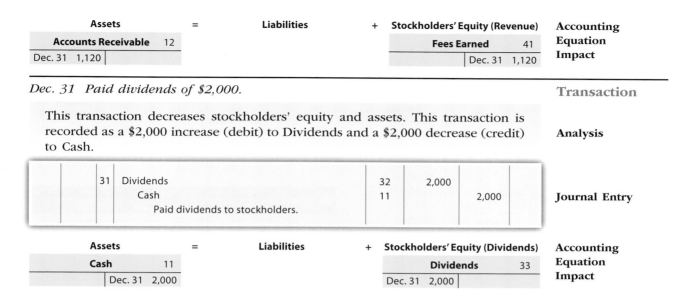

| Assets | = | Liabilities | + | Stockholders' Equity (Revenue) | Accounting |
|---|---|---|---|---|---|
| **Accounts Receivable** 12 | | | | **Fees Earned** 41 | Equation |
| Dec. 31  1,120 | | | | Dec. 31  1,120 | Impact |

**Dec. 31  Paid dividends of $2,000.**   *Transaction*

This transaction decreases stockholders' equity and assets. This transaction is recorded as a $2,000 increase (debit) to Dividends and a $2,000 decrease (credit) to Cash.   *Analysis*

| | 31 | Dividends | 32 | 2,000 | | *Journal Entry* |
|---|---|---|---|---|---|---|
| | | Cash | 11 | | 2,000 | |
| | | Paid dividends to stockholders. | | | | |

| Assets | = | Liabilities | + | Stockholders' Equity (Dividends) | Accounting |
|---|---|---|---|---|---|
| **Cash** 11 | | | | **Dividends** 33 | Equation |
| Dec. 31  2,000 | | | | Dec. 31  2,000 | Impact |

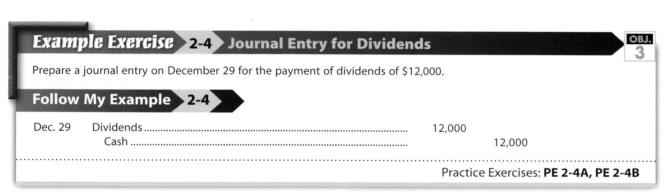

## Example Exercise 2-4  Journal Entry for Dividends    OBJ. 3

Prepare a journal entry on December 29 for the payment of dividends of $12,000.

### Follow My Example 2-4

| Dec. 29 | Dividends ......................................................................................... | 12,000 | |
|---|---|---|---|
| | Cash ......................................................................................... | | 12,000 |

Practice Exercises: **PE 2-4A, PE 2-4B**

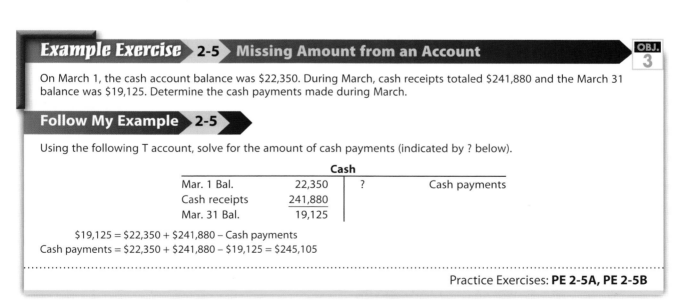

## Example Exercise 2-5  Missing Amount from an Account    OBJ. 3

On March 1, the cash account balance was $22,350. During March, cash receipts totaled $241,880 and the March 31 balance was $19,125. Determine the cash payments made during March.

### Follow My Example 2-5

Using the following T account, solve for the amount of cash payments (indicated by ? below).

| | Cash | | |
|---|---|---|---|
| Mar. 1 Bal. | 22,350 | ? | Cash payments |
| Cash receipts | 241,880 | | |
| Mar. 31 Bal. | 19,125 | | |

$19,125 = $22,350 + $241,880 − Cash payments
Cash payments = $22,350 + $241,880 − $19,125 = $245,105

Practice Exercises: **PE 2-5A, PE 2-5B**

Exhibit 5 shows the ledger for NetSolutions after the transactions for both November and December have been posted.

**EXHIBIT 5** **Ledger—NetSolutions**

### Ledger

#### Account Cash — Account No. 11

| Date | Item | Post. Ref. | Debit | Credit | Balance Debit | Balance Credit |
|---|---|---|---|---|---|---|
| 2011 | | | | | | |
| Nov. 1 | | 1 | 25,000 | | 25,000 | |
| 5 | | 1 | | 20,000 | 5,000 | |
| 18 | | 1 | 7,500 | | 12,500 | |
| 30 | | 1 | | 3,650 | 8,850 | |
| 30 | | 1 | | 950 | 7,900 | |
| 30 | | 2 | | 2,000 | 5,900 | |
| Dec. 1 | | 2 | | 2,400 | 3,500 | |
| 1 | | 2 | | 800 | 2,700 | |
| 1 | | 2 | 360 | | 3,060 | |
| 6 | | 2 | | 180 | 2,880 | |
| 11 | | 2 | | 400 | 2,480 | |
| 13 | | 3 | | 950 | 1,530 | |
| 16 | | 3 | 3,100 | | 4,630 | |
| 20 | | 3 | | 900 | 3,730 | |
| 21 | | 3 | 650 | | 4,380 | |
| 23 | | 3 | | 1,450 | 2,930 | |
| 27 | | 3 | | 1,200 | 1,730 | |
| 31 | | 3 | | 310 | 1,420 | |
| 31 | | 4 | | 225 | 1,195 | |
| 31 | | 4 | 2,870 | | 4,065 | |
| 31 | | 4 | | 2,000 | 2,065 | |

#### Account Accounts Receivable — Account No. 12

| Date | Item | Post. Ref. | Debit | Credit | Balance Debit | Balance Credit |
|---|---|---|---|---|---|---|
| 2011 | | | | | | |
| Dec. 16 | | 3 | 1,750 | | 1,750 | |
| 21 | | 3 | | 650 | 1,100 | |
| 31 | | 4 | 1,120 | | 2,220 | |

#### Account Supplies — Account No. 14

| Date | Item | Post. Ref. | Debit | Credit | Balance Debit | Balance Credit |
|---|---|---|---|---|---|---|
| 2011 | | | | | | |
| Nov. 10 | | 1 | 1,350 | | 1,350 | |
| 30 | | 1 | | 800 | 550 | |
| Dec. 23 | | 3 | 1,450 | | 2,000 | |

#### Account Prepaid Insurance — Account No. 15

| Date | Item | Post. Ref. | Debit | Credit | Balance Debit | Balance Credit |
|---|---|---|---|---|---|---|
| 2011 | | | | | | |
| Dec. 1 | | 2 | 2,400 | | 2,400 | |

#### Account Land — Account No. 17

| Date | Item | Post. Ref. | Debit | Credit | Balance Debit | Balance Credit |
|---|---|---|---|---|---|---|
| 2011 | | | | | | |
| Nov. 5 | | 1 | 20,000 | | 20,000 | |

#### Account Office Equipment — Account No. 18

| Date | Item | Post. Ref. | Debit | Credit | Balance Debit | Balance Credit |
|---|---|---|---|---|---|---|
| 2011 | | | | | | |
| Dec. 4 | | 2 | 1,800 | | 1,800 | |

#### Account Accounts Payable — Account No. 21

| Date | Item | Post. Ref. | Debit | Credit | Balance Debit | Balance Credit |
|---|---|---|---|---|---|---|
| 2011 | | | | | | |
| Nov. 10 | | 1 | | 1,350 | | 1,350 |
| 30 | | 1 | 950 | | | 400 |
| Dec. 4 | | 2 | | 1,800 | | 2,200 |
| 11 | | 2 | 400 | | | 1,800 |
| 20 | | 3 | 900 | | | 900 |

#### Account Unearned Rent — Account No. 23

| Date | Item | Post. Ref. | Debit | Credit | Balance Debit | Balance Credit |
|---|---|---|---|---|---|---|
| 2011 | | | | | | |
| Dec. 1 | | 2 | | 360 | | 360 |

#### Account Capital Stock — Account No. 31

| Date | Item | Post. Ref. | Debit | Credit | Balance Debit | Balance Credit |
|---|---|---|---|---|---|---|
| 2011 | | | | | | |
| Nov. 1 | | 1 | | 25,000 | | 25,000 |

#### Account Dividends — Account No. 33

| Date | Item | Post. Ref. | Debit | Credit | Balance Debit | Balance Credit |
|---|---|---|---|---|---|---|
| 2011 | | | | | | |
| Nov. 30 | | 2 | 2,000 | | 2,000 | |
| Dec. 31 | | 4 | 2,000 | | 4,000 | |

(continued)

## EXHIBIT 5    Ledger NetSolutions *(concluded)*

**Account** *Fees Earned*                    Account No. 41

| Date | Item | Post. Ref. | Debit | Credit | Balance Debit | Balance Credit |
|------|------|-----------|-------|--------|-------|--------|
| 2011 | | | | | | |
| Nov. 18 | | 1 | | 7,500 | | 7,500 |
| Dec. 16 | | 3 | | 3,100 | | 10,600 |
| 16 | | 3 | | 1,750 | | 12,350 |
| 31 | | 4 | | 2,870 | | 15,220 |
| 31 | | 4 | | 1,120 | | 16,340 |

**Account** *Wages Expense*                    Account No. 51

| Date | Item | Post. Ref. | Debit | Credit | Balance Debit | Balance Credit |
|------|------|-----------|-------|--------|-------|--------|
| 2011 | | | | | | |
| Nov. 30 | | 1 | 2,125 | | 2,125 | |
| Dec. 13 | | 3 | 950 | | 3,075 | |
| 27 | | 3 | 1,200 | | 4,275 | |

**Account** *Rent Expense*                    Account No. 52

| Date | Item | Post. Ref. | Debit | Credit | Balance Debit | Balance Credit |
|------|------|-----------|-------|--------|-------|--------|
| 2011 | | | | | | |
| Nov. 30 | | 1 | 800 | | 800 | |
| Dec. 1 | | 2 | 800 | | 1,600 | |

**Account** *Utilities Expense*                    Account No. 54

| Date | Item | Post. Ref. | Debit | Credit | Balance Debit | Balance Credit |
|------|------|-----------|-------|--------|-------|--------|
| 2011 | | | | | | |
| Nov. 30 | | 1 | 450 | | 450 | |
| Dec. 31 | | 3 | 310 | | 760 | |
| 31 | | 4 | 225 | | 985 | |

**Account** *Supplies Expense*                    Account No. 55

| Date | Item | Post. Ref. | Debit | Credit | Balance Debit | Balance Credit |
|------|------|-----------|-------|--------|-------|--------|
| 2011 | | | | | | |
| Nov. 30 | | 1 | 800 | | 800 | |

**Account** *Miscellaneous Expense*                    Account No. 59

| Date | Item | Post. Ref. | Debit | Credit | Balance Debit | Balance Credit |
|------|------|-----------|-------|--------|-------|--------|
| 2011 | | | | | | |
| Nov. 30 | | 1 | 275 | | 275 | |
| Dec. 6 | | 2 | 180 | | 455 | |

# Trial Balance

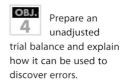

**OBJ. 4**  Prepare an unadjusted trial balance and explain how it can be used to discover errors.

Errors may occur in posting debits and credits from the journal to the ledger. One way to detect such errors is by preparing a **trial balance**. Double-entry accounting requires that debits must always equal credits. The trial balance verifies this equality. The steps in preparing a trial balance are as follows:

Step 1.  List the name of the company, the title of the trial balance, and the date the trial balance is prepared.

Step 2.  List the accounts from the ledger and enter their debit or credit balance in the Debit or Credit column of the trial balance.

Step 3.  Total the Debit and Credit columns of the trial balance.

Step 4.  Verify that the total of the Debit column equals the total of the Credit column.

The trial balance for NetSolutions as of December 31, 2011, is shown in Exhibit 6. The account balances in Exhibit 6 are taken from the ledger shown in Exhibit 5. Before a trial balance is prepared, each account balance in the ledger must be determined. When the standard account form is used as in Exhibit 5, the balance of each account appears in the balance column on the same line as the last posting to the account.

**EXHIBIT 6**

**Trial Balance**

Step 1

Step 2

| NetSolutions<br>Unadjusted Trial Balance<br>December 31, 2011 | Debit<br>Balances | Credit<br>Balances |
|---|---|---|
| Cash .......................................................... | 2,065 | |
| Accounts Receivable ................................... | 2,220 | |
| Supplies ..................................................... | 2,000 | |
| Prepaid Insurance ...................................... | 2,400 | |
| Land ........................................................... | 20,000 | |
| Office Equipment ....................................... | 1,800 | |
| Accounts Payable ....................................... | | 900 |
| Unearned Rent ........................................... | | 360 |
| Capital Stock .............................................. | | 25,000 |
| Dividends ................................................... | 4,000 | |
| Fees Earned ............................................... | | 16,340 |
| Wages Expense .......................................... | 4,275 | |
| Rent Expense ............................................. | 1,600 | |
| Utilities Expense ........................................ | 985 | |
| Supplies Expense ....................................... | 800 | |
| Miscellaneous Expense .............................. | 455 | |
| | 42,600 | 42,600 |

Steps 3–4

The trial balance shown in Exhibit 6 is titled an **unadjusted trial balance**. This is to distinguish it from other trial balances that will be prepared in later chapters. These other trial balances include an adjusted trial balance and a post-closing trial balance.[3]

## Errors Affecting the Trial Balance

If the trial balance totals are not equal, an error has occurred. In this case, the error must be found and corrected. A method useful in discovering errors is as follows:

1. If the difference between the Debit and Credit column totals is 10, 100, or 1,000, an error in addition may have occurred. In this case, re-add the trial balance column totals. If the error still exists, recompute the account balances.

2. If the difference between the Debit and Credit column totals can be evenly divisible by 2, the error may be due to the entering of a debit balance as a credit balance, or vice versa. In this case, review the trial balance for account balances of one-half the difference that may have been entered in the wrong column. For example, if the Debit column total is $20,640 and the Credit column total is $20,236, the difference of $404 ($20,640 – $20,236) may be due to a credit account balance of $202 that was entered as a debit account balance.

3. If the difference between the Debit and Credit column totals is evenly divisible by 9, trace the account balances back to the ledger to see if an account balance was incorrectly copied from the ledger. Two common types of copying errors are transpositions and slides. A **transposition** occurs when the order of the digits is copied incorrectly, such as writing $542 as $452 or $524. In a **slide**, the entire number is copied incorrectly one or more spaces to the right or the left, such as writing $542.00 as $54.20 or $5,420.00. In both cases, the resulting error will be evenly divisible by 9.

4. If the difference between the Debit and Credit column totals is not evenly divisible by 2 or 9, review the ledger to see if an account balance in the amount of the error has been omitted from the trial balance. If the error is not discovered, review the journal postings to see if a posting of a debit or credit may have been omitted.

3 The adjusted trial balance is discussed in Chapter 3, and the post-closing trial balance is discussed in Chapter 4.

5. If an error is not discovered by the preceding steps, the accounting process must be retraced, beginning with the last journal entry.

The trial balance does not provide complete proof of the accuracy of the ledger. It indicates only that the debits and the credits are equal. This proof is of value, however, because errors often affect the equality of debits and credits.

The unadjusted trial balance can be created on a spreadsheet. The unadjusted trial balance references the ledger account balances. To illustrate, the relationship between the Accounts Receivable account and unadjusted trial balance is as follows:

| | A | B | C | D | E | F | G |
|---|---|---|---|---|---|---|---|
| 1 | | | | | | | |
| 2 | **Account** | *Accounts Receivable* | | | | **Account No.** | *15* |
| 3 | | | | | | | **Balance** |
| 4 | **Date** | **Item** | **Post. Ref.** | **Debit** | **Credit** | **Debit** | **Credit** |
| 5 | 2011 | | | | | | |
| 6 | 16-Dec | | 3 | 1,750 | | =F5+D6-E6 | |
| 7 | 21-Dec | | 3 | | 650 | =F6+D7-E7 | }  b. |
| 8 | 31-Dec | | 4 | 1,120 | | =F7+D8-E8 | |
| 9 | | | | | | | |

| | A | B | C | D |
|---|---|---|---|---|
| 1 | | NetSolutions | | |
| 2 | | Unadjusted Trial Balance | | |
| 3 | | 31-Dec-11 | | |
| 4 | | Debit | Credit | |
| 5 | | Balances | Balances | |
| 6 | Cash | 2,065 | | |
| 7 | Accounts Receivable | =GL!F8 | | c. |
| 20 | Supplies Expense | 2,000 | | |
| 21 | Miscellaneous Expense | 455 | | |
| 22 | | =SUM(B6:B21) | =SUM(C6:C21) | d. |
| 23 | | | | |
| 24 | | | | |
| 25 | | | | |
| 26 | | | | |
| 27 | | | | |
| 28 | | | | |
| 29 | | | | |
| 30 | | | | |

a. ⌐

|◄ ◄ ► ►| \ JE / GL / **UTB** /        ◄

a.    Label the third worksheet "UTB" for unadjusted trial balance.

b.    Previously, a formula that computes the account balance was created. This formula is copied down to create a cumulative balance.  As of December 31st, the value in cell F8 represents the total. This formula computes the total from December 21st plus any debit amounts less any credit amounts.

c.    In cell B7 (of the UTB worksheet), a cell reference is created for the December 31st balance in the Accounts Receivable ledger account. This balance is in cell F8 (of the GL worksheet). The reference is =GL!F8.

d.    The debit and credit columns of the trial balance are summed using the auto sum. The sum formula for the **debit** column is   =SUM(B6:B21). Copy this formula to column C.

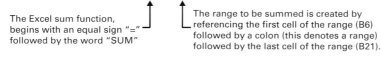

The Excel sum function, begins with an equal sign "=" followed by the word "SUM"

The range to be summed is created by referencing the first cell of the range (B6) followed by a colon (this denotes a range) followed by the last cell of the range (B21).

**Try***It*    Go to the hands-on ***Excel Tutor*** for this example!

**Try***It*    The Excel Success example shows the creation of journal entry transactions, posting to general ledger accounts, and the unadjusted trial balance.  Within that tutorial, accounting formatting is discussed. Go to the ***Excel Tutor*** titled **Accounting Formatting** for additional information!

**Example Exercise** ▶ **2-6** ▶ **Trial Balance Errors**

OBJ. 4

For each of the following errors, considered individually, indicate whether the error would cause the trial balance totals to be unequal. If the error would cause the trial balance totals to be unequal, indicate whether the debit or credit total is higher and by how much.

a. Payment of dividends of $5,600 was journalized and posted as a debit of $6,500 to Salary Expense and a credit of $6,500 to Cash.

b. A fee of $2,850 earned from a client was debited to Accounts Receivable for $2,580 and credited to Fees Earned for $2,850.

c. A payment of $3,500 to a creditor was posted as a debit of $3,500 to Accounts Payable and a debit of $3,500 to Cash.

**Follow My Example** ▶ **2-6** ▶

a. The totals are equal since both the debit and credit entries were journalized and posted for $6,500.

b. The totals are unequal. The credit total is higher by $270 ($2,850 − $2,580).

c. The totals are unequal. The debit total is higher by $7,000 ($3,500 + $3,500).

Practice Exercises: **PE 2-6A, PE 2-6B**

## Errors Not Affecting the Trial Balance

An error may occur that does not cause the trial balance totals to be unequal. Such an error may be discovered when preparing the trial balance or may be indicated by an unusual account balance. For example, a credit balance in the supplies account indicates an error has occurred. This is because a business cannot have "negative" supplies. When such errors are discovered, they should be corrected. If the error has already been journalized and posted to the ledger, a **correcting journal entry** is normally prepared.

To illustrate, assume that on May 5 a $12,500 purchase of office equipment on account was incorrectly journalized and posted as a debit to Supplies and a credit to Accounts Payable for $12,500. This posting of the incorrect entry is shown in the following T accounts:

*Incorrect:*

| Supplies | | Accounts Payable | |
|---|---|---|---|
| 12,500 | | | 12,500 |

Before making a correcting journal entry, it is best to determine the debit(s) and credit(s) that should have been recorded. These are shown in the following T accounts:

*Correct:*

| Office Equipment | | Accounts Payable | |
|---|---|---|---|
| 12,500 | | | 12,500 |

Comparing the two sets of T accounts shows that the incorrect debit to Supplies may be corrected by debiting Office Equipment for $12,500 and crediting Supplies for $12,500. The following correcting journal entry is then journalized and posted:

*Entry to Correct Error:*

| May | 31 | Office Equipment | 18 | 12,500 | |
|-----|----|------------------|----|--------|----|
| | | Supplies | 14 | | 12,500 |
| | | To correct erroneous debit | | | |
| | | to Supplies on May 5. See invoice | | | |
| | | from Bell Office Equipment Co. | | | |

## Example Exercise 2-7 Correcting Entries

**OBJ. 4**

The following errors took place in journalizing and posting transactions:

a. Dividends of $6,000 were recorded as a debit to Office Salaries Expense and a credit to Cash.

b. Utilities Expense of $4,500 paid for the current month was recorded as a debit to Miscellaneous Expense and a credit to Accounts Payable.

Journalize the entries to correct the errors. Omit explanations.

### Follow My Example 2-7

| | | | |
|---|---|---|---|
| a. | Dividends ................................................................ | 6,000 | |
| | Office Salaries Expense................................. | | 6,000 |
| b. | Accounts Payable.................................................... | 4,500 | |
| | Miscellaneous Expense................................. | | 4,500 |
| | Utilities Expense .................................................... | 4,500 | |
| | Cash.............................................................. | | 4,500 |

*Note:* The first entry in (b) reverses the incorrect entry, and the second entry records the correct entry. These two entries could also be combined into one entry; however, preparing two entries will make it easier for someone later to understand what had happened and why the entries were necessary.

Practice Exercises: **PE 2-7A, PE 2-7B**

# Financial Analysis and Interpretation: Horizontal Analysis

A single item in a financial statement, such as net income, is often useful in interpreting the financial performance of a company. However, a comparison with prior periods often makes the financial information even more useful. For example, comparing net income of the current period with the net income of the prior period will indicate whether the company's operating performance has improved.

In **horizontal analysis**, the amount of each item on a current financial statement is compared with the same item on an earlier statement. The increase or decrease in the *amount* of the item is computed together with the *percent* of increase or decrease. When two statements are being compared, the earlier statement is used as the base for computing the amount and the percent of change.

**OBJ. 5** Describe and illustrate the use of horizontal analysis in evaluating a company's performance and financial condition.

To illustrate, the horizontal analysis of two income statements for J. Holmes, Attorney-at-Law, P.C. (a professional corporation) is shown below.

**J. Holmes, Attorney-at-Law, P.C.**
**Income Statements**
**For the Years Ended December 31**

| | 2012 | 2011 | Increase (Decrease) Amount | Increase (Decrease) Percent |
|---|---|---|---|---|
| Fees earned | $187,500 | $150,000 | $37,500 | 25.0%* |
| Operating expenses: | | | | |
| Wages expense | $ 60,000 | $ 45,000 | $15,000 | 33.3 |
| Rent expense | 15,000 | 12,000 | 3,000 | 25.0 |
| Utilities expense | 12,500 | 9,000 | 3,500 | 38.9 |
| Supplies expense | 2,700 | 3,000 | (300) | (10.0) |
| Miscellaneous expense | 2,300 | 1,800 | 500 | 27.8 |
| Total operating expenses | $ 92,500 | $ 70,800 | $21,700 | 30.6 |
| Net income | $ 95,000 | $ 79,200 | $15,800 | 19.9 |

*$37,500 ÷ $150,000

The horizontal analysis for J. Holmes, Attorney-at-Law, P.C. indicates both favorable and unfavorable trends. The increase in fees earned is a favorable trend, as is the decrease in supplies expense. Unfavorable trends include the increase in wages expense, utilities expense, and miscellaneous expense. These expenses increased the same as or faster than the increase in revenues, with total operating expenses increasing by 30.6%. Overall, net income increased by $15,800, or 19.9%, a favorable trend.

The significance of the various increases and decreases in the revenue and expense items should be investigated to see if operations could be further improved. For example, the increase in utilities expense of 38.9% was the result of renting additional office space for use by a part-time law student in performing paralegal services. This explains the increase in rent expense of 25% and the increase in wages expense of 33.3%. The increase in revenues of 25% reflects the fees generated by the new paralegal.

The preceding example illustrates how horizontal analysis can be useful in interpreting and analyzing the income statement. Horizontal analyses can also be performed for the balance sheet, the retained earnings statement, and the statement of cash flows.

To illustrate, horizontal analysis for Apple Inc.'s 2009 and 2008 statements of cash flows (in millions) is shown below.

**Apple Inc.**
**Statements of Cash Flows**
**For the Years Ended**

| | Sept. 26, 2009 | Sept. 27, 2008 | Increase (Decrease) Amount | Increase (Decrease) Percent |
|---|---|---|---|---|
| Cash flows from operating activities | $ 10,159 | $ 9,596 | $ 563 | 5.9% |
| Cash flows used for investing activities | (17,434) | (8,189) | (9,245) | (112.9) |
| Cash flows from financing activities | 663 | 1,116 | (453) | (40.6) |
| Net increase (decrease) in cash | $ (6,612) | $ 2,523 | $(9,135) | (362.1) |
| Beginning of the year balance of cash | 11,875 | 9,352 | 2,523 | 27.0 |
| End of the year balance of cash | $ 5,263 | $11,875 | $(6,612) | (55.7) |

The horizontal analysis of cash flows for Apple Inc. indicates an increase in cash flows from operating activities of 5.9%, which is a favorable trend. At the same time, Apple increased the cash used in its investing activities by over 112.9% and decreased the cash it received from financing activities by 40.6%. Overall, Apple had a 362.1%

decrease in cash for the year, which decreased the end of the year cash balance by 55.7%. In contrast, in the prior year Apple increased its ending cash balance, which is the beginning cash balance of the current year, by 27%.

---

**Example Exercise** **2-8** **Horizontal Analysis** OBJ. 5

Two income statements for McCorkle Company are shown below.

**McCorkle Company**
**Income Statements**
**For the Years Ended December 31**

|  | 2012 | 2011 |
|---|---|---|
| Fees earned | $210,000 | $175,000 |
| Operating expenses | 172,500 | 150,000 |
| Net income | $ 37,500 | $ 25,000 |

Prepare a horizontal analysis of McCorkle Company's income statements.

**Follow My Example** **2-8**

**McCorkle Company**
**Income Statements**
**For the Years Ended December 31**

|  | 2012 | 2011 | Increase (Decrease) Amount | Percent |
|---|---|---|---|---|
| Fees earned | $210,000 | $175,000 | $35,000 | 20% |
| Operating expenses | 172,500 | 150,000 | 22,500 | 15 |
| Net income | $ 37,500 | $ 25,000 | $12,500 | 50 |

Practice Exercises: **PE 2-8A, PE 2-8B**

---

# At a Glance 2

OBJ. 1

**Describe the characteristics of an account and a chart of accounts.**

**Key Points**    The simplest form of an account, a T account, has three parts: (1) a title, which is the name of the item recorded in the account; (2) a left side, called the debit side; and (3) a right side, called the credit side. Periodically, the debits in an account are added, the credits in the account are added, and the balance of the account is determined.

The system of accounts that make up a ledger is called a chart of accounts.

| Learning Outcomes | Example Exercises | Practice Exercises |
|---|---|---|
| • Record transactions in T accounts. |  |  |
| • Determine the balance of a T account. |  |  |
| • Prepare a chart of accounts for a corporation. |  |  |

**OBJ. 2**

**Describe and illustrate journalizing transactions using the double-entry accounting system.**

**Key Points**    Transactions are initially entered in a record called a journal. The rules of debit and credit for recording increases or decreases in accounts are shown in Exhibit 3. Each transaction is recorded so that the sum of the debits is always equal to the sum of the credits. The normal balance of an account is indicated by the side of the account (debit or credit) that receives the increases.

| Learning Outcomes | Example Exercises | Practice Exercises |
|---|---|---|
| • Indicate the normal balance of an account. | EE2-1 | PE2-1A, 2-1B |
| • Journalize transactions using the rules of debit and credit. | EE2-2 | PE2-2A, 2-2B |

**OBJ. 3**

**Describe and illustrate the journalizing and posting of transactions to accounts.**

**Key Points**    Transactions are journalized and posted to the ledger using the rules of debit and credit. The debits and credits for each journal entry are posted to the accounts in the order in which they occur in the journal.

| Learning Outcomes | Example Exercises | Practice Exercises |
|---|---|---|
| • Journalize transactions using the rules of debit and credit. | EE2-3 | PE2-3A, 2-3B |
| • Given other account data, determine the missing amount of an account entry. | EE2-4 | PE2-4A, 2-4B |
|  | EE2-5 | PE2-5A, 2-5B |
| • Post journal entries to a standard account. |  |  |
| • Post journal entries to a T account. |  |  |

**OBJ. 4**

**Prepare an unadjusted trial balance and explain how it can be used to discover errors.**

**Key Points**    A trial balance is prepared by listing the accounts from the ledger and their balances. The totals of the Debit column and Credit column of the trial balance must be equal. If the two totals are not equal, an error has occurred. Errors may occur even though the trial balance totals are equal. Such errors may require a correcting journal entry.

| Learning Outcomes | Example Exercises | Practice Exercises |
|---|---|---|
| • Prepare an unadjusted trial balance. |  |  |
| • Discover errors that cause unequal totals in the trial balance. | EE2-6 | PE2-6A, 2-6B |
| • Prepare correcting journal entries for various errors. | EE2-7 | PE2-7A, 2-7B |

**OBJ. 5**

**Describe and illustrate the use of horizontal analysis in evaluating a company's performance and financial condition.**

**Key Points** In horizontal analysis, the amount of each item on a current financial statement is compared with the same item on an earlier statement. The increase or decrease in the *amount* of the item is computed together with the *percent* of increase or decrease. When two statements are being compared, the earlier statement is used as the base for computing the amount and the percent of change.

| Learning Outcomes | Example Exercises | Practice Exercises |
|---|---|---|
| • Describe horizontal analysis. | | |
| • Prepare a horizontal analysis report of a financial statement. | EE2-8 | PE2-8A, 2-8B |

# Key Terms

account (50)

account receivable (64)

assets (52)

balance of the account (51)

chart of accounts (52)

correcting journal entry (72)

credit (51)

debit (51)

dividends (52)

double-entry accounting system (53)

expenses (53)

horizontal analysis (73)

journal (55)

journal entry (56)

journalizing (56)

ledger (52)

liabilities (52)

normal balance of an account (54)

posting (59)

revenues (52)

rules of debit and credit (53)

slide (70)

stockholders' equity (52)

T account (50)

transposition (70)

trial balance (69)

unadjusted trial balance (70)

unearned revenue (62)

# Illustrative Problem

J. F. Outz, M.D., has been practicing as a cardiologist for three years in a professional corporation known as Hearts, P.C. During April 2011, Hearts, P.C. completed the following transactions:

Apr. 1. Paid office rent for April, $800.

3. Purchased equipment on account, $2,100.

5. Received cash on account from patients, $3,150.

8. Purchased X-ray film and other supplies on account, $245.

9. One of the items of equipment purchased on April 3 was defective. It was returned with the permission of the supplier, who agreed to reduce the account for the amount charged for the item, $325.

12. Paid cash to creditors on account, $1,250.

17. Paid cash for renewal of a six-month property insurance policy, $370.

20. Discovered that the balances of the cash account and the accounts payable account as of April 1 were overstated by $200. A payment of that amount to a creditor in March had not been recorded. Journalize the $200 payment as of April 20.

24. Paid cash for laboratory analysis, $545.

Apr. 27. Paid dividends, $1,250.

    30. Recorded the cash received in payment of services (on a cash basis) to patients during April, $1,720.

    30. Paid salaries of receptionist and nurses, $1,725.

    30. Paid various utility expenses, $360.

    30. Recorded fees charged to patients on account for services performed in April, $5,145.

    30. Paid miscellaneous expenses, $132.

Hearts, P.C.'s account titles, numbers, and balances as of April 1 (all normal balances) are listed as follows: Cash, 11, $4,123; Accounts Receivable, 12, $6,725; Supplies, 13, $290; Prepaid Insurance, 14, $465; Equipment, 18, $19,745; Accounts Payable, 22, $765; Capital Stock, 31, $10,000; Retained Earnings, 32, $20,583; Dividends, 33, $0; Professional Fees, 41, $0; Salary Expense, 51, $0; Rent Expense, 53, $0; Laboratory Expense, 55, $0; Utilities Expense, 56, $0; Miscellaneous Expense, 59, $0.

## Instructions

1. Open a ledger of standard four-column accounts for Hearts, P.C., as of April 1. Enter the balances in the appropriate balance columns and place a check mark (✓) in the Posting Reference column. (*Hint:* Verify the equality of the debit and credit balances in the ledger before proceeding with the next instruction.)

2. Journalize each transaction in a two-column journal.

3. Post the journal to the ledger, extending the month-end balances to the appropriate balance columns after each posting.

4. Prepare an unadjusted trial balance as of April 30.

**Solution** 1., 2., and 3.

### Journal — Page 27

| Date | Description | Post. Ref. | Debit | Credit |
|---|---|---|---|---|
| 2011 | | | | |
| Apr. 1 | Rent Expense | 53 | 800 | |
| | Cash | 11 | | 800 |
| | Paid office rent for April. | | | |
| 3 | Equipment | 18 | 2,100 | |
| | Accounts Payable | 22 | | 2,100 |
| | Purchased equipment on account. | | | |
| 5 | Cash | 11 | 3,150 | |
| | Accounts Receivable | 12 | | 3,150 |
| | Received cash on account. | | | |
| 8 | Supplies | 13 | 245 | |
| | Accounts Payable | 22 | | 245 |
| | Purchased supplies. | | | |
| 9 | Accounts Payable | 22 | 325 | |
| | Equipment | 18 | | 325 |
| | Returned defective equipment. | | | |
| 12 | Accounts Payable | 22 | 1,250 | |
| | Cash | 11 | | 1,250 |
| | Paid creditors on account. | | | |
| 17 | Prepaid Insurance | 14 | 370 | |
| | Cash | 11 | | 370 |
| | Renewed six-month property policy. | | | |
| 20 | Accounts Payable | 22 | 200 | |
| | Cash | 11 | | 200 |
| | Recorded March payment to creditor. | | | |

### Journal — Page 28

| Date | Description | Post. Ref. | Debit | Credit |
|---|---|---|---|---|
| 2011 | | | | |
| Apr. 24 | Laboratory Expense | 55 | 545 | |
| | Cash | 11 | | 545 |
| | Paid for laboratory analysis. | | | |
| 27 | Dividends | 33 | 1,250 | |
| | Cash | 11 | | 1,250 |
| | Paid dividends. | | | |
| 30 | Cash | 11 | 1,720 | |
| | Professional Fees | 41 | | 1,720 |
| | Received fees from patients. | | | |
| 30 | Salary Expense | 51 | 1,725 | |
| | Cash | 11 | | 1,725 |
| | Paid salaries. | | | |
| 30 | Utilities Expense | 56 | 360 | |
| | Cash | 11 | | 360 |
| | Paid utilities. | | | |
| 30 | Accounts Receivable | 12 | 5,145 | |
| | Professional Fees | 41 | | 5,145 |
| | Recorded fees earned on account. | | | |
| 30 | Miscellaneous Expense | 59 | 132 | |
| | Cash | 11 | | 132 |
| | Paid expenses. | | | |

### Account Cash — Account No. 11

| Date | Item | Post. Ref. | Debit | Credit | Balance Debit | Balance Credit |
|---|---|---|---|---|---|---|
| 2011 | | | | | | |
| Apr. 1 | Balance | ✓ | | | 4,123 | |
| 1 | | 27 | | 800 | 3,323 | |
| 5 | | 27 | 3,150 | | 6,473 | |
| 12 | | 27 | | 1,250 | 5,223 | |
| 17 | | 27 | | 370 | 4,853 | |
| 20 | | 27 | | 200 | 4,653 | |
| 24 | | 28 | | 545 | 4,108 | |
| 27 | | 28 | | 1,250 | 2,858 | |
| 30 | | 28 | 1,720 | | 4,578 | |
| 30 | | 28 | | 1,725 | 2,853 | |
| 30 | | 28 | | 360 | 2,493 | |
| 30 | | 28 | | 132 | 2,361 | |

### Account Accounts Receivable — Account No. 12

| Date | Item | Post. Ref. | Debit | Credit | Balance Debit | Balance Credit |
|---|---|---|---|---|---|---|
| 2011 | | | | | | |
| Apr. 1 | Balance | ✓ | | | 6,725 | |
| 5 | | 27 | | 3,150 | 3,575 | |
| 30 | | 28 | 5,145 | | 8,720 | |

### Account Supplies — Account No. 13

| Date | Item | Post. Ref. | Debit | Credit | Balance Debit | Balance Credit |
|---|---|---|---|---|---|---|
| 2011 | | | | | | |
| Apr. 1 | Balance | ✓ | | | 290 | |
| 8 | | 27 | 245 | | 535 | |

**Account** *Prepaid Insurance* — Account No. *14*

| Date | Item | Post. Ref. | Debit | Credit | Balance Debit | Balance Credit |
|------|------|-----------|-------|--------|------|------|
| 2011 Apr. 1 | Balance | ✓ | | | | 465 |
| 17 | | 27 | 370 | | | 835 |

**Account** *Equipment* — Account No. *18*

| Date | Item | Post. Ref. | Debit | Credit | Balance Debit | Balance Credit |
|------|------|-----------|-------|--------|------|------|
| 2011 Apr. 1 | Balance | ✓ | | | 19,745 | |
| 3 | | 27 | 2,100 | | 21,845 | |
| 9 | | 27 | | 325 | 21,520 | |

**Account** *Accounts Payable* — Account No. *22*

| Date | Item | Post. Ref. | Debit | Credit | Balance Debit | Balance Credit |
|------|------|-----------|-------|--------|------|------|
| 2011 Apr. 1 | Balance | ✓ | | | | 765 |
| 3 | | 27 | | 2,100 | | 2,865 |
| 8 | | 27 | | 245 | | 3,110 |
| 9 | | 27 | 325 | | | 2,785 |
| 12 | | 27 | 1,250 | | | 1,535 |
| 20 | | 27 | 200 | | | 1,335 |

**Account** *Capital Stock* — Account No. *31*

| Date | Item | Post. Ref. | Debit | Credit | Balance Debit | Balance Credit |
|------|------|-----------|-------|--------|------|------|
| 2011 Apr. 1 | Balance | ✓ | | | | 10,000 |

**Account** *Retained Earnings* — Account No. *32*

| Date | Item | Post. Ref. | Debit | Credit | Balance Debit | Balance Credit |
|------|------|-----------|-------|--------|------|------|
| 2011 Apr. 1 | Balance | ✓ | | | | 20,583 |

**Account** *Dividends* — Account No. *33*

| Date | Item | Post. Ref. | Debit | Credit | Balance Debit | Balance Credit |
|------|------|-----------|-------|--------|------|------|
| 2011 Apr. 27 | | 28 | 1,250 | | 1,250 | |

**Account** *Professional Fees* — Account No. *41*

| Date | Item | Post. Ref. | Debit | Credit | Balance Debit | Balance Credit |
|------|------|-----------|-------|--------|------|------|
| 2011 Apr. 30 | | 28 | | 1,720 | | 1,720 |
| 30 | | 28 | | 5,145 | | 6,865 |

**Account** *Salary Expense* — Account No. *51*

| Date | Item | Post. Ref. | Debit | Credit | Balance Debit | Balance Credit |
|------|------|-----------|-------|--------|------|------|
| 2011 Apr. 30 | | 28 | 1,725 | | 1,725 | |

**Account** *Rent Expense* — Account No. *53*

| Date | Item | Post. Ref. | Debit | Credit | Balance Debit | Balance Credit |
|------|------|-----------|-------|--------|------|------|
| 2011 Apr. 1 | | 27 | 800 | | 800 | |

**Account** *Laboratory Expense* — Account No. *55*

| Date | Item | Post. Ref. | Debit | Credit | Balance Debit | Balance Credit |
|------|------|-----------|-------|--------|------|------|
| 2011 Apr. 24 | | 28 | 545 | | 545 | |

**Account** *Utilities Expanse* — Account No. *56*

| Date | Item | Post. Ref. | Debit | Credit | Balance Debit | Balance Credit |
|------|------|-----------|-------|--------|------|------|
| 2011 Apr. 30 | | 28 | 360 | | 360 | |

**Account** *Miscellaneous Expense* — Account No. *59*

| Date | Item | Post. Ref. | Debit | Credit | Balance Debit | Balance Credit |
|------|------|-----------|-------|--------|------|------|
| 2011 Apr. 30 | | 28 | 132 | | 132 | |

4.

| Hearts, P.C. Unadjusted Trial Balance April 30, 2011 | | |
| --- | --- | --- |
| | **Debit Balances** | **Credit Balances** |
| Cash ............................................................... | 2,361 | |
| Accounts Receivable.......................................... | 8,720 | |
| Supplies .......................................................... | 535 | |
| Prepaid Insurance ............................................. | 835 | |
| Equipment....................................................... | 21,520 | |
| Accounts Payable ............................................. | | 1,335 |
| Capital Stock ................................................... | | 10,000 |
| Retained Earnings ............................................ | | 20,583 |
| Dividends........................................................ | 1,250 | |
| Professional Fees.............................................. | | 6,865 |
| Salary Expense.................................................. | 1,725 | |
| Rent Expense ................................................... | 800 | |
| Laboratory Expense .......................................... | 545 | |
| Utilities Expense .............................................. | 360 | |
| Miscellaneous Expense ..................................... | 132 | |
| | 38,783 | 38,783 |

# Discussion Questions

1. What is the difference between an account and a ledger?

2. Do the terms *debit* and *credit* signify increase or decrease or can they signify either? Explain.

3. Weir Company adheres to a policy of depositing all cash receipts in a bank account and making all payments by check. The cash account as of December 31 has a credit balance of $3,190, and there is no undeposited cash on hand. (a) Assuming no errors occurred during journalizing or posting, what caused this unusual balance? (b) Is the $3,190 credit balance in the cash account an asset, a liability, stockholders' equity, a revenue, or an expense?

4. Resource Services Company performed services in February for a specific customer, for a fee of $11,250. Payment was received the following March. (a) Was the revenue earned in February or March? (b) What accounts should be debited and credited in (1) February and (2) March?

5. If the two totals of a trial balance are equal, does it mean that there are no errors in the accounting records? Explain.

6. Assume that a trial balance is prepared with an account balance of $21,740 listed as $2,174 and an account balance of $4,500 listed as $5,400. Identify the transposition and the slide.

7. Assume that when a purchase of supplies of $3,100 for cash was recorded, both the debit and the credit were journalized and posted as $1,300. (a) Would this error cause the trial balance to be out of balance? (b) Would the trial balance be out of balance if the $3,100 entry had been journalized correctly but the credit to Cash had been posted as $1,300?

8. Assume that Timberline Consulting erroneously recorded the payment of $9,000 of dividends as a debit to Salary Expense. (a) How would this error affect the equality of the trial balance? (b) How would this error affect the income statement, retained earnings statement, and balance sheet?

9. Assume that Western Realty Co. borrowed $200,000 from Mountain First Bank and Trust. In recording the transaction, Western erroneously recorded the receipt as a debit to Cash, $200,000, and a credit to Fees Earned, $200,000. (a) How would this error affect the equality of the trial balance? (b) How would this error affect the income statement, retained earnings statement, and balance sheet?

10. Checking accounts are the most common form of deposits for banks. Assume that Village Storage has a checking account at Camino Savings Bank. What type of account (asset, liability, capital stock, retained earnings, dividends, revenue, expense) does the account balance of $8,750 represent from the viewpoint of (a) Village Storage and (b) Camino Savings Bank?

# Practice Exercises

| Learning Objectives | Example Exercises | |
|---|---|---|
| OBJ. 2 | EE 2-1 *p. 54* | **PE 2-1A** **Rules of debit and credit and normal balances** |

State for each account whether it is likely to have (a) debit entries only, (b) credit entries only, or (c) both debit and credit entries. Also, indicate its normal balance.

1. Accounts Receivable      4. Notes Payable
2. Capital Stock      5. Rent Revenue
3. Commissions Earned      6. Wages Expense

**OBJ. 2**   **EE 2-1** *p. 54*   **PE 2-1B** **Rules of debit and credit and normal balances**

State for each account whether it is likely to have (a) debit entries only, (b) credit entries only, or (c) both debit and credit entries. Also, indicate its normal balance.

1. Accounts Payable      4. Miscellaneous Expense
2. Cash      5. Insurance Expense
3. Dividends      6. Fees Earned

**OBJ. 2**   **EE 2-2** *p. 59*   **PE 2-2A** **Journal entry for asset purchase**

Prepare a journal entry for the purchase of office equipment on March 4 for $27,150, paying $5,000 cash and the remainder on account.

**OBJ. 2**   **EE 2-2** *p. 59*   **PE 2-2B** **Journal entry for asset purchase**

Prepare a journal entry for the purchase of office supplies on August 7 for $4,000, paying $1,000 cash and the remainder on account.

**OBJ. 3**   **EE 2-3** *p. 64*   **PE 2-3A** **Journal entry for fees earned**

Prepare a journal entry on September 6 for fees earned on account, $8,000.

**OBJ. 3**   **EE 2-3** *p. 64*   **PE 2-3B** **Journal entry for fees earned**

Prepare a journal entry on May 29 for cash received for services rendered, $5,000.

**OBJ. 3**   **EE 2-4** *p. 67*   **PE 2-4A** **Journal entry for dividends**

Prepare a journal entry on December 22 for the payment of dividends of $10,000.

**OBJ. 3**   **EE 2-4** *p. 67*   **PE 2-4B** **Journal entry for dividends**

Prepare a journal entry on February 3 for the payment of dividends of $7,500.

| Learning Objectives | Example Exercises | |
| --- | --- | --- |
| OBJ. 3 | EE 2-5 *p. 67* | **PE 2-5A** **Missing amount from an account** |

On June 1, the cash account balance was $17,200. During June, cash payments totaled $178,300, and the June 30 balance was $23,900. Determine the cash receipts during June.

| OBJ. 3 | EE 2-5 *p. 67* | **PE 2-5B** **Missing amount from an account** |

On October 1, the supplies account balance was $900. During October, supplies of $2,750 were purchased, and $1,025 of supplies were on hand as of October 31. Determine supplies expense for October.

| OBJ. 4 | EE 2-6 *p. 72* | **PE 2-6A** **Trial balance errors** |

For each of the following errors, considered individually, indicate whether the error would cause the trial balance totals to be unequal. If the error would cause the trial balance totals to be unequal, indicate whether the debit or credit total is higher and by how much.

a. The payment of an insurance premium of $4,800 for a two-year policy was debited to Prepaid Insurance for $4,800 and credited to Cash for $8,400.

b. A payment of $318 on account was debited to Accounts Payable for $381 and credited to Cash for $381.

c. A purchase of supplies on account for $1,200 was debited to Supplies for $1,200 and debited to Accounts Payable for $1,200.

| OBJ. 4 | EE 2-6 *p. 72* | **PE 2-6B** **Trial balance errors** |

For each of the following errors, considered individually, indicate whether the error would cause the trial balance totals to be unequal. If the error would cause the trial balance totals to be unequal, indicate whether the debit or credit total is higher and by how much.

a. The payment of cash for the purchase of office equipment of $15,000 was debited to Land for $15,000 and credited to Cash for $15,000.

b. The payment of $5,200 on account was debited to Accounts Payable for $520 and credited to Cash for $5,200.

c. The receipt of cash on account of $1,270 was recorded as a debit to Cash for $1,720 and a credit to Accounts Receivable for $1,270.

| OBJ. 4 | EE 2-7 *p. 73* | **PE 2-7A** **Correcting entries** |

The following errors took place in journalizing and posting transactions:

a. Advertising expense of $2,700 paid for the current month was recorded as a debit to Miscellaneous Expense and a credit to Advertising Expense.

b. The payment of $3,950 from a customer on account was recorded as a debit to Cash and a credit to Accounts Payable.

Journalize the entries to correct the errors. Omit explanations.

| OBJ. 4 | EE 2-7 *p. 73* | **PE 2-7B** **Correcting entries** |

The following errors took place in journalizing and posting transactions:

a. The receipt of $5,800 for services rendered was recorded as a debit to Accounts Receivable and a credit to Fees Earned.

b. The purchase of supplies of $1,800 on account was recorded as a debit to Office Equipment and a credit to Supplies.

Journalize the entries to correct the errors. Omit explanations.

| OBJ. 5 | EE 2-8 *p. 75* | **PE 2-8A** **Horizontal analysis** |

Two income statements for Boyer Company are shown on the following page.

*Learning
Objectives*    *Example
Exercises*

| Boyer Company Income Statements For Years Ended December 31 | | |
|---|---|---|
| | **2012** | **2011** |
| Fees earned | $315,000 | $300,000 |
| Operating expenses | 176,400 | 180,000 |
| Net income | $138,600 | $120,000 |

Prepare a horizontal analysis of Boyer Company's income statements.

**OBJ. 5**    **EE 2-8** *p. 75*    **PE 2-8B    Horizontal analysis**

Two income statements for Hitt Company are shown below.

| Hitt Company Income Statements For Years Ended December 31 | | |
|---|---|---|
| | **2012** | **2011** |
| Fees earned | $937,500 | $750,000 |
| Operating expenses | 612,500 | 500,000 |
| Net income | $325.000 | $250,000 |

Prepare a horizontal analysis of Hitt Company's income statements.

# Exercises

**OBJ. 1**

**EX 2-1    Chart of accounts**

The following accounts appeared in recent financial statements of Continental Airlines:

Accounts Payable                Flight Equipment
Air Traffic Liability           Landing Fees (Expense)
Aircraft Fuel Expense           Passenger Revenue
Cargo and Mail Revenue          Purchase Deposits for Flight Equipment
Commissions (Expense)           Spare Parts and Supplies

Identify each account as either a balance sheet account or an income statement account. For each balance sheet account, identify it as an asset, a liability, or stockholders' equity. For each income statement account, identify it as a revenue or an expense.

**OBJ. 1**

**EX 2-2    Chart of accounts**

Innerscape Interiors is owned and operated by Jean Cartier, an interior decorator. In the ledger of Innerscape Interiors, the first digit of the account number indicates its major account classification (1—assets, 2—liabilities, 3—stockholders' equity, 4—revenues, 5—expenses). The second digit of the account number indicates the specific account within each of the preceding major account classifications.

Match each account number with its most likely account in the list below. The account numbers are 11, 12, 13, 21, 31, 32, 41, 51, 52, and 53.

Accounts Payable                Land
Accounts Receivable             Miscellaneous Expense
Capital Stock                   Retained Earnings
Cash                            Supplies Expense
Dividends                       Wages Expense
Fees Earned

**OBJ. 1**

**EX 2-3    Chart of accounts**

Alpha School is a newly organized business that teaches people how to inspire and influence others. The list of accounts to be opened in the general ledger is as follows:

| | |
|---|---|
| Accounts Payable | Prepaid Insurance |
| Accounts Receivable | Rent Expense |
| Capital Stock | Retained Earnings |
| Cash | Supplies |
| Dividends | Supplies Expense |
| Equipment | Unearned Rent |
| Fees Earned | Wages Expense |
| Miscellaneous Expense | |

List the accounts in the order in which they should appear in the ledger of Alpha School and assign account numbers. Each account number is to have two digits: the first digit is to indicate the major classification (1 for assets, etc.), and the second digit is to identify the specific account within each major classification (11 for Cash, etc.).

OBJ. 1, 2

### EX 2-4 Rules of debit and credit

The following table summarizes the rules of debit and credit. For each of the items (a) through (l), indicate whether the proper answer is a debit or a credit.

| | Increase | Decrease | Normal Balance |
|---|---|---|---|
| Balance sheet accounts: | | | |
| Asset | (a) | Credit | (b) |
| Liability | Credit | (c) | (d) |
| Stockholders' equity: | | | |
| Capital Stock | Credit | (e) | (f) |
| Retained Earnings | (g) | Debit | Credit |
| Dividends | Debit | (h) | (i) |
| Income statement accounts: | | | |
| Revenue | Credit | (j) | (k) |
| Expense | (l) | Credit | Debit |

OBJ. 2

### EX 2-5 Normal entries for accounts

During the month, Iris Labs Co. has a substantial number of transactions affecting each of the following accounts. State for each account whether it is likely to have (a) debit entries only, (b) credit entries only, or (c) both debit and credit entries.

1. Accounts Payable
2. Accounts Receivable
3. Cash
4. Dividends
5. Fees Earned
6. Insurance Expense
7. Utilities Expense

OBJ. 1, 2

### EX 2-6 Normal balances of accounts

Identify each of the following accounts of Advanced Services Co. as asset, liability, stockholders' equity, revenue, or expense, and state in each case whether the normal balance is a debit or a credit.

a. Accounts Payable
b. Accounts Receivable
c. Capital Stock
d. Cash
e. Dividends
f. Fees Earned
g. Office Equipment
h. Rent Expense
i. Supplies
j. Wages Expense

OBJ. 2

### EX 2-7 Transactions

Chalet Co. has the following accounts in its ledger: Cash; Accounts Receivable; Supplies; Office Equipment; Accounts Payable; Capital Stock; Retained Earnings; Dividends; Fees Earned; Rent Expense; Advertising Expense; Utilities Expense; Miscellaneous Expense.

Journalize the following selected transactions for October 2012 in a two-column journal. Journal entry explanations may be omitted.

Oct. 1. Paid rent for the month, $2,000.

2. Paid advertising expense, $900.

5. Paid cash for supplies, $1,300.

6. Purchased office equipment on account, $16,000.

10. Received cash from customers on account, $6,700.

15. Paid creditor on account, $1,200.

27. Paid cash for repairs to office equipment, $600.

30. Paid telephone bill for the month, $180.

31. Fees earned and billed to customers for the month, $26,800.

31. Paid electricity bill for the month, $400.

31. Paid dividends, $3,000.

---

**OBJ. 2,3**

### EX 2-8   Journalizing and posting

On February 3, 2012, Wilco Co. purchased $3,250 of supplies on account. In Wilco Co.'s chart of accounts, the supplies account is No. 15, and the accounts payable account is No. 21.

a. Journalize the February 3, 2012, transaction on page 19 of Wilco Co.'s two-column journal. Include an explanation of the entry.

b. Prepare a four-column account for Supplies. Enter a debit balance of $975 as of February 1, 2012. Place a check mark (✓) in the Posting Reference column.

c. Prepare a four-column account for Accounts Payable. Enter a credit balance of $13,150 as of February 1, 2012. Place a check mark (✓) in the Posting Reference column.

d. Post the February 3, 2012, transaction to the accounts.

e. Do the rules of debit and credit apply to all companies?

---

**OBJ. 2,3**

### EX 2-9   Transactions and T accounts

The following selected transactions were completed during August of the current year:

1. Billed customers for fees earned, $35,700.

2. Purchased supplies on account, $2,000.

3. Received cash from customers on account, $26,150.

4. Paid creditors on account, $800.

a. Journalize the above transactions in a two-column journal, using the appropriate number to identify the transactions. Journal entry explanations may be omitted.

b. Post the entries prepared in (a) to the following T accounts: Cash, Supplies, Accounts Receivable, Accounts Payable, Fees Earned. To the left of each amount posted in the accounts, place the appropriate number to identify the transactions.

c. Assume that the unadjusted trial balance on August 31 shows a credit balance for Accounts Receivable. Does this credit balance mean an error has occurred?

---

**OBJ. 1,2,3**

### EX 2-10   Cash account balance

During the month, Lathers Co. received $400,000 in cash and paid out $290,000 in cash.

a. Do the data indicate that Lathers Co. had net income of $110,000 during the month? Explain.

b. If the balance of the cash account is $185,000 at the end of the month, what was the cash balance at the beginning of the month?

---

**OBJ. 1,2,3**

✔ c. $284,175

### EX 2-11   Account balances

a. During October, $90,000 was paid to creditors on account, and purchases on account were $125,000. Assuming the October 31 balance of Accounts Payable was $40,000, determine the account balance on October 1.

b. On May 1, the accounts receivable account balance was $25,000. During May, $240,000 was collected from customers on account. Assuming the May 31 balance was $36,000, determine the fees billed to customers on account during May.

c. On November 1, the cash account balance was $18,275. During November, cash receipts totaled $279,100 and the November 30 balance was $13,200. Determine the cash payments made during November.

OBJ. 1,2

### EX 2-12 Retained earnings account balance

As of January 1, retained earnings had a credit balance of $125,000. During the year, dividends totaled $7,000, and the business incurred a net loss of $130,000.

a. Compute the balance of retained earnings as of the end of the year.

b. Assuming that there have been no recording errors, will the balance sheet prepared at December 31 balance? Explain.

OBJ. 1,2

### EX 2-13 Identifying transactions

Southwest Tours Co. is a travel agency. The nine transactions recorded by Southwest Tours during May 2012, its first month of operations, are indicated in the following T accounts:

| Cash | | | | Equipment | | Dividends | | |
|---|---|---|---|---|---|---|---|---|
| (1) | 40,000 | (2) | 2,000 | (3) | 18,000 | (9) | 4,000 | |
| (7) | 10,000 | (3) | 3,600 | | | | | |
| | | (4) | 2,700 | | | | | |
| | | (6) | 9,000 | | | | | |
| | | (9) | 4,000 | | | | | |

| Accounts Receivable | | | | Accounts Payable | | | Service Revenue | | |
|---|---|---|---|---|---|---|---|---|---|
| (5) | 18,500 | (7) | 10,000 | (6) | 9,000 | (3) | 14,400 | (5) | 18,500 |

| Supplies | | | | Capital Stock | | Operating Expenses | | |
|---|---|---|---|---|---|---|---|---|
| (2) | 2,000 | (8) | 1,050 | | (1) | 40,000 | (4) | 2,700 |
| | | | | | | | (8) | 1,050 |

Indicate for each debit and each credit: (a) whether an asset, liability, capital stock, dividends, revenue, or expense account was affected and (b) whether the account was increased (+) or decreased (–). Present your answers in the following form, with transaction (1) given as an example:

| | Account Debited | | Account Credited | |
|---|---|---|---|---|
| Transaction | Type | Effect | Type | Effect |
| (1) | asset | + | capital stock | + |

OBJ. 1,2

### EX 2-14 Journal entries

Based upon the T accounts in Exercise 2-13, prepare the nine journal entries from which the postings were made. Journal entry explanations may be omitted.

OBJ. 4

### EX 2-15 Trial balance

Based upon the data presented in Exercise 2-13, (a) prepare an unadjusted trial balance, listing the accounts in their proper order. (b) Based upon the unadjusted trial balance, determine the net income or net loss.

✔ Total Debit column: $63,900

OBJ. 4

✔ Total of Credit column: $491,400

### EX 2-16 Trial balance

The accounts in the ledger of Diva Co. as of July 31, 2012, are listed in alphabetical order as follows. All accounts have normal balances. The balance of the cash account has been intentionally omitted.

| | | | |
|---|---|---|---|
| Accounts Payable | $ 28,000 | Notes Payable | $ 50,000 |
| Accounts Receivable | 40,000 | Prepaid Insurance | 6,400 |
| Capital Stock | 20,000 | Rent Expense | 36,000 |
| Cash | ? | Retained Earnings | 29,900 |
| Dividends | 25,000 | Supplies | 4,000 |
| Fees Earned | 350,000 | Supplies Expense | 9,000 |
| Insurance Expense | 6,000 | Unearned Rent | 13,500 |
| Land | 125,000 | Utilities Expense | 18,000 |
| Miscellaneous Expense | 12,000 | Wages Expense | 195,000 |

Prepare an unadjusted trial balance, listing the accounts in their normal order and inserting the missing figure for cash.

OBJ. 4

### EX 2-17 Effect of errors on trial balance

Indicate which of the following errors, each considered individually, would cause the trial balance totals to be unequal:

a. A fee of $15,000 earned and due from a client was not debited to Accounts Receivable or credited to a revenue account, because the cash had not been received.

b. A receipt of $6,000 from an account receivable was journalized and posted as a debit of $6,000 to Cash and a credit of $6,000 to Fees Earned.

c. A payment of $1,200 to a creditor was posted as a debit of $1,200 to Accounts Payable and a debit of $1,200 to Cash.

d. A payment of $10,000 for equipment purchased was posted as a debit of $1,000 to Equipment and a credit of $1,000 to Cash.

e. Payment of dividends of $10,000 was journalized and posted as a debit of $1,000 to Salary Expense and a credit of $10,000 to Cash.

Indicate which of the preceding errors would require a correcting entry.

OBJ. 4

✔ Total of Credit column: $225,000

### EX 2-18 Errors in trial balance

The following preliminary unadjusted trial balance of Seats-For-You Co., a sports ticket agency, does not balance:

**Seats-For-You Co.**
**Unadjusted Trial Balance**
**March 31, 2012**

| | Debit Balances | Credit Balances |
|---|---|---|
| Cash ..................................................... | 98,000 | |
| Accounts Receivable...................................... | 17,800 | |
| Prepaid Insurance ....................................... | | 9,000 |
| Equipment................................................ | 7,500 | |
| Accounts Payable ........................................ | | 16,500 |
| Unearned Rent............................................ | | 11,600 |
| Capital Stock ............................................ | 30,000 | |
| Retained Earnings ....................................... | 51,700 | |
| Dividends ................................................ | 13,000 | |
| Service Revenue .......................................... | | 125,000 |
| Wages Expense .......................................... | | 60,000 |
| Advertising Expense....................................... | 11,300 | |
| Miscellaneous Expense .................................... | | 15,400 |
| | 229,300 | 237,500 |

When the ledger and other records are reviewed, you discover the following: (1) the debits and credits in the cash account total $98,000 and $82,500, respectively; (2) a billing of $8,000 to a customer on account was not posted to the accounts receivable account; (3) a payment of $3,600 made to a creditor on account was not posted to the accounts payable account; (4) the balance of the unearned rent account is $5,400; (5) the correct balance of the equipment account is $75,000; and (6) each account has a normal balance.
    Prepare a corrected unadjusted trial balance.

OBJ. 4

### EX 2-19 Effect of errors on trial balance

The following errors occurred in posting from a two-column journal:

1. A credit of $7,150 to Accounts Payable was not posted.
2. An entry debiting Accounts Receivable and crediting Fees Earned for $11,000 was not posted.
3. A debit of $1,000 to Accounts Payable was posted as a credit.
4. A debit of $800 to Supplies was posted twice.
5. A debit of $900 to Cash was posted to Miscellaneous Expense.
6. A credit of $360 to Cash was posted as $630.
7. A debit of $9,420 to Wages Expense was posted as $9,240.

Considering each case individually (i.e., assuming that no other errors had occurred), indicate: (a) by "yes" or "no" whether the trial balance would be out of balance; (b) if answer to (a) is "yes," the amount by which the trial balance totals would differ; and (c) whether the Debit or Credit column of the trial balance would have the larger total. Answers should be presented in the following form, with error (1) given as an example:

| Error | (a)<br>Out of Balance | (b)<br>Difference | (c)<br>Larger Total |
|---|---|---|---|
| 1. | yes | $7,150 | debit |

OBJ. 4

✔ Total of Credit column: $750,000

### EX 2-20 Errors in trial balance

Identify the errors in the following trial balance. All accounts have normal balances.

**Bluefin Co.**
**Unadjusted Trial Balance**
**For the Month Ending August 31, 2012**

| | Debit<br>Balances | Credit<br>Balances |
|---|---|---|
| Cash .......................................................... | 45,000 | |
| Accounts Receivable........................................... | | 98,400 |
| Prepaid Insurance ............................................. | 21,600 | |
| Equipment...................................................... | 300,000 | |
| Accounts Payable .............................................. | 11,100 | |
| Salaries Payable ............................................... | | 7,500 |
| Capital Stock .................................................. | | 75,000 |
| Retained Earnings ............................................. | | 184,200 |
| Dividends...................................................... | | 36,000 |
| Service Revenue ............................................... | | 472,200 |
| Salary Expense................................................. | 196,860 | |
| Advertising Expense........................................... | | 43,200 |
| Miscellaneous Expense ........................................ | 8,940 | |
| | 916,500 | 916,500 |

OBJ. 4

### EX 2-21 Entries to correct errors

The following errors took place in journalizing and posting transactions:

a. Rent of $12,500 paid for the current month was recorded as a debit to Rent Expense and a credit to Prepaid Rent.

b. Dividends of $7,500 were recorded as a debit to Wages Expense and a credit to Cash.

Journalize the entries to correct the errors. Omit explanations.

OBJ. 4

### EX 2-22 Entries to correct errors

The following errors took place in journalizing and posting transactions:

a. Cash of $12,975 received on account was recorded as a debit to Fees Earned and a credit to Cash.

b. A $3,200 purchase of supplies for cash was recorded as a debit to Supplies Expense and a credit to Accounts Payable.

Journalize the entries to correct the errors. Omit explanations.

OBJ. 5

### EX 2-23    Horizontal analysis of income statement

The following data (in millions) is taken from the financial statements of Target Corporation.

|  | 2009 | 2008 |
|---|---|---|
| Net sales (revenues) | $64,948 | $63,367 |
| Total operating expenses | 60,546 | 58,095 |

a.  For Target Corporation, comparing 2009 with 2008, determine the amount of change in millions and the percent of change for:

   1.  Net sales (revenues)

   2.  Total operating expenses

b.  ———►What conclusions can you draw from your analysis of the net sales and the total operating expenses?

OBJ. 5

### EX 2-24    Horizontal analysis of income statement

The following data were adapted from the financial statements of Kmart Corporation, prior to its filing for bankruptcy:

|  | In millions | |
|---|---|---|
| **For years ending January 31** | **2000** | **1999** |
| Sales | $ 37,028 | $ 35,925 |
| Cost of sales (expense) | (29,658) | (28,111) |
| Selling, general, and administrative expenses | (7,415) | (6,514) |
| Operating income (loss) | $    (45) | $  1,300 |

a.  Prepare a horizontal analysis for the income statement showing the amount and percent of change in each of the following:

   1.  Sales

   2.  Cost of sales

   3.  Selling, general, and administrative expenses

   4.  Operating income (loss)

b.  Comment on the results of your horizontal analysis in part (a).

## Problems Series A

OBJ. 1,2,3,4

✔ 3. Total of Debit column: $78,350

### PR 2-1A    Entries into T accounts and trial balance

Leila Durkin, an architect, opened an office on May 1, 2012. During the month, she completed the following transactions connected with her professional corporation, Lelia Durkin Architect, P.C.

a.  Transferred cash from a personal bank account to an account to be used for the business in exchange for capital stock, $30,000.

b.  Paid May rent for office and workroom, $3,500.

c.  Purchased used automobile for $25,000, paying $5,000 cash and giving a note payable for the remainder.

d.  Purchased office and computer equipment on account, $9,000.

e.  Paid cash for supplies, $1,200.

f.  Paid cash for annual insurance policies, $2,400.

g.  Received cash from client for plans delivered, $8,150.

h.  Paid cash for miscellaneous expenses, $300.

i.  Paid cash to creditors on account, $2,500.

j.  Paid installment due on note payable, $400.

k.  Received invoice for blueprint service, due in June, $1,200.

l.  Recorded fee earned on plans delivered, payment to be received in June, $12,900.

m.  Paid salary of assistant, $1,800.

n.  Paid gas, oil, and repairs on automobile for May, $600.

## Instructions

1. Record the above transactions directly in the following T accounts, without journalizing: Cash; Accounts Receivable; Supplies; Prepaid Insurance; Automobiles; Equipment; Notes Payable; Accounts Payable; Capital Stock; Professional Fees; Rent Expense; Salary Expense; Blueprint Expense; Automobile Expense; Miscellaneous Expense. To the left of the amount entered in the accounts, place the appropriate letter to identify the transaction.

2. Determine account balances of the T accounts. Accounts containing a single entry only (such as Prepaid Insurance) do not need a balance.

3. Prepare an unadjusted trial balance for Leila Durkin, Architect, P.C., as of May 31, 2012.

4. Determine the net income or net loss for May.

---

**OBJ. 1,2,3,4**

✔ 4. c. $8,550

### PR 2-2A   Journal entries and trial balance

On October 1, 2012, Faith Schultz established Heavenly Realty, which completed the following transactions during the month:

a. Faith Schultz transferred cash from a personal bank account to an account to be used for the business in exchange for capital stock, $20,000.

b. Paid rent on office and equipment for the month, $3,750.

c. Purchased supplies on account, $1,100.

d. Paid creditor on account, $400.

e. Earned sales commissions, receiving cash, $16,750.

f. Paid automobile expenses (including rental charge) for month, $1,000, and miscellaneous expenses, $700.

g. Paid office salaries, $2,150.

h. Determined that the cost of supplies used was $600.

i. Paid dividends, $1,000.

## Instructions

1. Journalize entries for transactions (a) through (i), using the following account titles: Cash; Supplies; Accounts Payable; Capital Stock; Dividends; Sales Commissions; Rent Expense; Office Salaries Expense; Automobile Expense; Supplies Expense; Miscellaneous Expense. Explanations may be omitted.

2. Prepare T accounts, using the account titles in (1). Post the journal entries to these accounts, placing the appropriate letter to the left of each amount to identify the transactions. Determine the account balances, after all posting is complete. Accounts containing only a single entry do not need a balance.

3. Prepare an unadjusted trial balance as of October 31, 2012.

4. Determine the following:

   a. Amount of total revenue recorded in the ledger.

   b. Amount of total expenses recorded in the ledger.

   c. Amount of net income for October.

5. Determine the increase or decrease in retained earnings for October.

---

**OBJ. 1,2,3,4**

✔ 3. Total of Credit column: $66,500

### PR 2-3A   Journal entries and trial balance

On April 1, 2012, Kathleen Alvarez established an interior decorating business, Intrex Designs. During the month, Kathleen completed the following transactions related to the business:

Apr.  1. Kathleen transferred cash from a personal bank account to an account to be used for the business in exchange for capital stock, $17,000.

   2. Paid rent for period of April 2 to end of month, $3,400.

   6. Purchased office equipment on account, $10,000.

   8. Purchased a used truck for $21,000, paying $2,000 cash and giving a note payable for the remainder.

   10. Purchased supplies for cash, $1,800.

   12. Received cash for job completed, $13,000.

Apr. 15. Paid annual premiums on property and casualty insurance, $1,800.

23. Recorded jobs completed on account and sent invoices to customers, $9,000.

24. Received an invoice for truck expenses, to be paid in April, $1,000.

*Enter the following transactions on Page 2 of the two-column journal.*

29. Paid utilities expense, $1,500.

29. Paid miscellaneous expenses, $750.

30. Received cash from customers on account, $7,800.

30. Paid wages of employees, $4,000.

30. Paid creditor a portion of the amount owed for equipment purchased on April 6, $2,500.

30. Paid dividends, $2,000.

**Instructions**

1. Journalize each transaction in a two-column journal beginning on Page 1, referring to the following chart of accounts in selecting the accounts to be debited and credited. (Do not insert the account numbers in the journal at this time.) Explanations may be omitted.

| | | | |
|---|---|---|---|
| 11 | Cash | 31 | Capital Stock |
| 12 | Accounts Receivable | 33 | Dividends |
| 13 | Supplies | 41 | Fees Earned |
| 14 | Prepaid Insurance | 51 | Wages Expense |
| 16 | Equipment | 53 | Rent Expense |
| 18 | Truck | 54 | Utilities Expense |
| 21 | Notes Payable | 55 | Truck Expense |
| 22 | Accounts Payable | 59 | Miscellaneous Expense |

2. Post the journal to a ledger of four-column accounts, inserting appropriate posting references as each item is posted. Extend the balances to the appropriate balance columns after each transaction is posted.

3. Prepare an unadjusted trial balance for Intrex Designs as of April 30, 2012.

4. Determine the excess of revenues over expenses for April.

5. Can you think of any reason why the amount determined in (4) might not be the net income for April?

---

**OBJ. 1,2,3,4**

✔ 4. Total of Debit column: $259,600

**PR 2-4A   Journal entries and trial balance**

Utopia Realty acts as an agent in buying, selling, renting, and managing real estate. The unadjusted trial balance on October 31, 2012, is shown below.

**Utopia Realty**
**Unadjusted Trial Balance**
**October 31, 2012**

| | | Debit Balances | Credit Balances |
|---|---|---|---|
| 11 | Cash | 13,150 | |
| 12 | Accounts Receivable | 30,750 | |
| 13 | Prepaid Insurance | 1,500 | |
| 14 | Office Supplies | 900 | |
| 16 | Land | — | |
| 21 | Accounts Payable | | 7,000 |
| 22 | Unearned Rent | | — |
| 23 | Notes Payable | | — |
| 31 | Capital Stock | | 5,000 |
| 32 | Retained Earnings | | 18,000 |
| 33 | Dividends | 1,000 | |
| 41 | Fees Earned | | 120,000 |
| 51 | Salary and Commission Expense | 74,100 | |
| 52 | Rent Expense | 15,000 | |
| 53 | Advertising Expense | 8,900 | |
| 54 | Automobile Expense | 2,750 | |
| 59 | Miscellaneous Expense | 1,950 | |
| | | 150,000 | 150,000 |

The following business transactions were completed by Utopia Realty during November 2012:

Nov.  1.  Paid rent on office for month, $5,000.

2.  Purchased office supplies on account, $1,300.

5.  Paid annual insurance premiums, $3,600.

10.  Received cash from clients on account, $25,000.

15.  Purchased land for a future building site for $90,000, paying $10,000 in cash and giving a note payable for the remainder.

17.  Paid creditors on account, $4,500.

20.  Returned a portion of the office supplies purchased on November 2, receiving full credit for their cost, $200.

23.  Paid advertising expense, $2,000.

*Enter the following transactions on Page 19 of the two-column journal.*

27.  Discovered an error in computing a commission; received cash from the salesperson for the overpayment, $1,000.

28.  Paid automobile expense (including rental charges for an automobile), $1,500.

29.  Paid miscellaneous expenses, $450.

30.  Recorded revenue earned and billed to clients during the month, $30,000.

30.  Paid salaries and commissions for the month, $7,500.

30.  Paid dividends, $1,000.

30.  Rented land purchased on November 15 to local merchants association for use as a parking lot in December and January, during a street rebuilding program; received advance payment of $3,000.

### Instructions

1.  Record the November 1, 2010, balance of each account in the appropriate balance column of a four-column account, write *Balance* in the item section, and place a check mark (✓) in the Posting Reference column.

2.  Journalize the transactions for November in a two-column journal beginning on Page 18. Journal entry explanations may be omitted.

3.  Post to the ledger, extending the account balance to the appropriate balance column after each posting.

4.  Prepare an unadjusted trial balance of the ledger as of November 30, 2012.

5.  Assume that the November 30 transaction for salaries and commissions should have been $5,700. (a) Why did the unadjusted trial balance in (4) balance? (b) Journalize the correcting entry. (c) Is this error a transposition or slide?

---

**OBJ. 4**

✔ 7. Total of Debit column: $43,338.10

### PR 2-5A   Errors in trial balance

*If the working papers correlating with this textbook are not used, omit Problem 2-5A.*

The following records of A-Aall Electronic Repair are presented in the working papers:

• Journal containing entries for the period May 1–31.

• Ledger to which the May entries have been posted.

• Preliminary trial balance as of May 31, which does not balance.

Locate the errors, supply the information requested, and prepare a corrected trial balance according to the following instructions. The balances recorded in the accounts as of May 1 and the entries in the journal are correctly stated. If it is necessary to correct any posted amounts in the ledger, a line should be drawn through the erroneous figure and the correct amount inserted above. Corrections or notations may be inserted on the preliminary trial balance in any manner desired. It is not necessary to complete all of the instructions if equal trial balance totals can be obtained earlier. However, the requirements of instructions (6) and (7) should be completed in any event.

### Instructions

1.  Verify the totals of the preliminary trial balance, inserting the correct amounts in the schedule provided in the working papers.

(*Continued*)

2. Compute the difference between the trial balance totals.

3. Compare the listings in the trial balance with the balances appearing in the ledger, and list the errors in the space provided in the working papers.

4. Verify the accuracy of the balance of each account in the ledger, and list the errors in the space provided in the working papers.

5. Trace the postings in the ledger back to the journal, using small check marks to identify items traced. Correct any amounts in the ledger that may be necessitated by errors in posting, and list the errors in the space provided in the working papers.

6. Journalize as of May 31 the payment of $100 for advertising expense. The bill had been paid on May 31 but was inadvertently omitted from the journal. Post to the ledger. (Revise any amounts necessitated by posting this entry.)

7. Prepare a new unadjusted trial balance.

**OBJ. 4**

✔ 1. Total of Debit column: $1,400,000

**PR 2-6A   Corrected trial balance**

Imperial Carpet has the following unadjusted trial balance as of March 31, 2012.

**Imperial Carpet**
**Unadjusted Trial Balance**
**March 31, 2012**

| | Debit Balances | Credit Balances |
|---|---|---|
| Cash ......................................................... | 38,200 | |
| Accounts Receivable........................................ | 81,000 | |
| Supplies..................................................... | 16,690 | |
| Prepaid Insurance ......................................... | 3,600 | |
| Equipment.................................................. | 392,000 | |
| Notes Payable.............................................. | | 200,000 |
| Accounts Payable .......................................... | | 54,000 |
| Capital Stock................................................ | | 95,000 |
| Retained Earnings.......................................... | | 159,300 |
| Dividends .................................................. | 116,000 | |
| Fees Earned................................................. | | 858,900 |
| Wages Expense ............................................ | 490,000 | |
| Rent Expense .............................................. | 112,600 | |
| Advertising Expense....................................... | 50,400 | |
| Miscellaneous Expense .................................... | 10,200 | |
| | 1,310,690 | 1,367,200 |

The debit and credit totals are not equal as a result of the following errors:

a.  The balance of cash was understated by $12,000.

b.  A cash receipt of $13,900 was posted as a debit to Cash of $19,300.

c.  A debit of $15,000 to Accounts Receivable was not posted.

d.  A return of $90 of defective supplies was erroneously posted as a $900 credit to Supplies.

e.  An insurance policy acquired at a cost of $2,500 was posted as a credit to Prepaid Insurance.

f.  The balance of Notes Payable was understated by $35,200.

g.  A credit of $7,600 in Accounts Payable was overlooked when determining the balance of the account.

h.  A debit of $10,000 for dividends was posted as a credit to Retained Earnings.

i.  The balance of $116,200 in Rent Expense was entered as $112,600 in the trial balance.

j.  Gas, Electricity, and Water Expense, with a balance of $48,300 was omitted from the trial balance.

**Instructions**

1. Prepare a corrected unadjusted trial balance as of March 31, 2012.

2. ━━━▶ Does the fact that the unadjusted trial balance in (1) is balanced mean that there are no errors in the accounts? Explain.

## Problems Series B

OBJ. 1,2,3,4

✔ 3. Total of Debit column: $74,700

### PR 2-1B Entries into T accounts and trial balance

April Layton, an architect, opened an office on June 1, 2012. During the month, she completed the following transactions connected with her professional corporation, April Layton, Architect, P.C.:

a. Transferred cash from a personal bank account to an account to be used for the business in exchange for capital stock, $25,000.

b. Purchased used automobile for $24,000, paying $5,000 cash and giving a note payable for the remainder.

c. Paid June rent for office and workroom, $2,000.

d. Paid cash for supplies, $1,450.

e. Purchased office and computer equipment on account, $8,000.

f. Paid cash for annual insurance policies on automobile and equipment, $3,600.

g. Received cash from a client for plans delivered, $10,500.

h. Paid cash to creditors on account, $1,750.

i. Paid cash for miscellaneous expenses, $600.

j. Received invoice for blueprint service, due in July, $1,500.

k. Recorded fee earned on plans delivered, payment to be received in July, $12,800.

l. Paid salary of assistant, $1,600.

m. Paid cash for miscellaneous expenses, $200.

n. Paid installment due on note payable, $350.

o. Paid gas, oil, and repairs on automobile for June, $550.

#### Instructions

1. Record the above transactions directly in the following T accounts, without journalizing: Cash; Accounts Receivable; Supplies; Prepaid Insurance; Automobiles; Equipment; Notes Payable; Accounts Payable; Capital Stock; Professional Fees; Rent Expense; Salary Expense; Blueprint Expense; Automobile Expense; Miscellaneous Expense. To the left of each amount entered in the accounts, place the appropriate letter to identify the transaction.

2. Determine account balances of the T accounts. Accounts containing a single entry only (such as Prepaid Insurance) do not need a balance.

3. Prepare an unadjusted trial balance for April Layton, Architect, P.C. as of June 30, 2012.

4. Determine the net income or net loss for June.

OBJ. 1,2,3,4

✔ 4. c. $5,500

### PR 2-2B Journal entries and trial balance

On March 1, 2012, Mitch Quade established Marine Realty, which completed the following transactions during the month:

a. Mitch Quade transferred cash from a personal bank account to an account to be used for the business in exchange for capital stock, $18,000.

b. Purchased supplies on account, $1,200.

c. Earned sales commissions, receiving cash, $14,000.

d. Paid rent on office and equipment for the month, $3,000.

e. Paid creditor on account, $750.

f. Paid dividends, $2,000.

g. Paid automobile expenses (including rental charge) for month, $1,500, and miscellaneous expenses, $400.

h. Paid office salaries, $2,800.

i. Determined that the cost of supplies used was $800.

#### Instructions

1. Journalize entries for transactions (a) through (i), using the following account titles: Cash; Supplies; Accounts Payable; Capital Stock; Dividends; Sales Commissions; Rent Expense; Office Salaries Expense; Automobile Expense; Supplies Expense; Miscellaneous Expense. Journal entry explanations may be omitted.

*(Continued)*

2. Prepare T accounts, using the account titles in (1). Post the journal entries to these accounts, placing the appropriate letter to the left of each amount to identify the transactions. Determine the account balances, after all posting is complete. Accounts containing only a single entry do not need a balance.

3. Prepare an unadjusted trial balance as of March 31, 2012.

4. Determine the following:

   a. Amount of total revenue recorded in the ledger.

   b. Amount of total expenses recorded in the ledger.

   c. Amount of net income for March.

5. Determine the increase or decrease in retained earnings for March

---

OBJ. 1,2,3,4

✔ 3. Total of Credit column: $64,500

**PR 2-3B Journal entries and trial balance**

On July 1, 2012, Kim Wheeler established an interior decorating business, Aztec Designs. During the month, Kim completed the following transactions related to the business:

July  1. Kim transferred cash from a personal bank account to an account to be used for the business in exchange for capital stock, $21,000.

     4. Paid rent for period of July 4 to end of month, $2,750.

    10. Purchased a used truck for $18,000, paying $4,000 cash and giving a note payable for the remainder.

    13. Purchased equipment on account, $9,000.

    14. Purchased supplies for cash, $1,500.

    15. Paid annual premiums on property and casualty insurance, $3,600.

    15. Received cash for job completed, $12,000.

*Enter the following transactions on Page 2 of the two-column journal.*

    21. Paid creditor a portion of the amount owed for equipment purchased on July 13, $2,000.

    24. Recorded jobs completed on account and sent invoices to customers, $9,800.

    26. Received an invoice for truck expenses, to be paid in August, $700.

    27. Paid utilities expense, $1,000.

    27. Paid miscellaneous expenses, $300.

    29. Received cash from customers on account, $4,600.

    30. Paid wages of employees, $2,800.

    31. Paid dividends, $2,500.

**Instructions**

1. Journalize each transaction in a two-column journal beginning on Page 1, referring to the following chart of accounts in selecting the accounts to be debited and credited. (Do not insert the account numbers in the journal at this time.) Journal entry explanations may be omitted.

   | | |
   |---|---|
   | 11 Cash | 31 Capital Stock |
   | 12 Accounts Receivable | 33 Dividends |
   | 13 Supplies | 41 Fees Earned |
   | 14 Prepaid Insurance | 51 Wages Expense |
   | 16 Equipment | 53 Rent Expense |
   | 18 Truck | 54 Utilities Expense |
   | 21 Notes Payable | 55 Truck Expense |
   | 22 Accounts Payable | 59 Miscellaneous Expense |

2. Post the journal to a ledger of four-column accounts, inserting appropriate posting references as each item is posted. Extend the balances to the appropriate balance columns after each transaction is posted.

3. Prepare an unadjusted trial balance for Aztec Designs as of July 31, 2012.

4. Determine the excess of revenues over expenses for July.

5. Can you think of any reason why the amount determined in (4) might not be the net income for July?

OBJ. 1,2,3,4

✔ 4. Total of Debit
column: $575,400

### PR 2-4B   Journal entries and trial balance

Prime Time Realty acts as an agent in buying, selling, renting, and managing real estate. The unadjusted trial balance on July 31, 2012, is shown below.

**Prime Time Realty**
**Unadjusted Trial Balance**
**July 31, 2012**

| | | Debit Balances | Credit Balances |
|---|---|---:|---:|
| 11 | Cash. . . . . . . . . . . . . . . . . . . . . . . . . . . . . . . . . . . . . . . . . . . . . . . . . . . . . | 30,000 | |
| 12 | Accounts Receivable . . . . . . . . . . . . . . . . . . . . . . . . . . . . . . . . . . . . . . . . . | 57,200 | |
| 13 | Prepaid Insurance. . . . . . . . . . . . . . . . . . . . . . . . . . . . . . . . . . . . . . . . . . . . | 7,200 | |
| 14 | Office Supplies . . . . . . . . . . . . . . . . . . . . . . . . . . . . . . . . . . . . . . . . . . . . . . | 1,600 | |
| 16 | Land. . . . . . . . . . . . . . . . . . . . . . . . . . . . . . . . . . . . . . . . . . . . . . . . . . . . . . . | — | |
| 21 | Accounts Payable. . . . . . . . . . . . . . . . . . . . . . . . . . . . . . . . . . . . . . . . . . . . | | 12,000 |
| 22 | Unearned Rent . . . . . . . . . . . . . . . . . . . . . . . . . . . . . . . . . . . . . . . . . . . . . . | | — |
| 23 | Notes Payable . . . . . . . . . . . . . . . . . . . . . . . . . . . . . . . . . . . . . . . . . . . . . . | | — |
| 31 | Capital Stock . . . . . . . . . . . . . . . . . . . . . . . . . . . . . . . . . . . . . . . . . . . . . . . | | 6,000 |
| 32 | Retained Earnings . . . . . . . . . . . . . . . . . . . . . . . . . . . . . . . . . . . . . . . . . . . | | 44,000 |
| 33 | Dividends. . . . . . . . . . . . . . . . . . . . . . . . . . . . . . . . . . . . . . . . . . . . . . . . . . . | 25,600 | |
| 41 | Fees Earned . . . . . . . . . . . . . . . . . . . . . . . . . . . . . . . . . . . . . . . . . . . . . . . . | | 338,000 |
| 51 | Salary and Commission Expense . . . . . . . . . . . . . . . . . . . . . . . . . . . . . . . | 220,000 | |
| 52 | Rent Expense. . . . . . . . . . . . . . . . . . . . . . . . . . . . . . . . . . . . . . . . . . . . . . . . | 28,000 | |
| 53 | Advertising Expense . . . . . . . . . . . . . . . . . . . . . . . . . . . . . . . . . . . . . . . . . . | 18,400 | |
| 54 | Automobile Expense. . . . . . . . . . . . . . . . . . . . . . . . . . . . . . . . . . . . . . . . . . | 9,000 | |
| 59 | Miscellaneous Expense. . . . . . . . . . . . . . . . . . . . . . . . . . . . . . . . . . . . . . . . | 3,000 | |
| | | 400,000 | 400,000 |

The following business transactions were completed by Prime Time Realty during August 2012:

Aug.   1. Purchased office supplies on account, $1,800.

2. Paid rent on office for month, $5,000.

3. Received cash from clients on account, $40,000.

5. Paid annual insurance premiums, $6,000.

9. Returned a portion of the office supplies purchased on August 1, receiving full credit for their cost, $400.

17. Paid advertising expense, $5,500.

23. Paid creditors on account, $7,000

*Enter the following transactions on Page 19 of the two-column journal.*

29. Paid miscellaneous expenses, $500.

30. Paid automobile expense (including rental charges for an automobile), $2,500.

31. Discovered an error in computing a commission; received cash from the salesperson for the overpayment, $8,000.

31. Paid salaries and commissions for the month, $18,000.

31. Recorded revenue earned and billed to clients during the month, $112,000.

31. Purchased land for a future building site for $75,000, paying $10,000 in cash and giving a note payable for the remainder.

31. Paid dividends, $12,000.

31. Rented land purchased on August 31 to a local university for use as a parking lot during football season (September, October, and November); received advance payment of $4,000.

**Instructions**

1. Record the August 1 balance of each account in the appropriate balance column of a four-column account, write *Balance* in the item section, and place a check mark (✓) in the Posting Reference column.

2. Journalize the transactions for August in a two-column journal beginning on Page 18. Journal entry explanations may be omitted.

3. Post to the ledger, extending the account balance to the appropriate balance column after each posting.

(*Continued*)

4. Prepare an unadjusted trial balance of the ledger as of August 31, 2012.

5. Assume that the August 31 transaction for dividends should have been $1,200. (a) Why did the unadjusted trial balance in (4) balance? (b) Journalize the correcting entry. (c) Is this error a transposition or slide?

OBJ. 4

✔ 7. Total of Credit column: $43,338.10

**PR 2-5B   Errors in trial balance**

*If the working papers correlating with this textbook are not used, omit Problem 2-5B.*

The following records of A-Aall Electronic Repair are presented in the working papers:

• Journal containing entries for the period May 1–31.

• Ledger to which the May entries have been posted.

• Preliminary trial balance as of May 31, which does not balance.

Locate the errors, supply the information requested, and prepare a corrected trial balance according to the following instructions. The balances recorded in the accounts as of May 1 and the entries in the journal are correctly stated. If it is necessary to correct any posted amounts in the ledger, a line should be drawn through the erroneous figure and the correct amount inserted above. Corrections or notations may be inserted on the preliminary trial balance in any manner desired. It is not necessary to complete all of the instructions if equal trial balance totals can be obtained earlier. However, the requirements of instructions (6) and (7) should be completed in any event.

**Instructions**

1. Verify the totals of the preliminary trial balance, inserting the correct amounts in the schedule provided in the working papers.

2. Compute the difference between the trial balance totals.

3. Compare the listings in the trial balance with the balances appearing in the ledger, and list the errors in the space provided in the working papers.

4. Verify the accuracy of the balance of each account in the ledger, and list the errors in the space provided in the working papers.

5. Trace the postings in the ledger back to the journal, using small check marks to identify items traced. Correct any amounts in the ledger that may be necessitated by errors in posting, and list the errors in the space provided in the working papers.

6. Journalize as of May 31 the payment of $275 for gas and electricity. The bill had been paid on May 31 but was inadvertently omitted from the journal. Post to the ledger. (Revise any amounts necessitated by posting this entry.)

7. Prepare a new unadjusted trial balance.

OBJ. 4

✔ 1. Total of Debit column: $285,000

**PR 2-6B   Corrected trial balance**

Elite Video has the following unadjusted trial balance as of October 31, 2012.

**Elite Video**
**Unadjusted Trial Balance**
**October 31, 2012**

| | Debit Balances | Credit Balances |
|---|---|---|
| Cash | 11,100 | |
| Accounts Receivable | 17,560 | |
| Supplies | 2,520 | |
| Prepaid Insurance | 1,840 | |
| Equipment | 64,800 | |
| Notes Payable | | 31,600 |
| Accounts Payable | | 6,160 |
| Capital Stock | | 7,500 |
| Retained Earnings | | 31,640 |
| Dividends | 11,600 | |
| Fees Earned | | 213,600 |
| Wages Expense | 122,400 | |
| Rent Expense | 25,020 | |
| Advertising Expense | 13,140 | |
| Gas, Electricity, and Water Expense | 6,800 | |
| | 276,780 | 290,500 |

The debit and credit totals are not equal as a result of the following errors:

a. The balance of cash was overstated by $7,500.

b. A cash receipt of $7,200 was posted as a debit to Cash of $2,700.

c. A debit of $5,000 to Accounts Receivable was not posted.

d. A return of $350 of defective supplies was erroneously posted as a $530 credit to Supplies.

e. An insurance policy acquired at a cost of $1,000 was posted as a credit to Prepaid Insurance.

f. The balance of Notes Payable was overstated by $10,000.

g. A credit of $500 in Accounts Payable was overlooked when the balance of the account was determined.

h. A debit of $4,000 for dividends was posted as a debit to Capital Stock.

i. The balance of $11,340 in Advertising Expense was entered as $13,140 in the trial balance.

j. Miscellaneous Expense, with a balance of $1,840, was omitted from the trial balance.

**Instructions**

1. Prepare a corrected unadjusted trial balance as of October 31 of the current year.

2. ➤ Does the fact that the unadjusted trial balance in (1) is balanced mean that there are no errors in the accounts? Explain.

## Continuing Problem

✔ 4. Total of Debit
column: $40,030

The transactions completed by PS Music during June 2012 were described at the end of Chapter 1. The following transactions were completed during July, the second month of the business's operations:

July 1. Pat Sharpe made an additional investment in PS Music in exchange for capital stock by depositing $4,000 in PS Music's checking account.

1. Instead of continuing to share office space with a local real estate agency, Pat decided to rent office space near a local music store. Paid rent for July, $1,800.

1. Paid a premium of $2,700 for a comprehensive insurance policy covering liability, theft, and fire. The policy covers a one-year period.

2. Received $1,250 on account.

3. On behalf of PS Music, Pat signed a contract with a local radio station, WHBD, to provide guest spots for the next three months. The contract requires PS Music to provide a guest disc jockey for 80 hours per month for a monthly fee of $3,600. Any additional hours beyond 80 will be billed to WHBD at $40 per hour. In accordance with the contract, Pat received $7,200 from WHBD as an advance payment for the first two months.

3. Paid $250 on account.

4. Paid an attorney $800 for reviewing the July 3rd contract with WHBD. (Record as Miscellaneous Expense.)

5. Purchased office equipment on account from One-Stop Office Mart, $6,000.

8. Paid for a newspaper advertisement, $200.

11. Received $900 for serving as a disc jockey for a party.

13. Paid $600 to a local audio electronics store for rental of digital recording equipment.

14. Paid wages of $1,200 to receptionist and part-time assistant.

*Enter the following transactions on Page 2 of the two-column journal.*

July 16. Received $2,100 for serving as a disc jockey for a wedding reception.

18. Purchased supplies on account, $1,080.

21. Paid $620 to Upload Music for use of its current music demos in making various music sets.

22. Paid $800 to a local radio station to advertise the services of PS Music twice daily for the remainder of July.

23. Served as disc jockey for a party for $2,500. Received $750, with the remainder due August 4, 2012.

27. Paid electric bill, $760.

28. Paid wages of $1,200 to receptionist and part-time assistant.

29. Paid miscellaneous expenses, $370.

30. Served as a disc jockey for a charity ball for $1,800. Received $400, with the remainder due on August 9, 2012.

31. Received $2,800 for serving as a disc jockey for a party.

31. Paid $1,400 royalties (music expense) to National Music Clearing for use of various artists' music during July.

31. Paid dividends of $1,500.

PS Music's chart of accounts and the balance of accounts as of July 1, 2012 (all normal balances), are as follows:

| | | | | | |
|---|---|---|---|---|---|
| 11 | Cash | $5,310 | 41 | Fees Earned | $6,650 |
| 12 | Accounts Receivable | 1,250 | 50 | Wages Expense | 400 |
| 14 | Supplies | 170 | 51 | Office Rent Expense | 750 |
| 15 | Prepaid Insurance | — | 52 | Equipment Rent Expense | 700 |
| 17 | Office Equipment | — | 53 | Utilities Expense | 300 |
| 21 | Accounts Payable | 250 | 54 | Music Expense | 1,590 |
| 23 | Unearned Revenue | — | 55 | Advertising Expense | 450 |
| 31 | Capital Stock | 5,000 | 56 | Supplies Expense | 180 |
| 33 | Dividends | 500 | 59 | Miscellaneous Expense | 300 |

### Instructions

1. Enter the July 1, 2012, account balances in the appropriate balance column of a four-column account. Write *Balance* in the Item column, and place a check mark (✓) in the Posting Reference column. (*Hint:* Verify the equality of the debit and credit balances in the ledger before proceeding with the next instruction.)

2. Analyze and journalize each transaction in a two-column journal beginning on Page 1, omitting journal entry explanations.

3. Post the journal to the ledger, extending the account balance to the appropriate balance column after each posting.

4. Prepare an unadjusted trial balance as of July 31, 2012.

## Cases & Projects

You can access the Cases & Projects online at **www.cengage.com/accounting/reeve**

## Excel Success Special Activities

### SA 2-1   ImagePress—Journalize transactions

a. Open the Excel file *SA2-1,2,3_1e*. On the Sheet labeled *JE*, journalize the following selected April 2011 transactions for ImagePress Printing. Omit posting references and journal entry explanations.

Apr. 1. Paid advertising expense, $460. [This has been entered for you.]

2. Paid rent for the month, $2,500.

6. Purchased office equipment on account, $9,450.

9. Paid cash for supplies, $300.

13. Paid creditor on account, $340.

16. Received cash from customers on account, $1,080.

20. Fees earned and billed to customers, $9,570.

30. Paid salaries to employees, $1,900.

30. Paid electricity bill for the month, $440.

30. Paid dividends, $2,400.

b. When you have completed the journal transactions, perform a "save as," replacing the entire file name with the following:

*SA2-1,2,3_1e[your first name initial]_[your last name]*

---

### SA 2-2    ImagePress—Post transactions

a. Open your *SA2-1,2,3_1e[your first name initial]_[your last name]* file. Label Sheet2 as **GL** (for general ledger). Post the journal entries for ImagePress Printing from *SA2-1* to the appropriate accounts in the ledger, worksheet **GL**.

Insert the appropriate posting references as each item is posted. Extend the balances using spreadsheet formulas to the appropriate balance columns after each transaction is posted.

Using the following chart of accounts, place the beginning balance in the first row of each account in the appropriate balance column.

**ImagePress Printing**
**Unadjusted Trial Balance**
**March 31, 2011**

| Accounts | Debit Balances | Credit Balances |
|---|---|---|
| 11   Cash ..................................................... | 15,500 | |
| 12   Accounts Receivable ...................................... | 7,300 | |
| 13   Supplies ............................................... | 2,000 | |
| 14   Office Equipment........................................ | 12,400 | |
| 21   Accounts Payable........................................ | | 1,300 |
| 31   Capital Stock .......................................... | | 23,800 |
| 33   Dividends.............................................. | 3,500 | |
| 41   Fees Earned ............................................ | | 25,600 |
| 51   Advertising Expense ..................................... | 200 | |
| 52   Rent Expense........................................... | 5,000 | |
| 53   Salaries Expense......................................... | 3,600 | |
| 54   Utilities Expense ........................................ | 1,200 | |
| | 50,700 | 50,700 |

b. Save your file using the **same file name**.

---

### SA 2-3    ImagePress—Prepare a trial balance

a. Open your *SA2-1,2,3_1e[your first name initial]_[your last name]* file. Label Sheet3 as **UTB** (for Unadjusted Trial Balance). Within this worksheet, use cell references to prepare an unadjusted trial balance for the April 30 balances of ImagePress Printing, from the ledger accounts of *SA2-2*.

b. Save your file using the **same file name**.

### SA 2-4   Journalize transactions

a. Open the Excel file *SA2-4,5,6_1e*. On Sheet **JE**, journalize the following selected September 2011 transactions for Artscape in this worksheet. Omit posting references and journal entry explanations.

Sept.   1. Paid rent for the month, $1,150.

   3. Paid advertising expense, $670.

   8. Paid cash for supplies, $230.

   11. Purchased office equipment on account, $5,200.

   15. Paid creditor on account, $920.

   19. Fees earned and billed to customers, $7,200.

   25. Received cash from customers on account, $2,380.

   30. Paid telephone bill for the month, $240.

   30. Paid wages to employees, $1,450.

   30. Paid dividends, $1,100.

b. When you have completed the journal transactions, perform a "save as," replacing the entire file name with the following:

   *SA2-4,5,6_1e[your first name initial]_[your last name]*

### SA 2-5   Post transactions

a. Open your *SA2-4,5,6_1e[your first name initial]_[your last name]* file. Label Sheet2, **GL**. Post the journal entries to the appropriate accounts in the general ledger, worksheet **GL**.

Insert the appropriate posting references as each item is posted. Extend the balances using spreadsheet formulas to the appropriate balance columns after each transaction is posted.

Use the following chart of accounts by placing the beginning balance in the first row of each account in the appropriate balance column.

Artscape
Trial Balance
August 31, 2011

|    |    | Debit Balances | Credit Balances |
|----|----|---------------:|----------------:|
| 11 | Cash | 12,700 | |
| 12 | Accounts Receivable | 9,100 | |
| 13 | Supplies | 1,500 | |
| 14 | Office Equipment | 11,900 | |
| 21 | Accounts Payable | | 2,700 |
| 31 | Capital Stock | | 21,400 |
| 33 | Dividends | 3,100 | |
| 41 | Fees Earned | | 23,100 |
| 51 | Advertising Expense | 300 | |
| 52 | Rent Expense | 4,200 | |
| 53 | Utilities Expense | 3,500 | |
| 54 | Wages Expense | 900 | |
|    |    | 47,200 | 47,200 |

b. Save your file using the ***same file name***.

### SA 2-6   Prepare a trial balance

a. Open your *SA2-4,5,6_1e[your first name initial]_[your last name]* file. Label Sheet3, **UTB**. Use this worksheet to prepare an unadjusted trial balance for the September 30 balances of Artscape.

b. Save your file using the ***same file name***.

Search for music

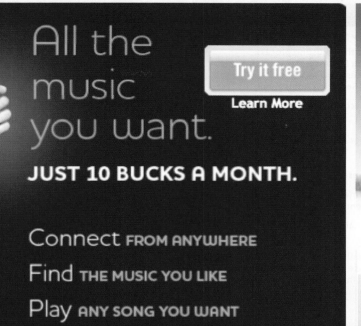

All the
music
you want.

**JUST 10 BUCKS A MONTH.**

Try it free

Learn More

Connect FROM ANYWHERE

Find THE MUSIC YOU LIKE

Play ANY SONG YOU WANT

Your opini...
a chance...

TAKE A SURVE...

safecount.net

Start »

**10 Essential Disney Soundtracks**

From the Lion King to Toy Story 3, we look back at the greatest Disney songs.

 More

**New Releases**

**What Members Are Listening To**

Tracks          Albums          Artists

# The Adjusting Process

## Rhapsody

**D**o you subscribe to an Internet-based music service such as Rhapsody®? Rhapsody began by providing digital music to its subscribers through Internet audio streaming. You can subscribe to "Rhapsody Premier" for $10.00 per month and listen to music by New Boyz, Coldplay, Flo Rida, or Carrie Underwood. Rhapsody, which is partially owned by RealNetworks®, has also expanded its services to include games and video content.

When should a company such as RealNetworks record revenue from its subscriptions? Subscriptions revenue is recorded when it is earned. Subscriptions revenue is earned when the service has been delivered to the customer. However, in many cases cash is received before the service is delivered. For example, the subscription to "Rhapsody Premier" is paid at the beginning of

the month. In this case, the cash received represents unearned revenue. As time passes and the services are delivered, the unearned revenue becomes earned and, thus, becomes revenue. As a result, companies like RealNetworks must update their accounting records for items such as unearned subscriptions before preparing their financial statements. For example, RealNetworks reported in its financial statements that it had unearned (deferred) revenue of approximately $33 million as of December 31, 2009.

This chapter describes and illustrates the process by which companies update their accounting records before preparing financial statements. This discussion includes the adjustments for unearned revenues made at the end of the accounting period.

**OBJ. 1** Describe the nature of the adjusting process.

# Nature of the Adjusting Process

When preparing financial statements, the economic life of the business is divided into time periods. This **accounting period concept** requires that revenues and expenses be reported in the proper period. To determine the proper period, accountants use generally accepted accounting principles (GAAP), which requires the **accrual basis of accounting**.

Under the accrual basis of accounting, revenues are reported on the income statement in the period in which they are earned. For example, revenue is reported when the services are provided to customers. Cash may or may not be received from customers during this period. The accounting concept supporting this reporting of revenues is called the **revenue recognition concept**.

Under the accrual basis, expenses are reported in the same period as the revenues to which they relate. For example, utility expenses incurred in December are reported as an expense and matched against December's revenues even though the utility bill may not be paid until January. The accounting concept supporting reporting revenues and related expenses in the same period is called the **matching concept**, or **matching principle**. By matching revenues and expenses, net income or loss for the period is properly reported on the income statement.

Although GAAP requires the accrual basis of accounting, some businesses use the **cash basis of accounting**. Under the cash basis of accounting, revenues and expenses are reported on the income statement in the period in which cash is received or paid. For example, fees are recorded when cash is received from clients; likewise, wages are recorded when cash is paid to employees. The net income (or net loss) is the difference between the cash receipts (revenues) and the cash payments (expenses).

Small service businesses may use the cash basis, because they have few receivables and payables. For example, attorneys, physicians, and real estate agents often use the cash basis. For them, the cash basis provides financial statements similar to those of the accrual basis. For most large businesses, however, the cash basis will not provide accurate financial statements for user needs. For this reason, the accrual basis is used in this text.

American Airlines uses the accrual basis of accounting. Revenues are recognized when passengers take flights, not when the passenger makes the reservation or pays for the ticket.

## The Adjusting Process

At the end of the accounting period, many of the account balances in the ledger are reported in the financial statements without change. For example, the balances of the cash and land accounts are normally the amount reported on the balance sheet.

Some accounts, however, require updating for the following reasons:[1]

1. Some expenses are not recorded daily. For example, the daily use of supplies would require many entries with small amounts. Also, the amount of supplies on hand on a day-to-day basis is normally not needed.

2. Some revenues and expenses are incurred as time passes rather than as separate transactions. For example, rent received in advance (unearned rent) expires and becomes revenue with the passage of time. Likewise, prepaid insurance expires and becomes an expense with the passage of time.

3. Some revenues and expenses may be unrecorded. For example, a company may have provided services to customers that it has not billed or recorded at the end of the accounting period. Likewise, a company may not pay its employees until the next accounting period even though the employees have earned their wages in the current period.

The analysis and updating of accounts at the end of the period before the financial statements are prepared is called the **adjusting process**. The journal entries that bring the accounts up to date at the end of the accounting period are called **adjusting entries**. All adjusting entries affect at least one income statement account and one balance sheet account. Thus, an adjusting entry will *always* involve a revenue or an expense account *and* an asset or a liability account.

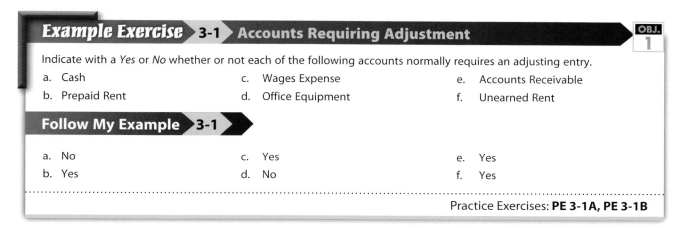

## Types of Accounts Requiring Adjustment

Four basic types of accounts require adjusting entries as shown below.

1. Prepaid expenses
2. Unearned revenues
3. Accrued revenues
4. Accrued expenses

**Prepaid expenses** are the advance payment of *future* expenses and are recorded as assets when cash is paid. Prepaid expenses become expenses over time or during normal operations. To illustrate, the following transaction of NetSolutions from Chapter 2 is used.

Dec. 1    NetSolutions paid $2,400 as a premium on a one-year insurance policy.

On December 1, the cash payment of $2,400 was recorded as a debit to Prepaid Insurance and credit to Cash for $2,400. At the end of December, only $200 ($2,400 divided by 12 months) of the insurance premium is expired and has become an expense. The remaining $2,200 of prepaid insurance will become an expense in future months. Thus, the $200 is insurance expense of December and should be recorded with an adjusting entry.

---

1 Under the cash basis of accounting, accounts do not require adjusting. This is because transactions are recorded only when cash is received or paid. Thus, the matching concept is not used under the cash basis.

Other examples of prepaid expenses include supplies, prepaid advertising, and prepaid interest.

Exhibit 1 summarizes the nature of prepaid expenses.

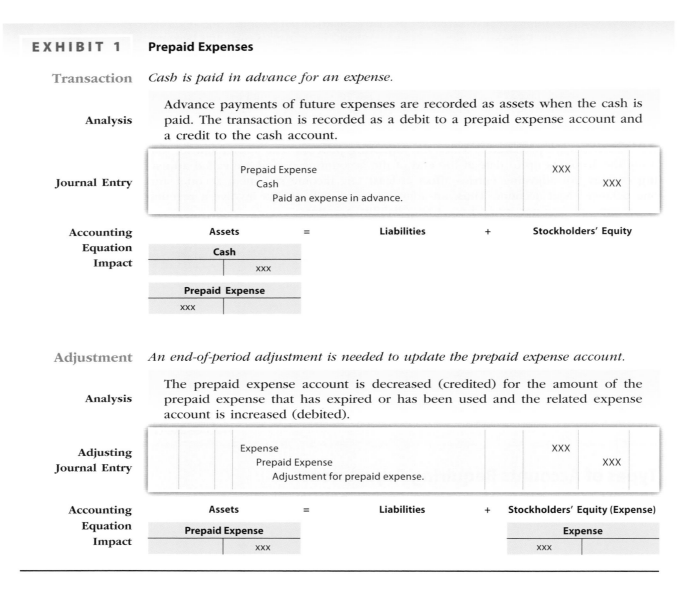

**EXHIBIT 1** **Prepaid Expenses**

**Transaction** *Cash is paid in advance for an expense.*

**Analysis** Advance payments of future expenses are recorded as assets when the cash is paid. The transaction is recorded as a debit to a prepaid expense account and a credit to the cash account.

**Journal Entry**

| | | Prepaid Expense | | XXX | |
| | | Cash | | | XXX |
| | | Paid an expense in advance. | | | |

**Accounting Equation Impact**

Assets = Liabilities + Stockholders' Equity

| Cash | |
| --- | --- |
| | XXX |

| Prepaid Expense | |
| --- | --- |
| XXX | |

**Adjustment** *An end-of-period adjustment is needed to update the prepaid expense account.*

**Analysis** The prepaid expense account is decreased (credited) for the amount of the prepaid expense that has expired or has been used and the related expense account is increased (debited).

**Adjusting Journal Entry**

| | | Expense | | XXX | |
| | | Prepaid Expense | | | XXX |
| | | Adjustment for prepaid expense. | | | |

**Accounting Equation Impact**

Assets = Liabilities + Stockholders' Equity (Expense)

| Prepaid Expense | |
| --- | --- |
| | XXX |

| Expense | |
| --- | --- |
| XXX | |

**Unearned revenues** are the advance receipt of *future* revenues and are recorded as liabilities when cash is received. Unearned revenues become earned revenues over time or during normal operations. To illustrate, the following December 1 transaction of NetSolutions is used.

> Dec. 1    NetSolutions received $360 from a local retailer to rent land for three months.

On December 1, the cash receipt of $360 was recorded as a debit to Cash and a credit to Unearned Rent for $360. At the end of December, $120 ($360 divided by 3 months) of the unearned rent has been earned. The remaining $240 will become rent revenue in future months. Thus, the $120 is rent revenue of December and should be recorded with an adjusting entry.

Other examples of unearned revenues include tuition received in advance by a school, an annual retainer fee received by an attorney, premiums received in advance by an insurance company, and magazine subscriptions received in advance by a publisher.

Exhibit 2 summarizes the nature of unearned revenues.

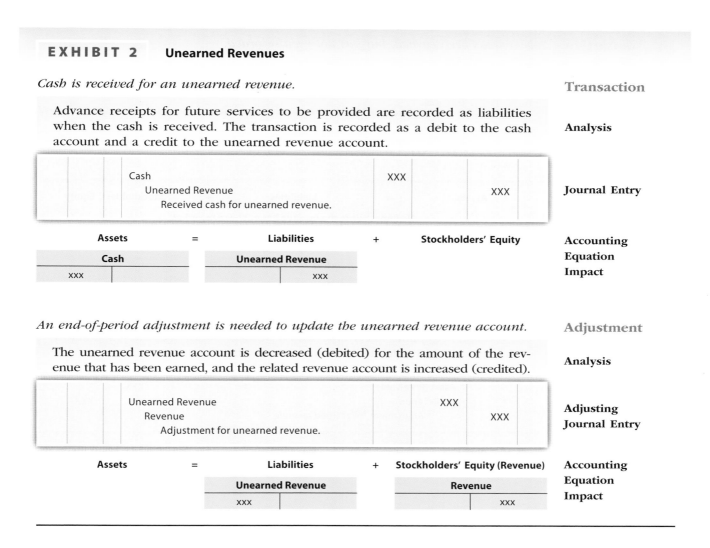

## EXHIBIT 2    Unearned Revenues

*Cash is received for an unearned revenue.*    Transaction

Advance receipts for future services to be provided are recorded as liabilities when the cash is received. The transaction is recorded as a debit to the cash account and a credit to the unearned revenue account.    Analysis

Cash                                         XXX
   Unearned Revenue                              XXX    Journal Entry
      Received cash for unearned revenue.

| Assets | = | Liabilities | + | Stockholders' Equity | Accounting |
| Cash | | Unearned Revenue | | | Equity |
| XXX | | XXX | | | Impact |

*An end-of-period adjustment is needed to update the unearned revenue account.*    Adjustment

The unearned revenue account is decreased (debited) for the amount of the revenue that has been earned, and the related revenue account is increased (credited).    Analysis

Unearned Revenue                             XXX
   Revenue                                       XXX    Adjusting Journal Entry
      Adjustment for unearned revenue.

| Assets | = | Liabilities | + | Stockholders' Equity (Revenue) | Accounting |
| | | Unearned Revenue | | Revenue | Equation |
| | | XXX | | XXX | Impact |

**Accrued revenues** are unrecorded revenues that have been earned and for which cash has yet to be received. Fees for services that an attorney or a doctor has provided but not yet billed are accrued revenues. To illustrate, the following example involving NetSolutions and one of its customers is used.

Dec. 15    NetSolutions signed an agreement with Dankner Co. under which NetSolutions will bill Dankner Co. on the fifteenth of each month for services rendered at the rate of $20 per hour.

From December 16–31, NetSolutions provided 25 hours of service to Dankner Co. Although the revenue of $500 (25 hours × $20) has been earned, it will not be billed until January 15. Likewise, cash of $500 will not be received until Dankner pays its bill. Thus, the $500 of accrued revenue and the $500 of fees earned should be recorded with an adjusting entry on December 31.

Other examples of accrued revenues include accrued interest on notes receivable and accrued rent on property rented to others.

Exhibit 3 summarizes the nature of accrued revenues.

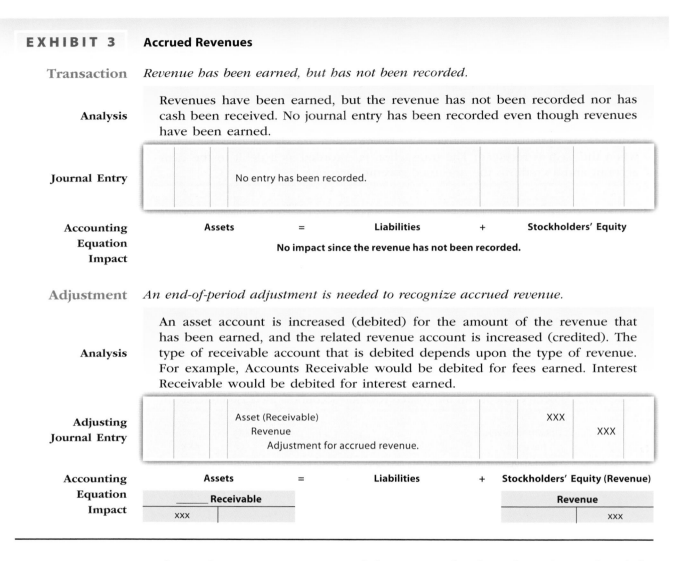

**EXHIBIT 3** **Accrued Revenues**

| | |
|---|---|
| **Transaction** | *Revenue has been earned, but has not been recorded.* |
| **Analysis** | Revenues have been earned, but the revenue has not been recorded nor has cash been received. No journal entry has been recorded even though revenues have been earned. |
| **Journal Entry** | No entry has been recorded. |

**Accounting Equation Impact**

| Assets | = | Liabilities | + | Stockholders' Equity |
|---|---|---|---|---|

No impact since the revenue has not been recorded.

| | |
|---|---|
| **Adjustment** | *An end-of-period adjustment is needed to recognize accrued revenue.* |
| **Analysis** | An asset account is increased (debited) for the amount of the revenue that has been earned, and the related revenue account is increased (credited). The type of receivable account that is debited depends upon the type of revenue. For example, Accounts Receivable would be debited for fees earned. Interest Receivable would be debited for interest earned. |

**Adjusting Journal Entry**

Asset (Receivable)     XXX
   Revenue     XXX
     Adjustment for accrued revenue.

**Accounting Equation Impact**

| Assets | = | Liabilities | + | Stockholders' Equity (Revenue) |
|---|---|---|---|---|

| _____ Receivable | | | Revenue | |
|---|---|---|---|---|
| XXX | | | | XXX |

**Accrued expenses** are unrecorded expenses that have been incurred and for which cash has yet to be paid. Wages owed to employees at the end of a period but not yet paid are an accrued expense. To illustrate, the following example involving NetSolutions and its employees is used.

> Dec. 31    NetSolutions owes its employees wages of $250 for Monday and Tuesday, December 30 and 31.

NetSolutions paid wages of $950 on December 13 and $1,200 on December 27, 2011. These payments covered the biweekly pay periods that ended on those days. As of December 31, 2011, NetSolutions owes its employees wages of $250 for Monday and Tuesday, December 30 and 31. The wages of $250 will be paid on January 10, 2012; however, they are an expense of December. Thus, $250 of accrued wages should be recorded with an adjusting entry on December 31.

Other examples of accrued expenses include accrued interest on notes payable and accrued taxes.

Exhibit 4 summarizes the nature of accrued expenses.

**EXHIBIT 4    Accrued Expenses**

*An expense has been incurred, but has not been recorded.*                                    Transaction

An expense has been incurred, but the expense has not been recorded nor has cash been paid. No journal entry has been recorded even though an expense has been incurred.                                                                   Analysis

| | | |
|---|---|---|
| | No entry has been recorded. | |

Journal Entry

| Assets | = | Liabilities | + | Stockholders' Equity |
|---|---|---|---|---|

No impact since the expense has not been recorded.

Accounting Equation Impact

*An end-of-period adjustment is needed to recognize the accrued expense.*                      Adjustment

An expense account is increased (debited) for the amount of the expense that has been incurred and the related liability account is increased (credited). The liability account that is credited depends upon the type of expense. For example, Wages Payable would be credited for wages expense. Interest Payable would be credited for interest expense.                                    Analysis

| | Expense | | XXX | |
|---|---|---|---|---|
| | Liability (Payable) | | | XXX |
| | Adjustment for accrued expense. | | | |

Adjusting Journal Entry

| Assets | = | Liabilities | + | Stockholders' Equity (Expense) |
|---|---|---|---|---|

| _____ Payable | | Expense |
|---|---|---|
| | XXX | XXX |

Accounting Equation Impact

As illustrated in Exhibit 4, accrued revenues are earned revenues that are unrecorded. The cash receipts for accrued revenues are normally received in the next accounting period. Accrued expenses are expenses that have been incurred, but are unrecorded. The cash payments for accrued expenses are normally paid in the next accounting period.

Prepaid expenses and unearned revenues are sometimes referred to as *deferrals*. This is because the recording of the related expense or revenue is deferred to a future period. Accrued revenues and accrued expenses are sometimes referred to as *accruals*. This is because the related revenue or expense should be recorded or accrued in the current period.

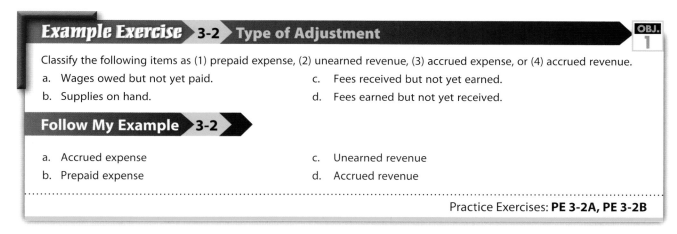

**Example Exercise  3-2  Type of Adjustment**                                          OBJ. 1

Classify the following items as (1) prepaid expense, (2) unearned revenue, (3) accrued expense, or (4) accrued revenue.

a.  Wages owed but not yet paid.              c.  Fees received but not yet earned.
b.  Supplies on hand.                         d.  Fees earned but not yet received.

**Follow My Example  3-2**

a.  Accrued expense                           c.  Unearned revenue
b.  Prepaid expense                           d.  Accrued revenue

Practice Exercises: **PE 3-2A, PE 3-2B**

Journalize entries for accounts requiring adjustment.

# Adjusting Entries

To illustrate adjusting entries, the December 31, 2011, unadjusted trial balance of NetSolutions shown in Exhibit 5 is used. An expanded chart of accounts for NetSolutions is shown in Exhibit 6. The additional accounts used in this chapter are shown in color. The rules of debit and credit shown in Exhibit 3 of Chapter 2 are used to record the adjusting entries.

**EXHIBIT 5**

**Unadusted Trial Balance for NetSolutions**

| NetSolutions<br>Unadusted Trial Balance<br>December 31, 2011 | | |
| --- | --- | --- |
| | Debit<br>Balances | Credit<br>Balances |
| Cash | 2,065 | |
| Accounts Receivable | 2,220 | |
| Supplies | 2,000 | |
| Prepaid Insurance | 2,400 | |
| Land | 20,000 | |
| Office Equipment | 1,800 | |
| Accounts Payable | | 900 |
| Unearned Rent | | 360 |
| Capital Stock | | 25,000 |
| Dividends | 4,000 | |
| Fees Earned | | 16,340 |
| Wages Expense | 4,275 | |
| Rent Expense | 1,600 | |
| Utilities Expense | 985 | |
| Supplies Expense | 800 | |
| Miscellaneous Expense | 455 | |
| | 42,600 | 42,600 |

**EXHIBIT 6**

**Expanded Chart of Accounts for NetSolutions**

**Balance Sheet Accounts**

**1. Assets**
11 Cash
12 Accounts Receivable
14 Supplies
15 Prepaid Insurance
17 Land
18 Office Equipment
19 Accumulated Depreciation—Office Equipment

**2. Liabilities**
21 Accounts Payable
22 Wages Payable
23 Unearned Rent

**3. Stockholders' Equity**
31 Capital Stock
33 Dividends

**Income Statement Accounts**

**4. Revenue**
41 Fees Earned
42 Rent Revenue

**5. Expenses**
51 Wages Expense
52 Rent Expense
53 Depreciation Expense
54 Utilities Expense
55 Supplies Expense
56 Insurance Expense
59 Miscellaneous Expense

## Prepaid Expenses

**Supplies** The December 31, 2011, unadjusted trial balance of NetSolutions indicates a balance in the supplies account of $2,000. In addition, the prepaid insurance account has a balance of $2,400. Each of these accounts requires an adjusting entry.

The balance in NetSolutions' supplies account on December 31 is $2,000. Some of these supplies (CDs, paper, envelopes, etc.) were used during December, and some are still on hand (not used). If either amount is known, the other can be determined. It is normally easier to determine the cost of the supplies on hand at the end of the month than to record daily supplies used.

Assuming that on December 31 the amount of supplies on hand is $760, the amount to be transferred from the asset account to the expense account is $1,240, computed as follows:

| | |
|---|---:|
| Supplies available during December (balance of account) | $2,000 |
| Supplies on hand, December 31 | 760 |
| Supplies used (amount of adjustment) | $1,240 |

At the end of December, the supplies expense account is increased (debited) for $1,240, and the supplies account is decreased (credited) for $1,240 to record the supplies used during December. The adjusting journal entry and T accounts for Supplies and Supplies Expense are as follows:

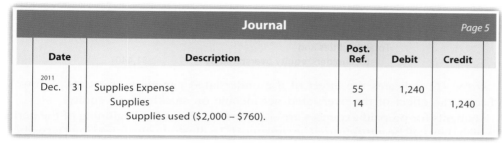

Adjusting Journal Entry

Accounting Equation Impact

The adjusting entry is shown in color in the T accounts to separate it from other transactions. After the adjusting entry is recorded and posted, the supplies account has a debit balance of $760. This balance is an asset that will become an expense in a future period.

**Prepaid Insurance** The debit balance of $2,400 in NetSolutions' prepaid insurance account represents a December 1 prepayment of insurance for 12 months. At the end of December, the insurance expense account is increased (debited), and the prepaid insurance account is decreased (credited) by $200, the insurance for one month. The adjusting journal entry and T accounts for Prepaid Insurance and Insurance Expense are as follows:

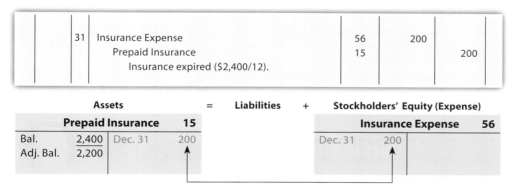

Adjusting Journal Entry

Accounting Equation Impact

After the adjusting entry is recorded and posted, the prepaid insurance account has a debit balance of $2,200. This balance is an asset that will become an expense in future periods. The insurance expense account has a debit balance of $200, which is an expense of the current period.

If the preceding adjustments for supplies ($1,240) and insurance ($200) are not recorded, the financial statements prepared as of December 31 will be misstated. On the income statement, Supplies Expense and Insurance Expense will be understated by a total of $1,440 ($1,240 + $200), and net income will be overstated by $1,440. On the balance sheet, Supplies and Prepaid Insurance will be overstated by a total of $1,440. Since net income increases Retained Earnings, stockholders' equity will also be overstated by $1,440 on the balance sheet. The effects of omitting these adjusting entries on the income statement and balance sheet are as follows:

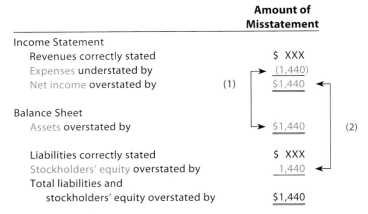

|  | Amount of Misstatement |  |
|---|---|---|
| **Income Statement** |  |  |
| Revenues correctly stated | $ XXX |  |
| Expenses understated by | (1,440) |  |
| Net income overstated by (1) | $1,440 |  |
| **Balance Sheet** |  |  |
| Assets overstated by | $1,440 | (2) |
| Liabilities correctly stated | $ XXX |  |
| Stockholders' equity overstated by | 1,440 |  |
| Total liabilities and stockholders' equity overstated by | $1,440 |  |

Arrow (1) indicates the effect of the understated expenses on assets. Arrow (2) indicates the effect of the overstated net income on stockholders' equity.

Payments for prepaid expenses are sometimes made at the beginning of the period in which they will be *entirely used or consumed*. To illustrate, the following December 1 transaction of NetSolutions is used.

Dec. 1    NetSolutions paid rent of $800 for the month.

On December 1, the rent payment of $800 represents Prepaid Rent. However, the Prepaid Rent expires daily, and at the end of December there will be no asset left. In such cases, the payment of $800 is recorded as Rent Expense rather than as Prepaid Rent. In this way, no adjusting entry is needed at the end of the period.[2]

**Example Exercise  3-3  Adjustment for Prepaid Expense**          OBJ. 2

The prepaid insurance account had a beginning balance of $6,400 and was debited for $3,600 of premiums paid during the year. Journalize the adjusting entry required at the end of the year assuming the amount of unexpired insurance related to future periods is $3,250.

**Follow My Example  3-3**

| Insurance Expense | 6,750 |  |
|---|---|---|
| Prepaid Insurance |  | 6,750 |
| Insurance expired ($6,400 + $3,600 − $3,250). |  |  |

Practice Exercises: **PE 3-3A, PE 3-3B**

## Integrity, Objectivity, and Ethics in Business

**FREE ISSUE**

Office supplies are often available to employees on a "free issue" basis. This means that employees do not have to "sign" for the release of office supplies but merely obtain the necessary supplies from a local storage area as needed. Just because supplies are easily available, however, doesn't mean they can be taken for personal use. There are many instances where employees have been terminated for taking supplies home for personal use.

2 An alternative treatment of recording the cost of supplies, rent, and other prepayments of expenses is discussed in an appendix that can be downloaded from the book's companion Web site (**www.cengage.com/accounting/reeve**).

# Unearned Revenues

The December 31 unadjusted trial balance of NetSolutions indicates a balance in the unearned rent account of $360. This balance represents the receipt of three months' rent on December 1 for December, January, and February. At the end of December, one months' rent has been earned. Thus, the unearned rent account is decreased (debited) by $120, and the rent revenue account is increased (credited) by $120. The $120 represents the rental revenue for one month ($360/3). The adjusting journal entry and T accounts are shown below.

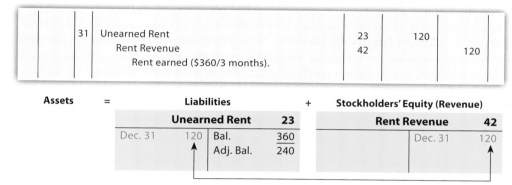

| | | 31 | Unearned Rent | 23 | 120 | |
| | | | Rent Revenue | 42 | | 120 |
| | | | Rent earned ($360/3 months). | | | |

**Adjusting Journal Entry**

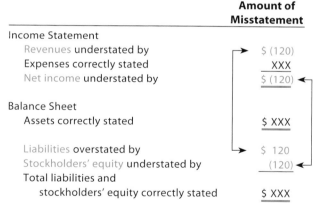

Assets = Liabilities + Stockholders' Equity (Revenue)

| Unearned Rent | 23 | | | Rent Revenue | 42 |
| Dec. 31 | 120 | Bal. | 360 | | Dec. 31 | 120 |
| | | Adj. Bal. | 240 | | | |

**Accounting Equation Impact**

After the adjusting entry is recorded and posted, the unearned rent account has a credit balance of $240. This balance is a liability that will become revenue in a future period. Rent Revenue has a balance of $120, which is revenue of the current period.[3]

If the preceding adjustment of unearned rent and rent revenue is not recorded, the financial statements prepared on December 31 will be misstated. On the income statement, Rent Revenue and the net income will be understated by $120. On the balance sheet, liabilities (Unearned Rent) will be overstated by $120, and stockholders' equity (Retained Earnings) will be understated by $120. The effects of omitting this adjusting entry are shown below.

Best Buy sells extended warranty contracts with terms between 12 and 36 months. The receipts from sales of these contracts are reported as unearned revenue on Best Buy's balance sheet. Revenue is recorded as the contracts expire.

| | Amount of Misstatement |
|---|---|
| Income Statement | |
| Revenues understated by | $ (120) |
| Expenses correctly stated | XXX |
| Net income understated by | $ (120) |
| | |
| Balance Sheet | |
| Assets correctly stated | $ XXX |
| | |
| Liabilities overstated by | $ 120 |
| Stockholders' equity understated by | (120) |
| Total liabilities and | |
| stockholders' equity correctly stated | $ XXX |

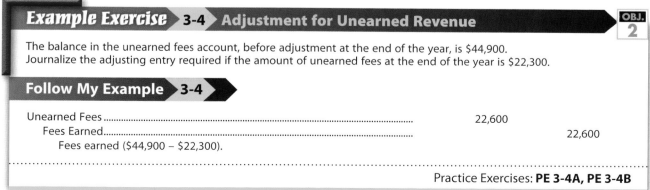

## Example Exercise 3-4 ▶ Adjustment for Unearned Revenue

**OBJ. 2**

The balance in the unearned fees account, before adjustment at the end of the year, is $44,900. Journalize the adjusting entry required if the amount of unearned fees at the end of the year is $22,300.

### Follow My Example 3-4

| Unearned Fees ........................................................................................ | 22,600 | |
| Fees Earned ........................................................................................ | | 22,600 |
| Fees earned ($44,900 – $22,300). | | |

Practice Exercises: **PE 3-4A, PE 3-4B**

3 An alternative treatment of recording revenues received in advance of their being earned is discussed in an appendix that can be downloaded from the book's companion Web site (**www.cengage.com/accounting/reeve**).

## Accrued Revenues

During an accounting period, some revenues are recorded only when cash is received. Thus, at the end of an accounting period, there may be revenue that has been earned *but has not been recorded*. In such cases, the revenue is recorded by increasing (debiting) an asset account and increasing (crediting) a revenue account.

To illustrate, assume that NetSolutions signed an agreement with Dankner Co. on December 15. The agreement provides that NetSolutions will answer computer questions and render assistance to Dankner Co.'s employees. The services will be billed to Dankner Co. on the fifteenth of each month at a rate of $20 per hour. As of December 31, NetSolutions had provided 25 hours of assistance to Dankner Co. The revenue of $500 (25 hours × $20) will be billed on January 15. However, NetSolutions earned the revenue in December.

The claim against the customer for payment of the $500 is an account receivable (*an asset*). Thus, the accounts receivable account is increased (debited) by $500 and the fees earned account is increased (credited) by $500. The adjusting journal entry and T accounts are shown below.

**Adjusting Journal Entry**

| | | | | | | |
|---|---|---|---|---|---|---|
| | | 31 | Accounts Receivable | 12 | 500 | |
| | | | Fees Earned | 41 | | 500 |
| | | | Accrued fees (25 hrs. × $20). | | | |

**Accounting Equation Impact**

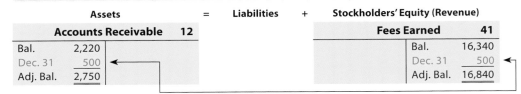

If the adjustment for the accrued revenue ($500) is not recorded, Fees Earned and the net income will be understated by $500 on the income statement. On the balance sheet, assets (Accounts Receivable) and stockholders' equity (Retained Earnings) will be understated by $500. The effects of omitting this adjusting entry are shown below.

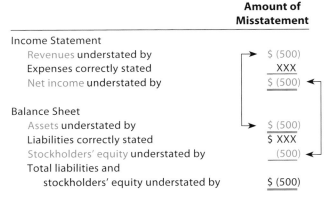

| | Amount of Misstatement |
|---|---|
| Income Statement | |
| Revenues understated by | $ (500) |
| Expenses correctly stated | XXX |
| Net income understated by | $ (500) |
| | |
| Balance Sheet | |
| Assets understated by | $ (500) |
| Liabilities correctly stated | $ XXX |
| Stockholders' equity understated by | (500) |
| Total liabilities and | |
| stockholders' equity understated by | $ (500) |

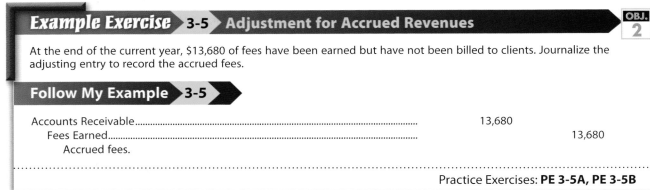

**Example Exercise** ▶ **3-5** ▶ **Adjustment for Accrued Revenues**    OBJ. 2

At the end of the current year, $13,680 of fees have been earned but have not been billed to clients. Journalize the adjusting entry to record the accrued fees.

**Follow My Example** ▶ **3-5**

| | | |
|---|---|---|
| Accounts Receivable.................................................................................................................. | 13,680 | |
| Fees Earned........................................................................................................................ | | 13,680 |
| Accrued fees. | | |

Practice Exercises: **PE 3-5A, PE 3-5B**

## Accrued Expenses

Some types of services used in earning revenues are paid for *after* the service has been performed. For example, wages expense is used hour by hour, but is paid only daily, weekly, biweekly, or monthly. At the end of the accounting period, the amount of such *accrued* but unpaid items is an expense and a liability.

For example, if the last day of the employees' pay period is not the last day of the accounting period, an accrued expense (wages expense) and the related liability (wages payable) must be recorded by an adjusting entry. This adjusting entry is necessary so that expenses are properly matched to the period in which they were incurred in earning revenue.

To illustrate, NetSolutions pays its employees biweekly. During December, NetSolutions paid wages of $950 on December 13 and $1,200 on December 27. These payments covered pay periods ending on those days as shown in Exhibit 7.

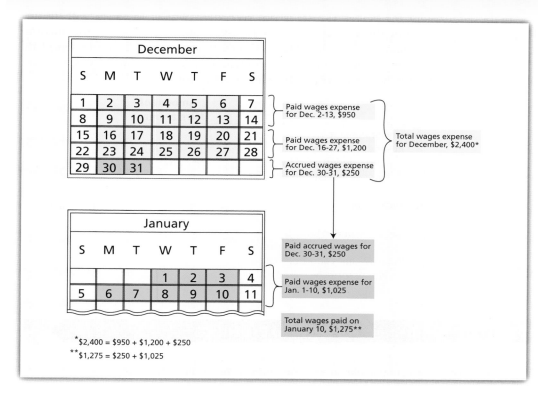

**EXHIBIT 7**

**Accrued Wages**

As of December 31, NetSolutions owes $250 of wages to employees for Monday and Tuesday, December 30 and 31. Thus, the wages expense account is increased (debited) by $250 and the wages payable account is increased (credited) by $250. The adjusting journal entry and T accounts are shown below.

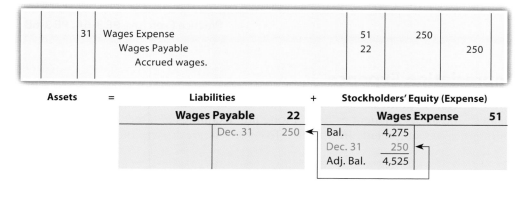

**Adjusting Journal Entry**

**Accounting Equation Impact**

Callaway Golf Company, a manufacturer of such innovative golf clubs as the "Big Bertha" driver, reports accrued warranty expense on its balance sheet.

After the adjusting entry is recorded and posted, the debit balance of the wages expense account is $4,525. This balance of $4,525 is the wages expense for two months, November and December. The credit balance of $250 in Wages Payable is the liability for wages owed on December 31.

As shown in Exhibit 7, NetSolutions paid wages of $1,275 on January 10. This payment includes the $250 of accrued wages recorded on December 31. Thus, on January 10, the wages payable account is decreased (debited) by $250. Also, the wages expense account is increased (debited) by $1,025 ($1,275 – $250), which is the wages expense for January 1–10. Finally, the cash account is decreased (credited) by $1,275. The journal entry for the payment of wages on January 10 is shown below.[4]

| | | | | | |
|---|---|---|---|---|---|
| Jan | 10 | Wages Expense | 51 | 1,025 | |
| | | Wages Payable | 22 | 250 | |
| | | Cash | 11 | | 1,275 |

If the adjustment for wages ($250) is not recorded, Wages Expense will be understated by $250, and the net income will be overstated by $250 on the income statement. On the balance sheet, liabilities (Wages Payable) will be understated by $250, and stockholders' equity (Retained Earnings) will be overstated by $250. The effects of omitting this adjusting entry are shown as follows:

| | Amount of Misstatement |
|---|---|
| Income Statement | |
| Revenues correctly stated | $ XXX |
| Expenses understated by | (250) |
| Net income overstated by | $ 250 |
| | |
| Balance Sheet | |
| Assets correctly stated | $ XXX |
| Liabilities understated by | $ (250) |
| Stockholders' equity overstated by | 250 |
| Total liabilities and stockholders' equity correctly stated | $ XXX |

## Example Exercise 3-6 ► Adjustment for Accrued Expense

**OBJ. 2**

Sanregret Realty Co. pays weekly salaries of $12,500 on Friday for a five-day week ending on that day. Journalize the necessary adjusting entry at the end of the accounting period, assuming that the period ends on Thursday.

### Follow My Example 3-6

| | | |
|---|---|---|
| Salaries Expense ........................................................................................................... | 10,000 | |
| Salaries Payable ......................................................................................................... | | 10,000 |
| Accrued salaries [($12,500/5 days) × 4 days]. | | |

Practice Exercises: **PE 3-6A, PE 3-6B**

## Depreciation Expense

**Fixed assets**, or **plant assets**, are physical resources that are owned and used by a business and are permanent or have a long life. Examples of fixed assets include land, buildings, and equipment. In a sense, fixed assets are a type of *long-term* prepaid

4 To simplify the subsequent recording of the following period's transactions, some accountants use what is known as reversing entries for certain types of adjustments. Reversing entries are discussed and illustrated in Appendix B at the end of the textbook.

## BusinessConnection

### FORD MOTOR COMPANY WARRANTIES

Ford Motor Company provides warranties on the vehicles that it sells. For example, Ford offers "bumper-to-bumper" coverage in the United States for five years or 60,000 miles on its Ford brand. A bumper-to-bumper warranty normally implies that every part of a new car will be repaired or replaced if it is defective during the term of the warranty.

When Ford sells a new car, it estimates the future warranty costs that it will incur on the vehicle and accrues a warranty expense. Accruals for estimated warranty costs are based on historical warranty claim experience, which is adjusted for changes such as offering new types of vehicles. For example, Ford adjusted its warranty costs when it began selling its new fuel efficient Ford Escape Hybrid. The Ford Escape Hybrid has a gas-electric engine that automatically shuts off when the vehicle is stopped. The Escape also uses an electric motor to assist in accelerating or when the vehicle is coasting or slowing down.

Ford's warranty cost accruals (in millions) for the years ended December 31, 2009 and 2008 are as follows:

|  | 2009 | 2008 |
|---|---|---|
| Beginning balance | $ 3,346 | $ 4,209 |
| Payments during the year | (2,481) | (2,747) |
| Warranties issued during year | 2,233 | 2,122 |
| Other | 121 | (238) |
| Ending balance of accrued warranties | $ 3,219 | $ 3,346 |

expense. However, because of their unique nature and long life, they are discussed separately from other prepaid expenses.

Fixed assets, such as office equipment, are used to generate revenue much like supplies are used to generate revenue. Unlike supplies, however, there is no visible reduction in the quantity of the equipment. Instead, as time passes, the equipment loses its ability to provide useful services. This decrease in usefulness is called **depreciation**.

All fixed assets, except land, lose their usefulness and, thus, are said to **depreciate**. As a fixed asset depreciates, a portion of its cost should be recorded as an expense. This periodic expense is called **depreciation expense**.

The adjusting entry to record depreciation expense is similar to the adjusting entry for supplies used. The depreciation expense account is increased (debited) for the amount of depreciation. However, the fixed asset account is not decreased (credited). This is because both the original cost of a fixed asset and the depreciation recorded since its purchase are reported on the balance sheet. Instead, an account entitled **Accumulated Depreciation** is increased (credited).

Accumulated depreciation accounts are called **contra accounts**, or **contra asset accounts**. This is because accumulated depreciation accounts are deducted from their related fixed asset accounts on the balance sheet. The normal balance of a contra account is opposite to the account from which it is deducted. Since the normal balance of a fixed asset account is a debit, the normal balance of an accumulated depreciation account is a credit.

The normal titles for fixed asset accounts and their related contra asset accounts are as follows:

Lowe's Companies, Inc., reported land, buildings, and store equipment at a cost of over $18 billion and accumulated depreciation of over $4.1 billion.

| **Fixed Asset Account** | **Contra Asset Account** |
|---|---|
| Land | None—Land is not depreciated. |
| Buildings | Accumulated Depreciation—Buildings |
| Store Equipment | Accumulated Depreciation—Store Equipment |
| Office Equipment | Accumulated Depreciation—Office Equipment |

The December 31, 2011, unadjusted trial balance of NetSolutions (Exhibit 5) indicates that NetSolutions owns two fixed assets: land and office equipment. Land does not depreciate; however, an adjusting entry is recorded for the depreciation of the office equipment for December. Assume that the office equipment depreciates $50 during December. The depreciation expense account is increased (debited) by $50, and the accumulated depreciation—office equipment account is increased (credited) by $50.[5] The adjusting journal entry and T accounts are shown below.

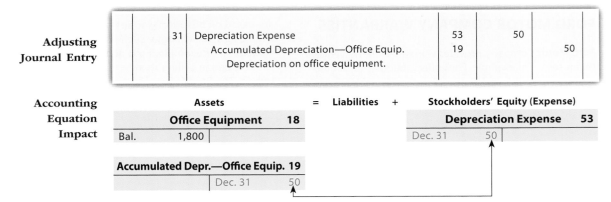

**Adjusting Journal Entry**

| | 31 | Depreciation Expense | 53 | 50 | |
| | | Accumulated Depreciation—Office Equip. | 19 | | 50 |
| | | Depreciation on office equipment. | | | |

**Accounting Equation Impact**

Assets = Liabilities + Stockholders' Equity (Expense)

| Office Equipment | 18 | | Depreciation Expense | 53 |
| Bal. | 1,800 | | Dec. 31 | 50 |

| Accumulated Depr.—Office Equip. | 19 |
| | Dec. 31 | 50 |

After the adjusting journal entry is recorded and posted, the office equipment account still has a debit balance of $1,800. This is the original cost of the office equipment that was purchased on December 4. The accumulated depreciation—office equipment account has a credit balance of $50. The difference between these two balances is the cost of the office equipment that has not yet been depreciated. This amount, called the **book value of the asset** (or **net book value**), is computed as shown below.

Book Value of Asset = Cost of the Asset – Accumulated Depreciation of Asset
Book Value of Office Equipment = Cost of Office Equipment – Accumulated Depr. of Office Equipment
Book Value of Office Equipment = $1,800 – $50
Book Value of Office Equipment = $1,750

The office equipment and its related accumulated depreciation are reported on the December 31, 2011, balance sheet as follows:

| Office equipment | | $1,800 | |
| Less accumulated depreciation | | 50 | $1,750 |

The market value of a fixed asset usually differs from its book value. This is because depreciation is an *allocation* method, not a *valuation* method. That is, depreciation allocates the cost of a fixed asset to expense over its estimated life. Depreciation does not measure changes in market values, which vary from year to year. Thus, on December 31, 2011, the market value of NetSolutions' office equipment could be more or less than $1,750.

If the adjustment for depreciation ($50) is not recorded, Depreciation Expense on the income statement will be understated by $50, and the net income will be overstated by $50. On the balance sheet, assets (the book value of the Office Equipment) and stockholders' equity (Retained Earnings) will be overstated by $50. The effects of omitting the adjustment for depreciation are shown below.

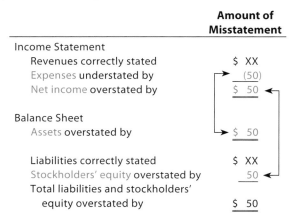

| | Amount of Misstatement |
|---|---|
| Income Statement | |
| Revenues correctly stated | $  XX |
| Expenses understated by | (50) |
| Net income overstated by | $  50 |
| | |
| Balance Sheet | |
| Assets overstated by | $  50 |
| | |
| Liabilities correctly stated | $  XX |
| Stockholders' equity overstated by | 50 |
| Total liabilities and stockholders' | |
| equity overstated by | $  50 |

5 Methods of computing depreciation expense are described and illustrated in Chapter 9.

**Example Exercise** 3-7 **Adjustment for Depreciation**

OBJ. 2

The estimated amount of depreciation on equipment for the current year is $4,250. Journalize the adjusting entry to record the depreciation.

**Follow My Example** 3-7

| | | |
|---|---|---|
| Depreciation Expense ............................................................................................................. | 4,250 | |
| Accumulated Depreciation—Equipment ................................................................ | | 4,250 |
| Depreciation on equipment. | | |

Practice Exercises: **PE 3-7A, PE 3-7B**

# Summary of Adjustment Process

OBJ. 3 Summarize the adjustment process.

A summary of the basic types of adjusting entries is shown in Exhibit 8 on page 120.

The adjusting entries for NetSolutions are shown in Exhibit 9 on page 121. The adjusting entries are dated as of the last day of the period. However, because collecting the adjustment data requires time, the entries are usually recorded at a later date. An explanation is normally included with each adjusting entry.

NetSolutions' adjusting entries are posted to the ledger shown in Exhibit 10 on pages 122–123. The adjustments are shown in color in Exhibit 10 to distinguish them from other transactions.

**Example Exercise** 3-8 **Effect of Omitting Adjustments**

OBJ. 3

For the year ending December 31, 2012, Mann Medical Co. mistakenly omitted adjusting entries for (1) $8,600 of unearned revenue that was earned, (2) earned revenue that was not billed of $12,500, and (3) accrued wages of $2,900. Indicate the combined effect of the errors on (a) revenues, (b) expenses, and (c) net income for the year ended December 31, 2012.

**Follow My Example** 3-8

a.  Revenues were understated by $21,100 ($8,600 + $12,500).
b.  Expenses were understated by $2,900.
c.  Net income was understated by $18,200 ($8,600 + $12,500 − $2,900).

Practice Exercises: **PE 3-8A, PE 3-8B**

**EXHIBIT 8**   **Summary of Adjustments**

| | | | | PREPAID EXPENSES | | | |
|---|---|---|---|---|---|---|---|
| **Examples** | **Reason for Adjustment** | **Adjusting Entry** | | **Examples from NetSolutions** | | **Financial Statement Impact if Adjusting Entry Is Omitted** | |
| Supplies, prepaid insurance | Prepaid expenses (assets) have been used or consumed in the business operations. | Expense    Dr.<br>  Asset        Cr. | | Supplies Expense    1,240<br>  Supplies                       1,240<br>Insurance Expense    200<br>  Prepaid Insurance            200 | | Income Statement:<br>  Revenues      No effect<br>  Expenses      Understated<br>  Net income    Overstated<br>Balance Sheet:<br>  Assets          Overstated<br>  Liabilities     No effect<br>  Stockholders'  Overstated<br>    equity (Retained<br>    Earnings) | |

| | | | | UNEARNED REVENUES | | | |
|---|---|---|---|---|---|---|---|
| Unearned rent, magazine subscriptions received in advance, fees received in advance of services | Cash received before the services have been provided is recorded as a liability. Some services have been provided to customer before the end of the accounting period. | Liability    Dr.<br>  Revenue       Cr. | | Unearned Rent    120<br>  Rent Revenue          120 | | Income Statement:<br>  Revenues      Understated<br>  Expenses      No effect<br>  Net income    Understated<br>Balance Sheet:<br>  Assets          No effect<br>  Liabilities     Overstated<br>  Stockholders'  Understated<br>    equity (Retained<br>    Earnings) | |

| | | | | ACCRUED REVENUES | | | |
|---|---|---|---|---|---|---|---|
| Services performed but not billed, interest to be received | Services have been provided to the customer, but have not been billed or recorded. Interest has been earned, but has not been received or recorded. | Asset    Dr.<br>  Revenue    Cr. | | Accounts Receivable    500<br>  Fees Earned                  500 | | Income Statement:<br>  Revenues      Understated<br>  Expenses      No effect<br>  Net income    Understated<br>Balance Sheet:<br>  Assets          Understated<br>  Liabilities     No effect<br>  Stockholders'  Understated<br>    equity (Retained<br>    Earnings) | |

| | | | | ACCRUED EXPENSES | | | |
|---|---|---|---|---|---|---|---|
| Wages or salaries incurred but not paid, interest incurred but not paid | Expenses have been incurred, but have not been paid or recorded. | Expense    Dr.<br>  Liability     Cr. | | Wages Expense    250<br>  Wages Payable        250 | | Income Statement:<br>  Revenues      No effect<br>  Expenses      Understated<br>  Net income    Overstated<br>Balance Sheet:<br>  Assets          No effect<br>  Liabilities     Understated<br>  Stockholders'  Overstated<br>    equity (Retained<br>    Earnings) | |

| | | | | DEPRECIATION | | | |
|---|---|---|---|---|---|---|---|
| Depreciation of equipment and buildings | Fixed assets depreciate as they are used or consumed in the business operations. | Expense          Dr.<br>  Contra Asset    Cr. | | Depreciation Expense    50<br>  Accum. Depreciation—<br>    Office Equipment       50 | | Income Statement:<br>  Revenues      No effect<br>  Expenses      Understated<br>  Net income    Overstated<br>Balance Sheet:<br>  Assets          Overstated<br>  Liabilities     No effect<br>  Stockholders'  Overstated<br>    equity (Retained<br>    Earnings) | |

**EXHIBIT 9**

**Adjusting
Entries—
NetSolutions**

| Journal | | | | | Page 5 |
|---|---|---|---|---|---|
| **Date** | | **Description** | **Post. Ref.** | **Debit** | **Credit** |
| 2011 | | Adjusting Entries | | | |
| Dec | 31 | Supplies Expense | 55 | 1,240 | |
| | | Supplies | 14 | | 1,240 |
| | | Supplies used ($2,000 – $760). | | | |
| | 31 | Insurance Expense | 56 | 200 | |
| | | Prepaid Insurance | 15 | | 200 |
| | | Insurance expired ($2,400/12 months). | | | |
| | 31 | Unearned Rent | 23 | 120 | |
| | | Rent Revenue | 42 | | 120 |
| | | Rent earned ($360/3 months). | | | |
| | 31 | Accounts Receivable | 12 | 500 | |
| | | Fees Earned | 41 | | 500 |
| | | Accrued fees (25 hrs. × $20). | | | |
| | 31 | Wages Expense | 51 | 250 | |
| | | Wages Payable | 22 | | 250 |
| | | Accrued wages. | | | |
| | 31 | Depreciation Expense | 53 | 50 | |
| | | Accum. Depreciation—Office Equipment | 19 | | 50 |
| | | Depreciation on office equipment. | | | |

An accountant may check whether all adjustments have been made by comparing current period adjustments with those of the prior period.

# BusinessConnection

## MICROSOFT CORPORATION

Microsoft Corporation develops, manufactures, licenses, and supports a wide range of computer software products, including Windows Vista, Windows 7, Windows XP, Word, Excel, and the Xbox® gaming system. When Microsoft sells its products, it incurs an obligation to support its software with technical support and periodic updates. As a result, not all the revenue is earned on the date of sale; some of the revenue on the date of sale is unearned. The portion of revenue related to support services, such as updates and technical support, is earned as time passes and support is provided to customers. Thus, each year Microsoft makes adjusting entries transferring some of its unearned revenue to revenue. The following excerpts were taken from Microsoft's financial statements:

The percentage of revenue recorded as unearned . . . ranges from approximately 15% to 25% of the sales price for Windows XP Home, approximately 5% to 15% of the sales price for Windows XP Professional, . . .

Unearned Revenue:

| | June 30, 2009 | June 30, 2008 |
|---|---|---|
| Unearned revenue (in millions) | $14,284 | $15,297 |

During the year ending June 30, 2010, Microsoft expects to record over $13,003 million of unearned revenue as revenue. At the same time, Microsoft will record additional unearned revenue from current period sales.

Source: Taken from Microsoft's June 30, 2009, annual report.

**EXHIBIT 10**    **Ledger with Adjusting Entries—NetSolutions**

**Account** *Cash*                               Account No. *11*

| Date | Item | Post. Ref. | Debit | Credit | Balance Debit | Balance Credit |
|------|------|-----------|-------|--------|-------|--------|
| 2011 | | | | | | |
| Nov. 1 | | 1 | 25,000 | | 25,000 | |
| 5 | | 1 | | 20,000 | 5,000 | |
| 18 | | 1 | 7,500 | | 12,500 | |
| 30 | | 1 | | 3,650 | 8,850 | |
| 30 | | 1 | | 950 | 7,900 | |
| 30 | | 2 | | 2,000 | 5,900 | |
| Dec. 1 | | 2 | | 2,400 | 3,500 | |
| 1 | | 2 | | 800 | 2,700 | |
| 1 | | 2 | 360 | | 3,060 | |
| 6 | | 2 | | 180 | 2,880 | |
| 11 | | 2 | | 400 | 2,480 | |
| 13 | | 3 | | 950 | 1,530 | |
| 16 | | 3 | 3,100 | | 4,630 | |
| 20 | | 3 | | 900 | 3,730 | |
| 21 | | 3 | 650 | | 4,380 | |
| 23 | | 3 | | 1,450 | 2,930 | |
| 27 | | 3 | | 1,200 | 1,730 | |
| 31 | | 3 | | 310 | 1,420 | |
| 31 | | 4 | | 225 | 1,195 | |
| 31 | | 4 | 2,870 | | 4,065 | |
| 31 | | 4 | | 2,000 | 2,065 | |

**Account** *Accounts Receivable*                 Account No. *12*

| Date | Item | Post. Ref. | Debit | Credit | Balance Debit | Balance Credit |
|------|------|-----------|-------|--------|-------|--------|
| 2011 | | | | | | |
| Dec. 16 | | 3 | 1,750 | | 1,750 | |
| 21 | | 3 | | 650 | 1,100 | |
| 31 | | 4 | 1,120 | | 2,220 | |
| 31 | Adjusting | 5 | 500 | | 2,720 | |

**Account** *Supplies*                            Account No. *14*

| Date | Item | Post. Ref. | Debit | Credit | Balance Debit | Balance Credit |
|------|------|-----------|-------|--------|-------|--------|
| 2011 | | | | | | |
| Nov. 10 | | 1 | 1,350 | | 1,350 | |
| 30 | | 1 | | 800 | 550 | |
| Dec. 23 | | 3 | 1,450 | | 2,000 | |
| 31 | Adjusting | 5 | | 1,240 | 760 | |

**Account** *Prepaid Insurance*                   Account No. *15*

| Date | Item | Post. Ref. | Debit | Credit | Balance Debit | Balance Credit |
|------|------|-----------|-------|--------|-------|--------|
| 2011 | | | | | | |
| Dec. 1 | | 2 | 2,400 | | 2,400 | |
| 31 | Adjusting | 5 | | 200 | 2,200 | |

**Account** *Land*                                Account No. *17*

| Date | Item | Post. Ref. | Debit | Credit | Balance Debit | Balance Credit |
|------|------|-----------|-------|--------|-------|--------|
| 2011 | | | | | | |
| Nov. 5 | | 1 | 20,000 | | 20,000 | |

**Account** *Office Equipment*                    Account No. *18*

| Date | Item | Post. Ref. | Debit | Credit | Balance Debit | Balance Credit |
|------|------|-----------|-------|--------|-------|--------|
| 2011 | | | | | | |
| Dec. 4 | | 2 | 1,800 | | 1,800 | |

**Account** *Accum. Depr.—Office Equip.*          Account No. *19*

| Date | Item | Post. Ref. | Debit | Credit | Balance Debit | Balance Credit |
|------|------|-----------|-------|--------|-------|--------|
| 2011 | | | | | | |
| Dec. 1 | Adjusting | 5 | | 50 | | 50 |

**Account** *Accounts Payable*                    Account No. *21*

| Date | Item | Post. Ref. | Debit | Credit | Balance Debit | Balance Credit |
|------|------|-----------|-------|--------|-------|--------|
| 2011 | | | | | | |
| Nov. 10 | | 1 | | 1,350 | | 1,350 |
| 30 | | 1 | 950 | | | 400 |
| Dec. 4 | | 2 | | 1,800 | | 2,200 |
| 11 | | 2 | 400 | | | 1,800 |
| 20 | | 3 | 900 | | | 900 |

**Account** *Wages Payable*                       Account No. *22*

| Date | Item | Post. Ref. | Debit | Credit | Balance Debit | Balance Credit |
|------|------|-----------|-------|--------|-------|--------|
| 2011 | | | | | | |
| Dec. 31 | Adjusting | 5 | | 250 | | 250 |

**Account** *Unearned Rent*                       Account No. *23*

| Date | Item | Post. Ref. | Debit | Credit | Balance Debit | Balance Credit |
|------|------|-----------|-------|--------|-------|--------|
| 2011 | | | | | | |
| Dec. 1 | | 2 | | 360 | | 360 |
| 31 | Adjusting | 5 | 120 | | | 240 |

**Account** *Capital Stock*                       Account No. *31*

| Date | Item | Post. Ref. | Debit | Credit | Balance Debit | Balance Credit |
|------|------|-----------|-------|--------|-------|--------|
| 2011 | | | | | | |
| Nov. 1 | | 1 | | 25,000 | | 25,000 |

**EXHIBIT 10**   **Ledger with Adjusting Entries—NetSolutions (*Concluded*)**

**Account** Dividends — Account No. 33

| Date | Item | Post. Ref. | Debit | Credit | Balance Debit | Balance Credit |
|---|---|---|---|---|---|---|
| 2011 | | | | | | |
| Nov. 30 | | 2 | 2,000 | | 2,000 | |
| Dec. 31 | | 4 | 2,000 | | 4,000 | |

**Account** Depreciation Expense — Account No. 53

| Date | Item | Post. Ref. | Debit | Credit | Balance Debit | Balance Credit |
|---|---|---|---|---|---|---|
| 2011 | | | | | | |
| Dec. 31 | Adjusting | 5 | 50 | | 50 | |

**Account** Fees Earned — Account No. 41

| Date | Item | Post. Ref. | Debit | Credit | Balance Debit | Balance Credit |
|---|---|---|---|---|---|---|
| 2011 | | | | | | |
| Nov. 18 | | 1 | | 7,500 | | 7,500 |
| Dec. 16 | | 3 | | 3,100 | | 10,600 |
| 16 | | 3 | | 1,750 | | 12,350 |
| 31 | | 4 | | 2,870 | | 15,220 |
| 31 | | 4 | | 1,120 | | 16,340 |
| 31 | Adjusting | 5 | | 500 | | 16,840 |

**Account** Utilities Expense — Account No. 54

| Date | Item | Post. Ref. | Debit | Credit | Balance Debit | Balance Credit |
|---|---|---|---|---|---|---|
| 2011 | | | | | | |
| Nov. 30 | | 1 | 450 | | 450 | |
| Dec. 31 | | 3 | 310 | | 760 | |
| 31 | | 4 | 225 | | 985 | |

**Account** Rent Revenue — Account No. 42

| Date | Item | Post. Ref. | Debit | Credit | Balance Debit | Balance Credit |
|---|---|---|---|---|---|---|
| 2011 | | | | | | |
| Dec. 31 | Adjusting | 5 | | 120 | | 120 |

**Account** Supplies Expense — Account No. 55

| Date | Item | Post. Ref. | Debit | Credit | Balance Debit | Balance Credit |
|---|---|---|---|---|---|---|
| 2011 | | | | | | |
| Nov. 30 | | 1 | 800 | | 800 | |
| Dec. 31 | Adjusting | 5 | 1,240 | | 2,040 | |

**Account** Wages Expense — Account No. 51

| Date | Item | Post. Ref. | Debit | Credit | Balance Debit | Balance Credit |
|---|---|---|---|---|---|---|
| 2011 | | | | | | |
| Nov. 30 | | 1 | 2,125 | | 2,125 | |
| Dec. 13 | | 3 | 950 | | 3,075 | |
| 27 | | 3 | 1,200 | | 4,275 | |
| 31 | Adjusting | 5 | 250 | | 4,525 | |

**Account** Insurance Expense — Account No. 56

| Date | Item | Post. Ref. | Debit | Credit | Balance Debit | Balance Credit |
|---|---|---|---|---|---|---|
| 2011 | | | | | | |
| Dec. 31 | Adjusting | 5 | 200 | | 200 | |

**Account** Rent Expense — Account No. 52

| Date | Item | Post. Ref. | Debit | Credit | Balance Debit | Balance Credit |
|---|---|---|---|---|---|---|
| 2011 | | | | | | |
| Nov. 30 | | 1 | 800 | | 800 | |
| Dec. 1 | | 2 | 800 | | 1,600 | |

**Account** Miscellaneous Expense — Account No. 59

| Date | Item | Post. Ref. | Debit | Credit | Balance Debit | Balance Credit |
|---|---|---|---|---|---|---|
| 2011 | | | | | | |
| Nov. 30 | | 1 | 275 | | 275 | |
| Dec. 6 | | 2 | 180 | | 455 | |

# Adjusted Trial Balance

OBJ. 4  Prepare an adjusted trial balance.

After the adjusting entries are posted, an **adjusted trial balance** is prepared. The adjusted trial balance verifies the equality of the total debit and credit balances before the financial statements are prepared. If the adjusted trial balance does not balance, an error has occurred. However, as discussed in Chapter 2, errors may occur even though the adjusted trial balance totals agree. For example, if an adjusting entry were omitted, the adjusted trial balance totals would still agree.

Exhibit 11 shows the adjusted trial balance for NetSolutions as of December 31, 2011. Chapter 4 discusses how financial statements, including a classified balance sheet, are prepared from an adjusted trial balance.

**EXHIBIT 11**

**Adjusted Trial Balance**

| NetSolutions Adjusted Trial Balance December 31, 2011 | Debit Balances | Credit Balances |
|---|---|---|
| Cash | 2,065 | |
| Accounts Receivable | 2,720 | |
| Supplies | 760 | |
| Prepaid Insurance | 2,200 | |
| Land | 20,000 | |
| Office Equipment | 1,800 | |
| Accumulated Depreciation—Office Equipment | | 50 |
| Accounts Payable | | 900 |
| Wages Payable | | 250 |
| Unearned Rent | | 240 |
| Capital Stock | | 25,000 |
| Dividends | 4,000 | |
| Fees Earned | | 16,840 |
| Rent Revenue | | 120 |
| Wages Expense | 4,525 | |
| Rent Expense | 1,600 | |
| Depreciation Expense | 50 | |
| Utilities Expense | 985 | |
| Supplies Expense | 2,040 | |
| Insurance Expense | 200 | |
| Miscellaneous Expense | 455 | |
| | 43,400 | 43,400 |

A spreadsheet can be used to prepare adjusting entries, post adjustments to ledger accounts, and prepare an adjusted trial balance. This is illustrated for a single adjusting entry, NetSolutions' December 31 adjustment for supplies used.

**a.**    Posting adjusting entry to ledger.

|  | A | B | C | D | E |
|---|---|---|---|---|---|
| 113 |  |  |  |  |  |
| 114 |  | **Journal** |  |  | Page 5 |
| 115 | **Date** | **Description** | **Post. Ref.** | **Debit** | **Credit** |
| 116 | 2011 |  |  |  |  |
| 117 | 31-Dec | Supplies Expense | 55 | 1,240 |  |
| 118 |  | Supplies | 14 |  | 1,240 |
| 119 |  | Supplies used ($2,000 – $760) |  |  |  |
| 120 |  |  |  |  |  |

⏮ ◀ ▶ ⏭ \ **JE** ⟨ GL ⟨UTB ⟩

a.  b.  c.

|  | A | B | C | D | E | F | G |
|---|---|---|---|---|---|---|---|
| 174 | **Account** | *Supplies Expense* |  |  |  | **Account No.** | 55 |
| 175 |  |  |  |  |  | **Balance** |  |
| 176 | **Date** | **Item** | **Post. Ref.** | **Debit** | **Credit** | **Debit** | **Credit** |
| 177 | 2011 |  |  |  |  |  |  |
| 178 | 30-Nov |  | 1 | 800 |  | 800 |  |
| 179 | 31-Dec | Adjusting | 5 | =JE!D117 |  | =F178+D179-E179 | ⬅ **d.** |

⏮ ◀ ▶ ⏭ \ JE ⟨ **GL** ⟨UTB ⟩

|  | A | B | C | D | E | F | G |
|---|---|---|---|---|---|---|---|
| 38 |  |  |  |  |  |  |  |
| 39 | **Account** | *Supplies* |  |  |  | **Account No.** | 14 |
| 40 |  |  |  |  |  | **Balance** |  |
| 41 | **Date** | **Item** | **Post. Ref.** | **Debit** | **Credit** | **Debit** | **Credit** |
| 42 | 2011 |  |  |  |  |  |  |
| 43 | 10-Nov |  | 1 | 1,350 |  | 1,350 |  |
| 44 | 30-Nov |  | 1 |  | 800 | 550 |  |
| 45 | 23-Dec |  | 3 | 1,450 |  | 2,000 |  |
| 46 | 31-Dec | Adjusting | 5 |  | =JE!E118 | =F45+D46-E46 | ⬅ **e.** |

⏮ ◀ ▶ ⏭ \ JE ⟨ **GL** ⟨UTB ⟩

**b.**    Enter into cell D179 (GL worksheet) the cell reference for the debit to *Supplies Expense* (Journal worksheet), =JE!D117

**c.**    Enter into cell E46 (GL worksheet) the cell reference for the debit to *Supplies* (Journal worksheet), =JE!E118

**d.**    Copy (GL worksheet) the formula for the cumulative balance from cell F178 to F179. (The formula is =F178+D179-E179)

**e.**    Copy (GL worksheet) the formula for the cumulative balance from cell F45 to F46. (The formula is =F45+D46-E46)

Prepare the adjusted trial balance by referencing the cell addresses from the GL:

| | A | B | C |
|---|---|---|---|
| 1 | | NetSolutions | |
| 2 | | Adjusted Trial Balance | |
| 3 | | December 31, 2011 | |
| 4 | | Debit | Credit |
| 5 | | Balances | Balances |
| 6 | Cash | 2.065 | |
| 7 | Accounts Receivable | 2,720 | |
| 8 | Supplies | =GL!F46 ← **g.** | |
| 9 | Prepaid Insurance | 2,200 | |
| 10 | Land | 20,000 | |
| 11 | Office Equipment | 1,800 | |
| 12 | Accumulated Depreciation | | 50 |
| 13 | Accounts Payable | | 900 |
| 14 | Wages Payable | | 250 |
| 15 | Unearned Rent | | 240 |
| 16 | Capital Stock | | 25,000 |
| 17 | Dividends | 4,000 | |
| 18 | Fees Earned | | 16,840 |
| 19 | Rent Revenue | | 120 |
| 20 | Wages Expense | 4,525 | |
| 21 | Rent Expense | 1,600 | |
| 22 | Depreciation Expense | 50 | |
| 23 | Utilities Expense | 985 | |
| 24 | Supplies Expense | =GL!F179 ← **g.** | |
| 25 | Insurance Expense | 200 | |
| 26 | Miscellaneous Expense | 455 | |
| 27 | | =SUM(B6:B26) | =SUM(B6:B26) } **h.** |
| 28 | | | |
| 29 | | | |

**f.** ───────→

⊲ ◄ ► ►⊳ \ JE \ GL / UTB \ ATB /        ◄

f.    Insert a new worksheet and label "ATB" for adjusted trial balance.
g.    Enter into the appropriate cell the account balance cell references from the GL worksheet. (As illustrated for *Supplies*, =GL!F46; *Supplies Expense*, =GL!F179)
h.    Enter the formula =SUM to total both the debit and credit balances for the adjusted trial balance.

**Try***It*    Go to the hands-on **Excel Tutor** for this example!

---

**Example Exercise** ▶ **3-9** ▶ **Effect of Errors on Adjusted Trial Balance**    **OBJ. 4**

For each of the following errors, considered individually, indicate whether the error would cause the adjusted trial balance totals to be unequal. If the error would cause the adjusted trial balance totals to be unequal, indicate whether the debit or credit total is higher and by how much.

a.   The adjustment for accrued fees of $5,340 was journalized as a debit to Accounts Payable for $5,340 and a credit to Fees Earned of $5,340.

b.   The adjustment for depreciation of $3,260 was journalized as a debit to Depreciation Expense for $3,620 and a credit to Accumulated Depreciation for $3,260.

**Follow My Example** ▶ **3-9** ▶

a.   The totals are equal even though the debit should have been to Accounts Receivable instead of Accounts Payable.

b.   The totals are unequal. The debit total is higher by $360 ($3,620 − $3,260).

Practice Exercises: **PE 3-9A, PE 3-9B**

# Financial Analysis and Interpretation: Vertical Analysis

**F·A·I**

Comparing each item in a financial statement with a total amount from the same statement is useful in analyzing relationships within the financial statement. **Vertical analysis** is the term used to describe such comparisons.

In vertical analysis of a balance sheet, each asset item is stated as a percent of the total assets. Each liability and stockholders' equity item is stated as a percent of total liabilities and stockholders' equity. In vertical analysis of an income statement, each item is stated as a percent of revenues or fees earned.

Vertical analysis is also useful for analyzing changes in financial statements over time. To illustrate, a vertical analysis of two years of income statements for J. Holmes, Attorney-at-Law, P.C., a professional corporation, is shown below.

**OBJ. 5** Describe and illustrate the use of vertical analysis in evaluating a company's performance and financial condition.

**J. Holmes, Attorney-at-Law, P.C.**
**Income Statements**
**For the Years Ended December 31, 2012 and 2011**

| | 2012 | | 2011 | |
| --- | --- | --- | --- | --- |
| | Amount | Percent | Amount | Percent |
| Fees earned | $187,500 | 100.0% | $150,000 | 100.0% |
| Operating expenses: | | | | |
| Wages expense | $ 60,000 | 32.0%* | $ 45,000 | 30.0%** |
| Rent expense | 15,000 | 8.0 | 12,000 | 8.0 |
| Utilities expense | 12,500 | 6.7 | 9,000 | 6.0 |
| Supplies expense | 2,700 | 1.4 | 3,000 | 2.0 |
| Miscellaneous expense | 2,300 | 1.2 | 1,800 | 1.2 |
| Total operating expenses | $ 92,500 | 49.3% | $ 70,800 | 47.2% |
| Net income | $ 95,000 | 50.7% | $ 79,200 | 52.8% |

*Rounded to one decimal place.
**$45,000 ÷ $150,000

The preceding vertical analysis indicates both favorable and unfavorable trends affecting the income statement of J. Holmes, Attorney-at-Law, P.C. The increase in wages expense of 2% (32.0% – 30.0%) is an unfavorable trend, as is the increase in utilities expense of 0.7% (6.7% – 6.0%). A favorable trend is the decrease in supplies expense of 0.6% (2.0% – 1.4%). Rent expense and miscellaneous expense as a percent of fees earned were constant. The net result of these trends is that net income decreased as a percent of fees earned from 52.8% to 50.7%.

The analysis of the various percentages shown for J. Holmes, Attorney-at-Law, P.C., can be enhanced by comparisons with industry averages. Such averages are published by trade associations and financial information services. Any major differences between industry averages should be investigated.

Vertical analysis of operating income taken from two years of income statements for RealNetworks is shown below.

**RealNetworks**
**Income Statements**
**For the Years Ended December 31, 2009 and 2008**

| | 2009 | | 2008 | |
| --- | --- | --- | --- | --- |
| | Amount | Percent | Amount | Percent |
| Revenues | $562,264* | 100.0% | $604,810 | 100.0% |
| Expenses: | | | | |
| Cost of revenues | $ 222,142 | 39.5% | $233,244 | 38.6% |
| Selling expenses | 199,148 | 35.4 | 256,135 | 42.3 |
| Administrative expenses | 79,164 | 14.1 | 69,981 | 11.6 |
| Other expenses (net) | 299,048 | 53.2 | 332,855 | 55.0 |
| Total operating expenses | $799,502 | 142.2% | $892,215 | 147.5% |
| Operating income (loss) | $(237,238) | (42.2)% | $(287,405) | (47.5)% |

*In millions

The preceding analysis indicates that RealNetworks experienced an operating loss of 42.2% of revenues in 2009. The analysis indicates that the cost of revenues was comparable across both years. Selling expenses decreased from 42.3% to 35.4%, while administrative expenses increased from 11.6% to 14.1%. The major cause of the losses in 2009 and 2008 was due to the other expenses, which were 53.2% and 55.0% of revenues for 2009 and 2008, respectively. The cause of these other expenses should be investigated. An examination of RealNetworks' annual report indicates that a large portion of these expenses was caused by the loss in value of some of its long-term assets due to the depressed economic conditions of the last several years.

**Example Exercise** **3-10** **Vertical Analysis** **OBJ. 5**

Two income statements for Fortson Company are shown below.

**Fortson Company**
**Income Statements**
**For the Years Ended December 31, 2012 and 2011**

|  | 2012 | 2011 |
|---|---|---|
| Fees earned | $425,000 | $375,000 |
| Operating expenses | 263,500 | 210,000 |
| Operating income | $161,500 | $165,000 |

a. Prepare a vertical analysis of Fortson Company's income statements.

b. Does the vertical analysis indicate a favorable or unfavorable trend?

**Follow My Example** **3-10**

a.

**Fortson Company**
**Income Statements**
**For the Years Ended December 31, 2012 and 2011**

|  | 2012 | | 2011 | |
|---|---|---|---|---|
|  | **Amount** | **Percent** | **Amount** | **Percent** |
| Fees earned | $425,000 | 100% | $375,000 | 100% |
| Operating expenses | 263,500 | 62 | 210,000 | 56 |
| Operating income | $161,500 | 38% | $165,000 | 44% |

b. An unfavorable trend of increasing operating expenses and decreasing operating income is indicated.

Practice Exercises: **PE 3-10A, PE 3-10B**

**At a Glance 3**

**OBJ. 1**

**Describe the nature of the adjusting process.**

**Key Points** The accrual basis of accounting requires that revenues are reported in the period in which they are earned and expenses are matched with the revenues they generate. The updating of accounts at the end of the accounting period is called the adjusting process. Each adjusting entry affects an income statement and balance sheet account. The four types of accounts requiring adjusting entries are prepaid expenses, unearned revenues, accrued revenues, and accrued expenses.

| Learning Outcomes | Example Exercises | Practice Exercises |
|---|---|---|
| • Explain why accrual accounting requires adjusting entries. | | |
| • List accounts that do and do NOT require adjusting entries at the end of the accounting period. | EE3-1 | PE3-1A, 3-1B |
| • Give an example of a prepaid expense, unearned revenue, accrued revenue, and accrued expense. | EE3-2 | PE3-2A, 3-2B |

**OBJ. 2**

### Journalize entries for accounts requiring adjustment.

**Key Points**   At the end of the period, adjusting entries are needed for prepaid expenses, unearned revenues, accrued revenues, and accrued expenses. In addition, an adjusting entry is necessary to record depreciation on fixed assets.

| Learning Outcomes | Example Exercises | Practice Exercises |
|---|---|---|
| • Prepare an adjusting entry for a prepaid expense. | EE3-3 | PE3-3A, 3-3B |
| • Prepare an adjusting entry for an unearned revenue. | EE3-4 | PE3-4A, 3-4B |
| • Prepare an adjusting entry for an accrued revenue. | EE3-5 | PE3-5A, 3-5B |
| • Prepare an adjusting entry for an accrued expense. | EE3-6 | PE3-6A, 3-6B |
| • Prepare an adjusting entry for depreciation expense. | EE3-7 | PE3-7A, 3-7B |

**OBJ. 3**

### Summarize the adjustment process.

**Key Points**   A summary of adjustments, including the type of adjustment, reason for the adjustment, the adjusting entry, and the effect of omitting an adjustment on the financial statements, is shown in Exhibit 8.

| Learning Outcomes | Example Exercises | Practice Exercises |
|---|---|---|
| • Determine the effect on the income statement and balance sheet of omitting an adjusting entry for prepaid expense, unearned revenue, accrued revenue, accrued expense, and depreciation. | EE3-8 | PE3-8A, 3-8B |

**OBJ. 4**

### Prepare an adjusted trial balance.

**Key Points**   After all the adjusting entries have been posted, the equality of the total debit balances and total credit balances is verified by an adjusted trial balance.

| Learning Outcomes | Example Exercises | Practice Exercises |
|---|---|---|
| • Prepare an adjusted trial balance. | | |
| • Determine the effect of errors on the equality of the adjusted trial balance. | EE3-9 | PE3-9A, 3-9B |

**OBJ. 5**

### Describe and illustrate the use of vertical analysis in evaluating a company's performance and financial condition.

**Key Points**   Comparing each item on a financial statement with a total amount from the same statement is called vertical analysis. On the balance sheet, each asset is expressed as a percent of total assets and each liability and stockholders' equity is expressed as a percent of total liabilities and stockholders' equity. On the income statement, each revenue and expense is expressed as a percent of total revenues or fees earned.

| Learning Outcomes | Example Exercises | Practice Exercises |
|---|---|---|
| • Describe vertical analysis. | | |
| • Prepare a vertical analysis report of a financial statement. | EE3-10 | PE3-10A, 3-10B |

## Key Terms

accounting period concept (104)

accrual basis of accounting (104)

accrued expenses (108)

accrued revenues (107)

Accumulated Depreciation (117)

adjusted trial balance (123)

adjusting entries (105)

adjusting process (105)

book value of the asset (or net book value) (118)

cash basis of accounting (104)

contra accounts (or contra asset accounts) (117)

depreciate (117)

depreciation (117)

depreciation expense (117)

fixed assets (or plant assets) (116)

matching concept (or matching principle) (104)

prepaid expenses (105)

revenue recognition concept (104)

unearned revenues (106)

vertical analysis (127)

## Illustrative Problem

Three years ago, T. Roderick organized Harbor Realty, Inc. At July 31, 2012, the end of the current year, the unadjusted trial balance of Harbor Realty appears as shown below.

**Harbor Realty, Inc.**
**Unadjusted Trial Balance**
**July 31, 2012**

|  | Debit Balances | Credit Balances |
|---|---|---|
| Cash ......................................................... | 3,425 | |
| Accounts Receivable.................................... | 7,000 | |
| Supplies ..................................................... | 1,270 | |
| Prepaid Insurance ...................................... | 620 | |
| Office Equipment ....................................... | 51,650 | |
| Accumulated Depreciation—Office Equipment........................... | | 9,700 |
| Accounts Payable ....................................... | | 925 |
| Wages Payable ........................................... | | 0 |
| Unearned Fees............................................ | | 1,250 |
| Capital Stock............................................... | | 5,000 |
| Retained Earnings...................................... | | 24,000 |
| Dividends.................................................... | 5,200 | |
| Fees Earned................................................ | | 59,125 |
| Wages Expense .......................................... | 22,415 | |
| Depreciation Expense ................................ | 0 | |
| Rent Expense ............................................. | 4,200 | |
| Utilities Expense ........................................ | 2,715 | |
| Supplies Expense........................................ | 0 | |
| Insurance Expense ..................................... | 0 | |
| Miscellaneous Expense .............................. | 1,505 | |
| | 100,000 | 100,000 |

The data needed to determine year-end adjustments are as follows:

a. Supplies on hand at July 31, 2012, $380.

b. Insurance premiums expired during the year, $315.

c. Depreciation of equipment during the year, $4,950.

d. Wages accrued but not paid at July 31, 2012, $440.

e. Accrued fees earned but not recorded at July 31, 2012, $1,000.

f. Unearned fees on July 31, 2012, $750.

## Instructions

1. Prepare the necessary adjusting journal entries. Include journal entry explanations.

2. Determine the balance of the accounts affected by the adjusting entries, and prepare an adjusted trial balance.

## Solution

1.

| Journal | | | | | |
|---|---|---|---|---|---|
| **Date** | | **Description** | **Post. Ref.** | **Debit** | **Credit** |
| 2012 | | | | | |
| July | 31 | Supplies Expense | | 890 | |
| | |    Supplies | | | 890 |
| | |       Supplies used ($1,270 – $380). | | | |
| | 31 | Insurance Expense | | 315 | |
| | |    Prepaid Insurance | | | 315 |
| | |       Insurance expired. | | | |
| | 31 | Depreciation Expense | | 4,950 | |
| | |    Accumulated Depreciation—Office Equipment | | | 4,950 |
| | |       Depreciation expense. | | | |
| | 31 | Wages Expense | | 440 | |
| | |    Wages Payable | | | 440 |
| | |       Accrued wages. | | | |
| | 31 | Accounts Receivable | | 1,000 | |
| | |    Fees Earned | | | 1,000 |
| | |       Accrued fees. | | | |
| | 31 | Unearned Fees | | 500 | |
| | |    Fees Earned | | | 500 |
| | |       Fees earned ($1,250 – $750). | | | |

2.

| Harbor Realty, Inc.<br>Adjusted Trial Balance<br>July 31, 2012 | | |
|---|---|---|
| | Debit<br>Balances | Credit<br>Balances |
| Cash ............................................................. | 3,425 | |
| Accounts Receivable.......................................... | 8,000 | |
| Supplies........................................................ | 380 | |
| Prepaid Insurance ............................................ | 305 | |
| Office Equipment ............................................ | 51,650 | |
| Accumulated Depreciation—Office Equipment........... | | 14,650 |
| Accounts Payable ............................................ | | 925 |
| Wages Payable ................................................ | | 440 |
| Unearned Fees ................................................ | | 750 |
| Capital Stock................................................... | | 5,000 |
| Retained Earnings............................................ | | 24,000 |
| Dividends....................................................... | 5,200 | |
| Fees Earned.................................................... | | 60,625 |
| Wages Expense ............................................... | 22,855 | |
| Depreciation Expense ....................................... | 4,950 | |
| Rent Expense .................................................. | 4,200 | |
| Utilities Expense ............................................. | 2,715 | |
| Supplies Expense.............................................. | 890 | |
| Insurance Expense ........................................... | 315 | |
| Miscellaneous Expense ...................................... | 1,505 | |
| | 106,390 | 106,390 |

# Discussion Questions

1. How are revenues and expenses reported on the income statement under (a) the cash basis of accounting and (b) the accrual basis of accounting?

2. Is the matching concept related to (a) the cash basis of accounting or (b) the accrual basis of accounting?

3. Why are adjusting entries needed at the end of an accounting period?

4. What is the difference between *adjusting entries* and *correcting entries*?

5. Identify the four different categories of adjusting entries frequently required at the end of an accounting period.

6. If the effect of the debit portion of an adjusting entry is to increase the balance of an asset account, which of the following statements describes the effect of the credit portion of the entry?

   a. Increases the balance of a revenue account.

   b. Increases the balance of an expense account.

   c. Increases the balance of a liability account.

7. If the effect of the credit portion of an adjusting entry is to increase the balance of a liability account, which of the following statements describes the effect of the debit portion of the entry?

   a. Increases the balance of a revenue account.

   b. Increases the balance of an expense account.

   c. Increases the balance of an asset account.

8. Does every adjusting entry have an effect on determining the amount of net income for a period? Explain.

9. On November 1 of the current year, a business paid the November rent on the building that it occupies. (a) Do the rights acquired at November 1 represent an asset or an expense? (b) What is the justification for debiting Rent Expense at the time of payment?

10. (a) Explain the purpose of the two accounts: Depreciation Expense and Accumulated Depreciation. (b) What is the normal balance of each account? (c) Is it customary for the balances of the two accounts to be equal in amount? (d) In what financial statements, if any, will each account appear?

# Practice Exercises

| Learning Objectives | Example Exercises | |
|---|---|---|
| OBJ. 1 | EE 3-1 *p. 105* | **PE 3-1A   Accounts requiring adjustment** |

Indicate with a Yes or No whether or not each of the following accounts normally requires an adjusting entry.

a.  Accumulated Depreciation     c.  Office Equipment     e.  Supplies

b.  Dividends     d.  Salaries Payable     f.  Unearned Rent

---

| | | |
|---|---|---|
| OBJ. 1 | EE 3-1 *p. 105* | **PE 3-1B   Accounts requiring adjustment** |

Indicate with a Yes or No whether or not each of the following accounts normally requires an adjusting entry.

a.  Building     c.  Cash     e.  Miscellaneous Expense

b.  Capital Stock     d.  Interest Expense     f.  Prepaid Insurance

---

| | | |
|---|---|---|
| OBJ. 1 | EE 3-2 *p. 109* | **PE 3-2A   Type of adjustment** |

Classify the following items as (1) prepaid expense, (2) unearned revenue, (3) accrued revenue, or (4) accrued expense.

a.  Cash received for services not yet rendered     c.  Rent revenue earned but not received

b.  Insurance paid     d.  Salaries owed but not yet paid

---

| | | |
|---|---|---|
| OBJ. 1 | EE 3-2 *p. 109* | **PE 3-2B   Type of adjustment** |

Classify the following items as (1) prepaid expense, (2) unearned revenue, (3) accrued revenue, or (4) accrued expense.

a.  Cash received for use of land next month     c.  Rent expense owed but not yet paid

b.  Fees earned but not received     d.  Supplies on hand

---

| | | |
|---|---|---|
| OBJ. 2 | EE 3-3 *p. 112* | **PE 3-3A   Adjustment for prepaid expense** |

The supplies account had a beginning balance of $2,400 and was debited for $3,975 for supplies purchased during the year. Journalize the adjusting entry required at the end of the year assuming the amount of supplies on hand is $1,375.

---

| | | |
|---|---|---|
| OBJ. 2 | EE 3-3 *p. 112* | **PE 3-3B   Adjustment for prepaid expense** |

The prepaid insurance account had a beginning balance of $7,200 and was debited for $4,800 of premiums paid during the year. Journalize the adjusting entry required at the end of the year assuming the amount of unexpired insurance related to future periods is $8,000.

---

| | | |
|---|---|---|
| OBJ. 2 | EE 3-4 *p. 113* | **PE 3-4A   Adjustment for unearned revenue** |

The balance in the unearned fees account, before adjustment at the end of the year, is $178,900. Journalize the adjusting entry required assuming the amount of unearned fees at the end of the year is $18,650.

---

| | | |
|---|---|---|
| OBJ. 2 | EE 3-4 *p. 113* | **PE 3-4B   Adjustment for unearned revenue** |

On August 1, 2012, Treadwell Co. received $10,500 for the rent of land for 12 months. Journalize the adjusting entry required for unearned rent on December 31, 2012.

---

| | | |
|---|---|---|
| OBJ. 2 | EE 3-5 *p. 114* | **PE 3-5A   Adjustment for accrued revenues** |

At the end of the current year, $11,600 of fees have been earned but have not been billed to clients. Journalize the adjusting entry to record the accrued fees.

| *Learning Objectives* | *Example Exercises* | |
|---|---|---|

**OBJ. 2**    **EE 3-5** *p. 114*

**PE 3-5B    Adjustment for accrued revenues**

At the end of the current year, $21,750 of fees have been earned but have not been billed to clients. Journalize the adjusting entry to record the accrued fees.

**OBJ. 2**    **EE 3-6** *p. 116*

**PE 3-6A    Adjustment for accrued expense**

Stress Free Realty Co. pays weekly salaries of $18,000 on Friday for a five-day workweek ending on that day. Journalize the necessary adjusting entry at the end of the accounting period assuming that the period ends on Thursday.

**OBJ. 2**    **EE 3-6** *p. 116*

**PE 3-6B    Adjustment for accrued expense**

ABC Realty Co. pays weekly salaries of $34,500 on Monday for a six-day workweek ending the preceding Saturday. Journalize the necessary adjusting entry at the end of the accounting period assuming that the period ends on Wednesday.

**OBJ. 2**    **EE 3-7** *p. 119*

**PE 3-7A    Adjustment for depreciation**

The estimated amount of depreciation on equipment for the current year is $11,500. Journalize the adjusting entry to record the depreciation.

**OBJ. 3**    **EE 3-7** *p. 119*

**PE 3-7B    Adjustment for depreciation**

The estimated amount of depreciation on equipment for the current year is $3,800. Journalize the adjusting entry to record the depreciation.

**OBJ. 3**    **EE 3-8** *p. 119*

**PE 3-8A    Effect of omitting adjustments**

For the year ending January 31, 2012, Balboa Medical Co. mistakenly omitted adjusting entries for (1) depreciation of $7,200, (2) fees earned that were not billed of $33,300, and (3) accrued wages of $6,000. Indicate the combined effect of the errors on (a) revenues, (b) expenses, and (c) net income for the year ended January 31, 2012.

**OBJ. 4**    **EE 3-8** *p. 119*

**PE 3-8B    Effect of omitting adjustments**

For the year ending June 30, 2012, Aspen Medical Services Co. mistakenly omitted adjusting entries for (1) $2,100 of supplies that were used, (2) unearned revenue of $13,900 that was earned, and (3) insurance of $12,000 that expired. Indicate the combined effect of the errors on (a) revenues, (b) expenses, and (c) net income for the year ended June 30, 2012.

**OBJ. 4**    **EE 3-9** *p. 126*

**PE 3-9A    Effect of errors on adjusted trial balance**

For each of the following errors, considered individually, indicate whether the error would cause the adjusted trial balance totals to be unequal. If the error would cause the adjusted trial balance totals to be unequal, indicate whether the debit or credit total is higher and by how much.

a. The adjustment of $17,520 for accrued fees earned was journalized as a debit to Accounts Receivable for $17,520 and a credit to Fees Earned for $17,250.

b. The adjustment of depreciation of $4,000 was omitted from the end-of-period adjusting entries.

**OBJ. 4**    **EE 3-9** *p. 126*

**PE 3-9B    Effect of errors on adjusted trial balance**

For each of the following errors, considered individually, indicate whether the error would cause the adjusted trial balance totals to be unequal. If the error would cause the adjusted trial balance totals to be unequal, indicate whether the debit or credit total is higher and by how much.

a. The adjustment for accrued wages of $3,600 was journalized as a debit to Wages Expense for $3,600 and a credit to Accounts Payable for $3,600.

b. The entry for $1,480 of supplies used during the period was journalized as a debit to Supplies Expense of $1,480 and a credit to Supplies of $1,840.

Learning
Objectives

Example
Exercises

OBJ. 5   EE 3-10   p. 128

## PE 3-10A   Vertical analysis

Two income statements for Newman Company are shown below.

**Newman Company**
**Income Statements**
**For Years Ended December 31**

|  | 2012 | 2011 |
|---|---|---|
| Fees earned | $405,000 | $375,000 |
| Operating expenses | 263,500 | 225,000 |
| Operating income | $141,500 | $150,000 |

a. Prepare a vertical analysis of Newman Company's income statements.

b. Does the vertical analysis indicate a favorable or unfavorable trend?

OBJ. 5   EE 3-10   p. 128

## PE 3-10B   Vertical analysis

Two income statements for Bradford Company are shown below.

**Bradford Company**
**Income Statements**
**For Years Ended December 31**

|  | 2012 | 2011 |
|---|---|---|
| Fees earned | $825,000 | $700,000 |
| Operating expenses | 684,750 | 602,000 |
| Operating income | $140,250 | $ 98,000 |

a. Prepare a vertical analysis of Bradford Company's income statements.

b. Does the vertical analysis indicate a favorable or unfavorable trend?

# Exercises

OBJ. 1

## EX 3-1   Classifying types of adjustments

Classify the following items as (a) prepaid expense, (b) unearned revenue, (c) accrued revenue, or (d) accrued expense.

1. A three-year premium paid on a fire insurance policy.

2. Fees earned but not yet received.

3. Fees received but not yet earned.

4. Salary owed but not yet paid.

5. Subscriptions received in advance by a magazine publisher.

6. Supplies on hand.

7. Taxes owed but payable in the following period.

8. Utilities owed but not yet paid.

OBJ. 1

## EX 3-2   Classifying adjusting entries

The following accounts were taken from the unadjusted trial balance of Orion Co., a congressional lobbying firm. Indicate whether or not each account would normally require an adjusting entry. If the account normally requires an adjusting entry, use the following notation to indicate the type of adjustment:

AE—Accrued Expense

AR—Accrued Revenue

PE—Prepaid Expense

UR—Unearned Revenue

To illustrate, the answer for the first account is shown below.

| Account | Answer |
|---|---|
| Accounts Receivable | Normally requires adjustment (AR). |
| Capital Stock | |
| Cash | |
| Interest Expense | |
| Interest Receivable | |
| Land | |
| Office Equipment | |
| Prepaid Rent | |
| Supplies | |
| Unearned Fees | |
| Wages Expense | |

OBJ. 2

## EX 3-3  Adjusting entry for supplies

The balance in the supplies account, before adjustment at the end of the year, is $3,915. Journalize the adjusting entry required if the amount of supplies on hand at the end of the year is $1,750.

OBJ. 2

## EX 3-4  Determining supplies purchased

The supplies and supplies expense accounts at December 31, after adjusting entries have been posted at the end of the first year of operations, are shown in the following T accounts:

| Supplies | | Supplies Expense | |
|---|---|---|---|
| Bal. | 900 | Bal. | 2,750 |

Determine the amount of supplies purchased during the year.

OBJ. 2, 3

## EX 3-5  Effect of omitting adjusting entry

At August 31, the end of the first month of operations, the usual adjusting entry transferring prepaid insurance expired to an expense account is omitted. Which items will be incorrectly stated, because of the error, on (a) the income statement for August and (b) the balance sheet as of August 31? Also indicate whether the items in error will be overstated or understated.

OBJ. 2

## EX 3-6  Adjusting entries for prepaid insurance

The balance in the prepaid insurance account, before adjustment at the end of the year, is $14,800. Journalize the adjusting entry required under each of the following *alternatives* for determining the amount of the adjustment: (a) the amount of insurance expired during the year is $11,200; (b) the amount of unexpired insurance applicable to future periods is $3,600.

OBJ. 2

## EX 3-7  Adjusting entries for prepaid insurance

The prepaid insurance account had a balance of $4,800 at the beginning of the year. The account was debited for $15,000 for premiums on policies purchased during the year. Journalize the adjusting entry required at the end of the year for each of the following situations: (a) the amount of unexpired insurance applicable to future periods is $5,000; (b) the amount of insurance expired during the year is $14,800.

OBJ. 2

✔ Amount of entry:
$36,000

## EX 3-8  Adjusting entries for unearned fees

The balance in the unearned fees account, before adjustment at the end of the year, is $45,000. Journalize the adjusting entry required if the amount of unearned fees at the end of the year is $9,000.

OBJ. 2, 3

## EX 3-9  Effect of omitting adjusting entry

At the end of October, the first month of the business year, the usual adjusting entry transferring rent earned to a revenue account from the unearned rent account was omitted. Indicate which items will be incorrectly stated, because of the error, on (a) the income statement for October and (b) the balance sheet as of October 31. Also indicate whether the items in error will be overstated or understated.

OBJ. 2

### EX 3-10  Adjusting entry for accrued fees

At the end of the current year, $12,300 of fees have been earned but have not been billed to clients.

a.  Journalize the adjusting entry to record the accrued fees.

b.  If the cash basis rather than the accrual basis had been used, would an adjusting entry have been necessary? Explain.

OBJ. 2

### EX 3-11  Adjusting entries for unearned and accrued fees

The balance in the unearned fees account, before adjustment at the end of the year, is $96,000. Of these fees, $78,500 have been earned. In addition, $23,600 of fees have been earned but have not been billed. Journalize the adjusting entries (a) to adjust the unearned fees account and (b) to record the accrued fees.

OBJ. 2, 3

### EX 3-12  Effect of omitting adjusting entry

The adjusting entry for accrued fees was omitted at July 31, the end of the current year. Indicate which items will be in error, because of the omission, on (a) the income statement for the current year and (b) the balance sheet as of July 31. Also indicate whether the items in error will be overstated or understated.

OBJ. 2

✔ a. Amount of entry: $3,750

### EX 3-13  Adjusting entries for accrued salaries

Torrey Realty Co. pays weekly salaries of $9,375 on Friday for a five-day workweek ending on that day. Journalize the necessary adjusting entry at the end of the accounting period assuming that the period ends (a) on Tuesday and (b) on Thursday.

OBJ. 2

### EX 3-14  Determining wages paid

The wages payable and wages expense accounts at January 31, after adjusting entries have been posted at the end of the first month of operations, are shown in the following T accounts:

| Wages Payable | | Wages Expense | |
|---|---|---|---|
| | Bal.   3,750 | Bal.   41,250 | |

Determine the amount of wages paid during the month.

OBJ. 2, 3

### EX 3-15  Effect of omitting adjusting entry

Accrued salaries owed to employees for December 30 and 31 are not considered in preparing the financial statements for the year ended December 31. Indicate which items will be erroneously stated, because of the error, on (a) the income statement for the year and (b) the balance sheet as of December 31. Also indicate whether the items in error will be overstated or understated.

OBJ. 2, 3

### EX 3-16  Effect of omitting adjusting entry

Assume that the error in Exercise 3-15 was not corrected and that the accrued salaries were included in the first salary payment in January. Indicate which items will be erroneously stated, because of failure to correct the initial error, on (a) the income statement for the month of January and (b) the balance sheet as of January 31.

OBJ. 2

✔ b. $41,250

### EX 3-17  Adjusting entries for prepaid and accrued taxes

Andular Financial Services was organized on April 1 of the current year. On April 2, Andular prepaid $9,000 to the city for taxes (license fees) for the *next* 12 months and debited the prepaid taxes account. Andular is also required to pay in January an annual tax (on property) for the *previous* calendar year. The estimated amount of the property tax for the current year (April 1 to December 31) is $34,500.

a.  Journalize the two adjusting entries required to bring the accounts affected by the two taxes up to date as of December 31, the end of the current year.

b.  What is the amount of tax expense for the current year?

OBJ. 2

### EX 3-18  Adjustment for depreciation

The estimated amount of depreciation on equipment for the current year is $2,900. Journalize the adjusting entry to record the depreciation.

OBJ. 2

### EX 3-19    Determining fixed asset's book value

The balance in the equipment account is $750,000, and the balance in the accumulated depreciation—equipment account is $425,000.

a. What is the book value of the equipment?

b. Does the balance in the accumulated depreciation account mean that the equipment's loss of value is $425,000? Explain.

OBJ. 2

### EX 3-20    Book value of fixed assets

In a recent balance sheet, Microsoft Corporation reported *Property, Plant, and Equipment* of $15,082 million and *Accumulated Depreciation* of $7,547 million.

a. What was the book value of the fixed assets?

b. Would the book value of Microsoft Corporation's fixed assets normally approximate their fair market values?

OBJ. 2, 3

### EX 3-21    Effects of errors on financial statements

For a recent period, the balance sheet for Costco Wholesale Corporation reported accrued expenses of $1,720 million. For the same period, Costco reported income before income taxes of $1,714 million. Assume that the adjusting entry for $1,720 million of accrued expenses was not recorded at the end of the current period. What would have been the income (loss) before income taxes?

OBJ. 2, 3

### EX 3-22    Effects of errors on financial statements

For a recent year, the balance sheet for The Campbell Soup Company includes accrued expenses of $579 million. The income before taxes for The Campbell Soup Company for the year was $1,079 million.

a. Assume the adjusting entry for $579 million of accrued expenses was not recorded at the end of the year. By how much would income before taxes have been misstated?

b. What is the percentage of the misstatement in (a) to the reported income of $1,079 million? Round to one decimal place.

OBJ. 2, 3

✔ 1. a. Revenue
understated, $18,000

### EX 3-23    Effects of errors on financial statements

The accountant for Hallmark Medical Co., a medical services consulting firm, mistakenly omitted adjusting entries for (a) unearned revenue earned during the year ($18,000) and (b) accrued wages ($3,000). Indicate the effect of each error, considered individually, on the income statement for the current year ended May 31. Also indicate the effect of each error on the May 31 balance sheet. Set up a table similar to the following, and record your answers by inserting the dollar amount in the appropriate spaces. Insert a zero if the error does not affect the item.

|  | Error (a) | | Error (b) | |
|---|---|---|---|---|
|  | Over-<br>stated | Under-<br>stated | Over-<br>stated | Under-<br>stated |
| 1. Revenue for the year would be | $ ____ | $ ____ | $ ____ | $ ____ |
| 2. Expenses for the year would be | $ ____ | $ ____ | $ ____ | $ ____ |
| 3. Net income for the year would be | $ ____ | $ ____ | $ ____ | $ ____ |
| 4. Assets at May 31 would be | $ ____ | $ ____ | $ ____ | $ ____ |
| 5. Liabilities at May 31 would be | $ ____ | $ ____ | $ ____ | $ ____ |
| 6. Stockholders' equity at May 31 would be | $ ____ | $ ____ | $ ____ | $ ____ |

OBJ. 2, 3

### EX 3-24    Effects of errors on financial statements

If the net income for the current year had been $240,000 in Exercise 3-23, what would have been the correct net income if the proper adjusting entries had been made?

OBJ. 2, 3

### EX 3-25    Adjusting entries for depreciation; effect of error

On December 31, a business estimates depreciation on equipment used during the first year of operations to be $14,500.

a. Journalize the adjusting entry required as of December 31.

b. If the adjusting entry in (a) were omitted, which items would be erroneously stated on (1) the income statement for the year and (2) the balance sheet as of December 31?

OBJ. 4

## EX 3-26   Adjusting entries from trial balances

The unadjusted and adjusted trial balances for McWay Services Co. on August 31, 2012, are shown below.

**McWay Services Co.**
**Trial Balance**
**August 31, 2012**

| | Unadjusted | | Adjusted | |
|---|---|---|---|---|
| | Debit Balances | Credit Balances | Debit Balances | Credit Balances |
| Cash ..................................................... | 8 | | 8 | |
| Accounts Receivable................................... | 19 | | 21 | |
| Supplies ................................................ | 6 | | 5 | |
| Prepaid Insurance ..................................... | 10 | | 6 | |
| Land .................................................... | 13 | | 13 | |
| Equipment............................................... | 20 | | 20 | |
| Accumulated Depreciation—Equipment ................... | | 4 | | 5 |
| Accounts Payable ...................................... | | 13 | | 13 |
| Wages Payable ......................................... | | 0 | | 1 |
| Capital Stock .......................................... | | 17 | | 17 |
| Retained Earnings ..................................... | | 29 | | 29 |
| Dividends............................................... | 4 | | 4 | |
| Fees Earned............................................ | | 37 | | 39 |
| Wages Expense ......................................... | 12 | | 13 | |
| Rent Expense ........................................... | 4 | | 4 | |
| Insurance Expense ..................................... | 0 | | 4 | |
| Utilities Expense ...................................... | 2 | | 2 | |
| Depreciation Expense .................................. | 0 | | 1 | |
| Supplies Expense....................................... | 0 | | 1 | |
| Miscellaneous Expense ................................. | 2 | | 2 | |
| | 100 | 100 | 104 | 104 |

Journalize the five entries that adjusted the accounts at August 31, 2012. None of the accounts were affected by more than one adjusting entry.

OBJ. 4

✔ Corrected trial balance totals, $360,950

## EX 3-27   Adjusting entries from trial balances

The accountant for E-Z Laundry prepared the following unadjusted and adjusted trial balances. Assume that all balances in the unadjusted trial balance and the amounts of the adjustments are correct. Identify the errors in the accountant's adjusting entries assuming that none of the accounts were affected by more than one adjusting entry.

**E-Z Laundry**
**Trial Balance**
**July 31, 2012**

| | Unadjusted | | Adjusted | |
|---|---|---|---|---|
| | Debit Balances | Credit Balances | Debit Balances | Credit Balances |
| Cash ................................................. | 7,500 | | 7,500 | |
| Accounts Receivable................................... | 18,250 | | 22,000 | |
| Laundry Supplies...................................... | 3,750 | | 5,500 | |
| Prepaid Insurance* .................................... | 5,200 | | 1,400 | |
| Laundry Equipment ..................................... | 190,000 | | 184,000 | |
| Accumulated Depreciation—Laundry Equipment.......... | | 48,000 | | 48,000 |
| Accounts Payable ...................................... | | 9,600 | | 9,600 |
| Wages Payable ......................................... | | | | 1,200 |
| Capital Stock.......................................... | | 40,000 | | 40,000 |
| Retained Earnings ..................................... | | 70,300 | | 70,300 |
| Dividends............................................. | 28,775 | | 28,775 | |
| Laundry Revenue....................................... | | 182,100 | | 182,100 |
| Wages Expense ......................................... | 49,200 | | 49,200 | |
| Rent Expense .......................................... | 25,575 | | 25,575 | |
| Utilities Expense ..................................... | 18,500 | | 18,500 | |
| Depreciation Expense ................................. | | | 6,000 | |
| Laundry Supplies Expense ............................. | | | 1,750 | |
| Insurance Expense .................................... | | | 800 | |
| Miscellaneous Expense ................................ | 3,250 | | 3,250 | |
| | 350,000 | 350,000 | 354,250 | 351,200 |

\* 3,800 of insurance expired during the year.

### EX 3-28   Vertical analysis of income statement

The following data (in millions) are taken from the financial statements of Nike Inc. for the years ending May 31, 2009 and 2008:

|                     | 2009    | 2008    |
|---------------------|---------|---------|
| Net sales (revenues) | $19,176 | $18,627 |
| Net income          | 1,487   | 1,883   |

a.  Determine the amount of change (in millions) and percent of change in net income for 2009. Round to one decimal place.

b.  Determine the percentage relationship between net income and net sales (net income divided by net sales) for 2009 and 2008. Round to one decimal place.

c.  What conclusions can you draw from your analysis?

### EX 3-29   Vertical analysis of income statement

The following income statement data (in millions) for Dell Inc. and Hewlett-Packard Company (HP) were taken from their recent annual reports:

|                            | Dell      | Hewlett-Packard |
|----------------------------|-----------|-----------------|
| Net sales                  | $ 61,101  | $118,364        |
| Cost of goods sold (expense) | (50,144)  | (89,592)        |
| Operating expenses         | (7,767)   | (17,970)        |
| Operating income (loss)    | $  3,190  | $  10,802       |

a.  Prepare a vertical analysis of the income statement for Dell. Round to one decimal place.

b.  Prepare a vertical analysis of the income statement for HP. Round to one decimal place.

c.  Based on (a) and (b), how does Dell compare to HP?

## Problems Series A

### PR 3-1A   Adjusting entries

On October 31, 2012, the following data were accumulated to assist the accountant in preparing the adjusting entries for Dependable Realty:

a.  The supplies account balance on October 31 is $3,975. The supplies on hand on October 31 are $1,050.

b.  The unearned rent account balance on October 31 is $11,000, representing the receipt of an advance payment on October 1 of four months' rent from tenants.

c.  Wages accrued but not paid at October 31 are $2,500.

d.  Fees accrued but unbilled at October 31 are $4,900.

e.  Depreciation of office equipment is $1,100.

**Instructions**

1.  Journalize the adjusting entries required at October 31, 2012.

2.  Briefly explain the difference between adjusting entries and entries that would be made to correct errors.

### PR 3-2A   Adjusting entries

Selected account balances before adjustment for Newhouse Realty at March 31, 2012, the end of the current year, are as follows:

|                          | Debits   | Credits  |
|--------------------------|----------|----------|
| Accounts Receivable      | $ 80,000 |          |
| Equipment                | 150,000  |          |
| Accumulated Depreciation |          | $ 28,000 |
| Prepaid Rent             | 6,000    |          |

*(Continued)*

|  | Debits | Credits |
|---|---|---|
| Supplies | $ 3,000 | |
| Wages Payable | — | |
| Unearned Fees | | $ 10,500 |
| Fees Earned | | 410,000 |
| Wages Expense | 190,000 | |
| Rent Expense | — | |
| Depreciation Expense | — | |
| Supplies Expense | — | |

Data needed for year-end adjustments are as follows:

a. Unbilled fees at March 31, $13,500.

b. Supplies on hand at March 31, $950.

c. Rent expired, $4,000.

d. Depreciation of equipment during year, $1,500.

e. Unearned fees at March 31, $2,500.

f. Wages accrued but not paid at March 31, $2,200.

## Instructions

1. Journalize the six adjusting entries required at March 31, based on the data presented.

2. What would be the effect on the income statement if adjustments (a) and (f) were omitted at the end of the year?

3. What would be the effect on the balance sheet if adjustments (a) and (f) were omitted at the end of the year?

4. What would be the effect on the "Net increase or decrease in cash" on the statement of cash flows if adjustments (a) and (f) were omitted at the end of the year?

**OBJ. 2**

## PR 3-3A   Adjusting entries

Econo Company, an electronics repair store, prepared the unadjusted trial balance shown below at the end of its first year of operations.

**Econo Company**
**Unadjusted Trial Balance**
**April 30, 2012**

|  | Debit Balances | Credit Balances |
|---|---|---|
| Cash | 13,800 | |
| Accounts Receivable | 90,000 | |
| Supplies | 21,600 | |
| Equipment | 454,800 | |
| Accounts Payable | | 21,000 |
| Unearned Fees | | 24,000 |
| Capital Stock | | 55,000 |
| Retained Earnings | | 257,000 |
| Dividends | 18,000 | |
| Fees Earned | | 543,000 |
| Wages Expense | 126,000 | |
| Rent Expense | 96,000 | |
| Utilities Expense | 69,000 | |
| Miscellaneous Expense | 10,800 | |
| | 900,000 | 900,000 |

For preparing the adjusting entries, the following data were assembled:

a. Fees earned but unbilled on April 30 were $10,000.

b. Supplies on hand on April 30 were $8,150.

c. Depreciation of equipment was estimated to be $13,800 for the year.

d. The balance in unearned fees represented the April 1 receipt in advance for services to be provided. Only $19,000 of the services was provided between April 1 and April 30.

e. Unpaid wages accrued on April 30 were $1,770.

**Instructions**

1. Journalize the adjusting entries necessary on April 30, 2012.

2. Determine the revenues, expenses, and net income of Econo Company before the adjusting entries.

3. Determine the revenues, expense, and net income of Econo Company after the adjusting entries.

4. Determine the effect on retained earnings of the adjusting entries.

---

OBJ. 2, 3, 4

### PR 3-4A    Adjusting entries

Timken Company specializes in the repair of music equipment and is owned and operated by Secilia Timken. On April 30, 2012, the end of the current year, the accountant for Timken Company prepared the following trial balances:

**Timken Company**
**Trial Balance**
**April 30, 2012**

|  | Unadjusted | | Adjusted | |
| --- | --- | --- | --- | --- |
|  | Debit Balances | Credit Balances | Debit Balances | Credit Balances |
| Cash | 38,250 | | 38,250 | |
| Accounts Receivable | 109,500 | | 109,500 | |
| Supplies | 11,250 | | 3,500 | |
| Prepaid Insurance | 14,250 | | 2,700 | |
| Equipment | 360,450 | | 360,450 | |
| Accumulated Depreciation—Equipment | | 94,500 | | 107,000 |
| Automobiles | 109,500 | | 109,500 | |
| Accumulated Depreciation—Automobiles | | 54,750 | | 57,500 |
| Accounts Payable | | 24,930 | | 26,000 |
| Salaries Payable | | — | | 7,500 |
| Unearned Service Fees | | 18,000 | | 6,000 |
| Capital Stock | | 125,000 | | 125,000 |
| Retained Earnings | | 269,020 | | 269,020 |
| Dividends | 75,000 | | 75,000 | |
| Service Fees Earned | | 733,800 | | 745,800 |
| Salary Expense | 516,900 | | 524,400 | |
| Rent Expense | 54,000 | | 54,000 | |
| Supplies Expense | — | | 7,750 | |
| Depreciation Expense—Equipment | — | | 12,500 | |
| Depreciation Expense—Automobiles | — | | 2,750 | |
| Utilities Expense | 12,900 | | 13,970 | |
| Taxes Expense | 8,175 | | 8,175 | |
| Insurance Expense | — | | 11,550 | |
| Miscellaneous Expense | 9,825 | | 9,825 | |
| | 1,320,000 | 1,320,000 | 1,343,820 | 1,343,820 |

**Instructions**

Journalize the seven entries that adjusted the accounts at June 30. None of the accounts were affected by more than one adjusting entry.

---

OBJ. 2, 3, 4

✔ 2. Total of Debit column: $819,550

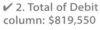

### PR 3-5A    Adjusting entries and adjusted trial balances

Galloway Company is a small editorial services company owned and operated by Fran Briggs. On July 31, 2012, the end of the current year, Galloway Company's accounting clerk prepared the unadjusted trial balance shown on the next page.

The data needed to determine year-end adjustments are as follows:

a. Unexpired insurance at July 31, $4,800.

b. Supplies on hand at July 31, $600.

c. Depreciation of building for the year, $3,100.

d. Depreciation of equipment for the year, $2,700.

e. Rent unearned at July 31, $1,750.

f. Accrued salaries and wages at July 31, $3,000.

g. Fees earned but unbilled on July 31, $10,750.

**Galloway Company**
**Unadjusted Trial Balance**
**July 31, 2012**

| | Debit Balances | Credit Balances |
|---|---|---|
| Cash ......................................................... | 7,500 | |
| Accounts Receivable. .......................................... | 38,400 | |
| Prepaid Insurance .............................................. | 7,200 | |
| Supplies........................................................ | 1,980 | |
| Land .......................................................... | 112,500 | |
| Building ....................................................... | 200,250 | |
| Accumulated Depreciation—Building. ........................... | | 137,550 |
| Equipment...................................................... | 135,300 | |
| Accumulated Depreciation—Equipment .......................... | | 97,950 |
| Accounts Payable .............................................. | | 12,150 |
| Unearned Rent.................................................. | | 6,750 |
| Capital Stock................................................... | | 80,000 |
| Retained Earnings.............................................. | | 141,000 |
| Dividends...................................................... | 15,000 | |
| Fees Earned.................................................... | | 324,600 |
| Salaries and Wages Expense..................................... | 193,370 | |
| Utilities Expense ............................................... | 42,375 | |
| Advertising Expense............................................ | 22,800 | |
| Repairs Expense................................................ | 17,250 | |
| Miscellaneous Expense ......................................... | 6,075 | |
| | 800,000 | 800,000 |

**Instructions**

1. Journalize the adjusting entries using the following additional accounts: Salaries and Wages Payable; Rent Revenue; Insurance Expense; Depreciation Expense—Building; Depreciation Expense—Equipment; and Supplies Expense.

2. Determine the balances of the accounts affected by the adjusting entries, and prepare an adjusted trial balance.

---

OBJ. 2, 3

✔ 2. Corrected net income: $92,300

### PR 3-6A  Adjusting entries and errors

At the end of June, the first month of operations, the following selected data were taken from the financial statements of Beth Cato, an attorney:

| | |
|---|---|
| Net income for June | $ 80,000 |
| Total assets at June 30 | 500,000 |
| Total liabilities at June 30 | 200,000 |
| Total stockholders' equity at June 30 | 300,000 |

In preparing the financial statements, adjustments for the following data were overlooked:

a. Supplies used during June, $1,500.

b. Unbilled fees earned at June 30, $18,000.

c. Depreciation of equipment for June, $3,000.

d. Accrued wages at June 30, $1,200.

**Instructions**

1. Journalize the entries to record the omitted adjustments.

2. Determine the correct amount of net income for June and the total assets, liabilities, and stockholders' equity at June 30. In addition to indicating the corrected amounts, indicate the effect of each omitted adjustment by setting up and completing a columnar table similar to the following. Adjustment (a) is presented as an example.

*(Continued)*

| | Net Income | Total Assets | = | Total Liabilities | + | Total Stockholders' Equity |
|---|---|---|---|---|---|---|
| Reported amounts | $80,000 | $500,000 | | $200,000 | | $300,000 |
| Corrections: | | | | | | |
| Adjustment (a) | –1,500 | –1,500 | | 0 | | –1,500 |
| Adjustment (b) | _____ | _____ | | _____ | | _____ |
| Adjustment (c) | _____ | _____ | | _____ | | _____ |
| Adjustment (d) | _____ | _____ | | _____ | | _____ |
| Corrected amounts | _____ | _____ | | _____ | | _____ |

## Problems Series B

OBJ. 2

### PR 3-1B   Adjusting entries

On January 31, 2012, the following data were accumulated to assist the accountant in preparing the adjusting entries for Oceanside Realty:

a. Fees accrued but unbilled at January 31 are $10,280.

b. The supplies account balance on January 31 is $6,100. The supplies on hand at January 31 are $1,300.

c. Wages accrued but not paid at January 31 are $3,000.

d. The unearned rent account balance at January 31 is $4,500, representing the receipt of an advance payment on January 1 of three months' rent from tenants.

e. Depreciation of office equipment is $1,400.

**Instructions**

1. Journalize the adjusting entries required at January 31, 2012.

2. Briefly explain the difference between adjusting entries and entries that would be made to correct errors.

OBJ. 2, 3

### PR 3-2B   Adjusting entries

Selected account balances before adjustment for Skylight Realty at June 30, 2012, the end of the current year, are shown below.

| | Debits | Credits |
|---|---|---|
| Accounts Receivable | $ 75,000 | |
| Accumulated Depreciation | | $ 12,000 |
| Depreciation Expense | — | |
| Equipment | 250,000 | |
| Fees Earned | | 400,000 |
| Prepaid Rent | 12,000 | |
| Rent Expense | — | |
| Supplies | 3,170 | |
| Supplies Expense | — | |
| Unearned Fees | | 10,000 |
| Wages Expense | 140,000 | |
| Wages Payable | — | |

Data needed for year-end adjustments are as follows:

a. Supplies on hand at June 30, $800.

b. Depreciation of equipment during year, $750.

c. Rent expired during year, $9,000.

d. Wages accrued but not paid at June 30, $1,700.

e. Unearned fees at June 30, $6,500.

f. Unbilled fees at June 30, $15,000.

**Instructions**

1. Journalize the six adjusting entries required at June 30, based on the data presented.

2. What would be the effect on the income statement if adjustments (b) and (e) were omitted at the end of the year?

3. What would be the effect on the balance sheet if adjustments (b) and (e) were omitted at the end of the year?

4. What would be the effect on the "Net increase or decrease in cash" on the statement of cash flows if adjustments (b) and (e) were omitted at the end of the year?

**OBJ. 2**

**PR 3-3B    Adjusting entries**

Brown Trout Outfitters Co., an outfitter store for fishing treks, prepared the following unadjusted trial balance at the end of its first year of operations:

**Brown Trout Outfitters Co.**
**Unadjusted Trial Balance**
**September 30, 2012**

|  | Debit Balances | Credit Balances |
|---|---|---|
| Cash | 26,400 | |
| Accounts Receivable | 87,600 | |
| Supplies | 7,200 | |
| Equipment | 162,000 | |
| Accounts Payable | | 12,200 |
| Unearned Fees | | 19,200 |
| Capital Stock | | 80,000 |
| Retained Earnings | | 142,800 |
| Dividends | 10,000 | |
| Fees Earned | | 295,800 |
| Wages Expense | 152,800 | |
| Rent Expense | 55,000 | |
| Utilities Expense | 42,000 | |
| Miscellaneous Expense | 7,000 | |
| | 550,000 | 550,000 |

For preparing the adjusting entries, the following data were assembled:

a. Supplies on hand on September 30 were $1,850.

b. Fees earned but unbilled on September 30 were $6,500.

c. Depreciation of equipment was estimated to be $2,800 for the year.

d. Unpaid wages accrued on September 30 were $1,275.

e. The balance in unearned fees represented the September 1 receipt in advance for services to be provided. Only $3,000 of the services was provided between September 1 and September 30.

**Instructions**

1. Journalize the adjusting entries necessary on September 30, 2012.

2. Determine the revenues, expenses, and net income of Brown Trout Outfitters Co. before the adjusting entries.

3. Determine the revenues, expense, and net income of Brown Trout Outfitters Co. after the adjusting entries.

4. Determine the effect on retained earnings of the adjusting entries.

**OBJ. 2, 3, 4**

**PR 3-4B    Adjusting entries**

Goldfinch Company specializes in the maintenance and repair of signs, such as billboards. On January 31, 2012, the accountant for Goldfinch Company prepared the following trial balances:

(Continued)

**Goldfinch Company**
**Trial Balance**
**January 31, 2012**

| | Unadjusted | | Adjusted | |
| --- | --- | --- | --- | --- |
| | Debit Balances | Credit Balances | Debit Balances | Credit Balances |
| Cash . . . . . . . . . . . . . . . . . . . . . . . . . . . . . . . . . . . . . | 4,750 | | 4,750 | |
| Accounts Receivable. . . . . . . . . . . . . . . . . . . . . . . . . . | 17,400 | | 17,400 | |
| Supplies . . . . . . . . . . . . . . . . . . . . . . . . . . . . . . . . . . | 6,200 | | 1,475 | |
| Prepaid Insurance . . . . . . . . . . . . . . . . . . . . . . . . . . . . | 9,000 | | 2,700 | |
| Land . . . . . . . . . . . . . . . . . . . . . . . . . . . . . . . . . . . . . | 50,000 | | 50,000 | |
| Buildings . . . . . . . . . . . . . . . . . . . . . . . . . . . . . . . . . . | 120,000 | | 120,000 | |
| Accumulated Depreciation—Buildings. . . . . . . . . . . . . . . . . | | 51,500 | | 60,000 |
| Trucks . . . . . . . . . . . . . . . . . . . . . . . . . . . . . . . . . . . . | 75,000 | | 75,000 | |
| Accumulated Depreciation—Trucks. . . . . . . . . . . . . . . . . . | | 12,000 | | 13,550 |
| Accounts Payable . . . . . . . . . . . . . . . . . . . . . . . . . . . . | | 6,920 | | 8,000 |
| Salaries Payable . . . . . . . . . . . . . . . . . . . . . . . . . . . . . | | — | | 750 |
| Unearned Service Fees. . . . . . . . . . . . . . . . . . . . . . . . . | | 10,500 | | 6,000 |
| Capital Stock. . . . . . . . . . . . . . . . . . . . . . . . . . . . . . . . | | 30,000 | | 30,000 |
| Retained Earnings . . . . . . . . . . . . . . . . . . . . . . . . . . . . | | 126,400 | | 126,400 |
| Dividends. . . . . . . . . . . . . . . . . . . . . . . . . . . . . . . . . . | 7,500 | | 7,500 | |
| Service Fees Earned . . . . . . . . . . . . . . . . . . . . . . . . . . | | 162,680 | | 167,180 |
| Salary Expense. . . . . . . . . . . . . . . . . . . . . . . . . . . . . . | 80,000 | | 80,750 | |
| Depreciation Expense—Trucks . . . . . . . . . . . . . . . . . . . . | — | | 1,550 | |
| Rent Expense . . . . . . . . . . . . . . . . . . . . . . . . . . . . . . . | 11,900 | | 11,900 | |
| Supplies Expense. . . . . . . . . . . . . . . . . . . . . . . . . . . . . | — | | 4,725 | |
| Utilities Expense . . . . . . . . . . . . . . . . . . . . . . . . . . . . . | 6,200 | | 7,280 | |
| Depreciation Expense—Buildings . . . . . . . . . . . . . . . . . . . | — | | 8,500 | |
| Taxes Expense . . . . . . . . . . . . . . . . . . . . . . . . . . . . . . | 2,900 | | 2,900 | |
| Insurance Expense . . . . . . . . . . . . . . . . . . . . . . . . . . . . | — | | 6,300 | |
| Miscellaneous Expense . . . . . . . . . . . . . . . . . . . . . . . . . | 9,150 | | 9,150 | |
| | 400,000 | 400,000 | 411,880 | 411,880 |

**Instructions**
Journalize the seven entries that adjusted the accounts at January 31. None of the accounts were affected by more than one adjusting entry.

---

OBJ. 2, 3, 4

✔ 2. Total of Debit column: $340,075

### PR 3-5B   Adjusting entries and adjusted trial balances

Pacific Financial Services Co., which specializes in appliance repair services, is owned and operated by Eileen Hastings. Pacific Financial Services Co.'s accounting clerk prepared the unadjusted trial balance at October 31, 2012, shown below.

**Pacific Financial Services Co.**
**Unadjusted Trial Balance**
**October 31, 2012**

| | Debit Balances | Credit Balances |
| --- | --- | --- |
| Cash . . . . . . . . . . . . . . . . . . . . . . . . . . . . . . . . . . . . . . . . . . . . . . . | 10,200 | |
| Accounts Receivable. . . . . . . . . . . . . . . . . . . . . . . . . . . . . . . . . . . . . | 34,750 | |
| Prepaid Insurance . . . . . . . . . . . . . . . . . . . . . . . . . . . . . . . . . . . . . . | 6,000 | |
| Supplies . . . . . . . . . . . . . . . . . . . . . . . . . . . . . . . . . . . . . . . . . . . . . | 1,725 | |
| Land . . . . . . . . . . . . . . . . . . . . . . . . . . . . . . . . . . . . . . . . . . . . . . . . | 50,000 | |
| Building . . . . . . . . . . . . . . . . . . . . . . . . . . . . . . . . . . . . . . . . . . . . . | 80,750 | |
| Accumulated Depreciation—Building. . . . . . . . . . . . . . . . . . . . . . . . . | | 37,850 |
| Equipment. . . . . . . . . . . . . . . . . . . . . . . . . . . . . . . . . . . . . . . . . . . . | 45,000 | |
| Accumulated Depreciation—Equipment . . . . . . . . . . . . . . . . . . . . . . . | | 17,650 |
| Accounts Payable . . . . . . . . . . . . . . . . . . . . . . . . . . . . . . . . . . . . . . | | 3,750 |
| Unearned Rent . . . . . . . . . . . . . . . . . . . . . . . . . . . . . . . . . . . . . . . . | | 3,600 |
| Capital Stock. . . . . . . . . . . . . . . . . . . . . . . . . . . . . . . . . . . . . . . . . . | | 22,500 |
| Retained Earnings . . . . . . . . . . . . . . . . . . . . . . . . . . . . . . . . . . . . . . | | 81,050 |
| Dividends . . . . . . . . . . . . . . . . . . . . . . . . . . . . . . . . . . . . . . . . . . . . | 8,000 | |
| Fees Earned. . . . . . . . . . . . . . . . . . . . . . . . . . . . . . . . . . . . . . . . . . | | 158,600 |
| Salaries and Wages Expense. . . . . . . . . . . . . . . . . . . . . . . . . . . . . . . | 56,850 | |
| Utilities Expense . . . . . . . . . . . . . . . . . . . . . . . . . . . . . . . . . . . . . . . | 14,100 | |
| Advertising Expense . . . . . . . . . . . . . . . . . . . . . . . . . . . . . . . . . . . . | 7,500 | |
| Repairs Expense. . . . . . . . . . . . . . . . . . . . . . . . . . . . . . . . . . . . . . . | 6,100 | |
| Miscellaneous Expense . . . . . . . . . . . . . . . . . . . . . . . . . . . . . . . . . . | 4,025 | |
| | 325,000 | 325,000 |

The data needed to determine year-end adjustments are as follows:

a. Depreciation of building for the year, $1,900.

b. Depreciation of equipment for the year, $2,400.

c. Accrued salaries and wages at October 31, $1,375.

d. Unexpired insurance at October 31, $2,700.

e. Fees earned but unbilled on October 31, $9,400.

f. Supplies on hand at October 31, $325.

g. Rent unearned at October 31, $1,800.

**Instructions**

1. Journalize the adjusting entries using the following additional accounts: Salaries and Wages Payable; Rent Revenue; Insurance Expense; Depreciation Expense—Building; Depreciation Expense—Equipment; and Supplies Expense.

2. Determine the balances of the accounts affected by the adjusting entries and prepare an adjusted trial balance.

---

**OBJ. 2, 3**

✔ 2. Corrected net income: $150,500

**PR 3-6B   Adjusting entries and errors**

At the end of March, the first month of operations, the following selected data were taken from the financial statements of Kurt Reibel, an attorney:

| | |
|---|---|
| Net income for March | $ 150,000 |
| Total assets at March 31 | 1,000,000 |
| Total liabilities at March 31 | 350,000 |
| Total stockholders' equity at March 31 | 650,000 |

In preparing the financial statements, adjustments for the following data were overlooked:

a. Unbilled fees earned at March 31, $15,000.

b. Depreciation of equipment for March, $9,000.

c. Accrued wages at March 31, $3,500.

d. Supplies used during March, $2,000.

**Instructions**

1. Journalize the entries to record the omitted adjustments.

2. Determine the correct amount of net income for March and the total assets, liabilities, and stockholders' equity at March 31. In addition to indicating the corrected amounts, indicate the effect of each omitted adjustment by setting up and completing a columnar table similar to the following. Adjustment (a) is presented as an example.

| | Net Income | Total Assets | + Total Liabilities | = Total Stockholders' Equity |
|---|---|---|---|---|
| Reported amounts | $150,000 | $1,000,000 | $350,000 | $650,000 |
| Corrections: | | | | |
| Adjustment (a) | +15,000 | +15,000 | 0 | +15,000 |
| Adjustment (b) | _____ | _____ | _____ | _____ |
| Adjustment (c) | _____ | _____ | _____ | _____ |
| Adjustment (d) | _____ | _____ | _____ | _____ |
| Corrected amounts | _____ | _____ | _____ | _____ |

---

## Continuing Problem

✔ 3. Total of Debit column: $41,875

The unadjusted trial balance that you prepared for PS Music at the end of Chapter 2 should appear as shown on the following page.

**PS Music**
**Unadjusted Trial Balance**
**July 31, 2012**

| | Debit Balances | Credit Balances |
|---|---|---|
| Cash | 10,510 | |
| Accounts Receivable | 3,150 | |
| Supplies | 1,250 | |
| Prepaid Insurance | 2,700 | |
| Office Equipment | 6,000 | |
| Accounts Payable | | 7,080 |
| Unearned Revenue | | 7,200 |
| Capital Stock | | 9,000 |
| Dividends | 2,000 | |
| Fees Earned | | 16,750 |
| Music Expense | 3,610 | |
| Wages Expense | 2,800 | |
| Office Rent Expense | 2,550 | |
| Advertising Expense | 1,450 | |
| Equipment Rent Expense | 1,300 | |
| Utilities Expense | 1,060 | |
| Supplies Expense | 180 | |
| Miscellaneous Expense | 1,470 | |
| | 40,030 | 40,030 |

The data needed to determine adjustments for the two-month period ending July 31, 2012, are as follows:

a. During July, PS Music provided guest disc jockeys for WHBD for a total of 120 hours. For information on the amount of the accrued revenue to be billed to WHBD, see the contract described in the July 3, 2012, transaction at the end of Chapter 2.

b. Supplies on hand at July 31, $400.

c. The balance of the prepaid insurance account relates to the July 1, 2012, transaction at the end of Chapter 2.

d. Depreciation of the office equipment is $75.

e. The balance of the unearned revenue account relates to the contract between PS Music and WHBD, described in the July 3, 2012, transaction at the end of Chapter 2.

f. Accrued wages as of July 31, 2012, were $170.

**Instructions**

1. Prepare adjusting journal entries. You will need the following additional accounts:

    18 Accumulated Depreciation—Office Equipment

    22 Wages Payable

    57 Insurance Expense

    58 Depreciation Expense

2. Post the adjusting entries, inserting balances in the accounts affected.

3. Prepare an adjusted trial balance.

## Cases & Projects

You can access the Cases & Projects online at **www.cengage.com/accounting/reeve**

## Excel Success Special Activities

### SA 3-1   Adjusting entries

Holly Company purchased a two-year insurance policy on January 2, 2012, for $1,800.

a. Open the Excel file *SA3-1_1e*.

b. Journalize in a spreadsheet (spreadsheet labeled J5) the adjusting entry to record insurance expired for the year on December 31, 2012.

c. Post the adjusting entry to the four-column general ledger on the GL worksheet.

|   | A | B | C | D | E | F | G |
|---|---|---|---|---|---|---|---|
| 1 | | | | | | | |
| 2 | Account | Prepaid Insurance | | | | Account No. | 18 |
| 3 | | | | | | **Balance** | |
| 4 | **Date** | **Item** | **Post. Ref.** | **Debit** | **Credit** | **Debit** | **Credit** |
| 5 | Jan 2 | | 5 | 1,800 | | 1,800 | |
| 6 | Dec. 31 | Adjusting | 5 | | | | |
| 7 | | | | | | | |
| 8 | | | | | | | |
| 9 | Account | Insurance Expense | | | | Account No. | 56 |
| 10 | | | | | | **Balance** | |
| 11 | **Date** | **Item** | **Post. Ref.** | **Debit** | **Credit** | **Debit** | **Credit** |
| 12 | Dec. 31 | Adjusting | 5 | | | | |
| 13 | | | | | | | |
| 14 | | | | | | | |
| 15 | | | | | | | |
| 16 | | | | | | | |

⏮ ◀ ▶ ⏭ \ J5 \ GL / \ Sheet3 /    ◀

d. When you have completed the journal entry and posted to the general ledger, perform a "save as," replacing the entire file name with the following:

*SA3-1_1e[your first name initial]_[your last name]*

### SA 3-2   Adjusting entries

The accrued wages for Darrin Company at October 31, 2013, are $14,300.

a. Open the Excel file *SA3-2_1e*.

b. Journalize in a spreadsheet the adjusting entry for accrued wages on October 31, 2013. On worksheet J5, journalize the adjusting entry.

c. Post the adjusting entry to the four-column general ledger on the GL worksheet.

|   | A | B | C | D | E | F | G |
|---|---|---|---|---|---|---|---|
| 1 | | | | | | | |
| 2 | Account | Cash | | | | Account No. | 10 |
| 3 | | | | | | **Balance** | |
| 4 | **Date** | **Item** | **Post. Ref.** | **Debit** | **Credit** | **Debit** | **Credit** |
| 5 | Oct. 15 | Payroll | | | 13,800 | | 13,800 |
| 6 | | | | | | | |
| 7 | | | | | | | |
| 8 | Account | Wages Payable | | | | Account No. | 34 |
| 9 | | | | | | **Balance** | |
| 10 | **Date** | **Item** | **Post. Ref.** | **Debit** | **Credit** | **Debit** | **Credit** |
| 11 | Oct. 31 | Adjusting | | | | | |
| 12 | | | | | | | |
| 13 | | | | | | | |
| 14 | Account | Wages Expense | | | | Account No. | 52 |
| 15 | | | | | | **Balance** | |
| 16 | **Date** | **Item** | **Post. Ref.** | **Debit** | **Credit** | **Debit** | **Credit** |
| 17 | Oct. 15 | Payroll | | 13,800 | | 13,800 | |
| 18 | Oct. 31 | Adjusting | | | | | |
| 19 | | | | | | | |
| 20 | | | | | | | |

⏮ ◀ ▶ ⏭ \ J5 \ GL / \ Sheet3 /    ◀

d. When you have completed the journal entry and posted to the general ledger, perform a "save as," replacing the entire file name with the following:

*SA3-2_1e[your first name initial]_[your last name]*

---

### SA 3-3    ImagePress—Adjusting entries

Open the previously saved file, *SA2-1,2,3_1e[your first name initial]_[your last name]*. (Note: This is the file saved in Chapter 2.)

ImagePress Printing (from *SA2-1,2,3*) prepared an unadjusted trial balance for the end of ImagePress's first year of operations.

In addition, the following adjustments were assembled:

- Supplies on hand on April 30 were $600.
- Fees earned but unbilled on April 30 were $1,380.
- Depreciation of office equipment was estimated to be $4,250.
- Utility expenses accrued on April 30 were $900.

a. Journalize on the JE worksheet for ImagePress Printing the necessary adjusting entries on April 30.

b. Post adjustments to the GL worksheet for ImagePress Printing. Add accounts to the ledger for those adjustments requiring new accounts.

c. On the worksheet, labeled ATB (adjusted trial balance), use cell references to complete the adjusted trial balance.

d. When you have completed the adjustments, postings, and adjusted trial balance, perform a "save as," replacing the entire file name with the following:

*SA3-3_1e[your first name initial]_[your last name]*

# Completing the Accounting Cycle

## Electronic Arts Inc.

Most of us have had to file a personal tax return. At the beginning of the year, you estimate your upcoming income and decide whether you need to increase your payroll tax withholdings or perhaps pay estimated taxes. During the year, you earn income and enter into tax-related transactions, such as making charitable contributions. At the end of the year, your employer sends you a tax withholding information (W-2) form, and you collect the tax records needed for completing your yearly tax forms. As the next year begins, you start the cycle all over again.

Businesses also go through a cycle of activities. For example, **Electronic Arts Inc.**, the world's largest developer and marketer of electronic game software, begins its cycle by developing new or revised game titles, such as Madden NFL Football®, Need for Speed®, The Sims®, and The Lord of the Rings®. These games are marketed and sold throughout the year. During the year, operating transactions of the business are recorded. For Electronic Arts, such

transactions include the salaries of game developers, advertising expenditures, costs for producing and packaging games, and game revenues. At the end of the year, financial statements are prepared that summarize the operating activities for the year. Electronic Arts publishes these statements on its Web site at **http:// investor .ea.com**. Finally, before the start of the next year, the accounts are readied for recording the operations of the next year.

In Chapter 1, the initial cycle for NetSolutions began with Chris Clark's investment in the business on November 1, 2011. The cycle continued with recording NetSolutions' transactions for November and December, as we discussed and illustrated in Chapters 1 and 2. In Chapter 3, the cycle continued when the adjusting entries for the two months ending December 31, 2011, were recorded. In this chapter, the cycle is completed for NetSolutions by preparing financial statements and getting the accounts ready for recording transactions of the next period.

**OBJ. 1** Describe the flow of accounting information from the unadjusted trial balance into the adjusted trial balance and financial statements.

Many companies use Microsoft's Excel® software to prepare end-of-period spreadsheets.

# Flow of Accounting Information

The process of adjusting the accounts and preparing financial statements is one of the most important in accounting. Using the **NetSolutions** illustration from Chapters 1–3, the end-of-period spreadsheet and flow of accounting data in adjusting accounts and preparing financial statements are summarized in Exhibit 1.

The end-of-period spreadsheet in Exhibit 1 begins with the unadjusted trial balance. The unadjusted trial balance verifies that the total of the debit balances equals the total of the credit balances. If the trial balance totals are unequal, an error has occurred. Any errors must be found and corrected before the end-of-period process can continue.

The adjustments for NetSolutions from Chapter 3 are shown in the Adjustments columns of the spreadsheet. Cross-referencing (by letters) the debit and credit of each adjustment is useful in reviewing the effect of the adjustments on the unadjusted account balances. The adjustments are normally entered in the order in which the data are assembled. If the titles of the accounts to be adjusted do not appear in the unadjusted trial balance, the accounts are inserted in their proper order in the Account Title column. The total of the Adjustments columns verifies that the total debits equal the total credits for the adjusting entries. The total of the Debit column must equal the total of the Credit column.

The adjustments in the spreadsheet are added to or subtracted from the amounts in the Unadjusted Trial Balance columns to arrive at the amounts inserted in the Adjusted Trial Balance columns. In this way, the Adjusted Trial Balance columns of the spreadsheet illustrate the effect of the adjusting entries on the unadjusted accounts. The totals of the Adjusted Trial Balance columns verify that the totals of the debit and credit balances are equal after adjustment.

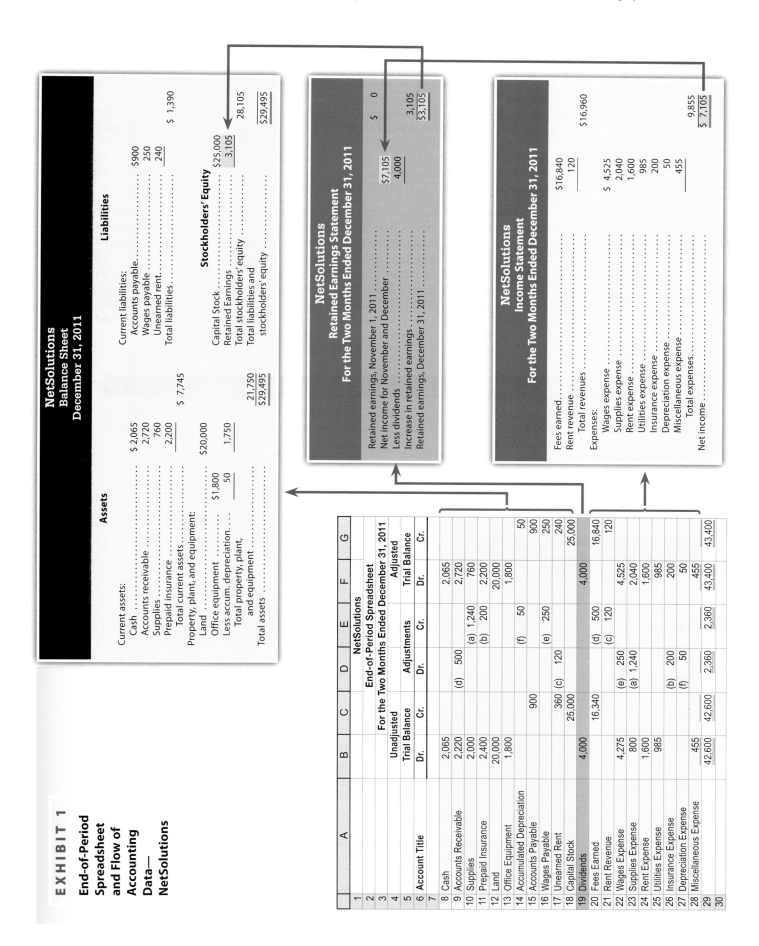

**EXHIBIT 1**

**End-of-Period Spreadsheet and Flow of Accounting Data—NetSolutions**

**NetSolutions**
**Balance Sheet**
**December 31, 2011**

**Assets**

| | | |
|---|---|---|
| Current assets: | | |
| Cash | | $ 2,065 |
| Accounts receivable | | 2,720 |
| Supplies | | 760 |
| Prepaid insurance | | 2,200 |
| Total current assets | | $ 7,745 |
| Property, plant, and equipment: | | |
| Land | | $20,000 |
| Office equipment | $1,800 | |
| Less accum. depreciation | 50 | 1,750 |
| Total property, plant, and equipment | | 21,750 |
| Total assets | | $29,495 |

**Liabilities**

| | | |
|---|---|---|
| Current liabilities: | | |
| Accounts payable | | $900 |
| Wages payable | | 250 |
| Unearned rent | | 240 |
| Total liabilities | | $ 1,390 |

**Stockholders' Equity**

| | | |
|---|---|---|
| Capital Stock | $25,000 | |
| Retained Earnings | 3,105 | |
| Total stockholders' equity | | 28,105 |
| Total liabilities and stockholders' equity | | $29,495 |

**NetSolutions**
**Retained Earnings Statement**
**For the Two Months Ended December 31, 2011**

| | | |
|---|---|---|
| Retained earnings, November 1, 2011 | | $ 0 |
| Net income for November and December | $7,105 | |
| Less dividends | 4,000 | |
| Increase in retained earnings | | 3,105 |
| Retained earnings, December 31, 2011 | | $3,105 |

**NetSolutions**
**Income Statement**
**For the Two Months Ended December 31, 2011**

| | | |
|---|---|---|
| Fees earned | | $16,840 |
| Rent revenue | | 120 |
| Total revenues | | $16,960 |
| Expenses: | | |
| Wages expense | $ 4,525 | |
| Supplies expense | 2,040 | |
| Rent expense | 1,600 | |
| Utilities expense | 985 | |
| Insurance expense | 200 | |
| Depreciation expense | 50 | |
| Miscellaneous expense | 455 | |
| Total expenses | | 9,855 |
| Net income | | $ 7,105 |

**NetSolutions**
**End-of-Period Spreadsheet**
**For the Two Months Ended December 31, 2011**

| | A | B C | D E | F G |
|---|---|---|---|---|
| | | Unadjusted Trial Balance | Adjustments | Adjusted Trial Balance |
| 6 | Account Title | Dr. | Cr. | Dr. | Cr. | Dr. | Cr. |
| 8 | Cash | 2,065 | | | | 2,065 | |
| 9 | Accounts Receivable | 2,220 | | (d) 500 | | 2,720 | |
| 10 | Supplies | 2,000 | | | (a) 1,240 | 760 | |
| 11 | Prepaid Insurance | 2,400 | | | (b) 200 | 2,200 | |
| 12 | Land | 20,000 | | | | 20,000 | |
| 13 | Office Equipment | 1,800 | | | | 1,800 | |
| 14 | Accumulated Depreciation | | | | (f) 50 | | 50 |
| 15 | Accounts Payable | | 900 | | | | 900 |
| 16 | Wages Payable | | | | (e) 250 | | 250 |
| 17 | Unearned Rent | | 360 | (c) 120 | | | 240 |
| 18 | Capital Stock | | 25,000 | | | | 25,000 |
| 19 | Dividends | 4,000 | | | | 4,000 | |
| 20 | Fees Earned | | 16,340 | | (d) 500 | | 16,840 |
| 21 | Rent Revenue | | | | (c) 120 | | 120 |
| 22 | Wages Expense | 4,275 | | (e) 250 | | 4,525 | |
| 23 | Supplies Expense | 800 | | (a) 1,240 | | 2,040 | |
| 24 | Rent Expense | 1,600 | | | | 1,600 | |
| 25 | Utilities Expense | 985 | | | | 985 | |
| 26 | Insurance Expense | | | (b) 200 | | 200 | |
| 27 | Depreciation Expense | | | (f) 50 | | 50 | |
| 28 | Miscellaneous Expense | 455 | | | | 455 | |
| 29 | | 42,600 | 42,600 | 2,360 | 2,360 | 43,400 | 43,400 |

Exhibit 1 also illustrates the flow of accounts from the adjusted trial balance into the financial statements as follows:

1. The revenue and expense accounts (spreadsheet lines 20–28) flow into the income statement.

2. The dividends account (spreadsheet line 19) flows into the retained earnings statement. The net income of $7,105 also flows into the retained earnings statement from the income statement.

3. The asset, liability, and capital stock accounts (spreadsheet lines 8–18) flow into the balance sheet. The end-of-the-period retained earnings of $3,105 also flows into the balance sheet from the retained earnings statement.

To summarize, Exhibit 1 illustrates the process by which accounts are adjusted. In addition, Exhibit 1 illustrates how the adjusted accounts flow into the financial statements. The financial statements for NetSolutions can be prepared directly from Exhibit 1.

The spreadsheet in Exhibit 1 is not required. However, many accountants prepare such a spreadsheet, sometimes called a work sheet, as part of the normal end-of-period process. The primary advantage in doing so is that it allows managers and accountants to see the effect of adjustments on the financial statements. This is especially useful for adjustments that depend upon estimates. Such estimates and their effect on the financial statements are discussed in later chapters.[1]

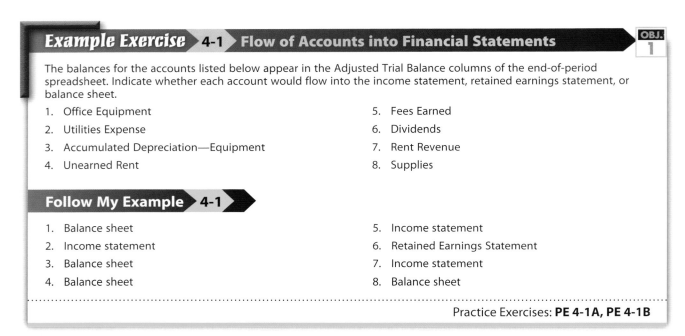

**Example Exercise** ▶ **4-1** ▶ **Flow of Accounts into Financial Statements**

OBJ. 1

The balances for the accounts listed below appear in the Adjusted Trial Balance columns of the end-of-period spreadsheet. Indicate whether each account would flow into the income statement, retained earnings statement, or balance sheet.

1. Office Equipment
2. Utilities Expense
3. Accumulated Depreciation—Equipment
4. Unearned Rent

5. Fees Earned
6. Dividends
7. Rent Revenue
8. Supplies

**Follow My Example** ▶ **4-1**

1. Balance sheet
2. Income statement
3. Balance sheet
4. Balance sheet

5. Income statement
6. Retained Earnings Statement
7. Income statement
8. Balance sheet

Practice Exercises: **PE 4-1A, PE 4-1B**

OBJ. **2** Prepare financial statements from adjusted account balances.

# Financial Statements

Using the adjusted trial balance shown in Exhibit 1, the financial statements for **NetSolutions** can be prepared. The income statement, the retained earnings statement, and the balance sheet are shown in Exhibit 2.

## Income Statement

The income statement is prepared directly from the Adjusted Trial Balance columns of the Exhibit 1 spreadsheet, beginning with fees earned of $16,840. The expenses in the income statement in Exhibit 2 are listed in order of size, beginning with the larger items. Miscellaneous expense is the last item, regardless of its amount.

1 The appendix to this chapter describes and illustrates how to prepare an end-of-period spreadsheet (work sheet) that includes financial statement columns.

**EXHIBIT 2**   **Financial Statements—NetSolutions**

### NetSolutions
### Income Statement
### For the Two Months Ended December 31, 2011

| | | |
|---|---:|---:|
| Fees earned............................................................ | $16,840 | |
| Rent revenue ......................................................... | 120 | |
|     Total revenues .................................................. | | $16,960 |
| Expenses: | | |
|     Wages expense................................................. | $ 4,525 | |
|     Supplies expense............................................... | 2,040 | |
|     Rent expense .................................................. | 1,600 | |
|     Utilities expense............................................... | 985 | |
|     Insurance expense.............................................. | 200 | |
|     Depreciation expense........................................... | 50 | |
|     Miscellaneous expense ......................................... | 455 | |
|        Total expenses ........................................... | | 9,855 |
| Net income ........................................................... | | $ 7,105 |

### NetSolutions
### Retained Earnings Statement
### For the Two Months Ended December 31, 2011

| | | |
|---|---:|---:|
| Retained earnings, November 1, 2011.................................. | | $  0 |
| Net income for November and December ............................... | $7,105 | |
| Less dividends ....................................................... | 4,000 | |
| Increase in retained earnings ........................................ | | 3,105 |
| Retained earnings, December 31, 2011................................. | | $3,105 |

### NetSolutions
### Balance Sheet
### December 31, 2011

| **Assets** | | | **Liabilities** | | |
|---|---:|---:|---|---:|---:|
| Current assets: | | | Current liabilities: | | |
|   Cash..................................... | $ 2,065 | |   Accounts payable.................... | $900 | |
|   Accounts receivable .................... | 2,720 | |   Wages payable ...................... | 250 | |
|   Supplies ............................... | 760 | |   Unearned rent....................... | 240 | |
|   Prepaid insurance ...................... | 2,200 | |   Total liabilities......................... | | $ 1,390 |
|     Total current assets................... | | $ 7,745 | | | |
| Property, plant, and equipment: | | | | | |
|   Land.................................... | $20,000 | | **Stockholders' Equity** | | |
|   Office equipment............ $1,800 | | | Capital stock........................... | $25,000 | |
|   Less accum. depreciation..... 50 | 1,750 | | Retained earnings..................... | 3,105 | |
|     Total property, plant, | | | Total stockholders' equity.............. | | 28,105 |
|     and equipment .................... | | 21,750 | Total liabilities and | | |
| Total assets.............................. | | $29,495 |   stockholders' equity................. | | $29,495 |

## Integrity, Objectivity, and Ethics in Business

**CEO'S HEALTH?**

How much and what information to disclose in financial statements and to investors presents a common ethical dilemma for managers and accountants. For example, Steve Jobs, co-founder and CEO of Apple Inc., has been diagnosed and treated for pancreatic cancer. Apple Inc., has insisted that the status of Steve Jobs's health is a "private" matter and does not have to be disclosed to investors. Apple maintains

this position even though Jobs is a driving force behind Apple's innovation and financial success.

In January 2009, however, in response to increasing investor concerns and speculation, Jobs released a letter to investors on his health. The letter indicated that his recent weight loss was due to a hormone imbalance and not due to the recurrence of cancer.

## Retained Earnings Statement

The first item normally presented on the retained earnings statement is the balance of the retained earnings account at the beginning of the period. Since NetSolutions began operations on November 1, this balance is zero in Exhibit 2. Then, the retained earnings statement shows the net income for the two months ended December 31, 2011. The amount of dividends is deducted from the net income to arrive at the retained earnings as of December 31, 2011.

For the following period, the beginning balance of retained earnings for NetSolutions is the ending balance that was reported for the previous period. For example, assume that during 2012, NetSolutions earned net income of $149,695 and paid dividends of $24,000. The retained earnings statement for the year ending December 31, 2012, for NetSolutions is as follows:

| NetSolutions Retained Earnings Statement For the Year Ended December 31, 2012 | | |
|---|---:|---:|
| Retained earnings, January 1, 2012 | | $ 3,105 |
| Net income for the year | $149,695 | |
| Less dividends | 24,000 | |
| Increase in retained earnings | | 125,695 |
| Retained earnings, December 31, 2012 | | $128,800 |

For NetSolutions, the amount of dividends was less than the net income. If the dividends had exceeded the net income, the order of the net income and the dividends would have been reversed. The difference between the two items would then be deducted from the beginning Retained Earnings balance. Other factors, such as a net loss, may also require some change in the form of the retained earnings statement, as shown in the following example:

| | | |
|---|---:|---:|
| Retained earnings, January 1, 20— | | $45,000 |
| Net loss for the year | $5,600 | |
| Dividends | 9,500 | |
| Decrease in retained earnings | | 15,100 |
| Retained earnings, December 31, 20— | | $29,900 |

## Example Exercise 4-2 Retained Earnings Statement

OBJ. 2

Zack Gaddis owns and operates Gaddis Employment Services. On January 1, 2011, Retained Earnings had a balance of $186,000. During the year, Zack invested an additional $40,000 in the business in exchange for capital stock. In addition, dividends of $25,000 were paid during the year. For the year ended December 31, 2011, Gaddis Employment Services reported a net income of $18,750. Prepare a retained earnings statement for the year ended December 31, 2011.

*(continued)*

**Follow My Example 4-2**

**Gaddis Employment Services**
**Retained Earnings Statement**
**For the Year Ended December 31, 2011**

| | | |
|---|---|---|
| Retained earnings, January 1, 2011 | | $186,000 |
| Dividends | $25,000 | |
| Less net income | 18,750 | |
| Decrease in retained earnings | | 6,250 |
| Retained earnings, December 31, 2011 | | $179,750 |

Practice Exercises: **PE 4-2A, PE 4-2B**

## Balance Sheet

The balance sheet is prepared directly from the Adjusted Trial Balance columns of the Exhibit 1 spreadsheet, beginning with Cash of $2,065. The asset, liability, and capital stock amounts are taken from the spreadsheet. The retained earnings amount, however, is taken from the retained earnings statement, as illustrated in Exhibit 2.

The balance sheet in Exhibit 2 shows subsections for assets and liabilities. Such a balance sheet is a *classified balance sheet*. These subsections are described next.

**Assets** Assets are commonly divided into two sections on the balance sheet: (1) current assets and (2) property, plant, and equipment.

*Current Assets* Cash and other assets that are expected to be converted to cash or sold or used up usually within one year or less, through the normal operations of the business, are called **current assets**. In addition to cash, the current assets may include notes receivable, accounts receivable, supplies, and other prepaid expenses.

**Notes receivable** are amounts that customers owe. They are written promises to pay the amount of the note and interest. Accounts receivable are also amounts customers owe, but they are less formal than notes. Accounts receivable normally result from providing services or selling merchandise on account. Notes receivable and accounts receivable are current assets because they are usually converted to cash within one year or less.

*Property, Plant, and Equipment* The property, plant, and equipment section may also be described as **fixed assets** or **plant assets**. These assets include equipment, machinery, buildings, and land. With the exception of land, as discussed in Chapter 3, fixed assets depreciate over a period of time. The original cost, accumulated depreciation, and book value of each major type of fixed asset are normally reported on the balance sheet or in the notes to the financial statements.

**Liabilities** Liabilities are the amounts the business owes to creditors. Liabilities are commonly divided into two sections on the balance sheet: (1) current liabilities and (2) long-term liabilities.

*Current Liabilities* Liabilities that will be due within a short time (usually one year or less) and that are to be paid out of current assets are called **current liabilities**. The most common liabilities in this group are notes payable and accounts payable. Other current liabilities may include Wages Payable, Interest Payable, Taxes Payable, and Unearned Fees.

*Long-Term Liabilities* Liabilities that will not be due for a long time (usually more than one year) are called **long-term liabilities**. If NetSolutions had long-term liabilities, they would be reported below the current liabilities. As long-term liabilities come due and are to be paid within one year, they are reported as current liabilities. If they are to be renewed rather than paid, they would continue to be reported as long term. When an asset is pledged as security for a liability, the obligation may be called a *mortgage note payable* or a *mortgage payable*.

**Note:**
Two common classes of assets are current assets and property, plant, and equipment.

**Note:**
Two common classes of liabilities are current liabilities and long-term liabilities.

**Stockholders' Equity** The stockholders' right to the assets of the business is presented on the balance sheet below the liabilities section. The stockholders' equity consists of capital stock and retained earnings. The stockholders' equity is added to the total liabilities, and this total must be equal to the total assets.

**Example Exercise** ▶ **4-3** ▶ **Classified Balance Sheet**                                         OBJ. 2

The following accounts appear in an adjusted trial balance of Hindsight Consulting. Indicate whether each account would be reported in the (a) current asset; (b) property, plant, and equipment; (c) current liability; (d) long-term liability; or (e) stockholders' equity section of the December 31, 2011, balance sheet of Hindsight Consulting.

1. Capital Stock
2. Notes Receivable (due in 6 months)
3. Notes Payable (due in 2013)
4. Land

5. Cash
6. Unearned Rent (3 months)
7. Accumulated Depreciation—Equipment
8. Accounts Payable

**Follow My Example** ▶ **4-3** ▶

1. Stockholders' equity
2. Current asset
3. Long-term liability
4. Property, plant, and equipment

5. Current asset
6. Current liability
7. Property, plant, and equipment
8. Current liability

Practice Exercises: **PE 4-3A, PE 4-3B**

 **IFRS**

# InternationalConnection

## INTERNATIONAL DIFFERENCES

Financial statements prepared under accounting practices in other countries often differ from those prepared under generally accepted accounting principles in the United States. This is to be expected, since cultures and market structures differ from country to country.

To illustrate, BMW Group prepares its financial statements under International Financial Reporting Standards as adopted by the European Union. In doing so, BMW's balance sheet reports fixed assets first, followed by current assets. It also reports stockholders' equity before the liabilities. In contrast, balance sheets prepared under U.S. accounting principles report current assets followed by fixed assets

and current liabilities followed by long-term liabilities and stockholders' equity. The U.S. form of balance sheet is organized to emphasize creditor interpretation and analysis. For example, current assets and current liabilities are presented first to facilitate their interpretation and analysis by creditors. Likewise, to emphasize their importance, liabilities are reported before stockholders' equity.*

Regardless of these differences, the basic principles underlying the accounting equation and the double-entry accounting system are the same in Germany and the United States. Even though differences in recording and reporting exist, the accounting equation holds true: the total assets still equal the total liabilities and stockholders' equity.

*Examples of U.S. and IFRS financial statement reporting differences are further discussed and illustrated in Appendix E.

OBJ. 3 Prepare closing entries.

# Closing Entries

As discussed in Chapter 3, the adjusting entries are recorded in the journal at the end of the accounting period. For NetSolutions, the adjusting entries are shown in Exhibit 9 of Chapter 3.

After the adjusting entries are posted to NetSolutions' ledger, shown in Exhibit 6 (on pages 162–163), the ledger agrees with the data reported on the financial statements.

The balances of the accounts reported on the balance sheet are carried forward from year to year. Because they are relatively permanent, these accounts are called **permanent accounts** or **real accounts**. For example, Cash, Accounts Receivable, Equipment, Accumulated Depreciation, Accounts Payable, Capital Stock, and Retained Earnings are permanent accounts.

The balances of the accounts reported on the income statement are not carried forward from year to year. Also, the balance of the dividends account, which is reported on the retained earnings statement, is not carried forward. Because these accounts report amounts for only one period, they are called **temporary accounts** or **nominal accounts**. Temporary accounts are not carried forward because they relate only to one period. For example, the Fees Earned of $16,840 and Wages Expense of $4,525 for NetSolutions shown in Exhibit 2 are for the two months ending December 31, 2011, and should not be carried forward to 2012.

At the beginning of the next period, temporary accounts should have zero balances. To achieve this, temporary account balances are transferred to permanent accounts at the end of the accounting period. The entries that transfer these balances are called **closing entries**. The transfer process is called the **closing process** and is sometimes referred to as **closing the books**.

The closing process involves the following four steps:

1. Revenue account balances are transferred to an account called Income Summary.
2. Expense account balances are transferred to an account called Income Summary.
3. The balance of Income Summary (net income or net loss) is transferred to the retained earnings account.
4. The balance of the dividends account is transferred to the retained earnings account.

Exhibit 3 diagrams the closing process.

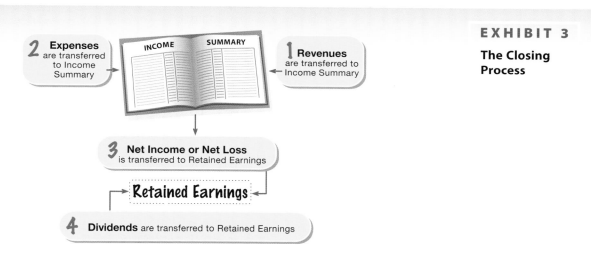

**EXHIBIT 3**

**The Closing Process**

**Income Summary** is a temporary account that is only used during the closing process. At the beginning of the closing process, Income Summary has no balance. During the closing process, Income Summary will be debited and credited for various amounts. At the end of the closing process, Income Summary will again have no balance. Because Income Summary has the effect of clearing the revenue and expense accounts of their balances, it is sometimes called a **clearing account**. Other titles used for this account include Revenue and Expense Summary, Profit and Loss Summary, and Income and Expense Summary.

The four closing entries required in the closing process are as follows:

1. Debit each revenue account for its balance and credit Income Summary for the total revenue.
2. Credit each expense account for its balance and debit Income Summary for the total expenses.
3. Debit Income Summary for its balance and credit the retained earnings account.
4. Debit the retained earnings account for the balance of the dividends account and credit the dividends account.

**Note:**
The income summary account does not appear on the financial statements.

**Note:**
Closing entries transfer the balances of temporary accounts to the retained earnings account.

In the case of a net loss, Income Summary will have a debit balance after the first two closing entries. In this case, credit Income Summary for the amount of its balance and debit the retained earnings account for the amount of the net loss.

Closing entries are recorded in the journal and are dated as of the last day of the accounting period. In the journal, closing entries are recorded immediately following the adjusting entries. The caption, *Closing Entries*, is often inserted above the closing entries to separate them from the adjusting entries.

It is possible to close the temporary revenue and expense accounts without using a clearing account such as Income Summary. In this case, the balances of the revenue and expense accounts are closed directly to the retained earnings account. This process may be used in a computerized accounting system.

## Journalizing and Posting Closing Entries

A flowchart of the four closing entries for NetSolutions is shown in Exhibit 4. The balances in the accounts are those shown in the Adjusted Trial Balance columns of the end-of-period spreadsheet shown in Exhibit 1.

**EXHIBIT 4** **Flowchart of Closing Entries for NetSolutions**

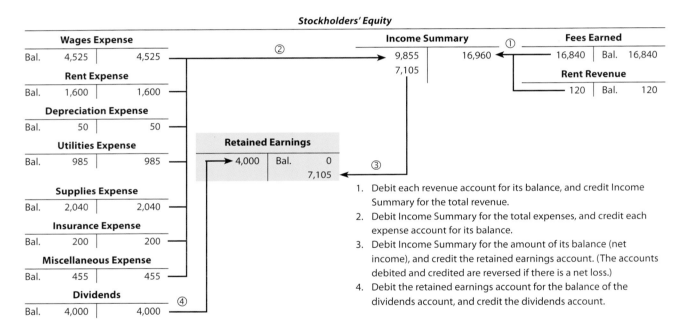

The closing entries for NetSolutions are shown in Exhibit 5. The account titles and balances for these entries may be obtained from the end-of-period spreadsheet, the adjusted trial balance, the income statement, the retained earnings statement, or the ledger.

The closing entries are posted to NetSolutions' ledger as shown in Exhibit 6 (pages 162–163). Income Summary has been added to NetSolutions' ledger in Exhibit 6 as account number 34. After the closing entries are posted, NetSolutions' ledger has the following characteristics:

1. The balance of Retained Earnings of $3,105 agrees with the amount reported on the retained earnings statement and the balance sheet.
2. The revenue, expense, and dividends accounts will have zero balances.

As shown in Exhibit 6, the closing entries are normally identified in the ledger as "Closing." In addition, a line is often inserted in both balance columns after a closing entry is posted. This separates the next period's revenue, expense, and dividend transactions from those of the current period. The next period's transactions will be posted directly below the closing entry.

**EXHIBIT 5**

**Closing Entries— NetSolutions**

| Journal | | | | | Page 6 |
|---|---|---|---|---|---|
| **Date** | | **Description** | **Post. Ref.** | **Debit** | **Credit** |
| 2011 | | Closing Entries | | | |
| Dec. | 31 | Fees Earned | 41 | 16,840 | |
| | | Rent Revenue | 42 | 120 | |
| | |    Income Summary | 34 | | 16,960 |
| | | | | | |
| | 31 | Income Summary | 34 | 9,855 | |
| | |    Wages Expense | 51 | | 4,525 |
| | |    Rent Expense | 52 | | 1,600 |
| | |    Depreciation Expense | 53 | | 50 |
| | |    Utilities Expense | 54 | | 985 |
| | |    Supplies Expense | 55 | | 2,040 |
| | |    Insurance Expense | 56 | | 200 |
| | |    Miscellaneous Expense | 59 | | 455 |
| | | | | | |
| | 31 | Income Summary | 34 | 7,105 | |
| | |    Retained Earnings | 32 | | 7,105 |
| | | | | | |
| | 31 | Retained Earnings | 32 | 4,000 | |
| | |    Dividends | 33 | | 4,000 |

## Example Exercise 4-4   Closing Entries

**OBJ. 3**

After the accounts have been adjusted at July 31, the end of the fiscal year, the following balances are taken from the ledger of Cabriolet Services Co.:

| | |
|---|---|
| Retained Earnings | $615,850 |
| Dividends | 25,000 |
| Fees Earned | 380,450 |
| Wages Expense | 250,000 |
| Rent Expense | 65,000 |
| Supplies Expense | 18,250 |
| Miscellaneous Expense | 6,200 |

Journalize the four entries required to close the accounts.

## Follow My Example 4-4

| | | | | |
|---|---|---|---|---|
| July | 31 | Fees Earned | 380,450 | |
| | |    Income Summary | | 380,450 |
| | | | | |
| | 31 | Income Summary | 339,450 | |
| | |    Wages Expense | | 250,000 |
| | |    Rent Expense | | 65,000 |
| | |    Supplies Expense | | 18,250 |
| | |    Miscellaneous Expense | | 6,200 |
| | | | | |
| | 31 | Income Summary | 41,000 | |
| | |    Retained Earnings | | 41,000 |
| | | | | |
| | 31 | Retained Earnings | 25,000 | |
| | |    Dividends | | 25,000 |

Practice Exercises: **PE 4-4A, PE 4-4B**

## EXHIBIT 6   Ledger—NetSolutions

### Account Cash                                    Account No. 11

| Date | Item | Post. Ref. | Debit | Credit | Balance Debit | Balance Credit |
|------|------|-----------|-------|--------|-------|--------|
| 2011 | | | | | | |
| Nov. 1 | | 1 | 25,000 | | 25,000 | |
| 5 | | 1 | | 20,000 | 5,000 | |
| 18 | | 1 | 7,500 | | 12,500 | |
| 30 | | 1 | | 3,650 | 8,850 | |
| 30 | | 1 | | 950 | 7,900 | |
| 30 | | 2 | | 2,000 | 5,900 | |
| Dec. 1 | | 2 | | 2,400 | 3,500 | |
| 1 | | 2 | | 800 | 2,700 | |
| 1 | | 2 | 360 | | 3,060 | |
| 6 | | 2 | | 180 | 2,880 | |
| 11 | | 2 | | 400 | 2,480 | |
| 13 | | 3 | | 950 | 1,530 | |
| 16 | | 3 | 3,100 | | 4,630 | |
| 20 | | 3 | | 900 | 3,730 | |
| 21 | | 3 | 650 | | 4,380 | |
| 23 | | 3 | | 1,450 | 2,930 | |
| 27 | | 3 | | 1,200 | 1,730 | |
| 31 | | 3 | | 310 | 1,420 | |
| 31 | | 4 | | 225 | 1,195 | |
| 31 | | 4 | 2,870 | | 4,065 | |
| 31 | | 4 | | 2,000 | 2,065 | |

### Account Accounts Receivable                     Account No. 12

| Date | Item | Post. Ref. | Debit | Credit | Balance Debit | Balance Credit |
|------|------|-----------|-------|--------|-------|--------|
| 2011 | | | | | | |
| Dec. 16 | | 3 | 1,750 | | 1,750 | |
| 21 | | 3 | | 650 | 1,100 | |
| 31 | | 4 | 1,120 | | 2,220 | |
| 31 | Adjusting | 5 | 500 | | 2,720 | |

### Account Supplies                                Account No. 14

| Date | Item | Post. Ref. | Debit | Credit | Balance Debit | Balance Credit |
|------|------|-----------|-------|--------|-------|--------|
| 2011 | | | | | | |
| Nov. 10 | | 1 | 1,350 | | 1,350 | |
| 30 | | 1 | | 800 | 550 | |
| Dec. 23 | | 3 | 1,450 | | 2,000 | |
| 31 | Adjusting | 5 | | 1,240 | 760 | |

### Account Prepaid Insurance                       Account No. 15

| Date | Item | Post. Ref. | Debit | Credit | Balance Debit | Balance Credit |
|------|------|-----------|-------|--------|-------|--------|
| 2011 | | | | | | |
| Dec. 1 | | 2 | 2,400 | | 2,400 | |
| 31 | Adjusting | 5 | | 200 | 2,200 | |

### Account Land                                    Account No. 17

| Date | Item | Post. Ref. | Debit | Credit | Balance Debit | Balance Credit |
|------|------|-----------|-------|--------|-------|--------|
| 2011 | | | | | | |
| Nov. 5 | | 1 | 20,000 | | 20,000 | |

### Account Office Equipment                        Account No. 18

| Date | Item | Post. Ref. | Debit | Credit | Balance Debit | Balance Credit |
|------|------|-----------|-------|--------|-------|--------|
| 2011 | | | | | | |
| Dec. 4 | | 2 | 1,800 | | 1,800 | |

### Account Accumulated Depreciation                Account No. 19

| Date | Item | Post. Ref. | Debit | Credit | Balance Debit | Balance Credit |
|------|------|-----------|-------|--------|-------|--------|
| 2011 | | | | | | |
| Dec. 31 | Adjusting | 5 | | 50 | | 50 |

### Account Accounts Payable                        Account No. 21

| Date | Item | Post. Ref. | Debit | Credit | Balance Debit | Balance Credit |
|------|------|-----------|-------|--------|-------|--------|
| 2011 | | | | | | |
| Nov. 10 | | 1 | | 1,350 | | 1,350 |
| 30 | | 1 | 950 | | | 400 |
| Dec. 4 | | 2 | | 1,800 | | 2,200 |
| 11 | | 2 | 400 | | | 1,800 |
| 20 | | 3 | 900 | | | 900 |

### Account Wages Payable                           Account No. 22

| Date | Item | Post. Ref. | Debit | Credit | Balance Debit | Balance Credit |
|------|------|-----------|-------|--------|-------|--------|
| 2011 | | | | | | |
| Dec. 31 | Adjusting | 5 | | 250 | | 250 |

### Account Unearned Rent                           Account No. 23

| Date | Item | Post. Ref. | Debit | Credit | Balance Debit | Balance Credit |
|------|------|-----------|-------|--------|-------|--------|
| 2011 | | | | | | |
| Dec. 1 | | 2 | | 360 | | 360 |
| 31 | Adjusting | 5 | 120 | | | 240 |

### Account Capital Stock                           Account No. 31

| Date | Item | Post. Ref. | Debit | Credit | Balance Debit | Balance Credit |
|------|------|-----------|-------|--------|-------|--------|
| 2011 | | | | | | |
| Nov. 1 | | 1 | | 25,000 | | 25,000 |

### Account Retained Earnings                        Account No. 32

| Date | Item | Post. Ref. | Debit | Credit | Balance Debit | Balance Credit |
|------|------|-----------|-------|--------|-------|--------|
| 2011 | | | | | | |
| Dec. 31 | Closing | 6 | | 7,105 | | 7,105 |
| 31 | Closing | 6 | 4,000 | | | 3,105 |

**EXHIBIT 6**   Ledger—NetSolutions (*concluded*)

**Account** *Dividends* — Account No. 33

| Date | Item | Post. Ref. | Debit | Credit | Balance Debit | Balance Credit |
|---|---|---|---|---|---|---|
| 2011 | | | | | | |
| Nov. 30 | | 2 | 2,000 | | 2,000 | |
| Dec. 31 | | 4 | 2,000 | | 4,000 | |
| 31 | Closing | 6 | | 4,000 | — | — |

**Account** *Income Summary* — Account No. 34

| Date | Item | Post. Ref. | Debit | Credit | Balance Debit | Balance Credit |
|---|---|---|---|---|---|---|
| 2011 | | | | | | |
| Dec. 31 | Closing | 6 | | 16,960 | | 16,960 |
| 31 | Closing | 6 | 9,855 | | | 7,105 |
| 31 | Closing | 6 | 7,105 | | — | |

**Account** *Fees Earned* — Account No. 41

| Date | Item | Post. Ref. | Debit | Credit | Balance Debit | Balance Credit |
|---|---|---|---|---|---|---|
| 2011 | | | | | | |
| Nov. 18 | | 1 | | 7,500 | | 7,500 |
| Dec. 16 | | 3 | | 3,100 | | 10,600 |
| 16 | | 3 | | 1,750 | | 12,350 |
| 31 | | 4 | | 2,870 | | 15,220 |
| 31 | | 4 | | 1,120 | | 16,340 |
| 31 | Adjusting | 5 | | 500 | | 16,840 |
| 31 | Closing | 6 | 16,840 | | — | — |

**Account** *Rent Revenue* — Account No. 42

| Date | Item | Post. Ref. | Debit | Credit | Balance Debit | Balance Credit |
|---|---|---|---|---|---|---|
| 2011 | | | | | | |
| Dec. 31 | Adjusting | 5 | | 120 | | 120 |
| 31 | Closing | 6 | 120 | | — | — |

**Account** *Wages Expense* — Account No. 51

| Date | Item | Post. Ref. | Debit | Credit | Balance Debit | Balance Credit |
|---|---|---|---|---|---|---|
| 2011 | | | | | | |
| Nov. 30 | | 1 | 2,125 | | 2,125 | |
| Dec. 13 | | 3 | 950 | | 3,075 | |
| 27 | | 3 | 1,200 | | 4,275 | |
| 31 | Adjusting | 5 | 250 | | 4,525 | |
| 31 | Closing | 6 | | 4,525 | — | — |

**Account** *Rent Expense* — Account No. 52

| Date | Item | Post. Ref. | Debit | Credit | Balance Debit | Balance Credit |
|---|---|---|---|---|---|---|
| 2011 | | | | | | |
| Nov. 30 | | 1 | 800 | | 800 | |
| Dec. 1 | | 2 | 800 | | 1,600 | |
| 31 | Closing | 6 | | 1,600 | — | — |

**Account** *Depreciation Expense* — Account No. 53

| Date | Item | Post. Ref. | Debit | Credit | Balance Debit | Balance Credit |
|---|---|---|---|---|---|---|
| 2011 | | | | | | |
| Dec. 31 | Adjusting | 5 | 50 | | 50 | |
| 31 | Closing | 6 | | 50 | — | — |

**Account** *Utilities Expense* — Account No. 54

| Date | Item | Post. Ref. | Debit | Credit | Balance Debit | Balance Credit |
|---|---|---|---|---|---|---|
| 2011 | | | | | | |
| Nov. 30 | | 1 | 450 | | 450 | |
| Dec. 31 | | 3 | 310 | | 760 | |
| 31 | | 4 | 225 | | 985 | |
| 31 | Closing | 6 | | 985 | — | — |

**Account** *Supplies Expense* — Account No. 55

| Date | Item | Post. Ref. | Debit | Credit | Balance Debit | Balance Credit |
|---|---|---|---|---|---|---|
| 2011 | | | | | | |
| Nov. 30 | | 1 | 800 | | 800 | |
| Dec. 31 | Adjusting | 5 | 1,240 | | 2,040 | |
| 31 | Closing | 6 | | 2,040 | — | — |

**Account** *Insurance Expense* — Account No. 56

| Date | Item | Post. Ref. | Debit | Credit | Balance Debit | Balance Credit |
|---|---|---|---|---|---|---|
| 2011 | | | | | | |
| Dec. 31 | Adjusting | 5 | 200 | | 200 | |
| 31 | Closing | 6 | | 200 | — | — |

**Account** *Miscellaneous Expense* — Account No. 59

| Date | Item | Post. Ref. | Debit | Credit | Balance Debit | Balance Credit |
|---|---|---|---|---|---|---|
| 2011 | | | | | | |
| Nov. 30 | | 1 | 275 | | 275 | |
| Dec. 6 | | 2 | 180 | | 455 | |
| 31 | Closing | 6 | | 455 | — | — |

## Post-Closing Trial Balance

A post-closing trial balance is prepared after the closing entries have been posted. The purpose of the post-closing (after closing) trial balance is to verify that the ledger is in balance at the beginning of the next period. The accounts and amounts should agree exactly with the accounts and amounts listed on the balance sheet at the end of the period. The post-closing trial balance for NetSolutions is shown in Exhibit 7.

**EXHIBIT 7**

**Post-Closing Trial Balance— NetSolutions**

| NetSolutions<br>Post-Closing Trial Balance<br>December 31, 2011 | | |
|---|---|---|
| | Debit<br>Balances | Credit<br>Balances |
| Cash........................................................ | 2,065 | |
| Accounts Receivable ...................................... | 2,720 | |
| Supplies ................................................... | 760 | |
| Prepaid Insurance......................................... | 2,200 | |
| Land........................................................ | 20,000 | |
| Office Equipment ......................................... | 1,800 | |
| Accumulated Depreciation............................... | | 50 |
| Accounts Payable ......................................... | | 900 |
| Wages Payable............................................. | | 250 |
| Unearned Rent ............................................ | | 240 |
| Capital Stock.............................................. | | 25,000 |
| Retained Earnings........................................ | | 3,105 |
| | 29,545 | 29,545 |

**4**
Describe the accounting cycle.

# Accounting Cycle

The accounting process that begins with analyzing and journalizing transactions and ends with the post-closing trial balance is called the **accounting cycle**. The steps in the accounting cycle are as follows:

1. Transactions are analyzed and recorded in the journal.
2. Transactions are posted to the ledger.
3. An unadjusted trial balance is prepared.
4. Adjustment data are assembled and analyzed.
5. An optional end-of-period spreadsheet is prepared.
6. Adjusting entries are journalized and posted to the ledger.
7. An adjusted trial balance is prepared.
8. Financial statements are prepared.
9. Closing entries are journalized and posted to the ledger.
10. A post-closing trial balance is prepared.[2]

**Example Exercise** ▶ **4-5** ▶ **Accounting Cycle**   **OBJ. 4**

From the following list of steps in the accounting cycle, identify what two steps are missing.
a. Transactions are analyzed and recorded in the journal.
b. Transactions are posted to the ledger.
c. Adjustment data are assembled and analyzed.
d. An optional end-of-period spreadsheet is prepared.
e. Adjusting entries are journalized and posted to the ledger.
f. Financial statements are prepared.
g. Closing entries are journalized and posted to the ledger.
h. A post-closing trial balance is prepared.

*(continued)*

**Follow My Example 4-5**

The following two steps are missing: (1) the preparation of an unadjusted trial balance and (2) the preparation of the adjusted trial balance. The unadjusted trial balance should be prepared after step (b). The adjusted trial balance should be prepared after step (e).

Practice Exercises: **PE 4-5A, PE 4-5B**

Exhibit 8 illustrates the accounting cycle in graphic form. It also illustrates how the accounting cycle begins with the source documents for a transaction and flows through the accounting system and into the financial statements.

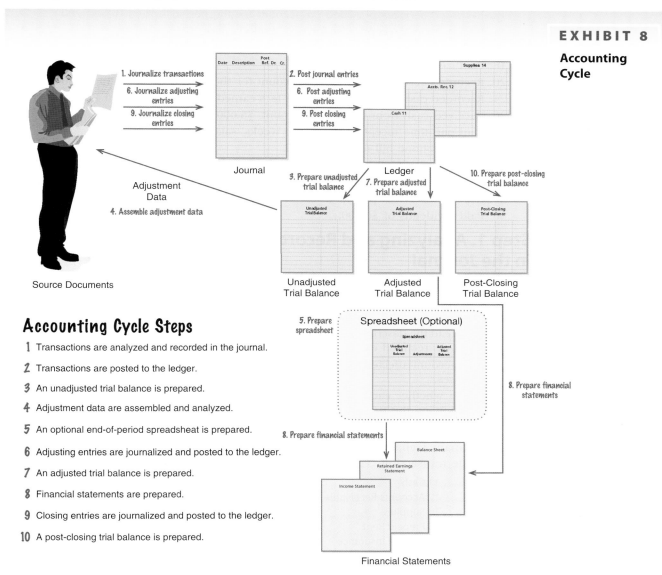

**EXHIBIT 8**

**Accounting Cycle**

## Accounting Cycle Steps

1 Transactions are analyzed and recorded in the journal.

2 Transactions are posted to the ledger.

3 An unadjusted trial balance is prepared.

4 Adjustment data are assembled and analyzed.

5 An optional end-of-period spreadsheet is prepared.

6 Adjusting entries are journalized and posted to the ledger.

7 An adjusted trial balance is prepared.

8 Financial statements are prepared.

9 Closing entries are journalized and posted to the ledger.

10 A post-closing trial balance is prepared.

# Illustration of the Accounting Cycle

**OBJ. 5** Illustrate the accounting cycle for one period.

In this section, the complete accounting cycle for one period is illustrated. Assume that for several years Kelly Pitney has operated a part-time consulting business from her home. As of April 1, 2012, Kelly decided to move to rented quarters and to operate the business on a full-time basis as a professional corporation. The business will be known as Kelly Consulting, P.C. During April, Kelly Consulting entered into the following transactions:

2 Some accountants include the journalizing and posting of "reversing entries" as the last step in the accounting cycle. Because reversing entries are not required, they are described and illustrated in Appendix B at the end of the book.

Apr. 1. The following assets were received from Kelly Pitney in exchange for capital stock: cash, $13,100; accounts receivable, $3,000; supplies, $1,400; and office equipment, $12,500. There were no liabilities received.

1. Paid three months' rent on a lease rental contract, $4,800.

2. Paid the premiums on property and casualty insurance policies, $1,800.

4. Received cash from clients as an advance payment for services to be provided and recorded it as unearned fees, $5,000.

5. Purchased additional office equipment on account from Office Station Co., $2,000.

6. Received cash from clients on account, $1,800.

10. Paid cash for a newspaper advertisement, $120.

12. Paid Office Station Co. for part of the debt incurred on April 5, $1,200.

12. Recorded services provided on account for the period April 1–12, $4,200.

14. Paid part-time receptionist for two weeks' salary, $750.

17. Recorded cash from cash clients for fees earned during the period April 1–16, $6,250.

18. Paid cash for supplies, $800.

20. Recorded services provided on account for the period April 13–20, $2,100.

24. Recorded cash from cash clients for fees earned for the period April 17–24, $3,850.

26. Received cash from clients on account, $5,600.

27. Paid part-time receptionist for two weeks' salary, $750.

29. Paid telephone bill for April, $130.

30. Paid electricity bill for April, $200.

30. Recorded cash from cash clients for fees earned for the period April 25–30, $3,050.

30. Recorded services provided on account for the remainder of April, $1,500.

30. Paid dividends of $6,000.

## Step 1. Analyzing and Recording Transactions in the Journal

The first step in the accounting cycle is to analyze and record transactions in the journal using the double-entry accounting system. As illustrated in Chapter 2, transactions are analyzed and journalized using the following steps:

1. Carefully read the description of the transaction to determine whether an asset, liability, capital stock, retained earnings, revenue, expense, or dividends account is affected.

2. For each account affected by the transaction, determine whether the account increases or decreases.

3. Determine whether each increase or decrease should be recorded as a debit or a credit, following the rules of debit and credit shown in Exhibit 3 of Chapter 2.

4. Record the transaction using a journal entry.

The company's chart of accounts is useful in determining which accounts are affected by the transaction. The chart of accounts for Kelly Consulting is as follows:

| | |
|---|---|
| 11 Cash | 32 Retained Earnings |
| 12 Accounts Receivable | 33 Dividends |
| 14 Supplies | 34 Income Summary |
| 15 Prepaid Rent | 41 Fees Earned |
| 16 Prepaid Insurance | 51 Salary Expense |
| 18 Office Equipment | 52 Rent Expense |
| 19 Accumulated Depreciation | 53 Supplies Expense |
| 21 Accounts Payable | 54 Depreciation Expense |
| 22 Salaries Payable | 55 Insurance Expense |
| 23 Unearned Fees | 59 Miscellaneous Expense |
| 31 Capital Stock | |

After analyzing each of Kelly Consulting's transactions for April, the journal entries are recorded as shown in Exhibit 9.

## Step 2. Posting Transactions to the Ledger

Periodically, the transactions recorded in the journal are posted to the accounts in the ledger. The debits and credits for each journal entry are posted to the accounts in the

**EXHIBIT 9**

**Journal Entries for April—Kelly Consulting**

| Date | | Description | Post. Ref. | Debit | Credit |
|---|---|---|---|---|---|
| **Journal** | | | | | Page 1 |
| 2012 Apr. | 1 | Cash | 11 | 13,100 | |
| | | Accounts Receivable | 12 | 3,000 | |
| | | Supplies | 14 | 1,400 | |
| | | Office Equipment | 18 | 12,500 | |
| | | Capital Stock | 31 | | 30,000 |
| | 1 | Prepaid Rent | 15 | 4,800 | |
| | | Cash | 11 | | 4,800 |
| | 2 | Prepaid Insurance | 16 | 1,800 | |
| | | Cash | 11 | | 1,800 |
| | 4 | Cash | 11 | 5,000 | |
| | | Unearned Fees | 23 | | 5,000 |
| | 5 | Office Equipment | 18 | 2,000 | |
| | | Accounts Payable | 21 | | 2,000 |
| | 6 | Cash | 11 | 1,800 | |
| | | Accounts Receivable | 12 | | 1,800 |
| | 10 | Miscellaneous Expense | 59 | 120 | |
| | | Cash | 11 | | 120 |
| | 12 | Accounts Payable | 21 | 1,200 | |
| | | Cash | 11 | | 1,200 |
| | 12 | Accounts Receivable | 12 | 4,200 | |
| | | Fees Earned | 41 | | 4,200 |
| | 14 | Salary Expense | 51 | 750 | |
| | | Cash | 11 | | 750 |

| Date | | Description | Post. Ref. | Debit | Credit |
|---|---|---|---|---|---|
| **Journal** | | | | | Page 2 |
| 2012 Apr. | 17 | Cash | 11 | 6,250 | |
| | | Fees Earned | 41 | | 6,250 |
| | 18 | Supplies | 14 | 800 | |
| | | Cash | 11 | | 800 |
| | 20 | Accounts Receivable | 12 | 2,100 | |
| | | Fees Earned | 41 | | 2,100 |
| | 24 | Cash | 11 | 3,850 | |
| | | Fees Earned | 41 | | 3,850 |
| | 26 | Cash | 11 | 5,600 | |
| | | Accounts Receivable | 12 | | 5,600 |
| | 27 | Salary Expense | 51 | 750 | |
| | | Cash | 11 | | 750 |
| | 29 | Miscellaneous Expense | 59 | 130 | |
| | | Cash | 11 | | 130 |

*(continued)*

| Journal | | | | | Page 2 |
|---|---|---|---|---|---|
| **Date** | | **Description** | **Post. Ref.** | **Debit** | **Credit** |
| 2012 Apr. | 30 | Miscellaneous Expense | 59 | 200 | |
| | | Cash | 11 | | 200 |
| | 30 | Cash | 11 | 3,050 | |
| | | Fees Earned | 41 | | 3,050 |
| | 30 | Accounts Receivable | 12 | 1,500 | |
| | | Fees Earned | 41 | | 1,500 |
| | 30 | Dividends | 33 | 6,000 | |
| | | Cash | 11 | | 6,000 |

order in which they occur in the journal. As illustrated in Chapters 2 and 3, journal entries are posted to the accounts using the following four steps:

1. The date is entered in the Date column of the account.
2. The amount is entered into the Debit or Credit column of the account.
3. The journal page number is entered in the Posting Reference column.
4. The account number is entered in the Posting Reference (Post. Ref.) column in the journal.

The journal entries for Kelly Consulting have been posted to the ledger shown in Exhibit 17 on pages 174–175.

## Step 3. Preparing an Unadjusted Trial Balance

An unadjusted trial balance is prepared to determine whether any errors have been made in posting the debits and credits to the ledger. The unadjusted trial balance shown in Exhibit 10 does not provide complete proof of the accuracy of the ledger. It indicates only that the debits and the credits are equal. This proof is of value, however, because errors often affect the equality of debits and credits. If the two totals of a trial balance are not equal, an error has occurred that must be discovered and corrected.

The unadjusted account balances shown in Exhibit 10 were taken from Kelly Consulting's ledger shown in Exhibit 17, on pages 174–175, before any adjusting entries were recorded.

## Step 4. Assembling and Analyzing Adjustment Data

Before the financial statements can be prepared, the accounts must be updated. The four types of accounts that normally require adjustment include prepaid expenses, unearned revenue, accrued revenue, and accrued expenses. In addition, depreciation expense must be recorded for fixed assets other than land. The following data have been assembled on April 30, 2012, for analysis of possible adjustments for Kelly Consulting:

a. Insurance expired during April is $300.
b. Supplies on hand on April 30 are $1,350.
c. Depreciation of office equipment for April is $330.
d. Accrued receptionist salary on April 30 is $120.
e. Rent expired during April is $1,600.
f. Unearned fees on April 30 are $2,500.

## Step 5. Preparing an Optional End-of-Period Spreadsheet

Although an end-of-period spreadsheet is not required, it is useful in showing the flow of accounting information from the unadjusted trial balance to the adjusted trial

| Kelly Consulting, P.C. Unadjusted Trial Balance April 30, 2012 | Debit Balances | Credit Balances |
|---|---|---|
| Cash | 22,100 | |
| Accounts Receivable | 3,400 | |
| Supplies | 2,200 | |
| Prepaid Rent | 4,800 | |
| Prepaid Insurance | 1,800 | |
| Office Equipment | 14,500 | |
| Accumulated Depreciation | | 0 |
| Accounts Payable | | 800 |
| Salaries Payable | | 0 |
| Unearned Fees | | 5,000 |
| Capital Stock | | 30,000 |
| Dividends | 6,000 | |
| Fees Earned | | 20,950 |
| Salary Expense | 1,500 | |
| Rent Expense | 0 | |
| Supplies Expense | 0 | |
| Depreciation Expense | 0 | |
| Insurance Expense | 0 | |
| Miscellaneous Expense | 450 | |
| | 56,750 | 56,750 |

**EXHIBIT 10**

**Unadjusted Trial Balance—Kelly Consulting, P.C.**

balance. In addition, an end-of-period spreadsheet is useful in analyzing the impact of proposed adjustments on the financial statements. The end-of-period spreadsheet for Kelly Consulting is shown in Exhibit 11.

**EXHIBIT 11**

**End-of-Period Spreadsheet—Kelly Consulting**

| | A | B | C | D | E | F | G |
|---|---|---|---|---|---|---|---|
| 1 | | | | Kelly Consulting, P.C. | | | |
| 2 | | | | End-of-Period Spreadsheet | | | |
| 3 | | | | For the Month Ended April 30, 2012 | | | |
| 4 | | Unadjusted | | | | Adjusted | |
| 5 | | Trial Balance | | Adjustments | | Trial Balance | |
| 6 | Account Title | Dr. | Cr. | Dr. | Cr. | Dr. | Cr. |
| 7 | | | | | | | |
| 8 | Cash | 22,100 | | | | 22,100 | |
| 9 | Accounts Receivable | 3,400 | | | | 3,400 | |
| 10 | Supplies | 2,200 | | | (b) 850 | 1,350 | |
| 11 | Prepaid Rent | 4,800 | | | (e) 1,600 | 3,200 | |
| 12 | Prepaid Insurance | 1,800 | | | (a) 300 | 1,500 | |
| 13 | Office Equipment | 14,500 | | | | 14,500 | |
| 14 | Accum. Depreciation | | | | (c) 330 | | 330 |
| 15 | Accounts Payable | | 800 | | | | 800 |
| 16 | Salaries Payable | | | | (d) 120 | | 120 |
| 17 | Unearned Fees | | 5,000 | (f) 2,500 | | | 2,500 |
| 18 | Capital Stock | | 30,000 | | | | 30,000 |
| 19 | Dividends | 6,000 | | | | 6,000 | |
| 20 | Fees Earned | | 20,950 | | (f) 2,500 | | 23,450 |
| 21 | Salary Expense | 1,500 | | (d) 120 | | 1,620 | |
| 22 | Rent Expense | | | (e) 1,600 | | 1,600 | |
| 23 | Supplies Expense | | | (b) 850 | | 850 | |
| 24 | Depreciation Expense | | | (c) 330 | | 330 | |
| 25 | Insurance Expense | | | (a) 300 | | 300 | |
| 26 | Miscellaneous Expense | 450 | | | | 450 | |
| 27 | | 56,750 | 56,750 | 5,700 | 5,700 | 57,200 | 57,200 |
| 28 | | | | | | | |

# Step 6. Journalizing and Posting Adjusting Entries

Based on the adjustment data shown in Step 4, adjusting entries for Kelly Consulting are prepared as shown in Exhibit 12. Each adjusting entry affects at least one income statement account and one balance sheet account. Explanations for each adjustment including any computations are normally included with each adjusting entry.

Each of the adjusting entries shown in Exhibit 12 is posted to Kelly Consulting's ledger shown in Exhibit 17 on pages 174–175. The adjusting entries are identified in the ledger as "Adjusting."

**EXHIBIT 12**

**Adjusting Entries—Kelly Consulting**

| | | Journal | | | | Page 3 |
|---|---|---|---|---|---|---|
| Date | | Description | Post. Ref. | Debit | Credit | |
| | | Adjusting Entries | | | | |
| 2012 Apr. | 30 | Insurance Expense | 55 | 300 | | |
| | | Prepaid Insurance | 16 | | 300 | |
| | | Expired Insurance. | | | | |
| | 30 | Supplies Expense | 53 | 850 | | |
| | | Supplies | 14 | | 850 | |
| | | Supplies used ($2,200 – $1,350). | | | | |
| | 30 | Depreciation Expense | 54 | 330 | | |
| | | Accumulated Depreciation | 19 | | 330 | |
| | | Depreciation of office equipment. | | | | |
| | 30 | Salary Expense | 51 | 120 | | |
| | | Salaries Payable | 22 | | 120 | |
| | | Accrued salary. | | | | |
| | 30 | Rent Expense | 52 | 1,600 | | |
| | | Prepaid Rent | 15 | | 1,600 | |
| | | Rent expired during April. | | | | |
| | 30 | Unearned Fees | 23 | 2,500 | | |
| | | Fees Earned | 41 | | 2,500 | |
| | | Fees earned ($5,000 – $2,500). | | | | |

# Step 7. Preparing an Adjusted Trial Balance

After the adjustments have been journalized and posted, an adjusted trial balance is prepared to verify the equality of the total of the debit and credit balances. This is the last step before preparing the financial statements. If the adjusted trial balance does not balance, an error has occurred and must be found and corrected. The adjusted trial balance for Kelly Consulting as of April 30, 2012, is shown in Exhibit 13.

# Step 8. Preparing the Financial Statements

The most important outcome of the accounting cycle is the financial statements. The income statement is prepared first, followed by the retained earnings statement and then the balance sheet. The statements can be prepared directly from the adjusted trial balance, the end-of-period spreadsheet, or the ledger. The net income or net loss shown on the income statement is reported on the retained earnings statement along with any dividends. The ending retained earnings is reported on the balance sheet. The total stockholders' equity (capital stock plus retained earnings) is added with total liabilities to equal total assets.

**EXHIBIT 13**

**Adjusted Trial Balance—Kelly Consulting, P.C.**

**Kelly Consulting, P.C.**
**Adjusted Trial Balance**
**April 30, 2012**

| | Debit Balances | Credit Balances |
|---|---|---|
| Cash | 22,100 | |
| Accounts Receivable | 3,400 | |
| Supplies | 1,350 | |
| Prepaid Rent | 3,200 | |
| Prepaid Insurance | 1,500 | |
| Office Equipment | 14,500 | |
| Accumulated Depreciation | | 330 |
| Accounts Payable | | 800 |
| Salaries Payable | | 120 |
| Unearned Fees | | 2,500 |
| Capital Stock | | 30,000 |
| Dividends | 6,000 | |
| Fees Earned | | 23,450 |
| Salary Expense | 1,620 | |
| Rent Expense | 1,600 | |
| Supplies Expense | 850 | |
| Depreciation Expense | 330 | |
| Insurance Expense | 300 | |
| Miscellaneous Expense | 450 | |
| | 57,200 | 57,200 |

The financial statements for Kelly Consulting are shown in Exhibit 14. Kelly Consulting earned net income of $18,300 for April. As of April 30, 2012, Kelly Consulting has total assets of $45,720, total liabilities of $3,420, and total stockholders' equity of $42,300.

## Step 9. Journalizing and Posting Closing Entries

As described earlier in this chapter, four closing entries are required at the end of an accounting period. These four closing entries are as follows:

1. Debit each revenue account for its balance and credit Income Summary for the total revenue.
2. Credit each expense account for its balance and debit Income Summary for the total expenses.
3. Debit Income Summary for its balance and credit the retained earnings account.
4. Debit the retained earnings account for the balance of the dividends account and credit the dividends account.

**EXHIBIT 14**

**Financial Statements— Kelly Consulting, P.C.**

**Kelly Consulting, P.C.**
**Income Statement**
**For the Month Ended April 30, 2012**

| | | |
|---|---|---|
| Fees earned | | $23,450 |
| Expenses: | | |
| Salary expense | $1,620 | |
| Rent expense | 1,600 | |
| Supplies expense | 850 | |
| Depreciation expense | 330 | |
| Insurance expense | 300 | |
| Miscellaneous expense | 450 | |
| Total expenses | | 5,150 |
| Net income | | $18,300 |

*(continued)*

**EXHIBIT 14** **Financial Statements—Kelly Consulting (*concluded*)**

**Kelly Consulting, P.C.**
**Retained Earnings Statement**
**For the Month Ended April 30, 2012**

| | | |
|---|---:|---:|
| Retained earnings, April 1, 2012 | | $    0 |
| Net income for April | $18,300 | |
| Less dividends | 6,000 | |
| Increase in retained earnings | | 12,300 |
| Retained earnings, April 30, 2012 | | $12,300 |

**Kelly Consulting, P.C.**
**Balance Sheet**
**April 30, 2012**

| Assets | | | Liabilities | | |
|---|---:|---:|---|---:|---:|
| Current assets: | | | Current liabilities: | | |
| Cash | $22,100 | | Accounts payable | $  800 | |
| Accounts receivable | 3,400 | | Salaries payable | 120 | |
| Supplies | 1,350 | | Unearned fees | 2,500 | |
| Prepaid rent | 3,200 | | Total liabilities | | $  3,420 |
| Prepaid insurance | 1,500 | $31,550 | | | |
| Total current assets | | | | | |
| Property, plant, and equipment: | | | **Stockholders' Equity** | | |
| Office equipment | $14,500 | | Capital stock | $30,000 | |
| Less accumulated depreciation | 330 | | Retained earnings | 12,300 | |
| Total property, plant, | | | Total stockholders' equity | | 42,300 |
| and equipment | | 14,170 | Total liabilities and | | |
| Total assets | | $45,720 | stockholders' equity | | $45,720 |

The four closing entries for Kelly Consulting are shown in Exhibit 15. The closing entries are posted to Kelly Consulting's ledger as shown in Exhibit 17 (pages 174–175). After the closing entries are posted, Kelly Consulting's ledger has the following characteristics:

1. The balance of Retained Earnings of $12,300 agrees with the amount reported on the retained earnings statement and the balance sheet.
2. The revenue, expense, and dividends accounts will have zero balances.

The closing entries are normally identified in the ledger as "Closing." In addition, a line is often inserted in both balance columns after a closing entry is posted. This separates next period's revenue, expense, and dividend transactions from those of the current period.

## Step 10. Preparing a Post-Closing Trial Balance

A post-closing trial balance is prepared after the closing entries have been posted. The purpose of the post-closing trial balance is to verify that the ledger is in balance at the beginning of the next period. The accounts and amounts in the post-closing trial balance should agree exactly with the accounts and amounts listed on the balance sheet at the end of the period.

| Journal | | | | | Page 4 |
|---|---|---|---|---|---|
| **Date** | | **Description** | **Post. Ref.** | **Debit** | **Credit** |
| | | Closing Entries | | | |
| 2012 Apr. | 30 | Fees Earned | 41 | 23,450 | |
| | | Income Summary | 34 | | 23,450 |
| | 30 | Income Summary | 34 | 5,150 | |
| | | Salary Expense | 51 | | 1,620 |
| | | Rent Expense | 52 | | 1,600 |
| | | Supplies Expense | 53 | | 850 |
| | | Depreciation Expense | 54 | | 330 |
| | | Insurance Expense | 55 | | 300 |
| | | Miscellaneous Expense | 59 | | 450 |
| | 30 | Income Summary | 34 | 18,300 | |
| | | Retained Earnings | 32 | | 18,300 |
| | 30 | Retained Earnings | 32 | 6,000 | |
| | | Dividends | 33 | | 6,000 |

**EXHIBIT 15**

**Closing Entries—Kelly Consulting, P.C.**

The post-closing trial balance for Kelly Consulting is shown in Exhibit 16. The balances shown in the post-closing trial balance are taken from the ending balances in the ledger shown in Exhibit 17. These balances agree with the amounts shown on Kelly Consulting's balance sheet in Exhibit 14.

| Kelly Consulting, P. C. Post-Closing Trial Balance April 30, 2012 | | |
|---|---|---|
| | **Debit Balances** | **Credit Balances** |
| Cash | 22,100 | |
| Accounts Receivable | 3,400 | |
| Supplies | 1,350 | |
| Prepaid Rent | 3,200 | |
| Prepaid Insurance | 1,500 | |
| Office Equipment | 14,500 | |
| Accumulated Depreciation | | 330 |
| Accounts Payable | | 800 |
| Salaries Payable | | 120 |
| Unearned Fees | | 2,500 |
| Capital Stock | | 30,000 |
| Retained Earnings | | 12,300 |
| | 46,050 | 46,050 |

**EXHIBIT 16**

**Post-Closing Trial Balance—Kelly Consulting, P.C.**

**EXHIBIT 17** **Ledger—Kelly Consulting, P.C.**

## Ledger

### Account Cash — Account No. 11

| Date | Item | Post. Ref. | Debit | Credit | Balance Debit | Balance Credit |
|------|------|-----------|-------|--------|-------|--------|
| 2012 |      |     |        |       |        |   |
| Apr. 1 |    | 1   | 13,100 |       | 13,100 |   |
| 1    |      | 1   |        | 4,800 | 8,300  |   |
| 2    |      | 1   |        | 1,800 | 6,500  |   |
| 4    |      | 1   | 5,000  |       | 11,500 |   |
| 6    |      | 1   | 1,800  |       | 13,300 |   |
| 10   |      | 1   |        | 120   | 13,180 |   |
| 12   |      | 1   |        | 1,200 | 11,980 |   |
| 14   |      | 1   |        | 750   | 11,230 |   |
| 17   |      | 2   | 6,250  |       | 17,480 |   |
| 18   |      | 2   |        | 800   | 16,680 |   |
| 24   |      | 2   | 3,850  |       | 20,530 |   |
| 26   |      | 2   | 5,600  |       | 26,130 |   |
| 27   |      | 2   |        | 750   | 25,380 |   |
| 29   |      | 2   |        | 130   | 25,250 |   |
| 30   |      | 2   |        | 200   | 25,050 |   |
| 30   |      | 2   | 3,050  |       | 28,100 |   |
| 30   |      | 2   |        | 6,000 | 22,100 |   |

### Account Accounts Receivable — Account No. 12

| Date | Item | Post. Ref. | Debit | Credit | Balance Debit | Balance Credit |
|------|------|-----------|-------|--------|-------|--------|
| 2012 |      |     |       |       |       |   |
| Apr. 1 |    | 1   | 3,000 |       | 3,000 |   |
| 6    |      | 1   |       | 1,800 | 1,200 |   |
| 12   |      | 1   | 4,200 |       | 5,400 |   |
| 20   |      | 2   | 2,100 |       | 7,500 |   |
| 26   |      | 2   |       | 5,600 | 1,900 |   |
| 30   |      | 2   | 1,500 |       | 3,400 |   |

### Account Supplies — Account No. 14

| Date | Item | Post. Ref. | Debit | Credit | Balance Debit | Balance Credit |
|------|------|-----------|-------|--------|-------|--------|
| 2012 |      |     |       |     |       |   |
| Apr. 1 |    | 1   | 1,400 |     | 1,400 |   |
| 18   |      | 2   | 800   |     | 2,200 |   |
| 30   | Adjusting | 3 |   | 850 | 1,350 |   |

### Account Prepaid Rent — Account No. 15

| Date | Item | Post. Ref. | Debit | Credit | Balance Debit | Balance Credit |
|------|------|-----------|-------|--------|-------|--------|
| 2012 |      |     |       |       |       |   |
| Apr. 1 |    | 1   | 4,800 |       | 4,800 |   |
| 30   | Adjusting | 3 |    | 1,600 | 3,200 |   |

### Account Prepaid Insurance — Account No. 16

| Date | Item | Post. Ref. | Debit | Credit | Balance Debit | Balance Credit |
|------|------|-----------|-------|--------|-------|--------|
| 2012 |      |     |       |     |       |   |
| Apr. 2 |    | 1   | 1,800 |     | 1,800 |   |
| 30   | Adjusting | 3 |   | 300 | 1,500 |   |

### Account Office Equipment — Account No. 18

| Date | Item | Post. Ref. | Debit | Credit | Balance Debit | Balance Credit |
|------|------|-----------|-------|--------|-------|--------|
| 2012 |      |     |        |     |        |   |
| Apr. 1 |    | 1   | 12,500 |     | 12,500 |   |
| 5    |      | 1   | 2,000  |     | 14,500 |   |

### Account Accumulated Depreciation — Account No. 19

| Date | Item | Post. Ref. | Debit | Credit | Balance Debit | Balance Credit |
|------|------|-----------|-------|--------|-------|--------|
| 2012 |      |     |     |     |   |     |
| Apr. 30 | Adjusting | 3 |  | 330 |  | 330 |

### Account Accounts Payable — Account No. 21

| Date | Item | Post. Ref. | Debit | Credit | Balance Debit | Balance Credit |
|------|------|-----------|-------|--------|-------|--------|
| 2012 |      |     |       |       |   |       |
| Apr. 5 |    | 1   |       | 2,000 |   | 2,000 |
| 12   |      | 1   | 1,200 |       |   | 800   |

### Account Salaries Payable — Account No. 22

| Date | Item | Post. Ref. | Debit | Credit | Balance Debit | Balance Credit |
|------|------|-----------|-------|--------|-------|--------|
| 2012 |      |     |     |     |   |     |
| Apr. 30 | Adjusting | 3 |  | 120 |  | 120 |

### Account Unearned Fees — Account No. 23

| Date | Item | Post. Ref. | Debit | Credit | Balance Debit | Balance Credit |
|------|------|-----------|-------|--------|-------|--------|
| 2012 |      |     |       |       |   |       |
| Apr. 4 |    | 1   |       | 5,000 |   | 5,000 |
| 30   | Adjusting | 3 | 2,500 |   |   | 2,500 |

### Account Capital Stock — Account No. 31

| Date | Item | Post. Ref. | Debit | Credit | Balance Debit | Balance Credit |
|------|------|-----------|-------|--------|-------|--------|
| 2012 |      |     |     |        |   |        |
| Apr. 1 |    | 1   |     | 30,000 |   | 30,000 |

### Account Retained Earnings — Account No. 32

| Date | Item | Post. Ref. | Debit | Credit | Balance Debit | Balance Credit |
|------|------|-----------|-------|--------|-------|--------|
| 2012 |      |     |       |        |   |        |
| Apr. 30 | Closing | 4 |   | 18,300 |   | 18,300 |
| 30   | Closing | 4 | 6,000 |   |   | 12,300 |

**EXHIBIT 17** Ledger—Kelly Consulting, P.C. (*concluded*)

**Account** *Dividends* — Account No. 33

| Date | Item | Post. Ref. | Debit | Credit | Balance Debit | Balance Credit |
|---|---|---|---|---|---|---|
| 2012 Apr. 30 |  | 2 | 6,000 |  | 6,000 |  |
| 30 | Closing | 4 |  | 6,000 | — | — |

**Account** *Income Summary* — Account No. 34

| Date | Item | Post. Ref. | Debit | Credit | Balance Debit | Balance Credit |
|---|---|---|---|---|---|---|
| 2012 Apr. 30 | Closing | 4 |  | 23,450 |  | 23,450 |
| 30 | Closing | 4 | 5,150 |  |  | 18,300 |
| 30 | Closing | 4 | 18,300 |  | — | — |

**Account** *Fees Earned* — Account No. 41

| Date | Item | Post. Ref. | Debit | Credit | Balance Debit | Balance Credit |
|---|---|---|---|---|---|---|
| 2012 Apr. 12 |  | 1 |  | 4,200 |  | 4,200 |
| 17 |  | 2 |  | 6,250 |  | 10,450 |
| 20 |  | 2 |  | 2,100 |  | 12,550 |
| 24 |  | 2 |  | 3,850 |  | 16,400 |
| 30 |  | 2 |  | 3,050 |  | 19,450 |
| 30 |  | 2 |  | 1,500 |  | 20,950 |
| 30 | Adjusting | 3 |  | 2,500 |  | 23,450 |
| 30 | Closing | 4 | 23,450 |  | — | — |

**Account** *Salary Expense* — Account No. 51

| Date | Item | Post. Ref. | Debit | Credit | Balance Debit | Balance Credit |
|---|---|---|---|---|---|---|
| 2012 Apr. 14 |  | 1 | 750 |  | 750 |  |
| 27 |  | 2 | 750 |  | 1,500 |  |
| 30 | Adjusting | 3 | 120 |  | 1,620 |  |
| 30 | Closing | 4 |  | 1,620 | — | — |

**Account** *Rent Expense* — Account No. 52

| Date | Item | Post. Ref. | Debit | Credit | Balance Debit | Balance Credit |
|---|---|---|---|---|---|---|
| 2012 Apr. 30 | Adjusting | 3 | 1,600 |  | 1,600 |  |
| 30 | Closing | 4 |  | 1,600 | — | — |

**Account** *Supplies Expense* — Account No. 53

| Date | Item | Post. Ref. | Debit | Credit | Balance Debit | Balance Credit |
|---|---|---|---|---|---|---|
| 2012 Apr. 30 | Adjusting | 3 | 850 |  | 850 |  |
| 30 | Closing | 4 |  | 850 | — | — |

**Account** *Depreciation Expense* — Account No. 54

| Date | Item | Post. Ref. | Debit | Credit | Balance Debit | Balance Credit |
|---|---|---|---|---|---|---|
| 2012 Apr. 30 | Adjusting | 3 | 330 |  | 330 |  |
| 30 | Closing | 4 |  | 330 | — | — |

**Account** *Insurance Expense* — Account No. 55

| Date | Item | Post. Ref. | Debit | Credit | Balance Debit | Balance Credit |
|---|---|---|---|---|---|---|
| 2012 Apr. 30 | Adjusting | 3 | 300 |  | 300 |  |
| 30 | Closing | 4 |  | 300 | — | — |

**Account** *Miscellaneous Expense* — Account No. 59

| Date | Item | Post. Ref. | Debit | Credit | Balance Debit | Balance Credit |
|---|---|---|---|---|---|---|
| 2012 Apr. 10 |  | 1 | 120 |  | 120 |  |
| 29 |  | 2 | 130 |  | 250 |  |
| 30 |  | 2 | 200 |  | 450 |  |
| 30 | Closing | 4 |  | 450 | — | — |

The financial statements can be developed on a spreadsheet using the cell references from the adjusted trial balance. The adjusted trial balance for NetSolutions is prepared in a worksheet from Chapter 3, labeled ATB, as follows:

| | A | B | C |
|---|---|---|---|
| 1 | | NetSolutions | |
| 2 | | Adjusted Trial Balance | |
| 3 | | December 31, 2011 | |
| 4 | | Debit | Credit |
| 5 | | Balances | Balances |
| 6 | Cash | 2.065 | |
| 7 | Accounts Receivable | 2,720 | |
| 8 | Supplies | 760 | |
| 9 | Prepaid Insurance | 2,200 | |
| 10 | Land | 20,000 | |
| 11 | Office Equipment | 1,800 | |
| 12 | Accumulated Depreciation | | 50 |
| 13 | Accounts Payable | | 900 |
| 14 | Wages Payable | | 250 |
| 15 | Unearned Rent | | 240 |
| 16 | Capital Stock | | 25,000 |
| 17 | Dividends | 4,000 | |
| 18 | Fees Earned | | 16,840 |
| 19 | Rent Revenue | | 120 |
| 20 | Wages Expense | 4,525 | |
| 21 | Rent Expense | 1,600 | |
| 22 | Depreciation Expense | 50 | |
| 23 | Utilities Expense | 985 | |
| 24 | Supplies Expense | 2,040 | |
| 25 | Insurance Expense | 200 | |
| 26 | Miscellaneous Expense | 455 | |
| 27 | | 43,400 | 43,400 |
| 28 | | | |

⊩ ◀ ▶ ▶⏐ **ATB** ◀

The financial statements are prepared in a separate worksheet labeled FS. Each financial statement could have its own separate worksheet; however, we'll combine the financial statements on to one worksheet in this text.

| | A | B | C | D |
|---|---|---|---|---|
| 1 | | NetSolutions | | |
| 2 | | Income Statement | | |
| 3 | | For the Two Months Ended December 31, 2011 | | |
| 4 | | | | |
| 5 | Fees earned | a. → | =ATB!C18 | |
| 6 | Rent revenue | | =ATB!C19 | |
| 7 | Total revenues | | | =C5+C6 |
| 8 | Expenses: | | | |
| 9 | Wages expense | | =ATB!B20 | |
| 10 | Supplies expense | | =ATB!B24 | |
| 11 | Rent expense | | =ATB!B21 | |
| 12 | Utilities expense | | =ATB!B23 | |
| 13 | Insurance expense | | =ATB!B25 | |
| 14 | Depreciation expense | | =ATB!B22 | |
| 15 | Miscellaneous expense | | =ATB!B26 | |
| 16 | Total expenses | | | =SUM(C9:C15) |
| 17 | Net income | | | =D7–D16 |
| 18 | | | | |

⊩ ◀ ▶ ▶⏐ **FS** ◀

**a.**    The *income statement* is prepared first by referencing the appropriate adjusted trial balance cell locations.

For example, insert in cell C5 the adjusted trial balance cell reference for Fees Earned, =ATB!C18. The reference =ATB!C18 tells the spreadsheet software to insert into cell C5 the contents of cell C18 in worksheet ATB. The expenses can be done in the same way. The appropriate arithmetic spreadsheet formulas are entered to calculate the total expenses and net income.

**b.** Next, the retained earnings statement is prepared by referencing the net income from the income statement, dividends from the ATB, and making the appropriate arithmetic formulas to determine the ending balance of retained earnings as follows:

| | A | B | C | D |
|---|---|---|---|---|
| 1 | | | NetSolutions | |
| 2 | | | Income Statement | |
| 3 | | | For the Two Months Ended December 31, 2011 | |
| 4 | | | | |
| 5 | Fees earned | | =ATB!C18 | |
| 6 | Rent revenue | | =ATB!C19 | |
| 7 | Total revenues | | | =C5+C6 |
| 8 | Expenses: | | | |
| 9 | Wages expense | | =ATB!B20 | |
| 10 | Supplies expense | | =ATB!B24 | |
| 11 | Rent expense | | =ATB!B21 | |
| 12 | Utilities expense | | =ATB!B23 | |
| 13 | Insurance expense | | =ATB!B25 | |
| 14 | Depreciation expense | | =ATB!B22 | |
| 15 | Miscellaneous expense | | =ATB!B26 | |
| 16 | Total expenses | | | =SUM(C9:C15) |
| 17 | Net income | | | =D7–D16 |
| 18 | | | | |
| 19 | | | | |
| 20 | | | NetSolutions | |
| 21 | | | Statement of Retained Earnings | |
| 22 | | | For the Two Months Ended December 31, 2011 | |
| 23 | | | | |
| 24 | Beginning Balance November 1, 2011 | | | 0 |
| 25 | Net income for November and December | | | =D17 |
| 26 | | | | =SUM(D24:D25) |
| 27 | Less: dividends | | | =ATB!B17 |
| 28 | Ending Balance December 31, 2011 | | | =D26–D27 |
| 29 | | | | |

FS

**b.** Net income cell reference

**c.** The third financial statement prepared is the balance sheet. It is prepared by referencing the adjusted trial balance for all account balances except for the ending balance of retained earnings. The retained earnings in cell G43 references the ending balance of the retained earnings statement, =D28. Appropriate spreadsheet formulas are then entered for subtotals and totals, as follows:

| | A | B | C | D | E | F | G |
|---|---|---|---|---|---|---|---|
| 19 | | | | | | | |
| 20 | | | NetSolutions | | | | |
| 21 | | | Statement of Retained Earnings | | | | |
| 22 | | | For the Two Months Ended December 31, 2011 | | | | |
| 23 | | | | | | | |
| 24 | Beginning Balance November 1, 2011 | | | 0 | | | |
| 25 | Net income for November and December | | | =D17 | | | Ending balance |
| 26 | | | | =SUM(D24:D25) | | | from the *Statement* |
| 27 | Less: dividends | | | =ATB!B17 | | | *of Retained Earnings.* |
| 28 | Ending Balance December 31, 2011 | | | =D26–D27 | | | |
| 29 | | | | | | | |
| 29 | | | | | | | |
| 30 | | | | | | | |
| 31 | | | NetSolutions | | | | |
| 32 | | | Balance Sheet | | | | |
| 33 | | | December 31, 2011 | | | | |
| 34 | **Assets** | | | | | **Liabilities** | |
| 35 | Current assets: | | | | | Current liabilities: | |
| 36 | Cash | | =ATB!B6 | | | Accounts payable | =ATB!C13 |
| 37 | Accounts receivable | | =ATB!B7 | | | Wages payable | =ATB!C14 |
| 38 | Supplies | | =ATB!B8 | | | Unearned rent | =ATB!C15 |
| 39 | Prepaid insurance | | =ATB!B9 | | | Total liabilities | =SUM(G36:G38) |
| 40 | Total current assets | | | =SUM(D36:C39) | | | |
| 41 | Property, plant, and equipment: | | | | | **Stockholders' Equity** | |
| 42 | Land | | =ATB!B10 | | | Capital stock | ATB!C16 |
| 43 | Office equipment | =ATB!B11 | | | | Retained earnings | =D28 |
| 44 | Less accum. depreciation | =ATB!C12 | =B43-B44 | | | Total stockholders' equity | =G42+G43 |
| 45 | Total prop., plant, and equip. | | | =SUM(C42:C44) | | Total liabilities and | |
| 46 | Total assets | | | =D40+D45 | | stockholders' equity | =G39+G44 |
| 47 | | | | | | | |

FS

**c.**

|   | A | B | C | D | E | F | G |
|---|---|---|---|---|---|---|---|
| 1 | NetSolutions | | | | | | |
| 2 | Income Statement | | | | | | |
| 3 | For the Two Months Ended December 31, 2011 | | | | | | |
| 4 | | | | | | | |
| 5 | Fees earned | | $ 16,840 | | | | |
| 6 | Rent revenue | | 120 | | | | |
| 7 | Total revenues | | | $16,960 | | | |
| 8 | Expenses: | | | | | | |
| 9 | Wages expense | | $ 4,525 | | | | |
| 10 | Supplies expense | | 2,040 | | | | |
| 11 | Rent expense | | 1,600 | | | | |
| 12 | Utilities expense | | 985 | | | | |
| 13 | Insurance expense | | 200 | | | | |
| 14 | Depreciation expense | | 50 | | | | |
| 15 | Miscellaneous expense | | 455 | | | | |
| 16 | Total expenses | | | 9,855 | | | |
| 17 | Net income | | | $ 7,105 | | | |
| 18 | | | | | | | |
| 19 | | | | | | | |
| 20 | NetSolutions | | | | | | |
| 21 | Statement of Retained Earnings | | | | | | |
| 22 | For the Two Months Ended December 31, 2011 | | | | | | |
| 23 | | | | | | | |
| 24 | Beginning Balance, November 1, 2011 | | | $ 0 | | | |
| 25 | Net income for November and December | | | 7,105 | | | |
| 26 | | | | $7,105 | | | |
| 27 | Less: dividends | | | 4,000 | | | |
| 28 | Ending Balance, December 31, 2011 | | | $3,105 | | | |
| 29 | | | | | | | |
| 30 | | | | | | | |
| 31 | NetSolutions | | | | | | |
| 32 | Balance Sheet | | | | | | |
| 33 | December 31, 2011 | | | | | | |
| 34 | **Assets** | | | | | **Liabilities** | |
| 35 | Current assets: | | $ 2,065 | | | Current liabilities: | |
| 36 | Cash | | 2,720 | | | Accounts payable | $ 900 |
| 37 | Accounts receivable | | 760 | | | Wages payable | 250 |
| 38 | Supplies | | 2,200 | | | Unearned rent | 240 |
| 39 | Prepaid insurance | | | $ 7,745 | | Total liabilities | $ 1,390 |
| 40 | Total current assets | | | | | | |
| 41 | Property, plant, and equipment: | | | | | **Stockholders' Equity** | |
| 42 | Land | | $ 20,000 | | | Capital stock | $ 25,000 |
| 43 | Office equipment | $ 1,800 | | | | Retained earnings | 3,105 |
| 44 | Less accum. depreciation | 50 | 1,750 | | | Total stockholders' equity | $ 28,105 |
| 45 | Total prop., plant, and equip. | | | 21,750 | | Total liabilities and | |
| 46 | Total assets | | | $ 29,495 | | stockholders' equity | $ 29,495 |
| 47 | | | | | | | |

FS

**Try**_It_   Go to the hands-on **Excel Tutor** for this example!

OBJ. 6 Explain what is meant by the fiscal year and the natural business year.

# Fiscal Year

The annual accounting period adopted by a business is known as its **fiscal year**. Fiscal years begin with the first day of the month selected and end on the last day of the following twelfth month. The period most commonly used is the calendar year. Other periods are not unusual, especially for businesses organized as corporations. For example, a corporation may adopt a fiscal year that ends when business activities have reached the lowest point in its annual operating cycle. Such a fiscal year is called the **natural business year**. At the low point in its operating cycle, a business has more time to analyze the results of operations and to prepare financial statements.

Because companies with fiscal years often have highly seasonal operations, investors and others should be careful in interpreting partial-year reports for such companies. That is, you should expect the results of operations for these companies to vary significantly throughout the fiscal year.

The financial history of a business may be shown by a series of balance sheets and income statements for several fiscal years. If the life of a business is expressed by a line moving from left to right, the series of balance sheets and income statements may be graphed as follows:

| **Percentage of Companies with Fiscal Years Ending in:** | | | |
|---|---|---|---|
| January | 5% | July | 2% |
| February | 2 | August | 3 |
| March | 3 | September | 6 |
| April | 2 | October | 3 |
| May | 3 | November | 2 |
| June | 6 | December | 63 |

Source: *Accounting Trends & Techniques*, 63rd edition, 2009 (New York: American Institute of Certified Public Accountants).

**Financial History of a Business**

**CHOOSING A FISCAL YEAR**

CVS Caremark Corporation (CVS) operates over 7,000 pharmacies throughout the United States and fills more than one billion prescriptions annually. CVS recently chose December 31 as its fiscal year-end described as follows:

*.... our Board of Directors approved a change in our fiscal year-end ... to December 31 of each year to better reflect our position in the health care ... industry.*

In contrast, most large retailers such as Walmart and Target use fiscal years ending January 31, when their operations are the slowest following the December holidays.

# Financial Analysis and Interpretation: Working Capital and Current Ratio

The ability to convert assets into cash is called **liquidity**, while the ability of a business to pay its debts is called **solvency**. Two financial measures for evaluating a business's short-term liquidity and solvency are working capital and the current ratio.

**Working capital** is the excess of the current assets of a business over its current liabilities, as shown below.

 **OBJ. 7** Describe and illustrate the use of working capital and the current ratio in evaluating a company's financial condition.

Working Capital = Current Assets – Current Liabilities

Current assets are more liquid than long-term assets. Thus, an increase in a company's current assets increases or improves its liquidity. An increase in working capital increases or improves liquidity in the sense that current assets are available for uses other than paying current liabilities.

A positive working capital implies that the business is able to pay its current liabilities and is solvent. Thus, an increase in working capital increases or improves a company's solvency.

To illustrate, NetSolutions' working capital at the end of 2011 is $675 as computed below. This amount of working capital implies that NetSolutions is able to pay its current liabilities.

$$\text{Working Capital} = \text{Current Assets} - \text{Current Liabilities}$$
$$= \$7,745 - \$1,390$$
$$= \$6,355$$

The **current ratio** is another means of expressing the relationship between current assets and current liabilities. The current ratio is computed by dividing current assets by current liabilities, as shown below.

$$\text{Current Ratio} = \frac{\text{Current Assets}}{\text{Current Liabilities}}$$

To illustrate, the current ratio for NetSolutions at the end of 2011 is 1.5, computed as follows:

$$\text{Current Ratio} = \frac{\text{Current Assets}}{\text{Current Liabilities}}$$

$$= \frac{\$7,745}{\$1,390}$$

$$= 5.6 \text{ (Rounded)}$$

The current ratio is more useful than working capital in making comparisons across companies or with industry averages. To illustrate, the following data (in millions) were taken from the financial statements of Electronic Arts Inc. and Take-Two Interactive Software, Inc.

| | Electronic Arts | | Take-Two | |
| --- | --- | --- | --- | --- |
| | **Mar. 31, 2009** | **Mar. 31, 2008** | **Oct. 31, 2009** | **Oct. 31, 2008** |
| Current assets | $3,120 | $3,925 | $628 | $724 |
| Current liabilities | 1,136 | 1,299 | 354 | 365 |
| Working capital | $1,984 | $2,626 | $274 | $359 |
| Current ratio | 2.75 | 3.02 | 1.77 | 1.98 |
| Operating income (loss) | ($3,120 ÷ $1,136) | ($3,925 ÷ $1,299) | ($628 ÷ $354) | ($724 ÷ $365) |

Electronic Arts is larger than Take-Two and has 2009 working capital of $1,984 as compared to Take-Two's 2009 working capital of $274. Such size differences make comparisons across companies difficult. In contrast, the current ratio allows comparability across companies.

To illustrate, Electronic Arts has over seven times more working capital ($1,984) than does Take-Two's ($274). However, by using the current ratio the changes in liquidity of both companies can be directly compared. Specifically, Electronic Arts' current ratio declined from 3.02 to 2.75, or 0.27. Take-Two's current ratio also declined from 1.98 to 1.77, or 0.21. Thus, both companies experienced a small decline in their liquidity in 2009.

**Example Exercise** **4-6** **Working Capital and Current Ratio** OBJ. 7

The current assets and current liabilities for Fortson Company are shown below.

| | **2012** | **2011** |
| --- | --- | --- |
| Current assets | $310,500 | $262,500 |
| Current liabilities | 172,500 | 150,000 |

a. Determine the working capital and current ratio for 2012 and 2011.

b. Does the change in the current ratio from 2011 to 2012 indicate a favorable or an unfavorable trend?

(*continued*)

**Follow My Example 4-6**

a.

|  | **2012** | **2011** |
|---|---|---|
| Current assets | $310,500 | $262,500 |
| Current liabilities | 172,500 | 150,000 |
| Working capital | $138,000 | $112,500 |
| Current ratio | 1.80 | 1.75 |
|  | ($310,500 ÷ $172,500) | ($262,500 ÷ $150,000) |

b.  The change from 1.75 to 1.80 indicates a favorable trend.

Practice Exercises: **PE 4-6A, PE 4-6B**

# A P P E N D I X

# End-of-Period Spreadsheet (Work Sheet)

Accountants often use working papers for analyzing and summarizing data. Such working papers are not a formal part of the accounting records. This is in contrast to the chart of accounts, the journal, and the ledger, which are essential parts of an accounting system. Working papers are usually prepared by using a computer spreadsheet program such as Microsoft's Excel.™

The end-of-period spreadsheet shown in Exhibit 1 is a working paper used to summarize adjusting entries and their effects on the accounts. As illustrated in the chapter, the financial statements for **NetSolutions** can be prepared directly from the spreadsheet's Adjusted Trial Balance columns.

Some accountants prefer to expand the end-of-period spreadsheet shown in Exhibit 1 to include financial statement columns. Exhibits 18 through 22 illustrate the step-by-step process of how to prepare this expanded spreadsheet. As a basis for illustration, NetSolutions is used.

## Step 1. Enter the Title

The spreadsheet is started by entering the following data:

1.  Name of the business: *NetSolutions*
2.  Type of working paper: *End-of-Period Spreadsheet*
3.  The period of time: *For the Two Months Ended December 31, 2011*

Exhibit 18 shows the preceding data entered for NetSolutions.

## Step 2. Enter the Unadjusted Trial Balance

Enter the unadjusted trial balance on the spreadsheet. The spreadsheet in Exhibit 18 shows the unadjusted trial balance for NetSolutions at December 31, 2011.

**EXHIBIT 18** **Spreadsheet (Work Sheet) with Unadjusted Trial Balance Entered**

| | A | B | C | D | E | F | G | H | I | J | K |
|---|---|---|---|---|---|---|---|---|---|---|---|
| 1 | | | | | NetSolutions | | | | | | |
| 2 | | | | End-of-Period Spreadsheet (Work Sheet) | | | | | | | |
| 3 | | | | For the Two Months Ended December 31, 2011 | | | | | | | |
| 4 | | Unadjusted | | | | Adjusted | | | | | |
| 5 | | Trial Balance | | Adjustments | | Trial Balance | | Income Statement | | Balance Sheet | |
| 6 | Account Title | Dr. | Cr. | Dr. | Cr. | Dr. | Cr. | Dr. | Cr. | Dr. | Cr. |
| 7 | | | | | | | | | | | |
| 8 | Cash | 2,065 | | | | | | | | | |
| 9 | Accounts Receivable | 2,220 | | | | | | | | | |
| 10 | Supplies | 2,000 | | | | | | | | | |
| 11 | Prepaid Insurance | 2,400 | | | | | | | | | |
| 12 | Land | 20,000 | | | | | | | | | |
| 13 | Office Equipment | 1,800 | | | | | | | | | |
| 14 | Accumulated Depreciation | | | | | | | | | | |
| 15 | Accounts Payable | | 900 | | | | | | | | |
| 16 | Wages Payable | | | | | | | | | | |
| 17 | Unearned Rent | | 360 | | | | | | | | |
| 18 | Capital Stock | | 25,000 | | | | | | | | |
| 19 | Dividends | 4,000 | | | | | | | | | |
| 20 | Fees Earned | | 16,340 | | | | | | | | |
| 21 | Rent Revenue | | | | | | | | | | |
| 22 | Wages Expense | 4,275 | | | | | | | | | |
| 23 | Supplies Expense | 800 | | | | | | | | | |
| 24 | Rent Expense | 1,600 | | | | | | | | | |
| 25 | Utilities Expense | 985 | | | | | | | | | |
| 26 | Insurance Expense | | | | | | | | | | |
| 27 | Depreciation Expense | | | | | | | | | | |
| 28 | Miscellaneous Expense | 455 | | | | | | | | | |
| 29 | | 42,600 | 42,600 | | | | | | | | |
| 30 | | | | | | | | | | | |
| 31 | | | | | | | | | | | |
| 32 | | | | | | | | | | | |

> The spreadsheet (work sheet) is used for summarizing the effects of adjusting entries. It also aids in preparing financial statements.

# Step 3. Enter the Adjustments

The adjustments for NetSolutions from Chapter 3 are entered in the Adjustments columns, as shown in Exhibit 19. Cross-referencing (by letters) the debit and credit of each adjustment is useful in reviewing the spreadsheet. It is also helpful for identifying the adjusting entries that need to be recorded in the journal. This cross-referencing process is sometimes referred to as *keying* the adjustments.

The adjustments are normally entered in the order in which the data are assembled. If the titles of the accounts to be adjusted do not appear in the unadjusted trial balance, the accounts are inserted in their proper order in the Account Title column.

The adjusting entries for NetSolutions that are entered in the Adjustments columns are as follows:

(a) **Supplies**. The supplies account has a debit balance of $2,000. The cost of the supplies on hand at the end of the period is $760. The supplies expense for December is the difference between the two amounts, or $1,240 ($2,000 − $760). The adjustment is entered as (1) $1,240 in the Adjustments Debit column on the same line as Supplies Expense and (2) $1,240 in the Adjustments Credit column on the same line as Supplies.

(b) **Prepaid Insurance**. The prepaid insurance account has a debit balance of $2,400. This balance represents the prepayment of insurance for 12 months beginning December 1. Thus, the insurance expense for December is $200 ($2,400 ÷ 12). The adjustment is entered as (1) $200 in the Adjustments Debit column on the same line as Insurance Expense and (2) $200 in the Adjustments Credit column on the same line as Prepaid Insurance.

**EXHIBIT 19** **Spreadsheet (Work Sheet) with Unadjusted Trial Balance and Adjustments**

| | A | B | C | D | E | F | G | H | I | J | K |
|---|---|---|---|---|---|---|---|---|---|---|---|
| 1 | | | | NetSolutions | | | | | | | |
| 2 | | | | End-of-Period Spreadsheet (Work Sheet) | | | | | | | |
| 3 | | | | For the Two Months Ended December 31, 2011 | | | | | | | |
| 4 | | Unadjusted | | | | Adjusted | | | | | |
| 5 | | Trial Balance | | Adjustments | | Trial Balance | | Income Statement | | Balance Sheet | |
| 6 | Account Title | Dr. | Cr. | Dr. | Cr. | Dr. | Cr. | Dr. | Cr. | Dr. | Cr. |
| 7 | | | | | | | | | | | |
| 8 | Cash | 2,065 | | | | | | | | | |
| 9 | Accounts Receivable | 2,220 | | (d) 500 | | | | | | | |
| 10 | Supplies | 2,000 | | | (a) 1,240 | | | | | | |
| 11 | Prepaid Insurance | 2,400 | | | (b) 200 | | | | | | |
| 12 | Land | 20,000 | | | | | | | | | |
| 13 | Office Equipment | 1,800 | | | | | | | | | |
| 14 | Accumulated Depreciation | | | | (f) 50 | | | | | | |
| 15 | Accounts Payable | | 900 | | | | | | | | |
| 16 | Wages Payable | | | | (e) 250 | | | | | | |
| 17 | Unearned Rent | | 360 | (c) 120 | | | | | | | |
| 18 | Capital Stock | | 25,000 | | | | | | | | |
| 19 | Dividends | 4,000 | | | | | | | | | |
| 20 | Fees Earned | | 16,340 | | (d) 500 | | | | | | |
| 21 | Rent Revenue | | | | (c) 120 | | | | | | |
| 22 | Wages Expense | 4,275 | | (e) 250 | | | | | | | |
| 23 | Supplies Expense | 800 | | (a) 1,240 | | | | | | | |
| 24 | Rent Expense | 1,600 | | | | | | | | | |
| 25 | Utilities Expense | 985 | | | | | | | | | |
| 26 | Insurance Expense | | | (b) 200 | | | | | | | |
| 27 | Depreciation Expense | | | (f) 50 | | | | | | | |
| 28 | Miscellaneous Expense | 455 | | | | | | | | | |
| 29 | | 42,600 | 42,600 | 2,360 | 2,360 | | | | | | |
| 30 | | | | | | | | | | | |
| 31 | | | | | | | | | | | |
| 32 | | | | | | | | | | | |

The adjustments on the spreadsheet (work sheet) are used in preparing the adjusting journal entries.

(c) **Unearned Rent**. The unearned rent account has a credit balance of $360. This balance represents the receipt of three months' rent, beginning with December. Thus, the rent revenue for December is $120 ($360 ÷ 3). The adjustment is entered as (1) $120 in the Adjustments Debit column on the same line as Unearned Rent and (2) $120 in the Adjustments Credit column on the same line as Rent Revenue.

(d) **Accrued Fees**. Fees accrued at the end of December but not recorded total $500. This amount is an increase in an asset and an increase in revenue. The adjustment is entered as (1) $500 in the Adjustments Debit column on the same line as Accounts Receivable and (2) $500 in the Adjustments Credit column on the same line as Fees Earned.

(e) **Wages**. Wages accrued but not paid at the end of December total $250. This amount is an increase in expenses and an increase in liabilities. The adjustment is entered as (1) $250 in the Adjustments Debit column on the same line as Wages Expense and (2) $250 in the Adjustments Credit column on the same line as Wages Payable.

(f) **Depreciation**. Depreciation of the office equipment is $50 for December. The adjustment is entered as (1) $50 in the Adjustments Debit column on the same line as Depreciation Expense and (2) $50 in the Adjustments Credit column on the same line as Accumulated Depreciation.

After the adjustments have been entered, the Adjustments columns are totaled to verify the equality of the debits and credits. The total of the Debit column must equal the total of the Credit column.

## Step 4. Enter the Adjusted Trial Balance

The adjusted trial balance is entered by combining the adjustments with the unadjusted balances for each account. The adjusted amounts are then extended to the Adjusted Trial Balance columns, as shown in Exhibit 20.

**EXHIBIT 20**    **Spreadsheet (Work Sheet) with Unadjusted Trial Balance, Adjustments, and Adjusted Trial Balance Entered**

| | A | B | C | D | E | F | G | H | I | J | K |
|---|---|---|---|---|---|---|---|---|---|---|---|
| 1 | | | | NetSolutions | | | | | | | |
| 2 | | | | End-of-Period Spreadsheet (Work Sheet) | | | | | | | |
| 3 | | | | For the Two Months Ended December 31, 2011 | | | | | | | |
| 4 | | Unadjusted | | | | Adjusted | | | | | |
| 5 | | Trial Balance | | Adjustments | | Trial Balance | | Income Statement | | Balance Sheet | |
| 6 | Account Title | Dr. | Cr. | Dr. | Cr. | Dr. | Cr. | Dr. | Cr. | Dr. | Cr. |
| 7 | | | | | | | | | | | |
| 8 | Cash | 2,065 | | | | 2,065 | | | | | |
| 9 | Accounts Receivable | 2,220 | | (d)    500 | | 2,720 | | | | | |
| 10 | Supplies | 2,000 | | | (a) 1,240 | 760 | | | | | |
| 11 | Prepaid Insurance | 2,400 | | | (b)    200 | 2,200 | | | | | |
| 12 | Land | 20,000 | | | | 20,000 | | | | | |
| 13 | Office Equipment | 1,800 | | | | 1,800 | | | | | |
| 14 | Accumulated Depreciation | | | | (f)    50 | | 50 | | | | |
| 15 | Accounts Payable | | 900 | | | | 900 | | | | |
| 16 | Wages Payable | | | | (e)    250 | | 250 | | | | |
| 17 | Unearned Rent | | 360 | (c)    120 | | | 240 | | | | |
| 18 | Capital Stock | | 25,000 | | | | 25,000 | | | | |
| 19 | Dividends | 4,000 | | | | 4,000 | | | | | |
| 20 | Fees Earned | | 16,340 | | (d)    500 | | 16,840 | | | | |
| 21 | Rent Revenue | | | | (c)    120 | | 120 | | | | |
| 22 | Wages Expense | 4,275 | | (e)    250 | | 4,525 | | | | | |
| 23 | Supplies Expense | 800 | | (a) 1,240 | | 2,040 | | | | | |
| 24 | Rent Expense | 1,600 | | | | 1,600 | | | | | |
| 25 | Utilities Expense | 985 | | | | 985 | | | | | |
| 26 | Insurance Expense | | | (b)    200 | | 200 | | | | | |
| 27 | Depreciation Expense | | | (f)    50 | | 50 | | | | | |
| 28 | Miscellaneous Expense | 455 | | | | 455 | | | | | |
| 29 | | 42,600 | 42,600 | 2,360 | 2,360 | 43,400 | 43,400 | | | | |
| 30 | | | | | | | | | | | |
| 31 | | | | | | | | | | | |
| 32 | | | | | | | | | | | |

> The adjusted trial balance amounts are determined by adding the adjustments to or subtracting the adjustments from the trial balance amounts. For example, the Wages Expense debit of $4,525 is the trial balance amount of $4,275 plus the $250 adjustment debit.

To illustrate, the cash amount of $2,065 is extended to the Adjusted Trial Balance Debit column since no adjustments affected Cash. Accounts Receivable has an initial balance of $2,220 and a debit adjustment of $500. Thus, $2,720 ($2,220 + $500) is entered in the Adjusted Trial Balance Debit column for Accounts Receivable. The same process continues until all account balances are extended to the Adjusted Trial Balance columns.

After the accounts and adjustments have been extended, the Adjusted Trial Balance columns are totaled to verify the equality of debits and credits. The total of the Debit column must equal the total of the Credit column.

## Step 5. Extend the Accounts to the Income Statement and Balance Sheet Columns

The adjusted trial balance amounts are extended to the Income Statement and Balance Sheet columns. The amounts for revenues and expenses are extended to the Income Statement column. The amounts for assets, liabilities, capital stock, and dividends are extended to the Balance Sheet columns.[3]

3 The balance of the dividends account is extended to the Balance Sheet columns because the spreadsheet does not have separate Retained Earnings Statement columns.

The first account listed in the Adjusted Trial Balance columns is Cash with a debit balance of $2,065. Cash is an asset, is listed on the balance sheet, and has a debit balance. Therefore, $2,065 is extended to the Balance Sheet Debit column. The Fees Earned balance of $16,840 is extended to the Income Statement Credit column. The same process continues until all account balances have been extended to the proper columns, as shown in Exhibit 21.

**EXHIBIT 21**   **Spreadsheet (Work Sheet) with Amounts Extended to Income Statement and Balance Sheet Columns**

| | A | B | C | D | E | F | G | H | I | J | K |
|---|---|---|---|---|---|---|---|---|---|---|---|
| 1 | | | | NetSolutions | | | | | | | |
| 2 | | | | End-of-Period Spreadsheet (Work Sheet) | | | | | | | |
| 3 | | | | For the Two Months Ended December 31, 2011 | | | | | | | |
| 4 | | Unadjusted | | | | Adjusted | | | | | |
| 5 | | Trial Balance | | Adjustments | | Trial Balance | | Income Statement | | Balance Sheet | |
| 6 | **Account Title** | Dr. | Cr. | Dr. | Cr. | Dr. | Cr. | Dr. | Cr. | Dr. | Cr. |
| 7 | | | | | | | | | | | |
| 8 | Cash | 2,065 | | | | 2,065 | | | | 2,065 | |
| 9 | Accounts Receivable | 2,220 | | (d)   500 | | 2,720 | | | | 2,720 | |
| 10 | Supplies | 2,000 | | | (a) 1,240 | 760 | | | | 760 | |
| 11 | Prepaid Insurance | 2,400 | | | (b)   200 | 2,200 | | | | 2,200 | |
| 12 | Land | 20,000 | | | | 20,000 | | | | 20,000 | |
| 13 | Office Equipment | 1,800 | | | | 1,800 | | | | 1,800 | |
| 14 | Accumulated Depreciation | | | | (f)    50 | | 50 | | | | 50 |
| 15 | Accounts Payable | | 900 | | | | 900 | | | | 900 |
| 16 | Wages Payable | | | | (e)   250 | | 250 | | | | 250 |
| 17 | Unearned Rent | | 360 | (c)   120 | | | 240 | | | | 240 |
| 18 | Capital Stock | | 25,000 | | | | 25,000 | | | | 25,000 |
| 19 | Dividends | 4,000 | | | | 4,000 | | | | 4,000 | |
| 20 | Fees Earned | | 16,340 | | (d)   500 | | 16,840 | | 16,840 | | |
| 21 | Rent Revenue | | | | (c)   120 | | 120 | | 120 | | |
| 22 | Wages Expense | 4,275 | | (e)   250 | | 4,525 | | 4,525 | | | |
| 23 | Supplies Expense | 800 | | (a) 1,240 | | 2,040 | | 2,040 | | | |
| 24 | Rent Expense | 1,600 | | | | 1,600 | | 1,600 | | | |
| 25 | Utilities Expense | 985 | | | | 985 | | 985 | | | |
| 26 | Insurance Expense | | | (b)   200 | | 200 | | 200 | | | |
| 27 | Depreciation Expense | | | (f)    50 | | 50 | | 50 | | | |
| 28 | Miscellaneous Expense | 455 | | | | 455 | | 455 | | | |
| 29 | | 42,600 | 42,600 | 2,360 | 2,360 | 43,400 | 43,400 | | | | |
| 30 | | | | | | | | | | | |
| 31 | | | | | | | | | | | |
| 32 | | | | | | | | | | | |

The revenue and expense amounts are extended to (entered in) the Income Statement columns.

The asset, liability, capital stock, and dividend amounts are extended to (entered in) the Balance Sheet columns.

# Step 6. Total the Income Statement and Balance Sheet Columns, Compute the Net Income or Net Loss, and Complete the Spreadsheet

After the account balances are extended to the Income Statement and Balance Sheet columns, each of the columns is totaled. The difference between the two Income Statement column totals is the amount of the net income or the net loss for the period. This difference (net income or net loss) will also be the difference between the two Balance Sheet column totals.

If the Income Statement Credit column total (total revenue) is greater than the Income Statement Debit column total (total expenses), the difference is the net income. If the Income Statement Debit column total is greater than the Income Statement Credit column total, the difference is a net loss.

As shown in Exhibit 22, the total of the Income Statement Credit column is $16,960, and the total of the Income Statement Debit column is $9,855. Thus, the net income for NetSolutions is $7,105 as shown below.

| | |
|---|---|
| Total of Income Statement Credit column (revenues) | $16,960 |
| Total of Income Statement Debit column (expenses) | 9,855 |
| Net income (excess of revenues over expenses) | $ 7,105 |

The amount of the net income, $7,105, is entered in the Income Statement Debit column and the Balance Sheet Credit column. *Net income* is also entered in the Account Title column. Entering the net income of $7,105 in the Balance Sheet Credit

**EXHIBIT 22**    **Completed Spreadsheet (Work Sheet) with Net Income Shown**

| | A | B | C | D | E | F | G | H | I | J | K |
|---|---|---|---|---|---|---|---|---|---|---|---|
| 1 | | | | | NetSolutions | | | | | | |
| 2 | | | | | End-of-Period Spreadsheet (Work Sheet) | | | | | | |
| 3 | | | | | For the Two Months Ended December 31, 2011 | | | | | | |
| 4 | | Unadjusted | | | | Adjusted | | | | | |
| 5 | | Trial Balance | | Adjustments | | Trial Balance | | Income Statement | | Balance Sheet | |
| 6 | Account Title | Dr. | Cr. | Dr. | Cr. | Dr. | Cr. | Dr. | Cr. | Dr. | Cr. |
| 7 | | | | | | | | | | | |
| 8 | Cash | 2,065 | | | | 2,065 | | | | 2,065 | |
| 9 | Accounts Receivable | 2,220 | | (d)    500 | | 2,720 | | | | 2,720 | |
| 10 | Supplies | 2,000 | | | (a)  1,240 | 760 | | | | 760 | |
| 11 | Prepaid Insurance | 2,400 | | | (b)    200 | 2,200 | | | | 2,200 | |
| 12 | Land | 20,000 | | | | 20,000 | | | | 20,000 | |
| 13 | Office Equipment | 1,800 | | | | 1,800 | | | | 1,800 | |
| 14 | Accumulated Depreciation | | | | (f)     50 | | 50 | | | | 50 |
| 15 | Accounts Payable | | 900 | | | | 900 | | | | 900 |
| 16 | Wages Payable | | | | (e)    250 | | 250 | | | | 250 |
| 17 | Unearned Rent | | 360 | (c)    120 | | | 240 | | | | 240 |
| 18 | Capital Stock | | 25,000 | | | | 25,000 | | | | 25,000 |
| 19 | Dividends | 4,000 | | | | 4,000 | | | | 4,000 | |
| 20 | Fees Earned | | 16,340 | | (d)    500 | | 16,840 | | 16,840 | | |
| 21 | Rent Revenue | | | | (c)    120 | | 120 | | 120 | | |
| 22 | Wages Expense | 4,275 | | (e)    250 | | 4,525 | | 4,525 | | | |
| 23 | Supplies Expense | 800 | | (a)  1,240 | | 2,040 | | 2,040 | | | |
| 24 | Rent Expense | 1,600 | | | | 1,600 | | 1,600 | | | |
| 25 | Utilities Expense | 985 | | | | 985 | | 985 | | | |
| 26 | Insurance Expense | | | (b)    200 | | 200 | | 200 | | | |
| 27 | Depreciation Expense | | | (f)     50 | | 50 | | 50 | | | |
| 28 | Miscellaneous Expense | 455 | | | | 455 | | 455 | | | |
| 29 | | 42,600 | 42,600 | 2,360 | 2,360 | 43,400 | 43,400 | 9,855 | 16,960 | 33,545 | 26,440 |
| 30 | Net income | | | | | | | 7,105 | | | 7,105 |
| 31 | | | | | | | | 16,960 | 16,960 | 33,545 | 33,545 |
| 32 | | | | | | | | | | | |

The difference between the Income Statement column totals is the net income (or net loss) for the period. The difference between the Balance Sheet column totals is also the net income (or net loss) for the period.

column has the effect of transferring the net balance of the revenue and expense accounts to the retained earnings account.

If there was a net loss instead of net income, the amount of the net loss would be entered in the Income Statement Credit column and the Balance Sheet Debit column. *Net loss* would also be entered in the Account Title column.

After the net income or net loss is entered on the spreadsheet, the Income Statement and Balance Sheet columns are totaled. The totals of the two Income Statement columns must now be equal. The totals of the two Balance Sheet columns must also be equal.

## Preparing the Financial Statements from the Spreadsheet

The spreadsheet can be used to prepare the income statement, the retained earnings statement, and the balance sheet shown in Exhibit 2. The income statement is normally prepared directly from the spreadsheet. The expenses are listed in the income statement in Exhibit 2 in order of size, beginning with the larger items. Miscellaneous expense is the last item, regardless of its amount.

The first item normally presented on the retained earnings statement is the balance of the retained earnings account at the beginning of the period. This amount along with the net income (or net loss) and the dividends amount shown in the spreadsheet, are used to determine the ending retained earnings account balance.

The balance sheet can be prepared directly from the spreadsheet columns except for the ending balance of retained earnings. The ending balance of retained earnings is taken from the retained earnings statement.

When a spreadsheet is used, the adjusting and closing entries are normally not journalized or posted until after the spreadsheet and financial statements have been prepared. The data for the adjusting entries are taken from the Adjustments columns of the spreadsheet. The data for the first two closing entries are taken from the Income Statement columns of the spreadsheet. The amount for the third closing entry is the net income or net loss appearing at the bottom of the spreadsheet. The amount for the fourth closing entry is the dividends account balance that appears in the Balance Sheet Debit column of the spreadsheet.

## At a Glance 4

**OBJ. 1**

**Describe the flow of accounting information from the unadjusted trial balance into the adjusted trial balance and financial statements.**

**Key Points** Exhibit 1 illustrates the end-of-period process by which accounts are adjusted and how the adjusted accounts flow into the financial statements.

| Learning Outcomes | Example Exercises | Practice Exercises |
|---|---|---|
| • Using an end-of-period spreadsheet, describe how the unadjusted trial balance accounts are affected by adjustments and how the adjusted trial balance accounts flow into the income statement, retained earnings statement, and balance sheet. | EE4-1 | PE4-1A, 4-1B |

**OBJ. 2**

**Prepare financial statements from adjusted account balances.**

**Key Points** Using the end-of-period spreadsheet shown in Exhibit 1, the income statement, retained earnings statement, and balance sheet for NetSolutions can be prepared. A classified balance sheet has sections for current assets; property, plant, and equipment; current liabilities; long-term liabilities; and stockholders' equity.

| Learning Outcomes | Example Exercises | Practice Exercises |
|---|---|---|
| • Describe how the net income or net loss from the period can be determined from an end-of-period spreadsheet. | | |
| • Prepare an income statement, retained earnings statement, and a balance sheet. | EE4-2 | PE4-2A, 4-2B |
| • Indicate how accounts would be reported on a classified balance sheet. | EE4-3 | PE4-3A, 4-3B |

**OBJ. 3**

**Prepare closing entries.**

**Key Points** Four entries are required in closing the temporary accounts. The first entry closes the revenue accounts to Income Summary. The second entry closes the expense accounts to Income Summary. The third entry closes the balance of Income Summary (net income or net loss) to the retained earnings account. The fourth entry closes the dividends account to the retained earnings account.

After the closing entries have been posted to the ledger, the balance in the retained earnings agrees with the amount reported on the retained earnings statement and balance sheet. In addition, the revenue, expense, and dividend accounts will have zero balances.

| Learning Outcomes | Example Exercises | Practice Exercises |
|---|---|---|
| • Prepare the closing entry for revenues. | EE4-4 | PE4-4A, 4-4B |
| • Prepare the closing entry for expenses. | EE4-4 | PE4-4A, 4-4B |
| • Prepare the closing entry for transferring the balance of Income Summary to the retained earnings account. | EE4-4 | PE4-4A, 4-4B |
| • Prepare the closing entry for the dividends account. | EE4-4 | PE4-4A, 4-4B |

## 4 Describe the accounting cycle.

**Key Points**   The 10 basic steps of the accounting cycle are as follows:

1. Transactions are analyzed and recorded in the journal.
2. Transactions are posted to the ledger.
3. An unadjusted trial balance is prepared.
4. Adjustment data are assembled and analyzed.
5. An optional end-of-period spreadsheet is prepared.
6. Adjusting entries are journalized and posted to the ledger.
7. An adjusted trial balance is prepared.
8. Financial statements are prepared.
9. Closing entries are journalized and posted to the ledger.
10. A post-closing trial balance is prepared.

| Learning Outcomes | Example Exercises | Practice Exercises |
|---|---|---|
| • List the 10 steps of the accounting cycle. | | |
| • Determine whether any steps are out of order in a listing of accounting cycle steps. | | |
| • Determine whether there are any missing steps in a listing of accounting cycle steps. | **EE4-5** | **PE4-5A, 4-5B** |

## 5 Illustrate the accounting cycle for one period.

**Key Points**   The complete accounting cycle for Kelly Consulting for the month of April is described and illustrated on pages 165–175.

**Learning Outcomes**

• Complete the accounting cycle for a period from beginning to end.

## 6 Explain what is meant by the fiscal year and the natural business year.

**Key Points**   The annual accounting period adopted by a business is its fiscal year. A company's fiscal year that ends when business activities have reached the lowest point in its annual operating cycle is called the natural business year.

**Learning Outcomes**

• Explain why companies use a fiscal year that is different from the calendar year.

## 7 Describe and illustrate the use of working capital and the current ratio in evaluating a company's financial condition.

**Key Points**   The ability to convert assets into cash is called liquidity, while the ability of a business to pay its debts is called solvency. Two financial measures for evaluating a business's short-term liquidity and solvency are working capital and the current ratio. Working capital is computed by subtracting current liabilities from current assets. An excess of current assets over current liabilities implies that the business is able to pay its current liabilities. The current ratio is computed by dividing current assets by current liabilities. The current ratio is more useful than working capital in making comparisons across companies or with industry averages.

| Learning Outcomes | Example Exercises | Practice Exercises |
|---|---|---|
| • Define liquidity and solvency. | | |
| • Compute working capital. | **EE4-6** | **PE4-6A, 4-6B** |
| • Compute the current ratio. | **EE4-6** | **PE4-6A, 4-6B** |

## Key Terms

accounting cycle (164)

clearing account (159)

closing entries (159)

closing process (159)

closing the books (159)

current assets (157)

current liabilities (157)

current ratio (180)

fiscal year (178)

fixed (plant) assets (157)

Income Summary (159)

liquidity (179)

long-term liabilities (157)

natural business year (179)

notes receivable (157)

real (permanent) accounts (158)

solvency (179)

temporary (nominal) accounts (159)

working capital (179)

## Illustrative Problem

Three years ago, T. Roderick organized Harbor Realty Inc. At July 31, 2012, the end of the current fiscal year, the following end-of-period spreadsheet was prepared:

| | A | B | C | D | E | F | G |
|---|---|---|---|---|---|---|---|
| 1 | | Harbor Realty Inc. | | | | | |
| 2 | | End-of-Period Spreadsheet | | | | | |
| 3 | | For the Year Ended July 31, 2012 | | | | | |
| 4 | | Unadjusted | | | | Adjusted | |
| 5 | | Trial Balance | | Adjustments | | Trial Balance | |
| 6 | Account Title | Dr. | Cr. | Dr. | Cr. | Dr. | Cr. |
| 7 | | | | | | | |
| 8 | Cash | 3,425 | | | | 3,425 | |
| 9 | Accounts Receivable | 7,000 | | (e) 1,000 | | 8,000 | |
| 10 | Supplies | 1,270 | | | (a)   890 | 380 | |
| 11 | Prepaid Insurance | 620 | | | (b)   315 | 305 | |
| 12 | Office Equipment | 51,650 | | | | 51,650 | |
| 13 | Accum. Depreciation | | 9,700 | | (c) 4,950 | | 14,650 |
| 14 | Accounts Payable | | 925 | | | | 925 |
| 15 | Unearned Fees | | 1,250 | (f)   500 | | | 750 |
| 16 | Wages Payable | | | | (d)   440 | | 440 |
| 17 | Capital Stock | | 5,000 | | | | 5,000 |
| 18 | Retained Earnings | | 24,000 | | | | 24,000 |
| 19 | Dividends | 5,200 | | | | 5,200 | |
| 20 | Fees Earned | | 59,125 | | (e) 1,000 | | 60,625 |
| 21 | | | | | (f)   500 | | |
| 22 | Wages Expense | 22,415 | | (d)   440 | | 22,855 | |
| 23 | Depreciation Expense | | | (c) 4,950 | | 4,950 | |
| 24 | Rent Expense | 4,200 | | | | 4,200 | |
| 25 | Utilities Expense | 2,715 | | | | 2,715 | |
| 26 | Supplies Expense | | | (a)   890 | | 890 | |
| 27 | Insurance Expense | | | (b)   315 | | 315 | |
| 28 | Miscellaneous Expense | 1,505 | | | | 1,505 | |
| 29 | | 100,000 | 100,000 | 8,095 | 8,095 | 106,390 | 106,390 |

## Instructions

1. Prepare an income statement, a retained earnings statement, and a balance sheet.

2. On the basis of the data in the end-of-period spreadsheet, journalize the closing entries.

### Solution

1.

| Harbor Realty Inc.<br>Income Statement<br>For the Year Ended July 31, 2012 | | |
|---|---:|---:|
| Fees earned........................................................ | | $60,625 |
| Expenses: | | |
| Wages expense ..................................................... | $22,855 | |
| Depreciation expense ................................................ | 4,950 | |
| Rent expense ....................................................... | 4,200 | |
| Utilities expense .................................................... | 2,715 | |
| Supplies expense ................................................... | 890 | |
| Insurance expense .................................................. | 315 | |
| Miscellaneous expense .............................................. | 1,505 | |
| Total expenses..................................................... | | 37,430 |
| Net income ......................................................... | | $23,195 |

| Harbor Realty Inc.<br>Retained Earnings Statement<br>For the Year Ended July 31, 2012 | | |
|---|---:|---:|
| Retained earnings, August 1, 2011............................................ | | $24,000 |
| Net income for the year..................................................... | $23,195 | |
| Less dividends ........................................................... | 5,200 | |
| Increase in retained earnings ............................................... | | 17,995 |
| Retained earnings, July 31, 2012............................................. | | $41,995 |

| Harbor Realty Inc.<br>Balance Sheet<br>July 31, 2012 | | | | | |
|---|---|---|---|---|---|
| **Assets** | | | **Liabilities** | | |
| Current assets: | | | Current liabilities: | | |
| Cash..................................... | $ 3,425 | | Accounts payable..................... | $925 | |
| Accounts receivable .................... | 8,000 | | Unearned fees ...................... | 750 | |
| Supplies .............................. | 380 | | Wages payable ....................... | 440 | |
| Prepaid insurance ..................... | 305 | | Total liabilities......................... | | $ 2,115 |
| Total current assets................... | | $12,110 | | | |
| Property, plant, and equipment: | | | **Stockholders' Equity** | | |
| Office equipment...................... | $51,650 | | Capital stock ........................... | $ 5,000 | |
| Less accum. depreciation............... | 14,650 | | Retained earnings ...................... | 41,995 | |
| Total property, plant, | | | Total stockholders' equity .............. | | 46,995 |
| and equipment .................... | | 37,000 | Total liabilities and | | |
| Total assets............................... | | $49,110 | stockholders' equity ................. | | $49,110 |

2.

| | | | Journal | Post. Ref. | Debit | Credit | Page |
|---|---|---|---|---|---|---|---|
| **Date** | | | **Description** | | **Debit** | **Credit** | |
| | | | Closing Entries | | | | |
| 2012 July | 31 | | Fees Earned | | 60,625 | | |
| | | | Income Summary | | | 60,625 | |
| | 31 | | Income Summary | | 37,430 | | |
| | | | Wages Expense | | | 22,855 | |
| | | | Depreciation Expense | | | 4,950 | |
| | | | Rent Expense | | | 4,200 | |
| | | | Utilities Expense | | | 2,715 | |
| | | | Supplies Expense | | | 890 | |
| | | | Insurance Expense | | | 315 | |
| | | | Miscellaneous Expense | | | 1,505 | |
| | 31 | | Income Summary | | 23,195 | | |
| | | | Retained Earnings | | | 23,195 | |
| | 31 | | Retained Earnings | | 5,200 | | |
| | | | Dividends | | | 5,200 | |

# Discussion Questions

1. Why do some accountants prepare an end-of-period spreadsheet?

2. Describe the nature of the assets that compose the following sections of a balance sheet: (a) current assets, (b) property, plant, and equipment.

3. What is the difference between a current liability and a long-term liability?

4. What types of accounts are referred to as temporary accounts?

5. Why are closing entries required at the end of an accounting period?

6. What is the difference between adjusting entries and closing entries?

7. What is the purpose of the post-closing trial balance?

8. (a) What is the most important output of the accounting cycle? (b) Do all companies have an accounting cycle? Explain.

9. What is the natural business year?

10. The fiscal years for several well-known companies are as follows:

| Company | Fiscal Year Ending | Company | Fiscal Year Ending |
|---|---|---|---|
| Sears | January 30 | Home Depot | January 31 |
| JCPenney | January 30 | Tiffany & Co. | January 31 |
| Target Corp. | January 30 | Limited Brands, Inc. | January 31 |

What general characteristic shared by these companies explains why they do not have fiscal years ending December 31?

# Practice Exercises

| Learning Objectives | Example Exercises | |
|---|---|---|
| OBJ. 1 | EE 4-1 *p. 154* | **PE 4-1A   Flow of accounts into financial statements** |

The balances for the accounts listed below appear in the Adjusted Trial Balance columns of the end-of-period spreadsheet. Indicate whether each account would flow into the income statement, retained earnings statement, or balance sheet.

1. Accounts Receivable
2. Capital Stock
3. Depreciation Expense—Equipment
4. Office Equipment
5. Rent Revenue
6. Supplies Expense
7. Unearned Revenue
8. Wages Payable

| | | |
|---|---|---|
| OBJ. 1 | EE 4-1 *p. 154* | **PE 4-1B   Flow of accounts into financial statements** |

The balances for the accounts listed below appear in the Adjusted Trial Balance columns of the end-of-period spreadsheet. Indicate whether each account would flow into the income statement, retained earnings statement, or balance sheet.

1. Accumulated Depreciation—Building
2. Cash
3. Dividends
4. Fees Earned
5. Insurance Expense
6. Prepaid Rent
7. Supplies
8. Wages Expense

| | | |
|---|---|---|
| OBJ. 2 | EE 4-2 *p. 156* | **PE 4-2A   Retained earnings statement** |

Judy Flint owns and operates Derby Advertising Services. On January 1, 2011, Retained Earnings had a balance of $290,000. During the year, Judy invested an additional $100,000 in exchange for capital stock. In addition, $40,000 of dividends were paid during the year. For the year ended December 31, 2011, Derby Advertising Services reported a net income of $93,750. Prepare a retained earnings statement for the year ended December 31, 2011.

| | | |
|---|---|---|
| OBJ. 2 | EE 4-2 *p. 156* | **PE 4-2B   Retained earnings statement** |

Mavis Curry owns and operates A2Z Delivery Services. On January 1, 2011, Retained Earnings had a balance of $600,000. During the year, Mavis made no additional investments and $45,000 of dividends were paid. For the year ended December 31, 2011, A2Z Delivery Services reported a net loss of $13,500. Prepare a retained earnings statement for the year ended December 31, 2011.

| | | |
|---|---|---|
| OBJ. 2 | EE 4-3 *p. 158* | **PE 4-3A   Classified balance sheet** |

The following accounts appear in an adjusted trial balance of Pilot Consulting. Indicate whether each account would be reported in the (a) current asset; (b) property, plant, and equipment; (c) current liability; (d) long-term liability; or (e) stockholders' equity section of the December 31, 2011, balance sheet of Pilot Consulting.

1. Building
2. Capital Stock
3. Notes Payable (due in 2017)
4. Prepaid Rent
5. Salaries Payable
6. Supplies
7. Taxes Payable
8. Unearned Service Fees

| Learning Objectives | Example Exercises | |
|---|---|---|
| OBJ. 2 | EE 4-3 *p. 158* | **PE 4-3B  Classified balance sheet** |

The following accounts appear in an adjusted trial balance of F-18 Consulting. Indicate whether each account would be reported in the (a) current asset; (b) property, plant, and equipment; (c) current liability; (d) long-term liability; or (e) stockholders' equity section of the December 31, 2011, balance sheet of F-18 Consulting.

1. Accounts Payable
2. Accounts Receivable
3. Accumulated Depreciation—Building
4. Capital Stock

5. Cash
6. Note Payable (due in 2018)
7. Supplies
8. Wages Payable

---

**OBJ. 3**  **EE 4-4** *p. 161*  **PE 4-4A  Closing entries**

After the accounts have been adjusted at October 31, the end of the fiscal year, the following balances were taken from the ledger of Silver Gate Delivery Services Co.:

| | |
|---|---|
| Retained Earnings | $800,000 |
| Dividends | 125,000 |
| Fees Earned | 700,000 |
| Wages Expense | 400,000 |
| Rent Expense | 75,000 |
| Supplies Expense | 16,000 |
| Miscellaneous Expense | 5,000 |

Journalize the four entries required to close the accounts.

---

**OBJ. 3**  **EE 4-4** *p. 161*  **PE 4-4B  Closing entries**

After the accounts have been adjusted at June 30, the end of the fiscal year, the following balances were taken from the ledger of Hillcrest Landscaping Co.:

| | |
|---|---|
| Retained Earnings | $275,000 |
| Dividends | 25,000 |
| Fees Earned | 400,000 |
| Wages Expense | 280,000 |
| Rent Expense | 40,000 |
| Supplies Expense | 3,000 |
| Miscellaneous Expense | 12,000 |

Journalize the four entries required to close the accounts.

---

**OBJ. 4**  **EE 4-5** *p. 164*  **PE 4-5A  Accounting cycle**

From the following list of steps in the accounting cycle, identify what two steps are missing.

a. Transactions are analyzed and recorded in the journal.
b. An unadjusted trial balance is prepared.
c. Adjustment data are assembled and analyzed.
d. An optional end-of-period spreadsheet is prepared.
e. Adjusting entries are journalized and posted to the ledger.
f. An adjusted trial balance is prepared.
g. Closing entries are journalized and posted to the ledger.
h. A post-closing trial balance is prepared.

---

**OBJ. 4**  **EE 4-5** *p. 164*  **PE 4-5B  Accounting cycle**

From the following list of steps in the accounting cycle, identify what two steps are missing.

a. Transactions are analyzed and recorded in the journal.
b. Transactions are posted to the ledger.

c. An unadjusted trial balance is prepared.

d. An optional end-of-period spreadsheet is prepared.

e. Adjusting entries are journalized and posted to the ledger.

f. An adjusted trial balance is prepared.

g. Financial statements are prepared.

h. A post-closing trial balance is prepared.

---

**OBJ. 7**  **EE 4-6** *p. 180*  **PE 4-6A**  **Working capital and current ratio**

**F·A·I**

The following balance sheet data for Mayer Company are shown below.

|  | 2012 | 2011 |
|---|---|---|
| Current assets | $840,000 | $1,430,000 |
| Current liabilities | 600,000 | 550,000 |

a. Determine the working capital and current ratio for 2012 and 2011.

b. Does the change in the current ratio from 2011 to 2012 indicate a favorable or an unfavorable trend?

---

**OBJ. 7**  **EE 4-6** *p. 180*  **PE 4-6B**  **Working capital and current ratio**

**F·A·I**

The following balance sheet data for Finn Company are shown below.

|  | 2012 | 2011 |
|---|---|---|
| Current assets | $288,000 | $171,000 |
| Current liabilities | 120,000 | 90,000 |

a. Determine the working capital and current ratio for 2012 and 2011.

b. Does the change in the current ratio from 2011 to 2012 indicate a favorable or an unfavorable trend?

# Exercises

---

**OBJ. 1, 2**

**EX 4-1**  **Flow of accounts into financial statements**

The balances for the accounts listed below appear in the Adjusted Trial Balance columns of the end-of-period spreadsheet. Indicate whether each account would flow into the income statement, retained earnings statement, or balance sheet.

1. Accounts Payable
2. Accounts Receivable
3. Cash
4. Dividends
5. Fees Earned

6. Supplies
7. Unearned Rent
8. Utilities Expense
9. Wages Expense
10. Wages Payable

---

**OBJ. 1, 2**

**EX 4-2**  **Classifying accounts**

Balances for each of the following accounts appear in an adjusted trial balance. Identify each as (a) asset, (b) liability, (c) revenue, or (d) expense.

1. Accounts Receivable
2. Equipment
3. Fees Earned
4. Insurance Expense
5. Prepaid Advertising
6. Prepaid Rent

7. Rent Revenue
8. Salary Expense
9. Salary Payable
10. Supplies
11. Supplies Expense
12. Unearned Rent

OBJ. 1, 2

**EX 4-3   Financial statements from the end-of-period spreadsheet**

Pacifica Consulting is a consulting firm owned and operated by Tara Milsap. The end-of-period spreadsheet shown below was prepared for the year ended August 31, 2012.

| | A | B | C | D | E | F | G |
|---|---|---|---|---|---|---|---|
| 1 | | Pacifica Consulting | | | | | |
| 2 | | End-of-Period Spreadsheet | | | | | |
| 3 | | For the Year Ended August 31, 2012 | | | | | |
| 4 | | Unadjusted | | | | Adjusted | |
| 5 | | Trial Balance | | Adjustments | | Trial Balance | |
| 6 | Account Title | Dr. | Cr. | Dr. | Cr. | Dr. | Cr. |
| 7 | | | | | | | |
| 8 | Cash | 9,500 | | | | 9,500 | |
| 9 | Accounts Receivable | 22,500 | | | | 22,500 | |
| 10 | Supplies | 2,400 | | | (a) 2,000 | 400 | |
| 11 | Office Equipment | 18,500 | | | | 18,500 | |
| 12 | Accumulated Depreciation | | 2,500 | | (b) 1,200 | | 3,700 |
| 13 | Accounts Payable | | 6,100 | | | | 6,100 |
| 14 | Salaries Payable | | | | (c) 300 | | 300 |
| 15 | Capital Stock | | 7,500 | | | | 7,500 |
| 16 | Retained Earnings | | 15,100 | | | | 15,100 |
| 17 | Dividends | 3,000 | | | | 3,000 | |
| 18 | Fees Earned | | 43,800 | | | | 43,800 |
| 19 | Salary Expense | 17,250 | | (c) 300 | | 17,550 | |
| 20 | Supplies Expense | | | (a) 2,000 | | 2,000 | |
| 21 | Depreciation Expense | | | (b) 1,200 | | 1,200 | |
| 22 | Miscellaneous Expense | 1,850 | | | | 1,850 | |
| 23 | | 75,000 | 75,000 | 3,500 | 3,500 | 76,500 | 76,500 |

Based on the preceding spreadsheet, prepare an income statement, retained earnings statement, and balance sheet for Pacifica Consulting.

OBJ. 1, 2

**EX 4-4   Financial statements from the end-of-period spreadsheet**

Three Winds Consulting is a consulting firm owned and operated by Gabriel Brull. The following end-of-period spreadsheet was prepared for the year ended June 30, 2012.

| | A | B | C | D | E | F | G |
|---|---|---|---|---|---|---|---|
| 1 | | Three Winds Consulting | | | | | |
| 2 | | End-of-Period Spreadsheet | | | | | |
| 3 | | For the Year Ended June 30, 2012 | | | | | |
| 4 | | Unadjusted | | | | Adjusted | |
| 5 | | Trial Balance | | Adjustments | | Trial Balance | |
| 6 | Account Title | Dr. | Cr. | Dr. | Cr. | Dr. | Cr. |
| 7 | | | | | | | |
| 8 | Cash | 7,500 | | | | 7,500 | |
| 9 | Accounts Receivable | 23,500 | | | | 23,500 | |
| 10 | Supplies | 3,000 | | | (a) 2,400 | 600 | |
| 11 | Office Equipment | 30,500 | | | | 30,500 | |
| 12 | Accumulated Depreciation | | 4,500 | | (b) 800 | | 5,300 |
| 13 | Accounts Payable | | 3,300 | | | | 3,300 |
| 14 | Salaries Payable | | | | (c) 500 | | 500 |
| 15 | Capital Stock | | 10,000 | | | | 10,000 |
| 16 | Retained Earnings | | 22,200 | | | | 22,200 |
| 17 | Dividends | 2,000 | | | | 2,000 | |
| 18 | Fees Earned | | 60,000 | | | | 60,000 |
| 19 | Salary Expense | 32,000 | | (c) 500 | | 32,500 | |
| 20 | Supplies Expense | | | (a) 2,400 | | 2,400 | |
| 21 | Depreciation Expense | | | (b) 800 | | 800 | |
| 22 | Miscellaneous Expense | 1,500 | | | | 1,500 | |
| 23 | | 100,000 | 100,000 | 3,700 | 3,700 | 101,300 | 101,300 |

Based on the preceding spreadsheet, prepare an income statement, retained earnings statement, and balance sheet for Three Winds Consulting.

**OBJ. 2**

✔ Net income,
$89,600

### EX 4-5  Income statement

The following account balances were taken from the adjusted trial balance for On-Time Messenger Service, a delivery service firm, for the current fiscal year ended April 30, 2012:

| Depreciation Expense | $ 6,400 | Rent Expense | $ 48,400 |
|---|---|---|---|
| Fees Earned | 340,000 | Salaries Expense | 171,040 |
| Insurance Expense | 1,200 | Supplies Expense | 2,200 |
| Miscellaneous Expense | 2,600 | Utilities Expense | 18,560 |

Prepare an income statement.

**OBJ. 2**

✔ Net loss, $36,600

### EX 4-6  Income statement; net loss

The following revenue and expense account balances were taken from the ledger of Graphics Services Co. after the accounts had been adjusted on February 29, 2012, the end of the current fiscal year:

| Depreciation Expense | $ 9,000 | Service Revenue | $250,000 |
|---|---|---|---|
| Insurance Expense | 4,000 | Supplies Expense | 3,000 |
| Miscellaneous Expense | 5,000 | Utilities Expense | 14,600 |
| Rent Expense | 36,000 | Wages Expense | 215,000 |

Prepare an income statement.

**OBJ. 2**

**Internet Project**

✔ a. Net income: $98

### EX 4-7  Income statement

FedEx Corporation had the following revenue and expense account balances (in millions) at its fiscal year-end of May 31, 2009:

| Depreciation | $1,975 | Purchased Transportation | $ 4,534 |
|---|---|---|---|
| Fuel | 3,811 | Rentals and Landing Fees | 2,429 |
| Maintenance and Repairs | 1,898 | Revenues | 35,497 |
| Other Expense (Income) Net | 6,406 | Salaries and Employee Benefits | 13,767 |
| Provision for Income Taxes | 579 | | |

a. Prepare an income statement.

b. ━━━▶ Compare your income statement with the related income statement that is available at the FedEx Corporation Web site, which is linked to the text's Web site at **www.cengage.com/accounting/reeve**. What similarities and differences do you see?

**OBJ. 2**

✔ Retained earnings, Oct. 31, 2012: $635,000

### EX 4-8  Retained earnings statement

Fouts Systems Co. offers its services to residents in the Chicago area. Selected accounts from the ledger of Fouts Systems Co. for the current fiscal year ended October 31, 2012, are as follows:

| **Retained Earnings** | | | | **Dividends** | | | |
|---|---|---|---|---|---|---|---|
| Oct. 31 | 20,000 | Nov. 1 (2011) | 550,000 | Jan. 31 | 5,000 | Oct. 31 | 20,000 |
| | | Oct. 31 | 105,000 | Apr. 30 | 5,000 | | |
| | | | | July 31 | 5,000 | | |
| | | | | Oct. 31 | 5,000 | | |

| **Income Summary** | | | |
|---|---|---|---|
| Oct. 31 | 375,000 | Oct. 31 | 480,000 |
| 31 | 105,000 | | |

Prepare a retained earnings statement for the year.

**OBJ. 2**

✔ Retained earnings, June 30, 2012: $346,500

### EX 4-9  Retained earnings statement; net loss

Selected accounts from the ledger of Balboa Sports for the current fiscal year ended June 30, 2012, are as follows:

| **Retained Earnings** | | | | **Dividends** | | | |
|---|---|---|---|---|---|---|---|
| June 30 | 42,000 | July 1 (2011) | 398,500 | Sept. 30 | 2,500 | June 30 | 10,000 |
| 30 | 10,000 | | | Dec. 31 | 2,500 | | |
| | | | | May 31 | 2,500 | | |
| | | | | June 30 | 2,500 | | |

**Income Summary**

| | | | |
|---|---|---|---|
| June 30 | 402,000 | June 30 | 360,000 |
| | | 30 | 42,000 |

Prepare a retained earnings statement for the year.

---

OBJ. 2

**EX 4-10    Classifying assets**

Identify each of the following as (a) a current asset or (b) property, plant, and equipment:

1. Accounts Receivable
2. Building
3. Cash
4. Equipment
5. Prepaid Insurance
6. Supplies

---

OBJ. 2

**EX 4-11    Balance sheet classification**

At the balance sheet date, a business owes a mortgage note payable of $480,000, the terms of which provide for monthly payments of $2,500.

➤ Explain how the liability should be classified on the balance sheet.

---

OBJ. 2

✔ Total assets: $750,000

**EX 4-12    Balance sheet**

My-Best Weight Co. offers personal weight reduction consulting services to individuals. After all the accounts have been closed on November 30, 2012, the end of the current fiscal year, the balances of selected accounts from the ledger of My-Best Weight Co. are as follows:

| | | | |
|---|---|---|---|
| Accounts Payable | $ 34,500 | Prepaid Insurance | $ 19,200 |
| Accounts Receivable | 83,120 | Prepaid Rent | 12,000 |
| Accumulated Depreciation—Equipment | 103,900 | Retained Earnings | 512,000 |
| Capital Stock | 180,000 | Salaries Payable | 13,500 |
| Cash | ? | Supplies | 2,080 |
| Equipment | 300,000 | Unearned Fees | 10,000 |
| Land | 400,000 | | |

Prepare a classified balance sheet that includes the correct balance for Cash.

---

OBJ. 2

✔ Corrected balance sheet, total assets: $525,000

**EX 4-13    Balance sheet**

List the errors you find in the following balance sheet. Prepare a corrected balance sheet.

**Poshe Services Co.**
**Balance Sheet**
**For the Year Ended May 31, 2012**

| Assets | | | Liabilities | | |
|---|---|---|---|---|---|
| Current assets: | | | Current liabilities: | | |
| Cash | $ 14,000 | | Accounts receivable | $ 32,500 | |
| Accounts payable | 24,000 | | Accum. depr.—building | 155,000 | |
| Supplies | 6,500 | | Accum. depr.—equipment | 25,000 | |
| Prepaid insurance | 12,000 | | Net income | 135,000 | |
| Land | 180,000 | | Total liabilities | | $347,500 |
| Total current assets | | $236,500 | | | |
| Property, plant, and equipment: | | | **Stockholders' Equity** | | |
| | | | Wages payable | $ 2,500 | |
| Building | $375,000 | | Capital stock | 150,000 | |
| Equipment | 85,000 | | Retained earnings | 348,500 | |
| Total property, plant, and equipment | | 612,000 | Total stockholders' equity | | 501,000 |
| | | | Total liabilities and | | |
| Total assets | | $848,500 | stockholders' equity | | $848,500 |

---

OBJ. 3

**EX 4-14    Identifying accounts to be closed**

From the list at the top of the next page, identify the accounts that should be closed to Income Summary at the end of the fiscal year:

a. Accounts Payable

b. Accumulated Depreciation—Equipment

c. Capital Stock

d. Depreciation Expense—Equipment

e. Dividends

f. Equipment

g. Fees Earned

h. Land

i. Supplies

j. Supplies Expense

k. Wages Expense

l. Wages Payable

**OBJ. 3**

### EX 4-15   Closing entries

Prior to its closing, Income Summary had total debits of $815,000 and total credits of $1,280,000.

➤ Briefly explain the purpose served by the income summary account and the nature of the entries that resulted in the $815,000 and the $1,280,000.

**OBJ. 3**

### EX 4-16   Closing entries with net income

After all revenue and expense accounts have been closed at the end of the fiscal year, Income Summary has a debit of $315,000 and a credit of $449,500. At the same date, Retained Earnings has a credit balance of $750,000, and Dividends has a balance of $40,000. (a) Journalize the entries required to complete the closing of the accounts. (b) Determine the amount of Retained Earnings at the end of the period.

**OBJ. 3**

### EX 4-17   Closing entries with net loss

Imex Services Co. offers its services to individuals desiring to improve their personal images. After the accounts have been adjusted at March 31, the end of the fiscal year, the following balances were taken from the ledger of Imex Services Co.

| | | | |
|---|---|---|---|
| Retained Earnings | $300,000 | Rent Expense | $40,000 |
| Dividends | 15,000 | Supplies Expense | 20,000 |
| Fees Earned | 180,000 | Miscellaneous Expense | 7,500 |
| Wages Expense | 90,000 | | |

Journalize the four entries required to close the accounts.

**OBJ. 3**

### EX 4-18   Identifying permanent accounts

Which of the following accounts will usually appear in the post-closing trial balance?

a. Accounts Payable

b. Accumulated Depreciation

c. Capital Stock

d. Cash

e. Dividends

f. Depreciation Expense

g. Fees Earned

h. Office Equipment

i. Salaries Expense

j. Salaries Payable

k. Supplies

**OBJ. 3**

✔ Correct column totals, $129,500

### EX 4-19   Post-closing trial balance

An accountant prepared the following post-closing trial balance:

**Gypsy Treasures Co.**
**Post-Closing Trial Balance**
**March 31, 2012**

| | Debit Balances | Credit Balances |
|---|---|---|
| Cash | 18,000 | |
| Accounts Receivable | 31,000 | |
| Supplies | | 5,500 |
| Equipment | | 75,000 |
| Accumulated Depreciation—Equipment | 19,000 | |
| Accounts Payable | 11,000 | |
| Salaries Payable | | 1,000 |
| Unearned Rent | 6,000 | |
| Capital Stock | 13,500 | |
| Retained Earnings | | 79,000 |
| | 98,500 | 160,500 |

Prepare a corrected post-closing trial balance. Assume that all accounts have normal balances and that the amounts shown are correct.

**OBJ. 4**

**EX 4-20 Steps in the accounting cycle**

Rearrange the following steps in the accounting cycle in proper sequence:

a. Financial statements are prepared.

b. An adjusted trial balance is prepared.

c. Adjustment data are asssembled and analyzed.

d. Adjusting entries are journalized and posted to the ledger.

e. Closing entries are journalized and posted to the ledger.

f. An unadjusted trial balance is prepared.

g. Transactions are posted to the ledger.

h. Transactions are analyzed and recorded in the journal.

i. An optional end-of-period spreadsheet (work sheet) is prepared.

j. A post-closing trial balance is prepared.

**OBJ. 7**

**EX 4-21 Working capital and current ratio**

The following data (in thousands) were taken from recent financial statements of Under Armour, Inc.:

| | December 31 | |
| | 2008 | 2007 |
|---|---|---|
| Current assets | $396,423 | $322,245 |
| Current liabilities | 113,110 | 95,699 |

a. Compute the working capital and the current ratio as of December 31, 2008 and 2007. Round to two decimal places.

b. What conclusions concerning the company's ability to meet its financial obligations can you draw from part (a)?

**OBJ. 7**

**EX 4-22 Working capital and current ratio**

The following data (in thousands) were taken from recent financial statements of Starbucks Corporation:

| | Sept. 27, 2009 | Sept. 28, 2008 |
|---|---|---|
| Current assets | $2,035,800 | $1,748,000 |
| Current liabilities | 1,581,000 | 2,189,700 |

a. Compute the working capital and the current ratio as of September 27, 2009, and September 28, 2008. Round to two decimal places.

b. What conclusions concerning the company's ability to meet its financial obligations can you draw from part (a)?

**Appendix**

**EX 4-23 Completing an end-of-period spreadsheet (work sheet)**

List (a) through (j) in the order they would be performed in preparing and completing an end-of-period spreadsheet (work sheet).

a. Add the Debit and Credit columns of the Unadjusted Trial Balance columns of the spreadsheet (work sheet) to verify that the totals are equal.

b. Add the Debit and Credit columns of the Balance Sheet and Income Statement columns of the spreadsheet (work sheet) to verify that the totals are equal.

c. Add or deduct adjusting entry data to trial balance amounts, and extend amounts to the Adjusted Trial Balance columns.

d. Add the Debit and Credit columns of the Adjustments columns of the spreadsheet (work sheet) to verify that the totals are equal.

e. Add the Debit and Credit columns of the Balance Sheet and Income Statement columns of the spreadsheet (work sheet) to determine the amount of net income or net loss for the period.

f. Add the Debit and Credit columns of the Adjusted Trial Balance columns of the spreadsheet (work sheet) to verify that the totals are equal.

g. Enter the adjusting entries into the spreadsheet (work sheet), based on the adjustment data.

h. Enter the amount of net income or net loss for the period in the proper Income Statement column and Balance Sheet column.

i. Enter the unadjusted account balances from the general ledger into the Unadjusted Trial Balance columns of the spreadsheet (work sheet).

j. Extend the adjusted trial balance amounts to the Income Statement columns and the Balance Sheet columns.

✔ Total debits of Adjustments column: $27

## Appendix
### EX 4-24  Adjustment data on an end-of-period spreadsheet (work sheet)

Zeidman Security Services Co. offers security services to business clients. The trial balance for Zeidman Security Services Co. has been prepared on the end-of-period spreadsheet (work sheet) for the year ended July 31, 2012, shown below.

**Zeidman Security Services Co.**
**End-of-Period Spreadsheet (Work Sheet)**
**For the Year Ended July 31, 2012**

| Account Title | Unadjusted Trial Balance | | Adjustments | | Adjusted Trial Balance | |
|---|---|---|---|---|---|---|
| | Dr. | Cr. | Dr. | Cr. | Dr. | Cr. |
| Cash | 12 | | | | | |
| Accounts Receivable | 80 | | | | | |
| Supplies | 8 | | | | | |
| Prepaid Insurance | 12 | | | | | |
| Land | 100 | | | | | |
| Equipment | 40 | | | | | |
| Accum. Depr.—Equipment | | 4 | | | | |
| Accounts Payable | | 36 | | | | |
| Wages Payable | | 0 | | | | |
| Capital Stock | | 40 | | | | |
| Retained Earnings | | 130 | | | | |
| Dividends | 8 | | | | | |
| Fees Earned | | 90 | | | | |
| Wages Expense | 20 | | | | | |
| Rent Expense | 12 | | | | | |
| Insurance Expense | 0 | | | | | |
| Utilities Expense | 6 | | | | | |
| Supplies Expense | 0 | | | | | |
| Depreciation Expense | 0 | | | | | |
| Miscellaneous Expense | 2 | | | | | |
| | 300 | 300 | | | | |

The data for year-end adjustments are as follows:

a. Fees earned, but not yet billed, $9.

b. Supplies on hand, $3.

c. Insurance premiums expired, $8.

d. Depreciation expense, $4.

e. Wages accrued, but not paid, $1.

Enter the adjustment data, and place the balances in the Adjusted Trial Balance columns.

✔ Net income: $41

## Appendix
### EX 4-25  Completing an end-of-period spreadsheet (work sheet)

Zeidman Security Services Co. offers security services to business clients. Complete the following end-of-period spreadsheet (work sheet) for Zeidman Security Services Co.

**Zeidman Security Services Co.**
**End-of-Period Spreadsheet (Work Sheet)**
**For the Year Ended July 31, 2012**

| Account Title | Adjusted Trial Balance | | Income Statement | | Balance Sheet | |
| --- | --- | --- | --- | --- | --- | --- |
| | Dr. | Cr. | Dr. | Cr. | Dr. | Cr. |
| Cash | 12 | | | | | |
| Accounts Receivable | 89 | | | | | |
| Supplies | 3 | | | | | |
| Prepaid Insurance | 4 | | | | | |
| Land | 100 | | | | | |
| Equipment | 40 | | | | | |
| Accum. Depr.—Equipment | | 8 | | | | |
| Accounts Payable | | 36 | | | | |
| Wages Payable | | 1 | | | | |
| Capital Stock | | 40 | | | | |
| Retained Earnings | | 130 | | | | |
| Dividends | 8 | | | | | |
| Fees Earned | | 99 | | | | |
| Wages Expense | 21 | | | | | |
| Rent Expense | 12 | | | | | |
| Insurance Expense | 8 | | | | | |
| Utilities Expense | 6 | | | | | |
| Supplies Expense | 5 | | | | | |
| Depreciation Expense | 4 | | | | | |
| Miscellaneous Expense | 2 | | | | | |
| | 314 | 314 | | | | |
| Net income (loss) | | | | | | |

✔ Retained earnings, July 31, 2012: $163

**Appendix**

**EX 4-26    Financial statements from an end-of-period spreadsheet (work sheet)**

Based on the data in Exercise 4-25, prepare an income statement, retained earnings statement, and balance sheet for Zeidman Security Services Co.

**Appendix**

**EX 4-27    Adjusting entries from an end-of-period spreadsheet (work sheet)**

Based on the data in Exercise 4-24, prepare the adjusting entries for Zeidman Security Services Co.

**Appendix**

**EX 4-28    Closing entries from an end-of-period spreadsheet (work sheet)**

Based on the data in Exercise 4-25, prepare the closing entries for Zeidman Security Services Co.

## Problems Series A

OBJ. 1, 2 , 3

✔ 3. Total assets: $239,500

**PR 4-1A    Financial statements and closing entries**

Beacon Company maintains and repairs warning lights, such as those found on radio towers and lighthouses. Beacon Company prepared the end-of-period spreadsheet shown on the next page at October 31, 2012, the end of the current fiscal year.

**Instructions**

1. Prepare an income statement for the year ended October 31.
2. Prepare a retained earnings statement for the year ended October 31.
3. Prepare a balance sheet as of October 31.
4. Based upon the end-of-period spreadsheet, journalize the closing entries.

5. Prepare a post-closing trial balance.

| | A | B | C | D | E | F | G |
|---|---|---|---|---|---|---|---|
| 1 | | | | | Beacon Company | | |
| 2 | | | | | End-of-Period Spreadsheet | | |
| 3 | | | | | For the Year Ended October 31, 2012 | | |
| 4 | | Unadjusted | | | | Adjusted | |
| 5 | | Trial Balance | | Adjustments | | Trial Balance | |
| 6 | Account Title | Dr. | Cr. | Dr. | Cr. | Dr. | Cr. |
| 7 | Cash | 5,800 | | | | 5,800 | |
| 8 | Accounts Receivable | 18,900 | | (a) 3,300 | | 22,200 | |
| 9 | Prepaid Insurance | 4,200 | | | (b) 2,500 | 1,700 | |
| 10 | Supplies | 2,730 | | | (c) 1,730 | 1,000 | |
| 11 | Land | 98,000 | | | | 98,000 | |
| 12 | Building | 200,000 | | | | 200,000 | |
| 13 | Accum. Depr.—Building | | 100,300 | | (d) 1,600 | | 101,900 |
| 14 | Equipment | 101,000 | | | | 101,000 | |
| 15 | Accum. Depr.—Equipment | | 85,100 | | (e) 3,200 | | 88,300 |
| 16 | Accounts Payable | | 5,700 | | | | 5,700 |
| 17 | Salaries & Wages Payable | | | | (f) 1,800 | | 1,800 |
| 18 | Unearned Rent | | 2,100 | (g) 1,000 | | | 1,100 |
| 19 | Capital Stock | | 25,000 | | | | 25,000 |
| 20 | Retained Earnings | | 78,100 | | | | 78,100 |
| 21 | Dividends | 10,000 | | | | 10,000 | |
| 22 | Fees Revenue | | 303,700 | | (a) 3,300 | | 307,000 |
| 23 | Rent Revenue | | | | (g) 1,000 | | 1,000 |
| 24 | Salaries & Wages Expense | 113,100 | | (f) 1,800 | | 114,900 | |
| 25 | Advertising Expense | 21,700 | | | | 21,700 | |
| 26 | Utilities Expense | 11,400 | | | | 11,400 | |
| 27 | Repairs Expense | 8,850 | | | | 8,850 | |
| 28 | Depr. Exp.—Equipment | | | (e) 3,200 | | 3,200 | |
| 29 | Insurance Expense | | | (b) 2,500 | | 2,500 | |
| 30 | Supplies Expense | | | (c) 1,730 | | 1,730 | |
| 31 | Depr. Exp.—Building | | | (d) 1,600 | | 1,600 | |
| 32 | Misc. Expense | 4,320 | | | | 4,320 | |
| 33 | | 600,000 | 600,000 | 15,130 | 15,130 | 609,900 | 609,900 |

OBJ. 2, 3

✔ 1. Retained
earnings, June 30:
$209,300

### PR 4-2A  Financial statements and closing entries

Info-Mart Company is an investigative services firm that is owned and operated by Tom Wagner. On June 30, 2012, the end of the current fiscal year, the accountant for Info-Mart Company prepared an end-of-period spreadsheet, a part of which is shown below.

| | A | F | G |
|---|---|---|---|
| 1 | | Info-Mart Company | |
| 2 | | End-of-Period Spreadsheet | |
| 3 | | For the Year Ended June 30, 2012 | |
| 4 | | Adjusted | |
| 5 | | Trial Balance | |
| 6 | Account Title | Dr. | Cr. |
| 7 | Cash | 20,000 | |
| 8 | Accounts Receivable | 47,200 | |
| 9 | Supplies | 7,500 | |
| 10 | Prepaid Insurance | 4,800 | |
| 11 | Building | 270,500 | |
| 12 | Accumulated Depreciation—Building | | 55,200 |
| 13 | Accounts Payable | | 6,000 |
| 14 | Salaries Payable | | 1,500 |
| 15 | Unearned Rent | | 3,000 |
| 16 | Capital Stock | | 75,000 |
| 17 | Retained Earnings | | 180,300 |
| 18 | Dividends | 50,000 | |
| 19 | Service Fees | | 500,000 |
| 20 | Rent Revenue | | 25,000 |
| 21 | Salaries Expense | 350,000 | |
| 22 | Rent Expense | 62,500 | |
| 23 | Supplies Expense | 12,000 | |
| 24 | Depreciation Expense—Building | 6,000 | |
| 25 | Utilities Expense | 4,400 | |
| 26 | Repairs Expense | 3,200 | |
| 27 | Insurance Expense | 2,800 | |
| 28 | Miscellaneous Expense | 5,100 | |
| 29 | | 846,000 | 846,000 |

**Instructions**

1. Prepare an income statement, retained earnings statement, and a balance sheet.

2. Journalize the entries that were required to close the accounts at June 30.

3. If Retained Earnings decreased $75,000 after the closing entries were posted, and the dividends remained the same, what was the amount of net income or net loss?

---

OBJ. 2, 3

✔ 2. Net income: $39,300

**PR 4-3A  T accounts, adjusting entries, financial statements, and closing entries; optional end-of-period spreadsheet (work sheet)**

The unadjusted trial balance of Launderland at November 30, 2012, the end of the current fiscal year, is shown below.

**Launderland**
**Unadjusted Trial Balance**
**November 30, 2012**

|  | Debit Balances | Credit Balances |
|---|---|---|
| Cash ...................................................... | 9,000 | |
| Laundry Supplies....................................... | 20,900 | |
| Prepaid Insurance ..................................... | 9,600 | |
| Laundry Equipment ................................... | 290,000 | |
| Accumulated Depreciation.......................... | | 150,400 |
| Accounts Payable ..................................... | | 11,800 |
| Capital Stock............................................ | | 15,000 |
| Retained Earnings..................................... | | 90,600 |
| Dividends ................................................ | 8,400 | |
| Laundry Revenue....................................... | | 232,200 |
| Wages Expense ........................................ | 97,000 | |
| Rent Expense ........................................... | 40,000 | |
| Utilities Expense ...................................... | 19,700 | |
| Miscellaneous Expense ............................. | 5,400 | |
| | 500,000 | 500,000 |

The data needed to determine year-end adjustments are as follows:

a. Laundry supplies on hand at November 30 are $5,000.

b. Insurance premiums expired during the year are $6,400.

c. Depreciation of equipment during the year is $7,000.

d. Wages accrued but not paid at November 30 are $1,500.

**Instructions**

1. For each account listed in the unadjusted trial balance, enter the balance in a T account. Identify the balance as "November 30 Bal." In addition, add T accounts for Wages Payable, Depreciation Expense, Laundry Supplies Expense, Insurance Expense, and Income Summary.

2. **Optional:** Enter the unadjusted trial balance on an end-of-period spreadsheet (work sheet) and complete the spreadsheet. Add the accounts listed in part (1) as needed.

3. Journalize and post the adjusting entries. Identify the adjustments by "Adj." and the new balances as "Adj. Bal."

4. Prepare an adjusted trial balance.

5. Prepare an income statement, a retained earnings statement, and a balance sheet.

6. Journalize and post the closing entries. Identify the closing entries by "Clos."

7. Prepare a post-closing trial balance.

---

OBJ. 2, 3

✔ 4. Net income: $22,350

**PR 4-4A  Ledger accounts, adjusting entries, financial statements, and closing entries; optional end-of-period spreadsheet (work sheet)**

*If the working papers correlating with this textbook are not used, omit Problem 4-4A.*

The ledger and trial balance of Wizard Services Co. as of July 31, 2012, the end of the first month of its current fiscal year, are presented in the working papers.

Data needed to determine the necessary adjusting entries are as follows:

a. Service revenue accrued at July 31 is $1,000.

b. Supplies on hand at July 31 are $3,900.

c. Insurance premiums expired during July are $1,100.

d. Depreciation of the building during July is $1,400.

e. Depreciation of equipment during July is $900.

f. Unearned rent at July 31 is $700.

g. Wages accrued at July 31 are $100.

**Instructions**

1. **Optional:** Complete the end-of-period spreadsheet (work sheet) using the adjustment data shown above.

2. Journalize and post the adjusting entries, inserting balances in the accounts affected.

3. Prepare an adjusted trial balance.

4. Prepare an income statement, a retained earnings statement, and a balance sheet.

5. Journalize and post the closing entries. Indicate closed accounts by inserting a line in both Balance columns opposite the closing entry. Insert the new balance of the retained earnings account.

6. Prepare a post-closing trial balance.

**OBJ. 2, 3**

✔ **5. Net income:**
**$63,700**

**PR 4-5A** **Ledger accounts, adjusting entries, financial statements, and closing entries; optional spreadsheet (work sheet)**

The unadjusted trial balance of Bruno's Hauling at February 29, 2012, the end of the current year, is shown below.

**Bruno's Hauling**
**Unadjusted Trial Balance**
**February 29, 2012**

| | | Debit Balances | Credit Balances |
|---|---|---|---|
| 11 | Cash | 5,000 | |
| 13 | Supplies | 12,000 | |
| 14 | Prepaid Insurance | 3,600 | |
| 16 | Equipment | 110,000 | |
| 17 | Accumulated Depreciation—Equipment | | 25,000 |
| 18 | Trucks | 60,000 | |
| 19 | Accumulated Depreciation—Trucks | | 15,000 |
| 21 | Accounts Payable | | 4,000 |
| 31 | Capital Stock | | 18,000 |
| 32 | Retained Earnings | | 53,000 |
| 33 | Dividends | 15,000 | |
| 41 | Service Revenue | | 160,000 |
| 51 | Wages Expense | 45,000 | |
| 53 | Rent Expense | 10,600 | |
| 54 | Truck Expense | 9,000 | |
| 59 | Miscellaneous Expense | 4,800 | |
| | | 275,000 | 275,000 |

The data needed to determine year-end adjustments are as follows:

a. Supplies on hand at February 29 are $1,000.

b. Insurance premiums expired during year are $2,400.

c. Depreciation of equipment during year is $8,000.

d. Depreciation of trucks during year is $5,000.

e. Wages accrued but not paid at February 29 are $500.

**Instructions**

1. For each account listed in the trial balance, enter the balance in the appropriate Balance column of a four-column account and place a check mark (✓) in the Posting Reference column.

*(Continued)*

2. **Optional:** Enter the unadjusted trial balance on an end-of-period spreadsheet (work sheet) and complete the spreadsheet. Add the accounts listed in part (3) as needed.

3. Journalize and post the adjusting entries, inserting balances in the accounts affected. Record the adjusting entries on Page 26 of the journal. The following additional accounts from Bruno's Hauling's chart of accounts should be used: Wages Payable, 22; Supplies Expense, 52; Depreciation Expense—Equipment, 55; Depreciation Expense—Trucks, 56; Insurance Expense, 57.

4. Prepare an adjusted trial balance.

5. Prepare an income statement, a retained earnings statement, and a balance sheet.

6. Journalize and post the closing entries. Record the closing entries on Page 27 of the journal. (Income Summary is account #34 in the chart of accounts.) Indicate closed accounts by inserting a line in both Balance columns opposite the closing entry.

7. Prepare a post-closing trial balance.

---

**OBJ. 4, 5**

✔ 8. Net income: $23,500

### PR 4-6A  Complete accounting cycle

For the past several years, Shane Banovich has operated a part-time consulting business from his home. As of October 1, 2012, Shane decided to move to rented quarters and to operate the business as a professional corporation, which was to be known as Epic Consulting, P.C., on a full-time basis. Epic Consulting entered into the following transactions during October:

Oct. 1. The following assets were received from Shane Banovich in exchange for capital stock: cash, $12,000; accounts receivable, $6,000; supplies, $1,500; and office equipment, $9,000. There were no liabilities received.

1. Paid three months' rent on a lease rental contract, $4,800.

2. Paid the premiums on property and casualty insurance policies, $3,000.

4. Received cash from clients as an advance payment for services to be provided and recorded it as unearned fees, $4,000.

5. Purchased additional office equipment on account from Office Station Co., $2,000.

6. Received cash from clients on account, $3,500.

10. Paid cash for a newspaper advertisement, $400.

12. Paid Office Station Co. for part of the debt incurred on October 5, $1,000.

12. Recorded services provided on account for the period October 1–12, $6,000.

14. Paid part-time receptionist for two weeks' salary, $1,000.

*Record the following transactions on Page 2 of the journal.*

17. Recorded cash from cash clients for fees earned during the period October 1–17, $7,500.

18. Paid cash for supplies, $750.

20. Recorded services provided on account for the period October 13–20, $5,200.

24. Recorded cash from cash clients for fees earned for the period October 17–24, $3,700.

26. Received cash from clients on account, $5,500.

27. Paid part-time receptionist for two weeks' salary, $1,000.

29. Paid telephone bill for October, $250.

31. Paid electricity bill for October, $300.

31. Recorded cash from cash clients for fees earned for the period October 25–31, $2,800.

31. Recorded services provided on account for the remainder of October, $3,000.

31. Paid dividends of $8,000.

**Instructions**

1. Journalize each transaction in a two-column journal starting on Page 1, referring to the following chart of accounts in selecting the accounts to be debited and credited. (Do not insert the account numbers in the journal at this time.)

| | |
|---|---|
| 11 Cash | 31 Capital Stock |
| 12 Accounts Receivable | 32 Retained Earnings |
| 14 Supplies | 33 Dividends |
| 15 Prepaid Rent | 41 Fees Earned |
| 16 Prepaid Insurance | 51 Salary Expense |
| 18 Office Equipment | 52 Rent Expense |
| 19 Accumulated Depreciation | 53 Supplies Expense |
| 21 Accounts Payable | 54 Depreciation Expense |
| 22 Salaries Payable | 55 Insurance Expense |
| 23 Unearned Fees | 59 Miscellaneous Expense |

2. Post the journal to a ledger of four-column accounts.

3. Prepare an unadjusted trial balance.

4. At the end of October, the following adjustment data were assembled. Analyze and use these data to complete parts (5) and (6).

   a. Insurance expired during October is $250.

   b. Supplies on hand on October 31 are $700.

   c. Depreciation of office equipment for October is $300.

   d. Accrued receptionist salary on October 31 is $250.

   e. Rent expired during October is $1,600.

   f. Unearned fees on October 31 are $1,800.

5. **Optional:** Enter the unadjusted trial balance on an end-of-period spreadsheet (work sheet) and complete the spreadsheet.

6. Journalize and post the adjusting entries. Record the adjusting entries on Page 3 of the journal.

7. Prepare an adjusted trial balance.

8. Prepare an income statement, a retained earnings statement, and a balance sheet.

9. Prepare and post the closing entries. (Income Summary is account #34 in the chart of accounts.) Record the closing entries on Page 4 of the journal. Indicate closed accounts by inserting a line in both the Balance columns opposite the closing entry.

10. Prepare a post-closing trial balance.

## Problems Series B

OBJ. 1, 2, 3

✔ 3. Total assets: $290,175

**PR 4-1B    Financial statements and closing entries**

DNA 4 U Company offers legal consulting advice to prison inmates. DNA 4 U Company prepared the end-of-period spreadsheet at the top of the following page at April 30, 2012, the end of the current fiscal year.

**Instructions**

1. Prepare an income statement for the year ended April 30.

2. Prepare a retained earnings statement for the year ended April 30.

3. Prepare a balance sheet as of April 30.

4. On the basis of the end-of-period spreadsheet, journalize the closing entries.

5. Prepare a post-closing trial balance.

| | A | B | C | D | E | F | G |
|---|---|---|---|---|---|---|---|
| 1 | | | | DNA 4 U Company | | | |
| 2 | | | | End-of-Period Spreadsheet | | | |
| 3 | | | | For the Year Ended April 30, 2012 | | | |
| 4 | | Unadjusted | | | | Adjusted | |
| 5 | | Trial Balance | | Adjustments | | Trial Balance | |
| 6 | Account Title | Dr. | Cr. | Dr. | Cr. | Dr. | Cr. |
| 7 | Cash | 5,100 | | | | 5,100 | |
| 8 | Accounts Receivable | 12,750 | | (a) 1,250 | | 14,000 | |
| 9 | Prepaid Insurance | 3,600 | | | (b) 1,200 | 2,400 | |
| 10 | Supplies | 2,025 | | | (c) 1,400 | 625 | |
| 11 | Land | 80,000 | | | | 80,000 | |
| 12 | Building | 200,000 | | | | 200,000 | |
| 13 | Accum. Depr.—Building | | 90,000 | | (d) 2,500 | | 92,500 |
| 14 | Equipment | 140,000 | | | | 140,000 | |
| 15 | Accum. Depr.—Equipment | | 54,450 | | (e) 5,000 | | 59,450 |
| 16 | Accounts Payable | | 9,750 | | | | 9,750 |
| 17 | Sal. & Wages Payable | | | | (f) 1,900 | | 1,900 |
| 18 | Unearned Rent | | 4,500 | (g) 3,000 | | | 1,500 |
| 19 | Capital Stock | | 100,000 | | | | 100,000 |
| 20 | Retained Earnings | | 211,300 | | | | 211,300 |
| 21 | Dividends | 20,000 | | | | 20,000 | |
| 22 | Fees Revenue | | 280,000 | | (a) 1,250 | | 281,250 |
| 23 | Rent Revenue | | | | (g) 3,000 | | 3,000 |
| 24 | Salaries & Wages Expense | 145,100 | | (f) 1,900 | | 147,000 | |
| 25 | Advertising Expense | 86,800 | | | | 86,800 | |
| 26 | Utilities Expense | 30,000 | | | | 30,000 | |
| 27 | Travel Expense | 18,750 | | | | 18,750 | |
| 28 | Depr. Exp.—Equipment | | | (e) 5,000 | | 5,000 | |
| 29 | Depr. Exp.—Building | | | (d) 2,500 | | 2,500 | |
| 30 | Supplies Expense | | | (c) 1,400 | | 1,400 | |
| 31 | Insurance Expense | | | (b) 1,200 | | 1,200 | |
| 32 | Misc. Expense | 5,875 | | | | 5,875 | |
| 33 | | 750,000 | 750,000 | 16,250 | 16,250 | 760,650 | 760,650 |

OBJ. 2, 3

✔ 1. Retained earnings, July 31: $408,000

## PR 4-2B Financial statements and closing entries

Mather Services Company is a financial planning services firm owned and operated by Lee Mather. As of July 31, 2012, the end of the current fiscal year, the accountant for Mather Services Company prepared an end-of-period spreadsheet (work sheet), part of which is shown below.

| | A | F | G |
|---|---|---|---|
| 1 | Mather Services Company | | |
| 2 | End-of-Period Spreadsheet | | |
| 3 | For the Year Ended July 31, 2012 | | |
| 4 | | Adjusted | |
| 5 | | Trial Balance | |
| 6 | Account Title | Dr. | Cr. |
| 7 | Cash | 11,000 | |
| 8 | Accounts Receivable | 28,150 | |
| 9 | Supplies | 6,350 | |
| 10 | Prepaid Insurance | 9,500 | |
| 11 | Land | 100,000 | |
| 12 | Buildings | 360,000 | |
| 13 | Accumulated Depreciation—Buildings | | 117,200 |
| 14 | Equipment | 260,000 | |
| 15 | Accumulated Depreciation—Equipment | | 151,700 |
| 16 | Accounts Payable | | 33,300 |
| 17 | Salaries Payable | | 3,300 |
| 18 | Unearned Rent | | 1,500 |
| 19 | Capital Stock | | 60,000 |
| 20 | Retained Earnings | | 347,000 |
| 21 | Dividends | 25,000 | |
| 22 | Service Fees | | |
| 23 | Rent Revenue | | 475,000 |
| 24 | Salaries Expense | 325,000 | 5,000 |
| 25 | Depreciation Expense—Equipment | 17,500 | |
| 26 | Rent Expense | 15,500 | |
| 27 | Supplies Expense | 9,000 | |
| 28 | Utilities Expense | 8,500 | |
| 29 | Depreciation Expense—Buildings | 6,600 | |
| 30 | Repairs Expense | 3,450 | |
| 31 | Insurance Expense | 3,000 | |
| 32 | Miscellaneous Expense | 5,450 | |
| 33 | | 1,194,000 | 1,194,000 |

### Instructions

1. Prepare an income statement, a retained earnings statement, and a balance sheet.
2. Journalize the entries that were required to close the accounts at July 31.
3. If the balance of Retained Earnings increased $40,000 after the closing entries were posted, and the dividends remained the same, what was the amount of net income or net loss?

OBJ. 2 , 3

✔ 2. Net income: $30,640

GENERAL
·· LEDGER:·

### PR 4-3B   T accounts, adjusting entries, financial statements, and closing entries; optional end-of-period spreadsheet (work sheet)

The unadjusted trial balance of Laundry Basket at January 31, 2012, the end of the current fiscal year, is shown below.

**Laundry Basket**
**Unadjusted Trial Balance**
**January 31, 2012**

| | Debit Balances | Credit Balances |
|---|---|---|
| Cash ..................................................... | 3,480 | |
| Laundry Supplies..................................... | 9,000 | |
| Prepaid Insurance .................................. | 5,760 | |
| Laundry Equipment ................................ | 130,800 | |
| Accumulated Depreciation........................ | | 49,200 |
| Accounts Payable .................................. | | 7,440 |
| Capital Stock......................................... | | 8,000 |
| Retained Earnings.................................. | | 37,360 |
| Dividends ............................................. | 2,400 | |
| Laundry Revenue.................................... | | 198,000 |
| Wages Expense ..................................... | 85,800 | |
| Rent Expense ........................................ | 43,200 | |
| Utilities Expense .................................... | 16,320 | |
| Miscellaneous Expense ........................... | 3,240 | |
| | 300,000 | 300,000 |

The data needed to determine year-end adjustments are as follows:

a.  Wages accrued but not paid at January 31 are $900.

b.  Depreciation of equipment during the year is $7,000.

c.  Laundry supplies on hand at January 31 are $2,100.

d.  Insurance premiums expired during the year are $4,000.

### Instructions

1.  For each account listed in the unadjusted trial balance, enter the balance in a T account. Identify the balance as "Jan. 31 Bal." In addition, add T accounts for Wages Payable, Depreciation Expense, Laundry Supplies Expense, Insurance Expense, and Income Summary.

2.  **Optional:** Enter the unadjusted trial balance on an end-of-period spreadsheet (work sheet) and complete the spreadsheet. Add the accounts listed in part (1) as needed.

3.  Journalize and post the adjusting entries. Identify the adjustments by "Adj." and the new balances as "Adj. Bal."

4.  Prepare an adjusted trial balance.

5.  Prepare an income statement, a retained earnings statement, and a balance sheet.

6.  Journalize and post the closing entries. Identify the closing entries by "Clos."

7.  Prepare a post-closing trial balance.

OBJ. 2

✔ 4. Net income: $22,150

### PR 4-4B   Ledger accounts, adjusting entries, financial statements, and closing entries; optional end-of-period spreadsheet (work sheet)

*If the working papers correlating with this textbook are not used, omit Problem 4-4B.*

The ledger and trial balance of Sweetwater Services Co. as of July 31, 2012, the end of the first month of its current fiscal year, are presented in the working papers.
   Data needed to determine the necessary adjusting entries are as follows:

a.  Service revenue accrued at July 31 is $1,500.

b.  Supplies on hand at July 31 are $3,800.

c.  Insurance premiums expired during July are $1,200.

d.  Depreciation of the building during July is $1,400.

e.  Depreciation of equipment during July is $1,100.

f.   Unearned rent at July 31 is $900.

g.  Wages accrued but not paid at July 31 are $200.

**Instructions**

1. **Optional:** Complete the end-of-period spreadsheet (work sheet) using the adjustment data shown on the previous page.

2. Journalize and post the adjusting entries, inserting balances in the accounts affected.

3. Prepare an adjusted trial balance.

4. Prepare an income statement, a retained earnings statement, and a balance sheet.

5. Journalize and post the closing entries. Indicate closed accounts by inserting a line in both Balance columns opposite the closing entry. Insert the new balance of the retained earnings account.

6. Prepare a post-closing trial balance.

OBJ. 2, 3

✔ 5. Net income: $35,150

**PR 4-5B  Ledger accounts, adjusting entries, financial statements, and closing entries; optional end-of-period spreadsheet (work sheet)**

The unadjusted trial balance of Oak and Brass Interiors at December 31, 2012, the end of the current year, is shown below.

**Oak and Brass Interiors**
**Unadjusted Trial Balance**
**December 31, 2012**

| | | Debit Balances | Credit Balances |
|---|---|---|---|
| 11 | Cash | 3,100 | |
| 13 | Supplies | 6,000 | |
| 14 | Prepaid Insurance | 7,500 | |
| 16 | Equipment | 90,000 | |
| 17 | Accumulated Depreciation—Equipment | | 12,000 |
| 18 | Trucks | 50,000 | |
| 19 | Accumulated Depreciation—Trucks | | 27,100 |
| 21 | Accounts Payable | | 4,500 |
| 31 | Capital Stock | | 10,000 |
| 32 | Retained Earnings | | 56,400 |
| 33 | Dividends | 3,000 | |
| 41 | Service Revenue | | 140,000 |
| 51 | Wages Expense | 72,000 | |
| 52 | Rent Expense | 7,600 | |
| 53 | Truck Expense | 5,350 | |
| 59 | Miscellaneous Expense | 5,450 | |
| | | 250,000 | 250,000 |

The data needed to determine year-end adjustments are as follows:

a. Supplies on hand at December 31 are $1,750.

b. Insurance premiums expired during the year are $2,000.

c. Depreciation of equipment during the year is $5,000.

d. Depreciation of trucks during the year is $2,200.

e. Wages accrued but not paid at December 31 are $1,000.

**Instructions**

1. For each account listed in the unadjusted trial balance, enter the balance in the appropriate Balance column of a four-column account and place a check mark (✓) in the Posting Reference column.

2. **Optional:** Enter the unadjusted trial balance on an end-of-period spreadsheet (work sheet) and complete the spreadsheet. Add the accounts listed in part (3) as needed.

3. Journalize and post the adjusting entries, inserting balances in the accounts affected. Record the adjusting entries on Page 26 of the journal. The following additional accounts from Oak and Brass Interiors' chart of accounts should be used: Wages Payable, 22; Depreciation Expense—Equipment, 54; Supplies Expense, 55; Depreciation Expense—Trucks, 56; Insurance Expense, 57.

4. Prepare an adjusted trial balance.

5. Prepare an income statement, a retained earnings statement, and a balance sheet.

6. Journalize and post the closing entries. Record the closing entries on Page 27 of the journal. (Income Summary is account #34 in the chart of accounts.) Indicate closed accounts by inserting a line in both Balance columns opposite the closing entry.

7. Prepare a post-closing trial balance.

**OBJ. 4, 5**

✔ 8. Net income: $35,150

### PR 4-6B   Complete accounting cycle

For the past several years, Abby Brown has operated a part-time consulting business from her home. As of June 1, 2012, Abby decided to move to rented quarters and to operate the business as a professional corporation, which was to be known as Square One Consulting, P.C., on a full-time basis. Square One Consulting entered into the following transactions during June:

June  1. The following assets were received from Abby Brown in exchange for capital stock: cash, $30,000; accounts receivable, $7,500; supplies, $2,000; and office equipment, $15,000. There were no liabilities received.

1. Paid three months' rent on a lease rental contract, $6,000.

2. Paid the premiums on property and casualty insurance policies, $3,600.

4. Received cash from clients as an advance payment for services to be provided and recorded it as unearned fees, $5,000.

5. Purchased additional office equipment on account from Office Depot Co., $6,000.

6. Received cash from clients on account, $4,000.

10. Paid cash for a newspaper advertisement, $200.

12. Paid Office Depot Co. for part of the debt incurred on June 5, $1,200.

12. Recorded services provided on account for the period June 1–12, $13,000.

14. Paid part-time receptionist for two weeks' salary, $1,500.

*Record the following transactions on Page 2 of the journal.*

17. Recorded cash from cash clients for fees earned during the period June 1–16, $9,000.

18. Paid cash for supplies, $1,400.

20. Recorded services provided on account for the period June 13–20, $8,500.

24. Recorded cash from cash clients for fees earned for the period June 17–24, $6,300.

26. Received cash from clients on account, $12,100.

27. Paid part-time receptionist for two weeks' salary, $1,500.

29. Paid telephone bill for June, $150.

30. Paid electricity bill for June, $400.

30. Recorded cash from cash clients for fees earned for the period June 25–30, $3,900.

30. Recorded services provided on account for the remainder of June, $2,500.

30. Paid dividends of $10,000.

### Instructions

1. Journalize each transaction in a two-column journal starting on Page 1, referring to the following chart of accounts in selecting the accounts to be debited and credited. (Do not insert the account numbers in the journal at this time.)

| | | | |
|---|---|---|---|
| 11 | Cash | 31 | Capital Stock |
| 12 | Accounts Receivable | 32 | Retained Earnings |
| 14 | Supplies | 33 | Dividends |
| 15 | Prepaid Rent | 41 | Fees Earned |
| 16 | Prepaid Insurance | 51 | Salary Expense |
| 18 | Office Equipment | 52 | Supplies Expense |
| 19 | Accumulated Depreciation | 53 | Rent Expense |
| 21 | Accounts Payable | 54 | Depreciation Expense |
| 22 | Salaries Payable | 55 | Insurance Expense |
| 23 | Unearned Fees | 59 | Miscellaneous Expense |

*(Continued)*

2. Post the journal to a ledger of four-column accounts.

3. Prepare an unadjusted trial balance.

4. At the end of June, the following adjustment data were assembled. Analyze and use these data to complete parts (5) and (6).

   a. Insurance expired during June is $200.

   b. Supplies on hand on June 30 are $600.

   c. Depreciation of office equipment for June is $250.

   d. Accrued receptionist salary on June 30 is $350.

   e. Rent expired during June is $2,500.

   f. Unearned fees on June 30 are $3,200.

5. **Optional:** Enter the unadjusted trial balance on an end-of-period spreadsheet (work sheet) and complete the spreadsheet.

6. Journalize and post the adjusting entries. Record the adjusting entries on Page 3 of the journal.

7. Prepare an adjusted trial balance.

8. Prepare an income statement, a retained earnings statement, and a balance sheet.

9. Prepare and post the closing entries. Record the closing entries on Page 4 of the journal. (Income Summary is account #34 in the chart of accounts.) Indicate closed accounts by inserting a line in both the Balance columns opposite the closing entry.

10. Prepare a post-closing trial balance.

## Continuing Problem

✔ 2. Net income: $6,210

The unadjusted trial balance of PS Music as of July 31, 2012, along with the adjustment data for the two months ended July 31, 2012, are shown in Chapter 3.

Based upon the adjustment data, the adjusted trial balance shown below was prepared.

**PS Music**
**Adjusted Trial Balance**
**July 31, 2012**

|  | Debit Balances | Credit Balances |
|---|---|---|
| Cash | 10,510 | |
| Accounts Receivable | 4,750 | |
| Supplies | 400 | |
| Prepaid Insurance | 2,475 | |
| Office Equipment | 6,000 | |
| Accumulated Depreciation—Office Equipment | | 75 |
| Accounts Payable | | 7,080 |
| Wages Payable | | 170 |
| Unearned Revenue | | 3,600 |
| Capital Stock | | 9,000 |
| Dividends | 2,000 | |
| Fees Earned | | 21,950 |
| Wages Expense | 2,970 | |
| Office Rent Expense | 2,550 | |
| Equipment Rent Expense | 1,300 | |
| Utilities Expense | 1,060 | |
| Music Expense | 3,610 | |
| Advertising Expense | 1,450 | |
| Supplies Expense | 1,030 | |
| Insurance Expense | 225 | |
| Depreciation Expense | 75 | |
| Miscellaneous Expense | 1,470 | |
| | 41,875 | 41,875 |

## Instructions

1. **Optional.** Using the data from Chapter 3, prepare an end-of-period spreadsheet (work sheet).

2. Prepare an income statement, a retained earnings statement, and a balance sheet.

3. Journalize and post the closing entries. The income summary account is #34 in the ledger of PS Music. Indicate closed accounts by inserting a line in both Balance columns opposite the closing entry.

4. Prepare a post-closing trial balance.

# Comprehensive Problem 1

✔ 8. Net income, $25,680

Kelly Pitney began her consulting business, Kelly Consulting, P.C., on April 1, 2012. The accounting cycle for Kelly Consulting for April, including financial statements, was illustrated on pages 165–175. During May, Kelly Consulting entered into the following transactions:

May 3. Received cash from clients as an advance payment for services to be provided and recorded it as unearned fees, $3,000.

5. Received cash from clients on account, $2,100.

9. Paid cash for a newspaper advertisement, $300.

13. Paid Office Station Co. for part of the debt incurred on April 5, $400.

15. Recorded services provided on account for the period May 1–15, $7,350.

16. Paid part-time receptionist for two weeks' salary including the amount owed on April 30, $750.

*Record the following transactions on Page 6 of the journal.*

17. Recorded cash from cash clients for fees earned during the period May 1–16, $6,150.

20. Purchased supplies on account, $600.

21. Recorded services provided on account for the period May 16–20, $6,175.

25. Recorded cash from cash clients for fees earned for the period May 17–23, $3,125.

27. Received cash from clients on account, $11,250.

28. Paid part-time receptionist for two weeks' salary, $750.

30. Paid telephone bill for May, $120.

31. Paid electricity bill for May, $290.

31. Recorded cash from cash clients for fees earned for the period May 26–31, $2,800.

31. Recorded services provided on account for the remainder of May, $1,900.

31. Paid dividends of $15,000.

## Instructions

1. The chart of accounts for Kelly Consulting is shown on page 166, and the post-closing trial balance as of April 30, 2012, is shown on page 173. For each account in the post-closing trial balance, enter the balance in the appropriate Balance column of a four-column account. Date the balances May 1, 2012, and place a check mark (✓) in the Posting Reference column. Journalize each of the May transactions in a two-column journal starting on Page 5 of the journal and using Kelly Consulting's chart of accounts. (Do not insert the account numbers in the journal at this time.)

2. Post the journal to a ledger of four-column accounts.

3. Prepare an unadjusted trial balance.

4. At the end of May, the following adjustment data were assembled. Analyze and use these data to complete parts (5) and (6).

a. Insurance expired during May is $300.

b. Supplies on hand on May 31 are $750.

c. Depreciation of office equipment for May is $330.

*(Continued)*

    d. Accrued receptionist salary on May 31 is $300.

    e. Rent expired during May is $1,600.

    f. Unearned fees on May 31 are $1,500.

5. **Optional:** Enter the unadjusted trial balance on an end-of-period spreadsheet (work sheet) and complete the spreadsheet.

6. Journalize and post the adjusting entries. Record the adjusting entries on Page 7 of the journal.

7. Prepare an adjusted trial balance.

8. Prepare an income statement, a retained earnings statement, and a balance sheet.

9. Prepare and post the closing entries. Record the closing entries on Page 8 of the journal. (Income Summary is account #34 in the chart of accounts.) Indicate closed accounts by inserting a line in both the Balance columns opposite the closing entry.

10. Prepare a post-closing trial balance.

# Cases & Projects

You can access Cases & Projects online at **www.cengage.com/accounting/reeve**

# Excel Success Special Activities

*success*

## SA 4-1 Financial statements

The end-of-month adjusted trial balance for Impact Tools was as follows:

| | A | B | C |
|---|---|---|---|
| 1 | | **Impact Tools** | |
| 2 | | **Adjusted Trial Balance** | |
| 3 | | **August 31, 2011** | |
| 4 | | | |
| 5 | | **Debit** | **Credit** |
| 6 | | **Balance** | **Balance** |
| 7 | Cash | 12,400 | |
| 8 | Accounts Receivable | 2,450 | |
| 9 | Supplies | 980 | |
| 10 | Prepaid Rent | 3,600 | |
| 11 | Equipment | 12,800 | |
| 12 | Accumulated Depreciation | | 3,260 |
| 13 | Accounts Payable | | 1,050 |
| 14 | Salaries Payable | | 490 |
| 15 | Capital | | 22,570 |
| 16 | Dividends | 7,500 | |
| 17 | Fees Earned | | 21,300 |
| 18 | Salary Expense | 5,270 | |
| 19 | Rent Expense | 1,200 | |
| 20 | Supplies Expense | 1,140 | |
| 21 | Depreciation Expense | 820 | |
| 22 | Miscellaneous Expense | 510 | |
| 23 | | 48,670 | 48,670 |
| 24 | | | |

FS

a. Open the Excel file *SA4-1_1e*.

b. On the worksheet labeled FS, complete the income statement, statement of retained earnings, and balance sheet from the adjusted trial balance.

c. When you have completed the financial statements, perform a "save as," replacing the entire file name with the following:

    *SA4-1_1e[your first name initial]_[your last name]*

### SA 4-2    Financial statements

The end-of-month adjusted trial balance for Fauna and Flowers was as follows:

|  | A | B | C |
|---|---|---|---|
| 1 | **Fauna and Flowers** | | |
| 2 | **Adjusted Trial Balance** | | |
| 3 | **March 31, 2013** | | |
| 4 | | | |
| 5 | | **Debit** | **Credit** |
| 6 | | **Balance** | **Balance** |
| 7 | Cash | 12,700 | |
| 8 | Accounts Receivable | 3,650 | |
| 9 | Supplies | 1,230 | |
| 10 | Equipment | 9,410 | |
| 11 | Accumulated Depreciation | | 1,250 |
| 12 | Accounts Payable | | 1,460 |
| 13 | Salaries Payable | | 940 |
| 14 | Unearned Revenue | | 560 |
| 15 | Capital | | 21,820 |
| 16 | Dividends | 5,230 | |
| 17 | Fees Earned | | 16,530 |
| 18 | Salary Expense | 6,790 | |
| 19 | Rent Expense | 1,800 | |
| 20 | Supplies Expense | 940 | |
| 21 | Depreciation Expense | 580 | |
| 22 | Miscellaneous Expense | 230 | |
| 23 | | 42,560 | 42,560 |
| 24 | | | |

FS

a.  Open the Excel file *SA4-2_1e*.

b.  On the worksheet labeled FS, complete the income statement, statement of retained earnings, and balance sheet from the adjusted trial balance.

c.  When you have completed creating the financial statements, perform a "save as," replacing the entire file name with the following:

 *SA4-2_1e[your first name initial]_[your last name]*

### SA 4-3    ImagePress—Financial Statements

ImagePress Printing's adjusted trial balance from SA3-3 is as follows:

|  | A | B | C |
|---|---|---|---|
| 1 | **ImagePress Printing** | | |
| 2 | **Adjusted Trial Balance** | | |
| 3 | **April 30, 2011** | | |
| 4 | | **Debit** | **Credit** |
| 5 | | **Balances** | **Balances** |
| 6 | Cash | 8,240 | |
| 7 | Accounts Receivable | 17,170 | |
| 8 | Supplies | 600 | |
| 9 | Office Equipment | 21,850 | |
| 10 | Accumulated Depreciation | | 4,250 |
| 11 | Accounts Payable | | 11,310 |
| 12 | Capital | | 23,800 |
| 13 | Dividends | 5,900 | |
| 14 | Fees Earned | | 36,550 |
| 15 | Advertising Expense | 660 | |
| 16 | Rent Expense | 7,500 | |
| 17 | Salaries Expense | 5,500 | |
| 18 | Utilities Expense | 2,540 | |
| 19 | Depreciation Expense | 4,250 | |
| 20 | Supplies Expense | 1,700 | |
| 21 | | 75,910 | 75,910 |
| 22 | | | |

FS

a.  Open the Excel file *SA4-3_1e*.

b.  On the worksheet labeled FS, prepare the income statement, retained earnings statement, and balance sheet from the adjusted trial balance.

c.  When you have completed creating the financial statements, perform a "save as," replacing the entire file name with the following:

 *SA4-3_1e[your first name initial]_[your last name]*

# Accounting for Merchandising Businesses

© Susan Van Etten

## Dollar Tree Stores, Inc.

**W**hen you are low on cash but need to pick up party supplies, housewares, or other consumer items, where do you go? Many shoppers are turning to **Dollar Tree Stores, Inc.**, the nation's largest single price-point dollar retailer with over 3,400 stores in 48 states. For the fixed price of $1 on merchandise in its stores, Dollar Tree has worked hard providing "new treasures" every week for the entire family.

Despite the fact that items cost only $1, the accounting for a merchandiser, like Dollar Tree, is more complex than for a service company. This is because a service company sells only services and has no inventory. With Dollar Tree's locations and merchandise, the company must design its accounting system to

not only record the receipt of goods for resale, but also to keep track of what merchandise is available for sale as well as where the merchandise is located. In addition, Dollar Tree must record the sales and costs of the goods sold for each of its stores. Finally, Dollar Tree must record such data as delivery costs, merchandise discounts, and merchandise returns.

This chapter focuses on the accounting principles and concepts for a merchandising business. In doing so, the basic differences between merchandiser and service company activities are highlighted. The financial statements of a merchandising business and accounting for merchandise transactions are also described and illustrated.

**OBJ. 1** Distinguish between the activities and financial statements of service and merchandising businesses.

# Nature of Merchandising Businesses

The activities of a service business differ from those of a merchandising business. These differences are illustrated in the following condensed income statements:

| Service Business | | Merchandising Business | |
|---|---|---|---|
| Fees earned | $XXX | Sales | $XXX |
| Operating expenses | –XXX | Cost of merchandise sold | –XXX |
| Net income | $XXX | Gross profit | $XXX |
| | | Operating expenses | –XXX |
| | | Net income | $XXX |

The revenue activities of a service business involve providing services to customers. On the income statement for a service business, the revenues from services are reported as *fees earned*. The operating expenses incurred in providing the services are subtracted from the fees earned to arrive at *net income*.

In contrast, the revenue activities of a merchandising business involve the buying and selling of merchandise. A merchandising business first purchases merchandise to sell to its customers. When this merchandise is sold, the revenue is reported as sales, and its cost is recognized as an expense. This expense is called the **cost of merchandise sold**. The cost of merchandise sold is subtracted from sales to arrive at gross profit. This amount is called **gross profit** because it is the profit *before* deducting operating expenses.

Merchandise on hand (not sold) at the end of an accounting period is called **merchandise inventory**. Merchandise inventory is reported as a current asset on the balance sheet.

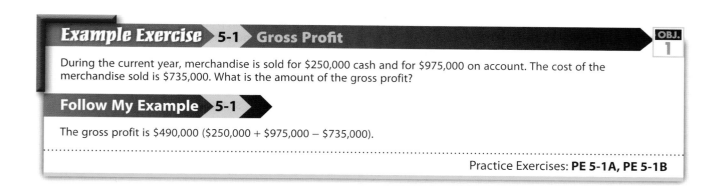

**Example Exercise 5-1 Gross Profit**
OBJ. 1

During the current year, merchandise is sold for $250,000 cash and for $975,000 on account. The cost of the merchandise sold is $735,000. What is the amount of the gross profit?

**Follow My Example 5-1**

The gross profit is $490,000 ($250,000 + $975,000 − $735,000).

Practice Exercises: **PE 5-1A, PE 5-1B**

---

## The Operating Cycle

The operations of a merchandising business involve the purchase of merchandise for sale (purchasing), the sale of the products to customers (sales), and the receipt of cash from customers (collection). This overall process is referred to as the *operating cycle*. Thus, the operating cycle begins with spending cash, and it ends with receiving cash from customers. The operating cycle for a merchandising business is shown to the right.

Operating cycles for retailers are usually shorter than for manufacturers because retailers purchase goods in a form ready for sale to the customer. Of course, some retailers will have shorter

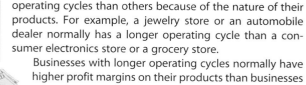

operating cycles than others because of the nature of their products. For example, a jewelry store or an automobile dealer normally has a longer operating cycle than a consumer electronics store or a grocery store.

Businesses with longer operating cycles normally have higher profit margins on their products than businesses with shorter operating cycles. For example, it is not unusual for jewelry stores to price their jewelry at 30%–50% above cost. In contrast, grocery stores operate on very small profit margins, often below 5%. Grocery stores make up the difference by selling their products more quickly.

---

# Financial Statements for a Merchandising Business

OBJ. 2 Describe and illustrate the financial statements of a merchandising business.

This section illustrates the financial statements for **NetSolutions** after it becomes a retailer of computer hardware and software. During 2011, Chris Clark implemented the second phase of NetSolutions' business plan. In doing so, Chris notified clients that beginning July 1, 2012, NetSolutions would no longer offer consulting services. Instead, it would become a retailer.

NetSolutions' business strategy is to offer personalized service to individuals and small businesses who are upgrading or purchasing new computer systems. NetSolutions' personal service includes a no-obligation, on-site assessment of the customer's computer needs. By providing personalized service and follow-up, Chris feels that Net-Solutions can compete effectively against such retailers as Best Buy and Office Depot, Inc.

## Multiple-Step Income Statement

The 2013 income statement for NetSolutions is shown in Exhibit 1.[1] This form of income statement, called a **multiple-step income statement**, contains several sections, subsections, and subtotals.

---

1 The NetSolutions income statement for 2013 is used because it allows a better illustration of the computation of the cost of merchandise sold in the appendix to this chapter.

**Revenue from Sales** This section of the multiple-step income statement consists of sales, sales returns and allowances, sales discounts, and net sales. This section, as shown in Exhibit 1, is as follows:

| Revenue from sales: | | | |
|---|---|---|---|
| Sales . . . . . . . . . . . . . . . . . . . . . . . . . . . . . . . . . . . . . . . . . | | $720,185 | |
| Less: Sales returns and allowances . . . . . . . . . . . . . . . . | $6,140 | | |
| Sales discounts . . . . . . . . . . . . . . . . . . . . . . . . . . . . | 5,790 | 11,930 | |
| Net sales . . . . . . . . . . . . . . . . . . . . . . . . . . . . . . . . . . . . . | | | $708,255 |

**Sales** is the total amount charged customers for merchandise sold, including cash sales and sales on account. During 2013, NetSolutions sold merchandise of $720,185 for cash or on account.

**Sales returns and allowances** are granted by the seller to customers for damaged or defective merchandise. In such cases, the customer may either return the merchandise or accept an allowance from the seller. NetSolutions reported $6,140 of sales returns and allowances during 2013.

**Sales discounts** are granted by the seller to customers for early payment of amounts owed. For example, a seller may offer a customer a 2% discount on a sale of $10,000 if the customer pays within 10 days. If the customer pays within the 10-day period, the seller receives cash of $9,800, and the buyer receives a discount of $200 ($10,000 × 2%). NetSolutions reported $5,790 of sales discounts during 2013.

**EXHIBIT 1**

**Multiple-Step Income Statement**

**NetSolutions**
**Income Statement**
**For the Year Ended December 31, 2013**

| | | | |
|---|---|---|---|
| Revenue from sales: | | | |
| Sales . . . . . . . . . . . . . . . . . . . . . . . . . . . . . . . . . . . . . | | $720,185 | |
| Less: Sales returns and allowances . . . . . . . . . . . . . | $ 6,140 | | |
| Sales discounts . . . . . . . . . . . . . . . . . . . . . . . | 5,790 | 11,930 | |
| Net sales . . . . . . . . . . . . . . . . . . . . . . . . . . . . . . . . | | | $708,255 |
| Cost of merchandise sold . . . . . . . . . . . . . . . . . . . . . . . | | | 525,305 |
| Gross profit . . . . . . . . . . . . . . . . . . . . . . . . . . . . . . . . . | | | $182,950 |
| Operating expenses: | | | |
| Selling expenses: | | | |
| Sales salaries expense . . . . . . . . . . . . . . . . . . . . . | $53,430 | | |
| Advertising expense . . . . . . . . . . . . . . . . . . . . . . | 10,860 | | |
| Depreciation expense—store equipment . . . . | 3,100 | | |
| Delivery expense . . . . . . . . . . . . . . . . . . . . . . . . | 2,800 | | |
| Miscellaneous selling expense . . . . . . . . . . . . . | 630 | | |
| Total selling expenses . . . . . . . . . . . . . . . . . . | | $ 70,820 | |
| Administrative expenses: | | | |
| Office salaries expense . . . . . . . . . . . . . . . . . . . . | $21,020 | | |
| Rent expense . . . . . . . . . . . . . . . . . . . . . . . . . . . | 8,100 | | |
| Depreciation expense—office equipment . . . | 2,490 | | |
| Insurance expense . . . . . . . . . . . . . . . . . . . . . . . | 1,910 | | |
| Office supplies expense . . . . . . . . . . . . . . . . . . . | 610 | | |
| Miscellaneous administrative expense . . . . . . . | 760 | | |
| Total administrative expenses . . . . . . . . . . . | | 34,890 | |
| Total operating expenses . . . . . . . . . . . . . . . . . . . . . | | | 105,710 |
| Income from operations . . . . . . . . . . . . . . . . . . . . . . . . | | | $ 77,240 |
| Other income and expense: | | | |
| Rent revenue . . . . . . . . . . . . . . . . . . . . . . . . . . . . . | | $ 600 | |
| Interest expense . . . . . . . . . . . . . . . . . . . . . . . . . . . | | (2,440) | (1,840) |
| Net income . . . . . . . . . . . . . . . . . . . . . . . . . . . . . . . . . | | | $ 75,400 |

**Net sales** is determined by subtracting sales returns and allowances and sales discounts from sales. As shown in Exhibit 1, NetSolutions reported $708,255 of net sales during 2013. Some companies report only net sales and report sales, sales returns and allowances, and sales discounts in notes to the financial statements.

**Cost of Merchandise Sold** As shown in Exhibit 1, NetSolutions reported cost of merchandise sold of $525,305 during 2013. The cost of merchandise sold is the cost of merchandise sold to customers. Merchandise costs consist of all the costs of acquiring the merchandise and readying it for sale, such as purchase and freight costs. Recording these costs is described and illustrated later in this chapter.

Two systems of accounting for recording and reporting the cost of merchandise sold are:

1. Periodic inventory system
2. Perpetual inventory system

Under the **periodic inventory system**, the inventory records do not show the amount available for sale or the amount sold during the period. Instead, the cost of merchandise sold and the merchandise on hand are determined at the end of the period by physically counting the inventory. The periodic inventory system is described and illustrated in the appendix to this chapter.

Under the **perpetual inventory system**, each purchase and sale of merchandise is recorded in the inventory and the cost of merchandise sold accounts. As a result, the amounts of merchandise available for sale and sold are continuously (perpetually) updated in the inventory records. Because many retailers use computerized systems, the perpetual inventory system is widely used.

Under a perpetual inventory system, the cost of merchandise sold is reported as a single line on the income statement. An example of such reporting is illustrated in Exhibit 1 for NetSolutions. Because of its wide use, the perpetual inventory system is used in the remainder of this chapter.

**Gross Profit** Gross profit is computed by subtracting the cost of merchandise sold from net sales, as shown below.

| | |
|---|---|
| Net sales | $708,255 |
| Cost of merchandise sold | 525,305 |
| Gross profit | $182,950 |

As shown above and in Exhibit 1, NetSolutions has gross profit of $182,950 in 2013.

**Income from Operations** **Income from operations**, sometimes called operating income, is determined by subtracting operating expenses from gross profit. Operating expenses are normally classified as either selling expenses or administrative expenses.

**Selling expenses** are incurred directly in the selling of merchandise. Examples of selling expenses include sales salaries, store supplies used, depreciation of store equipment, delivery expense, and advertising.

**Administrative expenses**, sometimes called **general expenses**, are incurred in the administration or general operations of the business. Examples of administrative expenses include office salaries, depreciation of office equipment, and office supplies used.

Each selling and administrative expense may be reported separately as shown in Exhibit 1. However, many companies report selling, administrative, and operating expenses as single line items as shown below for NetSolutions.

| | | |
|---|---|---|
| Gross profit | | $182,950 |
| Operating expenses: | | |
| Selling expenses | $70,820 | |
| Administrative expenses | 34,890 | |
| Total operating expenses | | 105,710 |
| Income from operations | | $ 77,240 |

For many merchandising businesses, the cost of merchandise sold is usually the largest expense. For example, the approximate percentage of cost of merchandise sold to sales is 63% for JCPenney and 66% for The Home Depot.

Retailers, such as Best Buy, Sears Holding Corporation, and Walmart, and grocery store chains, such as Winn-Dixie Stores, Inc. and Kroger, use bar codes and optical scanners as part of their computerized inventory systems.

See Appendix E for more information

**Other Income and Expense**  Other income and expense items are not related to the primary operations of the business. **Other income** is revenue from sources other than the primary operating activity of a business. Examples of other income include income from interest, rent, and gains resulting from the sale of fixed assets. **Other expense** is an expense that cannot be traced directly to the normal operations of the business. Examples of other expenses include interest expense and losses from disposing of fixed assets.

Other income and other expense are offset against each other on the income statement. If the total of other income exceeds the total of other expense, the difference is added to income from operations to determine net income. If the reverse is true, the difference is subtracted from income from operations. The other income and expense items of NetSolutions are reported as shown below and in Exhibit 1.

| | | |
|---|---|---|
| Income from operations | | $77,240 |
| Other income and expense: | | |
| Rent revenue | $  600 | |
| Interest expense | (2,440) | (1,840) |
| Net income | | $75,400 |

# Single-Step Income Statement

An alternate form of income statement is the **single-step income statement.** As shown in Exhibit 2, the income statement for NetSolutions deducts the total of all expenses *in one step* from the total of all revenues.

The single-step form emphasizes total revenues and total expenses in determining net income. A criticism of the single-step form is that gross profit and income from operations are not reported.

# Retained Earnings Statement

The retained earnings statement for NetSolutions is shown in Exhibit 3. This statement is prepared in the same manner as for a service business.

# Balance Sheet

The balance sheet may be presented with assets on the left-hand side and the liabilities and stockholders' equity on the right-hand side. This form of the balance sheet is called the **account form.** The balance sheet may also be presented in a downward

**EXHIBIT 2**

**Single-Step Income Statement**

| NetSolutions Income Statement For the Year Ended December 31, 2013 | | |
|---|---|---|
| Revenues: | | |
| Net sales. . . . . . . . . . . . . . . . . . . . . . . . . . . . . . . . . . . . . . . . . . . | | $708,255 |
| Rent revenue  . . . . . . . . . . . . . . . . . . . . . . . . . . . . . . . . . . . . . | | 600 |
| Total revenues . . . . . . . . . . . . . . . . . . . . . . . . . . . . . . . . . | | $708,855 |
| Expenses: | | |
| Cost of merchandise sold . . . . . . . . . . . . . . . . . . . . . . . . . . . . . | $525,305 | |
| Selling expenses . . . . . . . . . . . . . . . . . . . . . . . . . . . . . . . . . . . | 70,820 | |
| Administrative expenses . . . . . . . . . . . . . . . . . . . . . . . . . . . . . . | 34,890 | |
| Interest expense. . . . . . . . . . . . . . . . . . . . . . . . . . . . . . . . . . . . | 2,440 | |
| Total expenses . . . . . . . . . . . . . . . . . . . . . . . . . . . . . . . . . . | | 633,455 |
| Net income . . . . . . . . . . . . . . . . . . . . . . . . . . . . . . . . . . . . . . . . . | | $ 75,400 |

**EXHIBIT 3**

**Retained Earnings Statement for Merchandising Business**

**NetSolutions**
**Retained Earnings Statement**
**For the Year Ended December 31, 2013**

| | | |
|---|---:|---:|
| Retained earnings, January 1, 2013 ............................... | | $128,800 |
| Net income for the year............................................ | $75,400 | |
| Less dividends .................................................... | 18,000 | |
| Increase in retained earnings....................................... | | 57,400 |
| Retained earnings, December 31, 2013............................. | | $186,200 |

sequence in three sections. This form of balance sheet is called the **report form.** The report form of balance sheet for NetSolutions is shown in Exhibit 4. In Exhibit 4, merchandise inventory is reported as a current asset and the current portion of the note payable of $5,000 is reported as a current liability.

**EXHIBIT 4**

**Report Form of Balance Sheet**

**NetSolutions**
**Balance Sheet**
**December 31, 2013**

| | | | |
|---|---:|---:|---:|
| **Assets** | | | |
| Current assets: | | | |
| Cash.......................................... | | $ 52,950 | |
| Accounts receivable ........................... | | 91,080 | |
| Merchandise inventory ......................... | | 62,150 | |
| Office supplies ................................ | | 480 | |
| Prepaid insurance ............................. | | 2,650 | |
| Total current assets........................ | | | $209,310 |
| Property, plant, and equipment: | | | |
| Land ......................................... | | $ 20,000 | |
| Store equipment ............................. | $27,100 | | |
| Less accumulated depreciation................ | 5,700 | 21,400 | |
| Office equipment.............................. | $15,570 | | |
| Less accumulated depreciation................ | 4,720 | 10,850 | |
| Total property, plant, and equipment....... | | | 52,250 |
| Total assets ...................................... | | | $261,560 |
| **Liabilities** | | | |
| Current liabilities: | | | |
| Accounts payable ............................. | | $ 22,420 | |
| Note payable (current portion) ................... | | 5,000 | |
| Salaries payable ............................... | | 1,140 | |
| Unearned rent ................................ | | 1,800 | |
| Total current liabilities....................... | | | $ 30,360 |
| Long-term liabilities: | | | |
| Note payable (final payment due 2023) .......... | | | 20,000 |
| Total liabilities ................................... | | | $ 50,360 |
| **Stockholders' Equity** | | | |
| Capital stock..................................... | | $ 25,000 | |
| Retained earnings................................. | | 186,200 | |
| Total stockholders' equity ...................... | | | 211,200 |
| Total liabilities and stockholders' equity.............. | | | $261,560 |

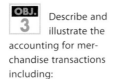

Describe and illustrate the accounting for merchandise transactions including:

- sale of merchandise
- purchase of merchandise
- freight
- sales taxes and trade discounts
- dual nature of merchandising transactions

# Merchandising Transactions

The prior section described and illustrated the financial statements of a merchandising business, **NetSolutions**. This section describes and illustrates the recording of merchandise transactions, including the use of a chart of accounts for a merchandising business.

## Chart of Accounts for a Merchandising Business

The chart of accounts for a merchandising business should reflect the elements of the financial statements. The chart of accounts for NetSolutions is shown in Exhibit 5. The accounts related to merchandising transactions are shown in color.

As shown in Exhibit 5, NetSolutions' chart of accounts consists of three-digit account numbers. The first digit indicates the major financial statement classification (1 for assets, 2 for liabilities, and so on). The second digit indicates the subclassification (e.g., 11 for current assets, 12 for noncurrent assets). The third digit identifies the specific account (e.g., 110 for Cash, 123 for Store Equipment). Using a three-digit numbering system makes it easier to add new accounts as they are needed.

**EXHIBIT 5**

**Chart of Accounts for NetSolutions, a Merchandising Business**

| Balance Sheet Accounts | Income Statement Accounts |
|---|---|
| **100 Assets** | **400 Revenues** |
| 110 Cash | 410 Sales |
| 112 Accounts Receivable | 411 Sales Returns and Allowances |
| 115 Merchandise Inventory | 412 Sales Discounts |
| 116 Office Supplies | **500 Costs and Expenses** |
| 117 Prepaid Insurance | 510 Cost of Merchandise Sold |
| 120 Land | 520 Sales Salaries Expense |
| 123 Store Equipment | 521 Advertising Expense |
| 124 Accumulated Depreciation— Store Equipment | 522 Depreciation Expense— Store Equipment |
| 125 Office Equipment | 523 Delivery Expense |
| 126 Accumulated Depreciation— Office Equipment | 529 Miscellaneous Selling Expense |
| **200 Liabilities** | 530 Office Salaries Expense |
| 210 Accounts Payable | 531 Rent Expense |
| 211 Salaries Payable | 532 Depreciation Expense— Office Equipment |
| 212 Unearned Rent | 533 Insurance Expense |
| 215 Notes Payable | 534 Office Supplies Expense |
| **300 Stockholders' Equity** | 539 Misc. Administrative Expense |
| 310 Capital Stock | **600 Other Income** |
| 311 Retained Earnings | 610 Rent Revenue |
| 312 Dividends | **700 Other Expense** |
| 313 Income Summary | 710 Interest Expense |

## Sales Transactions

Merchandise transactions are recorded using the rules of debit and credit that we described and illustrated in Chapter 2. Exhibit 3, shown on page 55 of Chapter 2, summarizes these rules.

The accounting system used in the preceding chapters is often modified to more efficiently record transactions. For example, an accounting system should be designed to provide information on the amounts due from various customers (accounts receivable) and amounts owed to various creditors (accounts payable). A separate account for each customer and creditor could be added to the ledger. However, as the number of customers and creditors increases, the ledger would become large and awkward to use.

A large number of individual accounts with a common characteristic can be grouped together in a separate ledger, called a **subsidiary ledger**. The primary ledger, which contains all of the balance sheet and income statement accounts, is then called the **general ledger**. Each subsidiary ledger is represented in the general ledger by a summarizing account, called a **controlling account**. The sum of the balances of the accounts in the subsidiary ledger must equal the balance of the related controlling account. Thus, a subsidiary ledger is a secondary ledger that supports a controlling account in the general ledger. Common subsidiary ledgers are:[2]

1. The **accounts receivable subsidiary ledger**, or *customers ledger*, lists the individual customer accounts in alphabetical order. The controlling account in the general ledger is Accounts Receivable.
2. The **accounts payable subsidiary ledger**, or *creditors ledger*, lists individual creditor accounts in alphabetical order. The controlling account in the general ledger is Accounts Payable.
3. The **inventory subsidiary ledger**, or *inventory ledger*, lists individual inventory by item (bar code) number. The controlling account in the general ledger is Inventory. An inventory subsidiary ledger is used in a perpetual inventory system.

In this section, sales transactions involving cash sales and sales on account are illustrated. In addition, sales discounts and sales returns transactions are illustrated.

**Cash Sales** A business may sell merchandise for cash. Cash sales are normally entered (rung up) on a cash register and recorded in the accounts. To illustrate, assume that on January 3, NetSolutions sells merchandise for $1,800. These cash sales are recorded as follows:

| | Journal | | | Page 25 |
|---|---|---|---|---|
| **Date** | **Description** | **Post. Ref.** | **Debit** | **Credit** |
| 2013 Jan. 3 | Cash | | 1,800 | |
| | Sales | | | 1,800 |
| | To record cash sales. | | | |

Using the perpetual inventory system, the cost of merchandise sold and the decrease in merchandise inventory are also recorded. In this way, the merchandise inventory account indicates the amount of merchandise on hand (not sold).

To illustrate, assume that the cost of merchandise sold on January 3 is $1,200. The entry to record the cost of merchandise sold and the decrease in the merchandise inventory is as follows:

| | | | | |
|---|---|---|---|---|
| Jan. 3 | Cost of Merchandise Sold | | 1,200 | |
| | Merchandise Inventory | | | 1,200 |
| | To record the cost of merchandise sold. | | | |

---

2 Subsidiary ledgers are further described and illustrated in Appendix C.

Sales may be made to customers using credit cards such as MasterCard or VISA. Such sales are recorded as cash sales. This is because these sales are normally processed by a clearing-house that contacts the bank that issued the card. The issuing bank then electronically transfers cash directly to the retailer's bank account.[3] Thus, the retailer normally receives cash within a few days of making the credit card sale.

If the customers in the preceding sales had used MasterCards to pay for their purchases, the sales would be recorded exactly as shown in the preceding entry. Any processing fees charged by the clearing-house or issuing bank are periodically recorded as an expense. This expense is normally reported on the income statement as an administrative expense. To illustrate, assume that NetSolutions paid credit card processing fees of $48 on January 31. These fees would be recorded as follows:

| | | | | |
|---|---|---|---|---|
| Jan. | 31 | Credit Card Expense | 48 | |
| | | Cash | | 48 |
| | | To record service charges on credit card sales for the month. | | |

A retailer may accept MasterCard or VISA but not American Express. Why? American Express Co.'s service fees are normally higher than MasterCard's or VISA's. As a result, some retailers choose not to accept American Express cards. The disadvantage of this practice is that the retailer may lose customers to competitors who do accept American Express cards.

Instead of using MasterCard or VISA, a customer may use a credit card that is not issued by a bank. For example, a customer might use an American Express card. If the seller uses a clearing-house, the clearing-house will collect the receivable and transfer the cash to the retailer's bank account similar to the way it would have if the customer had used MasterCard or VISA. Large businesses, however, may not use a clearing-house. In such cases, nonbank credit card sales must first be reported to the card company before cash is received. Thus, a receivable is created with the nonbank credit card company. However, since most retailers use clearing-houses to process both bank and nonbank credit cards, all credit card sales will be recorded as cash sales.

**Sales on Account** A business may sell merchandise on account. The seller records such sales as a debit to Accounts Receivable and a credit to Sales. An example of an entry for a NetSolutions sale on account of $510 follows. The cost of merchandise sold was $280.

| | | | | |
|---|---|---|---|---|
| Jan. | 12 | Accounts Receivable—Sims Co. | 510 | |
| | | Sales | | 510 |
| | | Invoice No. 7172. | | |
| | 12 | Cost of Merchandise Sold | 280 | |
| | | Merchandise Inventory | | 280 |
| | | Cost of merch. sold on Invoice No. 7172. | | |

**Sales Discounts** The terms of a sale are normally indicated on the **invoice** or bill that the seller sends to the buyer. An example of a sales invoice for NetSolutions is shown in Exhibit 6.

The terms for when payments for merchandise are to be made are called the **credit terms.** If payment is required on delivery, the terms are *cash* or *net cash.* Otherwise, the buyer is allowed an amount of time, known as the **credit period,** in which to pay.

The credit period usually begins with the date of the sale as shown on the invoice. If payment is due within a stated number of days after the invoice date, such as 30 days, the terms are *net 30 days.* These terms may be written as *n/30.*[4] If payment

3 CyberSource is one of the major credit card clearing-houses. For a more detailed description of how credit card sales are processed, see the following CyberSource Web page: **http://www.cybersource.com/products_and_services/global_payment_services/credit_card_processing/howitworks.xml**.

4 The word *net* as used here does not have the usual meaning of a number after deductions have been subtracted, as in *net income.*

**EXHIBIT 6**

**Invoice**

| | | |
|---|---|---|
| **NetSolutions** | | 106-8 |
| 5101 Washington Ave. | | |
| Cincinnati, OH 45227-5101 | | |

Invoice

Made in U.S.A.

| **SOLD TO** | **CUSTOMER'S ORDER NO. & DATE** |
|---|---|
| Omega Technologies | 412 Jan. 4, 2013 |
| 1000 Matrix Blvd. | |
| San Jose, CA. 95116-1000 | |

| **DATE SHIPPED** | **HOW SHIPPED AND ROUTE** | **TERMS** | **INVOICE DATE** |
|---|---|---|---|
| Jan. 7, 2013 | US Express Trucking Co. | 2/10, n/30 | Jan. 7, 2013 |

| **FROM** | **F.O.B.** |
|---|---|
| Cincinnati | Cincinnati |

| **QUANTITY** | **DESCRIPTION** | **UNIT PRICE** | **AMOUNT** |
|---|---|---|---|
| 10 | 3COM Wireless PC Card | 150.00 | 1,500.00 |

is due by the end of the month in which the sale was made, the terms are written as *n/eom*.

To encourage the buyer to pay before the end of the credit period, the seller may offer a discount. For example, a seller may offer a 2% discount if the buyer pays within 10 days of the invoice date. If the buyer does not take the discount, the total amount is due within 30 days. These terms are expressed as *2/10, n/30* and are read as *2% discount if paid within 10 days, net amount due within 30 days*. The credit terms of 2/10, n/30 are summarized in Exhibit 7, using the invoice in Exhibit 6.

Discounts taken by the buyer for early payment are recorded as sales discounts by the seller. Managers usually want to know the amount of the sales discounts for a period. For this reason, sales discounts are recorded in a separate sales discounts account, which is a *contra* (or *offsetting*) account to Sales.

To illustrate, assume that NetSolutions receives $1,470 on January 17 for the invoice shown in Exhibit 6. Since the invoice was paid within the discount period (10 days), the buyer deducted $30 ($1,500 × 2%) from the invoice amount. NetSolutions would record the receipt of the cash as follows:

| Jan. | 17 | Cash | | 1,470 | |
|---|---|---|---|---|---|
| | | Sales Discounts | | 30 | |
| | |     Accounts Receivable—Omega Technologies | | | 1,500 |
| | |     Collection on Invoice No. 106-8, less 2% | | | |
| | |     discount. | | | |

**Sales Returns and Allowances** Merchandise sold may be returned to the seller (sales return). In other cases, the seller may reduce the initial selling price (sales allowance). This might occur if the merchandise is defective, damaged during shipment, or does not meet the buyer's expectations.

If the return or allowance is for a sale on account, the seller usually issues the buyer a **credit memorandum**, often called a **credit memo**. A credit memo authorizes

**EXHIBIT 7**

**Credit Terms**

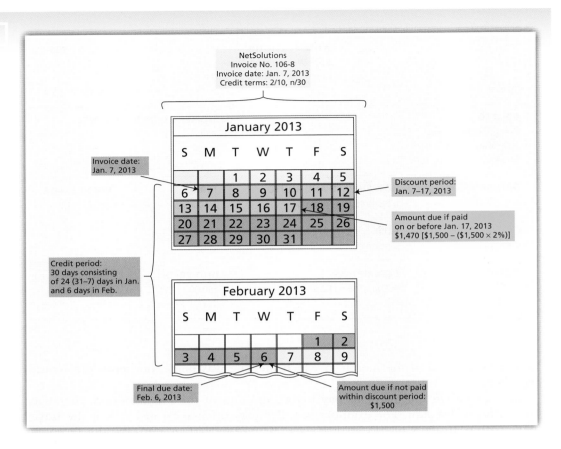

a credit to (decreases) the buyer's account receivable. A credit memo indicates the amount and reason for the credit. An example of a credit memo issued by NetSolutions is shown in Exhibit 8.

Like sales discounts, sales returns and allowances reduce sales revenue. Also, returns often result in additional shipping and handling expenses. Thus, managers usually want to know the amount of returns and allowances for a period. For this reason, sales returns and allowances are recorded in a separate sales returns and allowances account, which is a *contra* (or *offsetting*) account to Sales.

The seller debits Sales Returns and Allowances for the amount of the return or allowance. If the sale was on account, the seller credits Accounts Receivable. Using a perpetual inventory system, the seller must also debit (increase) Merchandise

**EXHIBIT 8**

**Credit Memo**

| **NetSolutions** | | **No. 32** |
|---|---|---|
| 5101 Washington Ave. | | |
| Cincinnati, OH 45227-5101 | | |

**CREDIT MEMO**

| **TO** | **DATE** |
|---|---|
| Krier Company | January 13, 2013 |
| 7608 Melton Avenue | |
| Los Angeles, CA 90025-3942 | |

**WE CREDIT YOUR ACCOUNT AS FOLLOWS**

| 1 | Graphic Video Card | 225.00 |
|---|---|---|

Inventory and decrease (credit) Cost of Merchandise Sold for the cost of the returned merchandise.

To illustrate, the credit memo shown in Exhibit 8 is used. The selling price of the merchandise returned in Exhibit 8 is $225. Assuming that the cost of the merchandise returned is $140, the sales return and allowance would be recorded as follows:

| Jan. | 13 | Sales Returns and Allowances | 225 | |
| | |     Accounts Receivable—Krier Company | | 225 |
| | |       Credit Memo No. 32. | | |
| | | | | |
| | 13 | Merchandise Inventory | 140 | |
| | |     Cost of Merchandise Sold | | 140 |
| | |       Cost of merchandise returned, Credit | | |
| | |       Memo No. 32. | | |

A buyer may pay for merchandise and then later return it. In this case, the seller may do one of the following:

1. Issue a credit that is applied against the buyer's other receivables.
2. Issue a cash refund.

If the credit is applied against the buyer's other receivables, the seller records the credit with entries similar to those shown above. If cash is refunded, the seller debits Sales Returns and Allowances and credits Cash.

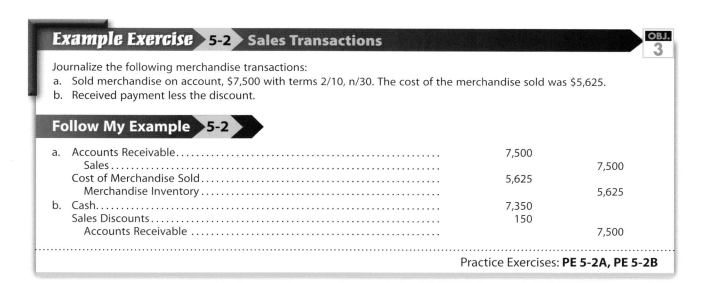

**Example Exercise 5-2 Sales Transactions**    OBJ. 3

Journalize the following merchandise transactions:
a.  Sold merchandise on account, $7,500 with terms 2/10, n/30. The cost of the merchandise sold was $5,625.
b.  Received payment less the discount.

**Follow My Example 5-2**

| | | | |
|---|---|---|---|
| a. | Accounts Receivable......................................... | 7,500 | |
| |   Sales.................................................... | | 7,500 |
| | Cost of Merchandise Sold................................. | 5,625 | |
| |   Merchandise Inventory................................. | | 5,625 |
| b. | Cash............................................................ | 7,350 | |
| | Sales Discounts............................................. | 150 | |
| |   Accounts Receivable................................... | | 7,500 |

Practice Exercises: **PE 5-2A, PE 5-2B**

## Integrity, Objectivity, and Ethics in Business

**THE CASE OF THE FRAUDULENT PRICE TAGS**

One of the challenges for a retailer is policing its sales return policy. There are many ways in which customers can unethically or illegally abuse such policies. In one case, a couple was accused of attaching **Marshalls'** store price tags to cheaper merchandise bought or obtained elsewhere. The couple then returned the cheaper goods and received the substantially higher refund amount. Company security officials discovered the fraud and had the couple arrested after they had allegedly bilked the company for over $1 million.

# Purchase Transactions

Under the perpetual inventory system, cash purchases of merchandise are recorded as follows:

| | Journal | | | | Page 24 |
|---|---|---|---|---|---|
| **Date** | **Description** | **Post. Ref.** | **Debit** | **Credit** | |
| 2013 Jan. 3 | Merchandise Inventory | | 2,510 | | |
| | Cash | | | 2,510 | |
| | Purchased inventory from Bowen Co. | | | | |

Purchases of merchandise on account are recorded as follows:

| Jan. 4 | Merchandise Inventory | | 9,250 | | |
|---|---|---|---|---|---|
| | Accounts Payable—Thomas Corporation | | | 9,250 | |
| | Purchased inventory on account. | | | | |

**Purchases Discounts** A buyer may receive a discount from the seller (sales discount) for early payment of the amount owed. From the buyer's perspective, such discounts are called **purchases discounts**.

Purchases discounts taken by a buyer reduce the cost of the merchandise purchased. Even if the buyer has to borrow to pay within a discount period, it is normally to the buyer's advantage to do so. For this reason, accounting systems are normally designed so that all available discounts are taken.

To illustrate, assume that NetSolutions purchased merchandise from Alpha Technologies as follows:

| Invoice Date | Invoice Amount | Terms |
|---|---|---|
| March 12 | $3,000 | 2/10, n/30 |

The last day of the discount period is March 22 (March 12 + 10 days). Assume that in order to pay the invoice on March 22, NetSolutions borrows $2,940, which is $3,000 less the discount of $60 ($3,000 × 2%). If we also assume an annual interest rate of 6% and a 360-day year, the interest on the loan of $2,940 for the remaining 20 days of the credit period is $9.80 ($2,940 × 6% × 20/360).

The net savings to NetSolutions of taking the discount is $50.20, computed as follows:

| | |
|---|---|
| Discount of 2% on $3,000 | $60.00 |
| Interest for 20 days at a rate of 6% on $2,940 | 9.80 |
| Savings from taking the discount | $50.20 |

The savings can also be seen by comparing the interest rate on the money *saved* by taking the discount and the interest rate on the money *borrowed* to take the discount. The interest rate on the money saved in the prior example is estimated by converting 2% for 20 days to a yearly rate, as follows:

$$2\% \times \frac{360 \text{ days}}{20 \text{ days}} = 2\% \times 18 = 36\%$$

NetSolutions borrowed $2,940 at 6% to take the discount. If NetSolutions does not take the discount, it *pays* an estimated interest rate of 36% for using the $2,940 for the remaining 20 days of the credit period. Thus, buyers should normally take all available purchase discounts.

Under the perpetual inventory system, the buyer initially debits Merchandise Inventory for the amount of the invoice. When paying the invoice within the discount period, the buyer credits Merchandise Inventory for the amount of the discount. In this way, Merchandise Inventory shows the *net* cost to the buyer.

To illustrate, NetSolutions would record the Alpha Technologies invoice and its payment at the end of the discount period as follows:

| | | | | |
|---|---|---|---|---|
| Mar. | 12 | Merchandise Inventory | 3,000 | |
| | | Accounts Payable—Alpha Technologies | | 3,000 |
| | 22 | Accounts Payable—Alpha Technologies | 3,000 | |
| | | Cash | | 2,940 |
| | | Merchandise Inventory | | 60 |

Assume that NetSolutions does not take the discount, but instead pays the invoice on April 11. In this case, NetSolutions would record the payment on April 11 as follows:

| | | | | |
|---|---|---|---|---|
| Apr. | 11 | Accounts Payable--Alpha Technologies | 3,000 | |
| | | Cash | | 3,000 |

**Purchases Returns and Allowances** A buyer may receive an allowance for merchandise that is returned (purchases return) or a price allowance (purchases allowance) for damaged or defective merchandise. From a buyer's perspective, such sales returns and allowances are called **purchases returns and allowances**. In both cases, the buyer normally sends the seller a debit memorandum.

A **debit memorandum**, often called a **debit memo**, is shown in Exhibit 9. A debit memo informs the seller of the amount the buyer proposes to *debit* to the account payable due the seller. It also states the reasons for the return or the request for the price allowance.

The buyer may use the debit memo as the basis for recording the return or allowance or wait for approval from the seller (creditor). In either case, the buyer debits Accounts Payable and credits Merchandise Inventory.

**NetSolutions** No. 18
5101 Washington Ave.
Cincinnati, OH 45227-5101

**DEBIT MEMO**

**TO** **DATE**
Maxim Systems March 7, 2013
7519 East Wilson Ave.
Seattle, WA 98101-7519

**WE DEBITED YOUR ACCOUNT AS FOLLOWS**

| | | | |
|---|---|---|---|
| 10 | Server Network Interface Cards, your invoice No. 7291, are being returned via parcel post. Our order specified No. 825X. | @90.00 | 900.00 |

To illustrate, NetSolutions records the return of the merchandise indicated in the debit memo in Exhibit 9 as follows:

| | | | | | |
|---|---|---|---|---|---|
| Mar. | 7 | Accounts Payable—Maxim Systems | | 900 | |
| | | Merchandise Inventory | | | 900 |
| | | Debit Memo No. 18. | | | |

A buyer may return merchandise or be granted a price allowance before paying an invoice. In this case, the amount of the debit memo is deducted from the invoice. The amount is deducted before the purchase discount is computed.

To illustrate, assume the following data concerning a purchase of merchandise by NetSolutions on May 2:

May 2. Purchased $5,000 of merchandise on account from Delta Data Link, terms 2/10, n/30.

    4. Returned $3,000 of the merchandise purchased on March 2.

   12. Paid for the purchase of May 2 less the return and discount.

NetSolutions would record these transactions as follows:

| | | | | | |
|---|---|---|---|---|---|
| May | 2 | Merchandise Inventory | | 5,000 | |
| | | Accounts Payable—Delta Data Link | | | 5,000 |
| | | Purchased merchandise. | | | |
| | 4 | Accounts Payable—Delta Data Link | | 3,000 | |
| | | Merchandise Inventory | | | 3,000 |
| | | Returned portion of merch. purchased. | | | |
| | 12 | Accounts Payable—Delta Data Link | | 2,000 | |
| | | Cash | | | 1,960 |
| | | Merchandise Inventory | | | 40 |
| | | Paid invoice [($5,000 – $3,000) × 2% | | | |
| | | = $40; $2,000 – $40 = $1,960]. | | | |

## Example Exercise 5-3 Purchase Transactions

OBJ. 3

Rofles Company purchased merchandise on account from a supplier for $11,500, terms 2/10, n/30. Rofles Company returned $3,000 of the merchandise and received full credit.

a. If Rofles Company pays the invoice within the discount period, what is the amount of cash required for the payment?

b. Under a perpetual inventory system, what account is credited by Rofles Company to record the return?

## Follow My Example 5-3

a. $8,330. Purchase of $11,500 less the return of $3,000 less the discount of $170 [($11,500 – $3,000) × 2%].

b. Merchandise Inventory

Practice Exercises: **PE 5-3A, PE 5-3B**

## Freight

Purchases and sales of merchandise often involve freight. The terms of a sale indicate when ownership (title) of the merchandise passes from the seller to the buyer. This point determines whether the buyer or the seller pays the freight costs.[5]

5 The passage of title also determines bwhether the buyer or seller must pay other costs, such as the cost of insurance, while the merchandise is in transit.

The ownership of the merchandise may pass to the buyer when the seller delivers the merchandise to the freight carrier. In this case, the terms are said to be **FOB (free on board) shipping point**. This term means that the buyer pays the freight costs from the shipping point to the final destination. Such costs are part of the buyer's total cost of purchasing inventory and are added to the cost of the inventory by debiting Merchandise Inventory.

To illustrate, assume that on June 10, NetSolutions purchased merchandise as follows:

June 10.  Purchased merchandise from Magna Data, $900, terms FOB shipping point.
   10.  Paid freight of $50 on June 10 purchase from Magna Data.

NetSolutions would record these two transactions as follows:

| | | | | | |
|---|---|---|---|---|---|
| June | 10 | Merchandise Inventory | | 900 | |
| | | Accounts Payable—Magna Data | | | 900 |
| | | Purchased merchandise, terms FOB | | | |
| | | shipping point. | | | |
| | 10 | Merchandise Inventory | | 50 | |
| | | Cash | | | 50 |
| | | Paid shipping cost on merchandise | | | |
| | | purchased. | | | |

The ownership of the merchandise may pass to the buyer when the buyer receives the merchandise. In this case, the terms are said to be **FOB (free on board) destination**. This term means that the seller pays the freight costs from the shipping point to the buyer's final destination. When the seller pays the delivery charges, the seller debits Delivery Expense or Freight Out. Delivery Expense is reported on the seller's income statement as a selling expense.

To illustrate, assume that NetSolutions sells merchandise as follows:

June 15.  Sold merchandise to Kranz Company on account, $700, terms FOB destination. The cost of the merchandise sold is $480.
   15.  NetSolutions pays freight of $40 on the sale of June 15.

NetSolutions records the sale, the cost of the sale, and the freight cost as follows:

| | | | | | |
|---|---|---|---|---|---|
| June | 15 | Accounts Receivable—Kranz Company | | 700 | |
| | | Sales | | | 700 |
| | | Sold merchandise, terms FOB destination. | | | |
| | 15 | Cost of Merchandise Sold | | 480 | |
| | | Merchandise Inventory | | | 480 |
| | | Recorded cost of merchandise sold to | | | |
| | | Kranz Company. | | | |
| | 15 | Delivery Expense | | 40 | |
| | | Cash | | | 40 |
| | | Paid shipping cost on merch. sold. | | | |

The seller may prepay the freight, even though the terms are FOB shipping point. The seller will then add the freight to the invoice. The buyer debits Merchandise Inventory for the total amount of the invoice, including the freight. Any discount terms would not apply to the prepaid freight.

**Note:**
**The buyer bears the freight costs if the shipping terms are FOB shipping point.**

Sometimes FOB shipping point and FOB destination are expressed in terms of a specific location at which the title to the merchandise passes to the buyer. For example, if Toyota Motor Corporation's assembly plant in Osaka, Japan, sells automobiles to a dealer in Chicago, FOB shipping point is expressed as FOB Osaka. Likewise, FOB destination is expressed as FOB Chicago.

**Note:**
**The seller bears the freight costs if the shipping terms are FOB destination.**

To illustrate, assume that NetSolutions sells merchandise as follows:

June 20.    Sold merchandise to Planter Company on account, $800, terms FOB shipping point. NetSolutions paid freight of $45, which was added to the invoice. The cost of the merchandise sold is $360.

NetSolutions records the sale, the cost of the sale, and the freight as follows:

| | | | | |
|---|---|---|---|---|
| June | 20 | Accounts Receivable—Planter Company | 800 | |
| | | Sales | | 800 |
| | | Sold merch., terms FOB shipping point. | | |
| | 20 | Cost of Merchandise Sold | 360 | |
| | | Merchandise Inventory | | 360 |
| | | Recorded cost of merchandise sold to Planter Company. | | |
| | 20 | Accounts Receivable—Planter Company | 45 | |
| | | Cash | | 45 |
| | | Prepaid shipping cost on merch. sold. | | |

Shipping terms, the passage of title, and whether the buyer or seller is to pay the freight costs are summarized in Exhibit 10.

**EXHIBIT 10    Freight Terms**

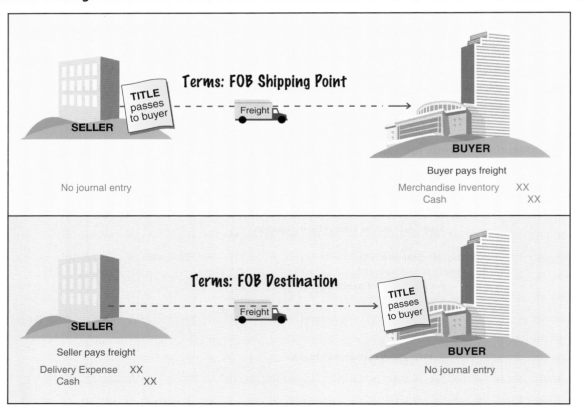

## Example Exercise 5-4 Freight Terms

**OBJ. 3**

Determine the amount to be paid in full settlement of each of invoices (a) and (b), assuming that credit for returns and allowances was received prior to payment and that all invoices were paid within the discount period.

| | Merchandise | Freight Paid by Seller | Freight Terms | Returns and Allowances |
|---|---|---|---|---|
| a. | $4,500 | $200 | FOB shipping point, 1/10, n/30 | $ 800 |
| b. | 5,000 | 60 | FOB destination, 2/10, n/30 | 2,500 |

### Follow My Example 5-4

a.  $3,863. Purchase of $4,500 less return of $800 less the discount of $37 [($4,500 – $800) × 1%] plus $200 of shipping.

b.  $2,450. Purchase of $5,000 less return of $2,500 less the discount of $50 [($5,000 – $2,500) × 2%].

Practice Exercises: **PE 5-4A, PE 5-4B**

## Summary: Recording Merchandise Inventory

Recording merchandise inventory transactions under the perpetual inventory system has been described and illustrated in the preceding sections. These transactions involved purchases, purchases discounts, purchases returns and allowances, freight, sales, and sales returns from customers. Exhibit 11 summarizes how these transactions are recorded in T account form.

**EXHIBIT 11**

**Recording Merchandise Inventory**

**Merchandise Inventory**

| | | | |
|---|---|---|---|
| Purchases of merchandise for sale | XXX | Purchases discounts | XXX |
| Freight for merchandise purchased FOB shipping point | XXX | Purchases returns and allowances | XXX |
| | | Cost of merchandise sold | XXX |
| Merchandise returned from customer | XXX | | |

**Cost of Merchandise Sold**

| | | | |
|---|---|---|---|
| Cost of merchandise sold | XXX | Merchandise returned from customer | XXX |

## Sales Taxes and Trade Discounts

Sales of merchandise often involve sales taxes. Also, the seller may offer buyers trade discounts.

**Sales Taxes**  Almost all states levy a tax on sales of merchandise.[6] The liability for the sales tax is incurred when the sale is made.

At the time of a cash sale, the seller collects the sales tax. When a sale is made on account, the seller charges the tax to the buyer by debiting Accounts Receivable. The seller credits the sales account for the amount of the sale and credits the tax to Sales Tax Payable. For example, the seller would record a sale of $100 on account, subject to a tax of 6%, as follows:

6 Businesses that purchase merchandise for resale to others are normally exempt from paying sales taxes on their purchases. Only final buyers of merchandise normally pay sales taxes.

| | | | | | |
|---|---|---|---|---|---|
| Aug. | 12 | Accounts Receivable—Lemon Co. | | 106 | |
| | | Sales | | | 100 |
| | | Sales Tax Payable | | | 6 |
| | | Invoice No. 339. | | | |

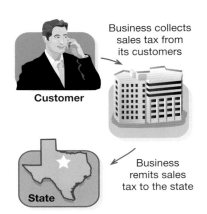

**Customer**

**State**

Business collects sales tax from its customers

Business remits sales tax to the state

On a regular basis, the seller pays to the taxing authority (state) the amount of the sales tax collected. The seller records such a payment as follows:

| | | | | | |
|---|---|---|---|---|---|
| Sept. | 15 | Sales Tax Payable | | 2,900 | |
| | | Cash | | | 2,900 |
| | | Payment for sales taxes collected | | | |
| | | during August. | | | |

*success*

The calculation for sales tax can be accomplished within a spreadsheet. A spreadsheet is often used if there are sales from many different states with different sales tax rates. We will simplify by illustrating the calculation for only one state.

| | A | B | |
|---|---|---|---|
| 1 | Inputs: | | |
| 2 | Sales tax rate | 6% | ← **a.** |
| 3 | Total sales | $ 100 | ← **b.** |
| 4 | | | |
| 5 | Output: | | |
| 6 | Sales tax | =B2*B3 | ← **c.** |
| 7 | | | |

The spreadsheet is developed with two inputs and one output. The sales tax rate is entered in cell B2 as .06, and then formatted as a percent. You can't simply type 6%, because that won't be interpreted as a number.

**a.** Insert the sales tax rate .06, and format as a percent, in cell B2.
**b.** Insert the total sales, and format as currency, in cell B3.
**c.** Insert the formula for the sales tax calculation in cell = B6, B2*B3. Note that Excel uses the asterisk (*) to denote multiplication.

**Try***It*   Go to the hands-on ***Excel Tutor*** for this example!

# BusinessConnection

## SALES TAXES

While there is no federal sales tax, most states have enacted state-wide sales taxes. In addition, many states allow counties and cities to collect a "local option" sales taxes. Delaware, Montana, New Hampshire, and Oregon have no state or local sales taxes. Tennessee (9.4%), California (9.15%), Washington (8.75%), and Louisiana (8.75%) have the highest average combined rates (including state and local option taxes). Several towns in Tuscaloosa County, Alabama, have the highest combined rates in the United States of 11%, while Chicago, Illinois, has the highest combined city rate of 10.25%.

What about companies that sell merchandise through the Internet? The general rule is that if the company ships merchandise to a customer in a state where the company does not have a physical location, no sales tax is due. For example, a customer in Montana who purchases merchandise online from a New York retailer (and no physical location in Montana) does not have to pay sales tax to either Montana or New York.

Source: The Sales Tax Clearinghouse at **www.thestc.com/FAQ.stm** (accessed May 6, 2010).

**Trade Discounts** Wholesalers are companies that sell merchandise to other businesses rather than to the public. Many wholesalers publish sales catalogs. Rather than updating their catalogs, wholesalers may publish price updates. These updates may include large discounts from the catalog list prices. In addition, wholesalers often offer special discounts to government agencies or businesses that order large quantities. Such discounts are called **trade discounts**.

Sellers and buyers do not normally record the list prices of merchandise and trade discounts in their accounts. For example, assume that an item has a list price of $1,000 and a 40% trade discount. The seller records the sale of the item at $600 [$1,000 less the trade discount of $400 ($1,000 × 40%)]. Likewise, the buyer records the purchase at $600.

## Dual Nature of Merchandise Transactions

Each merchandising transaction affects a buyer and a seller. In the following illustration, the same transactions for a seller and buyer are recorded. In this example, the seller is Scully Company and the buyer is Burton Co.

| Transaction | Scully Company (Seller) | | Burton Co. (Buyer) | |
|---|---|---|---|---|
| **July 1.** Scully Company sold merchandise on account to Burton Co., $7,500, terms FOB shipping point, n/45. The cost of the merchandise sold was $4,500. | Accounts Receivable—Burton Co.... 7,500<br>  Sales........................ <br><br>Cost of Merchandise Sold......... 4,500<br>  Merchandise Inventory......... | 7,500<br><br><br>4,500 | Merchandise Inventory........... 7,500<br>  Accounts Payable—Scully Co. .. | 7,500 |
| **July 2.** Burton Co. paid freight of $150 on July 1 purchase from Scully Company. | No journal entry. | | Merchandise Inventory .......... 150<br>  Cash........................ | 150 |
| **July 5.** Scully Company sold merchandise on account to Burton Co., $5,000, terms FOB destination, n/30. The cost of the merchandise sold was $3,500. | Accounts Receivable—Burton Co..... 5,000<br>  Sales........................ <br><br>Cost of Merchandise Sold......... 3,500<br>  Merchandise Inventory......... | 5,000<br><br><br>3,500 | Merchandise Inventory........... 5,000<br>  Accounts Payable—Scully Co. .. | 5,000 |
| **July 7.** Scully Company paid freight of $250 for delivery of merchandise sold to Burton Co. on July 5. | Delivery Expense .................. 250<br>  Cash........................ | 250 | No journal entry. | |
| **July 13.** Scully Company issued Burton Co. a credit memo for merchandise returned, $1,000. The merchandise had been purchased by Burton Co. on account on July 5. The cost of the merchandise returned was $700. | Sales Returns and Allowances...... 1,000<br>  Accounts Receivable—Burton Co. <br><br>Merchandise Inventory ............ 700<br>  Cost of Merchandise Sold........ | 1,000<br><br><br>700 | Accounts Payable—Scully Co. .... 1,000<br>  Merchandise Inventory......... | 1,000 |
| **July 15.** Scully Company received payment from Burton Co. for purchase of July 5. | Cash ............................. 4,000<br>  Accounts Receivable—Burton Co. | 4,000 | Accounts Payable—Scully Co. .... 4,000<br>  Cash........................ | 4,000 |
| **July 18.** Scully Company sold merchandise on account to Burton Co., $12,000, terms FOB shipping point, 2/10, n/eom. Scully Company prepaid freight of $500, which was added to the invoice. The cost of the merchandise sold was $7,200. | Accounts Receivable—Burton Co..... 12,000<br>  Sales........................ <br><br>Accounts Receivable—Burton Co. ... 500<br>  Cash........................ <br><br>Cost of Merchandise Sold.......... 7,200<br>  Merchandise Inventory......... | 12,000<br><br><br>500<br><br><br>7,200 | Merchandise Inventory........... 12,500<br>  Accounts Payable—Scully Co. .. | 12,500 |
| **July 28.** Scully Company received payment from Burton Co. for purchase of July 18, less discount (2% × $12,000). | Cash ............................. 12,260<br>Sales Discounts.................... 240<br>  Accounts Receivable—Burton Co. | 12,500 | Accounts Payable—Scully Co. .... 12,500<br>  Merchandise Inventory......... <br>  Cash........................ | 240<br>12,260 |

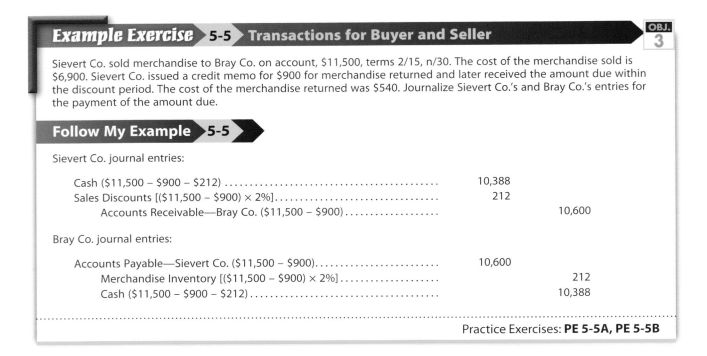

**Example Exercise** 5-5 **Transactions for Buyer and Seller** OBJ. 3

Sievert Co. sold merchandise to Bray Co. on account, $11,500, terms 2/15, n/30. The cost of the merchandise sold is $6,900. Sievert Co. issued a credit memo for $900 for merchandise returned and later received the amount due within the discount period. The cost of the merchandise returned was $540. Journalize Sievert Co.'s and Bray Co.'s entries for the payment of the amount due.

**Follow My Example** 5-5

Sievert Co. journal entries:

| | | |
|---|---|---|
| Cash ($11,500 – $900 – $212) . . . . . . . . . . . . . . . . . . . . . . . . . . . . . . . . . . . . . . . . . . | 10,388 | |
| Sales Discounts [($11,500 – $900) × 2%] . . . . . . . . . . . . . . . . . . . . . . . . . . . . . . . . . | 212 | |
| Accounts Receivable—Bray Co. ($11,500 – $900) . . . . . . . . . . . . . . . . . . | | 10,600 |

Bray Co. journal entries:

| | | |
|---|---|---|
| Accounts Payable—Sievert Co. ($11,500 – $900) . . . . . . . . . . . . . . . . . . . . . . . | 10,600 | |
| Merchandise Inventory [($11,500 – $900) × 2%] . . . . . . . . . . . . . . . . . . . . | | 212 |
| Cash ($11,500 – $900 – $212) . . . . . . . . . . . . . . . . . . . . . . . . . . . . . . . . . . . | | 10,388 |

Practice Exercises: **PE 5-5A, PE 5-5B**

---

OBJ. 4 Describe the adjusting and closing process for a merchandising business.

# The Adjusting and Closing Process

Thus far, the chart of accounts and the recording of transactions for a merchandising business have been described and illustrated. The preparation of financial statements for **NetSolutions** has also been illustrated. In the remainder of this chapter, the adjusting and closing process for a merchandising business will be described. In this discussion, the focus will be on the elements of the accounting cycle that differ from those of a service business.

## Adjusting Entry for Inventory Shrinkage

Under the perpetual inventory system, the merchandise inventory account is continually updated for purchase and sales transactions. As a result, the balance of the merchandise inventory account is the amount of merchandise available for sale at that point in time. However, retailers normally experience some loss of inventory due to shoplifting, employee theft, or errors. Thus, the physical inventory on hand at the end of the accounting period is usually less than the balance of Merchandise Inventory. This difference is called **inventory shrinkage** or **inventory shortage**.

To illustrate, NetSolutions' inventory records indicate the following on December 31, 2013:

**$62,150** Actual Inventory per Physical Count

**$1,800** Shrinkage

**$63,950** Available for Sale per Records

| | Dec. 31, 2013 |
|---|---|
| Account balance of Merchandise Inventory | $63,950 |
| Physical merchandise inventory on hand | 62,150 |
| Inventory shrinkage | $ 1,800 |

At the end of the accounting period, inventory shrinkage is recorded by the following adjusting entry:

| | | Adjusting Entry | | |
|---|---|---|---|---|
| Dec. | 31 | Cost of Merchandise Sold | 1,800 | |
| | | Merchandise Inventory | | 1,800 |
| | | Inventory shrinkage ($63,950 – $62,150). | | |

After the preceding entry is recorded, the balance of Merchandise Inventory agrees with the physical inventory on hand at the end of the period. Since inventory shrinkage cannot be totally eliminated, it is considered a normal cost of operations. If, however, the amount of the shrinkage is unusually large, it may be disclosed separately on the income statement. In such cases, the shrinkage may be recorded in a separate account, such as Loss from Merchandise Inventory Shrinkage.[7]

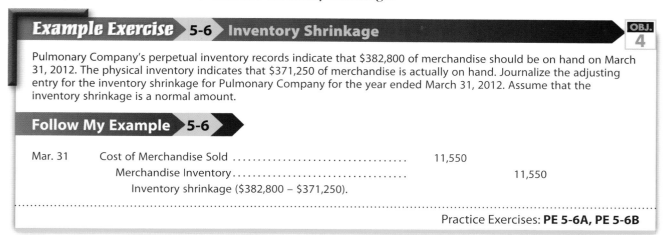

**Example Exercise** ▷ **5-6** ▷ **Inventory Shrinkage**    **OBJ. 4**

Pulmonary Company's perpetual inventory records indicate that $382,800 of merchandise should be on hand on March 31, 2012. The physical inventory indicates that $371,250 of merchandise is actually on hand. Journalize the adjusting entry for the inventory shrinkage for Pulmonary Company for the year ended March 31, 2012. Assume that the inventory shrinkage is a normal amount.

**Follow My Example** ▷ **5-6**

| | | | |
|---|---|---|---|
| Mar. 31 | Cost of Merchandise Sold ................................... | 11,550 | |
| | Merchandise Inventory.................................. | | 11,550 |
| | Inventory shrinkage ($382,800 − $371,250). | | |

Practice Exercises: **PE 5-6A, PE 5-6B**

## Closing Entries

The closing entries for a merchandising business are similar to those for a service business. The four closing entries for a merchandising business are as follows:

1. Debit each temporary account with a credit balance, such as Sales, for its balance and credit Income Summary.

2. Credit each temporary account with a debit balance, such as the various expenses, and credit Income Summary. Since Sales Returns and Allowances, Sales Discounts, and Cost of Merchandise Sold are temporary accounts with debit balances, they are credited for their balances.

3. Debit Income Summary for the amount of its balance (net income) and credit the retained earnings account. The accounts debited and credited are reversed if there is a net loss.

4. Debit the retained earnings account for the balance of the dividends account and credit the dividends account.

The four closing entries for NetSolutions are shown at the top of the following page.

NetSolutions' income summary account after the closing entries have been posted is as follows:

| **Account** *Income Summary* | | | | | Account No. *313* | |
|---|---|---|---|---|---|---|
| | | | | | **Balance** | |
| **Date** | **Item** | **Post. Ref.** | **Debit** | **Credit** | **Debit** | **Credit** |
| 2013 Dec. 31 | Revenues | 29 | | 720,785 | | 720,785 |
| 31 | Expenses | 29 | 645,385 | | | 75,400 |
| 31 | Net income | 29 | 75,400 | | — | — |

After the closing entries are posted to the accounts, a post-closing trial balance is prepared. The only accounts that should appear on the post-closing trial balance are the asset, contra asset, liability, and stockholders' accounts with balances. These are the same accounts that appear on the end-of-period balance sheet. If the two totals of the trial balance columns are not equal, an error has occurred that must be found and corrected.

7 The adjusting process for a merchandising business may be aided by preparing an end-of-period spreadsheet (work sheet). An end-of-period spreadsheet (work sheet) for a merchandising business is described and illustrated in an online appendix at **www. cengage.com/accounting/reeve**.

| Journal | | | | | Page 29 |
|---|---|---|---|---|---|
| **Date** | | **Item** | **Post. Ref.** | **Debit** | **Credit** |
| | | Closing Entries | | | |
| 2013 Dec. | 31 | Sales | 410 | 720,185 | |
| | | Rent Revenue | 610 | 600 | |
| | | Income Summary | 313 | | 720,785 |
| | | | | | |
| | 31 | Income Summary | 313 | 645,385 | |
| | | Sales Returns and Allowances | 411 | | 6,140 |
| | | Sales Discounts | 412 | | 5,790 |
| | | Cost of Merchandise Sold | 510 | | 525,305 |
| | | Sales Salaries Expense | 520 | | 53,430 |
| | | Advertising Expense | 521 | | 10,860 |
| | | Depr. Expense—Store Equipment | 522 | | 3,100 |
| | | Delivery Expense | 523 | | 2,800 |
| | | Miscellaneous Selling Expense | 529 | | 630 |
| | | Office Salaries Expense | 530 | | 21,020 |
| | | Rent Expense | 531 | | 8,100 |
| | | Depr. Expense—Office Equipment | 532 | | 2,490 |
| | | Insurance Expense | 533 | | 1,910 |
| | | Office Supplies Expense | 534 | | 610 |
| | | Misc. Administrative Expense | 539 | | 760 |
| | | Interest Expense | 710 | | 2,440 |
| | | | | | |
| | 31 | Income Summary | 313 | 75,400 | |
| | | Retained Earnings | 311 | | 75,400 |
| | | | | | |
| | 31 | Retained Earnings | 311 | 18,000 | |
| | | Dividends | 312 | | 18,000 |

# Financial Analysis and Interpretation: Ratio of Net Sales to Assets

**OBJ. 5** Describe and illustrate the use of the ratio of net sales to assets in evaluating a company's operating performance.

The **ratio of net sales to assets** measures how effectively a business is using its assets to generate sales. A high ratio indicates an effective use of assets. The assets used in computing the ratio may be the total assets at the end of the year, the average of the total assets at the beginning and end of the year, or the average of the monthly assets. For our purposes, the average of the total assets at the beginning and end of the year is used.

The ratio of net sales to assets is computed as follows:

$$\text{Ratio of Net Sales to Assets} = \frac{\text{Net Sales}}{\text{Average Total Assets}}$$

To illustrate the use of this ratio, the following data (in millions) were taken from the annual reports of Dollar Tree, Inc.:

| | **For Years Ended** | |
|---|---|---|
| | **January 31, 2009** | **February 2, 2008** |
| Total revenues (net sales) | $4,645 | $4,243 |
| Total assets: | | |
| Beginning of year | 1,788 | 1,873 |
| End of year | 2,036 | 1,788 |

The ratios of net sales to assets for each year are as follows:

| | For Years Ended | |
|---|---|---|
| | **January 31, 2009** | **February 2, 2008** |
| Ratio of net sales to assets | 2.43 | 2.32 |
| | $4,645/[($1,788 + $2,036)/2] | $4,243/[($1,873 + $1,788)/2] |

Based on the preceding ratios, Dollar Tree improved its ratio of net sales to assets from 2.32 in 2008 to 2.43 in 2009. Thus, Dollar Tree improved the utilization of its assets to generate sales in 2009.

Using the ratio of net sales to assets for comparisons to competitors and with industry averages could also be beneficial in interpreting Dollar Tree's use of its assets. For example, the following data (in millions) were taken from the annual reports of Dollar General Corporation for the year ended January 30, 2009:

| | For Year Ended January 30, 2009 |
|---|---|
| Total revenues (net sales) | $10,458 |
| Total assets: | |
| Beginning of year | 8,656 |
| End of year | 8,889 |

Dollar General's ratio of net sales to assets for 2009 is as follows:

| | For Year Ended January 30, 2009 |
|---|---|
| Ratio of net sales to assets | 1.19 |
| | $10,458/[($8,656 + $8,889)/2] |

Comparing Dollar General's 2009 ratio of 1.19 to Dollar Tree's 2009 ratio of 2.43 implies Dollar Tree is using its assets more efficiently than Dollar General.

---

## Example Exercise 5-7 Ratio of Net Sales to Assets

**OBJ. 5**

The following financial statement data for the years ending December 31, 2012 and 2011, for Gilbert Company are shown below.

| | 2012 | 2011 |
|---|---|---|
| Net sales | $1,305,000 | $962,500 |
| Total assets: | | |
| Beginning of year | 840,000 | 700,000 |
| End of year | 900,000 | 840,000 |

a. Determine the ratio of net sales to assets for 2012 and 2011.

b. Does the change in the current ratio from 2011 to 2012 indicate a favorable or an unfavorable trend?

### Follow My Example 5-7

a.

| | 2012 | 2011 |
|---|---|---|
| Ratio of net sales to assets | 1.50 | 1.25 |
| | $1,305,000/[($840,000 + $900,000)/2] | $962,500/[($840,000 + $700,000)/2] |

b. The change from 1.25 to 1.50 indicates a favorable trend in using assets to generate sales.

Practice Exercises: **PE 5-7A, PE 5-7B**

## Integrity, Objectivity, and Ethics in Business

**THE COST OF EMPLOYEE THEFT**

One survey reported that the 22 largest U.S. retail store chains have lost over $6 billion to shoplifting and employee theft. The stores apprehended over 900,000 shoplifters and dishonest employees and recovered more than $182 million from these thieves. Approximately 1 out of every 30 employees was apprehended for theft from his or her employer. Each dishonest employee stole approximately 7 times the amount stolen by shoplifters ($969 vs. $136).

Source: Jack L. Hayes International, 21st Annual Retail Theft Survey, 2009.

# A P P E N D I X

# The Periodic Inventory System

Throughout this chapter, the perpetual inventory system was used to record purchases and sales of merchandise. Not all merchandise businesses, however, use the perpetual inventory system. For example, small merchandise businesses, such as a local hardware store, may use a manual accounting system. A manual perpetual inventory system is time consuming and costly to maintain. In this case, the periodic inventory system may be used.

## Cost of Merchandise Sold Using the Periodic Inventory System

In the periodic inventory system, sales are recorded in the same manner as in the perpetual inventory system. However, cost of merchandise sold is not recorded on the date of sale. Instead, cost of merchandise sold is determined at the end of the period as shown in Exhibit 12 for **NetSolutions**.

**EXHIBIT 12**

**Determining Cost of Merchandise Sold Using the Periodic System**

| | | | |
|---|---|---:|---:|
| Merchandise inventory, January 1, 2013 | | | $ 59,700 |
| Purchases | | $521,980 | |
| Less: Purchases returns and allowances | $9,100 | | |
| Purchases discounts | 2,525 | 11,625 | |
| Net purchases | | $510,355 | |
| Add freight in | | 17,400 | |
| Cost of merchandise purchased | | | 527,755 |
| Merchandise available for sale | | | $587,455 |
| Less merchandise inventory, December 31, 2013 | | | 62,150 |
| Cost of merchandise sold | | | $525,305 |

# Chart of Accounts Under the Periodic Inventory System

The chart of accounts under a periodic inventory system is shown in Exhibit 13. The accounts used to record transactions under the periodic inventory system are highlighted in Exhibit 13.

| Balance Sheet Accounts | Income Statement Accounts |
|---|---|
| 100 Assets | 400 Revenues |
|    110  Cash |    410  Sales |
|    111  Notes Receivable |    411  Sales Returns and Allowances |
|    112  Accounts Receivable |    412  Sales Discounts |
|    115  Merchandise Inventory | 500 Costs and Expenses |
|    116  Office Supplies |    510  Purchases |
|    117  Prepaid Insurance |    511  Purchases Returns and Allowances |
|    120  Land |    512  Purchases Discounts |
|    123  Store Equipment |    513  Freight In |
|    124  Accumulated Depreciation—Store Equipment |    520  Sales Salaries Expense |
|    125  Office Equipment |    521  Advertising Expense |
|    126  Accumulated Depreciation—Office Equipment |    522  Depreciation Expense—Store Equipment |
| 200 Liabilities |    523  Delivery Expense |
|    210  Accounts Payable |    529  Miscellaneous Selling Expense |
|    211  Salaries Payable |    530  Office Salaries Expense |
|    212  Unearned Rent |    531  Rent Expense |
|    215  Notes Payable |    532  Depreciation Expense—Office Equipment |
| 300 Stockholders' Equity |    533  Insurance Expense |
|    310  Capital Stock |    534  Office Supplies Expense |
|    311  Retained Earnings |    539  Misc. Administrative Expense |
|    312  Dividends | 600 Other Income |
|    313  Income Summary |    610  Rent Revenue |
| | 700 Other Expense |
| |    710  Interest Expense |

**EXHIBIT 13**

**Chart of Accounts Under the Periodic Inventory System**

# Recording Merchandise Transactions Under the Periodic Inventory System

Using the periodic inventory system, purchases of inventory are not recorded in the merchandise inventory account. Instead, purchases, purchases discounts, and purchases returns and allowances accounts are used. In addition, the sales of merchandise are not recorded in the inventory account. Thus, there is no detailed record of the amount of inventory on hand at any given time. At the end of the period, a physical count of merchandise inventory on hand is taken. This physical count is used to determine the cost of merchandise sold as shown in Exhibit 12.

The use of purchases, purchases discounts, purchases returns and allowances, and freight in accounts are described below.

**Purchases** Purchases of inventory are recorded in a purchases account rather than in the merchandise inventory account. Purchases is debited for the invoice amount of a purchase.

**Purchases Discounts** Purchases discounts are normally recorded in a separate purchases discounts account. The balance of the purchases discounts account is reported as a deduction from Purchases for the period. Thus, Purchases Discounts is a contra (or offsetting) account to Purchases.

**Purchases Returns and Allowances** Purchases returns and allowances are recorded in a similar manner as purchases discounts. A separate purchases returns and allowances account is used to record returns and allowances. Purchases returns and allowances are reported as a deduction from Purchases for the period. Thus, Purchases Returns and Allowances is a contra (or offsetting) account to Purchases.

**Freight In** When merchandise is purchased FOB shipping point, the buyer pays for the freight. Under the periodic inventory system, freight paid when purchasing merchandise FOB shipping point is debited to Freight In, Transportation In, or a similar account.

The preceding periodic inventory accounts and their effect on the cost of merchandise purchased are summarized below.

| Account | Entry to Increase | Normal Balance | Effect on Cost of Merchandise Purchased |
|---|---|---|---|
| Purchases | Debit | Debit | Increases |
| Purchases Discounts | Credit | Credit | Decreases |
| Purchases Returns and Allowances | Credit | Credit | Decreases |
| Freight In | Debit | Debit | Increases |

Exhibit 14 illustrates the recording of merchandise transactions using the periodic system. As a review, Exhibit 14 also illustrates how each transaction would have been recorded using the perpetual system.

**EXHIBIT 14** **Transactions Using the Periodic and Perpetual Inventory Systems**

| Transaction | Periodic Inventory System | | Perpetual Inventory System | |
|---|---|---|---|---|
| **June 5.** Purchased $30,000 of merchandise on account, terms 2/10, n/30. | Purchases .................... 30,000<br>   Accounts Payable ........... | <br>30,000 | Merchandise Inventory ........ 30,000<br>   Accounts Payable ........... | <br>30,000 |
| **June 8.** Returned merchandise purchased on account on June 5, $500. | Accounts Payable.............. 500<br>   Purchases Returns and<br>     Allowances................ | <br><br>500 | Accounts Payable.............. 500<br>   Merchandise Inventory ..... | <br>500 |
| **June 15.** Paid for purchase of June 5, less return of $500 and discount of $590 [($30,000 – $500) × 2%]. | Accounts Payable.............. 29,500<br>   Cash........................<br>   Purchases Discounts ........ | <br>28,910<br>590 | Accounts Payable.............. 29,500<br>   Cash........................<br>   Merchandise Inventory ..... | <br>28,910<br>590 |
| **June 18.** Sold merchandise on account, $12,500, 1/10, n/30. The cost of the merchandise sold was $9,000. | Accounts Receivable........... 12,500<br>   Sales ...................... | <br>12,500 | Accounts Receivable........... 12,500<br>   Sales ......................<br>Cost of Merchandise Sold...... 9,000<br>   Merchandise Inventory ..... | <br>12,500<br><br>9,000 |
| **June 21.** Received merchandise returned on account, $4,000. The cost of the merchandise returned was $2,800. | Sales Returns and Allowances.. 4,000<br>   Accounts Receivable ........ | <br>4,000 | Sales Returns and Allowances.... 4,000<br>   Accounts Receivable........<br>Merchandise Inventory ........ 2,800<br>   Cost of Merchandise Sold ... | <br>4,000<br><br>2,800 |
| **June 22.** Purchased merchandise, $15,000, terms FOB shipping point, 2/15, n/30, with prepaid freight of $750 added to the invoice. | Purchases .................... 15,000<br>Freight In....................... 750<br>   Accounts Payable ........... | <br><br>15,750 | Merchandise Inventory ........ 15,750<br>   Accounts Payable ........... | <br>15,750 |
| **June 28.** Received $8,415 as payment on account from June 18 sale less return of June 21 and less discount of $85 [($12,500 – $4,000) × 1%]. | Cash ......................... 8,415<br>Sales Discounts................ 85<br>   Accounts Receivable ........ | <br><br>8,500 | Cash ......................... 8,415<br>Sales Discounts................ 85<br>   Accounts Receivable........ | <br><br>8,500 |
| **June 29.** Received $19,600 from cash sales. The cost of the merchandise sold was $13,800. | Cash ......................... 19,600<br>   Sales ...................... | <br>19,600 | Cash ......................... 19,600<br>   Sales ......................<br>Cost of Merchandise Sold...... 13,800<br>   Merchandise Inventory ..... | <br>19,600<br><br>13,800 |

## Adjusting Process Under the Periodic Inventory System

The adjusting process is the same under the periodic and perpetual inventory systems except for the inventory shrinkage adjustment. The ending merchandise inventory is determined by a physical count under both systems.

Under the perpetual inventory system, the ending inventory physical count is compared to the balance of Merchandise Inventory. The difference is the amount of inventory shrinkage. The inventory shrinkage is then recorded as a debit to Cost of Merchandise Sold and a credit to Merchandise Inventory.

Under the periodic inventory system, the merchandise inventory account is not kept up to date for purchases and sales. As a result, the inventory shrinkage cannot be directly determined. Instead, any inventory shrinkage is included indirectly in the computation of cost of merchandise sold as shown in Exhibit 12. This is a major disadvantage of the periodic inventory system. That is, under the periodic inventory system, inventory shrinkage is not separately determined.

## Financial Statements Under the Periodic Inventory System

The financial statements are similar under the perpetual and periodic inventory systems. When the multiple-step format of income statement is used, cost of merchandise sold may be reported as shown in Exhibit 12.

## Closing Entries Under the Periodic Inventory System

The closing entries differ in the periodic inventory system in that there is no cost of merchandise sold account to close to Income Summary. Instead, the purchases, purchases discounts, purchases returns and allowances, and freight in accounts are closed to Income Summary. In addition, the merchandise inventory account is adjusted to the end-of-period physical inventory count during the closing process.

The four closing entries under the periodic inventory system are as follows:

1. Debit each temporary account with a credit balance, such as Sales, for its balance and credit Income Summary. Since Purchases Discounts and Purchases Returns and Allowances are temporary accounts with credit balances, they are debited for their balances. In addition, Merchandise Inventory is debited for its end-of-period balance based on the end-of-period physical inventory.

2. Credit each temporary account with a debit balance, such as the various expenses, and debit Income Summary. Since Sales Returns and Allowances, Sales Discounts, Purchases, and Freight In are temporary accounts with debit balances, they are credited for their balances. In addition, Merchandise Inventory is credited for its balance as of the beginning of the period.

3. Debit Income Summary for the amount of its balance (net income) and credit the retained earnings account. The accounts debited and credited are reversed if there is a net loss.

4. Debit the retained earnings account for the balance of the dividends account and credit the dividends account.

The four closing entries for NetSolutions under the periodic inventory system are shown on the next page.

| | Journal | | | |
|---|---|---|---|---|
| **Date** | **Item** | **Post. Ref.** | **Debit** | **Credit** |
| 2013 | Closing Entries | | | |
| Dec. 31 | Merchandise Inventory | 115 | 62,150 | |
| | Sales | 410 | 720,185 | |
| | Purchases Returns and Allowances | 511 | 9,100 | |
| | Purchases Discounts | 512 | 2,525 | |
| | Rent Revenue | 610 | 600 | |
| | Income Summary | 313 | | 794,560 |
| | | | | |
| 31 | Income Summary | 313 | 719,160 | |
| | Merchandise Inventory | 115 | | 59,700 |
| | Sales Returns and Allowances | 411 | | 6,140 |
| | Sales Discounts | 412 | | 5,790 |
| | Purchases | 510 | | 521,980 |
| | Freight In | 513 | | 17,400 |
| | Sales Salaries Expense | 520 | | 53,430 |
| | Advertising Expense | 521 | | 10,860 |
| | Depreciation Expense—Store Equipment | 522 | | 3,100 |
| | Delivery Expense | 523 | | 2,800 |
| | Miscellaneous Selling Expense | 529 | | 630 |
| | Office Salaries Expense | 530 | | 21,020 |
| | Rent Expense | 531 | | 8,100 |
| | Depreciation Expense—Office Equipment | 532 | | 2,490 |
| | Insurance Expense | 533 | | 1,910 |
| | Office Supplies Expense | 534 | | 610 |
| | Miscellaneous Administrative Expense | 539 | | 760 |
| | Interest Expense | 710 | | 2,440 |
| | | | | |
| 31 | Income Summary | 313 | 75,400 | |
| | Retained Earnings | 311 | | 75,400 |
| | | | | |
| 31 | Retained Earnings | 311 | 18,000 | |
| | Dividends | 312 | | 18,000 |

In the first closing entry, Merchandise Inventory is debited for $62,150. This is the ending physical inventory count on December 31, 2013. In the second closing entry, Merchandise Inventory is credited for its January 1, 2013, balance of $59,700. In this way, the closing entries highlight the importance of the beginning and ending balances of Merchandise Inventory in determining cost of merchandise sold, as shown in Exhibit 12. After the closing entries are posted, Merchandise Inventory will have a balance of $62,150. This is the amount reported on the December 31, 2013, balance sheet.

In the preceding closing entries, the periodic accounts are highlighted in color. Under the perpetual inventory system, the highlighted periodic inventory accounts are replaced by the cost of merchandise sold account.

# At a Glance 5

**Distinguish between the activities and financial statements of service and merchandising businesses.**

**Key Points**   Merchandising businesses purchase merchandise for selling to customers.
On a merchandising business's income statement, revenue from selling merchandise is reported as sales. The cost of the merchandise sold is subtracted from sales to arrive at gross profit. The operating expenses are subtracted from gross profit to arrive at net income. Merchandise inventory, which is merchandise not sold, is reported as a current asset on the balance sheet.

| Learning Outcomes | Example Exercises | Practice Exercises |
|---|---|---|
| • Describe how the activities of a service and a merchandising business differ. | | |
| • Describe the differences between the income statements of a service and a merchandising business. | | |
| • Compute gross profit. | EE5-1 | PE5-1A, 5-1B |
| • Describe how merchandise inventory is reported on the balance sheet. | | |

**Describe and illustrate the financial statements of a merchandising business.**

**Key Points**   The multiple-step income statement of a merchandiser reports sales, sales returns and allowances, sales discounts, and net sales. The cost of the merchandise sold is subtracted from net sales to determine the gross profit. Operating income is determined by subtracting selling and administrative expenses from gross profit. Net income is determined by adding or subtracting the net of other income and expense. The income statement may also be reported in a single-step form.
The retained earnings statement is similar to that for a service business.
The balance sheet reports merchandise inventory at the end of the period as a current asset.

| Learning Outcomes | Example Exercises | Practice Exercises |
|---|---|---|
| • Prepare a multiple-step income statement for a merchandising business. | | |
| • Prepare a single-step income statement. | | |
| • Prepare a retained earnings statement for a merchandising business. | | |
| • Prepare a balance sheet for a merchandising business. | | |

**Describe and illustrate the accounting for merchandise transactions including:**
  - **sale of merchandise**
  - **purchase of merchandise**
  - **freight**
  - **sales taxes and trade discounts**
  - **dual nature of merchandising transactions**

**Key Points**   The chart of accounts for a merchandising business (NetSolutions) is shown in Exhibit 5. Sales of merchandise for cash or on account are recorded as sales. The cost of merchandise sold and the reduction in merchandise inventory are also recorded at the time of sale. Discounts for early payment of sales on account are recorded as sales discounts. Price adjustments and returned merchandise are recorded as sales returns and allowances.

Purchases of merchandise for cash or on account are recorded as merchandise inventory. Discounts for early payment of purchases on account are recorded as purchases discounts. Price adjustments or returned merchandise are recorded as purchases returns and allowances.

When merchandise is shipped FOB shipping point, the buyer pays the freight and debits Merchandise Inventory. When merchandise is shipped FOB destination, the seller pays the freight and debits Delivery Expense or Freight Out.

The liability for sales tax is incurred when the sale is made and is recorded by the seller as a credit to the sales tax payable account. Trade discounts are discounts off the list price of merchandise.

Each merchandising transaction affects a buyer and a seller.

| Learning Outcomes | Example Exercises | Practice Exercises |
|---|---|---|
| • Prepare journal entries to record sales of merchandise for cash or using a credit card. | | |
| • Prepare journal entries to record sales of merchandise on account. | EE5-2 | PE5-2A, 5-2B |
| • Prepare journal entries to record sales discounts and sales returns and allowances. | EE5-2 | PE5-2A, 5-2B |
| • Prepare journal entries to record the purchase of merchandise for cash. | | |
| • Prepare journal entries to record the purchase of merchandise on account. | EE5-3 | PE5-3A, 5-3B |
| • Prepare journal entries to record purchases discounts and purchases returns and allowances. | EE5-3 | PE5-3A, 5-3B |
| • Prepare journal entries for freight from the point of view of the buyer and seller. | | |
| • Determine the total cost of the purchase of merchandise under differing freight terms. | EE5-4 | PE5-4A, 5-4B |
| • Prepare journal entries for the collection and payment of sales taxes by the seller. | | |
| • Determine the cost of merchandise purchased when a trade discount is offered by the seller. | | |
| • Record the same merchandise transactions for the buyer and seller. | EE5-5 | PE5-5A, 5-5B |

**OBJ. 4**

## Describe the adjusting and closing process for a merchandising business.

**Key Points**   The normal adjusting entry for inventory shrinkage is to debit Cost of Merchandise Sold and credit Merchandise Inventory.

The closing entries for a merchandising business are similar to those for a service business except that the cost of merchandise sold, sales discounts, and sales returns and allowances accounts are also closed to Income Summary.

| Learning Outcomes | Example Exercises | Practice Exercises |
|---|---|---|
| • Prepare the adjusting journal entry for inventory shrinkage. | EE5-6 | PE5-6A, 5-6B |
| • Prepare the closing entries for a merchandising business. | | |

## OBJ. 5

**Describe and illustrate the use of the ratio of net sales to assets in evaluating a company's operating performance.**

**Key Points** The ratio of net sales to assets measures how effectively a business is using its assets to generate sales. A high ratio indicates an effective use of assets. Using the average of the total assets at the beginning and end of the year, the ratio is computed as follows:

$$\text{Ratio of Net Sales to Assets} = \frac{\text{Net Sales}}{\text{Average Total Assets}}$$

| Learning Outcomes | *Example Exercises* | *Practice Exercises* |
|---|---|---|
| • Interpret a high ratio of net sales to assets. | | |
| • Compute the ratio of net sales to assets. | **EE5-7** | **PE5-7A, 5-7B** |

# Key Terms

account form (222)

accounts payable subsidiary ledger (225)

accounts receivable subsidiary ledger (225)

administrative expenses (general expenses) (221)

controlling account (225)

cost of merchandise sold (218)

credit memorandum (credit memo) (227)

credit period (226)

credit terms (226)

debit memorandum (debit memo) (231)

FOB (free on board) destination (233)

FOB (free on board) shipping point (233)

general ledger (225)

gross profit (218)

income from operations (operating income) (221)

inventory shrinkage (inventory shortage) (238)

inventory subsidiary ledger (225)

invoice (226)

merchandise inventory (218)

multiple-step income statement (219)

net sales (221)

other expense (222)

other income (222)

periodic inventory system (221)

perpetual inventory system (221)

purchases discounts (230)

purchases returns and allowances (231)

ratio of net sales to assets (240)

report form (223)

sales (220)

sales discounts (220)

sales returns and allowances (220)

selling expenses (221)

single-step income statement (222)

subsidiary ledger (225)

trade discounts (236)

# Illustrative Problem

The following transactions were completed by Montrose Company during May of the current year. Montrose Company uses a perpetual inventory system.

May 3. Purchased merchandise on account from Floyd Co., $4,000, terms FOB shipping point, 2/10, n/30, with prepaid freight of $120 added to the invoice.

5. Purchased merchandise on account from Kramer Co., $8,500, terms FOB destination, 1/10, n/30.

6. Sold merchandise on account to C. F. Howell Co., list price $4,000, trade discount 30%, terms 2/10, n/30. The cost of the merchandise sold was $1,125.

8. Purchased office supplies for cash, $150.

10. Returned merchandise purchased on May 5 from Kramer Co., $1,300.

13. Paid Floyd Co. on account for purchase of May 3, less discount.

May 14. Purchased merchandise for cash, $10,500.

15. Paid Kramer Co. on account for purchase of May 5, less return of May 10 and discount.

16. Received cash on account from sale of May 6 to C. F. Howell Co., less discount.

19. Sold merchandise on MasterCard credit cards, $2,450. The cost of the merchandise sold was $980.

22. Sold merchandise on account to Comer Co., $3,480, terms 2/10, n/30. The cost of the merchandise sold was $1,400.

24. Sold merchandise for cash, $4,350. The cost of the merchandise sold was $1,750.

25. Received merchandise returned by Comer Co. from sale on May 22, $1,480. The cost of the returned merchandise was $600.

31. Paid a service processing fee of $140 for MasterCard sales.

### Instructions

1. Journalize the preceding transactions.

2. Journalize the adjusting entry for merchandise inventory shrinkage, $3,750.

### Solution

| | | | | | |
|---|---|---|---|---|---|
| 1. | May | 3 | Merchandise Inventory | 4,120 | |
| | | | Accounts Payable—Floyd Co. | | 4,120 |
| | | 5 | Merchandise Inventory | 8,500 | |
| | | | Accounts Payable—Kramer Co. | | 8,500 |
| | | 6 | Accounts Receivable—C. F. Howell Co. | 2,800 | |
| | | | Sales | | 2,800 |
| | | | [$4,000 – (30% × $4,000)] | | |
| | | 6 | Cost of Merchandise Sold | 1,125 | |
| | | | Merchandise Inventory | | 1,125 |
| | | 8 | Office Supplies | 150 | |
| | | | Cash | | 150 |
| | | 10 | Accounts Payable—Kramer Co. | 1,300 | |
| | | | Merchandise Inventory | | 1,300 |
| | | 13 | Accounts Payable—Floyd Co. | 4,120 | |
| | | | Merchandise Inventory | | 80 |
| | | | Cash | | 4,040 |
| | | | [$4,000 – (2% × $4,000) + $120] | | |
| | | 14 | Merchandise Inventory | 10,500 | |
| | | | Cash | | 10,500 |
| | | 15 | Accounts Payable—Kramer Co. | 7,200 | |
| | | | Merchandise Inventory | | 72 |
| | | | Cash | | 7,128 |
| | | | [($8,500 – $1,300) × 1% = $72; $8,500 – $1,300 – $72 = $7,128] | | |
| | | 16 | Cash | 2,744 | |
| | | | Sales Discounts | 56 | |
| | | | Accounts Receivable—C. F. Howell Co. | | 2,800 |
| | | 19 | Cash | 2,450 | |
| | | | Sales | | 2,450 |
| | | 19 | Cost of Merchandise Sold | 980 | |
| | | | Merchandise Inventory | | 980 |
| | | 22 | Accounts Receivable—Comer Co. | 3,480 | |
| | | | Sales | | 3,480 |
| | | 22 | Cost of Merchandise Sold | 1,400 | |
| | | | Merchandise Inventory | | 1,400 |
| | | 24 | Cash | 4,350 | |
| | | | Sales | | 4,350 |

| | May | 24 | Cost of Merchandise Sold | 1,750 | |
|---|---|---|---|---|---|
| | | | Merchandise Inventory | | 1,750 |
| | | 25 | Sales Returns and Allowances | 1,480 | |
| | | | Accounts Receivable—Comer Co. | | 1,480 |
| | | 25 | Merchandise Inventory | 600 | |
| | | | Cost of Merchandise Sold | | 600 |
| | | 31 | Credit Card Expense | 140 | |
| | | | Cash | | 140 |
| 2. | May | 31 | Cost of Merchandise Sold | 3,750 | |
| | | | Merchandise Inventory | | 3,750 |
| | | | Inventory shrinkage. | | |

# Discussion Questions

1. What distinguishes a merchandising business from a service business?

2. Can a business earn a gross profit but incur a net loss? Explain.

3. Name at least three accounts that would normally appear in the chart of accounts of a merchandising business but would not appear in the chart of accounts of a service business.

4. How are sales to customers using MasterCard and VISA recorded?

5. The credit period during which the buyer of merchandise is allowed to pay usually begins with what date?

6. What is the meaning of (a) 1/15, n/60; (b) n/30; (c) n/eom?

7. What is the nature of (a) a credit memo issued by the seller of merchandise, (b) a debit memo issued by the buyer of merchandise?

8. Who bears the freight when the terms of sale are (a) FOB shipping point, (b) FOB destination?

9. Mountain Gear Inc., which uses a perpetual inventory system, experienced a normal inventory shrinkage of $21,950. What accounts would be debited and credited to record the adjustment for the inventory shrinkage at the end of the accounting period?

10. Assume that Mountain Gear Inc. in Discussion Question 9 experienced an abnormal inventory shrinkage of $263,750. Mountain Gear Inc. has decided to record the abnormal inventory shrinkage so that it would be separately disclosed on the income statement. What account would be debited for the abnormal inventory shrinkage?

# Practice Exercises

| Learning Objectives | Example Exercises | |
|---|---|---|

**OBJ. 1**  **EE 5-1** *p. 219*  **PE 5-1A  Gross profit**

During the current year, merchandise is sold for $275,000 cash and $990,000 on account. The cost of the merchandise sold is $950,000. What is the amount of the gross profit?

**OBJ. 1**  **EE 5-1** *p. 219*  **PE 5-1B  Gross profit**

During the current year, merchandise is sold for $40,000 cash and $415,000 on account. The cost of the merchandise sold is $360,000. What is the amount of the gross profit?

**OBJ. 3**  **EE 5-2** *p. 229*  **PE 5-2A  Sales transactions**

Journalize the following merchandise transactions:

a. Sold merchandise on account, $29,000 with terms 2/10, n/30. The cost of the merchandise sold was $21,750.

b. Received payment less the discount.

**OBJ. 3**  **EE 5-2** *p. 229*  **PE 5-2B  Sales transactions**

Journalize the following merchandise transactions:

a. Sold merchandise on account, $60,000 with terms 1/10, n/30. The cost of the merchandise sold was $40,000.

b. Received payment less the discount.

**OBJ. 3**  **EE 5-3** *p. 232*  **PE 5-3A  Purchase transactions**

MR Tile Company purchased merchandise on account from a supplier for $9,000, terms 2/10, n/30. MR Tile Company returned $1,500 of the merchandise and received full credit.

a. If MR Tile Company pays the invoice within the discount period, what is the amount of cash required for the payment?

b. Under a perpetual inventory system, what account is credited by MR Tile Company to record the return?

**OBJ. 3**  **EE 5-3** *p. 232*  **PE 5-3B  Purchase transactions**

Piedmont Company purchased merchandise on account from a supplier for $30,000, terms 1/10, n/30. Piedmont Company returned $4,000 of the merchandise and received full credit.

a. If Piedmont Company pays the invoice within the discount period, what is the amount of cash required for the payment?

b. Under a perpetual inventory system, what account is debited by Piedmont Company to record the return?

**OBJ. 3**  **EE 5-4** *p. 235*  **PE 5-4A  Freight terms**

Determine the amount to be paid in full settlement of each of invoices (a) and (b), assuming that credit for returns and allowances was received prior to payment and that all invoices were paid within the discount period.

| | | Merchandise | Freight Paid by Seller | Freight Terms | Returns and Allowances |
|---|---|---|---|---|---|
| | a. | $120,000 | $5,000 | FOB shipping point, 1/10, n/30 | $15,000 |
| | b. | 90,000 | 1,000 | FOB destination, 2/10, n/30 | 2,000 |

**OBJ. 3**  **EE 5-4** *p. 235*

### PE 5-4B  Freight terms

Determine the amount to be paid in full settlement of each of invoices (a) and (b), assuming that credit for returns and allowances was received prior to payment and that all invoices were paid within the discount period.

| | | Merchandise | Freight Paid by Seller | Freight Terms | Returns and Allowances |
|---|---|---|---|---|---|
| | a. | $20,000 | $500 | FOB destination, 1/10, n/30 | $2,000 |
| | b. | 18,000 | 250 | FOB shipping point, 2/10, n/30 | 1,000 |

**OBJ. 3**  **EE 5-5** *p. 238*

### PE 5-5A  Transactions for buyer and seller

Storall Co. sold merchandise to Bunting Co. on account, $8,000, terms 2/15, n/30. The cost of the merchandise sold is $3,000. Storall Co. issued a credit memo for $1,000 for merchandise returned and later received the amount due within the discount period. The cost of the merchandise returned was $400. Journalize Storall Co.'s and Bunting Co.'s entries for the payment of the amount due.

**OBJ. 3**  **EE 5-5** *p. 238*

### PE 5-5B  Transactions for buyer and seller

SPA Co. sold merchandise to Boyd Co. on account, $25,000, terms FOB shipping point, 2/10, n/30. The cost of the merchandise sold is $16,000. SPA Co. paid freight of $675 and later received the amount due within the discount period. Journalize SPA Co.'s and Boyd Co.'s entries for the payment of the amount due.

**OBJ. 4**  **EE 5-6** *p. 239*

### PE 5-6A  Inventory shrinkage

House of Clean Company's perpetual inventory records indicate that $375,000 of merchandise should be on hand on June 30, 2012. The physical inventory indicates that $366,500 of merchandise is actually on hand. Journalize the adjusting entry for the inventory shrinkage for House of Clean Company for the year ended June 30, 2012. Assume that the inventory shrinkage is a normal amount.

**OBJ. 4**  **EE 5-6** *p. 239*

### PE 5-6B  Inventory shrinkage

Zurich Company's perpetual inventory records indicate that $1,380,000 of merchandise should be on hand on August 31, 2012. The physical inventory indicates that $1,315,900 of merchandise is actually on hand. Journalize the adjusting entry for the inventory shrinkage for Zurich Company for the year ended August 31, 2012. Assume that the inventory shrinkage is a normal amount.

**OBJ. 5**  **EE 5-7** *p. 241*

### PE 5-7A  Ratio of net sales to assets

The following financial statement data for years ending December 31 for Foodworks Company are shown below.

| | 2012 | 2011 |
|---|---|---|
| Net sales | $880,000 | $787,500 |
| Total assets: | | |
| Beginning of year | 500,000 | 375,000 |
| End of year | 600,000 | 500,000 |

a. Determine the ratio of net sales to assets for 2012 and 2011.

b. Does the change in the ratio of net sales to assets from 2011 to 2012 indicate a favorable or an unfavorable trend?

OBJ. 5     EE 5-7  *p. 241*

## PE 5-7B   Ratio of net sales to assets

The following financial Statement data for years ending December 31 for Beading Company are shown below.

|                   | 2012      | 2011      |
|-------------------|-----------|-----------|
| Net sales         | $675,000  | $475,000  |
| Total assets:     |           |           |
| Beginning of year | 200,000   | 180,000   |
| End of year       | 250,000   | 200,000   |

a. Determine the ratio of net sales to assets for 2012 and 2011.

b. Does the change in the ratio of net sales to assets from 2011 to 2012 indicate a favorable or an unfavorable trend?

# Exercises

OBJ. 1

## EX 5-1   Determining gross profit

During the current year, merchandise is sold for $775,000. The cost of the merchandise sold is $426,250.

a. What is the amount of the gross profit?

b. Compute the gross profit percentage (gross profit divided by sales).

c. ➤ Will the income statement necessarily report a net income? Explain.

OBJ. 1

## EX 5-2   Determining cost of merchandise sold

For the year ended February 28, 2009, Best Buy reported revenue of $45,015 million. Its gross profit was $10,998 million. What was the amount of Best Buy's cost of merchandise sold?

OBJ. 2

## EX 5-3   Income statement for merchandiser

For the fiscal year, sales were $6,750,000, sales discounts were $120,000, sales returns and allowances were $90,000, and the cost of merchandise sold was $4,000,000.

a. What was the amount of net sales?

b. What was the amount of gross profit?

c. If total operating expenses were $1,200,000, could you determine net income?

OBJ. 2

## EX 5-4   Income statement for merchandiser

The following expenses were incurred by a merchandising business during the year. In which expense section of the income statement should each be reported: (a) selling, (b) administrative, or (c) other?

1. Advertising expense

2. Depreciation expense on store equipment

3. Insurance expense on office equipment

4. Interest expense on notes payable

5. Rent expense on office building

6. Salaries of office personnel

7. Salary of sales manager

8. Sales supplies used

OBJ. 2

✔ Net income:
$1,075,000

## EX 5-5   Single-step income statement

Summary operating data for Heartland Company during the current year ended November 30, 2012, are as follows: cost of merchandise sold, $2,500,000; administrative expenses, $300,000; interest expense, $20,000; rent revenue, $95,000; net sales, $4,200,000; and selling expenses, $400,000. Prepare a single-step income statement.

OBJ. 2

### EX 5-6 Multiple-step income statement

Identify the errors in the following income statement:

**Keepsakes Company**
**Income Statement**
**For the Year Ended February 29, 2012**

| | | | |
|---|---|---|---|
| Revenue from sales: | | | |
| Sales...................................................... | | $7,200,000 | |
| Add: Sales returns and allowances ...................... | $275,000 | | |
| Sales discounts ................................. | 130,000 | 405,000 | |
| Gross sales ........................................... | | $7,605,000 | |
| Cost of merchandise sold............................ | | 4,075,000 | |
| Income from operations ................................ | | $3,530,000 | |
| Expenses: | | | |
| Selling expenses........................................ | $ 950,000 | | |
| Administrative expenses ............................... | 475,000 | | |
| Delivery expense ...................................... | 125,000 | | |
| Total expenses ...................................... | | 1,550,000 | |
| | | $1,980,000 | |
| Other expense: | | | |
| Interest revenue ....................................... | | 30,000 | |
| Gross profit ........................................... | | $1,950,000 | |

OBJ. 2

✔ a. $30,000
✔ h. $515,000

### EX 5-7 Determining amounts for items omitted from income statement

Two items are omitted in each of the following four lists of income statement data. Determine the amounts of the missing items, identifying them by letter.

| | | | | |
|---|---|---|---|---|
| Sales | $300,000 | $600,000 | $850,000 | $    (g) |
| Sales returns and allowances | (a) | 30,000 | (e) | 10,000 |
| Sales discounts | 20,000 | 18,000 | 70,000 | 25,000 |
| Net sales | 250,000 | (c) | 775,000 | (h) |
| Cost of merchandise sold | (b) | 330,000 | (f) | 400,000 |
| Gross profit | 100,000 | (d) | 300,000 | 115,000 |

OBJ. 2

✔ a. Net income:
$370,000

### EX 5-8 Multiple-step income statement

On December 31, 2012, the balances of the accounts appearing in the ledger of Warm Place Furnishings Company, a furniture wholesaler, are as follows:

| | | | |
|---|---|---|---|
| Administrative Expenses | $ 250,000 | Office Supplies | $   20,000 |
| Building | 1,025,000 | Retained Earnings | 591,000 |
| Capital Stock | 150,000 | Salaries Payable | 6,000 |
| Cash | 97,000 | Sales | 3,000,000 |
| Cost of Merchandise Sold | 1,700,000 | Sales Discounts | 40,000 |
| Dividends | 50,000 | Sales Returns and Allowances | 160,000 |
| Interest Expense | 30,000 | Selling Expenses | 450,000 |
| Merchandise Inventory | 260,000 | Store Supplies | 65,000 |
| Notes Payable | 400,000 | | |

a. Prepare a multiple-step income statement for the year ended December 31, 2012.

b. Compare the major advantages and disadvantages of the multiple-step and single-step forms of income statements.

OBJ. 3

## EX 5-9 Chart of accounts

Do-Right Paints Co. is a newly organized business with a list of accounts arranged in alphabetical order below.

| | |
|---|---|
| Accounts Payable | Miscellaneous Selling Expense |
| Accounts Receivable | Notes Payable |
| Accumulated Depreciation—Office Equipment | Office Equipment |
| Accumulated Depreciation—Store Equipment | Office Salaries Expense |
| Advertising Expense | Office Supplies |
| Capital Stock | Office Supplies Expense |
| Cash | Prepaid Insurance |
| Cost of Merchandise Sold | Rent Expense |
| Delivery Expense | Retained Earnings |
| Depreciation Expense—Office Equipment | Salaries Payable |
| Depreciation Expense—Store Equipment | Sales |
| Dividends | Sales Discounts |
| Income Summary | Sales Returns and Allowances |
| Insurance Expense | Sales Salaries Expense |
| Interest Expense | Store Equipment |
| Land | Store Supplies |
| Merchandise Inventory | Store Supplies Expense |
| Miscellaneous Administrative Expense | |

Construct a chart of accounts, assigning account numbers and arranging the accounts in balance sheet and income statement order, as illustrated in Exhibit 5. Each account number is three digits: the first digit is to indicate the major classification ("1" for assets, and so on); the second digit is to indicate the subclassification ("11" for current assets, and so on); and the third digit is to identify the specific account ("110" for Cash, "112" for Accounts Receivable, "114" for Merchandise Inventory, "115" for Store Supplies, and so on).

OBJ. 3

## EX 5-10 Sales-related transactions, including the use of credit cards

Journalize the entries for the following transactions:

a. Sold merchandise for cash, $30,000. The cost of the merchandise sold was $18,000.

b. Sold merchandise on account, $120,000. The cost of the merchandise sold was $72,000.

c. Sold merchandise to customers who used MasterCard and VISA, $100,000. The cost of the merchandise sold was $70,000.

d. Sold merchandise to customers who used American Express, $45,000. The cost of the merchandise sold was $27,000.

e. Received an invoice from National Credit Co. for $9,000, representing a service fee paid for processing MasterCard, VISA, and American Express sales.

OBJ. 3

## EX 5-11 Sales returns and allowances

During the year, sales returns and allowances totaled $80,000. The cost of the merchandise returned was $48,000. The accountant recorded all the returns and allowances by debiting the sales account and crediting Cost of Merchandise Sold for $80,000.

Was the accountant's method of recording returns acceptable? Explain. In your explanation, include the advantages of using a sales returns and allowances account.

OBJ. 3

## EX 5-12 Sales-related transactions

After the amount due on a sale of $40,000, terms 2/10, n/eom, is received from a customer within the discount period, the seller consents to the return of the entire shipment. The cost of the merchandise returned was $24,000. (a) What is the amount of the refund owed to the customer? (b) Journalize the entries made by the seller to record the return and the refund.

**OBJ. 3**

### EX 5-13   Sales-related transactions

The debits and credits for three related transactions are presented in the following T accounts. Describe each transaction.

| Cash | | | | Sales | | |
|---|---|---|---|---|---|---|
| (5) | 32,340 | | | | (1) | 35,000 |

| Accounts Receivable | | | | Sales Discounts | | |
|---|---|---|---|---|---|---|
| (1) | 35,000 | (3) | 2,000 | (5) | 660 | |
| | | (5) | 33,000 | | | |

| Merchandise Inventory | | | | Sales Returns and Allowances | | |
|---|---|---|---|---|---|---|
| (4) | 1,200 | (2) | 21,000 | (3) | 2,000 | |

| | | | | Cost of Merchandise Sold | | |
|---|---|---|---|---|---|---|
| | | | | (2) | 21,000 | (4) | 1,200 |

**OBJ. 3**

✔ d. $18,240

### EX 5-14   Sales-related transactions

Merchandise is sold on account to a customer for $18,000, terms FOB shipping point, 2/10, n/30. The seller paid the freight of $600. Determine the following: (a) amount of the sale, (b) amount debited to Accounts Receivable, (c) amount of the discount for early payment, and (d) amount due within the discount period.

**OBJ. 3**

### EX 5-15   Purchase-related transaction

Bergquist Company purchased merchandise on account from a supplier for $12,000, terms 1/10, n/30. Bergquist Company returned $3,000 of the merchandise and received full credit.

a. If Bergquist Company pays the invoice within the discount period, what is the amount of cash required for the payment?

b. Under a perpetual inventory system, what account is credited by Bergquist Company to record the return?

**OBJ. 3**

### EX 5-16   Purchase-related transactions

A retailer is considering the purchase of 100 units of a specific item from either of two suppliers. Their offers are as follows:

E: $300 a unit, total of $30,000, 1/10, n/30, no charge for freight.

F: $295 a unit, total of $29,500, 2/10, n/30, plus freight of $375.

Which of the two offers, E or F, yields the lower price?

**OBJ. 3**

### EX 5-17   Purchase-related transactions

The debits and credits from four related transactions are presented in the following T accounts. Describe each transaction.

| Cash | | | | Accounts Payable | | |
|---|---|---|---|---|---|---|
| | | (2) | 400 | (3) | 3,000 | (1) | 15,000 |
| | | (4) | 11,760 | (4) | 12,000 | | |

| Merchandise Inventory | | | |
|---|---|---|---|
| (1) | 15,000 | (3) | 3,000 |
| (2) | 400 | (4) | 240 |

**OBJ. 3**

✔ (c) Cash, cr. $31,360

### EX 5-18   Purchase-related transactions

Mayn Co., a women's clothing store, purchased $36,000 of merchandise from a supplier on account, terms FOB destination, 2/10, n/30. Mayn Co. returned $4,000 of the merchandise, receiving a credit memo, and then paid the amount due within the discount period. Journalize Mayn Co.'s entries to record (a) the purchase, (b) the merchandise return, and (c) the payment.

OBJ. 3

✔ (e) Cash, dr. $2,400

**EX 5-19   Purchase-related transactions**

Journalize entries for the following related transactions of Blue Moon Company:

a.  Purchased $60,000 of merchandise from Sierra Co. on account, terms 1/10, n/30.

b.  Paid the amount owed on the invoice within the discount period.

c.  Discovered that $10,000 of the merchandise was defective and returned items, receiving credit.

d.  Purchased $7,500 of merchandise from Sierra Co. on account, terms n/30.

e.  Received a check for the balance owed from the return in (c), after deducting for the purchase in (d).

OBJ. 3

✔ a. $35,000

**EX 5-20   Determining amounts to be paid on invoices**

Determine the amount to be paid in full settlement of each of the following invoices, assuming that credit for returns and allowances was received prior to payment and that all invoices were paid within the discount period.

| | Merchandise | Freight Paid by Seller | | Returns an Allowance |
|---|---|---|---|---|
| a. | $36,000 | — | FOB destination, n/30 | $1,000 |
| b. | 10,000 | $375 | FOB shipping point, 2/10, n/30 | 1,200 |
| c. | 8,250 | — | FOB shipping point, 1/10, n/30 | 750 |
| d. | 4,000 | 200 | FOB shipping point, 2/10, n/30 | 500 |
| e. | 8,500 | — | FOB destination, 1/10, n/30 | — |

OBJ. 3

✔ c. $29,960

**EX 5-21   Sales tax**

A sale of merchandise on account for $28,000 is subject to a 7% sales tax. (a) Should the sales tax be recorded at the time of sale or when payment is received? (b) What is the amount of the sale? (c) What is the amount debited to Accounts Receivable? (d) What is the title of the account to which the $1,960 ($28,000 × 7%) is credited?

OBJ. 3

**EX 5-22   Sales tax transactions**

Journalize the entries to record the following selected transactions:

a.  Sold $12,900 of merchandise on account, subject to a sales tax of 4%. The cost of the merchandise sold was $7,800.

b.  Paid $32,750 to the state sales tax department for taxes collected.

OBJ. 3

**EX 5-23   Sales-related transactions**

Skycrest Co., a furniture wholesaler, sells merchandise to Boyle Co. on account, $45,000, terms 2/10, n/30. The cost of the merchandise sold is $27,000. Skycrest Co. issues a credit memo for $9,000 for merchandise returned and subsequently receives the amount due within the discount period. The cost of the merchandise returned is $5,400. Journalize Skycrest Co.'s entries for (a) the sale, including the cost of the merchandise sold, (b) the credit memo, including the cost of the returned merchandise, and (c) the receipt of the check for the amount due from Boyle Co.

OBJ. 3

**EX 5-24   Purchase-related transactions**

Based on the data presented in Exercise 5-23, journalize Boyle Co.'s entries for (a) the purchase, (b) the return of the merchandise for credit, and (c) the payment of the invoice within the discount period.

OBJ. 3

**EX 5-25   Normal balances of merchandise accounts**

What is the normal balance of the following accounts: (a) Cost of Merchandise Sold, (b) Delivery Expense, (c) Merchandise Inventory, (d) Sales, (e) Sales Discounts, (f) Sales Returns and Allowances, (g) Sales Tax Payable?

OBJ. 4

### EX 5-26 Adjusting entry for merchandise inventory shrinkage

Old Faithful Tile Co.'s perpetual inventory records indicate that $715,950 of merchandise should be on hand on December 31, 2012. The physical inventory indicates that $693,675 of merchandise is actually on hand. Journalize the adjusting entry for the inventory shrinkage for Old Faithful Tile Co. for the year ended December 31, 2012.

OBJ. 4

### EX 5-27 Closing the accounts of a merchandiser

From the following list, identify the accounts that should be closed to Income Summary at the end of the fiscal year under a perpetual inventory system: (a) Accounts Payable, (b) Advertising Expense, (c) Cost of Merchandise Sold, (d) Merchandise Inventory, (e) Sales, (f) Sales Discounts, (g) Sales Returns and Allowances, (h) Supplies, (i) Supplies Expense, (j) Dividends, (k) Wages Payable.

OBJ. 4

### EX 5-28 Closing entries; net income

Based on the data presented in Exercise 5-8, journalize the closing entries.

OBJ. 4

### EX 5-29 Closing entries

On August 31, 2012, the balances of the accounts appearing in the ledger of Wood Interiors Company, a furniture wholesaler, are as follows:

| | | | |
|---|---|---|---|
| Accumulated Depr.—Building | $142,000 | Notes Payable | $ 25,000 |
| Administrative Expenses | 90,000 | Retained Earnings | 162,000 |
| Building | 400,000 | Sales | 800,000 |
| Capital Stock | 10,000 | Sales Discounts | 18,000 |
| Cash | 55,000 | Sales Returns and Allow. | 12,000 |
| Cost of Merchandise Sold | 350,000 | Sales Tax Payable | 3,000 |
| Dividends | 5,000 | Selling Expenses | 150,000 |
| Interest Expense | 1,000 | Store Supplies | 15,000 |
| Merchandise Inventory | 26,000 | Store Supplies Expenses | 20,000 |

Prepare the August 31, 2012, closing entries for Wood Interiors Company.

OBJ. 5

### EX 5-30 Ratio of net sales to assets

The Home Depot reported the following data (in millions) in its financial statements:

| | 2009 | 2008 |
|---|---|---|
| Net sales | $71,288 | $77,349 |
| Total assets at the end of the year | 41,164 | 44,324 |
| Total assets at the beginning of the year | 44,324 | 52,263 |

a. Determine the ratio of net sales to assets for The Home Depot for 2009 and 2008. Round to two decimal places.

b. What conclusions can be drawn from these ratios concerning the trend in the ability of The Home Depot to effectively use its assets to generate sales?

OBJ. 5

### EX 5-31 Ratio of net sales to assets

Kroger, a national supermarket chain, reported the following data (in millions) in its financial statements for the year ended January 31, 2009:

| | |
|---|---|
| Total revenue | $76,000 |
| Total assets at end of year | 23,211 |
| Total assets at beginning of year | 22,299 |

a. Compute the ratio of net sales to assets for 2009. Round to two decimal places.

b. ▬▬▬▶ Tiffany & Co. is a large North American retailer of jewelry, with a ratio of net sales to assets of 0.95. Why would Tiffany's ratio of net sales to assets be lower than that of Kroger?

**Appendix**
## EX 5-32 Identify items missing in determining cost of merchandise sold

For (a) through (d), identify the items designated by "X" and "Y."

a. Purchases − (X + Y) = Net purchases.

b. Net purchases + X = Cost of merchandise purchased.

c. Merchandise inventory (beginning) + Cost of merchandise purchased = X.

d. Merchandise available for sale − X = Cost of merchandise sold.

**✔ a. Cost of merchandise sold, $1,948,500**

**Appendix**
## EX 5-33 Cost of merchandise sold and related items

The following data were extracted from the accounting records of Danhof Company for the year ended June 30, 2012:

| | |
|---|---:|
| Merchandise inventory, July 1, 2011 | $ 250,000 |
| Merchandise inventory, June 30, 2012 | 325,000 |
| Purchases | 2,100,000 |
| Purchases returns and allowances | 50,000 |
| Purchases discounts | 39,000 |
| Sales | 3,250,000 |
| Freight in | 12,500 |

a. Prepare the cost of merchandise sold section of the income statement for the year ended June 30, 2012, using the periodic inventory system.

b. Determine the gross profit to be reported on the income statement for the year ended June 30, 2012.

c. Would gross profit be different if the perpetual inventory system was used instead of the periodic inventory system?

**Appendix**
## EX 5-34 Cost of merchandise sold

Based on the following data, determine the cost of merchandise sold for April:

| | |
|---|---:|
| Merchandise inventory, April 1 | $ 15,000 |
| Merchandise inventory, April 30 | 28,000 |
| Purchases | 290,000 |
| Purchases returns and allowances | 10,000 |
| Purchases discounts | 5,800 |
| Freight in | 4,200 |

**Appendix**
## EX 5-35 Cost of merchandise sold

Based on the following data, determine the cost of merchandise sold for March:

| | |
|---|---:|
| Merchandise inventory, March 1 | $100,000 |
| Merchandise inventory, March 31 | 90,000 |
| Purchases | 800,000 |
| Purchases returns and allowances | 15,000 |
| Purchases discounts | 12,000 |
| Freight in | 8,000 |

**✔ Correct cost of merchandise sold, $885,000**

**Appendix**
## EX 5-36 Cost of merchandise sold

Identify the errors in the following schedule of cost of merchandise sold for the current year ended March 31, 2012:

| | | | |
|---|---:|---:|---:|
| Cost of merchandise sold: | | | |
| Merchandise inventory, March 31, 2012 | | | $ 75,000 |
| Purchases | | $900,000 | |
| Plus: Purchases returns and allowances | $18,000 | | |
| Purchases discounts | 12,000 | 30,000 | |
| Gross purchases | | $930,000 | |
| Less freight in | | 10,000 | |
| Cost of merchandise purchased | | | 920,000 |
| Merchandise available for sale | | | $995,000 |
| Less merchandise inventory, April 1, 2011 | | | 80,000 |
| Cost of merchandise sold | | | $915,000 |

**Appendix**
### EX 5-37   Rules of debit and credit for periodic inventory accounts

Complete the following table by indicating for (a) through (g) whether the proper answer is debit or credit.

| Account | Increase | Decrease | Normal Balance |
|---|---|---|---|
| Purchases | (a) | credit | (b) |
| Purchases Discounts | (c) | debit | credit |
| Purchases Returns and Allowances | (d) | debit | (e) |
| Freight in | (f) | (g) | debit |

**Appendix**
### EX 5-38   Journal entries using the periodic inventory system

The following selected transactions were completed by Burton Company during July of the current year. Burton Company uses the periodic inventory system.

July  2.  Purchased $24,000 of merchandise on account, FOB shipping point, terms 2/15, n/30.

  5.  Paid freight of $500 on the July 2 purchase.

  6.  Returned $4,000 of the merchandise purchased on July 2.

  13.  Sold merchandise on account, $15,000, FOB destination, 1/10, n/30. The cost of merchandise sold was $9,000.

  15.  Paid freight of $100 for the merchandise sold on July 13.

  17.  Paid for the purchase of July 2 less the return and discount.

  23.  Received payment on account for the sale of July 13 less the discount.

Journalize the entries to record the transactions of Burton Company.

**Appendix**
### Ex 5-39   Journal entries using perpetual inventory system

Using the data shown in Exercise 5-38, journalize the entries for the transactions assuming that Burton Company uses the perpetual inventory system.

**Appendix**
### Ex 5-40   Closing entries using periodic inventory system

Pyramid Company is a small rug retailer owned and operated by Rosemary Endecott. After the accounts have been adjusted on January 31, the following selected account balances were taken from the ledger:

| | |
|---|---:|
| Advertising Expense | $ 40,000 |
| Depreciation Expense | 15,000 |
| Dividends | 60,000 |
| Freight In | 8,000 |
| Merchandise Inventory, January 1 | 250,000 |
| Merchandise Inventory, January 31 | 300,000 |
| Miscellaneous Expense | 29,000 |
| Purchases | 750,000 |
| Purchases Discounts | 12,000 |
| Purchases Returns and Allowances | 8,000 |
| Salaries Expense | 175,000 |
| Sales | 1,200,000 |
| Sales Discounts | 20,000 |
| Sales Returns and Allowances | 30,000 |

Journalize the closing entries on January 31.

## Problems Series A

OBJ. 1, 2

✔ 1. Net income:
$775,000

### PR 5-1A   Multiple-step income statement and report form of balance sheet

The following selected accounts and their current balances appear in the ledger of Carpet Land Co. for the fiscal year ended October 31, 2012:

| | | | |
|---|---|---|---|
| Cash | $274,000 | Sales | $6,155,000 |
| Accounts Receivable | 425,000 | Sales Returns and Allowances | 70,000 |
| Merchandise Inventory | 525,000 | Sales Discounts | 55,000 |
| Office Supplies | 12,000 | Cost of Merchandise Sold | 3,600,000 |
| Prepaid Insurance | 9,000 | Sales Salaries Expense | 925,000 |
| Office Equipment | 315,000 | Advertising Expense | 150,000 |
| Accumulated Depreciation— | | Depreciation Expense— | |
| Office Equipment | 187,000 | Store Equipment | 35,000 |
| Store Equipment | 900,000 | Miscellaneous Selling Expense | 40,000 |
| Accumulated Depreciation— | | Office Salaries Expense | 315,000 |
| Store Equipment | 293,000 | Rent Expense | 115,000 |
| Accounts Payable | 193,000 | Depreciation Expense— | |
| Salaries Payable | 12,000 | Office Equipment | 22,000 |
| Note Payable | | Insurance Expense | 18,000 |
| (final payment due 2037) | 400,000 | Office Supplies Expense | 9,000 |
| Capital Stock | 250,000 | Miscellaneous Administrative Exp. | 11,000 |
| Retained Earnings | 500,000 | Interest Expense | 15,000 |
| Dividends | 150,000 | | |

**Instructions**

1. Prepare a multiple-step income statement.

2. Prepare a retained earnings statement.

3. Prepare a report form of balance sheet, assuming that the current portion of the note payable is $16,000.

4. Briefly explain (a) how multiple-step and single-step income statements differ and (b) how report-form and account-form balance sheets differ.

---

**OBJ. 2, 4**

✔ 3. Total assets: $1,980,000

### PR 5-2A Single-step income statement and account form of balance sheet

Selected accounts and related amounts for Carpet Land Co. for the fiscal year ended October 31, 2012, are presented in Problem 5-1A.

**Instructions**

1. Prepare a single-step income statement in the format shown in Exhibit 2.

2. Prepare a retained earnings statement.

3. Prepare an account form of balance sheet, assuming that the current portion of the note payable is $16,000.

4. Prepare closing entries as of October 31, 2012.

---

**OBJ. 3**

### PR 5-3A Sales-related transactions

The following selected transactions were completed by Artic Supply Co., which sells office supplies primarily to wholesalers and occasionally to retail customers:

Jan. 2. Sold merchandise on account to Mammoth Co., $15,000, terms FOB destination, 1/10, n/30. The cost of the merchandise sold was $9,000.

3. Sold merchandise for $8,000 plus 8% sales tax to retail cash customers. The cost of merchandise sold was $6,000.

4. Sold merchandise on account to Sando Co., $12,500, terms FOB shipping point, n/eom. The cost of merchandise sold was $7,500.

5. Sold merchandise for $10,000 plus 8% sales tax to retail customers who used MasterCard. The cost of merchandise sold was $6,000.

12. Received check for amount due from Mammoth Co. for sale on January 2.

14. Sold merchandise to customers who used American Express cards, $9,000. The cost of merchandise sold was $5,500.

16. Sold merchandise on account to Malloy Co., $18,700, terms FOB shipping point, 1/10, n/30. The cost of merchandise sold was $11,250.

Jan. 18. Issued credit memo for $2,700 to Malloy Co. for merchandise returned from sale on January 16. The cost of the merchandise returned was $1,600.

19. Sold merchandise on account to Savin Co., $21,500, terms FOB shipping point, 2/10, n/30. Added $500 to the invoice for prepaid freight. The cost of merchandise sold was $12,900.

26. Received check for amount due from Malloy Co. for sale on January 16 less credit memo of January 18 and discount.

28. Received check for amount due from Savin Co. for sale of January 19.

31. Received check for amount due from Sando Co. for sale of January 4.

31. Paid Eagle Delivery Service $6,190 for merchandise delivered during January to customers under shipping terms of FOB destination.

Feb. 3. Paid City Bank $1,350 for service fees for handling MasterCard and American Express sales during January.

15. Paid $2,100 to state sales tax division for taxes owed on sales.

**Instructions**

Journalize the entries to record the transactions of Artic Supply Co.

---

OBJ. 3

### PR 5-4A  Purchase-related transactions

The following selected transactions were completed by Gourmet Company during January of the current year:

Jan. 1. Purchased merchandise from Bearcat Co., $19,000, terms FOB destination, n/30.

3. Purchased merchandise from Alvarado Co., $28,500, terms FOB shipping point, 2/10, n/eom. Prepaid freight of $650 was added to the invoice.

4. Purchased merchandise from Fogel Co., $11,000, terms FOB destination, 2/10, n/30.

6. Issued debit memo to Fogel Co. for $1,000 of merchandise returned from purchase on January 4.

13. Paid Alvarado Co. for invoice of January 3, less discount.

14. Paid Fogel Co. for invoice of January 4, less debit memo of January 6 and discount.

19. Purchased merchandise from Unitrust Co., $32,900, terms FOB shipping point, n/eom.

19. Paid freight of $750 on January 19 purchase from Unitrust Co.

20. Purchased merchandise from Lenn Co., $10,000, terms FOB destination, 1/10, n/30.

30. Paid Lenn Co. for invoice of January 20, less discount.

31. Paid Bearcat Co. for invoice of January 1.

31. Paid Unitrust Co. for invoice of January 19.

**Instructions**

Journalize the entries to record the transactions of Gourmet Company for January.

---

OBJ. 3

### PR 5-5A  Sales-related and purchase-related transactions

The following were selected from among the transactions completed by The Grill Company during April of the current year:

Apr. 3. Purchased merchandise on account from Grizzly Co., list price $60,000, trade discount 30%, terms FOB destination, 2/10, n/30.

4. Sold merchandise for cash, $23,750. The cost of the merchandise sold was $14,000.

Apr. 5. Purchased merchandise on account from Ferraro Co., $26,000, terms FOB shipping point, 2/10, n/30, with prepaid freight of $600 added to the invoice.

6. Returned $7,000 ($10,000 list price less trade discount of 30%) of merchandise purchased on April 3 from Grizzly Co.

11. Sold merchandise on account to Logan Co., list price $12,000, trade discount 25%, terms 1/10, n/30. The cost of the merchandise sold was $5,000.

13. Paid Grizzly Co. on account for purchase of April 3, less return of April 6 and discount.

14. Sold merchandise on VISA, $90,000. The cost of the merchandise sold was $55,000.

15. Paid Ferraro Co. on account for purchase of April 5, less discount.

21. Received cash on account from sale of April 11 to Logan Co., less discount.

24. Sold merchandise on account to Half Moon Co., $17,500, terms 1/10, n/30. The cost of the merchandise sold was $10,000.

28. Paid VISA service fee of $4,000.

30. Received merchandise returned by Half Moon Co. from sale on April 24, $2,500. The cost of the returned merchandise was $1,400.

**Instructions**
Journalize the transactions.

---

**PR 5-6A   Sales-related and purchase-related transactions for seller and buyer**

The following selected transactions were completed during May between Sky Company and Big Co.:

May 1. Sky Company sold merchandise on account to Big Co., $72,000, terms FOB destination, 2/15, n/eom. The cost of the merchandise sold was $43,200.

2. Sky Company paid freight of $3,000 for delivery of merchandise sold to Big Co. on May 1.

5. Sky Company sold merchandise on account to Big Co., $48,500, terms FOB shipping point, n/eom. The cost of the merchandise sold was $30,000.

6. Big Co. returned $12,000 of merchandise purchased on account on May 1 from Sky Company. The cost of the merchandise returned was $7,200.

9. Big Co. paid freight of $1,800 on May 5 purchase from Sky Company.

15. Sky Company sold merchandise on account to Big Co., $64,000, terms FOB shipping point, 1/10, n/30. Sky Company paid freight of $2,500, which was added to the invoice. The cost of the merchandise sold was $38,400.

16. Big Co. paid Sky Company for purchase of May 1, less discount and less return of May 6.

25. Big Co. paid Sky Company on account for purchase of May 15, less discount.

31. Big Co. paid Sky Company on account for purchase of May 5.

**Instructions**
Journalize the May transactions for (1) Sky Company and (2) Big Co.

---

**Appendix**
**PR 5-7A   Purchase-related transactions using periodic inventory system**

Selected transactions for Gourmet Company during January of the current year are listed in Problem 5-4A.

**Instructions**
Journalize the entries to record the transactions of Gourmet Company for January using the periodic inventory system.

## Appendix
### PR 5-8A   Sales-related and purchase-related transactions using periodic inventory system

Selected transactions for The Grill Company during April of the current year are listed in Problem 5-5A.

#### Instructions
Journalize the entries to record the transactions of The Grill Company for April using the periodic inventory system.

## Appendix
### PR 5-9A   Sales-related and purchase-related transactions for buyer and seller using periodic inventory system

Selected transactions during May between Sky Company and Big Co. are listed in Problem 5-6A.

#### Instructions
Journalize the entries to record the transactions for (1) Sky Company and (2) Big Co. assuming that both companies use the periodic inventory system.

✔ 2. Net income, $345,000

## Appendix
### PR 5-10A   Periodic inventory accounts, multiple-step income statement, closing entries

On July 31, 2012, the balances of the accounts appearing in the ledger of Sagebrush Company are as follows:

| | | | |
|---|---:|---|---:|
| Cash | $ 18,300 | Sales Returns and Allowances | $ 12,000 |
| Accounts Receivable | 72,000 | Sales Discounts | 8,000 |
| Merchandise Inventory, | | Purchases | 700,000 |
|   August 1, 2011 | 90,000 | Purchases Returns and Allowances | 6,000 |
| Office Supplies | 3,000 | Purchases Discounts | 4,000 |
| Prepaid Insurance | 4,500 | Freight In | 30,000 |
| Land | 300,000 | Sales Salaries Expense | 300,000 |
| Store Equipment | 270,000 | Advertising Expense | 55,000 |
| Accumulated Depreciation— | | Delivery Expense | 9,000 |
|   Store Equipment | 55,900 | Depreciation Expense— | |
| Office Equipment | 78,500 |   Store Equipment | 6,000 |
| Accumulated Depreciation— | | Miscellaneous Selling Expense | 10,000 |
|   Office Equipment | 16,000 | Office Salaries Expense | 150,000 |
| Accounts Payable | 27,800 | Rent Expense | 30,000 |
| Salaries Payable | 3,000 | Insurance Expense | 3,000 |
| Unearned Rent | 8,300 | Office Supplies Expense | 2,000 |
| Notes Payable | 50,000 | Depreciation Expense— | |
| Capital Stock | 80,000 |   Office Equipment | 1,500 |
| Retained Earnings | 275,300 | Miscellaneous Administrative Expense | 3,500 |
| Dividends | 35,000 | Rent Revenue | 7,000 |
| Sales | 1,660,000 | Interest Expense | 2,000 |

#### Instructions
1. Does Sagebrush Company use a periodic or perpetual inventory system? Explain.
2. Prepare a multiple-step income statement for Sagebrush Company for the year ended July 31, 2012. The merchandise inventory as of July 31, 2012, was $80,000.
3. Prepare the closing entries for Sagebrush Company as of July 31, 2012.
4. What would be the net income if the perpetual inventory system had been used?

## Problems Series B

OBJ. 1, 2

✔ 1. Net income:
$360,000

### PR 5-1B  Multiple-step income statement and report form of balance sheet

The following selected accounts and their current balances appear in the ledger of Black Lab Co. for the fiscal year ended April 30, 2012:

| | | | |
|---|---:|---|---:|
| Cash | $ 42,000 | Sales | $3,150,000 |
| Accounts Receivable | 150,000 | Sales Returns and Allowances | 40,000 |
| Merchandise Inventory | 180,000 | Sales Discounts | 15,000 |
| Office Supplies | 5,000 | Cost of Merchandise Sold | 1,855,000 |
| Prepaid Insurance | 12,000 | Sales Salaries Expense | 400,000 |
| Office Equipment | 120,000 | Advertising Expense | 120,000 |
| Accumulated Depreciation— | | Depreciation Expense— | |
|   Office Equipment | 28,000 |   Store Equipment | 15,000 |
| Store Equipment | 500,000 | Miscellaneous Selling Expense | 18,000 |
| Accumulated Depreciation— | | Office Salaries Expense | 240,000 |
|   Store Equipment | 87,500 | Rent Expense | 38,000 |
| Accounts Payable | 48,500 | Insurance Expense | 24,000 |
| Salaries Payable | 4,000 | Depreciation Expense— | |
| Note Payable | |   Office Equipment | 7,000 |
|   (final payment due 2032) | 140,000 | Office Supplies Expense | 4,000 |
| Capital Stock | 125,000 | Miscellaneous Administrative Exp. | 6,000 |
| Retained Earnings | 261,000 | Interest Expense | 8,000 |
| Dividends | 45,000 | | |

**Instructions**

1.  Prepare a multiple-step income statement.

2.  Prepare a retained earnings statement.

3.  Prepare a report form of balance sheet, assuming that the current portion of the note payable is $7,000.

4.  Briefly explain (a) how multiple-step and single-step income statements differ and (b) how report-form and account-form balance sheets differ.

OBJ. 2, 4

✔ 3. Total assets:
$893,500

### PR 5-2B  Single-step income statement and account form of balance sheet

Selected accounts and related amounts for Black Lab Co. for the fiscal year ended April 30, 2012, are presented in Problem 5-1B.

**Instructions**

1.  Prepare a single-step income statement in the format shown in Exhibit 2.

2.  Prepare a retained earnings statement.

3.  Prepare an account form of balance sheet, assuming that the current portion of the note payable is $7,000.

4.  Prepare closing entries as of April 30, 2012.

OBJ. 3

### PR 5-3B  Sales-related transactions

The following selected transactions were completed by Lawn Supplies Co., which sells irrigation supplies primarily to wholesalers and occasionally to retail customers:

Mar. 1.  Sold merchandise on account to Green Grass Co., $18,000, terms FOB shipping point, n/eom. The cost of merchandise sold was $11,000.

    2.  Sold merchandise for $42,000 plus 7% sales tax to retail cash customers. The cost of merchandise sold was $25,200.

    5.  Sold merchandise on account to Jones Company, $30,000, terms FOB destination, 1/10, n/30. The cost of merchandise sold was $19,500.

Mar. 8. Sold merchandise for $20,000 plus 7% sales tax to retail customers who used VISA cards. The cost of merchandise sold was $14,000.

13. Sold merchandise to customers who used MasterCard $15,800. The cost of merchandise sold was $9,500.

14. Sold merchandise on account to Haynes Co., $8,000, terms FOB shipping point, 1/10, n/30. The cost of merchandise sold was $5,000.

15. Received check for amount due from Jones Company for sale on March 5.

16. Issued credit memo for $1,800 to Haynes Co. for merchandise returned from sale on March 14. The cost of the merchandise returned was $1,000.

18. Sold merchandise on account to Horton Company, $6,850, terms FOB shipping point, 2/10, n/30. Paid $210 for freight and added it to the invoice. The cost of merchandise sold was $4,100.

24. Received check for amount due from Haynes Co. for sale on March 14 less credit memo of March 16 and discount.

28. Received check for amount due from Horton Company for sale of March 18.

31. Paid First Delivery Service $5,750 for merchandise delivered during March to customers under shipping terms of FOB destination.

31. Received check for amount due from Green Grass Co. for sale of March 1.

Apr. 3. Paid First Federal Bank $1,650 for service fees for handling MasterCard and VISA sales during March.

10. Paid $6,175 to state sales tax division for taxes owed on sales.

**Instructions**
Journalize the entries to record the transactions of Lawn Supplies Co.

---

OBJ. 3

### PR 5-4B  Purchase-related transactions

The following selected transactions were completed by Britt Co. during October of the current year:

Oct. 1. Purchased merchandise from Mable Co., $17,500, terms FOB shipping point, 2/10, n/eom. Prepaid freight of $300 was added to the invoice.

5. Purchased merchandise from Conway Co., $22,600, terms FOB destination, n/30.

10. Paid Mable Co. for invoice of October 1, less discount.

13. Purchased merchandise from Larson Co., $12,750, terms FOB destination, 2/10, n/30.

14. Issued debit memo to Larson Co. for $1,500 of merchandise returned from purchase on October 13.

18. Purchased merchandise from Lakey Company, $12,250, terms FOB shipping point, n/eom.

18. Paid freight of $275 on October 18 purchase from Lakey Company.

19. Purchased merchandise from Adler Co., $14,200, terms FOB destination, 2/10, n/30.

23. Paid Larson Co. for invoice of October 13, less debit memo of October 14 and discount.

29. Paid Adler Co. for invoice of October 19, less discount.

31. Paid Lakey Company for invoice of October 18.

31. Paid Conway Co. for invoice of October 5.

**Instructions**
Journalize the entries to record the transactions of Britt Co. for October.

OBJ. 3

### PR 5-5B   Sales-related and purchase-related transactions

The following were selected from among the transactions completed by Wild Adventures Company during December of the current year:

Dec. 3.  Purchased merchandise on account from Miramar Co., list price $45,000, trade discount 20%, terms FOB shipping point, 2/10, n/30, with prepaid freight of $1,200 added to the invoice.

5.  Purchased merchandise on account from Grand Canyon Co., $19,000, terms FOB destination, 2/10, n/30.

6.  Sold merchandise on account to Arches Co., list price $30,000, trade discount 25%, terms 2/10, n/30. The cost of the merchandise sold was $14,000.

7.  Returned $3,000 of merchandise purchased on December 5 from Grand Canyon Co.

13.  Paid Miramar Co. on account for purchase of December 3, less discount.

15.  Paid Grand Canyon Co. on account for purchase of December 5, less return of December 7 and discount.

16.  Received cash on account from sale of December 6 to Arches Co., less discount.

19.  Sold merchandise on MasterCard, $41,950. The cost of the merchandise sold was $25,000.

22.  Sold merchandise on account to Yellowstone River Co., $20,000, terms 2/10, n/30. The cost of the merchandise sold was $9,000.

23.  Sold merchandise for cash, $57,500. The cost of the merchandise sold was $34,500.

28.  Received merchandise returned by Yellowstone River Co. from sale on December 22, $4,000. The cost of the returned merchandise was $1,800.

31.  Paid MasterCard service fee of $1,700.

**Instructions**
Journalize the transactions.

---

OBJ. 3

### PR 5-6B   Sales-related and purchase-related transactions for seller and buyer

The following selected transactions were completed during June between Salinas Company and Brokaw Company:

June 2.  Salinas Company sold merchandise on account to Brokaw Company, $20,000, terms FOB shipping point, 2/10, n/30. Salinas Company paid freight of $675, which was added to the invoice. The cost of the merchandise sold was $12,000.

8.  Salinas Company sold merchandise on account to Brokaw Company, $34,750, terms FOB destination, 1/15, n/eom. The cost of the merchandise sold was $19,850.

8.  Salinas Company paid freight of $800 for delivery of merchandise sold to Brokaw Company on June 8.

12.  Brokaw Company returned $5,750 of merchandise purchased on account on June 8 from Salinas Company. The cost of the merchandise returned was $3,000.

12.  Brokaw Company paid Salinas Company for purchase of June 2, less discount.

23.  Brokaw Company paid Salinas Company for purchase of June 8, less discount and less return of June 12.

24.  Salinas Company sold merchandise on account to Brokaw Company, $31,800, terms FOB shipping point, n/eom. The cost of the merchandise sold was $20,500.

26.  Brokaw Company paid freight of $475 on June 24 purchase from Salinas Company.

30.  Brokaw Company paid Salinas Company on account for purchase of June 24.

**Instructions**
Journalize the June transactions for (1) Salinas Company and (2) Brokaw Company.

## Appendix
### PR 5-7B   Purchase-related transactions using periodic inventory system

Selected transactions for Britt Co. during October of the current year are listed in Problem 5-4B.

**Instructions**

Journalize the entries to record the transactions of Britt Co. for October using the periodic inventory system.

## Appendix
### PR 5-8B   Sales-related and purchase-related transactions using periodic inventory system

Selected transactions for Wild Adventures Company during December of the current year are listed in Problem 5-5B.

**Instructions**

Journalize the entries to record the transactions of Wild Adventures Company for December using the periodic inventory system.

## Appendix
### PR 5-9B   Sales-related and purchase-related transactions for buyer and seller using periodic inventory system

Selected transactions during June between Salinas Company and Brokaw Company are listed in Problem 5-6B.

**Instructions**

Journalize the entries to record the transactions for (1) Salinas Company and (2) Brokaw Company assuming that both companies use the periodic inventory system.

✔ 2. Net income,
$395,000

## Appendix
### PR 5-10B   Periodic inventory accounts, multiple-step income statement, closing entries

On April 30, 2012, the balances of the accounts appearing in the ledger of Heritage Company are as follows:

| | | | |
|---|---|---|---|
| Cash | $  60,000 | Sales Discounts | $  35,000 |
| Accounts Receivable | 150,000 | Purchases | 1,770,000 |
| Merchandise Inventory, May 1, 2011 | 290,000 | Purchases Returns and Allowances | 12,000 |
| Office Supplies | 7,000 | Purchases Discounts | 8,000 |
| Prepaid Insurance | 18,000 | Freight In | 25,000 |
| Land | 70,000 | Sales Salaries Expense | 450,000 |
| Store Equipment | 400,000 | Advertising Expense | 200,000 |
| Accumulated Depreciation— | | Delivery Expense | 18,000 |
|   Store Equipment | 190,000 | Depreciation Expense— | |
| Office Equipment | 250,000 |   Store Equipment | 12,000 |
| Accumulated Depreciation— | | Miscellaneous Selling Expense | 28,000 |
|   Office Equipment | 110,000 | Office Salaries Expense | 200,000 |
| Accounts Payable | 85,000 | Rent Expense | 45,000 |
| Salaries Payable | 9,000 | Insurance Expense | 6,000 |
| Unearned Rent | 6,000 | Office Supplies Expense | 5,000 |
| Notes Payable | 50,000 | Depreciation Expense— | |
| Capital Stock | 40,000 |   Office Equipment | 3,000 |
| Retained Earnings | 485,000 | Miscellaneous Administrative Expense | 13,000 |
| Dividends | 100,000 | Rent Revenue | 27,000 |
| Sales | 3,175,000 | Interest Expense | 2,000 |
| Sales Returns and Allowances | 40,000 | | |

**Instructions**

1. Does Heritage Company use a periodic or perpetual inventory system? Explain.

2. Prepare a multiple-step income statement for Heritage Company for the year ended April 30, 2012. The merchandise inventory as of April 30, 2012, was $315,000.

3. Prepare the closing entries for Heritage Company as of April 30, 2012.

4. What would be the net income if the perpetual inventory system had been used?

## Comprehensive Problem 2

✔ 8. Net income:
$710,760

Ocean Atlantic Co. is a merchandising business. The account balances for Ocean Atlantic Co. as of July 1, 2012 (unless otherwise indicated), are as follows:

| | | |
|---|---|---|
| 110 | Cash | $ 63,600 |
| 112 | Accounts Receivable | 153,900 |
| 115 | Merchandise Inventory | 602,400 |
| 116 | Prepaid Insurance | 16,800 |
| 117 | Store Supplies | 11,400 |
| 123 | Store Equipment | 469,500 |
| 124 | Accumulated Depreciation—Store Equipment | 56,700 |
| 210 | Accounts Payable | 96,600 |
| 211 | Salaries Payable | — |
| 310 | Capital Stock | 75,000 |
| 311 | Retained Earnings, August 1, 2011 | 480,300 |
| 312 | Dividends | 135,000 |
| 313 | Income Summary | — |
| 410 | Sales | 3,221,100 |
| 411 | Sales Returns and Allowances | 92,700 |
| 412 | Sales Discounts | 59,400 |
| 510 | Cost of Merchandise Sold | 1,623,000 |
| 520 | Sales Salaries Expense | 334,800 |
| 521 | Advertising Expense | 81,000 |
| 522 | Depreciation Expense | — |
| 523 | Store Supplies Expense | — |
| 529 | Miscellaneous Selling Expense | 12,600 |
| 530 | Office Salaries Expense | 182,100 |
| 531 | Rent Expense | 83,700 |
| 532 | Insurance Expense | — |
| 539 | Miscellaneous Administrative Expense | 7,800 |

During July, the last month of the fiscal year, the following transactions were completed:

July  1. Paid rent for July, $4,000.

 3. Purchased merchandise on account from Lingard Co., terms 2/10, n/30, FOB shipping point, $25,000.

 4. Paid freight on purchase of July 3, $1,000.

 6. Sold merchandise on account to Holt Co., terms 2/10, n/30, FOB shipping point, $40,000. The cost of the merchandise sold was $24,000.

 7. Received $18,000 cash from Flatt Co. on account, no discount.

 10. Sold merchandise for cash, $90,000. The cost of the merchandise sold was $50,000.

 13. Paid for merchandise purchased on July 3, less discount.

 14. Received merchandise returned on sale of July 6, $7,000. The cost of the merchandise returned was $4,500.

 15. Paid advertising expense for last half of July, $9,000.

 16. Received cash from sale of July 6, less return of July 14 and discount.

 19. Purchased merchandise for cash, $22,000.

 19. Paid $23,100 to Carino Co. on account, no discount.

*Record the following transactions on Page 21 of the journal.*

 20. Sold merchandise on account to Reedley Co., terms 1/10, n/30, FOB shipping point, $40,000. The cost of the merchandise sold was $25,000.

 21. For the convenience of the customer, paid freight on sale of July 20, $1,100.

July 21. Received $17,600 cash from Owen Co. on account, no discount.

21. Purchased merchandise on account from Munson Co., terms 1/10, n/30, FOB destination, $32,000.

24. Returned $5,000 of damaged merchandise purchased on July 21, receiving credit from the seller.

26. Refunded cash on sales made for cash, $12,000. The cost of the merchandise returned was $7,200.

28. Paid sales salaries of $22,800 and office salaries of $15,200.

29. Purchased store supplies for cash, $2,400.

30. Sold merchandise on account to Dix Co., terms 2/10, n/30, FOB shipping point, $18,750. The cost of the merchandise sold was $11,250.

30. Received cash from sale of July 20, less discount, plus freight paid on July 21.

31. Paid for purchase of July 21, less return of July 24 and discount.

## Instructions

1. Enter the balances of each of the accounts in the appropriate balance column of a four-column account. Write *Balance* in the item section, and place a check mark (✓) in the Posting Reference column. Journalize the transactions for July starting on page 20 of the journal.

2. Post the journal to the general ledger, extending the month-end balances to the appropriate balance columns after all posting is completed. In this problem, you are not required to update or post to the accounts receivable and accounts payable subsidiary ledgers.

3. Prepare an unadjusted trial balance.

4. At the end of July, the following adjustment data were assembled. Analyze and use these data to complete (5) and (6).

| | | | | |
|---|---|---|---|---|
| a. | Merchandise inventory on July 31 | | | $565,000 |
| b. | Insurance expired during the year | | | 13,400 |
| c. | Store supplies on hand on July 31 | | | 3,900 |
| d. | Depreciation for the current year | | | 11,500 |
| e. | Accrued salaries on July 31: | | | |
| | Sales salaries | | $3,200 | |
| | Office salaries | | 1,300 | 4,500 |

5. **Optional:** Enter the unadjusted trial balance on a 10-column end-of-period spreadsheet (work sheet), and complete the spreadsheet.

6. Journalize and post the adjusting entries. Record the adjusting entries on page 22 of the journal.

7. Prepare an adjusted trial balance.

8. Prepare an income statement, a retained earnings statement, and a balance sheet.

9. Prepare and post the closing entries. Record the closing entries on page 23 of the journal. Indicate closed accounts by inserting a line in both the Balance columns opposite the closing entry. Insert the new balance in the retained earnings account.

10. Prepare a post-closing trial balance.

## Cases & Projects

You can access the Cases & Projects online at **www.cengage.com/accounting/reeve**

## Excel Success Special Activities

### SA 5-1    Computing sales tax, multiple states

Jerrod Corporation had sales in several states. The total sales for each state is summarized in a spreadsheet. Sales tax rates of 6, 4, and 5.5 for Iowa, Missouri, and Nebraska, respectively, should be added to the spreadsheet.

| | A | B | C | D |
|---|---|---|---|---|
| 1 | | Total Sales | Sales Tax Rate | Sales Tax |
| 2 | Illinois | $ 318,000 | 6.5% | |
| 3 | Iowa | 194,100 | | |
| 4 | Missouri | 241,200 | | |
| 5 | Nebraska | 86,200 | | |
| 6 | Total | $ 839,500 | | |
| 7 | | | | |

a. Open the Excel file *SA5-1_1e*.

b. Finalize the spreadsheet by entering the sales tax for each state and properly formatting the percentage.

   Use percent formatting for the sales tax rates. For example, cell C2 is entered as .065 and formatted using the percent format with one decimal place.

c. Create a formula that determines the amount of sales tax due, by state, for the total sales shown.

d. When you have completed the sales tax table, perform a "save as," replacing the entire file name with the following:

   *SA5-1_1e[your first name initial]_[your last name]*

### SA 5-2    Computing sales tax, multiple locations

U Store It, Inc., has multiple storage locations throughout the state of Colorado. The total sales for each storage location is summarized in a spreadsheet as follows:

| | A | B | C | D |
|---|---|---|---|---|
| 1 | Sales tax rate | 3.5% | | |
| 2 | | | | |
| 3 | | Total Sales | Sales Tax Rate | Sales Tax |
| 4 | North Denver | $ 24,200 | | |
| 5 | Central Denver | 17,800 | | |
| 6 | Colorado Springs | 8,400 | | |
| 7 | Ft. Collins | 12,000 | | |
| 8 | Boulder | 6,400 | | |
| 9 | Total | $ 68,800 | | |
| 10 | | | | |

a. Open the Excel file *SA5-2_1e*.

b. Assume the sales tax rate for Colorado is 3.5%. Insert .035. Format as a percentage amount rounded to one decimal place in the cells C4:C8.

c. Finalize the spreadsheet by determining the sales tax for each location and total sales tax for U Store It, Inc.

d. When you have completed the sales tax table, perform a "save as," replacing the entire file name with the following:

   *SA5-2_1e[your first name initial]_[your last name]*

### SA 5-3    Computing sales tax, multiple cities

Cities in many states may add an additional city sales tax rate in addition to the state tax rate. Assume that cities in the state of New York can add an additional sales tax. Timely Blessings, Inc., has sales in various cities in New York. The sales and assumed total sales tax rate (city plus state rates) are summarized in a spreadsheet as follows:

| | A | B | C | D |
|---|---|---|---|---|
| 1 | | Total Sales | Sales Tax Rate | Sales Tax |
| 2 | New York City | $ 243,200 | 8.0% | |
| 3 | Rochester | 98,200 | 7.5% | |
| 4 | White Plains | 31,400 | 7.0% | |
| 5 | Buffalo | 54,000 | 7.2% | |
| 6 | Albany | 14,200 | 6.5% | |
| 7 | Total | $ 441,000 | | |
| 8 | | | | |
| 9 | | | | |

a. Open the Excel file *SA5-3_1e*.

b. The New York City combined rate of 8.0% has been entered. Input the combined rates for Rochester, White Plains, Buffalo, and Albany as 7.5, 7.0, 7.2, and 6.5 percent, respectively.

c. Finalize the spreadsheet by creating a formula in column D to compute the total sales tax for each city.

d. When you have completed the sales tax table, perform a "save as," replacing the entire file name with the following:

*SA5-3_1e[your first name initial]_[your last name]*

© Ryan McVay/Digital Vision/Getty Images

# Inventories

## Best Buy

**A**ssume that in September you purchased a Sony HDTV plasma television from **Best Buy**. At the same time, you purchased a Denon surround sound system for $399.99. You liked your surround sound so well that in November you purchased an identical Denon system on sale for $349.99 for your bedroom TV. Over the holidays, you moved to a new apartment and in the process of unpacking discovered that one of the Denon surround sound systems was missing. Luckily, your renters/homeowners insurance policy will cover the theft, but the insurance company needs to know the cost of the system that was stolen.

The Denon systems were identical. However, to respond to the insurance company, you will need to identify which system was stolen. Was it the first system, which cost $399.99, or was it the second system, which cost $349.99? Whichever assumption you make may determine the amount that you receive from the insurance company.

Merchandising businesses such as Best Buy make similar assumptions when identical merchandise is purchased at different costs. For example, Best Buy may have purchased thousands of Denon surround sound systems over the past year at different costs. At the end of a period, some of the Denon systems will still be in inventory, and some will have been sold. But which costs relate to the sold systems, and which costs relate to the Denon systems still in inventory? Best Buy's assumption about inventory costs can involve large dollar amounts and, thus, can have a significant impact on the financial statements. For example, Best Buy reported $4,753 million of inventory on February 28, 2009, and net income of $1,003 million for the year.

This chapter discusses such issues as how to determine the cost of merchandise in inventory and the cost of merchandise sold. However, this chapter begins by discussing the importance of control over inventory.

**OBJ. 1** Describe the importance of control over inventory.

# Control of Inventory

Two primary objectives of control over inventory are as follows:[1]

1. Safeguarding the inventory from damage or theft.
2. Reporting inventory in the financial statements.

## Safeguarding Inventory

Controls for safeguarding inventory begin as soon as the inventory is ordered. The following documents are often used for inventory control:

Purchase order
Receiving report
Vendor's invoice

The **purchase order** authorizes the purchase of the inventory from an approved vendor. As soon as the inventory is received, a receiving report is completed. The **receiving report** establishes an initial record of the receipt of the inventory. To make sure the inventory received is what was ordered, the receiving report is compared

---

1 Additional controls used by businesses are described and illustrated in Chapter 7, "Sarbanes-Oxley, Internal Control, and Cash."

with the company's purchase order. The price, quantity, and description of the item on the purchase order and receiving report are then compared to the vendor's invoice. If the receiving report, purchase order, and vendor's invoice agree, the inventory is recorded in the accounting records. If any differences exist, they should be investigated and reconciled.

Recording inventory using a perpetual inventory system is also an effective means of control. The amount of inventory is always available in the **subsidiary inventory ledger**. This helps keep inventory quantities at proper levels. For example, comparing inventory quantities with maximum and minimum levels allows for the timely reordering of inventory and prevents ordering excess inventory.

Finally, controls for safeguarding inventory should include security measures to prevent damage and customer or employee theft. Some examples of security measures include the following:

1. Storing inventory in areas that are restricted to only authorized employees.
2. Locking high-priced inventory in cabinets.
3. Using two-way mirrors, cameras, security tags, and guards.

Best Buy uses scanners to screen customers as they leave the store for merchandise that has not been purchased. In addition, Best Buy stations greeters at the store's entrance to keep customers from bringing in bags that can be used to shoplift merchandise.

## Reporting Inventory

A **physical inventory** or count of inventory should be taken near year-end to make sure that the quantity of inventory reported in the financial statements is accurate. After the quantity of inventory on hand is determined, the cost of the inventory is assigned for reporting in the financial statements. Most companies assign costs to inventory using one of three inventory cost flow assumptions. If a physical count is not possible or inventory records are not available, the inventory cost may be estimated as described in the appendix at the end of this chapter.

# Inventory Cost Flow Assumptions

 Describe three inventory cost flow assumptions and how they impact the income statement and balance sheet.

**OBJ. 2**

An accounting issue arises when identical units of merchandise are acquired at different unit costs during a period. In such cases, when an item is sold, it is necessary to determine its cost using a cost flow assumption and related inventory cost flow method. Three common cost flow assumptions and related inventory cost flow methods are shown below.

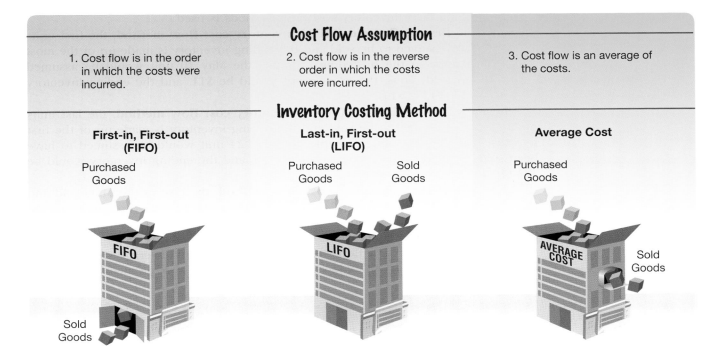

To illustrate, assume that three identical units of merchandise are purchased during May, as follows:

|  |  |  | Units | Cost |
|---|---|---|---|---|
| May | 10 | Purchase | 1 | $ 9 |
|  | 18 | Purchase | 1 | 13 |
|  | 24 | Purchase | 1 | 14 |
| Total |  |  | 3 | $36 |

Average cost per unit: $12 ($36 ÷ 3 units)

Assume that one unit is sold on May 30 for $20. Depending upon which unit was sold, the gross profit varies from $11 to $6 as shown below.

|  | May 10 Unit Sold | May 18 Unit Sold | May 24 Unit Sold |
|---|---|---|---|
| Sales | $20 | $20 | $20 |
| Cost of merchandise sold | 9 | 13 | 14 |
| Gross profit | $11 | $ 7 | $ 6 |
| Ending inventory | $27 | $23 | $22 |
|  | ($13 + $14) | ($9 + $14) | ($9 + $13) |

The specific identification method is normally used by automobile dealerships, jewelry stores, and art galleries.

Under the **specific identification inventory cost flow method**, the unit sold is identified with a specific purchase. The ending inventory is made up of the remaining units on hand. Thus, the gross profit, cost of merchandise sold, and ending inventory can vary as shown above. For example, if the May 18 unit was sold, the cost of merchandise sold is $13, the gross profit is $7, and the ending inventory is $23.

The specific identification method is not practical unless each inventory unit can be separately identified. For example, an automobile dealer may use the specific identification method since each automobile has a unique serial number. However, most businesses cannot identify each inventory unit separately. In such cases, one of the following three inventory cost flow methods is used.

Under the **first-in, first-out (FIFO) inventory cost flow method**, the first units purchased are assumed to be sold and the ending inventory is made up of the most recent purchases. In the preceding example, the May 10 unit would be assumed to have been sold. Thus, the gross profit would be $11, and the ending inventory would be $27 ($13 + $14).

Under the **last-in, first-out (LIFO) inventory cost flow method**, the last units purchased are assumed to be sold and the ending inventory is made up of the first purchases. In the preceding example, the May 24 unit would be assumed to have been sold. Thus, the gross profit would be $6, and the ending inventory would be $22 ($9 + $13).

Under the **average inventory cost flow method**, the cost of the units sold and in ending inventory is an average of the purchase costs. In the preceding example, the cost of the unit sold would be $12 ($36 ÷ 3 units), the gross profit would be $8 ($20 – $12), and the ending inventory would be $24 ($12 × 2 units).

The three inventory cost flow methods, FIFO, LIFO, and average, are shown in Exhibit 1. The frequency with which the FIFO, LIFO, and average methods are used is shown in Exhibit 2.

**EXHIBIT 1** **Inventory Costing Methods**

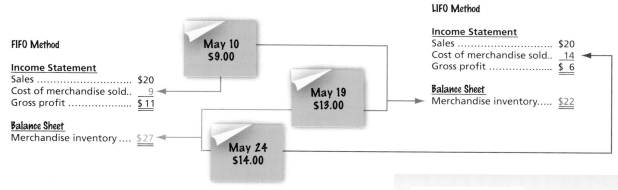

Purchases

**FIFO Method**

**Income Statement**
Sales .......................... $20
Cost of merchandise sold.. 9
Gross profit ................... $11

**Balance Sheet**
Merchandise inventory .... $27

**May 10 $9.00**

**May 19 $13.00**

**May 24 $14.00**

**LIFO Method**

**Income Statement**
Sales ........................... $20
Cost of merchandise sold.. 14
Gross profit ................... $ 6

**Balance Sheet**
Merchandise inventory..... $22

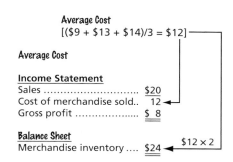

Average Cost
[($9 + $13 + $14)/3 = $12]

**Average Cost**

**Income Statement**
Sales ........................... $20
Cost of merchandise sold.. 12
Gross profit ................... $ 8

**Balance Sheet**
Merchandise inventory .... $24     $12 × 2

**EXHIBIT 2** **Use of Inventory Costing Methods***

Source: *Accounting Trends and Techniques*, 63rd edition, 2009 (New York: American Institute of Certified Public Accountants).
*Firms may be counted more than once for using multiple methods.

## Example Exercise 6-1 ▸ Cost Flow Methods

**OBJ. 2**

Three identical units of Item QBM are purchased during February, as shown below.

|       |    | Item QBM | Units | Cost |
|-------|----|----------|-------|------|
| Feb.  | 8  | Purchase | 1     | $ 45 |
|       | 15 | Purchase | 1     | 48   |
|       | 26 | Purchase | 1     | 51   |
|       |    | Total    | 3     | $144 |
|       |    | Average cost per unit |  | $ 48 ($144 ÷ 3 units) |

Assume that one unit is sold on February 27 for $70.

Determine the gross profit for February and ending inventory on February 28 using the (a) first-in, first-out (FIFO); (b) last-in, first-out (LIFO); and (c) average cost methods.

### Follow My Example 6-1

|                               | Gross Profit      | Ending Inventory   |
|-------------------------------|-------------------|--------------------|
| a. First-in, first-out (FIFO)...............  | $25 ($70 − $45)   | $99 ($48 + $51)    |
| b. Last-in, first-out (LIFO)...............   | $19 ($70 − $51)   | $93 ($45 + $48)    |
| c. Average cost ........................      | $22 ($70 − $48)   | $96 ($48 × 2)      |

Practice Exercises: **PE 6-1A, PE 6-1B**

**OBJ.**
**3** Determine the cost of inventory under the perpetual inventory system, using the FIFO, LIFO, and average cost methods.

# Inventory Costing Methods Under a Perpetual Inventory System

As illustrated in the prior section, when identical units of an item are purchased at different unit costs, an inventory cost flow method must be used. This is true regardless of whether the perpetual or periodic inventory system is used.

In this section, the FIFO, LIFO, and average cost methods are illustrated under a perpetual inventory system. For purposes of illustration, the data for Item 127B are used, as shown below.

Although e-tailers, such as eToys.com, Amazon.com, and Furniture.com, Inc., don't have retail stores, they still take possession of inventory in warehouses. Thus, they must account for inventory as illustrated in this chapter.

| Item 127B | | Units | Cost |
|---|---|---|---|
| Jan. 1 | Inventory | 100 | $20 |
| 4 | Sale at $30 per unit | 70 | |
| 10 | Purchase | 80 | 21 |
| 22 | Sale at $30 per unit | 40 | |
| 28 | Sale at $30 per unit | 20 | |
| 30 | Purchase | 100 | 22 |

## First-In, First-Out Method

When the FIFO method is used, costs are included in cost of merchandise sold in the order in which they were purchased. This is often the same as the physical flow of the merchandise. Thus, the FIFO method often provides results that are about the same as those that would have been obtained using the specific identification method. For example, grocery stores shelve milk and other perishable products by expiration dates. Products with early expiration dates are stocked in front. In this way, the oldest products (earliest purchases) are sold first.

To illustrate, Exhibit 3 shows use of FIFO under a perpetual inventory system for Item 127B. The journal entries and the subsidiary inventory ledger for Item 127B are shown in Exhibit 3 as follows:

1. The beginning balance on January 1 is $2,000 (100 units at a unit cost of $20).
2. On January 4, 70 units were sold at a price of $30 each for sales of $2,100 (70 units × $30). The cost of merchandise sold is $1,400 (70 units at a unit cost of $20). After the sale, there remains $600 of inventory (30 units at a unit cost of $20).

**EXHIBIT 3** **Entries and Perpetual Inventory Account (FIFO)**

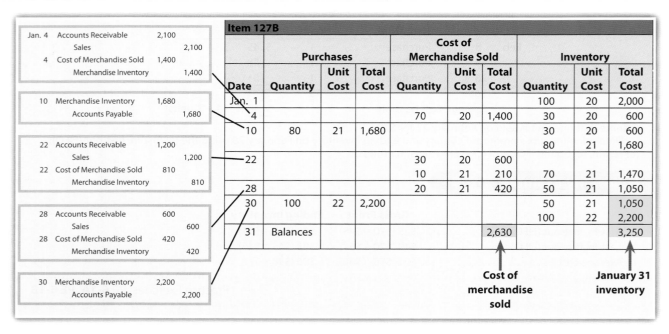

| Jan. 4 | Accounts Receivable | 2,100 | |
|---|---|---|---|
| | Sales | | 2,100 |
| 4 | Cost of Merchandise Sold | 1,400 | |
| | Merchandise Inventory | | 1,400 |

| 10 | Merchandise Inventory | 1,680 | |
|---|---|---|---|
| | Accounts Payable | | 1,680 |

| 22 | Accounts Receivable | 1,200 | |
|---|---|---|---|
| | Sales | | 1,200 |
| 22 | Cost of Merchandise Sold | 810 | |
| | Merchandise Inventory | | 810 |

| 28 | Accounts Receivable | 600 | |
|---|---|---|---|
| | Sales | | 600 |
| 28 | Cost of Merchandise Sold | 420 | |
| | Merchandise Inventory | | 420 |

| 30 | Merchandise Inventory | 2,200 | |
|---|---|---|---|
| | Accounts Payable | | 2,200 |

**Item 127B**

| | Purchases | | | Cost of Merchandise Sold | | | Inventory | | |
|---|---|---|---|---|---|---|---|---|---|
| Date | Quantity | Unit Cost | Total Cost | Quantity | Unit Cost | Total Cost | Quantity | Unit Cost | Total Cost |
| Jan. 1 | | | | | | | 100 | 20 | 2,000 |
| 4 | | | | 70 | 20 | 1,400 | 30 | 20 | 600 |
| 10 | 80 | 21 | 1,680 | | | | 30 | 20 | 600 |
| | | | | | | | 80 | 21 | 1,680 |
| 22 | | | | 30 | 20 | 600 | | | |
| | | | | 10 | 21 | 210 | 70 | 21 | 1,470 |
| 28 | | | | 20 | 21 | 420 | 50 | 21 | 1,050 |
| 30 | 100 | 22 | 2,200 | | | | 50 | 21 | 1,050 |
| | | | | | | | 100 | 22 | 2,200 |
| 31 | Balances | | | | | 2,630 | | | 3,250 |

Cost of merchandise sold

January 31 inventory

3. On January 10, $1,680 is purchased (80 units at a unit cost of $21). After the purchase, the inventory is reported on two lines, $600 (30 units at a unit cost of $20) from the beginning inventory and $1,680 (80 units at a unit cost of $21) from the January 10 purchase.

4. On January 22, 40 units are sold at a price of $30 each for sales of $1,200 (40 units × $30). Using FIFO, the cost of merchandise sold of $810 consists of $600 (30 units at a unit cost of $20) from the beginning inventory plus $210 (10 units at a unit cost of $21) from the January 10 purchase. After the sale, there remains $1,470 of inventory (70 units at a unit cost of $21) from the January 10 purchase.

5. The January 28 sale and January 30 purchase are recorded in a similar manner.

6. The ending balance on January 31 is $3,250. This balance is made up of two layers of inventory as follows:

| | Date of Purchase | Quantity | Unit Cost | Total Cost |
|---|---|---|---|---|
| Layer 1: | Jan. 10 | 50 | $21 | $1,050 |
| Layer 2: | Jan. 30 | 100 | 22 | 2,200 |
| Total | | 150 | | $3,250 |

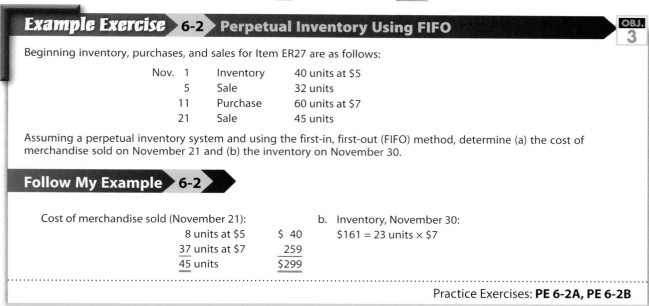

**Example Exercise 6-2** Perpetual Inventory Using FIFO OBJ. 3

Beginning inventory, purchases, and sales for Item ER27 are as follows:

| Nov. | 1 | Inventory | 40 units at $5 |
|---|---|---|---|
| | 5 | Sale | 32 units |
| | 11 | Purchase | 60 units at $7 |
| | 21 | Sale | 45 units |

Assuming a perpetual inventory system and using the first-in, first-out (FIFO) method, determine (a) the cost of merchandise sold on November 21 and (b) the inventory on November 30.

**Follow My Example 6-2**

Cost of merchandise sold (November 21):

| 8 units at $5 | $ 40 |
|---|---|
| 37 units at $7 | 259 |
| 45 units | $299 |

b. Inventory, November 30:
$161 = 23 units × $7

Practice Exercises: **PE 6-2A, PE 6-2B**

## Last-In, First-Out Method

When the LIFO method is used, the cost of the units sold is the cost of the most recent purchases. The LIFO method was originally used in those rare cases where the units sold were taken from the most recently purchased units. However, for tax purposes, LIFO is now widely used even when it does not represent the physical flow of units. The tax impact of LIFO is discussed later in this chapter.

See Appendix E for more information

To illustrate, Exhibit 4 shows the use of LIFO under a perpetual inventory system for Item 127B. The journal entries and the subsidiary inventory ledger for Item 127B are shown in Exhibit 4 as follows:

1. The beginning balance on January 1 is $2,000 (100 units at a unit of cost of $20).

2. On January 4, 70 units were sold at a price of $30 each for sales of $2,100 (70 units × $30). The cost of merchandise sold is $1,400 (70 units at a unit cost of $20). After the sale, there remains $600 of inventory (30 units at a unit cost of $20).

3. On January 10, $1,680 is purchased (80 units at a unit cost of $21). After the purchase, the inventory is reported on two lines, $600 (30 units at a unit cost of $20) from the beginning inventory and $1,680 (80 units at $21 per unit) from the January 10 purchase.

4. On January 22, 40 units are sold at a price of $30 each for sales of $1,200 (40 units × $30). Using LIFO, the cost of merchandise sold is $840 (40 units at unit cost of $21) from the January 10 purchase. After the sale, there remains $1,440 of inventory consisting of $600 (30 units at a unit cost of $20) from the beginning inventory and $840 (40 units at a unit cost of $21) from the January 10 purchase.

**EXHIBIT 4** **Entries and Perpetual Inventory Account (LIFO)**

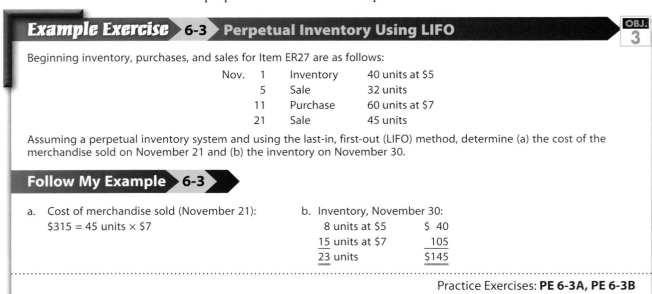

| Jan. 4 | Accounts Receivable | 2,100 | |
| | Sales | | 2,100 |
| 4 | Cost of Merchandise Sold | 1,400 | |
| | Merchandise Inventory | | 1,400 |
| 10 | Merchandise Inventory | 1,680 | |
| | Accounts Payable | | 1,680 |
| 22 | Accounts Receivable | 1,200 | |
| | Sales | | 1,200 |
| 22 | Cost of Merchandise Sold | 840 | |
| | Merchandise Inventory | | 840 |
| 28 | Accounts Receivable | 600 | |
| | Sales | | 600 |
| 28 | Cost of Merchandise Sold | 420 | |
| | Merchandise Inventory | | 420 |
| 30 | Merchandise Inventory | 2,200 | |
| | Accounts Payable | | 2,200 |

**Item 127B**

| Date | Purchases Quantity | Purchases Unit Cost | Purchases Total Cost | Cost of Merchandise Sold Quantity | Cost of Merchandise Sold Unit Cost | Cost of Merchandise Sold Total Cost | Inventory Quantity | Inventory Unit Cost | Inventory Total Cost |
|---|---|---|---|---|---|---|---|---|---|
| Jan. 1 | | | | | | | 100 | 20 | 2,000 |
| 4 | | | | 70 | 20 | 1,400 | 30 | 20 | 600 |
| 10 | 80 | 21 | 1,680 | | | | 30 | 20 | 600 |
| | | | | | | | 80 | 21 | 1,680 |
| 22 | | | | 40 | 21 | 840 | 30 | 20 | 600 |
| | | | | | | | 40 | 21 | 840 |
| 28 | | | | 20 | 21 | 420 | 30 | 20 | 600 |
| | | | | | | | 20 | 21 | 420 |
| 30 | 100 | 22 | 2,200 | | | | 30 | 20 | 600 |
| | | | | | | | 20 | 21 | 420 |
| | | | | | | | 100 | 22 | 2,200 |
| 31 | Balances | | | | | 2,660 | | | 3,220 |

Cost of merchandise sold

January 31 inventory

5. The January 28 sale and January 30 purchase are recorded in a similar manner.

6. The ending balance on January 31 is $3,220. This balance is made up of three layers of inventory as follows:

| | Date of Purchase | Quantity | Unit Cost | Total Cost |
|---|---|---|---|---|
| Layer 1: | Beg. inv. (Jan. 1) | 30 | $20 | $ 600 |
| Layer 2: | Jan. 10 | 20 | 21 | 420 |
| Layer 3: | Jan. 30 | 100 | 22 | 2,200 |
| Total | | 150 | | $3,220 |

When the LIFO method is used, the subsidiary inventory ledger is sometimes maintained in units only. The units are converted to dollars when the financial statements are prepared at the end of the period.

**Example Exercise 6-3 Perpetual Inventory Using LIFO**

OBJ. 3

Beginning inventory, purchases, and sales for Item ER27 are as follows:

| Nov. | 1 | Inventory | 40 units at $5 |
| | 5 | Sale | 32 units |
| | 11 | Purchase | 60 units at $7 |
| | 21 | Sale | 45 units |

Assuming a perpetual inventory system and using the last-in, first-out (LIFO) method, determine (a) the cost of the merchandise sold on November 21 and (b) the inventory on November 30.

**Follow My Example 6-3**

a. Cost of merchandise sold (November 21):
$315 = 45 units × $7

b. Inventory, November 30:
| 8 units at $5 | $ 40 |
| 15 units at $7 | 105 |
| 23 units | $145 |

Practice Exercises: **PE 6-3A, PE 6-3B**

# InternationalConnection

### INTERNATIONAL FINANCIAL REPORTING STANDARDS (IFRS)

IFRS permit the first-in, first-out and average cost methods but prohibit the last-in, first-out (LIFO) method for determining inventory costs. Since LIFO is used in the United States, adoption of IFRS could have a significant impact on many U.S. companies. For example, Caterpillar Inc. uses LIFO and reported that its inventories would have been $3,003 million higher in 2009 if FIFO had been used. Since Caterpillar reported profits of only $895 million in 2009, the adoption of IFRS would have resulted in a loss in 2009 if IFRS and FIFO had been used.*

* Differences between U.S. GAAP and IFRS are further discussed and illustrated in Appendix E.

## Average Cost Method

When the average cost method is used in a perpetual inventory system, an average unit cost for each item is computed each time a purchase is made. This unit cost is used to determine the cost of each sale until another purchase is made and a new average is computed. This technique is called a *moving average.* Since the average cost method is rarely used in a perpetual inventory system, it is not illustrated.

## Computerized Perpetual Inventory Systems

A perpetual inventory system may be used in a manual accounting system. However, if there are many inventory transactions, such a system is costly and time consuming. In most cases, perpetual inventory systems are computerized.

Computerized perpetual inventory systems are useful to managers in controlling and managing inventory. For example, fast-selling items can be reordered before the stock runs out. Sales patterns can also be analyzed to determine when to mark down merchandise or when to restock seasonal merchandise. Finally, inventory data can be used in evaluating advertising campaigns and sales promotions.

## Inventory Costing Methods Under a Periodic Inventory System

**OBJ. 4** Determine the cost of inventory under the periodic inventory system, using the FIFO, LIFO, and average cost methods.

When the periodic inventory system is used, only revenue is recorded each time a sale is made. No entry is made at the time of the sale to record the cost of the merchandise sold. At the end of the accounting period, a physical inventory is taken to determine the cost of the inventory and the cost of the merchandise sold.[2]

Like the perpetual inventory system, a cost flow assumption must be made when identical units are acquired at different unit costs during a period. In such cases, the FIFO, LIFO, or average cost method is used.

### First-In, First-Out Method

To illustrate the use of the FIFO method in a periodic inventory system, we use the same data for Item 127B as in the perpetual inventory example. The beginning inventory entry and purchases of Item 127B in January are as follows:

| | | | | |
|---|---|---|---|---|
| Jan. 1 | Inventory | 100 units at | $20 | $2,000 |
| 10 | Purchase | 80 units at | 21 | 1,680 |
| 30 | Purchase | 100 units at | 22 | 2,200 |
| Available for sale during month | | 280 | | $5,880 |

2 Determining the cost of merchandise sold using the periodic system was illustrated in the appendix to Chapter 5.

The physical count on January 31 shows that 150 units are on hand. Using the FIFO method, the cost of the merchandise on hand at the end of the period is made up of the most recent costs. The cost of the 150 units in ending inventory on January 31 is determined as follows:

| | | | |
|---|---|---|---|
| Most recent costs, January 30 purchase | 100 units at | $22 | $2,200 |
| Next most recent costs, January 10 purchase | 50 units at | $21 | 1,050 |
| Inventory, January 31 | 150 units | | $3,250 |

Deducting the cost of the January 31 inventory of $3,250 from the cost of merchandise available for sale of $5,880 yields the cost of merchandise sold of $2,630, as shown below.

| | |
|---|---|
| Beginning inventory, January 1 | $2,000 |
| Purchases ($1,680 + $2,200) | 3,880 |
| Cost of merchandise available for sale in January | $5,880 |
| Less ending inventory, January 31 | 3,250 |
| Cost of merchandise sold | $2,630 |

The $3,250 cost of the ending merchandise inventory on January 31 is made up of the most recent costs. The $2,630 cost of merchandise sold is made up of the beginning inventory and the earliest costs. Exhibit 5 shows the relationship of the cost of merchandise sold for January and the ending inventory on January 31.

**EXHIBIT 5**

**First-In, First-Out Flow of Costs**

Purchases

Merchandise Available for Sale

Cost of Merchandise Sold

Jan. 1
100 units at $20
$2,000
100 units at $20
$2,000

630

$2,630

Jan. 10
80 units at $21
1,680
30 units at $21

Merchandise Inventory

50 units at $21
$1,050

Jan. 30
100 units at $22
2,200
100 units at $22
2,200

$5,880

$3,250

## Last-In, First-Out Method

See Appendix E for more information

When the LIFO method is used, the cost of merchandise on hand at the end of the period is made up of the earliest costs. Based on the same data as in the FIFO example, the cost of the 150 units in ending inventory on January 31 is determined as follows:

| Beginning inventory, January 1 | 100 units at | $20 | $2,000 |
| Next earliest costs, January 10 | 50 units at | $21 | 1,050 |
| Inventory, January 31 | 150 units | | $3,050 |

Deducting the cost of the January 31 inventory of $3,050 from the cost of merchandise available for sale of $5,880 yields the cost of merchandise sold of $2,830, as shown below.

| Beginning inventory, January 1 | $2,000 |
| Purchases ($1,680 + $2,200) | 3,880 |
| Cost of merchandise available for sale in January | $5,880 |
| Less ending inventory, January 31 | 3,050 |
| Cost of merchandise sold | $2,830 |

The $3,050 cost of the ending merchandise inventory on January 31 is made up of the earliest costs. The $2,830 cost of merchandise sold is made up of the most recent costs. Exhibit 6 shows the relationship of the cost of merchandise sold for January and the ending inventory on January 31.

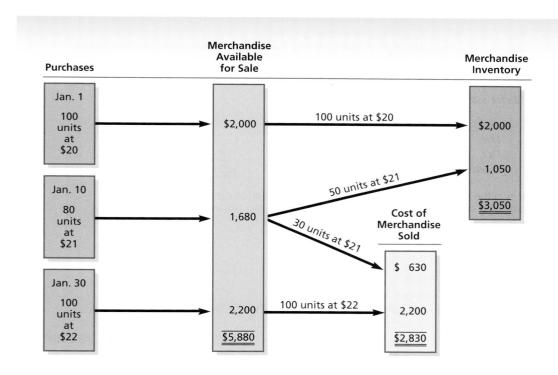

**EXHIBIT 6**

**Last-In, First-Out Flow of Costs**

## Average Cost Method

The average cost method is sometimes called the *weighted average method*. The average cost method uses the average unit cost for determining cost of merchandise sold and the ending merchandise inventory. If purchases are relatively uniform during a period, the average cost method provides results that are similar to the physical flow of goods.

The weighted average unit cost is determined as follows:

$$\text{Average Unit Cost} = \frac{\text{Total Cost of Units Available for Sale}}{\text{Units Available for Sale}}$$

To illustrate, we use the data for Item 127B as follows:

$$\text{Average Unit Cost} = \frac{\text{Total Cost of Units Available for Sale}}{\text{Units Available for Sale}} = \frac{\$5,880}{280 \text{ units}}$$

$$= \$21 \text{ per unit}$$

The cost of the January 31 ending inventory is as follows:

Inventory, January 31: $3,150 (150 units × $21)

Deducting the cost of the January 31 inventory of $3,150 from the cost of merchandise available for sale of $5,880 yields the cost of merchandise sold of $2,730, as shown below.

| | |
|---|---|
| Beginning inventory, January 1 | $2,000 |
| Purchases ($1,680 + $2,200) | 3,880 |
| Cost of merchandise available for sale in January | $5,880 |
| Less ending inventory, January 31 | 3,150 |
| Cost of merchandise sold | $2,730 |

The cost of merchandise sold could also be computed by multiplying the number of units sold by the average cost as follows:

Cost of merchandise sold: $2,730 (130 units × $21)

---

## Example Exercise 6-4 Periodic Inventory Using FIFO, LIFO, Average Cost Methods

**OBJ. 4**

The units of an item available for sale during the year were as follows:

| | | | | |
|---|---|---|---|---|
| Jan. | 1 | Inventory | 6 units at $50 | $ 300 |
| Mar. | 20 | Purchase | 14 units at $55 | 770 |
| Oct. | 30 | Purchase | 20 units at $62 | 1,240 |
| | | Available for sale | 40 units | $2,310 |

There are 16 units of the item in the physical inventory at December 31. The periodic inventory system is used. Determine the inventory cost using (a) the first-in, first-out (FIFO) method, (b) the last-in, first-out (LIFO) method, and (c) the average cost method.

### Follow My Example 6-4

a. First-in, first-out (FIFO) method: $992 = 16 units × $62
b. Last-in, first-out (LIFO) method: $850 = (6 units × $50) + (10 units × $55)
c. Average cost method: $924 (16 units × $57.75), where average cost = $57.75 = $2,310/40 units

Practice Exercises: **PE 6-4A, PE 6-4B**

---

**OBJ. 5** Compare and contrast the use of the three inventory costing methods.

# Comparing Inventory Costing Methods

A different cost flow is assumed for the FIFO, LIFO, and average inventory cost flow methods. As a result, the three methods normally yield different amounts for the following:

1. Cost of merchandise sold
2. Gross profit
3. Net income
4. Ending merchandise inventory

Using the periodic inventory system illustration with sales of $3,900 (130 units × $30), these differences are illustrated below.[3]

See Appendix E for more information

**Partial Income Statements**

| | First-In, First-Out | | Average Cost | | Last-In, First-Out | |
|---|---|---|---|---|---|---|
| Net sales | | $3,900 | | $3,900 | | $3,900 |
| Cost of merchandise sold: | | | | | | |
| Beginning inventory | $2,000 | | $2,000 | | $2,000 | |
| Purchases | 3,880 | | 3,880 | | 3,880 | |
| Merchandise available for sale | $5,880 | | $5,880 | | $5,880 | |
| Less ending inventory | 3,250 | | 3,150 | | 3,050 | |
| Cost of merchandise sold | | 2,630 | | 2,730 | | 2,830 |
| Gross profit | | $1,270 | | $1,170 | | $1,070 |

The preceding differences show the effect of increasing costs (prices). If costs (prices) remain the same, all three methods would yield the same results. However, costs (prices) normally do change. The effects of changing costs (prices) on the FIFO and LIFO methods are summarized in Exhibit 7. The average cost method will always yield results between those of FIFO and LIFO.

FIFO reports higher gross profit and net income than the LIFO method when costs (prices) are increasing, as shown in Exhibit 7. However, in periods of rapidly rising costs, the inventory that is sold must be replaced at increasingly higher costs. In such cases, the larger FIFO gross profit and net income are sometimes called *inventory profits* or *illusory profits*.

During a period of increasing costs, LIFO matches more recent costs against sales on the income statement. Thus, it can be argued that the LIFO method more nearly matches current costs with current revenues. LIFO also offers an income tax savings during periods of increasing costs. This is because LIFO reports the lowest amount of gross profit and, thus, taxable net income.[4] However, under LIFO, the ending inventory on the balance sheet may be quite different from its current replacement cost. In such cases, the financial statements normally include a note that estimates what the inventory would have been if FIFO had been used.

The average cost method is, in a sense, a compromise between FIFO and LIFO. The effect of cost (price) trends is averaged in determining the cost of merchandise sold and the ending inventory. For a series of purchases, the average cost will be the same, regardless of whether costs are increasing or decreasing. For example, reversing the sequence of unit costs presented in the prior illustration does not affect the average unit cost nor the amounts reported for cost of merchandise sold, gross profit, or ending inventory.

**EXHIBIT 7**

**Effects of Changing Costs (Prices): FIFO and LIFO Cost Methods**

| | Increasing Costs (Prices) | | Decreasing Costs (Prices) | |
|---|---|---|---|---|
| | Highest Amount | Lowest Amount | Highest Amount | Lowest Amount |
| Cost of merchandise sold | LIFO | FIFO | FIFO | LIFO |
| Gross profit | FIFO | LIFO | LIFO | FIFO |
| Net income | FIFO | LIFO | LIFO | FIFO |
| Ending merchandise inventory | FIFO | LIFO | LIFO | FIFO |

3 Similar results would also occur when comparing inventory costing methods under a perpetual inventory system.

4 A proposal currently exists before the U.S. Congress to not allow the use of LIFO for tax purposes.

## Integrity, Objectivity, and Ethics in Business

### WHERE'S THE BONUS?

Managers are often given bonuses based on reported earnings numbers. This can create a conflict. LIFO can improve the value of the company through lower taxes. However, in periods of rising costs (prices), LIFO also produces a lower earnings number and, therefore, lower management bonuses. Ethically, managers should select accounting procedures that will maximize the value of the firm, rather than their own compensation. Compensation specialists can help avoid this ethical dilemma by adjusting the bonus plan for the accounting procedure differences.

Describe and illustrate the reporting of merchandise inventory in the financial statements.

# Reporting Merchandise Inventory in the Financial Statements

Cost is the primary basis for valuing and reporting inventories in the financial statements. However, inventory may be valued at other than cost in the following cases:

1. The cost of replacing items in inventory is below the recorded cost.
2. The inventory cannot be sold at normal prices due to imperfections, style changes, or other causes.

## Valuation at Lower of Cost or Market

See Appendix E for more information

If the cost of replacing inventory is lower than its recorded purchase cost, the **lower-of-cost-or-market (LCM) method** is used to value the inventory. *Market,* as used in *lower of cost or market,* is the cost to replace the inventory. The market value is based on normal quantities that would be purchased from suppliers.

The lower-of-cost-or-market method can be applied in one of three ways. The cost, market price, and any declines could be determined for the following:

1. Each item in the inventory.
2. Each major class or category of inventory.
3. Total inventory as a whole.

The amount of any price decline is included in the cost of merchandise sold. This, in turn, reduces gross profit and net income in the period in which the price declines occur. This matching of price declines to the period in which they occur is the primary advantage of using the lower-of-cost-or-market method.

To illustrate, assume the following data for 400 identical units of Item A in inventory on December 31, 2012:

| | |
|---|---|
| Unit purchased cost | $10.25 |
| Replacement cost on December 31, 2012 | 9.50 |

Since Item A could be replaced at $9.50 a unit, $9.50 is used under the lower-of-cost-or-market method.

Exhibit 8 illustrates applying the lower-of-cost-or-market method to each inventory item (A, B, C, and D). As applied on an item-by-item basis, the total lower-of-cost-or-market is $15,070, which is a market decline of $450 ($15,520 − $15,070). This market decline of $450 is included in the cost of merchandise sold.

In Exhibit 8, Items A, B, C, and D could be viewed as a class of inventory items. If the lower of cost or market is applied to the class, the inventory would be valued at $15,472, which is a market decline of $48 ($15,520 − $15,472). Likewise, if Items A, B, C, and D make up the total inventory, the lower of cost or market as applied to the total inventory would be the same amount, $15,472.

|   | A | B | C | D | E | F | G |
|---|---|---|---|---|---|---|---|
| 1 | | | Unit | Unit | Total | | |
| 2 | | Inventory | Cost | Market | | | Lower |
| 3 | Item | Quantity | Price | Price | Cost | Market | of C or M |
| 4 | A | 400 | $10.25 | $ 9.50 | $ 4,100 | $ 3,800 | $ 3,800 |
| 5 | B | 120 | 22.50 | 24.10 | 2,700 | 2,892 | 2,700 |
| 6 | C | 600 | 8.00 | 7.75 | 4,800 | 4,650 | 4,650 |
| 7 | D | 280 | 14.00 | 14.75 | 3,920 | 4,130 | 3,920 |
| 8 | Total | | | | $15,520 | $15,472 | $15,070 |
| 9 | | | | | | | |

**EXHIBIT 8**

**Determining Inventory at Lower of Cost or Market**

The lower of cost or market inventory schedule from Exhibit 8 can be developed on a spreadsheet as follows:

|   | A | B | C | D | E | F | G |
|---|---|---|---|---|---|---|---|
| | | | | | **a.** | **b.** | **c.** |
| 1 | | | | | | | |
| 2 | | | | | | Total | |
| 3 | Item | Inventory Quantity | Unit Cost Price | Unit Market Price | Cost | Market | Lower of C or M |
| 4 | A | 400 | $   10.25 | $   9.50 | =B4*C4 | =B4*D4 | =MIN(E4:F4) |
| 5 | B | 120 | 22.50 | 24.10 | =B5*C5 | =B5*D5 | =MIN(E5:F5) |
| 6 | C | 600 | 8.00 | 7.75 | =B6*C6 | =B6*D6 | =MIN(E6:F6) |
| 7 | D | 280 | 14.00 | 14.75 | =B7*C7 | =B7*D7 | =MIN(E7:F7) |
| 8 | Total | | | e.⟶ | =SUM(E4:E7) | =SUM(F4:F7) | =SUM(G4:G7) |
| 9 | | | | | f. | | |

**d.**

Copy cells by using the fill handle in the corner of the cell to be copied and dragging to the target cells.

Develop the formulas by the following steps:

a. Enter in cell E4 the formula for the total at cost, =B4*C4.
b. Enter in cell F4 the formula for the total at market, =B4*D4.
c. Enter in cell G4 a =MIN function to calculate the lower of cost or market, as follows:

$$=MIN(E4:F4)$$

**Note**: This function will return the minimum value within the range of designated cells (E4 to F4).

d. Copy E4:G4 to E5:G7.
e. Enter in E8 a formula to sum the column, =SUM(E4:E7)
f. Copy E8 to F8:G8

**Try***It*   Go to the hands-on **Excel Tutor** for this example!

**Example Exercise  6-5  Lower-of-Cost-or-Market Method**    OBJ. 6

On the basis of the following data, determine the value of the inventory at the lower of cost or market. Apply lower of cost or market to each inventory item as shown in Exhibit 8.

| Item | Inventory Quantity | Unit Cost Price | Unit Market Price |
|---|---|---|---|
| C17Y | 10 | $ 39 | $40 |
| B563 | 7 | 110 | 98 |

**Follow My Example  6-5**

|   | A | B | C | D | E | F | G |
|---|---|---|---|---|---|---|---|
| 1 | | | Unit | Unit | Total | | |
| 2 | | Inventory | Cost | Market | | | Lower |
| 3 | Item | Quantity | Price | Price | Cost | Market | of C or M |
| 4 | C17Y | 10 | $ 39 | $ 40 | $ 390 | $ 400 | $ 390 |
| 5 | B563 | 7 | 110 | 98 | 770 | 686 | 686 |
| 6 | Total | | | | $1,160 | $1,086 | $1,076 |
| 7 | | | | | | | |

Practice Exercises: **PE 6-5A, PE 6-5B**

## Valuation at Net Realizable Value

Merchandise that is out of date, spoiled, or damaged can often be sold only at a price below its original cost. Such merchandise should be valued at its **net realizable value**. Net realizable value is determined as follows:

Net Realizable Value = Estimated Selling Price – Direct Costs of Disposal

Direct costs of disposal include selling expenses such as special advertising or sales commissions. To illustrate, assume the following data about an item of damaged merchandise:

| | |
|---|---|
| Original cost | $1,000 |
| Estimated selling price | 800 |
| Selling expenses | 150 |

The merchandise should be valued at its net realizable value of $650 as shown:

Net Realizable Value = $800 – $150 = $650

## Merchandise Inventory on the Balance Sheet

||IFRS▶    ◀IFRS|||

See Appendix E for
more information

Merchandise inventory is usually reported in the Current Assets section of the balance sheet. In addition to this amount, the following are reported:

1. The method of determining the cost of the inventory (FIFO, LIFO, or average)
2. The method of valuing the inventory (cost or the lower of cost or market)

The financial statement reporting for the topics covered in Chapters 6–13 are illustrated using excerpts from the financial statements of Mornin' Joe. Mornin' Joe is a fictitious company that offers drip and espresso coffee in a coffeehouse setting. The complete financial statements of Mornin' Joe are illustrated at the end of Chapter 13 (pages 627–629).

The balance sheet presentation for merchandise inventory for Mornin' Joe is as follows:

| Mornin' Joe Balance Sheet December 31, 2012 | | |
|---|---|---|
| **Current assets:** | | |
| Cash and cash equivalents | | $235,000 |
| Trading investments (at cost) | $420,000 | |
| Plus valuation allowance on trading investments | 45,000 | 465,000 |
| Accounts receivable | $305,000 | |
| Less allowance for doubtful accounts | 12,300 | 292,700 |
| Merchandise inventory—at lower of cost (first-in, first-out method) or market | | 120,000 |

It is not unusual for a large business to use different costing methods for segments of its inventories. Also, a business may change its inventory costing method. In such cases, the effect of the change and the reason for the change are disclosed in the financial statements.

See pages 630-634

## IFRS Reporting

Mornin' Joe plans to expand operations to various places around the world. We will call the international version of the company, Mornin' Joe International. Mornin' Joe International will prepare financial statements using International Financial Reporting Standards (IFRS) for their international users. Excerpts from the Mornin' Joe International statements (IFRS) will be illustrated parallel to Mornin' Joe financial statement (U.S. GAAP) in several following chapters. The financial statement excerpts are presented in euros (€) for demonstration purposes only. The euro is the standard currency of the European Union. To simplify comparisons, the euro is translated at a 1:1 ratio from the dollar. The full financial statements for Mornin' Joe (U.S. GAAP) and Mornin' Joe International (IFRS) are provided on pages 630–634.

The statement of financial position (balance sheet) presentation for merchandise inventory for Mornin' Joe International under IFRS is as follows:

**Mornin' Joe International**
**Statement of Financial Position**
**December 31, 2012**

**Current assets**

| | |
|---|---|
| Merchandise inventory—**at lower of cost (first in, first out)** **or realizable value** ................................................... | €120,000 |

Under IFRS, the balance sheet is termed the Statement of Financial Position. Merchandise inventory is listed under current assets, similar to U.S. GAAP. However, under IFRS, LIFO is prohibited. Thus, Mornin' Joe International uses FIFO for determining the cost of its merchandise inventory. Similar to U.S. GAAP, IFRS also uses lower of cost or market to value merchandise inventories. However, U.S. GAAP defines "market" as replacement cost in most circumstances, while IFRS defines "market" as net realizable value. The net realizable value is the selling price of the inventory less costs to dispose. Net realizable value would be less than cost when the inventory is obsolete.

## Effect of Inventory Errors on the Financial Statements

Any errors in merchandise inventory will affect the balance sheet and income statement. Some reasons that inventory errors may occur include the following:

1. Physical inventory on hand was miscounted.
2. Costs were incorrectly assigned to inventory. For example, the FIFO, LIFO, or average cost method was incorrectly applied.
3. Inventory in transit was incorrectly included or excluded from inventory.
4. Consigned inventory was incorrectly included or excluded from inventory.

Inventory errors often arise from merchandise that is in transit at year-end. As discussed in Chapter 5, shipping terms determine when the title to merchandise passes. When goods are purchased or sold *FOB shipping point*, title passes to the buyer when the goods are shipped. When the terms are *FOB destination*, title passes to the buyer when the goods are received.

To illustrate, assume SysExpress ordered this merchandise from American Products:

| | |
|---|---|
| Date ordered: | December 27, 2011 |
| Amount: | $10,000 |
| Terms: | FOB shipping point, 2/10, n/30 |
| Date shipped by seller: | December 30, 2011 |
| Date delivered: | January 3, 2012 |

When SysExpress counts its physical inventory on December 31, 2011, the merchandise is still in transit. In such cases, it would be easy for SysExpress to not include the $10,000 of merchandise in its December 31 physical inventory. However, since the merchandise was purchased *FOB shipping point*, SysExpress owns the merchandise. Thus, it should be included in the ending December 31 inventory even though it is not on hand. Likewise, any merchandise *sold* by SysExpress *FOB destination* is still SysExpress's inventory even if it is in transit to the buyer on December 31.

Inventory errors often arise from **consigned inventory**. Manufacturers sometimes ship merchandise to retailers who act as the manufacturer's selling agent. The manufacturer, called the **consignor**, retains title until the goods are sold. Such merchandise is said to be shipped *on consignment* to the retailer, called the **consignee**. Any unsold merchandise at year-end is a part of the manufacturer's (consignor's) inventory, even though the merchandise is in the hands of the retailer (consignee). At year-end, it would be easy for the retailer (consignee) to incorrectly include the consigned merchandise in its physical inventory. Likewise, the manufacturer (consignor) should include consigned inventory in its physical inventory even though the inventory is not on hand.

**Income Statement Effects** Inventory errors will misstate the income statement amounts for cost of merchandise sold, gross profit, and net income. The effects of inventory errors on the current period's income statement are summarized in Exhibit 9.

To illustrate, the income statements of SysExpress shown in Exhibit 10 are used.[5] On December 31, 2011, assume that SysExpress incorrectly records its physical inventory as $50,000 instead of the correct amount of $60,000. Thus, the December 31, 2011, inventory

## EXHIBIT 9

**Effect of Inventory Errors on Current Period's Income Statement**

| | Income Statement Effect | | |
|---|---|---|---|
| **Inventory Error** | **Cost of Merchandise Sold** | **Gross Profit** | **Net Income** |
| Beginning inventory is: | | | |
| *Understated* | *Understated* | *Overstated* | *Overstated* |
| *Overstated* | *Overstated* | *Understated* | *Understated* |
| Ending inventory is: | | | |
| *Understated* | *Overstated* | *Understated* | *Understated* |
| *Overstated* | *Understated* | *Overstated* | *Overstated* |

## EXHIBIT 10  Effects of Inventory Errors on Two Years' Income Statements

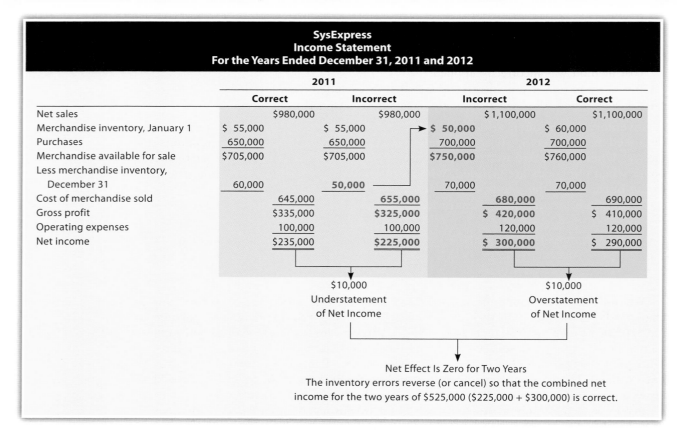

| SysExpress Income Statement For the Years Ended December 31, 2011 and 2012 | | | | |
|---|---|---|---|---|
| | **2011** | | **2012** | |
| | **Correct** | **Incorrect** | **Incorrect** | **Correct** |
| Net sales | $980,000 | $980,000 | $1,100,000 | $1,100,000 |
| Merchandise inventory, January 1 | $ 55,000 | $ 55,000 | $ 50,000 | $ 60,000 |
| Purchases | 650,000 | 650,000 | 700,000 | 700,000 |
| Merchandise available for sale | $705,000 | $705,000 | $750,000 | $760,000 |
| Less merchandise inventory, December 31 | 60,000 | 50,000 | 70,000 | 70,000 |
| Cost of merchandise sold | 645,000 | 655,000 | 680,000 | 690,000 |
| Gross profit | $335,000 | $325,000 | $ 420,000 | $ 410,000 |
| Operating expenses | 100,000 | 100,000 | 120,000 | 120,000 |
| Net income | $235,000 | $225,000 | $ 300,000 | $ 290,000 |

$10,000
Understatement
of Net Income

$10,000
Overstatement
of Net Income

Net Effect Is Zero for Two Years
The inventory errors reverse (or cancel) so that the combined net income for the two years of $525,000 ($225,000 + $300,000) is correct.

[5] The effect of inventory errors is illustrated using the periodic system because it is easier to see the impact of inventory errors on the income statement using this system. The effect of inventory errors would be the same under the perpetual inventory system.

is understated by $10,000 ($60,000 – $50,000). As a result, the cost of merchandise sold is overstated by $10,000. The gross profit and the net income for the year will also be understated by $10,000.

The December 31, 2011, merchandise inventory becomes the January 1, 2012, inventory. Thus, the beginning inventory for 2012 is understated by $10,000. As a result, the cost of merchandise sold is understated by $10,000 for 2012. The gross profit and net income for 2012 will be overstated by $10,000.

As shown in Exhibit 10, since the ending inventory of one period is the beginning inventory of the next period, the effects of inventory errors carry forward to the next period. Specifically, if uncorrected, the effects of inventory errors reverse themselves in the next period. In Exhibit 10, the combined net income for the two years of $525,000 is correct even though the 2011 and 2012 income statements were incorrect.

## Summary Effects of Inventory Errors

**Balance Sheet Effects** Inventory errors misstate the merchandise inventory, current assets, total assets, and stockholders' equity (retained earnings) on the balance sheet. The effects of inventory errors on the current period's balance sheet are summarized in Exhibit 11.

| Ending Inventory Error | Merchandise Inventory | Current Assets | Total Assets | Stockholders' Equity (Retained Earnings) |
|---|---|---|---|---|
| | | **Balance Sheet Effect** | | |
| Understated | Understated | Understated | Understated | Understated |
| Overstated | Overstated | Overstated | Overstated | Overstated |

**EXHIBIT 11**

**Effect of Inventory Errors on Current Period's Balance Sheet**

For the SysExpress illustration shown in Exhibit 10, the December 31, 2011, ending inventory was understated by $10,000. As a result, the merchandise inventory, current assets, and total assets would be understated by $10,000 on the December 31, 2011, balance sheet. Because the ending physical inventory is understated, the cost of merchandise sold for 2011 will be overstated by $10,000. Thus, the gross profit and the net income for 2011 are understated by $10,000. Since the net income is closed to Retained Earnings at the end of the period, the stockholders' equity on the December 31, 2011, balance sheet is also understated by $10,000.

As discussed on previous page, inventory errors reverse themselves within two years. As a result, the balance sheet will be correct as of December 31, 2012. Using the SysExpress illustration from Exhibit 10, these effects are summarized as follows:

| | **Amount of Misstatement** | |
|---|---|---|
| Balance Sheet: | December 31, 2011 | December 31, 2012 |
| Merchandise inventory overstated (understated) | $(10,000) | Correct |
| Current assets overstated (understated) | (10,000) | Correct |
| Total assets overstated (understated) | (10,000) | Correct |
| Stockholders' equity overstated (understated) | (10,000) | Correct |
| Income Statement: | 2011 | 2012 |
| Cost of merchandise sold overstated (understated) | $ 10,000 | $(10,000) |
| Gross profit overstated (understated) | (10,000) | 10,000 |
| Net income overstated (understated) | (10,000) | 10,000 |

**Example Exercise** ❯ **6-6** ❯ **Effect of Inventory Errors** OBJ. 6

Zula Repair Shop incorrectly counted its December 31, 2012, inventory as $250,000 instead of the correct amount of $220,000. Indicate the effect of the misstatement on Zula's December 31, 2012, balance sheet and income statement for the year ended December 31, 2012.

*(continued)*

**Follow My Example > 6-6 >**

| | Amount of Overstatement (Understatement) |
|---|---|
| Balance Sheet: | |
| Merchandise inventory overstated ........................................ | $ 30,000 |
| Current assets overstated ................................................. | 30,000 |
| Total assets overstated.................................................. | 30,000 |
| Stockholders' equity overstated ......................................... | 30,000 |
| Income Statement: | |
| Cost of merchandise sold understated................................... | $(30,000) |
| Gross profit overstated................................................... | 30,000 |
| Net income overstated................................................... | 30,000 |

Practice Exercises: **PE 6-6A, PE 6-6B**

## BusinessConnection

### RAPID INVENTORY AT COSTCO

Costco Wholesale Corporation operates over 500 membership warehouses that offer members low prices on a limited selection of nationally branded and selected private label products. Costco emphasizes high sales volumes and rapid inventory turnover. This enables Costco to operate profitably at lower gross margins than traditional wholesalers, discount retailers, and supermarkets. In addition, Costco's rapid inventory turnover allows it to conserve its working capital, as described below.

*Because of our high sales volume and rapid inventory turnover, we generally have the opportunity to sell and be paid for inventory before we are required to pay … our merchandise vendors…. As sales increase and inventory turnover becomes more rapid, a greater percentage of inventory is financed through*

*payment terms provided by suppliers rather than by our working capital.*

Source: Costco Wholesale Corporation, Annual Report on Form 10-K for the fiscal year ended August 31, 2009.

© Don Ryan/AP Images

**OBJ. 7**
Describe and illustrate the inventory turnover and the number of days' sales in inventory in analyzing the efficiency and effectiveness of inventory management.

## Financial Analysis and Interpretation: Inventory Turnover and Number of Days' Sales in Inventory

A merchandising business should keep enough inventory on hand to meet its customers' needs. A failure to do so may result in lost sales. However, too much inventory ties up funds that could be used to improve operations. Also, excess inventory increases expenses such as storage and property taxes. Finally, excess inventory increases the risk of losses due to price declines, damage, or changes in customer tastes.

Two measures to analyze the efficiency and effectiveness of inventory management are:

1. inventory turnover and
2. number of days' sales in inventory.

**Inventory turnover** measures the relationship between cost of merchandise sold and the amount of inventory carried during the period. It is computed as follows:

$$\text{Inventory Turnover} = \frac{\text{Cost of Merchandise Sold}}{\text{Average Inventory}}$$

To illustrate, inventory turnover for Best Buy is computed from the following data (in millions) taken from two recent annual reports.

| | For the Year Ended | |
| --- | --- | --- |
| | **February 28, 2009** | **March 1, 2008** |
| Cost of merchandise sold | $34,017 | $30,477 |
| Inventories: | | |
| Beginning of year | 4,708 | 4,028 |
| End of year | 4,753 | 4,708 |
| Average inventory: | | |
| ($4,708 + $4,753) ÷ 2 | 4,731 | |
| ($4,028 + $4,708) ÷ 2 | | 4,368 |
| Inventory turnover: | | |
| $34,017 ÷ $4,731 | 7.2 | |
| $30,477 ÷ $4,368 | | 7.0 |

Generally, the larger the inventory turnover the more efficient and effective the company is managing inventory. As shown above, inventory turnover increased from 7.0 to 7.2 during 2009, and thus Best Buy improved its inventory efficiency.

The **number of days' sales in inventory** measures the length of time it takes to acquire, sell, and replace the inventory. It is computed as follows:

$$\text{Number of Days' Sales in Inventory} = \frac{\text{Average Inventory}}{\text{Average Daily Cost of Merchandise Sold}}$$

The average daily cost of merchandise sold is determined by dividing the cost of merchandise sold by 365. Based upon the preceding data, the number of days' sales in inventory for Best Buy is computed below.

| | For the Year Ended | |
| --- | --- | --- |
| | **February 28, 2009** | **March 1, 2008** |
| Cost of merchandise sold | $34,017 | $30,477 |
| Average daily cost of merchandise sold: | | |
| $34,017 ÷ 365 days | 93 | |
| $30,477 ÷ 365 days | | 84 |
| Average inventory: | | |
| ($4,708 + $4,753) ÷ 2 | 4,731 | |
| ($4,028 + $4,708) ÷ 2 | | 4,368 |
| Number of days' sales in inventory: | | |
| $4,731 ÷ $93 | 51 days | |
| $4,368 ÷ $84 | | 52 days |

Generally, the lower the number of days' sales in inventory, the more efficient and effective the company is in managing inventory. As shown above, the number of days' sales in inventory decreased from 52 to 51 during 2009, and thus Best Buy improved its inventory management. This is consistent with the increase in inventory during the year.

As with most financial ratios, differences exist among industries. To illustrate, Zale Corporation is a large retailer of fine jewelry in the United States. Since jewelry doesn't sell as rapidly as Best Buy's consumer electronics, Zale's inventory turnover and number of days' sales in inventory should be significantly different than Best Buy's. For 2009, this is confirmed as shown below.

| | **Best Buy** | **Zale** |
| --- | --- | --- |
| Inventory turnover | 7.2 | 1.3 |
| Number of days' sales in inventory | 51 days | 292 days |

**Example Exercise** ▶ **6-7** ▶ **Inventory Turnover and Number of Days'**
**Sales in Inventory**

OBJ. 7

Financial statement data for years ending December 31 for Beadle Company are shown below.

|  | 2012 | 2011 |
|---|---|---|
| Cost of merchandise sold | $877,500 | $615,000 |
| Inventories: |  |  |
|    Beginning of year | 225,000 | 225,000 |
|    End of year | 315,000 | 185,000 |

a. Determine inventory turnover for 2012 and 2011.
b. Determine the number of days' sales in inventory for 2012 and 2011.
c. Does the change in inventory turnover and the number of days' sales in inventory from 2011 to 2012 indicate a favorable or an unfavorable trend?

**Follow My Example** ▶ **6-7** ▶

a. Inventory turnover:

|  | 2012 | 2011 |
|---|---|---|
| Average inventory: |  |  |
|   ($225,000 + $315,000) ÷ 2 | $270,000 |  |
|   ($185,000 + $225,000) ÷ 2 |  | $205,000 |
| Inventory turnover: |  |  |
|   $877,500 ÷ $270,000 | 3.25 |  |
|   $615,000 ÷ $205,000 |  | 3.00 |

b. Number of days' sales in inventory:

|  | 2012 | 2011 |
|---|---|---|
| Average daily cost of merchandise sold: |  |  |
|   $877,500 ÷ 365 days | $2,404 |  |
|   $615,000 ÷ 365 days |  | $1,685 |
| Average inventory: |  |  |
|   ($225,000 + $315,000) ÷ 2 | $270,000 |  |
|   ($185,000 + $225,000) ÷ 2 |  | $205,000 |
| Number of days' sales in inventory: |  |  |
|   $270,000 ÷ $2,404 | 112.3 days |  |
|   $205,000 ÷ $1,685 |  | 121.7 days |

c. The increase in the inventory turnover from 3.00 to 3.25 and the decrease in the number of days' sales in inventory from 121.7 days to 112.3 days indicate favorable trends in managing inventory.

Practice Exercises: **PE 6-7A, PE 6-7B**

# A P P E N D I X

# Estimating Inventory Cost

A business may need to estimate the amount of inventory for the following reasons:

1. Perpetual inventory records are not maintained.
2. A disaster such as a fire or flood has destroyed the inventory records and the inventory.
3. Monthly or quarterly financial statements are needed, but a physical inventory is taken only once a year.

This appendix describes and illustrates two widely used methods of estimating inventory cost.

# Retail Method of Inventory Costing

The **retail inventory method** of estimating inventory cost requires costs and retail prices to be maintained for the merchandise available for sale. A ratio of cost to retail price is then used to convert ending inventory at retail to estimate the ending inventory cost.

The retail inventory method is applied as follows:

Step 1. Determine the total merchandise available for sale at cost and retail.
Step 2. Determine the ratio of the cost to retail of the merchandise available for sale.
Step 3. Determine the ending inventory at retail by deducting the net sales from the merchandise available for sale at retail.
Step 4. Estimate the ending inventory cost by multiplying the ending inventory at retail by the cost to retail ratio.

Exhibit 12 illustrates the retail inventory method.

| | A | B Cost | C Retail |
|---|---|---|---|
| 1 | | Cost | Retail |
| 2 | Merchandise inventory, January 1 | $19,400 | $ 36,000 |
| 3 | Purchases in January (net) | 42,600 | 64,000 |
| Step 1 → 4 | Merchandise available for sale | $62,000 | $100,000 |
| Step 2 → 5 | Ratio of cost to retail price: $\frac{\$62,000}{\$100,000} = 62\%$ | | |
| 6 | Sales for January (net) | | 70,000 |
| Step 3 → 7 | Merchandise inventory, January 31, at retail | | $ 30,000 |
| Step 4 → 8 | Merchandise inventory, January 31, at estimated cost | | |
| 9 | ($30,000 × 62%) | | $ 18,600 |
| 10 | | | |

**EXHIBIT 12**

**Determining Inventory by the Retail Method**

When estimating the cost to retail ratio, the mix of items in the ending inventory is assumed to be the same as the merchandise available for sale. If the ending inventory is made up of different classes of merchandise, cost to retail ratios may be developed for each class of inventory.

An advantage of the retail method is that it provides inventory figures for preparing monthly statements. Department stores and similar retailers often determine gross profit and operating income each month, but may take a physical inventory only once or twice a year. Thus, the retail method allows management to monitor operations more closely.

The retail method may also be used as an aid in taking a physical inventory. In this case, the items are counted and recorded at their retail (selling) prices instead of their costs. The physical inventory at retail is then converted to cost by using the cost to retail ratio.

# Gross Profit Method of Inventory Costing

The **gross profit method** uses the estimated gross profit for the period to estimate the inventory at the end of the period. The gross profit is estimated from the preceding year, adjusted for any current-period changes in the cost and sales prices.

The gross profit method is applied as follows:

Step 1. Determine the merchandise available for sale at cost.

Step 2. Determine the estimated gross profit by multiplying the net sales by the gross profit percentage.

Step 3. Determine the estimated cost of merchandise sold by deducting the estimated gross profit from the net sales.

Step 4. Estimate the ending inventory cost by deducting the estimated cost of merchandise sold from the merchandise available for sale.

Exhibit 13 illustrates the gross profit method.

**EXHIBIT 13**

**Estimating Inventory by Gross Profit Method**

| | A | B | C |
|---|---|---|---|
| 1 | | | Cost |
| 2 | Merchandise inventory, January 1 | | $ 57,000 |
| 3 | Purchases in January (net) | | 180,000 |
| Step 1 → 4 | Merchandise available for sale | | $237,000 |
| 5 | Sales for January (net) | $250,000 | |
| Step 2 → 6 | Less estimated gross profit ($250,000 × 30%) | 75,000 | |
| Step 3 → 7 | Estimated cost of merchandise sold | | 175,000 |
| Step 4 → 8 | Estimated merchandise inventory, January 31 | | $ 62,000 |
| 9 | | | |

The gross profit method is useful for estimating inventories for monthly or quarterly financial statements. It is also useful in estimating the cost of merchandise destroyed by fire or other disasters.

# At a Glance 6

**OBJ. 1**

## Describe the importance of control over inventory.

**Key Points** Two objectives of inventory control are safeguarding the inventory and properly reporting it in the financial statements. The perpetual inventory system and physical count enhance control over inventory.

| Learning Outcomes | Example Exercises | Practice Exercises |
|---|---|---|
| • Describe controls for safeguarding inventory. | | |
| • Describe how a perpetual inventory system enhances control over inventory. | | |
| • Describe why taking a physical inventory enhances control over inventory. | | |

**OBJ. 2**

## Describe three inventory cost flow assumptions and how they impact the income statement and balance sheet.

**Key Points** The three common inventory cost flow assumptions used in business are the (1) first-in, first-out method (FIFO); (2) last-in, first-out method (LIFO); and (3) average cost method. The cost flow assumption affects the income statement and balance sheet.

| Learning Outcomes | Example Exercises | Practice Exercises |
|---|---|---|
| • Describe the FIFO, LIFO, and average cost flow methods. | | |
| • Describe how choice of a cost flow method affects the income statement and balance sheet. | EE6-1 | PE6-1A, 6-1B |

**OBJ. 3**

**Determine the cost of inventory under the perpetual inventory system, using the FIFO, LIFO, and average cost methods.**

**Key Points** In a perpetual inventory system, the number of units and the cost of each type of merchandise are recorded in a subsidiary inventory ledger, with a separate account for each type of merchandise.

| Learning Outcomes | Example Exercises | Practice Exercises |
|---|---|---|
| • Determine the cost of inventory and cost of merchandise sold using a perpetual inventory system under the FIFO method. | **EE6-2** | **PE6-2A, 6-2B** |
| • Determine the cost of inventory and cost of merchandise sold using a perpetual inventory system under the LIFO method. | **EE6-3** | **PE6-3A, 6-3B** |

**OBJ. 4**

**Determine the cost of inventory under the periodic inventory system, using the FIFO, LIFO, and average cost methods.**

**Key Points** In a periodic inventory system, a physical inventory is taken to determine the cost of the inventory and the cost of merchandise sold.

| Learning Outcomes | Example Exercises | Practice Exercises |
|---|---|---|
| • Determine the cost of inventory and cost of merchandise sold using a periodic inventory system under the FIFO method. | **EE6-4** | **PE6-4A, 6-4B** |
| • Determine the cost of inventory and cost of merchandise sold using a periodic inventory system under the LIFO method. | **EE6-4** | **PE6-4A, 6-4B** |
| • Determine the cost of inventory and cost of merchandise sold using a periodic inventory system under the average cost method. | **EE6-4** | **PE6-4A, 6-4B** |

**OBJ. 5**

**Compare and contrast the use of the three inventory costing methods.**

**Key Points** The three inventory costing methods will normally yield different amounts for (1) the ending inventory, (2) the cost of merchandise sold for the period, and (3) the gross profit (and net income) for the period.

| Learning Outcomes | Example Exercises | Practice Exercises |
|---|---|---|
| • Indicate which inventory cost flow method will yield the highest and lowest ending inventory and net income during periods of increasing prices. | | |
| • Indicate which inventory cost flow method will yield the highest and lowest ending inventory and net income during periods of decreasing prices. | | |

**OBJ. 6**

**Describe and illustrate the reporting of merchandise inventory in the financial statements.**

**Key Points** The lower of cost or market is used to value inventory. Inventory that is out of date, spoiled, or damaged is valued at its net realizable value.

Merchandise inventory is usually presented in the Current Assets section of the balance sheet, following receivables. The method of determining the cost and valuing the inventory is reported.

Errors in reporting inventory based on the physical inventory will affect the balance sheet and income statement.

| Learning Outcomes | Example Exercises | Practice Exercises |
|---|---|---|
| • Determine inventory using lower of cost or market. | **EE6-5** | **PE6-5A, 6-5B** |
| • Illustrate the use of net realizable value for spoiled or damaged inventory. | | |
| • Prepare the Current Assets section of the balance sheet that includes inventory. | | |
| • Determine the effect of inventory errors on the balance sheet and income statement. | **EE6-6** | **PE6-6A, 6-6B** |

**OBJ. 7**

**Describe and illustrate the inventory turnover and the number of days' sales in inventory in analyzing the efficiency and effectiveness of inventory management.**

**Key Points** Two measures to analyze the efficiency and effectiveness of inventory management are (1) inventory turnover and (2) number of days' sales in inventory

| Learning Outcomes | Example Exercises | Practice Exercises |
|---|---|---|
| • Describe the use of inventory turnover and number of days' sales in inventory in analyzing how well a company manages inventory. | | |
| • Compute the inventory turnover. | **EE6-7** | **PE6-7A, 6-7B** |
| • Compute the number of days' sales in inventory. | **EE6-7** | **PE6-7A, 6-7B** |

# Key Terms

average inventory cost flow method (278)
consigned inventory (291)
consignee (291)
consignor (291)
first-in, first-out (FIFO) inventory cost flow method (278)
gross profit method (297)

inventory turnover (294)
last-in, first-out (LIFO) inventory cost flow method (278)
lower-of-cost-or-market (LCM) method (288)
net realizable value (290)
number of days' sales in inventory (295)

physical inventory (277)
purchase order (276)
receiving report (276)
retail inventory method (297)
specific identification inventory cost flow method (278)
subsidiary inventory ledger (277)

## Illustrative Problem

Stewart Co.'s beginning inventory and purchases during the year ended December 31, 2012, were as follows:

|  |  | Unit | Unit Costs | Total Cost |
|---|---|---|---|---|
| January 1 | Inventory | 1,000 | $50.00 | $ 50,000 |
| March 10 | Purchase | 1,200 | 52.50 | 63,000 |
| June 25 | Sold 800 units |  |  |  |
| August 30 | Purchase | 800 | 55.00 | 44,000 |
| October 5 | Sold 1,500 units |  |  |  |
| November 26 | Purchase | 2,000 | 56.00 | 112,000 |
| December 31 | Sold 1,000 units |  |  |  |
| Total |  | 5,000 |  | $269,000 |

### Instructions

1. Determine the cost of inventory on December 31, 2012, using the perpetual inventory system and each of the following inventory costing methods:
   a. first-in, first-out
   b. last-in, first-out

2. Determine the cost of inventory on December 31, 2012, using the periodic inventory system and each of the following inventory costing methods:
   a. first-in, first-out
   b. last-in, first-out
   c. average cost

3. Appendix: Assume that during the fiscal year ended December 31, 2012, sales were $290,000 and the estimated gross profit rate was 40%. Estimate the ending inventory at December 31, 2012, using the gross profit method.

### Solution

1. a. First-in, first-out method: $95,200
   b. Last-in, first-out method: $91,000 ($35,000 + $56,000)

2. a. First-in, first-out method:
      1,700 units at $56 = $95,200

   b. Last-in, first-out method:

| 1,000 units at $50.00 | $50,000 |
|---|---|
| 700 units at $52.50 | 36,750 |
| 1,700 units | $86,750 |

1. a. First-in, first-out method: $95,200

| Date | Purchases | | | Cost of Merchandise Sold | | | Inventory | | |
|---|---|---|---|---|---|---|---|---|---|
| | Quantity | Unit Cost | Total Cost | Quantity | Unit Cost | Total Cost | Quantity | Unit Cost | Total Cost |
| 2012 Jan. 1 | | | | | | | 1,000 | 50.00 | 50,000 |
| Mar. 10 | 1,200 | 52.50 | 63,000 | | | | 1,000 | 50.00 | 50,000 |
| | | | | | | | 1,200 | 52.50 | 63,000 |
| June 25 | | | | 800 | 50.00 | 40,000 | 200 | 50.00 | 10,000 |
| | | | | | | | 1,200 | 52.50 | 63,000 |
| Aug. 30 | 800 | 55.00 | 44,000 | | | | 200 | 50.00 | 10,000 |
| | | | | | | | 1,200 | 52.50 | 63,000 |
| | | | | | | | 800 | 55.00 | 44,000 |
| Oct. 5 | | | | 200 | 50.00 | 10,000 | 700 | 55.00 | 38,500 |
| | | | | 1,200 | 52.50 | 63,000 | | | |
| | | | | 100 | 55.00 | 5,500 | | | |
| Nov. 26 | 2,000 | 56.00 | 112,000 | | | | 700 | 55.00 | 38,500 |
| | | | | | | | 2,000 | 56.00 | 112,000 |
| Dec. 31 | | | | 700 | 55.00 | 38,500 | 1,700 | 56.00 | 95,200 |
| | | | | 300 | 56.00 | 16,800 | | | |
| 31 | Balances | | | | | 173,800 | | | 95,200 |

b. Last-in, first-out method: $91,000 ($35,000 + $56,000)

| Date | Purchases | | | Cost of Merchandise Sold | | | Inventory | | |
|---|---|---|---|---|---|---|---|---|---|
| | Quantity | Unit Cost | Total Cost | Quantity | Unit Cost | Total Cost | Quantity | Unit Cost | Total Cost |
| 2012 Jan. 1 | | | | | | | 1,000 | 50.00 | 50,000 |
| Mar. 10 | 1,200 | 52.50 | 63,000 | | | | 1,000 | 50.00 | 50,000 |
| | | | | | | | 1,200 | 52.50 | 63,000 |
| June 25 | | | | 800 | 52.50 | 42,000 | 1,000 | 50.00 | 50,000 |
| | | | | | | | 400 | 52.50 | 21,000 |
| Aug. 30 | 800 | 55.00 | 44,000 | | | | 1,000 | 50.00 | 50,000 |
| | | | | | | | 400 | 52.50 | 21,000 |
| | | | | | | | 800 | 55.00 | 44,000 |
| Oct. 5 | | | | 800 | 55.00 | 44,000 | 700 | 50.00 | 35,000 |
| | | | | 400 | 52.50 | 21,000 | | | |
| | | | | 300 | 50.00 | 15,000 | | | |
| Nov. 26 | 2,000 | 56.00 | 112,000 | | | | 700 | 50.00 | 35,000 |
| | | | | | | | 2,000 | 56.00 | 112,000 |
| Dec. 31 | | | | 1,000 | 56.00 | 56,000 | 700 | 50.00 | 35,000 |
| | | | | | | | 1,000 | 56.00 | 56,000 |
| 31 | Balances | | | | | 178,000 | | | 91,000 |

c. Average cost method:

        Average cost per unit:        $269,000/5,000 units = $53.80

        Inventory, December 31, 2012:    1,700 units at $53.80 = $91,460

3. Appendix:

| | | |
|---|---|---|
| Merchandise inventory, January 1, 2012 ..................... | | $ 50,000 |
| Purchases (net).............................................. | | 219,000 |
| Merchandise available for sale............................... | | $269,000 |
| Sales (net)................................................. | $290,000 | |
| Less estimated gross profit ($290,000 × 40%) ................ | 116,000 | |
| Estimated cost of merchandise sold ......................... | | 174,000 |
| Estimated merchandise inventory, December 31, 2012........ | | $ 95,000 |

# Discussion Questions

1. Before inventory purchases are recorded, the receiving report should be reconciled to what documents?

2. Why is it important to periodically take a physical inventory when using a perpetual inventory system?

3. Do the terms *FIFO* and *LIFO* refer to techniques used in determining quantities of the various classes of merchandise on hand? Explain.

4. If merchandise inventory is being valued at cost and the price level is decreasing, which of the three methods of costing—FIFO, LIFO, or average cost—will yield (a) the highest inventory cost, (b) the lowest inventory cost, (c) the highest gross profit, and (d) the lowest gross profit?

5. Which of the three methods of inventory costing—FIFO, LIFO, or average cost—will in general yield an inventory cost most nearly approximating current replacement cost?

6. If inventory is being valued at cost and the price level is steadily rising, which of the three methods of costing—FIFO, LIFO, or average cost—will yield the lowest annual income tax expense? Explain.

7. Because of imperfections, an item of merchandise cannot be sold at its normal selling price. How should this item be valued for financial statement purposes?

8. The inventory at the end of the year was understated by $23,950. (a) Did the error cause an overstatement or an understatement of the gross profit for the year? (b) Which items on the balance sheet at the end of the year were overstated or understated as a result of the error?

9. X-mas Co. sold merchandise to Mistletoe Company on October 31, FOB shipping point. If the merchandise is in transit on October 31, the end of the fiscal year, which company would report it in its financial statements? Explain.

10. A manufacturer shipped merchandise to a retailer on a consignment basis. If the merchandise is unsold at the end of the period, in whose inventory should the merchandise be included?

# Practice Exercises

Learning
Objectives

Example
Exercises

OBJ. 2    EE 6-1  *p. 279*    **PE 6-1A   Cost flow methods**

Three identical units of Item K113 are purchased during July, as shown below.

|       |    | Item JC07 | Units | Cost |
|-------|----|-----------|-------|------|
| July  | 9  | Purchase  | 1     | $160 |
|       | 17 | Purchase  | 1     | 168  |
|       | 26 | Purchase  | 1     | 176  |
|       | Total |        | 3     | $504 |
|       | Average cost per unit | | | $168  ($504 ÷ 3 units) |

Assume that one unit is sold on July 31 for $225.

Determine the gross profit for July and ending inventory on July 31 using the
(a) first-in, first-out (FIFO); (b) last-in, first-out (LIFO); and (c) average cost methods.

OBJ. 2    EE 6-1  *p. 279*    **PE 6-1B   Cost flow methods**

Three identical units of Item ZE9 are purchased during April, as shown below.

|      |    | Item WH4 | Units | Cost |
|------|----|----------|-------|------|
| Apr. | 2  | Purchase | 1     | $10  |
|      | 12 | Purchase | 1     | 12   |
|      | 23 | Purchase | 1     | 14   |
|      | Total |       | 3     | $36  |
|      | Average cost per unit | | | $12  ($36 ÷ 3 units) |

Assume that one unit is sold on April 27 for $29.

Determine the gross profit for April and ending inventory on April 30 using the
(a) first-in, first-out (FIFO); (b) last-in, first-out (LIFO); and (c) average cost methods.

OBJ. 3    EE 6-2  *p. 281*    **PE 6-2A   Perpetual inventory using FIFO**

Beginning inventory, purchases, and sales for Item B901 are as follows:

|      |    |           |                  |
|------|----|-----------|------------------|
| Aug. | 1  | Inventory | 50 units at $80  |
|      | 9  | Sale      | 30 units         |
|      | 13 | Purchase  | 40 units at $85  |
|      | 28 | Sale      | 25 units         |

Assuming a perpetual inventory system and using the first-in, first-out (FIFO) method, determine (a) the cost of merchandise sold on August 28 and (b) the inventory on August 31.

OBJ. 3    EE 6-2  *p. 281*    **PE 6-2B   Perpetual inventory using FIFO**

Beginning inventory, purchases, and sales for Item CSW15 are as follows:

|      |    |           |                   |
|------|----|-----------|-------------------|
| Mar. | 1  | Inventory | 100 units at $15  |
|      | 7  | Sale      | 88 units          |
|      | 15 | Purchase  | 125 units at $18  |
|      | 24 | Sale      | 75 units          |

Assuming a perpetual inventory system and using the first-in, first-out (FIFO) method, determine (a) the cost of merchandise sold on March 24 and (b) the inventory on March 31.

| Learning Objectives | Example Exercises | |
|---|---|---|
| OBJ. 3 | EE 6-3  *p. 282* | **PE 6-3A    Perpetual inventory using LIFO** |

Beginning inventory, purchases, and sales for Item QED9 are as follows:

| | | | |
|---|---|---|---|
| Nov. | 1 | Inventory | 90 units at $50 |
| | 4 | Sale | 72 units |
| | 23 | Purchase | 100 units at $60 |
| | 26 | Sale | 84 units |

Assuming a perpetual inventory system and using the last-in, first-out (LIFO) method, determine (a) the cost of merchandise sold on November 26 and (b) the inventory on November 30.

| OBJ. 3 | EE 6-3  *p. 282* | **PE 6-3B    Perpetual inventory using LIFO** |
|---|---|---|

Beginning inventory, purchases, and sales for Item MMM8 are as follows:

| | | | |
|---|---|---|---|
| Jan. | 1 | Inventory | 90 units at $17 |
| | 8 | Sale | 75 units |
| | 15 | Purchase | 125 units at $18 |
| | 27 | Sale | 80 units |

Assuming a perpetual inventory system and using the last-in, first-out (LIFO) method, determine (a) the cost of merchandise sold on January 27 and (b) the inventory on January 31.

| OBJ. 4 | EE 6-4  *p. 286* | **PE 6-4A    Periodic inventory using FIFO, LIFO, average cost methods** |
|---|---|---|

The units of an item available for sale during the year were as follows:

| | | | | |
|---|---|---|---|---|
| Jan. | 1 | Inventory | 12 units at $45 | $ 540 |
| July | 7 | Purchase | 18 units at $50 | 900 |
| Nov. | 23 | Purchase | 15 units at $54 | 810 |
| | | Available for sale | 45 units | $2,250 |

There are 11 units of the item in the physical inventory at December 31. The periodic inventory system is used. Determine the inventory cost using (a) the first-in, first-out (FIFO) method; (b) the last-in, first-out (LIFO) method; and (c) the average cost method.

| OBJ. 4 | EE 6-4  *p. 286* | **PE 6-4B    Periodic inventory using FIFO, LIFO, average cost methods** |
|---|---|---|

The units of an item available for sale during the year were as follows:

| | | | | |
|---|---|---|---|---|
| Jan. | 1 | Inventory | 10 units at $120 | $ 1,200 |
| Apr. | 13 | Purchase | 130 units at $114 | 14,820 |
| Sept. | 30 | Purchase | 20 units at $119 | 2,380 |
| | | Available for sale | 160 units | $18,400 |

There are 23 units of the item in the physical inventory at December 31. The periodic inventory system is used. Determine the inventory cost using (a) the first-in, first-out (FIFO) method; (b) the last-in, first-out (LIFO) method; and (c) the average cost method.

| OBJ. 6 | EE 6-5  *p. 289* | **PE 6-5A    Lower-of-cost-or-market method** |
|---|---|---|

On the basis of the following data, determine the value of the inventory at the lower of cost or market. Apply lower of cost or market to each inventory item as shown in Exhibit 8.

| Item | Inventory Quantity | Unit Cost Price | Unit Market Price |
|---|---|---|---|
| IA17 | 200 | $40 | $38 |
| TX24 | 150 | 55 | 60 |

| OBJ. 6 | EE 6-5  *p. 289* | **PE 6-5B    Lower-of-cost-or-market method** |
|---|---|---|

On the basis of the following data, determine the value of the inventory at the lower of cost or market. Apply lower of cost or market to each inventory item as shown in Exhibit 8.

| Item | Inventory Quantity | Unit Cost Price | Unit Market Price |
|---|---|---|---|
| MT22 | 1,500 | $ 7 | $ 4 |
| WY09 | 900 | 22 | 25 |

| | |
|---|---|
| *Learning Objectives* | *Example Exercises* |

**OBJ. 6**   **EE 6-6** *p. 293*

### PE 6-6A   Effect of inventory errors

During the taking of its physical inventory on December 31, 2012, Kate's Interiors Company incorrectly counted its inventory as $83,175 instead of the correct amount of $90,700. Indicate the effect of the misstatement on Kate's Interiors' December 31, 2012, balance sheet and income statement for the year ended December 31, 2012.

**OBJ. 6**   **EE 6-6** *p. 294*

### PE 6-6B   Effect of inventory errors

During the taking of its physical inventory on December 31, 2012, Russian Bath Company incorrectly counted its inventory as $580,000 instead of the correct amount of $545,000. Indicate the effect of the misstatement on Russian Bath's December 31, 2012, balance sheet and income statement for the year ended December 31, 2012.

**OBJ. 7**   **EE 6-7** *p. 296*

### PE 6-7A   Inventory turnover and number of days' sales in inventory

The following financial statement data for years ending December 31 for Gillispie Company are shown below.

| | 2012 | 2011 |
|---|---|---|
| Cost of merchandise sold | $882,000 | $680,000 |
| Inventories: | | |
|    Beginning of year | $200,000 | $140,000 |
|    End of year | 290,000 | 200,000 |

a. Determine inventory turnover for 2012 and 2011.

b. Determine the number of days' sales in inventory for 2012 and 2011. Round to one decimal place.

c. Does the change in inventory turnover and the number of days' sales in inventory from 2011 to 2012 indicate a favorable or unfavorable trend?

**OBJ. 7**   **EE 6-7** *p. 296*

### PE 6-7B   Inventory turnover and number of days' sales in inventory

The following financial statement data for years ending December 31 for Pinnell Company are shown below.

| | 2012 | 2011 |
|---|---|---|
| Cost of merchandise sold | $1,800,000 | $1,428,000 |
| Inventories: | | |
|    Beginning of year | $570,000 | $450,000 |
|    End of year | 630,000 | 570,000 |

a. Determine inventory turnover for 2012 and 2011.

b. Determine the number of days' sales in inventory for 2012 and 2011. Round to one decimal place.

c. Does the change in inventory turnover and the number of days' sales in inventory from 2011 to 2012 indicate a favorable or unfavorable trend?

## Exercises

**OBJ. 1**

### EX 6-1   Control of inventories

A4A Hardware Store currently uses a periodic inventory system. Ray Ballard, the owner, is considering the purchase of a computer system that would make it feasible to switch to a perpetual inventory system.

Ray is unhappy with the periodic inventory system because it does not provide timely information on inventory levels. Ray has noticed on several occasions that the store runs out of good-selling items, while too many poor-selling items are on hand.

Ray is also concerned about lost sales while a physical inventory is being taken. A4A Hardware currently takes a physical inventory twice a year. To minimize distractions, the store is closed on the day inventory is taken. Ray believes that closing the store is the only way to get an accurate inventory count.

Will switching to a perpetual inventory system strengthen A4A Hardware's control over inventory items? Will switching to a perpetual inventory system eliminate the need for a physical inventory count? Explain.

---

**OBJ. 1**

### EX 6-2   Control of inventories

Lincoln Luggage Shop is a small retail establishment located in a large shopping mall. This shop has implemented the following procedures regarding inventory items:

a. Since the shop carries mostly high-quality, designer luggage, all inventory items are tagged with a control device that activates an alarm if a tagged item is removed from the store.

b. Since the display area of the store is limited, only a sample of each piece of luggage is kept on the selling floor. Whenever a customer selects a piece of luggage, the salesclerk gets the appropriate piece from the store's stockroom. Since all salesclerks need access to the stockroom, it is not locked. The stockroom is adjacent to the break room used by all mall employees.

c. Whenever Lincoln receives a shipment of new inventory, the items are taken directly to the stockroom. Lincoln's accountant uses the vendor's invoice to record the amount of inventory received.

State whether each of these procedures is appropriate or inappropriate. If it is inappropriate, state why.

---

**OBJ. 2, 3**

✔ Inventory balance, June 30, $5,070

### EX 6-3   Perpetual inventory using FIFO

Beginning inventory, purchases, and sales data for portable DVD players are as follows:

| June | 1 | Inventory | 75 units at $40 |
|---|---|---|---|
|  | 6 | Sale | 60 units |
|  | 14 | Purchase | 90 units at $42 |
|  | 19 | Sale | 50 units |
|  | 25 | Sale | 20 units |
|  | 30 | Purchase | 80 units at $45 |

The business maintains a perpetual inventory system, costing by the first-in, first-out method.

a. Determine the cost of the merchandise sold for each sale and the inventory balance after each sale, presenting the data in the form illustrated in Exhibit 3.

b. Based upon the preceding data, would you expect the inventory to be higher or lower using the last-in, first-out method?

---

**OBJ. 2, 3**

✔ Inventory balance, June 30, $5,040

### EX 6-4   Perpetual inventory using LIFO

Assume that the business in Exercise 6-3 maintains a perpetual inventory system, costing by the last-in, first-out method. Determine the cost of merchandise sold for each sale and the inventory balance after each sale, presenting the data in the form illustrated in Exhibit 4.

---

**OBJ. 2, 3**

✔ Inventory balance, July 31, $23,900

### EX 6-5   Perpetual inventory using LIFO

Beginning inventory, purchases, and sales data for prepaid cell phones for July are as follows:

| Inventory | | Purchases | | Sales | |
|---|---|---|---|---|---|
| July 1 | 800 units at $45 | July 10 | 500 units at $50 | July 12 | 700 units |
|  |  | 20 | 450 units at $52 | 14 | 300 units |
|  |  |  |  | 31 | 250 units |

a. Assuming that the perpetual inventory system is used, costing by the LIFO method, determine the cost of merchandise sold for each sale and the inventory balance after each sale, presenting the data in the form illustrated in Exhibit 4.

b. Based upon the preceding data, would you expect the inventory to be higher or lower using the first-in, first-out method?

OBJ. 2, 3
✔ Inventory balance, July 31, $25,900

### EX 6-6   Perpetual inventory using FIFO

Assume that the business in Exercise 6-5 maintains a perpetual inventory system, costing by the first-in, first-out method. Determine the cost of merchandise sold for each sale and the inventory balance after each sale, presenting the data in the form illustrated in Exhibit 3.

OBJ. 2, 3
✔ b. $15,100

### EX 6-7   FIFO, LIFO costs under perpetual inventory system

The following units of a particular item were available for sale during the year:

| | |
|---|---|
| Beginning inventory | 180 units at $80 |
| Sale | 120 units at $125 |
| First purchase | 400 units at $82 |
| Sale | 300 units at $125 |
| Second purchase | 300 units at $84 |
| Sale | 275 units at $125 |

The firm uses the perpetual inventory system, and there are 185 units of the item on hand at the end of the year. What is the total cost of the ending inventory according to (a) FIFO, (b) LIFO?

OBJ. 2, 4
✔ b. $6,138

### EX 6-8   Periodic inventory by three methods

The units of an item available for sale during the year were as follows:

| | | | |
|---|---|---|---|
| Jan. | 1 | Inventory | 9 units at $360 |
| Feb. | 17 | Purchase | 18 units at $414 |
| July | 21 | Purchase | 21 units at $468 |
| Nov. | 23 | Purchase | 12 units at $495 |

There are 16 units of the item in the physical inventory at December 31. The periodic inventory system is used. Determine the inventory cost by (a) the first-in, first-out method, (b) the last-in, first-out method, and (c) the average cost method.

OBJ. 2, 4
✔ a. Inventory, $4,986

### EX 6-9   Periodic inventory by three methods; cost of merchandise sold

The units of an item available for sale during the year were as follows:

| | | | |
|---|---|---|---|
| Jan. | 1 | Inventory | 21 units at $180 |
| Mar. | 10 | Purchase | 29 units at $195 |
| Aug. | 30 | Purchase | 10 units at $204 |
| Dec. | 12 | Purchase | 15 units at $210 |

There are 24 units of the item in the physical inventory at December 31. The periodic inventory system is used. Determine the inventory cost and the cost of merchandise sold by three methods, presenting your answers in the following form:

| | Cost | |
|---|---|---|
| Inventory Method | Merchandise Inventory | Merchandise Sold |
| a. First-in, first-out | $ | $ |
| b. Last-in, first-out | | |
| c. Average cost | | |

OBJ. 5

### EX 6-10   Comparing inventory methods

Assume that a firm separately determined inventory under FIFO and LIFO and then compared the results.

a. In each space below, place the correct sign [less than (<), greater than (>), or equal (=)] for each comparison, assuming periods of rising prices.

| | | |
|---|---|---|
| 1. FIFO inventory | _____ | LIFO inventory |
| 2. FIFO cost of goods sold | _____ | LIFO cost of goods sold |
| 3. FIFO net income | _____ | LIFO net income |
| 4. FIFO income tax | _____ | LIFO income tax |

b. Why would management prefer to use LIFO over FIFO in periods of rising prices?

### EX 6-11 Lower-of-cost-or-market inventory

On the basis of the following data, determine the value of the inventory at the lower of cost or market. Assemble the data in the form illustrated in Exhibit 8.

| Commodity | Inventory Quantity | Unit Cost Price | Unit Market Price |
|-----------|--------------------|-----------------|-------------------|
| AL65 | 40 | $28 | $30 |
| CA22 | 50 | 70 | 65 |
| LA98 | 110 | 6 | 5 |
| SC16 | 30 | 40 | 30 |
| UT28 | 75 | 60 | 62 |

OBJ. 6

### EX 6-12 Merchandise inventory on the balance sheet

Based on the data in Exercise 6-11 and assuming that cost was determined by the FIFO method, show how the merchandise inventory would appear on the balance sheet.

OBJ. 6

### EX 6-13 Effect of errors in physical inventory

Hydro White Water Co. sells canoes, kayaks, whitewater rafts, and other boating supplies. During the taking of its physical inventory on December 31, 2012, Hydro White Water incorrectly counted its inventory as $439,650 instead of the correct amount of $451,000.

a. State the effect of the error on the December 31, 2012, balance sheet of Hydro White Water.

b. State the effect of the error on the income statement of Hydro White Water for the year ended December 31, 2012.

c. If uncorrected, what would be the effect of the error on the 2013 income statement?

d. If uncorrected, what would be the effect of the error on the December 31, 2013, balance sheet?

OBJ. 6

### EX 6-14 Effect of errors in physical inventory

Eclipse Motorcycle Shop sells motorcycles, ATVs, and other related supplies and accessories. During the taking of its physical inventory on December 31, 2012, Eclipse Motorcycle Shop incorrectly counted its inventory as $350,000 instead of the correct amount of $338,000.

a. State the effect of the error on the December 31, 2012, balance sheet of Eclipse Motorcycle Shop.

b. State the effect of the error on the income statement of Eclipse Motorcycle Shop for the year ended December 31, 2012.

c. If uncorrected, what would be the effect of the error on the 2013 income statement?

d. If uncorrected, what would be the effect of the error on the December 31, 2013, balance sheet?

OBJ. 6

### EX 6-15 Error in inventory

During 2012, the accountant discovered that the physical inventory at the end of 2011 had been understated by $18,000. Instead of correcting the error, however, the accountant assumed that an $18,000 overstatement of the physical inventory in 2012 would balance out the error.

➤ Are there any flaws in the accountant's assumption? Explain.

OBJ. 7

### EX 6-16 Inventory turnover

The following data were taken from recent annual reports of Apple Inc., a manufacturer of personal computers and related products, and American Greetings Corporation, a manufacturer and distributor of greeting cards and related products:

|  | Apple | American Greetings |
|---|-------|---------------------|
| Cost of goods sold | $23,397,000,000 | $809,956,000 |
| Inventory, end of year | 455,000,000 | 203,873,000 |
| Inventory, beginning of the year | 509,000,000 | 216,671,000 |

a. Determine the inventory turnover for Apple and American Greetings. Round to one decimal place.

b. Would you expect American Greetings' inventory turnover to be higher or lower than Apple's? Why?

---

OBJ. 7

✔ a. Kroger, 30 days' sales in inventory

**EX 6-17    Inventory turnover and number of days' sales in inventory**

Kroger, Safeway Inc., and Winn-Dixie Stores Inc. are three grocery chains in the United States. Inventory management is an important aspect of the grocery retail business. Recent balance sheets for these three companies indicated the following merchandise inventory information:

|  | **Merchandise Inventory** | |
|---|---|---|
|  | **End of Year (in millions)** | **Beginning of Year (in millions)** |
| Kroger | $4,859 | $4,855 |
| Safeway | 2,591 | 2,798 |
| Winn-Dixie | 665 | 649 |

The cost of goods sold for each company were:

|  | **Cost of Goods Sold (in millions)** |
|---|---|
| Kroger | $58,564 |
| Safeway | 31,589 |
| Winn-Dixie | 5,269 |

a. Determine the number of days' sales in inventory and inventory turnover for the three companies. Round to the nearest day and one decimal place.

b. Interpret your results in part (a).

c. If Winn-Dixie had Kroger's number of days' sales in inventory, how much additional cash flow (round to nearest million) would have been generated from the smaller inventory relative to its actual average inventory position?

---

**Appendix**
**EX 6-18    Retail inventory method**

A business using the retail method of inventory costing determines that merchandise inventory at retail is $780,000. If the ratio of cost to retail price is 65%, what is the amount of inventory to be reported on the financial statements?

---

**Appendix**
**EX 6-19    Retail inventory method**

A business using the retail method of inventory costing determines that merchandise inventory at retail is $475,000. If the ratio of cost to retail price is 80%, what is the amount of inventory to be reported on the financial statements?

---

**Appendix**
**EX 6-20    Retail inventory method**

A business using the retail method of inventory costing determines that merchandise inventory at retail is $900,000. If the ratio of cost to retail price is 72%, what is the amount of inventory to be reported on the financial statements?

---

✔ Inventory, November 30: $337,500

**Appendix**
**EX 6-21    Retail inventory method**

On the basis of the following data, estimate the cost of the merchandise inventory at November 30 by the retail method:

|  |  | **Cost** | **Retail** |
|---|---|---|---|
| November 1 | Merchandise inventory | $ 300,000 | $ 400,000 |
| November 1–30 | Purchases (net) | 2,100,000 | 2,800,000 |
| November 1–30 | Sales (net) |  | 2,750,000 |

✔ a. Merchandise
destroyed: $620,000

**Appendix**
**EX 6-22 Gross profit inventory method**

The merchandise inventory was destroyed by fire on December 13. The following data were obtained from the accounting records:

| | | |
|---|---|---|
| Jan. 1 | Merchandise inventory | $ 500,000 |
| Jan. 1–Dec. 13 | Purchases (net) | 4,280,000 |
| | Sales (net) | 6,500,000 |
| | Estimated gross profit rate | 36% |

a. Estimate the cost of the merchandise destroyed.

b. Briefly describe the situations in which the gross profit method is useful.

**Appendix**
**EX 6-23 Gross profit method**

Based on the following data, estimate the cost of ending merchandise inventory:

| | |
|---|---|
| Sales (net) | $5,260,000 |
| Estimated gross profit rate | 40% |
| Beginning merchandise inventory | $ 180,000 |
| Purchases (net) | 3,200,000 |
| Merchandise available for sale | $3,380,000 |

**Appendix**
**EX 6-24 Gross profit method**

Based on the following data, estimate the cost of ending merchandise inventory:

| | |
|---|---|
| Sales (net) | $2,080,000 |
| Estimated gross profit rate | 37% |
| Beginning merchandise inventory | $ 75,000 |
| Purchases (net) | 1,325,000 |
| Merchandise available for sale | $1,400,000 |

# Problems Series A

OBJ. 2, 3
✔ 3. $28,725

**PR 6-1A FIFO perpetual inventory**

The beginning inventory at Keats Office Supplies and data on purchases and sales for a three-month period are as follows:

| Date | | Transaction | Number of Units | Per Unit | Total |
|---|---|---|---|---|---|
| Mar. | 1 | Inventory | 300 | $20 | $ 6,000 |
| | 10 | Purchase | 500 | 21 | 10,500 |
| | 28 | Sale | 400 | 35 | 14,000 |
| | 30 | Sale | 250 | 40 | 10,000 |
| Apr. | 5 | Sale | 80 | 40 | 3,200 |
| | 10 | Purchase | 450 | 22 | 9,900 |
| | 16 | Sale | 250 | 42 | 10,500 |
| | 28 | Sale | 150 | 45 | 6,750 |
| May | 5 | Purchase | 175 | 24 | 4,200 |
| | 14 | Sale | 160 | 50 | 8,000 |
| | 25 | Purchase | 150 | 25 | 3,750 |
| | 30 | Sale | 140 | 50 | 7,000 |

## Instructions

1. Record the inventory, purchases, and cost of merchandise sold data in a perpetual inventory record similar to the one illustrated in Exhibit 3, using the first-in, first-out method.

2. Determine the total sales and the total cost of merchandise sold for the period. Journalize the entries in the sales and cost of merchandise sold accounts. Assume that all sales were on account.

3. Determine the gross profit from sales for the period.

4. Determine the ending inventory cost.

5. Based upon the preceding data, would you expect the inventory using the last-in, first-out method to be higher or lower?

---

**OBJ. 2, 3**

✔ 2. Gross profit, $28,210

### PR 6-2A   LIFO perpetual inventory

The beginning inventory at Keats Office Supplies and data on purchases and sales for a three-month period are shown in Problem 6-1A.

### Instructions

1. Record the inventory, purchases, and cost of merchandise sold data in a perpetual inventory record similar to the one illustrated in Exhibit 4, using the last-in, first-out method.

2. Determine the total sales, the total cost of merchandise sold, and the gross profit from sales for the period.

3. Determine the ending inventory cost.

---

**OBJ. 2, 4**

✔ 1. $6,756

### PR 6-3A   Periodic inventory by three methods

Bulldog Appliances uses the periodic inventory system. Details regarding the inventory of appliances at September 1, 2011, purchases invoices during the next 12 months, and the inventory count at August 31, 2012, are summarized as follows:

| | | Purchases Invoices | | | |
|---|---|---|---|---|---|
| Model | Inventory, September 1 | 1st | 2nd | 3rd | Inventory Count, August 31 |
| AZ09 | — | 4 at $ 32 | 4 at $ 35 | 4 at $ 38 | 5 |
| GA85 | 8 at $ 88 | 4 at $ 79 | 3 at $ 85 | 6 at $ 92 | 7 |
| HI71 | 3 at 75 | 3 at 65 | 15 at 68 | 9 at 70 | 5 |
| KS32 | 7 at 242 | 6 at 250 | 5 at 260 | 10 at 259 | 9 |
| MS17 | 12 at 80 | 10 at 82 | 16 at 89 | 16 at 90 | 13 |
| ND52 | 2 at 108 | 2 at 110 | 3 at 128 | 3 at 130 | 5 |
| WV63 | 5 at 160 | 4 at 170 | 4 at 175 | 7 at 180 | 8 |

### Instructions

1. Determine the cost of the inventory on August 31, 2012, by the first-in, first-out method. Present data in columnar form, using the following headings:

| Model | Quantity | Unit Cost | Total Cost |
|---|---|---|---|

   If the inventory of a particular model comprises one entire purchase plus a portion of another purchase acquired at a different unit cost, use a separate line for each purchase.

2. Determine the cost of the inventory on August 31, 2012, by the last-in, first-out method, following the procedures indicated in (1).

3. Determine the cost of the inventory on August 31, 2012, by the average cost method, using the columnar headings indicated in (1).

4. ━━━━ Discuss which method (FIFO or LIFO) would be preferred for income tax purposes in periods of (a) rising prices and (b) declining prices.

OBJ. 6

✔ Total LCM, $44,621

### PR 6-4A Lower-of-cost-or-market inventory

*If the working papers correlating with this textbook are not used, omit Problem 6-4A.*

Data on the physical inventory of Rhino Company as of December 31, 2012, are presented in the working papers. The quantity of each commodity on hand has been determined and recorded on the inventory sheet. Unit market prices have also been determined as of December 31 and recorded on the sheet. The inventory is to be determined at cost and also at the lower of cost or market, using the first-in, first-out method. Quantity and cost data from the last purchases invoice of the year and the next-to-the-last purchases invoice are summarized as follows:

| Description | Last Purchases Invoice | | Next-to-the-Last Purchases Invoice | |
|---|---|---|---|---|
| | Quantity Purchased | Unit Cost | Quantity Purchased | Unit Cost |
| Alpha | 30 | $ 60 | 30 | $ 59 |
| Beta | 35 | 175 | 20 | 180 |
| Charlie | 20 | 130 | 25 | 129 |
| Echo | 130 | 24 | 100 | 25 |
| Frank | 10 | 565 | 10 | 560 |
| George | 100 | 15 | 100 | 14 |
| Killo | 10 | 385 | 5 | 384 |
| Quebec | 500 | 8 | 500 | 7 |
| Romeo | 80 | 22 | 50 | 21 |
| Sierra | 5 | 250 | 4 | 260 |
| Whiskey | 100 | 21 | 100 | 19 |
| X-Ray | 10 | 750 | 9 | 745 |

### Instructions

Record the appropriate unit costs on the inventory sheet, and complete the pricing of the inventory. When there are two different unit costs applicable to an item, proceed as follows:

1. Draw a line through the quantity, and insert the quantity and unit cost of the last purchase.

2. On the following line, insert the quantity and unit cost of the next-to-the-last purchase.

3. Total the cost and market columns and insert the lower of the two totals in the Lower of C or M column. The first item on the inventory sheet has been completed as an example.

✔ 1. $175,000

### Appendix
### PR 6-5A Retail method; gross profit method

Selected data on merchandise inventory, purchases, and sales for Myrina Co. and Lemnos Co. are as follows:

| | Cost | Retail |
|---|---|---|
| **Myrina Co.** | | |
| Merchandise inventory, May 1 | $ 130,000 | $ 185,000 |
| Transactions during May: | | |
| Purchases (net) | 1,382,000 | 1,975,000 |
| Sales | | 1,950,000 |
| Sales returns and allowances | | 40,000 |
| | | |
| **Lemnos Co.** | | |
| Merchandise inventory, July 1 | $ 280,000 | |
| Transactions during July through September: | | |
| Purchases (net) | 3,400,000 | |
| Sales | 5,300,000 | |
| Sales returns and allowances | 100,000 | |
| Estimated gross profit rate | 35% | |

## Instructions

1. Determine the estimated cost of the merchandise inventory of Myrina Co. on May 31 by the retail method, presenting details of the computations.

2. a. Estimate the cost of the merchandise inventory of Lemnos Co. on September 30 by the gross profit method, presenting details of the computations.

   b. Assume that Lemnos Co. took a physical inventory on September 30 and discovered that $269,750 of merchandise was on hand. What was the estimated loss of inventory due to theft or damage during July through September?

## Problems Series B

OBJ. 2, 3

✔ 3. $642,500

### PR 6-1B  FIFO perpetual inventory

The beginning inventory of merchandise at Francesca Co. and data on purchases and sales for a three-month period are as follows:

| Date | | Transaction | Number of Units | Per Unit | Total |
|---|---|---|---|---|---|
| July | 3 | Inventory | 75 | $1,500 | $112,500 |
| | 8 | Purchase | 150 | 1,800 | 270,000 |
| | 11 | Sale | 90 | 3,000 | 270,000 |
| | 30 | Sale | 45 | 3,000 | 135,000 |
| Aug. | 8 | Purchase | 125 | 2,000 | 250,000 |
| | 10 | Sale | 110 | 3,000 | 330,000 |
| | 19 | Sale | 80 | 3,000 | 240,000 |
| | 28 | Purchase | 100 | 2,200 | 220,000 |
| Sept. | 5 | Sale | 60 | 3,500 | 210,000 |
| | 16 | Sale | 50 | 3,500 | 175,000 |
| | 21 | Purchase | 180 | 2,400 | 432,000 |
| | 28 | Sale | 90 | 3,500 | 315,000 |

## Instructions

1. Record the inventory, purchases, and cost of merchandise sold data in a perpetual inventory record similar to the one illustrated in Exhibit 3, using the first-in, first-out method.

2. Determine the total sales and the total cost of merchandise sold for the period. Journalize the entries in the sales and cost of merchandise sold accounts. Assume that all sales were on account.

3. Determine the gross profit from sales for the period.

4. Determine the ending inventory cost.

5. Based upon the preceding data, would you expect the inventory using the last-in, first-out method to be higher or lower?

OBJ. 2, 3

✔ 2. Gross profit, $629,000

### PR 6-2B  LIFO perpetual inventory

The beginning inventory for Francesca Co and data on purchases and sales for a three-month period are shown in Problem 6-1B.

## Instructions

1. Record the inventory, purchases, and cost of merchandise sold data in a perpetual inventory record similar to the one illustrated in Exhibit 4, using the last-in, first-out method.

2. Determine the total sales, the total cost of merchandise sold, and the gross profit from sales for the period.

3. Determine the ending inventory cost.

## PR 6-3B  Periodic inventory by three methods

Artic Appliances uses the periodic inventory system. Details regarding the inventory of appliances at January 1, 2012, purchases invoices during the year, and the inventory count at December 31, 2012, are summarized as follows:

| Model | Inventory, January 1 | Purchases Invoices | | | Inventory Count, December 31 |
|---|---|---|---|---|---|
| | | 1st | 2nd | 3rd | |
| AK82 | 3 at $520 | 3 at $527 | 3 at $530 | 3 at $535 | 5 |
| CO62 | 9 at 213 | 7 at 215 | 6 at 222 | 6 at 225 | 12 |
| DE03 | 5 at 60 | 3 at 65 | 1 at 65 | 1 at 70 | 2 |
| FL12 | 6 at 305 | 3 at 310 | 3 at 316 | 4 at 317 | 4 |
| ME09 | 6 at 520 | 8 at 531 | 4 at 549 | 6 at 542 | 7 |
| NM57 | — | 4 at 222 | 4 at 232 | — | 2 |
| TN33 | 4 at 35 | 6 at 36 | 8 at 37 | 7 at 39 | 5 |

### Instructions

1. Determine the cost of the inventory on December 31, 2012, by the first-in, first-out method. Present data in columnar form, using the following headings:

| Model | Quantity | Unit Cost | Total Cost |
|---|---|---|---|

 If the inventory of a particular model comprises one entire purchase plus a portion of another purchase acquired at a different unit cost, use a separate line for each purchase.

2. Determine the cost of the inventory on December 31, 2012, by the last-in, first-out method, following the procedures indicated in (1).

3. Determine the cost of the inventory on December 31, 2012, by the average cost method, using the columnar headings indicated in (1).

4. ▬▬▬➤ Discuss which method (FIFO or LIFO) would be preferred for income tax purposes in periods of (a) rising prices and (b) declining prices.

## PR 6-4B  Lower-of-cost-or-market inventory

*If the working papers correlating with this textbook are not used, omit Problem 6-4B.*

Data on the physical inventory of Chiron Co. as of December 31, 2012, are presented in the working papers. The quantity of each commodity on hand has been determined and recorded on the inventory sheet. Unit market prices have also been determined as of December 31 and recorded on the sheet. The inventory is to be determined at cost and also at the lower of cost or market, using the first-in, first-out method. Quantity and cost data from the last purchases invoice of the year and the next-to-the-last purchases invoice are summarized as follows:

| Description | Last Purchases Invoice | | Next-to-the-Last Purchases Invoice | |
|---|---|---|---|---|
| | Quantity Purchased | Unit Cost | Quantity Purchased | Unit Cost |
| Alpha | 30 | $ 60 | 40 | $ 59 |
| Beta | 25 | 170 | 15 | 180 |
| Charlie | 20 | 130 | 15 | 128 |
| Echo | 150 | 25 | 100 | 27 |
| Frank | 6 | 550 | 15 | 540 |
| George | 90 | 16 | 100 | 15 |
| Killo | 8 | 395 | 4 | 394 |
| Quebec | 500 | 6 | 500 | 7 |
| Romeo | 75 | 25 | 80 | 26 |
| Sierra | 5 | 250 | 4 | 260 |
| Whiskey | 100 | 17 | 115 | 16 |
| X-Ray | 10 | 750 | 8 | 740 |

**Instructions**

Record the appropriate unit costs on the inventory sheet, and complete the pricing of the inventory. When there are two different unit costs applicable to an item:

1. Draw a line through the quantity, and insert the quantity and unit cost of the last purchase.

2. On the following line, insert the quantity and unit cost of the next-to-the-last purchase.

3. Total the cost and market columns and insert the lower of the two totals in the Lower of C or M column. The first item on the inventory sheet has been completed as an example.

✔ 1. $409,500

**Appendix**
**PR 6-5B    Retail method; gross profit method**

Selected data on merchandise inventory, purchases, and sales for Segal Co. and Iroquois Co. are as follows:

|  | Cost | Retail |
|---|---|---|
| **Segal Co.** | | |
| Merchandise inventory, March 1 | $  298,000 | $  375,000 |
| Transactions during March: | | |
|    Purchases (net) | 4,850,000 | 6,225,000 |
|    Sales | | 6,320,000 |
|    Sales returns and allowances | | 245,000 |
| | | |
| **Iroquois Co.** | | |
| Merchandise inventory, January 1 | $  300,000 | |
| Transactions during January thru March: | | |
|    Purchases (net) | 4,150,000 | |
|    Sales | 6,900,000 | |
|    Sales returns and allowances | 175,000 | |
| Estimated gross profit rate | 40% | |

**Instructions**

1. Determine the estimated cost of the merchandise inventory of Segal Co. on March 31 by the retail method, presenting details of the computations.

2. a. Estimate the cost of the merchandise inventory of Iroquois Co. on March 31 by the gross profit method, presenting details of the computations.

    b. Assume that Iroquois Co. took a physical inventory on March 31 and discovered that $396,500 of merchandise was on hand. What was the estimated loss of inventory due to theft or damage during January thru March?

## Cases & Projects

You can access the Cases & Projects online at **www.cengage.com/accounting/reeve**

## Excel Success Special Activities

### SA 6-1 Lower of cost or market

All-Tech, Inc., has five inventory items with the following quantities, unit costs, and unit market values:

|  | A | B | C | D |
|---|---|---|---|---|
| 1 |  |  | Unit | Unit |
| 2 |  | Inventory | Cost | Market |
| 3 | Item | Quantity | Price | Price |
| 4 | A | 250 | $ 4.50 | $ 4.20 |
| 5 | B | 340 | 9.20 | 8.90 |
| 6 | C | 90 | 12.90 | 13.50 |
| 7 | D | 125 | 18.90 | 21.80 |
| 8 | E | 440 | 11.30 | 11.40 |
| 9 | Total |  |  |  |
| 10 |  |  |  |  |

a. Open the Excel file *SA6-1_1e*.

b. Complete the spreadsheet by determining the lower of cost or market valuation for inventory.

c. When you have completed the inventory table, perform a "save as," replacing the entire file name with the following:

*SA6-1_1e[your first name initial]_[your last name]*

### SA 6-2 Lower of cost or market

New Way Industries, Inc., has the following inventory items and quantities:

| Item | Inventory Item |
|---|---|
| DJ-12 | 15 |
| KB-10 | 32 |
| MM-1 | 65 |
| PD-16 | 50 |
| QR-5 | 120 |

The unit cost and market value information for the inventory items is as follows:

|  | DJ-12 | KB-10 | MM-1 | PD-16 | QR-5 |
|---|---|---|---|---|---|
| Unit cost price | $145 | $225 | $90 | $235 | $32 |
| Unit market price | 150 | 208 | 94 | 244 | 30 |

a. Open the Excel file *SA6-2_1e*.

b. Complete the spreadsheet to determine the lower of cost or market valuation for inventory, as illustrated in the Excel Success example.

c. When you have completed the inventory table, perform a "save as," replacing the entire file name with the following:

*SA6-2_1e[your first name initial]_[your last name]*

© Kemie Guaida/iStockphoto.com

# Sarbanes-Oxley, Internal Control, and Cash

## eBay Inc.

**C**ontrols are a part of your everyday life. At one extreme, laws are used to limit your behavior. For example, speed limits are designed to control your driving for traffic safety. In addition, you are also affected by many nonlegal controls. For example, you can keep credit card receipts in order to compare your transactions to the monthly credit card statement. Comparing receipts to the monthly statement is a control designed to catch mistakes made by the credit card company. In addition, banks give you a personal identification number (PIN) as a control against unauthorized access to your cash if you lose your automated teller machine (ATM) card. Dairies use freshness dating on their milk containers as a control to prevent the purchase or sale of soured milk. As you can see, you use and encounter controls every day.

Just as there are many examples of controls throughout society, businesses must also implement controls to help guide the behavior of their managers, employees, and customers. For example, **eBay Inc.** maintains an Internet-based marketplace for the sale of goods and services. Using eBay's online platform, buyers and sellers can browse, buy, and sell a wide variety of items including antiques and used cars. However, in order to maintain the integrity and trust of its buyers and sellers, eBay must have controls to ensure that buyers pay for their items and sellers don't misrepresent their items or fail to deliver sales. One such control eBay uses is a feedback forum that establishes buyer and seller reputations. A prospective buyer or seller can view the member's reputation and feedback comments before completing a transaction. Dishonest or unfair trading can lead to a negative reputation and even suspension or cancellation of the member's ability to trade on eBay.

This chapter discusses controls that can be included in accounting systems to provide reasonable assurance that the financial statements are reliable. Controls to discover and prevent errors to a bank account are also discussed. This chapter begins by discussing the Sarbanes-Oxley Act of 2002 and its impact on controls and financial reporting.

**OBJ. 1** Describe the Sarbanes-Oxley Act of 2002 and its impact on internal controls and financial reporting.

# Sarbanes-Oxley Act of 2002

During the financial scandals of the early 2000s, stockholders, creditors, and other investors lost billions of dollars.[1] As a result, the U.S. Congress passed the **Sarbanes-Oxley Act of 2002**. This act, often referred to as *Sarbanes-Oxley*, is one of the most important laws affecting U.S. companies in recent history. The purpose of Sarbanes-Oxley is to restore public confidence and trust in the financial reporting of companies.

Sarbanes-Oxley applies only to companies whose stock is traded on public exchanges, referred to as *publicly held companies*. However, Sarbanes-Oxley highlighted the importance of assessing the financial controls and reporting of all companies. As a result, companies of all sizes have been influenced by Sarbanes-Oxley.

Sarbanes-Oxley emphasizes the importance of effective internal control.[2] **Internal control** is defined as the procedures and processes used by a company to:

1. Safeguard its assets.
2. Process information accurately.
3. Ensure compliance with laws and regulations.

Sarbanes-Oxley requires companies to maintain effective internal controls over the recording of transactions and the preparing of financial statements. Such controls are important because they deter fraud and prevent misleading financial statements as shown on the next page.

1 Exhibit 2 in Chapter 1 briefly summarizes these scandals.

2 Sarbanes-Oxley also has important implications for corporate governance and the regulation of the public accounting profession. This chapter, however, focuses on the internal control implications of Sarbanes-Oxley.

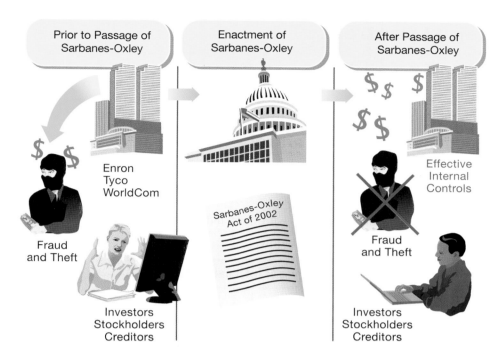

Sarbanes-Oxley also requires companies and their independent accountants to report on the effectiveness of the company's internal controls.[3] These reports are required to be filed with the company's annual 10-K report with the Securities and Exchange Commission. Companies are also encouraged to include these reports in their annual reports to stockholders. An example of such a report by the management of Nike is shown in Exhibit 1.

---

**Management's Annual Report on Internal Control Over Financial Reporting**

Management is responsible for establishing and maintaining adequate internal control over financial reporting . . . , Under the supervision and with the participation of our Chief Executive Officer and Chief Financial Officer, our management conducted an evaluation of the effectiveness of our internal control over financial reporting based upon the framework in *Internal Control—Integrated Framework* issued by the Committee of Sponsoring Organizations of the Treadway Commission. Based on that evaluation, our management concluded that our internal control over financial reporting is effective as of May 31, 2009. . . .

PricewaterhouseCoopers LLP, an independent registered public accounting firm, has audited . . . management's assessment of the effectiveness of our internal control over financial reporting . . . and . . . the effectiveness of our internal control over financial reporting . . . as stated in their report. . . .

MARK G. PARKER                                                 DONALD W. BLAIR
Chief Executive Officer and President                          Chief Financial Officer

**EXHIBIT 1**

**Sarbanes-Oxley Report of Nike**

Exhibit 1 indicates that Nike based its evaluation of internal controls on *Internal Control—Integrated Framework*, which was issued by the Committee of Sponsoring Organizations (COSO) of the Treadway Commission. This framework is the standard by which companies design, analyze, and evaluate internal controls. For this reason, this framework is used as the basis for discussing internal controls.

Information on *Internal Control—Integrated Framework* can be found on COSO's Web site at **http://www.coso.org/.**

3 These reporting requirements are required under Section 404 of the act. As a result, these requirements and reports are often referred to as 404 requirements and 404 reports.

**OBJ. 2** Describe and illustrate the objectives and elements of internal control.

# Internal Control

*Internal Control—Integrated Framework* is the standard by which companies design, analyze, and evaluate internal control.[4] In this section, the objectives of internal control are described, followed by a discussion of how these objectives can be achieved through the *Integrated Framework's* five elements of internal control.

## Objectives of Internal Control

The objectives of internal control are to provide reasonable assurance that:

1. Assets are safeguarded and used for business purposes.
2. Business information is accurate.
3. Employees and managers comply with laws and regulations.

These objectives are illustrated below.

Safeguarded Assets          Accurate Information          Compliance with Laws and Regulations

Internal control can safeguard assets by preventing theft, fraud, misuse, or misplacement. A serious concern of internal control is preventing employee fraud. **Employee fraud** is the intentional act of deceiving an employer for personal gain. Such fraud may range from minor overstating of a travel expense report to stealing millions of dollars. Employees stealing from a business often adjust the accounting records in order to hide their fraud. Thus, employee fraud usually affects the accuracy of business information.

Accurate information is necessary to successfully operate a business. Businesses must also comply with laws, regulations, and financial reporting standards. Examples of such standards include environmental regulations, safety regulations, and generally accepted accounting principles (GAAP).

# BusinessConnection

## EMPLOYEE FRAUD

The Association of Fraud Examiners estimates that 7% of annual revenues or about $994 billion is lost to employee fraud in the United States. The most common cash receipts employee fraud is where employees accept cash payments from customers, do not record the sale, and then pocket the cash. A common cash payments employee fraud is where employees bill their employer for false services or personal items.

Source: 2008 *Report to the Nation on Occupational Fraud and Abuse*, Association of Fraud Examiners.

## Elements of Internal Control

The three internal control objectives can be achieved by applying the five **elements of internal control** set forth by the *Integrated Framework*.[5] These elements are as follows:

1. Control environment
2. Risk assessment

4 *Internal Control—Integrated Framework* by the Committee of Sponsoring Organizations of the Treadway Commission, 1992.

5 Ibid., pp. 12–14.

3. Control procedures
4. Monitoring
5. Information and communication

The elements of internal control are illustrated in Exhibit 2.

**EXHIBIT 2**

**Elements of Internal Control**

In Exhibit 2, the elements of internal control form an umbrella over the business to protect it from control threats. The control environment is the size of the umbrella. Risk assessment, control procedures, and monitoring are the fabric of the umbrella, which keep it from leaking. Information and communication connect the umbrella to management.

## Control Environment

The **control environment** is the overall attitude of management and employees about the importance of controls. Three factors influencing a company's control environment are as follows:

1. Management's philosophy and operating style
2. The company's organizational structure
3. The company's personnel policies

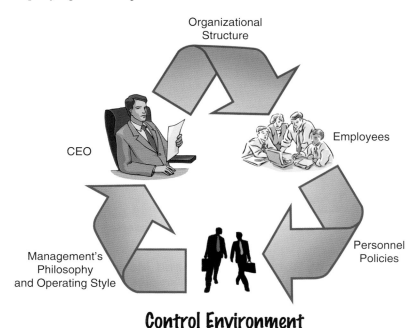

Management's philosophy and operating style relates to whether management emphasizes the importance of internal controls. An emphasis on controls and adherence to control policies creates an effective control environment. In contrast, overemphasizing operating goals and tolerating deviations from control policies creates an ineffective control environment.

The business's organizational structure is the framework for planning and controlling operations. For example, a retail store chain might organize each of its stores as separate business units. Each store manager has full authority over pricing and other operating activities. In such a structure, each store manager has the responsibility for establishing an effective control environment.

The business's personnel policies involve the hiring, training, evaluation, compensation, and promotion of employees. In addition, job descriptions, employee codes of ethics, and conflict-of-interest policies are part of the personnel policies. Such policies can enhance the internal control environment if they provide reasonable assurance that only competent, honest employees are hired and retained.

## Risk Assessment

All businesses face risks such as changes in customer requirements, competitive threats, regulatory changes, and changes in economic factors. Management should identify such risks, analyze their significance, assess their likelihood of occurring, and take any necessary actions to minimize them.

## Control Procedures

Control procedures provide reasonable assurance that business goals will be achieved, including the prevention of fraud. Control procedures, which constitute one of the most important elements of internal control, include the following as shown in Exhibit 3.

1. Competent personnel, rotating duties, and mandatory vacations
2. Separating responsibilities for related operations
3. Separating operations, custody of assets, and accounting
4. Proofs and security measures

**EXHIBIT 3**

**Internal Control Procedures**

**Control Threats**

**Control Procedures**
Competent personnel, rotating duties, and mandatory vacations
Separating responsibilities for related operations
Separating operations, custody of assets, and accounting
Proofs and security measures

Management

Business

**Competent Personnel, Rotating Duties, and Mandatory Vacations** A successful company needs competent employees who are able to perform the duties that they are assigned. Procedures should be established for properly training and supervising employees. It is also advisable to rotate duties of accounting personnel and mandate vacations for all employees. In this way, employees are encouraged to adhere to procedures. Cases of employee fraud are often discovered when a long-term employee, who never took vacations, missed work because of an illness or another unavoidable reason.

### Separating Responsibilities for Related Operations

The responsibility for related operations should be divided among two or more persons. This decreases the possibility of errors and fraud. For example, if the same person orders supplies, verifies the receipt of the supplies, and pays the supplier, the following abuses may occur:

1. Orders may be placed on the basis of friendship with a supplier, rather than on price, quality, and other objective factors.
2. The quantity and quality of supplies received may not be verified; thus, the company may pay for supplies not received or that are of poor quality.
3. Supplies may be stolen by the employee.
4. The validity and accuracy of invoices may not be verified; hence, the company may pay false or inaccurate invoices.

For the preceding reasons, the responsibilities for purchasing, receiving, and paying for supplies should be divided among three persons or departments.

### Separating Operations, Custody of Assets, and Accounting

The responsibilities for operations, custody of assets, and accounting should be separated. In this way, the accounting records serve as an independent check on the operating managers and the employees who have custody of assets.

To illustrate, employees who handle cash receipts should not record cash receipts in the accounting records. To do so would allow employees to borrow or steal cash and hide the theft in the accounting records. Likewise, operating managers should not also record the results of operations. To do so would allow the managers to distort the accounting reports to show favorable results, which might allow them to receive larger bonuses.

### Proofs and Security Measures

Proofs and security measures are used to safeguard assets and ensure reliable accounting data. Proofs involve procedures such as authorization, approval, and reconciliation. For example, an employee planning to travel on company business may be required to complete a "travel request" form for a manager's authorization and approval.

Documents used for authorization and approval should be prenumbered, accounted for, and safeguarded. Prenumbering of documents helps prevent transactions from being recorded more than once or not at all. In addition, accounting for and

## Integrity, Objectivity, and Ethics in Business

**TIPS ON PREVENTING EMPLOYEE FRAUD IN SMALL COMPANIES**

- Do not have the same employee write company checks and keep the books. Look for payments to vendors you don't know or payments to vendors whose names appear to be misspelled.
- If your business has a computer system, restrict access to accounting files as much as possible. Also, keep a backup copy of your accounting files and store it at an off-site location.
- Be wary of anybody working in finance that declines to take vacations. They may be afraid that a replacement will uncover fraud.
- Require and monitor supporting documentation (such as vendor invoices) before signing checks.

- Track the number of credit card bills you sign monthly.
- Limit and monitor access to important documents and supplies, such as blank checks and signature stamps.
- Check W-2 forms against your payroll annually to make sure you're not carrying any fictitious employees.
- Rely on yourself, not on your accountant, to spot fraud.

Source: Steve Kaufman, "Embezzlement Common at Small Companies," Knight-Ridder Newspapers, reported in *Athens Daily News/Athens Banner-Herald,* March 10, 1996, p. 4D.

safeguarding prenumbered documents helps prevent fraudulent transactions from being recorded. For example, blank checks are prenumbered and safeguarded. Once a payment has been properly authorized and approved, the checks are filled out and issued.

Reconciliations are also an important control. Later in this chapter, the use of bank reconciliations as an aid in controlling cash is described and illustrated.

Security measures involve measures to safeguard assets. For example, cash on hand should be kept in a cash register or safe. Inventory not on display should be stored in a locked storeroom or warehouse. Accounting records such as the accounts receivable subsidiary ledger should also be safeguarded to prevent their loss. For example, electronically maintained accounting records should be safeguarded with access codes and backed up so that any lost or damaged files could be recovered if necessary.

## Monitoring

Monitoring the internal control system is used to locate weaknesses and improve controls. Monitoring often includes observing employee behavior and the accounting system for indicators of control problems. Some such indicators are shown in Exhibit 4.[6]

**EXHIBIT 4**

**Warning Signs of Internal Control Problems**

**Warning signs with regard to people**

1. Abrupt change in lifestyle (without winning the lottery).
2. Close social relationships with suppliers.
3. Refusing to take a vacation.
4. Frequent borrowing from other employees.
5. Excessive use of alcohol or drugs.

**Warning signs from the accounting system**

1. Missing documents or gaps in transaction numbers (could mean documents are being used for fraudulent transactions).
2. An unusual increase in customer refunds (refunds may be phony).
3. Differences between daily cash receipts and bank deposits (could mean receipts are being pocketed before being deposited).
4. Sudden increase in slow payments (employee may be pocketing the payments).
5. Backlog in recording transactions (possibly an attempt to delay detection of fraud).

Evaluations of controls are often performed when there are major changes in strategy, senior management, business structure, or operations. Internal auditors, who are independent of operations, usually perform such evaluations. Internal auditors are also responsible for day-to-day monitoring of controls. External auditors also evaluate and report on internal control as part of their annual financial statement audit.

## Information and Communication

Information and communication is an essential element of internal control. Information about the control environment, risk assessment, control procedures, and monitoring is used by management for guiding operations and ensuring compliance with reporting, legal, and regulatory requirements. Management also uses external information to assess events and conditions that impact decision making and external

6 Edwin C. Bliss, "Employee Theft," *Boardroom Reports,* July 15, 1994, pp. 5–6.

reporting. For example, management uses pronouncements of the Financial Accounting Standards Board (FASB) to assess the impact of changes in reporting standards on the financial statements.

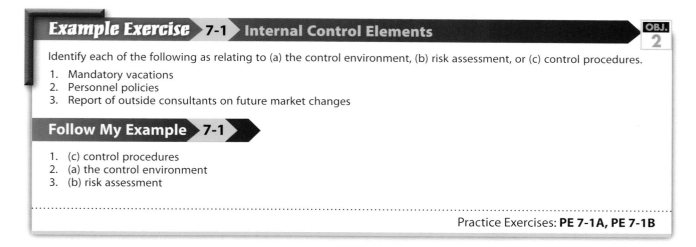

**Example Exercise** **7-1** **Internal Control Elements**

OBJ. **2**

Identify each of the following as relating to (a) the control environment, (b) risk assessment, or (c) control procedures.

1. Mandatory vacations
2. Personnel policies
3. Report of outside consultants on future market changes

**Follow My Example** **7-1**

1. (c) control procedures
2. (a) the control environment
3. (b) risk assessment

Practice Exercises: **PE 7-1A, PE 7-1B**

## Limitations of Internal Control

Internal control systems can provide only reasonable assurance for safeguarding assets, processing accurate information, and compliance with laws and regulations. In other words, internal controls are not a guarantee. This is due to the following factors:

1. The human element of controls
2. Cost-benefit considerations

The *human element* recognizes that controls are applied and used by humans. As a result, human errors can occur because of fatigue, carelessness, confusion, or misjudgment. For example, an employee may unintentionally shortchange a customer or miscount the amount of inventory received from a supplier. In addition, two or more employees may collude together to defeat or circumvent internal controls. This latter case often involves fraud and the theft of assets. For example, the cashier and the accounts receivable clerk might collude to steal customer payments on account.

*Cost-benefit considerations* recognize that cost of internal controls should not exceed their benefits. For example, retail stores could eliminate shoplifting by searching all customers before they leave the store. However, such a control procedure would upset customers and result in lost sales. Instead, retailers use cameras or signs saying *We prosecute all shoplifters.*

## Cash Controls Over Receipts and Payments

OBJ. **3** Describe and illustrate the application of internal controls to cash.

**Cash** includes coins, currency (paper money), checks, and money orders. Money on deposit with a bank or other financial institution that is available for withdrawal is also considered cash. Normally, you can think of cash as anything that a bank would accept for deposit in your account. For example, a check made payable to you could normally be deposited in a bank and, thus, is considered cash.

Businesses usually have several bank accounts. For example, a business might have one bank account for general cash payments and another for payroll. A separate ledger account is normally used for each bank account. For example, a bank account at City Bank could be identified in the ledger as *Cash in Bank—City Bank.* To simplify, this chapter assumes that a company has only *one* bank account, which is identified in the ledger as *Cash.*

Cash is the asset most likely to be stolen or used improperly in a business. For this reason, businesses must carefully control cash and cash transactions.

# Control of Cash Receipts

To protect cash from theft and misuse, a business must control cash from the time it is received until it is deposited in a bank. Businesses normally receive cash from two main sources.

1. Customers purchasing products or services
2. Customers making payments on account

**Cash Received from Cash Sales** An important control to protect cash received in over-the-counter sales is a cash register. The use of a cash register to control cash is shown below.

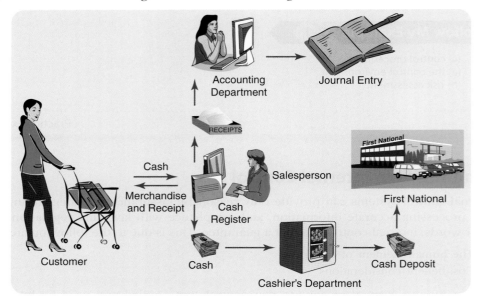

A cash register controls cash as follows:

1. At the beginning of every work shift, each cash register clerk is given a cash drawer containing a predetermined amount of cash. This amount is used for making change for customers and is sometimes called a *change fund*.
2. When a salesperson enters the amount of a sale, the cash register displays the amount to the customer. This allows the customer to verify that the clerk has charged the correct amount. The customer also receives a cash receipt.
3. At the end of the shift, the clerk and the supervisor count the cash in the clerk's cash drawer. The amount of cash in each drawer should equal the beginning amount of cash plus the cash sales for the day.
4. The supervisor takes the cash to the Cashier's Department where it is placed in a safe.
5. The supervisor forwards the clerk's cash register receipts to the Accounting Department.
6. The cashier prepares a bank deposit ticket.
7. The cashier deposits the cash in the bank, or the cash is picked up by an armored car service, such as Wells Fargo.
8. The Accounting Department summarizes the cash receipts and records the day's cash sales.
9. When cash is deposited in the bank, the bank normally stamps a duplicate copy of the deposit ticket with the amount received. This bank receipt is returned to the Accounting Department, where it is compared to the total amount that should have been deposited. This control helps ensure that all the cash is deposited and that no cash is lost or stolen on the way to the bank. Any shortages are thus promptly detected.

Salespersons may make errors in making change for customers or in ringing up cash sales. As a result, the amount of cash on hand may differ from the amount of cash sales. Such differences are recorded in a **cash short and over account**.

To illustrate, assume the following cash register data for May 3:

| | |
|---|---|
| Cash register total for cash sales | $35,690 |
| Cash receipts from cash sales | 35,668 |

The cash sales, receipts, and shortage of $22 ($35,690 – $35,668) would be recorded as follows:

| | | | | |
|---|---|---|---|---|
| May | 3 | Cash | 35,668 | |
| | | Cash Short and Over | 22 | |
| | | Sales | | 35,690 |

If there had been cash over, Cash Short and Over would have been credited for the overage. At the end of the accounting period, a debit balance in Cash Short and Over is included in miscellaneous expense on the income statement. A credit balance is included in the Other Income section. If a salesperson consistently has large cash short and over amounts, the supervisor may require the clerk to take additional training.

**Cash Received in the Mail** Cash is received in the mail when customers pay their bills. This cash is usually in the form of checks and money orders. Most companies design their invoices so that customers return a portion of the invoice, called a *remittance advice*, with their payment. Remittance advices may be used to control cash received in the mail as follows:

1. An employee opens the incoming mail and compares the amount of cash received with the amount shown on the remittance advice. If a customer does not return a remittance advice, the employee prepares one. The remittance advice serves as a record of the cash initially received. It also helps ensure that the posting to the customer's account is for the amount of cash received.
2. The employee opening the mail stamps checks and money orders "For Deposit Only" in the bank account of the business.
3. The remittance advices and their summary totals are delivered to the Accounting Department.
4. All cash and money orders are delivered to the Cashier's Department.
5. The cashier prepares a bank deposit ticket.
6. The cashier deposits the cash in the bank, or the cash is picked up by an armored car service, such as Wells Fargo.
7. An accounting clerk records the cash received and posts the amounts to the customer accounts.
8. When cash is deposited in the bank, the bank normally stamps a duplicate copy of the deposit ticket with the amount received. This bank receipt is returned to the Accounting Department, where it is compared to the total amount that should have been deposited. This control helps ensure that all cash is deposited and that no cash is lost or stolen on the way to the bank. Any shortages are thus promptly detected.

Separating the duties of the Cashier's Department, which handles cash, and the Accounting Department, which records cash, is a control. If Accounting Department employees both handle and record cash, an employee could steal cash and change the accounting records to hide the theft.

**Cash Received by EFT** Cash may also be received from customers through **electronic funds transfer (EFT)**. For example, customers may authorize automatic electronic transfers from their checking accounts to pay monthly bills for such items as cell phone, Internet, and electric services. In such cases, the company sends the customer's bank a signed form from the customer authorizing the monthly electronic transfers. Each month, the company notifies the customer's bank of the amount of the transfer and the date the transfer should take place. On the due date, the company records the electronic transfer as a receipt of cash to its bank account and posts the amount paid to the customer's account.

Companies encourage customers to use EFT for the following reasons:

1. EFTs cost less than receiving cash payments through the mail.
2. EFTs enhance internal controls over cash since the cash is received directly by the bank without any employees handling cash.
3. EFTs reduce late payments from customers and speed up the processing of cash receipts.

## Control of Cash Payments

The control of cash payments should provide reasonable assurance that:

1. Payments are made for only authorized transactions.
2. Cash is used effectively and efficiently. For example, controls should ensure that all available purchase discounts are taken.

Howard Schultz & Associates (HS&A) specializes in reviewing cash payments for its clients. HS&A searches for errors, such as duplicate payments, failures to take discounts, and inaccurate computations. Amounts recovered for clients range from thousands to millions of dollars.

In a small business, an owner/manager may authorize payments based on personal knowledge. In a large business, however, purchasing goods, inspecting the goods received, and verifying the invoices are usually performed by different employees. These duties must be coordinated to ensure that proper payments are made to creditors. One system used for this purpose is the voucher system.

**Voucher System** A **voucher system** is a set of procedures for authorizing and recording liabilities and cash payments. A **voucher** is any document that serves as proof of authority to pay cash or issue an electronic funds transfer. An invoice that has been approved for payment could be considered a voucher. In many businesses, however, a voucher is a special form used to record data about a liability and the details of its payment.

In a manual system, a voucher is normally prepared after all necessary supporting documents have been received. For the purchase of goods, a voucher is supported by the supplier's invoice, a purchase order, and a receiving report. After a voucher is prepared, it is submitted for approval. Once approved, the voucher is recorded in the accounts and filed by due date. Upon payment, the voucher is recorded in the same manner as the payment of an account payable.

In a computerized system, data from the supporting documents (such as purchase orders, receiving reports, and suppliers' invoices) are entered directly into computer files. At the due date, the checks are automatically generated and mailed to creditors. At that time, the voucher is electronically transferred to a paid voucher file.

**Cash Paid by EFT** Cash can also be paid by electronic funds transfer (EFT) systems. For example, you can withdraw cash from your bank account using an ATM machine. Your withdrawal is a type of EFT transfer.

Companies also use EFT transfers. For example, many companies pay their employees via EFT. Under such a system, employees authorize the deposit of their payroll checks directly into their checking accounts. Each pay period, the company transfers the employees' net pay to their checking accounts through the use of EFT. Many companies also use EFT systems to pay their suppliers and other vendors.

# Bank Accounts

Describe the nature of a bank account and its use in controlling cash.

A major reason that companies use bank accounts is for internal control. Some of the control advantages of using bank accounts are as follows:

1. Bank accounts reduce the amount of cash on hand.
2. Bank accounts provide an independent recording of cash transactions. Reconciling the balance of the cash account in the company's records with the cash balance according to the bank is an important control.
3. Use of bank accounts facilitates the transfer of funds using EFT systems.

## Bank Statement

Banks usually maintain a record of all checking account transactions. A summary of all transactions, called a **bank statement**, is mailed to the company (depositor) or made available online, usually each month. The bank statement shows the beginning balance, additions, deductions, and the ending balance. A typical bank statement is shown in Exhibit 5.

Checks or copies of the checks listed in the order that they were paid by the bank may accompany the bank statement. If paid checks are returned, they are stamped "Paid," together with the date of payment. Many banks no longer return checks or check copies. Instead, the check payment information is available online.

**EXHIBIT 5**

**Bank Statement**

MEMBER FDIC

PAGE 1

**VALLEY NATIONAL BANK**
**OF LOS ANGELES**

LOS ANGELES, CA 90020-4253    (310)555-5151

POWER NETWORKING
1000 Belkin Street
Los Angeles, CA 90014-1000

| | | |
|---|---|---|
| ACCOUNT NUMBER | 1627042 | |
| FROM 6/30/11 | TO 7/31/11 | |
| BALANCE | 4,218.60 | |
| 22 DEPOSITS | 13,749.75 | |
| 52 WITHDRAWALS | 14,698.57 | |
| 3 OTHER DEBITS AND CREDITS | 90.00CR | |
| NEW BALANCE | 3,359.78 | |

\* – – CHECKS AND OTHER DEBITS – – – – – – – – \* – – – – – – – – DEPOSITS – \* – DATE \* BALANCE \*

| | | | | DEPOSITS | DATE | BALANCE |
|---|---|---|---|---|---|---|
| No. 850 | 819.40 | No. 852 | 122.54 | 585.75 | 07/01 | 3,862.41 |
| No. 854 | 369.50 | No. 853 | 20.15 | 421.53 | 07/02 | 3,894.29 |
| No. 851 | 600.00 | No. 856 | 190.70 | 781.30 | 07/03 | 3,884.89 |
| No. 855 | 25.93 | No. 857 | 52.50 | | 07/04 | 3,806.46 |
| No. 860 | 921.20 | No. 858 | 160.00 | 662.50 | 07/05 | 3,387.76 |
| No. 862 | 91.07 | NSF | 300.00 | 503.18 | 07/07 | 3,499.87 |

| | | | | | | |
|---|---|---|---|---|---|---|
| No. 880 | 32.26 | No. 877 | 535.09 | ACH 932.00 | 07/29 | 4,136.66 |
| No. 881 | 21.10 | No. 879 | 732.26 | 705.21 | 07/30 | 4,088.51 |
| No. 882 | 126.20 | SC | 18.00 | MS 408.00 | 07/30 | 4,352.31 |
| No. 874 | 26.12 | ACH | 1,615.13 | 648.72 | 07/31 | 3,359.78 |

EC — ERROR CORRECTION    ACH — AUTOMATED CLEARING HOUSE
MS — MISCELLANEOUS
NSF — NOT SUFFICIENT FUNDS    SC — SERVICE CHARGE

\* \* \*    \* \* \*    \* \* \*

THE RECONCILEMENT OF THIS STATEMENT WITH YOUR RECORDS IS ESSENTIAL.
ANY ERROR OR EXCEPTION SHOULD BE REPORTED IMMEDIATELY.

The company's checking account balance *in the bank records* is a liability. Thus, in the bank's records, the company's account has a credit balance. Since the bank statement is prepared from the bank's point of view, a credit memo entry on the bank statement indicates an increase (a credit) to the company's account. Likewise, a debit memo entry on the bank statement indicates a decrease (a debit) in the company's account. This relationship is shown below.

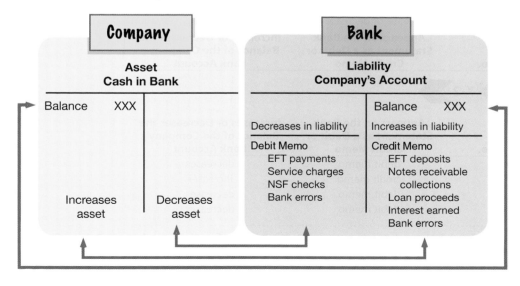

A bank makes credit entries (issues credit memos) for the following:

1. Deposits made by electronic funds transfer (EFT)
2. Collections of note receivable for the company
3. Proceeds for a loan made to the company by the bank
4. Interest earned on the company's account
5. Correction (if any) of bank errors

A bank makes debit entries (issues debit memos) for the following:

1. Payments made by electronic funds transfer (EFT)
2. Service charges
3. Customer checks returned for not sufficient funds
4. Correction (if any) of bank errors

Customers' checks returned for not sufficient funds, called *NSF checks*, are customer checks that were initially deposited, but were not paid by the customer's bank. Since the company's bank credited the customer's check to the company's account when it was deposited, the bank debits the company's account (issues a debit memo) when the check is returned without payment.

The reason for a credit or debit memo entry is indicated on the bank statement. Exhibit 5 identifies the following types of credit and debit memo entries:

| | |
|---|---|
| EC: | Error correction to correct bank error |
| NSF: | Not sufficient funds check |
| SC: | Service charge |
| ACH: | Automated clearing-house entry for electronic funds transfer |
| MS: | Miscellaneous item such as collection of a note receivable on behalf of the company or receipt of a loan by the company from the bank |

The above list includes the notation "ACH" for electronic funds transfers. ACH is a network for clearing electronic funds transfers among individuals, companies, and banks.[7] Because electronic funds transfers may be either deposits or payments, ACH entries may indicate either a debit or credit entry to the company's account. Likewise, entries to correct bank errors and miscellaneous items may indicate a debit or credit entry to the company's account.

## Example Exercise 7-2  Items on Company's Bank Statement
**OBJ. 4**

The following items may appear on a bank statement:

1. NSF check
2. EFT deposit
3. Service charge
4. Bank correction of an error from recording a $400 check as $40

Using the format shown below, indicate whether the item would appear as a debit or credit memo on the bank statement and whether the item would increase or decrease the balance of the company's account.

| Item No. | Appears on the Bank Statement as a Debit or Credit Memo | Increases or Decreases the Balance of the Company's Bank Account |
|---|---|---|

### Follow My Example 7-2

| Item No. | Appears on the Bank Statement as a Debit or Credit Memo | Increases or Decreases the Balance of the Company's Bank Account |
|---|---|---|
| 1 | debit memo | decreases |
| 2 | credit memo | increases |
| 3 | debit memo | decreases |
| 4 | debit memo | decreases |

Practice Exercises: **PE 7-2A, PE 7-2B**

7 For further information on ACH, go to **http://www.nacha.org/**. Click on "About Us," and then click on "Intro to NACHA".

## Using the Bank Statement as a Control Over Cash

The bank statement is a primary control that a company uses over cash. A company uses the bank's statement as a control by comparing the company's recording of cash transactions to those recorded by the bank.

The cash balance shown by a bank statement is usually different from the company's cash balance, as shown in Exhibit 6.

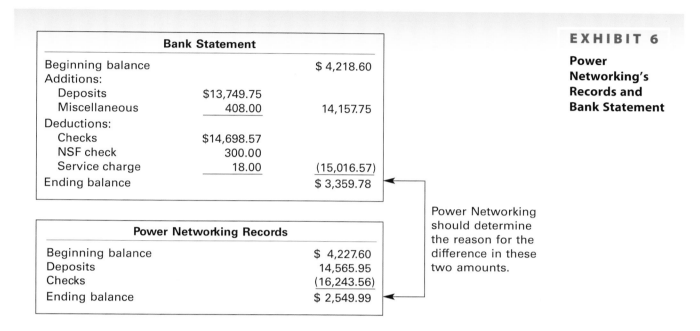

**EXHIBIT 6**

**Power Networking's Records and Bank Statement**

| Bank Statement | | |
|---|---:|---:|
| Beginning balance | | $ 4,218.60 |
| Additions: | | |
| Deposits | $13,749.75 | |
| Miscellaneous | 408.00 | 14,157.75 |
| Deductions: | | |
| Checks | $14,698.57 | |
| NSF check | 300.00 | |
| Service charge | 18.00 | (15,016.57) |
| Ending balance | | $ 3,359.78 |

| Power Networking Records | |
|---|---:|
| Beginning balance | $ 4,227.60 |
| Deposits | 14,565.95 |
| Checks | (16,243.56) |
| Ending balance | $ 2,549.99 |

Power Networking should determine the reason for the difference in these two amounts.

Differences between the company and bank balance may arise because of a delay by either the company or bank in recording transactions. For example, there is normally a time lag of one or more days between the date a check is written and the date that it is paid by the bank. Likewise, there is normally a time lag between when the company mails a deposit to the bank (or uses the night depository) and when the bank receives and records the deposit.

Differences may also arise because the bank has debited or credited the company's account for transactions that the company will not know about until the bank statement is received. Finally, differences may arise from errors made by either the company or the bank. For example, the company may incorrectly post to Cash a check written for $4,500 as $450. Likewise, a bank may incorrectly record the amount of a check.

# Bank Reconciliation

**OBJ. 5** Describe and illustrate the use of a bank reconciliation in controlling cash.

A **bank reconciliation** is an analysis of the items and amounts that result in the cash balance reported in the bank statement to differ from the balance of the cash account in the ledger. The adjusted cash balance determined in the bank reconciliation is reported on the balance sheet.

A bank reconciliation is usually divided into two sections as follows:

1. The *bank section* begins with the cash balance according to the bank statement and ends with the *adjusted balance*.
2. The *company section* begins with the cash balance according to the company's records and ends with the *adjusted balance*.

The *adjusted balance* from bank and company sections must be equal. The format of the bank reconciliation is shown below.

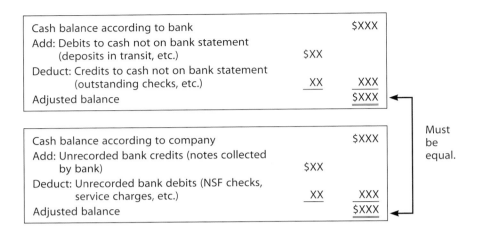

A bank reconciliation is prepared using the following steps:

**Bank Section of Reconciliation**

Step 1. Enter the *Cash balance according to bank* from the ending cash balance according to the bank statement.

Step 2. *Add deposits not recorded by the bank.*

Identify deposits not recorded by the bank by comparing each deposit listed on the bank statement with unrecorded deposits appearing in the preceding period's reconciliation and with the current period's deposits.

Examples: Deposits in transit at the end of the period.

Step 3. *Deduct outstanding checks that have not been paid by the bank.*

Identify outstanding checks by comparing paid checks with outstanding checks appearing on the preceding period's reconciliation and with recorded checks.

Examples: Outstanding checks at the end of the period.

Step 4. Determine the *Adjusted balance* by adding Step 2 and deducting Step 3.

**Company Section of Reconciliation**

Step 5. Enter the *Cash balance according to company* from the ending cash balance in the ledger.

Step 6. *Add credit memos that have not been recorded.*

Identify the bank credit memos that have not been recorded by comparing the bank statement credit memos to entries in the journal.

Examples: A note receivable and interest that the bank has collected for the company.

Step 7. *Deduct debit memos that have not been recorded.*

Identify the bank debit memos that have not been recorded by comparing the bank statement debit memos to entries in the journal.

Examples: Customers' not sufficient funds (NSF) checks; bank service charges.

Step 8. Determine the *Adjusted balance* by adding Step 6 and deducting Step 7.

Step 9. Verify that the adjusted balances determined in Steps 4 and 8 are equal.

The adjusted balances in the bank and company sections of the reconciliation must be equal. If the balances are not equal, an item has been overlooked and must be found.

Sometimes, the adjusted balances are not equal because either the company or the bank has made an error. In such cases, the error is often discovered by comparing the amount of each item (deposit and check) on the bank statement with that in the company's records.

Any bank or company errors discovered should be added or deducted from the bank or company section of the reconciliation depending on the nature of the error. For example, assume that the bank incorrectly recorded a company check for $50 as $500. This bank error of $450 ($500 – $50) would be added to the bank balance in the bank section of the reconciliation. In addition, the bank would be notified of the error so that it could be corrected. On the other hand, assume that the company recorded a deposit of $1,200 as $2,100. This company error of $900 ($2,100 – $1,200) would be deducted from the cash balance in the company section of the bank reconciliation. The company would later correct the error using a journal entry.

To illustrate, the bank statement for Power Networking in Exhibit 5 on page 331 is used. This bank statement shows a balance of $3,359.78 as of July 31. The cash balance in Power Networking's ledger on the same date is $2,549.99. Using the preceding steps, the following reconciling items were identified:

Step 2.  Deposit of July 31, not recorded on bank statement: $816.20
Step 3.  Outstanding checks:

| | |
|---|---:|
| Check No. 812 | $1,061.00 |
| Check No. 878 | 435.39 |
| Check No. 883 | 48.60 |
| Total | $1,544.99 |

Step 6.  Note receivable of $400 plus interest of $8 collected by bank not recorded in the journal as indicated by a credit memo of $408.
Step 7.  Check from customer (Thomas Ivey) for $300 returned by bank because of insufficient funds (NSF) as indicated by a debit memo of $300.00.
Bank service charges of $18, not recorded in the journal as indicated by a debit memo of $18.00.

In addition, an error of $9 was discovered. This error occurred when Check No. 879 for $732.26 to Taylor Co., on account, was recorded in the company's journal as $723.26.

The bank reconciliation, based on the Exhibit 5 bank statement and the preceding reconciling items, is shown in Exhibit 7.

The company's records do not need to be updated for any items in the *bank section* of the reconciliation. This section begins with the cash balance according to the bank statement. However, the bank should be notified of any errors that need to be corrected.

The company's records do need to be updated for any items in the *company section* of the bank reconciliation. The company's records are updated using journal entries. For example, journal entries should be made for any unrecorded bank memos and any company errors.

The journal entries for Power Networking, based on the bank reconciliation shown in Exhibit 7, are as follows:

| | | | | | |
|---|---|---|---|---:|---:|
| July | 31 | Cash | | 408 | |
| | | Notes Receivable | | | 400 |
| | | Interest Revenue | | | 8 |
| | | | | | |
| | 31 | Accounts Receivable—Thomas Ivey | | 300 | |
| | | Miscellaneous Expense | | 18 | |
| | | Accounts Payable—Taylor Co. | | 9 | |
| | | Cash | | | 327 |

**EXHIBIT 7    Bank Reconciliation for Power Networking**

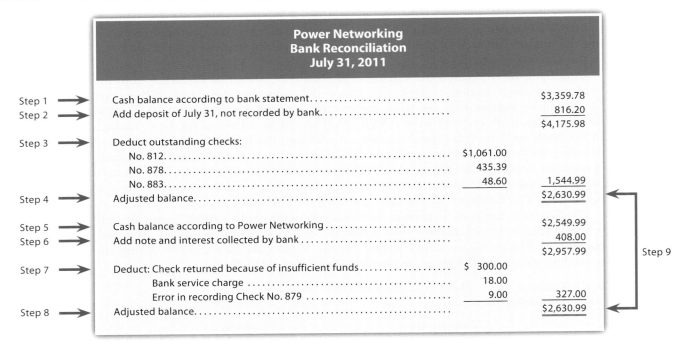

|  | Power Networking<br>Bank Reconciliation<br>July 31, 2011 |  |  |
|---|---|---|---|
| Step 1 → | Cash balance according to bank statement............................. |  | $3,359.78 |
| Step 2 → | Add deposit of July 31, not recorded by bank......................... |  | 816.20 |
|  |  |  | $4,175.98 |
| Step 3 → | Deduct outstanding checks: |  |  |
|  | No. 812...................................................... | $1,061.00 |  |
|  | No. 878...................................................... | 435.39 |  |
|  | No. 883...................................................... | 48.60 | 1,544.99 |
| Step 4 → | Adjusted balance............................................ |  | $2,630.99 |
| Step 5 → | Cash balance according to Power Networking......................... |  | $2,549.99 |
| Step 6 → | Add note and interest collected by bank............................ |  | 408.00 |
|  |  |  | $2,957.99 |
| Step 7 → | Deduct: Check returned because of insufficient funds.................. | $ 300.00 |  |
|  | Bank service charge......................................... | 18.00 |  |
|  | Error in recording Check No. 879.............................. | 9.00 | 327.00 |
| Step 8 → | Adjusted balance........................................... |  | $2,630.99 |

Step 9

After the preceding journal entries are recorded and posted, the cash account will have a debit balance of $2,630.99. This cash balance agrees with the adjusted balance shown on the bank reconciliation. This is the amount of cash on July 31 and is the amount that is reported on Power Networking's July 31 balance sheet.

Businesses may reconcile their bank accounts in a slightly different format from that shown in Exhibit 7. Regardless, the objective is to control cash by reconciling the company's records with the bank statement. In doing so, any errors or misuse of cash may be detected.

To enhance internal control, the bank reconciliation should be prepared by an employee who does not take part in or record cash transactions. Otherwise, mistakes may occur, and it is more likely that cash will be stolen or misapplied. For example, an employee who handles cash and also reconciles the bank statement could steal a cash deposit, omit the deposit from the accounts, and omit it from the reconciliation.

Bank reconciliations are also an important part of computerized systems where deposits and checks are stored in electronic files and records. Some systems use computer software to determine the difference between the bank statement and company cash balances. The software then adjusts for deposits in transit and outstanding checks. Any remaining differences are reported for further analysis.

**Example Exercise › 7-3 › Bank Reconciliation**

OBJ. 5

The following data were gathered to use in reconciling the bank account of Photo Op:

| | |
|---|---|
| Balance per bank............................................................ | $14,500 |
| Balance per company records................................................ | 13,875 |
| Bank service charges ....................................................... | 75 |
| Deposit in transit .......................................................... | 3,750 |
| NSF check................................................................. | 800 |
| Outstanding checks ........................................................ | 5,250 |

a.  What is the adjusted balance on the bank reconciliation?

b.  Journalize any necessary entries for Photo Op based on the bank reconciliation.

*(continued)*

**Follow My Example** 7-3

a. $13,000, as shown below.
   Bank section of reconciliation: $14,500 + $3,750 – $5,250 = $13,000
   Company section of reconciliation: $13,875 – $75 – $800 = $13,000

b. Accounts Receivable.................................................... 800
   Miscellaneous Expense ................................................ 75
      Cash................................................................ 875

Practice Exercises: **PE 7-3A, PE 7-3B**

## Integrity, Objectivity, and Ethics in Business

**BANK ERROR IN YOUR FAVOR**

You may sometime have a bank error in your favor, such as a misposted deposit. Such errors are not a case of "found money," as in the Monopoly® game. Bank control systems quickly discover most errors and make automatic adjustments. Even so, you have a legal responsibility to report the error and return the money to the bank.

# Special-Purpose Cash Funds

**OBJ. 6** Describe the accounting for special-purpose cash funds.

A company often has to pay small amounts for such items as postage, office supplies, or minor repairs. Although small, such payments may occur often enough to total a significant amount. Thus, it is desirable to control such payments. However, writing a check for each small payment is not practical. Instead, a special cash fund, called a **petty cash fund**, is used.

A petty cash fund is established by estimating the amount of payments needed from the fund during a period, such as a week or a month. A check is then written and cashed for this amount. The money obtained from cashing the check is then given to an employee, called the *petty cash custodian*. The petty cash custodian disburses monies from the fund as needed. For control purposes, the company may place restrictions on the maximum amount and the types of payments that can be made from the fund. Each time money is paid from petty cash, the custodian records the details on a petty cash receipts form.

The petty cash fund is normally replenished at periodic intervals, when it is depleted, or reaches a minimum amount. When a petty cash fund is replenished, the accounts debited are determined by summarizing the petty cash receipts. A check is then written for this amount, payable to Petty Cash.

To illustrate, assume that a petty cash fund of $500 is established on August 1. The entry to record this transaction is as follows:

| | | | | |
|---|---|---|---|---|
| Aug. | 1 | Petty Cash | 500 | |
| | | Cash | | 500 |

The only time Petty Cash is debited is when the fund is initially established, as shown in the preceding entry, or when the fund is being increased. The only time Petty Cash is credited is when the fund is being decreased.

At the end of August, the petty cash receipts indicate expenditures for the following items:

| | |
|---|---|
| Office supplies | $380 |
| Postage (debit Office Supplies) | 22 |
| Store supplies | 35 |
| Miscellaneous administrative expense | 30 |
| Total | $467 |

The entry to replenish the petty cash fund on August 31 is as follows:

| | | | | | |
|---|---|---|---|---|---|
| Aug. | 31 | Office Supplies | | 402 | |
| | | Store Supplies | | 35 | |
| | | Miscellaneous Administrative Expense | | 30 | |
| | | Cash | | | 467 |

Petty Cash is not debited when the fund is replenished. Instead, the accounts affected by the petty cash disbursements are debited, as shown in the preceding entry. Replenishing the petty cash fund restores the fund to its original amount of $500.

Companies often use other cash funds for special needs, such as payroll or travel expenses. Such funds are called **special-purpose funds**. For example, each salesperson might be given $1,000 for travel-related expenses. Periodically, each salesperson submits an expense report, and the fund is replenished. Special-purpose funds are established and controlled in a manner similar to that of the petty cash fund.

---

**Example Exercise** ▶ **7-4** ▶ **Petty Cash Fund** **OBJ. 6**

Prepare journal entries for each of the following:

a. Issued a check to establish a petty cash fund of $500.

b. The amount of cash in the petty cash fund is $120. Issued a check to replenish the fund, based on the following summary of petty cash receipts: office supplies, $300, and miscellaneous administrative expense, $75. Record any missing funds in the cash short and over account.

**Follow My Example** ▶ **7-4**

| | | | |
|---|---|---|---|
| a. | Petty Cash.......................................................... | 500 | |
| | Cash ......................................................... | | 500 |
| b. | Office Supplies ..................................................... | 300 | |
| | Miscellaneous Administrative Expense ................................. | 75 | |
| | Cash Short and Over.................................................. | 5 | |
| | Cash ......................................................... | | 380 |

Practice Exercises: **PE 7-4A, PE 7-4B**

---

**OBJ. 7** Describe and illustrate the reporting of cash and cash equivalents in the financial statements.

# Financial Statement Reporting of Cash

Cash is normally listed as the first asset in the Current Assets section of the balance sheet. Most companies present only a single cash amount on the balance sheet by combining all their bank and cash fund accounts.

A company may temporarily have excess cash. In such cases, the company normally invests in highly liquid investments in order to earn interest. These investments are called **cash equivalents**.[8] Examples of cash equivalents include U.S. Treasury bills,

---

8 To be classified a cash equivalent, according to FASB Statement No. 95, the investment is expected to be converted to cash within 90 days.

notes issued by major corporations (referred to as commercial paper), and money market funds. In such cases, companies usually report *Cash and cash equivalents* as one amount on the balance sheet.

The balance sheet presentation for cash for Mornin' Joe is shown below.

| Mornin' Joe<br>Balance Sheet<br>December 31, 2012 | |
| --- | --- |
| **Assets** | |
| Current assets: | |
| Cash and cash equivalents ................................... | $235,000 |

Banks may require that companies maintain minimum cash balances in their bank accounts. Such a balance is called a **compensating balance**. This is often required by the bank as part of a loan agreement or line of credit. A *line of credit* is a preapproved amount the bank is willing to lend to a customer upon request. Compensating balance requirements are normally disclosed in notes to the financial statements.

## IFRS Reporting

The statement of financial position (balance sheet) presentation for cash for Mornin' Joe International under IFRS is as follows:

See pages 630-634

| Mornin' Joe International<br>Statement of Financial Position<br>December 31, 2012 | | |
| --- | --- | --- |
| **Current assets** | | |
| Prepaid insurance ...................................................... | € 24,000 | |
| Merchandise inventory—at lower of cost | | |
|   (first in first out) or realizable value ..................................... | 120,000 | |
| Accounts receivable (net of allowance for doubtful accounts) ............. | 292,700 | |
| Financial assets at fair value through profit or loss ......................... | 465,000 | |
| **Cash and cash equivalents** ............................................. | 235,000 | |
|   Total current assets ................................................ | | €1,136,700 |

IFRS provides flexibility in the order in which the balance sheet accounts are presented. However, assets are normally presented from the least liquid to the most liquid. Liquidity is the ability to turn an asset into cash; thus, cash is the most liquid asset, and is presented last. Presenting current assets from least liquid to most liquid is intended to emphasize the going concern concept, which assumes that the company will remain in business. In contrast, U.S. GAAP presents current assets in order of their liquidity beginning with cash.

# Financial Analysis and Interpretation: Ratio of Cash to Monthly Cash Expenses

**OBJ. 8**
Describe and illustrate the use of the ratio of cash to monthly cash expenses to assess the ability of a company to continue in business.

For startup companies or companies in financial distress, cash is critical for survival. In their first few years, startup companies often report losses and negative net cash flows from operations. Moreover, companies in financial distress can also report losses and negative cash flows from operations. In such cases, the **ratio of cash to monthly cash expenses** is useful for assessing how long a company can continue to operate without:

1. Additional financing, or
2. Generating positive cash flows from operations

The ratio of cash to monthly cash expenses is computed as follows:

$$\text{Ratio of Cash to Monthly Cash Expenses} = \frac{\text{Cash as of Year-End}}{\text{Monthly Cash Expenses}}$$

The cash, including any cash equivalents, is taken from the balance sheet as of year-end. The monthly cash expenses, sometimes called *cash burn*, are estimated from the operating activities section of the statement of cash flows as follows:

$$\text{Monthly Cash Expenses} = \frac{\text{Negative Cash Flow from Operations}}{12}$$

To illustrate, Evergreen Solar, Inc., manufactures solar products including solar panels that convert sunlight into electricity. The following data (in thousands) were taken from the financial statements of Evergreen Solar:

|  | For Years Ending December 31 | | | |
| --- | --- | --- | --- | --- |
|  | **2009** | **2008** | **2007** | **2006** |
| Cash and cash equivalents at year-end | $112,368 | $100,888 | $ 70,428 | $ 6,828 |
| Cash flow from operations | (37,094) | (65,881) | (11,996) | (10,328) |

Based on the preceding data, the monthly cash expenses and ratio of cash to monthly expenses are computed below.

|  | For Years Ending December 31 | | | |
| --- | --- | --- | --- | --- |
|  | **2009** | **2008** | **2007** | **2006** |
| Monthly cash expenses: |  |  |  |  |
| $37,094 ÷ 12 . . . . . . . . . . . . . . . . . . . . . . . . . . . . . | $3,091 |  |  |  |
| $65,881 ÷ 12 . . . . . . . . . . . . . . . . . . . . . . . . . . . . . |  | $5,490 |  |  |
| $11,996 ÷ 12 . . . . . . . . . . . . . . . . . . . . . . . . . . . . . |  |  | $1,000 |  |
| $10,328 ÷ 12 . . . . . . . . . . . . . . . . . . . . . . . . . . . . . |  |  |  | $861 |
| Ratio of cash to monthly cash expenses: |  |  |  |  |
| $112,368 ÷ $3,091. . . . . . . . . . . . . . . . . . . . . . . . . | 36.4 months |  |  |  |
| $100,888 ÷ $5,490. . . . . . . . . . . . . . . . . . . . . . . . . |  | 18.4 months |  |  |
| $70,428 ÷ $1,000. . . . . . . . . . . . . . . . . . . . . . . . . |  |  | 70.4 months |  |
| $6,828 ÷ $861. . . . . . . . . . . . . . . . . . . . . . . . . . . . . |  |  |  | 7.9 months |

The preceding computations indicate that Evergreen Solar had only 7.9 months of cash available as of December 31, 2006. During 2007, Evergreen raised additional cash of approximately $175 million by issuing stock. This enabled Evergreen to continue to operate in 2007 and resulted in Evergreen having 70.4 months of cash available as of December 31, 2007.

During 2008, Evergreen's monthly cash expenses (cash burn) increased to $5,490 from $1,000 in 2007. Evergreen also raised additional cash of approximately $490 million while investing approximately $350 million in plant and equipment. The result is that as of December 31, 2008, Evergreen had 18.4 months of cash with which to continue to operate.

During 2009, Evergreen decreased its monthly cash expenses from $5,490 in 2008 to $3,091. In addition, Evergreen raised additional cash of $105 million by issuing stock and obtaining a loan. As a result, at the end of 2009 Evergreen had 36.4 months of cash with which to continue to operate. In the long-term, however, Evergreen will need to generate positive cash flows from operations to survive.

## Example Exercise 7-5 Ratio of Cash to Monthly Cash Expenses

**OBJ. 8**

Financial data for Chapman Company are as follows:

| | For Year Ending December 31, 2012 |
|---|---|
| Cash on December 31, 2012 | $ 102,000 |
| Cash flow from operations | (144,000) |

a. Compute the ratio of cash to monthly cash expenses.
b. Interpret the results computed in (a).

### Follow My Example 7-5

a. $\text{Monthly Cash Expenses} = \dfrac{\text{Negative Cash Flow from Operations}}{12} = \dfrac{\$144,000}{12} = \$12,000 \text{ per month}$

$\dfrac{\text{Ratio of Cash to}}{\text{Monthly Cash Expenses}} = \dfrac{\text{Cash as of Year-End}}{\text{Monthly Cash Expenses}} = \dfrac{\$102,000}{\$12,000 \text{ per month}} = 8.5 \text{ months}$

b. The preceding computations indicate that Chapman Company has 8.5 months of cash remaining as of December 31, 2012. To continue operations beyond 8.5 months, Chapman Company will need to generate positive cash flows from operations or raise additional financing from its owners or issue debt.

Practice Exercises: **PE 7-5A, PE 7-5B**

## Business Connection

### MICROSOFT CORPORATION

Microsoft Corporation develops, manufactures, licenses, and supports software products for computing devices. Microsoft software products include computer operating systems, such as Windows®, and application software, such as Microsoft Word® and Excel®. Microsoft is actively involved in the video game market through its Xbox® and is also involved in online products and services.

Microsoft is known for its strong cash position. Microsoft's June 30, 2009, balance sheet reported over $31 billion of cash and short-term investments, as shown below.

**Balance Sheet**
**June 30, 2009**
**(In millions)**

**Assets**

| | |
|---|---|
| Current assets: | |
| Cash and equivalents............................................ | $ 6,076 |
| Short-term investments .......................................... | 25,371 |
| Total cash and short-term investments...................... | $31,447 |

The cash and cash equivalents of $6,076 million are further described in the notes to the financial statements, as shown below.

| | |
|---|---|
| Cash and equivalents: | |
| Cash ............................................................ | $2,064 |
| Mutual funds.................................................... | 900 |
| Commercial paper .............................................. | 400 |
| U.S. government and agency securities......................... | 2,369 |
| Certificates of deposit .......................................... | 275 |
| Municipal securities ............................................ | 68 |
| Total cash and equivalents................................... | $6,076 |

# At a Glance 7

**Describe the Sarbanes-Oxley Act of 2002 and its impact on internal controls and financial reporting.**

**Key Points** Sarbanes-Oxley requires companies to maintain strong and effective internal controls and to report on the effectiveness of the internal controls.

| Learning Outcomes | Example Exercises | Practice Exercises |
|---|---|---|
| • Describe why Congress passed Sarbanes-Oxley. | | |
| • Describe the purpose of Sarbanes-Oxley. | | |
| • Define internal control. | | |

**Describe and illustrate the objectives and elements of internal control.**

**Key Points** The objectives of internal control are to provide reasonable assurance that (1) assets are safeguarded and used for business purposes, (2) business information is accurate, and (3) laws and regulations are complied with. The elements of internal control are the control environment, risk assessment, control procedures, monitoring, and information and communication.

| Learning Outcomes | Example Exercises | Practice Exercises |
|---|---|---|
| • List the objectives of internal control. | | |
| • List the elements of internal control. | | |
| • Describe each element of internal control and factors influencing each element. | EE7-1 | PE7-1A, 7-1B |

**Describe and illustrate the application of internal controls to cash.**

**Key Points** A cash register is a control for protecting cash received in over-the-counter sales. A remittance advice is a control for cash received through the mail. Separating the duties of handling cash and recording cash is also a control. A voucher system is a control system for cash payments. Many companies use electronic funds transfers for cash receipts and cash payments.

| Learning Outcomes | Example Exercises | Practice Exercises |
|---|---|---|
| • Describe and give examples of controls for cash received from cash sales, cash received in the mail, and cash received by EFT. | | |
| • Describe and give examples of controls for cash payments made using a voucher system and cash payments made by EFT. | | |

**Describe the nature of a bank account and its use in controlling cash.**

**Key Points** Bank accounts control cash by reducing the amount of cash on hand and facilitating the transfer of cash between businesses and locations. In addition, the bank statement allows a business to reconcile the cash transactions recorded in the accounting records to those recorded by the bank.

| Learning Outcomes | Example Exercises | Practice Exercises |
|---|---|---|
| • Describe how the use of bank accounts helps control cash. | | |
| • Describe a bank statement and provide examples of items that appear on a bank statement as debit and credit memos. | EE7-2 | PE7-2A, 7-2B |

**OBJ. 5**

## Describe and illustrate the use of a bank reconciliation in controlling cash.

**Key Points**  A bank reconciliation is prepared using nine steps as summarized on page 334. The items in the company section of a bank reconciliation must be journalized on the company's records.

| Learning Outcomes | Example Exercises | Practice Exercises |
|---|---|---|
| • Describe a bank reconciliation. | | |
| • Prepare a bank reconciliation. | EE7-3 | PE7-3A, 7-3B |
| • Journalize any necessary entries on the company's records based on the bank reconciliation. | EE7-3 | PE7-3A, 7-3B |

**OBJ. 6**

## Describe the accounting for special-purpose cash funds.

**Key Points**  Special-purpose cash funds, such as a petty cash fund or travel funds, are used by businesses to meet specific needs. Each fund is established by cashing a check for the amount of cash needed. At periodic intervals, the fund is replenished and the disbursements recorded.

| Learning Outcomes | Example Exercises | Practice Exercises |
|---|---|---|
| • Describe the use of special-purpose cash funds. | | |
| • Journalize the entry to establish a petty cash fund. | EE7-4 | PE7-4A, 7-4B |
| • Journalize the entry to replenish a petty cash fund. | EE7-4 | PE7-4A, 7-4B |

**OBJ. 7**

## Describe and illustrate the reporting of cash and cash equivalents in the financial statements.

**Key Points**  Cash is listed as the first asset in the Current assets section of the balance sheet. Companies that have invested excess cash in highly liquid investments usually report *Cash and cash equivalents* on the balance sheet.

| Learning Outcomes | Example Exercises | Practice Exercises |
|---|---|---|
| • Describe the reporting of cash and cash equivalents in the financial statements. | | |
| • Illustrate the reporting of cash and cash equivalents in the financial statements. | | |

**OBJ. 8**

## Describe and illustrate the use of the ratio of cash to monthly cash expenses to assess the ability of a company to continue in business.

**Key Points**  The ratio of cash to monthly cash expenses is useful for assessing how long a company can continue to operate without (1) additional financing or (2) generating positive cash flows from operations.

| Learning Outcomes | Example Exercises | Practice Exercises |
|---|---|---|
| • Describe the use of the ratio of cash to monthly cash expenses. | | |
| • Compute the ratio of cash to monthly cash expenses. | EE7-5 | PE 7-5A, 7-5B |

## Key Terms

bank reconciliation (333)
bank statement (330)
cash (327)
cash equivalents (338)
cash short and over account (328)
compensating balance (339)

control environment (323)
electronic funds transfer (EFT) (329)
elements of internal control (322)
employee fraud (322)
internal control (320)
petty cash fund (337)

ratio of cash to monthly
    cash expenses (340)
Sarbanes-Oxley Act of 2002 (320)
special-purpose funds (338)
voucher (330)
voucher system (330)

## Illustrative Problem

The bank statement for Urethane Company for June 30, 2011, indicates a balance of $9,143.11. All cash receipts are deposited each evening in a night depository, after banking hours. The accounting records indicate the following summary data for cash receipts and payments for June:

| | |
|---|---|
| Cash balance as of June 1 | $ 3,943.50 |
| Total cash receipts for June | 28,971.60 |
| Total amount of checks issued in June | 28,388.85 |

Comparing the bank statement and the accompanying canceled checks and memos with the records reveals the following reconciling items:

a. The bank had collected for Urethane Company $1,030 on a note left for collection. The face amount of the note was $1,000.

b. A deposit of $1,852.21, representing receipts of June 30, had been made too late to appear on the bank statement.

c. Checks outstanding totaled $5,265.27.

d. A check drawn for $139 had been incorrectly charged by the bank as $157.

e. A check for $30 returned with the statement had been recorded in the company's records as $240. The check was for the payment of an obligation to Avery Equipment Company for the purchase of office supplies on account.

f. Bank service charges for June amounted to $18.20.

### Instructions

1. Prepare a bank reconciliation for June.

2. Journalize the entries that should be made by Urethane Company.

**Solution**

1.

| Urethane Company<br>Bank Reconciliation<br>June 30, 2011 | | |
|---|---|---|
| Cash balance according to bank statement ............................. | | $ 9,143.11 |
| Add: Deposit of June 30 not recorded by bank ......................... | $1,852.21 | |
| Bank error in charging check as $157 | | |
| instead of $139 .............................................. | 18.00 | 1,870.21 |
| | | $11,013.32 |
| Deduct: Outstanding checks.......................................... | | 5,265.27 |
| Adjusted balance .................................................. | | $ 5,748.05 |
| | | |
| Cash balance according to company's records ......................... | | $ 4,526.25* |
| Add: Proceeds of note collected by bank, | | |
| including $30 interest......................................... | $1,030.00 | |
| Error in recording check....................................... | 210.00 | 1,240.00 |
| | | $ 5,766.25 |
| Deduct: Bank service charges ........................................ | | 18.20 |
| Adjusted balance .................................................. | | $ 5,748.05 |
| *$3,943.50 + $28,971.60 − $28,388.85 | | |

2.

| | | | | | |
|---|---|---|---|---|---|
| June | 30 | Cash | | 1,240.00 | |
| | | Notes Receivable | | | 1,000.00 |
| | | Interest Revenue | | | 30.00 |
| | | Accounts Payable—Avery Equipment Company | | | 210.00 |
| | | | | | |
| | 30 | Miscellaneous Administrative Expense | | 18.20 | |
| | | Cash | | | 18.20 |

# Discussion Questions

1. (a) Name and describe the five elements of internal control. (b) Is any one element of internal control more important than another?

2. Why should the employee who handles cash receipts not have the responsibility for maintaining the accounts receivable records? Explain.

3. The ticket seller at a movie theater doubles as a ticket taker for a few minutes each day while the ticket taker is on a break. Which control procedure of a business's system of internal control is violated in this situation?

4. Why should the responsibility for maintaining the accounting records be separated from the responsibility for operations? Explain.

5. Assume that Peggy Gyger, accounts payable clerk for Patmen Inc., stole $193,750 by paying fictitious invoices for goods that were never received. The clerk set up accounts in the names of the fictitious companies and cashed the checks at a local

bank. Describe a control procedure that would have prevented or detected the fraud.

6. Before a voucher for the purchase of merchandise is approved for payment, supporting documents should be compared to verify the accuracy of the liability. Give an example of supporting documents for the purchase of merchandise.

7. The balance of Cash is likely to differ from the bank statement balance. What two factors are likely to be responsible for the difference?

8. What is the purpose of preparing a bank reconciliation?

9. Smyrna Inc. has a petty cash fund of $900. (a) Since the petty cash fund is only $900, should Smyrna Inc. implement controls over petty cash? (b) What controls, if any, could be used for the petty cash fund?

10. (a) How are cash equivalents reported in the financial statements? (b) What are some examples of cash equivalents?

# Practice Exercises

**OBJ. 2**    **EE 7-1** *p. 327*

## PE 7-1A   Internal control elements

Identify each of the following as relating to (a) the control environment, (b) control procedures, or (c) information and communication.

1. Separating related operations
2. Report of internal auditors
3. Management's philosophy and operating style

**OBJ. 2**    **EE 7-1** *p. 327*

## PE 7-1B   Internal control elements

Identify each of the following as relating to (a) the control environment, (b) control procedures, or (c) monitoring.

1. Personnel policies
2. Safeguarding inventory in a locked warehouse
3. Hiring of external auditors to review the adequacy of controls

**OBJ. 4**    **EE 7-2** *p. 332*

## PE 7-2A   Items on company's bank statement

The following items may appear on a bank statement:

1. EFT payment
2. Note collected for company
3. Bank correction of an error from recording a $7,200 deposit as $2,700
4. Service charge

Using the format shown below, indicate whether each item would appear as a debit or credit memo on the bank statement and whether the item would increase or decrease the balance of the company's account.

| Item No. | Appears on the Bank Statement as a Debit or Credit Memo | Increases or Decreases the Balance of the Company's Bank Account |
|---|---|---|

**OBJ. 4**    **EE 7-2** *p. 332*

## PE 7-2B   Items on company's bank statement

The following items may appear on a bank statement:

1. NSF check
2. Bank correction of an error from posting another customer's check to the company's account
3. Loan proceeds
4. EFT deposit

Using the format shown below, indicate whether each item would appear as a debit or credit memo on the bank statement and whether the item would increase or decrease the balance of the company's account.

| Item No. | Appears on the Bank Statement as a Debit or Credit Memo | Increases or Decreases the Balance of the Company's Bank Account |
|---|---|---|

| Learning Objectives | Example Exercises | |
|---|---|---|

**OBJ. 5**    **EE 7-3** *p. 336*

### PE 7-3A   Bank reconciliation

The following data were gathered to use in reconciling the bank account of Azalea Company:

| | |
|---|---:|
| Balance per bank | $25,500 |
| Balance per company records | 27,475 |
| Bank service charges | 75 |
| Deposit in transit | 7,500 |
| NSF check | 3,400 |
| Outstanding checks | 9,000 |

a. What is the adjusted balance on the bank reconciliation?

b. Journalize any necessary entries for Azalea Company based on the bank reconciliation.

**OBJ. 5**    **EE 7-3** *p. 336*

### PE 7-3B   Bank reconciliation

The following data were gathered to use in reconciling the bank account of Bradford Company:

| | |
|---|---:|
| Balance per bank | $17,400 |
| Balance per company records | 5,765 |
| Bank service charges | 125 |
| Deposit in transit | 3,000 |
| Note collected by bank with $360 interest | 9,360 |
| Outstanding checks | 5,400 |

a. What is the adjusted balance on the bank reconciliation?

b. Journalize any necessary entries for Bradford Company based on the bank reconciliation.

**OBJ. 6**    **EE 7-4** *p. 338*

### PE 7-4A   Petty cash fund

Prepare journal entries for each of the following:

a. Issued a check to establish a petty cash fund of $800.

b. The amount of cash in the petty cash fund is $225. Issued a check to replenish the fund, based on the following summary of petty cash receipts: repair expense, $450, and miscellaneous selling expense, $75. Record any missing funds in the cash short and over account.

**OBJ. 6**    **EE 7-4** *p. 338*

### PE 7-4B   Petty cash fund

Prepare journal entries for each of the following:

a. Issued a check to establish a petty cash fund of $750.

b. The amount of cash in the petty cash fund is $325. Issued a check to replenish the fund, based on the following summary of petty cash receipts: store supplies, $300, and miscellaneous selling expense, $100. Record any missing funds in the cash short and over account.

**OBJ. 8**    **EE 7-5** *p. 341*

**FAI**

### PE 7-5A   Ratio of cash to monthly cash expenses

Financial data for Hauser Company are shown below.

| | For Year Ending December 31, 2012 |
|---|---:|
| Cash on December 31, 2012 | $ 58,800 |
| Cash flow from operations | (72,000) |

a. Compute the ratio of cash to monthly cash expenses.

b. Interpret the results computed in (a).

**OBJ. 8**    **EE 7-5** *p. 341*

**FAI**

### PE 7-5B   Ratio of cash to monthly cash expenses

Financial data for Preston Company are shown below.

| | For Year Ending December 31, 2012 |
|---|---:|
| Cash on December 31, 2012 | $ 184,800 |
| Cash flow from operations | (158,400) |

a. Compute the ratio of cash to monthly cash expenses.

b. Interpret the results computed in (a).

## Exercises

OBJ. 1

### EX 7-1 Sarbanes-Oxley internal control report

Using Wikipedia (**www.wikipedia.org**), look up the entry for Sarbanes-Oxley Act. Look over the table of contents and find the section that describes Section 404.

➤ What does Section 404 require of management's internal control report?

OBJ. 2, 3

### EX 7-2 Internal controls

Joan Whalen has recently been hired as the manager of Jittery Coffee Shop. Jittery Coffee Shop is a national chain of franchised coffee shops. During her first month as store manager, Joan encountered the following internal control situations:

a. Since only one employee uses the cash register, that employee is responsible for counting the cash at the end of the shift and verifying that the cash in the drawer matches the amount of cash sales recorded by the cash register. Joan expects each cashier to balance the drawer to the penny *every* time—no exceptions.

b. Joan caught an employee putting a case of 400 single-serving tea bags in her car. Not wanting to create a scene, Joan smiled and said, "I don't think you're putting those tea bags on the right shelf. Don't they belong inside the coffee shop?" The employee returned the tea bags to the stockroom.

c. Jittery Coffee Shop has one cash register. Prior to Joan's joining the coffee shop, each employee working on a shift would take a customer order, accept payment, and then prepare the order. Joan made one employee on each shift responsible for taking orders and accepting the customer's payment. Other employees prepare the orders.

➤ State whether you agree or disagree with Joan's method of handling each situation and explain your answer.

OBJ. 2, 3

### EX 7-3 Internal controls

Meridian Clothing is a retail store specializing in women's clothing. The store has established a liberal return policy for the holiday season in order to encourage gift purchases. Any item purchased during November and December may be returned through January 31, with a receipt, for cash or exchange. If the customer does not have a receipt, cash will still be refunded for any item under $50. If the item is more than $50, a check is mailed to the customer.

Whenever an item is returned, a store clerk completes a return slip, which the customer signs. The return slip is placed in a special box. The store manager visits the return counter approximately once every two hours to authorize the return slips. Clerks are instructed to place the returned merchandise on the proper rack on the selling floor as soon as possible.

This year, returns at Meridian Clothing have reached an all-time high. There are a large number of returns under $50 without receipts.

a. ➤ How can sales clerks employed at Meridian Clothing use the store's return policy to steal money from the cash register?

b. ➤ What internal control weaknesses do you see in the return policy that make cash thefts easier?

c. ➤ Would issuing a store credit in place of a cash refund for all merchandise returned without a receipt reduce the possibility of theft? List some advantages and disadvantages of issuing a store credit in place of a cash refund.

d. ➤ Assume that Meridian Clothing is committed to the current policy of issuing cash refunds without a receipt. What changes could be made in the store's procedures regarding customer refunds in order to improve internal control?

OBJ. 2, 3

### EX 7-4 Internal controls for bank lending

Evergreen Bank provides loans to businesses in the community through its Commercial Lending Department. Small loans (less than $250,000) may be approved by an individual loan officer, while larger loans (greater than $250,000) must be approved by a board of loan officers. Once a loan is approved, the funds are made available to the loan applicant under agreed-upon terms. The president of Evergreen Bank has instituted a policy whereby he has the individual authority to approve loans up to $10,000,000. The president believes that this policy will allow flexibility to approve loans to valued clients much quicker than under the previous policy.

▬▬▶ As an internal auditor of Evergreen Bank, how would you respond to this change in policy?

---

**OBJ. 2, 3**

### EX 7-5 Internal controls

One of the largest losses in history from unauthorized securities trading involved a securities trader for the French bank, Société Générale. The trader was able to circumvent internal controls and create over $7 billion in trading losses in six months. The trader apparently escaped detection by using knowledge of the bank's internal control systems learned from a previous back-office monitoring job. Much of this monitoring involved the use of software to monitor trades. In addition, traders were usually kept to tight trading limits. Apparently, these controls failed in this case.

▬▬▶ What general weaknesses in Societe Generale's internal controls contributed to the occurrence and size of the losses?

---

**OBJ. 2, 3**

### EX 7-6 Internal controls

An employee of JHT Holdings, Inc., a trucking company, was responsible for resolving roadway accident claims under $25,000. The employee created fake accident claims and wrote settlement checks of between $5,000 and $25,000 to friends or acquaintances acting as phony "victims." One friend recruited subordinates at his place of work to cash some of the checks. Beyond this, the JHT employee also recruited lawyers, who he paid to represent both the trucking company and the fake victims in the bogus accident settlements. When the lawyers cashed the checks, they allegedly split the money with the corrupt JHT employee. This fraud went undetected for two years.

▬▬▶ Why would it take so long to discover such a fraud?

---

**OBJ. 2, 3**

### EX 7-7 Internal controls

Frog Sound Co. discovered a fraud whereby one of its front office administrative employees used company funds to purchase goods, such as computers, digital cameras, compact disk players, and other electronic items for her own use. The fraud was discovered when employees noticed an increase in delivery frequency from vendors and the use of unusual vendors. After some investigation, it was discovered that the employee would alter the description or change the quantity on an invoice in order to explain the cost on the bill.

▬▬▶ What general internal control weaknesses contributed to this fraud?

---

**OBJ. 2, 3**

### EX 7-8 Financial statement fraud

A former chairman, CFO, and controller of Donnkenny, Inc., an apparel company that makes sportswear for Pierre Cardin and Victoria Jones, pleaded guilty to financial statement fraud. These managers used false journal entries to record fictitious sales, hid inventory in public warehouses so that it could be recorded as "sold," and required sales orders to be backdated so that the sale could be moved back to an earlier period. The combined effect of these actions caused $25 million out of $40 million in quarterly sales to be phony.

a. ▬▬▶ Why might control procedures listed in this chapter be insufficient in stopping this type of fraud?

b. ▬▬▶ How could this type of fraud be stopped?

---

**OBJ. 2, 3**

### EX 7-9 Internal control of cash receipts

The procedures used for over-the-counter receipts are as follows. At the close of each day's business, the sales clerks count the cash in their respective cash drawers, after which they determine the amount recorded by the cash register and prepare the memo cash form, noting any discrepancies. An employee from the cashier's office counts the cash, compares the total with the memo, and takes the cash to the cashier's office.

a. ▬▬▶ Indicate the weak link in internal control.

b. ▬▬▶ How can the weakness be corrected?

OBJ. 2, 3

### EX 7-10   Internal control of cash receipts

Mel Lane works at the drive-through window of Bison Burgers. Occasionally, when a drive-through customer orders, Mel fills the order and pockets the customer's money. He does not ring up the order on the cash register.

➤ Identify the internal control weaknesses that exist at Bison Burgers, and discuss what can be done to prevent this theft.

OBJ. 2, 3

### EX 7-11   Internal control of cash receipts

The mailroom employees send all remittances and remittance advices to the cashier. The cashier deposits the cash in the bank and forwards the remittance advices and duplicate deposit slips to the Accounting Department.

a. ➤ Indicate the weak link in internal control in the handling of cash receipts.

b. ➤ How can the weakness be corrected?

OBJ. 2, 3

### EX 7-12   Entry for cash sales; cash short

The actual cash received from cash sales was $27,943, and the amount indicated by the cash register total was $28,000. Journalize the entry to record the cash receipts and cash sales.

OBJ. 2, 3

### EX 7-13   Entry for cash sales; cash over

The actual cash received from cash sales was $13,590, and the amount indicated by the cash register total was $13,540. Journalize the entry to record the cash receipts and cash sales.

OBJ. 2, 3

### EX 7-14   Internal control of cash payments

Signs-A-Rama Co. is a small merchandising company with a manual accounting system. An investigation revealed that in spite of a sufficient bank balance, a significant amount of available cash discounts had been lost because of failure to make timely payments. In addition, it was discovered that the invoices for several purchases had been paid twice.

➤ Outline procedures for the payment of vendors' invoices, so that the possibilities of losing available cash discounts and of paying an invoice a second time will be minimized.

OBJ. 2, 3

### EX 7-15   Internal control of cash payments

Digit Tech Company, a communications equipment manufacturer, recently fell victim to a fraud scheme developed by one of its employees. To understand the scheme, it is necessary to review Digit Tech's procedures for the purchase of services.

The purchasing agent is responsible for ordering services (such as repairs to a photocopy machine or office cleaning) after receiving a service requisition from an authorized manager. However, since no tangible goods are delivered, a receiving report is not prepared. When the Accounting Department receives an invoice billing Digit Tech for a service call, the accounts payable clerk calls the manager who requested the service in order to verify that it was performed.

The fraud scheme involves Loretta Trent, the manager of plant and facilities. Loretta arranged for her uncle's company, Laser Systems, to be placed on Digit Tech's approved vendor list. Loretta did not disclose the family relationship.

On several occasions, Loretta would submit a requisition for services to be provided by Laser Systems. However, the service requested was really not needed, and it was never performed. Laser Systems would bill Digit Tech for the service and then split the cash payment with Loretta.

➤ Explain what changes should be made to Digit Tech's procedures for ordering and paying for services in order to prevent such occurrences in the future.

**OBJ. 5**

### EX 7-16  Bank reconciliation

Identify each of the following reconciling items as: (a) an addition to the cash balance according to the bank statement, (b) a deduction from the cash balance according to the bank statement, (c) an addition to the cash balance according to the company's records, or (d) a deduction from the cash balance according to the company's records. (None of the transactions reported by bank debit and credit memos have been recorded by the company.)

1.  Bank service charges, $120.
2.  Check of a customer returned by bank to company because of insufficient funds, $4,200.
3.  Check for $240 incorrectly recorded by the company as $420.
4.  Check for $1,000 incorrectly charged by bank as $10,000.
5.  Deposit in transit, $24,950.
6.  Outstanding checks, $18,100.
7.  Note collected by bank, $15,600.

**OBJ. 5**

### EX 7-17  Entries based on bank reconciliation

Which of the reconciling items listed in Exercise 7-16 require an entry in the company's accounts?

**OBJ. 5**

✔ Adjusted balance: $16,000

### EX 7-18  Bank reconciliation

The following data were accumulated for use in reconciling the bank account of Maplewood Co. for July:

1.  Cash balance according to the company's records at July 31, $15,600.
2.  Cash balance according to the bank statement at July 31, $16,230.
3.  Checks outstanding, $3,180.
4.  Deposit in transit, not recorded by bank, $2,950.
5.  A check for $270 in payment of an account was erroneously recorded in the check register as $720.
6.  Bank debit memo for service charges, $50.

a.  Prepare a bank reconciliation, using the format shown in Exhibit 7.
b.  If the balance sheet were prepared for Maplewood Co. on July 31, what amount should be reported for cash?
c.  Must a bank reconciliation always balance (reconcile)?

**OBJ. 5**

### EX 7-19  Entries for bank reconciliation

Using the data presented in Exercise 7-18, journalize the entry or entries that should be made by the company.

**OBJ. 5**

### EX 7-20  Entries for note collected by bank

Accompanying a bank statement for O'Fallon Company is a credit memo for $21,200, representing the principal ($20,000) and interest ($1,200) on a note that had been collected by the bank. The company had been notified by the bank at the time of the collection, but had made no entries. Journalize the entry that should be made by the company to bring the accounting records up to date.

**OBJ. 5**

✔ Adjusted balance: $14,000

### EX 7-21  Bank reconciliation

An accounting clerk for Muskegon Co. prepared the following bank reconciliation:

**Muskegon Co.**
**Bank Reconciliation**
**May 31, 2012**

| | | |
|---|---:|---:|
| Cash balance according to company's records . . . . . . . . . . . . . . . . . . . . . . . . | | $ 5,110 |
| Add: Outstanding checks . . . . . . . . . . . . . . . . . . . . . . . . . . . . . . . . . . . . . . . | $2,500 | |
| Error by Muskegon Co. in recording Check | | |
| No. 2219 as $810 instead of $180 . . . . . . . . . . . . . . . . . . . . . . . . . . | 630 | |
| Note for $8,000 collected by bank, including interest. . . . . . . . . . . . | 8,320 | 11,450 |
| | | $16,560 |
| Deduct: Deposit in transit on May 31 . . . . . . . . . . . . . . . . . . . . . . . . . . . . | $5,200 | |
| Bank service charges . . . . . . . . . . . . . . . . . . . . . . . . . . . . . . . . . . . | 60 | 5,260 |
| Cash balance according to bank statement. . . . . . . . . . . . . . . . . . . . . . . . | | $11,300 |

a. From the data in the above bank reconciliation, prepare a new bank reconciliation for Muskegon Co., using the format shown in the Illustrative Problem.

b. If a balance sheet were prepared for Muskegon Co. on May 31, 2012, what amount should be reported for cash?

---

OBJ. 5

✔ Corrected adjusted balance: $13,000

**EX 7-22  Bank reconciliation**

Identify the errors in the following bank reconciliation:

**Alma Co.**
**Bank Reconciliation**
**For the Month Ended November 30, 2012**

| | | | |
|---|---:|---:|---:|
| Cash balance according to bank statement. . . . . . . . . . . . . . . . . . . . . . . . . | | | $12,090 |
| Add outstanding checks: | | | |
| No. 915. . . . . . . . . . . . . . . . . . . . . . . . . . . . . . . . . . . . . . . . . . . . . . . . . . . | | $ 850 | |
| 960. . . . . . . . . . . . . . . . . . . . . . . . . . . . . . . . . . . . . . . . . . . . . . . . . . . | | 615 | |
| 964. . . . . . . . . . . . . . . . . . . . . . . . . . . . . . . . . . . . . . . . . . . . . . . . . . . | | 850 | |
| 965. . . . . . . . . . . . . . . . . . . . . . . . . . . . . . . . . . . . . . . . . . . . . . . . . . . | | 775 | 3,090 |
| | | | $15,180 |
| Deduct deposit of November 30, not recorded by bank . . . . . . . . . . . . . . | | | 4,000 |
| Adjusted balance. . . . . . . . . . . . . . . . . . . . . . . . . . . . . . . . . . . . . . . . . . . . | | | $11,180 |
| Cash balance according to company's records . . . . . . . . . . . . . . . . . . . . . . | | | $ 4,430 |
| Add: Proceeds of note collected by bank: | | | |
| Principal. . . . . . . . . . . . . . . . . . . . . . . . . . . . . . . . . . . . . . . . . . . . . . . | $5,000 | | |
| Interest. . . . . . . . . . . . . . . . . . . . . . . . . . . . . . . . . . . . . . . . . . . . . . . | 200 | $5,200 | |
| Service charges . . . . . . . . . . . . . . . . . . . . . . . . . . . . . . . . . . . . . . . . | | 30 | 5,230 |
| | | | $ 9,660 |
| Deduct: Check returned because of insufficient funds. . . . . . . . . . . . . . . | | $1,100 | |
| Error in recording November 23 deposit of $6,100 as $1,600 . . | | 4,500 | 5,600 |
| Adjusted balance. . . . . . . . . . . . . . . . . . . . . . . . . . . . . . . . . . . . . . . . . . . . | | | $ 4,060 |

---

OBJ. 2, 3, 5

**EX 7-23  Using bank reconciliation to determine cash receipts stolen**

Lasting Impressions Co. records all cash receipts on the basis of its cash register tapes. Lasting Impressions Co. discovered during April 2012 that one of its sales clerks had stolen an undetermined amount of cash receipts when she took the daily deposits to the bank. The following data have been gathered for April:

| | |
|---|---:|
| Cash in bank according to the general ledger | $ 8,900 |
| Cash according to the April 30, 2012, bank statement | 20,500 |
| Outstanding checks as of April 30, 2012 | 6,800 |
| Bank service charge for April | 100 |
| Note receivable, including interest collected by bank in April | 10,400 |

No deposits were in transit on April 30.

a. Determine the amount of cash receipts stolen by the sales clerk.

b. ━━━━▶ What accounting controls would have prevented or detected this theft?

OBJ. 6

### EX 7-24   Petty cash fund entries

Journalize the entries to record the following:

a.  Check No. 6300 is issued to establish a petty cash fund of $1,200.

b.  The amount of cash in the petty cash fund is now $200. Check No. 6527 is issued to replenish the fund, based on the following summary of petty cash receipts: office supplies, $650; miscellaneous selling expense, $230; miscellaneous administrative expense, $90. (Since the amount of the check to replenish the fund plus the balance in the fund do not equal $1,200, record the discrepancy in the cash short and over account.)

OBJ. 7

### EX 7-25   Variation in cash flows

Mattel, Inc., designs, manufactures, and markets toy products worldwide. Mattel's toys include Barbie™ fashion dolls and accessories, Hot Wheels™, and Fisher-Price brands. For a recent year, Mattel reported the following net cash flows from operating activities (in thousands):

| | |
|---|---:|
| First quarter ending March 31 | $ (214,807) |
| Second quarter ending June 30 | (135,003) |
| Third quarter ending September 30 | 31,003 |
| Fourth quarter December 31 | 1,102,915 |

 Explain why Mattel reported negative net cash flows from operating activities during the first two quarters, a small positive net cash flow in the third quarter, and a large positive cash flow for the fourth quarter with overall net positive cash flow for the year.

OBJ. 8

### EX 7-26   Cash to monthly cash expenses ratio

During 2012, Pierport Inc. has monthly cash expenses of $400,000. On December 31, 2012, the cash balance is $3,600,000.

a.  Compute the ratio of cash to monthly cash expenses.

b.  Based on (a), what are the implications for Pierport Inc.?

OBJ. 8

### EX 7-27   Cash to monthly cash expenses ratio

Delta Air Lines, one of the world's largest airlines, provides passenger and cargo services throughout the United States and the world. Delta reported the following financial data (in millions) for the year ended December 31, 2008:

| | |
|---|---:|
| Net cash flows from operating activities | $(1,7 07) |
| Cash and cash equivalents, December 31, 2008 | 4,255 |

a.  Determine the monthly cash expenses. Round to one decimal place.

b.  Determine the ratio of cash to monthly cash expenses. Round to one decimal place.

c.  Based on your analysis, do you believe that Delta will remain in business?

OBJ. 8

### EX 7-28   Cash to monthly cash expenses ratio

Allos Therapeutics, Inc., is a biopharmaceutical company that develops drugs for the treatment of cancer. Allos Therapeutics reported the following financial data (in thousands) for the years ending December 31, 2008, 2007, and 2006.

| | For Years Ending December 31 | | |
|---|---:|---:|---:|
| | **2008** | **2007** | **2006** |
| Cash and cash equivalents | $ 30,696 | $ 16,103 | $ 10,437 |
| Net cash flows from operations | (42,850) | (30,823) | (25,147) |

a. Determine the monthly cash expenses for 2008, 2007, and 2006. Round to one decimal place.

b. Determine the ratio of cash to monthly cash expenses as of December 31, 2008, 2007, and 2006. Round to one decimal place.

c. ➤ Based on (a) and (b), comment on Allos Therapeutics' ratio of cash to monthly operating expenses for 2008, 2007, and 2006.

## Problems Series A

OBJ. 2, 3

**PR 7-1A    Evaluating internal control of cash**

The following procedures were recently installed by Pine Creek Company:

a. Along with petty cash expense receipts for postage, office supplies, etc., several post-dated employee checks are in the petty cash fund.

b. After necessary approvals have been obtained for the payment of a voucher, the treasurer signs and mails the check. The treasurer then stamps the voucher and supporting documentation as paid and returns the voucher and supporting documentation to the accounts payable clerk for filing.

c. At the end of each day, all cash receipts are placed in the bank's night depository.

d. The accounts payable clerk prepares a voucher for each disbursement. The voucher along with the supporting documentation is forwarded to the treasurer's office for approval.

e. At the end of each day, an accounting clerk compares the duplicate copy of the daily cash deposit slip with the deposit receipt obtained from the bank.

f. The bank reconciliation is prepared by the cashier, who works under the supervision of the treasurer.

g. All mail is opened by the mail clerk, who forwards all cash remittances to the cashier. The cashier prepares a listing of the cash receipts and forwards a copy of the list to the accounts receivable clerk for recording in the accounts.

h. At the end of the day, cash register clerks are required to use their own funds to make up any cash shortages in their registers.

### Instructions

➤ Indicate whether each of the procedures of internal control over cash represents (1) a strength or (2) a weakness. For each weakness, indicate why it exists.

OBJ. 3, 6

**PR 7-2A    Transactions for petty cash, cash short and over**

Picasso Restoration Company completed the following selected transactions during August 2012:

Aug.   1.  Established a petty cash fund of $750.

10.  The cash sales for the day, according to the cash register records, totaled $9,780. The actual cash received from cash sales was $9,800.

31.  Petty cash on hand was $240. Replenished the petty cash fund for the following disbursements, each evidenced by a petty cash receipt:

Aug.   3.  Store supplies, $251.

7.  Express charges on merchandise sold, $60 (Delivery Expense).

9.  Office supplies, $20.

13.  Office supplies, $30.

19.  Postage stamps, $11 (Office Supplies).

21.  Repair to office file cabinet lock, $40 (Miscellaneous Administrative Expense).

Aug. 22. Postage due on special delivery letter, $18 (Miscellaneous Administrative Expense).

24. Express charges on merchandise sold, $50 (Delivery Expense).

30. Office supplies, $15.

31. The cash sales for the day, according to the cash register records, totaled $11,200. The actual cash received from cash sales was $11,130.

31. Decreased the petty cash fund by $100.

**Instructions**

Journalize the transactions.

---

OBJ. 5

✔ 1. Adjusted
balance: $11,400

### PR 7-3A Bank reconciliation and entries

The cash account for Online Medical Co. at June 30, 2012, indicated a balance of $9,375. The bank statement indicated a balance of $10,760 on June 30, 2012. Comparing the bank statement and the accompanying canceled checks and memos with the records revealed the following reconciling items:

a. Checks outstanding totaled $3,900.

b. A deposit of $4,000, representing receipts of June 30, had been made too late to appear on the bank statement.

c. The bank had collected $2,100 on a note left for collection. The face of the note was $2,000.

d. A check for $550 returned with the statement had been incorrectly recorded by Online Medical Co. as $500. The check was for the payment of an obligation to Hirsch Co. for the purchase on account.

e. A check drawn for $60 had been erroneously charged by the bank as $600.

f. Bank service charges for June amounted to $25.

**Instructions**

1. Prepare a bank reconciliation.

2. Journalize the necessary entries. The accounts have not been closed.

3. If a balance sheet were prepared for Online Medical Co. on June 30, 2012, what amount should be reported as cash?

---

OBJ. 5

✔ 1. Adjusted
balance: $23,750

### PR 7-4A Bank reconciliation and entries

The cash account for Bravo Bike Co. at May 1, 2012, indicated a balance of $15,085. During May, the total cash deposited was $75,100 and checks written totaled $69,750. The bank statement indicated a balance of $25,460 on May 31. Comparing the bank statement, the canceled checks, and the accompanying memos with the records revealed the following reconciling items:

a. Checks outstanding totaled $11,360.

b. A deposit of $9,200, representing receipts of May 31, had been made too late to appear on the bank statement.

c. The bank had collected for Bravo Bike Co. $4,725 on a note left for collection. The face of the note was $4,500.

d. A check for $490 returned with the statement had been incorrectly charged by the bank as $940.

e. A check for $410 returned with the statement had been recorded by Bravo Bike Co. as $140. The check was for the payment of an obligation to Portage Co. on account.

f. Bank service charges for July amounted to $40.

g. A check for $1,100 from Elkhart Co. was returned by the bank because of insufficient funds.

**Instructions**

1. Prepare a bank reconciliation as of May 31.

2. Journalize the necessary entries. The accounts have not been closed.

3. If a balance sheet were prepared for Bravo Bike Co. on May 31, 2012, what amount should be reported as cash?

OBJ. 5

✔ 1. Adjusted
balance: $13,900.50

**PR 7-5A   Bank reconciliation and entries**

Oneida Furniture Company deposits all cash receipts each Wednesday and Friday in a night depository, after banking hours. The data required to reconcile the bank statement as of June 30 have been taken from various documents and records and are reproduced as follows. The sources of the data are printed in capital letters. All checks were written for payments on account.

CASH ACCOUNT:

| | |
|---|---:|
| Balance as of June 1 | $9,317.40 |
| CASH RECEIPTS FOR MONTH OF JUNE | $9,524.16 |

DUPLICATE DEPOSIT TICKETS:
  Date and amount of each deposit in June:

| Date | Amount | Date | Amount | Date | Amount |
|---|---|---|---|---|---|
| June 1 | $1,080.50 | June 10 | $ 896.61 | June 22 | $ 897.34 |
| 3 | 854.17 | 15 | 882.95 | 24 | 942.71 |
| 8 | 845.00 | 17 | 1,607.64 | 30 | 1,517.24 |

CHECKS WRITTEN:
  Number and amount of each check issued in June:

| Check No. | Amount | Check No. | Amount | Check No. | Amount |
|---|---|---|---|---|---|
| 740 | $237.50 | 747 | Void | 754 | $ 449.75 |
| 741 | 495.15 | 748 | $450.90 | 755 | 272.75 |
| 742 | 501.90 | 749 | 640.13 | 756 | 113.95 |
| 743 | 671.30 | 750 | 276.77 | 757 | 407.95 |
| 744 | 560.88 | 751 | 299.37 | 758 | 259.60 |
| 745 | 117.25 | 752 | 537.01 | 759 | 901.50 |
| 746 | 298.66 | 753 | 380.95 | 760 | 486.39 |
| Total amount of checks issued in June | | | | | $8,359.66 |

BANK RECONCILIATION FOR PRECEDING MONTH:

**Oneida Furniture Company**
**Bank Reconciliation**
**May 31, 20—**

| | | |
|---|---:|---:|
| Cash balance according to bank statement.......................... | | $ 9,447.20 |
| Add deposit for May 31, not recorded by bank....................... | | 690.25 |
| | | $10,137.45 |
| Deduct outstanding checks: | | |
| No. 731 ...................................................... | $162.15 | |
| 736 ...................................................... | 345.95 | |
| 738 ...................................................... | 251.40 | |
| 739 ...................................................... | 60.55 | 820.05 |
| Adjusted balance............................................... | | $ 9,317.40 |
| Cash balance according to company's records ...................... | | $ 9,352.50 |
| Deduct service charges ......................................... | | 35.10 |
| Adjusted balance............................................... | | $ 9,317.40 |

JUNE BANK STATEMENT:

```
                                    MEMBER FDIC                        PAGE   1

    AMERICAN NATIONAL BANK           ACCOUNT NUMBER
         OF CHICAGO                   FROM 6/01/20–    TO 6/30/20–

 CHICAGO, IL 60603   (312)441-1239    BALANCE           9,447.20

                                    9 DEPOSITS          8,691.77

                                   20 WITHDRAWALS       8,014.37

   ONEIDA FURNITURE COMPANY         4 OTHER DEBITS
                                      AND CREDITS       3,370.00CR

                                      NEW BALANCE      13,494.60
```

| * – – – CHECKS AND OTHER DEBITS – – – * | | | | * – DEPOSITS – – * | – DATE – * | – – BALANCE– – * |
|---|---|---|---|---|---|---|
| No.731 | 162.15 | No.736 | 345.95 | 690.25 | 6/01 | 9,629.35 |
| No.739 | 60.55 | No.740 | 237.50 | 1,080.50 | 6/02 | 10,411.80 |
| No.741 | 495.15 | No.742 | 501.90 | 854.17 | 6/04 | 10,268.92 |
| No.743 | 671.30 | No.744 | 506.88 | 840.50 | 6/09 | 9,931.24 |
| No.745 | 117.25 | No.746 | 298.66 | MS 3,500.00 | 6/09 | 13,015.33 |
| No.748 | 450.90 | No.749 | 640.13 | MS 210.00 | 6/09 | 12,134.30 |
| No.750 | 276.77 | No.751 | 299.37 | 896.61 | 6/11 | 12,454.77 |
| No.752 | 537.01 | No.753 | 380.95 | 882.95 | 6/16 | 12,419.76 |
| No.754 | 449.75 | No.755 | 272.75 | 1,606.74 | 6/18 | 13,304.00 |
| No.757 | 407.95 | No.759 | 901.50 | 897.34 | 6/23 | 12,891.89 |
| | | | | 942.71 | 6/25 | 13,834.60 |
| | | | NSF 300.00 | | 6/28 | 13,534.60 |
| | | | SC 40.00 | | 6/30 | 13,494.60 |

```
   EC — ERROR CORRECTION           OD — OVERDRAFT
   MS — MISCELLANEOUS              PS — PAYMENT STOPPED
   NSF — NOT SUFFICIENT FUNDS      SC — SERVICE CHARGE

   * * *                  * * *                  * * *

      THE RECONCILEMENT OF THIS STATEMENT WITH YOUR RECORDS IS ESSENTIAL.
         ANY ERROR OR EXCEPTION SHOULD BE REPORTED IMMEDIATELY.
```

## Instructions

1. Prepare a bank reconciliation as of June 30. If errors in recording deposits or checks are discovered, assume that the errors were made by the company. Assume that all deposits are from cash sales. All checks are written to satisfy accounts payable.

2. Journalize the necessary entries. The accounts have not been closed.

3. What is the amount of Cash that should appear on the balance sheet as of June 30?

4. ➤ Assume that a canceled check for $270 has been incorrectly recorded by the bank as $720. Briefly explain how the error would be included in a bank reconciliation and how it should be corrected.

# Problems Series B

OBJ. 2, 3

### PR 7-1B    Evaluate internal control of cash

The following procedures were recently installed by The Blind Shop:

a. At the end of a shift, each cashier counts the cash in his or her cash register, unlocks the cash register record, and compares the amount of cash with the amount on the record to determine cash shortages and overages.

b. Checks received through the mail are given daily to the accounts receivable clerk for recording collections on account and for depositing in the bank.

c. Each cashier is assigned a separate cash register drawer to which no other cashier has access.

d. Vouchers and all supporting documents are perforated with a PAID designation after being paid by the treasurer.

e.  All sales are rung up on the cash register, and a receipt is given to the customer. All sales are recorded on a record locked inside the cash register.

f.  Disbursements are made from the petty cash fund only after a petty cash receipt has been completed and signed by the payee.

g.  The bank reconciliation is prepared by the cashier.

**Instructions**

Indicate whether each of the procedures of internal control over cash represents (1) a strength or (2) a weakness. For each weakness, indicate why it exists.

OBJ. 3, 6

**PR 7-2B    Transactions for petty cash, cash short and over**

Cedar Springs Company completed the following selected transactions during November 2012:

Nov.  1.  Established a petty cash fund of $850.

12.  The cash sales for the day, according to the cash register records, totaled $16,100. The actual cash received from cash sales was $16,175.

30.  Petty cash on hand was $70. Replenished the petty cash fund for the following disbursements, each evidenced by a petty cash receipt:

Nov.  2.  Store supplies, $100.

10.  Express charges on merchandise purchased, $260 (Merchandise Inventory).

14.  Office supplies, $125.

15.  Office supplies, $80.

18.  Postage stamps, $70 (Office Supplies).

20.  Repair to fax, $35 (Miscellaneous Administrative Expense).

21.  Repair to office door lock, $15 (Miscellaneous Administrative Expense).

22.  Postage due on special delivery letter, $40 (Miscellaneous Administrative Expense).

28.  Express charges on merchandise purchased, $40 (Merchandise Inventory).

30.  The cash sales for the day, according to the cash register records, totaled $19,415. The actual cash received from cash sales was $19,350.

30.  Increased the petty cash fund by $150.

**Instructions**

Journalize the transactions.

OBJ. 5

✔ 1. Adjusted balance: $27,000

**PR 7-3B    Bank reconciliation and entries**

The cash account for Ambulance Systems at February 29, 2012, indicated a balance of $20,580. The bank statement indicated a balance of $24,750 on February 29, 2012. Comparing the bank statement and the accompanying canceled checks and memos with the records reveals the following reconciling items:

a.  Checks outstanding totaled $9,300.

b.  A deposit of $12,000, representing receipts of February 29, had been made too late to appear on the bank statement.

c.  The bank had collected $6,240 on a note left for collection. The face of the note was $6,000.

d.  A check for $140 returned with the statement had been incorrectly recorded by Ambulance Systems as $410. The check was for the payment of an obligation to Holland Co. for the purchase of office supplies on account.

e.  A check drawn for $725 had been incorrectly charged by the bank as $275.

f.  Bank service charges for February amounted to $90.

**Instructions**

1.  Prepare a bank reconciliation.

2.  Journalize the necessary entries. The accounts have not been closed.

3.  If a balance sheet were prepared for Ambulance Systems on February 29, 2012, what amount should be reported as cash?

**OBJ. 5**

✔ 1. Adjusted
balance: $30,175

### PR 7-4B Bank reconciliation and entries

The cash account for South Bay Sports Co. on April 1, 2012, indicated a balance of $35,025. During April, the total cash deposited was $83,150, and checks written totaled $90,000. The bank statement indicated a balance of $34,345 on April 30, 2012. Comparing the bank statement, the canceled checks, and the accompanying memos with the records revealed the following reconciling items:

a. Checks outstanding totaled $7,700.

b. A deposit of $3,800, representing receipts of April 30, had been made too late to appear on the bank statement.

c. A check for $960 had been incorrectly charged by the bank as $690.

d. A check for $150 returned with the statement had been recorded by South Bay Sports Co. as $1,500. The check was for the payment of an obligation to Jones Co. on account.

e. The bank had collected for South Bay Sports Co. $2,600 on a note left for collection. The face of the note was $2,500.

f. Bank service charges for June amounted to $50.

g. A check for $1,900 from Valley Schools Academy was returned by the bank because of insufficient funds.

### Instructions

1. Prepare a bank reconciliation as of April 30.

2. Journalize the necessary entries. The accounts have not been closed.

3. If a balance sheet were prepared for South Bay Sports Co. on April 30, 2012, what amount should be reported as cash?

**OBJ. 5**

✔ 1. Adjusted
balance: $11,200.00

### PR 7-5B Bank reconciliation and entries

La Casa Interiors deposits all cash receipts each Wednesday and Friday in a night depository, after banking hours. The data required to reconcile the bank statement as of July 31 have been taken from various documents and records and are reproduced as follows. The sources of the data are printed in capital letters. All checks were written for payments on account.

BANK RECONCILIATION FOR PRECEDING MONTH (DATED JUNE 30):

| | | |
|---|---:|---:|
| Cash balance according to bank statement.......................... | | $ 9,422.80 |
| Add deposit of June 30, not recorded by bank....................... | | 780.80 |
| | | $10,203.60 |
| Deduct outstanding checks: | | |
| No. 580 ................................................ | $310.10 | |
| No. 602 ................................................ | 85.50 | |
| No. 612 ................................................ | 92.50 | |
| No. 613 ................................................ | 137.50 | 625.60 |
| Adjusted balance...................................... | | $ 9,578.00 |
| Cash balance according to company's records ...................... | | $ 9,605.70 |
| Deduct service charges ............................................ | | 27.70 |
| Adjusted balance...................................... | | $ 9,578.00 |
| CASH ACCOUNT: | | |
| Balance as of July 1 | | $ 9,578.00 |

CHECKS WRITTEN:

Number and amount of each check issued in July:

| Check No. | Amount | Check No. | Amount | Check No. | Amount |
|---|---|---|---|---|---|
| 614 | $243.50 | 621 | $309.50 | 628 | $ 837.70 |
| 615 | 350.10 | 622 | Void | 629 | 329.90 |
| 616 | 279.90 | 623 | Void | 630 | 882.80 |
| 617 | 395.50 | 624 | 707.01 | 631 | 1,081.56 |
| 618 | 435.40 | 625 | 185.63 | 632 | 325.40 |
| 619 | 320.10 | 626 | 550.03 | 633 | 310.08 |
| 620 | 238.87 | 627 | 318.73 | 634 | 241.71 |
| Total amount of checks issued in July | | | | | $8,343.42 |

CASH RECEIPTS FOR MONTH OF JULY                                                        6,247.12
DUPLICATE DEPOSIT TICKETS:

Date and amount of each deposit in July:

| Date | Amount | Date | Amount | Date | Amount |
|------|--------|------|--------|------|--------|
| July 2 | $569.50 | July 12 | $580.70 | July 23 | $731.45 |
| 5 | 701.80 | 16 | 600.10 | 26 | 601.50 |
| 9 | 812.94 | 19 | 701.26 | 31 | 947.87 |

JULY BANK STATEMENT:

```
                                    MEMBER FDIC                             PAGE   1

     A  AMERICAN NATIONAL BANK          ACCOUNT NUMBER
    NB     OF DETROIT                   FROM   7/01/20–  TO  7/31/20–

     DETROIT, MI 48201-2500  (313)933-8547   BALANCE            9,422.80

                                         9 DEPOSITS              6,086.35

                                        20 WITHDRAWALS           8,237.41

              LA CASA INTERIORS          4 OTHER DEBITS
                                           AND CREDITS           3,685.00CR

                                           NEW BALANCE          10,956.74

     *– – – – – CHECKS AND OTHER DEBITS – – – – – *– DEPOSITS –*– DATE –*– BALANCE– *
      No.580  310.10   No.612    92.50          780.80   07/01    9,801.00
      No.602   85.50   No.614   243.50          569.50   07/03   10,041.50
      No.615  350.10   No.616   279.90          701.80   07/06   10,113.30
      No.617  395.50   No.618   435.40          819.24   07/11   10,101.64
      No.619  320.10   No.620   238.87          580.70   07/13   10,123.37
      No.621  309.50   No.624   707.01   MS 4,000.00     07/14   13,106.86
      No.625  158.63   No.626   550.03   MS   160.00     07/14   12,558.20
      No.627  318.73   No.629   329.90          600.10   07/17   12,509.67
      No.630  882.80   No.631 1,081.56 NSF 450.00        07/20   10,095.31
      No.628  837.70   No.633   310.08          701.26   07/21    9,648.79
                                                731.45   07/24   10,380.24
                                                601.50   07/28   10,981.74
                             SC    25.00                 07/31   10,956.74

        EC — ERROR CORRECTION              OD — OVERDRAFT
        MS — MISCELLANEOUS                 PS — PAYMENT STOPPED
        NSF — NOT SUFFICIENT FUNDS         SC — SERVICE CHARGE
      * * *                         * * *                        * * *
          THE RECONCILEMENT OF THIS STATEMENT WITH YOUR RECORDS IS ESSENTIAL.
            ANY ERROR OR EXCEPTION SHOULD BE REPORTED IMMEDIATELY.
```

## Instructions

1. Prepare a bank reconciliation as of July 31. If errors in recording deposits or checks are discovered, assume that the errors were made by the company. Assume that all deposits are from cash sales. All checks are written to satisfy accounts payable.

2. Journalize the necessary entries. The accounts have not been closed.

3. What is the amount of Cash that should appear on the balance sheet as of July 31?

4. ➤ Assume that a canceled check for $325 has been incorrectly recorded by the bank as $3,250. Briefly explain how the error would be included in a bank reconciliation and how it should be corrected.

## Cases & Projects

You can access Cases & Projects online at **www.cengage.com/accounting/reeve**

© Erik Isakson/Tetra Images/Jupiter Images

# Receivables

## Oakley, Inc.

**T**he sale and purchase of merchandise involves the exchange of goods for cash. However, the point at which cash actually changes hands varies with the transaction. Consider transactions by **Oakley, Inc.**, a worldwide leader in the design, development, manufacture, and distribution of premium sunglasses, goggles, prescription eyewear, apparel, footwear, and accessories. Not only does the company sell its products through three different company-owned retail chains, but it also has approximately 10,000 independent distributors.

If you were to buy a pair of sunglasses at an Oakley Vault, which is one of the company's retail outlet stores, you would have to pay cash or use a credit card to pay for the glasses before you left the store. However, Oakley allows its distributors to purchase sunglasses "on account." These sales on account are recorded as receivables due from the distributors.

As an individual, you also might build up a trusted financial history with a local company or department store that would allow you to purchase merchandise on account. Like Oakley's distributors, your purchase on account would be recorded as an account receivable. Such credit transactions facilitate sales and are a significant current asset for many businesses.

This chapter describes common classifications of receivables, illustrates how to account for uncollectible receivables, and demonstrates the reporting of receivables on the balance sheet.

---

**OBJ. 1** Describe the common classes of receivables.

# Classification of Receivables

The receivables that result from sales on account are normally accounts receivable or notes receivable. The term **receivables** includes all money claims against other entities, including people, companies, and other organizations. Receivables are usually a significant portion of the total current assets.

## Accounts Receivable

The most common transaction creating a receivable is selling merchandise or services on account (on credit). The receivable is recorded as a debit to Accounts Receivable. Such **accounts receivable** are normally collected within a short period, such as 30 or 60 days. They are classified on the balance sheet as a current asset.

An annual report of La-Z-Boy Incorporated reported that receivables made up over 46% of La-Z-Boy's current assets.

## Notes Receivable

**Notes receivable** are amounts that customers owe for which a formal, written instrument of credit has been issued. If notes receivable are expected to be collected within a year, they are classified on the balance sheet as a current asset.

Notes are often used for credit periods of more than 60 days. For example, an automobile dealer may require a down payment at the time of sale and accept a note or a series of notes for the remainder. Such notes usually provide for monthly payments.

Notes may also be used to settle a customer's account receivable. Notes and accounts receivable that result from sales transactions are sometimes called *trade receivables*. In this chapter, all notes and accounts receivable are from sales transactions.

## Other Receivables

*Other receivables* include interest receivable, taxes receivable, and receivables from officers or employees. Other receivables are normally reported separately on the balance sheet. If they are expected to be collected within one year, they are classified as current assets. If collection is expected beyond one year, they are classified as noncurrent assets and reported under the caption *Investments*.

# Uncollectible Receivables

**OBJ. 2** Describe the accounting for uncollectible receivables.

In prior chapters, the accounting for sales of merchandise or services on account (on credit) was described and illustrated. A major issue that has not yet been discussed is that some customers will not pay their accounts. That is, some accounts receivable will be uncollectible.

Companies may shift the risk of uncollectible receivables to other companies. For example, some retailers do not accept sales on account, but will only accept cash or credit cards. Such policies shift the risk to the credit card companies.

Companies may also sell their receivables. This is often the case when a company issues its own credit card. For example, Macy's and JCPenney issue their own credit cards. Selling receivables is called *factoring* the receivables. The buyer of the receivables is called a *factor*. An advantage of factoring is that the company selling its receivables immediately receives cash for operating and other needs. Also, depending on the factoring agreement, some of the risk of uncollectible accounts is shifted to the factor.

Regardless of how careful a company is in granting credit, some credit sales will be uncollectible. The operating expense recorded from uncollectible receivables is called **bad debt expense**, *uncollectible accounts expense*, or *doubtful accounts expense*.

There is no general rule for when an account becomes uncollectible. Some indications that an account may be uncollectible include the following:

1. The receivable is past due.
2. The customer does not respond to the company's attempts to collect.
3. The customer files for bankruptcy.
4. The customer closes its business.
5. The company cannot locate the customer.

Adams, Stevens & Bradley, Ltd. is a collection agency that operates on a contingency basis. That is, its fees are based on what it collects.

If a customer doesn't pay, a company may turn the account over to a collection agency. After the collection agency attempts to collect payment, any remaining balance in the account is considered worthless.

The two methods of accounting for uncollectible receivables are as follows:

1. The **direct write-off method** records bad debt expense only when an account is determined to be worthless.
2. The **allowance method** records bad debt expense by estimating uncollectible accounts at the end of the accounting period.

The direct write-off method is often used by small companies and companies with few receivables.[1] Generally accepted accounting principles (GAAP), however, require companies with a large amount of receivables to use the allowance method. As a result, most well-known companies such as General Electric, Pepsi, Intel, and FedEx use the allowance method.

# Direct Write-Off Method for Uncollectible Accounts

**OBJ. 3** Describe the direct write-off method of accounting for uncollectible receivables.

Under the direct write-off method, Bad Debt Expense is not recorded until the customer's account is determined to be worthless. At that time, the customer's account receivable is written off.

1 The direct write-off method is also required for federal income tax purposes.

To illustrate, assume that a $4,200 account receivable from D. L. Ross has been determined to be uncollectible. The entry to write off the account is as follows:

| | | | | |
|---|---|---|---|---|
| May | 10 | Bad Debt Expense | 4,200 | |
| | | Accounts Receivable—D. L. Ross | | 4,200 |

An account receivable that has been written off may be collected later. In such cases, the account is reinstated by an entry that reverses the write-off entry. The cash received in payment is then recorded as a receipt on account.

To illustrate, assume that the D. L. Ross account of $4,200 written off on May 10 is later collected on November 21. The reinstatement and receipt of cash is recorded as follows:

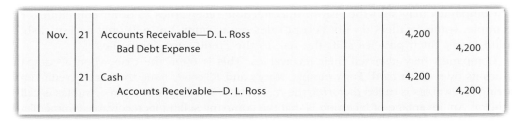

| | | | | |
|---|---|---|---|---|
| Nov. | 21 | Accounts Receivable—D. L. Ross | 4,200 | |
| | | Bad Debt Expense | | 4,200 |
| | 21 | Cash | 4,200 | |
| | | Accounts Receivable—D. L. Ross | | 4,200 |

The direct write-off method is used by businesses that sell most of their goods or services for cash or through the acceptance of MasterCard or VISA, which are recorded as cash sales. In such cases, receivables are a small part of the current assets and any bad debt expense is small. Examples of such businesses are a restaurant, a convenience store, and a small retail store.

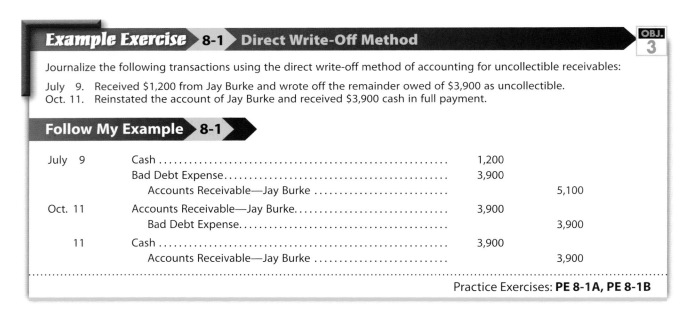

**Example Exercise** ▶ **8-1** ▶ **Direct Write-Off Method**

OBJ. 3

Journalize the following transactions using the direct write-off method of accounting for uncollectible receivables:

July 9. Received $1,200 from Jay Burke and wrote off the remainder owed of $3,900 as uncollectible.
Oct. 11. Reinstated the account of Jay Burke and received $3,900 cash in full payment.

**Follow My Example** ▶ **8-1** ▶

| | | | |
|---|---|---|---|
| July 9 | Cash ............................................................. | 1,200 | |
| | Bad Debt Expense............................................. | 3,900 | |
| | Accounts Receivable—Jay Burke ........................... | | 5,100 |
| Oct. 11 | Accounts Receivable—Jay Burke............................. | 3,900 | |
| | Bad Debt Expense............................................. | | 3,900 |
| 11 | Cash ............................................................. | 3,900 | |
| | Accounts Receivable—Jay Burke ........................... | | 3,900 |

Practice Exercises: **PE 8-1A, PE 8-1B**

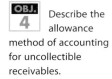

OBJ. 4 Describe the allowance method of accounting for uncollectible receivables.

# Allowance Method for Uncollectible Accounts

The allowance method estimates the uncollectible accounts receivable at the end of the accounting period. Based on this estimate, Bad Debt Expense is recorded by an adjusting entry.

To illustrate, assume that ExTone Company began operations August 1. As of the end of its accounting period on December 31, 2011, ExTone has an accounts receivable balance of $200,000. This balance includes some past due accounts. Based on industry averages, ExTone estimates that $30,000 of the December 31 accounts receivable will be uncollectible. However, on December 31, ExTone doesn't know which customer accounts will be uncollectible. Thus, specific customer accounts cannot be decreased or credited. Instead, a contra asset account, **Allowance for Doubtful Accounts**, is credited for the estimated bad debts.

Using the $30,000 estimate, the following adjusting entry is made on December 31:

| 2011 | | | | | |
|------|----|------------------------------------|--------|--------|
| Dec. | 31 | Bad Debt Expense | 30,000 | |
| | | Allowance for Doubtful Accounts | | 30,000 |
| | | Uncollectible accounts estimate. | | |

The preceding adjusting entry affects the income statement and balance sheet. On the income statement, the $30,000 of Bad Debt Expense will be matched against the related revenues of the period. On the balance sheet, the value of the receivables is reduced to the amount that is expected to be collected or realized. This amount, $170,000 ($200,000 – $30,000), is called the **net realizable value** of the receivables.

After the preceding adjusting entry is recorded, Accounts Receivable still has a debit balance of $200,000. This balance is the total amount owed by customers on account on December 31 as supported by the accounts receivable subsidiary ledger. The accounts receivable contra account, Allowance for Doubtful Accounts, has a credit balance of $30,000.

**Note:**
The adjusting entry reduces receivables to their net realizable value and matches the uncollectible expense with revenues.

## Integrity, Objectivity, and Ethics in Business

**SELLER BEWARE**

A company in financial distress will still try to purchase goods and services on account. In these cases, rather than "buyer beware," it is more like "seller beware." Sellers must be careful in advancing credit to such companies, because trade creditors have low priority for cash payments in the event of bankruptcy. To help suppliers, third-party services specialize in evaluating court actions and payment decisions of financially distressed companies.

## Write-Offs to the Allowance Account

When a customer's account is identified as uncollectible, it is written off against the allowance account. This requires the company to remove the specific accounts receivable and an equal amount from the allowance account.

To illustrate, on January 21, 2012, John Parker's account of $6,000 with ExTone Company is written off as follows:

| 2012 | | | | | |
|------|----|------------------------------------|-------|-------|
| Jan. | 21 | Allowance for Doubtful Accounts | 6,000 | |
| | | Accounts Receivable—John Parker | | 6,000 |

At the end of a period, Allowance for Doubtful Accounts will normally have a balance. This is because Allowance for Doubtful Accounts is based on an estimate. As a result, the total write-offs to the allowance account during the period will rarely equal the balance of the account at the beginning of the period. The allowance account will have a credit balance at the end of the period if the write-offs during the period are less than the beginning balance. It will have a debit balance if the write-offs exceed the beginning balance.

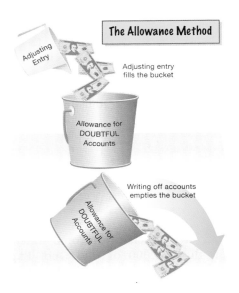

To illustrate, assume that during 2012 ExTone Company writes off $26,750 of uncollectible accounts, including the $6,000 account of John Parker recorded on January 21. Allowance for Doubtful Accounts will have a credit balance of $3,250 ($30,000 – $26,750), as shown below.

**ALLOWANCE FOR DOUBTFUL ACCOUNTS**

| | | | | | | |
|---|---|---|---|---|---|---|
| | | | | Jan. 1 | Balance | 30,000 |
| Total accounts written off $26,750 | Jan. | 21 | 6,000 | | | |
| | Feb. | 2 | 3,900 | | | |
| | ⋮ | | ⋮ | | | |
| | | | | Dec. 31 | Unadjusted balance | 3,250 |

If ExTone Company had written off $32,100 in accounts receivable during 2012, Allowance for Doubtful Accounts would have a debit balance of $2,100, as shown below.

**ALLOWANCE FOR DOUBTFUL ACCOUNTS**

| | | | | | | |
|---|---|---|---|---|---|---|
| | | | | Jan. 1 | Balance | 30,000 |
| Total accounts written off $32,100 | Jan. | 21 | 6,000 | | | |
| | Feb. | 2 | 3,900 | | | |
| | ⋮ | | ⋮ | | | |
| Dec. 31 | Unadjusted balance | | 2,100 | | | |

The allowance account balances (credit balance of $3,250 and debit balance of $2,100) in the preceding illustrations are *before* the end-of-period adjusting entry. After the end-of-period adjusting entry is recorded, Allowance for Doubtful Accounts should always have a credit balance.

An account receivable that has been written off against the allowance account may be collected later. Like the direct write-off method, the account is reinstated by an entry that reverses the write-off entry. The cash received in payment is then recorded as a receipt on account.

To illustrate, assume that Nancy Smith's account of $5,000 which was written off on April 2 is collected later on June 10. ExTone Company records the reinstatement and the collection as follows:

| | | | | |
|---|---|---|---|---|
| June | 10 | Accounts Receivable—Nancy Smith | 5,000 | |
| | | Allowance for Doubtful Accounts | | 5,000 |
| | 10 | Cash | 5,000 | |
| | | Accounts Receivable—Nancy Smith | | 5,000 |

## Example Exercise 8-2 Allowance Method

Journalize the following transactions using the allowance method of accounting for uncollectible receivables.

July 9. Received $1,200 from Jay Burke and wrote off the remainder owed of $3,900 as uncollectible.
Oct. 11. Reinstated the account of Jay Burke and received $3,900 cash in full payment.

### Follow My Example 8-2

| | | | |
|---|---|---|---|
| July 9 | Cash ...................................................... | 1,200 | |
| | Allowance for Doubtful Accounts............................ | 3,900 | |
| | Accounts Receivable—Jay Burke .......................... | | 5,100 |
| Oct. 11 | Accounts Receivable—Jay Burke............................ | 3,900 | |
| | Allowance for Doubtful Accounts......................... | | 3,900 |
| 11 | Cash ...................................................... | 3,900 | |
| | Accounts Receivable—Jay Burke .......................... | | 3,900 |

Practice Exercises: **PE 8-2A, PE 8-2B**

## Estimating Uncollectibles

The allowance method requires an estimate of uncollectible accounts at the end of the period. This estimate is normally based on past experience, industry averages, and forecasts of the future.

The two methods used to estimate uncollectible accounts are as follows:

1. Percent of sales method.
2. Analysis of receivables method.

**Percent of Sales Method** Since accounts receivable are created by credit sales, uncollectible accounts can be estimated as a percent of credit sales. If the portion of credit sales to sales is relatively constant, the percent may be applied to total sales or net sales.

# BusinessConnection

### ALLOWANCE PERCENTAGES ACROSS COMPANIES

The percent of the allowance for doubtful accounts to total accounts receivable will vary across companies and industries. For example, the following percentages were computed from recent annual reports:

HCA's higher percent of allowance for doubtful accounts to total accounts receivable is due in part because Medicare reimbursements are often less than the amounts billed patients.

| Company | Industry | Percent of Allowance for Doubtful Accounts to Total Accounts Receivable |
|---|---|---|
| Apple Inc. | Computer/technology products | 1.5% |
| Deere & Company | Farm machinery & equipment | 17.1 |
| Delta Air Lines | Transportation services | 2.8 |
| HCA Inc. | Health services | 59.0 |
| Sears | Retail | 4.8 |

To illustrate, assume the following data for ExTone Company on December 31, 2012, before any adjustments:

| | |
|---|---|
| Balance of Accounts Receivable | $ 240,000 |
| Balance of Allowance for Doubtful Accounts | 3,250 (Cr.) |
| Total credit sales | 3,000,000 |
| Bad debt as a percent of credit sales | ¾% |

Bad Debt Expense of $22,500 is estimated as follows:

Bad Debt Expense = Credit Sales × Bad Debt as a Percent of Credit Sales
Bad Debt Expense = $3,000,000 × ¾% = $22,500

The adjusting entry for uncollectible accounts on December 31, 2012, is as follows:

| | | | | |
|---|---|---|---|---|
| Dec. | 31 | Bad Debt Expense | 22,500 | |
| | | Allowance for Doubtful Accounts | | 22,500 |
| | | Uncollectible accounts estimate | | |
| | | ($3,000,000 × ¾% = $22,500). | | |

After the adjusting entry is posted to the ledger, Bad Debt Expense will have an adjusted balance of $22,500. Allowance for Doubtful Accounts will have an adjusted balance of $25,750 ($3,250 + $22,500). Both T accounts are shown below.

**BAD DEBT EXPENSE**

| | | |
|---|---|---|
| Dec. 31 | Adjusting entry | 22,500 |
| Dec. 31 | Adjusted balance | 22,500 |

**ALLOWANCE FOR DOUBTFUL ACCOUNTS**

| | | | | | | |
|---|---|---|---|---|---|---|
| | | | | Jan. 1 | Balance | 30,000 |
| Total accounts | Jan. 21 | 6,000 | | | | |
| written off $26,750 | Feb. 2 | 3,900 | | | | |
| | ⋮ | ⋮ | | | | |
| | | | | Dec. 31 | Unadjusted balance | 3,250 |
| | | | | Dec. 31 | Adjusting entry | 22,500 |
| | | | | Dec. 31 | Adjusted balance | 25,750 |

Under the percent of sales method, the amount of the adjusting entry is the amount estimated for Bad Debt Expense. This estimate is credited to whatever the unadjusted balance is for Allowance for Doubtful Accounts.

To illustrate, assume that in the preceding example the unadjusted balance of Allowance for Doubtful Accounts on December 31, 2012, had been a $2,100 debit balance instead of a $3,250 credit balance. The adjustment would still have been $22,500. However, the December 31, 2012, ending adjusted balance of Allowance for Doubtful Accounts would have been $20,400 ($22,500 − $2,100).

**Note:**
The estimate based on sales is added to any balance in Allowance for Doubtful Accounts.

## Example Exercise 8-3 > Percent of Sales Method

**OBJ. 4**

At the end of the current year, Accounts Receivable has a balance of $800,000; Allowance for Doubtful Accounts has a credit balance of $7,500; and net sales for the year total $3,500,000. Bad debt expense is estimated at ½ of 1% of net sales.

Determine (a) the amount of the adjusting entry for uncollectible accounts; (b) the adjusted balances of Accounts Receivable, Allowance for Doubtful Accounts, and Bad Debt Expense; and (c) the net realizable value of accounts receivable.

## Follow My Example 8-3

a.  $17,500 ($3,500,000 × 0.005)

| | Adjusted Balance |
|---|---|
| b.  Accounts Receivable .................................................. | $800,000 |
| Allowance for Doubtful Accounts ($7,500 + $17,500) ...................... | 25,000 |
| Bad Debt Expense....................................................... | 17,500 |

c.  $775,000 ($800,000 − $25,000)

Practice Exercises: **PE 8-3A, PE 8-3B**

**Analysis of Receivables Method** The analysis of receivables method is based on the assumption that the longer an account receivable is outstanding, the less likely that it will be collected. The analysis of receivables method is applied as follows:

Step 1. The due date of each account receivable is determined.

Step 2. The number of days each account is past due is determined. This is the number of days between the due date of the account and the date of the analysis.

Step 3. Each account is placed in an aged class according to its days past due. Typical aged classes include the following:

> Not past due
>
> 1–30 days past due
>
> 31–60 days past due
>
> 61–90 days past due
>
> 91–180 days past due
>
> 181–365 days past due
>
> Over 365 days past due

Step 4. The totals for each aged class are determined.

Step 5. The total for each aged class is multiplied by an estimated percentage of uncollectible accounts for that class.

Step 6. The estimated total of uncollectible accounts is determined as the sum of the uncollectible accounts for each aged class.

The preceding steps are summarized in an aging schedule, and this overall process is called **aging the receivables**.

To illustrate, assume that ExTone Company uses the analysis of receivables method instead of the percent of sales method. ExTone prepared an aging schedule for its accounts receivable of $240,000 as of December 31, 2012, as shown in Exhibit 1.

**EXHIBIT 1** **Aging of Receivables Schedule, December 31, 2012**

| | A | B | C | D | E | F | G | H | I |
|---|---|---|---|---|---|---|---|---|---|
| | | | Not | | | Days Past Due | | | |
| | | | Past | | | | | | Over |
| | Customer | Balance | Due | 1–30 | 31–60 | 61–90 | 91–180 | 181–365 | 365 |
| 4 | Ashby & Co. | 1,500 | | | 1,500 | | | | |
| 5 | B. T. Barr | 6,100 | | | | | 3,500 | 2,600 | |
| 6 | Brock Co. | 4,700 | 4,700 | | | | | | |
| 21 | | | | | | | | | |
| 22 | Saxon Woods Co. | 600 | | | | | 600 | | |
| 23 | Total | 240,000 | 125,000 | 64,000 | 13,100 | 8,900 | 5,000 | 10,000 | 14,000 |
| 24 | Percent uncollectible | | | 2% | 5% | 10% | 20% | 30% | 50% | 80% |
| 25 | Estimate of uncollectible accounts | 26,490 | 2,500 | 3,200 | 1,310 | 1,780 | 1,500 | 5,000 | 11,200 |

Steps 1–3 · Step 4 → 23 · Step 5 → 24 · Step 6 → 25

Assume that ExTone Company sold merchandise to Saxon Woods Co. on August 29 with terms 2/10, n/30. Thus, the due date (Step 1) of Saxon Woods' account is September 28, as shown below.

| Credit terms, net | 30 days |
|---|---|
| Less: Aug. 29 to Aug. 31 | 2 days |
| Days in September | 28 days |

As of December 31, Saxon Woods' account is 94 days past due (Step 2), as shown below.

| | |
|---|---|
| Number of days past due in September | 2 days (30 – 28) |
| Number of days past due in October | 31 days |
| Number of days past due in November | 30 days |
| Number of days past due in December | 31 days |
| Total number of days past due | 94 days |

Exhibit 1 shows that the $600 account receivable for Saxon Woods Co. was placed in the 91–180 days past due class (Step 3).

The total for each of the aged classes is determined (Step 4). Exhibit 1 shows that $125,000 of the accounts receivable are not past due, while $64,000 are 1–30 days past due. ExTone Company applies a different estimated percentage of uncollectible accounts to the totals of each of the aged classes (Step 5). As shown in Exhibit 1, the percent is 2% for accounts not past due, while the percent is 80% for accounts over 365 days past due.

The sum of the estimated uncollectible accounts for each aged class (Step 6) is the estimated uncollectible accounts on December 31, 2012. This is the desired adjusted balance for Allowance for Doubtful Accounts. For ExTone Company, this amount is $26,490, as shown in Exhibit 1.

Comparing the estimate of $26,490 with the unadjusted balance of the allowance account determines the amount of the adjustment for Bad Debt Expense. For ExTone, the unadjusted balance of the allowance account is a credit balance of $3,250. The amount to be added to this balance is therefore $23,240 ($26,490 – $3,250). The adjusting entry is as follows:

**Note:**
The estimate based on receivables is compared to the balance in the allowance account to determine the amount of the adjusting entry.

| | | | | |
|---|---|---|---|---|
| Dec. | 31 | Bad Debt Expense | 23,240 | |
| | | Allowance for Doubtful Accounts | | 23,240 |
| | | Uncollectible accounts estimate | | |
| | | ($26,490 – $3,250). | | |

After the preceding adjusting entry is posted to the ledger, Bad Debt Expense will have an adjusted balance of $23,240. Allowance for Doubtful Accounts will have an adjusted balance of $26,490, and the net realizable value of the receivables is $213,510 ($240,000 – $26,490). Both T accounts are shown below.

**BAD DEBT EXPENSE**

| | | |
|---|---|---|
| Dec. 31 | Adjusting entry | 23,240 |
| Dec. 31 | Adjusted balance | 23,240 |

**ALLOWANCE FOR DOUBTFUL ACCOUNTS**

| | | |
|---|---|---|
| Dec. 31 | Unadjusted balance | 3,250 |
| Dec. 31 | Adjusting entry | 23,240 |
| Dec. 31 | Adjusted balance | 26,490 |

Under the analysis of receivable method, the amount of the adjusting entry is the amount that will yield an adjusted balance for Allowance for Doubtful Accounts equal to that estimated by the aging schedule.

To illustrate, if the unadjusted balance of the allowance account had been a debit balance of $2,100, the amount of the adjustment would have been $28,590 ($26,490 + $2,100). In this case, Bad Debt Expense would have an adjusted balance of $28,590. However, the adjusted balance of Allowance for Doubtful Accounts would still have been $26,490. After the adjusting entry is posted, both T accounts are shown below.

**BAD DEBT EXPENSE**

| | | |
|---|---|---|
| Dec. 31 | Adjusting entry | 28,590 |
| Dec. 31 | Adjusted balance | 28,590 |

**ALLOWANCE FOR DOUBTFUL ACCOUNTS**

| | | | | | |
|---|---|---|---|---|---|
| Dec. 31 | Unadjusted balance | 2,100 | | | |
| | | | Dec. 31 | Adjusting entry | 28,590 |
| | | | Dec. 31 | Adjusted balance | 26,490 |

success

The aging of receivables schedule from *Exhibit 1* can be developed using spreadsheet software as follows:

| | A | B | C | D | E | F | G | H | I |
|---|---|---|---|---|---|---|---|---|---|
| 1 | | | | | | Days Past Due | | | |
| 2 | Customer | Balance | Not Past Due | 1-30 | 31-60 | 61-90 | 91-180 | 181-365 | Over 365 |
| 3 | Ashby & Co. | 1,500 | - | | 1,500 | | | | |
| 4 | B.T. Barr | 6,100 | - | | | | | 3,500 | 2,600 |
| 5 | Brock Co. | 4,700 | 4,700 | | | | | | |
| 21 | Saxon Woods Co. | 600 | - | - | - | 600 | | | |
| 22 | Total  a. | =SUM(B3:B21) | =SUM(C3:C21) | =SUM(D3:D21) | =SUM(E3:E21) | =SUM(F3:F21) | =SUM(G3:G21) | =SUM(H3:H21) | =SUM(I3:I21) |
| 23 | Percent uncollectible | | 2% | 5% | 10% b. | 20% | 30% | 50% | 80% |
| 24 | Estimate of uncollectible accounts | =SUM(C24:I24) | =C22*C23 | =D22*D23 | =E22*E23 | =F22*F23 | =G22*G23 | =H22*H23 | =I22*I23 |
| 25 | | | | | | | | | |

c.

d.

A spreadsheet uses the asterisk symbol (*) for multiplication.

Develop the formulas using the following steps:

a.  Enter a formula in B22 to sum the "Balance" column, =SUM(B3:B21).
b.  Copy the formula from B22 to C22:I22 so that the sum formula applies to all *Days Past Due* categories.
c.  Enter a formula in C24 to multiply the sum in C22 by the percent uncollectible in C23, =C22*C23.
d.  Copy the formula from C24 to D24:I24 so that the multiplication formula applies to all *Days Past Due* categories.
e.  Enter a formula in B24 to sum the total estimated uncollectible for each period, =SUM(C24:I24).

**Try***It*  Go to the hands-on **Excel Tutor** for this example!

## Example Exercise ▶ 8-4 ▶ Analysis of Receivables Method

**OBJ. 4**

At the end of the current year, Accounts Receivable has a balance of $800,000; Allowance for Doubtful Accounts has a credit balance of $7,500; and net sales for the year total $3,500,000. Using the aging method, the balance of Allowance for Doubtful Accounts is estimated as $30,000.

Determine (a) the amount of the adjusting entry for uncollectible accounts; (b) the adjusted balances of Accounts Receivable, Allowance for Doubtful Accounts, and Bad Debt Expense; and (c) the net realizable value of accounts receivable.

## Follow My Example ▶ 8-4

a.  $22,500 ($30,000 – $7,500)

| | Adjusted Balance |
|---|---|
| b.  Accounts Receivable | $800,000 |
| Allowance for Doubtful Accounts | 30,000 |
| Bad Debt Expense | 22,500 |

c.  $770,000 ($800,000 – $30,000)

Practice Exercises: **PE 8-4A, PE 8-4B**

**Comparing Estimation Methods** Both the percent of sales and analysis of receivables methods estimate uncollectible accounts. However, each method has a slightly different focus and financial statement emphasis.

Under the percent of sales method, Bad Debt Expense is the focus of the estimation process. The percent of sales method places more emphasis on matching revenues and expenses and, thus, emphasizes the income statement. That is, the amount of the adjusting entry is based on the estimate of Bad Debt Expense for the period. Allowance for Doubtful Accounts is then credited for this amount.

Under the analysis of receivables method, Allowance for Doubtful Accounts is the focus of the estimation process. The analysis of receivables method places more emphasis on the net realizable value of the receivables and, thus, emphasizes the balance sheet. That is, the amount of the adjusting entry is the amount that will yield an adjusted balance for Allowance for Doubtful Accounts equal to that estimated by the aging schedule. Bad Debt Expense is then debited for this amount.

Exhibit 2 summarizes these differences between the percent of sales and the analysis of receivables methods. Exhibit 2 also shows the results of the ExTone Company illustration for the percent of sales and analysis of receivables methods. The amounts shown in Exhibit 2 assume an unadjusted credit balance of $3,250 for Allowance for

**EXHIBIT 2**

**Difference
Between
Estimation
Methods**

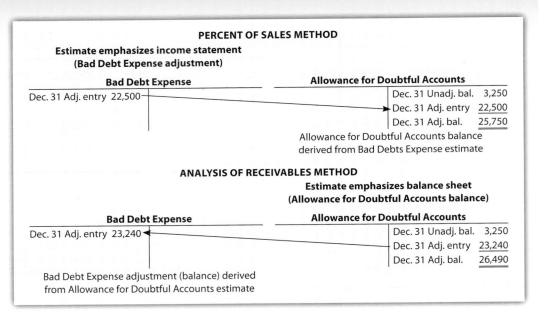

Doubtful Accounts. While the methods normally yield different amounts for any one period, over several periods the amounts should be similar.

**OBJ.
5**
Compare the direct write-off and allowance methods of accounting for uncollectible accounts.

# Comparing Direct Write-Off and Allowance Methods

Journal entries for the direct write-off and allowance methods are illustrated and compared in this section. As a basis for illustration, the following transactions, taken from the records of Hobbs Co. for the year ending December 31, 2011, are used:

Mar. 1. Wrote off account of C. York, $3,650.

Apr. 12. Received $2,250 as partial payment on the $5,500 account of Cary Bradshaw. Wrote off the remaining balance as uncollectible.

June 22. Received the $3,650 from C. York, which had been written off on March 1. Reinstated the account and recorded the cash receipt.

Sept. 7. Wrote off the following accounts as uncollectible (record as one journal entry):

| | | | |
|---|---|---|---|
| Jason Bigg | $1,100 | Stanford Noonan | $1,360 |
| Steve Bradey | 2,220 | Aiden Wyman | 990 |
| Samantha Neeley | 775 | | |

Dec. 31. Hobbs Company uses the percent of credit sales method of estimating uncollectible expenses. Based on past history and industry averages, 1.25% of credit sales are expected to be uncollectible. Hobbs recorded $3,400,000 of credit sales during 2011.

Exhibit 3 illustrates the journal entries for Hobbs Co. using the direct write-off and allowance methods. Using the direct write-off method, there is no adjusting entry on December 31 for uncollectible accounts. In contrast, the allowance method records an adjusting entry for estimated uncollectible accounts of $42,500.

The primary differences between the direct write-off and allowance methods are summarized below.

| | Direct Write-Off Method | Allowance Method |
|---|---|---|
| Bad debt expense is recorded | When the specific customer accounts are determined to be uncollectible. | Using estimate based on (1) a percent of sales or (2) an analysis of receivables. |
| Allowance account | No allowance account is used. | The allowance account is used. |
| Primary users | Small companies and companies with few receivables. | Large companies and those with a large amount of receivables. |

## EXHIBIT 3  Comparing Direct Write-Off and Allowance Methods

| 2011 | | | Direct Write-Off Method | | | Allowance Method | | |
|---|---|---|---|---|---|---|---|---|
| Mar. | 1 | | Bad Debt Expense | 3,650 | | Allowance for Doubtful Accounts | 3,650 | |
| | | | Accounts Receivable—C. York | | 3,650 | Accounts Receivable—C. York | | 3,650 |
| Apr. | 12 | | Cash | 2,250 | | Cash | 2,250 | |
| | | | Bad Debt Expense | 3,250 | | Allowance for Doubtful Accounts | 3,250 | |
| | | | Accounts Receivable—Cary Bradshaw | | 5,500 | Accounts Receivable—Cary Bradshaw | | 5,500 |
| June | 22 | | Accounts Receivable—C. York | 3,650 | | Accounts Receivable—C. York | 3,650 | |
| | | | Bad Debt Expense | | 3,650 | Allowance for Doubtful Accounts | | 3,650 |
| | 22 | | Cash | 3,650 | | Cash | 3,650 | |
| | | | Accounts Receivable—C. York | | 3,650 | Accounts Receivable—C. York | | 3,650 |
| Sept. | 7 | | Bad Debt Expense | 6,445 | | Allowance for Doubtful Accounts | 6,445 | |
| | | | Accounts Receivable—Jason Bigg | | 1,100 | Accounts Receivable—Jason Bigg | | 1,100 |
| | | | Accounts Receivable—Steve Bradey | | 2,220 | Accounts Receivable—Steve Bradey | | 2,220 |
| | | | Accounts Receivable—Samantha Neeley | | 775 | Accounts Receivable—Samantha Neeley | | 775 |
| | | | Accounts Receivable—Stanford Noonan | | 1,360 | Accounts Receivable—Stanford Noonan | | 1,360 |
| | | | Accounts Receivable—Aiden Wyman | | 990 | Accounts Receivable—Aiden Wyman | | 990 |
| Dec. | 31 | | No Entry | | | Bad Debt Expense | 42,500 | |
| | | | | | | Allowance for Doubtful Accounts | | 42,500 |
| | | | | | | Uncollectible accounts estimate ($3,400,000 × 0.0125 = $42,500). | | |

# Notes Receivable

**OBJ. 6** Describe the accounting for notes receivable.

A note has some advantages over an account receivable. By signing a note, the debtor recognizes the debt and agrees to pay it according to its terms. Thus, a note is a stronger legal claim.

## Characteristics of Notes Receivable

A promissory note is a written promise to pay the face amount, usually with interest, on demand or at a date in the future.[2] Characteristics of a promissory note are as follows:

1. The *maker* is the party making the promise to pay.
2. The *payee* is the party to whom the note is payable.
3. The *face amount* is the amount for which the note is written on its face.
4. The *issuance date* is the date a note is issued.
5. The *due date* or *maturity date* is the date the note is to be paid.
6. The *term* of a note is the amount of time between the issuance and due dates.
7. The *interest rate* is that rate of interest that must be paid on the face amount for the term of the note.

Exhibit 4 illustrates a promissory note. The maker of the note is Selig Company, and the payee is Pearland Company. The face value of the note is $2,000, and the

2 You may see references to noninterest-bearing notes. Such notes are not widely used and carry an assumed or implicit interest rate.

### EXHIBIT 4 Promissory Note

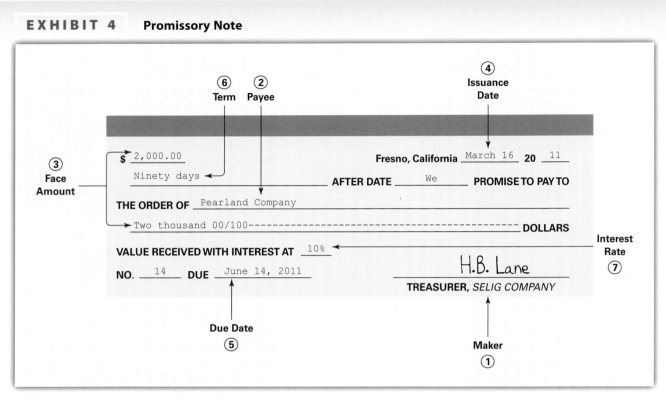

issuance date is March 16, 2011. The term of the note is 90 days, which results in a due date of June 14, 2011, as shown below.

| | |
|---|---|
| Days in March | 31 days |
| Minus issuance date of note | 16 |
| Days remaining in March | 15 days |
| Add days in April | 30 |
| Add days in May | 31 |
| Add days in June (due date of June 14) | 14 |
| Term of note | 90 days |

## Due Date of 90-Day Note

In Exhibit 4, the term of the note is 90 days and has an interest rate of 10%. The interest on a note is computed as follows:

$$\text{Interest} = \text{Face Amount} \times \text{Interest Rate} \times (\text{Term}/360 \text{ days})$$

The interest rate is stated on an annual (yearly) basis, while the term is expressed as days. Thus, the interest on the note in Exhibit 4 is computed as follows:

$$\text{Interest} = \$2,000 \times 10\% \times (90/360) = \$50$$

To simplify, 360 days per year will be used. In practice, companies such as banks and mortgage companies use the exact number of days in a year, 365.

The **maturity value** is the amount that must be paid at the due date of the note, which is the sum of the face amount and the interest. The maturity value of the note in Exhibit 4 is $2,050 ($2,000 + $50).

The interest on a note can be computed using a simple spreadsheet formula shown as follows:

|     | A            | B              | C    |      |
| --- | ------------ | -------------- | ---- | ---- |
| 1   |              |                |      |      |
| 2   | *Inputs*     |                |      |      |
| 3   | Face amount  | $ 2,000        |      | a.   |
| 4   | Interest rate | 10%           |      | b.   |
| 5   | Term         | 90             | days | c.   |
| 6   |              |                |      |      |
| 7   | *Output*     |                |      | d.   |
| 8   | Interest     | =B3*B4*(B5/360) |     |      |
| 9   |              |                |      |      |
| 10  |              |                |      |      |

Also, although the parentheses are not required, it is good programming practice.

There are three *inputs to* enter as follows:

a. Enter the face amount in cell B3 (in this example, 2,000).
b. Enter the interest rate in cell B4 (in this example, 10%, entered as .10 and formatted as a percent).
c. Enter the term in cell B5 (in this example, 90 expressed in days).
d. The output is a formula entered in B8 that determines the interest, =B3*B4*(B5/360).

**Try***It* Go to the hands-on **Excel Tutor** for this example!

## Accounting for Notes Receivable

A promissory note may be received by a company from a customer to replace an account receivable. In such cases, the promissory note is recorded as a note receivable.[3]

To illustrate, assume that a company accepts a 30-day, 12% note dated November 21, 2012, in settlement of the account of W. A. Bunn Co., which is past due and has a balance of $6,000. The company records the receipt of the note as follows:

| Nov. | 21 | Notes Receivable—W. A. Bunn Co. | 6,000 | |
| | | Accounts Receivable—W. A. Bunn Co. | | 6,000 |

At the due date, the company records the receipt of $6,060 ($6,000 face amount plus $60 interest) as follows:

| Dec. | 21 | Cash | 6,060 | |
| | | Notes Receivable—W. A. Bunn Co. | | 6,000 |
| | | Interest Revenue | | 60 |
| | | [$6,060 = $6,000 + ($6,000 × 12% × 30/360)]. | | |

If the maker of a note fails to pay the note on the due date, the note is a **dishonored note receivable**. A company that holds a dishonored note transfers the face amount of the note plus any interest due back to an accounts receivable account. For example, assume that the $6,000, 30-day, 12% note received from W. A. Bunn Co. and recorded on November 21 is dishonored. The company holding the note transfers the note and interest back to the customer's account as follows:

| Dec. | 21 | Accounts Receivable—W. A. Bunn Co. | 6,060 | |
| | | Notes Receivable—W. A. Bunn Co. | | 6,000 |
| | | Interest Revenue | | 60 |

3 The accounting for notes payable is described and illustrated in Chapter 12.

The company has earned the interest of $60, even though the note is dishonored. If the account receivable is uncollectible, the company will write off $6,060 against Allowance for Doubtful Accounts.

A company receiving a note should record an adjusting entry for any accrued interest at the end of the period. For example, assume that Crawford Company issues a $4,000, 90-day, 12% note dated December 1, 2012, to settle its account receivable. If the accounting period ends on December 31, the company receiving the note would record the following entries:

| 2012 | | | | |
|---|---|---|---|---|
| Dec. | 1 | Notes Receivable—Crawford Company | 4,000 | |
| | | Accounts Receivable—Crawford Company | | 4,000 |
| | 31 | Interest Receivable | 40 | |
| | | Interest Revenue | | 40 |
| | | Accrued interest | | |
| | | ($4,000 × 12% × 30/360). | | |
| 2013 | | | | |
| Mar. | 1 | Cash | 4,120 | |
| | | Notes Receivable—Crawford Company | | 4,000 |
| | | Interest Receivable | | 40 |
| | | Interest Revenue | | 80 |
| | | Total interest of $120 | | |
| | | ($4,000 × 12% × 90/360). | | |

The interest revenue account is closed at the end of each accounting period. The amount of interest revenue is normally reported in the Other Income section of the income statement.

## Example Exercise 8-5　Note Receivable

**OBJ. 6**

Same Day Surgery Center received a 120-day, 6% note for $40,000, dated March 14 from a patient on account.

a. Determine the due date of the note.
b. Determine the maturity value of the note.
c. Journalize the entry to record the receipt of the payment of the note at maturity.

### Follow My Example 8-5

a. The due date of the note is July 12, determined as follows:

| March | 17 days (31 – 14) |
|---|---|
| April | 30 days |
| May | 31 days |
| June | 30 days |
| July | 12 days |
| Total | 120 days |

b. $40,800 [$40,000 + ($40,000 × 6% × 120/360)]

c. July 12　Cash ....................................................... 40,800
　　　　　Notes Receivable......................................... 40,000
　　　　　Interest Revenue......................................... 800

Practice Exercises: **PE 8-5A, PE 8-5B**

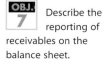

**OBJ. 7**

Describe the reporting of receivables on the balance sheet.

# Reporting Receivables on the Balance Sheet

All receivables that are expected to be realized in cash within a year are reported in the Current Assets section of the balance sheet. Current assets are normally reported in the order of their liquidity, beginning with cash and cash equivalents.

The balance sheet presentation for receivables for Mornin' Joe is shown below.

### Mornin' Joe
### Balance Sheet
### December 31, 2012

#### Assets

| | | |
|---|---:|---:|
| Current assets: | | |
| Cash and cash equivalents .................................. | | $235,000 |
| Trading investments (at cost).............................. | $420,000 | |
|    Plus valuation allowance for trading investments......... | 45,000 | 465,000 |
| Accounts receivable ........................................ | $305,000 | |
|    Less allowance for doubtful accounts.................... | 12,300 | 292,700 |

In Mornin' Joe's financial statements, the allowance for doubtful accounts is subtracted from accounts receivable. Some companies report receivables at their net realizable value with a note showing the amount of the allowance.

Other disclosures related to receivables are reported either on the face of the financial statements or in the financial statement notes. Such disclosures include the market (fair) value of the receivables. In addition, if unusual credit risks exist within the receivables, the nature of the risks are disclosed. For example, if the majority of the receivables are due from one customer or are due from customers located in one area of the country or one industry, these facts are disclosed.[4]

## IFRS Reporting

The statement of financial position (balance sheet) presentation for accounts receivable for Mornin' Joe International under IFRS is as follows:

See pages 630–634

### Mornin' Joe International
### Statement of Financial Position
### December 31, 2012

#### Current assets

| | | |
|---|---:|---:|
| Prepaid insurance ..................................................... | € 24,000 | |
| Merchandise inventory—at lower of cost (first in first out) or | | |
|    realizable value ..................................................... | 120,000 | |
| **Accounts receivable (net of allowance for doubtful accounts)** ....... | 292,700 | |
| Financial assets at fair value through profit or loss ...................... | 465,000 | |
| Cash and cash equivalents............................................. | 235,000 | |
|    Total current assets ................................................. | | €1,136,700 |

As discussed in Chapter 7, IFRS provides flexibility in the order in which the balance sheet accounts are presented. However, assets are normally presented from the least liquid to the most liquid. Thus, accounts receivable is normally presented after merchandise inventory, but prior to cash.

Under IFRS, the Allowance for Doubtful Accounts is disclosed in a footnote. In contrast, U.S. companies can either present Allowance for Doubtful Accounts on the face of the balance sheet or use a footnote.

 Describe and illustrate the use of accounts receivable turnover and number of days' sales in receivables to evaluate a company's efficiency in collecting its receivables.

# Financial Analysis and Interpretation: Accounts Receivable Turnover and Number of Days' Sales in Receivables

Two financial measures that are especially useful in evaluating efficiency in collecting receivables are (1) the accounts receivable turnover and (2) the number of days' sales in receivables.

The **accounts receivable turnover** measures how frequently during the year the accounts receivable are being converted to cash. For example, with credit terms of n/30, the accounts receivable should turn over about 12 times per year.

The accounts receivable turnover is computed as follows:[5]

$$\text{Accounts Receivable Turnover} = \frac{\text{Net Sales}}{\text{Average Accounts Receivable}}$$

The average accounts receivable can be determined by using monthly data or by simply adding the beginning and ending accounts receivable balances and dividing by two. For example, using the following financial data (in millions) for FedEx, the 2009 and 2008 accounts receivable turnover is computed as 8.1 as shown below.

|  | 2009 | 2008 |
|---|---|---|
| Net sales | $35,497 | $37,953 |
| Accounts receivable: | | |
|   Beginning of year | 4,903 | 4,478 |
|   End of year | 3,902 | 4,903 |
| Average accounts receivable: | | |
|   ($3,902 + $4,903)/2 | 4,403 | |
|   ($4,903 + $4,478)/2 | | 4,691 |
| Accounts receivable turnover: | | |
|   $35,497/$4,403 | 8.1 | |
|   $37,953/$4,691 | | 8.1 |

The **number of days' sales in receivables** is an estimate of the length of time the accounts receivable have been outstanding. With credit terms of n/30, the number of days' sales in receivables should be about 30 days. It is computed as follows:

$$\text{Number of Days' Sales in Receivables} = \frac{\text{Average Accounts Receivable}}{\text{Average Daily Sales}}$$

Average daily sales are determined by dividing net sales by 365 days. For example, using the preceding data for FedEx, the number of days' sales in receivables is 45.3 and 45.1 for 2009 and 2008, as shown below.

|  | 2009 | 2008 |
|---|---|---|
| Average daily sales: | | |
|   $35,497/365 | 97.3 | |
|   $37,953/365 | | 104.0 |
| Number of days' sales in receivables: | | |
|   $4,403/97.3 | 45.3 | |
|   $4,691/104.0 | | 45.1 |

5 If known, credit sales can be used in the numerator. However, because credit sales are not normally disclosed to external users, most analysts use net sales in the numerator.

## Example Exercise ▸ 8-6 ▸ Accounts Receivable Turnover and Number of Days' Sales in Receivables

OBJ.
8

Financial statement data for years ending December 31 for Osterman Company are as follows:

|  | **2012** | **2011** |
|---|---|---|
| Net sales ........................................ | $4,284,000 | $3,040,000 |
| Accounts receivable: | | |
| Beginning of year ............................ | 550,000 | 400,000 |
| End of year..................................... | 640,000 | 550,000 |

a.  Determine accounts receivable turnover for 2012 and 2011.

b.  Determine the number of days' sales in receivables for 2012 and 2011.

c.  Does the change in accounts receivable turnover and the number of days' sales in receivable from 2011 to 2012 indicate a favorable or an unfavorable trend?

## Follow My Example ▸ 8-6

a.  Accounts receivable turnover:

|  | **2012** | **2011** |
|---|---|---|
| Average accounts receivable: | | |
| ($550,000 + $640,000)/2...................... | $595,000 | |
| ($400,000 + $550,000)/2...................... | | $475,000 |
| Accounts receivable turnover: | | |
| $4,284,000/$595,000 .......................... | 7.2 | |
| $3,040,000/$475,000 .......................... | | 6.4 |

b.  Number of days' sales in receivables:

|  | **2012** | **2011** |
|---|---|---|
| Average daily sales: | | |
| $4,284,000/365 days ......................... | $11,737 | |
| $3,040,000/365 days ......................... | | $8,329 |
| Number of days' sales in receivables: | | |
| $595,000/$11,737............................. | 50.7 days | |
| $475,000/$8,329 ............................. | | 57.0 days |

c.  The increase in the accounts receivable turnover from 6.4 to 7.2 and the decrease in the number of days' sales in receivables from 57.0 days to 50.7 days indicate favorable trends in the efficiency of collecting accounts receivable.

Practice Exercises: **PE 8-6A, PE 8-6B**

The number of days' sales in receivables confirms that FedEx's efficiency in collecting accounts receivable has remained the same during 2009 and 2008. Generally, the efficiency in collecting accounts receivable has improved when the accounts receivable turnover increases or the number of days' sales in receivables decreases.

# BusinessConnection

## DELTA AIR LINES

Delta Air Lines is a major air carrier that services cities throughout the United States and the world. In its operations, Delta generates accounts receivable as reported in the following note to its financial statements:

*Our accounts receivable are generated largely from the sale of passenger airline tickets and cargo transportation services.*

*The majority of these sales are processed through major credit card companies, resulting in accounts receivable...*

*We also have receivables from the sale of mileage credits under our Sky-Miles and WorldPerks*

*Programs to participating airlines and nonairline businesses such as credit card companies, hotels, and car rental agencies. We believe the credit risk associated with these receivables is minimal and that the allowance for uncollectible accounts that we have provided is appropriate.*

In its December 31, 2008, balance sheet, Delta reported the following accounts receivable (in millions):

|  | Dec. 31, 2009 | Dec. 31, 2008 |
|---|---|---|
| Current Assets: | | |
| ... | | |
| Accounts receivable, net of an allowance for uncollectible accounts of $47 at December 31, 2009 and $42 at December 31, 2008 . . . . . . . . . . . | $1,353 | $1,513 |

# At a Glance 8

### OBJ. 1

## Describe the common classes of receivables.

**Key Points** *Receivables* includes all money claims against other entities. Receivables are normally classified as accounts receivable, notes receivable, or other receivables.

| Learning Outcomes | Example Exercises | Practice Exercises |
|---|---|---|
| • Define the term *receivables*. | | |
| • List some common classifications of receivables. | | |

### OBJ. 2

## Describe the accounting for uncollectible receivables.

**Key Points** The operating expense recorded from uncollectible receivables is called *bad debt expense*. The two methods of accounting for uncollectible receivables are the direct write-off method and the allowance method.

| Learning Outcomes | Example Exercises | Practice Exercises |
|---|---|---|
| • Describe how a company may shift the risk of uncollectible receivables to other companies. | | |
| • List factors that indicate an account receivable is uncollectible | | |
| • Describe two methods of accounting for uncollectible accounts receivable. | | |

**OBJ. 3**

### Describe the direct write-off method of accounting for uncollectible receivables.

**Key Points**   Under the direct write-off method, the entry to write off an account debits Bad Debt Expense and credits Accounts Receivable. Neither an allowance account nor an adjusting entry is needed at the end of the period.

| Learning Outcomes | Example Exercises | Practice Exercises |
|---|---|---|
| • Prepare journal entries to write off an account using the direct write-off method. | EE8-1 | PE8-1A, 8-1B |
| • Prepare journal entries for the reinstatement and collection of an account previously written off. | EE8-1 | PE8-1A, 8-1B |

**OBJ. 4**

### Describe the allowance method of accounting for uncollectible receivables.

**Key Points**   Under the allowance method, an adjusting entry is made for uncollectible accounts. When an account is determined to be uncollectible, it is written off against the allowance account. The allowance account normally has a credit balance after the adjusting entry has been posted and is a contra asset account.

   The estimate of uncollectibles may be based on a percent of sales or an analysis of receivables. Exhibit 2 compares and contrasts these two methods..

| Learning Outcomes | Example Exercises | Practice Exercises |
|---|---|---|
| • Prepare journal entries to write off an account using the allowance method. | EE8-2 | PE8-2A, 8-2B |
| • Prepare journal entries for the reinstatement and collection of an account previously written off. | EE8-2 | PE8-2A, 8-2B |
| • Determine the adjustment, bad debt expense, and net realizable value of accounts receivable using the percent of sales method. | EE8-3 | PE8-3A, 8-3B |
| • Determine the adjustment, bad debt expense, and net realizable value of accounts receivable using the analysis of receivables method. | EE8-4 | PE8-4A, 8-4B |

**OBJ. 5**

### Compare the direct write-off and allowance methods of accounting for uncollectible accounts.

**Key Points**   Exhibit 3 illustrates the differences between the direct write-off and allowance methods of accounting for uncollectible accounts.

| Learning Outcomes | Example Exercises | Practice Exercises |
|---|---|---|
| • Describe the differences in accounting for uncollectible accounts under the direct write-off and allowance methods. | | |
| • Record journal entries using the direct write-off and allowance methods. | | |

**OBJ. 6**

### Describe the accounting for notes receivable.

**Key Points**   A note received to settle an account receivable is recorded as a debit to Notes Receivable and a credit to Accounts Receivable. When a note is paid at maturity, Cash is debited, Notes Receivable is credited, and Interest Revenue is credited. If the maker of a note fails to pay, the dishonored note is recorded by debiting an accounts receivable account for the amount due from the maker of the note.

| Learning Outcomes | Example Exercises | Practice Exercises |
|---|---|---|
| • Describe the characteristics of a note receivable. | | |
| • Determine the due date and maturity value of a note receivable. | EE8-5 | PE8-5A, 8-5B |
| • Prepare journal entries for the receipt of the payment of a note receivable. | EE8-5 | PE8-5A, 8-5B |
| • Prepare a journal entry for the dishonored note receivable. | | |

**OBJ. 7**

**Describe the reporting of receivables on the balance sheet.**

**Key Points**  All receivables that are expected to be realized in cash within a year are reported in the Current Assets section of the balance sheet. In addition to the allowance for doubtful accounts, additional receivable disclosures include the market (fair) value and unusual credit risks.

| Learning Outcomes | Example Exercises | Practice Exercises |
|---|---|---|
| • Describe how receivables are reported in the Current Assets section of the balance sheet. | | |
| • Describe disclosures related to receivables that should be reported in the financial statements. | | |

**OBJ. 8**

**Describe and illustrate the use of accounts receivable turnover and number of days' sales in receivables to evaluate a company's efficiency in collecting its receivables.**

**Key Points**  Two financial measures that are especially useful in evaluating efficiency in collecting receivables are (1) the accounts receivable turnover and (2) the number of days' sales in receivables. Generally, the efficiency in collecting accounts receivable has improved when the accounts receivable turnover increases or there is a decrease in the number of days' sales in receivables.

| Learning Outcomes | Example Exercises | Practice Exercises |
|---|---|---|
| • Describe two measures of the efficiency of managing receivables. | | |
| • Compute and interpret the accounts receivable turnover and number of days' sales in receivables. | EE8-6 | PE8-6A, 8-6B |

## Key Terms

accounts receivable (362)
accounts receivable turnover (378)
aging the receivables (369)
Allowance for Doubtful
 Accounts (365)

allowance method (363)
bad debt expense (363)
direct write-off method (363)
dishonored note receivable (375)
maturity value (374)

net realizable value (365)
notes receivable (362)
number of days' sales in
 receivables (378)
receivables (362)

## Illustrative Problem

Ditzler Company, a construction supply company, uses the allowance method of accounting for uncollectible accounts receivable. Selected transactions completed by Ditzler Company are as follows:

Feb.  1.  Sold merchandise on account to Ames Co., $8,000. The cost of the merchandise sold was $4,500.

Mar. 15.  Accepted a 60-day, 12% note for $8,000 from Ames Co. on account.

Apr.  9.  Wrote off a $2,500 account from Dorset Co. as uncollectible.

     21.  Loaned $7,500 cash to Jill Klein, receiving a 90-day, 14% note.

May 14. Received the interest due from Ames Co. and a new 90-day, 14% note as a renewal of the loan. (Record both the debit and the credit to the notes receivable account.)

June 13. Reinstated the account of Dorset Co., written off on April 9, and received $2,500 in full payment.

July 20. Jill Klein dishonored her note.

Aug. 12. Received from Ames Co. the amount due on its note of May 14.

19. Received from Jill Klein the amount owed on the dishonored note, plus interest for 30 days at 15%, computed on the maturity value of the note.

Dec. 16. Accepted a 60-day, 12% note for $12,000 from Global Company on account.

31. It is estimated that 3% of the credit sales of $1,375,000 for the year ended December 31 will be uncollectible.

## Instructions

1. Journalize the transactions.

2. Journalize the adjusting entry to record the accrued interest on December 31 on the Global Company note.

## Solution

1.

| | | | | |
|---|---|---|---|---|
| Feb. | 1 | Accounts Receivable—Ames Co. | 8,000.00 | |
| | | Sales | | 8,000.00 |
| | 1 | Cost of Merchandise Sold | 4,500.00 | |
| | | Merchandise Inventory | | 4,500.00 |
| Mar. | 15 | Notes Receivable—Ames Co. | 8,000.00 | |
| | | Accounts Receivable—Ames Co. | | 8,000.00 |
| Apr. | 9 | Allowance for Doubtful Accounts | 2,500.00 | |
| | | Accounts Receivable—Dorset Co. | | 2,500.00 |
| | 21 | Notes Receivable—Jill Klein | 7,500.00 | |
| | | Cash | | 7,500.00 |
| May | 14 | Notes Receivable—Ames Co. | 8,000.00 | |
| | | Cash | 160.00 | |
| | | Notes Receivable—Ames Co. | | 8,000.00 |
| | | Interest Revenue | | 160.00 |
| June | 13 | Accounts Receivable—Dorset Co. | 2,500.00 | |
| | | Allowance for Doubtful Accounts | | 2,500.00 |
| | 13 | Cash | 2,500.00 | |
| | | Accounts Receivable—Dorset Co. | | 2,500.00 |
| July | 20 | Accounts Receivable—Jill Klein | 7,762.50 | |
| | | Notes Receivable—Jill Klein | | 7,500.00 |
| | | Interest Revenue | | 262.50 |

| Aug. | 12 | Cash | | 8,280.00 | |
|------|----|------|--|----------|--|
| | | Notes Receivable—Ames Co. | | | 8,000.00 |
| | | Interest Revenue | | | 280.00 |
| | 19 | Cash | | 7,859.53 | |
| | | Accounts Receivable—Jill Klein | | | 7,762.50 |
| | | Interest Revenue | | | 97.03 |
| | | ($7,762.50 × 15% × 30/360). | | | |
| Dec. | 16 | Notes Receivable—Global Company | | 12,000.00 | |
| | | Accounts Receivable—Global Company | | | 12,000.00 |
| | 31 | Bad Debt Expense | | 41,250.00 | |
| | | Allowance for Doubtful Accounts | | | 41,250.00 |
| | | Uncollectible accounts estimate | | | |
| | | ($1,375,000 × 3%). | | | |

2.

| Dec. | 31 | Interest Receivable | | 60.00 | |
|------|----|---------------------|--|-------|--|
| | | Interest Revenue | | | 60.00 |
| | | Accrued interest | | | |
| | | ($12,000 × 12% × 15/360). | | | |

# Discussion Questions

1. What are the three classifications of receivables?

2. Elite Hardware is a small hardware store in the rural township of Rexburg that rarely extends credit to its customers in the form of an account receivable. The few customers that are allowed to carry accounts receivable are long-time residents of Rexburg and have a history of doing business at Elite Hardware. What method of accounting for uncollectible receivables should Elite Hardware use? Why?

3. What kind of an account (asset, liability, etc.) is Allowance for Doubtful Accounts, and is its normal balance a debit or a credit?

4. After the accounts are adjusted and closed at the end of the fiscal year, Accounts Receivable has a balance of $471,200 and Allowance for Doubtful Accounts has a balance of $27,500. Describe how the accounts receivable and the allowance for doubtful accounts are reported on the balance sheet.

5. A firm has consistently adjusted its allowance account at the end of the fiscal year by adding a fixed percent of the period's net sales on account. After seven years, the balance in Allowance for Doubtful Accounts has become very large in relationship to the balance in Accounts Receivable. Give two possible explanations.

6. Which of the two methods of estimating uncollectibles provides for the most accurate estimate of the current net realizable value of the receivables?

7. Calypso Company issued a note receivable to Kearny Company. (a) Who is the payee? (b) What is the title of the account used by Kearny Company in recording the note?

8. If a note provides for payment of principal of $150,000 and interest at the rate of 4%, will the interest amount to $6,000? Explain.

9. The maker of a $60,000, 5%, 90-day note receivable failed to pay the note on the due date of April 30. What accounts should be debited and credited by the payee to record the dishonored note receivable?

10. The note receivable dishonored in Discussion Question 9 is paid on May 30 by the maker, plus interest for 30 days, 8%. What entry should be made to record the receipt of the payment?

# Practice Exercises

| Learning Objectives | Example Exercises | |
|---|---|---|
| OBJ. 3 | EE 8-1 *p. 364* | **PE 8-1A   Direct write-off method** |

Journalize the following transactions using the direct write-off method of accounting for uncollectible receivables:

Jan. 17. Received $250 from Ian Kearns and wrote off the remainder owed of $750 as uncollectible.

Apr. 6. Reinstated the account of Ian Kearns and received $750 cash in full payment.

**OBJ. 3**   **EE 8-1** *p. 364*   **PE 8-1B   Direct write-off method**

Journalize the following transactions using the direct write-off method of accounting for uncollectible receivables:

July 7. Received $500 from Betty Williams and wrote off the remainder owed of $2,000 as uncollectible.

Nov. 13. Reinstated the account of Betty Williams and received $2,000 cash in full payment.

**OBJ. 4**   **EE 8-2** *p. 367*   **PE 8-2A   Allowance method**

Journalize the following transactions using the allowance method of accounting for uncollectible receivables:

Jan. 17. Received $250 from Ian Kearns and wrote off the remainder owed of $750 as uncollectible.

Apr. 6. Reinstated the account of Ian Kearns and received $750 cash in full payment.

**OBJ. 4**   **EE 8-2** *p. 367*   **PE 8-2B   Allowance method**

Journalize the following transactions using the allowance method of accounting for uncollectible receivables:

July 7. Received $500 from Betty Williams and wrote off the remainder owed of $2,000 as uncollectible.

Nov. 13. Reinstated the account of Betty Williams and received $2,000 cash in full payment.

**OBJ. 4**   **EE 8-3** *p. 368*   **PE 8-3A   Percent of sales method**

At the end of the current year, Accounts Receivable has a balance of $325,000; Allowance for Doubtful Accounts has a credit balance of $3,900; and net sales for the year total $4,500,000. Bad debt expense is estimated at ½ of 1% of net sales.

Determine (a) the amount of the adjusting entry for uncollectible accounts; (b) the adjusted balances of Accounts Receivable, Allowance for Doubtful Accounts, and Bad Debt Expense; and (c) the net realizable value of accounts receivable.

**OBJ. 4**   **EE 8-3** *p. 368*   **PE 8-3B   Percent of sales method**

At the end of the current year, Accounts Receivable has a balance of $2,500,000; Allowance for Doubtful Accounts has a debit balance of $9,000; and net sales for the year total $32,000,000. Bad debt expense is estimated at ¼ of 1% of net sales.

Determine (a) the amount of the adjusting entry for uncollectible accounts; (b) the adjusted balances of Accounts Receivable, Allowance for Doubtful Accounts, and Bad Debt Expense; and (c) the net realizable value of accounts receivable.

**PE 8-4A**  **Analysis of receivables method**

At the end of the current year, Accounts Receivable has a balance of $325,000; Allowance for Doubtful Accounts has a credit balance of $3,900; and net sales for the year total $4,500,000. Using the aging method, the balance of Allowance for Doubtful Accounts is estimated as $25,000.

Determine (a) the amount of the adjusting entry for uncollectible accounts; (b) the adjusted balances of Accounts Receivable, Allowance for Doubtful Accounts, and Bad Debt Expense; and (c) the net realizable value of accounts receivable.

**PE 8-4B**  **Analysis of receivables method**

At the end of the current year, Accounts Receivable has a balance of $2,500,000; Allowance for Doubtful Accounts has a debit balance of $9,000; and net sales for the year total $32,000,000. Using the aging method, the balance of Allowance for Doubtful Accounts is estimated as $76,000.

Determine (a) the amount of the adjusting entry for uncollectible accounts; (b) the adjusted balances of Accounts Receivable, Allowance for Doubtful Accounts, and Bad Debt Expense; and (c) the net realizable value of accounts receivable.

**PE 8-5A**  **Note receivable**

Vista Supply Company received a 30-day, 4% note for $90,000, dated September 8 from a customer on account.

a.  Determine the due date of the note.

b.  Determine the maturity value of the note.

c.  Journalize the entry to record the receipt of the payment of the note at maturity.

**PE 8-5B**  **Note receivable**

Gorilla Supply Company received a 120-day, 5% note for $150,000, dated March 27 from a customer on account.

a.  Determine the due date of the note.

b.  Determine the maturity value of the note.

c.  Journalize the entry to record the receipt of the payment of the note at maturity.

**F·A·I**

**PE 8-6A**  **Accounts receivable turnover and number of days' sales in receivables**

Financial statement data for years ending December 31 for Blum Company are shown below.

|                      | 2012        | 2011        |
|----------------------|-------------|-------------|
| Net sales            | $2,430,000  | $1,920,000  |
| Accounts receivable: |             |             |
| Beginning of year    | 180,000     | 120,000     |
| End of year          | 225,000     | 180,000     |

a.  Determine the accounts receivable turnover for 2012 and 2011.

b.  Determine the number of days' sales in receivables for 2012 and 2011. Round to one decimal place.

c.  Does the change in accounts receivable turnover and the number of days' sales in receivables from 2011 to 2012 indicate a favorable or an unfavorable trend?

**F·A·I**

**PE 8-6B**  **Accounts receivable turnover and number of days' sales in receivables**

Financial statement data for years ending December 31 for Sherick Company are shown below.

|                      | 2012        | 2011        |
|----------------------|-------------|-------------|
| Net sales            | $4,514,000  | $4,200,000  |
| Accounts receivable: |             |             |
| Beginning of year    | 280,000     | 320,000     |
| End of year          | 330,000     | 280,000     |

a.  Determine the accounts receivable turnover for 2012 and 2011.

b.  Determine the number of days' sales in receivables for 2012 and 2011. Round to one decimal place.

c.  Does the change in accounts receivable turnover and the number of days' sales in receivables from 2011 to 2012 indicate a favorable or an unfavorable trend?

## Exercises

OBJ. 1

### EX 8-1 Classifications of receivables

Boeing is one of the world's major aerospace firms, with operations involving commercial aircraft, military aircraft, missiles, satellite systems, and information and battle management systems. As of December 31, 2009, Boeing had $3,090 million of receivables involving U.S. government contracts and $1,206 million of receivables involving commercial aircraft customers, such as Delta Air Lines and United Airlines.

▬▬▶ Should Boeing report these receivables separately in the financial statements, or combine them into one overall accounts receivable amount? Explain.

OBJ. 2
✔ a. 20.9%

### EX 8-2 Nature of uncollectible accounts

The MGM Mirage owns and operates casinos including the MGM Grand and the Bellagio in Las Vegas, Nevada. As of December 31, 2009, The MGM Mirage reported accounts and notes receivable of $465,580,000 and allowance for doubtful accounts of $97,106,000. Johnson & Johnson manufactures and sells a wide range of health care products including Band-Aids and Tylenol. As of December 31, 2009, Johnson & Johnson reported accounts receivable of $9,979,000,000 and allowance for doubtful accounts of $333,000,000.

a. Compute the percentage of the allowance for doubtful accounts to the accounts and notes receivable as of December 31, 2009, for The MGM Mirage. Round to one decimal place.

b. Compute the percentage of the allowance for doubtful accounts to the accounts receivable as of December 31, 2009, for Johnson & Johnson. Round to one decimal place.

c. ▬▬▶ Discuss possible reasons for the difference in the two ratios computed in (a) and (b).

OBJ. 3

### EX 8-3 Entries for uncollectible accounts, using direct write-off method

Journalize the following transactions in the accounts of Cecena Medical Co., a medical equipment company that uses the direct write-off method of accounting for uncollectible receivables:

Feb. 13. Sold merchandise on account to Dr. Ben Katz, $120,000. The cost of the merchandise sold was $72,000.

May 4. Received $90,000 from Dr. Ben Katz and wrote off the remainder owed on the sale of February 13 as uncollectible.

Nov. 19. Reinstated the account of Dr. Ben Katz that had been written off on May 4 and received $30,000 cash in full payment.

OBJ. 4

### EX 8-4 Entries for uncollectible receivables, using allowance method

Journalize the following transactions in the accounts of Metromark Company, a restaurant supply company that uses the allowance method of accounting for uncollectible receivables:

Feb. 11. Sold merchandise on account to Dakota Co., $29,000. The cost of the merchandise sold was $17,400.

Apr. 15. Received $7,500 from Dakota Co. and wrote off the remainder owed on the sale of February 11 as uncollectible.

Sept. 3. Reinstated the account of Dakota Co. that had been written off on April 15 and received $21,500 cash in full payment.

OBJ. 3, 4

### EX 8-5 Entries to write off accounts receivable

Acropolis Company, a computer consulting firm, has decided to write off the $12,950 balance of an account owed by a customer, Aaron Guzman. Journalize the entry to record the write-off, assuming that (a) the direct write-off method is used and (b) the allowance method is used.

OBJ. 4
✔ a. $80,000
✔ b. $82,000

### EX 8-6 Providing for doubtful accounts

At the end of the current year, the accounts receivable account has a debit balance of $1,275,000 and net sales for the year total $16,000,000. Determine the amount of the adjusting entry to provide for doubtful accounts under each of the following assumptions:

a. The allowance account before adjustment has a debit balance of $5,000. Bad debt expense is estimated at ½ of 1% of net sales.

b. The allowance account before adjustment has a debit balance of $5,000. An aging of the accounts in the customer ledger indicates estimated doubtful accounts of $77,000.

c. The allowance account before adjustment has a credit balance of $7,500. Bad debt expense is estimated at ¼ of 1% of net sales.

d. The allowance account before adjustment has a credit balance of $7,500. An aging of the accounts in the customer ledger indicates estimated doubtful accounts of $43,500.

---

**OBJ. 4**

✔ Alpha Auto, 77 days

### EX 8-7 Number of days past due

Honest Abe's Auto Supply distributes new and used automobile parts to local dealers throughout the Northeast. Honest Abe's credit terms are n/30. As of the end of business on July 31, the following accounts receivable were past due:

| Account | Due Date | Amount |
|---|---|---|
| Alpha Auto | May 15 | $ 9,000 |
| Best Auto | July 8 | 3,000 |
| Downtown Repair | March 18 | 7,500 |
| Lucky's Auto Repair | June 1 | 5,000 |
| Pit Stop Auto | June 3 | 750 |
| Sally's | April 12 | 13,000 |
| Trident Auto | May 31 | 1,500 |
| Washburn Repair & Tow | March 2 | 1,500 |

Determine the number of days each account is past due.

---

**OBJ. 4**

### EX 8-8 Aging of receivables schedule

The accounts receivable clerk for Quigley Industries prepared the following partially completed aging of receivables schedule as of the end of business on November 30:

| | A | B | C | D | E | F | G |
|---|---|---|---|---|---|---|---|
| 1 | | | Not | | Days Past Due | | |
| 2 | | | Past | | | | Over |
| 3 | Customer | Balance | Due | 1–30 | 31–60 | 61–90 | 90 |
| 4 | Able Brothers Inc. | 3,000 | 3,000 | | | | |
| 5 | Accent Company | 4,500 | | 4,500 | | | |
| 21 | Zumpano Company | 5,000 | | | 5,000 | | |
| 22 | Subtotals | 830,000 | 500,000 | 180,000 | 80,000 | 45,000 | 25,000 |

The following accounts were unintentionally omitted from the aging schedule and not included in the subtotals above:

| Customer | Balance | Due Date |
|---|---|---|
| Beltran Industries | $12,000 | July 10 |
| Doodle Company | 8,000 | September 20 |
| La Corp Inc. | 17,000 | October 17 |
| VIP Sales Company | 10,000 | November 4 |
| We-Go Company | 23,000 | December 21 |

a. Determine the number of days past due for each of the preceding accounts.

b. Complete the aging-of-receivables schedule by adding the omitted accounts to the bottom of the schedule and updating the totals.

---

**OBJ. 4**

✔ $68,130

### EX 8-9 Estimating allowance for doubtful accounts

Quigley Industries has a past history of uncollectible accounts, shown at the top of the next page. Estimate the allowance for doubtful accounts, based on the aging of receivables schedule you completed in Exercise 8-8.

| Age Class | Percent Uncollectible |
|---|---|
| Not past due | 1% |
| 1–30 days past due | 4 |
| 31–60 days past due | 15 |
| 61–90 days past due | 35 |
| Over 90 days past due | 60 |

**OBJ. 4**

### EX 8-10   Adjustment for uncollectible accounts

Using data in Exercise 8-9, assume that the allowance for doubtful accounts for Quigley Industries has a credit balance of $14,280 before adjustment on November 30. Journalize the adjusting entry for uncollectible accounts as of November 30.

**OBJ. 4**

### EX 8-11   Estimating doubtful accounts

Imperial Bikes Co. is a wholesaler of motorcycle supplies. An aging of the company's accounts receivable on December 31, 2012, and a historical analysis of the percentage of uncollectible accounts in each age category are as follows:

| Age Interval | Balance | Percent Uncollectible |
|---|---|---|
| Not past due | $600,000 | ¼% |
| 1–30 days past due | 120,000 | 2 |
| 31–60 days past due | 60,000 | 3 |
| 61–90 days past due | 45,000 | 10 |
| 91–180 days past due | 26,000 | 40 |
| Over 180 days past due | 24,000 | 75 |
| | $875,000 | |

Estimate what the proper balance of the allowance for doubtful accounts should be as of December 31, 2012.

**OBJ. 4**

### EX 8-12   Entry for uncollectible accounts

Using the data in Exercise 8-11, assume that the allowance for doubtful accounts for Imperial Bikes Co. had a debit balance of $1,400 as of December 31, 2012.

Journalize the adjusting entry for uncollectible accounts as of December 31, 2012.

**OBJ. 5**

✔ **c. $14,900 higher**

### EX 8-13   Entries for bad debt expense under the direct write-off and allowance methods

The following selected transactions were taken from the records of Aprilla Company for the first year of its operations ending December 31, 2012:

Jan.  27.  Wrote off account of C. Knoll, $6,000.

Feb.  17.  Received $1,000 as partial payment on the $3,000 account of Joni Lester. Wrote off the remaining balance as uncollectible.

Mar.  3.  Received $6,000 from C. Knoll, which had been written off on January 27. Reinstated the account and recorded the cash receipt.

Dec.  31.  Wrote off the following accounts as uncollectible (record as one journal entry):

| | |
|---|---|
| Jason Short | $4,500 |
| Kim Snider | 1,500 |
| Sue Pascall | 1,100 |
| Tracy Lane | 3,500 |
| Randy Pape | 500 |

31.  If necessary, record the year-end adjusting entry for uncollectible accounts.

a.  Journalize the transactions for 2012 under the direct write-off method.

b.  Journalize the transactions for 2012 under the allowance method. Aprilla Company uses the percent of credit sales method of estimating uncollectible accounts expense. Based on past history and industry averages, 1¾% of credit sales are expected to be uncollectible. Aprilla Company recorded $1,600,000 of credit sales during 2012.

c.  ▬▬▶ How much higher (lower) would Aprilla Company's net income have been under the direct write-off method than under the allowance method?

**EX 8-14   Entries for bad debt expense under the direct write-off and allowance methods**

The following selected transactions were taken from the records of Silhouette Company for the year ending December 31, 2012:

Mar.   4.   Wrote off account of Myron Rimando, $7,500.

May  19.   Received $2,000 as partial payment on the $10,000 account of Shirley Mason. Wrote off the remaining balance as uncollectible.

Aug.   7.   Received the $7,500 from Myron Rimando, which had been written off on March 4. Reinstated the account and recorded the cash receipt.

Dec. 31.   Wrote off the following accounts as uncollectible (record as one journal entry):

| | |
|---|---|
| Brandon Peele | $ 5,000 |
| Clyde Stringer | 9,000 |
| Ned Berry | 13,000 |
| Mary Adams | 2,000 |
| Gina Bowers | 4,500 |

Dec. 31.   If necessary, record the year-end adjusting entry for uncollectible accounts.

a.   Journalize the transactions for 2012 under the direct write-off method.

b.   Journalize the transactions for 2012 under the allowance method, assuming that the allowance account had a beginning balance of $45,000 on January 1, 2012, and the company uses the analysis of receivables method. Silhouette Company prepared the following aging schedule for its accounts receivable:

| Aging Class (Number of Days Past Due) | Receivables Balance on December 31 | Estimated Percent of Uncollectible Accounts |
|---|---|---|
| 0–30 days | $300,000 | 1% |
| 31–60 days | 80,000 | 4 |
| 61–90 days | 20,000 | 15 |
| 91–120 days | 10,000 | 40 |
| More than 120 days | 40,000 | 80 |
| Total receivables | $450,000 | |

c.   ▬▬▬▶ How much higher (lower) would Silhouette's 2012 net income have been under the direct write-off method than under the allowance method?

**EX 8-15   Effect of doubtful accounts on net income**

During its first year of operations, Filippi's Plumbing Supply Co. had net sales of $4,800,000, wrote off $65,000 of accounts as uncollectible using the direct write-off method, and reported net income of $375,000. Determine what the net income would have been if the allowance method had been used, and the company estimated that 1½% of net sales would be uncollectible.

**EX 8-16   Effect of doubtful accounts on net income**

Using the data in Exercise 8-15, assume that during the second year of operations Filippi's Plumbing Supply Co. had net sales of $5,500,000, wrote off $70,000 of accounts as uncollectible using the direct write-off method, and reported net income of $450,000.

a.   Determine what net income would have been in the second year if the allowance method (using 1½% of net sales) had been used in both the first and second years.

b.   Determine what the balance of the allowance for doubtful accounts would have been at the end of the second year if the allowance method had been used in both the first and second years.

**EX 8-17   Entries for bad debt expense under the direct write-off and allowance methods**

Spangler Company wrote off the following accounts receivable as uncollectible for the first year of its operations ending December 31, 2012:

| Customer | Amount |
|---|---|
| Will Boyette | $10,000 |
| Stan Frey | 8,000 |
| Tammy Imes | 5,000 |
| Shana Wagner | 6,000 |
| Total | $29,000 |

a. Journalize the write-offs for 2012 under the direct write-off method.

b. Journalize the write-offs for 2012 under the allowance method. Also, journalize the adjusting entry for uncollectible accounts. The company recorded $3,000,000 of credit sales during 2012. Based on past history and industry averages, 1½% of credit sales are expected to be uncollectible.

c. How much higher (lower) would Spangler Company's 2012 net income have been under the direct write-off method than under the allowance method?

---

**OBJ. 5**

**EX 8-18   Entries for bad debt expense under the direct write-off and allowance methods**

Magnetics International wrote off the following accounts receivable as uncollectible for the year ending December 31, 2012:

| Customer | Amount |
|---|---|
| Trey Betts | $15,500 |
| Cheryl Carson | 9,000 |
| Irene Harris | 29,700 |
| Renee Putman | 3,100 |
| Total | $57,300 |

The company prepared the following aging schedule for its accounts receivable on December 31, 2012:

| Aging Class (Number of Days Past Due) | Receivables Balance on December 31 | Estimated Percent of Uncollectible Accounts |
|---|---|---|
| 0–30 days | $600,000 | 1% |
| 31–60 days | 150,000 | 2 |
| 61–90 days | 75,000 | 18 |
| 91–120 days | 50,000 | 30 |
| More than 120 days | 60,000 | 50 |
| Total receivables | $935,000 | |

a. Journalize the write-offs for 2012 under the direct write-off method.

b. Journalize the write-offs and the year-end adjusting entry for 2012 under the allowance method, assuming that the allowance account had a beginning balance of $55,000 on January 1, 2012, and the company uses the analysis of receivables method.

c. How much higher (lower) would Magnetics International's 2012 net income have been under the allowance method than under the direct write-off method?

---

**OBJ. 6**

✔ a. Aug. 13, $600

**EX 8-19   Determine due date and interest on notes**

Determine the due date and the amount of interest due at maturity on the following notes:

| | Date of Note | Face Amount | Interest Rate | Term of Note |
|---|---|---|---|---|
| a. | May 15 | $40,000 | 6% | 90 days |
| b. | March 20 | 15,000 | 4 | 60 days |
| c. | May 19 | 24,000 | 3 | 60 days |
| d. | October 1 | 10,500 | 8 | 60 days |
| e. | August 30 | 18,000 | 5 | 120 days |

**OBJ. 6**
✔ b. $91,350

**EX 8-20** **Entries for notes receivable**

Oregon Interior Decorators issued a 90-day, 6% note for $90,000, dated April 9, to Corvallis Furniture Company on account.

a. Determine the due date of the note.

b. Determine the maturity value of the note.

c. Journalize the entries to record the following: (1) receipt of the note by Corvallis Furniture and (2) receipt of payment of the note at maturity.

**OBJ. 6**

**EX 8-21** **Entries for notes receivable**

The series of seven transactions recorded in the following T accounts were related to a sale to a customer on account and the receipt of the amount owed. Briefly describe each transaction.

| CASH | | NOTES RECEIVABLE | | | |
|---|---|---|---|---|---|
| (7) | 40,602 | (5) | 40,000 | (6) | 40,000 |

| ACCOUNTS RECEIVABLE | | | | SALES RETURNS AND ALLOWANCES | |
|---|---|---|---|---|---|
| (1) | 50,000 | (3) | 10,000 | (3) | 10,000 |
| (6) | 40,400 | (5) | 40,000 | | |
| | | (7) | 40,400 | | |

| MERCHANDISE INVENTORY | | | | COST OF MERCHANDISE SOLD | |
|---|---|---|---|---|---|
| (4) | 6,000 | (2) | 30,000 | (2) | 30,000 | (4) | 6,000 |

| SALES | | INTEREST REVENUE | |
|---|---|---|---|
| | (1) | 50,000 | (6) | 400 |
| | | | (7) | 202 |

**OBJ. 6**

**EX 8-22** **Entries for notes receivable, including year-end entries**

The following selected transactions were completed by Zip-Up Co., a supplier of zippers for clothing:

2011

Dec. 10. Received from Point Loma Clothing & Bags Co., on account, a $36,000, 90-day, 4% note dated December 10.

31. Recorded an adjusting entry for accrued interest on the note of December 10.

31. Recorded the closing entry for interest revenue.

2012

Mar. 9. Received payment of note and interest from Point Loma Clothing & Bags Co.

Journalize the transactions.

**OBJ. 6**

**EX 8-23** **Entries for receipt and dishonor of note receivable**

Journalize the following transactions of Frankenstein Productions:

May 3. Received a $150,000, 120-day, 6% note dated May 3 from Sunrider Co. on account.

Aug. 31. The note is dishonored by Sunrider Co.

Oct. 30. Received the amount due on the dishonored note plus interest for 60 days at 9% on the total amount charged to Sunrider Co. on August 31.

**OBJ. 4, 6**

**EX 8-24   Entries for receipt and dishonor of notes receivable**

Journalize the following transactions in the accounts of Jamba Co., which operates a riverboat casino:

Mar.   1.   Received an $80,000, 60-day, 6% note dated March 1 from Tomekia Co. on account.

18.   Received a $75,000, 60-day, 8% note dated March 18 from Mystic Co. on account.

Apr.  30.   The note dated March 1 from Tomekia Co. is dishonored, and the customer's account is charged for the note, including interest.

May  17.   The note dated March 18 from Mystic Co. is dishonored, and the customer's account is charged for the note, including interest.

July  29.   Cash is received for the amount due on the dishonored note dated March 1 plus interest for 90 days at 8% on the total amount debited to Tomekia Co. on April 30.

Aug.  23.   Wrote off against the allowance account the amount charged to Mystic Co. on May 17 for the dishonored note dated March 18.

**OBJ. 7**

**EX 8-25   Receivables on the balance sheet**

List any errors you can find in the following partial balance sheet:

**Tulips Company**
**Balance Sheet**
**December 31, 2012**

| Assets | | |
|---|---:|---:|
| Current assets: | | |
| Cash | | $138,000 |
| Notes receivable | $400,000 | |
| Less interest receivable | 20,000 | 380,000 |
| Accounts receivable | $795,000 | |
| Plus allowance for doubtful accounts | 14,500 | 809,500 |

**OBJ. 8**

✔ a. 2009: 8.6

**EX 8-26   Accounts receivable turnover and days' sales in receivables**

Polo Ralph Lauren Corporation designs, markets, and distributes a variety of apparel, home decor, accessory, and fragrance products. The company's products include such brands as Polo Ralph Lauren, Ralph Lauren Purple Label, Ralph Lauren, Ralph Lauren Polo Jeans Co., and Chaps. Polo Ralph Lauren reported the following (in thousands):

| | For the Period Ending | |
|---|---|---|
| | **March 29, 2009** | **March 29, 2008** |
| Net sales | $5,018,900 | $4,880,100 |
| Accounts receivable | 576,700 | 585,000 |

Assume that accounts receivable (in millions) were $511,900 at the beginning of the 2008 fiscal year.

a.   Compute the accounts receivable turnover for 2009 and 2008. Round to one decimal place.

b.   Compute the days' sales in receivables for 2009 and 2008. Round to one decimal place.

c.   ➤ What conclusions can be drawn from these analyses regarding Ralph Lauren's efficiency in collecting receivables?

**OBJ. 8**

✔a. 2009: 8.7

**EX 8-27   Accounts receivable turnover and days' sales in receivables**

H.J. Heinz Company was founded in 1869 at Sharpsburg, Pennsylvania, by Henry J. Heinz. The company manufactures and markets food products throughout the world, including ketchup, condiments and sauces, frozen food, pet food, soups, and tuna. For the fiscal years 2009 and 2008, H.J. Heinz reported the following (in thousands):

| | Year Ending | |
|---|---|---|
| | **April 29, 2009** | **April 30, 2008** |
| Net sales | $10,148,082 | $10,070,778 |
| Accounts receivable | 1,171,797 | 1,161,481 |

Assume that the accounts receivable (in thousands) were $996,852 at the beginning of fiscal year 2008.

a. Compute the accounts receivable turnover for 2009 and 2008. Round to one decimal place.

b. Compute the days' sales in receivables at the end of 2009 and 2008. Round to one decimal place.

c.  What conclusions can be drawn from these analyses regarding Heinz's efficiency in collecting receivables?

---

**OBJ. 8**

**EX 8-28   Accounts receivable turnover and days' sales in receivables**

The Limited Brands Inc. sells women's clothing and personal health care products through specialty retail stores including Victoria's Secret and Bath & Body Works stores. The Limited Brands reported the following (in millions):

| | For the Period Ending | |
|---|---|---|
| | **Jan. 31, 2010** | **Jan. 31, 2009** |
| Net sales | $8,632 | $9,043 |
| Accounts receivable | 249 | 313 |

Assume that accounts receivable (in millions) were $355 at the beginning of fiscal year 2009.

a. Compute the accounts receivable turnover for 2010 and 2009. Round to one decimal place.

b. Compute the days sales in receivables for 2010 and 2009. Round to one decimal place.

c. What conclusions can be drawn from these analyses regarding The Limited Brands' efficiency in collecting receivables?

---

**OBJ. 8**

**EX 8-29   Accounts receivable turnover**

Use the data in Exercises 8-27 and 8-28 to analyze the accounts receivable turnover ratios of H.J. Heinz Company and The Limited Brands Inc.

a. Compute the average accounts receivable turnover ratio for The Limited Brands Inc. and H.J. Heinz Company for the years shown in Exercises 8-27 and 8-28.

b. ■■■■ Does The Limited Brands or H.J. Heinz Company have the higher average accounts receivable turnover ratio?

c. ■■■■ Explain the logic underlying your answer in (b).

# Problems Series A

---

**OBJ. 4**

✔ 3. $1,140,000

**PR 8-1A   Entries related to uncollectible accounts**

The following transactions were completed by Axiom Management Company during the current fiscal year ended December 31:

Feb.   17. Received 25% of the $30,000 balance owed by Gillespie Co., a bankrupt business, and wrote off the remainder as uncollectible.

Apr.   11. Reinstated the account of Colleen Bertram, which had been written off in the preceding year as uncollectible. Journalized the receipt of $4,250 cash in full payment of Colleen's account.

July   6. Wrote off the $9,000 balance owed by Covered Wagon Co., which has no assets.

Nov. 20. Reinstated the account of Dugan Co., which had been written off in the preceding year as uncollectible. Journalized the receipt of $5,900 cash in full payment of the account.

Dec. 31. Wrote off the following accounts as uncollectible (compound entry): Kipp Co., $3,000; Moore Co., $4,000; Butte Distributors, $8,000; Parker Towers, $6,700.

31. Based on an analysis of the $1,200,000 of accounts receivable, it was estimated that $60,000 will be uncollectible. Journalized the adjusting entry.

**Instructions**

1. Record the January 1 credit balance of $40,000 in a T account for Allowance for Doubtful Accounts.

2. Journalize the transactions. Post each entry that affects the following selected T accounts and determine the new balances:

Allowance for Doubtful Accounts
Bad Debt Expense

3. Determine the expected net realizable value of the accounts receivable as of December 31.

4. Assuming that instead of basing the provision for uncollectible accounts on an analysis of receivables, the adjusting entry on December 31 had been based on an estimated expense of ¾ of 1% of the net sales of $7,500,000 for the year, determine the following:

a. Bad debt expense for the year.

b. Balance in the allowance account after the adjustment of December 31.

c. Expected net realizable value of the accounts receivable as of December 31.

OBJ. 4

✔ 3. $111,095

**PR 8-2A   Aging of receivables; estimating allowance for doubtful accounts**

Angler's Dream Company supplies flies and fishing gear to sporting goods stores and outfitters throughout the western United States. The accounts receivable clerk for Angler's Dream prepared the following partially completed aging of receivables schedule as of the end of business on December 31, 2011:

| | A | B | C | D | E | F | G | H |
|---|---|---|---|---|---|---|---|---|
| | | | Not | | | Days Past Due | | |
| 1 | | | Past | | | | | |
| 2 | Customer | Balance | Due | 1–30 | 31–60 | 61–90 | 91–120 | Over 120 |
| 3 | | | | | | | | |
| 4 | AAA Fishery | 20,000 | 20,000 | | | | | |
| 5 | Blue Ribbon Flies | 7,500 | | | | 7,500 | | |
| 30 | Z Fish Co. | 4,000 | | 4,000 | | | | |
| 31 | Subtotals | 1,060,000 | 500,000 | 315,000 | 120,000 | 40,000 | 25,000 | 60,000 |

The following accounts were unintentionally omitted from the aging schedule:

| Customer | Due Date | Balance |
|---|---|---|
| Antelope Sports & Flies | June 21, 2011 | $ 3,000 |
| Big Hole Flies | Aug. 30, 2011 | 6,500 |
| Charlie's Fish Co. | Sept. 8, 2011 | 12,000 |
| Deschutes Sports | Oct. 20, 2011 | 4,000 |
| Green River Sports | Nov. 7, 2011 | 3,500 |
| Smith River Co. | Nov. 28, 2011 | 1,500 |
| Wild Trout Company | Dec. 5, 2011 | 5,000 |
| Wolfe Sports | Jan. 7, 2012 | 4,500 |

Angler's Dream has a past history of uncollectible accounts by age category, as follows:

| Age Class | Percent Uncollectible |
|---|---|
| Not past due | 1% |
| 1–30 days past due | 4 |
| 31–60 days past due | 8 |
| 61–90 days past due | 25 |
| 91–120 days past due | 45 |
| Over 120 days past due | 80 |

**Instructions**

1. Determine the number of days past due for each of the preceding accounts.

2. Complete the aging of receivables schedule by adding the omitted accounts to the bottom of the schedule and updating the totals.

3. Estimate the allowance for doubtful accounts, based on the aging of receivables schedule.

4. Assume that the allowance for doubtful accounts for Angler's Dream Company has a debit balance of $1,405 before adjustment on December 31, 2011. Journalize the adjusting entry for uncollectible accounts.

5. Assume that the adjusting entry in (4) was inadvertently omitted, how would the omission affect the balance sheet and income statement?

OBJ. 3, 4, 5

✔ 1. Year 4: Balance of allowance account, end of year, $14,950

**PR 8-3A   Compare two methods of accounting for uncollectible receivables**

Tel-Com Company, a telephone service and supply company, has just completed its fourth year of operations. The direct write-off method of recording bad debt expense has been used during the entire period. Because of substantial increases in sales volume and the amount of uncollectible accounts, the company is considering changing to the allowance method. Information is requested as to the effect that an annual provision of ¾% of sales would have had on the amount of bad debt expense reported for each of the past four years. It is also considered desirable to know what the balance of Allowance for Doubtful Accounts would have been at the end of each year. The following data have been obtained from the accounts:

| | | | Year of Origin of Accounts Receivable Written Off as Uncollectible | | | |
|---|---|---|---|---|---|---|
| Year | Sales | Uncollectible Accounts Written off | 1st | 2nd | 3rd | 4th |
| 1st | $  700,000 | $2,000 | $2,000 | | | |
| 2nd | 900,000 | 3,400 | 1,800 | $1,600 | | |
| 3rd | 1,200,000 | 6,450 | 1,000 | 3,700 | $1,750 | |
| 4th | 2,000,000 | 9,200 | | 1,260 | 3,700 | $4,240 |

**Instructions**

1. Assemble the desired data, using the following column headings:

| | Bad Debt Expense | | | |
|---|---|---|---|---|
| Year | Expense Actually Reported | Expense Based on Estimate | Increase (Decrease) in Amount of Expense | Balance of Allowance Account, End of Year |

2. ━━━━▶ Experience during the first four years of operations indicated that the receivables were either collected within two years or had to be written off as uncollectible. Does the estimate of ¾% of sales appear to be reasonably close to the actual experience with uncollectible accounts originating during the first two years? Explain.

### PR 8-4A   Details of notes receivable and related entries

Old Town Co. wholesales bathroom fixtures. During the current fiscal year, Old Town Co. received the following notes:

|  | Date | Face Amount | Term | Interest Rate |
|---|---|---|---|---|
| 1. | Apr. 10 | $45,000 | 60 days | 4% |
| 2. | June 24 | 18,000 | 30 days | 6 |
| 3. | July 1 | 36,000 | 120 days | 6 |
| 4. | Oct. 31 | 36,000 | 60 days | 9 |
| 5. | Nov. 15 | 54,000 | 60 days | 6 |
| 6. | Dec. 27 | 40,500 | 30 days | 4 |

### Instructions

1. Determine for each note (a) the due date and (b) the amount of interest due at maturity, identifying each note by number.
2. Journalize the entry to record the dishonor of Note (3) on its due date.
3. Journalize the adjusting entry to record the accrued interest on Notes (5) and (6) on December 31.
4. Journalize the entries to record the receipt of the amounts due on Notes (5) and (6) in January.

---

### PR 8-5A   Notes receivable entries

The following data relate to notes receivable and interest for Viking Co., a cable manufacturer and supplier. (All notes are dated as of the day they are received.)

June   3.  Received a $24,000, 4%, 60-day note on account.

July   26.  Received a $27,000, 5%, 120-day note on account.

Aug.   2.  Received $24,160 on note of June 3.

Sept.   4.  Received a $60,000, 3%, 60-day note on account.

Nov.   3.  Received $60,300 on note of September 4.

   5.  Received a $36,000, 7%, 30-day note on account.

   23.  Received $27,450 on note of July 26.

   30.  Received an $18,000, 5%, 30-day note on account.

Dec.   5.  Received $36,210 on note of November 5.

   30.  Received $18,075 on note of November 30.

### Instructions
Journalize entries to record the transactions.

---

### PR 8-6A   Sales and notes receivable transactions

The following were selected from among the transactions completed by Sorento Co. during the current year. Sorento Co. sells and installs home and business security systems.

Jan.   5.  Loaned $17,500 cash to Marc Jager, receiving a 90-day, 8% note.

Feb.   4.  Sold merchandise on account to Tedra & Co., $19,000. The cost of the merchandise sold was $11,000.

   13.  Sold merchandise on account to Centennial Co., $30,000. The cost of merchandise sold was $17,600.

Mar.   6.  Accepted a 60-day, 6% note for $19,000 from Tedra & Co. on account.

   14.  Accepted a 60-day, 9% note for $30,000 from Centennial Co. on account.

Apr.   5.   Received the interest due from Marc Jager and a new 120-day, 9% note as a renewal of the loan of January 5. (Record both the debit and the credit to the notes receivable account.)

May   5.   Received from Tedra & Co. the amount due on the note of March 6.

      13.   Centennial Co. dishonored its note dated March 14.

July   12.   Received from Centennial Co. the amount owed on the dishonored note, plus interest for 60 days at 12% computed on the maturity value of the note.

Aug.   3.   Received from Marc Jager the amount due on his note of April 5.

Sept.   7.   Sold merchandise on account to Lock-It Co., $9,000. The cost of the merchandise sold was $5,000.

      17.   Received from Lock-It Co. the amount of the invoice of September 7, less 1% discount.

**Instructions**
Journalize the transactions.

# Problems Series B

OBJ. 4

✔ 3. $1,830,000

**PR 8-1B   Entries related to uncollectible accounts**

The following transactions were completed by The Spencer Gallery during the current fiscal year ended December 31:

Mar.   15.   Reinstated the account of Brad Atwell, which had been written off in the preceding year as uncollectible. Journalized the receipt of $3,750 cash in full payment of Brad's account.

May   20.   Wrote off the $15,000 balance owed by Glory Rigging Co., which is bankrupt.

Aug.   13.   Received 40% of the $18,000 balance owed by Coastal Co., a bankrupt business, and wrote off the remainder as uncollectible.

Sept.   2.   Reinstated the account of Lorie Kidd, which had been written off two years earlier as uncollectible. Recorded the receipt of $6,500 cash in full payment.

Dec.   31.   Wrote off the following accounts as uncollectible (compound entry): Kimbro Co., $9,000; McHale Co., $2,500; Summit Furniture, $7,500; Wes Riggs, $2,000.

      31.   Based on an analysis of the $1,880,000 of accounts receivable, it was estimated that $50,000 will be uncollectible. Journalized the adjusting entry.

**Instructions**

1.   Record the January 1 credit balance of $38,500 in a T account for Allowance for Doubtful Accounts.

2.   Journalize the transactions. Post each entry that affects the following T accounts and determine the new balances:

Allowance for Doubtful Accounts<br>Bad Debt Expense

3.   Determine the expected net realizable value of the accounts receivable as of December 31.

4.   Assuming that instead of basing the provision for uncollectible accounts on an analysis of receivables, the adjusting entry on December 31 had been based on an estimated expense of ½ of 1% of the net sales of $9,600,000 for the year, determine the following:

a.   Bad debt expense for the year.

b.   Balance in the allowance account after the adjustment of December 31.

c.   Expected net realizable value of the accounts receivable as of December 31.

OBJ. 4

✔ 3. $72,290

**PR 8-2B   Aging of receivables; estimating allowance for doubtful accounts**

Capri Wigs Company supplies wigs and hair care products to beauty salons throughout California and the Pacific Northwest. The accounts receivable clerk for Capri Wigs prepared the following partially completed aging of receivables schedule as of the end of business on December 31, 2011:

| | A | B | C | D | E | F | G | H |
|---|---|---|---|---|---|---|---|---|
| 1 | | | Not | | | Days Past Due | | |
| 2 | | | Past | | | | | |
| 3 | Customer | Balance | Due | 1–30 | 31–60 | 61–90 | 91–120 | Over 120 |
| 4 | Absolute Beauty | 15,000 | 15,000 | | | | | |
| 5 | Blonde Wigs | 8,000 | | | 8,000 | | | |
| 30 | Zensational Beauty | 3,000 | | 3,000 | | | | |
| 31 | Subtotals | 700,000 | 287,000 | 180,000 | 150,000 | 40,000 | 18,000 | 25,000 |

The following accounts were unintentionally omitted from the aging schedule:

| Customer | Due Date | Balance |
|---|---|---|
| All About Hair | Dec. 2, 2011 | $4,000 |
| Amazing Hair Products | Oct. 17, 2011 | 1,000 |
| Golden Images | Nov. 23, 2011 | 1,600 |
| Harry's Hair Care | Oct. 24, 2011 | 1,500 |
| Lasting Images | Jan. 5, 2012 | 9,400 |
| Oh The Hair | Nov. 29, 2011 | 3,500 |
| Paradise Beauty Store | Sept. 7, 2011 | 7,000 |
| Shining Beauty | May 28, 2011 | 4,000 |

Capri Wigs has a past history of uncollectible accounts by age category, as follows:

| Age Class | Percent Uncollectible |
|---|---|
| Not past due | 2% |
| 1–30 days past due | 5 |
| 31–60 days past due | 12 |
| 61–90 days past due | 16 |
| 91–120 days past due | 40 |
| Over 120 days past due | 75 |

**Instructions**

1. Determine the number of days past due for each of the preceding accounts.

2. Complete the aging of receivables schedule by adding the omitted accounts to the bottom of the schedule and updating the totals.

3. Estimate the allowance for doubtful accounts, based on the aging of receivables schedule.

4. Assume that the allowance for doubtful accounts for Capri Wigs has a credit balance of $3,040 before adjustment on December 31, 2011. Journalize the adjustment for uncollectible accounts.

5. Assume that the adjusting entry in (4) was inadvertently omitted, how would the omission affect the balance sheet and income statement?

OBJ. 3, 4, 5

✔ 1. Year 4: Balance of allowance account, end of year, $13,900

**PR 8-3B   Compare two methods of accounting for uncollectible receivables**

Cyber Tech Company, which operates a chain of 25 electronics supply stores, has just completed its fourth year of operations. The direct write-off method of recording bad debt expense has been used during the entire period. Because of substantial increases in sales volume and the amount of uncollectible accounts, the firm is considering changing to the allowance method. Information is requested as to the effect that an annual provision of ½% of sales would have had on the amount of bad debt expense reported for each of the past four years. It is also considered desirable to know what the balance of Allowance for Doubtful Accounts would have been at the end of each year. The following data have been obtained from the accounts:

| | | | Year of Origin of Accounts Receivable Written Off as Uncollectible | | | |
|---|---|---|---|---|---|---|
| Year | Sales | Uncollectible Accounts Written Off | 1st | 2nd | 3rd | 4th |
| 1st | $1,400,000 | $ 1,300 | $1,300 | | | |
| 2nd | 2,000,000 | 3,600 | 1,500 | $2,100 | | |
| 3rd | 3,000,000 | 13,500 | 4,000 | 3,300 | $6,200 | |
| 4th | 3,600,000 | 17,700 | | 4,000 | 6,100 | $7,600 |

**Instructions**

1. Assemble the desired data, using the following column headings:

| | Bad Debt Expense | | | |
|---|---|---|---|---|
| Year | Expense Actually Reported | Expense Based on Estimate | Increase (Decrease) in Amount of Expense | Balance of Allowance Account, End of Year |

2. ▬▬▬▶ Experience during the first four years of operations indicated that the receivables were either collected within two years or had to be written off as uncollectible. Does the estimate of ½% of sales appear to be reasonably close to the actual experience with uncollectible accounts originating during the first two years? Explain.

---

OBJ. 6

✔ 1. Note 1: Due date, June 2; Interest due at maturity, $100

**PR 8-4B** **Details of notes receivable and related entries**

Media Ads Co. produces advertising videos. During the last six months of the current fiscal year, Media Ads Co. received the following notes:

| | Date | Face Amount | Term | Interest Rate |
|---|---|---|---|---|
| 1. | Apr. 3 | $15,000 | 60 days | 4% |
| 2. | May 19 | 57,600 | 45 days | 6 |
| 3. | Aug. 7 | 50,000 | 90 days | 5 |
| 4. | Sept. 4 | 20,000 | 90 days | 6 |
| 5. | Nov. 21 | 27,000 | 60 days | 8 |
| 6. | Dec. 16 | 21,600 | 60 days | 6 |

**Instructions**

1. Determine for each note (a) the due date and (b) the amount of interest due at maturity, identifying each note by number.

2. Journalize the entry to record the dishonor of Note (3) on its due date.

3. Journalize the adjusting entry to record the accrued interest on Notes (5) and (6) on December 31.

4. Journalize the entries to record the receipt of the amounts due on Notes (5) and (6) in January and February.

---

OBJ. 6

**PR 8-5B** **Notes receivable entries**

The following data relate to notes receivable and interest for El Rayo Co., a financial services company. (All notes are dated as of the day they are received.)

Mar.  1.  Received a $90,000, 6%, 60-day note on account.

25.  Received a $10,000, 4%, 90-day note on account.

Apr. 30.  Received $90,900 on note of March 1.

May 16.  Received a $36,000, 7%, 90-day note on account.

31.  Received a $25,000, 6%, 30-day note on account.

June 23. Received $10,100 on note of March 25.

30. Received $25,125 on note of May 31.

July 1. Received a $28,000, 9%, 30-day note on account.

31. Received $28,210 on note of July 1.

Aug. 14. Received $36,630 on note of May 16.

**Instructions**
Journalize the entries to record the transactions.

OBJ. 6

### PR 8-6B    Sales and notes receivable transactions

The following were selected from among the transactions completed during the current year by Indigo Co., an appliance wholesale company:

Jan. 13. Sold merchandise on account to Boylan Co., $32,000. The cost of merchandise sold was $19,200.

Mar. 10. Accepted a 60-day, 6% note for $32,000 from Boylan Co. on account.

May 9. Received from Boylan Co. the amount due on the note of March 10.

June 10. Sold merchandise on account to Holen for $18,000. The cost of merchandise sold was $10,000.

15. Loaned $24,000 cash to Angie Jones, receiving a 30-day, 7% note.

20. Received from Holen the amount due on the invoice of June 10, less 2% discount.

July 15. Received the interest due from Angie Jones and a new 60-day, 9% note as a renewal of the loan of June 15. (Record both the debit and the credit to the notes receivable account.)

Sept. 13. Received from Angie Jones the amount due on her note of July 15.

13. Sold merchandise on account to Aztec Co., $40,000. The cost of merchandise sold was $25,000.

Oct. 12. Accepted a 60-day, 6% note for $40,000 from Aztec Co. on account.

Dec. 11. Aztec Co. dishonored the note dated October 12.

26. Received from Aztec Co. the amount owed on the dishonored note, plus interest for 15 days at 12% computed on the maturity value of the note.

**Instructions**
Journalize the transactions.

## Cases & Projects

You can access Cases & Projects online at **www.cengage.com/accounting/reeve**

## Excel Success Special Activities

### SA 8-1    Aging of receivables schedule

Brandy Company wholesales grocery food products to grocery stores. The accounts receivable clerk for Brandy Company prepared a partial aging of receivables schedule for December 31, 2011. The uncollectible totals have not been completed.

| | A | B | C | D | E | F | G | H |
|---|---|---|---|---|---|---|---|---|
| 1 | | | **Not** | | | **Days Past Due** | | |
| 2 | | | **Past** | | | | | **Over** |
| 3 | **Customer** | **Balance** | **Due** | **1-30** | **31-60** | **61-90** | **91-180** | **180** |
| 4 | Aslan, T.L. | 580 | 500 | 80 | | | | |
| 5 | Cheney, M. | 930 | 130 | | | 800 | | |
| 6 | Field Stores Inc. | 2,400 | 2,000 | 400 | | | | |
| 7 | Oakland City Stores | 1,500 | 1,250 | 50 | 50 | | | 150 |
| 8 | River Grocery | 1,480 | 580 | 500 | 400 | | | |
| 9 | Whitley, D. | 960 | 300 | | | | 660 | |
| 10 | Total | | | | | | | |

Brandy Company has a past history of uncollectible accounts by age category, as follows:

| Age Class | Percent Uncollectible |
|---|---|
| Not past due | 1% |
| 1–30 days past due | 3% |
| 31–60 days past due | 7% |
| 61–90 days past due | 10% |
| 91–180 days past due | 15% |
| Over 180 days past due | 20% |

a. Open the Excel file *SA8-1_1e*.

b. Complete the aging of receivables schedule using spreadsheet provided.

c. Estimate the allowance for doubtful accounts, based on the aging of receivables schedule.

d. Assume that after additional historical analysis, the accounts receivable clerk revised the percent uncollectible as follows:

| Age Class | Percent Uncollectible |
|---|---|
| Not past due | 1% |
| 1–30 days past due | 2% |
| 31–60 days past due | 7% |
| 61–90 days past due | 12% |
| 91–180 days past due | 20% |
| Over 180 days past due | 40% |

e. Determine the allowance for doubtful accounts under the revised percent uncollectible assumptions.

f. When you have completed the receivables aging schedule, perform a "save as," replacing the entire file name with the following:

*SA8-1_1e[your first name initial]_[your last name]*

---

### SA 8-2   Aging of receivables schedule

The Lawson Company accounts receivable clerk assembled customer data at year-end as follows:

| Customer Name | Accounts Receivable Balance | Number of Days Past Due |
|---|---|---|
| Kress, T. | $2,400 | Not past due |
| Bradley, V. | 1,580 | 14 |
| Silver, K. | 500 | 123 |
| Ng, N. | 950 | 75 |
| Horowitz, S. | 670 | 41 |
| Stevens, K. | 3,100 | Not past due |
| Wilde, P. | 240 | 68 |
| Total | $9,440 | |

Lawson's past history of uncollectible accounts is as follows:

| Age Class | Percent Uncollectible |
|---|---|
| Not past due | 3% |
| 1–30 days past due | 8% |
| 31–60 days past due | 14% |
| 61–90 days past due | 20% |
| Over 90 days past due | 30% |

a. Open the Excel file *SA8-2_1e*.

b. Complete an aging of receivables schedule spreadsheet provided.

c. Determine the allowance for doubtful accounts, based on the completed aging of receivables schedule.

d. When you have completed the schedule, perform a "save as," replacing the entire file name with the following:

*SA8-2_ 1e[your first name initial]_[your last name]*

---

### SA 8-3   Determine interest on notes

Determine the amount of interest due at maturity on the following notes:

| | Face Amount | Interest Rate | Term of Note |
|---|---|---|---|
| alpha | $24,000 | 5% | 60 days |
| bravo | 94,000 | 4% | 45 days |
| charlie | 49,000 | 6% | 90 days |
| delta | 16,000 | 7% | 36 days |
| echo | 55,000 | 6% | 30 days |

a. Open the Excel file *SA8-3_1e*.

b. When you have determined the interest on each of the notes, perform a "save as," replacing the entire file name with the following:

*SA8-3_ 1e[your first name initial]_[your last name]*

---

### SA 8-4

Entries for notes receivable, including year-end interest adjustment, is as follows:

**2011**

Dec. 11.   Received a $56,000, 45-day, 4.5% noted dated Dec. 11 from Kimberly Co. on account.

   31.   Recorded an adjusting entry for accrued interest on the note of December 11.

   31.   Recorded the closing entry for interest revenue.

**2012**

Jan.  25.   Received payment of note and interest from Kimberly Co.

a. Open the Excel file *SA8-4_1e*.

b. Complete the spreadsheet to determine the accrued interest on December 31, 2011, and interest earned on January 25, 2012.

c. When you have determined the interest calculation, perform a "save as," replacing the entire file name with the following:

*SA8-4_ 1e[your first name initial]_[your last name]*

© AP Photo/W. A. Harewood

# Fixed Assets and Intangible Assets

## Fatburger Inc.

**D**o you remember purchasing your first car? You probably didn't buy your first car like you would buy a CD. Purchasing a new or used car is expensive. In addition, you would drive (use) the car for the next 3–5 years or longer. As a result, you might spend hours or weeks considering different makes and models, safety ratings, warranties, and operating costs before deciding on the final purchase.

Like buying her first car, Lovie Yancey spent a lot of time before deciding to open her first restaurant. In 1952, she created the biggest, juiciest hamburger that anyone had ever seen. She called it a Fatburger. The restaurant initially started as a 24-hour operation to cater to the schedules of professional musicians. As a fan of popular music and its performers, Yancey played rhythm and blues, jazz, and blues recordings for her customers. Fatburger's popularity with entertainers was illustrated when its name was used in a 1992 rap by Ice Cube. "Two in the mornin' got the Fatburger," Cube said, in "It Was a Good Day," a track on his *Predator* album.

The demand for this incredible burger was such that, in 1980, Ms. Yancey decided to offer Fatburger franchise opportunities. In 1990, with the goal of expanding Fatburger throughout the world, **Fatburger Inc.** purchased the business from Yancey. Today, Fatburger has grown to a multi-restaurant chain with owners and investors such as talk show host Montel Williams, former Cincinnati Bengals' tackle Willie Anderson, comedian David Spade, and musicians Cher, Janet Jackson, and Pharrell.

So, how much would it cost you to open a Fatburger restaurant? On average, the total investment begins at over $700,000 per restaurant. Thus, in starting a Fatburger restaurant, you would be making a significant investment that would affect your life for years to come.

This chapter discusses the accounting for investments in fixed assets such as those used to open a Fatburger restaurant. How to determine the portion of the fixed asset that becomes an expense over time is also discussed. Finally, the accounting for the disposal of fixed assets and accounting for intangible assets such as patents and copyrights are discussed.

**OBJ. 1** Define, classify, and account for the cost of fixed assets.

# Nature of Fixed Assets

**Fixed assets** are long-term or relatively permanent assets such as equipment, machinery, buildings, and land. Other descriptive titles for fixed assets are *plant assets* or *property, plant, and equipment*. Fixed assets have the following characteristics:

1. They exist physically and, thus, are *tangible* assets.
2. They are owned and used by the company in its normal operations.
3. They are not offered for sale as part of normal operations.

Exhibit 1 shows the percent of fixed assets to total assets for some select companies. As shown in Exhibit 1, fixed assets are often a significant portion of the total assets of a company.

**EXHIBIT 1**    **Fixed Assets as a Percent of Total Assets—Selected Companies**

|  | Fixed Assets as a Percent of Total Assets |
|---|---|
| Alcoa Inc. | 47% |
| ExxonMobil Corporation | 53 |
| Ford Motor Company | 25 |
| Kroger | 57 |
| Office Depot Inc. | 30 |
| United Parcel Service, Inc. | 57 |
| Verizon Communications | 43 |
| Walgreen Co. | 43 |
| Wal-Mart | 59 |

## Classifying Costs

A cost that has been incurred may be classified as a fixed asset, an investment, or an expense. Exhibit 2 shows how to determine the proper classification of a cost and how it should be recorded. As shown in Exhibit 2, classifying a cost involves the following steps:

See Appendix E for more information

Step 1.   Is the purchased item long-lived?

If *yes*, the item is recorded as an asset on the balance sheet, either as a fixed asset or an investment. Proceed to Step 2.

If *no*, the item is classified and recorded as an *expense*.

Step 2.   Is the asset used in normal operations?

If *yes*, the asset is classified and recorded as a *fixed asset*.

If *no*, the asset is classified and recorded as an *investment*.

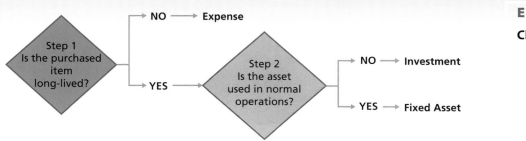

**EXHIBIT 2**

**Classifying Costs**

Items that are classified and recorded as fixed assets include land, buildings, or equipment. Such assets normally last more than a year and are used in the normal operations. However, standby equipment for use during peak periods or when other equipment breaks down is still classified as a fixed asset even though it is not used very often. In contrast, fixed assets that have been abandoned or are no longer used in operations are not classified as fixed assets.

Although fixed assets may be sold, they should not be offered for sale as part of normal operations. For example, cars and trucks offered for sale by an automotive dealership are not fixed assets of the dealership. On the other hand, a tow truck used in the normal operations of the dealership is a fixed asset of the dealership.

Investments are long-lived assets that are not used in the normal operations and are held for future resale. Such assets are reported on the balance sheet in a section entitled *Investments*. For example, undeveloped land acquired for future resale would be classified and reported as an investment, not land.

## The Cost of Fixed Assets

In addition to purchase price, costs of acquiring fixed assets include all amounts spent getting the asset in place and ready for use. For example, freight costs and the costs of installing equipment are part of the asset's total cost.

Exhibit 3 summarizes some of the common costs of acquiring fixed assets. These costs are recorded by debiting the related fixed asset account, such as Land,[1] Building, Land Improvements, or Machinery and Equipment.

**EXHIBIT 3**   **Costs of Acquiring Fixed Assets**

| **Building** | **Machinery & Equipment** | **Land** |
|---|---|---|
| • Architects' fees | • Sales taxes | • Purchase price |
| • Engineers' fees | • Freight | • Sales taxes |
| • Insurance costs incurred during construction | • Installation | • Permits from government agencies |
| • Interest on money borrowed to finance construction | • Repairs (purchase of used equipment) | • Broker's commissions |
| • Walkways to and around the building | • Reconditioning (purchase of used equipment) | • Title fees |
| • Sales taxes | • Insurance while in transit | • Surveying fees |
| • Repairs (purchase of existing building) | • Assembly | • Delinquent real estate taxes |
| • Reconditioning (purchase of existing building) | • Modifying for use | • Removing unwanted building less any salvage |
| • Modifying for use | • Testing for use | • Grading and leveling |
| • Permits from government agencies | • Permits from government agencies | • Paving a public street bordering the land |

**Land Improvements**
• Trees and shrubs
• Fences
• Outdoor lighting
• Paved parking areas

Only costs necessary for preparing the fixed asset for use are included as a cost of the asset. Unnecessary costs that do not increase the asset's usefulness are recorded as an expense. For example, the following costs are included as an expense:

1. Vandalism
2. Mistakes in installation
3. Uninsured theft
4. Damage during unpacking and installing
5. Fines for not obtaining proper permits from governmental agencies

A company may incur costs associated with constructing a fixed asset such as a new building. The direct costs incurred in the construction, such as labor and

1 As discussed here, land is assumed to be used only as a location or site and not for its mineral deposits or other natural resources.

materials, should be capitalized as a debit to an account entitled Construction in Progress. When the construction is complete, the costs are reclassified by crediting Construction in Progress and debiting the proper fixed asset account such as Building. For some companies, construction in progress can be significant.

## Capital and Revenue Expenditures

Once a fixed asset has been acquired and placed in service, costs may be incurred for ordinary maintenance and repairs. In addition, costs may be incurred for improving an asset or for extraordinary repairs that extend the asset's useful life. Costs that benefit only the current period are called **revenue expenditures**. Costs that improve the asset or extend its useful life are **capital expenditures**.

Intel Corporation reported in a recent annual report construction in progress of $2.7 billion, which was 16% of its total fixed assets.

See Appendix E for more information

**Ordinary Maintenance and Repairs**  Costs related to the ordinary maintenance and repairs of a fixed asset are recorded as an expense of the current period. Such expenditures are *revenue expenditures* and are recorded as increases to Repairs and Maintenance Expense. For example, $300 paid for a tune-up of a delivery truck is recorded as follows:

| | | | |
|---|---|---|---|
| Repairs and Maintenance Expense | | 300 | |
| Cash | | | 300 |

**Asset Improvements**  After a fixed asset has been placed in service, costs may be incurred to improve the asset. For example, the service value of a delivery truck might be improved by adding a $5,500 hydraulic lift to allow for easier and quicker loading of cargo. Such costs are *capital expenditures* and are recorded as increases to the fixed asset account. In the case of the hydraulic lift, the expenditure is recorded as follows:

| | | | |
|---|---|---|---|
| Delivery Truck | | 5,500 | |
| Cash | | | 5,500 |

Because the cost of the delivery truck has increased, depreciation for the truck would also change over its remaining useful life.

**Extraordinary Repairs**  After a fixed asset has been placed in service, costs may be incurred to extend the asset's useful life. For example, the engine of a forklift that is near the end of its useful life may be overhauled at a cost of $4,500, extending its useful life by eight years. Such costs are *capital expenditures* and are recorded as a decrease in an accumulated depreciation account. In the case of the forklift, the expenditure is recorded as follows:

| | | | |
|---|---|---|---|
| Accumulated Depreciation—Forklift | | 4,500 | |
| Cash | | | 4,500 |

## Integrity, Objectivity, and Ethics in Business

**CAPITAL CRIME**

One of the largest alleged accounting frauds in history involved the improper accounting for capital expenditures. WorldCom, the second largest telecommunications company in the United States at the time, improperly treated maintenance expenditures on its telecommunications network as capital expenditures. As a result, the company had to restate its prior years' earnings downward by nearly $4 billion to correct this error. The company declared bankruptcy within months of disclosing the error, and the CEO was sentenced to 25 years in prison.

Because the forklift's remaining useful life has changed, depreciation for the forklift would also change based on the new book value of the forklift.

The accounting for revenue and capital expenditures is summarized below.

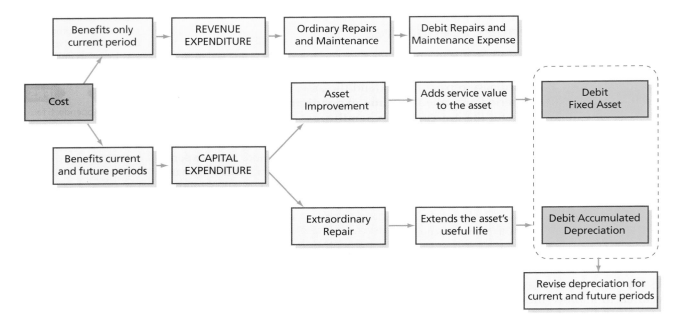

## Example Exercise 9-1 Capital and Revenue Expenditures

**OBJ. 1**

On June 18, GTS Co. paid $1,200 to upgrade a hydraulic lift and $45 for an oil change for one of its delivery trucks. Journalize the entries for the hydraulic lift upgrade and oil change expenditures.

### Follow My Example 9-1

| June 18 | Delivery Truck ............................................................ | 1,200 | |
| |     Cash.............................................................. | | 1,200 |
| | | | |
| 18 | Repairs and Maintenance Expense ........................................... | 45 | |
| |     Cash.............................................................. | | 45 |

Practice Exercises: **PE 9-1A, PE 9-1B**

## Leasing Fixed Assets

A *lease* is a contract for the use of an asset for a period of time. Leases are often used in business. For example, automobiles, computers, medical equipment, buildings, and airplanes are often leased.

The two parties to a lease contract are as follows:

1. The *lessor* is the party who owns the asset.
2. The *lessee* is the party to whom the rights to use the asset are granted by the lessor.

Delta Air Lines leases facilities, aircraft, and equipment using both capital and operating leases.

Under a lease contract, the lessee pays rent on a periodic basis for the lease term. The lessee accounts for a lease contract in one of two ways depending on how the lease contract is classified. A lease contract can be classified as either:

1. *A capital lease* or
2. *An operating lease*

A **capital lease** is accounted for as if the lessee has purchased the asset. The lessee debits an asset account for the fair market value of the asset and credits a long-term lease liability account. The asset is then written off as an expense (amortized) over the life of the capital lease. The accounting for capital leases is discussed in more advanced accounting texts.

An **operating lease** is accounted for as if the lessee is renting the asset for the lease term. The lessee records operating lease payments by debiting *Rent Expense* and crediting *Cash*. The lessee's future lease obligations are not recorded in the accounts. However, such obligations are disclosed in notes to the financial statements.

The asset rentals described in earlier chapters of this text were accounted for as operating leases. To simplify, all leases are assumed to be operating leases throughout this text.

# Accounting for Depreciation

Compute depreciation, using the following methods: straight-line method, units-of-production method, and double-declining-balance method.

Over time, fixed assets, with the exception of land, lose their ability to provide services. Thus, the costs of fixed assets such as equipment and buildings should be recorded as an expense over their useful lives. This periodic recording of the cost of fixed assets as an expense is called **depreciation**. Because land has an unlimited life, it is not depreciated.

The adjusting entry to record depreciation debits *Depreciation Expense* and credits a *contra asset* account entitled *Accumulated Depreciation* or *Allowance for Depreciation*. The use of a contra asset account allows the original cost to remain unchanged in the fixed asset account.

Depreciation can be caused by physical or functional factors.

1. *Physical depreciation* factors include wear and tear during use or from exposure to weather.
2. *Functional depreciation* factors include obsolescence and changes in customer needs that cause the asset to no longer provide services for which it was intended. For example, equipment may become obsolete due to changing technology.

Two common misunderstandings that exist about *depreciation* as used in accounting include:

1. Depreciation does not measure a decline in the market value of a fixed asset. Instead, depreciation is an allocation of a fixed asset's cost to expense over the asset's useful life. Thus, the book value of a fixed asset (cost less accumulated depreciation) usually does not agree with the asset's market value. This is justified in accounting because a fixed asset is for use in a company's operations rather than for resale.
2. Depreciation does not provide cash to replace fixed assets as they wear out. This misunderstanding may occur because depreciation, unlike most expenses, does not require an outlay of cash when it is recorded.

**Note:**
The adjusting entry to record depreciation debits Depreciation Expense and credits Accumulated Depreciation.

## Factors in Computing Depreciation Expense

Three factors determine the depreciation expense for a fixed asset. These three factors are as follows:

1. The asset's initial cost
2. The asset's expected useful life
3. The asset's estimated residual value

The initial *cost* of a fixed asset is determined using the concepts discussed and illustrated earlier in this chapter.

The *expected useful life* of a fixed asset is estimated at the time the asset is placed into service. Estimates of expected useful lives are available from industry trade associations. The Internal Revenue Service also publishes guidelines for useful lives, which may be helpful for financial reporting purposes. However, it is not uncommon for different companies to use a different useful life for similar assets.

The **residual value** of a fixed asset at the end of its useful life is estimated at the time the asset is placed into service. Residual value is sometimes referred to as *scrap* *value, salvage value*, or *trade-in value*. The difference between a fixed asset's initial cost and its residual value is called the asset's *depreciable cost*. The depreciable cost is the amount of the asset's cost that is allocated over its useful life as depreciation expense. If a fixed asset has no residual value, then its entire cost should be allocated to depreciation.

Exhibit 4 shows the relationship between depreciation expense and a fixed asset's initial cost, expected useful life, and estimated residual value.

**EXHIBIT 4**

**Depreciation Expense Factors**

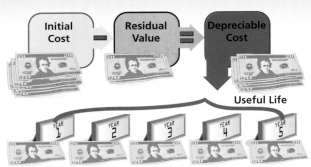

For an asset placed into or taken out of service during the first half of a month, many companies compute depreciation on the asset for the entire month. That is, the asset is treated as having been purchased or sold on the first day of *that* month. Likewise, purchases and sales during the second half of a month are treated as having occurred on the first day of the *next* month. To simplify, this practice is used in this chapter.

The three depreciation methods used most often are as follows:[2]

1. Straight-line depreciation
2. Units-of-production depreciation
3. Double-declining-balance depreciation

Exhibit 5 shows how often these methods are used in financial statements.

**EXHIBIT 5**

**Use of Depreciation Methods**

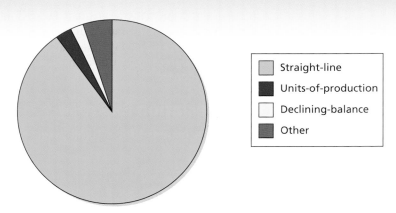

Source: *Accounting Trends & Techniques*, 63rd ed., American Institute of Certified Public Accountants, New York, 2009.

It is not necessary for a company to use only one method of computing depreciation for all of its fixed assets. For example, a company may use one method for depreciating equipment and another method for depreciating buildings.

2 Another method not often used today, called the *sum-of-the-years-digits method*, is described and illustrated in an online appendix located at **www.cengage.com/accounting/reeve**.

A company may also use different methods for determining income and property taxes.

## Straight-Line Method

The **straight-line method** provides for the same amount of depreciation expense for each year of the asset's useful life. As shown in Exhibit 5, the straight-line method is by far the most widely used depreciation method.

To illustrate, assume that equipment was purchased on January 1 as follows:

| | |
|---|---|
| Initial cost | $24,000 |
| Expected useful life | 5 years |
| Estimated residual value | $2,000 |

The annual straight-line depreciation of $4,400 is computed below.

$$\text{Annual Depreciation} = \frac{\text{Cost} - \text{Residual Value}}{\text{Useful Life}} = \frac{\$24,000 - \$2,000}{5 \text{ Years}} = \$4,400$$

If an asset is used for only part of a year, the annual depreciation is prorated. For example, assume that the preceding equipment was purchased and placed into service on October 1. The depreciation for the year ending December 31 would be **$1,100**, computed as follows:

$$\text{First-Year Partial Depreciation} = \$4,400 \times 3/12 = \$1,100$$

The computation of straight-line depreciation may be simplified by converting the annual depreciation to a percentage of depreciable cost.[3] The straight-line percentage is determined by dividing 100% by the number of years of expected useful life, as shown below.

| Expected Years of Useful Life | Straight-Line Percentage |
|---|---|
| 5 years | 20% (100%/5) |
| 8 years | 12.5% (100%/8) |
| 10 years | 10% (100%/10) |
| 20 years | 5% (100%/20) |
| 25 years | 4% (100%/25) |

For the preceding equipment, the annual depreciation of $4,400 can be computed by multiplying the depreciable cost of $22,000 by 20% (100%/5).

The straight-line method of depreciation can be calculated on a spreadsheet as follows:

| | A | B | C | |
|---|---|---|---|---|
| 1 | *Inputs* | | | |
| 2 | Initial cost | $ 24,000 | | |
| 3 | Expected useful life | 5 | years | Inputs |
| 4 | Estimated residual value | $ 2,000 | | |
| 5 | | | | |
| 6 | *Output* | | | |
| 7 | Annual depreciation | =(B2–B4)/B3 | | Outputs |
| 8 | | | | |

Rather than using a formula, periodic depreciation can also be calculated using Excel depreciation functions. For example, straight-line depreciation can be determined using the =SLN function.

The spreadsheet is divided into inputs and outputs. The formula in B7 is the straight-line depreciation formula using cell references of the input variables, =(B2-B4)/B3. Use parentheses as shown here so that the calculation is ordered properly.

**Try***It*   Go to the hands-on ***Excel Tutor*** for this example!

**Example Exercise** 9-2 **Straight-Line Depreciation**

Equipment acquired at the beginning of the year at a cost of $125,000 has an estimated residual value of $5,000 and an estimated useful life of 10 years. Determine (a) the depreciable cost, (b) the straight-line rate, and (c) the annual straight-line depreciation.

**Follow My Example** 9-2

a.  $120,000 ($125,000 – $5,000)

b.  10% = 1/10

c.  $12,000 ($120,000 × 10%), or ($120,000/10 years)

Practice Exercises: **PE 9-2A, PE 9-2B**

As shown on the previous page, the straight-line method is simple to use. When an asset's revenues are about the same from period to period, straight-line depreciation provides a good matching of depreciation expense with the asset's revenues.

Norfolk Southern Corporation depreciates its train engines based on hours of operation.

# Units-of-Production Method

The **units-of-production method** provides the same amount of depreciation expense for each unit of production. Depending on the asset, the units of production can be expressed in terms of hours, miles driven, or quantity produced.

The units-of-production method is applied in two steps.

Step 1.    Determine the depreciation per unit as:

$$\text{Depreciation per Unit} = \frac{\text{Cost} - \text{Residual Value}}{\text{Total Units of Production}}$$

Step 2.    Compute the depreciation expense as:

$$\text{Depreciation Expense} = \text{Depreciation per Unit} \times \text{Total Units of Production Used}$$

To illustrate, assume that the equipment in the preceding example is expected to have a useful life of 10,000 operating hours. During the year, the equipment was operated 2,100 hours. The units-of-production depreciation for the year is $4,620, as shown below.

Step 1.    Determine the depreciation per hour as:

$$\text{Depreciation per Hour} = \frac{\text{Cost} - \text{Residual Value}}{\text{Total Units of Production}} = \frac{\$24,000 - \$2,000}{10,000 \text{ Hours}} = \$2.20 \text{ per Hour}$$

Step 2.    Compute the depreciation expense as:

$$\text{Depreciation Expense} = \text{Depreciation per Unit} \times \text{Total Units of Production Used}$$
$$\text{Depreciation Expense} = \$2.20 \text{ per Hour} \times 2,100 \text{ Hours} = \$4,620$$

The units-of-production method is often used when a fixed asset's in-service time (or use) varies from year to year. In such cases, the units-of-production method matches depreciation expense with the asset's revenues.

3 The depreciation rate may also be expressed as a fraction. For example, the annual straight-line rate for an asset with a three-year useful life is 1/3.

The units of production method of depreciation can be calculated on a spreadsheet as follows:

| | A | B | C |
|---|---|---|---|
| 1 | *Inputs:* | | |
| 2 | Initial cost | $ 24,000 | |
| 3 | Estimated residual value | $ 2,000 | |
| 4 | Total units of production | 10,000 | hours |
| 5 | Total units of production used during the period | 2,100 | hours |
| 6 | | | |
| 7 | *Outputs* | | |
| 8 | Depreciation per unit | =(B2–B3)/B4 | ← a. |
| 9 | Depreciation expense for the period | =B8*B5 | ← b. |
| 10 | | | |

a.  Enter the formula for the depreciation per unit in cell B8, =(B2-B3)/B4. Use parentheses as shown here so that the calculation is ordered properly.

b.  Enter in B9 the formula for determining the depreciation for the period. The formula multiplies the rate in B8 by the units of production used during the period in B5, =B8*B5.

**Try***It*   Go to the hands-on *Excel Tutor* for this example!

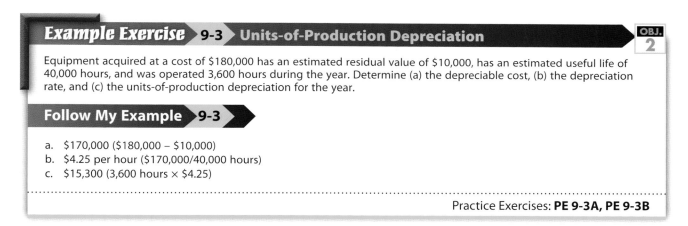

**Example Exercise** **9-3**  **Units-of-Production Depreciation**     **OBJ. 2**

Equipment acquired at a cost of $180,000 has an estimated residual value of $10,000, has an estimated useful life of 40,000 hours, and was operated 3,600 hours during the year. Determine (a) the depreciable cost, (b) the depreciation rate, and (c) the units-of-production depreciation for the year.

**Follow My Example** **9-3**

a.  $170,000 ($180,000 – $10,000)
b.  $4.25 per hour ($170,000/40,000 hours)
c.  $15,300 (3,600 hours × $4.25)

Practice Exercises: **PE 9-3A, PE 9-3B**

## Double-Declining-Balance Method

The **double-declining-balance method** provides for a declining periodic expense over the expected useful life of the asset. The double-declining-balance method is applied in three steps.

Step 1.   Determine the straight-line percentage using the expected useful life.
Step 2.   Determine the double-declining-balance rate by multiplying the straight-line rate from Step 1 by 2.
Step 3.   Compute the depreciation expense by multiplying the double-declining-balance rate from Step 2 times the book value of the asset.

To illustrate, the equipment purchased in the preceding example is used to compute double-declining-balance depreciation. For the first year, the depreciation is **$9,600**, as shown below.

Step 1.   Straight-line percentage = 20% (100%/5)
Step 2.   Double-declining-balance rate = 40% (20% × 2)
Step 3.   Depreciation expense = $9,600 ($24,000 × 40%)

For the first year, the book value of the equipment is its initial cost of $24,000. After the first year, the **book value** (cost minus accumulated depreciation) declines and, thus, the depreciation also declines. The double-declining-balance depreciation for the full five-year life of the equipment is shown below.

| Year | Cost | Acc. Dep. at Beginning of Year | Book Value at Beginning of Year | | Double-Declining-Balance Rate | Depreciation for Year | Book Value at End of Year |
|---|---|---|---|---|---|---|---|
| 1 | $24,000 | | $24,000.00 | × | 40% | $9,600.00 | $14,400.00 |
| 2 | 24,000 | $ 9,600.00 | 14,400.00 | × | 40% | 5,760.00 | 8,640.00 |
| 3 | 24,000 | 15,360.00 | 8,640.00 | × | 40% | 3,456.00 | 5,184.00 |
| 4 | 24,000 | 18,816.00 | 5,184.00 | × | 40% | 2,073.60 | 3,110.40 |
| 5 | 24,000 | 20,889.60 | 3,110.40 | | — | 1,110.40 | 2,000.00 |

When the double-declining-balance method is used, the estimated residual value is *not* considered. However, the asset should not be depreciated below its estimated residual value. In the above example, the estimated residual value was $2,000. Therefore, the depreciation for the fifth year is $1,110.40 ($3,110.40 − $2,000.00) instead of $1,244.16 (40% × $3,110.40).

Like straight-line depreciation, if an asset is used for only part of a year, the annual depreciation is prorated. For example, assume that the preceding equipment was purchased and placed into service on October 1. The depreciation for the year ending December 31 would be $2,400, computed as follows:

First-Year Partial Depreciation = $9,600 × 3/12 = $2,400

The depreciation for the second year would then be $8,640, computed as follows:

Second-Year Depreciation = $8,640 = [40% × ($24,000 − $2,400)]

The double-declining-balance method provides a higher depreciation in the first year of the asset's use, followed by declining depreciation amounts. For this reason, the double-declining-balance method is called an **accelerated depreciation method**.

An asset's revenues are often greater in the early years of its use than in later years. In such cases, the double-declining-balance method provides a good matching of depreciation expense with the asset's revenues.

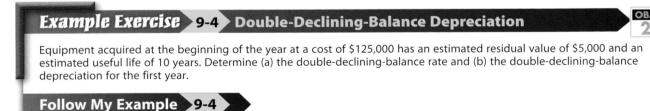

**Example Exercise ▶ 9-4 ▶ Double-Declining-Balance Depreciation** **OBJ. 2**

Equipment acquired at the beginning of the year at a cost of $125,000 has an estimated residual value of $5,000 and an estimated useful life of 10 years. Determine (a) the double-declining-balance rate and (b) the double-declining-balance depreciation for the first year.

**Follow My Example ▶ 9-4**

a. 20% [(1/10) × 2]
b. $25,000 ($125,000 × 20%)

Practice Exercises: **PE 9-4A, PE 9-4B**

## Comparing Depreciation Methods

The three depreciation methods are summarized in Exhibit 6. All three methods allocate a portion of the total cost of an asset to an accounting period, while never depreciating an asset below its residual value.

**EXHIBIT 6**

**Summary of Depreciation Methods**

| Method | Useful Life | Depreciable Cost | Depreciation Rate | Depreciation Expense |
|---|---|---|---|---|
| Straight-line | Years | Cost less residual value | Straight-line rate* | Constant |
| Units-of-production | Total units of production | Cost less residual value | $\dfrac{\text{Cost} - \text{Residual value}}{\text{Total units of production}}$ | Variable |
| Double-declining-balance | Years | Declining book value, but not below residual value | Straight-line rate* × 2 | Declining |

*Straight-line rate = (1/Useful life)

The straight-line method provides for the same periodic amounts of depreciation expense over the life of the asset. The units-of-production method provides for periodic amounts of depreciation expense that vary, depending on the amount the asset is used. The double-declining-balance method provides for a higher depreciation amount in the first year of the asset's use, followed by declining amounts.

The depreciation for the straight-line, units-of-production, and double-declining-balance methods is shown in Exhibit 7. The depreciation in Exhibit 7 is based on the equipment purchased in our prior illustrations. For the units-of-production method, we assume that the equipment was used as follows:

| | |
|---|---|
| Year 1 | 2,100 hours |
| Year 2 | 1,500 |
| Year 3 | 2,600 |
| Year 4 | 1,800 |
| Year 5 | 2,000 |
| Total | 10,000 hours |

**EXHIBIT 7**

**Comparing Depreciation Methods**

**Depreciation Expense**

| Year | Straight-Line Method | Units-of-Production Method | Double-Declining-Balance Method |
|---|---|---|---|
| 1 | $ 4,400* | $ 4,620 ($2.20 × 2,100 hrs.) | $ 9,600.00 ($24,000 × 40%) |
| 2 | 4,400 | 3,300 ($2.20 × 1,500 hrs.) | 5,760.00 ($14,400 × 40%) |
| 3 | 4,400 | 5,720 ($2.20 × 2,600 hrs.) | 3,456.00  ($8,640 × 40%) |
| 4 | 4,400 | 3,960 ($2.20 × 1,800 hrs.) | 2,073.60  ($5,184 × 40%) |
| 5 | 4,400 | 4,400 ($2.20 × 2,000 hrs.) | 1,110.40** |
| Total | $22,000 | $22,000 | $22,000.00 |

*$4,400 = ($24,000 – $2,000)/5 years
**$3,110.40 – $2,000.00 because the equipment cannot be depreciated below its residual value of $2,000.

## Depreciation for Federal Income Tax

The Internal Revenue Code uses the *Modified Accelerated Cost Recovery System (MACRS)* to compute depreciation for tax purposes. MACRS has eight classes of useful life and depreciation rates for each class. Two of the most common classes are the five-year class and the seven-year class.[4] The five-year class includes automobiles and light-duty trucks. The seven-year class includes most machinery and equipment. Depreciation for these two classes is similar to that computed using the double-declining-balance method.

4 Real estate is in either a 27½-year or a 31½-year class and is depreciated by the straight-line method.

In using the MACRS rates, residual value is ignored. Also, all fixed assets are assumed to be put in and taken out of service in the middle of the year. For the five-year-class assets, depreciation is spread over six years, as shown below.

| Year | MACRS 5-Year-Class Depreciation Rates |
|------|------|
| 1 | 20.0% |
| 2 | 32.0 |
| 3 | 19.2 |
| 4 | 11.5 |
| 5 | 11.5 |
| 6 | 5.8 |
| | 100.0% |

To simplify, a company will sometimes use MACRS for both financial statement and tax purposes. This is acceptable if MACRS does not result in significantly different amounts than would have been reported using one of the three depreciation methods discussed in this chapter.

# BusinessConnection

## DEPRECIATING ANIMALS?

Under MACRS, various farm animals may be depreciated. The period (years) over which some common classes of farm animals may be depreciated are shown in the table to the right.

Depreciation for farm animals begins when the animal reaches the age of maturity, which is normally when it can be worked, milked, or bred. For race horses, depreciation begins when a horse is put into training.

| Class of Animal | Years |
|------|------|
| Dairy or breeding cattle | 7–10 |
| Goats and sheep | 5 |
| Hogs | 3 |
| Horses | 3–12 |

## Revising Depreciation Estimates

Estimates of residual values and useful lives of fixed assets may change due to abnormal wear and tear or obsolescence. When new estimates are determined, they are used to determine the depreciation expense in future periods. The depreciation expense recorded in earlier years is not affected.[5]

To illustrate, assume the following data for a machine that was purchased on January 1, 2011.

| | |
|------|------|
| Initial machine cost | $140,000 |
| Expected useful life | 5 years |
| Estimated residual value | $10,000 |
| Annual depreciation using the straight-line method [($140,000 − $10,000)/5 years] | $26,000 |

At the end of 2012, the machine's book value (undepreciated cost) is $88,000, as shown below.

| | |
|------|------|
| Initial machine cost | $140,000 |
| Less accumulated depreciation ($26,000 per year × 2 years) | 52,000 |
| Book value (undepreciated cost), end of second year | $ 88,000 |

5 *FASB Accounting Standards Codification*, Section 250-10-05.

During 2013, the company estimates that the machine's remaining useful life is eight years (instead of three) and that its residual value is $8,000 (instead of $10,000). The depreciation expense for each of the remaining eight years is $10,000, computed as follows:

| | |
|---|---:|
| Book value (undepreciated cost), end of second year | $88,000 |
| Less revised estimated residual value | 8,000 |
| Revised remaining depreciable cost | $80,000 |
| | |
| Revised annual depreciation expense [($88,000 – $8,000)/8 years] | $10,000 |

Exhibit 8 shows the book value of the asset over its original and revised lives. After the depreciation is revised at the end of 2012, book value declines at a slower rate. At the end of year 2020, the book value reaches the revised residual value of $8,000.

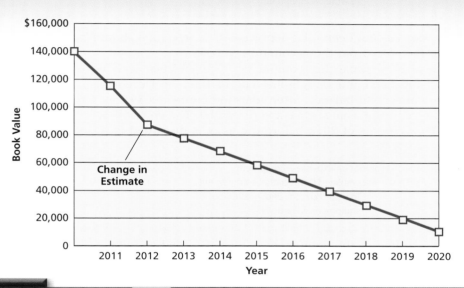

**EXHIBIT 8**

**Book Value of Asset with Change in Estimate**

---

## Example Exercise 9-5 ▸ Revision of Depreciation

**OBJ. 2**

A warehouse with a cost of $500,000 has an estimated residual value of $120,000, has an estimated useful life of 40 years, and is depreciated by the straight-line method. (a) Determine the amount of the annual depreciation. (b) Determine the book value at the end of the twentieth year of use. (c) Assuming that at the start of the twenty-first year the remaining life is estimated to be 25 years and the residual value is estimated to be $150,000, determine the depreciation expense for each of the remaining 25 years.

### Follow My Example 9-5

a. $9,500 [($500,000 – $120,000)/40]
b. $310,000 [$500,000 – ($9,500 × 20)]
c. $6,400 [($310,000 – $150,000)/25]

Practice Exercises: **PE 9-5A, PE 9-5B**

---

# Disposal of Fixed Assets

 **OBJ. 3** Journalize entries for the disposal of fixed assets.

Fixed assets that are no longer useful may be discarded or sold.[6] In such cases, the fixed asset is removed from the accounts. Just because a fixed asset is fully depreciated, however, does not mean that it should be removed from the accounts.

If a fixed asset is still being used, its cost and accumulated depreciation should remain in the ledger even if the asset is fully depreciated. This maintains accountability for the asset in the ledger. If the asset was removed from the ledger, the accounts would contain no evidence of the continued existence of the asset. In addition, cost and accumulated depreciation data on such assets are often needed for property tax and income tax reports.

6 The accounting for the exchange of fixed assets is described and illustrated in the appendix at the end of this chapter.

# Discarding Fixed Assets

If a fixed asset is no longer used and has no residual value, it is discarded. For example, assume that a fixed asset that is fully depreciated and has no residual value is discarded. The entry to record the discarding removes the asset and its related accumulated depreciation from the ledger.

To illustrate, assume that equipment acquired at a cost of $25,000 is fully depreciated at December 31, 2011. On February 14, 2012, the equipment is discarded. The entry to record the discard is as follows:

| | | | | | |
|---|---|---|---|---|---|
| Feb. | 14 | Accumulated Depreciation—Equipment | | 25,000 | |
| | | Equipment | | | 25,000 |
| | | To write off equipment discarded. | | | |

If an asset has not been fully depreciated, depreciation should be recorded before removing the asset from the accounting records.

To illustrate, assume that equipment costing $6,000 with no estimated residual value is depreciated at a straight-line rate of 10%. On December 31, 2011, the accumulated depreciation balance, after adjusting entries, is $4,750. On March 24, 2012, the asset is removed from service and discarded. The entry to record the depreciation for the three months of 2012 before the asset is discarded is as follows:

| | | | | | |
|---|---|---|---|---|---|
| Mar. | 24 | Depreciation Expense—Equipment | | 150 | |
| | | Accumulated Depreciation—Equipment | | | 150 |
| | | To record current depreciation on | | | |
| | | equipment discarded ($600 × 3/12). | | | |

The discarding of the equipment is then recorded as follows:

| | | | | | |
|---|---|---|---|---|---|
| Mar. | 24 | Accumulated Depreciation—Equipment | | 4,900 | |
| | | Loss on Disposal of Equipment | | 1,100 | |
| | | Equipment | | | 6,000 |
| | | To write off equipment discarded. | | | |

The loss of $1,100 is recorded because the balance of the accumulated depreciation account ($4,900) is less than the balance in the equipment account ($6,000). Losses on the discarding of fixed assets are nonoperating items and are normally reported in the Other Expense section of the income statement.

# Selling Fixed Assets

The entry to record the sale of a fixed asset is similar to the entries for discarding an asset. The only difference is that the receipt of cash is also recorded. If the selling price is more than the book value of the asset, a gain is recorded. If the selling price is less than the book value, a loss is recorded.

To illustrate, assume that equipment is purchased at a cost of $10,000 with no estimated residual value and is depreciated at a straight-line rate of 10%. The equipment is sold for cash on October 12 of the eighth year of its use. The balance of the accumulated depreciation account as of the preceding December 31 is $7,000. The entry to update the depreciation for the nine months of the current year is as follows:

| | | | | | |
|---|---|---|---|---|---|
| Oct. | 12 | Depreciation Expense—Equipment | | 750 | |
| | | Accumulated Depreciation—Equipment | | | 750 |
| | | To record current depreciation on | | | |
| | | equipment sold ($10,000 × 9/12 × 10%). | | | |

After the current depreciation is recorded, the book value of the asset is $2,250 ($10,000 − $7,750). The entries to record the sale, assuming three different selling prices, are as follows:

Sold at book value, for $2,250. No gain or loss.

| Oct. | 12 | Cash | 2,250 | |
|---|---|---|---|---|
| | | Accumulated Depreciation—Equipment | 7,750 | |
| | | Equipment | | 10,000 |

Sold below book value, for $1,000. Loss of $1,250.

| Oct. | 12 | Cash | 1,000 | |
|---|---|---|---|---|
| | | Accumulated Depreciation—Equipment | 7,750 | |
| | | Loss on Sale of Equipment | 1,250 | |
| | | Equipment | | 10,000 |

Sold above book value, for $2,800. Gain of $550.

| Oct. | 12 | Cash | 2,800 | |
|---|---|---|---|---|
| | | Accumulated Depreciation—Equipment | 7,750 | |
| | | Equipment | | 10,000 |
| | | Gain on Sale of Equipment | | 550 |

## Example Exercise 9-6  Sale of Equipment

**OBJ. 3**

Equipment was acquired at the beginning of the year at a cost of $91,000. The equipment was depreciated using the straight-line method based on an estimated useful life of nine years and an estimated residual value of $10,000.

a.  What was the depreciation for the first year?

b.  Assuming the equipment was sold at the end of the second year for $78,000, determine the gain or loss on sale of the equipment.

c.  Journalize the entry to record the sale.

### Follow My Example 9-6

a.  $9,000 [($91,000 − $10,000)/9]

b.  $5,000 gain {$78,000 − [$91,000 − ($9,000 × 2)]}

c.  Cash ................................................................................. 78,000
    Accumulated Depreciation—Equipment ........................................... 18,000
        Equipment ...................................................................... 91,000
        Gain on Sale of Equipment ..................................................... 5,000

Practice Exercises: **PE 9-6A, PE 9-6B**

# Natural Resources

**OBJ. 4**  Compute depletion and journalize the entry for depletion.

The fixed assets of some companies include timber, metal ores, minerals, or other natural resources. As these resources are harvested or mined and then sold, a portion of their cost is debited to an expense account. This process of transferring the cost of natural resources to an expense account is called **depletion**.

Depletion is determined as follows:[7]

Step 1.   Determine the depletion rate as:

$$\text{Depletion Rate} = \frac{\text{Cost of Resource}}{\text{Estimated Total Units of Resource}}$$

7 We assume that there is no significant residual value left after all the natural resource is extracted.

Step 2. Multiply the depletion rate by the quantity extracted from the resource during the period.

$$\text{Depletion Expense} = \text{Depletion Rate} \times \text{Quantity Extracted}$$

To illustrate, assume that Karst Company purchased mining rights as follows:

| | |
|---|---|
| Cost of mineral deposit | $400,000 |
| Estimated total units of resource | 1,000,000 tons |
| Tons mined during year | 90,000 tons |

The depletion expense of $36,000 for the year is computed, as shown below.

Step 1.

$$\text{Depletion Rate} = \frac{\text{Cost of Resource}}{\text{Estimated Total Units of Resource}} = \frac{\$400,000}{1,000,000 \text{ Tons}} = \$0.40 \text{ per Ton}$$

Step 2.

$$\text{Depletion Expense} = \$0.40 \text{ per Ton} \times 90,000 \text{ Tons} = \$36,000$$

The adjusting entry to record the depletion is shown below.

| | | | | | |
|---|---|---|---|---|---|
| Dec. | 31 | Depletion Expense | | 36,000 | |
| | | Accumulated Depletion | | | 36,000 |
| | | Depletion of mineral deposit. | | | |

Like the accumulated depreciation account, Accumulated Depletion is a *contra asset* account. It is reported on the balance sheet as a deduction from the cost of the mineral deposit.

---

## Example Exercise 9-7 Depletion

**OBJ. 4**

Earth's Treasures Mining Co. acquired mineral rights for $45,000,000. The mineral deposit is estimated at 50,000,000 tons. During the current year, 12,600,000 tons were mined and sold.

a. Determine the depletion rate.

b. Determine the amount of depletion expense for the current year.

c. Journalize the adjusting entry on December 31 to recognize the depletion expense.

### Follow My Example 9-7

a. $0.90 per ton ($45,000,000/50,000,000 tons)

b. $11,340,000 (12,600,000 tons × $0.90 per ton)

c. Dec. 31  Depletion Expense ................................................. 11,340,000
              Accumulated Depreciation ........................................... 11,340,000
                  Depletion of mineral deposit.

Practice Exercises: **PE 9-7A, PE 9-7B**

---

**OBJ. 5** Describe the accounting for intangible assets, such as patents, copyrights, and goodwill.

# Intangible Assets

Patents, copyrights, trademarks, and goodwill are long-lived assets that are used in the operations of a business and are not held for sale. These assets are called **intangible assets** because they do not exist physically.

The accounting for intangible assets is similar to that for fixed assets. The major issues are:

See Appendix E for more information

1. Determining the initial cost.

2. Determining the **amortization**, which is the amount of cost to transfer to expense.

Amortization results from the passage of time or a decline in the usefulness of the intangible asset.

## Patents

Manufacturers may acquire exclusive rights to produce and sell goods with one or more unique features. Such rights are granted by **patents,** which the federal government issues to inventors. These rights continue in effect for 20 years. A business may purchase patent rights from others, or it may obtain patents developed by its own research and development.

The initial cost of a purchased patent, including any legal fees, is debited to an asset account. This cost is written off, or amortized, over the years of the patent's expected useful life. The expected useful life of a patent may be less than its legal life. For example, a patent may become worthless due to changing technology or consumer tastes.

Patent amortization is normally computed using the straight-line method. The amortization is recorded by debiting an amortization expense account and crediting the patents account. A separate contra asset account is usually *not* used for intangible assets.

To illustrate, assume that at the beginning of its fiscal year, a company acquires patent rights for $100,000. Although the patent will not expire for 14 years, its remaining useful life is estimated as five years. The adjusting entry to amortize the patent at the end of the year is as follows:

| | | | | | |
|---|---|---|---|---|---|
| Dec. | 31 | Amortization Expense—Patents | | 20,000 | |
| | | Patents | | | 20,000 |
| | | Patent amortization ($100,000/5). | | | |

Some companies develop their own patents through research and development. In such cases, any *research and development costs* are usually recorded as current operating expenses in the period in which they are incurred. This accounting for research and development costs is justified on the basis that any future benefits from research and development are highly uncertain.

**IFRS**

## International Connection

### INTERNATIONAL FINANCIAL REPORTING STANDARDS (IFRS)

IFRS allow certain research and development (R&D) costs to be recorded as assets when incurred. Typically, R&D costs are classified as either research costs or development costs. If certain criteria are met, research costs can be recorded as an expense, while development costs can be recorded as an asset. This criterion includes such considerations as the company's intent to use or to sell the intangible asset. For example, Nokia Corporation (Finland) reported capitalized development costs of €143 million on its December 31, 2009, statement of financial position (balance sheet), where € represents the euro, the common currency of the European Economic Union.*

*Differences between U.S. GAAP and IFRS are further discussed and illustrated in Appendix E.

## Copyrights and Trademarks

The exclusive right to publish and sell a literary, artistic, or musical composition is granted by a **copyright**. Copyrights are issued by the federal government and extend for 70 years beyond the author's death. The costs of a copyright include all costs of creating the work plus any other costs of obtaining the copyright. A copyright that is purchased is recorded at the price paid for it. Copyrights are amortized over their estimated useful lives.

A **trademark** is a name, term, or symbol used to identify a business and its products. Most businesses identify their trademarks with ® in their advertisements and on their products.

Under federal law, businesses can protect their trademarks by registering them for 10 years and renewing the registration for 10-year periods. Like a copyright, the legal costs of registering a trademark are recorded as an asset.

If a trademark is purchased from another business, its cost is recorded as an asset. In such cases, the cost of the trademark is considered to have an indefinite useful life. Thus, trademarks are not amortized. Instead, trademarks are reviewed periodically for impaired value. When a trademark is impaired, the trademark should be written down and a loss recognized.

## Goodwill

**Goodwill** refers to an intangible asset of a business that is created from such favorable factors as location, product quality, reputation, and managerial skill. Goodwill allows a business to earn a greater rate of return than normal.

Generally accepted accounting principles (GAAP) allow goodwill to be recorded only if it is objectively determined by a transaction. An example of such a transaction is the purchase of a business at a price in excess of the fair value of its net assets (assets – liabilities). The excess is recorded as goodwill and reported as an intangible asset.

Unlike patents and copyrights, goodwill is not amortized. However, a loss should be recorded if the future prospects of the purchased firm become impaired. This loss would normally be disclosed in the Other Expense section of the income statement.

To illustrate, assume that on December 31 FaceCard Company has determined that $250,000 of the goodwill created from the purchase of Electronic Systems is impaired. The entry to record the impairment is as follows:

| Dec. | 31 | Loss from Impaired Goodwill | 250,000 | |
| | | Goodwill | | 250,000 |
| | | Impaired goodwill. | | |

Exhibit 9 shows intangible asset disclosures for 500 large firms. Goodwill is the most often reported intangible asset. This is because goodwill arises from merger transactions, which are common.

**EXHIBIT 9**

**Frequency of Intangible Asset Disclosures for 500 Firms**

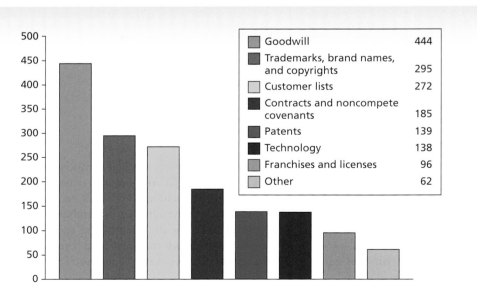

| | |
| --- | --- |
| Goodwill | 444 |
| Trademarks, brand names, and copyrights | 295 |
| Customer lists | 272 |
| Contracts and noncompete covenants | 185 |
| Patents | 139 |
| Technology | 138 |
| Franchises and licenses | 96 |
| Other | 62 |

Source: *Accounting Trends & Techniques,* 63rd ed., American Institute of Certified Public Accountants, New York, 2009.
Note: Some firms have multiple disclosures.

Exhibit 10 summarizes the characteristics of intangible assets.

**EXHIBIT 10**

**Comparison of Intangible Assets**

| Intangible Asset | Description | Amortization Period | Periodic Expense |
|---|---|---|---|
| Patent | Exclusive right to benefit from an innovation. | Estimated useful life not to exceed legal life. | Amortization expense. |
| Copyright | Exclusive right to benefit from a literary, artistic, or musical composition. | Estimated useful life not to exceed legal life. | Amortization expense. |
| Trademark | Exclusive use of a name, term, or symbol. | None | Impairment loss if fair value less than carrying value (impaired). |
| Goodwill | Excess of purchase price of a business over the fair value of its net assets (assets − liabilities). | None | Impairment loss if fair value less than carrying value (impaired). |

**Example Exercise** ▶ **9-8** ▶ **Impaired Goodwill and Amortization of Patent** ▶ **OBJ. 5**

On December 31, it was estimated that goodwill of $40,000 was impaired. In addition, a patent with an estimated useful economic life of 12 years was acquired for $84,000 on July 1.

a. Journalize the adjusting entry on December 31 for the impaired goodwill.

b. Journalize the adjusting entry on December 31 for the amortization of the patent rights.

**Follow My Example** ▶ **9-8** ▶

| | | | | |
|---|---|---|---|---|
| a. | Dec. 31 | Loss from Impaired Goodwill .................................... | 40,000 | |
| | | Goodwill ................................................... | | 40,000 |
| | | Impaired goodwill. | | |
| b. | Dec. 31 | Amortization Expense—Patents ............................... | 3,500 | |
| | | Patents .................................................... | | 3,500 |
| | | Amortized patent rights [($84,000/12) × (6/12)]. | | |

Practice Exercises: **PE 9-8A, PE 9-8B**

# Financial Reporting for Fixed Assets and Intangible Assets

**OBJ. 6** Describe how depreciation expense is reported in an income statement and prepare a balance sheet that includes fixed assets and intangible assets.

In the income statement, depreciation and amortization expense should be reported separately or disclosed in a note. A description of the methods used in computing depreciation should also be reported.

In the balance sheet, each class of fixed assets should be disclosed on the face of the statement or in the notes. The related accumulated depreciation should also be disclosed, either by class or in total. The fixed assets may be shown at their *book value* (cost less accumulated depreciation), which can also be described as their *net* amount.

If there are many classes of fixed assets, a single amount may be presented in the balance sheet, supported by a note with a separate listing. Fixed assets may be reported under the more descriptive caption of property, plant, and equipment.

Intangible assets are usually reported in the balance sheet in a separate section following fixed assets. The balance of each class of intangible assets should be disclosed net of any amortization.

The balance sheet presentation for Mornin' Joe's fixed and intangible assets is shown on the next page.

**Mornin' Joe**
**Balance Sheet**
**December 31, 2012**

| | | |
|---|---|---|
| Property, plant, and equipment: | | |
| Land | | $1,850,000 |
| Buildings | $2,650,000 | |
| Less accumulated depreciation | 420,000 | 2,230,000 |
| Office equipment | $ 350,000 | |
| Less accumulated depreciation | 102,000 | 248,000 |
| Total property, plant, and equipment | | $4,328,000 |
| Intangible assets: | | |
| Patents | | 140,000 |

The cost and related accumulated depletion of mineral rights are normally shown as part of the Fixed Assets section of the balance sheet. The mineral rights may be shown net of depletion on the face of the balance sheet. In such cases, a supporting note discloses the accumulated depletion.

See pages 630-634

### IFRS Reporting

The statement of financial position (balance sheet) presentation for fixed assets and intangible assets for Mornin' Joe International under IFRS is as follows:

**Mornin' Joe International**
**Statement of Financial Position**
**December 31, 2012**

| | | |
|---|---|---|
| **Noncurrent assets** | | |
| Property, plant, and equipment | | |
| Land and buildings **at fair value** | €4,180,000 | |
| Less: Accumulated depreciation | 375,200 | €3,804,800 |
| Office equipment at cost | € 350,000 | |
| Less: Accumulated depreciation | 102,000 | 248,000 |
| **Biological assets at fair value** | | 320,000 |
| Patents at amortized cost | | 140,000 |

The fixed and intangible assets disclosures are similar to U.S. GAAP except for the following two differences:

1. Under IFRS, property, plant, and equipment (PP&E) may be measured at historical cost or fair value. Fair value is the market value for the asset. If fair value is used, the revaluation must be for similar classifications of PP&E, but need not be for all PP&E. This departs from U.S. GAAP, which requires PP&E to be measured at historical cost.

    Mornin' Joe International restated its Land and Buildings to fair value since the café sites have readily available real estate market prices. Land and buildings are included together because their fair values are not separable. The office equipment remains at historical cost since it does not have a readily available market price. Intangible assets can also be disclosed at fair value if they have ready market prices; however, this is not the case for Mornin' Joe International's patents, which are stated at historical cost.

2. IFRS requires agricultural assets, termed biological assets, to be separately disclosed and valued at fair value. Mornin' Joe owns a coffee plantation, which is disclosed as a biological asset.

# Financial Analysis and Interpretation: Fixed Asset Turnover Ratio

A measure of a company's efficiency in using its fixed assets to generate revenue is the fixed asset turnover ratio. The **fixed asset turnover ratio** measures the number of dollars of sales earned per dollar of fixed assets. It is computed as follows:

**OBJ. 7** Describe and illustrate the fixed asset turnover ratio to assess the efficiency of a company's use of its fixed assets.

$$\text{Fixed Asset Turnover Ratio} = \frac{\text{Net Sales}}{\text{Average Book Value of Fixed Assets}}$$

To illustrate, the following data (in millions) are used for Starbucks Corp.

|  | Sept. 27, 2009 | Sept. 28, 2008 |
| --- | --- | --- |
| Net sales | $9,775 | $10,383 |
| Fixed assets (net): |  |  |
| Beginning of year | 2,956 | 2,890 |
| End of year | 2,536 | 2,956 |

Starbucks' fixed asset turnover ratios for 2009 and 2008 are computed as follows:

|  | 2009 | 2008 |
| --- | --- | --- |
| Net sales | $9,775 | $10,383 |
| Average fixed assets | $2,746 | $ 2,923 |
|  | [($2,536 + $2,956) ÷ 2] | [($2,956 + $2,890) ÷ 2] |
| Fixed asset turnover ratio | 3.56 | 3.55 |
|  | ($9,775 ÷ $2,746) | ($10,383 ÷ $2,923) |

The higher the fixed asset turnover, the more efficiently a company is using its fixed assets in generating sales. For example, in 2009 Starbucks earned $3.56 of sales for every dollar of fixed assets, which is slightly more than $3.55 of sales for every dollar of fixed assets it earned in 2008. Thus, Starbucks used its fixed assets slightly more efficiently in 2009.

As illustrated above, the fixed asset turnover ratio can be compared across time for a single company. In addition, the ratio can be compared across companies. For example, the fixed asset turnover ratio for a number of different companies and industries is shown below.

| Company (industry) | Fixed Asset Turnover Ratio |
| --- | --- |
| Comcast Corporation (cable) | 1.43 |
| Google (Internet) | 4.70 |
| Manpower Inc. (temporary employment) | 99.32 |
| Norfolk Southern Corporation (railroad) | 0.49 |
| Ruby Tuesday, Inc. (restaurant) | 1.20 |
| Southwest Airlines Co. (airline) | 1.01 |

The smaller ratios are associated with companies that require large fixed asset investments. The larger fixed asset turnover ratios are associated with firms that are more labor-intensive and require smaller fixed asset investments.

# BusinessConnection

## HUB-AND-SPOKE OR POINT-TO-POINT?

Southwest Airlines Co. uses a simple fare structure, featuring low, unrestricted, unlimited, everyday coach fares. These fares are made possible by Southwest's use of a point-to-point, rather than a hub-and-spoke, business approach. United Airlines, Inc., Delta Air Lines, and American Airlines employ a hub-and-spoke approach in which an airline establishes major hubs that serve as connecting links to other cities. For example, Delta has major connecting hubs in Atlanta and Salt Lake City.

In contrast, Southwest focuses on nonstop, point-to-point service between selected cities. As a result, Southwest minimizes connections, delays, and total trip time. This operating approach permits Southwest to achieve high utilization of its fixed assets, such as its 737 aircraft.

**Example Exercise** 9-9 Fixed Asset Turnover Ratio

OBJ. 7

Financial statement data for years ending December 31 for Broadwater Company are shown below.

|  | 2012 | 2011 |
|---|---|---|
| Net sales | $2,862,000 | $2,025,000 |
| Fixed assets: |  |  |
| Beginning of year | 750,000 | 600,000 |
| End of year | 840,000 | 750,000 |

a. Determine the fixed asset turnover ratio for 2012 and 2011.

b. Does the change in the fixed asset turnover ratio from 2011 to 2012 indicate a favorable or an unfavorable trend?

**Follow My Example** 9-9

a. Fixed asset turnover:

|  | 2012 | 2011 |
|---|---|---|
| Net sales | $2,862,000 | $2,025,000 |
| Fixed assets: |  |  |
| Beginning of year | $750,000 | $600,000 |
| End of year | $840,000 | $750,000 |
| Average fixed assets | $795,000 | $675,000 |
|  | [($750,000 + $840,000) ÷ 2] | [($600,000 + $750,000) ÷ 2] |
| Fixed asset turnover | 3.6 | 3.0 |
|  | ($2,862,000 ÷ $795,000) | ($2,025,000 ÷ $675,000) |

b. The increase in the fixed asset turnover ratio from 3.0 to 3.6 indicates a favorable trend in the efficiency of using fixed assets to generate sales.

Practice Exercises: **PE 9-9A, PE 9-9B**

# A P P E N D I X

# Exchanging Similar Fixed Assets

Old equipment is often traded in for new equipment having a similar use. In such cases, the seller allows the buyer an amount for the old equipment traded in. This amount, called the **trade-in allowance**, may be either greater or less than the book value of the old equipment. The remaining balance—the amount owed—is either paid in cash or recorded as a liability. It is normally called **boot**, which is its tax name.

Accounting for the exchange of similar assets depends on whether the transaction has *commercial substance*.[8] An exchange has commercial substance if future cash flows change as a result of the exchange. If an exchange of similar assets has commercial substance, a gain or loss is recognized based on the difference between the book value of the asset given up (exchanged) and the fair market value of the asset received. In such cases, the exchange is accounted for similar to that of a sale of a fixed asset.

## Gain on Exchange

To illustrate a gain on an exchange of similar assets, assume the following:

8 *FASB Accounting Standards Codification*, Section 360-10-30.

*Similar equipment acquired (new):*

Price (fair market value) of new equipment .................................................. $5,000
Trade-in allowance on old equipment .................................................... 1,100
Cash paid at June 19, date of exchange ................................................ $3,900

*Equipment traded in (old):*

Cost of old equipment ................................................................ $4,000
Accumulated depreciation at date of exchange ........................................... 3,200
Book value at June 19, date of exchange................................................ $ 800

The entry to record this exchange and payment of cash is as follows:

| | | | |
|---|---|---|---|
| June 19 | Accumulated Depreciation—Equipment.............. | 3,200 | |
| | Equipment (new equipment)........................ | 5,000 | |
| |    Equipment (old equipment) ..................... | | 4,000 |
| |    Cash ........................................... | | 3,900 |
| |    Gain on Exchange of Equipment ................. | | 300 |

The gain on the exchange, $300, is the difference between the fair market value of the new asset of $5,000 and the book value of the old asset traded in of $800 plus the cash paid of $3,900 as shown below.

Price (fair market value) of new equipment ...................... $5,000
Less assets given up in exchange:
   Book value of old equipment ($4,000 – $3,200) ............... $ 800
   Cash paid on the exchange ................................... 3,900   4,700
Gain on exchange of assets...................................... $ 300

## Loss on Exchange

To illustrate a loss on an exchange of similar assets, assume that instead of a trade-in allowance of $1,100, a trade-in allowance of only $675 was allowed in the preceding example. In this case, the cash paid on the exchange is $4,325 as shown below.

Price (fair market value) of new equipment ...................... $5,000
Trade-in allowance of old equipment............................. 675
Cash paid at June 19, date of exchange ......................... $4,325

The entry to record this exchange and payment of cash is as follows:

| | | | |
|---|---|---|---|
| June 19 | Accumulated Depreciation—Equipment.............. | 3,200 | |
| | Equipment (new equipment)........................ | 5,000 | |
| | Loss on Exchange of Equipment...................... | 125 | |
| |    Equipment (old equipment) ...................... | | 4,000 |
| |    Cash ........................................... | | 4,325 |

The loss on the exchange, $125, is the difference between the fair market value of the new asset ($5,000) and the book value of the old asset traded in ($800) plus the cash paid ($4,325), as shown below.

Price (fair market value) of new equipment ...................... $5,000
Less assets given up in exchange:
   Book value of old equipment ($4,000 – $3,200) ............... $ 800
   Cash paid on the exchange ................................... 4,325   5,125
Loss on exchange of assets...................................... $ (125)

In those cases where an asset exchange *lacks commercial substance*, no gain is recognized on the exchange. Instead, the cost of the new asset is adjusted for any gain. For example, in the first illustration, the gain of $300 would be subtracted from the purchase price of $5,000 and the new asset would be recorded at $4,700. Accounting for the exchange of assets that lack commercial substance is discussed in more advanced accounting texts.[9]

9 The exchange of similar assets also involves complex tax issues which are discussed in advanced accounting courses.

# At a Glance 9

**Key Points** Fixed assets are long-term tangible assets used in the normal operations of the business such as equipment, buildings, and land. The initial cost of a fixed asset includes all amounts spent to get the asset in place and ready for use. Revenue expenditures include ordinary repairs and maintenance. Capital expenditures include asset improvements and extraordinary repairs.

| Learning Outcomes | Example Exercises | Practice Exercises |
|---|---|---|
| • Define *fixed assets*. | | |
| • List types of costs that should be included in the cost of a fixed asset. | | |
| • Provide examples of ordinary repairs, asset improvements, and extraordinary repairs. | | |
| • Prepare journal entries for ordinary repairs, asset improvements, and extraordinary repairs. | EE9-1 | PE9-1A, 9-1B |

**Key Points** All fixed assets except land should be depreciated over time. Three factors are considered in determining depreciation: (1) the fixed asset's initial cost, (2) the useful life of the asset, and (3) the residual value of the asset.

Depreciation may be determined using the straight-line, units-of-production, and double-declining-balance methods.

Depreciation may be revised into the future for changes in an asset's useful life or residual value.

| Learning Outcomes | Example Exercises | Practice Exercises |
|---|---|---|
| • Define and describe *depreciation*. | | |
| • List the factors used in determining depreciation. | | |
| • Compute straight-line depreciation. | EE9-2 | PE9-2A, 9-2B |
| • Compute units-of-production depreciation. | EE9-3 | PE9-3A, 9-3B |
| • Compute double-declining-balance depreciation. | EE9-4 | PE9-4A, 9-4B |
| • Compute revised depreciation for a change in an asset's useful life and residual value. | EE9-5 | PE9-5A, 9-5B |

**Key Points** When discarding a fixed asset, any depreciation for the current period should be recorded, and the book value of the asset is then removed from the accounts.

When a fixed asset is sold, the book value is removed, and the cash or other asset received is recorded. If the selling price is more than the book value of the asset, the transaction results in a gain. If the selling price is less than the book value, there is a loss.

| Learning Outcomes | Example Exercises | Practice Exercises |
|---|---|---|
| • Prepare the journal entry for discarding a fixed asset. | | |
| • Prepare journal entries for the sale of a fixed asset. | EE9-6 | PE9-6A, 9-6B |

**OBJ. 4**

## Compute depletion and journalize the entry for depletion.

**Key Points**    The amount of periodic depletion is computed by multiplying the quantity of minerals extracted during the period by a depletion rate. The depletion rate is computed by dividing the cost of the mineral deposit by its estimated total units of resource. The entry to record depletion debits a depletion expense account and credits an accumulated depletion account.

| Learning Outcomes | Example Exercises | Practice Exercises |
|---|---|---|
| • Define and describe *depletion*. | | |
| • Compute a depletion rate. | EE9-7 | PE9-7A, 9-7B |
| • Prepare the journal entry to record depletion. | EE9-7 | PE9-7A, 9-7B |

**OBJ. 5**

## Describe the accounting for intangible assets, such as patents, copyrights, and goodwill.

**Key Points**    Long-term assets such as patents, copyrights, trademarks, and goodwill are intangible assets. The cost of patents and copyrights should be amortized over the years of the asset's expected usefulness by debiting an expense account and crediting the intangible asset account. Trademarks and goodwill are not amortized, but are written down only upon impairment.

| Learning Outcomes | Example Exercises | Practice Exercises |
|---|---|---|
| • Define, describe, and provide examples of intangible assets. | | |
| • Prepare a journal entry for the purchase of an intangible asset. | | |
| • Prepare a journal entry to amortize the costs of patents and copyrights. | EE9-8 | PE9-8A, 9-8B |
| • Prepare the journal entry to record the impairment of goodwill. | EE9-8 | PE9-8A, 9-8B |

**OBJ. 6**

## Describe how depreciation expense is reported in an income statement and prepare a balance sheet that includes fixed assets and intangible assets.

**Key Points**    The amount of depreciation expense and depreciation methods should be disclosed in the financial statements. Each major class of fixed assets should be disclosed, along with the related accumulated depreciation. Intangible assets are usually presented in a separate section following fixed assets. Each major class of intangible assets should be disclosed net of the amortization recorded to date.

| Learning Outcomes | Example Exercises | Practice Exercises |
|---|---|---|
| • Describe and illustrate how fixed assets are reported on the income statement and balance sheet. | | |
| • Describe and illustrate how intangible assets are reported on the income statement and balance sheet. | | |

**OBJ. 7**

## Describe and illustrate the fixed asset turnover ratio to assess the efficiency of a company's use of its fixed assets.

**Key Points**    A measure of a company's efficiency in using its fixed assets to generate sales is the fixed asset turnover ratio. The fixed asset turnover ratio measures the number of dollars of sales earned per dollar of fixed assets and is computed by dividing net sales by the average book value of fixed assets.

| Learning Outcomes | Example Exercises | Practice Exercises |
|---|---|---|
| • Describe a measure of the efficiency of a company's use of fixed assets to generate revenue. | | |
| • Compute and interpret the fixed asset turnover ratio. | EE9-9 | PE9-9A, 9-9B |

# Key Terms

accelerated depreciation
   method (416)
amortization (422)
book value (416)
boot (428)
capital expenditures (409)
capital lease (410)
copyright (423)

depletion (421)
depreciation (411)
double-declining-balance
   method (415)
fixed asset turnover ratio (427)
fixed assets (406)
goodwill (424)
intangible assets (422)

operating lease (411)
patents (423)
residual value (411)
revenue expenditures (409)
straight-line method (413)
trade-in allowance (428)
trademark (423)
units-of-production method (414)

# Illustrative Problem

McCollum Company, a furniture wholesaler, acquired new equipment at a cost of $150,000 at the beginning of the fiscal year. The equipment has an estimated life of five years and an estimated residual value of $12,000. Ellen McCollum, the president, has requested information regarding alternative depreciation methods.

## Instructions

1. Determine the annual depreciation for each of the five years of estimated useful life of the equipment, the accumulated depreciation at the end of each year, and the book value of the equipment at the end of each year by (a) the straight-line method and (b) the double-declining-balance method.

2. Assume that the equipment was depreciated under the double-declining-balance method. In the first week of the fifth year, the equipment was sold for $10,000. Journalize the entry to record the sale.

## Solution

1.

|  | Year | Depreciation Expense | Accumulated Depreciation, End of Year | Book Value, End of Year |
|---|---|---|---|---|
| a. | 1 | $27,600* | $ 27,600 | $122,400 |
|  | 2 | 27,600 | 55,200 | 94,800 |
|  | 3 | 27,600 | 82,800 | 67,200 |
|  | 4 | 27,600 | 110,400 | 39,600 |
|  | 5 | 27,600 | 138,000 | 12,000 |

*$27,600 = ($150,000 − $12,000) ÷ 5

|  | Year | Depreciation Expense | Accumulated Depreciation, End of Year | Book Value, End of Year |
|---|---|---|---|---|
| b. | 1 | $60,000** | $ 60,000 | $ 90,000 |
|  | 2 | 36,000 | 96,000 | 54,000 |
|  | 3 | 21,600 | 117,600 | 32,400 |
|  | 4 | 12,960 | 130,560 | 19,440 |
|  | 5 | 7,440*** | 138,000 | 12,000 |

**$60,000 = $150,000 × 40%

***The asset is not depreciated below the estimated residual value of $12,000.
   $7,440 = $150,000 − $130,560 − $12,000

2.

| | | Cash | 10,000 | |
|---|---|---|---|---|
| | | Accumulated Depreciation—Equipment | 130,560 | |
| | | Loss on Sale of Equipment | 9,440 | |
| | | Equipment | | 150,000 |

# Discussion Questions

1. Arentz Office Supplies has a fleet of automobiles and trucks for use by salespersons and for delivery of office supplies and equipment. Universal Auto Sales Co. has automobiles and trucks for sale. Under what caption would the automobiles and trucks be reported in the balance sheet of (a) Arentz Office Supplies and (b) Universal Auto Sales Co.?

2. Cleanway Co. acquired an adjacent vacant lot with the hope of selling it in the future at a gain. The lot is not intended to be used in Cleanway's business operations. Where should such real estate be listed in the balance sheet?

3. Airy Company solicited bids from several contractors to construct an addition to its office building. The lowest bid received was for $575,000. Airy Company decided to construct the addition itself at a cost of $435,000. What amount should be recorded in the building account?

4. Distinguish between the accounting for capital expenditures and revenue expenditures.

5. Immediately after a used truck is acquired, a new motor is installed at a total cost of $4,150. Is this a capital expenditure or a revenue expenditure?

6. Biggest Company purchased a machine that has a manufacturer's suggested life of 18 years. The company plans to use the machine on a special project that will last 10 years. At the completion of the project, the machine will be sold. Over how many years should the machine be depreciated?

7. Is it necessary for a business to use the same method of computing depreciation (a) for all classes of its depreciable assets and (b) for financial statement purposes and in determining income taxes?

8. a. Under what conditions is the use of an accelerated depreciation method most appropriate?
   b. Why is an accelerated depreciation method often used for income tax purposes?
   c. What is the Modified Accelerated Cost Recovery System (MACRS), and under what conditions is it used?

9. For some of the fixed assets of a business, the balance in Accumulated Depreciation is exactly equal to the cost of the asset. (a) Is it permissible to record additional depreciation on the assets if they are still useful to the business? Explain. (b) When should an entry be made to remove the cost and the accumulated depreciation from the accounts?

10. a. Over what period of time should the cost of a patent acquired by purchase be amortized?
    b. In general, what is the required accounting treatment for research and development costs?
    c. How should goodwill be amortized?

# Practice Exercises

OBJ. 1    EE 9-1  *p. 410*

### PE 9-1A    Capital and revenue expenditures

On September 30, Madison River Inflatables Co. paid $1,425 to install a hydraulic lift and $35 for an air filter for one of its delivery trucks. Journalize the entries for the new lift and air filter expenditures.

OBJ. 1    EE 9-1  *p. 410*

### PE 9-1B    Capital and revenue expenditures

On June 9, Martin Associates Co. paid $1,300 to repair the transmission on one of its delivery vans. In addition, Martin Associates paid $600 to install a GPS system in its van. Journalize the entries for the transmission and GPS system expenditures.

OBJ. 2    EE 9-2  *p. 414*

### PE 9-2A    Straight-line depreciation

Equipment acquired at the beginning of the year at a cost of $275,000 has an estimated residual value of $30,000 and an estimated useful life of 10 years. Determine (a) the depreciable cost, (b) the straight-line rate, and (c) the annual straight-line depreciation.

OBJ. 2    EE 9-2  *p. 414*

### PE 9-2B    Straight-line depreciation

A building acquired at the beginning of the year at a cost of $980,000 has an estimated residual value of $60,000 and an estimated useful life of 20 years. Determine (a) the depreciable cost, (b) the straight-line rate, and (c) the annual straight-line depreciation.

OBJ. 2    EE 9-3  *p. 415*

### PE 9-3A    Units-of-production depreciation

A tractor acquired at a cost of $315,000 has an estimated residual value of $27,000, has an estimated useful life of 90,000 hours, and was operated 3,700 hours during the year. Determine (a) the depreciable cost, (b) the depreciation rate, and (c) the units-of-production depreciation for the year.

OBJ. 2    EE 9-3  *p. 415*

### PE 9-3B    Units-of-production depreciation

A truck acquired at a cost of $150,000 has an estimated residual value of $40,000, has an estimated useful life of 400,000 miles, and was driven 80,000 miles during the year. Determine (a) the depreciable cost, (b) the depreciation rate, and (c) the units-of-production depreciation for the year.

OBJ. 2    EE 9-4  *p. 416*

### PE 9-4A    Double-declining-balance depreciation

Equipment acquired at the beginning of the year at a cost of $190,000 has an estimated residual value of $30,000 and an estimated useful life of eight years. Determine (a) the double-declining-balance rate and (b) the double-declining-balance depreciation for the first year.

OBJ. 2    EE 9-4  *p. 416*

### PE 9-4B    Double-declining-balance depreciation

A building acquired at the beginning of the year at a cost of $820,000 has an estimated residual value of $100,000 and an estimated useful life of 50 years. Determine (a) the double-declining-balance rate and (b) the double-declining-balance depreciation for the first year.

| Learning Objectives | Example Exercises | |
|---|---|---|
| OBJ. 2 | EE 9-5 *p. 419* | **PE 9-5A Revision of depreciation** |

A truck with a cost of $94,000 has an estimated residual value of $20,500, has an estimated useful life of 15 years, and is depreciated by the straight-line method. (a) Determine the amount of the annual depreciation. (b) Determine the book value at the end of the seventh year of use. (c) Assuming that at the start of the eighth year the remaining life is estimated to be six years and the residual value is estimated to be $15,000, determine the depreciation expense for each of the remaining six years.

| OBJ. 2 | EE 9-5 *p. 419* | **PE 9-5B Revision of depreciation** |
|---|---|---|

Equipment with a cost of $300,000 has an estimated residual value of $42,000, has an estimated useful life of 24 years, and is depreciated by the straight-line method. (a) Determine the amount of the annual depreciation. (b) Determine the book value at the end of the fourteenth year of use. (c) Assuming that at the start of the fifteenth year the remaining life is estimated to be five years and the residual value is estimated to be $20,000, determine the depreciation expense for each of the remaining five years.

| OBJ. 3 | EE 9-6 *p. 421* | **PE 9-6A Sale of equipment** |
|---|---|---|

Equipment was acquired at the beginning of the year at a cost of $215,000. The equipment was depreciated using the straight-line method based on an estimated useful life of 18 years and an estimated residual value of $39,500.

a. What was the depreciation for the first year?

b. Assuming the equipment was sold at the end of the eighth year for $128,000, determine the gain or loss on the sale of the equipment.

c. Journalize the entry to record the sale.

| OBJ. 3 | EE 9-6 *p. 421* | **PE 9-6B Sale of equipment** |
|---|---|---|

Equipment was acquired at the beginning of the year at a cost of $450,000. The equipment was depreciated using the double-declining-balance method based on an estimated useful life of 10 years and an estimated residual value of $60,000.

a. What was the depreciation for the first year?

b. Assuming the equipment was sold at the end of the second year for $319,500, determine the gain or loss on the sale of the equipment.

c. Journalize the entry to record the sale.

| OBJ. 4 | EE 9-7 *p. 422* | **PE 9-7A Depletion** |
|---|---|---|

Big Horn Mining Co. acquired mineral rights for $90,000,000. The mineral deposit is estimated at 250,000,000 tons. During the current year, 30,000,000 tons were mined and sold.

a. Determine the depletion rate.

b. Determine the amount of depletion expense for the current year.

c. Journalize the adjusting entry on December 31 to recognize the depletion expense.

| OBJ. 4 | EE 9-7 *p. 422* | **PE 9-7B Depletion** |
|---|---|---|

Silver Tip Mining Co. acquired mineral rights for $300,000,000. The mineral deposit is estimated at 400,000,000 tons. During the current year, 84,000,000 tons were mined and sold.

a. Determine the depletion rate.

b. Determine the amount of depletion expense for the current year.

c. Journalize the adjusting entry on December 31 to recognize the depletion expense.

| Learning Objectives | Example Exercises |
|---|---|
| OBJ. 5 | EE 9-8 *p. 425* |

**PE 9-8A  Impaired goodwill and amortization of patent**

On December 31, it was estimated that goodwill of $750,000 was impaired. In addition, a patent with an estimated useful economic life of 18 years was acquired for $864,000 on August 1.

a. Journalize the adjusting entry on December 31 for the impaired goodwill.

b. Journalize the adjusting entry on December 31 for the amortization of the patent rights.

---

| | |
|---|---|
| OBJ. 5 | EE 9-8 *p. 425* |

**PE 9-8B  Impaired goodwill and amortization of patent**

On December 31, it was estimated that goodwill of $1,200,000 was impaired. In addition, a patent with an estimated useful economic life of 12 years was acquired for $288,000 on April 1.

a. Journalize the adjusting entry on December 31 for the impaired goodwill.

b. Journalize the adjusting entry on December 31 for the amortization of the patent rights.

---

| | |
|---|---|
| OBJ. 7 | EE 9-9 *p. 428* |

**PE 9-9A  Fixed asset turnover ratio**

Financial statement data for years ending December 31 for Winnett Company are shown below.

| | 2012 | 2011 |
|---|---|---|
| Net sales | $3,572,000 | $3,526,000 |
| Fixed assets: | | |
| Beginning of year | 900,000 | 820,000 |
| End of year | 980,000 | 900,000 |

a. Determine the fixed asset turnover ratio for 2012 and 2011.

b. Does the change in the fixed asset turnover ratio from 2011 to 2012 indicate a favorable or an unfavorable trend?

---

| | |
|---|---|
| OBJ. 7 | EE 9-9 *p. 428* |

**PE 9-9B  Fixed asset turnover ratio**

Financial statement data for years ending December 31 for Fallon Company are shown below.

| | 2012 | 2011 |
|---|---|---|
| Net sales | $740,000 | $520,000 |
| Fixed assets: | | |
| Beginning of year | 425,000 | 375,000 |
| End of year | 500,000 | 425,000 |

a. Determine the fixed asset turnover ratio for 2012 and 2011.

b. Does the change in the fixed asset turnover ratio from 2011 to 2012 indicate a favorable or an unfavorable trend?

---

# Exercises

| | |
|---|---|
| OBJ. 1 | |

**EX 9-1  Costs of acquiring fixed assets**

Les Bancroft owns and operates Crown Print Co. During January, Crown Print Co. incurred the following costs in acquiring two printing presses. One printing press was new, and the other was used by a business that recently filed for bankruptcy.

Costs related to new printing press:

1. Sales tax on purchase price
2. Insurance while in transit
3. Freight
4. Special foundation

5. Fee paid to factory representative for installation

6. New parts to replace those damaged in unloading

Costs related to used printing press:

7. Fees paid to attorney to review purchase agreement

8. Freight

9. Installation

10. Replacement of worn-out parts

11. Repair of damage incurred in reconditioning the press

12. Repair of vandalism during installation

a.  Indicate which costs incurred in acquiring the new printing press should be debited to the asset account.

b.  Indicate which costs incurred in acquiring the used printing press should be debited to the asset account.

---

**OBJ. 1**

### EX 9-2  Determine cost of land

Alpine Ski Co. has developed a tract of land into a ski resort. The company has cut the trees, cleared and graded the land and hills, and constructed ski lifts. (a) Should the tree cutting, land clearing, and grading costs of constructing the ski slopes be debited to the land account? (b) If such costs are debited to Land, should they be depreciated?

---

**OBJ. 1**

✔ $346,600

### EX 9-3  Determine cost of land

Discount Delivery Company acquired an adjacent lot to construct a new warehouse, paying $25,000 and giving a short-term note for $300,000. Legal fees paid were $2,100, delinquent taxes assumed were $14,000, and fees paid to remove an old building from the land were $9,000. Materials salvaged from the demolition of the building were sold for $3,500. A contractor was paid $800,000 to construct a new warehouse. Determine the cost of the land to be reported on the balance sheet.

---

**OBJ. 1**

### EX 9-4  Capital and revenue expenditures

Emerald Lines Co. incurred the following costs related to trucks and vans used in operating its delivery service:

1.  Installed security systems on four of the newer trucks.

2.  Rebuilt the transmission on one of the vans that had been driven 40,000 miles. The van was no longer under warranty.

3.  Installed a hydraulic lift to a van.

4.  Replaced a truck's suspension system with a new suspension system that allows for the delivery of heavier loads.

5.  Removed a two-way radio from one of the trucks and installed a new radio with a greater range of communication.

6.  Repaired a flat tire on one of the vans.

7.  Changed the radiator fluid on a truck that had been in service for the past four years.

8.  Tinted the back and side windows of one of the vans to discourage theft of contents.

9.  Changed the oil and greased the joints of all the trucks and vans.

10.  Overhauled the engine on one of the trucks purchased three years ago.

Classify each of the costs as a capital expenditure or a revenue expenditure.

OBJ. 1

### EX 9-5 Capital and revenue expenditures

Aubrey Seagars owns and operates Diamond Transport Co. During the past year, Aubrey incurred the following costs related to an 18-wheel truck:

1. Installed a television in the sleeping compartment of the truck.
2. Replaced the old radar detector with a newer model that is fastened to the truck with a locking device that prevents its removal.
3. Installed a wind deflector on top of the cab to increase fuel mileage.
4. Modified the factory-installed turbo charger with a special-order kit designed to add 50 more horsepower to the engine performance.
5. Replaced a headlight that had burned out.
6. Replaced the hydraulic brake system that had begun to fail during his latest trip through the Rocky Mountains.
7. Changed engine oil.
8. Replaced a shock absorber that had worn out.
9. Replaced fog and cab light bulbs.
10. Removed the old CB radio and replaced it with a newer model with a greater range.

Classify each of the costs as a capital expenditure or a revenue expenditure.

OBJ. 1

### EX 9-6 Capital and revenue expenditures

Reliable Move Company made the following expenditures on one of its delivery trucks:

Feb.   4. Replaced transmission at a cost of $4,300.

May    6. Paid $1,900 for installation of a hydraulic lift.

Sept. 10. Paid $60 to change the oil and air filter.

Prepare journal entries for each expenditure.

OBJ. 2

### EX 9-7 Nature of depreciation

Butte Ironworks Co. reported $7,500,000 for equipment and $6,175,000 for accumulated depreciation—equipment on its balance sheet.

➤ Does this mean (a) that the replacement cost of the equipment is $7,500,000 and (b) that $6,175,000 is set aside in a special fund for the replacement of the equipment? Explain.

OBJ. 2
✔ c. 10%

### EX 9-8 Straight-line depreciation rates

Convert each of the following estimates of useful life to a straight-line depreciation rate, stated as a percentage: (a) 4 years, (b) 8 years, (c) 10 years, (d) 16 years, (e) 25 years, (f) 40 years, (g) 50 years.

OBJ. 2
✔ $6,625

### EX 9-9 Straight-line depreciation

A refrigerator used by a meat processor has a cost of $120,000, an estimated residual value of $14,000, and an estimated useful life of 16 years. What is the amount of the annual depreciation computed by the straight-line method?

OBJ. 2
✔ $518

### EX 9-10 Depreciation by units-of-production method

A diesel-powered tractor with a cost of $185,000 and estimated residual value of $37,000 is expected to have a useful operating life of 40,000 hours. During February, the tractor was operated 140 hours. Determine the depreciation for the month.

### EX 9-11 Depreciation by units-of-production method

Prior to adjustment at the end of the year, the balance in Trucks is $275,900 and the balance in Accumulated Depreciation—Trucks is $91,350. Details of the subsidiary ledger are as follows:

| Truck No. | Cost | Estimated Residual Value | Estimated Useful Life | Accumulated Depreciation at Beginning of Year | Miles Operated During Year |
|---|---|---|---|---|---|
| 1 | $75,000 | $15,000 | 200,000 miles | — | 19,500 miles |
| 2 | 38,000 | 3,000 | 200,000 | $ 8,050 | 36,000 |
| 3 | 72,900 | 9,900 | 300,000 | 60,900 | 25,000 |
| 4 | 90,000 | 20,000 | 250,000 | 22,400 | 26,000 |

a. Determine the depreciation rates per mile and the amount to be credited to the accumulated depreciation section of each of the subsidiary accounts for the miles operated during the current year.

b. Journalize the entry to record depreciation for the year.

### EX 9-12 Depreciation by two methods

A Kubota tractor acquired on January 9 at a cost of $80,000 has an estimated useful life of 25 years. Assuming that it will have no residual value, determine the depreciation for each of the first two years (a) by the straight-line method and (b) by the double-declining-balance method.

### EX 9-13 Depreciation by two methods

A storage tank acquired at the beginning of the fiscal year at a cost of $344,000 has an estimated residual value of $50,000 and an estimated useful life of 16 years. Determine the following: (a) the amount of annual depreciation by the straight-line method and (b) the amount of depreciation for the first and second years computed by the double-declining-balance method.

### EX 9-14 Partial-year depreciation

Sandblasting equipment acquired at a cost of $64,000 has an estimated residual value of $4,000 and an estimated useful life of eight years. It was placed in service on April 1 of the current fiscal year, which ends on December 31. Determine the depreciation for the current fiscal year and for the following fiscal year by (a) the straight-line method and (b) the double-declining-balance method.

### EX 9-15 Revision of depreciation

A building with a cost of $900,000 has an estimated residual value of $250,000, has an estimated useful life of 40 years, and is depreciated by the straight-line method. (a) What is the amount of the annual depreciation? (b) What is the book value at the end of the twenty-fourth year of use? (c) If at the start of the twenty-fifth year it is estimated that the remaining life is nine years and that the residual value is $240,000, what is the depreciation expense for each of the remaining nine years?

### EX 9-16 Capital expenditure and depreciation

Viking Company purchased and installed carpet in its new general offices on June 30 for a total cost of $15,000. The carpet is estimated to have a 12-year useful life and no residual value.

a. Prepare the journal entries necessary for recording the purchase of the new carpet.

b. Record the December 31 adjusting entry for the partial-year depreciation expense for the carpet, assuming that Viking Company uses the straight-line method.

OBJ. 3

**EX 9-17    Entries for sale of fixed asset**

Equipment acquired on January 5, 2009, at a cost of $380,000, has an estimated useful life of 16 years, has an estimated residual value of $40,000, and is depreciated by the straight-line method.

a. What was the book value of the equipment at December 31, 2012, the end of the year?

b. Assuming that the equipment was sold on July 1, 2013, for $270,000, journalize the entries to record (1) depreciation for the six months until the sale date, and (2) the sale of the equipment.

OBJ. 3

✔ b. $305,000

**EX 9-18    Disposal of fixed asset**

Equipment acquired on January 4, 2009, at a cost of $425,000, has an estimated useful life of nine years and an estimated residual value of $65,000.

a. What was the annual amount of depreciation for the years 2009, 2010, and 2011, using the straight-line method of depreciation?

b. What was the book value of the equipment on January 1, 2012?

c. Assuming that the equipment was sold on January 9, 2012, for $290,000, journalize the entry to record the sale.

d. Assuming that the equipment had been sold on January 9, 2012, for $310,000 instead of $290,000, journalize the entry to record the sale.

OBJ. 4

✔ a. $3,000,000

**EX 9-19    Depletion entries**

Ashwood Mining Co. acquired mineral rights for $15,000,000. The mineral deposit is estimated at 120,000,000 tons. During the current year, 24,000,000 tons were mined and sold.

a. Determine the amount of depletion expense for the current year.

b. Journalize the adjusting entry to recognize the depletion expense.

OBJ. 5

✔ a. $33,000

**EX 9-20    Amortization entries**

Greenleaf Company acquired patent rights on January 6, 2009, for $300,000. The patent has a useful life equal to its legal life of 12 years. On January 3, 2012, Greenleaf successfully defended the patent in a lawsuit at a cost of $72,000.

a. Determine the patent amortization expense for the current year ended December 31, 2012.

b. Journalize the adjusting entry to recognize the amortization.

OBJ. 6

**EX 9-21    Book value of fixed assets**

Apple Inc. designs, manufactures, and markets personal computers and related software. Apple also manufactures and distributes music players (iPod) and mobile phones (iPhone) along with related accessories and services including online distribution of third-party music, videos, and applications. The following information was taken from a recent annual report of Apple:

Property, Plant, and Equipment (in millions):

|  | Current Year | Preceding Year |
|---|---|---|
| Land and buildings | $ 955 | $ 810 |
| Machinery, equipment, and internal-use software | 1,932 | 1,491 |
| Office furniture and equipment | 115 | 122 |
| Other fixed assets related to leases | 1,665 | 1,324 |
| Accumulated depreciation and amortization | 1,713 | 1,292 |

a. Compute the book value of the fixed assets for the current year and the preceding year and explain the differences, if any.

b. 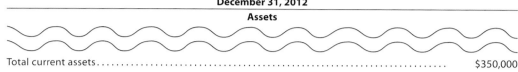 Would you normally expect the book value of fixed assets to increase or decrease during the year?

**OBJ. 6**

### EX 9-22 Balance sheet presentation

List the errors you find in the following partial balance sheet:

**Contours Company**
**Balance Sheet**
**December 31, 2012**

**Assets**

Total current assets.................................................. $350,000

| | Replacement Cost | Accumulated Depreciation | Book Value | |
|---|---|---|---|---|
| Property, plant, and equipment: | | | | |
| Land...................................... | $100,000 | $ 25,000 | $ 75,000 | |
| Buildings................................. | 256,000 | 90,000 | 166,000 | |
| Factory equipment ....................... | 297,000 | 110,000 | 187,000 | |
| Office equipment......................... | 72,000 | 48,000 | 24,000 | |
| Patents .................................. | 48,000 | — | 48,000 | |
| Goodwill................................. | 27,000 | 7,000 | 20,000 | |
| Total property, plant, and equipment........ | $800,000 | $280,000 | | $520,000 |

**OBJ. 7**

### EX 9-23 Fixed asset turnover ratio

Verizon Communications is a major telecommunications company in the United States. Verizon's balance sheet disclosed the following information regarding fixed assets:

| | Dec. 31, 2009 (in millions) | Dec. 31, 2008 (in millions) |
|---|---|---|
| Plant, property, and equipment | $228,518 | $215,605 |
| Less accumulated depreciation | 137,052 | 129,059 |
| | $ 91,466 | $ 86,546 |

Verizon's revenue for 2009 was $107,808 million. The fixed asset turnover for the telecommunications industry averages 1.10.

a. Determine Verizon's fixed asset turnover ratio. Round to two decimal places.

b. 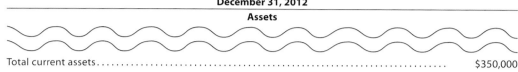 Interpret Verizon's fixed asset turnover ratio.

**OBJ. 7**

### EX 9-24 Fixed asset turnover ratio

The following table shows the revenue and average net fixed assets (in millions) for a recent fiscal year for Best Buy and RadioShack:

| | Revenue | Average Net Fixed Assets |
|---|---|---|
| Best Buy | $45,015 | $3,740 |
| RadioShack | 4,225 | 312 |

a. Compute the fixed asset turnover for each company. Round to two decimal places.

b. Which company uses its fixed assets more efficiently? Explain.

✔ a. $225,000

### Appendix
### EX 9-25 Asset traded for similar asset

A printing press priced at a fair market value of $400,000 is acquired in a transaction that has commercial substance by trading in a similar press and paying cash for the difference between the trade-in allowance and the price of the new press.

a. Assuming that the trade-in allowance is $175,000, what is the amount of cash given?

b. Assuming that the book value of the press traded in is $160,000, what is the gain or loss on the exchange?

✔ b. $10,000 loss

**Appendix**
**EX 9-26   Asset traded for similar asset**

Assume the same facts as in Exercise 9-25, except that the book value of the press traded in is $185,000. (a) What is the amount of cash given? (b) What is the gain or loss on the exchange?

**Appendix**
**EX 9-27   Entries for trade of fixed asset**

On April 1, Clear Water Co., a water distiller, acquired new bottling equipment with a list price (fair market value) of $350,000. Clear Water received a trade-in allowance of $50,000 on the old equipment of a similar type and paid cash of $300,000. The following information about the old equipment is obtained from the account in the equipment ledger: cost, $280,000; accumulated depreciation on December 31, the end of the preceding fiscal year, $216,000; annual depreciation, $18,000. Assuming the exchange has commercial substance, journalize the entries to record (a) the current depreciation of the old equipment to the date of trade-in and (b) the exchange transaction on April 1.

**Appendix**
**EX 9-28   Entries for trade of fixed asset**

On July 1, Potts Delivery Services acquired a new truck with a list price (fair market value) of $80,000. Potts received a trade-in allowance of $15,000 on an old truck of similar type and paid cash of $65,000. The following information about the old truck is obtained from the account in the equipment ledger: cost, $60,000; accumulated depreciation on December 31, the end of the preceding fiscal year, $42,000; annual depreciation, $7,500. Assuming the exchange has commercial substance, journalize the entries to record (a) the current depreciation of the old truck to the date of trade-in and (b) the transaction on July 1.

## Problems Series A

OBJ. 1

✔ Land, $402,500

**PR 9-1A   Allocate payments and receipts to fixed asset accounts**

The following payments and receipts are related to land, land improvements, and buildings acquired for use in a wholesale ceramic business. The receipts are identified by an asterisk.

| | | |
|---|---|---|
| a. | Fee paid to attorney for title search | $    3,000 |
| b. | Cost of real estate acquired as a plant site: Land | 320,000 |
| | Building | 30,000 |
| c. | Special assessment paid to city for extension of water main to the property | 18,000 |
| d. | Cost of razing and removing building | 5,000 |
| e. | Proceeds from sale of salvage materials from old building | 3,000* |
| f. | Delinquent real estate taxes on property, assumed by purchaser | 12,000 |
| g. | Premium on one-year insurance policy during construction | 4,200 |
| h. | Cost of filling and grading land | 17,500 |
| i. | Architect's and engineer's fees for plans and supervision | 44,000 |
| j. | Money borrowed to pay building contractor | 750,000* |
| k. | Cost of repairing windstorm damage during construction | 5,500 |
| l. | Cost of paving parking lot to be used by customers | 15,000 |
| m. | Cost of trees and shrubbery planted | 9,000 |
| n. | Cost of floodlights installed on parking lot | 1,000 |
| o. | Cost of repairing vandalism damage during construction | 2,500 |
| p. | Proceeds from insurance company for windstorm and vandalism damage | 6,000* |
| q. | Payment to building contractor for new building | 800,000 |
| r. | Interest incurred on building loan during construction | 37,500 |
| s. | Refund of premium on insurance policy (g) canceled after 11 months | 350* |

## Instructions

1. Assign each payment and receipt to Land (unlimited life), Land Improvements (limited life), Building, or Other Accounts. Indicate receipts by an asterisk. Identify each item by letter and list the amounts in columnar form, as follows:

| Item | Land | Land Improvements | Building | Other Accounts |
| --- | --- | --- | --- | --- |

2. Determine the amount debited to Land, Land Improvements, and Building.

3. ➤ The costs assigned to the land, which is used as a plant site, will not be depreciated, while the costs assigned to land improvements will be depreciated. Explain this seemingly contradictory application of the concept of depreciation.

4. What would be the effect on the income statement and balance sheet if the cost of filling and grading land of $17,500 [payment (h)] was incorrectly classified as Land Improvements rather than Land? Assume Land Improvements are depreciated over a 20-year life using the double-declining-balance method.

---

**OBJ. 2**

✔ a. 2010: straight-line depreciation, $31,250

### PR 9-2A  Compare three depreciation methods

Breyer Company purchased packaging equipment on January 3, 2010, for $101,250. The equipment was expected to have a useful life of three years, or 25,000 operating hours, and a residual value of $7,500. The equipment was used for 9,500 hours during 2010, 8,400 hours in 2011, and 7,100 hours in 2012.

#### Instructions

1. Determine the amount of depreciation expense for the years ended December 31, 2010, 2011, and 2012, by (a) the straight-line method, (b) the units-of-production method, and (c) the double-declining-balance method. Also determine the total depreciation expense for the three years by each method. The following columnar headings are suggested for recording the depreciation expense amounts:

| | Depreciation Expense | | |
| --- | --- | --- | --- |
| Year | Straight-Line Method | Units-of-Production Method | Double-Declining-Balance Method |

2. What method yields the highest depreciation expense for 2010?

3. What method yields the most depreciation over the three–year life of the equipment?

---

**OBJ. 2**

✔ a. 2010: $21,500

### PR 9-3A  Depreciation by three methods; partial years

Security IDs Company purchased equipment on July 1, 2010, for $135,000. The equipment was expected to have a useful life of three years, or 12,000 operating hours, and a residual value of $6,000. The equipment was used for 1,500 hours during 2010, 3,500 hours in 2011, 5,000 hours in 2012, and 2,000 hours in 2013.

#### Instructions

Determine the amount of depreciation expense for the years ended December 31, 2010, 2011, 2012, and 2013, by (a) the straight-line method, (b) the units-of-production method, and (c) the double-declining-balance method. Round to the nearest dollar.

---

**OBJ. 2, 3**

✔ b. Year 1: $315,000 depreciation expense

### PR 9-4A  Depreciation by two methods; sale of fixed asset

New lithographic equipment, acquired at a cost of $787,500 at the beginning of a fiscal year, has an estimated useful life of five years and an estimated residual value of $67,500. The manager requested information regarding the effect of alternative methods on the amount of depreciation expense each year. On the basis of the data presented to the manager, the double-declining-balance method was selected.

In the first week of the fifth year, the equipment was sold for $115,000.

#### Instructions

1. Determine the annual depreciation expense for each of the estimated five years of use, the accumulated depreciation at the end of each year, and the book value of the equipment at the end of each year by (a) the straight-line method and (b) the

double-declining-balance method. The following columnar headings are suggested for each schedule:

| Year | Depreciation Expense | Accumulated Depreciation, End of Year | Book Value, End of Year |
|------|---------------------|--------------------------------------|------------------------|

2. Journalize the entry to record the sale.

3. Journalize the entry to record the sale, assuming that the equipment was sold for $98,900 instead of $115,000.

---

OBJ. 1, 2, 3

### PR 9-5A   Transactions for fixed assets, including sale

The following transactions, adjusting entries, and closing entries were completed by D. Hurd Furniture Co. during a three-year period. All are related to the use of delivery equipment. The double-declining-balance method of depreciation is used.

**2010**

Jan.   9.   Purchased a used delivery truck for $30,000, paying cash.

Mar. 17.   Paid garage $400 for miscellaneous repairs to the truck.

Dec. 31.   Recorded depreciation on the truck for the year. The estimated useful life of the truck is four years, with a residual value of $6,000 for the truck.

**2011**

Jan.   2.   Purchased a new truck for $48,000, paying cash.

Aug.   1.   Sold the used truck for $12,500. (Record depreciation to date in 2011 for the truck.)

Sept. 23.   Paid garage $325 for miscellaneous repairs to the truck.

Dec. 31.   Record depreciation for the new truck. It has an estimated residual value of $11,000 and an estimated life of five years.

**2012**

July   1.   Purchased a new truck for $52,000, paying cash.

Oct.   2.   Sold the truck purchased January 2, 2011, for $17,000. (Record depreciation for the year.)

Dec. 31.   Recorded depreciation on the remaining truck. It has an estimated residual value of $14,000 and an estimated useful life of eight years.

**Instructions**

Journalize the transactions and the adjusting entries.

---

OBJ. 4, 5

✔ 1. a. $360,000

### PR 9-6A   Amortization and depletion entries

Data related to the acquisition of timber rights and intangible assets during the current year ended December 31 are as follows:

a.   Timber rights on a tract of land were purchased for $864,000 on July 10. The stand of timber is estimated at 3,600,000 board feet. During the current year, 1,500,000 board feet of timber were cut and sold.

b.   On December 31, the company determined that $4,000,000 of goodwill was impaired.

c.   Governmental and legal costs of $1,170,000 were incurred on April 10 in obtaining a patent with an estimated economic life of 12 years. Amortization is to be for three-fourths of a year.

**Instructions**

1. Determine the amount of the amortization, depletion, or impairment for the current year for each of the foregoing items.

2. Journalize the adjusting entries required to record the amortization, depletion, or impairment for each item.

## Problems Series B

**OBJ. 1**

✔ Land, $597,500

### PR 9-1B   Allocate payments and receipts to fixed asset accounts

The following payments and receipts are related to land, land improvements, and buildings acquired for use in a wholesale apparel business. The receipts are identified by an asterisk.

| | | |
|---|---|---:|
| a. | Finder's fee paid to real estate agency | $ 5,000 |
| b. | Cost of real estate acquired as a plant site: Land | 500,000 |
| | Building | 40,000 |
| c. | Fee paid to attorney for title search | 2,500 |
| d. | Delinquent real estate taxes on property, assumed by purchaser | 15,000 |
| e. | Architect's and engineer's fees for plans and supervision | 36,000 |
| f. | Cost of removing building purchased with land in (b) | 10,000 |
| g. | Proceeds from sale of salvage materials from old building | 4,000* |
| h. | Cost of filling and grading land | 20,000 |
| i. | Premium on one-year insurance policy during construction | 6,000 |
| j. | Money borrowed to pay building contractor | 750,000* |
| k. | Special assessment paid to city for extension of water main to the property | 9,000 |
| l. | Cost of repairing windstorm damage during construction | 3,000 |
| m. | Cost of repairing vandalism damage during construction | 2,000 |
| n. | Cost of trees and shrubbery planted | 12,000 |
| o. | Cost of paving parking lot to be used by customers | 14,500 |
| p. | Interest incurred on building loan during construction | 45,000 |
| q. | Proceeds from insurance company for windstorm and vandalism damage | 3,000* |
| r. | Payment to building contractor for new building | 800,000 |
| s. | Refund of premium on insurance policy (i) canceled after 10 months | 1,000* |

### Instructions

1. Assign each payment and receipt to Land (unlimited life), Land Improvements (limited life), Building, or Other Accounts. Indicate receipts by an asterisk. Identify each item by letter and list the amounts in columnar form, as follows:

| Item | Land | Land Improvements | Building | Other Accounts |
|---|---|---|---|---|

2. Determine the amount debited to Land, Land Improvements, and Building.

3. ➤ The costs assigned to the land, which is used as a plant site, will not be depreciated, while the costs assigned to land improvements will be depreciated. Explain this seemingly contradictory application of the concept of depreciation.

4. What would be the effect on the income statement and balance sheet if the cost of paving the parking lot of $14,500 [payment (o)] was incorrectly classified as Land rather than Land Improvements? Assume Land Improvements are depreciated over a 10-year life using the double-declining-balance method.

**OBJ. 2**

✔ a. 2011: straight-line depreciation, $100,000

### PR 9-2B   Compare three depreciation methods

Plum Coatings Company purchased waterproofing equipment on January 2, 2011, for $450,000. The equipment was expected to have a useful life of four years, or 10,000 operating hours, and a residual value of $50,000. The equipment was used for 3,000 hours during 2011, 4,000 hours in 2012, 2,500 hours in 2013, and 500 hours in 2014.

### Instructions

1. Determine the amount of depreciation expense for the years ended December 31, 2011, 2012, 2013, and 2014, by (a) the straight-line method, (b) the units-of-production method, and (c) the double-declining-balance method. Also determine the total depreciation expense for the four years by each method. The following columnar headings are suggested for recording the depreciation expense amounts:

| | Depreciation Expense | | |
|---|---|---|---|
| Year | Straight-Line Method | Units-of-Production Method | Double-Declining-Balance Method |

2.  What method yields the highest depreciation expense for 2011?

3.  What method yields the most depreciation over the four-year life of the equipment?

---

OBJ. 2

✔ a. 2010, $17,325

### PR 9-3B Depreciation by three methods; partial years

Helix Company purchased tool sharpening equipment on April 1, 2010, for $72,000. The equipment was expected to have a useful life of three years, or 9,000 operating hours, and a residual value of $2,700. The equipment was used for 2,400 hours during 2010, 4,000 hours in 2011, 2,000 hours in 2012, and 600 hours in 2013.

#### Instructions

Determine the amount of depreciation expense for the years ended December 31, 2010, 2011, 2012, and 2013, by (a) the straight-line method, (b) the units-of-production method, and (c) the double-declining-balance method.

---

OBJ. 2, 3

✔ 1. b. Year 1, $36,000 depreciation expense

### PR 9-4B Depreciation by two methods; sale of fixed asset

New tire retreading equipment, acquired at a cost of $72,000 at the beginning of a fiscal year, has an estimated useful life of four years and an estimated residual value of $5,400. The manager requested information regarding the effect of alternative methods on the amount of depreciation expense each year. On the basis of the data presented to the manager, the double-declining-balance method was selected.

In the first week of the fourth year, the equipment was sold for $13,750.

#### Instructions

1.  Determine the annual depreciation expense for each of the estimated four years of use, the accumulated depreciation at the end of each year, and the book value of the equipment at the end of each year by (a) the straight-line method and (b) the double-declining-balance method. The following columnar headings are suggested for each schedule:

| Year | Depreciation Expense | Accumulated Depreciation, End of Year | Book Value, End of Year |
| --- | --- | --- | --- |

2.  Journalize the entry to record the sale.

3.  Journalize the entry to record the sale, assuming that the equipment sold for $3,700 instead of $13,750.

---

OBJ. 1, 2, 3

### PR 9-5B Transactions for fixed assets, including sale

The following transactions, adjusting entries, and closing entries were completed by McHenry Furniture Co. during a three-year period. All are related to the use of delivery equipment. The double-declining-balance method of depreciation is used.

**2010**

Jan.  4.  Purchased a used delivery truck for $54,000, paying cash.

Feb. 24.  Paid garage $275 for changing the oil, replacing the oil filter, and tuning the engine on the delivery truck.

Dec. 31.  Recorded depreciation on the truck for the fiscal year. The estimated useful life of the truck is eight years, with a residual value of $12,000 for the truck.

**2011**

Jan.  3.  Purchased a new truck for $60,000, paying cash.

Mar.  7.  Paid garage $300 to tune the engine and make other minor repairs on the used truck.

Apr. 30.  Sold the used truck for $35,000. (Record depreciation to date in 2011 for the truck.)

Dec. 31.  Record depreciation for the new truck. It has an estimated residual value of $16,000 and an estimated life of 10 years.

2012

July   1.  Purchased a new truck for $64,000, paying cash.

Oct.   7.  Sold the truck purchased January 3, 2011, for $45,000. (Record depreciation for the year.)

Dec. 31.  Recorded depreciation on the remaining truck. It has an estimated residual value of $17,500 and an estimated useful life of 10 years.

**Instructions**
Journalize the transactions and the adjusting entries.

---

**OBJ. 4, 5**

✔ b. $45,000

**PR 9-6B   Amortization and depletion entries**

Data related to the acquisition of timber rights and intangible assets during the current year ended December 31 are as follows:

a.  On December 31, the company determined that $1,800,000 of goodwill was impaired.

b.  Governmental and legal costs of $900,000 were incurred on June 30 in obtaining a patent with an estimated economic life of 10 years. Amortization is to be for one-half year.

c.  Timber rights on a tract of land were purchased for $1,560,000 on February 4. The stand of timber is estimated at 12,000,000 board feet. During the current year, 3,200,000 board feet of timber were cut and sold.

**Instructions**
1.  Determine the amount of the amortization, depletion, or impairment for the current year for each of the foregoing items.

2.  Journalize the adjusting entries to record the amortization, depletion, or impairment for each item.

## Cases & Projects

You can access Cases & Projects online at **www.cengage.com/accounting/reeve**

## Excel Success Special Activities

**SA 9-1   Straight-line depreciation, multiple assets**
The fixed asset details for Hydro-Link, Inc., are as follows:

| Asset | Initial Cost | Estimated Residual Value | Estimated Useful Life (in years) |
|---|---|---|---|
| Computers | $36,000 | $ 5,800 | 4 |
| Conveyors | 58,000 | 16,000 | 12 |
| Cutting machine | 7,600 | 1,200 | 8 |
| Extruding machine | 9,000 | 1,500 | 10 |
| Forklift | 16,000 | 3,400 | 7 |
| Furnace | 22,000 | 4,500 | 20 |

a.  Open the Excel file *SA9-1_1e*.

b.  Develop a spreadsheet to determine the annual straight-line depreciation for each asset.

c.  When you have completed the depreciation table, perform a "save as," replacing the entire file name with the following:

*SA9-1_ 1e[your first name initial]_[your last name]*

### SA 9-2   Straight-line depreciation, revised estimates

The Better Bakery Company has a baking oven that has a book value at the beginning of the current year of $95,000 and an estimated residual value of $3,000. The remaining useful life of the baking oven is estimated to be five years.

a.  Open the Excel file *SA9-2_1e*.

b.  Prepare a spreadsheet to determine the depreciation expense under the straight-line method for the current year.

c.  When you have completed the depreciation table, perform a "save as," replacing the entire file name with the following:

   *SA9-2_1e[your first name initial]_[your last name]*

### SA 9-3   Units-of-production method, multiple assets

Details of the subsidiary ledger for the delivery trucks of Klondike Delivery, Inc., are as follows:

| Truck No. | Initial Cost | Estimated Residual Value | Estimated Useful Life (in miles) | Miles Operated in the Current Year |
|---|---|---|---|---|
| 1 | $37,500 | $1,100 | 140,000 | 35,000 |
| 2 | 29,650 | 900 | 125,000 | 32,000 |
| 3 | 32,800 | 1,300 | 150,000 | 40,000 |
| 4 | 45,900 | 900 | 180,000 | 38,000 |
| 5 | 36,700 | 1,500 | 160,000 | 28,000 |
| 6 | 48,400 | 2,400 | 200,000 | 42,000 |

a.  Open the Excel file *SA9-3_1e*.

b.  Develop a spreadsheet to determine the deprecation per mile and the current year depreciation expense for each truck using the units-of-production method.

c.  When you have completed the depreciation table, perform a "save as," replacing the entire file name with the following:

   *SA9-3_1e[your first name initial]_[your last name]*

### SA 9-4   Units-of-production method, multiple assets

Daniels Construction Company purchased a bulldozer, backhoe, and grader at the beginning of the current year. The bulldozer has an initial cost of $120,000 with an estimated salvage value of $12,000. The backhoe has an initial cost of $62,000 and an estimated salvage value of $6,000. Lastly, the grader has an initial cost of $75,000 and an estimated salvage value of $8,000. The estimated useful life and hours operated in the current year are as follows:

| Equipment | Estimated Useful Life (in hours) | Hours Operated in the Current Year |
|---|---|---|
| Bulldozer | 24,000 | 2,200 |
| Backhoe | 22,400 | 1,850 |
| Grader | 20,000 | 2,160 |

a.  Open the Excel file *SA9-4_1e*.

b.  Develop a spreadsheet to determine the depreciation per hour and the current year depreciation expense for each piece of equipment using the units-of-production method.

c.  When you have completed the depreciation table, perform a "save as," replacing the entire file name with the following:

   *SA9-4_1e[your first name initial]_[your last name]*

© AP Photo/Tom Gannam

# Current Liabilities and Payroll

## Panera Bread

**B**uying goods on credit is probably as old as business itself. In fact, the ancient Babylonians were lending money to support trade as early as 1300 B.C. The use of credit makes transactions more convenient and improves buying power. For *individuals*, the most common form of short-term credit is a credit card. Credit cards allow individuals to purchase items before they are paid for, while removing the need for individuals to carry large amounts of cash. They also provide documentation of purchases through a monthly credit card statement.

Short-term credit is also used by *businesses* to make purchasing items for manufacture or resale more convenient. Short-term credit also gives a business control over the payment for goods and services. For example, **Panera Bread**, a chain of bakery-cafés

located throughout the United States, uses short-term trade credit, or accounts payable, to purchase ingredients for making bread products in its bakeries. Short-term trade credit gives Panera control over cash payments by separating the purchase function from the payment function. Thus, the employee responsible for purchasing the bakery ingredients is separated from the employee responsible for paying for the purchase. This separation of duties can help prevent unauthorized purchases or payments.

In addition to accounts payable, a business like Panera Bread can also have current liabilities related to payroll, payroll taxes, employee benefits, short-term notes, unearned revenue, and contingencies. This chapter discusses each of these types of current liabilities.

**OBJ. 1** Describe and illustrate current liabilities related to accounts payable, current portion of long-term debt, and notes payable.

# Current Liabilities

When a company or a bank advances *credit*, it is making a loan. The company or bank is called a *creditor* (or *lender*). The individuals or companies receiving the loan are called *debtors* (or *borrowers*).

Debt is recorded as a liability by the debtor. *Long-term liabilities* are debts due beyond one year. Thus, a 30-year mortgage used to purchase property is a long-term liability. *Current liabilities* are debts that will be paid out of current assets and are due within one year.

Three types of current liabilities are discussed in this section—accounts payable, the current portion of long-term debt, and short-term notes payable.

## Accounts Payable

Accounts payable transactions have been described and illustrated in earlier chapters. These transactions involved a variety of purchases on account, including the purchase of merchandise and supplies. For most companies, accounts payable is the largest current liability. Exhibit 1 shows the accounts payable balance as a percent of total current liabilities for a number of companies.

| Company | Accounts Payable as a Percent of Total Current Liabilities |
|---|---|
| Alcoa Inc. | 36% |
| AT&T | 57 |
| Chevron Corp. | 52 |
| Gap Inc. | 47 |
| IBM | 17 |
| Rite Aid Corp. | 55 |

**EXHIBIT 1**

**Accounts Payable as a Percent of Total Current Liabilities**

## Current Portion of Long-Term Debt

Long-term liabilities are often paid back in periodic payments, called *installments*. Such installments that are due *within* the coming year are classified as a current liability. The installments due *after* the coming year are classified as a long-term liability.

To illustrate, The Coca-Cola Company reported the following debt payments schedule in its December 31, 2009, annual report to shareholders:

| Fiscal year ending | |
|---|---|
| 2010 | $ 51,000,000 |
| 2011 | 573,000,000 |
| 2012 | 153,000,000 |
| 2013 | 178,000,000 |
| 2014 | 912,000,000 |
| Thereafter | 3,243,000,000 |
| Total principal payments | $5,110,000,000 |

The debt of $51,000,000 due in 2010 would be reported as a current liability on the December 31, 2009, balance sheet. The remaining debt of $5,059,000,000 ($5,110,000,000 – $51,000,000) would be reported as a long-term liability on the balance sheet.

## Short-Term Notes Payable

Notes may be issued to purchase merchandise or other assets. Notes may also be issued to creditors to satisfy an account payable created earlier.[1]

To illustrate, assume that Nature's Sunshine Company issued a 90-day, 12% note for $1,000, dated August 1, 2011, to Murray Co. for a $1,000 overdue account. The entry to record the issuance of the note is as follows:

| | | | | |
|---|---|---|---|---|
| Aug. | 1 | Accounts Payable—Murray Co. | 1,000 | |
| | | Notes Payable | | 1,000 |
| | | Issued a 90-day, 12% note on account. | | |

When the note matures, the entry to record the payment of $1,000 plus $30 interest ($1,000 × 12% × 90/360) is as follows:

| | | | | |
|---|---|---|---|---|
| Oct. | 30 | Notes Payable | 1,000 | |
| | | Interest Expense | 30 | |
| | | Cash | | 1,030 |
| | | Paid principal and interest due on note. | | |

1 The accounting for notes received to satisfy an account receivable was described and illustrated in Chapter 8, Receivables.

The interest expense is reported in the Other Expense section of the income statement for the year ended December 31, 2011. The interest expense account is closed at December 31.

Each note transaction affects a debtor (borrower) and creditor (lender). The following illustration shows how the same transactions are recorded by the debtor and creditor. In this illustration, the debtor (borrower) is Bowden Co., and the creditor (lender) is Coker Co.

|  | Bowden Co. (Borrower) | | Coker Co. (Creditor) | |
|---|---|---|---|---|
| **May 1.** Bowden Co. purchased merchandise on account from Coker Co., $10,000, 2/10, n/30. The merchandise cost Coker Co. $7,500. | Merchandise Inventory 10,000<br>    Accounts Payable | 10,000 | Accounts Receivable 10,000<br>    Sales<br><br>Cost of Merchandise Sold 7,500<br>    Merchandise Inventory | 10,000<br><br><br>7,500 |
| **May 31.** Bowden Co. issued a 60-day, 12% note for $10,000 to Coker Co. on account. | Accounts Payable 10,000<br>    Notes Payable | 10,000 | Notes Receivable 10,000<br>    Accounts Receivable | 10,000 |
| **July 30.** Bowden Co. paid Coker Co. the amount due on the note of May 31. Interest: $10,000 × 12% × 60/360. | Notes Payable 10,000<br>Interest Expense 200<br>    Cash | 10,200 | Cash 10,200<br>    Interest Revenue<br>    Notes Receivable | 200<br>10,000 |

A company may also borrow from a bank by issuing a note. To illustrate, assume that on September 19 Iceburg Company borrowed cash from First National Bank by issuing a $4,000, 90-day, 15% note to the bank. The entry to record the issuance of the note and the cash proceeds is as follows:

| Sept. | 19 | Cash | 4,000 | |
|---|---|---|---|---|
| | | Notes Payable | | 4,000 |
| | | Issued a 90-day, 15% note to | | |
| | | First National Bank. | | |

On the due date of the note (December 18), Iceburg Company owes First National Bank $4,000 plus interest of $150 ($4,000 × 15% × 90/360). The entry to record the payment of the note is as follows:

| Dec. | 18 | Notes Payable | 4,000 | |
|---|---|---|---|---|
| | | Interest Expense | 150 | |
| | | Cash | | 4,150 |
| | | Paid principal and interest due on note. | | |

In some cases, a *discounted note* may be issued rather than an interest-bearing note. A discounted note has the following characteristics:

1. The interest rate on the note is called the *discount rate*.
2. The amount of interest on the note, called the *discount*, is computed by multiplying the discount rate times the face amount of the note.
3. The debtor (borrower) receives the face amount of the note less the discount, called the *proceeds*.
4. The debtor must repay the face amount of the note on the due date.

To illustrate, assume that on August 10, Cary Company issues a $20,000, 90-day discounted note to Western National Bank. The discount rate is 15%, and the amount of the discount is $750 ($20,000 × 15% × 90/360). Thus, the proceeds received by Cary Company are $19,250. The entry by Cary Company is as follows:

| | | | | | |
|---|---|---|---|---|---|
| Aug. | 10 | Cash | | 19,250 | |
| | | Interest Expense | | 750 | |
| | | Notes Payable | | | 20,000 |
| | | Issued a 90-day discounted note to Western | | | |
| | | National Bank at a 15% discount rate. | | | |

The entry when Cary Company pays the discounted note on November 8 is as follows:[2]

| | | | | | |
|---|---|---|---|---|---|
| Nov. | 8 | Notes Payable | | 20,000 | |
| | | Cash | | | 20,000 |
| | | Paid note due. | | | |

Other current liabilities that have been discussed in earlier chapters include accrued expenses, unearned revenue, and interest payable. The accounting for wages and salaries, termed *payroll accounting*, is discussed next.

## Example Exercise 10-1 ▶ Proceeds from Notes Payable

**OBJ. 1**

On July 1, Bella Salon Company issued a 60-day note with a face amount of $60,000 to Delilah Hair Products Company for merchandise inventory.

a. Determine the proceeds of the note, assuming the note carries an interest rate of 6%.

b. Determine the proceeds of the note, assuming the note is discounted at 6%.

### Follow My Example 10-1 ▶

a. $60,000

b. $59,400 [$60,000 − ($60,000 × 6% × 60/360)]

Practice Exercises: **PE 10-1A, PE 10-1B**

# Payroll and Payroll Taxes

**OBJ. 2** Determine employer liabilities for payroll, including liabilities arising from employee earnings and deductions from earnings.

In accounting, **payroll** refers to the amount paid to employees for services they provided during the period. A company's payroll is important for the following reasons:

1. Payroll and related payroll taxes significantly affect the net income of most companies.
2. Payroll is subject to federal and state regulations.
3. Good employee morale requires payroll to be paid timely and accurately.

## Liability for Employee Earnings

*Salary* usually refers to payment for managerial and administrative services. Salary is normally expressed in terms of a month or a year. *Wages* usually refers to payment for employee manual labor. The rate of wages is normally stated on an hourly or a weekly basis. The salary or wage of an employee may be increased by bonuses, commissions, profit sharing, or cost-of-living adjustments.

**Note:** Employee salaries and wages are expenses to an employer.

2 If the accounting period ends before a discounted note is paid, an adjusting entry should record the prepaid (deferred) interest that is not yet an expense. This deferred interest would be deducted from Notes Payable in the Current Liabilities section of the balance sheet.

Companies engaged in interstate commerce must follow the Fair Labor Standards Act. This act, sometimes called the Federal Wage and Hour Law, requires employers to pay a minimum rate of 1½ times the regular rate for all hours worked in excess of 40 hours per week. Exemptions are provided for executive, administrative, and some supervisory positions. Increased rates for working overtime, nights, or holidays are common, even when not required by law. These rates may be as much as twice the regular rate.

To illustrate computing an employee's earnings, assume that John T. McGrath is a salesperson employed by McDermott Supply Co. McGrath's regular rate is $34 per hour, and any hours worked in excess of 40 hours per week are paid at 1½ times the regular rate. McGrath worked 42 hours for the week ended December 27. His earnings of **$1,462** for the week are computed as follows:

| | |
|---|---|
| Earnings at regular rate (40 hrs. × $34) | $1,360 |
| Earnings at overtime rate [2 hrs. × ($34 × 1½)] | 102 |
| Total earnings | $1,462 |

## Deductions from Employee Earnings

The total earnings of an employee for a payroll period, including any overtime pay, are called **gross pay**. From this amount is subtracted one or more *deductions* to arrive at the **net pay**. Net pay is the amount paid the employee. The deductions normally include federal, state, and local income taxes, medical insurance, and pension contributions.

**Income Taxes** Employers normally withhold a portion of employee earnings for payment of the employees' federal income tax. Each employee authorizes the amount to be withheld by completing an "Employee's Withholding Allowance Certificate," called a W-4. Exhibit 2 is the W-4 form submitted by John T. McGrath.

On the W-4, an employee indicates marital status and the number of withholding allowances. A single employee may claim one withholding allowance. A married employee may claim an additional allowance for a spouse. An employee may also claim an allowance for each dependent other than a spouse. Each allowance reduces the federal income tax withheld from the employee's pay. Exhibit 2 indicates that John T. McGrath is single and, thus, claimed one withholding allowance.

The federal income tax withheld depends on each employee's gross pay and W-4 allowance. Withholding tables issued by the Internal Revenue Service (IRS) are used to determine amounts to withhold. Exhibit 3 is an example of an IRS wage withholding table for a single person who is paid weekly.[3]

**EXHIBIT 2**

Employee's Withholding Allowance Certificate (W-4 Form)

3 IRS withholding tables are also available for married employees and for pay periods other than weekly.

In Exhibit 3, each row is the employee's wages after deducting the employee's withholding allowances. Each year, the amount of the standard withholding allowance is determined by the IRS. For ease of computation and because this amount changes each year, we assume that the standard withholding allowance to be deducted in Exhibit 3 for a single person paid weekly is $70.[4] Thus, if two withholding allowances are claimed, $140 ($70 × 2) is deducted.

To illustrate, John T. McGrath made $1,462 for the week ended December 27. McGrath's W-4 claims one withholding allowance of $70. Thus, the wages used in determining McGrath's withholding bracket in Exhibit 3 are $1,392 ($1,462 − $70).

After the person's withholding wage bracket has been computed, the federal income tax to be withheld is determined as follows:

Step 1. Locate the proper withholding wage bracket in Exhibit 3.

*McGrath's wages after deducting one standard IRS withholding allowance are $1,392 ($1,462 − $70). Therefore, the wage bracket for McGrath is $1,302–$1,624.*

Step 2. Compute the withholding for the proper wage bracket using the directions in the two right-hand columns in Exhibit 3.

*For McGrath's wage bracket, the withholding is computed as "$234.60. plus 27% of the excess over $1,302." Hence, McGrath's withholding is $258.90, as shown below.*

| | |
|---|---|
| *Initial withholding from wage bracket* | *$234.60* |
| *Plus [27% × ($1,392 − $1,302)]* | *24.30* |
| *Total withholding* | *$258.90* |

---

**EXHIBIT 3** Wage Bracket Withholding Table

**Table for Percentage Method of Withholding WEEKLY Payroll Period**

**(a) SINGLE** person (including head of household)—

If the amount of wages (after subtracting withholding allowances) is: The amount of income tax to withhold is:

Not over $116 . . . . . . . . . . . . . . . .$0

| Over— | But not over— | | of excess over — | |
|---|---|---|---|---|
| $116 | − $200 | . . . 10% | | − $116 |
| $200 | − $693 | . . . $8.40 plus 15% | | − $200 |
| $693 | − $1,302 | . . . $82.35 plus 25% | | − $693 |
| $1,302 | − $1,624 | . . . $234.60 plus 27% | | − $1,302 | ← McGrath wage bracket |
| $1,624 | − $1,687 | . . . $321.54 plus 30% | | − $1,624 |
| $1,687 | − $3,344 | . . . $340.44 plus 28% | | − $1,687 |
| $3,344 | − $7,225 | . . . $804.40 plus 33% | | − $3,344 |
| $7,225 | . . . . . . . . . . . . . | $2,085.13 plus 35% | | − $7,225 |

Source: Publication 15, *Employer's Tax Guide*, Internal Revenue Service, 2010.

Employers may also be required to withhold state or city income taxes. The amounts to be withheld are determined on state-by-state and city-by-city bases.

Residents of New York City must pay federal, state, and city income taxes.

---

**Example Exercise** ▶ **10-2** ▶ **Federal Income Tax Withholding**

**OBJ. 2**

Karen Dunn's weekly gross earnings for the present week were $2,250. Dunn has two exemptions. Using the wage bracket withholding table in Exhibit 3 with a $70 standard withholding allowance for each exemption, what is Dunn's federal income tax withholding?

*(continued)*

4 The actual IRS standard withholding allowance changes every year and was $70.19 for 2010.

**Follow My Example  10-2**

| | | |
|---|---:|---:|
| Total wage payment............................................................... | | $ 2,250 |
| One allowance (provided by IRS)............................................. | $70 | |
| Multiplied by allowances claimed on Form W-4 ......................... | × 2 | 140 |
| Amount subject to withholding............................................... | | $ 2,110 |
| | | |
| Initial withholding from wage bracket in Exhibit 3...................... | | $340.44 |
| Plus additional withholding: 28% of excess over $1,687 .............. | | 118.44* |
| Federal income tax withholding.............................................. | | $458.88 |

*28% × ($2,110 – $1,687)

Practice Exercises: **PE 10-2A, PE 10-2B**

**FICA Tax**  Employers are required by the Federal Insurance Contributions Act (FICA) to withhold a portion of the earnings of each employee. The **FICA tax** withheld contributes to the following two federal programs:

1. *Social security*, which provides payments for retirees, survivors, and disability insurance.
2. *Medicare*, which provides health insurance for senior citizens.

The amount withheld from each employee is based on the employee's earnings *paid* in the *calendar* year. The withholding tax rates and maximum earnings subject to tax are often revised by Congress.[5] To simplify, this chapter assumes the following rates and earnings subject to tax:

1. Social security: 6% on all earnings
2. Medicare: 1.5% on all earnings

To illustrate, assume that John T. McGrath's earnings for the week ending December 27 are $1,462 and the total FICA tax to be withheld is **$109.65**, as shown below.

| | | |
|---|---:|---:|
| Earnings subject to 6% social security tax........................ | $1,462 | |
| Social security tax rate ............................................. | × 6% | |
| Social security tax ............................................. | | $ 87.72 |
| | | |
| Earnings subject to 1.5% Medicare tax............................ | $1,462 | |
| Medicare tax rate ................................................ | × 1.5% | |
| Medicare tax ................................................. | | 21.93 |
| Total FICA tax.................................................... | | $109.65 |

**Other Deductions**  Employees may choose to have additional amounts deducted from their gross pay. For example, an employee may authorize deductions for retirement savings, for charitable contributions, or life insurance. A union contract may also require the deduction of union dues.

## Computing Employee Net Pay

Gross earnings less payroll deductions equals *net pay*, sometimes called *take-home pay*. Assuming that John T. McGrath authorized deductions for retirement savings and for a United Fund contribution, McGrath's net pay for the week ended December 27 is $1,068.45, as shown below.

5 As of January 1, 2010, the social security tax rate was 6.2% and the Medicare tax rate was 1.45%. Earnings subject to the social security tax are limited to an annual threshold amount, but for text examples and problems, assume all accumulated annual earnings are below this threshold and subject to the tax.

| | | |
|---|---:|---:|
| Gross earnings for the week | | $1,462.00 |
| Deductions: | | |
| Social security tax | $ 87.72 | |
| Medicare tax | 21.93 | |
| Federal income tax | 258.90 | |
| Retirement savings | 20.00 | |
| United Fund | 5.00 | |
| Total deductions | | 393.55 |
| Net pay | | $1,068.45 |

## Example Exercise 10-3 Employee Net Pay

**OBJ. 2**

Karen Dunn's weekly gross earnings for the week ending December 3 were $2,250, and her federal income tax withholding was $458.88. Assuming the social security rate is 6% and Medicare is 1.5%, what is Dunn's net pay?

### Follow My Example 10-3

| | | |
|---|---:|---:|
| Total wage payment .......................................................... | | $2,250.00 |
| Less: Federal income tax withholding....................................... | $458.88 | |
| Social security tax ($2,250 × 6%) ....................................... | 135.00 | |
| Medicare tax ($2,250 × 1.5%)............................................. | 33.75 | 627.63 |
| Net pay ......................................................................... | | $1,622.37 |

Practice Exercises: **PE 10-3A, PE 10-3B**

Employee net pay can be computed using a spreadsheet, as follows.

| | A | B | C |
|---|---|---|---|
| 1 | *Inputs:* | *T. McGrath* | |
| 2 | Hours worked straight-time | 40 | |
| 3 | Hours worked overtime | 2 | |
| 4 | Hourly rate | $ 34.00 | |
| 5 | Overtime premium | 150% | |
| 6 | Federal income tax (weekly withholding) | $ 258.90 | |
| 7 | Social security rate | 6% | |
| 8 | Medicare rate | 1.5% | |
| 9 | Retirement savings (weekly) | $ 20.00 | |
| 10 | United Way | $ 5.00 | |
| 11 | | | |
| 12 | *Outputs:* | | |
| 13 | Gross earnings for the week | | =(B2*B4)+(B3*B4*B5) ◄— **a.** |
| 14 | Deductions: | | |
| 15 | Social security tax | =C13*B7 ◄— **b.** | |
| 16 | Medicare tax | =C13*B8 ◄— **c.** | |
| 17 | Federal income tax | =B6 ⎤ | |
| 18 | Retirement savings | =B9 ⎬◄— **d.** | |
| 19 | United Fund | =B10 ⎦ | |
| 20 | Total deductions | | =SUM(B15:B19) ◄— **e.** |
| 21 | Net Pay | | =C13-C20 ◄— **f.** |
| 22 | | | |
| 23 | | | |
| 24 | | | |

The spreadsheet should be developed with an input and output section. The outputs build formulas based on the inputs.

**a.** Enter in C13 the gross earnings:
=(B2*B4)+(B3*B4*B5)

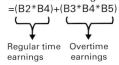

Regular time    Overtime
earnings         earnings

  **b.** Enter in B15 the formula for the social security tax, =C13*B7.
  **c.** Enter in B16 the formula for the Medicare tax, =C13*B8.
  **d.** Enter in B17, B18, and B19, the cell references for the federal income tax,
    retirement savings, and United Fund, respectively.
  **e.** Enter in C20 the formula to sum the deductions, =SUM(B15:B19).
  **f.** Enter in C21 the formula for the net pay, =C13-C20.

### Absolute Cell References

Many employers have more than one employee. Spreadsheets are very useful for summarizing payroll information for many employees. We will illustrate multiple employees in order to introduce the Excel concept of absolute cell references. Absolute cell references are often used in Excel formula design. For example, assume Dandridge Company has three employees who are paid $15 per hour with an overtime premium of 150% for hours in excess of 40 hours per week. Payroll information for a recent week is as follows:

|   | A | B | C | D |
|---|---|---|---|---|
| 1 | *Inputs:* | | | |
| 2 | Hourly rate | $ 15.00 | | |
| 3 | Overtime premium | 150% | | |
| 4 | Regular time hours | 40 | | |
| 5 | | | | |
| 6 | | Chambers, T. | Knox, J. | Little, B. |
| 7 | Hours worked | 42 | 45 | 48 |
| 8 | | | | |

The inputs include three columns of hours worked information for three employees. The formula for the straight-time, overtime, and gross earnings are first determined for T. Chambers as follows:

| 9 | *Output:* | | | |
|---|---|---|---|---|
| 10 | | Chambers, T. | Knox, J | Little, B. |
| 11 | Straight-time earnings | =$B4*$B2 | | |
| 12 | Overtime earnings | =(B7-$B4)*$B2*$B3 | Copied to | |
| 13 | Gross earnings | =SUM(B11:B12) | two remaining | |
| 14 | | | employees | |

The straight-time earnings formula is entered as,

=$B4*$B2

The dollar sign in front of both lettered columns indicates that the column references is to remain fixed when copying across the columns. That is, the formula is the same for all three employees, and the columns don't adjust during copying.

The overtime earnings formula is entered as:

=(B7-$B4)*$B2*$B3

In this case, the column reference for B4, B2, and B3 remains fixed in copying. However, B7 does adjust the column reference when copied. The sum formula is entered last. This formula requires no absolute cell references because the columns adjust in copying.

Once the three formulas are entered, they are copied to the two other employees. The formulas for all three employees after copying would appear as follows:

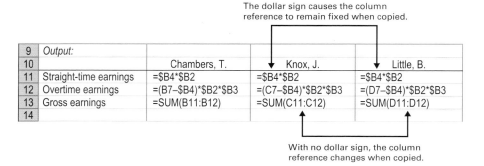

The dollar sign causes the column reference to remain fixed when copied.

| 9 | *Output:* | | | |
|---|---|---|---|---|
| 10 | | Chambers, T. | Knox, J. | Little, B. |
| 11 | Straight-time earnings | =$B4*$B2 | =$B4*$B2 | =$B4*$B2 |
| 12 | Overtime earnings | =(B7–$B4)*$B2*$B3 | =(C7–$B4)*$B2*$B3 | =(D7–$B4)*$B2*$B3 |
| 13 | Gross earnings | =SUM(B11:B12) | =SUM(C11:C12) | =SUM(D11:D12) |
| 14 | | | | |

With no dollar sign, the column reference changes when copied.

In the same way that the dollar sign is used in front of columns, the dollar sign can also be placed in front of the row reference when the row is to remain fixed when copying down rows. The use of absolute cell references ($ sign) is an important Excel formula design concept. You will use them often.

**Try**_It_   Go to the hands-on **Excel Tutor** for this example!

**Try**_It_   This Excel Success example uses an Excel function referred to as cell referencing. Go to the **Excel Tutor** titled **Absolute & Relative Cell References** for additional help on this useful Excel function!

## Liability for Employer's Payroll Taxes

Employers are subject to the following payroll taxes for amounts paid their employees:

1. *FICA Tax:* Employers must match the employee's FICA tax contribution.
2. *Federal Unemployment Compensation Tax (FUTA):* This employer tax provides for temporary payments to those who become unemployed. The tax collected by the federal government is allocated among the states for use in state programs rather than paid directly to employees. Congress often revises the FUTA tax rate and maximum earnings subject to tax.
3. *State Unemployment Compensation Tax (SUTA):* This employer tax also provides temporary payments to those who become unemployed. The FUTA and SUTA programs are closely coordinated, with the states distributing the unemployment checks.[6] SUTA tax rates and earnings subject to tax vary by state.[7]

The preceding employer taxes are an operating expense of the company. Exhibit 4 summarizes the responsibility for employee and employer payroll taxes.

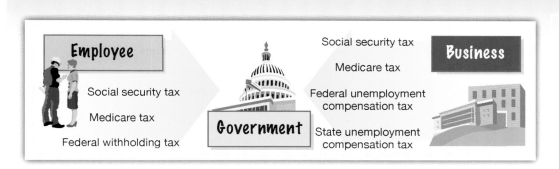

**EXHIBIT 4**

**Responsibility for Tax Payments**

## BusinessConnection

### THE MOST YOU WILL EVER PAY

In 1936, the Social Security Board described how the tax was expected to affect a worker's pay, as follows:

*The taxes called for in this law will be paid both by your employer and by you. For the next 3 years you will pay maybe 15 cents a week, maybe 25 cents a week, maybe 30 cents or more, according to what you earn. That is to say, during the next 3 years, beginning January 1, 1937, you will pay 1 cent for every dollar you earn, and at the same time your employer will pay 1 cent for every dollar you earn, up to $3,000 a year. . . .*

*. . . Beginning in 1940 you will pay, and your employer will pay, 1½ cents for each dollar you earn, up to $3,000 a year . . . and then beginning in 1943, you will pay 2 cents, and so will your employer, for every dollar you earn for the next three years. After that, you and your employer will each pay half a cent more for 3 years, and finally, beginning in 1949, . . . you and your employer will each pay 3 cents on each dollar you earn, up to $3,000 a year. That is the most you will ever pay.*

The rate on January 1, 2010, was 7.65 cents per dollar earned (7.65%). The social security portion was 6.20% on the first $106,800 of earnings. The Medicare portion was 1.45% on all earnings.

Source: Arthur Lodge, "That Is the Most You Will Ever Pay," *Journal of Accountancy*, October 1985, p. 44.

---

6 This rate may be reduced to 0.8% for credits for state unemployment compensation tax.

7 As of January 1, 2010, the maximum state rate credited against the federal unemployment rate was 5.4% of the first $7,000 of each employee's earnings during a calendar year.

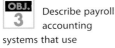

**OBJ. 3** Describe payroll accounting systems that use a payroll register, employee earnings records, and a general journal.

# Accounting Systems for Payroll and Payroll Taxes

Payroll systems should be designed to:

1. Pay employees accurately and timely.
2. Meet regulatory requirements of federal, state, and local agencies.
3. Provide useful data for management decision-making needs.

Although payroll systems differ among companies, the major elements of most payroll systems are:

1. Payroll register
2. Employee's earnings record
3. Payroll checks

## Payroll Register

The **payroll register** is a multicolumn report used for summarizing the data for each payroll period. Although payroll registers vary by company, a payroll register normally includes the following columns:

1. Employee name
2. Total hours worked
3. Regular earnings
4. Overtime earnings
5. Total gross earnings
6. Social security tax withheld
7. Medicare tax withheld
8. Federal income tax withheld
9. Retirement savings withheld
10. Miscellaneous items withheld
11. Total withholdings
12. Net pay
13. Check number of payroll check issued
14. Accounts debited for payroll expense

Exhibit 5, on pages 462–463, illustrates a payroll register. The two right-hand columns of the payroll register indicate the accounts debited for the payroll expense. These columns are often referred to as the *payroll distribution*.

**Recording Employees' Earnings** The column totals of the payroll register provide the basis for recording the journal entry for payroll. The entry based on the payroll register in Exhibit 5 is shown on the next page.

**Note:**
**Payroll taxes become a liability to the employer when the payroll is paid.**

**Recording and Paying Payroll Taxes** Payroll taxes are recorded as liabilities when the payroll is *paid* to employees. In addition, employers compute and report payroll taxes on a *calendar-year* basis, which may differ from the company's fiscal year.

| | | | | |
|---|---|---|---|---|
| Dec. | 27 | Sales Salaries Expense | 11,122.00 | |
| | | Office Salaries Expense | 2,780.00 | |
| | | Social Security Tax Payable | | 834.12 |
| | | Medicare Tax Payable | | 208.53 |
| | | Employees Federal Income Tax Payable | | 3,332.00 |
| | | Retirement Savings Deductions Payable | | 680.00 |
| | | United Fund Deductions Payable | | 520.00 |
| | | Salaries Payable | | 8,327.35 |
| | | Payroll for week ended December 27. | | |

**Example Exercise** 10-4 **Journalize Period Payroll** OBJ. 3

The payroll register of Chen Engineering Services indicates $900 of social security withheld and $225 of Medicare tax withheld on total salaries of $15,000 for the period. Federal withholding for the period totaled $2,925.
Provide the journal entry for the period's payroll.

**Follow My Example** 10-4

| | | |
|---|---|---|
| Salaries Expense............................................................... | 15,000 | |
| Social Security Tax Payable................................................. | | 900 |
| Medicare Tax Payable ....................................................... | | 225 |
| Employees Federal Withholding Tax Payable ................................ | | 2,925 |
| Salaries Payable............................................................. | | 10,950 |

Practice Exercises: **PE 10-4A, PE 10-4B**

On December 27, McDermott Supply has the following payroll data:

| | |
|---|---|
| Sales salaries ............................................. | $11,122 |
| Office salaries owed ...................................... | 2,780 |
| Wages owed employees on December 27.............. | $13,902 |
| | |
| Wages subject to payroll taxes: | |
| Social security tax (6%)................................. | $13,902 |
| Medicare tax (1.5%) ..................................... | 13,902 |
| State (5.4%) and federal (0.8%) | |
| unemployment compensation tax ................... | 2,710 |

Employers must match the employees' social security and Medicare tax contributions. In addition, the employer must pay state unemployment compensation tax (SUTA) of 5.4% and federal unemployment compensation tax (FUTA) of 0.8%. When payroll is paid on December 27, these payroll taxes are computed as follows:

| | |
|---|---|
| Social security tax | $ 834.12 ($13,902 × 6%, and from Social Security Tax column of Exhibit 5) |
| Medicare tax | 208.53 ($13,902 × 1.5%, and from Medicare Tax column of Exhibit 5) |
| SUTA | 146.34 ($2,710 × 5.4%) |
| FUTA | 21.68 ($2,710 × 0.8%) |
| Total payroll taxes | $1,210.67 |

The entry to journalize the payroll tax expense for Exhibit 5 is shown below.

| | | | | |
|---|---|---|---|---|
| Dec. | 27 | Payroll Tax Expense | 1,210.67 | |
| | | Social Security Tax Payable | | 834.12 |
| | | Medicare Tax Payable | | 208.53 |
| | | State Unemployment Tax Payable | | 146.34 |
| | | Federal Unemployment Tax Payable | | 21.68 |
| | | Payroll taxes for week ended December 27. | | |

**EXHIBIT 5** **Payroll Register**

| | Employee Name | Total Hours | Earnings | | | |
|---|---|---|---|---|---|---|
| | | | Regular | Overtime | Total | |
| 1 | Abrams, Julie S. | 40 | 500.00 | | 500.00 | 1 |
| 2 | Elrod, Fred G. | 44 | 392.00 | 58.80 | 450.80 | 2 |
| 3 | Gomez, Jose C. | 40 | 840.00 | | 840.00 | 3 |
| 4 | McGrath, John T. | 42 | 1,360.00 | 102.00 | 1,462.00 | 4 |
| 25 | Wilkes, Glenn K. | 40 | 480.00 | | 480.00 | 25 |
| 26 | Zumpano, Michael W. | 40 | 600.00 | | 600.00 | 26 |
| 27 | Total | | 13,328.00 | 574.00 | 13,902.00 | 27 |
| 28 | | | | | | 28 |

The preceding entry records a liability for each payroll tax. When the payroll taxes are paid, an entry is recorded debiting the payroll tax liability accounts and crediting Cash.

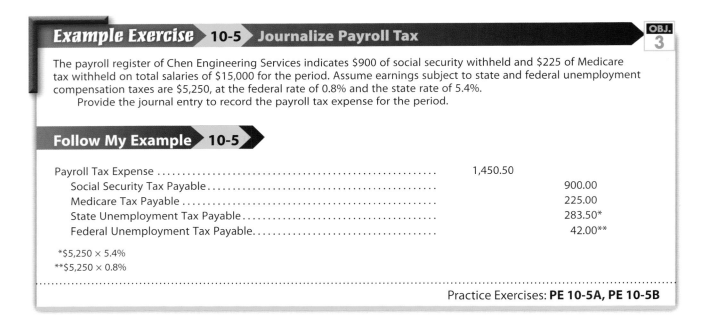

**Example Exercise** ▶ **10-5** ▶ **Journalize Payroll Tax** | **OBJ. 3**

The payroll register of Chen Engineering Services indicates $900 of social security withheld and $225 of Medicare tax withheld on total salaries of $15,000 for the period. Assume earnings subject to state and federal unemployment compensation taxes are $5,250, at the federal rate of 0.8% and the state rate of 5.4%.
   Provide the journal entry to record the payroll tax expense for the period.

**Follow My Example** ▶ **10-5**

| | | |
|---|---|---|
| Payroll Tax Expense . . . . . . . . . . . . . . . . . . . . . . . . . . . . . . . . . . . . . . . . . . . . . . . . | 1,450.50 | |
|    Social Security Tax Payable . . . . . . . . . . . . . . . . . . . . . . . . . . . . . . . . . . . . . . . . | | 900.00 |
|    Medicare Tax Payable . . . . . . . . . . . . . . . . . . . . . . . . . . . . . . . . . . . . . . . . . . . . | | 225.00 |
|    State Unemployment Tax Payable . . . . . . . . . . . . . . . . . . . . . . . . . . . . . . . . . . | | 283.50* |
|    Federal Unemployment Tax Payable . . . . . . . . . . . . . . . . . . . . . . . . . . . . . . . | | 42.00** |

*$5,250 × 5.4%
**$5,250 × 0.8%

Practice Exercises: **PE 10-5A, PE 10-5B**

## Employee's Earnings Record

Each employee's earnings to date must be determined at the end of each payroll period. This total is necessary for computing the employee's social security tax withholding and the employer's payroll taxes. Thus, detailed payroll records must be kept for each employee. This record is called an **employee's earnings record**.

Exhibit 6, on pages 456–457, shows a portion of John T. McGrath's employee's earnings record. An employee's earnings record and the payroll register are interrelated. For example, McGrath's earnings record for December 27 can be traced to the fourth line of the payroll register in Exhibit 5.

As shown in Exhibit 6, an employee's earnings record has quarterly and yearly totals. These totals are used for tax, insurance, and other reports. For example, one such report is the Wage and Tax Statement, commonly called a *W-2*. This form is

**EXHIBIT 5**    (Concluded)

| | Social Security Tax | Medicare Tax | Federal Income Tax | Retirement Savings | Misc. | | Total | Net Pay | Check No. | Sales Salaries Expense | Office Salaries Expense | |
|---|---|---|---|---|---|---|---|---|---|---|---|---|
| 1 | 30.00 | 7.50 | 74.00 | 20.00 | UF | 10.00 | 141.50 | 358.50 | 6857 | 500.00 | | 1 |
| 2 | 27.05 | 6.76 | 62.00 | | UF | 50.00 | 145.81 | 304.99 | 6858 | | 450.80 | 2 |
| 3 | 50.40 | 12.60 | 131.00 | 25.00 | UF | 10.00 | 229.00 | 611.00 | 6859 | 840.00 | | 3 |
| 4 | 87.72 | 21.93 | 258.90 | 20.00 | UF | 5.00 | 393.55 | 1,068.45 | 6860 | 1,462.00 | | 4 |
| 25 | 28.80 | 7.20 | 69.00 | 10.00 | | | 115.00 | 365.00 | 6880 | 480.00 | | 25 |
| 26 | 36.00 | 9.00 | 79.00 | 5.00 | UF | 2.00 | 131.00 | 469.00 | 6881 | | 600.00 | 26 |
| 27 | 834.12 | 208.53 | 3,332.00 | 680.00 | UF | 520.00 | 5,574.65 | 8,327.35 | | 11,122.00 | 2,780.00 | 27 |
| 28 | | | | | | | | | | | | 28 |

The header spans: "Deductions Withheld" over Social Security Tax, Medicare Tax, Federal Income Tax, Retirement Savings, Misc., Total. "Paid" over Net Pay, Check No. "Accounts Debited" over Sales Salaries Expense, Office Salaries Expense.

Miscellaneous Deductions: UF—United Fund

provided annually to each employee as well as to the Social Security Administration. The W-2 shown below is based on John T. McGrath's employee's earnings record shown in Exhibit 6.

| 22222 | Void ☐ | **a** Employee's social security number  381-48-9120 | For Official Use Only ▶  OMB No. 1545-0008 | |
|---|---|---|---|---|

**b** Employer identification number (EIN)
61-8436524

**c** Employer's name, address, and ZIP code
McDermott Supply Co.
415 5th Ave. So.
Dubuque, IA 52736-0142

**d** Control number

**e** Employee's first name and initial    Last name    Suff.
John T.                McGrath

1830 4th St.
Clinton, IA 52732-6142

**f** Employee's address and ZIP code

| **1** Wages, tips, other compensation  100,500.00 | **2** Federal income tax withheld  21,387.65 |
|---|---|
| **3** Social security wages  100,500.00 | **4** Social security tax withheld  6,030.00 |
| **5** Medicare wages and tips  100,500.00 | **6** Medicare tax withheld  1,507.50 |
| **7** Social security tips | **8** Allocated tips |
| **9** Advance EIC payment | **10** Dependent care benefits |
| **11** Nonqualified plans | **12a** See instructions for box 12 |
| **13** Statutory employee / Retirement plan / Third-party sick pay | **12b** |
| **14** Other | **12c** |
| | **12d** |

| **15** State   Employer's state ID number  IA | **16** State wages, tips, etc. | **17** State income tax | **18** Local wages, tips, etc. | **19** Local income tax | **20** Locality name  Dubuque |
|---|---|---|---|---|---|

Form **W-2**   Wage and Tax Statement   **2011**

Department of the Treasury—Internal Revenue Service
For Privacy Act and Paperwork Reduction
Act Notice, see back of Copy D.
Cat. No. 10134D

**Copy A For Social Security Administration** — Send this entire page with Form W-3 to the Social Security Administration; photocopies are **not** acceptable.
**Do Not Cut, Fold, or Staple Forms on This Page — Do Not Cut, Fold, or Staple Forms on This Page**

## Payroll Checks

Companies may pay employees, especially part-time employees, by issuing *payroll checks*. Each check includes a detachable statement showing how the net pay was computed. Exhibit 7, on page 466, illustrates a payroll check for John T. McGrath.

Most companies issuing payroll checks use a special payroll bank account. In such cases, payroll is processed as follows:

1. The total net pay for the period is determined from the payroll register.
2. The company authorizes an electronic funds transfer (EFT) from its regular bank account to the special payroll bank account for the total net pay.
3. Individual payroll checks are written from the payroll account.
4. The numbers of the payroll checks are inserted in the payroll register.

**EXHIBIT 6**

**Employee's Earnings Record**

John T. McGrath
1830 4th St.
Clinton, IA 52732-6142                                    PHONE: 555-3148

| SINGLE | NUMBER OF WITHHOLDING ALLOWANCES: 1 | PAY RATE: | $1,360.00 Per Week |
|---|---|---|---|
| OCCUPATION: | Salesperson | EQUIVALENT HOURLY RATE: $34 | |

| | Period Ending | Total Hours | Regular Earnings | Overtime Earnings | Total Earnings | Total | |
|---|---|---|---|---|---|---|---|
| 42 | SEPT. 27 | 53 | 1,360.00 | 663.00 | 2,023.00 | 75,565.00 | 42 |
| 43 | THIRD QUARTER | | 17,680.00 | 7,605.00 | 25,285.00 | | 43 |
| 44 | OCT. 4 | 51 | 1,360.00 | 561.00 | 1,921.00 | 77,486.00 | 44 |
| 50 | NOV. 15 | 50 | 1,360.00 | 510.00 | 1,870.00 | 89,382.00 | 50 |
| 51 | NOV. 22 | 53 | 1,360.00 | 663.00 | 2,023.00 | 91,405.00 | 51 |
| 52 | NOV. 29 | 47 | 1,360.00 | 357.00 | 1,717.00 | 93,122.00 | 52 |
| 53 | DEC. 6 | 53 | 1,360.00 | 663.00 | 2,023.00 | 95,145.00 | 53 |
| 54 | DEC.13 | 52 | 1,360.00 | 612.00 | 1,972.00 | 97,117.00 | 54 |
| 55 | DEC. 20 | 51 | 1,360.00 | 561.00 | 1,921.00 | 99,038.00 | 55 |
| 56 | DEC. 27 | 42 | 1,360.00 | 102.00 | 1,462.00 | 100,500.00 | 56 |
| 57 | FOURTH QUARTER | | 17,680.00 | 7,255.00 | 24,935.00 | | 57 |
| 58 | YEARLY TOTAL | | 70,720.00 | 29,780.00 | 100,500.00 | | 58 |

An advantage of using a separate payroll bank account is that reconciling the bank statements is simplified. In addition, a payroll bank account establishes control over payroll checks and, thus, prevents their theft or misuse.

Many companies use electronic funds transfer to pay their employees. In such cases, each pay period an employee's net pay is deposited directly into the employee checking account. Later, employees receive a payroll statement summarizing how the net pay was computed.

## Payroll System Diagram

The inputs into a payroll system may be classified as:

1. Constants, which are data that remain unchanged from payroll to payroll.

    Examples: Employee names, social security numbers, marital status, number of income tax withholding allowances, rates of pay, tax rates, and withholding tables.

2. Variables, which are data that change from payroll to payroll.

    Examples: Number of hours or days worked for each employee, accrued days of sick leave, vacation credits, total earnings to date, and total taxes withheld.

In a computerized accounting system, constants are stored within a payroll file. The variables are input each pay period by a payroll clerk. In some systems, employees swipe their identification (ID) cards when they report for and leave work. In such cases, the hours worked by each employee are automatically updated.

A computerized payroll system also maintains electronic versions of the payroll register and employee earnings records. Payroll system outputs, such as payroll checks, EFTs, and tax records, are automatically produced each pay period.

**EXHIBIT 6**   **(Concluded)**

SOC. SEC. NO.: 381-48-9120                                                   EMPLOYEE NO.: 814

DATE OF BIRTH: February 15, 1982

DATE EMPLOYMENT TERMINATED:

| | Deductions | | | | | | Paid | | |
| | Social Security Tax | Medicare Tax | Federal Income Tax | Retirement Savings | Other | | Total | Net Amount | Check No. | |
|---|---|---|---|---|---|---|---|---|---|---|
| 42 | 121.38 | 30.35 | 429.83 | 20.00 | | | 601.56 | 1,421.44 | 6175 | 42 |
| 43 | 1,517.10 | 379.28 | 5,391.71 | 260.00 | UF | 40.00 | 7,588.09 | 17,696.91 | | 43 |
| 44 | 115.26 | 28.82 | 401.27 | 20.00 | | | 565.35 | 1,355.65 | 6225 | 44 |
| 50 | 112.20 | 28.05 | 386.99 | 20.00 | | | 547.24 | 1,322.76 | 6530 | 50 |
| 51 | 121.38 | 30.35 | 429.83 | 20.00 | | | 601.56 | 1,421.44 | 6582 | 51 |
| 52 | 103.02 | 25.76 | 344.15 | 20.00 | | | 492.93 | 1,224.07 | 6640 | 52 |
| 53 | 121.38 | 30.35 | 429.83 | 20.00 | UF | 5.00 | 606.56 | 1,416.44 | 6688 | 53 |
| 54 | 118.32 | 29.58 | 415.55 | 20.00 | | | 583.45 | 1,388.55 | 6743 | 54 |
| 55 | 115.26 | 28.82 | 401.27 | 20.00 | | | 565.35 | 1,355.65 | 6801 | 55 |
| 56 | 87.72 | 21.93 | 258.90 | 20.00 | UF | 5.00 | 393.55 | 1,068.45 | 6860 | 56 |
| 57 | 1,496.10 | 374.03 | 5,293.71 | 260.00 | UF | 15.00 | 7,438.84 | 17,496.16 | | 57 |
| 58 | 6,030.00 | 1,507.50 | 21,387.65 | 1,040.00 | UF | 100.00 | 30,065.15 | 70,434.85 | | 58 |

## Internal Controls for Payroll Systems

The cash payment controls described in Chapter 7, *Sarbanes-Oxley, Internal Control, and Cash*, also apply to payrolls. Some examples of payroll controls include the following:

1. If a check-signing machine is used, blank payroll checks and access to the machine should be restricted to prevent their theft or misuse.
2. The hiring and firing of employees should be properly authorized and approved in writing.
3. All changes in pay rates should be properly authorized and approved in writing.
4. Employees should be observed when arriving for work to verify that employees are "checking in" for work only once and only for themselves. Employees may "check in" for work by using a time card or by swiping their employee ID card.
5. Payroll checks should be distributed by someone other than employee supervisors.
6. A special payroll bank account should be used.

## Integrity, Objectivity, and Ethics in Business

### $8 MILLION FOR 18 MINUTES OF WORK

Computer system controls can be very important in issuing payroll checks. In one case, a Detroit schoolteacher was paid $4,015,625 after deducting $3,884,375 in payroll deductions for 18 minutes of overtime work. The error was caused by a computer glitch when the teacher's employee identification number was substituted incorrectly in the "hourly wage" field and wasn't caught by the payroll software. After six days, the error was discovered and the money was returned. "One of the things that came with (the software) is a fail-safe that prevents that. It doesn't work," a financial officer said. The district has since installed a program to flag any paycheck exceeding $10,000.

Source: Associated Press, September 27, 2002.

**EXHIBIT 7**

**Payroll Check**

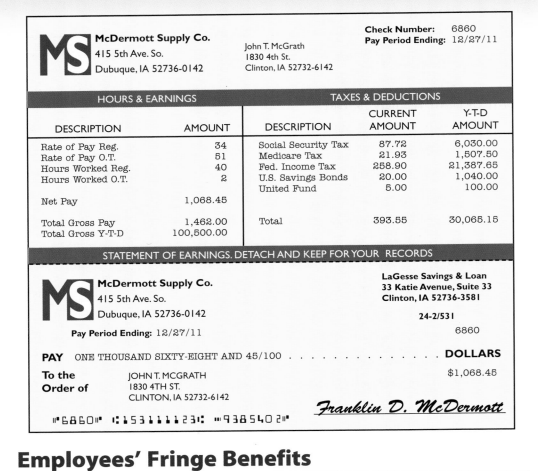

Journalize entries for employee fringe benefits, including vacation pay and pensions.

# Employees' Fringe Benefits

Many companies provide their employees benefits in addition to salary and wages earned. Such **fringe benefits** may include vacation, medical, and retirement benefits.

The cost of employee fringe benefits is recorded as an expense by the employer. To match revenues and expenses, the estimated cost of fringe benefits is recorded as an expense during the period in which the employees earn the benefits.

## Vacation Pay

**Note:**

**Vacation pay becomes the employer's liability as the employee earns vacation rights.**

Most employers provide employees vacations, sometimes called *compensated absences*. The liability to pay for employee vacations could be accrued as a liability at the end of each pay period. However, many companies wait and record an adjusting entry for accrued vacation at the end of the year.

To illustrate, assume that employees earn one day of vacation for each month worked. The estimated vacation pay for the year ending December 31 is $325,000. The adjusting entry for the accrued vacation is shown below.

| | | | | | |
|---|---|---|---|---|---|
| Dec. | 31 | Vacation Pay Expense | | 325,000 | |
| | | Vacation Pay Payable | | | 325,000 |
| | | Accrued vacation pay for the year. | | | |

Employees may be required to take all their vacation time within one year. In such cases, any accrued vacation pay will be paid within one year. Thus, the vacation pay payable is reported as a current liability on the balance sheet. If employees are allowed to accumulate their vacation pay, the estimated vacation pay payable that will *not* be taken within a year is reported as a long-term liability.

When employees take vacations, the liability for vacation pay is decreased by debiting Vacation Pay Payable. Salaries or Wages Payable and the other related payroll accounts for taxes and withholdings are credited.

# Pensions

A **pension** is a cash payment to retired employees. Pension rights are accrued by employees as they work, based on the employer's pension plan. Two basic types of pension plans are:

1. Defined contribution plan
2. Defined benefit plan

In a **defined contribution plan**, the company invests contributions on behalf of the employee during the employee's working years. Normally, the employee and employer contribute to the plan. The employee's pension depends on the total contributions and the investment returns earned on those contributions.

One of the more popular defined contribution plans is the 401k plan. Under this plan, employees contribute a portion of their gross pay to investments, such as mutual funds. A 401k plan offers employees two advantages.

1. The employee contribution is deducted before taxes.
2. The contributions and related earnings are not taxed until withdrawn at retirement.

In most cases, the employer matches some portion of the employee's contribution. The employer's cost is debited to *Pension Expense*. To illustrate, assume that Heaven Scent Perfumes Company contributes 10% of employee monthly salaries to an employee 401k plan. Assuming $500,000 of monthly salaries, the journal entry to record the monthly contribution is shown below.

| | | | | |
|---|---|---|---|---|
| Dec. | 31 | Pension Expense | 50,000 | |
| | | Cash | | 50,000 |
| | | Contributed 10% of monthly salaries to pension plan. | | |

In a **defined benefit plan**, the company pays the employee a fixed annual pension based on a formula. The formula is normally based on such factors as the employee's years of service, age, and past salary.

$$\text{Annual Pension} = 1.5\% \times \text{Years of Service} \times \text{Highest 3-Year Average Salary}$$

In a defined benefit plan, the employer is obligated to pay for (fund) the employee's future pension benefits. As a result, many companies are replacing their defined benefit plans with defined contribution plans.

The pension cost of a defined benefit plan is debited to *Pension Expense*. Cash is credited for the amount contributed (funded) by the employer. Any unfunded amount is credited to *Unfunded Pension Liability*.

To illustrate, assume that the defined benefit plan of Hinkle Co. requires an annual pension cost of $80,000. This annual contribution is based on estimates of Hinkle's future pension liabilities. On December 31, Hinkle Co. pays $60,000 to the pension fund. The entry to record the payment and unfunded liability is shown below.

| | | | | |
|---|---|---|---|---|
| Dec. | 31 | Pension Expense | 80,000 | |
| | | Cash | | 60,000 |
| | | Unfunded Pension Liability | | 20,000 |
| | | Annual pension cost and contribution. | | |

If the unfunded pension liability is to be paid within one year, it is reported as a current liability on the balance sheet. Any portion of the unfunded pension liability that will be paid beyond one year is a long-term liability.

The accounting for pensions is complex due to the uncertainties of estimating future pension liabilities. These estimates depend on such factors as employee life expectancies, employee turnover, expected employee compensation levels, and investment income on pension contributions. Additional accounting and disclosures related to pensions are covered in advanced accounting courses.

---

**Example Exercise** ❯ **10-6** ❯ **Vacation Pay and Pension Benefits**　　　　　　**OBJ. 4**

Manfield Services Company provides its employees vacation benefits and a defined contribution pension plan. Employees earned vacation pay of $44,000 for the period. The pension plan requires a contribution to the plan administrator equal to 8% of employee salaries. Salaries were $450,000 during the period.
　　Provide the journal entry for the (a) vacation pay and (b) pension benefit.

**Follow My Example** ❯ **10-6** ❯

| | | | |
|---|---|---|---|
| a. | Vacation Pay Expense .......................................................... | 44,000 | |
| | 　Vacation Pay Payable........................................................ | | 44,000 |
| | 　　Vacation pay accrued for the period. | | |
| b. | Pension Expense ............................................................... | 36,000 | |
| | 　Cash ............................................................................ | | 36,000 |
| | 　　Pension contribution, 8% of $450,000 salary. | | |

Practice Exercises: **PE 10-6A, PE 10-6B**

---

## Postretirement Benefits Other than Pensions

Employees may earn rights to other postretirement benefits from their employer. Such benefits may include dental care, eye care, medical care, life insurance, tuition assistance, tax services, and legal services.

The accounting for other postretirement benefits is similar to that of defined benefit pension plans. The estimate of the annual benefits expense is recorded by debiting *Postretirement Benefits Expense*. If the benefits are fully funded, Cash is credited for the same amount. If the benefits are not fully funded, a postretirement benefits plan liability account is also credited.

The financial statements should disclose the nature of the postretirement benefit liabilities. These disclosures are usually included as notes to the financial statements. Additional accounting and disclosures for postretirement benefits are covered in advanced accounting courses.

## Current Liabilities on the Balance Sheet

Accounts payable, the current portion of long-term debt, notes payable, and any other debts that are due within one year are reported as current liabilities on the balance sheet. The balance sheet presentation of current liabilities for Mornin' Joe is shown below.

| Mornin' Joe<br>Balance Sheet<br>December 31, 2012 | | |
|---|---|---|
| **Liabilities** | | |
| Current liabilities: | | |
| 　Accounts payable ......................................... | $133,000 | |
| 　Notes payable (current portion) ........................... | 200,000 | |
| 　Salaries and wages payable ............................... | 42,000 | |
| 　Payroll taxes payable .................................... | 16,400 | |
| 　Interest payable......................................... | 40,000 | |
| 　　Total current liabilities................................. | | $431,400 |

## IFRS Reporting

The statement of financial position (balance sheet) presentation for current liabilities for Mornin' Joe International under IFRS is as follows:

See pages 630–634

| Mornin' Joe International<br>Statement of Financial Position<br>December 31, 2012 | | |
|---|---:|---:|
| **Current liabilities** | | |
| Accounts payable.......................... | €133,000 | |
| Loans................................... | 200,000 | |
| Employee provisions...................... | 58,400 | |
| Interest payable ........................ | 40,000 | |
| Total current liabilities ................ | | 431,400 |
| Total liabilities ....................... | | €2,315,400 |
| **Total equity and liabilities** ......... | | €6,214,500 |

The current liabilities disclosure is similar to U.S. GAAP. The term "provision" is a term used to denote a liability under IFRS, whereas this term often indicates an expense under U.S. GAAP. Thus, "employee provisions" are the combined wages and salaries payable and payroll taxes payable from Mornin' Joe (U.S.). Loans are the same as notes payable due currently.

## BusinessConnection

### GENERAL MOTORS PENSION PROBLEMS

In June 2009, General Motors Company, the world's second-largest automaker, filed for bankruptcy. The company's troubles began decades earlier when the company agreed to provide employees with large pension benefits instead of giving them wage increases. While this strategy was initially successful, by the mid-1990s large numbers of employees began to retire, and the increasing pension costs began to put a financial strain on the company. In 2003, the company issued $18.5 billion in debt to fund its growing unfunded pension liability, but this only provided a temporary fix. From 1993 to 2007, General Motors spent $103 billion on pension and health care benefits for retirees, and the company had 4.61 retired union employees for every one active union employee. By June 2009, the combination of growing pension obligations and deteriorating sales forced the company into bankruptcy.

Source: R. Lowenstein, "Siphoning GM's Future," *The New York Times*, July 10, 2008.

# Contingent Liabilities

Some liabilities may arise from past transactions if certain events occur in the future. These *potential* liabilities are called **contingent liabilities**.

The accounting for contingent liabilities depends on the following two factors:

1. Likelihood of occurring: Probable, reasonably possible, or remote
2. Measurement: Estimable or not estimable

**OBJ. 5** Describe the accounting treatment for contingent liabilities and journalize entries for product warranties.

The likelihood that the event creating the liability occurring is classified as *probable*, *reasonably possible*, or *remote*. The ability to estimate the potential liability is classified as *estimable* or *not estimable*.

## Probable and Estimable

If a contingent liability is *probable* and the amount of the liability can be *reasonably estimated*, it is recorded and disclosed. The liability is recorded by debiting an expense and crediting a liability.

To illustrate, assume that during June a company sold a product for $60,000 that includes a 36-month warranty for repairs. The average cost of repairs over the warranty period is 5% of the sales price. The entry to record the estimated product warranty expense for June is as shown below.

| June | 30 | Product Warranty Expense | 3,000 | |
| | | Product Warranty Payable | | 3,000 |
| | | Warranty expense for June, 5% × $60,000. | | |

The estimated costs of warranty work on new car sales are a contingent liability for Ford Motor Company.

The preceding entry records warranty expense in the same period in which the sale is recorded. In this way, warranty expense is matched with the related revenue (sales).

If the product is repaired under warranty, the costs are recorded by debiting *Product Warranty Payable* and crediting *Cash, Supplies, Wages Payable*, or other appropriate accounts. Thus, if a $200 part is replaced under warranty on Aug. 16, the entry is:

| Aug. | 16 | Product Warranty Payable | 200 | |
| | | Supplies | | 200 |
| | | Replaced defective part under warranty. | | |

## Example Exercise 10-7    Estimated Warranty Liability

**OBJ. 5**

Cook-Rite Co. sold $140,000 of kitchen appliances during August under a six-month warranty. The cost to repair defects under the warranty is estimated at 6% of the sales price. On September 11, a customer required a $200 part replacement plus $90 of labor under the warranty.

Provide the journal entry for (a) the estimated warranty expense on August 31 and (b) the September 11 warranty work.

### Follow My Example 10-7

| a. | Product Warranty Expense .................................................... | 8,400 | |
| | Product Warranty Payable.................................................... | | 8,400 |
| | To record warranty expense for August, 6% × $140,000. | | |
| b. | Product Warranty Payable.................................................... | 290 | |
| | Supplies ..................................................................... | | 200 |
| | Wages Payable............................................................... | | 90 |
| | Replaced defective part under warranty. | | |

Practice Exercises: **PE 10-7A, PE 10-7B**

## Probable and Not Estimable

A contingent liability may be probable, but cannot be estimated. In this case, the contingent liability is disclosed in the notes to the financial statements. For example, a company may have accidentally polluted a local river by dumping waste products. At the end of the period, the cost of the cleanup and any fines may not be able to be estimated.

## Reasonably Possible

A contingent liability may be only possible. For example, a company may have lost a lawsuit for infringing on another company's patent rights. However, the verdict is under appeal and the company's lawyers feel that the verdict will be reversed or significantly reduced. In this case, the contingent liability is disclosed in the notes to the financial statements.

## Remote

A contingent liability may be remote. For example, a ski resort may be sued for injuries incurred by skiers. In most cases, the courts have found that a skier accepts the risk of injury when participating in the activity. Thus, unless the ski resort is grossly negligent, the resort will not incur a liability for ski injuries. In such cases, no disclosure needs to be made in the notes to the financial statements.

The accounting treatment of contingent liabilities is summarized in Exhibit 8.

**EXHIBIT 8** **Accounting Treatment of Contingent Liabilities**

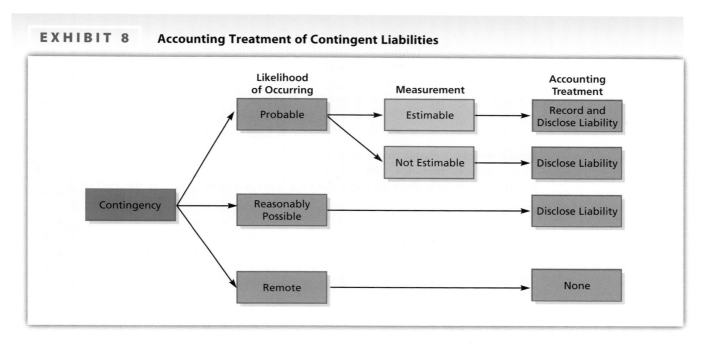

Common examples of contingent liabilities disclosed in notes to the financial statements are litigation, environmental matters, guarantees, and contingencies from the sale of receivables.

An example of a contingent liability disclosure from a recent annual report of Google Inc. is shown below.

> *We have also had copyright claims filed against us alleging that features of certain of our products and services, including Google Web Search, Google News, Google Video, Google Image Search, Google Book Search and YouTube, infringe their rights. Adverse results in these lawsuits may include awards of substantial monetary damages, costly royalty or licensing agreements or orders preventing us from offering certain functionalities, and may also result in a change in our business practices, which could result in a loss of revenue for us or otherwise harm our business. . . .*
>
> *Although the results of litigation and claims cannot be predicted with certainty, we believe that the final outcome of the matters discussed above will not have a material adverse effect on our business . . .*

Professional judgment is necessary in distinguishing between classes of contingent liabilities. This is especially the case when distinguishing between probable and reasonably possible contingent liabilities.

# Financial Analysis and Interpretation: Quick Ratio

**OBJ.**
**6**

Describe and illustrate the use of the quick ratio in analyzing a company's ability to pay its current liabilities.

**Current position analysis** helps creditors evaluate a company's ability to pay its current liabilities. This analysis is based on the following three measures:

1. Working capital
2. Current ratio
3. Quick ratio

Working capital and the current ratio were discussed in Chapter 4, and are computed as follows:

$$\text{Working Capital} = \text{Current Assets} - \text{Current Liabilities}$$

$$\text{Current Ratio} = \frac{\text{Current Assets}}{\text{Current Liabilities}}$$

While these two measures can be used to evaluate a company's ability to pay its current liabilities, they do not provide insight into the company's ability to pay its current liabilities *within a short period of time*. This is because some current assets, such as inventory, cannot be converted into cash as quickly as other current assets, such as cash and accounts receivable.

The **quick ratio** overcomes this limitation by measuring the "instant" debt-paying ability of a company and is computed as follows:

$$\text{Quick Ratio} = \frac{\text{Quick Assets}}{\text{Current Liabilities}}$$

**Quick assets** are cash and other current assets that can be easily converted to cash. This normally includes cash, temporary investments, and accounts receivable. To illustrate, consider the following data for TechSolutions, Inc., at the end of 2011:

| | |
|---|---:|
| Current assets: | |
| Cash | $2,020 |
| Temporary investments | 3,400 |
| Accounts receivable | 1,600 |
| Inventory | 2,000 |
| Other current assets | 160 |
| Total current assets | $9,180 |
| | |
| Current liabilities: | |
| Accounts payable | $3,000 |
| Other current liabilities | 2,400 |
| Total current liabilities | $5,400 |
| | |
| Working capital (current assets – current liabilities) | $3,780 |
| Current ratio (current assets/current liabilities) | 1.7 |

The quick ratio for TechSolutions, Inc., is computed as follows:

$$\text{Quick Ratio} = \frac{\$2,020 + \$3,400 + \$1,600}{\$5,400} = 1.3$$

The quick ratio of 1.3 indicates that the company has more than enough quick assets to pay its current liabilities in a short period of time. A quick ratio below 1.0 would indicate that the company does not have enough quick assets to cover its current liabilities.

Like the current ratio, the quick ratio is particularly useful in making comparisons across companies. To illustrate, the following selected balance sheet data (excluding ratios) were taken from the 2008 financial statements of Panera Bread Company and Starbucks Corporation (in thousands):

| | Panera Bread | Starbucks |
|---|---|---|
| Current assets: | | |
| Cash and cash equivalents | $ 74,710 | $ 599,800 |
| Temporary investments | 2,400 | 66,300 |
| Accounts receivable | 35,079 | 557,600 |
| Inventory | 11,959 | 664,900 |
| Other current assets | 14,265 | 147,200 |
| Total current assets | $138,413 | $2,035,800 |
| | | |
| Current liabilities: | | |
| Accounts payable | $114,014 | $1,192,100 |
| Other current liabilities | — | 388,900 |
| Total current liabilities | $114,014 | $1,581,000 |
| | | |
| Working capital (current assets – current liabilities) | $ 24,399 | $ 454,800 |
| Current ratio (current assets/current liabilities) | 1.2 | 1.3 |
| Quick ratio (quick assets/current liabilities)* | 1.0 | 0.8 |

*The quick ratio for each company is computed as follows:
 Panera Bread: ($74,710 + $2,400 + $35,079)/$114,014 = 1.0
 Starbucks: ($599,800 + $66,300 + $557,600)/$1,581,000 = 0.8

Starbucks is larger than Panera Bread and has over 18 times the amount of working capital. Such size differences make working capital comparisons between companies difficult. In contrast, the current and quick ratios provide better comparisons across companies. In this example, Panera Bread has a slightly lower current ratio than Starbucks. However, Starbucks' 0.8 quick ratio reveals that it does not have enough quick assets to cover its current liabilities, while Panera Bread's quick ratio of 1.0 indicates that the company has just enough quick assets to meet its current liabilities.

**Example Exercise 10-8 Quick Ratio** OBJ. 6

Sayer Company reported the following current assets and current liabilities for the years ended December 31, 2012 and 2011:

| | 2012 | 2011 |
|---|---|---|
| Cash | $1,250 | $1,000 |
| Temporary investments | 1,925 | 1,650 |
| Accounts receivable | 1,775 | 1,350 |
| Inventory | 1,900 | 1,700 |
| Accounts payable | 2,750 | 2,500 |

a. Compute the quick ratio for 2012 and 2011.

b. Interpret the company's quick ratio across the two time periods.

**Follow My Example 10-8**

a. December 31, 2012:
 Quick Ratio = Quick Assets/Current Liabilities
 Quick Ratio = ($1,250 + $1,925 + $1,775)/$2,750
 Quick Ratio = 1.8

 December 31, 2011:
 Quick Ratio = Quick Assets/Current Liabilities
 Quick Ratio = ($1,000 + $1,650 + $1,350)/$2,500
 Quick Ratio = 1.6

b. The quick ratio of Sayer Company has improved from 1.6 in 2011 to 1.8 in 2012. This increase is the result of a large increase in the three types of quick assets (cash, temporary investments, and accounts receivable) compared to a relatively smaller increase in the current liability, accounts payable.

Practice Exercises: **PE 10-8A, PE 10-8B**

# *At a Glance* 10

**OBJ. 1**

### Describe and illustrate current liabilities related to accounts payable, current portion of long-term debt, and notes payable.

**Key Points**   Current liabilities are obligations that are to be paid out of current assets and are due within a short time, usually within one year. The three primary types of current liabilities are accounts payable, notes payable, and current portion of long-term debt.

| Learning Outcomes | Example Exercises | Practice Exercises |
|---|---|---|
| • Identify and define the most frequently reported current liabilities on the balance sheet. | | |
| • Determine the interest from interest-bearing and discounted notes payable. | EE10-1 | PE10-1A, 10-1B |

**OBJ. 2**

### Determine employer liabilities for payroll, including liabilities arising from employee earnings and deductions from earnings.

**Key Points**   An employer's liability for payroll is determined from employee total earnings, including overtime pay. From this amount, employee deductions are subtracted to arrive at the net pay to be paid to each employee. Most employers also incur liabilities for payroll taxes, such as social security tax, Medicare tax, federal unemployment compensation tax, and state unemployment compensation tax.

| Learning Outcomes | Example Exercises | Practice Exercises |
|---|---|---|
| • Compute the federal withholding tax from a wage bracket withholding table. | EE10-2 | PE10-2A, 10-2B |
| • Compute employee net pay, including deductions for social security and Medicare tax. | EE10-3 | PE10-3A, 10-3B |

**OBJ. 3**

### Describe payroll accounting systems that use a payroll register, employee earnings records, and a general journal.

**Key Points**   The payroll register is used in assembling and summarizing the data needed for each payroll period. The payroll register is supported by a detailed payroll record for each employee, called an *employee's earnings record*.

| Learning Outcomes | Example Exercises | Practice Exercises |
|---|---|---|
| • Journalize the employee's earnings, net pay, and payroll liabilities from the payroll register. | EE10-4 | PE10-4A, 10-4B |
| • Journalize the payroll tax expense. | EE10-5 | PE10-5A, 10-5B |
| • Describe elements of a payroll system, including the employee's earnings record, payroll checks, and internal controls. | | |

**OBJ. 4**

## Journalize entries for employee fringe benefits, including vacation pay and pensions.

**Key Points** Fringe benefits are expenses of the period in which the employees earn the benefits. Fringe benefits are recorded by debiting an expense account and crediting a liability account.

| Learning Outcomes | Example Exercises | Practice Exercises |
|---|---|---|
| • Journalize vacation pay. | EE10-6 | PE10-6A, 10-6B |
| • Distinguish and journalize defined contribution and defined benefit pension plans. | EE10-6 | PE10-6A, 10-6B |

**OBJ. 5**

## Describe the accounting treatment for contingent liabilities and journalize entries for product warranties.

**Key Points** A contingent liability is a potential obligation that results from a past transaction but depends on a future event. The accounting for contingent liabilities is summarized in Exhibit 8.

| Learning Outcomes | Example Exercises | Practice Exercises |
|---|---|---|
| • Describe the accounting for contingent liabilities. | | |
| • Journalize estimated warranty obligations and services granted under warranty. | EE10-7 | PE10-7A, 10-7B |

**OBJ. 6**

## Describe and illustrate the use of the quick ratio in analyzing a company's ability to pay its current liabilities.

**Key Points** The quick ratio is a measure of a company's ability to pay current liabilities within a short period of time. The quick ratio is computed by dividing quick assets by current liabilities. Quick assets include cash, temporary investments, accounts receivable, and other current assets that can be easily converted into cash. A quick ratio exceeding 1.0 is usually desirable.

| Learning Outcomes | Example Exercises | Practice Exercises |
|---|---|---|
| • Describe the quick ratio. | | |
| • Compute and evaluate the quick ratio. | EE10-8 | PE10-8A, 10-8B |

## Key Terms

contingent liabilities (469)
current position analysis (472)
defined benefit plan (467)
defined contribution plan (467)
employee's earnings record (462)

FICA tax (456)
fringe benefits (466)
gross pay (454)
net pay (454)
payroll (453)

payroll register (460)
pension (467)
quick assets (472)
quick ratio (472)

## Illustrative Problem

Selected transactions of Taylor Company, completed during the fiscal year ended December 31, are as follows:

Mar.  1.  Purchased merchandise on account from Kelvin Co., $20,000.

Apr.  10.  Issued a 60-day, 12% note for $20,000 to Kelvin Co. on account.

June  9.  Paid Kelvin Co. the amount owed on the note of April 10.

Aug.  1.  Issued a $50,000, 90-day note to Harold Co. in exchange for a building. Harold Co. discounted the note at 15%.

Oct.  30.  Paid Harold Co. the amount due on the note of August 1.

Dec.  27.  Journalized the entry to record the biweekly payroll. A summary of the payroll record follows:

| | | |
|---|---:|---:|
| Salary distribution: | | |
|    Sales | $63,400 | |
|    Officers | 36,600 | |
|    Office | 10,000 | $110,000 |
| Deductions: | | |
|    Social security tax | $ 6,600 | |
|    Medicare tax | 1,650 | |
|    Federal income tax withheld | 17,600 | |
|    State income tax withheld | 4,950 | |
|    Savings bond deductions | 850 | |
|    Medical insurance deductions | 1,120 | 32,770 |
| Net amount | | $ 77,230 |

27.  Journalized the entry to record payroll taxes for social security and Medicare from the biweekly payroll.

30.  Issued a check in payment of liabilities for employees' federal income tax of $17,600, social security tax of $13,200, and Medicare tax of $3,300.

31.  Issued a check for $9,500 to the pension fund trustee to fully fund the pension cost for December.

31.  Journalized an entry to record the employees' accrued vacation pay, $36,100.

31.  Journalized an entry to record the estimated accrued product warranty liability, $37,240.

### Instructions

Journalize the preceding transactions.

## Solution

| | | | | | |
|---|---|---|---|---:|---:|
| Mar. | 1 | Merchandise Inventory | | 20,000 | |
| | |     Accounts Payable—Kelvin Co. | | | 20,000 |
| | | | | | |
| Apr. | 10 | Accounts Payable—Kelvin Co. | | 20,000 | |
| | |     Notes Payable | | | 20,000 |
| | | | | | |
| June | 9 | Notes Payable | | 20,000 | |
| | | Interest Expense | | 400 | |
| | |     Cash | | | 20,400 |
| | | | | | |
| Aug. | 1 | Building | | 48,125 | |
| | | Interest Expense | | 1,875 | |
| | |     Notes Payable | | | 50,000 |
| | | | | | |
| Oct. | 30 | Notes Payable | | 50,000 | |
| | |     Cash | | | 50,000 |
| | | | | | |
| Dec. | 27 | Sales Salaries Expense | | 63,400 | |
| | | Officers Salaries Expense | | 36,600 | |
| | | Office Salaries Expense | | 10,000 | |
| | |     Social Security Tax Payable | | | 6,600 |
| | |     Medicare Tax Payable | | | 1,650 |
| | |     Employees Federal Income Tax Payable | | | 17,600 |
| | |     Employees State Income Tax Payable | | | 4,950 |
| | |     Bond Deductions Payable | | | 850 |
| | |     Medical Insurance Payable | | | 1,120 |
| | |     Salaries Payable | | | 77,230 |
| | | | | | |
| | 27 | Payroll Tax Expense | | 8,250 | |
| | |     Social Security Tax Payable | | | 6,600 |
| | |     Medicare Tax Payable | | | 1,650 |
| | | | | | |
| | 30 | Employees Federal Income Tax Payable | | 17,600 | |
| | | Social Security Tax Payable | | 13,200 | |
| | | Medicare Tax Payable | | 3,300 | |
| | |     Cash | | | 34,100 |
| | | | | | |
| | 31 | Pension Expense | | 9,500 | |
| | |     Cash | | | 9,500 |
| | |         Fund pension cost. | | | |
| | | | | | |
| | 31 | Vacation Pay Expense | | 36,100 | |
| | |     Vacation Pay Payable | | | 36,100 |
| | |         Accrue vacation pay. | | | |
| | | | | | |
| | 31 | Product Warranty Expense | | 37,240 | |
| | |     Product Warranty Payable | | | 37,240 |
| | |         Accrue warranty expense. | | | |

## Discussion Questions

1. Does a discounted note payable provide credit without interest? Discuss.

2. Employees are subject to taxes withheld from their paychecks.

   a. List the federal taxes withheld from most employee paychecks.
   b. Give the title of the accounts credited by amounts withheld.

3. Why are deductions from employees' earnings classified as liabilities for the employer?

4. For each of the following payroll-related taxes, indicate whether they generally apply to (a) employees only, (b) employers only, or (c) both employees and employers:

   1. Federal income tax
   2. Medicare tax
   3. Social security tax
   4. Federal unemployment compensation tax
   5. State unemployment compensation tax

5. What are the principal reasons for using a special payroll checking account?

6. Explain how a payroll system that is properly designed and operated tends to ensure that wages paid are based on hours actually worked.

7. To match revenues and expenses properly, should the expense for employee vacation pay be recorded in the period during which the vacation privilege is earned or during the period in which the vacation is taken? Discuss.

8. Identify several factors that influence the future pension obligation of an employer under a defined benefit pension plan.

9. When should the liability associated with a product warranty be recorded? Discuss.

10. General Motors Corporation reported $7.0 billion of product warranties in the Current Liabilities section of a recent balance sheet. How would costs of repairing a defective product be recorded?

# Practice Exercises

**OBJ. 1**   EE 10-1 *p. 453*   **PE 10-1A**   **Proceeds from notes payable**

On September 1, Rongo Co. issued a 45-day note with a face amount of $80,000 to Simone Co. for merchandise inventory.

a. Determine the proceeds of the note, assuming the note carries an interest rate of 8%.

b. Determine the proceeds of the note, assuming the note is discounted at 8%.

**OBJ. 1**   EE 10-1 *p. 453*   **PE 10-1B**   **Proceeds from notes payable**

On February 1, Tectronic Co. issued a 60-day note with a face amount of $120,000 to Tokai Warehouse Co. for cash.

a. Determine the proceeds of the note, assuming the note carries an interest rate of 9%.

b. Determine the proceeds of the note, assuming the note is discounted at 9%.

**OBJ. 2**   EE 10-2 *p. 455*   **PE 10-2A**   **Federal income tax withholding**

Bob Tappert's weekly gross earnings for the present week were $1,600. Tappert has one exemption. Using the wage bracket withholding table in Exhibit 3 with a $70 standard withholding allowance for each exemption, what is Tappert's federal income tax withholding?

**OBJ. 2**   EE 10-2 *p. 455*   **PE 10-2B**   **Federal income tax withholding**

John Wolfe's weekly gross earnings for the present week were $2,200. Wolfe has two exemptions. Using the wage bracket withholding table in Exhibit 3 with a $70 standard withholding allowance for each exemption, what is Wolfe's federal income tax withholding?

**OBJ. 2**   EE 10-3 *p. 457*   **PE 10-3A**   **Employee net pay**

Bob Tappert's weekly gross earnings for the week ending December 18 were $1,600, and his federal income tax withholding was $296.16. Assuming the social security rate is 6% and Medicare is 1.5% of all earnings, what is Tappert's net pay?

**OBJ. 2**   EE 10-3 *p. 457*   **PE 10-3B**   **Employee net pay**

John Wolfe's weekly gross earnings for the week ending September 5 were $2,200, and his federal income tax withholding was $444.88. Assuming the social security rate is 6% and Medicare is 1.5% of all earnings, what is Wolfe's net pay?

**OBJ. 3**   EE 10-4 *p. 461*   **PE 10-4A**   **Journalize period payroll**

The payroll register of Gregory Communications Co. indicates $4,080 of social security withheld and $1,020 of Medicare tax withheld on total salaries of $68,000 for the period. Federal withholding for the period totaled $13,464.

     Provide the journal entry for the period's payroll.

**OBJ. 3**   EE 10-4 *p. 461*   **PE 10-4B**   **Journalize period payroll**

The payroll register of Russert Construction Co. indicates $18,000 of social security withheld and $4,500 of Medicare tax withheld on total salaries of $300,000 for the period.

Retirement savings withheld from employee paychecks were $18,000 for the period. Federal withholding for the period totaled $59,400.

Provide the journal entry for the period's payroll.

---

OBJ. 3   EE 10-5 *p. 462*   **PE 10-5A**   **Journalize payroll tax**

The payroll register of Gregory Communications Co. indicates $4,080 of social security withheld and $1,020 of Medicare tax withheld on total salaries of $68,000 for the period. Assume earnings subject to state and federal unemployment compensation taxes are $12,500, at the federal rate of 0.8% and the state rate of 5.4%.

Provide the journal entry to record the payroll tax expense for the period.

---

OBJ. 3   EE 10-5 *p. 462*   **PE 10-5B**   **Journalize payroll tax**

The payroll register of Russert Construction Co. indicates $18,000 of social security withheld and $4,500 of Medicare tax withheld on total salaries of $300,000 for the period. Assume earnings subject to state and federal unemployment compensation taxes are $13,000, at the federal rate of 0.8% and the state rate of 5.4%.

Provide the journal entry to record the payroll tax expense for the period.

---

OBJ. 4   EE 10-6 *p. 468*   **PE 10-6A**   **Vacation pay and pension benefits**

Lutes Company provides its employees with vacation benefits and a defined contribution pension plan. Employees earned vacation pay of $25,500 for the period. The pension plan requires a contribution to the plan administrator equal to 8% of employee salaries. Salaries were $340,000 during the period.

Provide the journal entry for the (a) vacation pay and (b) pension benefit.

---

OBJ. 4   EE 10-6 *p. 468*   **PE 10-6B**   **Vacation pay and pension benefits**

Wang Equipment Company provides its employees vacation benefits and a defined benefit pension plan. Employees earned vacation pay of $42,000 for the period. The pension formula calculated a pension cost of $273,000. Only $210,000 was contributed to the pension plan administrator.

Provide the journal entry for the (a) vacation pay and (b) pension benefit.

---

OBJ. 5   EE 10-7 *p. 470*   **PE 10-7A**   **Estimated warranty liability**

Zinn Co. sold $500,000 of equipment during May under a one-year warranty. The cost to repair defects under the warranty is estimated at 5% of the sales price. On October 10, a customer required a $100 part replacement, plus $65 of labor under the warranty.

Provide the journal entry for (a) the estimated warranty expense on May 31 and (b) the October 10 warranty work.

---

OBJ. 5   EE 10-7 *p. 470*   **PE 10-7B**   **Estimated warranty liability**

Caldwell Industries sold $410,000 of consumer electronics during August under a nine-month warranty. The cost to repair defects under the warranty is estimated at 4% of the sales price. On October 15, a customer was given $110 cash under terms of the warranty.

Provide the journal entry for (a) the estimated warranty expense on August 31 and (b) the October 15 cash payment.

---

OBJ. 6   EE 10-8 *p. 473*   **PE 10-8A**   **Quick ratio**

**F·A·I**

Grangel Company reported the following current assets and liabilities for December 31, 2012 and 2011:

*Learning Objectives*    *Example Exercises*

|  | Dec. 31, 2012 | Dec. 31, 2011 |
|---|---|---|
| Cash | $ 620 | $ 560 |
| Temporary investments | 1,330 | 1,250 |
| Accounts receivable | 850 | 830 |
| Inventory | 1,000 | 1,000 |
| Accounts payable | 2,800 | 2,200 |

a. Compute the quick ratio for December 31, 2012 and 2011.

b. Interpret the company's quick ratio. Is the quick ratio improving or declining?

**OBJ. 6**   **EE 10-8** *p. 473*   **PE 10-8B**   **Quick ratio**

Tappert Company reported the following current assets and liabilities for December 31, 2012 and 2011:

|  | Dec. 31, 2012 | Dec. 31, 2011 |
|---|---|---|
| Cash | $ 990 | $ 860 |
| Temporary investments | 1,910 | 1,500 |
| Accounts receivable | 1,600 | 1,280 |
| Inventory | 2,000 | 1,400 |
| Accounts payable | 3,000 | 2,800 |

a. Compute the quick ratio for December 31, 2012 and 2011.

b. Interpret the company's quick ratio. Is the quick ratio improving or declining?

# Exercises

**OBJ. 1**

✔ Total current liabilities, $782,500

### EX 10-1   Current liabilities

New Wave Co. sold 10,000 annual subscriptions of *Game Life* for $75 during December 2012. These new subscribers will receive monthly issues, beginning in January 2013. In addition, the business had taxable income of $550,000 during the first calendar quarter of 2013. The federal tax rate is 40%. A quarterly tax payment will be made on April 7, 2013.

Prepare the Current Liabilities section of the balance sheet for New Wave Co. on March 31, 2013.

**OBJ. 1**

### EX 10-2   Entries for discounting notes payable

TKR Enterprises issues a 30-day note for $570,000 to Sweeney Industries for merchandise inventory. Sweeney Industries discounts the note at 8%.

a. Journalize TKR Enterprises' entries to record:

   1. the issuance of the note.

   2. the payment of the note at maturity.

b. Journalize Sweeney Industries' entries to record:

   1. the receipt of the note.

   2. the receipt of the payment of the note at maturity.

**OBJ. 1**

### EX 10-3   Evaluate alternative notes

A borrower has two alternatives for a loan: (1) issue a $180,000, 45-day, 10% note or (2) issue a $180,000, 45-day note that the creditor discounts at 10%.

a. Calculate the amount of the interest expense for each option.

b. Determine the proceeds received by the borrower in each situation.

c. ━━━▶ Which alternative is more favorable to the borrower? Explain.

OBJ. 1

### EX 10-4   Entries for notes payable

A business issued a 45-day, 6% note for $80,000 to a creditor on account. Journalize the entries to record (a) the issuance of the note and (b) the payment of the note at maturity, including interest.

OBJ. 1

### EX 10-5   Entries for discounted note payable

A business issued a 30-day note for $72,000 to a creditor on account. The note was discounted at 7%. Journalize the entries to record (a) the issuance of the note and (b) the payment of the note at maturity.

OBJ. 1

### EX 10-6   Fixed asset purchases with note

On June 30, Beahm Management Company purchased land for $250,000 and a building for $350,000, paying $300,000 cash and issuing an 8% note for the balance, secured by a mortgage on the property. The terms of the note provide for 20 semiannual payments of $15,000 on the principal plus the interest accrued from the date of the preceding payment. Journalize the entry to record (a) the transaction on June 30, (b) the payment of the first installment on December 31, and (c) the payment of the second installment the following June 30.

OBJ. 1

### EX 10-7   Current portion of long-term debt

Burger King Holdings, Inc., the operator and franchisor of Burger King restaurants, reported the following information about its long-term debt in the notes to a recent financial statement:

Long-term debt is comprised of the following:

| | June 30 | |
|---|---|---|
| | **2009** | **2008** |
| Notes payable | $823,100,000 | $876,200,000 |
| Less current portion | (67,500,000) | (7,400,000) |
| Long-term debt | $755,600,000 | $868,800,000 |

a. How much of the notes payable was disclosed as a current liability on the June 30, 2009, balance sheet?

b. How much did the total current liabilities change between 2008 and 2009 as a result of the current portion of long-term debt?

c. If Burger King did not issue additional notes payable during 2010, what would be the total notes payable on June 30, 2010?

OBJ. 2
✔ b. Net pay, 2,725.75

### EX 10-8   Calculate payroll

An employee earns $60 per hour and 1.5 times that rate for all hours in excess of 40 hours per week. Assume that the employee worked 55 hours during the week, Assume further that the social security tax rate was 6.0%, the Medicare tax rate was 1.5%, and federal income tax to be withheld was $743.

a. Determine the gross pay for the week.

b. Determine the net pay for the week.

OBJ. 2
✔ Administrator net pay, $1,776.92

### EX 10-9   Calculate payroll

Donohue Professional Services has three employees—a consultant, a computer programmer, and an administrator. The following payroll information is available for each employee:

| | Consultant | Computer Programmer | Administrator |
|---|---|---|---|
| Regular earnings rate | $2,800 per week | $30 per hour | $42 per hour |
| Overtime earnings rate | Not applicable | 1.5 times hourly rate | 2 times hourly rate |
| Number of withholding allowances | 3 | 2 | 1 |

For the current pay period, the computer programmer worked 60 hours and the administrator worked 50 hours. The federal income tax withheld for all three employees, who are single, can be determined from the wage bracket withholding table in Exhibit 3 in the chapter. Assume further that the social security tax rate was 6.0%, the Medicare tax rate was 1.5%, and one withholding allowance is $70.

Determine the gross pay and the net pay for each of the three employees for the current pay period.

---

**OBJ. 2, 3**

✔ a. (3) Total earnings, $900,000

**EX 10-10  Summary payroll data**

In the following summary of data for a payroll period, some amounts have been intentionally omitted:

| Earnings: | |
|---|---|
| 1. At regular rate | ? |
| 2. At overtime rate | $135,000 |
| 3. Total earnings | ? |
| Deductions: | |
| 4. Social security tax | 54,000 |
| 5. Medicare tax | 13,500 |
| 6. Income tax withheld | 225,000 |
| 7. Medical insurance | 31,500 |
| 8. Union dues | ? |
| 9. Total deductions | 335,250 |
| 10. Net amount paid | 564,750 |
| Accounts debited: | |
| 11. Factory Wages | 475,000 |
| 12. Sales Salaries | ? |
| 13. Office Salaries | 200,000 |

a. Calculate the amounts omitted in lines (1), (3), (8), and (12).

b. Journalize the entry to record the payroll accrual.

c. Journalize the entry to record the payment of the payroll.

---

**OBJ. 3**

✔ a. $85,000

**EX 10-11  Payroll tax entries**

According to a summary of the payroll of Brooks Industries Co., $1,100,000 was subject to the 6.0% social security tax and the 1.5% Medicare tax. Also, $50,000 was subject to state and federal unemployment taxes.

a. Calculate the employer's payroll taxes, using the following rates: state unemployment, 4.2%; federal unemployment, 0.8%.

b. Journalize the entry to record the accrual of payroll taxes.

---

**OBJ. 3**

**EX 10-12  Payroll entries**

The payroll register for Robinson Company for the week ended November 18 indicated the following:

| | |
|---|---|
| Salaries | $1,300,000 |
| Social security tax withheld | 61,100 |
| Medicare tax withheld | 19,500 |
| Federal income tax withheld | 260,000 |

In addition, state and federal unemployment taxes were calculated at the rate of 5.2% and 0.8%, respectively, on $240,000 of salaries.

a. Journalize the entry to record the payroll for the week of November 18.

b. Journalize the entry to record the payroll tax expense incurred for the week of November 18.

OBJ. 3

### EX 10-13 Payroll entries

Faber Company had gross wages of $110,000 during the week ended June 17. The amount of wages subject to social security tax was $110,000, while the amount of wages subject to federal and state unemployment taxes was $15,000. Tax rates are as follows:

| | |
|---|---|
| Social security | 6.0% |
| Medicare | 1.5% |
| State unemployment | 5.4% |
| Federal unemployment | 0.8% |

The total amount withheld from employee wages for federal taxes was $22,000.

a. Journalize the entry to record the payroll for the week of June 17.

b. Journalize the entry to record the payroll tax expense incurred for the week of June 17.

OBJ. 3

### EX 10-14 Payroll internal control procedures

Big Dave's Pizza is a pizza restaurant specializing in the sale of pizza by the slice. The store employs 10 full-time and 15 part-time workers. The store's weekly payroll averages $5,600 for all 25 workers.

Big Dave's Pizza uses a personal computer to assist in preparing paychecks. Each week, the store's accountant collects employee time cards and enters the hours worked into the payroll program. The payroll program calculates each employee's pay and prints a paycheck. The accountant uses a check-signing machine to sign the paychecks. Next, the restaurant's owner authorizes the transfer of funds from the restaurant's regular bank account to the payroll account.

For the week of June 11, the accountant accidentally recorded 200 hours worked instead of 40 hours for one of the full-time employees.

➤ Does Big Dave's Pizza have internal controls in place to catch this error? If so, how will this error be detected?

OBJ. 3

### EX 10-15 Internal control procedures

Matt's Bikes is a small manufacturer of specialty bicycles. The company employs 18 production workers and four administrative persons. The following procedures are used to process the company's weekly payroll:

a. Whenever an employee receives a pay raise, the supervisor must fill out a wage adjustment form, which is signed by the company president. This form is used to change the employee's wage rate in the payroll system.

b. All employees are required to record their hours worked by clocking in and out on a time clock. Employees must clock out for lunch break. Due to congestion around the time clock area at lunch time, management has not objected to having one employee clock in and out for an entire department.

c. Whenever a salaried employee is terminated, Personnel authorizes Payroll to remove the employee from the payroll system. However, this procedure is not required when an hourly worker is terminated. Hourly employees only receive a paycheck if their time cards show hours worked. The computer automatically drops an employee from the payroll system when that employee has six consecutive weeks with no hours worked.

d. Paychecks are signed by using a check-signing machine. This machine is located in the main office so that it can be easily accessed by anyone needing a check signed.

e. Matt's Bikes maintains a separate checking account for payroll checks. Each week, the total net pay for all employees is transferred from the company's regular bank account to the payroll account.

➤ State whether each of the procedures is appropriate or inappropriate after considering the principles of internal control. If a procedure is inappropriate, describe the appropriate procedure.

**OBJ. 4**

**EX 10-16   Accrued vacation pay**

A business provides its employees with varying amounts of vacation per year, depending on the length of employment. The estimated amount of the current year's vacation pay is $61,200.

a. Journalize the adjusting entry required on January 31, the end of the first month of the current year, to record the accrued vacation pay.

b. How is the vacation pay reported on the company's balance sheet? When is this amount removed from the company's balance sheet?

**OBJ. 4**

**EX 10-17   Pension plan entries**

Wren Co. operates a chain of gift shops. The company maintains a defined contribution pension plan for its employees. The plan requires quarterly installments to be paid to the funding agent, Whims Funds, by the fifteenth of the month following the end of each quarter. Assume that the pension cost is $141,500 for the quarter ended March 31.

a. Journalize the entries to record the accrued pension liability on March 31 and the payment to the funding agent on April 15.

b. How does a defined contribution plan differ from a defined benefit plan?

**OBJ. 4**

**EX 10-18   Defined benefit pension plan terms**

In a recent year's financial statements, Procter & Gamble showed an unfunded pension liability of $3,706 million and a periodic pension cost of $341 million.

Explain the meaning of the $3,706 million unfunded pension liability and the $341 million periodic pension cost.

**OBJ. 5**

**EX 10-19   Accrued product warranty**

Parker Products Co. warrants its products for one year. The estimated product warranty is 3% of sales. Assume that sales were $442,000 for September. In October, a customer received warranty repairs requiring $110 of parts and $86 of labor.

a. Journalize the adjusting entry required at September 30, the end of the first month of the current fiscal year, to record the accrued product warranty.

b. Journalize the entry to record the warranty work provided in October.

**OBJ. 5**

**EX 10-20   Accrued product warranty**

General Motors Corporation disclosed estimated product warranty payable for comparative years as follows:

|  | (in millions) | |
|---|---|---|
|  | **12/31/08** | **12/31/07** |
| Current estimated product warranty payable | $3,792 | $4,655 |
| Noncurrent estimated product warranty payable | 4,699 | 4,960 |
| Total | $8,491 | $9,615 |

GM's sales were $177,594 million in 2007 and decreased to $147,732 million in 2008. Assume that the total paid on warranty claims during 2008 was $5,000 million.

a. ▬▬▶ Why are short- and long-term estimated warranty liabilities separately disclosed?

b. Provide the journal entry for the 2008 product warranty expense.

c. What two conditions must be met in order for a product warranty liability to be reported in the financial statements?

OBJ. 5

### EX 10-21 Contingent liabilities

Several months ago, Reiltz Industries, Inc., experienced a hazardous materials spill at one of its plants. As a result, the Environmental Protection Agency (EPA) fined the company $570,000. The company is contesting the fine. In addition, an employee is seeking $560,000 in damages related to the spill. Lastly, a homeowner has sued the company for $364,000. The homeowner lives 35 miles from the plant, but believes that the incident has reduced the home's resale value by $364,000.

Reiltz's legal counsel believes that it is probable that the EPA fine will stand. In addition, counsel indicates that an out-of-court settlement of $238,000 has recently been reached with the employee. The final papers will be signed next week. Counsel believes that the homeowner's case is much weaker and will be decided in favor of Reiltz. Other litigation related to the spill is possible, but the damage amounts are uncertain.

a. Journalize the contingent liabilities associated with the hazardous materials spill. Use the account "Damage Awards and Fines" to recognize the expense for the period.

b.  Prepare a note disclosure relating to this incident.

OBJ. 6

✔ a. 2012: 1.0

### EX 10-22 Quick ratio

CCB Co. had the following current assets and liabilities for two comparative years:

|  | Dec. 31, 2012 | Dec. 31, 2011 |
|---|---|---|
| Current assets: |  |  |
| Cash | $ 506,000 | $ 524,000 |
| Accounts receivable | 354,000 | 364,000 |
| Inventory | 240,000 | 200,000 |
| Total current assets | $1,100,000 | $1,088,000 |
| Current liabilities: |  |  |
| Current portion of long-term debt | $ 160,000 | $ 120,000 |
| Accounts payable | 265,000 | 220,000 |
| Accrued and other current liabilities | 435,000 | 400,000 |
| Total current liabilities | $ 860,000 | $ 740,000 |

a. Determine the quick ratio for December 31, 2012 and 2011.

b.  Interpret the change in the quick ratio between the two balance sheet dates.

OBJ. 6

✔ a. Apple, 2.4

### EX 10-23 Quick ratio

The current assets and current liabilities for Apple Inc. and Dell Inc. are shown as follows at the end of a recent fiscal period:

|  | Apple Inc. (in millions) Sept. 26, 2009 | Dell Inc. (in millions) Jan. 29, 2010 |
|---|---|---|
| Current assets: |  |  |
| Cash and cash equivalents | $ 5,263 | $10,635 |
| Short-term investments | 18,201 | 373 |
| Accounts receivable | 4,496 | 8,543 |
| Inventories | 455 | 1,051 |
| Other current assets* | 3,140 | 3,643 |
| Total current assets | $31,555 | $24,245 |
| Current liabilities: |  |  |
| Accounts payable | $ 9,453 | $15,257 |
| Accrued and other current liabilities | 2,053 | 3,703 |
| Total current liabilities | $11,506 | $18,960 |

*These represent prepaid expense and other nonquick current assets.

a. Determine the quick ratio for both companies.

b. Interpret the quick ratio difference between the two companies.

## Problems Series A

OBJ. 1, 5

OBJ. 1, 5

### PR 10-1A   Liability transactions

The following items were selected from among the transactions completed by Isis Co. during the current year:

Feb  15.  Purchased merchandise on account from Viper Co., $260,000, terms n/30.

Mar. 17.  Issued a 45-day, 5% note for $260,000 to Viper Co., on account.

May   1.  Paid Viper Co. the amount owed on the note of March 17.

June 15.  Borrowed $300,000 from Ima Bank, issuing a 60-day, 9% note.

July  21.  Purchased tools by issuing a $240,000, 60-day note to Charger Co., which discounted the note at the rate of 7%.

Aug. 14.  Paid Ima Bank the interest due on the note of June 15 and renewed the loan by issuing a new 30-day, 10% note for $300,000. (Journalize both the debit and credit to the notes payable account.)

Sept. 13.  Paid Ima Bank the amount due on the note of August 14.

      19.  Paid Charger Co. the amount due on the note of July 21.

Dec.   1.  Purchased office equipment from Challenger Co. for $235,000, paying $35,000 and issuing a series of ten 7.5% notes for $20,000 each, coming due at 30-day intervals.

      12.  Settled a product liability lawsuit with a customer for $121,600, payable in January. Isis accrued the loss in a litigation claims payable account.

      31.  Paid the amount due Challenger Co. on the first note in the series issued on December 1.

### Instructions

1. Journalize the transactions.

2. Journalize the adjusting entry for each of the following accrued expenses at the end of the current year: (a) product warranty cost, $26,240; (b) interest on the nine remaining notes owed to Challenger Co.

---

OBJ. 2, 3

✔ 1. (b) Dr. Payroll
Tax Expense, $42,465

### PR 10-2A   Entries for payroll and payroll taxes

The following information about the payroll for the week ended December 30 was obtained from the records of Arnsparger Equipment Co.:

| Salaries: | | Deductions: | |
|---|---:|---|---:|
| Sales salaries | $270,000 | Income tax withheld | $ 95,920 |
| Warehouse salaries | 142,000 | Social security tax withheld | 32,700 |
| Office salaries | 133,000 | Medicare tax withheld | 8,175 |
| | $545,000 | U.S. savings bonds | 11,990 |
| | | Group insurance | 9,810 |
| | | | $158,595 |

Tax rates assumed:

   Social security, 6%

   Medicare, 1.5%

   State unemployment (employer only), 4.5%

   Federal unemployment (employer only), 0.8%

### Instructions

1. Assuming that the payroll for the last week of the year is to be paid on December 31, journalize the following entries:

   a. December 30, to record the payroll.

   b. December 30, to record the employer's payroll taxes on the payroll to be paid on December 31. Of the total payroll for the last week of the year, $30,000 is subject to unemployment compensation taxes.

*(continued)*

2. Assuming that the payroll for the last week of the year is to be paid on January 5 of the following fiscal year, journalize the following entries:

 a. December 30, to record the payroll.

 b. January 5, to record the employer's payroll taxes on the payroll to be paid on January 5. Since it is a new fiscal year, all $545,000 in salaries is subject to unemployment compensation taxes.

OBJ. 2, 3

✔ 2. (e) $32,274

**PR 10-3A   Wage and tax statement data on employer FICA tax**

Courtside Concepts Co. began business on January 2, 2011. Salaries were paid to employees on the last day of each month, and social security tax, Medicare tax, and federal income tax were withheld in the required amounts. An employee who is hired in the middle of the month receives half the monthly salary for that month. All required payroll tax reports were filed, and the correct amount of payroll taxes was remitted by the company for the calendar year. Early in 2012, before the Wage and Tax Statements (Form W-2) could be prepared for distribution to employees and for filing with the Social Security Administration, the employees' earnings records were inadvertently destroyed.

None of the employees resigned or were discharged during the year, and there were no changes in salary rates. The social security tax was withheld at the rate of 6.0% and Medicare tax at the rate of 1.5% on salary. Data on dates of employment, salary rates, and employees' income taxes withheld, which are summarized as follows, were obtained from personnel records and payroll records:

| Employee | Date First Employed | Monthly Salary | Monthly Income Tax Withheld |
|---|---|---|---|
| Garnett | Jan. 2 | $ 4,400 | $ 706 |
| Kidd | Oct. 1 | 7,200 | 1,442 |
| J. O'Neal | Apr. 16 | 3,600 | 506 |
| Bryant | Nov. 1 | 3,000 | 356 |
| S. O'Neal | Jan. 16 | 12,800 | 3,012 |
| Marbury | Dec. 1 | 5,000 | 856 |
| Duncan | Feb. 1 | 11,200 | 2,564 |

**Instructions**

1. Calculate the amounts to be reported on each employee's Wage and Tax Statement (Form W-2) for 2011, arranging the data in the following form:

| Employee | Gross Earnings | Federal Income Tax Withheld | Social Security Tax Withheld | Medicare Tax Withheld |
|---|---|---|---|---|

2. Calculate the following employer payroll taxes for the year: (a) social security; (b) Medicare; (c) state unemployment compensation at 4.6% on the first $10,000 of each employee's earnings; (d) federal unemployment compensation at 0.8% on the first $10,000 of each employee's earnings; (e) total.

OBJ. 2, 3

✔ 3. Dr. Payroll Tax Expense, $1,002.93

**PR 10-4A   Payroll register**

*If the working papers correlating with this textbook are not used, omit Problem 10-4A.*

The payroll register for Knapp Co. for the week ended September 14, 2012, is presented in the working papers.

**Instructions**

1. Journalize the entry to record the payroll for the week.

2. Journalize the entry to record the issuance of the checks to employees.

3. Journalize the entry to record the employer's payroll taxes for the week. Assume the following tax rates: state unemployment, 3.6%; federal unemployment, 0.8%. Of the earnings, $2,000 is subject to unemployment taxes.

4. Journalize the entry to record a check issued on September 17 to Fourth National Bank in payment of employees' income taxes, $2,062.17, social security taxes, $1,463.88, and Medicare taxes, $365.98.

OBJ. 2, 3

✔ 1. Total net amount
payable, $11,180.93

### PR 10-5A   Payroll register

The following data for Throwback Industries, Inc., relate to the payroll for the week ended December 7, 2012:

| Employee | Hours Worked | Hourly Rate | Weekly Salary | Federal Income Tax | U.S. Savings Bonds |
|---|---|---|---|---|---|
| Blanda | 48 | $44.00 | | $526.24 | $ 45 |
| Dawson | 42 | 38.00 | | 351.31 | 50 |
| Fouts | 44 | 46.00 | | 402.04 | 55 |
| Griese | 36 | 32.00 | | 241.92 | 65 |
| Namath | 45 | 40.00 | | 399.00 | 0 |
| Marino | | | $2,200 | 528.00 | 44 |
| Staubach | 35 | 29.00 | | 152.25 | 110 |
| Starr | | | 2,450 | 539.00 | 102 |
| Unitas | 41 | 38.00 | | 315.40 | 0 |

Employees Marino and Starr are office staff, and all of the other employees are sales personnel. All sales personnel are paid 1½ times the regular rate for all hours in excess of 40 hours per week. The social security tax rate is 6.0%, and Medicare tax is 1.5% of each employee's annual earnings. The next payroll check to be used is No. 625.

### Instructions

1.  Prepare a payroll register for Throwback Industries, Inc., for the week ended December 7, 2012. Use the following columns for the payroll register: Name, Total Hours, Regular Earnings, Overtime Earnings, Total Earnings, Social Security Tax, Medicare Tax, Federal Income Tax, U.S. Savings Bonds, Total Deductions, Net Pay, Ck. No., Sales Salaries Expense, and Office Salaries Expense.

2.  Journalize the entry to record the payroll sales for the week.

OBJ. 2, 3, 4

### PR 10-6A   Payroll accounts and year-end entries

The following accounts, with the balances indicated, appear in the ledger of Quinn Co. on December 1 of the current year:

| | | | | | |
|---|---|---|---|---|---|
| 311 | Salaries Payable | — | 318 | Bond Deductions Payable | $ 4,200 |
| 312 | Social Security Tax Payable | $10,830 | 319 | Medical Insurance Payable | 33,000 |
| 313 | Medicare Tax Payable | 2,850 | 511 | Operations Salaries Expense | 1,150,000 |
| 314 | Employees Federal Income Tax Payable | 17,575 | 611 | Officers Salaries Expense | 750,000 |
| 315 | Employees State Income Tax Payable | 17,100 | 612 | Office Salaries Expense | 190,000 |
| 316 | State Unemployment Tax Payable | 1,800 | 619 | Payroll Tax Expense | 163,680 |
| 317 | Federal Unemployment Tax Payable | 600 | | | |

The following transactions relating to payroll, payroll deductions, and payroll taxes occurred during December:

Dec.  2.  Issued Check No. 210 for $4,200 to Ace Bank to purchase U.S. savings bonds for employees.

   5.  Issued Check No. 211 to Ace Bank for $31,255 in payment of $10,830 of social security tax, $2,850 of Medicare tax, and $17,575 of employees' federal income tax due.

   16.  Journalized the entry to record the biweekly payroll. A summary of the payroll record follows:

| | | | |
|---|---|---|---|
| Salary distribution: | | | |
| | Operations | $52,200 | |
| | Officers | 34,100 | |
| | Office | 8,650 | $94,950 |
| Deductions: | | | |
| | Social security tax | $ 5,697 | |
| | Medicare tax | 1,424 | |
| | Federal income tax withheld | 17,566 | |
| | State income tax withheld | 4,273 | |
| | Savings bond deductions | 2,100 | |
| | Medical insurance deductions | 5,500 | 36,560 |
| Net amount | | | $58,390 |

Dec. 16. Issued Check No. 220 in payment of the net amount of the biweekly payroll.

16. Journalized the entry to record payroll taxes on employees' earnings of December 16: social security tax, $5,697; Medicare tax, $1,424; state unemployment tax, $450; federal unemployment tax, $150.

19. Issued Check No. 224 to Ace Bank for $31,048, in payment of $11,394 of social security tax, $2,848 of Medicare tax, and $17,566 of employees' federal income tax due.

19. Issued Check No. 229 to Blackwood Insurance Company for $33,000, in payment of the semiannual premium on the group medical insurance policy.

30. Journalized the entry to record the biweekly payroll. A summary of the payroll record follows:

| | | |
|---|---:|---:|
| Salary distribution: | | |
| Operations | $51,400 | |
| Officers | 34,100 | |
| Office | 8,400 | $93,900 |
| Deductions: | | |
| Social security tax | $ 5,634 | |
| Medicare tax | 1,409 | |
| Federal income tax withheld | 17,184 | |
| State income tax withheld | 4,226 | |
| Savings bond deductions | 2,100 | 30,553 |
| Net amount | | $63,347 |

30. Issued Check No. 341 in payment of the net amount of the biweekly payroll.

30. Journalized the entry to record payroll taxes on employees' earnings of December 30: social security tax, $5,634; Medicare tax, $1,409; state unemployment tax, $225; federal unemployment tax, $75.

30. Issued Check No. 243 for $25,599 to State Department of Revenue in payment of employees' state income tax due on December 31.

30. Issued Check No. 245 to Ace Bank for $4,200 to purchase U.S. savings bonds for employees.

31. Paid $50,000 to the employee pension plan. The annual pension cost is $65,000. (Record both the payment and unfunded pension liability.)

### Instructions

1. Journalize the transactions.
2. Journalize the following adjusting entries on December 31:
   a. Salaries accrued: operations salaries, $5,140; officers salaries, $3,410; office salaries, $840. The payroll taxes are immaterial and are not accrued.
   b. Vacation pay, $17,500.

## Problems Series B

OBJ. 1, 5

**PR 10-1B　Liability transactions**

The following items were selected from among the transactions completed by Javelin, Inc., during the current year:

Mar. 1. Borrowed $80,000 from Nova Company, issuing a 30-day, 9% note for that amount.

15. Purchased equipment by issuing a $180,000, 180-day note to Shelby Manufacturing Co., which discounted the note at the rate of 7.5%.

31. Paid Nova Company the interest due on the note of March 1 and renewed the loan by issuing a new 60-day, 9% note for $80,000. (Record both the debit and credit to the notes payable account.)

May 30. Paid Nova Company the amount due on the note of March 31.

July   6.  Purchased merchandise on account from Pacer Co., $56,000, terms, n/30.

Aug.   5.  Issued a 45-day, 8% note for $56,000 to Pacer Co., on account.

Sept. 11.  Paid Shelby Manufacturing Co. the amount due on the note of March 15.

      19.  Paid Pacer Co. the amount owed on the note of August 5.

Nov. 16.  Purchased store equipment from Gremlin Co. for $190,000, paying $40,000 and issuing a series of fifteen 6% notes for $10,000 each, coming due at 30-day intervals.

Dec. 16.  Paid the amount due Gremlin Co. on the first note in the series issued on November 16.

      21.  Settled a personal injury lawsuit with a customer for $55,250, to be paid in January. Javelin, Inc., accrued the loss in a litigation claims payable account.

### Instructions

1.  Journalize the transactions.

2.  Journalize the adjusting entry for each of the following accrued expenses at the end of the current year:

      a.  Product warranty cost, $13,520.

      b.  Interest on the 14 remaining notes owed to Gremlin Co.

---

**OBJ. 2, 3**

✔ 1. (b) Dr. Payroll Tax Expense, $67,248

### PR 10-2B   Entries for payroll and payroll taxes

The following information about the payroll for the week ended December 30 was obtained from the records of Dart Co.:

| Salaries: | | Deductions: | |
|---|---|---|---|
| Sales salaries | $546,000 | Income tax withheld | $172,480 |
| Warehouse salaries | 116,000 | Social security tax withheld | 52,800 |
| Office salaries | 218,000 | Medicare tax withheld | 13,200 |
| | $880,000 | U.S. savings bonds | 26,400 |
| | | Group insurance | 39,600 |
| | | | $304,480 |

Tax rates assumed:

    Social security, 6%

    Medicare, 1.5%

    State unemployment (employer only), 4.0%

    Federal unemployment (employer only), 0.8%

### Instructions

1.  Assuming that the payroll for the last week of the year is to be paid on December 31, journalize the following entries:

      a.  December 30, to record the payroll.

      b.  December 30, to record the employer's payroll taxes on the payroll to be paid on December 31. Of the total payroll for the last week of the year, $26,000 is subject to unemployment compensation taxes.

2.  Assuming that the payroll for the last week of the year is to be paid on January 4 of the following fiscal year, journalize the following entries:

      a.  December 30, to record the payroll.

      b.  January 4, to record the employer's payroll taxes on the payroll to be paid on January 4. Since it is a new fiscal year, all $880,000 in salaries is subject to unemployment compensation taxes.

---

**OBJ. 2, 3**

✔ 2. (e) $23,977.00

### PR 10-3B   Wage and tax statement data and employer FICA tax

Diamond Industries, Inc., began business on January 2, 2011. Salaries were paid to employees on the last day of each month, and social security tax, Medicare tax, and federal income tax were withheld in the required amounts. An employee who is hired in the middle of the month receives half the monthly salary for that month. All required payroll tax reports were filed, and the correct amount of payroll taxes was remitted by the company for the calendar year. Early in 2012, before the Wage and Tax Statements

(Form W-2) could be prepared for distribution to employees and for filing with the Social Security Administration, the employees' earnings records were inadvertently destroyed.

None of the employees resigned or were discharged during the year, and there were no changes in salary rates. The social security tax was withheld at the rate of 6.0% and Medicare tax at the rate of 1.5% on salary. Data on dates of employment, salary rates, and employees' income taxes withheld, which are summarized as follows, were obtained from personnel records and payroll records:

| Employee | Date First Employed | Monthly Salary | Monthly Income Tax Withheld |
|---|---|---|---|
| Beltran | Jan. 1 | $ 4,300 | $ 681 |
| Jeter | Apr. 16 | 11,000 | 2,508 |
| Lee | Aug. 1 | 7,800 | 1,612 |
| Rodriguez | Nov. 16 | 3,000 | 356 |
| Santana | Mar. 1 | 6,120 | 1,145 |
| Ramirez | May 16 | 3,840 | 566 |
| Ordonez | Dec. 1 | 4,000 | 606 |

### Instructions

1. Calculate the amounts to be reported on each employee's Wage and Tax Statement (Form W-2) for 2011, arranging the data in the following form:

| Employee | Gross Earnings | Federal Income Tax Withheld | Social Security Tax Withheld | Medicare Tax Withheld |
|---|---|---|---|---|

2. Calculate the following employer payroll taxes for the year: (a) social security; (b) Medicare; (c) state unemployment compensation at 4.4% on the first $9,000 of each employee's earnings; (d) federal unemployment compensation at 0.8% on the first $9,000 of each employee's earnings; (e) total.

---

OBJ. 2, 3

✔ 3. Dr. Payroll Tax Expense, $1,188.61

### PR 10-4B  Payroll register

*If the working papers correlating with this textbook are not used, omit Problem 10-4B.*

The payroll register for Ritchie Manufacturing Co. for the week ended September 14, 2012, is presented in the working papers.

### Instructions

1. Journalize the entry to record the payroll for the week.

2. Journalize the entry to record the issuance of the checks to employees.

3. Journalize the entry to record the employer's payroll taxes for the week. Assume the following tax rates: state unemployment, 3.4%; federal unemployment, 0.8%. Of the earnings, $2,200 is subject to unemployment taxes.

4. Journalize the entry to record a check issued on September 17 to Second National Bank in payment of employees' income taxes, $2,464.97, social security taxes, $1,753.92, and Medicare taxes, $438.50.

---

OBJ. 2, 3

✔ 1. Total net amount payable, $9,583.80

### PR 10-5B  Payroll register

The following data for Gridiron Industries, Inc., relate to the payroll for the week ended December 7, 2012:

| Employee | Hours Worked | Hourly Rate | Weekly Salary | Federal Income Tax | U.S. Savings Bonds |
|---|---|---|---|---|---|
| Aikman | 50 | $26.00 | | $328.90 | $45 |
| Csonka | | | $3,400 | 731.00 | 0 |
| Dickerson | 35 | 28.00 | | 186.20 | 38 |
| Elway | 44 | 34.00 | | 328.44 | 30 |
| Harris | 38 | 22.00 | | 175.56 | 45 |
| Motley | | | 2,000 | 480.00 | 68 |
| Nagurski | 45 | 26.00 | | 185.25 | 0 |
| Sanders | 45 | 27.00 | | 282.15 | 45 |
| Swann | 42 | 25.00 | | 215.00 | 0 |

Employees Csonka and Motley are office staff, and all of the other employees are sales personnel. All sales personnel are paid 1½ times the regular rate for all hours in excess of 40 hours per week. The social security tax rate is 6.0% of each employee's annual earnings, and Medicare tax is 1.5% of each employee's annual earnings. The next payroll check to be used is No. 328.

### Instructions

1. Prepare a payroll register for Gridiron Industries, Inc., for the week ended December 7, 2012. Use the following columns for the payroll register: Name, Total Hours, Regular Earnings, Overtime Earnings, Total Earnings, Social Security Tax, Medicare Tax, Federal Income Tax, U.S. Savings Bonds, Total Deductions, Net Pay, Ck. No., Sales Salaries Expense, and Office Salaries Expense.

2. Journalize the entry to record the payroll sales for the week.

---

**OBJ. 2, 3, 4**

### PR 10-6B    Payroll accounts and year-end entries

The following accounts, with the balances indicated, appear in the ledger of Codigo Co. on December 1 of the current year:

| | | | | | |
|---|---|---|---|---|---|
| 111 | Salaries Payable | — | 118 | Bond Deductions Payable | $ 2,520 |
| 112 | Social Security Tax Payable | $ 6,847 | 119 | Medical Insurance Payable | 2,800 |
| 113 | Medicare Tax Payable | 1,763 | 411 | Sales Salaries Expense | 778,000 |
| 114 | Employees Federal Income Tax Payable | 10,873 | 511 | Officers Salaries Expense | 375,000 |
| 115 | Employees State Income Tax Payable | 9,874 | 611 | Office Salaries Expense | 140,000 |
| 116 | State Unemployment Tax Payable | 1,400 | 618 | Payroll Tax Expense | 104,610 |
| 117 | Federal Unemployment Tax Payable | 400 | | | |

The following transactions relating to payroll, payroll deductions, and payroll taxes occurred during December:

Dec.   1. Issued Check No. 615 to Canal Insurance Company for $2,800, in payment of the semiannual premium on the group medical insurance policy.

      1. Issued Check No. 616 to Green Bank for $19,483, in payment for $6,847 of social security tax, $1,763 of Medicare tax, and $10,873 of employees' federal income tax due.

      2. Issued Check No. 617 for $2,520 to Green Bank to purchase U.S. savings bonds for employees.

    12. Journalized the entry to record the biweekly payroll. A summary of the payroll record follows:

| | | |
|---|---|---|
| Salary distribution: | | |
|   Sales | $35,300 | |
|   Officers | 17,000 | |
|   Office | 6,300 | $58,600 |
| Deductions: | | |
|   Social security tax | $ 3,516 | |
|   Medicare tax | 879 | |
|   Federal income tax withheld | 10,431 | |
|   State income tax withheld | 2,637 | |
|   Savings bond deductions | 1,260 | |
|   Medical insurance deductions | 467 | 19,190 |
| Net amount | | $39,410 |

    12. Issued Check No. 622 in payment of the net amount of the biweekly payroll.

    12. Journalized the entry to record payroll taxes on employees' earnings of December 12: social security tax, $3,516; Medicare tax, $879; state unemployment tax, $350; federal unemployment tax, $100.

    15. Issued Check No. 630 to Green Bank for $18,635, in payment for $7,032 of social security tax, $1,758 of Medicare tax, and $10,431 of employees' federal income tax due.

Dec. 26. Journalized the entry to record the biweekly payroll. A summary of the payroll record follows:

| Salary distribution: | | |
|---|---|---|
| Sales | $35,400 | |
| Officers | 17,250 | |
| Office | 6,400 | $59,050 |
| Deductions: | | |
| Social security tax | $ 3,543 | |
| Medicare tax | 886 | |
| Federal income tax withheld | 10,511 | |
| State income tax withheld | 2,657 | |
| Savings bond deductions | 1,260 | 18,857 |
| Net amount | | $40,193 |

26. Issued Check No. 640 for the net amount of the biweekly payroll.

26. Journalized the entry to record payroll taxes on employees' earnings of December 26: social security tax, $3,543; Medicare tax, $886; state unemployment tax, $170; federal unemployment tax, $45.

30. Issued Check No. 651 for $15,168 to State Department of Revenue, in payment of employees' state income tax due on December 31.

30. Issued Check No. 652 to Green Bank for $2,520 to purchase U.S. savings bonds for employees.

31. Paid $61,600 to the employee pension plan. The annual pension cost is $72,800. (Record both the payment and the unfunded pension liability.)

## Instructions

1. Journalize the transactions.

2. Journalize the following adjusting entries on December 31:

  a. Salaries accrued: sales salaries, $10,620; officers salaries, $5,175; office salaries, $1,920. The payroll taxes are immaterial and are not accrued.

  b. Vacation pay, $14,840.

## Comprehensive Problem 3

✔ 5. Total assets,
$2,563,840

GENERAL
LEDGER

Selected transactions completed by Gampfer Company during its first fiscal year ending December 31 were as follows:

Jan.   2. Issued a check to establish a petty cash fund of $3,200.

Mar. 14. Replenished the petty cash fund, based on the following summary of petty cash receipts: office supplies, $1,200; miscellaneous selling expense, $410; miscellaneous administrative expense, $620.

Apr. 21. Purchased $22,400 of merchandise on account, terms 1/10, n/30. The perpetual inventory system is used to account for inventory.

May 20. Paid the invoice of April 21 after the discount period had passed.

       23. Received cash from daily cash sales for $15,120. The amount indicated by the cash register was $15,152.

June 15. Received a 60-day, 10% note for $127,500 on the Cady account.

Aug. 14. Received amount owed on June 15 note, plus interest at the maturity date.

       18. Received $5,440 on the Yoder account and wrote off the remainder owed on a $6,400 accounts receivable balance. (The allowance method is used in accounting for uncollectible receivables.)

Sept. 9. Reinstated the Yoder account written off on August 18 and received $960 cash in full payment.

       15. Purchased land by issuing a $480,000, 90-day note to Ace Development Co., which discounted it at 8%.

Oct. 17. Sold office equipment in exchange for $96,000 cash plus receipt of a $64,000, 90-day, 6% note. The equipment had a cost of $224,000 and accumulated depreciation of $44,800 as of October 17.

Nov. 30. Journalized the monthly payroll for November, based on the following data:

| Salaries | | Deductions | |
|---|---|---|---|
| Sales salaries | $ 96,640 | Income tax withheld | $28,090 |
| Office salaries | 55,200 | Social security tax withheld | 9,110 |
| | $151,840 | Medicare tax withheld | 2,278 |

| Unemployment tax rates: | |
|---|---|
| State unemployment | 4.0% |
| Federal unemployment | 0.8% |
| Amount subject to unemployment taxes: | |
| State unemployment | $5,000 |
| Federal unemployment | 5,000 |

       30. Journalized the employer's payroll taxes on the payroll.

Dec. 14. Journalized the payment of the September 15 note at maturity.

       31. The pension cost for the year was $136,000, of which $99,840 was paid to the pension plan trustee.

### Instructions

1. Journalize the selected transactions.

2. Based on the following data, prepare a bank reconciliation for December of the current year:

   a. Balance according to the bank statement at December 31, $202,240.

   b. Balance according to the ledger at December 31, $175,440.

   c. Checks outstanding at December 31, $48,960.

   d. Deposit in transit, not recorded by bank, $21,120.

   e. Bank debit memo for service charges, $540.

   f. A check for $11,520 in payment of an invoice was incorrectly recorded in the accounts as $11,020.

(*continued*)

3. Based on the bank reconciliation prepared in (2), journalize the entry or entries to be made by Gampfer Company.

4. Based on the following selected data, journalize the adjusting entries as of December 31 of the current year:

   a. Estimated uncollectible accounts at December 31, $11,520, based on an aging of accounts receivable. The balance of Allowance for Doubtful Accounts at December 31 was $1,200 (debit).

   b. The physical inventory on December 31 indicated an inventory shrinkage of $2,360.

   c. Prepaid insurance expired during the year, $16,300.

   d. Office supplies used during the year, $2,800.

   e. Depreciation is computed as follows:

   | Asset | Cost | Residual Value | Acquisition Date | Useful Life in Years | Depreciation Method Used |
   |---|---|---|---|---|---|
   | Buildings | $650,000 | $ 0 | January 2 | 50 | Double-declining-balance |
   | Office Equip. | 176,000 | 16,000 | January 3 | 5 | Straight-line |
   | Store Equip. | 80,000 | 8,000 | July 1 | 10 | Straight-line |

   f. A patent costing $36,000 when acquired on January 2 has a remaining legal life of eight years and is expected to have value for six years.

   g. The cost of mineral rights was $390,000. Of the estimated deposit of 650,000 tons of ore, 38,400 tons were mined and sold during the year.

   h. Vacation pay expense for December, $7,500.

   i. A product warranty was granted beginning December 1 and covering a one-year period. The estimated cost is 3% of sales, which totaled $1,350,000 in December.

   j. Interest was accrued on the note receivable received on October 17.

5. Based on the following information and the post-closing trial balance shown on the following page, prepare a balance sheet in report form at December 31 of the current year.

   The merchandise inventory is stated at cost by the LIFO method.
   The product warranty payable is a current liability.

   Vacation pay payable:
   | | |
   |---|---|
   | Current liability | $5,100 |
   | Long-term liability | 2,400 |

   The unfunded pension liability is a long-term liability.

   Notes payable:
   | | |
   |---|---|
   | Current liability | $ 50,000 |
   | Long-term liability | 450,000 |

**Gampfer Company**
**Post-Closing Trial Balance**
**December 31, 2012**

| | Debit Balances | Credit Balances |
|---|---|---|
| Petty Cash | 3,200 | |
| Cash | 174,400 | |
| Notes Receivable | 64,000 | |
| Accounts Receivable | 336,000 | |
| Allowance for Doubtful Accounts | | 11,520 |
| Merchandise Inventory | 230,000 | |
| Interest Receivable | 800 | |
| Prepaid Insurance | 32,600 | |
| Office Supplies | 9,600 | |
| Land | 470,400 | |
| Buildings | 650,000 | |
| Accumulated Depreciation—Buildings | | 26,000 |
| Office Equipment | 176,000 | |
| Accumulated Depreciation—Office Equipment | | 32,000 |
| Store Equipment | 80,000 | |
| Accumulated Depreciation—Store Equipment | | 3,600 |
| Mineral Rights | 390,000 | |
| Accumulated Depletion | | 23,040 |
| Patents | 30,000 | |
| Social Security Tax Payable | | 13,513 |
| Medicare Tax Payable | | 3,378 |
| Employees Federal Income Tax Payable | | 28,090 |
| State Unemployment Tax Payable | | 40 |
| Federal Unemployment Tax Payable | | 200 |
| Salaries Payable | | 112,612 |
| Accounts Payable | | 224,000 |
| Interest Payable | | 20,207 |
| Product Warranty Payable | | 40,500 |
| Vacation Pay Payable | | 7,500 |
| Unfunded Pension Liability | | 36,160 |
| Notes Payable | | 500,000 |
| Capital Stock | | 250,000 |
| Retained Earnings | | 1,314,640 |
| | 2,647,000 | 2,647,000 |

## Cases & Projects

You can access Cases & Projects online at **www.cengage.com/accounting/reeve**

## Excel Success Special Activities

### SA10-1   Computing employee net pay

JK Flowers Corporation has a single employee, S. Singh. Singh worked for 47 hours during the week, of which seven hours were overtime. Singh is paid $19.40 per hour. Overtime hours are paid at a rate of 150% of straight time. Additional information for Singh is as follows:

| | |
|---|---|
| Federal income tax (weekly withholding) | $201.30 |
| Retirement savings (weekly) | 75.00 |
| Earnings prior to payroll period | 27,950 |

The social security tax rate is assumed to be 6% on all employee earnings. The Medicare rate is assumed to be 1.5% on all employee earnings.

a. Open the Excel file *SA10-1_1e.xls*.

b. Prepare a spreadsheet to compute the weekly gross pay, deductions, and net pay for S. Singh.

c. When you have completed the pay calculations, perform a "save as," replacing the entire file name with the following:

*SA10-1_1e[your first name initial]_[your last name]*

### SA10-2   Computing employee net pay, multiple employees

The Myatt Companies prepared the following weekly schedule for its three employees:

| | A | B | C | D |
|---|---|---|---|---|
| 1 | *Inputs:* | M. Todd | J. Kress | V. Johns |
| 2 | Hours worked straight-time | 40 | 40 | 40 |
| 3 | Hours worked overtime | 6 | 12 | 0 |
| 4 | Hourly rate | $   24.00 | $   30.00 | $   16.50 |
| 5 | Overtime premium | 200% | 150% | 150% |
| 6 | Weekly withholding | $   218.42 | $   278.32 | $   186.45 |
| 7 | Earnings prior to payroll period | $   68,915 | $   71,725 | $   32,710 |
| 8 | Retirement savings | $   60.00 | $   150.00 | $   50.00 |
| 9 | | | | |

The social security rate is assumed to be 6% on all employee annual earnings. The Medicare rate is assumed to be 1.5%.

a. Open the Excel file *SA10-2_1e.xls*.

b. Prepare a spreadsheet to compute the weekly gross pay, deductions, and net pay for each employee.

c. When you have completed the pay calculations, perform a "save as," replacing the entire file name with the following:

*SA10-2_1e[your first name initial]_[your last name]*

**SA10-3   Computing employee net pay, multiple time periods**

Repair-It-for-U has a single employee, Josh Reed, who has the following weekly payroll information for four weeks:

| | A | B | C | D | E |
|---|---|---|---|---|---|
| 1 | | Week 1 | Week 2 | Week 3 | Week 4 |
| 2 | Hours worked straight-time | 40 | 39 | 40 | 36 |
| 3 | Hours worked overtime | 5 | 0 | 3 | 0 |
| 4 | Weekly withholding | $   145.00 | $   121.00 | $   138.00 | $   109.00 |
| 5 | | | | | |

Reed had a pay rate of $16 per hour and an overtime premium of 150%. The social security tax rate is assumed to be 6% of employee earnings. The Medicare tax rate is assumed to be 1.5% of employee earnings.

a. Open the Excel file *SA10-3_1e.xls*.

b. Prepare a spreadsheet to compute the weekly gross pay, deductions, and net pay for each week.

c. When you have completed the pay calculations, perform a "save as," replacing the entire file name with the following:

*SA10-3_ 1e[your first name initial]_[your last name]*

# Corporations: Organization, Stock Transactions, and Dividends

## Hasbro

If you purchase a share of stock from **Hasbro**, you own a small interest in the company. You may request a Hasbro stock certificate as an indication of your ownership.

As you may know, Hasbro is one of the world's largest toy manufacturers and produces popular children's toys such as G.I. Joe, Play-Doh, Tonka toys, Mr. Potato Head, and NERF. In addition, Hasbro manufactures family entertainment products such as Monopoly, Scrabble, and Trivial Pursuit under the Milton Bradley and Parker Brothers labels. In fact, the stock certificate of Hasbro has a picture of Mr. Monopoly, the Monopoly game icon, printed on it.

Purchasing a share of stock from Hasbro may be a great gift idea for the "hard-to-shop-for person." However, a stock certificate represents more than just a picture that you can frame. In fact, the stock certificate is a document that reflects legal ownership of the future financial prospects of Hasbro. In addition, as a shareholder, it represents your claim against the assets and earnings of the corporation.

If you are purchasing Hasbro stock as an investment, you should analyze Hasbro's financial statements and management's plans for the future. For example, Hasbro has a unique relationship with Disney that allows it to produce and sell licensed Disney products. Should this Disney relationship affect how much you are willing to pay for the stock? Also, you might want to know if Hasbro plans to pay cash dividends or whether management is considering issuing additional shares of stock.

This chapter describes and illustrates the nature of corporations including the accounting for stock and dividends. This discussion will aid you in making decisions such as whether or not to buy Hasbro stock.

**OBJ. 1** Describe the nature of the corporate form of organization.

# Nature of a Corporation

Most large businesses are organized as corporations. As a result, corporations generate more than 90% of the total business dollars in the United States. In contrast, most small businesses are organized as proprietorships, partnerships, or limited liability companies.

## Characteristics of a Corporation

A corporation was defined in the Dartmouth College case of 1819, in which Chief Justice Marshall of the U.S. Supreme Court stated: "A corporation is an artificial being, invisible, intangible, and existing only in contemplation of the law."

A *corporation* is a legal entity, distinct and separate from the individuals who create and operate it. As a legal entity, a corporation may acquire, own, and dispose of property in its own name. It may also incur liabilities and enter into contracts. Most importantly, it can sell shares of ownership, called **stock**. This characteristic gives corporations the ability to raise large amounts of capital.

The **stockholders** or *shareholders* who own the stock own the corporation. They can buy and sell stock without affecting the corporation's operations or continued existence. Corporations whose shares of stock are traded in public markets are called *public corporations*. Corporations whose shares are not traded publicly are usually owned by a small group of investors and are called *nonpublic* or *private corporations*.

The stockholders of a corporation have *limited liability*. This means that creditors usually may not go beyond the assets of the corporation to satisfy their claims. Thus, the financial loss that a stockholder may suffer is limited to the amount invested.

The stockholders control a corporation by electing a *board of directors*. This board meets periodically to establish corporate policies. It also selects the chief executive officer (CEO) and other major officers to manage the corporation's day-to-day affairs. Exhibit 1 shows the organizational structure of a corporation.

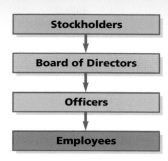

**EXHIBIT 1**

**Organizational Structure of a Corporation**

As a separate entity, a corporation is subject to taxes. For example, corporations must pay federal income taxes on their income.[1] Thus, corporate income that is distributed to stockholders in the form of *dividends* has already been taxed. In turn, stockholders must pay income taxes on the dividends they receive. This *double taxation* of corporate earnings is a major disadvantage of the corporate form. The advantages and disadvantages of the corporate form are listed in Exhibit 2.

**Note:**
Corporations have a separate legal existence, transferable units of ownership, and limited stockholder liability.

**EXHIBIT 2**   **Advantages and Disadvantages of the Corporate Form**

| Advantages | Explanation |
| --- | --- |
| Separate legal existence | A corporation exists separately from its owners. |
| Continuous life | A corporation's life is separate from its owners; therefore, it exists indefinitely. |
| Raising large amounts of capital | The corporate form is suited for raising large amounts of money from shareholders. |
| Ownership rights are easily transferable | A corporation sells shares of ownership, called *stock*. The stockholders of a public company can transfer their shares of stock to other stockholders through stock markets, such as the New York Stock Exchange. |
| Limited liability | A corporation's creditors usually may not go beyond the assets of the corporation to satisfy their claims. Thus, the financial loss that a stockholder may suffer is limited to the amount invested. |

| Disadvantages | Explanation |
| --- | --- |
| Owner is separate from management | Stockholders control management through a board of directors. The board of directors should represent shareholder interests; however, the board is often more closely tied to management than to shareholders. As a result, the board of directors and management may not always behave in the best interests of stockholders. |
| Double taxation of dividends | As a separate legal entity, a corporation is subject to taxation. Thus, net income distributed as dividends will be taxed once at the corporation level, and then again at the individual level. |
| Regulatory costs | Corporations must satisfy many requirements such as those required by the Sarbanes-Oxley Act of 2002. |

# Forming a Corporation

The first step in forming a corporation is to file an *application of incorporation* with the state. State incorporation laws differ, and corporations often organize in those states with the more favorable laws. For this reason, more than half of the largest companies are incorporated in Delaware. Exhibit 3 lists some corporations, their states of incorporation, and the location of their headquarters.

After the application of incorporation has been approved, the state grants a *charter* or *articles of incorporation*. The articles of incorporation formally create the corporation.[2]

1 A majority of states also require corporations to pay income taxes.

2 The articles of incorporation may also restrict a corporation's activities in certain areas, such as owning certain types of real estate, conducting certain types of business activities, or purchasing its own stock.

**EXHIBIT 3**

**Examples of Corporations and Their States of Incorporation**

| Corporation | State of Incorporation | Headquarters |
|---|---|---|
| Caterpillar | Delaware | Peoria, Ill. |
| Delta Air Lines | Delaware | Atlanta, Ga. |
| The Dow Chemical Company | Delaware | Midland, Mich. |
| General Electric Company | New York | Fairfield, Conn. |
| The Home Depot | Delaware | Atlanta, Ga. |
| Kellogg Company | Delaware | Battle Creek, Mich. |
| 3M | Delaware | St. Paul, Minn. |
| R.J. Reynolds Tobacco Company | Delaware | Winston-Salem, N.C. |
| Starbucks Corporation | Washington | Seattle, Wash. |
| Sun Microsystems, Inc. | Delaware | Palo Alto, Calif. |
| The Washington Post Company | Delaware | Washington, D.C. |
| Whirlpool Corporation | Delaware | Benton Harbor, Mich. |

The corporate management and board of directors then prepare a set of *bylaws*, which are the rules and procedures for conducting the corporation's affairs.

Costs may be incurred in organizing a corporation. These costs include legal fees, taxes, state incorporation fees, license fees, and promotional costs. Such costs are debited to an expense account entitled *Organizational Expenses*.

To illustrate, a corporation's organizing costs of $8,500 on January 5 are recorded as shown below.

| | | | | | |
|---|---|---|---|---|---|
| Jan. | 5 | Organizational Expenses | | 8,500 | |
| | | Cash | | | 8,500 |
| | | Paid costs of organizing the corporation. | | | |

**OBJ. 2**

Describe and illustrate the characteristics of stock, classes of stock, and entries for issuing stock.

# Paid-In Capital from Issuing Stock

As described and illustrated in earlier chapters, the two main sources of stockholders' equity are **paid-in capital** (or contributed capital) and retained earnings. The main source of paid-in capital is from issuing stock.

## Characteristics of Stock

The number of shares of stock that a corporation is *authorized* to issue is stated in its charter. The term *issued* refers to the shares issued to the stockholders. A corporation may reacquire some of the stock that it has issued. The stock remaining in the hands of stockholders is then called **outstanding stock**. The relationship between authorized, issued, and outstanding stock is shown in the graphic at the left.

Upon request, corporations may issue stock certificates to stockholders to document their ownership. Printed on a stock certificate is the name of the company, the name of the stockholder, and the number of shares owned. The stock certificate may also indicate a dollar amount assigned to each share of stock, called **par** value. Stock may be issued without par, in which case it is called *no-par stock.* In some states, the board of directors of a corporation is required to assign a *stated value* to no-par stock.

Authorized
Issued
Outstanding

**Number of shares authorized, issued, and outstanding**

Corporations have limited liability and, thus, creditors have no claim against stockholders' personal assets. To protect creditors, however, some states require corporations to maintain a minimum amount of paid-in capital. This minimum amount, called *legal capital,* usually includes the par or stated value of the shares issued.

The major rights that accompany ownership of a share of stock are as follows:

1. The right to vote in matters concerning the corporation.
2. The right to share in distributions of earnings.
3. The right to share in assets upon liquidation.

These stock rights normally vary with the class of stock.

## Classes of Stock

When only one class of stock is issued, it is called **common stock**. Each share of common stock has equal rights.

A corporation may also issue one or more classes of stock with various preference rights such as a preference to dividends. Such a stock is called a **preferred stock**. The dividend rights of preferred stock are stated either as dollars per share or as a percent of par. For example, a $50 par value preferred stock with a $4 per share dividend may be described as either:[3]

**Note:**
The two primary classes of paid-in capital are common stock and preferred stock.

$4 preferred stock, $50 par

or

8% preferred stock, $50 par

Because they have first rights (preference) to any dividends, preferred stockholders have a greater chance of receiving dividends than common stockholders. However, since dividends are normally based on earnings, a corporation cannot guarantee dividends even to preferred stockholders.

The payment of dividends is authorized by the corporation's board of directors. When authorized, the directors are said to have *declared* a dividend.

**Cumulative preferred stock** has a right to receive regular dividends that were not declared (paid) in prior years. Noncumulative preferred stock does not have this right.

Cumulative preferred stock dividends that have not been paid in prior years are said to be **in arrears**. Any preferred dividends in arrears must be paid before any common stock dividends are paid. In addition, any dividends in arrears are normally disclosed in notes to the financial statements.

To illustrate, assume that a corporation has issued the following preferred and common stock:

1,000 shares of $4 cumulative preferred stock, $50 par
4,000 shares of common stock, $15 par

The corporation was organized on January 1, 2010, and paid no dividends in 2010 and 2011. In 2012, the corporation paid $22,000 in dividends, of which $12,000 was paid to preferred stockholders and $10,000 was paid to common stockholders as shown below.

| | | |
|---|---:|---:|
| Total dividends paid . . . . . . . . . . . . . . . . . . . . . . . . . . . . . . . . . . . . . . . . . | | $ 22,000 |
| Preferred stockholders: | | |
|   2010 dividends in arrears (1,000 shares × $4) . . . . . . . . . . . . . . . . | $4,000 | |
|   2011 dividends in arrears (1,000 shares × $4) . . . . . . . . . . . . . . . . | 4,000 | |
|   2012 dividend (1,000 shares × $4) . . . . . . . . . . . . . . . . . . . . . . . . . | 4,000 | |
|     Total preferred dividends paid . . . . . . . . . . . . . . . . . . . . . . . . . | | (12,000) |
| Dividends available to common stockholders . . . . . . . . . . . . . . . . . . | | $10,000 |

As a result, preferred stockholders received $12.00 per share ($12,000 ÷ 1,000 shares) in dividends, while common stockholders received $2.50 per share ($10,000 ÷ 4,000 shares).

In addition to dividend preference, preferred stock may be given preferences to assets if the corporation goes out of business and is liquidated. However, claims of

3 In some cases, preferred stock may receive additional dividends if certain conditions are met. Such stock, called *participating preferred stock*, is not often issued.

**e×cel** *success*

The calculation for the dividends per share can be accomplished using a spreadsheet as follows:

| | A | B | C | |
|---|---|---|---|---|
| 1 | *Inputs:* | | | |
| 2 | | Number of shares | Dividend per share | |
| 3 | Preferred stock | 1,000 | $ 4.00 | |
| 4 | Common stock | 4,000 | | |
| 5 | | | | |
| 6 | Preferred dividends in arrears: | 2010 and 2011 | | |
| 7 | | | | |
| 8 | Dividend paid in 2012: | $ 22,000 | | |
| 9 | | | | |
| 10 | *Outputs:* | | | |
| 11 | | | | |
| 12 | Total amount to be distributed: | | =B8 | a. |
| 13 | Preferred dividend: | | | b. |
| 14 | 2010 dividend in arrears | =$B$3*$C$3 | | |
| 15 | 2011 dividend in arrears | =$B$3*$C$3 | | |
| 16 | 2012 dividend | =$B$3*$C$3 | =SUM(B14:B16) | c. |
| 17 | Common dividend | | =C12-C16 | d. |
| 18 | Dividends per share | | | |
| 19 | Preferred stock | | =C16/B3 | e. |
| 20 | Common stock | | =C17/B4 | |
| 21 | | | | |

The spreadsheet is designed with inputs and outputs. The inputs are the stock and dividend information, and the output is the distribution of the dividend to the two classes of stock.

**a.** Enter in cell C12 the cell reference for the dividend paid in 2010, =B8.

**b.** Enter in cell B14 the formula for the 2008 dividend in arrears, =$B$3*$C$3. Use the dollar sign ($) to fix the cell reference. This will allow you to copy this formula from B14 to B15:B16.

**c.** Enter in cell C16 the formula for the sum of the preferred dividends to be distributed, =SUM(B14:B16).

**d.** Enter in cell C17 the formula for the remaining common dividend, =C12-C16.

**e.** Enter in cells C19 and 20 the dividends per share for the two classes of stock by dividing the total dividend by the number of shares. The formula from C19 can be copied to C20.

**Try**It Go to the hands-on **Excel Tutor** for this example!

**Try**It This Excel Success example uses an Excel function referred to as cell referencing. Go to the **Excel Tutor** titled **Absolute & Relative Cell References** for additional help on this useful Excel function!

**Example Exercise** 11-1 **Dividends per Share**

OBJ. 2

Sandpiper Company has 20,000 shares of 1% cumulative preferred stock of $100 par and 100,000 shares of $50 par common stock. The following amounts were distributed as dividends:

| Year 1 | $10,000 |
|---|---|
| Year 2 | 45,000 |
| Year 3 | 80,000 |

Determine the dividends per share for preferred and common stock for each year.

**Follow My Example** 11-1

| | Year 1 | Year 2 | Year 3 |
|---|---|---|---|
| Amount distributed | $10,000 | $45,000 | $80,000 |
| Preferred dividend (20,000 shares) | 10,000 | 30,000* | 20,000 |
| Common dividend (100,000 shares) | $ 0 | $15,000 | $60,000 |
| *($10,000 + $20,000) | | | |
| Dividends per share: | | | |
| Preferred stock | $0.50 | $1.50 | $1.00 |
| Common stock | None | $0.15 | $0.60 |

Practice Exercises: **PE 11-1A, PE 11-1B**

creditors must be satisfied first. Preferred stockholders are next in line to receive any remaining assets, followed by the common stockholders.

## Issuing Stock

A separate account is used for recording the amount of each class of stock issued to investors in a corporation. For example, assume that a corporation is authorized to issue 10,000 shares of $100 par preferred stock and 100,000 shares of $20 par common stock. The corporation issued 5,000 shares of preferred stock and 50,000 shares of common stock at par for cash. The corporation's entry to record the stock issue is as follows:[4]

| | | | |
|---|---|---:|---:|
| Cash | | 1,500,000 | |
| Preferred Stock | | | 500,000 |
| Common Stock | | | 1,000,000 |
| Issued preferred stock and common | | | |
| stock at par for cash. | | | |

Stock is often issued by a corporation at a price other than its par. The price at which stock is sold depends on a variety of factors, such as the following:

1. The financial condition, earnings record, and dividend record of the corporation.
2. Investor expectations of the corporation's potential earning power.
3. General business and economic conditions and expectations.

If stock is issued (sold) for a price that is more than its par, the stock has been sold at a **premium**. For example, if common stock with a par of $50 is sold for $60 per share, the stock has sold at a premium of $10.

If stock is issued (sold) for a price that is less than its par, the stock has been sold at a **discount**. For example, if common stock with a par of $50 is sold for $45 per share, the stock has sold at a discount of $5. Many states do not permit stock to be sold at a discount. In other states, stock may be sold at a discount in only unusual cases. Since stock is rarely sold at a discount, it is not illustrated.

In order to distribute dividends, financial statements, and other reports, a corporation must keep track of its stockholders. Large public corporations normally use a financial institution, such as a bank, for this purpose.[5] In such cases, the financial institution is referred to as a *transfer agent* or *registrar*.

## Premium on Stock

When stock is issued at a premium, Cash is debited for the amount received. Common Stock or Preferred Stock is credited for the par amount. The excess of the amount paid over par is part of the paid-in capital. An account entitled *Paid-In Capital in Excess of Par* is credited for this amount.

To illustrate, assume that Caldwell Company issues 2,000 shares of $50 par preferred stock for cash at $55. The entry to record this transaction is as follows:

| | | | |
|---|---|---:|---:|
| Cash | | 110,000 | |
| Preferred Stock | | | 100,000 |
| Paid-In Capital in Excess of Par—Preferred Stock | | | 10,000 |
| Issued $50 par preferred stock at $55. | | | |

When stock is issued in exchange for assets other than cash, such as land, buildings, and equipment, the assets acquired are recorded at their fair market value. If this value cannot be determined, the fair market price of the stock issued is used.

4 The accounting for investments in stocks from the point of view of the investor is discussed in Chapter 13.

5 Small corporations may use a subsidiary ledger, called a *stockholders ledger*. in this case, the stock accounts (Preferred Stock and Common Stock) are controlling accounts for the subsidiary ledger.

To illustrate, assume that a corporation acquired land with a fair market value that cannot be determined. In exchange, the corporation issued 10,000 shares of its $10 par common. If the stock has a market price of $12 per share, the transaction is recorded as follows:

| | | | | |
|---|---|---|---|---|
| | Land | | 120,000 | |
| | Common Stock | | | 100,000 |
| | Paid-In Capital in Excess of Par | | | 20,000 |
| | Issued $10 par common stock, valued at $12 per share, for land. | | | |

## No-Par Stock

In most states, no-par preferred and common stock may be issued. When no-par stock is issued, Cash is debited and Common Stock is credited for the proceeds. As no-par stock is issued over time, this entry is the same even if the issuing price varies.

To illustrate, assume that on January 9 a corporation issues 10,000 shares of no-par common stock at $40 a share. On June 27, the corporation issues an additional 1,000 shares at $36. The entries to record these issuances of the no-par stock are as follows:

| | | | | | |
|---|---|---|---|---|---|
| Jan. | 9 | Cash | | 400,000 | |
| | | Common Stock | | | 400,000 |
| | | Issued 10,000 shares of no-par common at $40. | | | |
| June | 27 | Cash | | 36,000 | |
| | | Common Stock | | | 36,000 |
| | | Issued 1,000 shares of no-par common at $36. | | | |

In some states, no-par stock may be assigned a *stated value per share*. The stated value is recorded like a par value. Any excess of the proceeds over the stated value is credited to *Paid-In Capital in Excess of Stated Value*.

# BusinessConnection

### CISCO SYSTEMS, INC.

Cisco Systems, Inc., manufactures and sells networking and communications products worldwide. Some excerpts of its bylaws are shown below.

*ARTICLE 2*
*SHAREHOLDERS' MEETINGS*
*Section 2.01 Annual Meetings. The annual meeting of the shareholders of the Corporation . . . shall be held each year on the second Thursday in November at 10:00 A.M. . . .*

*ARTICLE 3*
*BOARD OF DIRECTORS*
*Section 3.02 Number and Qualification of Directors. The number of authorized directors of this Corporation shall be not less than eight (8) nor more than fifteen (15), . . . to be (determined) by . . . the Board of Directors or shareholders.*

*ARTICLE 4*
*OFFICERS*
*Section 4.01 Number and Term. The officers of the Corporation shall include a President, a Secretary and a Chief Financial Officer, all of which shall be chosen by the Board of Directors. . . .*

*Section 4.06 President. The President shall be the general manager and chief executive officer of the Corporation, . . . shall preside at all meetings of shareholders, shall have general supervision of the affairs of the Corporation. . . .*

To illustrate, assume that in the preceding example the no-par common stock is assigned a stated value of $25. The issuance of the stock on January 9 and June 27 is recorded as follows:

| | | | | | |
|---|---|---|---|---|---|
| Jan. | 9 | Cash | | 400,000 | |
| | | Common Stock | | | 250,000 |
| | | Paid-In Capital in Excess of Stated Value | | | 150,000 |
| | | Issued 10,000 shares of no-par common at $40; stated value, $25. | | | |
| June | 27 | Cash | | 36,000 | |
| | | Common Stock | | | 25,000 |
| | | Paid-In Capital in Excess of Stated Value | | | 11,000 |
| | | Issued 1,000 shares of no-par common at $36; stated value, $25. | | | |

## Example Exercise 11-2 Entries for Issuing Stock

**OBJ. 2**

On March 6, Limerick Corporation issued for cash 15,000 shares of no-par common stock at $30. On April 13, Limerick issued at par 1,000 shares of 4%, $40 par preferred stock for cash. On May 19, Limerick issued for cash 15,000 shares of 4%, $40 par preferred stock at $42.

Journalize the entries to record the March 6, April 13, and May 19 transactions.

### Follow My Example 11-2

| | | | |
|---|---|---|---|
| Mar. 6 | Cash ................................................ | 450,000 | |
| | Common Stock ..................................... | | 450,000 |
| | (15,000 shares × $30). | | |
| Apr. 13 | Cash ................................................ | 40,000 | |
| | Preferred Stock .................................... | | 40,000 |
| | (1,000 shares × $40). | | |
| May 19 | Cash ................................................ | 630,000 | |
| | Preferred Stock..................................... | | 600,000 |
| | Paid-In Capital in Excess of Par ..................... | | 30,000 |
| | (15,000 shares × $42). | | |

Practice Exercises: **PE 11-2A, PE 11-2B**

---

**IFRS**

# International Connection

## IFRS FOR SMES

In 2010, the International Accounting Standards Board (IASB) issued a set of accounting standards specifically designed for small- and medium-sized enterprises (SMEs) called International Financial Reporting Standards (IFRS) for SMEs. SMEs in the United States are private companies and such small corporations that they do not report to the Securities and Exchange Commission (SEC). IFRS for SMEs consist of only 230 pages, compared to 2,700 pages for full IFRS. These standards are designed to be cost effective for SMEs. Thus, IFRS for SMEs require fewer disclosures and contain no industry-specific standards or exceptions.

The American Institute of CPAs (AICPA) has accepted IFRS for SMEs as part of U.S. generally accepted accounting principles (GAAP) for private companies not reporting to the SEC. If users, such as bankers and investors, accept these financial statements, IFRS for SMEs may become popular in the United States.*

*Differences between U.S. GAAP and IFRS are further discussed and illustrated in Appendix E.

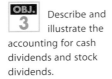

**OBJ. 3** Describe and illustrate the accounting for cash dividends and stock dividends.

# Accounting for Dividends

When a board of directors declares a cash dividend, it authorizes the distribution of cash to stockholders. When a board of directors declares a stock dividend, it authorizes the distribution of its stock. In both cases, declaring a dividend reduces the retained earnings of the corporation.[6]

## Cash Dividends

A cash distribution of earnings by a corporation to its shareholders is a **cash dividend**. Although dividends may be paid in other assets, cash dividends are the most common.

Three conditions for a cash dividend are as follows:

1. Sufficient retained earnings
2. Sufficient cash
3. Formal action by the board of directors

There must be a sufficient (large enough) balance in Retained Earnings to declare a cash dividend. That is, the balance of Retained Earnings must be large enough so that the dividend does not create a debit balance in the retained earnings account. However, a large Retained Earnings balance does not mean that there is cash available to pay dividends. This is because the balances of Cash and Retained Earnings are often unrelated.

Even if there are sufficient retained earnings and cash, a corporation's board of directors is not required to pay dividends. Nevertheless, many corporations pay quarterly cash dividends to make their stock more attractive to investors. *Special* or *extra* dividends may also be paid when a corporation experiences higher than normal profits.

Three dates included in a dividend announcement are as follows:

1. Date of declaration
2. Date of record
3. Date of payment

The *date of declaration* is the date the board of directors formally authorizes the payment of the dividend. On this date, the corporation incurs the liability to pay the amount of the dividend.

Microsoft Corporation declared a dividend of $0.13 per share on December 9, 2009, to common stockholders of record as of February 18, 2010, payable on March 11, 2010.

The *date of record* is the date the corporation uses to determine which stockholders will receive the dividend. During the period of time between the date of declaration and the date of record, the stock price is quoted as selling *with-dividends*. This means that any investors purchasing the stock before the date of record will receive the dividend.

The *date of payment* is the date the corporation will pay the dividend to the stockholders who owned the stock on the date of record. During the period of time between the record date and the payment date, the stock price is quoted as selling *ex-dividends*. This means that since the date of record has passed, any new investors will not receive the dividend.

To illustrate, assume that on October 1 Hiber Corporation declares the cash dividends shown below with a date of record of November 10 and a date of payment of December 2.

|  | Dividend per Share | Total Dividends |
|---|---|---|
| Preferred stock, $100 par, 5,000 shares outstanding..................... | $2.50 | $12,500 |
| Common stock, $10 par, 100,000 shares outstanding ................... | $0.30 | 30,000 |
| Total ........................................................................... |  | $42,500 |

On October 1, the declaration date, Hiber Corporation records the following entry:

*Declaration Date*

| | | | | | |
|---|---|---|---|---|---|
| Oct. | 1 | Cash Dividends | | 42,500 | |
| | |     Cash Dividends Payable | | | 42,500 |
| | |       Declared cash dividends. | | | |

6 In rare cases, when a corporation is reducing its operations or going out of business, a dividend may be a distribution of paid-in capital. Such a dividend is called a *liquidating dividend*.

On November 10, the date of record, no entry is necessary. This date merely *Date of Record* determines which stockholders will receive the dividends.

On December 2, the date of payment, Hiber Corporation records the payment of the dividends as follows:

| | | | | |
|---|---|---|---|---|
| Dec. | 2 | Cash Dividends Payable | 42,500 | |
| | | Cash | | 42,500 |
| | | Paid cash dividends. | | |

*Date of Payment*

At the end of the accounting period, the balance in Cash Dividends will be transferred to Retained Earnings as part of the closing process. This closing entry debits Retained Earnings and credits Cash Dividends for the balance of the cash dividends account. If the cash dividends have not been paid by the end of the period, Cash Dividends Payable will be reported on the balance sheet as a current liability.

---

## Example Exercise 11-3 ▶ Entries for Cash Dividends

The important dates in connection with a cash dividend of $75,000 on a corporation's common stock are February 26, March 30, and April 2. Journalize the entries required on each date.

### Follow My Example 11-3

| | | | |
|---|---|---|---|
| Feb. 26 | Cash Dividends........................................... | 75,000 | |
| | Cash Dividends Payable............................... | | 75,000 |
| Mar. 30 | No entry required. | | |
| Apr. 2 | Cash Dividends Payable ................................ | 75,000 | |
| | Cash ................................................. | | 75,000 |

Practice Exercises: **PE 11-3A, PE 11-3B**

---

## Integrity, Objectivity, and Ethics in Business

**THE PROFESSOR WHO KNEW TOO MUCH**

A major Midwestern university released a quarterly "American Customer Satisfaction Index" based on its research of customers of popular U.S. products and services. Before the release of the index to the public, the professor in charge of the research bought and sold stocks of some of the companies in the report. The professor was quoted as saying that he thought it was important to test his theories of customer satisfaction with "real" [his own] money.

Is this proper or ethical? Apparently, the dean of the Business School didn't think so. In a statement to the press,

the dean stated: "I have instructed anyone affiliated with the (index) not to make personal use of information gathered in the course of producing the quarterly index, prior to the index's release to the general public, and they [the researchers] have agreed."

Sources: Jon E. Hilsenrath and Dan Morse, "Researcher Uses Index to Buy, Short Stocks," *The Wall Street Journal*, February 18, 2003; and Jon E. Hilsenrath, "Satisfaction Theory: Mixed Results," *The Wall Street Journal*, February 19, 2003.

---

## Stock Dividends

A **stock dividend** is a distribution of shares of stock to stockholders. Stock dividends are normally declared only on common stock and issued to common stockholders.

A stock dividend affects only stockholders' equity. Specifically, the amount of the stock dividend is transferred from Retained Earnings to Paid-In Capital. The amount transferred is normally the fair value (market price) of the shares issued in the stock dividend.[7]

---

7 The use of fair market value is justified as long as the number of shares issued for the stock dividend is small (less than 25% of the shares outstanding).

To illustrate, assume that the stockholders' equity accounts of Hendrix Corporation as of December 15 are as follows:

| | |
|---|---|
| Common Stock, $20 par (2,000,000 shares issued) | $40,000,000 |
| Paid-In Capital in Excess of Par—Common Stock | 9,000,000 |
| Retained Earnings | 26,600,000 |

On December 15, Hendrix Corporation declares a stock dividend of 5% or 100,000 shares (2,000,000 shares × 5%) to be issued on January 10 to stockholders of record on December 31. The market price of the stock on December 15 (the date of declaration) is $31 per share.

The entry to record the stock dividend is as follows:

| | | | | |
|---|---|---|---|---|
| Dec. | 15 | Stock Dividends | 3,100,000 | |
| | | Stock Dividends Distributable | | 2,000,000 |
| | | Paid-In Capital in Excess of Par—Common Stock | | 1,100,000 |
| | | Declared 5% (100,000 share) stock | | |
| | | dividend on $20 par common stock | | |
| | | with a market price of $31 per share. | | |

After the preceding entry is recorded, Stock Dividends will have a debit balance of $3,100,000. Like cash dividends, the stock dividends account is closed to Retained Earnings at the end of the accounting period. This closing entry debits Retained Earnings and credits Stock Dividends.

At the end of the period, the *stock dividends distributable* and *paid-in capital in excess of par—common stock* accounts are reported in the Paid-In Capital section of the balance sheet. Thus, the effect of the preceding stock dividend is to transfer $3,100,000 of retained earnings to paid-in capital.

On January 10, the stock dividend is distributed to stockholders by issuing 100,000 shares of common stock. The issuance of the stock is recorded by the following entry:

| | | | | |
|---|---|---|---|---|
| Jan. | 10 | Stock Dividends Distributable | 2,000,000 | |
| | | Common Stock | | 2,000,000 |
| | | Issued stock as stock dividend. | | |

A stock dividend does not change the assets, liabilities, or total stockholders' equity of a corporation. Likewise, a stock dividend does not change an individual stockholder's proportionate interest (equity) in the corporation.

**Example Exercise** 11-4 **Entries for Stock Dividends**

OBJ. 3

Vienna Highlights Corporation has 150,000 shares of $100 par common stock outstanding. On June 14, Vienna Highlights declared a 4% stock dividend to be issued August 15 to stockholders of record on July 1. The market price of the stock was $110 per share on June 14.

Journalize the entries required on June 14, July 1, and August 15.

**Follow My Example** 11-4

| | | | |
|---|---|---|---|
| June 14 | Stock Dividends (150,000 × 4% × $110)......................... | 660,000 | |
| | Stock Dividends Distributable (6,000 × $100) ................. | | 600,000 |
| | Paid-In Capital in Excess of Par—Common Stock | | |
| | ($660,000 – $600,000)........................................ | | 60,000 |
| July 1 | No entry required. | | |
| Aug. 15 | Stock Dividends Distributable .................................. | 600,000 | |
| | Common Stock ............................................... | | 600,000 |

Practice Exercises: **PE 11-4A, PE 11-4B**

To illustrate, assume a stockholder owns 1,000 of a corporation's 10,000 shares outstanding. If the corporation declares a 6% stock dividend, the stockholder's proportionate interest will not change as shown below.

| | Before<br>Stock Dividend | After<br>Stock Dividend |
|---|---|---|
| Total shares issued | 10,000 | 10,600 [10,000 + (10,000 × 6%)] |
| Number of shares owned | 1,000 | 1,060 [1,000 + (1,000 × 6%)] |
| Proportionate ownership | 10% (1,000/10,000) | 10% (1,060/10,600) |

# Treasury Stock Transactions

**OBJ.**
**4**
Describe and illustrate the accounting for treasury stock transactions.

**Treasury stock** is stock that a corporation has issued and then reacquired. A corporation may reacquire (purchase) its own stock for a variety of reasons, including the following:

1. To provide shares for resale to employees
2. To reissue as bonuses to employees, or
3. To support the market price of the stock

The *cost method* is normally used for recording the purchase and resale of treasury stock.[8] Using the cost method, *Treasury Stock* is debited for the cost (purchase price) of the stock. When the stock is resold, Treasury Stock is credited for its cost. Any difference between the cost and the selling price is debited or credited to *Paid-In Capital from Sale of Treasury Stock.*

The 2009 edition of *Accounting Trends & Techniques* indicated that over 70% of the companies surveyed reported treasury stock.

To illustrate, assume that a corporation has the following paid-in capital on January 1:

| | |
|---|---|
| Common stock, $25 par (20,000 shares authorized and issued) | $500,000 |
| Excess of issue price over par | 150,000 |
| | $650,000 |

On February 13, the corporation purchases 1,000 shares of its common stock at $45 per share. The entry to record the purchase of the treasury stock is as follows:

| Feb. | 13 | Treasury Stock | 45,000 | |
|---|---|---|---|---|
| | | Cash | | 45,000 |
| | | Purchased 1,000 shares of treasury stock at $45. | | |

On April 29, the corporation sells 600 shares of the treasury stock for $60. The entry to record the sale is as follows:

| Apr. | 29 | Cash | 36,000 | |
|---|---|---|---|---|
| | | Treasury Stock | | 27,000 |
| | | Paid-In Capital from Sale of Treasury Stock | | 9,000 |
| | | Sold 600 shares of treasury stock at $60. | | |

A sale of treasury stock may result in a decrease in paid-in capital. To the extent that Paid-In Capital from Sale of Treasury Stock has a credit balance, it is debited for any such decrease. Any remaining decrease is then debited to the retained earnings account.

To illustrate, assume that on October 4, the corporation sells the remaining 400 shares of treasury stock for $40 per share. The entry to record the sale is as follows:

| Oct. | 4 | Cash | 16,000 | |
|---|---|---|---|---|
| | | Paid-In Capital from Sale of Treasury Stock | 2,000 | |
| | | Treasury Stock | | 18,000 |
| | | Sold 400 shares of treasury stock at $40. | | |

8 Another method that is infrequently used, called the *par value method*, is discussed in advanced accounting texts.

The October 4 entry shown above decreases paid-in capital by $2,000. Since Paid-In Capital from Sale of Treasury Stock has a credit balance of $9,000, the entire $2,000 was debited to Paid-In Capital from Sale of Treasury Stock.

No dividends (cash or stock) are paid on the shares of treasury stock. To do so would result in the corporation earning dividend revenue from itself.

---

**Example Exercise** ▶ **11-5** ▶ **Entries for Treasury Stock** ▶ **OBJ. 4**

On May 3, Buzz Off Corporation reacquired 3,200 shares of its common stock at $42 per share. On July 22, Buzz Off sold 2,000 of the reacquired shares at $47 per share. On August 30, Buzz Off sold the remaining shares at $40 per share. Journalize the transactions of May 3, July 22, and August 30.

**Follow My Example** ▶ **11-5** ▶

| | | | |
|---|---|---:|---:|
| May 3 | Treasury Stock (3,200 × $42). . . . . . . . . . . . . . . . . . . . . . . . . . . . . . . . . . . . . . . . . . . . . | 134,400 | |
| | Cash . . . . . . . . . . . . . . . . . . . . . . . . . . . . . . . . . . . . . . . . . . . . . . . . . . . . . . . . . . . . . . . | | 134,400 |
| July 22 | Cash (2,000 × $47) . . . . . . . . . . . . . . . . . . . . . . . . . . . . . . . . . . . . . . . . . . . . . . . . . . . | 94,000 | |
| | Treasury Stock (2,000 × $42). . . . . . . . . . . . . . . . . . . . . . . . . . . . . . . . . . . . . . . . . | | 84,000 |
| | Paid-In Capital from Sale of Treasury Stock [2,000 × ($47 − $42)] . . . . . . . . . . . . . . . . . . . . | | 10,000 |
| Aug. 30 | Cash (1,200 × $40) . . . . . . . . . . . . . . . . . . . . . . . . . . . . . . . . . . . . . . . . . . . . . . . . . . | 48,000 | |
| | Paid-In Capital from Sale of Treasury Stock [1,200 × ($42 − $40)] . . . . . . . . . . . . . . . . . . . . | 2,400 | |
| | Treasury Stock (1,200 × $42). . . . . . . . . . . . . . . . . . . . . . . . . . . . . . . . . . . . . . . . . . | | 50,400 |

Practice Exercises: **PE 11-5A, PE 11-5B**

---

 **OBJ. 5** Describe and illustrate the reporting of stockholders' equity.

# Reporting Stockholders' Equity

As with other sections of the balance sheet, alternative terms and formats may be used in reporting stockholders' equity. Also, changes in retained earnings and paid-in capital may be reported in separate statements or notes to the financial statements.

## Stockholders' Equity on the Balance Sheet

Exhibit 4 shows two methods for reporting stockholders' equity for the December 31, 2012, balance sheet for Telex Inc.

Method 1.   Each class of stock is reported, followed by its related paid-in capital accounts. Retained earnings is then reported followed by a deduction for treasury stock.

Method 2.   The stock accounts are reported, followed by the paid-in capital reported as a single item, Additional paid-in capital. Retained earnings is then reported followed by a deduction for treasury stock.

Significant changes in stockholders' equity during a period may also be presented in a statement of stockholders' equity or in the notes to the financial statements. The statement of stockholders' equity is illustrated later in this section.

Relevant rights and privileges of the various classes of stock outstanding should also be reported.[9] Examples include dividend and liquidation preferences, conversion rights, and redemption rights. Such information may be disclosed on the face of the balance sheet or in the notes to the financial statements.

---

9 *FASB Accounting Standards Codification*, Section 505-10-50.

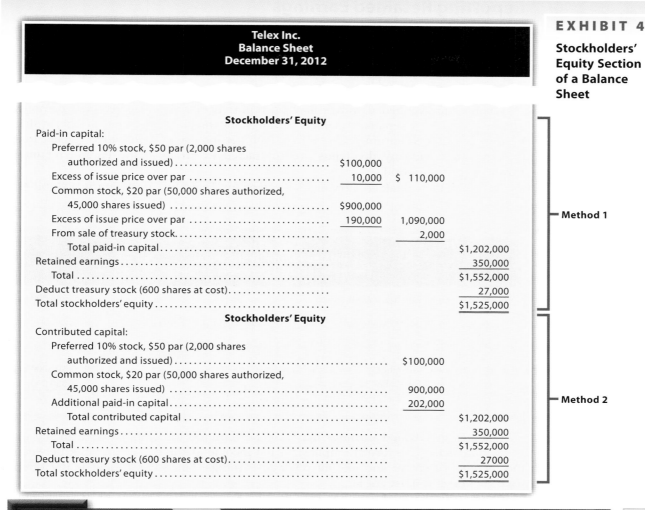

**EXHIBIT 4**

**Stockholders' Equity Section of a Balance Sheet**

**Telex Inc.**
**Balance Sheet**
**December 31, 2012**

**Stockholders' Equity**

Paid-in capital:

| | | | |
|---|---|---:|---:|
| Preferred 10% stock, $50 par (2,000 shares authorized and issued) | | $100,000 | |
| Excess of issue price over par | | 10,000 | $ 110,000 |
| Common stock, $20 par (50,000 shares authorized, 45,000 shares issued) | | $900,000 | |
| Excess of issue price over par | | 190,000 | 1,090,000 |
| From sale of treasury stock | | | 2,000 |
| Total paid-in capital | | | $1,202,000 |
| Retained earnings | | | 350,000 |
| Total | | | $1,552,000 |
| Deduct treasury stock (600 shares at cost) | | | 27,000 |
| Total stockholders' equity | | | $1,525,000 |

— Method 1

**Stockholders' Equity**

Contributed capital:

| | | |
|---|---:|---:|
| Preferred 10% stock, $50 par (2,000 shares authorized and issued) | $100,000 | |
| Common stock, $20 par (50,000 shares authorized, 45,000 shares issued) | 900,000 | |
| Additional paid-in capital | 202,000 | |
| Total contributed capital | | $1,202,000 |
| Retained earnings | | 350,000 |
| Total | | $1,552,000 |
| Deduct treasury stock (600 shares at cost) | | 27000 |
| Total stockholders' equity | | $1,525,000 |

— Method 2

---

## Example Exercise  11-6  Reporting Stockholders' Equity

OBJ. 5

Using the following accounts and balances, prepare the Stockholders' Equity section of the balance sheet. Forty thousand shares of common stock are authorized, and 5,000 shares have been reacquired.

| | |
|---|---:|
| Common Stock, $50 par | $1,500,000 |
| Paid-In Capital in Excess of Par | 160,000 |
| Paid-In Capital from Sale of Treasury Stock | 44,000 |
| Retained Earnings | 4,395,000 |
| Treasury Stock | 120,000 |

## Follow My Example  11-6

**Stockholders' Equity**

| | | |
|---|---:|---:|
| Paid-in capital: | | |
| Common stock, $50 par (40,000 shares authorized, 30,000 shares issued) | $1,500,000 | |
| Excess of issue price over par | 160,000 | $1,660,000 |
| From sale of treasury stock | | 44,000 |
| Total paid-in capital | | $1,704,000 |
| Retained earnings | | 4,395,000 |
| Total | | $6,099,000 |
| Deduct treasury stock (5,000 shares at cost) | | 120,000 |
| Total stockholders' equity | | $5,979,000 |

Practice Exercises: **PE 11-6A, PE 11-6B**

## Reporting Retained Earnings

Changes in retained earnings may be reported using one of the following:

1. Separate retained earnings statement
2. Combined income and retained earnings statement
3. Statement of stockholders' equity

Changes in retained earnings may be reported in a separate retained earnings statement. When a separate retained earnings statement is prepared, the beginning balance of retained earnings is reported. The net income is then added (or net loss is subtracted) and any dividends are subtracted to arrive at the ending retained earnings for the period.

To illustrate, a retained earnings statement for Telex Inc. is shown in Exhibit 5.

**EXHIBIT 5**

**Retained Earnings Statement**

| Telex Inc. | | | |
| --- | --- | --- | --- |
| Retained Earnings Statement | | | |
| For the Year Ended December 31, 2012 | | | |
| Retained earnings, January 1, 2012 | | | $245,000 |
| Net income | | $180,000 | |
| Less dividends: | | | |
| Preferred stock | $10,000 | | |
| Common stock | 65,000 | 75,000 | |
| Increase in retained earnings | | | 105,000 |
| Retained earnings, December 31, 2012 | | | $350,000 |

Changes in retained earnings may also be reported in combination with the income statement. This format emphasizes net income as the connecting link between the income statement and ending retained earnings. Since this format is not often used, we do not illustrate it.

Changes in retained earnings may also be reported in a statement of stockholders' equity. An example of reporting changes in retained earnings in a statement of stockholders' equity for Telex Inc. is shown in Exhibit 6.

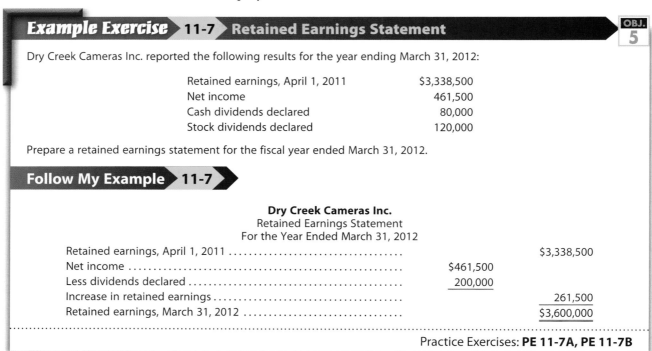

**Example Exercise 11-7 Retained Earnings Statement** **OBJ. 5**

Dry Creek Cameras Inc. reported the following results for the year ending March 31, 2012:

| | |
| --- | --- |
| Retained earnings, April 1, 2011 | $3,338,500 |
| Net income | 461,500 |
| Cash dividends declared | 80,000 |
| Stock dividends declared | 120,000 |

Prepare a retained earnings statement for the fiscal year ended March 31, 2012.

**Follow My Example 11-7**

| Dry Creek Cameras Inc. | | |
| --- | --- | --- |
| Retained Earnings Statement | | |
| For the Year Ended March 31, 2012 | | |
| Retained earnings, April 1, 2011 | | $3,338,500 |
| Net income | $461,500 | |
| Less dividends declared | 200,000 | |
| Increase in retained earnings | | 261,500 |
| Retained earnings, March 31, 2012 | | $3,600,000 |

Practice Exercises: **PE 11-7A, PE 11-7B**

**Restrictions**  The use of retained earnings for payment of dividends may be restricted by action of a corporation's board of directors. Such **restrictions,** sometimes called *appropriations,* remain part of the retained earnings.

Restrictions of retained earnings are classified as:

1. *Legal.* State laws may require a restriction of retained earnings.

> Example: States may restrict retained earnings by the amount of treasury stock purchased. In this way, legal capital cannot be used for dividends.

2. *Contractual.* A corporation may enter into contracts that require restrictions of retained earnings.

> Example: A bank loan may restrict retained earnings so that money for repaying the loan cannot be used for dividends.

3. *Discretionary.* A corporation's board of directors may restrict retained earnings voluntarily.

> Example: The board may restrict retained earnings and, thus, limit dividend distributions so that more money is available for expanding the business.

Restrictions of retained earnings must be disclosed in the financial statements. Such disclosures are usually included in the notes to the financial statements.

**Prior Period Adjustments**  An error may arise from a mathematical mistake or from a mistake in applying accounting principles. Such errors may not be discovered within the same period in which they occur. In such cases, the effect of the error should not affect the current period's net income. Instead, the correction of the error, called a **prior period adjustment**, is reported in the retained earnings statement. Such corrections are reported as an adjustment to the beginning balance of retained earnings.[10]

# Statement of Stockholders' Equity

When the only change in stockholders' equity is due to net income or net loss and dividends, a retained earnings statement is sufficient. However, when a corporation also has changes in stock and paid-in capital accounts, a **statement of stockholders' equity** is normally prepared.

A statement of stockholders' equity is normally prepared in a columnar format. Each column is a major stockholders' equity classification. Changes in each classification are then described in the left-hand column. Exhibit 6 illustrates a statement of stockholders' equity for Telex Inc.

**Statement of Stockholders' Equity    EXHIBIT 6**

**Telex Inc.**
**Statement of Stockholders' Equity**
**For the Year Ended December 31, 2012**

|  | Preferred Stock | Common Stock | Additional Paid-In Capital | Retained Earnings | Treasury Stock | Total |
|---|---|---|---|---|---|---|
| Balance, January 1, 2012 . . . . . . . . . . . . . . . . | $100,000 | $850,000 | $177,000 | $245,000 | $(17,000) | $1,355,000 |
| Net income . . . . . . . . . . . . . . . . . . . . . . . . . . . |  |  |  | 180,000 |  | 180,000 |
| Dividends on preferred stock . . . . . . . . . . . |  |  |  | (10,000) |  | (10,000) |
| Dividends on common stock . . . . . . . . . . . . |  |  |  | (65,000) |  | (65,000) |
| Issuance of additional common stock . . . . |  | 50,000 | 25,000 |  |  | 75,000 |
| Purchase of treasury stock . . . . . . . . . . . . . . |  |  |  |  | (10,000) | (10,000) |
| Balance, December 31, 2012 . . . . . . . . . . . . | $100,000 | $900,000 | $202,000 | $350,000 | $(27,000) | $1,525,000 |

10 Prior period adjustments are illustrated in advanced texts.

# Reporting Stockholders' Equity for Mornin' Joe

Mornin' Joe reports stockholders' equity in its balance sheet. Mornin' Joe also includes a retained earnings statement and statement of stockholders' equity in its financial statements.

The Stockholders' Equity section of Mornin' Joe's balance sheet as of December 31, 2012, is shown below.

**Mornin' Joe**
**Balance Sheet**
**December 31, 2012**

### Stockholders' Equity

| | | |
|---|---:|---:|
| Paid-in capital: | | |
| Preferred 10% stock, $50 par (6,000 shares authorized and issued) | $ 300,000 | |
| Excess of issue price over par | 50,000 | $ 350,000 |
| Common stock, $20 par (50,000 shares authorized, 45,000 shares issued) | $ 900,000 | |
| Excess of issue price over par | 1,450,000 | 2,350,000 |
| Total paid-in capital | | $2,700,000 |
| Retained earnings | | 1,200,300 |
| Total | | $3,900,300 |
| Deduct treasury stock (1,000 shares at cost) | | 46,000 |
| Total stockholders' equity | | $3,854,300 |
| Total liabilities and stockholders' equity | | $6,169,700 |

Mornin' Joe's retained earnings statement for the year ended Dec. 31, 2012, is:

**Mornin' Joe**
**Retained Earnings Statment**
**For the Year Ended December 31, 2012**

| | | | |
|---|---:|---:|---:|
| Retained earnings, January 1, 2012 | | | $ 852,700 |
| Net income | | $421,600 | |
| Less dividends: | | | |
| Preferred stock | $30,000 | | |
| Common stock | 44,000 | 74,000 | |
| Increase in retained earnings | | | 347,600 |
| Retained earnings, December 31, 2012 | | | $1,200,300 |

The statement of stockholders' equity for Mornin' Joe is shown below.

**Mornin' Joe**
**Statement of Stockholders' Equity**
**For the Year Ended December 31, 2012**

| | Preferred Stock | Common Stock | Additional Paid-In Capital | Retained Earnings | Treasury Stock | Total |
|---|---:|---:|---:|---:|---:|---:|
| Balance, January 1, 2012 | $300,000 | $800,000 | $1,325,000 | $ 852,700 | $(36,000) | $3,241,700 |
| Net income | | | | 421,600 | | 421,600 |
| Dividends on preferred stock | | | | (30,000) | | (30,000) |
| Dividends on common stock | | | | (44,000) | | (44,000) |
| Issuance of additional common stock | | 100,000 | 175,000 | | | 275,000 |
| Purchase of treasury stock | | | | | (10,000) | (10,000) |
| Balance, December 31, 2012 | $300,000 | $900,000 | $1,500,000 | $1,200,300 | $(46,000) | $3,854,300 |

See pages 630-634

### IFRS Reporting

The statement of financial position (balance sheet) presentation of stockholders' equity for Mornin' Joe International under IFRS is as follows:

| Mornin' Joe International<br>Statement of Financial Position<br>December 31, 2012 | | |
| --- | --- | --- |
| **Equity attributable to owners** | | |
| Preferred 10% stock, $50 par (6,000 shares authorized and issued)* | € 300,000 | |
| common stock, $20 par (50,000) shares authorized, 45,000 shares issued)* | 900,000 | |
| Share premium* | 1,500,000 | |
| Reserves* | (1,200) | |
| Retained earnings* | 1,200,300 | |
| Total equity attributable to owners* | | €3,899,100 |

As discussed in Chapter 7, IFRS provides flexibility in the order in which the balance sheet accounts are presented. Stockholders' equity, termed under IFRS "Equity attributable to owners," is often listed prior to liabilities. Listing equity before liabilities emphasizes the going concern nature of the entity and the long-term financial interest of the owners in the business.

The term "Share premium" is the same as "Excess of issue price over par." Reserves are additional stockholders' equity items other than paid in capital or retained earnings. Unlike IFRS, "reserve" is often used to denote a liability under U.S. GAAP.

The retained earnings statement is rarely disclosed as a separate statement under IFRS. The statement of stockholders' equity is termed the "statement of changes in equity" and is similar to U.S. GAAP, and thus, is not illustrated here.

## Stock Splits

**OBJ. 6** Describe the effect of stock splits on corporate financial statements.

A **stock split** is a process by which a corporation reduces the par or stated value of its common stock and issues a proportionate number of additional shares. A stock split applies to all common shares including the unissued, issued, and treasury shares.

A major objective of a stock split is to reduce the market price per share of the stock. This attracts more investors and broadens the types and numbers of stockholders.

To illustrate, assume that Rojek Corporation has 10,000 shares of $100 par common stock outstanding with a current market price of $150 per share. The board of directors declares the following stock split:

1. Each common shareholder will receive 5 shares for each share held. This is called a 5-for-1 stock split. As a result, 50,000 shares (10,000 shares × 5) will be outstanding.
2. The par of each share of common stock will be reduced to $20 ($100/5).

The par value of the common stock outstanding is $1,000,000 both before and after the stock split as shown below.

| | Before Split | After Split |
| --- | --- | --- |
| Number of shares | 10,000 | 50,000 |
| Par value per share | × $100 | × $20 |
| Total | $1,000,000 | $1,000,000 |

In addition, each Rojek Corporation shareholder owns the same total par amount of stock before and after the stock split. For example, a stockholder who owned 4 shares of $100 par stock before the split (total par of $400) would own 20 shares of

**Before Stock Split**

4 shares, $100 par

$400 total par value

**After 5:1 Stock Split**

20 shares, $20 par

$400 total par value

$20 par stock after the split (total par of $400). Only the number of shares and the par value per share have changed.

Since there are more shares outstanding after the stock split, the market price of the stock should decrease. For example, in the preceding example, there would be 5 times as many shares outstanding after the split. Thus, the market price of the stock would be expected to fall from $150 to about $30 ($150/5).

Stock splits do not require a journal entry since only the par (or stated) value and number of shares outstanding have changed. However, the details of stock splits are normally disclosed in the notes to the financial statements.

## BusinessConnection

### BUFFETT ON STOCK SPLITS

Warren E. Buffett, chairman and chief executive officer of Berkshire Hathaway Inc., opposes stock splits on the basis that they add no value to the company. Since its inception, Berkshire Hathaway has never declared a stock split on its primary (Class A) common stock. As a result, Berkshire Hathaway's Class A common stock sells well above $100,000 per share, which is the most expensive stock on the New York Stock Exchange. Such a high price doesn't bother Buffet since he believes that high stock prices attract more sophisticated and long-term investors and discourage stock speculators and short-term investors.

In contrast, Microsoft Corporation has split its stock nine times since it went public in 1986. As a result, one share of Microsoft purchased in 1986 is equivalent to 288 shares today, which would be worth approximately $7,500.

## F·A·I

# Financial Analysis and Interpretation: Earnings per Share

**OBJ. 7**
Describe and illustrate the use of earnings per share in evaluating a company's profitability.

Net income is often used by investors and creditors in evaluating a company's profitability. However, net income by itself is difficult to use in comparing companies of different sizes. Also, trends in net income may be difficult to evaluate if there have been significant changes in a company's stockholders' equity. Thus, the profitability of companies is often expressed as earnings per share.

**Earnings per common share (EPS)**, sometimes called *basic earnings per share,* is the net income per share of common stock outstanding during a period.[11] Corporations whose stock is traded in a public market must report earnings per common share on their income statements.

Earnings per share is computed as follows:

$$\text{Earnings per Share} = \frac{\text{Net Income} - \text{Preferred Dividends}}{\text{Average Number of Common Shares Outstanding}}$$

If a company has preferred stock outstanding, any preferred dividends are subtracted from net income. This is because the numerator represents only those earnings available to the common shareholders.

To illustrate, the following data (in thousands) were taken from Hasbro's financial statements:

|  | 2009 | 2008 |
|---|---|---|
| Net income............................. | $374,930 | $306,766 |
| Average number of common shares outstanding ........................... | 139,487 shares | 140,877 shares |
| Earnings per share....................... | $2.69 | $2.18 |
|  | ($374,930 ÷ 139,487 shares) | ($306,766 ÷ 140,877 shares) |

11 For complex capital structures, earnings per share assuming dilution may also be reported as described in Chapter 15.

Hasbro had no preferred stock outstanding during 2008; thus, no preferred dividends were subtracted in computing earnings per share. As shown above, Hasbro's earnings per share increased from $2.18 in 2008 to $2.69 in 2009. An increase in earnings per share is generally considered a favorable trend.

Earnings per share can be used to compare two companies with different net incomes. For example, the following data (in millions) were taken from a recent year's financial statements for Bank of America Corporation and JP Morgan Chase & Co.

| | Bank of America | JP Morgan Chase |
|---|---|---|
| Net income................................ | $4,008 | $5,605 |
| Preferred dividends......................... | $1,452 | $674 |
| Average number of common shares outstanding........................ | 4,592 shares | 3,501 shares |

Bank of America:

$$\text{Earnings per Share} = \frac{\text{Net Income} - \text{Preferred Dividends}}{\text{Average Number of Common Shares Outstanding}} = \frac{\$4,008 - \$1,452}{4,592 \text{ shares}} = \frac{\$2,556}{4,592 \text{ shares}} = \$0.56$$

JP Morgan Chase:

$$\text{Earnings per Share} = \frac{\text{Net Income} - \text{Preferred Dividends}}{\text{Average Number of Common Shares Outstanding}} = \frac{\$5,605 - \$674}{3,501 \text{ shares}} = \frac{\$4,931}{3,501 \text{ shares}} = \$1.41$$

On the bases of net income and earnings per share, JP Morgan Chase is more profitable than Bank of America.

---

## Example Exercise 11-8 Earnings per Share

**OBJ. 7**

Financial statement data for years ending December 31 for Finnegan Company are shown below.

| | 2012 | 2011 |
|---|---|---|
| Net income ............................................ | $350,000 | $195,000 |
| Preferred dividends ..................................... | $20,000 | $15,000 |
| Average number of common shares outstanding ........ | 75,000 shares | 50,000 shares |

a. Determine earnings per share for 2012 and 2011.
b. Does the change in the earnings per share from 2011 to 2012 indicate a favorable or an unfavorable trend?

### Follow My Example 11-8

a.

2012:

$$\text{Earnings per Share} = \frac{\text{Net Income} - \text{Preferred Dividends}}{\text{Average Number of Common Shares Outstanding}} = \frac{\$350,000 - \$20,000}{75,000 \text{ shares}} = \frac{\$330,000}{75,000 \text{ shares}} = \$4.40$$

2011:

$$\text{Earnings per Share} = \frac{\text{Net Income} - \text{Preferred Dividends}}{\text{Average Number of Common Shares Outstanding}} = \frac{\$195,000 - \$15,000}{50,000 \text{ shares}} = \frac{\$180,000}{50,000 \text{ shares}} = \$3.60$$

b. The increase in the earnings per share from $3.60 to $4.40 indicates a favorable trend in the company's profitability.

Practice Exercises: **PE 11-8A, PE 11-8B**

# At a Glance 11

### OBJ. 1 Describe the nature of the corporate form of organization.

**Key Points** Corporations have a separate legal existence, transferable units of stock, unlimited life, and limited stockholders' liability. The advantages and disadvantages of the corporate form are summarized in Exhibit 2. Costs incurred in organizing a corporation are debited to Organizational Expenses.

| Learning Outcomes | Example Exercises | Practice Exercises |
|---|---|---|
| • Describe the characteristics of corporations. | | |
| • List the advantages and disadvantages of the corporate form. | | |
| • Prepare a journal entry for the costs of organizing a corporation. | | |

### OBJ. 2 Describe and illustrate the characteristics of stock, classes of stock, and entries for issuing stock.

**Key Points** The main source of paid-in capital is from issuing common and preferred stock. Stock issued at par is recorded by debiting Cash and crediting the class of stock issued for its par amount. Stock issued for more than par is recorded by debiting Cash, crediting the class of stock for its par, and crediting Paid-In Capital in Excess of Par for the difference. When no-par stock is issued, the entire proceeds are credited to the stock account. No-par stock may be assigned a stated value per share, and the excess of the proceeds over the stated value may be credited to Paid-In Capital in Excess of Stated Value.

| Learning Outcomes | Example Exercises | Practice Exercises |
|---|---|---|
| • Describe the characteristics of common and preferred stock including rights to dividends. | EE11-1 | 11-1A, 11-1B |
| • Journalize the entry for common and preferred stock issued at par. | EE11-2 | 11-2A, 11-2B |
| • Journalize the entry for common and preferred stock issued at more than par. | EE11-2 | 11-2A, 11-2B |
| • Journalize the entry for issuing no-par stock. | EE11-2 | 11-2A, 11-2B |

### OBJ. 3 Describe and illustrate the accounting for cash dividends and stock dividends.

**Key Points** The entry to record a declaration of cash dividends debits Dividends and credits Dividends Payable. When a stock dividend is declared, Stock Dividends is debited for the fair value of the stock to be issued. Stock Dividends Distributable is credited for the par or stated value of the common stock to be issued. The difference between the fair value of the stock and its par or stated value is credited to Paid-In Capital in Excess of Par—Common Stock. When the stock is issued on the date of payment, Stock Dividends Distributable is debited and Common Stock is credited for the par or stated value of the stock issued.

| Learning Outcomes | Example Exercises | Practice Exercises |
|---|---|---|
| • Journalize the entries for the declaration and payment of cash dividends. | EE11-3 | PE11-3A, 11-3B |
| • Journalize the entries for the declaration and payment of stock dividends. | EE11-4 | PE11-4A, 11-4B |

## 4 Describe and illustrate the accounting for treasury stock transactions.

**Key Points** When a corporation buys its own stock, the cost method of accounting is normally used. Treasury Stock is debited for its cost, and Cash is credited. If the stock is resold, Treasury Stock is credited for its cost and any difference between the cost and the selling price is normally debited or credited to Paid-In Capital from Sale of Treasury Stock.

| Learning Outcomes | Example Exercises | Practice Exercises |
|---|---|---|
| • Define treasury stock. | | |
| • Describe the accounting for treasury stock. | | |
| • Journalize entries for the purchase and sale of treasury stock. | **EE11-5** | **PE11-5A, 11-5B** |

## 5 Describe and illustrate the reporting of stockholders' equity.

**Key Points** Two alternatives for reporting stockholders' equity are shown in Exhibit 4. Changes in retained earnings are reported in a retained earnings statement, as shown in Exhibit 5. Restrictions to retained earnings should be disclosed. Any prior period adjustments are reported in the retained earnings statement. Changes in stockholders' equity may be reported on a statement of stockholders' equity, as shown in Exhibit 6.

| Learning Outcomes | Example Exercises | Practice Exercises |
|---|---|---|
| • Prepare the Stockholders' Equity section of the balance sheet. | **EE11-6** | **PE11-6A, 11-6B** |
| • Prepare a retained earnings statement. | **EE11-7** | **PE11-7A, 11-7B** |
| • Describe retained earnings restrictions and prior period adjustments. | | |
| • Prepare a statement of stockholders' equity. | | |

## 6 Describe the effect of stock splits on corporate financial statements.

**Key Points** When a corporation reduces the par or stated value of its common stock and issues a proportionate number of additional shares, a stock split has occurred. There are no changes in the balances of any accounts, and no entry is required for a stock split.

| Learning Outcomes | Example Exercises | Practice Exercises |
|---|---|---|
| • Define and give an example of a stock split. | | |
| • Describe the accounting for and effects of a stock split on the financial statements. | | |

## 7 Describe and illustrate the use of earnings per share in evaluating a company's profitability.

**Key Points** The profitability of companies is often expressed as earnings per share. Earnings per share is computed by subtracting preferred dividends from net income and dividing by the average number of common shares outstanding.

| Learning Outcomes | Example Exercises | Practice Exercises |
|---|---|---|
| • Describe the use of earnings per share in evaluating a company's profitability. | | |
| • Compute and interpret earnings per share. | **EE11-8** | **PE11-8A, 11-8B** |

## Key Terms

cash dividend (510)

common stock (505)

cumulative preferred
stock (505)

discount (507)

earnings per common
share (EPS) (520)

in arrears (505)

outstanding stock (504)

paid-in capital (504)

par (504)

preferred stock (505)

premium (507)

prior period
adjustment (517)

restrictions (517)

statement of stockholders'
equity (517)

stock (502)

stock dividend (511)

stock split (519)

stockholders (502)

treasury stock (513)

## Illustrative Problem

Altenburg Inc. is a lighting fixture wholesaler located in Arizona. During its current fiscal year, ended December 31, 2012, Altenburg Inc. completed the following selected transactions:

Feb.   3.  Purchased 2,500 shares of its own common stock at $26, recording the stock at cost. (Prior to the purchase, there were 40,000 shares of $20 par common stock outstanding.)

May   1.  Declared a semiannual dividend of $1 on the 10,000 shares of preferred stock and a 30¢ dividend on the common stock to stockholders of record on May 31, payable on June 15.

June  15.  Paid the cash dividends.

Sept.  23.  Sold 1,000 shares of treasury stock at $28, receiving cash.

Nov.   1.  Declared semiannual dividends of $1 on the preferred stock and 30¢ on the common stock. In addition, a 5% common stock dividend was declared on the common stock outstanding, to be capitalized at the fair market value of the common stock, which is estimated at $30.

Dec.   1.  Paid the cash dividends and issued the certificates for the common stock dividend.

### Instructions

Journalize the entries to record the transactions for Altenburg Inc.

### Solution

| 2012 | | | | | |
|---|---|---|---|---|---|
| Feb. | 3 | Treasury Stock | | 65,000 | |
| | |     Cash | | | 65,000 |
| | | | | | |
| May | 1 | Cash Dividends | | 21,250 | |
| | |     Cash Dividends Payable | | | 21,250 |
| | |       (10,000 × $1) + [(40,000 − 2,500) × $0.30]. | | | |
| | | | | | |
| June | 15 | Cash Dividends Payable | | 21,250 | |
| | |     Cash | | | 21,250 |
| | | | | | |
| Sept. | 23 | Cash | | 28,000 | |
| | |     Treasury Stock | | | 26,000 |
| | |     Paid-In Capital from Sale of Treasury Stock | | | 2,000 |

| Nov. | 1 | Cash Dividends | 21,550 | |
| | |     Cash Dividends Payable | | 21,550 |
| | |        (10,000 × $1) + [(40,000 – 1,500) × $0.30]. | | |
| | | | | |
| | 1 | Stock Dividends | 57,750* | |
| | |     Stock Dividends Distributable | | 38,500 |
| | |     Paid-In Capital in Excess of | | |
| | |     Par—Common Stock | | 19,250 |
| | |        *(40,000 – 1,500) × 5% × $30. | | |
| | | | | |
| Dec. | 1 | Cash Dividends Payable | 21,550 | |
| | | Stock Dividends Distributable | 38,500 | |
| | |     Cash | | 21,550 |
| | |     Common Stock | | 38,500 |

# Discussion Questions

1. Of two corporations organized at approximately the same time and engaged in competing businesses, one issued $150 par common stock, and the other issued $1.00 par common stock. Do the par designations provide any indication as to which stock is preferable as an investment? Explain.

2. A stockbroker advises a client to "buy preferred stock. . . . With that type of stock, . . . [you] will never have to worry about losing the dividends." Is the broker right?

3. A corporation with both preferred stock and common stock outstanding has a substantial credit balance in its retained earnings account at the beginning of the current fiscal year. Although net income for the current year is sufficient to pay the preferred dividend of $90,000 each quarter and a common dividend of $275,000 each quarter, the board of directors declares dividends only on the preferred stock. Suggest possible reasons for passing the dividends on the common stock.

4. An owner of 1,000 shares of Simmons Company common stock receives a stock dividend of 6 shares.

   a. What is the effect of the stock dividend on the stockholder's proportionate interest (equity) in the corporation?

   b. How does the total equity of 1,006 shares compare with the total equity of 1,000 shares before the stock dividend?

5. a. Where should a declared but unpaid cash dividend be reported on the balance sheet?

   b. Where should a declared but unissued stock dividend be reported on the balance sheet?

6. A corporation reacquires 25,000 shares of its own $10 par common stock for $1,000,000, recording it at cost.

   a. What effect does this transaction have on revenue or expense of the period?

   b. What effect does it have on stockholders' equity?

7. The treasury stock in Discussion Question 6 is resold for $1,200,000.

   a. What is the effect on the corporation's revenue of the period?

   b. What is the effect on stockholders' equity?

8. What are the three classifications of restrictions of retained earnings, and how are such restrictions normally reported on the financial statements?

9. Indicate how prior period adjustments would be reported on the financial statements presented only for the current period.

10. What is the primary purpose of a stock split?

# Practice Exercises

### PE 11-1A    Dividends per share

Hays-Smith Company has 18,000 shares of 4% cumulative preferred stock of $125 par and 50,000 shares of $40 par common stock. The following amounts were distributed as dividends:

| | |
|---|---|
| Year 1 | $ 72,000 |
| Year 2 | 125,000 |
| Year 3 | 160,000 |

Determine the dividends per share for preferred and common stock for each year.

### PE 11-1B    Dividends per share

Lasers4U Company has 10,000 shares of 2% cumulative preferred stock of $50 par and 25,000 shares of $100 par common stock. The following amounts were distributed as dividends:

| | |
|---|---|
| Year 1 | $18,000 |
| Year 2 | 7,500 |
| Year 3 | 35,000 |

Determine the dividends per share for preferred and common stock for each year.

### PE 11-2A    Entries for issuing stock

On February 23, Muir Corporation issued for cash 75,000 shares of no-par common stock (with a stated value of $80) at $125. On October 6, Muir issued 20,000 shares of 1%, $50 preferred stock at par for cash. On November 4, Muir issued for cash 12,000 shares of 1%, $50 par preferred stock at $59.

Journalize the entries to record the February 23, October 6, and November 4 transactions.

### PE 11-2B    Entries for issuing stock

On August 7, Asian Artifacts Corporation issued for cash 300,000 shares of no-par common stock at $1.75. On September 1, Asian Artifacts issued 25,000 shares of 2%, $40 preferred stock at par for cash. On November 2, Asian Artifacts issued for cash 10,000 shares of 2%, $40 par preferred stock at $52.

Journalize the entries to record the August 7, September 1, and November 2 transactions.

### PE 11-3A    Entries for cash dividends

The declaration, record, and payment dates in connection with a cash dividend of $115,000 on a corporation's common stock are October 15, November 14, and December 14. Journalize the entries required on each date.

### PE 11-3B    Entries for cash dividends

The declaration, record, and payment dates in connection with a cash dividend of $275,000 on a corporation's common stock are March 3, April 2, and May 2. Journalize the entries required on each date.

### PE 11-4A    Entries for stock dividends

Arroyo Corporation has 100,000 shares of $60 par common stock outstanding. On February 8, Arroyo Corporation declared a 6% stock dividend to be issued April 11 to stockholders of record on March 10. The market price of the stock was $94 per share on February 8.

Journalize the entries required on February 8, March 10, and April 11.

### PE 11-4B  Entries for stock dividends

U-Store Corporation has 250,000 shares of $15 par common stock outstanding. On July 20, U-Store Corporation declared a 3% stock dividend to be issued September 18 to stockholders of record on August 19. The market price of the stock was $54 per share on July 20.

Journalize the entries required on July 20, August 19, and September 18.

### PE 11-5A  Entries for treasury stock

On March 8, Golf Resorts Inc. reacquired 13,000 shares of its common stock at $42 per share. On May 16, Golf Resorts sold 9,500 of the reacquired shares at $50 per share. On August 30, Golf Resorts sold the remaining shares at $40 per share.

Journalize the transactions of March 8, May 16, and August 30.

### PE 11-5B  Entries for treasury stock

On September 9, Palin Clothing Inc. reacquired 9,000 shares of its common stock at $24 per share. On October 7, Palin Clothing sold 4,800 of the reacquired shares at $29 per share. On December 20, Palin Clothing sold the remaining shares at $22 per share.

Journalize the transactions of September 9, October 7, and December 20.

### PE 11-6A  Reporting stockholders' equity

Using the following accounts and balances, prepare the Stockholders' Equity section of the balance sheet. Fifty thousand shares of common stock are authorized, and 2,500 shares have been reacquired.

| | |
|---|---|
| Common Stock, $120 par | $4,800,000 |
| Paid-In Capital in Excess of Par | 600,000 |
| Paid-In Capital from Sale of Treasury Stock | 59,000 |
| Retained Earnings | 7,138,500 |
| Treasury Stock | 287,500 |

### PE 11-6B  Reporting stockholders' equity

Using the following accounts and balances, prepare the Stockholders' Equity section of the balance sheet. Two-hundred thousand shares of common stock are authorized, and 24,000 shares have been reacquired.

| | |
|---|---|
| Common Stock, $15 par | $2,400,000 |
| Paid-In Capital in Excess of Par | 480,000 |
| Paid-In Capital from Sale of Treasury Stock | 100,000 |
| Retained Earnings | 5,275,000 |
| Treasury Stock | 336,000 |

### PE 11-7A  Retained earnings statement

Emmy Leaders Inc. reported the following results for the year ending August 31, 2012:

| | |
|---|---|
| Retained earnings, September 1, 2011 | $740,000 |
| Net income | 145,000 |
| Cash dividends declared | 5,000 |
| Stock dividends declared | 30,000 |

Prepare a retained earnings statement for the fiscal year ended August 31, 2012.

### PE 11-7B  Retained earnings statement

Auckland Cruises Inc. reported the following results for the year ending April 30, 2012:

| | |
|---|---|
| Retained earnings, May 1, 2011 | $3,180,000 |
| Net income | 515,000 |
| Cash dividends declared | 100,000 |
| Stock dividends declared | 125,000 |

Prepare a retained earnings statement for the fiscal year ended April 30, 2012.

| *Learning* | *Example* |
| *Objectives* | *Exercises* |

**OBJ. 7**   **EE 11-8** *p. 521*

**PE 11-8A   Earnings per share**

Financial statement data for years ending December 31 for Jardine Company are shown below.

| | 2012 | 2011 |
|---|---|---|
| Net income | $117,000 | $104,000 |
| Preferred dividends | $18,000 | $18,000 |
| Average number of common shares outstanding | 50,000 shares | 40,000 shares |

a. Determine the earnings per share for 2012 and 2011.

b. Does the change in the earnings per share from 2011 to 2012 indicate a favorable or an unfavorable trend?

**OBJ. 7**   **EE 11-8** *p. 521*

**F·A·I**

**PE 11-8B   Earnings per share**

Financial statement data for years ending December 31 for Duffner Company are shown below.

| | 2012 | 2011 |
|---|---|---|
| Net income | $971,000 | $692,000 |
| Preferred dividends | $35,000 | $35,000 |
| Average number of common shares outstanding | 120,000 shares | 90,000 shares |

a. Determine the earnings per share for 2012 and 2011.

b. Does the change in the earnings per share from 2011 to 2012 indicate a favorable or an unfavorable trend?

# Exercises

**OBJ. 2**

✔ Preferred stock,
1st year: $1.25

**EX 11-1   Dividends per share**

Baxter Inc., a developer of radiology equipment, has stock outstanding as follows: 18,000 shares of cumulative 2%, preferred stock of $75 par, and 40,000 shares of $10 par common. During its first four years of operations, the following amounts were distributed as dividends: first year, $22,500; second year, $28,800; third year, $40,100; fourth year, $77,000. Calculate the dividends per share on each class of stock for each of the four years.

**OBJ. 2**

✔ Preferred stock,
1st year: $0.30

**EX 11-2   Dividends per share**

Wings Inc., a software development firm, has stock outstanding as follows: 25,000 shares of cumulative 1%, preferred stock of $40 par, and 50,000 shares of $120 par common. During its first four years of operations, the following amounts were distributed as dividends: first year, $7,500; second year, $10,500; third year, $25,000; fourth year, $60,000. Calculate the dividends per share on each class of stock for each of the four years.

**OBJ. 2**

**EX 11-3   Entries for issuing par stock**

On January 14, Mountain Rocks Inc., a marble contractor, issued for cash 24,000 shares of $25 par common stock at $32, and on March 17, it issued for cash 60,000 shares of $10 par preferred stock at $11.

a. Journalize the entries for January 14 and March 17.

b. What is the total amount invested (total paid-in capital) by all stockholders as of March 17?

**OBJ. 2**

**EX 11-4   Entries for issuing no-par stock**

On July 12, Lasting Carpet Inc., a carpet wholesaler, issued for cash 300,000 shares of no-par common stock (with a stated value of $4) at $9, and on November 18, it issued for cash 40,000 shares of $90 par preferred stock at $100.

a. Journalize the entries for July 12 and November 18, assuming that the common stock is to be credited with the stated value.

b. What is the total amount invested (total paid-in capital) by all stockholders as of November 18?

OBJ. 2

### EX 11-5  Issuing stock for assets other than cash

On April 15, Hass Corporation, a wholesaler of hydraulic lifts, acquired land in exchange for 17,500 shares of $20 par common stock with a current market price of $30. Journalize the entry to record the transaction.

OBJ. 2

### EX 11-6  Selected stock transactions

Fantastic Sounds Corp., an electric guitar retailer, was organized by Pam Mikhail, Jane Lo, and Dale Nadal. The charter authorized 400,000 shares of common stock with a par of $50. The following transactions affecting stockholders' equity were completed during the first year of operations:

a. Issued 20,000 shares of stock at par to Pam Mikhail for cash.

b. Issued 1,000 shares of stock at par to Dale Nadal for promotional services provided in connection with the organization of the corporation, and issued 15,000 shares of stock at par to Dale Nadal for cash.

c. Purchased land and a building from Jane Lo. The building is mortgaged for $300,000 for 20 years at 5%, and there is accrued interest of $2,500 on the mortgage note at the time of the purchase. It is agreed that the land is to be priced at $200,000 and the building at $500,000, and that Jane Lo's equity will be exchanged for stock at par. The corporation agreed to assume responsibility for paying the mortgage note and the accrued interest.

Journalize the entries to record the transactions.

OBJ. 2

### EX 11-7  Issuing stock

Wildwood Nursery, with an authorization of 50,000 shares of preferred stock and 400,000 shares of common stock, completed several transactions involving its stock on June 1, the first day of operations. The trial balance at the close of the day follows:

| | | |
|---|---:|---:|
| Cash | 1,584,000 | |
| Land | 350,000 | |
| Buildings | 910,000 | |
| Preferred 3% Stock, $120 par | | 1,200,000 |
| Paid-In Capital in Excess of Par—Preferred Stock | | 60,000 |
| Common Stock, $50 par | | 1,500,000 |
| Paid-In Capital in Excess of Par—Common Stock | | 84,000 |
| | 2,844,000 | 2,844,000 |

All shares within each class of stock were sold at the same price. The preferred stock was issued in exchange for the land and buildings.

Journalize the two entries to record the transactions summarized in the trial balance.

OBJ. 2

### EX 11-8  Issuing stock

Baird Products Inc., a wholesaler of office products, was organized on January 30 of the current year, with an authorization of 80,000 shares of 2% preferred stock, $75 par and 800,000 shares of $20 par common stock. The following selected transactions were completed during the first year of operations:

Jan.  30.  Issued 300,000 shares of common stock at par for cash.

    31.  Issued 750 shares of common stock at par to an attorney in payment of legal fees for organizing the corporation.

Feb.  21.  Issued 32,000 shares of common stock in exchange for land, buildings, and equipment with fair market prices of $150,000, $460,000, and $90,000, respectively.

Mar.   2.  Issued 15,000 shares of preferred stock at $77.50 for cash.

Journalize the transactions.

OBJ. 3

### EX 11-9 Entries for cash dividends

The declaration, record, and payment dates in connection with a cash dividend of $365,850 on a corporation's common stock are April 1, May 1, and June 3. Journalize the entries required on each date.

OBJ. 3

✔ b. (1) $18,060,000
(3) $93,556,000

### EX 11-10 Entries for stock dividends

Organic Life Co. is an HMO for businesses in the Portland area. The following account balances appear on the balance sheet of Organic Life Co.: Common stock (250,000 shares authorized), $125 par, $17,500,000; Paid-in capital in excess of par—common stock, $560,000; and Retained earnings, $75,496,000. The board of directors declared a 3% stock dividend when the market price of the stock was $132 a share. Organic Life Co. reported no income or loss for the current year.

a. Journalize the entries to record (1) the declaration of the dividend, capitalizing an amount equal to market value, and (2) the issuance of the stock certificates.

b. Determine the following amounts before the stock dividend was declared: (1) total paid-in capital, (2) total retained earnings, and (3) total stockholders' equity.

c. Determine the following amounts after the stock dividend was declared and closing entries were recorded at the end of the year: (1) total paid-in capital, (2) total retained earnings, and (3) total stockholders' equity.

OBJ. 4

✔ b. $102,000 credit

### EX 11-11 Treasury stock transactions

Deer Creek Inc. bottles and distributes spring water. On April 27 of the current year, Deer Creek reacquired 15,000 shares of its common stock at $60 per share. On July 13, Deer Creek sold 9,000 of the reacquired shares at $72 per share. The remaining 6,000 shares were sold at $59 per share on October 8.

a. Journalize the transactions of April 27, July 13, and October 8.

b. What is the balance in Paid-In Capital from Sale of Treasury Stock on December 31 of the current year?

c. ⬛➤ For what reasons might Deer Creek have purchased the treasury stock?

OBJ. 4, 5

✔ b. $94,000 credit

### EX 11-12 Treasury stock transactions

Golden Gardens Inc. develops and produces spraying equipment for lawn maintenance and industrial uses. On June 19 of the current year, Golden Gardens Inc. reacquired 24,000 shares of its common stock at $64 per share. On August 30, 19,000 of the reacquired shares were sold at $68 per share, and on September 6, 3,000 of the reacquired shares were sold at $70.

a. Journalize the transactions of June 19, August 30, and September 6.

b. What is the balance in Paid-In Capital from Sale of Treasury Stock on December 31 of the current year?

c. What is the balance in Treasury Stock on December 31 of the current year?

d. How will the balance in Treasury Stock be reported on the balance sheet?

OBJ. 4, 5

✔ b. $24,000 credit

### EX 11-13 Treasury stock transactions

Conyers Water Inc. bottles and distributes spring water. On July 5 of the current year, Conyers Water Inc. reacquired 12,500 shares of its common stock at $80 per share. On November 3, Conyers Water Inc. sold 7,000 of the reacquired shares at $85 per share. The remaining 5,500 shares were sold at $78 per share on December 10.

a. Journalize the transactions of July 5, November 3, and December 10.

b. What is the balance in Paid-In Capital from Sale of Treasury Stock on December 31 of the current year?

c. Where will the balance in Paid-In Capital from Sale of Treasury Stock be reported on the balance sheet?

d. ⬛➤ For what reasons might Conyers Water Inc. have purchased the treasury stock?

**OBJ. 5**

✔ Total paid-in capital, $7,720,000

### EX 11-14 Reporting paid-in capital

The following accounts and their balances were selected from the unadjusted trial balance of CW Group Inc., a freight forwarder, at March 31, the end of the current fiscal year:

| | |
|---|---|
| Preferred 1% Stock, $75 par | $ 4,500,000 |
| Paid-In Capital in Excess of Par—Preferred Stock | 180,000 |
| Common Stock, no par, $8 stated value | 2,400,000 |
| Paid-In Capital in Excess of Stated Value—Common Stock | 450,000 |
| Paid-In Capital from Sale of Treasury Stock | 190,000 |
| Retained Earnings | 11,570,000 |

Prepare the Paid-In Capital portion of the Stockholders' Equity section of the balance sheet. There are 500,000 shares of common stock authorized and 100,000 shares of preferred stock authorized.

**OBJ. 5**

✔ Total stockholders' equity, $11,677,000

### EX 11-15 Stockholders' equity section of balance sheet

The following accounts and their balances appear in the ledger of Cline Properties Inc. on April 30 of the current year:

| | |
|---|---|
| Common Stock, $90 par | $2,700,000 |
| Paid-In Capital in Excess of Par | 120,000 |
| Paid-In Capital from Sale of Treasury Stock | 36,000 |
| Retained Earnings | 9,173,000 |
| Treasury Stock | 352,000 |

Prepare the Stockholders' Equity section of the balance sheet as of April 30. Fifty thousand shares of common stock are authorized, and 4,000 shares have been reacquired.

**OBJ. 5**

✔ Total stockholders' equity, $31,308,000

### EX 11-16 Stockholders' equity section of balance sheet

Furious and Fast Car Inc. retails racing products for BMWs, Porsches, and Ferraris. The following accounts and their balances appear in the ledger of Furious and Fast Car Inc. on November 30, the end of the current year:

| | |
|---|---|
| Common Stock, $8 par | $ 3,000,000 |
| Paid-In Capital in Excess of Par—Common Stock | 525,000 |
| Paid-In Capital in Excess of Par—Preferred Stock | 280,000 |
| Paid-In Capital from Sale of Treasury Stock—Common | 175,000 |
| Preferred 2% Stock, $125 par | 5,000,000 |
| Retained Earnings | 23,120,000 |
| Treasury Stock—Common | 792,000 |

Sixty thousand shares of preferred and 500,000 shares of common stock are authorized. There are 88,000 shares of common stock held as treasury stock.

Prepare the Stockholders' Equity section of the balance sheet as of November 30, the end of the current year.

**OBJ. 5**

✔ Retained earnings, October 31, $966,750

### EX 11-17 Retained earnings statement

Sandusky Corporation, a manufacturer of industrial pumps, reports the following results for the year ending October 31, 2012:

| | |
|---|---|
| Retained earnings, November 1, 2011 | $796,750 |
| Net income | 215,000 |
| Cash dividends declared | 15,000 |
| Stock dividends declared | 30,000 |

Prepare a retained earnings statement for the fiscal year ended October 31, 2012.

**OBJ. 5**

✔ Corrected total stockholders' equity, $53,527,000

### EX 11-18 Stockholders' equity section of balance sheet

List the errors in the following Stockholders' Equity section of the balance sheet prepared as of the end of the current year.

**Stockholders' Equity**

| | | |
|---|---|---|
| Paid-in capital: | | |
| Preferred 1% stock, $200 par | | |
| (25,000 shares authorized and issued)................... | $5,000,000 | |
| Excess of issue price over par .............................. | 75,000 | $ 5,075,000 |
| Retained earnings ........................................... | | 41,750,000 |
| Treasury stock (45,000 shares at cost) ..................... | | 648,000 |
| Dividends payable........................................... | | 175,000 |
| Total paid-in capital ..................................... | | $47,648,000 |
| Common stock, $14 par (800,000 shares | | |
| authorized, 500,000 shares issued)...................... | | 7,600,000 |
| Organizing costs ................................................ | | 250,000 |
| Total stockholders' equity ........................................ | | $55,498,000 |

---

**EX 11-19   Statement of stockholders' equity**

The stockholders' equity T accounts of Life's Greeting Cards Inc. for the current fiscal year ended December 31, 2012, are as follows. Prepare a statement of stockholders' equity for the fiscal year ended December 31, 2012.

**COMMON STOCK**

| | | | |
|---|---|---|---|
| | Jan.  1 | Balance | 3,000,000 |
| | Mar.  7 | Issued | |
| | | 27,000 shares | 1,350,000 |
| | Dec. 31 | Balance | 4,350,000 |

**PAID-IN CAPITAL IN EXCESS OF PAR**

| | | | |
|---|---|---|---|
| | Jan.  1 | Balance | 480,000 |
| | Mar.  7 | Issued | |
| | | 27,000 shares | 324,000 |
| | Dec. 31 | Balance | 804,000 |

**TREASURY STOCK**

| | | | |
|---|---|---|---|
| Aug.  7 | Purchased | | |
| | 4,500 shares | 216,000 | |

**RETAINED EARNINGS**

| | | | | | |
|---|---|---|---|---|---|
| Mar.  31 | Dividend | 37,500 | Jan.  1 | Balance | 5,220,000 |
| June 30 | Dividend | 37,500 | Dec. 31 | Closing | |
| Sept. 30 | Dividend | 37,500 | | (net income) | 765,000 |
| Dec.  31 | Dividend | 37,500 | Dec. 31 | Balance | 5,835,000 |

---

OBJ. 6

**EX 11-20   Effect of stock split**

Gino's Restaurant Corporation wholesales ovens and ranges to restaurants throughout the Midwest. Gino's Restaurant Corporation, which had 100,000 shares of common stock outstanding, declared a 5-for-1 stock split (4 additional shares for each share issued).

a.  What will be the number of shares outstanding after the split?

b.  If the common stock had a market price of $200 per share before the stock split, what would be an approximate market price per share after the split?

---

OBJ. 3, 6

**EX 11-21   Effect of cash dividend and stock split**

Indicate whether the following actions would (+) increase, (–) decrease, or (0) not affect Indigo Inc.'s total assets, liabilities, and stockholders' equity:

| | Assets | Liabilities | Stockholders' Equity |
|---|---|---|---|
| (1)  Authorizing and issuing stock certificates in a stock split | _____ | _____ | _____ |
| (2)  Declaring a stock dividend | _____ | _____ | _____ |
| (3)  Issuing stock certificates for the stock dividend declared in (2) | _____ | _____ | _____ |
| (4)  Declaring a cash dividend | _____ | _____ | _____ |
| (5)  Paying the cash dividend declared in (4) | _____ | _____ | _____ |

OBJ. 3, 6

### EX 11-22 Selected dividend transactions, stock split

Selected transactions completed by Gene's Boating Corporation during the current fiscal year are as follows:

Feb. 10. Split the common stock 3 for 1 and reduced the par from $60 to $20 per share. After the split, there were 300,000 common shares outstanding.

May 1. Declared semiannual dividends of $2.00 on 40,000 shares of preferred stock and $0.12 on the common stock payable on June 15.

June 15. Paid the cash dividends.

Nov. 1. Declared semiannual dividends of $2.00 on the preferred stock and $0.08 on the common stock (before the stock dividend). In addition, a 2% common stock dividend was declared on the common stock outstanding. The fair market value of the common stock is estimated at $28.

Dec. 15. Paid the cash dividends and issued the certificates for the common stock dividend.

Journalize the transactions.

OBJ. 7

### EX 11-23 EPS

Malen Arts, Inc., had earnings of $133,750 for 2012. The company had 25,000 shares of common stock outstanding during the year. In addition, the company issued 10,000 shares of $100 par value preferred stock on January 3, 2012. The preferred stock has a dividend of $4 per share. There were no transactions in either common or preferred stock during 2012.

Determine the basic earnings per share for Malen Arts.

OBJ. 7

### EX 11-24 EPS

Procter & Gamble (P&G) is one of the largest consumer products companies in the world, famous for such brands as Crest® and Tide®. Financial information for the company for three recent years is as follows:

| | Fiscal Years Ended (in millions) | | |
| --- | --- | --- | --- |
| | 2009 | 2008 | 2007 |
| Net income | $11,293 | $11,798 | $10,063 |
| Preferred dividends | $192 | $176 | $161 |
| Average number of common shares outstanding | 2,952 | 3,081 | 3,159 |

a. Determine the earnings per share for fiscal years 2009, 2008, and 2007. Round to the nearest cent.

b. Evaluate the growth in earnings per share for the three years in comparison to the growth in net income for the three years.

OBJ. 7

### EX 11-25 EPS

OfficeMax and Staples are two companies competing in the retail office supply business. OfficeMax had a net income of $667,000 for a recent year, while Staples had a net income of $738,671,000. OfficeMax had preferred stock of $36,479,000 with preferred dividends of $2,818,000. Staples had no preferred stock. The outstanding common shares for each company were as follows:

| | Average Number of Common Shares Outstanding |
| --- | --- |
| OfficeMax | 77,483,000 |
| Staples | 721,838,000 |

a. Determine the earnings per share for each company. Round to the nearest cent.

b. Evaluate the relative profitability of the two companies.

## Problems Series A

---

OBJ. 2

✔ 1. Common
dividends in 2009:
$9,000

### PR 11-1A  Dividends on preferred and common stock

Love Theatre Inc. owns and operates movie theaters throughout New Mexico and Utah. Love Theatre has declared the following annual dividends over a six-year period: 2007, $16,000; 2008, $48,000; 2009, $65,000; 2010, $90,000; 2011, $115,000; and 2012, $140,000. During the entire period ending December 31 of each year, the outstanding stock of the company was composed of 25,000 shares of cumulative, 2% preferred stock, $80 par, and 100,000 shares of common stock, $4 par.

#### Instructions

1. Calculate the total dividends and the per-share dividends declared on each class of stock for each of the six years. There were no dividends in arrears on January 1, 2007. Summarize the data in tabular form, using the following column headings:

| Year | Total Dividends | Preferred Dividends Total | Preferred Dividends Per Share | Common Dividends Total | Common Dividends Per Share |
|------|-----------------|---------------------------|-------------------------------|------------------------|----------------------------|
| 2007 | $ 16,000 | | | | |
| 2008 | 48,000 | | | | |
| 2009 | 65,000 | | | | |
| 2010 | 90,000 | | | | |
| 2011 | 115,000 | | | | |
| 2012 | 140,000 | | | | |

2. Calculate the average annual dividend per share for each class of stock for the six-year period.

3. Assuming a market price per share of $128 for the preferred stock and $7.80 for the common stock, calculate the average annual percentage return on initial shareholders' investment, based on the average annual dividend per share (a) for preferred stock and (b) for common stock.

---

OBJ. 2

GENERAL
LEDGER

### PR 11-2A  Stock transactions for corporate expansion

On March 1 of the current year, the following accounts and their balances appear in the ledger of Mocha Corp., a coffee processor:

| | |
|---|---|
| Preferred 2% Stock, $25 par (300,000 shares authorized, 120,000 shares issued)............................................... | $ 3,000,000 |
| Paid-In Capital in Excess of Par—Preferred Stock ........................... | 480,000 |
| Common Stock, $100 par (800,000 shares authorized, 250,000 shares issued)............................................... | 25,000,000 |
| Paid-In Capital in Excess of Par—Common Stock .......................... | 2,000,000 |
| Retained Earnings..................................................... | 50,000,000 |

At the annual stockholders' meeting on April 18, the board of directors presented a plan for modernizing and expanding plant operations at a cost of approximately $14,000,000. The plan provided (a) that a building, valued at $3,500,000, and the land on which it is located, valued at $5,000,000, be acquired in accordance with preliminary negotiations by the issuance of 80,000 shares of common stock, (b) that 85,000 shares of the unissued preferred stock be issued through an underwriter, and (c) that the corporation borrow $3,000,000. The plan was approved by the stockholders and accomplished by the following transactions:

June   5. Issued 80,000 shares of common stock in exchange for land and a building, according to the plan.

16. Issued 85,000 shares of preferred stock, receiving $30 per share in cash.

29. Borrowed $3,000,000 from First City Bank, giving a 6% mortgage note.

No other transactions occurred during June.

#### Instructions

Journalize the entries to record the foregoing transactions.

**OBJ. 2, 3, 4**

✔ f. Cash dividends, $57,200

### PR 11-3A  Selected stock transactions

The following selected accounts appear in the ledger of Patton Environmental Inc. on July 1, 2012, the beginning of the current fiscal year:

| | |
|---|---:|
| Preferred 2% Stock, $75 par (40,000 shares authorized, 20,000 shares issued) | $ 1,500,000 |
| Paid-In Capital in Excess of Par—Preferred Stock | 240,000 |
| Common Stock, $15 par (500,000 shares authorized, 260,000 shares issued) | 3,900,000 |
| Paid-In Capital in Excess of Par—Common Stock | 400,000 |
| Retained Earnings | 12,750,000 |

During the year, the corporation completed a number of transactions affecting the stockholders' equity. They are summarized as follows:

a.  Issued 50,000 shares of common stock at $20, receiving cash.

b.  Issued 10,000 shares of preferred 2% stock at $92.

c.  Purchased 30,000 shares of treasury common for $480,000.

d.  Sold 15,000 shares of treasury common for $322,500.

e.  Sold 10,000 shares of treasury common for $155,000.

f.  Declared cash dividends of $1.50 per share on preferred stock and $0.04 per share on common stock.

g.  Paid the cash dividends.

### Instructions

Journalize the entries to record the transactions. Identify each entry by letter.

**OBJ. 2, 3, 4, 5**

✔ 4. Total stockholders' equity, $15,599,960

### PR 11-4A  Entries for selected corporate transactions

Tolbert Enterprises Inc. manufactures bathroom fixtures. The stockholders' equity accounts of Tolbert Enterprises Inc., with balances on January 1, 2012, are as follows:

| | |
|---|---:|
| Common Stock, $10 stated value (600,000 shares authorized, 400,000 shares issued) | $4,000,000 |
| Paid-In Capital in Excess of Stated Value | 750,000 |
| Retained Earnings | 9,150,000 |
| Treasury Stock (40,000 shares, at cost) | 600,000 |

The following selected transactions occurred during the year:

Jan.  4.  Paid cash dividends of $0.13 per share on the common stock. The dividend had been properly recorded when declared on December 1 of the preceding fiscal year for $46,800.

Apr.  3.  Issued 75,000 shares of common stock for $1,200,000.

June  6.  Sold all of the treasury stock for $725,000.

July  1.  Declared a 4% stock dividend on common stock, to be capitalized at the market price of the stock, which is $18 per share.

Aug.  15.  Issued the certificates for the dividend declared on July 1.

Nov.  10.  Purchased 25,000 shares of treasury stock for $500,000.

Dec.  27.  Declared a $0.16-per-share dividend on common stock.

31.  Closed the credit balance of the income summary account, $950,000.

31.  Closed the two dividends accounts to Retained Earnings.

### Instructions

1.  Enter the January 1 balances in T accounts for the stockholders' equity accounts listed. Also prepare T accounts for the following: Paid-In Capital from Sale of Treasury Stock; Stock Dividends Distributable; Stock Dividends; Cash Dividends.

2.  Journalize the entries to record the transactions, and post to the eight selected accounts.

3. Prepare a retained earnings statement for the year ended December 31, 2012.

4. Prepare the Stockholders' Equity section of the December 31, 2012, balance sheet.

OBJ. 2, 3, 4, 6

✔ Nov. 15, cash
dividends, $159,400

### PR 11-5A   Entries for selected corporate transactions

Selected transactions completed by Big Water Boating Corporation during the current fiscal year are as follows:

Jan.  3. Split the common stock 3 for 1 and reduced the par from $90 to $30 per share. After the split, there were 750,000 common shares outstanding.

Apr.  7. Purchased 50,000 shares of the corporation's own common stock at $33, recording the stock at cost.

May  1. Declared semiannual dividends of $1.40 on 35,000 shares of preferred stock and $0.09 on the common stock to stockholders of record on May 15, payable on June 1.

June  1. Paid the cash dividends.

July  29. Sold 36,000 shares of treasury stock at $40, receiving cash.

Nov.  15. Declared semiannual dividends of $1.40 on the preferred stock and $0.15 on the common stock (before the stock dividend). In addition, a 2% common stock dividend was declared on the common stock outstanding. The fair market value of the common stock is estimated at $41.

Dec.  31. Paid the cash dividends and issued the certificates for the common stock dividend.

**Instructions**
Journalize the transactions.

## Problems Series B

OBJ. 2

✔ 1. Common
dividends in 2009:
$2,000

### PR 11-1B   Dividends on preferred and common stock

Boise Bike Corp. manufactures mountain bikes and distributes them through retail outlets in Montana, Idaho, Oregon, and Washington. Boise Bike Corp. has declared the following annual dividends over a six-year period ending December 31 of each year: 2007, $8,000; 2008, $24,000; 2009, $60,000; 2010, $75,000; 2011, $80,000; and 2012, $98,000. During the entire period, the outstanding stock of the company was composed of 20,000 shares of 2% cumulative preferred stock, $75 par, and 50,000 shares of common stock, $5 par.

**Instructions**

1. Determine the total dividends and the per-share dividends declared on each class of stock for each of the six years. There were no dividends in arrears on January 1, 2007. Summarize the data in tabular form, using the following column headings:

| Year | Total Dividends | Preferred Dividends | | Common Dividends | |
|------|-----------------|---------------------|-----------|------------------|-----------|
| | | Total | Per Share | Total | Per Share |
| 2007 | $ 8,000 | | | | |
| 2008 | 24,000 | | | | |
| 2009 | 60,000 | | | | |
| 2010 | 75,000 | | | | |
| 2011 | 80,000 | | | | |
| 2012 | 98,000 | | | | |

2. Determine the average annual dividend per share for each class of stock for the six-year period.

3. Assuming a market price of $125 for the preferred stock and $13.75 for the common stock, calculate the average annual percentage return on initial shareholders' investment, based on the average annual dividend per share (a) for preferred stock and (b) for common stock.

### PR 11-2B   Stock transaction for corporate expansion

Picasso Optics produces medical lasers for use in hospitals. The accounts and their balances appear in the ledger of Picasso Optics on November 30 of the current year as follows:

| | |
|---|---|
| Preferred 2% Stock, $80 par (150,000 shares authorized, 75,000 shares issued) | $ 6,000,000 |
| Paid-In Capital in Excess of Par—Preferred Stock | 225,000 |
| Common Stock, $100 par (500,000 shares authorized, 150,000 shares issued) | 15,000,000 |
| Paid-In Capital in Excess of Par—Common Stock | 1,800,000 |
| Retained Earnings | 50,250,000 |

At the annual stockholders' meeting on December 10, the board of directors presented a plan for modernizing and expanding plant operations at a cost of approximately $15,500,000. The plan provided (a) that the corporation borrow $6,000,000, (b) that 45,000 shares of the unissued preferred stock be issued through an underwriter, and (c) that a building, valued at $5,000,000, and the land on which it is located, valued at $487,500, be acquired in accordance with preliminary negotiations by the issuance of 52,500 shares of common stock. The plan was approved by the stockholders and accomplished by the following transactions:

Jan.  12.  Borrowed $6,000,000 from Livingston National Bank, giving a 5% mortgage note.

18.  Issued 45,000 shares of preferred stock, receiving $85 per share in cash.

25.  Issued 52,500 shares of common stock in exchange for land and a building, according to the plan.

No other transactions occurred during January.

### Instructions
Journalize the entries to record the foregoing transactions.

---

### PR 11-3B   Selected stock transactions

Daley Welding Corporation sells and services pipe welding equipment in Illinois. The following selected accounts appear in the ledger of Daley Welding Corporation on May 1, 2012, the beginning of the current fiscal year:

| | |
|---|---|
| Preferred 2% Stock, $40 par (50,000 shares authorized, 40,000 shares issued) | $ 1,600,000 |
| Paid-In Capital in Excess of Par—Preferred Stock | 240,000 |
| Common Stock, $8 par (1,000,000 shares authorized, 750,000 shares issued) | 6,000,000 |
| Paid-In Capital in Excess of Par—Common Stock | 2,500,000 |
| Retained Earnings | 43,175,000 |

During the year, the corporation completed a number of transactions affecting the stockholders' equity. They are summarized as follows:

a.  Purchased 100,000 shares of treasury common for $1,500,000.

b.  Sold 60,000 shares of treasury common for $1,080,000.

c.  Issued 8,000 shares of preferred 2% stock at $50.

d.  Issued 150,000 shares of common stock at $21, receiving cash.

e.  Sold 25,000 shares of treasury common for $362,500.

f.  Declared cash dividends of $0.80 per share on preferred stock and $0.11 per share on common stock.

g.  Paid the cash dividends.

### Instructions
Journalize the entries to record the transactions. Identify each entry by letter.

OBJ. 2, 3, 4, 5

✔ 4. Total stockholders' equity, $5,190,460

### PR 11-4B Entries for selected corporate transactions

Ruffalo Enterprises Inc. produces aeronautical navigation equipment. The stockholders' equity accounts of Ruffalo Enterprises Inc., with balances on January 1, 2012, are as follows:

| | |
|---|---:|
| Common Stock, $8 stated value (250,000 shares authorized, 175,000 shares issued) | $1,400,000 |
| Paid-In Capital in Excess of Stated Value | 700,000 |
| Retained Earnings | 1,840,000 |
| Treasury Stock (40,000 shares, at cost) | 400,000 |

The following selected transactions occurred during the year:

Jan.  9. Paid cash dividends of $0.10 per share on the common stock. The dividend had been properly recorded when declared on November 30 of the preceding fiscal year for $13,500.

Mar. 15. Sold all of the treasury stock for $540,000.

May 13. Issued 50,000 shares of common stock for $680,000.

June 14. Declared a 2% stock dividend on common stock, to be capitalized at the market price of the stock, which is $15 per share.

July 16. Issued the certificates for the dividend declared on June 14.

Oct. 30. Purchased 25,000 shares of treasury stock for $320,000.

Dec. 30. Declared a $0.12-per-share dividend on common stock.

31. Closed the credit balance of the income summary account, $775,000.

31. Closed the two dividends accounts to Retained Earnings.

#### Instructions

1. Enter the January 1 balances in T accounts for the stockholders' equity accounts listed. Also prepare T accounts for the following: Paid-In Capital from Sale of Treasury Stock; Stock Dividends Distributable; Stock Dividends; Cash Dividends.

2. Journalize the entries to record the transactions, and post to the eight selected accounts.

3. Prepare a retained earnings statement for the year ended December 31, 2012.

4. Prepare the Stockholders' Equity section of the December 31, 2012, balance sheet.

OBJ. 2, 3, 4, 6

✔ Sept. 1, Cash dividends, $156,000

### PR 11-5B Entries for selected corporate transactions

Maui Outfitters Corporation manufactures and distributes leisure clothing. Selected transactions completed by Maui Outfitters during the current fiscal year are as follows:

Feb. 19. Split the common stock 4 for 1 and reduced the par from $80 to $20 per share. After the split, there were 600,000 common shares outstanding.

Mar.  1. Declared semiannual dividends of $1.20 on 75,000 shares of preferred stock and $0.08 on the 600,000 shares of $20 par common stock to stockholders of record on March 31, payable on April 30.

Apr. 30. Paid the cash dividends.

June 27. Purchased 90,000 shares of the corporation's own common stock at $24, recording the stock at cost.

Aug. 17. Sold 40,000 shares of treasury stock at $30, receiving cash.

Sept. 1. Declared semiannual dividends of $1.20 on the preferred stock and $0.12 on the common stock (before the stock dividend). In addition, a 1% common stock dividend was declared on the common stock outstanding, to be capitalized at the fair market value of the common stock, which is estimated at $28.

Oct. 31. Paid the cash dividends and issued the certificates for the common stock dividend.

#### Instructions

Journalize the transactions.

## Cases & Projects

You can access Cases & Projects online at **www.cengage.com/accounting/reeve**

## Excel Success Special Activities

### SA 11-1 Dividends per share

Truett Company issued 100,000 shares of $1 par value common stock and 12,000 shares of $100 par value cumulative preferred stock. The preferred stock has a dividend rate of $6.50 per share. The preferred dividend is in arrears for 2010 and 2011. Truett is able to pay a total dividend of $420,000 in 2012.

a. Open file *SA11-1_1e* and determine the dividend and dividend per share for common and preferred stock in 2012.

b. When you have completed the dividend calculations, perform a "save as," replacing the entire file name with the following:

*SA11-1_1e[your first name initial]_[your last name]*

### SA 11-2 Dividends per share

Daniels Company began business on January 1, 2009, by issuing 50,000 shares of $1 par value common stock. On January 1, 2010, Daniels issued 4,000 shares of $120 par value, 5% cumulative preferred stock. A dividend was paid on the preferred stock in 2010, but not in 2011. A total dividend of $68,000 was paid in 2012.

a. Open file *SA11-2_1e* and determine the dividend and dividend per share for common and preferred stock in 2012.

b. When you have completed the dividend calculations, perform a "save as," replacing the entire file name with the following:

*SA11-2_1e[your first name initial]_[your last name]*

### SA 11-3 Dividends per share

Sable Company has two classes of stock issued on January 1, 2010, as follows:

• Common stock, $1 par value, 150,000 issued and outstanding

• $2 cumulative preferred stock, $25 par value, 8,000 shares issued and outstanding

The cumulative preferred stock paid no dividends in 2010. The total dividends paid in 2011 and 2012 were $4,000 and $56,000, respectively.

a. Open file *SA11-3_1e* and determine the dividend and dividend per share for common and preferred stock in 2012.

b. When you have completed the dividend calculations, perform a "save as," replacing the entire file name with the following:

*SA11-3_1e[your first name initial]_[your last name]*

© Under Armour®/PRNewsFoto/AP Photos Publicity

# Long-Term Liabilities: Bonds and Notes

## Under Armour®

**M**ost of us don't have enough money in our bank accounts to buy a house or a car by simply writing a check. Just imagine if you had to save the entire purchase price of a house before you could buy it! To help us make these types of purchases, banks will typically lend us the money, as long as we agree to repay the loan with interest in smaller future payments. Loans such as this, or long-term debt, allow us to purchase assets such as houses and cars today, which benefit us over the long term.

The use of debt can also help a business reach its objectives. Most businesses have to borrow money in order to acquire assets that they will use to generate income. For example, **Under Armour®**, a maker of performance athletic clothing, uses debt to

acquire assets that it needs to manufacture and sell its products. Since it began in 1995, the company has used long-term debt to transform itself from a small business to a leading athletic wear company. The company now sells products in over 8,000 retail stores across the world. In addition, Under Armour® products are used by a number of teams in the National Football League, Major League Baseball, the National Hockey League, and in Olympic sports.

While debt can help companies like Under Armour® grow to achieve financial success, too much debt can be a financial burden that may even lead to bankruptcy. Just like individuals, businesses must manage debt wisely. In this chapter, we will discuss the nature of, accounting for, analysis of, and investments in long-term debt.

## Learning Objectives

After studying this chapter, you should be able to:

| | | Example Exercises | Page |
|---|---|---|---|
| **OBJ. 1** | Compute the potential impact of long-term borrowing on earnings per share.<br>Financing Corporations | EE 12-1 | 544 |
| **OBJ. 2** | Describe the characteristics and terminology of bonds payable.<br>Nature of Bonds Payable<br>　　Bond Characteristics and Terminology<br>　　Proceeds from Issuing Bonds | | |
| **OBJ. 3** | Journalize entries for bonds payable.<br>Accounting for Bonds Payable<br>　　Bonds Issued at Face Amount<br>　　Bonds Issued at a Discount<br>　　Amortizing a Bond Discount<br>　　Bonds Issued at a Premium<br>　　Amortizing a Bond Premium<br>　　Bond Redemption | EE 12-2<br>EE 12-3<br>EE 12-4<br>EE 12-5<br>EE 12-6 | 547<br>548<br>549<br>550<br>551 |
| **OBJ. 4** | Describe and illustrate the accounting for installment notes.<br>Installment Notes<br>　　Issuing an Installment Note<br>　　Annual Payments | EE 12-7 | 554 |
| **OBJ. 5** | Describe and illustrate the reporting of long-term liabilities including bonds and notes payable.<br>Reporting Long-Term Liabilities | | |
| **OBJ. 6** | Describe and illustrate how the number of times interest charges are earned is used to evaluate a company's financial condition.<br>Financial Analysis and Interpretation: Number of Times Interest Charges Are Earned | EE 12-8 | 557 |

**At a Glance 12** Page 564

---

**OBJ. 1** Compute the potential impact of long-term borrowing on earnings per share.

# Financing Corporations

Corporations finance their operations using the following sources:

1. Short-term debt, such as purchasing goods or services on account.
2. Long-term debt, such as issuing bonds or notes payable.
3. Equity, such as issuing common or preferred stock.

Short-term debt including the purchase of goods and services on account and the issuance of short-term notes payable was discussed in Chapter 10, while issuing equity in the form of common or preferred stock was discussed in Chapter 11. This chapter focuses on the use of long-term debt such as bonds and notes payable to finance a company's operations.

A **bond** is a form of an interest-bearing note. Like a note, a bond requires periodic interest payments with the face amount to be repaid at the maturity date. As creditors of the corporation, bondholder claims on the corporation's assets rank ahead of stockholders.

To illustrate the effects of long-term financing, assume Huckadee Corporation is considering the following plans to issue debt and equity:

| | Plan 1 | | Plan 2 | | Plan 3 | |
|---|---|---|---|---|---|---|
| | **Amount** | **Percent** | **Amount** | **Percent** | **Amount** | **Percent** |
| Issue 12% bonds | — | 0% | — | 0% | $2,000,000 | 50% |
| Issue 9% preferred stock, $50 par value | — | 0 | $2,000,000 | 50 | 1,000,000 | 25 |
| Issue common stock, $10 par value | $4,000,000 | 100 | 2,000,000 | 50 | 1,000,000 | 25 |
| Total amount of financing | $4,000,000 | 100% | $4,000,000 | 100% | $4,000,000 | 100% |

Each of the preceding plans finances some of the corporation's operations by issuing common stock. However, the percentage financed by common stock varies from 100% (Plan 1) to 25% (Plan 3). In deciding among financing plans, the effect on earnings per share is often considered.

**Earnings per share (EPS)** measures the income earned by each share of common stock. It is computed as follows:[1]

$$\text{Earnings per Share} = \frac{\text{Net Income} - \text{Preferred Dividends}}{\text{Number of Common Shares Outstanding}}$$

To illustrate, assume the following data for Huckadee Corporation:

1. Earnings before interest and income taxes are $800,000.
2. The tax rate is 40%.
3. All bonds or stocks are issued at their par or face amount.

The effect of the preceding financing plans on Huckadee's net income and earnings per share is shown in Exhibit 1.

| | Plan 1 | Plan 2 | Plan 3 |
|---|---|---|---|
| 12% bonds | — | — | $2,000,000 |
| Preferred 9% stock, $50 par | — | $2,000,000 | 1,000,000 |
| Common stock, $10 par | $4,000,000 | 2,000,000 | 1,000,000 |
| Total | $4,000,000 | $4,000,000 | $4,000,000 |
| Earnings before interest and income tax | $ 800,000 | $ 800,000 | $ 800,000 |
| Deduct interest on bonds | — | — | 240,000 |
| Income before income tax | $ 800,000 | $ 800,000 | $ 560,000 |
| Deduct income tax | 320,000 | 320,000 | 224,000 |
| Net income | $ 480,000 | $ 480,000 | $ 336,000 |
| Dividends on preferred stock | — | 180,000 | 90,000 |
| Available for dividends on common stock | $ 480,000 | $ 300,000 | $ 246,000 |
| Shares of common stock outstanding | ÷ 400,000 | ÷ 200,000 | ÷ 100,000 |
| Earnings per share on common stock | $ 1.20 | $ 1.50 | $ 2.46 |

**EXHIBIT 1**

**Effect of Alternative Financing Plans—$800,000 Earnings**

Exhibit 1 indicates that Plan 3 yields the highest earnings per share on common stock and, thus, is the most attractive for common stockholders. If the estimated earnings are more than $800,000, the difference between the earnings per share to common stockholders under Plans 1 and 3 is even greater.[2]

If smaller earnings occur, however, Plans 1 and 2 become more attractive to common stockholders. To illustrate, Exhibit 2 shows the effect on earnings per share if estimated earnings are $440,000 rather than $800,000 as estimated in Exhibit 1.

| | Plan 1 | Plan 2 | Plan 3 |
|---|---|---|---|
| 12% bonds | — | — | $2,000,000 |
| Preferred 9% stock, $50 par | — | $2,000,000 | 1,000,000 |
| Common stock, $10 par | $4,000,000 | 2,000,000 | 1,000,000 |
| Total | $4,000,000 | $4,000,000 | $4,000,000 |
| Earnings before interest and income tax | $ 440,000 | $ 440,000 | $ 440,000 |
| Deduct interest on bonds | — | — | 240,000 |
| Income before income tax | $ 440,000 | $ 440,000 | $ 200,000 |
| Deduct income tax | 176,000 | 176,000 | 80,000 |
| Net income | $ 264,000 | $ 264,000 | $ 120,000 |
| Dividends on preferred stock | — | 180,000 | 90,000 |
| Available for dividends on common stock | $ 264,000 | $ 84,000 | $ 30,000 |
| Shares of common stock outstanding | ÷ 400,000 | ÷ 200,000 | ÷ 100,000 |
| Earnings per share on common stock | $ 0.66 | $ 0.42 | $ 0.30 |

**EXHIBIT 2**

**Effect of Alternative Financing Plans—$440,000 Earnings**

1 Earnings per share is also discussed in the *Financial Analysis and Interpretation* section of Chapter 11 and in Chapter 15.

2 The higher earnings per share under Plan 3 is due to a finance concept known as *leverage*. This concept is discussed further in Chapter 15.

In addition to earnings per share, the corporation should consider other factors in deciding among the financing plans. For example, if bonds are issued, the interest and the face value of the bonds at maturity must be paid. If these payments are not made, the bondholders could seek court action and force the company into bankruptcy. In contrast, a corporation is not legally obligated to pay dividends on preferred or common stock.

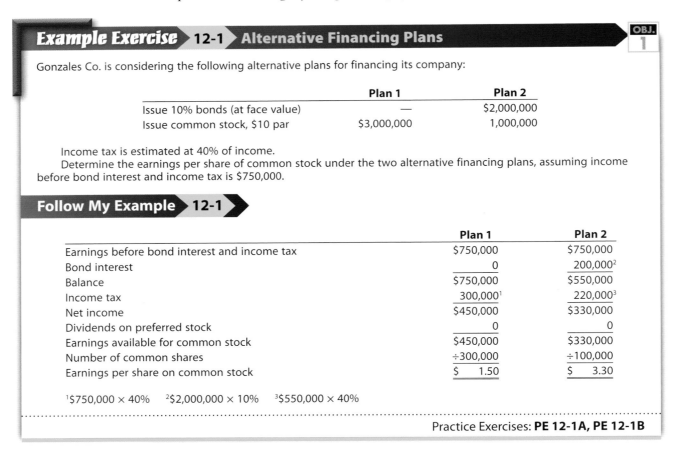

**Example Exercise** > **12-1** > **Alternative Financing Plans**

OBJ. 1

Gonzales Co. is considering the following alternative plans for financing its company:

|  | Plan 1 | Plan 2 |
|---|---|---|
| Issue 10% bonds (at face value) | — | $2,000,000 |
| Issue common stock, $10 par | $3,000,000 | 1,000,000 |

Income tax is estimated at 40% of income.

Determine the earnings per share of common stock under the two alternative financing plans, assuming income before bond interest and income tax is $750,000.

**Follow My Example** > **12-1** >

|  | Plan 1 | Plan 2 |
|---|---|---|
| Earnings before bond interest and income tax | $750,000 | $750,000 |
| Bond interest | 0 | 200,000[2] |
| Balance | $750,000 | $550,000 |
| Income tax | 300,000[1] | 220,000[3] |
| Net income | $450,000 | $330,000 |
| Dividends on preferred stock | 0 | 0 |
| Earnings available for common stock | $450,000 | $330,000 |
| Number of common shares | ÷300,000 | ÷100,000 |
| Earnings per share on common stock | $ 1.50 | $ 3.30 |

[1]$750,000 × 40%    [2]$2,000,000 × 10%    [3]$550,000 × 40%

Practice Exercises: **PE 12-1A, PE 12-1B**

---

OBJ. 2 Describe the characteristics and terminology of bonds payable.

# Nature of Bonds Payable

Corporate bonds normally differ in face amount, interest rates, interest payment dates, and maturity dates. Bonds also differ in other ways such as whether corporate assets are pledged in support of the bonds.

## Bond Characteristics and Terminology

Dow Chemical Company's 8.55% bonds, maturing in 2019, sold for 119.753 on January 19, 2010.

The underlying contract between the company issuing bonds and the bondholders is called a **bond indenture** or *trust indenture*. A bond issue is normally divided into a number of individual bonds. The face amount of each bond is called the principal. This is the amount that must be repaid on the dates the bonds mature. The principal is usually $1,000, or a multiple of $1,000. The interest on bonds may be payable annually, semiannually, or quarterly. Most bonds pay interest semiannually.

When all bonds of an issue mature at the same time, they are called *term bonds*. If the bonds mature over several dates, they are called *serial bonds*. For example, one-tenth of an issue of $1,000,000 bonds, or $100,000, may mature 16 years from the issue date, another $100,000 in the 17th year, and so on.

Bonds that may be exchanged for other securities, such as common stock, are called *convertible bonds*. Bonds that a corporation reserves the right to redeem before their maturity are called *callable bonds*. Bonds issued on the basis of the general credit of the corporation are called *debenture bonds*.

## Proceeds from Issuing Bonds

When a corporation issues bonds, the proceeds received for the bonds depend on:

1. The face amount of the bonds, which is the amount due at the maturity date.
2. The interest rate on the bonds.
3. The market rate of interest for similar bonds.

The face amount and the interest rate on the bonds are identified in the bond indenture. The interest rate to be paid on the face amount of the bond is called the **contract rate** or *coupon rate*.

The **market rate of interest**, sometimes called the **effective rate of interest**, is the rate determined from sales and purchases of similar bonds. The market rate of interest is affected by a variety of factors, including investors' expectations of current and future economic conditions.

By comparing the market and contract rates of interest, it can be determined whether the bonds will sell for more than, less than, or at their face amount, as shown below.

If the market rate equals the contract rate, bonds will sell at the **face amount**.

If the market rate is greater than the contract rate, the bonds will sell for less than their face value. The face amount of the bonds less the selling price is called a **discount**. A bond sells at a discount because buyers are not willing to pay the full face amount for bonds whose contract rate is lower than the market rate.

If the market rate is less than the contract rate, the bonds will sell for more than their face value. The selling price of the bonds less the face amount is called a **premium**. A bond sells at a premium because buyers are willing to pay more than the face amount for bonds whose contract rate is higher than the market rate.

The price of a bond is quoted as a percentage of the bond's face value. For example, a $1,000 bond quoted at 98 could be purchased or sold for $980 ($1,000 × 0.98). Likewise, bonds quoted at 109 could be purchased or sold for $1,090 ($1,000 × 1.09).

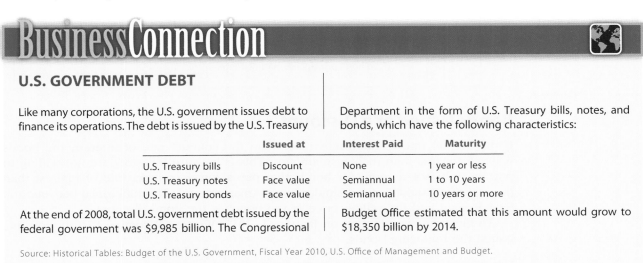

## BusinessConnection

### U.S. GOVERNMENT DEBT

Like many corporations, the U.S. government issues debt to finance its operations. The debt is issued by the U.S. Treasury Department in the form of U.S. Treasury bills, notes, and bonds, which have the following characteristics:

| | Issued at | Interest Paid | Maturity |
|---|---|---|---|
| U.S. Treasury bills | Discount | None | 1 year or less |
| U.S. Treasury notes | Face value | Semiannual | 1 to 10 years |
| U.S. Treasury bonds | Face value | Semiannual | 10 years or more |

At the end of 2008, total U.S. government debt issued by the federal government was $9,985 billion. The Congressional Budget Office estimated that this amount would grow to $18,350 billion by 2014.

Source: Historical Tables: Budget of the U.S. Government, Fiscal Year 2010, U.S. Office of Management and Budget.

Journalize entries for bonds payable.

# Accounting for Bonds Payable

Bonds may be issued at their face amount, a discount, or a premium. When bonds are issued at less or more than their face amount, the discount or premium must be amortized over the life of the bonds. At the maturity date, the face amount must be repaid. In some situations, a corporation may redeem bonds before their maturity date by repurchasing them from investors.

## Bonds Issued at Face Amount

If the market rate of interest is equal to the contract rate of interest, the bonds will sell for their face amount or a price of 100. To illustrate, assume that on January 1, 2011, Eastern Montana Communications Inc. issued the following bonds:

| | |
|---|---|
| Face amount ................................... | $100,000 |
| Contract rate of interest ......................... | 12% |
| Interest paid semiannually on June 30 and December 31. | |
| Term of bonds ................................. | 5 years |
| Market rate of interest .......................... | 12% |

Since the contract rate of interest and the market rate of interest are the same, the bonds will sell at their face amount. The entry to record the issuance of the bonds is as follows:

| 2011 | | | | |
|---|---|---|---|---|
| Jan. | 1 | Cash | 100,000 | |
| | | Bonds Payable | | 100,000 |
| | | Issued $100,000 bonds payable at face amount. | | |

Every six months (on June 30 and December 31) after the bonds are issued, interest of $6,000 ($100,000 × 12% × ½) is paid. The first interest payment on June 30, 2011, is recorded as follows:

| 2011 | | | | |
|---|---|---|---|---|
| June | 30 | Interest Expense | 6,000 | |
| | | Cash | | 6,000 |
| | | Paid six months' interest on bonds. | | |

At the maturity date, the payment of the principal of $100,000 is recorded as follows:

| 2015 | | | | |
|---|---|---|---|---|
| Dec. | 31 | Bonds Payable | 100,000 | |
| | | Cash | | 100,000 |
| | | Paid bond principal at maturity date. | | |

## Bonds Issued at a Discount

If the market rate of interest is more than the contract rate of interest, the bonds will sell for less than their face amount. This is because investors are not willing to pay the full face amount for bonds that pay a lower contract rate of interest than the rate they could earn on similar bonds (market rate). The difference between the face amount and the selling price of the bonds is the bond discount.[3]

To illustrate, assume that on January 1, 2011, Western Wyoming Distribution Inc. issued the following bonds:

[3] The price that investors are willing to pay for the bonds depends on present value concepts. Present value concepts, including the computation of bond prices, are described and illustrated in Appendix 1 at the end of this chapter.

| Face amount . . . . . . . . . . . . . . . . . . . . . . . . . . . . | $100,000 |
| Contract rate of interest . . . . . . . . . . . . . . . . . | 12% |
| Interest paid semiannually on June 30 and December 31. | |
| Term of bonds. . . . . . . . . . . . . . . . . . . . . . . . . . | 5 years |
| Market rate of interest . . . . . . . . . . . . . . . . . . | 13% |

**Note:**
Bonds will sell at a discount when the market rate of interest is higher than the contract rate.

Since the contract rate of interest is less than the market rate of interest, the bonds will sell at less than their face amount. Assuming the bonds sell for $96,406, the entry to record the issuance of the bonds is as follows:

| 2011 Jan. | 1 | Cash | | 96,406 | |
| | | Discount on Bonds Payable | | 3,594 | |
| | | Bonds Payable | | | 100,000 |
| | | Issued $100,000 bonds at discount. | | | |

The $96,406 may be viewed as the amount investors are willing to pay for bonds that have a lower contract rate of interest (12%) than the market rate (13%). The discount is the market's way of adjusting the contract rate of interest to the higher market rate of interest.

The account, Discount on Bonds Payable, is a contra account to Bonds Payable and has a normal debit balance. It is subtracted from Bonds Payable to determine the carrying amount (or book value) of the bonds payable. Thus, after the preceding entry, the carrying amount of the bonds payable is $96,406 ($100,000 – $3,594).

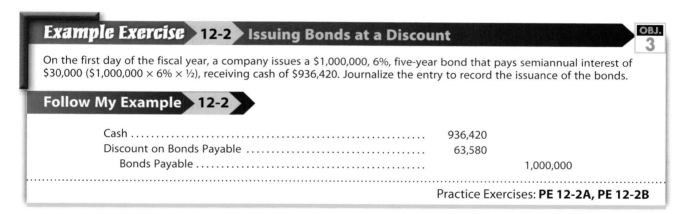

**Example Exercise** 12-2 **Issuing Bonds at a Discount**  OBJ. 3

On the first day of the fiscal year, a company issues a $1,000,000, 6%, five-year bond that pays semiannual interest of $30,000 ($1,000,000 × 6% × ½), receiving cash of $936,420. Journalize the entry to record the issuance of the bonds.

**Follow My Example** 12-2

| Cash . . . . . . . . . . . . . . . . . . . . . . . . . . . . . . . . . . . . . . . . . . . . . . . . . . . | 936,420 | |
| Discount on Bonds Payable . . . . . . . . . . . . . . . . . . . . . . . . . . . . . . . | 63,580 | |
| Bonds Payable . . . . . . . . . . . . . . . . . . . . . . . . . . . . . . . . . . . . . . . . . | | 1,000,000 |

Practice Exercises: **PE 12-2A, PE 12-2B**

## Amortizing a Bond Discount

A bond discount must be amortized to interest expense over the life of the bond. The entry to amortize a bond discount is shown below.

| | | Interest Expense | | XXX | |
| | | Discount on Bonds Payable | | | XXX |

The preceding entry may be made annually as an adjusting entry, or it may be combined with the semiannual interest payment. In the latter case, the entry would be as follows:

| | | Interest Expense | | XXX | |
| | | Discount on Bonds Payable | | | XXX |
| | | Cash (amount of semiannual interest) | | | XXX |

The two methods of computing the amortization of a bond discount are:

1. *Straight-line method*
2. *Effective interest rate method,* sometimes called the *interest method*

The **effective interest rate method** is required by generally accepted accounting principles. However, the straight-line method may be used if the results do not differ significantly from the interest method. The straight-line method is used in this chapter. The effective interest rate method is described and illustrated in Appendix 2 at the end of this chapter.

The straight-line method provides equal amounts of amortization. To illustrate, amortization of the Western Wyoming Distribution bond discount of $3,594 is computed below.

| | |
|---|---|
| Discount on bonds payable ................. | $3,594 |
| Term of bonds ............................ | 5 years |
| Semiannual amortization ................... | $359.40 ($3,594/10 periods) |

The combined entry to record the first interest payment and the amortization of the discount is as follows:

| 2011 | | | | | |
|---|---|---|---|---|---|
| June | 30 | Interest Expense | | 6,359.40 | |
| | | Discount on Bonds Payable | | | 359.40 |
| | | Cash | | | 6,000.00 |
| | | Paid semiannual interest and | | | |
| | | amortized ¹⁄₁₀ of bond discount. | | | |

The preceding entry is made on each interest payment date. Thus, the amount of the semiannual interest expense on the bonds ($6,359.40) remains the same over the life of the bonds.

The effect of the discount amortization is to increase the interest expense from $6,000.00 to $6,359.40 on every semiannual interest payment date. In effect, this increases the contract rate of interest from 12% to a rate of interest that approximates the market rate of 13%. In addition, as the discount is amortized, the carrying amount of the bonds increases until it equals the face amount of the bonds on the maturity date.

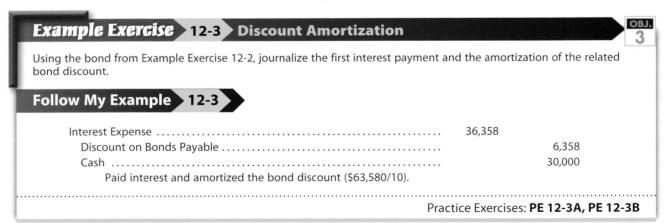

**Example Exercise** ▶ **12-3** ▶ **Discount Amortization**          OBJ. 3

Using the bond from Example Exercise 12-2, journalize the first interest payment and the amortization of the related bond discount.

**Follow My Example** ▶ **12-3** ▶

| | | |
|---|---|---|
| Interest Expense ..................................................... | 36,358 | |
| Discount on Bonds Payable ......................................... | | 6,358 |
| Cash ................................................................. | | 30,000 |
| Paid interest and amortized the bond discount ($63,580/10). | | |

Practice Exercises: **PE 12-3A, PE 12-3B**

## Bonds Issued at a Premium

**Note:**
Bonds will sell at a premium when the market rate of interest is less than the contract rate.

If the market rate of interest is less than the contract rate of interest, the bonds will sell for more than their face amount. This is because investors are willing to pay more for bonds that pay a higher contract rate of interest than the rate they could earn on similar bonds (market rate).

To illustrate, assume that on January 1, 2011, Northern Idaho Transportation Inc. issued the following bonds:

| | |
|---|---|
| Face amount .................................. | $100,000 |
| Contract rate of interest ...................... | 12% |
| Interest paid semiannually on<br>June 30 and December 31. | |
| Term of bonds ............................. | 5 years |
| Market rate of interest ....................... | 11% |

Since the contract rate of interest is more than the market rate of interest, the bonds will sell at more than their face amount. Assuming the bonds sell for $103,769, the entry to record the issuance of the bonds is as follows:

| 2011 | | | | | |
|---|---|---|---|---|---|
| Jan. | 1 | Cash | | 103,769 | |
| | | Bonds Payable | | | 100,000 |
| | | Premium on Bonds Payable | | | 3,769 |
| | | Issued $100,000 bonds at a premium. | | | |

The $3,769 premium may be viewed as the extra amount investors are willing to pay for bonds that have a higher contract rate of interest (12%) than the market rate (11%). The premium is the market's way of adjusting the contract rate of interest to the lower market rate of interest.

The account, Premium on Bonds Payable, has a normal credit balance. It is added to Bonds Payable to determine the carrying amount (or book value) of the bonds payable. Thus, after the preceding entry, the carrying amount of the bonds payable is $103,769 ($100,000 + $3,769).

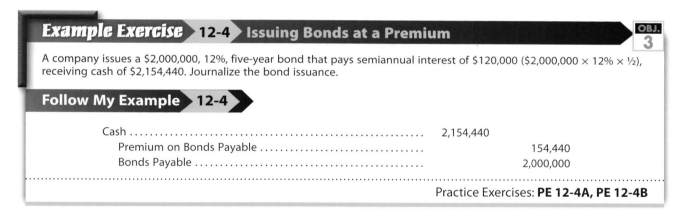

**Example Exercise 12-4 Issuing Bonds at a Premium** OBJ. 3

A company issues a $2,000,000, 12%, five-year bond that pays semiannual interest of $120,000 ($2,000,000 × 12% × ½), receiving cash of $2,154,440. Journalize the bond issuance.

**Follow My Example 12-4**

| | | |
|---|---|---|
| Cash ........................................................ | 2,154,440 | |
| Premium on Bonds Payable ................................ | | 154,440 |
| Bonds Payable ............................................ | | 2,000,000 |

Practice Exercises: **PE 12-4A, PE 12-4B**

## Amortizing a Bond Premium

Like bond discounts, a bond premium must be amortized over the life of the bond. The amortization can be computed using either the straight-line or the effective interest rate method. The entry to amortize a bond premium is shown below.

| | | | | | |
|---|---|---|---|---|---|
| | | Premium on Bonds Payable | | XXX | |
| | | Interest Expense | | | XXX |

The preceding entry may be made annually as an adjusting entry, or it may be combined with the semiannual interest payment. In the latter case, it would be:

| | | | | | |
|---|---|---|---|---|---|
| | | Interest Expense | | XXX | |
| | | Premium on Bonds Payable | | XXX | |
| | | Cash (amount of semiannual interest) | | | XXX |

To illustrate, amortization of the preceding premium of $3,769 is computed using the straight-line method as shown below.

| | |
|---|---|
| Premium on bonds payable................... | $3,769 |
| Term of bonds............................... | 5 years |
| Semiannual amortization.................... | $376.90 ($3,769/10 periods) |

The combined entry to record the first interest payment and the amortization of the discount is as follows:

| | | | | | |
|---|---|---|---|---|---|
| 2011 June | 30 | Interest Expense | | 5,623.10 | |
| | | Premium on Bonds Payable | | 376.90 | |
| | |   Cash | | | 6,000.00 |
| | |     Paid semiannual interest and | | | |
| | |     amortized $^{1}/_{10}$ of bond discount. | | | |

The preceding entry is made on each interest payment date. Thus, the amount of the semiannual interest expense ($5,623.10) on the bonds remains the same over the life of the bonds.

The effect of the premium amortization is to decrease the interest expense from $6,000.00 to $5,623.10. In effect, this decreases the rate of interest from 12% to a rate of interest that approximates the market rate of 11%. In addition, as the premium is amortized, the carrying amount of the bonds decreases until it equals the face amount of bonds on the maturity date.

---

**Example Exercise** ❯ **12-5** ❯ **Premium Amortization**

OBJ. 3

Using the bond from Example Exercise 12-4, journalize the first interest payment and the amortization of the related bond premium.

**Follow My Example** ❯ **12-5** ❯

| | | |
|---|---|---|
| Interest Expense ....................................................... | 104,556 | |
| Premium on Bonds Payable ............................................ | 15,444 | |
|   Cash...................................................................... | | 120,000 |
|     Paid interest and amortized the bond premium ($154,440/10). | | |

Practice Exercises: **PE 12-5A, PE 12-5B**

---

# BusinessConnection

## GENERAL MOTORS BONDS

In June 2009, after years of losses and weakening financial condition, General Motors Corporation, maker of Chevrolet, Saturn, Pontiac, and Saab cars and trucks, was forced to file for bankruptcy. As part of the bankruptcy and restructuring plan, the U.S. government made a multibillion-dollar cash investment in the company in exchange for 60% of the restructured company's common stock. In addition, General Motors' bondholders were forced to exchange their bonds for the remaining common shares in the restructured company, which were worth only a fraction of the bonds' face value. Bondholders also lost the security of interest payments and repayment of the bonds' face value at maturity.

Source: C. Isidore, "GM Bankruptcy: End of an Era," *CNNMoney.com*, June 2, 2009.

# Bond Redemption

A corporation may redeem or call bonds before they mature. This is often done when the market rate of interest declines below the contract rate of interest. In such cases, the corporation may issue new bonds at a lower interest rate and use the proceeds to redeem the original bond issue.

*Callable bonds* can be redeemed by the issuing corporation within the period of time and at the price stated in the bond indenture. Normally, the call price is above the face value. A corporation may also redeem its bonds by purchasing them on the open market.[4]

A corporation usually redeems its bonds at a price different from the carrying amount (or book value) of the bonds. The **carrying amount** of bonds payable is the face amount of the bonds less any unamortized discount or plus any unamortized premium. A gain or loss may be realized on a bond redemption as follows:

1. A *gain* is recorded if the price paid for redemption is below the bond carrying amount.
2. A *loss* is recorded if the price paid for the redemption is above the carrying amount.

Gains and losses on the redemption of bonds are reported in the *Other income (loss)* section of the income statement.

To illustrate, assume that on June 30, 2011, a corporation has the following bond issue:

| | |
|---|---|
| Face amount of bonds | $100,000 |
| Premium on bonds payable | 4,000 |

On June 30, 2011, the corporation redeemed one-fourth ($25,000) of these bonds in the market for $24,000. The entry to record the redemption is as follows:

| 2011 | | | | |
|---|---|---|---|---|
| June | 30 | Bonds Payable | 25,000 | |
| | | Premium on Bonds Payable | 1,000 | |
| | | Cash | | 24,000 |
| | | Gain on Redemption of Bonds | | 2,000 |
| | | Redeemed $25,000 bonds for $24,000. | | |

In the preceding entry, only the portion of the premium related to the redeemed bonds ($4,000 × 25% = $1,000) is written off. The difference between the carrying amount of the bonds redeemed, $26,000 ($25,000 + $1,000), and the redemption price, $24,000, is recorded as a gain.

Assume that the corporation calls the remaining $75,000 of outstanding bonds, which are held by a private investor, for $79,500 on July 1, 2011. The entry to record the redemption is as follows:

| 2011 | | | | |
|---|---|---|---|---|
| July | 1 | Bonds Payable | 75,000 | |
| | | Premium on Bonds Payable | 3,000 | |
| | | Loss on Redemption of Bonds | 1,500 | |
| | | Cash | | 79,500 |
| | | Redeemed $75,000 bonds for $79,500. | | |

## Example Exercise 12-6 Redemption of Bonds Payable OBJ. 3

A $500,000 bond issue on which there is an unamortized discount of $40,000 is redeemed for $475,000. Journalize the redemption of the bonds.

*(Continued)*

4 Some bond indentures require the corporation issuing the bonds to transfer cash to a special cash fund, called a *sinking fund,* over the life of the bond. Such funds help assure investors that there will be adequate cash to pay the bonds at their maturity date.

**OBJ. 4**  Describe and illustrate the accounting for installment notes.

# Installment Notes

Corporations often finance their operations by issuing bonds payable. As an alternative, corporations may issue installment notes. An **installment note** is a debt that requires the borrower to make equal periodic payments to the lender for the term of the note. Unlike bonds, each note payment includes the following:

Individuals typically use mortgage notes when buying a house or car.

1. Payment of a portion of the amount initially borrowed, called the *principal*
2. Payment of interest on the outstanding balance

At the end of the note's term, the principal will have been repaid in full.

Installment notes are often used to purchase specific assets such as equipment, and are often secured by the purchased asset. When a note is secured by an asset, it is called a **mortgage note**. If the borrower fails to pay a mortgage note, the lender has the right to take possession of the pledged asset and sell it to pay off the debt. Mortgage notes are typically issued by an individual bank.

## Issuing an Installment Note

When an installment note is issued, an entry is recorded debiting Cash and crediting Notes Payable. To illustrate, assume that Lewis Company issues the following installment note to City National Bank on January 1, 2010.

| | |
|---|---|
| Principal amount of note ........................... | $24,000 |
| Interest rate ........................................ | 6% |
| Term of note ....................................... | 5 years |
| Annual payments ................................... | $5,698[5] |

The entry to record the issuance of the note is as follows:

| 2010 | | | | | |
|---|---|---|---|---|---|
| Jan. | 1 | Cash | | 24,000 | |
| | |    Notes Payable | | | 24,000 |
| | |     Issued installment note for cash. | | | |

## Annual Payments

The preceding note payable requires Lewis Company to repay the principal and interest in equal payments of $5,698 beginning December 3, 2010, for each of the next five years. Unlike bonds, however, each installment note payment includes an interest and principal component.

The interest portion of an installment note payment is computed by multiplying the interest rate by the carrying amount (book value) of the note at the beginning of the period. The principal portion of the payment is then computed as the difference between the total installment note payment (cash paid) and the interest component. These computations are illustrated in Exhibit 3 as follows:

[5] The amount of the annual payment is calculated by using the present value concepts discussed in Appendix 1. The annual payment of $5,698 is computed by dividing the $24,000 loan amount by the present value of an annuity of $1 for 5 periods at 6% (4.21236) from Exhibit 5 (rounded to the nearest dollar).

**EXHIBIT 3**     **Amortization of Installment Notes**

| For the Year Ending | A<br>January 1<br>Carrying<br>Amount | B<br>Note<br>Payment<br>(Cash Paid) | C<br>Interest Expense<br>(6% of January 1<br>Note Carrying Amount) | D<br>Decrease<br>in Notes<br>Payable<br>(B – C) | E<br>December 31<br>Carrying<br>Amount<br>(A – D) |
|---|---|---|---|---|---|
| December 31, 2010 | $24,000 | $ 5,698 | $ 1,440  (6% of $24,000) | $ 4,258 | $19,742 |
| December 31, 2011 | 19,742 | 5,698 | 1,185  (6% of $19,742) | 4,513 | 15,229 |
| December 31, 2012 | 15,229 | 5,698 | 914  (6% of $15,229) | 4,784 | 10,445 |
| December 31, 2013 | 10,445 | 5,698 | 627  (6% of $10,445) | 5,071 | 5,374 |
| December 31, 2014 | 5,374 | 5,698 | 324* (6% of  $5,374) | 5,374 | 0 |
| | | $28,490 | $4,490 | $24,000 | |

*Rounded ($5,374 – $5,698).

1. The January 1, 2010, carrying value (Column A) equals the amount borrowed from the bank. The January 1 balance in the following years equals the December 31 balance from the prior year.

2. The note payment (Column B) remains constant at $5,698, the annual cash payments required by the bank.

3. The interest expense (Column C) is computed at 6% of the installment note carrying amount at the beginning of each year. As a result, the interest expense decreases each year.

4. Notes payable decreases each year by the amount of the principal repayment (Column D). The principal repayment is computed by subtracting the interest expense (Column C) from the total payment (Column B). The principal repayment (Column D) increases each year as the interest expense decreases (Column C).

5. The carrying amount on December 31 (Column E) of the note decreases from $24,000, the initial amount borrowed, to $0 at the end of the five years.

The entry to record the first payment on December 31, 2010, is as follows:

| 2010 | | | | |
|---|---|---|---|---|
| Dec. | 31 | Interest Expense | 1,440 | |
| | | Notes Payable | 4,258 | |
| | | Cash | | 5,698 |
| | | Paid principal and interest on installment note. | | |

The entry to record the second payment on December 31, 2011, is as follows:

| 2011 | | | | |
|---|---|---|---|---|
| Dec. | 31 | Interest Expense | 1,185 | |
| | | Notes Payable | 4,513 | |
| | | Cash | | 5,698 |
| | | Paid principal and interest on installment note. | | |

As the prior entries show, the cash payment is the same in each year. The interest and principal repayment, however, change each year. This is because the carrying amount (book value) of the note decreases each year as principal is repaid, which decreases the interest component the next period.

The entry to record the final payment on December 31, 2014, is as follows:

| 2014 | | | | |
|---|---|---|---|---|
| Dec. | 31 | Interest Expense | 324 | |
| | | Notes Payable | 5,374 | |
| | | Cash | | 5,698 |
| | | Paid principal and interest on installment note. | | |

After the final payment, the carrying amount on the note is zero, indicating that the note has been paid in full. Any assets that secure the note would then be released by the bank.

## e**x**cel
*success*

Spreadsheet software can be used to develop an amortization table for installment notes as follows:

You can fill cells according to a sequence of numbers or dates by highlighting the cells containing the fill sequence, then using the fill handle to drag to the empty cells to be filled.

| | A | B | C | D | E | F |
|---|---|---|---|---|---|---|
| 1 | *Inputs:* | | | | | |
| 2 | Principal amount on note | $ 24,000.00 | | | | |
| 3 | Interest rate | 6% | | | | |
| 4 | Term of note | 5 | years | | | |
| 5 | Annual payments | $ 5,698 | | | | |
| 6 | | | | | | |
| 7 | | | | | | |
| 8 | *Output:* | b. | c. | d. | e. | f. |
| 9 | For the year ending: | January 1 Carrying Amount | Note Payment (cash paid) | Interest Expense at 6% | Decrease in Notes Payable | December 31 Carrying Amount |
| 10 | December 31, 2010 | =B2 | =$B$5 | =B$3*B10 | =C10-D10 | =B10-E10 |
| 11 | December 31, 2011 | =F10 | =$B$5 | =B$3*B11 | =C11-D11 | =B11-E11 |
| 12 | December 31, 2012 | =F11 | =$B$5 | =B$3*B12 | =C12-D12 | =B12-E12 |
| 13 | December 31, 2013 | =F12 | =$B$5 | =B$3*B13 | =C13-D13 | =B13-E13 |
| 14 | December 31, 2014 | =F13 | =$B$5 | =B$3*B14 | =C14-D14 | =B14-E14 |

a. (pointing to A10)
g. (pointing to B11)
h.
i.

The spreadsheet is developed by creating input and output areas. The four inputs are the principal amount of the note, interest rate, term of note, and annual payments, as shown in the chapter illustration. Use the following steps in formulating the output table.

**a.** Enter the dates for December 31, 2010 and 2011, in cells A10 and A11. You may need to reformat the date in these two cells to appear as shown. Highlight these two cells, then drag the fill handle over the range that you want to fill, or A12:A14. The dates will automatically fill in with correct annual spacing.

**b.** Enter in cell B10 the cell reference for principal amount of the note, =B2.

**c.** Enter in cell C10 the cell reference for the annual payment, =$B$5. The dollar sign makes the cell absolute, so that the installment is fixed when copied.

**d.** Enter in cell D10 the formula for the interest expense, =B$3*B10. The interest rate row must also remain fixed (absolute) for copying.

**e.** Enter in cell E10 the formula for the decrease in notes payable, =C10-D10.

**f.** Enter in cell F10 the formula for the December 31 carrying amount, =B10-E10.

**g.** Enter in cell B11 the cell reference for the January 1 carrying amount, =F10.

**h.** Copy B11 to B12:B14.

**i.** Copy cells C10:F10 to C11:F14.

**Try**It   Go to the hands-on **Excel Tutor** for this example!

**Try**It   This Excel Success example shows the use of an Excel function referred to as cell referencing. Go to the **Excel Tutor** titled **Absolute & Relative Cell References** for additional help on this useful Excel function!

## Example Exercise  12-7  Journalizing Installment Notes
OBJ. 4

On the first day of the fiscal year, a company issues a $30,000, 10%, five-year installment note that has annual payments of $7,914. The first note payment consists of $3,000 of interest and $4,914 of principal repayment.

a. Journalize the entry to record the issuance of the installment note.
b. Journalize the first annual note payment.

## Follow My Example  12-7

a.

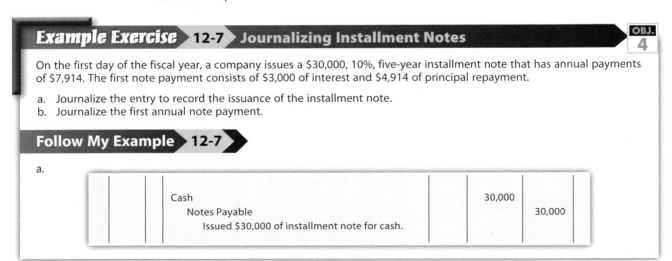

| | | |
|---|---|---|
| Cash | 30,000 | |
| Notes Payable | | 30,000 |
| Issued $30,000 of installment note for cash. | | |

b.

| | | | | |
|---|---|---|---|---|
| Interest Expense | | 3,000 | | |
| Notes Payable | | 4,914 | | |
|   Cash | | | 7,914 | |
|     Paid principal and interest on installment note. | | | | |

Practice Exercises: **PE 12-7A, PE 12-7B**

# Integrity, Objectivity, and Ethics in Business

### LIAR'S LOANS

One of the main causes of the 2008 financial crisis was a widespread inability of homeowners to repay their home mortgages. While the weak economy contributed to these problems, many mortgage defaults were the result of unethical lending practices in the form of "stated income" or "liar's" loans. In a conventional home mortgage, lenders base the amount of a loan on the borrower's income, expenses, and total assets. These amounts are verified by reviewing the borrower's tax returns, bank statements, and payroll records. Liar's loans, however, based the amount of the loan on the borrower's "stated income," without verifying it through sources such as tax returns, W-2 statements, or payroll records. Without independent verification, borrowers often falsified or lied about their "stated income" in order to obtain a larger loan than they were qualified for. Once in their homes, many of these borrowers were unable to make their loan payments, causing them to default on their home mortgages.

# Reporting Long-Term Liabilities

**OBJ. 5** Describe and illustrate the reporting of long-term liabilities including bonds and notes payable.

Bonds payable and notes payable are reported as liabilities on the balance sheet. Any portion of the bonds or notes that is due within one year is reported as a current liability. Any remaining bonds or notes are reported as a long-term liability.

Any unamortized premium is reported as an addition to the face amount of the bonds. Any unamortized discount is reported as a deduction from the face amount of the bonds. A description of the bonds and notes should also be reported either on the face of the financial statements or in the accompanying notes.

The reporting of bonds and notes payable for Mornin' Joe is shown below.

**Mornin' Joe**
**Balance Sheet**
**December 31, 2012**

| | | |
|---|---|---|
| Current liabilities: | | |
|   Accounts payable | $133,000 | |
|   Notes payable (current portion) | 200,000 | |
|   Salaries and wages payable | 42,000 | |
|   Payroll taxes payable | 16,400 | |
|   Interest payable | 40,000 | |
|     Total current liabilities | | $  431,400 |
| Long-term liabilities: | | |
|   Bonds payable, 8%, due December 31, 2030 | $500,000 | |
|     Less unamortized discount | 16,000 | $  484,000 |
|   Notes payable | | 1,400,000 |
|     Total long-term liabilities | | $1,884,000 |
| Total liabilities | | $2,315,400 |

See pages 630–634

See pages 630–634

### IFRS Reporting

The statement of financial position (balance sheet) presentation of stockholders' equity for Mornin' Joe International under IFRS is as follows:

| Mornin' Joe International |
| :---: |
| **Statement of Financial Position** |
| **December 31, 2012** |

**Noncurrent liabilities**

| | | |
| --- | ---: | ---: |
| Bonds payable, 8%, due December 31, 2030 | | |
| (net of discount) | € 484,000 | |
| Notes payable | 1,400,000 | |
| Total noncurrent liabilities | | €1,884,000 |

As discussed in Chapter 7, IFRS provides flexibility in the order in which the statement of financial position (balance sheet) accounts are presented. Liabilities typically follow the equity disclosure. Within liabilities, long-term liabilities, or what is termed here as noncurrent liabilities, precede current liabilities. This ordering is the reverse of Mornin' Joe (U.S.). IFRS ordering emphasizes the going concern nature of the business. In addition, details of the bond discount are provided in the footnotes.

## Financial Analysis and Interpretation: Number of Times Interest Charges Are Earned

**OBJ. 6** Describe and illustrate how the number of times interest charges are earned is used to evaluate a company's financial condition.

As we have discussed, the assets of a company are subject to the (1) claims of creditors and (2) the rights of owners. As creditors, bondholders are primarily concerned with the company's ability to make its periodic interest payments and repay the face amount of the bonds at maturity.

Analysts assess the risk that bondholders will not receive their interest payments by computing the **number of times interest charges are earned** during the year:

$$\text{Number of Times Interest Charges Are Earned} = \frac{\text{Income Before Income Tax} + \text{Interest Expense}}{\text{Interest Expense}}$$

This ratio computes the number of times interest payments could be paid out of current period earnings, measuring the company's ability to make its interest payments. Because interest payments reduce income tax expense, the ratio is computed using income before tax.

To illustrate, the following data were taken from the 2008 annual report of Under Armour, Inc. (in thousands):

| | |
| --- | ---: |
| Interest expense | $ 850 |
| Income before income tax | 69,900 |

The number of times interest charges are earned for Under Armour, Inc., is computed as follows:

$$\text{Number of Times Interest Charges Are Earned} = \frac{\$69,900 + \$850}{\$850} = 83.24$$

Compare this to the number of times interest charges are earned for Southwest Airlines (an airline), and Verizon Communications (a telecommunications company) shown below (in thousands):

| | Under Armour | Southwest Airlines | Verizon Communications |
| --- | ---: | ---: | ---: |
| Interest expense | $850 | $105,000 | $1,819,000 |
| Income before income tax expense | $69,900 | $278,000 | $9,759,000 |
| Number of times interest charges are earned | 83.24 | 3.65 | 6.37 |

Under Armour's number of times interest charges are earned is 83.24, indicating that the company generates enough income before taxes to pay (cover) its interest payments 83.24 times. As a result, debtholders have extremely good protection in the event of an earnings decline. Compare this to Southwest Airlines, which only generates enough income before taxes to pay (cover) its interest payments 3.65 times. A small decrease in Southwest Airlines' earnings could jeopardize the payment of interest. Verizon Communications falls in between, with a ratio of 6.37.

**Example Exercise** ⟩ **12-8** ⟩ **Number of Times Interest Charges Are Earned**

**OBJ. 6**

Harris Industries reported the following on the company's income statement in 2012 and 2011:

|  | 2012 | 2011 |
| --- | --- | --- |
| Interest expense | $ 200,000 | $180,000 |
| Income before income tax expense | 1,000,000 | 720,000 |

a. Determine the number of times interest charges were earned for 2012 and 2011. Round to one decimal place.
b. Is the number of times interest charges are earned improving or declining?

**Follow My Example** ⟩ **12-8** ⟩

a. 2012:

$$\text{Number of times interest charges are earned: } 6.0 = \frac{\$1,000,000 + \$200,000}{\$200,000}$$

2011:

$$\text{Number of times interest charges are earned: } 5.0 = \frac{\$720,000 + \$180,000}{\$180,000}$$

b. The number of times interest charges are earned has increased from 5.0 in 2011 to 6.0 in 2012. Thus, the debtholders have improved confidence in the company's ability to make its interest payments.

Practice Exercises: **PE 12-8A, PE 12-8B**

# A P P E N D I X  1

# Present Value Concepts and Pricing Bonds Payable

When a corporation issues bonds, the price that investors are willing to pay for the bonds depends on the following:

1. The face amount of the bonds, which is the amount due at the maturity date.
2. The periodic interest to be paid on the bonds.
3. The market rate of interest.

An investor determines how much to pay for the bonds by computing the present value of the bond's future cash receipts, using the market rate of interest. A bond's future cash receipts include its face value at maturity and the periodic interest payments.

## Present Value Concepts

The concept of present value is based on the time value of money. The *time value of money concept* recognizes that cash received today is worth more than the same amount of cash to be received in the future.

To illustrate, what would you rather have: $1,000 today or $1,000 one year from now? You would rather have the $1,000 today because it could be invested to earn interest. For example, if the $1,000 could be invested to earn 10% per year, the $1,000 will accumulate to $1,100 ($1,000 plus $100 interest) in one year. In this sense, you can think of the $1,000 in hand today as the **present value** of $1,100 to be received a year from today. This present value is illustrated below.

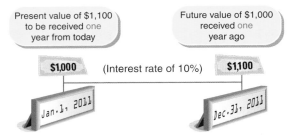

A related concept to present value is **future value**. To illustrate, using the preceding example, the $1,100 to be received on December 31, 2011, is the *future value* of $1,000 on January 1, 2011, assuming an interest rate of 10%.

## Present Value of an Amount

To illustrate the present value of an amount, assume that $1,000 is to be received in one year. If the market rate of interest is 10%, the present value of the $1,000 is $909.09 ($1,000/1.10). This present value is illustrated below.

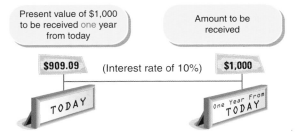

If the $1,000 is to be received in two years, with interest of 10% compounded at the end of the first year, the present value is $826.45 ($909.09/1.10).[6] This present value is illustrated below.

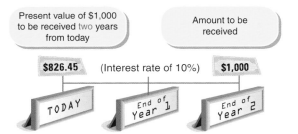

Spreadsheet software with built-in present value functions can be used to calculate present values.

The present value of an amount to be received in the future can be determined by a series of divisions such as illustrated on the previous page. In practice, however, it is easier to use a table of present values.

The *present value of $1* table is used to find the present value factor for $1 to be received after a number of periods in the future. The amount to be received is then multiplied by this factor to determine its present value.

To illustrate, Exhibit 4 is a partial table of the present value of $1.[7] Exhibit 4 indicates that the present value of $1 to be received in two years with a market rate of interest of 10% a year is 0.82645. Multiplying $1,000 to be received in two years by 0.82645 yields

6 Note that the future value of $826.45 in two years, at an interest rate of 10% compounded annually, is $1,000.

7 To simplify the illustrations bond homework assignments, the tables presented in this chapter are limited to 10 periods for a small number of interest rates, and the amounts are carried to only five decimal places. Computer programs are available for determining present value factors for any number of interest rates, decimal places, or periods. More complete interest tables are presented in Appendix A of the text.

$826.45 ($1,000 × 0.82645). This amount is the same amount computed earlier. In Exhibit 4, the Periods column represents the number of compounding periods, and the percentage columns represent the compound interest rate per period. Thus, the present value factor from Exhibit 4 for 12% for five years is 0.56743. If the interest is compounded semiannually, the interest rate is 6% (12% divided by 2), and the number of periods is 10 (5 years × 2 times per year). Thus, the present value factor from Exhibit 4 for 6% and 10 periods is 0.55840. Some additional examples using Exhibit 4 are shown below.

**EXHIBIT 4**     **Present Value of $1 at Compound Interest**

| Periods | 5% | 5½% | 6% | 6½% | 7% | 10% | 11% | 12% | 13% | 14% |
|---|---|---|---|---|---|---|---|---|---|---|
| 1 | 0.95238 | 0.94787 | 0.94340 | 0.93897 | 0.93458 | 0.90909 | 0.90090 | 0.89286 | 0.88496 | 0.87719 |
| 2 | 0.90703 | 0.89845 | 0.89000 | 0.88166 | 0.87344 | 0.82645 | 0.81162 | 0.79719 | 0.78315 | 0.76947 |
| 3 | 0.86384 | 0.85161 | 0.83962 | 0.82785 | 0.81630 | 0.75132 | 0.73119 | 0.71178 | 0.69305 | 0.67497 |
| 4 | 0.82270 | 0.80722 | 0.79209 | 0.77732 | 0.76290 | 0.68301 | 0.65873 | 0.63552 | 0.61332 | 0.59208 |
| 5 | 0.78353 | 0.76513 | 0.74726 | 0.72988 | 0.71299 | 0.62092 | 0.59345 | 0.56743 | 0.54276 | 0.51937 |
| 6 | 0.74622 | 0.72525 | 0.70496 | 0.68533 | 0.66634 | 0.56447 | 0.53464 | 0.50663 | 0.48032 | 0.45559 |
| 7 | 0.71068 | 0.68744 | 0.66506 | 0.64351 | 0.62275 | 0.51316 | 0.48166 | 0.45235 | 0.42506 | 0.39964 |
| 8 | 0.67684 | 0.65160 | 0.62741 | 0.60423 | 0.58201 | 0.46651 | 0.43393 | 0.40388 | 0.37616 | 0.35056 |
| 9 | 0.64461 | 0.61763 | 0.59190 | 0.56735 | 0.54393 | 0.42410 | 0.39092 | 0.36061 | 0.33288 | 0.30751 |
| 10 | 0.61391 | 0.58543 | 0.55840 | 0.53273 | 0.50835 | 0.38554 | 0.35218 | 0.32197 | 0.29459 | 0.26974 |

| | Number of Periods | Interest Rate | Present Value of $1 Factor from Exhibit 4 |
|---|---|---|---|
| 10% for *two* years compounded *annually* | 2 | 10% | 0.82645 |
| 10% for *two* years compounded *semiannually* | 4 | 5% | 0.82270 |
| 10% for *three* years compounded *semiannually* | 6 | 5% | 0.74622 |
| 12% for *five* years compounded *semiannually* | 10 | 6% | 0.55840 |

**Present Value of the Periodic Receipts** A series of equal cash receipts spaced equally in time is called an **annuity**. The **present value of an annuity** is the sum of the present values of each cash receipt. To illustrate, assume that $100 is to be received annually for two years and that the market rate of interest is 10%. Using Exhibit 4, the present value of the receipt of the two amounts of $100 is $173.55, as shown below.

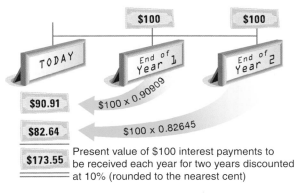

$90.91 ← $100 × 0.90909

$82.64 ← $100 × 0.82645

$173.55 — Present value of $100 interest payments to be received each year for two years discounted at 10% (rounded to the nearest cent)

Instead of using present value of $1 tables to determine the present value of each cash flow separately, such as Exhibit 4, the present value of an annuity can be computed in a single step. Using a value from the present value of an annuity of $1 table in Exhibit 5, the present value of the entire annuity can be calculated by multiplying the equal cash payment times the appropriate present value of an annuity of $1.

To illustrate, the present value of $100 to be received at the end of each of the next two years at 10% compound interest per period is $173.55 ($100 × 1.73554). This amount is the same amount computed above using the present value of $1.

**EXHIBIT 5**    **Present Value of an Annuity of $1 at Compound Interest**

| Periods | 5% | 5½% | 6% | 6½% | 7% | 10% | 11% | 12% | 13% | 14% |
|---|---|---|---|---|---|---|---|---|---|---|
| 1 | 0.95238 | 0.94787 | 0.94340 | 0.93897 | 0.93458 | 0.90909 | 0.90090 | 0.89286 | 0.88496 | 0.87719 |
| 2 | 1.85941 | 1.84632 | 1.83339 | 1.82063 | 1.80802 | 1.73554 | 1.71252 | 1.69005 | 1.66810 | 1.64666 |
| 3 | 2.72325 | 2.69793 | 2.67301 | 2.64848 | 2.62432 | 2.48685 | 2.44371 | 2.40183 | 2.36115 | 2.32163 |
| 4 | 3.54595 | 3.50515 | 3.46511 | 3.42580 | 3.38721 | 3.16987 | 3.10245 | 3.03735 | 2.97447 | 2.91371 |
| 5 | 4.32948 | 4.27028 | 4.21236 | 4.15568 | 4.10020 | 3.79079 | 3.69590 | 3.60478 | 3.51723 | 3.43308 |
| 6 | 5.07569 | 4.99553 | 4.91732 | 4.84101 | 4.76654 | 4.35526 | 4.23054 | 4.11141 | 3.99755 | 3.88867 |
| 7 | 5.78637 | 5.68297 | 5.58238 | 5.48452 | 5.38929 | 4.86842 | 4.71220 | 4.56376 | 4.42261 | 4.28830 |
| 8 | 6.46321 | 6.33457 | 6.20979 | 6.08875 | 5.97130 | 5.33493 | 5.14612 | 4.96764 | 4.79677 | 4.63886 |
| 9 | 7.10782 | 6.95220 | 6.80169 | 6.65610 | 6.51523 | 5.75902 | 5.53705 | 5.32825 | 5.13166 | 4.94637 |
| 10 | 7.72174 | 7.53763 | 7.36009 | 7.18883 | 7.02358 | 6.14457 | 5.88923 | 5.65022 | 5.42624 | 5.21612 |

## Pricing Bonds

The selling price of a bond is the sum of the present values of:

1. The face amount of the bonds due at the maturity date
2. The periodic interest to be paid on the bonds

The market rate of interest is used to compute the present value of both the face amount and the periodic interest.

To illustrate the pricing of bonds, assume that Southern Utah Communications Inc. issued the following bond on January 1, 2011:

| | |
|---|---|
| Face amount . . . . . . . . . . . . . . . . . . . . . . . . . . . . . . . . . . . . . . . . . . . . . . . . . . . . . . | $100,000 |
| Contract rate of interest . . . . . . . . . . . . . . . . . . . . . . . . . . . . . . . . . . . . . . . | 12% |
| Interest paid semiannually on June 30 and December 31. | |
| Term of bonds. . . . . . . . . . . . . . . . . . . . . . . . . . . . . . . . . . . . . . . . . . . . . . . . . . . | 5 years |

**Market Rate of Interest of 12%**   Assuming a market rate of interest of 12%, the bonds would sell for their face amount. As shown by the following present value computations, the bonds would sell for $100,000.

| | |
|---|---|
| Present value of face amount of $100,000 due in 5 years, at 12% compounded semiannually: $100,000 × 0.55840 (present value of $1 for 10 periods at 6% from Exhibit 4). . . . . . . . . . . . . . . . . . . . . . . . . . . . . | $ 55,840 |
| Present value of 10 semiannual interest payments of $6,000, at 12% compounded semiannually: $6,000 × 7.36009 (present value of an annuity of $1 for 10 periods at 6% from Exhibit 5) . . . . . . . . . . . . . . . . . . . | 44,160 |
| Total present value of bonds . . . . . . . . . . . . . . . . . . . . . . . . . . . . . . . . . . . . . . . . . . . . . . . . . . . . . | $100,000 |

**Market Rate of Interest of 13%**   Assuming a market rate of interest of 13%, the bonds would sell at a discount. As shown by the following present value computations, the bonds would sell for $96,406.[8]

| | |
|---|---|
| Present value of face amount of $100,000 due in 5 years, at 13% compounded semiannually: $100,000 × 0.53273 (present value of $1 for 10 periods at 6½% from Exhibit 4) . . . . . . . . . . . . . . . . . . . . . . . . . | $53,273 |
| Present value of 10 semiannual interest payments of $6,000, at 13% compounded semiannually: $6,000 × 7.18883 (present value of an annuity of $1 for 10 periods at 6½% from Exhibit 5) . . . . . . . . . . . . . . . . | 43,133 |
| Total present value of bonds . . . . . . . . . . . . . . . . . . . . . . . . . . . . . . . . . . . . . . . . . . . . . . . . . . . . . | $96,406 |

**Market Rate of Interest of 11%**   Assuming a market rate of interest of 11%, the bonds would sell at a premium. As shown by the following present value computations, the bonds would sell for $103,769.

8 Some corporations issue bonds called **zero-coupon bonds** that provide for only the payment of the face amount at maturity. Such bonds sell for large discounts. In this example, such a bond would sell for $53,273, which is the present value of the face amount.

Present value of face amount of $100,000 due in 5 years,
   at 11% compounded semiannually: $100,000 × 0.58543
      (present value of $1 for 10 periods at 5½% from Exhibit 4) . . . . . . . . . . . . . . . . . . . . . . . . . . . . .    $ 58,543
Present value of 10 semiannual interest payments of $6,000,
   at 11% compounded semiannually: $6,000 × 7.53763
      (present value of an annuity of $1 for 10 periods at 5½% from Exhibit 5) . . . . . . . . . . . . . . . .    45,226
Total present value of bonds . . . . . . . . . . . . . . . . . . . . . . . . . . . . . . . . . . . . . . . . . . . . . . . . . . . . . . . . . .    $103,769

As shown above, the selling price of the bond varies with the present value of the bond's face amount at maturity, interest payments, and the market rate of interest.

# A P P E N D I X   2

# Effective Interest Rate Method of Amortization

The effective interest rate method of amortization provides for a constant *rate* of interest over the life of the bonds. As the discount or premium is amortized, the carrying amount of the bonds changes. As a result, interest expense also changes each period. This is in contrast to the straight-line method, which provides for a constant *amount* of interest expense each period.

The interest rate used in the effective interest rate method of amortization, sometimes called the *interest method*, is the market rate on the date the bonds are issued. The carrying amount of the bonds is multiplied by this interest rate to determine the interest expense for the period. The difference between the interest expense and the interest payment is the amount of discount or premium to be amortized for the period.

## Amortization of Discount by the Interest Method

To illustrate, the following data taken from the chapter illustration of issuing bonds at a discount are used:

Face value of 12%, 5-year bonds, interest compounded semiannually . . . . . . . . . . . . . . . . . . . . . .    $100,000
Present value of bonds at effective (market) rate of interest of 13% . . . . . . . . . . . . . . . . . . . . . . .    96,406
Discount on bonds payable . . . . . . . . . . . . . . . . . . . . . . . . . . . . . . . . . . . . . . . . . . . . . . . . . . . . . . . . . . . .    $ 3,594

Exhibit 6 illustrates the interest method for the preceding bonds. Exhibit 6 begins with six columns. The first column is not lettered. The remaining columns are lettered A through E. The exhibit is then prepared as follows:

Step 1. List the interest payment dates in the first column, which for the preceding bond are 10 interest payment dates (semiannual interest over five years). Also, list on the first line the initial amount of discount in Column D and the initial carrying amount (selling price) of the bonds in Column E.

Step 2. List in Column A the semiannual interest payments, which for the preceding bond is $6,000 ($100,000 × 6%).

Step 3. Compute the interest expense in Column B by multiplying the bond carrying amount at the beginning of each period times 6½%, which is the effective interest (market) rate.

Step 4. Compute the discount to be amortized each period in Column C by subtracting the interest payment in Column A ($6,000) from the interest expense for the period shown in Column B.

Step 5. Compute the remaining unamortized discount by subtracting the amortized discount for the period in Column C from the unamortized discount at the beginning of the period in Column D.

Step 6. Compute the bond carrying amount at the end of the period by subtracting the unamortized discount at the end of the period in Column D from the face amount of the bonds ($100,000).

**EXHIBIT 6**  **Amortization of Discount on Bonds Payable**

| Interest Payment Date | A Interest Paid (6% of Face Amount) | B Interest Expense (6½% of Bond Carrying Amount) | C Discount Amortization (B – A) | D Unamortized Discount (D – C) | E Bond Carrying Amount ($100,000 – D) |
|---|---|---|---|---|---|
| | | | | $3,594 | $ 96,406 |
| June 30, 2011 | $6,000 | $6,266 (6½% of $96,406) | $266 | 3,328 | 96,672 |
| Dec. 31, 2011 | 6,000 | 6,284 (6½% of $96,672) | 284 | 3,044 | 96,956 |
| June 30, 2012 | 6,000 | 6,302 (6½% of $96,956) | 302 | 2,742 | 97,258 |
| Dec. 31, 2012 | 6,000 | 6,322 (6½% of $97,258) | 322 | 2,420 | 97,580 |
| June 30, 2013 | 6,000 | 6,343 (6½% of $97,580) | 343 | 2,077 | 97,923 |
| Dec. 31, 2013 | 6,000 | 6,365 (6½% of $97,923) | 365 | 1,712 | 98,288 |
| June 30, 2014 | 6,000 | 6,389 (6½% of $98,288) | 389 | 1,323 | 98,677 |
| Dec. 31, 2014 | 6,000 | 6,414 (6½% of $98,677) | 414 | 909 | 99,091 |
| June 30, 2015 | 6,000 | 6,441 (6½% of $99,091) | 441 | 468 | 99,532 |
| Dec. 31, 2015 | 6,000 | 6,470 (6½% of $99,532) | 468* | — | 100,000 |

*Cannot exceed unamortized discount.

Steps 3–6 are repeated for each interest payment.

As shown in Exhibit 6, the interest expense increases each period as the carrying amount of the bond increases. Also, the unamortized discount decreases each period to zero at the maturity date. Finally, the carrying amount of the bonds increases from $96,406 to $100,000 (the face amount) at maturity.

The entry to record the first interest payment on June 30, 2011, and the related discount amortization is as follows:

| | | | | | |
|---|---|---|---|---|---|
| 2011 June | 30 | Interest Expense | | 6,266 | |
| | | Discount on Bonds Payable | | | 266 |
| | | Cash | | | 6,000 |
| | | Paid semiannual interest and amortized bond discount for ½ year. | | | |

If the amortization is recorded only at the end of the year, the amount of the discount amortized on December 31, 2011, would be $550. This is the sum of the first two semiannual amortization amounts ($266 and $284) from Exhibit 6.

## Amortization of Premium by the Interest Method

To illustrate, the following data taken from the chapter illustration of issuing bonds at a premium are used:

Present value of bonds at effective (market) rate of interest of 11%.......................... $103,769
Face value of 12%, 5-year bonds, interest compounded semiannually ....................... 100,000
Premium on bonds payable........................................................... $   3,769

Exhibit 7 illustrates the interest method for the preceding bonds. Exhibit 7 begins with six columns. The first column is not lettered. The remaining columns are lettered A through E. The exhibit is then prepared as follows:

Step 1. List the number of interest payments in the first column, which for the preceding bond are 10 interest payments (semiannual interest over 5 years). Also, list on the first line the initial amount of premium in Column D and the initial carrying amount of the bonds in Column E.

Step 2. List in Column A the semiannual interest payments, which for the preceding bond is $6,000 ($100,000 × 6%).

**EXHIBIT 7**    **Amortization of Premium on Bonds Payable**

| Interest Payment Date | A Interest Paid (6% of Face Amount) | B Interest Expense (5½% of Bond Carrying Amount) | C Premium Amortization (A − B) | D Unamortized Premium (D − C) | E Bond Carrying Amount ($100,000 + D) |
|---|---|---|---|---|---|
| | | | | $3,769 | $103,769 |
| June 30, 2011 | $6,000 | $5,707 (5½% of $103,769) | $293 | 3,476 | 103,476 |
| Dec. 31, 2011 | 6,000 | 5,691 (5½% of $103,476) | 309 | 3,167 | 103,167 |
| June 30, 2012 | 6,000 | 5,674 (5½% of $103,167) | 326 | 2,841 | 102,841 |
| Dec. 31, 2012 | 6,000 | 5,656 (5½% of $102,841) | 344 | 2,497 | 102,497 |
| June 30, 2013 | 6,000 | 5,637 (5½% of $102,497) | 363 | 2,134 | 102,134 |
| Dec. 31, 2013 | 6,000 | 5,617 (5½% of $102,134) | 383 | 1,751 | 101,751 |
| June 30, 2014 | 6,000 | 5,596 (5½% of $101,751) | 404 | 1,347 | 101,347 |
| Dec. 31, 2014 | 6,000 | 5,574 (5½% of $101,347) | 426 | 921 | 100,921 |
| June 30, 2015 | 6,000 | 5,551 (5½% of $100,921) | 449 | 472 | 100,472 |
| Dec. 31, 2015 | 6,000 | 5,526 (5½% of $100,472) | 472* | — | 100,000 |

*Cannot exceed unamortized premium.

Step 3. Compute the interest expense in Column B by multiplying the bond carrying amount at the beginning of each period times 5½%, which is the effective interest (market) rate.

Step 4. Compute the premium to be amortized each period in Column C by subtracting the interest expense for the period shown in Column B from the interest payment in Column A ($6,000).

Step 5. Compute the remaining unamortized premium by subtracting the amortized premium for the period in Column C from the unamortized premium at the beginning of the period in Column D.

Step 6. Compute the bond carrying amount at the end of the period in Column D by adding the unamortized premium at the end of the period to the face amount of the bonds ($100,000).

Steps 3–6 are repeated for each interest payment.

As shown in Exhibit 7, the interest expense decreases each period as the carrying amount of the bond decreases. Also, the unamortized premium decreases each period to zero at the maturity date. Finally, the carrying amount of the bonds decreases from $103,769 to $100,000 (the face amount) at maturity.

The entry to record the first interest payment on June 30, 2011, and the related premium amortization is as follows:

| 2011 | | | | |
|---|---|---|---|---|
| June | 30 | Interest Expense | 5,707 | |
| | | Premium on Bonds Payable | 293 | |
| | | Cash | | 6,000 |
| | | Paid semiannual interest and amortized bond premium for ½ year. | | |

If the amortization is recorded only at the end of the year, the amount of the premium amortized on December 31, 2011, would be $602. This is the sum of the first two semiannual amortization amounts ($293 and $309) from Exhibit 7.

# At a Glance 12

OBJ.
**1** **Compute the potential impact of long-term borrowing on earnings per share.**

**Key Points** Corporations can finance their operations by issuing short-term debt, long-term debt, or equity. One of the many factors that influence a corporation's decision on whether it should issue long-term debt or equity is the effect each alternative has on earnings per share.

| Learning Outcomes | Example Exercises | Practice Exercises |
|---|---|---|
| • Define the concept of a bond. | | |
| • Calculate and compare the effect of alternative long-term financing plans on earnings per share. | EE12-1 | PE12-1A, 12-1B |

OBJ.
**2** **Describe the characteristics and terminology of bonds payable.**

**Key Points** A corporation that issues bonds enters into a contract, or bond indenture.

When a corporation issues bonds, the price that buyers are willing to pay for the bonds depends on (1) the face amount of the bonds, (2) the periodic interest to be paid on the bonds, and (3) the market rate of interest.

| Learning Outcomes | Example Exercises | Practice Exercises |
|---|---|---|
| • Define the characteristics of a bond. | | |
| • Describe the various types of bonds. | | |
| • Describe the factors that determine the price of a bond. | | |

OBJ.
**3** **Journalize entries for bonds payable.**

**Key Points** The journal entry for issuing bonds payable debits Cash and credits Bonds Payable. Any difference between the face amount of the bonds and the selling price is debited to Discount on Bonds Payable or credited to Premium on Bonds Payable when the bonds are issued. The discount or premium on bonds payable is amortized to interest expense over the life of the bonds.

At the maturity date, the entry to record the repayment of the face value of a bond is a debit to Bonds Payable and a credit to Cash.

When a corporation redeems bonds before they mature, Bonds Payable is debited for the face amount of the bonds, the premium (discount) on bonds payable account is debited (credited) for its unamoritized balance, Cash is credited, and any gain or loss on the redemption is recorded.

| Learning Outcomes | Example Exercises | Practice Exercises |
|---|---|---|
| • Journalize the issuance of bonds at face value and the payment of periodic interest. | | |
| • Journalize the issuance of bonds at a discount. | EE12-2 | PE12-2A, 12-2B |
| • Journalize the amortization of a bond discount. | EE12-3 | PE12-3A, 12-3B |
| • Journalize the issuance of bonds at a premium. | EE12-4 | PE12-4A, 12-4B |
| • Journalize the amortization of a bond premium. | EE12-5 | PE12-5A, 12-5B |
| • Describe bond redemptions. | | |
| • Journalize the redemption of bonds payable. | EE12-6 | PE12-6A, 12-6B |

**OBJ. 4 Describe and illustrate the accounting for installment notes.**

**Key Points** An installment note requires the borrower to make equal periodic payments to the lender for the term of the note. Unlike bonds, the annual payment in an installment note consists of both principal and interest. The journal entry for the annual payment debits Interest Expense and Notes Payable and credits Cash for the amount of the payment. After the final payment, the carrying amount on the note is zero.

| Learning Outcomes | Example Exercises | Practice Exercises |
|---|---|---|
| • Define the characteristics of an installment note. | | |
| • Journalize the issuance of installment notes. | EE12-7 | PE12-7A, 12-7B |
| • Journalize the annual payment for an installment note. | | |

**OBJ. 5 Describe and illustrate the reporting of long-term liabilities including bonds and notes payable.**

**Key Points** Bonds payable and notes payable are usually reported as long-term liabilities. If the balance sheet date is within one year, they are reported as a current liability. A discount on bonds should be reported as a deduction from the related bonds payable. A premium on bonds should be reported as an addition to the related bonds payable.

| Learning Outcome | Example Exercises | Practice Exercises |
|---|---|---|
| • Illustrate the balance sheet presentation of bonds payable and notes payable. | | |

**OBJ. 6 Describe and illustrate how the number of times interest charges are earned is used to evaluate a company's financial condition.**

**Key Points** The number of times interest charges are earned measures the risk to bondholders that a company will not be able to make its interest payments. It is computed by dividing income before income tax plus interest expense by interest expense. This ratio measures the number of times interest payments could be paid (covered) by current period earnings.

| Learning Outcomes | Example Exercises | Practice Exercises |
|---|---|---|
| • Describe and compute the number of times interest charges are earned. | EE12-8 | PE12-8A, 12-8B |
| • Interpret the number of times interest charges are earned. | | |

# Key Terms

bond (542)
bond indenture (544)
carrying amount (551)
contract rate (545)
discount (545)

earnings per share (EPS) (543)
effective interest rate method (548)
effective rate of interest (545)
face amount (545)
installment note (552)

market rate of interest (545)
mortgage note (552)
number of times interest charges are earned (556)
premium (545)

## Illustrative Problem

The fiscal year of Russell Inc., a manufacturer of acoustical supplies, ends December 31. Selected transactions for the period 2011 through 2018, involving bonds payable issued by Russell Inc., are as follows:

**2011**

June 30.  Issued $2,000,000 of 25-year, 7% callable bonds dated June 30, 2011, for cash of $1,920,000. Interest is payable semiannually on June 30 and December 31.

Dec. 31.  Paid the semiannual interest on the bonds.

     31.  Recorded straight-line amortization of $1,600 of discount on the bonds.

     31.  Closed the interest expense account.

**2012**

June 30.  Paid the semiannual interest on the bonds.

Dec. 31.  Paid the semiannual interest on the bonds.

     31.  Recorded straight-line amortization of $3,200 of discount on the bonds.

     31.  Closed the interest expense account.

**2018**

June 30.  Recorded the redemption of the bonds, which were called at 101.5. The balance in the bond discount account is $57,600 after the payment of interest and amortization of discount have been recorded. (Record the redemption only.)

### Instructions

1.  Journalize entries to record the preceding transactions.

2.  Determine the amount of interest expense for 2011 and 2012.

3.  Determine the carrying amount of the bonds as of December 31, 2012.

### Solution

1.

| 2011 | | | | |
|---|---|---|---|---|
| June | 30 | Cash | 1,920,000 | |
| | | Discount on Bonds Payable | 80,000 | |
| | | Bonds Payable | | 2,000,000 |
| | | | | |
| Dec. | 31 | Interest Expense | 70,000 | |
| | | Cash | | 70,000 |
| | | | | |
| | 31 | Interest Expense | 1,600 | |
| | | Discount on Bonds Payable | | 1,600 |
| | | Amortization of discount from July 1 | | |
| | | to December 31. | | |
| | | | | |
| | 31 | Income Summary | 71,600 | |
| | | Interest Expense | | 71,600 |
| 2012 | | | | |
| June | 30 | Interest Expense | 70,000 | |
| | | Cash | | 70,000 |
| | | | | |
| Dec. | 31 | Interest Expense | 70,000 | |
| | | Cash | | 70,000 |

| | 31 | Interest Expense | | 3,200 | |
|---|---|---|---|---|---|
| | | Discount on Bonds Payable | | | 3,200 |
| | | Amortization of discount from | | | |
| | | January 1 to December 31. | | | |
| | | | | | |
| | 31 | Income Summary | | 143,200 | |
| | | Interest Expense | | | 143,200 |
| 2018 | | | | | |
| June | 30 | Bonds Payable | | 2,000,000 | |
| | | Loss on Redemption of Bonds Payable | | 87,600 | |
| | | Discount on Bonds Payable | | | 57,600 |
| | | Cash | | | 2,030,000 |

2.  a.  2011: $71,600 = $70,000 + $1,600

    b.  2012: $143,200 = $70,000 + $70,000 + $3,200

3.  Initial carrying amount of bonds                 $1,920,000

    Discount amortized on December 31, 2011         1,600

    Discount amortized on December 31, 2012         3,200

    Carrying amount of bonds, December 31, 2012    $1,924,800

# Discussion Questions

1.  Describe the two distinct obligations incurred by a corporation when issuing bonds.

2.  Explain the meaning of each of the following terms as they relate to a bond issue: (a) convertible, (b) callable, and (c) debenture.

3.  If you asked your broker to purchase for you a 12% bond when the market interest rate for such bonds was 11%, would you expect to pay more or less than the face amount for the bond? Explain.

4.  A corporation issues $18,000,000 of 10% bonds to yield interest at the rate of 8%. (a) Was the amount of cash received from the sale of the bonds greater or less than $18,000,000? (b) Identify the following terms related to the bond issue: (1) face amount, (2) market or effective rate of interest, (3) contract rate of interest, and (4) maturity amount.

5.  If bonds issued by a corporation are sold at a premium, is the market rate of interest greater or less than the contract rate?

6.  The following data relate to a $200,000,000, 5% bond issued for a selected semiannual interest period:

| | |
|---|---|
| Bond carrying amount at beginning of period | $216,221,792 |
| Interest paid during period | 5,000,000 |
| Interest expense allocable to the period | 4,864,990 |

(a) Were the bonds issued at a discount or at a premium? (b) What is the unamortized amount of the discount or premium account at the beginning of the period? (c) What account was debited to amortize the discount or premium?

7.  Bonds Payable has a balance of $3,500,000 and Discount on Bonds Payable has a balance of $125,000. If the issuing corporation redeems the bonds at 97, is there a gain or loss on the bond redemption?

8.  What is a mortgage note?

9.  Fleeson Company needs additional funds to purchase equipment for a new production facility and is considering either issuing bonds payable or borrowing the money from a local bank in the form of an installment note. How does an installment note differ from a bond payable?

10.  How would a bond payable be reported on the balance sheet if: (a) it is payable within one year and (b) it is payable beyond one year?

# Practice Exercises

**OBJ. 1**   **EE 12-1**  *p. 544*   **PE 12-1A**   **Alternative financing plans**

Baker Co. is considering the following alternative financing plans:

|  | Plan 1 | Plan 2 |
|---|---|---|
| Issue 5% bonds (at face value) | $3,000,000 | $1,500,000 |
| Issue preferred $4 stock, $25 par | — | 2,500,000 |
| Issue common stock, $40 par | 3,000,000 | 2,000,000 |

Income tax is estimated at 40% of income.

Determine the earnings per share of common stock, assuming income before bond interest and income tax is $1,000,000.

**OBJ. 1**   **EE 12-1**  *p. 544*   **PE 12-1B**   **Alternative financing plans**

Fly Co. is considering the following alternative financing plans:

|  | Plan 1 | Plan 2 |
|---|---|---|
| Issue 12% bonds (at face value) | $10,000,000 | $5,000,000 |
| Issue preferred $1.75 stock, $20 par | — | 8,000,000 |
| Issue common stock, $20 par | 10,000,000 | 7,000,000 |

Income tax is estimated at 40% of income.

Determine the earnings per share of common stock, assuming income before bond interest and income tax is $2,000,000.

**OBJ. 3**   **EE 12-2**  *p. 547*   **PE 12-2A**   **Issuing bonds at a discount**

On the first day of the fiscal year, a company issues a $4,000,000, 10%, 10-year bond that pays semiannual interest of $200,000 ($4,000,000 × 10% × ½), receiving cash of $3,760,992. Journalize the bond issuance.

**OBJ. 3**   **EE 12-2**  *p. 547*   **PE 12-2B**   **Issuing bonds at a discount**

On the first day of the fiscal year, a company issues a $1,500,000, 9%, five-year bond that pays semiannual interest of $67,500 ($1,500,000 × 9% × ½), receiving cash of $1,334,398. Journalize the bond issuance.

**OBJ. 3**   **EE 12-3**  *p. 548*   **PE 12-3A**   **Discount amortization**

Using the bond from Practice Exercise 12-2A, journalize the first interest payment and the amortization of the related bond discount. Round to the nearest dollar.

**OBJ. 3**   **EE 12-3**  *p. 548*   **PE 12-3B**   **Discount amortization**

Using the bond from Practice Exercise 12-2B, journalize the first interest payment and the amortization of the related bond discount. Round to the nearest dollar.

**OBJ. 3**   **EE 12-4**  *p. 549*   **PE 12-4A**   **Issuing bonds at a premium**

A company issues a $2,000,000, 9%, five-year bond that pays semiannual interest of $90,000 ($2,000,000 × 9% × ½), receiving cash of $2,166,332. Journalize the bond issuance.

**OBJ. 3**   **EE 12-4**  *p. 549*   **PE 12-4B**   **Issuing bonds at a premium**

A company issues a $6,000,000, 12%, five-year bond that pays semiannual interest of $360,000 ($6,000,000 × 12% × ½), receiving cash of $6,463,304. Journalize the bond issuance.

| Learning Objectives | Example Exercises | |
|---|---|---|
| OBJ. 3 | EE 12-5 *p. 550* | **PE 12-5A   Premium amortization** |

Using the bond from Practice Exercise 12-4A, journalize the first interest payment and the amortization of the related bond premium. Round to the nearest dollar.

| OBJ. 3 | EE 12-5 *p. 550* | **PE 12-5B   Premium amortization** |
|---|---|---|

Using the bond from Practice Exercise 12-4B, journalize the first interest payment and the amortization of the related bond premium. Round to the nearest dollar.

| OBJ. 3 | EE 12-6 *p. 551* | **PE 12-6A   Redemption of bonds payable** |
|---|---|---|

An $800,000 bond issue on which there is an unamortized discount of $60,000 is redeemed for $760,000. Journalize the redemption of the bonds.

| OBJ. 3 | EE 12-6 *p. 551* | **PE 12-6B   Redemption of bonds payable** |
|---|---|---|

A $450,000 bond issue on which there is an unamortized premium of $25,000 is redeemed for $441,000. Journalize the redemption of the bonds.

| OBJ. 4 | EE 12-7 *p. 554* | **PE 12-7A   Journalizing installment notes** |
|---|---|---|

On the first day of the fiscal year, a company issues $100,000, 8%, six-year installment notes that have annual payments of $21,632. The first note payment consists of $8,000 of interest and $13,632 of principal repayment.

a. Journalize the entry to record the issuance of the installment notes.

b. Journalize the first annual note payment.

| OBJ. 4 | EE 12-7 *p. 554* | **PE 12-7B   Journalizing installment notes** |
|---|---|---|

On the first day of the fiscal year, a company issues $55,000, 9%, five-year installment notes that have annual payments of $14,140. The first note payment consists of $4,950 of interest and $9,190 of principal repayment.

a. Journalize the entry to record the issuance of the installment notes.

b. Journalize the first annual note payment.

| OBJ. 6 | EE 12-8 *p. 557* | **PE 12-8A   Number of times interest charges are earned** |
|---|---|---|

Katula Company reported the following on the company's income statement in 2012 and 2011:

| | 2012 | 2011 |
|---|---|---|
| Interest expense | $ 250,000 | $ 275,000 |
| Income before income tax expense | 3,100,000 | 4,400,000 |

a. Determine the number of times interest charges were earned for 2011 and 2012. Round to one decimal place.

b. Is the number of times interest charges are earned improving or declining?

| OBJ. 6 | EE 12-8 *p. 557* | **PE 12-8B   Number of times interest charges are earned** |
|---|---|---|

Marsh Products, Inc., reported the following on the company's income statement in 2012 and 2011:

| | 2012 | 2011 |
|---|---|---|
| Interest expense | $ 420,000 | $ 375,000 |
| Income before income tax expense | 4,200,000 | 3,000,000 |

a. Determine the number of times interest charges were earned for 2011 and 2012. Round to one decimal place.

b. Is the number of times interest charges are earned improving or declining?

# Exercises

OBJ. 1

✔ a. $1.30

### EX 12-1  Effect of financing on earnings per share

Kelton Co., which produces and sells skiing equipment, is financed as follows:

| | |
|---|---|
| Bonds payable, 8% (issued at face amount) | $20,000,000 |
| Preferred $2 stock, $10 par | 20,000,000 |
| Common stock, $25 par | 20,000,000 |

Income tax is estimated at 40% of income.

Determine the earnings per share of common stock, assuming that the income before bond interest and income tax is (a) $10,000,000, (b) $12,000,000, and (c) $14,000,000.

OBJ. 1

### EX 12-2  Evaluate alternative financing plans

Based on the data in Exercise 12-1, what factors other than earnings per share should be considered in evaluating these alternative financing plans?

OBJ. 1

### EX 12-3  Corporate financing

The financial statements for Nike, Inc., are presented in Appendix D at the end of the text. What is the major source of financing for Nike?

OBJ. 3

### EX 12-4  Bond price

Procter and Gamble's 4.7% bonds due in 2019 were reported as selling for 104.797.

Were the bonds selling at a premium or at a discount? Why is Proctor & Gamble able to sell its bonds at this price?

OBJ. 3

### EX 12-5  Entries for issuing bonds

Austin Co. produces and distributes semiconductors for use by computer manufacturers. Austin Co. issued $15,000,000 of 12-year, 12% bonds on May 1 of the current year, with interest payable on May 1 and November 1. The fiscal year of the company is the calendar year. Journalize the entries to record the following selected transactions for the current year:

May   1.  Issued the bonds for cash at their face amount.

Nov.   1.  Paid the interest on the bonds.

Dec. 31.  Recorded accrued interest for two months.

OBJ. 2, 3

✔ b. $2,867,977

### EX 12-6  Entries for issuing bonds and amortizing discount by straight-line method

On the first day of its fiscal year, Keller Company issued $25,000,000 of five-year, 10% bonds to finance its operations of producing and selling home improvement products. Interest is payable semiannually. The bonds were issued at a market (effective) interest rate of 12%, resulting in Keller Company receiving cash of $23,160,113.

a.  Journalize the entries to record the following:

   1.  Sale of the bonds.

   2.  First semiannual interest payment. (Amortization of discount is to be recorded annually.)

   3.  Second semiannual interest payment.

   4.  Amortization of discount at the end of the first year, using the straight-line method. (Round to the nearest dollar.)

b.  Determine the amount of the bond interest expense for the first year.

c.  Explain why the company was able to issue the bonds for only $23,160,113 rather than for the face amount of $25,000,000.

**OBJ. 2, 3**

### EX 12-7 Entries for issuing bonds and amortizing premium by straight-line method

McCool Corporation wholesales repair products to equipment manufacturers. On April 1, 2010, McCool Corporation issued $30,000,000 of five-year, 10% bonds at a market (effective) interest rate of 8%, receiving cash of $32,446,500. Interest is payable semiannually on April 1 and October 1. Journalize the entries to record the following:

a. Sale of bonds on April 1, 2012.

b. First interest payment on October 1, 2012, and amortization of bond premium for six months, using the straight-line method. (Round to the nearest dollar.)

c. Explain why the company was able to issue the bonds for $32,446,500 rather than for the face amount of $30,000,000.

**OBJ. 3**

### EX 12-8 Entries for issuing and calling bonds; loss

Dillip Corp., a wholesaler of office equipment, issued $45,000,000 of 10-year, 10% callable bonds on March 1, 2012, with interest payable on March 1 and September 1. The fiscal year of the company is the calendar year. Journalize the entries to record the following selected transactions:

2012

Mar. 1. Issued the bonds for cash at their face amount.

Sept. 1. Paid the interest on the bonds.

2016

Sept. 1. Called the bond issue at 103, the rate provided in the bond indenture. (Omit entry for payment of interest.)

**OBJ. 3**

### EX 12-9 Entries for issuing and calling bonds; gain

Fogel Corp. produces and sells renewable energy equipment. To finance its operations, Fogel Corp. issued $32,000,000 of 20-year, 11% callable bonds on January 1, 2012, with interest payable on January 1 and July 1. The fiscal year of the company is the calendar year. Journalize the entries to record the following selected transactions:

2012

Jan. 1. Issued the bonds for cash at their face amount.

July 1. Paid the interest on the bonds.

2018

July 1. Called the bond issue at 97, the rate provided in the bond indenture. (Omit entry for payment of interest.)

**OBJ. 4**

### EX 12-10 Entries for issuing installment note transactions

On the first day of the fiscal year, Harris Company borrowed $65,000 by giving a 10-year, 6% installment note to Cuba Bank. The note requires annual payments of $8,832, with the first payment occurring on the last day of the fiscal year. The first payment consists of interest of $3,900 and principal repayment of $4,932.

a. Journalize the entries to record the following:

1. Issued the installment note for cash on the first day of the fiscal year.

2. Paid the first annual payment on the note.

b. Explain how the notes payable would be reported on the balance sheet at the end of the first year.

**OBJ. 4**

### EX 12-11 Entries for issuing installment note transactions

On January 1, 2012, Averill Company issued a $120,000, 8-year, 10% installment note from Deacon Bank. The note requires annual payments of $22,493, beginning on December 31, 2012. Journalize the entries to record the following:

2012

Jan. 1. Issued the notes for cash at their face amount.

Dec. 31. Paid the annual payment on the note, which consisted of interest of $12,000 and principal of $10,493.

2017

Dec. 31. Paid the annual payment on the note, which consisted of interest of $5,594 and principal of $16,899.

---

OBJ. 4

**EX 12-12   Entries for issuing installment note transactions**

On January 1, 2012, Daan Company obtained a $28,000, four-year, 9% installment note from Poklers Bank. The note requires annual payments of $8,642, beginning on December 31, 2012.

a. Prepare an amortization table for this installment note, similar to the one presented in Exhibit 3.

b. Journalize the entries for the issuance of the note and the four annual note payments.

c. Describe how the annual note payment would be reported in the 2012 income statement.

---

OBJ. 5

**EX 12-13   Reporting bonds**

At the beginning of the current year, two bond issues (Putnam Industries 5% 10-year bonds and Rucker Corporation 6% five-year bonds) were outstanding. During the year, the Putnam Industries bonds were redeemed and a significant loss on the redemption of bonds was reported as an extraordinary item on the income statement. At the end of the year, the Rucker Corporation bonds were reported as a noncurrent liability. The maturity date on the Rucker Corporation bonds was early in the following year.

Identify the flaws in the reporting practices related to the two bond issues.

---

OBJ. 6

**EX 12-14   Number of times interest charges are earned**

The following data were taken from recent annual reports of Southwest Airlines, which operates a low-fare airline service to over 50 cities in the United States.

|  | Current Year | Preceding Year |
|---|---|---|
| Interest expense | $105,000,000 | $69,000,000 |
| Income before income tax | 278,000,000 | 1,058,000 |

a. Determine the number of times interest charges were earned for the current and preceding years. Round to one decimal place.

b.  What conclusions can you draw?

---

OBJ. 6

**FAI**

**EX 12-15   Number of times interest charges are earned**

Quansi, Inc., reported the following on the company's income statement in 2012 and 2011:

|  | 2012 | 2011 |
|---|---|---|
| Interest expense | $ 10,000,000 | $ 12,500,000 |
| Income before income tax expense | 240,000,000 | 375,000,000 |

a. Determine the number of times interest charges were earned for 2011 and 2012. Round to one decimal place.

b.  Is the number of times interest charges are earned improving or declining?

---

OBJ. 6

**FAI**

**EX 12-16   Number of times interest charges are earned**

Vixeron Company reported the following on the company's income statement for 2012 and 2011:

|  | 2012 | 2011 |
|---|---|---|
| Interest expense | $3,000,000 | $3,000,000 |
| Income before income tax | 1,200,000 | 3,600,000 |

a. Determine the number of times interest charges were earned for 2011 and 2012. Round to one decimal place.

b.  What conclusions can you draw?

**Appendix 1**
**EX 12-17   Present value of amount due**

Determine the present value of $750,000 to be received in three years, using an interest rate of 12%, compounded annually.

a.  Use the present value table in Exhibit 4.

b.  Why is the present value less than the $750,000 to be received in the future?

**Appendix 1**
**EX 12-18   Present value of an annuity**

Determine the present value of $150,000 to be received at the end of each of four years, using an interest rate of 7%, compounded annually, as follows:

a.  By successive computations, using the present value table in Exhibit 4.

b.  By using the present value table in Exhibit 5.

c.  Why is the present value of the four $150,000 cash receipts less than the $600,000 to be received in the future?

✔ $79,077,130

**Appendix 1**
**EX 12-19   Present value of an annuity**

On January 1, 2012, you win $110,000,000 in the state lottery. The $110,000,000 prize will be paid in equal installments of $11,000,000 over 10 years. The payments will be made on December 31 of each year, beginning on December 31, 2012. If the current interest rate is 6.5%, determine the present value of your winnings. Use the present value tables in Appendix A.

**Appendix 1**
**EX 12-20   Present value of an annuity**

Assume the same data as in Appendix 1 Exercise 12-19, except that the current interest rate is 13%.

━━━▶ Will the present value of your winnings using an interest rate of 13% be one-half the present value of your winnings using an interest rate of 6.5%? Why or why not?

**Appendix 1**
**EX 12-21   Present value of bonds payable; discount**

Baliga Co. produces and sells high-quality audio equipment. To finance its operations, Baliga Co. issued $18,000,000 of five-year, 8% bonds with interest payable semiannually at a market (effective) interest rate of 10%. Determine the present value of the bonds payable, using the present value tables in Exhibits 4 and 5. Round to the nearest dollar.

✔ $86,030,076

**Appendix 1**
**EX 12-22   Present value of bonds payable; premium**

Herbst Co. issued $80,000,000 of five-year, 13% bonds with interest payable semiannually, at a market (effective) interest rate of 11%. Determine the present value of the bonds payable, using the present value tables in Exhibits 4 and 5. Round to the nearest dollar.

✔ b. $3,396,512

**Appendix 2**
**EX 12-23   Amortize discount by interest method**

On the first day of its fiscal year, Ramsey Company issued $35,000,000 of 10-year, 9% bonds to finance its operations. Interest is payable semiannually. The bonds were issued at a market (effective) interest rate of 11%, resulting in Ramsey Company receiving cash of $30,817,399. The company uses the interest method.

a.  Journalize the entries to record the following:

   1.  Sale of the bonds.

   2.  First semiannual interest payment, including amortization of discount. Round to the nearest dollar.

(*continued*)

3. Second semiannual interest payment, including amortization of discount. Round to the nearest dollar.

b. Compute the amount of the bond interest expense for the first year.

c. Explain why the company was able to issue the bonds for only $30,817,399 rather than for the face amount of $35,000,000.

✔ b. $1,879,754

**Appendix 2**
**EX 12-24  Amortize premium by interest method**

Knight Corporation wholesales auto parts to auto manufacturers. On March 1, 2012, Knight Corporation issued $17,500,000 of five-year, 12% bonds at a market (effective) interest rate of 10%, receiving cash of $18,851,252. Interest is payable semiannually. Knight Corporation's fiscal year begins on March 1. The company uses the interest method.

a. Journalize the entries to record the following:

1. Sale of the bonds.

2. First semiannual interest payment, including amortization of premium. Round to the nearest dollar.

3. Second semiannual interest payment, including amortization of premium. Round to the nearest dollar.

b. Determine the bond interest expense for the first year.

c. Explain why the company was able to issue the bonds for $18,851,252 rather than for the face amount of $17,500,000.

✔ a. $53,680,315
✔ c. $295,932

**Appendix 1 and Appendix 2**
**EX 12-25  Compute bond proceeds, amortizing premium by interest method, and interest expense**

Evans Co. produces and sells motorcycle parts. On the first day of its fiscal year, Evans Co. issued $50,000,000 of five-year, 14% bonds at a market (effective) interest rate of 12%, with interest payable semiannually. Compute the following, presenting figures used in your computations.

a. The amount of cash proceeds from the sale of the bonds. Use the tables of present values in Exhibits 4 and 5. Round to the nearest dollar.

b. The amount of premium to be amortized for the first semiannual interest payment period, using the interest method. Round to the nearest dollar.

c. The amount of premium to be amortized for the second semiannual interest payment period, using the interest method. Round to the nearest dollar.

d. The amount of the bond interest expense for the first year.

✔ a. $53,530,290
✔ b. $479,469

**Appendix 1 and Appendix 2**
**EX 12-26  Compute bond proceeds, amortizing discount by interest method, and interest expense**

Lewis Co. produces and sells aviation equipment. On the first day of its fiscal year, Lewis Co. issued $60,000,000 of five-year, 10% bonds at a market (effective) interest rate of 13%, with interest payable semiannually. Compute the following, presenting figures used in your computations.

a. The amount of cash proceeds from the sale of the bonds. Use the tables of present values in Exhibits 4 and 5. Round to the nearest dollar.

b. The amount of discount to be amortized for the first semiannual interest payment period, using the interest method. Round to the nearest dollar.

c. The amount of discount to be amortized for the second semiannual interest payment period, using the interest method. Round to the nearest dollar.

d. The amount of the bond interest expense for the first year.

## Problems Series A

### PR 12-1A  Effect of financing on earnings per share

Three different plans for financing a $200,000,000 corporation are under consideration by its organizers. Under each of the following plans, the securities will be issued at their par or face amount, and the income tax rate is estimated at 40% of income.

|  | Plan 1 | Plan 2 | Plan 3 |
|---|---|---|---|
| 11% bonds | — | — | $100,000,000 |
| Preferred 5% stock, $40 par | — | $100,000,000 | 50,000,000 |
| Common stock, $25 par | $200,000,000 | 100,000,000 | 50,000,000 |
| Total | $200,000,000 | $200,000,000 | $200,000,000 |

**Instructions**

1. Determine for each plan the earnings per share of common stock, assuming that the income before bond interest and income tax is $30,000,000.

2. Determine for each plan the earnings per share of common stock, assuming that the income before bond interest and income tax is $16,000,000.

3. ▬▬▬▬▶ Discuss the advantages and disadvantages of each plan.

### PR 12-2A  Bond discount, entries for bonds payable transactions

On July 1, 2012, Bliss Industries Inc. issued $24,000,000 of 20-year, 11% bonds at a market (effective) interest rate of 14%, receiving cash of $19,200,577. Interest on the bonds is payable semiannually on December 31 and June 30. The fiscal year of the company is the calendar year.

**Instructions**

1. Journalize the entry to record the amount of cash proceeds from the sale of the bonds.

2. Journalize the entries to record the following:

   a. The first semiannual interest payment on December 31, 2012, and the amortization of the bond discount, using the straight-line method. (Round to the nearest dollar.)

   b. The interest payment on June 30, 2013, and the amortization of the bond discount, using the straight-line method. (Round to the nearest dollar.)

3. Determine the total interest expense for 2012.

4. Will the bond proceeds always be less than the face amount of the bonds when the contract rate is less than the market rate of interest?

5. (Appendix 1) Compute the price of $19,200,577 received for the bonds by using the tables of present value in Appendix A at the end of the text. (Round to the nearest dollar.)

### PR 12-3A  Bond premium, entries for bonds payable transactions

Fabulator, Inc. produces and sells fashion clothing. On July 1, 2012, Fabulator, Inc. issued $120,000,000 of 20-year, 14% bonds at a market (effective) interest rate of 11%, receiving cash of $148,882,608. Interest on the bonds is payable semiannually on December 31 and June 30. The fiscal year of the company is the calendar year.

**Instructions**

1. Journalize the entry to record the amount of cash proceeds from the sale of the bonds.

2. Journalize the entries to record the following:

   a. The first semiannual interest payment on December 31, 2012, and the amortization of the bond premium, using the straight-line method. (Round to the nearest dollar.)

   b. The interest payment on June 30, 2013, and the amortization of the bond premium, using the straight-line method. (Round to the nearest dollar.)

3. Determine the total interest expense for 2012.

4. Will the bond proceeds always be greater than the face amount of the bonds when the contract rate is greater than the market rate of interest?

*(continued)*

5. (Appendix 1) Compute the price of $148,882,608 received for the bonds by using the tables of present value in Appendix A at the end of the text. (Round to the nearest dollar.)

OBJ. 3, 4

✔ 3. $58,236,896

### PR 12-4A   Entries for bonds payable and installment note transactions

The following transactions were completed by Simmons Inc., whose fiscal year is the calendar year:

**2012**

July   1. Issued $64,000,000 of 10-year, 12% callable bonds dated July 1, 2012, at a market (effective) rate of 14%, receiving cash of $57,219,878. Interest is payable semiannually on December 31 and June 30.

Oct.   1. Borrowed $320,000 as a five-year, 6% installment note from Ibis Bank. The note requires annual payments of $75,967, with the first payment occurring on September 30, 2013.

Dec. 31. Accrued $4,800 of interest on the installment note. The interest is payable on the date of the next installment note payment.

     31. Paid the semiannual interest on the bonds. The bond discount is amortized annually in a separate journal entry.

     31. Recorded bond discount amortization of $339,006, which was determined using the straight-line method.

     31. Closed the interest expense account.

**2013**

June 30. Paid the semiannual interest on the bonds.

Sept. 30. Paid the annual payment on the note, which consisted of interest of $19,200 and principal of $56,767.

Dec. 31. Accrued $3,948 of interest on the installment note. The interest is payable on the date of the next installment note payment.

     31. Paid the semiannual interest on the bonds. The bond discount is amortized annually in a separate journal entry.

     31. Recorded bond discount amortization of $678,012, which was determined using the straight-line method.

     31. Closed the interest expense account.

**2014**

June 30. Recorded the redemption of the bonds, which were called at 98. The balance in the bond discount account is $5,424,098 after payment of interest and amortization of discount have been recorded. (Record the redemption only.)

Sept. 30. Paid the second annual payment on the note, which consisted of interest of $15,794 and principal of $60,173.

**Instructions**

1. Journalize the entries to record the foregoing transactions.

2. Indicate the amount of the interest expense in (a) 2012 and (b) 2013.

3. Determine the carrying amount of the bonds as of December 31, 2013.

✔ 3. $1,344,040

### Appendix 1 and Appendix 2
### PR 12-5A   Bond discount, entries for bonds payable transactions, interest method of amortizing bond discount

On July 1, 2012, Bliss Industries, Inc. issued $24,000,000 of 20-year, 11% bonds at a market (effective) interest rate of 14%, receiving cash of $19,200,577. Interest on the bonds is payable semiannually on December 31 and June 30. The fiscal year of the company is the calendar year.

**Instructions**

1. Journalize the entry to record the amount of cash proceeds from the sale of the bonds.

2. Journalize the entries to record the following:

a. The first semiannual interest payment on December 31, 2012, and the amortization of the bond discount, using the interest method. (Round to the nearest dollar.)

b. The interest payment on June 30, 2013, and the amortization of the bond discount, using the interest method. (Round to the nearest dollar.)

3. Determine the total interest expense for 2012.

✔ 3. $8,188,543

**Appendix 1 and Appendix 2**
**PR 12-6A   Bond premium, entries for bonds payable transactions, interest method of amortizing bond discount**

Fabulator, Inc. produces and sells fashion clothing. On July 1, 2012, Fabulator, Inc. issued $120,000,000 of 20-year, 14% bonds at a market (effective) interest rate of 11%, receiving cash of $148,882,608. Interest on the bonds is payable semiannually on December 31 and June 30. The fiscal year of the company is the calendar year.

**Instructions**

1. Journalize the entry to record the amount of cash proceeds from the sale of the bonds.

2. Journalize the entries to record the following:

   a. The first semiannual interest payment on December 31, 2012, and the amortization of the bond discount, using the interest method. (Round to the nearest dollar.)

   b. The interest payment on June 30, 2013, and the amortization of the bond discount, using the interest method. (Round to the nearest dollar.)

3. Determine the total interest expense for 2012.

## Problems Series B

OBJ. 1

✔ 1. Plan 3: $4.75

**PR 12-1B   Effect of financing on earnings per share**

Three different plans for financing a $40,000,000 corporation are under consideration by its organizers. Under each of the following plans, the securities will be issued at their par or face amount, and the income tax rate is estimated at 40% of income.

|  | Plan 1 | Plan 2 | Plan 3 |
|---|---|---|---|
| 10% bonds | — | — | $20,000,000 |
| Preferred $2.50 stock, $50 par | — | $20,000,000 | 10,000,000 |
| Common stock, $25 par | $40,000,000 | 20,000,000 | 10,000,000 |
| Total | $40,000,000 | $40,000,000 | $40,000,000 |

**Instructions**

1. Determine for each plan the earnings per share of common stock, assuming that the income before bond interest and income tax is $6,000,000.

2. Determine for each plan the earnings per share of common stock, assuming that the income before bond interest and income tax is $3,200,000.

3. ➡ Discuss the advantages and disadvantages of each plan.

OBJ. 2, 3

✔ 3. $2,100,119

**PR 12-2B   Bond discount, entries for bonds payable transactions**

On July 1, 2012, Hallo Corporation, a wholesaler of communication equipment, issued $34,000,000 of 20-year, 12% bonds at a market (effective) interest rate of 13%, receiving cash of $31,595,241. Interest on the bonds is payable semiannually on December 31 and June 30. The fiscal year of the company is the calendar year.

**Instructions**

1. Journalize the entry to record the amount of cash proceeds from the sale of the bonds.

2. Journalize the entries to record the following:

   a. The first semiannual interest payment on December 31, 2012, and the amortization of the bond discount, using the straight-line method. (Round to the nearest dollar.)

(*continued*)

b. The interest payment on June 30, 2013, and the amortization of the bond discount, using the straight-line method. (Round to the nearest dollar.)

3. Determine the total interest expense for 2012.

4. Will the bond proceeds always be less than the face amount of the bonds when the contract rate is less than the market rate of interest?

5. (Appendix 1) Compute the price of $31,595,241 received for the bonds by using the tables of present value in Appendix A at the end of the text. (Round to the nearest dollar.)

---

**OBJ. 2, 3**

✔ 3. $803,316

### PR 12-3B   Bond premium, entries for bonds payable transactions

Buddie Corporation produces and sells baseball gloves. On July 1, 2012, Buddie Corporation issued $12,500,000 of 10-year, 14% bonds at a market (effective) interest rate of 12%, receiving cash of $13,933,680. Interest on the bonds is payable semiannually on December 31 and June 30. The fiscal year of the company is the calendar year.

**Instructions**

1. Journalize the entry to record the amount of cash proceeds from the sale of the bonds.

2. Journalize the entries to record the following:

    a. The first semiannual interest payment on December 31, 2012, and the amortization of the bond premium, using the straight-line method. (Round to the nearest dollar.)

    b. The interest payment on June 30, 2013, and the amortization of the bond premium, using the straight-line method. (Round to the nearest dollar.)

3. Determine the total interest expense for 2012.

4. Will the bond proceeds always be greater than the face amount of the bonds when the contract rate is greater than the market rate of interest?

5. (Appendix 1) Compute the price of $13,933,680 received for the bonds by using the tables of present value in Appendix A at the end of the text. (Round to the nearest dollar.)

---

**OBJ. 3, 4**

✔ 3. $48,673,530

### PR 12-4B   Entries for bonds payable and installment note transactions

The following transactions were completed by Wilkerson Inc., whose fiscal year is the calendar year:

**2012**

July   1.  Issued $42,000,000 of 10-year, 13% callable bonds dated July 1, 2012, at a market (effective) rate of 10%, receiving cash of $49,851,213. Interest is payable semiannually on December 31 and June 30.

Oct.   1.  Borrowed $510,000 as a six-year, 9% installment note from Challenger Bank. The note requires annual payments of $113,689, with the first payment occurring on September 30, 2013.

Dec. 31.  Accrued $11,475 of interest on the installment note. The interest is payable on the date of the next installment note payment.

    31.  Paid the semiannual interest on the bonds. The bond premium is amortized annually in a separate journal entry.

    31.  Recorded bond premium amortization of $392,561, which was determined using the straight-line method.

    31.  Closed the interest expense account.

**2013**

June 30.  Paid the semiannual interest on the bonds.

Sept. 30.  Paid the annual payment on the note, which consisted of interest of $45,900 and principal of $67,789.

Dec. 31.  Accrued $9,950 of interest on the installment note. The interest is payable on the date of the next installment note payment.

Dec. 31.  Paid the semiannual interest on the bonds. The bond discount is amortized annually in a separate journal entry.

    31.  Recorded bond premium amortization of $785,122, which was determined using the straight-line method.

    31.  Closed the interest expense account.

2014

June 30.  Recorded the redemption of the bonds, which were called at 102. The balance in the bond premium account is $6,280,969 after payment of interest and amortization of premium have been recorded. (Record the redemption only.)

Sept. 30.  Paid the second annual payment on the note, which consisted of interest of $39,799 and principal of $73,890.

**Instructions**

1.  Journalize the entries to record the foregoing transactions.

2.  Indicate the amount of the interest expense in (a) 2012 and (b) 2013.

3.  Determine the carrying amount of the bonds as of December 31, 2013.

---

✔ 3. $2,053,691

**Appendix 1 and Appendix 2**
**PR 12-5B    Bond discount, entries for bonds payable transactions, interest method of amortizing bond discount**

On July 1, 2012, Hallo Corporation, a wholesaler of communication equipment, issued $34,000,000 of 20-year, 12% bonds at a market (effective) interest rate of 13%, receiving cash of $31,595,241. Interest on the bonds is payable semiannually on December 31 and June 30. The fiscal year of the company is the calendar year.

**Instructions**

1.  Journalize the entry to record the amount of cash proceeds from the sale of the bonds.

2.  Journalize the entries to record the following:

    a.  The first semiannual interest payment on December 31, 2012, and the amortization of the bond discount, using the interest method. (Round to the nearest dollar.)

    b.  The interest payment on June 30, 2013, and the amortization of the bond discount, using the interest method. (Round to the nearest dollar.)

3.  Determine the total interest expense for 2012.

---

✔ 3. $836,021

**Appendix 1 and Appendix 2**
**PR 12-6B    Bond premium, entries for bonds payable transactions, interest method of amortizing bond premium**

Buddie Corporation produces and sells baseball gloves. On July 1, 2012, Buddie Corporation issued $12,500,000 of 10-year, 14% bonds at a market (effective) interest rate of 12%, receiving cash of $13,933,680. Interest on the bonds is payable semiannually on December 31 and June 30. The fiscal year of the company is the calendar year.

**Instructions**

1.  Journalize the entry to record the amount of cash proceeds from the sale of the bonds.

2.  Journalize the entries to record the following:

    a.  The first semiannual interest payment on December 31, 2012, and the amortization of the bond premium, using the interest method. (Round to the nearest dollar.)

    b.  The interest payment on June 30, 2013, and the amortization of the bond premium, using the interest method. (Round to the nearest dollar.)

3.  Determine the total interest expense for 2012.

## Cases & Projects

You can access Cases & Projects online at **www.cengage.com/accounting/reeve**

## Excel Success Special Activities

### SA 12-1   Interest amortization table

On July 1, 2010 the beginning of Egan Enterprises' fiscal year, the company borrowed $15,000 from Claymore Bank by signing a 6% installment note. The note calls for annual payments of $3,561 at the end of each calendar year during the note's 5-year term.

a.  Open the Excel file *SA12-1_1e*.

b.  Use your spreadsheet program to prepare an amortization table for the note.

c.  When you have completed the amortization table, perform a "save as," replacing the entire file name with the following:

   *SA12-1_1e[your first name initial]_[your last name]*

### SA 12-2   Interest amortization table

Amad Mosan is a realtor who is arranging for $35,000 of financing for the purchase of a new automobile. Amad is considering two financing options.

**Option 1:** A 7% 4-year installment note dated January 1, 2010, requiring 4 annual payments of $10,333 at the end of each of the four years.

**Option 2:** An 8% 6-year installment note dated January 1, 2010, requiring 6 annual payments of $7,571 at the end of each of the six years.

a.  Open the Excel file *SA12-2_1e*.

b.  Use your spreadsheet program to prepare an amortization table for each of the installment notes described above.

c.  When you have completed the amortization tables perform a "save as," replacing the entire file name with the following:

   *SA12-2_1e[your first name initial]_[your last name]*

### SA 12-3   Interest amortization table

Use your spreadsheet program to prepare interest amortization tables for each of the installment notes listed below.

|  | Principal Amount | Date of Note | Annual Interest Rate | Term (Years) | Annual Payment |
|---|---|---|---|---|---|
| Note A | $9,000 | 01/01/2011 | 10% | 3 | $3,619 |
| Note B | 4,500 | 07/01/2010 | 5% | 4 | 1,269 |
| Note C | 3,800 | 07/01/2010 | 9% | 7 | 755 |

a.  Open the Excel file *SA12-3_1e*.

b.  Use your spreadsheet program to prepare an amortization table for each note.

c.  When you have completed the amortization tables perform a "save as," replacing the entire file name with the following:

   *SA12-3_1e[your first name initial]_[your last name]*

## CHAPTER 13

© Fred Prouser/Reuters/Landov

# Investments and Fair Value Accounting

## News Corporation

**Y**ou invest cash to earn more cash. For example, you could deposit cash in a bank account to earn interest. You could also invest cash in preferred or common stocks and in corporate or U.S. government notes and bonds.

Preferred and common stock can be purchased through a stock exchange, such as the **New York Stock Exchange (NYSE)**. Preferred stock is purchased primarily with the expectation of earning dividends. Common stock is purchased with the expectation of earning dividends or realizing gains from a price increase in the stock.

Corporate and U.S. government bonds can also be purchased through a bond exchange. Bonds are purchased with the primary expectation of earning interest revenue.

Companies make investments for many of the same reasons that you would as an individual. For example, **News Corporation**,

a diversified media company, which produces such popular television shows as *The Simpsons* and *American Idol*, has invested $150 million of available cash in stocks and bonds. These investments are held by News Corporation for interest, dividends, and expected price increases.

Unlike most individuals, however, companies also purchase significant amounts of the outstanding common stock of other companies for strategic reasons. For example, News Corporation invested in 32% of the Hulu, an online video joint venture with other major media companies.

Investments in debt and equity securities give rise to a number of accounting issues. These issues are described and illustrated in this chapter.

**OBJ. 1** Describe why companies invest in debt and equity securities.

# Why Companies Invest

Most companies generate cash from their operations. This cash can be used for the following purposes:

1. Investing in current operations
2. Investing in temporary investments to earn additional revenue
3. Investing in long-term investments in stock of other companies for strategic reasons

## Investing Cash in Current Operations

Cash is often used to support the current operating activities of a company. For example, cash may be used to replace worn-out equipment or to purchase new, more efficient, and productive equipment. In addition, cash may be reinvested in the company to expand its current operations. For example, a retailer based in the northwest United States might decide to expand by opening stores in the midwest.

To support its current level of operations, a company also uses cash to pay:

1. expenses.
2. suppliers of merchandise and other assets.
3. interest to creditors.
4. dividends to stockholders.

The accounting for the use of cash in current operations has been described and illustrated in earlier chapters. For example, Chapter 9, "Fixed Assets and Intangible

Assets," illustrated the use of cash for purchasing property, plant, and equipment. In this chapter, we describe and illustrate the use of cash for investing in temporary investments and stock of other companies.

## Investing Cash in Temporary Investments

A company may temporarily have excess cash that is not needed for use in its current operations. This is often the case when a company has a seasonal operating cycle. For example, a significant portion of the annual merchandise sales of a retailer occurs during the fall holiday season. As a result, retailers often experience a large increase in cash during this period, which is not needed until the spring buying season.

Instead of letting excess cash remain idle in a checking account, most companies invest their excess cash in temporary investments. In doing so, companies invest in securities such as:

1. **Debt securities**, which are notes and bonds that pay interest and have a fixed maturity date.
2. **Equity securities**, which are preferred and common stock that represent ownership in a company and do not have a fixed maturity date.

Investments in debt and equity securities, termed **Investments** or *Temporary Investments*, are reported in the Current Assets section of the balance sheet.

The primary objective of investing in temporary investments is to:

1. earn interest revenue
2. receive dividends
3. realize gains from increases in the market price of the securities.

Investments in certificates of deposit and other securities that do not normally change in value are disclosed on the balance sheet as *cash and cash equivalents*. Such investments are held primarily for their interest revenue.

## Investing Cash in Long-Term Investments

A company may invest cash in the debt or equity of another company as a long-term investment. Long-term investments may be held for the same investment objectives as temporary investments. However, long-term investments often involve the purchase of a significant portion of the stock of another company. Such investments usually have a strategic purpose, such as:

1. *Reduction of costs*: When one company buys another company, the combined company may be able to reduce administrative expenses. For example, a combined company does not need two chief executive officers (CEOs) or chief financial officers (CFOs).
2. *Replacement of management*: If the purchased company has been mismanaged, the acquiring company may replace the company's management and, thus, improve operations and profits.
3. *Expansion*: The acquiring company may purchase a company because it has a complementary product line, territory, or customer base. The new combined company may be able to serve customers better than the two companies could separately.
4. *Integration*: A company may integrate operations by acquiring a supplier or customer. Acquiring a supplier may provide a more stable or uninterrupted supply of resources. Acquiring a customer may also provide a market for the company's products or services.

The Walt Disney Company purchased Marvel Entertainment in order to expand into action/adventure characters, movies, and products.

## Accounting for Debt Investments

**OBJ. 2** Describe and illustrate the accounting for debt investments.

Debt securities include notes and bonds, issued by corporations and governmental organizations. Most companies invest excess cash in bonds as investments to earn interest revenue.

The accounting for bond investments[1] includes recording the following:

1. Purchase of bonds
2. Interest revenue
3. Sale of bonds

## Purchase of Bonds

The purchase of bonds is recorded by debiting an investments account for the purchase price of the bonds, including any brokerage commissions. If the bonds are purchased between interest dates, the purchase price includes accrued interest since the last interest payment. This is because the seller has earned the accrued interest, but the buyer will receive the accrued interest when it is paid.

To illustrate, assume that Homer Company purchases $18,000 of U.S. Treasury bonds at their par value on March 17, 2012, plus accrued interest for 45 days. The bonds have an interest rate of 6%, payable on July 31 and January 31.

The entry to record the purchase of Treasury bonds is as follows:

| 2012 | | | | | |
|---|---|---|---|---|---|
| Mar. | 17 | Investments—U.S. Treasury Bonds | 18,000 | | |
| | | Interest Receivable | 135 | | |
| | | Cash | | 18,135 | |
| | | Purchased $18,000, 6% Treasury bonds. | | | |

Since Homer Company purchased the bonds on March 17, it is also purchasing the accrued interest for 45 days (January 31 to March 17) as shown in Exhibit 1. The accrued interest of $135 is computed as follows:[2]

$$\text{Accrued Interest} = \$18,000 \times 6\% \times (45/360) = \$135$$

The accrued interest is recorded by debiting Interest Receivable for $135. Investments is debited for the purchase price of the bonds of $18,000.

## Interest Revenue

On July 31, Homer Company receives a semiannual interest payment of $540 ($18,000 × 6% × 1 ½). The $540 interest includes the $135 accrued interest that Homer Company purchased with the bonds on March 17. Thus, Homer Company has earned $405 ($540 − $135) of interest revenue since purchasing the bonds as shown in Exhibit 1.

The receipt of the interest on July 31 is recorded as follows:

| 2012 | | | | | |
|---|---|---|---|---|---|
| July | 31 | Cash | 540 | | |
| | | Interest Receivable | | 135 | |
| | | Interest Revenue | | 405 | |
| | | Received semiannual interest. | | | |

Homer Company's accounting period ends on December 31. Thus, an adjusting entry must be made to accrue interest for five months (August 1 to December 31) of $450 ($18,000 × 6% × 5/12) as shown in Exhibit 1. The adjusting entry to record the accrued interest is as follows:

| 2012 | | | | | |
|---|---|---|---|---|---|
| Dec. | 31 | Interest Receivable | 450 | | |
| | | Interest Revenue | | 450 | |
| | | Accrue interest. | | | |

1 Debt investments may also include installment notes and short-term notes. The basic accounting for notes is similar to bonds and, thus, is not illustrated.

2 To simplify, a 360-day year is used to compute interest.

**EXHIBIT 1** **Interest Timeline**

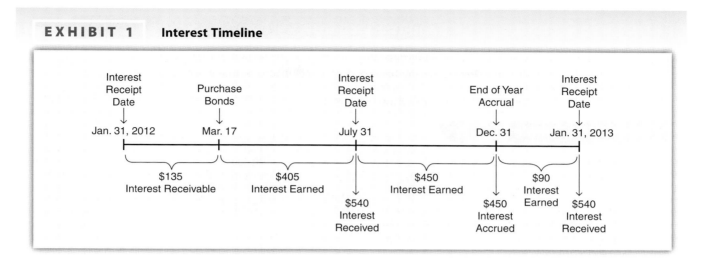

For the year ended December 31, 2012, Homer Company would report *Interest revenue* of $855 ($405 + $450) as part of *Other income* on its income statement.

The receipt of the semiannual interest of $540 on January 31, 2013, is recorded as follows:

| 2013 | | | | | |
|------|-----|------|------|------|------|
| Jan. | 31 | Cash | | 540 | |
| | | Interest Revenue | | | 90 |
| | | Interest Receivable | | | 450 |
| | | Received interest on Treasury bonds. | | | |

## Sale of Bonds

The sale of a bond investment normally results in a gain or loss. If the proceeds from the sale exceed the book value (cost) of the bonds, then a gain is recorded. If the proceeds are less than the book value (cost) of the bonds, a loss is recorded.

To illustrate, on January 31, 2013, Homer Company sells the Treasury bonds at 98, which is a price equal to 98% of par value. The sale results in a loss of $360, as shown below.

| | |
|---|---|
| Proceeds from sale | $17,640* |
| Less book value (cost) of the bonds | 18,000 |
| Loss on sale of bonds | $ (360) |

*($18,000 × 98%)

The entry to record the sale is as follows:

| 2013 | | | | | |
|------|-----|------|------|------|------|
| Jan. | 31 | Cash | | 17,640 | |
| | | Loss on Sale of Investment | | 360 | |
| | | Investments—U.S. Treasury Bonds | | | 18,000 |
| | | Sale of U.S. Treasury bonds. | | | |

There is no accrued interest upon the sale since the interest payment date is also January 31. If the sale were between interest dates, interest accrued since the last interest payment date would be added to the sale proceeds and credited to Interest Revenue. The loss on the sale of bond investments is reported as part of *Other income (loss)* on Homer Company's income statement.

**Example Exercise** **13-1** **Bond Transactions** **OBJ. 2**

Journalize the entries to record the following selected bond investment transactions for Tyler Company:

1. Purchased for cash $40,000 of Tyler Company 10% bonds at 100 plus accrued interest of $320.
2. Received the first semiannual interest.
3. Sold $30,000 of the bonds at 102 plus accrued interest of $110.

**Follow My Example** **13-1**

| | | | |
|---|---|---|---|
| 1. | Investments—Tyler Company Bonds . . . . . . . . . . . . . . . . . . . . . . . . . . . . | 40,000 | |
| | Interest Receivable . . . . . . . . . . . . . . . . . . . . . . . . . . . . . . . . . . . . . . . . . . | 320 | |
| | Cash . . . . . . . . . . . . . . . . . . . . . . . . . . . . . . . . . . . . . . . . . . . . . . . . . . . . | | 40,320 |
| 2. | Cash . . . . . . . . . . . . . . . . . . . . . . . . . . . . . . . . . . . . . . . . . . . . . . . . . . . . . . | 2,000* | |
| | Interest Receivable . . . . . . . . . . . . . . . . . . . . . . . . . . . . . . . . . . . . . . . . . | | 320 |
| | Interest Revenue . . . . . . . . . . . . . . . . . . . . . . . . . . . . . . . . . . . . . . . . . . . | | 1,680 |
| | *$40,000 × 10% × ½ | | |
| 3. | Cash . . . . . . . . . . . . . . . . . . . . . . . . . . . . . . . . . . . . . . . . . . . . . . . . . . . . . . | 30,710* | |
| | Interest Revenue . . . . . . . . . . . . . . . . . . . . . . . . . . . . . . . . . . . . . . . . . . . | | 110 |
| | Gain on Sale of Investments . . . . . . . . . . . . . . . . . . . . . . . . . . . . . . . . . . | | 600 |
| | Investments—Tyler Company Bonds . . . . . . . . . . . . . . . . . . . . . . . . . . | | 30,000 |
| | | | |
| | *Sale proceeds ($30,000 × 102%) . . . . . . . . . . . . . . . . . . . . . . . . . . . . . . | $30,600 | |
| | Accrued interest . . . . . . . . . . . . . . . . . . . . . . . . . . . . . . . . . . . . . . . . . . . | 110 | |
| | Total proceeds from sale . . . . . . . . . . . . . . . . . . . . . . . . . . . . . . . . . . . . | $30,710 | |

Practice Exercises: **PE 13-1A, PE 13-1B**

**OBJ. 3** Describe and illustrate the accounting for equity investments.

# Accounting for Equity Investments

A company may invest in the preferred or common stock of another company. The company investing in another company's stock is the **investor**. The company whose stock is purchased is the **investee**.

The percent of the investee's outstanding stock purchased by the investor determines the degree of control that the investor has over the investee. This, in turn, determines the accounting method used to record the stock investment as shown in Exhibit 2.

**EXHIBIT 2**

**Stock Investments**

| Percent of Outstanding Stock Owned by Investor | Degree of Control of Investor over Investee | Accounting Method |
|---|---|---|
| Less than 20% | No control | Cost method |
| Between 20% and 50% | Significant influence | Equity method |
| Greater than 50% | Control | Consolidation |

## Less Than 20% Ownership

If the investor purchases less than 20% of the outstanding stock of the investee, the investor is considered to have no control over the investee. In this case, it is assumed that the investor purchased the stock primarily to earn dividends or realize gains on price increases of the stock.

Investments of less than 20% of the investee's outstanding stock are accounted for using the **cost method**. Under the cost method, entries are recorded for the following transactions:

1. Purchase of stock
2. Receipt of dividends
3. Sale of stock

**Purchase of Stock**   The purchase of stock is recorded at its cost. Any brokerage commissions are included as part of the cost.

To illustrate, assume that on May 1, Bart Company purchases 2,000 shares of Lisa Company common stock at $49.90 per share plus a brokerage fee of $200. The entry to record the purchase of the stock is as follows:

| | | | | |
|---|---|---|---|---|
| May | 1 | Investments—Lisa Company Stock | 100,000 | |
| | | Cash | | 100,000 |
| | | Purchased 2,000 shares of Lisa Company common stock [($49.90 × 2,000 shares) + $200]. | | |

**Receipt of Dividends**   On July 31, Bart Company receives a dividend of $0.40 per share from Lisa Company. The entry to record the receipt of the dividend is as follows:

| | | | | |
|---|---|---|---|---|
| July | 31 | Cash | 800 | |
| | | Dividend Revenue | | 800 |
| | | Received dividend on Lisa Company common stock (2,000 shares × $0.40). | | |

*Dividend revenue* is reported as part of *Other income* on Bart Company's income statement.

**Sale of Stock**   The sale of a stock investment normally results in a gain or loss. A gain is recorded if the proceeds from the sale exceed the book value (cost) of the stock. A loss is recorded if the proceeds from the sale are less than the book value (cost).

To illustrate, on September 1, Bart Company sells 1,500 shares of Lisa Company stock for $54.50 per share, less a $160 commission. The sale results in a gain of $6,590, as shown below.

| | |
|---|---|
| Proceeds from sale | $81,590* |
| Book value (cost) of the stock | 75,000** |
| Gain on sale | $ 6,590 |

*($54.50 × 1,500 shares) – $160
**($100,000/2,000 shares) × 1,500 shares

The entry to record the sale is as follows:

| | | | | |
|---|---|---|---|---|
| Sept. | 1 | Cash | 81,590 | |
| | | Gain on Sale of Investments | | 6,590 |
| | | Investments—Lisa Company Stock | | 75,000 |
| | | Sale of 1,500 shares of Lisa Company common stock. | | |

The gain on the sale of investments is reported as part of *Other income* on Bart Company's income statement.

**Example Exercise** 13-2 **Stock Transactions**

OBJ. 3

On September 1, 1,500 shares of Monroe Company are acquired at a price of $24 per share plus a $40 brokerage fee. On October 14, a $0.60 per share dividend was received on the Monroe Company stock. On November 11, 750 shares (half) of Monroe Company stock were sold for $20 per share, less a $45 brokerage fee. Prepare the journal entries for the original purchase, dividend, and sale.

**Follow My Example** 13-2

| | | | |
|---|---|---|---|
| Sept. 1 | Investments—Monroe Company Stock ................... | 36,040* | |
| | Cash ................................................. | | 36,040 |
| | *(1,500 shares × $24 per share) + $40 | | |
| Oct. 14 | Cash .................................................. | 900* | |
| | Dividend Revenue ...................................... | | 900 |
| | *$0.60 per share × 1,500 shares | | |
| Nov. 11 | Cash .................................................. | 14,955* | |
| | Loss on Sale of Investments ............................. | 3,065 | |
| | Investments—Monroe Company Stock ................. | | 18,020** |

*(750 shares × $20) − $45
**$36,040 × ½

Practice Exercises: **PE 13-2A, PE 13-2B**

## Between 20%–50% Ownership

If the investor purchases between 20% and 50% of the outstanding stock of the investee, the investor is considered to have a significant influence over the investee. In this case, it is assumed that the investor purchased the stock primarily for strategic reasons such as developing a supplier relationship.

Investments of between 20% and 50% of the investee's outstanding stock are accounted for using the **equity method**. Under the equity method, the stock is recorded initially at its cost, including any brokerage commissions. This is the same as under the cost method.

Under the equity method, the investment account is adjusted for the investor's share of the *net income* and *dividends* of the investee. These adjustments are as follows:

1. *Net Income:* The investor records its share of the net income of the investee as an increase in the investment account. Its share of any net loss is recorded as a decrease in the investment account.

2. *Dividends:* The investor's share of cash dividends received from the investee decreases the investment account.

**Purchase of Stock**  To illustrate, assume that Simpson Inc. purchased its 40% interest in Flanders Corporation's common stock on January 2, 2012, for $350,000. The entry to record the purchase is as follows:

| 2012 | | | | | | | |
|---|---|---|---|---|---|---|---|
| Jan. | 2 | Investment in Flanders Corporation Stock | | 350,000 | | | |
| | | Cash | | | 350,000 | | |
| | | Purchased 40% of Flanders | | | | | |
| | | Corporation stock. | | | | | |

**Recording Investee Net Income**  For the year ended December 31, 2012, Flanders Corporation reported net income of $105,000. Under the equity method, Simpson Inc. (the investor) records its share of Flanders net income as shown on the next page.

| 2012 | | | | | |
|---|---|---|---|---|---|
| Dec. | 31 | Investment in Flanders Corporation Stock | | 42,000 | |
| | | Income of Flanders Corporation | | | 42,000 |
| | | Record 40% share of Flanders | | | |
| | | Corporation net income, $105,000 × 40%. | | | |

*Income of Flanders Corporation* is reported on Simpson Inc.'s income statement. Depending on its significance, it may be reported separately or as part of *Other income*. If Flanders Corporation had a loss during the period, then the journal entry would be a debit to Loss of Flanders Corporation and a credit to the investment account.

**Recording Investee Dividends** During the year, Flanders declared and paid cash dividends of $45,000. Under the equity method, Simpson Inc. (the investor) records its share of Flanders dividends as follows:

| 2012 | | | | | |
|---|---|---|---|---|---|
| Dec. | 31 | Cash | | 18,000 | |
| | | Investment in Flanders Corporation Stock | | | 18,000 |
| | | Record 40% share of Flanders | | | |
| | | Corporation dividends, $45,000 × 40%. | | | |

The effect of recording 40% of Flanders Corporation's net income and dividends is to increase the investment account by $24,000 ($42,000 − $18,000). Thus, Investment in Flanders Corporation Stock increases from $350,000 to $374,000, as shown below.

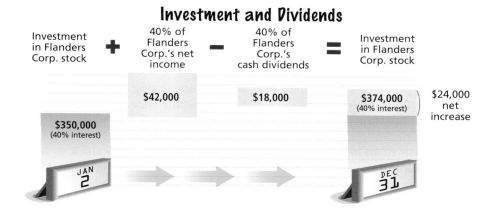

**Investment and Dividends**

Under the equity method, the investment account reflects the investor's proportional changes in the net book value of the investee. For example, Flanders Corporation's net book value increased by $60,000 (net income of $105,000 less dividends of $45,000) during the year. As a result, Simpson's share of Flanders' net book value increased by $24,000 ($60,000 × 40%). Investments accounted for under the equity method are classified on the balance sheet as noncurrent assets.

**Sale of Stock** Under the equity method, a gain or loss is normally recorded from the sale of an investment. A gain is recorded if the proceeds exceed the *book value* of the investment. A loss is recorded if the proceeds are less than the *book value* of the investment.

To illlustrate, if Simpson Inc. sold Flanders Corporation's stock on January 1, 2013, for $400,000, a gain of $26,000 would be reported, as shown below.

| | |
|---|---|
| Proceeds from sale | $400,000 |
| Book value of stock investment | 374,000 |
| Gain on sale | $ 26,000 |

The entry to record the sale is as follows:

| 2013 | | | | | |
|------|---|---|---|---|---|
| Jan. | 1 | Cash | | 400,000 | |
| | | Investment in Flanders Corporation Stock | | | 374,000 |
| | | Gain on Sale of Flanders Corporation Stock | | | 26,000 |
| | | Sale of Flanders Corporation stock. | | | |

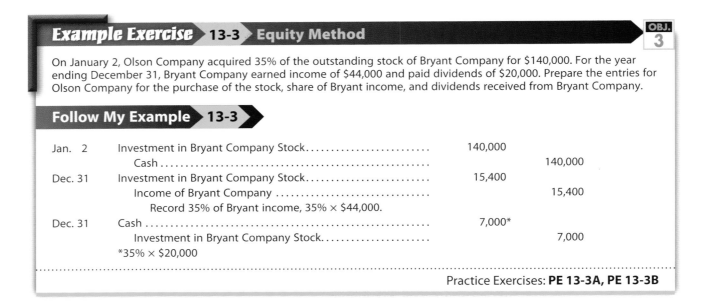

**Example Exercise** 13-3 **Equity Method**

OBJ. 3

On January 2, Olson Company acquired 35% of the outstanding stock of Bryant Company for $140,000. For the year ending December 31, Bryant Company earned income of $44,000 and paid dividends of $20,000. Prepare the entries for Olson Company for the purchase of the stock, share of Bryant income, and dividends received from Bryant Company.

**Follow My Example** 13-3

| Jan. 2 | Investment in Bryant Company Stock........................ | 140,000 | |
|--------|--------|--------|--------|
| | Cash...................................................... | | 140,000 |
| Dec. 31 | Investment in Bryant Company Stock........................ | 15,400 | |
| | Income of Bryant Company .............................. | | 15,400 |
| | Record 35% of Bryant income, 35% × $44,000. | | |
| Dec. 31 | Cash ...................................................... | 7,000* | |
| | Investment in Bryant Company Stock..................... | | 7,000 |
| | *35% × $20,000 | | |

Practice Exercises: **PE 13-3A, PE 13-3B**

## More Than 50% Ownership

If the investor purchases more than 50% of the outstanding stock of the investee, the investor is considered to have control over the investee. In this case, it is assumed that the investor purchased the stock of the investee primarily for strategic reasons.

The purchase of more than 50% ownership of the investee's stock is termed a **business combination**. Companies may combine in order to produce more efficiently, diversify product lines, expand geographically, or acquire know-how.

A corporation owning all or a majority of the voting stock of another corporation is called a **parent company**. The corporation that is controlled is called the **subsidiary company**.

Parent and subsidiary corporations often continue to maintain separate accounting records and prepare their own financial statements. In such cases, at the end of the year, the financial statements of the parent and subsidiary are combined and reported as a single company. These combined financial statements are called **consolidated financial statements**. Such statements are normally identified by adding *and Subsidiary(ies)* to the name of the parent corporation or by adding *Consolidated* to the statement title.

To the external stakeholders of the parent company, consolidated financial statements are more meaningful than separate statements for each corporation. This is because the parent company, in substance, controls the subsidiaries. The accounting for business combinations, including preparing consolidated financial statements, is decribed and illustrated in advanced accounting courses and textbooks.

# BusinessConnection

### APPLE'S ENTRANCE TO STREAMING MUSIC

Apple's iTunes is the dominant provider of music downloads. However, companies such as Pandora, Lala, and Grooveshark are challenging iTunes by providing permanent access to web songs that can be streamed live from a web browser, but cannot be downloaded onto a device. These companies can stream customized radio stations for free, or individual songs for as little as 10 cents. This compares to downloading a song from iTunes for $0.99 or more.

In late 2009, Apple acquired Lala in order to establish a presence in streaming music. Apparently, Apple believed that it was easier to acquire this technology by purchasing Lala, rather than build it in-house. While Apple has not declared its intentions, it may use Lala's technology to stream web songs through its iTunes store to iPhone®, iTouch®, and other online devices.

Source: Ethan Smith and Yakari Iwatani Kane, "Apple Acquires Lala Media," *The Wall Street Journal*, December 6, 2009.

# Valuing and Reporting Investments

Debt and equity securities are *financial assets* that are often traded on public exchanges such as the New York Stock Exchange. As a result, their market value can be observed and, thus, objectively determined.

For this reason, generally accepted accounting principles (GAAP) allow some debt and equity securities to be valued in the accounting records and financial statements at their fair market values. In contrast, GAAP requires tangible assets such as property, plant, and equipment to be valued and reported at their net book values (cost less accumulated depreciation).

For purposes of valuing and reporting, debt and equity securities are classified as follows:

1. Trading securities
2. Available-for-sale securities
3. Held-to-maturity securities

## Trading Securities

**Trading securities** are debt and equity securities that are purchased and sold to earn short-term profits from changes in their market prices. Trading securities are often held by banks, mutual funds, insurance companies, and other financial institutions.

Since trading securities are held as a short-term investment, they are reported as a current asset on the balance sheet. Trading securities are valued as a portfolio (group) of securities using the securities' fair values. **Fair value** is the market price that the company would receive for a security if it were sold. Changes in fair value of the portfolio (group) of trading securities are recognized as an **unrealized gain or loss** for the period.

SunTrust Banks Inc. holds $10 billion in trading securities as current assets.

To illustrate, assume Maggie Company purchased a portfolio of trading securities during 2012. On December 31, 2012, the cost and fair values of the securities were as follows:

| Name | Number of Shares | Total Cost | Total Fair Value |
|---|---|---|---|
| Armour Company | 400 | $ 5,000 | $ 7,200 |
| Maven, Inc. | 500 | 11,000 | 7,500 |
| Polaris Co. | 200 | 8,000 | 10,600 |
| Total | | $24,000 | $25,300 |

The portfolio of trading securities is reported at its fair value of $25,300. An adjusting entry is made to record the increase in fair value of $1,300 ($25,300 − $24,000). In order to maintain a record of the original cost of the securities, a valuation account, called *Valuation Allowance for Trading Investments*, is debited for $1,300 and *Unrealized Gain on Trading Investments* is credited for $1,300.[3] The adjusting entry on December 31, 2012, to record the fair value of the portfolio of trading securities is shown below.

| 2012 | | | | | |
|---|---|---|---|---|---|
| Dec. | 31 | Valuation Allowance for Trading Investments | | 1,300 | |
| | | Unrealized Gain on Trading Investments | | | 1,300 |
| | | To record increase in fair value of | | | |
| | | trading securities. | | | |

The *Unrealized Gain on Trading Investments* is reported on the income statement. Depending on its significance, it may be reported separately or as *Other income* on the income statement. The valuation allowance is reported on the December 31, 2012, balance sheet as follows:

**Maggie Company**
**Balance Sheet (selected items)**
**December 31, 2012**

| | | |
|---|---|---|
| Current assets: | | |
| Cash...................................................... | | $120,000 |
| Trading investments (at cost)................................ | $24,000 | |
| Plus valuation allowance for trading investments............ | 1,300 | |
| Trading investments (at fair value)......................... | | 25,300 |

If the fair value was less than the cost, then the adjustment would debit *Unrealized Loss on Trading Investments* and credit *Valuation Allowance for Trading Investments* for the difference. Unrealized Loss on Trading Investments would be reported on the income statement as Other expenses. Valuation Allowance for Trading Investments would be shown on the balance sheet as a *deduction* from Trading Investments (at cost).

Over time, the valuation allowance account is adjusted to reflect the difference between the cost and fair value of the portfolio. Thus, increases in the valuation allowance account from the beginning of the period will result in an adjustment to record an unrealized gain, similar to the journal entry illustrated above. Likewise, decreases in the valuation allowance account from the beginning of the period will result in an adjustment to record an unrealized loss.

**Example Exercise** ▶ **13-4** ▶ **Valuing Trading Securities at Fair Value**    OBJ. 4

On January 1, 2012, Valuation Allowance for Trading Investments had a zero balance. On December 31, 2012, the cost of the trading securities portfolio was $79,200, and the fair value was $76,800. Prepare the December 31, 2012, adjusting journal entry to record the unrealized gain or loss on trading investments.

*(Continued)*

---

[3] We assume that the valuation allowance account has a beginning balance of zero to simplify our illustrations.

**Follow My Example 13-4**

| 2012 | | | |
|---|---|---|---|
| Dec. 31 | Unrealized Loss on Trading Investments...................... | 2,400 | |
| |     Valuation Allowance for Trading Investments............... | | 2,400* |
| |       To record decrease in fair value of trading investments. | | |

| *Trading investments at fair value, December 31, 2012 | $ 76,800 |
|---|---|
| Less: Trading investments at cost, December 31, 2012 | 79,200 |
| Unrealized loss on trading investments | $ (2,400) |

Practice Exercises: **PE 13-4A, PE 13-4B**

## Integrity, Objectivity, and Ethics in Business

**LOAN LOSS WOES**

During the economic crisis of 2008, many of the largest U.S. banks were accused of having provided mortgages to marginally qualified borrowers. Such loans, called "sub-prime" and "Alt-A" loans, were made to earn mortgage fees. When the borrowers were unable to pay their mortgages, the banks incurred large losses on defaulted loans. These losses were so large that the U.S. government had to provide money (TARP funds) to many banks to bail them out of their financial distress.

During the middle of the crisis, the FASB voted to provide banks more flexibility in applying fair value accounting for bank assets, such as defaulted loans. These FASB rule changes allowed banks to minimize the impact of their defaulted loan write-downs and improve their earnings. Some criticized the FASB as succumbing to political pressure, and reducing overall financial statement fairness.

Source: Ian Katz, "FASB Eases Fair-Value Rules Amid Lawmaker Pressure," *Bloomberg*, April 2, 2009.

## Available-for-Sale Securities

**Available-for-sale securities** are debt and equity securities that are neither held for trading, held to maturity, or held for strategic reasons.

The accounting for available-for-sale securities is similar to the accounting for trading securities except for the reporting of changes in fair values. Specifically, changes in the fair values of *trading securities* are reported as an unrealized gain or loss on the income statement. In contrast, changes in the fair values of *available-for-sale securities* are reported as part of stockholders' equity and, thus, excluded from the income statement.

To illustrate, assume that Maggie Company purchased the three securities during 2012 as available-for-sale securities instead of trading securities. On December 31, 2012, the cost and fair values of the securities were as follows:

| Name | Number of Shares | Total Cost | Total Fair Value |
|---|---|---|---|
| Armour Company | 400 | $ 5,000 | $ 7,200 |
| Maven, Inc. | 500 | 11,000 | 7,500 |
| Polaris Co. | 200 | 8,000 | 10,600 |
|    Total | | $24,000 | $25,300 |

Microsoft Corporation holds over $25 billion in available-for-sale securities as current assets.

The portfolio of available-for-sale securities is reported at its fair value of $25,300. An adjusting entry is made to record the increase in fair value of $1,300 ($25,300 – $24,000). In order to maintain a record of the original cost of the securities, a valuation account, called *Valuation Allowance for Available-for-Sale Investments*, is debited for $1,300. This account is similar to the valuation account used for trading securities.

Unlike trading securities, the December 31, 2012, adjusting entry credits a stockholders' equity account instead of an income statement account.[4] The $1,300 increase in fair value is credited to *Unrealized Gain (Loss) on Available-for-Sale Investments.*

The adjusting entry on December 31, 2012, to record the fair value of the portfolio of available-for-sale securities is as follows:

| 2012 | | | | |
|---|---|---|---|---|
| Dec. | 31 | Valuation Allowance for Available-for-Sale Investments | 1,300 | |
| | |    Unrealized Gain (Loss) on Available-for-Sale Investments | | 1,300 |
| | |      To record increase in fair value of available-for-sale investments. | | |

A credit balance in Unrealized Gain (Loss) on Available-for-Sale Investments is added to stockholders' equity, while a debit balance is subtracted from stockholders' equity.

The valuation allowance and the unrealized gain are reported on the December 31, 2012, balance sheet as follows:

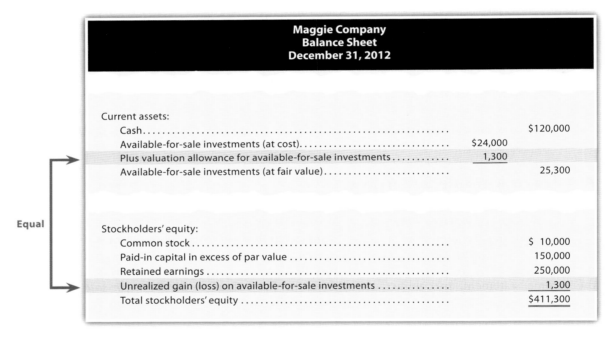

**Maggie Company**
**Balance Sheet**
**December 31, 2012**

Current assets:
| | | |
|---|---|---|
| Cash | | $120,000 |
| Available-for-sale investments (at cost) | $24,000 | |
| Plus valuation allowance for available-for-sale investments | 1,300 | |
| Available-for-sale investments (at fair value) | | 25,300 |

Stockholders' equity:
| | |
|---|---|
| Common stock | $ 10,000 |
| Paid-in capital in excess of par value | 150,000 |
| Retained earnings | 250,000 |
| Unrealized gain (loss) on available-for-sale investments | 1,300 |
| Total stockholders' equity | $411,300 |

**Equal**

As shown above, Unrealized Gain (Loss) on Available-for-Sale Investments is reported as an addition to stockholders' equity. In future years, the cumulative effects of unrealized gains and losses are reported in this account. Since 2012 was the first year that Maggie Company purchased available-for-sale securities, the unrealized gain is reported as the balance of *Unrealized Gain (Loss) on Available-for-Sale Investments.* This treatment is supported under the theory that available-for-sale securities will be held longer than trading securities, so changes in fair value over time have a greater opportunity to cancel out. Thus, these changes are not reported on the income statement as is the case with trading securities.

If the fair value was less than the cost, then the adjustment would debit Unrealized Gain (Loss) on Available-for-Sale Investments and credit Valuation Allowance for Available-for-Sale Investments for the difference. Unrealized Gain (Loss) on Trading Investments would be reported in the Stockholders' Equity section as

4 This is a rare exception to the rule that every adjusting entry must affect an income statement and a balance sheet account.

a negative item. Valuation Allowance for Available-for-Sale Investments would be shown on the balance sheet as a deduction from Available-for-Sale Investments (at cost).

Over time, the valuation allowance account is adjusted to reflect the difference between the cost and fair value of the portfolio. Thus, increases in the valuation allowance from the beginning of the period will result in an adjustment to record an increase in the valuation and unrealized gain (loss) accounts, similar to the journal entry illustrated earlier. Likewise, decreases in the valuation allowance from the beginning of the period will result in an adjustment to record decreases in the valuation and unrealized gain (loss) accounts.

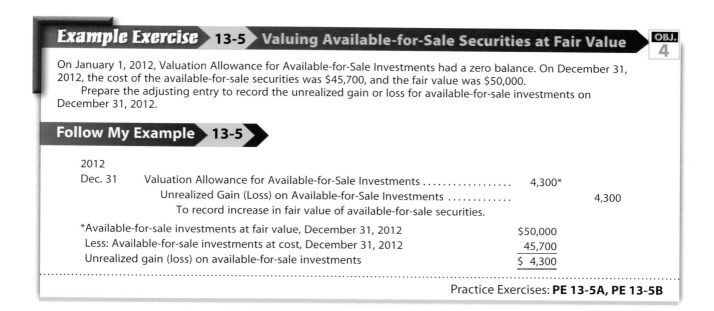

**Example Exercise 13-5 Valuing Available-for-Sale Securities at Fair Value** | **OBJ. 4**

On January 1, 2012, Valuation Allowance for Available-for-Sale Investments had a zero balance. On December 31, 2012, the cost of the available-for-sale securities was $45,700, and the fair value was $50,000.

Prepare the adjusting entry to record the unrealized gain or loss for available-for-sale investments on December 31, 2012.

**Follow My Example 13-5**

2012
Dec. 31  Valuation Allowance for Available-for-Sale Investments . . . . . . . . . . . . . . . . . .   4,300*
              Unrealized Gain (Loss) on Available-for-Sale Investments . . . . . . . . . . . . .            4,300
              To record increase in fair value of available-for-sale securities.

| *Available-for-sale investments at fair value, December 31, 2012 | $50,000 |
| Less: Available-for-sale investments at cost, December 31, 2012 | 45,700 |
| Unrealized gain (loss) on available-for-sale investments | $ 4,300 |

Practice Exercises: **PE 13-5A, PE 13-5B**

## Held-to-Maturity Securities

**Held-to-maturity securities** are debt investments, such as notes or bonds, that a company intends to hold until their maturity date. Held-to-maturity securities are primarily purchased to earn interest revenue.

If a held-to-maturity security will mature within a year, it is reported as a current asset on the balance sheet. Held-to-maturity securities maturing beyond a year are reported as noncurrent assets.

Only securities with maturity dates such as corporate notes and bonds are classified as held-to-maturity securities. Equity securities are not held-to-maturity securities because they have no maturity date.

Held-to-maturity bond investments are recorded at their cost, including any brokerage commissions, as illustrated earlier in this chapter. If the interest rate on the bonds differs from the market rate of interest, the bonds may be purchased at a premium or discount. In such cases, the premium or discount is amortized over the life of the bonds.

Held-to-maturity bond investments are reported on the balance sheet at their amortized cost. The accounting for held-to-maturity investments, including premium and discount amortization, is described in advanced accounting texts.

## Summary

Exhibit 3 summarizes the valuation and balance sheet reporting of trading, available-for-sale, and held-to-maturity securities.

**EXHIBIT 3**

**Summary of Valuing and Reporting of Investments**

|  | Trading Securities | Available-for-Sale Securities | Held-to-Maturity Securities |
|---|---|---|---|
| Valued at: | **Fair Value** | **Fair Value** | **Amortized Cost** |
| Changes in valuation are reported as: | Unrealized gain or loss is reported on income statement as Other income (loss). | Accumulated unrealized gain or loss is reported in stockholders' equity on the balance sheet. | Premium or discount amortization is reported as part of interest revenue on the income statement. |
| Reported on the balance sheet as: | Cost of investments plus or minus valuation allowance. | Cost of investments plus or minus valuation allowance. | Amortized cost of investment. |
| Classified on balance sheet as: | A current asset. | Either as a current or noncurrent asset, depending on management's intent. | Either as a current or noncurrent asset, depending on remaining term to maturity. |

Common stock investments in trading and available-for-sale securities are normally less than 20% of the outstanding common stock of the investee. The portfolios are reported at fair value using the valuation allowance account, while the individual securities are accounted for using the cost method. Investments between 20% and 50% of the outstanding common stock of the investee are accounted for using the equity method illustrated earlier in this chapter. Equity method investments are classified as noncurrent assets on the balance sheet. Moreover, such investments are permitted to be valued using fair values. To simplify, it is assumed that the investor does not elect this option.

The balance sheet reporting for the investments of Mornin' Joe is shown below.

| **Mornin' Joe** | | |
|---|---|---|
| **Balance Sheet** | | |
| **December 31, 2012** | | |
| **Assets** | | |
| Current assets: | | |
| Cash and cash equivalents ............................ | | $235,000 |
| Trading investments (at cost) ........................... | $420,000 | |
| Plus valuation allowance for trading investments ..... | 45,000 | 465,000 |
| Accounts receivable .................................... | $305,000 | |
| Less allowance for doubtful accounts ............... | 12,300 | 292,700 |
| Merchandise inventory—at lower of cost | | |
| (first-in, first-out method) or market ................. | | 120,000 |
| Prepaid insurance ...................................... | | 24,000 |
| Total current assets................................ | | $1,136,700 |
| Investments: | | |
| Investment in AM Coffee (equity method) ............... | | 565,000 |
| Property, plant, and equipment: | | |

Mornin' Joe invests in trading securities and does not have investments in held-to-maturity or available-for-sale securities. Mornin' Joe also owns 40% of AM Coffee Corporation, which is accounted for using the equity method. Mornin' Joe intends to keep its investment in AM Coffee indefinitely for strategic reasons; thus, its investment in AM Coffee is classified as a noncurrent asset. Such investments are normally reported before property, plant, and equipment.

Mornin' Joe reported an unrealized gain on trading investments of $5,000 and equity income in AM Coffee of $57,000 in the *Other income and expense* section of its income statement, as shown below.

| Mornin' Joe Income Statement For the Year Ended December 31, 2012 | | | |
|---|---|---|---|
| Revenue from sales: | | | |
| Sales | | $5,450,000 | |
| Less: Sales returns and allowances | $26,500 | | |
| Sales discounts | 21,400 | 47,900 | |
| Net sales | | | $5,402,100 |
| Cost of merchandise sold | | | 2,160,000 |
| Gross profit | | | $3,242,100 |
| Total operating expenses | | | 2,608,700 |
| Income from operations | | | $ 633,400 |
| Other income and expense: | | | |
| Interest revenue | | $ 18,000 | |
| Interest expense | | (136,000) | |
| Loss on disposal of fixed asset | | (23,000) | |
| Unrealized gain on trading investments | | 5,000 | |
| Equity income in AM Coffee | | 57,000 | (79,000) |
| Income before income taxes | | | $ 554,400 |
| Income tax expense | | | 132,800 |
| Net income | | | $ 421,600 |

## IFRS Reporting

See pages 630-634

The statement of financial position (balance sheet) presentation for trading investments for Mornin' Joe International under IFRS is as follows:

| Mornin' Joe International Statement of Financial Position December 31, 2012 | |
|---|---|
| **Current assets** | |
| Prepaid insurance | € 24,000 |
| Merchandise inventory—at lower of cost (first-in, first-out) or realizable value | 120,000 |
| Accounts receivable (net of allowance for doubtful accounts) | 292,700 |
| **Financial assets at fair value through profit or loss** | 465,000 |
| Cash and cash equivalents | 235,000 |
| Total current assets | 1,136,700 |

The trading investments are termed "financial assets at fair value through profit or loss" under IFRS. The financial assets are listed prior to cash in reverse liquidity order to emphasize the going concern nature of the business. The cost of the financial assets would be disclosed in the footnotes. The treatment of trading, available-for-sale, and held-to-maturity investments under IFRS is similar to U.S. GAAP.

## BusinessConnection

### WARREN BUFFETT: THE SAGE OF OMAHA

Beginning in 1962, Warren Buffett, one of the world's wealthiest and most successful investors, began buying shares of Berkshire Hathaway. He eventually took control of the company and transformed it from a textile manufacturing company into an investment holding company. Today, Berkshire Hathaway holds over $125 billion in cash and cash equivalents, equity securities, and debt securities. Berkshire's largest holdings include The Coca-Cola Company, American Express, Wells Fargo, and Procter & Gamble. Berkshire Class A common stock trades near $115,000 per share, the highest priced share on the New York Stock Exchange. These shares would have given an investor a nearly 1,400% return since 1990.

Buffett compares his investment style to hitting a baseball: "Ted Williams, one of the greatest hitters in the game, stated, 'my argument is, to be a good hitter, you've got to get a good ball to hit. It's the first rule of the book. If I have to bite at stuff that is out of my happy zone, I'm not a .344 hitter. I might only be a .250 hitter.'" Buffett states, "Charlie (Buffett's partner) and I agree and will try to wait for (investment) opportunities that are well within our 'happy zone.'"[5] One of Buffet's recent "happy zone" investments was the acquisition of Burlington Northern Santa Fe Railroad for $34 billion.

Warren Buffett as the CEO of Berkshire Hathaway earns a salary of only $100,000 per year, which is the lowest CEO salary for a company of its size in the United States. However, he personally owns approximately 38% of the company, making him worth over $40 billion. What will Buffett do with this wealth? He has decided to give nearly all of it to philanthropic causes through the Bill and Melinda Gates Foundation.

**OBJ. 5** Describe fair value accounting and its implications for the future.

# Fair Value Accounting

Fair value is the price that would be received for selling an asset or paying off a liability. Fair value assumes that the asset is sold or the liability paid off under *normal* rather than under distressed conditions.

As illustrated earlier, generally accepted accounting principles require the use of fair values for valuing and reporting debt and equity securities held as trading or available-for-sale investments. In addition, accounts receivable is recorded and reported at an amount that approximates its fair value. Likewise, accounts payable are recorded and reported at approximately their fair value.

In contrast, many assets and liabilities are recorded and reported at amounts that differ significantly from their fair values. For example, when equipment or other property, plant, and equipment assets are purchased, they are initially recorded at their fair values. That is, they are recorded at their purchase price, called *historical cost*, and depreciated over their useful lives. As a result, the book value of property, plant, and equipment normally differs significantly from its fair value. Likewise, held-to-maturity securities are valued at their amortized cost rather than at their fair values.

## Trend to Fair Value Accounting

A current trend is for the Financial Accounting Standards Board (FASB) and other accounting regulators to adopt accounting principles using fair values for valuing and reporting assets and liabilities. Factors contributing to this trend include the following:

1. Current generally accepted accounting principles are a hybrid of varying measurement methods that often conflict with one another. For example, property, plant, and equipment are normally reported at their depreciated book values. However, GAAP require that if a fixed asset value is *impaired*, it be written down to its fair value. Such conflicting accounting principles could confuse users of financial statements.

2. A greater percentage of the total assets of many companies consists of financial assets such as receivables and securities. Fair values for such assets can often be readily obtained from stock market quotations or computed using current interest rates and present values. Likewise, many liabilities can be readily valued using market quotations or current interest rates and present values.

5 Warren E. Buffett, *The Essays of Warren Buffett: Lessons for Corporate America*, edited by Lawrence A. Cunningham, p. 234.

3. The world economy has compelled accounting regulators to adopt a worldwide set of accounting principles and standards. *International Financial Reporting Standards (IFRSs)* are issued by the International Accounting Standards Board *(IASB)* and are used by the European Economic Union (EU). As a result, the FASB is under increasing pressure to conform U.S. accounting standards to international standards. One area where differences exist is in the use of fair values, which are more often used by International Financial Reporting Standards.

See Appendix E for more information

While there is an increasing trend to fair value accounting, using fair values has several potential disadvantages. Some of these disadvantages include the following:

1. Fair values may not be readily obtainable for some assets or liabilities. As a result, accounting reports may become more subjective and less reliable. For example, fair values (market quotations) are normally available for trading and available-for-sale securities. However, fair values may not be as available for assets such as property, plant, and equipment or intangible assets such as goodwill.

2. Fair values make it more difficult to compare companies if companies use different methods of determining (measuring) fair values. This would be especially true for assets and liabilities for which fair values are not readily available.

3. Using fair values could result in more fluctuations in accounting reports because fair values normally change from year to year. Such volatility may confuse users of the financial statements. It may also make it more difficult for users to determine current operating trends and to predict future trends.

## Effect of Fair Value Accounting on the Financial Statements

The use of fair values for valuing assets and liabilities affects the financial statements. Specifically, the balance sheet and income statement could be affected.

**Balance Sheet** When an asset or a liability is reported at its fair value, any difference between the asset's original cost or prior period's fair value must be recorded. As we illustrated for trading and available-for-sale securities, one method for doing this is to use a valuation allowance. The account, *Valuation Allowance for Trading Investments,* was used earlier in this chapter to adjust trading securities to their fair values.

Available-for-sale securities are recorded at fair value. Changes in their fair values are not recognized on the income statement, but are included as part of stockholders' equity.

**Income Statement** Instead of recording the unrealized gain or loss on changes in fair values as part of stockholders' equity, the unrealized gains or losses may be reported on the income statement. This method was illustrated earlier in this chapter for *trading* securities.

As shown above, differences exist as to how to best report changes in fair values—that is, whether to report gains or losses on fair values on the income statement or the balance sheet.

In an attempt to bridge these differences, the FASB introduced the concepts of *comprehensive income* and *accumulated other comprehensive income.* These concepts are described in the appendix to this chapter.

## Financial Analysis and Interpretation: Dividend Yield

The **dividend yield** measures the rate of return to stockholders based on cash dividends. Dividend yield is most often computed for common stock because preferred stock has a stated dividend rate. In contrast, the cash dividends paid on common stock normally varies with the profitability of the corporation.

**OBJ. 6** Describe and illustrate the computation of dividend yield.

The dividend yield is computed as follows:

$$\text{Dividend Yield} = \frac{\text{Dividends per Share of Common Stock}}{\text{Market Price per Share of Common Stock}}$$

To illustrate, the market price of News Corporation was $15.50 on February 12, 2010. During the preceding year, News Corporation had paid dividends of $0.12 per share. Thus, the dividend yield of News Corporation's common stock is computed as follows:

$$\text{Dividend Yield} = \frac{\text{Dividends per Share of Common Stock}}{\text{Market Price per Share of Common Stock}} = \frac{\$0.12}{\$15.50} = 0.77\%$$

News Corporation pays a dividend yield of less than 1%. The dividend yield is first a function of a company's profitability, or ability to pay a dividend. For example, many banks nearly eliminated their dividends during the banking crisis of the late 2000s because they had significant losses. News Corporation has sufficient profitability to pay a dividend. Secondly, a company's dividend yield is a function of management's alternative use of funds. If a company has sufficient growth opportunities, funds may be directed toward internal investment, rather than toward paying dividends. This would explain News Corporation's small dividend yield.

The dividend yield will vary from day to day, because the market price of a corporation's stock varies day to day. Current dividend yields are provided with newspaper listings of market prices and most Internet quotation services, such as from either Yahoo's or Google's Finance Web site.

Recent dividend yields for some selected companies are as follows:

| Company | Dividend Yield (%) |
| --- | --- |
| Apple | None |
| Best Buy | 1.57 |
| Coca-Cola Company | 3.04 |
| Duke Energy | 5.94 |
| Hewlett-Packard | 0.48 |
| Microsoft | 1.86 |
| Starbucks | None |
| Verizon Communications | 6.57 |

As can be seen, the dividend yield varies widely across firms. Growth firms tend to retain their earnings to fund future growth. Thus, Apple and Starbucks pay no dividends, and Hewlett-Packard has a very small dividend. Common stockholders of these companies expect to earn most of their return from stock price appreciation. In contrast, Duke Energy and Verizon Communications are regulated utilities that provide a return to common stockholders mostly through their dividend. Best Buy, Coca-Cola, and Microsoft provide a mix of dividend and expected stock price appreciation to their common stockholders.

---

**Example Exercise 13-6 ▶ Dividend Yield**  OBJ. 6

On March 11, 2012, Sheldon Corporation had a market price per share of common stock of $58. For the previous year, Sheldon paid an annual dividend of $2.90. Compute the dividend yield for Sheldon Corporation.

**Follow My Example 13-6**

$$\text{Dividend Yield} = \frac{\text{Dividends per Share of Common Stock}}{\text{Market Price per Share of Common Stock}}$$

$$\text{Dividend Yield} = \frac{\$2.90}{\$58} = 0.05, \text{ or } 5\%$$

Practice Exercises: **PE 13-6A, PE 13-6B**

# A P P E N D I X

# Comprehensive Income

**Comprehensive income** is defined as all changes in stockholders' equity during a period, except those resulting from dividends and stockholders' investments. Comprehensive income is computed by adding or subtracting *other comprehensive income* from net income as follows:

| | |
|---|---|
| Net income | $XXX |
| Other comprehensive income | XXX |
| Comprehensive income | $XXX |

**Other comprehensive income** items include unrealized gains and losses on available-for-sale securities as well as other items such as foreign currency and pension liability adjustments. The *cumulative* effect of other comprehensive income is reported on the balance sheet, as **accumulated other comprehensive income**.

Companies may report comprehensive income in the financial statements as follows:

1. On the income statement
2. In a separate statement of comprehensive income
3. In the statement of stockholders' equity

Companies may use terms other than comprehensive income, such as *total nonowner changes in equity*.

In the earlier illustration, Maggie Company had reported an unrealized gain on available-for-sale investments of $1,300. This unrealized gain would be reported in the Stockholders' Equity section of its 2012 balance sheet as follows:

**Maggie Company**
**Balance Sheet**
**December 31, 2012**

| | |
|---|---:|
| Stockholders' equity: | |
| Common stock. . . . . . . . . . . . . . . . . . . . . . . . . . . . . . . . . . . . . . . . . . . . . . . . | $ 10,000 |
| Paid-in capital in excess of par value. . . . . . . . . . . . . . . . . . . . . . . . . . . . . . . . | 150,000 |
| Retained earnings. . . . . . . . . . . . . . . . . . . . . . . . . . . . . . . . . . . . . . . . . . . . . . | 250,000 |
| Unrealized gain (loss) on available-for-sale investments. . . . . . . . . . . . . . . . . . | 1,300 |
| Total stockholders' equity . . . . . . . . . . . . . . . . . . . . . . . . . . . . . . . . . . . . . . . . | $411,300 |

Alternatively, Maggie Company could have reported the unrealized gain as part of accumulated other comprehensive income as follows:

**Maggie Company**
**Balance Sheet**
**December 31, 2012**

| | |
|---|---:|
| Stockholders' equity: | |
| Common stock. . . . . . . . . . . . . . . . . . . . . . . . . . . . . . . . . . . . . . . . . . . . . . . . | $ 10,000 |
| Paid-in capital in excess of par value. . . . . . . . . . . . . . . . . . . . . . . . . . . . . . . . | 150,000 |
| Retained earnings. . . . . . . . . . . . . . . . . . . . . . . . . . . . . . . . . . . . . . . . . . . . . . | 250,000 |
| Accumulated other comprehensive income: | |
| Unrealized gain on available-for-sale investments. . . . . . . . . . . . . . . . . . . . . . . | 1,300 |
| Total stockholders' equity . . . . . . . . . . . . . . . . . . . . . . . . . . . . . . . . . . . . . . . . | $411,300 |

# At a Glance 13

**OBJ. 1**

## Describe why companies invest in debt and equity securities.

**Key Points**  Cash can be used to (1) invest in current operations, (2) invest to earn additional revenue in marketable securities, or (3) invest in marketable securities for strategic reasons.

| Learning Outcomes | Example Exercises | Practice Exercises |
|---|---|---|
| • Describe the ways excess cash is used by a business. | | |
| • Describe the purpose of temporary investments. | | |
| • Describe the strategic purpose of long-term investments. | | |

**OBJ. 2**

## Describe and illustrate the accounting for debt investments.

**Key Points**  The accounting for debt investments includes recording the purchase, interest revenue, and sale of the debt. Both the purchase and sale date may include accrued interest.

| Learning Outcomes | Example Exercises | Practice Exercises |
|---|---|---|
| • Prepare journal entries to record the purchase of a debt investment, including accrued interest. | EE13-1 | PE13-1A, 13-1B |
| • Prepare journal entries for interest revenue from debt investments. | EE13-1 | PE13-1A, 13-1B |
| • Prepare journal entries to record the sale of a debt investment at a gain or loss. | EE13-1 | PE13-1A, 13-1B |

**OBJ. 3**

## Describe and illustrate the accounting for equity investments.

**Key Points**  The accounting for equity investments differs depending on the degree of control. Accounting for investments of less than 20% of the outstanding stock (no control) of the investee includes recording the purchase of stock, receipt of dividends, and sale of stock at a gain or loss. Influential investments of 20%–50% of the outstanding stock of an investee are accounted for under the *equity method*. An investment of more than 50% of the outstanding stock of an investee is treated as a *business combination* and accounted for using *consolidated financial statements*.

| Learning Outcomes | Example Exercises | Practice Exercises |
|---|---|---|
| • Describe the accounting for less than 20%, 20%–50%, and greater than 50% investments. | | |
| • Prepare journal entries to record the purchase of a stock investment. | EE13-2 | PE13-2A, 13-2B |
| • Prepare journal entries for receipt of dividends. | EE13-2 | PE13-2A, 13-2B |
| • Prepare journal entries for the sale of a stock investment at a gain or loss. | EE13-2 | PE13-2A, 13-2B |
| • Prepare journal entries for the equity earnings of an equity method investee. | EE13-3 | PE13-3A, 13-3B |
| • Prepare journal entries for the dividends received from an equity method investee. | EE13-3 | PE13-3A, 13-3B |
| • Describe a business combination, parent company, and subsidiary company. | | |
| • Describe consolidated financial statements. | | |

**OBJ. 4**

### Describe and illustrate valuing and reporting investments in the financial statements.

**Key Points**   Debt and equity securities are classified as (1) trading securities, (2) available-for-sale securities, and (3) held-to-maturity securities for reporting and valuation purposes. *Trading securities* are valued at *fair value*, with unrealized gains and losses reported on the income statement. *Available-for-sale securities* are debt and equity securities that are not classified as trading or held-to-maturity. Available-for-sale securities are reported at fair value with unrealized gains or losses reported in the Stockholders' Equity section of the balance sheet. *Held-to-maturity* investments are debt securities that are intended to be held until their maturity date. Held-to-maturity debt investments are valued at amortized cost.

| Learning Outcomes | Example Exercises | Practice Exercises |
|---|---|---|
| • Describe trading securities, held-to-maturity securities, and available-for-sale securities. | | |
| • Prepare journal entries to record the change in the fair value of a trading security portfolio. | **EE13-4** | **PE13-4A, 13-4B** |
| • Describe and illustrate the reporting of trading securities on the balance sheet. | | |
| • Prepare journal entries to record the change in fair value of an available-for-sale security portfolio. | **EE13-5** | **PE13-5A, 13-5B** |
| • Describe and illustrate the reporting of available-for-sale securities on the balance sheet. | | |
| • Describe the accounting for held-to-maturity debt securities. | | |

**OBJ. 5**

### Describe fair value accounting and its implications for the future.

**Key Points**   There is a trend toward fair value accounting in generally accepted accounting principles (GAAP). Fair value provides relevance at the sacrifice of objectivity for assets without established market prices.

| Learning Outcomes | Example Exercises | Practice Exercises |
|---|---|---|
| • Describe the reasons why there is a trend toward fair value accounting. | | |
| • Describe the disadvantages of fair value accounting. | | |
| • Describe how fair value accounting impacts the balance sheet and income statement. | | |
| • Describe the future of fair value accounting. | | |

**OBJ. 6**

### Describe and illustrate the computation of dividend yield.

**Key Points**   The dividend yield measures the cash return from common dividends as a percent of the market price. The ratio is computed as dividends per share of common stock divided by the market price per share of common stock.

| Learning Outcomes | Example Exercises | Practice Exercises |
|---|---|---|
| • Compute dividend yield. | **EE13-6** | **PE13-6A, 13-6B** |
| • Describe how dividend yield measures the return to stockholders from dividends. | | |

## Key Terms

accumulated other comprehensive income (601)

available-for-sale securities (593)

business combination (590)

comprehensive income (601)

consolidated financial statements (590)

cost method (587)

debt securities (583)

dividend yield (599)

equity method (588)

equity securities (583)

fair value (591)

held-to-maturity securities (595)

investee (586)

investments (583)

investor (586)

other comprehensive income (601)

parent company (590)

subsidiary company (590)

trading securities (591)

unrealized gain or loss (591)

## Illustrative Problem

The following selected investment transactions were completed by Rosewell Company during 2012, its first year of operations:

2012

Jan. 11. Purchased 800 shares of Bryan Company stock as an available-for-sale security at $23 per share plus an $80 brokerage commission.

Feb. 6. Purchased $40,000 of 8% U.S. Treasury bonds at par value plus accrued interest for 36 days. The bonds pay interest on January 1 and July 1. The bonds were classified as held-to-maturity securities.

Mar. 3. Purchased 1,900 shares of Cohen Company stock as a trading security at $48 per share plus a $152 brokerage commission.

Apr. 5. Purchased 2,400 shares of Lyons Inc. stock as an available-for-sale security at $68 per share plus a $120 brokerage commission.

May 12. Purchased 200,000 shares of Myers Company at $37 per share plus an $8,000 brokerage commission. Myers Company has 800,000 common shares issued and outstanding. The equity method was used for this investment.

July 1. Received semiannual interest on bonds purchased on February 6.

Aug. 29. Sold 1,200 shares of Cohen Company stock at $61 per share less a $90 brokerage commission.

Oct. 5. Received an $0.80-per-share dividend on Bryan Company stock.

Nov. 11. Received a $1.10-per-share dividend on Myers Company stock.

16. Purchased 3,000 shares of Morningside Company stock as a trading security for $52 per share plus a $150 brokerage commission.

Dec. 31. Accrued interest on February 6 bonds.

31. Myers Company earned $1,200,000 during the year. Rosewell recorded its share of Myers Company earnings using the equity method.

31. Prepared adjusting entries for the portfolios of trading and available-for-sale securities based upon the following fair values (stock prices):

| | |
|---|---|
| Bryan Company | $21 |
| Cohen Company | 43 |
| Lyons Inc. | 88 |
| Myers Company | 40 |
| Morningside Company | 45 |

## Instructions

1. Journalize the preceding transactions.

2. Prepare the balance sheet disclosure for Rosewell Company's investments on December 31, 2012. Assume held-to-maturity investments are classified as noncurrent assets.

## Solution

1.

| 2012 | | | | | |
|------|---|---|---|---|---|
| Jan. | 11 | Available-for-Sale Investments—Bryan Company | 18,480* | | |
| | | Cash | | | 18,480 |
| | | *(800 shares × $23 per share) + $80 | | | |

| | | | | | |
|------|---|---|---|---|---|
| Feb. | 6 | Investments—U.S. Treasury Bonds | 40,000 | | |
| | | Interest Receivable | 320* | | |
| | | Cash | | | 40,320 |
| | | *$40,000 × 8% × (36 days/360 days) | | | |

| | | | | | |
|------|---|---|---|---|---|
| Mar. | 3 | Trading Investments—Cohen Company | 91,352* | | |
| | | Cash | | | 91,352 |
| | | *(1,900 shares × $48 per share) + $152 | | | |

| | | | | | |
|------|---|---|---|---|---|
| Apr. | 5 | Available-for-Sale Investments—Lyons Inc. | 163,320* | | |
| | | Cash | | | 163,320 |
| | | *(2,400 shares × $68 per share) + $120 | | | |

| | | | | | |
|------|---|---|---|---|---|
| May | 12 | Investment in Myers Company | 7,408,000* | | |
| | | Cash | | | 7,408,000 |
| | | *(200,000 shares × $37 per share) + $8,000 | | | |

| | | | | | |
|------|---|---|---|---|---|
| July | 1 | Cash | 1,600* | | |
| | | Interest Receivable | | | 320 |
| | | Interest Revenue | | | 1,280 |
| | | *$40,000 × 8% × ½ | | | |

| | | | | | |
|------|---|---|---|---|---|
| Aug. | 29 | Cash | 73,110* | | |
| | | Trading Investments—Cohen Company | | | 57,696** |
| | | Gain on Sale of Investments | | | 15,414 |
| | | *(1,200 shares × $61 per share) – $90 | | | |
| | | **1,200 shares × ($91,352/1,900 shares) | | | |

| 2012 | | | | | |
|---|---|---|---|---|---|
| Oct. | 5 | Cash | | 640 | |
| | | Dividend Revenue | | | 640 |
| | | *800 shares × $0.80 per share | | | |

| | | | | | |
|---|---|---|---|---|---|
| Nov. | 11 | Cash | | 220,000 | |
| | | Investment in Myers Company Stock | | | 220,000 |
| | | *200,000 shares × $1.10 per share | | | |

| | | | | | |
|---|---|---|---|---|---|
| Nov. | 16 | Trading Investments—Morningside Company | | 156,150* | |
| | | Cash | | | 156,150 |
| | | *(3,000 shares × $52 per share) + $150 | | | |

| | | | | | |
|---|---|---|---|---|---|
| Dec. | 31 | Interest Receivable | | 1,600 | |
| | | Interest Revenue | | | 1,600 |
| | | Accrue interest, $40,000 × 8% × ½. | | | |

| | | | | | |
|---|---|---|---|---|---|
| Dec. | 31 | Investment in Myers Company Stock | | 300,000 | |
| | | Income of Myers Company | | | 300,000 |
| | | Record equity income, | | | |
| | | $1,200,000 × (200,000 shares/800,000 shares). | | | |

| | | | | | |
|---|---|---|---|---|---|
| Dec. | 31 | Unrealized Loss on Trading Investments | | 24,706 | |
| | | Valuation Allowance for Trading Investments | | | 24,706 |
| | | Record decease in fair value of trading | | | |
| | | investments, $165,100 –$189,806. | | | |

| Name | Number of Shares | Total Cost | Total Fair Value |
|---|---|---|---|
| Cohen Company | 700 | $ 33,656 | $ 30,100* |
| Morningside Company | 3,000 | 156,150 | 135,000** |
| Total | | $189,806 | $165,100 |

*700 shares × $43 per share
**3,000 shares × $45 per share

*Note*: Myers Company is valued using the equity method; thus, the fair value is not used.

| | | | | | |
|---|---|---|---|---|---|
| Dec. | 31 | Valuation Allowance for Available-for-Sale | | | |
| | | Investments | | 46,200 | |
| | | Unrealized Gain (Loss) on Available-for- | | | |
| | | Sale Investments | | | 46,200 |
| | | Record increase in fair value of available-for- | | | |
| | | sale investments, $228,000 – $181,800. | | | |

| Name | Number of Shares | Total Cost | Total Fair Value |
|---|---|---|---|
| Bryan Company | 800 | $ 18,480 | $ 16,800* |
| Lyons Inc. | 2,400 | 163,320 | 211,200** |
| Total | | $181,800 | $228,000 |

*800 shares × $21 per share
**2,400 shares × $88 per share

2.

**Rosewell Company**
**Balance Sheet (Selected)**
**December 31, 2012**

| | | |
|---|---|---|
| Current assets: | | |
| Cash.................................................... | | $ XXX,XXX |
| Trading investments (at cost) .............................. | $189,806 | |
| Less valuation allowance for trading investments ............. | 24,706 | |
| Trading investments at fair value............................ | | 165,100 |
| Available-for-sale investments (at cost)...................... | $181,800 | |
| Plus valuation allowance for available-for-sale investments .... | 46,200 | |
| Available-for-sale investments at fair value ................... | | 228,000 |
| Noncurrent investments: | | |
| Held-to-maturity investments ............................... | | $ 40,000 |
| Investments in Myers Company (equity method).............. | | 7,488,000 |
| | | |
| Stockholders' equity: | | |
| Common stock ............................................ | | $ XX,XXX |
| Paid-in capital in excess of par value ........................ | | XXX,XXX |
| Retained earnings ......................................... | | XXX,XXX |
| Plus unrealized gain (loss) on available-for-sale investments ... | | 46,200 |
| Total stockholders' equity....................................... | | $ XXX,XXX |

# Discussion Questions

1. Why might a business invest in another company's stock?

2. Why would there be a gain or loss on the sale of a bond investment?

3. When is using the cost method the appropriate accounting for equity investments?

4. How does the accounting for a dividend received differ between the cost method and the equity method?

5. If an investor owns more than 50% of an investee, how is this treated on the investor's financial statements?

6. What is the major difference in the accounting for a portfolio of trading securities and a portfolio of available-for-sale securities?

7. If Valuation Allowance for Trading Investments has a credit balance, how is it treated on the balance sheet?

8. How would a debit balance in Unrealized Gain (Loss) on Available-for-Sale Investments be disclosed in the financial statements?

9. What is the evidence of the trend toward fair value accounting?

10. What are some potential disadvantages of fair value accounting?

# Practice Exercises

| Learning Objectives | Example Exercises | |
|---|---|---|
| OBJ. 2 | EE 13-1 p. 586 | **PE 13-1A** **Bond transactions** |

Journalize the entries to record the following selected bond investment transactions for Capital Trust:

a. Purchased for cash $250,000 of Belmont City 4% bonds at 100 plus accrued interest of $1,500.

b. Received first semiannual interest.

c. Sold $80,000 of the bonds at 97 plus accrued interest of $500.

| Learning Objectives | Example Exercises | |
|---|---|---|
| OBJ. 2 | EE 13-1 p. 586 | **PE 13-1B** **Bond transactions** |

Journalize the entries to record the following selected bond investment transactions for Jennings Products:

a. Purchased for cash $40,000 of Tech Grove, Inc. 6% bonds at 100 plus accrued interest of $850.

b. Received first semiannual interest.

c. Sold $15,000 of the bonds at 102 plus accrued interest of $150.

| Learning Objectives | Example Exercises | |
|---|---|---|
| OBJ. 3 | EE 13-2 p. 588 | **PE 13-2A** **Stock transactions** |

On February 12, 5,000 shares of Mid-Ex Company are acquired at a price of $24 per share plus a $200 brokerage fee. On April 22, a $0.36-per-share dividend was received on the Mid-Ex Company stock. On May 10, 4,000 shares of the Mid-Ex Company stock were sold for $31 per share less a $160 brokerage fee. Prepare the journal entries for the original purchase, dividend, and sale.

| Learning Objectives | Example Exercises | |
|---|---|---|
| OBJ. 3 | EE 13-2 p. 588 | **PE 13-2B** **Stock transactions** |

On August 15, 1,600 shares of Birch Company are acquired at a price of $44 per share plus a $160 brokerage fee. On September 10, a $0.75-per-share dividend was received on the Birch Company stock. On October 5, 500 shares of the Birch Company stock were sold for $35 per share less a $50 brokerage fee. Prepare the journal entries for the original purchase, dividend, and sale.

| Learning Objectives | Example Exercises | |
|---|---|---|
| OBJ. 3 | EE 13-3 p. 590 | **PE 13-3A** **Equity method** |

On January 2, THT Company acquired 40% of the outstanding stock of First Alert Company for $155,000. For the year ending December 31, First Alert Company earned income of $42,000 and paid dividends of $12,000. Prepare the entries for THT Company for the purchase of the stock, share of First Alert income, and dividends received from First Alert Company.

| Learning Objectives | Example Exercises | |
|---|---|---|
| OBJ. 3 | EE 13-3 p. 590 | **PE 13-3B** **Equity method** |

On January 2, Bassett Company acquired 30% of the outstanding stock of Nassim Company for $400,000. For the year ending December 31, Nassim Company earned income of $110,000 and paid dividends of $46,000. Prepare the entries for Bassett Company for the purchase of the stock, share of Nassim income, and dividends received from Nassim Company.

| *Learning Objectives* | *Example Exercises* | |
|---|---|---|
| OBJ. 4 | EE 13-4 *p. 592* | **PE 13-4A   Valuing trading securities at fair value** |

On January 1, 2012, Valuation Allowance for Trading Investments had a zero balance. On December 31, 2012, the cost of the trading securities portfolio was $105,800 and the fair value was $101,600. Prepare the December 31, 2012, adjusting journal entry to record the unrealized gain or loss on trading investments.

| OBJ. 4 | EE 13-4 *p. 592* | **PE 13-4B   Valuing trading securities at fair value** |
|---|---|---|

On January 1, 2012, Valuation Allowance for Trading Investments had a zero balance. On December 31, 2012, the cost of the trading securities portfolio was $33,200, and the fair value was $39,500. Prepare the December 31, 2012, adjusting journal entry to record the unrealized gain or loss on trading investments.

| OBJ. 4 | EE 13-5 *p. 595* | **PE 13-5A   Valuing available-for-sale securities at fair value** |
|---|---|---|

On January 1, 2012, Valuation Allowance for Available-for-Sale Securities had a zero balance. On December 31, 2012, the cost of the available-for-sale securities was $62,400, and the fair value was $56,900. Prepare the adjusting entry to record the unrealized gain or loss for available-for-sale securities on December 31, 2012.

| OBJ. 4 | EE 13-5 *p. 595* | **PE 13-5B   Valuing available-for-sale securities at fair value** |
|---|---|---|

On January 1, 2012, Valuation Allowance for Available-for-Sale Securities had a zero balance. On December 31, 2012, the cost of the available-for-sale securities was $7,600, and the fair value was $9,500. Prepare the adjusting entry to record the unrealized gain or loss for available-for-sale securities on December 31, 2012.

| OBJ. 6 | EE 13-6 *p. 600* | **PE 13-6A   Dividend yield** |
|---|---|---|

On September 25, 2012, Lucas Corporation had a market price per share of common stock of $8. For the previous year, Lucas paid an annual dividend of $0.16. Compute the dividend yield for Lucas Corporation.

| OBJ. 6 | EE 13-6 *p. 600* | **PE 13-6B   Dividend yield** |
|---|---|---|

On June 12, 2012, Mid State Power and Electric Company had a market price per share of common stock of $48. For the previous year, Mid State paid an annual dividend of $2.88. Compute the dividend yield for Mid State Power and Electric Company.

## Exercises

**OBJ. 2**

**EX 13-1   Entries for investment in bonds, interest, and sale of bonds**

Dristol Company acquired $56,000 Reynolds Company, 4.5% bonds on April 1, 2012, at par value. Interest is paid semiannually on April 1 and October 1. On October 1, 2012, Dristol sold $20,000 of the bonds for 99.

Journalize entries to record the following:

a.  The initial acquisition of the bonds on April 1.

b.  The semiannual interest received on October 1.

c.  The sale of the bonds on October 1.

d.  The accrual of $637 interest on December 31, 2012.

OBJ. 2

### EX 13-2   Entries for investments in bonds, interest, and sale of bonds

Jupiter Investments acquired $40,000 Carlisle Corp., 9% bonds at par value on September 1, 2012. The bonds pay interest on September 1 and March 1. On March 1, 2013, Jupiter sold $40,000 par value Carlisle Corp. bonds at 103.

Journalize the entries to record the following:

a. The initial acquisition of the Carlisle Corp. bonds on September 1, 2012.

b. The adjusting entry for four months of accrued interest earned on the Carlisle Corp. bonds on December 31, 2012.

c. The receipt of semiannual interest on March 1, 2013.

d. The sale of $10,000 Carlisle Corp. bonds on March 1, 2013, at 103.

OBJ. 2

✔ Dec. 1, Loss on
sale of investments,
$220

### EX 13-3   Entries for investment in bonds, interest, and sale of bonds

Afton Co. purchased $24,000 of 4%, 10-year Davis County bonds on July 12, 2012, directly from the county at par value. The bonds pay semiannual interest on May 1 and November 1. On December 1, 2012, Afton Co. sold $6,000 of the Davis County bonds at 98 plus $20 accrued interest, less a $100 brokerage commission.

Provide the journal entries for:

a. the purchase of the bonds on July 12, plus 72 days of accrued interest.

b. semiannual interest on November 1.

c. sale of the bonds on December 1.

d. adjusting entry for accrued interest of $120 on December 31, 2012.

OBJ. 2

✔ Sept. 5, Loss on
sale of investments,
$720

### EX 13-4   Entries for investment in bonds, interest, and sale of bonds

The following bond investment transactions were completed during 2012 by Mission Company:

Jan.  21.  Purchased 50, $1,000 par value government bonds at 100 plus 20 days' accrued interest. The bonds pay 4.5% annual interest on June 30 and January 1.

June 30.  Received semiannual interest on bond investment.

Sept.  5.  Sold 24, $1,000 par value bonds at 97 plus $201 accrued interest.

a. Journalize the entries for these transactions.

b. Provide the December 31, 2012, adjusting journal entry for semiannual interest earned from the bond.

OBJ. 2

### EX 13-5   Interest on bond investments

On May 1, 2012, Todd Company purchased $66,000 of 5%, 12-year Lincoln Company bonds at par plus two months' accrued interest. The bonds pay interest on March 1 and September 1. On October 1, 2012, Todd Company sold $24,000 of the Lincoln Company bonds acquired on May 1, plus one month's accrued interest. On December 31, 2012, four months' interest was accrued for the remaining bonds.

Determine the interest earned by Todd Company on Lincoln Company bonds for 2012.

OBJ. 3

✔ c. Gain on sale
of investments,
$5,625

### EX 13-6   Entries for investment in stock, receipt of dividends, and sale of shares

On February 17, Walters Corporation acquired 4,000 shares of the 100,000 outstanding shares of Lycore Co. common stock at $22.50 plus commission charges of $200. On July 11, a cash dividend of $0.80 per share was received. On December 4, 1,000 shares were sold at $28.30, less commission charges of $125.

Record the entries for (a) the purchase of stock, (b) the receipt of dividends, and (c) the sale of 1,000 shares.

OBJ. 3

✔ June 3, Loss on
sale of investments,
$4,097

**EX 13-7**   **Entries for investment in stock, receipt of dividends, and sale of shares**

The following equity investment-related transactions were completed by Kindle Company in 2012:

Jan. 12.   Purchased 1,400 shares of Inskip Company for a price of $48.90 per share plus a brokerage commission of $112.

Apr. 10.   Received a quarterly dividend of $0.22 per share on the Inskip Company investment.

June 3.   Sold 900 shares for a price of $44.50 per share less a brokerage commission of $65.

Journalize the entries for these transactions.

OBJ. 3

✔ Nov. 14, Dividend
revenue, $60

**EX 13-8**   **Entries for stock investments, dividends, and sale of stock**

Archway Tech Corp. manufactures surveying equipment. Journalize the entries to record the following selected equity investment transactions completed by Archway during 2012:

Feb.   2.   Purchased for cash 800 shares of Parr Inc. stock for $28 per share plus a $120 brokerage commission.

Apr.  16.   Received dividends of $0.12 per share on Parr Inc. stock.

June 17.   Purchased 600 shares of Parr Inc. stock for $33 per share plus a $150 brokerage commission.

Aug. 19.   Sold 1,000 shares of Parr Inc. stock for $41 per share less a $200 brokerage commission. Archway assumes that the first investments purchased are the first investments sold.

Nov. 14.   Received dividends of $0.15 per share on Parr Inc. stock.

OBJ. 3

**EX 13-9**   **Entries for stock investments, dividends, and sale of stock**

Hombolt Industries, Inc. buys and sells investments as part of its ongoing cash management. The following investment transactions were completed during the year:

Feb.   6.   Acquired 500 shares of Randolph Co. stock for $112 per share plus a $125 brokerage commission.

Apr.  21.   Acquired 1,400 shares of Sterling Co. stock for $28 per share plus a $98 commission.

Aug. 15.   Sold 200 shares of Randolph Co. stock for $124 per share less an $80 brokerage commission.

Sept.  8.   Sold 500 shares of Sterling Co. stock for $22.50 per share less a $70 brokerage commission.

Oct.  31.   Received dividends of $0.26 per share on Randolph Co. stock.

Journalize the entries for these transactions.

OBJ. 3

**EX 13-10**   **Equity method for stock investment**

At a total cost of $660,000, Penn Corporation acquired 60,000 shares of Teller Corp. common stock as a long-term investment. Penn Corporation uses the equity method of accounting for this investment. Teller Corp. has 200,000 shares of common stock outstanding, including the shares acquired by Penn Corporation.

Journalize the entries by Penn Corporation to record the following information:

a.   Teller Corp. reports net income of $940,000 for the current period.

b.   A cash dividend of $2.50 per common share is paid by Teller Corp. during the current period.

c.   Why is the equity method appropriate for the Teller Corp. investment?

### EX 13-11 Equity method for stock investment

On January 15, 2012, Outdoor Life Inc. purchased 94,500 shares of Escape Tours Inc. directly from one of the founders for a price of $38 per share. Escape Tours has 225,000 shares outstanding, including the Outdoor Life shares. On July 2, 2012, Escape Tours paid $230,000 in total dividends to its shareholders. On December 31, 2012, Escape Tours reported a net income of $695,000 for the year. Outdoor Life uses the equity method in accounting for its investment in Escape Tours.

a. Provide the Outdoor Life Inc. journal entries for the transactions involving its investment in Escape Tours Inc. during 2012.

b. Determine the December 31, 2012, balance of Investment in Escape Tours Inc. Stock.

### EX 13-12 Equity method for stock investment with loss

On January 10, 2012, Badger Co. purchased 30% of the outstanding stock of Crest Co. for $123,000. Crest paid total dividends to all shareholders of $15,000 on July 15. Crest had a net loss of $25,000 for 2012.

a. Journalize Badger's purchase of the stock, receipt of dividends, and adjusting entry for the equity loss in Crest Co. stock.

b. Compute the balance of Investment in Crest Co. Stock for December 31, 2012.

c. How does valuing an investment under the equity method differ from valuing an investment at fair value?

### EX 13-13 Equity method for stock investment

Jarvis Company's balance sheet disclosed its long-term investment in Moss Company under the equity method for comparative years as follows:

|  | Dec. 31, 2013 | Dec. 31, 2012 |
|---|---|---|
| Investment in Moss Company stock (in millions) | $105 | $116 |

In addition, the 2013 Jarvis Company income statement disclosed equity earnings in the Moss Company investment as $15 million. Jarvis Company neither purchased nor sold Moss Company stock during 2013. The fair value of the Moss Company stock investment on December 31, 2013, was $125 million.

Explain the change in the Investment in Moss Company Stock balance sheet account from December 31, 2012, to December 31, 2013.

### EX 13-14 Missing statement items, trading investments

KVS Capital, Inc., makes investments in trading securities. Selected income statement items for the years ended December 31, 2012 and 2013, plus selected items from comparative balance sheets, are as follows:

**KVS Capital, Inc.**
**Selected Income Statement Items**
**For the Years Ended December 31, 2012 and 2013**

|  | 2012 | 2013 |
|---|---|---|
| Operating income | a. | e. |
| Unrealized gain (loss) | b. | $(3,000) |
| Net income | c. | 19,000 |

**KVS Capital, Inc.**
**Selected Balance Sheet Items**
**December 31, 2011, 2012, and 2013**

| | Dec. 31, 2011 | Dec. 31, 2012 | Dec. 31, 2013 |
|---|---|---|---|
| Trading investments, at cost | $123,000 | $146,000 | $172,000 |
| Valuation allowance for trading investments | (4,000) | 9,000 | g. |
| Trading investments, at fair value | d. | f. | h. |
| Retained earnings | $156,000 | $192,000 | i. |

There were no dividends.

Determine the missing lettered items.

---

**OBJ. 3, 4**

**EX 13-15  Fair value journal entries, trading investments**

The investments of Giving Tree, Inc., include a single investment: 9,000 shares of Cardio Solutions, Inc. common stock purchased on March 3, 2012, for $22 per share including brokerage commission. These shares were classified as trading securities. As of the December 31, 2012, balance sheet date, the share price increased to $29 per share.

a.  Journalize the entries to acquire the investment on March 3, and record the adjustment to fair value on December 31, 2012.

b.  How is the unrealized gain or loss for trading investments disclosed on the financial statements?

---

**OBJ. 3, 4**

**EX 13-16  Fair value journal entries, trading investments**

Acorn Bancorp Inc. purchased a portfolio of trading securities during 2012. The cost and fair value of this portfolio on December 31, 2012, was as follows:

| Name | Number of Shares | Total Cost | Total Fair Value |
|---|---|---|---|
| Apex, Inc. | 1,200 | $16,000 | $17,500 |
| Evans Company | 700 | 23,000 | 19,000 |
| Quaker Company | 300 | 9,000 | 8,600 |
| Total | | $48,000 | $45,100 |

On April 3, 2013, Acorn Bancorp Inc. purchased 500 shares of Luke, Inc., at $36 per share plus a $100 brokerage fee.

Provide the journal entries to record the following:

a.  The adjustment of the trading security portfolio to fair value on December 31, 2012.

b.  The April 3, 2013, purchase of Luke, Inc., stock.

---

**OBJ. 3, 4**

✔ **a. Dec. 31, 2012,**
**Unrealized gain on**
**trading investments,**
**$12,600**

**EX 13-17  Fair value journal entries, trading investments**

First Guarantee Financial, Inc., purchased the following trading securities during 2012, its first year of operations:

| Name | Number of Shares | Cost |
|---|---|---|
| B&T Transportation, Inc. | 3,400 | $ 74,200 |
| Citrus Foods, Inc. | 1,500 | 26,500 |
| Stuart Housewares, Inc. | 800 | 45,200 |
| Total | | $145,900 |

The market price per share for the trading security portfolio on December 31, 2012, was as follows:

| | Market Price per Share Dec. 31, 2012 |
|---|---|
| B&T Transportation, Inc. | $26 |
| Citrus Foods, Inc. | 19 |
| Stuart Housewares, Inc. | 52 |

a. Provide the journal entry to adjust the trading security portfolio to fair value on December 31, 2012.

b. Assume the market prices of the portfolio were the same on December 31, 2013, as they were on December 31, 2012. What would be the journal entry to adjust the portfolio to fair value?

OBJ. 4

### EX 13-18   Financial statement disclosure, trading investments

The income statement for Tri-Con, Inc., for the year ended December 31, 2012, was as follows:

**Tri-Con, Inc.**
**Income Statement (selected items)**
**For the Year Ended December 31, 2012**

| | |
|---|---|
| Income from operations | $148,000 |
| Gain on sale of investments | 12,000 |
| Less unrealized loss on trading investments | 34,000 |
| Net income | $126,000 |

The balance sheet dated December 31, 2011, showed a Retained Earnings balance of $614,000. During 2012, the company purchased trading investments for the first time at a cost of $166,000. In addition, trading investments with a cost of $45,000 were sold at a gain during 2012. The company paid $35,000 in dividends during 2012.

a. Determine the December 31, 2012, Retained Earnings balance.

b. Provide the December 31, 2012, balance sheet disclosure for Trading Investments.

OBJ. 4
✔ f. ($9,000)

### EX 13-19   Missing statement items, available-for-sale securities

Oceanic Airways makes investments in available-for-sale securities. Selected income statement items for the years ended December 31, 2012 and 2013, plus selected items from comparative balance sheets, are as follows:

**Oceanic Airways**
**Selected Income Statement Items**
**For the Years Ended December 31, 2012 and 2013**

| | 2012 | 2013 |
|---|---|---|
| Operating income | a. | g. |
| Gain (loss) from sale of investments | $4,000 | $ (8,000) |
| Net income (loss) | b. | (15,000) |

**Oceanic Airways**
**Selected Balance Sheet Items**
**December 31, 2011, 2012, and 2013**

| | Dec. 31, 2011 | Dec. 31, 2012 | Dec. 31, 2013 |
|---|---|---|---|
| **Assets** | | | |
| Available-for-sale investments, at cost | $ 78,000 | $ 68,000 | $95,000 |
| Valuation allowance for available-for-sale investments | 6,000 | (9,000) | h. |
| Available-for-sale investments, at fair value | c. | e. | i. |
| **Stockholders' Equity** | | | |
| Unrealized gain (loss) on available-for- sale investments | d. | f. | (11,000) |
| Retained earnings | $151,000 | $201,000 | j. |

There were no dividends.
Determine the missing lettered items.

OBJ. 3, 4

### EX 13-20   Fair value journal entries, available-for-sale investments

The investments of Macon, Inc., include a single investment: 8,000 shares of Pacific Wave, Inc. common stock purchased on August 10, 2012, for $8 per share including brokerage commission. These shares were classified as available-for-sale securities. As of the December 31, 2012, balance sheet date, the share price declined to $6 per share.

a.  Journalize the entries to acquire the investment on August 10, and record the adjustment to fair value on December 31, 2012.

b.  How is the unrealized gain or loss for available-for-sale investments disclosed on the financial statements?

---

OBJ. 3, 4

### EX 13-21 Fair value journal entries, available-for-sale investments

Arnott Inc. purchased a portfolio of available-for-sale securities in 2012, its first year of operations. The cost and fair value of this portfolio on December 31, 2012, was as follows:

| Name | Number of Shares | Total Cost | Total Fair Value |
|---|---|---|---|
| Jasper, Inc. | 600 | $ 9,000 | $10,500 |
| Parker Corp. | 900 | 21,000 | 23,400 |
| Smithfield Corp. | 1,800 | 32,500 | 31,900 |
| Total | | $62,500 | $65,800 |

On May 10, 2013, Arnott purchased 900 shares of Violet Inc. at $42 per share plus a $125 brokerage fee.

a.  Provide the journal entries to record the following:

1.  The adjustment of the available-for-sale security portfolio to fair value on December 31, 2012.

2.  The May 10, 2013, purchase of Violet Inc. stock.

b.  How are unrealized gains and losses treated differently for available-for-sale securities than for trading securities?

---

OBJ. 3, 4

### EX 13-22 Fair value journal entries, available-for-sale investments

Cumberland, Inc., purchased the following available-for-sale securities during 2012, its first year of operations:

| Name | Number of Shares | Cost |
|---|---|---|
| Abbotford Electronics, Inc. | 1,500 | $ 42,500 |
| Ryan Co. | 400 | 28,200 |
| Sharon Co. | 2,200 | 66,100 |
| Total | | $136,800 |

The market price per share for the available-for-sale security portfolio on December 31, 2012, was as follows:

| | Market Price per Share Dec. 31, 2012 |
|---|---|
| Abbotford Electronics, Inc. | $22 |
| Ryan Co. | 65 |
| Sharon Co. | 32 |

a.  Provide the journal entry to adjust the available-for-sale security portfolio to fair value on December 31, 2012.

b.  Describe the income statement impact from the December 31, 2012, journal entry.

---

OBJ. 4

### EX 13-23 Balance sheet presentation of available-for-sale investments

During 2012, its first year of operations, Newton Company purchased two available-for-sale investments as follows:

| Security | Shares Purchased | Cost |
|---|---|---|
| Starlight Products, Inc. | 700 | $31,000 |
| Reynolds Co. | 1,900 | 41,000 |

Assume that as of December 31, 2012, the Starlight Products, Inc., stock had a market value of $55 per share and the Reynolds Co. stock had a market value of $18 per share. Newton Company had net income of $250,000, and paid no dividends for the year ending December 31, 2012.

a. Prepare the Current Assets section of the balance sheet presentation for the available-for-sale investments.

b. Prepare the Stockholders' Equity section of the balance sheet to reflect the earnings and unrealized gain (loss) for the available-for-sale investments.

OBJ. 4

### EX 13-24 Balance sheet presentation of available-for-sale investments

During 2012, Norcross Corporation held a portfolio of available-for-sale securities having a cost of $175,000. There were no purchases or sales of investments during the year. The market values at the beginning and end of the year were $215,000 and $150,000, respectively. The net income for 2012 was $110,000, and no dividends were paid during the year. The Stockholders' Equity section of the balance sheet was as follows on December 31, 2011:

**Norcross Corporation**
**Stockholders' Equity**
**December 31, 2011**

| | |
|---|---:|
| Common stock | $ 50,000 |
| Paid-in capital in excess of par value | 350,000 |
| Retained earnings | 265,000 |
| Unrealized gain (loss) on available-for- sale investments | 40,000 |
| Total | $705,000 |

Prepare the Stockholders' Equity section of the balance sheet for December 31, 2012.

### Appendix
### EX 13-25 Comprehensive income

On April 23, 2012, Frost Co. purchased 1,500 shares of Apex, Inc., for $88 per share including the brokerage commission. The Apex investment was classified as an available-for-sale security. On December 31, 2012, the fair value of Apex, Inc., was $101 per share. The net income of Frost Co. was $60,000 for 2012.

Compute the comprehensive income for Frost Co. for the year ended December 31, 2012.

### Appendix
### EX 13-26 Comprehensive income

On December 31, 2011, Memphis Co. had the following available-for-sale investment disclosure within the Current Assets section of the balance sheet:

| | |
|---|---:|
| Available-for-sale investments (at cost) | $105,000 |
| Plus valuation allowance for available-for-sale investments | 15,000 |
| Available-for-sale investments (at fair value) | $120,000 |

There were no purchases or sales of available-for-sale investments during 2012. On December 31, 2012, the fair value of the available-for-sale investment portfolio was $94,000. The net income of Memphis Co. was $150,000 for 2012.

Compute the comprehensive income for Memphis Co. for the year ended December 31, 2012.

OBJ. 6

### EX 13-27 Dividend yield

**FAI**

At the market close on February 19, 2010, McDonald's Corporation had a closing stock price of $64.74. In addition, McDonald's Corporation had a dividend per share of $2.05 over the previous year.

Determine McDonald's Corporation's dividend yield. (Round to one decimal place.)

OBJ. 6

✔ a. Dec. 31, 2008, 2.37%

### EX 13-28 Dividend yield

The market price for Microsoft Corporation closed at $19.40 and $30.48 on December 31, 2008, and 2009, respectively. The dividends per share were $0.46 for 2008 and $0.52 for 2009.

a. Determine the dividend yield for Microsoft on December 31, 2008, and 2009. (Round percentages to two decimal places.)

b. Interpret these measures.

OBJ. 6

### EX 13-29 Dividend yield

eBay Inc. developed a Web-based marketplace at **http://www.ebay.com**, in which individuals can buy and sell a variety of items. eBay also acquired PayPal, an online payments system that allows businesses and individuals to send and receive online payments securely. In a recent annual report, eBay published the following dividend policy:

*We have never paid cash dividends on our stock and currently anticipate that we will continue to retain any future earnings for the foreseeable future.*

Given eBay's dividend policy, why would an investor be attracted to its stock?

## Problems Series A

OBJ. 2, 4

### PR 13-1A Debt investment transactions, available-for-sale valuation

Fleet Inc. is an athletic footware company that began operations on January 1, 2012. The following transactions relate to debt investments acquired by Fleet Inc., which has a fiscal year ending on December 31:

2012

Mar. 1. Purchased $36,000 of Madison Co. 5%, 10-year bonds at face value plus accrued interest of $150. The bonds pay interest semiannually on February 1 and August 1.

Apr. 16. Purchased $45,000 of Westville 4%, 15-year bonds at face value plus accrued interest of $75. The bonds pay interest semiannually on April 1 and October 1.

Aug. 1. Received semiannual interest on the Madison Co. bonds.

Sept. 1. Sold $12,000 of Madison Co. bonds at 98 plus accrued interest of $50.

Oct. 1. Received semiannual interest on Westville bonds.

Dec. 31. Accrued $500 interest on Madison Co. bonds.

31. Accrued $450 interest on Westville bonds.

2013

Feb. 1. Received semiannual interest on the Madison Co. bonds.

Apr. 1. Received semiannual interest on the Westville bonds.

**Instructions**

1. Journalize the entries to record these transactions.

2. If the bond portfolio was classified as available-for-sale, what impact would this have on financial statement disclosure?

OBJ. 3, 4

### PR 13-2A Stock investment transactions, trading securities

Heritage Insurance Co. is a regional insurance company that began operations on January 1, 2012. The following transactions relate to trading securities acquired by Heritage Insurance Co., which has a fiscal year ending on December 31:

2012

Feb. 21. Purchased 4,000 shares of Astor Inc. as a trading security at $30 per share plus a brokerage commission of $600.

Mar. 9. Purchased 800 shares of Millsaps Inc. as a trading security at $41 per share plus a brokerage commission of $160.

May 3. Sold 600 shares of Astor Inc. for $27.50 per share less an $80 brokerage commission.

June 8. Received an annual dividend of $0.22 per share on Astor Inc. stock.

Dec. 31. The portfolio of trading securities was adjusted to fair values of $32 and $30 per share for Astor Inc. and Millsaps Inc., respectively.

2013

May 21. Purchased 2,000 shares of Essex Inc. as a trading security at $21 per share plus a $200 brokerage commission.

June 11. Received an annual dividend of $0.25 per share on Astor Inc. stock.

Aug. 16. Sold 400 shares of Essex Inc. for $25 per share less an $80 brokerage commission.

Dec. 31. The portfolio of trading securities had a cost of $169,230 and fair value of $170,560, requiring a debit balance in Valuation Allowance for Trading Investments of $1,330 ($170,560 − $169,230). Thus, the credit balance from December 31, 2012, is to be adjusted to the new balance.

**Instructions**

1. Journalize the entries to record these transactions.

2. Prepare the investment-related current asset balance sheet disclosures for Heritage Insurance Co. on December 31, 2013.

3. How are unrealized gains or losses on trading investments disclosed on the financial statements of Heritage Insurance Co.?

---

OBJ. 3, 4

**PR 13-3A    Stock investment transactions, equity method and available-for-sale securities**

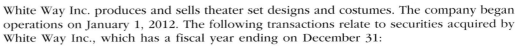

White Way Inc. produces and sells theater set designs and costumes. The company began operations on January 1, 2012. The following transactions relate to securities acquired by White Way Inc., which has a fiscal year ending on December 31:

2012

Jan. 10. Purchased 8,000 shares of Lott Inc. as an available-for-sale security at $14 per share, including the brokerage commission.

Mar. 10. Received the regular cash dividend of $0.12 per share on Lott Inc. stock.

Sept. 9. Lott Inc. stock was split two for one. The regular cash dividend of $0.06 per share was received on the stock after the stock split.

Oct. 16. Sold 2,000 shares of Lott Inc. stock at $5 per share, less a brokerage commission of $100.

Dec. 31. Lott Inc. is classified as an available-for-sale investment and is adjusted to a fair value of $8.50 per share. Use the valuation allowance for available-for-sale investments account in making the adjustment.

2013

Jan. 5. Purchased an influential interest in Stage Hand Inc. for $235,000 by purchasing 50,000 shares directly from the estate of the founder of Stage Hand Inc. There are 200,000 shares of Stage Hand Inc. stock outstanding.

Mar. 9. Received the regular cash divided of $0.07 per share on Lott Inc. stock.

Sept. 10. Received the regular cash dividend of $0.07 per share plus an extra dividend of $0.03 per share on Lott Inc. stock.

Dec. 31. Received $21,500 of cash dividends on Stage Hand Inc. stock. Stage Hand Inc. reported net income of $136,000 in 2013. White Way Inc. uses the equity method of accounting for its investment in Stage Hand Inc.

31. Lott Inc. is classified as an available-for-sale investment and is adjusted to a fair value of $8 per share. Use the valuation allowance for available-for-sale investments account in making the adjustment for the decrease in fair value from $8.50 to $8.00 per share.

**Instructions**

1. Journalize the entries to record these transactions.

2. Prepare the investment-related asset and stockholders' equity balance sheet disclosures for White Way Inc. on December 31, 2013, assuming the Retained Earnings balance on December 31, 2013, is $310,000.

OBJ. 2, 3, 4

✔ h. $(4,500)

### PR 13-4A Investment reporting

Luminous Publishing, Inc., is a book publisher. The comparative unclassified balance sheets for December 31, 2013 and 2012 are provided below. Selected missing balances are shown by letters.

**Luminous Publishing, Inc.**
**Balance Sheet**
**December 31, 2013 and 2012**

|  | Dec. 31, 2013 | Dec. 31, 2012 |
|---|---|---|
| Cash | $178,000 | $157,000 |
| Accounts receivable (net) | 106,000 | 98,000 |
| Available-for-sale investments (at cost)—Note 1 | a. | 53,400 |
| Less valuation allowance for available-for-sale investments | b. | 3,900 |
| Available-for-sale investments (fair value) | $  c. | $ 49,500 |
| Interest receivable | $  d. | — |
| Investment in Quest Co. stock—Note 2 | e. | $ 55,000 |
| Office equipment (net) | 90,000 | 95,000 |
| Total assets | $   f. | $454,500 |
| Accounts payable | $ 56,900 | $ 51,400 |
| Common stock | 50,000 | 50,000 |
| Excess of issue price over par | 160,000 | 160,000 |
| Retained earnings | g. | 197,000 |
| Less unrealized gain (loss) on available-for-sale investments | h. | 3,900 |
| Total liabilities and stockholders' equity | $   i. | $454,500 |

Note 1. Investments are classified as available for sale. The investments at cost and fair value on December 31, 2012, are as follows:

|  | No. of Shares | Cost per Share | Total Cost | Total Fair Value |
|---|---|---|---|---|
| Barns Co. Stock | 1,600 | $12 | $19,200 | $17,500 |
| Dynasty Co. Stock | 900 | 38 | 34,200 | 32,000 |
|  |  |  | $53,400 | $49,500 |

Note 2. The investment in Quest Co. stock is an equity method investment representing 32% of the outstanding shares of Quest Co.

The following selected investment transactions occurred during 2013:

May 5. Purchased 2,200 shares of Gypsy, Inc., at $22 per share including brokerage commission. Gypsy, Inc., is classified as an available-for-sale security.

Sept. 1. Purchased $30,000 of Norton Co. 5%, 10-year bonds at 100. The bonds are classified as available for sale. The bonds pay interest on September 1 and March 1.

9. Dividends of $9,000 are received on the Quest Co. investment.

Dec. 31.  Quest Co. reported a total net income of $80,000 for 2013. Luminous record-ed equity earnings for its share of Quest Co. net income.

31.  Accrued four months of interest on the Norton bonds.

31.  Adjusted the available-for-sale investment portfolio to fair value using the following fair value per-share amounts:

| Available-for-Sale Investments | Fair Value |
| --- | --- |
| Barns Co. stock | $11 per share |
| Dynasty Co. stock | $33 per share |
| Gypsy Inc. stock | $23 per share |
| Norton Co. bonds | 98 per $100 of face value |

Dec. 31.  Closed the Luminous Publishing, Inc. net income of $114,000 for 2013. Lumi-nous paid no dividends during 2013.

**Instructions**
Determine the missing letters in the unclassified balance sheet. Provide appropriate sup-porting calculations.

## Problems Series B

OBJ. 2, 4

**PR 13-1B    Debt investment transactions, available-for-sale valuation**

Savers Mart Inc. is a general merchandise retail company that began operations on January 1, 2012. The following transactions relate to debt investments acquired by Savers Mart Inc., which has a fiscal year ending on December 31:

2012

May   1.  Purchased $80,000 of Northridge City 4.5%, 10-year bonds at face value plus accrued interest of $600. The bonds pay interest semiannually on March 1 and September 1.

June 16.  Purchased $38,000 of Hancock Co. 6%, 12-year bonds at face value plus ac-crued interest of $95. The bonds pay interest semiannually on June 1 and December 1.

Sept.  1.  Received semiannual interest on the Northridge City bonds.

Oct.   1.  Sold $24,000 of Northridge City bonds at 102 plus accrued interest of $90.

Dec.   1.  Received semiannual interest on Hancock Co. bonds.

31.  Accrued $840 interest on Northridge City bonds.

31.  Accrued $190 interest on Hancock Co. bonds.

2013

Mar.   1.  Received semiannual interest on the Northridge City bonds.

June   1.  Received semiannual interest on the Hancock Co. bonds.

**Instructions**
1.  Journalize the entries to record these transactions.
2.  If the bond portfolio was classified as available-for-sale, what impact would this have on financial statement disclosure?

OBJ. 3, 4

**PR 13-2B    Stock investment transactions, trading securities**

Ophir Investments Inc. is a regional investment company that began operations on Janu-ary 1, 2012. The following transactions relate to trading securities acquired by Ophir Investments Inc., which has a fiscal year ending on December 31:

2012

Feb.   3.  Purchased 2,000 shares of Mapco Inc. as a trading security at $42 per share plus a brokerage commission of $500.

Mar. 23. Purchased 1,400 shares of Swift Inc. as a trading security at $23 per share plus a brokerage commission of $210.

May 19. Sold 500 shares of Mapco Inc. for $46 per share less an $80 brokerage commission.

June 12. Received an annual dividend of $0.14 per share on Mapco stock.

Dec. 31. The portfolio of trading securities was adjusted to fair values of $40 and $29 per share for Mapco Inc. and Swift Inc., respectively.

2013

Apr. 9. Purchased 900 shares of Corvair Inc. as a trading security at $62 per share plus a $90 brokerage commission.

June 15. Received an annual dividend of $0.16 per share on Mapco Inc. stock.

Aug. 30. Sold 200 shares of Corvair Inc. for $51 per share less a $60 brokerage commission.

Dec. 31. The portfolio of trading securities had a cost of $139,255 and fair value of $133,470, requiring a credit balance in Valuation Allowance for Trading Investments of $5,785 ($139,255 − $133,470). Thus, the debit balance from December 31, 2012, is to be adjusted to the new balance.

### Instructions

1. Journalize the entries to record these transactions.

2. Prepare the investment-related current asset balance sheet disclosures for Ophir Investments Inc. on December 31, 2013.

3. How are unrealized gains or losses on trading investments disclosed on the financial statements of Ophir Investments Inc.?

OBJ. 3, 4

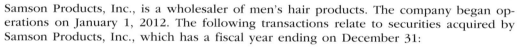

**PR 13-3B    Stock investment transactions, equity method and available-for-sale securities**

Samson Products, Inc., is a wholesaler of men's hair products. The company began operations on January 1, 2012. The following transactions relate to securities acquired by Samson Products, Inc., which has a fiscal year ending on December 31:

2012

Jan. 3. Purchased 5,000 shares of Merlin Inc. as an available-for-sale investment at $22 per share, including the brokerage commission.

July 8. Merlin Inc. stock was split two for one. The regular cash dividend of $0.40 per share was received on the stock after the stock split.

Oct. 19. Sold 1,200 shares of Merlin Inc. stock at $13 per share, less a brokerage commission of $50.

Dec. 12. Received the regular cash dividend of $0.40 per share.

31. Merlin Inc. is classified as an available-for-sale investment and is adjusted to a fair value of $9.50 per share. Use the valuation allowance for available-for-sale investments account in making the adjustment.

2013

Jan. 5. Purchased an influential interest in Juarez Co. for $540,000 by purchasing 60,000 shares directly from the estate of the founder of Juarez. There are 150,000 shares of Juarez Co. stock outstanding.

July 9. Received the regular cash divided of $0.50 per share on Merlin Inc. stock.

Dec. 8. Received the regular cash dividend of $0.50 per share plus an extra dividend of $0.05 per share on Merlin Inc. stock.

Dec. 31. Received $21,000 of cash dividends on Juarez Co. stock. Juarez Co. reported net income of $96,000 in 2013. Samson Products uses the equity method of accounting for its investment in Juarez Co.

31. Merlin Inc. is classified as an available-for-sale investment and is adjusted to a fair value of $10 per share. Use the valuation allowance for available-for-sale investments account in making the adjustment for the increase in fair value from $9.50 to $10 per share.

**Instructions**

1. Journalize the entries to record the preceding transactions.

2. Prepare the investment-related asset and stockholders' equity balance sheet disclosures for Samson Products, Inc., on December 31, 2013, assuming the Retained Earnings balance on December 31, 2013, is $395,000.

OBJ. 2, 3, 4

✔ b. $250

**PR 13-4B   Investment reporting**

Guardian Devices, Inc., manufactures and sells commercial and residential security equipment. The comparative unclassified balance sheets for December 31, 2013 and 2012 are provided below. Selected missing balances are shown by letters.

**Guardian Devices, Inc.**
**Balance Sheet**
**December 31, 2013 and 2012**

|  | Dec. 31, 2013 | Dec. 31, 2012 |
|---|---|---|
| Cash | $104,000 | $ 98,000 |
| Accounts receivable (net) | 71,000 | 67,500 |
| Available-for-sale investments (at cost)—Note 1 | a. | 36,000 |
| Plus valuation allowance for available-for-sale investments | b. | 6,000 |
| Available-for-sale investments (fair value) | $    c. | $ 42,000 |
| Interest receivable | $    d. | — |
| Investment in Omaha Co. stock—Note 2 | e. | $ 62,000 |
| Office equipment (net) | 60,000 | 65,000 |
| Total assets | $    f. | $334,500 |
| Accounts payable | $ 56,900 | $ 45,100 |
| Common stock | 50,000 | 50,000 |
| Excess of issue price over par | 160,000 | 160,000 |
| Retained earnings | g. | 73,400 |
| Plus unrealized gain (loss) on available-for-sale investments | h. | 6,000 |
| Total liabilities and stockholders' equity | $    i. | $334,500 |

Note 1. Investments are classified as available for sale. The investments at cost and fair value on December 31, 2012, are as follows:

|  | No. of Shares | Cost per Share | Total Cost | Total Fair Value |
|---|---|---|---|---|
| Tyndale Inc. Stock | 600 | $24 | $14,400 | $17,000 |
| UR-Smart Inc. Stock | 1,200 | 18 | 21,600 | 25,000 |
|  |  |  | $36,000 | $42,000 |

Note 2. The Investment in Omaha Co. stock is an equity method investment representing 32% of the outstanding shares of Omaha Co.

The following selected investment transactions occurred during 2013:

Apr. 21. Purchased 500 shares of Walton Winery, Inc., at $25 including brokerage commission. Walton Winery is classified as an available-for-sale security.

Sept. 9. Dividends of $7,500 are received on the Omaha Co. investment.

Oct. 1. Purchased $15,000 of Yokohama Co. 6%, 10-year bonds at 100. The bonds are classified as available for sale. The bonds pay interest on October 1 and April 1.

Dec. 31. Omaha Co. reported a total net income of $50,000 for 2013. Guardian recorded equity earnings for its share of Omaha Co. net income.

Dec. 31. Accrued interest for three months on Yokohama bonds purchased on October 1.

31. Adjusted the available-for-sale investment portfolio to fair value using the following fair value per-share amounts:

| Available-for-Sale Investments | Fair Value |
| --- | --- |
| Tyndale Inc. stock | $26 per share |
| UR-Smart, Inc., stock | $15 per share |
| Walton Winery, Inc., stock | $30 per share |
| Yokohama Co. bonds | 101 per $100 of face value |

31. Closed the Guardian Devices, Inc., net income of $28,925 for 2013. Guardian paid no dividends during 2013.

**Instructions**

Determine the missing letters in the unclassified balance sheet. Provide appropriate supporting calculations.

## Comprehensive Problem 4

Selected transactions completed by Everyday Products Inc. during the fiscal year ending December 31, 2012, were as follows:

a.  Issued 12,500 shares of $25 par common stock at $32, receiving cash.

b.  Issued 2,000 shares of $100 par preferred 5% stock at $105, receiving cash.

c.  Issued $400,000 of 10-year, 6% bonds at 105, with interest payable semiannually.

d.  Declared a quarterly dividend of $0.45 per share on common stock and $1.25 per share on preferred stock. On the date of record, 85,000 shares of common stock were outstanding, no treasury shares were held, and 17,000 shares of preferred stock were outstanding.

e.  Paid the cash dividends declared in (d).

f.  Purchased 5,500 shares of Kress Corp. at $22 per share, plus a $275 brokerage commission. The investment is classified as an available-for-sale investment.

g.  Purchased 6,500 shares of treasury common stock at $35 per share.

h.  Purchased 36,000 shares of Lifecare Co. stock directly from the founders for $18 per share. Lifecare has 112,500 shares issued and outstanding. Everyday Products Inc. treated the investment as an equity method investment.

i.  Declared a 2% stock dividend on common stock and a $1.25 quarterly cash dividend per share on preferred stock. On the date of declaration, the market value of the common stock was $40 per share. On the date of record, 85,000 shares of common stock had been issued, 6,500 shares of treasury common stock were held, and 17,000 shares of preferred stock had been issued.

j.  Issued the stock certificates for the stock dividends declared in (h) and paid the cash dividends to the preferred stockholders.

k.  Received $24,500 dividend from Lifecare Co. investment in (h).

l.  Purchased $62,000 of Nordic Wear Inc. 10-year, 6% bonds, directly from the issuing company at par value, plus accrued interest of $550. The bonds are classifed as a held-to-maturity long-term investment.

m.  Sold, at $42 per share, 2,600 shares of treasury common stock purchased in (g).

n.  Received a dividend of $0.65 per share from the Kress Corp. investment in (f).

o.  Sold 500 shares of Kress Corp. at $26.50, including commission.

p.  Recorded the payment of semiannual interest on the bonds issued in (c) and the amortization of the premium for six months. The amortization was determined using the straight-line method.

q.  Accrued interest for three months on the Nordic Wear Inc. bonds purchased in (l).

r.  Lifecare Co. recorded total earnings of $205,000. Everyday Products recorded equity earnings for its share of Lifecare Co. net income.

s.  The fair value for Kress Corp. stock was $18.50 per share on December 31, 2012. The investment is adjusted to fair value using a valuation allowance account. Assume Valuation Allowance for Available-for-Sale Investments had a beginning balance of zero.

### Instructions

1.  Journalize the selected transactions.

2.  After all of the transactions for the year ended December 31, 2012, had been posted [including the transactions recorded in part (1) and all adjusting entries], the data on the following page were taken from the records of Everyday Products Inc.

    a.  Prepare a multiple-step income statement for the year ended December 31, 2012, concluding with earnings per share. In computing earnings per share, assume that the average number of common shares outstanding was 84,000 and preferred dividends were $85,000. (Round earnings per share to the nearest cent.)

    b.  Prepare a retained earnings statement for the year ended December 31, 2012.

    c.  Prepare a balance sheet in report form as of December 31, 2012.

**Income statement data:**

| | |
|---|---:|
| Advertising expense | $ 125,000 |
| Cost of merchandise sold | 3,650,000 |
| Delivery expense | 29,000 |
| Depreciation expense—office buildings and equipment | 26,000 |
| Depreciation expense—store buildings and equipment | 95,000 |
| Dividend revenue | 3,575 |
| Gain on sale of investment | 2,225 |
| Income from Lifecare Co. investment | 65,600 |
| Income tax expense | 128,500 |
| Interest expense | 19,000 |
| Interest revenue | 1,800 |
| Miscellaneous administrative expense | 7,500 |
| Miscellaneous selling expense | 13,750 |
| Office rent expense | 50,000 |
| Office salaries expense | 165,000 |
| Office supplies expense | 10,000 |
| Sales | 5,145,000 |
| Sales commissions | 182,000 |
| Sales salaries expense | 365,000 |
| Store supplies expense | 22,000 |

**Retained earnings and balance sheet data:**

| | |
|---|---:|
| Accounts payable | $ 195,000 |
| Accounts receivable | 543,000 |
| Accumulated depreciation—office buildings and equipment | 1,580,000 |
| Accumulated depreciation—store buildings and equipment | 4,126,000 |
| Allowance for doubtful accounts | 8,150 |
| Available-for-sale investments (at cost) | 110,250 |
| Bonds payable, 6%, due 2022 | 400,000 |
| Cash | 240,000 |
| Common stock, $25 par (400,000 shares authorized; 86,570 shares issued, 82,670 outstanding) | 2,164,250 |
| Dividends: | |
|   Cash dividends for common stock | 155,120 |
|   Cash dividends for preferred stock | 85,000 |
|   Stock dividends for common stock | 62,800 |
| Goodwill | 510,000 |
| Income tax payable | 40,000 |
| Interest receivable | 930 |
| Investment in Lifecare Co. stock (equity method) | 689,100 |
| Investment in Nordic Wear Inc. bonds (long term) | 62,000 |
| Merchandise inventory (December 31, 2012), at lower of cost (FIFO) or market | 780,000 |
| Office buildings and equipment | 4,320,000 |
| Paid-in capital from sale of treasury stock | 18,200 |
| Paid-in capital in excess of par—common stock | 842,000 |
| Paid-in capital in excess of par—preferred stock | 150,000 |
| Preferred 5% stock, $100 par (30,000 shares authorized; 17,000 shares issued) | 1,700,000 |
| Premium on bonds payable | 19,000 |
| Prepaid expenses | 26,500 |
| Retained earnings, January 1, 2012 | 8,708,150 |
| Store buildings and equipment | 12,560,000 |
| Treasury stock (3,900 shares of common stock at cost of $35 per share) | 136,500 |
| Unrealized gain (loss) on available-for-sale investments | (17,750) |
| Valuation allowance for available-for-sale investments | (17,750) |

## Cases & Projects

You can access Cases & Projects online at **www.cengage.com/accounting/reeve**

# Financial Statements for Mornin' Joe

The financial statements of Mornin' Joe are provided in the following pages. Mornin' Joe is a fictitious coffeehouse chain featuring drip and espresso coffee in a café setting. The financial statements of Mornin' Joe are provided to illustrate the complete financial statements of a corporation using the terms, formats, and reporting illustrated throughout this text. In addition, excerpts of the Mornin' Joe financial statements are used to illustrate the financial reporting presentation for the topics discussed in Chapters 6–13. Thus, you can refer to the complete financial statements shown here or the excerpts in Chapters 6–13. A set of real world financial statements by Nike, Inc., is provided in Appendix D.

### Mornin' Joe
### Income Statement
### For the Year Ended December 31, 2012

| | | | |
|---|---|---|---|
| Revenue from sales: | | | |
| Sales | | $5,450,000 | |
| Less: Sales returns and allowances | $ 26,500 | | |
| Sales discounts | 21,400 | 47,900 | |
| Net sales | | | $5,402,100 |
| Cost of merchandise sold | | | 2,160,000 |
| Gross profit | | | $3,242,100 |
| Operating expenses | | | |
| Selling expenses: | | | |
| Wages expense | $825,000 | | |
| Advertising expense | 678,900 | | |
| Depreciation expense—buildings | 124,300 | | |
| Miscellaneous selling expense | 26,500 | | |
| Total selling expenses | | $1,654,700 | |
| Administrative expenses: | | | |
| Office salaries expense | $325,000 | | |
| Rent expense | 425,600 | | |
| Payroll tax expense | 110,000 | | |
| Depreciation expense—office equipment | 68,900 | | |
| Bad debt expense | 14,000 | | |
| Amortization expense | 10,500 | | |
| Total administrative expenses | | 954,000 | |
| Total operating expenses | | | 2,608,700 |
| Income from operations | | | $ 633,400 |
| Other income and expense: | | | |
| Interest revenue | | $ 18,000 | |
| Interest expense | | (136,000) | |
| Loss on disposal of fixed asset | | (23,000) | |
| Unrealized gain on trading investments | | 5,000 | |
| Equity income in AM Coffee | | 57,000 | (79,000) |
| Income before income taxes | | | $ 554,400 |
| Income tax expense | | | 132,800 |
| Net income | | | $ 421,600 |
| | | | |
| Basic earnings per share [($421,600 − $30,000)/44,000 shares issued and outstanding] | | | $ 8.90 |

**Mornin' Joe**
**Balance Sheet**
**December 31, 2012**

### Assets

| | | | |
|---|---|---|---|
| Current assets: | | | |
| Cash and cash equivalents | | $ 235,000 | |
| Trading investments (at cost) | $ 420,000 | | |
| Plus valuation allowance for trading investments | 45,000 | 465,000 | |
| Accounts receivable | $ 305,000 | | |
| Less allowance for doubtful accounts | 12,300 | 292,700 | |
| Merchandise inventory—at lower of cost | | | |
| (first-in, first-out method) or market | | 120,000 | |
| Prepaid insurance | | 24,000 | |
| Total current assets | | | $1,136,700 |
| Investments: | | | |
| Investment in AM Coffee (equity method) | | | 565,000 |
| Property, plant, and equipment: | | | |
| Land | | $1,850,000 | |
| Buildings | $2,650,000 | | |
| Less accumulated depreciation | 420,000 | 2,230,000 | |
| Office equipment | $ 350,000 | | |
| Less accumulated depreciation | 102,000 | 248,000 | |
| Total property, plant, and equipment | | | 4,328,000 |
| Intangible assets: | | | |
| Patents | | | 140,000 |
| Total assets | | | $6,169,700 |

### Liabilities

| | | | |
|---|---|---|---|
| Current liabilities: | | | |
| Accounts payable | | $ 133,000 | |
| Notes payable (current portion) | | 200,000 | |
| Salaries and wages payable | | 42,000 | |
| Payroll taxes payable | | 16,400 | |
| Interest payable | | 40,000 | |
| Total current liabilities | | | $ 431,400 |
| Long-term liabilities: | | | |
| Bonds payable, 8%, due December 31, 2030 | | $ 500,000 | |
| Less unamortized discount | | 16,000 | $ 484,000 |
| Notes payable | | | 1,400,000 |
| Total long-term liabilities | | | $1,884,000 |
| Total liabilities | | | $2,315,400 |

### Stockholders' Equity

| | | | |
|---|---|---|---|
| Paid-in capital: | | | |
| Preferred 10% stock, $50 par (6,000 shares | | | |
| authorized and issued) | | $ 300,000 | |
| Excess of issue price over par | | 50,000 | $ 350,000 |
| Common stock, $20 par (50,000 shares | | | |
| authorized, 45,000 shares issued) | | $ 900,000 | |
| Excess of issue price over par | | 1,450,000 | 2,350,000 |
| Total paid-in capital | | | $2,700,000 |
| Retained earnings | | | 1,200,300 |
| Total | | | $3,900,300 |
| Deduct treasury stock (1,000 shares at cost) | | | 46,000 |
| Total stockholders' equity | | | $3,854,300 |
| Total liabilities and stockholders' equity | | | $6,169,700 |

**Mornin' Joe**
**Retained Earnings Statement**
**For the Year Ended December 31, 2012**

| | | | |
|---|---:|---:|---:|
| Retained earnings, January 1, 2012 | | | $ 852,700 |
| Net income | | $421,600 | |
| Less dividends: | | | |
| Preferred stock | $30,000 | | |
| Common stock | 44,000 | 74,000 | |
| Increase in retained earnings | | | 347,600 |
| Retained earnings, December 31, 2012 | | | $1,200,300 |

**Mornin' Joe**
**Statement of Stockholders' Equity**
**For the Year Ended December 31, 2012**

| | Preferred Stock | Common Stock | Additional Paid-In Capital | Retained Earnings | Treasury Stock | Total |
|---|---:|---:|---:|---:|---:|---:|
| Balance, January 1, 2012 | $300,000 | $800,000 | $1,325,000 | $ 852,700 | $(36,000) | $3,241,700 |
| Net income | | | | 421,600 | | 421,600 |
| Dividends on preferred stock | | | | (30,000) | | (30,000) |
| Dividends on common stock | | | | (44,000) | | (44,000) |
| Issuance of additional common stock ... | | 100,000 | 175,000 | | | 275,000 |
| Purchase of treasury stock | | | | | (10,000) | (10,000) |
| Balance, December 31, 2012 | $300,000 | $900,000 | $1,500,000 | $1,200,300 | $(46,000) | $3,854,300 |

# Mornin' Joe International

Mornin' Joe is planning to expand operations to various places around the world. Financing for this expansion will come from foreign banks. While financial statements prepared under U.S. GAAP may be appropriate for U.S. operations, financial statements prepared for foreign bankers should be prepared using international accounting standards.

The European Union (EU) has developed accounting standards similar in structure to U.S. standards. Its accounting standards board is called the International Accounting Standards Board (IASB). The IASB issues accounting standards that are termed *International Financial Reporting Standards* (IFRS). The intent of the IASB is to create a set of financial standards that can be used by public companies worldwide, not just in the EU.

Currently, the EU countries and over 100 other countries around the world have adopted or are planning to adopt IFRS. As a result, there are efforts under way to converge U.S. GAAP with IFRS so as to harmonize accounting standards around the world.

The following pages illustrate the financial statements of Mornin' Joe International using IFRS. This illustration highlights reporting and terminology differences between IFRS and U.S. GAAP. Differences in recording transactions under IFRS and U.S. GAAP are discussed in Appendix D and in various International Connection boxes throughout the text.

The following Mornin' Joe International financial statements are simplified and illustrate only portions of IFRS that are appropriate for introductory accounting. The financial statements are presented in euros (€) for demonstration purposes only. The euro is the standard currency of the European Union. The euro is translated at a 1:1 ratio from the dollar to simplify comparisons. Throughout the illustration, call-outs and end notes to each statement are used to highlight the differences between financial statements prepared under IFRS and under U.S. GAAP.

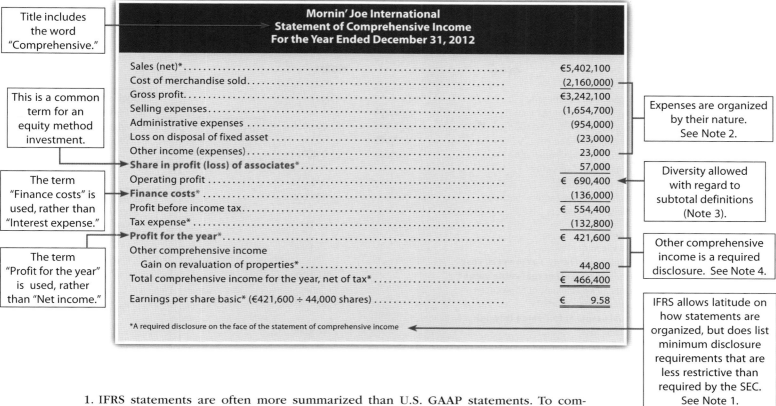

Title includes the word "Comprehensive."

This is a common term for an equity method investment.

The term "Finance costs" is used, rather than "Interest expense."

The term "Profit for the year" is used, rather than "Net income."

Expenses are organized by their nature. See Note 2.

Diversity allowed with regard to subtotal definitions (Note 3).

Other comprehensive income is a required disclosure. See Note 4.

IFRS allows latitude on how statements are organized, but does list minimum disclosure requirements that are less restrictive than required by the SEC. See Note 1.

**Mornin' Joe International**
**Statement of Comprehensive Income**
**For the Year Ended December 31, 2012**

| | |
|---|---:|
| Sales (net)* | €5,402,100 |
| Cost of merchandise sold | (2,160,000) |
| Gross profit | €3,242,100 |
| Selling expenses | (1,654,700) |
| Administrative expenses | (954,000) |
| Loss on disposal of fixed asset | (23,000) |
| Other income (expenses) | 23,000 |
| Share in profit (loss) of associates* | 57,000 |
| Operating profit | € 690,400 |
| Finance costs* | (136,000) |
| Profit before income tax | € 554,400 |
| Tax expense* | (132,800) |
| Profit for the year* | € 421,600 |
| Other comprehensive income | |
|    Gain on revaluation of properties* | 44,800 |
| Total comprehensive income for the year, net of tax* | € 466,400 |
| Earnings per share basic* (€421,600 ÷ 44,000 shares) | € 9.58 |

*A required disclosure on the face of the statement of comprehensive income

1. IFRS statements are often more summarized than U.S. GAAP statements. To compensate, IFRS requires specific disclosures on the face of the financial statements (denoted *) and additional disclosures in the footnotes to the financial statements. Since additions and subtractions are grouped together in sections of IFRS statements, parentheses are used to indicate subtractions.

2. Expenses in an IFRS income statement are classified by either their nature or function. The nature of an expense is how the expense would naturally be recorded in a journal entry reflecting the economic benefit received for that expense. Examples include salaries, depreciation, advertising, and utilities. The function of an expense identifies the purpose of the expense, such as a selling expense or an administrative expense.

   IFRS does not permit the natural and functional classifications to be mixed together on the same statement. That is, all expenses must be classified by either nature or function. However, if a functional classification of expenses is used, a footnote to the income statement must show the natural classification of expenses. To illustrate, because Mornin' Joe International uses the functional classification of expenses in its income statement, it must also show the following natural classification of expenses in a footnote:

| | | |
|---|---:|---|
| Cost of product | €2,100,000 | The cost of product purchased for resale |
| Employee benefits expense | 1,260,000 | Required natural disclosure |
| Depreciation and amortization expense | 203,700 | Required natural disclosure |
| Rent expense | 425,600 | |
| Advertising expense | 678,900 | |
| Other expenses | 58,500 | |
| Total natural expenses | €4,726,700 | |

3. IFRS provides flexibility with regard to line items, headings, and subtotals on the income statement. There is less flexibility under U.S. GAAP for public companies.

4. IFRS requires the reporting of other comprehensive income (see appendix to Chapter 13) either on the income statement (illustrated) or in a separate statement. In contrast, other comprehensive income is often disclosed on the statement of changes in stockholders' equity under U.S. GAAP. For Mornin' Joe International, other comprehensive income consists of the restatement of café locations to fair value (see Note 6 for more details).

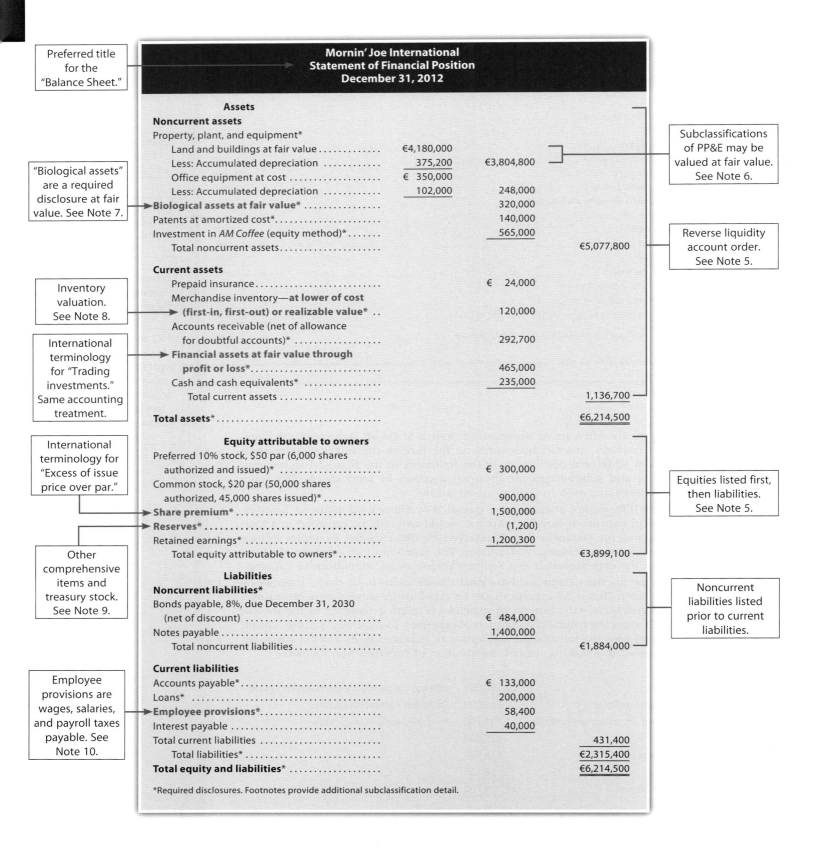

Preferred title for the "Balance Sheet."

"Biological assets" are a required disclosure at fair value. See Note 7.

Inventory valuation. See Note 8.

International terminology for "Trading investments." Same accounting treatment.

International terminology for "Excess of issue price over par."

Other comprehensive items and treasury stock. See Note 9.

Employee provisions are wages, salaries, and payroll taxes payable. See Note 10.

Subclassifications of PP&E may be valued at fair value. See Note 6.

Reverse liquidity account order. See Note 5.

Equities listed first, then liabilities. See Note 5.

Noncurrent liabilities listed prior to current liabilities.

**Mornin' Joe International**
**Statement of Financial Position**
**December 31, 2012**

### Assets
**Noncurrent assets**
Property, plant, and equipment*

| | | |
|---|---|---|
| Land and buildings at fair value | €4,180,000 | |
| Less: Accumulated depreciation | 375,200 | €3,804,800 |
| Office equipment at cost | € 350,000 | |
| Less: Accumulated depreciation | 102,000 | 248,000 |
| Biological assets at fair value* | | 320,000 |
| Patents at amortized cost* | | 140,000 |
| Investment in *AM Coffee* (equity method)* | | 565,000 |
| Total noncurrent assets | | €5,077,800 |

**Current assets**

| | | |
|---|---|---|
| Prepaid insurance | € 24,000 | |
| Merchandise inventory—at lower of cost (first-in, first-out) or realizable value* | 120,000 | |
| Accounts receivable (net of allowance for doubtful accounts)* | 292,700 | |
| Financial assets at fair value through profit or loss* | 465,000 | |
| Cash and cash equivalents* | 235,000 | |
| Total current assets | | 1,136,700 |
| **Total assets*** | | €6,214,500 |

### Equity attributable to owners

| | | |
|---|---|---|
| Preferred 10% stock, $50 par (6,000 shares authorized and issued)* | € 300,000 | |
| Common stock, $20 par (50,000 shares authorized, 45,000 shares issued)* | 900,000 | |
| Share premium* | 1,500,000 | |
| Reserves* | (1,200) | |
| Retained earnings* | 1,200,300 | |
| Total equity attributable to owners* | | €3,899,100 |

### Liabilities
**Noncurrent liabilities***

| | | |
|---|---|---|
| Bonds payable, 8%, due December 31, 2030 (net of discount) | € 484,000 | |
| Notes payable | 1,400,000 | |
| Total noncurrent liabilities | | €1,884,000 |

**Current liabilities**

| | | |
|---|---|---|
| Accounts payable* | € 133,000 | |
| Loans* | 200,000 | |
| Employee provisions* | 58,400 | |
| Interest payable | 40,000 | |
| Total current liabilities | | 431,400 |
| Total liabilities* | | €2,315,400 |
| **Total equity and liabilities*** | | €6,214,500 |

*Required disclosures. Footnotes provide additional subclassification detail.

5. Under IFRS, there is no standard format for the balance sheet (statement of financial position). A typical format for European Union companies is to begin the asset section of the balance sheet with noncurrent assets. This is followed by current assets listed in reverse order of liquidity. That is, the asset side of the balance sheet is reported

in reverse order of liquidity from least liquid to most liquid. Listing noncurrent assets first emphasizes the going concern nature of the entity.

The liability and owners' equity side of the balance sheet is also reported differently than under U.S. GAAP. Specifically, owners' equity is reported first followed by noncurrent liabilities and current liabilities. Listing equity first emphasizes the going concern nature of the entity and the long-term financial interest of the owners in the business.

6. Under IFRS, property, plant, and equipment (PP&E) may be measured at historical cost or fair value. If fair value is used, the revaluation must be for similar classifications of PP&E, but need not be for all PP&E. This departs from U.S. GAAP which requires PP&E to be measured at historical cost. Mornin' Joe International restated its Land and Buildings to fair value since the café sites have readily available real estate market prices. Land and buildings are included together because their fair values are not separable. The office equipment remains at historical cost since its does not have a readily available market price. The increase in fair value is recorded by reducing accumulated depreciation and recognizing the gain as other comprehensive income. This element of other comprehensive income is accumulated in stockholders' equity under the heading Property revaluation reserve.* This treatment is similar (with different titles) to the U.S. GAAP treatment of unrealized gains (losses) from available-for-sale securities. For Mornin' Joe International, there is an increase in the property revaluation reserve of €44,800. This amount is the only difference between Mornin' Joe's U.S. GAAP net income, total assets, and total stockholders' equity and Mornin' Joe International's IFRS total comprehensive income, total assets, and total stockholders' equity.

7. Mornin' Joe International recently acquired a coffee plantation. This is an example of a biological asset. IFRS requires separate reporting of biological assets (principally agricultural assets) at fair value.

8. Inventories are valued at lower of cost or market; however, "market" is defined as net realizable value under IFRS. U.S. GAAP defines "market" as replacement cost under most conditions. In addition, IFRS prohibits LIFO cost valuation.

9. Under IFRS, some elements of other comprehensive income and owner's equity are often aggregated under the term "reserves." In contrast, under U.S. GAAP "reserve" is used to identify a liability. IFRS also does not require separate disclosure of treasury stock as does U.S. GAAP. Specifically, treasury stock may be reported as a reduction of a reserve, a reduction of a stock premium, or as a separate item.

10. The term "provision" is used to denote a liability under IFRS, whereas this term often indicates an expense under U.S. GAAP. For example, "Provision for income taxes" means "Income tax expense" under U.S. GAAP, whereas it would mean "Income taxes payable" under IFRS.

---

* The term "property revaluation surplus" is also used.

**Mornin' Joe International**
**Statement of Changes in Equity**
**For the Year Ended December 31, 2012**

| | Preferred Stock | Common Stock | Share Premium | Property Revaluation Reserve | Reserve for Own Shares | Retained Earnings | Total Equity Attributable to Owners |
|---|---|---|---|---|---|---|---|
| | | | | | **Reserves** | | |
| **Balance, January 1, 2012**........ | €300,000 | €800,000 | €1,325,000 | € 0 | (€36,000) | € 852,700 | €3,241,700 |
| Profit for the year ............... | | | | | | 421,600 | 421,600 |
| **Other comprehensive income** | | | | | | | |
| Property revaluation (gain) ....... | | | | 44,800 | | | 44,800 |
| **Total comprehensive income** ... | | | | €44,800 | | € 421,600 | € 466,400 |
| **Contributions by and distributions to owners** | | | | | | | |
| Dividends on preferred stock ..... | | | | | | (30,000) | (30,000) |
| Dividends on common stock...... | | | | | | (44,000) | (44,000) |
| Issuance of additional common stock ............... | | 100,000 | 175,000 | | | | 275,000 |
| Purchase of own shares .......... | | | | | (10,000) | | (10,000) |
| **Total contributions and distributions to owners**....... | € 0 | €100,000 | € 175,000 | € 0 | (€10,000) | (€ 74,000) | € 191,000 |
| Balance, December 31, 2012 | €300,000 | €900,000 | €1,500,000 | €44,800 | (€46,000) | €1,200,300 | €3,899,100 |

"Reserves", see Notes 9 and 11.

11. The statement of changes in equity under IFRS is similar to U.S. GAAP. For example, both IFRS and GAAP include other comprehensive income items and total comprehensive income disclosures in the statement of changes in equity. In this illustration, treasury stock is included as part a reserve (Reserve for Own Shares). As discussed in Note 9, under U.S. GAAP the term "reserve" denotes a liability.

# DiscussionQuestions

1. Contrast U.S. GAAP income statement terms with their differing IFRS terms, starting with the name of the statement.

2. What is the difference between classifying an expense by nature or function?

3. If a functional expense classification is used for the statement of comprehensive income, what must also be disclosed?

4. What is an example of "Other comprehensive income"? How would it be reported on the statement of comprehensive income?

5. How is the term "provision" used differently under IFRS than under U.S. GAAP?

6. What are two main differences in inventory valuation under IFRS compared to U.S. GAAP?

7. What is a "biological asset"?

8. What is the most significant IFRS departure from U.S. GAAP for valuing property, plant, and equipment?

9. What is a "share premium"?

10. How is the term "reserve" used under IFRS, and how does it differ from its meaning under U.S. GAAP?

11. How is treasury stock reported under IFRS? How does this differ from its treatment under U.S. GAAP?

**IFRS Activity 1**

Unilever Group is a global company that markets a wide variety of products, including Lever® soap, Breyer's® ice cream, and Hellman's® mayonnaise. The income statement and statement of comprehensive income for the Dutch company, Unilever Group is shown below.

**Unilever Group**
**Consolidated Income Statement**
**For the Year Ended December 31, 2009**
**(in millions of euros)**

| | |
|---|---:|
| Turnover | €39,823 |
| Operating profit | 5,020 |
| | |
| After (charging)/crediting: | |
| Restructuring | (897) |
| Business disposals, impairments, other | 29 |
| | |
| Net finance costs | (593) |
| Finance income | 75 |
| Finance costs | (504) |
| Pensions and similar obligations | (164) |
| | |
| Share of net profit/(loss) of joint ventures | 111 |
| Share of net profit/(loss) of associates | 4 |
| Other income from non-current investments | 374 |
| | |
| Profit before taxation | € 4,916 |
| Taxation | (1,257) |
| Net profit | € 3,659 |
| | |
| Earnings per share—basic | € 1.21 |
| Earnings per share—diluted | € 1.17 |

**Consolidated Statement of Comprehensive Income**
**For the Year Ended December 31, 2009**

| | |
|---|---:|
| Fair value gains (losses), net of tax | € 65 |
| Actuarial gains (losses) on pensions, net of tax | 18 |
| Currency retranslation gains (losses), net of tax | 396 |
| Net income (expense) recognized directly into equity | € 519 |
| | |
| Net profit | 3,659 |
| Total comprehensive income | €4,178 |

a. What do you think is meant by "turnover"?

b. How does Unilever's income statement presentation differ significantly from that of Mornin' Joe?

c. How is the total for net finance costs presented differently than would be typically found under U.S. GAAP?

d. What are two ways in which other comprehensive income items can be disclosed under IFRS, and how does this differ from U.S. GAAP?

**IFRS Activity 2**

The following is the consolidated statement of financial position for LVMH, a French company that markets the Louis Vuitton® and Moët Hennessy® brands.

| LVMH<br>Statement of Financial Position<br>December 31, 2009<br>(in millions of euros) | |
| --- | --- |
| **Assets** | |
| Brands and other intangible assets—net | € 8,697 |
| Goodwill—net | 4,270 |
| Property, plant, and equipment—net | 6,140 |
| Investment in associates | 213 |
| Non-current available for sale financial assets | 540 |
| Other non-current assets | 750 |
| Deferred tax | 521 |
| **Non-current assets** | €21,131 |
| | |
| Inventories | € 5,644 |
| Trade accounts receivable | 1,455 |
| Income taxes receivable | 217 |
| Other current assets | 1,213 |
| Cash and cash equivalents | 2,446 |
| **Current assets** | €10,975 |
| **TOTAL ASSETS** | €32,106 |
| | |
| **Liabilities and Equity** | |
| Share capital | € 147 |
| Share premium | 1,763 |
| Treasury shares | (929) |
| Revaluation reserves | 871 |
| Other reserves | 10,684 |
| Net profit, group share | 1,755 |
| Equity, group share | €13,796 |
| Minority interests | 989 |
| **Total equity** | €14,785 |
| | |
| Long-term borrowings | € 4,077 |
| Provisions | 990 |
| Deferred tax | 3,117 |
| Other non-current liabilities | 3,089 |
| **Total non-current liabilities** | €11,273 |
| | |
| Short-term borrowings | 1,708 |
| Trade accounts payable | 1,911 |
| Income taxes payable | 221 |
| Provisions | 334 |
| Other current liabilities | 1,874 |
| **Total current liabilities** | € 6,048 |
| **TOTAL LIABILITIES AND EQUITY** | €32,106 |

a. Identify presentation differences between the balance sheet of LVMH and a balance sheet prepared under U.S. GAAP. Use the Mornin' Joe balance sheet on page 628 as an example of a U.S. GAAP balance sheet. (Ignore minority interests.)

b. Compare the terms used in this balance sheet with the terms used by Mornin' Joe (page 628), using the table below.

| LVMH Term | U.S. GAAP Term as Used by Mornin' Joe |
|---|---|
| Statement of financial position | |
| Share capital | |
| Share premium | |
| Other reserves | |
| Provisions | |

c. What does the "Revaluation reserves" in the equity section of the balance sheet represent?

**IFRS Activity 3**

Under U.S. GAAP, LIFO is an acceptable inventory method. Listed below is financial statement information for three companies that use LIFO. All table numbers are in millions of dollars.

| | LIFO Inventory | FIFO Inventory (from footnotes) | Impact on Net Income from Using LIFO Rather than FIFO (from footnotes) | Total Current Assets | Net Income as Reported |
|---|---|---|---|---|---|
| ExxonMobil | $11,553 | $28,653 | $207 | $55,235 | $19,280 |
| Kroger | 4,902 | 5,705 | (49) | 7,450 | 70 |
| Ford Motor* | 5,450 | 6,248 | 33 | 40,560 | 1,212 |

*Autos and trucks only

Assume these companies adopted IFRS, and thus were required to use FIFO, rather than LIFO. Prepare a table with the following columns as shown below.

(1) Difference between FIFO and LIFO inventory valuation.

(2) Revised IFRS net income using FIFO.

(3) Difference between FIFO and LIFO inventory valuation as a percent of total current assets.

(4) Revised IFRS net income as a percent of the reported net income.

| (1) | (2) | (3) | (4) |
|---|---|---|---|
| FIFO less LIFO | IFRS Net Income | $\dfrac{\text{(FIFO less LIFO)}}{\text{Total Current Assets}}$ | $\dfrac{\text{IFRS Net Income Col. (2)}}{\text{Reported Net Income}}$ |

a. Complete the table.

b. For which company would a change to IFRS for inventory valuation have the largest percentage impact on total current assets (Col. 3)?

c. For which company would a change to IFRS for inventory valuation have the largest percentage impact on net income (Col. 4)?

d. Why might Kroger have a negative impact on net income from using LIFO, while the other two companies have a positive impact on net income from using LIFO?

# Statement of Cash Flows

## *Jones Soda Co.*

**S**uppose you were to receive $100 from an event. Would it make a difference what the event was? Yes, it would! If you received $100 for your birthday, then it's a gift. If you received $100 as a result of working part time for a week, then it's the result of your effort. If you received $100 as a loan, then it's money that you will have to pay back in the future. If you received $100 as a result of selling your iPod, then it's the result of giving up something tangible. Thus, $100 received can be associated with different types of events, and these events have different meanings to you, and different implications for your future. You would much rather receive a $100 gift than take out a $100 loan. Likewise, company stakeholders view inflows and outflows of cash differently depending on their source.

Companies are required to report information about the events causing a change in cash over a period of time. This information is reported in the statement of cash flows. One such company is

Jones Soda Co. Jones began in the late 1980s as an alternative beverage company, known for its customer-provided labels, unique flavors, and support for extreme sports. You have probably seen Jones Soda at **Barnes & Noble**, **Panera Bread**, or **Starbucks**, or maybe sampled some of its unique flavors, such as Fufu Berry®, Blue Bubblegum®, or Lemon Drop®. As with any company, cash is important to Jones Soda. Without cash, Jones would be unable to expand its brands, distribute its product, support extreme sports, or provide a return for its owners. Thus, its managers are concerned about the sources and uses of cash.

In previous chapters, we have used the income statement, balance sheet, statement of retained earnings, and other information to analyze the effects of management decisions on a business's financial position and operating performance. In this chapter, we focus on the events causing a change in cash by presenting the preparation and use of the statement of cash flows.

# Reporting Cash Flows

**OBJ. 1** Describe the cash flow activities reported in the statement of cash flows.

The **statement of cash flows** reports a company's cash inflows and outflows for a period.[1] The statement of cash flows provides useful information about a company's ability to do the following:

1. Generate cash from operations
2. Maintain and expand its operating capacity
3. Meet its financial obligations
4. Pay dividends

The statement of cash flows is used by managers in evaluating past operations and in planning future investing and financing activities. It is also used by external users such as investors and creditors to assess a company's profit potential and ability to pay its debt and pay dividends.

The statement of cash flows reports three types of cash flow activities as follows:

**Cash flows from operating activities** are cash flows from transactions that affect the net income of the company.

    Example: Purchase and sale of merchandise by a retailer.

**Cash flows from investing activities** are cash flows from transactions that affect investments in the noncurrent assets of the company.

    Example: Purchase and sale of fixed assets, such as equipment and buildings.

---

1 As used in this chapter, *cash* refers to cash and cash equivalents. Examples of cash equivalents include short-term, highly liquid investments, such as money market accounts, bank certificates of deposit, and U.S. Treasury bills.

**Cash flows from financing activities** are cash flows from transactions that affect the debt and equity of the company.

Example: Issuing or retiring equity and debt securities.

The cash flows are reported in the statement of cash flows as follows:

| | |
|---|---|
| Cash flows from operating activities | $XXX |
| Cash flows from investing activities | XXX |
| Cash flows from financing activities | XXX |
| Net increase or decrease in cash for the period | $XXX |
| Cash at the beginning of the period | XXX |
| Cash at the end of the period | $XXX |

The ending cash on the statement of cash flows equals the cash reported on the company's balance sheet at the end of the year.

Exhibit 1 illustrates the sources (increases) and uses (decreases) of cash by each of the three cash flow activities. A *source* of cash causes the cash flow to increase and is called a *cash inflow*. A *use* of cash causes cash flow to decrease and is called *cash outflow*.

**Note:**
**The statement of cash flows reports cash flows from operating, investing, and financing activities.**

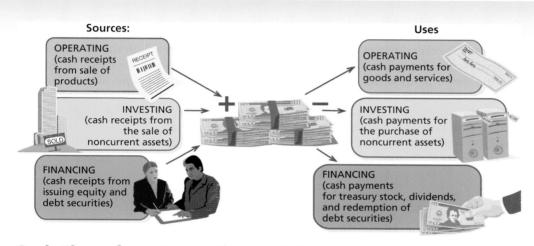

**EXHIBIT 1**

**Cash Flows**

## Cash Flows from Operating Activities

Cash flows from operating activities is the cash inflow or outflow from a company's day-to-day operations. Companies may select one of two alternative methods for reporting cash flows from operating activities in the statement of cash flows:

1. The direct method
2. The indirect method

Both methods result in the same amount of cash flows from operating activities. They differ in the way they report cash flow from operating activities as discussed below.

The **direct method** reports operating cash inflows (receipts) and cash outflows (payments) as follows:

| | | |
|---|---|---|
| Cash flows from operating activities: | | |
| Cash received from customers | | $XXX |
| Less: Cash payments for merchandise | $XXX | |
| Cash payments for operating expenses | XXX | |
| Cash payments for interest | XXX | |
| Cash payments for income taxes | XXX | XXX |
| Net cash flows from operating activities | | $XXX |

The primary operating cash inflow is cash received from customers. The primary operating cash outflows are cash payments for merchandise, operating expenses, interest, and income tax payments. The cash received from operating activities less the cash payments for operating activities is the net cash flow from operating activities.

The primary advantage of the direct method is that it *directly* reports cash receipts and cash payments in the statement of cash flows. Its primary disadvantage is that these data may not be readily available in the accounting records. Thus, the direct method is normally more costly to prepare and, as a result, is used by less than 1% of companies.[2]

The **indirect method** reports cash flows from operating activities by beginning with net income and adjusting it for revenues and expenses that do not involve the receipt or payment of cash as follows:

| | |
|---|---|
| Cash flows from operating activities: | |
| Net income | $XXX |
| Adjustments to reconcile net income to net cash flow from operating activities | XXX |
| Net cash flow from operating activities | $XXX |

The adjustments to reconcile net income to net cash flow from operating activities include such items as depreciation and gains or losses on fixed assets. Changes in current operating assets and liabilities such as accounts receivable or accounts payable are also added or deducted depending on their effect on cash flows. In effect, these additions and deductions adjust net income, which is reported on an accrual accounting basis, to cash flows from operating activities, which uses a cash basis.

A primary advantage of the indirect method is that it reconciles the differences between net income and net cash flows from operations. In doing so, it shows how net income is related to the ending cash balance that is reported on the balance sheet.

Because the data are readily available, the indirect method is less costly to prepare than the direct method. As a result, over 99% of companies use the indirect method of reporting cash flows from operations.

Exhibit 2 illustrates the Cash Flows from Operating Activities section of the statement of cash flows for **NetSolutions**. Exhibit 2 shows the direct and indirect methods using the NetSolutions data from Chapter 1. As Exhibit 2 illustrates, both methods report the same amount of net cash flow from operating activities, $2,900.

---

**EXHIBIT 2** **Cash Flow from Operations: Direct and Indirect Methods—NetSolutions**

**Direct Method**

| | |
|---|---|
| Cash flows from operating activities: | |
| Cash received from customers | $7,500 |
| Deduct cash payments for expenses and payments to creditors | 4,600 |
| Net cash flow from operating activities | $2,900 |

**Indirect Method**

| | |
|---|---|
| Cash flows from operating activities: | |
| Net income | $3,050 |
| Add increase in accounts payable | 400 |
| | $3,450 |
| Deduct increase in supplies | 550 |
| Net cash flow from operating activities | $2,900 |

the same

---

# Cash Flows from Investing Activities

Cash flows from investing activities show the cash inflows and outflows related to changes in a company's long-term assets. Cash flows from investing activities are reported on the statement of cash flows as follows:

In October 2008, the U.S. government invested $250 billion of cash into U.S. banks to help stabilize the financial system.

| | |
|---|---|
| Cash flows from investing activities: | |
| Cash inflows from investing activities | $XXX |
| Less cash used for investing activities | XXX |
| Net cash flows from investing activities | $XXX |

Cash inflows from investing activities normally arise from selling fixed assets, investments, and intangible assets. Cash outflows normally include payments to purchase fixed assets, investments, and intangible assets.

## Cash Flows from Financing Activities

Cash flows from financing activities show the cash inflows and outflows related to changes in a company's long-term liabilities and stockholders' equity. Cash flows from financing activities are reported on the statement of cash flows as follows:

| | | |
|---|---|---|
| Cash flows from financing activities: | | |
| Cash inflows from financing activities | $XXX | |
| Less cash used for financing activities | XXX | |
| Net cash flows from financing activities | | $XXX |

Cash inflows from financing activities normally arise from issuing long-term debt or equity securities. For example, issuing bonds, notes payable, preferred stock, and common stock creates cash inflows from financing activities. Cash outflows from financing activities include paying cash dividends, repaying long-term debt, and acquiring treasury stock.

## Noncash Investing and Financing Activities

A company may enter into transactions involving investing and financing activities that do not *directly* affect cash. For example, a company may issue common stock to retire long-term debt. Although this transaction does not directly affect cash, it does eliminate future cash payments for interest and for paying the bonds when they mature. Because such transactions *indirectly* affect cash flows, they are reported in a separate section of the statement of cash flows. This section usually appears at the bottom of the statement of cash flows.

In fiscal 2009, Apple, Inc., generated $10.1 billion in cash flow from operating activities.

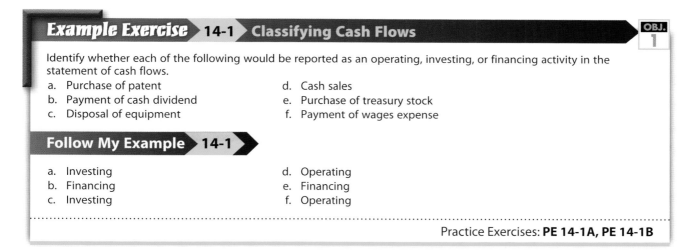

**Example Exercise 14-1** **Classifying Cash Flows** **OBJ. 1**

Identify whether each of the following would be reported as an operating, investing, or financing activity in the statement of cash flows.
a. Purchase of patent
b. Payment of cash dividend
c. Disposal of equipment
d. Cash sales
e. Purchase of treasury stock
f. Payment of wages expense

**Follow My Example 14-1**

a. Investing
b. Financing
c. Investing
d. Operating
e. Financing
f. Operating

Practice Exercises: **PE 14-1A, PE 14-1B**

## No Cash Flow per Share

**Cash flow per share** is sometimes reported in the financial press. As reported, cash flow per share is normally computed as *cash flow from operations per share*. However, such reporting may be misleading because of the following:

1. Users may misinterpret cash flow per share as the per-share amount available for dividends. This would not be the case if the cash generated by operations is required for repaying loans or for reinvesting in the business.

2. Users may misinterpret cash flow per share as equivalent to (or better than) earnings per share.

For these reasons, the financial statements, including the statement of cash flows, should not report cash flow per share.

Prepare a statement of cash flows, using the indirect method.

# Statement of Cash Flows— The Indirect Method

The indirect method of reporting cash flows from operating activities uses the logic that a change in any balance sheet account (including cash) can be analyzed in terms of changes in the other balance sheet accounts. Thus, by analyzing changes in noncash balance sheet accounts, any change in the cash account can be *indirectly* determined.

To illustrate, the accounting equation can be solved for cash as shown below.

$$\text{Assets} = \text{Liabilities} + \text{Stockholders' Equity}$$
$$\text{Cash} + \text{Noncash Assets} = \text{Liabilities} + \text{Stockholders' Equity}$$
$$\text{Cash} = \text{Liabilities} + \text{Stockholders' Equity} - \text{Noncash Assets}$$

Therefore, any change in the cash account can be determined by analyzing changes in the liability, stockholders' equity, and noncash asset accounts as shown below.

$$\text{\textit{Change} in Cash} = \text{\textit{Change} in Liabilities} + \text{\textit{Change} in Stockholders' Equity}$$
$$- \text{\textit{Change} in Noncash Assets}$$

Under the indirect method, there is no order in which the balance sheet accounts must be analyzed. However, net income (or net loss) is the first amount reported on the statement of cash flows. Since net income (or net loss) is a component of any change in Retained Earnings, the first account normally analyzed is Retained Earnings.

To illustrate the indirect method, the income statement and comparative balance sheets for Rundell Inc. shown in Exhibit 3 are used. Ledger accounts and other data supporting the income statement and balance sheet are presented as needed.[3]

---

**EXHIBIT 3** **Income Statement and Comparative Balance Sheet**

### Rundell Inc.
### Income Statement
### For the Year Ended December 31, 2012

| | | |
|---|---:|---:|
| Sales | | $1,180,000 |
| Cost of merchandise sold | | 790,000 |
| Gross profit | | $ 390,000 |
| Operating expenses: | | |
|    Depreciation expense | $ 7,000 | |
|    Other operating expenses | 196,000 | |
|       Total operating expenses | | 203,000 |
| Income from operations | | $ 187,000 |
| Other income: | | |
|    Gain on sale of land | $ 12,000 | |
| Other expense: | | |
|    Interest expense | 8,000 | 4,000 |
| Income before income tax | | $ 191,000 |
| Income tax expense | | 83,000 |
| Net income | | $ 108,000 |

---

3 An appendix that discusses using a spreadsheet (work sheet) as an aid in assembling data for the statement of cash flows is presented at the end of this chapter. This appendix illustrates the use of this spreadsheet in reporting cash flows from operating activities using the indirect method.

**EXHIBIT 3** Income Statement and Comparative Balance Sheet *(concluded)*

**Rundell Inc.**
**Comparative Balance Sheet**
**December 31, 2012 and 2011**

| | 2012 | 2011 | Increase Decrease* |
|---|---|---|---|
| **Assets** | | | |
| Cash ................................................. | $ 97,500 | $ 26,000 | $ 71,500 |
| Accounts receivable (net) ............................ | 74,000 | 65,000 | 9,000 |
| Inventories ......................................... | 172,000 | 180,000 | 8,000* |
| Land ............................................... | 80,000 | 125,000 | 45,000* |
| Building ............................................ | 260,000 | 200,000 | 60,000 |
| Accumulated depreciation—building.................. | (65,300) | (58,300) | 7,000** |
| Total assets ........................................ | $618,200 | $537,700 | $ 80,500 |
| **Liabilities** | | | |
| Accounts payable (merchandise creditors) ............. | $ 43,500 | $ 46,700 | $ 3,200* |
| Accrued expenses payable (operating expenses) ....... | 26,500 | 24,300 | 2,200 |
| Income taxes payable ............................... | 7,900 | 8,400 | 500* |
| Dividends payable ................................... | 14,000 | 10,000 | 4,000 |
| Bonds payable ...................................... | 100,000 | 150,000 | 50,000* |
| Total liabilities ..................................... | $191,900 | $239,400 | $ 47,500* |
| **Stockholders' Equity** | | | |
| Common stock ($2 par) .............................. | $ 24,000 | $ 16,000 | $ 8,000 |
| Paid-in capital in excess of par...................... | 120,000 | 80,000 | 40,000 |
| Retained earnings................................... | 282,300 | 202,300 | 80,000 |
| Total stockholders' equity ........................... | $426,300 | $298,300 | $128,000 |
| Total liabilities and stockholders' equity............... | $618,200 | $537,700 | $ 80,500 |

**There is a $7,000 increase to Accumulated Depreciation—Building, which is a contra asset account. As a result, the $7,000 increase in this account must be subtracted in summing to the increase in Total assets of $80,500.

## Retained Earnings

The comparative balance sheet for Rundell Inc. shows that retained earnings increased $80,000 during the year. The retained earnings account shown below indicates how this change occurred.

| **Account** *Retained Earnings* | | | | | Account No. | |
|---|---|---|---|---|---|---|
| | | | | | **Balance** | |
| **Date** | | **Item** | **Debit** | **Credit** | **Debit** | **Credit** |
| 2012 Jan. | 1 | Balance | | | | 202,300 |
| Dec. | 31 | Net income | | 108,000 | | 310,300 |
| | 31 | Cash dividends | 28,000 | | | 282,300 |

The retained earnings account indicates that the $80,000 ($108,000 − $28,000) change resulted from net income of $108,000 and cash dividends of $28,000. The net income of $108,000 is the first amount reported in the Cash Flows from Operating Activities section.

## Adjustments to Net Income

The net income of $108,000 reported by Rundell Inc. does not equal the cash flows from operating activities for the period. This is because net income is determined using the accrual method of accounting.

Under the accrual method of accounting, revenues and expenses are recorded at different times from when cash is received or paid. For example, merchandise may be sold on account and the cash received at a later date. Likewise, insurance premiums may be paid in the current period, but expensed in a following period.

Thus, under the indirect method, adjustments to net income must be made to determine cash flows from operating activities. The typical adjustments to net income are shown in Exhibit 4.[4]

Net income is normally adjusted to cash flows from operating activities using the following steps:

Step 1.   Expenses that do not affect cash are added. Such expenses decrease net income but do not involve cash payments and, thus, are added to net income.

Examples: *Depreciation* of fixed assets and *amortization* of intangible assets are added to net income.

Step 2.   Losses and gains on disposal of assets are added or deducted. The disposal (sale) of assets is an investing activity rather than an operating activity. However, such losses and gains are reported as part of net income. As a result, any *losses* on disposal of assets are *added* back to net income. Likewise, any *gains* on disposal of assets are *deducted* from net income.

Example: Land costing $100,000 is sold for $90,000. The loss of $10,000 is added back to net income.

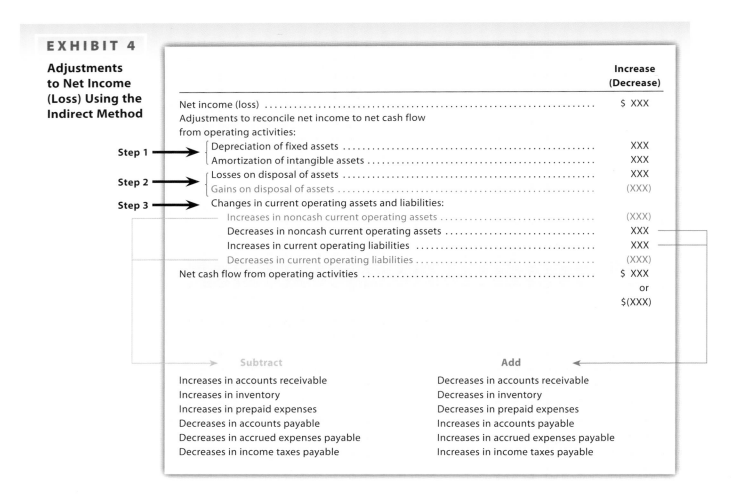

**EXHIBIT 4**

**Adjustments to Net Income (Loss) Using the Indirect Method**

|  | Increase (Decrease) |
| --- | --- |
| Net income (loss) | $ XXX |
| Adjustments to reconcile net income to net cash flow from operating activities: |  |
| Depreciation of fixed assets | XXX |
| Amortization of intangible assets | XXX |
| Losses on disposal of assets | XXX |
| Gains on disposal of assets | (XXX) |
| Changes in current operating assets and liabilities: |  |
| Increases in noncash current operating assets | (XXX) |
| Decreases in noncash current operating assets | XXX |
| Increases in current operating liabilities | XXX |
| Decreases in current operating liabilities | (XXX) |
| Net cash flow from operating activities | $ XXX |
|  | or |
|  | $(XXX) |

Step 1 — Depreciation of fixed assets; Amortization of intangible assets
Step 2 — Losses on disposal of assets; Gains on disposal of assets
Step 3 — Changes in current operating assets and liabilities

| Subtract | Add |
| --- | --- |
| Increases in accounts receivable | Decreases in accounts receivable |
| Increases in inventory | Decreases in inventory |
| Increases in prepaid expenses | Decreases in prepaid expenses |
| Decreases in accounts payable | Increases in accounts payable |
| Decreases in accrued expenses payable | Increases in accrued expenses payable |
| Decreases in income taxes payable | Increases in income taxes payable |

4 Other items that also require adjustments to net income to obtain cash flows from operating activities include amortization of bonds payable discounts (add), losses on debt retirement (add), amortization of bonds payable premiums (deduct), and gains on retirement of debt (deduct).

Step 3. Changes in current operating assets and liabilities are added or deducted as follows:

> Increases in noncash current operating assets are deducted.
> Decreases in noncash current operating assets are added.
> Increases in current operating liabilities are added.
> Decreases in current operating liabilities are deducted.

Example: A sale of $10,000 on account increases sales, accounts receivable, and net income by $10,000. However, cash is not affected. Thus, an increase in accounts receivable of $10,000 is deducted. Similar adjustments are required for the changes in the other current asset and liability accounts such as inventory, prepaid expenses, accounts payable, accrued expenses payable, and income taxes payable as shown in Exhibit 4.

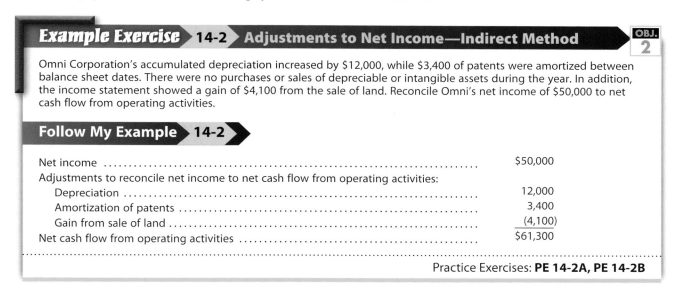

**Example Exercise** 14-2 **Adjustments to Net Income—Indirect Method** OBJ. 2

Omni Corporation's accumulated depreciation increased by $12,000, while $3,400 of patents were amortized between balance sheet dates. There were no purchases or sales of depreciable or intangible assets during the year. In addition, the income statement showed a gain of $4,100 from the sale of land. Reconcile Omni's net income of $50,000 to net cash flow from operating activities.

**Follow My Example** 14-2

| | |
|---|---:|
| Net income | $50,000 |
| Adjustments to reconcile net income to net cash flow from operating activities: | |
|   Depreciation | 12,000 |
|   Amortization of patents | 3,400 |
|   Gain from sale of land | (4,100) |
| Net cash flow from operating activities | $61,300 |

Practice Exercises: **PE 14-2A, PE 14-2B**

To illustrate, the Cash Flows from Operating Activities section of Rundell's statement of cash flows is shown in Exhibit 5. Rundell's net income of $108,000 is converted to cash flows from operating activities of $100,500 as follows:

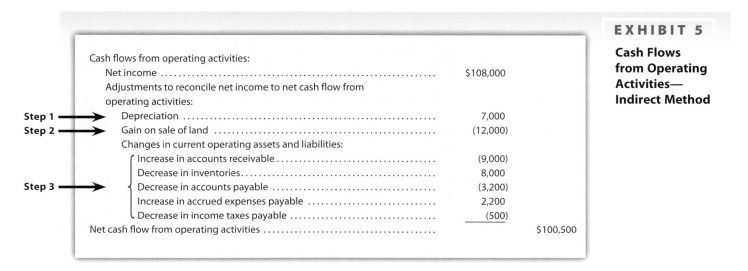

**EXHIBIT 5**

**Cash Flows from Operating Activities— Indirect Method**

| | | |
|---|---:|---:|
| Cash flows from operating activities: | | |
|   Net income | $108,000 | |
|   Adjustments to reconcile net income to net cash flow from operating activities: | | |
| Step 1 →     Depreciation | 7,000 | |
| Step 2 →     Gain on sale of land | (12,000) | |
|     Changes in current operating assets and liabilities: | | |
|      Increase in accounts receivable | (9,000) | |
|      Decrease in inventories | 8,000 | |
| Step 3 →      Decrease in accounts payable | (3,200) | |
|      Increase in accrued expenses payable | 2,200 | |
|      Decrease in income taxes payable | (500) | |
|   Net cash flow from operating activities | | $100,500 |

Step 1. Add depreciation of $7,000.

> Analysis: The comparative balance sheet in Exhibit 3 indicates that Accumulated Depreciation—Building increased by $7,000. The account, shown on the following page, indicates that depreciation for the year was $7,000 for the building.

| **Account** Accumulated Depreciation—Building | | | | | Account No. | |
|---|---|---|---|---|---|---|
| | | | | | **Balance** | |
| **Date** | **Item** | **Debit** | **Credit** | **Debit** | **Credit** | |
| 2012 Jan. 1 | Balance | | | | 58,300 | |
| Dec. 31 | Depreciation for year | | 7,000 | | 65,300 | |

Step 2. Deduct the gain on the sale of land of $12,000.

Analysis: The income statement in Exhibit 3 reports a gain from the sale of land of $12,000. The proceeds, which include the gain, are reported in the Investing section of the statement of cash flows.[5] Thus, the gain of $12,000 is deducted from net income in determining cash flows from operating activities.

Step 3. Add and deduct changes in current operating assets and liabilities.

Analysis: The increases and decreases in the current operating asset and current liability accounts are shown below.

| | **December 31** | | **Increase** |
|---|---|---|---|
| **Accounts** | **2012** | **2011** | **Decrease*** |
| Accounts Receivable (net) | $ 74,000 | $ 65,000 | $9,000 |
| Inventories | 172,000 | 180,000 | 8,000* |
| Accounts Payable (merchandise creditors) | 43,500 | 46,700 | 3,200* |
| Accrued Expenses Payable (operating expenses) | 26,500 | 24,300 | 2,200 |
| Income Taxes Payable | 7,900 | 8,400 | 500* |

*Accounts receivable (net)*: The $9,000 increase is deducted from net income. This is because the $9,000 increase in accounts receivable indicates that sales on account were $9,000 more than the cash received from customers. Thus, sales (and net income) includes $9,000 that was not received in cash during the year.

*Inventories*: The $8,000 decrease is added to net income. This is because the $8,000 decrease in inventories indicates that the cost of merchandise *sold* exceeds the cost of the merchandise *purchased* during the year by $8,000. In other words, cost of merchandise sold includes $8,000 of goods from inventory that was not purchased (used cash) during the year.

*Accounts payable (merchandise creditors)*: The $3,200 decrease is deducted from net income. This is because a decrease in accounts payable indicates that the cash *payments* to merchandise creditors exceed the merchandise *purchased on account* by $3,200. Therefore, the cost of merchandise sold is $3,200 less than the cash paid to merchandise creditors during the year.

*Accrued expenses payable (operating expenses)*: The $2,200 increase is added to net income. This is because an increase in accrued expenses payable indicates that operating expenses exceed the cash payments for operating expenses by $2,200. In other words, operating expenses reported on the income statement include $2,200 that did not require a cash outflow during the year.

*Income taxes payable*: The $500 decrease is deducted from net income. This is because a decrease in income taxes payable indicates that taxes paid exceed the amount of taxes incurred during the year by $500. In other words, the amount reported on the income statement for income tax expense is less than the amount paid by $500.

Using the preceding analyses, Rundell's net income of $108,000 is converted to cash flows from operating activities of $100,500 as shown in Exhibit 5, on page 647.

---

5 The reporting of the proceeds (cash flows) from the sale of land as part of investing activities is discussed later in this chapter.

Spreadsheet software can be used to develop the complete statement of cash flows using the worksheet approach illustrated in the appendix to this chapter. Here we illustrate the use of spreadsheet software for developing the cash flows from operating activities section of the statement of cash flows.

| | A | B | C | D | E |
|---|---|---|---|---|---|
| 1 | *Inputs:* | | | | |
| 2 | | | | | |
| 3 | Selected income statement items: | | | | |
| 4 | Net income | $    108,000 | | | |
| 5 | Depreciation expense | 7,000 | | | |
| 6 | Gain on sale of land | 12,000 | | | |
| 7 | | | | | |
| 8 | Comparative noncash current assets and liabilities | | | | |
| 9 | | | | | |
| 10 | | December 31, 2012 | December 31, 2011 | Increase/ (Decrease) | 1 = Current asset 2 = Current liability |
| 11 | Accounts receivable | $    74,000 | $    65,000 | =B11-C11 | 1 |
| 12 | Inventories | 172,000 | 180,000 | =B12-C12 | 1 |
| 13 | Accounts payable | 43,500 | 46,700 | =B13-C13 | 2 |
| 14 | Accrued expenses | 26,500 | 24,300 | =B14-C14 | 2 |
| 15 | Income taxes payable | 7,900 | 8,400 | =B15-C15 | 2 |
| 16 | | | | ↑ | ↑ |
| 17 | | | | | |
| 18 | *Output:* | | | a. | b. |
| 19 | | | | | |
| 20 | Cash flows from operating activities: | | | | |
| 21 | Net income | =B4 ⎤ | | | |
| 22 | Adjustments to reconcile net income to net cash flow: | ⎬ c. | | | |
| 23 | Depreciation | =B5 ⎥ | | | |
| 24 | Gain on sale of land | =-B6 ⎦ | | | |
| 25 | Changes in current operating assets and liabilities: | | | | |
| 26 |     Increase in accounts receivable | =IF(E11=1,-D11,D11) ← d. | | | |
| 27 |     Decrease in inventory | =IF(E12=1,-D12,D12) ⎤ | | | |
| 28 |     Decrease in accounts payable | =IF(E13=1,-D13,D13) | | | |
| 29 |     Increase in accrued expense payable | =IF(E14=1,-D14,D14) ← e. | | | |
| 30 |     Decrease in income taxes payable | =IF(E15=1,-D15,D15) ⎦ | | | |
| 31 |     Net cash flow from operating activities | | =SUM(B21:B30) ← f. | | |

The **input** section of the spreadsheet includes the selected income statement items that are required on the cash flows from operating activities. These include the net income, depreciation expense, and gain on sale of land in this example, B4, B5, and B6.

The input section also contains the comparative noncash current assets and current liabilities from the balance sheet. Begin by computing the Increase/Decrease in current assets and current liabilities in the input section:

a.   Enter in D11 the formula for the increase or decrease in accounts receivable, =B11-C11. Copy this formula for the remaining current assets and liabilities.

b.   Enter into cells E11 through E16, a number "1" for current assets and a number "2" for current liabilities. This is termed an *indicator* variable, which we will use in a formula below. Indicator variables can be any number. For example, 0 or 1 would also work.

The **output** section contains the cash flows from operating activities, which is the first section of the complete statement of cash flows. The output section is prepared using cell references from the input section. It is important to insert cell references with the correct sign.

c.  Enter in cell B21 the cell reference for net income, =B4. Enter in cell B23 the cell reference for depreciation, =B5. Enter in cell B24 the cell reference for gain on sale of land as a minus, =-B6.

d.  Enter in cell B26 a formula for calculating the impact of changes in current assets and current liabilities on net income in determining net cash flows from operating activities. We will use the =IF function to develop a formula that works for all current items. The =IF function is used to program your spreadsheet to test for conditions illustrated as follows:

B26:                    =IF(E11=1,-D11,D11)

| The logical condition that is being tested. Must include a logical operator, such as =, <, or >. Is E11=1? Or in English, is this reference (E11) a current asset? | The value that is entered into cell B26 if the answer to the logical statement is True. In this case, if the reference (E11) is a current asset, then -D11 is entered in B26. | The value that is entered in cell B26 if the answer to the logical statement is False. In this case, if reference (E11) is not a current asset (thus, a current liability), then D11 is entered in B26. |

After you enter this formula in cell B26, you should see that -D11, or (9,000), is entered in cell B26. This is what we want. For current assets, increases are subtracted and decreases are added, when adjusting net income to cash flows from operating activities. For the current liabilities, the increases and decreases keep their sign in adjusting net income to cash flows from operating activities.

Thus, we have created a single formula that will work for all current assets and current liabilities. We only needed to add the indicator variable in the input section for the =IF function to work.

We can now copy this formula to the remaining current assets and liabilities:

e.  Copy B26 to B27:B30.
f.  Enter in C31 the formula to sum cells B21:B30, =SUM(B21:B30).

**Try**_It_  Go to the hands-on **Excel Tutor** for this example!

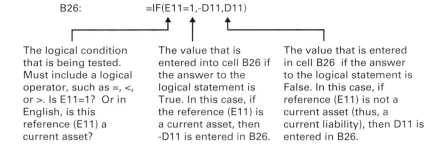

**Example Exercise** ▶ **14-3** ▶ **Changes in Current Operating Assets and Liabilities—Indirect Method**  **OBJ. 2**

Victor Corporation's current operating assets and liabilities from the company's comparative balance sheet were as follows:

|  | Dec. 31, 2013 | Dec. 31, 2012 |
|---|---|---|
| Accounts receivable | $ 6,500 | $ 4,900 |
| Inventory | 12,300 | 15,000 |
| Accounts payable | 4,800 | 5,200 |
| Dividends payable | 5,000 | 4,000 |

Adjust Victor's net income of $70,000 for changes in operating assets and liabilities to arrive at cash flows from operating activities.

**Follow My Example** ▶ **14-3** ▶

| | |
|---|---|
| Net income ................................................................ | $70,000 |
| Adjustments to reconcile net income to net cash flow from operating activities: | |
| Changes in current operating assets and liabilities: | |
|    Increase in accounts receivable ................................................ | (1,600) |
|    Decrease in inventory ......................................................... | 2,700 |
|    Decrease in accounts payable .................................................. | (400) |
| Net cash flow from operating activities ............................................. | $70,700 |

*Note:* The change in dividends payable impacts the cash paid for dividends, which is disclosed under financing activities.

Practice Exercises: **PE 14-3A, PE 14-3B**

## Integrity, Objectivity, and Ethics in Business

### CREDIT POLICY AND CASH FLOW

One would expect customers to pay for products and services sold on account. Unfortunately, that is not always the case. Collecting accounts receivable efficiently is the key to turning a current asset into positive cash flow. Most entrepreneurs would rather think about the exciting aspects of their business—such as product development, marketing, sales, and advertising—than credit collection. This can be a mistake. Hugh McHugh of Overhill Flowers, Inc., decided that he would have no more trade accounts after dealing with Christmas orders that weren't paid for until late February, or sometimes not paid at all. As stated by one collection service, "One thing business owners always tell me is that they never thought about [collections] when they started their own business." To the small business owner, the collection of accounts receivable may mean the difference between succeeding and failing.

Source: Paulette Thomas, "Making Them Pay: The Last Thing Most Entrepreneurs Want to Think About Is Bill Collection; It Should Be One of the First Things," *The Wall Street Journal*, September 19, 2005, p. R6.

---

## Example Exercise  14-4  Cash Flows from Operating Activities—Indirect Method

**OBJ. 2**

Omicron Inc. reported the following data:

| | |
|---|---|
| Net income | $120,000 |
| Depreciation expense | 12,000 |
| Loss on disposal of equipment | 15,000 |
| Increase in accounts receivable | 5,000 |
| Decrease in accounts payable | 2,000 |

Prepare the Cash Flows from Operating Activities section of the statement of cash flows using the indirect method.

### Follow My Example  14-4

Cash flows from operating activities:

| | | |
|---|---|---|
| Net income ...................................................... | | $120,000 |
| Adjustments to reconcile net income to net cash flow from operating activities: | | |
|     Depreciation expense.................................................. | 12,000 | |
|     Loss on disposal of equipment......................................... | 15,000 | |
|     Changes in current operating assets and liabilities: | | |
|         Increase in accounts receivable ..................................... | (5,000) | |
|         Decrease in accounts payable........................................ | (2,000) | |
| Net cash flow from operating activities......................................... | | $140,000 |

Practice Exercises: **PE 14-4A, PE 14-4B**

---

## BusinessConnection

### CASH CRUNCH!

Automobile manufacturers such as Chrysler Group LLC sell their cars and trucks through a network of independently owned and operated dealerships. The vehicles are sold to the dealerships on credit by issuing a trade receivable, which is repaid to Chrysler Group LLC after the vehicles are sold by the dealership. The economic crisis of 2008 created a slump in car sales that lasted well into 2009.

By spring 2009, Chrysler dealers around the world found themselves with large inventories of unsold cars and trucks, resulting in their inability to repay their trade receivables from Chrysler Group LLC. This led to a significant decline in Chrysler's cash flow from operating activities that forced the company into a financial restructuring. Ultimately, the company was rescued by a significant investment (cash inflow from financing activities) from Fiat and the U.S. and Canadian governments.

Source: "Chrysler Restructuring Plan for Long-Term Viability," Chrysler Group LLC, February 17, 2009.

# Dividends

The retained earnings account of Rundell Inc., shown on page 645, indicates cash dividends of $28,000 declared during the year. However, the dividends payable account, shown below, indicates that only $24,000 of dividends were paid during the year.

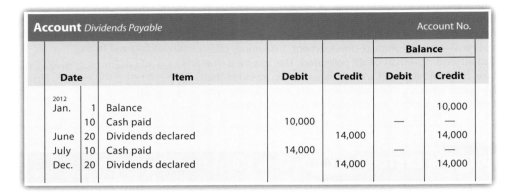

| Account Dividends Payable | | | | | Account No. | |
|---|---|---|---|---|---|---|
| | | | | | **Balance** | |
| **Date** | **Item** | **Debit** | **Credit** | **Debit** | **Credit** | |
| 2012 | | | | | | |
| Jan. 1 | Balance | | | | 10,000 | |
| 10 | Cash paid | 10,000 | | — | — | |
| June 20 | Dividends declared | | 14,000 | | 14,000 | |
| July 10 | Cash paid | 14,000 | | — | — | |
| Dec. 20 | Dividends declared | | 14,000 | | 14,000 | |

Since dividend payments are a financing activity, the dividend payment of $24,000 is reported in the Financing Activities section of the statement of cash flows, as shown below.

Cash flows from financing activities:
    Cash paid for dividends . . . . . . . . . . . . . . . . . . . . . . . . . . . . . . . . . . . . . . .     $24,000

# Common Stock

The common stock account increased by $8,000, and the paid-in capital in excess of par—common stock account increased by $40,000, as shown below. These increases were from issuing 4,000 shares of common stock for $12 per share.

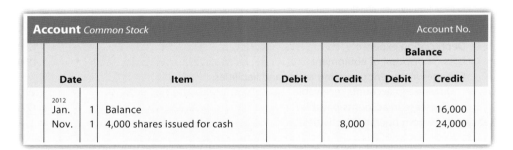

| Account Common Stock | | | | | Account No. | |
|---|---|---|---|---|---|---|
| | | | | | **Balance** | |
| **Date** | **Item** | **Debit** | **Credit** | **Debit** | **Credit** | |
| 2012 | | | | | | |
| Jan. 1 | Balance | | | | 16,000 | |
| Nov. 1 | 4,000 shares issued for cash | | 8,000 | | 24,000 | |

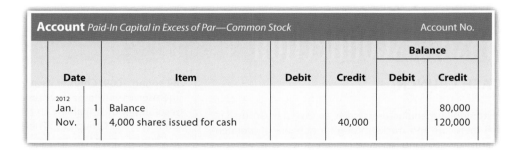

| Account Paid-In Capital in Excess of Par—Common Stock | | | | | Account No. | |
|---|---|---|---|---|---|---|
| | | | | | **Balance** | |
| **Date** | **Item** | **Debit** | **Credit** | **Debit** | **Credit** | |
| 2012 | | | | | | |
| Jan. 1 | Balance | | | | 80,000 | |
| Nov. 1 | 4,000 shares issued for cash | | 40,000 | | 120,000 | |

This cash inflow is reported in the Financing Activities section as follows:

Cash flows from financing activities:
    Cash received from sale of common stock . . . . . . . . . . . . . . . . . . .     $48,000

# Bonds Payable

The bonds payable account decreased by $50,000, as shown below. This decrease is from retiring the bonds by a cash payment for their face amount.

| **Account** Bonds Payable | | | | | | Account No. | |
|---|---|---|---|---|---|---|---|
| | | | | | | **Balance** | |
| **Date** | | **Item** | **Debit** | **Credit** | **Debit** | **Credit** | |
| 2012 Jan. | 1 | Balance | | | | 150,000 | |
| June | 1 | Retired by payment of cash at face amount | 50,000 | | | 100,000 | |

This cash outflow is reported in the Financing Activities section as follows:

Cash flows from financing activities:
Cash paid to retire bonds payable . . . . . . . . . . . . . . . . . . . . . . . . . . .       $50,000

# Building

The building account increased by $60,000, and the accumulated depreciation—building account increased by $7,000, as shown below.

| **Account** Building | | | | | | Account No. | |
|---|---|---|---|---|---|---|---|
| | | | | | | **Balance** | |
| **Date** | | **Item** | **Debit** | **Credit** | **Debit** | **Credit** | |
| 2012 Jan. | 1 | Balance | | | 200,000 | | |
| Dec. | 27 | Purchased for cash | 60,000 | | 260,000 | | |

| **Account** Accumulated Depreciation—Building | | | | | | Account No. | |
|---|---|---|---|---|---|---|---|
| | | | | | | **Balance** | |
| **Date** | | **Item** | **Debit** | **Credit** | **Debit** | **Credit** | |
| 2012 Jan. | 1 | Balance | | | | 58,300 | |
| Dec. | 31 | Depreciation for the year | | 7,000 | | 65,300 | |

The purchase of a building for cash of $60,000 is reported as an outflow of cash in the Investing Activities section as follows:

Cash flows from investing activities:
Cash paid for purchase of building . . . . . . . . . . . . . . . . . . . . . . . . . . .       $60,000

The credit in the accumulated depreciation—building account represents depreciation expense for the year. This depreciation expense of $7,000 on the building was added to net income in determining cash flows from operating activities, as reported in Exhibit 5, on page 647.

## Land

The $45,000 decline in the land account was from two transactions, as shown below.

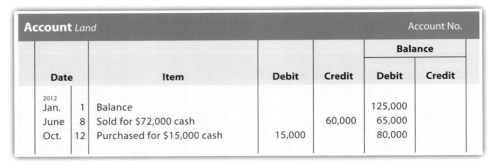

| Account *Land* | | | | | Account No. | |
|---|---|---|---|---|---|---|
| | | | | | **Balance** | |
| **Date** | | **Item** | **Debit** | **Credit** | **Debit** | **Credit** |
| 2012 Jan. | 1 | Balance | | | 125,000 | |
| June | 8 | Sold for $72,000 cash | | 60,000 | 65,000 | |
| Oct. | 12 | Purchased for $15,000 cash | 15,000 | | 80,000 | |

The June 8 transaction is the sale of land with a cost of $60,000 for $72,000 in cash. The $72,000 proceeds from the sale are reported in the Investing Activities section, as follows:

Cash flows from investing activities:
Cash received from sale of land .............................. $72,000

The proceeds of $72,000 include the $12,000 gain on the sale of land and the $60,000 cost (book value) of the land. As shown in Exhibit 5, on page 647, the $12,000 gain is deducted from net income in the Cash Flows from Operating Activities section. This is so that the $12,000 cash inflow related to the gain is not included twice as a cash inflow.

The October 12 transaction is the purchase of land for cash of $15,000. This transaction is reported as an outflow of cash in the Investing Activities section, as follows:

Cash flows from investing activities:
Cash paid for purchase of land .............................. $15,000

---

**Example Exercise** › **14-5** › **Land Transactions on the Statement of Cash Flows** **OBJ. 2**

Alpha Corporation purchased land for $125,000. Later in the year, the company sold a different piece of land with a book value of $165,000 for $200,000. How are the effects of these transactions reported on the statement of cash flows?

**Follow My Example** › **14-5** ›

The gain on sale of land is deducted from net income as shown below.

Gain on sale of land ........................................................ $ (35,000)

The purchase and sale of land is reported as part of cash flows from investing activities as shown below.

Cash received from sale of land ................................................ 200,000
Cash paid for purchase of land ................................................ (125,000)

Practice Exercises: **PE 14-5A, PE 14-5B**

---

## Preparing the Statement of Cash Flows

The statement of cash flows for Rundell Inc. using the indirect method is shown in Exhibit 6. The statement of cash flows indicates that cash increased by $71,500 during the year. The most significant increase in net cash flows ($100,500) was from operating activities. The most significant use of cash ($26,000) was for financing activities. The ending balance of cash on December 31, 2012, is $97,500. This ending cash balance is also reported on the December 31, 2012, balance sheet shown in Exhibit 3 on page 645.

**EXHIBIT 6**

**Statement of Cash Flows— Indirect Method**

**Rundell Inc.**
**Statement of Cash Flows**
**For the Year Ended December 31, 2012**

| | | | |
|---|---|---|---|
| Cash flows from operating activities: | | | |
| Net income................................... | | $108,000 | |
| Adjustments to reconcile net income to net cash flow from operating activities: | | | |
| Depreciation ...................................... | | 7,000 | |
| Gain on sale of land............................. | | (12,000) | |
| Changes in current operating assets and liabilities: | | | |
| Increase in accounts receivable................. | | (9,000) | |
| Decrease in inventories......................... | | 8,000 | |
| Decrease in accounts payable ................... | | (3,200) | |
| Increase in accrued expenses payable........... | | 2,200 | |
| Decrease in income taxes payable .............. | | (500) | |
| Net cash flow from operating activities ................ | | | $100,500 |
| Cash flows from investing activities: | | | |
| Cash from sale of land................................ | | $ 72,000 | |
| Less: Cash paid to purchase land ...................... | $15,000 | | |
| Cash paid for purchase of building ................ | 60,000 | 75,000 | |
| Net cash flow used for investing activities.............. | | | (3,000) |
| Cash flows from financing activities: | | | |
| Cash received from sale of common stock.............. | | $ 48,000 | |
| Less: Cash paid to retire bonds payable ................ | $50,000 | | |
| Cash paid for dividends......................... | 24,000 | 74,000 | |
| Net cash flow used for financing activities ............. | | | (26,000) |
| Increase in cash ......................................... | | | $ 71,500 |
| Cash at the beginning of the year........................ | | | 26,000 |
| Cash at the end of the year.............................. | | | $ 97,500 |

# Statement of Cash Flows—The Direct Method

OBJ. 3 Prepare a statement of cash flows, using the direct method.

The direct method reports cash flows from operating activities as follows:

| | | |
|---|---|---|
| Cash flows from operating activities: | | |
| Cash received from customers ......................................... | | $ XXX |
| Less: Cash payments for merchandise ................................. | $ XXX | |
| Cash payments for operating expenses........................... | XXX | |
| Cash payments for interest ....................................... | XXX | |
| Cash payments for income taxes ................................. | XXX | XXX |
| Net cash flows from operating activities .............................. | | $ XXX |

The Cash Flows from Investing and Financing Activities sections of the statement of cash flows are exactly the same under both the direct and indirect methods. The amount of cash flows from operating activities is also the same, but the manner in which it is reported is different.

Under the direct method, the income statement is adjusted to cash flows from operating activities as follows:

| Income Statement | Adjusted to | Cash Flows from Operating Activities |
|---|:---:|---|
| Sales | → | Cash received from customers |
| Cost of merchandise sold | → | Cash payments for merchandise |
| Operating expenses: | | |
| Depreciation expense | N/A | N/A |
| Other operating expenses | → | Cash payments for operating expenses |
| Gain on sale of land | N/A | N/A |
| Interest expense | → | Cash payments for interest |
| Income tax expense | → | Cash payments for income taxes |
| Net income | → | Cash flows from operating activities |

N/A—Not applicable

As shown above, depreciation expense is not adjusted or reported as part of cash flows from operating activities. This is because deprecation expense does not involve a cash outflow. The gain on sale of land is also not adjusted and is not reported as part of cash flows from operating activities. This is because the cash flow from operating activities is determined directly, rather than by reconciling net income. The cash proceeds from the sale of land are reported as an investing activity.

To illustrate the direct method, the income statement and comparative balance sheet for Rundell Inc. shown in Exhibit 3, on pages 644–645, are used.

## Cash Received from Customers

The income statement (shown in Exhibit 3) of Rundell Inc. reports sales of $1,180,000. To determine the *cash received from customers*, the $1,180,000 is adjusted for any increase or decrease in accounts receivable. The adjustment is summarized below.

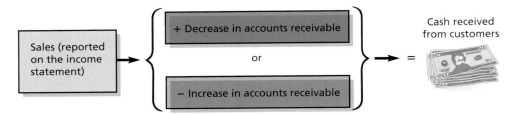

The cash received from customers is $1,171,000, computed as follows:

| | |
|---|---|
| Sales | $ 1,180,000 |
| Less increase in accounts receivable | 9,000 |
| Cash received from customers | $1,171,000 |

The increase of $9,000 in accounts receivable (shown in Exhibit 3) during 2012 indicates that sales on account exceeded cash received from customers by $9,000. In other words, sales include $9,000 that did not result in a cash inflow during the year. Thus, $9,000 is deducted from sales to determine the *cash received from customers*.

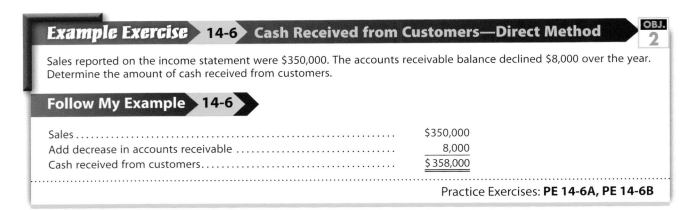

**Example Exercise 14-6 Cash Received from Customers—Direct Method**

OBJ. 2

Sales reported on the income statement were $350,000. The accounts receivable balance declined $8,000 over the year. Determine the amount of cash received from customers.

**Follow My Example 14-6**

| | |
|---|---|
| Sales | $350,000 |
| Add decrease in accounts receivable | 8,000 |
| Cash received from customers | $ 358,000 |

Practice Exercises: **PE 14-6A, PE 14-6B**

## Cash Payments for Merchandise

The income statement (shown in Exhibit 3) for Rundell Inc. reports cost of merchandise sold of $790,000. To determine the *cash payments for merchandise*, the $790,000 is adjusted for any increases or decreases in inventories and accounts payable. Assuming the accounts payable are owed to merchandise suppliers, the adjustment is summarized below.

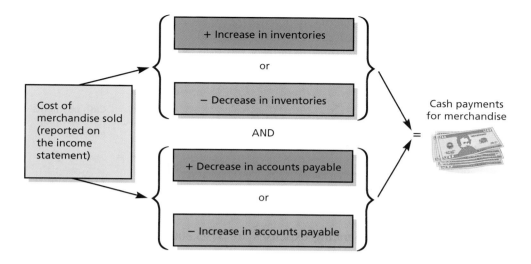

The cash payments for merchandise are $785,200, computed as follows:

| | |
|---|---|
| Cost of merchandise sold | $790,000 |
| Deduct decrease in inventories | (8,000) |
| Add decrease in accounts payable | 3,200 |
| Cash payments for merchandise | $785,200 |

The $8,000 decrease in inventories (from Exhibit 3) indicates that the merchandise sold exceeded the cost of the merchandise purchased by $8,000. In other words, the cost of merchandise sold includes $8,000 of goods sold from inventory that did not require a cash outflow during the year. Thus, $8,000 is deducted from the cost of merchandise sold in determining the *cash payments for merchandise*.

The $3,200 decrease in accounts payable (from Exhibit 3) indicates that cash payments for merchandise were $3,200 more than the purchases on account during 2012. Therefore, $3,200 is added to the cost of merchandise sold in determining the *cash payments for merchandise*.

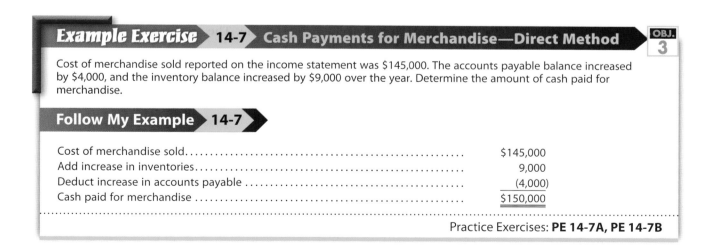

*Example Exercise* **14-7** **Cash Payments for Merchandise—Direct Method** OBJ. 3

Cost of merchandise sold reported on the income statement was $145,000. The accounts payable balance increased by $4,000, and the inventory balance increased by $9,000 over the year. Determine the amount of cash paid for merchandise.

**Follow My Example 14-7**

| | |
|---|---|
| Cost of merchandise sold | $145,000 |
| Add increase in inventories | 9,000 |
| Deduct increase in accounts payable | (4,000) |
| Cash paid for merchandise | $150,000 |

Practice Exercises: **PE 14-7A, PE 14-7B**

## Cash Payments for Operating Expenses

The income statement (from Exhibit 3) for Rundell Inc. reports total operating expenses of $203,000, which includes depreciation expense of $7,000. Since depreciation expense does not require a cash outflow, it is omitted from *cash payments for operating expenses*.

To determine the *cash payments for operating expenses*, the other operating expenses (excluding depreciation) of $196,000 ($203,000 − $7,000) are adjusted for any increase or decrease in accrued expenses payable. Assuming that the accrued expenses payable are all operating expenses, this adjustment is summarized below.

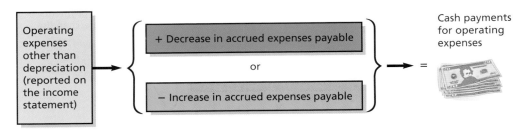

The cash payments for operating expenses are $193,800, computed as follows:

| | |
|---|---:|
| Operating expenses other than depreciation | $196,000 |
| Deduct increase in accrued expenses payable | (2,200) |
| Cash payments for operating expenses | $193,800 |

The increase in accrued expenses payable (from Exhibit 3) indicates that the cash payments for operating expenses were $2,200 less than the amount reported for operating expenses during the year. Thus, $2,200 is deducted from the operating expenses in determining the *cash payments for operating expenses*.

## Gain on Sale of Land

The income statement for Rundell Inc. (from Exhibit 3) reports a gain of $12,000 on the sale of land. The sale of land is an investing activity. Thus, the proceeds from the sale, which include the gain, are reported as part of the cash flows from investing activities.

## Interest Expense

The income statement (from Exhibit 3) for Rundell Inc. reports interest expense of $8,000. To determine the *cash payments for interest*, the $8,000 is adjusted for any increases or decreases in interest payable. The adjustment is summarized as follows:

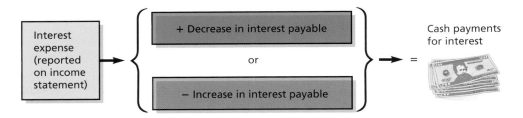

The comparative balance sheet of Rundell Inc. in Exhibit 3 indicates no interest payable. This is because the interest expense on the bonds payable is paid on June 1 and December 31. Since there is no interest payable, no adjustment of the interest expense of $8,000 is necessary.

## Cash Payments for Income Taxes

The income statement (from Exhibit 3) for Rundell Inc. reports income tax expense of $83,000. To determine the *cash payments for income taxes*, the $83,000 is adjusted for any increases or decreases in income taxes payable. The adjustment is summarized below.

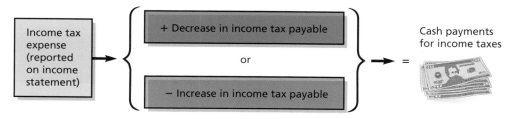

The cash payments for income taxes are $83,500, computed as follows:

| | |
|---|---|
| Income tax expense | $83,000 |
| Add decrease in income taxes payable | 500 |
| Cash payments for income taxes | $83,500 |

The $500 decrease in income taxes payable (from Exhibit 3) indicates that the cash payments for income taxes were $500 more than the amount reported for income tax expense during 2012. Thus, $500 is added to the income tax expense in determining the *cash payments for income taxes*.

# Reporting Cash Flows from Operating Activities—Direct Method

The statement of cash flows for Rundell Inc. using the direct method for reporting cash flows from operating activities is shown in Exhibit 7. The portions of the statement that differ from those prepared under the indirect method are highlighted in color.

---

**EXHIBIT 7**

**Statement of Cash Flows— Direct Method**

**Rundell Inc.**
**Statement of Cash Flows**
**For the Year Ended December 31, 2012**

| | | | |
|---|---|---|---|
| Cash flows from operating activities: | | | |
| Cash received from customers ......................... | | $1,171,000 | |
| Deduct: Cash payments for merchandise.............. | $785,200 | | |
| Cash payments for operating expenses........ | 193,800 | | |
| Cash payments for interest ................... | 8,000 | | |
| Cash payments for income taxes ............. | 83,500 | 1,070,500 | |
| Net cash flow from operating activities ............... | | | $100,500 |
| Cash flows from investing activities: | | | |
| Cash from sale of land................................ | | $ 72,000 | |
| Less: Cash paid to purchase land ..................... | $ 15,000 | | |
| Cash paid for purchase of building .............. | 60,000 | 75,000 | |
| Net cash flow used for investing activities............. | | | (3,000) |
| Cash flows from financing activities: | | | |
| Cash received from sale of common stock............. | | $ 48,000 | |
| Less: Cash paid to retire bonds payable ............... | $ 50,000 | | |
| Cash paid for dividends ........................ | 24,000 | 74,000 | |
| Net cash flow used for financing activities ........... | | | (26,000) |
| Increase in cash ........................................ | | | $ 71,500 |
| Cash at the beginning of the year....................... | | | 26,000 |
| Cash at the end of the year............................. | | | $ 97,500 |
| **Schedule Reconciling Net Income with Cash** | | | |
| **Flows from Operating Activities:** | | | |
| Cash flows from operating activities: | | | |
| Net income......................................... | | | $108,000 |

*(continued)*

| Rundell Inc. Statement of Cash Flows For the Year Ended December 31, 2012 | |
|---|---|
| Adjustments to reconcile net income to net cash flow from operating activities: | |
| Depreciation | 7,000 |
| Gain on sale of land | (12,000) |
| Changes in current operating assets and liabilities: | |
| Increase in accounts receivable | (9,000) |
| Decrease in inventory | 8,000 |
| Decrease in accounts payable | (3,200) |
| Increase in accrued expenses payable | 2,200 |
| Decrease in income taxes payable | (500) |
| Net cash flow from operating activities | $100,500 |

Exhibit 7 also includes the separate schedule reconciling net income and net cash flow from operating activities. This schedule is included in the statement of cash flows when the direct method is used. This schedule is similar to the Cash Flows from Operating Activities section prepared under the indirect method.

## InternationalConnection

### IFRS FOR STATEMENT OF CASH FLOWS

The statement of cash flows is required under International Financial Reporting Standards (IFRS). The statement of cash flows under IFRS is similar to that reported under U.S. GAAP in that the statement has separate sections for operating, investing, and financing activities. Like U.S. GAAP, IFRS also allow the use of either the indirect or direct method of reporting cash flows from operating activities. IFRS differ from U.S. GAAP in some minor areas, including:

- Interest paid can be reported as either an operating or a financing activity, while interest received can be reported as either an operating or an investing activity. In contrast, U.S. GAAP reports interest paid or received as an operating activity.
- Dividends paid can be reported as either an operating or a financing activity, while dividends received can be reported as either an operating or an investing activity. In contrast, U.S. GAAP reports dividends paid as a financing activity and dividends received as an operating activity.
- Cash flows to pay taxes are reported as a separate line in the operating activities, in contrast to U.S. GAAP, which does not require a separate line disclosure.

*\* IFRS are further discussed and illustrated in Appendix E.*

# Financial Analysis and Interpretation: Free Cash Flow

A valuable tool for evaluating the cash flows of a business is free cash flow. **Free cash flow** measures the operating cash flow available to a company to use after purchasing the property, plant, and equipment (PP&E) necessary to maintain current productive capacity.[6] It is computed as follows:

6 Productive capacity is the number of goods the company is currently producing and selling.

| Cash flow from operating activities | $XXX |
|---|---|
| Less: Investments in PP&E needed to maintain current production | XXX |
| Free cash flow | $XXX |

Analysts often use free cash flow, rather than cash flows from operating activities, to measure the financial strength of a business. Industries such as airlines, railroads, and telecommunications companies must invest heavily in new equipment to remain competitive. Such investments can significantly reduce free cash flow. For example, Verizon Communications Inc.'s free cash flow is less than 35% of the cash flow from operating activities. In contrast, The Coca-Cola Company's free cash flow is approximately 74% of the cash flow from operating activities.

To illustrate, the cash flow from operating activities for Research in Motion, Inc., maker of BlackBerry® smartphones, was $1,452 million in a recent fiscal year. The statement of cash flows indicated that the cash invested in property, plant, and equipment was $834 million. Assuming that the amount invested in property, plant, and equipment is necessary to maintain productive capacity, free cash flow would be computed as follows (in millions):

| Cash flow from operating activities | $1,452 |
|---|---|
| Less: Investments in PP&E needed to maintain current production | 834 |
| Free cash flow | $ 618 |

Research in Motion's free cash flow was 43% of cash flow from operations and over 5% of sales. Compare this to the calculation of free cash flows for Apple, Inc. (a computer company), The Coca-Cola Company (a beverage company), and Verizon Communications, Inc. (a telecommunications company) shown below (in millions):

| | Apple, Inc. | The Coca-Cola Company | Verizon Communications, Inc. |
|---|---|---|---|
| Sales | $36,537 | $31,944 | $97,354 |
| Cash flow from operating activities | $10,159 | $ 7,571 | $26,620 |
| Less: Investments in PP&E needed to maintain current production | 1,144 | 1,968 | 17,238 |
| Free cash flow | $ 9,015 | $ 5,603 | $ 9,382 |
| Free cash flow as a percentage of cash flow from operations | 89% | 74% | 35% |
| Free cash flow as a percentage of sales | 25% | 18% | 10% |

Positive free cash flow is considered favorable. A company that has free cash flow is able to fund internal growth, retire debt, pay dividends, and benefit from financial flexibility. A company with no free cash flow is unable to maintain current productive capacity. Lack of free cash flow can be an early indicator of liquidity problems. As one analyst notes, "Free cash flow gives the company firepower to reduce debt and ultimately generate consistent, actual income."[7]

7 Jill Krutick, *Fortune*, March 30, 1998, p. 106.

**Example Exercise** **14-8** **Free Cash Flow** OBJ. 4

Omnicron Inc. reported the following on the company's cash flow statement in 2012 and 2011:

|  | 2012 | 2011 |
|---|---|---|
| Net cash flow from operating activities | $140,000 | $120,000 |
| Net cash flow used for investing activities | (120,000) | (80,000) |
| Net cash flow used for financing activities | (20,000) | (32,000) |

Seventy-five percent of the cash flow used for investing activities was used to replace existing capacity.

a. Determine Omnicron's free cash flow.

b. Has Omnicron's free cash flow improved or declined from 2011 to 2012?

**Follow My Example** **14-8**

a.

|  | 2012 | 2011 |
|---|---|---|
| Cash flow from operating activities | $140,000 | $120,000 |
| Less: Investments in fixed assets to maintain current production | 90,000[1] | 60,000[2] |
| Free cash flow | $ 50,000 | $ 60,000 |

[1] $120,000 × 75%
[2] $80,000 × 75%

b. The change from $60,000 to $50,000 indicates an unfavorable trend.

Practice Exercises: **PE 14-8A, PE 14-8B**

# A P P E N D I X

# Spreadsheet (Work Sheet) for Statement of Cash Flows—The Indirect Method

A spreadsheet (work sheet) may used in preparing the statement of cash flows. However, whether or not a spreadsheet (work sheet) is used, the concepts presented in this chapter are not affected.

The data for Rundell Inc., presented in Exhibit 3 on pages 644–645, are used as a basis for illustrating the spreadsheet (work sheet) for the indirect method. The steps in preparing this spreadsheet (work sheet), shown in Exhibit 8, are as follows:

Step 1. List the title of each balance sheet account in the Accounts column.

Step 2. For each balance sheet account, enter its balance as of December 31, 2011, in the first column and its balance as of December 31, 2012, in the last column. Place the credit balances in parentheses.

Step 3. Add the December 31, 2011 and 2012 column totals, which should total to zero.

Step 4. Analyze the change during the year in each noncash account to determine its net increase (decrease) and classify the change as affecting cash flows from operating activities, investing activities, financing activities, or noncash investing and financing activities.

**EXHIBIT 8**    **End-of-Period Spreadsheet (Work Sheet) for Statement of Cash Flows—Indirect Method**

Step 2

| | A | B | C | D | E | F | G |
|---|---|---|---|---|---|---|---|
| 1 | | Rundell Inc. | | | | | |
| 2 | | End-of-Period Spreadsheet (Work Sheet) for Statement of Cash Flows | | | | | |
| 3 | | For the Year Ended December 31, 2012 | | | | | |
| 4 | Accounts | Balance, | Transactions | | | | Balance, |
| 5 | | Dec. 31, 2011 | Debit | | | Credit | Dec. 31, 2012 |
| 6 | Cash | 26,000 | (o) | 71,500 | | | 97,500 |
| 7 | Accounts receivable (net) | 65,000 | (n) | 9,000 | | | 74,000 |
| 8 | Inventories | 180,000 | | | (m) | 8,000 | 172,000 |
| 9 | Land | 125,000 | (k) | 15,000 | (l) | 60,000 | 80,000 |
| 10 | Building | 200,000 | (j) | 60,000 | | | 260,000 |
| 11 | Accumulated depreciation—building | (58,300) | | | (i) | 7,000 | (65,300) |
| 12 | Accounts payable (merchandise creditors) | (46,700) | (h) | 3,200 | | | (43,500) |
| 13 | Accrued expenses payable (operating expenses) | (24,300) | | | (g) | 2,200 | (26,500) |
| 14 | Income taxes payable | (8,400) | (f) | 500 | | | (7,900) |
| 15 | Dividends payable | (10,000) | | | (e) | 4,000 | (14,000) |
| 16 | Bonds payable | (150,000) | (d) | 50,000 | | | (100,000) |
| 17 | Common stock | (16,000) | | | (c) | 8,000 | (24,000) |
| 18 | Paid-in capital in excess of par | (80,000) | | | (c) | 40,000 | (120,000) |
| 19 | Retained earnings | (202,300) | (b) | 28,000 | (a) | 108,000 | (282,300) |
| 20 | Totals | 0 | | 237,200 | | 237,200 | 0 |
| 21 | Operating activities: | | | | | | |
| 22 |   Net income | | (a) | 108,000 | | | |
| 23 |   Depreciation of building | | (i) | 7,000 | | | |
| 24 |   Gain on sale of land | | | | (l) | 12,000 | |
| 25 |   Increase in accounts receivable | | | | (n) | 9,000 | |
| 26 |   Decrease in inventories | | (m) | 8,000 | | | |
| 27 |   Decrease in accounts payable | | | | (h) | 3,200 | |
| 28 |   Increase in accrued expenses payable | | (g) | 2,200 | | | |
| 29 |   Decrease in income taxes payable | | | | (f) | 500 | |
| 30 | Investing activities: | | | | | | |
| 31 |   Sale of land | | (l) | 72,000 | | | |
| 32 |   Purchase of land | | | | (k) | 15,000 | |
| 33 |   Purchase of building | | | | (j) | 60,000 | |
| 34 | Financing activities: | | | | | | |
| 35 |   Issued common stock | | (c) | 48,000 | | | |
| 36 |   Retired bonds payable | | | | (d) | 50,000 | |
| 37 |   Declared cash dividends | | | | (b) | 28,000 | |
| 38 |   Increase in dividends payable | | (e) | 4,000 | | | |
| 39 | Net increase in cash | | | | (o) | 71,500 | |
| 40 | Totals | | | 249,200 | | 249,200 | |

Step 3 (row 20, column B and column G)

Steps 4–7

Step 5. Indicate the effect of the change on cash flows by making entries in the Transactions columns.

Step 6. After all noncash accounts have been analyzed, enter the net increase (decrease) in cash during the period.

Step 7. Add the Debit and Credit Transactions columns. The totals should be equal.

## Analyzing Accounts

In analyzing the noncash accounts (Step 4), try to determine the type of cash flow activity (operating, investing, or financing) that led to the change in account. As each noncash account is analyzed, an entry (Step 5) is made on the spreadsheet (work sheet) for the type of cash flow activity that caused the change. After all noncash accounts have been analyzed, an entry (Step 6) is made for the increase (decrease) in cash during the period.

The entries made on the spreadsheet are not posted to the ledger. They are only used in preparing and summarizing the data on the spreadsheet.

The order in which the accounts are analyzed is not important. However, it is more efficient to begin with Retained Earnings and proceed upward in the account listing.

## Retained Earnings

The spreadsheet (work sheet) shows a Retained Earnings balance of $202,300 at December 31, 2011, and $282,300 at December 31, 2012. Thus, Retained Earnings increased $80,000 during the year. This increase is from the following:

1. Net income of $108,000
2. Declaring cash dividends of $28,000

To identify the cash flows from these activities, two entries are made on the spreadsheet.

The $108,000 is reported on the statement of cash flows as part of "cash flows from operating activities." Thus, an entry is made in the Transactions columns on the spreadsheet as follows:

| | | | |
|---|---|---|---|
| (a) | Operating Activities—Net Income............................. | 108,000 | |
| | Retained Earnings............................................ | | 108,000 |

The preceding entry accounts for the net income portion of the change to Retained Earnings. It also identifies the cash flow in the bottom portion of the spreadsheet as related to operating activities.

The $28,000 of dividends is reported as a financing activity on the statement of cash flows. Thus, an entry is made in the Transactions columns on the spreadsheet as follows:

| | | | |
|---|---|---|---|
| (b) | Retained Earnings............................................ | 28,000 | |
| | Financing Activities—Declared Cash Dividends ................ | | 28,000 |

The preceding entry accounts for the dividends portion of the change to Retained Earnings. It also identifies the cash flow in the bottom portion of the spreadsheet as related to financing activities. The $28,000 of declared dividends will be adjusted later for the actual amount of cash dividends paid during the year.

## Other Accounts

The entries for the other noncash accounts are made in the spreadsheet in a manner similar to entries (a) and (b). A summary of these entries is as follows:

| | | | |
|---|---|---|---|
| (c) | Financing Activities—Issued Common Stock...................... | 48,000 | |
| | Common Stock ............................................... | | 8,000 |
| | Paid-In Capital in Excess of Par—Common Stock ................ | | 40,000 |
| (d) | Bonds Payable ................................................ | 50,000 | |
| | Financing Activities—Retired Bonds Payable.................... | | 50,000 |
| (e) | Financing Activities—Increase in Dividends Payable................ | 4,000 | |
| | Dividends Payable ........................................... | | 4,000 |
| (f) | Income Taxes Payable ........................................ | 500 | |
| | Operating Activities—Decrease in Income Taxes Payable ........ | | 500 |
| (g) | Operating Activities—Increase in Accrued Expenses Payable ....... | 2,200 | |
| | Accrued Expenses Payable .................................... | | 2,200 |

| | | | |
|---|---|---|---|
| (h) | Accounts Payable .............................................. | 3,200 | |
| | Operating Activities—Decrease in Accounts Payable ............ | | 3,200 |
| (i) | Operating Activities—Depreciation of Building .................... | 7,000 | |
| | Accumulated Depreciation—Building ......................... | | 7,000 |
| (j) | Building ...................................................... | 60,000 | |
| | Investing Activities—Purchase of Building ..................... | | 60,000 |
| (k) | Land.......................................................... | 15,000 | |
| | Investing Activities—Purchase of Land......................... | | 15,000 |
| (l) | Investing Activities—Sale of Land............................... | 72,000 | |
| | Operating Activities—Gain on Sale of Land .................... | | 12,000 |
| | Land.......................................................... | | 60,000 |
| (m) | Operating Activities—Decrease in Inventories..................... | 8,000 | |
| | Inventories................................................... | | 8,000 |
| (n) | Accounts Receivable ........................................... | 9,000 | |
| | Operating Activities—Increase in Accounts Receivable .......... | | 9,000 |
| (o) | Cash.......................................................... | 71,500 | |
| | Net Increase in Cash.......................................... | | 71,500 |

After all the balance sheet accounts are analyzed and the entries made on the spreadsheet (work sheet), all the operating, investing, and financing activities are identified in the bottom portion of the spreadsheet. The accuracy of the entries is verified by totaling the Debit and Credit Transactions columns. The totals of the columns should be equal.

## Preparing the Statement of Cash Flows

The statement of cash flows prepared from the spreadsheet is identical to the statement in Exhibit 6 on page 655. The data for the three sections of the statement are obtained from the bottom portion of the spreadsheet.

## At a Glance 14

**OBJ. 1**

**Describe the cash flow activities reported in the statement of cash flows.**

**Key Points**   The statement of cash flows reports cash receipts and cash payments by three types of activities: operating activities, investing activities, and financing activities. Cash flows from operating activities are the cash inflow or outflow from a company's day-to-day operations. Cash flows from investing activities show the cash inflows and outflows related to changes in a company's long-term assets. Cash flows from financing activities show the cash inflows and outflows related to changes in a company's long-term liabilities and stockholders' equity. Investing and financing for a business may be affected by transactions that do not involve cash. The effect of such transactions should be reported in a separate schedule accompanying the statement of cash flows.

| Learning Outcomes | Example Exercises | Practice Exercises |
|---|---|---|
| • Classify transactions that either provide or use cash into either operating, investing, or financing activities. | EE14-1 | PE14-1A, 14-1B |

**OBJ. 2**

## Prepare a statement of cash flows, using the indirect method.

**Key Points** The indirect method reports cash flow from operating activities by adjusting net income for revenues and expenses that do not involve the receipt or payment of cash. Noncash expenses such as depreciation are added back to net income. Gains and losses on the disposal of assets are added to or deducted from net income. Changes in current operating assets and liabilities are added to or subtracted from net income depending on their effect on cash. Cash flow from investing activities and cash flow from financing activities are reported below cash flow from operating activities in the statement of cash flows.

| Learning Outcomes | Example Exercises | Practice Exercises |
|---|---|---|
| • Determine cash flow from operating activities under the indirect method by adjusting net income for noncash expenses and gains and losses from asset disposals. | EE14-2 | PE14-2A, 14-2B |
| • Determine cash flow from operating activities under the indirect method by adjusting net income for changes in current operating assets and liabilities. | EE14-3 | PE14-3A, 14-3B |
| • Prepare the Cash Flows from Operating Activities section of the statement of cash flows using the indirect method. | EE14-4 | PE14-4A, 14-4B |
| • Prepare the Cash Flows from Investing Activities and Cash Flows from Financing Activities sections of the statement of cash flows. | EE14-5 | PE14-5A, 14-5B |

**OBJ. 3**

## Prepare a statement of cash flows, using the direct method.

**Key Points** The amount of cash flows from operating activities is the same under both the direct and indirect methods, but the manner in which cash flow from operating activities is reported is different. The direct method reports cash flows from operating activities by major classes of operating cash receipts and cash payments. The difference between the major classes of total operating cash receipts and total operating cash payments is the net cash flow from operating activities. The Cash Flows from Investing and Financing Activities sections of the statement are the same under both the direct and indirect methods.

| Learning Outcomes | Example Exercises | Practice Exercises |
|---|---|---|
| • Prepare the cash flows from operating activities and the remainder of the statement of cash flows under the direct method. | EE14-6<br>EE14-7 | PE14-6A, 14-6B<br>PE14-7A, 14-7B |

**OBJ. 4**

## Describe and illustrate the use of free cash flow in evaluating a company's cash flow.

**Key Points** Free cash flow measures the operating cash flow available for company use after purchasing the fixed assets that are necessary to maintain current productive capacity. It is calculated by subtracting these fixed asset purchases from cash flow from operating activities. A company with strong free cash flow is able to fund internal growth, retire debt, pay dividends, and enjoy financial flexibility. A company with weak free cash flow has much less financial flexibility for such activities.

| Learning Outcomes | Example Exercises | Practice Exercises |
|---|---|---|
| • Describe free cash flow. | | |
| • Calculate and evaluate free cash flow. | EE14-8 | PE14-8A, 14-8B |

## Key Terms

cash flow per share (643)

cash flows from financing
activities (641)

cash flows from investing
activities (640)

cash flows from operating
activities (640)

direct method (641)

free cash flow (660)

indirect method (642)

statement of cash
flows (640)

## Illustrative Problem

The comparative balance sheet of Dowling Company for December 31, 2012 and 2011, is
as follows:

### Dowling Company
### Comparative Balance Sheet
### December 31, 2012 and 2011

|  | 2012 | 2011 |
|---|---|---|
| **Assets** | | |
| Cash ..................................................... | $ 140,350 | $ 95,900 |
| Accounts receivable (net) ..................................... | 95,300 | 102,300 |
| Inventories ............................................... | 165,200 | 157,900 |
| Prepaid expenses .......................................... | 6,240 | 5,860 |
| Investments (long-term) ..................................... | 35,700 | 84,700 |
| Land ..................................................... | 75,000 | 90,000 |
| Buildings ................................................. | 375,000 | 260,000 |
| Accumulated depreciation—buildings......................... | (71,300) | (58,300) |
| Machinery and equipment..................................... | 428,300 | 428,300 |
| Accumulated depreciation—machinery and equipment.......... | (148,500) | (138,000) |
| Patents ................................................... | 58,000 | 65,000 |
| Total assets ............................................... | $1,159,290 | $1,093,660 |
| | | |
| **Liabilities and Stockholders' Equity** | | |
| Accounts payable (merchandise creditors) ..................... | $ 43,500 | $ 46,700 |
| Accrued expenses payable (operating expenses) ............... | 14,000 | 12,500 |
| Income taxes payable........................................ | 7,900 | 8,400 |
| Dividends payable........................................... | 14,000 | 10,000 |
| Mortgage note payable, due 2023 ............................ | 40,000 | 0 |
| Bonds payable ............................................. | 150,000 | 250,000 |
| Common stock, $30 par....................................... | 450,000 | 375,000 |
| Excess of issue price over par—common stock ................. | 66,250 | 41,250 |
| Retained earnings........................................... | 373,640 | 349,810 |
| Total liabilities and stockholders' equity........................ | $1,159,290 | $1,093,660 |

The income statement for Dowling Company is shown here.

### Dowling Company
### Income Statement
### For the Year Ended December 31, 2012

| | | |
|---|---:|---:|
| Sales . . . . . . . . . . . . . . . . . . . . . . . . . . . . . . . . . . . . . . . . . . . . . . . . . . . . | | $1,100,000 |
| Cost of merchandise sold . . . . . . . . . . . . . . . . . . . . . . . . . . . . . . . . . . . . | | 710,000 |
| Gross profit . . . . . . . . . . . . . . . . . . . . . . . . . . . . . . . . . . . . . . . . . . . . . . . | | $ 390,000 |
| Operating expenses: | | |
|    Depreciation expense . . . . . . . . . . . . . . . . . . . . . . . . . . . . . . . . . | $ 23,500 | |
|    Patent amortization . . . . . . . . . . . . . . . . . . . . . . . . . . . . . . . . . . . | 7,000 | |
|    Other operating expenses . . . . . . . . . . . . . . . . . . . . . . . . . . . . . . | 196,000 | |
|       Total operating expenses . . . . . . . . . . . . . . . . . . . . . . . . | | 226,500 |
| Income from operations . . . . . . . . . . . . . . . . . . . . . . . . . . . . . . . . . . . | | $ 163,500 |
| Other income: | | |
|    Gain on sale of investments . . . . . . . . . . . . . . . . . . . . . . . . . . . . . | $ 11,000 | |
| Other expense: | | |
|    Interest expense . . . . . . . . . . . . . . . . . . . . . . . . . . . . . . . . . . . . . . | 26,000 | (15,000) |
| Income before income tax . . . . . . . . . . . . . . . . . . . . . . . . . . . . . . . . . . | | $ 148,500 |
| Income tax expense . . . . . . . . . . . . . . . . . . . . . . . . . . . . . . . . . . . . . . . . | | 50,000 |
| Net income . . . . . . . . . . . . . . . . . . . . . . . . . . . . . . . . . . . . . . . . . . . . . . . | | $ 98,500 |

An examination of the accounting records revealed the following additional information applicable to 2012:

a. Land costing $15,000 was sold for $15,000.

b. A mortgage note was issued for $40,000.

c. A building costing $115,000 was constructed.

d. 2,500 shares of common stock were issued at $40 in exchange for the bonds payable.

e. Cash dividends declared were $74,670.

### Instructions

1. Prepare a statement of cash flows, using the indirect method of reporting cash flows from operating activities.

2. Prepare a statement of cash flows, using the direct method of reporting cash flows from operating activities.

## Solution

1.

| Dowling Company |
|---|
| **Statement of Cash Flows—Indirect Method** |
| **For the Year Ended December 31, 2012** |

| | | | |
|---|---|---|---|
| Cash flows from operating activities: | | | |
| Net income | | $ 98,500 | |
| Adjustments to reconcile net income to net cash flow from operating activities: | | | |
| Depreciation | | 23,500 | |
| Amortization of patents | | 7,000 | |
| Gain on sale of investments | | (11,000) | |
| Changes in current operating assets and liabilities: | | | |
| Decrease in accounts receivable | | 7,000 | |
| Increase in inventories | | (7,300) | |
| Increase in prepaid expenses | | (380) | |
| Decrease in accounts payable | | (3,200) | |
| Increase in accrued expenses payable | | 1,500 | |
| Decrease in income taxes payable | | (500) | |
| Net cash flow from operating activities | | | $115,120 |
| Cash flows from investing activities: | | | |
| Cash received from sale of: | | | |
| Investments | $60,000[1] | | |
| Land | 15,000 | $ 75,000 | |
| Less: Cash paid for construction of building | | 115,000 | |
| Net cash flow used for investing activities | | | (40,000) |
| Cash flows from financing activities: | | | |
| Cash received from issuing mortgage note payable | | $ 40,000 | |
| Less: Cash paid for dividends | | 70,670[2] | |
| Net cash flow used for financing activities | | | (30,670) |
| Increase in cash | | | $ 44,450 |
| Cash at the beginning of the year | | | 95,900 |
| Cash at the end of the year | | | $140,350 |
| | | | |
| **Schedule of Noncash Investing and Financing Activities:** | | | |
| Issued common stock to retire bonds payable | | | $100,000 |

[1] $60,000 = $11,000 gain + $49,000 (decrease in investments)
[2] $70,670 = $74,670 − $4,000 (increase in dividends)

2.

---

**Dowling Company**
**Statement of Cash Flows—Direct Method**
**For the Year Ended December 31, 2012**

| | | | |
|---|---|---|---|
| Cash flows from operating activities: | | | |
| Cash received from customers[1]...................... | | $1,107,000 | |
| Deduct: Cash paid for merchandise[2].................. | $720,500 | | |
| Cash paid for operating expenses[3]............. | 194,880 | | |
| Cash paid for interest expense ............... | 26,000 | | |
| Cash paid for income tax[4].................... | 50,500 | 991,880 | |
| Net cash flow from operating activities ............... | | | $115,120 |
| Cash flows from investing activities: | | | |
| Cash received from sale of: | | | |
| Investments..................................... | $ 60,000[5] | | |
| Land........................................... | 15,000 | $ 75,000 | |
| Less: Cash paid for construction of building ........... | | 115,000 | |
| Net cash flow used for investing activities............. | | | (40,000) |
| Cash flows from financing activities: | | | |
| Cash received from issuing mortgage note payable..... | | $ 40,000 | |
| Less: Cash paid for dividends[6]....................... | | 70,670 | |
| Net cash flow used for financing activities ............. | | | (30,670) |
| Increase in cash ........................................ | | | $ 44,450 |
| Cash at the beginning of the year....................... | | | 95,900 |
| Cash at the end of the year............................. | | | $140,350 |

**Schedule of Noncash Investing and Financing Activities:**

| | |
|---|---|
| Issued common stock to retire bonds payable.......... | $100,000 |

**Schedule Reconciling Net Income with Cash Flows from Operating Activities[7]**

**Computations:**

[1]$1,100,000 + $7,000 = $1,107,000
[2]$710,000 + $3,200 + $7,300 = $720,500
[3]$196,000 + $380 – $1,500 = $194,880
[4]$50,000 + $500 = $50,500
[5]$60,000 = $11,000 gain + $49,000 (decrease in investments)

[6]$74,670 + $10,000 – $14,000 = $70,670
[7]The content of this schedule is the same as the Operating Activities section of part (1) of this solution and is not reproduced here for the sake of brevity.

# Discussion Questions

1. What is the principal disadvantage of the direct method of reporting cash flows from operating activities?

2. What are the major advantages of the indirect method of reporting cash flows from operating activities?

3. A corporation issued $1,000,000 of common stock in exchange for $1,000,000 of fixed assets. Where would this transaction be reported on the statement of cash flows?

4. A retail business, using the accrual method of accounting, owed merchandise creditors (accounts payable) $240,000 at the beginning of the year and $265,000 at the end of the year. How would the $25,000 increase be used to adjust net income in determining the amount of cash flows from operating activities by the indirect method? Explain.

5. If salaries payable was $75,000 at the beginning of the year and $40,000 at the end of the year, should $35,000 be added to or deducted from income to determine the amount of cash flows from operating activities by the indirect method? Explain.

6. A long-term investment in bonds with a cost of $800,000 was sold for $910,000 cash. (a) What was

the gain or loss on the sale? (b) What was the effect of the transaction on cash flows? (c) How should the transaction be reported in the statement of cash flows if cash flows from operating activities are reported by the indirect method?

7. A corporation issued $10,000,000 of 20-year bonds for cash at 102. How would the transaction be reported on the statement of cash flows?

8. Fully depreciated equipment costing $25,000 was discarded. What was the effect of the transaction on cash flows if (a) $10,000 cash is received, (b) no cash is received?

9. For the current year, Bearings Company decided to switch from the indirect method to the direct method for reporting cash flows from operating activities on the statement of cash flows. Will the change cause the amount of net cash flow from operating activities to be (a) larger, (b) smaller, or (c) the same as if the indirect method had been used? Explain.

10. Name five common major classes of operating cash receipts or operating cash payments presented on the statement of cash flows when the cash flows from operating activities are reported by the direct method.

# Practice Exercises

| Learning Objectives | Example Exercises | |
|---|---|---|
| OBJ. 1 | EE 14-1 p. 643 | **PE 14-1A   Classifying cash flows** |

Identify whether each of the following would be reported as an operating, investing, or financing activity in the statement of cash flows.

a. Retirement of bonds payable

b. Payment of accounts payable

c. Issuance of common stock

d. Payment for administrative expenses

e. Cash received from customers

f. Purchase of land

---

**OBJ. 1    EE 14-1** p. 643

**PE 14-1B   Classifying cash flows**

Identify whether each of the following would be reported as an operating, investing, or financing activity in the statement of cash flows.

a. Issuance of bonds payable

b. Cash sales

c. Collection of accounts receivable

d. Payment for selling expenses

e. Disposal of equipment

f. Purchase of investments

---

**OBJ. 2    EE 14-2** p. 647

**PE 14-2A   Adjustments to net income—indirect method**

Martin Corporation's accumulated depreciation—furniture increased by $10,500, while $3,850 of patents were amortized between balance sheet dates. There were no purchases or sales of depreciable or intangible assets during the year. In addition, the income statement showed a loss of $5,600 from the sale of land. Reconcile a net income of $150,500 to net cash flow from operating activities.

---

**OBJ. 2    EE 14-2** p. 647

**PE 14-2B   Adjustments to net income—indirect method**

Chu Corporation's accumulated depreciation—equipment increased by $5,600, while $2,080 of patents were amortized between balance sheet dates. There were no purchases or sales of depreciable or intangible assets during the year. In addition, the income statement showed a gain of $12,000 from the sale of investments. Reconcile a net income of $112,000 to net cash flow from operating activities.

---

**OBJ. 2    EE 14-3** p. 650

**PE 14-3A   Changes in current operating assets and liabilities—indirect method**

Phelps Corporation's comparative balance sheet for current assets and liabilities was as follows:

|  | Dec. 31, 2013 | Dec. 31, 2012 |
|---|---|---|
| Accounts receivable | $22,500 | $27,000 |
| Inventory | 15,000 | 12,900 |
| Accounts payable | 13,500 | 11,850 |
| Dividends payable | 41,250 | 44,250 |

Adjust net income of $138,000 for changes in operating assets and liabilities to arrive at net cash flow from operating activities.

**OBJ. 2**    **EE 14-3**   *p. 650*

### PE 14-3B   Changes in current operating assets and liabilities—indirect method

Dali Corporation's comparative balance sheet for current assets and liabilities was as follows:

|  | Dec. 31, 2013 | Dec. 31, 2012 |
|---|---|---|
| Accounts receivable | $25,500 | $20,400 |
| Inventory | 49,300 | 42,075 |
| Accounts payable | 39,100 | 29,325 |
| Dividends payable | 11,900 | 15,300 |

Adjust net income of $240,000 for changes in operating assets and liabilities to arrive at net cash flow from operating activities.

**OBJ. 2**    **EE 14-4**   *p. 651*

### PE 14-4A   Cash flows from operating activities—indirect method

Salem Inc. reported the following data:

| | |
|---|---|
| Net income | $168,750 |
| Depreciation expense | 18,750 |
| Gain on disposal of equipment | 15,375 |
| Decrease in accounts receivable | 10,500 |
| Decrease in accounts payable | 2,700 |

Prepare the Cash Flows from Operating Activities section of the statement of cash flows using the indirect method.

**OBJ. 2**    **EE 14-4**   *p. 651*

### PE 14-4B   Cash flows from operating activities—indirect method

Malibu Inc. reported the following data:

| | |
|---|---|
| Net income | $393,750 |
| Depreciation expense | 67,500 |
| Loss on disposal of equipment | 27,450 |
| Increase in accounts receivable | 24,300 |
| Increase in accounts payable | 12,600 |

Prepare the Cash Flows from Operating Activities section of the statement of cash flows using the indirect method.

**OBJ. 2**    **EE 14-5**   *p. 654*

### PE 14-5A   Land transactions on the statement of cash flows

Seeing Double Corporation purchased land for $510,000. Later in the year, the company sold land with a book value of $217,500 for $165,000. How are the effects of these transactions reported on the statement of cash flows?

**OBJ. 2**    **EE 14-5**   *p. 654*

### PE 14-5B   Land transactions on the statement of cash flows

Pilot Corporation purchased land for $480,000. Later in the year, the company sold land with a book value of $288,000 for $328,000. How are the effects of these transactions reported on the statement of cash flows?

**OBJ. 3**    **EE 14-6**   *p. 656*

### PE 14-6A   Cash received from customers—direct method

Sales reported on the income statement were $450,000. The accounts receivable balance increased $47,000 over the year. Determine the amount of cash received from customers.

**OBJ. 3**    **EE 14-6**   *p. 656*

### PE 14-6B   Cash received from customers—direct method

Sales reported on the income statement were $85,600. The accounts receivable balance decreased $7,400 over the year. Determine the amount of cash received from customers.

**OBJ. 3** **EE 14-7** *p. 657*

### PE 14-7A Cash payments for merchandise—direct method

Cost of merchandise sold reported on the income statement was $360,000. The accounts payable balance decreased $17,800, and the inventory balance decreased by $28,000 over the year. Determine the amount of cash paid for merchandise.

**OBJ. 3** **EE 14-7** *p. 657*

### PE 14-7B Cash payments for merchandise—direct method

Cost of merchandise sold reported on the income statement was $210,000. The accounts payable balance increased $8,600, and the inventory balance increased by $16,900 over the year. Determine the amount of cash paid for merchandise.

**OBJ. 4** **EE 14-8** *p. 662*

### PE 14-8A Free cash flow

Totson Inc. reported the following on the company's statement of cash flows in 2012 and 2011:

|  | 2012 | 2011 |
| --- | --- | --- |
| Net cash flow from operating activities | $ 210,000 | $ 200,000 |
| Net cash flow used for investing activities | (160,000) | (180,000) |
| Net cash flow used for financing activities | (45,000) | (30,000) |

Eighty percent of the cash flow used for investing activities was used to replace existing capacity.

a. Determine Totson's free cash flow.

b. Has Totson's free cash flow improved or declined from 2011 to 2012?

**OBJ. 4** **EE 14-8** *p. 662*

### PE 14-8B Free cash flow

Burkenfelt Inc. reported the following on the company's statement of cash flows in 2012 and 2011:

|  | 2012 | 2011 |
| --- | --- | --- |
| Net cash flow from operating activities | $ 340,000 | $ 325,000 |
| Net cash flow used for investing activities | (305,000) | (270,000) |
| Net cash flow used for financing activities | (30,000) | (42,000) |

Seventy percent of the cash flow used for investing activities was used to replace existing capacity.

a. Determine Burkenfelt's free cash flow.

b. Has Burkenfelt's free cash flow improved or declined from 2011 to 2012?

## Exercises

**OBJ. 1**

### EX 14-1 Cash flows from operating activities—net loss

On its income statement for a recent year, Continental Airlines, Inc. reported a net *loss* of $68 million from operations. On its statement of cash flows, it reported $457 million of cash flows from operating activities.

Explain this apparent contradiction between the loss and the positive cash flows.

**OBJ. 1**

✔ c. Cash payment,
$560,000

### EX 14-2 Effect of transactions on cash flows

State the effect (cash receipt or payment and amount) of each of the following transactions, considered individually, on cash flows:

a. Sold equipment with a book value of $65,000 for $83,000.

b. Sold a new issue of $400,000 of bonds at 98.

c. Retired $550,000 of bonds, on which there was $5,000 of unamortized discount, for $560,000.

d. Purchased 2,000 shares of $25 par common stock as treasury stock at $50 per share.

e. Sold 5,000 shares of $20 par common stock for $100 per share.

f. Paid dividends of $1.00 per share. There were 50,000 shares issued and 6,000 shares of treasury stock.

g. Purchased land for $320,000 cash.

h. Purchased a building by paying $40,000 cash and issuing a $60,000 mortgage note payable.

---

**OBJ. 1**

### EX 14-3 Classifying cash flows

Identify the type of cash flow activity for each of the following events (operating, investing, or financing):

a. Sold equipment.

b. Issued bonds.

c. Issued common stock.

d. Paid cash dividends.

e. Purchased treasury stock.

f. Redeemed bonds.

g. Purchased patents.

h. Purchased buildings.

i. Sold long-term investments.

j. Issued preferred stock.

k. Net income.

---

**OBJ. 2**

### EX 14-4 Cash flows from operating activities—indirect method

Indicate whether each of the following would be added to or deducted from net income in determining net cash flow from operating activities by the indirect method:

a. Decrease in accounts payable

b. Increase in notes receivable due in 90 days from customers

c. Decrease in accounts receivable

d. Loss on disposal of fixed assets

e. Increase in notes payable due in 90 days to vendors

f. Amortization of patent

g. Depreciation of fixed assets

h. Gain on retirement of long-term debt

i. Decrease in salaries payable

j. Increase in merchandise inventory

k. Decrease in prepaid expenses

---

**OBJ. 1, 2**

✔ Net cash flow from operating activities, $752,880

### EX 14-5 Cash flows from operating activities—indirect method

The net income reported on the income statement for the current year was $720,000. Depreciation recorded on store equipment for the year amounted to $32,700. Balances of the current asset and current liability accounts at the beginning and end of the year are as follows:

|  | End of Year | Beginning of Year |
|---|---|---|
| Cash | $78,450 | $72,300 |
| Accounts receivable (net) | 56,250 | 53,400 |
| Merchandise inventory | 76,800 | 81,330 |
| Prepaid expenses | 9,000 | 6,900 |
| Accounts payable (merchandise creditors) | 73,500 | 68,400 |
| Wages payable | 40,200 | 44,700 |

a. Prepare the Cash Flows from Operating Activities section of the statement of cash flows, using the indirect method.

b. ▬▬▶ Briefly explain why cash flows from operating activities is different than net income.

---

**OBJ. 1, 2**

✔ Net cash flow from operating activities, $466,110

### EX 14-6 Cash flows from operating activities—indirect method

The net income reported on the income statement for the current year was $378,000. Depreciation recorded on equipment and a building amounted to $112,500 for the year. Balances of the current asset and current liability accounts at the beginning and end of the year are as follows:

| | End of Year | Beginning of Year |
|---|---|---|
| Cash | $100,800 | $107,100 |
| Accounts receivable (net) | 127,800 | 132,120 |
| Inventories | 252,000 | 227,700 |
| Prepaid expenses | 14,040 | 15,120 |
| Accounts payable (merchandise creditors) | 112,680 | 119,520 |
| Salaries payable | 16,200 | 14,850 |

a. Prepare the Cash Flows from Operating Activities section of the statement of cash flows, using the indirect method.

b. ➤ If the direct method had been used, would the net cash flow from operating activities have been the same? Explain.

---

**OBJ. 1, 2**

✔ Net cash flow from operating activities, $197,220

### EX 14-7 Cash flows from operating activities—indirect method

The income statement disclosed the following items for 2013:

| | |
|---|---|
| Depreciation expense | $ 21,600 |
| Gain on disposal of equipment | 12,600 |
| Net income | 190,500 |

Balances of the current asset and current liability accounts changed between December 31, 2012, and December 31, 2013, as follows:

| | |
|---|---|
| Accounts receivable | $3,360 |
| Inventory | 1,920* |
| Prepaid insurance | 720* |
| Accounts payable | 2,280* |
| Income taxes payable | 720 |
| Dividends payable | 510 |

*Decrease

a. Prepare the Cash Flows from Operating Activities section of the statement of cash flows, using the indirect method.

b. Briefly explain why cash flows from operating activities is different than net income.

---

**OBJ. 2**

### EX 14-8 Determining cash payments to stockholders

The board of directors declared cash dividends totaling $260,000 during the current year. The comparative balance sheet indicates dividends payable of $74,500 at the beginning of the year and $65,000 at the end of the year. What was the amount of cash payments to stockholders during the year?

---

**OBJ. 2**

### EX 14-9 Reporting changes in equipment on statement of cash flows

An analysis of the general ledger accounts indicates that office equipment, which cost $89,000 and on which accumulated depreciation totaled $36,000 on the date of sale, was sold for $43,500 during the year. Using this information, indicate the items to be reported on the statement of cash flows.

---

**OBJ. 2**

### EX 14-10 Reporting changes in equipment on statement of cash flows

An analysis of the general ledger accounts indicates that delivery equipment, which cost $246,000 and on which accumulated depreciation totaled $124,500 on the date of sale, was sold for $110,500 during the year. Using this information, indicate the items to be reported on the statement of cash flows.

OBJ. 2

**EX 14-11   Reporting land transactions on statement of cash flows**

On the basis of the details of the following fixed asset account, indicate the items to be reported on the statement of cash flows:

ACCOUNT *Land*                                    ACCOUNT NO.

| Date | | Item | Debit | Credit | Balance Debit | Balance Credit |
|------|--|------|-------|--------|--------|--------|
| 2012 | | | | | | |
| Jan. | 1 | Balance | | | 620,000 | |
| Apr. | 6 | Purchased for cash | 74,500 | | 694,500 | |
| Nov. | 23 | Sold for $68,250 | | 45,600 | 648,900 | |

OBJ. 2

**EX 14-12   Reporting stockholders' equity items on statement of cash flows**

On the basis of the following stockholders' equity accounts, indicate the items, exclusive of net income, to be reported on the statement of cash flows. There were no unpaid dividends at either the beginning or the end of the year.

ACCOUNT *Common Stock, $30 par*                  ACCOUNT NO.

| Date | | Item | Debit | Credit | Balance Debit | Balance Credit |
|------|--|------|-------|--------|--------|--------|
| 2012 | | | | | | |
| Jan. | 1 | Balance, 90,000 shares | | | | 2,700,000 |
| Mar. | 7 | 22,500 shares issued for cash | | 675,000 | | 3,375,000 |
| June | 30 | 3,300-share stock dividend | | 99,000 | | 3,474,000 |

ACCOUNT *Paid-In Capital in Excess of Par—Common Stock*      ACCOUNT NO.

| Date | | Item | Debit | Credit | Balance Debit | Balance Credit |
|------|--|------|-------|--------|--------|--------|
| 2012 | | | | | | |
| Jan. | 1 | Balance | | | | 300,000 |
| Mar. | 7 | 22,500 shares issued for cash | | 1,080,000 | | 1,380,000 |
| June | 30 | Stock dividend | | 178,200 | | 1,558,200 |

ACCOUNT *Retained Earnings*                       ACCOUNT NO.

| Date | | Item | Debit | Credit | Balance Debit | Balance Credit |
|------|--|------|-------|--------|--------|--------|
| 2012 | | | | | | |
| Jan. | 1 | Balance | | | | 1,500,000 |
| June | 30 | Stock dividend | 277,200 | | | 1,222,800 |
| Dec. | 30 | Cash dividend | 260,550 | | | 962,250 |
| | 31 | Net income | | 1,080,000 | | 2,042,250 |

OBJ. 2

**EX 14-13   Reporting land acquisition for cash and mortgage note on statement of cash flows**

On the basis of the details of the following fixed asset account, indicate the items to be reported on the statement of cash flows:

ACCOUNT *Land*                                    ACCOUNT NO.

| Date | | Item | Debit | Credit | Balance Debit | Balance Credit |
|------|--|------|-------|--------|--------|--------|
| 2012 | | | | | | |
| Jan. | 1 | Balance | | | 195,000 | |
| Feb. | 10 | Purchased for cash | 307,500 | | 502,500 | |
| Nov. | 20 | Purchased with long-term mortgage note | 405,000 | | 907,500 | |

OBJ. 2

### EX 14-14 Reporting issuance and retirement of long-term debt

On the basis of the details of the following bonds payable and related discount accounts, indicate the items to be reported in the Financing Activities section of the statement of cash flows, assuming no gain or loss on retiring the bonds:

**ACCOUNT** Bonds Payable    **ACCOUNT NO.**

| Date | | Item | Debit | Credit | Balance Debit | Balance Credit |
|------|---|------|-------|--------|-------|--------|
| 2012 | | | | | | |
| Jan. | 1 | Balance | | | | 800,000 |
| | 2 | Retire bonds | 160,000 | | | 640,000 |
| June | 30 | Issue bonds | | 480,000 | | 1,120,000 |

**ACCOUNT** Discount on Bond Payable    **ACCOUNT NO.**

| Date | | Item | Debit | Credit | Balance Debit | Balance Credit |
|------|---|------|-------|--------|-------|--------|
| 2012 | | | | | | |
| Jan. | 1 | Balance | | | 36,000 | |
| | 2 | Retire bonds | | 12,800 | 23,200 | |
| June | 30 | Issue bonds | 32,000 | | 55,200 | |
| Dec. | 31 | Amortize discount | | 2,800 | 52,400 | |

OBJ. 1, 2

✔ Net income, $233,025

### EX 14-15 Determining net income from net cash flow from operating activities

Shinlund, Inc., reported a net cash flow from operating activities of $243,750 on its statement of cash flows for the year ended December 31, 2012. The following information was reported in the Cash Flows from Operating Activities section of the statement of cash flows, using the indirect method:

| | |
|---|---|
| Decrease in income taxes payable | $ 5,250 |
| Decrease in inventories | 13,050 |
| Depreciation | 20,100 |
| Gain on sale of investments | 9,000 |
| Increase in accounts payable | 3,600 |
| Increase in prepaid expenses | 2,025 |
| Increase in accounts receivable | 9,750 |

a. Determine the net income reported by Shinlund, Inc., for the year ended December 31, 2012.

b. Briefly explain why Shinlund's net income is different than cash flows from operating activities.

OBJ. 2

✔ Net cash flow from operating activities, $(7,263)

### EX 14-16 Cash flows from operating activities—indirect method

Selected data derived from the income statement and balance sheet of Jones Soda Co. for a recent year are as follows:

| | |
|---|---|
| Income statement data (in thousands): | |
| Net earnings | $(10,547) |
| Losses on inventory write-down and fixed assets | 2,248 |
| Depreciation expense | 811 |
| Stock-based compensation expense (noncash) | 727 |
| Balance sheet data (in thousands): | |
| Decrease in accounts receivable | 364 |
| Decrease in inventory | 210 |
| Decrease in prepaid expenses | 206 |
| Decrease in accounts payable | (165) |
| Decrease in accrued liabilities | (1,117) |

a. Prepare the Cash Flows from Operating Activities section of the statement of cash flows using the indirect method for Jones Soda Co. for the year.

b. ➤ Interpret your results in part (a).

### EX 14-17 Statement of cash flows—indirect method

The comparative balance sheet of Hobson Medical Equipment Inc. for December 31, 2013 and 2012, is as follows:

|  | Dec. 31, 2013 | Dec. 31, 2012 |
|---|---|---|
| **Assets** | | |
| Cash | $294 | $ 96 |
| Accounts receivable (net) | 168 | 120 |
| Inventories | 105 | 66 |
| Land | 240 | 270 |
| Equipment | 135 | 105 |
| Accumulated depreciation—equipment | (36) | (18) |
| Total | $906 | $639 |
| **Liabilities and Stockholders' Equity** | | |
| Accounts payable (merchandise creditors) | $105 | $ 96 |
| Dividends payable | 18 | — |
| Common stock, $10 par | 60 | 30 |
| Paid-in capital in excess of par—common stock | 150 | 75 |
| Retained earnings | 573 | 438 |
| Total | $906 | $639 |

The following additional information is taken from the records:

    a. Land was sold for $75.

    b. Equipment was acquired for cash.

    c. There were no disposals of equipment during the year.

    d. The common stock was issued for cash.

    e. There was a $195 credit to Retained Earnings for net income.

    f. There was a $60 debit to Retained Earnings for cash dividends declared.

Respond to the following:

a. Prepare a statement of cash flows, using the indirect method of presenting cash flows from operating activities.

b. Was Hobson Medical Equipment's cash flow from operations more or less than net income? What is the source of this difference?

OBJ. 2

### EX 14-18 Statement of cash flows—indirect method

List the errors you find in the following statement of cash flows. The cash balance at the beginning of the year was $180,576. All other amounts are correct, except the cash balance at the end of the year.

**Hough Inc.**
**Statement of Cash Flows**
**For the Year Ended December 31, 2012**

| | | |
|---|---|---|
| Cash flows from operating activities: | | |
| Net income | $266,544 | |
| Adjustments to reconcile net income to net cash flow from operating activities: | | |
| Depreciation | 75,600 | |
| Gain on sale of investements | 12,960 | |
| Changes in current operating assets and liabilities: | | |
| Increase in accounts receivable | 20,520 | |
| Increase in inventories | (26,568) | |
| Increase in accounts payable | (7,992) | |
| Decrease in accrued expenses payable | (1,944) | |
| Net cash flow from operating activities | | $339,120 |

*(continued)*

| Cash flows from investing activities: | | | |
|---|---|---|---|
| Cash received from sale of investments .................. | | $183,600 | |
| Less: Cash paid for purchase of land ...................... | $194,400 | | |
| Cash paid for purchase of equipment................ | 324,360 | 518,760 | |
| Net cash flow used for investing activities................. | | | (335,160) |
| Cash flows from financing activities: | | | |
| Cash received from sale of common stock................. | | $231,120 | |
| Cash paid for dividends..................................... | | 97,200 | |
| Net cash flow provided by financing activities............. | | | 133,920 |
| Increase in cash .......................................... | | | $ 86,904 |
| Cash at the end of the year................................ | | | 180,576 |
| Cash at the beginning of the year........................... | | | $267,480 |

---

OBJ. 3

✔ a. $546,375

### EX 14-19  Cash flows from operating activities—direct method

The cash flows from operating activities are reported by the direct method on the statement of cash flows. Determine the following:

a. If sales for the current year were $513,750 and accounts receivable decreased by $32,625 during the year, what was the amount of cash received from customers?

b. If income tax expense for the current year was $34,500 and income tax payable decreased by $3,900 during the year, what was the amount of cash payments for income tax?

c. Briefly explain why the cash received from customers in (a) is different than sales.

---

OBJ. 3

### EX 14-20  Cash paid for merchandise purchases

The cost of merchandise sold for Kohl's Corporation for a recent year was $10,680 million. The balance sheet showed the following current account balances (in millions):

| | Balance, End of Year | Balance, Beginning of Year |
|---|---|---|
| Merchandise inventories | $2,923 | $2,799 |
| Accounts payable | 2,374 | 1,827 |

Determine the amount of cash payments for merchandise.

---

OBJ. 3

✔ a. $624,442

### EX 14-21  Determining selected amounts for cash flows from operating activities—direct method

Selected data taken from the accounting records of Bentson Inc. for the current year ended December 31 are as follows:

| | Balance, December 31 | Balance, January 1 |
|---|---|---|
| Accrued expenses payable (operating expenses) | $ 7,826 | $ 8,554 |
| Accounts payable (merchandise creditors) | 58,422 | 64,428 |
| Inventories | 108,290 | 117,754 |
| Prepaid expenses | 4,550 | 5,460 |

During the current year, the cost of merchandise sold was $627,900, and the operating expenses other than depreciation were $109,200. The direct method is used for presenting the cash flows from operating activities on the statement of cash flows.

Determine the amount reported on the statement of cash flows for (a) cash payments for merchandise and (b) cash payments for operating expenses.

**EX 14-22 Cash flows from operating activities—direct method**

The income statement of Goliath Industries Inc. for the current year ended June 30 is as follows:

| | | |
|---|---|---|
| Sales .............................................. | | $273,600 |
| Cost of merchandise sold ................................. | | 155,400 |
| Gross profit ........................................... | | $118,200 |
| Operating expenses: | | |
|    Depreciation expense ..................... | $21,000 | |
|    Other operating expenses ........................... | 55,440 | |
|       Total operating expenses .......................... | | 76,440 |
| Income before income tax ............................... | | $ 41,760 |
| Income tax expense ..................................... | | 11,580 |
| Net income .......................................... | | $ 30,180 |

Changes in the balances of selected accounts from the beginning to the end of the current year are as follows:

| | Increase Decrease* |
|---|---|
| Accounts receivable (net) ......................................... | $6,300* |
| Inventories ..................................................... | 2,100 |
| Prepaid expenses ............................................... | 2,040* |
| Accounts payable (merchandise creditors) ......................... | 4,320* |
| Accrued expenses payable (operating expenses) ................... | 660 |
| Income tax payable............................................ | 1,440* |

a. Prepare the Cash Flows from Operating Activities section of the statement of cash flows, using the direct method.

b. What does the direct method show about a company's cash flow from operating activities that is not shown using the indirect method?

**EX 14-23 Cash flows from operating activities—direct method**

The income statement for Kipitz Company for the current year ended June 30 and balances of selected accounts at the beginning and the end of the year are as follows:

| | | |
|---|---|---|
| Sales ................................................. | | $657,800 |
| Cost of merchandise sold ................................. | | 227,500 |
| Gross profit ........................................... | | $430,300 |
| Operating expenses: | | |
|    Depreciation expense ..................................... | $ 56,875 | |
|    Other operating expenses ............................. | 170,300 | |
|       Total operating expenses .............................. | | 227,175 |
| Income before income tax ................................ | | $203,125 |
| Income tax expense ..................................... | | 58,500 |
| Net income ............................................. | | $144,625 |

| | End of Year | Beginning of Year |
|---|---|---|
| Accounts receivable (net) .................................... | $ 52,975 | $ 46,085 |
| Inventories ............................................... | 136,500 | 118,625 |
| Prepaid expenses ......................................... | 21,450 | 23,595 |
| Accounts payable (merchandise creditors) ................... | 99,775 | 92,625 |
| Accrued expenses payable (operating expenses) ............. | 28,275 | 30,875 |
| Income tax payable......................................... | 6,500 | 6,500 |

Prepare the Cash Flows from Operating Activities section of the statement of cash flows, using the direct method.

OBJ. 4

**EX 14-24    Free cash flow**

Iglesias Enterprises, Inc. has cash flows from operating activities of $385,000. Cash flows used for investments in property, plant, and equipment totaled $145,000, of which 80% of this investment was used to replace existing capacity.

a.  Determine the free cash flow for Iglesias Enterprises, Inc.

b.  How might a lender use free cash flow to determine whether or not to give Iglesias Enterprises, Inc. a loan?

OBJ. 4

**EX 14-25    Free cash flow**

The financial statements for Nike, Inc., are provided in Appendix D at the end of the text.

a.  Determine the free cash flow for the year ended May 31, 2010. Assume that 90% of additions to property, plant and equipment were used to maintain productive capacity.

b.  How might a lender use free cash flow to determine whether or not to give Nike, Inc. a loan?

c.  Would you feel comfortable giving Nike a loan based on the free cash flow calculated in (a)?

OBJ. 4

**EX 14-26    Free cash flow**

Matthias Motors, Inc. has cash flows from operating activities of $900,000. Cash flows used for investments in property, plant, and equipment totaled $550,000, of which 75% of this investment was used to replace existing capacity.

Determine the free cash flow for Matthias Motors, Inc.

## Problems Series A

OBJ. 2

✔ Net cash flow from operating activities, $37,140

**PR 14-1A    Statement of cash flows—indirect method**

The comparative balance sheet of Flack Inc. for December 31, 2013 and 2012, is shown as follows:

|  | Dec. 31, 2013 | Dec. 31, 2012 |
|---|---|---|
| **Assets** | | |
| Cash | $234,660 | $219,720 |
| Accounts receivable (net) | 85,440 | 78,360 |
| Inventories | 240,660 | 231,420 |
| Investments | 0 | 90,000 |
| Land | 123,000 | 0 |
| Equipment | 264,420 | 207,420 |
| Accumulated depreciation—equipment | (62,400) | (55,500) |
| | $885,780 | $771,420 |
| **Liabilities and Stockholders' Equity** | | |
| Accounts payable (merchandise creditors) | $159,180 | $151,860 |
| Accrued expenses payable (operating expenses) | 15,840 | 19,740 |
| Dividends payable | 9,000 | 7,200 |
| Common stock, $1 par | 48,000 | 36,000 |
| Paid-in capital in excess of par—common stock | 180,000 | 105,000 |
| Retained earnings | 473,760 | 451,620 |
| | $885,780 | $771,420 |

The following additional information was taken from the records:

a.  The investments were sold for $105,000 cash.

b.  Equipment and land were acquired for cash.

c.  There were no disposals of equipment during the year.

d.  The common stock was issued for cash.

e.  There was a $58,140 credit to Retained Earnings for net income.

f.  There was a $36,000 debit to Retained Earnings for cash dividends declared.

## Instructions

Prepare a statement of cash flows, using the indirect method of presenting cash flows from operating activities.

---

### PR 14-2A  Statement of cash flows—indirect method

The comparative balance sheet of Hinson Enterprises, Inc. at December 31, 2013 and 2012, is as follows:

|  | Dec. 31, 2013 | Dec. 31, 2012 |
|---|---|---|
| **Assets** | | |
| Cash | $ 128,275 | $ 157,325 |
| Accounts receivable (net) | 196,525 | 211,750 |
| Merchandise inventory | 281,400 | 261,800 |
| Prepaid expenses | 11,725 | 8,400 |
| Equipment | 573,125 | 469,875 |
| Accumulated depreciation—equipment | (149,450) | (115,675) |
| | $1,041,600 | $ 993,475 |
| **Liabilities and Stockholders' Equity** | | |
| Accounts payable (merchandise creditors) | $ 218,925 | $ 207,900 |
| Mortgage note payable | 0 | 294,000 |
| Common stock, $1 par | 91,000 | 21,000 |
| Paid-in capital in excess of par—common stock | 455,000 | 280,000 |
| Retained earnings | 276,675 | 190,575 |
| | $1,041,600 | $ 993,475 |

Additional data obtained from the income statement and from an examination of the accounts in the ledger for 2012 are as follows:

a. Net income, $220,500.

b. Depreciation reported on the income statement, $72,975.

c. Equipment was purchased at a cost of $142,450, and fully depreciated equipment costing $39,200 was discarded, with no salvage realized.

d. The mortgage note payable was not due until 2014, but the terms permitted earlier payment without penalty.

e. 7,000 shares of common stock were issued at $35 for cash.

f. Cash dividends declared and paid, $134,400.

## Instructions

Prepare a statement of cash flows, using the indirect method of presenting cash flows from operating activities.

---

### PR 14-3A  Statement of cash flows—indirect method

The comparative balance sheet of Mills Engine Co. at December 31, 2013 and 2012, is as follows:

|  | Dec. 31, 2013 | Dec. 31, 2012 |
|---|---|---|
| **Assets** | | |
| Cash | $ 714,000 | $ 750,400 |
| Accounts receivable (net) | 644,700 | 592,620 |
| Inventories | 986,580 | 904,540 |
| Prepaid expenses | 22,820 | 27,300 |
| Land | 245,700 | 373,100 |
| Buildings | 1,137,500 | 700,700 |
| Accumulated depreciation—buildings | (317,800) | (297,360) |
| Equipment | 398,440 | 353,640 |
| Accumulated depreciation—equipment | (109,900) | (123,480) |
| | $3,722,040 | $3,281,460 |

*(continued)*

**Liabilities and Stockholders' Equity**

| | | |
|---|---:|---:|
| Accounts payable (merchandise creditors) ...................... | $ 717,500 | $ 745,360 |
| Bonds payable .................................................. | 210,000 | 0 |
| Common stock, $20 par......................................... | 245,000 | 91,000 |
| Paid-in capital in excess of par—common stock ................. | 588,000 | 434,000 |
| Retained earnings.............................................. | 1,961,540 | 2,011,100 |
| | $3,722,040 | $3,281,460 |

The noncurrent asset, noncurrent liability, and stockholders' equity accounts for 2010 are as follows:

**ACCOUNT** *Land*                                                     ACCOUNT NO.

| Date | | Item | Debit | Credit | Balance Debit | Balance Credit |
|---|---|---|---|---|---|---|
| 2013 | | | | | | |
| Jan. | 1 | Balance | | | 373,100 | |
| Apr. | 20 | Realized $117,600 cash | | | | |
| | | from sale | | 127,400 | 245,700 | |

**ACCOUNT** *Buildings*                                                ACCOUNT NO.

| Date | | Item | Debit | Credit | Balance Debit | Balance Credit |
|---|---|---|---|---|---|---|
| 2013 | | | | | | |
| Jan. | 1 | Balance | | | 700,700 | |
| Apr. | 20 | Acquired for cash | 436,800 | | 1,137,500 | |

**ACCOUNT** *Accumulated Depreciation—Buildings*                       ACCOUNT NO.

| Date | | Item | Debit | Credit | Balance Debit | Balance Credit |
|---|---|---|---|---|---|---|
| 2013 | | | | | | |
| Jan. | 1 | Balance | | | | 297,360 |
| Dec. | 31 | Depreciation for year | | 20,440 | | 317,800 |

**ACCOUNT** *Equipment*                                                ACCOUNT NO.

| Date | | Item | Debit | Credit | Balance Debit | Balance Credit |
|---|---|---|---|---|---|---|
| 2013 | | | | | | |
| Jan. | 1 | Balance | | | 353,640 | |
| | 26 | Discarded, no salvage | | 36,400 | 317,240 | |
| Aug. | 11 | Purchased for cash | 81,200 | | 398,440 | |

**ACCOUNT** *Accumulated Depreciation—Equipment*                      ACCOUNT NO.

| Date | | Item | Debit | Credit | Balance Debit | Balance Credit |
|---|---|---|---|---|---|---|
| 2013 | | | | | | |
| Jan. | 1 | Balance | | | | 123,480 |
| | 26 | Equipment discarded | 36,400 | | | 87,080 |
| Dec. | 31 | Depreciation for year | | 22,820 | | 109,900 |

ACCOUNT *Bonds Payable*                                          ACCOUNT NO.

| Date | | Item | Debit | Credit | Balance Debit | Balance Credit |
|---|---|---|---|---|---|---|
| 2013 | | | | | | |
| May | 1 | Issued 20-year bonds | | 210,000 | | 210,000 |

ACCOUNT *Common Stock, $20 par*                                 ACCOUNT NO.

| Date | | Item | Debit | Credit | Balance Debit | Balance Credit |
|---|---|---|---|---|---|---|
| 2013 | | | | | | |
| Jan. | 1 | Balance | | | | 91,000 |
| Dec. | 7 | Issued 7,700 shares of common stock for $40 per share | | 154,000 | | 245,000 |

ACCOUNT *Paid-In Capital in Excess of Par—Common Stock*         ACCOUNT NO.

| Date | | Item | Debit | Credit | Balance Debit | Balance Credit |
|---|---|---|---|---|---|---|
| 2013 | | | | | | |
| Jan. | 1 | Balance | | | | 434,000 |
| Dec. | 7 | Issued 7,700 shares of common stock for $40 per share | | 154,000 | | 588,000 |

ACCOUNT *Retained Earnings*                                      ACCOUNT NO.

| Date | | Item | Debit | Credit | Balance Debit | Balance Credit |
|---|---|---|---|---|---|---|
| 2013 | | | | | | |
| Jan. | 1 | Balance | | | | 2,011,100 |
| Dec. | 31 | Net loss | 24,360 | | | 1,986,740 |
| | 31 | Cash dividends | 25,200 | | | 1,961,540 |

## Instructions

Prepare a statement of cash flows, using the indirect method of presenting cash flows from operating activities.

---

**OBJ. 3**

✔ Net cash flow from operating activities, $352,320

### PR 14-4A   Statement of cash flows—direct method

The comparative balance sheet of Rowe Products Inc. for December 31, 2013 and 2012, is as follows:

| | Dec. 31, 2013 | Dec. 31, 2012 |
|---|---|---|
| **Assets** | | |
| Cash ............................................... | $ 772,080 | $ 815,280 |
| Accounts receivable (net) ......................... | 680,160 | 656,880 |
| Inventories ....................................... | 1,213,200 | 1,179,360 |
| Investments ....................................... | 0 | 288,000 |
| Land .............................................. | 624,000 | 0 |
| Equipment.......................................... | 1,056,000 | 816,000 |
| Accumulated depreciation .......................... | (293,280) | (240,480) |
| | $4,052,160 | $3,515,040 |

*(continued)*

**Liabilities and Stockholders' Equity**

| | | |
|---|---:|---:|
| Accounts payable (merchandise creditors) ....................... | $ 926,160 | $ 898,080 |
| Accrued expenses payable (operating expenses) ................. | 76,080 | 84,960 |
| Dividends payable....................................... | 10,560 | 7,680 |
| Common stock, $10 par...................................... | 177,600 | 38,400 |
| Paid-in capital in excess of par—common stock ................. | 369,600 | 230,400 |
| Retained earnings........................................... | 2,492,160 | 2,255,520 |
| | $4,052,160 | $3,515,040 |

The income statement for the year ended December 31, 2012, is as follows:

| | | |
|---|---:|---:|
| Sales .................................................. | | $7,176,000 |
| Cost of merchandise sold ....................................... | | 2,942,400 |
| Gross profit ............................................. | | $4,233,600 |
| Operating expenses: | | |
|    Depreciation expense ...................................... | $ 52,800 | |
|    Other operating expenses ..................................... | 3,720,000 | |
|      Total operating expenses ................................ | | 3,772,800 |
| Operating income.......................................... | | $ 460,800 |
| Other expense: | | |
|    Loss on sale of investments .................................. | | (76,800) |
| Income before income tax ...................................... | | $ 384,000 |
| Income tax expense ........................................ | | 123,360 |
| Net income ............................................. | | $ 260,640 |

The following additional information was taken from the records:

a. Equipment and land were acquired for cash.

b. There were no disposals of equipment during the year.

c. The investments were sold for $211,200 cash.

d. The common stock was issued for cash.

e. There was a $24,000 debit to Retained Earnings for cash dividends declared.

**Instructions**

Prepare a statement of cash flows, using the direct method of presenting cash flows from operating activities.

---

OBJ. 3

✔ Net cash flow from operating activities, $37,140

**PR 14-5A** **Statement of cash flows—direct method applied to PR 14-1A**

The comparative balance sheet of Flack Inc. for December 31, 2013 and 2012, is as follows:

| | Dec. 31, 2013 | Dec. 31, 2012 |
|---|---:|---:|
| **Assets** | | |
| Cash ....................................................... | $234,660 | $219,720 |
| Accounts receivable (net) ....................................... | 85,440 | 78,360 |
| Inventories ................................................. | 240,660 | 231,420 |
| Investments ................................................. | 0 | 90,000 |
| Land ....................................................... | 123,000 | 0 |
| Equipment.................................................. | 264,420 | 207,420 |
| Accumulated depreciation—equipment ........................ | (62,400) | (55,500) |
| | $885,780 | $771,420 |
| **Liabilities and Stockholders' Equity** | | |
| Accounts payable (merchandise creditors) ..................... | $159,180 | $151,860 |
| Accrued expenses payable (operating expenses) ................ | 15,840 | 19,740 |
| Dividends payable........................................... | 9,000 | 7,200 |
| Common stock, $1 par........................................ | 48,000 | 36,000 |
| Paid-in capital in excess of par—common stock ................ | 180,000 | 105,000 |
| Retained earnings............................................ | 473,760 | 451,620 |
| | $885,780 | $771,420 |

The income statement for the year ended December 31, 2013, is as follows:

| | | |
|---|---:|---:|
| Sales | | $1,508,520 |
| Cost of merchandise sold | | 928,320 |
| Gross profit | | $ 580,200 |
| Operating expenses: | | |
| Depreciation expense | $ 6,900 | |
| Other operating expenses | 491,400 | |
| Total operating expenses | | 498,300 |
| Operating income | | $ 81,900 |
| Other income: | | |
| Gain on sale of investments | | 15,000 |
| Income before income tax | | $ 96,900 |
| Income tax expense | | 38,760 |
| Net income | | $ 58,140 |

The following additional information was taken from the records:

a. The investments were sold for $105,000 cash.

b. Equipment and land were acquired for cash.

c. There were no disposals of equipment during the year.

d. The common stock was issued for cash.

e. There was a $36,000 debit to Retained Earnings for cash dividends declared.

**Instructions**

Prepare a statement of cash flows, using the direct method of presenting cash flows from operating activities.

## Problems Series B

OBJ. 2

✔ Net cash flow from operating activities, $246,720

**PR 14-1B    Statement of cash flows—indirect method**

The comparative balance sheet of Juras Equipment Co. for December 31, 2013 and 2012, is as follows:

| | Dec. 31, 2013 | Dec. 31, 2012 |
|---|---:|---:|
| **Assets** | | |
| Cash | $ 99,840 | $ 67,680 |
| Accounts receivable (net) | 292,560 | 265,680 |
| Inventories | 421,440 | 409,200 |
| Investments | 0 | 144,000 |
| Land | 417,600 | 0 |
| Equipment | 619,200 | 505,440 |
| Accumulated depreciation | (139,920) | (119,040) |
| | $1,710,720 | $1,272,960 |
| **Liabilities and Stockholders' Equity** | | |
| Accounts payable (merchandise creditors) | $ 290,400 | $ 274,080 |
| Accrued expenses payable (operating expenses) | 43,200 | 37,920 |
| Dividends payable | 36,000 | 28,800 |
| Common stock, $1 par | 162,000 | 144,000 |
| Paid-in capital in excess of par—common stock | 594,000 | 288,000 |
| Retained earnings | 585,120 | 500,160 |
| | $1,710,720 | $1,272,960 |

The following additional information was taken from the records of Juras Equipment:

a. Equipment and land were acquired for cash.

b. There were no disposals of equipment during the year.

c. The investments were sold for $129,600 cash.

d. The common stock was issued for cash.

e. There was a $228,960 credit to Retained Earnings for net income.

f. There was a $144,000 debit to Retained Earnings for cash dividends declared.

**Instructions**

Prepare a statement of cash flows, using the indirect method of presenting cash flows from operating activities.

---

OBJ. 2

✔ Net cash flow from operating activities, $481,200

**PR 14-2B   Statement of cash flows—indirect method**

The comparative balance sheet of Beets Industries, Inc., at December 31, 2013 and 2012, is as follows:

|  | Dec. 31, 2013 | Dec. 31, 2012 |
|---|---|---|
| **Assets** | | |
| Cash | $   379,920 | $   309,360 |
| Accounts receivable (net) | 570,240 | 507,600 |
| Inventories | 761,040 | 876,480 |
| Prepaid expenses | 27,120 | 21,600 |
| Land | 259,200 | 259,200 |
| Buildings | 1,468,800 | 972,000 |
| Accumulated depreciation—buildings | (399,600) | (355,320) |
| Machinery and equipment | 669,600 | 669,600 |
| Accumulated depreciation—machinery and equipment | (183,600) | (164,160) |
| Patents | 91,680 | 103,680 |
|  | $3,644,400 | $3,200,040 |
| **Liabilities and Stockholders' Equity** | | |
| Accounts payable (merchandise creditors) | $   717,840 | $   794,640 |
| Dividends payable | 28,080 | 21,600 |
| Salaries payable | 67,680 | 74,640 |
| Mortgage note payable, due 2017 | 192,000 | 0 |
| Bonds payable | 0 | 336,000 |
| Common stock, $2 par | 99,200 | 43,200 |
| Paid-in capital in excess of par—common stock | 388,000 | 108,000 |
| Retained earnings | 2,151,600 | 1,821,960 |
|  | $3,644,400 | $3,200,040 |

An examination of the income statement and the accounting records revealed the following additional information applicable to 2013:

a. Net income, $441,960.

b. Depreciation expense reported on the income statement: buildings, $44,280; machinery and equipment, $19,440.

c. Patent amortization reported on the income statement, $12,000.

d. A building was constructed for $496,800.

e. A mortgage note for $192,000 was issued for cash.

f. 28,000 shares of common stock were issued at $12 in exchange for the bonds payable.

g. Cash dividends declared, $112,320.

**Instructions**

Prepare a statement of cash flows, using the indirect method of presenting cash flows from operating activities.

---

OBJ. 2

✔ Net cash flow from operating activities, $70,200

**PR 14-3B   Statement of cash flows—indirect method**

The comparative balance sheet of Wen Technology, Inc., at December 31, 2013 and 2012, is as follows:

| | | Dec. 31, 2013 | Dec. 31, 2012 |
|---|---|---|---|
| **Assets** | | | |
| Cash ................................................... | | $ 450,900 | $ 506,700 |
| Accounts receivable (net) ................................ | | 1,056,600 | 914,400 |
| Inventories ............................................. | | 1,377,900 | 1,298,700 |
| Prepaid expenses ....................................... | | 27,900 | 39,600 |
| Land .................................................... | | 1,485,000 | 2,079,000 |
| Buildings ............................................... | | 2,970,000 | 1,485,000 |
| Accumulated depreciation—buildings..................... | | (595,800) | (549,000) |
| Equipment .............................................. | | 990,900 | 794,700 |
| Accumulated depreciation—equipment ................... | | (199,800) | (243,000) |
| | | $7,563,600 | $6,326,100 |
| **Liabilities and Stockholders' Equity** | | | |
| Accounts payable (merchandise creditors) ................. | | $ 891,000 | $ 946,800 |
| Income tax payable ..................................... | | 39,600 | 32,400 |
| Bonds payable .......................................... | | 495,000 | 0 |
| Common stock, $10 par................................... | | 378,000 | 270,000 |
| Paid-in capital in excess of par—common stock ............. | | 1,701,000 | 1,215,000 |
| Retained earnings....................................... | | 4,059,000 | 3,861,900 |
| | | $7,563,600 | $6,326,100 |

The noncurrent asset, noncurrent liability, and stockholders' equity accounts for 2013 are as follows:

**ACCOUNT** *Land*  **ACCOUNT NO.**

| Date | | Item | Debit | Credit | Balance Debit | Balance Credit |
|---|---|---|---|---|---|---|
| 2013 | | | | | | |
| Jan. | 1 | Balance | | | 2,079,000 | |
| Apr. | 20 | Realized $684,000 cash from sale | | 594,000 | 1,485,000 | |

**ACCOUNT** *Buildings*  **ACCOUNT NO.**

| Date | | Item | Debit | Credit | Balance Debit | Balance Credit |
|---|---|---|---|---|---|---|
| 2013 | | | | | | |
| Jan. | 1 | Balance | | | 1,485,000 | |
| Apr. | 20 | Acquired for cash | 1,485,000 | | 2,970,000 | |

**ACCOUNT** *Accumulated Depreciation—Buildings*  **ACCOUNT NO.**

| Date | | Item | Debit | Credit | Balance Debit | Balance Credit |
|---|---|---|---|---|---|---|
| 2013 | | | | | | |
| Jan. | 1 | Balance | | | | 549,000 |
| Dec. | 31 | Depreciation for year | | 46,800 | | 595,800 |

**ACCOUNT** *Equipment*                                                    ACCOUNT NO.

| Date | | Item | Debit | Credit | Balance Debit | Balance Credit |
|---|---|---|---|---|---|---|
| 2013 | | | | | | |
| Jan. | 1 | Balance | | | 794,700 | |
| | 26 | Discarded, no salvage | | 99,000 | 695,700 | |
| Aug. | 11 | Purchased for cash | 295,200 | | 990,900 | |

**ACCOUNT** *Accumulated Depreciation—Equipment*                ACCOUNT NO.

| Date | | Item | Debit | Credit | Balance Debit | Balance Credit |
|---|---|---|---|---|---|---|
| 2013 | | | | | | |
| Jan. | 1 | Balance | | | | 243,000 |
| | 26 | Equipment discarded | 99,000 | | | 144,000 |
| Dec. | 31 | Depreciation for year | | 55,800 | | 199,800 |

**ACCOUNT** *Bonds Payable*                                               ACCOUNT NO.

| Date | | Item | Debit | Credit | Balance Debit | Balance Credit |
|---|---|---|---|---|---|---|
| 2013 | | | | | | |
| May | 1 | Issued 20-year bonds | | 495,000 | | 495,000 |

**ACCOUNT** *Common Stock, $10 par*                                       ACCOUNT NO.

| Date | | Item | Debit | Credit | Balance Debit | Balance Credit |
|---|---|---|---|---|---|---|
| 2013 | | | | | | |
| Jan. | 1 | Balance | | | | 270,000 |
| Dec. | 7 | Issued 10,800 shares of common stock for $10 per share | | 108,000 | | 378,000 |

**ACCOUNT** *Paid-In Capital in Excess of Par—Common Stock*        ACCOUNT NO.

| Date | | Item | Debit | Credit | Balance Debit | Balance Credit |
|---|---|---|---|---|---|---|
| 2013 | | | | | | |
| Jan. | 1 | Balance | | | | 1,215,000 |
| Dec. | 7 | Issued 10,800 shares of common stock for $10 per share | | 486,000 | | 1,701,000 |

**ACCOUNT** *Retained Earnings*                                          ACCOUNT NO.

| Date | | Item | Debit | Credit | Balance Debit | Balance Credit |
|---|---|---|---|---|---|---|
| 2013 | | | | | | |
| Jan. | 1 | Balance | | | | 3,861,900 |
| Dec. | 31 | Net income | | 315,900 | | 4,177,800 |
| | 31 | Cash dividends | 118,800 | | | 4,059,000 |

## Instructions

Prepare a statement of cash flows, using the indirect method of presenting cash flows from operating activities.

OBJ. 3

✔ Net cash flow from operating activities, $254,610

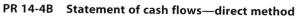

### PR 14-4B    Statement of cash flows—direct method

The comparative balance sheet of Middaugh Restaurant Supplies Inc. for December 31, 2013 and 2012, is as follows:

|  | Dec. 31, 2013 | Dec. 31, 2012 |
|---|---|---|
| **Assets** | | |
| Cash | $ 330,960 | $ 341,550 |
| Accounts receivable (net) | 496,320 | 457,200 |
| Inventories | 697,200 | 681,900 |
| Investments | 0 | 216,000 |
| Land | 480,000 | 0 |
| Equipment | 612,000 | 492,000 |
| Accumulated depreciation | (240,750) | (184,200) |
| | $2,375,730 | $2,004,450 |
| **Liabilities and Stockholders' Equity** | | |
| Accounts payable (merchandise creditors) | $ 540,000 | $ 483,300 |
| Accrued expenses payable (operating expenses) | 33,900 | 39,600 |
| Dividends payable | 50,400 | 45,600 |
| Common stock, $10 par | 108,000 | 15,000 |
| Paid-in capital in excess of par—common stock | 364,500 | 225,000 |
| Retained earnings | 1,278,930 | 1,195,950 |
| | $2,375,730 | $2,004,450 |

The income statement for the year ended December 31, 2012, is as follows:

| | | |
|---|---|---|
| Sales | | $2,256,000 |
| Cost of merchandise sold | | 1,176,000 |
| Gross profit | | $1,080,000 |
| Operating expenses: | | |
| Depreciation expense | $ 56,550 | |
| Other operating expenses | 672,420 | |
| Total operating expenses | | 728,970 |
| Operating income | | $ 351,030 |
| Other income: | | |
| Gain on sale of investments | | 78,000 |
| Income before income tax | | $ 429,030 |
| Income tax expense | | 149,550 |
| Net income | | $ 279,480 |

The following additional information was taken from the records:

a. Equipment and land were acquired for cash.

b. There were no disposals of equipment during the year.

c. The investments were sold for $294,000 cash.

d. The common stock was issued for cash.

e. There was a $196,500 debit to Retained Earnings for cash dividends declared.

## Instructions

Prepare a statement of cash flows, using the direct method of presenting cash flows from operating activities.

**OBJ. 3**

✔ Net cash flow from operating activities, $246,720

### PR 14-5B   Statement of cash flows—direct method applied to PR 14-1B

The comparative balance sheet of Juras Equipment Co. for Dec. 31, 2013 and 2012, is:

| | Dec. 31, 2013 | Dec. 31, 2012 |
|---|---|---|
| **Assets** | | |
| Cash | $ 99,840 | $ 67,680 |
| Accounts receivable (net) | 292,560 | 265,680 |
| Inventories | 421,440 | 409,200 |
| Investments | 0 | 144,000 |
| Land | 417,600 | 0 |
| Equipment | 619,200 | 505,440 |
| Accumulated depreciation | (139,920) | (119,040) |
| | $1,710,720 | $1,272,960 |
| **Liabilities and Stockholders' Equity** | | |
| Accounts payable (merchandise creditors) | $ 290,400 | $ 274,080 |
| Accrued expenses payable (operating expenses) | 43,200 | 37,920 |
| Dividends payable | 36,000 | 28,800 |
| Common stock, $1 par | 162,000 | 144,000 |
| Paid-in capital in excess of par—common stock | 594,000 | 288,000 |
| Retained earnings | 585,120 | 500,160 |
| | $1,710,720 | $1,272,960 |

The income statement for the year ended December 31, 2013, is as follows:

| | | |
|---|---|---|
| Sales | | $3,246,048 |
| Cost of merchandise sold | | 1,997,568 |
| Gross profit | | $1,248,480 |
| Operating expenses: | | |
| Depreciation expense | $ 20,880 | |
| Other operating expenses | 831,600 | |
| Total operating expenses | | 852,480 |
| Operating income | | $ 396,000 |
| Other expenses: | | |
| Loss on sale of investments | | (14,400) |
| Income before income tax | | $ 381,600 |
| Income tax expense | | 152,640 |
| Net income | | $ 228,960 |

The following additional information was taken from the records:

a.  Equipment and land were acquired for cash.

b.  There were no disposals of equipment during the year.

c.  The investments were sold for $129,600 cash.

d.  The common stock was issued for cash.

e.  There was a $144,000 debit to Retained Earnings for cash dividends declared.

**Instructions**

Prepare a statement of cash flows, using the direct method of presenting cash flows from operating activities.

## Cases & Projects

You can access Cases & Projects online at **www.cengage.com/accounting/reeve**

## Excel Success Special Activities

### SA 14-1   Cash flow from operating activities

Omar Company had the following selected income statement information for the year ended December 31, 2013:

| | |
|---|---:|
| Net income. | $310,000 |
| Depreciation expense | 48,000 |
| Loss on sale of land. | 21,000 |

Comparative noncash current assets and current liabilities for December 31, 2013 and 2012, are as follows:

| | 2013 | 2012 |
|---|---:|---:|
| Accounts receivable. | 132,400 | 145,200 |
| Inventories. | 256,000 | 231,900 |
| Accounts payable. | 194,600 | 209,800 |
| Accrued expenses. | 89,200 | 94,200 |
| Interest payable | 24,500 | 20,000 |

a.  Open the Excel file *SA14-1_1e*.

b.  Use your spreadsheet to prepare the cash flows from operating activities section of the statement of cash flows.

c.  When you have completed the section, perform a "save as," replacing the entire file name with the following:

*SA14-1_1e[your first name initial]_[your last name]*

### SA 14-2   Cash flow from operating activities

Troy Company had the following selected income statement information for the year ended December 31, 2013:

| | |
|---|---:|
| Net income. | $79,000 |
| Amortization expense | 14,500 |
| Gain on sale of land | 5,600 |

Comparative noncash current assets and current liabilities at the end of the two latest years are as follows:

| | 2013 | 2012 |
|---|---:|---:|
| Accounts receivable. | 57,300 | 68,900 |
| Inventories. | 42,100 | 47,300 |
| Prepaid expenses | 12,300 | 10,100 |
| Accounts payable. | 37,900 | 35,100 |
| Accrued expenses. | 21,500 | 24,600 |
| Income taxes payable | 15,400 | 13,200 |

Use your spreadsheet to prepare the cash flows from operating activities section of the statement of cash flows.

a.  Open the Excel file *SA14-2_1e*.

b.  Use your spreadsheet to prepare the cash flows from operating activities section of the statement of cash flows.

c.  When you have completed the section, perform a "save as," replacing the entire file name with the following:

*SA14-2_1e[your first name initial]_[your last name]*

### SA 14-3    Cash flow from operating activities

The income statement for the McIntyre Company is as follows for the year ended December 31, 2013:

**McIntyre Company**
**Income Statement**
**For the Year Ended December 31, 2013**

| | | |
|---|---:|---:|
| Sales | | $325,000 |
| Cost of merchandise sold | | 143,000 |
| Gross profit | | $182,000 |
| | | |
| Operating expenses: | | |
| Salaries expense | $45,600 | |
| Sales expenses | 34,100 | |
| Depreciation expense | 13,200 | |
| Total operating expenses | | 92,900 |
| Income from operations | | $ 89,100 |
| Other expense | | |
| Loss on sale of investments | | 22,000 |
| Income before income tax | | $ 67,100 |
| Income tax expense | | 25,000 |
| Net income | | $ 42,100 |

Increases and decreases in noncash current assets and liabilities for the comparative balances sheets dated December 31, 2013 and 2012, are as follows:

| | Increase/(Decrease) |
|---|---:|
| Accounts receivable | $ (2,900) |
| Inventories | 5,800 |
| Prepaid expenses | (2,100) |
| Accounts payable | (12,400) |
| Accrued expenses | (3,400) |
| Income taxes payable | 1,500 |

a. Open the Excel file *SA14-3_1e*.

b. Use your spreadsheet to prepare the cash flows from operating activities section of the statement of cash flows.

c. When you have completed the section, perform a "save as," replacing the entire file name with the following:

*SA14-3_1e[your first name initial]_[your last name]*

© AP Photo/Matt York

# Financial Statement Analysis

## Nike, Inc.

"**J**ust do it." These three words identify one of the most recognizable brands in the world, **Nike**. While this phrase inspires athletes to "compete and achieve their potential," it also defines the company.

Nike began in 1964 as a partnership between University of Oregon track coach Bill Bowerman and one of his former student-athletes, Phil Knight. The two began by selling shoes imported from Japan out of the back of Knight's car to athletes at track and field events. As sales grew, the company opened retail outlets, calling itself **Blue Ribbon Sports**. The company also began to develop its own shoes. In 1971, the company commissioned a graphic design student at Portland State University to develop the swoosh logo for a fee of $35. In 1978, the company changed its name to Nike, and in 1980, it sold its first shares of stock to the public.

Nike would have been a great company to invest in at the time. If you had invested in Nike's common stock back in 1990,

you would have paid $5.00 per share. As of July 2010, Nike's stock was worth $70.15 per share. Unfortunately, you can't invest using hindsight.

How can you select companies in which to invest? Like any significant purchase, you should do some research to guide your investment decision. If you were buying a car, for example, you might go to **Edmunds.com** to obtain reviews, ratings, prices, specifications, options, and fuel economies to evaluate different vehicles. In selecting companies to invest in, you can use financial analysis to gain insight into a company's past performance and future prospects. This chapter describes and illustrates common financial data that can be analyzed to assist you in making investment decisions such as whether or not to invest in Nike's stock.

*Source:* http://www.nikebiz.com/.

**OBJ. 1** Describe basic financial statement analytical methods.

# Basic Analytical Methods

Users analyze a company's financial statements using a variety of analytical methods. Three such methods are as follows:

1. Horizontal analysis
2. Vertical analysis
3. Common-sized statements

## Horizontal Analysis

The percentage analysis of increases and decreases in related items in comparative financial statements is called **horizontal analysis**. Each item on the most recent statement is compared with the same item on one or more earlier statements in terms of the following:

1. *Amount* of increase or decrease
2. *Percent* of increase or decrease

When comparing statements, the earlier statement is normally used as the base year for computing increases and decreases.

Exhibit 1 illustrates horizontal analysis for the December 31, 2012 and 2011, balance sheets of Lincoln Company. In Exhibit 1, the December 31, 2011, balance sheet (the earliest year presented) is used as the base year.

Exhibit 1 indicates that total assets decreased by $91,000 (7.4%), liabilities decreased by $133,000 (30.0%), and stockholders' equity increased by $42,000 (5.3%).

**EXHIBIT 1**

Comparative
Balance Sheet—
Horizontal
Analysis

**Lincoln Company**
**Comparative Balance Sheet**
**December 31, 2012 and 2011**

| | Dec. 31, 2012 | Dec. 31, 2011 | Increase (Decrease) Amount | Percent |
|---|---|---|---|---|
| **Assets** | | | | |
| Current assets.................................... | $ 550,000 | $ 533,000 | $ 17,000 | 3.2% |
| Long-term investments........................... | 95,000 | 177,500 | (82,500) | (46.5%) |
| Property, plant, and equipment (net) ............. | 444,500 | 470,000 | (25,500) | (5.4%) |
| Intangible assets ................................ | 50,000 | 50,000 | — | — |
| Total assets .................................... | $1,139,500 | $1,230,500 | $ (91,000) | (7.4%) |
| **Liabilities** | | | | |
| Current liabilities............................... | $ 210,000 | $ 243,000 | $ (33,000) | (13.6%) |
| Long-term liabilities............................ | 100,000 | 200,000 | (100,000) | (50.0%) |
| Total liabilities ................................ | $ 310,000 | $ 443,000 | $(133,000) | (30.0%) |
| **Stockholders' Equity** | | | | |
| Preferred 6% stock, $100 par .................... | $ 150,000 | $ 150,000 | — | — |
| Common stock, $10 par.......................... | 500,000 | 500,000 | — | — |
| Retained earnings............................... | 179,500 | 137,500 | $ 42,000 | 30.5% |
| Total stockholders' equity........................ | $ 829,500 | $ 787,500 | $ 42,000 | 5.3% |
| Total liabilities and stockholders' equity............ | $1,139,500 | $1,230,500 | $ (91,000) | (7.4%) |

Since the long-term investments account decreased by $82,500, it appears that most of the decrease in long-term liabilities of $100,000 was achieved through the sale of long-term investments.

The balance sheets in Exhibit 1 may be expanded or supported by a separate schedule that includes the individual asset and liability accounts. For example, Exhibit 2 is a supporting schedule of Lincoln's current asset accounts.

Exhibit 2 indicates that while cash and temporary investments increased, accounts receivable and inventories decreased. The decrease in accounts receivable could be caused by improved collection policies, which would increase cash. The decrease in inventories could be caused by increased sales.

**EXHIBIT 2**

Comparative
Schedule of
Current Assets—
Horizontal
Analysis

**Lincoln Company**
**Comparative Schedule of Current Assets**
**December 31, 2012 and 2011**

| | Dec. 31, 2012 | Dec. 31, 2011 | Increase (Decrease) Amount | Percent |
|---|---|---|---|---|
| Cash ............................................ | $ 90,500 | $ 64,700 | $ 25,800 | 39.9% |
| Temporary investments........................... | 75,000 | 60,000 | 15,000 | 25.0% |
| Accounts receivable (net) ........................ | 115,000 | 120,000 | (5,000) | (4.2%) |
| Inventories ..................................... | 264,000 | 283,000 | (19,000) | (6.7%) |
| Prepaid expenses ............................... | 5,500 | 5,300 | 200 | 3.8% |
| Total current assets.............................. | $550,000 | $533,000 | $ 17,000 | 3.2% |

Exhibit 3 illustrates horizontal analysis for the 2012 and 2011 income statements of Lincoln Company. Exhibit 3 indicates an increase in sales of $296,500, or 24.0%. However, the percentage increase in sales of 24.0% was accompanied by an even greater percentage increase in the cost of goods (merchandise) sold of 27.2%.[1] Thus, gross profit increased by only 19.7% rather than by the 24.0% increase in sales.

---

1 The term *cost of goods sold* is often used in practice in place of *cost of merchandise sold*. Such usage is followed in this chapter.

**EXHIBIT 3**

**Comparative Income Statement— Horizontal Analysis**

| | | | Increase (Decrease) | |
|---|---|---|---|---|
| **Lincoln Company** **Comparative Income Statement** **For the Years Ended December 31, 2012 and 2011** | | | | |
| | **2012** | **2011** | **Amount** | **Percent** |
| Sales ........................................... | $1,530,500 | $1,234,000 | $296,500 | 24.0% |
| Sales returns and allowances...................... | 32,500 | 34,000 | (1,500) | (4.4%) |
| Net sales......................................... | $1,498,000 | $1,200,000 | $298,000 | 24.8% |
| Cost of goods sold............................... | 1,043,000 | 820,000 | 223,000 | 27.2% |
| Gross profit ..................................... | $ 455,000 | $ 380,000 | $ 75,000 | 19.7% |
| Selling expenses ................................. | $ 191,000 | $ 147,000 | $ 44,000 | 29.9% |
| Administrative expenses.......................... | 104,000 | 97,400 | 6,600 | 6.8% |
| Total operating expenses ........................ | $ 295,000 | $ 244,400 | $ 50,600 | 20.7% |
| Income from operations ......................... | $ 160,000 | $ 135,600 | $ 24,400 | 18.0% |
| Other income.................................... | 8,500 | 11,000 | (2,500) | (22.7%) |
| | $ 168,500 | $ 146,600 | $ 21,900 | 14.9% |
| Other expense (interest) .......................... | 6,000 | 12,000 | (6,000) | (50.0%) |
| Income before income tax ....................... | $ 162,500 | $ 134,600 | $ 27,900 | 20.7% |
| Income tax expense .............................. | 71,500 | 58,100 | 13,400 | 23.1% |
| Net income ..................................... | $ 91,000 | $ 76,500 | $ 14,500 | 19.0% |

Exhibit 3 also indicates that selling expenses increased by 29.9%. Thus, the 24.0% increases in sales could have been caused by an advertising campaign, which increased selling expenses. Administrative expenses increased by only 6.8%, total operating expenses increased by 20.7%, and income from operations increased by 18.0%. Interest expense decreased by 50.0%. This decrease was probably caused by the 50.0% decrease in long-term liabilities (Exhibit 1). Overall, net income increased by 19.0%, a favorable result.

Exhibit 4 illustrates horizontal analysis for the 2012 and 2011 retained earnings statements of Lincoln Company. Exhibit 4 indicates that retained earnings increased by 30.5% for the year. The increase is due to net income of $91,000 for the year, less dividends of $49,000.

**EXHIBIT 4**

**Comparative Retained Earnings Statement— Horizontal Analysis**

| | | | Increase (Decrease) | |
|---|---|---|---|---|
| **Lincoln Company** **Comparative Retained Earnings Statement** **For the Years Ended December 31, 2012 and 2011** | | | | |
| | **2012** | **2011** | **Amount** | **Percent** |
| Retained earnings, January 1.................. | $137,500 | $100,000 | $37,500 | 37.5% |
| Net income for the year...................... | 91,000 | 76,500 | 14,500 | 19.0% |
| Total ....................................... | $228,500 | $176,500 | $52,000 | 29.5% |
| Dividends: | | | | |
| On preferred stock ....................... | $ 9,000 | $ 9,000 | — | — |
| On common stock........................ | 40,000 | 30,000 | $10,000 | 33.3% |
| Total ....................................... | $ 49,000 | $ 39,000 | $10,000 | 25.6% |
| Retained earnings, December 31 ............. | $179,500 | $137,500 | $42,000 | 30.5% |

**Example Exercise > 15-1 > Horizontal Analysis**

**OBJ. 1**

The comparative cash and accounts receivable balances for a company are provided below.

| | Dec. 31, 2012 | Dec. 31, 2011 |
|---|---|---|
| Cash | $62,500 | $50,000 |
| Accounts receivable (net) | 74,400 | 80,000 |

Based on this information, what is the amount and percentage of increase or decrease that would be shown on a balance sheet with horizontal analysis?

**Follow My Example > 15-1 >**

Cash $12,500 increase ($62,500 – $50,000), or 25%
Accounts receivable $5,600 decrease ($74,400 – $80,000), or (7%)

Practice Exercises: **PE 15-1A, PE 15-1B**

## Vertical Analysis

The percentage analysis of the relationship of each component in a financial statement to a total within the statement is called **vertical analysis**. Although vertical analysis is applied to a single statement, it may be applied on the same statement over time. This enhances the analysis by showing how the percentages of each item have changed over time.

In vertical analysis of the balance sheet, the percentages are computed as follows:

1. Each asset item is stated as a percent of the total assets.
2. Each liability and stockholders' equity item is stated as a percent of the total liabilities and stockholders' equity.

Exhibit 5 illustrates the vertical analysis of the December 31, 2012 and 2011, balance sheets of Lincoln Company. Exhibit 5 indicates that current assets have increased from 43.3% to 48.3% of total assets. Long-term investments decreased from 14.4% to 8.3% of total assets. Stockholders' equity increased from 64.0% to 72.8% with a comparable decrease in liabilities.

**EXHIBIT 5**

**Comparative Balance Sheet— Vertical Analysis**

**Lincoln Company**
**Comparative Balance Sheet**
**December 31, 2012 and 2011**

| | Dec. 31, 2012 | | Dec. 31, 2011 | |
|---|---|---|---|---|
| | Amount | Percent | Amount | Percent |
| **Assets** | | | | |
| Current assets.............................. | $ 550,000 | 48.3% | $ 533,000 | 43.3% |
| Long-term investments..................... | 95,000 | 8.3 | 177,500 | 14.4 |
| Property, plant, and equipment (net) ......... | 444,500 | 39.0 | 470,000 | 38.2 |
| Intangible assets ........................... | 50,000 | 4.4 | 50,000 | 4.1 |
| Total assets ................................ | $1,139,500 | 100.0% | $1,230,500 | 100.0% |
| **Liabilities** | | | | |
| Current liabilities........................... | $ 210,000 | 18.4% | $ 243,000 | 19.7% |
| Long-term liabilities........................ | 100,000 | 8.8 | 200,000 | 16.3 |
| Total liabilities ............................ | $ 310,000 | 27.2% | $ 443,000 | 36.0% |
| **Stockholders' Equity** | | | | |
| Preferred 6% stock, $100 par ................ | $ 150,000 | 13.2% | $ 150,000 | 12.2% |
| Common stock, $10 par..................... | 500,000 | 43.9 | 500,000 | 40.6 |
| Retained earnings.......................... | 179,500 | 15.7 | 137,500 | 11.2 |
| Total stockholders' equity................... | $ 829,500 | 72.8% | $ 787,500 | 64.0% |
| Total liabilities and stockholders' equity....... | $1,139,500 | 100.0% | $1,230,500 | 100.0% |

In a vertical analysis of the income statement, each item is stated as a percent of net sales. Exhibit 6 illustrates the vertical analysis of the 2012 and 2011 income statements of Lincoln Company.

Exhibit 6 indicates a decrease in the gross profit rate from 31.7% in 2011 to 30.4% in 2012. Although this is only a 1.3 percentage point (31.7% – 30.4%) decrease, in dollars of potential gross profit, it represents a decrease of about $19,500 (1.3% × $1,498,000). Thus, a small percentage decrease can have a large dollar effect.

**EXHIBIT 6**

**Comparative Income Statement— Vertical Analysis**

| | Lincoln Company Comparative Income Statement For the Years Ended December 31, 2012 and 2011 | | | | |
|---|---|---|---|---|---|
| | **2012** | | **2011** | | |
| | **Amount** | **Percent** | **Amount** | **Percent** | |
| Sales ...................................... | $1,530,500 | 102.2% | $1,234,000 | 102.8% | |
| Sales returns and allowances................ | 32,500 | 2.2 | 34,000 | 2.8 | |
| Net sales.................................... | $1,498,000 | 100.0% | $1,200,000 | 100.0% | |
| Cost of goods sold.......................... | 1,043,000 | 69.6 | 820,000 | 68.3 | |
| Gross profit ................................ | $ 455,000 | 30.4% | $ 380,000 | 31.7% | |
| Selling expenses ........................... | $ 191,000 | 12.8% | $ 147,000 | 12.3% | |
| Administrative expenses..................... | 104,000 | 6.9 | 97,400 | 8.1 | |
| Total operating expenses ................... | $ 295,000 | 19.7% | $ 244,400 | 20.4% | |
| Income from operations ..................... | $ 160,000 | 10.7% | $ 135,600 | 11.3% | |
| Other income ............................... | 8,500 | 0.6 | 11,000 | 0.9 | |
| | $ 168,500 | 11.3% | $ 146,600 | 12.2% | |
| Other expense (interest) .................... | 6,000 | 0.4 | 12,000 | 1.0 | |
| Income before income tax ................... | $ 162,500 | 10.9% | $ 134,600 | 11.2% | |
| Income tax expense ......................... | 71,500 | 4.8 | 58,100 | 4.8 | |
| Net income ................................. | $ 91,000 | 6.1% | $ 76,500 | 6.4% | |

All of the analyses illustrated in this objective are well suited to a spreadsheet solution approach because of the repetitive calculations across rows and columns. However, for brevity we will illustrate only the vertical analysis of comparative income statements. The formulas are as follows:

a.          b.

| | A | B | C | D | E | F |
|---|---|---|---|---|---|---|
| 1 | | Lincoln Company | | | | |
| 2 | | Comparative Income Statement | | | | |
| 3 | | For the Years Ended December 31, 2012 and 2011 | | | | |
| 4 | | | | | | |
| 5 | | | 2012 | | 2011 | |
| 6 | | Amount | Percent | | Amount | Percent |
| 7 | Sales | $ 1,530,500 | =B7/B$9 | | $ 1,234,000 | =E7/E$9 |
| 8 | Sales returns and allowances | 32,500 | =B8/B$9 | | 34,000 | =E8/E$9 |
| 9 | Net sales | =B7-B8 | =B9/B$9 | | =E7-E8 | =E9/E$9 |
| 10 | Cost of goods sold | 1,043,000 | =B10/B$9 | | 820,000 | =E10/E$9 |
| 11 | Gross profit | =B9-B10 | =B11/B$9 | | =E9-E10 | =E11/E$9 |
| 12 | Selling expenses | 191,000 | =B12/B$9 | | 147,000 | =E12/E$9 |
| 13 | Administrative expenses | 104,000 | =B13/B$9 | | 97,400 | =E13/E$9 |
| 14 | Total operating expenses | =B12+B13 | =B14/B$9 | | =E12+E13 | =E14/E$9 |
| 15 | Income from operations | =B11-B14 | =B15/B$9 | | =E11-E14 | =E15/E$9 |
| 16 | Other income | 8,500 | =B16/B$9 | | 11,000 | =E16/E$9 |
| 17 | | =B15+B16 | =B17/B$9 | | =E15+E16 | =E17/E$9 |
| 18 | Other expense (interest) | 6,000 | =B18/B$9 | | 12,000 | =E18/E$9 |
| 19 | Income before income tax | =B17-B18 | =B19/B$9 | | =E17-E18 | =E19/E$9 |
| 20 | Income tax expense | 71,500 | =B20/B$9 | | 58,100 | =E20/E$9 |
| 21 | Net Income | =B19-B20 | =B21/B$9 | | =E19-E20 | =E21/E$9 |

c.                                c.

a.   Enter the formulas for the sub-totals and totals within the income statement at appropriate cell locations, such as B9. The formulas entered in column B can be copied into the adjacent cell location in column E, one-by-one, to save time. For example, the formula in B9 can be copied to E9; B11 copied to E11; and so on.

b.   Insert the formula in cell C7 for the vertical percentage computation, =B7/B$9. The absolute cell address ($ sign) is placed in front of the row 9 number. This is because the sales denominator remains fixed when the formula is copied across the rows.

c.   Copy the formula in cell C7 to C8:C21 and F7:F21. Column C and F calculations are formatted as a percent with one decimal place.

**Try***It*   Go to the hands-on ***Excel Tutor*** for this example!
(Note: The example here and throughout this chapter are contained in a **single** tutorial.)

**Try***It*   This Excel Success example uses an Excel function referred to as cell referencing. Go to the ***Excel Tutor*** titled **Absolute & Relative Cell References** for additional help with this useful Excel function!

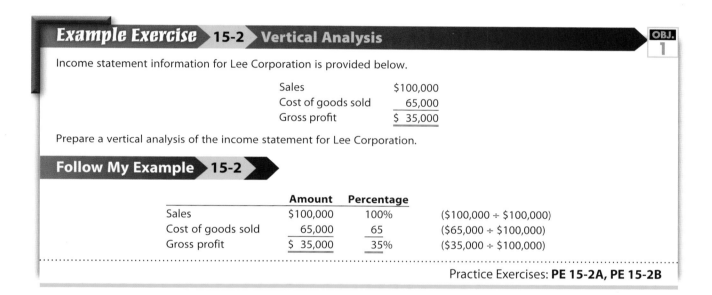

**Example Exercise** 15-2 **Vertical Analysis**   OBJ. 1

Income statement information for Lee Corporation is provided below.

| Sales | $100,000 |
|---|---|
| Cost of goods sold | 65,000 |
| Gross profit | $ 35,000 |

Prepare a vertical analysis of the income statement for Lee Corporation.

**Follow My Example** 15-2

| | Amount | Percentage | |
|---|---|---|---|
| Sales | $100,000 | 100% | ($100,000 ÷ $100,000) |
| Cost of goods sold | 65,000 | 65 | ($65,000 ÷ $100,000) |
| Gross profit | $ 35,000 | 35% | ($35,000 ÷ $100,000) |

Practice Exercises: **PE 15-2A, PE 15-2B**

## Common-Sized Statements

In a **common-sized statement**, all items are expressed as percentages with no dollar amounts shown. Common-sized statements are often useful for comparing one company with another or for comparing a company with industry averages.

Exhibit 7 illustrates common-sized income statements for Lincoln Company and Madison Corporation. Exhibit 7 indicates that Lincoln Company has a slightly higher rate of gross profit (30.4%) than Madison Corporation (30.0%). However, Lincoln has a higher percentage of selling expenses (12.8%) and administrative expenses (6.9%) than does Madison (11.5% and 4.1%). As a result, the income from operations of Lincoln (10.7%) is less than that of Madison (14.4%).

The unfavorable difference of 3.7 (14.4% − 10.7%) percentage points in income from operations would concern the managers and other stakeholders of Lincoln. The underlying causes of the difference should be investigated and possibly corrected. For example, Lincoln Company may decide to outsource some of its administrative duties so that its administrative expenses are more comparative to those of Madison Corporation.

| **EXHIBIT 7** | | **Lincoln Company** | **Madison Corporation** |
|---|---|---|---|
| **Common-Sized Income Statement** | Sales | 102.2% | 102.3% |
| | Sales returns and allowances | 2.2 | 2.3 |
| | Net sales | 100.0% | 100.0% |
| | Cost of goods sold | 69.6 | 70.0 |
| | Gross profit | 30.4% | 30.0% |
| | Selling expenses | 12.8% | 11.5% |
| | Administrative expenses | 6.9 | 4.1 |
| | Total operating expenses | 19.7% | 15.6% |
| | Income from operations | 10.7% | 14.4% |
| | Other income | 0.6 | 0.6 |
| | | 11.3% | 15.0% |
| | Other expense (interest) | 0.4 | 0.5 |
| | Income before income tax | 10.9% | 14.5% |
| | Income tax expense | 4.8 | 5.5 |
| | Net income | 6.1% | 9.0% |

## Other Analytical Measures

Other relationships may be expressed in ratios and percentages. Often, these relationships are compared within the same statement and, thus, are a type of vertical analysis. Comparing these items with items from earlier periods is a type of horizontal analysis.

Analytical measures are not a definitive conclusion. They are only guides in evaluating financial and operating data. Many other factors, such as trends in the industry and general economic conditions, should also be considered when analyzing a company.

**OBJ. 2** Use financial statement analysis to assess the liquidity and solvency of a business.

# Liquidity and Solvency Analysis

All users of financial statements are interested in the ability of a company to do the following:

1. Maintain **liquidity** and **solvency**.
2. Earn income, called **profitability**.

The ability to convert assets into cash is called *liquidity*, while the ability of a business to pay its debts is called *solvency*. Liquidity, solvency, and profitability are interrelated. For example, a company that cannot convert assets into cash may have difficulty taking advantage of profitable courses of action requiring immediate cash outlays. Likewise, a company that cannot pay its debts will have difficulty obtaining credit. A lack of credit will, in turn, limit the company's ability to purchase merchandise or expand operations, which decreases its profitability.

Liquidity and solvency are normally assessed using the following:

1. Current position analysis
   Working capital
   Current ratio
   Quick ratio

2. Accounts receivable analysis
   Accounts receivable turnover
   Number of days' sales in receivables

3. Inventory analysis
   Inventory turnover
   Number of days' sales in inventory

4. The ratio of fixed assets to long-term liabilities
5. The ratio of liabilities to stockholders' equity
6. The number of times interest charges are earned

The Lincoln Company financial statements presented earlier are used to illustrate the preceding analyses.

One popular printed source for industry ratios is *Annual Statement Studies* from Risk Management Association. Online analysis is available from Zacks Investment Research site, which is linked to the text's Web site at **www.cengage.com/accounting/reeve.**

## Current Position Analysis

A company's ability to pay its current liabilities is called **current position analysis**. It is a solvency measure of special interest to short-term creditors and includes the computation and analysis of the following:

1. Working capital
2. Current ratio
3. Quick ratio

**Working Capital**  A company's **working capital** is computed as follows:

Working Capital = Current Assets – Current Liabilities

To illustrate, the working capital for Lincoln Company for 2012 and 2011 is computed below.

|  | 2012 | 2011 |
| --- | --- | --- |
| Current assets | $550,000 | $533,000 |
| Less current liabilities | 210,000 | 243,000 |
| Working capital | $340,000 | $290,000 |

The working capital is used to evaluate a company's ability to pay current liabilities. A company's working capital is often monitored monthly, quarterly, or yearly by creditors and other debtors. However, it is difficult to use working capital to compare companies of different sizes. For example, working capital of $250,000 may be adequate for a local hardware store, but it would be inadequate for The Home Depot.

**Current Ratio**  The **current ratio**, sometimes called the *working capital ratio* is computed as follows:

$$\text{Current Ratio} = \frac{\text{Current Assets}}{\text{Current Liabilities}}$$

To illustrate, the current ratio for Lincoln Company is computed below.

|  | 2012 | 2011 |
| --- | --- | --- |
| Current assets | $550,000 | $533,000 |
| Current liabilities | $210,000 | $243,000 |
| Current ratio | 2.6 ($550,000/$210,000) | 2.2 ($533,000/$243,000) |

The current ratio is a more reliable indicator of a company's ability to pay its current liabilities than is working capital, and it is much easier to compare across companies. To illustrate, assume that as of December 31, 2012, the working capital of a competitor is much greater than $340,000, but its current ratio is only 1.3. Considering these facts alone, Lincoln Company, with its current ratio of 2.6, is in a more favorable position to obtain short-term credit than the competitor, which has the greater amount of working capital.

The ratios illustrated in the chapter can all be computed using spreadsheet software. To simplify, we will illustrate only the use of spreadsheet software for the current ratio and rate earned on total assets in this chapter. At the end of the chapter a comprehensive spreadsheet illustration is provided to show the calculations of all of the ratios using spreadsheet software. The working capital and current ratio can be computed using spreadsheet software as follows:

|   | A | B | C |
|---|---|---|---|
| 1 | *Inputs:* | | |
| 2 | | 2012 | 2011 |
| 3 | Current assets | $ 550,000 | $ 533,000 |
| 4 | Current liabilities | 210,000 | 243,000 |
| 5 | | | |
| 6 | *Outputs* | | |
| 7 | Working capital | =B3-B4 | =C3-C4 |
| 8 | | | |
| 9 | Current ratio | =B3/B4 | =C3/C4 |
| 10 | | | |

a. (arrow pointing to row 7)
b. (arrow pointing to row 9)

The two calculations in column B can be copied simultaneously (B7:B9 to C7:C9) rather than copying one at a time.

The inputs could be the financial statements or a section of the financial statements. Here we illustrate just two separate lines, current assets and current liabilities. The outputs are two analyses, working capital and the current ratio.

**a.** Enter the formula for working capital in B7, =B3-B4, then copy to C7.

**b.** Enter the formula for the current ratio in B9, =B3/B4, then copy to C9.

Format this ratio with one decimal place.

**Try***It* Go to the hands-on **Excel Tutor** for this example!
(Note: The example here and throughout this chapter are contained in a **single** tutorial.)

**Quick Ratio** One limitation of working capital and the current ratio is that they do not consider the types of current assets a company has and how easily they can be turned into cash. Because of this, two companies may have the same working capital and current ratios, but differ significantly in their ability to pay their current liabilities.

To illustrate, the current assets and liabilities for Lincoln Company and Jefferson Corporation as of December 31, 2012, are as follows:

| | Lincoln Company | Jefferson Corporation |
|---|---|---|
| Current assets: | | |
| Cash | $ 90,500 | $ 45,500 |
| Temporary investments | 75,000 | 25,000 |
| Accounts receivable (net) | 115,000 | 90,000 |
| Inventories | 264,000 | 380,000 |
| Prepaid expenses | 5,500 | 9,500 |
| Total current assets | $550,000 | $550,000 |
| Total current assets | $550,000 | $550,000 |
| Less current liabilities | 210,000 | 210,000 |
| Working capital | $340,000 | $340,000 |
| Current ratio ($550,000/$210,000) | 2.6 | 2.6 |

Lincoln and Jefferson both have a working capital of $340,000 and current ratios of 2.6. Jefferson, however, has more of its current assets in inventories. These inventories must be sold and the receivables collected before all the current liabilities can be paid. This takes time. In addition, if the market for its product declines, Jefferson may have difficulty selling its inventory. This, in turn, could impair its ability to pay its current liabilities.

In contrast, Lincoln's current assets contain more cash, temporary investments, and accounts receivable, which can easily be converted to cash. Thus, Lincoln is in a stronger current position than Jefferson to pay its current liabilities.

A ratio that measures the "instant" debt-paying ability of a company is the **quick ratio**, sometimes called the *acid-test ratio*. The quick ratio is computed as follows:

$$\text{Quick Ratio} = \frac{\text{Quick Assets}}{\text{Current Liabilities}}$$

**Quick assets** are cash and other current assets that can be easily converted to cash. Quick assets normally include cash, temporary investments, and receivables but exclude inventories and prepaid assets.

To illustrate, the quick ratio for Lincoln Company is computed below.

|  | 2012 | 2011 |
|---|---|---|
| Quick assets: |  |  |
| Cash | $ 90,500 | $ 64,700 |
| Temporary investments | 75,000 | 60,000 |
| Accounts receivable (net) | 115,000 | 120,000 |
| Total quick assets | $280,500 | $244,700 |
| Current liabilities | $210,000 | $243,000 |
| Quick ratio | 1.3 ($280,500 ÷ $210,000) | 1.0 ($244,700 ÷ $243,000) |

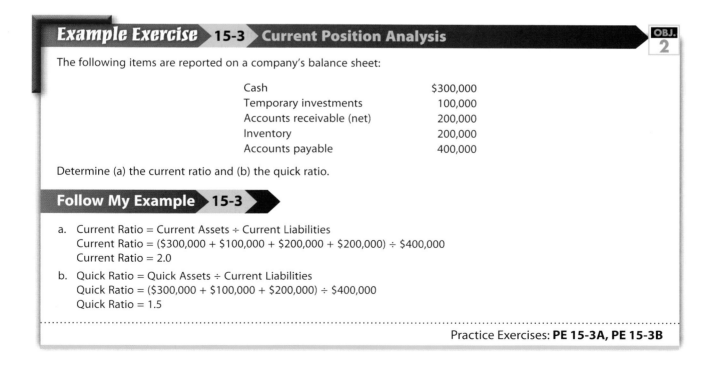

**Example Exercise** ▶ **15-3** ▶ **Current Position Analysis**   **OBJ. 2**

The following items are reported on a company's balance sheet:

| Cash | $300,000 |
|---|---|
| Temporary investments | 100,000 |
| Accounts receivable (net) | 200,000 |
| Inventory | 200,000 |
| Accounts payable | 400,000 |

Determine (a) the current ratio and (b) the quick ratio.

**Follow My Example** ▶ **15-3** ▶

a.  Current Ratio = Current Assets ÷ Current Liabilities
    Current Ratio = ($300,000 + $100,000 + $200,000 + $200,000) ÷ $400,000
    Current Ratio = 2.0

b.  Quick Ratio = Quick Assets ÷ Current Liabilities
    Quick Ratio = ($300,000 + $100,000 + $200,000) ÷ $400,000
    Quick Ratio = 1.5

Practice Exercises: **PE 15-3A, PE 15-3B**

## Accounts Receivable Analysis

A company's ability to collect its accounts receivable is called **accounts receivable analysis**. It includes the computation and analysis of the following:

1. Accounts receivable turnover
2. Number of days' sales in receivables

Collecting accounts receivable as quickly as possible improves a company's liquidity. In addition, the cash collected from receivables may be used to improve or expand operations. Quick collection of receivables also reduces the risk of uncollectible accounts.

**Accounts Receivable Turnover**   The **accounts receivable turnover** is computed as follows:

$$\text{Accounts Receivable Turnover} = \frac{\text{Net Sales}^2}{\text{Average Accounts Receivable}}$$

To illustrate, the accounts receivable turnover for Lincoln Company for 2012 and 2011 is computed below. Lincoln's accounts receivable balance at the beginning of 2011 is $140,000.

|  | 2012 | 2011 |
|---|---|---|
| Net sales | $1,498,000 | $1,200,000 |
| Accounts receivable (net): |  |  |
| Beginning of year | $ 120,000 | $ 140,000 |
| End of year | 115,000 | 120,000 |
| Total | $ 235,000 | $ 260,000 |
| Average accounts receivable | $117,500 ($235,000 ÷ 2) | $130,000 ($260,000 ÷ 2) |
| Accounts receivable turnover | 12.7 ($1,498,000 ÷ $117,500) | 9.2 ($1,200,000 ÷ $130,000) |

The increase in Lincoln's accounts receivable turnover from 9.2 to 12.7 indicates that the collection of receivables has improved during 2012. This may be due to a change in how credit is granted, collection practices, or both.

For Lincoln Company, the average accounts receivable was computed using the accounts receivable balance at the beginning and the end of the year. When sales are seasonal and, thus, vary throughout the year, monthly balances of receivables are often used. Also, if sales on account include notes receivable as well as accounts receivable, notes and accounts receivables are normally combined for analysis.

**Number of Days' Sales in Receivables**   The **number of days' sales in receivables** is computed as follows:

$$\text{Number of Days' Sales in Receivables} = \frac{\text{Average Accounts Receivable}}{\text{Average Daily Sales}}$$

where

$$\text{Average Daily Sales} = \frac{\text{Net Sales}}{365 \text{ days}}$$

To illustrate, the number of days' sales in receivables for Lincoln Company is computed below.

|  | 2012 | 2011 |
|---|---|---|
| Average accounts receivable | $117,500 ($235,000 ÷ 2) | $130,000 ($260,000 ÷ 2) |
| Average daily sales | $4,104 ($1,498,000 ÷ 365) | $3,288 ($1,200,000 ÷ 365) |
| Number of days' sales in receivables | 28.6 ($117,500 ÷ $4,104) | 39.5 ($130,000 ÷ $3,288) |

---

2 If known, *credit* sales should be used in the numerator. Because credit sales are not normally known by external users, we use net sales in the numerator.

The number of days' sales in receivables is an estimate of the time (in days) that the accounts receivable have been outstanding. The number of days' sales in receivables is often compared with a company's credit terms to evaluate the efficiency of the collection of receivables.

To illustrate, if Lincoln's credit terms are 2/10, n/30, then Lincoln was very *inefficient* in collecting receivables in 2011. In other words, receivables should have been collected in 30 days or less, but were being collected in 39.5 days. Although collections improved during 2012 to 28.6 days, there is probably still room for improvement. On the other hand, if Lincoln's credit terms are n/45, then there is probably little room for improving collections.

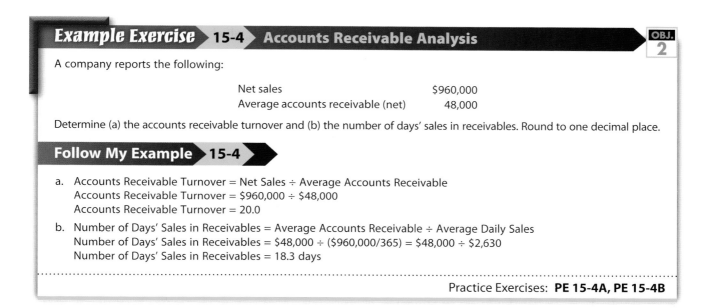

**Example Exercise** 15-4 **Accounts Receivable Analysis** OBJ. 2

A company reports the following:

| | |
|---|---|
| Net sales | $960,000 |
| Average accounts receivable (net) | 48,000 |

Determine (a) the accounts receivable turnover and (b) the number of days' sales in receivables. Round to one decimal place.

**Follow My Example** 15-4

a.  Accounts Receivable Turnover = Net Sales ÷ Average Accounts Receivable
    Accounts Receivable Turnover = $960,000 ÷ $48,000
    Accounts Receivable Turnover = 20.0

b.  Number of Days' Sales in Receivables = Average Accounts Receivable ÷ Average Daily Sales
    Number of Days' Sales in Receivables = $48,000 ÷ ($960,000/365) = $48,000 ÷ $2,630
    Number of Days' Sales in Receivables = 18.3 days

Practice Exercises: **PE 15-4A, PE 15-4B**

## Inventory Analysis

A company's ability to manage its inventory effectively is evaluated using **inventory analysis**. It includes the computation and analysis of the following:

1. Inventory turnover
2. Number of days' sales in inventory

Excess inventory decreases liquidity by tying up funds (cash) in inventory. In addition, excess inventory increases insurance expense, property taxes, storage costs, and other related expenses. These expenses further reduce funds that could be used elsewhere to improve or expand operations.

Excess inventory also increases the risk of losses because of price declines or obsolescence of the inventory. On the other hand, a company should keep enough inventory in stock so that it doesn't lose sales because of lack of inventory.

**Inventory Turnover** The **inventory turnover** is computed as follows:

$$\text{Inventory Turnover} = \frac{\text{Cost of Goods Sold}}{\text{Average Inventory}}$$

To illustrate, the inventory turnover for Lincoln Company for 2012 and 2011 is computed below. Lincoln's inventory balance at the beginning of 2011 is $311,000.

|  | **2012** | **2011** |
|---|---|---|
| Cost of goods sold | $1,043,000 | $820,000 |
| Inventories: |  |  |
| Beginning of year | $ 283,000 | $311,000 |
| End of year | 264,000 | 283,000 |
| Total | $ 547,000 | $594,000 |
| Average inventory | $273,500 ($547,000 ÷ 2) | $297,000 ($594,000 ÷ 2) |
| Inventory turnover | 3.8 ($1,043,000 ÷ $273,500) | 2.8 ($820,000 ÷ $297,000) |

The increase in Lincoln's inventory turnover from 2.8 to 3.8 indicates that the management of inventory has improved in 2012. The inventory turnover improved because of an increase in the cost of goods sold, which indicates more sales, and a decrease in the average inventories.

What is considered a good inventory turnover varies by type of inventory, companies, and industries. For example, grocery stores have a higher inventory turnover than jewelers or furniture stores. Likewise, within a grocery store, perishable foods have a higher turnover than the soaps and cleansers.

**Number of Days' Sales in Inventory** The **number of days' sales in inventory** is computed as follows:

$$\text{Number of Days' Sales in Inventory} = \frac{\text{Average Inventory}}{\text{Average Daily Cost of Goods Sold}}$$

where

$$\text{Average Daily Cost of Goods Sold} = \frac{\text{Cost of Goods Sold}}{365 \text{ days}}$$

To illustrate, the number of days' sales in inventory for Lincoln Company is computed below.

|  | **2012** | **2011** |
|---|---|---|
| Average inventory | $273,500 ($547,000 ÷ 2) | $297,000 ($594,000 ÷ 2) |
| Average daily cost of goods sold | $2,858 ($1,043,000 ÷ 365) | $2,247 ($820,000 ÷ 365) |
| Number of days' sales in inventory | 95.7 ($273,500 ÷ $2,858) | 132.2 ($297,000 ÷ $2,247) |

The number of days' sales in inventory is a rough measure of the length of time it takes to purchase, sell, and replace the inventory. Lincoln's number of days' sales in inventory improved from 132.2 days to 95.7 days during 2012. This is a major improvement in managing inventory.

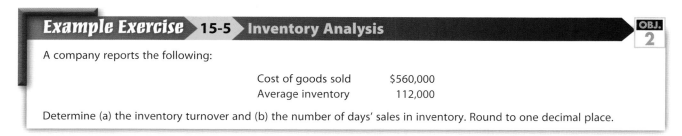

**Example Exercise** **15-5** **Inventory Analysis**

**OBJ. 2**

A company reports the following:

| Cost of goods sold | $560,000 |
|---|---|
| Average inventory | 112,000 |

Determine (a) the inventory turnover and (b) the number of days' sales in inventory. Round to one decimal place.

*(Continued)*

**Follow My Example 15-5**

a.  Inventory Turnover = Cost of Goods Sold ÷ Average Inventory
    Inventory Turnover = $560,000 ÷ $112,000
    Inventory Turnover = 5.0

b.  Number of Days' Sales in Inventory = Average Inventory ÷ Average Daily Cost of Goods Sold
    Number of Days' Sales in Inventory = $112,000 ÷ ($560,000/365) = $112,000 ÷ $1,534
    Number of Days' Sales in Inventory = 73.0 days

Practice Exercises: **PE 15-5A, PE 15-5B**

## Ratio of Fixed Assets to Long-Term Liabilities

The **ratio of fixed assets to long-term liabilities** provides a solvency measure of whether noteholders or bondholders will be paid. Since fixed assets are often pledged as security for long-term notes and bonds, it is computed as follows:

$$\text{Ratio of Fixed Assets to Long-Term Liabilities} = \frac{\text{Fixed Assets (net)}}{\text{Long-Term Liabilities}}$$

To illustrate, the ratio of fixed assets to long-term liabilities for Lincoln Company is computed below.

|  | 2012 | 2011 |
|---|---|---|
| Fixed assets (net) | $444,500 | $470,000 |
| Long-term liabilities | $100,000 | $200,000 |
| Ratio of fixed assets to long-term liabilities | 4.4 ($444,500 ÷ $100,000) | 2.4 ($470,000 ÷ $200,000) |

During 2012, Lincoln's ratio of fixed assets to long-term liabilities increased from 2.4 to 4.4. This increase was due primarily to Lincoln paying off one-half of its long-term liabilities in 2012.

## Ratio of Liabilities to Stockholders' Equity

The **ratio of liabilities to stockholders' equity** is a solvency measure that determines how much of the company is financed by debt and equity. It is computed as follows:

$$\text{Ratio of Liabilities to Stockholders' Equity} = \frac{\text{Total Liabilities}}{\text{Total Stockholders' Equity}}$$

To illustrate, the ratio of liabilities to stockholders' equity for Lincoln Company is computed below.

|  | 2012 | 2011 |
|---|---|---|
| Total liabilities | $310,000 | $443,000 |
| Total stockholders' equity | $829,500 | $787,500 |
| Ratio of liabilities to stockholders' equity | 0.4 ($310,000 ÷ $829,500) | 0.6 ($443,000 ÷ $787,500) |

Lincoln's ratio of liabilities to stockholders' equity decreased from 0.6 to 0.4 during 2012. This is an improvement and indicates that Lincoln's creditors have an adequate margin of safety that their debt will be paid.

**Example Exercise** **15-6** **Long-Term Solvency Analysis**

OBJ. 2

The following information was taken from Acme Company's balance sheet:

| | |
|---|---|
| Fixed assets (net) | $1,400,000 |
| Long-term liabilities | 400,000 |
| Total liabilities | 560,000 |
| Total stockholders' equity | 1,400,000 |

Determine the company's (a) ratio of fixed assets to long-term liabilities and (b) ratio of liabilities to total stockholders' equity.

**Follow My Example** **15-6**

a. Ratio of Fixed Assets to Long-Term Liabilities = Fixed Assets ÷ Long-Term Liabilities
   Ratio of Fixed Assets to Long-Term Liabilities = $1,400,000 ÷ $400,000
   Ratio of Fixed Assets to Long-Term Liabilities = 3.5

b. Ratio of Liabilities to Total Stockholders' Equity = Total Liabilities ÷ Total Stockholders' Equity
   Ratio of Liabilities to Total Stockholders' Equity = $560,000 ÷ $1,400,000
   Ratio of Liabilities to Total Stockholders' Equity = 0.4

Practice Exercises: **PE 15-6A, PE 15-6B**

## Number of Times Interest Charges Earned

The **number of times interest charges are earned**, sometimes called the *fixed charge coverage ratio*, is a solvency measure that determines the risk that interest payments will not be made if earnings decrease. It is computed as follows:

$$\text{Number of Times Interest Charges Are Earned} = \frac{\text{Income Before Income Tax} + \text{Interest Expense}}{\text{Interest Expense}}$$

Interest expense is paid before income taxes. In other words, interest expense is deducted in determining taxable income and, thus, income tax. For this reason, income *before taxes* is used in computing the number of times interest charges are earned.

The *higher* the ratio the more likely interest payments will be paid if earnings decrease. To illustrate, the number of times interest charges are earned for Lincoln Company is computed below.

| | 2012 | 2011 |
|---|---|---|
| Income before income tax | $162,500 | $134,600 |
| Add interest expense | 6,000 | 12,000 |
| Amount available to pay interest | $168,500 | $146,600 |
| Number of times interest charges earned | 28.1 ($168,500 ÷ $6,000) | 12.2 ($146,600 ÷ $12,000) |

The number of times interest charges are earned improved from 12.2 to 28.1 during 2012. This indicates that Lincoln Company has sufficient earnings to pay interest expense.

The number of times interest charges are earned can be adapted for use with dividends on preferred stock. In this case, the *number of times preferred dividends are earned* is computed as follows:

$$\text{Number of Times Preferred Dividends Are Earned} = \frac{\text{Net Income}}{\text{Preferred Dividends}}$$

Since dividends are paid after taxes, net income is used in computing the number of times preferred dividends are earned. The *higher* the ratio, the more likely preferred dividends payments will be paid if earnings decrease.

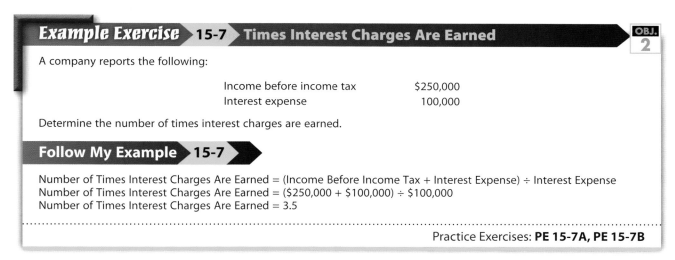

**Example Exercise** 15-7 **Times Interest Charges Are Earned**

OBJ. 2

A company reports the following:

| | |
|---|---|
| Income before income tax | $250,000 |
| Interest expense | 100,000 |

Determine the number of times interest charges are earned.

**Follow My Example** 15-7

Number of Times Interest Charges Are Earned = (Income Before Income Tax + Interest Expense) ÷ Interest Expense
Number of Times Interest Charges Are Earned = ($250,000 + $100,000) ÷ $100,000
Number of Times Interest Charges Are Earned = 3.5

Practice Exercises: **PE 15-7A, PE 15-7B**

# Profitability Analysis

OBJ. **3** Use financial statement analysis to assess the profitability of a business.

Profitability analysis focuses on the ability of a company to earn profits. This ability is reflected in the company's operating results, as reported in its income statement. The ability to earn profits also depends on the assets the company has available for use in its operations, as reported in its balance sheet. Thus, income statement and balance sheet relationships are often used in evaluating profitability.

Common profitability analyses include the following:

1. Ratio of net sales to assets
2. Rate earned on total assets
3. Rate earned on stockholders' equity
4. Rate earned on common stockholders' equity
5. Earnings per share on common stock
6. Price-earnings ratio
7. Dividends per share
8. Dividend yield

**Note:**
**Profitability analysis focuses on the relationship between operating results and the resources available to a business.**

## Ratio of Net Sales to Assets

The **ratio of net sales to assets** measures how effectively a company uses its assets. It is computed as follows:

$$\text{Ratio of Net Sales to Assets} = \frac{\text{Net Sales}}{\text{Average Total Assets}}$$
$$\text{(excluding long-term investments)}$$

As shown above, any long-term investments are excluded in computing the ratio of net sales to assets. This is because long-term investments are unrelated to normal operations and net sales.

To illustrate, the ratio of net sales to assets for Lincoln Company is computed below. Total assets (excluding long-term investments) are $1,010,000 at the beginning of 2011.

| | 2012 | 2011 |
|---|---|---|
| Net sales | $1,498,000 | $1,200,000 |
| Total assets (excluding long-term investments): | | |
| Beginning of year | $1,053,000* | $1,010,000 |
| End of year | 1,044,500** | 1,053,000*** |
| Total | $2,097,500 | $2,063,000 |
| | | |
| Average total assets | $1,048,750 ($2,097,500 ÷ 2) | $1,031,500 ($2,063,000 ÷ 2) |
| Ratio of net sales to assets | 1.4 ($1,498,000 ÷ $1,048,750) | 1.2 ($1,200,000 ÷ $1,031,500) |

\*($1,230,500 − $177,500)
\*\*($1,139,500 − $95,000)
\*\*\*($1,230,500 − $177,500)

For Lincoln Company, the average total assets was computed using total assets (excluding long-term investments) at the beginning and the end of the year. The average total assets could also be based on monthly or quarterly averages.

The ratio of net sales to assets indicates that Lincoln's use of its operating assets has improved in 2012. This was primarily due to the increase in net sales in 2012.

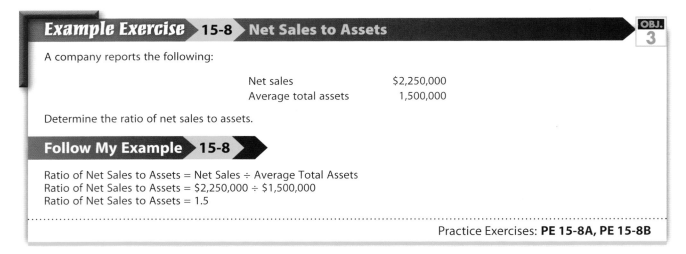

**Example Exercise** **15-8** **Net Sales to Assets**                          **OBJ. 3**

A company reports the following:

|  |  |
|---|---|
| Net sales | $2,250,000 |
| Average total assets | 1,500,000 |

Determine the ratio of net sales to assets.

**Follow My Example** **15-8**

Ratio of Net Sales to Assets = Net Sales ÷ Average Total Assets
Ratio of Net Sales to Assets = $2,250,000 ÷ $1,500,000
Ratio of Net Sales to Assets = 1.5

Practice Exercises: **PE 15-8A, PE 15-8B**

## Rate Earned on Total Assets

The **rate earned on total assets** measures the profitability of total assets, without considering how the assets are financed. In other words, this rate is not affected by the portion of assets financed by creditors or stockholders. It is computed as follows:

$$\text{Rate Earned on Total Assets} = \frac{\text{Net Income} + \text{Interest Expense}}{\text{Average Total Assets}}$$

The rate earned on total assets is computed by adding interest expense to net income. By adding interest expense to net income, the effect of whether the assets are financed by creditors (debt) or stockholders (equity) is eliminated. Because net income includes any income earned from long-term investments, the average total assets includes long-term investments as well as the net operating assets.

To illustrate, the rate earned on total assets by Lincoln Company is computed below. Total assets are $1,187,500 at the beginning of 2011.

|  | 2012 | 2011 |
|---|---|---|
| Net income | $ 91,000 | $ 76,500 |
| Plus interest expense | 6,000 | 12,000 |
| Total | $ 97,000 | $ 88,500 |
| Total assets: |  |  |
| Beginning of year | $1,230,500 | $1,187,500 |
| End of year | 1,139,500 | 1,230,500 |
| Total | $2,370,000 | $2,418,000 |
| Average total assets | $1,185,000 ($2,370,000 ÷ 2) | $1,209,000 ($2,418,000 ÷ 2) |
| Rate earned on total assets | 8.2% ($97,000 ÷ $1,185,000) | 7.3% ($88,500 ÷ $1,209,000) |

The rate earned on total assets improved from 7.3% to 8.2% during 2012.

The *rate earned on operating assets* is sometimes computed when there are large amounts of nonoperating income and expense. It is computed as follows:

$$\text{Rate Earned on Operating Assets} = \frac{\text{Income from Operations}}{\text{Average Operating Assets}}$$

Since Lincoln Company does not have a significant amount of nonoperating income and expense, the rate earned on operating assets is not illustrated.

The rate earned on total assets can be computed using spreadsheet software as follows:

| | A | B | C |
|---|---|---|---|
| 1 | *Inputs:* | | |
| 2 | | 2012 | 2011 |
| 3 | Net income | $          91,000 | $          76,500 |
| 4 | Interest expense | 6,000 | 12,000 |
| 5 | | | |
| 6 | Total assets: | | |
| 7 | Beginning of year | $     1,230,500 | $     1,187,500 |
| 8 | End of year | 1,139,500 | 1,230,500 |
| 9 | | | |
| 10 | *Outputs:* | | |
| 11 | Rate earned on total assets | =(B3+B4)/((B7+B8)/2) | =(C3+C4)/((C7+C8)/2) |

a.                    ➝ b.

The inputs could be the financial statements or a section of the financial statements. Here we illustrate only the data needed to compute the ratio. The output is the rate earned on total assets for the two years.

a.   Enter the formula for the rate earned on total assets in B11 as follows:

=(B3+B4)/((B7+B8)/2)

Numerator, using parentheses to force calculation order. ↑    ↑ Denominator, using parentheses to force calculation order.

b.   Copy the formula from B11 to C11.

**Try**It   Go to the hands-on **Excel Tutor** for this example!
(Note: The example here and throughout this chapter are contained in a **single** tutorial.)

**Try**It   This Excel Success example shows the use of parentheses.
Go to the **Excel Tutor** titled **Using Parentheses** for additional help!

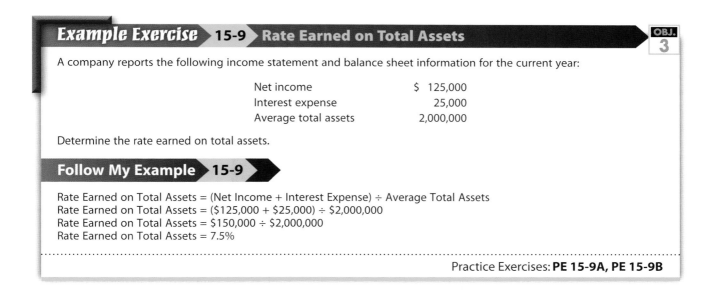

**Example Exercise** ▸ **15-9** ▸ **Rate Earned on Total Assets**                    OBJ. 3

A company reports the following income statement and balance sheet information for the current year:

| | |
|---|---|
| Net income | $  125,000 |
| Interest expense | 25,000 |
| Average total assets | 2,000,000 |

Determine the rate earned on total assets.

**Follow My Example** ▸ **15-9**

Rate Earned on Total Assets = (Net Income + Interest Expense) ÷ Average Total Assets
Rate Earned on Total Assets = ($125,000 + $25,000) ÷ $2,000,000
Rate Earned on Total Assets = $150,000 ÷ $2,000,000
Rate Earned on Total Assets = 7.5%

Practice Exercises: **PE 15-9A, PE 15-9B**

## Rate Earned on Stockholders' Equity

The **rate earned on stockholders' equity** measures the rate of income earned on the amount invested by the stockholders. It is computed as follows:

$$\text{Rate Earned on Stockholders' Equity} = \frac{\text{Net Income}}{\text{Average Total Stockholders' Equity}}$$

To illustrate, the rate earned on stockholders' equity for Lincoln Company is computed below. Total stockholders' equity is $750,000 at the beginning of 2011.

| | 2012 | 2011 |
|---|---|---|
| Net income | $     91,000 | $     76,500 |
| Stockholders' equity: | | |
| Beginning of year | $  787,500 | $  750,000 |
| End of year | 829,500 | 787,500 |
| Total | $1,617,000 | $1,537,500 |
| | | |
| Average stockholders' equity | $808,500 ($1,617,000 ÷ 2) | $768,750 ($1,537,500 ÷ 2) |
| Rate earned on stockholders' equity | 11.3% ($91,000 ÷ $808,500) | 10.0% ($76,500 ÷ $768,750) |

The rate earned on stockholders' equity improved from 10.0% to 11.3% during 2012.

Leverage involves using debt to increase the return on an investment. The rate earned on stockholders' equity is normally higher than the rate earned on total assets. This is because of the effect of leverage.

For Lincoln Company, the effect of leverage for 2012 is 3.1% and for 2011 is 2.7% computed as follows:

| | 2012 | 2011 |
|---|---|---|
| Rate earned on stockholders' equity | 11.3% | 10.0% |
| Less rate earned on total assets | 8.2 | 7.3 |
| Effect of leverage | 3.1% | 2.7% |

Exhibit 8 shows the 2012 and 2011 effects of leverage for Lincoln Company.

## Rate Earned on Common Stockholders' Equity

The **rate earned on common stockholders' equity** measures the rate of profits earned on the amount invested by the common stockholders. It is computed as follows:

$$\frac{\text{Rate Earned on Common}}{\text{Stockholders' Equity}} = \frac{\text{Net Income} - \text{Preferred Dividends}}{\text{Average Common Stockholders' Equity}}$$

**EXHIBIT 8**

**Effect of Leverage**

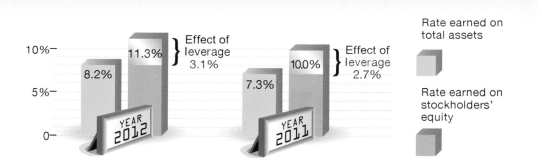

Because preferred stockholders rank ahead of the common stockholders in their claim on earnings, any preferred dividends are subtracted from net income in computing the rate earned on common stockholders' equity.

Lincoln Company had $150,000 of 6% preferred stock outstanding on December 31, 2012 and 2011. Thus, preferred dividends of $9,000 ($150,000 × 6%) are deducted from net income. Lincoln's common stockholders' equity is determined as follows:

| | December 31 | | |
|---|---|---|---|
| | 2012 | 2011 | 2010 |
| Common stock, $10 par | $500,000 | $500,000 | $500,000 |
| Retained earnings | 179,500 | 137,500 | 100,000 |
| Common stockholders' equity | $679,500 | $637,500 | $600,000 |

The retained earnings on December 31, 2010, of $100,000 is the same as the retained earnings on January 1, 2011, as shown in Lincoln's retained earnings statement in Exhibit 4.

Using this information, the rate earned on common stockholders' equity for Lincoln Company is computed below.

|  | 2012 | 2011 |
|---|---|---|
| Net income | $ 91,000 | $ 76,500 |
| Less preferred dividends | 9,000 | 9,000 |
| Total | $ 82,000 | $ 67,500 |
| Common stockholders' equity: |  |  |
| Beginning of year | $ 637,500 | $ 600,000 |
| End of year | 679,500* | 637,500** |
| Total | $1,317,000 | $1,237,500 |
| Average common stockholders' equity | $ 658,500 ($1,317,000 ÷ 2) | $618,750 ($1,237,500 ÷ 2) |
| Rate earned on common stockholders' equity | 12.5% ($82,000 ÷ $658,500) | 10.9% ($67,500 ÷ $618,750) |

*($829,500 – $150,000)
**($787,500 – $150,000)

Lincoln Company's rate earned on common stockholders' equity improved from 10.9% to 12.5% in 2012. This rate differs from the rates earned by Lincoln Company on total assets and stockholders' equity as shown below.

|  | 2012 | 2011 |
|---|---|---|
| Rate earned on total assets | 8.2% | 7.3% |
| Rate earned on stockholders' equity | 11.3% | 10.0% |
| Rate earned on common stockholders' equity | 12.5% | 10.9% |

These rates differ because of leverage, as discussed in the preceding section.

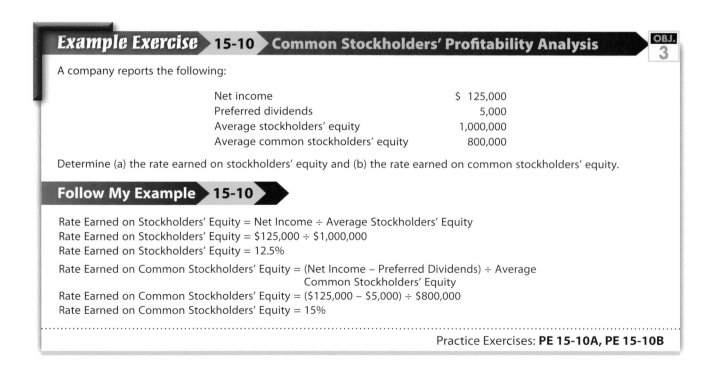

**Example Exercise 15-10 Common Stockholders' Profitability Analysis** OBJ. 3

A company reports the following:

| Net income | $ 125,000 |
|---|---|
| Preferred dividends | 5,000 |
| Average stockholders' equity | 1,000,000 |
| Average common stockholders' equity | 800,000 |

Determine (a) the rate earned on stockholders' equity and (b) the rate earned on common stockholders' equity.

**Follow My Example 15-10**

Rate Earned on Stockholders' Equity = Net Income ÷ Average Stockholders' Equity
Rate Earned on Stockholders' Equity = $125,000 ÷ $1,000,000
Rate Earned on Stockholders' Equity = 12.5%

Rate Earned on Common Stockholders' Equity = (Net Income – Preferred Dividends) ÷ Average Common Stockholders' Equity
Rate Earned on Common Stockholders' Equity = ($125,000 – $5,000) ÷ $800,000
Rate Earned on Common Stockholders' Equity = 15%

Practice Exercises: **PE 15-10A, PE 15-10B**

## Earnings per Share on Common Stock

**Earnings per share (EPS) on common stock** measures the share of profits that are earned by a share of common stock. Earnings per share must be reported in the income statement. As a result, earnings per share (EPS) is often reported in the financial press. It is computed as follows:

$$\text{Earnings per Share (EPS) on Common Stock} = \frac{\text{Net Income} - \text{Preferred Dividends}}{\text{Shares of Common Stock Outstanding}}$$

When preferred and common stock are outstanding, preferred dividends are subtracted from net income to determine the income related to the common shares.

To illustrate, the earnings per share (EPS) of common stock for Lincoln Company is computed below.

|  | 2012 | 2011 |
|---|---|---|
| Net income | $91,000 | $76,500 |
| Preferred dividends | 9,000 | 9,000 |
| Total | $82,000 | $67,500 |
| Shares of common stock outstanding | 50,000 | 50,000 |
| Earnings per share on common stock | $1.64 ($82,000 ÷ 50,000) | $1.35 ($67,500 ÷ 50,000) |

Lincoln Company had $150,000 of 6% preferred stock outstanding on December 31, 2012 and 2011. Thus, preferred dividends of $9,000 ($150,000 × 6%) are deducted from net income in computing earnings per share on common stock.

Lincoln did not issue any additional shares of common stock in 2012. If Lincoln had issued additional shares in 2012, a weighted average of common shares outstanding during the year would have been used.

Lincoln's earnings per share (EPS) on common stock improved from $1.35 to $1.64 during 2012.

Lincoln Company has a simple capital structure with only common stock and preferred stock outstanding. Many corporations, however, have complex capital structures with various types of equity securities outstanding, such as convertible preferred stock, stock options, and stock warrants. In such cases, the possible effects of such securities on the shares of common stock outstanding are considered in reporting earnings per share. These possible effects are reported separately as *earnings per common share assuming dilution* or *diluted earnings per share*. This topic is described and illustrated in advanced accounting courses and textbooks.

## Price-Earnings Ratio

The **price-earnings (P/E) ratio** on common stock measures a company's future earnings prospects. It is often quoted in the financial press and is computed as follows:

$$\text{Price-Earnings (P/E) Ratio} = \frac{\text{Market Price per Share of Common Stock}}{\text{Earnings per Share on Common Stock}}$$

To illustrate, the price-earnings (P/E) ratio for Lincoln Company is computed below.

|  | 2012 | 2011 |
|---|---|---|
| Market price per share of common stock | $41.00 | $27.00 |
| Earnings per share on common stock | $1.64 | $1.35 |
| Price-earnings ratio on common stock | 25 ($41 ÷ $1.64) | 20 ($27 ÷ $1.35) |

**Example Exercise** ▶ **15-11** ▶ **Earnings per Share and Price-Earnings Ratio** OBJ. 3

A company reports the following:

| | |
|---|---:|
| Net income | $250,000 |
| Preferred dividends | $15,000 |
| Shares of common stock outstanding | 20,000 |
| Market price per share of common stock | $35.00 |

a. Determine the company's earnings per share on common stock.
b. Determine the company's price-earnings ratio. Round to one decimal place.

**Follow My Example** ▶ **15-11** ▶

a. Earnings per Share on Common Stock = (Net Income – Preferred Dividends) ÷ Shares of Common Stock
   Outstanding
   Earnings per Share = ($250,000 – $15,000) ÷ 20,000
   Earnings per Share = $11.75

b. Price-Earnings Ratio = Market Price per Share of Common Stock ÷ Earnings per Share on Common Stock
   Price-Earnings Ratio = $35.00 ÷ $11.75
   Price-Earnings Ratio = 3.0

Practice Exercises: **PE 15-11A, PE 15-11B**

The price-earnings ratio improved from 20 to 25 during 2012. In other words, a share of common stock of Lincoln Company was selling for 20 times earnings per share at the end of 2011. At the end of 2012, the common stock was selling for 25 times earnings per share. This indicates that the market expects Lincoln to experience favorable earnings in the future.

## Dividends per Share

**Dividends per share** measures the extent to which earnings are being distributed to common shareholders. It is computed as follows:

$$\text{Dividends per Share} = \frac{\text{Dividends on Common Stock}}{\text{Shares of Common Stock Outstanding}}$$

To illustrate, the dividends per share for Lincoln Company are computed below.

| | 2012 | 2011 |
|---|---|---|
| Dividends on common stock | $40,000 | $30,000 |
| Shares of common stock outstanding | 50,000 | 50,000 |
| Dividends per share of common stock | $0.80 ($40,000 ÷ 50,000) | $0.60 ($30,000 ÷ 50,000) |

The dividends per share of common stock increased from $0.60 to $0.80 during 2012.

Dividends per share are often reported with earnings per share. Comparing the two per-share amounts indicates the extent to which earnings are being retained for use in operations. To illustrate, the dividends and earnings per share for Lincoln Company are shown in Exhibit 9.

**EXHIBIT 9**

**Dividends and Earnings per Share of Common Stock**

## Dividend Yield

The **dividend yield** on common stock measures the rate of return to common stockholders from cash dividends. It is of special interest to investors whose objective is to earn revenue (dividends) from their investment. It is computed as follows:

The dividends per share, dividend yield, and P/E ratio of a common stock are normally quoted on the daily listing of stock prices in *The Wall Street Journal* and on Yahoo!'s finance Web site.

$$\text{Dividend Yield} = \frac{\text{Dividends per Share of Common Stock}}{\text{Market Price per Share of Common Stock}}$$

To illustrate, the dividend yield for Lincoln Company is computed below.

|  | 2012 | 2011 |
|---|---|---|
| Dividends per share of common stock | $0.80 | $0.60 |
| Market price per share of common stock | $41.00 | $27.00 |
| Dividend yield on common stock | 2.0% ($0.80 ÷ $41) | 2.2% ($0.60 ÷ $27) |

The dividend yield declined slightly from 2.2% to 2.0% in 2012. This decline was primarily due to the increase in the market price of Lincoln's common stock.

## Summary of Analytical Measures

Exhibit 10 shows a summary of the liquidity, solvency, and profitability measures discussed in this chapter. The type of industry and the company's operations usually affect which measures are used. In many cases, additional measures are used for a specific industry. For example, airlines use *revenue per passenger mile* and *cost per available seat* as profitability measures. Likewise, hotels use *occupancy rates* as a profitability measure.

The analytical measures shown in Exhibit 10 are a useful starting point for analyzing a company's liquidity, solvency, and profitability. However, they are not a substitute for sound judgment. For example, the general economic and business environment should always be considered in analyzing a company's future prospects. In addition, any trends and interrelationships among the measures should be carefully studied.

---

## Integrity, Objectivity, and Ethics in Business

### CHIEF FINANCIAL OFFICER BONUSES

A recent study by compensation experts at Temple University found that chief financial officer salaries are correlated with the complexity of a company's operations, but chief financial officer bonuses are correlated with the company's ability to meet analysts' earnings forecasts. These results suggest that financial bonuses may provide chief financial officers with an incentive to use questionable accounting practices to improve earnings. While the study doesn't conclude that bonuses lead to accounting fraud, it does suggest that bonuses give chief financial officers a reason to find ways to use accounting to increase apparent earnings.

Source: E. Jelesiewicz, "Today's CFO: More Challenge but Higher Compensation," *News Communications* (Temple University, August 2009).

**EXHIBIT 10** **Summary of Analytical Measures**

| *Liquidity and solvency measures:* | **Method of Computation** | **Use** |
|---|---|---|
| Working Capital | Current Assets – Current Liabilities | To indicate the ability to meet currently maturing obligations (measures solvency) |
| Current Ratio | $\dfrac{\text{Current Assets}}{\text{Current Liabilities}}$ | |
| Quick Ratio | $\dfrac{\text{Quick Assets}}{\text{Current Liabilities}}$ | To indicate instant debt-paying ability (measures solvency) |
| Accounts Receivable Turnover | $\dfrac{\text{Net Sales}}{\text{Average Accounts Receivable}}$ | To assess the efficiency in collecting receivables and in the management of credit (measures liquidity) |
| Numbers of Days' Sales in Receivables | $\dfrac{\text{Average Accounts Receivable}}{\text{Average Daily Sales}}$ | |
| Inventory Turnover | $\dfrac{\text{Cost of Goods Sold}}{\text{Average Inventory}}$ | To assess the efficiency in the management of inventory (measures liquidity) |
| Number of Days' Sales in Inventory | $\dfrac{\text{Average Inventory}}{\text{Average Daily Cost of Goods Sold}}$ | |
| Ratio of Fixed Assets to Long-Term Liabilities | $\dfrac{\text{Fixed Assets (net)}}{\text{Long-Term Liabilities}}$ | To indicate the margin of safety to long-term creditors (measures solvency) |
| Ratio of Liabilities to Stockholders' Equity | $\dfrac{\text{Total Liabilities}}{\text{Total Stockholders' Equity}}$ | To indicate the margin of safety to creditors (measures solvency) |
| Number of Times Interest Charges Are Earned | $\dfrac{\text{Income Before Income Tax + Interest Expense}}{\text{Interest Expense}}$ | To assess the risk to debtholders in terms of number of times interest charges were earned (measures solvency) |
| *Profitability measures:* | | |
| Ratio of Net Sales to Assets | $\dfrac{\text{Net Sales}}{\text{Average Total Assets (excluding long-term investments)}}$ | To assess the effectiveness in the use of assets |
| Rate Earned on Total Assets | $\dfrac{\text{Net Income + Interest Expense}}{\text{Average Total Assets}}$ | To assess the profitability of the assets |
| Rate Earned on Stockholders' Equity | $\dfrac{\text{Net Income}}{\text{Average Total Stockholders' Equity}}$ | To assess the profitability of the investment by stockholders |
| Rate Earned on Common Stockholders' Equity | $\dfrac{\text{Net Income – Preferred Dividends}}{\text{Average Common Stockholders' Equity}}$ | To assess the profitability of the investment by common stockholders |
| Earnings per Share (EPS) on Common Stock | $\dfrac{\text{Net Income – Preferred Dividends}}{\text{Shares of Common Stock Outstanding}}$ | |
| Price-Earnings (P/E) Ratio | $\dfrac{\text{Market Price per Share of Common Stock}}{\text{Earnings per Share on Common Stock}}$ | To indicate future earnings prospects, based on the relationship between market value of common stock and earnings |
| Dividends per Share | $\dfrac{\text{Dividends on Common Stock}}{\text{Shares of Common Stock Outstanding}}$ | To indicate the extent to which earnings are being distributed to common stockholders |
| Dividend Yield | $\dfrac{\text{Dividends per Share of Common Stock}}{\text{Market Price per Share of Common Stock}}$ | To indicate the rate of return to common stockholders in terms of dividends |

OBJ. **4** Describe the contents of corporate annual reports.

# Corporate Annual Reports

Public corporations issue annual reports summarizing their operating activities for the past year and plans for the future. Such annual reports include the financial statements and the accompanying notes. In addition, annual reports normally include the following sections:

See Appendix E for more information

- Management discussion and analysis
- Report on internal control
- Report on fairness of the financial statements

## Management's Discussion and Analysis

**Management's Discussion and Analysis (MD&A)** is required in annual reports filed with the Securities and Exchange Commission. It includes management's analysis of current operations and its plans for the future. Typical items included in the MD&A are as follows:

- Management's analysis and explanations of any significant changes between the current and prior years' financial statements.
- Important accounting principles or policies that could affect interpretation of the financial statements, including the effect of changes in accounting principles or the adoption of new accounting principles.
- Management's assessment of the company's liquidity and the availability of capital to the company.
- Significant risk exposures that might affect the company.
- Any "off-balance-sheet" arrangements such as leases not included directly in the financial statements. Such arrangements are discussed in advanced accounting courses and textbooks.

## Report on Internal Control

The Sarbanes-Oxley Act of 2002 requires a report on internal control by management. The report states management's responsibility for establishing and maintaining internal control. In addition, management's assessment of the effectiveness of internal controls over financial reporting is included in the report.

Sarbanes-Oxley also requires a public accounting firm to verify management's conclusions on internal control. Thus, two reports on internal control, one by management and one by a public accounting firm, are included in the annual report. In some situations, these may be combined into a single report on internal control.

## Report on Fairness of the Financial Statements

All publicly held corporations are required to have an independent audit (examination) of their financial statements. The Certified Public Accounting (CPA) firm that conducts the audit renders an opinion, called the *Report of Independent Registered Public Accounting Firm*, on the fairness of the statements.

An opinion stating that the financial statements present fairly the financial position, results of operations, and cash flows of the company is said to be an *unqualified opinion*, sometimes called a *clean opinion*. Any report other than an unqualified opinion raises a "red flag" for financial statement users and requires further investigation as to its cause.[3]

The annual report of Nike Inc. is shown in Appendix D. The Nike report includes the financial statements as well as the MD&A Report on Internal Control and Report on Fairness of the Financial Statements.

---

3 Earnings per share related to discontinued operations and extraordinary items should be reported separately. The reporting of these items is discussed in this chapter's appendix.

# Integrity, Objectivity, and Ethics in Business

**BUY LOW, SELL HIGH**

Research analysts work for banks, brokerages, or other financial institutions. Their job is to estimate the value of a company's common stock by reviewing and evaluating the company's business model, strategic plan, and financial performance. Based on this analysis, the analyst develops an estimate of a stock's value, which is called its *fundamental value*. Analysts then advise their clients to "buy" or "sell" a company's stock based on the following guidelines:

| | |
|---|---|
| Current market price is greater than fundamental value | Sell |
| Current market price is lower than fundamental value | Buy |

If analysts are doing their job well, their clients will enjoy large returns by buying stocks at low prices and selling them at high prices.

Comprehensive Spreadsheet Illustration:
Rainbow Paint Co.'s comparative financial statement for the years ending December 31, 2012 and 2011, in spreadsheet form are shown below. The market price of Rainbow Paint Co.'s common stock was $30 on December 31, 2012.

| | A | B | C |
|---|---|---|---|
| 1 | Rainbow Paint Co. | | |
| 2 | Comparative Income Statements | | |
| 3 | For the Years Ended December 31, 2012 and 2011 | | |
| 4 | | | |
| 5 | | 2012 | 2011 |
| 6 | Sales | $ 5,125,000 | $ 3,257,600 |
| 7 | Sales returns and allowances | 125,000 | 57,600 |
| 8 | Net sales | $ 5,000,000 | $ 3,200,000 |
| 9 | Cost of goods sold | 3,400,000 | 2,080,000 |
| 10 | Gross profit | $ 1,600,000 | $ 1,120,000 |
| 11 | Selling expenses | 650,000 | 464,000 |
| 12 | Administrative expenses | 325,000 | 224,000 |
| 13 | Total operating expenses | $ 975,000 | $ 688,000 |
| 14 | Income from operations | $ 625,000 | $ 432,000 |
| 15 | Other income | 25,000 | 19,200 |
| 16 | | $ 650,000 | $ 451,200 |
| 17 | Other expense (interest) | 105,000 | 64,000 |
| 18 | Income before income tax | $ 545,000 | $ 387,200 |
| 19 | Income tax expense | 300,000 | 176,000 |
| 20 | Net Income | $ 245,000 | $ 211,200 |
| 21 | | | |

| | A | B | C |
|---|---|---|---|
| 23 | Rainbow Paint Co. | | |
| 24 | Comparative Retained Earnings Statement | | |
| 25 | For the Years Ended December 31, 2012 and 2011 | | |
| 26 | | | |
| 27 | | 2012 | 2011 |
| 28 | Retained earnings, January 1 | $ 723,000 | $ 581,800 |
| 29 | Add net income for year | 245,000 | 211,200 |
| 30 | Total | $ 968,000 | $ 793,000 |
| 31 | Deduct dividends: | | |
| 32 | On preferred stock | $ 40,000 | $ 40,000 |
| 33 | On common stock | 45,000 | 30,000 |
| 34 | Total | $ 85,000 | $ 70,000 |
| 35 | Retained earnings, December 31 | $ 883,000 | $ 723,000 |

| | A | B | C |
|---|---|---|---|
| 38 | Rainbow Paint Co. | | |
| 39 | Comparative Balance Sheet | | |
| 40 | For the Years Ended December 31, 2012 and 2011 | | |
| 41 | | | |
| 42 | | Dec. 31, 2012 | Dec. 31, 2011 |
| 43 | **Assets** | | |
| 44 | Current assets: | | |
| 45 | Cash | $ 175,000 | $ 125,000 |
| 46 | Temporary investments | 150,000 | 50,000 |
| 47 | Accounts receivable (net) | 425,000 | 325,000 |
| 48 | Inventories | 720,000 | 480,000 |
| 49 | Prepaid expenses | 30,000 | 20,000 |
| 50 | Total current assets | $ 1,500,000 | $ 1,000,000 |
| 51 | Long-term investments | 250,000 | 225,000 |
| 52 | Property, plant, and equipment | 2,093,000 | 1,948,000 |
| 53 | Total assets | $ 3,843,000 | $ 3,173,000 |
| 54 | | | |
| 55 | **Liabilities** | | |
| 56 | Current liabilities | $ 750,000 | $ 650,000 |
| 57 | Long-term liabilities: | | |
| 58 | Mortgage note payable, 10% due 2015 | 410,000 | - |
| 59 | Bonds payable, 8%, due 2018 | 800,000 | 800,000 |
| 60 | Total long-term liabilities | $ 1,210,000 | $ 800,000 |
| 61 | Total liabilities | $ 1,960,000 | $ 1,450,000 |
| 62 | | | |
| 63 | **Stockholders' Equity** | | |
| 64 | Preferred 8% stock, $100 par | $ 500,000 | $ 500,000 |
| 65 | Common stock, $10 par | 500,000 | 500,000 |
| 66 | Retained earnings | 883,000 | 723,000 |
| 67 | Total stockholders' equity | $ 1,883,000 | $ 1,723,000 |
| 68 | Total liabilities and stockholders' equity | $ 3,843,000 | $ 3,173,000 |
| 69 | | | |
| 70 | | Dec. 31, 2012 | |
| 71 | Common stock market price | $ 25.00 | |
| 72 | Number of common shares outstanding | $ 50,000 | |

Working Capital, =B50-B56

**Solution**

Ratio formulas are illustrated for Rainbow Paint Co. for 2012. The Excel formulas refer to the cell references shown in the financial statements for Rainbow Paint Co. For example, the working capital is computed as the difference between cells B50 and B56, or =B50-B56. This formula is computed based on the balance sheet data. The remaining formulas reference financial statement cells for 2012.

The parentheses in the Excel formulas are required to force proper calculation order. Proper use of parenthesis is important when developing complex Excel formulas.

| | A | B | C |
|---|---|---|---|
| 1 | | Ratio solution and numerical formula | Excel formula |
| 2 | 1. | Working capital: $750,000<br>$1,500,000 - $750,000 | =B50-B56 |
| 3 | 2. | Current ratio: 2.0<br> $1,500,000 ÷ $750,000 | =B50/B56 |
| 4 | 3. | Quick ratio: 1.0<br>$750,000 ÷ $750,000 | =SUM(B45:B47)/B56 |
| 5 | 4. | Accounts receivable turnover: 13.3<br>$5,000,000 ÷ [($425,000 + 325,000) ÷ 2] | =B8/((B47+C47)/2) |
| 6 | 5. | Number of days' sales in receivables: 27.4 days<br>$5,000,000 ÷ 365 days = $13,699<br>$375,000 ÷ $13,699 | =((B47+C47)/2)/(B8/365) |
| 7 | 6. | Inventory turnover: 5.7<br>$3,400,000 ÷ [($720,000 + $480,000) ÷ 2] | =B9/((B48+C48)/2) |
| 8 | 7. | Number of days' sales in inventory: 64.4 days<br>$3,400,000 ÷ 365 days = $9,315<br>$600,000 ÷ $9,315 | =((B48+C48)/2)/(B9/365) |
| 9 | 8. | Ratio of fixed assets to long-term liabilities: 1.7<br>$2,093,000 ÷ $1,210,000 | =B52/B60 |

| | A | B | C |
|---|---|---|---|
| 10 | 9. | Ratio of liabilities to stockholders' equity: 1.0<br>$1,960,000 + $1,883,000 | =B61/B67 |
| 11 | 10. | Number of times interest charges are earned: 6.2<br>($545,000 + $105,000) ÷ $105,000 | =(B18+B17)/B17 |
| 12 | 11. | Number of times preferred dividends are earned: 6.1<br>$245,000 ÷ $40,000 | =B20/B32 |
| 13 | 12. | Ratio of net sales to assets: 1.5<br>$5,000,000 ÷ [($3,593,000 + $2,948,000) ÷ 2] | =B8/((($53-B51)+(C53-C51))/2) |
| 14 | 13. | Rate earned on total assets: 10.0%<br>($245,000 + $105,000) ÷ [($3,843,000 + $3,173,000) ÷ 2] | =(B20+B17)/((B53+C53)/2) |
| 15 | 14. | Rate earned on stockholders' equity: 13.6%<br>$245,000 + [($1,883,000 + $1,723,000) ÷ 2] | =B20/((B67+C67)/2) |
| 16 | 15. | Rate earned on common stockholders' equity: 15.7%<br>($245,000 - $40,000) ÷ [($1,383,000 + $1,223,000) ÷ 2] | =(B20-B32)/(((B67-B64)+(C67-C64))/2) |
| 17 | 16. | Earnings per share on common stock: $4.10<br>($245,000 - $40,000) ÷ 50,000 shares | =(B20-B32)/B72 |
| 18 | 17. | Price-earnings ratio: 6.1<br>$25 ÷ [($245,000 - $40,000) ÷ 50,000 shares] | =B71/((B20-B32)/B72) |
| 19 | 18. | Dividends per share: $0.90<br>$45,000 ÷ 50,000 shares | =B33/B72 |
| 20 | 19. | Dividend yield: 3.6%<br>(45,000 ÷ 50,000 shares) ÷ $25 | =(B33/B72)/B71 |

**Try***It*  Reminder: Go to the **Excel Tutor** titled **Using Parentheses** for additional help!

# A P P E N D I X

# Unusual Items on the Income Statement

Generally accepted accounting principles require that unusual items be reported separately on the income statement. This is because such items do not occur frequently and are typically unrelated to current operations. Without separate reporting of these items, users of the financial statements might be misled about current and future operations.

Unusual items on the income statement are classified as one of the following:

1. Affecting the *current period* income statement
2. Affecting a *prior period* income statement

## Unusual Items Affecting the Current Period's Income Statement

Unusual items affecting the current period's income statement include the following:

1. Discontinued operations
2. Extraordinary items

These items are reported separately on the income statement for any period in which they occur.

**Discontinued Operations**  A company may discontinue a segment of its operations by selling or abandoning the segment's operations. For example, a retailer might decide to sell its product only online and, thus, discontinue selling its merchandise at its retail outlets (stores).

Any gain or loss on discontinued operations is reported on the income statement as a *Gain (or loss) from discontinued operations*. It is reported immediately following *Income from continuing operations*.

To illustrate, assume that Jones Corporation produces and sells electrical products, hardware supplies, and lawn equipment. Because of lack of profits, Jones discontinues its electrical products operation and sells the remaining inventory and other assets at a loss of $100,000. Exhibit 11 illustrates the reporting of the loss on discontinued operations.[4]

**EXHIBIT 11**

**Unusual Items in the Income Statement**

**Jones Corporation**
**Income Statement**
**For the Year Ended December 31, 2012**

| | |
|---|---|
| Net sales.......................................................................... | $12,350,000 |
| Cost of merchandise sold ................................................... | 5,800,000 |
| Gross profit ....................................................................... | $ 6,550,000 |
| Selling and administrative expenses ..................................... | 5,240,000 |
| Income from continuing operations before income tax............. | $ 1,310,000 |
| Income tax expense .......................................................... | 620,000 |
| Income from continuing operations ..................................... | $ 690,000 |
| Loss on discontinued operations ......................................... | 100,000 |
| Income before extraordinary items ...................................... | $ 590,000 |
| Extraordinary items: | |
|    Gain on condemnation of land ........................................ | 150,000 |
| Net income ....................................................................... | $ 740,000 |

In addition, a note accompanying the income statement should describe the operations sold including such details as the date operations were discontinued, the assets sold, and the effect (if any) on current and future operations.

**Extraordinary Items** An **extraordinary item** is defined as an event or a transaction that has both of the following characteristics:

1. Unusual in nature
2. Infrequent in occurrence

Gains and losses from natural disasters such as floods, earthquakes, and fires are normally reported as extraordinary items, provided that they occur infrequently. Gains or losses from land or buildings taken (condemned) for public use are also reported as extraordinary items.

Any gain or loss from extraordinary items is reported on the income statement as *Gain (or loss) from extraordinary item*. It is reported immediately following *Income from continuing operations* and any *Gain (or loss) on discontinued operations*.

To illustrate, assume that land owned by Jones Corporation was taken for public use (condemned) by the local government. The condemnation of the land resulted in a gain of $150,000. Exhibit 11 illustrates the reporting of the extraordinary gain.[5]

**Reporting Earnings per Share** Earnings per common share should be reported separately for discontinued operations and extraordinary items. To illustrate, a partial income statement for Jones Corporation is shown in Exhibit 12.

Exhibit 12 reports earnings per common share for income from continuing operations, discontinued operations, and extraordinary items. However, only earnings per share for income from continuing operations and net income are required by generally accepted accounting principles. The other per-share amounts may be presented in the notes to the financial statements.

---

4 The gain or loss on discontinued operations is reported net of any tax effects. To simplify, the tax effects are not specifically identified in Exhibit 11.

5 The gain or loss on extraordinary operations is reported net of any tax effects.

**EXHIBIT 12**

**Income Statement with Earnings per Share**

**Jones Corporation**
**Income Statement**
**For the Year Ended December 31, 2012**

| Earnings per common share: | |
| --- | --- |
| Income from continuing operations............................................... | $3.45 |
| Loss on discontinued operations ...................................... | 0.50 |
| Income before extraordinary items ................................. | $2.95 |
| Extraordinary items: | |
| Gain on condemnation of land ................................. | 0.75 |
| Net income .................................................... | $3.70 |

## Unusual Items Affecting the Prior Period's Income Statement

An unusual item may occur that affects a prior period's income statement. Two such items are as follows:

1. Errors in applying generally accepted accounting principles
2. Changes from one generally accepted accounting principle to another

If an error is discovered in a prior period's financial statement, the prior-period statement and all following statements are restated and thus corrected.

A company may change from one generally accepted accounting principle to another. In this case, the prior-period financial statements are restated as if the new accounting principle had always been used.[6]

For both of the preceding items, the current-period earnings are not affected. That is, only the earnings reported in prior periods are restated. However, because the prior earnings are restated, the beginning balance of Retained Earnings may also have to be restated. This, in turn, may cause the restatement of other balance sheet accounts. Illustrations of these types of adjustments and restatements are provided in advanced accounting courses.

6 Changes from one acceptable depreciation method to another acceptable depreciation method are an exception to this general rule and are to be treated prospectively as a change in estimate, as discussed in Chapter 9.

# At a Glance 15

**OBJ.**
**1**  **Describe basic financial statement analytical methods.**

**Key Points**    The basic financial statements provide much of the information users need to make economic decisions. Analytical procedures are used to compare items on a current financial statement with related items on earlier statements, or to examine relationships within a financial statement.

| Learning Outcomes | Example Exercises | Practice Exercises |
| --- | --- | --- |
| • Prepare a vertical analysis from a company's financial statements. | EE15-1 | PE15-1A, 15-1B |
| • Prepare a horizontal analysis from a company's financial statements. | EE15-2 | PE15-2A, 15-2B |
| • Prepare common-sized financial statements. | | |

**OBJ. 2** Use financial statement analysis to assess the liquidity and solvency of a business.

**Key Points** All users of financial statements are interested in the ability of a business to convert assets into cash (liquidity), pay its debts (solvency), and earn income (profitability). Liquidity, solvency, and profitability are interrelated. Liquidity and solvency are normally assessed by examining the following: current position analysis, accounts receivable analysis, inventory analysis, the ratio of fixed assets to long-term liabilities, the ratio of liabilities to stockholders' equity, and the number of times interest charges are earned.

| Learning Outcomes | Example Exercises | Practice Exercises |
|---|---|---|
| • Determine working capital. | | |
| • Compute and interpret the current ratio. | EE15-3 | PE15-3A, 15-3B |
| • Compute and interpret the quick ratio. | EE15-3 | PE15-3A, 15-3B |
| • Compute and interpret accounts receivable turnover. | EE15-4 | PE15-4A, 15-4B |
| • Compute and interpret number of days' sales in receivables. | EE15-4 | PE15-4A, 15-4B |
| • Compute and interpret inventory turnover. | EE15-5 | PE15-5A, 15-5B |
| • Compute and interpret number of days' sales in inventory. | EE15-5 | PE15-5A, 15-5B |
| • Compute and interpret the ratio of fixed assets to long-term liabilities. | EE15-6 | PE15-6A, 15-6B |
| • Compute and interpret the ratio of liabilities to stockholders' equity. | EE15-6 | PE15-6A, 15-6B |
| • Compute and interpret the number of times interest charges are earned. | EE15-7 | PE15-7A, 15-7B |

**OBJ. 3** Use financial statement analysis to assess the profitability of a business.

**Key Points** Profitability analysis focuses on the ability of a company to earn profits. This ability is reflected in the company's operating results as reported on the income statement and resources available as reported on the balance sheet. Major analyses include the ratio of net sales to assets, the rate earned on total assets, the rate earned on stockholders' equity, the rate earned on common stockholders' equity, earnings per share on common stock, the price-earnings ratio, dividends per share, and dividend yield.

| Learning Outcomes | Example Exercises | Practice Exercises |
|---|---|---|
| • Compute and interpret the ratio of net sales to assets. | EE15-8 | PE15-8A, 15-8B |
| • Compute and interpret the rate earned on total assets. | EE15-9 | PE15-9A, 15-9B |
| • Compute and interpret the rate earned on stockholders' equity. | EE15-10 | PE15-10A, 15-10B |
| • Compute and interpret the rate earned on common stockholders' equity. | EE15-10 | PE15-10A, 15-10B |
| • Compute and interpret the earnings per share on common stock. | EE15-11 | PE15-11A, 15-11B |
| • Compute and interpret the price-earnings ratio. | EE15-11 | PE15-11A, 15-11B |
| • Compute and interpret the dividends per share and dividend yield. | | |
| • Describe the uses and limitations of analytical measures. | | |

**OBJ. 4** Describe the contents of corporate annual reports.

**Key Points** Corporations normally issue annual reports to their stockholders and other interested parties. Such reports summarize the corporation's operating activities for the past year and plans for the future.

| Learning Outcomes | Example Exercises | Practice Exercises |
|---|---|---|
| • Describe the elements of a corporate annual report. | | |

# Key Terms

accounts receivable analysis (706)

accounts receivable turnover (706)

common-sized statement (701)

current position analysis (703)

current ratio (703)

dividend yield (718)

dividends per share (717)

earnings per share (EPS) on common stock (716)

extraordinary item (724)

horizontal analysis (696)

inventory analysis (707)

inventory turnover (707)

liquidity (702)

Management's Discussion and Analysis (MD&A) (720)

number of days' sales in inventory (708)

number of days' sales in receivables (706)

number of times interest charges are earned (710)

price-earnings (P/E) ratio (716)

profitability (702)

quick assets (705)

quick ratio (705)

rate earned on common stockholders' equity (714)

rate earned on stockholders' equity (713)

rate earned on total assets (712)

ratio of fixed assets to long-term liabilities (709)

ratio of liabilities to stockholders' equity (709)

ratio of net sales to assets (711)

solvency (702)

vertical analysis (699)

working capital (703)

# Illustrative Problem

Rainbow Paint Co.'s comparative financial statements for the years ending December 31, 2012 and 2011, are as follows. The market price of Rainbow Paint Co.'s common stock was $25 on December 31, 2012, and $30 on December 31, 2011.

| Rainbow Paint Co. Comparative Income Statement For the Years Ended December 31, 2012 and 2011 | 2012 | 2011 |
|---|---|---|
| Sales | $5,125,000 | $3,257,600 |
| Sales returns and allowances | 125,000 | 57,600 |
| Net sales | $5,000,000 | $3,200,000 |
| Cost of goods sold | 3,400,000 | 2,080,000 |
| Gross profit | $1,600,000 | $1,120,000 |
| Selling expenses | $ 650,000 | $ 464,000 |
| Administrative expenses | 325,000 | 224,000 |
| Total operating expenses | $ 975,000 | $ 688,000 |
| Income from operations | $ 625,000 | $ 432,000 |
| Other income | 25,000 | 19,200 |
| | $ 650,000 | $ 451,200 |
| Other expense (interest) | 105,000 | 64,000 |
| Income before income tax | $ 545,000 | $ 387,200 |
| Income tax expense | 300,000 | 176,000 |
| Net income | $ 245,000 | $ 211,200 |

| **Rainbow Paint Co.**<br>**Comparative Retained Earnings Statement**<br>**For the Years Ended December 31, 2012 and 2011** | | |
|---|---|---|
| | **2012** | **2011** |
| Retained earnings, January 1 | $723,000 | $581,800 |
| Add net income for year | 245,000 | 211,200 |
| Total | $968,000 | $793,000 |
| Deduct dividends: | | |
| On preferred stock | $ 40,000 | $ 40,000 |
| On common stock | 45,000 | 30,000 |
| Total | $ 85,000 | $ 70,000 |
| Retained earnings, December 31 | $883,000 | $723,000 |

| **Rainbow Paint Co.**<br>**Comparative Balance Sheet**<br>**December 31, 2012 and 2011** | | |
|---|---|---|
| | **Dec. 31,**<br>**2012** | **Dec. 31,**<br>**2011** |
| **Assets** | | |
| Current assets: | | |
| Cash | $ 175,000 | $ 125,000 |
| Temporary investments | 150,000 | 50,000 |
| Accounts receivable (net) | 425,000 | 325,000 |
| Inventories | 720,000 | 480,000 |
| Prepaid expenses | 30,000 | 20,000 |
| Total current assets | $1,500,000 | $1,000,000 |
| Long-term investments | 250,000 | 225,000 |
| Property, plant, and equipment (net) | 2,093,000 | 1,948,000 |
| Total assets | $3,843,000 | $3,173,000 |
| **Liabilities** | | |
| Current liabilities | $ 750,000 | $ 650,000 |
| Long-term liabilities: | | |
| Mortgage note payable, 10%, due 2015 | $ 410,000 | — |
| Bonds payable, 8%, due 2018 | 800,000 | $ 800,000 |
| Total long-term liabilities | $1,210,000 | $ 800,000 |
| Total liabilities | $1,960,000 | $1,450,000 |
| **Stockholders' Equity** | | |
| Preferred 8% stock, $100 par | $ 500,000 | $ 500,000 |
| Common stock, $10 par | 500,000 | 500,000 |
| Retained earnings | 883,000 | 723,000 |
| Total stockholders' equity | $1,883,000 | $1,723,000 |
| Total liabilities and stockholders' equity | $3,843,000 | $3,173,000 |

## Instructions

Determine the following measures for 2012:

1. Working capital

2. Current ratio

3. Quick ratio

4. Accounts receivable turnover

5. Number of days' sales in receivables

6. Inventory turnover

7. Number of days' sales in inventory

8.  Ratio of fixed assets to long-term liabilities

9.  Ratio of liabilities to stockholders' equity

10.  Number of times interest charges are earned

11.  Number of times preferred dividends earned

12.  Ratio of net sales to assets

13.  Rate earned on total assets

14.  Rate earned on stockholders' equity

15.  Rate earned on common stockholders' equity

16.  Earnings per share on common stock

17.  Price-earnings ratio

18.  Dividends per share

19.  Dividend yield

## Solution

(Ratios are rounded to the nearest single digit after the decimal point.)

1.  Working capital: $750,000
    $1,500,000 − $750,000

2.  Current ratio: 2.0
    $1,500,000 ÷ $750,000

3.  Quick ratio: 1.0
    $750,000 ÷ $750,000

4.  Accounts receivable turnover: 13.3
    $5,000,000 ÷ [($425,000 + $325,000) ÷ 2]

5.  Number of days' sales in receivables: 27.4 days
    $5,000,000 ÷ 365 days = $13,699
    $375,000 ÷ $13,699

6.  Inventory turnover: 5.7
    $3,400,000 ÷ [($720,000 + $480,000) ÷ 2]

7.  Number of days' sales in inventory: 64.4 days
    $3,400,000 ÷ 365 days = $9,315
    $600,000 ÷ $9,315

8.  Ratio of fixed assets to long-term liabilities: 1.7
    $2,093,000 ÷ $1,210,000

9.  Ratio of liabilities to stockholders' equity: 1.0
    $1,960,000 ÷ $1,883,000

10.  Number of times interest charges are earned: 6.2
    ($545,000 + $105,000) ÷ $105,000

11.  Number of times preferred dividends earned: 6.1
    $245,000 ÷ $40,000

12.  Ratio of net sales to assets: 1.5
    $5,000,000 ÷ [($3,593,000 + $2,948,000) ÷ 2]

13.  Rate earned on total assets: 10.0%
    ($245,000 + $105,000) ÷ [($3,843,000 + $3,173,000) ÷ 2]

14.  Rate earned on stockholders' equity: 13.6%
    $245,000 ÷ [($1,883,000 + $1,723,000) ÷ 2]

15.  Rate earned on common stockholders' equity: 15.7%
    ($245,000 − $40,000) ÷ [($1,383,000 + $1,223,000) ÷ 2]

16. Earnings per share on common stock: $4.10
    ($245,000 – $40,000) ÷ 50,000 shares

17. Price-earnings ratio: 6.1
    $25 ÷ $4.10

18. Dividends per share: $0.90
    $45,000 ÷ 50,000 shares

19. Dividend yield: 3.6%
    $0.90 ÷ $25

## Discussion Questions

1. What is the difference between horizontal and vertical analysis of financial statements?

2. What is the advantage of using comparative statements for financial analysis rather than statements for a single date or period?

3. The current year's amount of net income (after income tax) is 20% larger than that of the preceding year. Does this indicate an improved operating performance? Discuss.

4. How would the current and quick ratios of a service business compare?

5. a. Why is it advantageous to have a high inventory turnover?
   b. Is it possible for the inventory turnover to be too high? Discuss.
   c. Is it possible to have a high inventory turnover and a high number of days' sales in inventory? Discuss.

6. What do the following data taken from a comparative balance sheet indicate about the company's ability to borrow additional funds on a long-term basis in the current year as compared to the preceding year?

|  | Current Year | Preceding Year |
| --- | --- | --- |
| Fixed assets (net) | $600,000 | $720,000 |
| Total long-term liabilities | 120,000 | 180,000 |

7. a. How does the rate earned on total assets differ from the rate earned on stockholders' equity?
   b. Which ratio is normally higher? Explain.

8. a. Why is the rate earned on stockholders' equity by a thriving business ordinarily higher than the rate earned on total assets?
   b. Should the rate earned on common stockholders' equity normally be higher or lower than the rate earned on total stockholders' equity? Explain.

9. The net income (after income tax) of McCants Inc. was $40 per common share in the latest year and $100 per common share for the preceding year. At the beginning of the latest year, the number of shares outstanding was doubled by a stock split. There were no other changes in the amount of stock outstanding. What were the earnings per share in the preceding year, adjusted for comparison with the latest year?

10. Describe two reports provided by independent auditors in the annual report to shareholders.

# Practice Exercises

**PE 15-1A   Horizontal analysis**

The comparative accounts payable and long-term debt balances of a company are provided below.

|  | 2012 | 2011 |
| --- | --- | --- |
| Accounts payable | $114,000 | $100,000 |
| Long-term debt | 143,000 | 130,000 |

Based on this information, what is the amount and percentage of increase or decrease that would be shown in a balance sheet with horizontal analysis?

**PE 15-1B   Horizontal analysis**

The comparative temporary investments and inventory balances for a company are provided below.

|  | 2012 | 2011 |
| --- | --- | --- |
| Temporary investments | $218,400 | $240,000 |
| Inventory | 269,800 | 284,000 |

Based on this information, what is the amount and percentage of increase or decrease that would be shown in a balance sheet with horizontal analysis?

**PE 15-2A   Vertical analysis**

Income statement information for Battus Corporation is provided below.

| Sales | $680,000 |
| --- | --- |
| Gross profit | 231,200 |
| Net income | 74,800 |

Prepare a vertical analysis of the income statement for Battus Corporation.

**PE 15-2B   Vertical analysis**

Income statement information for Canace Corporation is provided below.

| Sales | $1,400,000 |
| --- | --- |
| Cost of goods sold | 910,000 |
| Gross profit | 490,000 |

Prepare a vertical analysis of the income statement for Canace Corporation.

**PE 15-3A   Current position analysis**

The following items are reported on a company's balance sheet:

| Cash | $200,000 |
| --- | --- |
| Temporary investments | 100,000 |
| Accounts receivable (net) | 60,000 |
| Inventory | 100,000 |
| Accounts payable | 200,000 |

Determine (a) the current ratio and (b) the quick ratio. Round to one decimal place.

**OBJ. 2**   **EE 15-3** *p. 705*    **PE 15-3B**   **Current position analysis**

The following items are reported on a company's balance sheet:

| | |
|---|---|
| Cash | $250,000 |
| Temporary investments | 180,000 |
| Accounts receivable (net) | 220,000 |
| Inventory | 200,000 |
| Accounts payable | 500,000 |

Determine (a) the current ratio and (b) the quick ratio. Round to one decimal place.

---

**OBJ. 2**   **EE 15-4** *p. 707*    **PE 15-4A**   **Accounts receivable analysis**

A company reports the following:

| | |
|---|---|
| Net sales | $1,600,000 |
| Average accounts receivable (net) | 100,000 |

Determine (a) the accounts receivable turnover and (b) the number of days' sales in receivables. Round to one decimal place.

---

**OBJ. 2**   **EE 15-4** *p. 707*    **PE 15-4B**   **Accounts receivable analysis**

A company reports the following:

| | |
|---|---|
| Net sales | $700,000 |
| Average accounts receivable (net) | 50,000 |

Determine (a) the accounts receivable turnover and (b) the number of days' sales in receivables. Round to one decimal place.

---

**OBJ. 2**   **EE 15-5** *p. 708*    **PE 15-5A**   **Inventory analysis**

A company reports the following:

| | |
|---|---|
| Cost of goods sold | $880,000 |
| Average inventory | 110,000 |

Determine (a) the inventory turnover and (b) the number of days' sales in inventory. Round to one decimal place.

---

**OBJ. 2**   **EE 15-5** *p. 708*    **PE 15-5B**   **Inventory analysis**

A company reports the following:

| | |
|---|---|
| Cost of goods sold | $360,000 |
| Average inventory | 50,000 |

Determine (a) the inventory turnover and (b) the number of days' sales in inventory. Round to one decimal place.

---

**OBJ. 2**   **EE 15-6** *p. 710*    **PE 15-6A**   **Solvency analysis**

The following information was taken from Wheat Company's balance sheet:

| | |
|---|---|
| Fixed assets (net) | $836,000 |
| Long-term liabilities | 380,000 |
| Total liabilities | 550,000 |
| Total stockholders' equity | 500,000 |

Determine the company's (a) ratio of fixed assets to long-term liabilities and (b) ratio of liabilities to stockholders' equity.

**OBJ. 2**   **EE 15-6**  *p. 710*

### PE 15-6B   Solvency analysis

The following information was taken from Chaff Company's balance sheet:

| | |
|---|---|
| Fixed assets (net) | $1,000,000 |
| Long-term liabilities | 625,000 |
| Total liabilities | 840,000 |
| Total stockholders' equity | 600,000 |

Determine the company's (a) ratio of fixed assets to long-term liabilities and (b) ratio of liabilities to stockholders' equity.

**OBJ. 2**   **EE 15-7**  *p. 711*

### PE 15-7A   Times interest charges are earned

A company reports the following:

| | |
|---|---|
| Income before income tax | $4,000,000 |
| Interest expense | 500,000 |

Determine the number of times interest charges are earned.

**OBJ. 2**   **EE 15-7**  *p. 711*

### PE 15-7B   Times interest charges are earned

A company reports the following:

| | |
|---|---|
| Income before income tax | $10,000,000 |
| Interest expense | 800,000 |

Determine the number of times interest charges are earned.

**OBJ. 3**   **EE 15-8**  *p. 712*

### PE 15-8A   Net sales to assets

A company reports the following:

| | |
|---|---|
| Net sales | $1,200,000 |
| Average total assets | 750,000 |

Determine the ratio of net sales to assets.

**OBJ. 3**   **EE 15-8**  *p. 712*

### PE 15-8B   Net sales to assets

A company reports the following:

| | |
|---|---|
| Net sales | $3,500,000 |
| Average total assets | 2,500,000 |

Determine the ratio of net sales to assets.

**OBJ. 3**   **EE 15-9**  *p. 713*

### PE 15-9A   Rate earned on total assets

A company reports the following income statement and balance sheet information for the current year:

| | |
|---|---|
| Net income | $ 820,000 |
| Interest expense | 80,000 |
| Average total assets | 5,000,000 |

Determine the rate earned on total assets.

**OBJ. 3**   **EE 15-9**  *p. 713*

### PE 15-9B   Rate earned on total assets

A company reports the following income statement and balance sheet information for the current year:

| | |
|---|---|
| Net income | $ 700,000 |
| Interest expense | 50,000 |
| Average total assets | 4,687,500 |

Determine the rate earned on total assets.

OBJ. 3   EE 15-10  p. 715

### PE 15-10A   Common stockholders' profitability analysis

A company reports the following:

| | |
| --- | --- |
| Net income | $ 210,000 |
| Preferred dividends | 30,000 |
| Average stockholders' equity | 1,750,000 |
| Average common stockholders' equity | 1,000,000 |

Determine (a) the rate earned on stockholders' equity and (b) the rate earned on common stockholders' equity. Round to one decimal place.

OBJ. 3   EE 15-10  p. 715

### PE 15-10B   Common stockholders' profitability analysis

A company reports the following:

| | |
| --- | --- |
| Net income | $ 600,000 |
| Preferred dividends | 50,000 |
| Average stockholders' equity | 6,000,000 |
| Average common stockholders' equity | 5,000,000 |

Determine (a) the rate earned on stockholders' equity and (b) the rate earned on common stockholders' equity. Round to one decimal place.

OBJ. 3   EE 15-11  p. 717

### PE 15-11A   Earnings per share and price-earnings ratio

A company reports the following:

| | |
| --- | --- |
| Net income | $440,000 |
| Preferred dividends | $40,000 |
| Shares of common stock outstanding | 50,000 |
| Market price per share of common stock | $100 |

a. Determine the company's earnings per share on common stock.

b. Determine the company's price-earnings ratio.

OBJ. 3   EE 15-11  p. 717

### PE 15-11B   Earnings per share and price-earnings ratio

A company reports the following:

| | |
| --- | --- |
| Net income | $650,000 |
| Preferred dividends | $50,000 |
| Shares of common stock outstanding | 120,000 |
| Market price per share of common stock | $75 |

a. Determine the company's earnings per share on common stock.

b. Determine the company's price-earnings ratio.

## Exercises

OBJ. 1

✔ a. 2012 net income: $4,000; 0.5% of sales

### EX 15-1   Vertical analysis of income statement

Revenue and expense data for Mandell Technologies Co. are as follows:

| | 2012 | 2011 |
| --- | --- | --- |
| Sales | $800,000 | $740,000 |
| Cost of goods sold | 504,000 | 407,000 |
| Selling expenses | 120,000 | 140,600 |
| Administrative expenses | 128,000 | 125,800 |
| Income tax expense | 33,600 | 48,100 |

a. Prepare an income statement in comparative form, stating each item for both 2012 and 2011 as a percent of sales. Round to one decimal place.

b. ➤ Comment on the significant changes disclosed by the comparative income statement.

---

**OBJ. 1**

✔ a. Fiscal year 2008 income from continuing operations, 29.2% of revenues

### EX 15-2   Vertical analysis of income statement

The following comparative income statement (in thousands of dollars) for the fiscal years 2008 and 2007 was adapted from the annual report of Speedway Motorsports, Inc., owner and operator of several major motor speedways, such as the Atlanta, Texas, and Las Vegas Motor Speedways.

| | Fiscal Year 2008 | Fiscal Year 2007 |
|---|---|---|
| Revenues: | | |
| Admissions | $188,036 | $179,765 |
| Event-related revenue | 211,630 | 197,321 |
| NASCAR broadcasting revenue | 168,159 | 142,517 |
| Other operating revenue | 43,168 | 42,030 |
| Total revenue | $610,993 | $561,633 |
| Expenses and other: | | |
| Direct expense of events | $113,477 | $100,414 |
| NASCAR purse and sanction fees | 118,766 | 100,608 |
| Other direct expenses | 116,376 | 163,222 |
| General and administrative | 84,029 | 80,913 |
| Total expenses and other | $432,648 | $445,157 |
| Income from continuing operations | $178,345 | $116,476 |

a. Prepare a comparative income statement for fiscal years 2007 and 2008 in vertical form, stating each item as a percent of revenues. Round to one decimal place.

b. ➤ Comment on the significant changes.

---

**OBJ. 1**

✔ a. Shoesmith net income: $144,000; 3.6% of sales

### EX 15-3   Common-sized income statement

Revenue and expense data for the current calendar year for Shoesmith Electronics Company and for the electronics industry are as follows. The Shoesmith Electronics Company data are expressed in dollars. The electronics industry averages are expressed in percentages.

| | Shoesmith Electronics Company | Electronics Industry Average |
|---|---|---|
| Sales | $4,200,000 | 105.0% |
| Sales returns and allowances | 200,000 | 5.0 |
| Net sales | $4,000,000 | 100.0% |
| Cost of goods sold | 2,120,000 | 59.0 |
| Gross profit | $1,880,000 | 41.0% |
| Selling expenses | $1,160,000 | 24.0% |
| Administrative expenses | 480,000 | 10.5 |
| Total operating expenses | $1,640,000 | 34.5% |
| Operating income | $ 240,000 | 6.5% |
| Other income | 84,000 | 2.1 |
| | $ 324,000 | 8.6% |
| Other expense | 60,000 | 1.5 |
| Income before income tax | $ 264,000 | 7.1% |
| Income tax | 120,000 | 6.0 |
| Net income | $ 144,000 | 1.1% |

a. Prepare a common-sized income statement comparing the results of operations for Shoesmith Electronics Company with the industry average. Round to one decimal place.

b. ➤ As far as the data permit, comment on significant relationships revealed by the comparisons.

### EX 15-4    Vertical analysis of balance sheet

Balance sheet data for Bryant Company on December 31, the end of the fiscal year, are shown below.

|  | 2012 | 2011 |
|---|---|---|
| Current assets | $ 775,000 | $ 585,000 |
| Property, plant, and equipment | 1,425,000 | 1,597,500 |
| Intangible assets | 300,000 | 67,500 |
| Current liabilities | 525,000 | 360,000 |
| Long-term liabilities | 900,000 | 855,000 |
| Common stock | 250,000 | 270,000 |
| Retained earnings | 825,000 | 765,000 |

Prepare a comparative balance sheet for 2012 and 2011, stating each asset as a percent of total assets and each liability and stockholders' equity item as a percent of the total liabilities and stockholders' equity. Round to one decimal place.

### EX 15-5    Horizontal analysis of the income statement

Income statement data for Boone Company for the years ended December 31, 2012 and 2011, are as follows:

|  | 2012 | 2011 |
|---|---|---|
| Sales | $446,400 | $360,000 |
| Cost of goods sold | 387,450 | 315,000 |
| Gross profit | $ 58,950 | $ 45,000 |
| Selling expenses | $ 27,900 | $ 22,500 |
| Administrative expenses | 21,960 | 18,000 |
| Total operating expenses | $ 49,860 | $ 40,500 |
| Income before income tax | $ 9,090 | $ 4,500 |
| Income tax expenses | 5,400 | 2,700 |
| Net income | $ 3,690 | $ 1,800 |

a. Prepare a comparative income statement with horizontal analysis, indicating the increase (decrease) for 2012 when compared with 2011. Round to one decimal place.

b. ━━━━━ What conclusions can be drawn from the horizontal analysis?

### EX 15-6    Current position analysis

The following data were taken from the balance sheet of Beatty Company:

|  | Dec. 31, 2012 | Dec. 31, 2011 |
|---|---|---|
| Cash | $ 330,000 | $ 238,000 |
| Temporary investments | 465,000 | 385,000 |
| Accounts and notes receivable (net) | 425,000 | 295,000 |
| Inventories | 420,000 | 291,000 |
| Prepaid expenses | 312,000 | 141,000 |
| Total current assets | $1,952,000 | $1,350,000 |
| Accounts and notes payable (short-term) | $ 420,000 | $ 400,000 |
| Accrued liabilities | 190,000 | 140,000 |
| Total current liabilities | $ 610,000 | $ 540,000 |

a. Determine for each year (1) the working capital, (2) the current ratio, and (3) the quick ratio. Round ratios to one decimal place.

b. ━━━━━ What conclusions can be drawn from these data as to the company's ability to meet its currently maturing debts?

**OBJ. 2**

✔ a. (1) Dec. 27, 2008
current ratio, 1.2

### EX 15-7   Current position analysis

PepsiCo, Inc., the parent company of Frito-Lay snack foods and Pepsi beverages, had the following current assets and current liabilities at the end of two recent years:

| | Dec. 26, 2009 (in millions) | Dec. 27, 2008 (in millions) |
|---|---|---|
| Cash and cash equivalents | $3,943 | $2,064 |
| Short-term investments, at cost | 192 | 213 |
| Accounts and notes receivable, net | 4,624 | 4,683 |
| Inventories | 2,618 | 2,522 |
| Prepaid expenses and other current assets | 1,194 | 1,324 |
| Short-term obligations | 464 | 369 |
| Accounts payable | 8,292 | 6,494 |
| Other current liabilities | 0 | 1,924 |

a. Determine the (1) current ratio and (2) quick ratio for both years. Round to one decimal place.

b. ━━━▶ What conclusions can you draw from these data?

**OBJ. 2**

### EX 15-8   Current position analysis

The bond indenture for the 10-year, 10% debenture bonds dated January 2, 2011, required working capital of $700,000, a current ratio of 1.7, and a quick ratio of 1.2 at the end of each calendar year until the bonds mature. At December 31, 2012, the three measures were computed as follows:

1. Current assets:

| | | |
|---|---|---|
| Cash...................................... | $302,400 | |
| Temporary investments ...................... | 144,000 | |
| Accounts and notes receivable (net)........... | 353,600 | |
| Inventories................................. | 114,400 | |
| Prepaid expenses........................... | 45,600 | |
| Intangible assets ........................... | 388,000 | |
| Property, plant, and equipment............... | 172,000 | |
| Total current assets (net) ................. | | $1,520,000 |
| Current liabilities: | | |
| Accounts and short-term notes payable ....... | $256,000 | |
| Accrued liabilities.......................... | 544,000 | |
| Total current liabilities .................... | | 800,000 |
| Working capital ............................. | | $ 720,000 |
| 2.  Current ratio ...................................... | 1.9 | $1,520,000 ÷ $800,000 |
| 3.  Quick ratio...................................... | 1.3 | $ 332,000 ÷ $256,000 |

a. List the errors in the determination of the three measures of current position analysis.

b. ━━━▶ Is the company satisfying the terms of the bond indenture?

**OBJ. 2**

✔ a. Accounts
receivable turnover,
2012, 6.6

### EX 15-9   Accounts receivable analysis

The following data are taken from the financial statements of Saladin Inc. Terms of all sales are 2/10, n/60.

| | 2012 | 2011 | 2010 |
|---|---|---|---|
| Accounts receivable, end of year | $ 221,250 | $ 237,000 | $247,500 |
| Net sales on account | 1,512,225 | 1,380,825 | |

a. Determine for each year (1) the accounts receivable turnover and (2) the number of days' sales in receivables. Round to the nearest dollar and one decimal place.

b. ━━━▶ What conclusions can be drawn from these data concerning accounts receivable and credit policies?

OBJ. 2

### EX 15-10 Accounts receivable analysis

Klick Company and Klack Inc., are large retail department stores. Both companies offer credit to their customers through their own credit card operations. Information from the financial statements for both companies for two recent years is as follows (all numbers are in millions):

|  | Klick | Klack |
|---|---|---|
| Merchandise sales | $18,000 | $70,980 |
| Credit card receivables—beginning | 3,300 | 9,000 |
| Credit card receviables—ending | 2,700 | 6,600 |

a. Determine the (1) accounts receivable turnover and (2) the number of days' sales in receivables for both companies. Round to one decimal place.

b. ▬▬▬ Compare the two companies with regard to their credit card policies.

OBJ. 2

✔ a. Inventory turnover, current year, 8.2

### EX 15-11 Inventory analysis

The following data were extracted from the income statement of Hestia Systems Inc.:

|  | Current Year | Preceding Year |
|---|---|---|
| Sales | $2,443,600 | $2,592,000 |
| Beginning inventories | 158,000 | 130,000 |
| Cost of goods sold | 1,221,800 | 1,440,000 |
| Ending inventories | 140,000 | 158,000 |

a. Determine for each year (1) the inventory turnover and (2) the number of days' sales in inventory. Round to the nearest dollar and one decimal place.

b. ▬▬▬ What conclusions can be drawn from these data concerning the inventories?

OBJ. 2

✔ a. Dell inventory turnover, 49.0

### EX 15-12 Inventory analysis

Dell Inc. and Hewlett-Packard Company (HP) compete with each other in the personal computer market. Dell's primary strategy is to assemble computers to customer orders, rather than for inventory. Thus, for example, Dell will build and deliver a computer within four days of a customer entering an order on a Web page. Hewlett-Packard, on the other hand, builds some computers prior to receiving an order, then sells from this inventory once an order is received. Below is selected financial information for both companies from a recent year's financial statements (in millions):

|  | Dell Inc. | Hewlett-Packard Company |
|---|---|---|
| Sales | $61,101 | $74,051 |
| Cost of goods sold | 50,144 | 56,503 |
| Inventory, beginning of period | 1,180 | 7,879 |
| Inventory, end of period | 867 | 6,128 |

a. Determine for both companies (1) the inventory turnover and (2) the number of days' sales in inventory. Round to one decimal place.

b. ▬▬▬ Interpret the inventory ratios by considering Dell's and Hewlett-Packard's operating strategies.

OBJ. 2

✔ a. Ratio of liabilities to stockholders' equity, Dec. 31, 2012, 0.7

### EX 15-13 Ratio of liabilities to stockholders' equity and number of times interest charges earned

The following data were taken from the financial statements of Hermes Inc. for December 31, 2012 and 2011:

|  | Dec. 31, 2012 | Dec. 31, 2011 |
|---|---|---|
| Accounts payable | $ 473,960 | $ 325,000 |
| Current maturities of serial bonds payable | 500,000 | 500,000 |
| Serial bonds payable, 9%, issued 2007, due 2017 | 2,500,000 | 3,000,000 |
| Common stock, $1 par value | 100,000 | 100,000 |
| Paid-in capital in excess of par | 1,200,000 | 1,200,000 |
| Retained earnings | 3,662,800 | 2,950,000 |

The income before income tax was $891,000 and $787,500 for the years 2012 and 2011, respectively.

a.  Determine the ratio of liabilities to stockholders' equity at the end of each year. Round to one decimal place.

b.  Determine the number of times the bond interest charges are earned during the year for both years. Round to one decimal place.

c.  ➡️ What conclusions can be drawn from these data as to the company's ability to meet its currently maturing debts?

---

**OBJ. 2**

✔ a. Hasbro, 1.3

### EX 15-14 Ratio of liabilities to stockholders' equity and number of times interest charges earned

Hasbro and Mattel, Inc., are the two largest toy companies in North America. Condensed liabilities and stockholders' equity from a recent balance sheet are shown for each company as follows (in thousands):

|  | Hasbro | Mattel |
|---|---|---|
| Current liabilities | $ 799,892 | $ 1,259,974 |
| Long-term debt | 709,723 | 750,000 |
| Other liabilities | 268,396 | 547,930 |
| Total liabilities | $ 1,778,011 | $ 2,557,904 |
| Shareholders' equity: |  |  |
| Common stock | $ 104,847 | $ 441,369 |
| Additional paid in capital | 450,155 | 1,642,092 |
| Retained earnings | 2,456,650 | 2,085,573 |
| Accumulated other comprehensive loss and other equity items | 62,256 | (430,635) |
| Treasury stock, at cost | (1,683,122) | (1,621,264) |
| Total stockholders' equity | $ 1,390,786 | $ 2,117,135 |
| Total liabilities and stockholders' equity | $ 3,168,797 | $ 4,675,039 |

The income from operations and interest expense from the income statement for both companies were as follows (in thousands):

|  | Hasbro | Mattel |
|---|---|---|
| Income from operations | $494,296 | $541,792 |
| Interest expense | 47,143 | 81,944 |

a.  Determine the ratio of liabilities to stockholders' equity for both companies. Round to one decimal place.

b.  Determine the number of times interest charges are earned for both companies. Round to one decimal place.

c.  ➡️ Interpret the ratio differences between the two companies.

---

**OBJ. 2**

✔ a. H.J. Heinz, 6.9

### EX 15-15 Ratio of liabilities to stockholders' equity and ratio of fixed assets to long-term liabilities

Recent balance sheet information for two companies in the food industry, H.J. Heinz Company and The Hershey Company, is as follows (in thousands of dollars):

|  | H.J. Heinz | Hershey |
|---|---|---|
| Net property, plant, and equipment | $1,978,302 | $1,458,949 |
| Current liabilities | 2,062,846 | 1,270,212 |
| Long-term debt | 5,076,186 | 1,505,954 |
| Other long-term liabilities | 1,305,214 | 540,354 |
| Stockholders' equity | 1,219,938 | 318,199 |

a.  Determine the ratio of liabilities to stockholders' equity for both companies. Round to one decimal place.

b.  Determine the ratio of fixed assets to long-term liabilities for both companies. Round to one decimal place.

c.  ➡️ Interpret the ratio differences between the two companies.

## EX 15-16   Ratio of net sales to assets

Three major segments of the transportation industry are motor carriers, such as YRC World-wide; railroads, such as Union Pacific; and transportation arrangement services, such as C.H. Robinson Worldwide Inc. Recent financial statement information for these three companies is shown as follows (in thousands of dollars):

| | YRC Worldwide | Union Pacific | C.H. Robinson Worldwide Inc. |
|---|---|---|---|
| Net sales | $8,940,401 | $17,970,000 | $8,578,614 |
| Average total assets | 4,514,368 | 38,877,500 | 1,813,514 |

a.  Determine the ratio of net sales to assets for all three companies. Round to one decimal place.

b.  ━━━━━▶ Assume that the ratio of net sales to assets for each company represents their respective industry segment. Interpret the differences in the ratio of net sales to assets in terms of the operating characteristics of each of the respective segments.

## EX 15-17   Profitability ratios

The following selected data were taken from the financial statements of Preslar Inc. for December 31, 2012, 2011, and 2010:

| | December 31 | | |
|---|---|---|---|
| | **2012** | **2011** | **2010** |
| Total assets . . . . . . . . . . . . . . . . . . . . . . . . . . . . . . . . . . . . | $4,500,000 | $4,050,000 | $3,600,000 |
| Notes payable (8% interest) . . . . . . . . . . . . . . . . . . . . . . . . | 1,500,000 | 1,500,000 | 1,500,000 |
| Common stock. . . . . . . . . . . . . . . . . . . . . . . . . . . . . . . . . | 600,000 | 600,000 | 600,000 |
| Preferred 4% stock, $100 par (no change during year) . . . . . . . . . . . . . . . . . . . . . . . . | 300,000 | 300,000 | 300,000 |
| Retained earnings. . . . . . . . . . . . . . . . . . . . . . . . . . . . . . | 1,765,500 | 1,341,750 | 900,000 |

The 2012 net income was $435,750, and the 2011 net income was $453,750. No dividends on common stock were declared between 2010 and 2012.

a.  Determine the rate earned on total assets, the rate earned on stockholders' equity, and the rate earned on common stockholders' equity for the years 2011 and 2012. Round to one decimal place.

b.  ━━━━━▶ What conclusions can be drawn from these data as to the company's profitability?

## EX 15-18   Profitability ratios

Ann Taylor Retail, Inc., sells professional women's apparel through company-owned retail stores. Recent financial information for Ann Taylor is provided below (all numbers in thousands).

| | Fiscal Year Ended | | |
|---|---|---|---|
| | **February 2, 2008** | **February 3, 2007** | |
| Net income | $97,235 | $142,982 | |
| Interest expense | 2,172 | 2,230 | |
| | **February 2, 2008** | **February 3, 2007** | **January 28, 2006** |
| Total assets | $1,393,755 | $1,568,503 | $1,492,906 |
| Total stockholders' equity | 839,484 | 1,049,911 | 1,034,482 |

Assume the apparel industry average rate earned on total assets is 5.0%, and the average rate earned on stockholders' equity is 8.0% for the year ended February 2, 2008 (fiscal year 2007).

a.  Determine the rate earned on total assets for Ann Taylor for the fiscal years ended February 2, 2008, and February 3, 2007. Round to one digit after the decimal place.

b.  Determine the rate earned on stockholders' equity for Ann Taylor for the fiscal years ended February 2, 2008, and February 3, 2007. Round to one decimal place.

c.  ━━━━━▶ Evaluate the two-year trend for the profitability ratios determined in (a) and (b).

d.  ━━━━━▶ Evaluate Ann Taylor's profit performance relative to the industry.

OBJ. 2, 3

✔ c. Ratio of net
sales to assets, 4.5

### EX 15-19  Six measures of solvency or profitability

The following data were taken from the financial statements of Ares Inc. for the current fiscal year. Assuming that long-term investments totaled $3,000,000 throughout the year and that total assets were $6,250,000 at the beginning of the current fiscal year, determine the following: (a) ratio of fixed assets to long-term liabilities, (b) ratio of liabilities to stockholders' equity, (c) ratio of net sales to assets, (d) rate earned on total assets, (e) rate earned on stockholders' equity, and (f) rate earned on common stockholders' equity. Round to one decimal place.

| | | | |
|---|---|---|---|
| Property, plant, and equipment (net) ..................... | | | $ 2,700,000 |
| Liabilities: | | | |
|     Current liabilities....................................... | | $ 666,500 | |
|     Mortgage note payable, 8%, issued 2001, due 2017...... | | 1,800,000 | |
|     Total liabilities ...................................... | | | $ 2,466,500 |
| Stockholders' equity: | | | |
|     Preferred $10 stock, $100 par (no change during year) ... | | | $ 1,200,000 |
|     Common stock, $10 par (no change during year) ........ | | | 1,000,000 |
|     Retained earnings: | | | |
|         Balance, beginning of year........................... | $2,203,000 | | |
|         Net income......................................... | 750,000 | $2,953,000 | |
|         Preferred dividends ................................. | $ 120,000 | | |
|         Common dividends .................................. | 100,000 | 220,000 | |
|         Balance, end of year ................................ | | | 2,733,000 |
| Total stockholders' equity ............................... | | | $ 4,933,000 |
| Net sales.............................................. | | | $17,211,375 |
| Interest expense ...................................... | | | $ 144,000 |

OBJ. 2, 3

✔ d. Price-earnings
ratio, 14.4

### EX 15-20  Six measures of solvency or profitability

The balance sheet for Kronos Inc. at the end of the current fiscal year indicated the following:

| | |
|---|---|
| Bonds payable, 10% (issued in 2002, due in 2022) | $3,750,000 |
| Preferred $4 stock, $40 par | 2,000,000 |
| Common stock, $10 par | 3,600,000 |

Income before income tax was $2,400,000, and income taxes were $400,000 for the current year. Cash dividends paid on common stock during the current year totaled $720,000. The common stock was selling for $72 per share at the end of the year. Determine each of the following: (a) number of times bond interest charges are earned, (b) number of times preferred dividends are earned, (c) earnings per share on common stock, (d) price-earnings ratio, (e) dividends per share of common stock, and (f) dividend yield. Round to one decimal place except earnings per share, which should be rounded to two decimal places.

OBJ. 3

✔ b. Price-earnings
ratio, 16.0

### EX 15-21  Earnings per share, price-earnings ratio, dividend yield

The following information was taken from the financial statements of Bailey Inc. for December 31 of the current fiscal year:

| | |
|---|---|
| Common stock, $10 par value (no change during the year) | $4,000,000 |
| Preferred $5 stock, $25 par (no change during the year) | 1,250,000 |

The net income was $1,250,000 and the declared dividends on the common stock were $800,000 for the current year. The market price of the common stock is $40 per share.

For the common stock, determine (a) the earnings per share, (b) the price-earnings ratio, (c) the dividends per share, and (d) the dividend yield. Round to one decimal place except earnings per share, which should be rounded to two decimal places.

OBJ. 3

### EX 15-22   Price-earnings ratio; dividend yield

The table below shows the stock price, earnings per share, and dividends per share for three companies as of May 2010:

|  | Price | Earnings per Share | Dividends per Share |
|---|---|---|---|
| The Home Depot | $ 33.43 | $ 1.57 | $0.95 |
| Google | 493.14 | 21.99 | 0.00 |
| The Coca-Cola Company | 52.67 | 3.04 | 1.76 |

a.  Determine the price-earnings ratio and dividend yield for the three companies. Round to one decimal place.

b.  ━━━━▶ Explain the differences in these ratios across the three companies.

✔ b. Earnings per share on common stock, $11.80

**Appendix**
### EX 15-23   Earnings per share, extraordinary item

The net income reported on the income statement of Styx Co. was $3,200,000. There were 250,000 shares of $5 par common stock and 250,000 shares of $1 preferred stock outstanding throughout the current year. The income statement included two extraordinary items: a $700,000 gain from condemnation of land and a $350,000 loss arising from flood damage, both after applicable income tax. Determine the per-share figures for common stock for (a) income before extraordinary items and (b) net income.

**Appendix**
### EX 15-24   Extraordinary item

Assume that the amount of each of the following items is material to the financial statements. Classify each item as either normally recurring (NR) or extraordinary (E).

a.  Gain on sale of land condemned by the local government for a public works project.

b.  Uninsured flood loss. (Flood insurance is unavailable because of periodic flooding in the area.)

c.  Loss on the disposal of equipment considered to be obsolete because of the development of new technology.

d.  Uncollectible accounts expense.

e.  Loss on sale of investments in stocks and bonds.

f.  Uninsured loss on building due to hurricane damage. The building was purchased by the company in 1910 and had not previously incurred hurricane damage.

g.  Interest revenue on notes receivable.

**Appendix**
### EX 15-25   Income statement and earnings per share for extraordinary items and discontinued operations

Eris, Inc., reports the following for 2012:

| | |
|---|---|
| Income from continuing operations before income tax | $800,000 |
| Extraordinary property loss from hurricane | $100,000* |
| Loss from discontinued operations | $120,000* |
| Weighted average number of shares outstanding | 50,000 |
| Applicable tax rate | 40% |

*Net of any tax effect.

a.  Prepare a partial income statement for Eris, Inc., beginning with income from continuing operations before income tax.

b.  Calculate the earnings per common share for Eris, Inc., including per-share amounts for unusual items.

**Appendix**
**EX 15-26    Unusual items**

Discuss whether Daphne Company correctly reported the following items in the financial statements:

a. In 2012, the company discovered a clerical error in the prior year's accounting records. As a result, the reported net income for 2011 was overstated by $30,000. The company corrected this error by restating the prior-year financial statements.

b. In 2012, the company voluntarily changed its method of accounting for long-term construction contracts from the percentage of completion method to the completed contract method. Both methods are acceptable under generally acceptable accounting principles. The cumulative effect of this change was reported as a separate component of income in the 2012 income statement.

# Problems Series A

OBJ. 1

✔ 1. Net sales, 14.4% increase

**PR 15-1A    Horizontal analysis for income statement**

For 2012, Eurie Company reported its most significant decline in net income in years. At the end of the year, H. Finn, the president, is presented with the following condensed comparative income statement:

**Eurie Company**
**Comparative Income Statement**
**For the Years Ended December 31, 2012 and 2011**

|  | 2012 | 2011 |
|---|---|---|
| Sales | $928,000 | $800,000 |
| Sales returns and allowances | 70,000 | 50,000 |
| Net sales | $858,000 | $750,000 |
| Cost of goods sold | 640,000 | 500,000 |
| Gross profit | $218,000 | $250,000 |
| Selling expenses | $ 85,800 | $ 65,000 |
| Administrative expenses | 43,400 | 35,000 |
| Total operating expenses | $129,200 | $100,000 |
| Income from operations | $ 88,800 | $150,000 |
| Other income | 16,000 | 10,000 |
| Income before income tax | $104,800 | $160,000 |
| Income tax expense | 9,200 | 8,000 |
| Net income | $ 95,600 | $152,000 |

**Instructions**

1. Prepare a comparative income statement with horizontal analysis for the two-year period, using 2011 as the base year. Round to one decimal place.

2. ▬▬▬▶ To the extent the data permit, comment on the significant relationships revealed by the horizontal analysis prepared in (1).

OBJ. 1

✔ 1. Net income, 2012, 14.0%

**PR 15-2A    Vertical analysis for income statement**

For 2012, Selene Company initiated a sales promotion campaign that included the expenditure of an additional $25,000 for advertising. At the end of the year, Scott Brown, the president, is presented with the following condensed comparative income statement:

**Selene Company**
**Comparative Income Statement**
**For the Years Ended December 31, 2012 and 2011**

| | 2012 | 2011 |
|---|---|---|
| Sales | $999,600 | $867,000 |
| Sales returns and allowances | 19,600 | 17,000 |
| Net sales | $980,000 | $850,000 |
| Cost of goods sold | 460,600 | 433,500 |
| Gross profit | $519,400 | $416,500 |
| Selling expenses | $225,400 | $178,500 |
| Administrative expenses | 107,800 | 102,000 |
| Total operating expenses | $333,200 | $280,500 |
| Income from operations | $186,200 | $136,000 |
| Other income | 49,000 | 42,500 |
| Income before income tax | $235,200 | $178,500 |
| Income tax expense | 98,000 | 85,000 |
| Net income | $137,200 | $ 93,500 |

**Instructions**

1. Prepare a comparative income statement for the two-year period, presenting an analysis of each item in relationship to net sales for each of the years. Round to one decimal place.

2. ━━━━▶ To the extent the data permit, comment on the significant relationships revealed by the vertical analysis prepared in (1).

---

**OBJ. 2**

✔ 2. c. Current ratio, 2.2

**PR 15-3A  Effect of transactions on current position analysis**

Data pertaining to the current position of Brin Company are as follows:

| | |
|---|---|
| Cash | $520,000 |
| Temporary investments | 380,000 |
| Accounts and notes receivable (net) | 700,000 |
| Inventories | 720,000 |
| Prepaid expenses | 80,000 |
| Accounts payable | 300,000 |
| Notes payable (short-term) | 360,000 |
| Accrued expenses | 340,000 |

**Instructions**

1. Compute (a) the working capital, (b) the current ratio, and (c) the quick ratio. Round to one decimal place.

2. List the following captions on a sheet of paper:

| Transaction | Working Capital | Current Ratio | Quick Ratio |
|---|---|---|---|

Compute the working capital, the current ratio, and the quick ratio after each of the following transactions, and record the results in the appropriate columns. *Consider each transaction separately* and assume that only that transaction affects the data given above. Round to one decimal place.

a. Sold temporary investments at no gain or loss, $90,000.

b. Paid accounts payable, $175,000.

c. Purchased goods on account, $125,000.

d. Paid notes payable, $200,000.

e. Declared a cash dividend, $160,000.

f. Declared a common stock dividend on common stock, $45,000.

g. Borrowed cash from bank on a long-term note, $300,000.

h. Received cash on account, $140,000.

i. Issued additional shares of stock for cash, $700,000.

j. Paid cash for prepaid expenses, $80,000.

**OBJ. 2, 3**

✔ 5. Number of days' sales in receivables, 68.4

### PR 15-4A  Nineteen measures of liquidity, solvency, and profitability

The comparative financial statements of Blige Inc. are as follows. The market price of Blige Inc. common stock was $60 on December 31, 2012.

**Blige Inc.**
**Comparative Retained Earnings Statement**
**For the Years Ended December 31, 2012 and 2011**

|  | 2012 | 2011 |
|---|---|---|
| Retained earnings, January 1 | $1,810,000 | $1,526,000 |
| Add net income for year | 410,750 | 322,000 |
| Total | $2,220,750 | $1,848,000 |
| Deduct dividends: |  |  |
| On preferred stock | $ 16,000 | $ 16,000 |
| On common stock | 22,000 | 22,000 |
| Total | $ 38,000 | $ 38,000 |
| Retained earnings, December 31 | $2,182,750 | $1,810,000 |

**Blige Inc.**
**Comparative Income Statement**
**For the Years Ended December 31, 2012 and 2011**

|  | 2012 | 2011 |
|---|---|---|
| Sales | $2,211,000 | $2,037,200 |
| Sales returns and allowances | 11,000 | 7,200 |
| Net sales | $2,200,000 | $2,030,000 |
| Cost of goods sold | 825,000 | 811,200 |
| Gross profit | $1,375,000 | $1,218,800 |
| Selling expenses | $ 445,500 | $ 484,000 |
| Administrative expenses | 321,750 | 290,400 |
| Total operating expenses | $ 767,250 | $ 774,400 |
| Income from operations | $ 607,750 | $ 444,400 |
| Other income | 33,000 | 26,400 |
|  | $ 640,750 | $ 470,800 |
| Other expense (interest) | 176,000 | 96,000 |
| Income before income tax | $ 464,750 | $ 374,800 |
| Income tax expense | 54,000 | 52,800 |
| Net income | $ 410,750 | $ 322,000 |

**Blige Inc.**
**Comparative Balance Sheet**
**December 31, 2012 and 2011**

|  | Dec. 31, 2012 | Dec. 31, 2011 |
|---|---|---|
| **Assets** |  |  |
| Current assets: |  |  |
| Cash | $ 528,000 | $ 410,000 |
| Temporary investments | 800,000 | 725,000 |
| Accounts receivable (net) | 425,000 | 400,000 |
| Inventories | 310,000 | 240,000 |
| Prepaid expenses | 100,000 | 75,000 |
| Total current assets | $2,163,000 | $1,850,000 |
| Long-term investments | 633,000 | 560,000 |
| Property, plant, and equipment (net) | 3,146,750 | 2,150,000 |
| Total assets | $5,942,750 | $4,560,000 |
| **Liabilities** |  |  |
| Current liabilities | $ 720,000 | $ 710,000 |
| Long-term liabilities: |  |  |
| Mortgage note payable, 8%, due 2017 | $1,000,000 | $ 0 |
| Bonds payable, 8%, due 2021 | 1,200,000 | 1,200,000 |
| Total long-term liabilities | $2,200,000 | $1,200,000 |
| Total liabilities | $2,920,000 | $1,910,000 |
| **Stockholders' Equity** |  |  |
| Preferred $0.80 stock, $20 par | $ 400,000 | $ 400,000 |
| Common stock, $10 par | 440,000 | 440,000 |
| Retained earnings | 2,182,750 | 1,810,000 |
| Total stockholders' equity | $3,022,750 | $2,650,000 |
| Total liabilities and stockholders' equity | $5,942,750 | $4,560,000 |

**Instructions**

Determine the following measures for 2012, rounding to one decimal place:

1. Working capital
2. Current ratio
3. Quick ratio
4. Accounts receivable turnover
5. Number of days' sales in receivables
6. Inventory turnover
7. Number of days' sales in inventory
8. Ratio of fixed assets to long-term liabilities
9. Ratio of liabilities to stockholders' equity
10. Number of times interest charges earned
11. Number of times preferred dividends earned
12. Ratio of net sales to assets
13. Rate earned on total assets
14. Rate earned on stockholders' equity
15. Rate earned on common stockholders' equity
16. Earnings per share on common stock
17. Price-earnings ratio
18. Dividends per share of common stock
19. Dividend yield

---

OBJ. 2, 3

**PR 15-5A   Solvency and profitability trend analysis**

Itzkoff Company has provided the following comparative information:

| | 2012 | 2011 | 2010 | 2009 | 2008 |
|---|---|---|---|---|---|
| Net income | $ 170,879 | $ 229,985 | $ 394,485 | $ 552,500 | $ 500,000 |
| Interest expense | 350,027 | 325,002 | 300,094 | 281,250 | 250,000 |
| Income tax expense | 49,492 | 83,179 | 166,358 | 124,800 | 156,000 |
| Total assets (ending balance) | 6,023,425 | 5,624,113 | 5,089,695 | 4,552,500 | 3,750,000 |
| Total stockholders' equity | | | | | |
| (ending balance) | 2,647,848 | 2,476,970 | 2,246,985 | 1,852,500 | 1,300,000 |
| Average total assets | 5,823,769 | 5,356,904 | 4,821,098 | 4,151,250 | 3,375,000 |
| Average stockholders' equity | 2,562,409 | 2,361,977 | 2,049,743 | 1,576,250 | 1,050,000 |

You have been asked to evaluate the historical performance of the company over the last five years.

Selected industry ratios have remained relatively steady at the following levels for the last five years:

| | 2008–2012 |
|---|---|
| Rate earned on total assets | 11% |
| Rate earned on stockholders' equity | 16% |
| Number of times interest charges earned | 3.1 |
| Ratio of liabilities to stockholders' equity | 1.5 |

**Instructions**

1. Prepare four line graphs with the ratio on the vertical axis and the years on the horizontal axis for the following four ratios (rounded to one decimal place):

   a. Rate earned on total assets

   b. Rate earned on stockholders' equity

   c. Number of times interest charges earned

   d. Ratio of liabilities to stockholders' equity

Display both the company ratio and the industry benchmark on each graph. That is, each graph should have two lines.

2. ━━━▶ Prepare an analysis of the graphs in (1).

## Problems Series B

### PR 15-1B    Horizontal analysis for income statement

For 2012, McFadden Inc. reported its most significant increase in net income in years. At the end of the year, John Mayer, the president, is presented with the following condensed comparative income statement:

**McFadden Inc.**
**Comparative Income Statement**
**For the Years Ended December 31, 2012 and 2011**

|  | 2012 | 2011 |
|---|---|---|
| Sales | $516,600 | $410,000 |
| Sales returns and allowances | 12,200 | 10,000 |
| Net sales | $504,400 | $400,000 |
| Cost of goods sold | 240,000 | 200,000 |
| Gross profit | $264,400 | $200,000 |
| Selling expenses | $ 69,600 | $ 60,000 |
| Administrative expenses | 44,800 | 40,000 |
| Total operating expenses | $114,400 | $100,000 |
| Income from operations | $150,000 | $100,000 |
| Other income | 12,600 | 10,000 |
| Income before income tax | $162,600 | $110,000 |
| Income tax expense | 9,000 | 5,000 |
| Net income | $153,600 | $105,000 |

### Instructions

1. Prepare a comparative income statement with horizontal analysis for the two-year period, using 2011 as the base year. Round to one decimal place.

2. ▬▬▶ To the extent the data permit, comment on the significant relationships revealed by the horizontal analysis prepared in (1).

### PR 15-2B    Vertical analysis for income statement

For 2012, Avatar Industries Inc. initiated a sales promotion campaign that included the expenditure of an additional $35,000 for advertising. At the end of the year, Leif Grando, the president, is presented with the following condensed comparative income statement:

**Avatar Industries Inc.**
**Comparative Income Statement**
**For the Years Ended December 31, 2012 and 2011**

|  | 2012 | 2011 |
|---|---|---|
| Sales | $630,000 | $504,000 |
| Sales returns and allowances | 30,000 | 24,000 |
| Net sales | $600,000 | $480,000 |
| Cost of goods sold | 330,000 | 259,200 |
| Gross profit | $270,000 | $220,800 |
| Selling expenses | $144,000 | $ 86,400 |
| Adminstrative expenses | 72,000 | 62,400 |
| Total operating expenses | $216,000 | $148,800 |
| Income from operations | $ 54,000 | $ 72,000 |
| Other income | 24,000 | 19,200 |
| Income before income tax | $ 78,000 | $ 91,200 |
| Income tax expense (benefit) | 48,000 | 38,400 |
| Net income (loss) | $ 30,000 | $ 52,800 |

### Instructions

1. Prepare a comparative income statement for the two-year period, presenting an analysis of each item in relationship to net sales for each of the years. Round to one decimal place.

2. ▬▬▶ To the extent the data permit, comment on the significant relationships revealed by the vertical analysis prepared in (1).

**PR 15-3B    Effect of transactions on current position analysis**

Data pertaining to the current position of Diaz Industries, Inc., are as follows:

| | |
|---|---:|
| Cash | $560,000 |
| Temporary investments | 520,000 |
| Accounts and notes receivable (net) | 800,000 |
| Inventories | 900,000 |
| Prepaid expenses | 100,000 |
| Accounts payable | 800,000 |
| Notes payable (short-term) | 700,000 |
| Accrued expenses | 300,000 |

**Instructions**

1. Compute (a) the working capital, (b) the current ratio, and (c) the quick ratio. Round to one decimal place.

2. List the following captions on a sheet of paper:

| Transaction | Working Capital | Current Ratio | Quick Ratio |
|---|---|---|---|

Compute the working capital, the current ratio, and the quick ratio after each of the following transactions, and record the results in the appropriate columns. *Consider each transaction separately* and assume that only that transaction affects the data given above. Round to one decimal place.

a. Sold temporary investments at no gain or loss, $200,000.

b. Paid accounts payable, $400,000.

c. Purchased goods on account, $150,000.

d. Paid notes payable, $380,000.

e. Declared a cash dividend, $220,000.

f. Declared a common stock dividend on common stock, $200,000.

g. Borrowed cash from bank on a long-term note, $680,000.

h. Received cash on account, $110,000.

i. Issued additional shares of stock for cash, $1,400,000.

j. Paid cash for prepaid expenses, $50,000.

**PR 15-4B    Nineteen measures of liquidity, solvency, and profitability**

The comparative financial statements of Chattah Inc. are as follows. The market price of Chattah Inc. common stock was $25 on December 31, 2012.

**Chattah Inc.**
**Comparative Retained Earnings Statement**
**For the Years Ended December 31, 2012 and 2011**

| | 2012 | 2011 |
|---|---:|---:|
| Retained earnings, January 1 | $1,646,120 | $ 976,120 |
| Add net income for year | 847,000 | 850,000 |
| Total | $2,493,120 | $1,826,120 |
| Deduct dividends: | | |
| On preferred stock | $   30,000 | $   30,000 |
| On common stock | 150,000 | 150,000 |
| Total | $ 180,000 | $ 180,000 |
| Retained earnings, December 31 | $2,313,120 | $1,646,120 |

**Chattah Inc.**
**Comparative Income Statement**
**For the Years Ended December 31, 2012 and 2011**

| | 2012 | 2011 |
|---|---|---|
| Sales (all on account) . . . . . . . . . . . . . . . . . . . . . . . . . . . . . . . . . . . . . . . . . . . . . . . . . | $9,056,000 | $7,840,000 |
| Sales returns and allowances. . . . . . . . . . . . . . . . . . . . . . . . . . . . . . . . . . . . . . . . . . | 56,000 | 40,000 |
| Net sales. . . . . . . . . . . . . . . . . . . . . . . . . . . . . . . . . . . . . . . . . . . . . . . . . . . . . . . . . . . . | $9,000,000 | $7,800,000 |
| Cost of goods sold. . . . . . . . . . . . . . . . . . . . . . . . . . . . . . . . . . . . . . . . . . . . . . . . . . . . | 4,500,000 | 3,680,000 |
| Gross profit . . . . . . . . . . . . . . . . . . . . . . . . . . . . . . . . . . . . . . . . . . . . . . . . . . . . . . . . . . | $4,500,000 | $4,120,000 |
| Selling expenses . . . . . . . . . . . . . . . . . . . . . . . . . . . . . . . . . . . . . . . . . . . . . . . . . . . . . | $1,936,000 | $1,840,000 |
| Administrative expenses. . . . . . . . . . . . . . . . . . . . . . . . . . . . . . . . . . . . . . . . . . . . . . . | 1,296,000 | 1,216,000 |
| Total operating expenses . . . . . . . . . . . . . . . . . . . . . . . . . . . . . . . . . . . . . . . . . . . . . | $3,232,000 | $3,056,000 |
| Income from operations . . . . . . . . . . . . . . . . . . . . . . . . . . . . . . . . . . . . . . . . . . . . . . | $1,268,000 | $1,064,000 |
| Other income. . . . . . . . . . . . . . . . . . . . . . . . . . . . . . . . . . . . . . . . . . . . . . . . . . . . . . . . | 128,000 | 96,000 |
| | $1,396,000 | $1,160,000 |
| Other expense (interest) . . . . . . . . . . . . . . . . . . . . . . . . . . . . . . . . . . . . . . . . . . . . . . | 309,000 | 110,000 |
| Income before income tax . . . . . . . . . . . . . . . . . . . . . . . . . . . . . . . . . . . . . . . . . . . . | $1,087,000 | $1,050,000 |
| Income tax expense . . . . . . . . . . . . . . . . . . . . . . . . . . . . . . . . . . . . . . . . . . . . . . . . . . | 240,000 | 200,000 |
| Net income . . . . . . . . . . . . . . . . . . . . . . . . . . . . . . . . . . . . . . . . . . . . . . . . . . . . . . . . . | $ 847,000 | $ 850,000 |

**Chattah Inc.**
**Comparative Balance Sheet**
**December 31, 2012 and 2011**

| | Dec. 31, 2012 | Dec. 31, 2011 |
|---|---|---|
| **Assets** | | |
| Current assets: | | |
| Cash . . . . . . . . . . . . . . . . . . . . . . . . . . . . . . . . . . . . . . . . . . . . . . . . . . . . . . . . . . . . . . . | $ 420,000 | $ 306,000 |
| Temporary investments . . . . . . . . . . . . . . . . . . . . . . . . . . . . . . . . . . . . . . . . . . . . . | 760,000 | 408,000 |
| Accounts receivable (net). . . . . . . . . . . . . . . . . . . . . . . . . . . . . . . . . . . . . . . . . . . . | 663,000 | 482,120 |
| Inventories. . . . . . . . . . . . . . . . . . . . . . . . . . . . . . . . . . . . . . . . . . . . . . . . . . . . . . . . . | 1,072,700 | 850,000 |
| Prepaid expenses . . . . . . . . . . . . . . . . . . . . . . . . . . . . . . . . . . . . . . . . . . . . . . . . . . . | 92,400 | 89,250 |
| Total current assets. . . . . . . . . . . . . . . . . . . . . . . . . . . . . . . . . . . . . . . . . . . . . . . | $ 3,008,100 | $2,135,370 |
| Long-term investments. . . . . . . . . . . . . . . . . . . . . . . . . . . . . . . . . . . . . . . . . . . . . . . | 825,000 | 637,500 |
| Property, plant, and equipment (net) . . . . . . . . . . . . . . . . . . . . . . . . . . . . . . . . . . | 6,450,020 | 5,100,000 |
| Total assets . . . . . . . . . . . . . . . . . . . . . . . . . . . . . . . . . . . . . . . . . . . . . . . . . . . . . . . . | $10,283,120 | $7,872,870 |
| **Liabilities** | | |
| Current liabilities. . . . . . . . . . . . . . . . . . . . . . . . . . . . . . . . . . . . . . . . . . . . . . . . . . . . | $ 770,000 | $ 726,750 |
| Long-term liabilities: | | |
| Mortgage note payable, 12%, due 2017 . . . . . . . . . . . . . . . . . . . . . . . . . . . . . | $ 1,200,000 | $ 0 |
| Bonds payable, 11%, due 2021. . . . . . . . . . . . . . . . . . . . . . . . . . . . . . . . . . . . . . | 1,500,000 | 1,000,000 |
| Total long-term liabilities . . . . . . . . . . . . . . . . . . . . . . . . . . . . . . . . . . . . . . . . . | $ 2,700,000 | $1,000,000 |
| Total liabilities . . . . . . . . . . . . . . . . . . . . . . . . . . . . . . . . . . . . . . . . . . . . . . . . . . . . . | $ 3,470,000 | $1,726,750 |
| **Stockholders' Equity** | | |
| Preferred $2.00 stock, $100 par. . . . . . . . . . . . . . . . . . . . . . . . . . . . . . . . . . . . . . . | $ 1,500,000 | $1,500,000 |
| Common stock, $5 par. . . . . . . . . . . . . . . . . . . . . . . . . . . . . . . . . . . . . . . . . . . . . . . | 3,000,000 | 3,000,000 |
| Retained earnings. . . . . . . . . . . . . . . . . . . . . . . . . . . . . . . . . . . . . . . . . . . . . . . . . . . | 2,313,120 | 1,646,120 |
| Total stockholders' equity. . . . . . . . . . . . . . . . . . . . . . . . . . . . . . . . . . . . . . . . . . | $ 6,813,120 | $6,146,120 |
| Total liabilities and stockholders' equity. . . . . . . . . . . . . . . . . . . . . . . . . . . . . . . | $10,283,120 | $7,872,870 |

**Instructions**

Determine the following measures for 2012, rounding to one decimal place:

1. Working capital
2. Current ratio
3. Quick ratio
4. Accounts receivable turnover
5. Number of days' sales in receivables
6. Inventory turnover
7. Number of days' sales in inventory
8. Ratio of fixed assets to long-term liabilities

9. Ratio of liabilities to stockholders' equity

10. Number of times interest charges earned

11. Number of times preferred dividends earned

12. Ratio of net sales to assets

13. Rate earned on total assets

14. Rate earned on stockholders' equity

15. Rate earned on common stockholders' equity

16. Earnings per share on common stock

17. Price-earnings ratio

18. Dividends per share of common stock

19. Dividend yield

OBJ. 2, 3

## PR 15-5B  Solvency and profitability trend analysis

Haviland Company has provided the following comparative information:

| | 2012 | 2011 | 2010 | 2009 | 2008 |
|---|---|---|---|---|---|
| Net income | $ 2,785,860 | $ 1,857,240 | $1,386,000 | $ 924,000 | $ 700,000 |
| Interest expense | 736,442 | 624,103 | 538,020 | 427,000 | 350,000 |
| Income tax expense | 612,786 | 422,611 | 320,160 | 220,800 | 160,000 |
| Total assets (ending balance) | 16,321,384 | 12,554,911 | 9,511,296 | 6,993,600 | 5,640,000 |
| Total stockholders' equity (ending balance) | 9,653,100 | 6,867,240 | 5,010,000 | 3,624,000 | 2,700,000 |
| Average total assets | 14,438,147 | 11,033,103 | 8,252,448 | 6,316,800 | 4,820,000 |
| Average stockholders' equity | 8,260,170 | 5,938,620 | 4,317,000 | 3,162,000 | 2,350,000 |

You have been asked to evaluate the historical performance of the company over the last five years.

Selected industry ratios have remained relatively steady at the following levels for the last five years:

| | 2008–2012 |
|---|---|
| Rate earned on total assets | 18% |
| Rate earned on stockholders' equity | 22% |
| Number of times interest charges earned | 3.0 |
| Ratio of liabilities to stockholders' equity | 1.5 |

### Instructions

1. Prepare four line graphs with the ratio on the vertical axis and the years on the horizontal axis for the following four ratios (rounded to one decimal place):

   a. Rate earned on total assets

   b. Rate earned on stockholders' equity

   c. Number of times interest charges earned

   d. Ratio of liabilities to stockholders' equity

   Display both the company ratio and the industry benchmark on each graph. That is, each graph should have two lines.

2. ➤ Prepare an analysis of the graphs in (1).

## Nike, Inc., Problem

### Financial Statement Analysis

The financial statements for Nike, Inc., are presented in Appendix D at the end of the text. The following additional information (in millions) is available:

| | |
|---|---|
| Accounts receivable at May 31, 2008 | $ 2,795.3 |
| Inventories at May 31, 2008 | 2,438.4 |
| Total assets at May 31, 2008 | 12,442.7 |
| Stockholders' equity at May 31, 2008 | 7,825.3 |

### Instructions

1. Determine the following measures for the fiscal years ended May 31, 2010, and May 31, 2009, rounding to one decimal place.

   a. Working capital

   b. Current ratio

   c. Quick ratio

   d. Accounts receivable turnover

   e. Number of days' sales in receivables

   f. Inventory turnover

   g. Number of days' sales in inventory

   h. Ratio of liabilities to stockholders' equity

   i. Ratio of net sales to average total assets

   j. Rate earned on average total assets, assuming interest expense is $36.4 million for the year ending May 31, 2010, and $40.2 million for the year ending May 31, 2009

   k. Rate earned on average common stockholders' equity

   l. Price-earnings ratio, assuming that the market price was $57.05 per share on May 31, 2010, and $68.37 per share on May 31, 2009

   m. Percentage relationship of net income to net sales

2. ➤ What conclusions can be drawn from these analyses?

## Cases & Projects

You can access Cases & Projects online at **www.cengage.com/accounting/reeve**

## Excel Success Special Activities

**SA 15-1 Horizontal analysis**

The comparative income statement for Ironside, Inc., is provided below.

| | A | B | C |
|---|---|---|---|
| 1 | Ironside, Inc. | | |
| 2 | Comparative Income Statement | | |
| 3 | For the Years Ended December 31, 2013 and 2012 | | |
| 4 | | | |
| 5 | | 2013 | 2012 |
| 6 | Sales | $ 425,000 | $ 460,000 |
| 7 | Sales returns and allowances | 25,000 | 30,000 |
| 8 | Net sales | $ 400,000 | $ 430,000 |
| 9 | Cost of goods sold | 205,000 | 227,000 |
| 10 | Gross profit | $ 195,000 | $ 203,000 |
| 11 | Selling expenses | 82,400 | 99,500 |
| 12 | Administrative expenses | 31,900 | 34,600 |
| 13 | Total operating expenses | 114,300 | 134,100 |
| 14 | Income from operations | $ 80,700 | $ 68,900 |
| 15 | Other income | 5,000 | 5,000 |
| 16 | | $ 85,700 | $ 73,900 |
| 17 | Other expense (interest) | 10,000 | 12,000 |
| 18 | Income before income tax | $ 75,700 | $ 61,900 |
| 19 | Income tax expense | 25,700 | 31,400 |
| 20 | Net Income | $ 50,000 | $ 30,500 |
| 21 | | | |

a. Open the Excel file *SA15-1_1e*.

b. Prepare a horizontal analysis using 2012 as the base year. Round percentages to one tenth of a percent (for example, 10.47% rounds to 10.5%).

c. When you have completed the horizontal analysis, perform a "save as," replacing the entire file name with the following:

*SA15-1_1e[your first name initial]_[your last name]*

**SA 15-2 Vertical analysis**

The comparative balance sheet for Ironside, Inc., is provided below.

| | A | B | C | D | E |
|---|---|---|---|---|---|
| 1 | Ironside, Inc. | | | | |
| 2 | Comparative Balance Sheet | | | | |
| 3 | For the Years Ended December 31, 2013 and 2012 | | | | |
| 4 | | | | | |
| 5 | | Dec. 31, 2013 | Percent | Dec. 31, 2012 | Percent |
| 6 | Assets | | | | |
| 7 | Current assets: | | | | |
| 8 | Cash | $ 27,000 | | $ 25,000 | |
| 9 | Temporary investments | 32,000 | | 35,000 | |
| 10 | Accounts receivable (net) | 55,000 | | 50,000 | |
| 11 | Inventories | 51,000 | | 55,000 | |
| 12 | Prepaid expenses | 5,000 | | 5,000 | |
| 13 | Total current assets | $ 170,000 | | $ 170,000 | |
| 14 | Long-term investments | 55,000 | | 60,000 | |
| 15 | Property, plant, and equipment (net) | 305,000 | | 290,000 | |
| 16 | Total assets | $ 530,000 | | $ 520,000 | |
| 17 | | | | | |

| | A | B | | C | D | | E |
|---|---|---|---|---|---|---|---|
| 18 | **Liabilities** | | | | | | |
| 19 | Current liabilities | $ | 60,000 | | $ | 70,000 | |
| 20 | Bonds payable, 6%, due 2020 | | 170,000 | | | 200,000 | |
| 21 | Total liabilities | $ | 230,000 | | $ | 270,000 | |
| 22 | | | | | | | |
| 23 | **Stockholders' Equity** | | | | | | |
| 24 | Common stock, $10 par | $ | 50,000 | | $ | 50,000 | |
| 25 | Retained earnings | | 250,000 | | | 200,000 | |
| 26 | Total stockholders' equity | $ | 300,000 | | $ | 250,000 | |
| 27 | Total liabilities and stockholders' equity | $ | 530,000 | | $ | 520,000 | |
| 28 | | | | | | | |

a. Open the Excel file *SA15-2_1e.*

b. Prepare a vertical analysis for December 31, 2012 and 2013, balance sheets. Round percentages to one tenth of a percent (for example, 10.47% rounds to 10.5%).

c. When you have completed the vertical analysis, perform a "save as," replacing the entire file name with the following:

   *SA15-2_1e[your first name initial]_[your last name]*

---

**SA 15-3 Financial ratios**

In addition to the financial statements in **SA 15-1** and **SA 15-2,** the following information is available for Ironside, Inc.

| | A | B | C |
|---|---|---|---|
| 50 | | | |
| 51 | | Dec. 31, 2013 | Dec. 31, 2012 |
| 52 | Common stock market price | $ 20.00 | $ 15.00 |
| 53 | Number of common shares outstanding | 25,000 | 25,000 |
| 54 | | | |

a. Open the Excel file *SA15-3_1e.*

b. Using the financial statements for Ironside, Inc., in the file provided, determine the following ratios for 2013

- Working capital
- Current ratio
- Inventory turnover
- Number of days' sales in inventory
- Ratio of fixed assets to long-term liabilities
- Number of times interest charges are earned
- Rate earned on total assets
- Earnings per share

c. When you have completed computing the ratios listed, perform a "save as," replacing the entire file name with the following:

   *SA15-3_1e[your first name initial]_[your last name]*

**SA 15-4    Financial ratios**

In addition to the financial statements in **SA 15-1** and **SA 15-2,** the following information is available for Ironside, Inc.

|  | A | B | C |
|---|---|---|---|
| 50 |  |  |  |
| 51 |  | Dec. 31, 2013 | Dec. 31, 2012 |
| 52 | Common stock market price | $        20.00 | $        15.00 |
| 53 | Number of common shares outstanding | 25,000 | 25,000 |
| 54 |  |  |  |
| 55 | Earnings per share on common stock | 2.0 |  |
| 56 |  |  |  |

a.  Open the Excel file *SA15-4_1e.*

b.  Using the financial statements for Ironside, Inc., in the file provided, determine the following ratios for 2013:

  • Quick ratio

  • Accounts receivable turnover

  • Number of days' sales in receivables

  • Ratio of liabilities to stockholders' equity

  • Ratio of net sales to assets

  • Rate earned on common stockholders' equity

  • Price-earnings ratio

c.  When you have completed computing the ratios listed, perform a "save as," replacing the entire file name with the following:

  *SA15-4_1e[your first name initial]_[your last name]*

© AP Photo/Greg Brown/Waterloo Courier

# Managerial Accounting Concepts and Principles

## Washburn Guitars

**P**aul Stanley, guitarist for the legendary rock band **KISS**, has entertained millions of fans playing his guitar. His guitar was built by quality craftsmen at **Washburn Guitars** in Chicago. Washburn Guitars is well-known in the music industry and has been in business for over 120 years.

Staying in business for 120 years requires a thorough understanding of how to manufacture high-quality guitars. In addition, it requires knowledge of how to account for the costs of making guitars. For example, Washburn needs cost information to answer the following questions:

How much should be charged for its guitars?

How many guitars does it have to sell in a year to cover its costs and earn a profit?

How many employees should the company have working on each stage of the manufacturing process?

How would purchasing automated equipment affect the costs of its guitars?

This chapter introduces managerial accounting concepts that are useful in addressing the preceding questions.

This chapter begins by describing managerial accounting and its relationship to financial accounting. Following this overview, the management process is described along with the role of managerial accounting in this process. Finally, characteristics of managerial accounting reports, managerial accounting terms, and uses of managerial accounting information are described and illustrated.

**OBJ. 1** Describe managerial accounting and the role of managerial accounting in a business.

# Managerial Accounting

Managers make numerous decisions during the day-to-day operations of a business and in planning for the future. Managerial accounting provides much of the information used for these decisions.

Some examples of managerial accounting information along with the chapter in which it is described and illustrated are listed below.

1. Classifying manufacturing and other costs and reporting them in the financial statements (Chapter 16)
2. Determining the cost of manufacturing a product or providing a service (Chapters 17 and 18)
3. Estimating the behavior of costs for various levels of activity and assessing cost-volume-profit relationships (Chapter 19)
4. Analyzing changes in operating income (Chapter 20).
5. Planning for the future by preparing budgets (Chapter 21)
6. Evaluating manufacturing costs by comparing actual with expected results (Chapter 22)
7. Evaluating decentralized operations by comparing actual and budgeted costs as well as computing various measures of profitability (Chapter 23)
8. Evaluating special decision-making situations by comparing differential revenues and costs, and allocating product costs (Chapter 24)
9. Evaluating alternative proposals for long-term investments in fixed assets (Chapter 25)
10. Evaluating the impact of cost allocation on pricing products and services and activity-based costing (Chapter 26)
11. Planning operations using just-in-time concepts (Chapter 27)

## Differences Between Managerial and Financial Accounting

Accounting information is often divided into two types: financial and managerial. Exhibit 1 shows the relationship between financial accounting and managerial accounting.

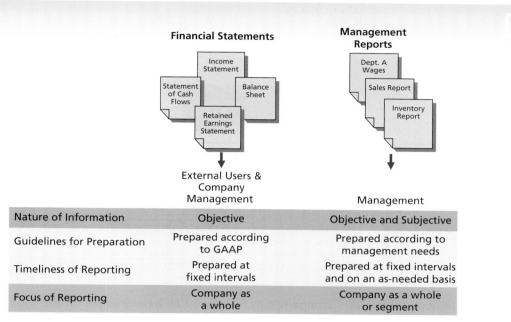

**EXHIBIT 1**

**Financial Accounting and Managerial Accounting**

**Financial accounting** information is reported at fixed intervals (monthly, quarterly, yearly) in general-purpose financial statements. These financial statements—the income statement, retained earnings statement, balance sheet, and statement of cash flows—are prepared according to generally accepted accounting principles (GAAP). These statements are used by external users such as the following:

1. Shareholders
2. Creditors
3. Government agencies
4. The general public

Managers of a company also use general-purpose financial statements. For example, in planning future operations, managers often begin by evaluating the current income statement and statement of cash flows.

**Managerial accounting** information is designed to meet the specific needs of a company's management. This information includes the following:

1. Historical data, which provide *objective measures* of past operations
2. Estimated data, which provide *subjective estimates* about future decisions

Management uses both types of information in directing daily operations, planning future operations, and developing business strategies.

Unlike the financial statements prepared in financial accounting, managerial accounting reports do *not* always have to be:

1. Prepared according to generally accepted accounting principles (GAAP). This is because *only* the company's management uses the information. Also, in many cases, GAAP are not relevant to the specific decision-making needs of management.
2. Prepared at fixed intervals (monthly, quarterly, yearly). Although some management reports are prepared at fixed intervals, most reports are prepared as management needs the information.
3. Prepared for the business as a whole. Most management reports are prepared for products, projects, sales territories, or other segments of the company.

## The Management Accountant in the Organization

In most companies, departments or similar organizational units are assigned responsibilities for specific functions or activities. The operating structure of a company can be shown in an *organization chart*.

Exhibit 2 is a partial organization chart for Callaway Golf Company, the manufacturer and distributor of golf clubs, clothing, and other products.

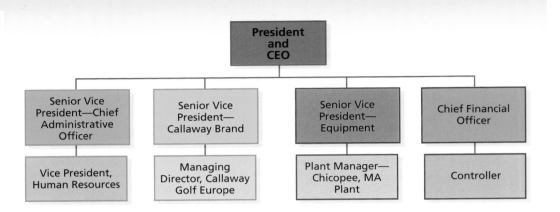

**EXHIBIT 2**

**Partial Organization Chart for Callaway Golf Company**

The departments in a company can be viewed as having either of the following:

1. Line responsibilities                    2. Staff responsibilities

A **line department** is directly involved in providing goods or services to the customers of the company. For Callaway Golf (shown in Exhibit 2), the following occupy line positions:

1. Senior Vice President—Equipment          3. Senior Vice President—Callaway Brand
2. Plant Manager—Chicopee, MA Plant         4. Managing Director, Callaway Golf Europe

The preceding occupy line positions because they are responsible for manufacturing and selling Callaway's products.

A **staff department** provides services, assistance, and advice to the departments with line or other staff responsibilities. A staff department has no direct authority over a line department. For Callaway Golf (Exhibit 2), these occupy staff positions:

1. Senior VP—Chief Administrative Officer   3. Chief Financial Officer
2. Vice President, Human Resources          4. Controller

The terms *line* and *staff* may be applied to service organizations. For example, the line positions in a hospital would be the nurses, doctors, and other caregivers. Staff positions would include admissions and records.

As shown above, the chief financial officer (CFO) and the controller occupy staff positions. In most companies, the **controller** is the chief management accountant. The controller's staff consists of a variety of other accountants who are responsible for specialized accounting functions such as the following:

1. Systems and procedures    4. Special reports and analysis
2. General accounting        5. Taxes
3. Budgets and budget analysis  6. Cost accounting

Experience in managerial accounting is often an excellent training ground for senior management positions. This is not surprising, since accounting touches all phases of a company's operations.

## Managerial Accounting in the Management Process

As a staff department, managerial accounting supports management and the management process. The **management process** has the following five basic phases as shown in Exhibit 3.

1. Planning        4. Improving
2. Directing       5. Decision making
3. Controlling

As Exhibit 3 illustrates, the five phases interact with one another.

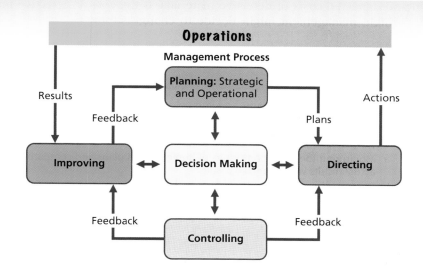

**EXHIBIT 3**

**The Management Process**

**Planning**  Management uses **planning** in developing the company's **objectives (goals)** and translating these objectives into courses of action. For example, a company may set an objective to increase market share by 15% by introducing three new products. The actions to achieve this objective might be as follows:

1. Increase the advertising budget
2. Open a new sales territory
3. Increase the research and development budget

   Planning may be classified as follows:

1. **Strategic planning**, which is developing long-term actions to achieve the company's objectives. These long-term actions are called **strategies**, which often involve periods of 5 to 10 years.
2. **Operational planning**, which develops short-term actions for managing the day-to-day operations of the company.

**Directing**  The process by which managers run day-to-day operations is called **directing.** An example of directing is a production supervisor's efforts to keep the production line moving without interruption (downtime). A credit manager's development of guidelines for assessing the ability of potential customers to pay their bills is also an example of directing.

**Controlling**  Monitoring operating results and comparing actual results with the expected results is **controlling.** This **feedback** allows management to isolate areas for further investigation and possible remedial action. It may also lead to revising future plans. This philosophy of controlling by comparing actual and expected results is called **management by exception**.

**Improving**  Feedback is also used by managers to support continuous process improvement. **Continuous process improvement** is the philosophy of continually improving employees, business processes, and products. The objective of continuous improvement is to eliminate the *source* of problems in a process. In this way, the right products (services) are delivered in the right quantities at the right time.

**Decision Making**  Inherent in each of the preceding management processes is **decision making.** In managing a company, management must continually decide among alternative actions. For example, in directing operations, managers must decide on an operating structure, training procedures, and staffing of day-to-day operations.

Managerial accounting supports managers in all phases of the management process. For example, accounting reports comparing actual and expected operating results help managers plan and improve current operations. Such a report might compare the actual and expected costs of defective materials. If the cost of defective materials is unusually high, management might decide to change suppliers.

---

## Example Exercise ▶ 16-1 ▶ Management Process                                    OBJ. 1

Three phases of the management process are planning, controlling, and improving. Match the following descriptions to the proper phase:

| Phase of management process | Description |
|---|---|
| Planning | a. Monitoring the operating results of implemented plans and comparing the actual results with expected results. |
| Controlling | b. Rejects solving individual problems with temporary solutions that fail to address the root cause of the problem. |
| Improving | c. Used by management to develop the company's objectives. |

### Follow My Example ▶ 16-1

Phase of management process

Planning (c)
Controlling (a)
Improving (b)

Practice Exercises: **PE 16-1A, PE 16-1B**

---

## Integrity, Objectivity, and Ethics in Business

### ENVIRONMENTAL ACCOUNTING

In recent years, multinational agreements such as the Kyoto Accord have raised public awareness of environmental issues and introduced guidelines for reducing the effect that businesses have on the environment. As a result, managers must now consider the environmental impact of their business decisions in the same way that they would consider other operational issues. To help managers make environmentally conscious decisions, the emerging field of environmental management accounting focuses on calculating the environmental-related costs of business decisions. Environmental managerial accountants evaluate a variety of issues such as the volume and level of emissions, the estimated costs of different levels of emissions, and the impact that environmental costs have on product cost. Managers can then use the results of these analyses to clearly consider the environmental effects of their business decisions.

---

**OBJ. 2** Describe and illustrate the following costs:
1. direct and indirect costs
2. direct materials, direct labor, and factory overhead costs
3. product and period costs

# Manufacturing Operations: Costs and Terminology

The operations of a business can be classified as service, merchandising, or manufacturing. The accounting for service and merchandising businesses has been described and illustrated in earlier chapters. For this reason, the remaining chapters of this text focus primarily on manufacturing businesses. Most of the managerial accounting concepts discussed, however, also apply to service and merchandising businesses.

As a basis for illustration of manufacturing operations, a guitar manufacturer, Legend Guitars, is used. Exhibit 4 is an overview of Legend's guitar manufacturing operations.

Legend's guitar-making process begins when a customer places an order for a guitar. Once the order is accepted, the manufacturing process begins by obtaining the

**EXHIBIT 4**    **Guitar-Making Operations of Legend Guitars**

Legend Guitars

Wood • Guitar Strings • Guitar Bridge

**Customer Places Order**    **Materials**    **Cutting Function**    **Assembly Function**    **Finished Guitar**

necessary materials. An employee then cuts the body and neck of the guitar out of raw lumber. Once the wood is cut, the body and neck of the guitar are assembled. When the assembly is complete, the guitar is painted and finished.

## Direct and Indirect Costs

A **cost** is a payment of cash or the commitment to pay cash in the future for the purpose of generating revenues. For example, cash (or credit) used to purchase equipment is the cost of the equipment. If equipment is purchased by exchanging assets other than cash, the current market value of the assets given up is the cost of the equipment purchased.

In managerial accounting, costs are classified according to the decision-making needs of management. For example, costs are often classified by their relationship to a segment of operations, called a **cost object**. A cost object may be a product, a sales territory, a department, or an activity, such as research and development. Costs identified with cost objects are either direct costs or indirect costs.

**Direct costs** are identified with and can be traced to a cost object. For example, the cost of wood (materials) used by Legend Guitars in manufacturing a guitar is a direct cost of the guitar.

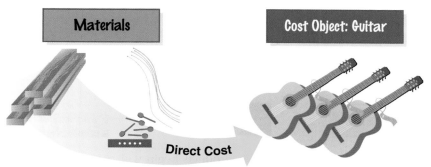

**Materials** → **Direct Cost** → **Cost Object: Guitar**

**Indirect costs** cannot be identified with or traced to a cost object. For example, the salaries of the Legend Guitars production supervisors are indirect costs of producing a guitar. While the production supervisors contribute to the production of a guitar, their salaries cannot be identified with or traced to any individual guitar.

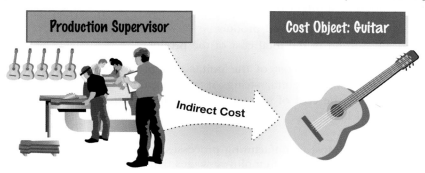

**Production Supervisor** → **Indirect Cost** → **Cost Object: Guitar**

Depending on the cost object, a cost may be either a direct or an indirect cost. For example, the salaries of production supervisors are indirect costs when the cost object is an individual guitar. If, however, the cost object is Legend Guitars' overall production process, then the salaries of production supervisors are direct costs.

This process of classifying a cost as direct or indirect is illustrated in Exhibit 5.

**EXHIBIT 5**

**Classifying Direct and Indirect Costs**

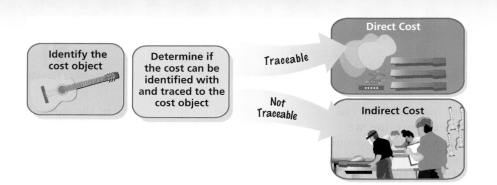

## Manufacturing Costs

The cost of a manufactured product includes the cost of materials used in making the product. In addition, the cost of a manufactured product includes the cost of converting the materials into a finished product. For example, Legend Guitars uses employees and machines to convert wood (and other supplies) into finished guitars. Thus, the cost of a finished guitar (the cost object) includes the following:

1. Direct materials cost
2. Direct labor cost
3. Factory overhead cost

**Direct Materials Cost**   Manufactured products begin with raw materials that are converted into finished products. The cost of any material that is an integral part of the finished product is classified as a **direct materials cost**. For Legend Guitars, direct materials cost includes the cost of the wood used in producing each guitar. Other examples of direct materials costs include the cost of electronic components for a television, silicon wafers for microcomputer chips, and tires for an automobile.

To be classified as a direct materials cost, the cost must be *both* of the following:

1. An integral part of the finished product
2. A significant portion of the total cost of the product

For Legend Guitars, the cost of the guitar strings is not a direct materials cost. This is because the cost of guitar strings is an insignificant part of the total cost of each guitar. Instead, the cost of guitar string is classified as a factory overhead cost, which is discussed later.

**Direct Labor Cost**   Most manufacturing processes use employees to convert materials into finished products. The cost of employee wages that is an integral part of the finished product is classified as **direct labor cost**. For Legend Guitars, direct labor cost includes the wages of the employees who cut each guitar out of raw lumber and assemble it. Other examples of direct labor costs include mechanics' wages for repairing an automobile, machine operators' wages for manufacturing tools, and assemblers' wages for assembling a laptop computer.

Like a direct materials cost, a direct labor cost must meet *both* of the following criteria:

1. An integral part of the finished product
2. A significant portion of the total cost of the product

For Legend Guitars, the wages of the janitors who clean the factory are not a direct labor cost. This is because janitorial costs are not an integral part or a significant cost of each guitar. Instead, janitorial costs are classified as a factory overhead cost, which is discussed next.

### Factory Overhead Cost

Costs other than direct materials cost and direct labor cost that are incurred in the manufacturing process are combined and classified as **factory overhead cost**. Factory overhead is sometimes called **manufacturing overhead** or **factory burden.**

All factory overhead costs are indirect costs of the product. Some factory overhead costs include the following:

1. Heating and lighting the factory
2. Repairing and maintaining factory equipment
3. Property taxes on factory buildings and land
4. Insurance on factory buildings
5. Depreciation on factory plant and equipment

Factory overhead cost also includes materials and labor costs that do not enter directly into the finished product. Examples include the cost of oil used to lubricate machinery and the wages of janitorial and supervisory employees. Also, if the costs of direct materials or direct labor are not a significant portion of the total product cost, these costs may be classified as factory overhead costs.

For Legend Guitars, the costs of guitar strings and janitorial wages are factory overhead costs. Additional factory overhead costs of making guitars are as follows:

1. Sandpaper
2. Buffing compound
3. Glue

4. Power (electricity) to run the machines
5. Depreciation of the machines and building
6. Salaries of production supervisors

As manufacturing processes have become more automated, direct labor costs have become so small that in some situations they are included as part of factory overhead.

---

**Example Exercise** 16-2 **Direct Materials, Direct Labor, and Factory Overhead** **OBJ. 2**

Identify the following costs as direct materials (DM), direct labor (DL), or factory overhead (FO) for a baseball glove manufacturer.

a. Leather used to make a baseball glove
b. Coolants for machines that sew baseball gloves
c. Wages of assembly line employees
d. Ink used to print a player's autograph on a baseball glove

**Follow My Example** 16-2

a. DM
b. FO
c. DL
d. FO

Practice Exercises: **PE 16-2A, PE 16-2B**

**Prime Costs and Conversion Costs** Direct materials, direct labor, and factory overhead costs may be grouped together for analysis and reporting. Two such common groupings are as follows:

1. **Prime costs**, which consist of direct materials and direct labor costs
2. **Conversion costs**, which consist of direct labor and factory overhead costs

Conversion costs are the costs of converting the materials into a finished product. Direct labor is both a prime cost and a conversion cost, as shown in Exhibit 6.

**EXHIBIT 6**

**Prime Costs and Conversion Costs**

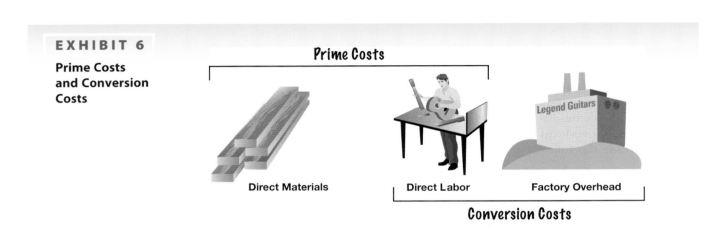

**Example Exercise 16-3 Prime and Conversion Costs** OBJ. 2

Identify the following costs as a prime cost (P), conversion cost (C), or both (B) for a baseball glove manufacturer.

a.   Leather used to make a baseball glove
b.   Coolants for machines that sew baseball gloves
c.   Wages of assembly line employees
d.   Ink used to print a player's autograph on a baseball glove

**Follow My Example 16-3**

a.   P
b.   C
c.   B
d.   C

Practice Exercises: **PE 16-3A, PE 16-3B**

**Product Costs and Period Costs** For financial reporting purposes, costs are classified as product costs or period costs.

1. **Product costs** consist of manufacturing costs: direct materials, direct labor, and factory overhead.
2. **Period costs** consist of selling and administrative expenses. *Selling expenses* are incurred in marketing the product and delivering the product to customers. *Administrative expenses* are incurred in managing the company and are not directly related to the manufacturing or selling functions.

Examples of product costs and period costs for Legend Guitars are presented in Exhibit 7.

**EXHIBIT 7**   **Examples of Product Costs and Period Costs—Legend Guitars**

# Product (Manufacturing) Costs

**Direct Materials Cost**
Wood used in neck and
body

**Direct Labor Cost**
Wages of saw operator
Wages of employees who
assemble the guitar

**Factory Overhead**
Guitar strings
Wages of janitor
Power to run the machines
Depreciation expense—factory building
Sandpaper and buffing materials
Glue used in assembly of the guitar
Salary of production supervisors

# Period (Nonmanufacturing) Costs

**Selling Expenses**
Advertising expenses
Sales salaries expenses
Commissions expenses

**Administrative Expenses**
Office salaries expense
Office supplies expense
Depreciation expense—
office building
and equipment

To facilitate control, selling and administrative expenses may be reported by level of responsibility. For example, selling expenses may be reported by products, salespersons, departments, divisions, or territories. Likewise, administrative expenses may be reported by areas such as human resources, computer services, legal, accounting, or finance.

The impact on the financial statements of product and period costs is summarized in Exhibit 8. As product costs are incurred, they are recorded and reported on the balance sheet as *inventory*. When the inventory is sold, the cost of the manufactured product sold is reported as *cost of goods sold* on the income statement. Period costs are reported as *expenses* on the income statement in the period in which they are incurred and, thus, never appear on the balance sheet.

**Note:**
Product costs consist of direct materials, direct labor, and factory overhead costs.

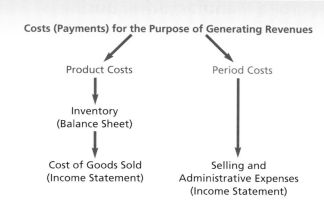

Costs (Payments) for the Purpose of Generating Revenues

Product Costs

Period Costs

Inventory
(Balance Sheet)

Cost of Goods Sold
(Income Statement)

Selling and
Administrative Expenses
(Income Statement)

**EXHIBIT 8**

**Product Costs, Period Costs, and the Financial Statements**

## Example Exercise ▶ 16-4 ▶ Product and Period Costs

OBJ.
2

Identify the following costs as a product cost or a period cost for a baseball glove manufacturer.

a.  Leather used to make a baseball glove
b.  Cost of endorsement from a professional baseball player
c.  Office supplies used at the company headquarters
d.  Ink used to print a player's autograph on the baseball glove

### Follow My Example ▶ 16-4 ▶

a.  Product cost
b.  Period cost
c.  Period cost
d.  Product cost

Practice Exercises: **PE 16-4A, PE 16-4B**

## BusinessConnection

### BUILD-TO-ORDER

Dell Inc. manufactures computers based on specific customer orders. In this build-to-order manufacturing process, customers select the exact features they want before the computer is built. Once the order is placed, the parts required for each feature are removed from inventory, which initiates the manufacturing process. Inventory items are scanned as they are removed from inventory to keep track of inventory levels and help the manufacturer determine when to reorder. This efficient process allows Dell to manufacture and ship the computer within days of the order being placed and has helped the company become one of the largest computer manufacturers in the world.

OBJ.
3

Describe and illustrate the following statements for a manufacturing business:
1. balance sheet
2. statement of cost of goods manufactured
3. income statement

# Financial Statements for a Manufacturing Business

The retained earnings and cash flow statements for a manufacturing business are similar to those illustrated in earlier chapters for service and merchandising businesses. However, the balance sheet and income statement for a manufacturing business are more complex. This is because a manufacturer makes the products that it sells and, thus, must record and report product costs. The reporting of product costs primarily affects the balance sheet and the income statement.

## Balance Sheet for a Manufacturing Business

A manufacturing business reports three types of inventory on its balance sheet as follows:

1. **Materials inventory** (sometimes called raw materials inventory). This inventory consists of the costs of the direct and indirect materials that have not entered the manufacturing process.

    Examples for Legend Guitars: Wood, guitar strings, glue, sandpaper

2. **Work in process inventory**. This inventory consists of the direct materials, direct labor, and factory overhead costs for products that have entered the manufacturing process, but are not yet completed (in process).

    Example for Legend Guitars: Unfinished (partially assembled) guitars

3. **Finished goods inventory**. This inventory consists of completed (or finished) products that have not been sold.

    Example for Legend Guitars: Unsold guitars

Exhibit 9 illustrates the reporting of inventory on the balance sheet for a merchandising and a manufacturing business. MusicLand Stores, Inc., a retailer of musical instruments, reports only *Merchandise Inventory*. In contrast, Legend Guitars, a manufacturer of guitars, reports *Finished Goods*, *Work in Process*, and *Materials* inventories. In both balance sheets, inventory is reported in the *Current Assets* section.

**EXHIBIT 9**

**Balance Sheet Presentation of Inventory in Manufacturing and Merchandising Companies**

**MusicLand Stores, Inc.**
**Balance Sheet**
**December 31, 2012**

| | |
|---|---:|
| Current assets: | |
| Cash..... | $ 25,000 |
| Accounts receivable (net) ..... | 85,000 |
| **Merchandise inventory**..... | **142,000** |
| Supplies ..... | 10,000 |
| Total current assets..... | $ 262,000 |

**Legend Guitars**
**Balance Sheet**
**December 31, 2012**

| | | |
|---|---:|---:|
| Current assets: | | |
| Cash..... | | $ 21,000 |
| Accounts receivable (net) ..... | | 120,000 |
| **Inventories:** | | |
| **Finished goods**..... | $62,500 | |
| **Work in process** ..... | 24,000 | |
| **Materials**..... | 35,000 | 121,500 |
| Supplies ..... | | 2,000 |
| Total current assets..... | | $ 264,500 |

## Income Statement for a Manufacturing Company

The income statements for merchandising and manufacturing businesses differ primarily in the reporting of the cost of merchandise (goods) *available for sale* and *sold* during the period. These differences are shown below.

| **Merchandising Business** | | |
|---|---:|---:|
| Sales | | $XXX |
| Beginning merchandise inventory | $XXX | |
| Plus net purchases | XXX | |
| **Merchandise available for sale** | $XXX | |
| Less ending merchandise inventory | XXX | |
| **Cost of merchandise sold** | | XXX |
| Gross profit | | $XXX |

| **Manufacturing Business** | | |
|---|---:|---:|
| Sales | | $XXX |
| Beginning finished goods inventory | $XXX | |
| Plus **cost of goods manufactured** | XXX | |
| **Cost of finished goods available for sale** | $XXX | |
| Less ending finished goods inventory | XXX | |
| **Cost of goods sold** | | XXX |
| Gross profit | | $XXX |

A merchandising business purchases merchandise ready for resale to customers. The total cost of the **merchandise available for sale** during the period is determined by adding the beginning merchandise inventory to the net purchases. The **cost of merchandise sold** is determined by subtracting the ending merchandise inventory from the cost of merchandise available for sale.

A manufacturer makes the products it sells, using direct materials, direct labor, and factory overhead. The total cost of making products that are available for sale during the period is called the **cost of goods manufactured**. The **cost of finished goods available** for sale is determined by adding the beginning finished goods inventory to the cost of goods manufactured during the period. The **cost of goods sold** is determined by subtracting the ending finished goods inventory from the cost of finished goods available for sale.

*Cost of goods manufactured* is required to determine the *cost of goods sold* and, thus, to prepare the income statement. The cost of goods manufactured is often determined by preparing a **statement of cost of goods manufactured**.[1] This statement summarizes the cost of goods manufactured during the period as shown below.

**Statement of Cost of Goods Manufactured**

| | | |
|---|---:|---:|
| Beginning work in process inventory........... | | $XXX |
| Direct materials: | | |
|     Beginning materials inventory.............. | $XXX | |
|     Purchases................................. | XXX | |
|     Cost of materials available for use........... | $XXX | |
|     Less ending materials inventory ............ | XXX | |
|         Cost of direct materials used ............ | $XXX | |
| Direct labor .................................... | XXX | |
| Factory overhead............................. | XXX | |
| Total manufacturing costs incurred ............ | | XXX |
| Total manufacturing costs ..................... | | $XXX |
| Less ending work in process inventory ......... | | XXX |
| **Cost of goods manufactured** ................. | | $XXX |

To illustrate, the following data for Legend Guitars are used:

| | Jan. 1, 2012 | Dec. 31, 2012 |
|---|---:|---:|
| Inventories: | | |
|     Materials.................................. | $ 65,000 | $ 35,000 |
|     Work in process ........................... | 30,000 | 24,000 |
|     Finished goods............................ | 60,000 | 62,500 |
| Total inventories............................. | $155,000 | $121,500 |
| Manufacturing costs incurred during 2012: | | |
|     Materials purchased....................... | | $100,000 |
|     Direct labor .............................. | | 110,000 |
|     Factory overhead: | | |
|         Indirect labor........................... | $ 24,000 | |
|         Depreciation on factory equipment ..... | 10,000 | |
|         Factory supplies and utility costs ........ | 10,000 | 44,000 |
| Total ....................................... | | $254,000 |
| Sales........................................ | | $366,000 |
| Selling expenses.............................. | | 20,000 |
| Administrative expenses...................... | | 15,000 |

The statement of cost of goods manufactured is prepared using the following three steps:

Step 1. Determine the *cost of materials used*.

Step 2. Determine the *total manufacturing costs incurred*.

Step 3. Determine the *cost of goods manufactured*.

---

[1] Chapters 17 and 18 describe and illustrate the use of job order and process cost systems. As will be discussed, these systems do not require a statement of cost of goods manufactured.

Exhibit 10 summarizes how manufacturing costs flow to the income statement and balance sheet of a manufacturing business.

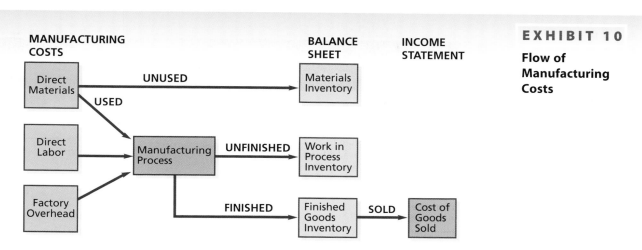

**EXHIBIT 10**

Flow of Manufacturing Costs

Using the data for Legend Guitars, the steps for determining the cost of materials used, total manufacturing costs incurred, and cost of goods manufactured are shown below.

Step 1. The *cost of materials used* in production is determined as follows:

| | |
|---|---|
| Materials inventory, January 1, 2012 | $ 65,000 |
| Add materials purchased | 100,000 |
| Cost of materials available for use | $ 165,000 |
| Less materials inventory, December 31, 2012 | 35,000 |
| Cost of direct materials used | $130,000 |

The January 1, 2012 (beginning), materials inventory of $65,000 is added to the cost of materials purchased of $100,000 to yield the total cost of materials that are available for use during 2012 of $165,000. Deducting the December 31, 2012 (ending), materials inventory of $35,000 yields the cost of direct materials used in production of $130,000.

Step 2. The *total manufacturing costs incurred* is determined as follows:

| | |
|---|---|
| Direct materials used in production (Step 1) | $ 130,000 |
| Direct labor | 110,000 |
| Factory overhead | 44,000 |
| Total manufacturing costs incurred | $284,000 |

The total manufacturing costs of $284,000 incurred in 2012 are determined by adding the direct materials used in production (Step 1), the direct labor cost, and the factory overhead costs.

Step 3. The *cost of goods manufactured* is determined as follows:

| | |
|---|---|
| Work in process inventory, January 1, 2012 | $ 30,000 |
| Total manufacturing costs incurred (Step 2) | 284,000 |
| Total manufacturing costs | $ 314,000 |
| Less work in process inventory, December 31, 2012 | 24,000 |
| Cost of goods manufactured | $290,000 |

The cost of goods manufactured of $290,000 is determined by adding the total manufacturing costs incurred (Step 2) to the January 1, 2012 (beginning), work in process inventory of $30,000. This yields total manufacturing costs of $314,000. The December 31, 2012 (ending), work in process of $24,000 is then deducted to determine the cost of goods manufactured of $290,000.

The income statement and statement of cost of goods manufactured for Legend Guitars is shown in Exhibit 11.

**EXHIBIT 11**

**Manufacturing Company— Income Statement with Statement of Cost of Goods Manufactured**

**Legend Guitars**
**Income Statement**
**For the Year Ended December 31, 2012**

| | | |
|---|---:|---:|
| Sales . . . . . . . . . . . . . . . . . . . . . . . . . . . . . . . . . . . . . . . . . . . . . . . . . . . . . . . . . | | $366,000 |
| Cost of goods sold: | | |
| Finished goods inventory, January 1, 2012. . . . . . . . . . . . . . . . . . . . . . . . . | $ 60,000 | |
| Cost of goods manufactured . . . . . . . . . . . . . . . . . . . . . . . . . . . . . . . . . . . . | 290,000 | |
| Cost of finished goods available for sale. . . . . . . . . . . . . . . . . . . . . . . . . | $350,000 | |
| Less finished goods inventory, December 31, 2012. . . . . . . . . . . . . . . . . | 62,500 | |
| Cost of goods sold . . . . . . . . . . . . . . . . . . . . . . . . . . . . . . . . . . . . . | | 287,500 |
| Gross profit . . . . . . . . . . . . . . . . . . . . . . . . . . . . . . . . . . . . . . . . . . . . . . . . . . . . . . | | $ 78,500 |
| Operating expenses: | | |
| Selling expenses . . . . . . . . . . . . . . . . . . . . . . . . . . . . . . . . . . . . . . . . . . . . . . . | $ 20,000 | |
| Administrative expenses . . . . . . . . . . . . . . . . . . . . . . . . . . . . . . . . . . . . . . . | 15,000 | |
| Total operating expenses . . . . . . . . . . . . . . . . . . . . . . . . . . . . . . . . . . . | | 35,000 |
| Net income . . . . . . . . . . . . . . . . . . . . . . . . . . . . . . . . . . . . . . . . . . . . . . . . . . . . . . . | | $ 43,500 |

**Legend Guitars**
**Statement of Cost of Goods Manufactured**
**For the Year Ended December 31, 2012**

| | | | |
|---|---:|---:|---:|
| Work in process inventory, January 1, 2012. . . . . . . . . . . . . . . . . . | | | $ 30,000 |
| Direct materials: | | | |
| Materials inventory, January 1, 2012 . . . . . . . . . . . . . . . . . . . . | $ 65,000 | | |
| Purchases. . . . . . . . . . . . . . . . . . . . . . . . . . . . . . . . . . . . . . . . . . . . . | 100,000 | | |
| Cost of materials available for use. . . . . . . . . . . . . . . . . . . . . . | $165,000 | | |
| Less materials inventory, December 31, 2012 . . . . . . . . . . . . | 35,000 | | |
| Cost of direct materials used . . . . . . . . . . . . . . . . . . . . . . . . | | $130,000 | |
| Direct labor. . . . . . . . . . . . . . . . . . . . . . . . . . . . . . . . . . . . . . . . . . . . . . . . | | 110,000 | |
| Factory overhead: | | | |
| Indirect labor . . . . . . . . . . . . . . . . . . . . . . . . . . . . . . . . . . . . . . . . . | $ 24,000 | | |
| Depreciation on factory equipment. . . . . . . . . . . . . . . . . . . . . | 10,000 | | |
| Factory supplies and utility costs . . . . . . . . . . . . . . . . . . . . . . | 10,000 | | |
| Total factory overhead. . . . . . . . . . . . . . . . . . . . . . . . . . . . . . | | 44,000 | |
| Total manufacturing costs incurred . . . . . . . . . . . . . . . . . . . . . . . . | | | 284,000 |
| Total manufacturing costs . . . . . . . . . . . . . . . . . . . . . . . . . . . . . . . . . . | | | $314,000 |
| Less work in process inventory, December 31, 2012 . . . . . . . . . . | | | 24,000 |
| Cost of goods manufactured . . . . . . . . . . . . . . . . . . . . . . . . . . . . . . . . | | | $290,000 |

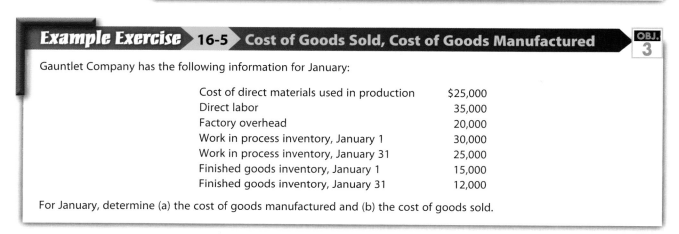

**Example Exercise** ▸ **16-5** ▸ **Cost of Goods Sold, Cost of Goods Manufactured** **OBJ. 3**

Gauntlet Company has the following information for January:

| | |
|---|---:|
| Cost of direct materials used in production | $25,000 |
| Direct labor | 35,000 |
| Factory overhead | 20,000 |
| Work in process inventory, January 1 | 30,000 |
| Work in process inventory, January 31 | 25,000 |
| Finished goods inventory, January 1 | 15,000 |
| Finished goods inventory, January 31 | 12,000 |

For January, determine (a) the cost of goods manufactured and (b) the cost of goods sold.

*(continued)*

## Follow My Example 16-5

| | | | |
|---|---|---|---:|
| a. | Work in process inventory, January 1.................................. | | $ 30,000 |
| | Cost of direct materials used in production......................... | $ 25,000 | |
| | Direct labor...................................................... | 35,000 | |
| | Factory overhead ................................................ | 20,000 | |
| | Total manufacturing costs incurred during January.................. | | 80,000 |
| | Total manufacturing costs ........................................ | | $110,000 |
| | Less work in process inventory, January 31........................ | | 25,000 |
| | Cost of goods manufactured....................................... | | $ 85,000 |
| | | | |
| b. | Finished goods inventory, January 1 .............................. | | $ 15,000 |
| | Cost of goods manufactured....................................... | | 85,000 |
| | Cost of finished goods available for sale.......................... | | $100,000 |
| | Less finished goods inventory, January 31......................... | | 12,000 |
| | Cost of goods sold............................................... | | $ 88,000 |

Practice Exercises: **PE 16-5A, PE 16-5B**

# Uses of Managerial Accounting

**OBJ. 4** Describe the uses of managerial accounting information.

As mentioned earlier, managerial accounting provides information and reports for managers to use in operating a business. Some examples of how managerial accounting could be used by Legend Guitars include the following:

1. The cost of manufacturing each guitar could be used to determine its selling price.
2. Comparing the costs of guitars over time can be used to monitor and control the cost of direct materials, direct labor, and factory overhead.
3. Performance reports could be used to identify any large amounts of scrap or employee downtime. For example, large amounts of unusable wood (scrap) after the cutting process should be investigated to determine the underlying cause. Such scrap may be caused by saws that have not been properly maintained.
4. A report could analyze the potential efficiencies and dollar savings of purchasing a new computerized saw to speed up the production process.
5. A report could analyze how many guitars need to be sold to cover operating costs and expenses. Such information could be used to set monthly selling targets and bonuses for sales personnel.

As the prior examples illustrate, managerial accounting information can be used for a variety of purposes. In the remaining chapters of this text, we examine these and other areas of managerial accounting.

# BusinessConnection

### OVERHEAD COSTS

Defense contractors such as General Dynamics, Boeing, and Lockheed Martin sell products that include airplanes, ships, and military equipment to the U.S. Department of Defense. Building large products such as these requires a significant investment in facilities and tools, all of which are classified as factory overhead costs. As a result, factory overhead costs are a much larger portion of cost of goods sold for defense contractors than it is in other industries. For example, a U.S. General Accounting Office study of six defense contractors found that overhead costs were almost one-third of the price of the final product. This is over three times greater than the factory overhead costs for a laptop computer, which are typically about 10% of the price of the final product.

# At a Glance 16

**OBJ. 1** Describe managerial accounting and the role of managerial accounting in a business.

**Key Points** Managerial accounting is a staff function that supports the management process by providing reports to aid management in planning, directing, controlling, improving, and decision making. This differs from financial accounting, which provides information to users outside of the organization. Managerial accounting reports are designed to meet the specific needs of management and aid management in planning long-term strategies and running the day-to-day operations.

| Learning Outcomes | Example Exercises | Practice Exercises |
|---|---|---|
| • Describe the differences between financial accounting and managerial accounting. | | |
| • Describe the role of the management accountant in the organization. | | |
| • Describe the role of managerial accounting in the management process. | EE16-1 | PE16-1A, 16-1B |

**OBJ. 2** Describe and illustrate the following costs: (1) direct and indirect costs; (2) direct materials, direct labor, and factory overhead costs; and (3) product and period costs.

**Key Points** Manufacturing companies use machinery and labor to convert materials into a finished product. A direct cost can be directly traced to a finished product, while an indirect cost cannot. The cost of a finished product is made up of three components: (1) direct materials, (2) direct labor, and (3) factory overhead.

These three manufacturing costs can be categorized into prime costs (direct materials and direct labor) or conversion costs (direct labor and factory overhead). Product costs consist of the elements of manufacturing cost—direct materials, direct labor, and factory overhead—while period costs consist of selling and administrative expenses.

| Learning Outcomes | Example Exercises | Practice Exercises |
|---|---|---|
| • Describe a cost object. | | |
| • Classify a cost as a direct or an indirect cost for a cost object. | | |
| • Describe direct materials cost. | EE16-2 | PE16-2A, 16-2B |
| • Describe direct labor cost. | EE16-2 | PE16-2A, 16-2B |
| • Describe factory overhead cost. | EE16-2 | PE16-2A, 16-2B |
| • Describe prime costs and conversion costs. | EE16-3 | PE16-3A, 16-3B |
| • Describe product costs and period costs. | EE16-4 | PE16-4A, 16-4B |

## OBJ. 3

**Describe and illustrate the following statements for a manufacturing business: (1) balance sheet, (2) statement of cost of goods manufactured, and (3) income statement.**

**Key Points** The financial statements of manufacturing companies differ from those of merchandising companies. Manufacturing company balance sheets report three types of inventory: materials, work in process, and finished goods. The income statement of manufacturing companies reports cost of goods sold, which is the total manufacturing cost of the goods sold. The income statement is supported by the statement of cost of goods manufactured, which provides the details of the cost of goods manufactured during the period.

| Learning Outcomes | Example Exercises | Practice Exercises |
|---|---|---|
| • Describe materials inventory. | | |
| • Describe work in process inventory. | | |
| • Describe finished goods inventory. | | |
| • Describe the differences between merchandising and manufacturing company balance sheets. | | |
| • Prepare a statement of cost of goods manufactured. | EE16-5 | PE16-5A, 16-5B |
| • Prepare an income statement for a manufacturing company. | EE16-5 | PE16-5A, 16-5B |

## OBJ. 4

**Describe the uses of managerial accounting information.**

**Key Points** Managers need information to guide their decision making. Managerial accounting provides a variety of information and reports that help managers run the operations of their business.

| Learning Outcomes | Example Exercises | Practice Exercises |
|---|---|---|
| • Describe examples of how managerial accounting aids managers in decision making. | | |

# Key Terms

continuous process improvement (759)
controller (758)
controlling (759)
conversion costs (764)
cost (761)
cost object (761)
cost of finished goods available (768)
cost of goods manufactured (768)
cost of goods sold (768)
cost of merchandise sold (767)
decision making (759)
direct costs (761)
direct labor cost (763)

direct materials cost (762)
directing (759)
factory burden (763)
factory overhead cost (763)
feedback (759)
financial accounting (757)
finished goods inventory (766)
indirect costs (761)
line department (758)
management by exception (759)
management process (758)
managerial accounting (757)
manufacturing overhead (763)
materials inventory (766)

merchandise available for sale (767)
objectives (goals) (759)
operational planning (759)
period costs (764)
planning (759)
prime costs (764)
product costs (764)
staff department (758)
statement of cost of goods manufactured (768)
strategic planning (759)
strategies (759)
work in process inventory (766)

## Illustrative Problem

The following is a list of costs that were incurred in producing this textbook:

a. Insurance on the factory building and equipment

b. Salary of the vice president of finance

c. Hourly wages of printing press operators during production

d. Straight-line depreciation on the printing presses used to manufacture the text

e. Electricity used to run the presses during the printing of the text

f. Sales commissions paid to textbook representatives for each text sold

g. Paper on which the text is printed

h. Book covers used to bind the pages

i. Straight-line depreciation on an office building

j. Salaries of staff used to develop artwork for the text

k. Glue used to bind pages to cover

### Instructions

With respect to the manufacture and sale of this text, classify each cost as either a product cost or a period cost. Indicate whether each product cost is a direct materials cost, a direct labor cost, or a factory overhead cost. Indicate whether each period cost is a selling expense or an administrative expense.

### Solution

| | Product Cost | | | Period Cost | |
| --- | --- | --- | --- | --- | --- |
| Cost | Direct Materials Cost | Direct Labor Cost | Factory Overhead Cost | Selling Expense | Administrative Expense |
| a. | | | X | | |
| b. | | | | | X |
| c. | | X | | | |
| d. | | | X | | |
| e. | | | X | | |
| f. | | | | X | |
| g. | X | | | | |
| h. | X | | | | |
| i. | | | | | X |
| j. | | | X | | |
| k. | | | X | | |

## Discussion Questions

1. What are the major differences between managerial accounting and financial accounting?

2. a. Differentiate between a department with line responsibility and a department with staff responsibility.

   b. In an organization that has a Sales Department and a Personnel Department, among others, which of the two departments has (1) line responsibility and (2) staff responsibility?

3. What manufacturing cost term is used to describe the cost of materials that are an integral part of the manufactured end product?

4. Distinguish between prime costs and conversion costs.

5. What is the difference between a product cost and a period cost?

6. Name the three inventory accounts for a manufacturing business, and describe what each balance represents at the end of an accounting period.

7. In what order should the three inventories of a manufacturing business be presented on the balance sheet?

8. What are the three categories of manufacturing costs included in the cost of finished goods and the cost of work in process?

9. For a manufacturer, what is the description of the account that is comparable to a merchandising business's cost of merchandise sold?

10. How does the Cost of Goods Sold section of the income statement differ between merchandising and manufacturing companies?

# Practice Exercises

| Learning Objectives | Example Exercises | |
|---|---|---|

**OBJ. 1**  **EE 16-1** *p. 760*

### PE 16-1A  Management process

Three phases of the management process are controlling, planning, and decision making. Match the following descriptions to the proper phase.

| Phase of management process | Description |
|---|---|
| Controlling | a. Long-range courses of action. |
| Decision making | b. Inherent in planning, directing, controlling, and improving. |
| Planning | c. Monitoring the operating results of implemented plans and comparing the actual results with expected results. |

**OBJ. 1**  **EE 16-1** *p. 760*

### PE 16-1B  Management process

Three phases of the management process are planning, directing, and controlling. Match the following descriptions to the proper phase.

| Phase of management process | Description |
|---|---|
| Directing | a. Isolating significant departures from plans for further investigation and possible remedial action. It may lead to a revision of future plans. |
| Controlling | b. Developing long-range courses of action to achieve goals. |
| Planning | c. Process by which managers, given their assigned levels of responsibilities, run day-to-day operations. |

**OBJ. 2**  **EE 16-2** *p. 763*

### PE 16-2A  Direct materials, direct labor, and factory overhead

Identify the following costs as direct materials (DM), direct labor (DL), or factory overhead (FO) for an automobile manufacturer.

a. Steel

b. Wages of employees that operate painting equipment

c. Oil used for assembly line machinery

d. Wages of the plant supervisor

**OBJ. 2**  **EE 16-2** *p. 763*

### PE 16-2B  Direct materials, direct labor, and factory overhead

Identify the following costs as direct materials (DM), direct labor (DL), or factory overhead (FO) for a magazine publisher.

a. Paper used in the magazine

b. Maintenance on printing machines

c. Wages of printing machine employees

d. Staples used to bind magazines

**OBJ. 2**  **EE 16-3** *p. 764*

### PE 16-3A  Prime and conversion costs

Identify the following costs as a prime cost (P), conversion cost (C), or both (B) for an automobile manufacturer.

a. Steel

b. Wages of employees that operate painting equipment

c. Oil used for assembly line machinery

d. Wages of the plant manager

**OBJ. 2**    **EE 16-3**  *p. 764*

### PE 16-3B    Prime and conversion costs

Identify the following costs as a prime cost (P), conversion cost (C), or both (B) for a magazine publisher.

a. Maintenance on printing machines

b. Glue used to bind magazine

c. Wages of printing machine employees

d. Paper used for the magazine

**OBJ. 2**    **EE 16-4**  *p. 766*

### PE 16-4A    Product and period costs

Identify the following costs as a product cost or a period cost for an automobile manufacturer.

a. Sales staff salaries

b. Rent on office building

c. Wages of employees that operate painting equipment

d. Steel

**OBJ. 2**    **EE 16-4**  *p. 766*

### PE 16-4B    Product and period costs

Identify the following costs as a product cost or a period cost for a magazine publisher.

a. Maintenance on printing machines

b. Sales salaries

c. Depreciation expense—corporate headquarters

d. Paper used for the magazine

**OBJ. 3**    **EE 16-5**  *p. 770*

### PE 16-5A    Cost of goods sold, cost of goods manufactured

Swain Company has the following information for January:

| | |
|---|---|
| Cost of direct materials used in production | $12,000 |
| Direct labor | 31,000 |
| Factory overhead | 20,000 |
| Work in process inventory, January 1 | 50,000 |
| Work in process inventory, January 31 | 53,000 |
| Finished goods inventory, January 1 | 21,000 |
| Finished goods inventory, January 31 | 24,000 |

For January, determine (a) the cost of goods manufactured and (b) the cost of goods sold.

**OBJ. 3**    **EE 16-5**  *p. 770*

### PE 16-5B    Cost of goods sold, cost of goods manufactured

Dandee Company has the following information for July:

| | |
|---|---|
| Cost of direct materials used in production | $ 84,000 |
| Direct labor | 110,000 |
| Factory overhead | 56,000 |
| Work in process inventory, July 1 | 41,000 |
| Work in process inventory, July 31 | 37,000 |
| Finished goods inventory, July 1 | 47,000 |
| Finished goods inventory, July 31 | 34,000 |

For July, determine (a) the cost of goods manufactured and (b) the cost of goods sold.

## Exercises

OBJ. 2

**EX 16-1 Classifying costs as materials, labor, or factory overhead**

Indicate whether each of the following costs of an automobile manufacturer would be classified as direct materials cost, direct labor cost, or factory overhead cost:

a. Depreciation of welding equipment

b. Assembly machinery lubricants

c. Steering wheel

d. Wages of assembly line worker

e. Tires

f. V8 automobile engine

g. Salary of test driver

h. Steel used in body

OBJ. 2

**EX 16-2 Classifying costs as materials, labor, or factory overhead**

Indicate whether the following costs of Colgate-Palmolive Company, a maker of consumer products, would be classified as direct materials cost, direct labor cost, or factory overhead cost:

a. Scents and fragrances

b. Wages paid to Packaging Department employees

c. Resins for soap and shampoo products

d. Maintenance supplies

e. Depreciation on production machinery

f. Salary of process engineers

g. Plant manager salary for the Clarksville, Indiana, soap plant

h. Packaging materials

i. Depreciation on the Morristown, Tennessee, toothpaste plant

j. Wages of production line employees

OBJ. 2

**EX 16-3 Classifying costs as factory overhead**

Which of the following items are properly classified as part of factory overhead for Caterpillar, a maker of heavy machinery and equipment?

a. Sales incentive fees to dealers

b. Factory supplies used in the Danville, Kentucky, tractor tread plant

c. Depreciation on Peoria, Illinois, headquarters building

d. Interest expense on debt

e. Amortization of patents on new assembly process

f. Steel plate

g. Vice president of finance's salary

h. Property taxes on the Aurora, Illinois, manufacturing plant

i. Plant manager's salary at Aurora, Illinois, manufacturing plant

j. Consultant fees for a study of production line employee productivity

OBJ. 2

**EX 16-4 Classifying costs as product or period costs**

For apparel manufacturer Ann Taylor, Inc., classify each of the following costs as either a product cost or a period cost:

a. Advertising expenses

b. Salaries of distribution center personnel

c. Factory janitorial supplies

d. Repairs and maintenance costs for sewing machines

e. Travel costs of media relations employees

f. Fabric used during production

g. Depreciation on office equipment

h. Salary of production quality control supervisor

i. Utility costs for office building

j. Depreciation on sewing machines

k. Factory supervisors' salaries

l. Wages of sewing machine operators

m. Property taxes on factory building and equipment

n. Research and development costs

o. Chief financial officer's salary

p. Sales commissions

q. Oil used to lubricate sewing machines

---

**OBJ. 1, 2**

### EX 16-5 Concepts and terminology

From the choices presented in parentheses, choose the appropriate term for completing each of the following sentences:

a. The implementation of automatic, robotic factory equipment normally (increases, decreases) the direct labor component of product costs.

b. Payments of cash or the commitment to pay cash in the future for the purpose of generating revenues are (costs, expenses).

c. Feedback is often used to (improve, direct) operations.

d. Advertising costs are usually viewed as (period, product) costs.

e. The balance sheet of a manufacturer would include an account for (cost of goods sold, work in process inventory).

f. A product, sales territory, department, or activity to which costs are traced is called a (direct cost, cost object).

g. Factory overhead costs combined with direct labor costs are called (prime, conversion) costs.

---

**OBJ. 1, 2**

### EX 16-6 Concepts and terminology

From the choices presented in parentheses, choose the appropriate term for completing each of the following sentences:

a. An example of factory overhead is (sales office depreciation, plant depreciation).

b. The plant manager's salary would be considered (direct, indirect) to the product.

c. Materials for use in production are called (supplies, materials inventory).

d. Direct materials costs combined with direct labor costs are called (prime, conversion) costs.

e. The phase of the management process that uses process information to eliminate the source of problems in a process so that the process delivers the correct product in the correct quantities is called (directing, improving).

f. The wages of an assembly worker are normally considered a (period, product) cost.

g. Short-term plans are called (strategic, operational) plans.

---

**OBJ. 2**

### EX 16-7 Classifying costs in a service company

A partial list of the costs for Wisconsin and Minnesota Railroad, a short hauler of freight, is provided below. Classify each cost as either indirect or direct. For purposes of classifying each cost as direct or indirect, use the train as the cost object.

a. Fuel costs

b. Maintenance costs of right of way, bridges, and buildings

c. Wages of switch and classification yard personnel

*(continued)*

d. Cost to lease (rent) train locomotives

e. Wages of train engineers

f. Cost to lease (rent) railroad cars

g. Depreciation of terminal facilities

h. Payroll clerk salaries

i. Safety training costs

j. Cost of track and bed (ballast) replacement

k. Salaries of dispatching and communications personnel

l. Costs of accident cleanup

---

**OBJ. 2, 3**

### EX 16-8 Classifying costs

The following report was prepared for evaluating the performance of the plant manager of Nuuman Inc. Evaluate and correct this report.

**Nuuman Inc.**
**Manufacturing Costs**
**For the Quarter Ended June 30, 2012**

| | |
|---|---:|
| Materials used in production (including $70,000 of indirect materials) ........................... | $ 760,000 |
| Direct labor (including $80,000 maintenance salaries)........ | 700,000 |
| Factory overhead: | |
|    Supervisor salaries ..................................... | 510,000 |
|    Heat, light, and power.................................. | 135,000 |
|    Sales salaries ......................................... | 327,000 |
|    Promotional expenses.................................... | 304,000 |
|    Insurance and property taxes—plant ..................... | 143,000 |
|    Insurance and property taxes—corporate offices .......... | 208,000 |
|    Depreciation—plant and equipment ..................... | 119,000 |
|    Depreciation—corporate offices ........................ | 92,000 |
| Total ................................................... | $3,298,000 |

---

**OBJ. 3**

✔ a. Net income, $36,000

### EX 16-9 Financial statements of a manufacturing firm

The following events took place for Air Temp Manufacturing Company during January, the first month of its operations as a producer of digital thermometers:

a. Purchased $68,000 of materials.

b. Used $48,000 of direct materials in production.

c. Incurred $92,000 of direct labor wages.

d. Incurred $108,000 of factory overhead.

e. Transferred $217,000 of work in process to finished goods.

f. Sold goods with a cost of $170,000.

g. Earned revenues of $325,000.

h. Incurred $80,000 of selling expense.

i. Incurred $39,000 of administrative expense.

Using the above information, complete the following:

a. Prepare the January income statement for Air Temp Manufacturing Company.

b. Determine the inventory balances at the end of the first month of operations.

---

**OBJ. 3**

### EX 16-10 Manufacturing company balance sheet

Partial balance sheet data for Lawler Company at December 31, 2012, are as follows:

| | | | |
|---|---:|---|---:|
| Finished goods inventory | $23,000 | Supplies | $41,000 |
| Prepaid insurance | 23,000 | Materials inventory | 50,000 |
| Accounts receivable | 60,000 | Cash | 64,000 |
| Work in process inventory | 90,000 | | |

Prepare the Current Assets section of Lawler Company's balance sheet at December 31, 2012.

---

OBJ. 3

**EX 16-11  Cost of direct materials used in production for a manufacturing company**

Saron Manufacturing Company reported the following materials data for the month ending April 30, 2012:

| | |
|---|---|
| Materials purchased | $860,000 |
| Materials inventory, April 1 | 350,000 |
| Materials inventory, April 30 | 300,000 |

Determine the cost of direct materials used in production by Saron during the month ended April 30, 2012.

---

OBJ. 3

✔ e. $7,000

**EX 16-12  Cost of goods manufactured for a manufacturing company**

Two items are omitted from each of the following three lists of cost of goods manufactured statement data. Determine the amounts of the missing items, identifying them by letter.

| | | | |
|---|---|---|---|
| Work in process inventory, November 1 | $ 16,000 | $ 36,000 | (e) |
| Total manufacturing costs incurred during November | 112,000 | (c) | 42,000 |
| Total manufacturing costs | (a) | $210,000 | $49,000 |
| Work in process inventory, November 30 | 24,000 | 48,000 | (f) |
| Cost of goods manufactured | (b) | (d) | $43,000 |

---

OBJ. 3

**EX 16-13  Cost of goods manufactured for a manufacturing company**

The following information is available for Neaves Manufacturing Company for the month ending January 31, 2012:

| | |
|---|---|
| Cost of direct materials used in production | $215,000 |
| Direct labor | 185,000 |
| Work in process inventory, January 1 | 85,000 |
| Work in process inventory, January 31 | 94,000 |
| Total factory overhead | 130,000 |

Determine Neaves' cost of goods manufactured for the month ended January 31, 2012.

---

OBJ. 3

✔ d. $142,000

**EX 16-14  Income statement for a manufacturing company**

Two items are omitted from each of the following three lists of cost of goods sold data from a manufacturing company income statement. Determine the amounts of the missing items, identifying them by letter.

| | | | |
|---|---|---|---|
| Finished goods inventory, November 1 | $ 44,000 | $ 33,000 | (e) |
| Cost of goods manufactured | 235,000 | (c) | 404,000 |
| Cost of finished goods available for sale | (a) | $186,000 | $450,000 |
| Finished goods inventory, November 30 | 52,000 | 44,000 | (f) |
| Cost of goods sold | (b) | (d) | $428,000 |

**OBJ. 3**

✔ a. Total manufacturing costs, $1,190,200

**EX 16-15** **Statement of cost of goods manufactured for a manufacturing company**

Cost data for Bedford Manufacturing Company for the month ending May 31, 2012, are as follows:

| Inventories | May 1 | May 31 |
|---|---|---|
| Materials | $168,000 | $139,000 |
| Work in process | 240,000 | 260,000 |
| Finished goods | 182,000 | 214,200 |

| | |
|---|---|
| Direct labor | $475,000 |
| Materials purchased during May | 302,000 |
| Factory overhead incurred during May: | |
| Indirect labor | 57,200 |
| Machinery depreciation | 36,000 |
| Heat, light, and power | 13,000 |
| Supplies | 10,000 |
| Property taxes | 9,800 |
| Miscellaneous cost | 18,200 |

a. Prepare a cost of goods manufactured statement for May 2012.

b. Determine the cost of goods sold for May 2012.

**OBJ. 3**

✔ a. Cost of goods sold, $274,000

**EX 16-16** **Cost of goods sold, profit margin, and net income for a manufacturing company**

The following information is available for Vega Manufacturing Company for the month ending July 31, 2012:

| | |
|---|---|
| Cost of goods manufactured | $270,000 |
| Selling expenses | 58,000 |
| Administrative expenses | 46,000 |
| Sales | 515,000 |
| Finished goods inventory, July 1 | 66,000 |
| Finished goods inventory, July 31 | 62,000 |

For the month ended July 31, 2012, determine Vega's (a) cost of goods sold, (b) gross profit, and (c) net income.

**OBJ. 3**

✔ a. $260,000

**EX 16-17** **Cost flow relationships**

The following information is available for the first month of operations of Enders Company, a manufacturer of mechanical pencils:

| | |
|---|---|
| Sales | $630,000 |
| Gross profit | 370,000 |
| Cost of goods manufactured | 315,000 |
| Indirect labor | 84,000 |
| Factory depreciation | 22,000 |
| Materials purchased | 164,000 |
| Total manufacturing costs for the period | 362,000 |
| Materials inventory | 22,000 |

Using the above information, determine the following missing amounts:

a. Cost of goods sold

b. Finished goods inventory

c. Direct materials cost

d. Direct labor cost

e. Work in process inventory

## Problems Series A

OBJ. 2

### PR 16-1A Classifying costs

The following is a list of costs that were incurred in the production and sale of boats:

a. Annual bonus paid to top executives of the company.

b. Cost of paving the headquarters employee parking lot.

c. Steering wheels.

d. Salary of shop supervisor.

e. Power used by sanding equipment.

f. Cost of electrical wiring for boats.

g. Commissions to sales representatives, based upon the number of boats sold.

h. Legal department costs for the year.

i. Memberships for key executives in the Bass World Association.

j. Yearly cost maintenance contract for robotic equipment.

k. Cost of normal scrap from defective hulls.

l. Masks for use by sanders in smoothing boat hulls.

m. Decals for boat hull.

n. Salary of president of company.

o. Cost of boat for "grand prize" promotion in local bass tournament.

p. Special advertising campaign in *Bass World*.

q. Wood paneling for use in interior boat trim.

r. Cost of metal hardware for boats, such as ornaments and tie-down grasps.

s. Annual fee to pro-fisherman Bill Tennessee to promote the boats.

t. Canvas top for boats.

u. Straight-line depreciation on factory equipment.

v. Oil to lubricate factory equipment.

w. Fiberglass for producing the boat hull.

x. Salary of chief financial officer.

y. Hourly wages of assembly line workers.

z. Boat chairs.

### Instructions

Classify each cost as either a product cost or a period cost. Indicate whether each product cost is a direct materials cost, a direct labor cost, or a factory overhead cost. Indicate whether each period cost is a selling expense or an administrative expense. Use the following tabular headings for your answer, placing an "X" in the appropriate column.

| | Product Costs | | | Period Costs | |
|---|---|---|---|---|---|
| Cost | Direct Materials Cost | Direct Labor Cost | Factory Overhead Cost | Selling Expense | Administrative Expense |

OBJ. 2

### PR 16-2A Classifying costs

The following is a list of costs incurred by several businesses:

a. Cost of 30-second television commercial.

b. Fees charged by collection agency on past-due customer accounts.

c. Depreciation of robot used to assemble a product.

d. Rent for a warehouse used to store finished products.

e.  Cost of plastic for a telephone being manufactured.

f.  Wages of a machine operator on the production line.

g.  Cost of sewing machine needles used by a shirt manufacturer.

h.  Maintenance costs for factory equipment.

i.  Depreciation of microcomputers used in the factory to coordinate and monitor the production schedules.

j.  Charitable contribution to United Fund.

k.  Maintenance and repair costs for factory equipment.

l.  Telephone charges by president's office.

m.  Wages of production quality control personnel.

n.  Depreciation of copying machines used by the Marketing Department.

o.  Electricity used to operate factory machinery.

p.  Factory janitorial supplies.

q.  Travel costs of marketing executives to annual sales meeting.

r.  Oil lubricants for factory plant and equipment.

s.  Depreciation of tools used in production.

t.  Cost of fabric used by clothing manufacturer.

u.  Salary of the vice president of manufacturing logistics.

v.  Fees paid to lawn service for office grounds upkeep.

w.  Surgeon's fee for heart bypass surgery.

x.  Pens, paper, and other supplies used by the Accounting Department in preparing various managerial reports.

**Instructions**

Classify each of the preceding costs as a product cost or period cost. Indicate whether each product cost is a direct materials cost, a direct labor cost, or a factory overhead cost. Indicate whether each period cost is a selling expense or an administrative expense. Use the following tabular headings for preparing your answer, placing an "X" in the appropriate column.

| | Product Costs | | | Period Costs | |
|---|---|---|---|---|---|
| Cost | Direct Materials Cost | Direct Labor Cost | Factory Overhead Cost | Selling Expense | Administrative Expense |

**OBJ. 2**

**PR 16-3A    Cost classifications—service company**

A partial list of Cottonwood Medical Center's costs is provided below.

a.  Cost of patient meals.

b.  Training costs for nurses.

c.  Cost of intravenous solutions.

d.  Depreciation of X-ray equipment.

e.  Cost of blood tests.

f.  Cost of improvements on the employee parking lot.

g.  Salary of intensive care personnel.

h.  Cost of new heart wing.

i.  Nurses' salaries.

j.  Operating room supplies used on patients (catheters, sutures, etc.).

k.  Cost of advertising hospital services on television.

l.  Cost of maintaining the staff and visitors' cafeteria.

m.  Cost of laundry services for operating room personnel.

n.  Utility costs of the hospital.

o. Cost of drugs used for patients.

p. Doctor's fee.

q. Cost of X-ray test.

r. Overtime incurred in the Records Department due to a computer failure.

s. General maintenance of the hospital.

t. Salary of the nutritionist.

u. Depreciation on patient rooms.

**Instructions**

1. What would be Cottonwood's most logical definition for the final cost object?

2. Identify whether each of the costs is to be classified as direct or indirect. For purposes of classifying each cost as direct or indirect, use the patient as the cost object.

OBJ. 2, 3

✔ 1. b. Jerry
$344,000

**PR 16-4A    Manufacturing income statement, statement of cost of goods manufactured**

Several items are omitted from each of the following income statement and cost of goods manufactured statement data for the month of December 2012:

| | Tom Company | Jerry Company |
|---|---|---|
| Materials inventory, December 1 | $ 187,200 | $ 118,000 |
| Materials inventory, December 31 | (a) | 120,000 |
| Materials purchased | 475,200 | 228,000 |
| Cost of direct materials used in production | 501,600 | (a) |
| Direct labor | 705,600 | (b) |
| Factory overhead | 218,400 | 120,000 |
| Total manufacturing costs incurred during December | (b) | 690,000 |
| Total manufacturing costs | 1,785,600 | 985,000 |
| Work in process inventory, December 1 | 360,000 | 295,000 |
| Work in process inventory, December 31 | 302,400 | (c) |
| Cost of goods manufactured | (c) | 683,000 |
| Finished goods inventory, December 1 | 316,800 | 136,000 |
| Finished goods inventory, December 31 | 331,200 | (d) |
| Sales | 2,760,000 | 1,117,000 |
| Cost of goods sold | (d) | 701,000 |
| Gross profit | (e) | (e) |
| Operating expenses | 360,000 | (f) |
| Net income | (f) | 256,000 |

**Instructions**

1. Determine the amounts of the missing items, identifying them by letter.

2. Prepare a statement of cost of goods manufactured for Jerry Company.

3. Prepare an income statement for Jerry Company.

**OBJ. 2, 3**

✔ 1. Cost of goods
manufactured,
$742,000

### PR 16-5A Statement of cost of goods manufactured and income statement for a manufacturing company

The following information is available for The Green Hornet Corporation for 2012:

| Inventories | January 1 | December 31 |
|---|---|---|
| Materials | $165,000 | $210,000 |
| Work in process | 306,000 | 290,000 |
| Finished goods | 298,000 | 284,000 |

| | |
|---|---|
| Advertising expense | $ 148,000 |
| Depreciation expense—office equipment | 21,000 |
| Depreciation expense—factory equipment | 20,900 |
| Direct labor | 360,000 |
| Heat, light, and power—factory | 8,400 |
| Indirect labor | 29,100 |
| Materials purchased | 325,000 |
| Office salaries expense | 115,000 |
| Property taxes—factory | 6,800 |
| Property taxes—office building | 18,000 |
| Rent expense—factory | 11,500 |
| Sales | 1,530,000 |
| Sales salaries expense | 188,000 |
| Supplies—factory | 5,700 |
| Miscellaneous cost—factory | 3,600 |

**Instructions**

1. Prepare the 2012 statement of cost of goods manufactured.

2. Prepare the 2012 income statement.

## Problems Series B

**OBJ. 2**

### PR 16-1B Classifying costs

The following is a list of costs that were incurred in the production and sale of lawn mowers:

a. Salary of factory supervisor.

b. Steel used in producing the lawn mowers.

c. Commissions paid to sales representatives, based on the number of lawn mowers sold.

d. Tires for lawn mowers.

e. Property taxes on the factory building and equipment.

f. Maintenance costs for new robotic factory equipment, based on hours of usage.

g. Hourly wages of operators of robotic machinery used in production.

h. Salary of vice president of marketing.

i. Gasoline engines used for lawn mowers.

j. Telephone charges for company controller's office.

k. Factory cafeteria cashier's wages.

l. Plastic for outside housing of lawn mowers.

m. Electricity used to run the robotic machinery.

n. Attorney fees for drafting a new lease for headquarters offices.

o. Paint used to coat the lawn mowers.

p. License fees for use of patent for lawn mower blade, based on the number of lawn mowers produced.

q. Cash paid to outside firm for janitorial services for factory.

r. Straight-line depreciation on the robotic machinery used to manufacture the lawn mowers.

s. Steering wheels for lawn mowers.

t. Cost of advertising in a national magazine.

u. Engine oil used in mower engines prior to shipment.

v. Premiums on insurance policy for factory buildings.

w. Payroll taxes on hourly assembly line employees.

x. Salary of quality control supervisor who inspects each lawn mower before it is shipped.

y. Cost of boxes used in packaging lawn mowers.

z. Filter for spray gun used to paint the lawn mowers.

## Instructions

Classify each cost as either a product cost or a period cost. Indicate whether each product cost is a direct materials cost, a direct labor cost, or a factory overhead cost. Indicate whether each period cost is a selling expense or an administrative expense. Use the following tabular headings for your answer, placing an "X" in the appropriate column.

| | Product Costs | | | Period Costs | |
| --- | --- | --- | --- | --- | --- |
| Cost | Direct Materials Cost | Direct Labor Cost | Factory Overhead Cost | Selling Expense | Administrative Expense |

OBJ. 2

### PR 16-2B  Classifying costs

The following is a list of costs incurred by several businesses:

a. Hourly wages of warehouse laborers.

b. Wages of a machine operator on the production line.

c. Costs for television advertisement.

d. Wages of company controller's secretary.

e. Disk drives for a microcomputer manufacturer.

f. Packing supplies for products sold. These supplies are a very small portion of the total cost of the product.

g. Salary of quality control supervisor.

h. Executive bonus for vice president of marketing.

i. Protective glasses for factory machine operators.

j. Tires for an automobile manufacturer.

k. Cost of telephone operators for a toll-free hotline to help customers operate products.

l. Entertainment expenses for sales representatives.

m. Lumber used by furniture manufacturer.

n. Health insurance premiums paid for factory workers.

o. Seed for grain farmer.

p. Costs of operating a research laboratory.

q. Paper used by Computer Department in processing various managerial reports.

r. Factory operating supplies.

s. Cost of hogs for meat processor.

t. Maintenance and repair costs for factory equipment.

u. First-aid supplies for factory workers.

v. Sales commissions.

w. Paper used by commercial printer.

x. Depreciation of factory equipment.

### Instructions

Classify each of the preceding costs as a product cost or period cost. Indicate whether each product cost is a direct materials cost, a direct labor cost, or a factory overhead cost. Indicate whether each period cost is a selling expense or an administrative expense. Use the following tabular headings for preparing your answer. Place an "X" in the appropriate column.

| | Product Costs | | | Period Costs | |
|---|---|---|---|---|---|
| Cost | Direct Materials Cost | Direct Labor Cost | Factory Overhead Cost | Selling Expense | Administrative Expense |

OBJ. 2

### PR 16-3B   Cost classifications—service company

A partial list of Berry Hotel's costs is provided below.

a. Cost of laundering towels and bedding.

b. Cost of food.

c. Cost to paint lobby.

d. Cost of advertising in local newspaper.

e. Cost to mail a customer survey.

f. Training for hotel restaurant servers.

g. Champagne for guests.

h. Wages of convention setup employees.

i. Pay per view movie rental costs (in rooms).

j. Cost of soaps and shampoos for rooms.

k. Wages of desk clerks.

l. Wages of kitchen employees.

m. Salary of the hotel president.

n. Depreciation of the hotel.

o. Wages of maids.

p. Cost to replace lobby furniture.

q. Cost of room mini-bar supplies.

r. Utility cost.

s. Wages of bellhops.

t. Cost of valet parking.

u. Guest room telephone costs for long-distance calls.

v. General maintenance supplies.

w. Cost of new carpeting.

### Instructions

1. What would be Berry's most logical definition for the final cost object?

2. Identify whether each of the costs is to be classified as direct or indirect. For purposes of classifying each cost as direct or indirect, use the hotel guest as the cost object.

OBJ. 2, 3

✔1. Margo, c.
$572,000

**PR 16-4B** **Manufacturing income statement, statement of cost of goods manufactured**

Several items are omitted from each of the following income statement and cost of goods manufactured statement data for the month of December 2012:

| | Margo Company | Rita Company |
|---|---|---|
| Materials inventory, December 1 | $ 47,000 | $ 139,500 |
| Materials inventory, December 31 | (a) | 65,100 |
| Materials purchased | 202,000 | (a) |
| Cost of direct materials used in production | 227,000 | (b) |
| Direct labor | 277,000 | 412,300 |
| Factory overhead | 106,000 | 182,900 |
| Total manufacturing costs incurred in December | (b) | 1,085,000 |
| Total manufacturing costs | 695,000 | 1,233,800 |
| Work in process inventory, December 1 | 85,000 | 148,800 |
| Work in process inventory, December 31 | 123,000 | (c) |
| Cost of goods manufactured | (c) | 1,094,300 |
| Finished goods inventory, December 1 | 160,000 | 192,200 |
| Finished goods inventory, December 31 | 141,000 | (d) |
| Sales | 805,000 | 1,388,800 |
| Cost of goods sold | (d) | 1,103,600 |
| Gross profit | (e) | (e) |
| Operating expenses | 84,000 | (f) |
| Net income | (f) | 117,800 |

**Instructions**

1. Determine the amounts of the missing items, identifying them by letter.

2. Prepare a statement of cost of goods manufactured for Margo Company.

3. Prepare an income statement for Margo Company.

OBJ. 2, 3

✔1. Cost of goods manufactured, $226,000

**PR 16-5B** **Statement of cost of goods manufactured and income statement for a manufacturing company**

The following information is available for Yu Company for 2012:

| Inventories | January 1 | December 31 |
|---|---|---|
| Materials | $47,000 | $58,500 |
| Work in process | 67,000 | 59,000 |
| Finished goods | 70,000 | 62,000 |

| | |
|---|---|
| Advertising expense | $ 42,500 |
| Depreciation expense—office equipment | 13,800 |
| Depreciation expense—factory equipment | 9,000 |
| Direct labor | 115,000 |
| Heat, light, and power—factory | 3,600 |
| Indirect labor | 14,400 |
| Materials purchased | 76,000 |
| Office salaries expense | 46,800 |
| Property taxes—factory | 2,500 |
| Property taxes—headquarters building | 8,400 |
| Rent expense—factory | 4,000 |
| Sales | 529,000 |
| Sales salaries expense | 82,500 |
| Supplies—factory | 3,000 |
| Miscellaneous cost—factory | 2,000 |

**Instructions**

1. Prepare the 2012 statement of cost of goods manufactured.

2. Prepare the 2012 income statement.

## Cases & Projects

You can access Cases & Projects online at **www.cengage.com/accounting/reeve**

# Job Order Costing

## Paul Stanley's Guitar

**A**s we discussed in Chapter 16, Paul Stanley of the legendary rock band **KISS** uses a custom-made guitar purchased from **Washburn Guitars**. In fact, Paul Stanley designed his guitar in partnership with Washburn Guitars, as have other rock stars like Dan Donnegan of the rock band **Disturbed**. Washburn's guitars are precision instruments that require high-quality materials and careful craftsmanship. As a result, amateurs and professionals are willing to pay between $1,100 and $10,000 for a PS (Paul Stanley) Series guitar. In order for Washburn to stay in business, the purchase price of the guitar must be greater than the cost of producing the guitar. So, how does Washburn determine the cost of producing a guitar?

Costs associated with creating a guitar include materials such as wood and strings, the wages of employees who build the guitar, and factory overhead. To determine the purchase price of Paul Stanley's guitar, Washburn identifies and records the costs that go into the guitar during each step of the manufacturing process. As the guitar moves through the production process, the costs of direct materials, direct labor, and factory overhead are recorded. When the guitar is complete, the costs that have been recorded are added up to determine the cost of Paul Stanley's unique guitar. The company then prices the guitar to achieve a level of profit over the cost of the guitar. This chapter introduces the principles of accounting systems that accumulate costs in the same manner as they were for Paul Stanley's guitar.

---

**OBJ. 1** Describe cost accounting systems used by manufacturing businesses.

# Cost Accounting System Overview

**Cost accounting systems** measure, record, and report product costs. Managers use product costs for setting product prices, controlling operations, and developing financial statements.

The two main types of cost accounting systems for manufacturing operations are:

1. Job order cost systems
2. Process cost systems

Warner Bros. and other movie studios use job order cost systems to accumulate movie production and distribution costs. Costs such as actor salaries, production costs, movie print costs, and marketing costs are accumulated in a job account for a particular movie.

A **job order cost system** provides product costs for each quantity of product that is manufactured. Each quantity of product that is manufactured is called a *job*. Job order cost systems are often used by companies that manufacture custom products for customers or batches of similar products. Manufacturers that use a job order cost system are sometimes called *job shops*. An example of a job shop would be an apparel manufacturer, such as Levi Strauss & Co., or a guitar manufacturer such as Washburn Guitars.

A **process cost system** provides product costs for each manufacturing department or process. Process cost systems are often used by companies that manufacture units of a product that are indistinguishable from each other and are manufactured using a continuous production process. Examples would be oil refineries, paper producers, chemical processors, and food processors.

Job order and process cost systems are widely used. A company may use a job order cost system for some of its products and a process cost system for other products.

The process cost system is illustrated in Chapter 18. In this chapter, the job order cost system is illustrated. As a basis for illustration, Legend Guitars, a manufacturer of guitars, is used. Exhibit 1 provides a summary of Legend Guitars' manufacturing operations, which were described in Chapter 16.

**OBJ. 2** Describe and illustrate a job order cost accounting system.

# Job Order Cost Systems for Manufacturing Businesses

A job order cost system records and summarizes manufacturing costs by jobs. The flow of manufacturing costs in a job order system is illustrated in Exhibit 2.

**EXHIBIT 1**

**Summary of Legend Guitars' Manufacturing Operations**

**Manufacturing Operations**

| | |
|---|---|
| Cutting | Employees cut the body and neck of the guitar out of wood. |
| Assembling | Employees assemble and finish the guitars. |

**Product Costs**

| | |
|---|---|
| Direct materials | The cost of material that is an integral part of and a significant portion of the total cost of the final product. The cost of wood used in the neck and body of the guitars. |
| Direct labor | The cost of employee wages that is an integral part of and a significant portion of the total cost of the final product. The wages of the cutting and assembling employees. |
| Factory overhead | Costs other than direct materials and direct labor that are incurred in the manufacturing process. The cost of guitar strings, glue, sandpaper, buffing compound, paint, salaries of production supervisors, janitorial salaries, and factory utilities. |

**Inventories**

| | |
|---|---|
| Materials | Includes the cost of direct and indirect materials used to produce the guitars. Direct materials include the cost of wood used in the neck and body of the guitars. Indirect materials include guitar strings, glue, sandpaper, buffing compound, varnish, and paint. |
| Work in process | Includes the product costs of units that have entered the manufacturing process, but have not been completed. The product costs of guitars for which the neck and body have been cut, but not yet assembled. |
| Finished goods | Includes the cost of completed (or finished) products that have not been sold. The product costs assigned to completed guitars that have not yet been sold. |

Exhibit 2 indicates that although the materials for Jobs 71 and 72 have been added, both jobs are still in the production process. Thus, Jobs 71 and 72 are part of *Work in Process Inventory*. In contrast, Exhibit 2 indicates that Jobs 69 and 70 have been completed. Thus, Jobs 69 and 70 are part of *Finished Goods Inventory*. Exhibit 2 also indicates that when finished guitars are sold to music stores, their costs become part of *Cost of Goods Sold*.

In a job order cost accounting system, perpetual inventory controlling accounts and subsidiary ledgers are maintained for materials, work in process, and finished goods inventories as shown on the next page.

## Materials

The materials account in the general ledger is a controlling account. A separate account for each type of material is maintained in a subsidiary **materials ledger**.

**EXHIBIT 2**     **Flow of Manufacturing Costs**

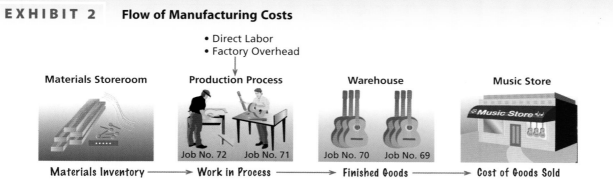

• Direct Labor
• Factory Overhead

| Materials Storeroom | Production Process | Warehouse | Music Store |
|---|---|---|---|
| | Job No. 72    Job No. 71 | Job No. 70    Job No. 69 | |
| Materials Inventory → | Work in Process → | Finished Goods → | Cost of Goods Sold |

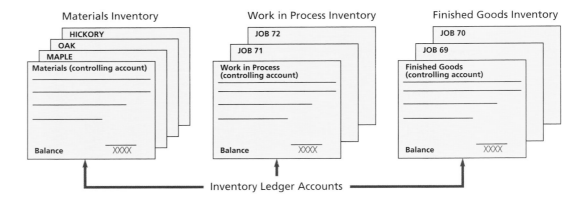

Exhibit 3 shows Legend Guitars' materials ledger account for maple. Increases (debits) and decreases (credits) to the account are as follows:

1. Increases (debits) are based on *receiving reports* such as Receiving Report No. 196 for $10,500, which is supported by the supplier's invoice.
2. Decreases (credits) are based on *materials requisitions* such as Requisition No. 672 for $2,000 for Job 71 and Requisition No. 704 for $11,000 for Job 72.

**EXHIBIT 3**

**Materials Information and Cost Flows**

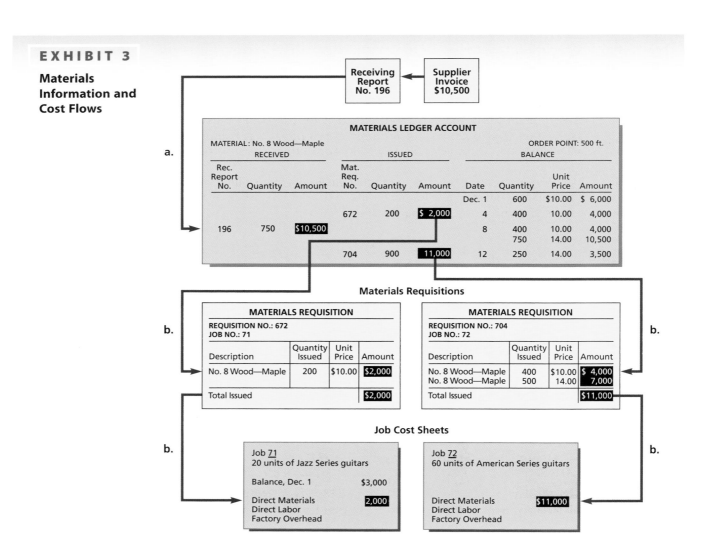

A **receiving report** is prepared when materials that have been ordered are received and inspected. The quantity received and the condition of the materials are entered on the receiving report. When the supplier's invoice is received, it is compared to the receiving report. If there are no discrepancies, a journal entry is made to record the purchase. The journal entry to record the supplier's invoice related to Receiving Report No. 196 in Exhibit 3 is as follows:

| a. | Materials | 10,500 | |
| | Accounts Payable | | 10,500 |
| | Materials purchased during December. | | |

The storeroom releases materials for use in manufacturing when a **materials requisition** is received. Examples of materials requisitions are shown in Exhibit 3.

The materials requisitions for each job serve as the basis for recording materials used. For direct materials, the quantities and amounts from the materials requisitions are posted to job cost sheets. **Job cost sheets**, which are also illustrated in Exhibit 3, make up the work in process subsidiary ledger.

Exhibit 3 shows the posting of $2,000 of direct materials to Job 71 and $11,000 of direct materials to Job 72.[1] Job 71 is an order for 20 units of Jazz Series guitars, while Job 72 is an order for 60 units of American Series guitars.

A summary of the materials requisitions is used as a basis for the journal entry recording the materials used for the month. For direct materials, this entry increases (debits) Work in Process and decreases (credits) Materials as shown below.

| b. | Work in Process | 13,000 | |
| | Materials | | 13,000 |
| | Materials requisitioned to jobs | | |
| | ($2,000 + $11,000). | | |

Many companies use computerized information processes to record the use of materials. In such cases, storeroom employees electronically record the release of materials, which automatically updates the materials ledger and job cost sheets.

## Integrity, Objectivity, and Ethics in Business

**PHONY INVOICE SCAMS**

A popular method for defrauding a company is to issue a phony invoice. The scam begins by initially contacting the target firm to discover details of key business contacts, business operations, and products. The swindler then uses this information to create a fictitious invoice. The invoice will include names, figures, and other details to give it the appearance of legitimacy. This type of scam can be avoided if invoices are matched with receiving documents prior to issuing a check.

## Example Exercise ▸ 17-1 ▸ Issuance of Materials    OBJ. 2

On March 5, Hatch Company purchased 400 units of raw materials at $14 per unit. On March 10, raw materials were requisitioned for production as follows: 200 units for Job 101 at $12 per unit and 300 units for Job 102 at $14 per unit. Journalize the entry on March 5 to record the purchase and on March 10 to record the requisition from the materials storeroom.

(continued)

---

1 To simplify, Exhibit 3 and this chapter use the first-in, first-out cost flow method.

**Follow My Example 17-1**

| Mar. 5 | Materials ..................................................... | 5,600 | |
| | Accounts Payable ................................................. | | 5,600 |
| | $5,600 = 400 × $14. | | |
| 10 | Work in Process ..................................................... | 6,600* | |
| | Materials ........................................................... | | 6,600 |

| *Job 101 | $2,400 = 200 × $12 |
| Job 102 | 4,200 = 300 × $14 |
| Total | $6,600 |

Practice Exercises: **PE 17-1A, PE 17-1B**

## Factory Labor

When employees report for work, they may use *clock cards*, *in-and-out cards*, or *electronic badges* to clock in. When employees work on an individual job, they use **time tickets**. Exhibit 4 illustrates time tickets for Jobs 71 and 72.

Exhibit 4 shows that on December 13, 2012, D. McInnis spent six hours working on Job 71 at an hourly rate of $10 for a cost of $60 (6 hrs. × $10). Exhibit 4 also indicates that a total of 350 hours was spent by employees on Job 71 during December for a total cost of $3,500. This total direct labor cost of $3,500 is posted to the job cost sheet for Job 71, as shown in Exhibit 4.

Likewise, Exhibit 4 shows that on December 26, 2012, S. Andrews spent eight hours on Job 72 at an hourly rate of $15 for a cost of $120 (8 hrs. × $15). A total of

**EXHIBIT 4**

**Labor Information and Cost Flows**

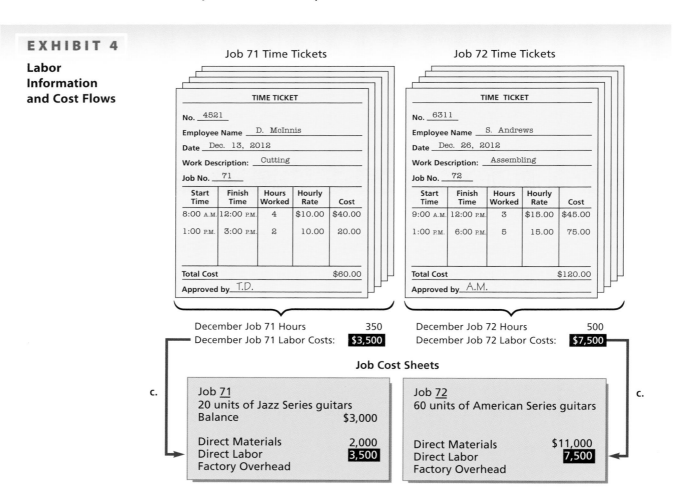

500 hours was spent by employees on Job 72 during December for a total cost of $7,500. This total direct labor cost of $7,500 is posted to the job cost sheet for Job 72, as shown in Exhibit 4.

A summary of the time tickets is used as the basis for the journal entry recording direct labor for the month. This entry increases (debits) Work in Process and increases (credits) Wages Payable, as shown below.

| | | | | |
|---|---|---|---|---|
| c. | Work in Process | | 11,000 | |
| | Wages Payable | | | 11,000 |
| | Factory labor used in production of jobs ($3,500 + $7,500). | | | |

As with direct materials, many businesses use computerized information processing to record direct labor. In such cases, employees may log their time directly into computer terminals at their workstations. In other cases, employees may be issued magnetic cards, much like credit cards, to log in and out of work assignments.

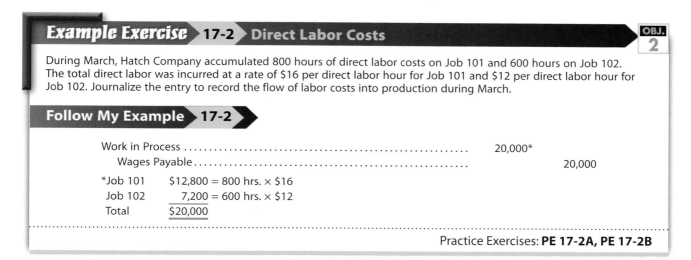

**Example Exercise 17-2 Direct Labor Costs**

OBJ. 2

During March, Hatch Company accumulated 800 hours of direct labor costs on Job 101 and 600 hours on Job 102. The total direct labor was incurred at a rate of $16 per direct labor hour for Job 101 and $12 per direct labor hour for Job 102. Journalize the entry to record the flow of labor costs into production during March.

**Follow My Example 17-2**

| | | |
|---|---|---|
| Work in Process ............................................................... | 20,000* | |
| Wages Payable ............................................................ | | 20,000 |

| | | |
|---|---|---|
| *Job 101 | $12,800 = 800 hrs. × $16 | |
| Job 102 | 7,200 = 600 hrs. × $12 | |
| Total | $20,000 | |

Practice Exercises: **PE 17-2A, PE 17-2B**

## BusinessConnection

### BMW'S FACTORY LABOR EXPERIMENT

In 2007, managers at Bavarian Motorworks (BMW) began to worry about the increasing age of their workforce. The average age of manufacturing plant workers was expected to increase from 39 to 47 by 2017. To plan for this change, BMW conducted an experiment by altering the age makeup of workers on one of the company's production lines to match the average age anticipated in 2017. In addition, the company made 70 changes to the production line to reduce the chance of error and physical strain. The changes resulted in a 7% improvement in productivity and a 2% decrease in employee absences from work. The company now uses the line as a model of quality and productivity for the rest of the company.

Source: C. Loch, F. Sting, N. Bauer, and H. Mauermann, "How BMW Is Defusing the Demographic Time Bomb," *Harvard Business Review*, March 2010.

## Factory Overhead Cost

Factory overhead includes all manufacturing costs except direct materials and direct labor.

Factory overhead costs come from a variety of sources including the following:

- *Indirect materials* comes from a summary of materials requisitions.
- *Indirect labor* comes from the salaries of production supervisors and the wages of other employees such as janitors.

3. *Factory power* comes from utility bills.

4. *Factory depreciation* comes from Accounting Department computations of depreciation.

To illustrate the recording of factory overhead, assume that Legend Guitars incurred $4,600 of overhead in December. The $500 of materials consisted of $200 of glue and $300 of sandpaper. The entry to record the factory overhead is shown below.

| | | | | | |
|---|---|---|---|---|---|
| d. | Factory Overhead | | | 4,600 | |
| | Materials | | | | 500 |
| | Wages Payable | | | | 2,000 |
| | Utilities Payable | | | | 900 |
| | Accumulated Depreciation | | | | 1,200 |
| | Factory overhead incurred in production. | | | | |

**Example Exercise** ▶ **17-3** ▶ **Factory Overhead Costs**
**OBJ. 2**

During March, Hatch Company incurred factory overhead costs as follows: indirect materials, $800; indirect labor, $3,400; utilities cost, $1,600; and factory depreciation, $2,500. Journalize the entry to record the factory overhead incurred during March.

**Follow My Example** ▶ **17-3** ▶

| | | |
|---|---|---|
| Factory Overhead ..................................................... | 8,300 | |
| Materials...................................................... | | 800 |
| Wages Payable..................................................... | | 3,400 |
| Utilities Payable..................................................... | | 1,600 |
| Accumulated Depreciation ......................................... | | 2,500 |

Practice Exercises: **PE 17-3A, PE 17-3B**

**Allocating Factory Overhead** Factory overhead is different from direct labor and direct materials in that it is *indirectly* related to the jobs. That is, factory overhead costs cannot be identified with or traced to specific jobs. For this reason, factory overhead costs are allocated to jobs. The process by which factory overhead or other costs are assigned to a cost object, such as a job, is called **cost allocation**.

The factory overhead costs are *allocated* to jobs using a common measure related to each job. This measure is called an **activity base**, *allocation base*, or *activity driver*. The activity base used to allocate overhead should reflect the consumption or use of factory overhead costs. For example, production supervisor salaries could be allocated on the basis of direct labor hours or direct labor cost of each job.

**Predetermined Factory Overhead Rate** Factory overhead costs are normally allocated or *applied* to jobs using a **predetermined factory overhead rate**. The predetermined factory overhead rate is computed as follows:

$$\text{Predetermined Factory Overhead Rate} = \frac{\text{Estimated Total Factory Overhead Costs}}{\text{Estimated Activity Base}}$$

To illustrate, assume that Legend Guitars estimates the total factory overhead cost as $50,000 for the year and the activity base as 10,000 direct labor hours. The predetermined factory overhead rate of $5 per direct labor hour is computed as follows:

$$\text{Predetermined Factory Overhead Rate} = \frac{\text{Estimated Total Factory Overhead Costs}}{\text{Estimated Activity Base}}$$

$$\text{Predetermined Factory} \atop \text{Overhead Rate} = \frac{\$50,000}{10,000 \text{ direct labor hours}} = \$5 \text{ per direct labor hour}$$

As shown above, the predetermined overhead rate is computed using *estimated* amounts at the beginning of the period. This is because managers need timely information on the product costs of each job. If a company waited until all overhead costs were known at the end of the period, the allocated factory overhead would be accurate, but not timely. Only through timely reporting can managers adjust manufacturing methods or product pricing.

Many companies are using a method for accumulating and allocating factory overhead costs. This method, called **activity-based costing**, uses a different overhead rate for each type of factory overhead activity, such as inspecting, moving, and machining. Activity-based costing is discussed and illustrated in Chapter 26.

A spreadsheet can be used to calculate the predetermined factory overhead rate, as follows:

| | A | B | C | D |
|---|---|---|---|---|
| 1 | Inputs: | | | |
| 2 | | | | |
| 3 | Estimated total factory overhead costs | $    50,000 | | |
| 4 | Estimated activity base | 10,000 | *direct labor hours* | |
| 5 | | | | |
| 6 | Output: | | | |
| 7 | | | | |
| 8 | Predetermined factory overhead rate | =B3/B4 | *per direct labor hour* | |

↑
a.

a.  The predetermined factory overhead rate is determined by dividing the two inputs, =B3/B4.

The spreadsheet might involve multiple factories, thus requiring the calculation of multiple rates across columns or rows. In addition, spreadsheets are particularly useful when determining multiple activity rates under activity-based costing.

**Try**It  Go to the hands-on **Excel Tutor** for this example!

**Applying Factory Overhead to Work in Process**  Legend Guitars applies factory overhead using a rate of $5 per direct labor hour. The factory overhead applied to each job is recorded in the job cost sheets, as shown in Exhibit 5.

Exhibit 5 shows that 850 direct labor hours were used in Legend Guitars' December operations. Based on the time tickets, 350 hours can be traced to Job 71, and 500 hours can be traced to Job 72.

Using a factory overhead rate of $5 per direct labor hour, $4,250 of factory overhead is applied as follows:

| | **Direct Labor Hours** | **Factory Overhead Rate** | **Factory Overhead Applied** |
|---|---|---|---|
| Job 71 | 350 | $5 | $1,750 (350 hrs. × $5) |
| Job 72 | 500 | $5 | 2,500 (500 hrs. × $5) |
| Total | 850 | | $4,250 |

As shown in Exhibit 5, the applied overhead is posted to each job cost sheet. Factory overhead of $1,750 is posted to Job 71, which results in a total product cost on December 31, 2012, of $10,250. Factory overhead of $2,500 is posted to Job 72, which results in a total product cost on December 31, 2012, of $21,000.

**EXHIBIT 5**

**Applying Factory Overhead to Jobs**

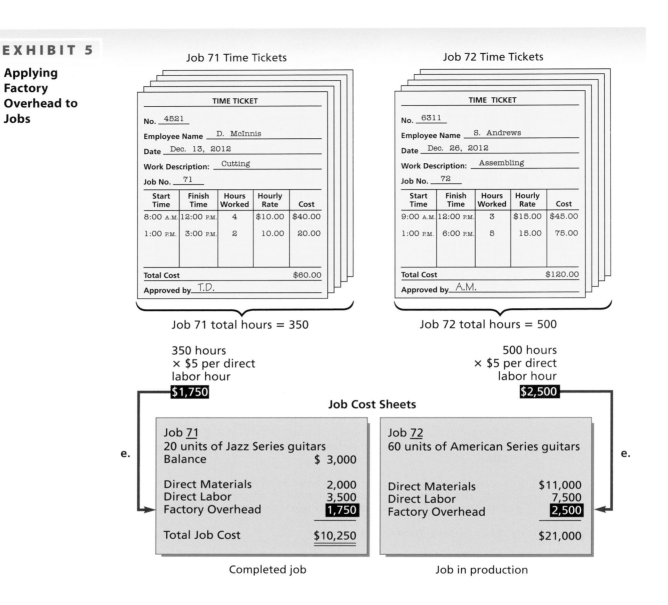

Job 71 Time Tickets

Job 72 Time Tickets

TIME TICKET

No. 4521

Employee Name D. McInnis

Date Dec. 13, 2012

Work Description: Cutting

Job No. 71

| Start Time | Finish Time | Hours Worked | Hourly Rate | Cost |
|---|---|---|---|---|
| 8:00 A.M. | 12:00 P.M. | 4 | $10.00 | $40.00 |
| 1:00 P.M. | 3:00 P.M. | 2 | 10.00 | 20.00 |

| Total Cost | | | | $60.00 |

Approved by T.D.

TIME TICKET

No. 6311

Employee Name S. Andrews

Date Dec. 26, 2012

Work Description: Assembling

Job No. 72

| Start Time | Finish Time | Hours Worked | Hourly Rate | Cost |
|---|---|---|---|---|
| 9:00 A.M. | 12:00 P.M. | 3 | $15.00 | $45.00 |
| 1:00 P.M. | 6:00 P.M. | 5 | 15.00 | 75.00 |

| Total Cost | | | | $120.00 |

Approved by A.M.

Job 71 total hours = 350

Job 72 total hours = 500

350 hours × $5 per direct labor hour
**$1,750**

500 hours × $5 per direct labor hour
**$2,500**

**Job Cost Sheets**

e.

| Job 71 20 units of Jazz Series guitars | |
|---|---|
| Balance | $ 3,000 |
| Direct Materials | 2,000 |
| Direct Labor | 3,500 |
| Factory Overhead | 1,750 |
| Total Job Cost | $10,250 |

Completed job

e.

| Job 72 60 units of American Series guitars | |
|---|---|
| Direct Materials | $11,000 |
| Direct Labor | 7,500 |
| Factory Overhead | 2,500 |
| | $21,000 |

Job in production

The journal entry to apply factory overhead increases (debits) Work in Process and decreases (credits) Factory Overhead. This journal entry to apply overhead to Jobs 71 and 72 is as follows:

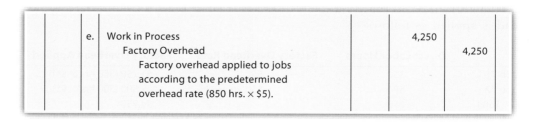

| e. | Work in Process | | 4,250 | |
|---|---|---|---|---|
| | Factory Overhead | | | 4,250 |
| | Factory overhead applied to jobs according to the predetermined overhead rate (850 hrs. × $5). | | | |

To summarize, the factory overhead account is:

1. Increased (debited) for the *actual overhead* costs incurred, as shown earlier for transaction (d) on page 798.
2. Decreased (credited) for the *applied overhead*, as shown above for transaction (e).

The actual and applied overhead usually differ because the actual overhead costs are normally different from the estimated overhead costs. Depending on whether actual overhead is greater or less than applied overhead, the factory overhead account will either have a debit or credit ending balance as follows:

1. If the applied overhead is *less than* the actual overhead incurred, the factory overhead account will have a debit balance. This debit balance is called **underapplied factory overhead** or *underabsorbed factory overhead*.

2. If the applied overhead is *more than* the actual overhead incurred, the factory overhead account will have a credit balance. This credit balance is called **overapplied factory overhead** or *overabsorbed factory overhead*.

The factory overhead account for Legend Guitars shown below illustrates both underapplied and overapplied factory overhead. Specifically, the December 1, 2012, credit balance of $200 represents overapplied factory overhead. In contrast, the December 31, 2012, debit balance of $150 represents underapplied factory overhead.

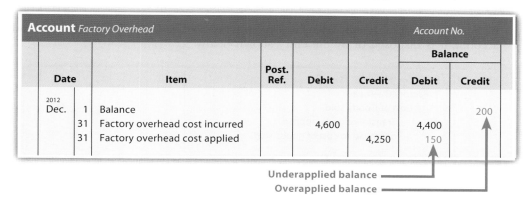

If the balance of factory overhead (either underapplied or overapplied) becomes large, the balance and related overhead rate should be investigated. For example, a large balance could be caused by changes in manufacturing methods. In this case, the factory overhead rate should be revised.

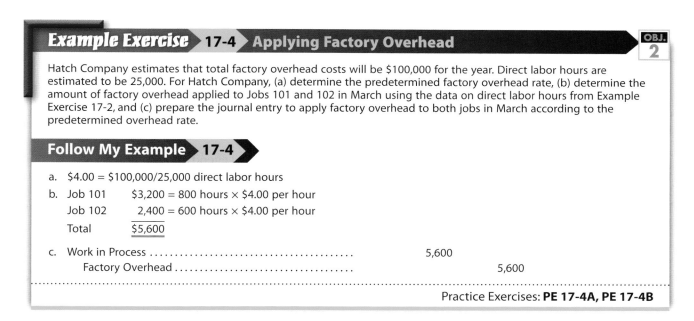

**Example Exercise 17-4 Applying Factory Overhead** OBJ. 2

Hatch Company estimates that total factory overhead costs will be $100,000 for the year. Direct labor hours are estimated to be 25,000. For Hatch Company, (a) determine the predetermined factory overhead rate, (b) determine the amount of factory overhead applied to Jobs 101 and 102 in March using the data on direct labor hours from Example Exercise 17-2, and (c) prepare the journal entry to apply factory overhead to both jobs in March according to the predetermined overhead rate.

**Follow My Example 17-4**

a. $4.00 = $100,000/25,000 direct labor hours
b. Job 101    $3,200 = 800 hours × $4.00 per hour
   Job 102     2,400 = 600 hours × $4.00 per hour
   Total      $5,600

c. Work in Process ........................................    5,600
      Factory Overhead ..................................           5,600

Practice Exercises: **PE 17-4A, PE 17-4B**

**Disposal of Factory Overhead Balance** During the year, the balance in the factory overhead account is carried forward and reported as a deferred debit or credit on the monthly (interim) balance sheets. However, any balance in the factory overhead account should not be carried over to the next year. This is because any such balance applies only to operations of the current year.

If the estimates for computing the predetermined overhead rate are reasonably accurate, the ending balance of Factory Overhead should be relatively small. For this reason, the balance of Factory Overhead at the end of the year is disposed of by transferring it to the cost of goods sold account as follows:[2]

1. If there is an ending debit balance (underapplied overhead) in the factory overhead account, it is disposed of by the entry shown below.

| | | | | |
|---|---|---|---|---|
| | Cost of Goods Sold | | XXX | |
| | Factory Overhead | | | XXX |
| | Transfer of underapplied | | | |
| | overhead to cost of goods sold. | | | |

2. If there is an ending credit balance (overapplied overhead) in the factory overhead account, it is disposed of by the entry shown below.

| | | | | |
|---|---|---|---|---|
| | Factory Overhead | | XXX | |
| | Cost of Goods Sold | | | XXX |
| | Transfer of underapplied | | | |
| | overhead to cost of goods sold. | | | |

To illustrate, the journal entry to dispose of Legend Guitars' December 31, 2012, underapplied overhead balance of $150 is as follows:

| | | | | |
|---|---|---|---|---|
| f. | Cost of Goods Sold | | 150 | |
| | Factory Overhead | | | 150 |
| | Closed underapplied factory | | | |
| | overhead to cost of goods sold. | | | |

## Work in Process

During the period, Work in Process is increased (debited) for the following:

1. Direct materials cost
2. Direct labor cost
3. Applied factory overhead cost

To illustrate, the work in process account for Legend Guitars is shown in Exhibit 6. The balance of Work in Process on December 1, 2012 (beginning balance), was $3,000. As shown in Exhibit 6, this balance relates to Job 71, which was the only job in process on this date. During December, Work in Process was debited for the following:

1. Direct materials cost of $13,000 [transaction (b)] based on materials requisitions.
2. Direct labor cost of $11,000 [transaction (c)] based on time tickets.
3. Applied factory overhead of $4,250 [transaction (e)] based on the predetermined overhead rate of $5 per direct labor hour.

The preceding Work in Process debits are supported by the detail postings to job cost sheets for Jobs 71 and 72, as shown in Exhibit 6.

---

2 An ending balance in the factory overhead account may also be allocated among the work in process, finished goods, and cost of goods sold accounts. This brings these accounts into agreement with the actual costs incurred. This approach is rarely used and is only required for large ending balances in the factory overhead account. For this reason, it will not be used in this text.

**Job Cost Sheets**

**EXHIBIT 6**

**Job Cost Sheets and the Work in Process Controlling Account**

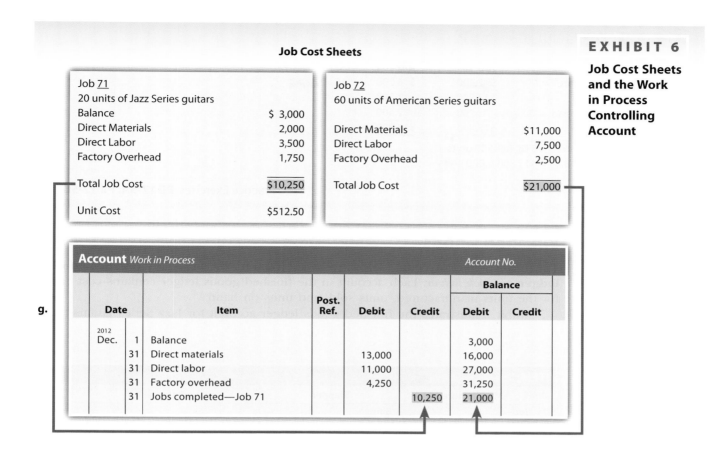

During December, Job 71 was completed. Upon completion, the product costs (direct materials, direct labor, factory overhead) are totaled. This total is divided by the number of units produced to determine the cost per unit. Thus, the 20 Jazz Series guitars produced as Job 71 cost $512.50 ($10,250/20) per guitar.

After completion, Job 71 is transferred from Work in Process to Finished Goods by the following entry:

| | | | | | |
|---|---|---|---|---|---|
| g. | Finished Goods | | | 10,250 | |
| | Work in Process | | | | 10,250 |
| | Job 71 completed in December. | | | | |

Job 72 was started in December, but was not completed by December 31, 2012. Thus, Job 72 is still part of work in process on December 31, 2012. As shown in Exhibit 6, the balance of the job cost sheet for Job 72 ($21,000) is also the December 31, 2012, balance of Work in Process.

**Example Exercise** **17-5** **Job Costs**

**OBJ. 2**

At the end of March, Hatch Company had completed Jobs 101 and 102. Job 101 is for 500 units, and Job 102 is for 1,000 units. Using the data from Example Exercises 17-1, 17-2, and 17-4, determine (a) the balance on the job cost sheets for Jobs 101 and 102 at the end of March and (b) the cost per unit for Jobs 101 and 102 at the end of March.

**Follow My Example** 17-5

a.

| | **Job 101** | **Job 102** |
|---|---|---|
| Direct materials | $ 2,400 | $ 4,200 |
| Direct labor | 12,800 | 7,200 |
| Factory overhead | 3,200 | 2,400 |
| Total costs | $18,400 | $13,800 |

b.  Job 101    $36.80 = $18,400/500 units
    Job 102    $13.80 = $13,800/1,000 units

Practice Exercises: **PE 17-5A, PE 17-5B**

## Finished Goods

The finished goods account is a controlling account for the subsidiary **finished goods ledger** or *stock ledger*. Each account in the finished goods ledger contains cost data for the units manufactured, units sold, and units on hand.

Exhibit 7 illustrates the finished goods ledger account for Jazz Series guitars.

**EXHIBIT 7**

**Finished Goods Ledger Account**

**ITEM:** *Jazz Series guitars*

| **Manufactured** | | | **Shipped** | | | **Balance** | | | |
|---|---|---|---|---|---|---|---|---|---|
| Job Order No. | Quantity | Amount | Ship Order No. | Quantity | Amount | Date | Quantity | Amount | Unit Cost |
| | | | | | | Dec. 1 | 40 | $20,000 | $500.00 |
| | | | 643 | 40 | $20,000 | 9 | — | — | — |
| 71 | 20 | $10,250 | | | | 31 | 20 | 10,250 | 512.50 |

Exhibit 7 indicates that there were 40 Jazz Series guitars on hand on December 1, 2012. During the month, 20 additional Jazz guitars were completed and transferred to Finished Goods from the completion of Job 71. In addition, the beginning inventory of 40 Jazz guitars were sold during the month.

## Sales and Cost of Goods Sold

During December, Legend Guitars sold 40 Jazz Series guitars for $850 each, generating total sales of $34,000 ($850 × 40 guitars). Exhibit 7 indicates that the cost of these guitars was $500 per guitar or a total cost of $20,000 ($500 × 40 guitars). The entries to record the sale and related cost of goods sold are as follows:

| | | | | |
|---|---|---|---|---|
| h. | Accounts Receivable | | 34,000 | |
| | Sales | | | 34,000 |
| | Revenue received from guitars sold on account. | | | |

| | | | | |
|---|---|---|---|---|
| i. | Cost of Goods Sold | | 20,000 | |
| | Finished Goods | | | 20,000 |
| | Cost of 40 Jazz Series guitars sold. | | | |

In a job order cost accounting system, the preparation of a statement of cost of goods manufactured, which was discussed in Chapter 16, is not necessary. This is because job order costing uses the perpetual inventory system and, thus, the cost of goods sold can be directly determined from the finished goods ledger as illustrated in Exhibit 7.

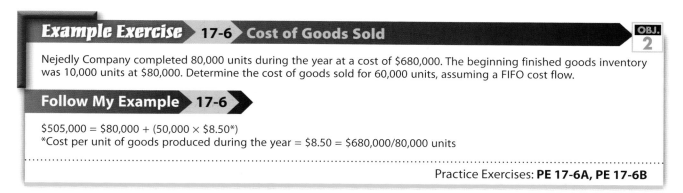

**Example Exercise** 17-6 **Cost of Goods Sold**   OBJ. 2

Nejedly Company completed 80,000 units during the year at a cost of $680,000. The beginning finished goods inventory was 10,000 units at $80,000. Determine the cost of goods sold for 60,000 units, assuming a FIFO cost flow.

**Follow My Example** 17-6

$505,000 = $80,000 + (50,000 × $8.50*)
*Cost per unit of goods produced during the year = $8.50 = $680,000/80,000 units

Practice Exercises: **PE 17-6A, PE 17-6B**

## Period Costs

Period costs are used in generating revenue during the current period, but are not involved in the manufacturing process. As discussed in Chapter 16, *period costs* are recorded as expenses of the current period as either selling or administrative expenses.

Selling expenses are incurred in marketing the product and delivering sold products to customers. Administrative expenses are incurred in managing the company, but are not related to the manufacturing or selling functions. During December, Legend Guitars recorded the following selling and administrative expenses:

| | | | | | |
|---|---|---|---|---|---|
| j. | Sales Salaries Expense | | 2,000 | | |
| | Office Salaries Expense | | 1,500 | | |
| | Salaries Payable | | | 3,500 | |
| | Recorded December period costs. | | | | |

## Summary of Cost Flows for Legend Guitars

Exhibit 8 shows the cost flows through the manufacturing accounts of Legend Guitars for December.

In addition, summary details of the following subsidiary ledgers are shown:

1. *Materials Ledger*—the subsidiary ledger for Materials.
2. *Job Cost Sheets*—the subsidiary ledger for Work in Process.
3. *Finished Goods Ledger*—the subsidiary ledger for Finished Goods.

Entries in the accounts shown in Exhibit 8 are identified by letters. These letters refer to the journal entries described and illustrated in the chapter. Entries (h) and (j) are not shown because they do not involve a flow of manufacturing costs.

As shown in Exhibit 8, the balances of Materials, Work in Process, and Finished Goods are supported by their subsidiary ledgers. These balances are as follows:

| Controlling Account | Balance and Total of Related Subsidiary Ledger |
|---|---|
| Materials | $ 3,500 |
| Work in Process | 21,000 |
| Finished Goods | 10,250 |

The income statement for Legend Guitars is shown in Exhibit 9.

**EXHIBIT 8** **Flow of Manufacturing Costs for Legend Guitars**

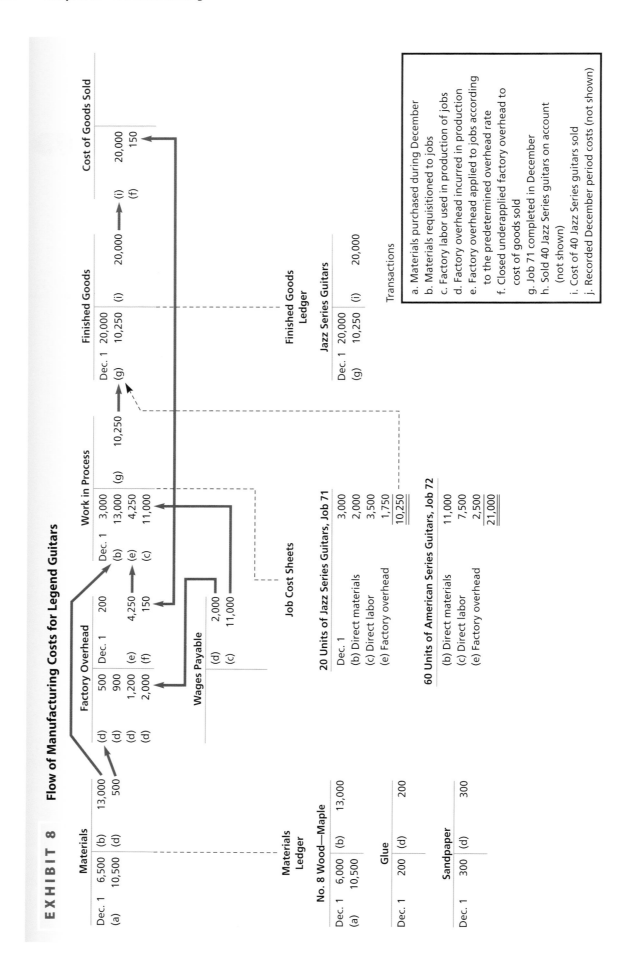

**Materials**

| | | | |
|---|---|---|---|
| Dec. 1 | 6,500 | (b) | 13,000 |
| (a) | 10,500 | (d) | 500 |

**Materials Ledger**

**No. 8 Wood—Maple**

| | | | |
|---|---|---|---|
| Dec. 1 | 6,000 | (b) | 13,000 |
| (a) | 10,500 | | |

**Glue**

| | | | |
|---|---|---|---|
| Dec. 1 | 200 | (d) | 200 |

**Sandpaper**

| | | | |
|---|---|---|---|
| Dec. 1 | 300 | (d) | 300 |

**Factory Overhead**

| | | | |
|---|---|---|---|
| | Dec. 1 | 500 | |
| (d) | | 500 | |
| (d) | | 900 | |
| (d) | | 1,200 | |
| (d) | | 2,000 | |
| (e) | 4,250 | | |
| (f) | 150 | | |

**Wages Payable**

| | | |
|---|---|---|
| (d) | 2,000 | |
| (c) | 11,000 | |

**Work in Process**

| | | | |
|---|---|---|---|
| Dec. 1 | 3,000 | (g) | 10,250 |
| (b) | 13,000 | | |
| (e) | 4,250 | | |
| (c) | 11,000 | | |

**Job Cost Sheets**

**20 Units of Jazz Series Guitars, Job 71**

| | |
|---|---|
| Dec. 1 | 3,000 |
| (b) Direct materials | 2,000 |
| (c) Direct labor | 3,500 |
| (e) Factory overhead | 1,750 |
| | 10,250 |

**60 Units of American Series Guitars, Job 72**

| | |
|---|---|
| (b) Direct materials | 11,000 |
| (c) Direct labor | 7,500 |
| (e) Factory overhead | 2,500 |
| | 21,000 |

**Finished Goods**

| | | | |
|---|---|---|---|
| Dec. 1 | 20,000 | (i) | 20,000 |
| (g) | 10,250 | | |

**Finished Goods Ledger**

**Jazz Series Guitars**

| | | | |
|---|---|---|---|
| Dec. 1 | 20,000 | (i) | 20,000 |
| (g) | 10,250 | | |

**Cost of Goods Sold**

| | |
|---|---|
| (i) | 20,000 |
| (f) | 150 |

**Transactions**

a. Materials purchased during December
b. Materials requisitioned to jobs
c. Factory labor used in production of jobs
d. Factory overhead incurred in production
e. Factory overhead applied to jobs according to the predetermined overhead rate
f. Closed underapplied factory overhead to cost of goods sold
g. Job 71 completed in December
h. Sold 40 Jazz Series guitars on account (not shown)
i. Cost of 40 Jazz Series guitars sold
j. Recorded December period costs (not shown)

**EXHIBIT 9**

**Income Statement of Legend Guitars**

**Legend Guitars**
**Income Statement**
**For the Month Ended December 31, 2012**

| | | |
|---|---|---|
| Sales | | $34,000 |
| Cost of goods sold | | 20,150* |
| Gross profit | | $13,850 |
| Selling and administrative expenses: | | |
| Sales salaries expense | $2,000 | |
| Office salaries expense | 1,500 | |
| Total selling and administrative expenses | | 3,500 |
| Income from operations | | $10,350 |

*$20,150 = ($500 × 40 guitars) + $150 underapplied factory overhead

# Job Order Costing for Decision Making

**OBJ. 3** Describe the use of job order cost information for decision making.

A job order cost accounting system accumulates and records product costs by jobs. The resulting total and unit product costs can be compared to similar jobs, compared over time, or compared to expected costs. In this way, a job order cost system can be used by managers for cost evaluation and control.

To illustrate, Exhibit 10 shows the direct materials used for Jobs 54 and 63 for Legend Guitars. The wood used in manufacturing guitars is measured in board feet. Since Jobs 54 and 63 produced the same type and number of guitars, the direct materials cost per unit should be about the same. However, the materials cost per guitar for Job 54 is $100, while for Job 63 it is $125. Thus, the materials costs are significantly more for Job 63.

The job cost sheets shown in Exhibit 10 can be analyzed for possible reasons for the increased materials cost for Job 63. Since the materials price did not change ($10 per board foot), the increased materials cost must be related to wood consumption.

Comparing wood consumed for Jobs 54 and 63 shows that 400 board feet were used in Job 54 to produce 40 guitars. In contrast, Job 63 used 500 board feet to

**EXHIBIT 10**

**Comparing Data from Job Cost Sheets**

**Job 54**
Item: 40 Jazz Series guitars

| | Materials Quantity (board feet) | Materials Price | Materials Amount |
|---|---|---|---|
| Direct materials: | | | |
| No. 8 Wood—Maple | 400 | $10.00 | $4,000 |
| Direct materials per guitar | | | $ 100* |

*$4,000/40

**Job 63**
Item: 40 Jazz Series guitars

| | Materials Quantity (board feet) | Materials Price | Materials Amount |
|---|---|---|---|
| Direct materials: | | | |
| No. 8 Wood—Maple | 500 | $10.00 | $5,000 |
| Direct materials per guitar | | | $ 125* |

*$5,000/40

Major electric utilities such as Tennessee Valley Authority, Consolidated Edison Inc., and Pacific Gas and Electric Company use job order accounting to control the costs associated with major repairs and overhauls that occur during maintenance shutdowns.

**OBJ. 4** Describe the flow of costs for a service business that uses a job order cost accounting system.

produce the same number of guitars. Thus, an investigation should be undertaken to determine the cause of the extra 100 board feet used for Job 63. Possible explanations could include the following:

1. A new employee, who was not properly trained, cut the wood for Job 63. As a result, there was excess waste and scrap.
2. The wood used for Job 63 was purchased from a new supplier. The wood was of poor quality, which created excessive waste and scrap.
3. The cutting tools needed repair and were not properly maintained. As a result, the wood was miscut, which created excessive waste and scrap.
4. The instructions attached to the job were incorrect. The wood was cut according to the instructions. The incorrect instructions were discovered later in assembly. As a result, the wood had to be recut and the initial cuttings scrapped.

# Job Order Cost Systems for Professional Service Businesses

A job order cost accounting system may be used for a professional service business. For example, an advertising agency, an attorney, and a physician provide services to individual customers, clients, or patients. In such cases, the customer, client, or patient can be viewed as a job for which costs are accumulated and reported.

The primary product costs for a service business are direct labor and overhead costs. Any materials or supplies used in rendering services are normally insignificant. As a result, materials and supply costs are included as part of the overhead cost.

Like a manufacturing business, direct labor and overhead costs of rendering services to clients are accumulated in a work in process account. *Work in Process* is supported by a cost ledger with a job cost sheet for each client.

When a job is completed and the client is billed, the costs are transferred to a cost of services account. *Cost of Services* is similar to the cost of merchandise sold account for a merchandising business or the cost of goods sold account for a manufacturing business. A finished goods account and related finished goods ledger are not necessary. This is because the revenues for the services are recorded only after the services are provided.

The flow of costs through a service business using a job order cost accounting system is shown in Exhibit 11.

In practice, other considerations unique to service businesses may need to be considered. For example, a service business may bill clients on a weekly or monthly basis rather than when a job is completed. In such cases, a portion of the costs related to each billing is transferred from the work in process account to the cost of services account. A service business may also bill clients for services in advance, which would be accounted for as deferred revenue until the services are completed.

**EXHIBIT 11** **Flow of Costs Through a Service Business**

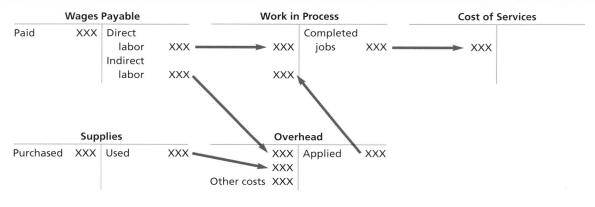

# BusinessConnection

## MAKING MONEY IN THE MOVIE BUSINESS

Movie making is a high risk venture. The movie must be produced and marketed before the first dollar is received from the box office. If the movie is a hit, then all is well; but if the movie is a bomb, money will be lost. This is termed a "blockbuster" business strategy and is common in businesses that have large up-front costs in the face of uncertain follow-up revenues.

The profitability of a movie depends on its revenue and cost. A movie's cost is determined using job order costing; however, how costs are assigned to a movie is often complex and may be subject to disagreement. For example, studios often negotiate payments to producers and actors based on a percentage of the film's gross revenues. This is termed "contingent compensation." As movies become hits, compensation costs increase in proportion to the movie's revenues.

As the dollars involved get bigger, disagreements often develop over the amount of contingent compensation. For example, the producer of the 2002 hit movie *Chicago* sued Miramax Film Corp. for failing to include foreign receipts and DVD sales in the revenue that was used to determine his payments. The controversial nature of contingent compensation is illustrated by the suit's claim that the accounting for contingent compensation leads to confusing and meaningless results.

# At a Glance 17

## OBJ. 1 Describe cost accounting systems used by manufacturing businesses.

**Key Points**   A cost accounting system accumulates product costs. The two primary cost accounting systems are job order and process cost systems. Job order cost systems accumulate costs for each quantity of product that passes through the factory. Process cost systems accumulate costs for each department or process within the factory.

| Learning Outcomes | Example Exercises | Practice Exercises |
|---|---|---|
| • Describe a cost accounting system. | | |
| • Describe a job order cost system. | | |
| • Describe a process cost system. | | |

## OBJ. 2 Describe and illustrate a job order cost accounting system.

**Key Points**   A job order cost system accumulates costs for each quantity of product, or "job," that passes through the factory. Direct materials, direct labor, and factory overhead are accumulated on the job cost sheet, which is the subsidiary cost ledger for each job. Direct materials and direct labor are assigned to individual jobs based on the quantity used. Factory overhead costs are assigned to each job based on an activity base that reflects the use of factory overhead costs.

| Learning Outcomes | Example Exercises | Practice Exercises |
|---|---|---|
| • Describe the flow of materials and how materials costs are assigned. | | |
| • Prepare the journal entry to record materials used in production. | EE17-1 | PE17-1A, 17-1B |
| • Describe how factory labor hours are recorded and how labor costs are assigned. | | |

| Learning Outcomes | Example Exercises | Practice Exercises |
|---|---|---|
| • Prepare the journal entry to record factory labor used in production. | EE17-2 | PE17-2A, 17-2B |
| • Describe and illustrate how factory overhead costs are accumulated and assigned. | EE17-3 EE17-4 | PE17-3A, 17-3B PE17-4A, 17-4B |
| • Compute the predetermined overhead rate. | EE17-4 | PE17-4A, 17-4B |
| • Describe and illustrate how to dispose of the balance in the factory overhead account. | | |
| • Describe and illustrate how costs are accumulated for work in process and finished goods inventory. | EE17-5 | PE17-5A, 17-5B |
| • Describe how costs are assigned to cost of goods sold. | EE17-6 | PE17-6A, 17-6B |
| • Describe and illustrate the flow of costs. | | |

**OBJ. 3**

### Describe the use of job order cost information for decision making.

**Key Points** Job order cost systems can be used to evaluate cost performance. Unit costs can be compared over time to determine if product costs are staying within expected ranges.

| Learning Outcomes | Example Exercises | Practice Exercises |
|---|---|---|
| • Describe and illustrate how job cost sheets can be used to investigate possible reasons for increased product costs. | | |

**OBJ. 4**

### Describe the flow of costs for a service business that uses a job order cost accounting system.

**Key Points** Job order cost accounting systems can be used by service businesses to plan and control operations. Since the product is a service, the focus is on direct labor and overhead costs. The costs of providing a service are accumulated in a work in process account and transferred to a cost of services account upon completion.

| Learning Outcomes | Example Exercises | Practice Exercises |
|---|---|---|
| • Describe how service businesses use a job order cost system. | | |

## Key Terms

activity base (798)

activity-based costing (799)

cost accounting systems (792)

cost allocation (798)

finished goods ledger (804)

job cost sheets (795)

job order cost system (792)

materials ledger (793)

materials requisition (795)

overapplied factory overhead (801)

predetermined factory
overhead rate (798)

process cost system (792)

receiving report (795)

time tickets (796)

underapplied factory
overhead (801)

## Illustrative Problem

Wildwing Entertainment, Inc., specializes in producing and packaging digital video discs (DVDs) for the video entertainment industry. Wildwing uses a job order cost system. The following data summarize the operations related to production for March, the first month of operations:

a. Materials purchased on account, $15,500.

b. Materials requisitioned and labor used:

|  | Materials | Factory Labor |
| --- | --- | --- |
| Job No. 100 | $2,650 | $1,770 |
| Job No. 101 | 1,240 | 650 |
| Job No. 102 | 980 | 420 |
| Job No. 103 | 3,420 | 1,900 |
| Job No. 104 | 1,000 | 500 |
| Job No. 105 | 2,100 | 1,760 |
| For general factory use | 450 | 650 |

c. Factory overhead costs incurred on account, $2,700.

d. Depreciation of machinery, $1,750.

e. Factory overhead is applied at a rate of 70% of direct labor cost.

f. Jobs completed: Nos. 100, 101, 102, 104.

g. Jobs 100, 101, and 102 were shipped, and customers were billed for $8,100, $3,800, and $3,500, respectively.

### Instructions

1. Journalize the entries to record the transactions identified above.

2. Determine the account balances for Work in Process and Finished Goods.

3. Prepare a schedule of unfinished jobs to support the balance in the work in process account.

4. Prepare a schedule of completed jobs on hand to support the balance in the finished goods account.

## Solution

1. a. Materials                                                    15,500
          Accounts Payable                                         15,500
   b. Work in Process                                              11,390
          Materials                                                11,390
        Work in Process                                   7,000
          Wages Payable                                            7,000
        Factory Overhead                                  1,100
          Materials                                                450
          Wages Payable                                            650
   c. Factory Overhead                                             2,700
          Accounts Payable                                         2,700
   d. Factory Overhead                                             1,750
          Accumulated Depreciation—Machinery                       1,750
   e. Work in Process                                              4,900
          Factory Overhead (70% of $7,000)                         4,900
   f. Finished Goods                                               11,548
          Work in Process                                          11,548

Computation of the cost of jobs finished:

| Job | Direct Materials | Direct Labor | Factory Overhead | Total |
|---|---|---|---|---|
| Job No. 100 | $2,650 | $1,770 | $1,239 | $ 5,659 |
| Job No. 101 | 1,240 | 650 | 455 | 2,345 |
| Job No. 102 | 980 | 420 | 294 | 1,694 |
| Job No. 104 | 1,000 | 500 | 350 | 1,850 |
| | | | | $11,548 |

g. Accounts Receivable                                            15,400
       Sales                                                       15,400
     Cost of Goods Sold                                   9,698
       Finished Goods                                              9,698

Cost of jobs sold computation:

| Job No. 100 | $5,659 |
|---|---|
| Job No. 101 | 2,345 |
| Job No. 102 | 1,694 |
| | $9,698 |

2. Work in Process: $11,742 ($11,390 + $7,000 + $4,900 − $11,548)

   Finished Goods: $1,850 ($11,548 − $9,698)

3.
| **Schedule of Unfinished Jobs** | | | | |
|---|---|---|---|---|
| Job | Direct Materials | Direct Labor | Factory Overhead | Total |
| Job No. 103 | $3,420 | $1,900 | $1,330 | $ 6,650 |
| Job No. 105 | 2,100 | 1,760 | 1,232 | 5,092 |
| Balance of Work in Process, March 31 | | | | $11,742 |

4.
**Schedule of Completed Jobs**

Job No. 104:

| Direct materials | $1,000 |
|---|---|
| Direct labor | 500 |
| Factory overhead | 350 |
| Balance of Finished Goods, March 31 | $1,850 |

## Discussion Questions

1. a. Name two principal types of cost accounting systems.

   b. Which system provides for a separate record of each particular quantity of product that passes through the factory?

   c. Which system accumulates the costs for each department or process within the factory?

2. What kind of firm would use a job order cost system?

3. How does the use of the materials requisition help control the issuance of materials from the storeroom?

4. What document is the source for (a) debiting the accounts in the materials ledger and (b) crediting the accounts in the materials ledger?

5. What is a job cost sheet?

6. a. Differentiate between the clock card and the time ticket.

   b. Why should the total time reported on an employee's time tickets for a payroll period be compared with the time reported on the employee's clock cards for the same period?

7. Discuss how the predetermined factory overhead rate can be used in job order cost accounting to assist management in pricing jobs.

8. a. How is a predetermined factory overhead rate calculated?

   b. Name three common bases used in calculating the rate.

9. a. What is (1) overapplied factory overhead and (2) underapplied factory overhead?

   b. If the factory overhead account has a debit balance, was factory overhead underapplied or overapplied?

   c. If the factory overhead account has a credit balance at the end of the first month of the fiscal year, where will the amount of this balance be reported on the interim balance sheet?

10. Describe how a job order cost system can be used for professional service businesses.

# Practice Exercises

| Learning Objectives | Example Exercises | |
|---|---|---|

**OBJ. 2**  **EE 17-1** *p. 795*

### PE 17-1A  Issuance of materials

On April 8, Darling Company purchased 65,000 units of raw materials at $7 per unit. On April 20, raw materials were requisitioned for production as follows: 26,000 units for Job 50 at $6 per unit and 30,000 units for Job 51 at $7 per unit. Journalize the entry on April 8 to record the purchase and on April 20 to record the requisition from the materials storeroom.

**OBJ. 2**  **EE 17-1** *p. 795*

### PE 17-1B  Issuance of materials

On June 3, Plowers Company purchased 8,000 units of raw materials at $10 per unit. On June 22, raw materials were requisitioned for production as follows: 2,400 units for Job 30 at $8 per unit and 2,600 units for Job 32 at $10 per unit. Journalize the entry on June 3 to record the purchase and on June 22 to record the requisition from the materials storeroom.

**OBJ. 2**  **EE 17-2** *p. 797*

### PE 17-2A  Direct labor costs

During April, Darling Company accumulated 12,000 hours of direct labor costs on Job 50 and 15,000 hours on Job 51. The total direct labor was incurred at a rate of $21.50 per direct labor hour for Job 50 and $24 per direct labor hour for Job 51. Journalize the entry to record the flow of labor costs into production during April.

**OBJ. 2**  **EE 17-2** *p. 797*

### PE 17-2B  Direct labor costs

During June, Plowers Company accumulated 2,400 hours of direct labor costs on Job 30 and 3,000 hours on Job 32. The total direct labor was incurred at a rate of $22 per direct labor hour for Job 30 and $20 per direct labor hour for Job 32. Journalize the entry to record the flow of labor costs into production during June.

**OBJ. 2**  **EE 17-3** *p. 798*

### PE 17-3A  Factory overhead costs

During April, Darling Company incurred factory overhead costs as follows: indirect materials, $30,000; indirect labor, $78,000; utilities cost, $7,000; and factory depreciation, $55,000. Journalize the entry to record the factory overhead incurred during April.

**OBJ. 2**  **EE 17-3** *p. 798*

### PE 17-3B  Factory overhead costs

During June, Plowers Company incurred factory overhead costs as follows: indirect materials, $14,000; indirect labor, $15,000; utilities cost, $6,500; and factory depreciation, $14,500. Journalize the entry to record the factory overhead incurred during June.

**OBJ. 2**  **EE 17-4** *p. 801*

### PE 17-4A  Applying factory overhead

Darling Company estimates that total factory overhead costs will be $750,000 for the year. Direct labor hours are estimated to be 300,000. For Darling Company, (a) determine the predetermined factory overhead rate, (b) determine the amount of factory overhead applied to Jobs 50 and 51 in April using the data on direct labor hours from Practice Exercise 17-2A, and (c) prepare the journal entry to apply factory overhead to both jobs in April according to the predetermined overhead rate.

**OBJ. 2**    **EE 17-4** *p. 801*

### PE 17-4B   Applying factory overhead

Plowers Company estimates that total factory overhead costs will be $480,000 for the year. Direct labor hours are estimated to be 60,000. For Plowers Company, (a) determine the predetermined factory overhead rate, (b) determine the amount of factory overhead applied to Jobs 30 and 32 in June using the data on direct labor hours from Practice Exercise 17-2B, and (c) prepare the journal entry to apply factory overhead to both jobs in June according to the predetermined overhead rate.

**OBJ. 2**    **EE 17-5** *p. 803*

### PE 17-5A   Job costs

At the end of April, Darling Company had completed Jobs 50 and 51. Job 50 is for 10,000 units, and Job 51 is for 12,500 units. Using the data from Practice Exercises 17-1A, 17-2A, and 17-4A, determine (a) the balance on the job cost sheets for Jobs 50 and 51 at the end of April and (b) the cost per unit for Jobs 50 and 51 at the end of April.

**OBJ. 2**    **EE 17-5** *p. 803*

### PE 17-5B   Job costs

At the end of June, Plowers Company had completed Jobs 30 and 32. Job 30 is for 6,000 units, and Job 32 is for 6,875 units. Using the data from Practice Exercises 17-1B, 17-2B, and 17-4B, determine (a) the balance on the job cost sheets for Jobs 30 and 32 at the end of June and (b) the cost per unit for Jobs 30 and 32 at the end of June.

**OBJ. 2**    **EE 17-6** *p. 805*

### PE 17-6A   Cost of goods sold

Curl Company completed 425,000 units during the year at a cost of $20,187,500. The beginning finished goods inventory was 35,000 units at $1,470,000. Determine the cost of goods sold for 435,000 units, assuming a FIFO cost flow.

**OBJ. 2**    **EE 17-6** *p. 805*

### PE 17-6B   Cost of goods sold

Skeleton Company completed 155,000 units during the year at a cost of $2,418,000. The beginning finished goods inventory was 15,000 units at $225,000. Determine the cost of goods sold for 160,000 units, assuming a FIFO cost flow.

# Exercises

**OBJ. 2**

### EX 17-1   Transactions in a job order cost system

Five selected transactions for the current month are indicated by letters in the following T accounts in a job order cost accounting system:

| Materials | | Work in Process | |
|---|---|---|---|
| | (a) | (a) | (d) |
| | | (b) | |
| | | (c) | |

| Wages Payable | | Finished Goods | |
|---|---|---|---|
| | (b) | (d) | (e) |

| Factory Overhead | | Cost of Goods Sold | |
|---|---|---|---|
| (a) | (c) | (e) | |
| (b) | | | |

Describe each of the five transactions.

OBJ. 2

✔ c. $883,000

## EX 17-2   Cost flow relationships

The following information is available for the first month of operations of Icahn Inc., a manufacturer of art and craft items:

| | |
|---|---:|
| Sales | $1,680,000 |
| Gross profit | 450,000 |
| Indirect labor | 150,000 |
| Indirect materials | 65,000 |
| Other factory overhead | 30,000 |
| Materials purchased | 850,000 |
| Total manufacturing costs for the period | 1,850,000 |
| Materials inventory, end of period | 63,000 |

Using the above information, determine the following missing amounts:

a.  Cost of goods sold

b.  Direct materials cost

c.  Direct labor cost

OBJ. 2

✔ b. $1,960

## EX 17-3   Cost of materials issuances under the FIFO method

An incomplete subsidiary ledger of wire cable for June is as follows:

| RECEIVED | | | ISSUED | | | BALANCE | | | |
|---|---|---|---|---|---|---|---|---|---|
| Receiving Report Number | Quantity | Unit Price | Materials Requisition Number | Quantity | Amount | Date | Quantity | Unit Price | Amount |
| | | | | | | June  1 | 350 | $10.00 | $3,500 |
| 26 | 250 | $12.00 | | | | June  2 | ___ | ___ | ___ |
| | | | 103 | 380 | | June  6 | ___ | ___ | ___ |
| 32 | 160 | 14.00 | | | | June 12 | ___ | ___ | ___ |
| | | | 111 | 240 | | June 21 | ___ | ___ | ___ |

a.  Complete the materials issuances and balances for the wire cable subsidiary ledger under FIFO.

b.  Determine the balance of wire cable at the end of June.

c.  Journalize the summary entry to transfer materials to work in process.

d.  ━━━► Explain how the materials ledger might be used as an aid in maintaining inventory quantities on hand.

OBJ. 2

## EX 17-4   Entry for issuing materials

Materials issued for the current month are as follows:

| Requisition No. | Material | Job No. | Amount |
|---|---|---|---:|
| 201 | Steel | 110 | $30,500 |
| 202 | Plastic | 112 | 23,500 |
| 203 | Glue | Indirect | 2,000 |
| 204 | Rubber | 123 | 1,750 |
| 205 | Aluminum | 128 | 55,000 |

Journalize the entry to record the issuance of materials.

OBJ. 2

✔ c. fabric, $53,200

## EX 17-5   Entries for materials

Gorman Furniture Company manufactures furniture. Gorman uses a job order cost system. Balances on April 1 from the materials ledger are as follows:

| | |
|---|---:|
| Fabric | $40,000 |
| Polyester filling | 12,000 |
| Lumber | 89,500 |
| Glue | 3,900 |

The materials purchased during April are summarized from the receiving reports as follows:

| | |
|---|---|
| Fabric | $201,600 |
| Polyester filling | 280,000 |
| Lumber | 550,000 |
| Glue | 19,500 |

Materials were requisitioned to individual jobs as follows:

| | Fabric | Polyester Filling | Lumber | Glue | Total |
|---|---|---|---|---|---|
| Job 101 | $ 76,000 | $ 96,000 | $256,000 | | $ 428,000 |
| Job 102 | 58,400 | 86,400 | 224,000 | | 368,800 |
| Job 103 | 54,000 | 70,500 | 125,000 | | 249,500 |
| Factory overhead—indirect materials | | | | $20,800 | 20,800 |
| Total | $188,400 | $252,900 | $605,000 | $20,800 | $1,067,100 |

The glue is not a significant cost, so it is treated as indirect materials (factory overhead).

a. Journalize the entry to record the purchase of materials in April.

b. Journalize the entry to record the requisition of materials in April.

c. Determine the April 30 balances that would be shown in the materials ledger accounts.

OBJ. 2

## EX 17-6   Entry for factory labor costs

A summary of the time tickets for the current month follows:

| Job No. | Amount | Job No. | Amount |
|---|---|---|---|
| 301 | $ 3,200 | Indirect | $ 4,500 |
| 302 | 2,450 | 312 | 3,450 |
| 304 | 3,875 | 314 | 3,760 |
| 306 | 14,500 | 315 | 12,500 |

Journalize the entry to record the factory labor costs.

OBJ. 2

## EX 17-7   Entry for factory labor costs

The weekly time tickets indicate the following distribution of labor hours for three direct labor employees:

| | Hours | | | |
|---|---|---|---|---|
| | Job 301 | Job 302 | Job 303 | Process Improvement |
| Ken Thain | 13 | 13 | 10 | 4 |
| Dick Lewis | 12 | 13 | 11 | 4 |
| John Fuld | 8 | 15 | 12 | 5 |

The direct labor rate earned per hour by the three employees is as follows:

| | |
|---|---|
| Ken Thain | $30.00 |
| Dick Lewis | 34.00 |
| John Fuld | 25.00 |

The process improvement category includes training, quality improvement, housekeeping, and other indirect tasks.

a. Journalize the entry to record the factory labor costs for the week.

b. Assume that Jobs 301 and 302 were completed but not sold during the week and that Job 303 remained incomplete at the end of the week. How would the direct labor costs for all three jobs be reflected on the financial statements at the end of the week?

OBJ. 2

### EX 17-8   Entries for direct labor and factory overhead

Kraus Industries Inc. manufactures recreational vehicles. Kraus uses a job order cost system. The time tickets from July jobs are summarized below.

| | |
|---|---|
| Job 501 | $4,200 |
| Job 502 | 3,200 |
| Job 503 | 2,870 |
| Job 504 | 3,650 |
| Factory supervision | 2,450 |

Factory overhead is applied to jobs on the basis of a predetermined overhead rate of $12 per direct labor hour. The direct labor rate is $30 per hour.

a. Journalize the entry to record the factory labor costs.

b. Journalize the entry to apply factory overhead to production for July.

OBJ. 2

✔ b. $38.00 per
direct labor hour

### EX 17-9   Factory overhead rates, entries, and account balance

Bryson Company operates two factories. The company applies factory overhead to jobs on the basis of machine hours in Factory 1 and on the basis of direct labor hours in Factory 2. Estimated factory overhead costs, direct labor hours, and machine hours are as follows:

| | Factory 1 | Factory 2 |
|---|---|---|
| Estimated factory overhead cost for fiscal year beginning November 1 | $660,000 | $798,000 |
| Estimated direct labor hours for year | | 21,000 |
| Estimated machine hours for year | 30,000 | |
| Actual factory overhead costs for November | $53,200 | $72,800 |
| Actual direct labor hours for November | | 2,000 |
| Actual machine hours for November | 2,184 | |

a. Determine the factory overhead rate for Factory 1.

b. Determine the factory overhead rate for Factory 2.

c. Journalize the entries to apply factory overhead to production in each factory for November.

d. Determine the balances of the factory accounts for each factory as of November 30, and indicate whether the amounts represent overapplied or underapplied factory overhead.

OBJ. 2

### EX 17-10   Predetermined factory overhead rate

Pierpont Engine Shop uses a job order cost system to determine the cost of performing engine repair work. Estimated costs and expenses for the coming period are as follows:

| | |
|---|---|
| Engine parts | $  700,000 |
| Shop direct labor | 520,000 |
| Shop and repair equipment depreciation | 38,000 |
| Shop supervisor salaries | 100,000 |
| Shop property tax | 18,000 |
| Shop supplies | 13,000 |
| Advertising expense | 14,240 |
| Administrative office salaries | 60,000 |
| Administrative office depreciation expense | 8,000 |
| Total costs and expenses | $1,471,240 |

The average shop direct labor rate is $20 per hour.

Determine the predetermined shop overhead rate per direct labor hour.

OBJ. 2

✔ a. $210 per hour

### EX 17-11   Predetermined factory overhead rate

Barley Medical Center has a single operating room that is used by local physicians to perform surgical procedures. The cost of using the operating room is accumulated by each patient procedure and includes the direct materials costs (drugs and medical devices), physician surgical time, and operating room overhead. On January 1 of the current year, the annual operating room overhead is estimated to be:

| | |
|---|---|
| Disposable supplies | $210,000 |
| Depreciation expense | 32,000 |
| Utilities | 16,000 |
| Nurse salaries | 248,000 |
| Technician wages | 82,000 |
| Total operating room overhead | $588,000 |

The overhead costs will be assigned to procedures based on the number of surgical room hours. Barley Medical Center expects to use the operating room an average of eight hours per day, seven days per week. In addition, the operating room will be shut down two weeks per year for general repairs.

a. Determine the predetermined operating room overhead rate for the year.

b. Dan Baliga had a four-hour procedure on January 15. How much operating room overhead would be charged to his procedure, using the rate determined in part (a)?

c. During January, the operating room was used 196 hours. The actual overhead costs incurred for January were $40,000. Determine the overhead under- or overapplied for the period.

OBJ. 2

✔ b. $23,100

### EX 17-12  Entry for jobs completed; cost of unfinished jobs

The following account appears in the ledger after only part of the postings have been completed for March:

| Work in Process | |
|---|---|
| Balance, March 1 | $ 18,000 |
| Direct materials | 122,500 |
| Direct labor | 145,000 |
| Factory overhead | 80,000 |

Jobs finished during March are summarized as follows:

| | | | |
|---|---|---|---|
| Job 320 | $72,400 | Job 327 | $ 46,200 |
| Job 326 | 79,200 | Job 350 | 144,600 |

a. Journalize the entry to record the jobs completed.

b. Determine the cost of the unfinished jobs at March 31.

OBJ. 2

✔ d. $29,305

### EX 17-13  Entries for factory costs and jobs completed

Cox Publishing Inc. began printing operations on August 1. Jobs 101 and 102 were completed during the month, and all costs applicable to them were recorded on the related cost sheets. Jobs 103 and 104 are still in process at the end of the month, and all applicable costs except factory overhead have been recorded on the related cost sheets. In addition to the materials and labor charged directly to the jobs, $1,000 of indirect materials and $12,000 of indirect labor were used during the month. The cost sheets for the four jobs entering production during the month are as follows, in summary form:

| Job 101 | | Job 102 | |
|---|---|---|---|
| Direct materials | 10,300 | Direct materials | 4,830 |
| Direct labor | 4,000 | Direct labor | 4,100 |
| Factory overhead | 3,000 | Factory overhead | 3,075 |
| Total | 17,300 | Total | 12,005 |

| Job 103 | | Job 104 | |
|---|---|---|---|
| Direct materials | 14,500 | Direct materials | 2,920 |
| Direct labor | 4,320 | Direct labor | 580 |
| Factory overhead | | Factory overhead | |

Journalize the summary entry to record each of the following operations for August (one entry for each operation):

a. Direct and indirect materials used.

b. Direct and indirect labor used.

c. Factory overhead applied to all four jobs (a single overhead rate is used based on direct labor cost).

d. Completion of Jobs 101 and 102.

---

**OBJ. 2**

✔ a. Income from operations, $151,800

**EX 17-14   Financial statements of a manufacturing firm**

The following events took place for Fed Inc. during October 2012, the first month of operations as a producer of road bikes:

• Purchased $427,000 of materials.

• Used $367,500 of direct materials in production.

• Incurred $315,000 of direct labor wages.

• Applied factory overhead at a rate of 80% of direct labor cost.

• Transferred $892,500 of work in process to finished goods.

• Sold goods with a cost of $848,750.

• Sold goods for $1,500,000.

• Incurred $367,500 of selling expenses.

• Incurred $131,950 of administrative expenses.

a. Prepare the October income statement for Fed. Assume that Fed uses the perpetual inventory method.

b. Determine the inventory balances at the end of the first month of operations.

---

**OBJ. 3**

**EX 17-15   Decision making with job order costs**

Moss Manufacturing Inc. is a job shop. The management of Moss Manufacturing uses the cost information from the job sheets to assess their cost performance. Information on the total cost, product type, and quantity of items produced is as follows:

| Date | Job No. | Product | Quantity | Amount |
|---|---|---|---|---|
| Jan. 2 | 1 | XKR1 | 300 | $ 6,600 |
| Jan. 15 | 26 | M-Z4 | 1,300 | 11,700 |
| Feb. 3 | 34 | M-Z4 | 1,100 | 14,300 |
| Mar. 7 | 44 | XKR1 | 460 | 7,360 |
| Mar. 24 | 51 | SL500 | 1,850 | 12,950 |
| May 19 | 62 | SL500 | 2,200 | 19,800 |
| June 12 | 76 | XKR1 | 400 | 4,800 |
| Aug. 18 | 80 | SL500 | 2,750 | 30,250 |
| Sept. 2 | 88 | M-Z4 | 900 | 9,000 |
| Nov. 14 | 96 | XKR1 | 540 | 4,320 |
| Dec. 12 | 102 | SL500 | 2,350 | 32,900 |

a. Develop a graph for *each* product (three graphs), with Job Number (in date order) on the horizontal axis and Unit Cost on the vertical axis. Use this information to determine Moss Manufacturing's cost performance over time for the three products.

b. ➤ What additional information would you require to investigate Moss Manufacturing's cost performance more precisely?

---

**OBJ. 3**

**EX 17-16   Decision making with job order costs**

Lightner Trophies Inc. uses a job order cost system for determining the cost to manufacture award products (plaques and trophies). Among the company's products is an engraved plaque that is awarded to participants who complete a training program at a local business. The company sells the plaque to the local business for $180 each.

Each plaque has a brass plate engraved with the name of the participant. Engraving requires approximately 30 minutes per name. Improperly engraved names must be redone. The plate is screwed to a walnut backboard. This assembly takes approximately 25 minutes per unit. Improper assembly must be redone using a new walnut backboard.

During the first half of the year, the university had two separate executive education classes. The job cost sheets for the two separate jobs indicated the following information:

| Job 101 | April 12 | | |
| --- | --- | --- | --- |
| | **Cost per Unit** | **Units** | **Job Cost** |
| Direct materials: | | | |
| Wood | $30.00/unit | 66 units | $1,980.00 |
| Brass | 25.00/unit | 66 units | 1,650.00 |
| Engraving labor | 75.00/hr. | 33 hrs. | 2,475.00 |
| Assembly labor | 50.00/hr. | 27.5 hrs. | 1,375.00 |
| Factory overhead | 40.00/hr. | 60.5 hrs. | 2,420.00 |
| | | | $9,900.00 |
| Plaques shipped | | | ÷ 66 |
| Cost per plaque | | | $ 150.00 |

| Job 105 | May 6 | | |
| --- | --- | --- | --- |
| | **Cost per Unit** | **Units** | **Job Cost** |
| Direct materials: | | | |
| Wood | $30.00/unit | 36 units | $1,080.00 |
| Brass | 25.00/unit | 36 units | 900.00 |
| Engraving labor | 75.00/hr. | 18 hrs. | 1,350.00 |
| Assembly labor | 50.00/hr. | 15 hrs. | 750.00 |
| Factory overhead | 40.00/hr. | 33 hrs. | 1,320.00 |
| | | | $5,400.00 |
| Plaques shipped | | | ÷ 30 |
| Cost per plaque | | | $ 180.00 |

a. Why did the cost per plaque increase from $150.00 to $180.00?

b. What improvements would you recommend for Lightner Trophies Inc.?

---

OBJ. 4

✔ b. Overapplied, $3,000

**EX 17-17 Job order cost accounting entries for a service business**

The law firm of Yoo and Sachs accumulates costs associated with individual cases, using a job order cost system. The following transactions occurred during July:

July 3. Charged 500 hours of professional (lawyer) time to the Liddy Co. breech of contract suit to prepare for the trial, at a rate of $150 per hour.

9. Reimbursed travel costs to employees for depositions related to the Liddy case, $18,500.

10. Charged 250 hours of professional time for the Liddy trial at a rate of $225 per hour.

15. Received invoice from consultants Mack and Corzine for $55,000 for expert testimony related to the Liddy trial.

22. Applied office overhead at a rate of $60 per professional hour charged to the Liddy case.

31. Paid secretarial and administrative salaries of $32,000 for the month.

31. Used office supplies for the month, $10,000.

31. Paid professional salaries of $126,000 for the month.

31. Billed Liddy $365,000 for successful defense of the case.

a. Provide the journal entries for each of the above transactions.

b. How much office overhead is over- or underapplied?

c. Determine the gross profit on the Liddy case, assuming that over- or underapplied office overhead is closed monthly to cost of services.

OBJ. 4

✔ d. Dr. Cost of Services, $1,225,500

**EX 17-18  Job order cost accounting entries for a service business**

The Pedersen Company provides advertising services for clients across the nation. The Pedersen Company is presently working on four projects, each for a different client. The Pedersen Company accumulates costs for each account (client) on the basis of both direct costs and allocated indirect costs. The direct costs include the charged time of professional personnel and media purchases (air time and ad space). Overhead is allocated to each project as a percentage of media purchases. The predetermined overhead rate is 60% of media purchases.

On March 1, the four advertising projects had the following accumulated costs:

|                  | March 1 Balances |
|------------------|------------------|
| Hedge Bank       | $120,000         |
| Sullivan Airlines| 36,000           |
| Tesley Hotels    | 84,000           |
| Wakelin Beverages| 51,000           |
|                  | $291,000         |

During March, The Pedersen Company incurred the following direct labor and media purchase costs related to preparing advertising for each of the four accounts:

|                  | Direct Labor | Media Purchases |
|------------------|-------------|-----------------|
| Hedge Bank       | $ 84,000    | $315,000        |
| Sullivan Airlines| 37,500      | 277,500         |
| Tesley Hotels    | 165,000     | 202,500         |
| Wakelin Beverages| 187,500     | 151,500         |
| Total            | $474,000    | $946,500        |

At the end of March, both the Hedge Bank and Sullivan Airlines campaigns were completed. The costs of completed campaigns are debited to the cost of services account.

Journalize the summary entry to record each of the following for the month:

a. Direct labor costs

b. Media purchases

c. Overhead applied

d. Completion of Hedge Bank and Sullivan Airlines campaigns

# Problems Series A

OBJ. 2

**PR 17-1A  Entries for costs in a job order cost system**

GIA Co. uses a job order cost system. The following data summarize the operations related to production for August:

a. Materials purchased on account, $660,000.

b. Materials requisitioned, $577,500, of which $73,500 was for general factory use.

c. Factory labor used, $681,500, of which $95,500 was indirect.

d. Other costs incurred on account were for factory overhead, $154,320; selling expenses, $244,440; and administrative expenses, $152,250.

e. Prepaid expenses expired for factory overhead were $30,450; for selling expenses, $25,830; and for administrative expenses, $18,690.

f. Depreciation of office building was $88,200; of office equipment, $45,150; and of factory equipment, $30,450.

g. Factory overhead costs applied to jobs, $375,500.

h. Jobs completed, $871,800.

i. Cost of goods sold, $860,000.

**Instructions**

Journalize the entries to record the summarized operations.

**PR 17-2A   Entries and schedules for unfinished jobs and completed jobs**

Sinatra Industries, Inc., uses a job order cost system. The following data summarize the operations related to production for June 2012, the first month of operations:

a. Materials purchased on account, $32,760.

b. Materials requisitioned and factory labor used:

| Job | Materials | Factory Labor |
| --- | --- | --- |
| 301 | $3,290 | $3,080 |
| 302 | 4,025 | 4,160 |
| 303 | 2,660 | 2,080 |
| 304 | 9,030 | 7,640 |
| 305 | 5,740 | 5,810 |
| 306 | 4,170 | 3,710 |
| For general factory use | 1,200 | 4,550 |

c. Factory overhead costs incurred on account, $6,300.

d. Depreciation of machinery and equipment, $2,200.

e. The factory overhead rate is $58 per machine hour. Machine hours used:

| Job | Machine Hours |
| --- | --- |
| 301 | 26 |
| 302 | 38 |
| 303 | 30 |
| 304 | 80 |
| 305 | 40 |
| 306 | 26 |
| Total | 240 |

f. Jobs completed: 301, 302, 303, and 305.

g. Jobs were shipped and customers were billed as follows: Job 301, $9,150; Job 302, $12,350; Job 303, $16,600.

**Instructions**

1. Journalize the entries to record the summarized operations.

2. Post the appropriate entries to T accounts for Work in Process and Finished Goods, using the identifying letters as dates. Insert memo account balances as of the end of the month.

3. Prepare a schedule of unfinished jobs to support the balance in the work in process account.

4. Prepare a schedule of completed jobs on hand to support the balance in the finished goods account.

---

**PR 17-3A   Job order cost sheet**

*If the working papers correlating with the textbook are not used, omit Problem 17-3A.*

Carlin Furniture Company refinishes and reupholsters furniture. Carlin uses a job order cost system. When a prospective customer asks for a price quote on a job, the estimated cost data are inserted on an unnumbered job cost sheet. If the offer is accepted, a number is assigned to the job, and the costs incurred are recorded in the usual manner on the job cost sheet. After the job is completed, reasons for the variances between the estimated and actual costs are noted on the sheet. The data are then available to management in evaluating the efficiency of operations and in preparing quotes on future jobs. On July 6, 2012, an estimate of $1,880.00 for reupholstering a sofa and loveseat was given to Justin Flannigan. The estimate was based on the following data:

Estimated direct materials:

| | |
|---|---:|
| 30 meters at $30 per meter ..................................... | $ 900.00 |
| Estimated direct labor: | |
| 20 hours at $28 per hour ....................................... | 560.00 |
| Estimated factory overhead (75% of direct labor cost) .............. | 420.00 |
| Total estimated costs ........................................... | $1,880.00 |
| Markup (30% of production costs) ................................ | 564.00 |
| Total estimate ................................................ | $2,444.00 |

On July 10, the sofa and loveseat were picked up from the residence of Justin Flannigan, 310 Suzuki Drive, Lubbock, TX, with a commitment to return it on September 7. The job was completed on September 3.

The related materials requisitions and time tickets are summarized as follows:

| Materials Requisition No. | Description | Amount |
|:---:|:---:|:---:|
| 310 | 15 meters at $30 | $450 |
| 312 | 19 meters at $30 | 570 |

| Time Ticket No. | Description | Amount |
|:---:|:---:|:---:|
| H50 | 10 hours at $28 | $280 |
| H55 | 14 hours at $28 | 392 |

## Instructions

1. Complete that portion of the job order cost sheet that would be prepared when the estimate is given to the customer.

2. ➤ Assign number 12-211 to the job, record the costs incurred, and complete the job order cost sheet. Comment on the reasons for the variances between actual costs and estimated costs. For this purpose, assume that four meters of materials were spoiled, the factory overhead rate has been proved to be satisfactory, and an inexperienced employee performed the work.

**OBJ. 2**

✔ G. $350,500

## PR 17-4A Analyzing manufacturing cost accounts

Long Board Company manufactures designer paddle boards in a wide variety of sizes and styles. The following incomplete ledger accounts refer to transactions that are summarized for May:

### Materials

| | | | | | | |
|---|---|---|---:|---|---|---|
| May | 1 | Balance | 37,500 | May 31 | Requisitions | (A) |
| | 31 | Purchases | 150,000 | | | |

### Work in Process

| | | | | | | |
|---|---|---|---|---|---|---|
| May | 1 | Balance | (B) | May 31 | Completed jobs | (F) |
| | 31 | Materials | (C) | | | |
| | 31 | Direct labor | (D) | | | |
| | 31 | Factory overhead applied | (E) | | | |

### Finished Goods

| | | | | | | |
|---|---|---|---|---|---|---|
| May | 1 | Balance | 0 | May 31 | Cost of goods sold | (G) |
| | 31 | Completed jobs | (F) | | | |

### Wages Payable

| | | | | |
|---|---|---|---|---:|
| | May 31 | Wages incurred | | 150,000 |

### Factory Overhead

| | | | | | | |
|---|---|---|---:|---|---|---|
| May | 1 | Balance | 15,000 | May 31 | Factory overhead applied | (E) |
| | 31 | Indirect labor | (H) | | | |
| | 31 | Indirect materials | 20,000 | | | |
| | 31 | Other overhead | 120,000 | | | |

In addition, the following information is available:

a. Materials and direct labor were applied to six jobs in May:

| Job No. | Style | Quantity | Direct Materials | Direct Labor |
|---|---|---|---|---|
| 15 | A-100 | 250 | $ 25,000 | $ 18,750 |
| 16 | A-200 | 500 | 42,500 | 32,500 |
| 17 | A-500 | 250 | 17,500 | 10,000 |
| 18 | X-2 | 300 | 37,500 | 31,500 |
| 19 | A-400 | 220 | 27,500 | 22,000 |
| 20 | X-1 | 175 | 10,000 | 5,620 |
| | Total | 1,695 | $160,000 | $120,370 |

b. Factory overhead is applied to each job at a rate of 150% of direct labor cost.

c. The May 1 Work in Process balance consisted of two jobs, as follows:

| Job No. | Style | Work in Process, May 1 |
|---|---|---|
| Job 15 | A-100 | $ 7,500 |
| Job 16 | A-200 | 20,000 |
| Total | | $27,500 |

d. Customer jobs completed and units sold in May were as follows:

| Job No. | Style | Completed in May | Units Sold in May |
|---|---|---|---|
| 15 | A-100 | X | 200 |
| 16 | A-200 | X | 400 |
| 17 | A-500 | | 0 |
| 18 | X-2 | X | 260 |
| 19 | A-400 | X | 190 |
| 20 | X-1 | | 0 |

## Instructions

1. Determine the missing amounts associated with each letter. Provide supporting calculations by completing a table with the following headings:

| Job No. | Quantity | May 1 Work in Process | Direct Materials | Direct Labor | Factory Overhead | Total Cost | Unit Cost | Units Sold | Cost of Goods Sold |
|---|---|---|---|---|---|---|---|---|---|

2. Determine the May 31 balances for each of the inventory accounts and factory overhead.

OBJ. 2

✔ 1. Income from operations, $2,030,000

### PR 17-5A Flow of costs and income statement

Kid Stuff Inc. is in the business of developing, promoting, and selling children's videos. The company developed a new DVD video, called *Jake the Sleepy Old Dog*, on January 1, 2012. For the first six months of 2012, the company spent $1,500,000 on a media campaign for *Jake the Sleepy Old Dog* and $650,000 in legal costs. The video production began on February 1, 2012.

Kid Stuff uses a job order cost system to accumulate costs associated with a DVD video title. The unit direct materials cost for the video is:

| DVD video | $1.00 |
|---|---|
| Case | 1.50 |
| Story booklet and stuffed animal | 3.50 |

The production process is straightforward. First, the blank DVDs are brought to a production area where the video is copied onto a DVD. The copying machine requires one hour per 2,000 DVDs.

After the DVDs are copied, they are brought to an assembly area where an employee packs the DVD in a case along with the story booklet and stuffed animal. The direct labor cost is $0.20 per unit.

The DVDs are sold to stores. Each store is given promotional materials, such as posters and aisle displays. Promotional materials cost $30 per store. In addition, shipping costs average $0.30 per DVD.

Total completed production was 800,000 units during the year. Other information is as follows:

| | |
|---|---|
| Number of customers (stores) | 50,000 |
| Number of DVDs sold | 710,000 |
| Wholesale price (to store) per DVD | $15 |

Factory overhead cost is applied to jobs at the rate of $1,000 per copy machine hour after the vidoes are copied to the DVDs. There were an additional 15,000 copied DVDs, cases, story booklets, and stuffed animals waiting to be assembled on December 31, 2012.

### Instructions

1. Prepare an annual income statement for the *Jake the Sleepy Old Dog* video, including supporting calculations, from the information above.

2. Determine the balances in the work in process and finished goods inventory for the *Jake the Sleepy Old Dog* video on December 31, 2012.

## Problems Series B

OBJ. 2

### PR 17-1B  Entries for costs in a job order cost system

Jester Company uses a job order cost system. The following data summarize the operations related to production for September:

a. Materials purchased on account, $550,000.

b. Materials requisitioned, $485,000, of which $54,200 was for general factory use.

c. Factory labor used, $540,000, of which $130,000 was indirect.

d. Other costs incurred on account were for factory overhead, $175,000; selling expenses, $122,500; and administrative expenses, $79,000.

e. Prepaid expenses expired for factory overhead were $17,500; for selling expenses, $20,300; and for administrative expenses, $11,900.

f. Depreciation of factory equipment was $35,400; of office equipment, $44,200; and of store equipment, $10,650.

g. Factory overhead costs applied to jobs, $385,000.

h. Jobs completed, $1,350,000.

i. Cost of goods sold, $1,325,000.

### Instruction

Journalize the entries to record the summarized operations.

OBJ. 2

✔ 3. Work in Process balance, $90,722

### PR 17-2B  Entries and schedules for unfinished jobs and completed jobs

Krall Company uses a job order cost system. The following data summarize the operations related to production for June 2012, the first month of operations:

a. Materials purchased on account, $105,000.

b. Materials requisitioned and factory labor used:

| Job No. | Materials | Factory Labor |
|---|---|---|
| 101 | $13,800 | $13,875 |
| 102 | 16,500 | 20,100 |
| 103 | 9,600 | 10,000 |
| 104 | 27,300 | 26,100 |
| 105 | 12,900 | 11,100 |
| 106 | 12,800 | 13,350 |
| For general factory use | 6,150 | 14,400 |

c. Factory overhead costs incurred on account, $4,125.

d. Depreciation of machinery and equipment, $2,800.

e. The factory overhead rate is $38 per machine hour. Machine hours used:

| Job | Machine Hours |
|---|---|
| 101 | 110 |
| 102 | 114 |
| 103 | 90 |
| 104 | 170 |
| 105 | 114 |
| 106 | 124 |
| Total | 722 |

f. Jobs completed: 101, 102, 103, and 105.

g. Jobs were shipped and customers were billed as follows: Job 101, $39,200; Job 102, $50,400; Job 105, $35,400.

**Instructions**

1. Journalize the entries to record the summarized operations.

2. Post the appropriate entries to T accounts for Work in Process and Finished Goods, using the identifying letters as dates. Insert memo account balances as of the end of the month.

3. Prepare a schedule of unfinished jobs to support the balance in the work in process account.

4. Prepare a schedule of completed jobs on hand to support the balance in the finished goods account.

---

OBJ. 2, 3

**PR 17-3B  Job order cost sheet**

*If the working papers correlating with the textbook are not used, omit Problem 17-3B.*

Tylee Furniture Company refinishes and reupholsters furniture. Tylee uses a job order cost system. When a prospective customer asks for a price quote on a job, the estimated cost data are inserted on an unnumbered job cost sheet. If the offer is accepted, a number is assigned to the job, and the costs incurred are recorded in the usual manner on the job cost sheet. After the job is completed, reasons for the variances between the estimated and actual costs are noted on the sheet. The data are then available to management in evaluating the efficiency of operations and in preparing quotes on future jobs. On April 15, 2012, an estimate of $684.00 for reupholstering a sofa and a loveseat was given to Jeff Tomcszak. The estimate was based on the following data:

| | |
|---|---|
| Estimated direct materials: | |
| 18 meters at $18 per meter ..................................... | $  324.00 |
| Estimated direct labor: | |
| 12 hours at $20 per hour....................................... | 240.00 |
| Estimated factory overhead (50% of direct labor cost)................ | 120.00 |
| Total estimated costs ............................................ | $  684.00 |
| Markup (50% of production costs).................................. | 342.00 |
| Total estimate............................................... | $1,026.00 |

On April 19, the sofa and loveseat were picked up from the residence of Jeff Tomcszak, 202 Bimmer Road, Mooresville, NC, with a commitment to return them on May 22. The job was completed on May 20.

The related materials requisitions and time tickets are summarized as follows:

| Materials Requisition No. | Description | Amount |
|---|---|---|
| 602 | 9 meters at $18 | $162 |
| 606 | 11 meters at $18 | 198 |

| Time Ticket No. | Description | Amount |
|---|---|---|
| H9 | 8 hours at $19 | $152 |
| H12 | 8 hours at $19 | 152 |

**Instructions**

1. Complete that portion of the job order cost sheet that would be prepared when the estimate is given to the customer.

2. ➤ Assign number 12-305 to the job, record the costs incurred, and complete the job order cost sheet. Comment on the reasons for the variances between actual costs and estimated costs. For this purpose, assume that two meters of materials were spoiled, the factory overhead rate has been proved to be satisfactory, and an inexperienced employee performed the work.

OBJ. 2

✔ G. $329,400

### PR 17-4B  Analyzing manufacturing cost accounts

Jagger and Richards Company manufactures custom guitars in a wide variety of styles. The following incomplete ledger accounts refer to transactions that are summarized for October:

**Materials**

| Oct. | 1 | Balance | 48,000 | Oct. 31 | Requisitions | (A) |
| | 31 | Purchases | 225,000 | | | |

**Work in Process**

| Oct. | 1 | Balance | (B) | Oct. 31 | Completed jobs | (F) |
| | 31 | Materials | (C) | | | |
| | 31 | Direct labor | (D) | | | |
| | 31 | Factory overhead applied | (E) | | | |

**Finished Goods**

| Oct. | 1 | Balance | 0 | Oct. 31 | Cost of goods sold | (G) |
| | 31 | Completed jobs | (F) | | | |

**Wages Payable**

| | | | | Oct. 31 | Wages incurred | 180,000 |

**Factory Overhead**

| Oct. | 1 | Balance | 12,000 | Oct. 31 | Factory overhead applied | (E) |
| | 31 | Indirect labor | (H) | | | |
| | 31 | Indirect materials | 7,000 | | | |
| | 31 | Other overhead | 77,500 | | | |

In addition, the following information is available:

a. Materials and direct labor were applied to six jobs in October:

| Job No. | Style | Quantity | Direct Materials | Direct Labor |
|---|---|---|---|---|
| 101 | X-1 | 150 | $ 37,500 | $ 27,000 |
| 102 | X-3 | 175 | 48,000 | 33,000 |
| 103 | X-2 | 225 | 60,000 | 50,000 |
| 104 | S-1 | 175 | 30,000 | 18,000 |
| 105 | S-2 | 300 | 54,000 | 30,000 |
| 106 | X-4 | 150 | 30,000 | 14,000 |
| | Total | 1,175 | $259,500 | $172,000 |

b. Factory overhead is applied to each job at a rate of 60% of direct labor cost.

c. The October Work in Process balance consisted of two jobs, as follows:

| Job No. | Style | Work in Process, October 1 |
|---|---|---|
| Job 101 | X-1 | $12,000 |
| Job 102 | X-3 | 21,000 |
| Total | | $33,000 |

d. Customer jobs completed and units sold in October were as follows:

| Job No. | Style | Completed in October | Units Sold in October |
|---|---|---|---|
| 101 | X-1 | X | 120 |
| 102 | X-3 | X | 165 |
| 103 | X-2 | | 0 |
| 104 | S-1 | X | 175 |
| 105 | S-2 | X | 240 |
| 106 | X-4 | | 0 |

**Instructions**

1. Determine the missing amounts associated with each letter. Provide supporting calculations by completing a table with the following headings:

| Job No. | Quantity | Oct. 1 Work in Process | Direct Materials | Direct Labor | Factory Overhead | Total Cost | Unit Cost | Units Sold | Cost of Goods Sold |
|---|---|---|---|---|---|---|---|---|---|

2. Determine the October 31 balances for each of the inventory accounts and factory overhead.

---

**OBJ. 2**

✔ **1. Income from operations, $3,590,000**

**PR 17-5B Flow of costs and income statement**

Designer Software Inc. is a designer, manufacturer, and distributor of software for microcomputers. A new product, *Design 2012*, was released for production and distribution in early 2012. In January, $1,250,000 was spent on developing marketing and advertising materials. For the first six months of 2012, the company spent $1,200,000 promoting *Design 2012* in trade magazines. The product was ready for manufacture on January 21, 2012.

Designer Software uses a job order cost system to accumulate costs associated with each software title. Direct materials unit costs are as follows:

| | |
|---|---|
| Blank CD | $0.60 |
| Packaging | 1.00 |
| Manual | 6.40 |
| Total | $8.00 |

The actual production process for the software product is fairly straightforward. First, blank CDs are brought to a CD copying machine. The copying machine requires one hour per 2,500 CDs.

After the program is copied onto the CD, the CD is brought to assembly, where assembly personnel pack the CD and manual for shipping. The direct labor cost for this work is $0.60 per unit.

The completed packages are then sold to retail outlets through a sales force. The sales force is compensated by a 20% commission on the wholesale price for all sales.

Total completed production was 250,000 units during the year. Other information is as follows:

| | |
|---|---|
| Number of software units sold in 2012 | 200,000 |
| Wholesale price per unit | $50 |

Factory overhead cost is applied to jobs at the rate of $3,000 per copy machine hour after the program is copied to the CDs. There were an additional 10,000 copied CDs, packaging, and manuals waiting to be assembled on December 31, 2012.

**Instructions**

1. Prepare an annual income statement for the *Design 2012* product, including supporting calculations, from the information above.

2. Determine the balances in the finished goods and work in process inventory for the *Design 2012* product on December 31, 2012.

## Cases & Projects

You can access Cases & Projects online at **www.cengage.com/accounting/reeve**

## Excel Success Special Activities

### SA 17-1  Calculation of predetermined overhead application rate

California Custom Design, LLC, is a business that customizes motorcycles and automobiles according to the customers' specifications. The company uses a job-order cost accounting system. Factory overhead is applied to production on the basis of direct labor hours. Estimated overhead costs for the coming year amount to $860,000. The company expects to operate at 80% of capacity, utilizing 16,000 direct labor hours.

a.  Open the Excel file *SA17-1_1e*.

b.  Calculate the predetermined overhead application rate.

c.  When you have completed determining the overhead application rate, perform a "save as," replacing the entire file name with the following:

*SA17-1_1e[your first name initial]_[your last name]*

### SA 17-2  Calculation of predetermined overhead application rate

Mendoza Home Builders, Inc., specializes in the construction of large family homes. The company applies overhead to each home it builds on the basis of the direct labor cost incurred on the job site. The budgeted total direct labor costs for the coming year amount to $5,000,000. A list of the budgeted overhead costs is presented below.

| Budgeted Overhead Costs | |
|---|---:|
| Indirect labor—hourly workers | $1,000,000 |
| Indirect labor—supervisor salaries | 400,000 |
| Equipment repairs and maintenance | 350,000 |
| Indirect materials | 250,000 |
| Licenses, permits, and taxes | 100,000 |
| Waste disposal | 75,000 |
| Equipment depreciation | 50,000 |
| Materials and equipment storage | 20,000 |
| Small tools lost or broken | 12,000 |
| Other miscellaneous overhead | 43,000 |

a.  Open the Excel file *SA17-2_1e*.

b.  Calculate the predetermined overhead application rate for the coming year.

c.  When you have completed determining the overhead application rate, perform a "save as," replacing the entire file name with the following:

*SA17-2_1e[your first name initial]_[your last name]*

### SA 17-3  Calculation of predetermined overhead application rate

Sandstone Manufacturing Company operates three production facilities in the state of New Mexico. Because manufacturing operations are heavily automated, the company uses machine hours as the factory overhead allocation base. The estimated annual overhead costs and the budgeted number of machine hours for each of these facilities are as follows:

| | Manufacturing Facility | | |
|---|---:|---:|---:|
| | **Santa Fe** | **Clovis** | **Roswell** |
| Estimated annual factory overhead cost | $1,670,000 | $1,394,000 | $1,200,000 |
| Estimated total machine hours | 1,000,000 | 820,000 | 750,000 |

Calculate the predetermined factory overhead application rates that would be used in each of these manufacturing plants during the coming year.

a. Open the Excel file *SA17-3_1e*.

b. Calculate the predetermined overhead rate for the coming year for each manufacturing plant.

c. When you have completed determining the overhead application rate, perform a "save as," replacing the entire file name with the following:

*SA17-3_1e[your first name initial]_[your last name]*

© Michael Strauch@streetcarmike.com

# Process Cost Systems

## Dreyer's Grand Ice Cream, Inc.

In making ice cream, an electric ice cream maker is used to mix ingredients, which include milk, cream, sugar, and flavoring. After the ingredients are added, the mixer is packed with ice and salt to cool the ingredients, and it is then turned on.

After mixing for half of the required time, would you have ice cream? Of course not, because the ice cream needs to mix longer to freeze. Now, assume that you ask the question:

What costs have I incurred so far in making ice cream?

The answer to this question requires knowing the cost of the ingredients and electricity. The ingredients are added at the beginning; thus, all the ingredient costs have been incurred. Since the mixing is only half complete, only 50% of the electricity costs has been incurred. Therefore, the answer to the preceding question is:

All the materials costs and half the electricity costs have been incurred.

These same cost concepts apply to larger ice cream processes like those of **Dreyer's Grand Ice Cream, Inc.,** manufacturer of Häagen-Dazs®, Edys®, Dreyer's®, and Nestle® ice cream. Dreyer's mixes ingredients in 3,000-gallon vats in much the same way you would with an electric ice cream maker. Dreyer's also records the costs of the ingredients, labor, and factory overhead used in making ice cream. These costs are used by managers for decisions such as setting prices and improving operations.

This chapter describes and illustrates process cost systems that are used by manufacturers such as Dreyer's. In addition, the use of cost of production reports in decision making is described. Finally, just-in-time cost systems are discussed.

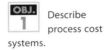
OBJ. 1 Describe process cost systems.

# Process Cost Systems

A **process manufacturer** produces products that are indistinguishable from each other using a continuous production process. For example, an oil refinery processes crude oil through a series of steps to produce a barrel of gasoline. One barrel of gasoline, the product, cannot be distinguished from another barrel. Other examples of process manufacturers include paper producers, chemical processors, aluminum smelters, and food processors.

The cost accounting system used by process manufacturers is called the **process cost system**. A process cost system records product costs for each manufacturing department or process.

In contrast, a job order manufacturer produces custom products for customers or batches of similar products. For example, a custom printer produces wedding invitations, graduation announcements, or other special print items that are tailored to the specifications of each customer. Each item manufactured is unique to itself. Other examples of job order manufacturers include furniture manufacturers, shipbuilders, and home builders.

As described and illustrated in Chapter 17, the cost accounting system used by job order manufacturers is called the *job order cost system*. A job order cost system records product cost for each job using job cost sheets.

Some examples of process and job order manufacturers are shown on the next page.

| Process Manufacturers | | Job Order Manufacturers | |
|---|---|---|---|
| **Company** | **Product** | **Company** | **Product** |
| Pepsi | soft drinks | Walt Disney | movies |
| Alcoa | aluminum | Nike, Inc. | athletic shoes |
| Intel | computer chip | Nicklaus Design | golf courses |
| Apple | iPhone | Heritage Log Homes | log homes |
| Hershey Foods | chocolate bars | DDB Advertising Agency | advertising |

## Comparing Job Order and Process Cost Systems

Process and job order cost systems are similar in that each system:

1. Records and summarizes product costs.
2. Classifies product costs as direct materials, direct labor, and factory overhead.
3. Allocates factory overhead costs to products.
4. Uses perpetual inventory system for materials, work in process, and finished goods.
5. Provides useful product cost information for decision making.

Process and job costing systems are different in several ways. As a basis for illustrating these differences, the cost systems for Frozen Delight and Legend Guitars are used.

## Integrity, Objectivity, and Ethics in Business

**ON BEING GREEN**

Building a world with environmentally sustainable resources is one of the largest challenges of today's corporate community. E.I. du Pont de Nemours and Company (DuPont) states: *As a science company, (we have) the experience and expertise to put our science to work in ways that can design in—at the early stages of product development—attributes that help protect or enhance human health, safety, and the environment.* As a result, DuPont has developed a set of product and manufacturing related goals for the year 2015.

Source: DuPont Web site.

- Double investment in R&D programs with direct and quantifiable environmental benefits.
- Grow annual revenues by $2 billion from products that reduce greenhouse emissions.
- Double revenues from nondepletable resources to at least $8 billion.
- Reduce greenhouse gas emissions from its processing facilities by 15%.
- Reduce air carcinogens from its processing facilities by 50%.

Exhibit 1 illustrates the process cost system for Frozen Delight, an ice cream manufacturer. As a basis for comparison, Exhibit 1 also illustrates the job order cost system for Legend Guitars, a custom guitar manufacturer. Legend Guitars was described and illustrated in Chapters 16 and 17.

Exhibit 1 indicates that Frozen Delight manufactures ice cream using two departments:

1. Mixing Department mixes the ingredients using large vats.
2. Packaging Department puts the ice cream into cartons for shipping to customers.

Since each gallon of ice cream is similar, product costs are recorded in each department's work in process account. As shown in Exhibit 1, Frozen Delight accumulates (records) the cost of making ice cream in *work in process accounts* for the Mixing and Packaging departments. The product costs of making a gallon of ice cream include:

1. *Direct materials cost,* which include milk, cream, sugar, and packing cartons. All materials costs are added at the beginning of the process for both the Mixing Department and the Packaging Department.

**EXHIBIT 1** **Process Cost and Job Order Cost Systems**

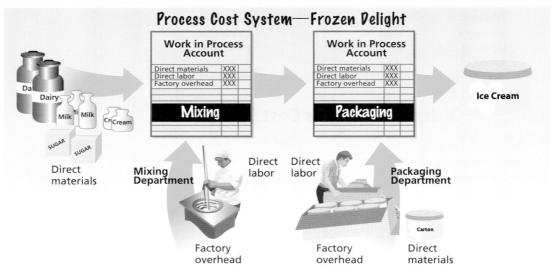

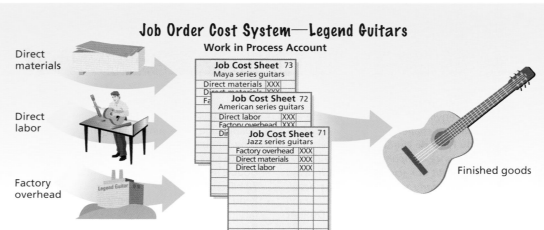

2. *Direct labor cost,* which is incurred by employees in each department who run the equipment and load and unload product.

3. *Factory overhead costs,* which include the utility costs (power) and depreciation on the equipment.

When the Mixing Department completes the mixing process, its product costs are transferred to the Packaging Department. When the Packaging Department completes its process, the product costs are transferred to Finished Goods. In this way, the cost of the product (a gallon of ice cream) accumulates across the entire production process.

In contrast, Exhibit 1 shows that Legend Guitars accumulates (records) product costs by jobs using a job cost sheet for each type of guitar. Thus, Legend Guitars uses just one work in process account. As each job is completed, its product costs are transferred to Finished Goods.

In a job order cost system, the work in process at the end of the period is the sum of the job cost sheets for partially completed jobs. In a process cost system, the work in process at the end of the period is the sum of the costs remaining in each department account at the end of the period.

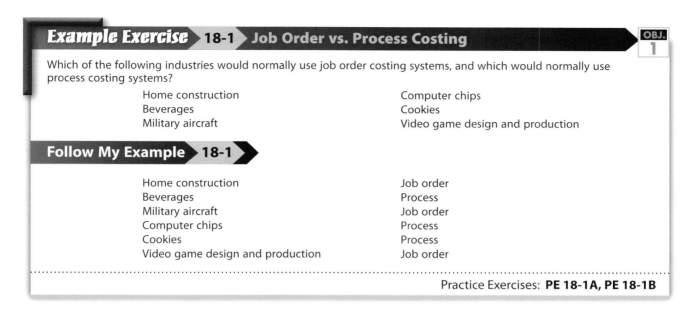

**Example Exercise** ▶ **18-1** ▶ **Job Order vs. Process Costing**    **OBJ. 1**

Which of the following industries would normally use job order costing systems, and which would normally use process costing systems?

| | |
|---|---|
| Home construction | Computer chips |
| Beverages | Cookies |
| Military aircraft | Video game design and production |

**Follow My Example** ▶ **18-1**

| | |
|---|---|
| Home construction | Job order |
| Beverages | Process |
| Military aircraft | Job order |
| Computer chips | Process |
| Cookies | Process |
| Video game design and production | Job order |

Practice Exercises: **PE 18-1A, PE 18-1B**

## Cost Flows for a Process Manufacturer

Exhibit 2 illustrates the *physical flow* of materials for Frozen Delight. Ice cream is made in a manufacturing plant in much the same way you would make it at home, except on a larger scale.

Materials costs can be as high as 70% of the total product costs for many process manufacturers.

In the Mixing Department, direct materials in the form of milk, cream, and sugar are placed into a vat. An employee (direct labor) fills each vat, sets the cooling temperature, and sets the mix speed. The vat is cooled (refrigerated) as the direct materials are being mixed by agitators (paddles). Factory overhead is incurred in the form of power (electricity) to run the vat and vat (equipment) depreciation.

In the Packaging Department, the ice cream is received from the Mixing Department in a form ready for packaging. The Packaging Department uses direct labor and factory overhead (conversion costs) to package the ice cream into one-gallon containers (direct materials). The ice cream is then transferred to finished goods where it is frozen and stored in refrigerators prior to shipment to customers (stores).

**EXHIBIT 2**    **Physical Flows for a Process Manufacturer**

The *cost flows* in a process cost accounting system are similar to the *physical flow* of materials described above. The cost flows for Frozen Delight are illustrated in Exhibit 3 (on page 839) as follows:

a. The cost of materials purchased is recorded in the materials account.

b. The cost of direct materials used by the Mixing and Packaging departments is recorded in the work in process accounts for each department.

c. The cost of direct labor used by the Mixing and Packaging departments is recorded in work in process accounts for each department.

d. The cost of factory overhead incurred for indirect materials and other factory overhead such as depreciation is recorded in the factory overhead accounts for each department.

e. The factory overhead incurred in the Mixing and Packaging departments is applied to the work in process accounts for each department.

f. The cost of units completed in the Mixing Department is transferred to the Packaging Department.

g. The cost of units completed in the Packaging Department is transferred to Finished Goods.

h. The cost of units sold is transferred to Cost of Goods Sold.

As shown in Exhibit 3, the Mixing and Packaging departments have separate factory overhead accounts. The factory overhead costs incurred for indirect materials, depreciation, and other overhead are debited to each department's factory overhead account. The overhead is applied to work in process by debiting each department's work in process account and crediting the department's factory overhead account.

Exhibit 3 illustrates how the Mixing and Packaging departments have separate work in process accounts. Each work in process account is debited for the direct materials, direct labor, and applied factory overhead. In addition, the work in process account for the Packaging Department is debited for the cost of the units transferred in from the Mixing Department. Each work in process account is credited for the cost of the units transferred to the next department.

Lastly, Exhibit 3 shows that the finished goods account is debited for the cost of the units transferred from the Packaging Department. The finished goods account is credited for the cost of the units sold, which is debited to the cost of goods sold account.

## BusinessConnection

### FRIDGE PACK

Go to any food store and you will see beverage cans sold in popular 12-can fridge packs. The fridge pack was introduced to the soft drink industry in 1998 by Alcoa Inc.

The fridge pack story began when Alcoa was looking for ways to sell more aluminum can sheet, one of its major products. After extensive market research, Alcoa thought of a fiberboard package design that would make it easier for consumers to store canned beverages in a refrigerator by taking up the "dead space." Alcoa believed if more cans

could be stored in the refrigerator it would result in more cans being consumed, and hence more overall sales.

The fridge pack was first adopted by Coca-Cola Australia, where they saw an instant increase in sales as Alcoa predicted. As a result, the remaining soft beverage industry quickly adopted the package design. Miller Brewing introduced the fridge pack for beer in 2004. The fridge pack is an excellent example of a process manufacturer, like Alcoa, creating innovations to benefit their customers (and themselves).

Source: Alcoa Recycling Company, "Fridge Vendor: A Cool Idea that Is Paying Off," Web site, 2010.

**OBJ. 2** Prepare a cost of production report.

# Cost of Production Report

In a process cost system, the cost of units transferred out of each processing department must be determined along with the cost of any partially completed units remaining in the department. The report that summarizes these costs is a cost of production report.

The **cost of production report** summarizes the production and cost data for a department as follows:

1. The units the department is accountable for and the disposition of those units.

2. The product costs incurred by the department and the allocation of those costs between completed (transferred out) and partially completed units.

**EXHIBIT 3** **Cost Flows for a Process Manufacturer—Frozen Delight**

**Materials**

| a. Purchased | Direct materials |
| | Indirect materials |

**Work in Process—Mixing Department**

| b. Direct materials | Costs of units transferred out |
| c. Direct labor | |
| e. Factory overhead applied | |

**Factory Overhead—Mixing Department**

| d. Factory overhead incurred | Factory Overhead applied |

**Work in Process—Packaging Department**

| b. Direct materials | Costs of units transferred out |
| f. Costs of units transferred in | |
| c. Direct labor | |
| e. Factory overhead applied | |

**Factory Overhead—Packaging Department**

| d. Factory overhead incurred | Factory overhead applied |

**Factory Overhead Costs Incurred**

Indirect materials
Depreciation of equipment
Other overhead (utilities, indirect labor)

**Finished Goods**

| g. Costs of units transferred In | Cost of goods sold |

**Cost of Goods Sold**

| h. Cost of goods sold |

**Cost Flows for Frozen Delight**

a. The cost of materials purchased is recorded in the materials account.

b. The cost of direct materials used by the Mixing and Packaging departments is recorded in the work in process accounts for each department.

c. The cost of direct labor used by the Mixing and Packaging departments is recorded in work in process accounts for each department.

d. The cost of factory overhead incurred for indirect materials and other factory overhead such as depreciation is recorded in the factory overhead accounts for each department.

e. The factory overhead incurred in the Mixing and Packaging departments is applied to the work in process accounts for each department.

f. The cost of units completed in the Mixing Department is transferred to the Packaging Department.

g. The cost of units completed in the Packaging Department is transferred to Finished Goods.

h. The cost of units sold is transferred to Cost of Goods Sold.

A cost of production report is prepared using the following four steps:

Step 1. Determine the units to be assigned costs.
Step 2. Compute equivalent units of production.
Step 3. Determine the cost per equivalent unit.
Step 4. Allocate costs to units transferred out and partially completed units.

Preparing a cost of production report requires making a cost flow assumption. Like merchandise inventory, costs can be assumed to flow through the manufacturing process using the first-in, first-out (FIFO), last in, first-out (LIFO), or average cost methods. Because the **first-in, first-out (FIFO) method** is often the same as the physical flow of units, the FIFO method is used in this chapter.[1]

To illustrate, a cost of production report for the Mixing Department of Frozen Delight for July 2012 is prepared. The July data for the Mixing Department are as follows:

| | | |
|---|---:|---:|
| Inventory in process, July 1, 5,000 gallons: | | |
|     Direct materials cost, for 5,000 gallons ..................... | $5,000 | |
|     Conversion costs, for 5,000 gallons, 70% completed ......... | 1,225 | |
|     Total inventory in process, July 1........................... | | $ 6,225 |
| Direct materials cost for July, 60,000 gallons .................. | | 66,000 |
| Direct labor cost for July...................................... | | 10,500 |
| Factory overhead applied for July ............................. | | 7,275 |
|     Total production costs to account for ...................... | | $90,000 |
| Gallons transferred to Packaging in July (includes | | |
|     units in process on July 1), 62,000 gallons .................. | | ? |
| Inventory in process, July 31, 3,000 gallons, | | |
|     25% completed as to conversion costs ..................... | | ? |

By preparing a cost of production report, the cost of the gallons transferred to the Packaging Department in July and the ending work in process inventory in the Mixing Department is determined. These amounts are indicated by question marks (?).

## Step 1: Determine the Units to Be Assigned Costs

The first step is to determine the units to be assigned costs. A unit can be any measure of completed production, such as tons, gallons, pounds, barrels, or cases. For Frozen Delight, a unit is a gallon of ice cream.

The Mixing Department is accountable for 65,000 gallons of direct materials during July, as shown below.

| | |
|---|---:|
| Total units (gallons) charged to production: | |
|   In process, July 1 | 5,000 gallons |
|     Received from materials storage | 60,000 |
|       Total units (gallons) accounted for | 65,000 gallons |

For July, the following three groups of units (gallons) are assigned costs:

Group 1. Units (gallons) in beginning work in process inventory on July 1.
Group 2. Units (gallons) started and completed during July.
Group 3. Units (gallons) in ending work in process inventory on July 31.

Exhibit 4 illustrates these groups of units (gallons) in the Mixing Department for July. The 5,000 gallons of beginning inventory were completed and transferred to the Packaging Department. During July, 60,000 gallons of material were started (entered into mixing). Of the 60,000 gallons started in July, 3,000 gallons were incomplete on July 31. Thus, 57,000 gallons (60,000 – 3,000) were started and completed in July.

The total units (gallons) to be assigned costs for July are summarized below.

| | | |
|---|---|---:|
| Group 1 | Inventory in process, July 1, completed in July | 5,000 gallons |
| Group 2 | Started and completed in July | 57,000 |
| |     Transferred out to the Packaging Department in July | 62,000 gallons |
| Group 3 | Inventory in process, July 31 | 3,000 |
| |     Total units (gallons) to be assigned costs | 65,000 gallons |

1 The average cost method is illustrated in an appendix to this chapter.

The total gallons to be assigned costs (65,000) equal the total gallons accounted for (65,000) by the Mixing Department.

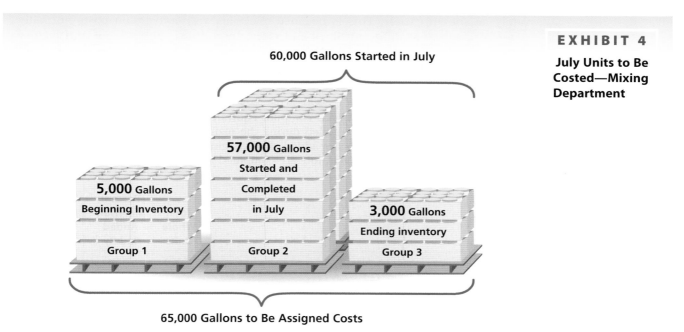

EXHIBIT 4

July Units to Be Costed—Mixing Department

60,000 Gallons Started in July

57,000 Gallons Started and Completed in July

Group 2

5,000 Gallons Beginning Inventory

Group 1

3,000 Gallons Ending inventory

Group 3

65,000 Gallons to Be Assigned Costs

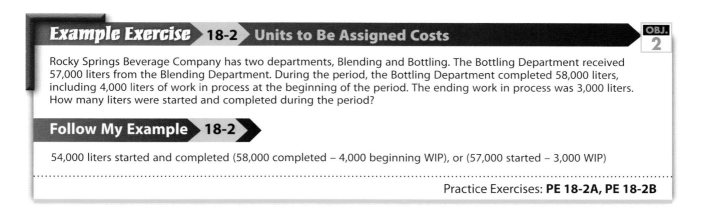

**Example Exercise** 18-2 **Units to Be Assigned Costs**

OBJ. 2

Rocky Springs Beverage Company has two departments, Blending and Bottling. The Bottling Department received 57,000 liters from the Blending Department. During the period, the Bottling Department completed 58,000 liters, including 4,000 liters of work in process at the beginning of the period. The ending work in process was 3,000 liters. How many liters were started and completed during the period?

**Follow My Example** 18-2

54,000 liters started and completed (58,000 completed – 4,000 beginning WIP), or (57,000 started – 3,000 WIP)

Practice Exercises: **PE 18-2A, PE 18-2B**

## Step 2: Compute Equivalent Units of Production

**Whole units** are the number of units in production during a period, whether completed or not. **Equivalent units of production** are the portion of whole units that are complete with respect to materials or conversion (direct labor and factory overhead) costs.

To illustrate, assume that a 1,000-gallon batch (vat) of ice cream is only 40% complete in the mixing process on May 31. Thus, the batch is only 40% complete as to conversion costs such as power. In this case, the whole units and equivalent units of production are as follows:

|  | Whole Units | Equivalent Units |
| --- | --- | --- |
| Materials costs | 1,000 gallons | 1,000 gallons |
| Conversion costs | 1,000 gallons | 400 gallons (1,000 × 40%) |

Since the materials costs are all added at the beginning of the process, the materials costs are 100% complete for the 1,000-gallon batch of ice cream. Thus, the whole units and equivalent units for materials costs are 1,000 gallons. However, since the batch is only 40% complete as to conversion costs, the equivalent units for conversion costs are 400 gallons.

Equivalent units for materials and conversion costs are usually determined separately as shown earlier. This is because materials and conversion costs normally enter production at different times and rates. In contrast, direct labor and factory overhead normally enter production at the same time and rate. For this reason, direct labor and factory overhead are combined as conversion costs in computing equivalent units.

**Materials Equivalent Units** To compute equivalent units for materials, it is necessary to know how materials are added during the manufacturing process. In the case of Frozen Delight, all the materials are added at the beginning of the mixing process. Thus, the equivalent units for materials in July are computed as follows:

|  |  | Total Whole Units | Percent Materials Added in July | Equivalent Units for Direct Materials |
|---|---|---|---|---|
| Group 1 | Inventory in process, July 1 .......................... | 5,000 | 0% | 0 |
| Group 2 | Started and completed in July |  |  |  |
|  | (62,000 − 5,000) ................................ | 57,000 | 100% | 57,000 |
|  | Transferred out to Packaging |  |  |  |
|  | Department in July ........................... | 62,000 | — | 57,000 |
| Group 3 | Inventory in process, July 31 ......................... | 3,000 | 100% | 3,000 |
|  | Total gallons to be assigned cost ................. | 65,000 |  | 60,000 |

As shown above, the whole units for the three groups of units determined in Step 1 are listed in the first column. The percent of materials added in July is then listed. The equivalent units are determined by multiplying the whole units by the percent of materials added.

To illustrate, the July 1 inventory (Group 1) has 5,000 gallons of whole units, which are complete as to materials. That is, all the direct materials for the 5,000 gallons in process on July 1 were added in June. Thus, the percent of materials added in July is zero, and the equivalent units added in July are zero.

The 57,000 gallons started and completed in July (Group 2) are 100% complete as to materials. Thus, the equivalent units for the gallons started and completed in July are 57,000 (57,000 × 100%) gallons. Therefore, the equivalent units for the inventory in process on July 31 are 3,000 (3,000 × 100%) gallons. The 3,000 gallons in process on July 31 (Group 3) are also 100% complete as to materials since all materials are added at the beginning of the process.

**Example Exercise 18-3 Equivalent Units of Materials Cost**

OBJ. 2

The Bottling Department of Rocky Springs Beverage Company had 4,000 liters in beginning work in process inventory (30% complete). During the period, 58,000 liters were completed. The ending work in process inventory was 3,000 liters (60% complete). What are the total equivalent units for direct materials if materials are added at the beginning of the process?

*(continued)*

**Follow My Example** 18-3

Total equivalent units for direct materials is 57,000, computed as follows:

| | Total Whole Units | Percent Materials Added in Period | Equivalent Units for Direct Materials |
|---|---|---|---|
| Inventory in process, beginning of period | 4,000 | 0% | 0 |
| Started and completed during the period | 54,000* | 100% | 54,000 |
| Transferred out of Bottling (completed) | 58,000 | — | 54,000 |
| Inventory in process, end of period | 3,000 | 100% | 3,000 |
| Total units to be assigned costs | 61,000 | | 57,000 |

*(58,000 – 4,000)

Practice Exercises: **PE 18-3A, PE 18-3B**

The equivalent units for direct materials are summarized in Exhibit 5.

**EXHIBIT 5** **Direct Materials Equivalent Units**

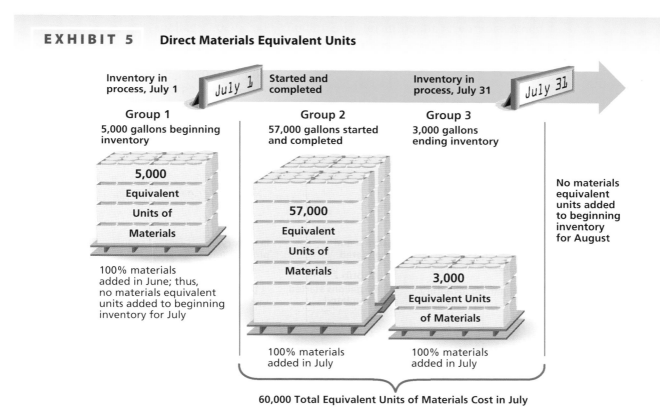

**Conversion Equivalent Units** To compute equivalent units for conversion costs, it is necessary to know how direct labor and factory overhead enter the manufacturing process. Direct labor, utilities, and equipment depreciation are often incurred uniformly during processing. For this reason, it is assumed that Frozen Delight incurs conversion costs evenly throughout its manufacturing process. Thus, the equivalent units for conversion costs in July are computed as follows:

| | | Total Whole Units | Percent Conversion Completed in July | Equivalent Units for Conversion |
|---|---|---|---|---|
| Group 1 | Inventory in process, July 1 (70% completed) .............................. | 5,000 | 30% | 1,500 |
| Group 2 | Started and completed in July (62,000 − 5,000) .............................. | 57,000 | 100% | 57,000 |
| | Transferred out to Packaging Department in July ......................... | 62,000 | — | 58,500 |
| Group 3 | Inventory in process, July 31 (25% completed) .............................. | 3,000 | 25% | 750 |
| | Total gallons to be assigned cost ............... | 65,000 | | 59,250 |

As shown above, the whole units for the three groups of units determined in Step 1 are listed in the first column. The percent of conversion costs added in July is then listed. The equivalent units are determined by multiplying the whole units by the percent of conversion costs added.

To illustrate, the July 1 inventory has 5,000 gallons of whole units (Group 1), which are 70% complete as to conversion costs. During July, the remaining 30% (100% − 70%) of conversion costs was added. Therefore, the equivalent units of conversion costs added in July are 1,500 (5,000 × 30%) gallons.

The 57,000 gallons started and completed in July (Group 2) are 100% complete as to conversion costs. Thus, the equivalent units of conversion costs for the gallons started and completed in July are 57,000 (57,000 × 100%) gallons.

The 3,000 gallons in process on July 31 (Group 3) are 25% complete as to conversion costs. Hence, the equivalent units for the inventory in process on July 31 are 750 (3,000 × 25%) gallons.

The equivalent units for conversion costs are summarized in Exhibit 6.

**EXHIBIT 6    Conversion Equivalent Units**

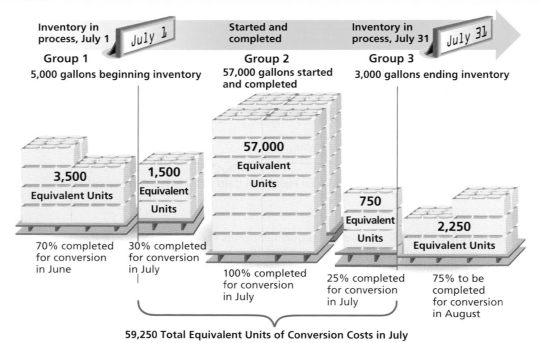

59,250 Total Equivalent Units of Conversion Costs in July

**Example Exercise** 18-4 **Equivalent Units of Conversion Costs**   OBJ. 2

The Bottling Department of Rocky Springs Beverage Company had 4,000 liters in beginning work in process inventory (30% complete). During the period, 58,000 liters were completed. The ending work in process inventory was 3,000 liters (60% complete). What are the total equivalent units for conversion costs?

**Follow My Example** 18-4

|  | Total Whole Units | Percent Conversion Completed in Period | Equivalent Units for Conversion |
|---|---|---|---|
| Inventory in process, beginning of period | 4,000 | 70% | 2,800 |
| Started and completed during the period | 54,000* | 100% | 54,000 |
| Transferred out of Bottling (completed) | 58,000 | — | 56,800 |
| Inventory in process, end of period | 3,000 | 60% | 1,800 |
| Total units to be assigned costs | 61,000 |  | 58,600 |

*(58,000 − 4,000)

Practice Exercises: **PE 18-4A, PE 18-4B**

## Step 3: Determine the Cost per Equivalent Unit

The next step in preparing the cost of production report is to compute the cost per equivalent unit for direct materials and conversion costs. The **cost per equivalent unit** for direct materials and conversion costs is computed as follows:

$$\text{Direct Materials Cost per Equivalent Unit} = \frac{\text{Total Direct Materials Cost for the Period}}{\text{Total Equivalent Units of Direct Materials}}$$

$$\text{Conversion Cost per Equivalent Unit} = \frac{\text{Total Conversion Costs for the Period}}{\text{Total Equivalent Units of Conversion Costs}}$$

The July direct materials and conversion cost equivalent units for Frozen Delight's Mixing Department from Step 2 are shown below.

|  |  | Equivalent Units | |
|---|---|---|---|
|  |  | Direct Materials | Conversion |
| Group 1 | Inventory in process, July 1 ................................. | 0 | 1,500 |
| Group 2 | Started and completed in July (62,000 – 5,000) ............. | 57,000 | 57,000 |
|  | Transferred out to Packaging Department in July ....... | 57,000 | 58,500 |
| Group 3 | Inventory in process, July 31 ............................... | 3,000 | 750 |
|  | Total gallons to be assigned cost ....................... | 60,000 | 59,250 |

The direct materials and conversion costs incurred by Frozen Delight in July are as follows:

| Direct materials ............................................... |  | $66,000 |
|---|---|---|
| Conversion costs: |  |  |
| Direct labor................................................ | $10,500 |  |
| Factory overhead .......................................... | 7,275 | 17,775 |
| Total product costs incurred in July....................... |  | $83,775 |

The direct materials and conversion costs per equivalent unit are $1.10 and $0.30 per gallon, computed as follows:

$$\text{Direct Materials Cost per Equivalent Unit} = \frac{\text{Total Direct Materials Cost for the Period}}{\text{Total Equivalent Units of Direct Materials}}$$

$$\text{Direct Materials Cost per Equivalent Unit} = \frac{\$66,000}{60,000 \text{ gallons}} = \$1.10 \text{ per gallon}$$

$$\text{Conversion Cost per Equivalent Unit} = \frac{\text{Total Conversion Costs for the Period}}{\text{Total Equivalent Units of Conversion Costs}}$$

$$\text{Conversion Cost per Equivalent Unit} = \frac{\$17,775}{59,250 \text{ gallons}} = \$0.30 \text{ per gallon}$$

The preceding costs per equivalent unit are used in Step 4 to allocate the direct materials and conversion costs to the completed and partially completed units.

The cost per equivalent unit can be determined using a spreadsheet as follows:

| | A | B | C | |
|---|---|---|---|---|
| 1 | | Equivalent Units | | |
| 2 | | Direct Materials | Conversion | |
| 3 | Inventory in process, July 1 | - | 1,500 | ← a. |
| 4 | Started and completed in July | 57,000 | 57,000 | |
| 5 | Transferred out to Packaging | =B3+B4 | =C3+C4 | |
| 6 | Inventory in process, July 31 | 3,000 | 750 | b. |
| 7 | Total gallons to be assigned cost | =B5+B6 | =C5+C6 | |
| 8 | | | | |
| 9 | | Direct Materials | Conversion | |
| 10 | Costs | $    66,000 | $    17,775 | |
| 11 | | | | |
| 12 | | Direct Materials | Conversion | |
| 13 | Cost per Equivalent Unit    c. → | =B10/B7 | =C10/C7 | ← d. |
| 14 | | **per gallon** | **per gallon** | |

a. Arrange the equivalent units and cost information in two columns, one for direct materials and one for conversion. Doing so will facilitate copying the cost per equivalent unit formula in step d.
b. Insert the appropriate sum formulas to compute the totals and subtotals of the equivalent units.
c. Insert in cell B13 a formula that divides the direct materials costs by the total gallons to be assigned, =B10/B7
d. Copy this formula to C13 to determine the cost per equivalent unit of conversion.

**Try**It    Go to the hands-on **Excel Tutor** for this example!

**Example Exercise** **18-5** **Cost per Equivalent Unit**                    OBJ. 2

The cost of direct materials transferred into the Bottling Department of Rocky Springs Beverage Company is $22,800. The conversion cost for the period in the Bottling Department is $8,790. The total equivalent units for direct materials and conversion are 57,000 liters and 58,600 liters, respectively. Determine the direct materials and conversion costs per equivalent unit.

**Follow My Example** **18-5**

$$\text{Direct Materials Cost per Equivalent Unit} = \frac{\$22,800}{57,000 \text{ liters}} = \$0.40 \text{ per liter}$$

$$\text{Conversion Cost per Equivalent Unit} = \frac{\$8,790}{58,600 \text{ liters}} = \$0.15 \text{ per liter}$$

Practice Exercises: **PE 18-5A, PE 18-5B**

# Step 4: Allocate Costs to Units Transferred Out and Partially Completed Units

Product costs must be allocated to the units transferred out and the partially completed units on hand at the end of the period. The product costs are allocated using the costs per equivalent unit for materials and conversion costs that were computed in Step 3.

The total production costs to be assigned for Frozen Delight in July are $90,000 as shown below and on page 840.

| | |
|---|---|
| Inventory in process, July 1, 5,000 gallons: | |
| Direct materials cost, for 5,000 gallons . . . . . . . . . . . . . . . . . . . . . . . . . . . . . . . . . . . | $ 5,000 |
| Conversion costs, for 5,000 gallons, 70% completed . . . . . . . . . . . . . . . . . . . . . . | 1,225 |
| Total inventory in process, July 1 . . . . . . . . . . . . . . . . . . . . . . . . . . . . . . . . . . . . . . . | $ 6,225 |
| Direct materials cost for July, 60,000 gallons . . . . . . . . . . . . . . . . . . . . . . . . . . . . . . . | 66,000 |
| Direct labor cost for July . . . . . . . . . . . . . . . . . . . . . . . . . . . . . . . . . . . . . . . . . . . . . . . . | 10,500 |
| Factory overhead applied for July . . . . . . . . . . . . . . . . . . . . . . . . . . . . . . . . . . . . . . . . | 7,275 |
| Total production costs to account for . . . . . . . . . . . . . . . . . . . . . . . . . . . . . . . . . . | $90,000 |

The units to be assigned these costs are shown below. The costs to be assigned these units are indicated by question marks (?).

| | | Units | Total Cost |
|---|---|---|---|
| Group 1 | Inventory in process, July 1, completed in July . . . . . . . . | 5,000 gallons | ? |
| Group 2 | Started and completed in July . . . . . . . . . . . . . . . . . . . . . . . | 57,000 | ? |
| | Transferred out to the Packaging | | |
| | Department in July . . . . . . . . . . . . . . . . . . . . . . . . . . . . . | 62,000 gallons | ? |
| Group 3 | Inventory in process, July 31 . . . . . . . . . . . . . . . . . . . . . . . . | 3,000 | ? |
| | Total . . . . . . . . . . . . . . . . . . . . . . . . . . . . . . . . . . . . . . . . . . . . | 65,000 gallons | $90,000 |

**Group 1: Inventory in Process on July 1** The 5,000 gallons of inventory in process on July 1 (Group 1) were completed and transferred out to the Packaging Department in July. The cost of these units, $6,675, is determined as follows:

| | Direct Materials Costs | Conversion Costs | Total Costs |
|---|---|---|---|
| Inventory in process, July 1 balance . . . . . . . . . . . . . . . . . . | | | $6,225 |
| Equivalent units for completing the | | | |
| July 1 in-process inventory . . . . . . . . . . . . . . . . . . . . . . . | 0 | 1,500 | |
| Cost per equivalent unit . . . . . . . . . . . . . . . . . . . . . . . . . . . . | × $1.10 | × $0.30 | |
| Cost of completed July 1 in-process inventory . . . . . . . . | 0 | $450 | 450 |
| Cost of July 1 in-process inventory | | | |
| transferred to Packaging Department . . . . . . . . . . . . | | | $6,675 |

As shown above, $6,225 of the cost of the July 1 in-process inventory of 5,000 gallons was carried over from June. This cost plus the cost of completing the 5,000 gallons in July was transferred to the Packaging Department during July. The cost of completing the 5,000 gallons during July is $450. The $450 represents the conversion costs necessary to complete the remaining 30% of the processing. There were no direct materials costs added in July because all the materials costs had been added in

June. Thus, the cost of the 5,000 gallons in process on July 1 (Group 1) transferred to the Packaging Department is $6,675.

### Group 2: Started and Completed

The 57,000 units started and completed in July (Group 2) incurred all (100%) of their direct materials and conversion costs in July. Thus, the cost of the 57,000 gallons started and completed is $79,800, computed by multiplying 57,000 gallons by the costs per equivalent unit for materials and conversion costs as shown below.

|  | Direct Materials Costs | Conversion Costs | Total Costs |
|---|---|---|---|
| Units started and completed in July.................. | 57,000 gallons | 57,000 gallons | |
| Cost per equivalent unit ............................. | × $1.10 | × $0.30 | |
| Cost of the units started and completed in July........................... | $62,700 | $17,100 | $79,800 |

The total cost transferred to the Packaging Department in July of $86,475 is the sum of the beginning inventory cost and the costs of the units started and completed in July as shown below.

| Group 1 | Cost of July 1 in-process inventory | $ 6,675 |
|---|---|---|
| Group 2 | Cost of the units started and completed in July | 79,800 |
| | Total costs transferred to Packaging Department in July | $86,475 |

### Group 3: Inventory in Process on July 31

The 3,000 gallons in process on July 31 (Group 3) incurred all their direct materials costs and 25% of their conversion costs in July. The cost of these partially completed units, $3,525, is computed below.

|  | Direct Materials Costs | Conversion Costs | Total Costs |
|---|---|---|---|
| Equivalent units in ending inventory ................. | 3,000 gallons | 750 gallons | |
| Cost per equivalent unit ............................. | × $1.10 | × $0.30 | |
| Cost of July 31 in-process inventory ................. | $3,300 | $225 | $3,525 |

The 3,000 gallons in process on July 31 received all (100%) of their materials in July. Therefore, the direct materials cost incurred in July is $3,300 (3,000 × $1.10). The conversion costs of $225 represent the cost of the 750 (3,000 × 25%) equivalent gallons times the cost per equivalent unit for conversion costs of $0.30. The sum of the direct materials cost ($3,300) and the conversion costs ($225) equals the total cost of the July 31 work in process inventory of $3,525 ($3,300 + $225).

To summarize, the total manufacturing costs for Frozen Delight in July were assigned as shown below. In doing so, the question marks (?) on page 840 have been answered.

|  | | Units | Total Cost |
|---|---|---|---|
| Group 1 | Inventory in process, July 1, completed in July ...... | 5,000 gallons | $ 6,675 |
| Group 2 | Started and completed in July ...................... | 57,000 | 79,800 |
| | Transferred out to the Packaging Department in July .......................... | 62,000 gallons | $86,475 |
| Group 3 | Inventory in process, July 31 ....................... | 3,000 | 3,525 |
| | Total......................................... | 65,000 gallons | $90,000 |

**Example Exercise** 18-6 **Cost of Units Transferred Out and Ending Work in Process**

OBJ. 2

The costs per equivalent unit of direct materials and conversion in the Bottling Department of Rocky Springs Beverage Company are $0.40 and $0.15, respectively. The equivalent units to be assigned costs are as follows:

|  | Equivalent Units | |
| --- | --- | --- |
|  | Direct Materials | Conversion |
| Inventory in process, beginning of period | 0 | 2,800 |
| Started and completed during the period | 54,000 | 54,000 |
| Transferred out of Bottling (completed) | 54,000 | 56,800 |
| Inventory in process, end of period | 3,000 | 1,800 |
| Total units to be assigned costs | 57,000 | 58,600 |

The beginning work in process inventory had a cost of $1,860. Determine the cost of units transferred out and the ending work in process inventory.

**Follow My Example** 18-6

|  | Direct Materials Costs | | Conversion Costs | Total Costs |
| --- | --- | --- | --- | --- |
| Inventory in process, beginning of period .......... |  |  |  | $ 1,860 |
| Inventory in process, beginning of period .......... | 0 | + | 2,800 × $0.15 | 420 |
| Started and completed during the period .......... | 54,000 × $0.40 | + | 54,000 × $0.15 | 29,700 |
| Transferred out of Bottling (completed)............ |  |  |  | $31,980 |
| Inventory in process, end of period................. | 3,000 × $0.40 | + | 1,800 × $0.15 | 1,470 |
| Total costs assigned by the Bottling Department ... |  |  |  | $33,450 |
| Completed and transferred out of production ...... | $31,980 |  |  |  |
| Inventory in process, ending...................... | $ 1,470 |  |  |  |

Practice Exercises: **PE 18-6A, PE 18-6B**

## Preparing the Cost of Production Report

A cost of production report is prepared for each processing department at periodic intervals. The report summarizes the following production quantity and cost data:

1. The units for which the department is accountable and the disposition of those units.
2. The production costs incurred by the department and the allocation of those costs between completed (transferred out) and partially completed units.

Using Steps 1–4, the July cost of production report for Frozen Delight's Mixing Department is shown in Exhibit 7.

As shown in Exhibit 7, the Mixing Department was accountable for 65,000 units (gallons). Of these units, 62,000 units were completed and transferred to the Packaging Department. The remaining 3,000 units are partially completed and are part of in-process inventory as of July 31.

The Mixing Department was responsible for $90,000 of production costs during July. The cost of goods transferred to the Packaging Department in July was $86,475. The remaining cost of $3,525 is part of in-process inventory as of July 31.

 e**X**cel *success* The cost of production report on a spreadsheet is illustrated at the end of the chapter in a comprehensive spreadsheet illustration.

**EXHIBIT 7**    **Cost of Production Report for Frozen Delight's Mixing Department—FIFO**

| | A | B | C | D | E |
|---|---|---|---|---|---|
| 1 | | Frozen Delight | | | |
| 2 | | Cost of Production Report—Mixing Department | | | |
| 3 | | For the Month Ended July 31, 2012 | | | |
| 4 | | | | | |
| 5 | | Whole Units | Equivalent Units | | |
| | | | Direct Materials | Conversion | |
| 6 | **UNITS** | | | | |
| 7 | Units charged to production: | | | | |
| 8 | Inventory in process, July 1 | 5,000 | | | |
| 9 | Received from materials storeroom | 60,000 | | | |
| 10 | Total units accounted for by the Mixing Department | 65,000 | | | |
| 11 | | | | | |
| 12 | Units to be assigned costs: | | | | |
| 13 | Inventory in process, July 1 (70% completed) | 5,000 | 0 | 1,500 | |
| 14 | Started and completed in July | 57,000 | 57,000 | 57,000 | |
| 15 | Transferred to Packaging Department in July | 62,000 | 57,000 | 58,500 | |
| 16 | Inventory in process, July 31 (25% completed) | 3,000 | 3,000 | 750 | |
| 17 | Total units to be assigned costs | 65,000 | 60,000 | 59,250 | |
| 18 | | | | | |
| 19 | | | Costs | | |
| 20 | **COSTS** | | Direct Materials | Conversion | Total |
| 21 | | | | | |
| 22 | Costs per equivalent unit: | | | | |
| 23 | Total costs for July in Mixing Department | | $ 66,000 | $ 17,775 | |
| 24 | Total equivalent units (from step 2 above) | | ÷60,000 | ÷59,250 | |
| 25 | Cost per equivalent unit | | $   1.10 | $   0.30 | |
| 26 | | | | | |
| 27 | Costs assigned to production: | | | | |
| 28 | Inventory in process, July 1 | | | | $ 6,225 |
| 29 | Costs incurred in July | | | | 83,775[a] |
| 30 | Total costs accounted for by the Mixing Department | | | | $90,000 |
| 31 | | | | | |
| 32 | | | | | |
| 33 | Cost allocated to completed and partially | | | | |
| 34 | completed units: | | | | |
| 35 | Inventory in process, July 1—balance | | | | $ 6,225 |
| 36 | To complete inventory in process, July 1 | | $     0  + | $    450[b]  = | 450 |
| 37 | Cost of completed July 1 work in process | | | | $ 6,675 |
| 38 | Started and completed in July | | 62,700[c]  + | 17,100[d]  = | 79,800 |
| 39 | Transferred to Packaging Department in July | | | | $86,475 |
| 40 | Inventory in process, July 31 | | $ 3,300[e]  + | $   225[f]  = | 3,525 |
| 41 | Total costs assigned by the Mixing Department | | | | $90,000 |
| 42 | | | | | |

Step 1
Step 2
Step 3
Step 4

[a]$66,000 + $10,500 + $7,275 = $83,775  [b]1,500 units × $0.30 = $450  [c]57,000 units × $1.10 = $62,700  [d]57,000 units × $0.30 = $17,100
[e]3,000 units × $1.10 = $3,300  [f]750 units × $0.30 = $225

**OBJ. 3** Journalize entries for transactions using a process cost system.

# Journal Entries for a Process Cost System

The journal entries to record the cost flows and transactions for a process cost system are illustrated in this section. As a basis for illustration, the July transactions for Frozen Delight are used. To simplify, the entries are shown in summary form, even though many of the transactions would be recorded daily.

   a. Purchased materials, including milk, cream, sugar, packaging, and indirect materials on account, $88,000.

| | | | | |
|---|---|---|---|---|
| | Materials | | 88,000 | |
| | Accounts Payable | | | 88,000 |

b. The Mixing Department requisitioned milk, cream, and sugar, $66,000. This is the amount indicated on page 840. Packaging materials of $8,000 were requisitioned by the Packaging Department. Indirect materials for the Mixing and Packaging departments were $4,125 and $3,000, respectively.

| | | | |
|---|---|---|---|
| Work in Process—Mixing | | 66,000 | |
| Work in Process—Packaging | | 8,000 | |
| Factory Overhead—Mixing | | 4,125 | |
| Factory Overhead—Packaging | | 3,000 | |
| Materials | | | 81,125 |

c. Incurred direct labor in the Mixing and Packaging departments of $10,500 and $12,000, respectively.

| | | | |
|---|---|---|---|
| Work in Process—Mixing | | 10,500 | |
| Work in Process—Packaging | | 12,000 | |
| Wages Payable | | | 22,500 |

d. Recognized equipment depreciation for the Mixing and Packaging departments of $3,350 and $1,000, respectively.

| | | | |
|---|---|---|---|
| Factory Overhead—Mixing | | 3,350 | |
| Factory Overhead—Packaging | | 1,000 | |
| Accumulated Depreciation—Equipment | | | 4,350 |

e. Applied factory overhead to Mixing and Packaging departments of $7,275 and $3,500, respectively.

| | | | |
|---|---|---|---|
| Work in Process—Mixing | | 7,275 | |
| Work in Process—Packaging | | 3,500 | |
| Factory Overhead—Mixing | | | 7,275 |
| Factory Overhead—Packaging | | | 3,500 |

f. Transferred costs of $86,475 from the Mixing Department to the Packaging Department per the cost of production report in Exhibit 7.

| | | | |
|---|---|---|---|
| Work in Process—Packaging | | 86,475 | |
| Work in Process—Mixing | | | 86,475 |

g. Transferred goods of $106,000 out of the Packaging Department to Finished Goods according to the Packaging Department cost of production report (not illustrated).

| | | | |
|---|---|---|---|
| Finished Goods—Ice Cream | | 106,000 | |
| Work in Process—Packaging | | | 106,000 |

h. Recorded cost of goods sold out of the finished goods inventory of $107,000.

| | | | |
|---|---|---|---|
| Cost of Goods Sold | | 107,000 | |
| Finished Goods—Ice Cream | | | 107,000 |

Exhibit 8 shows the flow of costs for each transaction. The highlighted amounts in Exhibit 8 were determined from assigning the costs in the Mixing Department. These amounts were computed and are shown at the bottom of the cost of production report for the Mixing Department in Exhibit 7 on page 850. Likewise, the amount transferred out of the Packaging Department to Finished Goods would have also been determined from a cost of production report for the Packaging Department.

**EXHIBIT 8**   **Frozen Delight's Cost Flows**

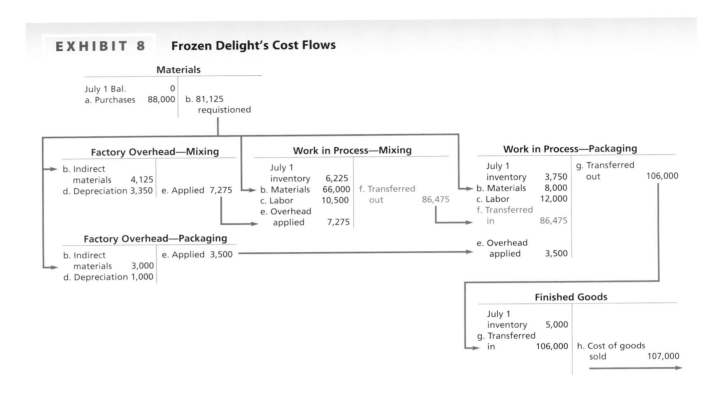

The ending inventories for Frozen Delight are reported on the July 31 balance sheet as follows:

| | |
|---|---:|
| Materials | $ 6,875 |
| Work in Process—Mixing Department | 3,525 |
| Work in Process—Packaging Department | 7,725 |
| Finished Goods | 4,000 |
| Total inventories | $22,125 |

The $3,525 of Work in Process—Mixing Department is the amount determined from the bottom of the cost of production report in Exhibit 7.

**Example Exercise** **18-7** **Process Cost Journal Entries**

OBJ. 2

The cost of materials transferred into the Bottling Department of Rocky Springs Beverage Company is $22,800, including $20,000 from the Blending Department and $2,800 from the materials storeroom. The conversion cost for the period in the Bottling Department is $8,790 ($3,790 factory overhead applied and $5,000 direct labor). The total cost transferred to Finished Goods for the period was $31,980. The Bottling Department had a beginning inventory of $1,860.

a.  Journalize (1) the cost of transferred-in materials, (2) conversion costs, and (3) the costs transferred out to Finished Goods.

b.  Determine the balance of Work in Process—Bottling at the end of the period.

*(continued)*

a. 1. Work in Process—Bottling............................................. 22,800
      Work in Process—Blending........................................ 20,000
      Materials....................................................... 2,800
   2. Work in Process—Bottling............................................. 8,790
      Factory Overhead—Bottling....................................... 3,790
      Wages Payable.................................................... 5,000
   3. Finished Goods....................................................... 31,980
      Work in Process—Bottling........................................ 31,980

b. $1,470 ($1,860 + $22,800 + $8,790 − $31,980)

Practice Exercises: **PE 18-7A, PE 18-7B**

# Using the Cost of Production Report for Decision Making

**OBJ. 4** Describe and illustrate the use of cost of production reports for decision making.

The cost of production report is often used by managers for decisions involving the control and improvement of operations. To illustrate, cost of production reports for Frozen Delight and Holland Beverage Company are used. Finally, the computation and use of yield is discussed.

## Frozen Delight

The cost of production report for the Mixing Department is shown in Exhibit 7 on page 850. The cost per equivalent unit for June can be determined from the beginning inventory. The Frozen Delight data on page 840 indicate that the July 1 inventory in process of $6,225 consists of the following costs:

| | |
|---|---|
| Direct materials cost, 5,000 gallons | $5,000 |
| Conversion costs, 5,000 gallons, 70% completed | 1,225 |
| Total inventory in process, July 1 | $6,225 |

Using the preceding data, the June costs per equivalent unit of materials and conversion costs can be determined as follows:

$$\text{Direct Materials Cost per Equivalent Unit} = \frac{\text{Total Direct Materials Cost for the Period}}{\text{Total Equivalent Units of Direct Materials}}$$

$$\text{Direct Materials Cost per Equivalent Unit} = \frac{\$5,000}{5,000 \text{ gallons}} = \$1.00 \text{ per gallon}$$

$$\text{Conversion Cost per Equivalent Unit} = \frac{\text{Total Conversion Costs for the Period}}{\text{Total Equivalent Units of Conversion Costs}}$$

$$\text{Conversion Cost per Equivalent Unit} = \frac{\$1,225}{(5,000 \times 70\%) \text{ gallons}} = \$0.35 \text{ per gallon}$$

In July, the cost per equivalent unit of materials increased by $0.10 per gallon, while the cost per equivalent unit for conversion costs decreased by $0.05 per gallon, as shown below.

| | July* | June | Increase (Decrease) |
|---|---|---|---|
| Cost per equivalent unit for direct materials | $1.10 | $1.00 | $0.10 |
| Cost per equivalent unit for conversion costs | 0.30 | 0.35 | (0.05) |

Frozen Delight's management could use the preceding analysis as a basis for investigating the increase in the direct materials cost per equivalent unit and the decrease in the conversion cost per equivalent unit.

# Holland Beverage Company

A cost of production report may be prepared showing more cost categories beyond just direct materials and conversion costs. This greater detail can help managers isolate problems and seek opportunities for improvement.

To illustrate, the Blending Department of Holland Beverage Company prepared cost of production reports for April and May. To simplify, assume that the Blending Department had no beginning or ending work in process inventory in either month. That is, all units started were completed in each month. The cost of production reports showing multiple cost categories for April and May in the Blending Department are as follows:

| | A | B | C |
|---|---|---|---|
| 1 | Cost of Production Reports | | |
| 2 | Holland Beverage Company—Blending Department | | |
| 3 | For the Months Ended April 30 and May 31, 2012 | | |
| 4 | | April | May |
| 5 | Direct materials | $ 20,000 | $ 40,600 |
| 6 | Direct labor | 15,000 | 29,400 |
| 7 | Energy | 8,000 | 20,000 |
| 8 | Repairs | 4,000 | 8,000 |
| 9 | Tank cleaning | 3,000 | 8,000 |
| 10 | Total | $ 50,000 | $106,000 |
| 11 | Units completed | ÷ 100,000 | ÷ 200,000 |
| 12 | Cost per unit | $    0.50 | $    0.53 |
| 13 | | | |

The May results indicate that total unit costs have increased from $0.50 to $0.53, or 6% from April. To determine the possible causes for this increase, the cost of production report is restated in per-unit terms by dividing the costs by the number of units completed, as shown below.

| | A | B | C | D |
|---|---|---|---|---|
| 1 | Blending Department | | | |
| 2 | Per-Unit Expense Comparisons | | | |
| 3 | | April | May | % Change |
| 4 | Direct materials | $0.200 | $0.203 | 1.50% |
| 5 | Direct labor | 0.150 | 0.147 | −2.00% |
| 6 | Energy | 0.080 | 0.100 | 25.00% |
| 7 | Repairs | 0.040 | 0.040 | 0.00% |
| 8 | Tank cleaning | 0.030 | 0.040 | 33.33% |
| 9 | Total | $0.500 | $0.530 | 6.00% |
| 10 | | | | |

Both energy and tank cleaning per-unit costs have increased significantly in May. These increases should be further investigated. For example, the increase in energy may be due to the machines losing fuel efficiency. This could lead management to repair the machines. The tank cleaning costs could be investigated in a similar fashion.

# Yield

In addition to unit costs, managers of process manufacturers are also concerned about yield. The **yield** is computed as follows:

$$\text{Yield} = \frac{\text{Quantity of Material Output}}{\text{Quantity of Material Input}}$$

To illustrate, assume that 1,000 pounds of sugar enter the Packaging Department, and 980 pounds of sugar were packed. The yield is 98% as computed below.

$$\text{Yield} = \frac{\text{Quantity of Material Output}}{\text{Quantity of Material Input}} = \frac{980 \text{ pounds}}{1,000 \text{ pounds}} = 98\%$$

Thus, two percent (100% − 98%) or 20 pounds of sugar was lost or spilled during the packing process. Managers can investigate significant changes in yield over time or significant differences in yield from industry standards.

**Example Exercise** 18-8 **Using Process Costs for Decision Making** OBJ. 4

The cost of energy consumed in producing good units in the Bottling Department of Rocky Springs Beverage Company was $4,200 and $3,700 for March and April, respectively. The number of equivalent units produced in March and April was 70,000 liters and 74,000 liters, respectively. Evaluate the change in the cost of energy between the two months.

**Follow My Example** 18-8

Energy cost per liter, March $= \dfrac{\$4,200}{70,000 \text{ liters}} = \$0.06$

Energy cost per liter, April $= \dfrac{\$3,700}{74,000 \text{ liters}} = \$0.05$

The cost of energy has improved by 1 cent per liter between March and April.

Practice Exercises: **PE 18-8A, PE 18-8B**

# Just-in-Time Processing

OBJ. 5 Compare just-in-time processing with traditional manufacturing processing.

The objective of most manufacturers is to produce products with high quality, low cost, and instant availability. In attempting to achieve this objective, many manufacturers have implemented just-in-time processing. **Just-in-time (JIT) processing** is a management approach that focuses on reducing time and cost and eliminating poor quality. A JIT system obtains efficiencies and flexibility by reorganizing the traditional production process.

A traditional manufacturing process for a furniture manufacturer is shown in Exhibit 9. The product (chair) moves through seven processes. In each process, workers are assigned a specific job, which is performed repeatedly as unfinished products are received from the preceding department. The product moves from process to process as each function or step is completed.

For the furniture maker in Exhibit 9, the product (chair) moves through the following processes:

1. In the Cutting Department, the wood is cut to design specifications.
2. In the Drilling Department, the wood is drilled to design specifications.
3. In the Sanding Department, the wood is sanded.
4. In the Staining Department, the wood is stained.
5. In the Varnishing Department, varnish and other protective coatings are applied.
6. In the Upholstery Department, fabric and other materials are added.
7. In the Assembly Department, the product (chair) is assembed.

**EXHIBIT 9** **Traditional Production Line**

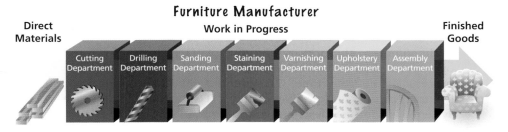

In the traditional production process, supervisors enter materials into manufacturing so as to keep all the manufacturing departments (processes) operating. Some departments, however, may process materials more rapidly than others. In addition, if one department stops because of machine breakdowns, for example, the preceding departments usually continue production in order to avoid idle time. In such cases, a buildup of work in process inventories results in some departments.

In a just-in-time system, processing functions are combined into work centers, sometimes called **manufacturing cells**. For example, the seven departments illustrated in Exhibit 9 might be reorganized into the following three work centers:

1. Work Center 1 performs the cutting, drilling, and sanding functions.
2. Work Center 2 performs the staining and varnishing functions.
3. Work Center 3 performs the upholstery and assembly functions.

The preceding JIT manufacturing process is illustrated in Exhibit 10.

In traditional manufacturing, a worker typically performs only one function. However, in JIT manufacturing, work centers complete several functions. Thus, workers

**EXHIBIT 10**

**Just-in-Time Production Line**

are often cross-trained to perform more than one function. Research has indicated that workers who perform several functions identify better with the end product. This creates pride in the product and improves quality and productivity.

The activities supporting the manufacturing process are called *service activities*. For example, repair and maintenance of manufacturing equipment are service activities. In a JIT manufacturing process, service activities may be assigned to individual work centers, rather than to centralized service departments. For example, each work center may be assigned responsibility for the repair and maintenance of its machinery and equipment. This creates an environment in which workers gain a better understanding of the production process and their machinery. In turn, workers tend to take better care of the machinery, which decreases repairs and maintenance costs, reduces machine downtime, and improves product quality.

In a JIT system, the product is often placed on a movable carrier that is centrally located in the work center. After the workers in a work center have completed their activities with the product, the entire carrier and any additional materials are moved just in time to satisfy the demand or need of the next work center. In this sense, the product is said to be "pulled through." Each work center is connected to other work centers through information contained on a Kanban, which is a Japanese term for cards.

In summary, the primary objective of JIT systems is to increase the efficiency of operations. This is achieved by eliminating waste and simplifying the production process. At the same time, JIT systems emphasize continually improving the manufacturing process and product quality. JIT systems, including cost management in JIT systems, are further described and illustrated in Chapter 27.

Before Caterpillar implemented JIT, a transmission traveled 10 miles through the factory and required 1,000 pieces of paper to support the manufacturing process. After implementing JIT, a transmission travels only 200 feet and requires only 10 pieces of paper.

# BusinessConnection

**RADICAL IMPROVEMENT: JUST IN TIME FOR PULASKI'S CUSTOMERS**

Pulaski Furniture Corporation embraced just-in-time manufacturing principles and revolutionized its business. The company wanted to "be easier to do business with" by offering its customers smaller shipments more frequently. It was able to accomplish this by taking the following steps:

- Mapping processes to properly align labor, machines, and materials.
- Eliminating 100 feet of conveyor line.

- Moving machines into manufacturing cells.
- Reducing manufacturing run sizes by simplifying the product design.
- Making every product more frequently in order to reduce the customer's waiting time for a product.

As a result of these just-in-time changes, the company significantly improved its inventory position while simultaneously improving its shipping times to the customer. Its lumber inventory was reduced by 25%, finished goods inventory was reduced by 40%, and work in process inventory was reduced by 50%. At the same time, customers' shipment waiting times were shortened from months to weeks.

Source: Jeff Linville, "Pulaski's Passion for Lean Plumps up Dealer Service," *Furniture Today,* June 2006.

## Comprehensive Spreadsheet Illustration

Southern Aggregate Company manufactures concrete through a series of processes. All materials are introduced in Crushing. From Crushing, the materials pass through Sifting, Baking, and Mixing, emerging as finished concrete. All inventories are costed by the first-in, first-out method.

The following information has been prepared on a spreadsheet as follows:

| | A | B | C | D |
|---|---|---|---|---|
| 1 | *Inputs:* | | | |
| 2 | | | | |
| 3 | Work in Process–Mixing Department | | | |
| 4 | | Units | Amount | Percent Complete |
| 5 | Work in Process, May 1, 2012 | 2,000 | $ 13,700 | 25% |
| 6 | Direct materials transferred from Baking | 15,200 | 98,800 | |
| 7 | Direct labor | | 17,200 | |
| 8 | Factory overhead | | 11,780 | |
| 9 | | | | |
| 10 | Work in Process, May 31, 2012 | 1,200 | | 50% |

### Instructions

Using the input information, prepare a cost of production report for the Mixing Department using a spreadsheet.

### Solution

| | A | B | C | D | E |
|---|---|---|---|---|---|
| 12 | *Output:* | | | | |
| 13 | | | | | |
| 14 | Southern Aggregate Company | | | | |
| 15 | Cost of Production Report–Mixing Department | | | | |
| 16 | For the Month Ended May 31, 2012 | | | | |
| 17 | | | Equivalent Units | | |
| 18 | UNITS | Whole Units | Direct Materials | Conversion | |
| 19 | Units charged to production: | | | | |
| 20 | Inventory in process, May 1 | 2,000 | | | |
| 21 | Received from Baking | 15,200 | | | |
| 22 | Total units accounted for by the Mixing Department | 17,200 | | | |
| 23 | | | | | |
| 24 | Units to be assigned costs: | | | | |

(*continued*)

| | | Whole Units | Direct Materials | Conversion | Total |
|---|---|---|---|---|---|
| 25 | Inventory in process, May 1 (25% completed) | 2,000 | - | 1,500 | |
| 26 | Started and completed in May | 14,000 | 14,000 | 14,000 | |
| 27 | Transferred to finished goods in May | 16,000 | 14,000 | 15,500 | |
| 28 | Inventory in process, May 31 (50% completed) | 1,200 | 1,200 | 600 | |
| 29 | Total units to be assigned costs | 17,200 | 15,200 | 16,100 | |
| 30 | | | | | |
| 31 | | | | Costs | |
| 32 | COSTS | | Direct Materials | Conversion | Total |
| 33 | Unit costs: | | | | |
| 34 | Total costs for May in Mixing Department | | $ 98,800 | $ 28,980 | |
| 35 | Total equivalent units (from row 29) | | 15,200 | 16,100 | |
| 36 | Cost per equivalent unit | | $ 6.50 | $ 1.80 | |
| 37 | | | | | |
| 38 | Costs assigned to production: | | | | |
| 39 | Inventory in process, May 1 | | | | $ 13,700 |
| 40 | Costs incurred in May | | | | 127,780 |
| 41 | Total costs accounted for by the Mixing Department | | | | $ 141,480 |
| 42 | | | | | |
| 43 | Cost allocated to completed and partially completed | | | | |
| 44 | units: | | | | |
| 45 | Inventory in process, May 1–balance | | | | $ 13,700 |
| 46 | To complete inventory in process, May 1 | | $ – | $ 2,700 | 2,700 |
| 47 | Cost of completed May 1 work in process | | | | $ 16,400 |
| 48 | Started and completed in May | | 91,000 | 25,200 | 116,200 |
| 49 | Transferred to finished goods in May | | | | $ 132,600 |
| 50 | Inventory in process, May 31 | | 7,800 | 1,080 | 8,880 |
| 51 | Total costs assigned by the Mixing Department | | | | $ 141,480 |

The formulas used to create the cost of production report are as follows:

| | A | B | C | D | E |
|---|---|---|---|---|---|
| 12 | *Output:* | | | | |
| 13 | | | | | |
| 14 | Southern Aggregate Company | | | | |
| 15 | Cost of Production Report–Mixing Department | | | | |
| 16 | For the Month Ended May 31, 2012 | | | | |
| 17 | | | Equivalent Units | | |
| 18 | UNITS | Whole Units | Direct Materials | Conversion | |
| 19 | Units charged to production: | | | | |
| 20 | Inventory in process, May 1 | =B5 | | | |
| 21 | Received from Baking | =B6 | | | |
| 22 | Total units accounted for by the Mixing Department | =SUM(B20:B21) | | | |
| 23 | | | | | |
| 24 | Units to be assigned costs: | | | | |
| 25 | Inventory in process, May 1 (25% completed) | =B20 | – | =B25*(1–D5) | |
| 26 | Started and completed in May | =B6-B28 | =B26 | =B26 | |
| 27 | Transferred to finished goods in May | =SUM(B25:B26) | =SUM(C25:C26) | =SUM(D25:D26) | |
| 28 | Inventory in process, May 31 (50% completed) | =B10 | =B28 | =B28*D10 | |
| 29 | Total units to be assigned costs | =B27+B28 | =C27+C28 | =D27+D28 | |
| 30 | | | | | |
| 31 | | | | Costs | |
| 32 | COSTS | | Direct Materials | Conversion | Total |
| 33 | Unit Costs: | | | | |
| 34 | Total costs for May in Mixing | | =C6 | =C7+C8 | |
| 35 | Total equivalent units (row 29) | | =C29 | =D29 | |
| 36 | Cost per equivalent unit | | =C34/C35 | =D34/D35 | |
| 37 | | | | | |
| 38 | Costs assigned to production: | | | | |
| 39 | Inventory in process, May 1 | | | | =C5 |
| 40 | Costs incurred in May | | | | =SUM(C6:C8) |
| 41 | Total costs accounted for by the Mixing Department | | | | =SUM(E39:E40) |

| 42 | | | | |
|---|---|---|---|---|
| 43 | Cost allocated to completed and partially completed | | | |
| 44 | units: | | | |
| 45 | Inventory in process, May 1–balance | | | =E39 |
| 46 | To complete inventory in process, May 1 | =C25*C36 | =D25*D36 | =C46+D46 |
| 47 | Cost of completed May 1 work in process | | | =SUM(E45:E46) |
| 48 | Started and completed in May | =C26*C36 | =D26*D36 | =C48+D48 |
| 49 | Transferred to finished goods in May 31 | | | =E47+E48 |
| 50 | Inventory in proccess, May 31 | =C28*C36 | =D28*D36 | =C50+D50 |
| 51 | Total costs assigned by the Mixing Department | | | =E49+E50 |

The cell formulas follow the steps outlined within the chapter for developing the cost of production report. Note that the complete cost of production report uses cell references. There are no number inputs into the report. Rather, the report will work for any and all input combinations.

# A P P E N D I X

# Average Cost Method

A cost flow assumption must be used as product costs flow through manufacturing processes. In this chapter, the first-in, first-out cost flow method was used for the Mixing Department of Frozen Delight. In this appendix, the average cost flow method is illustrated for S&W Ice Cream Company (S&W).

## Determining Costs Using the Average Cost Method

S&W's operations are similar to those of Frozen Delight. Like Frozen Delight, S&W mixes direct materials (milk, cream, sugar) in refrigerated vats and has two manufacturing departments, Mixing and Packaging.

The manufacturing data for the Mixing Department for July 2012 are as follows:

| | |
|---|---|
| Inventory in process, July 1, 5,000 gallons (70% completed)................ | $ 6,200 |
| Direct materials cost incurred in July, 60,000 gallons...................... | 66,000 |
| Direct labor cost incurred in July ......................................... | 10,500 |
| Factory overhead applied in July ......................................... | 6,405 |
| Total production costs to account for ................................ | $89,105 |
| | |
| Cost of goods transferred to Packaging in July (includes units in process on July 1), 62,000 gallons ........................................... | ? |
| Cost of work in process inventory, July 31, 3,000 gallons, 25% completed as to conversion costs........................................... | ? |

Using the average cost method, the objective is to allocate the total costs of production of $89,105 to the following:

1. The 62,000 gallons completed and transferred to the Packaging Department
2. The 3,000 gallons in the July 31 (ending) work in process inventory

The preceding costs show two question marks. These amounts are determined by preparing a cost of production report using the following four steps:

Step 1. Determine the units to be assigned costs.

Step 2. Compute equivalent units of production.

Step 3. Determine the cost per equivalent unit.

Step 4. Allocate costs to transferred out and partially completed units.

Under the average cost method, all production costs (materials and conversion costs) are combined together for determining equivalent units and cost per equivalent unit.

## Step 1: Determine the Units to Be Assigned Costs

The first step is to determine the units to be assigned costs. A unit can be any measure of completed production, such as tons, gallons, pounds, barrels, or cases. For S&W, a unit is a gallon of ice cream.

S&W's Mixing Department had 65,000 gallons of direct materials to account for during July, as shown here.

| Total gallons to account for: | |
|---|---|
| Inventory in process, July 1 | 5,000 gallons |
| Received from materials storeroom | 60,000 |
| Total units to account for by the Packaging Department | 65,000 gallons |

There are two groups of units to be assigned costs for the period.

| | |
|---|---|
| Group 1 | Units completed and transferred out |
| Group 2 | Units in the July 31 (ending) work in process inventory |

During July, the Mixing Department completed and transferred 62,000 gallons to the Packaging Department. Of the 60,000 gallons started in July, 57,000 (60,000 − 3,000) gallons were completed and transferred to the Packaging Department. Thus, the ending work in process inventory consists of 3,000 gallons.

The total units (gallons) to be assigned costs for S&W can be summarized as follows:

| Group 1 | Units transferred out to the Packaging Department in July | 62,000 gallons |
|---|---|---|
| Group 2 | Inventory in process, July 31 | 3,000 |
| | Total gallons to be assigned costs | 65,000 gallons |

The total units (gallons) to be assigned costs (65,000 gallons) equal the total units to account for (65,000 gallons).

## Step 2: Compute Equivalent Units of Production

S&W has 3,000 gallons of whole units in the work in process inventory for the Mixing Department on July 31. Since these units are 25% complete, the number of equivalent units in process in the Mixing Department on July 31 is 750 gallons (3,000 gallons × 25%). Since the units transferred to the Packaging Department have been completed, the whole units (62,000 gallons) transferred are the same as the equivalent units transferred.

The total equivalent units of production for the Mixing Department are determined by adding the equivalent units in the ending work in process inventory to the units transferred and completed during the period as shown below.

| Equivalent units completed and transferred to the Packaging Department during July | 62,000 gallons |
|---|---|
| Equivalent units in ending work in process, July 31 | 750 |
| Total equivalent units | 62,750 gallons |

## Step 3: Determine the Cost per Equivalent Unit

Since materials and conversion costs are combined under the average cost method, the cost per equivalent unit is determined by dividing the total production costs by the total equivalent units of production as follows:

$$\text{Cost per Equivalent Unit} = \frac{\text{Total Production Costs}}{\text{Total Equivalent Units}}$$

$$\text{Cost per Equivalent Unit} = \frac{\text{Total Production Costs}}{\text{Total Equivalent Units}} = \frac{\$89,105}{62,750 \text{ gallons}} = \$1.42$$

The cost per equivalent unit shown above is used in Step 4 to allocate the production costs to the completed and partially completed units.

## Step 4: Allocate Costs to Transferred Out and Partially Completed Units

The cost of transferred and partially completed units is determined by multiplying the cost per equivalent unit times the equivalent units of production. For the Mixing Department, these costs are determined as follows:

| | | |
|---|---|---|
| Group 1 | Transferred out to the Packaging Department (62,000 gallons × $1.42) ...... | $88,040 |
| Group 2 | Inventory in process, July 31 (3,000 gallons × 25% × $1.42)................. | 1,065 |
| | Total production costs assigned ........................................ | $89,105 |

# The Cost of Production Report

The July cost of production report for S&W's Mixing Department is shown in Exhibit 11. This cost of production report summarizes the following:

1. The units for which the department is accountable and the disposition of those units
2. The production costs incurred by the department and the allocation of those costs between completed and partially completed units

**EXHIBIT 11**    **Cost of Production Report for S&W's Mixing Department—Average Cost**

| | A | B | C |
|---|---|---|---|
| 1 | S&W Ice Cream Company | | |
| 2 | Cost of Production Report—Mixing Department | | |
| 3 | For the Month Ended July 31, 2012 | | |
| 4 | **UNITS** | | |
| 5 | | Whole Units | Equivalent Units |
| 6 | | | of Production |
| 7 | Units to account for during production: | | |
| 8 | Inventory in process, July 1 | 5,000 | |
| 9 | Received from materials storeroom | 60,000 | |
| 10 | Total units accounted for by the Mixing Department | 65,000 | |
| 11 | | | |
| 12 | Units to be assigned costs: | | |
| 13 | Transferred to Packaging Department in July | 62,000 | 62,000 |
| 14 | Inventory in process, July 31 (25% completed) | 3,000 | 750 |
| 15 | Total units to be assigned costs | 65,000 | 62,750 |
| 16 | | | |
| 17 | **COSTS** | | Costs |
| 18 | | | |
| 19 | Cost per equivalent unit: | | |
| 20 | Total production costs for July in Mixing Department | | $89,105 |
| 21 | Total equivalent units (from Step 2 above) | | ÷62,750 |
| 22 | Cost per equivalent unit | | $   1.42 |
| 23 | | | |
| 24 | Costs assigned to production: | | |
| 25 | Inventory in process, July 1 | | $  6,200 |
| 26 | Direct materials, direct labor, and factory overhead incurred in July | | 82,905 |
| 27 | Total costs accounted for by the Mixing Department | | $89,105 |
| 28 | | | |
| 29 | | | |
| 30 | Costs allocated to completed and partially completed units: | | |
| 31 | Transferred to Packaging Department in July (62,000 gallons × $1.42) | | $88,040 |
| 32 | Inventory in process, July 31 (3,000 gallons × 25% × $1.42) | | 1,065 |
| 33 | Total costs assigned by the Mixing Department | | $89,105 |
| 34 | | | |

Step 1
Step 2
Step 3
Step 4

# At a Glance 18

**Key Points** The process cost system is best suited for industries that mass produce identical units of a product. Costs are charged to processing departments, rather than to jobs as with the job order cost system. These costs are transferred from one department to the next until production is completed.

| Learning Outcomes | Example Exercises | Practice Exercises |
|---|---|---|
| • Identify the characteristics of a process manufacturer. | | |
| • Compare and contrast the job order cost system with the process cost system. | EE18-1 | PE18-1A, 18-1B |
| • Describe the physical and cost flows of a process manufacturer. | | |

**Key Points** Manufacturing costs must be allocated between the units that have been completed and those that remain within the department. This allocation is accomplished by allocating costs using equivalent units of production.

| Learning Outcomes | Example Exercises | Practice Exercises |
|---|---|---|
| • Determine the whole units charged to production and to be assigned costs. | EE18-2 | PE18-2A, 18-2B |
| • Compute the equivalent units with respect to materials. | EE18-3 | PE18-3A, 18-3B |
| • Compute the equivalent units with respect to conversion. | EE18-4 | PE18-4A, 18-4B |
| • Compute the costs per equivalent unit. | EE18-5 | PE18-5A, 18-5B |
| • Allocate the costs to beginning inventory, units started and completed, and ending inventory. | EE18-6 | PE18-6A, 18-6B |
| • Prepare a cost of production report. | | |

**Key Points** Prepare the summary journal entries for materials, labor, applied factory overhead, and transferred costs incurred in production.

| Learning Outcomes | Example Exercises | Practice Exercises |
|---|---|---|
| • Prepare journal entries for process costing transactions. | EE18-7 | PE18-7A, 18-7B |
| • Summarize cost flows in T account form. | | |
| • Compute the ending inventory balances. | | |

**Describe and illustrate the use of cost of production reports for decision making.**

**Key Points**  The cost of production report provides information for controlling and improving operations. The report(s) can provide details of a department for a single period, or over a period of time.
   Yield measures the quantity of output of production relative to the inputs.

| Learning Outcomes | Example Exercises | Practice Exercises |
|---|---|---|
| • Prepare and evaluate a report showing the change in costs per unit by cost category for comparative periods. | **EE18-8** | **PE18-8A, 18-8B** |
| • Compute and interpret yield. | | |

**Compare just-in-time processing with traditional manufacturing processing.**

**Key Points**  The just-in-time processing philosophy focuses on reducing time, cost, and poor quality within the process.

**Learning Outcome**

• Identify the characteristics of a just-in-time process.

## Key Terms

cost of production report (838)
cost per equivalent unit (845)
equivalent units of production (841)
first-in, first-out (FIFO) method (840)

just-in-time (JIT) processing (855)
manufacturing cells (856)
process cost system (834)
process manufacturer (834)

whole units (841)
yield (854)

## Illustrative Problem

Southern Aggregate Company manufactures concrete by a series of four processes. All materials are introduced in Crushing. From Crushing, the materials pass through Sifting, Baking, and Mixing, emerging as finished concrete. All inventories are costed by the first-in, first-out method.
   The balances in the accounts Work in Process—Mixing and Finished Goods were as follows on May 1, 2012:

| | |
|---|---|
| Inventory in Process—Mixing (2,000 units, 1/4 completed) | $13,700 |
| Finished Goods (1,800 units at $8.00 a unit) | 14,400 |

The following costs were charged to Work in Process—Mixing during May:

| | |
|---|---|
| Direct materials transferred from Baking: 15,200 units at | |
| $6.50 a unit | $98,800 |
| Direct labor | 17,200 |
| Factory overhead | 11,780 |

During May, 16,000 units of concrete were completed, and 15,800 units were sold. Inventories on May 31 were as follows:

Inventory in Process—Mixing: 1,200 units, 1/2 completed
Finished Goods: 2,000 units

### Instructions

1. Prepare a cost of production report for the Mixing Department.

2. Determine the cost of goods sold (indicate number of units and unit costs).

3. Determine the finished goods inventory, May 31, 2012.

### Solution

1. See below for the cost of production report.

2. Cost of goods sold:

| | | |
|---|---|---|
| 1,800 units at $8.00 | $ 14,400 | (from finished goods beginning inventory) |
| 2,000 units at $8.20* | 16,400 | (from inventory in process beginning inventory) |
| 12,000 units at $8.30** | 99,600 | (from May production started and completed) |
| 15,800 units | $130,400 | |

*($13,700 + $2,700)/2,000
**$116,200/14,000

3. Finished goods inventory, May 31:

2,000 units at $8.30   $16,600

| | A | B | C | D | E |
|---|---|---|---|---|---|
| 1 | | Southern Aggregate Company | | | |
| 2 | | Cost of Production Report—Mixing Department | | | |
| 3 | | For the Month Ended May 31, 2012 | | | |
| 4 | | | Equivalent Units | | |
| 5 | **UNITS** | Whole Units | Direct Materials | Conversion | |
| 6 | Units charged to production: | | | | |
| 7 | Inventory in process, May 1 | 2,000 | | | |
| 8 | Received from Baking | 15,200 | | | |
| 9 | Total units accounted for by the Mixing Department | 17,200 | | | |
| 10 | | | | | |
| 11 | Units to be assigned costs: | | | | |
| 12 | Inventory in process, May 1 (25% completed) | 2,000 | 0 | 1,500 | |
| 13 | Started and completed in May | 14,000 | 14,000 | 14,000 | |
| 14 | Transferred to finished goods in May | 16,000 | 14,000 | 15,500 | |
| 15 | Inventory in process, May 31 (50% completed) | 1,200 | 1,200 | 600 | |
| 16 | Total units to be assigned costs | 17,200 | 15,200 | 16,100 | |
| 17 | | | | | |
| 18 | | | Costs | | |
| 19 | **COSTS** | | Direct Materials | Conversion | Total |
| 20 | Unit costs: | | | | |
| 21 | Total costs for May in Mixing | | $ 98,800 | $ 28,980 | |
| 22 | Total equivalent units (row 16) | | ÷15,200 | ÷16,100 | |
| 23 | Cost per equivalent unit | | $ 6.50 | $ 1.80 | |
| 24 | | | | | |
| 25 | Costs assigned to production: | | | | |
| 26 | Inventory in process, May 1 | | | | $ 13,700 |
| 27 | Costs incurred in May | | | | 127,780 |
| 28 | Total costs accounted for by the Mixing Department | | | | $141,480 |
| 29 | | | | | |
| 30 | Cost allocated to completed and partially | | | | |
| 31 | completed units: | | | | |
| 32 | Inventory in process, May 1—balance | | | | $ 13,700 |
| 33 | To complete inventory in process, May 1 | | $ 0 | $ 2,700ᵃ | 2,700 |
| 34 | Cost of completed May 1 work in process | | | | $ 16,400 |
| 35 | Started and completed in May | | 91,000ᵇ | 25,200ᶜ | 116,200 |
| 36 | Transferred to finished goods in May | | | | $132,600 |
| 37 | Inventory in process, May 31 | | $ 7,800ᵈ | $ 1,080ᵉ | 8,880 |
| 38 | Total costs assigned by the Mixing Department | | | | $141,480 |
| 39 | | | | | |

ᵃ1,500 × $1.80 = $2,700  ᵇ14,000 × $6.50 = $91,000  ᶜ14,000 × $1.80 = $25,200  ᵈ1,200 × $6.50 = $7,800  ᵉ600 × $1.80 = $1,080

# Discussion Questions

1. Which type of cost system, process or job order, would be best suited for each of the following: (a) TV assembler, (b) building contractor, (c) automobile repair shop, (d) paper manufacturer, (e) custom jewelry manufacturer? Give reasons for your answers.

2. In job order cost accounting, the three elements of manufacturing cost are charged directly to job orders. Why is it not necessary to charge manufacturing costs in process cost accounting to job orders?

3. In a job order cost system, direct labor and factory overhead applied are debited to individual jobs. How are these items treated in a process cost system and why?

4. Why is the cost per equivalent unit often determined separately for direct materials and conversion costs?

5. What is the purpose for determining the cost per equivalent unit?

6. Rameriz Company is a process manufacturer with two production departments, Blending and Filling. All direct materials are introduced in Blending from the materials store area. What is included in the cost transferred to Filling?

7. What is the most important purpose of the cost of production report?

8. How are cost of production reports used for controlling and improving operations?

9. How is "yield" determined for a process manufacturer?

10. How does just-in-time processing differ from the conventional manufacturing process?

# Practice Exercises

OBJ. 1  EE 18-1  *p. 837*  **PE 18-1A  Job order vs. process costing**

Which of the following industries would typically use job order costing, and which would typically use process costing?

| | |
|---|---|
| Flour mill | Plastic manufacturing |
| Gasoline refining | Print shop |
| Movie studio | Home construction |

OBJ. 1  EE 18-1  *p. 837*  **PE 18-1B  Job order vs. process costing**

Which of the following industries would typically use job order costing, and which would typically use process costing?

| | |
|---|---|
| Designer clothes manufacturing | Web designer |
| Business consulting | Paper manufacturing |
| Computer chip manufacturing | Steel manufacturing |

OBJ. 2  EE 18-2  *p. 841*  **PE 18-2A  Units to be assigned costs**

Rose Petal Lotion Company consists of two departments, Blending and Filling. The Filling Department received 46,000 ounces from the Blending Department. During the period, the Filling Department completed 46,500 ounces, including 2,300 ounces of work in process at the beginning of the period. The ending work in process inventory was 1,800 ounces. How many ounces were started and completed during the period?

OBJ. 2  EE 18-2  *p. 841*  **PE 18-2B  Units to be assigned costs**

Matco Steel Company has two departments, Casting and Rolling. In the Rolling Department, ingots from the Casting Department are rolled into steel sheet. The Rolling Department received 9,200 tons from the Casting Department. During the period, the Rolling Department completed 9,050 tons, including 380 tons of work in process at the beginning of the period. The ending work in process inventory was 530 tons. How many tons were started and completed during the period?

OBJ. 2  EE 18-3  *p. 842*  **PE 18-3A  Equivalent units of materials cost**

The Filling Department of Rose Petal Lotion Company had 2,300 ounces in beginning work in process inventory (70% complete). During the period, 46,500 ounces were completed. The ending work in process inventory was 1,800 ounces (25% complete). What are the total equivalent units for direct materials if materials are added at the beginning of the process?

OBJ. 2  EE 18-3  *p. 842*  **PE 18-3B  Equivalent units of materials cost**

The Rolling Department of Matco Steel Company had 380 tons in beginning work in process inventory (40% complete). During the period, 9,050 tons were completed. The ending work in process inventory was 530 tons (30% complete). What are the total equivalent units for direct materials if materials are added at the beginning of the process?

*Learning* *Objectives*  *Example* *Exercises*

OBJ. 2  EE 18-4  *p. 845*

### PE 18-4A  Equivalent units of conversion costs

The Filling Department of Rose Petal Lotion Company had 2,300 ounces in beginning work in process inventory (70% complete). During the period, 46,500 ounces were completed. The ending work in process inventory was 1,800 ounces (25% complete). What are the total equivalent units for conversion costs?

OBJ. 2  EE 18-4  *p. 845*

### PE 18-4B  Equivalent units of conversion costs

The Rolling Department of Matco Steel Company had 380 tons in beginning work in process inventory (40% complete). During the period, 9,050 tons were completed. The ending work in process inventory was 530 tons (30% complete). What are the total equivalent units for conversion costs?

OBJ. 2  EE 18-5  *p. 846*

### PE 18-5A  Cost per equivalent unit

The cost of direct materials transferred into the Filling Department of Rose Petal Lotion Company is $18,400. The conversion cost for the period in the Filling Department is $4,534. The total equivalent units for direct materials and conversion are 46,000 ounces and 45,340 ounces, respectively. Determine the direct materials and conversion costs per equivalent unit.

OBJ. 2  EE 18-5  *p. 846*

### PE 18-5B  Cost per equivalent unit

The cost of direct materials transferred into the Rolling Department of Matco Steel Company is $506,000. The conversion cost for the period in the Rolling Department is $108,684. The total equivalent units for direct materials and conversion are 9,200 tons and 9,057 tons, respectively. Determine the direct materials and conversion costs per equivalent unit.

OBJ. 2  EE 18-6  *p. 849*

### PE 18-6A  Cost of units transferred out and ending work in process

The costs per equivalent unit of direct materials and conversion in the Filling Department of Rose Petal Lotion Company are $0.40 and $0.10, respectively. The equivalent units to be assigned costs are as follows:

| | Equivalent Units | |
| --- | --- | --- |
| | Direct Materials | Conversion |
| Inventory in process, beginning of period | 0 | 690 |
| Started and completed during the period | 44,200 | 44,200 |
| Transferred out of Filling (completed) | 44,200 | 44,890 |
| Inventory in process, end of period | 1,800 | 450 |
| Total units to be assigned costs | 46,000 | 45,340 |

The beginning work in process inventory had a cost of $1,100. Determine the cost of completed and transferred-out production and the ending work in process inventory.

OBJ. 2  EE 18-6  *p. 849*

### PE 18-6B  Cost of units transferred out and ending work in process

The costs per equivalent unit of direct materials and conversion in the Rolling Department of Matco Steel Company are $55 and $12, respectively. The equivalent units to be assigned costs are as follows:

| | Equivalent Units | |
| --- | --- | --- |
| | Direct Materials | Conversion |
| Inventory in process, beginning of period | 0 | 228 |
| Started and completed during the period | 8,670 | 8,670 |
| Transferred out of Rolling (completed) | 8,670 | 8,898 |
| Inventory in process, end of period | 530 | 159 |
| Total units to be assigned costs | 9,200 | 9,057 |

The beginning work in process inventory had a cost of $23,000. Determine the cost of completed and transferred-out production and the ending work in process inventory.

**PE 18-7A    Process cost journal entries**

The cost of materials transferred into the Filling Department of Rose Petal Lotion Company is $18,400, including $6,900 from the Blending Department and $11,500 from the materials storeroom. The conversion cost for the period in the Filling Department is $4,534 ($2,160 factory overhead applied and $2,374 direct labor). The total cost transferred to Finished Goods for the period was $23,269. The Filling Department had a beginning inventory of $1,100.

a. Journalize (1) the cost of transferred-in materials, (2) conversion costs, and (3) the costs transferred out to Finished Goods.

b. Determine the balance of Work in Process—Filling at the end of the period.

**PE 18-7B    Process cost journal entries**

The cost of materials transferred into the Rolling Department of Matco Steel Company is $506,000 from the Casting Department. The conversion cost for the period in the Rolling Department is $108,684 ($63,250 factory overhead applied and $45,434 direct labor). The total cost transferred to Finished Goods for the period was $606,626. The Rolling Department had a beginning inventory of $23,000.

a. Journalize (1) the cost of transferred-in materials, (2) conversion costs, and (3) the costs transferred out to Finished Goods.

b. Determine the balance of Work in Process—Rolling at the end of the period.

**PE 18-8A    Using process costs for decision making**

The costs of energy consumed in producing good units in the Baking Department were $15,680 and $15,400 for August and September, respectively. The number of equivalent units produced in August and September was 49,000 pounds and 44,000 pounds, respectively. Evaluate the change in the cost of energy between the two months.

**PE 18-8B    Using process costs for decision making**

The costs of materials consumed in producing good units in the Forming Department were $84,000 and $85,500 for May and June, respectively. The number of equivalent units produced in May and June was 700 tons and 750 tons, respectively. Evaluate the change in the cost of materials between the two months.

## Exercises

**EX 18-1    Entries for materials cost flows in a process cost system**

The Hershey Foods Company manufactures chocolate confectionery products. The three largest raw materials are cocoa, sugar, and dehydrated milk. These raw materials first go into the Blending Department. The blended product is then sent to the Molding Department, where the bars of candy are formed. The candy is then sent to the Packing Department, where the bars are wrapped and boxed. The boxed candy is then sent to the distribution center, where it is eventually sold to food brokers and retailers.

Show the accounts debited and credited for each of the following business events:

a. Materials used by the Blending Department.

b. Transfer of blended product to the Molding Department.

c. Transfer of chocolate to the Packing Department.

d. Transfer of boxed chocolate to the distribution center.

e. Sale of boxed chocolate.

OBJ. 1

### EX 18-2 Flowchart of accounts related to service and processing departments

Alcoa Inc. is the world's largest producer of aluminum products. One product that Alcoa manufactures is aluminum sheet products for the aerospace industry. The entire output of the Smelting Department is transferred to the Rolling Department. Part of the fully processed goods from the Rolling Department are sold as rolled sheet, and the remainder of the goods are transferred to the Converting Department for further processing into sheared sheet.

Prepare a chart of the flow of costs from the processing department accounts into the finished goods accounts and then into the cost of goods sold account. The relevant accounts are as follows:

Cost of Goods Sold

Materials

Factory Overhead—Smelting Department

Factory Overhead—Rolling Department

Factory Overhead—Converting Department

Finished Goods—Rolled Sheet

Finished Goods—Sheared Sheet

Work in Process—Smelting Department

Work in Process—Rolling Department

Work in Process—Converting Department

OBJ. 1, 3

### EX 18-3 Entries for flow of factory costs for process cost system

Domino Foods, Inc., manufactures a sugar product by a continuous process, involving three production departments—Refining, Sifting, and Packing. Assume that records indicate that direct materials, direct labor, and applied factory overhead for the first department, Refining, were $310,000, $118,000, and $81,400, respectively. Also, work in process in the Refining Department at the beginning of the period totaled $23,700, and work in process at the end of the period totaled $29,100.

Journalize the entries to record (a) the flow of costs into the Refining Department during the period for (1) direct materials, (2) direct labor, and (3) factory overhead, and (b) the transfer of production costs to the second department, Sifting.

OBJ. 1, 3

✔ a. 120%

### EX 18-4 Factory overhead rate, entry for applying factory overhead, and factory overhead account balance

The chief cost accountant for Dr. Cinnamon Beverage Co. estimated that total factory overhead cost for the Blending Department for the coming fiscal year beginning April 1 would be $106,800, and total direct labor costs would be $89,000. During April, the actual direct labor cost totaled $7,500, and factory overhead cost incurred totaled $9,150.

a. What is the predetermined factory overhead rate based on direct labor cost?

b. Journalize the entry to apply factory overhead to production for April.

c. What is the April 30 balance of the account Factory Overhead—Blending Department?

d. Does the balance in part (c) represent overapplied or underapplied factory overhead?

OBJ. 2

✔ Direct materials, 16,240 units

### EX 18-5 Equivalent units of production

The Converting Department of Soft N' Dry Towel and Tissue Company had 920 units in work in process at the beginning of the period, which were 75% complete. During the period, 16,200 units were completed and transferred to the Packing Department. There were 960 units in process at the end of the period, which were 25% complete. Direct materials are placed into the process at the beginning of production. Determine the number of equivalent units of production with respect to direct materials and conversion costs.

OBJ. 2

✔ a. Conversion, 82,270 units

### EX 18-6 Equivalent units of production

Units of production data for the two departments of Atlantic Cable and Wire Company for June of the current fiscal year are as follows:

|  | Drawing Department | Winding Department |
| --- | --- | --- |
| Work in process, June 1 | 6,200 units, 40% completed | 2,600 units, 70% completed |
| Completed and transferred to next processing department during June | 82,000 units | 81,600 units |
| Work in process, June 30 | 5,000 units, 55% completed | 3,000 units, 15% completed |

If all direct materials are placed in process at the beginning of production, determine the direct materials and conversion equivalent units of production for June for (a) the Drawing Department and (b) the Winding Department.

---

**OBJ. 2**

✔ b. Conversion, 137,180

### EX 18-7  Equivalent units of production

The following information concerns production in the Baking Department for May. All direct materials are placed in process at the beginning of production.

ACCOUNT *Work in Process—Baking Department*                    ACCOUNT NO.

| Date | | Item | Debit | Credit | Balance Debit | Balance Credit |
|---|---|---|---|---|---|---|
| May | 1 | Bal., 6,500 units, ⅖ completed | | | 12,480 | |
| | 31 | Direct materials, 135,000 units | 229,500 | | 241,980 | |
| | 31 | Direct labor | 62,300 | | 304,280 | |
| | 31 | Factory overhead | 20,008 | | 324,288 | |
| | 31 | Goods finished, 137,200 units | | 315,430 | 8,858 | |
| | 31 | Bal. ? units, ⅗ completed | | | 8,858 | |

a. Determine the number of units in work in process inventory at the end of the month.
b. Determine the equivalent units of production for direct materials and conversion costs in May.

---

**OBJ. 2, 4**

✔ a. 2. Conversion cost per equivalent unit, $0.60

### EX 18-8  Costs per equivalent unit

a. Based upon the data in Exercise 18-7, determine the following:
1. Direct materials cost per equivalent unit.
2. Conversion cost per equivalent unit.
3. Cost of the beginning work in process completed during May.
4. Cost of units started and completed during May.
5. Cost of the ending work in process.
b. Assuming that the direct materials cost is the same for April and May, did the conversion cost per equivalent unit increase, decrease, or remain the same in May?

---

**OBJ. 2**

### EX 18-9  Equivalent units of production

Kellogg Company manufactures cold cereal products, such as *Frosted Flakes*. Assume that the inventory in process on January 1 for the Packing Department included 750 pounds of cereal in the packing machine hopper, enough for 500 24-oz. boxes. In addition, there were 500 empty 24-oz. boxes held in the package carousel of the packing machine. During January, 41,500 boxes of 24-oz. cereal were packaged. Conversion costs are incurred when a box is filled with cereal. On January 31, the packing machine hopper held 960 pounds of cereal, and the package carousel held 640 empty 24-oz. (1½-pound) boxes. Assume that once a box is filled with cereal, it is immediately transferred to the finished goods warehouse.

Determine the equivalent units of production for cereal, boxes, and conversion costs for January. An equivalent unit is defined as "pounds" for cereal and "24-oz. boxes" for boxes and conversion costs.

---

**OBJ. 2**

✔ c. $3.60

### EX 18-10  Costs per equivalent unit

Pacific Products Inc. completed and transferred 55,000 particle board units of production from the Pressing Department. There was no beginning inventory in process in the department. The ending in-process inventory was 1,400 units, which were ⅗ complete as to conversion cost. All materials are added at the beginning of the process. Direct materials cost incurred was $203,040, direct labor cost incurred was $38,900, and factory overhead applied was $28,108.

Determine the following for the Pressing Department:

a. Total conversion cost

b. Conversion cost per equivalent unit

c. Direct materials cost per equivalent unit

---

**OBJ. 2**

✔ a. 7,500 units

### EX 18-11 Equivalent units of production and related costs

The charges to Work in Process—Assembly Department for a period, together with information concerning production, are as follows. All direct materials are placed in process at the beginning of production.

| Work in Process— Assembly Department | | | |
|---|---|---|---|
| Bal., 5,000 units, 35% completed | 10,475 | To Finished Goods, 105,500 units | ? |
| Direct materials, 108,000 units @ $1.50 | 162,000 | | |
| Direct labor | 145,300 | | |
| Factory overhead | 47,525 | | |
| Bal. ? units, 45% completed | ? | | |

Determine the following:

a. The number of units in work in process inventory at the end of the period.

b. Equivalent units of production for direct materials and conversion.

c. Costs per equivalent unit for direct materials and conversion.

d. Cost of the units started and completed during the period.

---

**OBJ. 2, 4**

✔ a. 1. $16,325

### EX 18-12 Cost of units completed and in process

a. Based on the data in Exercise 18-11, determine the following:

1. Cost of beginning work in process inventory completed this period.

2. Cost of units transferred to finished goods during the period.

3. Cost of ending work in process inventory.

4. Cost per unit of the completed beginning work in process inventory, rounded to the nearest cent.

b. Did the production costs change from the preceding period? Explain.

c. Assuming that the direct materials cost per unit did not change from the preceding period, did the conversion costs per equivalent unit increase, decrease, or remain the same for the current period?

---

**OBJ. 2**

### EX 18-13 Errors in equivalent unit computation

Golden Bear Refining Company processes gasoline. On April 1 of the current year, 5,000 units were ⅗ completed in the Blending Department. During April, 45,000 units entered the Blending Department from the Refining Department. During April, the units in process at the beginning of the month were completed. Of the 45,000 units entering the department, all were completed except 6,100 units that were ⅕ completed. The equivalent units for conversion costs for April for the Blending Department were computed as follows:

| Equivalent units of production in April: | |
|---|---|
| To process units in inventory on April 1: 5,000 × ⅗ | 3,000 |
| To process units started and completed in April : 45,000 – 5,000 | 40,000 |
| To process units in inventory on April 30: 6,100 × ⅕ | 1,220 |
| Equivalent units of production | 44,220 |

List the errors in the computation of equivalent units for conversion costs for the Blending Department for April.

---

**OBJ. 2**

✔ a. 7,450 units

### EX 18-14 Cost per equivalent unit

The following information concerns production in the Forging Department for September. All direct materials are placed into the process at the beginning of production, and conversion costs are incurred evenly throughout the process. The beginning inventory consists of $11,250 of direct materials.

ACCOUNT *Work in Process—Forging Department*                                        ACCOUNT NO.

| Date | | Item | Debit | Credit | Balance Debit | Balance Credit |
|---|---|---|---|---|---|---|
| Sept. | 1 | Bal., 750 units, 60% completed | | | 13,185 | |
| | 30 | Direct materials, 7,200 units | 100,800 | | 113,985 | |
| | 30 | Direct labor | 17,300 | | 131,285 | |
| | 30 | Factory overhead | 17,980 | ? | 149,265 | |
| | 30 | Goods transferred, ? units | | | ? | |
| | 30 | Bal., 500 units, 70% completed | | | ? | |

a. Determine the number of units transferred to the next department.

b. Determine the costs per equivalent unit of direct materials and conversion.

c. Determine the cost of units started and completed in September.

---

OBJ. 2, 4

✔ a. $14,625

### EX 18-15   Costs per equivalent unit and production costs

Based on the data in Exercise 18-14, determine the following:

a. Cost of beginning work in process inventory completed in September.

b. Cost of units transferred to the next department during September.

c. Cost of ending work in process inventory on September 30.

d. Costs per equivalent unit of direct materials and conversion included in the September 1 beginning work in process.

e. The September increase or decrease in costs per equivalent unit for direct materials and conversion from the previous month.

---

OBJ. 2, 4

✔ d. $4,104

### EX 18-16   Cost of production report

The debits to Work in Process—Roasting Department for St. Arbucks Coffee Company for July 2012, together with information concerning production, are as follows:

| | | |
|---|---|---|
| Work in process, July 1, 600 pounds, 20% completed | | $ 2,418* |
| *Direct materials (600 × $3.80) | $2,280 | |
| Conversion (600 × 20% × $1.15) | 138 | |
| | $2,418 | |
| Coffee beans added during July, 23,000 pounds | | 82,800 |
| Conversion costs during July | | 27,480 |
| Work in process, July 31, 1,000 pounds, 42% completed | | ? |
| Goods finished during July, 22,600 pounds | | ? |

All direct materials are placed in process at the beginning of production. Prepare a cost of production report, presenting the following computations:

a. Direct materials and conversion equivalent units of production for July.

b. Direct materials and conversion costs per equivalent unit for July.

c. Cost of goods finished during July.

d. Cost of work in process at July 31, 2012.

e. Compute and evaluate the change in cost per equivalent unit for direct materials and conversion from the previous month (June).

---

OBJ. 2, 4

✔ Conversion cost per equivalent unit, $4.00

### EX 18-17   Cost of production report

The Cutting Department of Tangu Carpet Company provides the following data for December 2012. Assume that all materials are added at the beginning of the process.

| | | |
|---|---|---|
| Work in process, December 1, 9,000 units, 75% completed | | $ 103,275* |
| *Direct materials (9,000 × $8.55) | $ 76,950 | |
| Conversion (9,000 × 75% × $3.90) | 26,325 | |
| | $103,275 | |
| Materials added during December from Weaving Department, 139,000 units | | $1,209,300 |
| Direct labor for December | | 289,300 |
| Factory overhead for December | | 260,300 |
| Goods finished during December (includes goods in process, December 1), 142,500 units | | — |
| Work in process, December 31, 5,500 units, 30% completed | | — |

a. Prepare a cost of production report for the Cutting Department.

b. Compute and evaluate the change in the cost per equivalent unit for direct materials and conversion from the previous month (November).

---

OBJ. 1, 2, 3, 4

✔ b. $6,800

### EX 18-18 Cost of production and journal entries

Airfoil Castings Inc. casts blades for turbine engines. Within the Casting Department, alloy is first melted in a crucible, then poured into molds to produce the castings. On March 1, there were 190 pounds of alloy in process, which were 60% complete as to conversion. The Work in Process balance for these 190 pounds was $25,536, determined as follows:

| | |
|---|---|
| Direct materials (190 × $120) | $22,800 |
| Conversion (190 × 60% × $24) | 2,736 |
| | $25,536 |

During March, the Casting Department was charged $237,500 for 1,900 pounds of alloy and $19,480 for direct labor. Factory overhead is applied to the department at a rate of 150% of direct labor. The department transferred out 2,040 pounds of finished castings to the Machining Department. The March 31 inventory in process was 44% complete as to conversion.

a. Prepare the following March journal entries for the Casting Department:

   1. The materials charged to production.

   2. The conversion costs charged to production.

   3. The completed production transferred to the Machining Department.

b. Determine the Work in Process—Casting Department March 31 balance.

c. Compute and evaluate the change in cost per equivalent unit for direct materials and conversion from the previous month (February).

---

OBJ. 1, 2, 3

✔ b. $22,806

### EX 18-19 Cost of production and journal entries

Beacon Paper Company manufactures newsprint. The product is manufactured in two departments, Papermaking and Converting. Pulp is first placed into a vessel at the beginning of papermaking production. The following information concerns production in the Papermaking Department for January.

ACCOUNT *Work in Process—Papermaking Department*          ACCOUNT NO.

| Date | | Item | Debit | Credit | Balance Debit | Balance Credit |
|---|---|---|---|---|---|---|
| Jan. | 1 | Bal., 3,400 units, 35% completed | | | 15,300 | |
| | 31 | Direct materials, 82,000 units | 307,500 | | 322,800 | |
| | 31 | Direct labor | 93,477 | | 416,277 | |
| | 31 | Factory overhead | 81,600 | | 497,877 | |
| | 31 | Goods transferred, 81,200 units | | ? | ? | |
| | 31 | Bal., 4,200 units, 80% completed | | | ? | |

a. Prepare the following January journal entries for the Papermaking Department:

   1. The materials charged to production.

   2. The conversion costs charged to production.

3. The completed production transferred to the Converting Department.

b. Determine the Work in Process—Papermaking Department January 31 balance.

---

**OBJ. 4**

### EX 18-20  Decision making

Cool Springs Bottling Company bottles popular beverages in the Bottling Department. The beverages are produced by blending concentrate with water and sugar. The concentrate is purchased from a concentrate producer. The concentrate producer sets higher prices for the more popular concentrate flavors. Below is a simplified Bottling Department cost of production report separating the costs of bottling the four flavors.

| | A | B | C | D | E |
|---|---|---|---|---|---|
| 1 | | Orange | Cola | Lemon-Lime | Root Beer |
| 2 | Concentrate | $ 3,700 | $107,500 | $ 84,000 | $ 5,700 |
| 3 | Water | 1,000 | 25,000 | 20,000 | 1,500 |
| 4 | Sugar | 2,000 | 50,000 | 40,000 | 3,000 |
| 5 | Bottles | 4,400 | 110,000 | 88,000 | 6,600 |
| 6 | Flavor changeover | 1,600 | 4,000 | 3,200 | 6,000 |
| 7 | Conversion cost | 1,400 | 20,000 | 16,000 | 2,100 |
| 8 | Total cost transferred to finished goods | $14,100 | $316,500 | $251,200 | $24,900 |
| 9 | Number of cases | 2,000 | 50,000 | 40,000 | 3,000 |
| 10 | | | | | |

Beginning and ending work in process inventories are negligible, so are omitted from the cost of production report. The flavor changeover cost represents the cost of cleaning the bottling machines between production runs of different flavors.

Prepare a memo to the production manager analyzing this comparative cost information. In your memo, provide recommendations for further action, along with supporting schedules showing the total cost per case and cost per case by cost element.

---

**OBJ. 4**

### EX 18-21  Decision making

Instant Pix Inc. produces photographic paper for printing digital images. One of the processes for this operation is a coating (solvent spreading) operation, where chemicals are coated on to paper stock. There has been some concern about the cost performance of this operation. As a result, you have begun an investigation. You first discover that all materials and conversion prices have been stable for the last six months. Thus, increases in prices for inputs are not an explanation for increasing costs. However, you have discovered three possible problems from some of the operating personnel whose quotes follow:

*Operator 1:* "I've been keeping an eye on my operating room instruments. I feel as though our energy consumption is becoming less efficient."

*Operator 2:* "Every time the coating machine goes down, we produce waste on shutdown and subsequent startup. It seems like during the last half year we have had more unscheduled machine shutdowns than in the past. Thus, I feel as though our yields must be dropping."

*Operator 3:* "My sense is that our coating costs are going up. It seems to me like we are spreading a thicker coating than we should. Perhaps the coating machine needs to be recalibrated."

The Coating Department had no beginning or ending inventories for any month during the study period. The following data from the cost of production report are made available:

| | A | B | C | D | E | F | G |
|---|---|---|---|---|---|---|---|
| 1 | | January | February | March | April | May | June |
| 2 | Paper stock | $67,200 | $63,840 | $60,480 | $64,512 | $57,120 | $53,760 |
| 3 | Coating | $14,400 | $16,416 | $17,280 | $20,275 | $20,400 | $23,040 |
| 4 | Conversion cost (incl. energy) | $48,000 | $45,600 | $43,200 | $46,080 | $40,800 | $38,400 |
| 5 | Pounds input to the process | 100,000 | 95,000 | 90,000 | 96,000 | 85,000 | 80,000 |
| 6 | Pounds transferred out | 96,000 | 91,200 | 86,400 | 92,160 | 81,600 | 76,800 |
| 7 | | | | | | | |

a. Prepare a table showing the paper cost per output pound, coating cost per output pound, conversion cost per output pound, and yield (pounds out/pounds input) for each month.

b. Interpret your table results.

**OBJ. 5**

### EX 18-22  Just-in-time manufacturing

The following are some quotes provided by a number of managers at Ken-Tex Machining Company regarding the company's planned move toward a just-in-time manufacturing system:

*Director of Sales:* I'm afraid we'll miss some sales if we don't keep a large stock of items on hand just in case demand increases. It only makes sense to me to keep large inventories in order to assure product availability for our customers.

*Director of Purchasing:* I'm very concerned about moving to a just-in-time system for materials. What would happen if one of our suppliers were unable to make a shipment? A supplier could fall behind in production or have a quality problem. Without some safety stock in our materials, our whole plant would shut down.

*Director of Manufacturing:* If we go to just-in-time, I think our factory output will drop. We need in-process inventory in order to "smooth out" the inevitable problems that occur during manufacturing. For example, if a machine that is used to process a product breaks down, it would starve the next machine if I don't have in-process inventory between the two machines. If I have in-process inventory, then I can keep the next operation busy while I fix the broken machine. Thus, the in-process inventories give me a safety valve that I can use to keep things running when things go wrong.

➤ How would you respond to these managers?

✔ a. 17,200

### Appendix
### EX 18-23  Equivalent units of production: average cost method

The Converting Department of Sydney Napkin Company uses the average cost method and had 1,600 units in work in process that were 60% complete at the beginning of the period. During the period, 16,200 units were completed and transferred to the Packing Department. There were 1,000 units in process that were 30% complete at the end of the period.

a.  Determine the number of whole units to be accounted for and to be assigned costs for the period.

b.  Determine the number of equivalent units of production for the period.

✔ a. 13,300 units to be accounted for

### Appendix
### EX 18-24  Equivalent units of production: average cost method

Units of production data for the two departments of Continental Cable and Wire Company for May of the current fiscal year are as follows:

|  | Drawing Department | Winding Department |
|---|---|---|
| Work in process, May 1 | 800 units, 50% completed | 250 units, 30% completed |
| Completed and transferred to next processing department during May | 12,700 units | 12,550 units |
| Work in process, May 31 | 600 units, 55% completed | 400 units, 25% completed |

Each department uses the average cost method.

a.  Determine the number of whole units to be accounted for and to be assigned costs and the equivalent units of production for the Drawing Department.

b.  Determine the number of whole units to be accounted for and to be assigned costs and the equivalent units of production for the Winding Department.

✔ a. 8,500

### Appendix
### EX 18-25  Equivalent units of production: average cost method

The following information concerns production in the Finishing Department for March. The Finishing Department uses the average cost method.

ACCOUNT *Work in Process—Finishing Department*  ACCOUNT NO.

| Date | | Item | Debit | Credit | Balance Debit | Balance Credit |
|---|---|---|---|---|---|---|
| Mar. | 1 | Bal., 12,500 units, 70% completed | | | 44,000 | |
| | 31 | Direct materials, 61,200 units | 130,650 | | 174,650 | |
| | 31 | Direct labor | 81,500 | | 256,150 | |
| | 31 | Factory overhead | 82,600 | | 338,750 | |
| | 31 | Goods transferred, 65,200 units | | 326,000 | 12,750 | |
| | 31 | Bal., ? units, 30% completed | | | 12,750 | |

a. Determine the number of units in work in process inventory at the end of the month.

b. Determine the number of whole units to be accounted for and to be assigned costs and the equivalent units of production for March.

✔ b. 14,200 units

**Appendix**

**EX 18-26 Equivalent units of production and related costs**

The charges to Work in Process—Baking Department for a period as well as information concerning production are as follows. The Baking Department uses the average cost method, and all direct materials are placed in process during production.

| Work in Process—Baking Department | | | |
|---|---|---|---|
| Bal., 1,800 units, 40% completed | 2,952 | To Finished Goods, 13,000 units | ? |
| Direct materials, 13,200 units | 32,100 | | |
| Direct labor | 16,160 | | |
| Factory overhead | 8,428 | | |
| Bal., 2,000 units, 60% completed | ? | | |

Determine the following:

a. The number of whole units to be accounted for and to be assigned costs.

b. The number of equivalent units of production.

c. The cost per equivalent unit.

d. The cost of units transferred to Finished Goods.

e. The cost of units in ending Work in Process.

✔ a. $22.50

**Appendix**

**EX 18-27 Cost per equivalent unit: average cost method**

The following information concerns production in the Forging Department for April. The Forging Department uses the average cost method.

**ACCOUNT** *Work in Process—Forging Department*  ACCOUNT NO.

| Date | | Item | Debit | Credit | Balance Debit | Balance Credit |
|---|---|---|---|---|---|---|
| Apr. | 1 | Bal., 500 units, 40% completed | | | 4,400 | |
| | 30 | Direct materials, 4,900 units | 56,075 | | 60,475 | |
| | 30 | Direct labor | 31,600 | | 92,075 | |
| | 30 | Factory overhead | 24,700 | | 116,775 | |
| | 30 | Goods transferred, 4,700 units | | ? | ? | |
| | 30 | Bal., 700 units, 70% completed | | | ? | |

a. Determine the cost per equivalent unit.

b. Determine the cost of units transferred to Finished Goods.

c. Determine the cost of units in ending Work in Process.

✔ Cost per equivalent unit, $4.00

**Appendix**

**EX 18-28 Cost of production report: average cost method**

The increases to Work in Process—Roasting Department for Boston Coffee Company for March 2012 as well as information concerning production are as follows:

| | |
|---|---|
| Work in process, March 1, 650 pounds, 40% completed | $ 1,050 |
| Coffee beans added during March, 12,300 pounds | 32,170 |
| Conversion costs during March | 17,860 |
| Work in process, March 31, 900 pounds, 80% completed | — |
| Goods finished during March, 12,050 pounds | — |

Prepare a cost of production report, using the average cost method.

✔ Cost per
equivalent unit,
$12.00

**Appendix**

**EX 18-29   Cost of production report: average cost method**

Prepare a cost of production report for the Cutting Department of Tanner Carpet Company for December 2012. Use the average cost method with the following data:

| | |
|---|---:|
| Work in process, December 1, 4,500 units, 75% completed | $ 40,000 |
| Materials added during December from Weaving Department, 85,000 units | 699,300 |
| Direct labor for December | 169,410 |
| Factory overhead for December | 98,330 |
| Goods finished during December (includes goods in process, December 1), 83,300 units | — |
| Work in process, December 31, 6,200 units, 10% completed | — |

## Problems Series A

OBJ. 1, 3

✔ 2. Materials July 31
balance, $5,600

GENERAL
·LEDGER·

**PR 18-1A   Entries for process cost system**

Design Flooring Carpet Company manufactures carpets. Fiber is placed in process in the Spinning Department, where it is spun into yarn. The output of the Spinning Department is transferred to the Tufting Department, where carpet backing is added at the beginning of the process and the process is completed. On July 1, Design Flooring Carpet Company had the following inventories:

| | |
|---|---:|
| Finished Goods | $5,600 |
| Work in Process—Spinning Department | 900 |
| Work in Process—Tufting Department | 1,400 |
| Materials | 4,200 |

Departmental accounts are maintained for factory overhead, and both have zero balances on July 1.

Manufacturing operations for July are summarized as follows:

| | |
|---|---:|
| a. Materials purchased on account . . . . . . . . . . . . . . . . . . . . . . . . . . . . . . . . . . . . . . . . . . . . . . . | $ 84,600 |
| b. Materials requisitioned for use: | |
|     Fiber—Spinning Department . . . . . . . . . . . . . . . . . . . . . . . . . . . . . . . . . . . . . . . . . . . . . . | $ 42,800 |
|     Carpet backing—Tufting Department . . . . . . . . . . . . . . . . . . . . . . . . . . . . . . . . . . . . . | 34,400 |
|     Indirect materials—Spinning Department . . . . . . . . . . . . . . . . . . . . . . . . . . . . . . . . . . | 3,200 |
|     Indirect materials—Tufting Department . . . . . . . . . . . . . . . . . . . . . . . . . . . . . . . . . . . | 2,800 |
| c. Labor used: | |
|     Direct labor—Spinning Department . . . . . . . . . . . . . . . . . . . . . . . . . . . . . . . . . . . . . . . | $ 24,200 |
|     Direct labor—Tufting Department . . . . . . . . . . . . . . . . . . . . . . . . . . . . . . . . . . . . . . . . | 18,700 |
|     Indirect labor—Spinning Department . . . . . . . . . . . . . . . . . . . . . . . . . . . . . . . . . . . . | 12,300 |
|     Indirect labor—Tufting Department . . . . . . . . . . . . . . . . . . . . . . . . . . . . . . . . . . . . . | 11,900 |
| d. Depreciation charged on fixed assets: | |
|     Spinning Department . . . . . . . . . . . . . . . . . . . . . . . . . . . . . . . . . . . . . . . . . . . . . . . . . . | $ 5,300 |
|     Tufting Department . . . . . . . . . . . . . . . . . . . . . . . . . . . . . . . . . . . . . . . . . . . . . . . . . . . | 3,100 |
| e. Expired prepaid factory insurance: | |
|     Spinning Department . . . . . . . . . . . . . . . . . . . . . . . . . . . . . . . . . . . . . . . . . . . . . . . . . . | $ 1,200 |
|     Tufting Department . . . . . . . . . . . . . . . . . . . . . . . . . . . . . . . . . . . . . . . . . . . . . . . . . . . | 900 |
| f. Applied factory overhead: | |
|     Spinning Department . . . . . . . . . . . . . . . . . . . . . . . . . . . . . . . . . . . . . . . . . . . . . . . . . . | $ 21,600 |
|     Tufting Department . . . . . . . . . . . . . . . . . . . . . . . . . . . . . . . . . . . . . . . . . . . . . . . . . . . | 19,500 |
| g. Production costs transferred from Spinning Department to Tufting Department . . . . . . . . | $ 87,200 |
| h. Production costs transferred from Tufting Department to Finished Goods . . . . . . . . . . . . . . | $159,200 |
| i. Cost of goods sold during the period . . . . . . . . . . . . . . . . . . . . . . . . . . . . . . . . . . . . . . . . . . . | $160,300 |

**Instructions**

1. Journalize the entries to record the operations, identifying each entry by letter.

2. Compute the July 31 balances of the inventory accounts.

3. Compute the July 31 balances of the factory overhead accounts.

OBJ. 2, 4

✔ 1. Conversion cost per equivalent unit, $1.20

### PR 18-2A  Cost of production report

Robusta Coffee Company roasts and packs coffee beans. The process begins by placing coffee beans into the Roasting Department. From the Roasting Department, coffee beans are then transferred to the Packing Department. The following is a partial work in process account of the Roasting Department at March 31, 2012:

**ACCOUNT** *Work in Process—Roasting Department*  **ACCOUNT NO.**

| Date | | Item | Debit | Credit | Balance Debit | Balance Credit |
|---|---|---|---|---|---|---|
| Mar. | 1 | Bal., 1,050 units, 30% completed | | | 4,997 | |
| | 31 | Direct materials,16,200 units | 72,900 | | 77,897 | |
| | 31 | Direct labor | 10,800 | | 88,697 | |
| | 31 | Factory overhead | 8,910 | | 97,607 | |
| | 31 | Goods transferred, 16,400 units | | ? | | |
| | 31 | Bal., ? units, 40% completed | | | ? | |

### Instructions

1. Prepare a cost of production report, and identify the missing amounts for Work in Process—Roasting Department.

2. Assuming that the March 1 work in process inventory includes $4,578 of direct materials, determine the increase or decrease in the cost per equivalent unit for direct materials and conversion between February and March.

OBJ. 2, 3, 4

✔ 2. Transferred to Packaging Dept., $42,569

### PR 18-3A  Equivalent units and related costs; cost of production report; entries

White Star Flour Company manufactures flour by a series of three processes, beginning with wheat grain being introduced in the Milling Department. From the Milling Department, the materials pass through the Sifting and Packaging departments, emerging as packaged refined flour.

The balance in the account Work in Process—Sifting Department was as follows on May 1, 2012:

Work in Process—Sifting Department (800 units, ⅗ completed):
| | | |
|---|---|---|
| Direct materials (800 × $2.25) | $1,800 | |
| Conversion (800 × ⅗ × $0.65) | 312 | |
| | $2,112 | |

The following costs were charged to Work in Process—Sifting Department during May:

Direct materials transferred from Milling Department:
| | | |
|---|---|---|
| 14,200 units at $2.35 a unit | $33,370 | |
| Direct labor | 6,100 | |
| Factory overhead | 3,924 | |

During May, 14,000 units of flour were completed. Work in Process—Sifting Department on May 31 was 1,000 units, ⅕ completed.

### Instructions

1. Prepare a cost of production report for the Sifting Department for May.

2. Journalize the entries for costs transferred from Milling to Sifting and the costs transferred from Sifting to Packaging.

3. Determine the increase or decrease in the cost per equivalent unit from April to May for direct materials and conversion costs.

4. ▬▬▬▶ Discuss the uses of the cost of production report and the results of part (3).

**PR 18-4A   Work in process account data for two months; cost of production reports**

HomeStyle Soup Co. uses a process cost system to record the costs of processing soup, which requires the cooking and filling processes. Materials are entered from the cooking process at the beginning of the filling process. The inventory of Work in Process—Filling on February 1 and debits to the account during February 2012 were as follows:

Bal., 400 units, 30% completed:

| | |
|---|---|
| Direct materials (400 × $3.70) | $ 1,480 |
| Conversion (400 × 30% × $1.55) | 186 |
| | $ 1,666 |
| | |
| From Cooking Department, 8,900 units | $33,820 |
| Direct labor | 9,450 |
| Factory overhead | 5,134 |

During February, 400 units in process on February 1 were completed, and of the 8,900 units entering the department, all were completed except 650 units that were 90% completed. Charges to Work in Process—Filling for March were as follows:

| | |
|---|---|
| From Cooking Department, 9,600 units | $38,400 |
| Direct labor | 10,890 |
| Factory overhead | 5,922 |

During March, the units in process at the beginning of the month were completed, and of the 9,600 units entering the department, all were completed except 500 units that were 35% completed.

**Instructions**

1.  Enter the balance as of February 1, 2012, in a four-column account for Work in Process—Filling. Record the debits and the credits in the account for February. Construct a cost of production report, and present computations for determining (a) equivalent units of production for materials and conversion, (b) costs per equivalent unit, (c) cost of goods finished, differentiating between units started in the prior period and units started and finished in February, and (d) work in process inventory.

2.  Provide the same information for March by recording the March transactions in the four-column work in process account. Construct a cost of production report, and present the March computations (a through d) listed in part (1).

3.  ━━━▶ Comment on the change in costs per equivalent unit for January through March for direct materials and conversion costs.

---

✔ Cost per equivalent
unit, $2.60

**Appendix**
**PR 18-5A   Cost of production report: average cost method**

AM Coffee Company roasts and packs coffee beans. The process begins in the Roasting Department. From the Roasting Department, the coffee beans are transferred to the Packing Department. The following is a partial work in process account of the Roasting Department at October 31, 2012:

**ACCOUNT** *Work in Process—Roasting Department*                    **ACCOUNT NO.**

| Date | | Item | Debit | Credit | Balance Debit | Balance Credit |
|---|---|---|---|---|---|---|
| Oct. | 1 | Bal., 12,400 units, 75% completed | | | 24,000 | |
| | 31 | Direct materials, 214,600 units | 235,700 | | 259,700 | |
| | 31 | Direct labor | 127,200 | | 386,900 | |
| | 31 | Factory overhead | 181,850 | | 568,750 | |
| | 31 | Goods transferred, 216,000 units | | ? | ? | |
| | 31 | Bal., ? units, 25% completed | | | ? | |

**Instructions**

Prepare a cost of production report, using the average cost method, and identify the missing amounts for Work in Process—Roasting Department.

## Problems Series B

**OBJ. 1, 3**

✔ 2. Materials
May 31 balance,
$7,480

### PR 18-1B    Entries for process cost system

G&P Soap Company manufactures powdered detergent. Phosphate is placed in process in the Making Department, where it is turned into granulars. The output of Making is transferred to the Packing Department, where packaging is added at the beginning of the process. On May 1, G&P Soap Company had the following inventories:

| | |
|---|---|
| Finished Goods | $11,200 |
| Work in Process—Making | 5,240 |
| Work in Process—Packing | 6,710 |
| Materials | 3,100 |

Departmental accounts are maintained for factory overhead, which both have zero balances on May 1.

Manufacturing operations for May are summarized as follows:

| | |
|---|---|
| a. Materials purchased on account .............................................. | $145,800 |
| b. Materials requisitioned for use: | |
|     Phosphate—Making Department ............................................ | $103,250 |
|     Packaging—Packing Department ............................................ | 32,600 |
|     Indirect materials—Making Department ...................................... | 4,320 |
|     Indirect materials—Packing Department...................................... | 1,250 |
| c. Labor used: | |
|     Direct labor—Making Department .......................................... | $ 28,200 |
|     Direct labor—Packing Department .......................................... | 37,200 |
|     Indirect labor—Making Department......................................... | 15,100 |
|     Indirect labor—Packing Department ........................................ | 16,700 |
| d. Depreciation charged on fixed assets: | |
|     Making Department....................................................... | $ 9,500 |
|     Packing Department ...................................................... | 6,300 |
| e. Expired prepaid factory insurance: | |
|     Making Department....................................................... | $ 2,400 |
|     Packing Department ...................................................... | 1,200 |
| f. Applied factory overhead: | |
|     Making Department....................................................... | $ 32,420 |
|     Packing Department ...................................................... | 24,150 |
| g. Production costs transferred from Making Department to Packing Department ..... | $164,320 |
| h. Production costs transferred from Packing Department to Finished Goods.......... | $257,900 |
| i. Cost of goods sold during the period ......................................... | $260,200 |

### Instructions

1. Journalize the entries to record the operations, identifying each entry by letter.
2. Compute the May 31 balances of the inventory accounts.
3. Compute the May 31 balances of the factory overhead accounts.

**OBJ. 2, 4**

✔ 1. Conversion cost
per equivalent unit,
$1.00

### PR 18-2B    Cost of production report

Swiss Velvet Chocolate Company processes chocolate into candy bars. The process begins by placing direct materials (raw chocolate, milk, and sugar) into the Blending Department. All materials are placed into production at the beginning of the blending process. After blending, the milk chocolate is then transferred to the Molding Department, where the milk chocolate is formed into candy bars. The following is a partial work in process account of the Blending Department at August 31, 2012:

**ACCOUNT** *Work in Process—Blending Department*                    **ACCOUNT NO.**

| Date | | Item | Debit | Credit | Balance Debit | Balance Credit |
|---|---|---|---|---|---|---|
| Aug. | 1 | Bal., 1,900 units, ⅗ completed | | | 7,657 | |
| | 31 | Direct materials, 22,000 units | 77,000 | | 84,657 | |
| | 31 | Direct labor | 14,200 | | 98,857 | |
| | 31 | Factory overhead | 6,880 | | 105,737 | |
| | 31 | Goods transferred, 21,800 units | | ? | | |
| | 31 | Bal., ? units, ⅕ completed | | | ? | |

**Instructions**

1. Prepare a cost of production report, and identify the missing amounts for Work in Process—Blending Department.

2. Assuming that the August 1 work in process inventory includes direct materials of $6,460, determine the increase or decrease in the cost per equivalent unit for direct materials and conversion between July and August.

---

OBJ. 2, 3, 4
✔ 2. Transferred
to finished goods,
$757,125

**PR 18-3B    Equivalent units and related costs; cost of production report; entries**

Meadowland Chemical Company manufactures specialty chemicals by a series of three processes, all materials being introduced in the Distilling Department. From the Distilling Department, the materials pass through the Reaction and Filling departments, emerging as finished chemicals.

The balance in the account Work in Process—Filling was as follows on December 1, 2012:

Work in Process—Filling Department
(2,500 units, 60% completed):

| Direct materials (2,500 × $13.10) | $32,750 |
|---|---|
| Conversion (2,500 × 60% × $5.65) | 8,475 |
| | $41,225 |

The following costs were charged to Work in Process—Filling during December:

| Direct materials transferred from Reaction Department: 42,100 units at $13.00 a unit | $547,300 |
|---|---|
| Direct labor | 143,200 |
| Factory overhead | 79,605 |

During December, 40,900 units of specialty chemicals were completed. Work in Process—Filling Department on December 31 was 3,700 units, 30% completed.

**Instructions**

1. Prepare a cost of production report for the Filling Department for December.

2. Journalize the entries for costs transferred from Reaction to Filling and the cost transferred from Filling to Finished Goods.

3. Determine the increase or decrease in the cost per equivalent unit from November to December for direct materials and conversion costs.

4. ━━━▶ Discuss the uses of the cost of production report and the results of part (3).

---

OBJ. 1, 2, 3, 4
✔ 1. c. Transferred
to finished goods in
June, $647,925

**PR 18-4B    Work in process account data for two months; cost of production reports**

Natco Aluminum Company uses a process cost system to record the costs of manufacturing rolled aluminum, which consists of the smelting and rolling processes. Materials are entered from smelting at the beginning of the rolling process. The inventory of Work in Process—Rolling on June 1, 2012, and debits to the account during June were as follows:

Bal., 3,300 units, ¼ completed:
| | |
|---|---|
| Direct materials (3,300 × $12.50) | $41,250 |
| Conversion (3,300 × ¼ × $7.40) | 6,105 |
| | $47,355 |

| | |
|---|---|
| From Smelting Department, 32,500 units | $409,500 |
| Direct labor | 142,400 |
| Factory overhead | 117,786 |

During June, 3,300 units in process on June 1 were completed, and of the 32,500 units entering the department, all were completed except 3,700 units that were ⅕ completed. Charges to Work in Process—Rolling for July were as follows:

| | |
|---|---|
| From Smelting Department, 33,000 units | $422,400 |
| Direct labor | 136,400 |
| Factory overhead | 111,600 |

During July, the units in process at the beginning of the month were completed, and of the 33,000 units entering the department, all were completed except 2,900 units that were ⅖ completed.

**Instructions**

1. Enter the balance as of June 1, 2012, in a four-column account for Work in Process—Rolling. Record the debits and the credits in the account for June. Construct a cost of production report and present computations for determining (a) equivalent units of production for materials and conversion, (b) costs per equivalent unit, (c) cost of goods finished, differentiating between units started in the prior period and units started and finished in June, and (d) work in process inventory.

2. Provide the same information for July by recording the July transactions in the four-column work in process account. Construct a cost of production report, and present the July computations (a through d) listed in part (1).

3. ━━━━➤ Comment on the change in costs per equivalent unit for May through July for direct materials and conversion cost.

---

✔ Transferred to Packaging Dept., $58,100

**Appendix**
**PR 18-5B   Equivalent units and related costs; Cost of production report: Average cost method**

State Fair Flour Company manufactures flour by a series of three processes, beginning in the Milling Department. From the Milling Department, the materials pass through the Sifting and Packaging departments, emerging as packaged refined flour.

The balance in the account Work in Process—Sifting Department was as follows on March 1, 2012:

| | |
|---|---|
| Work in Process—Sifting Department (1,000 units, 75% completed) | $2,600 |

The following costs were charged to Work in Process—Sifting Department during March:

| | |
|---|---|
| Direct materials transferred from Milling Department: 16,800 units | $31,000 |
| Direct labor | 13,250 |
| Factory overhead | 14,400 |

During March, 16,600 units of flour were completed and transferred to finished goods. Work in Process—Sifting Department on March 31 was 1,200 units, 75% completed.

**Instructions**

Prepare a cost of production report for the Sifting Department for March, using the average cost method.

## Cases & Projects

You can access Cases & Projects online at **www.cengage.com/accounting/reeve**

## Excel Success Special Activities

### SA 18-1   Cost per equivalent unit

Brazil Aluminum, Inc., processes aluminum. The Smelting Department had the following equivalent units with respect to direct materials and conversion:

|  | Equivalent Units | |
|---|---|---|
|  | Direct Materials | Conversion |
| Inventory in process, October 1 | — | 2,400 |
| Started and completed in October | 95,000 | 95,000 |
| Transferred out to Rolling | 95,000 | 97,400 |
| Inventory in process, October 31 | 6,000 | 1,200 |
| Total equivalent units to be assigned costs (tons) | 101,000 | 98,600 |

|  | Direct Materials | Conversion |
|---|---|---|
| Costs | $1,727,100 | $423,980 |

a. Open the Excel file *SA18-1_1e.*

b. Develop a spreadsheet to determine the cost per equivalent unit for direct materials and for conversion.

c. When you have completed the spreadsheet, perform a "save as," replacing the entire file name with the following:

*SA18-1_1e[your first name initial]_[your last name]*

### SA 18-2   Cost per equivalent unit

The Crumble Cookie Company makes cookies using two departments, Mixing and Baking. The Baking Department started and completed 56,000 units during August. The Baking Department had the following units of inventory on August 1 and August 31 of the current year.

| Aug. 1 Work in Process—Baking | 3,200 units | (³⁄₄ complete as to conversion costs) |
|---|---|---|
| Aug. 31 Work in Process—Baking | 1,600 units | (¹⁄₄ complete as to conversion costs) |

Total costs incurred during the month in the Baking Department were as follows:

| Direct materials | $1,238,400 |
|---|---|
| Conversion | 280,220 |

a. Open the Excel file *SA18-2_1e.*

b. Develop a spreadsheet to determine the cost per equivalent unit for direct materials and for conversion.

c. When you have completed the spreadsheet, perform a "save as," replacing the entire file name with the following:

*SA18-2_1e[your first name initial]_[your last name]*

### SA 18-3    Cost of production report using a spreadsheet

Atlantic Beverages, Inc., produces soft drinks. The Mixing Department had the following information with respect to the Work in Process—Mixing Department for June of the current year:

|  | Units | Amount | Percent Complete |
|---|---|---|---|
| Work in Process, June 1 | 5,000 | $ 41,000 | 60% |
| Direct materials received from Materials | 36,000 | 198,000 | |
| Direct labor | | 101,890 | |
| Factory overhead | | 61,640 | |
| Work in Process, June 30 | 3,500 | | 30% |

a. Open the Excel file *SA18-3_1e.*

b. Prepare a cost of production report using spreadsheet software for the Mixing Department for June.

c. When you have completed the spreadsheet, perform a "save as," replacing the entire file name with the following:

   *SA18-3_1e[your first name initial]_[your last name]*

### SA 18-4    Cost of production report using a spreadsheet

Alberta Paper Company produces paper. The Converting Department had the following information with respect to the Work in Process—Converting for April 1 of the current year:

| Work in Process—Converting (1,200 units, $2/5$ completed) | $35,800 |
|---|---|

The following costs were charged to Work in Process—Converting during April:

| Direct materials transferred from Rolling, 21,400 units | $175,480 |
|---|---|
| Direct labor | 53,600 |
| Factory overhead | 71,920 |

During April, 21,100 units of paper were completed in the Converting Department and transferred to finished goods. Inventories for April 30, were 1,500 whole units that were $1/5$ completed as to conversion costs.

Prepare a cost of production report using spreadsheet software for the Converting Department for April.

a. Open the Excel file *SA18-4_1e.*

b. Prepare a cost of production report using spreadsheet software for the Converting Department for April.

c. When you have completed the spreadsheet, perform a "save as," replacing the entire file name with the following:

   *SA18-4_1e[your first name initial]_[your last name]*

© AP Photo/Paul Sakuma

# Cost Behavior and Cost-Volume-Profit Analysis

## Netflix

**H**ow do you decide whether you are going to buy or rent a video game? It probably depends on how much you think you are going to use the game. If you are going to play the game a lot, you are probably better off buying the game than renting. The one-time cost of buying the game would be much less expensive than the cost of multiple rentals. If, on the other hand, you are uncertain about how frequently you are going to play the game, it may be less expensive to rent. The cost of an individual rental is much less than the cost of purchase. Understanding how the costs of rental and purchase behave affects your decision.

Understanding how costs behave is also important to companies like **Netflix**, an online movie rental service. For a fixed monthly fee, Netflix customers can watch movies and TV episodes online, or they can have DVDs delivered to their home along with a pre-paid return envelope. Customers can keep the DVDs as long as they want, but must return the DVDs before they rent additional

movies. The number of DVDs that members can check out at one time varies, depending on their subscription plan.

In order to entice customers to subscribe, Netflix had to invest in a well-stocked library of DVD titles and build a warehouse to hold and distribute these titles. These costs do not change with the number of subscriptions. But how many subscriptions does Netflix need in order to make a profit? That depends on the price of each subscription, the costs incurred with each DVD rental, and the costs associated with maintaining the DVD library.

As with Netflix, understanding how costs behave, and the relationship between costs, profits, and volume is important for all businesses. This chapter discusses commonly used methods for classifying costs according to how they change. Techniques that management can use to evaluate costs in order to make sound business decisions are also discussed.

**OBJ. 2** Classify costs as variable costs, fixed costs, or mixed costs.

# Cost Behavior

**Cost behavior** is the manner in which a cost changes as a related activity changes. The behavior of costs is useful to managers for a variety of reasons. For example, knowing how costs behave allows managers to predict profits as sales and production volumes change. Knowing how costs behave is also useful for estimating costs, which affects a variety of decisions such as whether to replace a machine.

Understanding the behavior of a cost depends on:

1. Identifying the activities that cause the cost to change. These activities are called **activity bases** (or *activity drivers*).
2. Specifying the range of activity over which the changes in the cost are of interest. This range of activity is called the **relevant range**.

To illustrate, assume that a hospital is concerned about planning and controlling patient food costs. A good activity base is the number of patients who *stay* overnight in the hospital. The number of patients who are *treated* is not as good an activity base since some patients are outpatients and, thus, do not consume food. Once an activity base is identified, food costs can then be analyzed over the range of the number of patients who normally stay in the hospital (the relevant range).

Costs are normally classified as variable costs, fixed costs, or mixed costs.

## Variable Costs

**Variable costs** are costs that vary in proportion to changes in the activity base. When the activity base is units produced, direct materials and direct labor costs are normally classified as variable costs.

To illustrate, assume that Jason Sound Inc. produces stereo systems. The parts for the stereo systems are purchased from suppliers for $10 per unit and are assembled by Jason Sound Inc. For Model JS-12, the direct materials costs for the relevant range of 5,000 to 30,000 units of production are shown below.

| Number of Units of Model JS-12 Produced | Direct Materials Cost per Unit | Total Direct Materials Cost |
|---|---|---|
| 5,000 units | $10 | $ 50,000 |
| 10,000 | 10 | 100,000 |
| 15,000 | 10 | 150,000 |
| 20,000 | 10 | 200,000 |
| 25,000 | 10 | 250,000 |
| 30,000 | 10 | 300,000 |

As shown above, variable costs have the following characteristics:

1. *Cost per unit* remains the same regardless of changes in the activity base. For Model JS-12, the cost per unit is $10.
2. *Total cost* changes in proportion to changes in the activity base. For Model JS-12, the direct materials cost for 10,000 units ($100,000) is twice the direct materials cost for 5,000 units ($50,000).

Exhibit 1 illustrates how the variable costs for direct materials for Model JS-12 behave in total and on a per-unit basis as production changes.

**EXHIBIT 1**  **Variable Cost Graphs**

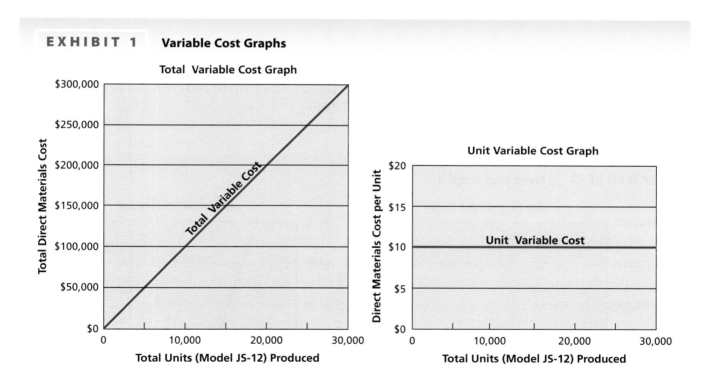

Some examples of variable costs and their related activity bases for various types of businesses are shown below.

| Type of Business | Cost | Activity Base |
|---|---|---|
| University | Instructor salaries | Number of classes |
| Passenger airline | Fuel | Number of miles flown |
| Manufacturing | Direct materials | Number of units produced |
| Hospital | Nurse wages | Number of patients |
| Hotel | Maid wages | Number of guests |
| Bank | Teller wages | Number of banking transactions |

# Fixed Costs

**Fixed costs** are costs that remain the same in total dollar amount as the activity base changes. When the activity base is units produced, many factory overhead costs such as straight-line depreciation are classified as fixed costs.

To illustrate, assume that Minton Inc. manufactures, bottles, and distributes perfume. The production supervisor is Jane Sovissi, who is paid a salary of $75,000 per year. For the relevant range of 50,000 to 300,000 bottles of perfume, the total fixed cost of $75,000 does not vary as production increases. However, the fixed cost per bottle decreases as the units produced increase; thus, the fixed cost is spread over a larger number of bottles, as shown below.

| Number of Bottles of Perfume Produced | Total Salary for Jane Sovissi | Salary per Bottle of Perfume Produced |
|---|---|---|
| 50,000 bottles | $75,000 | $1.500 |
| 100,000 | 75,000 | 0.750 |
| 150,000 | 75,000 | 0.500 |
| 200,000 | 75,000 | 0.375 |
| 250,000 | 75,000 | 0.300 |
| 300,000 | 75,000 | 0.250 |

As shown above, fixed costs have the following characteristics:

1. *Cost per unit* changes inversely to changes in the activity base. For Jane Sovissi's salary, the cost per unit decreased from $1.50 for 50,000 bottles produced to $0.25 for 300,000 bottles produced.

2. *Total cost* remains the same regardless of changes in the activity base. Jane Sovissi's salary of $75,000 remained the same regardless of whether 50,000 bottles or 300,000 bottles were produced.

Exhibit 2 illustrates how Jane Sovissi's salary (fixed cost) behaves in total and on a per-unit basis as production changes.

**EXHIBIT 2** **Fixed Cost Graphs**

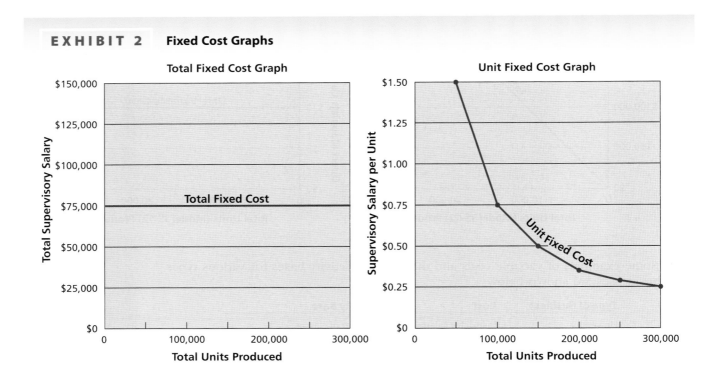

Some examples of fixed costs and their related activity bases for various types of businesses are shown below.

| Type of Business | Fixed Cost | Activity Base |
|---|---|---|
| University | Building (straight-line) depreciation | Number of students |
| Passenger airline | Airplane (straight-line) depreciation | Number of miles flown |
| Manufacturing | Plant manager salary | Number of units produced |
| Hospital | Property insurance | Number of patients |
| Hotel | Property taxes | Number of guests |
| Bank | Branch manager salary | Number of customer accounts |

## Mixed Costs

**Mixed costs** are costs that have characteristics of both a variable and a fixed cost. Mixed costs are sometimes called *semivariable* or *semifixed* costs.

To illustrate, assume that Simpson Inc. manufactures sails, using rented machinery. The rental charges are as follows:

A salesperson's compensation can be a mixed cost comprised of a salary (fixed portion) plus a commission as a percent of sales (variable portion).

Rental Charge = $15,000 per year + $1 times each machine hour over 10,000 hours

The rental charges for various hours used within the relevant range of 8,000 hours to 40,000 hours are as follows:

| Hours Used | Rental Charge |
|---|---|
| 8,000 hours | $15,000 |
| 12,000 | $17,000 {$15,000 + [(12,000 hrs. − 10,000 hrs.) × $1]} |
| 20,000 | $25,000 {$15,000 + [(20,000 hrs. − 10,000 hrs.) × $1]} |
| 40,000 | $45,000 {$15,000 + [(40,000 hrs. − 10,000 hrs.) × $1]} |

Exhibit 3 illustrates the preceding mixed cost behavior.

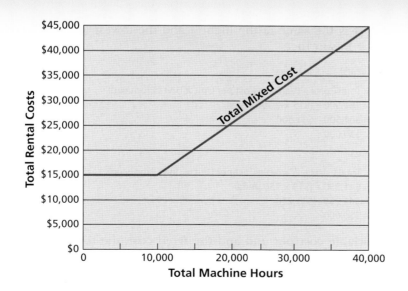

**EXHIBIT 3**

**Mixed Costs**

For purposes of analysis, mixed costs are usually separated into their fixed and variable components. The **high-low method** is a cost estimation method that may be used for this purpose.[1] The high-low method uses the highest and lowest activity levels and their related costs to estimate the variable cost per unit and the fixed cost.

1 Other methods of estimating costs, such as the scattergraph method and the least squares method, are discussed in cost accounting textbooks.

To illustrate, assume that the Equipment Maintenance Department of Kason Inc. incurred the following costs during the past five months:

| | Production | Total Cost |
|---|---|---|
| June | 1,000 units | $45,550 |
| July | 1,500 | 52,000 |
| August | 2,100 | 61,500 |
| September | 1,800 | 57,500 |
| October | 750 | 41,250 |

The number of units produced is the activity base, and the relevant range is the units produced between June and October. For Kason Inc., the difference between the units produced and total costs at the highest and lowest levels of production are as follows:

| | Production | Total Cost |
|---|---|---|
| Highest level | 2,100 units | $61,500 |
| Lowest level | 750 | 41,250 |
| Difference | 1,350 units | $20,250 |

The total fixed cost does not change with changes in production. Thus, the $20,250 difference in the total cost is the change in the total variable cost. Dividing this difference of $20,250 by the difference in production is an estimate of the variable cost per unit. For Kason Inc., this estimate is $15, as computed below.

$$\text{Variable Cost per Unit} = \frac{\text{Difference in Total Cost}}{\text{Difference in Production}}$$

$$\text{Variable Cost per Unit} = \frac{\$20,250}{1,350 \text{ units}} = \$15 \text{ per unit}$$

The fixed cost is estimated by subtracting the total variable costs from the total costs for the units produced as shown below.

$$\text{Fixed Cost} = \text{Total Costs} - (\text{Variable Cost per Unit} \times \text{Units Produced})$$

The fixed cost is the same at the highest and the lowest levels of production as shown below for Kason Inc.

Highest level (2,100 units)

Fixed Cost = Total Costs – (Variable Cost per Unit × Units Produced)
Fixed Cost = $61,500 – ($15 × 2,100 units)
Fixed Cost = $61,500 – $31,500
Fixed Cost = $30,000

Lowest level (750 units)

Fixed Cost = Total Costs – (Variable Cost per Unit × Units Produced)
Fixed Cost = $41,250 – ($15 × 750 units)
Fixed Cost = $41,250 – $11,250
Fixed Cost = $30,000

Using the variable cost per unit and the fixed cost, the total equipment maintenance cost for Kason Inc. can be computed for various levels of production as follows:

Total Cost = (Variable Cost per Unit × Units Produced) + Fixed Costs
Total Cost = ($15 × Units Produced) + $30,000

To illustrate, the estimated total cost of 2,000 units of production is $60,000, as computed below.

Total Cost = ($15 × Units Produced) + $30,000
Total Cost = ($15 × 2,000 units) + $30,000 = $30,000 + $30,000
Total Cost = $60,000

A spreadsheet can be used to determine the variable cost per unit and total fixed cost under the high-low method as follows:

| | A | B | C | D | E |
|---|---|---|---|---|---|
| 1 | | | | | |
| 2 | *Inputs* | Production | Total Cost | | |
| 3 | June | 1,000 | $ 45,550 | | |
| 4 | July | 1,500 | 52,000 | | |
| 5 | August | 2,100 | 61,500 | | |
| 6 | September | 1,800 | 57,500 | | |
| 7 | October | 750 | 41,250 | | |
| 8 | | | | | |
| 9 | *Outputs* | Production | Total Cost | | |
| 10 | Highest level  a. → | =MAX(B3:B7) | =VLOOKUP(B10,B$3:C$7,2,FALSE) ← d. | | |
| 11 | Lowest level  b. → | =MIN(B3:B7) | =VLOOKUP(B11,B$3:C$7,2,FALSE) ← e. | | |
| 12 | Difference  c. → | =B10-B11 | =C10-C11 ← f. | | |
| 13 | | | | | |
| 14 | Variable cost per unit | =C12/B12 ← g. | | | |
| 15 | | | | | |
| 16 | Fixed cost at the highest | | | | |
| 17 | level of production | =C5-(B14*B10) ← h. | | | |
| 18 | | | | | |

a. Enter in cell B10 the maximum production by using the =MAX function, =MAX(B3:B7). This function will return the maximum value in the stated range.

b. Enter in cell B11 the minimum production by using the =MIN function, =MIN(B3:B7). This function will return the minimum value in the stated range.

c. Enter in cell B12 the formula for the difference between the maximum and minimum, =B10-B11.

d. The total cost that is associated with the maximum value from the table must be inserted in C10. While you could do this by eye, there is a useful Excel function that can be used to find the matching cost. The VLOOKUP function finds a value in the first column and returns the value in the same row from the second column. For example, enter in C10 the following formula:

=VLOOKUP(B10,B$3:C$7,2,FALSE), where

  B10 is the value that is to be found in the first column of the production and total cost table. In this case, the maximum value is 2,100.

  B$3:C$7 is the table that contains the production and cost information. The dollar sign makes the rows absolute so that we can copy this formula when it is completed.

  "2" indicates the column number of the table from which the matching value is to be returned. We enter 2 for the second column, or Total Cost column. Thus, we want the function to return the number 61,500, which is the number in the second column that matches the maximum number from the first column, or 2,100.

  "False" tells Excel to find an exact match.

e. Copy the VLOOKUP function from cell C10 to C11.

f. Enter in cell C12 the difference, or copy from B12.

g. Enter in B14 the formula for the variable cost per unit, =C12/B12.

h. Enter in B16 the formula for the total fixed cost, =C5-(B14*B10) using the maximum level total cost and matching production level. The formula could also use the minimum cost and matching production level to yield the same result.

**Try***It*    Go to the hands-on ***Excel Tutor*** for this example!

---

**Example Exercise** 19-1  **High-Low Method**                                      OBJ. 1

The manufacturing costs of Alex Industries for the first three months of the year are provided below.

| | Total Cost | Production |
|---|---|---|
| January | $ 80,000 | 1,000 units |
| February | 125,000 | 2,500 |
| March | 100,000 | 1,800 |

Using the high-low method, determine (a) the variable cost per unit and (b) the total fixed cost.

**Follow My Example 19-1**

a. $30 per unit = ($125,000 − $80,000)/(2,500 − 1,000)
b. $50,000 = $125,000 − ($30 × 2,500), or $80,000 − ($30 × 1,000)

Practice Exercises: **PE 19-1A, PE 19-1B**

## Summary of Cost Behavior Concepts

The cost behavior of variable costs and fixed costs is summarized below.

| Cost | Effect of Changing Activity Level | |
| --- | --- | --- |
| | **Total Amount** | **Per-Unit Amount** |
| Variable | Increases and decreases proportionately with activity level. | Remains the same regardless of activity level. |
| Fixed | Remains the same regardless of activity level. | Increases and decreases inversely with activity level. |

Mixed costs contain a fixed cost component that is incurred even if nothing is produced. For analysis, the fixed and variable cost components of mixed costs are separated using the high-low method.

Some examples of variable, fixed, and mixed costs for the activity base *units produced* are as follows:

| **Variable Cost** | **Fixed Cost** | **Mixed Cost** |
| --- | --- | --- |
| Direct materials | Straight-line depreciation | Quality Control Department salaries |
| Direct labor | Property taxes | Purchasing Department salaries |
| Electricity expense | Production supervisor salaries | Maintenance expenses |
| Supplies | Insurance expense | Warehouse expenses |

One method of reporting variable and fixed costs is called **variable costing** or *direct costing*. Under variable costing, only the variable manufacturing costs (direct materials, direct labor, and variable factory overhead) are included in the product cost. The fixed factory overhead is treated as an expense of the period in which it is incurred. Variable costing is described and illustrated in Chapter 20.

# BusinessConnection

### FRANCHISING

Many restaurant chains such as McDonalds, Wendy's, Dunkin' Donuts, and Fatburger operate as franchises. In a franchise, the restaurant chain (called the franchisor) sells the right to sell products using its trademark or brand name to a franchisee. The franchisee typically pays an initial franchise fee, which is a fixed cost. In addition, the franchisee must normally make royalty payments to the franchisor based on a percentage of sales revenues, which is a variable cost. Prior to signing a franchise agreement, most franchisees conduct a break-even analysis to determine how much sales volume their franchise must generate to earn a profit. For example, McDonald's franchises require an initial investment of over $500,000 and typically take several years to break even.

Source: B. Beshel, *An Introduction to Franchising*, IFA Educational Foundation, 2000.

**OBJ. 2** Compute the contribution margin, the contribution margin ratio, and the unit contribution margin.

# Cost-Volume-Profit Relationships

**Cost-volume-profit analysis** is the examination of the relationships among selling prices, sales and production volume, costs, expenses, and profits. Cost-volume-profit analysis is useful for managerial decision making. Some of the ways cost-volume-profit analysis may be used include:

1. Analyzing the effects of changes in selling prices on profits
2. Analyzing the effects of changes in costs on profits
3. Analyzing the effects of changes in volume on profits
4. Setting selling prices
5. Selecting the mix of products to sell
6. Choosing among marketing strategies

## Contribution Margin

Contribution margin is especially useful because it provides insight into the profit potential of a company. **Contribution margin** is the excess of sales over variable costs, as shown below.

$$\text{Contribution Margin} = \text{Sales} - \text{Variable Costs}$$

To illustrate, assume the following data for Lambert Inc.:

| | |
|---|---|
| Sales | 50,000 units |
| Sales price per unit | $20 per unit |
| Variable cost per unit | $12 per unit |
| Fixed costs | $300,000 |

Exhibit 4 illustrates an income statement for Lambert Inc. prepared in a contribution margin format.

**EXHIBIT 4**

**Contribution Margin Income Statement**

| | |
|---|---|
| Sales (50,000 units × $20) | $1,000,000 |
| Variable costs (50,000 units × $12) | 600,000 |
| Contribution margin (50,000 units × $8) | $ 400,000 |
| Fixed costs | 300,000 |
| Income from operations | $ 100,000 |

Lambert's contribution margin of $400,000 is available to cover the fixed costs of $300,000. Once the fixed costs are covered, any additional contribution margin increases income from operations.

## Contribution Margin Ratio

The contribution margin can also be expressed as a percentage. The **contribution margin ratio**, sometimes called the *profit-volume ratio*, indicates the percentage of each sales dollar available to cover fixed costs and to provide income from operations. The contribution margin ratio is computed as follows:

$$\text{Contribution Margin Ratio} = \frac{\text{Contribution Margin}}{\text{Sales}}$$

The contribution margin ratio is 40% for Lambert Inc., computed as follows:

$$\text{Contribution Margin Ratio} = \frac{\text{Contribution Margin}}{\text{Sales}}$$

$$\text{Contribution Margin Ratio} = \frac{\$400,000}{\$1,000,000} = 40\%$$

The contribution margin ratio is most useful when the increase or decrease in sales volume is measured in sales *dollars*. In this case, the change in sales dollars multiplied by the contribution margin ratio equals the change in income from operations, as shown below.

Change in Income from Operations = Change in Sales Dollars × Contribution Margin Ratio

To illustrate, if Lambert Inc. adds $80,000 in sales from the sale of an additional 4,000 units, its income from operations will increase by $32,000, as computed below.

Change in Income from Operations = Change in Sales Dollars × Contribution Margin Ratio
Change in Income from Operations = $80,000 × 40% = $32,000

The preceding analysis is confirmed by the following contribution margin income statement of Lambert Inc.:

| | |
|---|---:|
| Sales......................................................................................... | $1,080,000 |
| Variable costs ($1,080,000 × 60%)....................................................... | 648,000* |
| Contribution margin ($1,080,000 × 40%).............................................. | $ 432,000 |
| Fixed costs................................................................................ | 300,000 |
| Income from operations................................................................ | $ 132,000 |

*54,000 × $12 per unit.

Income from operations increased from $100,000 to $132,000 when sales increased from $1,000,000 to $1,080,000. Variable costs as a percentage of sales are equal to 100% minus the contribution margin ratio. Thus, in the above income statement, the variable costs are 60% (100% − 40%) of sales, or $648,000 ($1,080,000 × 60%). The total contribution margin, $432,000, can also be computed directly by multiplying the total sales by the contribution margin ratio ($1,080,000 × 40%).

In the preceding analysis, factors other than sales volume, such as variable cost per unit and sales price, are assumed to remain constant. If such factors change, their effect must also be considered.

The contribution margin ratio is also useful in developing business strategies. For example, assume that a company has a high contribution margin ratio and is producing below 100% of capacity. In this case, a large increase in income from operations can be expected from an increase in sales volume. Therefore, the company might consider implementing a special sales campaign to increase sales. In contrast, a company with a small contribution margin ratio will probably want to give more attention to reducing costs before attempting to promote sales.

## Unit Contribution Margin

The unit contribution margin is also useful for analyzing the profit potential of proposed decisions. The **unit contribution margin** is computed as follows:

Unit Contribution Margin = Sales Price per Unit − Variable Cost per Unit

To illustrate, if Lambert Inc.'s unit selling price is $20 and its variable cost per unit is $12, the unit contribution margin is $8 as shown below.

Unit Contribution Margin = Sales Price per Unit − Variable Cost per Unit
Unit Contribution Margin = $20 − $12 = $8

The unit contribution margin is most useful when the increase or decrease in sales volume is measured in sales *units* (quantities). In this case, the change in sales volume (units) multiplied by the unit contribution margin equals the change in income from operations, as shown below.

Change in Income from Operations = Change in Sales Units × Unit Contribution Margin

To illustrate, assume that Lambert Inc.'s sales could be increased by 15,000 units, from 50,000 units to 65,000 units. Lambert's income from operations would increase by $120,000 (15,000 units × $8), as shown below.

Change in Income from Operations = Change in Sales Units × Unit Contribution Margin
Change in Income from Operations = 15,000 units × $8 = $120,000

The preceding analysis is confirmed by the following contribution margin income statement of Lambert Inc., which shows that income increased to $220,000 when 65,000 units are sold. The prior income statement on page 893 indicates income of $100,000 when 50,000 units are sold. Thus, selling an additional 15,000 units increases income by $120,000 ($220,000 − $100,000).

| | |
|---|---|
| Sales (65,000 units × $20) | $1,300,000 |
| Variable costs (65,000,units × $12) | 780,000 |
| Contribution margin (65,000 units × $8) | $ 520,000 |
| Fixed costs | 300,000 |
| Income from operations | $ 220,000 |

A room night at Hilton Hotels has a high contribution margin. The high contribution margin per room night is necessary to cover the high fixed costs for the hotel.

Unit contribution margin analysis is useful information for managers. For example, in the preceding illustration, Lambert Inc. could spend up to $120,000 for special advertising or other product promotions to increase sales by 15,000 units and still increase income by $100,000 ($220,000 − $120,000).

**Example Exercise** **19-2** **Contribution Margin** **OBJ. 2**

Molly Company sells 20,000 units at $12 per unit. Variable costs are $9 per unit, and fixed costs are $25,000. Determine the (a) contribution margin ratio, (b) unit contribution margin, and (c) income from operations.

**Follow My Example** **19-2**

a. 25% = ($12 − $9)/$12, or ($240,000 − $180,000)/$240,000
b. $3 per unit = $12 − $9
c.

| Sales | $240,000 | (20,000 units × $12 per unit) |
|---|---|---|
| Variable costs | 180,000 | (20,000 units × $9 per unit) |
| Contribution margin | $ 60,000 | [20,000 units × ($12 − $9)] |
| Fixed costs | 25,000 | |
| Income from operations | $ 35,000 | |

Practice Exercises: **PE 19-2A, PE 19-2B**

# Mathematical Approach to Cost-Volume-Profit Analysis

**OBJ. 3** Determine the break-even point and sales necessary to achieve a target profit.

The mathematical approach to cost-volume-profit analysis uses equations to determine the following:

1. Sales necessary to break even
2. Sales necessary to make a target or desired profit

## Break-Even Point

The **break-even point** is the level of operations at which a company's revenues and expenses are equal. At break-even, a company reports neither an income nor a loss from operations. The break-even point in *sales units* is computed as follows:

$$\text{Break-Even Sales (units)} = \frac{\text{Fixed Costs}}{\text{Unit Contribution Margin}}$$

To illustrate, assume the following data for Baker Corporation:

| | |
|---|---:|
| Fixed costs | $90,000 |
| Unit selling price | $25 |
| Unit variable cost | 15 |
| Unit contribution margin | $10 |

The break-even point is 9,000 units, as shown below.

$$\text{Break-Even Sales (units)} = \frac{\text{Fixed Costs}}{\text{Unit Contribution Margin}} = \frac{\$90,000}{\$10} = 9,000 \text{ units}$$

The following income statement verifies the break-even point of 9,000 units:

| | |
|---|---:|
| Sales (9,000 units × $25) ......................................................... | $225,000 |
| Variable costs (9,000 units × $15)................................................ | 135,000 |
| Contribution margin................................................................ | $ 90,000 |
| Fixed costs ........................................................................ | 90,000 |
| Income from operations ............................................................ | $    0 |

As shown in the preceding income statement, the break-even point is $225,000 (9,000 units × $25) of sales. The break-even point in *sales dollars* can be determined directly as follows:

$$\text{Break-Even Sales (dollars)} = \frac{\text{Fixed Costs}}{\text{Contribution Margin Ratio}}$$

The contribution margin ratio can be computed using the unit contribution margin and unit selling price as follows:

$$\text{Contribution Margin Ratio} = \frac{\text{Unit Contribution Margin}}{\text{Unit Selling Price}}$$

The contribution margin ratio for Baker Corporation is 40%, as shown below.

$$\text{Contribution Margin Ratio} = \frac{\text{Unit Contribution Margin}}{\text{Unit Selling Price}} = \frac{\$10}{\$25} = 40\%$$

Thus, the break-even sales dollars for Baker Corporation of $225,000 can be computed directly as follows:

$$\text{Break-Even Sales (dollars)} = \frac{\text{Fixed Costs}}{\text{Contribution Margin Ratio}} = \frac{\$90,000}{40\%} = \$225,000$$

The break-even point is affected by changes in the fixed costs, unit variable costs, and the unit selling price.

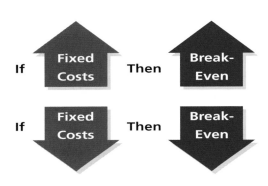

**Effect of Changes in Fixed Costs** Fixed costs do not change in total with changes in the level of activity. However, fixed costs may change because of other factors such as changes in property tax rates or factory supervisors' salaries.

Changes in fixed costs affect the break-even point as follows:

1. Increases in fixed costs increase the break-even point.
2. Decreases in fixed costs decrease the break-even point.

To illustrate, assume that Bishop Co. is evaluating a proposal to budget an additional $100,000 for advertising. The data for Bishop Co. are as follows:

|  | **Current** | **Proposed** |
|---|---|---|
| Unit selling price | $90 | $90 |
| Unit variable cost | 70 | 70 |
| Unit contribution margin | $20 | $20 |
| Fixed costs | $600,000 | $700,000 |

Bishop Co.'s break-even point *before* the additional advertising expense of $100,000 is 30,000 units, as shown below.

$$\text{Break-Even Sales (units)} = \frac{\text{Fixed Costs}}{\text{Unit Contribution Margin}} = \frac{\$600,000}{\$20} = 30,000 \text{ units}$$

Bishop Co.'s break-even point *after* the additional advertising expense of $100,000 is 35,000 units, as shown below.

$$\text{Break-Even Sales (units)} = \frac{\text{Fixed Costs}}{\text{Unit Contribution Margin}} = \frac{\$700,000}{\$20} = 35,000 \text{ units}$$

As shown above, the $100,000 increase in advertising (fixed costs) requires an additional 5,000 units (35,000 − 30,000) of sales to break even.[2] In other words, an increase in sales of 5,000 units is required in order to generate an additional $100,000 of total contribution margin (5,000 units × $20) to cover the increased fixed costs.

## Effect of Changes in Unit Variable Costs

Unit variable costs do not change with changes in the level of activity. However, unit variable costs may be affected by other factors such as changes in the cost per unit of direct materials.

Changes in unit variable costs affect the break-even point as follows:

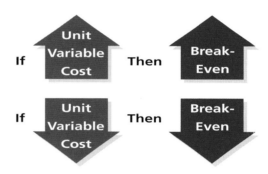

1. Increases in unit variable costs increase the break-even point.
2. Decreases in unit variable costs decrease the break-even point.

To illustrate, assume that Park Co. is evaluating a proposal to pay an additional 2% commission on sales to its salespeople as an incentive to increase sales. The data for Park Co. are as follows:

|  | **Current** | **Proposed** |
|---|---|---|
| Unit selling price | $250 | $250 |
| Unit variable cost | 145 | 150 |
| Unit contribution margin | $105 | $100 |
| Fixed costs | $840,000 | $840,000 |

Park Co.'s break-even point *before* the additional 2% commission is 8,000 units, as shown below.

$$\text{Break-Even Sales (units)} = \frac{\text{Fixed Costs}}{\text{Unit Contribution Margin}} = \frac{\$840,000}{\$105} = 8,000 \text{ units}$$

If the 2% sales commission proposal is adopted, unit variable costs will increase by $5 ($250 × 2%) from $145 to $150 per unit. This increase in unit variable costs will decrease the unit contribution margin from $105 to $100 ($250 − $150). Thus, Park Co.'s break-even point *after* the additional 2% commission is 8,400 units, as shown on the next page.

2 The increase of 5,000 units can also be computed by dividing the increase in fixed costs of $100,000 by the unit contribution margin, $20, as follows: 5,000 units = $100,000/$20.

$$\text{Break-Even Sales (units)} = \frac{\text{Fixed Costs}}{\text{Unit Contribution Margin}} = \frac{\$840,000}{\$100} = 8,400 \text{ units}$$

As shown above, an additional 400 units of sales will be required in order to break even. This is because if 8,000 units are sold, the new unit contribution margin of $100 provides only $800,000 (8,000 units × $100) of contribution margin. Thus, $40,000 more contribution margin is necessary to cover the total fixed costs of $840,000. This additional $40,000 of contribution margin is provided by selling 400 more units (400 units × $100).

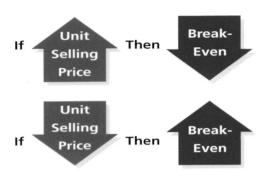

### Effect of Changes in Unit Selling Price

Changes in the unit selling price affect the unit contribution margin and, thus, the break-even point. Specifically, changes in the unit selling price affect the break-even point as follows:

1. Increases in the unit selling price decrease the break-even point.
2. Decreases in the unit selling price increase the break-even point.

To illustrate, assume that Graham Co. is evaluating a proposal to increase the unit selling price of its product from $50 to $60. The data for Graham Co. are as follows:

|                          | Current   | Proposed  |
|--------------------------|-----------|-----------|
| Unit selling price       | $50       | $60       |
| Unit variable cost       | 30        | 30        |
| Unit contribution margin | $20       | $30       |
|                          |           |           |
| Fixed costs              | $600,000  | $600,000  |

Graham Co.'s break-even point *before* the price increase is 30,000 units, as shown below.

$$\text{Break-Even Sales (units)} = \frac{\text{Fixed Costs}}{\text{Unit Contribution Margin}} = \frac{\$600,000}{\$20} = 30,000 \text{ units}$$

The increase of $10 per unit in the selling price increases the unit contribution margin by $10. Thus, Graham Co.'s break-even point *after* the price increase is 20,000 units, as shown below.

$$\text{Break-Even Sales (units)} = \frac{\text{Fixed Costs}}{\text{Unit Contribution Margin}} = \frac{\$600,000}{\$30} = 20,000 \text{ units}$$

As shown above, the price increase of $10 increased the unit contribution margin by $10, which decreased the break-even point by 10,000 units (30,000 units – 20,000 units).

### Summary of Effects of Changes on Break-Even Point

The break-even point in sales changes in the same direction as changes in the variable cost per unit and fixed costs. In contrast, the break-even point in sales changes in the opposite direction as changes in the unit selling price. These changes on the break-even point in sales are summarized below.

| Type of Change     | Direction of Change | Effect of Change on Break-Even Sales |
|--------------------|---------------------|--------------------------------------|
| Fixed cost         | Increase            | Increase                             |
|                    | Decrease            | Decrease                             |
| Unit variable cost | Increase            | Increase                             |
|                    | Decrease            | Decrease                             |
| Unit selling price | Increase            | Decrease                             |
|                    | Decrease            | Increase                             |

**Example Exercise** ▶ **19-3** ▶ **Break-Even Point**

Nicolas Enterprises sells a product for $60 per unit. The variable cost is $35 per unit, while fixed costs are $80,000. Determine the (a) break-even point in sales units and (b) break-even point if the selling price were increased to $67 per unit.

**Follow My Example** ▶ **19-3** ▶

  a.  3,200 units = $80,000/($60 − $35)
  b.  2,500 units = $80,000/($67 − $35)

Practice Exercises: **PE 19-3A, PE 19-3B**

# BusinessConnection

## BREAKING EVEN IN THE AIRLINE INDUSTRY

Airlines have high fixed costs and operate in a very competitive industry. As a result, many airlines struggle to break even. For example, of the five airlines shown below, only Delta is operating at a profit. As the below table shows, the increase in airfare needed to break even ranges from less than 1% to 17%. This indicates that a small increase in ticket prices could enable an airline to break even. However, the competitive nature of the airline industry makes increasing airfares difficult to implement and maintain.

| | United | Continental | Delta | American | US Air |
|---|---|---|---|---|---|
| Average one-way airfare per passenger* | $255 | $251 | $212 | $206 | $156 |
| Average cost per passenger* | $292 | $252 | $192 | $216 | $182 |
| Percentage increase in airfare needed to break even | 15% | Less than 1% | N/A | 5% | 17% |

*Source: R. Herbst, "What Will It Take for Airlines to Break Even on Airfares?" Airline Industry Commentary at AirlineFinancials.com, November 5, 2008.

## Target Profit

At the break-even point, sales and costs are exactly equal. However, the goal of most companies is to make a profit.

By modifying the break-even equation, the sales required to earn a target or desired amount of profit may be computed. For this purpose, target profit is added to the break-even equation as shown below.

$$\text{Sales (units)} = \frac{\text{Fixed Costs} + \text{Target Profit}}{\text{Unit Contribution Margin}}$$

To illustrate, assume the following data for Waltham Co.:

| | |
|---|---|
| Fixed costs | $200,000 |
| Target profit | 100,000 |
| Unit selling price | $75 |
| Unit variable cost | 45 |
| Unit contribution margin | $30 |

The sales necessary to earn the target profit of $100,000 would be 10,000 units, computed as follows:

$$\text{Sales (units)} = \frac{\text{Fixed Costs} + \text{Target Profit}}{\text{Unit Contribution Margin}} = \frac{\$200,000 + \$100,000}{\$30} = 10,000 \text{ units}$$

The following income statement verifies this computation:

| | |
|---|---|
| Sales (10,000 units × $75) | $750,000 |
| Variable costs (10,000 units × $45) | 450,000 |
| Contribution margin (10,000 units × $30) | $300,000 |
| Fixed costs | 200,000 |
| Income from operations | $100,000 |

**Target profit** → Income from operations

As shown in the preceding income statement, sales of $750,000 (10,000 units × $75) are necessary to earn the target profit of $100,000. The sales of $750,000 needed to earn the target profit of $100,000 can be computed directly using the contribution margin ratio, as shown below.

$$\text{Contribution Margin Ratio} = \frac{\text{Unit Contribution Margin}}{\text{Unit Selling Price}} = \frac{\$30}{\$75} = 40\%$$

$$\text{Sales (dollars)} = \frac{\text{Fixed Costs} + \text{Target Profit}}{\text{Contribution Margin Ratio}}$$

$$= \frac{\$200,000 + \$100,000}{40\%} = \frac{\$300,000}{40\%} = \$750,000$$

**Example Exercise** ▶ **19-4** ▶ **Target Profit** **OBJ. 3**

Forest Company sells a product for $140 per unit. The variable cost is $60 per unit, and fixed costs are $240,000. Determine the (a) break-even point in sales units and (b) the sales units required to achieve a target profit of $50,000.

**Follow My Example** ▶ **19-4**

a. 3,000 units = $240,000/($140 − $60)
b. 3,625 units = ($240,000 + $50,000)/($140 − $60)

Practice Exercises: **PE 19-4A, PE 19-4B**

## Integrity, Objectivity, and Ethics in Business

### ORPHAN DRUGS

Each year, pharmaceutical companies develop new drugs that cure a variety of physical conditions. In order to be profitable, drug companies must sell enough of a product to exceed break even for a reasonable selling price. Break-even points, however, create a problem for drugs targeted at rare diseases, called "orphan drugs." These drugs are typically expensive to develop and have low sales volumes, making it impossible to achieve break even. To ensure that orphan drugs are not overlooked, Congress passed the Orphan Drug Act that provides incentives for pharmaceutical companies to develop drugs for rare diseases that might not generate enough sales to reach break even. The program has been a great success. Since 1982, over 200 orphan drugs have come to market, including Jacobus Pharmaceuticals Company, Inc.'s drug for the treatment of tuberculosis and Novartis AG's drug for the treatment of Paget's disease.

**OBJ. 4** Using a cost-volume-profit chart and a profit-volume chart, determine the break-even point and sales necessary to achieve a target profit.

# Graphic Approach to Cost-Volume-Profit Analysis

Cost-volume-profit analysis can be presented graphically as well as in equation form. Many managers prefer the graphic form because the operating profit or loss for different levels of sales can readily be seen.

# Cost-Volume-Profit (Break-Even) Chart

A **cost-volume-profit chart**, sometimes called a *break-even chart*, graphically shows sales, costs, and the related profit or loss for various levels of units sold. It assists in understanding the relationship among sales, costs, and operating profit or loss.

To illustrate, the cost-volume-profit chart in Exhibit 5 is based on the following data:

| | |
|---|---:|
| Total fixed costs | $100,000 |
| Unit selling price | $50 |
| Unit variable cost | 30 |
| Unit contribution margin | $20 |

The cost-volume-profit chart in Exhibit 5 is constructed using the following steps:

Step 1. Volume in units of sales is indicated along the horizontal axis. The range of volume shown is the relevant range in which the company expects to operate. Dollar amounts of total sales and total costs are indicated along the vertical axis.

Step 2. A sales line is plotted by beginning at zero on the left corner of the graph. A second point is determined by multiplying any units of sales on the horizontal axis by the unit sales price of $50. For example, for 10,000 units of sales, the total sales would be $500,000 (10,000 units × $50). The sales line is drawn upward to the right from zero through the $500,000 point.

Step 3. A cost line is plotted by beginning with total fixed costs, $100,000, on the vertical axis. A second point is determined by multiplying any units of sales on the horizontal axis by the unit variable costs and adding the fixed costs. For example, for 10,000 units of sales, the total estimated costs would be $400,000 [(10,000 units × $30) + $100,000]. The cost line is drawn upward to the right from $100,000 on the vertical axis through the $400,000 point.

Step 4. The break-even point is the intersection point of the total sales and total cost lines. A vertical dotted line drawn downward at the intersection point indicates the units of sales at the break-even point. A horizontal dotted line drawn to the left at the intersection point indicates the sales dollars and costs at the break-even point.

In Exhibit 5, the break-even point is $250,000 of sales, which represents sales of 5,000 units. Operating profits will be earned when sales levels are to the right of the break-even point (*operating profit area*). Operating losses will be incurred when sales levels are to the left of the break-even point (*operating loss area*).

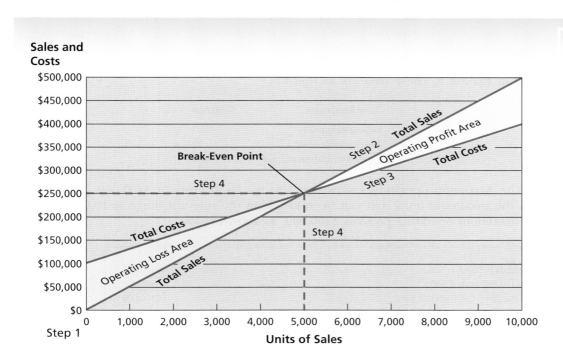

**EXHIBIT 5**

**Cost-Volume-Profit Chart**

Changes in the unit selling price, total fixed costs, and unit variable costs can be analyzed by using a cost-volume-profit chart. Using the data in Exhibit 5, assume that a proposal to reduce fixed costs by $20,000 is to be evaluated. In this case, the total fixed costs would be $80,000 ($100,000 – $20,000).

As shown in Exhibit 6, the total cost line is redrawn, starting at the $80,000 point (total fixed costs) on the vertical axis. A second point is determined by multiplying any units of sales on the horizontal axis by the unit variable costs and adding the fixed costs. For example, for 10,000 units of sales, the total estimated costs would be $380,000 [(10,000 units × $30) + $80,000]. The cost line is drawn upward to the right from $80,000 on the vertical axis through the $380,000 point. The revised cost-volume-profit chart in Exhibit 6 indicates that the break-even point decreases to $200,000 and 4,000 units of sales.

**EXHIBIT 6**

**Revised Cost-Volume-Profit Chart**

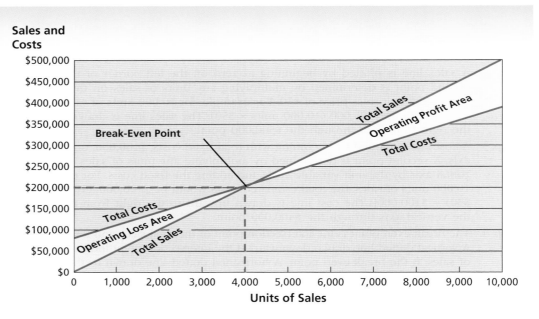

## Profit-Volume Chart

Another graphic approach to cost-volume-profit analysis is the profit-volume chart. The **profit-volume chart** plots only the difference between total sales and total costs (or profits). In this way, the profit-volume chart allows managers to determine the operating profit (or loss) for various levels of units sold.

To illustrate, the profit-volume chart in Exhibit 7 is based on the same data as used in Exhibit 5. These data are as follows:

| | |
|---|---|
| Total fixed costs | $100,000 |
| Unit selling price | $50 |
| Unit variable cost | 30 |
| Unit contribution margin | $20 |

The maximum operating loss is equal to the fixed costs of $100,000. Assuming that the maximum units that can be sold within the relevant range is 10,000 units, the maximum operating profit is $100,000, as shown below.

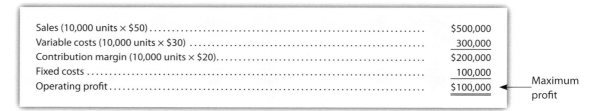

| | |
|---|---|
| Sales (10,000 units × $50) | $500,000 |
| Variable costs (10,000 units × $30) | 300,000 |
| Contribution margin (10,000 units × $20) | $200,000 |
| Fixed costs | 100,000 |
| Operating profit | $100,000 |

Maximum profit

The profit-volume chart in Exhibit 7 is constructed using the following steps:

Step 1. Volume in units of sales is indicated along the horizontal axis. The range of vol-ume shown is the relevant range in which the company expects to operate. In Exhibit 7, the maximum units of sales is 10,000 units. Dollar amounts indicating operating profits and losses are shown along the vertical axis.

Step 2. A point representing the maximum operating loss is plotted on the vertical axis at the left. This loss is equal to the total fixed costs at the zero level of sales. Thus, the maximum operating loss is equal to the fixed costs of $100,000.

Step 3. A point representing the maximum operating profit within the relevant range is plotted on the right. Assuming that the maximum unit sales within the relevant range is 10,000 units, the maximum operating profit is $100,000.

Step 4. A diagonal profit line is drawn connecting the maximum operating loss point with the maximum operating profit point.

Step 5. The profit line intersects the horizontal zero operating profit line at the break-even point in units of sales. The area indicating an operating profit is identified to the right of the intersection, and the area indicating an operating loss is identified to the left of the intersection.

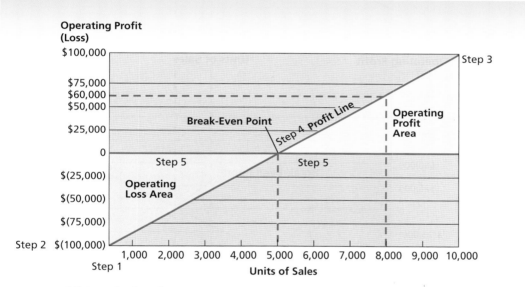

**EXHIBIT 7**

**Profit-Volume Chart**

In Exhibit 7, the break-even point is 5,000 units of sales, which is equal to total sales of $250,000 (5,000 units × $50). Operating profit will be earned when sales levels are to the right of the break-even point (*operating profit area*). Operating losses will be incurred when sales levels are to the left of the break-even point (*operating loss area*). For example, at sales of 8,000 units, an operating profit of $60,000 will be earned, as shown in Exhibit 7.

Changes in the unit selling price, total fixed costs, and unit variable costs on profit can be analyzed using a profit-volume chart. Using the data in Exhibit 7, assume the effect on profit of an increase of $20,000 in fixed costs is to be evaluated. In this case, the total fixed costs would be $120,000 ($100,000 + $20,000), and the maximum operating loss would also be $120,000. At the maximum sales of 10,000 units, the maximum operating profit would be $80,000, as shown below.

| | |
|---|---|
| Sales (10,000 units × $50)............................................. | $500,000 |
| Variable costs (10,000 units × $30) ............................... | 300,000 |
| Contribution margin (10,000 units × $20)......................... | $200,000 |
| Fixed costs ...................................................... | 120,000 |
| Operating profit.................................................. | $ 80,000 |

← Revised maximum profit

A revised profit-volume chart is constructed by plotting the maximum operating loss and maximum operating profit points and drawing the revised profit line. The original and the revised profit-volume charts are shown in Exhibit 8.

**EXHIBIT 8**

**Original Profit-Volume Chart and Revised Profit-Volume Chart**

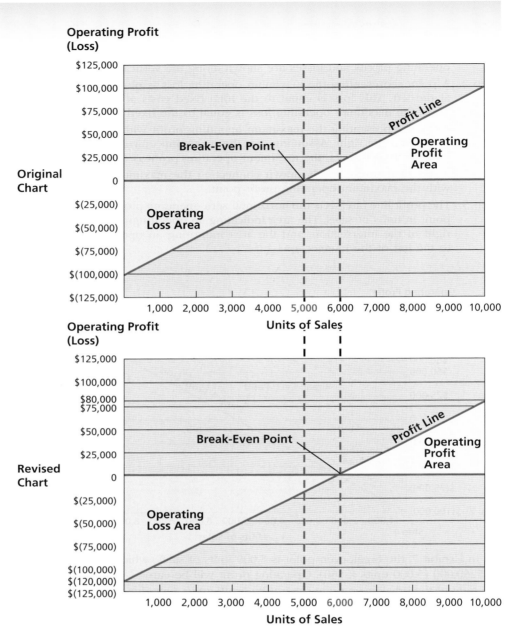

The revised profit-volume chart indicates that the break-even point is 6,000 units of sales. This is equal to total sales of $300,000 (6,000 units × $50). The operating loss area of the chart has increased, while the operating profit area has decreased.

## Use of Computers in Cost-Volume-Profit Analysis

With computers, the graphic approach and the mathematical approach to cost-volume-profit analysis are easy to use. Managers can vary assumptions regarding selling prices, costs, and volume and can observe the effects of each change on the break-even point and profit. Such an analysis is called a *"what if"* analysis or *sensitivity* analysis.

## Assumptions of Cost-Volume-Profit Analysis

Cost-volume-profit analysis depends on several assumptions. The primary assumptions are as follows:

1. Total sales and total costs can be represented by straight lines.
2. Within the relevant range of operating activity, the efficiency of operations does not change.

3. Costs can be divided into fixed and variable components.
4. The sales mix is constant.
5. There is no change in the inventory quantities during the period.

These assumptions simplify cost-volume-profit analysis. Since they are often valid for the relevant range of operations, cost-volume-profit analysis is useful for decision making.[3]

# Special Cost-Volume-Profit Relationships

**OBJ. 5** Compute the break-even point for a company selling more than one product, the operating leverage, and the margin of safety.

Cost-volume-profit analysis can also be used when a company sells several products with different costs and prices. In addition, operating leverage and the margin of safety are useful in analyzing cost-volume-profit relationships.

## Sales Mix Considerations

Many companies sell more than one product at different selling prices. In addition, the products normally have different unit variable costs and, thus, different unit contribution margins. In such cases, break-even analysis can still be performed by considering the sales mix. The **sales mix** is the relative distribution of sales among the products sold by a company.

To illustrate, assume that Cascade Company sold Products A and B during the past year as follows:

Total fixed costs $200,000

|  | **Product A** | **Product B** |
|---|---|---|
| Unit selling price ................. | $90 | $140 |
| Unit variable cost................ | 70 | 95 |
| Unit contribution margin ........ | $20 | $ 45 |
| Units sold ....................... | 8,000 | 2,000 |
| Sales mix........................ | 80% | 20% |

Sales Mix

The sales mix for Products A and B is expressed as a percentage of total units sold. For Cascade Company, a total of 10,000 (8,000 + 2,000) units were sold during the year. Therefore, the sales mix is 80% (8,000/10,000) for Product A and 20% for Product B (2,000/10,000) as shown above. The sales mix could also be expressed as the ratio 80:20.

For break-even analysis, it is useful to think of Products A and B as components of one overall enterprise product called E. The unit selling price of E equals the sum of the unit selling prices of each product multiplied by its sales mix percentage. Likewise, the unit variable cost and unit contribution margin of E equal the sum of the unit variable costs and unit contribution margins of each product multiplied by its sales mix percentage.

For Cascade Company, the unit selling price, unit variable cost, and unit contribution margin for E are computed as follows:

| **Product E** | **Product A** | **Product B** |
|---|---|---|
| Unit selling price of E | $100 = ($90 × 0.8) + | ($140 × 0.2) |
| Unit variable cost of E | 75 = ($70 × 0.8) + | ($95 × 0.2) |
| Unit contribution margin of E | $ 25 = ($20 × 0.8) + | ($45 × 0.2) |

The break-even point of 8,000 units of E can be determined in the normal manner as shown below.

$$\text{Break-Even Sales (units) for E} = \frac{\text{Fixed Costs}}{\text{Unit Contribution Margin}} = \frac{\$200,000}{\$25} = 8,000 \text{ units}$$

Since the sales mix for Products A and B is 80% and 20% respectively, the break-even quantity of A is 6,400 units (8,000 units × 80%) and B is 1,600 units (8,000 units × 20%).

The preceding break-even analysis is verified by the following income statement:

3 The impact of violating these assumptions is discussed in advanced accounting texts.

| | Product A | Product B | Total |
|---|---|---|---|
| Sales: | | | |
| 6,400 units × $90 ............................. | $576,000 | | $576,000 |
| 1,600 units × $140 ............................. | | $224,000 | 224,000 |
| Total sales ...................................... | $576,000 | $224,000 | $800,000 |
| Variable costs: | | | |
| 6,400 units × $70 ............................. | $448,000 | | $448,000 |
| 1,600 units × $95 ............................. | | $152,000 | 152,000 |
| Total variable costs ........................... | $448,000 | $152,000 | $600,000 |
| Contribution margin ............................. | $128,000 | $ 72,000 | $200,000 |
| Fixed costs ........................................ | | | 200,000 |
| Income from operations ........................... | | | $        0  ← Break-even point |

The effects of changes in the sales mix on the break-even point can be determined by assuming a different sales mix. The break-even point of E can then be recomputed.

## Example Exercise 19-5  Sales Mix and Break-Even Analysis

OBJ. 5

Megan Company has fixed costs of $180,000. The unit selling price, variable cost per unit, and contribution margin per unit for the company's two products are provided below.

| Product | Selling Price | Variable Cost per Unit | Contribution Margin per Unit |
|---|---|---|---|
| Q | $160 | $100 | $60 |
| Z | 100 | 80 | 20 |

The sales mix for products Q and Z is 75% and 25%, respectively. Determine the break-even point in units of Q and Z.

### Follow My Example 19-5

Unit selling price of E:      [($160 × 0.75) + ($100 × 0.25)] = $145
Unit variable cost of E:      [($100 × 0.75) + ($80 × 0.25)]  =   95
Unit contribution margin of E:                              $  50

Break-Even Sales (units) = 3,600 units = $180,000/$50

Practice Exercises: **PE 19-5A, PE 19-5B**

## Operating Leverage

The relationship of a company's contribution margin to income from operations is measured by **operating leverage**. A company's operating leverage is computed as follows:

$$\text{Operating Leverage} = \frac{\text{Contribution Margin}}{\text{Income from Operations}}$$

The difference between contribution margin and income from operations is fixed costs. Thus, companies with high fixed costs will normally have a high operating leverage. Examples of such companies include airline and automotive companies. Low operating leverage is normal for companies that are labor intensive, such as professional service companies, which have low fixed costs.

To illustrate operating leverage, assume the following data for Jones Inc. and Wilson Inc.:

| | Jones Inc. | Wilson Inc. |
|---|---|---|
| Sales........................................................ | $400,000 | $400,000 |
| Variable costs ............................................ | 300,000 | 300,000 |
| Contribution margin....................................... | $100,000 | $100,000 |
| Fixed costs ................................................. | 80,000 | 50,000 |
| Income from operations ................................... | $ 20,000 | $ 50,000 |

As shown above, Jones Inc. and Wilson Inc. have the same sales, the same variable costs, and the same contribution margin. However, Jones Inc. has larger fixed costs than Wilson Inc. and, thus, a higher operating leverage. The operating leverage for each company is computed as follows:

Jones Inc.

$$\text{Operating Leverage} = \frac{\text{Contribution Margin}}{\text{Income from Operations}} = \frac{\$100,000}{\$20,000} = 5$$

Wilson Inc.

$$\text{Operating Leverage} = \frac{\text{Contribution Margin}}{\text{Income from Operations}} = \frac{\$100,000}{\$50,000} = 2$$

Operating leverage can be used to measure the impact of changes in sales on income from operations. Using operating leverage, the effect of changes in sales on income from operations is computed as follows:

$$\frac{\text{Percent Change in}}{\text{Income from Operations}} = \frac{\text{Percent Change in}}{\text{Sales}} \times \frac{\text{Operating}}{\text{Leverage}}$$

To illustrate, assume that sales increased by 10%, or $40,000 ($400,000 × 10%), for Jones Inc. and Wilson Inc. The percent increase in income from operations for Jones Inc. and Wilson Inc. is computed below.

Jones Inc.

$$\frac{\text{Percent Change in}}{\text{Income from Operations}} = \frac{\text{Percent Change in}}{\text{Sales}} \times \frac{\text{Operating}}{\text{Leverage}}$$

$$\frac{\text{Percent Change in}}{\text{Income from Operations}} = 10\% \times 5 = 50\%$$

Wilson Inc.

$$\frac{\text{Percent Change in}}{\text{Income from Operations}} = \frac{\text{Percent Change in}}{\text{Sales}} \times \frac{\text{Operating}}{\text{Leverage}}$$

$$\frac{\text{Percent Change in}}{\text{Income from Operations}} = 10\% \times 2 = 20\%$$

As shown above, Jones Inc.'s income from operations increases by 50%, while Wilson Inc.'s income from operations increases by only 20%. The validity of this analysis is shown in the following income statements for Jones Inc. and Wilson Inc. based on the 10% increase in sales:

|  | Jones Inc. | Wilson Inc. |
|---|---|---|
| Sales | $440,000 | $440,000 |
| Variable costs | 330,000 | 330,000 |
| Contribution margin | $110,000 | $110,000 |
| Fixed costs | 80,000 | 50,000 |
| Income from operations | $ 30,000 | $ 60,000 |

The preceding income statements indicate that Jones Inc.'s income from operations increased from $20,000 to $30,000, a 50% increase ($10,000/$20,000). In contrast, Wilson Inc.'s income from operations increased from $50,000 to $60,000, a 20% increase ($10,000/$50,000).

Because even a small increase in sales will generate a large percentage increase in income from operations, Jones Inc. might consider ways to increase sales. Such actions could include special advertising or sales promotions. In contrast, Wilson Inc. might consider ways to increase operating leverage by reducing variable costs.

The impact of a change in sales on income from operations for companies with high and low operating leverage can be summarized as follows:

|  | **Percentage Impact on Income from Operations** |
|---|---|
| **Operating Leverage** | **from a Change in Sales** |
| High | Large |
| Low | Small |

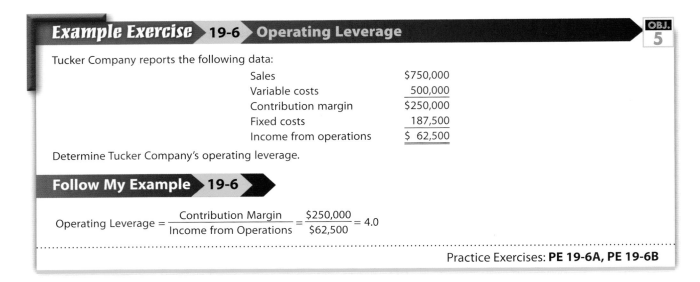

**Example Exercise** 19-6 ▶ Operating Leverage     OBJ. 5

Tucker Company reports the following data:

| | |
|---|---|
| Sales | $750,000 |
| Variable costs | 500,000 |
| Contribution margin | $250,000 |
| Fixed costs | 187,500 |
| Income from operations | $ 62,500 |

Determine Tucker Company's operating leverage.

**Follow My Example** 19-6

$$\text{Operating Leverage} = \frac{\text{Contribution Margin}}{\text{Income from Operations}} = \frac{\$250,000}{\$62,500} = 4.0$$

Practice Exercises: **PE 19-6A, PE 19-6B**

## Margin of Safety

The **margin of safety** indicates the possible decrease in sales that may occur before an operating loss results. Thus, if the margin of safety is low, even a small decline in sales revenue may result in an operating loss.

The margin of safety may be expressed in the following ways:

1. Dollars of sales
2. Units of sales
3. Percent of current sales

To illustrate, assume the following data:

| | |
|---|---|
| Sales | $250,000 |
| Sales at the break-even point | 200,000 |
| Unit selling price | 25 |

The margin of safety in dollars of sales is $50,000 ($250,000 – $200,000). The margin of safety in units is 2,000 units ($50,000/$25). The margin of safety expressed as a percent of current sales is 20%, as computed below.

$$\text{Margin of Safety} = \frac{\text{Sales – Sales at Break-Even Point}}{\text{Sales}}$$

$$= \frac{\$250,000 – \$200,000}{\$250,000} = \frac{\$50,000}{\$250,000} = 20\%$$

Therefore, the current sales may decline $50,000, 2,000 units, or 20% before an operating loss occurs.

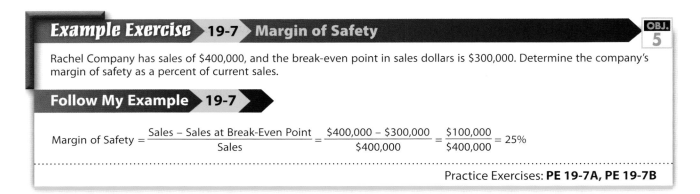

**Example Exercise** 19-7 ▶ Margin of Safety     OBJ. 5

Rachel Company has sales of $400,000, and the break-even point in sales dollars is $300,000. Determine the company's margin of safety as a percent of current sales.

**Follow My Example** 19-7

$$\text{Margin of Safety} = \frac{\text{Sales – Sales at Break-Even Point}}{\text{Sales}} = \frac{\$400,000 – \$300,000}{\$400,000} = \frac{\$100,000}{\$400,000} = 25\%$$

Practice Exercises: **PE 19-7A, PE 19-7B**

# At a Glance 19

**Classify costs as variable costs, fixed costs, or mixed costs.**

**Key Points**  Variable costs vary in proportion to changes in the level of activity. Fixed costs remain the same in total dollar amount as the level of activity changes. Mixed costs are comprised of both fixed and variable costs.

| Learning Outcomes | Example Exercises | Practice Exercises |
|---|---|---|
| • Describe variable costs. | | |
| • Describe fixed costs. | | |
| • Describe mixed costs. | | |
| • Separate mixed costs using the high-low method. | EE19-1 | PE19-1A, 19-1B |

**Compute the contribution margin, the contribution margin ratio, and the unit contribution margin.**

**Key Points**  Contribution margin is the excess of sales revenue over variable costs and can be expressed as a ratio (contribution margin ratio) or a dollar amount (unit contribution margin).

| Learning Outcomes | Example Exercises | Practice Exercises |
|---|---|---|
| • Describe contribution margin. | | |
| • Compute the contribution margin ratio. | EE19-2 | PE19-2A, 19-2B |
| • Compute the unit contribution margin. | EE19-2 | PE19-2A, 19-2B |

**Determine the break-even point and sales necessary to achieve a target profit.**

**Key Points**  The break-even point is the point at which a business's revenues exactly equal costs. The mathematical approach to cost-volume-profit analysis uses the unit contribution margin concept and mathematical equations to determine the break-even point and the volume necessary to achieve a target profit.

| Learning Outcomes | Example Exercises | Practice Exercises |
|---|---|---|
| • Compute the break-even point in units. | EE19-3 | PE19-3A, 19-3B |
| • Describe how changes in fixed costs affect the break-even point. | | |
| • Describe how changes in unit variable costs affect the break-even point. | | |
| • Describe how a change in the unit selling price affects the break-even point. | EE19-3 | PE19-3A, 19-3B |
| • Modify the break-even equation to compute the unit sales required to earn a target profit. | EE19-4 | PE19-4A, 19-4B |

**OBJ. 4**

**Using a cost-volume-profit chart and a profit-volume chart, determine the break-even point and sales necessary to achieve a target profit.**

**Key Points** Graphical methods can be used to determine the break-even point and the volume necessary to achieve a target profit. A cost-volume-profit chart focuses on the relationship among costs, sales, and operating profit or loss. The profit-volume chart focuses on profits rather than on revenues and costs.

| Learning Outcomes | Example Exercises | Practice Exercises |
|---|---|---|
| • Describe how to construct a cost-volume-profit chart. | | |
| • Determine the break-even point using a cost-volume-profit chart. | | |
| • Describe how to construct a profit-volume chart. | | |
| • Determine the break-even point using a profit-volume chart. | | |
| • Describe factors affecting the reliability of cost-volume-profit analysis. | | |

**OBJ. 5**

**Compute the break-even point for a company selling more than one product, the operating leverage, and the margin of safety.**

**Key Points** Cost-volume-profit relationships can be used for analyzing (1) sales mix, (2) operating leverage, and (3) margin of safety.

| Learning Outcomes | Example Exercises | Practice Exercises |
|---|---|---|
| • Compute the break-even point for a mix of products. | EE19-5 | PE19-5A, 19-5B |
| • Compute operating leverage. | EE19-6 | PE19-6A, 19-6B |
| • Compute the margin of safety. | EE19-7 | PE19-7A, 19-7B |

## Key Terms

activity bases (drivers) (886)
break-even point (895)
contribution margin (893)
contribution margin ratio (893)
cost behavior (886)
cost-volume-profit analysis (892)

cost-volume-profit chart (901)
fixed costs (888)
high-low method (889)
margin of safety (908)
mixed costs (889)
operating leverage (906)

profit-volume chart (902)
relevant range (886)
sales mix (905)
unit contribution margin (894)
variable costing (892)
variable costs (886)

## Illustrative Problem

Wyatt Inc. expects to maintain the same inventories at the end of the year as at the beginning of the year. The estimated fixed costs for the year are $288,000, and the estimated variable costs per unit are $14. It is expected that 60,000 units will be sold at a price of $20 per unit. Maximum sales within the relevant range are 70,000 units.

**Instructions**

1. What is (a) the contribution margin ratio and (b) the unit contribution margin?

2. Determine the break-even point in units.

3. Construct a cost-volume-profit chart, indicating the break-even point.

4. Construct a profit-volume chart, indicating the break-even point.

5. What is the margin of safety?

## Solution

1. a. Contribution Margin Ratio = $\dfrac{\text{Sales} - \text{Variable Costs}}{\text{Sales}}$

   Contribution Margin Ratio = $\dfrac{(60{,}000 \text{ units} \times \$20) - (60{,}000 \text{ units} \times \$14)}{(60{,}000 \text{ units} \times \$20)}$

   Contribution Margin Ratio = $\dfrac{\$1{,}200{,}000 - \$840{,}000}{\$1{,}200{,}000} = \dfrac{\$360{,}000}{\$1{,}200{,}000}$

   Contribution Margin Ratio = 30%

   b. Unit Contribution Margin = Unit Selling Price − Unit Variable Costs
   Unit Contribution Margin = $20 − $14 = $6

2. Break-Even Sales (units) = $\dfrac{\text{Fixed Costs}}{\text{Unit Contribution Margin}}$

   Break-Even Sales (units) = $\dfrac{\$288{,}000}{\$6}$ = 48,000 units

3. **Sales and Costs**

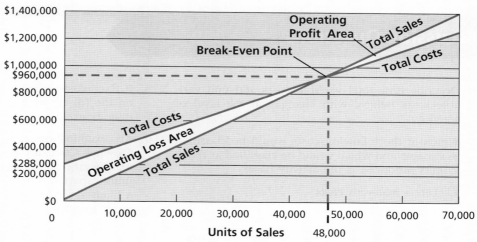

4. **Operating Profit (Loss)**

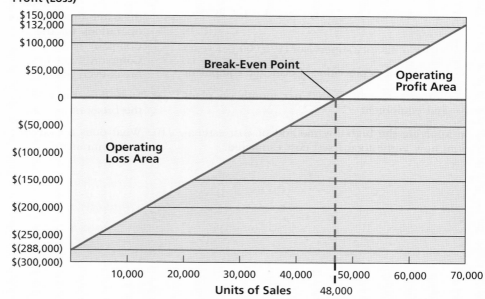

5. Margin of safety:

| | |
|---|---|
| Expected sales (60,000 units × $20) | $1,200,000 |
| Break-even point (48,000 units × $20) | 960,000 |
| Margin of safety | $ 240,000 |

or

$$\text{Margin of Safety (units)} = \frac{\text{Margin of Safety (dollars)}}{\text{Unit Selling Price}}$$

or

12,000 units ($240,000/$20)

or

$$\text{Margin of Safety} = \frac{\text{Sales} - \text{Sales at Break-Even Point}}{\text{Sales}}$$

$$\text{Margin of Safety} = \frac{\$240,000}{\$1,200,000} = 20\%$$

# Discussion Questions

1. Describe how total variable costs and unit variable costs behave with changes in the level of activity.

2. Which of the following costs would be classified as variable and which would be classified as fixed, if units produced is the activity base?

   a. Direct materials costs

   b. Direct labor costs

   c. Electricity costs of $0.35 per kilowatt-hour

3. How would each of the following fixed/variable costs be classified if units produced is the activity base?

   a. Salary of factory supervisor ($70,000 per year)

   b. Straight-line depreciation of plant and equipment

   c. Property rent of $6,000 per month on plant and equipment

4. In applying the high-low method of cost estimation, how is the total fixed cost estimated?

5. If fixed costs increase, what would be the impact on the (a) contribution margin? (b) income from operations?

6. An examination of the accounting records of Clowney Company disclosed a high contribution margin ratio and production at a level below maximum capacity. Based on this information, suggest a likely means of improving income from operations. Explain.

7. If the unit cost of direct materials is decreased, what effect will this change have on the break-even point?

8. Both Austin Company and Hill Company had the same unit sales, total costs, and income from operations for the current fiscal year; yet Austin Company had a lower break-even point than Hill Company. Explain the reason for this difference in break-even points.

9. How does the sales mix affect the calculation of the break-even point?

10. What does operating leverage measure, and how is it computed?

# Practice Exercises

| Learning Objectives | Example Exercises | |
|---|---|---|

**OBJ. 1**   **EE 19-1** *p. 891*

## PE 19-1A   High-low method

The manufacturing costs of Fuld Industries for three months of the year are provided below.

| | Total Costs | Production |
|---|---|---|
| January | $175,000 | 7,500 units |
| February | 390,000 | 20,000 |
| March | 490,000 | 25,000 |

Using the high-low method, determine (a) the variable cost per unit and (b) the total fixed cost.

**OBJ. 1**   **EE 19-1** *p. 891*

## PE 19-1B   High-low method

The manufacturing costs of Greenburg Enterprises for the first three months of the year are provided below.

| | Total Costs | Production |
|---|---|---|
| April | $210,000 | 2,000 units |
| May | 320,000 | 4,000 |
| June | 225,000 | 2,500 |

Using the high-low method, determine (a) the variable cost per unit and (b) the total fixed cost.

**OBJ. 2**   **EE 19-2** *p. 895*

## PE 19-2A   Contribution margin

United Merchants Company sells 4,000 units at $60 per unit. Variable costs are $45 per unit, and fixed costs are $40,000. Determine (a) the contribution margin ratio, (b) the unit contribution margin, and (c) income from operations.

**OBJ. 2**   **EE 19-2** *p. 895*

## PE 19-2B   Contribution margin

Gluxman Company sells 10,000 units at $25 per unit. Variable costs are $22 per unit, and fixed costs are $20,000. Determine (a) the contribution margin ratio, (b) the unit contribution margin, and (c) income from operations.

**OBJ. 3**   **EE 19-3** *p. 899*

## PE 19-3A   Break-even point

Gregory Enterprises sells a product for $80 per unit. The variable cost is $55 per unit, while fixed costs are $20,000. Determine (a) the break-even point in sales units and (b) the break-even point if the selling price were increased to $87 per unit.

**OBJ. 3**   **EE 19-3** *p. 899*

## PE 19-3B   Break-even point

Grobe Inc. sells a product for $50 per unit. The variable cost is $40 per unit, while fixed costs are $14,000. Determine (a) the break-even point in sales units and (b) the break-even point if the selling price were decreased to $45 per unit.

**PE 19-4A   Target profit**

Ivey Inc. sells a product for $100 per unit. The variable cost is $75 per unit, and fixed costs are $30,000. Determine (a) the break-even point in sales units and (b) the break-even point in sales units if the company desires a target profit of $10,000.

**PE 19-4B   Target profit**

Hofstra Company sells a product for $120 per unit. The variable cost is $100 per unit, and fixed costs are $120,000. Determine (a) the break-even point in sales units and (b) the break-even point in sales units if the company desires a target profit of $40,000.

**PE 19-5A   Sales mix and break-even analysis**

Figg Inc. has fixed costs of $420,000. The unit selling price, variable cost per unit, and contribution margin per unit for the company's two products are provided below.

| Product | Selling Price | Variable Cost per Unit | Contribution Margin per Unit |
|---------|---------------|------------------------|------------------------------|
| L | $100 | $80 | $20 |
| M | 80 | 62 | 18 |

The sales mix for products L and M is 60% and 40%, respectively. Determine the break-even point in units of L and M.

**PE 19-5B   Sales mix and break-even analysis**

Golub Company has fixed costs of $100,000. The unit selling price, variable cost per unit, and contribution margin per unit for the company's two products are provided below.

| Product | Selling Price | Variable Cost per Unit | Contribution Margin per Unit |
|---------|---------------|------------------------|------------------------------|
| X | $30 | $25 | $ 5 |
| Y | 20 | 10 | 10 |

The sales mix for products X and Y is 75% and 25%, respectively. Determine the break-even point in units of X and Y.

**PE 19-6A   Operating leverage**

Emily Enterprises reports the following data:

| | |
|---|---:|
| Sales | $180,000 |
| Variable costs | 100,000 |
| Contribution margin | $ 80,000 |
| Fixed costs | 30,000 |
| Income from operations | $ 50,000 |

Determine Emily Enterprises's operating leverage.

**PE 19-6B   Operating leverage**

Walker Co. reports the following data:

| | |
|---|---:|
| Sales | $600,000 |
| Variable costs | 250,000 |
| Contribution margin | $350,000 |
| Fixed costs | 150,000 |
| Income from operations | $200,000 |

Determine Walker Co.'s operating leverage.

**PE 19-7A   Margin of safety**

Mitra Inc. has sales of $910,000, and the break-even point in sales dollars is $746,200. Determine the company's margin of safety as a percent of current sales.

*Learning Objectives*

*Example Exercises*

**OBJ. 5**   **EE 19-7** *p. 908*

**PE 19-7B   Margin of safety**

Marsh Company has sales of $600,000, and the break-even point in sales dollars is $456,000. Determine the company's margin of safety as a percent of current sales.

# Exercises

**OBJ. 1**

**EX 19-1   Classify costs**

Following is a list of various costs incurred in producing toy robotic helicopters. With respect to the production and sale of these toy helicopters, classify each cost as either variable, fixed, or mixed.

1. Janitorial costs, $5,000 per month
2. Salary of plant manager
3. Oil used in manufacturing equipment
4. Property taxes, $210,000 per year on factory building and equipment
5. Hourly wages of inspectors
6. Plastic
7. Packaging
8. Metal
9. Electricity costs, $0.10 per kilowatt-hour
10. Rent on warehouse, $12,000 per month plus $20 per square foot of storage used
11. Property insurance premiums, $2,000 per month plus $0.008 for each dollar of property over $1,000,000
12. Straight-line depreciation on the production equipment
13. Hourly wages of machine operators
14. Pension cost, $0.75 per employee hour on the job
15. Computer chip (purchased from a vendor)

**OBJ. 1**

**EX 19-2   Identify cost graphs**

The following cost graphs illustrate various types of cost behavior:

**Cost Graph One**

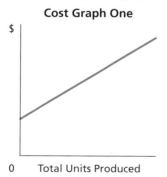

0    Total Units Produced

**Cost Graph Two**

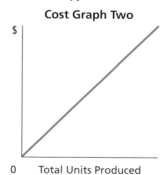

0    Total Units Produced

**Cost Graph Three**

0    Total Units Produced

**Cost Graph Four**

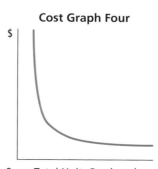

0    Total Units Produced

For each of the following costs, identify the cost graph that best illustrates its cost behavior as the number of units produced increases.

a. Electricity costs of $1,000 per month plus $0.10 per kilowatt-hour

b. Per-unit cost of straight-line depreciation on factory equipment

c. Total direct materials cost

d. Per-unit direct labor cost

e. Salary of quality control supervisor, $20,000 per month

---

### EX 19-3    Identify activity bases

For a major university, match each cost in the following table with the activity base most appropriate to it. An activity base may be used more than once, or not used at all.

| Cost: | Activity Base: |
|---|---|
| 1. Financial aid office salaries | a. Student credit hours |
| 2. School supplies | b. Number of students living on campus |
| 3. Instructor salaries | c. Number of enrollment applications |
| 4. Housing personnel wages | d. Number of financial aid applications |
| 5. Student records office salaries | e. Number of enrolled students and alumni |
| 6. Admissions office salaries | f. Number of student/athletes |

---

### EX 19-4    Identify activity bases

From the following list of activity bases for an automobile dealership, select the base that would be most appropriate for each of these costs: (1) preparation costs (cleaning, oil, and gasoline costs) for each car received, (2) salespersons' commission of 5% of the sales price for each car sold, and (3) administrative costs for ordering cars.

a. Dollar amount of cars ordered

b. Number of cars on hand

c. Dollar amount of cars sold

d. Number of cars sold

e. Dollar amount of cars received

f. Dollar amount of cars on hand

g. Number of cars received

h. Number of cars ordered

---

### EX 19-5    Identify fixed and variable costs

Intuit Inc. develops and sells software products for the personal finance market, including popular titles such as Quicken® and TurboTax®. Classify each of the following costs and expenses for this company as either variable or fixed to the number of units produced and sold:

a. Salaries of human resources personnel

b. User's guides

c. Shipping expenses

d. Advertising

e. Property taxes on general offices

f. Wages of telephone order assistants

g. President's salary

h. Straight-line depreciation of computer equipment

i. Sales commissions

j. CDs

k. Packaging costs

l. Salaries of software developers

OBJ. 1

✔ a. $0.25

### EX 19-6   Relevant range and fixed and variable costs

Fortress Inc. manufactures pistons for custom motorcycles within a relevant range of 300,000 to 375,000 pistons per year. Within this range, the following partially completed manufacturing cost schedule has been prepared:

| Components produced ............... | 300,000 | 360,000 | 375,000 |
|---|---|---|---|
| Total costs: | | | |
| Total variable costs ................. | $ 75,000 | (d) | (j) |
| Total fixed costs ................... | 90,000 | (e) | (k) |
| Total costs........................ | $165,000 | (f) | (l) |
| Cost per unit: | | | |
| Variable cost per unit ............... | (a) | (g) | (m) |
| Fixed cost per unit................. | (b) | (h) | (n) |
| Total cost per unit ................. | (c) | (i) | (o) |

Complete the cost schedule, identifying each cost by the appropriate letter (a) through (o).

OBJ. 1

✔ a. $17.60 per unit

### EX 19-7   High-low method

Crane Inc. has decided to use the high-low method to estimate the total cost and the fixed and variable cost components of the total cost. The data for various levels of production are as follows:

| Units Produced | Total Costs |
|---|---|
| 10,000 | $700,000 |
| 15,000 | 840,000 |
| 22,500 | 920,000 |

a.  Determine the variable cost per unit and the fixed cost.

b.  Based on part (a), estimate the total cost for 14,000 units of production.

OBJ. 1

✔ Fixed cost, $200,000

### EX 19-8   High-low method for service company

Diamond Railroad decided to use the high-low method and operating data from the past six months to estimate the fixed and variable components of transportation costs. The activity base used by Diamond Railroad is a measure of railroad operating activity, termed "gross-ton miles," which is the total number of tons multiplied by the miles moved.

| | Transportation Costs | Gross-Ton Miles |
|---|---|---|
| January | $1,190,000 | 385,000 |
| February | 1,043,000 | 434,000 |
| March | 900,000 | 350,000 |
| April | 1,015,000 | 420,000 |
| May | 920,000 | 360,000 |
| June | 1,250,000 | 525,000 |

Determine the variable cost per gross-ton mile and the fixed cost.

OBJ. 2

✔ a. 70%

### EX 19-9   Contribution margin ratio

a.  Bryan Company budgets sales of $1,800,000, fixed costs of $1,000,000, and variable costs of $1,080,000. What is the contribution margin ratio for Bryan Company?

b.  If the contribution margin ratio for Carnegie Company is 32%, sales were $900,000, and fixed costs were $210,000, what was the income from operations?

OBJ. 2

✔ b. 34.6%

### EX 19-10   Contribution margin and contribution margin ratio

For a recent year, McDonald's company-owned restaurants had the following sales and expenses (in millions):

| | |
|---|---|
| Sales | $16,561 |
| Food and packaging | $ 5,586 |
| Payroll | 4,300 |
| Occupancy (rent, depreciation, etc.) | 3,767 |
| General, selling, and administrative expenses | 2,355 |
| | $16,008 |
| Income from operations | $ 553 |

Assume that the variable costs consist of food and packaging, payroll, and 40% of the general, selling, and administrative expenses.

a. What is McDonald's contribution margin? Round to the nearest million.

b. What is McDonald's contribution margin ratio? Round to one decimal place.

c. How much would income from operations increase if same-store sales increased by $400 million for the coming year, with no change in the contribution margin ratio or fixed costs?

---

OBJ. 3

✔ b. 35,200 units

### EX 19-11 Break-even sales and sales to realize income from operations

For the current year ending March 31, Ewok Company expects fixed costs of $740,000, a unit variable cost of $55, and a unit selling price of $80.

a. Compute the anticipated break-even sales (units).

b. Compute the sales (units) required to realize income from operations of $140,000.

---

OBJ. 3

✔ a. 115,377,060 barrels

### EX 19-12 Break-even sales

Anheuser-Busch InBev Companies, Inc., reported the following operating information for a recent year (in millions):

| | |
|---|---|
| Net sales | $23,507 |
| Cost of goods sold | $10,336 |
| Selling, general and administration | 7,831 |
| | $18,167 |
| Income from operations | $ 5,340* |
| *Before special items | |

In addition, assume that Anheuser-Busch InBev sold 200 million barrels of beer during the year. Assume that variable costs were 75% of the cost of goods sold and 40% of selling, general and administration expenses. Assume that the remaining costs are fixed. For the following year, assume that Anheuser-Busch InBev expects pricing, variable costs per barrel, and fixed costs to remain constant, except that new distribution and general office facilities are expected to increase fixed costs by $225 million.

a. Compute the break-even number of barrels for the current year. *Note:* For the selling price per barrel and variable costs per barrel, round to the nearest cent. Also, round the break-even to the nearest barrel.

b. Compute the anticipated break-even number of barrels for the following year.

---

OBJ. 3

✔ a. 11,500 units

### EX 19-13 Break-even sales

Currently, the unit selling price of a product is $110, the unit variable cost is $80, and the total fixed costs are $345,000. A proposal is being evaluated to increase the unit selling price to $120.

a. Compute the current break-even sales (units).

b. Compute the anticipated break-even sales (units), assuming that the unit selling price is increased and all costs remain constant.

---

OBJ. 3

### EX 19-14 Break-even analysis

The Junior League of Kernersville, North Carolina, collected recipes from members and published a cookbook entitled *Food Is Love*. The book will sell for $15 per copy. The chairwoman of the cookbook development committee estimated that the club needed to sell 5,000 books to break even on its $25,000 investment. What is the variable cost per unit assumed in the Junior League's analysis?

---

**OBJ. 3**

### EX 19-15 Break-even analysis

Media outlets such as ESPN and Fox Sports often have Web sites that provide in-depth coverage of news and events. Portions of these Web sites are restricted to members who pay a monthly subscription to gain access to exclusive news and commentary. These Web sites typically offer a free trial period to introduce viewers to the Web site. Assume that during a recent fiscal year, ESPN.com spent $3,150,000 on a promotional campaign for the ESPN.com Web site that offered two free months of service for new subscribers. In addition, assume the following information:

| | |
|---|---|
| Number of months an average new customer stays with the service (including the two free months) | 23 months |
| Revenue per month per customer subscription | $15.00 |
| Variable cost per month per customer subscription | $5.00 |

Determine the number of new customer accounts needed to break even on the cost of the promotional campaign. In forming your answer, (1) treat the cost of the promotional campaign as a fixed cost, and (2) treat the revenue less variable cost per account for the subscription period as the unit contribution margin.

---

**OBJ. 3**

### EX 19-16 Break-even analysis

Sprint Nextel is one of the largest digital wireless service providers in the United States. In a recent year, it had approximately 36.7 million direct subscribers (accounts) that generated revenue of $35,635 million. Costs and expenses for the year were as follows (in millions):

| | |
|---|---|
| Cost of revenue | $16,746 |
| Selling, general, and administrative expenses | 11,355 |
| Depreciation | 5,953 |

Assume that 80% of the cost of revenue and 30% of the selling, general, and administrative expenses are variable to the number of direct subscribers (accounts).

a. What is Sprint Nextel's break-even number of accounts, using the data and assumptions above? Round units (accounts) to one decimal place.

b. How much revenue per account would be sufficient for Sprint Nextel to break even if the number of accounts remained constant?

---

**OBJ. 4**

✔ b. $720,000

### EX 19-17 Cost-volume-profit chart

For the coming year, Weill Inc. anticipates fixed costs of $240,000, a unit variable cost of $80, and a unit selling price of $120. The maximum sales within the relevant range are $1,200,000.

a. Construct a cost-volume-profit chart.

b. Estimate the break-even sales (dollars) by using the cost-volume-profit chart constructed in part (a).

c. ➤ What is the main advantage of presenting the cost-volume-profit analysis in graphic form rather than equation form?

---

**OBJ. 4**

✔ b. $160,000

### EX 19-18 Profit-volume chart

Using the data for Weill Inc. in Exercise 19-17, (a) determine the maximum possible operating loss, (b) compute the maximum possible income from operations, (c) construct a profit-volume chart, and (d) estimate the break-even sales (units) by using the profit-volume chart constructed in part (c).

**OBJ. 4**

**EX 19-19  Break-even chart**

Name the following chart, and identify the items represented by the letters (a) through (f).

**Sales and Costs**

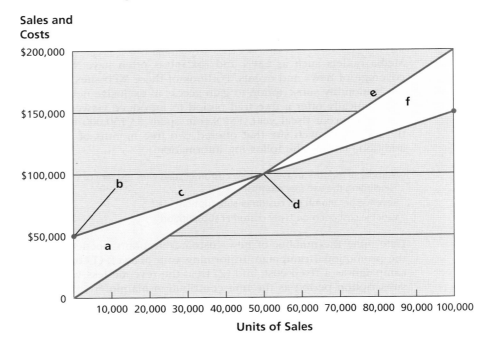

**OBJ. 4**

**EX 19-20  Break-even chart**

Name the following chart, and identify the items represented by the letters (a) through (f).

**Operating Profit (Loss)**

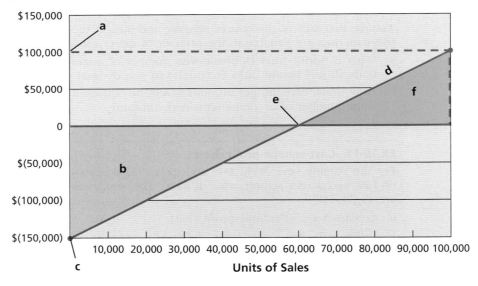

**OBJ. 5**

✔ a. 20,000 units

**EX 19-21  Sales mix and break-even sales**

Geitner Sports Inc. manufactures and sells two products, baseball bats and baseball gloves. The fixed costs are $460,000, and the sales mix is 60% bats and 40% gloves. The unit selling price and the unit variable cost for each product are as follows:

| Products | Unit Selling Price | Unit Variable Cost |
|----------|--------------------|--------------------|
| Bats     | $100.00            | $75.00             |
| Gloves   | 80.00              | 60.00              |

a. Compute the break-even sales (units) for the overall product, E.

b. How many units of each product, baseball bats and baseball gloves, would be sold at the break-even point?

---

**OBJ. 5**

✔ a. 100 seats

### EX 19-22  Break-even sales and sales mix for a service company

Sunshine Airways provides air transportation services between Philadelphia and Orlando. A single Philadelphia to Orlando round-trip flight has the following operating statistics:

| | |
|---|---:|
| Fuel | $8,200 |
| Flight crew salaries | 3,700 |
| Airplane depreciation | 3,450 |
| Variable cost per passenger—business class | 100 |
| Variable cost per passenger—economy class | 75 |
| Round-trip ticket price—business class | 600 |
| Round-trip ticket price—economy class | 190 |

It is assumed that the fuel, crew salaries, and airplane depreciation are fixed, regardless of the number of seats sold for the round-trip flight.

a. Compute the break-even number of seats sold on a single round-trip flight for the overall product. Assume that the overall product is 10% business class and 90% economy class tickets.

b. How many business class and economy class seats would be sold at the break-even point?

---

**OBJ. 5**

✔ a. (2) 30%

### EX 19-23  Margin of safety

a. If Steele Company, with a break-even point at $378,000 of sales, has actual sales of $540,000, what is the margin of safety expressed (1) in dollars and (2) as a percentage of sales?

b. If the margin of safety for Kramer Company was 20%, fixed costs were $900,000, and variable costs were 70% of sales, what was the amount of actual sales (dollars)? (*Hint:* Determine the break-even in sales dollars first.)

---

**OBJ. 5**

### EX 19-24  Break-even and margin of safety relationships

At a recent staff meeting, the management of Rocket Technologies, Inc., was considering discontinuing the Maestro line of electronic games from the product line. The chief financial analyst reported the following current monthly data for the Maestro:

| | |
|---|---:|
| Units of sales | 200,000 |
| Break-even units | 225,000 |
| Margin of safety in units | 14,000 |

➤ For what reason would you question the validity of these data?

---

**OBJ. 5**

✔ a. Fulp, 4.00

### EX 19-25  Operating leverage

Fulp Inc. and Baucom Inc. have the following operating data:

| | Fulp | Baucom |
|---|---:|---:|
| Sales | $3,000,000 | $1,600,000 |
| Variable costs | 1,400,000 | 600,000 |
| Contribution margin | $1,600,000 | $1,000,000 |
| Fixed costs | 1,200,000 | 600,000 |
| Income from operations | $ 400,000 | $ 400,000 |

a. Compute the operating leverage for Fulp Inc. and Baucom Inc.

b. How much would income from operations increase for each company if the sales of each increased by 25%?

c. ➤ Why is there a difference in the increase in income from operations for the two companies? Explain.

## Problems Series A

OBJ. 1

### PR 19-1A Classify costs

Olympic Clothing Co. manufactures a variety of clothing types for distribution to several major retail chains. The following costs are incurred in the production and sale of blue jeans:

a. Consulting fee of $200,000 paid to industry specialist for marketing advice

b. Brass buttons

c. Legal fees paid to attorneys in defense of the company in a patent infringement suit, $50,000 plus $87 per hour

d. Rental costs of warehouse, $5,000 per month plus $4 per square foot of storage used

e. Straight-line depreciation on sewing machines

f. Supplies

g. Insurance premiums on property, plant, and equipment, $70,000 per year plus $5 per $30,000 of insured value over $8,000,000

h. Salary of production vice president

i. Property taxes on property, plant, and equipment

j. Janitorial services, $2,200 per month

k. Shipping boxes used to ship orders

l. Electricity costs of $0.10 per kilowatt-hour

m. Hourly wages of machine operators

n. Leather for patches identifying the brand on individual pieces of apparel

o. Rent on experimental equipment, $50,000 per year

p. Salesperson's salary, $10,000 plus 2% of the total sales

q. Dye

r. Fabric

s. Thread

t. Salary of designers

### Instructions

Classify the preceding costs as either fixed, variable, or mixed. Use the following tabular headings and place an "X" in the appropriate column. Identify each cost by letter in the cost column.

| Cost | Fixed Cost | Variable Cost | Mixed Cost |
|------|-----------|--------------|-----------|

OBJ. 2, 3

✔ 2. (b) $50.00

### PR 19-2A Break-even sales under present and proposed conditions

Armstrong Company, operating at full capacity, sold 80,000 units at a price of $124 per unit during 2012. Its income statement for 2012 is as follows:

| | | |
|---|---|---|
| Sales ............................ | | $9,920,000 |
| Cost of goods sold .............. | | 5,000,000 |
| Gross profit ..................... | | $4,920,000 |
| Expenses: | | |
| Selling expenses.............. | $2,600,000 | |
| Administrative expenses...... | 1,220,000 | |
| Total expenses ............ | | 3,820,000 |
| Income from operations......... | | $1,100,000 |

The division of costs between fixed and variable is as follows:

|  | Fixed | Variable |
| --- | --- | --- |
| Cost of goods sold | 25% | 75% |
| Selling expenses | 40% | 60% |
| Administrative expenses | 50% | 50% |

Management is considering a plant expansion program that will permit an increase of $2,480,000 in yearly sales. The expansion will increase fixed costs by $272,000, but will not affect the relationship between sales and variable costs.

**Instructions**

1. Determine for 2012 the total fixed costs and the total variable costs.

2. Determine for 2012 (a) the unit variable cost and (b) the unit contribution margin.

3. Compute the break-even sales (units) for 2012.

4. Compute the break-even sales (units) under the proposed program.

5. Determine the amount of sales (units) that would be necessary under the proposed program to realize the $1,100,000 of income from operations that was earned in 2012.

6. Determine the maximum income from operations possible with the expanded plant.

7. If the proposal is accepted and sales remain at the 2012 level, what will the income or loss from operations be for 2013?

8. ━━━━━▶ Based on the data given, would you recommend accepting the proposal? Explain.

---

**OBJ. 3, 4**

✔ 1. 10,000 units

**PR 19-3A  Break-even sales and cost-volume-profit chart**

For the coming year, Sorkin Company anticipates a unit selling price of $80, a unit variable cost of $40, and fixed costs of $400,000.

**Instructions**

1. Compute the anticipated break-even sales (units).

2. Compute the sales (units) required to realize income from operations of $200,000.

3. Construct a cost-volume-profit chart, assuming maximum sales of 20,000 units within the relevant range.

4. Determine the probable income (loss) from operations if sales total 16,000 units.

---

**OBJ. 3, 4**

✔ 1. 1,400 units

**PR 19-4A  Break-even sales and cost-volume-profit chart**

Last year, Gelbin Inc. had sales of $240,000, based on a unit selling price of $120. The variable cost per unit was $90, and fixed costs were $42,000. The maximum sales within Gelbin's relevant range are 2,500 units. Gelbin is considering a proposal to spend an additional $12,000 on billboard advertising during the current year in an attempt to increase sales and utilize unused capacity.

**Instructions**

1. Construct a cost-volume-profit chart indicating the break-even sales for last year. Verify your answer, using the break-even equation.

2. Using the cost-volume-profit chart prepared in part (1), determine (a) the income from operations for last year and (b) the maximum income from operations that could have been realized during the year. Verify your answers arithmetically.

3. Construct a cost-volume-profit chart indicating the break-even sales for the current year, assuming that a noncancelable contract is signed for the additional billboard advertising. No changes are expected in the unit selling price or other costs. Verify your answer, using the break-even equation.

4. Using the cost-volume-profit chart prepared in part (3), determine (a) the income from operations if sales total 2,000 units and (b) the maximum income from operations that could be realized during the year. Verify your answers arithmetically.

OBJ. 5

✔ 1. 2,100 units

**PR 19-5A   Sales mix and break-even sales**

Data related to the expected sales of mountain bikes and road bikes for Cycle Sports Inc. for the current year, which is typical of recent years, are as follows:

| Products | Unit Selling Price | Unit Variable Cost | Sales Mix |
|---|---|---|---|
| Mountain bikes | $800 | $475 | 60% |
| Road bikes | 700 | 325 | 40% |

The estimated fixed costs for the current year are $724,500.

**Instructions**

1. Determine the estimated units of sales of the overall (total) product necessary to reach the break-even point for the current year.

2. Based on the break-even sales (units) in part (1), determine the unit sales of both mountain bikes and road bikes for the current year.

3. ━━━━➤ Assume that the sales mix was 50% mountain bikes and 50% road bikes. Compare the break-even point with that in part (1). Why is it so different?

OBJ. 2, 3, 4, 5

✔ 2. 62.5%

**PR 19-6A   Contribution margin, break-even sales, cost-volume-profit chart, margin of safety, and operating leverage**

Blythe Industries Inc. expects to maintain the same inventories at the end of 2012 as at the beginning of the year. The total of all production costs for the year is therefore assumed to be equal to the cost of goods sold. With this in mind, the various department heads were asked to submit estimates of the costs for their departments during 2012. A summary report of these estimates is as follows:

| | Estimated Fixed Cost | Estimated Variable Cost (per unit sold) |
|---|---|---|
| Production costs: | | |
| Direct materials.............................. | — | $30 |
| Direct labor ................................. | — | 20 |
| Factory overhead........................... | $340,000 | 11 |
| Selling expenses: | | |
| Sales salaries and commissions.............. | 80,000 | 5 |
| Advertising................................ | 32,000 | — |
| Travel ...................................... | 8,000 | — |
| Miscellaneous selling expense .............. | 7,600 | 5. |
| Administrative expenses: | | |
| Office and officers' salaries ................. | 120,000 | — |
| Supplies..................................... | 8,000 | 2 |
| Miscellaneous administrative expense........ | 4,400 | 2 |
| Total ...................................... | $600,000 | $75 |

It is expected that 8,000 units will be sold at a price of $200 a unit. Maximum sales within the relevant range are 9,000 units.

**Instructions**

1. Prepare an estimated income statement for 2012.

2. What is the expected contribution margin ratio?

3. Determine the break-even sales in units and dollars.

4. Construct a cost-volume-profit chart indicating the break-even sales.

5. What is the expected margin of safety in dollars and as a percentage of sales?

6. Determine the operating leverage.

## Problems Series B

OBJ. 1

### PR 19-1B Classify costs

Hand-Made Furniture Company manufactures sofas for distribution to several major retail chains. The following costs are incurred in the production and sale of sofas:

a. Wood for framing the sofas

b. Salary of production vice president

c. Rent on experimental equipment, $50 for every sofa produced

d. Rental costs of warehouse, $30,000 per month

e. Insurance premiums on property, plant, and equipment, $25,000 per year plus $25 per $25,000 of insured value over $16,000,000

f. Consulting fee of $120,000 paid to efficiency specialists

g. Salesperson's salary, $80,000 plus 4% of the selling price of each sofa sold

h. Janitorial supplies, $25 for each sofa produced

i. Employer's FICA taxes on controller's salary of $180,000

j. Fabric for sofa coverings

k. Hourly wages of sewing machine operators

l. Sewing supplies

m. Salary of designers

n. Foam rubber for cushion fillings

o. Electricity costs of $0.13 per kilowatt-hour

p. Springs

q. Property taxes on property, plant, and equipment

r. Straight-line depreciation on factory equipment

s. Cartons used to ship sofas

t. Legal fees paid to attorneys in defense of the company in a patent infringement suit, $25,000 plus $160 per hour

### Instructions

Classify the preceding costs as either fixed, variable, or mixed. Use the following tabular headings and place an "X" in the appropriate column. Identify each cost by letter in the cost column.

| Cost | Fixed Cost | Variable Cost | Mixed Cost |
|------|------------|---------------|------------|

OBJ. 2, 3

✔ 3. 13,000 units

### PR 19-2B Break-even sales under present and proposed conditions

Colt Industries Inc., operating at full capacity, sold 30,000 units at a price of $56 per unit during 2012. Its income statement for 2012 is as follows:

| | | |
|---|---|---|
| Sales .............................. | | $1,680,000 |
| Cost of goods sold ................... | | 740,000 |
| Gross profit ........................ | | $ 940,000 |
| Expenses: | | |
| Selling expenses ................... | $260,000 | |
| Administrative expenses............ | 136,000 | |
| Total expenses................... | | 396,000 |
| Income from operations .............. | | $ 544,000 |

The division of costs between fixed and variable is as follows:

|  | Fixed | Variable |
|---|---|---|
| Cost of goods sold | 40% | 60% |
| Selling expenses | 20% | 80% |
| Administrative expenses | 50% | 50% |

Management is considering a plant expansion program that will permit an increase of $1,120,000 in yearly sales. The expansion will increase fixed costs by $400,000, but will not affect the relationship between sales and variable costs.

**Instructions**

1. Determine for 2012 the total fixed costs and the total variable costs.

2. Determine for 2012 (a) the unit variable cost and (b) the unit contribution margin.

3. Compute the break-even sales (units) for 2012.

4. Compute the break-even sales (units) under the proposed program.

5. Determine the amount of sales (units) that would be necessary under the proposed program to realize the $544,000 of income from operations that was earned in 2012.

6. Determine the maximum income from operations possible with the expanded plant.

7. If the proposal is accepted and sales remain at the 2012 level, what will the income or loss from operations be for 2013?

8. ➤ Based on the data given, would you recommend accepting the proposal? Explain.

---

**OBJ. 3, 4**

✔ 1. 16,000 units

**PR 19-3B    Break-even sales and cost-volume-profit chart**

For the coming year, Viking Products Inc. anticipates a unit selling price of $125, a unit variable cost of $50, and fixed costs of $1,200,000.

**Instructions**

1. Compute the anticipated break-even sales (units).

2. Compute the sales (units) required to realize income from operations of $300,000.

3. Construct a cost-volume-profit chart, assuming maximum sales of 40,000 units within the relevant range.

4. Determine the probable income (loss) from operations if sales total 28,000 units.

---

**OBJ. 3, 4**

✔ 1. 3,600 units

**PR 19-4B    Break-even sales and cost-volume-profit chart**

Last year, O'Meara Co. had sales of $2,000,000, based on a unit selling price of $500. The variable cost per unit was $300, and fixed costs were $720,000. The maximum sales within O'Meara's relevant range are 5,000 units. O'Meara is considering a proposal to spend an additional $50,000 on billboard advertising during the current year in an attempt to increase sales and utilize unused capacity.

**Instructions**

1. Construct a cost-volume-profit chart indicating the break-even sales for last year. Verify your answer, using the break-even equation.

2. Using the cost-volume-profit chart prepared in part (1), determine (a) the income from operations for last year and (b) the maximum income from operations that could have been realized during the year. Verify your answers arithmetically.

3. Construct a cost-volume-profit chart indicating the break-even sales for the current year, assuming that a noncancelable contract is signed for the additional billboard advertising. No changes are expected in the selling price or other costs. Verify your answer, using the break-even equation.

4. Using the cost-volume-profit chart prepared in part (3), determine (a) the income from operations if sales total 4,000 units and (b) the maximum income from operations that could be realized during the year. Verify your answers arithmetically.

### PR 19-5B  Sales mix and break-even sales

Data related to the expected sales of two types of frozen pizzas for Delicious Frozen Foods Inc. for the current year, which is typical of recent years, are as follows:

| Products | Unit Selling Price | Unit Variable Cost | Sales Mix |
|---|---|---|---|
| 12" Pizza | $ 8.00 | $2.00 | 60% |
| 16" Pizza | 10.00 | 3.00 | 40% |

The estimated fixed costs for the current year are $26,400.

### Instructions

1. Determine the estimated units of sales of the overall product necessary to reach the break-even point for the current year.

2. Based on the break-even sales (units) in part (1), determine the unit sales of both the 12" pizza and 16" pizza for the current year.

3. ▬▬▬▶ Assume that the sales mix was 40% 12" pizza and 60% 16" pizza. Compare the break-even point with that in part (1). Why is it so different?

### PR 19-6B  Contribution margin, break-even sales, cost-volume-profit chart, margin of safety, and operating leverage

Baker Co. expects to maintain the same inventories at the end of 2012 as at the beginning of the year. The total of all production costs for the year is therefore assumed to be equal to the cost of goods sold. With this in mind, the various department heads were asked to submit estimates of the costs for their departments during 2012. A summary report of these estimates is as follows:

| | Estimated Fixed Cost | Estimated Variable Cost (per unit sold) |
|---|---|---|
| Production costs: | | |
| Direct materials . . . . . . . . . . . . . . . . . . . . . . . . . . . . . . . . | — | $30.00 |
| Direct labor . . . . . . . . . . . . . . . . . . . . . . . . . . . . . . . . . . . | — | 15.00 |
| Factory overhead  . . . . . . . . . . . . . . . . . . . . . . . . . . . . | $240,000 | 5.00 |
| Selling expenses: | | |
| Sales salaries and commissions . . . . . . . . . . . . . . . . . | 43,000 | 3.00 |
| Advertising . . . . . . . . . . . . . . . . . . . . . . . . . . . . . . . . . . . | 12,000 | — |
| Travel . . . . . . . . . . . . . . . . . . . . . . . . . . . . . . . . . . . . | 4,200 | — |
| Miscellaneous selling expense . . . . . . . . . . . . . . . . . | 2,300 | 2.50 |
| Administrative expenses: | | |
| Office and officers' salaries . . . . . . . . . . . . . . . . . . . . . | 110,000 | — |
| Supplies . . . . . . . . . . . . . . . . . . . . . . . . . . . . . . . . . . . . | 16,000 | 2.50 |
| Miscellaneous administrative expense . . . . . . . . . . . | 22,500 | 2.00 |
| Total . . . . . . . . . . . . . . . . . . . . . . . . . . . . . . . . . . . . . . . | $450,000 | $60.00 |

It is expected that 40,000 units will be sold at a price of $75 a unit. Maximum sales within the relevant range are 45,000 units.

### Instructions

1. Prepare an estimated income statement for 2012.

2. What is the expected contribution margin ratio?

3. Determine the break-even sales in units and dollars.

4. Construct a cost-volume-profit chart indicating the break-even sales.

5. What is the expected margin of safety in dollars and as a percentage of sales?

6. Determine the operating leverage.

## Cases & Projects

You can access Cases & Projects online at **www.cengage.com/accounting/reeve**

## Excel Success Special Activities

### SA 19-1 High-low method

Bi-Rize, Inc. incurred the following production volumes and costs for the last six months of the current year:

|  | Production Units | Total Cost |
|---|---|---|
| July | 3,000 | $111,700 |
| August | 2,980 | 110,600 |
| September | 3,250 | 118,250 |
| October | 2,520 | 100,200 |
| November | 2,260 | 93,500 |
| December | 3,110 | 114,800 |

a. Open the Excel file *SA19-1_1e*.

b. Prepare a spreadsheet to determine the variable cost per unit and total fixed cost using the high-low method. Use the VLOOKUP function to match the total cost to the minimum and maximum production in computing the variable cost per unit.

c. When you have completed the high-low analysis, perform a "save as," replacing the entire file name with the following:

   *SA19-1_1e[your first name initial]_[your last name]*

### SA 19-2 High-low method

Jeffries Industrial Products Company prepared production and total cost information for their Moline plant for seven months as follows:

|  | Production Units | Total Cost |
|---|---|---|
| April | 450 | $32,485 |
| May | 525 | 35,100 |
| June | 590 | 36,700 |
| July | 680 | 38,650 |
| August | 820 | 43,240 |
| September | 910 | 45,825 |
| October | 750 | 41,710 |

a. Open the Excel file *SA19-2_1e*.

b. Prepare a spreadsheet to determine the variable cost per unit and total fixed cost using the high-low method. Use the VLOOKUP function to match the total cost to the minimum and maximum production in computing the variable cost per unit.

c. When you have completed the high-low analysis, perform a "save as," replacing the entire file name with the following:

   *SA19-2_1e[your first name initial]_[your last name]*

### SA 19-3   High-low method

Barnstable Company prepared weekly production and total cost information for the Assembly Department for 12 weeks as follows:

| | Production Units | Total Cost |
|---|---|---|
| Week 1 | 1,930 | $46,790 |
| Week 2 | 1,240 | 33,710 |
| Week 3 | 1,760 | 42,490 |
| Week 4 | 980 | 28,740 |
| Week 5 | 1,130 | 31,740 |
| Week 6 | 1,520 | 39,400 |
| Week 7 | 1,690 | 42,350 |
| Week 8 | 1,420 | 37,240 |
| Week 9 | 1,550 | 38,540 |
| Week 10 | 1,300 | 34,990 |
| Week 11 | 1,750 | 42,870 |
| Week 12 | 1,890 | 46,320 |

a. Open the Excel file *SA19-3_1e*.

b. Prepare a spreadsheet to determine the variable cost per unit and total fixed cost using the high-low method. Use the VLOOKUP function to match the total cost to the minimum and maximum production in computing the variable cost per unit.

c. When you have completed the high-low analysis, perform a "save as," replacing the entire file name with the following:

*SA19-3_1e[your first name initial]_[your last name]*

# Variable Costing for Management Analysis

## Adobe Systems, Inc.

**A**ssume that you have three different options for a summer job. How would you evaluate these options? Naturally there are many things to consider, including how much you could earn from each job.

Determining how much you could earn from each job may not be as simple as comparing the wage rate per hour. For example, a job as an office clerk at a local company pays $7 per hour. A job delivering pizza pays $10 per hour (including estimated tips), although you must use your own transportation. Another job working in a beach resort over 500 miles away from your home pays $8 per hour. All three jobs offer 40 hours per week for the whole summer. If these options were ranked according to their pay per hour, the pizza delivery job would be the most attractive. However, the costs associated with each job must also be evaluated. For example, the office job may require that you pay for downtown parking and purchase office clothes. The pizza delivery job will require you to pay for gas and maintenance for your car. The resort job will require you to move to the resort city and incur additional living costs. Only by considering the costs for each job will you be able to determine which job will provide you with the most income.

Just as you should evaluate the relative income of various choices, a business also evaluates the income earned from its choices. Important choices include the products offered and the geographical regions to be served.

A company will often evaluate the profitability of products and regions. For example, **Adobe Systems Inc.**, one of the largest software companies in the world, determines the income earned from its various product lines, such as Acrobat®, Photoshop®, Premier®, and Dreamweaver® software. Adobe uses this information to establish product line pricing, as well as sales, support, and development effort. Likewise, Adobe evaluates the income earned in the geographic regions it serves, such as the United States, Europe, and Asia. Again, such information aids management in managing revenue and expenses within the regions.

In this chapter, how businesses measure profitability using absorption costing and variable costing is discussed. After illustrating and comparing these concepts, how businesses use them for controlling costs, pricing products, planning production, analyzing market segments, and analyzing contribution margins is described and illustrated.

**OBJ. 1** Describe and illustrate reporting income from operations under absorption and variable costing.

# Income from Operations Under Absorption Costing and Variable Costing

Income from operations is one of the most important items reported by a company. Depending on the decision-making needs of management, income from operations can be determined using absorption or variable costing.

## Absorption Costing

**Absorption costing** is required under generally accepted accounting principles for financial statements distributed to external users. Under absorption costing, the cost of goods manufactured includes direct materials, direct labor, and factory overhead costs. Both fixed and variable factory costs are included as part of factory overhead. In the financial statements, these costs are included in the cost of goods sold (income statement) and inventory (balance sheet).

The reporting of income from operations under absorption costing is as follows:

| | |
|---|---|
| Sales | $XXX |
| Cost of goods sold | XXX |
| Gross profit | $XXX |
| Selling and administrative expenses | XXX |
| Income from operations | $XXX |

The income statements illustrated in the preceding chapters of this text have used absorption costing.

## Variable Costing

For internal use in decision making, managers often use variable costing. Under **variable costing**, sometimes called *direct costing*, the cost of goods manufactured includes only variable manufacturing costs. Thus, the cost of goods manufactured consists of the following:

1. Direct materials
2. Direct labor
3. *Variable* factory overhead

Under variable costing, *fixed* factory overhead costs are not a part of the cost of goods manufactured. Instead, fixed factory overhead costs are treated as a period expense.

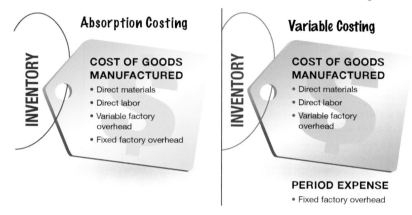

The reporting of income from operations under variable costing is as follows:

| | | |
|---|---:|---:|
| Sales | | $XXX |
| Variable cost of goods sold | | XXX |
| Manufacturing margin | | $XXX |
| Variable selling and administrative expenses | | XXX |
| Contribution margin | | $XXX |
| Fixed costs: | | |
|    Fixed manufacturing costs | $XXX | |
|    Fixed selling and administrative expenses | XXX | XXX |
| Income from operations | | $XXX |

**Manufacturing margin** is sales less variable cost of goods sold. **Variable cost of goods sold** consists of direct materials, direct labor, and variable factory overhead for the units sold. **Contribution margin** is manufacturing margin less variable selling and administrative expenses. Subtracting fixed costs from contribution margin yields income from operations.

To illustrate variable costing and absorption costing, assume that 15,000 units are manufactured and sold at a price of $50. The related costs and expenses are as follows:

| | Number of Units | Unit Cost | Total Cost |
|---|---:|---:|---:|
| Manufacturing costs: | | | |
|   Variable.......................................... | 15,000 | $25 | $375,000 |
|   Fixed ............................................ | 15,000 | 10 | 150,000 |
|     Total .......................................... | | $35 | $525,000 |
| Selling and administrative expenses: | | | |
|   Variable.......................................... | 15,000 | $ 5 | $ 75,000 |
|   Fixed ............................................ | 15,000 | — | 50,000 |
|     Total .......................................... | | | $125,000 |

Exhibit 1 illustrates the reporting of income from operations under absorption costing prepared from the data on the previous page. The computations are shown in parentheses.

**EXHIBIT 1**

**Absorption Costing Income Statement**

| | |
|---|---|
| Sales (15,000 × $50)............................................................ | $750,000 |
| Cost of goods sold (15,000 × $35)................................................ | 525,000 |
| Gross profit.................................................................. | $225,000 |
| Selling and administrative expenses ($75,000 + $50,000)............................ | 125,000 |
| Income from operations......................................................... | $100,000 |

Absorption costing does not distinguish between variable and fixed costs. All manufacturing costs are included in the cost of goods sold. Deducting the cost of goods sold of $525,000 from sales of $750,000 yields gross profit of $225,000. Deducting selling and administrative expenses of $125,000 from gross profit yields income from operations of $100,000.

Exhibit 2 shows the reporting of income from operations under variable costing prepared from the same data. The computations are shown in parentheses.

**EXHIBIT 2**

**Variable Costing Income Statement**

| | | |
|---|---|---|
| Sales (15,000 × $50) ........................................... | | $750,000 |
| Variable cost of goods sold (15,000 × $25)............................ | | 375,000 |
| Manufacturing margin........................................... | | $375,000 |
| Variable selling and administrative expenses (15,000 × $5).............. | | 75,000 |
| Contribution margin............................................. | | $300,000 |
| Fixed costs: | | |
|     Fixed manufacturing costs ...................................... | $150,000 | |
|     Fixed selling and administrative expenses ......................... | 50,000 | 200,000 |
| Income from operations.......................................... | | $100,000 |

**Note:**

The variable costing income statement includes only variable manufacturing costs in the cost of goods sold.

Variable costing income reports variable costs separately from fixed costs. Deducting the variable cost of goods sold of $375,000 from sales of $750,000 yields the manufacturing margin of $375,000. Deducting variable selling and administrative expenses of $75,000 from the manufacturing margin yields the contribution margin of $300,000. Deducting fixed costs of $200,000 from the contribution margin yields income from operations of $100,000.

The contribution margin reported in Exhibit 2 is the same as that used in Chapter 19. That is, the contribution margin is sales less variable costs and expenses. The only difference is that Exhibit 2 reports manufacturing margin before deducting variable selling and administrative expenses.

**Example Exercise 20-1 Variable Costing** OBJ. 1

Leone Company has the following information for March:

| | |
|---|---|
| Sales | $450,000 |
| Variable cost of goods sold | 220,000 |
| Fixed manufacturing costs | 80,000 |
| Variable selling and administrative expenses | 50,000 |
| Fixed selling and administrative expenses | 35,000 |

Determine (a) the manufacturing margin, (b) the contribution margin, and (c) income from operations for Leone Company for the month of March.

(continued)

## Units Manufactured Equal Units Sold

In Exhibits 1 and 2, 15,000 units were manufactured and sold. Both variable and absorption costing reported the same income from operations of $100,000. Thus, when the number of units manufactured equals the number of units sold, income from operations will be the same under both methods.

## Units Manufactured Exceed Units Sold

When units manufactured exceed the units sold, the variable costing income from operations will be *less* than it is for absorption costing. To illustrate, assume that in the preceding example only 12,000 units of the 15,000 units manufactured were sold.

Exhibit 3 shows the reporting of income from operations under absorption and variable costing.

Different regions of the world emphasize different approaches to reporting income. For example, Scandinavian companies have a strong variable costing tradition, while German cost accountants have developed some of the most advanced absorption costing practices in the world.

**EXHIBIT 3**

**Units Manufactured Exceed Units Sold**

| Absorption Costing Income Statement | | |
|---|---|---|
| Sales (12,000 × $50) | | $600,000 |
| Cost of goods sold: | | |
|   Cost of goods manufactured (15,000 × $35) | $525,000 | |
|   Less ending inventory (3,000 × $35) | 105,000 | |
|     Cost of goods sold | | 420,000 |
| Gross profit | | $180,000 |
| Selling and administrative expenses [(12,000 × $5) + $50,000] | | 110,000 |
| Income from operations | | $ 70,000 |

| Variable Costing Income Statement | | |
|---|---|---|
| Sales (12,000 × $50) | | $600,000 |
| Variable cost of goods sold: | | |
|   Variable cost of goods manufactured (15,000 × $25) | $375,000 | |
|   Less ending inventory (3,000 × $25) | 75,000 | |
|     Variable cost of goods sold | | 300,000 |
| Manufacturing margin | | $300,000 |
| Variable selling and administrative expenses (12,000 × $5) | | 60,000 |
| Contribution margin | | $240,000 |
| Fixed costs: | | |
|   Fixed manufacturing costs | $150,000 | |
|   Fixed selling and administrative expenses | 50,000 | 200,000 |
| Income from operations | | $ 40,000 |

Exhibit 3 shows a $30,000 difference in income from operations ($70,000 – $40,000). This difference is due to the fixed manufacturing costs. All of the $150,000 of fixed manufacturing costs is included as a period expense in the variable costing statement. However, the 3,000 units of ending inventory in the absorption costing statement includes $30,000 (3,000 units × $10) of fixed manufacturing costs. By including the $30,000 in inventory, it is excluded from the cost of goods sold. Thus, the absorption costing income from operations is $30,000 higher than the income from operations for variable costing.

**Example Exercise 20-2 Variable Costing—Production Exceeds Sales** OBJ. 1

Fixed manufacturing costs are $40 per unit, and variable manufacturing costs are $120 per unit. Production was 125,000 units, while sales were 120,000 units. Determine (a) whether variable costing income from operations is less than or greater than absorption costing income from operations, and (b) the difference in variable costing and absorption costing income from operations.

**Follow My Example 20-2**

a. Variable costing income from operations is less than absorption costing income from operations.
b. $200,000 ($40 per unit × 5,000 units)

Practice Exercises: **PE 20-2A, PE 20-2B**

## Units Manufactured Less Than Units Sold

When the units manufactured are less than the number of units sold, the variable costing income from operations will be *greater* than that of absorption costing. To illustrate, assume that beginning inventory, units manufactured, and units sold were as follows:

| | |
|---|---|
| Beginning inventory...................................... | 5,000 units |
| Units manufactured during current period ................ | 10,000 units |
| Units sold during the current period at $50 per unit ....... | 15,000 units |

The manufacturing costs and selling and administrative expenses are as follows:

| | Number of Units | Unit Cost | Total Cost |
|---|---|---|---|
| Beginning inventory (5,000 units): | | | |
| Manufacturing costs: | | | |
| Variable .......................................... | 5,000 | $25 | $125,000 |
| Fixed............................................. | 5,000 | 10 | 50,000 |
| Total ........................................... | | $35 | $175,000 |
| Current period (10,000 units): | | | |
| Manufacturing costs: | | | |
| Variable .......................................... | 10,000 | $25 | $250,000 |
| Fixed............................................. | 10,000 | 15 | 150,000 |
| Total ........................................... | | $40 | $400,000 |
| Selling and administrative expenses: | | | |
| Variable .......................................... | 15,000 | $5 | $ 75,000 |
| Fixed............................................. | 15,000 | — | 50,000 |
| Total ........................................... | | | $125,000 |

Exhibit 4 shows the reporting of income from operations under absorption and variable costing based on the preceding data.

**EXHIBIT 4**

**Units Manufactured Are Less Than Units Sold**

| Absorption Costing Income Statement | | |
|---|---:|---:|
| Sales (15,000 × $50) ......................................................... | | $750,000 |
| Cost of goods sold: | | |
|     Beginning inventory (5,000 × $35)....................................... | $175,000 | |
|     Cost of goods manufactured (10,000 × $40)............................ | 400,000 | |
| Cost of goods sold......................................................... | | 575,000 |
| Gross profit.............................................................. | | $175,000 |
| Selling and administrative expenses ($75,000 + $50,000) ................... | | 125,000 |
| Income from operations .................................................. | | $ 50,000 |

| Variable Costing Income Statement | | |
|---|---:|---:|
| Sales (15,000 × $50) ........................................................ | | $750,000 |
| Variable cost of goods sold: | | |
|     Beginning inventory (5,000 × $25)......................................... | $125,000 | |
|     Variable cost of goods manufactured (10,000 × $25)...................... | 250,000 | |
|       Variable cost of goods sold.......................................... | | 375,000 |
| Manufacturing margin........................................................ | | $375,000 |
| Variable selling and administrative expenses (15,000 × $5)................. | | 75,000 |
| Contribution margin......................................................... | | $300,000 |
| Fixed costs: | | |
|     Fixed manufacturing costs ............................................... | $150,000 | |
|     Fixed selling and administrative expenses................................ | 50,000 | 200,000 |
| Income from operations ..................................................... | | $100,000 |

Exhibit 4 shows a $50,000 difference in income from operations ($100,000 – $50,000). This difference is due to the fixed manufacturing costs. The beginning inventory under absorption costing includes $50,000 (5,000 units × $10) of fixed manufacturing costs incurred in the preceding period. By being included in the beginning inventory, this $50,000 is included in the cost of goods sold for the current period. Under variable costing, this $50,000 was included as an expense in an income statement of a prior period. Thus, the variable costing income from operations is $50,000 higher than the income from operations for absorption costing.

---

**Example Exercise** 20-3  **Variable Costing—Sales Exceed Production**     **OBJ. 1**

The beginning inventory is 6,000 units. All of the units that were manufactured during the period and the 6,000 units of beginning inventory were sold. The beginning inventory fixed manufacturing costs are $60 per unit, and variable manufacturing costs are $300 per unit. Determine (a) whether variable costing income from operations is less than or greater than absorption costing income from operations, and (b) the difference in variable costing and absorption costing income from operations.

**Follow My Example** 20-3

a. Variable costing income from operations is greater than absorption costing income from operations.
b. $360,000 ($60 per unit × 6,000 units)

Practice Exercises: **PE 20-3A, PE 20-3B**

## Effects on Income from Operations

The preceding examples illustrate the effects on income from operations of using absorption and variable costing. These effects are summarized below.

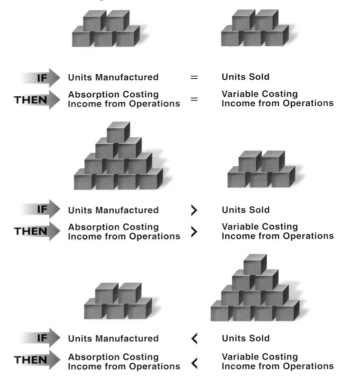

| | | | |
|---|---|---|---|
| **IF** | Units Manufactured | = | Units Sold |
| **THEN** | Absorption Costing Income from Operations | = | Variable Costing Income from Operations |

| | | | |
|---|---|---|---|
| **IF** | Units Manufactured | > | Units Sold |
| **THEN** | Absorption Costing Income from Operations | > | Variable Costing Income from Operations |

| | | | |
|---|---|---|---|
| **IF** | Units Manufactured | < | Units Sold |
| **THEN** | Absorption Costing Income from Operations | < | Variable Costing Income from Operations |

**OBJ. 2** Describe and illustrate the effects of absorption and variable costing on analyzing income from operations.

# Income Analysis Under Absorption and Variable Costing

Whenever the units manufactured differ from the units sold, finished goods inventory is affected. When the units manufactured are greater than the units sold, finished goods inventory increases. Under absorption costing, a portion of this increase is related to the allocation of fixed manufacturing overhead to ending inventory. As a result, increases or decreases in income from operations can be due to changes in inventory levels. In analyzing income from operations, such increases and decreases could be misinterpreted as operating efficiencies or inefficiencies.

To illustrate, assume that Frand Manufacturing Company has no beginning inventory and sales are estimated to be 20,000 units at $75 per unit. Also, assume that sales will not change if more than 20,000 units are manufactured.

The management of Frand Manufacturing Company is evaluating whether to manufacture 20,000 units (Proposal 1) or 25,000 units (Proposal 2). The costs and expenses related to each proposal are shown below.

Proposal 1: 20,000 Units to Be Manufactured and Sold

| | Number of Units | Unit Cost | Total Cost |
|---|---|---|---|
| Manufacturing costs: | | | |
| Variable........................................... | 20,000 | $35 | $ 700,000 |
| Fixed ............................................. | 20,000 | 20* | 400,000 |
| Total ........................................... | | $55 | $1,100,000 |
| Selling and administrative expenses: | | | |
| Variable........................................... | 20,000 | $ 5 | $ 100,000 |
| Fixed ............................................. | 20,000 | — | 100,000 |
| Total ........................................... | | | $ 200,000 |

*$400,000/20,000 units

Proposal 2: 25,000 Units to Be Manufactured and 20,000 Units to Be Sold

|  | Number of Units | Unit Cost | Total Cost |
|---|---|---|---|
| Manufacturing costs: | | | |
| Variable.......................................... | 25,000 | $35 | $ 875,000 |
| Fixed .......................................... | 25,000 | 16* | 400,000 |
| Total .......................................... | | $51 | $1,275,000 |
| Selling and administrative expenses: | | | |
| Variable.......................................... | 20,000 | $ 5 | $ 100,000 |
| Fixed .......................................... | 20,000 | — | 100,000 |
| Total .......................................... | | | $ 200,000 |

*$400,000/25,000 units

The absorption costing income statements for each proposal are shown in Exhibit 5.

**EXHIBIT 5**

**Absorption Costing Income Statements for Two Production Levels**

**Frand Manufacturing Company**
**Absorption Costing Income Statements**

|  | Proposal 1 20,000 Units Manufactured | Proposal 2 25,000 Units Manufactured |
|---|---|---|
| Sales (20,000 units × $75)............................................ | $1,500,000 | $1,500,000 |
| Cost of goods sold: | | |
| Cost of goods manufactured: | | |
| (20,000 units × $55) ........................................... | $1,100,000 | |
| (25,000 units × $51) ........................................... | | $1,275,000 |
| Less ending inventory: | | |
| (5,000 units × $51)............................................ | | 255,000 |
| Cost of goods sold ............................................. | $1,100,000 | $1,020,000 |
| Gross profit...................................................... | $ 400,000 | $ 480,000 |
| Selling and administrative expenses: | | |
| ($100,000 + $100,000)......................................... | 200,000 | 200,000 |
| Income from operations ........................................ | $ 200,000 | $ 280,000 |

Exhibit 5 shows that if Frand manufactures 25,000 units, sells 20,000 units, and adds the 5,000 units to finished goods inventory (Proposal 2), income from operations will be $280,000. In contrast, if Frand manufactures and sells 20,000 units (Proposal 1), income from operations will be $200,000. In other words, Frand can increase income from operations by $80,000 ($280,000 – $200,000) by simply increasing finished goods inventory by 5,000 units.

The $80,000 increase in income from operations under Proposal 2 is caused by the allocation of the fixed manufacturing costs of $400,000 over a greater number of units manufactured. Specifically, an increase in production from 20,000 units to 25,000 units means that the fixed manufacturing cost per unit decreases from $20 ($400,000/20,000 units) to $16 ($400,000/25,000 units). Thus, the cost of goods sold when 25,000 units are manufactured is $4 per unit less, or $80,000 less in total (20,000 units sold × $4). Since the cost of goods sold is less, income from operations is $80,000 more when 25,000 units rather than 20,000 units are manufactured.

Managers should be careful in analyzing income from operations under absorption costing when finished goods inventory changes. As shown above, increases in income from operations may be created by simply increasing finished goods inventory. Thus, managers could misinterpret such increases (or decreases) in income from operations as due to changes in sales volume, prices, or costs.

Under variable costing, income from operations is $200,000, regardless of whether 20,000 units or 25,000 units are manufactured. This is because no fixed manufacturing costs are allocated to the units manufactured. Instead, all fixed manufacturing costs are treated as a period expense.

To illustrate, Exhibit 6 shows the variable costing income statements for Frand Manufacturing Company for the production of 20,000 units, 25,000 units, and 30,000 units. In each case, the income from operations is $200,000.

**EXHIBIT 6**

**Variable Costing Income Statements for Three Production Levels**

| Frand Manufacturing Company Variable Costing Income Statements | | | |
|---|---|---|---|
| | **20,000 Units Manufactured** | **25,000 Units Manufactured** | **30,000 Units Manufactured** |
| Sales (20,000 units × $75) . . . . . . . . . . . . . . . . . . | $1,500,000 | $1,500,000 | $1,500,000 |
| Variable cost of goods sold: | | | |
| Variable cost of goods manufactured: | | | |
| (20,000 units × $35) . . . . . . . . . . . . . . . . | $ 700,000 | | |
| (25,000 units × $35) . . . . . . . . . . . . . . . . | | $ 875,000 | |
| (30,000 units × $35) . . . . . . . . . . . . . . . . | | | $1,050,000 |
| Less ending inventory: | | | |
| (0 units × $35) . . . . . . . . . . . . . . . . . . . . . . | 0 | | |
| (5,000 units × $35) . . . . . . . . . . . . . . . . . . | | 175,000 | |
| (10,000 units × $35) . . . . . . . . . . . . . . . . | | | 350,000 |
| Variable cost of goods sold . . . . . . . . . . . . . | $ 700,000 | $ 700,000 | $ 700,000 |
| Manufacturing margin. . . . . . . . . . . . . . . . . . . . | $ 800,000 | $ 800,000 | $ 800,000 |
| Variable selling and administrative | | | |
| expenses . . . . . . . . . . . . . . . . . . . . . . . . . . . . . | 100,000 | 100,000 | 100,000 |
| Contribution margin. . . . . . . . . . . . . . . . . . . . . | $ 700,000 | $ 700,000 | $ 700,000 |
| Fixed costs: | | | |
| Fixed manufacturing costs . . . . . . . . . . . . . . | $ 400,000 | $ 400,000 | $ 400,000 |
| Fixed selling and administrative | | | |
| expenses . . . . . . . . . . . . . . . . . . . . . . . . . . | 100,000 | 100,000 | 100,000 |
| Total fixed costs . . . . . . . . . . . . . . . . . . . . | $ 500,000 | $ 500,000 | $ 500,000 |
| Income from operations . . . . . . . . . . . . . . . . . | $ 200,000 | $ 200,000 | $ 200,000 |

## Integrity, Objectivity, and Ethics in Business

**TAKING AN "ABSORPTION HIT"**

Aligning production to demand is a critical decision in business. Managers must not allow the temporary benefits of excess production through higher absorption of fixed costs to guide their decisions. Likewise, if demand falls, production should be dropped and inventory liquidated to match the new demand level, even though earnings will be penalized. The following interchange provides an example of an appropriate response to lowered demand for H.J. Heinz Company:

**Analyst's question:** *Could you talk for a moment about manufacturing costs during the quarter? You had highlighted that they were up and that gross margins at Heinz USA were down. Why was that the case?*

**Heinz executive's response:** *Yeah. The manufacturing costs were somewhat up . . . as we improve our inventory position, obviously you've got less inventory to spread your fixed costs over, so you'll take what accountants would call an absorption hit as we reduce costs. And that will be something that as we pull down inventory over the years, that will be an additional P&L cost hurdle that we need to overcome.*

Management operating with integrity will seek the tangible benefits of reducing inventory, even though there may be an adverse impact on published financial statements caused by absorption costing.

As shown previously, absorption costing may encourage managers to produce inventory. This is because producing inventory absorbs fixed manufacturing costs, which increases income from operations. However, producing inventory leads to higher handling, storage, financing, and obsolescence costs. For this reason, many accountants believe that variable costing should be used by management for evaluating operating performance.

---

**Example Exercise** ▶ **20-4** ▶ **Analyzing Income Under Absorption and Variable Costing**   **OBJ. 2**

Variable manufacturing costs are $100 per unit, and fixed manufacturing costs are $50,000. Sales are estimated to be 4,000 units.

a.  How much would absorption costing income from operations differ between a plan to produce 4,000 units and a plan to produce 5,000 units?

b.  How much would variable costing income from operations differ between the two production plans?

**Follow My Example** ▶ **20-4** ▶

a.  $10,000 greater in producing 5,000 units. 4,000 units × ($12.50[1] − $10.00[2]), or [1,000 units × ($50,000/5,000 units)].

b.  There would be no difference in variable costing income from operations between the two plans.

[1]$50,000/4,000 units
[2]$50,000/5,000 units

Practice Exercises: **PE 20-4A, PE 20-4B**

---

# Using Absorption and Variable Costing

**OBJ. 3**  Describe management's use of absorption and variable costing.

Each decision-making situation should be carefully analyzed in deciding whether absorption or variable costing reporting would be more useful. As a basis for discussion, the use of absorption and variable costing in the following decision-making situations is described:

1. Controlling costs
2. Pricing products
3. Planning production
4. Analyzing contribution margins
5. Analyzing market segments

The role of accounting reports in these decision-making situations is shown in Exhibit 7.

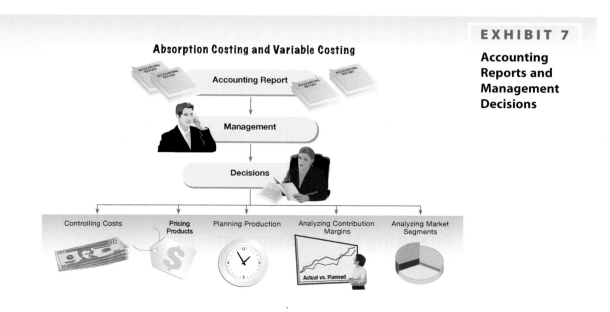

**EXHIBIT 7**

**Accounting Reports and Management Decisions**

## Controlling Costs

All costs are controllable in the long run by someone within a business. However, not all costs are controllable at the same level of management. For example, plant supervisors control the use of direct materials in their departments. They have no control, though, over insurance costs related to the property, plant, and equipment.

For a level of management, **controllable costs** are costs that can be influenced (increased or decreased) by management at that level. **Noncontrollable costs** are costs that another level of management controls. This distinction is useful for reporting costs to those responsible for their control.

Variable manufacturing costs are controlled by operating management. In contrast, fixed manufacturing overhead costs such as the salaries of production supervisors are normally controlled at a higher level of management. Likewise, control of the variable and fixed operating expenses usually involves different levels of management. Since fixed costs and expenses are reported separately under variable costing, variable costing reports are normally more useful than absorption costing reports for controlling costs.

Major hotel chains, such as Marriott, Hilton, and Hyatt, often provide "weekend getaway" packages, which provide discounts for weekend stays in their city hotels. As long as the weekend rates exceed the variable costs, the "weekend getaway" pricing will contribute to the hotel's short-run profitability.

## Pricing Products

Many factors enter into determining the selling price of a product. However, the cost of making the product is significant in all pricing decisions.

In the short run, fixed costs cannot be avoided. Thus, the selling price of a product should at least be equal to the variable costs of making and selling it. Any price above this minimum selling price contributes to covering fixed costs and generating income. Since variable costing reports variable and fixed costs and expenses separately, it is often more useful than absorption costing for setting short-run prices.

In the long run, a company must set its selling price high enough to cover all costs and expenses (variable and fixed) and generate income. Since absorption costing includes fixed and variable costs in the cost of manufacturing a product, absorption costing is often more useful than variable costing for setting long-term prices.

## Planning Production

In the short run, planning production is limited to existing capacity. In many cases, operating decisions must be made quickly before opportunities are lost.

To illustrate, a company with seasonal demand for its products may have an opportunity to obtain an off-season order that will not interfere with its current production schedule. The relevant factors for such a short-run decision are the additional revenues and the additional variable costs associated with the order. If the revenues from the order exceed the related variable costs, the order will increase contribution margin and, thus, increase the company's income from operations. Since variable costing reports contribution margin, it is often more useful than absorption costing in such cases.

In the long run, planning production can include expanding existing capacity. Thus, when analyzing and evaluating long-run sales and operating decisions, absorption costing, which considers fixed and variable costs, is often more useful.

## Analyzing Contribution Margins

For planning and control purposes, managers often compare planned and actual contribution margins. For example, an increase in the price of fuel could have a significant impact on the planned contribution margins of an airline. The use of variable costing as a basis for such analyses is described and illustrated later in this chapter.

## Analyzing Market Segments

Market analysis determines the profit contributed by the market segments of a company. A **market segment** is a portion of a company that can be analyzed using sales,

# BusinessConnection

### APPLE'S IPOD NANO

Apple has become one of the most financially successful companies of the past decade by using variable cost information to carefully price its iPod family of products. The cost of an iPod consists almost entirely of direct materials and other variable costs. For example, Apple's recently released sixth generation iPod nano is estimated to have a total cost of $45.10, of which $43.73 is direct materials.

Thus, when designing a new iPod, Apple has to carefully balance product features with the variable cost of direct materials. For the sixth generation iPod nano, Apple added touch screen technology and a more powerful battery, while removing the camera feature. This careful balancing of cost and functionality allowed Apple to offer a new generation of iPod nano at an enticing price, highlighting how Apple's awareness and understanding of variable cost information has been a key element of the company's financial success.

Source: A. Rassweiler, "ISuppli Estimates New iPod Nano Bill of Materials at $43.73," iSuppli, Applied Market Intelligence.

costs, and expenses to determine its profitability. Examples of market segments include sales territories, products, salespersons, and customers. Variable costing as an aid in decision making regarding market segments is discussed next.

# Analyzing Market Segments

**OBJ. 4** Use variable costing for analyzing market segments, including product, territories, and salespersons segments.

Companies can report income for internal decision making using either absorption or variable costing. Absorption costing is often used for long-term analysis of market segments. This type of analysis is illustrated in Chapter 26, "Cost Allocation and Activity-Based Costing." Variable costing is often used for short-term analysis of market segments. In this section, segment profitability reporting using variable costing is described and illustrated.

Most companies prepare variable costing reports for each product. These reports are often used for product pricing and deciding whether to discontinue a product. In addition, variable costing reports may be prepared for geographic areas, customers, distribution channels, or salespersons. A distribution channel is the method for selling a product to a customer.

To illustrate analysis of market segments using variable costing, the following data for the month ending March 31, 2012, for Camelot Fragrance Company are used:

McDonald's Corporation evaluates the profitability of its geographic segments. For example, it compares the profitability of its restaurants in the United States with those in Asia and Europe.

**Camelot Fragrance Company**
**Sales and Production Data**
**For the Month Ended March 31, 2012**

| | Northern Territory | Southern Territory | Total |
|---|---|---|---|
| Sales: | | | |
| Gwenevere .......................................... | $60,000 | $30,000 | $ 90,000 |
| Lancelot ............................................. | 20,000 | 50,000 | 70,000 |
| Total territory sales ................................ | $80,000 | $80,000 | $160,000 |
| Variable production costs: | | | |
| Gwenevere (12% of sales) ........................... | $ 7,200 | $ 3,600 | $ 10,800 |
| Lancelot (12% of sales) .............................. | 2,400 | 6,000 | 8,400 |
| Total variable production cost by territory .......... | $ 9,600 | $ 9,600 | $ 19,200 |
| Promotion costs: | | | |
| Gwenevere (variable at 30% of sales) ................. | $18,000 | $ 9,000 | $ 27,000 |
| Lancelot (variable at 20% of sales) .................... | 4,000 | 10,000 | 14,000 |
| Total promotion cost by territory ................... | $22,000 | $19,000 | $ 41,000 |
| Sales commissions: | | | |
| Gwenevere (variable at 20% of sales) ................. | $12,000 | $ 6,000 | $ 18,000 |
| Lancelot (variable at 10% of sales) .................... | 2,000 | 5,000 | 7,000 |
| Total sales commissions by territory ............... | $14,000 | $11,000 | $ 25,000 |

Camelot Fragrance Company manufactures and sells the Gwenevere perfume for women and the Lancelot cologne for men. To simplify, no inventories are assumed to exist at the beginning or end of March.

## Sales Territory Profitability Analysis

An income statement presenting the contribution margin by sales territories is often used in evaluating past performance and in directing future sales efforts. Sales territory profitability analysis may lead management to do the following:

1. Reduce costs in lower-profit sales territories
2. Increase sales efforts in higher-profit territories

To illustrate sales territory profitability analysis, Exhibit 8 shows the contribution margin for the Northern and Southern territories of Camelot Fragrance Company. As Exhibit 8 indicates, the Northern Territory is generating $34,400 of contribution margin, while the Southern Territory is generating $40,400 of contribution margin.

In addition to the contribution margin, the contribution margin ratio for each territory is shown in Exhibit 8. The contribution margin ratio is computed as follows:

$$\text{Contribution Margin Ratio} = \frac{\text{Contribution Margin}}{\text{Sales}}$$

Exhibit 8 indicates that the Northern Territory has a contribution margin ratio of 43% ($34,400/$80,000). In contrast, the Southern Territory has a contribution margin ratio of 50.5% ($40,400/$80,000).

**EXHIBIT 8**

**Contribution Margin by Sales Territory Report**

**Camelot Fragrance Company**
**Contribution Margin by Sales Territory**
**For the Month Ended March 31, 2012**

| | Northern Territory | | Southern Territory | |
|---|---|---|---|---|
| Sales .......................................... | | $80,000 | | $80,000 |
| Variable cost of goods sold ................. | | 9,600 | | 9,600 |
| Manufacturing margin ..................... | | $70,400 | | $70,400 |
| Variable selling expenses: | | | | |
| Promotion costs ......................... | $22,000 | | $19,000 | |
| Sales commissions ...................... | 14,000 | 36,000 | 11,000 | 30,000 |
| Contribution margin ...................... | | $34,400 | | $40,400 |
| Contribution margin ratio.................. | | 43% | | 50.5% |

The **Coca-Cola Company** earns over 75% of its total corporate profits outside of the United States. As a result, Coca-Cola management continues to expand operations and sales efforts around the world.

The difference in profit of the Northern and Southern territories is due to the difference in sales mix between the territories. **Sales mix**, sometimes referred to as *product mix*, is the relative amount of sales among the various products. The sales mix is computed by dividing the sales of each product by the total sales of each territory. Sales mix of the Northern and Southern territories is as follows:

| | Northern Territory | | Southern Territory | |
|---|---|---|---|---|
| **Product** | **Sales** | **Sales Mix** | **Sales** | **Sales Mix** |
| Gwenevere | $60,000 | 75% | $30,000 | 37.5% |
| Lancelot | 20,000 | 25 | 50,000 | 62.5 |
| Total | $80,000 | 100% | $80,000 | 100.0% |

As shown on the previous page, 62.5% of the Southern Territory's sales are sales of Lancelot. Since the Southern Territory's contribution margin ($40,400) is higher (as shown in Exhibit 8) than that of the Northern Territory ($34,400), Lancelot must be more profitable than Gwenevere. To verify this, product profitability analysis is performed.

## Product Profitability Analysis

A company should focus its sales efforts on products that will provide the maximum total contribution margin. In doing so, product profitability analysis is often used by management in making decisions regarding product sales and promotional efforts.

To illustrate product profitability analysis, Exhibit 9 shows the contribution margin by product for Camelot Fragrance Company.

**EXHIBIT 9**

**Contribution Margin by Product Line Report**

| Camelot Fragrance Company<br>Contribution Margin by Product Line<br>For the Month Ended March 31, 2012 | | | | |
|---|---|---|---|---|
| | **Gwenevere** | | **Lancelot** | |
| Sales ..................................... | | $90,000 | | $70,000 |
| Variable cost of goods sold ............... | | 10,800 | | 8,400 |
| Manufacturing margin ................... | | $79,200 | | $61,600 |
| Variable selling expenses: | | | | |
| Promotion costs ...................... | $27,000 | | $14,000 | |
| Sales commissions .................... | 18,000 | 45,000 | 7,000 | 21,000 |
| Contribution margin .................... | | $34,200 | | $40,600 |
| Contribution margin ratio ............... | | 38% | | 58% |

Exhibit 9 indicates that Lancelot's contribution margin ratio (58%) is greater than Gwenevere's (38%). Lancelot's higher contribution margin ratio is a result of its lower promotion and sales commissions costs. Thus, management should consider the following:

1. Emphasizing Lancelot in its marketing plans
2. Reducing Gwenevere's promotion and sales commissions costs
3. Increasing the price of Gwenevere

## Salesperson Profitability Analysis

A salesperson profitability report is useful in evaluating sales performance. Such a report normally includes total sales, variable cost of goods sold, variable selling expenses, contribution margin, and contribution margin ratio for each salesperson.

Exhibit 10 illustrates such a salesperson profitability report for three salespersons in the Northern Territory of Camelot Fragrance Company.

Exhibit 10 indicates that Beth Williams produced the greatest contribution margin ($15,200), but had the lowest contribution margin ratio (38%). Beth sold $40,000 of product, which is twice as much product as the other two salespersons. However, Beth sold only Gwenevere, which has the lowest contribution margin ratio (from Exhibit 9). The other two salespersons sold equal amounts of Gwenevere and Lancelot. As a result, Inez Rodriguez and Tom Ginger had higher contribution margin

**EXHIBIT 10**

Contribution Margin by Salesperson Report

| | Inez Rodriguez | Tom Ginger | Beth Williams | Northern Territory— Total |
|---|---|---|---|---|
| **Camelot Fragrance Company** | | | | |
| **Contribution Margin by Salesperson—Northern Territory** | | | | |
| **For the Month Ended March 31, 2012** | | | | |
| Sales .................................... | $20,000 | $20,000 | $40,000 | $80,000 |
| Variable cost of goods sold .............. | 2,400 | 2,400 | 4,800 | 9,600 |
| Manufacturing margin ................... | $17,600 | $17,600 | $35,200 | $70,400 |
| Variable selling expenses: | | | | |
| Promotion costs....................... | $ 5,000 | $ 5,000 | $12,000 | $22,000 |
| Sales commissions ................... | 3,000 | 3,000 | 8,000 | 14,000 |
| | $ 8,000 | $ 8,000 | $20,000 | $36,000 |
| Contribution margin..................... | $ 9,600 | $ 9,600 | $15,200 | $34,400 |
| Contribution margin ratio................ | 48% | 48% | 38% | 43% |
| Sales mix (% Lancelot sales) ............. | 50% | 50% | 0 | 25% |

ratios because they sold more Lancelot. The Northern Territory manager could use this report to encourage Inez and Tom to sell more total product, while encouraging Beth to sell more Lancelot.

Other factors should also be considered in evaluating salespersons' performance. For example, sales growth rates, years of experience, customer service, territory size, and actual performance compared to budgeted performance may also be important.

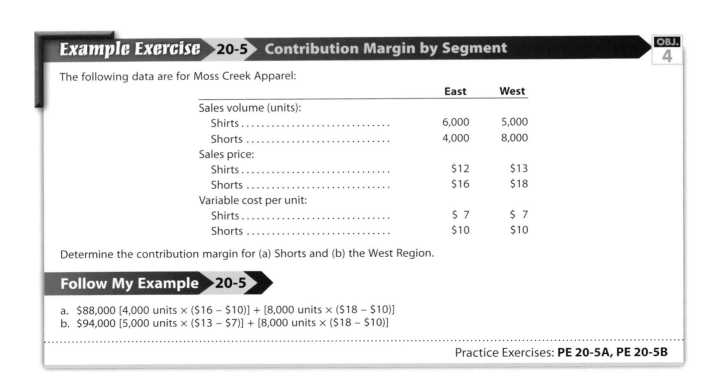

**Example Exercise** ▶ **20-5** ▶ **Contribution Margin by Segment**

OBJ. 4

The following data are for Moss Creek Apparel:

| | East | West |
|---|---|---|
| Sales volume (units): | | |
| Shirts ............................. | 6,000 | 5,000 |
| Shorts ............................ | 4,000 | 8,000 |
| Sales price: | | |
| Shirts ............................. | $12 | $13 |
| Shorts ............................ | $16 | $18 |
| Variable cost per unit: | | |
| Shirts ............................. | $ 7 | $ 7 |
| Shorts ............................ | $10 | $10 |

Determine the contribution margin for (a) Shorts and (b) the West Region.

**Follow My Example** ▶ **20-5** ▶

a. $88,000 [4,000 units × ($16 − $10)] + [8,000 units × ($18 − $10)]
b. $94,000 [5,000 units × ($13 − $7)] + [8,000 units × ($18 − $10)]

Practice Exercises: **PE 20-5A, PE 20-5B**

# BusinessConnection

## CHIPOTLE MEXICAN GRILL CONTRIBUTION MARGIN BY STORE

Chipotle Mexican Grill's annual report identifies revenues and costs for its company-owned restaurant operations. Assume that food, beverage, packaging, and labor are variable and that occupancy and other expenses are fixed. A contribution margin and income from operations can be constructed for the restaurants as follows for the year ended December 31, 2009 (in thousands):

| | | |
|---|---:|---:|
| Sales | | $1,518,417 |
| Variable restaurant expenses: | | |
| Food, beverage, and packaging | $466,027 | |
| Labor | 385,072 | |
| Total variable restaurant operating costs | | 851,099 |
| Contribution margin | | $ 667,318 |
| Occupancy and other expenses | | 288,799 |
| Income from operations | | $ 378,519 |

The annual report also indicates that Chipotle Mexican Grill has 956 restaurants, all company-owned. Dividing the numbers above by 956 yields the contribution margin and income from operations per restaurant as follows (in thousands):

| | |
|---|---:|
| Sales | $1,588 |
| Variable restaurant expenses | 890 |
| Contribution margin | $ 698 |
| Occupancy and other expenses | 302 |
| Income from operations | $ 396 |

Chipotle Mexican Grill can use this information for pricing products; evaluating the sensitivity of store profitability to changes in sales volume, prices, and costs; and analyzing profitability by geographic segment.

# Contribution Margin Analysis

**OBJ. 5** Use variable costing for analyzing and explaining changes in contribution margin as a result of quantity and price factors.

Managers often use contribution margin in planning and controlling operations. In doing so, managers use contribution margin analysis. **Contribution margin analysis** focuses on explaining the differences between planned and actual contribution margins.

Contribution margin is defined as sales less variable costs. Thus, a difference between the planned and actual contribution margin may be caused by an increase or a decrease in:

1. Sales
2. Variable costs

An increase or a decrease in sales or variable costs may in turn be due to an increase or a decrease in the:

1. Number of units sold
2. Unit sales price or unit cost

The effects of the preceding factors on sales or variable costs may be stated as follows:

1. **Quantity factor:** The effect of a difference in the number of units sold, assuming no change in unit sales price or unit cost. The *sales quantity factor* and the *variable cost quantity factor* are computed as follows:

   Sales Quantity Factor = (Actual Units Sold − Planned Units of Sales) × Planned Sales Price

   Variable Cost Quantity Factor = (Planned Units of Sales − Actual Units Sold) × Planned Unit Cost

   The preceding factors are computed so that a positive amount increases contribution margin and a negative amount decreases contribution margin.

2. **Unit price factor** or unit cost factor: The effect of a difference in unit sales price or unit cost on the number of units sold. The *unit price factor* and *unit cost factor* are computed as follows:

Unit Price Factor = (Actual Selling Price per Unit − Planned Selling Price per Unit) × Actual Units Sold

Unit Cost Factor = (Planned Cost per Unit − Actual Cost per Unit) × Actual Units Sold

The preceding factors are computed so that a positive amount increases contribution margin and a negative amount decreases contribution margin.

The effects of the preceding factors on contribution margin are summarized in Exhibit 11.

**EXHIBIT 11**

**Contribution Margin Analysis**

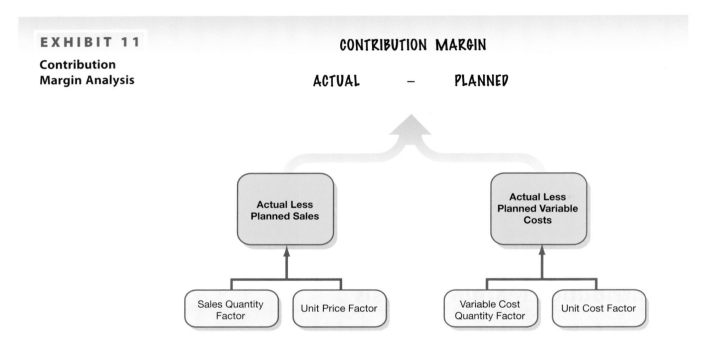

To illustrate, the following data for the year ended December 31, 2012 for Noble Inc., which sells a single product, are used.[1]

|  | Actual | Planned |
|---|---|---|
| Sales ............................................... | $937,500 | $800,000 |
| Less: Variable cost of goods sold ......................... | $425,000 | $350,000 |
| Variable selling and administrative expenses ........ | 162,500 | 125,000 |
| Total ......................................... | $587,500 | $475,000 |
| Contribution margin .................................... | $350,000 | $325,000 |
| Number of units sold .................................... | 125,000 | 100,000 |
| Per unit: |  |  |
| Sales price ........................................... | $7.50 | $8.00 |
| Variable cost of goods sold ........................... | 3.40 | 3.50 |
| Variable selling and administrative expenses ........... | 1.30 | 1.25 |

Exhibit 12 shows the contribution margin analysis report for Noble Inc. for the year ended December 31, 2012.

[1] To simplify, it is assumed that Noble Inc. sells a single product. The analysis would be more complex, but the principles would be the same, if more than one product were sold.

| Noble Inc.<br>Contribution Margin Analysis<br>For the Year Ended December 31, 2012 | | |
|---|---:|---:|
| Planned contribution margin ............................................... | | $325,000 |
| Effect of changes in sales: | | |
| Sales quantity factor (125,000 units – 100,000 units) × $8.00 ............. | $200,000 | |
| Unit price factor ($7.50 – $8.00) × 125,000 units ......................... | –62,500 | |
| Total effect of changes in sales ........................................ | | 137,500 |
| Effect of changes in variable cost of goods sold: | | |
| Variable cost quantity factor (100,000 units – 125,000 units) × $3.50 ...... | –$ 87,500 | |
| Unit cost factor ($3.50 – $3.40) × 125,000 units ......................... | 12,500 | |
| Total effect of changes in variable cost of goods sold .................. | | –75,000 |
| Effect of changes in selling and administrative expenses: | | |
| Variable cost quantity factor (100,000 units – 125,000 units) × $1.25 ......... | –$ 31,250 | |
| Unit cost factor ($1.25 – $1.30) × 125,000 units ......................... | –6,250 | |
| Total effect of changes in selling and administrative expenses.......... | | –37,500 |
| Actual contribution margin ................................................ | | $350,000 |

Exhibit 12 indicates that the favorable difference of $25,000 ($350,000 – $325,000) between the actual and planned contribution margins was due in large part to an increase in the quantity sold (sales quantity factor) of $200,000. This $200,000 increase was partially offset by a decrease in the unit sales price (unit price factor) of $62,500 and an increase in the amount of variable costs of $112,500 ($75,000 + $37,500).

The contribution margin analysis reports are useful to management in evaluating past performance and in planning future operations. For example, the impact of the $0.50 reduction in the unit sales price by Noble Inc. on the number of units sold and on the total sales for the year is useful information in determining whether further price reductions might be desirable.

The contribution margin analysis report also highlights the impact of changes in unit variable costs and expenses. For example, the $0.05 increase in the unit variable selling and administrative expenses might be a result of increased advertising expenditures. If so, the increase in the number of units sold in 2012 could be attributed to both the $0.50 price reduction and the increased advertising.

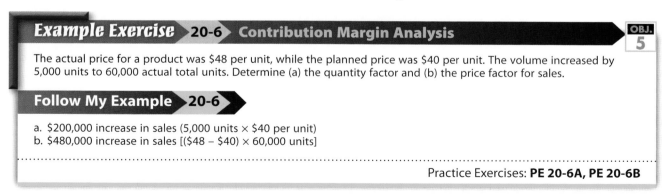

**Example Exercise** **20-6** **Contribution Margin Analysis**

**OBJ. 5**

The actual price for a product was $48 per unit, while the planned price was $40 per unit. The volume increased by 5,000 units to 60,000 actual total units. Determine (a) the quantity factor and (b) the price factor for sales.

**Follow My Example** **20-6**

a. $200,000 increase in sales (5,000 units × $40 per unit)
b. $480,000 increase in sales [($48 – $40) × 60,000 units]

Practice Exercises: **PE 20-6A, PE 20-6B**

# Variable Costing for Service Firms

**OBJ. 6** Describe and illustrate the use of variable costing for service firms.

Variable costing and the use of variable costing for manufacturing firms have been discussed earlier in this chapter. Service companies also use variable costing, contribution margin analysis, and segment analysis.

# Reporting Income from Operations Using Variable Costing for a Service Company

Unlike a manufacturing company, a service company does not make or sell a product. Thus, service companies do not have inventory. Since service companies have no inventory, they do not use absorption costing to allocate fixed costs. In addition, variable costing reports of service companies do not report a manufacturing margin.

To illustrate variable costing for a service company, Blue Skies Airlines Inc., which operates as a small commercial airline, is used. The variable and fixed costs of Blue Skies are shown in Exhibit 13.

**EXHIBIT 13**

**Costs of Blue Skies Airlines Inc.**

| Cost | Amount | Cost Behavior | Activity Base |
|------|--------|---------------|---------------|
| Depreciation expense .................... | $3,600,000 | Fixed | |
| Food and beverage service expense....... | 444,000 | Variable | Number of passengers |
| Fuel expense ........................... | 4,080,000 | Variable | Number of miles flown |
| Rental expense.......................... | 800,000 | Fixed | |
| Selling expense ........................ | 3,256,000 | Variable | Number of passengers |
| Wages expense.......................... | 6,120,000 | Variable | Number of miles flown |

As discussed in the prior chapter, a cost is classified as a fixed or variable cost according to how it changes relative to an activity base. A common activity for a manufacturing firm is the number of units produced. In contrast, most service companies use several activity bases.

To illustrate, Blue Skies Airlines uses the activity base *number of passengers* for food and beverage service and selling expenses. Blue Skies uses *number of miles flown* for fuel and wage expenses.

The variable costing income statement for Blue Skies, assuming revenue of $19,238,000, is shown in Exhibit 14.

**EXHIBIT 14**

**Variable Costing Income Statement**

| Blue Skies Airlines Inc. Variable Costing Income Statement For the Month Ended April 30, 2012 | | |
|---|---|---|
| Revenue ................................................ | | $19,238,000 |
| Variable costs: | | |
| Fuel expense ............................................. | $4,080,000 | |
| Wages expense ............................................. | 6,120,000 | |
| Food and beverage service expense ......................... | 444,000 | |
| Selling expense ............................................ | 3,256,000 | |
| Total variable costs ...................................... | | 13,900,000 |
| Contribution margin....................................... | | $ 5,338,000 |
| Fixed costs: | | |
| Depreciation expense....................................... | $3,600,000 | |
| Rental expense .......................................... | 800,000 | |
| Total fixed costs .......................................... | | 4,400,000 |
| Income from operations ...................................... | | $ 938,000 |

Unlike a manufacturing company, Exhibit 14 does not report cost of goods sold, inventory, or manufacturing margin. However, as shown in Exhibit 14, contribution margin is reported separately from income from operations.

# Market Segment Analysis for Service Company

A contribution margin report for service companies can be used to analyze and evaluate market segments. Typical segments for various service companies are shown below.

| Service Industry | Market Segments |
|---|---|
| Electric power | Regions, customer types (industrial, consumer) |
| Banking | Customer types (commercial, retail), products (loans, savings accounts) |
| Airlines | Products (passengers, cargo), routes |
| Railroads | Products (commodity type), routes |
| Hotels | Hotel properties |
| Telecommunications | Customer type (commercial, retail), service type (voice, data) |
| Health care | Procedure, payment type (Medicare, insured) |

To illustrate, a contribution margin report segmented by route is used for Blue Skies Airlines. In preparing the report, the following data for April 2012 are used:

|  | Chicago/Atlanta | Atlanta/LA | LA/Chicago |
|---|---|---|---|
| Average ticket price per passenger | $400 | $1,075 | $805 |
| Total passengers served | 16,000 | 7,000 | 6,600 |
| Total miles flown | 56,000 | 88,000 | 60,000 |

The variable costs per unit are as follows:

| Fuel | $ 20 per mile |
|---|---|
| Wages | 30 per mile |
| Food and beverage service | 15 per passenger |
| Selling | 110 per passenger |

A contribution margin report for Blue Skies Airlines is shown in Exhibit 15. The report is segmented by the routes (city pairs) flown.

**EXHIBIT 15**

Contribution Margin by Segment Report—Service Firm

| **Blue Skies Airlines Inc.** <br> **Contribution Margin by Route** <br> **For the Month Ended April 30, 2012** | | | | |
|---|---|---|---|---|
|  | Chicago/ Atlanta | Atlanta/ Los Angeles | Los Angeles/ Chicago | Total |
| Revenue |  |  |  |  |
| (Ticket price × No. of passengers) ..... | $ 6,400,000 | $ 7,525,000 | $5,313,000 | $19,238,000 |
| Aircraft fuel |  |  |  |  |
| ($20 × No. of miles flown) ............. | (1,120,000) | (1,760,000) | (1,200,000) | (4,080,000) |
| Wages and benefits |  |  |  |  |
| ($30 × No. of miles flown) ............. | (1,680,000) | (2,640,000) | (1,800,000) | (6,120,000) |
| Food and beverage service |  |  |  |  |
| ($15 × No. of passengers) ............. | (240,000) | (105,000) | (99,000) | (444,000) |
| Selling expenses |  |  |  |  |
| ($110 × No. of passengers) ............ | (1,760,000) | (770,000) | (726,000) | (3,256,000) |
| Contribution margin....................... | $ 1,600,000 | $ 2,250,000 | $ 1,488,000 | $ 5,338,000 |
| Contribution margin ratio* (rounded) ...... | 25% | 30% | 28% | 28% |

*Contribution margin/revenue

Exhibit 15 indicates that the Chicago/Atlanta route has the lowest contribution margin ratio of 25%. In contrast, the Atlanta/Los Angeles route has the highest contribution margin ratio of 30%.

# Contribution Margin Analysis

Blue Skies Airlines Inc. is also used to illustrate contribution margin analysis. Specifically, assume that Blue Skies decides to try to improve the contribution margin of its Chicago/Atlanta route during May by decreasing ticket prices. Thus, Blue Skies decreases the ticket price from $400 to $380 beginning May 1. As a result, the number of tickets sold (passengers) increased from 16,000 to 20,000. However, the cost per mile also increased during May from $20 to $22 due to increasing fuel prices.

The actual and planned results for the Chicago/Atlanta route during May are shown below. The planned amounts are based on the April results without considering the price change or cost per mile increase. The highlighted numbers indicate changes during May.

| | Chicago/Atlanta Route | |
|---|---|---|
| | **Actual, May** | **Planned, May** |
| Revenue .............................................. | $7,600,000 | $6,400,000 |
| Less variable expenses: | | |
| Aircraft fuel ......................................... | $1,232,000 | $1,120,000 |
| Wages and benefits ................................ | 1,680,000 | 1,680,000 |
| Food and beverage service ......................... | 300,000 | 240,000 |
| Selling expenses and commissions ................. | 2,200,000 | 1,760,000 |
| Total ................................................. | $5,412,000 | $4,800,000 |
| Contribution margin................................. | $2,188,000 | $1,600,000 |
| Contribution margin ratio........................... | 29% | 25% |
| Number of miles flown ............................. | 56,000 | 56,000 |
| Number of passengers flown........................ | 20,000 | 16,000 |
| Per unit: | | |
| Ticket price ......................................... | $380 | $400 |
| Fuel expense........................................ | 22 | 20 |
| Wages expense ..................................... | 30 | 30 |
| Food and beverage service expense ............... | 15 | 15 |
| Selling expense .................................... | 110 | 110 |

Using the preceding data, a contribution margin analysis report can be prepared for the Chicago/Atlanta route for May as shown in Exhibit 16. Since the planned and actual wages and benefits expense are the same ($1,680,000), its quantity and unit cost factors are not included in Exhibit 16.

**EXHIBIT 16**

**Contribution Margin Analysis Report—Service Company**

| Blue Skies Airlines Inc. Contribution Margin Analysis Chicago/Atlanta Route For the Month Ended May 31, 2012 | | |
|---|---|---|
| Planned contribution margin .............................................. | | $1,600,000 |
| Effect of changes in revenue: | | |
| Revenue quantity factor (20,000 pass. – 16,000 pass.) × $400 ............. | $1,600,000 | |
| Unit price factor ($380 – $400) × 20,000 passengers ...................... | –400,000 | |
| Total effect of changes in revenue ...................................... | | 1,200,000 |
| Effect of changes in fuel cost: | | |
| Variable cost quantity factor (56,000 miles – 56,000 miles) × $20 ......... | $ 0 | |
| Unit cost factor ($20 – $22) × 56,000 miles .............................. | –112,000 | |
| Total effect of changes in fuel costs .................................... | | –112,000 |
| Effect of changes in food and beverage expenses: | | |
| Variable cost quantity factor (16,000 pass. – 20,000 pass.) × $15........... | –$ 60,000 | |
| Unit cost factor ($15 – $15) × 20,000 passengers ......................... | 0 | |
| Total effect of changes in food and beverage expenses................. | | –60,000 |
| Effect of changes in selling and commission expenses: | | |
| Variable cost quantity factor (16,000 pass. – 20,000 pass.) × $110 ......... | –$ 440,000 | |
| Unit cost factor ($110 – $110) × 20,000 passengers ...................... | 0 | |
| Total effect of changes in selling and administrative expenses ......... | | –440,000 |
| Actual contribution margin ............................................... | | $2,188,000 |

Exhibit 16 indicates that the price decrease generated an additional $1,200,000 in revenue. This consists of $1,600,000 from an increased number of passengers (revenue quantity factor) and a $400,000 revenue reduction from the decrease in ticket price (unit price factor).

The increased fuel costs (by $2 per mile) reduced the contribution margin by $112,000 (unit cost factor). The increased number of passengers also increased the food and beverage service costs by $60,000 and the selling costs by $440,000 (variable cost quantity factors). The net increase in contribution margin is $588,000 ($2,188,000 − $1,600,000).

# At a Glance 20

**OBJ. 1**

**Describe and illustrate reporting income from operations under absorption and variable costing.**

**Key Points**   Under absorption costing, the cost of goods manufactured is comprised of all direct materials, direct labor, and factory overhead costs (both fixed and variable). Under variable costing, the cost of goods manufactured is composed of only variable costs: direct materials, direct labor, and variable factory overhead costs. Fixed factory overhead costs are considered a period expense.

The variable costing income statement is structured differently than a traditional absorption costing income statement. Sales less variable cost of goods sold is presented as manufacturing margin. Manufacturing margin less variable selling and administrative expenses is presented as contribution margin. Contribution margin less fixed costs is presented as income from operations.

| Learning Outcomes | Example Exercises | Practice Exercises |
|---|---|---|
| • Describe the difference between absorption and variable costing. | | |
| • Prepare a variable costing income statement for a manufacturer. | **EE20-1** | **PE20-1A, 20-1B** |
| • Evaluate the difference between the variable and absorption costing income statements when production exceeds sales. | **EE20-2** | **PE20-2A, 20-2B** |
| • Evaluate the difference between the variable and absorption costing income statements when sales exceed production. | **EE20-3** | **PE20-3A, 20-3B** |

**OBJ. 2**

**Describe and illustrate the effects of absorption and variable costing on analyzing income from operations.**

**Key Points**   Management should be aware of the effects of changes in inventory levels on income from operations reported under variable costing and absorption costing. If absorption costing is used, managers could misinterpret increases or decreases in income from operations due to changes in inventory levels to be the result of operating efficiencies or inefficiencies.

| Learning Outcomes | Example Exercises | Practice Exercises |
|---|---|---|
| • Determine absorption costing and variable costing income under different planned levels of production for a given sales level. | **EE20-4** | **PE20-4A, 20-4B** |

**OBJ. 3**

### Describe management's use of absorption and variable costing.

**Key Points**    Variable costing is especially useful at the operating level of management because the amount of variable manufacturing costs are controllable at this level. The fixed factory overhead costs are ordinarily controllable by a higher level of management.

In the short run, variable costing may be useful in establishing the selling price of a product. This price should be at least equal to the variable costs of making and selling the product. In the long run, however, absorption costing is useful in establishing selling prices because all costs must be covered and a reasonable amount of operating income earned.

| Learning Outcomes | Example Exercises | Practice Exercises |
|---|---|---|
| • Describe management's use of variable and absorption costing for controlling costs, pricing products, planning production, analyzing contribution margins, and analyzing market segments. | | |

**OBJ. 4**

### Use variable costing for analyzing market segments, including product, territories, and salespersons segments.

**Key Points**    Variable costing can support management decision making in analyzing and evaluating market segments, such as territories, products, salespersons, and customers. Contribution margin reports by segment can be used by managers to support price decisions, evaluate cost changes, and plan volume changes.

| Learning Outcomes | Example Exercises | Practice Exercises |
|---|---|---|
| • Describe management's uses of contribution margin reports by segment. | | |
| • Prepare a contribution margin report by sales territory | | |
| • Prepare a contribution margin report by product. | | |
| • Prepare a contribution margin report by salesperson. | **EE20-5** | **PE20-5A, 20-5B** |

**OBJ. 5**

### Use variable costing for analyzing and explaining changes in contribution margin as a result of quantity and price factors.

**Key Points**    Contribution margin analysis is the systematic examination of differences between planned and actual contribution margins. These differences can be caused by an increase/decrease in the amount of sales or variable costs, which can be caused by changes in the amount of units sold, unit sales price, or unit cost.

| Learning Outcomes | Example Exercises | Practice Exercises |
|---|---|---|
| • Prepare a contribution margin analysis identifying changes between actual and planned contribution margin by price/cost and quantity factors. | **EE20-6** | **PE20-6A, 20-6B** |

**OBJ. 6**

### Describe and illustrate the use of variable costing for service firms.

**Key Points**    Service firms will not have inventories, manufacturing margin, or cost of goods sold. Service firms can prepare variable costing income statements and contribution margin reports for market segments. In addition, service firms can use contribution margin analysis to plan and control operations.

| Learning Outcomes | Example Exercises | Practice Exercises |
|---|---|---|
| • Prepare a variable costing income statement for a service firm. | | |
| • Prepare contribution margin reports by market segments for a service firm. | | |
| • Prepare a contribution margin analysis for a service firm. | | |

## Key Terms

absorption costing (932)

contribution margin (933)

contribution margin analysis (947)

controllable costs (942)

manufacturing margin (933)

market segment (942)

noncontrollable costs (942)

quantity factor (947)

sales mix (944)

unit price (cost) factor (948)

variable cost of goods sold (933)

variable costing (933)

## Illustrative Problem

During the current period, McLaughlin Company sold 60,000 units of product at $30 per unit. At the beginning of the period, there were 10,000 units in inventory and McLaughlin Company manufactured 50,000 units during the period. The manufacturing costs and selling and administrative expenses were as follows:

|  | Total Cost | Number of Units | Unit Cost |
|---|---|---|---|
| Beginning inventory: |  |  |  |
|   Direct materials . . . . . . . . . . . . . . . . . . . . | $   67,000 | 10,000 | $  6.70 |
|   Direct labor   . . . . . . . . . . . . . . . . . . . . . | 155,000 | 10,000 | 15.50 |
|   Variable factory overhead   . . . . . . . . . . . . | 18,000 | 10,000 | 1.80 |
|   Fixed factory overhead   . . . . . . . . . . . . . . | 20,000 | 10,000 | 2.00 |
|     Total . . . . . . . . . . . . . . . . . . . . . . . . | $  260,000 |  | $26.00 |
| Current period costs: |  |  |  |
|   Direct materials . . . . . . . . . . . . . . . . . . . . | $  350,000 | 50,000 | $  7.00 |
|   Direct labor   . . . . . . . . . . . . . . . . . . . . . | 810,000 | 50,000 | 16.20 |
|   Variable factory overhead   . . . . . . . . . . . . | 90,000 | 50,000 | 1.80 |
|   Fixed factory overhead   . . . . . . . . . . . . . . | 100,000 | 50,000 | 2.00 |
|     Total . . . . . . . . . . . . . . . . . . . . . . . . | $1,350,000 |  | $27.00 |
| Selling and administrative expenses: |  |  |  |
|   Variable   . . . . . . . . . . . . . . . . . . . . . . . | $   65,000 |  |  |
|   Fixed   . . . . . . . . . . . . . . . . . . . . . . . . . | 45,000 |  |  |
|     Total . . . . . . . . . . . . . . . . . . . . . . . . | $  110,000 |  |  |

### Instructions

1. Prepare an income statement based on the absorption costing concept.

2. Prepare an income statement based on the variable costing concept.

3. Give the reason for the difference in the amount of income from operations in parts (1) and (2).

### Solution

1.

| Absorption Costing Income Statement | | |
|---|---|---|
| Sales (60,000 × $30) . . . . . . . . . . . . . . . . . . . . . . . . . . . . . . . . . . . . . . . . . . . . . | | $1,800,000 |
| Cost of goods sold: | | |
|   Beginning inventory (10,000 × $26) . . . . . . . . . . . . . . . . . . . . . . . . . . . | $  260,000 | |
|   Cost of goods manufactured (50,000 × $27) . . . . . . . . . . . . . . . . . . . . . | 1,350,000 | |
|     Cost of goods sold . . . . . . . . . . . . . . . . . . . . . . . . . . . . . . . . . . . . . . . | | 1,610,000 |
|   Gross profit. . . . . . . . . . . . . . . . . . . . . . . . . . . . . . . . . . . . . . . . . . . . . . . . | | $  190,000 |
| Selling and administrative expenses ($65,000 × $45,000) . . . . . . . . . . . . . | | 110,000 |
| Income from operations . . . . . . . . . . . . . . . . . . . . . . . . . . . . . . . . . . . . . . . . | | $   80,000 |

2.

| Variable Costing Income Statement | | |
|---|---:|---:|
| Sales (60,000 × $30) . . . . . . . . . . . . . . . . . . . . . . . . . . . . . . . . . . . . . . . . . . . . . . | | $1,800,000 |
| Variable cost of goods sold: | | |
|    Beginning inventory (10,000 × $24) . . . . . . . . . . . . . . . . . . . . . . . . . | $ 240,000 | |
|    Variable cost of goods manufactured (50,000 × $25) . . . . . . . . . . . | 1,250,000 | |
|      Variable cost of goods sold . . . . . . . . . . . . . . . . . . . . . . . . . . . . . . . | | 1,490,000 |
| Manufacturing margin. . . . . . . . . . . . . . . . . . . . . . . . . . . . . . . . . . . . . . . . . | | $ 310,000 |
| Variable selling and administrative expenses . . . . . . . . . . . . . . . . . . . . | | 65,000 |
| Contribution margin. . . . . . . . . . . . . . . . . . . . . . . . . . . . . . . . . . . . . . . . . . . | | $ 245,000 |
| Fixed costs: | | |
|    Fixed manufacturing costs. . . . . . . . . . . . . . . . . . . . . . . . . . . . . . . . . . . | $ 100,000 | |
|    Fixed selling and administrative expenses . . . . . . . . . . . . . . . . . . . | 45,000 | 145,000 |
| Income from operations . . . . . . . . . . . . . . . . . . . . . . . . . . . . . . . . . . . . . . | | $ 100,000 |

3.  The difference of $20,000 ($100,000 – $80,000) in the amount of income from opera-
    tions is attributable to the different treatment of the fixed manufacturing costs. The
    beginning inventory in the absorption costing income statement includes $20,000
    (10,000 units × $2) of fixed manufacturing costs incurred in the preceding period.
    This $20,000 was included as an expense in a variable costing income statement of
    a prior period. Therefore, none of it is included as an expense in the current period
    variable costing income statement.

# Discussion Questions

1.  What types of costs are customarily included in
    the cost of manufactured products under (a) the
    absorption costing concept and (b) the variable
    costing concept?

2.  Which type of manufacturing cost (direct mate-
    rials, direct labor, variable factory overhead,
    fixed factory overhead) is included in the cost
    of goods manufactured under the absorption
    costing concept but is excluded from the cost
    of goods manufactured under the variable cost-
    ing concept?

3.  Which of the following costs would be included
    in the cost of a manufactured product according
    to the variable costing concept: (a) rent on factory
    building, (b) direct materials, (c) property taxes on
    factory building, (d) electricity purchased to operate
    factory equipment, (e) salary of factory supervisor,
    (f) depreciation on factory building, (g) direct labor?

4.  In the variable costing income statement, how are the
    fixed manufacturing costs reported, and how are the
    fixed selling and administrative expenses reported?

5.  Since all costs of operating a business are control-
    lable, what is the significance of the term *noncon-
    trollable cost*?

6.  Discuss how financial data prepared on the basis
    of variable costing can assist management in the
    development of short-run pricing policies.

7.  Why might management analyze product profit-
    ability?

8.  Explain why rewarding sales personnel on the
    basis of total sales might not be in the best interests
    of a business whose goal is to maximize profits.

9.  Discuss the two factors affecting both sales and
    variable costs to which a change in contribution
    margin can be attributed.

10. How is the quantity factor for an increase or a
    decrease in the amount of sales computed in using
    contribution margin analysis?

11. How is the unit cost factor for an increase or a de-
    crease in the amount of variable cost of goods sold
    computed in using contribution margin analysis?

# Practice Exercises

| Learning Objectives | Example Exercises | |
|---|---|---|
| **OBJ. 1** | **EE 20-1** *p. 934* | **PE 20-1A  Variable costing** |

Tiffany Company has the following information for March:

| | |
|---|---|
| Sales | $360,000 |
| Variable cost of goods sold | 129,600 |
| Fixed manufacturing costs | 86,400 |
| Variable selling and administrative expenses | 28,800 |
| Fixed selling and administrative expenses | 21,600 |

Determine (a) the manufacturing margin, (b) the contribution margin, and (c) income from operations for Tiffany Company for the month of March.

| Learning Objectives | Example Exercises | |
|---|---|---|
| **OBJ. 1** | **EE 20-1** *p. 934* | **PE 20-1B  Variable costing** |

Hardin Company has the following information for July:

| | |
|---|---|
| Sales | $625,000 |
| Variable cost of goods sold | 325,000 |
| Fixed manufacturing costs | 56,250 |
| Variable selling and administrative expenses | 162,500 |
| Fixed selling and administrative expenses | 37,500 |

Determine (a) the manufacturing margin, (b) the contribution margin, and (c) income from operations for Hardin Company for the month of July.

| Learning Objectives | Example Exercises | |
|---|---|---|
| **OBJ. 1** | **EE 20-2** *p. 936* | **PE 20-2A  Variable costing—production exceeds sales** |

Fixed manufacturing costs are $60 per unit, and variable manufacturing costs are $110 per unit. Production was 320,000 units, while sales were 288,000 units. Determine (a) whether variable costing income from operations is less than or greater than absorption costing income from operations, and (b) the difference in variable costing and absorption costing income from operations.

| Learning Objectives | Example Exercises | |
|---|---|---|
| **OBJ. 1** | **EE 20-2** *p. 936* | **PE 20-2B  Variable costing—production exceeds sales** |

Fixed manufacturing costs are $36 per unit, and variable manufacturing costs are $84 per unit. Production was 56,000 units, while sales were 42,000 units. Determine (a) whether variable costing income from operations is less than or greater than absorption costing income from operations, and (b) the difference in variable costing and absorption costing income from operations.

| Learning Objectives | Example Exercises | |
|---|---|---|
| **OBJ. 1** | **EE 20-3** *p. 937* | **PE 20-3A  Variable costing—sales exceed production** |

The beginning inventory is 24,000 units. All of the units that were manufactured during the period and 8,000 units of the beginning inventory were sold. The beginning inventory fixed manufacturing costs are $30.80 per unit, and variable manufacturing costs are $88 per unit. Determine (a) whether variable costing income from operations is less than or greater than absorption costing income from operations, and (b) the difference in variable costing and absorption costing income from operations.

| Learning Objectives | Example Exercises | |
|---|---|---|
| **OBJ. 1** | **EE 20-3** *p. 937* | **PE 20-3B  Variable costing—sales exceed production** |

The beginning inventory is 80,000 units. All of the units that were manufactured during the period and 44,000 units of the beginning inventory were sold. The beginning inventory fixed manufacturing costs are $11.60 per unit, and variable manufacturing costs are $24 per unit. Determine (a) whether variable costing income from operations is less than or greater than absorption costing income from operations, and (b) the difference in variable costing and absorption costing income from operations.

**OBJ. 2** **EE 20-4** *p. 941*

**PE 20-4A  Analyzing income under absorption and variable costing**

Variable manufacturing costs are $11 per unit, and fixed manufacturing costs are $55,000. Sales are estimated to be 10,000 units.

a. How much would absorption costing income from operations differ between a plan to produce 10,000 units and a plan to produce 12,500 units?

b. How much would variable costing income from operations differ between the two production plans?

**OBJ. 2** **EE 20-4** *p. 941*

**PE 20-4B  Analyzing income under absorption and variable costing**

Variable manufacturing costs are $105 per unit, and fixed manufacturing costs are $126,000. Sales are estimated to be 9,000 units.

a. How much would absorption costing income from operations differ between a plan to produce 9,000 units and a plan to produce 12,000 units?

b. How much would variable costing income from operations differ between the two production plans?

**OBJ. 4** **EE 20-5** *p. 946*

**PE 20-5A  Contribution margin by segment**

The following information is for Shotz Snowboards, Inc.:

|  | North | South |
|---|---|---|
| Sales volume (units): | | |
| Eddie's Dream | 25,000 | 33,000 |
| Big T's Marauder | 56,000 | 70,000 |
| Sales price: | | |
| Eddie's Dream | $240.00 | $250.00 |
| Big T's Marauder | $280.00 | $300.00 |
| Variable cost per unit: | | |
| Eddie's Dream | $124.00 | $124.00 |
| Big T's Marauder | $130.00 | $130.00 |

Determine the contribution margin for (a) Eddie's Dream Skateboards and (b) North Region.

**OBJ. 4** **EE 20-5** *p. 946*

**PE 20-5B  Contribution margin by segment**

The following information is for Filimonov Industries, Inc.:

|  | East | West |
|---|---|---|
| Sales volume (units): | | |
| Sea | 22,500 | 19,000 |
| Cake | 30,000 | 25,000 |
| Sales price: | | |
| Sea | $350.00 | $330.00 |
| Cake | $364.00 | $360.00 |
| Variable cost per unit: | | |
| Sea | $168.00 | $168.00 |
| Cake | $180.00 | $180.00 |

Determine the contribution margin for (a) Cake hand-held video games and (b) West Region.

### PE 20-6A Contribution margin analysis

The actual price for a product was $56 per unit, while the planned price was $50 per unit. The volume decreased by 40,000 units to 820,000 actual total units. Determine (a) the sales quantity factor and (b) the unit price factor for sales.

### PE 20-6B Contribution margin analysis

The actual variable cost of goods sold for a product was $70 per unit, while the planned variable cost of goods sold was $68 per unit. The volume increased by 1,200 units to 7,000 actual total units. Determine (a) the variable cost quantity factor and (b) the unit cost factor for variable cost of goods sold.

## Exercises

OBJ. 1

✔ b. Inventory,
$633,000

### EX 20-1 Inventory valuation under absorption costing and variable costing

At the end of the first year of operations, 7,500 units remained in the finished goods inventory. The unit manufacturing costs during the year were as follows:

| | |
|---|---|
| Direct materials | $52.00 |
| Direct labor | 25.00 |
| Fixed factory overhead | 8.40 |
| Variable factory overhead | 7.40 |

Determine the cost of the finished goods inventory reported on the balance sheet under (a) the absorption costing concept and (b) the variable costing concept.

OBJ. 1

✔ a. Income from
operations, $490,000

### EX 20-2 Income statements under absorption costing and variable costing

The Duller Edge Inc. assembles and sells MP3 players. The company began operations on May 1, 2012, and operated at 100% of capacity during the first month. The following data summarize the results for May:

| | | |
|---|---|---|
| Sales (20,000 units) | | $4,000,000 |
| Production costs (27,000 units): | | |
| Direct materials | $1,998,000 | |
| Direct labor | 972,000 | |
| Variable factory overhead | 486,000 | |
| Fixed factory overhead | 324,000 | 3,780,000 |
| Selling and administrative expenses: | | |
| Variable selling and administrative expenses | $ 560,000 | |
| Fixed selling and administrative expenses | 150,000 | 710,000 |

a. Prepare an income statement according to the absorption costing concept.

b. Prepare an income statement according to the variable costing concept.

c. What is the reason for the difference in the amount of income from operations reported in (a) and (b)?

OBJ. 1

✔ b. Income from
operations, $2,346,000

### EX 20-3 Income statements under absorption costing and variable costing

Patagucci Inc. manufactures and sells athletic equipment. The company began operations on August 1, 2012, and operated at 100% of capacity (66,000 units) during the first month, creating an ending inventory of 6,000 units. During September, the company produced 60,000 garments during the month but sold 66,000 units at $165 per unit. The September manufacturing costs and selling and administrative expenses were as follows:

| | Number of Units | Unit Cost | Total Cost |
|---|---|---|---|
| Manufacturing costs in September beginning inventory: | | | |
| Variable................................................. | 6,000 | $66.00 | $ 396,000 |
| Fixed .................................................. | 6,000 | 24.00 | 144,000 |
| Total ............................................. | | $90.00 | $ 540,000 |
| September manufacturing costs: | | | |
| Variable................................................. | 60,000 | $66.00 | $3,960,000 |
| Fixed .................................................. | 60,000 | 26.40 | 1,584,000 |
| Total ............................................. | | $92.40 | $5,544,000 |
| Selling and administrative expenses: | | | |
| Variable ............................................... | | | $2,079,000 |
| Fixed .................................................. | | | 525,000 |
| Total ............................................. | | | $2,604,000 |

a. Prepare an income statement according to the absorption costing concept for September.

b. Prepare an income statement according to the variable costing concept for September.

c. What is the reason for the difference in the amount of income from operations reported in (a) and (b)?

---

OBJ. 1

✔ b. Unit cost of goods manufactured, $8,400

**EX 20-4  Cost of goods manufactured, using variable costing and absorption costing**

On June 30, the end of the first year of operations, Johnson Industries, Inc., manufactured 4,500 units and sold 4,000 units. The following income statement was prepared, based on the variable costing concept:

**Johnson Industries, Inc.**
**Variable Costing Income Statement**
**For the Year Ended June 30, 2013**

| | | |
|---|---|---|
| Sales ....................................................... | | $48,000,000 |
| Variable cost of goods sold: | | |
| Variable cost of goods manufactured .......................... | $25,920,000 | |
| Less inventory, July 31........................................ | 2,880,000 | |
| Variable cost of goods sold ...................................... | | 23,040,000 |
| Manufacturing margin......................................... | | $24,960,000 |
| Variable selling and administrative expenses ...................... | | 5,760,000 |
| Contribution margin.......................................... | | $19,200,000 |
| Fixed costs: | | |
| Fixed manufacturing costs ................................... | $11,880,000 | |
| Fixed selling and administrative expenses...................... | 3,840,000 | 15,720,000 |
| Income from operations ....................................... | | $ 3,480,000 |

Determine the unit cost of goods manufactured, based on (a) the variable costing concept and (b) the absorption costing concept.

---

OBJ. 1

✔ Income from operations, $64,320

**EX 20-5  Variable costing income statement**

On June 30, the end of the first month of operations, Clowney Company prepared the following income statement, based on the absorption costing concept:

**Clowney Company**
**Absorption Costing Income Statement**
**For the Month Ended June 30, 2013**

| | | |
|---|---|---|
| Sales (9,600 units) ............................................. | | $537,600 |
| Cost of goods sold: | | |
| Cost of goods manufactured (11,200 units) ..................... | $448,000 | |
| Less inventory, June 30 (1,600 units) .......................... | 64,000 | |
| Cost of goods sold............................................ | | 384,000 |
| Gross profit................................................... | | $153,600 |
| Selling and administrative expenses ............................ | | 82,080 |
| Income from operations ....................................... | | $ 71,520 |

If the fixed manufacturing costs were $50,400 and the variable selling and administrative expenses were $45,600, prepare an income statement according to the variable costing concept.

**OBJ. 1**

✔ Income from operations, $806,400

### EX 20-6 Absorption costing income statement

On May 31, the end of the first month of operations, Seger Equipment Company prepared the following income statement, based on the variable costing concept:

**Seger Equipment Company**
**Variable Costing Income Statement**
**For the Month Ended May 31, 2012**

| | | |
|---|---:|---:|
| Sales (36,000 units) ............................................... | | $4,320,000 |
| Variable cost of goods sold: | | |
|    Variable cost of goods manufactured ......................... | $2,073,600 | |
|    Less inventory, May 31 (7,200 units)........................... | 345,600 | |
| Variable cost of goods sold ...................................... | | 1,728,000 |
| Manufacturing margin............................................ | | $2,592,000 |
| Variable selling and administrative expenses ..................... | | 1,080,000 |
| Contribution margin............................................. | | $1,512,000 |
| Fixed costs: | | |
|    Fixed manufacturing costs ..................................... | $ 432,000 | |
|    Fixed selling and administrative expenses...................... | 345,600 | 777,600 |
| Income from operations .......................................... | | $ 734,400 |

Prepare an income statement under absorption costing.

**OBJ. 1**

✔ a. Income from operations, $16,021

### EX 20-7 Variable costing income statement

The following data were adapted from a recent income statement of Procter & Gamble Company:

| | (in millions) |
|---|---:|
| Net sales ........................................................... | $78,938 |
| Operating costs: | |
|    Cost of products sold....................................... | $37,919 |
|    Marketing, administrative, and other expenses............................ | 24,998 |
|       Total operating costs.................................... | $62,917 |
| Income from operations ........................................... | $16,021 |

Assume that the variable amount of each category of operating costs is as follows:

| | (in millions) |
|---|---:|
| Cost of products sold ........................................... | $21,230 |
| Marketing, administrative, and other expenses ............................. | 10,000 |

a. Based on the above data, prepare a variable costing income statement for Procter & Gamble Company, assuming that the company maintained constant inventory levels during the period.

b. If Procter & Gamble reduced its inventories during the period, what impact would that have on the income from operations determined under absorption costing?

### EX 20-8  Estimated income statements, using absorption and variable costing

Prior to the first month of operations ending April 30, 2012, Jadelis Industries Inc. estimated the following operating results:

| | |
|---|---:|
| Sales (36,000 × $124.00) | $4,464,000 |
| Manufacturing costs (36,000 units): | |
|     Direct materials | 2,736,000 |
|     Direct labor | 648,000 |
|     Variable factory overhead | 288,000 |
|     Fixed factory overhead | 360,000 |
|     Fixed selling and administrative expenses | 49,000 |
|     Variable selling and administrative expenses | 59,200 |

The company is evaluating a proposal to manufacture 45,000 units instead of 36,000 units, thus creating an ending inventory of 9,000 units. Manufacturing the additional units will not change sales, unit variable factory overhead costs, total fixed factory overhead cost, or total selling and administrative expenses.

a.  Prepare an estimated income statement, comparing operating results if 36,000 and 45,000 units are manufactured in (1) the absorption costing format and (2) the variable costing format.

b.  What is the reason for the difference in income from operations reported for the two levels of production by the absorption costing income statement?

### EX 20-9  Variable and absorption costing

Whirlpool Corporation had the following abbreviated income statement for a recent year:

| | (in millions) |
|---|---:|
| Net sales | $17,099 |
| Cost of goods sold | $14,713 |
| Selling administrative, and other expenses | 1,544 |
|     Total expenses | $16,257 |
| Income from operations | $    842 |

Assume that there were $3,680 million fixed manufacturing costs and $890 million fixed selling, administrative, and other costs for the year.

The finished goods inventories at the beginning and end of the year from the balance sheet were as follows:

| | |
|---|---|
| January 1 | $2,591 million |
| December 31 | $2,197 million |

Assume that 30% of the beginning and ending inventory consists of fixed costs. Assume work in process and materials inventory were unchanged during the period.

a.  Prepare an income statement according to the variable costing concept for Whirlpool Corporation for the recent year.

b.  Explain the difference between the amount of income from operations reported under the absorption costing and variable costing concepts.

### EX 20-10   Variable and absorption costing—three products

Shoes R' Us, Inc. manufactures and sells three types of shoes. The income statements prepared under absorption costing method for the three shoes are as follows:

**Shoes R' Us, Inc.**
**Product Income Statements—Absorption Costing**
**For the Year Ended December 31, 2012**

|  | Party Shoes | Play Shoes | Dress Shoes |
|---|---|---|---|
| Revenues ........................................ | $522,000 | $441,000 | $378,000 |
| Cost of goods sold............................... | 270,000 | 216,000 | 252,000 |
| Gross profit...................................... | $252,000 | $225,000 | $126,000 |
| Selling and administrative expenses .............. | 216,000 | 162,000 | 211,500 |
| Income from operations ......................... | $ 36,000 | $ 63,000 | $ (85,500) |

In addition, you have determined the following information with respect to allocated fixed costs:

|  | Party Shoes | Play Shoes | Dress Shoes |
|---|---|---|---|
| Fixed costs: |  |  |  |
| Cost of goods sold ............................ | $81,000 | $58,500 | $72,000 |
| Selling and administrative expenses ............ | 63,000 | 54,000 | 72,000 |

These fixed costs are used to support all three product lines. In addition, you have determined that the inventory is negligible.

The management of the company has deemed the profit performance of the dress shoe line as unacceptable. As a result, it has decided to eliminate the dress shoe line. Management does not expect to be able to increase sales in the other two lines. However, as a result of eliminating the dress shoe line, management expects the profits of the company to increase by $85,500.

a. Do you agree with management's decision and conclusions?

b. Prepare a variable costing income statement for the three products.

c. Use the report in (b) to determine the profit impact of eliminating the dress shoe line, assuming no other changes.

---

**OBJ. 4**

### EX 20-11   Change in sales mix and contribution margin

Life Sound Company manufactures two models of noise-canceling headphones: Noise Resistant and Total Silence models. The company is operating at less than full capacity. Market research indicates that 29,750 additional Noise Resistant and 33,000 additional Total Silence headphones could be sold. The income from operations by unit of product is as follows:

|  | Noise Resistant Headphone | Total Silence Headphone |
|---|---|---|
| Sales price | $50.00 | $70.00 |
| Variable cost of goods sold | 28.00 | 39.20 |
| Manufacturing margin | $22.00 | $30.80 |
| Variable selling and administrative expenses | 10.00 | 14.00 |
| Contribution margin | $12.00 | $16.80 |
| Fixed manufacturing costs | 5.00 | 7.00 |
| Income from operations | $ 7.00 | $ 9.80 |

Prepare an analysis indicating the increase or decrease in total profitability if 29,750 additional Noise Resistant and 33,000 additional Total Silence headphones are produced and sold, assuming that there is sufficient capacity for the additional production.

---

**OBJ. 4**

✔ a. 2WD
contribution margin,
$1,625,000

### EX 20-12   Product profitability analysis

Outdoor Motor Sports Inc. manufactures and sells two styles of ATVs, 4-wheel drive (4WD) and 2-wheel drive (2WD), from a single manufacturing facility. The manufacturing facility operates at 100% of capacity. The following per unit information is available for the two products:

*(Continued)*

|  | 4WD | 2WD |
|---|---|---|
| Sales price | $5,250 | $3,250 |
| Variable cost of goods sold | 3,100 | 2,100 |
| Manufacturing margin | $2,150 | $1,150 |
| Variable selling expenses | 890 | 500 |
| Contribution margin | $1,260 | $ 650 |
| Fixed expenses | 460 | 200 |
| Income from operations | $ 800 | $ 450 |

In addition, the following unit volume information for the period is as follows:

|  | 4WD | 2WD |
|---|---|---|
| Sales unit volume | 3,100 | 2,500 |

a. Prepare a contribution margin by product report. Calculate the contribution margin ratio for each product as a whole percent, rounded to two decimal places.

b. What advice would you give to the management of Outdoor Motor Sports Inc. regarding the relative profitability of the two products?

---

OBJ. 4

✔ a. Northern contribution margin, $500,000

**EX 20-13 Territory and product profitability analysis**

Zen Skateboards, Inc., manufactures and sells two styles of skateboards, Street Machine and Winter Warrior. These skateboards are sold in two regions, Southern and Northern. Information about the two skateboards is as follows:

|  | Street Machine | Winter Warrior |
|---|---|---|
| Sales price | $250 | $150 |
| Variable cost of goods sold per unit | 175 | 105 |
| Manufacturing margin per unit | $ 75 | $ 45 |
| Variable selling expense per unit | 50 | 25 |
| Contribution margin per unit | $ 25 | $ 20 |

The sales unit volume for the territories and products for the period is as follows:

|  | Southern | Northern |
|---|---|---|
| Street Machine | 25,000 | 12,500 |
| Winter Warrior | 0 | 12,500 |

a. Prepare a contribution margin by sales territory report. Calculate the contribution margin ratio for each territory as a whole percent, rounded to two decimal places.

b. What advice would you give to the management of Zen Skateboards, Inc., regarding the relative profitability of the two territories?

---

OBJ. 4

✔ a. Bart T. contribution margin, $231,840

**EX 20-14 Sales territory and salesperson profitability analysis**

Loom Industries, Inc., manufactures and sells a variety of commercial vehicles in the North and South regions. There are two salespersons assigned to each territory. Higher commission rates go to the most experienced salespersons. The following sales statistics are available for each salesperson:

|  | North | | South | |
|---|---|---|---|---|
|  | Kurt W. | Bart T. | Jody T. | Big T. |
| Average per unit: |  |  |  |  |
| Sales price ............................... | $48,000 | $42,000 | $54,000 | $39,000 |
| Variable cost of goods sold ............... | 28,800 | 16,800 | 32,400 | 15,600 |
| Commission rate .......................... | 10% | 14% | 14% | 10% |
| Units sold ................................ | 14 | 12 | 12 | 19 |
| Manufacturing margin ratio ............... | 40% | 60% | 40% | 60% |

a. 1. Prepare a contribution margin by salesperson report. Calculate the contribution margin ratio for each salesperson.

   2. Interpret the report.

b. 1. Prepare a contribution margin by territory report. Calculate the contribution margin for each territory as a whole percent, rounded to one decimal place.

   2. Interpret the report.

---

OBJ. 4

✔ a. Electric Power, $1,165.44

### EX 20-15 Segment profitability analysis

Provided below are the marketing segment sales for Caterpillar, Inc., for a recent year.

**Caterpillar, Inc.**
**Machinery and Engines Marketing Segment Sales**
**(in millions)**

|  | Building Construction Products | Europe/Africa/ Middle East (EAME) | Electric Power | Heavy Construction | Industrial Power Systems | Infra-structure Development | Large Power Systems | Marine & Petroleum Power | All Others |
|---|---|---|---|---|---|---|---|---|---|
| Sales | $3,415 | $961 | $3,632 | $9,751 | $2,016 | $9,583 | 3,125 | 4,061 | 11,313 |

In addition, assume the following information:

|  | Building Construction Products | Europe/Africa/ Middle East (EAME) | Electric Power | Heavy Construction | Industrial Power Systems | Infra-structure Development | Large Power Systems | Marine & Petroleum Power | All Others |
|---|---|---|---|---|---|---|---|---|---|
| Variable cost of goods sold as a percent of sales . . . . . . . . | 47% | 54% | 50% | 50% | 54% | 54% | 53% | 50% | 50% |
| Dealer commissions as a percent of sales . . . . . . . . . . . | 9% | 11% | 8% | 8% | 10% | 6% | 5% | 7% | 9% |
| Variable promotion expenses (in millions) . . . . . . | 350 | 100 | 360 | 970 | 190 | 950 | 300 | 410 | 1,100 |

a. Use the sales information and the additional assumed information to prepare a contribution margin by segment report. Round to two decimal places. In addition, calculate the contribution margin ratio for each segment as a whole percent, rounded to one decimal place.

b. Prepare a table showing the manufacturing margin, dealer commissions, and variable promotion expenses as a percent of sales for each segment. Round whole percents to one decimal place.

c. ➤ Use the information in (a) and (b) to interpret the segment performance.

---

OBJ. 4, 6

✔ a. Filmed entertainment, $7,524.9, 68%

### EX 20-16 Segment contribution margin analysis

The operating revenues of the three largest business segments for Time Warner, Inc., for a recent year are shown below. Each segment includes a number of businesses, examples of which are indicated in parentheses.

**Time Warner, Inc.**
**Segment Revenues**
**(in millions)**

| | |
|---|---|
| Filmed Entertainment (Warner Bros.) | $11,066 |
| Networks (CNN, HBO, WB) | 11,703 |
| Publishing (*Time, People, Sports Illustrated*) | 3,736 |

Assume that the variable costs as a percent of sales for each segment are as follows:

| | |
|---|---|
| Filmed Entertainment | 32% |
| Networks | 30% |
| Publishing | 72% |

a. Determine the contribution margin (round to whole millions) and contribution margin ratio (round to whole percents) for each segment from the above information.

*(Continued)*

b. Why is the contribution margin ratio for the Publishing segment smaller than for the other segments?

c. Does your answer to (b) mean that the other segments are more profitable businesses than the Publishing segment?

---

OBJ. 4

### EX 20-17 Contribution margin analysis—sales

Blueberry, Inc., sells computer equipment. Management decided early in the year to reduce the price of the speakers in order to increase sales volume. As a result, for the year ended December 31, 2013, the sales increased by $17,500 from the planned level of $1,182,500. The following information is available from the accounting records for the year ended December 31, 2013:

| | Actual | Planned | Increase or (Decrease) |
|---|---|---|---|
| Sales | $1,200,000 | $1,182,500 | $17,500 |
| Number of units sold | 48,000 | 43,000 | 5,000 |
| Sales price | $25.00 | $27.50 | $(2.50) |
| Variable cost per unit | $5.00 | $5.00 | 0 |

a. Prepare an analysis of the sales quantity and unit price factors.

b. Did the price decrease generate sufficient volume to result in a net increase in contribution margin if the actual variable cost per unit was $5, as planned?

---

OBJ. 4

✔ Sales quantity factor, −$305,500

### EX 20-18 Contribution margin analysis—sales

The following data for Gardot Products Inc. are available:

| For the Year Ended December 31, 2012 | Actual | Planned | Difference— Increase or (Decrease) |
|---|---|---|---|
| Sales........................................... | $6,875,000 | $6,768,000 | $107,000 |
| Less: | | | |
|   Variable cost of goods sold .................... | $3,630,000 | $3,513,600 | $116,400 |
|   Variable selling and administrative expenses.... | 715,000 | 806,400 | (91,400) |
|     Total variable costs......................... | $4,345,000 | $4,320,000 | $ 25,000 |
| Contribution margin............................. | $2,530,000 | $2,448,000 | $ 82,000 |
| Number of units sold ........................... | 27,500 | 28,800 | |
| Per unit: | | | |
|   Sales price ..................................... | $250.00 | $235.00 | |
|   Variable cost of goods sold .................... | 132.00 | 122.00 | |
|   Variable selling and administrative expenses.... | 26.00 | 28.00 | |

Prepare an analysis of the sales quantity and unit price factors.

---

OBJ. 4

✔ Variable cost of goods sold quantity factor, $158,600

### EX 20-19 Contribution margin analysis—variable costs

Based on the data in Exercise 20-18, prepare a contribution analysis of the variable costs for Gardot Products Inc. for the year ended December 31, 2012.

---

OBJ. 4, 6

### EX 20-20 Variable costing income statement—service company

Mid-Atlantic Railroad Company transports commodities among three routes (city-pairs): Boston/Philadelphia, Philadelphia/Buffalo, and Buffalo/Boston. Significant costs, their cost behavior, and activity rates for May 2012 are as follows:

| Cost | Amount | Cost Behavior | Activity Rate |
|---|---|---|---|
| Labor costs for loading and unloading railcars | $ 237,660 | Variable | $51.00 per railcar |
| Fuel costs | 572,950 | Variable | 14.00 per train-mile |
| Train crew labor costs | 327,400 | Variable | 8.00 per train-mile |
| Switchyard labor costs | 163,100 | Variable | 35.00 per railcar |
| Track and equipment depreciation | 216,000 | Fixed | |
| Maintenance | 144,000 | Fixed | |
| | $1,661,110 | | |

Operating statistics from the management information system reveal the following for May:

| | Boston/ Philadelphia | Philadelphia/ Buffalo | Buffalo/ Boston | Total |
|---|---|---|---|---|
| Number of train-miles | 14,345 | 11,220 | 15,360 | 40,925 |
| Number of railcars | 532 | 2,640 | 1,488 | 4,660 |
| Revenue per railcar | $614 | $308 | $490 | |

a. Prepare a contribution margin by route report for Mid-Atlantic Railroad Company for the month of May. Calculate the contribution margin ratio in whole percents, rounded to one decimal place.

b. Evaluate the route performance of the railroad using the report in (a).

---

OBJ. 5, 6

**EX 20-21  Contribution margin reporting and analysis—service company**

The management of Mid-Atlantic Railroad Company introduced in Exercise 20-20 improved the profitability of the Boston/Philadelphia route in June by reducing the price of a railcar from $614 to $556. This price reduction increased the demand for rail services. Thus, the number of railcars increased by 236 railcars to a total of 768 railcars. This was accomplished by increasing the size of each train but not the number of trains. Thus, the number of train-miles was unchanged. All the activity rates remained unchanged.

a. Prepare a contribution margin report for the Boston/Philadelphia route for June. Calculate the contribution margin ratio in percentage terms to one decimal place.

b. Prepare a contribution margin analysis to evaluate management's actions in June. Assume that the June planned quantity, price, and unit cost was the same as May.

---

OBJ. 5, 6

**EX 20-22  Variable costing income statement and contribution margin analysis—service company**

The actual and planned data for Fly University for the Fall term 2012 were as follows:

| | Actual | Planned |
|---|---|---|
| Enrollment | 6,010 | 5,500 |
| Tuition per credit hour | $160 | $180 |
| Credit hours | 80,600 | 57,600 |
| Registration, records, and marketing cost per enrolled student | $370 | $370 |
| Instructional costs per credit hour | $85 | $80 |
| Depreciation on classrooms and equipment | $1,100,800 | $1,100,800 |

Registration, records, and marketing costs vary by the number of enrolled students, while instructional costs vary by the number of credit hours. Depreciation is a fixed cost.

a. Prepare a variable costing income statement showing the contribution margin and income from operations for the Fall 2012 term.

b. Prepare a contribution margin analysis report comparing planned with actual performance for the Fall 2012 term.

## Problems Series A

OBJ. 1, 2

✔ 2. Income
from operations,
$195,950

### PR 20-1A Absorption and variable costing income statements

During the first month of operations ended May 31, 2012, Dorm Fridge Company manufactured 12,500 microwaves, of which 11,700 were sold. Operating data for the month are summarized as follows:

| | | |
|---|---:|---:|
| Sales | | $2,106,000 |
| Manufacturing costs: | | |
|     Direct materials | $1,050,000 | |
|     Direct labor | 312,500 | |
|     Variable manufacturing cost | 268,750 | |
|     Fixed manufacturing cost | 137,500 | 1,768,750 |
| Selling and administrative expenses: | | |
|     Variable | $ 169,650 | |
|     Fixed | 76,050 | 245,700 |

**Instructions**

1. Prepare an income statement based on the absorption costing concept.

2. Prepare an income statement based on the variable costing concept.

3. ➤ Explain the reason for the difference in the amount of income from operations reported in (1) and (2).

OBJ. 1, 2

✔ 2. Contribution
margin, $44,100

### PR 20-2A Income statements under absorption costing and variable costing

The demand for solvent, one of numerous products manufactured by Hipp Industries Inc., has dropped sharply because of recent competition from a similar product. The company's chemists are currently completing tests of various new formulas, and it is anticipated that the manufacture of a superior product can be started on June 1, one month in the future. No changes will be needed in the present production facilities to manufacture the new product because only the mixture of the various materials will be changed.

The controller has been asked by the president of the company for advice on whether to continue production during May or to suspend the manufacture of solvent until June 1. The controller has assembled the following pertinent data:

**Hipp Industries Inc.**
**Income Statement—Solvent**
**For the Month Ended April 31, 2013**

| | |
|---|---:|
| Sales (2,800 units) | $215,600 |
| Cost of goods sold | 187,320 |
| Gross profit | $ 28,280 |
| Selling and administrative expenses | 41,780 |
| Loss from operations | $ (13,500) |

The production costs and selling and administrative expenses, based on production of 2,800 units in April, are as follows:

| | |
|---|---|
| Direct materials | $30.00 per unit |
| Direct labor | 10.50 per unit |
| Variable manufacturing cost | 9.90 per unit |
| Variable selling and administrative expenses | 5.60 per unit |
| Fixed manufacturing cost | $46,200 for April |
| Fixed selling and administrative expenses | 26,100 for April |

Sales for May are expected to drop about 25% below those of the preceding month. No significant changes are anticipated in the fixed costs or variable costs per unit. No extra costs will be incurred in discontinuing operations in the portion of the plant associated with solvent. The inventory of solvent at the beginning and end of May is expected to be inconsequential.

## Instructions

1. Prepare an estimated income statement in absorption costing form for May for solvent, assuming that production continues during the month. Round amounts to two decimals.

2. Prepare an estimated income statement in variable costing form for May for solvent, assuming that production continues during the month. Round amounts to two decimals.

3. What would be the estimated loss in income from operations if the solvent production were temporarily suspended for May?

4. ➤ What advice should the controller give to management?

---

**OBJ. 1, 2**

✔ **1. b. Income from operations, $14,958**

**PR 20-3A    Absorption and variable costing income statements for two months and analysis**

During the first month of operations ended May 31, 2013, T-Shirt Express Company produced 37,000 designer T-Shirts, of which 34,300 were sold. Operating data for the month are summarized as follows:

| | | |
|---|---:|---:|
| Sales | | $343,000 |
| Manufacturing costs: | | |
| Direct materials | $210,900 | |
| Direct labor | 57,350 | |
| Variable manufacturing cost | 26,640 | |
| Fixed manufacturing cost | 24,420 | 319,310 |
| Selling and administrative expenses: | | |
| Variable | $ 16,464 | |
| Fixed | 12,005 | 28,469 |

During June, T-Shirt Express Company produced 31,600 designer T-shirts and sold 34,300 T-shirts. Operating data for June are summarized as follows:

| | | |
|---|---:|---:|
| Sales | | $343,000 |
| Manufacturing costs: | | |
| Direct materials | $180,120 | |
| Direct labor | 48,980 | |
| Variable manufacturing cost | 22,752 | |
| Fixed manufacturing cost | 24,420 | 276,272 |
| Selling and administrative expenses: | | |
| Variable | $ 16,464 | |
| Fixed | 12,005 | 28,469 |

## Instructions

1. Using the absorption costing concept, prepare income statements for (a) May and (b) June.

2. Using the variable costing concept, prepare income statements for (a) May and (b) June.

3. a. ➤ Explain the reason for the differences in the amount of income from operations in (1) and (2) for May.

   b. ➤ Explain the reason for the differences in the amount of income from operations in (1) and (2) for June.

4. Based on your answers to (1) and (2), did T-Shirt Express Company operate more profitably in May or in June? Explain.

OBJ. 4

✔ 1. Ainge
contribution margin
ratio, 25%

**PR 20-4A Salespersons' report and analysis**

Tavaris Instruments Company employs seven salespersons to sell and distribute its product throughout the state. Data taken from reports received from the salespersons during the year ended December 31, 2012, are as follows:

| Salesperson | Total Sales | Variable Cost of Goods Sold | Variable Selling Expenses |
|---|---|---|---|
| Ainge | $560,000 | $308,000 | $112,000 |
| Brohm | 565,000 | 310,750 | 124,300 |
| Carr | 460,000 | 234,600 | 82,800 |
| Harrell | 510,000 | 188,700 | 102,000 |
| Losman | 530,000 | 259,700 | 100,700 |
| Null | 695,000 | 236,300 | 118,150 |
| Skelton | 500,000 | 245,000 | 100,000 |

**Instructions**

1. Prepare a table indicating contribution margin, variable cost of goods sold as a percent of sales, variable selling expenses as a percent of sales, and contribution margin ratio by salesperson. Round whole percents to a single digit.

2. Which salesperson generated the highest contribution margin ratio for the year and why?

3. Briefly list factors other than contribution margin that should be considered in evaluating the performance of salespersons.

OBJ. 4

✔ 1. Income from
operations,
$107,200

**PR 20-5A Segment variable costing income statement and effect on income of change in operations**

Extreme Camping Company manufactures three sizes of extreme weather tents—small (S), medium (M), and large (L). The income statement has consistently indicated a net loss for the M size, and management is considering three proposals: (1) continue Size M, (2) discontinue Size M and reduce total output accordingly, or (3) discontinue Size M and conduct an advertising campaign to expand the sales of Size S so that the entire plant capacity can continue to be used.

If Proposal 2 is selected and Size M is discontinued and production curtailed, the annual fixed production costs and fixed operating expenses could be reduced by $57,600 and $40,300, respectively. If Proposal 3 is selected, it is anticipated that an additional annual expenditure of $43,200 for the rental of additional warehouse space would yield an increase of 130% in Size S sales volume. It is also assumed that the increased production of Size S would utilize the plant facilities released by the discontinuance of Size M.

The sales and costs have been relatively stable over the past few years, and they are expected to remain so for the foreseeable future. The income statement for the past year ended June 30, 2012, is as follows:

| | Size | | | |
|---|---|---|---|---|
| | S | M | L | Total |
| Sales ............................................. | $835,000 | $ 921,600 | $1,195,200 | $2,951,800 |
| Cost of goods sold: | | | | |
| Variable costs ................................ | $375,000 | $ 446,400 | $ 547,200 | $1,368,600 |
| Fixed costs .................................... | 93,600 | 172,800 | 216,000 | 482,400 |
| Total cost of goods sold ..................... | $468,600 | $ 619,200 | $ 763,200 | $1,851,000 |
| Gross profit .................................... | $366,400 | $ 302,400 | $ 432,000 | $1,100,800 |
| Less operating expenses: | | | | |
| Variable expenses ........................... | $165,600 | $ 194,400 | $ 244,800 | $ 604,800 |
| Fixed expenses .............................. | 115,200 | 129,600 | 144,000 | 388,800 |
| Total operating expenses ................... | $280,800 | $ 324,000 | $ 388,800 | $ 993,600 |
| Income from operations ....................... | $ 85,600 | $ (21,600) | $ 43,200 | $ 107,200 |

**Instructions**

1. Prepare an income statement for the past year in the variable costing format. Use the following headings:

| | Size | | |
|---|---|---|---|
| S | M | L | Total |

*(Continued)*

Data for each style should be reported through contribution margin. The fixed costs should be deducted from the total contribution margin, as reported in the "Total" column, to determine income from operations.

2. Based on the income statement prepared in (1) and the other data presented, determine the amount by which total annual income from operations would be reduced below its present level if Proposal 2 is accepted.

3. Prepare an income statement in the variable costing format, indicating the projected annual income from operations if Proposal 3 is accepted. Use the following headings:

| Size | | |
| --- | --- | --- |
| S | L | Total |

Data for each style should be reported through contribution margin. The fixed costs should be deducted from the total contribution margin as reported in the "Total" column. For purposes of this problem, the expenditure of $43,200 for the rental of additional warehouse space can be added to the fixed operating expenses.

4. By how much would total annual income increase above its present level if Proposal 3 is accepted? Explain.

---

**OBJ. 5**

1. Sales quantity factor, $(220,000)

### PR 20-6A  Contribution margin analysis

Costello Industries Inc. manufactures only one product. For the year ended December 31, 2012, the contribution margin increased by $19,800 from the planned level of $888,800. The president of Costello Industries Inc. has expressed some concern about such a small increase and has requested a follow-up report.

The following data have been gathered from the accounting records for the year ended December 31, 2012:

| | Actual | Planned | Difference—Increase (Decrease) |
| --- | --- | --- | --- |
| Sales | $1,771,000 | $1,760,000 | $ 11,000 |
| Less: | | | |
| Variable cost of goods sold | $ 677,600 | $ 712,800 | $ (35,200) |
| Variable selling and administrative expenses | 184,800 | 158,400 | 26,400 |
| Total | $ 862,400 | $ 871,200 | $ (8,800) |
| Contribution margin | $ 908,600 | $ 888,800 | $ 19,800 |
| Number of units sold | 15,400 | 17,600 | |
| Per unit: | | | |
| Sales price | $115.00 | $100.00 | |
| Variable cost of goods sold | 44.00 | 40.50 | |
| Variable selling and administrative expenses | 12.00 | 9.00 | |

**Instructions**

1. Prepare a contribution margin analysis report for the year ended December 31, 2012.

2. ━━━▶ At a meeting of the board of directors on January 30, 2013, the president, after reviewing the contribution margin analysis report, made the following comment:

*It looks as if the price increase of $15 had the effect of decreasing sales volume. However, this was a favorable tradeoff. The variable cost of goods sold was less than planned. Apparently, we are efficiently managing our variable cost of goods sold. However, the variable selling and administrative expenses appear out of control. Let's look into these expenses and get them under control! Also, let's consider increasing the sales price to $130 and continue this favorable tradeoff between higher price and lower volume.*

Do you agree with the president's comment? Explain.

## Problems Series B

### PR 20-1B   Absorption and variable costing income statements

During the first month of operations ended September 30, 2012, Sungsam Inc. manufactured 3,200 flat panel televisions, of which 3,000 were sold. Operating data for the month are summarized as follows:

| | | |
|---|---:|---:|
| Sales | | $4,275,000 |
| Manufacturing costs: | | |
| Direct materials | $1,680,000 | |
| Direct labor | 720,000 | |
| Variable manufacturing cost | 272,000 | |
| Fixed manufacturing cost | 505,600 | 3,177,600 |
| Selling and administrative expenses: | | |
| Variable | $ 408,000 | |
| Fixed | 195,000 | 603,000 |

### Instructions

1. Prepare an income statement based on the absorption costing concept.

2. Prepare an income statement based on the variable costing concept.

3. Explain the reason for the difference in the amount of income from operations reported in (1) and (2).

### PR 20-2B   Income statements under absorption costing and variable costing

The demand for shampoo, one of numerous products manufactured by Ziggy Hair Care Products Inc., has dropped sharply because of recent competition from a similar product. The company's chemists are currently completing tests of various new formulas, and it is anticipated that the manufacture of a superior product can be started on March 1, one month in the future. No changes will be needed in the present production facilities to manufacture the new product because only the mixture of the various materials will be changed.

The controller has been asked by the president of the company for advice on whether to continue production during February or to suspend the manufacture of shampoo until March 1. The controller has assembled the following pertinent data:

**Ziggy Hair Care Products Inc.**
**Income Statement—Shampoo**
**For the Month Ended January 31, 2012**

| | |
|---|---:|
| Sales (294,000 units) | $15,582,000 |
| Cost of goods sold | 14,250,000 |
| Gross profit | $ 1,332,000 |
| Selling and administrative expenses | 2,149,800 |
| Loss from operations | $  (817,800) |

The production costs and selling and administrative expenses, based on production of 294,000 units in January, are as follows:

| | |
|---|---|
| Direct materials | $     9.50 per unit |
| Direct labor | 12.00 per unit |
| Variable manufacturing cost | 23.50 per unit |
| Variable selling and administrative expenses | 6.70 per unit |
| Fixed manufacturing cost | 1,020,000 for January |
| Fixed selling and administrative expenses | 180,000 for January |

Sales for February are expected to drop about 30% below those of the preceding month. No significant changes are anticipated in the fixed costs or variable costs per unit. No extra costs will be incurred in discontinuing operations in the portion of the plant associated with shampoo. The inventory of shampoo at the beginning and end of February is expected to be inconsequential.

### Instructions

1. Prepare an estimated income statement in absorption costing form for February for shampoo, assuming that production continues during the month.

2. Prepare an estimated income statement in variable costing form for February for shampoo, assuming that production continues during the month.

3. What would be the estimated loss in income from operations if the shampoo production were temporarily suspended for February?

4. ▬▬▬▬▶ What advice should the controller give to management?

---

**OBJ. 1, 2**

✔ 2. a. Manufacturing margin, $58,500

**PR 20-3B   Absorption and variable costing income statements for two months and analysis**

During the first month of operations ended July 31, 2012, Lids R' Us Inc. manufactured 8,000 hats, of which 6,500 were sold. Operating data for the month are summarized as follows:

| | | |
|---|---:|---:|
| Sales | | $162,500 |
| Baking costs: | | |
| Direct materials | $73,600 | |
| Direct labor | 35,200 | |
| Variable manufacturing cost | 19,200 | |
| Fixed manufacturing cost | 24,000 | 152,000 |
| Selling and administrative expenses: | | |
| Variable | $16,900 | |
| Fixed | 7,800 | 24,700 |

During August, Lids R' Us Inc. manufactured 5,000 hats and sold 6,500 hats. Operating data for August are summarized as follows:

| | | |
|---|---:|---:|
| Sales | | $162,500 |
| Baking costs: | | |
| Direct materials | $46,000 | |
| Direct labor | 22,000 | |
| Variable manufacturing cost | 12,000 | |
| Fixed manufacturing cost | 24,000 | 104,000 |
| Selling and administrative expenses: | | |
| Variable | $16,900 | |
| Fixed | 7,800 | 24,700 |

**Instructions**

1. Using the absorption costing concept, prepare income statements for (a) July and (b) August.

2. Using the variable costing concept, prepare income statements for (a) July and (b) August.

3. a. ▬▬▬▶ Explain the reason for the differences in the amount of income from operations in (1) and (2) for July.

   b. ▬▬▬▶ Explain the reason for the differences in the amount of income from operations in (1) and (2) for August.

4. Based on your answers to (1) and (2), did Lids R' Us Inc. operate more profitably in July or in August? Explain.

---

**OBJ. 4**

✔ 1. Kitna contribution margin ratio, 40%

**PR 20-4B   Salespersons' report and analysis**

Kuhn Inc. employs seven salespersons to sell and distribute its product throughout the state. Data taken from reports received from the salespersons during the year ended June 30, 2012, are as follows:

| Salesperson | Total Sales | Variable Cost of Goods Sold | Variable Selling Expenses |
|---|---:|---:|---:|
| Boot | $350,000 | $150,500 | $ 63,000 |
| Canfield | 456,000 | 173,280 | 68,400 |
| Hamdan | 540,000 | 237,600 | 108,000 |
| Kitna | 470,000 | 188,000 | 94,000 |
| Martin | 420,000 | 163,800 | 96,600 |
| Palko | 470,000 | 188,000 | 75,200 |
| Shockley | 460,000 | 193,200 | 87,400 |

**Instructions**

1. Prepare a table indicating contribution margin, variable cost of goods sold as a percent of sales, variable selling expenses as a percent of sales, and contribution margin ratio by salesperson. (Round whole percent to one digit after decimal point).

2. Which salesperson generated the highest contribution margin ratio for the year and why?

3. Briefly list factors other than contribution margin that should be considered in evaluating the performance of salespersons.

---

**OBJ. 4**

✔ 3. Income from operations, $141,710

**PR 20-5B    Variable costing income statement and effect on income of change in operations**

Freebird, Inc., manufactures three sizes of industrial work benches—small (S), medium (M), and large (L). The income statement has consistently indicated a net loss for the M size, and management is considering three proposals: (1) continue Size M, (2) discontinue Size M and reduce total output accordingly, or (3) discontinue Size M and conduct an advertising campaign to expand the sales of Size S so that the entire plant capacity can continue to be used.

If Proposal 2 is selected and Size M is discontinued and production curtailed, the annual fixed production costs and fixed operating expenses could be reduced by $190,000 and $37,800, respectively. If Proposal 3 is selected, it is anticipated that an additional annual expenditure of $113,400 for the salary of an assistant brand manager (classified as a fixed operating expense) would yield an increase of 130% in Size S sales volume. It is also assumed that the increased production of Size S would utilize the plant facilities released by the discontinuance of Size M.

The sales and costs have been relatively stable over the past few years, and they are expected to remain so for the foreseeable future. The income statement for the past year ended January 31, 2013, is as follows:

|  | Size | | | |
|---|---|---|---|---|
|  | **S** | **M** | **L** | **Total** |
| Sales | $1,320,000 | $1,450,000 | $1,260,000 | $4,030,000 |
| Cost of goods sold: |  |  |  |  |
| Variable costs | $ 718,000 | $ 958,000 | $ 756,000 | $2,432,000 |
| Fixed costs | 321,300 | 384,000 | 334,000 | 1,039,300 |
| Total cost of goods sold | $1,039,300 | $1,342,000 | $1,090,000 | $3,471,300 |
| Gross profit | $ 280,700 | $ 108,000 | $ 170,000 | $ 558,700 |
| Less operating expenses: |  |  |  |  |
| Variable expenses | $ 157,500 | $ 145,000 | $ 113,400 | $ 415,900 |
| Fixed expenses | 42,840 | 56,700 | 19,000 | 118,540 |
| Total operating expenses | $ 200,340 | $ 201,700 | $ 132,400 | $ 534,440 |
| Income from operations | $ 80,360 | $ (93,700) | $ 37,600 | $ 24,260 |

**Instructions**

1. Prepare an income statement for the past year in the variable costing format. Use the following headings:

| Size | | |
|---|---|---|
| S | M | L | Total |

Data for each style should be reported through contribution margin. The fixed costs should be deducted from the total contribution margin, as reported in the "Total" column, to determine income from operations.

2. Based on the income statement prepared in (1) and the other data presented above, determine the amount by which total annual income from operations would be reduced below its present level if Proposal 2 is accepted.

3. Prepare an income statement in the variable costing format, indicating the projected annual income from operations if Proposal 3 is accepted. Use the following headings:

| Size | |
|---|---|
| S | L | Total |

Data for each style should be reported through contribution margin. The fixed costs should be deducted from the total contribution margin as reported in the "Total" column. For purposes of this problem, the additional expenditure of $113,400 for the assistant brand manager's salary can be added to the fixed operating expenses.

4. By how much would total annual income increase above its present level if Proposal 3 is accepted? Explain.

---

**OBJ. 5**

✔ 1. Sales quantity factor, $215,625

### PR 20-6B    Contribution margin analysis

Lawrence Company manufactures only one product. For the year ended December 31, 2012, the contribution margin decreased by $87,500 from the planned level of $375,000. The president of Lawrence Company has expressed some concern about this decrease and has requested a follow-up report.

The following data have been gathered from the accounting records for the year ended December 31, 2012:

|  | Actual | Planned | Difference—Increase or (Decrease) |
|---|---|---|---|
| Sales | $1,581,250 | $1,437,500 | $143,750 |
| Less: | | | |
| Variable cost of goods sold | $ 718,750 | $ 687,500 | $ 31,250 |
| Variable selling and administrative expenses | 575,000 | 375,000 | 200,000 |
| Total | $1,293,750 | $1,062,500 | $231,250 |
| Contribution margin | $ 287,500 | $ 375,000 | $ (87,500) |
| Number of units sold | 28,750 | 25,000 | |
| Per unit: | | | |
| Sales price | $55.00 | $57.50 | |
| Variable cost of goods sold | 25.00 | 27.50 | |
| Variable selling and administrative expenses | 20.00 | 15.00 | |

### Instructions

1. Prepare a contribution margin analysis report for the year ended December 31, 2012.

2. ━━━▶ At a meeting of the board of directors on January 30, 2013, the president, after reviewing the contribution margin analysis report, made the following comment:

*"It looks as if the price decrease of $2.50 had the effect of increasing sales. However, we lost control over the variable cost of goods sold and variable selling and administrative expenses. Let's look into these expenses and get them under control! Also, let's consider decreasing the sales price to $50 to increase sales further."*

Do you agree with the president's comment? Explain.

---

## Cases & Projects

You can access Cases & Projects online at **www.cengage.com/accounting/reeve**

© StockShot/Alamy

# Budgeting

## The North Face

**Y**ou may have financial goals for your life. To achieve these goals, it is necessary to plan for future expenses. For example, you may consider taking a part-time job to save money for school expenses for the coming school year. How much money would you need to earn and save in order to pay these expenses? One way to find an answer to this question would be to prepare a budget. A budget would show an estimate of your expenses associated with school, such as tuition, fees, and books. In addition, you would have expenses for day-to-day living, such as rent, food, and clothing. You might also have expenses for travel and entertainment. Once the school year begins, you can use the budget as a tool for guiding your spending priorities during the year.

The budget is used in businesses in much the same way as it can be used in personal life. For example, **The North Face** sponsors mountain climbing expeditions throughout the year for professional and amateur climbers. These events require budgeting to plan trip expenses, much like you might use a budget to plan a vacation.

Budgeting is also used by The North Face to plan the manufacturing costs associated with its outdoor clothing and equipment production. For example, budgets would be used to determine the number of coats to be produced, number of people to be employed, and amount of material to be purchased. The budget provides the company with a "game plan" for the year. In this chapter, you will see how budgets can be used for financial planning and control.

**OBJ. 1** Describe budgeting, its objectives, and its impact on human behavior.

The chart below shows the estimated portion of your total monthly income that should be budgeted for various living expenses according to the Consumer Credit Counseling Service.

- Savings 8%
- Entertainment 6%
- Housing 30%
- Transportation 15%
- Clothing 7%
- Utilities 5%
- Other essentials 4%
- Medical 5%
- Food 20%

# Nature and Objectives of Budgeting

**Budgets** play an important role for organizations of all sizes and forms. For example, budgets are used in managing the operations of government agencies, churches, hospitals, and other nonprofit organizations. Individuals and families also use budgeting in managing their financial affairs. This chapter describes and illustrates budgeting for a manufacturing company.

## Objectives of Budgeting

Budgeting involves (1) establishing specific goals, (2) executing plans to achieve the goals, and (3) periodically comparing actual results with the goals. In doing so, budgeting affects the following managerial functions:

1. Planning
2. Directing
3. Controlling

The relationships of these activities are illustrated in Exhibit 1.

*Planning* involves setting goals to guide decisions and help motivate employees. The planning process often identifies where operations can be improved.

**EXHIBIT 1**     **Planning, Directing, and Controlling**

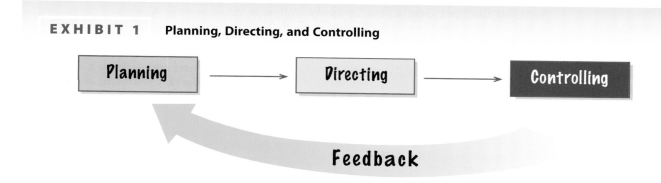

*Directing* involves decisions and actions to achieve budgeted goals. A budgetary unit of a company is called a **responsibility center**. Each responsibility center is led by a manager who has the authority and responsibility for achieving the center's budgeted goals.

*Controlling* involves comparing actual performance against the budgeted goals. Such comparisons provide feedback to managers and employees about their performance. If necessary, responsibility centers can use such feedback to adjust their activities in the future.

## Human Behavior and Budgeting

Human behavior problems can arise in the budgeting process in the following situations:

1. Budgeted goals are set too tight, which are very hard or impossible to achieve
2. Budgeted goals are set too loose, which are very easy to achieve
3. Budgeted goals conflict with the objectives of the company and employees

These behavior problems are illustrated in Exhibit 2.

**EXHIBIT 2**

**Human Behavior Problems in Budgeting**

**Setting Budget Goals Too Tightly**  Employees and managers may become discouraged if budgeted goals are set too high. That is, if budgeted goals are viewed as unrealistic or unachievable, the budget may have a negative effect on the ability of the company to achieve its goals.

Reasonable, attainable goals are more likely to motivate employees and managers. For this reason, it is important for employees and managers to be involved in the budgeting process. Involving employees in the budgeting process provides them with a sense of control and, thus, more of a commitment in meeting budgeted goals.

**Setting Budget Goals Too Loosely** Although it is desirable to establish attainable goals, it is undesirable to plan budget goals that are too easy. Such budget "padding" is termed **budgetary slack**. Managers may plan slack in their budgets to provide a "cushion" for unexpected events. However, if the budget is not spent by the end of the period, senior management may determine that the responsibility center should have a reduced budget. This may cause responsibility managers to spend budgetary resources at the end of the period rather than risk losing them. This can be wasteful.

**Setting Conflicting Budget Goals** **Goal conflict** occurs when the employees' or managers' self-interest differs from the company's objectives or goals. Goal conflict may also occur among responsibility centers such as departments. To illustrate, assume that the sales department manager is given an increased sales goal and as a result accepts customers who are poor credit risks. This, in turn, causes bad debt expense to increase and profitability to decline.

## Integrity, Objectivity, and Ethics in Business

**BUDGET GAMES**

The budgeting system is designed to plan and control a business. However, it is common for the budget to be "gamed" by its participants. For example, managers may pad their budgets with excess resources. In this way, the managers have additional resources for unexpected events during the period. If the budget is being used to establish the incentive plan, then sales managers have incentives to understate the sales potential of a territory to ensure hitting their quotas. Other times, managers engage in "land grabbing," which occurs when they overstate the sales potential of a territory to guarantee access to resources. If managers believe that unspent resources will not roll over to future periods, then they may be encouraged to "spend it or lose it," causing wasteful expenditures. These types of problems can be partially overcome by separating the budget into planning and incentive components. This is why many organizations have two budget processes, one for resource planning and another, more challenging budget, for motivating managers.

---

**OBJ. 2** Describe the basic elements of the budget process, the two major types of budgeting, and the use of computers in budgeting.

# Budgeting Systems

Budgeting systems vary among companies and industries. For example, the budget system used by Ford Motor Company differs from that used by Delta Air Lines. However, the basic budgeting concepts discussed in this section apply to all types of businesses and organizations.

The budgetary period for operating activities normally includes the fiscal year of a company. A year is short enough that future operations can be estimated fairly accurately, yet long enough that the future can be viewed in a broad context. However, for control purposes, annual budgets are usually subdivided into shorter time periods, such as quarters of the year, months, or weeks.

A variation of fiscal-year budgeting, called **continuous budgeting**, maintains a 12-month projection into the future. The 12-month budget is continually revised by replacing the data for the month just ended with the budget data for the same month in the next year. A continuous budget is illustrated in Exhibit 3.

Developing an annual budget usually begins several months prior to the end of the current year. This responsibility is normally assigned to a budget committee. Such a committee often consists of the budget director, the controller, the treasurer, the production manager, and the sales manager. The budget process is monitored and summarized by the Accounting Department, which reports to the committee.

**EXHIBIT 3** **Continuous Budgeting**

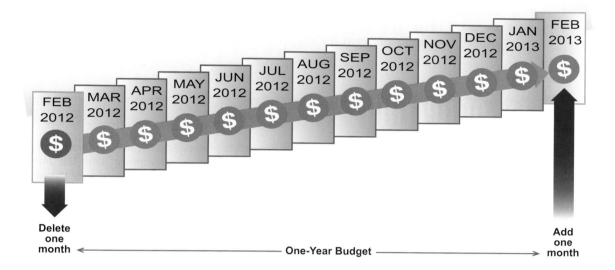

FEB 2012 — MAR 2012 — APR 2012 — MAY 2012 — JUN 2012 — JUL 2012 — AUG 2012 — SEP 2012 — OCT 2012 — NOV 2012 — DEC 2012 — JAN 2013 — FEB 2013

Delete one month ← —————— One-Year Budget —————— → Add one month

There are several methods of developing budget estimates. One method, termed **zero-based budgeting**, requires managers to estimate sales, production, and other operating data as though operations are being started for the first time. This approach has the benefit of taking a fresh view of operations each year. A more common approach is to start with last year's budget and revise it for actual results and expected changes for the coming year. Two major budgets using this approach are the static budget and the flexible budget.

## Static Budget

A **static budget** shows the expected results of a responsibility center for only one activity level. Once the budget has been determined, it is not changed, even if the activity changes. Static budgeting is used by many service companies, governmental entities, and for some functions of manufacturing companies, such as purchasing, engineering, and accounting.

To illustrate, the static budget for the Assembly Department of Colter Manufacturing Company is shown in Exhibit 4.

**Static Budget**

| | A | B |
|---|---|---|
| 1 | Colter Manufacturing Company | |
| 2 | Assembly Department Budget | |
| 3 | For the Year Ending July 31, 2012 | |
| 4 | Direct labor | $40,000 |
| 5 | Electric power | 5,000 |
| 6 | Supervisor salaries | 15,000 |
| 7 | Total department costs | $60,000 |
| 8 | | |

A disadvantage of static budgets is that they do not adjust for changes in activity levels. For example, assume that the Assembly Department of Colter Manufacturing spent $70,800 for the year ended July 31, 2012. Thus, the Assembly Department spent

$10,800 ($70,800 – $60,000), or 18% ($10,800/$60,000) more than budgeted. Is this good news or bad news?

The first reaction is that this is bad news and the Assembly Department was inefficient in spending more than budgeted. However, assume that the Assembly Department's budget was based on plans to assemble 8,000 units during the year. If 10,000 units were actually assembled, the additional $10,800 spent in excess of budget might be good news. That is, the Assembly Department assembled 25% (2,000 units/8,000 units) more than planned for only 18% more cost.

## BusinessConnection

### U.S. FEDERAL BUDGET DEFICIT

Budgeting is an important tool used by municipalities, states, and federal governments to control expenditures. Many states are required by law to have balanced budgets. That is, the amount of money received from taxes and other revenues must be greater than or equal to the planned expenditures for state services. The U.S. federal government, however, may run a budget deficit. A *deficit* is the excess of expenditures over revenues. The deficit is paid for by issuing government debt. The amount of deficit a nation can sustain is a function of the size of its economy. Thus, the deficit is often measured as a percentage of gross domestic product (GDP), a measure of the nation's output of goods and services. The deficit as a percent of GDP for the United States over the last several decades is as follows:

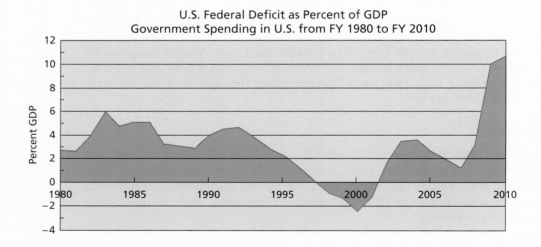

U.S. Federal Deficit as Percent of GDP
Government Spending in U.S. from FY 1980 to FY 2010

As can be seen, the budget deficit has jumped above 10% of GDP in response to the recession that began in 2008. While a nation may increase a deficit to above 10% of GDP temporarily, keeping a budget deficit above 10% for a long period of time typically slows a nation's economic growth.

Source: Carmen Reinhart and Kenneth Rogoff, *This Time Its Different: Eight Centuries of Financial Folly* (Princeton University Press, 2009).

## Flexible Budget

**Note:**
**Flexible budgets show expected results for several activity levels.**

Unlike static budgets, **flexible budgets** show the expected results of a responsibility center for several activity levels. A flexible budget is, in effect, a series of static budgets for different levels of activity.

To illustrate, a flexible budget for the Assembly Department of Colter Manufacturing Company is shown in Exhibit 5.

**EXHIBIT 5**

**Flexible Budget**

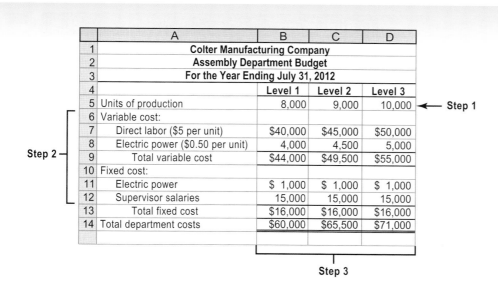

|  | A | B | C | D |
|---|---|---|---|---|
| 1 | Colter Manufacturing Company | | | |
| 2 | Assembly Department Budget | | | |
| 3 | For the Year Ending July 31, 2012 | | | |
| 4 |  | Level 1 | Level 2 | Level 3 |
| 5 | Units of production | 8,000 | 9,000 | 10,000 |
| 6 | Variable cost: | | | |
| 7 | Direct labor ($5 per unit) | $40,000 | $45,000 | $50,000 |
| 8 | Electric power ($0.50 per unit) | 4,000 | 4,500 | 5,000 |
| 9 | Total variable cost | $44,000 | $49,500 | $55,000 |
| 10 | Fixed cost: | | | |
| 11 | Electric power | $ 1,000 | $ 1,000 | $ 1,000 |
| 12 | Supervisor salaries | 15,000 | 15,000 | 15,000 |
| 13 | Total fixed cost | $16,000 | $16,000 | $16,000 |
| 14 | Total department costs | $60,000 | $65,500 | $71,000 |

A flexible budget is constructed as follows:

Step 1. Identify the relevant activity levels. The relevant levels of activity could be expressed in units, machine hours, direct labor hours, or some other activity base. In Exhibit 5, the levels of activity are 8,000, 9,000, and 10,000 units of production.

Step 2. Identify the fixed and variable cost components of the costs being budgeted. In Exhibit 5, the electric power cost is separated into its fixed cost ($1,000 per year) and variable cost ($0.50 per unit). The direct labor is a variable cost, and the supervisor salaries are all fixed costs.

Step 3. Prepare the budget for each activity level by multiplying the variable cost per unit by the activity level and then adding the monthly fixed cost.

With a flexible budget, actual costs can be compared to the budgeted costs for actual activity. To illustrate, assume that the Assembly Department spent $70,800 to produce 10,000 units. Exhibit 5 indicates that the Assembly Department was *under* budget by $200 ($71,000 – $70,800).

Under the static budget in Exhibit 4, the Assembly Department was $10,800 *over* budget. This comparison is illustrated in Exhibit 6.

The flexible budget for the Assembly Department is much more accurate and useful than the static budget. This is because the flexible budget adjusts for changes in the level of activity.

**EXHIBIT 6**  **Static and Flexible Budgets**

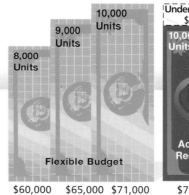

## Example Exercise ▶ 21-1 ▶ Flexible Budgeting

**OBJ. 2**

At the beginning of the period, the Assembly Department budgeted direct labor of $45,000 and supervisor salaries of $30,000 for 5,000 hours of production. The department actually completed 6,000 hours of production. Determine the budget for the department, assuming that it uses flexible budgeting.

### Follow My Example ▶ 21-1 ▶

| | |
|---|---:|
| Variable cost: | |
| Direct labor (6,000 hours × $9* per hour) ........................................ | $54,000 |
| Fixed cost: | |
| Supervisor salaries......................................................... | 30,000 |
| Total department costs ...................................................... | $84,000 |

*$45,000/5,000 hours

Practice Exercises: **PE 21-1A, PE 21-1B**

## Computerized Budgeting Systems

In developing budgets, companies use a variety of computerized approaches. Two of the most popular computerized approaches use:

1. Spreadsheet software such as Microsoft Excel
2. Integrated budget and planning (B&P) software systems

Fujitsu, a Japanese technology company, used B&P to reduce its budgeting process from 6–8 weeks down to 10–15 days.

Spreadsheets ease budget preparation by summarizing budget information in linked spreadsheets across the organization. In addition, the impact of proposed changes in various assumptions or operating alternatives can be analyzed on a speadsheet.

B&P software systems use the Web (Intranet) to link thousands of employees together during the budget process. Employees can input budget data onto Web pages that are integrated and summarized throughout the company. In this way, a company can quickly and consistently integrate top-level strategies and goals to lower-level operational goals.

# BusinessConnection

### BUILD VERSUS HARVEST

Budgeting systems are not "one size fits all" solutions but must adapt to the underlying business conditions. For example, a business can adopt either a build strategy or a harvest strategy. A *build* strategy is one where the business is designing, launching, and growing new products and markets. Build strategies often require short-term profit sacrifice in order to grow market share. Apple, Inc.'s iPad® is an example of a product managed under a build strategy. A *harvest* strategy is often employed for business units with mature products enjoying high market share in low-growth industries. H.J. Heinz Company's Ketchup® and P&G's *Ivory* soap are examples of such products. A build strategy often

has greater uncertainty, unpredictability, and change than a harvest strategy. The difference between these strategies implies different budgeting approaches.

The build strategy should employ a budget approach that is flexible to the uncertainty of the business. Thus, budgets should adapt to changing conditions by allowing periodic revisions and flexible targets. The budget serves as a short-term planning tool to guide management in executing an uncertain and evolving product market strategy.

In a harvest strategy, the business is often much more stable and is managed to maximize profitability and cash flow. Because cost control is much more important in this strategy, the budget is used to restrict the actions of managers.

# Master Budget

**OBJ. 3** Describe the master budget for a manufacturing company.

The **master budget** is an integrated set of operating, investing, and financing budgets for a period of time. Most companies prepare the master budget on a yearly basis.

For a manufacturing company, the master budget consists of the following integrated budgets:

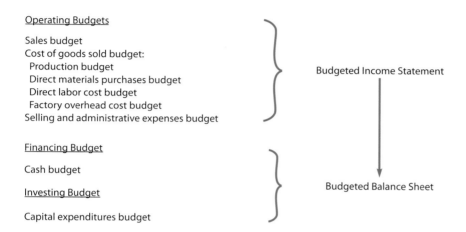

As shown above, the master budget is an integrated set of budgets that tie together a company's operating, financing, and investing activities into an integrated plan for the coming year.

The master budget begins with preparing the operating budgets, which form the budgeted income statement. The income statement budgets are normally prepared in the following order beginning with the sales budget:

1. Sales budget
2. Production budget
3. Direct materials purchases budget
4. Direct labor cost budget
5. Factory overhead cost budget
6. Cost of goods sold budget
7. Selling and administrative expenses budget
8. Budgeted income statement

After the budgeted income statement is prepared, the budgeted balance sheet is prepared. Two major budgets comprising the budgeted balance sheet are the cash budget and the capital expenditures budget.

Exhibit 7 shows the relationships among the income statement budgets.

**EXHIBIT 7**

**Income
Statement
Budgets**

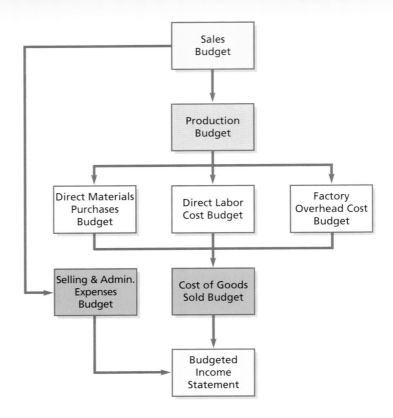

**OBJ.
4** Prepare the
basic income
statement budgets
for a manufacturing
company.

# Income Statement Budgets

The integrated budgets that support the income statement budget are described and illustrated in this section. Elite Accessories Inc., a small manufacturing company, is used as a basis for illustration.

## Sales Budget

The **sales budget** begins by estimating the quantity of sales. As a starting point, the prior year's sales quantities are often used. These sales quantities are then revised for such factors as the following:

1. Backlog of unfilled sales orders from the prior period
2. Planned advertising and promotion
3. Productive capacity
4. Projected pricing changes
5. Findings of market research studies
6. Expected industry and general economic conditions

Once sales quantities are estimated, the expected sales revenue can be determined by multiplying the volume by the expected unit sales price.

To illustrate, Elite Accessories Inc. manufactures wallets and handbags that are sold in two regions, the East and West regions. Elite Accessories estimates the following sales quantities and prices for 2012:

|  | East Region | West Region | Unit Selling Price |
|---|---|---|---|
| Wallets | 287,000 | 241,000 | $12 |
| Handbags | 156,400 | 123,600 | 25 |

Exhibit 8 illustrates the sales budget for Elite Accessories based on the preceding data.

EXHIBIT 8

Sales Budget

| | A | B | C | D |
|---|---|---|---|---|
| 1 | Elite Accessories Inc. | | | |
| 2 | Sales Budget | | | |
| 3 | For the Year Ending December 31, 2012 | | | |
| 4 | | Unit Sales | Unit Selling | |
| 5 | **Product and Region** | Volume | Price | Total Sales |
| 6 | Wallet: | 287,000 | $12.00 | $ 3,444,000 |
| 7 | East | 241,000 | 12.00 | 2,892,000 |
| 8 | West | 528,000 | | $ 6,336,000 |
| 9 | Total | | | |
| 10 | | | | |
| 11 | Handbag: | | | |
| 12 | East | 156,400 | $25.00 | $ 3,910,000 |
| 13 | West | 123,600 | 25.00 | 3,090,000 |
| 14 | Total | 280,000 | | $ 7,000,000 |
| 15 | | | | |
| 16 | Total revenue from sales | | | $13,336,000 |

## Production Budget

The production budget should be integrated with the sales budget to ensure that production and sales are kept in balance during the year. The **production budget** estimates the number of units to be manufactured to meet budgeted sales and desired inventory levels. The budgeted units to be produced are determined as follows:

| | |
|---|---|
| Expected units to be sold | XXX units |
| Plus desired units in ending inventory | + XXX |
| Less estimated units in beginning inventory | – XXX |
| Total units to be produced | XXX units |

Elite Accessories Inc. expects the following inventories of wallets and handbags:

| | Estimated Inventory January 1, 2012 | Desired Inventory December 31, 2012 |
|---|---|---|
| Wallets | 88,000 | 80,000 |
| Handbags | 48,000 | 60,000 |

Exhibit 9 illustrates the production budget for Elite Accessories Inc.

EXHIBIT 9

Production Budget

| | A | B | C |
|---|---|---|---|
| 1 | Elite Accessories Inc. | | |
| 2 | Production Budget | | |
| 3 | For the Year Ending December 31, 2012 | | |
| 4 | | Units | |
| 5 | | Wallet | Handbag |
| 6 | Expected units to be sold (from Exhibit 8) | 528,000 | 280,000 |
| 7 | Plus desired ending inventory, December 31, 2012 | 80,000 | 60,000 |
| 8 | Total | 608,000 | 340,000 |
| 9 | Less estimated beginning inventory, January 1, 2012 | 88,000 | 48,000 |
| 10 | Total units to be produced | 520,000 | 292,000 |

A spreadsheet can be used to create a sales budget, as illustrated below:

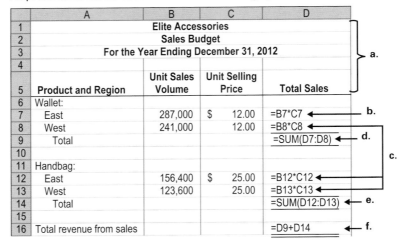

a. Format the budget in a spreadsheet, centering the heading in merged cells over four columns. Enter row text and data in the first three columns as shown.

b. Enter in cell D7 the formula that calculates the total sales for the first line of data (East region, wallet), =B7*C7.

c. Copy cell D7 to D8, D12, and D13. Thus, the product of the units sales volume and unit selling price are now calculated for each region.

d. Enter in D9 the formula to sum cells D7 and D8, =SUM(D7:D8).

e. Copy D9 to D14.

f. Enter in D16 the formula to sum the two region, =D9+D14.

The remaining budgets illustrated in this chapter can also be constructed on a spreadsheet using appropriate formulas and cell references. The complete master budget is shown on a spreadsheet at the end of this chapter illustrating selected formula entries.

**TryIt** Go to the hands-on **Excel Tutor** for this example!

**Example Exercise ▶ 21-2 ▶ Production Budget** **OBJ. 4**

Landon Awards Co. projected sales of 45,000 brass plaques for 2012. The estimated January 1, 2012, inventory is 3,000 units, and the desired December 31, 2012, inventory is 5,000 units. What is the budgeted production (in units) for 2012?

**Follow My Example ▶ 21-2 ▶**

| | |
|---|---:|
| Expected units to be sold . . . . . . . . . . . . . . . . . . . . . . . . . . . . . . . . . . . . . . . . . . . . . . . | 45,000 |
| Plus desired ending inventory, December 31, 2012 . . . . . . . . . . . . . . . . . . . . . . . . . . . . . | 5,000 |
| Total . . . . . . . . . . . . . . . . . . . . . . . . . . . . . . . . . . . . . . . . . . . . . . . . . . . . . . . . . . . . . . | 50,000 |
| Less estimated beginning inventory, January 1, 2012 . . . . . . . . . . . . . . . . . . . . . . . . . . . | 3,000 |
| Total units to be produced . . . . . . . . . . . . . . . . . . . . . . . . . . . . . . . . . . . . . . . . . . . . | 47,000 |

Practice Exercises: **PE 21-2A, PE 21-2B**

## Direct Materials Purchases Budget

The direct materials purchases budget should be integrated with the production budget to ensure that production is not interrupted during the year. The **direct materials purchases budget** estimates the quantities of direct materials to be purchased to support budgeted production and desired inventory levels.

The direct materials to be purchased are determined as follows:

| | |
|---|---:|
| Materials required for production | XXX |
| Plus desired ending materials inventory | + XXX |
| Less estimated beginning materials inventory | − XXX |
| Direct materials to be purchased | XXX |

Elite Accessories Inc. uses leather and lining in producing wallets and handbags. The quantity of direct materials expected to be used for each unit of product is as follows:

| **Wallet** | **Handbag** |
|---|---|
| Leather: 0.30 sq. yd. per unit | Leather: 1.25 sq. yds. per unit |
| Lining: 0.10 sq. yd. per unit | Lining: 0.50 sq. yd. per unit |

Elite Accessories Inc. expects the following direct materials inventories of leather and lining:

| | **Estimated Direct Materials Inventory January 1, 2012** | **Desired Direct Materials Inventory December 31, 2012** |
|---|---|---|
| Leather | 18,000 sq. yds. | 20,000 sq. yds. |
| Lining | 15,000 sq. yds. | 12,000 sq. yds. |

The estimated price per square yard of leather and lining during 2012 is shown below.

| | **Price per Square Yard** |
|---|---|
| Leather | $4.50 |
| Lining | 1.20 |

Exhibit 10 illustrates the direct materials purchases budget for Elite Accessories Inc. The timing of the direct materials purchases should be coordinated between the purchasing and production departments so that production is not interrupted.

| | A | B | C | D | E |
|---|---|---|---|---|---|
| 1 | | Elite Accessories Inc. | | | |
| 2 | | Direct Materials Purchases Budget | | | |
| 3 | | For the Year Ending December 31, 2012 | | | |
| 4 | | | Direct Materials | | |
| 5 | | | Leather | Lining | Total |
| 6 | Square yards required for production: | | | | |
| 7 | Wallet (Note A) | | 156,000 | 52,000 | |
| 8 | Handbag (Note B) | | 365,000 | 146,000 | |
| 9 | Plus desired inventory, December 31, 2012 | | 20,000 | 12,000 | |
| 10 | Total | | 541,000 | 210,000 | |
| 11 | Less estimated inventory, January 1, 2012 | | 18,000 | 15,000 | |
| 12 | Total square yards to be purchased | | 523,000 | 195,000 | |
| 13 | Unit price (per square yard) | | × $4.50 | × $1.20 | |
| 14 | Total direct materials to be purchased | | $2,353,500 | $234,000 | $2,587,500 |
| 15 | | | | | |
| 16 | Note A: | Leather: 520,000 units × 0.30 sq. yd. per unit = 156,000 sq. yds. | | | |
| 17 | | Lining: 520,000 units × 0.10 sq. yd. per unit = 52,000 sq. yds. | | | |
| 18 | | | | | |
| 19 | Note B: | Leather: 292,000 units × 1.25 sq. yds. per unit = 365,000 sq. yds. | | | |
| 20 | | Lining: 292,000 units × 0.50 sq. yd. per unit = 146,000 sq. yds. | | | |
| | | | | | |

**EXHIBIT 10**

**Direct Materials Purchases Budget**

*Example Exercise* **21-3** **Direct Materials Purchases Budget**

OBJ. 4

Landon Awards Co. budgeted production of 47,000 brass plaques in 2012. Brass sheet is required to produce a brass plaque. Assume 96 square inches of brass sheet are required for each brass plaque. The estimated January 1, 2012, brass sheet inventory is 240,000 square inches. The desired December 31, 2012, brass sheet inventory is 200,000 square inches. If brass sheet costs $0.12 per square inch, determine the direct materials purchases budget for 2012.

*(continued)*

**Follow My Example 21-3**

| | |
|---|---|
| Square inches required for production: | |
| Brass sheet (47,000 × 96 sq. in.) .......................................... | 4,512,000 |
| Plus desired ending inventory, December 31, 2012 ......................... | 200,000 |
| Total ...................................................................... | 4,712,000 |
| Less estimated beginning inventory, January 1, 2012 ...................... | 240,000 |
| Total square inches to be purchased ...................................... | 4,472,000 |
| Unit price (per square inch) .............................................. | × $0.12 |
| Total direct materials to be purchased ................................... | $ 536,640 |

Practice Exercises: **PE 21-3A, PE 21-3B**

## Direct Labor Cost Budget

The **direct labor cost budget** estimates the direct labor hours and related cost needed to support budgeted production.

Elite Accessories Inc. estimates that the following direct labor hours are needed to produce a wallet and handbag:

| Wallet | Handbag |
|---|---|
| Cutting Department: 0.10 hr. per unit | Cutting Department: 0.15 hr. per unit |
| Sewing Department: 0.25 hr. per unit | Sewing Department: 0.40 hr. per unit |

The estimated direct labor hourly rates for the Cutting and Sewing departments during 2012 are shown below.

| | Hourly Rate |
|---|---|
| Cutting Department | $12 |
| Sewing Department | 15 |

Exhibit 11 illustrates the direct labor cost budget for Elite Accessories Inc.

**EXHIBIT 11**

**Direct Labor Cost Budget**

| | A | B | C | D | E |
|---|---|---|---|---|---|
| 1 | | Elite Accessories Inc. | | | |
| 2 | | Direct Labor Cost Budget | | | |
| 3 | | For the Year Ending December 31, 2012 | | | |
| 4 | | | Cutting | Sewing | Total |
| 5 | Hours required for production: | | | | |
| 6 | Wallet (Note A) | | 52,000 | 130,000 | |
| 7 | Handbag (Note B) | | 43,800 | 116,800 | |
| 8 | Total | | 95,800 | 246,800 | |
| 9 | Hourly rate | | × $12.00 | × $15.00 | |
| 10 | Total direct labor cost | | $1,149,600 | $3,702,000 | $4,851,600 |
| 11 | | | | | |
| 12 | Note A: | Cutting Department: 520,000 units × 0.10 hr. per unit = 52,000 hrs. | | | |
| 13 | | Sewing Department: 520,000 units × 0.25 hr. per unit = 130,000 hrs. | | | |
| 14 | | | | | |
| 15 | Note B: | Cutting Department: 292,000 units × 0.15 hr. per unit = 43,800 hrs. | | | |
| 16 | | Sewing Department: 292,000 units × 0.40 hr. per unit = 116,800 hrs. | | | |

As shown in Exhibit 11, for Elite Accessories Inc. to produce 520,000 wallets, 52,000 hours (520,000 units × 0.10 hr. per unit) of labor are required in the Cutting Department. Likewise, to produce 292,000 handbags, 43,800 hours (292,000 units × 0.15 hour per unit) of labor are required in the Cutting Department. Thus, the estimated total direct labor cost for the Cutting Department is $1,149,600 [(52,000 hrs. + 43,800 hrs.) × $12 per hr.). In a similar manner, the direct labor hours and cost for the Sewing Department are determined.

The direct labor needs should be coordinated between the production and personnel departments so that there will be enough labor available for production.

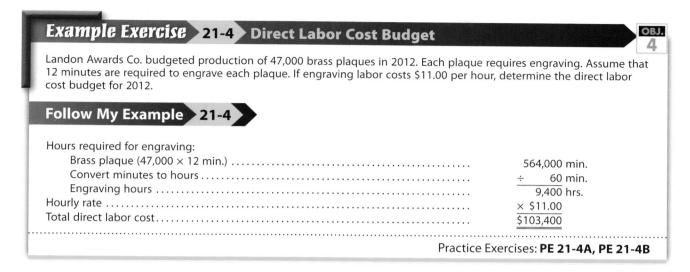

**Example Exercise** **21-4** **Direct Labor Cost Budget** OBJ. 4

Landon Awards Co. budgeted production of 47,000 brass plaques in 2012. Each plaque requires engraving. Assume that 12 minutes are required to engrave each plaque. If engraving labor costs $11.00 per hour, determine the direct labor cost budget for 2012.

**Follow My Example** **21-4**

Hours required for engraving:

| | |
|---|---:|
| Brass plaque (47,000 × 12 min.) | 564,000 min. |
| Convert minutes to hours | ÷ 60 min. |
| Engraving hours | 9,400 hrs. |
| Hourly rate | × $11.00 |
| Total direct labor cost | $103,400 |

Practice Exercises: **PE 21-4A, PE 21-4B**

## Factory Overhead Cost Budget

The **factory overhead cost budget** estimates the cost for each item of factory overhead needed to support budgeted production.

Exhibit 12 illustrates the factory overhead cost budget for Elite Accessories Inc.

| | A | B |
|---|---|---:|
| 1 | Elite Accessories Inc. | |
| 2 | Factory Overhead Cost Budget | |
| 3 | For the Year Ending December 31, 2012 | |
| 4 | Indirect factory wages | $ 732,800 |
| 5 | Supervisor salaries | 360,000 |
| 6 | Power and light | 306,000 |
| 7 | Depreciation of plant and equipment | 288,000 |
| 8 | Indirect materials | 182,800 |
| 9 | Maintenance | 140,280 |
| 10 | Insurance and property taxes | 79,200 |
| 11 | Total factory overhead cost | $2,089,080 |

**EXHIBIT 12**

**Factory Overhead Cost Budget**

The factory overhead cost budget shown in Exhibit 12 may be supported by departmental schedules. Such schedules normally separate factory overhead costs into fixed and variable costs to better enable department managers to monitor and evaluate costs during the year.

The factory overhead cost budget should be integrated with the production budget to ensure that production is not interrupted during the year.

## Cost of Goods Sold Budget

The **cost of goods sold budget** is prepared by integrating the following budgets:

1. Direct materials purchases budget (Exhibit 10)
2. Direct labor cost budget (Exhibit 11)
3. Factory overhead cost budget (Exhibit 12)

In addition, the estimated and desired inventories for direct materials, work in process, and finished goods must be integrated into the cost of goods sold budget.

Elite Accessories Inc. expects the following direct materials, work in process, and finished goods inventories:

| | Estimated Inventory Jan. 1, 2012 | Desired Inventory Dec. 31, 2012 |
|---|---|---|
| Direct materials: | | |
| Leather | $ 81,000 (18,000 sq. yds. × $4.50) | $ 90,000 (20,000 sq. yds. × $4.50) |
| Lining | 18,000 (15,000 sq. yds. × $1.20) | 14,400 (12,000 sq. yds. × $1.20) |
| Total direct materials | $ 99,000 | $ 104,400 |
| Work in process: | $ 214,400 | $ 220,000 |
| Finished goods: | $1,095,600 | $1,565,000 |

Exhibit 13 illustrates the cost of goods sold budget for Elite Accessories Inc. It indicates that total manufacturing costs of $9,522,780 are budgeted to be incurred in 2012. Of this total, $2,582,100 is budgeted for direct materials, $4,851,600 is budgeted for direct labor, and $2,089,080 is budgeted for factory overhead. After considering work in process inventories, the total budgeted cost of goods manufactured and transferred to finished goods during 2012 is $9,517,180. Based on expected sales, the budgeted cost of goods sold is $9,047,780.

**EXHIBIT 13**

**Cost of Goods Sold Budget**

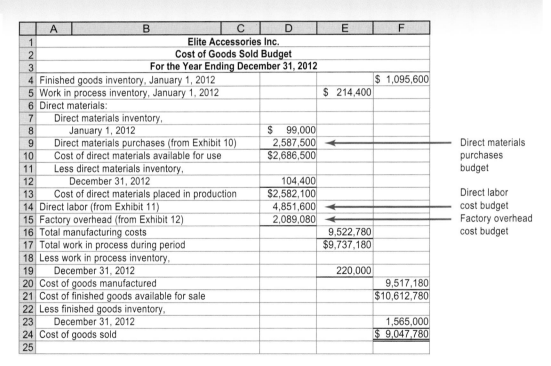

| | A | B | C | D | E | F | |
|---|---|---|---|---|---|---|---|
| 1 | | Elite Accessories Inc. | | | | | |
| 2 | | Cost of Goods Sold Budget | | | | | |
| 3 | | For the Year Ending December 31, 2012 | | | | | |
| 4 | Finished goods inventory, January 1, 2012 | | | | | $ 1,095,600 | |
| 5 | Work in process inventory, January 1, 2012 | | | | $ 214,400 | | |
| 6 | Direct materials: | | | | | | |
| 7 | Direct materials inventory, | | | | | | |
| 8 | January 1, 2012 | | | $ 99,000 | | | |
| 9 | Direct materials purchases (from Exhibit 10) | | | 2,587,500 | | | ← Direct materials purchases budget |
| 10 | Cost of direct materials available for use | | | $2,686,500 | | | |
| 11 | Less direct materials inventory, | | | | | | |
| 12 | December 31, 2012 | | | 104,400 | | | |
| 13 | Cost of direct materials placed in production | | | $2,582,100 | | | |
| 14 | Direct labor (from Exhibit 11) | | | 4,851,600 | | | ← Direct labor cost budget |
| 15 | Factory overhead (from Exhibit 12) | | | 2,089,080 | | | ← Factory overhead cost budget |
| 16 | Total manufacturing costs | | | | 9,522,780 | | |
| 17 | Total work in process during period | | | | $9,737,180 | | |
| 18 | Less work in process inventory, | | | | | | |
| 19 | December 31, 2012 | | | | 220,000 | | |
| 20 | Cost of goods manufactured | | | | | 9,517,180 | |
| 21 | Cost of finished goods available for sale | | | | | $10,612,780 | |
| 22 | Less finished goods inventory, | | | | | | |
| 23 | December 31, 2012 | | | | | 1,565,000 | |
| 24 | Cost of goods sold | | | | | $ 9,047,780 | |
| 25 | | | | | | | |

**Example Exercise** ▶ **21-5** ▶ **Cost of Goods Sold Budget**

OBJ. 4

Prepare a cost of goods sold budget for Landon Awards Co. using the information in Example Exercises 21-3 and 21-4. Assume the estimated inventories on January 1, 2012, for finished goods and work in process were $54,000 and $47,000, respectively. Also assume the desired inventories on December 31, 2012, for finished goods and work in process were $50,000 and $49,000, respectively. Factory overhead was budgeted for $126,000.

*(continued)*

**Follow My Example** 21-5

| | | |
|---|---:|---:|
| Finished goods inventory, January 1, 2012 .......................... | | $ 54,000 |
| Work in process inventory, January 1, 2012.......................... | $ 47,000 | |
| Direct materials: | | |
| Direct materials inventory, January 1, 2012 | | |
| (240,000 × $0.12, from EE 21-3)............................ | $ 28,800 | |
| Direct materials purchases (from EE 21-3)...................... | 536,640 | |
| Cost of direct materials available for use...................... | $565,440 | |
| Less direct materials inventory, December 31, 2012 | | |
| (200,000 × $0.12, from EE 21-3)............................ | 24,000 | |
| Cost of direct materials placed in production................... | $541,440 | |
| Direct labor (from EE 21-4) ........................................ | 103,400 | |
| Factory overhead .................................................. | 126,000 | |
| Total manufacturing costs......................................... | 770,840 | |
| Total work in process during period............................... | $817,840 | |
| Less work in process inventory, December 31, 2012 ................ | 49,000 | |
| Cost of goods manufactured....................................... | | 768,840 |
| Cost of finished goods available for sale........................... | | $822,840 |
| Less finished goods inventory, December 31, 2012 ................. | | 50,000 |
| Cost of goods sold................................................. | | $772,840 |

Practice Exercises: **PE 21-5A, PE 21-5B**

## Selling and Administrative Expenses Budget

The sales budget is often used as the starting point for the selling and administrative expenses budget. For example, a budgeted increase in sales may require more advertising expenses.

Exhibit 14 illustrates the selling and administrative expenses budget for Elite Accessories Inc.

| | A | B | C |
|---|---|---|---|
| 1 | Elite Accessories Inc. | | |
| 2 | Selling and Administrative Expenses Budget | | |
| 3 | For the Year Ending December 31, 2012 | | |
| 4 | Selling expenses: | | |
| 5 | Sales salaries expense | $715,000 | |
| 6 | Advertising expense | 360,000 | |
| 7 | Travel expense | 115,000 | |
| 8 | Total selling expenses | | $1,190,000 |
| 9 | Administrative expenses: | | |
| 10 | Officers' salaries expense | $360,000 | |
| 11 | Office salaries expense | 258,000 | |
| 12 | Office rent expense | 34,500 | |
| 13 | Office supplies expense | 17,500 | |
| 14 | Miscellaneous administrative expenses | 25,000 | |
| 15 | Total administrative expenses | | 695,000 |
| 16 | Total selling and administrative expenses | | $1,885,000 |

**EXHIBIT 14**

**Selling and Administrative Expenses Budget**

The selling and administrative expenses budget shown in Exhibit 14 is normally supported by departmental schedules. For example, an advertising expense schedule for the Marketing Department could include the advertising media to be used (newspaper, direct mail, television), quantities (column inches, number of pieces, minutes), and related costs per unit.

## Budgeted Income Statement

The budgeted income statement is prepared by integrating the following budgets:

1. Sales budget (Exhibit 8)
2. Cost of goods sold budget (Exhibit 13)
3. Selling and administrative expenses budget (Exhibit 14)

In addition, estimates of other income, other expense, and income tax are also integrated into the budgeted income statement.

Exhibit 15 illustrates the budgeted income statement for Elite Accessories Inc. This budget summarizes the budgeted operating activities of the company. In doing so, the budgeted income statement allows management to assess the effects of estimated sales, costs, and expenses on profits for the year.

**EXHIBIT 15    Budgeted Income Statement**

|  | A | B | C |  |
|---|---|---|---|---|
| 1 | Elite Accessories Inc. | | | |
| 2 | Budgeted Income Statement | | | |
| 3 | For the Year Ending December 31, 2012 | | | |
| 4 | Revenue from sales (from Exhibit 8) | | $13,336,000 | ← Sales budget |
| 5 | Cost of goods sold (from Exhibit 13) | | 9,047,780 | ← Cost of goods sold budget |
| 6 | | | | |
| 7 | Gross profit | | $ 4,288,220 | |
| 8 | Selling and administrative expenses: | | | |
| 9 | Selling expenses (from Exhibit 14) | $1,190,000 | | ← Selling and administrative expenses budget |
| 10 | | | | |
| 11 | Administrative expenses (from Exhibit 14) | 695,000 | | |
| 12 | Total selling and administrative expenses | | 1,885,000 | |
| 13 | Income from operations | | $ 2,403,220 | |
| 14 | Other income: | | | |
| 15 | Interest revenue | $   98,000 | | |
| 16 | Other expenses: | | | |
| 17 | Interest expense | 90,000 | 8,000 | |
| 18 | Income before income tax | | $ 2,411,220 | |
| 19 | Income tax | | 600,000 | |
| 20 | Net income | | $ 1,811,220 | |

**OBJ. 5** Prepare balance sheet budgets for a manufacturing company.

# Balance Sheet Budgets

While the income statement budgets reflect the operating activities of the company, the balance sheet budgets reflect the financing and investing activities. In this section, the following balance sheet budgets are described and illustrated:

1. Cash budget (financing activity)
2. Capital expenditures budget (investing activity)

## Cash Budget

**Note:**
The cash budget presents the expected receipts and payments of cash for a period of time.

The **cash budget** estimates the expected receipts (inflows) and payments (outflows) of cash for a period of time. The cash budget is integrated with the various operating budgets. In addition, the capital expenditures budget, dividends, and equity or long-term debt financing plans of the company affect the cash budget.

To illustrate, a monthly cash budget for January, February, and March 2012 for Elite Accessories Inc. is prepared. The preparation of the cash budget begins by estimating cash receipts.

**Estimated Cash Receipts** The primary source of estimated cash receipts is from cash sales and collections on account. In addition, cash receipts may be obtained from plans to issue equity or debt financing as well as other sources such as interest revenue.

To estimate cash receipts from cash sales and collections on account, a *schedule of collections from sales* is prepared. To illustrate, the following data for Elite Accessories Inc. are used:

| | January | February | March |
|---|---|---|---|
| Sales: | | | |
| Budgeted sales...................................... | $1,080,000 | $1,240,000 | $970,000 |
| Percent of cash sales .............................. | 10% | 10% | 10% |
| Accounts receivable, January 1, 2012 ................... | $ 370,000 | | |
| Receipts from sales on account: | | | |
| From prior month's sales on account ................. | 40% | | |
| From current month's sales on account.............. | 60 | | |
| | 100% | | |

Using the preceding data, the schedule of collections from sales is prepared, as shown in Exhibit 16. Cash sales are determined by multiplying the percent of cash sales by the monthly budgeted sales. The cash receipts from sales on account are determined by adding the cash received from the prior month's sales on account (40%) and the cash received from the current month's sales on account (60%). To simplify, it is assumed that all accounts receivable are collected.

| | A | B | C | D | E |
|---|---|---|---|---|---|
| 1 | | Elite Accessories Inc. | | | |
| 2 | | Schedule of Collections from Sales | | | |
| 3 | | For the Three Months Ending March 31, 2012 | | | |
| 4 | | | January | February | March |
| 5 | Receipts from cash sales: | | | | |
| 6 | | Cash sales (10% × current month's sales— | | | |
| 7 | | Note A) | $108,000 | $ 124,000 | $ 97,000 |
| 8 | | | | | |
| 9 | Receipts from sales on account: | | | | |
| 10 | | Collections from prior month's sales (40% of | | | |
| 11 | | previous month's credit sales—Note B) | $370,000 | $ 388,800 | $446,400 |
| 12 | | Collections from current month's sales (60% | | | |
| 13 | | of current month's credit sales—Note C) | 583,200 | 669,600 | 523,800 |
| 14 | Total receipts from sales on account | | $953,200 | $1,058,400 | $970,200 |
| 15 | | | | | |
| 16 | Note A: | $108,000 = $1,080,000 × 10% | | | |
| 17 | | $124,000 = $1,240,000 × 10% | | | |
| 18 | | $ 97,000 = $ 970,000 × 10% | | | |
| 19 | | | | | |
| 20 | Note B: | $370,000, given as January 1, 2012, Accounts Receivable balance | | | |
| 21 | | $388,800 = $1,080,000 × 90% × 40% | | | |
| 22 | | $446,400 = $1,240,000 × 90% × 40% | | | |
| 23 | | | | | |
| 24 | Note C: | $583,200 = $1,080,000 × 90% × 60% | | | |
| 25 | | $669,600 = $1,240,000 × 90% × 60% | | | |
| 26 | | $523,800 = $ 970,000 × 90% × 60% | | | |

**EXHIBIT 16**

**Schedule of Collections from Sales**

**Estimated Cash Payments** Estimated cash payments must be budgeted for operating costs and expenses such as manufacturing costs, selling expenses, and administrative expenses. In addition, estimated cash payments may be planned for capital expenditures, dividends, interest payments, or long-term debt payments.

To estimate cash payments for manufacturing costs, a *schedule of payments for manufacturing costs* is prepared. To illustrate, the following data for Elite Accessories Inc. are used:

|  | January | February | March |
|---|---|---|---|
| Manufacturing Costs: |  |  |  |
| Budgeted manufacturing costs . . . . . . . . . . . . . . . . . . . . . . . . . . . . | $840,000 | $780,000 | $812,000 |
| Depreciation on machines included |  |  |  |
| in manufacturing costs . . . . . . . . . . . . . . . . . . . . . . . . . . . . . . . . . . | 24,000 | 24,000 | 24,000 |
| Accounts Payable: |  |  |  |
| Accounts payable, January 1, 2012 . . . . . . . . . . . . . . . . . . . . . . . . | $190,000 |  |  |
| Payments of manufacturing costs on account: |  |  |  |
| From prior month's manufacturing costs . . . . . . . . . . . . . . . . . . | 25% |  |  |
| From current month's manufacturing costs . . . . . . . . . . . . . . . . | 75 |  |  |
|  | 100% |  |  |

Using the preceding data, the schedule of payments for manufacturing costs is prepared, as shown in Exhibit 17. The cash payments are determined by adding the cash paid on costs incurred from the prior month (25%) to the cash paid on costs incurred in the current month (75%). The $24,000 of depreciation is excluded from all computations, since depreciation does not require a cash payment.

**EXHIBIT 17**

**Schedule of Payments for Manufacturing Costs**

| | A | B | C | D | E |
|---|---|---|---|---|---|
| 1 | | Elite Accessories Inc. | | | |
| 2 | | Schedule of Payments for Manufacturing Costs | | | |
| 3 | | For the Three Months Ending March 31, 2012 | | | |
| 4 | | | January | February | March |
| 5 | Payments of prior month's manufacturing costs | | | | |
| 6 | {[25% × previous month's manufacturing costs | | | | |
| 7 | (less depreciation)]—Note A} | | $190,000 | $204,000 | $189,000 |
| 8 | Payments of current month's manufacturing costs | | | | |
| 9 | {[75% × current month's manufacturing costs | | | | |
| 10 | (less depreciation)]—Note B} | | 612,000 | 567,000 | 591,000 |
| 11 | Total payments | | $802,000 | $771,000 | $780,000 |
| 12 | | | | | |
| 13 | Note A: | $190,000, given as January 1, 2012, Accounts Payable balance | | | |
| 14 | | $204,000 = ($840,000 − $24,000) × 25% | | | |
| 15 | | $189,000 = ($780,000 − $24,000) × 25% | | | |
| 16 | | | | | |
| 17 | Note B: | $612,000 = ($840,000 − $24,000) × 75% | | | |
| 18 | | $567,000 = ($780,000 − $24,000) × 75% | | | |
| 19 | | $591,000 = ($812,000 − $24,000) × 75% | | | |

**Completing the Cash Budget** Assume the additional data for Elite Accessories Inc. shown below.

| | |
|---|---|
| Cash balance on January 1, 2012 | $280,000 |
| Quarterly taxes paid on March 31, 2012 | 150,000 |
| Quarterly interest expense paid on January 10, 2012 | 22,500 |
| Quarterly interest revenue received on March 21, 2012 | 24,500 |
| Sewing equipment purchased in February 2012 | 274,000 |
| Selling and administrative expenses (paid in month incurred): | |

| January | February | March |
|---|---|---|
| $160,000 | $165,000 | $145,000 |

Using the preceding data, the *cash budget* is prepared, as shown in Exhibit 18.

**EXHIBIT 18** **Cash Budget**

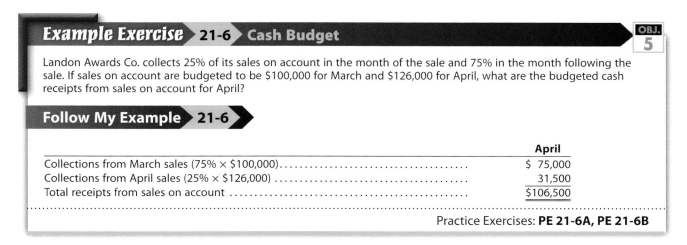

| | A | B | C | D |
|---|---|---|---|---|
| 1 | Elite Accessories Inc. | | | |
| 2 | Cash Budget | | | |
| 3 | For the Three Months Ending March 31, 2012 | | | |
| 4 | | January | February | March |
| 5 | Estimated cash receipts from: | | | |
| 6 | Cash sales (from Exhibit 16) | $ 108,000 | $ 124,000 | $ 97,000 |
| 7 | Collections of accounts receivable | | | |
| 8 | (from Exhibit 16) | 953,200 | 1,058,400 | 970,200 |
| 9 | Interest revenue | | | 24,500 |
| 10 | Total cash receipts | $1,061,200 | $1,182,400 | $1,091,700 |
| 11 | Estimated cash payments for: | | | |
| 12 | Manufacturing costs (from Exhibit 17) | $ 802,000 | $ 771,000 | $ 780,000 |
| 13 | Selling and administrative expenses | 160,000 | 165,000 | 145,000 |
| 14 | Capital additions (sewing equipment) | | 274,000 | |
| 15 | Interest expense | 22,500 | | |
| 16 | Income taxes | | | 150,000 |
| 17 | Total cash payments | $ 984,500 | $1,210,000 | $1,075,000 |
| 18 | Cash increase (decrease) | $ 76,700 | $ (27,600) | $ 16,700 |
| 19 | Cash balance at beginning of month | 280,000 | 356,700 | 329,100 |
| 20 | Cash balance at end of month | $ 356,700 | $ 329,100 | $ 345,800 |
| 21 | Minimum cash balance | 340,000 | 340,000 | 340,000 |
| 22 | Excess (deficiency) | $ 16,700 | $ (10,900) | $ 5,800 |

Schedule of collections from sales

Schedule of cash payments for manufacturing costs

As shown in Exhibit 18, Elite Accessories Inc. has estimated that a *minimum cash balance* of $340,000 is required at the end of each month to support its operations. This minimum cash balance is compared to the estimated ending cash balance for each month. In this way, any expected cash excess or deficiency is determined.

Exhibit 18 indicates that Elite Accessories expects a cash excess at the end of January of $16,700. This excess could be invested in temporary income-producing securities such as U.S. Treasury bills or notes. In contrast, the estimated cash deficiency at the end of February of $10,900 might require Elite Accessories to borrow cash from its bank.

**Example Exercise** ⟩ **21-6** ⟩ **Cash Budget**                          **OBJ. 5**

Landon Awards Co. collects 25% of its sales on account in the month of the sale and 75% in the month following the sale. If sales on account are budgeted to be $100,000 for March and $126,000 for April, what are the budgeted cash receipts from sales on account for April?

**Follow My Example** ⟩ **21-6** ⟩

| | April |
|---|---|
| Collections from March sales (75% × $100,000)....................................... | $ 75,000 |
| Collections from April sales (25% × $126,000) ...................................... | 31,500 |
| Total receipts from sales on account ............................................. | $106,500 |

Practice Exercises: **PE 21-6A, PE 21-6B**

## Capital Expenditures Budget

The **capital expenditures budget** summarizes plans for acquiring fixed assets. Such expenditures are necessary as machinery and other fixed assets wear out or become obsolete. In addition, purchasing additional fixed assets may be necessary to meet increasing demand for the company's product.

To illustrate, a five-year capital expenditures budget for Elite Accessories Inc. is shown in Exhibit 19.

**EXHIBIT 19**

**Capital Expenditures Budget**

| | A | B | C | D | E | F |
|---|---|---|---|---|---|---|
| 1 | Elite Accessories Inc. | | | | | |
| 2 | Capital Expenditures Budget | | | | | |
| 3 | For the Five Years Ending December 31, 2016 | | | | | |
| 4 | Item | 2012 | 2013 | 2014 | 2015 | 2016 |
| 5 | Machinery—Cutting Department | $400,000 | | | $280,000 | $360,000 |
| 6 | Machinery—Sewing Department | 274,000 | $260,000 | $560,000 | 200,000 | |
| 7 | Office equipment | | 90,000 | | | 60,000 |
| 8 | Total | $674,000 | $350,000 | $560,000 | $480,000 | $420,000 |

As shown in Exhibit 19, capital expenditures budgets are often prepared for five to ten years into the future. This is necessary since fixed assets often must be ordered years in advance. Likewise, it could take years to construct new buildings or other production facilities.

The capital expenditures budget should be integrated with the operating and financing budgets. For example, depreciation of new manufacturing equipment affects the factory overhead cost budget. The plans for financing the capital expenditures also affect the cash budget.

## Budgeted Balance Sheet

The budgeted balance sheet is prepared based on the operating, financing, and investing budgets of the master budget. The budgeted balance sheet is dated as of the end of the budget period and is similar to a normal balance sheet except that estimated amounts are used. For this reason, a budgeted balance sheet for Elite Accessories Inc. is not illustrated.

**Comprehensive Spreadsheet Illustration: Master Budget**
The master budget is often developed on a spreadsheet. A spreadsheet to create the master budget is shown below. Spreadsheet formulas in selected cells are identified to illustrate the relationships.

Selected information concerning estimated sales and production for Cabot Co. for July 2012 are summarized in a spreadsheet as follows:

**a.**　Estimated sales:

| | A | B | C |
|---|---|---|---|
| 1 | | | |
| 2 | Estimated Sales | Units | Price |
| 3 | Product K | 40,000 | $ 30 |
| 4 | Product L | 20,000 | $ 65 |
| 5 | Total | | |
| 6 | | | |

**b.**　Estimated inventories, July 1, 2012:

| | A | B | C | D | E |
|---|---|---|---|---|---|
| 7 | | | | | |
| 8 | Estimated Inventories, July 1, 2012 | Pounds | | Units | Price per Unit |
| 9 | Material A | 4,000 | Product K | 3,000 | $ 17 |
| 10 | Material B | 3,500 | Product L | 2,700 | $ 35 |
| 11 | | | | | |
| 12 | There were no work-in-process inventories estimated for July 1, 2012 | | | | |
| 13 | | | | | |

c. Desired inventories, July 31, 2012:

| | A | B | C | D | E |
|---|---|---|---|---|---|
| 14 | | | | | |
| 15 | **Desired Inventories, July 31, 2012** | **Pounds** | | **Units** | **Price per Unit** |
| 16 | Material A | 3,000 | Product K | 2,500 | $ 17 |
| 17 | Material B | 2,500 | Product L | 2,000 | $ 35 |
| 18 | | | | | |
| 19 | There were no work-in-process inventories desired for July 31, 2012 | | | | |
| 20 | | | | | |

d. Direct materials used in production:

| | A | B | C |
|---|---|---|---|
| 21 | | | |
| 22 | **Direct materials used in production (pounds per unit)** | **Product K** | **Product L** |
| 23 | Material A | 0.7 | 3.5 |
| 24 | Material B | 1.2 | 1.8 |
| 25 | | | |

e. Unit cost for direct materials (price per lb.):

| | A | B |
|---|---|---|
| 26 | | |
| 27 | **Unit costs for direct materials (per pound)** | |
| 28 | Material A | $ 4.00 |
| 29 | Material B | $ 2.00 |
| 30 | | |

f. Direct labor requirements per unit:

| | A | B | C |
|---|---|---|---|
| 31 | | | |
| 32 | **Direct labor requirements (hours per unit)** | **Department 1** | **Department 2** |
| 33 | Product K | 0.40 | 0.15 |
| 34 | Product L | 0.60 | 0.25 |
| 35 | | | |

g. Direct labor rate:

| | A | B | C |
|---|---|---|---|
| 36 | | | |
| 37 | | **Department 1** | **Department 2** |
| 38 | Direct labor rate (per hour) | $ 12.00 | $ 16.00 |
| 39 | | | |

h. Estimated factory overhead costs for July:

| | A | B |
|---|---|---|
| 40 | | |
| 41 | Estimated factory overhead costs for July: | |
| 42 | Indirect factory wages | $ 200,000 |
| 43 | Depreciation of plant and equipment | 40,000 |
| 44 | Power and light | 25,000 |
| 45 | Indirect materials | 34,000 |
| 46 | Total | $ 299,000 |
| 47 | | |

**Instructions:**
1. Prepare a sales budget for July.
2. Prepare a production budget for July.
3. Prepare a direct materials budget for July.
4. Prepare a direct labor cost budget for July.
5. Prepare a cost of goods sold budget for July.

*Note:* Numbers correlate to the solutions outlined in the following pages.

**Spreadsheet Solution**

Formulas are provided for selected cells. Many formulas are provided for Product L. Use the Product L formulas as a pattern to determine the correct Product K cell references and formulas.

1. Sales Budget:

| | A | B | C | D |
|---|---|---|---|---|
| 50 | | | | |
| 51 | Cabot Co. | | | |
| 52 | Sales Budget | | | |
| 53 | For the Month Ending July 31, 2012 | | | |
| 54 | **Product** | **Unit Sales Volume** | **Unit Selling Price** | **Total Sales** |
| 55 | Product K | 40,000 | $     30 | $  1,200,000 |
| 56 | Product L | =B4 | =C4 | =B56*C56 |
| 57 | Total revenue from sales | | | =SUM(D55:D56) |
| 58 | | | | |

2. Production Budget:

| | A | B | C |
|---|---|---|---|
| 60 | | | |
| 61 | Cabot Co. | | |
| 62 | Production Budget | | |
| 63 | For the Month Ending July 31, 2012 | | |
| 64 | | Product K | Product L |
| 65 | Expected units to be sold | 40,000 | =B4 |
| 66 | Plus desired units of inventory, July 31, 2012 | 2,500 | =D17 |
| 67 | Total | 42,500 | =SUM(C65:C66) |
| 68 | Less estimated units of inventory, July 1, 2012 | 3,000 | =D10 |
| 69 | Total units to be produced | 39,500 | =C67-C68 |
| 70 | | | |

3. Direct Materials Purchases Budget

| | A | B | C | D |
|---|---|---|---|---|
| 75 | | | | |
| 76 | Cabot Co. | | | |
| 77 | Direct Materials Purchases Budget | | | |
| 78 | For the Month Ending July 31, 2012 | | | |
| 79 | **Product** | **Material A** | **Material B** | **Total** |
| 80 | Pounds required for production: | | | |
| 81 | Product K (39,500 × lbs. per unit) | 27,650 | =B69*B24 | |
| 82 | Product L (19,300 × lbs. per unit) | 67,550 | C69*C24 | |
| 83 | Plus desired pounds of inventory, July 31, 2012 | 3,000 | =B17 | |
| 84 | Total | 98,200 | =SUM(C81:C83) | |
| 85 | Less estimated pounds of inventory, July 1, 2012 | 4,000 | =B10 | |
| 86 | Total pounds to be purchased | 94,200 | =C84-C85 | |
| 87 | Unit price (per pound) | $     4.00 | =B29 | |
| 88 | Total direct materials purchases | $  376,800 | =C86*C87 | =SUM(B88:C88) |
| 89 | | | | |

4. Direct Labor Cost Budget

| | A | B | C | D |
|---|---|---|---|---|
| 90 | | | | |
| 91 | | Cabot Co. | | |
| 92 | | Direct Labor Cost Budget | | |
| 93 | For the Month Ending July 31, 2012 | Department | Department | |
| 94 | | 1 | 2 | Total |
| 95 | Hours required for production: | | | |
| 96 | Product K | 15,800 | 5,925 | |
| 97 | Product L | 11,580 | =C69*C34 | |
| 98 | Total | 27,380 | 10,750 | |
| 99 | Hourly rate | $ 12.00 | $ 16.00 | |
| 100 | Total direct labor cost | $ 328,560 | =C38*C99 | $ 500,560 |
| 101 | | | | |

5. Cost of Goods Sold Budget

| | A | B | C | D |
|---|---|---|---|---|
| 102 | | | | |
| 103 | | Cabot Co. | | |
| 104 | | Cost of Goods Sold Budget | | |
| 105 | | For the Month Ending July 31, 2012 | | |
| 106 | Finished goods inventory, July 1, 2012 | | $ 145,500 | |
| 107 | Direct materials: | | | |
| 108 | Direct materials inventory, July 1, 2012 (Note A) | =D124 | | |
| 109 | Direct materials purchases | =D88 | | |
| 110 | Cost of direct materials available for use | =SUM(B108:B109) | | |
| 111 | Less direct materials inventory, July 31, 2012 (Note B) | =D129 | | |
| 112 | Cost of direct materials placed in production | =B110-B111 | | |
| 113 | Direct labor | =D100 | | |
| 114 | Factory overhead | =B46 | | |
| 115 | Cost of goods manufactured | | =SUM(B112:B114) | |
| 116 | Cost of finished goods available for sale | | =SUM(C106:C115) | |
| 117 | Less finished goods inventory, July 31, 2012 | | =(D16*E16)+(D17*E17) | |
| 118 | Cost of goods sold | | =C116-C117 | |
| 119 | | | | |
| 120 | | | | |
| 121 | Note A: | Pounds | Price per lb. | |
| 122 | Material A | 4,000 | $ 4.00 | $ 16,000 |
| 123 | Material B | 3,500 | $ 2.00 | 7,000 |
| 124 | Direct materials inventory, July 1, 2012 | | | $ 23,000 |
| 125 | | | | |
| 126 | Note B: | Pounds | Price per lb. | |
| 127 | Material A | 3,000 | $ 4.00 | $ 12,000 |
| 128 | Material B | 2,500 | $ 2.00 | 5,000 |
| 129 | Direct materials inventory, July 31, 2012 | | | $ 17,000 |
| 130 | | | | |

# At a Glance 21

## Describe budgeting, its objectives, and its impact on human behavior.

**Key Points** Budgeting involves (1) establishing plans (planning), (2) directing operations (directing), and (3) evaluating performance (controlling). In addition, budgets should be established to avoid human behavior problems.

| Learning Outcomes | Example Exercises | Practice Exercises |
|---|---|---|
| • Describe the planning, directing, controlling, and feedback elements of the budget process. | | |
| • Describe the behavioral issues associated with tight goals, loose goals, and goal conflict. | | |

## Describe the basic elements of the budget process, the two major types of budgeting, and the use of computers in budgeting.

**Key Points** The budget estimates received by the budget committee should be carefully studied, analyzed, revised, and integrated. The static and flexible budgets are two major budgeting approaches. Computers can be used to make the budget process more efficient and organizationally integrated.

| Learning Outcomes | Example Exercises | Practice Exercises |
|---|---|---|
| • Describe a static budget and explain when it might be used. | | |
| • Describe and prepare a flexible budget and explain when it might be used. | **EE21-1** | **PE21-1A, 21-1B** |
| • Describe the role of computers in the budget process. | | |

## Describe the master budget for a manufacturing company.

**Key Points** The master budget consists of the budgeted income statement and budgeted balance sheet.

| Learning Outcome | Example Exercises | Practice Exercises |
|---|---|---|
| • Illustrate the connection between the major income statement and balance sheet budgets. | | |

**OBJ. 4** **Prepare the basic income statement budgets for a manufacturing company.**

**Key Points**   The basic income statement budgets are the sales budget, production budget, direct materials purchases budget, direct labor cost budget, factory overhead cost budget, cost of goods sold budget, and selling and administrative expenses budget.

| Learning Outcomes | Example Exercises | Practice Exercises |
|---|---|---|
| • Prepare a sales budget. | | |
| • Prepare a production budget. | EE21-2 | PE21-2A, 21-2B |
| • Prepare a direct materials purchases budget. | EE21-3 | PE21-3A, 21-3B |
| • Prepare a direct labor cost budget. | EE21-4 | PE21-4A, 21-4B |
| • Prepare a factory overhead cost budget. | | |
| • Prepare a cost of goods sold budget. | EE21-5 | PE21-5A, 21-5B |
| • Prepare a selling and administrative expenses budget. | | |

**OBJ. 5** **Prepare balance sheet budgets for a manufacturing company.**

**Key Points**   The cash budget and capital expenditures budget can be used in preparing the budgeted balance sheet.

| Learning Outcomes | Example Exercises | Practice Exercises |
|---|---|---|
| • Prepare cash receipts and cash payments budgets. | EE21-6 | PE21-6A, 21-6B |
| • Prepare a capital expenditures budget. | | |

# Key Terms

budgets (978)

budgetary slack (980)

capital expenditures budget (997)

cash budget (994)

continuous budgeting (980)

cost of goods sold budget (991)

direct labor cost budget (990)

direct materials purchases budget (988)

factory overhead cost budget (991)

flexible budgets (982)

goal conflict (980)

master budget (985)

production budget (987)

responsibility center (979)

sales budget (986)

static budget (981)

zero-based budgeting (981)

# Illustrative Problem

Selected information concerning sales and production for Cabot Co. for July 2012 are summarized as follows:

a. Estimated sales:

Product K:   40,000 units at $30.00 per unit

Product L:   20,000 units at $65.00 per unit

b. Estimated inventories, July 1, 2012:

| Material A: | 4,000 lbs. | Product K: | 3,000 units at $17 per unit | $ 51,000 |
|---|---|---|---|---|
| Material B: | 3,500 lbs. | Product L: | 2,700 units at $35 per unit | 94,500 |
| | | Total | | $145,500 |

There were no work in process inventories estimated for July 1, 2012.

c. Desired inventories at July 31, 2012:

| Material A: | 3,000 lbs. | Product K: | 2,500 units at $17 per unit | $ 42,500 |
|---|---|---|---|---|
| Material B: | 2,500 lbs. | Product L: | 2,000 units at $35 per unit | 70,000 |
| | | Total | | $112,500 |

There were no work in process inventories desired for July 31, 2012.

d. Direct materials used in production:

| | Product K | Product L |
|---|---|---|
| Material A: | 0. 7 lb. per unit | 3.5 lbs. per unit |
| Material B: | 1.2 lbs. per unit | 1.8 lbs. per unit |

e. Unit costs for direct materials:

| Material A: | $4.00 per lb. |
|---|---|
| Material B: | $2.00 per lb. |

f. Direct labor requirements:

| | Department 1 | Department 2 |
|---|---|---|
| Product K | 0.4 hr. per unit | 0.15 hr. per unit |
| Product L | 0.6 hr. per unit | 0.25 hr. per unit |

g.

| | Department 1 | Department 2 |
|---|---|---|
| Direct labor rate | $12.00 per hr. | $16.00 per hr. |

h. Estimated factory overhead costs for July:

| Indirect factory wages | $200,000 |
|---|---|
| Depreciation of plant and equipment | 40,000 |
| Power and light | 25,000 |
| Indirect materials | 34,000 |
| Total | $299,000 |

## Instructions

1. Prepare a sales budget for July.

2. Prepare a production budget for July.

3. Prepare a direct materials purchases budget for July.

4. Prepare a direct labor cost budget for July.

5. Prepare a cost of goods sold budget for July.

## Solution

1.

| | A | B | C | D |
|---|---|---|---|---|
| 1 | | Cabot Co. | | |
| 2 | | Sales Budget | | |
| 3 | | For the Month Ending July 31, 2012 | | |
| 4 | Product | Unit Sales Volume | Unit Selling Price | Total Sales |
| 5 | Product K | 40,000 | $30.00 | $1,200,000 |
| 6 | Product L | 20,000 | 65.00 | 1,300,000 |
| 7 | Total revenue from sales | | | $2,500,000 |
| | | | | |

2.

| | A | B | C |
|---|---|---|---|
| 1 | Cabot Co. | | |
| 2 | Production Budget | | |
| 3 | For the Month Ending July 31, 2012 | | |
| 4 | | Units | |
| 5 | | Product K | Product L |
| 6 | Sales | 40,000 | 20,000 |
| 7 | Plus desired inventories at July 31, 2012 | 2,500 | 2,000 |
| 8 | Total | 42,500 | 22,000 |
| 9 | Less estimated inventories, July 1, 2012 | 3,000 | 2,700 |
| 10 | Total production | 39,500 | 19,300 |

3.

| | A | B | C | D | E | F | G |
|---|---|---|---|---|---|---|---|
| 1 | Cabot Co. | | | | | | |
| 2 | Direct Materials Purchases Budget | | | | | | |
| 3 | For the Month Ending July 31, 2012 | | | | | | |
| 4 | | | Direct Materials | | | | |
| 5 | | | Material A | | Material B | | Total |
| 6 | Units required for production: | | | | | | |
| 7 | Product K (39,500 × lbs. per unit) | | 27,650 | lbs.* | 47,400 | lbs.* | |
| 8 | Product L (19,300 × lbs. per unit) | | 67,550 | ** | 34,740 | ** | |
| 9 | Plus desired units of inventory, | | | | | | |
| 10 | July 31, 2012 | | 3,000 | | 2,500 | | |
| 11 | Total | | 98,200 | lbs. | 84,640 | lbs. | |
| 12 | Less estimated units of inventory, | | | | | | |
| 13 | July 1, 2012 | | 4,000 | | 3,500 | | |
| 14 | Total units to be purchased | | 94,200 | lbs. | 81,140 | lbs. | |
| 15 | Unit price | | × $4.00 | | × $2.00 | | |
| 16 | Total direct materials purchases | | $376,800 | | $162,280 | | $539,080 |
| 17 | | | | | | | |
| 18 | *27,650 = 39,500 × 0.7 | 47,400 = 39,500 × 1.2 | | | | | |
| 19 | **67,550 = 19,300 × 3.5 | 34,740 = 19,300 × 1.8 | | | | | |

4.

| | A | B | C | D | E | F | G |
|---|---|---|---|---|---|---|---|
| 1 | Cabot Co. | | | | | | |
| 2 | Direct Labor Cost Budget | | | | | | |
| 3 | For the Month Ending July 31, 2012 | | | | | | |
| 4 | | | Department 1 | | Department 2 | | Total |
| 5 | Hours required for production: | | | | | | |
| 6 | Product K (39,500 × hrs. per unit) | | 15,800 | * | 5,925 | * | |
| 7 | Product L (19,300 × hrs. per unit) | | 11,580 | ** | 4,825 | ** | |
| 8 | Total | | 27,380 | | 10,750 | | |
| 9 | Hourly rate | | ×$12.00 | | ×$16.00 | | |
| 10 | Total direct labor cost | | $328,560 | | $172,000 | | $500,560 |
| 11 | | | | | | | |
| 12 | *15,800 = 39,500 × 0.4 | 5,925 = 39,500 × 0.15 | | | | | |
| 13 | **11,580 = 19,300 × 0.6 | 4,825 = 19,300 × 0.25 | | | | | |

5.

| | A | B | C | D |
|---|---|---|---|---|
| 1 | Cabot Co. | | | |
| 2 | Cost of Goods Sold Budget | | | |
| 3 | For the Month Ending July 31, 2012 | | | |
| 4 | Finished goods inventory, July 1, 2012 | | | $ 145,500 |
| 5 | Direct materials: | | | |
| 6 |   Direct materials inventory, July 1, 2012—(Note A) | | $ 23,000 | |
| 7 |   Direct materials purchases | | 539,080 | |
| 8 |   Cost of direct materials available for use | | $562,080 | |
| 9 |   Less direct materials inventory, July 31, 2012—(Note B) | | 17,000 | |
| 10 |   Cost of direct materials placed in production | | $545,080 | |
| 11 | Direct labor | | 500,560 | |
| 12 | Factory overhead | | 299,000 | |
| 13 | Cost of goods manufactured | | | 1,344,640 |
| 14 | Cost of finished goods available for sale | | | $1,490,140 |
| 15 | Less finished goods inventory, July 31, 2012 | | | 112,500 |
| 16 | Cost of goods sold | | | $1,377,640 |
| 17 | | | | |
| 18 |   Note A: | | | |
| 19 |   Material A  4,000 lbs. at $4.00 per lb. | $16,000 | | |
| 20 |   Material B  3,500 lbs. at $2.00 per lb. | 7,000 | | |
| 21 |   Direct materials inventory, July 1, 2012 | $23,000 | | |
| 22 | | | | |
| 23 |   Note B: | | | |
| 24 |   Material A  3,000 lbs. at $4.00 per lb. | $12,000 | | |
| 25 |   Material B  2,500 lbs. at $2.00 per lb. | 5,000 | | |
| 26 |   Direct materials inventory, July 31, 2012 | $17,000 | | |

# Discussion Questions

1. What are the three major objectives of budgeting?

2. Briefly describe the type of human behavior problems that might arise if budget goals are set too tightly.

3. What behavioral problems are associated with setting a budget too loosely?

4. What behavioral problems are associated with establishing conflicting goals within the budget?

5. Under what circumstances would a static budget be appropriate?

6. How do computerized budgeting systems aid firms in the budgeting process?

7. Why should the production requirements set forth in the production budget be carefully coordinated with the sales budget?

8. Why should the timing of direct materials purchases be closely coordinated with the production budget?

9. a. Discuss the purpose of the cash budget.

   b. If the cash for the first quarter of the fiscal year indicates excess cash at the end of each of the first two months, how might the excess cash be used?

10. Give an example of how the capital expenditures budget affects other operating budgets.

# Practice Exercises

**PE 21-1A   Flexible budgeting**

At the beginning of the period, the Assembly Department budgeted direct labor of $166,500 and property tax of $12,000 for 9,000 hours of production. The department actually completed 11,200 hours of production. Determine the budget for the department, assuming that it uses flexible budgeting.

**PE 21-1B   Flexible budgeting**

At the beginning of the period, the Fabricating Department budgeted direct labor of $6,500 and equipment depreciation of $2,000 for 400 hours of production. The department actually completed 500 hours of production. Determine the budget for the department, assuming that it uses flexible budgeting.

**PE 21-2A   Production budget**

MyLife Publishers Inc. projected sales of 165,000 diaries for 2012. The estimated January 1, 2012, inventory is 24,200 units, and the desired December 31, 2012, inventory is 18,200 units. What is the budgeted production (in units) for 2012?

**PE 21-2B   Production budget**

Confederate Candle Co. projected sales of 64,000 candles for 2012. The estimated January 1, 2012, inventory is 2,900 units, and the desired December 31, 2012, inventory is 3,200 units. What is the budgeted production (in units) for 2012?

**PE 21-3A   Direct materials purchases budget**

MyLife Publishers Inc. budgeted production of 159,000 diaries in 2012. Paper is required to produce a diary. Assume eight square yards of paper are required for each diary. The estimated January 1, 2012, paper inventory is 30,500 square yards. The desired December 31, 2012, paper inventory is 27,000 square yards. If paper costs $0.70 per square yard, determine the direct materials purchases budget for 2012.

**PE 21-3B   Direct materials purchases budget**

Confederate Candle Co. budgeted production of 64,300 candles in 2012. Wax is required to produce a candle. Assume eight ounces (one-half of a pound) of wax is required for each candle. The estimated January 1, 2012, wax inventory is 3,000 pounds. The desired December 31, 2012, wax inventory is 3,200 pounds. If candle wax costs $3.60 per pound, determine the direct materials purchases budget for 2012.

**PE 21-4A   Direct labor cost budget**

MyLife Publishers Inc. budgeted production of 159,000 diaries in 2012. Each diary requires assembly. Assume that 12 minutes are required to assemble each diary. If assembly labor costs $14.50 per hour, determine the direct labor cost budget for 2012.

*Learning
Objectives*   *Example
Exercises*

**OBJ. 4**   **EE 21-4** p. 991   **PE 21-4B   Direct labor cost budget**

Confederate Candle Co. budgeted production of 64,300 candles in 2012. Each candle requires molding. Assume that 15 minutes are required to mold each candle. If molding labor costs $13.00 per hour, determine the direct labor cost budget for 2012.

**OBJ. 4**   **EE 21-5** p. 992   **PE 21-5A   Cost of goods sold budget**

Prepare a cost of goods sold budget for MyLife Publishers Inc. using the information in Practice Exercises 21-3A and 21-4A. Assume the estimated inventories on January 1, 2012, for finished goods and work in process were $32,000 and $15,000, respectively. Also assume the desired inventories on December 31, 2012, for finished goods and work in process were $34,500 and $14,000, respectively. Factory overhead was budgeted at $225,000.

**OBJ. 4**   **EE 21-5** p. 992   **PE 21-5B   Cost of goods sold budget**

Prepare a cost of goods sold budget for Confederate Candle Co. using the information in Practice Exercises 21-3B and 21-4B. Assume the estimated inventories on January 1, 2012, for finished goods and work in process were $11,500 and $3,200, respectively. Also assume the desired inventories on December 31, 2012, for finished goods and work in process were $7,200 and $4,000, respectively. Factory overhead was budgeted at $116,000.

**OBJ. 5**   **EE 21-6** p. 997   **PE 21-6A   Cash budget**

MyLife Publishers Inc. collects 25% of its sales on account in the month of the sale and 75% in the month following the sale. If sales on account are budgeted to be $340,000 for April and $300,000 for May, what are the budgeted cash receipts from sales on account for May?

**OBJ. 5**   **EE 21-6** p. 997   **PE 21-6B   Cash budget**

Confederate Candle Co. pays 20% of its purchases on account in the month of the purchase and 80% in the month following the purchase. If purchases are budgeted to be $18,000 for October and $19,500 for November, what are the budgeted cash payments for purchases on account for November?

## Exercises

**OBJ. 2, 5**

✔ a. December
31 cash balance,
$3,600

**EX 21-1   Personal budget**

At the beginning of the 2012 school year, Candace Thompson decided to prepare a cash budget for the months of September, October, November, and December. The budget must plan for enough cash on December 31 to pay the spring semester tuition, which is the same as the fall tuition. The following information relates to the budget:

| | |
|---|---:|
| Cash balance, September 1 (from a summer job)..................... | $6,500 |
| Purchase season football tickets in September...................... | 120 |
| Additional entertainment for each month........................... | 270 |
| Pay fall semester tuition in September ............................. | 4,000 |
| Pay rent at the beginning of each month........................... | 250 |
| Pay for food each month........................................... | 175 |
| Pay apartment deposit on September 2 (to be returned Dec. 15)...... | 500 |
| Part-time job earnings each month (net of taxes) ................... | 1,000 |

a.  Prepare a cash budget for September, October, November, and December.

b.  Are the four monthly budgets that are presented prepared as static budgets or flexible budgets?

c.  ➤ What are the budget implications for Candace Thompson?

### EX 21-2 Flexible budget for selling and administrative expenses

Net Vision uses flexible budgets that are based on the following data:

| | |
|---|---|
| Sales commissions ......................................... | 10% of sales |
| Advertising expense......................................... | 18% of sales |
| Miscellaneous selling expense ............................ | $2,800 per month plus 4% of sales |
| Office salaries expense ..................................... | $18,000 per month |
| Office supplies expense..................................... | 3% of sales |
| Miscellaneous administrative expense ...................... | $2,200 per month plus 2% of sales |

Prepare a flexible selling and administrative expenses budget for January 2012 for sales volumes of $100,000, $125,000, and $150,000. (Use Exhibit 5 as a model.)

### EX 21-3 Static budget vs. flexible budget

The production supervisor of the Machining Department for Cramer Company agreed to the following monthly static budget for the upcoming year:

**Cramer Company**
**Machining Department**
**Monthly Production Budget**

| | |
|---|---|
| Wages..................................................... | $552,000 |
| Utilities................................................... | 48,300 |
| Depreciation.............................................. | 60,000 |
| Total ................................................. | $660,300 |

The actual amount spent and the actual units produced in the first three months of 2012 in the Machining Department were as follows:

| | Amount Spent | Units Produced |
|---|---|---|
| January | $545,000 | 90,000 |
| February | 595,000 | 100,000 |
| March | 649,000 | 110,000 |

   The Machining Department supervisor has been very pleased with this performance, since actual expenditures have been less than the monthly budget. However, the plant manager believes that the budget should not remain fixed for every month but should "flex" or adjust to the volume of work that is produced in the Machining Department. Additional budget information for the Machining Department is as follows:

| | |
|---|---|
| Wages per hour | $16.00 |
| Utility cost per direct labor hour | $1.40 |
| Direct labor hours per unit | 0.30 |
| Planned monthly unit production | 115,000 |

a. Prepare a flexible budget for the actual units produced for January, February, and March in the Machining Department. Assume depreciation is a fixed cost.

b. ➤ Compare the flexible budget with the actual expenditures for the first three months. What does this comparison suggest?

### EX 21-4 Flexible budget for Fabrication Department

Steelcase Inc. is one of the largest manufacturers of office furniture in the United States. In Grand Rapids, Michigan, it produces filing cabinets in two departments: Fabrication and Trim Assembly. Assume the following information for the Fabrication Department:

| | |
|---|---|
| Steel per filing cabinet........................................... | 50 pounds |
| Direct labor per filing cabinet ...................................... | 18 minutes |
| Supervisor salaries ............................................... | $160,000 per month |
| Depreciation..................................................... | $25,000 per month |
| Direct labor rate................................................. | $23 per hour |
| Steel cost........................................................ | $1.85 per pound |

Prepare a flexible budget for 12,000, 15,000, and 18,000 filing cabinets for the month of October 2012, similar to Exhibit 5, assuming that inventories are not significant.

---

**EX 21-5    Production budget**

Rite Weight, Inc. produces a small and large version of its popular electronic scale. The anticipated unit sales for the scales by sales region are as follows:

|  | Small Scale | Large Scale |
|---|---|---|
| North Region unit sales | 29,000 | 46,000 |
| South Region unit sales | 31,000 | 55,000 |
| Total | 60,000 | 101,000 |

The finished goods inventory estimated for May 1, 2013, for the small and large scale models is 1,500 and 2,300 units, respectively. The desired finished goods inventory for May 31, 2013, for the small and large scale models is 1,100 and 2,500 units, respectively.

Prepare a production budget for the small and large scales for the month ended May 31, 2013.

---

**EX 21-6    Sales and production budgets**

Audio Mechanics, Inc. manufactures two models of speakers, DL and XL. Based on the following production and sales data for September 2012, prepare (a) a sales budget and (b) a production budget.

|  | DL | XL |
|---|---|---|
| Estimated inventory (units), September 1 .................... | 250 | 60 |
| Desired inventory (units), September 30 .................... | 275 | 48 |
| Expected sales volume (units): | | |
| East Region............................................ | 1,850 | 820 |
| West Region ........................................... | 1,540 | 710 |
| Unit sales price........................................... | $ 145 | $210 |

---

**EX 21-7    Professional fees earned budget**

Perez and Ford, CPAs, offer three types of services to clients: auditing, tax, and small business accounting. Based on experience and projected growth, the following billable hours have been estimated for the year ending December 31, 2012:

|  | Billable Hours |
|---|---|
| Audit Department: | |
| Staff...................................................... | 19,200 |
| Partners ................................................. | 6,200 |
| Tax Department: | |
| Staff...................................................... | 12,300 |
| Partners ................................................. | 4,100 |
| Small Business Accounting Department: | |
| Staff...................................................... | 4,900 |
| Partners ................................................. | 1,900 |

The average billing rate for staff is $120 per hour, and the average billing rate for partners is $280 per hour. Prepare a professional fees earned budget for Perez and Ford, CPAs, for the year ending December 31, 2012, using the following column headings and showing the estimated professional fees by type of service rendered:

| Billable Hours | Hourly Rate | Total Revenue |
|---|---|---|

**OBJ. 4**

✔ Staff total labor cost, $1,456,000

### EX 21-8 Professional labor cost budget

Based on the data in Exercise 21-7 and assuming that the average compensation per hour for staff is $40 and for partners is $150, prepare a professional labor cost budget for each department for Perez and Ford, CPAs, for the year ending December 31, 2012. Use the following column headings:

| Staff | Partners |
| --- | --- |

**OBJ. 4**

✔ Total cheese purchases, $43,904

### EX 21-9 Direct materials purchases budget

Romano's Frozen Pizza Inc. has determined from its production budget the following estimated production volumes for 12″ and 16″ frozen pizzas for June 2012:

| | Units | |
| --- | --- | --- |
| | 12″ Pizza | 16″ Pizza |
| Budgeted production volume | 5,200 | 9,400 |

There are three direct materials used in producing the two types of pizza. The quantities of direct materials expected to be used for each pizza are as follows:

| | 12″ Pizza | 16″ Pizza |
| --- | --- | --- |
| Direct materials: | | |
| Dough | 0.90 lb. per unit | 1.50 lbs. per unit |
| Tomato | 0.60 | 1.00 |
| Cheese | 0.75 | 1.25 |

In addition, Romano's has determined the following information about each material:

| | Dough | Tomato | Cheese |
| --- | --- | --- | --- |
| Estimated inventory, June 1, 2012 | 580 lbs. | 210 lbs. | 325 lbs. |
| Desired inventory, June 30, 2012 | 640 lbs. | 200 lbs. | 355 lbs. |
| Price per pound | $1.10 | $2.60 | $2.80 |

Prepare June's direct materials purchases budget for Romano's Frozen Pizza Inc.

**OBJ. 4**

✔ Concentrate budgeted purchases, $79,560

### EX 21-10 Direct materials purchases budget

Coca-Cola Enterprises is the largest bottler of Coca-Cola® in Western Europe. The company purchases Coke® and Sprite® concentrate from The Coca-Cola Company, dilutes and mixes the concentrate with carbonated water, and then fills the blended beverage into cans or plastic two-liter bottles. Assume that the estimated production for Coke and Sprite two-liter bottles at the Wakefield, UK, bottling plant are as follows for the month of March:

| Coke | 143,000 two-liter bottles |
| --- | --- |
| Sprite | 104,000 two-liter bottles |

In addition, assume that the concentrate costs $90 per pound for both Coke and Sprite and is used at a rate of 0.2 pound per 100 liters of carbonated water in blending Coke and 0.15 pound per 100 liters of carbonated water in blending Sprite. Assume that two liters of carbonated water are used for each two-liter bottle of finished product. Assume further that two-liter bottles cost $0.10 per bottle and carbonated water costs $0.08 per liter.

Prepare a direct materials purchases budget for March 2012, assuming no changes between beginning and ending inventories for concentrate, bottles, and carbonated water.

**OBJ. 4**

✔ Total steel belt purchases, $1,701,000

### EX 21-11 Direct materials purchases budget

Anticipated sales for Safe Ride Tire Company were 36,000 passenger car tires and 16,000 truck tires. Beginning and ending finished goods inventories for both products were negligible, and thus were omitted from the sales budget. Rubber and steel belts are used in producing passenger car and truck tires according to the following table:

| | Passenger Car | Truck |
|---|---|---|
| Rubber | 30 lbs. per unit | 70 lbs. per unit |
| Steel belts | 6 lbs. per unit | 10 lbs. per unit |

The purchase prices of rubber and steel are $3.60 and $4.50 per pound, respectively. The desired ending inventories of rubber and steel belts are 40,000 and 10,000 pounds, respectively. The estimated beginning inventories for rubber and steel belts are 46,000 and 8,000 pounds, respectively.

Prepare a direct materials purchases budget for Safe Ride Tire Company for the year ended December 31, 2012.

---

**OBJ. 4**

✔ Total direct labor cost, Assembly, $72,300

### EX 21-12 Direct labor cost budget

Ace Racket Company manufactures two types of tennis rackets, the Junior and Pro Striker models. The production budget for May for the two rackets is as follows:

| | Junior | Pro Striker |
|---|---|---|
| Production budget | 1,400 units | 7,100 units |

Both rackets are produced in two departments, Forming and Assembly. The direct labor hours required for each racket are estimated as follows:

| | Forming Department | Assembly Department |
|---|---|---|
| Junior | 0.30 hour per unit | 0.40 hour per unit |
| Pro Striker | 0.35 hour per unit | 0.60 hour per unit |

The direct labor rate for each department is as follows:

| Forming Department | $18.00 per hour |
|---|---|
| Assembly Department | $15.00 per hour |

Prepare the direct labor cost budget for May 2012.

---

**OBJ. 4**

✔ Average weekday total, $1,800

### EX 21-13 Direct labor budget—service business

Executive Inn, Inc., operates a downtown hotel property that has 200 rooms. On average, 90% of Executive Inn's rooms are occupied on weekdays, and 60% are occupied during the weekend. The manager has asked you to develop a direct labor budget for the housekeeping and restaurant staff for weekdays and weekends. You have determined that the housekeeping staff requires 30 minutes to clean each occupied room. The housekeeping staff is paid $12 per hour. The restaurant has six full-time staff (eight-hour day) on duty, regardless of occupancy. However, for every 60 occupied rooms, an additional person is brought in to work in the restaurant for the eight-hour day. The restaurant staff is paid $10 per hour.

Determine the estimated housekeeping, restaurant, and total direct labor cost for an average weekday and average weekend day. Format the budget in two columns, labeled as weekday and weekend day.

---

**OBJ. 4**

✔ a. Total production of 501 Jeans, 45,000

### EX 21-14 Production and direct labor cost budgets

Levi Strauss & Co. manufactures slacks and jeans under a variety of brand names, such as Dockers® and 501 Jeans®. Slacks and jeans are assembled by a variety of different sewing operations. Assume that the sales budget for Dockers and 501 Jeans shows estimated sales of 20,500 and 44,200 pairs, respectively, for March 2012. The finished goods inventory is assumed as follows:

| | Dockers | 501 Jeans |
|---|---|---|
| March 1 estimated inventory | 980 | 1,590 |
| March 31 desired inventory | 480 | 2,390 |

Assume the following direct labor data per 10 pairs of Dockers and 501 Jeans for four different sewing operations:

| | Direct Labor per 10 Pairs | |
|---|---|---|
| | **Dockers** | **501 Jeans** |
| Inseam | 18 minutes | 12 minutes |
| Outerseam | 21 | 15 |
| Pockets | 6 | 9 |
| Zipper | 12 | 6 |
| Total | 57 minutes | 42 minutes |

a. Prepare a production budget for March. Prepare the budget in two columns: Dockers® and 501 Jeans®.

b. Prepare the March direct labor cost budget for the four sewing operations, assuming a $13 wage per hour for the inseam and outerseam sewing operations and a $15 wage per hour for the pocket and zipper sewing operations. Prepare the direct labor cost budget in four columns: inseam, outerseam, pockets, and zipper.

---

**OBJ. 4**

✔ Total variable factory overhead costs, $242,000

### EX 21-15  Factory overhead cost budget

Blondie Candy Company budgeted the following costs for anticipated production for July 2012:

| | | | |
|---|---|---|---|
| Advertising expenses | $245,000 | Production supervisor wages | $126,000 |
| Manufacturing supplies | 12,000 | Production control wages | 29,000 |
| Power and light | 41,000 | Executive officer salaries | 272,000 |
| Sales commissions | 285,000 | Materials management wages | 34,000 |
| Factory insurance | 25,000 | Factory depreciation | 20,000 |

Prepare a factory overhead cost budget, separating variable and fixed costs. Assume that factory insurance and depreciation are the only fixed factory costs.

---

**OBJ. 4**

✔ Cost of goods sold, $2,954,700

### EX 21-16  Cost of goods sold budget

Dover Chemical Company uses oil to produce two types of plastic products, P1 and P2. Dover budgeted 30,000 barrels of oil for purchase in April for $78 per barrel. Direct labor budgeted in the chemical process was $240,000 for April. Factory overhead was budgeted $375,000 during April. The inventories on April 1 were estimated to be:

| | |
|---|---|
| Oil ................................... | $15,800 |
| P1.................................... | 9,800 |
| P2.................................... | 8,900 |
| Work in process ...................... | 12,100 |

The desired inventories on April 30 were:

| | |
|---|---|
| Oil ................................... | $16,100 |
| P1.................................... | 9,400 |
| P2.................................... | 7,900 |
| Work in process ...................... | 13,500 |

Use the preceding information to prepare a cost of goods sold budget for April 2013.

---

**OBJ. 4**

✔ Cost of goods sold, $449,690

### EX 21-17  Cost of goods sold budget

The controller of Oriental Ceramics Inc. wishes to prepare a cost of goods sold budget for June. The controller assembled the following information for constructing the cost of goods sold budget:

| Direct materials: | Enamel | Paint | Porcelain | Total |
|---|---|---|---|---|
| Total direct materials purchases budgeted for June | $33,840 | $6,940 | $134,200 | $174,980 |
| Estimated inventory, June 1, 2012 | 1,150 | 2,800 | 4,620 | 8,570 |
| Desired inventory, June 30, 2012 | 2,550 | 2,310 | 6,000 | 10,860 |

| Direct labor cost: | Kiln Department | Decorating Department | | Total |
|---|---|---|---|---|
| Total direct labor cost budgeted for June | $44,700 | $132,500 | | $177,200 |

| Finished goods inventories: | Dish | Bowl | Figurine | Total |
|---|---|---|---|---|
| Estimated inventory, June 1, 2012 | $5,240 | $2,970 | $2,470 | $10,680 |
| Desired inventory, June 30, 2012 | 3,350 | 4,150 | 3,920 | 11,420 |

| Work in process inventories: | |
|---|---|
| Estimated inventory, June 1, 2012 | $3,200 |
| Desired inventory, June 30, 2012 | 1,760 |

| Budgeted factory overhead costs for June: | |
|---|---|
| Indirect factory wages | $77,900 |
| Depreciation of plant and equipment | 12,600 |
| Power and light | 4,900 |
| Indirect materials | 3,700 |
| Total | $99,100 |

Use the preceding information to prepare a cost of goods sold budget for June 2012.

---

**OBJ. 5**

✔ Total cash collected in May, $191,400

**EX 21-18** **Schedule of cash collections of accounts receivable**

Pet Mart Wholesale Inc., a pet wholesale supplier, was organized on March 1, 2012. Projected sales for each of the first three months of operations are as follows:

| March | $ 90,000 |
|---|---|
| April | 150,000 |
| May | 240,000 |

The company expects to sell 10% of its merchandise for cash. Of sales on account, 50% are expected to be collected in the month of the sale, 35% in the month following the sale, and the remainder in the second month following the sale.

Prepare a schedule indicating cash collections from sales for March, April, and May.

---

**OBJ. 5**

✔ Total cash collected in August, $128,000

**EX 21-19** **Schedule of cash collections of accounts receivable**

Office Universe Supplies Inc. has "cash and carry" customers and credit customers. Office Universe estimates that 25% of monthly sales are to cash customers, while the remaining sales are to credit customers. Of the credit customers, 20% pay their accounts in the month of sale, while the remaining 80% pay their accounts in the month following the month of sale. Projected sales for the next three months of 2012 are as follows:

| August | $120,000 |
|---|---|
| September | 150,000 |
| October | 220,000 |

The Accounts Receivable balance on July 31, 2012, was $80,000.

Prepare a schedule of cash collections from sales for August, September, and October.

---

**OBJ. 5**

✔ Total cash payments in December, $73,940

**EX 21-20** **Schedule of cash payments**

Sage Learning Systems Inc. was organized on September 30, 2012. Projected selling and administrative expenses for each of the first three months of operations are as follows:

| October | $67,500 |
|---|---|
| November | 75,200 |
| December | 88,100 |

Depreciation, insurance, and property taxes represent $9,000 of the estimated monthly expenses. The annual insurance premium was paid on September 30, and property taxes for the year will be paid in June. Sixty percent of the remainder of the expenses are expected to be paid in the month in which they are incurred, with the balance to be paid in the following month.

Prepare a schedule indicating cash payments for selling and administrative expenses for October, November, and December.

OBJ. 5

✔ Total cash
payments in
September, $141,760

### EX 21-21 Schedule of cash payments

Select Physical Therapy Inc. is planning its cash payments for operations for the third quarter (July–September), 2013. The Accrued Expenses Payable balance on July 1 is $28,000. The budgeted expenses for the next three months are as follows:

| | July | August | September |
|---|---|---|---|
| Salaries | $ 63,200 | $ 78,100 | $ 84,900 |
| Utilities | 5,300 | 5,600 | 7,100 |
| Other operating expenses | 48,500 | 52,700 | 58,200 |
| Total | $117,000 | $136,400 | $150,200 |

Other operating expenses include $3,500 of monthly depreciation expense and $800 of monthly insurance expense that was prepaid for the year on March 1 of the current year. Of the remaining expenses, 70% are paid in the month in which they are incurred, with the remainder paid in the following month. The Accrued Expenses Payable balance on July 1 relates to the expenses incurred in June.

Prepare a schedule of cash payments for operations for July, August, and September.

OBJ. 5

✔ Total capital
expenditures in
2012, $5,500,000

### EX 21-22 Capital expenditures budget

On January 1, 2012, the controller of Med-Tek Inc. is planning capital expenditures for the years 2012–2015. The following interviews helped the controller collect the necessary information for the capital expenditures budget:

*Director of Facilities:* A construction contract was signed in late 2011 for the construction of a new factory building at a contract cost of $9,000,000. The construction is scheduled to begin in 2012 and be completed in 2013.

*Vice President of Manufacturing:* Once the new factory building is finished, we plan to purchase $1.2 million in equipment in late 2013. I expect that an additional $150,000 will be needed early in the following year (2014) to test and install the equipment before we can begin production. If sales continue to grow, I expect we'll need to invest another $900,000 in equipment in 2015.

*Vice President of Marketing:* We have really been growing lately. I wouldn't be surprised if we need to expand the size of our new factory building in 2015 by at least 40%. Fortunately, we expect inflation to have minimal impact on construction costs over the next four years. Additionally, I would expect the cost of the expansion to be proportional to the size of the expansion.

*Director of Information Systems:* We need to upgrade our information systems to wireless network technology. It doesn't make sense to do this until after the new factory building is completed and producing product. During 2014, once the factory is up and running, we should equip the whole facility with wireless technology. I think it would cost us $1,200,000 today to install the technology. However, prices have been dropping by 25% per year, so it should be less expensive at a later date.

*President:* I am excited about our long-term prospects. My only short-term concern is financing the $5,500,000 of construction costs on the portion of the new factory building scheduled to be completed in 2012.

Use the interview information above to prepare a capital expenditures budget for Med-Tek Inc. for the years 2012–2015.

## Problems Series A

OBJ. 4

✔ 3. Total revenue
from sales, $855,111

### PR 21-1A Forecast sales volume and sales budget

Da Vinci Frame Company prepared the following sales budget for the current year:

**Da Vinci Frame Company**
**Sales Budget**
**For the Year Ending December 31, 2012**

| Product and Area | Unit Sales Volume | Unit Selling Price | Total Sales |
|---|---|---|---|
| 8" × 10" Frame: | | | |
| East | 9,400 | $15.00 | $141,000 |
| Central | 6,900 | 15.00 | 103,500 |
| West | 13,200 | 15.00 | 198,000 |
| Total | 29,500 | | $442,500 |

12" × 16" Frame:

| | | | |
|---|---|---|---|
| East | 4,200 | $25.00 | $105,000 |
| Central | 3,100 | 25.00 | 77,500 |
| West | 5,900 | 25.00 | 147,500 |
| Total | 13,200 | | $330,000 |
| Total revenue from sales | | | $772,500 |

At the end of December 2012, the following unit sales data were reported for the year:

| | Unit Sales | |
|---|---|---|
| | 8" × 10" Frame | 12" × 16" Frame |
| East | 9,870 | 4,116 |
| Central | 7,107 | 3,224 |
| West | 13,068 | 6,018 |

For the year ending December 31, 2013, unit sales are expected to follow the patterns established during the year ending December 31, 2012. The unit selling price for the 8" × 10" frame is expected to increase to $16 and the unit selling price for the 12" × 16" frame is expected to increase to $27, effective January 1, 2013.

**Instructions**

1. Compute the increase or decrease of actual unit sales for the year ended December 31, 2012, over budget. Place your answers in a columnar table with the following format:

| | Unit Sales, Year Ended 2012 | | Increase (Decrease) Actual Over Budget | |
|---|---|---|---|---|
| | Budget | Actual Sales | Amount | Percent |
| 8" × 10" Frame: | | | | |
| East | | | | |
| Central | | | | |
| West | | | | |
| 12" × 16" Frame: | | | | |
| East | | | | |
| Central | | | | |
| West | | | | |

2. Assuming that the increase or decrease in actual sales to budget indicated in part (1) is to continue in 2013, compute the unit sales volume to be used for preparing the sales budget for the year ending December 31, 2013. Place your answers in a columnar table similar to that in part (1) above but with the following column heads. Round budgeted units to the nearest unit.

| 2012 Actual Units | Percentage Increase (Decrease) | 2013 Budgeted Units (rounded) |
|---|---|---|

3. Prepare a sales budget for the year ending December 31, 2013.

---

OBJ. 4

✔ 3. Total direct materials purchases, $939,065

**PR 21-2A  Sales, production, direct materials purchases, and direct labor cost budgets**

The budget director of Outdoor Chef Grill Company requests estimates of sales, production, and other operating data from the various administrative units every month. Selected information concerning sales and production for May 2012 is summarized as follows:

a. Estimated sales for May by sales territory:

Maine:

| Backyard Chef | 280 units at $750 per unit |
|---|---|
| Master Chef | 250 units at $1,500 per unit |

Vermont:

| Backyard Chef | 210 units at $800 per unit |
|---|---|
| Master Chef | 160 units at $1,600 per unit |

New Hampshire:

| Backyard Chef | 305 units at $850 per unit |
|---|---|
| Master Chef | 275 units at $1,700 per unit |

b. Estimated inventories at May 1:

| Direct materials: | | Finished products: | |
|---|---|---|---|
| Grates......................... | 300 units | Backyard Chef ............ | 36 units |
| Stainless steel.................. | 1,800 lbs. | Master Chef............... | 18 units |
| Burner subassemblies .......... | 150 units | | |
| Shelves....................... | 300 units | | |

c. Desired inventories at May 31:

| Direct materials: | | Finished products: | |
|---|---|---|---|
| Grates......................... | 320 units | Backyard Chef ............ | 31 units |
| Stainless steel.................. | 2,100 lbs. | Master Chef............... | 23 units |
| Burner subassemblies .......... | 135 units | | |
| Shelves....................... | 285 units | | |

d. Direct materials used in production:

In manufacture of Backyard Chef:

| | |
|---|---|
| Grates.............................................. | 3 units per unit of product |
| Stainless steel....................................... | 24 lbs. per unit of product |
| Burner subassemblies ................................. | 2 units per unit of product |
| Shelves............................................. | 4 units per unit of product |

In manufacture of Master Chef:

| | |
|---|---|
| Grates.............................................. | 6 units per unit of product |
| Stainless steel....................................... | 42 lbs. per unit of product |
| Burner subassemblies ................................. | 4 units per unit of product |
| Shelves............................................. | 5 units per unit of product |

e. Anticipated purchase price for direct materials:

| | | | |
|---|---|---|---|
| Grates..................... | $16 per unit | Burner subassemblies ......... | $125 per unit |
| Stainless steel.............. | $5 per lb. | Shelves...................... | $8 per unit |

f. Direct labor requirements:

Backyard Chef:

| | |
|---|---|
| Stamping Department........................................ | 0.60 hr. at $17 per hr. |
| Forming Department......................................... | 0.80 hr. at $14 per hr. |
| Assembly Department........................................ | 2.0 hrs. at $12 per hr. |

Master Chef:

| | |
|---|---|
| Stamping Department........................................ | 0.80 hr. at $17 per hr. |
| Forming Department......................................... | 1.50 hrs. at $14 per hr. |
| Assembly Department........................................ | 2.50 hrs. at $12 per hr. |

**Instructions**

1. Prepare a sales budget for May.
2. Prepare a production budget for May.
3. Prepare a direct materials purchases budget for May.
4. Prepare a direct labor cost budget for May.

OBJ. 4

✔ 4. Total direct labor cost in Fabrication Dept., $32,760

**PR 21-3A    Budgeted income statement and supporting budgets**

The budget director of Feathered Friends Inc., with the assistance of the controller, treasurer, production manager, and sales manager, has gathered the following data for use in developing the budgeted income statement for October 2012:

a. Estimated sales for October:

| | |
|---|---|
| Bird house........................................... | 3,500 units at $45 per unit |
| Bird feeder.......................................... | 3,700 units at $65 per unit |

b. Estimated inventories at October 1:

| Direct materials: | | | Finished products: | | |
|---|---|---|---|---|---|
| Wood ........ | 240 ft. | | Bird house ....... | 300 units at $22 per unit | |
| Plastic........ | 360 lbs. | | Bird feeder....... | 200 units at $33 per unit | |

c. Desired inventories at October 31:

| Direct materials: | | | Finished products: | | |
|---|---|---|---|---|---|
| Wood ........ | 290 ft. | | Bird house ....... | 360 units at $22 per unit | |
| Plastic........ | 340 lbs. | | Bird feeder....... | 180 units at $34 per unit | |

d. Direct materials used in production:

| In manufacture of bird house: | | In manufacture of bird feeder: | |
|---|---|---|---|
| Wood ............ | 0.80 ft. per unit of product | Wood ........... | 1.20 ft. per unit of product |
| Plastic............ | 0.50 lb. per unit of product | Plastic........... | 0.75 lb. per unit of product |

e. Anticipated cost of purchases and beginning and ending inventory of direct materials:

Wood ....................... $6.00 per ft.     Plastic................. $0.80 per lb.

f. Direct labor requirements:

Bird house:
| Fabrication Department ......................................... | 0.20 hr. at $15 per hr. |
|---|---|
| Assembly Department......................................... | 0.30 hr. at $11 per hr. |

Bird feeder:
| Fabrication Department ......................................... | 0.40 hr. at $15 per hr. |
|---|---|
| Assembly Department......................................... | 0.35 hr. at $11 per hr. |

g. Estimated factory overhead costs for October:

| Indirect factory wages | $70,000 | Power and light | $5,000 |
|---|---|---|---|
| Depreciation of plant and equipment | 18,000 | Insurance and property tax | 2,500 |

h. Estimated operating expenses for October:

| Sales salaries expense | $65,000 |
|---|---|
| Advertising expense | 15,000 |
| Office salaries expense | 22,000 |
| Depreciation expense—office equipment | 500 |
| Telephone expense—selling | 450 |
| Telephone expense—administrative | 150 |
| Travel expense—selling | 3,700 |
| Office supplies expense | 350 |
| Miscellaneous administrative expense | 500 |

i. Estimated other income and expense for October:

| Interest revenue | $170 |
|---|---|
| Interest expense | 118 |

j. Estimated tax rate: 30%

**Instructions**
1. Prepare a sales budget for October.
2. Prepare a production budget for October.
3. Prepare a direct materials purchases budget for October.
4. Prepare a direct labor cost budget for October.
5. Prepare a factory overhead cost budget for October.
6. Prepare a cost of goods sold budget for October. Work in process at the beginning of October is estimated to be $27,000, and work in process at the end of October is estimated to be $32,400.
7. Prepare a selling and administrative expenses budget for October.
8. Prepare a budgeted income statement for October.

**OBJ. 5**

✔ 1. May deficiency, $5,130

### PR 21-4A   Cash budget

The controller of Santa Fe Housewares Inc. instructs you to prepare a monthly cash budget for the next three months. You are presented with the following budget information:

| | March | April | May |
|---|---|---|---|
| Sales . . . . . . . . . . . . . . . . . . . . . . . . . . . . . . . . . . . . . . . . . . . . . . . . . . . . . . . | $70,000 | $84,000 | $92,000 |
| Manufacturing costs. . . . . . . . . . . . . . . . . . . . . . . . . . . . . . . . . . . . . . . . | 32,000 | 39,000 | 42,500 |
| Selling and administrative expenses . . . . . . . . . . . . . . . . . . . . . . . . | 12,000 | 18,000 | 21,000 |
| Capital expenditures . . . . . . . . . . . . . . . . . . . . . . . . . . . . . . . . . . . . . . . | | | 20,000 |

The company expects to sell about 10% of its merchandise for cash. Of sales on account, 70% are expected to be collected in full in the month following the sale and the remainder the following month. Depreciation, insurance, and property tax expense represent $3,000 of the estimated monthly manufacturing costs. The annual insurance premium is paid in July, and the annual property taxes are paid in November. Of the remainder of the manufacturing costs, 80% are expected to be paid in the month in which they are incurred and the balance in the following month.

Current assets as of March 1 include cash of $10,000, marketable securities of $40,000, and accounts receivable of $75,600 ($60,000 from February sales and $15,600 from January sales). Sales on account for January and February were $52,000 and $60,000, respectively. Current liabilities as of March 1 include a $12,000, 15%, 90-day note payable due May 20 and $4,000 of accounts payable incurred in February for manufacturing costs. All selling and administrative expenses are paid in cash in the period they are incurred. It is expected that $1,800 in dividends will be received in March. An estimated income tax payment of $16,000 will be made in April. Santa Fe's regular quarterly dividend of $3,000 is expected to be declared in April and paid in May. Management desires to maintain a minimum cash balance of $30,000.

**Instructions**

1. Prepare a monthly cash budget and supporting schedules for March, April, and May.

2. ━━━━▶ On the basis of the cash budget prepared in part (1), what recommendation should be made to the controller?

**OBJ. 4, 5**

✔ 1. Budgeted net income, $44,800

### PR 21-5A   Budgeted income statement and balance sheet

As a preliminary to requesting budget estimates of sales, costs, and expenses for the fiscal year beginning January 1, 2013, the following tentative trial balance as of December 31, 2012, is prepared by the Accounting Department of Tahiti Blossom Soap Co.:

| | | |
|---|---|---|
| Cash . . . . . . . . . . . . . . . . . . . . . . . . . . . . . . . . . . . . . . . . . . . . . . . . . . . . . . . | $100,000 | |
| Accounts Receivable. . . . . . . . . . . . . . . . . . . . . . . . . . . . . . . . . . . . . . . . | 112,300 | |
| Finished Goods . . . . . . . . . . . . . . . . . . . . . . . . . . . . . . . . . . . . . . . . . . . . | 76,700 | |
| Work in Process . . . . . . . . . . . . . . . . . . . . . . . . . . . . . . . . . . . . . . . . . . . | 24,300 | |
| Materials . . . . . . . . . . . . . . . . . . . . . . . . . . . . . . . . . . . . . . . . . . . . . . . . . | 54,100 | |
| Prepaid Expenses . . . . . . . . . . . . . . . . . . . . . . . . . . . . . . . . . . . . . . . . . | 3,400 | |
| Plant and Equipment . . . . . . . . . . . . . . . . . . . . . . . . . . . . . . . . . . . . . . . | 295,000 | |
| Accumulated Depreciation—Plant and Equipment . . . . . . . . . . . . . . . . . | | $140,400 |
| Accounts Payable . . . . . . . . . . . . . . . . . . . . . . . . . . . . . . . . . . . . . . . . . | | 59,000 |
| Common Stock, $10 par . . . . . . . . . . . . . . . . . . . . . . . . . . . . . . . . . . . . | | 210,000 |
| Retained Earnings . . . . . . . . . . . . . . . . . . . . . . . . . . . . . . . . . . . . . . . . | | 256,400 |
| | $665,800 | $665,800 |

Factory output and sales for 2013 are expected to total 160,000 units of product, which are to be sold at $4.50 per unit. The quantities and costs of the inventories at December 31, 2013, are expected to remain unchanged from the balances at the beginning of the year.

Budget estimates of manufacturing costs and operating expenses for the year are summarized as follows:

| | Estimated Costs and Expenses | |
|---|---|---|
| | Fixed (Total for Year) | Variable (Per Unit Sold) |
| Cost of goods manufactured and sold: | | |
| Direct materials ............................................. | — | $0.90 |
| Direct labor................................................... | — | 0.55 |
| Factory overhead: | | |
| Depreciation of plant and equipment......................... | $45,000 | — |
| Other factory overhead...................................... | 8,000 | 0.35 |
| Selling expenses: | | |
| Sales salaries and commissions............................... | 37,000 | 0.40 |
| Advertising ................................................. | 55,000 | — |
| Miscellaneous selling expense ............................... | 5,000 | 0.20 |
| Administrative expenses: | | |
| Office and officers salaries .................................... | 58,200 | 0.15 |
| Supplies....................................................... | 4,000 | 0.08 |
| Miscellaneous administrative expense ........................... | 3,000 | 0.12 |

Balances of accounts receivable, prepaid expenses, and accounts payable at the end of the year are not expected to differ significantly from the beginning balances. Federal income tax of $20,000 on 2013 taxable income will be paid during 2013. Regular quarterly cash dividends of $0.10 per share are expected to be declared and paid in March, June, September, and December on 21,000 shares of common stock outstanding. It is anticipated that fixed assets will be purchased for $60,000 cash in May.

**Instructions**

1. Prepare a budgeted income statement for 2013.

2. Prepare a budgeted balance sheet as of December 31, 2013, with supporting calculations.

## Problems Series B

OBJ. 4

✔ 3. Total revenue from sales, $20,373,510

**PR 21-1B   Forecast sales volume and sales budget**

Alert Systems Inc. prepared the following sales budget for the current year:

**Alert Systems Inc.**
**Sales Budget**
**For the Year Ending December 31, 2012**

| Product and Area | Unit Sales Volume | Unit Selling Price | Total Sales |
|---|---|---|---|
| Home Alert System: | | | |
| United States ...................................... | 18,900 | $250 | $ 4,725,000 |
| Europe ........................................... | 5,400 | 250 | 1,350,000 |
| Asia .............................................. | 4,500 | 250 | 1,125,000 |
| Total ........................................... | 28,800 | | $ 7,200,000 |
| Business Alert System: | | | |
| United States ...................................... | 9,500 | $800 | $ 7,600,000 |
| Europe ........................................... | 3,200 | 800 | 2,560,000 |
| Asia .............................................. | 2,700 | 800 | 2,160,000 |
| Total ........................................... | 15,400 | | $12,320,000 |
| Total revenue from sales ............................. | | | $19,520,000 |

At the end of December 2012, the following unit sales data were reported for the year:

| | Unit Sales | |
|---|---|---|
| | **Home Alert System** | **Business Alert System** |
| United States | 19,845 | 9,880 |
| Europe | 5,292 | 3,264 |
| Asia | 4,545 | 2,619 |

For the year ending December 31, 2013, unit sales are expected to follow the patterns established during the year ending December 31, 2012. The unit selling price for the Home Alert System is expected to increase to $270, and the unit selling price for the Business Alert System is expected to be decreased to $750, effective January 1, 2013.

### Instructions

1. Compute the increase or decrease of actual unit sales for the year ended December 31, 2012, over budget. Place your answers in a columnar table with the following format:

| | Unit Sales, Year Ended 2012 | | Increase (Decrease) Actual Over Budget | |
|---|---|---|---|---|
| | **Budget** | **Actual Sales** | **Amount** | **Percent** |
| Home Alert System: | | | | |
| United States .................. | | | | |
| Europe ....................... | | | | |
| Asia .......................... | | | | |
| Business Alert System: | | | | |
| United States .................. | | | | |
| Europe ....................... | | | | |
| Asia .......................... | | | | |

2. Assuming that the increase or decrease in actual sales to budget indicated in part (1) is to continue in 2013, compute the unit sales volume to be used for preparing the sales budget for the year ending December 31, 2013. Place your answers in a columnar table similar to that in part (1) above but with the following column heads. Round budgeted units to the nearest unit.

| 2012 Actual Units | Percentage Increase (Decrease) | 2013 Budgeted Units (rounded) |
|---|---|---|

3. Prepare a sales budget for the year ending December 31, 2013.

---

### PR 21-2B  Sales, production, direct materials purchases, and direct labor cost budgets

The budget director of Monarch Furniture Company requests estimates of sales, production, and other operating data from the various administrative units every month. Selected information concerning sales and production for November 2012 is summarized as follows:

a. Estimated sales of King and Prince chairs for November by sales territory:

Northern Domestic:

| | |
|---|---|
| King........................................ | 5,800 units at $750 per unit |
| Prince...................................... | 7,200 units at $570 per unit |

Southern Domestic:

| | |
|---|---|
| King........................................ | 3,600 units at $690 per unit |
| Prince...................................... | 4,100 units at $580 per unit |

International:

| | |
|---|---|
| King........................................ | 1,750 units at $780 per unit |
| Prince...................................... | 1,100 units at $610 per unit |

b. Estimated inventories at November 1:

| Direct materials: | | Finished products: | |
|---|---|---|---|
| Fabric .................. | 4,500 sq. yds. | King.................... | 950 units |
| Wood .................. | 6,000 linear ft. | Prince ................. | 280 units |
| Filler ................... | 2,800 cu. ft. | | |
| Springs................. | 6,700 units | | |

c. Desired inventories at November 30:

| Direct materials: | | Finished products: | |
|---|---|---|---|
| Fabric | 4,100 sq. yds. | King | 900 units |
| Wood | 6,200 linear ft. | Prince | 400 units |
| Filler | 3,100 cu. ft. | | |
| Springs | 7,200 units | | |

d. Direct materials used in production:

In manufacture of King:

| Fabric | 6.0 sq. yds. per unit of product |
|---|---|
| Wood | 38 linear ft. per unit of product |
| Filler | 4.2 cu. ft. per unit of product |
| Springs | 16 units per unit of product |

In manufacture of Prince:

| Fabric | 4.0 sq. yds. per unit of product |
|---|---|
| Wood | 26 linear ft. per unit of product |
| Filler | 3.4 cu. ft. per unit of product |
| Springs | 12 units per unit of product |

e. Anticipated purchase price for direct materials:

| Fabric | $14.00 per sq. yd. | Filler | $3.50 per cu. ft. |
|---|---|---|---|
| Wood | 8.00 per linear ft. | Springs | 4.00 per unit |

f. Direct labor requirements:

King:

| Framing Department | 2.6 hrs. at $12 per hr. |
|---|---|
| Cutting Department | 1.4 hrs. at $11 per hr. |
| Upholstery Department | 2.2 hrs. at $15 per hr. |

Prince:

| Framing Department | 2.0 hrs. at $12 per hr. |
|---|---|
| Cutting Department | 0.5 hr. at $11 per hr. |
| Upholstery Department | 1.8 hrs. at $15 per hr. |

**Instructions**

1. Prepare a sales budget for November.
2. Prepare a production budget for November.
3. Prepare a direct materials purchases budget for November.
4. Prepare a direct labor cost budget for November.

OBJ. 4

✔ 4. Total direct labor cost in Assembly Dept., $7,358

**PR 21-3B    Budgeted income statement and supporting budgets**

The budget director of Hi Performance Athletic Co., with the assistance of the controller, treasurer, production manager, and sales manager, has gathered the following data for use in developing the budgeted income statement for January 2012:

a. Estimated sales for January:

| Batting helmet | 305 units at $70 per unit |
|---|---|
| Football helmet | 630 units at $135 per unit |

b. Estimated inventories at January 1:

| Direct materials: | | Finished products: | |
|---|---|---|---|
| Plastic | 80 lbs. | Batting helmet | 35 units at $40 per unit |
| Foam lining | 60 lbs. | Football helmet | 40 units at $60 per unit |

c. Desired inventories at January 31:

| Direct materials: | | Finished products: | |
|---|---|---|---|
| Plastic............... | 90 lbs. | Batting helmet......... | 30 units at $40 per unit |
| Foam lining......... | 55 lbs. | Football helmet........ | 50 units at $58 per unit |

d. Direct materials used in production:

In manufacture of batting helmet:

| | |
|---|---|
| Plastic............................................. | 1.20 lbs. per unit of product |
| Foam lining........................................ | 0.50 lb. per unit of product |

In manufacture of football helmet:

| | |
|---|---|
| Plastic............................................. | 2.80 lbs. per unit of product |
| Foam lining........................................ | 1.40 lbs. per unit of product |

e. Anticipated cost of purchases and beginning and ending inventory of direct materials:

| | |
|---|---|
| Plastic...................................... | $5.50 per lb. |
| Foam lining................................. | $4.00 per lb. |

f. Direct labor requirements:

Batting helmet:

| | |
|---|---|
| Molding Department............................. | 0.20 hr. at $15 per hr. |
| Assembly Department............................ | 0.50 hr. at $13 per hr. |

Football helmet:

| | |
|---|---|
| Molding Department............................. | 0.30 hr. at $15 per hr. |
| Assembly Department............................ | 0.65 hr. at $13 per hr. |

g. Estimated factory overhead costs for January:

| | | | |
|---|---|---|---|
| Indirect factory wages | $14,500 | Power and light | $2,000 |
| Depreciation of plant and equipment | 4,200 | Insurance and property tax | 1,700 |

h. Estimated operating expenses for January:

| | |
|---|---|
| Sales salaries expense | $15,400 |
| Advertising expense | 8,500 |
| Office salaries expense | 11,500 |
| Depreciation expense—office equipment | 3,200 |
| Telephone expense—selling | 950 |
| Telephone expense—administrative | 600 |
| Travel expense—selling | 2,300 |
| Office supplies expense | 550 |
| Miscellaneous administrative expense | 400 |

i. Estimated other income and expense for January:

| | |
|---|---|
| Interest revenue | $140 |
| Interest expense | 172 |

j. Estimated tax rate: 30%

**Instructions**

1. Prepare a sales budget for January.
2. Prepare a production budget for January.
3. Prepare a direct materials purchases budget for January.
4. Prepare a direct labor cost budget for January.
5. Prepare a factory overhead cost budget for January.
6. Prepare a cost of goods sold budget for January. Work in process at the beginning of January is estimated to be $12,500, and work in process at the end of January is desired to be $13,500.
7. Prepare a selling and administrative expenses budget for January.
8. Prepare a budgeted income statement for January.

### PR 21-4B    Cash budget

The controller of Fleet Shoes Inc. instructs you to prepare a monthly cash budget for the next three months. You are presented with the following budget information:

|  | June | July | August |
|---|---|---|---|
| Sales | $140,000 | $176,000 | $240,000 |
| Manufacturing costs | 60,000 | 75,000 | 94,000 |
| Selling and administrative expenses | 35,000 | 40,000 | 45,000 |
| Capital expenditures | — | — | 55,000 |

The company expects to sell about 10% of its merchandise for cash. Of sales on account, 60% are expected to be collected in full in the month following the sale and the remainder the following month. Depreciation, insurance, and property tax expense represent $10,000 of the estimated monthly manufacturing costs. The annual insurance premium is paid in February, and the annual property taxes are paid in November. Of the remainder of the manufacturing costs, 80% are expected to be paid in the month in which they are incurred and the balance in the following month.

Current assets as of June 1 include cash of $48,000, marketable securities of $65,000, and accounts receivable of $168,000 ($124,000 from May sales and $44,000 from April sales). Sales on account in April and May were $110,000 and $124,000, respectively. Current liabilities as of June 1 include a $65,000, 8%, 90-day note payable due August 20 and $8,000 of accounts payable incurred in May for manufacturing costs. All selling and administrative expenses are paid in cash in the period they are incurred. It is expected that $4,000 in dividends will be received in June. An estimated income tax payment of $18,000 will be made in July. Fleet Shoes' regular quarterly dividend of $8,000 is expected to be declared in July and paid in August. Management desires to maintain a minimum cash balance of $45,000.

### Instructions

1. Prepare a monthly cash budget and supporting schedules for June, July, and August 2012.

2. ━━━▶ On the basis of the cash budget prepared in part (1), what recommendation should be made to the controller?

### PR 21-5B    Budgeted income statement and balance sheet

As a preliminary to requesting budget estimates of sales, costs, and expenses for the fiscal year beginning January 1, 2013, the following tentative trial balance as of December 31, 2012, is prepared by the Accounting Department of Franklin Publishing Co.:

| | | |
|---|---|---|
| Cash | $ 22,000 | |
| Accounts Receivable | 24,500 | |
| Finished Goods | 14,300 | |
| Work in Process | 3,500 | |
| Materials | 5,100 | |
| Prepaid Expenses | 400 | |
| Plant and Equipment | 55,000 | |
| Accumulated Depreciation—Plant and Equipment | | $ 26,000 |
| Accounts Payable | | 17,900 |
| Common Stock, $1.50 par | | 45,000 |
| Retained Earnings | | 35,900 |
| | $124,800 | $124,800 |

Factory output and sales for 2013 are expected to total 3,200 units of product, which are to be sold at $100 per unit. The quantities and costs of the inventories at December 31, 2013, are expected to remain unchanged from the balances at the beginning of the year.

Budget estimates of manufacturing costs and operating expenses for the year are summarized as follows:

| | Estimated Costsw and Expenses | |
| --- | --- | --- |
| | Fixed (Total for Year) | Variable (Per Unit Sold) |
| Cost of goods manufactured and sold: | | |
| Direct materials....................................... | — | $25.00 |
| Direct labor.......................................... | — | 7.80 |
| Factory overhead: | | |
| Depreciation of plant and equipment.................. | $ 3,200 | — |
| Other factory overhead............................... | 1,100 | 4.50 |
| Selling expenses: | | |
| Sales salaries and commissions......................... | 10,500 | 12.80 |
| Advertising......................................... | 11,800 | — |
| Miscellaneous selling expense ......................... | 900 | 2.00 |
| Administrative expenses: | | |
| Office and officers salaries ............................ | 7,400 | 6.25 |
| Supplies............................................ | 400 | 1.00 |
| Miscellaneous administrative expense ................... | 200 | 1.50 |

Balances of accounts receivable, prepaid expenses, and accounts payable at the end of the year are not expected to differ significantly from the beginning balances. Federal income tax of $26,000 on 2013 taxable income will be paid during 2013. Regular quarterly cash dividends of $0.15 per share are expected to be declared and paid in March, June, September, and December on 30,000 shares of common stock outstanding. It is anticipated that fixed assets will be purchased for $17,500 cash in May.

**Instructions**

1. Prepare a budgeted income statement for 2013.

2. Prepare a budgeted balance sheet as of December 31, 2013, with supporting calculations.

## Cases & Projects

You can access Cases & Projects online at **www.cengage.com/accounting/reeve**

## Excel Success Special Activities

**SA 21-1    Sales budget**

Cramden Talent Agency, Inc., books musical performances for the bands that it has under contract. The booking agent has partially completed a sales budget for two of the bands:

| | A | B | C | D |
| --- | --- | --- | --- | --- |
| 1 | Cramden Talent Agency, Inc. | | | |
| 2 | Sales Budget | | | |
| 3 | For November and December 2012 | | | |
| 4 | | | | |
| 5 | | Number | Fee | Total |
| 6 | | of | per | Performance |
| 7 | **Band and Month** | **Performances** | **Performance** | **Revenue** |
| 8 | The Saturn Five: | | | |
| 9 | November | 10 | $ 1,000 | $ 10,000 |
| 10 | December | 15 | 1,000 | 15,000 |
| 11 | Total | | | $ 25,000 |
| 12 | | | | |
| 13 | Alice and the Heartbeats: | | | |
| 14 | November | 8 | $ 800 | |
| 15 | December | 12 | 800 | |
| 16 | Total | | | |
| 17 | | | | |
| 18 | Total Revenue from Performances | | | |

a. Open Excel file *SA21-1_1e* and complete the sales budget.

b. If the Christmas season is unusually active, the number of performances for each of the bands will increase. Revise the sales budget, assuming that the number of performances for each of the bands increases by two performances in November and by three in December.

[*Hint:* Copy and paste the spreadsheet you created in part (a) into the Revised Sales Budget worksheet and then modify it.]

c. When you have completed the sales budget and revisions, perform a "save as," replacing the entire file name with the following:

*SA21-1_1e[your first name initial]_[your last name]*

---

### SA 21-2  Sales budget

Bluewater Sailing, Inc., manufactures and sells three cruising sailboats: the $200,000 *Nantucket*, the $350,000 *Circumnavigator*, and the $500,000 *Cape Horn*. Boats of this class require months to build; thus, long-range sales forecasts are critical in managing operations. The cruisers are manufactured in boatyards in California, North Carolina, and Italy. The estimated number of boats that will be delivered to customers during 2012 follows:

| Product | West Coast | East Coast | Italy | Total |
|---|---|---|---|---|
| Nantucket | 1 | 2 | 0 | 3 |
| Circumnavigator | 3 | 3 | 4 | 10 |
| Cape Horn | 2 | 2 | 2 | 6 |

a. Open Excel file *SA21-2_1e* to complete the sales budget.

b. Using the sales volume data and your spreadsheet software, prepare a sales budget that displays total sales volume and revenue for 2012. Your budget should display total estimated sales volume and revenue for each vessel and for all three boatyards.

c. When you have completed the sales budget and revisions, perform a "save as," replacing the entire file name with the following:

*SA21-2_1e[your first name initial]_[your last name]*

---

### SA 21-3  Sales budget

Completely Fit, Inc., sells exercise equipment through three retail outlets in California. Among the fitness equipment items are two elliptical trainers: the Enduro (priced at $1,500 per unit) and the Marathon (priced at $2,500 per unit).

a. Open Excel file *SA21-3_1e* to complete the sales budget.

b. Using the estimated sales volume data below and your spreadsheet software, prepare a sales budget that displays total estimated sales volume and revenue for the first quarter of 2012.

**Completely Fit, Inc.**
**Projected Unit Sales**
**For the Quarter Ending March 31, 2012**

| Outlet and Model | Estimated Sales Volume (Units) |
|---|---|
| Northern California Outlet: | |
|    Enduro | 10 |
|    Marathon | 7 |
| Bay Area Outlet: | |
|    Enduro | 23 |
|    Marathon | 18 |
| Southern California Outlet: | |
|    Enduro | 40 |
|    Marathon | 48 |
| Total | 146 |

(*continued*)

c. The marketing department has recommended that the price of the Enduro model be reduced by $150 in order to stimulate sales. If this is done, Enduro sales will increase by an estimated 6 units per quarter in Northern California, by 12 units per quarter in the Bay Area, and by 15 units per quarter in Southern California. Prepare a revised sales budget for the quarter.

[*Hint:* Copy and save the spreadsheet created in part (a) to another worksheet and then modify it.]

d. When you have completed the sales budget and revisions, perform a "save as," replacing the entire file name with the following:

*SA21-3_1e[your first name initial]_[your last name]*

© AP Photo/Alastair Grant

# Performance Evaluation Using Variances from Standard Costs

## BMW Group—Mini Cooper

**W**hen you play a sport, you are evaluated with respect to how well you perform compared to a standard or to a competitor. In bowling, for example, your score is compared to a perfect score of 300 or to the scores of your competitors. In this class, you are compared to performance standards. These standards are often described in terms of letter grades, which provide a measure of how well you achieved the class objectives. On your job, you are also evaluated according to performance standards.

Just as your class performance is evaluated, managers are evaluated according to goals and plans. For example, **BMW Group** uses manufacturing standards at its automobile assembly plants to guide performance. The Mini Cooper, a BMW Group car, is manufactured in a modern facility in Oxford, England. There are a

number of performance targets used in this plant. For example, the bodyshell is welded by over 250 robots so as to be two to three times stiffer than rival cars. In addition, the bodyshell dimensions are tested to the accuracy of the width of a human hair. Such performance standards are not surprising given the automotive racing background of John W. Cooper, the designer of the original Mini Cooper.

If you want to take an online tour of the Oxford plant to see how a Mini Cooper is manufactured, go to **http://www.mini .com/com/en/manufacturing.**

Performance is often measured as the difference between actual results and planned results. In this chapter, we will discuss and illustrate the ways in which business performance is evaluated.

Drivers for United Parcel Service (UPS) are expected to drive a standard distance per day. Salespersons for The Limited are expected to meet sales standards.

# Standards

**Standards** are performance goals. Manufacturing companies normally use **standard cost** for each of the three following product costs:

1. Direct materials
2. Direct labor
3. Factory overhead

Accounting systems that use standards for product costs are called **standard cost systems**. Standard cost systems enable management to determine the following:

1. How much a product *should* cost (standard cost)
2. How much it does cost (actual cost)

When actual costs are compared with standard costs, the exceptions or cost variances are reported. This reporting by the *principle of exceptions* allows management to focus on correcting the cost variances.

## Setting Standards

The standard-setting process normally requires the joint efforts of accountants, engineers, and other management personnel. The accountant converts the results of judgments and process studies into dollars and cents. Engineers with the aid of operation managers identify the materials, labor, and machine requirements needed to produce the product. For example, engineers estimate direct materials by studying the product specifications and estimating normal spoilage. Time and motion studies may be used to determine the direct labor required for each manufacturing operation. Engineering studies may also be used to determine standards for factory overhead, such as the amount of power needed to operate machinery.

## Types of Standards

Standards imply an acceptable level of production efficiency. One of the major objectives in setting standards is to motivate employees to achieve efficient operations.

**Ideal standards**, or *theoretical standards*, are standards that can be achieved only under perfect operating conditions, such as no idle time, no machine breakdowns, and no materials spoilage. Such standards may have a negative impact on performance, because they may be viewed by employees as unrealistic.

**Currently attainable standards**, sometimes called *normal standards*, are standards that can be attained with reasonable effort. Such standards, which are used by most companies, allow for normal production difficulties and mistakes. When reasonable standards are used, employees focus more on cost and are more likely to put forth their best efforts.

An example from the game of golf illustrates the distinction between ideal and normal standards. In golf, "par" is an ideal standard for most players. Each player's USGA (United States Golf Association) handicap is the player's normal standard. The motivation of average players is to beat their handicaps because beating par is unrealistic for most players.

## Reviewing and Revising Standards

Standard costs should be periodically reviewed to ensure that they reflect current operating conditions. Standards should not be revised, however, just because they differ from actual costs. For example, the direct labor standard would not be revised just because employees are unable to meet properly set standards. On the other hand, standards should be revised when prices, product designs, labor rates, or manufacturing methods change.

## Criticisms of Standard Costs

Some criticisms of using standard costs for performance evaluation include the following:

1. Standards limit operating improvements by discouraging improvement beyond the standard.
2. Standards are too difficult to maintain in a dynamic manufacturing environment, resulting in "stale standards."
3. Standards can cause employees to lose sight of the larger objectives of the organization by focusing only on efficiency improvement.
4. Standards can cause employees to unduly focus on their own operations to the possible harm of other operations that rely on them.

Regardless of these criticisms, standards are widely used. In addition, standard costs are only one part of the performance evaluation system used by most companies. As discussed in this chapter, other nonfinancial performance measures are often used to supplement standard costs, with the result that many of the preceding criticisms are overcome.

# BusinessConnection

## MAKING THE GRADE IN THE REAL WORLD—THE 360-DEGREE REVIEW

When you leave school and take your first job, you will likely be subject to an employee evaluation. These reviews provide feedback on performance that is often very detailed, providing insights to strengths and weaknesses that often go beyond mere grades.

One feedback trend is the 360-degree review. As stated by the human resources consulting firm Towers Perrin, the 360-degree review "is a huge wave that's just hitting—not only here, but all over the world." In a 360-degree review, six to twelve evaluators who encircle an employee's sphere of influence, such as superiors, peers, and subordinates, are selected to fill out anonymous questionnaires. These questionnaires rate the employee on various criteria including the ability to work in groups, form a consensus, make timely decisions, motivate employees, and achieve objectives. The results are summarized and used to identify and strengthen weaknesses.

For example, one individual at Intel Corporation was very vocal during team meetings. In the 360-degree

review, the manager thought this behavior was "refreshing." However, the employee's peers thought the vocal behavior monopolized conversations. Thus, what the manager viewed as a positive, the peer group viewed as a negative. The 360-degree review provided valuable information to both the manager and the employee to adjust behavior.

Sources: Llana DeBare, "360-Degrees of Evaluation: More Companies Turning to Full-Circle Job Reviews," *San Francisco Chronicle*, May 5, 1997; Francie Dalton, "Using 360 Degree Feedback Mechanisms," *Occupational Health and Safety*, Vol. 74, Issue 7, 2005.

# Integrity, Objectivity, and Ethics in Business

## COMPANY REPUTATION: THE BEST OF THE BEST

Harris Interactive annually ranks American corporations in terms of reputation. The ranking is based on how respondents rate corporations on 20 attributes in six major areas. The six areas are emotional appeal, products and services, financial performance, workplace environment, social responsibility,

and vision and leadership. What are the five highest ranked companies in its 2008 survey? The five highest (best) ranked companies were Johnson & Johnson, Google, Sony Corporation, The Coca-Cola Company, and Kraft Foods.

Source: Harris Interactive, February 2009.

---

**OBJ. 2** Describe and illustrate how standards are used in budgeting.

# Budgetary Performance Evaluation

As discussed in Chapter 21, the master budget assists a company in planning, directing, and controlling performance. The control function, or budgetary performance evaluation, compares the actual performance against the budget.

To illustrate, Western Rider Inc., a manufacturer of blue jeans, uses standard costs in its budgets. The standards for direct materials, direct labor, and factory overhead are separated into the following two components.

1. Standard price
2. Standard quantity

The standard cost per unit for direct materials, direct labor, and factory overhead is computed as follows:

Standard Cost per Unit = Standard Price × Standard Quantity

Western Rider's standard costs per unit for its XL jeans are shown in Exhibit 1.

**EXHIBIT 1**

**Standard Cost for XL Jeans**

| Manufacturing Costs | Standard Price | × | Standard Quantity per Pair | = | Standard Cost per Pair of XL Jeans |
|---|---|---|---|---|---|
| Direct materials | $5.00 per sq. yd. | | 1.5 sq. yds. | | $ 7.50 |
| Direct labor | $9.00 per hr. | | 0.80 hr. per pair | | 7.20 |
| Factory overhead | $6.00 per hr. | | 0.80 hr. per pair | | 4.80 |
| Total standard cost per pair | | | | | $19.50 |

As shown in Exhibit 1, the standard cost per pair of XL jeans is $19.50, which consists of $7.50 for direct materials, $7.20 for direct labor, and $4.80 for factory overhead.

The standard price and standard quantity are separated for each product cost. For example, Exhibit 1 indicates that for each pair of XL jeans, the standard price for direct materials is $5.00 per square yard and the standard quantity is 1.5 square yards. The standard price and quantity are separated because the department responsible for their control is normally different. For example, the direct materials price per square yard is controlled by the Purchasing Department, and the direct materials quantity per pair is controlled by the Production Department.

As illustrated in Chapter 21, the master budget is prepared based on planned sales and production. The budgeted costs for materials purchases, direct labor, and factory overhead are determined by multiplying their standard costs per unit by the planned level of production. Budgeted (standard) costs are then compared to actual costs during the year for control purposes.

## Budget Performance Report

The report that summarizes actual costs, standard costs, and the differences for the units produced is called a **budget performance report**. To illustrate, assume that Western Rider produced the following pairs of jeans during June:

| XL jeans produced and sold | 5,000 pairs |
|---|---|
| Actual costs incurred in June: | |
| Direct materials | $ 40,150 |
| Direct labor | 38,500 |
| Factory overhead | 22,400 |
| Total costs incurred | $101,050 |

Exhibit 2 illustrates the budget performance report for June for Western Rider Inc. The report summarizes the actual costs, standard costs, and the differences for each product cost. The differences between actual and standard costs are called **cost variances**. A **favorable cost variance** occurs when the actual cost is less than the standard cost. An **unfavorable cost variance** occurs when the actual cost exceeds the standard cost.

**Note:**
Favorable cost variance: Actual cost < Standard cost at actual volumes

Unfavorable cost variance: Actual cost > Standard cost at actual volumes

| Western Rider Inc. Budget Performance Report For the Month Ended June 30, 2012 | | | |
|---|---|---|---|
| **Manufacturing Costs** | **Actual Costs** | **Standard Cost at Actual Volume (5,000 pairs of XL Jeans)\*** | **Cost Variance— (Favorable) Unfavorable** |
| Direct materials............................. | $ 40,150 | $37,500 | $ 2,650 |
| Direct labor ............................... | 38,500 | 36,000 | 2,500 |
| Factory overhead ......................... | 22,400 | 24,000 | (1,600) |
| Total manufacturing costs.............. | $101,050 | $97,500 | $ 3,550 |

\*5,000 pairs × $7.50 per pair = $37,500
5,000 pairs × $7.20 per pair = $36,000
5,000 pairs × $4.80 per pair = $24,000

The budget performance report shown in Exhibit 2 is based on the actual units of 5,000 XL jeans produced in June. Even though 6,000 XL jeans might have been *planned* for production, the budget performance report is based on *actual* production.

## Manufacturing Cost Variances

The **total manufacturing cost variance** is the difference between total standard costs and total actual cost for the units produced. As shown in Exhibit 2, the total manufacturing cost unfavorable variance and the variance for each product cost is as follows:

| | **Cost Variance (Favorable) Unfavorable** |
|---|---|
| Direct materials | $ 2,650 |
| Direct labor | 2,500 |
| Factory overhead | (1,600) |
| Total manufacturing variance | $ 3,550 |

For control purposes, each product cost variance is separated into two additional variances as shown in Exhibit 3.

**Manufacturing Cost Variances**

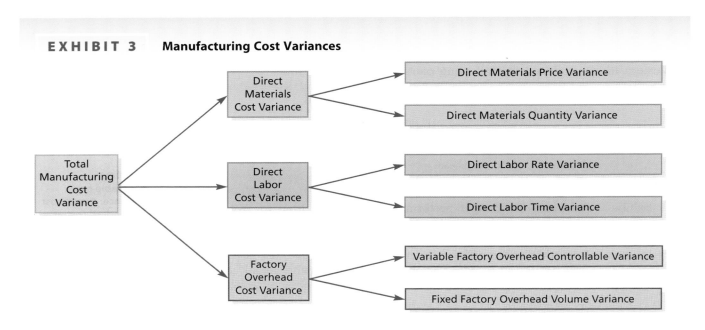

The total direct materials variance is separated into a *price* and *quantity* variance. This is because standard and actual direct materials costs are computed as follows:

Actual Direct Materials Cost  =  Actual Price  ×  Actual Quantity

Standard Direct Materials Cost  =  −Standard Price  × Standard Quantity

Direct Materials Cost Variance  =  Price Difference  +  Quantity Difference

Thus, the actual and standard direct materials costs may differ because of either a price difference (variance) or a quantity difference (variance).

Likewise, the total direct labor variance is separated into a *rate* and a *time* variance. This is because standard and actual direct labor costs are computed as follows:

Actual Direct Labor Cost  =  Actual Rate  ×  Actual Time

Standard Direct Labor Cost  =  −Standard Rate  × Standard Time

Direct Labor Cost Variance  =  Rate Difference  +  Time Difference

Therefore, the actual and standard direct labor costs may differ because of either a rate difference (variance) or a time difference (variance).

The total factory overhead variance is separated into a *controllable* and *volume* variance. Because factory overhead has fixed and variable cost elements, it uses different variances than direct materials and direct labor, which are variable costs.

In the next sections, the price and quantity variances for direct materials, the rate and time variances for direct labor, and the controllable and volume variances for factory overhead are further described and illustrated.

# Direct Materials and Direct Labor Variances

**OBJ. 3** Compute and interpret direct materials and direct labor variances.

As indicated in the prior section, the total direct materials and direct labor variances are separated into the following variances for analysis and control purposes:

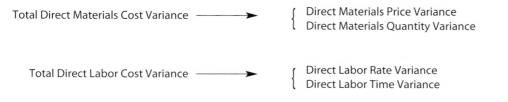

Total Direct Materials Cost Variance ⟶ { Direct Materials Price Variance / Direct Materials Quantity Variance

Total Direct Labor Cost Variance ⟶ { Direct Labor Rate Variance / Direct Labor Time Variance

As a basis for illustration, the variances for Western Rider Inc.'s June operations shown in Exhibit 2 are used.

## Direct Materials Variances

During June, Western Rider reported an unfavorable total direct materials cost variance of $2,650 for the production of 5,000 XL style jeans, as shown in Exhibit 2. This variance was based on the following actual and standard costs:

| | |
|---|---|
| Actual costs | $40,150 |
| Standard costs | 37,500 |
| Total direct materials cost variance | $ 2,650 |

The actual costs incurred of $40,150 consist of the following:

Actual Direct Materials Cost = Actual Price × Actual Quantity
Actual Direct Materials Cost = ($5.50 per sq. yd.) × (7,300 sq. yds.)
Actual Direct Materials Cost = $40,150

The standard costs of $37,500 consist of the following:

Standard Direct Materials Cost = Standard Price × Standard Quantity
Standard Direct Materials Cost = ($5.00 per sq. yd.) × (7,500 sq. yds.)
Standard Direct Materials Cost = $37,500

The standard price of $5.00 per square yard is taken from Exhibit 1. In addition, Exhibit 1 indicates that 1.5 square yards is the standard for producing one pair of XL jeans. Thus, 7,500 (5,000 × 1.5) square yards is the standard for producing 5,000 pairs of XL jeans.

Comparing the actual and standard cost computations shown above indicates that the total direct materials unfavorable cost variance of $2,650 is caused by the following:

1. A price per square yard of $0.50 ($5.50 − $5.00) more than standard
2. A quantity usage of 200 square yards (7,300 sq. yds. − 7,500 sq. yds.) less than standard

The impact of these differences from standard is reported and analyzed as a direct materials *price* variance and direct materials *quantity* variance.

### Direct Materials Price Variance
The **direct materials price variance** is computed as follows:

Direct Materials Price Variance = (Actual Price − Standard Price) × Actual Quantity

If the actual price per unit exceeds the standard price per unit, the variance is unfavorable. This positive amount (unfavorable variance) can be thought of as increasing costs (a debit). If the actual price per unit is less than the standard price per unit, the variance is favorable. This negative amount (favorable variance) can be thought of as decreasing costs (a credit).

To illustrate, the direct materials price variance for Western Rider Inc. is computed as follows:[1]

Direct Materials Price Variance = (Actual Price − Standard Price) × Actual Quantity
Direct Materials Price Variance = ($5.50 − $5.00) × 7,300 sq. yds.
Direct Materials Price Variance = $3,650 Unfavorable Variance

As shown above, Western Rider has an unfavorable direct materials price variance of $3,650 for June.

### Direct Materials Quantity Variance
The **direct materials quantity variance** is computed as follows:

Direct Materials Quantity Variance = (Actual Quantity − Standard Quantity) × Standard Price

If the actual quantity for the units produced exceeds the standard quantity, the variance is unfavorable. This positive amount (unfavorable variance) can be thought of as increasing costs (a debit). If the actual quantity for the units produced is less than the standard quantity, the variance is favorable. This negative amount (favorable variance) can be thought of as decreasing costs (a credit).

To illustrate, the direct materials quantity variance for Western Rider Inc. is computed as follows:

Direct Materials Quantity Variance = (Actual Quantity − Standard Quantity) × Standard Price
Direct Materials Quantity Variance = (7,300 sq. yds. − 7,500 sq. yds.) × $5.00
Direct Materials Quantity Variance = −$1,000 Favorable Variance

As shown above, Western Rider has a favorable direct materials quantity variance of $1,000 for June.

### Direct Materials Variance Relationships
The relationships among the *total* direct materials cost variance, the direct materials *price* variance, and the direct materials *quantity* variance are shown in Exhibit 4.

---

[1] To simplify, it is assumed that there is no change in the beginning and ending materials inventories. Thus, the amount of materials budgeted for production equals the amount purchased.

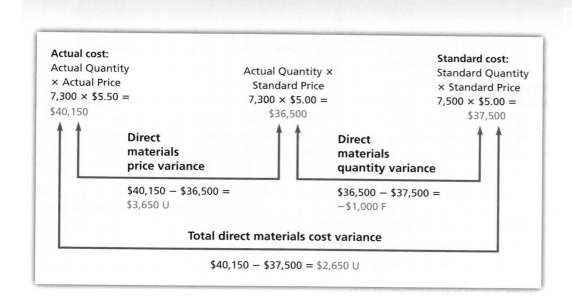

**EXHIBIT 4**

**Direct Materials Variance Relationships**

**Reporting Direct Materials Variances** The direct materials quantity variances should be reported to the manager responsible for the variance. For example, an unfavorable quantity variance might be caused by either of the following:

1. Equipment that has not been properly maintained
2. Low-quality (inferior) direct materials

In the first case, the operating department responsible for maintaining the equipment should be held responsible for the variance. In the second case, the Purchasing Department should be held responsible.

Not all variances are controllable. For example, an unfavorable materials price variance might be due to market-wide price increases. In this case, there is nothing the Purchasing Department might have done to avoid the unfavorable variance. On the other hand, if materials of the same quality could have been purchased from another supplier at the standard price, the variance was controllable.

## BusinessConnection

### WOULD YOU LIKE DESSERT?

Many restaurants use standards to manage the business. Food quantity standards are used to control the amount of food that is served to a customer. For example, Darden Restaurants, Inc., the operator of the Red Lobster chain, establishes food quantity standards for the number of shrimp, scallops, or clams on a seafood plate.

A food price variance can be used to control the price paid for food products. For example, Uno Restaurant Holdings Corp. controls food prices by using "forward contracts" for about 80% of its cheese and 50% of its wheat. Such a contract locks in the price for a period of time, thus eliminating materials price variances (favorable or unfavorable) for these items over the contract term.

Standards can also be used in innovative ways to monitor revenues. Brinker International, the operator of popular chains such as Chili's and On the Border, uses "theoretical food system" software that enables it to compare customer traffic and menu item volumes over a period of time. Thus, actual order revenue can be compared to expected (standard) revenues based on actual traffic volumes. In this way, the restaurant can monitor trends in check composition and size.

Source: Edward Teach, "Table Stakes," *CFO* (December 2008), pp. 44–49.

**Example Exercise** ▶ **22-1** ▶ **Direct Materials Variances**

Tip Top Corp. produces a product that requires six standard pounds per unit. The standard price is $4.50 per pound. If 3,000 units required 18,500 pounds, which were purchased at $4.35 per pound, what is the direct materials (a) price variance, (b) quantity variance, and (c) cost variance?

**Follow My Example** ▶ **22-1** ▶

a.  Direct materials price variance (favorable)
b.  Direct materials quantity variance (unfavorable)
c.  Direct materials cost variance (favorable)

−$2,775 [($4.35 − $4.50) × 18,500 pounds]
  $2,250 [(18,500 pounds − 18,000 pounds*) × $4.50]
−$525 [($2,775) + $2,250] or [($4.35 × 18,500 pounds)
  − ($4.50 × 18,000 pounds)] = $80,475 − $81,000

*3,000 units × 6 pounds

Practice Exercises: **PE 22-1A, PE 22-1B**

# Direct Labor Variances

During June, Western Rider reported an unfavorable total direct labor cost variance of $2,500 for the production of 5,000 XL style jeans, as shown in Exhibit 2. This variance was based on the following actual and standard costs:

| | |
|---|---|
| Actual costs | $38,500 |
| Standard costs | 36,000 |
| Total direct labor cost variance | $ 2,500 |

The actual costs incurred of $38,500 consist of the following:

Actual Direct Labor Cost = Actual Rate per Hour × Actual Time
Actual Direct Labor Cost = $10.00 per hr. × 3,850 hrs.
Actual Direct Labor Cost = $38,500

The standard costs of $36,000 consist of the following:

Standard Direct Labor Cost = Standard Rate per Hour × Standard Time
Standard Direct Labor Cost = $9.00 per hr. × 4,000 hrs.
Standard Direct Labor Cost = $36,000

The standard rate of $9.00 per direct labor hour is taken from Exhibit 1. In addition, Exhibit 1 indicates that 0.80 hour is the standard time required for producing one pair of XL jeans. Thus, 4,000 (5,000 × 0.80) direct labor hours is the standard for producing 5,000 pairs of XL jeans.

Comparing the actual and standard cost computations shown above indicates that the total direct labor unfavorable cost variance of $2,500 is caused by the following:

1.  A rate of $1.00 per hour ($10.00 − $9.00) more than standard
2.  A quantity of 150 hours (4,000 hrs. − 3,850 hrs.) less than standard

The impact of these differences from standard is reported and analyzed as a direct labor *rate* variance and a direct labor *time* variance.

**Direct Labor Rate Variance** The **direct labor rate variance** is computed as follows:

Direct Labor Rate Variance = (Actual Rate per Hour − Standard Rate per Hour) × Actual Hours

If the actual rate per hour exceeds the standard rate per hour, the variance is unfavorable. This positive amount (unfavorable variance) can be thought of as increasing costs (a debit). If the actual rate per hour is less than the standard rate per hour, the variance is favorable. This negative amount (favorable variance) can be thought of as decreasing costs (a credit).

To illustrate, the direct labor rate variance for Western Rider Inc. is computed as follows:

Direct Labor Rate Variance = (Actual Rate per Hour – Standard Rate per Hour)
× Actual Hours
Direct Labor Rate Variance = ($10.00 – $9.00) × 3,850 hours
Direct Labor Rate Variance = $3,850 Unfavorable Variance

As shown above, Western Rider has an unfavorable direct labor rate variance of $3,850 for June.

**Direct Labor Time Variance** The **direct labor time variance** is computed as follows:

Direct Labor Time Variance = (Actual Direct Labor Hours – Standard Direct Labor Hours)
× Standard Rate per Hour

If the actual direct labor hours for the units produced exceeds the standard direct labor hours, the variance is unfavorable. This positive amount (unfavorable variance) can be thought of as increasing costs (a debit). If the actual direct labor hours for the units produced is less than the standard direct labor hours, the variance is favorable. This negative amount (favorable variance) can be thought of as decreasing costs (a credit).

To illustrate, the direct labor time variance for Western Rider Inc. is computed as follows:

Direct Labor Time Variance = (Actual Direct Labor Hours – Standard Direct Labor Hours)
× Standard Rate per Hour
Direct Labor Time Variance = (3,850 hours – 4,000 direct labor hours) × $9.00
Direct Labor Time Variance = – $1,350 Favorable Variance

As shown above, Western Rider has a favorable direct labor time variance of $1,350 for June.

**Direct Labor Variance Relationships** The relationships among the *total* direct labor cost variance, the direct labor *rate* variance, and the direct labor *time* variance are shown in Exhibit 5.

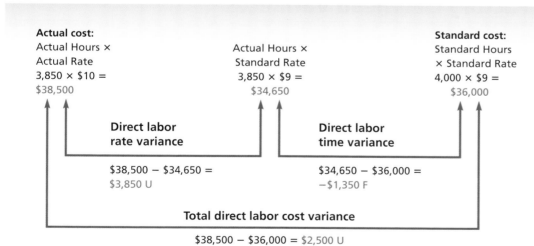

**EXHIBIT 5**

**Direct Labor Variance Relationships**

**Reporting Direct Labor Variances** Production supervisors are normally responsible for controlling direct labor cost. For example, an investigation could reveal the following causes for unfavorable rate and time variances:

1. An unfavorable rate variance may be caused by the improper scheduling and use of employees. In such cases, skilled, highly paid employees may be used in jobs that are normally performed by unskilled, lower-paid employees. In this case, the unfavorable rate variance should be reported to the managers who schedule work assignments.

2. An unfavorable time variance may be caused by a shortage of skilled employees. In such cases, there may be an abnormally high turnover rate among skilled employees. In this case, production supervisors with high turnover rates should be questioned as to why their employees are quitting.

**Direct Labor Standards for Nonmanufacturing Activities** Direct labor time standards can also be developed for use in administrative, selling, and service activities. This is most appropriate when the activity involves a repetitive task that produces a common output. In these cases, the use of standards is similar to that for a manufactured product.

To illustrate, standards could be developed for customer service personnel who process sales orders. A standard time for processing a sales order (the output) could be developed and used to control sales order processing costs. Similar standards could be developed for computer help desk operators, nurses, and insurance application processors.

When labor-related activities are not repetitive, direct labor time standards are less commonly used. For example, the time spent by a senior executive or the work of a research and development scientist would not normally be controlled using time standards.

---

**Example Exercise** **22-2** **Direct Labor Variances**     **OBJ. 3**

Tip Top Corp. produces a product that requires 2.5 standard hours per unit at a standard hourly rate of $12 per hour. If 3,000 units required 7,420 hours at an hourly rate of $12.30 per hour, what is the (a) direct labor rate variance, (b) direct labor time variance, and (c) total direct labor cost variance?

**Follow My Example** **22-2**

a.  Direct labor rate variance (unfavorable)         $2,226 [($12.30 – $12.00) × 7,420 hours]
b.  Direct labor time variance (favorable)            –$960 [(7,420 hours – 7,500 hours*) × $12.00]
c.  Total direct labor cost variance (unfavorable)   $1,266 [$2,226 + ($960)] or [($12.30 × 7,420 hours) –
                                                     ($12.00 × 7,500 hours)] = $91,266 – $90,000

*3,000 units × 2.5 hours

Practice Exercises: **PE 22-2A, PE 22-2B**

---

# Factory Overhead Variances

**OBJ. 4** Compute and interpret factory overhead controllable and volume variances.

Factory overhead costs are analyzed differently than direct labor and direct materials costs. This is because factory overhead costs have fixed and variable cost elements. For example, indirect materials and factory supplies normally behave as a variable cost as units produced changes. In contrast, straight-line plant depreciation on factory machinery is a fixed cost.

Factory overhead costs are budgeted and controlled by separating factory overhead into fixed and variable components. Doing so allows the preparation of flexible budgets and the analysis of factory overhead controllable and volume variances.

## The Factory Overhead Flexible Budget

The preparation of a flexible budget was described and illustrated in Chapter 21. Exhibit 6 illustrates a flexible factory overhead budget for Western Rider Inc. for June 2012.

Exhibit 6 indicates that the budgeted factory overhead rate for Western Rider is $6.00, as computed below.

$$\text{Factory Overhead Rate} = \frac{\text{Budgeted Factory Overhead at Normal Capacity}}{\text{Normal Productive Capacity}}$$

$$\text{Factory Overhead Rate} = \frac{\$30,000}{5,000 \text{ direct labor hrs.}} = \$6.00 \text{ per direct labor hr.}$$

The normal productive capacity is expressed in terms of an activity base such as direct labor hours, direct labor cost, or machine hours. For Western Rider, 100% of

|   | A | B | C | D | E |
|---|---|---|---|---|---|
| 1 | Western Rider Inc. | | | | |
| 2 | Factory Overhead Cost Budget | | | | |
| 3 | For the Month Ending June 30, 2012 | | | | |
| 4 | Percent of normal capacity | 80% | 90% | 100% | 110% |
| 5 | Units produced | 5,000 | 5,625 | 6,250 | 6,875 |
| 6 | Direct labor hours (0.80 hr. per unit) | 4,000 | 4,500 | 5,000 | 5,500 |
| 7 | Budgeted factory overhead: | | | | |
| 8 |    Variable costs: | | | | |
| 9 |       Indirect factory wages | $ 8,000 | $ 9,000 | $10,000 | $11,000 |
| 10 |       Power and light | 4,000 | 4,500 | 5,000 | 5,500 |
| 11 |       Indirect materials | 2,400 | 2,700 | 3,000 | 3,300 |
| 12 |       Total variable cost | $14,400 | $16,200 | $18,000 | $19,800 |
| 13 |    Fixed costs: | | | | |
| 14 |       Supervisory salaries | $ 5,500 | $ 5,500 | $ 5,500 | $ 5,500 |
| 15 |       Depreciation of plant | | | | |
| 16 |         and equipment | 4,500 | 4,500 | 4,500 | 4,500 |
| 17 |       Insurance and property taxes | 2,000 | 2,000 | 2,000 | 2,000 |
| 18 |       Total fixed cost | $12,000 | $12,000 | $12,000 | $12,000 |
| 19 |    Total factory overhead cost | $26,400 | $28,200 | $30,000 | $31,800 |
| 20 | | | | | |
| 21 | Factory overhead rate per direct labor hour, $30,000/5,000 hours = $6.00 | | | | |
| 22 | | | | | |

**EXHIBIT 6**

**Factory Overhead Cost Budget Indicating Standard Factory Overhead Rate**

normal capacity is 5,000 direct labor hours. The budgeted factory overhead cost at 100% of normal capacity is $30,000, which consists of variable overhead of $18,000 and fixed overhead of $12,000.

For analysis purposes, the budgeted factory overhead rate is subdivided into a variable factory overhead rate and a fixed factory overhead rate. For Western Rider, the variable overhead rate is $3.60 per direct labor hour, and the fixed overhead rate is $2.40 per direct labor hour, as computed below.

$$\text{Variable Factory Overhead Rate} = \frac{\text{Budgeted Variable Overhead at Normal Capacity}}{\text{Normal Productive Capacity}}$$

$$\text{Variable Factory Overhead Rate} = \frac{\$18,000}{5,000 \text{ direct labor hrs.}} = \$3.60 \text{ per direct labor hr.}$$

$$\text{Fixed Factory Overhead Rate} = \frac{\text{Budgeted Fixed Overhead at Normal Capacity}}{\text{Normal Productive Capacity}}$$

$$\text{Fixed Factory Overhead Rate} = \frac{\$12,000}{5,000 \text{ direct labor hrs.}} = \$2.40 \text{ per direct labor hr.}$$

To summarize, the budgeted factory overhead rates for Western Rider Inc. are as follows:

| | |
|---|---|
| Variable factory overhead rate | $3.60 |
| Fixed factory overhead rate | 2.40 |
| Total factory overhead rate | $6.00 |

As mentioned earlier, factory overhead variances can be separated into a controllable variance and a volume variance as discussed in the next sections.

# Variable Factory Overhead Controllable Variance

The variable factory overhead **controllable variance** is the difference between the actual variable overhead costs and the budgeted variable overhead for actual production. It is computed as shown below.

| Variable Factory Overhead | Actual | Budgeted |
|---|---|---|
| Controllable Variance | = Variable Factory Overhead − | Variable Factory Overhead |

If the actual variable overhead is less than the budgeted variable overhead, the variance is favorable. If the actual variable overhead exceeds the budgeted variable overhead, the variance is unfavorable.

The **budgeted variable factory overhead** is the standard variable overhead for the *actual* units produced. It is computed as follows:

$$\text{Budgeted Variable Factory Overhead} = \text{Standard Hours for Actual Units Produced} \times \text{Variable Factory Overhead Rate}$$

To illustrate, the budgeted variable overhead for Western Rider for June is $14,400, as computed below.

$$\text{Budgeted Variable Factory Overhead} = \text{Standard Hours for Actual Units Produced} \times \text{Variable Factory Overhead Rate}$$
$$\text{Budgeted Variable Factory Overhead} = 4,000 \text{ direct labor hrs.} \times \$3.60$$
$$\text{Budgeted Variable Factory Overhead} = \$14,400$$

The preceding computation is based on the fact that Western Rider produced 5,000 XL jeans, which requires a standard of 4,000 (5,000 × 0.8 hr.) direct labor hours. The variable factory overhead rate of $3.60 was computed earlier. Thus, the budgeted variable factory overhead is $14,400 (4,000 direct labor hrs. × $3.60).

During June, assume that Western Rider incurred the following actual factory overhead costs:

|  | **Actual Costs in June** |
|---|---|
| Variable factory overhead | $10,400 |
| Fixed factory overhead | 12,000 |
| Total actual factory overhead | $22,400 |

Based on the actual variable factory overhead incurred in June, the variable factory overhead controllable variance is a $4,000 favorable variance, as computed below.

Variable Factory Overhead Controllable Variance = Actual Variable Factory Overhead − Budgeted Variable Factory Overhead

Variable Factory Overhead Controllable Variance = $10,400 − $14,400

Variable Factory Overhead Controllable Variance = −$4,000 Favorable Variance

The variable factory overhead controllable variance indicates the ability to keep the factory overhead costs within the budget limits. Since variable factory overhead costs are normally controllable at the department level, responsibility for controlling this variance usually rests with department supervisors.

**Example Exercise 22-3 Factory Overhead Controllable Variance** OBJ. 4

Tip Top Corp. produced 3,000 units of product that required 2.5 standard hours per unit. The standard variable overhead cost per unit is $2.20 per hour. The actual variable factory overhead was $16,850. Determine the variable factory overhead controllable variance.

**Follow My Example 22-3**

Variable Factory Overhead Controllable Variance = Actual Variable Factory Overhead − Budgeted Variable Factory Overhead

Variable Factory Overhead Controllable Variance = $16,850 − [(3,000 units × 2.5 hrs.) × $2.20]

Variable Factory Overhead Controllable Variance = $16,850 − $16,500

Variable Factory Overhead Controllable Variance = $350 Unfavorable Variance

Practice Exercises: **PE 22-3A, PE 22-3B**

# Fixed Factory Overhead Volume Variance

Western Rider's budgeted factory overhead is based on a 100% normal capacity of 5,000 direct labor hours, as shown in Exhibit 6. This is the expected capacity that management believes will be used under normal business conditions. Exhibit 6 indicates that the 5,000 direct labor hours is less than the total available capacity of 110%, which is 5,500 direct labor hours.

The fixed factory overhead **volume variance** is the difference between the budgeted fixed overhead at 100% of normal capacity and the standard fixed overhead for the actual units produced. It is computed as follows:

$$
\begin{array}{c}
\text{Fixed Factory} \\
\text{Overhead} \\
\text{Volume Variance}
\end{array}
=
\left(
\begin{array}{c}
\text{Standard Hours} \\
\text{for 100\% of} \\
\text{Normal Capacity}
\end{array}
-
\begin{array}{c}
\text{Standard Hours for} \\
\text{Actual Units} \\
\text{Produced}
\end{array}
\right)
\times
\begin{array}{c}
\text{Fixed Factory} \\
\text{Overhead Rate}
\end{array}
$$

The volume variance measures the use of fixed overhead resources (plant and equipment). The interpretation of an unfavorable and a favorable fixed factory overhead volume variance is as follows:

1. *Unfavorable* fixed factory overhead variance. The actual units produced is *less than* 100% of normal capacity; thus, the company used its fixed overhead resources (plant and equipment) less than would be expected under normal operating conditions.
2. *Favorable* fixed factory overhead variance. The actual units produced is *more than* 100% of normal capacity; thus, the company used its fixed overhead resources (plant and equipment) more than would be expected under normal operating conditions.

To illustrate, the volume variance for Western Rider is a $2,400 unfavorable variance, as computed below.

$$
\begin{array}{c}
\text{Fixed Factory} \\
\text{Overhead} \\
\text{Volume Variance}
\end{array}
=
\left(
\begin{array}{c}
\text{Standard Hours} \\
\text{for 100\% of} \\
\text{Normal Capacity}
\end{array}
-
\begin{array}{c}
\text{Standard Hours for} \\
\text{Actual Units} \\
\text{Produced}
\end{array}
\right)
\times
\begin{array}{c}
\text{Fixed Factory} \\
\text{Overhead Rate}
\end{array}
$$

$$
\begin{array}{c}
\text{Fixed Factory} \\
\text{Overhead} \\
\text{Volume Variance}
\end{array}
=
\left(
\begin{array}{c}
\text{5,000 direct} \\
\text{labor hrs.}
\end{array}
-
\begin{array}{c}
\text{4,000 direct} \\
\text{labor hrs.}
\end{array}
\right)
\times \ \$2.40
$$

$$
\begin{array}{c}
\text{Fixed Factory} \\
\text{Overhead} \\
\text{Volume Variance}
\end{array}
= \$2,400 \text{ Unfavorable Variance}
$$

Since Western Rider produced 5,000 XL jeans during June, the standard for the actual units produced is 4,000 (5,000 × 0.80) direct labor hours. This is 1,000 hours less then the 5,000 standard hours of normal capacity. The fixed overhead rate of $2.40 was computed earlier. Thus, the unfavorable fixed factory overhead volume variance is $2,400 (1,000 direct labor hrs. × $2.40).

Exhibit 7 illustrates graphically the fixed factory overhead volume variance for Western Rider Inc. The budgeted fixed overhead does not change and is $12,000 at all levels of production. At 100% of normal capacity (5,000 direct labor hours), the standard fixed overhead line intersects the budgeted fixed costs line. For production levels *more than* 100% of normal capacity (5,000 direct labor hours), the volume variance is *favorable*. For production levels *less than* 100% of normal capacity (5,000 direct labor hours), the volume variance is *unfavorable*.

Exhibit 7 indicates that Western Rider's volume variance is unfavorable in June because the actual production is 4,000 direct labor hours, or 80% of normal volume. The unfavorable volume variance of $2,400 can be viewed as the cost of the unused capacity (1,000 direct labor hours).

**EXHIBIT 7**

**Graph of Fixed Overhead Volume Variance**

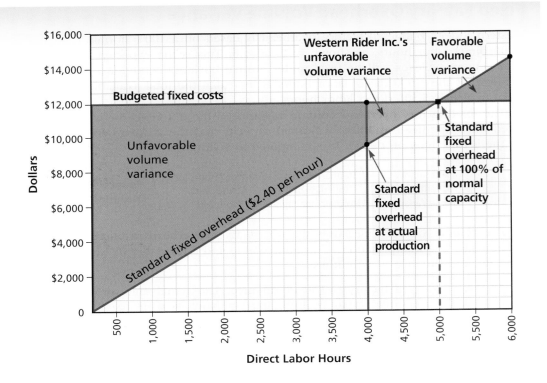

An unfavorable volume variance may be due to factors such as the following:

1. Failure to maintain an even flow of work
2. Machine breakdowns
3. Work stoppages caused by lack of materials or skilled labor
4. Lack of enough sales orders to keep the factory operating at normal capacity

Management should determine the causes of the unfavorable variance and consider taking corrective action. For example, a volume variance caused by an uneven flow of work could be remedied by changing operating procedures. Lack of sales orders may be corrected through increased advertising.

Favorable volume variances may not always be desirable. For example, in an attempt to create a favorable volume variance, manufacturing managers might run the factory above the normal capacity. However, if the additional production cannot be sold, it must be stored as inventory, which would incur storage costs.

---

**Example Exercise** 22-4   **Factory Overhead Volume Variance**          OBJ. 4

Tip Top Corp. produced 3,000 units of product that required 2.5 standard hours per unit. The standard fixed overhead cost per unit is $0.90 per hour at 8,000 hours, which is 100% of normal capacity. Determine the fixed factory overhead volume variance.

**Follow My Example** 22-4

Fixed Factory Overhead Volume Variance = (Standard Hours for 100% of Normal Capacity – Standard Hours
  for Actual Units Produced) × Fixed Factory Overhead Rate
Fixed Factory Overhead Volume Variance = [8,000 hrs. – (3,000 units × 2.5 hrs.)] × $0.90
Fixed Factory Overhead Volume Variance = (8,000 hrs. – 7,500 hrs.) × $0.90
Fixed Factory Overhead Volume Variance = $450 Unfavorable Variance

Practice Exercises: **PE 22-4A, PE 22-4B**

# Reporting Factory Overhead Variances

The total factory overhead cost variance can also be determined as the sum of the factory overhead controllable and volume variances, as shown below for Western Rider Inc.

| | |
|---|---|
| Variable factory overhead controllable variance | −$4,000 Favorable Variance |
| Fixed factory overhead volume variance | 2,400 Unfavorable Variance |
| Total factory overhead cost variance | −$1,600 Favorable Variance |

A **factory overhead cost variance report** is useful to management in controlling factory overhead costs. Budgeted and actual costs for variable and fixed factory overhead along with the related controllable and volume variances are reported by each cost element.

Exhibit 8 illustrates a factory overhead cost variance report for Western Rider Inc. for June.

**EXHIBIT 8**

**Factory Overhead Cost Variance Report**

| | A | B | C | D | E |
|---|---|---|---|---|---|
| 1 | | Western Rider Inc. | | | |
| 2 | | Factory Overhead Cost Variance Report | | | |
| 3 | | For the Month Ending June 30, 2012 | | | |
| 4 | Productive capacity for the month (100% of normal) | 5,000 hours | | | |
| 5 | Actual production for the month | 4,000 hours | | | |
| 6 | | | | | |
| 7 | | Budget | | | |
| 8 | | (at Actual | | Variances | |
| 9 | | Production) | Actual | Favorable | Unfavorable |
| 10 | Variable factory overhead costs: | | | | |
| 11 | Indirect factory wages | $ 8,000 | $ 5,100 | $2,900 | |
| 12 | Power and light | 4,000 | 4,200 | | $ 200 |
| 13 | Indirect materials | 2,400 | 1,100 | 1,300 | |
| 14 | Total variable factory | | | | |
| 15 | overhead cost | $14,400 | $10,400 | | |
| 16 | Fixed factory overhead costs: | | | | |
| 17 | Supervisory salaries | $ 5,500 | $ 5,500 | | |
| 18 | Depreciation of plant and | | | | |
| 19 | equipment | 4,500 | 4,500 | | |
| 20 | Insurance and property taxes | 2,000 | 2,000 | | |
| 21 | Total fixed factory | | | | |
| 22 | overhead cost | $12,000 | $12,000 | | |
| 23 | Total factory overhead cost | $26,400 | $22,400 | | |
| 24 | Total controllable variances | | | $4,200 | $ 200 |
| 25 | | | | | |
| 26 | | | | | |
| 27 | Net controllable variance—favorable | | | | $4,000 |
| 28 | Volume variance—unfavorable: | | | | |
| 29 | Capacity not used at the standard rate for fixed | | | | |
| 30 | factory overhead—1,000 × $2.40 | | | | 2,400 |
| 31 | Total factory overhead cost variance—favorable | | | | $1,600 |
| 32 | | | | | |

# Factory Overhead Account

The applied factory overhead for Western Rider for the 5,000 XL jeans produced in June is $24,000 is computed below.

$$\text{Applied Factory Overhead} = \frac{\text{Standard Hours for Actual}}{\text{Units Produced}} \times \frac{\text{Total Factory}}{\text{Overhead Rate}}$$

Applied Factory Overhead = (5,000 jeans × 0.80 direct labor hr. per pair of jeans) × $6.00

Applied Factory Overhead = 4,000 direct labor hrs. × $6.00 = $24,000

The total actual factory overhead for Western Rider, as shown in Exhibit 8, was $22,400. Thus, the total factory overhead cost variance for Western Rider for June is a $1,600 favorable variance, as computed on the next page.

$$\text{Total Factory Overhead Cost Variance} = \text{Actual Factory Overhead} - \text{Applied Factory Overhead}$$

$$\text{Total Factory Overhead Cost Variance} = \$22,400 - \$24,000 = -\$1,600 \text{ Favorable Variance}$$

At the end of the period, the factory overhead account normally has a balance. A debit balance in Factory Overhead represents underapplied overhead. Underapplied overhead occurs when actual factory overhead costs exceed the applied factory overhead. A credit balance in Factory Overhead represents overapplied overhead. Overapplied overhead occurs when actual factory overhead costs are less than the applied factory overhead.

The difference between the actual factory overhead and the applied factory overhead is the total factory overhead cost variance. Thus, underapplied and overapplied factory overhead account balances represent the following total factory overhead cost variances:

1. *Underapplied* Factory Overhead = *Unfavorable* Total Factory Overhead Cost Variance
2. *Overapplied* Factory Overhead = *Favorable* Total Factory Overhead Cost Variance

The factory overhead account for Western Rider Inc. for the month ending June 30, 2012, is shown below.

**Factory Overhead**

| | | | |
|---|---|---|---|
| Actual factory overhead | 22,400 | 24,000 | Applied factory overhead |
| ($10,400 + $12,000) | | | (4,000 hrs. × $6.00 per hr.) |
| | | Bal., June 30  1,600 | Overapplied factory overhead |

The $1,600 overapplied factory overhead account balance shown above and the favorable total factory overhead cost variance shown in Exhibit 8 are the same.

The variable factory overhead controllable variance and the volume variance can be computed by comparing the factory overhead account with the budgeted total overhead for the actual level produced, as shown below.

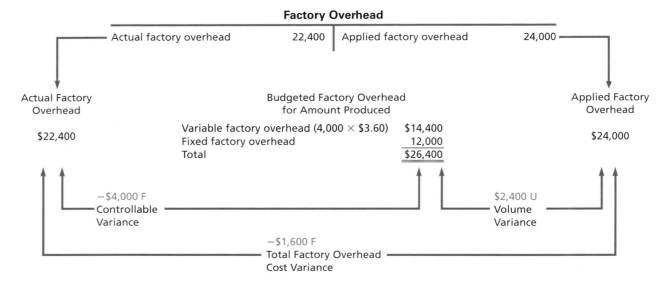

The controllable and volume variances are determined as follows:

1. The difference between the actual overhead incurred and the budgeted overhead is the *controllable* variance.
2. The difference between the applied overhead and the budgeted overhead is the *volume* variance.

If the actual factory overhead exceeds (is less than) the budgeted factory overhead, the controllable variance is unfavorable (favorable). In contrast, if the applied factory overhead is less than (exceeds) the budgeted factory overhead, the volume variance is unfavorable (favorable).

A spreadsheet can be used to compute the cost variances as follows:

| | A | B | C | D | E | F |
|---|---|---|---|---|---|---|
| 1 | Inputs: | | | | | |
| 2 | | Standard | Actual | | | |
| 3 | Direct Materials | | | | | |
| 4 | Square yards | 7,500 | 7,300 | | | |
| 5 | Price per square yard | $ 5.00 | $ 5.50 | | | |
| 6 | | | | | | |
| 7 | Direct Labor | | | | | |
| 8 | Hours | 4,000 | 3,850 | | | |
| 9 | Rate per hour | $ 9.00 | $ 10.00 | | | |
| 10 | | | | | | |
| 11 | Factory Overhead | | | | | |
| 12 | Variable cost | | $ 10,400 | | | |
| 13 | Fixed cost | | 12,000 | | | |
| 14 | Variable factory overhead rate | $ 3.60 | | | | |
| 15 | Fixed factory overhead rate | $ 2.40 | | | | |
| 16 | Normal productive capacity (hrs.) | 5,000 | | | | |
| 17 | | | | | | |
| 18 | Outputs: | | | | | |
| 19 | | | | | | |
| 20 | Direct Materials Variances | | | | | |
| 21 | Price variance | =(C5-B5)*C4 | (Actual Price - Standard Price) x Actual Quantity | | | |
| 22 | Quantity variance | =(C4-B4)*B5 | (Actual Quantity - Standard Quantity) x Standard Price | | | |
| 23 | Direct materials cost variance | =SUM(B21:B22) | Sum | | | |
| 24 | | | | | | |
| 25 | Direct Labor Variances | | | | | |
| 26 | Rate variance | =(C9-B9)*C8 | (Actual Rate per Hour - Standard Rate per Hour) x Actual Hours | | | |
| 27 | Time variance | =(C8-B8)*B9 | (Actual Hours - Standard Hours) x Standard Rate per Hour | | | |
| 28 | Direct labor cost variance | =SUM(B26:B27) | Sum | | | |
| 29 | | | | | | |
| 30 | Factory Overhead Variance | | | | | |
| 31 | Variable factory overhead controllable variance | =(C12-(B14*B8) | Actual Variable Factory Overhead - Budgeted Variable Factory Overhead | | | |
| 32 | Fixed factory overhead volume | =(B16-B8)*B15 | (Normal Capacity in Hours - Standard Hours for Actual Units) x Fixed Factory Overhead Rate | | | |
| 33 | Factory overhead cost variance | =SUM(B31:B32) | Sum | | | |

← **a.**

The spreadsheet is divided into inputs and outputs. The inputs provide the information needed to develop the cost variance formulas. The formulas for each variance are explained by the adjacent text explanation. Thus, for example, the direct materials price variance is determined as:

a.    (Actual Price - Standard Price)  x  Actual Quantity

The formula referencing cells from the input area is:

=(C5-B5)*C4

The remaining formulas reference the input cells in a similar manner.

**Try***It*    Go to the hands-on **Excel Tutor** for this example!

# Recording and Reporting Variances from Standards

**OBJ.**
**5**

Journalize the entries for recording standards in the accounts and prepare an income statement that includes variances from standard.

Standard costs may be used as a management tool to control costs separately from the accounts in the general ledger. However, many companies include standard costs in their accounts. One method for doing so records standard costs and variances at the same time the actual product costs are recorded.

To illustrate, assume that Western Rider Inc. purchased, on account, the 7,300 square yards of blue denim used at $5.50 per square yard. The standard price for direct materials is $5.00 per square yard. The entry to record the purchase and the unfavorable direct materials price variance is as follows:

| | | |
|---|---|---|
| Materials (7,300 sq. yds. × $5.00) | 36,500 | |
| Direct Materials Price Variance | 3,650 | |
| Accounts Payable (7,300 sq. yds. × $5.50) | | 40,150 |

The materials account is debited for the *actual quantity* purchased at the *standard price*, $36,500 (7,300 square yards × $5.00). Accounts Payable is credited for the $40,150 actual cost and the amount due the supplier. The difference of $3,650 is the unfavorable direct materials price variance [($5.50 – $5.00) × 7,300 sq. yds.]. It is recorded by debiting *Direct Materials Price Variance*. If the variance had been favorable, Direct Materials Price Variance would have been credited for the variance.

A debit balance in the direct materials price variance account represents an unfavorable variance. Likewise, a credit balance in the direct materials price variance account represents a favorable variance.

The direct materials quantity variance is recorded in a similar manner. For example, Western Rider Inc. used 7,300 square yards of blue denim to produce 5,000 pairs of XL jeans. The standard quantity of denim for the 5,000 jeans produced is 7,500 square yards. The entry to record the materials used is as follows:

| | | |
|---|---|---|
| Work in Process (7,500 sq. yds. × $5.00) | 37,500 | |
| Direct Materials Quantity Variance | | 1,000 |
| Materials (7,300 sq. yds. × $5.00) | | 36,500 |

Work in Process is debited for $37,500, which is the standard cost of the direct materials required to produce 5,000 XL jeans (7,500 sq. yds. × $5.00). Materials is credited for $36,500, which is the actual quantity of materials used at the standard price (7,300 sq. yds. × $5.00). The difference of $1,000 is the favorable direct materials quantity variance [(7,300 sq. yds. – 7,500 sq. yds.) × $5.00]. It is recorded by crediting *Direct Materials Quantity Variance*. If the variance had been unfavorable, Direct Materials Quantity Variance would have been debited for the variance.

A debit balance in the direct materials quantity variance account represents an unfavorable variance. Likewise, a credit balance in the direct materials quantity variance account represents a favorable variance.

## Example Exercise 22-5 Standard Cost Journal Entries

**OBJ. 5**

Tip Top Corp. produced 3,000 units that require six standard pounds per unit at the $4.50 standard price per pound. The company actually used 18,500 pounds in production. Journalize the entry to record the standard direct materials used in production.

### Follow My Example 22-5

| | | |
|---|---|---|
| Work in Process (18,000* pounds × $4.50) | 81,000 | |
| Direct Materials Quantity Variance [(18,500 pounds – 18,000 pounds) × $4.50] | 2,250 | |
| Materials (18,500 pounds × $4.50) | | 83,250 |

*3,000 units × 6 pounds per unit = 18,000 standard pounds for units produced

Practice Exercises: **PE 22-5A, PE 22-5B**

The journal entries to record the standard costs and variances for *direct labor* are similar to those for direct materials. These entries are summarized below.

1. Work in Process is debited for the standard cost of direct labor.
2. Wages Payable is credited for the actual direct labor cost incurred.
3. Direct Labor Rate Variance is debited for an unfavorable variance and credited for a favorable variance.
4. Direct Labor Time Variance is debited for an unfavorable variance and credited for a favorable variance.

As illustrated in the prior section, the factory overhead account already incorporates standard costs and variances into its journal entries. That is, Factory Overhead is debited for actual factory overhead and credited for applied (standard) factory overhead. The ending balance of factory overhead (overapplied or underapplied) is the total factory overhead cost variance. By comparing the actual factory overhead with the budgeted factory overhead, the controllable variance can be determined. By comparing the budgeted factory overhead with the applied factory overhead, the volume variance can be determined.

When goods are completed, Finished Goods is debited and Work in Process is credited for the standard cost of the product transferred.

At the end of the period, the balances of each of the variance accounts indicate the net favorable or unfavorable variance for the period. These variances may be reported in an income statement prepared for management's use.

Exhibit 9 is an example of an income statement for Western Rider Inc. that includes variances. In Exhibit 9, a sales price of $28 per pair of jeans, selling expenses of $14,500, and administrative expenses of $11,225 are assumed.

**EXHIBIT 9**

**Variance from Standards in Income Statement**

**Western Rider Inc.**
**Income Statement**
**For the Month Ended June 30, 2012**

| | Favorable | Unfavorable | |
|---|---|---|---|
| Sales .............................................. | | | $140,000[1] |
| Cost of goods sold—at standard......................... | | | 97,500[2] |
| Gross profit—at standard ............................. | | | $ 42,500 |
| Less variances from standard cost: | | | |
| Direct materials price .............................. | | $ 3,650 | |
| Direct materials quantity .......................... | $1,000 | | |
| Direct labor rate ................................... | | 3,850 | |
| Direct labor time................................... | 1,350 | | |
| Factory overhead controllable ...................... | 4,000 | | |
| Factory overhead volume............................ | | 2,400 | 3,550 |
| Gross profit ......................................... | | | $ 38,950 |
| Operating expenses: | | | |
| Selling expenses .................................... | | $14,500 | |
| Administrative expenses............................. | | 11,225 | 25,725 |
| Income before income tax ............................ | | | $ 13,225 |

[1]5,000 × $28
[2]$37,500 + $36,000 + $24,000 (from Exhibit 2), or 5,000 × $19.50 (from Exhibit 1)

The income statement shown in Exhibit 9 is for internal use by management. That is, variances are not reported to external users. Thus, the variances shown in Exhibit 9 must be transferred to other accounts in preparing an income statement for external users.

In preparing an income statement for external users, the balances of the variance accounts are normally transferred to Cost of Goods Sold. However, if the variances are significant or if many of the products manufactured are still in inventory, the variances should be allocated to Work in Process, Finished Goods, and Cost of Goods Sold. Such an allocation, in effect, converts these account balances from standard cost to actual cost.

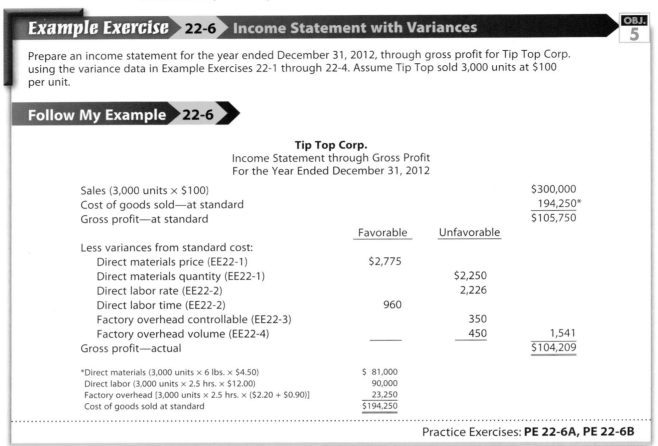

**Example Exercise** 22-6 **Income Statement with Variances** OBJ. 5

Prepare an income statement for the year ended December 31, 2012, through gross profit for Tip Top Corp. using the variance data in Example Exercises 22-1 through 22-4. Assume Tip Top sold 3,000 units at $100 per unit.

**Follow My Example** 22-6

**Tip Top Corp.**
Income Statement through Gross Profit
For the Year Ended December 31, 2012

| | Favorable | Unfavorable | |
|---|---|---|---|
| Sales (3,000 units × $100) | | | $300,000 |
| Cost of goods sold—at standard | | | 194,250* |
| Gross profit—at standard | | | $105,750 |
| Less variances from standard cost: | | | |
| Direct materials price (EE22-1) | $2,775 | | |
| Direct materials quantity (EE22-1) | | $2,250 | |
| Direct labor rate (EE22-2) | | 2,226 | |
| Direct labor time (EE22-2) | 960 | | |
| Factory overhead controllable (EE22-3) | | 350 | |
| Factory overhead volume (EE22-4) | | 450 | 1,541 |
| Gross profit—actual | | | $104,209 |

| | | |
|---|---|---|
| *Direct materials (3,000 units × 6 lbs. × $4.50) | $ 81,000 | |
| Direct labor (3,000 units × 2.5 hrs. × $12.00) | 90,000 | |
| Factory overhead [3,000 units × 2.5 hrs. × ($2.20 + $0.90)] | 23,250 | |
| Cost of goods sold at standard | $194,250 | |

Practice Exercises: **PE 22-6A, PE 22-6B**

 Describe and provide examples of nonfinancial performance measures.

# Nonfinancial Performance Measures

Many companies supplement standard costs and variances from standards with non-financial performance measures. A **nonfinancial performance measure** expresses performance in a measure other than dollars. For example, airlines use on-time performance, percent of bags lost, and number of customer complaints as nonfinancial performance measures. Such measures are often used to evaluate the time, quality, or quantity of a business activity.

Using financial and nonfinancial performance measures aids managers and employees in considering multiple performance objectives. Such measures often bring additional perspectives, such as quality of work, to evaluating performance. Some examples of nonfinancial performance measures include the following:

**Nonfinancial Performance Measures**

Inventory turnover
Percent on-time delivery
Elapsed time between a customer order and product delivery
Customer preference rankings compared to competitors
Response time to a service call
Time to develop new products
Employee satisfaction
Number of customer complaints

Nonfinancial measures are often linked to either the inputs or outputs of an activity or process. A **process** is a sequence of activities for performing a task. The relationship between an activity or a process and its inputs and outputs is on the next page.

To illustrate, the counter service activity of a fast-food restaurant is used. The following inputs/outputs could be identified for providing customer service:

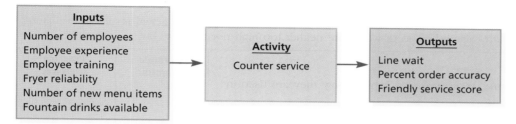

The customer service outputs of the counter service activity include the following:

1. Line wait for the customer
2. Percent order accuracy in serving the customer
3. Friendly service experience for the customer

Some of the inputs that impact the customer service outputs include the following:

1. Number of employees
2. Employee experience
3. Employee training
4. Fryer (and other cooking equipment) reliability
5. Number of new menu items
6. Fountain drink availability

A fast-food restaurant can develop a set of linked nonfinancial performance measures across inputs and outputs. The output measures tell management how the activity is performing, such as keeping the line wait to a minimum. The input measures are used to improve the output measures. For example, if the customer line wait is too long, then improving employee training or hiring more employees could improve the output (decrease customer line wait).

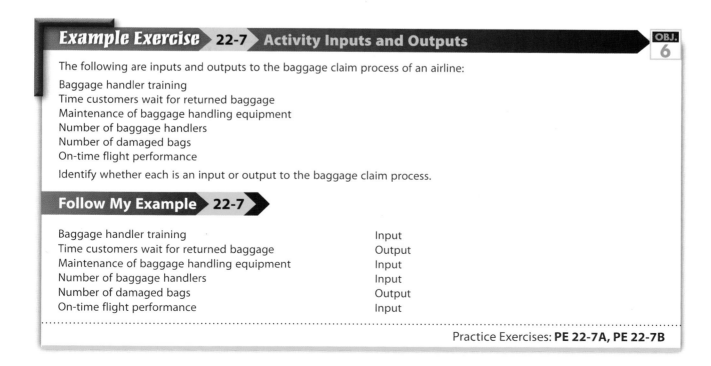

## Example Exercise ▶ 22-7 ▶ Activity Inputs and Outputs   OBJ. 6

The following are inputs and outputs to the baggage claim process of an airline:

Baggage handler training
Time customers wait for returned baggage
Maintenance of baggage handling equipment
Number of baggage handlers
Number of damaged bags
On-time flight performance

Identify whether each is an input or output to the baggage claim process.

## Follow My Example ▶ 22-7

| | |
|---|---|
| Baggage handler training | Input |
| Time customers wait for returned baggage | Output |
| Maintenance of baggage handling equipment | Input |
| Number of baggage handlers | Input |
| Number of damaged bags | Output |
| On-time flight performance | Input |

Practice Exercises: **PE 22-7A, PE 22-7B**

# At a Glance 22

**OBJ. 1**
## Describe the types of standards and how they are established.

**Key Points**   Standards represent performance benchmarks that can be compared to actual results in evaluating performance. Standards are established so that they are neither too high nor too low, but are attainable.

| Learning Outcomes | Example Exercises | Practice Exercises |
|---|---|---|
| • Define *ideal* and *normal standards* and explain how they are used in setting standards. | | |
| • Describe some of the criticisms of the use of standards. | | |

**OBJ. 2**
## Describe and illustrate how standards are used in budgeting.

**Key Points**   Budgets are prepared by multiplying the standard cost per unit by the planned production. To measure performance, the standard cost per unit is multiplied by the actual number of units produced, and the actual results are compared with the standard cost at actual volumes (cost variance).

| Learning Outcomes | Example Exercises | Practice Exercises |
|---|---|---|
| • Compute the standard cost per unit of production for materials, labor, and factory overhead. | | |
| • Compute the direct materials, direct labor, and factory overhead cost variances. | | |
| • Prepare a budget performance report. | | |

**OBJ. 3**
## Compute and interpret direct materials and direct labor variances.

**Key Points**   The direct materials cost variance can be separated into direct materials price and quantity variances. The direct labor cost variance can be separated into direct labor rate and time variances.

| Learning Outcomes | Example Exercises | Practice Exercises |
|---|---|---|
| • Compute and interpret direct materials price and quantity variances. | EE22-1 | PE22-1A, 22-1B |
| • Compute and interpret direct labor rate and time variances. | EE22-2 | PE22-2A, 22-2B |
| • Describe and illustrate how time standards are used in nonmanufacturing settings. | | |

**Compute and interpret factory overhead controllable and volume variances.**

**Key Points**   The factory overhead cost variance can be separated into a variable factory overhead controllable variance and a fixed factory overhead volume variance.

| Learning Outcomes | Example Exercises | Practice Exercises |
|---|---|---|
| • Prepare a factory overhead flexible budget. | | |
| • Compute and interpret the variable factory overhead controllable variance. | EE22-3 | PE22-3A, 22-3B |
| • Compute and interpret the fixed factory overhead volume variance. | EE22-4 | PE22-4A, 22-4B |
| • Prepare a factory overhead cost variance report. | | |
| • Evaluate factory overhead variances using a T account. | | |

**Journalize the entries for recording standards in the accounts and prepare an income statement that includes variances from standard.**

**Key Points**   Standard costs and variances can be recorded in the accounts at the same time the manufacturing costs are recorded in the accounts. Work in Process is debited at standard. Under a standard cost system, the cost of goods sold will be reported at standard cost. Manufacturing variances can be disclosed on the income statement to adjust the gross profit at standard to the actual gross profit.

| Learning Outcomes | Example Exercises | Practice Exercises |
|---|---|---|
| • Journalize the entries to record the purchase and use of direct materials at standard, recording favorable or unfavorable variances. | EE22-5 | PE22-5A, 22-5B |
| • Prepare an income statement, disclosing favorable and unfavorable direct materials, direct labor, and factory overhead variances. | EE22-6 | PE22-6A, 22-6B |

**Describe and provide examples of nonfinancial performance measures.**

**Key Points**   Many companies use a combination of financial and nonfinancial measures in order for multiple perspectives to be incorporated in evaluating performance. Nonfinancial measures are often used in conjunction with the inputs or outputs of a process or an activity.

| Learning Outcomes | Example Exercises | Practice Exercises |
|---|---|---|
| • Define, provide the rationale for, and provide examples of nonfinancial performance measures. | | |
| • Identify nonfinancial inputs and outputs of an activity. | EE22-7 | PE22-7A, 22-7B |

# Key Terms

budget performance report (1033)

budgeted variable factory overhead (1042)

controllable variance (1041)

cost variances (1033)

currently attainable standards (1031)

direct labor rate variance (1038)

direct labor time variance (1039)

direct materials price variance (1036)

direct materials quantity variance (1036)

factory overhead cost variance report (1045)

favorable cost variance (1033)

ideal standards (1031)

nonfinancial performance measure (1050)

process (1050)

standard cost (1030)

standard cost systems (1030)

standards (1030)

total manufacturing cost variance (1034)

unfavorable cost variance (1033)

volume variance (1043)

# Illustrative Problem

Hawley Inc. manufactures woven baskets for national distribution. The standard costs for the manufacture of Folk Art style baskets were as follows:

|  | **Standard Costs** | **Actual Costs** |
|---|---|---|
| Direct materials | 1,500 lbs. at $35 | 1,600 lbs. at $32 |
| Direct labor | 4,800 hrs. at $11 | 4,500 hrs. at $11.80 |
| Factory overhead | Rates per labor hour, based on 100% of normal capacity of 5,500 labor hrs.: |  |
|  | Variable cost, $2.40 | $12,300 variable cost |
|  | Fixed cost, $3.50 | $19,250 fixed cost |

## Instructions

1. Determine the quantity variance, price variance, and total direct materials cost variance for the Folk Art style baskets.

2. Determine the time variance, rate variance, and total direct labor cost variance for the Folk Art style baskets.

3. Determine the controllable variance, volume variance, and total factory overhead cost variance for the Folk Art style baskets.

## Solution

1.                              **Direct Materials Cost Variance**

**Quantity variance:**
> Direct Materials Quantity Variance = (Actual Quantity − Standard Quantity) × Standard Price
> Direct Materials Quantity Variance = (1,600 lbs. − 1,500 lbs.) × $35 per lb.
> Direct Materials Quantity Variance = $3,500 Unfavorable Variance

**Price variance:**
> Direct Materials Price Variance = (Actual Price − Standard Price) × Actual Quantity
> Direct Materials Price Variance = ($32 per lb. − $35 per lb.) × 1,600 lbs.
> Direct Materials Price Variance = −$4,800 Favorable Variance

**Total direct materials cost variance:**
> Direct Materials Cost Variance = Direct Materials Quantity Variance + Direct Materials Price Variance
> Direct Materials Cost Variance = $3,500 + ($4,800)
> Direct Materials Cost Variance = −$1,300 Favorable Variance

2.
## Direct Labor Cost Variance

**Time variance:**

Direct Labor Time Variance = (Actual Direct Labor Hours – Standard Direct Labor Hours) × Standard Rate per Hour

Direct Labor Time Variance = (4,500 hrs. – 4,800 hrs.) × $11 per hour

Direct Labor Time Variance = –$3,300 Favorable Variance

**Rate variance:**

Direct Labor Rate Variance = (Actual Rate per Hour – Standard Rate per Hour) × Actual Hours

Direct Labor Rate Variance = ($11.80 – $11.00) × 4,500 hrs.

Direct Labor Rate Variance = $3,600 Unfavorable Variance

**Total direct labor cost variance:**

Direct Labor Cost Variance = Direct Labor Time Variance + Direct Labor Rate Variance

Direct Labor Cost Variance = ($3,300) + $3,600

Direct Labor Cost Variance = $300 Unfavorable Variance

3.
## Factory Overhead Cost Variance

**Variable factory overhead controllable variance:**

$$\text{Variable Factory Overhead Controllable Variance} = \text{Actual Variable Factory Overhead} - \text{Budgeted Variable Factory Overhead}$$

$$\text{Variable Factory Overhead Controllable Variance} = \$12,300 - \$11,520^*$$

$$\text{Variable Factory Overhead Controllable Variance} = \$780 \text{ Unfavorable Variance}$$

*4,800 hrs. × $2.40 per hour

**Fixed factory overhead volume variance:**

$$\text{Fixed Factory Overhead Volume Variance} = \left( \begin{array}{c} \text{Standard Hours for 100\%} \\ \text{of Normal Capacity} \end{array} - \begin{array}{c} \text{Standard Hours for} \\ \text{Actual Units Produced} \end{array} \right) \times \begin{array}{c} \text{Fixed Factory} \\ \text{Overhead Rate} \end{array}$$

$$\text{Fixed Factory Overhead Volume Variance} = (5,500 \text{ hrs.} - 4,800 \text{ hrs.}) \times \$3.50 \text{ per hr.}$$

$$\text{Fixed Factory Overhead Volume Variance} = \$2,450 \text{ Unfavorable Variance}$$

**Total factory overhead cost variance:**

$$\text{Factory Overhead Cost Variance} = \begin{array}{c} \text{Variable Factory Overhead} \\ \text{Controllable Variance} \end{array} + \begin{array}{c} \text{Fixed Factory Overhead} \\ \text{Volume Variance} \end{array}$$

$$\text{Factory Overhead Cost Variance} = \$780 + \$2,450$$

$$\text{Factory Overhead Cost Variance} = \$3,230 \text{ Unfavorable Variance}$$

## Discussion Questions

1. What are the basic objectives in the use of standard costs?

2. What is meant by reporting by the "principle of exceptions," as the term is used in reference to cost control?

3. a. What are the two variances between the actual cost and the standard cost for direct materials?

   b. Discuss some possible causes of these variances.

4. The materials cost variance report for Nickols Inc. indicates a large favorable materials price variance and a significant unfavorable materials quantity variance. What might have caused these offsetting variances?

5. a. What are the two variances between the actual cost and the standard cost for direct labor?

   b. Who generally has control over the direct labor cost?

6. A new assistant controller recently was heard to remark: "All the assembly workers in this plant are covered by union contracts, so there should be no labor variances." Was the controller's remark correct? Discuss.

7. Would the use of standards be appropriate in a nonmanufacturing setting, such as a fast-food restaurant?

8. a. Describe the two variances between the actual costs and the standard costs for factory overhead.

   b. What is a factory overhead cost variance report?

9. If variances are recorded in the accounts at the time the manufacturing costs are incurred, what does a debit balance in Direct Materials Price Variance represent?

10. Briefly explain why firms might use nonfinancial performance measures.

# Practice Exercises

**PE 22-1A   Direct materials variances**

Primm Company produces a product that requires four standard gallons per unit. The standard price is $24.50 per gallon. If 2,500 units required 10,600 gallons, which were purchased at $23.75 per gallon, what is the direct materials (a) price variance, (b) quantity variance, and (c) cost variance?

**PE 22-1B   Direct materials variances**

Young Company produces a product that requires five standard pounds per unit. The standard price is $0.90 per pound. If 500 units required 2,350 pounds, which were purchased at $1.10 per pound, what is the direct materials (a) price variance, (b) quantity variance, and (c) cost variance?

**PE 22-2A   Direct labor variances**

Primm Company produces a product that requires three standard hours per unit at a standard hourly rate of $20 per hour. If 2,500 units required 7,900 hours at an hourly rate of $21.50 per hour, what is the direct labor (a) rate variance, (b) time variance, and (c) cost variance?

**PE 22-2B   Direct labor variances**

Young Company produces a product that requires 2.5 standard hours per unit at a standard hourly rate of $9 per hour. If 500 units required 1,200 hours at an hourly rate of $8.75 per hour, what is the direct labor (a) rate variance, (b) time variance, and (c) cost variance?

**PE 22-3A   Factory overhead controllable variance**

Primm Company produced 2,500 units of product that required three standard hours per unit. The standard variable overhead cost per unit is $2.50 per hour. The actual variable factory overhead was $19,050. Determine the variable factory overhead controllable variance.

**PE 22-3B   Factory overhead controllable variance**

Young Company produced 500 units of product that required 2.5 standard hours per unit. The standard variable overhead cost per unit is $0.70 per hour. The actual variable factory overhead was $840. Determine the variable factory overhead controllable variance.

**PE 22-4A   Factory overhead volume variance**

Primm Company produced 2,500 units of product that required three standard hours per unit. The standard fixed overhead cost per unit is $1.30 per hour at 7,000 hours, which is 100% of normal capacity. Determine the fixed factory overhead volume variance.

**PE 22-4B   Factory overhead volume variance**

Young Company produced 500 units of product that required 2.5 standard hours per unit. The standard fixed overhead cost per unit is $0.30 per hour at 1,500 hours, which is 100% of normal capacity. Determine the fixed factory overhead volume variance.

OBJ. 5    **EE 22-5**  *p. 1048*    **PE 22-5A    Standard cost journal entries**

Primm Company produced 2,500 units that require four standard gallons per unit at $24.50 standard price per gallon. The company actually used 10,600 gallons in production. Journalize the entry to record the standard direct materials used in production.

OBJ. 5    **EE 22-5**  *p. 1048*    **PE 22-5B    Standard cost journal entries**

Young Company produced 500 units that require five standard pounds per unit at $0.90 standard price per pound. The company actually used 2,350 pounds in production. Journalize the entry to record the standard direct materials used in production.

OBJ. 5    **EE 22-6**  *p. 1050*    **PE 22-6A    Income statement with variances**

Prepare a 2012 income statement through gross profit for Primm Company using the variance data in Practice Exercises 22-1A, 22-2A, 22-3A, and 22-4A. Assume Primm sold 2,500 units at $320 per unit.

OBJ. 5    **EE 22-6**  *p. 1050*    **PE 22-6B    Income statement with variances**

Prepare a 2012 income statement through gross profit for Young Company using the variance data in Practice Exercises 22-1B, 22-2B, 22-3B, and 22-4B. Assume Young sold 500 units at $82 per unit.

OBJ. 6    **EE 22-7**  *p. 1051*    **PE 22-7A    Activity inputs and outputs**

The following are inputs and outputs to the copying process of a copy shop:

Number of pages copied per hour
Number of customer complaints
Number of times paper supply runs out
Number of employee errors
Copy machine downtime (broken)
Percent jobs done on time

Identify whether each is an input or output to the copying process.

OBJ. 6    **EE 22-7**  *p. 1051*    **PE 22-7B    Activity inputs and outputs**

The following are inputs and outputs to the cooking process of a restaurant:

Number of unexpected cook absences
Number of server order mistakes
Percent of meals prepared on time
Number of times ingredients are missing
Number of customer complaints
Number of hours kitchen equipment is down for repairs

Identify whether each is an input or output to the cooking process.

## Exercises

OBJ. 2    **EX 22-1    Standard direct materials cost per unit**

Geneva Chocolate Company produces chocolate bars. The primary materials used in producing chocolate bars are cocoa, sugar, and milk. The standard costs for a batch of chocolate (5,000 bars) are as follows:

| Ingredient | Quantity | Price |
|---|---|---|
| Cocoa | 510 lbs. | $0.70 per lb. |
| Sugar | 150 lbs. | $1.18 per lb. |
| Milk | 120 gal. | $1.80 per gal. |

Determine the standard direct materials cost per bar of chocolate.

**OBJ. 2**

**EX 22-2 Standard product cost**

Cumberland Furniture Company manufactures unfinished oak furniture. Cumberland uses a standard cost system. The direct labor, direct materials, and factory overhead standards for an unfinished dining room table are as follows:

| | | |
|---|---|---|
| Direct labor: | standard rate | $16.00 per hr. |
| | standard time per unit | 1.8 hrs. |
| Direct materials (oak): | standard price | $12.50 per bd. ft. |
| | standard quantity | 17 bd. ft. |
| Variable factory overhead: | standard rate | $2.40 per direct labor hr. |
| Fixed factory overhead: | standard rate | $1.10 per direct labor hr. |

a. Determine the standard cost per dining room table.

b. ➤ Why would Cumberland use a standard cost system?

---

**OBJ. 2**

✔ **b. Direct labor cost variance, $700 F**

**EX 22-3 Budget performance report**

PET Bottle Company (PBC) manufactures plastic two-liter bottles for the beverage industry. The cost standards per 100 two-liter bottles are as follows:

| Cost Category | Standard Cost per 100 Two-Liter Bottles |
|---|---|
| Direct labor | $1.32 |
| Direct materials | 5.34 |
| Factory overhead | 0.34 |
| Total | $7.00 |

At the beginning of March, PBC management planned to produce 450,000 bottles. The actual number of bottles produced for March was 500,000 bottles. The actual costs for March of the current year were as follows:

| Cost Category | Actual Cost for the Month Ended March 31, 2012 |
|---|---|
| Direct labor | $ 5,900 |
| Direct materials | 25,300 |
| Factory overhead | 1,900 |
| Total | $33,100 |

a. Prepare the March manufacturing standard cost budget (direct labor, direct materials, and factory overhead) for PBC, assuming planned production.

b. Prepare a budget performance report for manufacturing costs, showing the total cost variances for direct materials, direct labor, and factory overhead for March.

c. ➤ Interpret the budget performance report.

---

**OBJ. 3**

✔ **a. Price variance, $2,155 U**

**EX 22-4 Direct materials variances**

The following data relate to the direct materials cost for the production of 2,000 automobile tires:

| | | |
|---|---|---|
| Actual: | 43,100 lbs. at $2.05 | $88,355 |
| Standard: | 44,100 lbs. at $2.00 | $88,200 |

a. Determine the price variance, quantity variance, and total direct materials cost variance.

b. ➤ To whom should the variances be reported for analysis and control?

---

**OBJ. 3**

✔ **Quantity variance, $258 U**

**EX 22-5 Direct materials variances**

MyTime, Inc., produces electronic timepieces. The company uses mini-LCD displays for its products. Each timepiece uses one display. The company produced 540 timepieces during October. However, due to LCD defects, the company actually used 570 LCD displays during October. Each display has a standard cost of $8.60. Five hundred seventy LCD displays were purchased for October production at a cost of $4,560.

Determine the price variance, quantity variance, and total direct materials cost variance for October.

---

OBJ. 2, 3

### EX 22-6 Standard direct materials cost per unit from variance data

The following data relating to direct materials cost for November of the current year are taken from the records of Tot Toys Inc., a manufacturer of plastic toys:

| | |
|---|---|
| Quantity of direct materials used | 2,000 lbs. |
| Actual unit price of direct materials | $2.40 per lb. |
| Units of finished product manufactured | 460 units |
| Standard direct materials per unit of finished product | 4 lbs. |
| Direct materials quantity variance—unfavorable | $500 |
| Direct materials price variance—favorable | $1,450 |

Determine the standard direct materials cost per unit of finished product, assuming that there was no inventory of work in process at either the beginning or the end of the month.

---

OBJ. 2, 3

### EX 22-7 Standard product cost, direct materials variance

H.J. Heinz Company uses standards to control its materials costs. Assume that a batch of ketchup (1,500 pounds) has the following standards:

| | Standard Quantity | Standard Price |
|---|---|---|
| Whole tomatoes | 2,400 lbs. | $0.45 per lb. |
| Vinegar | 160 gal. | 2.75 per gal. |
| Corn syrup | 14 gal. | 10.00 per gal. |
| Salt | 62 lbs. | 2.50 per lb. |

The actual materials in a batch may vary from the standard due to tomato characteristics. Assume that the actual quantities of materials for batch K-54 were as follows:

2,540 lbs. of tomatoes
164 gal. of vinegar
13 gal. of corn syrup
60 lbs. of salt

a. Determine the standard unit materials cost per pound for a standard batch.

b. Determine the direct materials quantity variance for batch K-54.

---

OBJ. 3

✔ a. Rate variance, $1,035 F

### EX 22-8 Direct labor variances

The following data relate to labor cost for production of 5,500 cellular telephones:

| | | | |
|---|---|---|---|
| Actual: | 3,450 hrs. at $16.40 | $56,580 |
| Standard: | 3,390 hrs. at $16.70 | $56,613 |

a. Determine the rate variance, time variance, and total direct labor cost variance.

b. ➤ Discuss what might have caused these variances.

---

OBJ. 3, 5

✔ a. Time variance, $284 U

### EX 22-9 Direct labor variances

Provence Bicycle Company manufactures road bikes. The following data for September of the current year are available:

| | |
|---|---|
| Quantity of direct labor used | 650 hrs. |
| Actual rate for direct labor | $14.00 per hr. |
| Bicycles completed in September | 280 |
| Standard direct labor per bicycle | 2.25 hrs. |
| Standard rate for direct labor | $14.20 per hr. |

a. Determine the direct labor rate and time variances.

b. How much direct labor should be debited to Work in Process?

---

**OBJ. 3**

✔ a. Cutting Department rate variance, $700 favorable

### EX 22-10 Direct labor variances

The New Day Clothes Company produced 18,000 units during June of the current year. The Cutting Department used 3,500 direct labor hours at an actual rate of $11.80 per hour. The Sewing Department used 5,800 direct labor hours at an actual rate of $12.15 per hour. Assume there were no work in process inventories in either department at the beginning or end of the month. The standard labor rate is $12.00. The standard labor time for the Cutting and Sewing departments is 0.19 hour and 0.33 hour per unit, respectively.

a. Determine the direct labor rate and time variances for the (1) Cutting Department and (2) Sewing Department.

b. ➡ Interpret your results.

---

**OBJ. 3**

✔ a. $960

### EX 22-11 Direct labor standards for nonmanufacturing expenses

Good Samaritan Hospital began using standards to evaluate its Admissions Department. The standard was broken into two types of admissions as follows:

| Type of Admission | Standard Time to Complete Admission Record |
|---|---|
| Unscheduled admission | 40 min. |
| Scheduled admission | 10 min. |

The unscheduled admission took longer, since name, address, and insurance information needed to be determined at the time of admission. Information was collected on scheduled admissions prior to the admissions, which was less time consuming.

The Admissions Department employs two full-time people (40 productive hours per week, with no overtime) at $12 per hour. For the most recent week, the department handled 60 unscheduled and 210 scheduled admissions.

a. How much was actually spent on labor for the week?

b. What are the standard hours for the actual volume for the week?

c. Calculate a time variance, and report how well the department performed for the week.

---

**OBJ. 2, 3**

### EX 22-12 Direct labor standards for nonmanufacturing operations

One of the operations in the United States Postal Service is a mechanical mail sorting operation. In this operation, letter mail is sorted at a rate of one letter per second. The letter is mechanically sorted from a three-digit code input by an operator sitting at a keyboard. The manager of the mechanical sorting operation wishes to determine the number of temporary employees to hire for December. The manager estimates that there will be an additional 35,100,000 pieces of mail in December, due to the upcoming holiday season.

Assume that the sorting operators are temporary employees. The union contract requires that temporary employees be hired for one month at a time. Each temporary employee is hired to work 150 hours in the month.

a. How many temporary employees should the manager hire for December?

b. If each employee earns a standard $16 per hour, what would be the labor time variance if the actual number of letters sorted in December was 34,020,000?

---

**OBJ. 3**

✔ Direct materials quantity variance, $300 U

### EX 22-13 Direct materials and direct labor variances

At the beginning of June, Marshall Printing Company budgeted 16,000 books to be printed in June at standard direct materials and direct labor costs as follows:

| | |
|---|---|
| Direct materials | $24,000 |
| Direct labor | 8,000 |
| Total | $32,000 |

The standard materials price is $0.75 per pound. The standard direct labor rate is $12.50 per hour. At the end of June, the actual direct materials and direct labor costs were as follows:

| | |
|---|---|
| Actual direct materials | $21,300 |
| Actual direct labor | 6,800 |
| Total | $28,100 |

There were no direct materials price or direct labor rate variances for June. In addition, assume no changes in the direct materials inventory balances in June. Marshall Printing Company actually produced 14,000 units during June.

Determine the direct materials quantity and direct labor time variances.

---

**OBJ. 4**

✔ Total factory overhead, 12,000 hrs., $218,760

### EX 22-14 Flexible overhead budget

Carson Wood Products Company prepared the following factory overhead cost budget for the Press Department for April 2012, during which it expected to require 10,000 hours of productive capacity in the department:

| | | |
|---|---|---|
| Variable overhead cost: | | |
| Indirect factory labor | $83,000 | |
| Power and light | 3,800 | |
| Indirect materials | 28,000 | |
| Total variable cost | | $114,800 |
| Fixed overhead cost: | | |
| Supervisory salaries | $40,000 | |
| Depreciation of plant and equipment | 25,000 | |
| Insurance and property taxes | 16,000 | |
| Total fixed cost | | 81,000 |
| Total factory overhead cost | | $195,800 |

Assuming that the estimated costs for May are the same as for April, prepare a flexible factory overhead cost budget for the Press Department for May for 8,000, 10,000, and 12,000 hours of production.

---

**OBJ. 4**

### EX 22-15 Flexible overhead budget

Van Dyck Company has determined that the variable overhead rate is $3.90 per direct labor hour in the Fabrication Department. The normal production capacity for the Fabrication Department is 14,000 hours for the month. Fixed costs are budgeted at $72,800 for the month.

a. Prepare a monthly factory overhead flexible budget for 13,000, 14,000, and 15,000 hours of production.

b. How much overhead would be applied to production if 15,000 hours were used in the department during the month?

---

**OBJ. 4**

✔ Volume variance, $7,125 U

### EX 22-16 Factory overhead cost variances

The following data relate to factory overhead cost for the production of 4,000 computers:

| | | |
|---|---|---|
| Actual: | Variable factory overhead | $130,000 |
| | Fixed factory overhead | 30,875 |
| Standard: | 5,000 hrs. at $32 | 160,000 |

If productive capacity of 100% was 6,500 hours and the factory overhead cost budgeted at the level of 5,000 standard hours was $167,125, determine the variable factory overhead controllable variance, fixed factory overhead volume variance, and total factory overhead cost variance. The fixed factory overhead rate was $4.75 per hour.

### EX 22-17   Factory overhead cost variances

Casual Comfort Textiles Corporation began January with a budget for 30,000 hours of production in the Weaving Department. The department has a full capacity of 40,000 hours under normal business conditions. The budgeted overhead at the planned volumes at the beginning of January was as follows:

| | |
|---|---|
| Variable overhead | $124,500 |
| Fixed overhead | 62,000 |
| Total | $186,500 |

The actual factory overhead was $178,900 for January. The actual fixed factory overhead was as budgeted. During January, the Weaving Department had standard hours at actual production volume of 31,000 hours.

a.  Determine the variable factory overhead controllable variance.

b.  Determine the fixed factory overhead volume variance.

### EX 22-18   Factory overhead variance corrections

The data related to Elite Sporting Goods Company's factory overhead cost for the production of 50,000 units of product are as follows:

| | | |
|---|---|---|
| Actual: | Variable factory overhead | $218,900 |
| | Fixed factory overhead | 157,500 |
| Standard: | 76,000 hrs. at $5.00 ($2.90 for variable factory overhead) | 380,000 |

Productive capacity at 100% of normal was 75,000 hours, and the factory overhead cost budgeted at the level of 76,000 standard hours was $377,900. Based on these data, the chief cost accountant prepared the following variance analysis:

| | | |
|---|---|---|
| Variable factory overhead controllable variance: | | |
| Actual variable factory overhead cost incurred | $218,900 | |
| Budgeted variable factory overhead for 76,000 hours | 220,400 | |
| Variance—favorable | | −$1,500 |
| Fixed factory overhead volume variance: | | |
| Normal productive capacity at 100% | 75,000 hrs. | |
| Standard for amount produced | 76,000 | |
| Productive capacity not used | 1,000 hrs. | |
| Standard variable factory overhead rate | × $5.00 | |
| Variance—unfavorable | | 5,000 |
| Total factory overhead cost variance—unfavorable | | $3,500 |

Identify the errors in the factory overhead cost variance analysis.

### EX 22-19   Factory overhead cost variance report

Medical Molded Products Inc. prepared the following factory overhead cost budget for the Trim Department for March 2012, during which it expected to use 10,000 hours for production:

| | | |
|---|---|---|
| Variable overhead cost: | | |
| Indirect factory labor | $29,000 | |
| Power and light | 7,500 | |
| Indirect materials | 13,000 | |
| Total variable cost | | $ 49,500 |
| Fixed overhead cost: | | |
| Supervisory salaries | $34,100 | |
| Depreciation of plant and equipment | 24,800 | |
| Insurance and property taxes | 22,100 | |
| Total fixed cost | | 81,000 |
| Total factory overhead cost | | $130,500 |

Medical Molded Products has available 15,000 hours of monthly productive capacity in the Trim Department under normal business conditions. During March, the Trim Department actually used 11,000 hours for production. The actual fixed costs were as budgeted. The actual variable overhead for March was as follows:

| Actual variable factory overhead cost: | |
|---|---|
| Indirect factory labor | $31,100 |
| Power and light | 8,100 |
| Indirect materials | 15,000 |
| Total variable cost | $54,200 |

Construct a factory overhead cost variance report for the Trim Department for March.

---

**OBJ. 5**

### EX 22-20 Recording standards in accounts

Gemini Manufacturing Company incorporates standards in its accounts and identifies variances at the time the manufacturing costs are incurred. Journalize the entries to record the following transactions:

a. Purchased 1,700 units of copper tubing on account at $68.90 per unit. The standard price is $65.00 per unit.

b. Used 1,000 units of copper tubing in the process of manufacturing 140 air conditioners. Eight units of copper tubing are required, at standard, to produce one air conditioner.

---

**OBJ. 5**

### EX 22-21 Recording standards in accounts

The Assembly Department produced 2,000 units of product during June. Each unit required 1.75 standard direct labor hours. There were 3,800 actual hours used in the Assembly Department during June at an actual rate of $14.60 per hour. The standard direct labor rate is $15 per hour. Assuming direct labor for a month is paid on the fifth day of the following month, journalize the direct labor in the Assembly Department on June 30.

---

**OBJ. 5**

✔ Income before income tax, $61,200

### EX 22-22 Income statement indicating standard cost variances

The following data were taken from the records of Gentry Company for December 2012:

| | |
|---|---|
| Administrative expenses | $ 72,000 |
| Cost of goods sold (at standard) | 390,000 |
| Direct materials price variance—unfavorable | 1,200 |
| Direct materials quantity variance—favorable | 400 |
| Direct labor rate variance—favorable | 800 |
| Direct labor time variance—unfavorable | 350 |
| Variable factory overhead controllable variance—favorable | 150 |
| Fixed factory overhead volume variance—unfavorable | 2,200 |
| Interest expense | 2,100 |
| Sales | 620,000 |
| Selling expenses | 92,300 |

Prepare an income statement for presentation to management.

---

**OBJ. 6**

### EX 22-23 Nonfinancial performance measures

Ace, Inc., is an Internet retailer of golf equipment. Customers order golf equipment from the company, using an online catalog. The company processes these orders and delivers the requested product from its warehouse. The company wants to provide customers with an excellent purchase experience in order to expand the business through favorable word-of-mouth advertising and to drive repeat business. To help monitor performance, the company developed a set of performance measures for its order placement and delivery process.

Average computer response time to customer "clicks"

Dollar amount of returned goods

Elapsed time between customer order and product delivery

Maintenance dollars divided by hardware investment

Number of customer complaints divided by the number of orders

Number of misfilled orders divided by the number of orders

Number of orders per warehouse employee

Number of page faults or errors due to software programming errors

Number of software fixes per week

Server (computer) downtime

Training dollars per programmer

a.  For each performance measure, identify it as either an input or output measure related to the "order placement and delivery" process.

b.  Provide an explanation for each performance measure.

---

**OBJ. 6**

### EX 22-24   Nonfinancial performance measures

Lake Area College wishes to monitor the efficiency and quality of its course registration process.

a.  Identify three input and three output measures for this process.

b.  Why would Lake Area College use nonfinancial measures for monitoring this process?

---

## Problems Series A

---

**OBJ. 2, 3**

✔ **c. Direct labor time variance, $2,900 U**

### PR 22-1A   Direct materials and direct labor variance analysis

Oasis Faucet Company manufactures faucets in a small manufacturing facility. The faucets are made from zinc. Manufacturing has 50 employees. Each employee presently provides 36 hours of labor per week. Information about a production week is as follows:

| | |
|---|---|
| Standard wage per hr. | $14.50 |
| Standard labor time per faucet | 12 min. |
| Standard number of lbs. of zinc | 1.8 lbs. |
| Standard price per lb. of zinc | $12.00 |
| Actual price per lb. of zinc | $11.75 |
| Actual lbs. of zinc used during the week | 15,100 lbs. |
| Number of faucets produced during the week | 8,000 |
| Actual wage per hr. | $15.10 |
| Actual hrs. per week | 1,800 hrs. |

### Instructions

Determine (a) the standard cost per unit for direct materials and direct labor; (b) the price variance, quantity variance, and total direct materials cost variance; and (c) the rate variance, time variance, and total direct labor cost variance.

---

**OBJ. 1, 2, 3**

✔ **1. a. Direct materials quantity variance, $350 F**

### PR 22-2A   Flexible budgeting and variance analysis

Belgian Chocolate Company makes dark chocolate and light chocolate. Both products require cocoa and sugar. The following planning information has been made available:

| | Standard Amount per Case | | |
|---|---|---|---|
| | **Dark Chocolate** | **Light Chocolate** | **Standard Price per Pound** |
| Cocoa | 10 lbs. | 7 lbs. | $4.50 |
| Sugar | 8 lbs. | 12 lbs. | 0.65 |
| Standard labor time | 0.35 hr. | 0.40 hr. | |

| | **Dark Chocolate** | **Light Chocolate** |
|---|---|---|
| Planned production | 4,200 cases | 10,500 cases |
| Standard labor rate | $14.50 per hr. | $14.50 per hr. |

Belgian Chocolate does not expect there to be any beginning or ending inventories of cocoa or sugar. At the end of the budget year, Belgian Chocolate had the following actual results:

|  | Dark Chocolate | Light Chocolate |
| --- | --- | --- |
| Actual production (cases) | 4,000 | 11,000 |
|  | **Actual Price per Pound** | **Actual Pounds Purchased and Used** |
| Cocoa | $4.60 | 117,500 |
| Sugar | 0.60 | 160,000 |
|  | **Actual Labor Rate** | **Actual Labor Hours Used** |
| Dark chocolate | $13.90 per hr. | 1,270 |
| Light chocolate | 14.90 per hr. | 4,500 |

### Instructions

1. Prepare the following variance analyses for both chocolates and total, based on the actual results and production levels at the end of the budget year:

   a. Direct materials price, quantity, and total variance.

   b. Direct labor rate, time, and total variance.

2. ➡ Why are the standard amounts in part (1) based on the actual production for the year instead of the planned production for the year?

---

**OBJ. 3, 4**

✔ c. Controllable
variance, $260 F

### PR 22-3A Direct materials, direct labor, and factory overhead cost variance analysis

Specialty Polymers, Inc., processes a base chemical into plastic. Standard costs and actual costs for direct materials, direct labor, and factory overhead incurred for the manufacture of 19,000 units of product were as follows:

|  | Standard Costs | Actual Costs |
| --- | --- | --- |
| Direct materials | 2,500 lbs. at $8.10 | 2,440 lbs. at $8.30 |
| Direct labor | 3,800 hrs. at $17.50 | 3,750 hrs. at $17.68 |
| Factory overhead | Rates per direct labor hr., based on 100% of normal capacity of 3,900 direct labor hrs.: |  |
|  | Variable cost, $2.20 | $8,100 variable cost |
|  | Fixed cost, $3.50 | $13,650 fixed cost |

Each unit requires 0.2 hour of direct labor.

### Instructions

Determine (a) the price variance, quantity variance, and total direct materials cost variance; (b) the rate variance, time variance, and total direct labor cost variance; and (c) variable factory overhead controllable variance, the fixed factory overhead volume variance, and total factory overhead cost variance.

---

**OBJ. 4**

✔ Controllable
variance, $280 U

### PR 22-4A Standard factory overhead variance report

Tiger Equipment Inc., a manufacturer of construction equipment, prepared the following factory overhead cost budget for the Welding Department for May 2012. The company expected to operate the department at 100% of normal capacity of 7,000 hours.

| Variable costs: | | |
| --- | --- | --- |
| Indirect factory wages | $22,050 | |
| Power and light | 12,600 | |
| Indirect materials | 10,500 | |
| Total variable cost | | $45,150 |

Fixed costs:

| | | |
|---|---|---|
| Supervisory salaries | $12,000 | |
| Depreciation of plant and equipment | 31,450 | |
| Insurance and property taxes | 9,750 | |
| Total fixed cost | | 53,200 |
| Total factory overhead cost | | $98,350 |

During May, the department operated at 7,400 standard hours, and the factory overhead costs incurred were indirect factory wages, $23,580; power and light, $13,120; indirect materials, $11,310; supervisory salaries, $12,000; depreciation of plant and equipment, $31,450; and insurance and property taxes, $9,750.

### Instructions

Prepare a factory overhead cost variance report for May. To be useful for cost control, the budgeted amounts should be based on 7,400 hours.

---

OBJ. 3, 6

✔ 3. $1,120 U

### PR 22-5A  Standards for nonmanufacturing expenses

Diamond Software, Inc., does software development. One important activity in software development is writing software code. The manager of the WordPro Development Team determined that the average software programmer could write 40 lines of code in an hour. The plan for the first week in May called for 6,200 lines of code to be written on the WordPro product. The WordPro Team has four programmers. Each programmer is hired from an employment firm that requires temporary employees to be hired for a minimum of a 40-hour week. Programmers are paid $25.00 per hour. The manager offered a bonus if the team could generate more lines for the week, without overtime. Due to a project emergency, the programmers wrote more code in the first week of May than planned. The actual amount of code written in the first week of May was 7,200 lines, without overtime. As a result, the bonus caused the average programmer's hourly rate to increase to $32.00 per hour during the first week in May.

### Instructions

1. If the team generated 6,200 lines of code according to the original plan, what would have been the labor time variance?

2. What was the actual labor time variance as a result of generating 7,200 lines of code?

3. What was the labor rate variance as a result of the bonus?

4. ━━━━━▶ Are there any performance-related issues that the labor time and rate variances fail to consider? Explain.

5. The manager is trying to determine if a better decision would have been to hire a temporary programmer to meet the higher programming demand in the first week of May, rather than paying out the bonus. If another employee was hired from the employment firm, what would have been the labor time variance in the first week?

6. ━━━━━▶ Which decision is better, paying the bonus or hiring another programmer?

## Problems Series B

---

OBJ. 2, 3

✔ c. Rate variance, $420 F

### PR 22-1B  Direct materials and direct labor variance analysis

Heart Dress Co. manufactures dresses in a small manufacturing facility. Manufacturing has 20 employees. Each employee presently provides 35 hours of productive labor per week. Information about a production week is as follows:

| | |
|---|---|
| Standard wage per hr. | $10.60 |
| Standard labor time per dress | 15 min. |
| Standard number of yds. of fabric per dress | 4.0 yds. |
| Standard price per yd. of fabric | $2.90 |
| Actual price per yd. of fabric | $3.05 |
| Actual yds. of fabric used during the week | 14,200 yds. |
| Number of dresses produced during the week | 3,500 |
| Actual wage per hr. | $10.00 |
| Actual hrs. per week | 700 hrs. |

## Instructions

Determine (a) the standard cost per dress for direct materials and direct labor; (b) the price variance, quantity variance, and total direct materials cost variance; and (c) the rate variance, time variance, and total direct labor cost variance.

OBJ. 1, 2, 3

✔ 1. a. Direct materials price variance, $11,645 U

### PR 22-2B   Flexible budgeting and variance analysis

Yukon Coat Company makes women's and men's coats. Both products require filler and lining material. The following planning information has been made available:

|  | **Standard Amount per Unit** | | **Standard Price per Unit** |
|---|---|---|---|
|  | **Women's Coats** | **Men's Coats** |  |
| Filler | 2.2 lbs. | 3.5 lbs. | $1.00 |
| Liner | 5.5 yds. | 8.0 yds. | 6.50 |
| Standard labor time | 0.30 hr. | 0.40 hr. |  |

|  | **Women's Coats** | **Men's Coats** |
|---|---|---|
| Planned production | 3,000 units | 5,000 units |
| Standard labor rate | $12.50 per hr. | $11.00 per hr. |

Yukon Coat does not expect there to be any beginning or ending inventories of filler and lining material. At the end of the budget year, Yukon Coat experienced the following actual results:

|  | **Women's Coats** | **Men's Coats** |
|---|---|---|
| Actual production | 3,200 | 4,900 |
|  | **Actual Price per Unit** | **Actual Quantity Purchased and Used** |
| Filler | $0.90 per lb. | 24,800 |
| Liner | 6.75 per yd. | 56,500 |
|  | **Actual Labor Rate** | **Actual Labor Hours Used** |
| Women's Coats | $12.70 per hr. | 1,000 |
| Men's Coats | 11.20 per hr. | 1,900 |

The expected beginning inventory and desired ending inventory were realized.

## Instructions

1. Prepare the following variance analyses for each coat and total, based on the actual results and production levels at the end of the budget year:

   a. Direct materials price, quantity, and total variance.

   b. Direct labor rate, time, and total variance.

2. ━━━━▶ Why are the standard amounts in part (1) based on the actual production at the end of the year instead of the planned production at the beginning of the year?

OBJ. 3, 4

✔ a. Direct materials price variance, $12,390 U

### PR 22-3B   Direct materials, direct labor, and factory overhead cost variance analysis

Roadmaster Tire Co. manufactures automobile tires. Standard costs and actual costs for direct materials, direct labor, and factory overhead incurred for the manufacture of 5,500 tires were as follows:

|  | **Standard Costs** | **Actual Costs** |
|---|---|---|
| Direct materials | 82,000 lbs. at $5.10 | 82,600 lbs. at $5.25 |
| Direct labor | 1,650 hrs. at $17.50 | 1,620 hrs. at $17.40 |
| Factory overhead | Rates per direct labor hr., based on 100% of normal capacity of 1,500 direct labor hrs.: |  |
|  | Variable cost, $3.10 | $5,000 variable cost |
|  | Fixed cost, $4.90 | $7,350 fixed cost |

Each tire requires 0.30 hour of direct labor.

## Instructions

Determine (a) the price variance, quantity variance, and total direct materials cost variance; (b) the rate variance, time variance, and total direct labor cost variance; and (c) variable factory overhead controllable variance, the fixed factory overhead volume variance, and total factory overhead cost variance.

**OBJ. 4**

✔ Controllable
variance, $950 F

### PR 22-4B   Standard factory overhead variance report

Star Medical, Inc., a manufacturer of disposable medical supplies, prepared the following factory overhead cost budget for the Assembly Department for October 2012. The company expected to operate the department at 100% of normal capacity of 24,000 hours.

| Variable costs: | | |
|---|---|---|
| Indirect factory wages | $180,000 | |
| Power and light | 124,800 | |
| Indirect materials | 33,600 | |
| Total variable cost | | $338,400 |
| Fixed costs: | | |
| Supervisory salaries | $ 72,000 | |
| Depreciation of plant and equipment | 51,500 | |
| Insurance and property taxes | 24,100 | |
| Total fixed cost | | 147,600 |
| Total factory overhead cost | | $486,000 |

During October, the department operated at 22,500 hours, and the factory overhead costs incurred were indirect factory wages, $167,550; power and light, $116,800; indirect materials, $31,950; supervisory salaries, $72,000; depreciation of plant and equipment, $51,500; and insurance and property taxes, $24,100.

## Instructions

Prepare a factory overhead cost variance report for October. To be useful for cost control, the budgeted amounts should be based on 22,500 hours.

**OBJ. 3, 6**

✔ 2. $210 F

### PR 22-5B   Standards for nonmanufacturing expenses

The Radiology Department provides imaging services for Brentmore Medical Center. One important activity in the Radiology Department is transcribing digitally recorded analyses of images into a written report. The manager of the Radiology Department determined that the average transcriptionist could type 750 lines of a report in an hour. The plan for the first week in May called for 58,500 typed lines to be written. The Radiology Department has two transcriptionists. Each transcriptionist is hired from an employment firm that requires temporary employees to be hired for a minimum of a 40-hour week. Transcriptionists are paid $15.00 per hour. The manager offered a bonus if the department could type more lines for the week, without overtime. Due to high service demands, the transcriptionists typed more lines in the first week of May than planned. The actual amount of lines typed in the first week of May was 70,500 lines, without overtime. As a result, the bonus caused the average transcriptionist hourly rate to increase to $20.00 per hour during the first week in May.

## Instructions

1.  If the department typed 58,500 lines according to the original plan, what would have been the labor time variance?

2.  What was the labor time variance as a result of typing 70,500 lines?

3.  What was the labor rate variance as a result of the bonus?

4.  The manager is trying to determine if a better decision would have been to hire a temporary transcriptionist to meet the higher typing demands in the first week of May, rather than paying out the bonus. If another employee was hired from the employment firm, what would have been the labor time variance in the first week?

5.  ➤ Which decision is better, paying the bonus or hiring another transcriptionist?

6.  ➤ Are there any performance-related issues that the labor time and rate variances fail to consider? Explain.

## Comprehensive Problem

Natural Fragrance, Inc., began operations on January 1, 2012. The company produces a hand and body lotion in an eight-ounce bottle called *Eternal Beauty*. The lotion is sold wholesale in 12-bottle cases for $80 per case. There is a selling commission of $16 per case. The January direct materials, direct labor, and factory overhead costs are as follows:

### DIRECT MATERIALS

| | Cost Behavior | Units per Case | Cost per Unit | Direct Materials Cost per Case |
|---|---|---|---|---|
| Cream base | Variable | 72 ozs. | $0.015 | $ 1.08 |
| Natural oils | Variable | 24 ozs. | 0.250 | 6.00 |
| Bottle (8-oz.) | Variable | 12 bottles | 0.400 | 4.80 |
| | | | | $11.88 |

### DIRECT LABOR

| Department | Cost Behavior | Time per Case | Labor Rate per Hour | Direct Labor Cost per Case |
|---|---|---|---|---|
| Mixing | Variable | 16.8 min. | $15.00 | $4.20 |
| Filling | Variable | 4.2 | 12.00 | 0.84 |
| | | 21.0 min. | | $5.04 |

### FACTORY OVERHEAD

| | Cost Behavior | Total Cost |
|---|---|---|
| Utilities | Mixed | $ 230 |
| Facility lease | Fixed | 12,043 |
| Equipment depreciation | Fixed | 3,600 |
| Supplies | Fixed | 600 |
| | | $16,473 |

### Part A—Break-Even Analysis

The management of Natural Fragrance, Inc., wishes to determine the number of cases required to break even per month. The utilities cost, which is part of factory overhead, is a mixed cost. The following information was gathered from the first six months of operation regarding this cost:

| 2012 | Case Production | Utility Total Cost |
|---|---|---|
| January | 300 | $230 |
| February | 600 | 263 |
| March | 1,000 | 300 |
| April | 900 | 292 |
| May | 750 | 280 |
| June | 825 | 285 |

### Instructions

1. Determine the fixed and variable portion of the utility cost using the high-low method.

✔ 2. $46.98

2. Determine the contribution margin per case.

3. Determine the fixed costs per month, including the utility fixed cost from part (1).

4. Determine the break-even number of cases per month.

### Part B—August Budgets

During July of the current year, the management of Natural Fragrance, Inc., asked the controller to prepare August manufacturing and income statement budgets. Demand was expected to be 1,300 cases at $80 per case for August. Inventory planning information is provided as follows:

Finished Goods Inventory:

| | Cases | Cost |
|---|---|---|
| Estimated finished goods inventory, August 1, 2012 | 200 | $6,000 |
| Desired finished goods inventory, August 31, 2012 | 100 | 3,000 |

Materials Inventory:

| | Cream Base (ozs.) | Oils (ozs.) | Bottles (bottles) |
|---|---|---|---|
| Estimated materials inventory, August 1, 2012 | 200 | 240 | 500 |
| Desired materials inventory, August 31, 2012 | 800 | 300 | 200 |

There was negligible work in process inventory assumed for either the beginning or end of the month; thus, none was assumed. In addition, there was no change in the cost per unit or estimated units per case operating data from January.

**Instructions**

5. Prepare the August production budget.

✔ **6. Bottles purchased, $5,640**

6. Prepare the August direct materials purchases budget.

7. Prepare the August direct labor budget.

8. Prepare the August factory overhead budget.

9. Prepare the August budgeted income statement, including selling expenses.

**Part C—August Variance Analysis**

During September of the current year, the controller was asked to perform variance analyses for August. The January operating data provided the standard prices, rates, times, and quantities per case. There were 1,300 actual cases produced during August, which was 100 more cases than planned at the beginning of the month. Actual data for August were as follows:

| | Actual Direct Materials Price per Unit | Actual Direct Materials Quantity per Case |
|---|---|---|
| Cream base | $0.014 per oz. | 74 ozs. |
| Natural oils | $0.27 per oz. | 26 ozs. |
| Bottle (8-oz.) | $0.35 per bottle | 12.6 bottles |

| | Actual Direct Labor Rate | Actual Direct Labor Time per Case |
|---|---|---|
| Mixing | $15.20 | 16.20 min. |
| Filling | 11.70 | 4.80 min. |

| | |
|---|---|
| Actual variable overhead | $162.00 |
| Normal volume | 1,350 cases |

The prices of the materials were different than standard due to fluctuations in market prices. The standard quantity of materials used per case was an ideal standard. The Mixing Department used a higher grade labor classification during the month, thus causing the actual labor rate to exceed standard. The Filling Department used a lower grade labor classification during the month, thus causing the actual labor rate to be less than standard.

**Instructions**

10. Determine and interpret the direct materials price and quantity variances for the three materials.

✔ **11. Mixing time variance, –$195 F**

11. Determine and interpret the direct labor rate and time variances for the two departments.

✔ **12. $32 U**

12. Determine and interpret the factory overhead controllable variance.

13. Determine and interpret the factory overhead volume variance.

14. Why are the standard direct labor and direct materials costs in the calculations for parts (10) and (11) based on the actual 1,300-case production volume rather than the planned 1,200 cases of production used in the budgets for parts (6) and (7)?

## Cases & Projects

You can access Cases & Projects online at **www.cengage.com/accounting/reeve**

## Excel Success Special Activities

### SA 22-1    Direct materials variances

The May Company manufactures plastic toy cars. Each toy car requires 16 standard pounds of resin (plastic). Each pound of resin has a standard cost of $3.25 per pound. Actual production information is as follows:

Volume: 800 toy cars
Actual material price per pound: $3.15
Actual pounds of resin used to produce each car: 16.2
Actual total pounds of used: 12,960 (800 cars × 16.2 pounds)

a.  Open the Excel file *SA22-1_1e*.
b.  Determine the direct materials price variance, direct materials quantity variance, and the direct materials cost variance.
c.  When you have completed the variances, perform a "save as," replacing the entire file name with the following:

    *SA22-1_1e[your first name initial]_[your last name]*

### SA 22-2    Direct labor variances

Each toy car produced by the May Company requires 0.35 standard direct labor hour. Each labor hour has a standard rate of $16 per hour. Actual production information is as follows:

Volume: 800 toy cars
Actual labor rate: $16.50 per hour
Actual direct labor hours per car: 0.32 hours
Actual total direct labor hours: 256 hours (800 cars × 0.32 hours)

a.  Open the Excel file *SA22-2_1e*.
b.  Determine the direct labor rate variance, direct labor time variance, and the direct labor cost variance.
c.  When you have completed the variances, perform a "save as," replacing the entire file name with the following:

    *SA22-2_1e[your first name initial]_[your last name]*

### SA 22-3    Factory overhead variances

The May Company produced 800 toy cars that required 0.32 standard hour per unit to manufacture. The standard variable factory overhead rate per unit is $15.00 per hour. The actual variable factory overhead was $3,775. The normal productive capacity is 300 direct labor hours, and the standard fixed factory overhead rate is $17.00 per direct labor hour. Thus, the budgeted amount of fixed factory overhead is $5,100 (300 direct labor hours × $17.00 per hour).

a.  Open the Excel file *SA22-3_1e*.
b.  Determine the variable factory overhead controllable variance and the fixed factory overhead volume variance.

c. When you have completed the variances, perform a "save as," replacing the entire file name with the following:

*SA22-3_1e[your first name initial]_[your last name]*

*success*

### SA 22-4 Direct materials, direct labor, and factory overhead variances

The Morgan Company produces bed sheets by cutting and sewing fabric. The following production information relates to a recent period:

| Inputs | Standard | Actual |
| --- | --- | --- |
| Direct Materials | | |
| Square yrds. | 34,500 | 35,200 |
| Price per sq. yrd. | $ 6.50 | $ 6.45 |
| | | |
| Direct Labor | | |
| Hours | 6,300 | 6,450 |
| Rate per hour | $ 11.50 | $ 11.62 |
| | | |
| Factory Overhead | | |
| Variable cost | | $47,900 |
| Fixed cost | | 42,000 |
| Variable factory overhead rate, per hour | $ 8.20 | |
| Fixed factory overhead rate, per hour | $ 6.00 | |
| Normal productive capacity (hours) | 7,000 | |

a. Open the Excel file *SA22-4_1e*.

b. Prepare a spreadsheet to calculate the direct materials, direct labor, and factory overhead variances.

c. When you have completed the variances, perform a "save as," replacing the entire files name with the following:

*SA22-4_1e[your first name initial]_[your last name]*

CHAPTER

23

© Horizon/Horizon International Images Limited/Alamy

# Performance Evaluation for Decentralized Operations

## E.W. Scripps

**H**ave you ever wondered why large retail stores like **Macy's, JC Penny**, and **Sears** are divided into departments? Organizing into departments allows retailers to provide products and expertise in specialized areas, while offering a wide range of products. Departments also allow companies to assign responsibility for financial performance. This information can be used to make product decisions, evaluate operations, and guide company strategy. Strong departmental performance might be attributable to a good department manager, while weak departmental performance may be the result of a product mix that has low customer appeal. By tracking departmental performance, companies can identify and reward excellent performance and take corrective action in departments that are performing poorly.

Like retailers, most businesses organize into operational units, such as divisions and departments. For example, **E.W. Scripps Company** operates a variety of media companies and is organized into three business segments: Newspapers, TV Stations,

and United Media. The Newspapers segment includes the Scripps Media Center and a variety of local newspapers such as the *Ventura County Star* and the *Knoxville News*. The TV Stations segment operates network-affiliated television stations. United Media licenses media brands and creative content, such as the comic strips *Peanuts* and *Dilbert*, and distributes many of these brands internationally.

Managers at E.W. Scripps are responsible for running their business segment. Each segment is evaluated on segment profit, which excludes certain expense items from the calculation of profit that are not within the control of the business segment. The company uses segment profit to determine how to allocate resources between business segments and to plan and control the company's operations.

In this chapter, the role of accounting in assisting managers in planning and controlling organizational units, such as departments, divisions, and stores, is described and illustrated.

---

**OBJ. 1** Describe the advantages and disadvantages of decentralized operations.

# Centralized and Decentralized Operations

In a *centralized* company, all major planning and operating decisions are made by top management. For example, a one-person, owner-manager-operated company is centralized because all plans and decisions are made by one person. In a small owner-manager-operated business, centralization may be desirable. This is because the owner-manager's close supervision ensures that the business will be operated in the way the owner-manager wishes.

In a *decentralized* company, managers of separate divisions or units are delegated operating responsibility. The division (unit) managers are responsible for planning and controlling the operations of their divisions. Divisions are often structured around products, customers, or regions.

The proper amount of decentralization for a company depends on the company's unique circumstances. For example, in some companies, division managers have authority over all operations, including fixed asset purchases. In other companies, division managers have authority over profits but not fixed asset purchases.

## Advantages of Decentralization

For large companies, it is difficult for top management to do the following:

1. Maintain daily contact with all operations
2. Maintain operating expertise in all product lines and services

In such cases, delegating authority to managers closest to the operations usually results in better decisions. These managers often anticipate and react to operating data more quickly than could top management. These managers also can focus their attention on becoming "experts" in their area of operation.

Decentralized operations provide excellent training for managers. Delegating responsibility allows managers to develop managerial experience early in their careers. This helps a company retain managers, some of whom may be later promoted to top management positions.

Managers of decentralized operations often work closely with customers. As a result, they tend to identify with customers and, thus, are often more creative in suggesting operating and product improvements. This helps create good customer relations.

## Disadvantages of Decentralization

A primary disadvantage of decentralized operations is that decisions made by one manager may negatively affect the profits of the company. For example, managers of divisions whose products compete with one another might start a price war that decreases the profits of both divisions and, thus, the overall company.

Another disadvantage of decentralized operations is that they may result in duplicate assets and expenses. For example, each manager of a product line might have a separate sales force and office support staff.

The advantages and disadvantages of decentralization are summarized in Exhibit 1.

**EXHIBIT 1**

**Advantages and Disadvantages of Decentralized Operations**

**Advantages of Decentralization**
Allows managers closest to the operations to make decisions
Provides excellent training for managers
Allows managers to become experts in their area of operation
Helps retain managers
Improves creativity and customer relations

**Disadvantages of Decentralization**
Decisions made by managers may negatively affect the profits of the company
Duplicates assets and expenses

### CENTRALIZED VS. DECENTRALIZED RESEARCH AND DEVELOPMENT

Companies use research and development (R&D) to search for ideas, processes, and technologies that result in new products. For many industries, research and development is the key to future growth and continued success. While most companies conduct research at both the corporate (centralized) and business segment (decentralized) levels, research and development strategies often differ depending on company strategy and product mix. Companies with a wide range of products that serve global markets tend to do most of their research and development on a centralized basis. In contrast, companies with a limited number of technologies that focus on local markets tend to conduct research and development on a decentralized basis.

Source: "Centralized versus Decentralized R&D: Benefits and Drawbacks," *Research Technology Management*, November 1, 2001.

## Responsibility Accounting

In a decentralized business, accounting assists managers in evaluating and controlling their areas of responsibility, called *responsibility centers*. **Responsibility accounting** is the process of measuring and reporting operating data by responsibility center.

Three types of responsibility centers are:

1. Cost centers, which have responsibility over costs
2. Profit centers, which have responsibility over revenues and costs
3. Investment centers, which have responsibility over revenues, costs, and investment in assets

# Responsibility Accounting for Cost Centers

A **cost center** manager has responsibility for controlling costs. For example, the supervisor of the Power Department has responsibility for the costs of providing power. A cost center manager does not make decisions concerning sales or the amount of fixed assets invested in the center.

Cost centers may vary in size from a small department to an entire manufacturing plant. In addition, cost centers may exist within other cost centers. For example, an entire university or college could be viewed as a cost center, and each college and department within the university could also be a cost center, as shown in Exhibit 2.

**EXHIBIT 2**    **Cost Centers in a University**

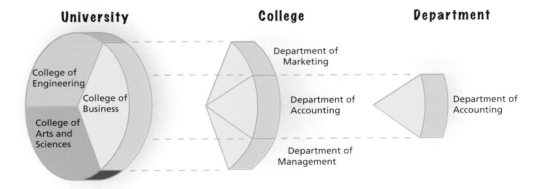

Responsibility accounting for cost centers focuses on controlling and reporting of costs. Budget performance reports that report budgeted and actual costs are normally prepared for each cost center.

Exhibit 3 illustrates budget performance reports for the following cost centers:

1. Vice President, Production
2. Manager, Plant A
3. Supervisor, Department 1—Plant A

Exhibit 3 shows how cost centers are often linked together within a company. For example, the budget performance report for Department 1—Plant A supports the report for Plant A, which supports the report for the vice president of production.

The reports in Exhibit 3 show the budgeted costs and actual costs along with the differences. Each difference is classified as either *over* budget or *under* budget. Such reports allow cost center managers to focus on areas of significant differences.

For example, the supervisor for Department 1 of Plant A can focus on why the materials cost was over budget. The supervisor might discover that excess materials were scrapped. This could be due to such factors as machine malfunctions, improperly trained employees, or low-quality materials.

As shown in Exhibit 3, responsibility accounting reports are usually more summarized for higher levels of management. For example, the budget performance report for the manager of Plant A shows only administration and departmental data. This report enables the plant manager to identify the departments responsible for major differences. Likewise, the report for the vice president of production summarizes the cost data for each plant.

EXHIBIT 3

Responsibility Accounting Reports for Cost Centers

**Budget Performance Report**
**Vice President, Production**
**For the Month Ended October 31, 2012**

| | Budget | Actual | Over Budget | Under Budget |
|---|---|---|---|---|
| Administration....................... | $ 19,500 | $ 19,700 | $ 200 | |
| Plant A ............................. | 467,475 | 470,330 | 2,855 | |
| Plant B ............................. | 395,225 | 394,300 | | $925 |
| | $882,200 | $884,330 | $3,055 | $925 |

**Budget Performance Report**
**Manager, Plant A**
**For the Month Ended October 31, 2012**

| | Budget | Actual | Over Budget | Under Budget |
|---|---|---|---|---|
| Administration....................... | $ 17,500 | $ 17,350 | | $150 |
| Department 1........................ | 109,725 | 111,280 | $1,555 | |
| Department 2........................ | 190,500 | 192,600 | 2,100 | |
| Department 3........................ | 149,750 | 149,100 | | 650 |
| | $467,475 | $470,330 | $3,655 | $800 |

**Budget Performance Report**
**Supervisor, Department 1 — Plant A**
**For the Month Ended October 31, 2012**

| | Budget | Actual | Over Budget | Under Budget |
|---|---|---|---|---|
| Factory wages ........................ | $ 58,100 | $ 58,000 | | $100 |
| Materials ............................ | 32,500 | 34,225 | $1,725 | |
| Supervisory salaries .................. | 6,400 | 6,400 | | |
| Power and light ...................... | 5,750 | 5,690 | | 60 |
| Depreciation of plant and equipment ........................ | 4,000 | 4,000 | | |
| Maintenance......................... | 2,000 | 1,990 | | 10 |
| Insurance and property taxes ......... | 975 | 975 | | |
| | $109,725 | $111,280 | $1,725 | $170 |

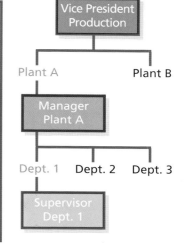

Vice President Production

Plant A          Plant B

Manager Plant A

Dept. 1    Dept. 2    Dept. 3

Supervisor Dept. 1

---

**Example Exercise** ▶ **23-1** ▶ **Budgetary Performance for Cost Center**    OBJ. **2**

Nuclear Power Company's costs were over budget by $24,000. The company is divided into North and South regions. The North Region's costs were under budget by $2,000. Determine the amount that the South Region's costs were over or under budget.

**Follow My Example** ▶ **23-1** ▶

$26,000 over budget ($24,000 + $2,000)

.................................................................................................

Practice Exercises: **PE 23-1A, PE 23-1B**

# Responsibility Accounting for Profit Centers

A **profit center** manager has the responsibility and authority for making decisions that affect revenues and costs and, thus, profits. Profit centers may be divisions, departments, or products.

The manager of a profit center does not make decisions concerning the fixed assets invested in the center. However, profit centers are an excellent training assignment for new managers.

Responsibility accounting for profit centers focuses on reporting revenues, expenses, and income from operations. Thus, responsibility accounting reports for profit centers take the form of income statements.

The profit center income statement should include only revenues and expenses that are controlled by the manager. **Controllable revenues** are revenues earned by the profit center. **Controllable expenses** are costs that can be influenced (controlled) by the decisions of profit center managers.

## Service Department Charges

The controllable expenses of profit centers include *direct operating expenses* such as sales salaries and utility expenses. In addition, a profit center may incur expenses provided by internal centralized *service departments*. Examples of such service departments include the following:

1. Research and Development
2. Legal
3. Telecommunications
4. Information and Computer Systems
5. Facilities Management
6. Purchasing
7. Publications and Graphics
8. Payroll Accounting
9. Transportation
10. Personnel Administration

Service department charges are *indirect* expenses to a profit center. They are similar to the expenses that would be incurred if the profit center purchased the services from outside the company. A profit center manager has control over service department expenses if the manager is free to choose how much service is used. In such cases, **service department charges** are allocated to profit centers based on the usage of the service by each profit center.

To illustrate, Nova Entertainment Group (NEG), a diversified entertainment company, is used. NEG has the following two operating divisions organized as profit centers:

1. Theme Park Division
2. Movie Production Division

The revenues and direct operating expenses for the two divisions are shown below. The operating expenses consist of direct expenses, such as the wages and salaries of a division's employees.

|  | Theme Park Division | Movie Production Division |
|---|---|---|
| Revenues | $6,000,000 | $2,500,000 |
| Operating expenses | 2,495,000 | 405,000 |

NEG's service departments and the expenses they incurred for the year ended December 31, 2012, are as follows:

| | |
|---|---|
| Purchasing | $400,000 |
| Payroll Accounting | 255,000 |
| Legal | 250,000 |
| Total | $905,000 |

An activity base for each service department is used to charge service department expenses to the Theme Park and Movie Production divisions. The activity base for each service department is a measure of the services performed. For NEG, the service department activity bases are as follows:

| Department | Activity Base |
|---|---|
| Purchasing | Number of purchase requisitions |
| Payroll Accounting | Number of payroll checks |
| Legal | Number of billed hours |

The use of services by the Theme Park and Movie Production divisions is as follows:

| Division | Service Usage Purchasing | Payroll Accounting | Legal |
|---|---|---|---|
| Theme Park | 25,000 purchase requisitions | 12,000 payroll checks | 100 billed hrs. |
| Movie Production | 15,000 | 3,000 | 900 |
| Total | 40,000 purchase requisitions | 15,000 payroll checks | 1,000 billed hrs. |

The rates at which services are charged to each division are called *service department charge rates*. These rates are computed as follows:

$$\text{Service Department Charge Rate} = \frac{\text{Service Department Expense}}{\text{Total Service Department Usage}}$$

NEG's service department charge rates are computed as follows:

$$\text{Purchasing Charge Rate} = \frac{\$400,000}{40,000 \text{ purchase requisitions}} = \$10 \text{ per purchase requisition}$$

$$\text{Payroll Charge Rate} = \frac{\$255,000}{15,000 \text{ payroll checks}} = \$17 \text{ per payroll check}$$

$$\text{Legal Charge Rate} = \frac{\$250,000}{1,000 \text{ billed hrs.}} = \$250 \text{ per hr.}$$

The services used by each division are multiplied by the service department charge rates to determine the service charges for each division, as shown below.

$$\text{Service Department Charge} = \text{Service Usage} \times \text{Service Department Charge Rate}$$

Exhibit 4 illustrates the service department charges and related computations for NEG's Theme Park and Movie Production divisions.

**EXHIBIT 4**

Service Department Charges to NEG Divisions

**Nova Entertainment Group**
**Service Department Charges to NEG Divisions**
**For the Year Ended December 31, 2012**

| Service Department | Theme Park Division | Movie Production Division |
|---|---|---|
| Purchasing (Note A) | $250,000 | $150,000 |
| Payroll Accounting (Note B) | 204,000 | 51,000 |
| Legal (Note C) | 25,000 | 225,000 |
| Total service department charges | $479,000 | $426,000 |

Note A:
25,000 purchase requisitions × $10 per purchase requisition = $250,000
15,000 purchase requisitions × $10 per purchase requisition = $150,000
Note B:
12,000 payroll checks × $17 per check = $204,000
3,000 payroll checks × $17 per check = $51,000
Note C:
100 hours × $250 per hour = $25,000
900 hours × $250 per hour = $225,000

The differences in the service department charges between the two divisions can be explained by the nature of their operations and, thus, usage of services. For example, the Theme Park Division employs many part-time employees who are paid weekly. As a result, the Theme Park Division requires 12,000 payroll checks and incurs a $204,000 payroll service department charge (12,000 × $17). In contrast, the Movie Production Division has more permanent employees who are paid monthly. Thus, the Movie Production Division requires only 3,000 payroll checks and incurs a payroll service department charge of $51,000 (3,000 × $17).

The service department charges can be determined using a spreadsheet as follows:

| | A | B | C | D | E |
|---|---|---|---|---|---|
| 1 | Inputs | | | | |
| 2 | | | | | |
| 3 | Purchasing | $          400,000 | | | |
| 4 | Payroll Accounting | 255,000 | | | |
| 5 | Legal | 250,000 | | | |
| 6 | Total | $          905,000 | | | |
| 7 | | | | | |
| 8 | | **Theme Park Division** | **Movie Production Division** | **Total** | |
| 9 | Purchasing | 25,000 | 15,000 | 40,000 | purch. reqs. |
| 10 | Payroll Accounting | 12,000 | 3,000 | 15,000 | payroll chks. |
| 11 | Legal | 100 | 900 | 1,000 | billed hrs. |
| 12 | | | | | |
| 13 | | | | | |
| 14 | | | | | |
| 15 | Output | | | | |
| 16 | | Nova Entertainment Group | | | |
| 17 | | Service Department Charges to NEG Division | | | |
| 18 | | For the Year Ended December 31, 2012 | | | |
| 19 | | | | | |
| 20 | **Service Department** | **Theme Park Division** | **Movie Production Division** | | |
| 21 | Purchasing          a. → | =$B3*(B9/$D9) | =$B3*(C9/$D9) | | |
| 22 | Payroll Accounting  b. → | =$B4*(B10/$D10) | =$B4*(C10/$D10)  ← c. | | |
| 23 | Legal | =$B5*(B11/$D11) | =$B5*(C11/$D11) | | |
| 24 | Total service department charges | =SUM(B21:B23) | =SUM(C21:C23) | | |

d.

The spreadsheet is divided into input and output sections. The inputs include the expense and activity base data for the service departments. The activity base information is transposed from the table shown in the text. A table is transposed when the columns and rows are reversed. This presentation facilitates copying formulas in the output table.

**a.**   Enter in cell B21 the formula for the purchasing department charge to the Theme Park Division:

=$B3*(B9/$D9)

The dollar sign ($) makes the column references absolute (doesn't change when copied).

**b.**   Copy the formula from B21 to cells B22:B23.

**c.**   Then copy the cells B21:B23 to C21:C23. If you place the dollar signs as shown in the formula, you will see that the formula copied correctly to all the cells.

**d.**   Enter in B24:C24 the =SUM function to total the columns.

**TryIt**   Go to the hands-on *Excel Tutor* for this example!

**TryIt**   This Excel Success example uses an Excel function referred to as cell referencing. Go to the *Excel Tutor* titled **Absolute & Relative Cell References** for additional help on this useful Excel function!

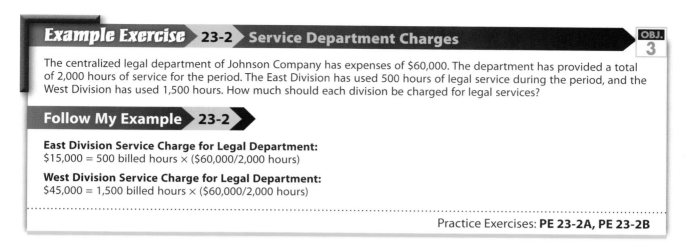

**Example Exercise** **23-2** **Service Department Charges**   OBJ. 3

The centralized legal department of Johnson Company has expenses of $60,000. The department has provided a total of 2,000 hours of service for the period. The East Division has used 500 hours of legal service during the period, and the West Division has used 1,500 hours. How much should each division be charged for legal services?

**Follow My Example** **23-2**

**East Division Service Charge for Legal Department:**
$15,000 = 500 billed hours × ($60,000/2,000 hours)

**West Division Service Charge for Legal Department:**
$45,000 = 1,500 billed hours × ($60,000/2,000 hours)

Practice Exercises: **PE 23-2A, PE 23-2B**

## Profit Center Reporting

The divisional income statements for NEG are shown in Exhibit 5.

| Nova Entertainment Group Divisional Income Statements For the Year Ended December 31, 2012 | | |
|---|---|---|
| | **Theme Park Division** | **Movie Production Division** |
| Revenues* | $6,000,000 | $2,500,000 |
| Operating expenses | 2,495,000 | 405,000 |
| Income from operations before service department charges | $3,505,000 | $2,095,000 |
| Less service department charges: | | |
| Purchasing | $  250,000 | $  150,000 |
| Payroll Accounting | 204,000 | 51,000 |
| Legal | 25,000 | 225,000 |
| Total service department charges | $  479,000 | $  426,000 |
| Income from operations | $3,026,000 | $1,669,000 |

*For a profit center that sells products, the income statement would show: Net sales – Cost of goods sold = Gross profit. The operating expenses would be deducted from the gross profit to get the income from operations before service department charges.

**EXHIBIT 5**

**Divisional Income Statements— NEG**

In evaluating the profit center manager, the income from operations should be compared over time to a budget. However, it should not be compared across profit centers, since the profit centers are usually different in terms of size, products, and customers.

**Example Exercise** **23-3** **Income from Operations for Profit Center**   OBJ. 3

Using the data for Johnson Company from Example Exercise 23-2 along with the data given below, determine the divisional income from operations for the East and West divisions.

| | **East Division** | **West Division** |
|---|---|---|
| Sales | $300,000 | $800,000 |
| Cost of goods sold | 165,000 | 420,000 |
| Selling expenses | 85,000 | 185,000 |

(Continued)

---

**Follow My Example 23-3**

| | East Division | West Division |
|---|---|---|
| Net sales......................................................... | $300,000 | $800,000 |
| Cost of goods sold ........................................ | 165,000 | 420,000 |
| Gross profit................................................... | $135,000 | $380,000 |
| Selling expenses .......................................... | 85,000 | 185,000 |
| Income from operations before service department charges .................... | $ 50,000 | $195,000 |
| Service department charges........................... | 15,000 | 45,000 |
| Income from operations.................................. | $ 35,000 | $150,000 |

Practice Exercises: **PE 23-3A, PE 23-3B**

---

**OBJ. 4** Compute and interpret the rate of return on investment, the residual income, and the balanced scorecard for an investment center.

# Responsibility Accounting for Investment Centers

An **investment center** manager has the responsibility and the authority to make decisions that affect not only costs and revenues but also the assets invested in the center. Investment centers are often used in diversified companies organized by divisions. In such cases, the divisional manager has authority similar to that of a chief operating officer or president of a company.

Since investment center managers have responsibility for revenues and expenses, *income from operations* is part of investment center reporting. In addition, because the manager has responsibility for the assets invested in the center, the following two additional measures of performance are used:

1. Rate of return on investment
2. Residual income

To illustrate, DataLink Inc., a cellular phone company with three regional divisions, is used. Condensed divisional income statements for the Northern, Central, and Southern divisions of DataLink are shown in Exhibit 6.

**EXHIBIT 6**

**Divisional Income Statements— DataLink Inc.**

| DataLink Inc. Divisional Income Statements For the Year Ended December 31, 2012 | | | |
|---|---|---|---|
| | Northern Division | Central Division | Southern Division |
| Revenues ...................................... | $560,000 | $672,000 | $750,000 |
| Operating expenses........................... | 336,000 | 470,400 | 562,500 |
| Income from operations before service department charges ........................ | $224,000 | $201,600 | $187,500 |
| Service department charges.................... | 154,000 | 117,600 | 112,500 |
| Income from operations....................... | $ 70,000 | $ 84,000 | $ 75,000 |

Using only income from operations, the Central Division is the most profitable division. However, income from operations does not reflect the amount of assets invested in each center. For example, the Central Division could have twice as many assets as the Northern Division. For this reason, performance measures that consider the amount of invested assets, such as the rate of return on investment and residual income, are used.

## Rate of Return on Investment

Since investment center managers control the amount of assets invested in their centers, they should be evaluated based on the use of these assets. One measure that considers the amount of assets invested is the **rate of return on investment (ROI)** or *rate of return on assets*. It is computed as follows:

$$\text{Rate of Return on Investment (ROI)} = \frac{\text{Income from Operations}}{\text{Invested Assets}}$$

The rate of return on investment is useful because the three factors subject to control by divisional managers (revenues, expenses, and invested assets) are considered. The higher the rate of return on investment, the better the division is using its assets to generate income. In effect, the rate of return on investment measures the income (return) on each dollar invested. As a result, the rate of return on investment can be used as a common basis for comparing divisions with each other.

To illustrate, the invested assets of DataLink's three divisions are as follows:

|  | **Invested Assets** |
| --- | --- |
| Northern Division | $350,000 |
| Central Division | 700,000 |
| Southern Division | 500,000 |

Using the income from operations for each division shown in Exhibit 6, the rate of return on investment for each division is computed below.

Northern Division:

$$\text{Rate of Return on Investment} = \frac{\text{Income from Operations}}{\text{Invested Assets}} = \frac{\$70,000}{\$350,000} = 20\%$$

Central Division:

$$\text{Rate of Return on Investment} = \frac{\text{Income from Operations}}{\text{Invested Assets}} = \frac{\$84,000}{\$700,000} = 12\%$$

Southern Division:

$$\text{Rate of Return on Investment} = \frac{\text{Income from Operations}}{\text{Invested Assets}} = \frac{\$75,000}{\$500,000} = 15\%$$

Although the Central Division generated the largest income from operations, its rate of return on investment (12%) is the lowest. Hence, relative to the assets invested, the Central Division is the least profitable division. In comparison, the rate of return on investment of the Northern Division is 20%, and the Southern Division is 15%.

To analyze differences in the rate of return on investment across divisions, the **DuPont formula** for the rate of return on investment is often used.[1] The DuPont formula views the rate of return on investment as the product of the following two factors:

1. **Profit margin**, which is the ratio of income from operations to sales.
2. **Investment turnover**, which is the ratio of sales to invested assets.

---

1 The DuPont formula was created by a financial executive of E. I. du Pont de Nemours and Company in 1919.

Using the DuPont formula, the rate of return on investment is expressed as follows:

$$\text{Rate of Return on Investment} = \text{Profit Margin} \times \text{Investment Turnover}$$

$$\text{Rate of Return on Investment} = \frac{\text{Income from Operations}}{\text{Sales}} \times \frac{\text{Sales}}{\text{Invested Assets}}$$

The DuPont formula is useful in evaluating divisions. This is because the profit margin and the investment turnover reflect the following underlying operating relationships of each division:

1. Profit margin indicates *operating profitability* by computing the rate of profit earned on each sales dollar.
2. Investment turnover indicates *operating efficiency* by computing the number of sales dollars generated by each dollar of invested assets.

If a division's profit margin increases, and all other factors remain the same, the division's rate of return on investment will increase. For example, a division might add more profitable products to its sales mix and, thus, increase its operating profit, profit margin, and rate of return on investment.

If a division's investment turnover increases, and all other factors remain the same, the division's rate of return on investment will increase. For example, a division might attempt to increase sales through special sales promotions and thus increase operating efficiency, investment turnover, and rate of return on investment.

The rate of return on investment, profit margin, and investment turnover operate in relationship to one another. Specifically, more income can be earned by either increasing the investment turnover, by increasing the profit margin, or both.

Using the DuPont formula yields the same rate of return on investment for each of DataLink's divisions, as shown below.

$$\text{Rate of Return on Investment} = \frac{\text{Income from Operations}}{\text{Sales}} \times \frac{\text{Sales}}{\text{Invested Assets}}$$

Northern Division:

$$\text{Rate of Return on Investment} = \frac{\$70,000}{\$560,000} \times \frac{\$560,000}{\$350,000} = 12.5\% \times 1.6 = 20\%$$

Central Division:

$$\text{Rate of Return on Investment} = \frac{\$84,000}{\$672,000} \times \frac{\$672,000}{\$700,000} = 12.5\% \times 0.96 = 12\%$$

Southern Division:

$$\text{Rate of Return on Investment} = \frac{\$75,000}{\$750,000} \times \frac{\$750,000}{\$500,000} = 10\% \times 1.5 = 15\%$$

The Northern and Central divisions have the same profit margins of 12.5%. However, the Northern Division's investment turnover of 1.6 is larger than that of the Central Division's turnover of 0.96. By using its invested assets more efficiently, the Northern Division's rate of return on investment of 20% is 8 percentage points higher than the Central Division's rate of return of 12%.

The Southern Division's profit margin of 10% and investment turnover of 1.5 are lower than those of the Northern Division. The product of these factors results in a return on investment of 15% for the Southern Division, compared to 20% for the Northern Division.

Even though the Southern Division's profit margin is lower than the Central Division's, its higher turnover of 1.5 results in a rate of return of 15%, which is greater than the Central Division's rate of return of 12%.

To increase the rate of return on investment, the profit margin and investment turnover for a division may be analyzed. For example, assume that the Northern Division is in a highly competitive industry in which the profit margin cannot be easily increased. As a result, the division manager might focus on increasing the investment turnover.

To illustrate, assume that the revenues of the Northern Division could be increased by $56,000 through increasing operating expenses, such as advertising, to $385,000. The Northern Division's income from operations will increase from $70,000 to $77,000, as shown below.

| | |
|---|---:|
| Revenues ($560,000 + $56,000) | $616,000 |
| Operating expenses | 385,000 |
| Income from operations before service department charges | $231,000 |
| Service department charges | 154,000 |
| Income from operations | $ 77,000 |

The rate of return on investment for the Northern Division, using the DuPont formula, is recomputed as follows:

$$\text{Rate of Return on Investment} = \frac{\text{Income from Operations}}{\text{Sales}} \times \frac{\text{Sales}}{\text{Invested Assets}}$$

$$\text{Rate of Return on Investment} = \frac{\$77,000}{\$616,000} \times \frac{\$616,000}{\$350,000} = 12.5\% \times 1.76 = 22\%$$

Although the Northern Division's profit margin remains the same (12.5%), the investment turnover has increased from 1.6 to 1.76, an increase of 10% (0.16 ÷ 1.6). The 10% increase in investment turnover increases the rate of return on investment by 10% (from 20% to 22%).

The rate of return on investment is also useful in deciding where to invest additional assets or expand operations. For example, DataLink should give priority to expanding operatons in the Northern Division because it earns the highest rate of return on investment. In other words, an investment in the Northern Division will return 20 cents (20%) on each dollar invested. In contrast, investments in the Central and Southern divisions will earn only 12 cents and 15 cents per dollar invested.

A disadvantage of the rate of return on investment as a performance measure is that it may lead divisional managers to reject new investments that could be profitable for the company as a whole. To illustrate, assume the following rates of return for the Northern Division of DataLink:

| | |
|---|---|
| Current rate of return on investment | 20% |
| Minimum acceptable rate of return | |
| on investment set by top management | 10% |
| Expected rate of return | |
| on investment for new project | 14% |

If the manager of the Northern Division invests in the new project, the Northern Division's overall rate of return will decrease from 20% due to averaging. Thus, the division manager might decide to reject the project, even though the new project's expected rate of return of 14% exceeds DataLink's minimum acceptable rate of return of 10%.

## Example Exercise 23-4   Profit Margin, Investment Turnover, and ROI

OBJ. 4

Campbell Company has income from operations of $35,000, invested assets of $140,000, and sales of $437,500. Use the DuPont formula to compute the rate of return on investment and show (a) the profit margin, (b) the investment turnover, and (c) the rate of return on investment.

## Follow My Example 23-4

a. Profit Margin = $35,000/$437,500 = 8%

b. Investment Turnover = $437,500/$140,000 = 3.125

c. Rate of Return on Investment = 8% × 3.125 = 25%

Practice Exercises: **PE 23-4A, PE 23-4B**

# Business Connection

## BOOSTING ROI

Investment centers can use the rate of return on investment (ROI) to identify operational and strategic decisions that improve their financial performance. For example, a group of consultants worked with a golf ball manufacturer to find ways to improve their rate of return on investment. After examining the company's operations, the consultants found that if the golf ball manufacturer outsourced a portion of the production process, changed the company's product mix, and slightly altered its brand strategy, they could increase the company's rate of return on investment by 70% (from 33% to 57%).

Source: M. Cvar and J. Quelch, "Which Levers Boost ROI?" *Harvard Business Review*, June 1, 2007.

## Residual Income

Residual income is useful in overcoming some of the disadvantages of the rate of return on investment. **Residual income** is the excess of income from operations over a minimum acceptable income from operations, as shown below.

| | |
|---|---|
| Income from operations | $XXX |
| Less minimum acceptable income from operations as a percent of invested assets | XXX |
| Residual income | $XXX |

The minimum acceptable income from operations is computed by multiplying the company minimum rate of return by the invested assets. The minimum rate is set by top management, based on such factors as the cost of financing.

To illustrate, assume that DataLink Inc. has established 10% as the minimum acceptable rate of return on divisional assets. The residual incomes for the three divisions are as follows:

| | Northern Division | Central Division | Southern Division |
|---|---|---|---|
| Income from operations | $70,000 | $84,000 | $75,000 |
| Less minimum acceptable income from operations as a percent of invested assets: | | | |
| $350,000 × 10% | 35,000 | | |
| $700,000 × 10% | | 70,000 | |
| $500,000 × 10% | | | 50,000 |
| Residual income | $35,000 | $14,000 | $25,000 |

The Northern Division has more residual income ($35,000) than the other divisions, even though it has the least amount of income from operations ($70,000). This is because the invested assets are less for the Northern Division than for the other divisions.

The major advantage of residual income as a performance measure is that it considers both the minimum acceptable rate of return, invested assets, and the income from operations for each division. In doing so, residual income encourages division managers to maximize income from operations in excess of the minimum. This provides an incentive to accept any project that is expected to have a rate of return in excess of the minimum.

To illustrate, assume the following rates of return for the Northern Division of DataLink:

| | |
|---|---|
| Current rate of return on investment | 20% |
| Minimum acceptable rate of return on investment set by top management | 10% |
| Expected rate of return on investment for new project | 14% |

If the manager of the Northern Division is evaluated using only return on investment, the division manager might decide to reject the new project. This is because investing in the new project will decrease Northern's current rate of return of 20%. Thus, the manager might reject the new project even though its expected rate of return of 14% exceeds DataLink's minimum acceptable rate of return of 10%.

In contrast, if the manager of the Northern Division is evaluated using residual income, the new project would probably be accepted because it will increase the Northern Division's residual income. In this way, residual income supports both divisional and overall company objectives.

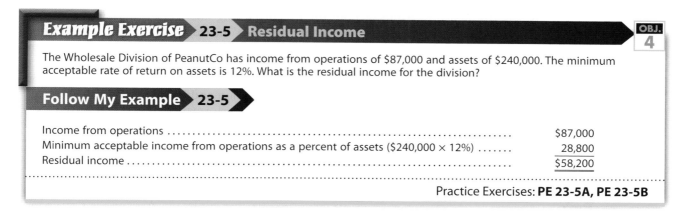

**Example Exercise** ❯ **23-5** ❯ **Residual Income**   OBJ. 4

The Wholesale Division of PeanutCo has income from operations of $87,000 and assets of $240,000. The minimum acceptable rate of return on assets is 12%. What is the residual income for the division?

**Follow My Example** ❯ **23-5** ❯

| | |
|---|---|
| Income from operations ............................................................ | $87,000 |
| Minimum acceptable income from operations as a percent of assets ($240,000 × 12%) ....... | 28,800 |
| Residual income .................................................................. | $58,200 |

Practice Exercises: **PE 23-5A, PE 23-5B**

## The Balanced Scorecard[2]

The **balanced scorecard** is a set of multiple performance measures for a company. In addition to financial performance, a balanced scorecard normally includes performance measures for customer service, innovation and learning, and internal processes, as shown in Exhibit 7.

Performance measures for learning and innovation often revolve around a company's research and development efforts. For example, the number of new products

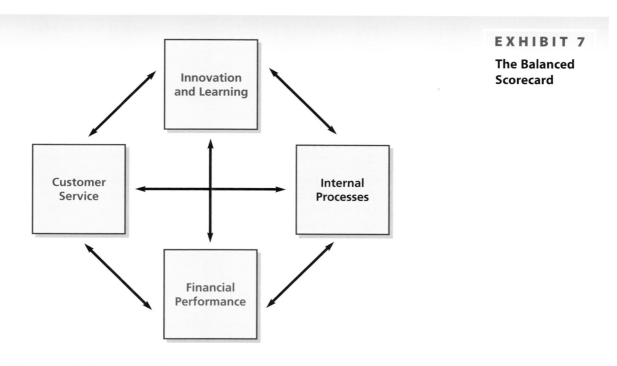

**EXHIBIT 7**

**The Balanced Scorecard**

2  The balanced scorecard was developed by R. S. Kaplan and D. P. Norton and explained in *The Balanced Scorecard: Translating Strategy into Action* (Cambridge: Harvard Business School Press, 1996).

developed during a year and the time it takes to bring new products to the market are performance measures for innovation. Performance measures for learning could include the number of employee training sessions and the number of employees who are cross-trained in several skills.

Performance measures for customer service include the number of customer complaints and the number of repeat customers. Customer surveys can also be used to gather measures of customer satisfaction with the company as compared to competitors.

Performance measures for internal processes include the length of time it takes to manufacture a product. The amount of scrap and waste is a measure of the efficiency of a company's manufacturing processes. The number of customer returns is a performance measure of both the manufacturing and sales ordering processes.

All companies will use financial performance measures. Some financial performance measures have been discussed earlier in this chapter and include income from operations, rate of return on investment, and residual income.

The balanced scorecard attempts to identify the underlying nonfinancial drivers, or causes, of financial performance related to innovation and learning, customer service, and internal processes. In this way, the financial performance may be improved. For example, customer satisfaction is often measured by the number of repeat customers. By increasing the number of repeat customers, sales and income from operations can be increased.

Some common performance measures used in the balanced scorecard approach are shown below.

Hilton Hotels Corporation uses a balanced scorecard to measure employee satisfaction, customer loyalty, and financial performance.

### Innovation and Learning

Number of new products
Number of new patents
Number of cross-trained employees
Number of training hours
Number of ethics violations
Employee turnover

### Internal Processes

Waste and scrap
Time to manufacture products
Number of defects
Number of rejected sales orders
Number of stockouts
Labor utilization

### Customer Service

Number of repeat customers
Customer brand recognition
Delivery time to customer
Customer satisfaction
Number of sales returns
Customer complaints

### Financial

Sales
Income from operations
Return on investment
Profit margin and investment turnover
Residual income
Actual versus budgeted (standard) costs

**OBJ. 5** Describe and illustrate how the market price, negotiated price, and cost price approaches to transfer pricing may be used by decentralized segments of a business.

# Transfer Pricing

When divisions transfer products or render services to each other, a **transfer price** is used to charge for the products or services.[3] Since transfer prices will affect a division's financial performance, setting a transfer price is a sensitive matter for the managers of both the selling and buying divisions.

Three common approaches to setting transfer prices are as follows:

1. Market price approach
2. Negotiated price approach
3. Cost approach

Transfer prices may be used for cost, profit, or investment centers. The objective of setting a transfer price is to motivate managers to behave in a manner that will

---

3 The discussion in this chapter highlights the essential concepts of transfer pricing. In-depth discussion of transfer pricing can be found in advanced texts.

increase the overall company income. As will be illustrated, however, transfer prices may be misused in such a way that overall company income suffers.

Transfer prices can be set as low as the variable cost per unit or as high as the market price. Often, transfer prices are negotiated at some point between variable cost per unit and market price. Exhibit 8 shows the possible range of transfer prices.

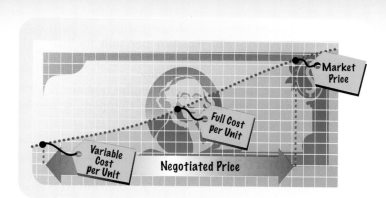

**EXHIBIT 8**

**Commonly Used Transfer Prices**

To illustrate, Wilson Company, a packaged snack food company with no service departments, is used. Wilson Company has two operating divisions (Eastern and Western) that are organized as investment centers. Condensed income statements for Wilson Company, assuming no transfers between divisions, are shown in Exhibit 9.

**EXHIBIT 9**

**Income Statements— No Transfers Between Divisions**

| Wilson Company Income Statements For the Year Ended December 31, 2012 | | | |
|---|---|---|---|
| | **Eastern Division** | **Western Division** | **Total Company** |
| Sales: | | | |
| 50,000 units × $20 per unit.............. | $1,000,000 | | $1,000,000 |
| 20,000 units × $40 per unit.............. | | $800,000 | 800,000 |
| | | | $1,800,000 |
| Expenses: | | | |
| Variable: | | | |
| 50,000 units × $10 per unit............ | $ 500,000 | | $ 500,000 |
| 20,000 units × $30* per unit........... | | $600,000 | 600,000 |
| Fixed ................................ | 300,000 | 100,000 | 400,000 |
| Total expenses ...................... | $ 800,000 | $700,000 | $1,500,000 |
| Income from operations................. | $ 200,000 | $100,000 | $ 300,000 |

*$20 of the $30 per unit represents materials costs, and the remaining $10 per unit represents other variable conversion expenses incurred within the Western Division.

## Market Price Approach

Using the **market price approach**, the transfer price is the price at which the product or service transferred could be sold to outside buyers. If an outside market exists for the product or service transferred, the current market price may be a proper transfer price.

Transfer Price = Market Price

To illustrate, assume that materials used by Wilson Company in producing snack food in the Western Division are currently purchased from an outside supplier at $20 per unit. The same materials are produced by the Eastern Division. The Eastern Division is operating at full capacity of 50,000 units and can sell all it produces to either the Western Division or to outside buyers.

A transfer price of $20 per unit (the market price) has no effect on the Eastern Division's income or total company income. The Eastern Division will earn revenues of $20 per unit on all its production and sales, regardless of who buys its product.

Likewise, the Western Division will pay $20 per unit for materials (the market price). Thus, the use of the market price as the transfer price has no effect on the Eastern Division's income or total company income.

In this situation, the use of the market price as the transfer price is proper. The condensed divisional income statements for Wilson Company would be the same as shown in Exhibit 9.

## Negotiated Price Approach

If unused or excess capacity exists in the supplying division (the Eastern Division), and the transfer price is equal to the market price, total company profit may not be maximized. This is because the manager of the Western Division will be indifferent toward purchasing materials from the Eastern Division or from outside suppliers. That is, in both cases the Western Division manager pays $20 per unit (the market price). As a result, the Western Division may purchase the materials from outside suppliers.

If, however, the Western Division purchases the materials from the Eastern Division, the difference between the market price of $20 and the variable costs of the Eastern Division of $10 per unit (from Exhibit 9) can cover fixed costs and contribute to overall company profits. Thus, the Western Division manager should be encouraged to purchase the materials from the Eastern Division.

The **negotiated price approach** allows the managers to agree (negotiate) among themselves on a transfer price. The only constraint is that the transfer price be less than the market price, but greater than the supplying division's variable costs per unit, as shown below.

Variable Costs per Unit < Transfer Price < Market Price

To illustrate, assume that instead of a capacity of 50,000 units, the Eastern Division's capacity is 70,000 units. In addition, assume that the Eastern Division can continue to sell only 50,000 units to outside buyers.

A transfer price less than $20 would encourage the manager of the Western Division to purchase from the Eastern Division. This is because the Western Division is currently purchasing its materials from outside suppliers at a cost of $20 per unit. Thus, its materials cost would decrease, and its income from operations would increase.

At the same time, a transfer price above the Eastern Division's variable costs per unit of $10 (from Exhibit 10) would encourage the manager of the Eastern Division to supply materials to the Western Division. In doing so, the Eastern Division's income from operations would also increase.

Exhibit 10 illustrates the divisional and company income statements, assuming that the Eastern and Western division managers agree to a transfer price of $15.

The Eastern Division increases its sales by $300,000 (20,000 units × $15 per unit) to $1,300,000. As a result, the Eastern Division's income from operations increases by $100,000 ($300,000 sales − $200,000 variable costs) to $300,000, as shown in Exhibit 10.

EXHIBIT 10

Income
Statements—
Negotiated
Transfer Price

**Wilson Company**
**Income Statements**
**For the Year Ended December 31, 2012**

| | Eastern Division | Western Division | Total Company |
|---|---|---|---|
| Sales: | | | |
| 50,000 units × $20 per unit.............. | $1,000,000 | | $1,000,000 |
| 20,000 units × $15 per unit.............. | 300,000 | | 300,000 |
| 20,000 units × $40 per unit.............. | | $800,000 | 800,000 |
| | $1,300,000 | $800,000 | $2,100,000 |
| Expenses: | | | |
| Variable: | | | |
| 70,000 units × $10 per unit............ | $ 700,000 | | $ 700,000 |
| 20,000 units × $25* per unit........... | | $500,000 | 500,000 |
| Fixed .................................. | 300,000 | 100,000 | 400,000 |
| Total expenses ...................... | $1,000,000 | $600,000 | $1,600,000 |
| Income from operations.................. | $ 300,000 | $200,000 | $ 500,000 |

*$10 of the $25 represents variable conversion expenses incurred solely within the Western Division, and $15 per unit represents the transfer price per unit from the Eastern Division.

The increase of $100,000 in the Eastern Division's income can also be computed as follows:

$$\text{Increase in Eastern (Supplying) Division's Income from Operations} = (\text{Transfer Price} - \text{Variable Cost per Unit}) \times \text{Units Transferred}$$

$$\text{Increase in Eastern (Supplying) Division's Income from Operations} = (\$15 - \$10) \times 20,000 \text{ units} = \$100,000$$

Western Division's materials cost decreases by $5 per unit ($20 – $15) for a total of $100,000 (20,000 units × $5 per unit). Thus, Western Division's income from operations increases by $100,000 to $200,000, as shown in Exhibit 10.

The increase of $100,000 in the Western Division's income can also be computed as follows:

$$\text{Increase in Western (Purchasing) Division's Income from Operations} = (\text{Market Price} - \text{Transfer Price}) \times \text{Units Transferred}$$

$$\text{Increase in Western (Purchasing) Division's Income from Operations} = (\$20 - \$15) \times 20,000 \text{ units} = \$100,000$$

Comparing Exhibits 9 and 10 shows that Wilson Company's income from operations increased by $200,000, as shown below.

**Income from Operations**

| | No Units Transferred (Exhibit 9) | 20,000 Units Transferred at $15 per Unit (Exhibit 10) | Increase (Decrease) |
|---|---|---|---|
| Eastern Division | $200,000 | $300,000 | $100,000 |
| Western Division | 100,000 | 200,000 | 100,000 |
| Wilson Company | $300,000 | $500,000 | $200,000 |

In the preceding illustration, any negotiated transfer price between $10 and $20 is acceptable, as shown below.

Variable Costs per Unit < Transfer Price < Market Price
$10 < Transfer Price < $20

Any transfer price within this range will increase the overall income from operations for Wilson Company by $200,000. However, the increases in the Eastern and Western divisions' income from operations will vary depending on the transfer price.

To illustrate, a transfer price of $16 would increase the Eastern Division's income from operations by $120,000, as shown below.

$$\text{Increase in Eastern (Supplying) Division's Income from Operations} = (\text{Transfer Price} - \text{Variable Cost per Unit}) \times \text{Units Transferred}$$

$$\text{Increase in Eastern (Supplying) Division's Income from Operations} = (\$16 - \$10) \times 20,000 \text{ units} = \$120,000$$

A transfer price of $16 would increase the Western Division's income from operations by $80,000, as shown below.

$$\text{Increase in Western (Purchasing) Division's Income from Operations} = (\text{Market Price} - \text{Transfer Price}) \times \text{Units Transferred}$$

$$\text{Increase in Western (Purchasing) Division's Income from Operations} = (\$20 - \$16) \times 20,000 \text{ units} = \$80,000$$

With a transfer price of $16, Wilson Company's income from operations still increases by $200,000, which consists of the Eastern Division's increase of $120,000 plus the Western Division's increase of $80,000.

As shown above, negotiated price provides each division manager with an incentive to negotiate the transfer of materials. At the same time, the overall company's income from operations will also increase. However, the negotiated approach only applies when the supplying division has excess capacity. In other words, the supplying division cannot sell all its production to outside buyers at the market price.

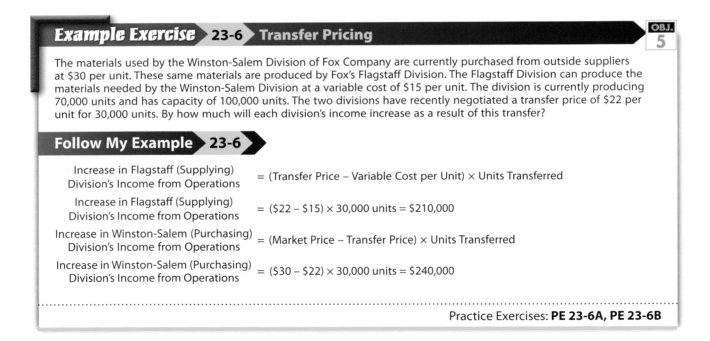

**Example Exercise** 23-6 **Transfer Pricing** OBJ. 5

The materials used by the Winston-Salem Division of Fox Company are currently purchased from outside suppliers at $30 per unit. These same materials are produced by Fox's Flagstaff Division. The Flagstaff Division can produce the materials needed by the Winston-Salem Division at a variable cost of $15 per unit. The division is currently producing 70,000 units and has capacity of 100,000 units. The two divisions have recently negotiated a transfer price of $22 per unit for 30,000 units. By how much will each division's income increase as a result of this transfer?

**Follow My Example** 23-6

$$\text{Increase in Flagstaff (Supplying) Division's Income from Operations} = (\text{Transfer Price} - \text{Variable Cost per Unit}) \times \text{Units Transferred}$$

$$\text{Increase in Flagstaff (Supplying) Division's Income from Operations} = (\$22 - \$15) \times 30,000 \text{ units} = \$210,000$$

$$\text{Increase in Winston-Salem (Purchasing) Division's Income from Operations} = (\text{Market Price} - \text{Transfer Price}) \times \text{Units Transferred}$$

$$\text{Increase in Winston-Salem (Purchasing) Division's Income from Operations} = (\$30 - \$22) \times 30,000 \text{ units} = \$240,000$$

Practice Exercises: **PE 23-6A, PE 23-6B**

## Cost Price Approach

Under the **cost price approach**, cost is used to set transfer prices. A variety of costs may be used in this approach, including the following:

1. Total product cost per unit
2. Variable product cost per unit

If total product cost per unit is used, direct materials, direct labor, and factory overhead are included in the transfer price. If variable product cost per unit is used, the fixed factory overhead cost is excluded from the transfer price.

Actual costs or standard (budgeted) costs may be used in applying the cost price approach. If actual costs are used, inefficiencies of the producing (supplying) division are transferred to the purchasing division. Thus, there is little incentive for the producing (supplying) division to control costs. For this reason, most companies use standard costs in the cost price approach. In this way, differences between actual and standard costs remain with the producing (supplying) division for cost control purposes.

The cost price approach is most often used when the responsibility centers are organized as cost centers. When the responsibility centers are organized as profit or investment centers, the cost price approach is normally not used.

For example, using the cost price approach when the supplying division is organized as a profit center ignores the supplying division manager's responsibility for earning profits. In this case, using the cost price approach prevents the supplying division from reporting any profit (revenues – costs) on the units transferred. As a result, the division manager has little incentive to transfer units to another division, even though it may be in the best interests of the company.

## Integrity, Objectivity, and Ethics in Business

### SHIFTING INCOME THROUGH TRANSFER PRICES

Transfer prices allow companies to minimize taxes by shifting taxable income from countries with high tax rates to countries with low taxes. For example, GlaxoSmithKline, a British company, and the second biggest drug maker in the world, had been in a dispute with the U.S. Internal Revenue Service (IRS) over international transfer prices since the early 1990s. The company pays U.S. taxes on income from its U.S. Division and British taxes on income from the British Division.

The IRS, however, claimed that the transfer prices on sales from the British Division to the U.S. Division were too high, which reduced profits and taxes in the U.S. Division. The company received a new tax bill from the IRS in 2005 for almost $1.9 billion related to the transfer pricing issue, raising the total bill to almost $5 billion. In January 2006, the company agreed to settle this dispute with the IRS for $3.4 billion, the largest tax settlement in history.

Source: J. Whalen, "Glaxo Gets New IRS Bill Seeking Another $1.9 Billion in BackTax," *The Wall Street Journal*, January 27, 2005.

## At a Glance 23

**OBJ. 1**

### Describe the advantages and disadvantages of decentralized operations.

**Key Points**   In a centralized business, all major planning and operating decisions are made by top management. In a decentralized business, these responsibilities are delegated to unit managers. Decentralization may be more effective because operational decisions are made by the managers closest to the operations.

| Learning Outcomes | Example Exercises | Practice Exercises |
|---|---|---|
| • Describe the advantages of decentralization. | | |
| • Describe the disadvantages of decentralization. | | |
| • Describe the common types of responsibility centers and the role of responsibility accounting. | | |

**OBJ. 2**

## Prepare a responsibility accounting report for a cost center.

**Key Points** Cost centers limit the responsibility and authority of managers to decisions related to the costs of their unit. The primary tools for planning and controlling are budgets and budget performance reports.

| Learning Outcomes | Example Exercises | Practice Exercises |
|---|---|---|
| • Describe cost centers. | | |
| • Describe the responsibility reporting for a cost center. | | |
| • Compute the over (under) budgeted costs for a cost center. | EE23-1 | PE23-1A, 23-1B |

**OBJ. 3**

## Prepare responsibility accounting reports for a profit center.

**Key Points** In a profit center, managers have the responsibility and authority to make decisions that affect both revenues and costs. Responsibility reports for a profit center usually show income from operations for the unit.

| Learning Outcomes | Example Exercises | Practice Exercises |
|---|---|---|
| • Describe profit centers. | | |
| • Determine how service department charges are allocated to profit centers. | EE23-2 | PE23-2A, 23-2B |
| • Describe the responsibility reporting for a profit center. | | |
| • Compute income from operations for a profit center. | EE23-3 | PE23-3A, 23-3B |

**OBJ. 4**

## Compute and interpret the rate of return on investment, the residual income, and the balanced scorecard for an investment center.

**Key Points** In an investment center, the unit manager has the responsibility and authority to make decisions that affect the unit's revenues, expenses, and assets invested in the center. Three measures are commonly used to assess investment center performance: return on investment (ROI), residual income, and the balanced scorecard. These measures are often used to compare investment center performance.

| Learning Outcomes | Example Exercises | Practice Exercises |
|---|---|---|
| • Describe investment centers. | | |
| • Describe the responsibility reporting for an investment center. | | |
| • Compute the profit margin, investment turnover, and rate of return on investment (ROI). | EE23-4 | PE23-4A, 23-4B |
| • Compute residual income. | EE23-5 | PE23-5A, 23-5B |
| • Describe the balanced scorecard approach. | | |

**Describe and illustrate how the market price, negotiated price, and cost price approaches to transfer pricing may be used by decentralized segments of a business.**

**Key Points** When divisions within a company transfer products or provide services to each other, a transfer price is used to charge for the products or services. Transfer prices should be set so that the overall company income is increased when goods are transferred between divisions. One of three approaches is typically used to establish transfer prices: market price, negotiated price, or cost price.

| Learning Outcomes | Example Exercises | Practice Exercises |
|---|---|---|
| • Describe how companies determine the price used to transfer products or services between divisions. | | |
| • Determine transfer prices using the market price approach. | | |
| • Determine transfer prices using the negotiated price approach. | **EE23-6** | **PE23-6A, 23-6B** |
| • Describe the cost price approach to determining transfer price. | | |

# Key Terms

balanced scorecard (1089)
controllable expenses (1080)
controllable revenues (1080)
cost center (1078)
cost price approach (1094)
DuPont formula (1085)

investment center (1084)
investment turnover (1085)
market price approach (1091)
negotiated price approach (1092)
profit center (1080)
profit margin (1085)

rate of return on investment (ROI) (1085)
residual income (1088)
responsibility accounting (1077)
service department charges (1080)
transfer price (1090)

# Illustrative Problem

Quinn Company has two divisions, Domestic and International. Invested assets and condensed income statement data for each division for the past year ended December 31 are as follows:

| | Domestic Division | International Division |
|---|---|---|
| Revenues | $675,000 | $480,000 |
| Operating expenses | 450,000 | 372,400 |
| Service department charges | 90,000 | 50,000 |
| Invested assets | 600,000 | 384,000 |

**Instructions**

1. Prepare condensed income statements for the past year for each division.

2. Using the DuPont formula, determine the profit margin, investment turnover, and rate of return on investment for each division.

3. If management's minimum acceptable rate of return is 10%, determine the residual income for each division.

**Solution**

1.

**Quinn Company**
**Divisional Income Statements**
**For the Year Ended December 31, 2012**

|  | Domestic Division | International Division |
|---|---|---|
| Revenues | $675,000 | $480,000 |
| Operating expenses | 450,000 | 372,400 |
| Income from operations before |  |  |
| service department charges | $225,000 | $107,600 |
| Service department charges | 90,000 | 50,000 |
| Income from operations | $135,000 | $ 57,600 |

2. Rate of Return on Investment = Profit Margin × Investment Turnover

$$\text{Rate of Return on Investment} = \frac{\text{Income from Operations}}{\text{Sales}} \times \frac{\text{Sales}}{\text{Invested Assets}}$$

$$\text{Domestic Division: ROI} = \frac{\$135,000}{\$675,000} \times \frac{\$675,000}{\$600,000}$$

$$\text{ROI} = 20\% \times 1.125$$

$$\text{ROI} = 22.5\%$$

$$\text{International Division: ROI} = \frac{\$57,600}{\$480,000} \times \frac{\$480,000}{\$384,000}$$

$$\text{ROI} = 12\% \times 1.25$$

$$\text{ROI} = 15\%$$

3. Domestic Division: $75,000 [$135,000 − (10% × $600,000)]
   International Division: $19,200 [$57,600 − (10% × $384,000)]

# Discussion Questions

1. Differentiate between a cost center and a profit center.

2. Differentiate between a profit center and an investment center.

3. Weyerhaeuser developed a system that assigns service department expenses to user divisions on the basis of actual services consumed by the division. Here are a number of Weyerhaeuser's activities in its central Financial Services Department:
   - Payroll
   - Accounts payable
   - Accounts receivable
   - Database administration—report preparation
   For each activity, identify an activity base that could be used to charge user divisions for service.

4. What is the major shortcoming of using income from operations as a performance measure for investment centers?

5. In a decentralized company in which the divisions are organized as investment centers, how could a division be considered the least profitable even though it earned the largest amount of income from operations?

6. How does using the rate of return on investment facilitate comparability between divisions of decentralized companies?

7. Why would a firm use a balanced scorecard in evaluating divisional performance?

8. What is the objective of transfer pricing?

9. When is the negotiated price approach preferred over the market price approach in setting transfer prices?

10. When using the negotiated price approach to transfer pricing, within what range should the transfer price be established?

# Practice Exercises

## PE 23-1A   Budgetary performance for cost center

Bahrke Company's costs were over budget by $300,000. The company is divided into West and East regions. The East Region's costs were under budget by $60,000. Determine the amount that the West Region's costs were over or under budget.

## PE 23-1B   Budgetary performance for cost center

Vonn Motion Company's costs were under budget by $175,000. The company is divided into North and South regions. The North Region's costs were over budget by $60,000. Determine the amount that the South Region's costs were over or under budget.

## PE 23-2A   Service department charges

The centralized employee travel department of Ohno Company has expenses of $210,000. The department has serviced a total of 3,000 travel reservations for the period. The Northeast Division has made 1,250 reservations during the period, and the Pacific Division has made 1,750 reservations. How much should each division be charged for travel services?

## PE 23-2B   Service department charges

The centralized computer technology department of Kearney Company has expenses of $170,000. The department has provided a total of 4,250 hours of service for the period. The Retail Division has used 2,250 hours of computer technology service during the period, and the Commercial Division has used 2,000 hours of computer technology service. How much should each division be charged for computer technology department services?

## PE 23-3A   Income from operations for profit center

Using the data for Ohno Company from Practice Exercise 23-2A along with the data provided below, determine the divisional income from operations for the Northeast and Pacific divisions.

|  | Northeast Division | Pacific Division |
|---|---|---|
| Sales | $825,000 | $860,000 |
| Cost of goods sold | 422,000 | 470,000 |
| Selling expenses | 165,000 | 180,000 |

## PE 23-3B   Income from operations for profit center

Using the data for Kearney Company from Practice Exercise 23-2B along with the data provided below, determine the divisional income from operations for the Retail Division and the Commercial Division.

|  | Retail Division | Commercial Division |
|---|---|---|
| Sales | $1,350,000 | $1,380,000 |
| Cost of goods sold | 720,000 | 799,000 |
| Selling expenses | 224,000 | 250,000 |

| *Learning Objectives* | *Example Exercises* | |
|---|---|---|

**OBJ. 4**  **EE 23-4** *p. 1087*  **PE 23-4A  Profit margin, investment turnover, and ROI**

Celski Company has income from operations of $60,000, invested assets of $250,000, and sales of $800,000. Use the DuPont formula to compute the rate of return on investment and show (a) the profit margin, (b) the investment turnover, and (c) the rate of return on investment.

**OBJ. 4**  **EE 23-4** *p. 1087*  **PE 23-4B  Profit margin, investment turnover, and ROI**

Roark Company has income from operations of $40,000, invested assets of $160,000, and sales of $320,000. Use the DuPont formula to compute the rate of return on investment and show (a) the profit margin, (b) the investment turnover, and (c) the rate of return on investment.

**OBJ. 4**  **EE 23-5** *p. 1089*  **PE 23-5A  Residual income**

The Consumer Division of McPhie Company has income from operations of $75,000 and assets of $500,000. The minimum acceptable rate of return on assets is 11%. What is the residual income for the division?

**OBJ. 4**  **EE 23-5** *p. 1089*  **PE 23-5B  Residual income**

The Commercial Division of Morse Company has income from operations of $160,000 and assets of $700,000. The minimum acceptable rate of return on assets is 9%. What is the residual income for the division?

**OBJ. 5**  **EE 23-6** *p. 1094*  **PE 23-6A  Transfer pricing**

The materials used by the Vancouver Division of Roberts Company are currently purchased from outside suppliers at $45 per unit. These same materials are produced by Roberts' Tucson Division. The Tucson Division can produce the materials needed by the Vancouver Division at a variable cost of $30 per unit. The division is currently producing 100,000 units and has capacity of 130,000 units. The two divisions have recently negotiated a transfer price of $38 per unit for 25,000 units. By how much will each division's income increase as a result of this transfer?

**OBJ. 5**  **EE 23-6** *p. 1094*  **PE 23-6B  Transfer pricing**

The materials used by the Burlington Division of Wilson Company are currently purchased from outside suppliers at $100 per unit. These same materials are produced by the Racine Division. The Racine Division can produce the materials needed by the Burlington Division at a variable cost of $70 per unit. The division is currently producing 160,000 units and has capacity of 200,000 units. The two divisions have recently negotiated a transfer price of $85 per unit for 40,000 units. By how much will each division's income increase as a result of this transfer?

## Exercises

**OBJ. 2**

✔ a. (c) $3,960

**EX 23-1  Budget performance reports for cost centers**

Partially completed budget performance reports for Gehring Company, a manufacturer of air conditioners, are provided on the following page.

**Gehring Company**
**Budget Performance Report—Vice President, Production**
**For the Month Ended April 30, 2012**

| Plant | Budget | Actual | Over Budget | Under Budget |
|---|---|---|---|---|
| Mid-Atlantic Region | $624,000 | $622,500 | | $1,500 |
| West Region | 446,400 | 444,000 | | 2,400 |
| South Region | (g) | (h) | (i) | |
| | (j) | (k) | $ (l) | $3,900 |

**Gehring Company**
**Budget Performance Report—Manager, South Region Plant**
**For the Month Ended April 30, 2012**

| Department | Budget | Actual | Over Budget | Under Budget |
|---|---|---|---|---|
| Chip Fabrication | (a) | (b) | (c) | |
| Electronic Assembly | $127,680 | $129,360 | $ 1,680 | |
| Final Assembly | 205,500 | 204,960 | | $540 |
| | (d) | (e) | $5,640 (f) | $540 |

**Gehring Company**
**Budget Performance Report—Supervisor, Chip Fabrication**
**For the Month Ended April 30, 2012**

| Department | Budget | Actual | Over Budget | Under Budget |
|---|---|---|---|---|
| Factory wages | $ 36,960 | $ 39,600 | $2,640 | |
| Materials | 104,400 | 103,680 | | $720 |
| Power and light | 5,760 | 6,840 | 1,080 | |
| Maintenance | 10,080 | 11,040 | 960 | |
| | $157,200 | $161,160 | $4,680 | $720 |

a. Complete the budget performance reports by determining the correct amounts for the lettered spaces.

b. ▬▬▬▬▶ Compose a memo to Tony Amoruso, vice president of production for Gehring Company, explaining the performance of the production division for April.

---

**OBJ. 3**

✔ Commercial
Division income from
operations, $101,080

**EX 23-2    Divisional income statements**

The following data were summarized from the accounting records for Jareau Construction Company for the year ended June 30, 2012:

Cost of goods sold:

| | | Service department charges: | |
|---|---|---|---|
| Commercial Division | $523,000 | Commercial Division | $ 64,320 |
| Residential Division | 242,100 | Residential Division | 38,760 |

Administrative expenses:

Net sales:

| | | | |
|---|---|---|---|
| Commercial Division | $ 85,600 | Commercial Division | $774,000 |
| Residential Division | 73,500 | Residential Division | 425,000 |

Prepare divisional income statements for Jareau Construction Company.

---

**OBJ. 3**

**EX 23-3    Service department charges and activity bases**

For each of the following service departments, identify an activity base that could be used for charging the expense to the profit center.

a. Electronic data processing

b. Central purchasing

c. Accounts receivable

d. Legal

e. Duplication services

f. Telecommunications

**OBJ. 3**

✔ c. 5

**EX 23-4 Activity bases for service department charges**

For each of the following service departments, select the activity base listed that is most appropriate for charging service expenses to responsible units.

| Service Department | Activity Base |
|---|---|
| a. Telecommunications | 1. Number of conference attendees |
| b. Accounts Receivable | 2. Number of computers |
| c. Central Purchasing | 3. Number of employees trained |
| d. Training | 4. Number of telephone lines |
| e. Computer Support | 5. Number of purchase requisitions |
| f. Conferences | 6. Number of sales invoices |
| g. Employee Travel | 7. Number of payroll checks |
| h. Payroll Accounting | 8. Number of travel claims |

**OBJ. 3**

✔ b. Commercial payroll, $21,560

**EX 23-5 Service department charges**

In divisional income statements prepared for Brooks Construction Company, the Payroll Department costs are charged back to user divisions on the basis of the number of payroll checks, and the Purchasing Department costs are charged back on the basis of the number of purchase requisitions. The Payroll Department had expenses of $84,000, and the Purchasing Department had expenses of $40,040 for the year. The following annual data for Residential, Commercial, and Government Contract divisions were obtained from corporate records:

| | Residential | Commercial | Government Contract |
|---|---|---|---|
| Sales | $720,000 | $975,000 | $2,240,000 |
| Number of employees: | | | |
| Weekly payroll (52 weeks per year) | 200 | 100 | 120 |
| Monthly payroll | 50 | 80 | 50 |
| Number of purchase requisitions per year | 3,000 | 2,500 | 2,200 |

a. Determine the total amount of payroll checks and purchase requisitions processed per year by the company and each division.

b. Using the activity base information in (a), determine the annual amount of payroll and purchasing costs charged back to the Residential, Commercial, and Government Contract divisions from payroll and purchasing services.

c. ➤ Why does the Residential Division have a larger service department charge than the other two divisions, even though its sales are lower?

**OBJ. 3**

✔ b. Help desk, $75,600

**EX 23-6 Service department charges and activity bases**

Harris Corporation, a manufacturer of electronics and communications systems, uses a service department charge system to charge profit centers with Computing and Communications Services (CCS) service department costs. The following table identifies an abbreviated list of service categories and activity bases used by the CCS department. The table also includes some assumed cost and activity base quantity information for each service for April.

| CCS Service Category | Activity Base | Assumed Cost | Assumed Activity Base Quantity |
|---|---|---|---|
| Help desk | Number of calls | $135,200 | 3,380 |
| Network center | Number of devices monitored | 893,200 | 12,760 |
| Electronic mail | Number of user accounts | 117,600 | 8,400 |
| Local voice support | Number of phone extensions | 263,120 | 11,960 |

One of the profit centers for Harris Corporation is the Communication Systems (COMM) sector. Assume the following information for the COMM sector:

• The sector has 3,500 employees, of whom 30% are office employees.

• All the office employees have a phone, and 90% of them have a computer on the network.

- One hundred percent of the employees with a computer also have an e-mail account.
- The average number of help desk calls for April was 2.0 calls per individual with a computer.
- There are 300 additional printers, servers, and peripherals on the network beyond the personal computers.

a. Determine the service charge rate for the four CCS service categories for April.

b. Determine the charges to the COMM sector for the four CCS service categories for April.

---

OBJ. 3

✔ Retail income from operations, $980,000

**EX 23-7** **Divisional income statements with service department charges**

Ryan Snow Sports Company has two divisions, Wholesale and Retail, and two corporate service departments, Tech Support and Accounts Payable. The corporate expenses for the year ended December 31, 2012, are as follows:

| | |
|---|---|
| Tech Support Department | $  845,000 |
| Accounts Payable Department | 320,000 |
| Other corporate administrative expenses | 502,300 |
| Total corporate expense | $1,667,300 |

The other corporate administrative expenses include officers' salaries and other expenses required by the corporation. The Tech Support Department charges the divisions for services rendered, based on the number of computers in the department, and the Accounts Payable Department charges divisions for services, based on the number of checks issued. The usage of service by the two divisions is as follows:

| | Tech Support | Accounts Payable |
|---|---|---|
| Wholesale Division | 400 computers | 5,600 checks |
| Retail Division | 250 | 10,400 |
| Total | 650 computers | 16,000 checks |

The service department charges of the Tech Support Department and the Accounts Payable Department are considered controllable by the divisions. Corporate administrative expenses are not considered controllable by the divisions. The revenues, cost of goods sold, and operating expenses for the two divisions are as follows:

| | Wholesale | Retail |
|---|---|---|
| Revenues | $7,430,000 | $6,184,000 |
| Cost of goods sold | 4,123,000 | 3,125,000 |
| Operating expenses | 1,465,000 | 1,546,000 |

Prepare the divisional income statements for the two divisions.

---

OBJ. 3

✔ b. Income from operations, Cargo Division, $62,500

**EX 23-8** **Corrections to service department charges**

Temasec Airlines, Inc., has two divisions organized as profit centers, the Passenger Division and the Cargo Division. The following divisional income statements were prepared:

**Temasec Airlines, Inc.**
**Divisional Income Statements**
**For the Year Ended June 30, 2012**

| | Passenger Division | | Cargo Division | |
|---|---|---|---|---|
| Revenues | | $2,100,000 | | $2,100,000 |
| Operating expenses | | 1,700,000 | | 1,900,000 |
| Income from operations before service department charges | | $  400,000 | | $  200,000 |
| Less service department charges: | | | | |
| Training | $ 87,500 | | $ 87,500 | |
| Flight scheduling | 75,000 | | 75,000 | |
| Reservations | 105,000 | 267,500 | 105,000 | 267,500 |
| Income from operations | | $  132,500 | | $   (67,500) |

The service department charge rate for the service department costs was based on revenues. Since the revenues of the two divisions were the same, the service department charges to each division were also the same.

The following additional information is available:

| | Passenger Division | Cargo Division | Total |
|---|---|---|---|
| Number of personnel trained | 250 | 100 | 350 |
| Number of flights | 300 | 420 | 720 |
| Number of reservations requested | 16,000 | 0 | 16,000 |

a. Does the income from operations for the two divisions accurately measure performance? Explain.

b. Correct the divisional income statements, using the activity bases provided above in revising the service department charges.

OBJ. 3

✔ Income from operations, Winter Sports Division, $1,020,000

### EX 23-9  Profit center responsibility reporting

O'Neill Sporting Goods Co. operates two divisions—the Winter Sports Division and the Summer Sports Division. The following income and expense accounts were provided from the trial balance as of June 30, 2012, the end of the current fiscal year, after all adjustments, including those for inventories, were recorded and posted:

| | |
|---|---|
| Sales—Winter Sports Division | $21,500,000 |
| Sales—Summer Sports Division | 24,210,000 |
| Cost of Goods Sold—Winter Sports Division | 12,900,000 |
| Cost of Goods Sold—Summer Sports Division | 14,041,800 |
| Sales Expense—Winter Sports Division | 3,440,000 |
| Sales Expense—Summer Sports Division | 3,389,400 |
| Administrative Expense—Winter Sports Division | 2,150,000 |
| Administrative Expense—Summer Sports Division | 2,154,690 |
| Advertising Expense | 989,000 |
| Transportation Expense | 411,600 |
| Accounts Receivable Collection Expense | 225,600 |
| Warehouse Expense | 2,100,000 |

The bases to be used in allocating expenses, together with other essential information, are as follows:

a. Advertising expense—incurred at headquarters, charged back to divisions on the basis of usage: Winter Sports Division, $465,000; Summer Sports Division, $524,000.

b. Transportation expense—charged back to divisions at a charge rate of $14.00 per bill of lading: Winter Sports Division, 14,000 bills of lading; Summer Sports Division, 15,400 bills of lading.

c. Accounts receivable collection expense—incurred at headquarters, charged back to divisions at a charge rate of $8.00 per invoice: Winter Sports Division, 13,000 sales invoices; Summer Sports Division, 15,200 sales invoices.

d. Warehouse expense—charged back to divisions on the basis of floor space used in storing division products: Winter Sports Division, 140,000 square feet; Summer Sports Division, 100,000 square feet.

Prepare a divisional income statement with two column headings: Winter Sports Division and Summer Sports Division. Provide supporting schedules for determining service department charges.

OBJ. 4

✔ a. Retail, 18%

### EX 23-10  Rate of return on investment

The income from operations and the amount of invested assets in each division of Steele Industries are as follows:

|  | Income from Operations | Invested Assets |
|---|---|---|
| Retail Division | $90,000 | $500,000 |
| Commercial Division | 49,000 | 350,000 |
| Internet Division | 85,000 | 425,000 |

a. Compute the rate of return on investment for each division.

b. Which division is the most profitable per dollar invested?

---

**OBJ. 4**

✔ **a. Internet Division, $46,750**

### EX 23-11  Residual income

Based on the data in Exercise 23-10, assume that management has established a 9% minimum acceptable rate of return for invested assets.

a. Determine the residual income for each division.

b. Which division has the most residual income?

---

**OBJ. 4**

✔ **d. 1.25**

### EX 23-12  Determining missing items in rate of return computation

One item is omitted from each of the following computations of the rate of return on investment:

| Rate of Return on Investment | = | Profit Margin | × | Investment Turnover |
|---|---|---|---|---|
| 10% | = | 8% | × | (a) |
| (b) | = | 15% | × | 0.80 |
| 14% | = | (c) | × | 2.00 |
| 20% | = | 16% | × | (d) |
| (e) | = | 10% | × | 1.50 |

Determine the missing items, identifying each by the appropriate letter.

---

**OBJ. 4**

✔ **a. ROI, 36%**

### EX 23-13  Profit margin, investment turnover, and rate of return on investment

The condensed income statement for the Domestic Division of Fahkahany Industries Inc. is as follows (assuming no service department charges):

| | |
|---|---|
| Sales | $4,500,000 |
| Cost of goods sold | 2,611,000 |
| Gross profit | $1,889,000 |
| Administrative expenses | 539,000 |
| Income from operations | $1,350,000 |

The manager of the Domestic Division is considering ways to increase the rate of return on investment.

a. Using the DuPont formula for rate of return on investment, determine the profit margin, investment turnover, and rate of return on investment of the Domestic Division, assuming that $3,750,000 of assets have been invested in the Domestic Division.

b. If expenses could be reduced by $450,000 without decreasing sales, what would be the impact on the profit margin, investment turnover, and rate of return on investment for the Domestic Division?

---

**OBJ. 4**

✔ **a. Media Networks ROI, 17.6%**

### EX 23-14  Rate of return on investment

The Walt Disney Company has four profitable business segments, described as follows:

- **Media Networks:** The ABC television and radio network, The Disney Channel, ESPN, A&E, E!, and Disney.com.

- **Parks and Resorts:** Walt Disney World Resort, Disneyland, Disney Cruise Line, and other resort properties.

- **Studio Entertainment:** Walt Disney Pictures, Touchstone Pictures, Hollywood Pictures, Miramax Films, and Buena Vista Theatrical Productions.

- **Consumer Products:** Character merchandising, Disney stores, books, and magazines.

Disney recently reported sector income from operations, revenue, and invested assets (in millions) as follows:

| | Income from Operations | Revenue | Invested Assets |
|---|---|---|---|
| Media Networks | $4,765 | $16,209 | $26,936 |
| Parks and Resorts | 1,418 | 10,667 | 16,945 |
| Studio Entertainment | 175 | 6,136 | 11,104 |
| Consumer Products | 609 | 2,425 | 1,278 |

a. Use the DuPont formula to determine the rate of return on investment for the four Disney sectors. Round whole percents to one decimal place and investment turnover to two decimal places.

b. ➤ How do the four sectors differ in their profit margin, investment turnover, and return on investment?

---

**EX 23-15  Determining missing items in rate of return and residual income computations**

Data for Magnum Company is presented in the following table of rates of return on investment and residual incomes:

| Invested Assets | Income from Operations | Rate of Return on Investment | Minimum Rate of Return | Minimum Acceptable Income from Operations | Residual Income |
|---|---|---|---|---|---|
| $920,000 | $202,400 | (a) | 15% | (b) | (c) |
| $610,000 | (d) | (e) | (f) | $67,100 | $24,400 |
| $440,000 | (g) | 16% | (h) | $57,200 | (i) |
| $280,000 | $50,400 | (j) | 14% | (k) | (l) |

Determine the missing items, identifying each item by the appropriate letter.

---

**EX 23-16  Determining missing items from computations**

Data for the North, South, East, and West divisions of Gateway Company are as follows:

| | Sales | Income from Operations | Invested Assets | Rate of Return on Investment | Profit Margin | Investment Turnover |
|---|---|---|---|---|---|---|
| North | $625,000 | (a) | (b) | 20% | 10% | (c) |
| South | (d) | $84,000 | (e) | (f) | 14% | 1.5 |
| East | $800,000 | (g) | $320,000 | 18% | (h) | (i) |
| West | $950,000 | $142,500 | $950,000 | (j) | (k) | (l) |

a. Determine the missing items, identifying each by the letters (a) through (l). Round percents and investment turnover to one decimal place.

b. Determine the residual income for each division, assuming that the minimum acceptable rate of return established by management is 11%.

c. Which division is the most profitable in terms of (1) return on investment and (2) residual income?

---

**EX 23-17  Rate of return on investment, residual income**

Starwood Hotels & Resorts Worldwide provides lodging services around the world. The company is separated into two major divisions.

• **Hotel Ownership:** Hotels owned and operated by Starwood.

• **Vacation Ownership:** Resort properties developed, owned, and operated for timeshare vacation owners.

Financial information for each division, from a recent annual report, is as follows (in millions):

|  | Hotel Ownership | Vacation Ownership |
|---|---|---|
| Revenues | $5,013 | $  894 |
| Income from operations | 785 | 136 |
| Total assets | 6,728 | 2,183 |

a. Use the DuPont formula to determine the return on investment for each of the Starwood business divisions. Round whole percents to one decimal place and investment turnover to two decimal places.

b. Determine the residual income for each division, assuming a minimum acceptable income of 8% of total assets. Round minimal acceptable return to the nearest million dollars.

c. ━━━━━ Interpret your results.

---

### EX 23-18  Balanced scorecard

American Express Company is a major financial services company, noted for its American Express® card. Below are some of the performance measures used by the company in its balanced scorecard.

| | |
|---|---|
| Average cardmember spending | Number of merchant signings |
| Cards in force | Number of card choices |
| Earnings growth | Number of new card launches |
| Hours of credit consultant training | Return on equity |
| Investment in information technology | Revenue growth |
| Number of Internet features | |

For each measure, identify whether the measure best fits the innovation, customer, internal process, or financial dimension of the balanced scorecard.

---

### EX 23-19  Balanced scorecard

Several years ago, United Parcel Service (UPS) believed that the Internet was going to change the parcel delivery market and would require UPS to become a more nimble and customer-focused organization. As a result, UPS replaced its old measurement system, which was 90% oriented toward financial performance, with a balanced scorecard. The scorecard emphasized four "point of arrival" measures, which were:

1. Customer satisfaction index—a measure of customer satisfaction.
2. Employee relations index—a measure of employee sentiment and morale.
3. Competitive position—delivery performance relative to competition.
4. Time in transit—the time from order entry to delivery.

a. ━━━━━ Why did UPS introduce a balanced scorecard and nonfinancial measures in its new performance measurement system?

b. ━━━━━ Why do you think UPS included a factor measuring employee sentiment?

---

✔ a. $1,500,000

### EX 23-20  Decision on transfer pricing

Materials used by the Truck Division of Goldman Motors are currently purchased from outside suppliers at a cost of $310 per unit. However, the same materials are available from the Components Division. The Components Division has unused capacity and can produce the materials needed by the Truck Division at a variable cost of $250 per unit.

a. If a transfer price of $272 per unit is established and 25,000 units of materials are transferred, with no reduction in the Components Division's current sales, how much would Goldman Motors' total income from operations increase?

b. How much would the Truck Division's income from operations increase?

c. How much would the Components Division's income from operations increase?

**OBJ. 5**

✔ b. $500,000

**EX 23-21   Decision on transfer pricing**

Based on Goldman Motors' data in Exercise 23-20, assume that a transfer price of $290 has been established and that 25,000 units of materials are transferred, with no reduction in the Components Division's current sales.

a.  How much would Goldmon Motors' total income from operations increase?

b.  How much would the Truck Division's income from operations increase?

c.  How much would the Components Division's income from operations increase?

d.  ━━━▶ If the negotiated price approach is used, what would be the range of acceptable transfer prices and why?

## Problems Series A

**OBJ. 2**

**PR 23-1A   Budget performance report for a cost center**

World-Tec Company sells electronics over the Internet. The International Division is organized as a cost center. The budget for the International Division for the month ended March 31, 2012, is as follows (in thousands):

| | |
|---|---:|
| Customer service salaries | $  325,500 |
| Insurance and property taxes | 68,250 |
| Distribution salaries | 519,250 |
| Marketing salaries | 612,125 |
| Engineer salaries | 498,125 |
| Warehouse wages | 348,800 |
| Equipment depreciation | 109,400 |
| Total | $2,481,450 |

During March, the costs incurred in the International Division were as follows:

| | |
|---|---:|
| Customer service salaries | $  416,700 |
| Insurance and property taxes | 66,200 |
| Distribution salaries | 514,000 |
| Marketing salaries | 685,500 |
| Engineer salaries | 488,100 |
| Warehouse wages | 334,900 |
| Equipment depreciation | 109,375 |
| Total | $2,614,775 |

**Instructions**

1.  Prepare a budget performance report for the director of the International Division for the month of March.

2.  For which costs might the director be expected to request supplemental reports?

**OBJ. 3**

✔ 1. Income from operations, Central Division, $390,000

**PR 23-2A   Profit center responsibility reporting**

Johnson Products Inc. has three regional divisions organized as profit centers. The chief executive officer (CEO) evaluates divisional performance, using income from operations as a percent of revenues. The following quarterly income and expense accounts were provided from the trial balance as of December 31, 2012:

| | |
|---|---:|
| Revenues—East | $  720,000 |
| Revenues—West | 860,000 |
| Revenues—Central | 1,560,000 |
| Operating Expenses—East | 456,150 |
| Operating Expenses—West | 511,700 |
| Operating Expenses—Central | 943,550 |
| Corporate Expenses—Shareholder Relations | 112,000 |
| Corporate Expenses—Customer Support | 385,000 |
| Corporate Expenses—Legal | 152,000 |
| General Corporate Officers' Salaries | 240,000 |

The company operates three service departments: Shareholder Relations, Customer Support, and Legal. The Shareholder Relations Department conducts a variety of services for shareholders of the company. The Customer Support Department is the company's point of contact for new service, complaints, and requests for repair. The department believes that the number of customer contacts is an activity base for this work. The Legal Department provides legal services for division management. The department believes that the number of hours billed is an activity base for this work. The following additional information has been gathered:

|  | East | West | Central |
|---|---|---|---|
| Number of customer contacts | 4,375 | 5,250 | 7,875 |
| Number of hours billed | 950 | 1,520 | 1,330 |

### Instructions

1. Prepare quarterly income statements showing income from operations for the three divisions. Use three column headings: East, West, and Central.
2. Identify the most successful division according to the profit margin.
3. ➤ Provide a recommendation to the CEO for a better method for evaluating the performance of the divisions. In your recommendation, identify the major weakness of the present method.

---

**OBJ. 4**

✔ 2. Mutual Fund Division, ROI, 18%

### PR 23-3A   Divisional income statements and rate of return on investment analysis

Edward Baird Company is a diversified investment company with three operating divisions organized as investment centers. Condensed data taken from the records of the three divisions for the year ended June 30, 2012, are as follows:

|  | Mutual Fund Division | Electronic Brokerage Division | Investment Banking Division |
|---|---|---|---|
| Fee revenue | $3,450,000 | $2,800,000 | $3,800,000 |
| Operating expenses | 2,415,000 | 2,632,000 | 2,850,000 |
| Invested assets | 5,750,000 | 800,000 | 4,750,000 |

The management of Edward Baird Company is evaluating each division as a basis for planning a future expansion of operations.

### Instructions

1. Prepare condensed divisional income statements for the three divisions, assuming that there were no service department charges.
2. Using the DuPont formula for rate of return on investment, compute the profit margin, investment turnover, and rate of return on investment for each division.
3. ➤ If available funds permit the expansion of operations of only one division, which of the divisions would you recommend for expansion, based on parts (1) and (2)? Explain.

---

**OBJ. 4**

✔ 1. ROI, 15.6%

### PR 23-4A   Effect of proposals on divisional performance

A condensed income statement for the Golf Division of Rewind Sports Inc. for the year ended December 31, 2012, is as follows:

| | |
|---|---|
| Sales | $2,400,000 |
| Cost of goods sold | 1,663,000 |
| Gross profit | $ 737,000 |
| Operating expenses | 425,000 |
| Income from operations | $ 312,000 |
| Invested assets | $2,000,000 |

Assume that the Golf Division received no charges from service departments. The president of Rewind Sports has indicated that the division's rate of return on a $2,000,000 investment must be increased to at least 18% by the end of the next year if operations are to continue. The division manager is considering the following three proposals:

*Proposal 1:* Transfer equipment with a book value of $400,000 to other divisions at no gain or loss and lease similar equipment. The annual lease payments would exceed the amount of depreciation expense on the old equipment by $72,000. This increase in expense would be included as part of the cost of goods sold. Sales would remain unchanged.

*Proposal 2:* Purchase new and more efficient machining equipment and thereby reduce the cost of goods sold by $264,000. Sales would remain unchanged, and the old equipment, which has no remaining book value, would be scrapped at no gain or loss. The new equipment would increase invested assets by an additional $1,000,000 for the year.

*Proposal 3:* Reduce invested assets by discontinuing a product line. This action would eliminate sales of $425,000, cost of goods sold of $284,250, and operating expenses of $125,000. Assets of $1,012,500 would be transferred to other divisions at no gain or loss.

### Instructions

1. Using the DuPont formula for rate of return on investment, determine the profit margin, investment turnover, and rate of return on investment for the Golf Division for the past year.

2. Prepare condensed estimated income statements and compute the invested assets for each proposal.

3. Using the DuPont formula for rate of return on investment, determine the profit margin, investment turnover, and rate of return on investment for each proposal.

4. Which of the three proposals would meet the required 18% rate of return on investment?

5. If the Golf Division were in an industry where the profit margin could not be increased, how much would the investment turnover have to increase to meet the president's required 18% rate of return on investment? Round to one decimal place.

---

**OBJ. 4**

✔ 2. Business
Division ROI, 24.0%

### PR 23-5A   Divisional performance analysis and evaluation

The vice president of operations of Avigi IQ Company is evaluating the performance of two divisions organized as investment centers. Invested assets and condensed income statement data for the past year for each division are as follows:

|  | Business Division | Consumer Division |
|---|---|---|
| Sales | $1,800,000 | $1,850,000 |
| Cost of goods sold | 940,000 | 950,000 |
| Operating expenses | 572,000 | 493,000 |
| Invested assets | 1,200,000 | 2,312,500 |

### Instructions

1. Prepare condensed divisional income statements for the year ended December 31, 2012, assuming that there were no service department charges.

2. Using the DuPont formula for rate of return on investment, determine the profit margin, investment turnover, and rate of return on investment for each division.

3. If management desires a minimum acceptable rate of return of 18%, determine the residual income for each division.

4.  Discuss the evaluation of the two divisions, using the performance measures determined in parts (1), (2), and (3).

---

**OBJ. 5**

✔ 3. Total income
from operations,
$1,092,000

### PR 23-6A   Transfer pricing

Eccles, Inc., manufactures electronic products, with two operating divisions, the Electronics and Instruments divisions. Condensed divisional income statements, which involve no intracompany transfers and which include a breakdown of expenses into variable and fixed components, are as follows:

**Eccles, Inc.**
**Divisional Income Statements**
**For the Year Ended December 31, 2012**

| | | Electronics Division | Instruments Division | Total |
|---|---|---|---|---|
| Sales: | | | | |
| 12,000 units @ | $120 per unit | $1,440,000 | | $1,440,000 |
| 18,000 units @ | $228 per unit | | $4,104,000 | 4,104,000 |
| | | $1,440,000 | $4,104,000 | $5,544,000 |
| Expenses: | | | | |
| Variable: | | | | |
| 12,000 units @ | $86 per unit | $1,032,000 | | $1,032,000 |
| 18,000 units @ | $162* per unit | | $2,916,000 | 2,916,000 |
| Fixed | | 168,000 | 432,000 | 600,000 |
| Total expenses | | $1,200,000 | $3,348,000 | $4,548,000 |
| Income from operations | | $ 240,000 | $ 756,000 | $ 996,000 |

*$126 of the $162 per unit represents materials costs, and the remaining $36 per unit represents other variable conversion expenses incurred within the Instruments Division.

The Electronics Division is presently producing 12,000 units out of a total capacity of 14,400 units. Materials used in producing the Instruments Division's product are currently purchased from outside suppliers at a price of $126 per unit. The Electronics Division is able to produce the materials used by the Instruments Division. Except for the possible transfer of materials between divisions, no changes are expected in sales and expenses.

**Instructions**

1. ➤ Would the market price of $126 per unit be an appropriate transfer price for Eccles, Inc.? Explain.

2. ➤ If the Instruments Division purchases 2,400 units from the Electronics Division, rather than externally, at a negotiated transfer price of $96 per unit, how much would the income from operations of each division and the total company income from operations increase?

3. Prepare condensed divisional income statements for Eccles, Inc., based on the data in part (2).

4. ➤ If a transfer price of $105 per unit is negotiated, how much would the income from operations of each division and the total company income from operations increase?

5. a. ➤ What is the range of possible negotiated transfer prices that would be acceptable for Eccles, Inc.?

   b. Assuming that the managers of the two divisions cannot agree on a transfer price, what price would you suggest as the transfer price?

## Problems Series B

OBJ. 2

**PR 23-1B   Budget performance report for a cost center**

The Eastern District of Blankfine Products, Inc., is organized as a cost center. The budget for the Eastern District of Blankfine Products, Inc., for the month ended October 31, 2012, is as follows:

| | |
|---|---|
| Sales salaries | $ 683,200 |
| System administration salaries | 373,460 |
| Customer service salaries | 127,200 |
| Billing salaries | 82,300 |
| Maintenance | 226,170 |
| Depreciation of plant and equipment | 76,860 |
| Insurance and property taxes | 34,400 |
| Total | $1,603,590 |

During October, the costs incurred in the Eastern District were as follows:

| | |
|---|---:|
| Sales salaries | $ 682,400 |
| System administration salaries | 373,100 |
| Customer service salaries | 150,100 |
| Billing salaries | 81,750 |
| Maintenance | 227,500 |
| Depreciation of plant and equipment | 76,860 |
| Insurance and property taxes | 34,500 |
| Total | $1,626,210 |

## Instructions

1. Prepare a budget performance report for the manager of the Eastern District of Blankfine Products for the month of October.

2. ━━━━➤ For which costs might the supervisor be expected to request supplemental reports?

---

**OBJ. 3**

✔ 1. Income from operations, West Region, $534,375

### PR 23-2B  Profit center responsibility reporting

Train-X Railroad Company organizes its three divisions, the North (N), South (S), and West (W) regions, as profit centers. The chief executive officer (CEO) evaluates divisional performance, using income from operations as a percent of revenues. The following quarterly income and expense accounts were provided from the trial balance as of December 31, 2012:

| | |
|---|---:|
| Revenues—N Region | $2,625,000 |
| Revenues—S Region | 3,940,000 |
| Revenues—W Region | 3,562,500 |
| Operating Expenses—N Region | 1,856,250 |
| Operating Expenses—S Region | 3,081,000 |
| Operating Expenses—W Region | 2,525,625 |
| Corporate Expenses—Dispatching | 180,000 |
| Corporate Expenses—Equipment Management | 1,110,000 |
| Corporate Expenses—Treasurer's | 510,000 |
| General Corporate Officers' Salaries | 960,000 |

The company operates three service departments: the Dispatching Department, the Equipment Management Department, and the Treasurer's Department. The Dispatching Department manages the scheduling and releasing of completed trains. The Equipment Management Department manages the railroad cars inventories. It makes sure the right freight cars are at the right place at the right time. The Treasurer's Department conducts a variety of services for the company as a whole. The following additional information has been gathered:

| | North | South | West |
|---|---:|---:|---:|
| Number of scheduled trains | 500 | 850 | 650 |
| Number of railroad cars in inventory | 4,625 | 6,475 | 7,400 |

## Instructions

1. Prepare quarterly income statements showing income from operations for the three regions. Use three column headings: North, South, and West.

2. Identify the most successful region according to the profit margin.

3. ━━━━➤ Provide a recommendation to the CEO for a better method for evaluating the performance of the regions. In your recommendation, identify the major weakness of the present method.

### PR 23-3B   Divisional income statements and rate of return on investment analysis

Earthy Grains Food Company is a diversified food company with three operating divisions organized as investment centers. Condensed data taken from the records of the three divisions for the year ended June 30, 2012, are as follows:

| | Cereal Division | Snack Cake Division | Retail Bakeries Division |
|---|---|---|---|
| Sales | $4,950,000 | $5,400,000 | $4,896,000 |
| Cost of goods sold | 3,725,000 | 3,800,000 | 3,400,000 |
| Operating expenses | 433,000 | 844,000 | 516,800 |
| Invested assets | 5,500,000 | 6,750,000 | 4,080,000 |

The management of Earthy Grains Food Company is evaluating each division as a basis for planning a future expansion of operations.

#### Instructions

1. Prepare condensed divisional income statements for the three divisions, assuming that there were no service department charges.

2. Using the DuPont formula for rate of return on investment, compute the profit margin, investment turnover, and rate of return on investment for each division.

3.  If available funds permit the expansion of operations of only one division, which of the divisions would you recommend for expansion, based on parts (1) and (2)? Explain.

---

### PR 23-4B   Effect of proposals on divisional performance

A condensed income statement for the Electronics Division of Fannie Industries Inc. for the year ended January 31, 2012, is as follows:

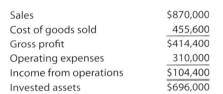

| | |
|---|---|
| Sales | $870,000 |
| Cost of goods sold | 455,600 |
| Gross profit | $414,400 |
| Operating expenses | 310,000 |
| Income from operations | $104,400 |
| Invested assets | $696,000 |

Assume that the Electronics Division received no charges from service departments.

The president of Fannie Industries Inc. has indicated that the division's rate of return on a $696,000 investment must be increased to at least 20% by the end of the next year if operations are to continue. The division manager is considering the following three proposals:

*Proposal 1:* Transfer equipment with a book value of $96,000 to other divisions at no gain or loss and lease similar equipment. The annual lease payments would be less than the amount of depreciation expense on the old equipment by $34,800. This decrease in expense would be included as part of the cost of goods sold. Sales would remain unchanged.

*Proposal 2:* Reduce invested assets by discontinuing a product line. This action would eliminate sales of $100,000, cost of goods sold of $42,600, and operating expenses of $30,000. Assets of $146,000 would be transferred to other divisions at no gain or loss.

*Proposal 3:* Purchase new and more efficient machinery and thereby reduce the cost of goods sold by $87,000. Sales would remain unchanged, and the old machinery, which has no remaining book value, would be scrapped at no gain or loss. The new machinery would increase invested assets by $754,000 for the year.

#### Instructions

1. Using the DuPont formula for rate of return on investment, determine the profit margin, investment turnover, and rate of return on investment for the Electronics Division for the past year. Round investment turnover to two decimal places.

2. Prepare condensed estimated income statements and compute the invested assets for each proposal.

3. Using the DuPont formula for rate of return on investment, determine the profit margin, investment turnover, and rate of return on investment for each proposal.

4. Which of the three proposals would meet the required 20% rate of return on investment?

5. If the Electronics Division were in an industry where the profit margin could not be increased, how much would the investment turnover have to increase to meet the president's required 20% rate of return on investment? Round to one decimal place.

---

**OBJ. 4**

✔ 2. Road Bike
Division ROI, 22.0%

### PR 23-5B    Divisional performance analysis and evaluation

The vice president of operations of Cantor Bike Company is evaluating the performance of two divisions organized as investment centers. Invested assets and condensed income statement data for the past year for each division are as follows:

|  | Road Bike Division | Mountain Bike Division |
|---|---|---|
| Sales | $1,210,000 | $1,440,000 |
| Cost of goods sold | 895,000 | 1,150,000 |
| Operating expenses | 194,000 | 74,000 |
| Invested assets | 550,000 | 1,200,000 |

### Instructions

1. Prepare condensed divisional income statements for the year ended December 31, 2012, assuming that there were no service department charges.

2. Using the DuPont formula for rate of return on investment, determine the profit margin, investment turnover, and rate of return on investment for each division.

3. If management's minimum acceptable rate of return is 16%, determine the residual income for each division.

4.  Discuss the evaluation of the two divisions, using the performance measures determined in parts (1), (2), and (3).

---

**OBJ. 5**

✔ 3. Navigational
Systems Division,
$210,750

### PR 23-6B    Transfer pricing

Lockhart Industries, Inc., is a diversified aerospace company, including two operating divisions, Semiconductors and Navigational Systems divisions. Condensed divisional income statements, which involve no intracompany transfers and which include a breakdown of expenses into variable and fixed components, are as follows:

**Lockhart Industries, Inc.**
**Divisional Income Statements**
**For the Year Ended December 31, 2012**

|  | Semiconductors Division | Navigational Systems Division | Total |
|---|---|---|---|
| Sales: |  |  |  |
| 1,200 units @  $990 per unit | $1,188,000 |  | $1,188,000 |
| 1,875 units @  $1,488 per unit |  | $2,790,000 | 2,790,000 |
|  | $1,188,000 | $2,790,000 | $3,978,000 |
| Expenses: |  |  |  |
| Variable: |  |  |  |
| 1,200 units @  $582 per unit | $  698,400 |  | $  698,400 |
| 1,875 units @  $1,170* per unit |  | $2,193,750 | 2,193,750 |
| Fixed | 366,000 | 477,000 | 843,000 |
| Total expenses | $1,064,400 | $2,670,750 | $3,735,150 |
| Income from operations | $  123,600 | $  119,250 | $  242,850 |

*$1,080 of the $1,170 per unit represents materials costs, and the remaining $90 per unit represents other variable conversion expenses incurred within the Navigational Systems Division.

The Semiconductors Division is presently producing 1,200 units out of a total capacity of 1,500 units. Materials used in producing the Navigational Systems Division's product are currently purchased from outside suppliers at a price of $1,080 per unit.

The Semiconductors Division is able to produce the components used by the Navigational Systems Division. Except for the possible transfer of materials between divisions, no changes are expected in sales and expenses.

**Instructions**

1. ━━━ Would the market price of $1,080 per unit be an appropriate transfer price for Lockhart Industries, Inc.? Explain.

2. ━━━ If the Navigational Systems Division purchases 300 units from the Semiconductors Division, rather than externally, at a negotiated transfer price of $775 per unit, how much would the income from operations of each division and total company income from operations increase?

3. Prepare condensed divisional income statements for Lockhart Industries, Inc., based on the data in part (2).

4. ━━━ If a transfer price of $850 per unit is negotiated, how much would the income from operations of each division and total company income from operations increase?

5. a. ━━━ What is the range of possible negotiated transfer prices that would be acceptable for Lockhart Industries, Inc.?

   b. Assuming that the managers of the two divisions cannot agree on a transfer price, what price would you suggest as the transfer price?

## Cases & Projects

You can access Cases & Projects online at **www.cengage.com/accounting/reeve**

## Excel Success Special Activities

### SA 23-1  Service department charges

The Kirkland Company has three central service departments: sales administration, credit, and human resources. The expenses for the three departments are as follows for the year ended December 31, 2012:

| | |
|---|---|
| Sales administration | $120,000 |
| Credit | 84,000 |
| Human resources | 185,000 |
| Total | $389,000 |

Service department expenses are allocated to divisions based on an appropriate activity base. The activity bases associated with each service department for each division during 2012 is as follows:

| Service Departments | Northern Division | Southern Division | Total |
|---|---|---|---|
| Sales administration | 1,650 | 3,850 | 5,500 sales orders |
| Credit | 4,900 | 9,100 | 14,000 customers |
| Human resources | 400 | 600 | 1,000 employees |

a. Open the Excel file *SA23-1_1e*.

b. Prepare a report showing the service department charges allocated to each division.

c. When you have completed the report, perform a "save as," replacing the entire file name with the following:

   *SA23-1_1e[your first name initial]_[your last name]*

### SA 23-2    Service department charges

Bass Company allocates central service department expenses from the accounting, travel, and purchasing departments to the Retail, Commercial, and Municipal Divisions. The expenses for the three service departments for the year ended December 31, 2012 are:

| | |
|---|---|
| Accounting | $264,000 |
| Travel | 94,000 |
| Purchasing | 192,000 |
| Total | $550,000 |

The activity base used by each service department in allocating service department expenses to the divisions was determined as follows:

| Department | Activity Base |
|---|---|
| Accounting | Number of transactions |
| Travel | Number of travel requests |
| Purchasing | Number of purchase orders |

The use of services by the three divisions is as follows:

| Division | Service Usage | | |
|---|---|---|---|
| | Accounting | Travel | Purchasing |
| Retail | 22,400 trans. | 250 trav. req. | 1,500 purch. ord. |
| Commercial | 12,500 | 190 | 900 |
| Municipal | 5,100 | 60 | 600 |
| Total | 40,000 trans. | 500 trav. req. | 3,000 purch. ord. |

a. Open the Excel file *SA23-2_1e*.

b. Prepare a report showing the service department charges allocated to each division.

c. When you have completed the report, perform a "save as," replacing the entire file name with the following:

   *SA23-2_1e[your first name initial]_[your last name]*

### SA 23-3    Divisional income statement

The revenues and direct operating expenses for the two divisions of the UniCast Cable Company for the year ended December 31, 2012, are as follows:

| | Eastern Division | Western Division |
|---|---|---|
| Revenues | $4,100,000 | $3,500,000 |
| Operating expenses | 2,450,000 | 2,200,000 |

There are three central service departments: billing, payroll, and service and repairs. The expenses associated with these central service departments for December 31, 2012, are as follows:

| | |
|---|---|
| Billing | $ 310,000 |
| Payroll | 265,000 |
| Service and repairs | 684,000 |
| Total | $1,259,000 |

The central service department expenses are allocated to the two divisions based on relevant activity bases. The billing, payroll, and service and repairs departments are allocated to the divisions on the basis of bills, payroll checks, and repair requests, respectively.

The consumption of activity by the two divisions from the three service departments for 2012 is as follows:

| | Eastern Division | Western Division | Total |
|---|---|---|---|
| Billing | 18,500 | 21,500 | 40,000 bills |
| Payroll | 1,530 | 1,870 | 3,400 payroll chks. |
| Service and repairs | 408 | 442 | 850 serv. requests |

a. Open the Excel file *SA23-3_1e*.

b. Prepare a divisional income statement for UniCast Cable Company for the year ended December 31, 2012.

c. When you have completed the statement, perform a "save as," replacing the entire file name with the following:

   *SA23-3_1e[your first name initial]_[your last name]*

© AP Photo/Paul Sakuma

# Differential Analysis and Product Pricing

## Facebook

**M**any of the decisions that you make depend on comparing the estimated costs of alternatives. The payoff from such comparisons is described in the following report from a University of Michigan study.

*Richard Nisbett and two colleagues quizzed Michigan faculty members and university seniors on such questions as how often they walk out on a bad movie, refuse to finish a bad meal, start over on a weak term paper, or abandon a research project that no longer looks promising. They believe that people who cut their losses this way are following sound economic rules: calculating the net benefits of alternative courses of action, writing off past costs that can't be recovered, and weighing the opportunity to use future time and effort more profitably elsewhere.*

*Among students, those who have learned to use cost-benefit analysis frequently are apt to have far better grades than their Scholastic Aptitude Test scores would have predicted. Again, the more economics courses the students have, the more likely they are to apply cost-benefit analysis outside the classroom.*

*Dr. Nisbett concedes that for many Americans, cost-benefit rules often appear to conflict with such traditional principles as "never give up" and "waste not, want not."*

Managers must also evaluate the costs and benefits of alternative actions. **Facebook**, the largest social networking site in the world, was cofounded by 26-year-old Mark Zuckerberg in 2004. Since then, it has grown to over 350 million users and made Zuckerberg a multibillionaire.

Facebook has plans to grow to over 1 billion users worldwide. Such growth involves decisions about where to expand. For example, expanding the site to new languages and countries involves software programming, marketing, and computer hardware costs. The benefits include adding new users to Facebook.

Analysis of the benefits and costs might lead Facebook to expand in some languages before others. For example, such an analysis might lead Facebook to expand in Spanish before it expands in Tok Pisin (language of Papua New Guinea).

In this chapter, differential analysis, which reports the effects of decisions on total revenues and costs, is discussed. Practical approaches to setting product prices are also described and illustrated. Finally, how production bottlenecks influence pricing and other decisions is also discussed.

*Source:* Alan L. Otten, "Economic Perspective Produces Steady Yields," from People Patterns, *The Wall Street Journal,* March 31,1992, p. B1.

## Learning Objectives

After studying this chapter, you should be able to:

| | Example Exercises | Page |
|---|---|---|

**OBJ. 1** Prepare differential analysis reports for a variety of managerial decisions.
Differential Analysis

| | Example Exercises | Page |
|---|---|---|
| Lease or Sell | EE 24-1 | 1123 |
| Discontinue a Segment or Product | EE 24-2 | 1125 |
| Make or Buy | EE 24-3 | 1126 |
| Replace Equipment | EE 24-4 | 1128 |
| Process or Sell | EE 24-5 | 1130 |
| Accept Business at a Special Price | EE 24-6 | 1131 |

**OBJ. 2** Determine the selling price of a product, using the product cost concept.
Setting Normal Product Selling Prices

| | Example Exercises | Page |
|---|---|---|
| Product Cost Concept | EE 24-7 | 1134 |
| Target Costing | | |

**OBJ. 3** Compute the relative profitability of products in bottleneck production processes.
Production Bottlenecks, Pricing, and Profits

| | Example Exercises | Page |
|---|---|---|
| Production Bottlenecks and Profits | EE 24-8 | 1137 |
| Production Bottlenecks and Pricing | | |

**At a Glance 24** Page 1141

**OBJ. 1** Prepare differential analysis reports for a variety of managerial decisions.

# Differential Analysis

Managerial decision making involves choosing between alternative courses of action. Although the managerial decision-making process varies by the type of decision, it normally involves the following steps:

Step 1.   Identify the objective of the decision, which is normally maximizing income.

Step 2.   Identify alternative courses of action.

Step 3.   Gather information and perform a differential analysis.

Step 4.   Make a decision.

Step 5.   Review, analyze, and assess the results of the decision.

To illustrate, assume Bryant Restaurants, Inc., is deciding whether to replace some of its customer seating (tables) with a salad bar. The differential analysis decision-making process is as follows:

**Step 1.**   Bryant Restaurants' objective is to increase its income.

**Step 2.**   The alternative courses of action are:

1. Use floor space for existing tables.
2. Replace the tables with a salad bar.

**Step 3.**   The following relevant data have been gathered:

| | Tables (Alternative 1) | Salad Bar (Alternative 2) |
|---|---|---|
| Revenues | $100,000 | $120,000 |
| Costs | 60,000 | 65,000 |
| Income (loss) | $ 40,000 | $ 55,000 |

The preceding information is used to perform differential analysis. **Differential analysis**, sometimes called *incremental analysis*, analyzes differential revenues and costs in order to determine the differential impact on income of two alternative courses of action.

**Differential revenue** is the amount of increase or decrease in revenue that is expected from a course of action compared to an alternative. **Differential cost** is the amount of increase or decrease in cost that is expected from a course of action as compared to an alternative. **Differential income (loss)** is the difference between the differential revenue and differential costs. Differential income indicates that a decision is expected to increase income, while a differential loss indicates the decision is expected to decrease income.

To illustrate, the differential analysis as of July 11, 2012, for Bryant Restaurants is shown below.

**EXHIBIT 1**

**Differential Analysis— Bryant Restaurants**

**Differential Analysis**
**Tables (Alternative 1) or Salad Bar (Alternative 2)**
**July 11, 2012**

| | Tables (Alternative 1) | Salad Bar (Alternative 2) | Differential Effect on Income (Alternative 2) |
|---|---|---|---|
| Revenues.................. | $100,000 | $120,000 | $20,000 |
| Costs..................... | –60,000 | –65,000 | –5,000 |
| Income (loss).............. | $ 40,000 | $ 55,000 | $15,000 |

The differential analysis is prepared in three columns where positive amounts indicate the effect is to increase income and negative amounts indicate the effect is to decrease income. The first column is the revenues, costs, and income for maintaining floor space for tables (Alternative 1). The second column is the revenues, costs, and income for using that floor space for a salad bar (Alternative 2). The third column is the difference between the revenue, costs, and income of one alternative over the other.

In Exhibit 1, the salad bar is being considered over retaining the existing tables. Thus, Column 3 in Exhibit 1 is expressed in terms of Alternative 2 (salad bar) over Alternative 1 (tables).

In Exhibit 1, the differential revenue of a salad bar over tables is $20,000 ($120,000 – $100,000). Since the increased revenue would increase income, it is entered as a positive $20,000 in the Differential Effect on Income column. The differential cost of a salad bar over tables is $5,000 ($65,000 – $60,000). Since the increased costs will decrease income, it is entered as a negative $5,000 in the Differential Effect on Income column.

The differential income (loss) of a salad bar over tables of $15,000 is determined by subtracting the differential costs from the differential revenues in the Differential Effect on Income column. Thus, installing a salad bar increases income by $15,000.

The preceding differential revenue, costs, and income can also be determined using the following formulas:

Differential Revenue = Revenue (Alt. 2) – Revenue (Alt. 1)
Differential Revenue = $120,000 – $100,000 = $20,000

Differential Costs = Costs (Alt. 2) – Costs (Alt. 1)
Differential Costs = –$65,000 – (–$60,000) = –$5,000

Differential Income (Loss) = Income (Alt. 2) – Income (Alt. 1)
Differential Income (Loss) = $55,000 – $40,000 = $15,000

**Step 4.** Based upon the differential analysis report shown in Exhibit 1, Bryant Restaurants should decide to replace some of its tables with a salad bar. Doing so will increase its income by $15,000.

**Step 5.** Over time, Bryant Restaurants' decision should be reviewed based upon actual revenues and costs. If the actual revenues and costs differ significantly from those gathered in Step 3, another differential analysis might be necessary to verify that the correct decision was made.

In this chapter, differential analysis is illustrated for the following common decisions:

1. Leasing or selling equipment
2. Discontinuing an unprofitable segment
3. Manufacturing or purchasing a needed part
4. Replacing fixed assets
5. Selling a product or processing further
6. Accepting additional business at a special price

*success*

Differential analysis can be performed using spreadsheet software. The spreadsheet solution for Bryant Restaurants is as follows:

| | A | B | C | D |
|---|---|---|---|---|
| 1 | | Differential Analysis | | |
| 2 | | Tables (Alternative 1) or Salad Bar (Alternative 2) | | |
| 3 | | July 11, 2012 | | |
| 4 | | Tables (Alternative 1) | Salad Bar (Alternative 2) | Differential Effect on Income (Alternative 2) |
| 5 | Revenues a. | $100,000 | $120,000 | =C5–B5 |
| 6 | Costs | –60,000 | –65,000 | =C6–B6 c. |
| 7 | Income (loss) b. | =SUM (B5:B6) | =SUM (C5:C6) | =C7–B7 |
| 8 | | | | |

The formulas for the output space would be developed as follows:

a.  Enter in cells B5:C6 the revenues and costs for both alternatives. Enter revenues as a plus and expenses as a minus.
b.  Enter in cell B7 the sum function, =SUM(B5:B6). Copy this formula to C7.
c.  Enter in cell D5 the formula for the difference between the revenues for the two alternatives, as Alternative 2 minus Alternative 1, or =C5–B5. Copy this formula to D6 and D7.

All of the differential analyses illustrated in this text can be solved with a spreadsheet using this general framework. However, it is important to remember that revenues must be entered as a plus and expenses as a minus for these formulas to provide a correct solution.

**Try**It    Go to the hands-on *Excel Tutor* for this example!

## Lease or Sell

Management may lease or sell a piece of equipment that is no longer needed. This may occur when a company changes its manufacturing process and can no longer use the equipment in the manufacturing process. In making a decision, differential analysis can be used.

**Marcus Company**

To illustrate, assume that on June 22, 2012, Marcus Company is considering leasing or disposing of the following equipment:

| | |
|---|---|
| Cost of equipment | $200,000 |
| Less accumulated depreciation | 120,000 |
| Book value | $ 80,000 |
| Lease (Alternative 1): | |
| Total revenue for five-year lease | $160,000 |
| Total estimated repair, insurance, and property tax expenses during life of lease | 35,000 |
| Residual value at end of fifth year of lease | 0 |
| Sell (Alternative 2): | |
| Sales price | $100,000 |
| Commission on sales | 6% |

Exhibit 2 shows the differential analysis of whether to lease (Alternative 1) or sell (Alternative 2) the equipment.

**EXHIBIT 2**

**Differential Analysis— Lease or Sell Equipment**

| | Differential Analysis Lease Equipment (Alternative 1) or Sell Equipment (Alternative 2) June 22, 2012 | | |
|---|---|---|---|
| | Lease Equipment (Alternative 1) | Sell Equipment (Alternative 2) | Differential Effect on Income (Alternative 2) |
| Revenues............... | $160,000 | $100,000 | –$60,000 |
| Costs.................. | –35,000 | –6,000 | 29,000 |
| Income (loss)........... | $125,000 | $ 94,000 | –$31,000 |

If the equipment is sold, differential revenues will decrease by $60,000, differential costs will decrease by $29,000, and the differential effect on income is a decrease of $31,000. Thus, the decision should be to lease the equipment.

Exhibit 2 includes only the differential revenues and differential costs associated with the lease-or-sell decision. The $80,000 book value ($200,000 – $120,000) of the equipment is a *sunk* cost and is not considered in the differential analysis. **Sunk costs** are costs that have been incurred in the past, cannot be recouped, and are not relevant to future decisions. That is, the $80,000 is not affected regardless of which decision is made. For example, if the $80,000 were included in Exhibit 2, the costs for each alternative would both increase by $80,000, but the differential effect on income of –$31,000 would remain unchanged.

Have you ever walked out on a bad movie? The cost of the ticket is a sunk cost and, thus, irrelevant to the decision to walk out early.

To simplify, the following factors were not considered in Exhibit 2:

1. Differential revenue from investing funds
2. Differential income tax

Differential revenue, such as interest revenue, could arise from investing the cash created by the two alternatives. Differential income tax could also arise from differences in income. These factors are discussed in Chapter 25.

---

**Example Exercise 24-1 Lease or Sell** **OBJ. 1**

Casper Company owns office space with a cost of $100,000 and accumulated depreciation of $30,000 that can be sold for $150,000, less a 6% broker commission. Alternatively, the office space can be leased by Casper Company for 10 years for a total of $170,000, at the end of which there is no residual value. In addition, repair, insurance, and property tax that would be incurred by Casper Company on the rented office space would total $24,000 over the 10 years. Prepare a differential analysis on May 30, 2012, as to whether Casper Company should lease (Alternative 1) or sell (Alternative 2) the office space.

**Follow My Example 24-1**

**Differential Analysis**
**Lease Office Space (Alternative 1) or Sell Office Space (Alternative 2)**
**May 30, 2012**

| | Lease Office Space (Alternative 1) | Sell Office Space (Alternative 2) | Differential Effect on Income (Alternative 2) |
|---|---|---|---|
| Revenues............................................ | $170,000 | $150,000 | –$20,000 |
| Costs.................................................. | –24,000 | –9,000* | 15,000 |
| Income (loss)..................................... | $146,000 | $141,000 | –$ 5,000 |

*$150,000 × 6%

Casper Company should lease the office space.

Practice Exercises: **PE 24-1A, PE 24-1B**

---

## Discontinue a Segment or Product

A product, department, branch, territory, or other segment of a business may be generating losses. As a result, management may consider discontinuing (eliminating) the product or segment. In such cases, it may be erroneously assumed that the total company income will increase by eliminating the operating loss.

Discontinuing the product or segment usually eliminates all of the product's or segment's variable costs. Such costs include direct materials, direct labor, variable factory overhead, and sales commissions. However, fixed costs such as depreciation, insurance, and property taxes may not be eliminated. Thus, it is possible for total company income to decrease rather than increase if the unprofitable product or segment is discontinued.

To illustrate, the income statement for Battle Creek Cereal Co. is shown in Exhibit 3. As shown in Exhibit 3, Bran Flakes incurred an operating loss of $11,000. Because Bran Flakes has incurred annual losses for several years, management is considering discontinuing it.

**EXHIBIT 3**

**Income (Loss) by Product**

| | Corn Flakes | Toasted Oats | Bran Flakes | Total Company |
|---|---|---|---|---|
| Sales..................................... | $500,000 | $400,000 | $100,000 | $1,000,000 |
| Cost of goods sold: | | | | |
| Variable costs........................ | $220,000 | $200,000 | $ 60,000 | $ 480,000 |
| Fixed costs ......................... | 120,000 | 80,000 | 20,000 | 220,000 |
| Total cost of goods sold............ | $340,000 | $280,000 | $ 80,000 | $ 700,000 |
| Gross profit............................. | $160,000 | $120,000 | $ 20,000 | $ 300,000 |
| Operating expenses: | | | | |
| Variable expenses.................... | $ 95,000 | $ 60,000 | $ 25,000 | $ 180,000 |
| Fixed expenses....................... | 25,000 | 20,000 | 6,000 | 51,000 |
| Total operating expenses .......... | $120,000 | $ 80,000 | $ 31,000 | $ 231,000 |
| Income (loss) from operations............. | $ 40,000 | $ 40,000 | $ (11,000) | $ 69,000 |

Battle Creek Cereal Co.
Condensed Income Statement
For the Year Ended August 31, 2012

If Bran Flakes is discontinued, what would be the total annual operating income of Battle Creek Cereal? The first impression is that total annual operating income would be $80,000, as shown below.

| | Corn Flakes | Toasted Oats | Total Company |
|---|---|---|---|
| Income from operations | $40,000 | $40,000 | $80,000 |

However, the differential analysis dated September 29, 2012, in Exhibit 4 indicates that discontinuing Bran Flakes (Alternative 2) actually decreases operating income by $15,000. This is because discontinuing Bran Flakes has no effect on fixed costs and expenses. This is confirmed by the income statement analysis in Exhibit 5, which indicates that income from operations would decrease from $69,000 to $54,000 if Bran Flakes were discontinued.

Exhibits 4 and 5 consider only the short-term (one-year) effects of discontinuing Bran Flakes. When discontinuing a product or segment, long-term effects should also be considered. For example, discontinuing Bran Flakes could decrease sales of other products. This might be the case if customers upset with the discontinuance of Bran Flakes quit buying other products from the company. Finally, employee morale and productivity might suffer if employees have to be laid off or relocated.

**EXHIBIT 4**

**Differential Analysis— Continue or Discontinue Bran Flakes**

Differential Analysis
Continue Bran Flakes (Alternative 1) or Discontinue Bran Flakes (Alternative 2)
September 29, 2012

| | Continue Bran Flakes (Alternative 1) | Discontinue Bran Flakes (Alternative 2) | Differential Effect on Income (Alternative 2) |
|---|---|---|---|
| Revenues.......................... | $100,000 | $ 0 | −$100,000 |
| Costs: | | | |
| Variable........................ | −$ 85,000 | $ 0 | $ 85,000 |
| Fixed ......................... | −26,000 | −26,000 | 0 |
| Total costs..................... | −$111,000 | −$26,000 | $ 85,000 |
| Income (loss)..................... | −$ 11,000 | −$26,000 | −$ 15,000 |

EXHIBIT 5

Income
Statement
Analysis

**Proposal to Discontinue Bran Flakes**
**September 29, 2012**

| | Bran Flakes, Toasted Oats, and Corn Flakes | Discontinue Bran Flakes* | Toasted Oats and Corn Flakes |
|---|---|---|---|
| Sales | $1,000,000 | $100,000 | $900,000 |
| Cost of goods sold: | | | |
| Variable costs | $ 480,000 | $ 60,000 | $420,000 |
| Fixed costs | 220,000 | 0 | 220,000 |
| Total cost of goods sold | $ 700,000 | $ 60,000 | $640,000 |
| Gross profit | $ 300,000 | $ 40,000 | $260,000 |
| Operating expenses: | | | |
| Variable expenses | $ 180,000 | $ 25,000 | $155,000 |
| Fixed expenses | 51,000 | 0 | 51,000 |
| Total operating expenses | $ 231,000 | $ 25,000 | $206,000 |
| **Income (loss) from operations** | **$ 69,000** | **$ 15,000** | **$ 54,000** |

*Fixed costs are assumed to remain unchanged with the discontinuance of Bran Flakes.

---

**Example Exercise** ❯ **24-2** ❯ **Discontinue a Segment**                    **OBJ. 1**

Product K has revenue of $65,000, variable cost of goods sold of $50,000, variable selling expenses of $12,000, and fixed costs of $25,000, creating a loss from operations of $22,000. Prepare a differential analysis dated February 22, 2012, to determine if Product K should be continued (Alternative 1) or discontinued (Alternative 2).

**Follow My Example** ❯ **24-2** ❯

**Differential Analysis**
**Continue K (Alternative 1) or Discontinue K (Alternative 2)**
**February 22, 2012**

| | Continue Product K (Alternative 1) | Discontinue Product K (Alternative 2) | Differential Effect on Income (Alternative 2) |
|---|---|---|---|
| Revenues | $65,000 | $ 0 | −$65,000 |
| Costs: | | | |
| Variable | −$62,000* | $ 0 | $62,000 |
| Fixed | −25,000 | −25,000 | 0 |
| Total costs | −$87,000 | −$25,000 | $62,000 |
| Income (loss) | −$22,000 | −$25,000 | −$ 3,000 |

*$50,000 + $12,000

Product K should be continued.

Practice Exercises: **PE 24-2A, PE 24-2B**

## Make or Buy

Companies often manufacture products made up of components that are assembled into a final product. For example, an automobile manufacturer assembles tires, radios, motors, interior seats, transmissions, and other parts into a finished automobile. In such cases, the manufacturer must decide whether to make a part or purchase it from a supplier.

Differential analysis can be used to decide whether to make or buy a part. The analysis is similar whether management is considering making a part that is currently being purchased or purchasing a part that is currently being made.

To illustrate, assume that an automobile manufacturer has been purchasing instrument panels for $240 a unit. The factory is currently operating at 80% of capacity, and no major increase in production is expected in the near future. The cost per unit of manufacturing an instrument panel internally is estimated on February 15, 2012, as follows:

| Direct materials | $ 80 |
|---|---|
| Direct labor | 80 |
| Variable factory overhead | 52 |
| Fixed factory overhead | 68 |
| Total cost per unit | $280 |

If the make price of $280 is simply compared with the buy price of $240, the decision is to buy the instrument panel. However, if unused capacity could be used in manufacturing the part, there would be no increase in the total fixed factory overhead costs. Thus, only the variable factory overhead costs would be incurred.

The differential analysis for this make (Alternative 1) or buy (Alternative 2) decision is shown in Exhibit 6. The fixed factory overhead cannot be eliminated by purchasing the panels; thus, both alternatives include the fixed factory overhead. The differential analysis indicates there is a loss of $28 per unit from buying the instrument panels. Thus, the instrument panels should be manufactured.

**EXHIBIT 6**

**Differential Analysis— Make or Buy Instrument Panels**

**Differential Analysis**
**Make Panels (Alternative 1) or Buy Panels (Alternative 2)**
**February 15, 2012**

| | Make Panels (Alternative 1) | Buy Panels (Alternative 2) | Differential Effect on Income (Alternative 2) |
|---|---|---|---|
| Costs: | | | |
| Purchase price .......................... | $ 0 | –$240 | –$240 |
| Direct materials ........................ | –80 | 0 | 80 |
| Direct labor ............................. | –80 | 0 | 80 |
| Variable factory overhead .............. | –52 | 0 | 52 |
| Fixed factory overhead ................. | –68 | –68 | 0 |
| Income (loss).......................... | –$280 | –$308 | –$ 28 |

Other factors should also be considered in the analysis. For example, productive capacity used to make the instrument panel would not be available for other production. The decision may also affect the future business relationship with the instrument panel supplier. For example, if the supplier provides other parts, the company's decision to make instrument panels might jeopardize the timely delivery of other parts.

**Example Exercise** **24-3** **Make or Buy** **OBJ. 1**

A company manufactures a subcomponent of an assembly for $80 per unit, including fixed costs of $25 per unit. A proposal is offered to purchase the subcomponent from an outside source for $60 per unit, plus $5 per unit freight. Prepare a differential analysis dated November 2, 2012, to determine whether the company should make (Alternative 1) or buy (Alternative 2) the subcomponent.

*(continued)*

**Follow My Example ⟩ 24-3 ⟩**

**Differential Analysis**
**Make Subcomponent (Alternative 1) or Buy Subcomponent (Alternative 2)**
**November 2, 2012**

|  | Make Subcomponent (Alternative 1) | Buy Subcomponent (Alternative 2) | Differential Effect on Income (Alternative 2) |
|---|---|---|---|
| Costs: |  |  |  |
| Purchase price............................................. | $ 0 | −$60 | −$60 |
| Freight............................................................. | 0 | −5 | −5 |
| Variable costs ($80 − $25)................................. | −55 | 0 | 55 |
| Fixed factory overhead................................. | −25 | −25 | 0 |
| Income (loss) ................................................. | −$80 | −$90 | −$10 |

The company should make the subcomponent.

Practice Exercises: **PE 24-3A, PE 24-3B**

## Replace Equipment

The usefulness of a fixed asset may decrease before it is worn out. For example, old equipment may no longer be as efficient as new equipment.

Differential analysis can be used for decisions to replace fixed assets such as equipment and machinery. The analysis normally focuses on the costs of continuing to use the old equipment versus replacing the equipment. The book value of the old equipment is a sunk cost and, thus, is irrelevant.

To illustrate, assume that on November 28, 2012, a business is considering replacing the following machine:

| | |
|---|---|
| Old Machine | |
| Book value | $100,000 |
| Estimated annual variable manufacturing costs | 225,000 |
| Estimated selling price | 25,000 |
| Estimated remaining useful life | 5 years |
| New Machine | |
| Cost of new machine | $250,000 |
| Estimated annual variable manufacturing costs | 150,000 |
| Estimated residual value | 0 |
| Estimated useful life | 5 years |

The differential analysis for whether to continue with the old machine (Alternative 1) or replace the old machine with a new machine (Alternative 2) is shown in Exhibit 7.

**EXHIBIT 7**

**Differential Analysis— Continue with or Replace Old Equipment**

**Differential Analysis**
**Continue with Old Machine (Alternative 1) or Replace Old Machine (Alternative 2)**
**November 28, 2012**

|  | Continue with Old Machine (Alternative 1) | Replace Old Machine (Alternative 2) | Differential Effect on Income (Alternative 2) |
|---|---|---|---|
| Revenues: |  |  |  |
| Proceeds from sale of old machine ......... | $        0 | $    25,000 | $  25,000 |
| Costs: |  |  |  |
| Purchase price  ........................... | $        0 | −$  250,000 | −$250,000 |
| Annual variable costs (5 years) ............. | −1,125,000 | −750,000 | 375,000 |
| Total costs................................. | −$1,125,000 | −$1,000,000 | $125,000 |
| Income (loss) ................................ | −$1,125,000 | −$  975,000 | $150,000 |

Differential effect on
income, $30,000 per year

As shown in Exhibit 7, there is five-year differential effect on income of $150,000 (or $30,000 per year) from replacing the machine. Thus, the decision should be to purchase the new machine and sell the old machine.

Other factors are often important in equipment replacement decisions. For example, differences between the remaining useful life of the old equipment and the estimated life of the new equipment could exist. In addition, the new equipment might improve the overall quality of the product and, thus, increase sales.

The time value of money and other uses for the cash needed to purchase the new equipment could also affect the decision to replace equipment.[1] The revenue that is forgone from an alternative use of an asset, such as cash, is called an **opportunity cost**. Although the opportunity cost is not recorded in the accounting records, it is useful in analyzing alternative courses of action.

To illustrate, assume that in the preceding illustration the cash outlay of $250,000 for the new machine, less the $25,000 proceeds from the sale of the old machine, could be invested to yield a 15% return. Thus, the annual opportunity cost related to the purchase of the new machine is $33,750 (15% × $225,000). Since the opportunity cost of $33,750 exceeds the annual cost savings of $30,000, the old machine should not be replaced.

---

## Example Exercise ▶ 24-4 ▶ Replace Equipment                    OBJ. 1

A machine with a book value of $32,000 has an estimated four-year life. A proposal is offered to sell the old machine for $10,000 and replace it with a new machine at a cost of $45,000. The new machine has a four-year life with no residual value. The new machine would reduce annual direct labor costs from $33,000 to $22,000. Prepare a differential analysis dated October 7, 2012, on whether to continue with the old machine (Alternative 1) or replace the old machine (Alternative 2).

## Follow My Example ▶ 24-4 ▶

**Differential Analysis**
**Continue with Old Machine (Alternative 1) or Replace Old Machine (Alternative 2)**
**October 7, 2012**

|  | Continue with Old Machine (Alternative 1) | Replace Old Machine (Alternative 2) | Differential Effect on Income (Alternative 2) |
|---|---|---|---|
| Revenues: |  |  |  |
|   Proceeds from sale of old machine | $ 0 | $ 10,000 | $10,000 |
| Costs: |  |  |  |
|   Purchase price | $ 0 | –$ 45,000 | –$45,000 |
|   Direct labor (4 years) | –132,000* | –88,000** | 44,000 |
|   Total costs | –$132,000 | –$133,000 | –$ 1,000 |
| Total income (loss) | –$132,000 | –$123,000 | $ 9,000 |

  *$33,000 × 4 years
**$22,000 × 4 years

The old machine should be sold and replaced with the new machine.

· · · · · · · · · · · · · · · · · · · · · · · · · · · · · · · · · · · · · · · · · · · · · · · · · · · · · · · · · · · · · · · · · · · · · · · · · · · · · · · · · · · · · · · · · · · · · · · · · · · · · · · · · · · · · · · · · · · · · · · · · · · · · · · · · · · · · · · · · · · · · · · · · · · · · ·

Practice Exercises: **PE 24-4A, PE 24-4B**

---

1 The time value of money in purchasing equipment (capital assets) is discussed in Chapter 25.

## Process or Sell

During manufacturing, a product normally progresses through various stages or processes. In some cases, a product can be sold at an intermediate stage of production, or it can be processed further and then sold.

Differential analysis can be used to decide whether to sell a product at an intermediate stage or to process it further. In doing so, the differential revenues and costs from further processing are compared. The costs of producing the intermediate product do not change, regardless of whether the intermediate product is sold or processed further.

To illustrate, assume that a business produces kerosene as follows:

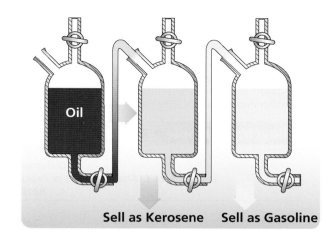

Kerosene:

|  |  |
|---|---|
| Batch size | 4,000 gallons |
| Cost of producing kerosene | $2,400 per batch |
| Selling price | $2.50 per gallon |

The kerosene can be processed further to yield gasoline as follows:

Gasoline:

|  |  |
|---|---|
| Input batch size | 4,000 gallons |
| Less evaporation (20%) | 800 (4,000 × 20%) |
| Output batch size | 3,200 gallons |
|  |  |
| Cost of producing gasoline | $3,050 per batch |
| Selling price | $3.50 per gallon |

Exhibit 8 shows the differential analysis dated October 1, 2012, for whether to sell kerosene (Alternative 1) or process it further into gasoline (Alternative 2).

**EXHIBIT 8**

**Differential Analysis—Sell Kerosene or Process Further into Gasoline**

**Differential Analysis**
**Sell Kerosene (Alternative 1) or Process Further into Gasoline (Alternative 2)**
**October 1, 2012**

|  | Sell Kerosene (Alternative 1) | Process Further into Gasoline (Alternative 2) | Differential Effect on Income (Alternative 2) |
|---|---|---|---|
| Revenues.......................... | $10,000* | $11,200** | $1,200 |
| Costs.............................. | −2,400 | −3,050 | −650 |
| Income (loss) ...................... | $ 7,600 | $ 8,150 | $ 550 |

*4,000 gallons × $2.50
**(4,000 gallons − 800 gallons) × $3.50

As shown in Exhibit 8, there is additional income from further processing the kerosene into gasoline of $550 per batch. Therefore, the decision should be to process the kerosene further into gasoline.

**Example Exercise** 24-5 **Process or Sell**

**OBJ.**
**1**

Product T is produced for $2.50 per gallon. Product T can be sold without additional processing for $3.50 per gallon, or processed further into Product V at an additional total cost of $0.70 per gallon. Product V can be sold for $4.00 per gallon. Prepare a differential analysis dated April 8, 2012, on whether to sell Product T (Alternative 1) or process it further into Product V (Alternative 2).

**Follow My Example** 24-5

**Differential Analysis**
**Sell Product T (Alternative 1) or Process Further into Product V (Alternative 2)**
**April 8, 2012**

|  | Sell Product T (Alternative 1) | Process Further into Product V (Alternative 2) | Differential Effect on Income (Alternative 2) |
|---|---|---|---|
| Revenues, per unit............................................................... | $3.50 | $4.00 | $0.50 |
| Costs, per unit .................................................................... | –2.50 | –3.20* | –0.70 |
| Income (loss), per unit ...................................................... | $1.00 | $0.80 | –$0.20 |

*$2.50 + $0.70

The decision should be to sell Product T.

Practice Exercises: **PE 24-5A, PE 24-5B**

## Accept Business at a Special Price

A company may be offered the opportunity to sell its products at prices other than normal prices. For example, an exporter may offer to sell a company's products overseas at special discount prices.

Differential analysis can be used to decide whether to accept additional business at a special price. The differential revenue from accepting the additional business is compared to the differential costs of producing and delivering the product to the customer.

The differential costs of accepting additional business depend on whether the company is operating at full capacity.

1. If the company is *operating at full capacity,* any additional production increases fixed and variable manufacturing costs. Selling and administrative expenses may also increase because of the additional business.

2. If the company is *operating below full capacity,* any additional production does not increase fixed manufacturing costs. In this case, the differential costs of the additional production are the variable manufacturing costs. Selling and administrative expenses may also increase because of the additional business.

To illustrate, assume that B-Ball Inc. manufactures basketballs as follows:

| | |
|---|---|
| Monthly productive capacity | 12,500 basketballs |
| Current monthly sales | 10,000 basketballs |
| Normal (domestic) selling price | $30.00 per basketball |
| Manufacturing costs: | |
|     Variable costs | $12.50 per basketball |
|     Fixed costs | 7.50 |
|        Total | $20.00 per basketball |

Order for 5,000 basketballs at $18 each

On March 10, 2012, B-Ball Inc. has received an offer from an exporter for 5,000 basketballs at $18 each. Production can be spread over three months without interfering with normal production or incurring overtime costs. Pricing policies in the domestic market will not be affected.

Comparing the special offer sales price of $18 with the manufacturing cost of $20 per basketball indicates that the offer should be rejected. However, as shown in Exhibit 9, a differential analysis on whether to reject the order (Alternative 1) or accept the order (Alternative 2) shows that the special order should be accepted. This is because the fixed costs are not affected by the decision and thus are omitted from the analysis.

**EXHIBIT 9**

**Differential Analysis— Accept Business at a Special Price**

**Differential Analysis**
**Reject Order (Alternative 1) or Accept Order (Alternative 2)**
**March 10, 2012**

|  | Reject Order (Alternative 1) | Accept Order (Alternative 2) | Differential Effect on Income (Alternative 2) |
|---|---|---|---|
| Revenues.................................. | $0 | $90,000* | $90,000 |
| Costs: |  |  |  |
|    Variable manufacturing costs........... | 0 | –62,500** | –62,500 |
| Income (loss) ............................. | $0 | $27,500 | $27,500 |

*5,000 units × $18
**5,000 units × $12.50 variable cost per unit

Proposals to sell products at special prices often require additional considerations. For example, special prices in one geographic area may result in price reductions in other areas with the result that total company sales revenues decrease. Manufacturers must also conform to the Robinson-Patman Act, which prohibits price discrimination within the United States unless price differences can be justified by different costs.

## BusinessConnection

### NAME YOUR OWN PRICE

Priceline.com Inc. was founded in the late 1990s and has become a successful survivor of the Internet revolution. Priceline developed the "name your price®" bidding format, which can provide price discounts of up to 60% for travel services. How does it work? For hotel services, Priceline has arrangements with hotels to provide discounted rooms. These rooms are sold to customers based on a name-your-own-price bid. Customers must identify a zone (approximate location for the hotel), quality level,

and dates; then submit a price bid for a hotel. If you place a bid that is rejected, you can try again after 24 hours. If your bid is accepted, you are committed to pay for the hotel that has been selected according to your criteria. Why do hotels provide rooms at such a large discount? The hotels are accepting business at a special price. If the hotel has unused rooms, the variable cost of an incremental guest is low relative to the fixed cost of the room. Thus, during low occupancy times, any price above the variable cost of providing the room can add to the profitability of the hotel.

### *Example Exercise* 24-6 ▶ Accept Business at Special Price

**OBJ. 1**

Product D is normally sold for $4.40 per unit. A special price of $3.60 is offered for the export market. The variable production cost is $3.00 per unit. An additional export tariff of 10% of revenue must be paid for all export products. Assume there is sufficient capacity for the special order. Prepare a differential analysis dated January 14, 2012, on whether to reject (Alternative 1) or accept (Alternative 2) the special order.

*(continued)*

**Follow My Example 24-6**

**Differential Analysis**
**Reject Order (Alternative 1) or Accept Order (Alternative 2)**
**January 14, 2012**

| | Reject Order (Alternative 1) | Accept Order (Alternative 2) | Differential Effect on Income (Alternative 2) |
|---|---|---|---|
| Revenues, per unit................................................................ | $0 | $3.60 | $3.60 |
| Costs: | | | |
| Variable manufacturing costs, per unit......................... | $0 | −$3.00 | −$3.00 |
| Export tariff, per unit........................................................ | 0 | −0.36* | −0.36 |
| Total costs.......................................................................... | $0 | −$3.36 | −$3.36 |
| Income (loss), per unit ..................................................... | $0 | $0.24 | $0.24 |

*$3.60 × 10%

The special order should be accepted.

Practice Exercises: **PE 24-6A, PE 24-6B**

**OBJ. 2** Determine the selling price of a product, using the product cost concept.

Hotels and motels use the demand-based concept in setting room rates. Room rates are set low during off-season travel periods (low demand) and high for peak-season travel periods (high demand) such as holidays.

# Setting Normal Product Selling Prices

The *normal* selling price is the target selling price to be achieved in the long term. The normal selling price must be set high enough to cover all costs and expenses (fixed and variable) and provide a reasonable profit. Otherwise, the business will not survive.

In contrast, in deciding whether to accept additional business at a special price, only differential costs are considered. Any price above the differential costs will increase profits in the short term. However, in the long term, products are sold at normal prices rather than special prices.

Managers can use one of two market methods to determine selling price:

1. Demand-based concept
2. Competition-based concept

The demand-based concept sets the price according to the demand for the product. If there is high demand for the product, then the price is set high. Likewise, if there is a low demand for the product, then the price is set low.

The competition-based concept sets the price according to the price offered by competitors. For example, if a competitor reduces the price, then management adjusts the price to meet the competition. The market-based pricing approaches are discussed in greater detail in marketing courses.

Managers can also use one of three cost-plus methods to determine the selling price:

1. Product cost concept
2. Total cost concept
3. Variable cost concept

The product cost concept is illustrated in this section. The total cost and variable cost concepts are illustrated in the appendix to this chapter.

## Integrity, Objectivity, and Ethics in Business

### PRICE FIXING

Federal law prevents companies competing in similar markets from sharing cost and price information, or what is commonly termed "price fixing." For example, the Federal Trade Commission brought a suit against the major record labels and music retailers for conspiring to set CD prices at a minimum level, or MAP (minimum advertised price). In settling the suit, the major labels ceased their MAP policies and provided $143 million in cash and CDs for consumers.

# Product Cost Concept

Cost-plus methods determine the normal selling price by estimating a cost amount per unit and adding a markup, as shown below.

Normal Selling Price = Cost Amount per Unit + Markup

Management determines the markup based on the desired profit for the product. The markup should be sufficient to earn the desired profit plus cover any costs and expenses that are not included in the cost amount.

Under the **product cost concept**, only the costs of manufacturing the product, termed the *product costs,* are included in the cost amount per unit to which the markup is added. Estimated selling expenses, administrative expenses, and desired profit are included in the markup. The markup per unit is then computed and added to the product cost per unit to determine the normal selling price.

The product cost concept is applied using the following steps:

Step 1. Estimate the total product costs as follows:

**PRODUCT COST CONCEPT**

| Product costs: | |
|---|---|
| Direct materials | $XXX |
| Direct labor | XXX |
| Factory overhead | XXX |
| Total product cost | $XXX |

Step 2. Estimate the total selling and administrative expenses.

Step 3. Divide the total product cost by the number of units expected to be produced and sold to determine the total product cost per unit, as shown below.

$$\text{Product Cost per Unit} = \frac{\text{Total Product Cost}}{\text{Estimated Units Produced and Sold}}$$

Step 4. Compute the markup percentage as follows:

$$\text{Markup Percentage} = \frac{\text{Desired Profit} + \text{Total Selling and Administrative Expenses}}{\text{Total Product Cost}}$$

The numerator of the markup percentage is the desired profit plus the total selling and administrative expenses. These expenses must be included in the markup percentage, since they are not included in the cost amount to which the markup is added.

The desired profit is normally computed based on a rate of return on assets as follows:

Desired Profit = Desired Rate of Return × Total Assets

Step 5. Determine the markup per unit by multiplying the markup percentage times the product cost per unit as follows:

Markup per Unit = Markup Percentage × Product Cost per Unit

Step 6. Determine the normal selling price by adding the markup per unit to the product cost per unit as follows:

| Product cost per unit | $XXX |
|---|---|
| Markup per unit | XXX |
| Normal selling price per unit | $XXX |

To illustrate, assume the following data for 100,000 calculators that Digital Solutions Inc. expects to produce and sell during the current year:

| | |
|---|---|
| Manufacturing costs: | |
| Direct materials ($3.00 × 100,000) | $ 300,000 |
| Direct labor ($10.00 × 100,000) | 1,000,000 |
| Factory overhead | 200,000 |
| Total manufacturing costs | $1,500,000 |
| Selling and administrative expenses | 170,000 |
| Total cost | $1,670,000 |
| Total assets | $800,000 |
| Desired rate of return | 20% |

The normal selling price of $18.30 is determined under the product cost concept as follows:

Step 1. Total product cost: $1,500,000

Step 2. Total selling and administrative expenses: $170,000

Step 3. Total product cost per unit: $15.00

$$\text{Total Cost per Unit} = \frac{\text{Total Product Cost}}{\text{Estimated Units Produced and Sold}} = \frac{\$1,500,000}{100,000 \text{ units}} = \$15.00 \text{ per unit}$$

Step 4. Markup percentage: 22%

$$\text{Desired Profit} = \text{Desired Rate of Return} \times \text{Total Assets} = 20\% \times \$800,000 = \$160,000$$

$$\text{Markup Percentage} = \frac{\text{Desired Profit} + \text{Total Selling and Administrative Expenses}}{\text{Total Product Cost}}$$

$$\text{Markup Percentage} = \frac{\$160,000 + \$170,000}{\$1,500,000} = \frac{\$330,000}{\$1,500,000} = 22\%$$

Step 5. Markup per unit: $3.30

$$\text{Markup per Unit} = \text{Markup Percentage} \times \text{Product Cost per Unit}$$
$$\text{Markup per Unit} = 22\% \times \$15.00 = \$3.30 \text{ per unit}$$

Step 6. Normal selling price: $18.30

| | |
|---|---:|
| Total product cost per unit | $15.00 |
| Markup per unit | 3.30 |
| Normal selling price per unit | $18.30 |

---

**Example Exercise 24-7 Product Cost Markup Percentage** OBJ. 2

Apex Corporation produces and sells Product Z at a total cost of $30 per unit, of which $20 is product cost and $10 is selling and administrative expenses. In addition, the total cost of $30 is made up of $18 variable cost and $12 fixed cost. The desired profit is $3 per unit. Determine the markup percentage on product cost.

**Follow My Example 24-7**

Markup percentage on product cost: $\dfrac{\$3 + \$10}{\$20} = 65.0\%$

Practice Exercises: **PE 24-7A, PE 24-7B**

---

# BusinessConnection

## iPAD PRODUCT COST

Market research firm iSuppli opened up an Apple iPad® to estimate its total variable manufacturing cost. After listing and analyzing all of the components, it determined that the iPad has a total variable production cost of $259.60. This is about 52% of the retail price, which is estimated to be in line with other Apple products. Of the $259.60, much of the costs went toward making the product easy and appealing to use. More than 40% of the iPad's cost is devoted to powering the touch screen interface, including the screen itself from LG Display Co., the touch-sensitive glass overlay from Wintek Corp., and the silicon chips from Texas Instruments that power the screen interactions. The unique aluminum casing is estimated to contribute $10.50 to the cost. The main processor chip is likely designed by PA Semi, an Apple acquisition, with an estimated production cost of $26.80 by Samsung. As illustrated with the iPad, sophisticated products require extensive collaboration across many different companies to provide exciting product features at a reasonable cost.

Source: A. Hesseldahl, "Apple iPad Components May Cost as Little as $260, iSuppli Says," *Bloomberg Business Week*, April 7, 2010.

Product cost estimates, rather than actual costs, may be used in computing the markup. Management should be careful, however, when using estimated or standard costs in applying the cost-plus approach. Specifically, estimates should be based on normal (attainable) operating levels and not theoretical (ideal) levels of performance. In product pricing, the use of estimates based on ideal operating performance could lead to setting product prices too low.

## Target Costing

**Target costing** is a method of setting prices that combines market-based pricing with a cost-reduction emphasis. Under target costing, a future selling price is anticipated, using the demand-based or the competition-based concepts. The target cost is then determined by subtracting a desired profit from the expected selling price, as shown below.

Target Cost = Expected Selling Price – Desired Profit

Target costing tries to reduce costs as shown in Exhibit 10. The bar at the left in Exhibit 10 shows the actual cost and profit that can be earned during the current period. The bar at the right shows that the market price is expected to decline in the future. The target cost is estimated as the difference between the expected market price and the desired profit.

The target cost is normally less than the current cost. Thus, managers must try to reduce costs from the design and manufacture of the product. The planned cost reduction is sometimes referred to as the cost "drift." Costs can be reduced in a variety of ways such as the following:

1. Simplifying the design
2. Reducing the cost of direct materials
3. Reducing the direct labor costs
4. Eliminating waste

Target costing is especially useful in highly competitive markets such as the market for personal computers. Such markets require continual product cost reductions to remain competitive.

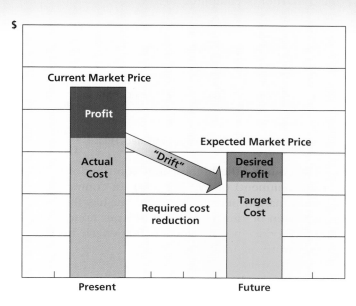

**EXHIBIT 10**

**Target Cost Concept**

## Production Bottlenecks, Pricing, and Profits

**OBJ. 3** Compute the relative profitability of products in bottleneck production processes.

A **production bottleneck** (or *constraint*) is a point in the manufacturing process where the demand for the company's product exceeds the ability to produce the product. The **theory of constraints (TOC)** is a manufacturing strategy that focuses on reducing the influence of bottlenecks on production processes.

## Production Bottlenecks and Profits

When a company has a production bottleneck in its production process, it should attempt to maximize its profits, subject to the production bottleneck. In doing so, the unit contribution margin of each product per production bottleneck constraint is used.

To illustrate, assume that PrideCraft Tool Company makes three types of wrenches: small, medium, and large. All three products are processed through a heat treatment operation, which hardens the steel tools. PrideCraft Tool's heat treatment process is operating at full capacity and is a production bottleneck. The product unit contribution margin and the number of hours of heat treatment used by each type of wrench are as follows:

The sand in the hourglass can pass only as fast as the narrowest point in the glass will allow.

Bottleneck

|  | Small Wrench | Medium Wrench | Large Wrench |
| --- | --- | --- | --- |
| Unit selling price | $130 | $140 | $160 |
| Unit variable cost | 40 | 40 | 40 |
| Unit contribution margin | $ 90 | $100 | $120 |
| Heat treatment hours per unit | 1 hr. | 4 hrs. | 8 hrs. |

The large wrench appears to be the most profitable product because its unit contribution margin of $120 is the greatest. However, the unit contribution margin can be misleading in a production bottleneck operation.

In a production bottleneck operation, the best measure of profitability is the unit contribution margin per production bottleneck constraint. For PrideCraft Tool, the production bottleneck constraint is heat treatment process hours. Therefore, the unit contribution margin per bottleneck constraint is expressed as follows:

$$\text{Unit Contribution Margin per Production Bottleneck Hour} = \frac{\text{Unit Contribution Margin}}{\text{Heat Treatment Hours per Unit}}$$

The unit contribution per production bottleneck hour for each of the wrenches produced by PrideCraft Tool is computed below.

Small Wrenches

$$\text{Unit Contribution Margin per Production Bottleneck Hour} = \frac{\$90}{1 \text{ hr.}} = \$90 \text{ per hr.}$$

Medium Wrenches

$$\text{Unit Contribution Margin per Production Bottleneck Hour} = \frac{\$100}{4 \text{ hrs.}} = \$25 \text{ per hr.}$$

Large Wrenches

$$\text{Unit Contribution Margin per Production Bottleneck Hour} = \frac{\$120}{8 \text{ hrs.}} = \$15 \text{ per hr.}$$

The small wrench produces the highest unit contribution margin per production bottleneck hour (heat treatment) of $90 per hour. In contrast, the large wrench has the largest contribution margin per unit of $120, but has the smallest unit contribution margin per production bottleneck hour of $15 per hour. Thus, the small wrench is the most profitable product per production bottleneck hour and is the one that should be emphasized in the market.

## Production Bottlenecks and Pricing

When a company has a production bottleneck, the unit contribution margin per bottleneck hour is a measure of each product's profitability. This measure can be used to adjust product prices to reflect the product's use of the bottleneck.

To illustrate, the large wrench produced by PrideCraft Tool Company uses eight bottleneck hours, but produces a contribution margin per unit of only $120. As a result, the large wrench is the least profitable of the wrenches per bottleneck hour ($15 per hour).

PrideCraft Tool Company can improve the profitability of producing large wrenches by any combination of the following:

1. Increase the selling price of the large wrenches.
2. Decrease the variable cost per unit of the large wrenches.
3. Decrease the heat treatment hours required for the large wrenches.

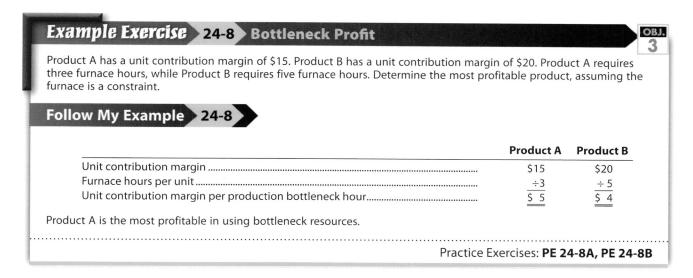

**Example Exercise** 24-8 **Bottleneck Profit**

OBJ. 3

Product A has a unit contribution margin of $15. Product B has a unit contribution margin of $20. Product A requires three furnace hours, while Product B requires five furnace hours. Determine the most profitable product, assuming the furnace is a constraint.

**Follow My Example** 24-8

|  | Product A | Product B |
| --- | --- | --- |
| Unit contribution margin ................................................................................................................ | $15 | $20 |
| Furnace hours per unit ..................................................................................................................... | ÷3 | ÷5 |
| Unit contribution margin per production bottleneck hour............................................. | $ 5 | $ 4 |

Product A is the most profitable in using bottleneck resources.

Practice Exercises: **PE 24-8A, PE 24-8B**

Assume that the variable cost per unit and the heat treatment hours for the large wrench cannot be decreased. In this case, PrideCraft Tool might be able to increase the selling price of the large wrenches.

The price of the large wrench that would make it as profitable as the small wrench is determined as follows:[2]

$$\text{Unit Contribution Margin per Bottleneck Hour for Small Wrench} = \frac{\text{Revised Price of Large Wrench} - \text{Unit Variable Cost for Large Wrench}}{\text{Bottleneck Hours per Unit for Large Wrench}}$$

$$\$90 = \frac{\text{Revised Price of Large Wrench} - \$40}{8}$$

$$\$720 = \text{Revised Price of Large Wrench} - \$40$$

$$\$760 = \text{Revised Price of Large Wrench}$$

If the large wrench's price is increased to $760, it would provide the same unit contribution margin per bottleneck hour as the small wrench, as shown below.

$$\text{Unit Contribution Margin per Bottleneck Hour} = \frac{\text{Unit Contribution Margin}}{\text{Heat Treatment Hours per Unit}}$$

$$\text{Unit Contribution Margin per Bottleneck Hour} = \frac{\$760 - \$40}{8 \text{ hrs.}} = \$90 \text{ per hr.}$$

At a price of $760, PrideCraft Tool Company would be indifferent between producing and selling the small wrench or the large wrench. This assumes that there is unlimited demand for the products. If the market were unwilling to purchase the large wrench at a price of $760, then the company should produce and sell the small wrenches.

---

2 Assuming that the selling price of the large wrench cannot be increased, the same approach (equation) could be used to determine the decrease in variable cost per unit or the decrease in bottleneck hours that is required to make the large wrench as profitable as the small wrench.

# A P P E N D I X

# Total and Variable Cost Concepts to Setting Normal Price

Recall from the chapter that cost-plus methods determine the normal selling price by estimating a cost amount per unit and adding a markup, as shown below.

$$\text{Normal Selling Price} = \text{Cost Amount per Unit} + \text{Markup}$$

Management determines the markup based on the desired profit for the product. The markup should be sufficient to earn the desired profit plus cover any cost and expenses that are not included in the cost amount. The product cost concept was discussed in the chapter, and the total and variable cost concepts are discussed in this appendix.

## Total Cost Concept

Under the **total cost concept**, manufacturing cost plus the selling and administrative expenses are included in the total cost per unit. The markup per unit is then computed and added to the total cost per unit to determine the normal selling price.

The total cost concept is applied using the following steps:

Step 1.   Estimate the total manufacturing cost as shown below.

| Manufacturing costs: | |
|---|---|
| Direct materials | $XXX |
| Direct labor | XXX |
| Factory overhead | XXX |
| Total manufacturing cost | $XXX |

Step 2.   Estimate the total selling and administrative expenses.
Step 3.   Estimate the total cost as shown below.

| Total manufacturing costs | $XXX |
|---|---|
| Selling and administrative expenses | XXX |
| Total cost | $XXX |

TOTAL COST CONCEPT

**MARKUP:**
Desired Profit

**TOTAL COST:**
Manufacturing Cost
**+**
Administrative Expense
**+**
Selling Expense

Step 4.   Divide the total cost by the number of units expected to be produced and sold to determine the total cost per unit, as shown below.

$$\text{Total Cost per Unit} = \frac{\text{Total Cost}}{\text{Estimated Units Produced and Sold}}$$

Step 5.   Compute the markup percentage as follows:

$$\text{Markup Percentage} = \frac{\text{Desired Profit}}{\text{Total Cost}}$$

The desired profit is normally computed based on a rate of return on assets as follows:

$$\text{Desired Profit} = \text{Desired Rate of Return} \times \text{Total Assets}$$

Step 6.   Determine the markup per unit by multiplying the markup percentage times the total cost per unit as follows:

$$\text{Markup per Unit} = \text{Markup Percentage} \times \text{Total Cost per Unit}$$

Step 7.  Determine the normal selling price by adding the markup per unit to the total cost per unit as follows:

| | |
|---|---|
| Total cost per unit | $XXX |
| Markup per unit | XXX |
| Normal selling price per unit | $XXX |

To illustrate, assume the following data for 100,000 calculators that Digital Solutions Inc. expects to produce and sell during the current year:

| | | |
|---|---|---|
| Manufacturing costs: | | |
| Direct materials ($3.00 × 100,000) | | $ 300,000 |
| Direct labor ($10.00 × 100,000) | | 1,000,000 |
| Factory overhead: | | |
| Variable costs ($1.50 × 100,000) | $150,000 | |
| Fixed costs | 50,000 | 200,000 |
| Total manufacturing cost | | $1,500,000 |
| Selling and administrative expenses: | | |
| Variable expenses ($1.50 × 100,000) | $150,000 | |
| Fixed costs | 20,000 | |
| Total selling and administrative expenses | | 170,000 |
| Total cost | | $1,670,000 |
| Desired rate of return | | 20% |
| Total assets | | $ 800,000 |

Using the total cost concept, the normal selling price of $18.30 is determined as follows:

Step 1.  Total manufacturing cost: $1,500,000

Step 2.  Total selling and administrative expenses: $170,000

Step 3.  Total cost: $1,670,000

Step 4.  Total cost per unit: $16.70

$$\text{Total Cost per Unit} = \frac{\text{Total Cost}}{\text{Estimated Units Produced and Sold}} = \frac{\$1,670,000}{100,000 \text{ units}} = \$16.70 \text{ per unit}$$

Step 5.  Markup percentage: 9.6% (rounded)

Desired Profit = Desired Rate of Return × Total Assets = 20% × $800,000 = $160,000

$$\text{Markup Percentage} = \frac{\text{Desired Profit}}{\text{Total Cost}} = \frac{\$160,000}{\$1,670,000} = 9.6\% \text{ (rounded)}$$

Step 6.  Markup per unit: $1.60

Markup per Unit = Markup Percentage × Total Cost per Unit
Markup per Unit = 9.6% × $16.70 = $1.60 per unit

Step 7.  Normal selling price: $18.30

| | |
|---|---|
| Total cost per unit | $16.70 |
| Markup per unit | 1.60 |
| Normal selling price per unit | $18.30 |

The ability of the selling price of $18.30 to generate the desired profit of $160,000 is illustrated by the income statement shown below.

**Digital Solutions Inc.**
**Income Statement**
**For the Year Ended December 31, 2012**

| | | |
|---|---|---|
| Sales (100,000 units × $18.30) | | $1,830,000 |
| Expenses: | | |
| Variable (100,000 units × $16.00) | $1,600,000 | |
| Fixed ($50,000 + $20,000) | 70,000 | 1,670,000 |
| Income from operations | | $ 160,000 |

The total cost concept is often used by contractors who sell products to government agencies. This is because in many cases government contractors are required by law to be reimbursed for their products on a total-cost-plus-profit basis.

## Variable Cost Concept

Under the **variable cost concept**, only variable costs are included in the cost amount per unit to which the markup is added. All variable manufacturing costs, as well as variable selling and administrative expenses, are included in the cost amount. Fixed manufacturing costs, fixed selling and administrative expenses, and desired profit are included in the markup. The markup per unit is then added to the variable cost per unit to determine the normal selling price.

The variable cost concept is applied using the following steps:

**Step 1.** Estimate the total variable product cost as follows:

| | |
|---|---|
| Variable product costs: | |
| Direct materials | $XXX |
| Direct labor | XXX |
| Variable factory overhead | XXX |
| Total variable product cost | $XXX |

**Step 2.** Estimate the total variable selling and administrative expenses.

**Step 3.** Determine the total variable cost as follows:

| | |
|---|---|
| Total variable product cost | $XXX |
| Total variable selling and administrative expenses | XXX |
| Total variable cost | $XXX |

**Step 4.** Compute the variable cost per unit as follows:

$$\text{Variable Cost per Unit} = \frac{\text{Total Variable Cost}}{\text{Estimated Units Produced and Sold}}$$

**Step 5.** Compute the markup percentage as follows:

$$\text{Markup Percentage} = \frac{\text{Desired Profit} + \text{Total Fixed Costs and Expenses}}{\text{Total Variable Cost}}$$

**VARIABLE COST CONCEPT**

**MARKUP:**
Total Fixed Costs
**+**
Desired Profit

**VARIABLE COST:**
Variable Manufacturing Cost
**+**
Variable Administrative and Selling Expenses

The numerator of the markup percentage is the desired profit plus the total fixed costs (fixed factory overhead) and expenses (selling and administrative). These fixed costs and expenses must be included in the markup percentage, since they are not included in the cost amount to which the markup is added.

As illustrated for the total and product cost concepts, the desired profit is normally computed based on a rate of return on assets as follows:

$$\text{Desired Profit} = \text{Desired Rate of Return} \times \text{Total Assets}$$

**Step 6.** Determine the markup per unit by multiplying the markup percentage times the variable cost per unit as follows:

$$\text{Markup per Unit} = \text{Markup Percentage} \times \text{Variable Cost per Unit}$$

**Step 7.** Determine the normal selling price by adding the markup per unit to the variable cost per unit as follows:

| | |
|---|---|
| Variable cost per unit | $XXX |
| Markup per unit | XXX |
| Normal selling price per unit | $XXX |

To illustrate, assume the same data for the production and sale of 100,000 calculators by Digital Solutions Inc. as in the preceding example. The normal selling price of $18.30 is determined under the variable cost concept as follows:

**Step 1.** Total variable product cost: $1,450,000

| Variable product costs: | |
|---|---|
| Direct materials ($3 × 100,000) | $ 300,000 |
| Direct labor ($10 × 100,000) | 1,000,000 |
| Variable factory overhead ($1.50 × 100,000) | 150,000 |
| Total variable product cost | $1,450,000 |

**Step 2.** Total variable selling and administrative expenses: $150,000 ($1.50 × 100,000)

**Step 3.** Total variable cost: $1,600,000 ($1,450,000 + $150,000)

**Step 4.** Variable cost per unit: $16.00

$$\text{Variable Cost per Unit} = \frac{\text{Total Variable Cost}}{\text{Estimated Units Produced and Sold}} = \frac{\$1,600,000}{100,000 \text{ units}} = \$16 \text{ per unit}$$

**Step 5.** Markup percentage: 14.4% (rounded)

Desired Profit = Desired Rate of Return × Total Assets = 20% × $800,000 = $160,000

$$\text{Markup Percentage} = \frac{\text{Desired Profit} + \text{Total Fixed Costs and Expenses}}{\text{Total Variable Cost}}$$

$$\text{Markup Percentage} = \frac{\$160,000 + \$50,000 + \$20,000}{\$1,600,000} = \frac{\$230,000}{\$1,600,000}$$

Markup Percentage = 14.4% (rounded)

**Step 6.** Markup per unit: $2.30

Markup per Unit = Markup Percentage × Variable Cost per Unit
Markup per Unit = 14.4% × $16.00 = $2.30 per unit

**Step 7.** Normal selling price: $18.30

| Total variable cost per unit | $16.00 |
|---|---|
| Markup per unit | 2.30 |
| Normal selling price per unit | $18.30 |

# At a Glance 24

**OBJ. 1**

**Prepare differential analysis reports for a variety of managerial decisions.**

**Key Points** Differential analysis reports for various decisions listed on page 1126 are illustrated in the text. Each analysis focuses on the differential effects on income (loss) for alternative courses of action.

| Learning Outcomes | Example Exercises | Practice Exercises |
|---|---|---|
| • Prepare a lease or sell differential analysis. | EE24-1 | PE24-1A, 24-1B |
| • Prepare a discontinued segment differential analysis. | EE24-2 | PE24-2A, 24-2B |
| • Prepare a make-or-buy differential analysis. | EE24-3 | PE24-3A, 24-3B |
| • Prepare an equipment replacement differential analysis. | EE24-4 | PE24-4A, 24-4B |
| • Prepare a process or sell differential analysis. | EE24-5 | PE24-5A, 24-5B |
| • Prepare an accept business at a special price differential analysis. | EE24-6 | PE24-6A, 24-6B |

# Key Terms

differential analysis (1120)
differential cost (1120)
differential income (loss) (1120)
differential revenue (1120)
opportunity cost (1128)

product cost concept (1133)
production bottleneck (1135)
sunk costs (1123)
target costing (1135)

theory of constraints
  (TOC) (1135)
total cost concept (1138)
variable cost concept (1140)

# Illustrative Problem

Inez Company recently began production of a new product, a digital clock, which required the investment of $1,600,000 in assets. The costs of producing and selling 80,000 units of the digital clock are estimated as follows:

| | |
|---|---|
| Variable costs: | |
| Direct materials | $10.00 per unit |
| Direct labor | 6.00 |
| Factory overhead | 4.00 |
| Selling and administrative expenses | 5.00 |
| Total | $25.00 per unit |
| Fixed costs: | |
| Factory overhead | $800,000 |
| Selling and administrative expenses | 400,000 |

Inez Company is considering a selling price for the digital clock. The president of Inez Company has decided to use the cost-plus approach to product pricing and has indicated that the digital clock must earn a 10% rate of return on invested assets.

## Instructions

1. Determine the amount of desired profit from the production and sale of the digital clock.

2. Assuming that the product cost concept is used, determine (a) the cost amount per unit, (b) the markup percentage, and (c) the selling price of the digital clock.

3. Assume the market price for similar digital clocks was estimated at $38. Compute the reduction in manufacturing cost per unit needed to maintain the desired profit and existing selling and administrative expenses under target costing.

4. Assume that for the current year, the selling price of the digital clock was $42 per unit. To date, 60,000 units have been produced and sold, and analysis of the domestic market indicates that 15,000 additional units are expected to be sold during the remainder of the year. On August 7, 2012, Inez Company received an offer from Wong Inc. for 4,000 units of the digital clock at $28 each. Wong Inc. will market the units in Korea under its own brand name, and no selling and administrative expenses associated with the sale will be incurred by Inez Company. The additional business is not expected to affect the domestic sales of the digital clock, and the additional units could be produced during the current year, using existing capacity. Prepare a differential analysis dated August 7, 2012, to determine whether to reject (Alternative 1) or accept (Alternative 2) the special order from Wong.

## Solution

1. $160,000 ($1,600,000 × 10%)

2. a. Total manufacturing costs:

| | |
|---|---|
| Variable ($20 × 80,000 units) | $1,600,000 |
| Fixed factory overhead | 800,000 |
| Total | $2,400,000 |

Cost amount per unit: $2,400,000/80,000 units = $30.00

$$\text{b. Markup Percentage} = \frac{\text{Desired Profit} + \text{Total Selling and Administrative Expenses}}{\text{Total Product Cost}}$$

$$\text{Markup Percentage} = \frac{\$160,000 + \$400,000 + (\$5 \times 80,000 \text{ units})}{\$2,400,000}$$

$$\text{Markup Percentage} = \frac{\$160,000 + \$400,000 + \$400,000}{\$2,400,000}$$

$$\text{Markup Percentage} = \frac{\$960,000}{\$2,400,000} = 40\%$$

c.

| | |
|---|---|
| Cost amount per unit | $30.00 |
| Markup ($30 × 40%) | 12.00 |
| Selling price | $42.00 |

3. 

| | |
|---|---:|
| Current selling price | $42 |
| Expected selling price | −38 |
| Required reduction in manufacturing cost to maintain same profit | $ 4 |

Revised revenue and cost figures:

| | Current | Desired |
|---|---:|---:|
| Selling price | $42 | $38 |
| Costs: | | |
| Variable selling and administrative expenses per unit | $ 5 | $ 5 |
| Fixed selling and administrative expenses per unit | | |
| ($400,000/80,000 units) | 5 | 5 |
| Existing manufacturing cost per unit [part (2)] | 30 | |
| Target manufacturing cost per unit ($30 − $4) | | 26 |
| Total costs | $40 | $36 |
| Profit | $ 2 | $ 2 |

4.

**Differential Analysis—Wong Inc. Special Order**
**Reject Order (Alternative 1) or Accept Order (Alternative 2)**
**August 7, 2012**

| | Reject Order (Alternative 1) | Accept Order (Alternative 2) | Differential Effect on Income (Alternative 2) |
|---|---:|---:|---:|
| Revenues | $0 | $112,000* | $112,000 |
| Costs: | | | |
| Variable manufacturing costs | 0 | −80,000** | −80,000 |
| Income (loss) | $0 | $ 32,000 | $ 32,000 |

*4,000 units × $28 per unit
**4,000 units × $20 per unit

The proposal should be accepted.

# Discussion Questions

1. Explain the meaning of (a) differential revenue, (b) differential cost, and (c) differential income.

2. A company could sell a building for $250,000 or lease it for $2,500 per month. What would need to be considered in determining if the lease option would be preferred?

3. A chemical company has a commodity-grade and premium-grade product. Why might the company elect to process the commodity-grade product further to the premium-grade product?

4. A company accepts incremental business at a special price that exceeds the variable cost. What other issues must the company consider in deciding whether to accept the business?

5. A company fabricates a component at a cost of $6.00. A supplier offers to supply the same component for $5.50. Under what circumstances is it reasonable to purchase from the supplier?

6. Many fast-food restaurant chains, such as McDonald's, will occasionally discontinue restaurants in their system. What are some financial considerations in deciding to eliminate a store?

7. In the long run, the normal selling price must be set high enough to cover what factors?

8. Although the cost-plus approach to product pricing may be used by management as a general guideline, what are some examples of other factors that managers should also consider in setting product prices?

9. How does the target cost concept differ from cost-plus approaches?

10. What is the appropriate measure of a product's value when a firm is operating under production bottlenecks?

# Practice Exercises

**PE 24-1A   Lease or sell**

Kincaid Company owns a machine with a cost of $365,000 and accumulated depreciation of $55,000 that can be sold for $276,000, less a 5% sales commission. Alternatively, the machine can be leased by Kincaid Company for three years for a total of $287,000, at the end of which there is no residual value. In addition, the repair, insurance, and property tax expense that would be incurred by Kincaid Company on the machine would total $15,900 over the three years. Prepare a differential analysis on January 12, 2012, as to whether Kincaid Company should lease (Alternative 1) or sell (Alternative 2) the equipment.

**PE 24-1B   Lease or sell**

Lassiter Company owns equipment with a cost of $140,000 and accumulated depreciation of $75,000 that can be sold for $55,000, less a 6% sales commission. Alternatively, the equipment can be leased by Lassiter Company for five years for a total of $51,000, at the end of which there is no residual value. In addition, the repair, insurance, and property tax expense that would be incurred by Lassiter Company on the equipment would total $6,400 over the five years. Prepare a differential analysis on March 23, 2012, as to whether Lassiter Company should lease (Alternative 1) or sell (Alternative 2) the equipment.

**PE 24-2A   Discontinue a segment**

Product T has revenue of $194,000, variable cost of goods sold of $115,000, variable selling expenses of $33,000, and fixed costs of $60,000, creating a loss from operations of $14,000. Prepare a differential analysis as of September 12, 2012, to determine if Product T should be continued (Alternative 1) or discontinued (Alternative 2).

**PE 24-2B   Discontinue a segment**

Product J has revenue of $49,000, variable cost of goods sold of $28,000, variable selling expenses of $15,000, and fixed costs of $14,000, creating a loss from operations of $8,000. Prepare a differential analysis as of May 9, 2012, to determine if Product J should be continued (Alternative 1) or discontinued (Alternative 2).

**PE 24-3A   Make or buy**

A restaurant bakes its own bread for $150 per unit (100 loaves), including fixed costs of $34 per unit. A proposal is offered to purchase bread from an outside source for $101 per unit, plus $9 per unit for delivery. Prepare a differential analysis dated August 16, 2012, to determine whether the company should make (Alternative 1) or buy (Alternative 2) the bread.

**PE 24-3B   Make or buy**

A company manufactures various sized plastic bottles for its medicinal product. The manufacturing cost for small bottles is $46 per unit (100 bottles), including fixed costs of $14 per unit. A proposal is offered to purchase small bottles from an outside source for $30 per unit, plus $6 per unit for freight. Prepare a differential analysis dated March 30, 2012, to determine whether the company should make (Alternative 1) or buy (Alternative 2) the bottles.

**PE 24-4A** **Replace equipment**

A machine with a book value of $250,000 has an estimated six-year life. A proposal is offered to sell the old machine for $216,000 and replace it with a new machine at a cost of $282,000. The new machine has a six-year life with no residual value. The new machine would reduce annual direct labor costs from $50,000 to $40,000. Prepare a differential analysis dated February 18, 2012, on whether to continue with the old machine (Alternative 1) or replace the old machine (Alternative 2).

**PE 24-4B** **Replace equipment**

A machine with a book value of $75,000 has an estimated five-year life. A proposal is offered to sell the old machine for $64,000 and replace it with a new machine at a cost of $80,000. The new machine has a five-year life with no residual value. The new machine would reduce annual direct labor costs from $9,500 to $5,500. Prepare a differential analysis dated April 11, 2012, on whether to continue with the old machine (Alternative 1) or replace the old machine (Alternative 2).

**PE 24-5A** **Process or sell**

Product T is produced for $3.50 per pound. Product T can be sold without additional processing for $4.15 per pound, or processed further into Product U at an additional cost of $0.44 per pound. Product U can be sold for $4.50 per pound. Prepare a differential analysis dated September 17, 2012, on whether to sell Product T (Alternative 1) or process further into Product U (Alternative 2).

**PE 24-5B** **Process or sell**

Product D is produced for $52 per gallon. Product D can be sold without additional processing for $80 per gallon, or processed further into Product E at an additional cost of $19 per gallon. Product E can be sold for $102 per gallon. Prepare a differential analysis dated June 9, 2012, on whether to sell Product D (Alternative 1) or process further into Product E (Alternative 2).

**PE 24-6A** **Accept business at special price**

Product R is normally sold for $45 per unit. A special price of $32 is offered for the export market. The variable production cost is $25 per unit. An additional export tariff of 15% of revenue must be paid for all export products. Assume there is sufficient capacity for the special order. Prepare a differential analysis dated July 7, 2012, on whether to reject (Alternative 1) or accept (Alternative 2) the special order.

**PE 24-6B** **Accept business at special price**

Product A is normally sold for $8.90 per unit. A special price of $6.60 is offered for the export market. The variable production cost is $5.10 per unit. An additional export tariff of 25% of revenue must be paid for all export products. Assume there is sufficient capacity for the special order. Prepare a differential analysis dated January 22, 2012, on whether to reject (Alternative 1) or accept (Alternative 2) the special order.

**PE 24-7A** **Product cost markup percentage**

Crescent Lighting Inc. produces and sells lighting fixtures. An entry light has a total cost of $60 per unit, of which $32 is product cost and $28 is selling and administrative expenses. In addition, the total cost of $60 is made up of $40 variable cost and $20 fixed cost. The desired profit is $12 per unit. Determine the markup percentage on product cost.

**PE 24-7B** **Product cost markup percentage**

Eden Garden Tools Inc. produces and sells home and garden tools and equipment. A lawnmower has a total cost of $200 per unit, of which $140 is product cost and $60 is selling and administrative expenses. In addition, the total cost of $200 is made up of $150 variable cost and $50 fixed cost. The desired profit is $38 per unit. Determine the markup percentage on product cost.

### PE 24-8A   Bottleneck profit

Product A has a unit contribution margin of $27. Product B has a unit contribution margin of $55. Product A requires three testing hours, while Product B requires five testing hours. Determine the most profitable product, assuming the testing is a constraint.

### PE 24-8B   Bottleneck profit

Product K has a unit contribution margin of $160. Product L has a unit contribution margin of $80. Product K requires eight furnace hours, while Product L requires five furnace hours. Determine the most profitable product, assuming the furnace is a constraint.

## Exercises

### EX 24-1   Differential analysis for a lease or sell decision

Sure-Bilt Construction Company is considering selling excess machinery with a book value of $280,000 (original cost of $400,000 less accumulated depreciation of $120,000) for $276,000, less a 5% brokerage commission. Alternatively, the machinery can be leased for a total of $285,000 for five years, after which it is expected to have no residual value. During the period of the lease, Sure-Bilt Construction Company's costs of repairs, insurance, and property tax expenses are expected to be $25,500.

a. Prepare a differential analysis, dated January 3, 2012, to determine whether Sure-Bilt should lease (Alternative 1) or sell (Alternative 2) the machinery.

b. ➤ On the basis of the data presented, would it be advisable to lease or sell the machinery? Explain.

### EX 24-2   Differential analysis for a lease or buy decision

Gilroy Corporation is considering new equipment. The equipment can be purchased from an overseas supplier for $3,200. The freight and installation costs for the equipment are $640. If purchased, annual repairs and maintenance are estimated to be $400 per year over the four-year useful life of the machine. Alternatively, Gilroy can lease the machine from a domestic supplier for $1,400 per year for four years, with no additional costs. Prepare a differential analysis dated October 3, 2012, to determine whether Gilroy should lease (Alternative 1) or purchase (Alternative 2) the machine. *Hint:* This is a "lease or buy" decision, which must be analyzed from the perspective of the equipment user, as opposed to the equipment owner.

### EX 24-3   Differential analysis for a discontinued product

A condensed income statement by product line for Crown Beverage Inc. indicated the following for King Cola for the past year:

| | |
|---|---:|
| Sales | $235,000 |
| Cost of goods sold | 110,000 |
| Gross profit | $125,000 |
| Operating expenses | 144,000 |
| Loss from operations | $ (19,000) |

It is estimated that 16% of the cost of goods sold represents fixed factory overhead costs and that 20% of the operating expenses are fixed. Since King Cola is only one of many products, the fixed costs will not be materially affected if the product is discontinued.

a. Prepare a differential analysis, dated March 3, 2012, to determine whether King Cola should be continued (Alternative 1) or discontinued (Alternative 2).

b. Should King Cola be retained? Explain.

### EX 24-4 Differential analysis for a discontinued product

The condensed product-line income statement for Porcelain Tableware Company for the month of December is as follows:

**Porcelain Tableware Company**
**Product-Line Income Statement**
**For the Month Ended December 31, 2012**

|  | Bowls | Plates | Cups |
|---|---|---|---|
| Sales | $65,000 | $89,400 | $26,900 |
| Cost of goods sold | 26,300 | 32,800 | 14,800 |
| Gross profit | $38,700 | $56,600 | $12,100 |
| Selling and administrative expenses | 29,400 | 34,900 | 15,400 |
| Income from operations | $ 9,300 | $21,700 | $ (3,300) |

Fixed costs are 15% of the cost of goods sold and 40% of the selling and administrative expenses. Porcelain Tableware assumes that fixed costs would not be materially affected if the Cups line were discontinued.

a. Prepare a differential analysis dated December 31, 2012, to determine if Cups should be continued (Alternative 1) or discontinued (Alternative 2).

b. Should the Cups line be retained? Explain.

### EX 24-5 Segment analysis, Charles Schwab Corporation

Charles Schwab Corporation is one of the more innovative brokerage and financial service companies in the United States. The company recently provided information about its major business segments as follows (in millions):

|  | Investor Services | Institutional Services |
|---|---|---|
| Revenues | $2,710 | $1,483 |
| Income from operations | 1,024 | 183 |
| Depreciation | 100 | 59 |

a. ━━━▶ How do you believe Schwab defines the difference between the "Investor Services" and "Institutional Services" segments?

b. Provide a specific example of a variable and fixed cost in the "Investor Services" segment.

c. Estimate the contribution margin for each segment, assuming depreciation represents the majority of fixed costs.

d. If Schwab decided to sell its "Institutional Services" accounts to another company, estimate how much operating income would decline.

### EX 24-6 Decision to discontinue a product

On the basis of the data at the top of the following page, the general manager of Glide Shoes Inc. decided to discontinue Children's Shoes because it reduced income from operations by $25,000. What is the flaw in this decision if it is assumed fixed costs would not be materially affected by the discontinuance?

**Glide Shoes Inc.**
**Product-Line Income Statement**
**For the Year Ended August 31, 2012**

| | Children's Shoes | Men's Shoes | Women's Shoes | Total |
|---|---|---|---|---|
| Sales | $200,000 | $300,000 | $500,000 | $1,000,000 |
| Costs of goods sold: | | | | |
| Variable costs | $125,000 | $150,000 | $220,000 | $ 495,000 |
| Fixed costs | 50,000 | 60,000 | 120,000 | 230,000 |
| Total cost of goods sold | $175,000 | $210,000 | $340,000 | $ 725,000 |
| Gross profit | $ 25,000 | $ 90,000 | $160,000 | $ 275,000 |
| Selling and adminstrative expenses: | | | | |
| Variable selling and admin. expenses | $ 28,000 | $ 45,000 | $ 95,000 | $ 168,000 |
| Fixed selling and admin. expenses | 22,000 | 20,000 | 25,000 | 67,000 |
| Total selling and admin. expenses | $ 50,000 | $ 65,000 | $120,000 | $ 235,000 |
| Income (loss) from operations | $ (25,000) | $ 25,000 | $ 40,000 | $ 40,000 |

OBJ. 1

✔ a. Differential loss from buying, $4.00 per case

### EX 24-7 Make-or-buy decision

Matchless Computer Company has been purchasing carrying cases for its portable computers at a delivered cost of $55 per unit. The company, which is currently operating below full capacity, charges factory overhead to production at the rate of 40% of direct labor cost. The fully absorbed unit costs to produce comparable carrying cases are expected to be as follows:

| | |
|---|---|
| Direct materials | $28.00 |
| Direct labor | 20.00 |
| Factory overhead (40% of direct labor) | 8.00 |
| Total cost per unit | $56.00 |

If Matchless Computer Company manufactures the carrying cases, fixed factory overhead costs will not increase and variable factory overhead costs associated with the cases are expected to be 15% of the direct labor costs.

a. Prepare a differential analysis, dated October 11, 2012, to determine whether the company should make (Alternative 1) or buy (Alternative 2) the carrying case.

b. ⬤➤ On the basis of the data presented, would it be advisable to make the carrying cases or to continue buying them? Explain.

OBJ. 1

### EX 24-8 Make-or-buy decision

The Theater Arts Guild of Miami (TAG-M) employs five people in its Publication Department. These people layout pages for pamphlets, brochures, magazines, and other publications for the TAG-M productions. The pages are delivered to an outside company for printing. The company is considering an outside publication service for the layout work. The outside service is quoting a price of $14 per layout page. The budget for the Publication Department for 2013 is as follows:

| | |
|---|---|
| Salaries | $185,000 |
| Benefits | 42,000 |
| Supplies | 23,000 |
| Office expenses | 28,000 |
| Office depreciation | 25,000 |
| Computer depreciation | 17,000 |
| Total | $320,000 |

The department expects to layout 20,000 pages for 2012. The computers used by the department have an estimated residual value of $9,000. The Publication Department office space would be used for future administrative needs, if the department's function were purchased from the outside.

a. Prepare a differential analysis dated December 15, 2012, to determine whether TAG-M should layout pages internally (Alternative 1) or purchase layout services from the outside (Alternative 2).

b. ➤ On the basis of your analysis in part (a), should the page layout work be purchased from an outside company?

c. ➤ What additional considerations might factor into the decision making?

---

OBJ. 1

**EX 24-9    Machine replacement decision**

A company is considering replacing an old piece of machinery, which cost $600,000 and has $350,000 of accumulated depreciation to date, with a new machine that costs $485,000. The old equipment could be sold for $63,000. The annual variable production costs associated with the old machine are estimated to be $157,000 per year for eight years. The annual variable production costs for the new machine are estimated to be $100,500 per year for eight years.

a. Prepare a differential analysis dated October 3, 2012, to determine whether to continue with (Alternative 1) or replace (Alternative 2) the old machine.

b. What is the sunk cost in this situation?

---

OBJ. 1
✔ a. Differential loss, $7,500

**EX 24-10    Differential analysis for machine replacement**

Taipei Digital Components Company assembles circuit boards by using a manually operated machine to insert electronic components. The original cost of the machine is $60,000, the accumulated depreciation is $24,000, its remaining useful life is five years, and its residual value is negligible. On September 27, 2012, a proposal was made to replace the present manufacturing procedure with a fully automatic machine that will cost $125,000. The automatic machine has an estimated useful life of five years and no significant residual value. For use in evaluating the proposal, the accountant accumulated the following annual data on present and proposed operations:

|  | Present Operations | Proposed Operations |
|---|---|---|
| Sales | $190,000 | $190,000 |
| Direct materials | $ 65,000 | $ 65,000 |
| Direct labor | 45,000 | — |
| Power and maintenance | 4,000 | 22,000 |
| Taxes, insurance, etc. | 1,500 | 5,000 |
| Selling and administrative expenses | 45,000 | 45,000 |
| Total expenses | $160,500 | $137,000 |

a. Prepare a differential analysis dated September 27, 2012, to determine whether to continue with the old machine (Alternative 1) or replace the old machine (Alternative 2). Prepare the analysis over the useful life of the new machine.

b. Based only on the data presented, should the proposal be accepted?

c. ➤ What are some of the other factors that should be considered before a final decision is made?

---

OBJ. 1

**EX 24-11    Sell or process further**

Jackson Lumber Company incurs a cost of $390 per hundred board feet in processing certain "rough-cut" lumber, which it sells for $555 per hundred board feet. An alternative is to produce a "finished cut" at a total processing cost of $525 per hundred board feet, which can be sold for $760 per hundred board feet. Prepare a differential analysis dated March 4, 2012, on whether to sell rough-cut lumber (Alternative 1) or process further into finished-cut lumber (Alternative 2).

---

OBJ. 1

**EX 24-12    Sell or process further**

Abica Roast Coffee Company produces Columbian coffee in batches of 6,000 pounds. The standard quantity of materials required in the process is 6,000 pounds, which cost $5.00

per pound. Columbian coffee can be sold without further processing for $8.40 per pound. Columbian coffee can also be processed further to yield Decaf Columbian, which can be sold for $10.00 per pound. The processing into Decaf Columbian requires additional processing costs of $9,450 per batch. The additional processing will also cause a 5% loss of product due to evaporation.

a. Prepare a differential analysis dated August 28, 2012, on whether to sell regular Columbian (Alternative 1) or process further into Decaf Columbian (Alternative 2).

b. ──────▶ Should Abica Roast sell Columbian coffee or process further and sell Decaf Columbian?

c. Determine the price of Decaf Columbian that would cause neither an advantage or disadvantage for processing further and selling Decaf Columbian.

---

**OBJ. 1**

✔ **a. Differential income, $30,000**

### EX 24-13 Decision on accepting additional business

Country Jeans Co. has an annual plant capacity of 65,000 units, and current production is 45,000 units. Monthly fixed costs are $40,000, and variable costs are $25 per unit. The present selling price is $35 per unit. On February 2, 2012, the company received an offer from Miller Company for 15,000 units of the product at $27 each. Miller Company will market the units in a foreign country under its own brand name. The additional business is not expected to affect the domestic selling price or quantity of sales of Country Jeans Co.

a. Prepare a differential analysis on whether to reject (Alternative 1) or accept (Alternative 2) the Miller order.

b. ──────▶ Briefly explain the reason why accepting this additional business will increase operating income.

c. What is the minimum price per unit that would produce a positive contribution margin?

---

**OBJ. 1**

### EX 24-14 Accepting business at a special price

Forever Ready Company expects to operate at 85% of productive capacity during May. The total manufacturing costs for May for the production of 25,000 batteries are budgeted as follows:

| | |
|---|---|
| Direct materials | $255,000 |
| Direct labor | 110,000 |
| Variable factory overhead | 35,000 |
| Fixed factory overhead | 57,000 |
| Total manufacturing costs | $457,000 |

The company has an opportunity to submit a bid for 2,000 batteries to be delivered by May 31 to a government agency. If the contract is obtained, it is anticipated that the additional activity will not interfere with normal production during May or increase the selling or administrative expenses. What is the unit cost below which Forever Ready Company should not go in bidding on the government contract?

---

**OBJ. 1**

✔ **a. Differential revenue, $1,440,000**

### EX 24-15 Decision on accepting additional business

Glide Ride Tire and Rubber Company has capacity to produce 170,000 tires. Glide Ride presently produces and sells 130,000 tires for the North American market at a price of $90 per tire. Glide Ride is evaluating a special order from a European automobile company, Euro Motors. Euro is offering to buy 20,000 tires for $72 per tire. Glide Ride's accounting system indicates that the total cost per tire is as follows:

| | |
|---|---|
| Direct materials | $34 |
| Direct labor | 12 |
| Factory overhead (60% variable) | 20 |
| Selling and administrative expenses (35% variable) | 18 |
| Total | $84 |

Glide Ride pays a selling commission equal to 5% of the selling price on North American orders, which is included in the variable portion of the selling and administrative expenses. However, this special order would not have a sales commission. If the order was accepted, the tires would be shipped overseas for an additional shipping cost of $5.00 per tire. In addition, Euro has made the order conditional on receiving European safety certification. Glide Ride estimates that this certification would cost $95,000.

a. Prepare a differential analysis dated May 4, 2012, on whether to reject (Alternative 1) or accept (Alternative 2) the special order from Euro Motors.

b. What is the minimum price per unit that would be financially acceptable to Glide Ride?

---

**OBJ. 2**
✔ b. $25

### EX 24-16  Product cost concept of product pricing

Mademoiselle Company produces women's handbags. The cost of producing 1,200 handbags is as follows:

| | |
|---|---|
| Direct materials | $16,000 |
| Direct labor | 8,000 |
| Factory overhead | 6,000 |
| Total manufacturing cost | $30,000 |

The selling and administrative expenses are $28,000. The management desires a profit equal to 16% of invested assets of $500,000.

a. Determine the amount of desired profit from the production and sale of 1,200 handbags.

b. Determine the product cost per unit for the production of 1,200 handbags.

c. Determine the product cost markup percentage for handbags.

d. Determine the selling price of handbags.

---

**OBJ. 2**
✔ d. $232

### EX 24-17  Product cost concept of product costing

Voice Com, Inc., uses the product cost concept of applying the cost-plus approach to product pricing. The costs of producing and selling 5,000 units of cellular phones are as follows:

| Variable costs: | | Fixed costs: | |
|---|---|---|---|
| Direct materials | $ 80 per unit | Factory overhead | $200,000 |
| Direct labor | 36 | Selling and admin. exp. | 70,000 |
| Factory overhead | 24 | | |
| Selling and admin. exp. | 20 | | |
| Total | $160 per unit | | |

Voice Com desires a profit equal to a 15% rate of return on invested assets of $600,000.

a. Determine the amount of desired profit from the production and sale of 5,000 units of cellular phones.

b. Determine the product cost and the cost amount per unit for the production of 5,000 units of cellular phones.

c. Determine the product cost markup percentage (rounded to two decimal places) for cellular phones.

d. Determine the selling price of cellular phones. Round to the nearest dollar.

---

**OBJ. 2**

### EX 24-18  Target costing

Toyota Motor Corporation uses target costing. Assume that Toyota marketing personnel estimate that the competitive selling price for the Camry in the upcoming model year will need to be $24,000. Assume further that the Camry's total unit cost for the upcoming model year is estimated to be $19,800 and that Toyota requires a 20% profit margin on selling price (which is equivalent to a 25% markup on total cost).

a. What price will Toyota establish for the Camry for the upcoming model year?

b. ➡ What impact will target costing have on Toyota, given the assumed information?

**OBJ. 2**

✔ b. $16

**EX 24-19 Target costing**

Laser Impressions, Inc., manufactures color laser printers. Model J20 presently sells for $360 and has a total product cost of $288, as follows:

| | |
|---|---|
| Direct materials | $218 |
| Direct labor | 50 |
| Factory overhead | 20 |
| Total | $288 |

It is estimated that the competitive selling price for color laser printers of this type will drop to $340 next year. Laser Impressions has established a target cost to maintain its historical markup percentage on product cost. Engineers have provided the following cost reduction ideas:

1. Purchase a plastic printer cover with snap-on assembly, rather than with screws. This will reduce the amount of direct labor by 12 minutes per unit.

2. Add an inspection step that will add six minutes per unit of direct labor but reduce the materials cost by $7 per unit.

3. Decrease the cycle time of the injection molding machine from four minutes to three minutes per part. Forty percent of the direct labor and 42% of the factory overhead are related to running injection molding machines.

The direct labor rate is $25 per hour.

a. Determine the target cost for Model J20 assuming that the historical markup on product cost is maintained.

b. Determine the required cost reduction.

c. Evaluate the three engineering improvements together to determine if the required cost reduction (drift) can be achieved.

**OBJ. 3**

**EX 24-20 Product decisions under bottlenecked operations**

Eagle Alloys Inc. has three grades of metal product, Type 5, Type 10, and Type 20. Financial data for the three grades are as follows:

| | Type 5 | Type 10 | Type 20 |
|---|---|---|---|
| Revenues | $39,000 | $41,000 | $26,500 |
| Variable cost | $25,000 | $20,500 | $13,500 |
| Fixed cost | 8,000 | 8,000 | 8,000 |
| Total cost | $33,000 | $28,500 | $21,500 |
| Income from operations | $ 6,000 | $12,500 | $ 5,000 |
| Number of units | ÷ 5,000 | ÷ 5,000 | ÷ 5,000 |
| Income from operations per unit | $ 1.20 | $ 2.50 | $ 1.00 |

Eagle's operations require all three grades to be melted in a furnace before being formed. The furnace runs 24 hours a day, 7 days a week, and is a production bottleneck. The furnace hours required per unit of each product are as follows:

| | |
|---|---|
| Type 5: | 5 hours |
| Type 10: | 10 hours |
| Type 20: | 5 hours |

The Marketing Department is considering a new marketing and sales campaign.
Which product should be emphasized in the marketing and sales campaign in order to maximize profitability?

**OBJ. 3**

✔ a. Total income from operations, $104,000

**EX 24-21 Product decisions under bottlenecked operations**

Pennsylvania Glass Company manufactures three types of safety plate glass: large, medium, and small. All three products have high demand. Thus, Pennsylvania Glass is able to sell all the safety glass that it can make. The production process includes an autoclave operation, which is a pressurized heat treatment. The autoclave is a production bottleneck. Total fixed costs are $85,000 for the company as a whole. In addition, the following information is available about the three products:

| | Large | Medium | Small |
|---|---|---|---|
| Unit selling price | $140 | $115 | $100 |
| Unit variable cost | 110 | 94 | 88 |
| Unit contribution margin | $ 30 | $ 21 | $ 12 |
| Autoclave hours per unit | 4 | 2 | 1 |
| Total process hours per unit | 8 | 6 | 3 |
| Budgeted units of production | 3,000 | 3,000 | 3,000 |

a. Determine the contribution margin by glass type and the total company income from operations for the budgeted units of production.

b. Prepare an analysis showing which product is the most profitable per bottleneck hour.

---

**OBJ. 3**
✔ **Medium, $118**

**EX 24-22  Product pricing under bottlenecked operations**

Based on the data presented in Exercise 24-21, assume that Pennsylvania Glass wanted to price all products so that they produced the same profit potential as the highest profit product. Thus, determine the prices for each of the products so that they would produce a profit equal to the highest profit product.

---

**Appendix**
✔ **b. 8.41%**

**EX 24-23  Total cost concept of product pricing**

Based on the data presented in Exercise 24-17, assume that Voice Com, Inc., uses the total cost concept of applying the cost-plus approach to product pricing.

a. Determine the total costs and the total cost amount per unit for the production and sale of 5,000 units of cellular phones.

b. Determine the total cost markup percentage (rounded to two decimal places) for cellular phones.

c. Determine the selling price of cellular phones. Round to the nearest dollar.

---

**Appendix**
✔ **a. Cost amount per unit, $160**

**EX 24-24  Variable cost concept of product pricing**

Based on the data presented in Exercise 24-17, assume that Voice Com, Inc., uses the variable cost concept of applying the cost-plus approach to product pricing.

a. Determine the variable costs and the variable cost amount per unit for the production and sale of 5,000 units of cellular phones.

b. Determine the variable cost markup percentage for cellular phones.

c. Determine the selling price of cellular phones. Round to the nearest dollar.

---

## Problems Series A

---

**OBJ. 1**

**PR 24-1A  Differential analysis involving opportunity costs**

On August 1, Matrix Stores Inc. is considering leasing a building and purchasing the necessary equipment to operate a retail store. Alternatively, the company could use the funds to invest in $150,000 of 6% U.S. Treasury bonds that mature in 16 years. The bonds could be purchased at face value. The following data have been assembled:

| | |
|---|---|
| Cost of store equipment | $150,000 |
| Life of store equipment | 16 years |
| Estimated residual value of store equipment | $18,000 |
| Yearly costs to operate the store, excluding depreciation of store equipment | $56,000 |
| Yearly expected revenues—years 1–8 | $75,000 |
| Yearly expected revenues—years 9–16 | $70,000 |

**Instructions**

1. Prepare a differential analysis as of August 1, 2012, presenting the proposed operation of the store for the 16 years (Alternative 1) as compared with investing in U.S. Treasury bonds (Alternative 2).

2. Based on the results disclosed by the differential analysis, should the proposal be accepted?

3. If the proposal is accepted, what would be the total estimated income from operations of the store for the 16 years?

OBJ. 1

### PR 24-2A   Differential analysis for machine replacement proposal

Franklin Printing Company is considering replacing a machine that has been used in its factory for four years. Relevant data associated with the operations of the old machine and the new machine, neither of which has any estimated residual value, are as follows:

| **Old Machine** | |
| --- | --- |
| Cost of machine, 10-year life | $108,000 |
| Annual depreciation (straight-line) | 10,800 |
| Annual manufacturing costs, excluding depreciation | 38,600 |
| Annual nonmanufacturing operating expenses | 12,300 |
| Annual revenue | 95,000 |
| Current estimated selling price of machine | 35,900 |

| **New Machine** | |
| --- | --- |
| Cost of machine, six-year life | $138,000 |
| Annual depreciation (straight-line) | 23,000 |
| Estimated annual manufacturing costs, exclusive of depreciation | 18,200 |

Annual nonmanufacturing operating expenses and revenue are not expected to be affected by purchase of the new machine.

**Instructions**

1. Prepare a differential analysis as of February 29, 2012, comparing operations using the present equipment (Alternative 1) with operations using the new equipment (Alternative 2). The analysis should indicate the total differential income that would result over the six-year period if the new machine is acquired.

2. ➤ List other factors that should be considered before a final decision is reached.

OBJ. 1

✔ 1. Moisturizer income, $330,000

### PR 24-3A   Differential analysis for sales promotion proposal

L'Essence Cosmetics Company is planning a one-month campaign for June to promote sales of one of its two cosmetics products. A total of $150,000 has been budgeted for advertising, contests, redeemable coupons, and other promotional activities. The following data have been assembled for their possible usefulness in deciding which of the products to select for the campaign:

| | Moisturizer | Perfume |
| --- | --- | --- |
| Unit selling price | $50 | $55 |
| Unit production costs: | | |
| Direct materials | $ 9 | $12 |
| Direct labor | 3 | 4 |
| Variable factory overhead | 2 | 3 |
| Fixed factory overhead | 5 | 6 |
| Total unit production costs | $19 | $25 |
| Unit variable selling expenses | 16 | 15 |
| Unit fixed selling expenses | 9 | 5 |
| Total unit costs | $44 | $45 |
| Operating income per unit | $ 6 | $10 |

No increase in facilities would be necessary to produce and sell the increased output. It is anticipated that 24,000 additional units of moisturizer or 20,000 additional units of perfume could be sold without changing the unit selling price of either product.

**Instructions**

1. Prepare a differential analysis as of June 15, 2012, to determine whether to promote moisturizer (Alternative 1) or perfume (Alternative 2).

2. ━━━▶ The sales manager had tentatively decided to promote perfume, estimating that operating income would be increased by $50,000 ($10 operating income per unit for 20,000 units, less promotion expenses of $150,000). The manager also believed that the selection of moisturizer would reduce operating income, ($6,000) ($6 operating income per unit for 24,000 units, less promotion expenses of $150,000). State briefly your reasons for supporting or opposing the tentative decision.

---

**OBJ. 1**

✔ 1. Raw sugar income, $16,200

**PR 24-4A   Differential analysis for further processing**

The management of Jamaican Sugar Company is considering whether to process further raw sugar into refined sugar. Refined sugar can be sold for $2.15 per pound, and raw sugar can be sold without further processing for $1.20 per pound. Raw sugar is produced in batches of 36,000 pounds by processing 90,000 pounds of sugar cane, which costs $0.30 per pound of cane. Refined sugar will require additional processing costs of $0.45 per pound of raw sugar, and 1.2 pounds of raw sugar will produce 1 pound of refined sugar.

**Instructions**

1. Prepare a differential analysis as of January 30, 2012, to determine whether to sell raw sugar (Alternative 1) or process further into refined sugar (Alternative 2).

2. ━━━▶ Briefly report your recommendations.

---

**OBJ. 1, 2, and Appendix**

✔ 2. b. Markup percentage, 50%

**PR 24-5A   Product pricing using the cost-plus approach concepts; differential analysis for accepting additional business**

Display Labs Inc. recently began production of a new product, flat panel displays, which required the investment of $1,800,000 in assets. The costs of producing and selling 9,000 units of flat panel displays are estimated as follows:

| Variable costs per unit: | | Fixed costs: | |
|---|---|---|---|
| Direct materials | $ 90 | Factory overhead | $360,000 |
| Direct labor | 20 | Selling and administrative expenses | 180,000 |
| Factory overhead | 40 | | |
| Selling and administrative expenses | 35 | | |
| Total | $185 | | |

Display Labs Inc. is currently considering establishing a selling price for flat panel displays. The president of Display Labs has decided to use the cost-plus approach to product pricing and has indicated that the displays must earn a 20% rate of return on invested assets.

**Instructions**

1. Determine the amount of desired profit from the production and sale of flat panel displays.

2. Assuming that the product cost concept is used, determine (a) the cost amount per unit, (b) the markup percentage, and (c) the selling price of flat panel displays.

3. **Appendix:** Assuming that the total cost concept is used, determine (a) the cost amount per unit, (b) the markup percentage (rounded to two decimal places), and (c) the selling price of flat panel displays (rounded to nearest whole dollar).

4. **Appendix:** Assuming that the variable cost concept is used, determine (a) the cost amount per unit, (b) the markup percentage (rounded to two decimal places), and (c) the selling price of flat panel displays (rounded to nearest whole dollar).

5. ━━━▶ Comment on any additional considerations that could influence establishing the selling price for flat panel displays.

6.  Assume that as of August 1, 2012, 5,000 units of flat panel displays have been pro-
    duced and sold during the current year. Analysis of the domestic market indicates that
    4,000 additional units are expected to be sold during the remainder of the year at the
    normal product price determined under the product cost concept. On August 3, Dis-
    play Labs Inc. received an offer from Video Systems Inc. for 1,500 units of flat panel
    displays at $225 each. Video Systems Inc. will market the units in Canada under its
    own brand name, and no selling and administrative expenses associated with the sale
    will be incurred by Display Labs Inc. The additional business is not expected to affect
    the domestic sales of flat panel displays, and the additional units could be produced
    using existing capacity.

    a.  Prepare a differential analysis of the proposed sale to Video Systems Inc.

    b.  Based on the differential analysis in part (a), should the proposal be accepted?

---

**OBJ. 3**

✔ 1. High Grade, $40

### PR 24-6A   Product pricing and profit analysis with bottleneck operations

Atlas Steel Company produces three grades of steel: high, good, and regular grade. Each of
these products (grades) has high demand in the market, and Atlas is able to sell as much
as it can produce of all three. The furnace operation is a bottleneck in the process and
is running at 100% of capacity. Atlas wants to improve steel operation profitability. The
variable conversion cost is $12 per process hour. The fixed cost is $410,000. In addition,
the cost analyst was able to determine the following information about the three products:

| | High Grade | Good Grade | Regular Grade |
|---|---|---|---|
| Budgeted units produced | 5,000 | 5,000 | 5,000 |
| Total process hours per unit | 15 | 15 | 12 |
| Furnace hours per unit | 5 | 4 | 3 |
| Unit selling price | $320 | $290 | $270 |
| Direct materials cost per unit | $100 | $105 | $96 |

The furnace operation is part of the total process for each of these three products.
Thus, for example, 5 of the 15 hours required to process High Grade steel are associated
with the furnace.

#### Instructions

1.  Determine the unit contribution margin for each product.

2.  Provide an analysis to determine the relative product profitability, assuming that the
    furnace is a bottleneck.

3.  Assume that management wishes to improve profitability by increasing prices on
    selected products. At what price would High and Good grades need to be offered in
    order to produce the same relative profitability as Regular Grade steel?

# Problems Series B

---

**OBJ. 1**

### PR 24-1B   Differential analysis involving opportunity costs

On May 1, Interstate Distribution Company is considering leasing a building and buying
the necessary equipment to operate a public warehouse. Alternatively, the company could
use the funds to invest in $800,000 of 5% U.S. Treasury bonds that mature in 14 years.
The bonds could be purchased at face value. The following data have been assembled:

| | |
|---|---|
| Cost of equipment | $800,000 |
| Life of equipment | 14 years |
| Estimated residual value of equipment | $75,000 |
| Yearly costs to operate the warehouse, excluding depreciation of equipment | $200,000 |
| Yearly expected revenues—years 1–7 | $325,000 |
| Yearly expected revenues—years 8–14 | $275,000 |

#### Instructions

1.  Prepare a differential analysis as of May 1, 2012, presenting the proposed operation
    of the warehouse for the 14 years (Alternative 1) as compared with investing in U.S.
    Treasury bonds (Alternative 2).

2. Based on the results disclosed by the differential analysis, should the proposal be accepted?

3. If the proposal is accepted, what is the total estimated income from operations of the warehouse for the 14 years?

---

OBJ. 1

### PR 24-2B    Differential analysis for machine replacement proposal

Saginaw Tooling Company is considering replacing a machine that has been used in its factory for two years. Relevant data associated with the operations of the old machine and the new machine, neither of which has any estimated residual value, are as follows:

| Old Machine | |
|---|---|
| Cost of machine, eight-year life | $44,000 |
| Annual depreciation (straight-line) | 5,500 |
| Annual manufacturing costs, excluding depreciation | 16,300 |
| Annual nonmanufacturing operating expenses | 3,100 |
| Annual revenue | 29,600 |
| Current estimated selling price of the machine | 21,000 |

| New Machine | |
|---|---|
| Cost of machine, six-year life | $72,000 |
| Annual depreciation (straight-line) | 12,000 |
| Estimated annual manufacturing costs, exclusive of depreciation | 5,900 |

Annual nonmanufacturing operating expenses and revenue are not expected to be affected by purchase of the new machine.

### Instructions

1. Prepare a differential analysis as of September 10, 2012, comparing operations using the present equipment (Alternative 1) with operations using the new equipment (Alternative 2). The analysis should indicate the differential income that would result over the six-year period if the new machine is acquired.

2. ➤ List other factors that should be considered before a final decision is reached.

---

OBJ. 1

✔ 1. Income, tennis shoe, $230,000

### PR 24-3B    Differential analysis for sales promotion proposal

Sole Mates Inc. is planning a one-month campaign for May to promote sales of one of its two shoe products. A total of $130,000 has been budgeted for advertising, contests, redeemable coupons, and other promotional activities. The following data have been assembled for their possible usefulness in deciding which of the products to select for the campaign.

| | Tennis Shoe | Walking Shoe |
|---|---|---|
| Unit selling price | $120 | $92 |
| Unit production costs: | | |
| Direct materials | $ 24 | $20 |
| Direct labor | 10 | 9 |
| Variable factory overhead | 6 | 5 |
| Fixed factory overhead | 14 | 12 |
| Total unit production costs | $ 54 | $46 |
| Unit variable selling expenses | 8 | 6 |
| Unit fixed selling expenses | 20 | 15 |
| Total unit costs | $ 82 | $67 |
| Operating income per unit | $ 38 | $25 |

No increase in facilities would be necessary to produce and sell the increased output. It is anticipated that 5,000 additional units of tennis shoes or 7,000 additional units of walking shoes could be sold without changing the unit selling price of either product.

### Instructions

1. Prepare a differential analysis as of May 13, 2012, to determine whether to promote tennis shoes (Alternative 1) or walking shoes (Alternative 2).

2. ➤ The sales manager had tentatively decided to promote tennis shoes, estimating that operating income would be increased by $60,000 ($38 operating income per unit for 5,000 units, less promotion expenses of $130,000). The manager also believed

that the selection of walking shoes would increase operating income by $45,000 ($25 operating income per unit for 7,000 units, less promotion expenses of $130,000). State briefly your reasons for supporting or opposing the tentative decision.

OBJ. 1

✔ 1. Ingot income, $36,000

### PR 24-4B   Differential analysis for further processing

The management of Pittsburgh Aluminum Co. is considering whether to process aluminum ingot further into rolled aluminum. Rolled aluminum can be sold for $1,800 per ton, and ingot can be sold without further processing for $1,000 per ton. Ingot is produced in batches of 72 tons by smelting 400 tons of bauxite, which costs $90 per ton of bauxite. Rolled aluminum will require additional processing costs of $525 per ton of ingot, and 1.2 tons of ingot will produce 1 ton of rolled aluminum (due to trim losses).

**Instructions**

1. Prepare a differential analysis as of December 20, 2012, to determine whether to sell aluminum ingot (Alternative 1) or process further into rolled aluminum (Alternative 2).

2. ━━━━▶ Briefly report your recommendations.

OBJ. 1, 2, and Appendix

✔ 2. b. Markup percentage, 34.69%

### PR 24-5B   Product pricing using the cost-plus approach concepts; differential analysis for accepting additional business

Safety Systems, Inc., recently began production of a new product, the halogen light, which required the investment of $600,000 in assets. The costs of producing and selling 10,000 halogen lights are estimated as follows:

| Variable costs per unit: | | Fixed costs: | |
|---|---|---|---|
| Direct materials | $24 | Factory overhead | $100,000 |
| Direct labor | 10 | Selling and administrative expenses | 50,000 |
| Factory overhead | 5 | | |
| Selling and administrative expenses | 6 | | |
| Total | $45 | | |

Safety Systems, Inc., is currently considering establishing a selling price for the halogen light. The president of Safety Systems, Inc., has decided to use the cost-plus approach to product pricing and has indicated that the halogen light must earn a 10% rate of return on invested assets.

**Instructions**

1. Determine the desired profit from the production and sale of the halogen light.

2. Assuming that the product cost concept is used, determine (a) the cost amount per unit, (b) the markup percentage (rounded to two decimal places), and (c) the selling price of the halogen light (rounded to nearest whole dollar).

3. **Appendix:** Assuming that the total cost concept is used, determine (a) the cost amount per unit, (b) the markup percentage, and (c) the selling price of the halogen light.

4. **Appendix:** Assuming that the variable cost concept is used, determine (a) the cost amount per unit, (b) the markup percentage (rounded to two decimal places), and (c) the selling price of the halogen light (rounded to nearest whole dollar).

5. ━━━━▶ Comment on any additional considerations that could influence establishing the selling price for the halogen light.

6. Assume that as of September 1, 2012, 7,000 units of halogen light have been produced and sold during the current year. Analysis of the domestic market indicates that 3,000 additional units of the halogen light are expected to be sold during the remainder of the year at the normal product price determined under the product cost concept. On September 5, Safety Systems, Inc., received an offer from International Lighting Inc. for 2,000 units of the halogen light at $42 each. International Lighting Inc. will market the units in Japan under its own brand name, and no selling and administrative expenses associated with the sale will be incurred by Safety Systems, Inc. The

additional business is not expected to affect the domestic sales of the halogen light, and the additional units could be produced using existing capacity.

a. Prepare a differential analysis of the proposed sale to International Lighting Inc.

b. Based on the differential analysis in part (a), should the proposal be accepted?

### PR 24-6B Product pricing and profit analysis with bottleneck operations

Dover Chemical Company produces three products: ethylene, butane, and ester. Each of these products has high demand in the market, and Dover Chemical is able to sell as much as it can produce of all three. The reaction operation is a bottleneck in the process and is running at 100% of capacity. Dover wants to improve chemical operation profitability. The variable conversion cost is $8 per process hour. The fixed cost is $550,000. In addition, the cost analyst was able to determine the following information about the three products:

|                              | Ethylene | Butane | Ester |
|------------------------------|----------|--------|-------|
| Budgeted units produced      | 9,000    | 9,000  | 9,000 |
| Total process hours per unit | 3        | 3      | 2     |
| Reactor hours per unit       | 0.75     | 0.5    | 1.0   |
| Unit selling price           | $165     | $132   | $128  |
| Direct materials cost per unit | $117   | $88    | $85   |

The reaction operation is part of the total process for each of these three products. Thus, for example, 1.0 of the 3 hours required to process ethylene is associated with the reactor.

### Instructions

1. Determine the unit contribution margin for each product.

2. Provide an analysis to determine the relative product profitabilities, assuming that the reactor is a bottleneck.

3. Assume that management wishes to improve profitability by increasing prices on selected products. At what price would ethylene and ester need to be offered in order to produce the same relative profitability as butane?

## Cases & Projects

You can access Cases & Projects online at **www.cengage.com/accounting/reeve**

## Excel Success Special Activities

### SA 24-1 Lease or sell

On April 4, 2012, Lane Company is considering whether to lease or sell equipment with an original cost of $150,000 and a current book value of $110,000. Lane can lease this equipment over six years for a total estimated revenue of $220,000 and estimated property tax and insurance expenses of $140,000. Alternatively, Lane could sell the equipment for $76,000 less a 5% sales commission.

a. Open the Excel file *SA24-1_1e*.

b. Prepare a differential analysis based on the example shown in the chapter.

c. When you have completed the analysis, perform a "save as," replacing the entire file name with the following:

*SA24-1_1e[your first name initial]_[your last name]*

### SA 24-2 Make or buy

V-Systems manufactures electronic test equipment. The test equipment uses an integrated circuit (IC) that can be purchased from an outside supplier for $46 per unit plus $4 per unit freight. Alternatively, the integrated circuit can be manufactured for $68 per unit, including variable costs of $42 per unit and fixed costs of $26 per unit. The fixed costs cannot be avoided by purchasing the part.

a. Open the Excel file *SA24-2_1e.*

b. Prepare a differential analysis dated August 21, 2012 based on the example shown in the chapter.

c. When you have completed the analysis, perform a "save as," replacing the entire file name with the following:

   *SA24-2_1e[your first name initial]_[your last name]*

---

### SA 24-3   Continue or replace equipment

Carlisle Company has a machine with a book value of $59,000 and a five-year remaining life. A proposal is offered to sell the machine for $65,000 and replace it with a new machine at a cost of $73,000. The new machine would have a five-year life. If replaced, the new machine would reduce annual energy costs from $7,000 to $4,000 per year and increase annual property taxes from $900 to $1,400 per year.

a. Open the Excel file *SA24-3_1e.*

b. Prepare a differential analysis dated January 17, 2012 based on the example shown in the chapter.

c. When you have completed the analysis, perform a "save as", replacing the entire file name with the following:

   *SA24-3_1e[your first name initial]_[your last name]*

---

### SA 24-4   Sell or process further

Norris Company produces ester for $4.90 per pound. Ester can be sold without additional processing for $8.00 per pound, or processed further into polyester at an additional total cost of $1.10 per pound. Polyester can be sold for $9.00 per pound.

a. Open the Excel file *SA24-4_1e.*

b. Prepare a differential analysis dated May 29, 2012 based on the example shown in the chapter.

c. When you have completed the analysis, perform a "save as," replacing the entire file name with the following:

   *SA24-4_1e[your first name initial]_[your last name]*

# Capital Investment Analysis

## Carnival Corporation

**W**hy are you paying tuition, studying this text, and spending time and money on a higher education? Most people believe that the money and time spent now will return them more earnings in the future. In other words, the cost of higher education is an investment in your future earning ability. How would you know if this investment is worth it?

One method would be for you to compare the cost of a higher education against the estimated increase in your future earning power. The bigger the difference between your expected future earnings and the cost of your education, the better the investment. A business also evaluates its investments in fixed assets by comparing the initial cost of the investment to its future earnings and cash flows.

For example, **Carnival Corporation** is the largest vacation cruise company in the world, with over 90 cruise ships that sail to locations around the world. Carnival's fleet required an investment of nearly $35 billion, with each new ship costing approximately $600 million. In deciding to build more ships, Carnival compares the cost of a ship with its future earnings and cash flows over its 30-year expected life. Carnival must be satisfied with its investments, because the company has signed agreements with shipyards to add an additional 13 cruise ships to its fleet from 2010–2012.

In this chapter, the methods used to make investment decisions, which may involve thousands, millions, or even billions of dollars, are described and illustrated. The similarities and differences among the most commonly used methods of evaluating investment proposals, as well as the benefits of each method, are emphasized. Factors that can complicate the analysis are also discussed.

**After studying this chapter, you should be able to:**

| | | Example Exercises | Page |
|---|---|---|---|
| **OBJ. 1** | **Explain the nature and importance of capital investment analysis.**<br>Nature of Capital Investment Analysis | | |
| **OBJ. 2** | **Evaluate capital investment proposals using the average rate of return and cash payback methods.**<br>Methods Not Using Present Values | | |
| | Average Rate of Return Method | EE 25-1 | 1166 |
| | Cash Payback Method | EE 25-2 | 1167 |
| **OBJ. 3** | **Evaluate capital investment proposals using the net present value and internal rate of return methods.**<br>Methods Using Present Values | | |
| | Present Value Concepts | | |
| | Net Present Value Method | EE 25-3 | 1173 |
| | Internal Rate of Return Method | EE 25-4 | 1177 |
| **OBJ. 4** | **List and describe factors that complicate capital investment analysis.**<br>Factors That Complicate Capital Investment Analysis | | |
| | Income Tax | | |
| | Unequal Proposal Lives | EE 25-5 | 1178 |
| | Lease versus Capital Investment | | |
| | Uncertainty | | |
| | Changes in Price Levels | | |
| | Qualitative Considerations | | |
| **OBJ. 5** | **Diagram the capital rationing process.**<br>Capital Rationing | | |

**At a Glance 25**  Page 1183

---

**OBJ. 1** Explain the nature and importance of capital investment analysis.

The Walt Disney Company committed over $1 billion of capital investment to expand Disney's California Adventure theme park, including new attractions: *Toy Story Mania* (2008), *Mickey's Fun Wheel* (2009), *World of Color* (2010), and *Ariel's Undersea Adventure* (2011).

# Nature of Capital Investment Analysis

Companies use capital investment analysis to evaluate long-term investments. **Capital investment analysis** (or *capital budgeting*) is the process by which management plans, evaluates, and controls investments in fixed assets. Capital investments use funds and affect operations for many years and must earn a reasonable rate of return. Thus, capital investment decisions are some of the most important decisions that management makes.

Capital investment evaluation methods can be grouped into the following categories:

**Methods That Do Not Use Present Values**
1. Average rate of return method
2. Cash payback method

**Methods That Use Present Values**
1. Net present value method
2. Internal rate of return method

The two methods that use present values consider the time value of money. The **time value of money concept** recognizes that a dollar today is worth more than a dollar tomorrow because today's dollar can earn interest.

**OBJ. 2** Evaluate capital investment proposals using the average rate of return and cash payback methods.

# Methods Not Using Present Values

The methods not using present values are often useful in evaluating capital investment proposals that have relatively short useful lives. In such cases, the timing of the cash flows (the time value of money) is less important.

Since the methods not using present values are easy to use, they are often used to screen proposals. Minimum standards for accepting proposals are set, and proposals not meeting these standards are dropped. If a proposal meets the minimum standards, it may be subject to further analysis using the present value methods.

## Average Rate of Return Method

The **average rate of return**, sometimes called the *accounting rate of return*, measures the average income as a percent of the average investment. The average rate of return is computed as follows:

$$\text{Average Rate of Return} = \frac{\text{Estimated Average Annual Income}}{\text{Average Investment}}$$

In the preceding equation, the numerator is the average of the annual income expected to be earned from the investment over its life, after deducting depreciation. The denominator is the average investment (book value) over the life of the investment. Assuming straight-line depreciation, the average investment is computed as follows:

$$\text{Average Investment} = \frac{\text{Initial Cost} + \text{Residual Value}}{2}$$

To illustrate, assume that management is evaluating the purchase of a new machine as follows:

A CFO survey of capital investment analysis methods used by large U.S. companies reported the following:

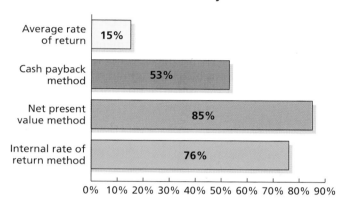

**Percentage of Respondents Reporting the Use of the Method as "Always" or "Often"**

| Method | Percentage |
|---|---|
| Average rate of return | 15% |
| Cash payback method | 53% |
| Net present value method | 85% |
| Internal rate of return method | 76% |

*Source:* Patricia A. Ryan and Glenn P. Ryan, "Capital Budgeting Practice of the Fortune 1000: How Have Things Changed?" *Journal of Business and Management* (Winter 2002).

| | |
|---|---|
| Cost of new machine | $500,000 |
| Residual value | 0 |
| Estimated total income from machine | 200,000 |
| Expected useful life | 4 years |

The average estimated annual income from the machine is $50,000 ($200,000/4 years). The average investment is $250,000, as computed below.

$$\text{Average Investment} = \frac{\text{Initial Cost} + \text{Residual Value}}{2} = \frac{\$500,000 + \$0}{2} = \$250,000$$

The average rate of return on the average investment is 20%, as computed below.

$$\text{Average Rate of Return} = \frac{\text{Estimated Average Annual Income}}{\text{Average Investment}} = \frac{\$50,000}{\$250,000} = 20\%$$

The average rate of return of 20% should be compared to the minimum rate of return required by management. If the average rate of return equals or exceeds the minimum rate, the machine should be purchased or considered for further analysis.

Several capital investment proposals can be ranked by their average rates of return. The higher the average rate of return, the more desirable the proposal.

The average rate of return has the following three advantages:

1. It is easy to compute.
2. It includes the entire amount of income earned over the life of the proposal.
3. It emphasizes accounting income, which is often used by investors and creditors in evaluating management performance.

The average rate of return has the following two disadvantages:

1. It does not directly consider the expected cash flows from the proposal.
2. It does not directly consider the timing of the expected cash flows.

**Note:**
The average rate of return method considers the amount of income earned over the life of a proposal.

**Example Exercise > 25-1 > Average Rate of Return**

OBJ.
2

Determine the average rate of return for a project that is estimated to yield total income of $273,600 over three years, has a cost of $690,000, and has a $70,000 residual value.

**Follow My Example > 25-1 >**

| | |
|---|---|
| Estimated average annual income | $91,200 ($273,600/3 years) |
| Average investment | $380,000 ($690,000 + $70,000)/2 |
| Average rate of return | 24% ($91,200/$380,000) |

Practice Exercises: **PE 25-1A, PE 25-1B**

## Cash Payback Method

A capital investment uses cash and must return cash in the future to be successful. The expected period of time between the date of an investment and the recovery in cash of the amount invested is the **cash payback period**.

When annual net cash inflows are equal, the cash payback period is computed as follows:

$$\text{Cash Payback Period} = \frac{\text{Initial Cost}}{\text{Annual Net Cash Inflow}}$$

To illustrate, assume that management is evaluating the purchase of the following new machine:

| | |
|---|---|
| Cost of new machine | $200,000 |
| Cash revenues from machine per year | 50,000 |
| Expenses of machine per year | 30,000 |
| Depreciation per year | 20,000 |

To simplify, the revenues and expenses other than depreciation are assumed to be in cash. Hence, the net cash inflow per year from use of the machine is as follows:

| | | |
|---|---|---|
| Net cash inflow per year: | | |
| Cash revenues from machine | | $50,000 |
| Less cash expenses of machine: | | |
| Expenses of machine | $30,000 | |
| Less depreciation | 20,000 | 10,000 |
| Net cash inflow per year | | $40,000 |

The time required for the net cash flow to equal the cost of the new machine is the payback period. Thus, the estimated cash payback period for the investment is five years, as computed below.

$$\text{Cash Payback Period} = \frac{\text{Initial Cost}}{\text{Annual Net Cash Inflow}} = \frac{\$200,000}{\$40,000} = 5 \text{ years}$$

In the preceding illustration, the annual net cash inflows are equal ($40,000 per year). When the annual net cash inflows are not equal, the cash payback period is determined by adding the annual net cash inflows until the cumulative total equals the initial cost of the proposed investment.

To illustrate, assume that a proposed investment has an initial cost of $400,000. The annual and cumulative net cash inflows over the proposal's six-year life are as follows:

| Year | Net Cash Flow | Cumulative Net Cash Flow |
|------|---------------|--------------------------|
| 1 | $ 60,000 | $ 60,000 |
| 2 | 80,000 | 140,000 |
| 3 | 105,000 | 245,000 |
| 4 | 155,000 | 400,000 |
| 5 | 100,000 | 500,000 |
| 6 | 90,000 | 590,000 |

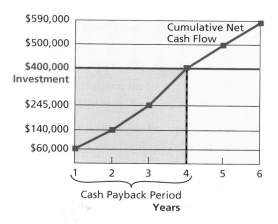

The cumulative net cash flow at the end of Year 4 equals the initial cost of the investment, $400,000. Thus, the payback period is four years.

If the initial cost of the proposed investment had been $450,000, the cash payback period would occur during Year 5. Since $100,000 of net cash flow is expected during Year 5, the additional $50,000 to increase the cumulative total to $450,000 occurs halfway through the year ($50,000/$100,000). Thus, the cash payback period would be 4½ years.[1]

A short cash payback period is desirable. This is because the sooner cash is recovered, the sooner it can be reinvested in other projects. In addition, there is less chance of losses from changing economic or business conditions. A short cash payback period is also desirable for quickly repaying any debt used to purchase the investment.

The cash payback method has the following two advantages:

1. It is simple to use and understand.
2. It analyzes cash flows.

The cash payback method has the following two disadvantages:

1. It ignores cash flows occurring after the payback period.
2. It does not use present value concepts in valuing cash flows occurring in different periods.

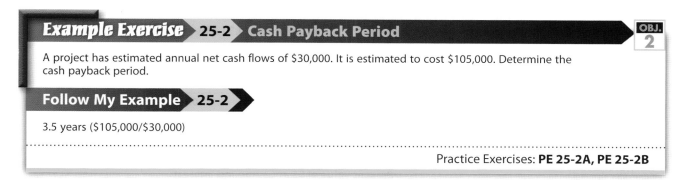

**Example Exercise** ⟩ **25-2** ⟩ **Cash Payback Period**   **OBJ. 2**

A project has estimated annual net cash flows of $30,000. It is estimated to cost $105,000. Determine the cash payback period.

**Follow My Example** ⟩ **25-2** ⟩

3.5 years ($105,000/$30,000)

Practice Exercises: **PE 25-2A, PE 25-2B**

# Methods Using Present Values

**OBJ. 3** Evaluate capital investment proposals using the net present value and internal rate of return methods.

An investment in fixed assets may be viewed as purchasing a series of net cash flows over a period of time. The timing of when the net cash flows will be received is important in determining the value of a proposed investment.

Present value methods use the amount and timing of the net cash flows in evaluating an investment. The two methods of evaluating capital investments using present values are as follows:

1. Net present value method
2. Internal rate of return method

1 Unless otherwise stated, net cash inflows are received uniformly throughout the year.

# Present Value Concepts

Both the net present value and the internal rate of return methods use the following two **present value concepts**:

1. Present value of an amount
2. Present value of an annuity

**Present Value of an Amount** If you were given the choice, would you prefer to receive $1 now or $1 three years from now? You should prefer to receive $1 now, because you could invest the $1 and earn interest for three years. As a result, the amount you would have after three years would be greater than $1.

To illustrate, assume that you have $1 to invest as follows:

| | |
|---|---|
| Amount to be invested | $1 |
| Period to be invested | 3 years |
| Interest rate | 12% |

After one year, the $1 earns interest of $0.12 ($1 × 12%) and, thus, will grow to $1.12 ($1 × 1.12). In the second year, the $1.12 earns 12% interest of $0.134 ($1.12 × 12%) and, thus, will grow to $1.254 ($1.12 × 1.12) by the end of the second year. This process of interest earning interest is called *compounding*. By the end of the third year, your $1 investment will grow to $1.404 as shown below.

On January 1, 2012, what is the present value of $1.404 to be received on December 31, 2014? This is a present value question. The answer can be determined with the aid of a present value of $1 table. For example, the partial table in Exhibit 1 indicates that the present value of $1 to be received in three years with earnings compounded at the rate of 12% per year is 0.712.[2] Multiplying 0.712 by $1.404 yields $1 as follows:

| Present Value | | Amount to Be Received in 3 Years | | Present Value of $1 to Be Received in 3 Years (from Exhibit 1) |
|---|---|---|---|---|
| $1 | = | $1.404 | × | 0.712 |

**EXHIBIT 1**

**Partial Present Value of $1 Table**

**Present Value of $1 at Compound Interest**

| Year | 6% | 10% | 12% | 15% | 20% |
|---|---|---|---|---|---|
| 1 | 0.943 | 0.909 | 0.893 | 0.870 | 0.833 |
| 2 | 0.890 | 0.826 | 0.797 | 0.756 | 0.694 |
| 3 | 0.840 | 0.751 | 0.712 | 0.658 | 0.579 |
| 4 | 0.792 | 0.683 | 0.636 | 0.572 | 0.482 |
| 5 | 0.747 | 0.621 | 0.567 | 0.497 | 0.402 |
| 6 | 0.705 | 0.564 | 0.507 | 0.432 | 0.335 |
| 7 | 0.665 | 0.513 | 0.452 | 0.376 | 0.279 |
| 8 | 0.627 | 0.467 | 0.404 | 0.327 | 0.233 |
| 9 | 0.592 | 0.424 | 0.361 | 0.284 | 0.194 |
| 10 | 0.558 | 0.386 | 0.322 | 0.247 | 0.162 |

2 The present value factors in the table are rounded to three decimal places. More complete tables of present values are in Appendix A.

That is, the present value of $1.404 to be received in three years using a compound interest rate of 12% is $1, as shown below.

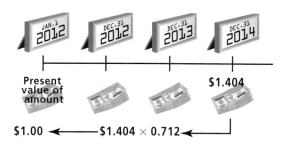

**Present Value of an Annuity** An **annuity** is a series of equal net cash flows at fixed time intervals. Annuities are very common in business. Cash payments for monthly rent, salaries, and bond interest are all examples of annuities.

The present value of an annuity is the sum of the present values of each cash flow. That is, the **present value of an annuity** is the amount of cash needed today to yield a series of equal net cash flows at fixed time intervals in the future.

To illustrate, the present value of a $100 annuity for five periods at 12% could be determined by using the present value factors in Exhibit 1. Each $100 net cash flow could be multiplied by the present value of $1 at a 12% factor for the appropriate period and summed to determine a present value of $360.50, as shown below.

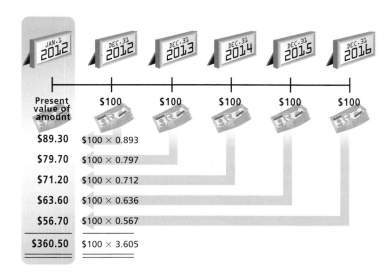

Using a present value of an annuity table is a simpler approach. Exhibit 2 is a partial table of present value annuity factors.[3]

The present value factors in the table shown in Exhibit 2 are the sum of the present value of $1 factors in Exhibit 1 for the number of annuity periods. Thus, 3.605 in the annuity table (Exhibit 2) is the sum of the five present value of $1 factors at 12%, as shown on the following page.

3 The present value factors in the table are rounded to three decimal places. More complete tables of present values are in Appendix A.

**EXHIBIT 2**

**Partial Present Value of an Annuity Table**

| | Present Value of an Annuity of $1 at Compound Interest | | | | |
| Year | 6% | 10% | 12% | 15% | 20% |
|---|---|---|---|---|---|
| 1 | 0.943 | 0.909 | 0.893 | 0.870 | 0.833 |
| 2 | 1.833 | 1.736 | 1.690 | 1.626 | 1.528 |
| 3 | 2.673 | 2.487 | 2.402 | 2.283 | 2.106 |
| 4 | 3.465 | 3.170 | 3.037 | 2.855 | 2.589 |
| 5 | 4.212 | 3.791 | 3.605 | 3.353 | 2.991 |
| 6 | 4.917 | 4.355 | 4.111 | 3.785 | 3.326 |
| 7 | 5.582 | 4.868 | 4.564 | 4.160 | 3.605 |
| 8 | 6.210 | 5.335 | 4.968 | 4.487 | 3.837 |
| 9 | 6.802 | 5.759 | 5.328 | 4.772 | 4.031 |
| 10 | 7.360 | 6.145 | 5.650 | 5.019 | 4.192 |

| | Present Value of $1 (Exhibit 1) |
|---|---|
| Present value of $1 for 1 year @12% | 0.893 |
| Present value of $1 for 2 years @12% | 0.797 |
| Present value of $1 for 3 years @12% | 0.712 |
| Present value of $1 for 4 years @12% | 0.636 |
| Present value of $1 for 5 years @12% | 0.567 |
| Present value of an annuity of $1 for 5 years (from Exhibit 2) | 3.605 |

Multiplying $100 by 3.605 yields the same amount ($360.50) as follows:

| Present Value | | Amount to Be Received Annually for 5 Years | | Present Value of an Annuity of $1 to Be Received for 5 Years (Exhibit 2) |
|---|---|---|---|---|
| $360.50 | = | $100 | × | 3.605 |

This is the same amount ($360.50) that was determined in the preceding illustration by five successive multiplications.

## Net Present Value Method

The **net present value method** compares the amount to be invested with the present value of the net cash inflows. It is sometimes called the *discounted cash flow method*.

The interest rate (return) used in net present value analysis is the company's minimum desired rate of return. This rate, sometimes termed the *hurdle rate*, is based on such factors as the purpose of the investment and the cost of obtaining funds for the investment. If the present value of the cash inflows equals or exceeds the amount to be invested, the proposal is desirable.

To illustrate, assume the following data for a proposed investment in new equipment:

| | |
|---|---|
| Cost of new equipment | $200,000 |
| Expected useful life | 5 years |
| Minimum desired rate of return | 10% |
| Expected cash flows to be received each year: | |
| Year 1 | $ 70,000 |
| Year 2 | 60,000 |
| Year 3 | 50,000 |
| Year 4 | 40,000 |
| Year 5 | 40,000 |
| Total expected cash flows | $260,000 |

A 55-year-old janitor won a $5 million lottery jackpot, payable in 21 annual installments of $240,245. Unfortunately, the janitor died after collecting only one payment. What happens to the remaining unclaimed payments? In this case, the lottery winnings were auctioned off for the benefit of the janitor's estate. The winning bid approximated the present value of the remaining cash flows, or about $2.1 million.

**Note:**
**The net present value method compares an investment's initial cash outflow with the present value of its cash inflows.**

The present value of the net cash flow for each year is computed by multiplying the net cash flow for the year by the present value factor of $1 for that year as shown below.

| Year | Present Value of $1 at 10% | Net Cash Flow | Present Value of Net Cash Flow |
|------|---------------------------|---------------|-------------------------------|
| 1 | 0.909 | $ 70,000 | $ 63,630 |
| 2 | 0.826 | 60,000 | 49,560 |
| 3 | 0.751 | 50,000 | 37,550 |
| 4 | 0.683 | 40,000 | 27,320 |
| 5 | 0.621 | 40,000 | 24,840 |
| Total | | $260,000 | $202,900 |
| Amount to be invested | | | 200,000 |
| Net present value | | | $ 2,900 |

The preceding computations are also graphically illustrated below.

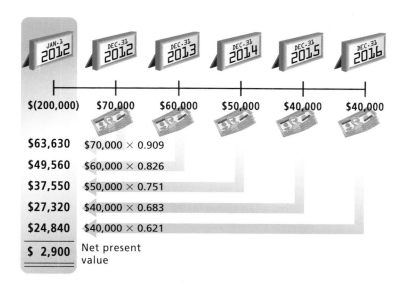

The net present value of $2,900 indicates that the purchase of the new equipment is expected to recover the investment and provide more than the minimum rate of return of 10%. Thus, the purchase of the new equipment is desirable.

When capital investment funds are limited and the proposals involve different investments, a ranking of the proposals can be prepared by using a present value index. The **present value index** is computed as follows:

$$\text{Present Value Index} = \frac{\text{Total Present Value of Net Cash Flow}}{\text{Amount to Be Invested}}$$

The present value index for the investment in the preceding illustration is 1.0145, as computed below.

$$\text{Present Value Index} = \frac{\text{Total Present Value of Net Cash Flow}}{\text{Amount to Be Invested}}$$

$$\text{Present Value Index} = \frac{\$202,900}{\$200,000} = 1.0145$$

**excel**
*success*

Spreadsheet software can be used to determine the net present value of a project using a specialized function, illustrated as follows:

| | A | B |
|---|---|---|
| 1 | Inputs: | |
| 2 | | |
| 3 | Minimum desired rate of return | 10% |
| 4 | | |
| 5 | | |
| 6 | Cost of new equipment | $ 200,000 |
| 7 | | |
| 8 | | Net Cash Flows |
| 9 | Year 1 | $70,000 |
| 10 | Year 2 | 60,000 |
| 11 | Year 3 | 50,000 |
| 12 | Year 4 | 40,000 |
| 13 | Year 5 | 40,000 |
| 14 | | |
| 15 | Output: | |
| 16 | | |
| 17 | Present value of cash flows | =NPV(B3,B9:B13) ◄—— **a.** |
| 18 | Less: amount to be invested | =B6 ◄—— **b.** |
| 19 | Net present value | =B17-B18 ◄—— **c.** |

The inputs include the minimum desired rate of return, cost of the new equipment (amount to be invested), and the end of each year net cash flows expected from the project.

The outputs consist of the following three steps:

**a.** Enter in B17 the formula for calculating the present value of the net cash flows of the project using the =NPV function as follows,

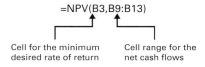

=NPV(B3,B9:B13)

Cell for the minimum          Cell range for the
desired rate of return        net cash flows

**b.** Enter in cell B18 the cell reference for the cost of the equipment (amount to be invested), B6.

**c.** Enter in cell B19 the difference between the net present value of cash flows and amount to be invested, =B17-B18. In your spreadsheet the net present value will calculate to $2,946. The amount shown in the text, $2,900, is rounded.

**Try**It    Go to the hands-on **Excel Tutor** for this example!

Assume that a company is considering three proposals. The net present value and the present value index for each proposal are as follows:

| | Proposal A | Proposal B | Proposal C |
|---|---|---|---|
| Total present value of net cash flow | $107,000 | $86,400 | $86,400 |
| Amount to be invested | 100,000 | 80,000 | 90,000 |
| Net present value | $ 7,000 | $ 6,400 | $ (3,600) |
| Present value index: | | | |
| Proposal A ($107,000/$100,000) | 1.07 | | |
| Proposal B ($86,400/$80,000) | | 1.08 | |
| Proposal C ($86,400/$90,000) | | | 0.96 |

A project will have a present value index greater than 1 when the net present value is positive. This is the case for Proposals A and B. When the net present value is negative, the present value index will be less than 1, as is the case for Proposal C.

Although Proposal A has the largest net present value, the present value indices indicate that it is not as desirable as Proposal B. That is, Proposal B returns $1.08 present value per dollar invested, whereas Proposal A returns only $1.07. Proposal B requires an investment of $80,000, compared to an investment of $100,000 for Proposal A. The possible use of the $20,000 difference between Proposals A and B investments should also be considered before making a final decision.

The use of spreadsheet software such as Microsoft Excel can simplify present value computations.

The net present value method has the following three advantages:

1. It considers the cash flows of the investment.
2. It considers the time value of money.
3. It can rank equal lived projects using the present value index.

The net present value method has the following two disadvantages:

1. It has more complex computations than methods that don't use present value.
2. It assumes the cash flows can be reinvested at the minimum desired rate of return, which may not be valid.

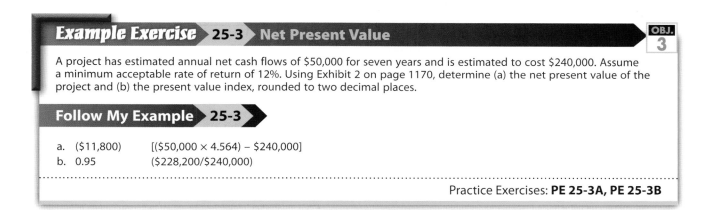

**Example Exercise** 25-3 **Net Present Value** OBJ. 3

A project has estimated annual net cash flows of $50,000 for seven years and is estimated to cost $240,000. Assume a minimum acceptable rate of return of 12%. Using Exhibit 2 on page 1170, determine (a) the net present value of the project and (b) the present value index, rounded to two decimal places.

**Follow My Example** 25-3

a. ($11,800)  [($50,000 × 4.564) – $240,000]
b. 0.95  ($228,200/$240,000)

Practice Exercises: **PE 25-3A, PE 25-3B**

## Internal Rate of Return Method

The **internal rate of return (IRR) method** uses present value concepts to compute the rate of return from a capital investment proposal based on its expected net cash flows. This method, sometimes called the *time-adjusted rate of return method*, starts with the proposal's net cash flows and works backward to estimate the proposal's expected rate of return.

To illustrate, assume that management is evaluating the following proposal to purchase new equipment:

| | |
|---|---|
| Cost of new equipment | $33,530 |
| Yearly expected cash flows to be received | 10,000 |
| Expected life | 5 years |
| Minimum desired rate of return | 12% |

The present value of the net cash flows, using the present value of an annuity table in Exhibit 2 on page 1170 is $2,520, as shown in Exhibit 3.

**EXHIBIT 3**

**Net Present Value Analysis at 12%**

| | |
|---|---:|
| Annual net cash flow (at the end of each of five years) | $10,000 |
| Present value of an annuity of $1 at 12% for five years (Exhibit 2) | × 3.605 |
| Present value of annual net cash flows | $36,050 |
| Less amount to be invested | 33,530 |
| Net present value | $ 2,520 |

In Exhibit 3, the $36,050 present value of the cash inflows, based on a 12% rate of return, is greater than the $33,530 to be invested. Thus, the internal rate of return must be greater than 12%. Through trial and error, the rate of return equating the $33,530 cost of the investment with the present value of the net cash flows can be determined to be 15%, as shown below.

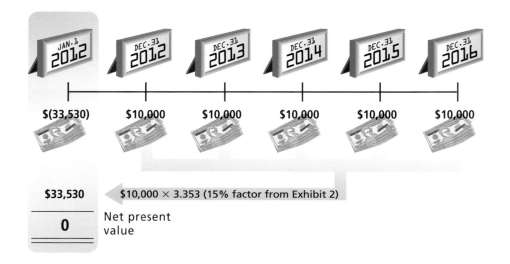

When equal annual net cash flows are expected from a proposal, as in the above example, the internal rate of return can be determined as follows:[4]

Step 1. Determine a present value factor for an annuity of $1 as follows:

$$\text{Present Value Factor for an Annuity of } \$1 = \frac{\text{Amount to Be Invested}}{\text{Equal Annual Net Cash Flows}}$$

Step 2. Locate the present value factor determined in Step 1 in the present value of an annuity of $1 table (Exhibit 2 on page 1170) as follows:

a. Locate the number of years of expected useful life of the investment in the Year column.

b. Proceed horizontally across the table until you find the present value factor computed in Step 1.

Step 3. Identify the internal rate of return by the heading of the column in which the present value factor in Step 2 is located.

---

4 To simplify, equal annual net cash flows are assumed. If the net cash flows are not equal, spreadsheet software can be used to determine the rate of return.

To illustrate, assume that management is evaluating the following proposal to purchase new equipment:

| | |
|---|---|
| Cost of new equipment | $97,360 |
| Yearly expected cash flows to be received | 20,000 |
| Expected useful life | 7 years |

The present value factor for an annuity of $1 is 4.868, as shown below.

$$\text{Present Value Factor for an Annuity of } \$1 = \frac{\text{Amount to Be Invested}}{\text{Equal Annual Net Cash Flows}}$$

$$\text{Present Value Factor for an Annuity of } \$1 = \frac{\$97,360}{\$20,000} = 4.868$$

Using the partial present value of an annuity of $1 table shown below and a period of seven years, the factor 4.868 is related to 10%. Thus, the internal rate of return for this proposal is 10%.

**Present Value of an Annuity of $1 at Compound Interest**

| Year | 6% | | 10% | 12% |
|---|---|---|---|---|
| 1 | 0.943 | | 0.909 | 0.893 |
| 2 | 1.833 | | 1.736 | 1.690 |
| 3 | 2.673 | | 2.487 | 2.402 |
| 4 | 3.465 | | 3.170 | 3.037 |
| 5 | 4.212 | | 3.791 | 3.605 |
| 6 | 4.917 | Step 2(b) | 4.355 | 4.111 |
| Step 2(a) 7 | 5.582 | | 4.868 | 4.564 |
| 8 | 6.210 | | 5.335 | 4.968 |
| 9 | 6.802 | | 5.759 | 5.328 |
| 10 | 7.360 | | 6.145 | 5.650 |

Step 3 → (above 10%)

**Step 1:** Determine present value factor for an annuity of $1 $= \dfrac{\$97,360}{\$20,000} = 4.868$

If the minimum acceptable rate of return is 10%, then the proposal is considered acceptable. Several proposals can be ranked by their internal rates of return. The proposal with the highest rate is the most desirable.

The internal rate of return method has the following three advantages:

1. It considers the cash flows of the investment.
2. It considers the time value of money.
3. It ranks proposals based upon the cash flows over their complete useful life, even if the project lives are not the same.

The internal rate of return method has the following two disadvantages:

1. It has complex computations, requiring a computer if the periodic cash flows are not equal (an annuity).
2. It assumes the cash received from a proposal can be reinvested at the internal rate of return, which may not be valid.

# BusinessConnection

## PANERA BREAD STORE RATE OF RETURN

Panera Bread owns, operates, and franchises bakery-cafes throughout the United States. A recent annual report to the Securities and Exchange Commission (SEC Form 10-K) disclosed the following information about an average company-owned store:

| | |
|---|---|
| Operating profit | $ 327,000 |
| Depreciation | 98,000 |
| Investment | 1,000,000 |

Assume that the operating profit and depreciation will remain unchanged for the next 10 years. Assume operating profit plus depreciation approximates annual net cash flows, and that the investment residual value will be zero. The average rate of return and internal rate of return can then be estimated. The average rate of return on a company-owned store is:

$$\frac{\$327,000}{\$1,000,000/2} = 65.4\%$$

The internal rate of return is calculated by first determining the present value of an annuity of $1:

$$\frac{\text{Present Value}}{\text{of an Annuity of \$1}} = \frac{\$1,000,000}{\$327,000 + \$98,000} = 2.35$$

For a period of three years, this factor implies an internal rate of return over 12% (from Exhibit 2). However, if we more realistically assumed these cash flows for 10 years, Panera's company-owned stores generate an estimated internal rate of return of approximately 41% (from a spreadsheet calculation). Clearly, both investment evaluation methods indicate a highly successful business.

© Jeff Greenberg/Alamy

---

*success*

The internal rate of return can be determined using a spreadsheet formula, as follows:

| | A | B |
|---|---|---|
| 1 | *Inputs:* | |
| 2 | | |
| 3 | | |
| 4 | | Net Cash Flows |
| 5 | Cost of new equipment | $ (97,360) |
| 6 | Year 1 | 20,000 |
| 7 | Year 2 | 20,000 |
| 8 | Year 3 | 20,000 |
| 9 | Year 4 | 20,000 |
| 10 | Year 5 | 20,000 |
| 11 | Year 6 | 20,000 |
| 12 | Year 7 | 20,000 |
| 13 | | |
| 14 | *Output:* | |
| 15 | | |
| 16 | Internal rate of return | =IRR(B5:B12) ← **a.** |

The inputs are the cash flows of the project, beginning with the initial investment entered as a negative number. In this case, the cost of the equipment is $97,360, which is entered in cell B5 as a negative number.

The remaining cash flows are entered individually for each of the years of the project life. The equipment will generate cash flows of $20,000 at the end of each year of the expected seven years of equipment life. These cash flows are entered in B6:B12.

**a.** The output is the internal rate of return. Enter in cell B16 the Excel =IRR function, as follows:

=IRR(B5:B12)

The range B5:B12 covers the cash flows of the project, including the first cash flow (initial investment) entered as a negative number. The internal rate of return calculated is 10%, the same rate using the table method.

One advantage of the spreadsheet approach is that the =IRR function can estimate the internal rate of return for a series of unequal cash flows, which is not possible to determine under the table method.

**TryIt**   Go to the hands-on **Excel Tutor** for this example!

---

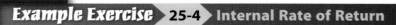

**Example Exercise** **25-4** **Internal Rate of Return**   **OBJ. 3**

A project is estimated to cost $208,175 and provide annual net cash flows of $55,000 for six years. Determine the internal rate of return for this project, using Exhibit 2 on page 1170.

**Follow My Example** **25-4**

15%   [($208,175/$55,000) = 3.785, the present value of an annuity factor for six periods at 15%, from Exhibit 2]

Practice Exercises: **PE 25-4A, PE 25-4B**

---

# Factors That Complicate Capital Investment Analysis

**OBJ. 4** List and describe factors that complicate capital investment analysis.

Four widely used methods of evaluating capital investment proposals have been described and illustrated in this chapter. In practice, additional factors such as the following may impact capital investment decisions:

1. Income tax
2. Proposals with unequal lives
3. Leasing versus purchasing
4. Uncertainty
5. Changes in price levels
6. Qualitative factors

## Income Tax

The impact of income taxes on capital investment decisions can be material. For example, in determining depreciation for federal income tax purposes, useful lives that are much shorter than the actual useful lives are often used. Also, depreciation for tax purposes often differs from depreciation for financial statement purposes. As a result, the timing of the cash flows for income taxes can have a significant impact on capital investment analysis.[5]

## Unequal Proposal Lives

The prior capital investment illustrations assumed that the alternative proposals had the same useful lives. In practice, however, proposals often have different lives.

---

5 The impact of taxes on capital investment analysis is covered in advanced accounting textbooks.

To illustrate, assume that a company is considering purchasing a new truck or a new computer network. The data for each proposal are shown below.

| | Truck | Computer Network |
|---|---|---|
| Cost | $100,000 | $100,000 |
| Minimum desired rate of return | 10% | 10% |
| Expected useful life | 8 years | 5 years |
| Yearly expected cash flows to be received: | | |
| Year 1 | $ 30,000 | $ 30,000 |
| Year 2 | 30,000 | 30,000 |
| Year 3 | 25,000 | 30,000 |
| Year 4 | 20,000 | 30,000 |
| Year 5 | 15,000 | 35,000 |
| Year 6 | 15,000 | 0 |
| Year 7 | 10,000 | 0 |
| Year 8 | 10,000 | 0 |
| Total | $155,000 | $155,000 |

The expected cash flows and net present value for each proposal are shown in Exhibit 4. Because of the unequal useful lives, however, the net present values in Exhibit 4 are not comparable.

To make the proposals comparable, the useful lives are adjusted to end at the same time. In this illustration, this is done by assuming that the truck will be sold at the end of five years. The selling price (residual value) of the truck at the end of five years is estimated and included in the cash inflows. Both proposals will then cover five years; thus, the net present value analyses will be comparable.

To illustrate, assume that the truck's estimated selling price (residual value) at the end of Year 5 is $40,000. Exhibit 5 shows the truck's revised present value analysis assuming a five-year life.

As shown in Exhibit 5, the net present value for the truck exceeds the net present value for the computer network by $1,835 ($18,640 – $16,805). Thus, the truck is the more attractive of the two proposals.

---

**Example Exercise** ❯ **25-5** ❯ **Net Present Value—Unequal Lives**
OBJ. 4

Project 1 requires an original investment of $50,000. The project will yield cash flows of $12,000 per year for seven years. Project 2 has a calculated net present value of $8,900 over a five-year life. Project 1 could be sold at the end of five years for a price of $30,000. (a) Determine the net present value of Project 1 over a five-year life with residual value, assuming a minimum rate of return of 12%. (b) Which project provides the greatest net present value?

**Follow My Example** ❯ **25-5** ❯

Project 1

a. Present value of $12,000 per year at 12% for 5 years    $43,260    [$12,000 × 3.605 (Exhibit 2, 12%, 5 years)]
    Present value of $30,000 at 12% at the end of 5 years    17,010    [$30,000 × 0.567 (Exhibit 1, 12%, 5 years)]
    Total present value of Project 1    $60,270
    Total cost of Project 1    50,000
    Net present value of Project 1    $10,270

b. Project 1—$10,270 is greater than the net present value of Project 2, $8,900.

Practice Exercises: **PE 25-5A, PE 25-5B**

**EXHIBIT 4**   Net Present Value Analysis—Unequal Lives of Proposals

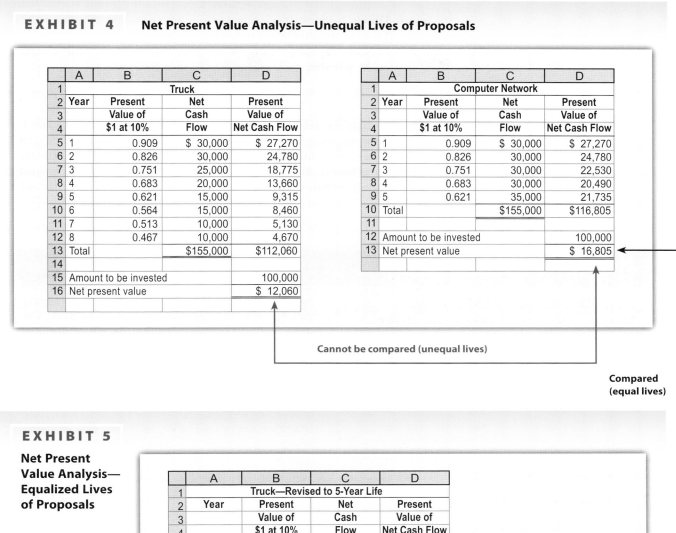

| | A | B | C | D |
|---|---|---|---|---|
| 1 | | Truck | | |
| 2 | Year | Present | Net | Present |
| 3 | | Value of | Cash | Value of |
| 4 | | $1 at 10% | Flow | Net Cash Flow |
| 5 | 1 | 0.909 | $ 30,000 | $ 27,270 |
| 6 | 2 | 0.826 | 30,000 | 24,780 |
| 7 | 3 | 0.751 | 25,000 | 18,775 |
| 8 | 4 | 0.683 | 20,000 | 13,660 |
| 9 | 5 | 0.621 | 15,000 | 9,315 |
| 10 | 6 | 0.564 | 15,000 | 8,460 |
| 11 | 7 | 0.513 | 10,000 | 5,130 |
| 12 | 8 | 0.467 | 10,000 | 4,670 |
| 13 | Total | | $155,000 | $112,060 |
| 14 | | | | |
| 15 | Amount to be invested | | | 100,000 |
| 16 | Net present value | | | $ 12,060 |

| | A | B | C | D |
|---|---|---|---|---|
| 1 | | Computer Network | | |
| 2 | Year | Present | Net | Present |
| 3 | | Value of | Cash | Value of |
| 4 | | $1 at 10% | Flow | Net Cash Flow |
| 5 | 1 | 0.909 | $ 30,000 | $ 27,270 |
| 6 | 2 | 0.826 | 30,000 | 24,780 |
| 7 | 3 | 0.751 | 30,000 | 22,530 |
| 8 | 4 | 0.683 | 30,000 | 20,490 |
| 9 | 5 | 0.621 | 35,000 | 21,735 |
| 10 | Total | | $155,000 | $116,805 |
| 11 | | | | |
| 12 | Amount to be invested | | | 100,000 |
| 13 | Net present value | | | $ 16,805 |

Cannot be compared (unequal lives)

Compared (equal lives)

**EXHIBIT 5**

**Net Present Value Analysis— Equalized Lives of Proposals**

| | A | B | C | D |
|---|---|---|---|---|
| 1 | | Truck—Revised to 5-Year Life | | |
| 2 | Year | Present | Net | Present |
| 3 | | Value of | Cash | Value of |
| 4 | | $1 at 10% | Flow | Net Cash Flow |
| 5 | 1 | 0.909 | $ 30,000 | $ 27,270 |
| 6 | 2 | 0.826 | 30,000 | 24,780 |
| 7 | 3 | 0.751 | 25,000 | 18,775 |
| 8 | 4 | 0.683 | 20,000 | 13,660 |
| 9 | 5 | 0.621 | 15,000 | 9,315 |
| 10 | 5 (Residual | | | |
| 11 | value) | 0.621 | 40,000 | 24,840 |
| 12 | Total | | $160,000 | $118,640 |
| 13 | | | | |
| 14 | Amount to be invested | | | 100,000 |
| 15 | Net present value | | | $ 18,640 |

Truck Net Present Value Greater than Computer Network Net Present Value by $1,835

# Lease versus Capital Investment

Leasing fixed assets is common in many industries. For example, hospitals often lease medical equipment. Some advantages of leasing a fixed asset include the following:

1. The company has use of the fixed asset without spending large amounts of cash to purchase the asset.
2. The company eliminates the risk of owning an obsolete asset.
3. The company may deduct the annual lease payments for income tax purposes.

A disadvantage of leasing a fixed asset is that it is normally more costly than purchasing the asset. This is because the lessor (owner of the asset) includes in the rental price not only the costs of owning the asset, but also a profit.

The methods of evaluating capital investment proposals illustrated in this chapter can also be used to decide whether to lease or purchase a fixed asset.

## Uncertainty

All capital investment analyses rely on factors that are uncertain. For example, estimates of revenues, expenses, and cash flows are uncertain. This is especially true for long-term capital investments. Errors in one or more of the estimates could lead to incorrect decisions. Methods that consider the impact of uncertainty on capital investment analysis are discussed in advanced accounting and finance textbooks.

## BusinessConnection

### AVATAR: THE MOST EXPENSIVE MOVIE EVER MADE (AND THE MOST SUCCESSFUL)

Prior to the release of the blockbuster *Avatar* in December 2009, many were skeptical that the movie's huge $500 million investment would pay off. After all, just to break even the movie would have to perform as one of the top 50 movies of all time. To provide a return that was double the investment, the movie would have to crack the top ten. Many thought this was a tall order, even though James Cameron, the force behind this movie, already had the number one grossing movie of all time: *Titanic*, at $1.8 billion in worldwide box office revenues. Could he do it again? That was the question.

So, how did the film do? Only eight weeks after its release, Avatar had become the number one grossing film of all time, with over $2.2 billion in worldwide box office revenue. Executives at Fox anticipated that the profit might double after the film was released on DVD in the summer of 2010. Needless to say, James Cameron, 20th Century Fox, and other investors are very pleased with their return on this investment.

Sources: Michael Cieply, "A Movie's Budget Pops from the Screen," *New York Times*, November 8, 2009; "Bulk of Avatar Profit Still to Come," *The Age*, February 3, 2010.

## Changes in Price Levels

Price levels normally change as the economy improves or deteriorates. General price levels often increase in a rapidly growing economy, which is called **inflation**. During such periods, the rate of return on an investment should exceed the rising price level. If this is not the case, the cash returned on the investment will be less than expected.

Price levels may also change for foreign investments. This occurs as currency exchange rates change. **Currency exchange rates** are the rates at which currency in another country can be exchanged for U.S. dollars.

If the amount of local currency that can be exchanged for one U.S. dollar increases, then the local currency is said to be weakening to the dollar. When a company has an investment in another country where the local currency is weakening, the return on the investment, as expressed in U.S. dollars, is adversely impacted. This is because the expected amount of local currency returned on the investment would purchase fewer U.S. dollars.[6]

6 Further discussion on accounting for foreign currency transactions is available on the companion Web site at **www.cengage.com/accounting/reeve**.

## Qualitative Considerations

Some benefits of capital investments are qualitative in nature and cannot be estimated in dollar terms. However, if a company does not consider qualitative considerations, an acceptable investment proposal could be rejected.

Some examples of qualitative considerations that may influence capital investment analysis include the impact of the investment proposal on the following:

1. Product quality
2. Manufacturing flexibility
3. Employee morale
4. Manufacturing productivity
5. Market (strategic) opportunities

Many qualitative factors, such as those listed above, may be as important as, if not more important than, quantitative factors.

## Integrity, Objectivity, and Ethics in Business

**ASSUMPTION FUDGING**

The results of any capital budgeting analysis depend on many subjective estimates, such as the cash flows, discount rate, time period, and total investment amount. The results of the analysis should be used to either support or reject a project. Capital budgeting should not be used to justify an assumed net present value. That is, the analyst should not work backwards, filling in assumed numbers that will produce the desired net present value. Such a reverse approach reduces the credibility of the entire process.

## Capital Rationing

**OBJ. 5** Diagram the capital rationing process.

**Capital rationing** is the process by which management allocates funds among competing capital investment proposals. In this process, management often uses a combination of the methods described in this chapter.

Exhibit 6 illustrates the capital rationing decision process. Alternative proposals are initially screened by establishing minimum standards using the cash payback and the average rate of return methods. The proposals that survive this screening are further analyzed, using the net present value and internal rate of return methods.

Qualitative factors related to each proposal should also be considered throughout the capital rationing process. For example, new equipment might improve the quality of the product and, thus, increase consumer satisfaction and sales.

At the end of the capital rationing process, accepted proposals are ranked and compared with the funds available. Proposals that are selected for funding are included in the capital expenditures budget. Unfunded proposals may be reconsidered if funds later become available.

**EXHIBIT 6**    **Capital Rationing Decision Process**

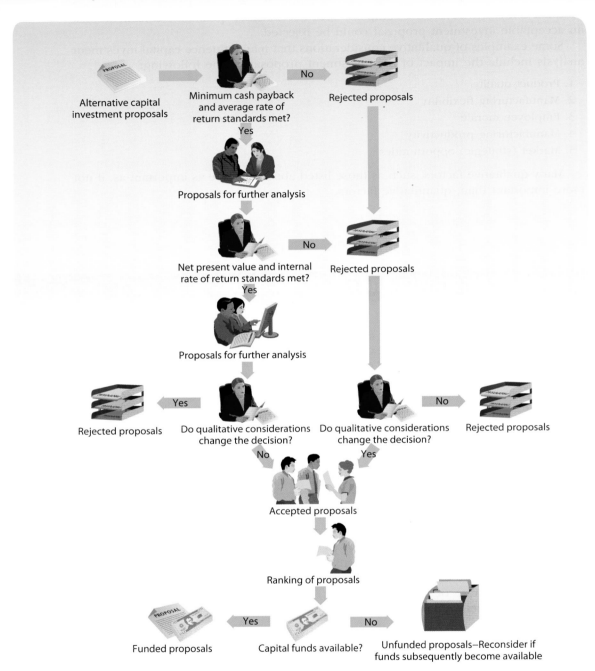

# At a Glance 25

**OBJ. 1**

### Explain the nature and importance of capital investment analysis.

**Key Points**   Capital investment analysis is the process by which management plans, evaluates, and controls investments involving fixed assets. Capital investment analysis is important to a business because such investments affect profitability for a long period of time.

| Learning Outcomes | Example Exercises | Practice Exercises |
|---|---|---|
| • Describe the purpose of capital investment analysis. | | |

**OBJ. 2**

### Evaluate capital investment proposals using the average rate of return and cash payback methods.

**Key Points**   The average rate of return method measures the expected profitability of an investment in fixed assets. The expected period of time that will pass between the date of an investment and the complete recovery in cash (or equivalent) of the amount invested is the cash payback period.

| Learning Outcomes | Example Exercises | Practice Exercises |
|---|---|---|
| • Compute the average rate of return of a project. | EE25-1 | PE25-1A, 25-1B |
| • Compute the cash payback period of a project. | EE25-2 | PE25-2A, 25-2B |

**OBJ. 3**

### Evaluate capital investment proposals using the net present value and internal rate of return methods.

**Key Points**   The net present value method uses present values to compute the net present value of the cash flows expected from a proposal. The internal rate of return method uses present values to compute the rate of return from the net cash flows expected from capital investment proposals.

| Learning Outcomes | Example Exercises | Practice Exercises |
|---|---|---|
| • Compute the net present value of a project. | EE25-3 | PE25-3A, 25-3B |
| • Compute the internal rate of return of a project. | EE25-4 | PE25-4A, 25-4B |

**OBJ. 4**

### List and describe factors that complicate capital investment analysis.

**Key Points**   Factors that may complicate capital investment analysis include the impact of income tax, unequal lives of alternative proposals, leasing, uncertainty, changes in price levels, and qualitative considerations.

| Learning Outcomes | Example Exercises | Practice Exercises |
|---|---|---|
| • Describe the impact of income taxes in capital investment analysis. | | |
| • Evaluate projects with unequal lives. | EE25-5 | PE25-5A, 25-5B |
| • Describe leasing versus capital investment. | | |
| • Describe uncertainty, changes in price levels, and qualitative considerations in capital investment analysis. | | |

**OBJ.**
**5**
**Diagram the capital rationing process.**

**Key Points** Capital rationing refers to the process by which management allocates available investment funds among competing capital investment proposals. A diagram of the capital rationing process appears in Exhibit 6.

| Learning Outcomes | Example Exercises | Practice Exercises |
|---|---|---|
| • Define *capital rationing*. | | |
| • Diagram the capital rationing process. | | |

## Key Terms

annuity (1169)
average rate of return (1165)
capital investment analysis (1164)
capital rationing (1181)
cash payback period (1166)

currency exchange rate (1180)
inflation (1180)
internal rate of return (IRR) method (1173)
net present value method (1170)
present value concepts (1168)

present value index (1171)
present value of an annuity (1169)
time value of money concept (1164)

## Illustrative Problem

The capital investment committee of Hopewell Company is currently considering two investments. The estimated income from operations and net cash flows expected from each investment are as follows:

| | Truck | | Equipment | |
|---|---|---|---|---|
| **Year** | **Income from Operations** | **Net Cash Flow** | **Income from Operations** | **Net Cash Flow** |
| 1 | $ 6,000 | $ 22,000 | $13,000 | $ 29,000 |
| 2 | 9,000 | 25,000 | 10,000 | 26,000 |
| 3 | 10,000 | 26,000 | 8,000 | 24,000 |
| 4 | 8,000 | 24,000 | 8,000 | 24,000 |
| 5 | 11,000 | 27,000 | 3,000 | 19,000 |
| | $44,000 | $124,000 | $42,000 | $122,000 |

Each investment requires $80,000. Straight-line depreciation will be used, and no residual value is expected. The committee has selected a rate of 15% for purposes of the net present value analysis.

### Instructions

1. Compute the following:

    a. The average rate of return for each investment.

    b. The net present value for each investment. Use the present value of $1 table appearing in this chapter (Exhibit 1).

2. Why is the net present value of the equipment greater than the truck, even though its average rate of return is less?

3. Prepare a summary for the capital investment committee, advising it on the relative merits of the two investments.

### Solution

1. a. Average rate of return for the truck:

$$\frac{\$44,000 \div 5}{(\$80,000 + \$0) \div 2} = 22\%$$

Average rate of return for the equipment:

$$\frac{\$42,000 \div 5}{(\$80,000 + \$0) \div 2} = 21\%$$

b. Net present value analysis:

| Year | Present Value of $1 at 15% | Net Cash Flow | | Present Value of Net Cash Flow | |
|------|------|------|------|------|------|
| | | Truck | Equipment | Truck | Equipment |
| 1 | 0.870 | $ 22,000 | $ 29,000 | $19,140 | $25,230 |
| 2 | 0.756 | 25,000 | 26,000 | 18,900 | 19,656 |
| 3 | 0.658 | 26,000 | 24,000 | 17,108 | 15,792 |
| 4 | 0.572 | 24,000 | 24,000 | 13,728 | 13,728 |
| 5 | 0.497 | 27,000 | 19,000 | 13,419 | 9,443 |
| Total | | $124,000 | $122,000 | $82,295 | $83,849 |
| Amount to be invested | | | | 80,000 | 80,000 |
| Net present value | | | | $ 2,295 | $ 3,849 |

2. The equipment has a lower average rate of return than the truck because the equipment's total income from operations for the five years is $42,000, which is $2,000 less than the truck's. Even so, the net present value of the equipment is greater than that of the truck, because the equipment has higher cash flows in the early years.

3. Both investments exceed the selected rate established for the net present value analysis. The truck has a higher average rate of return, but the equipment offers a larger net present value. Thus, if only one of the two investments can be accepted, the equipment would be the more attractive.

## Discussion Questions

1. What are the principal objections to the use of the average rate of return method in evaluating capital investment proposals?

2. Discuss the principal limitations of the cash payback method for evaluating capital investment proposals.

3. Why would the average rate of return differ from the internal rate of return on the same project?

4. Your boss has suggested that a one-year payback period is the same as a 100% average rate of return. Do you agree?

5. Why would the cash payback method understate the attractiveness of a project with a large residual value?

6. Why would the use of the cash payback period for analyzing the financial performance of theatrical releases from a motion picture production studio be supported over the net present value method?

7. A net present value analysis used to evaluate a proposed equipment acquisition indicated a $7,900 net present value. What is the meaning of the $7,900 as it relates to the desirability of the proposal?

8. Two projects have an identical net present value of $9,000. Are both projects equal in desirability?

9. What are the major disadvantages of the use of the net present value method of analyzing capital investment proposals?

10. What are the major disadvantages of the use of the internal rate of return method of analyzing capital investment proposals?

11. What are the major advantages of leasing a fixed asset rather than purchasing it?

12. Give an example of a qualitative factor that should be considered in a capital investment analysis related to acquiring automated factory equipment.

# Practice Exercises

| Learning Objectives | Example Exercises | |
|---|---|---|
| OBJ. 2 | EE 25-1 p. 1166 | **PE 25-1A** **Average rate of return** |

Determine the average rate of return for a project that is estimated to yield total income of $180,000 over five years, has a cost of $340,000, and has a $20,000 residual value.

| OBJ. 2 | EE 25-1 p. 1166 | **PE 25-1B** **Average rate of return** |
|---|---|---|

Determine the average rate of return for a project that is estimated to yield total income of $54,000 over three years, has a cost of $80,000, and has a $20,000 residual value.

| OBJ. 2 | EE 25-2 p. 1167 | **PE 25-2A** **Cash payback period** |
|---|---|---|

A project has estimated annual net cash flows of $121,000. It is estimated to cost $798,600. Determine the cash payback period. Round to one decimal place.

| OBJ. 2 | EE 25-2 p. 1167 | **PE 25-2B** **Cash payback period** |
|---|---|---|

A project has estimated annual net cash flows of $8,600. It is estimated to cost $47,300. Determine the cash payback period. Round to one decimal place.

| OBJ. 3 | EE 25-3 p. 1173 | **PE 25-3A** **Net present value** |
|---|---|---|

A project has estimated annual net cash flows of $86,400 for five years and is estimated to cost $259,000. Assume a minimum acceptable rate of return of 12%. Using Exhibit 2, determine (1) the net present value of the project and (2) the present value index, rounded to two decimal places.

| OBJ. 3 | EE 25-3 p. 1173 | **PE 25-3B** **Net present value** |
|---|---|---|

A project has estimated annual net cash flows of $8,200 for four years and is estimated to cost $30,050. Assume a minimum acceptable rate of return of 10%. Using Exhibit 2, determine (1) the net present value of the project and (2) the present value index, rounded to two decimal places.

| OBJ. 3 | EE 25-4 p. 1177 | **PE 25-4A** **Internal rate of return** |
|---|---|---|

A project is estimated to cost $71,580 and provide annual net cash flows of $15,000 for nine years. Determine the internal rate of return for this project, using Exhibit 2.

| OBJ. 3 | EE 25-4 p. 1177 | **PE 25-4B** **Internal rate of return** |
|---|---|---|

A project is estimated to cost $409,370 and provide annual net cash flows of $94,000 for six years. Determine the internal rate of return for this project, using Exhibit 2.

| OBJ. 4 | EE 25-5 p. 1178 | **PE 25-5A** **Net present value—unequal lives** |
|---|---|---|

Project A requires an original investment of $112,000. The project will yield cash flows of $22,000 per year for nine years. Project B has a calculated net present value of $2,400 over a six-year life. Project A could be sold at the end of six years for a price of $50,000. (a) Determine the net present value of Project A over a six-year life with residual value, assuming a minimum rate of return of 12%. (b) Which project provides the greatest net present value?

---

**OBJ. 4**  **EE 25-5** *p. 1178*  **PE 25-5B  Net present value—unequal lives**

Project 1 requires an original investment of $12,000. The project will yield cash flows of $4,000 per year for seven years. Project 2 has a calculated net present value of $6,500 over a four-year life. Project 1 could be sold at the end of four years for a price of $14,500. (a) Determine the net present value of Project 1 over a four-year life with residual value, assuming a minimum rate of return of 20%. (b) Which project provides the greatest net present value?

## Exercises

---

**OBJ. 2**

✔ Testing equipment, 9%

**EX 25-1  Average rate of return**

The following data are accumulated by ChemLabs, Inc. in evaluating two competing capital investment proposals:

|  | Testing Equipment | Vehicle |
| --- | --- | --- |
| Amount of investment | $90,000 | $25,000 |
| Useful life | 6 years | 8 years |
| Estimated residual value | 0 | 0 |
| Estimated total income over the useful life | $24,300 | $15,000 |

Determine the expected average rate of return for each proposal.

---

**OBJ. 2**

**EX 25-2  Average rate of return—cost savings**

Wisconsin Fabricators Inc. is considering an investment in equipment that will replace direct labor. The equipment has a cost of $90,000 with a $10,000 residual value and a 10-year life. The equipment will replace one employee who has an average wage of $30,000 per year. In addition, the equipment will have operating and energy costs of $4,500 per year.

Determine the average rate of return on the equipment, giving effect to straight-line depreciation on the investment.

---

**OBJ. 2**

✔ Average annual income, $252,000

**EX 25-3  Average rate of return—new product**

I-Mobile Inc. is considering an investment in new equipment that will be used to manufacture a mobile communications device. The device is expected to generate additional annual sales of 2,100 units at $370 per unit. The equipment has a cost of $920,000, residual value of $88,000, and an eight-year life. The equipment can only be used to manufacture the device. The cost to manufacture the device is shown below.

| Cost per unit: | |
| --- | --- |
| Direct labor | $ 45 |
| Direct materials | 170 |
| Factory overhead (including depreciation) | 35 |
| Total cost per unit | $250 |

Determine the average rate of return on the equipment.

---

**OBJ. 2**

Year 1: ($98,000)

**EX 25-4  Calculate cash flows**

Earth's Bounty, Inc., is planning to invest in new manufacturing equipment to make a new garden tool. The new garden tool is expected to generate additional annual sales of 10,000 units at $58 each. The new manufacturing equipment will cost $177,000 and is expected to have a 10-year life and $13,000 residual value. Selling expenses related to the new product are expected to be 5% of sales revenue. The cost to manufacture the product includes the following on a per-unit basis:

| | |
|---|---|
| Direct labor | $ 8.00 |
| Direct materials | 35.00 |
| Fixed factory overhead—depreciation | 1.64 |
| Variable factory overhead | 4.20 |
| Total | $48.84 |

Determine the net cash flows for the first year of the project, Years 2–9, and for the last year of the project.

---

OBJ. 2

✔ Location 1: 5 years

**EX 25-5   Cash payback period**

Nations Trust is evaluating two capital investment proposals for a drive-up ATM kiosk, each requiring an investment of $320,000 and each with an eight-year life and expected total net cash flows of $512,000. Location 1 is expected to provide equal annual net cash flows of $64,000, and Location 2 is expected to have the following unequal annual net cash flows:

| | | | |
|---|---|---|---|
| Year 1 | $110,000 | Year 5 | $48,000 |
| Year 2 | 80,000 | Year 6 | 48,000 |
| Year 3 | 70,000 | Year 7 | 48,000 |
| Year 4 | 60,000 | Year 8 | 48,000 |

Determine the cash payback period for both location proposals.

---

OBJ. 2

**EX 25-6   Cash payback method**

Bath Works Products Company is considering an investment in one of two new product lines. The investment required for either product line is $660,000. The net cash flows associated with each product are as follows:

| Year | Liquid Soap | Body Lotion |
|---|---|---|
| 1 | $110,000 | $210,000 |
| 2 | 110,000 | 180,000 |
| 3 | 110,000 | 150,000 |
| 4 | 110,000 | 120,000 |
| 5 | 110,000 | 80,000 |
| 6 | 110,000 | 50,000 |
| 7 | 110,000 | 50,000 |
| 8 | 110,000 | 40,000 |
| Total | $880,000 | $880,000 |

a. Recommend a product offering to Bath Works Products Company, based on the cash payback period for each product line.

b. ━━━━▶ Why is one product line preferred over the other, even though they both have the same total net cash flows through eight periods?

---

OBJ. 3

✔ a. NPV, $14,822

**EX 25-7   Net present value method**

The following data are accumulated by Parker Company in evaluating the purchase of $126,000 of equipment, having a four-year useful life:

| | Net Income | Net Cash Flow |
|---|---|---|
| Year 1 | $33,500 | $65,000 |
| Year 2 | 24,500 | 56,000 |
| Year 3 | 10,500 | 42,000 |
| Year 4 | (6,500) | 25,000 |

a. Assuming that the desired rate of return is 15%, determine the net present value for the proposal. Use the table of the present value of $1 appearing in Exhibit 1 of this chapter.

b. ▬▬▬▬ Would management be likely to look with favor on the proposal? Explain.

---

OBJ. 3

✔ a. 2012, $14,000

**EX 25-8   Net present value method**

Courier Express, Inc., is considering the purchase of an additional delivery vehicle for $48,000 on January 1, 2012. The truck is expected to have a five-year life with an expected residual value of $12,000 at the end of five years. The expected additional revenues from the added delivery capacity are anticipated to be $62,000 per year for each of the next five years. A driver will cost $45,000 in 2012, with an expected annual salary increase of $2,000 for each year thereafter. The insurance for the truck is estimated to cost $3,000 per year.

a. Determine the expected annual net cash flows from the delivery truck investment for 2012–2016.

b. Calculate the net present value of the investment, assuming that the minimum desired rate of return is 12%. Use the present value of $1 table appearing in Exhibit 1 of this chapter.

c. Is the additional truck a good investment based on your analysis?

---

OBJ. 3

✔ a. $33 million

**EX 25-9   Net present value method—annuity**

Luxmark Hotels is considering the construction of a new hotel for $210 million. The expected life of the hotel is 30 years with no residual value. The hotel is expected to earn revenues of $58 million per year. Total expenses, including depreciation, are expected to be $32 million per year. Luxmark management has set a minimum acceptable rate of return of 14%.

a. Determine the equal annual net cash flows from operating the hotel.

b. Calculate the net present value of the new hotel using the present value of an annuity of $1 table found in Appendix A. Round to the nearest million dollars.

c. Does your analysis support construction of the new hotel?

---

OBJ. 3

✔ a. $37,200

**EX 25-10   Net present value method—annuity**

Easton Excavation Company is planning an investment of $120,000 for a bulldozer. The bulldozer is expected to operate for 1,400 hours per year for five years. Customers will be charged $105 per hour for bulldozer work. The bulldozer operator costs $34 per hour in wages and benefits. The bulldozer is expected to require annual maintenance costing $9,000. The bulldozer uses fuel that is expected to cost $38 per hour of bulldozer operation.

a. Determine the equal annual net cash flows from operating the bulldozer.

b. Determine the net present value of the investment, assuming that the desired rate of return is 10%. Use the present value of an annuity of $1 table in the chapter (Exhibit 2). Round to the nearest dollar.

c. ▬▬▬▬ Should Easton invest in the bulldozer, based on this analysis?

d. Determine the number of operating hours such that the present value of cash flows equals the amount to be invested.

---

OBJ. 3

✔ a. $148,120,000

**EX 25-11   Net present value method**

Carnival Corporation has recently placed into service some of the largest cruise ships in the world. One of these ships, the *Carnival Dream*, can hold up to 3,600 passengers and cost $750 million to build. Assume the following additional information:

• There will be 320 cruise days per year operated at a full capacity of 3,600 passengers.

• The variable expenses per passenger are estimated to be $95 per cruise day.

• The revenue per passenger is expected to be $280 per cruise day.

- The fixed expenses for running the ship, other than depreciation, are estimated to be $65,000,000 per year.
- The ship has a service life of 10 years, with a residual value of $100,000,000 at the end of 10 years.

a. Determine the annual net cash flow from operating the cruise ship.

b. Determine the net present value of this investment, assuming a 12% minimum rate of return. Use the present value tables provided in the chapter in determining your answer.

---

OBJ. 3

✔ Cedar Rapids, 1.04

**EX 25-12 Present value index**

Dippin' Doughnuts has computed the net present value for capital expenditures at two locations. Relevant data related to the computation are as follows:

|  | Mason City | Cedar Rapids |
|---|---|---|
| Total present value of net cash flow | $455,900 | $565,760 |
| Amount to be invested | 485,000 | 544,000 |
| Net present value | $ (29,100) | $ 21,760 |

a. Determine the present value index for each proposal.

b. Which location does your analysis support?

---

OBJ. 3

✔ b. Packing
Machine, 1.50

**EX 25-13 Net present value method and present value index**

All-Star, Inc., is considering an investment in one of two machines. The sewing machine will increase productivity from sewing 150 baseballs per hour to sewing 260 per hour. The contribution margin per unit is $0.54 per baseball. Assume that any increased production of baseballs can be sold. The second machine is an automatic packing machine for the golf ball line. The packing machine will reduce packing labor cost. The labor cost saved is equivalent to $25 per hour. The sewing machine will cost $360,000, have an eight-year life, and will operate for 1,700 hours per year. The packing machine will cost $120,000, have an eight-year life, and will operate for 1,600 hours per year. All-Star seeks a minimum rate of return of 15% on its investments.

a. Determine the net present value for the two machines. Use the present value of an annuity of $1 table in the chapter (Exhibit 2). Round to the nearest dollar.

b. Determine the present value index for the two machines. Round to two decimal places.

c. ━━━━➤ If All-Star has sufficient funds for only one of the machines and qualitative factors are equal between the two machines, in which machine should it invest?

---

OBJ. 2, 3

✔ b. 6 years

**EX 25-14 Average rate of return, cash payback period, net present value method**

Continental Railroad Inc. is considering acquiring equipment at a cost of $552,000. The equipment has an estimated life of 10 years and no residual value. It is expected to provide yearly net cash flows of $92,000. The company's minimum desired rate of return for net present value analysis is 10%.

Compute the following:

a. The average rate of return, giving effect to straight-line depreciation on the investment. Round whole percent to one decimal place.

b. The cash payback period.

c. The net present value. Use the present value of an annuity of $1 table appearing in this chapter (Exhibit 2). Round to the nearest dollar.

---

OBJ. 2, 3, 4

✔ a. 5 years

**EX 25-15 Payback period, net present value analysis, and qualitative considerations**

The plant manager of Dublin Electronics Company is considering the purchase of new automated assembly equipment. The new equipment will cost $2,500,000. The manager believes that the new investment will result in direct labor savings of $500,000 per year for 10 years.

a. What is the payback period on this project?

b. What is the net present value, assuming a 10% rate of return? Use the present value of an annuity of $1 table in Exhibit 2.

c. ▬▬▶ What else should the manager consider in the analysis?

---

**OBJ. 3**
✔ a. 3.785

### EX 25-16 Internal rate of return method

The internal rate of return method is used by Maxwell Construction Co. in analyzing a capital expenditure proposal that involves an investment of $45,420 and annual net cash flows of $12,000 for each of the six years of its useful life.

a. Determine a present value factor for an annuity of $1 which can be used in determining the internal rate of return.

b. Using the factor determined in part (a) and the present value of an annuity of $1 table appearing in this chapter (Exhibit 2), determine the internal rate of return for the proposal.

---

**OBJ. 3, 4**

### EX 25-17 Internal rate of return method

The Canyons Resort, a Utah ski resort, recently announced a $400 million expansion to lodging properties, lifts, and terrain. Assume that this investment is estimated to produce $70.8 million in equal annual cash flows for each of the first 10 years of the project life.

a. Determine the expected internal rate of return of this project for 10 years, using the present value of an annuity of $1 table found in Exhibit 2.

b. What are some uncertainties that could reduce the internal rate of return of this project?

---

**OBJ. 3**
✔ a. Delivery truck, 12%

### EX 25-18 Internal rate of return method—two projects

Toasted Treats Snack Company is considering two possible investments: a delivery truck or a bagging machine. The delivery truck would cost $44,271 and could be used to deliver an additional 61,000 bags of pretzels per year. Each bag of pretzels can be sold for a contribution margin of $0.40. The delivery truck operating expenses, excluding depreciation, are $0.70 per mile for 21,000 miles per year. The bagging machine would replace an old bagging machine, and its net investment cost would be $49,920. The new machine would require three fewer hours of direct labor per day. Direct labor is $16 per hour. There are 250 operating days in the year. Both the truck and the bagging machine are estimated to have seven-year lives. The minimum rate of return is 13%. However, Toasted Treats has funds to invest in only one of the projects.

a. Compute the internal rate of return for each investment. Use the present value of an annuity of $1 table appearing in this chapter (Exhibit 2).

b. ▬▬▶ Provide a memo to management with a recommendation.

---

**OBJ. 3**
✔ a. ($12,987)

### EX 25-19 Net present value method and internal rate of return method

Hawkeye Healthcare Corp. is proposing to spend $134,136 on an eight-year project that has estimated net cash flows of $27,000 for each of the eight years.

a. Compute the net present value, using a rate of return of 15%. Use the present value of an annuity of $1 table in the chapter (Exhibit 2).

b. ▬▬▶ Based on the analysis prepared in part (a), is the rate of return (1) more than 15%, (2) 15%, or (3) less than 15%? Explain.

c. Determine the internal rate of return by computing a present value factor for an annuity of $1 and using the present value of an annuity of $1 table presented in the text (Exhibit 2).

---

**OBJ. 3**

### EX 25-20 Identify error in capital investment analysis calculations

Solid Solutions Inc. is considering the purchase of automated machinery that is expected to have a useful life of five years and no residual value. The average rate of return on the average investment has been computed to be 20%, and the cash payback period was computed to be 5.5 years.

▬▬▶ Do you see any reason to question the validity of the data presented? Explain.

OBJ. 3, 4

✔ Net present value,
Processing Mill,
$71,700

**EX 25-21  Net present value—unequal lives**

Gold Creek Mining Company has two competing proposals: a processing mill and an electric shovel. Both pieces of equipment have an initial investment of $840,000. The net cash flows estimated for the two proposals are as follows:

| | Net Cash Flow | |
|---|---|---|
| Year | Processing Mill | Electric Shovel |
| 1 | $280,000 | $350,000 |
| 2 | 250,000 | 325,000 |
| 3 | 250,000 | 300,000 |
| 4 | 200,000 | 300,000 |
| 5 | 150,000 | |
| 6 | 125,000 | |
| 7 | 100,000 | |
| 8 | 100,000 | |

The estimated residual value of the processing mill at the end of Year 4 is $350,000.

Determine which equipment should be favored, comparing the net present values of the two proposals and assuming a minimum rate of return of 15%. Use the present value tables presented in this chapter (Exhibits 1 and 2).

OBJ. 3, 4

**EX 25-22  Net present value—unequal lives**

Al a Mode, Inc., is considering one of two investment options. Option 1 is a $60,000 investment in new blending equipment that is expected to produce equal annual cash flows of $16,000 for each of seven years. Option 2 is a $70,000 investment in a new computer system that is expected to produce equal annual cash flows of $20,000 for each of five years. The residual value of the blending equipment at the end of the fifth year is estimated to be $10,000. The computer system has no expected residual value at the end of the fifth year.

For purposes of analysis, assume that the blending equipment is adjusted to a five-year life and assume there is sufficient capital to fund only one of these projects. Determine which project should be selected, comparing the (a) net present values and (b) present value indices of the two projects, assuming a minimum rate of return of 10%. Round the present value index to two decimal places. Use the present value tables presented in this chapter (Exhibits 1 and 2).

## Problems Series A

OBJ. 2, 3

✔ 1. a. 22.5%

**PR 25-1A  Average rate of return method, net present value method, and analysis**

The capital investment committee of Hampton Landscaping Company is considering two capital investments. The estimated income from operations and net cash flows from each investment are as follows:

| | Greenhouse | | Skid Loader | |
|---|---|---|---|---|
| Year | Income from Operations | Net Cash Flow | Income from Operations | Net Cash Flow |
| 1 | $22,200 | $ 35,000 | $ 7,200 | $ 20,000 |
| 2 | 12,200 | 25,000 | 7,200 | 20,000 |
| 3 | 7,200 | 20,000 | 7,200 | 20,000 |
| 4 | (2,800) | 10,000 | 7,200 | 20,000 |
| 5 | (2,800) | 10,000 | 7,200 | 20,000 |
| | $36,000 | $100,000 | $36,000 | $100,000 |

Each project requires an investment of $64,000. Straight-line depreciation will be used, and no residual value is expected. The committee has selected a rate of 12% for purposes of the net present value analysis.

**Instructions**

1. Compute the following:

    a. The average rate of return for each investment. Round to one decimal place.

    b. The net present value for each investment. Use the present value of $1 table appearing in this chapter (Exhibit 1).

2. ▬▬▬▶ Prepare a brief report for the capital investment committee, advising it on the relative merits of the two investments.

---

OBJ. 2, 3

✔ 1. b. Plant
Expansion, $47,490

### PR 25-2A Cash payback period, net present value method, and analysis

Runway Apparel Inc. is considering two investment projects. The estimated net cash flows from each project are as follows:

| Year | Plant Expansion | Retail Store Expansion |
|---|---|---|
| 1 | $ 350,000 | $ 360,000 |
| 2 | 350,000 | 340,000 |
| 3 | 140,000 | 140,000 |
| 4 | 90,000 | 100,000 |
| 5 | 70,000 | 60,000 |
| Total | $1,000,000 | $1,000,000 |

Each project requires an investment of $700,000. A rate of 15% has been selected for the net present value analysis.

**Instructions**

1. Compute the following for each product:

    a. Cash payback period.

    b. The net present value. Use the present value of $1 table appearing in this chapter (Exhibit 1).

2. ▬▬▬▶ Prepare a brief report advising management on the relative merits of each project.

---

OBJ. 3

✔ 2. Railcars, 1.12

### PR 25-3A Net present value method, present value index, and analysis

Mid-Continent Railroad Company wishes to evaluate three capital investment proposals by using the net present value method. Relevant data related to the proposals are summarized as follows:

| | New Maintenance Yard | Route Expansion | Acquire Railcars |
|---|---|---|---|
| Amount to be invested | $12,000,000 | $20,000,000 | $36,000,000 |
| Annual net cash flows: | | | |
| Year 1 .................... | 6,000,000 | 12,000,000 | 22,000,000 |
| Year 2 .................... | 4,800,000 | 11,000,000 | 18,500,000 |
| Year 3 .................... | 4,500,000 | 9,500,000 | 16,000,000 |

**Instructions**

1. Assuming that the desired rate of return is 20%, prepare a net present value analysis for each proposal. Use the present value of $1 table appearing in this chapter (Exhibit 1).

2. Determine a present value index for each proposal. Round to two decimal places.

3. ▬▬▬▶ Which proposal offers the largest amount of present value per dollar of investment? Explain.

---

OBJ. 3

✔ 1. a. Generating
unit, $109,150

### PR 25-4A Net present value method, internal rate of return method, and analysis

The management of Pacific Utilities Inc. is considering two capital investment projects. The estimated net cash flows from each project are as follows:

| Year | Generating Unit | Distribution Network Expansion |
|---|---|---|
| 1 | $370,000 | $280,000 |
| 2 | 370,000 | 280,000 |
| 3 | 370,000 | 280,000 |
| 4 | 370,000 | 280,000 |

The generating unit requires an investment of $1,172,900, while the distribution network expansion requires an investment of $850,360. No residual value is expected from either project.

**Instructions**

1. Compute the following for each project:

   a. The net present value. Use a rate of 6% and the present value of an annuity of $1 table appearing in this chapter (Exhibit 2).

   b. A present value index. Round to two decimal places.

2. Determine the internal rate of return for each project by (a) computing a present value factor for an annuity of $1 and (b) using the present value of an annuity of $1 table appearing in this chapter (Exhibit 2).

3. ━━━━━ What advantage does the internal rate of return method have over the net present value method in comparing projects?

---

**OBJ. 3, 4**

✔ 1. Servers, $27,770

**PR 25-5A  Evaluate alternative capital investment decisions**

The investment committee of Shield Insurance Co. is evaluating two projects, office expansion and upgrade to computer servers. The projects have different useful lives, but each requires an investment of $610,000. The estimated net cash flows from each project are as follows:

| | Net Cash Flows | |
|---|---|---|
| Year | Office Expansion | Servers |
| 1 | $160,000 | $210,000 |
| 2 | 160,000 | 210,000 |
| 3 | 160,000 | 210,000 |
| 4 | 160,000 | 210,000 |
| 5 | 160,000 | |
| 6 | 160,000 | |

The committee has selected a rate of 12% for purposes of net present value analysis. It also estimates that the residual value at the end of each project's useful life is $0, but at the end of the fourth year, the office expansion's residual value would be $200,000.

**Instructions**

1. For each project, compute the net present value. Use the present value of an annuity of $1 table appearing in this chapter (Exhibit 2). (Ignore the unequal lives of the projects.)

2. For each project, compute the net present value, assuming that the office expansion is adjusted to a four-year life for purposes of analysis. Use the present value of $1 table appearing in this chapter (Exhibit 1).

3. ━━━━━ Prepare a report to the investment committee, providing your advice on the relative merits of the two projects.

---

**OBJ. 2, 3, 5**

✔ 5. Proposal B, 1.26

**PR 25-6A  Capital rationing decision involving four proposals**

Renaissance Capital Group is considering allocating a limited amount of capital investment funds among four proposals. The amount of proposed investment, estimated income from operations, and net cash flow for each proposal are as follows:

| | Investment | Year | Income from Operations | Net Cash Flow |
|---|---|---|---|---|
| Proposal A: | $720,000 | 1 | $ 76,000 | $ 220,000 |
| | | 2 | 76,000 | 220,000 |
| | | 3 | 76,000 | 220,000 |
| | | 4 | 36,000 | 180,000 |
| | | 5 | 36,000 | 180,000 |
| | | | $300,000 | $1,020,000 |
| Proposal B: | $124,000 | 1 | $ 59,200 | $ 84,000 |
| | | 2 | 15,200 | 40,000 |
| | | 3 | 15,200 | 40,000 |
| | | 4 | 5,200 | 30,000 |
| | | 5 | (4,800) | 20,000 |
| | | | $ 90,000 | $ 214,000 |
| Proposal C: | $300,000 | 1 | $ 20,000 | $ 80,000 |
| | | 2 | 20,000 | 80,000 |
| | | 3 | 20,000 | 80,000 |
| | | 4 | 0 | 60,000 |
| | | 5 | 0 | 60,000 |
| | | | $ 60,000 | $ 360,000 |
| Proposal D: | $200,000 | 1 | $ 40,000 | $ 80,000 |
| | | 2 | 40,000 | 80,000 |
| | | 3 | 20,000 | 60,000 |
| | | 4 | 20,000 | 60,000 |
| | | 5 | 20,000 | 60,000 |
| | | | $140,000 | $ 340,000 |

The company's capital rationing policy requires a maximum cash payback period of three years. In addition, a minimum average rate of return of 12% is required on all projects. If the preceding standards are met, the net present value method and present value indexes are used to rank the remaining proposals.

**Instructions**

1. Compute the cash payback period for each of the four proposals.

2. Giving effect to straight-line depreciation on the investments and assuming no estimated residual value, compute the average rate of return for each of the four proposals. Round to one decimal place.

3. Using the following format, summarize the results of your computations in parts (1) and (2). By placing the calculated amounts in the first two columns on the left and by placing a check mark in the appropriate column to the right, indicate which proposals should be accepted for further analysis and which should be rejected.

| Proposal | Cash Payback Period | Average Rate of Return | Accept for Further Analysis | Reject |
|---|---|---|---|---|
| A | | | | |
| B | | | | |
| C | | | | |
| D | | | | |

4. For the proposals accepted for further analysis in part (3), compute the net present value. Use a rate of 15% and the present value of $1 table appearing in this chapter (Exhibit 1).

5. Compute the present value index for each of the proposals in part (4). Round to two decimal places.

6. Rank the proposals from most attractive to least attractive, based on the present values of net cash flows computed in part (4).

7. Rank the proposals from most attractive to least attractive, based on the present value indexes computed in part (5).

8. ⬛━━━▶ Based on the analyses, comment on the relative attractiveness of the proposals ranked in parts (6) and (7).

## Problems Series B

OBJ. 2, 3

✔ 1.a. 18%

### PR 25-1B    Average rate of return method, net present value method, and analysis

The capital investment committee of Safety Haul Trucking Inc. is considering two investment projects. The estimated income from operations and net cash flows from each investment are as follows:

| | Warehouse | | Tracking Technology | |
| Year | Income from Operations | Net Cash Flow | Income from Operations | Net Cash Flow |
|---|---|---|---|---|
| 1 | $ 90,000 | $170,000 | $ 36,000 | $116,000 |
| 2 | 80,000 | 160,000 | 36,000 | 116,000 |
| 3 | 30,000 | 110,000 | 36,000 | 116,000 |
| 4 | 0 | 80,000 | 36,000 | 116,000 |
| 5 | (20,000) | 60,000 | 36,000 | 116,000 |
| Total | $180,000 | $580,000 | $180,000 | $580,000 |

Each project requires an investment of $400,000. Straight-line depreciation will be used, and no residual value is expected. The committee has selected a rate of 15% for purposes of the net present value analysis.

**Instructions**

1. Compute the following:

   a. The average rate of return for each investment.

   b. The net present value for each investment. Use the present value of $1 table appearing in this chapter (Exhibit 1).

2. ➡ Prepare a brief report for the capital investment committee, advising it on the relative merits of the two projects.

OBJ. 2, 3

✔ 1. b. *At Home Chef,* $86,620

### PR 25-2B    Cash payback period, net present value method, and analysis

Lifestyle Publications Inc. is considering two new magazine products. The estimated net cash flows from each product are as follows:

| Year | At Home Chef | Music Beat |
|---|---|---|
| 1 | $170,000 | $140,000 |
| 2 | 150,000 | 180,000 |
| 3 | 100,000 | 90,000 |
| 4 | 55,000 | 60,000 |
| 5 | 25,000 | 30,000 |
| Total | $500,000 | $500,000 |

Each product requires an investment of $320,000. A rate of 10% has been selected for the net present value analysis.

**Instructions**

1. Compute the following for each product:

   a. Cash payback period.

   b. The net present value. Use the present value of $1 table appearing in this chapter (Exhibit 1).

2. ➡ Prepare a brief report advising management on the relative merits of each of the two products.

**OBJ. 3**

✔ 2. Branch office
expansion, 1.11

### PR 25-3B Net present value method, present value index, and analysis

Evergreen Security Bank, Inc., wishes to evaluate three capital investment projects by using the net present value method. Relevant data related to the projects are summarized as follows:

| | Branch Office Expansion | Computer System Upgrade | Install Internet Bill-Pay |
|---|---|---|---|
| Amount to be invested .............................. | $425,000 | $650,000 | $360,000 |
| Annual net cash flows: | | | |
| Year 1 ......................................... | 230,000 | 325,000 | 175,000 |
| Year 2 ......................................... | 210,000 | 300,000 | 155,000 |
| Year 3 ......................................... | 170,000 | 290,000 | 120,000 |

#### Instructions

1. Assuming that the desired rate of return is 15%, prepare a net present value analysis for each project. Use the present value of $1 table appearing in this chapter (Exhibit 1).

2. Determine a present value index for each project. Round to two decimal places.

3. ━━━▶ Which project offers the largest amount of present value per dollar of investment? Explain.

**OBJ. 3**

✔ 1. a. Radio station, $55,860

### PR 25-4B Net present value method, internal rate of return method, and analysis

The management of Saturn Networks Inc. is considering two capital investment projects. The estimated net cash flows from each project are as follows:

| Year | Radio Station | TV Station |
|---|---|---|
| 1 | $420,000 | $620,000 |
| 2 | 420,000 | 620,000 |
| 3 | 420,000 | 620,000 |
| 4 | 420,000 | 620,000 |

The radio station requires an investment of $1,275,540, while the TV station requires an investment of $1,770,100. No residual value is expected from either project.

#### Instructions

1. Compute the following for each project:

   a. The net present value. Use a rate of 10% and the present value of an annuity of $1 table appearing in this chapter (Exhibit 2).

   b. A present value index. Round to two decimal places.

2. Determine the internal rate of return for each project by (a) computing a present value factor for an annuity of $1 and (b) using the present value of an annuity of $1 table appearing in this chapter (Exhibit 2).

3. ━━━▶ What advantage does the internal rate of return method have over the net present value method in comparing projects?

**OBJ. 3, 4**

✔ 1. Pasadena, $126,150

### PR 25-5B Evaluate alternative capital investment decisions

The investment committee of Fiesta Cantina Restaurants Inc. is evaluating two restaurant sites. The sites have different useful lives, but each requires an investment of $780,000. The estimated net cash flows from each site are as follows:

| | Net Cash Flows | |
|---|---|---|
| Year | Burbank | Pasadena |
| 1 | $270,000 | $350,000 |
| 2 | 270,000 | 350,000 |
| 3 | 270,000 | 350,000 |
| 4 | 270,000 | 350,000 |
| 5 | 270,000 | |
| 6 | 270,000 | |

The committee has selected a rate of 20% for purposes of net present value analysis. It also estimates that the residual value at the end of each restaurant's useful life is $0, but at the end of the fourth year, Burbank's residual value would be $440,000.

**Instructions**

1. For each site, compute the net present value. Use the present value of an annuity of $1 table appearing in this chapter (Exhibit 2). (Ignore the unequal lives of the projects.)

2. For each site, compute the net present value, assuming that Burbank is adjusted to a four-year life for purposes of analysis. Use the present value of $1 table appearing in this chapter (Exhibit 1).

3. ━━━► Prepare a report to the investment committee, providing your advice on the relative merits of the two sites.

OBJ. 2, 3, 5

✔ 5. Proposal B, 1.19

**PR 25-6B    Capital rationing decision involving four proposals**

Nova Communications Inc. is considering allocating a limited amount of capital investment funds among four proposals. The amount of proposed investment, estimated income from operations, and net cash flow for each proposal are as follows:

|  | Investment | Year | Income from Operations | Net Cash Flow |
|---|---|---|---|---|
| Proposal A: | $500,000 | 1 | $ 40,000 | $140,000 |
|  |  | 2 | 40,000 | 140,000 |
|  |  | 3 | 20,000 | 120,000 |
|  |  | 4 | 0 | 100,000 |
|  |  | 5 | (40,000) | 60,000 |
|  |  |  | $ 60,000 | $560,000 |
| Proposal B: | $225,000 | 1 | $ 55,000 | $100,000 |
|  |  | 2 | 35,000 | 80,000 |
|  |  | 3 | 15,000 | 60,000 |
|  |  | 4 | 15,000 | 60,000 |
|  |  | 5 | 15,000 | 60,000 |
|  |  |  | $135,000 | $360,000 |
| Proposal C: | $600,000 | 1 | $100,000 | $220,000 |
|  |  | 2 | 80,000 | 200,000 |
|  |  | 3 | 60,000 | 180,000 |
|  |  | 4 | 60,000 | 180,000 |
|  |  | 5 | 30,000 | 150,000 |
|  |  |  | $330,000 | $930,000 |
| Proposal D: | $300,000 | 1 | $ 65,000 | $125,000 |
|  |  | 2 | 25,000 | 85,000 |
|  |  | 3 | 0 | 60,000 |
|  |  | 4 | 0 | 60,000 |
|  |  | 5 | 0 | 60,000 |
|  |  |  | $ 90,000 | $390,000 |

The company's capital rationing policy requires a maximum cash payback period of three years. In addition, a minimum average rate of return of 12% is required on all projects. If the preceding standards are met, the net present value method and present value indexes are used to rank the remaining proposals.

**Instructions**

1. Compute the cash payback period for each of the four proposals.

2. Giving effect to straight-line depreciation on the investments and assuming no estimated residual value, compute the average rate of return for each of the four proposals. Round to one decimal place.

3. Using the following format, summarize the results of your computations in parts (1) and (2). By placing the calculated amounts in the first two columns on the left and by placing a check mark in the appropriate column to the right, indicate which proposals should be accepted for further analysis and which should be rejected.

| Proposal | Cash Payback Period | Average Rate of Return | Accept for Further Analysis | Reject |
|---|---|---|---|---|
| A | | | | |
| B | | | | |
| C | | | | |
| D | | | | |

4. For the proposals accepted for further analysis in part (3), compute the net present value. Use a rate of 12% and the present value of $1 table appearing in this chapter (Exhibit 1).

5. Compute the present value index for each of the proposals in part (4). Round to two decimal places.

6. Rank the proposals from most attractive to least attractive, based on the present values of net cash flows computed in part (4).

7. Rank the proposals from most attractive to least attractive, based on the present value indexes computed in part (5). Round to two decimal places.

8. Based on the analyses, comment on the relative attractiveness of the proposals ranked in parts (6) and (7).

# Cases & Projects

You can access Cases & Projects online at **www.cengage.com/accounting/reeve**

# Excel Success Special Activities

### SA 25-1   Net present value

The Cambridge Company is considering expansion into the South. The expansion effort is expected to cost $215,000. The net cash flows expected from this investment are $25,000 per year for the first two years, and $40,000 per year for the remaining eight years of the project life.

a. Open the Excel file *SA25-1_1e*.

b. Determine the net present value of the expansion project assuming a minimum desired rate of return of 12%.

c. When you have completed the analysis, perform a "save as," replacing the entire file name with the following:

   *SA25-1_1e[your first name initial]_[your last name]*

### SA 25-2   Net present value

Gold Software, Inc., is considering an investment in a new game product titled *EagleGolf.* The project will require an investment of $3,800,000. The five-year revenues and cash expenses over the product's life are estimated as follows:

| | Revenues | Cash Expenditures |
|---|---|---|
| Year 1 | $ 500,000 | $ 750,000 |
| Year 2 | 2,600,000 | 1,500,000 |
| Year 3 | 3,400,000 | 1,700,000 |
| Year 4 | 3,000,000 | 1,000,000 |
| Year 5 | 2,100,000 | 800,000 |

a. Open the Excel file *SA25-2_1e*.

b. Assuming a minimum desired rate of return of 8%, determine the net present value of the project.

c. When you have completed the analysis, perform a "save as," replacing the entire file name with the following:

*SA25-2_1e[your first name initial]_[your last name]*

### SA 25-3   Internal rate of return

Celtic Pride Productions, Inc., produces movies. It is estimated that a new movie, *Kelly's Revenge*, will cost $70 million to produce. The movie is estimated to generate net cash flows from ticket, DVD, and cable sales over the next four years as follows:

| | |
|---|---|
| Year 1 | $80,000,000 |
| Year 2 | 45,000,000 |
| Year 3 | 15,000,000 |
| Year 4 | 10,000,000 |

a. Open the Excel file *SA25-3_1e*.

b. Determine the internal rate of return for this movie.

c. When you have completed the analysis, perform a "save as," replacing the entire file name with the following:

*SA25-3_1e[your first name initial]_[your last name]*

### SA 25-4   Internal rate of return

Ryder Company is planning one of two alternative investments. The first investment requires a $60,000 investment and will generate net cash flows of $24,000 per year for five years. The second investment requires an investment of $90,000 and will generate net cash flows as follows:

| | Net Cash Flows |
|---|---|
| Year 1 | 15,000 |
| Year 2 | 35,000 |
| Year 3 | 60,000 |
| Year 4 | 80,000 |
| Year 5 | 20,000 |

a. Open the Excel file *SA25-4_1e*.

b. Determine the internal rate of return for each alternative.

c. Indicate in the spreadsheet which alternative should be selected.

d. When you have completed the analysis, perform a "save as," replacing the entire file name with the following:

*SA25-4_1e[your first name initial]_[your last name]*

# Cost Allocation and Activity-Based Costing

## Cold Stone Creamery

**H**ave you ever had to request service repairs on an appliance at your home? The repair person may arrive and take five minutes to replace a part. Yet, the bill may indicate a minimum charge for more than five minutes of work.

Why might there be a minimum charge for a service call? The answer is that the service person must charge for the time and expense of coming to your house. In a sense, the bill reflects two elements of service: (1) the cost of coming to your house and (2) the cost of the repair. The first portion of the bill reflects the time required to "set up" the job. The second part of the bill reflects the cost of performing the repair. The setup charge will be the same, whether the repairs take five minutes or five hours. In contrast, the actual repair charge will vary with the time on the job.

Like the repair person, companies must be careful that the cost of their products and services accurately reflect the different activities involved in producing the product or service. Otherwise,

the cost of products and services may be distorted and lead to improper management decisions.

To illustrate, **Cold Stone Creamery**, a chain of super premium ice cream shops, uses activity-based costing to determine the cost of its ice cream products, such as cones, mixings, cakes, frozen yogurt, smoothies, and sorbets. The costs of activities, such as scooping and mixing, are added to the cost of the ingredients to determine the total cost of each product. As stated by Cold Stone's president:

". . . it only makes sense to have the price you pay for the product be reflective of the activities involved in making it for you."

In this chapter, three different methods of allocating factory overhead to products are described and illustrated. In addition, product cost distortions resulting from improper factory overhead allocations are discussed. The chapter concludes by describing activity-based costing for selling and administrative expenses and its use in service businesses.

**OBJ. 1** Identify three methods used for allocating factory overhead costs to products.

# Product Costing Allocation Methods

Determining the cost of a product is termed **product costing**. Product costs consist of direct materials, direct labor, and factory overhead. The direct materials and direct labor are direct costs that can be traced to the product. However, factory overhead includes indirect costs that must be allocated to the product.

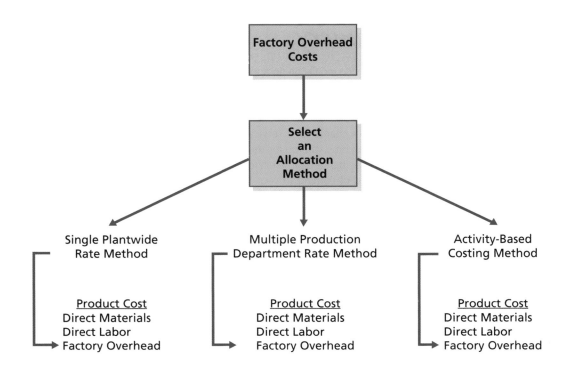

In Chapter 17, the allocation of factory overhead using a predetermined factory overhead rate was illustrated. The most common methods of allocating factory overhead using predetermined factory overhead rates are:

1. Single plantwide factory overhead rate method
2. Multiple production department factory overhead rate method
3. Activity-based costing method

The choice of allocation method is important to managers because the allocation affects the product cost, as shown in the illustration at the bottom of the previous page. Managers are concerned about the accuracy of product costs, which are used for decisions such as determining product mix, establishing product price, and determining whether to discontinue a product line.

# Single Plantwide Factory Overhead Rate Method

**OBJ. 2** Use a single plantwide factory overhead rate for product costing.

A company may use a predetermined factory overhead rate to allocate factory overhead costs to products. Under the **single plantwide factory overhead rate method**, factory overhead costs are allocated to products using only one rate.

To illustrate, assume the following data for Ruiz Company, which manufactures snowmobiles and riding mowers in a single factory.

Total budgeted factory overhead costs for the year ........................ $1,600,000
Total budgeted direct labor hours (as computed below) .................... 20,000 hours

|  | Snowmobiles | Riding Mowers | Total |
|---|---|---|---|
| Planned production for the year............ | 1,000 units | 1,000 units | |
| Direct labor hours per unit ................ | × 10 hours | × 10 hours | |
| Budgeted direct labor hours .............. | 10,000 hours | 10,000 hours | 20,000 hours |

Under the single plantwide factory overhead rate method, the $1,600,000 budgeted factory overhead is applied to all products by using one rate. This rate is computed as follows:

$$\text{Single Plantwide Factory Overhead Rate} = \frac{\text{Total Budgeted Factory Overhead}}{\text{Total Budgeted Plantwide Allocation Base}}$$

The budgeted allocation base is a measure of operating activity in the factory. Common allocation bases would include direct labor hours, direct labor dollars, and machine hours. Ruiz Company allocates factory overhead using budgeted direct labor hours as the plantwide allocation base. Thus, Ruiz's single plantwide factory overhead rate is $80 per direct labor hour, computed as follows:

$$\text{Single Plantwide Factory Overhead Rate} = \frac{\$1,600,000}{20,000 \text{ direct labor hours}}$$
$$\text{Single Plantwide Factory Overhead Rate} = \$80 \text{ per direct labor hours}$$

Ruiz uses the plantwide rate of $80 per direct labor hour to allocate factory overhead to snowmobiles and riding mowers as shown below.

| | Single Plantwide Factory Overhead Rate | × | Direct Labor Hours per Unit | = | Factory Overhead Cost per Unit |
|---|---|---|---|---|---|
| Snowmobile | $80 per direct labor hour | × | 10 direct labor hours | = | $800 |
| Riding movers | $80 per direct labor hour | × | 10 direct labor hours | = | $800 |

As shown above, the factory overhead allocated to each product is $800. This is because each product uses the same number of direct labor hours.

The effects of Ruiz Company using the single plantwide factory overhead rate method are summarized in Exhibit 1.

**EXHIBIT 1**

**Single Plantwide
Factory
Overhead Rate
Method—Ruiz
Company**

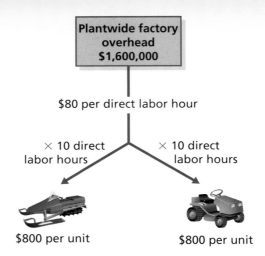

Many military contractors use a single plantwide rate for allocating factory overhead costs to products, such as jet fighters.

The primary advantage of using the single plantwide overhead rate method is that it is simple and inexpensive to use. However, the single plantwide rate assumes that the factory overhead costs are consumed in the same way by all products. For example, in the preceding illustration Ruiz Company assumes that factory overhead costs are consumed as each direct labor hour is incurred.

The preceding assumption may be valid for companies that manufacture one or a few products. If, however, a company manufactures products that consume factory overhead costs in different ways, a single plantwide rate may not accurately allocate factory overhead costs to the products.

**Example Exercise** ▶ **26-1** ▶ **Single Plantwide Overhead Rate**    OBJ. **2**

The total factory overhead for Morris Company is budgeted for the year at $650,000. Morris manufactures two office furniture products: a credenza and desk. The credenza and desk each require four direct labor hours (dlh) to manufacture. Each product is budgeted for 5,000 units of production for the year. Determine (a) the total number of budgeted direct labor hours for the year, (b) the single plantwide factory overhead rate, and (c) the factory overhead allocated per unit for each product using the single plantwide factory overhead rate.

**Follow My Example** ▶ **26-1** ▶

a.  Credenza: 5,000 units × 4 direct labor hours = 20,000 direct labor hours
    Desk: 5,000 units × 4 direct labor hours =      20,000
                                                    40,000 direct labor hours

b.  Single plantwide factory overhead rate: $650,000/40,000 dlh = $16.25 per dlh
c.  Credenza: $16.25 per direct labor hour × 4 dlh per unit = $65 per unit
    Desk: $16.25 per direct labor hour × 4 dlh per unit = $65 per unit

............................................................................................................

Practice Exercises: **PE 26-1A, PE 26-1B**

## Integrity, Objectivity, and Ethics in Business

**FRAUD AGAINST YOU AND ME**

The U.S. government makes a wide variety of purchases. Two of the largest are health care purchases under Medicare and military equipment. The purchase price for these and other items is often determined by the cost plus some profit. The cost is often the sum of direct costs plus allocated overhead. Due to the complexity of determining cost, government agencies review the amount charged for products and services. In the event of disagreement between the contractor and the government, the U.S. government may sue the contractor under the False Claims Act, which provides for three times the government's damages plus civil penalties. For example, Pfizer recently paid $1 billion in fines and penalties, the largest settlement under the False Claims Act to date, for false claims related to drug reimbursements.

Source: *Top 20 Cases*, The False Claims Act Legal Center of the TAF Education Fund.

# Multiple Production Department Factory Overhead Rate Method

**OBJ. 3** Use multiple production department factory overhead rates for product costing.

When production departments *differ significantly* in their manufacturing processes, factory overhead costs are normally incurred differently in each department. In such cases, factory overhead costs may be more accurately allocated using multiple production department factory overhead rates.

The **multiple production department factory overhead rate method** uses different rates for each production department to allocate factory overhead costs to products. In contrast, the single plantwide rate method uses only one rate to allocate factory overhead costs. Exhibit 2 illustrates how these two methods differ.

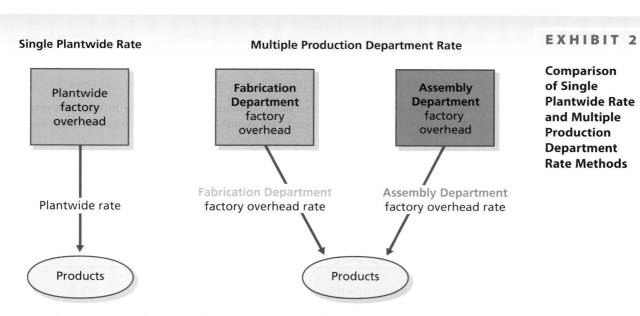

**Single Plantwide Rate**

Plantwide factory overhead

Plantwide rate

Products

**Multiple Production Department Rate**

Fabrication Department factory overhead

Assembly Department factory overhead

Fabrication Department factory overhead rate

Assembly Department factory overhead rate

Products

**EXHIBIT 2**

Comparison of Single Plantwide Rate and Multiple Production Department Rate Methods

To illustrate the multiple production department factory overhead rate method, the prior illustration for Ruiz Company is used. In doing so, assume that Ruiz uses the following two production departments in the manufacture of snowmobiles and riding mowers:

1. Fabrication Department, which cuts metal to the shape of the product.
2. Assembly Department, which manually assembles machined pieces into a final product.

The total budgeted factory overhead for Ruiz Co. is $1,600,000 divided into the Fabrication and Assembly departments as follows:[1]

---

1 Factory overhead costs are assigned to production departments using methods discussed in advanced cost accounting textbooks.

| | Budgeted Factory<br>Overhead Costs |
|---|---|
| Fabrication Department............................... | $1,030,000 |
| Assembly Department ................................ | 570,000 |
| Total budgeted factory overhead costs .............. | $1,600,000 |

As shown above, the Fabrication Department incurs nearly twice the factory overhead of the Assembly Department. This is because the Fabrication Department has more machinery and equipment that uses more power, incurs equipment depreciation, and uses factory supplies.

## Department Overhead Rates and Allocation

Each **production department factory overhead rate** is computed as follows:

$$\frac{\text{Production Department}}{\text{Factory Overhead Rate}} = \frac{\text{Budgeted Department Factory Overhead}}{\text{Budgeted Department Allocation Base}}$$

To illustrate, assume that Ruiz Company uses direct labor hours as the allocation base for the Fabrication and Assembly departments.[2] Each department uses 10,000 direct labor hours. Thus, the factory overhead rates are as follows:

$$\frac{\text{Fabrication Department}}{\text{Factory Overhead Rate}} = \frac{\$1,030,000}{10,000 \text{ direct labor hours}} = \$103 \text{ direct labor hours}$$

$$\frac{\text{Assembly Department}}{\text{Factory Overhead Rate}} = \frac{\$570,000}{10,000 \text{ direct labor hours}} = \$57 \text{ direct labor hours}$$

Ten direct labor hours are required for the manufacture of each snowmobile and riding mower. These 10 hours are consumed in the Fabrication and Assembly departments as follows:

| | Snowmobile | Riding Mower |
|---|---|---|
| Fabrication Department ................. | 8 hours | 2 hours |
| Assembly Department................... | 2 | 8 |
| Direct labor hours per unit............. | 10 hours | 10 hours |

The factory overhead allocated to each snowmobile and riding mower is shown in Exhibit 3. As shown in Exhibit 3, each snowmobile is allocated $938 of total factory

**EXHIBIT 3**   **Allocating Factory Overhead to Products—Ruiz Company**

| | Allocation Base<br>Usage per Unit | × | Production<br>Department Factory<br>Overhead Rate | = | Allocated Factory<br>Overhead per Unit<br>of Product |
|---|---|---|---|---|---|
| *Snowmobile* | | | | | |
| Fabrication Department | 8 direct labor hours | × | $103 per dlh | = | $824 |
| Assembly Department | 2 direct labor hours | × | $ 57 per dlh | = | 114 |
| Total factory overhead cost<br>per snowmobile | | | | | $938 |
| | | | | | |
| *Riding mower* | | | | | |
| Fabrication Department | 2 direct labor hours | × | $103 per dlh | = | $206 |
| Assembly Department | 8 direct labor hours | × | $ 57 per dlh | = | 456 |
| Total factory overhead cost<br>per riding mower | | | | | $662 |

2 Departments need not use the same allocation base. The allocation base should be associated with the operating activity of the department.

overhead costs. In contrast, each riding mower is allocated $662 of factory overhead costs.

Exhibit 4 summarizes the multiple production department rate allocation method for Ruiz Company. Exhibit 4 indicates that the Fabrication Department factory overhead rate is $103 per direct labor hour while the Assembly Department rate is $57 per direct labor hour. Since the snowmobile uses more Fabrication Department direct labor hours than does the riding mower, the total overhead allocated to each snowmobile is $276 greater ($938 − $662) than the amount allocated to each riding mower.

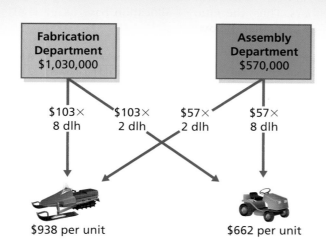

**EXHIBIT 4**

**Multiple Production Department Rate Method— Ruiz Company**

## Distortion of Product Costs

The differences in the factory overhead for each snowmobile and riding mower using the single plantwide and the multiple production department factory overhead rate methods are shown below.

| | Factory Overhead Cost per Unit | | |
| --- | --- | --- | --- |
| | Single Plantwide Method | Multiple Production Department Method | Difference |
| Snowmobile.............. | $800 | $938 | $(138) |
| Riding mower ............ | 800 | 662 | 138 |

The single plantwide factory overhead rate distorts the product cost of both the snowmobile and riding mower. That is, the snowmobile is not allocated enough cost and, thus, is undercosted by $138. In contrast, the riding mower is allocated too much cost and is overcosted by $138 ($800 − $662).

The preceding cost distortions are caused by averaging the differences between the high factory overhead costs in the Fabrication Department and the low factory overhead costs in the Assembly Department. Using the single plantwide rate, it is assumed that all factory overhead is directly related to a single allocation base for the entire plant. This assumption is not realistic for Ruiz Company. Thus, using a single plantwide rate distorted the product costs of snowmobiles and riding mowers.

The following conditions indicate that a single plantwide factory overhead rate may cause product cost distortions:

**Note:**
The single plantwide factory overhead rate distorts product cost by averaging high and low factory overhead costs.

**Condition 1**: *Differences in production department factory overhead rates.* Some departments have high rates, whereas others have low rates.

**Condition 2**: *Differences among products in the ratios of allocation base usage within a department and across departments.* Some products have a high ratio of allocation base usage within departments, whereas other products have a low ratio of allocation base usage within the same departments.

To illustrate, Condition 1 exists for Ruiz Company because the factory overhead rate for the Fabrication Department is $103 per direct labor hour, whereas the rate for the Assembly Department is only $57 per direct labor hour. However, this condition by itself will not cause product cost distortions.

Condition 2 also exists for Ruiz Company. The snowmobile consumes eight direct labor hours in the Fabrication Department, whereas the riding mower consumes only two direct labor hours. Thus, the ratio of allocation base usage is 4:1 in the Fabrication Department, as computed below.[3]

$$\frac{\text{Ratio of Allocation Base Usage}}{\text{in the Fabrication Department}} = \frac{\text{Direct Labor Hours for snowmobiles}}{\text{Direct Labor Hours for riding mowers}} = \frac{8 \text{ hours}}{2 \text{ hours}} = 4:1$$

In contrast, the ratio of allocation base usage is 1:4 in the Assembly Department, as computed below.

$$\frac{\text{Ratio of Allocation Base Usage}}{\text{in the Fabrication Department}} = \frac{\text{Direct Labor Hours for snowmobiles}}{\text{Direct Labor Hours for riding mowers}} = \frac{2 \text{ hours}}{8 \text{ hours}} = 1:4$$

Because both conditions exist for Ruiz Company, the product costs from using the single plantwide factory overhead rate are distorted. The preceding conditions and the resulting product cost distortions are summarized in Exhibit 5.

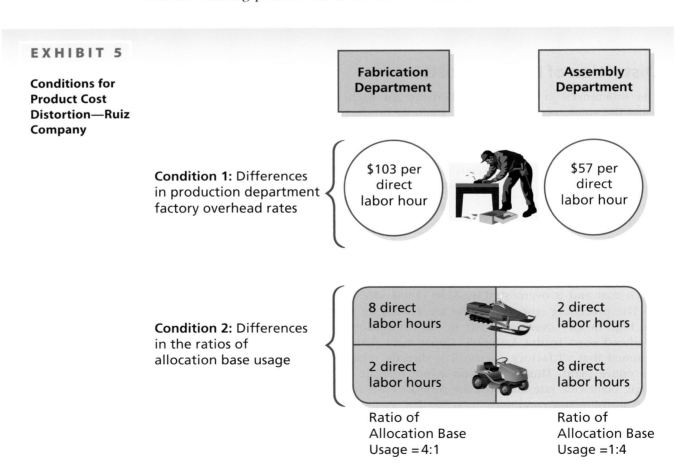

**EXHIBIT 5**

**Conditions for Product Cost Distortion—Ruiz Company**

**Condition 1:** Differences in production department factory overhead rates

**Condition 2:** Differences in the ratios of allocation base usage

Fabrication Department — $103 per direct labor hour

Assembly Department — $57 per direct labor hour

Fabrication Department: 8 direct labor hours / 2 direct labor hours — Ratio of Allocation Base Usage = 4:1

Assembly Department: 2 direct labor hours / 8 direct labor hours — Ratio of Allocation Base Usage = 1:4

3 The numerator and denominator could be switched as long as the ratio is computed the same for each department. This is because the objective is to compare whether differences exist in the ratio of allocation base usage across products and departments.

## Example Exercise 26-2 ▶ Multiple Production Department Overhead Rates

**OBJ. 3**

The total factory overhead for Morris Company is budgeted for the year at $600,000 and divided into two departments: Fabrication, $420,000 and Assembly, $180,000. Morris manufactures two office furniture products: credenzas and desks. Each credenza requires one direct labor hour (dlh) in Fabrication and three direct labor hours in Assembly. Each desk requires three direct labor hours in Fabrication and one direct labor hour in Assembly. Each product is budgeted for 5,000 units of production for the year. Determine (a) the total number of budgeted direct labor hours for the year in each department, (b) the departmental factory overhead rates for both departments, and (c) the factory overhead allocated per unit for each product, using the department factory overhead allocation rates.

### Follow My Example 26-2 ▶

a. Fabrication: (5,000 credenzas × 1 dlh) + (5,000 desks × 3 dlh) = 20,000 direct labor hours
   Assembly: (5,000 credenzas × 3 dlh) + (5,000 desks × 1 dlh) = 20,000 direct labor hours
b. Fabrication Department rate: $420,000/20,000 direct labor hours = $21.00 per dlh
   Assembly Department rate: $180,000/20,000 direct labor hours = $9.00 per dlh

c. Credenza:

| | |
|---|---|
| Fabrication Department . . . . . . . . . . . . . . . . . . . . | 1 dlh × $21.00 = $21.00 |
| Assembly Department. . . . . . . . . . . . . . . . . . . . . | 3 dlh × $ 9.00 = _27.00_ |
| Total factory overhead per credenza . . . . . . . . . | $48.00 |

Desk:

| | |
|---|---|
| Fabrication Department . . . . . . . . . . . . . . . . . . . . | 3 dlh × $21.00 = $63.00 |
| Assembly Department. . . . . . . . . . . . . . . . . . . . . | 1 dlh × $ 9.00 = _9.00_ |
| Total factory overhead per desk. . . . . . . . . . . . . . | $72.00 |

Practice Exercises: **PE 26-2A, PE 26-2B**

# Activity-Based Costing Method

**OBJ. 4** Use activity-based costing for product costing.

As illustrated in the preceding section, product costs may be distorted when a single plantwide factory overhead rate is used. However, product costs may also be distorted when multiple production department factory overhead rates are used. Activity-based costing further reduces the possibility of product cost distortions.

The **activity-based costing method** provides an alternative approach for allocating factory overhead that uses multiple factory overhead rates based on different activities. **Activities** are the types of work, or actions, involved in a manufacturing or service process. For example, the assembly, inspection, and engineering design functions are activities that might be used to allocate overhead.

Under activity-based costing, factory overhead costs are initially budgeted for activities, sometimes termed activity cost pools, such as machine usage, inspections, moving, production setups, and engineering activities.[4] In contrast, when multiple production department factory overhead rates are used, factory overhead costs are first accounted for in production departments.

Exhibit 6 illustrates how activity-based costing differs from the multiple production department method.

To illustrate the activity-based costing method, the prior illustration for Ruiz Company is used. Assume that the following activities have been identified for producing snowmobiles and riding mowers:

1. *Fabrication*, which consists of cutting metal to shape the product. This activity is machine-intensive.
2. *Assembly*, which consists of manually assembling machined pieces into a final product. This activity is labor-intensive.
3. *Setup*, which consists of changing tooling in machines in preparation for making a new product. Each production run requires a **setup**.

4 The activity rate is based on budgeted activity costs. Activity-based budgeting and the reconciliation of budgeted activity costs to actual costs are topics covered in advanced texts.

**EXHIBIT 6**  **Multiple Production Department Factory Overhead Rate Method vs. Activity-Based Costing**

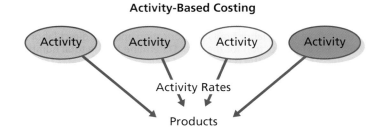

Multiple Production Department Factory Overhead Rate Method

Activity-Based Costing

4. *Quality-control inspections*, which consist of inspecting the product for conformance to specifications. Inspection requires product tear down and reassembly.
5. *Engineering changes*, which consist of processing changes in design or process specifications for a product. The document that initiates changing a product or process is called an **engineering change order (ECO)**.

Fabrication and assembly are now identified as *activities* rather than *departments*. As a result, the setup, quality-control inspections, and engineering change functions that were previously allocated to the fabrication and assembly departments are now classified as separate activities.

The budgeted cost for each activity is as follows:

| Activity | Budgeted Activity Cost |
|---|---|
| Fabrication ............................................... | $  530,000 |
| Assembly................................................. | 70,000 |
| Setup..................................................... | 480,000 |
| Quality-control inspections ............................... | 312,000 |
| Engineering changes ...................................... | 208,000 |
| Total budgeted activity costs............................ | $1,600,000 |

The costs for the fabrication and assembly activities shown above are less than the costs shown in the preceding section where these activities were identified as production departments. This is because the costs of setup, quality-control inspections, and engineering changes, which total $1,000,000 ($480,000 + $312,000 + $208,000), have now been separated into their own activity cost pools.

## Activity Rates and Allocation

The budgeted activity costs are assigned to products using factory overhead rates for each activity. These rates are called **activity rates** because they are related to activities. Activity rates are determined as follows:

$$\text{Activity Rate} = \frac{\text{Budgeted Activity Cost}}{\text{Total Activity Base Usage}}$$

**Note:**
Activity rates are determined by dividing the budgeted activity cost pool by the total estimated activity base usage.

The term **activity base**, rather than *allocation base*, is used because the base is related to an activity.

To illustrate, assume that snowmobiles are a new product for Ruiz Company, and engineers are still making minor design changes. Riding mowers have been produced by Ruiz Company for many years. Activity base usage for the two products are as follows:

| | Snowmobile | Riding Mower |
|---|---|---|
| Estimated units of total production ....................... | 1,000 units | 1,000 units |
| Estimated engineering change orders .................... | 12 change orders | 4 change orders |
| Estimated setups .................... | 100 setups | 20 setups |
| Quality-control inspections ........... | 100 inspections (10%) | 4 inspections (0.4%) |

The number of direct labor hours used by each product is 10,000 hours as shown below.

|  | Direct Labor Hours per Unit | Number of Units of Production | Total Direct Labor Hours |
|---|---|---|---|
| Snowmobile: |  |  |  |
| Fabrication Department.............. | 8 hours | 1,000 units | 8,000 hours |
| Assembly Department ............... | 2 hours | 1,000 units | 2,000 hours |
| Total................................ |  |  | 10,000 hours |
| Riding Mower: |  |  |  |
| Fabrication Department.............. | 2 hours | 1,000 units | 2,000 hours |
| Assembly Department ............... | 8 hours | 1,000 units | 8,000 hours |
| Total................................ |  |  | 10,000 hours |

Exhibit 7 summarizes the activity base usage quantities for each product.

**EXHIBIT 7**   Activity Bases—Ruiz Company

| Products | Activity Base Usage |  |  |  |  |
|---|---|---|---|---|---|
|  | Fabrication | Assembly | Setup | Quality-Control Inspections | Engineering Changes |
| Snowmobile ................... | 8,000 dlh | 2,000 dlh | 100 setups | 100 inspections | 12 ECOs |
| Riding mower................. | 2,000 | 8,000 | 20 | 4 | 4 |
| Total activity base usage...... | 10,000 dlh | 10,000 dlh | 120 setups | 104 inspections | 16 ECOs |

The activity rates for each activity are determined as follows:

$$\text{Activity Rate} = \frac{\text{Budgeted Activity Cost}}{\text{Total Activity Base Usage}}$$

The activity rates for Ruiz Company are shown in Exhibit 8.

**EXHIBIT 8**   Activity Rates—Ruiz Company

| Activity | Budgeted Activity Cost | ÷ | Total Activity-Base Usage | = | Activity Rate |
|---|---|---|---|---|---|
| Fabrication | $530,000 | ÷ | 10,000 direct labor hours | = | $53 per direct labor hour |
| Assembly | $ 70,000 | ÷ | 10,000 direct labor hours | = | $7 per direct labor hour |
| Setup | $480,000 | ÷ | 120 setups | = | $4,000 per setup |
| Quality-control inspections | $312,000 | ÷ | 104 inspections | = | $3,000 per inspection |
| Engineering changes | $208,000 | ÷ | 16 engineering changes | = | $13,000 per engineering change order |

The factory overhead costs are allocated to the snowmobile and riding mower by multiplying the activity-base usage by the activity rate. The sum of the costs for each product is the total factory overhead cost for the product. This amount, divided by the total number of units of estimated production, determines the factory overhead cost per unit. These computations are shown in Exhibit 9.

**EXHIBIT 9** **Activity-Based Product Cost Calculations**

| | A | B | C | D | E | F | G | H | I | J | K | L |
|---|---|---|---|---|---|---|---|---|---|---|---|---|
| 1 | | | | Snowmobile | | | | | | Riding Mower | | |
| 2 | | Activity-Base | | Activity | | Activity | | Activity-Base | | Activity | | Activity |
| 3 | Activity | Usage | × | Rate | = | Cost | | Usage | × | Rate | = | Cost |
| 4 | | | | | | | | | | | | |
| 5 | Fabrication | 8000 dlh | | $53/dlh | | $ 424,000 | | 2,000 dlh | | $53/dlh | | $106,000 |
| 6 | Assembly | 2000 dlh | | $7/dlh | | 14,000 | | 8,000 dlh | | $7/dlh | | 56,000 |
| 7 | Setup | 100 setups | | $4,000/setup | | 400,000 | | 20 setups | | $4,000/setup | | 80,000 |
| 8 | Quality control | | | | | | | | | | | |
| 9 | inspections | 100 inspections | | $3,000/insp. | | 300,000 | | 4 inspections | | $3,000/insp. | | 12,000 |
| 10 | Engineering | | | | | | | | | | | |
| 11 | changes | 12 ECOs | | $13,000/ECO | | 156,000 | | 4 ECOs | | $13,000/ECO | | 52,000 |
| 12 | Total factory | | | | | | | | | | | |
| 13 | overhead cost | | | | | $1,294,000 | | | | | | $306,000 |
| 14 | Budgeted units | | | | | | | | | | | |
| 15 | of production | | | | | ÷ 1,000 | | | | | | ÷ 1,000 |
| 16 | Factory overhead | | | | | | | | | | | |
| 17 | cost per unit | | | | | $ 1,294 | | | | | | $ 306 |
| 18 | | | | | | | | | | | | |

The activity-based costing calculations for Ruiz Company from Exhibit 9 are shown with their spreadsheet formulas below:

| | A | B | C | D | E | F | G | H | I | J | K | L |
|---|---|---|---|---|---|---|---|---|---|---|---|---|
| 1 | | | | Snowmobiles | | | | | | Lawnmowers | | |
| 2 | Activity | Activity-Base Usage | × | Activity Rate | = | Activity Cost | | Activity-Base Usage | × | Activity Rate | = | Activity Cost |
| 3 | Fabrication | 8000 | | 53 | | =B3*D3 | a. | 2000 | × | 53 | = | =H3*J3 | d. |
| 4 | Assembly | 2000 | | 7 | | =B4*D4 | | 8000 | × | 7 | = | =H4*J4 |
| 5 | Setup | 100 | | 4000 | | =B5*D5 | | 20 | × | 4000 | = | =H5*J5 |
| 6 | Quality control inspections | 100 | | 3000 | | =B6*D6 | | 4 | × | 3000 | = | =H6*J6 |
| 7 | Engineering changes | 12 | | 13000 | | =B7*D7 | | 4 | × | 13000 | = | =H7*J7 |
| 8 | Total factory overhead | | | b. → | | =SUM(F3:F7) | | | | | = | =SUM(L3:L7) |
| 9 | Budgeted units of production | | | | | 1000 | | | | | = | 1000 |
| 10 | Factory overhead per unit | | | c. → | | =F8/F9 | | | | | = | =L8/L9 | d. |
| 11 | | | | | | | | | | | | |

The formulas to determine the activity cost for each product are as follows:

a. Enter in cell F3 the formula to multiply the activity-based usage by the activity rate, =B3*D3. Copy this formula for the remaining activities, F4 through F7.
b. Enter in cell F8 the sum of the activity costs, =SUM(F3:F7).
c. Enter in cell F10 the formula for the cost per unit, =F8/F9.
d. Copy the formulas from F3:F8 to L3:L8 and copy F10 to L10.

The activity-based costing method for Ruiz Company is summarized in Exhibit 10.

## Distortion in Product Costs

The factory overhead costs per unit for Ruiz Company using the three allocation methods are shown below.

| | Factory Overhead Cost per Unit— Three Cost Allocation Methods | | |
|---|---|---|---|
| | Single Plantwide Rate | Multiple Production Department Rates | Activity-Based Costing |
| Snowmobile | $800 | $938 | $1,294 |
| Riding mower | 800 | 662 | 306 |

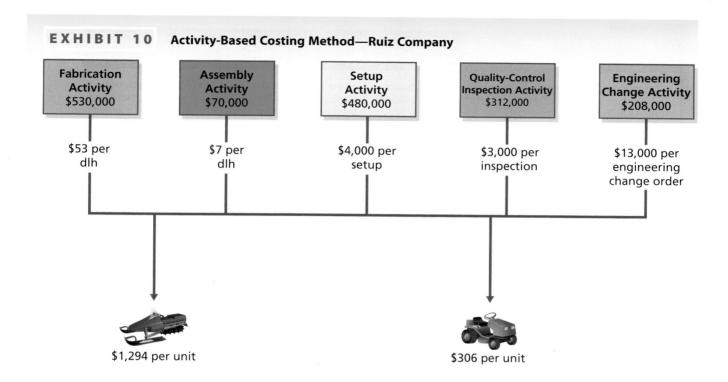

**EXHIBIT 10** **Activity-Based Costing Method—Ruiz Company**

| Fabrication Activity $530,000 | Assembly Activity $70,000 | Setup Activity $480,000 | Quality-Control Inspection Activity $312,000 | Engineering Change Activity $208,000 |
|---|---|---|---|---|
| $53 per dlh | $7 per dlh | $4,000 per setup | $3,000 per inspection | $13,000 per engineering change order |

$1,294 per unit          $306 per unit

The activity-based costing method produces different factory overhead costs per unit (product costs) than the multiple department factory overhead rate method. This difference is caused by how the $1,000,000 of setup, quality control, and engineering change activities are allocated.

Under the multiple production department factory overhead rate method, setup, quality control, and engineering change costs were allocated using departmental rates based on direct labor hours. However, snowmobiles and riding mowers did *not* consume these *activities* in proportion to direct labor hours. That is, each snowmobile consumed a larger portion of the setup, quality-control inspection, and engineering change activities. This was true even though each product consumed 10,000 direct labor hours. As a result, activity-based costing allocated more of the cost of these activities to the snowmobile. Only under the activity-based approach were these differences reflected in the factory overhead cost allocations and, thus, in the product costs.

## Dangers of Product Cost Distortion

If Ruiz Company used the $800 factory overhead cost allocation (single plantwide rate) instead of activity-based costing for pricing snowmobiles and riding mowers, the following would likely result:

1. The snowmobile would be *underpriced* because its factory overhead cost is understated by $494 ($1,294 − $800).
2. The riding mower would be *overpriced* because its factory overhead cost is overstated by $494 ($800 − $306).

As a result, Ruiz would likely lose sales of riding mowers because they are overpriced. In contrast, sale of snowmobiles would increase because they are underpriced. Due to these pricing errors, Ruiz might incorrectly decide to expand production of snowmobiles and discontinue making riding mowers.

If Ruiz uses the activity-based costing method, its product costs would be more accurate. Thus, Ruiz would have a better starting point for making proper pricing decisions. Although the product cost distortions are not as great, similar results would occur if Ruiz had used the multiple production department rate method.

ArvinMeritor, Inc., discovered that incorrect factory overhead cost allocations had "overcosted" some of its products by roughly 20%. As a result, these products were overpriced and began losing market share.

**Example Exercise** **26-3** **Activity-Based Costing:**
**Factory Overhead Costs**

**OBJ.**
**4**

The total factory overhead for Morris Company is budgeted for the year at $600,000, divided into four activities: fabrication, $300,000; assembly, $120,000; setup, $100,000; and materials handling, $80,000. Morris manufactures two office furniture products: a credenza and desk. The activity-base usage quantities for each product by each activity are estimated as follows:

|  | Fabrication | Assembly | Setup | Material Handling |
|---|---|---|---|---|
| Credenza | 5,000 dlh | 15,000 dlh | 30 setups | 50 moves |
| Desk | 15,000 | 5,000 | 220 | 350 |
| Total activity-base usage | 20,000 dlh | 20,000 dlh | 250 setups | 400 moves |

Each product is budgeted for 5,000 units of production for the year. Determine (a) the activity rates for each activity and (b) the activity-based factory overhead per unit for each product.

**Follow My Example** **26-3**

a. Fabrication: $300,000/20,000 direct labor hours = $15 per dlh
   Assembly: $120,000/20,000 direct labor hours = $6 per dlh
   Setup: $100,000/250 setups = $400 per setup
   Materials handling: $80,000/400 moves = $200 per move

| | A | B | C | D | E | F | G | H | I | J | K | L |
|---|---|---|---|---|---|---|---|---|---|---|---|---|
| 1 | | | | Credenza | | | | | | Desk | | |
| 2 | | Activity-Base | | Activity | | Activity | | Activity-Base | | Activity | | Activity |
| 3 | Activity | Usage | × | Rate | = | Cost | | Usage | × | Rate | = | Cost |
| 4 | | | | | | | | | | | | |
| 5 | Fabrication | 5,000 dlh | | $15 per dlh | | $ 75,000 | | 15,000 dlh | | $15 per dlh | | $225,000 |
| 6 | Assembly | 15,000 dlh | | $6 per dlh | | 90,000 | | 5,000 dlh | | $6 per dlh | | 30,000 |
| 7 | Setup | 30 setups | | $400/setup | | 12,000 | | 220 setups | | $400/setup | | 88,000 |
| 8 | Materials handling | 50 moves | | $200/move | | 10,000 | | 350 moves | | $200/move | | 70,000 |
| 9 | Total | | | | | $187,000 | | | | | | $413,000 |
| 10 | Budgeted units | | | | | ÷ 5,000 | | | | | | ÷ 5,000 |
| 11 | Factory overhead | | | | | | | | | | | |
| 12 | per unit | | | | | $ 37.40 | | | | | | $ 82.60 |
| 13 | | | | | | | | | | | | |

Practice Exercises: **PE 26-3A, PE 26-3B**

**OBJ.**
**5**
Use activity-based costing to allocate selling and administrative expenses to products.

# Activity-Based Costing for Selling and Administrative Expenses

Generally accepted accounting principles (GAAP) require that selling and administrative expenses be reported as period expenses on the income statement. However, selling and administrative expenses may be allocated to products for managerial decision making. For example, selling and administrative expenses may be allocated for analyzing product profitability.

One method of allocating selling and administrative expenses to the products is based on sales volumes. However, products may consume activities in ways that are unrelated to their sales volumes. When this occurs, activity-based costing may be a more accurate method of allocation.

To illustrate, assume that Abacus Company has two products, Ipso and Facto. Both products have the same total sales volume. However, Ipso and Facto consume selling and administrative activities differently, as shown in Exhibit 11.

If the selling and administrative expenses of Abacus Company are allocated on the basis of sales volumes, the same amount of expense would be allocated to Ipso

| Selling and Administrative Activities | Ipso | Facto |
|---|---|---|
| Post-sale technical support | Product is easy to use by the customer. | Product requires specialized training in order to be used by the customer. |
| Order writing | Product requires no technical information from the customer. | Product requires detailed technical information from the customer. |
| Promotional support | Product requires no promotional effort. | Product requires extensive promotional effort. |
| Order entry | Product is purchased in large volumes per order. | Product is purchased in small volumes per order. |
| Customer return processing | Product has few customer returns. | Product has many customer returns. |
| Shipping document preparation | Product is shipped domestically. | Product is shipped internationally, requiring customs and export documents. |
| Shipping and handling | Product is not hazardous. | Product is hazardous, requiring specialized shipping and handling. |
| Field service | Product has few warranty claims. | Product has many warranty claims. |

**EXHIBIT 11**

**Selling and Administrative Activity Product Differences**

and Facto. This is because Ipso and Facto have the same sales volume. However, as Exhibit 11 implies, such an allocation would be misleading.

The activity-based costing method can be used to allocate the selling and administrative activities to Ipso and Facto. Activity-based costing allocates selling and administrative expenses based on how each product consumes activities.

To illustrate, assume that the field warranty service activity of Abacus Company has a budgeted cost of $150,000. Additionally, assume that 100 warranty claims are estimated for the period. Using warranty claims as an activity base, the warranty claim activity rate is $1,500, as computed below.

ExxonMobil Corporation allocated selling and administrative activities, such as engineering calls, order taking, market research, and advertising, to its lubricant products.

$$\text{Activity Rate} = \frac{\text{Budgeted Activity Cost}}{\text{Total Activity-Base Usage}}$$

$$\text{Warranty Claim Activity Rate} = \frac{\text{Budgeted Warranty Claim Expenses}}{\text{Total Estimated Warranty Claim}}$$

$$= \frac{\$150,000}{100 \text{ claims}} = \$150,000 \text{ per warranty claim}$$

Assuming that Ipso had 10 warranty claims and Facto had 90 warranty claims, the field service activity expenses would be allocated to each product as follows:

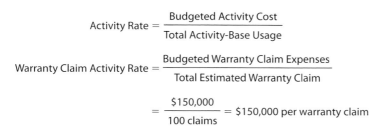

Ipso: $15,000 = 10 warranty claims × $1,500 per warranty claim
Facto: $135,000 = 90 warranty claims × $1,500 per warranty claim

The remaining selling and administrative activities could be allocated to Ipso and Facto in a similar manner.

In some cases, selling and administrative expenses may be more related to *customer* behaviors than to differences in products. That is, some customers may demand more service and selling activities than other customers. In such cases, activity-based costing would allocate selling and administrative expenses to customers.

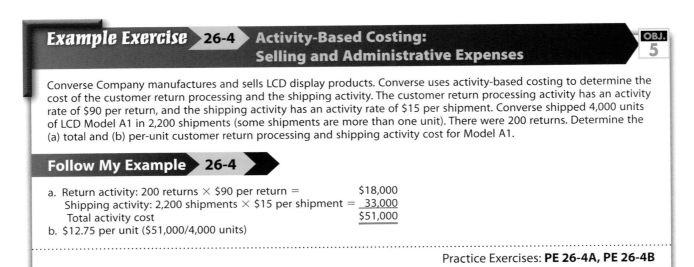

**Example Exercise** ▶ **26-4** ▶ **Activity-Based Costing:**
**Selling and Administrative Expenses**                OBJ. 5

Converse Company manufactures and sells LCD display products. Converse uses activity-based costing to determine the cost of the customer return processing and the shipping activity. The customer return processing activity has an activity rate of $90 per return, and the shipping activity has an activity rate of $15 per shipment. Converse shipped 4,000 units of LCD Model A1 in 2,200 shipments (some shipments are more than one unit). There were 200 returns. Determine the (a) total and (b) per-unit customer return processing and shipping activity cost for Model A1.

**Follow My Example** ▶ **26-4** ▶

a.  Return activity: 200 returns × $90 per return =         $18,000
    Shipping activity: 2,200 shipments × $15 per shipment = __33,000__
    Total activity cost                                      $51,000
b.  $12.75 per unit ($51,000/4,000 units)

Practice Exercises: **PE 26-4A, PE 26-4B**

---

**OBJ. 6** Use activity-based costing in a service business.

# Activity-Based Costing in Service Businesses

Service companies need to determine the cost of their services so that they can make pricing, promoting, and other decisions. The use of single and multiple department overhead rate methods may lead to distortions similar to those of manufacturing firms. Thus, many service companies use activity-based costing for determining the cost of services.

To illustrate, assume that Hopewell Hospital uses activity-based costing to allocate hospital overhead to patients. Hopewell Hospital applies activity-based costing by

1. Identifying activities.
2. Determining activity rates for each activity.
3. Allocating overhead costs to patients based upon activity base usage.

Hopewell Hospital has identified the following activities:

1. Admission
2. Radiological testing
3. Operating room
4. Pathological testing
5. Dietary and laundry

Each activity has an estimated patient activity-base usage. Based on the budgeted costs for each activity and related estimated activity base usage, the activity rates shown in Exhibit 12 were developed.

To illustrate, assume the following data for radiological testing:

Budgeted costs . . . . . . . . . . . . . . . . . . . . . . . . . . . . . . . . . . . . .   $96,000
Total estimated activity-base usage . . . . . . . . . . . . . . .   3,000 images

The activity rate of $320 per radiological image is computed as:

$$\text{Activity Rate} = \frac{\text{Budgeted Activity Cost}}{\text{Total Activity Base Usage}}$$

$$\text{Radiological Testing Activity Rate} = \frac{\text{Budgeted Radiological Testing}}{\text{Total Estimated Images}}$$

$$= \frac{\$960,000}{3,000 \text{ images}} = \$320 \text{ per image}$$

**EXHIBIT 12**   **Activity-Based Costing Method—Hopewell Hospital**

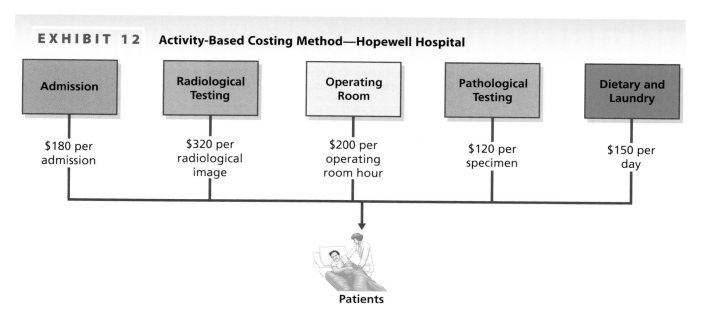

The activity rates for the other activities are determined in a similar manner. These activity rates along with the patient activity-base usage are used to allocate costs to patients as follows:

$$\text{Activity Cost Allocated to Patient} = \text{Patient Activity-Base Usage} \times \text{Activity Rate}$$

To illustrate, assume that Mia Wilson was a patient of the hospital. The hospital overhead services (activities) performed for Mia Wilson are shown below.

|  | **Patient (Mia Wilson) Activity-Base Usage** |
|---|---|
| Admission . . . . . . . . . . . . . . . . . . . . . . . . . . . | 1 admission |
| Radiological testing . . . . . . . . . . . . . . . . . . | 2 images |
| Operating room . . . . . . . . . . . . . . . . . . . . . . | 4 hours |
| Pathological testing . . . . . . . . . . . . . . . . . . | 1 specimen |
| Dietary and laundry . . . . . . . . . . . . . . . . . . | 7 days |

## BusinessConnection

### UNIVERSITY AND COMMUNITY PARTNERSHIP—LEARNING YOUR ABC'S

Students at Harvard's Kennedy School of Government joined with the city of Somerville, Massachusetts, in building an activity-based cost system for the city. The students volunteered several hours a week in four-person teams, interviewing city officials within 18 departments. The students were able to determine activity costs, such as the cost to fill a pothole, processing a building permit, or responding to a four-alarm fire. Their study was used by the city in forming the city budget. As stated by some of the students participating on this project: "It makes sense to use the resources of the university for community building. ...Real-world experience is a tremendous thing to have in your back pocket. We learned from the mayor and the fire chief, who are seasoned professionals in their own right."

Source: *Kennedy School Bulletin*, Spring 2005, "Easy as A-B-C: Students Take on the Somerville Budget Overhaul."

Based on the preceding services (activities), the Hopewell Hospital overhead costs allocated to Mia Wilson total $2,790, as computed below.

|  | A | B | C | D | E | F |
|---|---|---|---|---|---|---|
| 1 |  | Patient Name: Mia Wilson | | | | |
| 2 |  | Activity-Base | | Activity | | Activity |
| 3 | Activity | Usage | × | Rate | = | Cost |
| 4 |  |  |  |  |  |  |
| 5 | Admission | 1 admission |  | $180/admission |  | $ 180 |
| 6 | Radiological testing | 2 images |  | $320/image |  | 640 |
| 7 | Operating room | 4 hours |  | $200/hour |  | 800 |
| 8 | Pathological testing | 1 specimen |  | $120/specimen |  | 120 |
| 9 | Dietary and laundry | 7 days |  | $150/day |  | 1,050 |
| 10 | Total |  |  |  |  | $2,790 |
| 11 |  |  |  |  |  |  |

The patient activity costs can be combined with the direct costs, such as drugs and supplies. These costs and the related revenues can be reported for each patient in a patient (customer) profitability report. A partial patient profitability report for Hopewell Hospital is shown in Exhibit 13.

**EXHIBIT 13**

**Customer Profitability Report**

**Hopewell Hospital**
**Patient (Customer) Profitability Report**
**For the Period Ending December 31, 2012**

|  | Adcock, Kim | Birini, Brian | Conway, Don | Wilson, Mia |
|---|---|---|---|---|
| Revenues | $9,500 | $21,400 | $5,050 | $3,300 |
| Less patient costs: |  |  |  |  |
| Drugs and supplies | $ 400 | $ 1,000 | $ 300 | $ 200 |
| Admission | 180 | 180 | 180 | 180 |
| Radiological testing | 1,280 | 2,560 | 1,280 | 640 |
| Operating room | 2,400 | 6,400 | 1,600 | 800 |
| Pathological testing | 240 | 600 | 120 | 120 |
| Dietary and laundry | 4,200 | 14,700 | 1,050 | 1,050 |
| Total patient costs | $8,700 | $25,440 | $4,530 | $2,990 |
| Income from operations | $ 800 | $ (4,040) | $ 520 | $ 310 |

Exhibit 13 can be used by hospital administrators for decisions on pricing or services. For example, there was a large loss on services provided to Brian Birini. Investigation might reveal that some of the services provided to Birini were not reimbursed by insurance. As a result, Hopewell might lobby the insurance company to reimburse these services or request higher insurance reimbursement on other services.

**Example Exercise 26-5 Activity-Based Costing: Service Businesses** OBJ. 6

The Metro Radiology Clinic uses activity-based costing to determine the cost of servicing patients. There are three activities: patient administration, imaging, and diagnostic services. The activity rates associated with each activity are $45 per patient visit, $320 per X-ray image, and $450 per diagnosis. Julie Campbell went to the clinic and had two X-rays, each of which was read and interpreted by a doctor. Determine the total activity-based cost of Campbell's visit.

*(continued)*

**Follow My Example** 26-5

| | | |
|---|---|---|
| Imaging.................................... | $ 640 | (2 images × $320) |
| Diagnosis................................. | 900 | (2 diagnoses × $450) |
| Patient administration................... | 45 | (1 visit × $45) |
| Total activity cost ....................... | $1,585 | |

Practice Exercises: **PE 26-5A, PE 26-5B**

# BusinessConnection

## FINDING THE RIGHT NICHE

Businesses often attempt to divide a market into its unique characteristics, called market segmentation. Once a market segment is identified, product, price, promotion, and location strategies are tailored to fit that market. This is a better approach for many products and services than following a "one size fits all" strategy. Activity-based costing can be used to help tailor organizational effort toward different segments. For example, Fidelity Investments uses activity-based costing to tailor its sales and marketing strategies to different wealth segments. Thus, a higher wealth segment could rely on personal sales activities, while less wealthy segments would rely on less costly sales activities, such as mass mail. The following table lists popular forms of segmentation and their common characteristics:

| Form of Segmentation | Characteristics |
|---|---|
| Demographic | Age, education, gender, income, race |
| Geographic | Region, city, country |
| Psychographic | Lifestyle, values, attitudes |
| Benefit | Benefits provided |
| Volume | Light vs. heavy use |

Examples for each of these forms of segmentation are as follows:

*Demographic:* Fidelity Investments tailors sales and marketing strategies to different wealth segments.

© PAUL CONNORS/NEWSCOM

*Geographic:* Pro sports teams offer merchandise in their home cities.

*Psychographic:* The Body Shop markets all-natural beauty products to consumers who value cosmetic products that have not been animal-tested.

*Benefit:* Cold Stone Creamery sells a premium ice cream product with customized toppings.

*Volume:* Delta Air Lines provides additional benefits, such as class upgrades, free air travel, and boarding priority, to its frequent fliers.

# At a Glance 26

**OBJ. 1**

**Identify three methods used for allocating factory costs to products.**

**Key Points**    Three cost allocation methods used for determining product costs are the (1) single plantwide factory overhead rate method, (2) multiple production department rate method, and (3) activity-based costing method.

| Learning Outcomes | Example Exercises | Practice Exercises |
|---|---|---|
| • List the three methods for allocating factory overhead costs to products. | | |

**OBJ. 2**

## Use a single plantwide factory overhead rate for product costing.

**Key Points** A single plantwide factory overhead rate can be used to allocate all plant overhead to all products. The single plantwide factory overhead rate is simple to apply, but can lead to product cost distortions.

| Learning Outcomes | Example Exercises | Practice Exercises |
|---|---|---|
| • Compute the single plantwide factory overhead rate and use it to allocate factory overhead costs to products. | EE26-1 | PE26-1A, 26-1B |
| • Identify the conditions that favor the use of a single plantwide factory overhead rate for allocating factory overhead costs to products. | | |

**OBJ. 3**

## Use multiple production department factory overhead rates for product costing.

**Key Points** Product costing using multiple production department factory overhead rates requires identifying the factory overhead by each production department. Using these rates can result in greater accuracy than using single plantwide factory overhead rates when:
1. There are significant differences in the factory overhead rates across different production departments.
2. The products require different ratios of allocation-base usage in each production department.

| Learning Outcomes | Example Exercises | Practice Exercises |
|---|---|---|
| • Compute multiple production department overhead rates and use these rates to allocate factory overhead costs to products. | EE26-2 | PE26-2A, 26-2B |
| • Identify and describe the two conditions that favor the use of multiple production department factory overhead rates for allocating factory overhead costs to products as compared to the single plantwide factory overhead rate method. | | |

**OBJ. 4**

## Use activity-based costing for product costing.

**Key Points** Activity-based costing requires factory overhead to be budgeted to activities. The budgeted activity costs are allocated to products by multiplying activity rates by the activity-base quantity consumed for each product. Activity-based costing is more accurate when products consume activities in proportions unrelated to plantwide or departmental allocation bases.

| Learning Outcomes | Example Exercises | Practice Exercises |
|---|---|---|
| • Compute activity rates and use these rates to allocate factory overhead costs to products. | EE26-3 | PE26-3A, 26-3B |
| • Identify the conditions that favor the use of activity-based rates for allocating factory overhead costs to products, as compared to the other two methods of cost allocation. | | |
| • Compare the three factory overhead allocation methods and describe the causes of cost allocation distortion | | |

**OBJ. 5**

**Use activity-based costing to allocate selling and administrative expenses to products.**

**Key Points**   Selling and administrative expenses can be allocated to products for management profit reporting, using activity-based costing. Activity-based costing would be preferred when the products use selling and administrative activities in ratios that are unrelated to their sales volumes.

| Learning Outcomes | Example Exercises | Practice Exercises |
|---|---|---|
| • Compute selling and administrative activity rates and use these rates to allocate selling and administrative expenses to either a product or customer. | EE26-4 | PE26-4A, 26-4B |
| • Identify the conditions that would favor the use of activity-based costing for allocating selling and administrative expenses. | | |

**OBJ. 6**

**Use activity-based costing in a service business.**

**Key Points**   Activity-based costing may be applied in service settings to determine the cost of individual service offerings. Service costs are determined by multiplying activity rates by the amount of activity-base quantities consumed by the customer using the service offering.

| Learning Outcomes | Example Exercises | Practice Exercises |
|---|---|---|
| • Compute activity rates for service offerings and use these rates to allocate indirect costs to either a service product line or a customer. | EE26-5 | PE26-5A, 26-5B |
| • Prepare a customer profitability report using the cost of activities. | | |
| • Describe how activity-based cost information can be used in a service business for improved decision making. | | |

# Key Terms

activities (1209)

activity base (1210)

activity rates (1210)

activity-based costing (ABC) method (1209)

engineering change order (ECO) (1210)

multiple production department factory overhead rate method (1205)

product costing (1202)

production department factory overhead rates (1206)

setup (1209)

single plantwide factory overhead rate method (1203)

# Illustrative Problem

Hammer Company plans to use activity-based costing to determine its product costs. It presently uses a single plantwide factory overhead rate for allocating factory overhead to products, based on direct labor hours. The total factory overhead cost is as follows:

| Department | Factory Overhead |
|---|---|
| Production Support................................... | $1,225,000 |
| Production (factory overhead only).................... | 175,000 |
| Total cost......................................... | $1,400,000 |

The company determined that it performed four major activities in the Production Support Department. These activities, along with their budgeted activity costs, are as follows:

| Production Support Activities | Budgeted Activity Cost |
|---|---|
| Setup............................................. | $ 428,750 |
| Production control................................. | 245,000 |
| Quality control.................................... | 183,750 |
| Materials management ............................ | 367,500 |
| Total .......................................... | $1,225,000 |

Hammer Company estimated the following activity-base usage and units produced for each of its three products:

| Products | Number of Units | Direct Labor Hrs. | Setups | Production Orders | Inspections | Material Requisitions |
|---|---|---|---|---|---|---|
| TV ...................... | 10,000 | 25,000 | 80 | 80 | 35 | 320 |
| Computer............... | 2,000 | 10,000 | 40 | 40 | 40 | 400 |
| Cell phone ............. | 50,000 | 140,000 | 5 | 5 | 0 | 30 |
| Total cost ............. | 62,000 | 175,000 | 125 | 125 | 75 | 750 |

## Instructions

1. Determine the factory overhead cost per unit for the TV, computer, and cell phone under the single plantwide factory overhead rate method. Use direct labor hours as the activity base.

2. Determine the factory overhead cost per unit for the TV, computer, and cell phone under activity-based costing. Round to whole cents.

3. Which method provides more accurate product costing? Why?

## Solution

1. Single Plantwide Factory Overhead Rate $= \dfrac{\$1,400,000}{175,000 \text{ direct labor hours}}$

   $= \$8$ per direct labor hour

Factory overhead cost per unit:

| | TV | Computer | Cell Phone |
|---|---|---|---|
| Number of direct labor hours........................... | 25,000 | 10,000 | 140,000 |
| Single plantwide factory overhead rate................. | × $8/dlh | × $8/dlh | × $8/dlh |
| Total factory overhead ................................ | $200,000 | $ 80,000 | $ 1,120,000 |
| Number of units ...................................... | ÷ 10,000 | ÷ 2,000 | ÷ 50,000 |
| Factory overhead cost per unit ........................ | $ 20.00 | $ 40.00 | $ 22.40 |

2. Under activity-based costing, an activity rate must be determined for each activity pool:

| Activity | Budgeted Activity Cost | ÷ | Total Activity-Base Usage | = | Activity Rate |
|---|---|---|---|---|---|
| Setup ..................... | $428,750 | ÷ | 125 setups | = | $3,430 per setup |
| Production control......... | $245,000 | ÷ | 125 production orders | = | $1,960 per production order |
| Quality control............. | $183,750 | ÷ | 75 inspections | = | $2,450 per inspection |
| Materials management .... | $367,500 | ÷ | 750 requisitions | = | $490 per requisition |
| Production ................ | $175,000 | ÷ | 175,000 direct labor hours | = | $1 per direct labor hour |

These activity rates can be used to determine the activity-based factory overhead cost per unit as follows:

**TV**

| Activity | Activity-Base Usage | × | Activity Rate | = | Activity Cost |
|---|---|---|---|---|---|
| Setup ...................... | 80 setups | × | $3,430 | = | $274,400 |
| Production control........... | 80 production orders | × | $1,960 | = | 156,800 |
| Quality control............... | 35 inspections | × | $2,450 | = | 85,750 |
| Materials management ...... | 320 requisitions | × | $490 | = | 156,800 |
| Production ................. | 25,000 direct labor hrs. | × | $1 | = | 25,000 |
| Total factory overhead ....... | | | | | $698,750 |
| Unit volume ................. | | | | | ÷ 10,000 |
| Factory overhead cost per unit............... | | | | | $   69.88 |

**Computer**

| Activity | Activity-Base Usage | × | Activity Rate | = | Activity Cost |
|---|---|---|---|---|---|
| Setup ...................... | 40 setups | × | $3,430 | = | $137,200 |
| Production control........... | 40 production orders | × | $1,960 | = | 78,400 |
| Quality control............... | 40 inspections | × | $2,450 | = | 98,000 |
| Materials management ...... | 400 requisitions | × | $490 | = | 196,000 |
| Production ................. | 10,000 direct labor hrs. | × | $1 | = | 10,000 |
| Total factory overhead ....... | | | | | $519,600 |
| Unit volume ................. | | | | | ÷  2,000 |
| Factory overhead cost per unit............... | | | | | $ 259.80 |

**Cell phone**

| Activity | Activity-Base Usage | × | Activity Rate | = | Activity Cost |
|---|---|---|---|---|---|
| Setup ...................... | 5 setups | × | $3,430 | = | $ 17,150 |
| Production control........... | 5 production orders | × | $1,960 | = | 9,800 |
| Quality control............... | 0 inspections | × | $2,450 | = | 0 |
| Materials management ...... | 30 requisitions | × | $490 | = | 14,700 |
| Production ................. | 140,000 direct labor hrs. | × | $1 | = | 140,000 |
| Total factory overhead ....... | | | | | $181,650 |
| Unit volume ................. | | | | | ÷ 50,000 |
| Factory overhead cost per unit............... | | | | | $   3.63 |

3. Activity-based costing is more accurate, compared to the single plantwide factory overhead rate method. Activity-based costing properly shows that the cell phone is actually less expensive to make, while the other two products are more expensive to make. The reason is that the single plantwide factory overhead rate method fails to account for activity costs correctly. The setup, production control, quality-control, and materials management activities are all performed on products in amounts that are proportionately different than their volumes. For example, the computer requires many of these activities relative to its actual unit volume. The computer requires 40 setups over a volume of 2,000 units (average production run size = 50 units), while the cell phone has only 5 setups over 50,000 units (average production run size = 10,000 units). Thus, the computer requires greater support costs relative to the cell phone.

The cell phone requires minimum activity support because it is scheduled in large batches and requires no inspections (has high quality) and few requisitions. The other two products exhibit the opposite characteristics.

## Discussion Questions

1. Why would management be concerned about the accuracy of product costs?
2. Why would a manufacturing company with multiple production departments still prefer to use a single plantwide overhead rate?
3. How do the multiple production department and the single plantwide factory overhead rate methods differ?
4. Under what two conditions would the multiple production department factory overhead rate method provide more accurate product costs than the single plantwide factory overhead rate method?
5. How does activity-based costing differ from the multiple production department factory overhead rate method?
6. Shipping, selling, marketing, sales order processing, return processing, and advertising activities can be related to products by using activity-based costing. Would allocating these activities to products for financial statement reporting be acceptable according to GAAP?
7. What would happen to net income if the activities noted in Discussion Question 6 were allocated to products for financial statement reporting and the inventory increased?
8. Under what circumstances might the activity-based costing method provide more accurate product costs than the multiple production department factory overhead rate method?
9. When might activity-based costing be preferred over using a relative amount of product sales in allocating selling and administrative expenses to products?
10. How can activity-based costing be used in service companies?

# Practice Exercises

## PE 26-1A    Single plantwide overhead rate

The total factory overhead for Urban Styles, Inc., is budgeted for the year at $225,000. Urban Styles manufactures two types of men's pants: jeans and khakis. The jeans and khakis each require 0.15 direct labor hour for manufacture. Each product is budgeted for 15,000 units of production for the year. Determine (a) the total number of budgeted direct labor hours for the year, (b) the single plantwide factory overhead rate, and (c) the factory overhead allocated per unit for each product using the single plantwide factory overhead rate.

## PE 26-1B    Single plantwide overhead rate

The total factory overhead for Maritime Marine Company is budgeted for the year at $600,000. Maritime Marine manufactures two types of boats: speedboats and bass boats. The speedboat and bass boat each require 12 direct labor hours for manufacture. Each product is budgeted for 250 units of production for the year. Determine (a) the total number of budgeted direct labor hours for the year, (b) the single plantwide factory overhead rate, and (c) the factory overhead allocated per unit for each product using the single plantwide factory overhead rate.

## PE 26-2A    Multiple production department overhead rates

The total factory overhead for Urban Styles, Inc., is budgeted for the year at $225,000, divided into two departments: Cutting, $72,000, and Sewing, $153,000. Urban Styles manufactures two types of men's pants: jeans and khakis. The jeans require 0.05 direct labor hour in Cutting and 0.10 direct labor hour in Sewing. The khakis require 0.10 direct labor hour in Cutting and 0.05 direct labor hour in Sewing. Each product is budgeted for 15,000 units of production for the year. Determine (a) the total number of budgeted direct labor hours for the year in each department, (b) the departmental factory overhead rates for both departments, and (c) the factory overhead allocated per unit for each product using the department factory overhead allocation rates.

## PE 26-2B    Multiple production department overhead rates

The total factory overhead for Maritime Marine Company is budgeted for the year at $600,000, divided into two departments: Fabrication, $420,000, and Assembly, $180,000. Maritime manufactures two types of boats: speedboats and bass boats. The speedboats require 8 direct labor hours in Fabrication and 4 direct labor hours in Assembly. The bass boats require 4 direct labor hours in Fabrication and 8 direct labor hours in Assembly. Each product is budgeted for 250 units of production for the year. Determine (a) the total number of budgeted direct labor hours for the year in each department, (b) the departmental factory overhead rates for both departments, and (c) the factory overhead allocated per unit for each product using the department factory overhead allocation rates.

## PE 26-3A    Activity-based costing: factory overhead costs

The total factory overhead for Urban Styles, Inc., is budgeted for the year at $225,000, divided into four activities: cutting, $22,500; sewing, $45,000; setup, $100,000; and inspection, $57,500. Urban manufactures two types of men's pants: jeans and khakis. The activity-base usage quantities for each product by each activity are as follows:

|  | Cutting | Sewing | Setup | Inspection |
|---|---|---|---|---|
| Jeans | 750 dlh | 1,500 dlh | 1,600 setups | 4,000 inspections |
| Khakis | 1,500 | 750 | 400 | 1,750 |
|  | 2,250 dlh | 2,250 dlh | 2,000 setups | 5,750 inspections |

Each product is budgeted for 15,000 units of production for the year. Determine (a) the activity rates for each activity and (b) the activity-based factory overhead per unit for each product.

---

OBJ. 4    EE 26-3  *p. 1214*    **PE 26-3B    Activity-based costing: factory overhead costs**

The total factory overhead for Maritime Marine Company is budgeted for the year at $600,000, divided into four activities: fabrication, $204,000; assembly, $105,000; setup, $156,000; and inspection, $135,000. Maritime manufactures two types of boats: speedboats and bass boats. The activity-base usage quantities for each product by each activity are as follows:

|  | Fabrication | Assembly | Setup | Inspection |
|---|---|---|---|---|
| Speedboat | 2,000 dlh | 1,000 dlh | 300 setups | 1,100 inspections |
| Bass boat | 1,000 | 2,000 | 100 | 400 |
|  | 3,000 dlh | 3,000 dlh | 400 setups | 1,500 inspections |

Each product is budgeted for 250 units of production for the year. Determine (a) the activity rates for each activity and (b) the activity-based factory overhead per unit for each product.

---

OBJ. 5    EE 26-4  *p. 1216*    **PE 26-4A    Activity-based costing: selling and administrative expenses**

Comfort Step Company manufactures and sells shoes. Comfort Step uses activity-based costing to determine the cost of the sales order processing and the shipping activity. The sales order processing activity has an activity rate of $8 per sales order, and the shipping activity has an activity rate of $21 per shipment. Comfort Step sold 25,000 units of walking shoes, which consisted of 4,000 orders and 1,000 shipments. Determine (a) the total and (b) the per-unit sales order processing and shipping activity cost for walking shoes.

---

OBJ. 5    EE 26-4  *p. 1216*    **PE 26-4B    Activity-based costing: selling and administrative expenses**

PlayTyme Company manufactures and sells outdoor play equipment. PlayTyme uses activity-based costing to determine the cost of the sales order processing and the customer return activity. The sales order processing activity has an activity rate of $18 per sales order, and the customer return activity has an activity rate of $110 per return. PlayTyme sold 2,000 swing sets, which consisted of 600 orders and 50 returns. Determine (a) the total and (b) the per-unit sales order processing and customer return activity cost for swing sets.

---

OBJ. 6    EE 26-5  *p. 1218*    **PE 26-5A    Activity-based costing: service business**

Metropolitan Bank uses activity-based costing to determine the cost of servicing customers. There are three activity pools: teller transaction processing, check processing, and ATM transaction processing. The activity rates associated with each activity pool are $3.40 per teller transaction, $0.16 per canceled check, and $0.10 per ATM transaction. Corner Cleaners, Inc., had 10 teller transactions, 90 canceled checks, and 15 ATM transactions during the month. Determine the total monthly activity-based cost for Corner Cleaners, Inc., during the month.

---

OBJ. 6    EE 26-5  *p. 1218*    **PE 26-5B    Activity-based costing: service business**

Oasis Palms Hotel uses activity-based costing to determine the cost of servicing customers. There are three activity pools: guest check-in, room cleaning, and meal service. The activity rates associated with each activity pool are $9.40 per guest check-in, $22.50 per room cleaning, and $3.40 per served meal (not including food). Ginny Campbell visited the hotel for a 4-night stay. Campbell had three meals in the hotel during her visit. Determine the total activity-based cost for Campbell's visit.

# Exercises

OBJ. 2

### EX 26-1 Single plantwide factory overhead rate

Eaton Metal Fabricators Inc.'s Fabrication Department incurred $215,000 of factory overhead cost in producing gears and sprockets. The two products consumed a total of 4,000 direct machine hours. Of that amount, sprockets consumed 2,200 direct machine hours.

Determine the total amount of factory overhead that should be allocated to sprockets using machine hours as the allocation base.

OBJ. 2

✔ a. $62 per direct labor hour

### EX 26-2 Single plantwide factory overhead rate

Sousa Band Instruments Inc. makes three musical instruments: trumpets, tubas, and trombones. The budgeted factory overhead cost is $139,500. Factory overhead is allocated to the three products on the basis of direct labor hours. The products have the following budgeted production volume and direct labor hours per unit:

| | Budgeted Production Volume | Direct Labor Hours per Unit |
|---|---|---|
| Trumpets | 1,400 units | 0.5 |
| Tubas | 400 | 1.4 |
| Trombones | 900 | 1.1 |

a. Determine the single plantwide factory overhead rate.
b. Use the factory overhead rate in (a) to determine the amount of total and per-unit factory overhead allocated to each of the three products.

OBJ. 2

✔ a. $60 per processing hour

### EX 26-3 Single plantwide factory overhead rate

Krispy Treats Snack Food Company manufactures three types of snack foods: tortilla chips, potato chips, and pretzels. The company has budgeted the following costs for the upcoming period:

| | |
|---|---|
| Factory depreciation | $12,900 |
| Indirect labor | 32,150 |
| Factory electricity | 3,500 |
| Indirect materials | 6,650 |
| Selling expenses | 18,000 |
| Administrative expenses | 9,600 |
| Total costs | $82,800 |

Factory overhead is allocated to the three products on the basis of processing hours. The products had the following production budget and processing hours per case:

| | Budgeted Volume (Cases) | Processing Hours per Case |
|---|---|---|
| Tortilla chips | 2,500 | 0.12 |
| Potato chips | 4,400 | 0.10 |
| Pretzels | 1,200 | 0.15 |
| Total | 8,100 | |

a. Determine the single plantwide factory overhead rate.
b. Use the factory overhead rate in (a) to determine the amount of total and per-case factory overhead allocated to each of the three products under generally accepted accounting principles.

**EX 26-4** **Product costs and product profitability reports, using a single plantwide factory overhead rate**

Flint Engine Parts Inc. (FEP) produces three products—pistons, valves, and cams—for the heavy equipment industry. FEP has a very simple production process and product line and uses a single plantwide factory overhead rate to allocate overhead to the three products. The factory overhead rate is based on direct labor hours. Information about the three products for 2012 is as follows:

| | Budgeted Volume (Units) | Direct Labor Hours per Unit | Price per Unit | Direct Materials per Unit |
|---|---|---|---|---|
| Pistons | 6,000 | 0.15 | $42.00 | $20.50 |
| Valves | 24,000 | 0.10 | 8.50 | 3.25 |
| Cams | 1,000 | 0.30 | 56.00 | 24.00 |

The estimated direct labor rate is $25 per direct labor hour. Beginning and ending inventories are negligible and are, thus, assumed to be zero. The budgeted factory overhead for FEP is $108,000.

a. Determine the plantwide factory overhead rate.
b. Determine the factory overhead and direct labor cost per unit for each product.
c. Use the information above to construct a budgeted gross profit report by product line for the year ended December 31, 2012. Include the gross profit as a percent of sales in the last line of your report, rounded to one decimal place.
d. What does the report in (c) indicate to you?

**EX 26-5** **Multiple production department factory overhead rate method**

Home & Farm Glove Company produces three types of gloves: small, medium, and large. A glove pattern is first stenciled onto leather in the Pattern Department. The stenciled patterns are then sent to the Cut and Sew Department, where the final glove is cut and sewed together. Home & Farm uses the multiple production department factory overhead rate method of allocating factory overhead costs. Its factory overhead costs were budgeted as follows:

| | |
|---|---|
| Pattern Department overhead | $140,000 |
| Cut and Sew Department overhead | 207,000 |
| Total | $347,000 |

The direct labor estimated for each production department was as follows:

| | |
|---|---|
| Pattern Department | 2,000 direct labor hours |
| Cut and Sew Department | 2,300 |
| Total | 4,300 direct labor hours |

Direct labor hours are used to allocate the production department overhead to the products. The direct labor hours per unit for each product for each production department were obtained from the engineering records as follows:

| Production Departments | Small Glove | Medium Glove | Large Glove |
|---|---|---|---|
| Pattern Department | 0.05 | 0.06 | 0.07 |
| Cut and Sew Department | 0.07 | 0.09 | 0.11 |
| Direct labor hours per unit | 0.12 | 0.15 | 0.18 |

a. Determine the two production department factory overhead rates.
b. Use the two production department factory overhead rates to determine the factory overhead per unit for each product.

### EX 26-6  Single plantwide and multiple production department factory overhead rate methods and product cost distortion

Peach Computer Company manufactures a desktop and portable computer through two production departments, Assembly and Testing. Presently, the company uses a single plantwide factory overhead rate for allocating factory overhead to the two products. However, management is considering using the multiple production department factory overhead rate method. The following factory overhead was budgeted for Peach:

| | |
|---|---|
| Assembly Department | $210,000 |
| Testing Department | 600,000 |
| Total | $810,000 |

Direct machine hours were estimated as follows:

| | |
|---|---|
| Assembly Department | 3,000 hours |
| Testing Department | 6,000 |
| Total | 9,000 hours |

In addition, the direct machine hours (dmh) used to produce a unit of each product in each department were determined from engineering records, as follows:

| | Desktop | Portable |
|---|---|---|
| Assembly Department | 0.50 dmh | 1.00 dmh |
| Testing Department | 1.00 | 2.00 |
| Total machine hours per unit | 1.50 dmh | 3.00 dmh |

a. Determine the per-unit factory overhead allocated to the desktop and portable computers under the single plantwide factory overhead rate method, using direct machine hours as the allocation base.
b. Determine the per-unit factory overhead allocated to the desktop and portable computers under the multiple production department factory overhead rate method, using direct machine hours as the allocation base for each department.
c. Recommend to management a product costing approach, based on your analyses in (a) and (b). Support your recommendation.

### EX 26-7  Single plantwide and multiple production department factory overhead rate methods and product cost distortion

The management of Cobalt Engines Inc. manufactures gasoline and diesel engines through two production departments, Fabrication and Assembly. Management needs accurate product cost information in order to guide product strategy. Presently, the company uses a single plantwide factory overhead rate for allocating factory overhead to the two products. However, management is considering the multiple production department factory overhead rate method. The following factory overhead was budgeted for Cobalt:

| | |
|---|---|
| Fabrication Department factory overhead | $576,000 |
| Assembly Department factory overhead | 224,000 |
| Total | $800,000 |

Direct labor hours were estimated as follows:

| | |
|---|---|
| Fabrication Department | 3,200 hours |
| Assembly Department | 3,200 |
| Total | 6,400 hours |

In addition, the direct labor hours (dlh) used to produce a unit of each product in each department were determined from engineering records, as follows:

| Production Departments | Gasoline Engine | Diesel Engine |
|---|---|---|
| Fabrication Department | 0.8 dlh | 2.2 dlh |
| Assembly Department | 2.2 | 0.8 |
| Direct labor hours per unit | 3.0 dlh | 3.0 dlh |

a. Determine the per-unit factory overhead allocated to the gasoline and diesel engines under the single plantwide factory overhead rate method, using direct labor hours as the activity base.
b. Determine the per-unit factory overhead allocated to the gasoline and diesel engines under the multiple production department factory overhead rate method, using direct labor hours as the activity base for each department.
c. Recommend to management a product costing approach, based on your analyses in (a) and (b). Support your recommendation.

---

**OBJ. 4**

### EX 26-8   Identifying activity bases in an activity-based cost system

Select Foods Inc. uses activity-based costing to determine product costs. For each activity listed in the left column, match an appropriate activity-base from the right column. You may use items in the activity-base list more than once or not at all.

| Activity | Activity Base |
|---|---|
| Accounting reports | Engineering change orders |
| Customer return processing | Kilowatt hours used |
| Electric power | Number of accounting reports |
| Human resources | Number of customers |
| Inventory control | Number of customer orders |
| Invoice and collecting | Number of customer returns |
| Machine depreciation | Number of employees |
| Materials handling | Number of inspections |
| Order shipping | Number of inventory transactions |
| Payroll | Number of machine hours |
| Production control | Number of material moves |
| Production setup | Number of payroll checks processed |
| Purchasing | Number of production orders |
| Quality control | Number of purchase orders |
| Sales order processing | Number of sales orders |
| | Number of setups |

---

**OBJ. 4**

**✔ b. $32,220**

### EX 26-9   Product costs using activity rates

Elegant Occasions Inc. sells china and flatware over the Internet. For the next period, the budgeted cost of the sales order processing activity is $78,300, and 4,350 sales orders are estimated to be processed.

a. Determine the activity rate of the sales order processing activity.
b. Determine the amount of sales order processing cost that Elegant Occasions would receive if it had 1,790 sales orders.

---

**OBJ. 4**

**✔ Treadmill activity cost per unit, $212**

### EX 26-10   Product costs using activity rates

Cardio Care, Inc., manufactures stationary bicycles and treadmills. The products are produced in its Fabrication and Assembly production departments. In addition to production activities, several other activities are required to produce the two products. These activities and their associated activity rates are as follows:

| Activity | Activity Rate |
|---|---|
| Fabrication | $24 per machine hour |
| Assembly | $10 per direct labor hour |
| Setup | $50 per setup |
| Inspecting | $24 per inspection |
| Production scheduling | $11 per production order |
| Purchasing | $ 9 per purchase order |

The activity-base usage quantities and units produced for each product were as follows:

| Activity Base | Stationary Bicycle | Treadmill |
|---|---|---|
| Machine hours | 1,750 | 965 |
| Direct labor hours | 450 | 156 |
| Setups | 49 | 15 |
| Inspections | 320 | 310 |
| Production orders | 60 | 10 |
| Purchase orders | 190 | 100 |
| Units produced | 500 | 160 |

Use the activity rate and usage information to calculate the total activity cost and activity cost per unit for each product.

✔ b. Dining room lighting fixtures, $31.26 per unit

**EX 26-11   Activity rates and product costs using activity-based costing**

Contemporary Lighting Inc. manufactures entry and dining room lighting fixtures. Five activities are used in manufacturing the fixtures. These activities and their associated budgeted activity costs and activity bases are as follows:

| Activity | Budgeted Activity Cost | Activity Base |
|---|---|---|
| Casting | $106,400 | Machine hours |
| Assembly | 52,800 | Direct labor hours |
| Inspecting | 17,080 | Number of inspections |
| Setup | 33,600 | Number of setups |
| Materials handling | 35,700 | Number of loads |

Corporate records were obtained to estimate the amount of activity to be used by the two products. The estimated activity-base usage quantities and units produced are provided in the table below.

| Activity Base | Entry | Dining | Total |
|---|---|---|---|
| Machine hours | 2,600 | 1,200 | 3,800 |
| Direct labor hours | 1,000 | 2,300 | 3,300 |
| Number of inspections | 900 | 320 | 1,220 |
| Number of setups | 180 | 60 | 240 |
| Number of loads | 600 | 250 | 850 |
| Units produced | 7,500 | 3,000 | 10,500 |

a. Determine the activity rate for each activity.
b. Use the activity rates in (a) to determine the total and per-unit activity costs associated with each product.

✔ b. Ovens, $55.47 per unit

**EX 26-12   Activity cost pools, activity rates, and product costs using activity-based costing**

Kitchen Mate, Inc., is estimating the activity cost associated with producing ovens and refrigerators. The indirect labor can be traced into four separate activity pools, based on time records provided by the employees. The budgeted activity cost and activity-base information are provided as follows:

| Activity | Activity Pool Cost | Activity Base |
|---|---|---|
| Procurement | $121,000 | Number of purchase orders |
| Scheduling | 8,140 | Number of production orders |
| Materials handling | 21,000 | Number of moves |
| Product development | 22,440 | Number of engineering changes |
| Total cost | $172,580 | |

The estimated activity-base usage and unit information for Top Chef's two product lines was determined from corporate records as follows:

| | Number of Purchase Orders | Number of Production Orders | Number of Moves | Number of Engineering Changes | Units |
|---|---|---|---|---|---|
| Ovens | 700 | 250 | 420 | 120 | 2,000 |
| Refrigerators | 400 | 120 | 280 | 50 | 1,541 |
| Totals | 1,100 | 370 | 700 | 170 | 3,541 |

a. Determine the activity rate for each activity cost pool.
b. Determine the activity-based cost per unit of each product.

---

OBJ. 2, 4

✔ c. CDs,
$1.53 per unit

### EX 26-13   Activity-based costing and product cost distortion

Memory Disk Inc. is considering a change to activity-based product costing. The company produces two products, CDs and DVDs, in a single production department. The production department is estimated to require 3,000 direct labor hours. The total indirect labor is budgeted to be $270,000.

Time records from indirect labor employees revealed that they spent 40% of their time setting up production runs and 60% of their time supporting actual production.

The following information about CDs and DVDs was determined from the corporate records:

| | Number of Setups | Direct Labor Hours | Units |
|---|---|---|---|
| CDs | 500 | 1,500 | 75,000 |
| DVDs | 1,100 | 1,500 | 75,000 |
| Total | 1,600 | 3,000 | 150,000 |

a. Determine the indirect labor cost per unit allocated to CDs and DVDs under a single plantwide factory overhead rate system using the direct labor hours as the allocation base.
b. Determine the budgeted activity costs and activity rates for the indirect labor under activity-based costing. Assume two activities—one for setup and the other for production support.
c. Determine the activity cost per unit for indirect labor allocated to each product under activity-based costing.
d. Why are the per-unit allocated costs in (a) different from the per-unit activity cost assigned to the products in (c)?

---

OBJ. 3

✔ b. Blender, $15.90 per unit

### EX 26-14   Multiple production department factory overhead rate method

Gourmet Appliance Company manufactures small kitchen appliances. The product line consists of blenders and toaster ovens. Gourmet Appliance presently uses the multiple production department factory overhead rate method. The factory overhead is as follows:

| | |
|---|---|
| Assembly Department | $108,000 |
| Test and Pack Department | 70,000 |
| Total | $178,000 |

The direct labor information for the production of 5,000 units of each product is as follows:

| | Assembly Department | Test and Pack Department |
|---|---|---|
| Blender | 500 dlh | 1,500 dlh |
| Toaster oven | 1,500 | 500 |
| Total | 2,000 dlh | 2,000 dlh |

Gourmet Appliance used direct labor hours to allocate production department factory overhead to products.

a. Determine the two production department factory overhead rates.
b. Determine the total factory overhead and the factory overhead per unit allocated to each product.

---

**OBJ. 4**

✔ b. Blender, $19.70 per unit

### EX 26-15   Activity-based costing and product cost distortion

The management of Gourmet Appliance Company in Exercise 26-14 has asked you to use activity-based costing to allocate factory overhead costs to the two products. You have determined that $57,000 of factory overhead from each of the production departments can be associated with setup activity ($114,000 in total). Company records indicate that blenders required 100 setups, while the toaster ovens required only 50 setups. Each product has a production volume of 5,000 units.

a. Determine the three activity rates (assembly, test and pack, and setup).
b. Determine the total factory overhead and factory overhead per unit allocated to each product using the activity rates in (a).

---

**OBJ. 2, 4**

✔ a. Low, Col. C, 90.7%

### EX 26-16   Single plantwide rate and activity-based costing

Whirlpool Corporation conducted an activity-based costing study of its Evansville, Indiana, plant in order to identify its most profitable products. Assume that we select three representative refrigerators (out of 333): one low-, one medium-, and one high-volume refrigerator. Additionally, we assume the following activity-base information for each of the three refrigerators:

| Three Representative Refrigerators | Number of Machine Hours | Number of Setups | Number of Sales Orders | Number of Units |
|---|---|---|---|---|
| Refrigerator—Low Volume | 28 | 15 | 45 | 140 |
| Refrigerator—Medium Volume | 240 | 14 | 100 | 1,200 |
| Refrigerator—High Volume | 1,000 | 10 | 150 | 5,000 |

Prior to conducting the study, the factory overhead allocation was based on a single machine hour rate. The machine hour rate was $180 per hour. After conducting the activity-based costing study, assume that three activities were used to allocate the factory overhead. The new activity rate information is assumed to be as follows:

| | Machining Activity | Setup Activity | Sales Order Processing Activity |
|---|---|---|---|
| Activity rate | $145 | $220 | $50 |

a. Complete the following table, using the single machine hour rate to determine the per-unit factory overhead for each refrigerator (Column A) and the three activity-based rates to determine the activity-based factory overhead per unit (Column B). Finally, compute the percent change in per-unit allocation from the single to activity-based rate methods (Column C). Round per-unit overhead to nearest cent and whole percents to one decimal place.

| Product Volume Class | Column A Single Rate Overhead Allocation per Unit | Column B ABC Overhead Allocation per Unit | Column C Percent Change in Allocation (Col. B – Col. A)/Col. A |
|---|---|---|---|
| Low | | | |
| Medium | | | |
| High | | | |

b. Why is the traditional overhead rate per machine hour greater under the single rate method than under the activity-based method?
c. Interpret Column C in your table from part (a).

OBJ. 5

**EX 26-17 Evaluating selling and administrative cost allocations**

Empire Furniture Company has two major product lines with the following characteristics:

Commercial office furniture: Few large orders, little advertising support, shipments in full truckloads, and low handling complexity

Home office furniture: Many small orders, large advertising support, shipments in partial truckloads, and high handling complexity

The company produced the following profitability report for management:

**Office Comfort Furniture Company**
**Product Profitability Report**
**For the Year Ended December 31, 2012**

|  | Commercial Office Furniture | Home Office Furniture | Total |
|---|---|---|---|
| Revenue | $4,000,000 | $2,000,000 | $6,000,000 |
| Cost of goods sold | 1,500,000 | 700,000 | 2,200,000 |
| Gross profit | $2,500,000 | $1,300,000 | $3,800,000 |
| Selling and administrative expenses | 1,200,000 | 600,000 | 1,800,000 |
| Income from operations | $1,300,000 | $ 700,000 | $2,000,000 |

The selling and administrative expenses are allocated to the products on the basis of relative sales dollars.

Evaluate the accuracy of this report and recommend an alternative approach.

---

OBJ. 5

✔ b. Generators operating profit-to-sales, 22%

**EX 26-18 Construct and interpret a product profitability report, allocating selling and administrative expenses**

Volt-Gear, Inc., manufactures power equipment. Volt-Gear has two primary products—generators and air compressors. The following report was prepared by the controller for Volt-Gear senior marketing management:

|  | Generators | Air Compressors | Total |
|---|---|---|---|
| Revenue | $1,250,000 | $800,000 | $2,050,000 |
| Cost of goods sold | 900,000 | 600,000 | 1,500,000 |
| Gross profit | $ 350,000 | $200,000 | $ 550,000 |
| Selling and administrative expenses |  |  | 235,000 |
| Income from operations |  |  | $ 315,000 |

The marketing management team was concerned that the selling and administrative expenses were not traced to the products. Marketing management believed that some products consumed larger amounts of selling and administrative expense than did other products. To verify this, the controller was asked to prepare a complete product profitability report, using activity-based costing.

The controller determined that selling and administrative expenses consisted of two activities: sales order processing and post-sale customer service. The controller was able to determine the activity base and activity rate for each activity, as shown below.

| Activity | Activity Base | Activity Rate |
|---|---|---|
| Sales order processing | Sales orders | $ 50 per sales order |
| Post-sale customer service | Service requests | $225 per customer service request |

The controller determined the following activity-base usage information about each product:

|  | Generators | Air Compressors |
|---|---|---|
| Number of sales orders | 870 | 1,193 |
| Number of service requests | 140 | 446 |

a. Determine the activity cost of each product for sales order processing and post-sale customer service activities.

b. Use the information in (a) to prepare a complete product profitability report dated for the year ended December 31, 2012. Calculate the gross profit to sales and the income from operations to sales percentages for each product.

c. Interpret the product profitability report. How should management respond to the report?

---

### EX 26-19 Activity-based costing and customer profitability

Schneider Electric manufactures power distribution equipment for commercial customers, such as hospitals and manufacturers. Activity-based costing was used to determine customer profitability. Customer service activities were assigned to individual customers, using the following assumed customer service activities, activity base, and activity rate:

| Customer Service Activity | Activity Base | Activity Rate |
|---|---|---|
| Bid preparation | Number of bid requests | $220/request |
| Shipment | Number of shipments | $18/shipment |
| Support standard items | Number of standard items ordered | $24/std. item |
| Support nonstandard items | Number of nonstandard items ordered | $82/nonstd. item |

Assume that the company had the following gross profit information for three representative customers:

| | Customer 1 | Customer 2 | Customer 3 |
|---|---|---|---|
| Revenue | $32,300 | $21,500 | $26,000 |
| Cost of goods sold | 19,380 | 11,180 | 12,480 |
| Gross profit | $12,920 | $10,320 | $13,520 |
| Gross profit as a percent of sales | 40% | 48% | 52% |

The administrative records indicated that the activity-base usage quantities for each customer were as follows:

| Activity Base | Customer 1 | Customer 2 | Customer 3 |
|---|---|---|---|
| Number of bid requests | 10 | 6 | 22 |
| Number of shipments | 14 | 23 | 42 |
| Number of standard items ordered | 45 | 36 | 51 |
| Number of nonstandard items ordered | 16 | 26 | 50 |

a. Prepare a customer profitability report dated for the year ended December 31, 2012, showing (1) the income from operations after customer service activities, (2) the gross profit as a percent of sales, and (3) the income from operations after customer service activities as a percent of sales. Prepare the report with a column for each customer. Round percentages to the nearest whole percent.

b. Interpret the report in part (a).

---

### EX 26-20 Activity-based costing for a hospital

Valley Hospital plans to use activity-based costing to assign hospital indirect costs to the care of patients. The hospital has identified the following activities and activity rates for the hospital indirect costs:

| Activity | Activity Rate |
|---|---|
| Room and meals | $220 per day |
| Radiology | $290 per image |
| Pharmacy | $ 45 per physician order |
| Chemistry lab | $ 85 per test |
| Operating room | $920 per operating room hour |

The activity usage information associated with the two patients is as follows:

|  | Patient Barns | Patient Powell |
|---|---|---|
| Number of days | 8 days | 3 days |
| Number of images | 5 images | 2 images |
| Number of physician orders | 6 orders | 4 orders |
| Number of tests | 5 tests | 2 tests |
| Number of operating room hours | 5.5 hours | 1.5 hours |

a. Determine the activity cost associated with each patient.
b. Why is the total activity cost different for the two patients?

---

OBJ. 5, 6

✔ a. Auto, $797,000

**EX 26-21     Activity-based costing in an insurance company**

Safeguard Insurance Company carries three major lines of insurance: auto, workers' compensation, and homeowners. The company has prepared the following report for 2013:

**Safeguard Insurance Company**
**Product Profitability Report**
**For the Year Ended December 31, 2013**

|  | Auto | Workers' Compensation | Homeowners |
|---|---|---|---|
| Premium revenue | $4,800,000 | $5,200,000 | $6,800,000 |
| Less estimated claims | 3,360,000 | 3,640,000 | 4,760,000 |
| Underwriting income | $1,440,000 | $1,560,000 | $2,040,000 |
| Underwriting income as a percent of premium revenue | 30% | 30% | 30% |

Management is concerned that the administrative expenses may make some of the insurance lines unprofitable. However, the administrative expenses have not been allocated to the insurance lines. The controller has suggested that the administrative expenses could be assigned to the insurance lines using activity-based costing. The administrative expenses are comprised of five activities. The activities and their rates are as follows:

|  | Activity Rates |
|---|---|
| New policy processing | $150 per new policy |
| Cancellation processing | $220 per cancellation |
| Claim audits | $400 per claim audit |
| Claim disbursements processing | $130 per disbursement |
| Premium collection processing | $30 per premium collected |

Activity-base usage data for each line of insurance was retrieved from the corporate records and is shown below.

|  | Auto | Workers' Comp. | Homeowners |
|---|---|---|---|
| Number of new policies | 1,100 | 1,250 | 3,400 |
| Number of canceled policies | 400 | 200 | 1,800 |
| Number of audited claims | 320 | 100 | 800 |
| Number of claim disbursements | 400 | 180 | 700 |
| Number of premiums collected | 7,000 | 1,500 | 13,000 |

a. Complete the product profitability report through the administrative activities. Determine the income from operations as a percent of premium revenue, rounded to the nearest whole percent.
b. Interpret the report.

## Problems Series A

OBJ. 2

✔ 1. b. $60 per machine hour

### PR 26-1A Single plantwide factory overhead rate

California Chrome Company manufactures three chrome-plated products—automobile bumpers, valve covers, and wheels. These products are manufactured in two production departments (Stamping and Plating). The factory overhead for California Chrome is $338,400.

The three products consume both machine hours and direct labor hours in the two production departments as follows:

|  | Direct Labor Hours | Machine Hours |
|---|---|---|
| **Stamping Department** | | |
| Automobile bumpers | 700 | 940 |
| Valve covers | 380 | 680 |
| Wheels | 420 | 720 |
| | 1,500 | 2,340 |
| **Plating Department** | | |
| Automobile bumpers | 200 | 1,460 |
| Valve covers | 210 | 890 |
| Wheels | 205 | 950 |
| | 615 | 3,300 |
| Total | 2,115 | 5,640 |

**Instructions**

1. Determine the single plantwide factory overhead rate, using each of the following allocation bases: (a) direct labor hours and (b) machine hours.
2. Determine the product factory overhead costs, using (a) the direct labor hour plantwide factory overhead rate and (b) the machine hour plantwide factory overhead rate.

OBJ. 3

✔ 2. Wheels, $96,000

### PR 26-2A Multiple production department factor overhead rates

The management of California Chrome Company, described in Problem 26-1A, now plans to use the multiple production department factory overhead rate method. The total factory overhead associated with each department is as follows:

| | |
|---|---|
| Stamping Department | $180,000 |
| Plating Department | 158,400 |
| Total | $338,400 |

**Instructions**

1. Determine the multiple production department factory overhead rates, using direct labor hours for the Stamping Department and machine hours for the Plating Department.
2. Determine the product factory overhead costs, using the multiple production department rates in (1).

OBJ. 3, 4

✔ 4. Snowboards, $236,000 and $59

### PR 26-3A Activity-based and department rate product costing and product cost distortions

White Mountain Sports Inc. manufactures two products: snowboards and skis. The factory overhead incurred is as follows:

| | |
|---|---|
| Indirect labor | $200,000 |
| Cutting Department | 85,000 |
| Finishing Department | 95,000 |
| Total | $380,000 |

The activity base associated with the two production departments is direct labor hours. The indirect labor can be assigned to two different activities as follows:

| Activity | Budgeted Activity Cost | Activity Base |
|---|---|---|
| Production control | $ 80,000 | Number of production runs |
| Materials handling | 120,000 | Number of moves |
| Total | $200,000 | |

The activity-base usage quantities and units produced for the two products are shown below.

| | Number of Production Runs | Number of Moves | Direct Labor Hours—Cutting | Direct Labor Hours—Finishing | Units Produced |
|---|---|---|---|---|---|
| Snowboards | 340 | 4,000 | 3,500 | 1,500 | 4,000 |
| Skis | 60 | 2,000 | 1,500 | 3,500 | 4,000 |
| Total | 400 | 6,000 | 5,000 | 5,000 | 8,000 |

### Instructions

1. Determine the factory overhead rates under the multiple production department rate method. Assume that indirect labor is associated with the production departments, so that the total factory overhead is $175,000 and $205,000 for the Cutting and Finishing departments, respectively.
2. Determine the total and per-unit factory overhead costs allocated to each product, using the multiple production department overhead rates in (1).
3. Determine the activity rates, assuming that the indirect labor is associated with activities rather than with the production departments.
4. Determine the total and per-unit cost assigned to each product under activity-based costing.
5. Explain the difference in the per-unit overhead allocated to each product under the multiple production department factory overhead rate and activity-based costing methods.

---

OBJ. 4

✔ 2 . Newsprint total activity cost, $243,900

### PR 26-4A    Activity-based product costing

Alabama Paper Company manufactures three products (computer paper, newsprint, and specialty paper) in a continuous production process. Senior management has asked the controller to conduct an activity-based costing study. The controller identified the amount of factory overhead required by the critical activities of the organization as follows:

| Activity | Activity Cost Pool |
|---|---|
| Production | $437,400 |
| Setup | 176,000 |
| Moving | 31,200 |
| Shipping | 105,300 |
| Product engineering | 127,500 |
| Total | $877,400 |

The activity bases identified for each activity are as follows:

| Activity | Activity Base |
|---|---|
| Production | Machine hours |
| Setup | Number of setups |
| Moving | Number of moves |
| Shipping | Number of customer orders |
| Product engineering | Number of test runs |

The activity-base usage quantities and units produced for the three products were determined from corporate records and are as follows:

| | Machine Hours | Number of Setups | Number of Moves | Number of Customer Orders | Number of Test Runs | Units |
|---|---|---|---|---|---|---|
| Computer paper | 900 | 120 | 270 | 440 | 80 | 1,000 |
| Newsprint | 1,080 | 50 | 110 | 140 | 25 | 1,200 |
| Specialty paper | 450 | 270 | 400 | 590 | 150 | 500 |
| Total | 2,430 | 440 | 780 | 1,170 | 255 | 2,700 |

Each product requires 0.9 machine hour per unit.

### Instructions

1. Determine the activity rate for each activity.
2. Determine the total and per-unit activity cost for all three products.
3. Why aren't the activity unit costs equal across all three products since they require the same machine time per unit?

OBJ. 5

✔ 3. Hope Hospital loss from operations, ($4,150)

**PR 26-5A** **Allocating selling and administrative expenses using activity-based costing**

Western Mechancial Inc. manufactures cooling units for commercial buildings. The price and cost of goods sold for each unit are as follows:

| | |
|---|---|
| Price | $55,200 per unit |
| Cost of goods sold | 27,500 |
| Gross profit | $27,700 per unit |

In addition, the company incurs selling and administrative expenses of $199,800. The company wishes to assign these costs to its three major customers, Coastal Atlantic University, Celebrity Arena, and Hope Hospital. These expenses are related to three major nonmanufacturing activities: customer service, project bidding, and engineering support. The engineering support is in the form of engineering changes that are placed by the customer to change the design of a product. The budgeted activity costs and activity bases associated with these activities are:

| Activity | Budgeted Activity Cost | Activity Base |
|---|---|---|
| Customer service | $ 74,000 | Number of service requests |
| Project bidding | 48,800 | Number of bids |
| Engineering support | 77,000 | Number of customer design changes |
| Total costs | $199,800 | |

Activity-base usage and unit volume information for the three customers is as follows:

| | Coastal Atlantic University | Celebrity Arena | Hope Hospital | Total |
|---|---|---|---|---|
| Number of service requests | 40 | 35 | 125 | 200 |
| Number of bids | 25 | 12 | 24 | 61 |
| Number of customer design changes | 30 | 20 | 90 | 140 |
| Unit volume | 15 | 10 | 4 | 29 |

### Instructions

1. Determine the activity rates for each of the three nonmanufacturing activity pools.
2. Determine the activity costs allocated to the three customers, using the activity rates in (1).

(*Continued*)

3. Construct customer profitability reports for the three customers, dated for the year ended December 31, 2013, using the activity costs in (2). The reports should disclose the gross profit and income from operations associated with each customer.
4. Provide recommendations to management, based on the profitability reports in (3).

**PR 26-6A    Product costing and decision analysis for a hospital**

Healthmark Medical Inc. wishes to determine its product costs. Healthmark offers a variety of medical procedures (operations) that are considered its "products." The overhead has been separated into three major activities. The annual estimated activity costs and activity bases are provided below.

| Activity | Budgeted Activity Cost | Activity Base |
|---|---|---|
| Scheduling and admitting | $ 300,000 | Number of patients |
| Housekeeping | 2,925,000 | Number of patient days |
| Nursing | 3,840,000 | Weighted care unit |
| Total costs | $7,065,000 | |

Total "patient days" are determined by multiplying the number of patients by the average length of stay in the hospital. A weighted care unit (wcu) is a measure of nursing effort used to care for patients. There were 160,000 weighted care units estimated for the year. In addition, Healthmark estimated 5,000 patients and 22,500 patient days for the year. (The average patient is expected to have a a little more than a four-day stay in the hospital.)

During a portion of the year, Healthmark collected patient information for three selected procedures, as shown below.

| | Activity-Base Usage |
|---|---|
| **Procedure A** | |
| Number of patients | 230 |
| Average length of stay | × 5 days |
| Patient days | 1,150 |
| Weighted care units | 16,000 |
| **Procedure B** | |
| Number of patients | 540 |
| Average length of stay | × 4 days |
| Patient days | 2,160 |
| Weighted care units | 5,000 |
| **Procedure C** | |
| Number of patients | 1,000 |
| Average length of stay | × 3 days |
| Patient days | 3,000 |
| Weighted care units | 20,000 |

Private insurance reimburses the hospital for these activities at a fixed daily rate of $400 per patient day for all three procedures.

**Instructions**
1. Determine the activity rates.
2. Determine the activity cost for each procedure.
3. Determine the excess or deficiency of reimbursements to activity cost.
4. Interpret your results.

## Problems Series B

OBJ. 2

✔ 1. b. $120 per machine hour

### PR 26-1B Single plantwide factory overhead rate

Daisy Dairy Company manufactures three products—whole milk, skim milk, and cream—in two production departments, Blending and Packing. The factory overhead for Daisy Dairy is $360,000.

The three products consume both machine hours and direct labor hours in the two production departments as follows:

|  | Direct Labor Hours | Machine Hours |
| --- | --- | --- |
| **Blending Department** |  |  |
| Whole milk | 290 | 720 |
| Skim milk | 270 | 790 |
| Cream | 240 | 290 |
|  | 800 | 1,800 |
| **Packing Department** |  |  |
| Whole milk | 520 | 560 |
| Skim milk | 330 | 460 |
| Cream | 150 | 180 |
|  | 1,000 | 1,200 |
| Total | 1,800 | 3,000 |

### Instructions

1. Determine the single plantwide factory overhead rate, using each of the following allocation bases: (a) direct labor hours and (b) machine hours.
2. Determine the product factory overhead costs, using (a) the direct labor hour plantwide factory overhead rate and (b) the machine hour plantwide factory overhead rate.

OBJ. 3

✔ 2 . Cream, $56,400

### PR 26-2B Multiple production department factory overhead rates

The management of Daisy Dairy Company, described in Problem 26-1B, now plans to use the multiple production department factory overhead rate method. The total factory overhead associated with each department is as follows:

| | |
| --- | --- |
| Blending Department | $216,000 |
| Packing Department | 144,000 |
| Total | $360,000 |

### Instructions

1. Determine the multiple production department factory overhead rates, using machine hours for the Blending Department and direct labor hours for the Packing Department.
2. Determine the product factory overhead costs, using the multiple production department rates in (1).

OBJ. 3, 4

✔ 4. Loudspeakers, $321,300 and $64.26

### PR 26-3B Activity-based department rate product costing and product cost distortions

Pro Audio Inc. manufactures two products: receivers and loudspeakers. The factory overhead incurred is as follows:

| | |
| --- | --- |
| Indirect labor | $260,000 |
| Subassembly Department | 145,000 |
| Final Assembly Department | 95,000 |
| Total | $500,000 |

The activity base associated with the two production departments is direct labor hours. The indirect labor can be assigned to two different activities as follows:

| Activity | Budgeted Activity Cost | Activity Base |
|---|---|---|
| Setup | $119,000 | Number of setups |
| Quality control | 141,000 | Number of inspections |
| Total | $260,000 | |

The activity-base usage quantities and units produced for the two products are shown below.

| | Number of Setups | Number of Inspections | Direct Labor Hours— Subassembly | Direct Labor Hours— Final Assembly | Units Produced |
|---|---|---|---|---|---|
| Receivers | 60 | 300 | 600 | 400 | 5,000 |
| Loudspeakers | 220 | 1,200 | 400 | 600 | 5,000 |
| Total | 280 | 1,500 | 1,000 | 1,000 | 10,000 |

**Instructions**
1. Determine the factory overhead rates under the multiple production department rate method. Assume that indirect labor is associated with the production departments, so that the total factory overhead is $275,000 and $225,000 for the Subassembly and Final Assembly departments, respectively.
2. Determine the total and per-unit factory overhead costs allocated to each product, using the multiple production department overhead rates in (1).
3. Determine the activity rates, assuming that the indirect labor is associated with activities rather than with the production departments.
4. Determine the total and per-unit cost assigned to each product under activity-based costing.
5. Explain the difference in the per-unit overhead allocated to each product under the multiple production department factory overhead rate and activity-based costing methods.

---

OBJ. 4

✔ 2 . Brown sugar total activity cost, $274,300

**PR 26-4B   Activity-based product costing**

Jamaican Sugar Company manufactures three products (white sugar, brown sugar, and powdered sugar) in a continuous production process. Senior management has asked the controller to conduct an activity-based costing study. The controller identified the amount of factory overhead required by the critical activities of the organization as follows:

| Activity | Budgeted Activity Cost |
|---|---|
| Production | $480,000 |
| Setup | 133,000 |
| Inspection | 50,600 |
| Shipping | 84,600 |
| Customer service | 72,000 |
| Total | $820,200 |

The activity bases identified for each activity are as follows:

| Activity | Activity Base |
|---|---|
| Production | Machine hours |
| Setup | Number of setups |
| Inspection | Number of inspections |
| Shipping | Number of customer orders |
| Customer service | Number of customer service requests |

The activity-base usage quantities and units produced for the three products were determined from corporate records and are as follows:

| | Machine Hours | Number of Setups | Number of Inspections | Number of Customer Orders | Number of Customer Service Requests | Units |
|---|---|---|---|---|---|---|
| White sugar | 4,000 | 70 | 120 | 1,000 | 50 | 10,000 |
| Brown sugar | 2,000 | 140 | 300 | 2,200 | 300 | 5,000 |
| Powdered sugar | 2,000 | 140 | 500 | 1,500 | 130 | 5,000 |
| Total | 8,000 | 350 | 920 | 4,700 | 480 | 20,000 |

Each product requires 0.4 machine hour per unit.

**Instructions**

1. Determine the activity rate for each activity.
2. Determine the total and per-unit activity cost for all three products. Round to the nearest cent.
3. Why aren't the activity unit costs equal across all three products since they require the same machine time per unit?

---

**OBJ. 5**

✔ 3. Office Universe, income from operations, $199,280

**PR 26-5B   Allocating selling and administrative expenses using activity-based costing**

Z-Rox Inc. manufactures office copiers, which are sold to retailers. The price and cost of goods sold for each copier are as follows:

| | |
|---|---|
| Price | $890 per unit |
| Cost of goods sold | 510 |
| Gross profit | $380 per unit |

In addition, the company incurs selling and administrative expenses of $307,150. The company wishes to assign these costs to its three major retail customers, Office Warehouse, Office To-Go, and Office Universe. These expenses are related to its three major nonmanufacturing activities: customer service, sales order processing, and advertising support. The advertising support is in the form of advertisements that are placed by Z-Rox Inc. to support the retailer's sale of Z-Rox copiers to consumers. The budgeted activity costs and activity bases associated with these activities are:

| Activity | Budgeted Activity Cost | Activity Base |
|---|---|---|
| Customer service | $ 54,450 | Number of service requests |
| Sales order processing | 18,700 | Number of sales orders |
| Advertising support | 234,000 | Number of ads placed |
| Total activity cost | $307,150 | |

Activity-base usage and unit volume information for the three customers is as follows:

| | Office Warehouse | Office To-Go | Office Universe | Total |
|---|---|---|---|---|
| Number of service requests | 50 | 260 | 20 | 330 |
| Number of sales orders | 240 | 500 | 110 | 850 |
| Number of ads placed | 20 | 140 | 35 | 195 |
| Unit volume | 650 | 650 | 650 | 1,950 |

**Instructions**

1. Determine the activity rates for each of the three nonmanufacturing activities.
2. Determine the activity costs allocated to the three customers, using the activity rates in (1).
3. Construct customer profitability reports for the three customers, dated for the year ended December 31, 2012, using the activity costs in (2). The reports should disclose the gross profit and income from operations associated with each customer.
4. Provide recommendations to management, based on the profitability reports in (3).

OBJ. 6

✔ 3. Flight 102
income from
operations, $5,605

**PR 26-6B** **Product costing and decision analysis for a passenger airline**

Blue Skies Airline provides passenger airline service, using small jets. The airline connects four major cities: Atlanta, Cincinnati, Chicago, and Los Angeles. The company expects to fly 140,000 miles during a month. The following costs are budgeted for a month:

| | |
|---|---|
| Fuel | $1,450,000 |
| Ground personnel | 693,250 |
| Crew salaries | 710,000 |
| Depreciation | 360,000 |
| Total costs | $3,213,250 |

Blue Skies management wishes to assign these costs to individual flights in order to gauge the profitability of its service offerings. The following activity bases were identified with the budgeted costs:

| Airline Cost | Activity Base |
|---|---|
| Fuel, crew, and depreciation costs | Number of miles flown |
| Ground personnel | Number of arrivals and departures at an airport |

The size of the company's ground operation in each city is determined by the size of the workforce. The following monthly data are available from corporate records for each terminal operation:

| Terminal City | Ground Personnel Cost | Number of Arrivals/Departures |
|---|---|---|
| Atlanta | $224,750 | 290 |
| Cincinnati | 84,000 | 120 |
| Chicago | 114,800 | 140 |
| Los Angeles | 269,700 | 310 |
| Total | $693,250 | 860 |

Three recent representative flights have been selected for the profitability study. Their characteristics are as follows:

| | Description | Miles Flown | Number of Passengers | Ticket Price per Passenger |
|---|---|---|---|---|
| Flight 101 | Atlanta to LA | 1,850 | 70 | $650 |
| Flight 102 | Chicago to Atlanta | 600 | 45 | 400 |
| Flight 103 | Atlanta to Cincinnati | 350 | 20 | 350 |

**Instructions**

1. Determine the fuel, crew, and depreciation cost per mile flown.
2. Determine the cost per arrival or departure by terminal city.
3. Use the information in (1) and (2) to construct a profitability report for the three flights. Each flight has a single arrival and departure to its origin and destination city pairs.
4. Evaluate flight profitability by determining the break-even number of passengers required for each flight assuming all the costs of a flight are fixed. Round to the nearest whole number.

## Cases & Projects

You can access Cases & Projects online at **www.cengage.com/accounting/reeve**

## Excel Success Special Activities

### SA 26-1   Activity-based costing, manufacturing

Ming Cookie Company uses activity-based costing to allocate factory overhead. Four activities and their activity rates are as follows:

| Activity | Activity Rate |
|---|---|
| Cooking | $45 per cooking hour |
| Inspecting | $80 per inspection |
| Material control | $28 per move |
| Setup | $500 per setup |

Ming plans to make 10,000 units each of two different products, cookies and crackers. The activity-base usage quantities for each product is as follows:

| | Cooking | Inspecting | Material Control | Setup |
|---|---|---|---|---|
| Cookies | 1,200 | 80 | 50 | 10 |
| Crackers | 1,200 | 240 | 150 | 50 |
| Total | 2,400 | 320 | 200 | 60 |

a. Open the Excel file *SA26-1_1e.xls*.

b. Determine the activity-based cost for the cookies and crackers.

c. When you have completed the assignment, perform a "save as," replacing the entire file name with the following:

*SA26-1_1e[your first name initial]_[your last name]*

### SA 26-2   Activity-based costing, service

The total overhead for Jamestown Heart Clinic is divided into four activities: patient administration, imaging, testing, and consultation. The activity rates associated with the activities are as follows:

| Activity | Activity Rate |
|---|---|
| Patient administration | $38 per visit |
| Imaging | $260 per image |
| Testing | $145 per test |
| Consultation | $350 per hour |

The clinic has hundreds of patients. Three representative patients and their activity-base usage is as follows:

| | Activity-Based Usage Quantities | | |
|---|---|---|---|
| | P. Bellows | S. Ng | K. Santana |
| Patient administration | 4 visits | 8 visits | 1 visits |
| Imaging | 3 images | 4 images | 1 image |
| Testing | 6 tests | 16 tests | 2 tests |
| Consultation | 3 hours | 9 hours | 0. 5 hour |

a. Open the Excel file *SA26-2_1e.xls*.

b. Determine the activity-based cost for servicing the three representative patients.

c. When you have completed the assignment, perform a "save as," replacing the entire file name with the following:

*SA26-2_1e[your first name initial]_[your last name]*

**SA26-3   Activity rates and activity-based costing**

The total factory overhead for Engelhardt Company is budgeted for the year at $400,000, divided into four activities: machining, packing, setup, and quality control. The estimated cost and activity base associated with each activity is as follows:

| Activity | Activity Cost | Activity Base |
|---|---|---|
| Machining | $195,000 | Machine hours |
| Packing | 48,000 | Packing hours |
| Setup | 94,000 | Number of setups |
| Quality control | 63,000 | Inspection hours |
| Total | $400,000 | |

Engelhardt manufactures two machined products: levers and housings. The activity-base usage quantities for each product by each activity is as follows:

| | Machine Hours | Packing Hours | Number of Setups | Inspection Hours |
|---|---|---|---|---|
| Levers | 300 | 80 | 12 | 40 |
| Housings | 700 | 120 | 68 | 110 |
| Total | 1,000 | 200 | 80 | 150 |

There are 2,000 units of each product produced for the year.

a.  Open the Excel file *SA26-3_1e.xls*.

b.  Determine the activity rates for each activity.

c.  Determine the activity-based cost for each product using the rates in (b).

e.  When you have completed the assignment, perform a "save as," replacing the entire file name with the following:

   *SA26-3_1e[your first name initial]_[your last name]*

© Banana Stock/First Light

# Cost Management for Just-in-Time Environments

## Precor

**W**hen you order the salad bar at the local restaurant, you are able to serve yourself at your own pace. There is no waiting for the waitress to take the order or for the cook to prepare the meal. You are able to move directly to the salad bar and select from various offerings. You might wish to have salad with lettuce, cole slaw, bacon bits, croutons, and salad dressing. The offerings are arranged in a row so that you can build your salad as you move down the salad bar.

Many manufacturers are producing products in much the same way that the salad bar is designed to satisfy each customer's needs. Like customers at the salad bar, products move through a production process as they are built for each customer. Such a process eliminates many sources of waste, which is why it is termed *just in time*.

Using just-in-time practices can improve performance. For example, when **Precor**, a manufacturer of fitness equipment, used just-in-time principles, it improved its manufacturing operations and achieved the following results:

1. Increased on-time shipments from near 40% to above 90%.
2. Decreased direct labor costs by 30%.
3. Reduced the number of suppliers from 3,000 to under 250.
4. Reduced inventory by 40%.
5. Reduced warranty claims by almost 60%.

In this chapter, just-in-time practices are described and illustrated. The chapter concludes by describing and illustrating the accounting for quality costs and activity analysis.

**OBJ. 1** Describe just-in-time manufacturing practices.

# Just-in-Time Practices

The objective of most manufacturers is to produce products with high quality, low cost, and instant availability. In attempting to achieve this objective, many manufacturers have implemented just-in-time processing. **Just-in-time processing (JIT)**, sometimes called *lean manufacturing,* is a philosophy that focuses on reducing time and cost, and eliminating poor quality.

Exhibit 1 lists just-in-time manufacturing and the traditional manufacturing practices. Each of the just-in-time practices is discussed in this section.

**EXHIBIT 1**

**Operating Principles of Just-in-Time versus Traditional Manufacturing**

| Issue | Just-in-Time Manufacturing | Traditional Manufacturing |
|---|---|---|
| Inventory | Reduces inventory. | Increases inventory to protect against process problems. |
| Lead time | Reduces lead time. | Increases lead time to protect against uncertainty. |
| Setup time | Reduces setup time. | Disregards setup time as an improvement priority. |
| Production layout | Emphasizes product-oriented layout. | Emphasizes process-oriented layout. |
| Role of the employee | Emphasizes team-oriented employee involvement. | Emphasizes work of individuals, following manager instructions. |
| Production scheduling policy | Emphasizes pull manufacturing. | Emphasizes push manufacturing. |
| Quality | Emphasizes zero defects. | Tolerates defects. |
| Suppliers and customers | Emphasizes supply chain management. | Treats suppliers and customers as "arm's-length," independent entities. |

# Reducing Inventory

Just-in-time (JIT) manufacturing views inventory as wasteful and unnecessary. As a result, JIT emphasizes reducing or eliminating inventory.

Under traditional manufacturing, inventory often hides underlying production problems. For example, if machine breakdowns occur, work in process inventories can be used to keep production running in other departments while the machines are being repaired. Likewise, inventories can be used to hide problems caused by a shortage of trained employees, unreliable suppliers, or poor quality.

In contrast, just-in-time manufacturing attempts to solve and remove production problems. In this way, raw materials, work in process, and finished goods inventories are reduced or eliminated.

The role of inventory in manufacturing can be illustrated using a river. Inventory is the water in a river. The rocks at the bottom of the river are production problems. When the water level (inventory) is high, the rocks (production problems) at the bottom of the river are hidden. As the water level (inventory) level drops, the rocks (production problems) become visible, one by one. JIT manufacturing reduces the water level (inventory), exposes the rocks (production problems), and removes the rocks so that the river can flow smoothly.

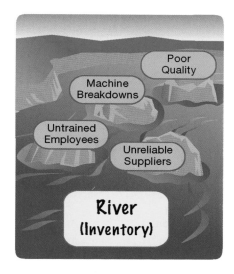

# Integrity, Objectivity, and Ethics in Business

**THE INVENTORY SHIFT**

Some managers take a shortcut to reducing inventory by shifting inventory to their suppliers. With this tactic, the hard work of improving processes is avoided. Enlightened managers realize that such tactics often have short-lived savings. Suppliers will eventually increase their prices to compensate for the additional inventory holding costs, thus resulting in no savings. Therefore, shifting a problem doesn't eliminate a problem.

# Reducing Lead Times

**Lead time**, sometimes called *throughput time*, measures the time interval between a product entering production (is started) and when it is completed (finished). That is, lead time measures how long it takes to manufacture a product. For example, if a product enters production at 1:00 P.M. and is completed at 5:00 P.M., the lead time is four hours.

The lead time can be classified as one of the following:

1. **Value-added lead time**, which is the time spent in converting raw materials into a finished unit of product
2. **Non-value-added lead time**, which is the time spent while the unit of product is waiting to enter the next production process or is moved from one process to another

Exhibit 2 illustrates value-added and non-value-added lead time.

The time spent drilling and packing the unit of product is value-added time. The time spent waiting to enter the next process or the time spent moving the unit of product from one process to another is non-value-added time.

The **value-added ratio** is computed as follows:

$$\text{Value-Added Ratio} = \frac{\text{Value-Added Lead Time}}{\text{Total Lead Time}}$$

**EXHIBIT 2**    **Components of Lead Time**

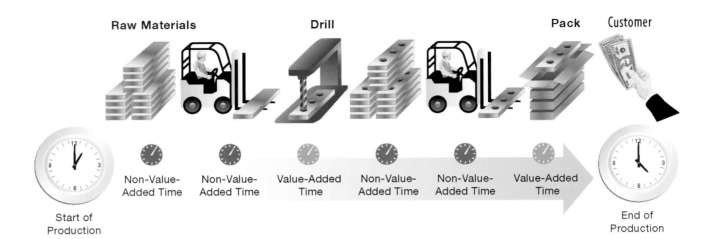

To illustrate, assume that the lead time to manufacture a unit of product is as follows:

| | |
|---|---|
| Move raw materials to machining ................................... | 5 minutes |
| **Machining** ...................................................... | **35** |
| Move time to assembly .............................................. | 10 |
| **Assembly** ........................................................ | **20** |
| Move time to packing ............................................... | 15 |
| Wait time for packing ............................................... | 30 |
| **Packing** ......................................................... | **10** |
| Total lead time .................................................. | 125 minutes |

The value-added ratio for the preceding product is 52%, as computed below:

$$\text{Value-Added Ratio} = \frac{\text{Value-Added Lead Time}}{\text{Total Lead Time}}$$

$$= \frac{(35 + 20 + 10) \text{ minutes}}{125 \text{ minutes}} = \frac{65 \text{ minutes}}{125 \text{ minutes}} = 52\%$$

Crown Audio reduced the lead time between receiving and delivering a customer order from 30 days to 12 hours by using just-in-time principles.

A low value-added ratio indicates a poor manufacturing process. A good manufacturing process will reduce non-value-added lead time to a minimum and, thus, have a high value-added ratio.

Just-in-time manufacturing reduces or eliminates non-value-added time. In contrast, traditional manufacturing processes may have a value-added ratio as small as 5%.

## Reducing Setup Time

A *setup* is the effort spent preparing an operation or process for a production run. If setups are long and costly, the batch size (number of units) for the related production run is normally large. Large batch sizes allow setup costs to be spread over more units and, thus, reduce the cost per unit. However, large batch sizes increase inventory and lead time.

Exhibit 3 shows the relationship between setup times and lead time.

**EXHIBIT 3** **Relationship between Setup Times and Lead Time**

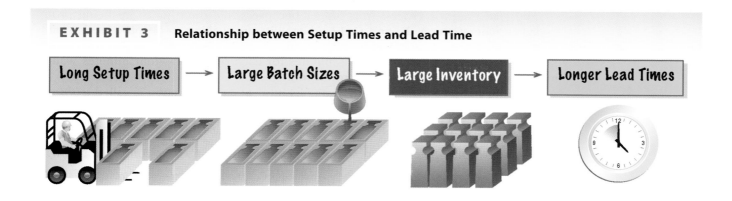

To illustrate, assume that a product can be manufactured in Process X or Process Y as follows:

|  | Process X | Process Y |
|---|---|---|
| Operation A ............... | 1 minute | 1 minute |
| Operation B ............... | 1 | 1 |
| Operation C ............... | 1 | 1 |
| Total ................... | 3 minutes | 3 minutes |
| Batch size ................ | 1 unit | 5 units |

Exhibit 4 shows that the lead time for Process X is three minutes. In contrast, the lead time for Process Y is 15 minutes.

**EXHIBIT 4** **Impact of Batch Sizes on Lead Times**

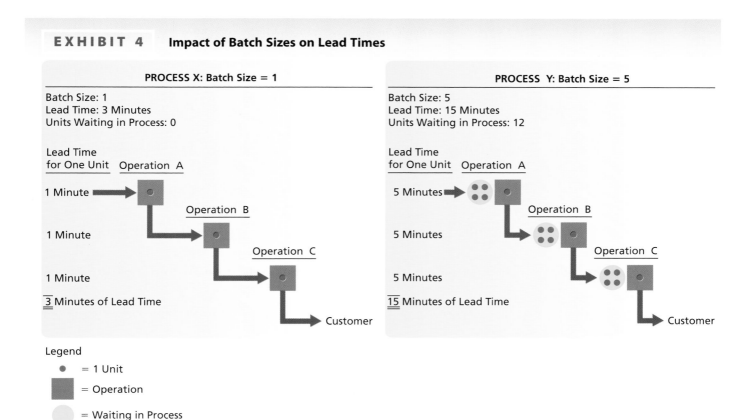

The lead time for Process Y is longer because while three units are being produced in Operations A, B, and C, 12 other units are waiting to be processed. That is, in Process Y each unit has to wait its "turn" while other units in the batch are processed. Thus, it takes a unit five minutes for each operation—four minutes waiting its "turn" and one minute in production.

The four minutes that each part "waits its turn" at each operation is called *within-batch wait time.* The total within-batch wait time is computed as follows:

$$\text{Total Within-Batch Wait Time} = (\text{Total Time to Perform Operations}) \times (\text{Batch Size} - 1)$$

The total within-batch wait time for Process Y is 12 minutes, as computed below.

$$\text{Total Within-Batch Wait Time} = (1+1+1) \text{ minutes} \times (5-1) = 3 \text{ minutes} \times 4 = 12 \text{ minutes}$$

The value-added ratio for Process Y is 20%, as computed below.

$$\text{Value-Added Ratio} = \frac{\text{Value-Added Lead Time}}{\text{Total Lead Time}}$$

$$= \frac{(1+1+1) \text{ minutes}}{(3+12) \text{ minutes}} = \frac{3 \text{ minutes}}{15 \text{ minutes}} = 20\%$$

Thus, 80% (100% − 20%) of the lead time in Process Y is non-value-added time.

Just-in-time manufacturing emphasizes decreasing setup times in order to reduce the batch size. By reducing batch sizes, work in process and wait time are decreased, thus reducing total lead time and increasing the value-added ratio.

To illustrate, assume that Automotive Components Inc. manufactures engine starters as follows:

| Operations | Processing Time per Unit |
|---|---|
| Move raw materials to Machining.......... | 5 minutes |
| **Machining** .............................. | **7** |
| Move time to Assembly ................... | 10 |
| **Assembly** ............................... | **9** |
| Move time to Testing ..................... | 10 |
| **Testing** ................................. | **8** |
| Total ................................. | 49 minutes |
| Batch size .............................. | 40 units |

The total within-batch wait time is 936 minutes, as computed below:

Total Within-Batch Wait Time = (Total Time to Perform Operations) × (Batch Size − 1)
Total Within-Batch Wait Time = (7 + 9 + 8) minutes × (40 − 1) = 24 minutes × 39
Total Within-Batch Wait Time = 936 minutes

The total lead time is 985 minutes, as shown below:

| | |
|---|---|
| Operations (7 + 9 + 8) ............. | 24 minutes |
| Move time (5 + 10 + 10) ........... | 25 |
| Total within-batch wait time ...... | 936 |
| Total time ..................... | 985 minutes |

Of the total lead time of 985 minutes, 24 minutes is value-added time and 961 minutes (985 − 24) is non-value-added time. The total non-value-added time of 961 minutes can also be determined as the sum of the total within-batch time of 936 minutes plus the move time of 25 minutes.

Based on the preceding data, the value-added ratio is approximately 2.4%, as computed below:

$$\text{Value-Added Ratio} = \frac{\text{Value-Added Lead Time}}{\text{Total Lead Time}}$$

$$= \frac{(7+9+8) \text{ minutes}}{985 \text{ minutes}} = \frac{24 \text{ minutes}}{985 \text{ minutes}} = 2.4\% \text{ (rounded)}$$

Thus, the non-value-added time for Automotive Components Inc. is approximately 97.6% (100% − 2.4%).

Automotive Components can increase its value-added ratio by reducing setups so that the batch size is one unit, termed *one-piece flow*. Automotive Components could also move the Machining, Assembly, and Testing operations closer to each other so that the move time could be reduced. With these changes, Automotive Components' value-added ratio would increase.

# BusinessConnection

## P&G'S "PIT STOPS"

What do Procter & Gamble and Formula One racing have in common? The answer begins with P&G's Packing Department, which is where detergents and other products are filled on a "pack line." Containers move down the pack line and are filled with products from a packing machine. When it was time to change from a 36-oz. to a 54-oz. *Tide* box, for example, the changeover involved stopping the line, adjusting guide rails, retrieving items from the tool room, placing items back in the tool room, changing and cleaning the pack heads, and performing routine maintenance. Changing the pack line could be a very difficult process and typically took up to several hours.

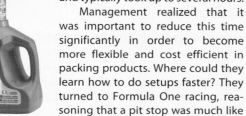

Management realized that it was important to reduce this time significantly in order to become more flexible and cost efficient in packing products. Where could they learn how to do setups faster? They turned to Formula One racing, reasoning that a pit stop was much like

a setup. As a result, P&G videotaped actual Formula One pit stops. These videos were used to form the following principles for conducting a fast setup:

- Position the tools near their point of use on the line prior to stopping the line, to reduce time going back and forth to the tool room.
- Arrange the tools in the exact order of work, so that no time is wasted looking for a tool.
- Have each employee perform a very specific task during the setup.
- Design the workflow so that employees don't interfere with each other.
- Have each employee in position at the moment the line is stopped.
- Train each employee, and practice, practice, practice.
- Put a stop watch on the setup process.
- Plot improvements over time on a visible chart.

As a result of these changes, P&G was able to reduce pack-line setup time from several hours to 20 minutes. This allowed it to reduce lead time and to improve cost performance of the Packing Department.

## Example Exercise 27-1 Lead Time

**OBJ. 1**

The Helping Hands glove company manufactures gloves in the cutting and assembly process. Gloves are manufactured in 50-glove batch sizes. The cutting time is 4 minutes per glove. The assembly time is 6 minutes per glove. It takes 12 minutes to move a batch of gloves from cutting to assembly.

a. Compute the value-added, non-value-added, and total lead time of this process.
b. Compute the value-added ratio. Round to one decimal.

## Follow My Example 27-1

a. Value-added lead time:             10 min. = (4 min. + 6 min.)
   Non-value-added lead time:
      Total within-batch wait time     490     = (4 + 6) minutes × (50 − 1)
      Move time                 12
   Total lead time             $\overline{512}$ min.

b. Value-added ratio: $\dfrac{10 \text{ min.}}{512 \text{ min.}}$ = 2% (rounded)

Practice Exercises: **PE 27-1A, PE 27-1B**

## Emphasizing Product-Oriented Layout

Manufacturing processes can be organized around a product, which is called a **product-oriented layout** (or *product cells*). Alternatively, manufacturing processes can be organized around a process, which is called a **process-oriented layout**.

Just-in-time normally organizes manufacturing around products rather than processes. Organizing work around products reduces:

1. Moving materials and products between processes
2. Work in process inventory
3. Lead time
4. Production costs

In addition, a product-oriented layout improves coordination among operations.

## Emphasizing Employee Involvement

**Employee involvement** is a management approach that grants employees the responsibility and authority to make decisions about operations. Employee involvement is often applied in a just-in-time operation by organizing employees into *product cells*. Within each product cell, employees are organized as teams where the employees are *cross-trained* to perform any operation within the product cell.

To illustrate, employees learn how to operate several different machines within their product cell. In addition, team members are trained to perform functions traditionally performed by centralized service departments. For example, product cell employees may perform their own equipment maintenance, quality control, and housekeeping.

## Emphasizing Pull Manufacturing

**Pull manufacturing** (or *make to order*) is an important just-in-time practice. In pull manufacturing, products are manufactured only as they are needed by the customer. Products can be thought of as being pulled through the manufacturing process. In other words, the status of the next operation determines when products are moved or produced. If the next operation is busy, production stops so that work in process does not pile up in front of the busy operation. When the next operation is ready, the product is moved to that operation.

A system used in pull manufacturing is *kanban*, which is Japanese for "cards." Electronic cards or containers signal production quantities to be filled by the preceding operation. The cards link the customer's order for a product back through each stage of production. In other words, when a consumer orders a product, a kanban card triggers the manufacture of the product.

In contrast, the traditional approach to manufacturing is based on estimated customer demand. This principle is called **push manufacturing** (or make to stock) manufacturing. In push manufacturing, products are manufactured according to a production schedule that is based upon estimated sales. The schedule "pushes" product into inventory before customer orders are received. As a result, push-manufacturers normally have more inventory than pull-manufacturers.

## Emphasizing Zero Defects

Just-in-time manufacturing attempts to eliminate poor quality. Poor quality creates:

1. Scrap
2. Rework, which is fixing product made wrong the first time
3. Disruption in the production process
4. Dissatisfied customers
5. Warranty costs and expenses

One way to improve product quality and manufacturing processes is Six Sigma. **Six Sigma** was developed by Motorola Corporation and consists of five steps: define, measure, analyze, improve, and control (DMAIC).[1] Since its development, Six Sigma has been adopted by thousands of organizations worldwide.

---

1 The term "six sigma" refers to a statistical property where a process has less than 3.4 defects per one million items.

## Emphasizing Supply Chain Management

**Supply chain management** coordinates and controls the flow of materials, services, information, and finances with suppliers, manufacturers, and customers. Supply chain management partners with suppliers using long-term agreements. These agreements ensure that products are delivered with the right quality, at the right cost, at the right time.

To enhance the interchange of information between suppliers and customers, supply chain management often uses:

1. **Electronic data interchange (EDI)**, which uses computers to electronically communicate orders, relay information, and make or receive payments from one organization to another
2. **Radio frequency identification devices (RFIDs)**, which are electronic tags (chips) placed on or embedded within products that can be read by radio waves that allow instant monitoring of product location
3. **Enterprise resource planning (ERP)** systems, which are used to plan and control internal and supply chain operations

## BusinessConnection

### JUST-IN-TIME IN ACTION

- **Yamaha** manufactures musical instruments such as trumpets, horns, saxophones, clarinets, and flutes using **product-oriented layouts**.
- **Sony** uses **employee involvement** to organize employees into small four-person teams to completely assemble a camcorder, doing everything from soldering to testing. This team-based approach reduces assembly time from 70 minutes to 15 minutes per camcorder.

- **Kenney Manufacturing Company**, a manufacturer of window shades, estimated that 50% of its window shade process was non-value-added. By using **pull manufacturing** and changing the line layout, it was able to reduce inventory by 82% and lead time by 84%.
- **Motorola** has claimed over $17 billion in savings from **Six Sigma**.
- **Hyundia/Kia Motors Group** will use 20 million RFID tags annually to track automotive parts from its suppliers, providing greater **supply chain** transparency and flexibility.

---

**Example Exercise 27-2 Just-In-Time Features**

Which of the following are features of a just-in-time manufacturing system?

a. Reduced space
b. Larger inventory
c. Longer lead times
d. Reduced setups

**Follow My Example 27-2**

a. Reduced space
d. Reduced setups

Practice Exercises: **PE 27-2A, PE 27-2B**

---

## Just-in-Time for Nonmanufacturing Processes

 **OBJ. 2** Apply just-in-time practices to a nonmanufacturing setting.

Just-in-time practices may also be applied to service businesses or administrative processes. Examples of service businesses that use just-in-time practices include hospitals, banks, insurance companies, and hotels. Examples of administrative processes that use just-in-time practices include processing of insurance applications, product

ITW Paslode, a manufacturer of specialty tools, used just-in-time principles to reduce steps in the sales order process by 86% and improve delivery time by 80%.

designs, and sales orders. In the case of a service business, the "product" is normally the customer or patient. In the case of administrative processes, the "product" is normally information.

To illustrate, a traditional process used by a hospital to treat patients is illustrated in Exhibit 5. As shown in Exhibit 5, four basic processes used by the hospital include:

1. Admission
2. Testing and Diagnosis
3. Treatment
4. Discharge

**EXHIBIT 5**   **Typical Hospital Process Flow**

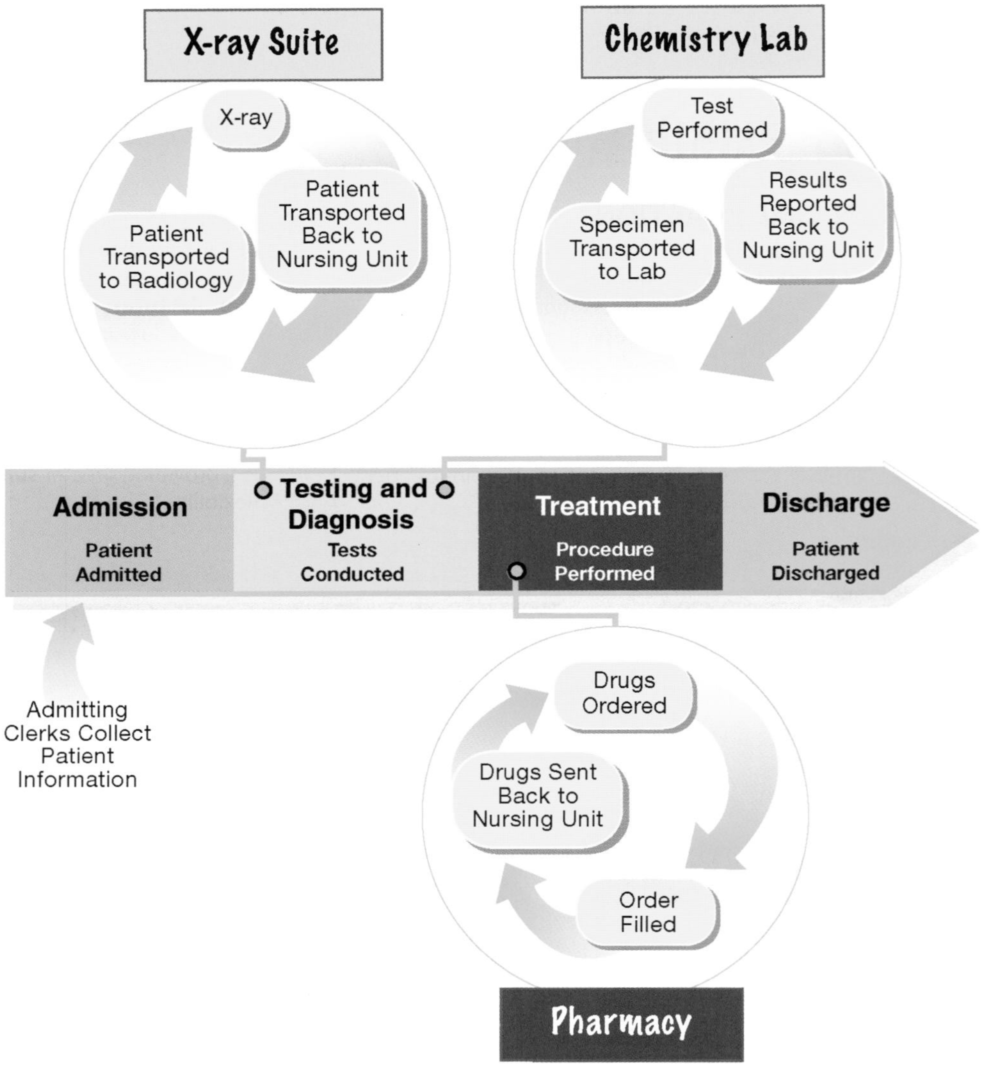

X-ray Suite

- X-ray
- Patient Transported Back to Nursing Unit
- Patient Transported to Radiology

Chemistry Lab

- Test Performed
- Results Reported Back to Nursing Unit
- Specimen Transported to Lab

**Admission** — Patient Admitted

**Testing and Diagnosis** — Tests Conducted

**Treatment** — Procedure Performed

**Discharge** — Patient Discharged

Admitting Clerks Collect Patient Information

Pharmacy

- Drugs Ordered
- Drugs Sent Back to Nursing Unit
- Order Filled

The traditional hospital layout consumes a great deal of time. The patient first spends time in Admission, providing patient and insurance information. Once admitted, the patient is transported (moved) to a room where a variety of tests are performed. These tests often require the patient to be moved to the testing location, such as radiology for an X-ray. If laboratory tests are required, the lab specimens are sent (moved) to a central chemistry lab. If drugs are ordered, they must be dispensed from the central pharmacy and delivered (moved) to the patient's room for nurses to administer.

Each of the prior processes consumes time and movement as the patient, specimen, test results, and drugs are processed. In each of the centralized departments, such as Admission and Radiology or Laboratory, the processing of any one patient requires waiting for other patients to be processed. Again, this also consumes time and is similar to within-batch wait time for a manufacturing business. As a result, an average patient's time in the hospital (lead time) is longer than it needs to be. In addition, the value-added ratio for each patient is low.

Exhibit 6 illustrates a just-in-time hospital layout.

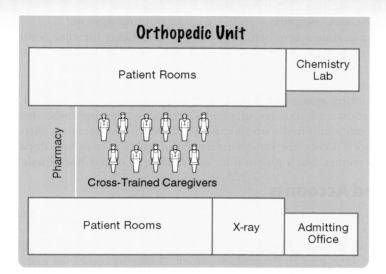

**EXHIBIT 6**

**Just-in-Time Hospital Unit Layout**

As shown in Exhibit 6, patients with common health problems are placed together on one floor of the hospital. Centralized services are distributed to each of the floors, so that each floor has its own minipharmacy, X-ray suite, chemistry lab, and admitting office.

In Exhibit 6, patients are served where they are, rather than moving around the hospital. This is similar to the product-oriented layout in a manufacturing business. Nurses are "cross-trained" to provide X-ray, laboratory, and other services. This provides much greater flexibility and faster treatment of patients.

A just-in-time hospital process reduces the "inventory" of orders, patients, and drugs as compared to that of the traditional hospital shown in Exhibit 5. As a result, the lead time to process orders and tests decreases along with the average stay in the hospital.

In a just-in-time hospital, the quality of the patient's experience should increase. This is because the same group of caregivers serves the patient from admittance to discharge. The caregivers should also have a more rewarding experience because they work as a team in serving each patient. Finally, the overall cost of patient care should decrease as the hospital becomes more efficient.

# Accounting for Just-in-Time Manufacturing

**OBJ. 3** Describe the implications of just-in-time manufacturing on cost accounting and performance measurement.

In just-in-time manufacturing, the accounting system has the following characteristics:

1. *Fewer transactions.* There are fewer transactions to record, thus simplifying the accounting system.
2. *Combined accounts.* All in-process work is combined with raw materials to form a new account, **Raw and In Process (RIP) Inventory**. Direct labor is also combined with other costs to form a new account titled **Conversion Costs**.

3. *Nonfinancial performance measures*. Nonfinancial performance measures are emphasized.

4. *Direct tracing of overhead*. Indirect labor is directly assigned to product cells; thus, less factory overhead is allocated to products.

## Fewer Transactions

The traditional process cost accounting system accumulates product costs by department. These costs are transferred from department to department as the product is manufactured. Thus, materials are recorded into and out of work in process inventories as the product moves through the factory.

The recording of product costs by departments facilitates the control of costs. However, this requires that many transactions and costs be recorded and reported. This adds cost and complexity to the cost accounting system.

In the just-in-time manufacturing, there is less need for cost control. This is because lower inventory levels make problems more visible. That is, managers don't need accounting reports to indicate problems because any problems become immediately known.

The accounting system for just-in-time manufacturing is simplified by eliminating the accumulation and transfer of product costs by departments. Instead, costs are transferred from combined material and conversion cost accounts directly to finished goods inventory. Costs are not transferred through intermediate departmental work in process accounts. Such just-in-time accounting is called **backflush accounting**.

## Combined Accounts

Materials are received directly by the product cells and enter immediately into production. Thus, there is no central materials inventory location (warehouse) or a materials account. Instead, just-in-time debits all materials and conversion costs to an account titled *Raw and In Process Inventory*. Doing so combines materials and work in process costs into one account.

Just-in-time manufacturing often does not use a separate direct labor cost classification. This is because the employees in product cells perform many tasks. Some of these tasks could be classified as direct, such as performing operations, and some as indirect, such as performing repairs. Thus, labor cost (direct and indirect) is combined with other product cell overhead costs and recorded in an account titled *Conversion Costs*.

To illustrate, assume the following data for Anderson Metal Fabricators, a manufacturer of metal covers for electronic test equipment:

Budgeted conversion cost ................. $2,400,000
Planned hours of production............... 1,920 hours

The cell conversion cost rate is determined as follows:

$$\text{Cell Conversion Cost Rate} = \frac{\text{Budgeted Conversion Cost}}{\text{Planned Hours of Production}}$$

$$= \frac{\$2,400,000}{1,920 \text{ hours}} = \$1,250 \text{ per hour}$$

The cell conversion rate is similar to a predetermined factory overhead rate, except that it includes all conversion costs in the numerator.

Assume that Anderson Metal's cover product cell is expected to require 0.02 hour of manufacturing time per unit. Thus, the conversion cost for the cover is $25 per unit, as shown below.

Conversion Cost for Cover = Manufacturing Time × Cell Conversion Cost Rate
Conversion Cost for Cover = 0.02 hour × $1,250 = $25 per unit

The recording of selected just-in-time transactions for Anderson Metal Fabricators for April is illustrated on the next page.

| Transaction | Journal Entry | | Comment |
|---|---|---|---|
| 1. Steel coil is purchased for producing 8,000 covers. The purchase cost was $120,000, or $15 per unit. | Raw and In Process Inventory<br>    Accounts Payable<br>        To record materials purchases. | 120,000<br>      120,000 | Note that the materials purchased are debited to the combined account, Raw and In Process Inventory. A separate materials account is not used, because materials are received directly in the product cells, rather than in an inventory location. |
| 2. Conversion costs are applied to 8,000 covers at a rate of $25 per cover. | Raw and In Process Inventory<br>    Conversion Costs<br>        To record applied conversion costs of<br>        the medium-cover line. | 200,000<br>      200,000 | The raw and in process inventory account is used to accumulate the applied cell conversion costs during the period. The credit to Conversion Costs is similar to the treatment of applied factory overhead. |
| 3. All 8,000 covers were completed in the cell. The raw and in process inventory account is reduced by the $15 per unit materials cost and the $25 per unit conversion cost. | Finished Goods Inventory<br>    Raw and In Process Inventory<br>        To transfer the cost of completed units<br>        to finished goods. | 320,000<br>      320,000 | Materials<br>($15 × 8,000 units)    $120,000<br>Conversion<br>($25 × 8,000 units)    200,000<br>    Total    $320,000<br><br>After the cost of the completed units is transferred from the raw and in process inventory account, the account's balance is zero. There are no units left in process within the cell.[1] This is a backflush transaction. |
| 4. Of the 8,000 units completed, 7,800 were sold and shipped to customers at $70 per unit, leaving 200 finished units in stock. Thus, the finished goods inventory account has a balance of $8,000 (200 × $40). | Accounts Receivable<br>    Sales<br>        To record sales.<br><br>Cost of Goods Sold<br>    Finished Goods<br>        To record cost of goods sold. | 546,000<br>      546,000<br><br>312,000<br>      312,000 | Units sold    7,800<br>Conversion and<br>  materials cost per<br>  unit    ×   $40<br>Transferred to<br>  Cost of Goods<br>  Sold    $312,000 |

2 The actual conversion cost per unit may be different from the budgeted conversion cost per unit due to cell inefficiency, improvements in processing methods, or excess scrap. These deviations from the budgeted cost can be accounted for as cost variances, as illustrated in more advanced texts.

**Example Exercise 27-3 Just-In-Time Journal Entries** OBJ. 3

The budgeted conversion costs for a just-in-time cell are $142,500 for 1,900 production hours. Each unit produced by the cell requires 10 minutes of cell process time. During the month, 1,050 units are manufactured in the cell. The estimated materials cost is $46 per unit. Provide the following journal entries:
a. Materials are purchased to produce 1,100 units.
b. Conversion costs are applied to 1,050 units of production.
c. 1,030 units are completed and placed into finished goods.

**Follow My Example 27-3**

| | | | |
|---|---|---|---|
| a. | Raw and In Process Inventory ............................................... | 50,600* | |
| | Accounts Payable ....................................................... | | 50,600 |

*$46 per unit × 1,100 units

| | | | |
|---|---|---|---|
| b. | Raw and In Process Inventory ............................................... | 13,125* | |
| | Conversion Costs ....................................................... | | 13,125 |

*[($142,500/1,900 hours) × (10 min./60 min.)] = $12.50 per unit; $12.50 × 1,050 units = $13,125

| | | | |
|---|---|---|---|
| c. | Finished Goods Inventory .................................................. | 60,255* | |
| | Raw and In Process Inventory .............................................. | | 60,255 |

*($46.00 + $12.50) × 1,030 units

Practice Exercises: **PE 27-3A, PE 27-3B**

## Nonfinancial Performance Measures

Just-in-time manufacturing normally uses nonfinancial measures to help guide short-term operating performance. A **nonfinancial measure** is operating information not stated in dollar terms. Examples of nonfinancial measures of performance include:

1. Lead time
2. Value-added ratio
3. Setup time
4. Number of production line stops
5. Number of units scrapped
6. Deviations from scheduled production
7. Number of failed inspections

Most companies use a combination of financial and nonfinancial operating measures, which are often referred to as *key performance indicators* (or *KPIs*). Nonfinancial measures are often available more quickly than financial measures. Thus, nonfinancial measures are often used for day-to-day operating decisions that require quick or instant feedback. In contrast, traditional financial accounting measures are often used for longer-term operating decisions.

## Direct Tracing of Overhead

In just-in-time manufacturing, many indirect tasks are assigned to a product cell. For example, maintenance department personnel may be assigned to a product cell and cross-trained to perform other operations. Thus, the salary of this person can be traced directly to the product cell.

In traditional manufacturing, maintenance personnel are part of the maintenance department. The cost of the maintenance department is then allocated to products based on service charges. Such allocations are not necessary when maintenance personnel are assigned directly to a product cell and, thus, to the product.

# Activity Analysis

**OBJ. 4**   Describe and illustrate activity analysis for improving operations.

In the previous chapter, we discussed activity-based costing for product costing. Activities can also be used to support operational improvement using activity analysis. **Activity analysis** determines the cost of activities. An activity analysis can be used to determine the cost of:

1. Quality
2. Value-added activities
3. Processes

## Costs of Quality

Competition encourages businesses to emphasize high-quality products, services, and processes. In doing so, businesses incur **costs of quality**, which can be classified as follows:

1. **Prevention costs**, which are costs of preventing defects before or during the manufacture of the product or delivery of services

   Examples: Costs of engineering good product design, controlling vendor quality, training equipment operators, maintaining equipment

2. **Appraisal costs**, which are costs of activities that detect, measure, evaluate, and inspect products and processes to ensure that they meet customer needs

   Examples: Costs of inspecting and testing products

3. **Internal failure costs**, which are costs associated with defects discovered before the product is delivered to the consumer

   Examples: Cost of scrap and rework

4. **External failure costs**, which are costs incurred after defective products have been delivered to consumers

   Examples: Cost of recalls and warranty work

Prevention and appraisal costs can be thought of as costs of controlling quality *before* any products are known to be defective. Internal and external failure costs can be thought of as the cost of controlling quality *after* products have become defective. Internal and external failure costs can also be thought of as the costs of "failing to control quality" through prevention and appraisal efforts.

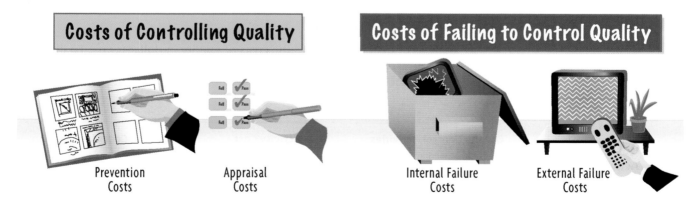

| Costs of Controlling Quality | | Costs of Failing to Control Quality | |
|---|---|---|---|
| Prevention Costs | Appraisal Costs | Internal Failure Costs | External Failure Costs |

Prevention and appraisal costs are incurred *before* the product is manufactured or delivered to the customer. Prevention costs are incurred in an attempt to permanently improve product quality. In contrast, appraisal costs are incurred in an attempt to limit the amount of defective products that "slip out the door."

Internal and external failure costs are incurred *after* the defective products have been discovered. In addition to costs of scrap and rework, internal failure costs may be incurred for lost equipment time because of rework and the costs of carrying additional inventory used for reworking. In addition to costs of recall and warranty work, external failure costs include the loss of customer goodwill. Although the loss

It is said that every dissatisfied customer tells at least ten people about an unhappy experience with a product.

of customer goodwill is difficult to measure, it may be the largest and most important quality control cost.

The relationship between the costs of quality is shown in Exhibit 7. The graph in Exhibit 7 indicates that as prevention and appraisal costs (blue line) increase, the percent of good units increases. In contrast, as internal and external failure costs (green line) decrease, the percent of good units increases. Total quality cost (red line) is the sum of the prevention/appraisal costs and internal/external failure costs.

**EXHIBIT 7**

**The Relationship between the Costs of Quality**

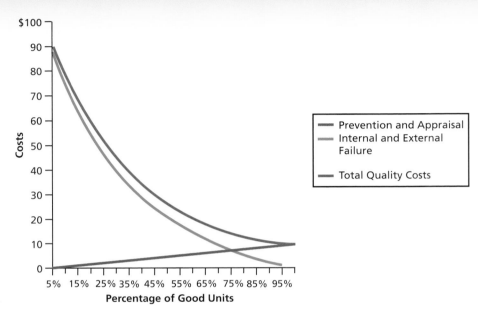

The optimal level of quality (percent of good units) is the one that minimizes the total quality costs. At this point, prevention and appraisal costs are balanced against internal and external failure costs. Exhibit 7 indicates that the optimal level of quality occurs at (or near) 100% quality. This is because prevention and appraisal costs grow moderately as quality increases. However, the costs of internal and external failure drop dramatically as quality increases.

## Quality Activity Analysis

An activity analysis of quality quantifies the costs of quality in dollar terms. To illustrate, the quality control activities, activity costs, and quality cost classifications for Gifford Company, a consumer electronics company, are shown in Exhibit 8.

**EXHIBIT 8**

**Quality Control Activity Analysis— Gifford Company**

| Quality Control Activities | Activity Cost | Quality Cost Classification |
|---|---|---|
| Design engineering | $ 55,000 | Prevention |
| Disposing of rejected materials | 160,000 | Internal Failure |
| Finished goods inspection | 140,000 | Appraisal |
| Materials inspection | 70,000 | Appraisal |
| Preventive maintenance | 80,000 | Prevention |
| Processing returned materials | 150,000 | External Failure |
| Disposing of scrap | 195,000 | Internal Failure |
| Assessing vendor quality | 45,000 | Prevention |
| Rework | 380,000 | Internal Failure |
| Warranty work | 225,000 | External Failure |
| Total activity cost | $1,500,000 | |

**Pareto Chart of Quality Costs** One method of reporting quality cost information is using a Pareto chart. A **Pareto chart** is a bar chart that shows the totals of an attribute for a number of categories. The categories are ranked and shown left to right, so that the largest total attribute is on the left and the smallest total is on the right.

To illustrate, Exhibit 9 is a Pareto chart for the quality control activities in Exhibit 8.

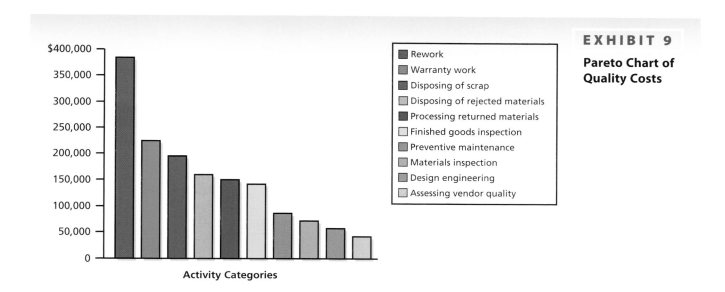

**EXHIBIT 9**

**Pareto Chart of Quality Costs**

In Exhibit 9, the vertical axis is dollars, which represents quality control costs. The horizontal axis represents activity categories, which are the ten quality control cost activities. The ten quality control cost categories are ranked from the one with the largest total on the left to the one with the smallest total on the right. Thus, the largest bar on the left is rework costs ($380,000), the second bar is warranty work ($225,000), and so on.

The Pareto chart gives managers a quick visual tool for identifying the most important quality control cost categories. Exhibit 9 indicates that Gifford Company should focus efforts on reducing rework and warranty costs.

**Cost of Quality Report** The costs of quality can also be summarized in a cost of quality report. A **cost of quality report** normally reports the:

1. Total activity cost for each quality cost classification
2. Percent of total quality costs associated with each classification
3. Percent of each quality cost classification to sales

Exhibit 10 is a cost of quality report for Gifford Company, based on assumed sales of $5,000,000. Exhibit 10 indicates that only 12% of the total quality cost is the cost of preventing quality problems while 14% is the cost of appraisal activities. Thus, prevention and appraisal costs make up only 26% of the total quality control costs. In contrast, 74% (49% + 25%) of the quality control costs are incurred for internal (49%) and external failure (25%) costs. In addition, internal and external failure costs are 22.2% (14.7% + 7.5%) of sales.

Exhibit 10 implies that Gifford Company is not spending enough on prevention and appraisal activities. By spending more on prevention and appraisal, internal and external failure costs will decrease, as was shown in Exhibit 7.

**EXHIBIT 10**

**Cost of Quality Report—Gifford Company**

**Gifford Company**
**Cost of Quality Report**

| Quality Cost Classification | Quality Cost | Percent of Total Quality Cost | Percent of Total Sales |
|---|---|---|---|
| Prevention | $ 180,000 | 12% | 3.6% |
| Appraisal | 210,000 | 14 | 4.2 |
| Internal failure | 735,000 | 49 | 14.7 |
| External failure | 375,000 | 25 | 7.5 |
| Total | $1,500,000 | 100% | 30.0% |

**Example Exercise 27-4 Cost of Quality Report**

**OBJ. 4**

A quality control activity analysis indicated the following four activity costs of an administrative department:

| | |
|---|---|
| Verifying the accuracy of a form | $ 50,000 |
| Responding to customer complaints | 100,000 |
| Correcting errors in forms | 75,000 |
| Redesigning forms to reduce errors | 25,000 |
| Total | $250,000 |

Sales are $2,000,000. Prepare a cost of quality report.

**Follow My Example 27-4**

**Cost of Quality Report**

| Quality Cost Classification | Quality Cost | Percent of Total Quality Cost | Percent of Total Sales |
|---|---|---|---|
| Prevention | $ 25,000 | 10% | 1.25% |
| Appraisal | 50,000 | 20 | 2.50 |
| Internal failure | 75,000 | 30 | 3.75 |
| External failure | 100,000 | 40 | 5.00 |
| Total | $250,000 | 100% | 12.50% |

Practice Exercises: **PE 27-4A, PE 27-4B**

## Value-Added Activity Analysis

In the preceding section, the quality control activities of Gifford Company were classified as prevention, appraisal, internal failure, and external failure activities. Activities may also be classified as:

1. Value-added
2. Non-value-added

A **value-added activity** is one that is necessary to meet customer requirements. A **non-value-added activity** is *not* required by the customer, but occurs because of mistakes, errors, omissions, and process failures.

To illustrate, Exhibit 11 shows the value-added and non-value-added classification for the quality control activities for Gifford Company.[3]

---

3 We use the quality control activities for illustrating the value-added and non-value-added activities in this section. However, a value-added/non-value-added activity analysis can be done for any activity in a business, not just quality control activities.

**EXHIBIT 11**

**Value-Added/
Non-Value-Added
Quality Control
Activities**

| Quality Control Activities | Activity Cost | Classification |
|---|---|---|
| Design engineering | $    55,000 | Value-added |
| Disposing of rejected materials | 160,000 | Non-value-added |
| Finished goods inspection | 140,000 | Value-added |
| Materials inspection | 70,000 | Value-added |
| Preventive maintenance | 80,000 | Value-added |
| Processing returned materials | 150,000 | Non-value-added |
| Disposing of scrap | 195,000 | Non-value-added |
| Assessing vendor quality | 45,000 | Value-added |
| Rework | 380,000 | Non-value-added |
| Warranty work | 225,000 | Non-value-added |
| Total activity cost | $1,500,000 | |

Exhibit 11 shows that internal and external failure costs are classified as non-value-added. In contrast, prevention and appraisal costs are classified as value-added.[4]

A summary of the value-added and non-value-added activities is shown below. The summary expresses value-added and non-value-added costs as a percent of total costs.

| Classification | Amount | Percent |
|---|---|---|
| Value-added | $   390,000 | 26% |
| Non-value-added | 1,110,000 | 74 |
| Total | $1,500,000 | 100% |

The preceding summary indicates that 74% of Gifford Company's quality control activities are non-value-added. This should motivate Gifford Company to make improvements to reduce non-value-added activities.

## Process Activity Analysis

Activity analysis can be used to evaluate business processes. A **process** is a series of activities that converts an input into an output. In other words, a process is a set of activities linked together by inputs and outputs. Common business processes include:

1. Procurement
2. Product development
3. Manufacturing
4. Distribution
5. Sales order fulfillment

Exhibit 12 shows a sales order fulfillment process for Masters Company. This process converts a customer order (the input) into a product received by the customer (the output).

**EXHIBIT 12    Sales Order Fulfillment Process**

Sales Order Submitted by Customer → Customer Credit Check → Order Entered into Computer System → Order Picked from Warehouse* → Order Shipped → Product Received by Customer

*Operators driving forklifts receive a list of orders, drive to stacking locations within the warehouse, pick the orders, and then transport them back to an area to prepare for shipment.

4 Some believe that appraisal costs are non-value-added. They argue that if the product had been made correctly, then no inspection would be required. We take a less strict view and assume that appraisal costs are value-added.

Exhibit 12 indicates that Masters Company's sales order fulfillment process has the following four activities:

1. Customer credit check
2. Order entered into computer system
3. Order picked from warehouse
4. Order shipped to customer

A process activity analysis can be used to determine the cost of the preceding activities. To illustrate, assume that a process activity analysis determines that the cost of the four activities is as follows:

| Sales Order Fulfillment Activities | Activity Cost | Percent of Total Process Cost |
|---|---|---|
| Customer credit check ............................ | $14,400 | 18% |
| Order entered into computer system .............. | 9,600 | 12 |
| Order picked from warehouse .................... | 36,000 | 45 |
| Order shipped to customer ...................... | 20,000 | 25 |
| Total sales order fulfillment process cost ........... | $80,000 | 100% |

If 10,000 sales orders are filled during the current period, the per-unit process cost is $8 per order ($80,000/10,000 orders).

Management can use process activity analysis to improve a process. To illustrate, assume that Masters Company sets a cost improvement target of $6 per order. A $2 reduction per order ($8 – $6) requires improving efficiency or eliminating unnecessary activities.

Masters Company determines that only *new* customers need to have a credit check. If this change is made, it is estimated that only 25% of sales orders would require credit checks. In addition, by revising the warehouse product layout, it is estimated that the cost of picking orders can be reduced by 35%.

Assuming that 10,000 orders will be filled, the cost savings from these two improvements are as follows:

| Sales Order Fulfillment Activities | Activity Cost Prior to Improvement | Activity Cost After Improvement | Activity Cost Savings |
|---|---|---|---|
| Customer credit check ................................. | $14,400 | $ 3,600* | $10,800 |
| Order entered in computer system ..................... | 9,600 | 9,600 | 0 |
| Order picked from warehouse ......................... | 36,000 | 23,400** | 12,600 |
| Order shipped ....................................... | 20,000 | 20,000 | 0 |
| Total sales order fulfillment process cost ................. | $80,000 | $56,600 | $23,400 |
| Cost per order (total cost divided by 10,000 orders)....................................... | $8.00 | $5.66 | |

*$14,400 × 25%
** $36,000 – ($36,000 × 35%)

As shown above, the activity changes generate a savings of $23,400.[5] In addition, the cost per order is reduced to $5.66, which is less than the $6.00 per order targeted cost.[6]

---

[5] This analysis assumes that the activity costs are variable to the inputs and outputs of the process. While this is likely true for processes primarily using labor, such as a sales order fulfillment process, other types of processes may have significant fixed costs that would not change with changes of inputs and outputs.

[6] Process activity analysis can also be integrated into a company's budgeting system using flexible budgets. Process activity analysis used in this way is discussed in advanced texts.

## Example Exercise  27-5  Process Activity Analysis

OBJ. 4

Mason Company incurred an activity cost of $120,000 for inspecting 50,000 units of production. Management determined that the inspecting objectives could be met without inspecting every unit. Therefore, rather than inspecting 50,000 units of production, the inspection activity was limited to 20% of the production. Determine the inspection activity cost per unit on 50,000 units of total production both before and after the improvement.

### Follow My Example  27-5

Inspection activity before improvement: $120,000/50,000 units = $2.40 per unit
Inspection activity after improvement:

| | |
|---|---|
| Revised inspection cost | (20% × 50,000 units) × $2.40 per unit = $24,000 |
| Revised inspection cost per unit | $24,000/50,000 units = $0.48 per unit |

Practice Exercises: **PE 27-5A, PE 27-5B**

## At a Glance 27

**1**  Describe just-in-time (JIT) manufacturing practices.

**Key Points**   Just-in-time emphasizes reduced lead time, a product-oriented production layout, a team-oriented work environment, setup time reduction, pull manufacturing, high quality, and supplier and customer partnering in order to improve the supply chain.

| Learning Outcomes | Example Exercises | Practice Exercises |
|---|---|---|
| • Describe the relationships among setup time, batch size, inventory, and lead time. | | |
| • Compute lead time and the value-added ratio. | **EE27-1** | **PE27-1A, 27-1B** |
| • Identify the characteristics of a just-in-time manufacturing environment and compare it to traditional approaches | **EE27-2** | **PE27-2A, 27-2B** |

**2**  Apply just-in-time practices to a nonmanufacturing setting.

**Key Points**   Just-in-time principles can be used in service businesses and administrative processes. In such processes, just-in-time principles are used to process information, such as an engineering design, or people, such as a patient.

| Learning Outcomes | Example Exercises | Practice Exercises |
|---|---|---|
| • Illustrate the use of just-in-time principles in a nonmanufacturing setting, such as a hospital. | | |

**OBJ. 3**

**Describe the implications of a just-in-time manufacturing on cost accounting and performance measurement.**

**Key Points** Under just-in-time, the cost accounting system will have fewer transactions, will combine the materials and work in process accounts, and will account for direct labor as a part of cell conversion cost. Just-in-time will use nonfinancial reporting measures and result in more direct tracing of factory overhead to product cells.

| Learning Outcomes | Example Exercises | Practice Exercises |
|---|---|---|
| • Identify the implications of the just-in-time philosophy for cost accounting. | | |
| • Prepare just-in-time journal entries for material purchases, application of cell conversion cost, and transfer of cell costs to finished goods. | EE27-3 | PE27-3A, 27-3B |
| • Describe nonfinancial performance measures. | | |

**OBJ. 4**

**Describe and illustrate activity analysis for improving operations.**

**Key Points** Companies use activity analysis to identify the costs of quality, which include prevention, appraisal, internal failure, and external failure costs. The quality cost activities may be reported on a Pareto chart or quality cost report. An alternative method for categorizing activities is by value-added and non-value-added classifications. An activity analysis can also be used to improve the cost of processes.

| Learning Outcomes | Example Exercises | Practice Exercises |
|---|---|---|
| • Define the costs of quality | | |
| • Define and prepare a Pareto chart. | | |
| • Prepare a cost of quality report. | EE27-4 | PE27-4A, 27-4B |
| • Identify value-added and non-value-added activity costs. | | |
| • Use process activity analysis to measure process improvement. | EE27-5 | PE27-5A, 27-5B |

# Key Terms

activity analysis (1261)
appraisal costs (1261)
backflush accounting (1258)
conversion costs (1257)
cost of quality report (1263)
costs of quality (1261)
electronic data interchange (EDI) (1255)
employee involvement (1254)
enterprise resource planning (ERP) (1255)
external failure costs (1261)

internal failure costs (1261)
just-in-time (JIT) processing (1248)
lead time (1249)
nonfinancial measure (1260)
non-value-added activity (1264)
non-value-added lead time (1249)
Pareto chart (1263)
prevention costs (1261)
process (1265)
process-oriented layout (1253)
product-oriented layout (1253)

pull manufacturing (1254)
push manufacturing (1254)
radio frequency identification devices (RFIDs) (1255)
Raw and In Process (RIP) Inventory (1257)
Six Sigma (1254)
supply chain management (1255)
value-added activity (1264)
value-added lead time (1249)
value-added ratio (1249)

## Illustrative Problem

Krisco Company operates under the just-in-time philosophy. As such, it has a production cell for its microwave ovens. The conversion cost for 2,400 hours of production is budgeted for the year at $4,800,000.

During January, 2,000 microwave ovens were started and completed. Each oven requires six minutes of cell processing time. The materials cost for each oven is $100.

### Instructions

1. Determine the budgeted cell conversion cost per hour.
2. Determine the manufacturing cost per unit.
3. Journalize the entry to record the costs charged to the production cell in January.
4. Journalize the entry to record the costs transferred to finished goods.

### Solution

1. Budgeted Cell Conversion Cost Rate $= \dfrac{\$4,800,000}{2,400 \text{ hours}} = \$2,000$ per cell hour

2. 
| | |
|---|---|
| Materials | $100 per unit |
| Conversion cost [($2,000 per hour/60 min.) × 6 min.] | 200 |
| Total | $300 per unit |

3. 
| | | |
|---|---|---|
| Raw and In Process Inventory | 200,000 | |
|     Accounts Payable | | 200,000 |
|         To record materials costs. | | |
|            (2,000 units × $100 per unit). | | |
| | | |
| Raw and In Process Inventory | 400,000 | |
|     Conversion Costs | | 400,000 |
|         To record conversion costs. | | |
|            (2,000 units × $200 per unit). | | |

4. 
| | | |
|---|---|---|
| Finished Goods (2,000 × $300 per unit) | 600,000 | |
|     Raw and In Process Inventory | | 600,000 |
|         To record finished production. | | |

## Discussion Questions

1. What is the benefit of just-in-time processing?

2. What are some examples of non-value-added lead time?

3. Why is a product-oriented layout preferred by just-in-time manufacturers over a process-oriented layout?

4. How is setup time related to lead time?

5. Why do just-in-time manufacturers favor pull or "make to order" manufacturing?

6. Why would a just-in-time manufacturer strive to produce zero defects?

7. How is supply chain management different from traditional supplier and customer relationships?

8. What just-in-time principles might a hospital use?

9. Why does accounting in a just-in-time environment result in fewer transactions?

10. Why is a "raw and in process inventory" account used by just-in-time manufacturers, rather than separately reporting materials and work in process?

11. Why is the direct labor cost category eliminated in many just-in-time environments?

12. How does a Pareto chart assist management?

13. What is the benefit of identifying non-value-added activities?

14. What ways can the cost of a process be improved?

# Practice Exercises

## PE 27-1A   Lead time

The High Altitude Ski Company manufactures skis in the finishing and assembly process. Skis are manufactured in 34-ski batch sizes. The finishing time is 20 minutes per ski. The assembly time is 16 minutes per ski. It takes 10 minutes to move a batch of skis from finishing to assembly.

a.  Compute the value-added, non-value-added, and total lead time of this process.

b.  Compute the value-added ratio. Round to one decimal.

## PE 27-1B   Lead time

The Nite Life Jean Company manufactures jeans in the cutting and sewing process. Jeans are manufactured in 90-jean batch sizes. The cutting time is 9 minutes per jean. The sewing time is 12 minutes per jean. It takes 14 minutes to move a batch of jeans from cutting to sewing.

a.  Compute the value-added, non-value-added, and total lead time of this process.

b.  Compute the value-added ratio. Round to one decimal.

## PE 27-2A   Just-in-time features

Which of the following are features of a just-in-time manufacturing system?

a.  Centralized maintenance areas

b.  Smaller batch sizes

c.  Employee involvement

d.  Less wasted movement of material and people

## PE 27-2B   Just-in-time features

Which of the following are features of a just-in-time manufacturing system?

a.  Production pace matches demand

b.  Centralized work in process inventory locations

c.  Push scheduling

d.  Receive raw materials directly to manufacturing cells

## PE 27-3A   Just-in-time journal entries

The budgeted conversion costs for a just-in-time cell are $1,267,500 for 1,950 production hours. Each unit produced by the cell requires 12 minutes of cell process time. During the month, 575 units are manufactured in the cell. The estimated materials costs are $840 per unit. Provide the following journal entries:

a.  Materials are purchased to produce 600 units.

b.  Conversion costs are applied to 575 units of production.

c.  565 units are completed and placed into finished goods.

## PE 27-3B   Just-in-time journal entries

The budgeted conversion costs for a just-in-time cell are $180,000 for 1,800 production hours. Each unit produced by the cell requires 24 minutes of cell process time. During the month, 450 units are manufactured in the cell. The estimated materials costs are $90 per unit. Provide the following journal entries:

a.  Materials are purchased to produce 465 units.

b.  Conversion costs are applied to 450 units of production.

c.  435 units are completed and placed into finished goods.

OBJ. 4    **EE 27-4** p. 1264    **PE 27-4A   Cost of quality report**

A quality control activity analysis indicated the following four activity costs of a manufacturing department:

| | |
|---|---:|
| Rework | $ 18,000 |
| Inspecting incoming raw materials | 24,000 |
| Warranty work | 9,000 |
| Process improvement effort | 99,000 |
| Total | $150,000 |

Sales are $1,000,000. Prepare a cost of quality report.

OBJ. 4    **EE 27-4** p. 1264    **PE 27-4B   Cost of quality report**

A quality control activity analysis indicated the following four activity costs of a hotel:

| | |
|---|---:|
| Inspecting cleanliness of rooms | $ 84,000 |
| Processing lost customer reservations | 330,000 |
| Rework incorrectly prepared room service meal | 30,000 |
| Employee training | 156,000 |
| Total | $600,000 |

Sales are $3,000,000. Prepare a cost of quality report.

OBJ. 4    **EE 27-5** p. 1267    **PE 27-5A   Process activity analysis**

Briggs Company incurred an activity cost of $250,000 for inspecting 25,000 units of production. Management determined that the inspecting objectives could be met without inspecting every unit. Therefore, rather than inspecting 25,000 units of production, the inspection activity was limited to 30% of the production. Determine the inspection activity cost per unit on 25,000 units of total production both before and after the improvement.

OBJ. 4    **EE 27-5** p. 1267    **PE 27-5B   Process activity analysis**

Lamont Company incurred an activity cost of $48,000 for inspecting 8,000 units of production. Management determined that the inspecting objectives could be met without inspecting every unit. Therefore, rather than inspecting 8,000 units of production, the inspection activity was limited to a random selection of 1,000 units out of the 8,000 units of production. Determine the inspection activity cost per unit on 8,000 units of total production both before and after the improvement.

# Exercises

OBJ. 1

### EX 27-1   Just-in-time principles

The chief executive officer (CEO) of Advent Inc. has just returned from a management seminar describing the benefits of the just-in-time philosophy. The CEO issued the following statement after returning from the conference:

*This company will become a just-in-time manufacturing company. Presently, we have too much inventory. To become just-in-time, we need to eliminate the excess inventory. Therefore, I want all employees to begin reducing inventories until we are just-in-time. Thank you for your cooperation.*

➤ How would you respond to the CEO's statement?

OBJ. 1

### EX 27-2   Just-in-time as a strategy

The American textile industry has moved much of its operations offshore in the pursuit of lower labor costs. Textile imports have risen from 2% of all textile production in 1962 to over 70% in 2010. Offshore manufacturers make long runs of standard mass-market apparel items. These are then brought to the United States in container ships, requiring significant time between original order and delivery. As a result, retail customers must accurately forecast market demands for imported apparel items.

Assuming that you work for a U.S.-based textile company, how would you recommend responding to the low-cost imports?

OBJ. 1

### EX 27-3   Just-in-time principles

Active Apparel Company manufactures various styles of men's casual wear. Shirts are cut and assembled by a workforce that is paid by piece rate. This means that they are paid according to the amount of work completed during a period of time. To illustrate, if the piece rate is $0.10 per sleeve assembled, and the worker assembles 700 sleeves during the day, then the worker would be paid $84 (700 × $0.12) for the day's work.

The company is considering adopting a just-in-time manufacturing philosophy by organizing work cells around various types of products and employing pull manufacturing. However, no change is expected in the compensation policy. On this point, the manufacturing manager stated the following:

*"Piecework compensation provides an incentive to work fast. Without it, the workers will just goof off and expect a full day's pay. We can't pay straight hourly wages—at least not in this industry."*

How would you respond to the manufacturing manager's comments?

OBJ. 1

### EX 27-4   Lead time analysis

Furry Friends Inc. manufactures toy stuffed animals. The direct labor time required to cut, sew, and stuff a toy is 10 minutes per unit. The company makes two types of stuffed toys—a lion and a bear. The lion is assembled in lot sizes of 60 units per batch, while the bear is assembled in lot sizes of 6 units per batch. Since each product has direct labor time of 10 minutes per unit, management has determined that the lead time for each product is 10 minutes.

Is management correct? What are the lead times for each product?

OBJ. 1

### EX 27-5   Reduce setup time

Jackson Inc. has analyzed the setup time on its computer-controlled lathe. The setup requires changing the type of fixture that holds a part. The average setup time has been 135 minutes, consisting of the following steps:

| | |
|---|---|
| Turn off machine and remove fixture from lathe | 10 minutes |
| Go to tool room with fixture | 20 |
| Record replacement of fixture to tool room | 18 |
| Return to lathe | 20 |
| Clean lathe | 20 |
| Return to tool room | 20 |
| Record withdrawal of new fixture from tool room | 12 |
| Return to lathe | 20 |
| Install new fixture and turn on machine | 10 |
| Total setup time | 150 minutes |

a.   Why should management be concerned about improving setup time?

b.   What do you recommend to Jackson Inc. for improving setup time?

c.   How much time would be required for a setup, using your suggestion in (b)?

OBJ. 1

### EX 27-6 Calculate lead time

Michigan Machining Company machines metal parts for the automotive industry. Under the traditional manufacturing approach, the parts are machined through two processes: milling and finishing. Parts are produced in batch sizes of 60 parts. A part requires 5 minutes in milling and 7 minutes in finishing. The move time between the two operations for a complete batch is 10 minutes.

Under the just-in-time philosophy, the part is produced in a cell that includes both the milling and finishing operations. The operating time is unchanged; however, the batch size is reduced to 5 parts and the move time is eliminated.

Determine the value-added, non-value-added, total lead time, and the value-added ratio under the traditional and just-in-time manufacturing methods. Round whole percentages to one decimal place.

OBJ. 1

### EX 27-7 Calculate lead time

Orion Devices Inc. is considering a new just-in-time product cell. The present manufacturing approach produces a product in four separate steps. The production batch sizes are 60 units. The process time for each step is as follows:

| | |
|---|---|
| Process Step 1 | 5 minutes |
| Process Step 2 | 8 minutes |
| Process Step 3 | 9 minutes |
| Process Step 4 | 6 minutes |

The time required to move each batch between steps is 12 minutes. In addition, the time to move raw materials to Process Step 1 is also 12 minutes, and the time to move completed units from Process Step 4 to finished goods inventory is 12 minutes.

The new just-in-time layout will allow the company to reduce the batch sizes from 60 units to 4 units. The time required to move each batch between steps and the inventory locations will be reduced to 2 minutes. The processing time in each step will stay the same.

Determine the value-added, non-value-added, total lead times, and the value-added ratio under the present and proposed production approaches. Round whole percentages to one decimal place.

OBJ. 1, 2

✔ b. 105 minutes

### EX 27-8 Lead time calculation—doctor's office

Carlton Maples caught the flu and needed to see the doctor. Maples called to set up an appointment and was told to come in at 1:00 P.M. Maples arrived at the doctor's office promptly at 1:00 P.M. The waiting room had 8 other people in it. Patients were admitted from the waiting room in FIFO (first-in, first-out) order at a rate of 5 minutes per patient. After waiting until his turn, a nurse finally invited Maples to an examining room. Once in the examining room, Maples waited another 15 minutes before a nurse arrived to take some basic readings (temperature, blood pressure). The nurse needed 10 minutes to collect the clinical information. After the nurse left, Maples waited 15 additional minutes before the doctor arrived. The doctor arrived and diagnosed the flu and provided a prescription for antibiotics. This took the doctor 10 minutes. Before leaving the doctor's office, Maples waited 10 minutes at the business office to pay for the office visit.

Maples spent 5 minutes walking next door to fill the prescription at the pharmacy. There were five people in front of Maples, each person requiring 5 minutes to fill and purchase a prescription. Maples finally arrived home 15 minutes after paying for his prescription.

a. What time does Maples arrive home?

b. How much of the total elapsed time from 1:00 P.M. until when Maples arrived home was non-value-added time?

c. What is the value-added ratio?

d. Why does the doctor require patients to wait so long for service?

OBJ. 1

### EX 27-9 Suppy chain management

The following is an excerpt from a recent article discussing supplier relationships with the Big Three North American automakers.

*"The Big Three select suppliers on the basis of lowest price and annual price reductions," said Neil De Koker, president of the Original Equipment Suppliers Association. "They look globally for the lowest parts prices from the lowest cost countries," De Koker said. "There is little trust and respect. Collaboration is missing." Japanese auto makers want long-term supplier relationships. They select suppliers as a person would a mate. The Big Three are quick to beat down prices with methods such as electronic auctions or rebidding work to a competitor. The Japanese are equally tough on price but are committed to maintaining supplier continuity. "They work with you to arrive at a competitive price, and they are willing to pay because they want long-term partnering," said Carl Code, a vice president at Ernie Green Industries. "They [Honda and Toyota] want suppliers to make enough money to stay in business, grow, and bring them innovation." The Big Three's supply chain model is not much different from the one set by Henry Ford. In 1913, he set up the system of independent supplier firms operating at arm's length on short-term contracts. One consequence of the Big Three's low-price-at-all-costs mentality is that suppliers are reluctant to offer them their cutting-edge technology out of fear the contract will be resourced before the research and development costs are recouped.*

a. Contrast the Japanese supply chain model with that of the Big Three.

b. Why might a supplier prefer the Japanese model?

c. What benefits might accrue to the Big Three by adopting the Japanese supply chain practices?

**Source:** Robert Sherefkin and Amy Wilson, "Suppliers Prefer Japanese Business Model," *Rubber & Plastics News*, March 17, 2003, Vol. 24, No. 11.

OBJ. 1

### EX 27-10 Employee involvement

Quickie Designs Inc. uses teams in the manufacture of lightweight wheelchairs. Two features of its team approach are team hiring and peer reviews. Under team hiring, the team recruits, interviews, and hires new team members from within the organization. Using peer reviews, the team evaluates each member of the team with regard to quality, knowledge, teamwork, goal performance, attendance, and safety. These reviews provide feedback to the team member for improvement.

➤ How do these two team approaches differ from using managers to hire and evaluate employees?

OBJ. 1, 2

### EX 27-11 Lead time reduction—service company

Tower Insurance Company takes ten days to make payments on insurance claims. Claims are processed through three departments: Data Input, Claims Audit, and Claims Adjustment. The three departments are on different floors, approximately one hour apart from each other. Claims are processed in batches of 100. Each batch of 100 claims moves through the three departments on a wheeled cart. Management is concerned about customer dissatisfaction caused by the long lead time for claim payments.

➤ How might this process be changed so that the lead time could be reduced significantly?

OBJ. 2

### EX 27-12 Just-in-time—fast-food restaurant

The management of Grid Iron Burger fast-food franchise wants to provide hamburgers quickly to customers. It has been using a process by which precooked hamburgers are prepared and placed under hot lamps. These hamburgers are then sold to customers. In this process, every customer receives the same type of hamburger and dressing (ketchup, onions, mustard). If a customer wants something different, then a "special order" must be cooked to the customer's requirements. This requires the customer to wait several minutes, which often slows down the service line. Grid Iron has been receiving more and more special orders from customers, which has been slowing service down considerably.

a. ➤ How would you describe the present Grid Iron service delivery system?

b ➤ How might you use just-in-time principles to provide customers quick service, yet still allow them to custom order their burgers?

---

**OBJ. 3**

### EX 27-13  Accounting issues in a just-in-time environment

Diamond Technologies has recently implemented a just-in-time manufacturing approach. A production department manager has approached the controller with the following comments:

*I am very upset with our accounting system now that we have implemented our new just-in-time manufacturing methods. It seems as if all I'm doing is paperwork. Our product is moving so fast through the manufacturing process that the paperwork can hardly keep up. For example, it just doesn't make sense to me to fill out daily labor reports. The employees are assigned to complete cells, performing many different tasks. I can't keep up with direct labor reports on each individual task. I thought we were trying to eliminate waste. Yet the information requirements of the accounting system are slowing us down and adding to overall lead time. Moreover, I'm still getting my monthly variance reports. I don't think that these are necessary. I have nonfinancial performance measures that are more timely than these reports. Besides, the employees don't really understand accounting variances. How about giving some information that I can really use?*

➤ What accounting system changes would you suggest in light of the production department manager's criticisms?

---

**OBJ. 3**
✔ b. $65

### EX 27-14  Just-in-time journal entries

Motion Media Inc. uses a just-in-time strategy to manufacture DVD players. The company manufactures DVD players through a single product cell. The budgeted conversion cost for the year is $760,500 for 1,950 production hours. Each unit requires 10 minutes of cell process time. During May, 950 DVD players are manufactured in the cell. The materials cost per unit is $85. The following summary transactions took place during May:

1. Materials are purchased for May production.
2. Conversion costs were applied to production.
3. 950 DVD players are assembled and placed in finished goods.
4. 900 DVD players are sold for $260 per unit.

    a.  Determine the budgeted cell conversion cost per hour.

    b.  Determine the budgeted cell conversion cost per unit.

    c.  Journalize the summary transactions (1)–(4) for May.

---

**OBJ. 3**
✔ a. $60

### EX 27-15  Just-in-time journal entries

Martin Lighting Inc. manufactures lighting fixtures, using just-in-time manufacturing methods. Style BB-01 has a materials cost per unit of $32. The budgeted conversion cost for the year is $126,000 for 2,100 production hours. A unit of Style BB-01 requires 15 minutes of cell production time. The following transactions took place during October:

1. Materials were acquired to assemble 700 Style BB-01 units for October.
2. Conversion costs were applied to 700 Style BB-01 units of production.
3. 675 units of Style BB-01 were completed in October.
4. 625 units of Style BB-01 were sold in October for $90 per unit.

    a.  Determine the budgeted cell conversion cost per hour.

    b.  Determine the budgeted cell conversion cost per unit.

    c.  Journalize the summary transactions (1)–(4) for October.

OBJ. 3

✔ b. Finished goods,
$6,900

**EX 27-16    Just-in-time journal entries**

Audio Master, Inc., manufactures audio speakers. Each speaker requires $125 per unit of direct materials. The speaker manufacturing assembly cell includes the following estimated costs for the period:

| Speaker assembly cell, estimated costs: | |
| --- | --- |
| Labor | $52,400 |
| Depreciation | 6,700 |
| Supplies | 2,500 |
| Power | 1,400 |
| Total cell costs for the period | $63,000 |

The operating plan calls for 180 operating hours for the period. Each speaker requires 18 minutes of cell process time. The unit selling price for each speaker is $450. During the period, the following transactions occurred:

1. Purchased materials to produce 600 speaker units.
2. Applied conversion costs to production of 550 speaker units.
3. Completed and transferred 530 speaker units to finished goods.
4. Sold 500 speaker units.

There were no inventories at the beginning of the period.

a. Journalize the summary transactions (1)–(4) for the period.
b. Determine the ending balance for raw and in process inventory and finished goods inventory.

OBJ. 4

**EX 27-17    Pareto chart**

Silicon Solutions Inc. manufactures RAM memory chips for personal computers. An activity analysis was conducted, and the following activity costs were identified with the manufacture and sale of memory chips:

| Activities | Activity Cost |
| --- | --- |
| Correct shipment errors | $ 84,000 |
| Disposing of scrap | 72,000 |
| Emergency equipment maintenance | 54,000 |
| Employee training | 30,000 |
| Final inspection | 72,000 |
| Inspecting incoming materials | 24,000 |
| Preventive equipment maintenance | 12,000 |
| Processing customer returns | 60,000 |
| Scrap reporting | 24,000 |
| Supplier development | 12,000 |
| Warranty claims | 156,000 |
| Total | $600,000 |

Prepare a Pareto chart of these activities.

OBJ. 4

✔ a. Appraisal, 16%
of total quality costs

**EX 27-18    Cost of quality report**

a. Using the information in Exercise 27-17, prepare a cost of quality report. Assume that the sales for the period were $3,000,000.
b. ━━━━▶ Interpret the cost of quality report.

**OBJ. 2, 4**

### EX 27-19  Pareto chart for a service company

Mountain States Cable Co. provides cable TV and Internet service to the local community. The activities and activity costs of Mountain States are identified as follows:

| Activities | Activity Cost |
|---|---|
| Billing error correction | $ 28,000 |
| Cable signal testing | 60,000 |
| Reinstalling service (installed incorrectly the first time) | 44,000 |
| Repairing satellite equipment | 24,000 |
| Repairing underground cable connections to the customer | 12,000 |
| Replacing old technology cable with higher quality cable | 100,000 |
| Replacing old technology signal switches with higher quality switches | 76,000 |
| Responding to customer home repair requests | 20,000 |
| Training employees | 36,000 |
| Total | $400,000 |

Prepare a Pareto chart of these activities.

**OBJ. 2, 4**

✔ a. External failure, 26% of total costs

### EX 27-20  Cost of quality and value-added/ non-value-added reports

a.  Using the activity data in Exercise 27-19, prepare a cost of quality report. Assume that sales are $2,000,000. Round percentages to one decimal place.

b.  Using the activity data in Exercise 27-19, prepare a value-added/non-value-added analysis.

c.  ━━━━▶  Interpret the information in (a) and (b).

**OBJ. 4**

✔ a. $0.10 per can

### EX 27-21  Process activity analysis

The Quench Beverage Company bottles soft drinks into aluminum cans. The manufacturing process consists of three activities:

1. **Mixing:** water, sugar, and beverage concentrate are mixed.
2. **Filling:** mixed beverage is filled into 12-oz. cans.
3. **Packaging:** properly filled cans are boxed into "fridge packs."

The activity costs associated with these activities for the period are as follows:

| | |
|---|---|
| Mixing | $352,000 |
| Filling | 280,000 |
| Packaging | 168,000 |
| Total | $800,000 |

Each can is expected to contain 12 ozs. of beverage. Thus, after being filled, each can is automatically weighed. If a can is too light, it is rejected, or "kicked," from the filling line prior to being packaged. The primary cause of kicks is heat expansion. With heat expansion, the beverage overflows during filling, resulting in underweight cans.

This process begins by mixing and filling 8,400,000 cans during the period, of which only 8,000,000 cans are actually packaged. Four hundred thousand cans are rejected due to underweight kicks.

A process improvement team has determined that cooling the cans prior to filling them will reduce the amount of overflows due to expansion. After this improvement, the number of kicks is expected to decline from 400,000 cans to 84,000 cans.

a.  Determine the total activity cost per packaged can under present operations.

b.  Determine the amount of increased packaging costs from the expected improvements.

c.  Determine the expected total activity cost per packaged can after improvements. Round to the nearest tenth of a cent.

OBJ. 2, 4

✔ b. $80 per claim payment

### EX 27-22 Process activity analysis

Columbia Insurance Company has a process for making payments on insurance claims as follows:

An activity analysis revealed that the cost of these activities was as follows:

| | |
|---|---|
| Receiving claim | $ 60,000 |
| Adjusting claim | 260,000 |
| Paying claim | 80,000 |
| Total | $400,000 |

This process includes only the cost of processing the claim payments, not the actual amount of the claim payments. The adjusting activity involves verifying and estimating the amount of the claim and is variable to the number of claims adjusted.

The process received, adjusted, and paid 5,000 claims during the period. All claims were treated identically in this process.

To improve the cost of this process, management has determined that claims should be segregated into two categories. Claims under $1,000 and claims greater than $1,000: claims under $1,000 would not be adjusted but would be accepted upon the insured's evidence of claim. Claims above $1,000 would be adjusted. It is estimated that 75% of the claims are under $1,000 and would thus be paid without adjustment. It is also estimated that the additional effort to segregate claims would add 10% to the "receiving claim" activity cost.

a. Develop a table showing the percent of individual activity cost to the total process cost.

b. Determine the average total process cost per claim payment, assuming 5,000 total claims.

c. Prepare a table showing the changes in the activity costs as a result of the changes proposed by management.

d. Estimate the average cost per claim payment, assuming that the changes proposed by management are enacted for 5,000 total claims.

OBJ. 2, 4

✔ b. $12.80 per payment

### EX 27-23 Process activity analysis

The procurement process for Li Wholesale Company includes a series of activities that transforms a materials requisition into a vendor check. The process begins with a request for materials. The requesting department prepares and sends a materials request form to the Purchasing Department. The Purchasing Department then places a request for a quote to vendors. Vendors prepare bids in response to the request for a quote. A vendor is selected based on the lowest bid. A purchase order to the low-bid vendor is prepared. The vendor delivers the materials to the company, whereupon a receiving ticket is prepared. Payment to the vendor is authorized if the materials request form, receiving ticket, and vendor invoice are in agreement. These three documents fail to agree 50% of the time, initiating effort to reconcile the differences. Once the three documents agree, a check is issued. The process can be diagrammed as follows:

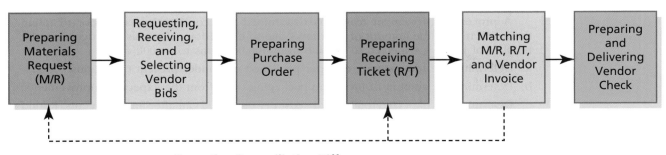

Correcting Reconciliation Differences

An activity analysis indicated the following activity costs with this process:

| | |
|---|---:|
| Preparing materials request | $ 25,600 |
| Requesting, receiving, and selecting vendor bids | 80,000 |
| Preparing purchase order | 16,000 |
| Preparing receiving ticket | 22,400 |
| Matching M/R, R/T, and invoice | 32,000 |
| Correcting reconciliation differences | 112,000 |
| Preparing and delivering vendor payment | 32,000 |
| Total process activity cost | $320,000 |

On average, the process handles 25,000 individual requests for materials that result in 25,000 individual payments to vendors.

Management proposes to improve this process in two ways. First, the Purchasing Department will develop a preapproved vendor list for which orders can be placed without a request for quote. It is expected that this will reduce the cost of requesting and receiving vendor bids by 70%. Second, additional training and standardization will be provided to reduce errors introduced into the materials requisition form and receiving tickets. It is expected that this will reduce the number of reconciliation differences from 50% to 15%, over an average of 25,000 payments.

a. Develop a table showing the percent of individual activity cost to the total process cost.

b. Determine the average total process cost per vendor payment, assuming 25,000 payments.

c. Prepare a table showing the improvements in the activity costs as a result of the changes proposed by management.

d. Estimate the average cost per vendor payment, assuming that the changes proposed by management are enacted for 25,000 total payments. Round to the nearest cent.

## Problems Series A

### PR 27-1A Just-in-time principles

Glow Bright Co. manufactures light bulbs. Glow Bright's purchasing policy requires that the purchasing agents place each quarter's purchasing requirements out for bid. This is because the Purchasing Department is evaluated solely by its ability to get the lowest purchase prices. The lowest cost bidder receives the order for the next quarter (90 working days).

To make its bulb products, Glow Bright requires 54,000 pounds of glass per quarter. Glow Bright received two glass bids for the third quarter, as follows:

- *Mid-States Glass Company:* $25.00 per pound of glass. Delivery schedule: 54,000 (600 lbs. × 90 days) pounds at the beginning of July to last for 3 months.
- *Akron Glass Company:* $25.15 per pound of glass. Delivery schedule: 600 pounds per working day (90 days in the quarter).

Glow Bright accepted Mid-States Glass Company's bid because it was the low-cost bid.

**Instructions**

1. Comment on Glow Bright's purchasing policy.

2. What are the additional (hidden) costs, beyond price, of Mid-States Glass Company's bid? Why weren't these costs considered?

3. Considering just inventory financing costs, what is the additional cost per pound of Mid-States Glass Company's bid if the cost of money is 10%? (*Hint:* Determine the average value of glass inventory held for the quarter and multiply by the quarterly interest charge, then divide by the number of pounds.)

## PR 27-2A   Lead time

Audio Max Electronics Company manufactures electronic stereo equipment. The manufacturing process includes printed circuit (PC) card assembly, final assembly, testing, and shipping. In the PC card assembly operation, a number of individuals are responsible for assembling electronic components into printed circuit boards. Each operator is responsible for soldering components according to a given set of instructions. Operators work on batches of 80 printed circuit boards. Each board requires 5 minutes of assembly time. After each batch is completed, the operator moves the assembled cards to the final assembly area. This move takes 10 minutes to complete.

The final assembly for each stereo unit requires 20 minutes and is also done in batches of 80 units. A batch of 80 stereos is moved into the test building, which is across the street. The move takes 20 minutes. Before conducting the test, the test equipment must be set up for the particular stereo model. The test setup requires 30 minutes. The units wait while the setup is performed. In the final test, the 80-unit batch is tested one at a time. Each test requires 7 minutes. The completed batch, after all testing, is sent to shipping for packaging and final shipment to customers. A complete batch of 80 units is sent from final assembly to shipping. The Shipping Department is located next to final assembly. Thus, there is no move time between these two operations. Packaging and labeling requires 8 minutes per unit.

### Instructions

1. Determine the amount of value-added and non-value-added lead time and the value-added ratio in this process for an average stereo unit in a batch of 80 units. Round percentages to one decimal place. Categorize the non-value-added time into wait and move time.

2. ➤ How could this process be improved so as to reduce the amount of waste in the process?

## PR 27-3A   Just-in-time accounting

Optic Matrix Inc. manufactures and assembles automobile instrument panels for both Yokohama Motors and Detroit Motors. The process consists of a just-in-time product cell for each customer's instrument assembly. The data that follow concern only the Yokohama just-in-time cell.

For the year, Optic Matrix Inc. budgeted the following costs for the Yokohama production cell:

| Conversion Cost Categories | Budget |
| --- | --- |
| Labor | $615,000 |
| Supplies | 96,000 |
| Utilities | 25,000 |
| Total | $736,000 |

Optic Matrix Inc. plans 3,200 hours of production for the Yokohama cell for the year. The materials cost is $125 per instrument assembly. Each assembly requires 24 minutes of cell assembly time. There was no November 1 inventory for either Raw and In Process Inventory or Finished Goods Inventory.

The following summary events took place in the Yokohama cell during November:

a. Electronic parts and wiring were purchased to produce 8,200 instrument assemblies in November.

b. Conversion costs were applied for the production of 8,000 units in November.

c. 7,850 units were started, completed, and transferred to finished goods in November.

d. 7,750 units were shipped to customers at a price of $400 per unit.

### Instructions

1. Determine the budgeted cell conversion cost per hour.

2. Determine the budgeted cell conversion cost per unit.

3. Journalize the summary transactions (a) through (d).

4. Determine the ending balance in Raw and In Process Inventory and Finished Goods Inventory.

5. ➤ How does the accounting in a JIT environment differ from traditional accounting?

OBJ. 2, 4

✔ 3. Non-value-added, 66%

### PR 27-4A Pareto chart and cost of quality report–municipality

The administrator of elections for the city of Madisonville has been asked to perform an activity analysis of its optical scanning center. The optical scanning center reads voter forms into the computer. The result of the activity analysis is summarized as follows:

| Activities | Activity Cost |
|---|---|
| Correcting errors identified by election commission | $130,000 |
| Correcting jams | 110,000 |
| Correcting scan errors | 60,000 |
| Loading | 25,000 |
| Logging-in control codes (for later reconciliation) | 20,000 |
| Program scanner | 30,000 |
| Rerunning job due to scan reading errors | 30,000 |
| Scanning | 60,000 |
| Verifying scan accuracy via reconciling totals | 20,000 |
| Verifying scanner accuracy with test run | 15,000 |
| Total | $500,000 |

#### Instructions

1. Prepare a Pareto chart of the department activities.

2. Use the activity cost information to determine the percentages of total department costs that are prevention, appraisal, internal failure, external failure, and not costs of quality.

3. Determine the percentages of the total department costs that are value- and non-value-added.

4. ▬▬▶ Interpret the information.

## Problems Series B

OBJ. 1

### PR 27-1B Just-in-time principles

David Harrelson Motorcycle Company manufactures a variety of motorcycles. Harrelson's purchasing policy requires that the purchasing agents place each quarter's purchasing requirements out for bid. This is because the Purchasing Department is evaluated solely by its ability to get the lowest purchase prices. The lowest cost bidder receives the order for the next quarter (90 days). To make its motorcycles, Harrelson requires 3,600 frames per quarter. Harrelson received two frame bids for the third quarter, as follows:

- *Famous Frames, Inc.:* $322 per frame. Delivery schedule: 40 frames per working day (90 days in the quarter).
- *Iron Horse Frames Inc.:* $320 per frame. Delivery schedule: 3,600 (40 frames × 90 days) frames at the beginning of July to last for three months.

Harrelson accepted Iron Horse Frames Inc.'s bid because it was the low-cost bid.

#### Instructions

1. ▬▬▶ Comment on Harrelson's purchasing policy.

2. ▬▬▶ What are the additional (hidden) costs, beyond price, of Iron Horse Frames Inc.'s bid? Why weren't these costs considered?

3. Considering just inventory financing costs, what is the additional cost per frame of Iron Horse Frames Inc.'s bid if the cost of money is 8%? (*Hint:* Determine the average value of frame inventory held for the quarter and multiply by the quarterly interest charge, then divide by the number of frames.)

OBJ. 1

✔ 1. Total wait time, 2,636 minutes

**PR 27-2B    Lead time**

Classic Chef Appliance Company manufactures home kitchen appliances. The manufacturing process includes stamping, final assembly, testing, and shipping. In the stamping operation, a number of individuals are responsible for stamping the steel outer surface of the appliance. The stamping operation is set up prior to each run. A run of 60 stampings is completed after each setup. A setup requires 40 minutes. The parts wait for the setup to be completed before stamping begins. Each stamping requires 6 minutes of operating time. After each batch is completed, the operator moves the stamped covers to the final assembly area. This move takes 10 minutes to complete.

The final assembly for each appliance unit requires 20 minutes and is also done in batches of 60 appliance units. The batch of 60 appliance units is moved into the test building, which is across the street. The move takes 25 minutes. In the final test, the 60-unit batch is tested one at a time. Each test requires 6 minutes. The completed units are sent to shipping for packaging and final shipment to customers. A complete batch of 60 units is sent from final assembly to shipping. The Shipping Department is located next to final assembly. Thus, there is no move time between these two operations. Packaging and shipment labeling requires 12 minutes per unit.

**Instructions**

1. Determine the amount of value-added and non-value-added lead time and the value-added ratio in this process for an average kitchen appliance in a batch of 60 units. Round percentages to one decimal place. Categorize the non-value-added time into wait and move time.

2. ➤ How could this process be improved so as to reduce the amount of waste in the process?

OBJ. 3

✔ 4. Raw and In Process Inventory, $17,520

**PR 27-3B    Just-in-time accounting**

Connect Tek Inc. manufactures and assembles two major types of telephone assemblies—a cordless phone and a cellular phone. The process consists of a just-in-time cell for each product. The data that follow concern only the cellular phone just-in-time cell.

For the year, Connect Tek Inc. budgeted the following costs for the cellular phone production cell:

| Conversion Cost Categories | Budget |
| --- | --- |
| Labor | $135,000 |
| Supplies | 55,000 |
| Utilities | 20,000 |
| Total | $210,000 |

Connect Tek plans 2,100 hours of production for the cellular phone cell for the year. The materials cost is $54 per unit. Each assembly requires 18 minutes of cell assembly time. There was no March 1 inventory for either Raw and In Process Inventory or Finished Goods Inventory.

The following summary events took place in the cellular phone cell during March:

a. Electronic parts were purchased to produce 7,200 cellular phone assemblies in March.

b. Conversion costs were applied for 7,000 units of production in March.

c. 6,920 units were completed and transferred to finished goods in March.

d. 6,840 units were shipped to customers at a price of $250 per unit.

**Instructions**

1. Determine the budgeted cell conversion cost per hour.

2. Determine the budgeted cell conversion cost per unit.

3. Journalize the summary transactions (a) through (d).

4. Determine the ending balance in Raw and In Process Inventory and Finished Goods Inventory.

5. ━━━➤ How does the accounting in a JIT environment differ from traditional accounting?

---

OBJ. 4

✔ 3. Non-value-added, 36%

### PR 27-4B   Pareto chart and cost of quality report-manufacturing company

The president of Cardio Care Exercise Equipment Co. has been concerned about the growth in costs over the last several years. The president asked the controller to perform an activity analysis to gain a better insight into these costs. The activity analysis revealed the following:

| Activities | Activity Cost |
|---|---|
| Correcting invoice errors | $ 7,200 |
| Disposing of incoming materials with poor quality | 21,600 |
| Disposing of scrap | 43,200 |
| Expediting late production | 36,000 |
| Final inspection | 28,800 |
| Inspecting incoming materials | 7,200 |
| Inspecting work in process | 32,400 |
| Preventive machine maintenance | 21,600 |
| Producing product | 140,400 |
| Responding to customer quality complaints | 21,600 |
| Total | $360,000 |

The production process is complicated by quality problems, requiring the production manager to expedite production and dispose of scrap.

### Instructions

1. Prepare a Pareto chart of the company activities.

2. Use the activity cost information to determine the percentages of total costs that are prevention, appraisal, internal failure, external failure, and not costs of quality (producing product).

3. Determine the percentages of total costs that are value- and non-value-added.

4. ━━━➤ Interpret the information.

---

## Cases & Projects

You can access Cases & Projects online at **www.cengage.com/accounting/reeve**

# Appendices

## Interest Tables

### Present Value of $1 at Compound Interest Due in *n* Periods

| Periods | 5% | 5.5% | 6% | 6.5% | 7% | 8% |
|---|---|---|---|---|---|---|
| 1 | 0.95238 | 0.94787 | 0.94334 | 0.93897 | 0.93458 | 0.92593 |
| 2 | 0.90703 | 0.89845 | 0.89000 | 0.88166 | 0.87344 | 0.85734 |
| 3 | 0.86384 | 0.85161 | 0.83962 | 0.82785 | 0.81630 | 0.79383 |
| 4 | 0.82270 | 0.80722 | 0.79209 | 0.77732 | 0.76290 | 0.73503 |
| 5 | 0.78353 | 0.76513 | 0.74726 | 0.72988 | 0.71290 | 0.68058 |
| 6 | 0.74622 | 0.72525 | 0.70496 | 0.68533 | 0.66634 | 0.63017 |
| 7 | 0.71068 | 0.68744 | 0.66506 | 0.64351 | 0.62275 | 0.58349 |
| 8 | 0.67684 | 0.65160 | 0.62741 | 0.60423 | 0.58201 | 0.54027 |
| 9 | 0.64461 | 0.61763 | 0.59190 | 0.56735 | 0.54393 | 0.50025 |
| 10 | 0.61391 | 0.58543 | 0.55840 | 0.53273 | 0.50835 | 0.46319 |
| 11 | 0.58468 | 0.55491 | 0.52679 | 0.50021 | 0.47509 | 0.42888 |
| 12 | 0.55684 | 0.52598 | 0.49697 | 0.46968 | 0.44401 | 0.39711 |
| 13 | 0.53032 | 0.49856 | 0.46884 | 0.44102 | 0.41496 | 0.36770 |
| 14 | 0.50507 | 0.47257 | 0.44230 | 0.41410 | 0.38782 | 0.34046 |
| 15 | 0.48102 | 0.44793 | 0.41726 | 0.38883 | 0.36245 | 0.31524 |
| 16 | 0.45811 | 0.42458 | 0.39365 | 0.36510 | 0.33874 | 0.29189 |
| 17 | 0.43630 | 0.40245 | 0.37136 | 0.34281 | 0.31657 | 0.27027 |
| 18 | 0.41552 | 0.38147 | 0.35034 | 0.32189 | 0.29586 | 0.25025 |
| 19 | 0.39573 | 0.36158 | 0.33051 | 0.30224 | 0.27651 | 0.23171 |
| 20 | 0.37689 | 0.34273 | 0.31180 | 0.28380 | 0.25842 | 0.21455 |
| 21 | 0.35894 | 0.32486 | 0.29416 | 0.26648 | 0.24151 | 0.19866 |
| 22 | 0.34185 | 0.30793 | 0.27750 | 0.25021 | 0.22571 | 0.18394 |
| 23 | 0.32557 | 0.29187 | 0.26180 | 0.23494 | 0.21095 | 0.17032 |
| 24 | 0.31007 | 0.27666 | 0.24698 | 0.22060 | 0.19715 | 0.15770 |
| 25 | 0.29530 | 0.26223 | 0.23300 | 0.20714 | 0.18425 | 0.14602 |
| 26 | 0.28124 | 0.24856 | 0.21981 | 0.19450 | 0.17211 | 0.13520 |
| 27 | 0.26785 | 0.23560 | 0.20737 | 0.18263 | 0.16093 | 0.12519 |
| 28 | 0.25509 | 0.22332 | 0.19563 | 0.17148 | 0.15040 | 0.11591 |
| 29 | 0.24295 | 0.21168 | 0.18456 | 0.16101 | 0.14056 | 0.10733 |
| 30 | 0.23138 | 0.20064 | 0.17411 | 0.15119 | 0.13137 | 0.09938 |
| 31 | 0.22036 | 0.19018 | 0.16426 | 0.14196 | 0.12277 | 0.09202 |
| 32 | 0.20987 | 0.18027 | 0.15496 | 0.13329 | 0.11474 | 0.08520 |
| 33 | 0.19987 | 0.17087 | 0.14619 | 0.12516 | 0.10724 | 0.07889 |
| 34 | 0.19036 | 0.16196 | 0.13791 | 0.11752 | 0.10022 | 0.07304 |
| 35 | 0.18129 | 0.15352 | 0.13010 | 0.11035 | 0.09366 | 0.06764 |
| 40 | 0.14205 | 0.11746 | 0.09722 | 0.08054 | 0.06678 | 0.04603 |
| 45 | 0.11130 | 0.08988 | 0.07265 | 0.05879 | 0.04761 | 0.03133 |
| 50 | 0.08720 | 0.06877 | 0.05429 | 0.04291 | 0.03395 | 0.02132 |

**Present Value of $1 at Compound Interest Due in _n_ Periods**

| Periods | 9% | 10% | 11% | 12% | 13% | 14% |
|---|---|---|---|---|---|---|
| 1 | 0.91743 | 0.90909 | 0.90090 | 0.89286 | 0.88496 | 0.87719 |
| 2 | 0.84168 | 0.82645 | 0.81162 | 0.79719 | 0.78315 | 0.76947 |
| 3 | 0.77218 | 0.75132 | 0.73119 | 0.71178 | 0.69305 | 0.67497 |
| 4 | 0.70842 | 0.68301 | 0.65873 | 0.63552 | 0.61332 | 0.59208 |
| 5 | 0.64993 | 0.62092 | 0.59345 | 0.56743 | 0.54276 | 0.51937 |
| 6 | 0.59627 | 0.56447 | 0.53464 | 0.50663 | 0.48032 | 0.45559 |
| 7 | 0.54703 | 0.51316 | 0.48166 | 0.45235 | 0.42506 | 0.39964 |
| 8 | 0.50187 | 0.46651 | 0.43393 | 0.40388 | 0.37616 | 0.35056 |
| 9 | 0.46043 | 0.42410 | 0.39092 | 0.36061 | 0.33288 | 0.30751 |
| 10 | 0.42241 | 0.38554 | 0.35218 | 0.32197 | 0.29459 | 0.26974 |
| 11 | 0.38753 | 0.35049 | 0.31728 | 0.28748 | 0.26070 | 0.23662 |
| 12 | 0.35554 | 0.31863 | 0.28584 | 0.25668 | 0.23071 | 0.20756 |
| 13 | 0.32618 | 0.28966 | 0.25751 | 0.22917 | 0.20416 | 0.18207 |
| 14 | 0.29925 | 0.26333 | 0.23199 | 0.20462 | 0.18068 | 0.15971 |
| 15 | 0.27454 | 0.23939 | 0.20900 | 0.18270 | 0.15989 | 0.14010 |
| 16 | 0.25187 | 0.21763 | 0.18829 | 0.16312 | 0.14150 | 0.12289 |
| 17 | 0.23107 | 0.19784 | 0.16963 | 0.14564 | 0.12522 | 0.10780 |
| 18 | 0.21199 | 0.17986 | 0.15282 | 0.13004 | 0.11081 | 0.09456 |
| 19 | 0.19449 | 0.16351 | 0.13768 | 0.11611 | 0.09806 | 0.08295 |
| 20 | 0.17843 | 0.14864 | 0.12403 | 0.10367 | 0.08678 | 0.07276 |
| 21 | 0.16370 | 0.13513 | 0.11174 | 0.09256 | 0.07680 | 0.06383 |
| 22 | 0.15018 | 0.12285 | 0.10067 | 0.08264 | 0.06796 | 0.05599 |
| 23 | 0.13778 | 0.11168 | 0.09069 | 0.07379 | 0.06014 | 0.04911 |
| 24 | 0.12640 | 0.10153 | 0.08170 | 0.06588 | 0.05323 | 0.04308 |
| 25 | 0.11597 | 0.09230 | 0.07361 | 0.05882 | 0.04710 | 0.03779 |
| 26 | 0.10639 | 0.08390 | 0.06631 | 0.05252 | 0.04168 | 0.03315 |
| 27 | 0.09761 | 0.07628 | 0.05974 | 0.04689 | 0.03689 | 0.02908 |
| 28 | 0.08955 | 0.06934 | 0.05382 | 0.04187 | 0.03264 | 0.02551 |
| 29 | 0.08216 | 0.06304 | 0.04849 | 0.03738 | 0.02889 | 0.02237 |
| 30 | 0.07537 | 0.05731 | 0.04368 | 0.03338 | 0.02557 | 0.01963 |
| 31 | 0.06915 | 0.05210 | 0.03935 | 0.02980 | 0.02262 | 0.01722 |
| 32 | 0.06344 | 0.04736 | 0.03545 | 0.02661 | 0.02002 | 0.01510 |
| 33 | 0.05820 | 0.04306 | 0.03194 | 0.02376 | 0.01772 | 0.01325 |
| 34 | 0.05331 | 0.03914 | 0.02878 | 0.02121 | 0.01568 | 0.01162 |
| 35 | 0.04899 | 0.03558 | 0.02592 | 0.01894 | 0.01388 | 0.01019 |
| 40 | 0.03184 | 0.02210 | 0.01538 | 0.01075 | 0.00753 | 0.00529 |
| 45 | 0.02069 | 0.01372 | 0.00913 | 0.00610 | 0.00409 | 0.00275 |
| 50 | 0.01345 | 0.00852 | 0.00542 | 0.00346 | 0.00222 | 0.00143 |

**Present Value of Ordinary Annuity of $1 per Period**

| Periods | 5% | 5.5% | 6% | 6.5% | 7% | 8% |
|---|---|---|---|---|---|---|
| 1 | 0.95238 | 0.94787 | 0.94340 | 0.93897 | 0.93458 | 0.92593 |
| 2 | 1.85941 | 1.84632 | 1.83339 | 1.82063 | 1.80802 | 1.78326 |
| 3 | 2.72325 | 2.69793 | 2.67301 | 2.64848 | 2.62432 | 2.57710 |
| 4 | 3.54595 | 3.50515 | 3.46511 | 3.42580 | 3.38721 | 3.31213 |
| 5 | 4.32948 | 4.27028 | 4.21236 | 4.15568 | 4.10020 | 3.99271 |
| 6 | 5.07569 | 4.99553 | 4.91732 | 4.84101 | 4.76654 | 4.62288 |
| 7 | 5.78637 | 5.68297 | 5.58238 | 5.48452 | 5.38923 | 5.20637 |
| 8 | 6.46321 | 6.33457 | 6.20979 | 6.08875 | 5.97130 | 5.74664 |
| 9 | 7.10782 | 6.95220 | 6.80169 | 6.65610 | 6.51523 | 6.24689 |
| 10 | 7.72174 | 7.53763 | 7.36009 | 7.18883 | 7.02358 | 6.71008 |
| 11 | 8.30641 | 8.09254 | 7.88688 | 7.68904 | 7.49867 | 7.13896 |
| 12 | 8.86325 | 8.61852 | 8.38384 | 8.15873 | 7.94269 | 7.53608 |
| 13 | 9.39357 | 9.11708 | 8.85268 | 8.59974 | 8.35765 | 7.90378 |
| 14 | 9.89864 | 9.58965 | 9.29498 | 9.01384 | 8.74547 | 8.22424 |
| 15 | 10.37966 | 10.03758 | 9.71225 | 9.40267 | 9.10791 | 8.55948 |
| 16 | 10.83777 | 10.46216 | 10.10590 | 9.76776 | 9.44665 | 8.85137 |
| 17 | 11.27407 | 10.86461 | 10.47726 | 10.11058 | 9.76322 | 9.12164 |
| 18 | 11.68959 | 11.24607 | 10.82760 | 10.43247 | 10.05909 | 9.37189 |
| 19 | 12.08532 | 11.60765 | 11.15812 | 10.73471 | 10.33560 | 9.60360 |
| 20 | 12.46221 | 11.95038 | 11.46992 | 11.01851 | 10.59401 | 9.81815 |
| 21 | 12.82115 | 12.27524 | 11.76408 | 11.28498 | 10.83553 | 10.01680 |
| 22 | 13.16300 | 12.58317 | 12.04158 | 11.53520 | 11.06124 | 10.20074 |
| 23 | 13.48857 | 12.87504 | 12.30338 | 11.77014 | 11.27219 | 10.37106 |
| 24 | 13.79864 | 13.15170 | 12.55036 | 11.99074 | 11.46933 | 10.52876 |
| 25 | 14.09394 | 13.41393 | 12.78336 | 12.19788 | 11.65358 | 10.67478 |
| 26 | 14.37518 | 13.66250 | 13.00317 | 12.39237 | 11.82578 | 10.80998 |
| 27 | 14.64303 | 13.89810 | 13.21053 | 12.57500 | 11.98671 | 10.93516 |
| 28 | 14.89813 | 14.12142 | 13.40616 | 12.74648 | 12.13711 | 11.05108 |
| 29 | 15.14107 | 14.33310 | 13.59072 | 12.90749 | 12.27767 | 11.15841 |
| 30 | 15.37245 | 14.53375 | 13.76483 | 13.05868 | 12.40904 | 11.25778 |
| 31 | 15.59281 | 14.72393 | 13.92909 | 13.20063 | 12.53181 | 11.34980 |
| 32 | 15.80268 | 14.90420 | 14.08404 | 13.33393 | 12.64656 | 11.43500 |
| 33 | 16.00255 | 15.07507 | 14.23023 | 13.45909 | 12.75379 | 11.51389 |
| 34 | 16.19290 | 15.23703 | 14.36814 | 13.57661 | 12.85401 | 11.58693 |
| 35 | 16.37420 | 15.39055 | 14.49825 | 13.68696 | 12.94767 | 11.65457 |
| 40 | 17.15909 | 16.04612 | 15.04630 | 14.14553 | 13.33171 | 11.92461 |
| 45 | 17.77407 | 16.54773 | 15.45583 | 14.48023 | 13.60552 | 12.10840 |
| 50 | 18.25592 | 16.93152 | 15.76186 | 14.72452 | 13.80075 | 12.23348 |

**Present Value of Ordinary Annuity of $1 per Period**

| Periods | 9% | 10% | 11% | 12% | 13% | 14% |
|---|---|---|---|---|---|---|
| 1 | 0.91743 | 0.90909 | 0.90090 | 0.89286 | 0.88496 | 0.87719 |
| 2 | 1.75911 | 1.73554 | 1.71252 | 1.69005 | 1.66810 | 1.64666 |
| 3 | 2.53130 | 2.48685 | 2.44371 | 2.40183 | 2.36115 | 2.32163 |
| 4 | 3.23972 | 3.16986 | 3.10245 | 3.03735 | 2.97447 | 2.91371 |
| 5 | 3.88965 | 3.79079 | 3.69590 | 3.60478 | 3.51723 | 3.43308 |
| 6 | 4.48592 | 4.35526 | 4.23054 | 4.11141 | 3.99755 | 3.88867 |
| 7 | 5.03295 | 4.86842 | 4.71220 | 4.56376 | 4.42261 | 4.28830 |
| 8 | 5.53482 | 5.33493 | 5.14612 | 4.96764 | 4.79677 | 4.63886 |
| 9 | 5.99525 | 5.75902 | 5.53705 | 5.32825 | 5.13166 | 4.94637 |
| 10 | 6.41766 | 6.14457 | 5.88923 | 5.65022 | 5.42624 | 5.21612 |
| 11 | 6.80519 | 6.49506 | 6.20652 | 5.93770 | 5.68694 | 5.45273 |
| 12 | 7.16072 | 6.81369 | 6.49236 | 6.19437 | 5.91765 | 5.66029 |
| 13 | 7.48690 | 7.10336 | 6.74987 | 6.42355 | 6.12181 | 5.84236 |
| 14 | 7.78615 | 7.36669 | 6.96187 | 6.62817 | 6.30249 | 6.00207 |
| 15 | 8.06069 | 7.60608 | 7.19087 | 6.81086 | 6.46238 | 6.14217 |
| 16 | 8.31256 | 7.82371 | 7.37916 | 6.97399 | 6.60388 | 6.26506 |
| 17 | 8.54363 | 8.02155 | 7.54879 | 7.11963 | 6.72909 | 6.37286 |
| 18 | 8.75562 | 8.20141 | 7.70162 | 7.24967 | 6.83991 | 6.46742 |
| 19 | 8.95012 | 8.36492 | 7.83929 | 7.36578 | 6.93797 | 6.55037 |
| 20 | 9.12855 | 8.51356 | 7.96333 | 7.46944 | 7.02475 | 6.62313 |
| 21 | 9.29224 | 8.64869 | 8.07507 | 7.56200 | 7.10155 | 6.68696 |
| 22 | 9.44242 | 8.77154 | 8.17574 | 7.64465 | 7.16951 | 6.74294 |
| 23 | 9.58021 | 8.88322 | 8.26643 | 7.71843 | 7.22966 | 6.79206 |
| 24 | 9.70661 | 8.98474 | 8.34814 | 7.78432 | 7.28288 | 6.83514 |
| 25 | 9.82258 | 9.07704 | 8.42174 | 7.84314 | 7.32998 | 6.87293 |
| 26 | 9.92897 | 9.16094 | 8.48806 | 7.89566 | 7.37167 | 6.90608 |
| 27 | 10.02658 | 9.23722 | 8.54780 | 7.94255 | 7.40856 | 6.93515 |
| 28 | 10.11613 | 9.30657 | 8.60162 | 7.98442 | 7.44120 | 6.96066 |
| 29 | 10.19828 | 9.36961 | 8.65011 | 8.02181 | 7.47009 | 6.98304 |
| 30 | 10.27365 | 9.42691 | 8.69379 | 8.05518 | 7.49565 | 7.00266 |
| 31 | 10.34280 | 9.47901 | 8.73315 | 8.08499 | 7.51828 | 7.01988 |
| 32 | 10.40624 | 9.52638 | 8.76860 | 8.11159 | 7.53830 | 7.03498 |
| 33 | 10.46444 | 9.56943 | 8.80054 | 8.13535 | 7.55602 | 7.04823 |
| 34 | 10.51784 | 9.60858 | 8.82932 | 8.15656 | 7.57170 | 7.05985 |
| 35 | 10.56682 | 9.64416 | 8.85524 | 8.17550 | 7.58557 | 7.07005 |
| 40 | 10.75736 | 9.77905 | 8.95105 | 8.24378 | 7.63438 | 7.10504 |
| 45 | 10.88118 | 9.86281 | 9.00791 | 8.28252 | 7.66086 | 7.12322 |
| 50 | 10.96168 | 9.91481 | 9.04165 | 8.30450 | 7.67524 | 7.13266 |

# Appendix B

## Reversing Entries

Some of the adjusting entries recorded at the end of the accounting period affect transactions that occur in the next period. In such cases, a reversing entry may be used to simplify the recording of the next period's transactions.

To illustrate, an adjusting entry for accrued wages expense affects the first payment of wages in the next period. Without using a reversing entry, Wages Payable must be debited for the accrued wages at the end of the preceding period. In addition, Wages Expense must also be debited for only that portion of the payroll that is an expense of the current period.

Using a reversing entry, however, simplifies the analysis and recording of the first wages payment in the next period. As the term implies, a *reversing entry* is the exact opposite of the related adjusting entry. The amounts and accounts are the same as the adjusting entry, but the debits and credits are reversed.

Reversing entries are illustrated by using the accrued wages for **NetSolutions** presented in Chapter 3. These data are summarized in Exhibit 1.

**EXHIBIT 1**

**Accrued Wages**

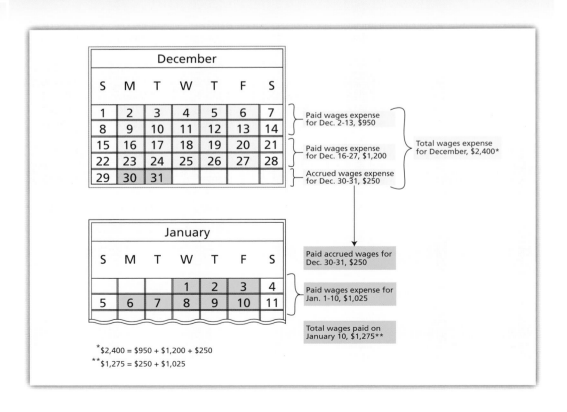

*$2,400 = $950 + $1,200 + $250

**$1,275 = $250 + $1,025

The adjusting entry for the accrued wages of December 30 and 31 is as follows:

| | 2011 | | | | | |
|---|---|---|---|---|---|---|
| Dec. | 31 | Wages Expense | 51 | 250 | | |
| | | Wages Payable | 22 | | 250 | |
| | | Accrued wages. | | | | |

After the adjusting entry is recorded, Wages Expense will have a debit balance of $4,525 ($4,275 + $250), as shown on the top of page B-3. Wages Payable will have a credit balance of $250, as shown on page B-3.

After the closing entries are recorded, Wages Expense will have a zero balance. However, since Wages Payable is a liability account, it is not closed. Thus, Wages Payable will have a credit balance of $250 as of January 1, 2012.

Without recording a reversing entry, the payment of the $1,275 payroll on January 10 would be recorded as follows:

| | 2012 | | | | | |
|---|---|---|---|---|---|---|
| Jan. | 10 | Wages Payable | 22 | 250 | | |
| | | Wages Expense | 51 | 1,025 | | |
| | | Cash | 11 | | 1,275 | |

As shown above, to record the January 10 payroll correctly Wages Payable must be debited for $250. This means that the employee who records the January 10 payroll must refer to the December 31, 2011, adjusting entry or to the ledger to determine the amount to debit Wages Payable.

Because the January 10 payroll is not recorded in the normal manner, there is a greater chance that an error may occur. This chance of error is reduced by recording a reversing entry as of the first day of the next period. For example, the reversing entry for the accrued wages expense would be recorded on January 1, 2012, as follows:

| | 2012 | | | | | |
|---|---|---|---|---|---|---|
| Jan. | 1 | Wages Payable | 22 | 250 | | |
| | | Wages Expense | 51 | | 250 | |
| | | Reversing entry. | | | | |

The preceding reversing entry transfers the $250 liability from Wages Payable to the credit side of Wages Expense. The nature of the $250 is unchanged—it is still a liability. However, because of its unusual nature, an explanation is written under the reversing entry.

When the payroll is paid on January 10, the following entry is recorded:

| | | | | | | |
|---|---|---|---|---|---|---|
| Jan. | 10 | Wages Expense | 51 | 1,275 | | |
| | | Cash | 11 | | 1,275 | |

After the January 10 payroll is recorded, Wages Expense has a debit balance of $1,025. This is the wages expense for the period January 1–10, 2012.

Wages Payable and Wages Expense after posting the adjusting, closing, and reversing entries are shown on the next page.

**Account** Wages Payable  Account No. 22

| Date | | Item | Post. Ref. | Debit | Credit | Balance Debit | Balance Credit |
|------|---|------|------------|-------|--------|-------|--------|
| 2011 Dec. | 31 | Adjusting | 5 | | 250 | | 250 |
| 2012 Jan. | 1 | Reversing | 7 | 250 | | — | — |

**Account** Wages Expense  Account No. 51

| Date | | Item | Post. Ref. | Debit | Credit | Balance Debit | Balance Credit |
|------|---|------|------------|-------|--------|-------|--------|
| 2011 Nov. | 30 | | 1 | 2,125 | | 2,125 | |
| Dec. | 13 | | 3 | 950 | | 3,075 | |
| | 27 | | 3 | 1,200 | | 4,275 | |
| | 31 | Adjusting | 5 | 250 | | 4,525 | |
| | 31 | Closing | 6 | | 4,525 | — | — |
| 2012 Jan. | 1 | Reversing | 7 | | 250 | | 250 |
| | 10 | | 7 | 1,275 | | 1,025 | |

In addition to accrued expenses (accrued liabilities), reversing entries are also used for accrued revenues (accrued assets). To illustrate, the reversing entry for NetSolutions' accrued fees earned as of December 31, 2011, is as follows:

| Jan. | 1 | Fees Earned | 41 | 500 | |
|------|---|-------------|----|-----|---|
| | | Accounts Receivable | 12 | | 500 |
| | | Reversing entry. | | | |

The use of reversing entries is optional. However, in computerized accounting systems, data entry employees often input routine accounting entries. In such cases, reversing entries may be useful in avoiding errors.

---

**EX B-1  Adjusting and reversing entries**

On the basis of the following data, (a) journalize the adjusting entries at December 31, the end of the current fiscal year, and (b) journalize the reversing entries on January 1, the first day of the following year.

1. Sales salaries are uniformly $21,000 for a five-day workweek, ending on Friday. The last payday of the year was Friday, December 26.

2. Accrued fees earned but not recorded at December 31, $33,750.

---

**EX B-2  Adjusting and reversing entries**

On the basis of the following data, (a) journalize the adjusting entries at June 30, the end of the current fiscal year, and (b) journalize the reversing entries on July 1, the first day of the following year.

1. Wages are uniformly $48,000 for a five-day workweek, ending on Friday. The last payday of the year was Friday, June 27.

2. Accrued fees earned but not recorded at June 30, $23,900.

## EX B-3   Entries posted to the wages expense account

Portions of the wages expense account of a business are shown below.

a. Indicate the nature of the entry (payment, adjusting, closing, reversing) from which each numbered posting was made.

b. Journalize the complete entry from which each numbered posting was made.

| Account | Wages Expense | | | | | | Account No. 53 |
|---|---|---|---|---|---|---|---|
| | | Post. | | | | Balance | |
| Date | Item | Ref. | Dr. | Cr. | Dr. | Cr. | |
| 2011 | | | | | | | |
| Dec. 26 | (1) | 125 | 32,000 | | 1,600,000 | | |
| 31 | (2) | 126 | 19,200 | | 1,619,200 | | |
| 31 | (3) | 127 | | 1,619,200 | — | — | |
| 2012 | | | | | | | |
| Jan. 1 | (4) | 128 | | 19,200 | | 19,200 | |
| 2 | (5) | 129 | 32,000 | | 12,800 | | |

## EX B-4   Entries posted to the salaries expense account

Portions of the salaries expense account of a business are shown below.

| Account | Salaries Expense | | | | | | Account No. 53 |
|---|---|---|---|---|---|---|---|
| | | Post. | | | | Balance | |
| Date | Item | Ref. | Dr. | Cr. | Dr. | Cr. | |
| 2011 | | | | | | | |
| Dec. 27 | (1) | 29 | 18,500 | | 897,800 | | |
| 31 | (2) | 30 | 7,400 | | 905,200 | | |
| 31 | (3) | 31 | | 905,200 | — | — | |
| 2012 | | | | | | | |
| Jan. 1 | (4) | 32 | | 7,400 | | 7,400 | |
| 2 | (5) | 33 | 18,500 | | 11,100 | | |

a. Indicate the nature of the entry (payment, adjusting, closing, reversing) from which each numbered posting was made.

b. Journalize the complete entry from which each numbered posting was made.

# Appendix C

## Special Journals and Subsidiary Ledgers

In the early chapters of this text, the transactions of NetSolutions were manually recorded in an all-purpose (two-column) journal. The journal entries were then posted individually to the accounts in the ledger. Such a system is simple to use and easy to understand when there are a small number of transactions. However, when a business has a large number of similar transactions, using an all-purpose journal is inefficient and impractical. In such cases, subsidiary ledgers and special journals are useful. Although the manual use of subsidiary ledgers and special journals is described and illustrated, the basic principles also apply to computerized accounting systems.

### Subsidiary Ledgers

A large number of individual accounts with a common characteristic can be grouped together in a separate ledger called a **subsidiary ledger**. The primary ledger, which contains all of the balance sheet and income statement accounts, is then called the **general ledger**. Each subsidiary ledger is represented in the general ledger by a summarizing account, called a **controlling account**. The sum of the balances of the accounts in a subsidiary ledger must equal the balance of the related controlling account. Thus, a subsidiary ledger is a secondary ledger that supports a controlling account in the general ledger.

Two of the most common subsidiary ledgers are as follows:

1. Accounts receivable subsidiary ledger
2. Accounts payable subsidiary ledger

The **accounts receivable subsidiary ledger**, or *customers ledger*, lists the individual customer accounts in alphabetical order. The controlling account in the general ledger that summarizes the debits and credits to the individual customer accounts is Accounts Receivable.

The **accounts payable subsidiary ledger**, or *creditors ledger*, lists individual creditor accounts in alphabetical order. The related controlling account in the general ledger is Accounts Payable.

The relationship between the general ledger and the accounts receivable and accounts payable subsidiary ledgers is illustrated in Exhibit 1.

Many businesses use subsidiary ledgers for other accounts in addition to Accounts Receivable and Accounts Payable. For example, businesses often use an equipment subsidiary ledger to keep track of each item of equipment purchased, its cost, location, and other data.

### Special Journals

One method of processing transactions more efficiently in a manual system is to use special journals. **Special journals** are designed to record a single kind of transaction

**EXHIBIT 1**   **General Ledger and Subsidiary Ledgers**

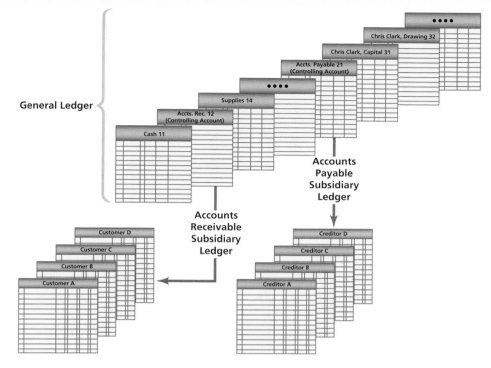

that occurs frequently. For example, since most businesses have many transactions in which cash is paid out, they will likely use a special journal for recording cash payments. Likewise, they will use another special journal for recording cash receipts.

The format and number of special journals that a business uses depends on the nature of the business. The common transactions and their related special journals used by small service businesses are as follows:

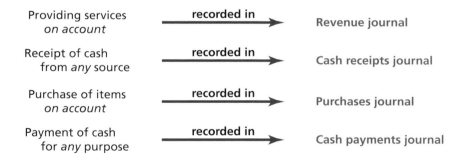

The all-purpose two-column journal, called the **general journal** or simply the *journal,* can be used for entries that do not fit into any of the special journals. For example, adjusting and closing entries are recorded in the general journal.

The following types of transactions, special journals, and subsidiary ledgers are described and illustrated for **NetSolutions**:

| Transaction | Special Journal | Subsidiary Ledger |
|---|---|---|
| Fees earned on account | Revenue journal | Accounts receivable subsidiary ledger |
| Cash receipts | Cash receipts journal | Accounts receivable subsidiary ledger |
| Purchases on account | Purchases journal | Accounts payable subsidiary ledger |
| Cash payments | Cash payments journal | Accounts payable subsidiary ledger |

As shown above, transactions that are recorded in the revenue and cash receipts journals will affect the accounts receivable subsidiary ledger. Likewise, transactions that are recorded in the purchases and cash payments journals will affect the accounts payable subsidiary ledger.

We will assume that NetSolutions had the following selected general ledger balances on March 1, 2012:

| Account Number | Account | Balance |
|---|---|---|
| 11 | Cash | $6,200 |
| 12 | Accounts Receivable | 3,400 |
| 14 | Supplies | 2,500 |
| 18 | Office Equipment | 2,500 |
| 21 | Accounts Payable | 1,230 |

## Revenue Journal

*Fees earned on account* would be recorded in the **revenue journal**. *Cash fees earned* would be recorded in the cash receipts journal.

To illustrate the efficiency of using a revenue journal, an example for NetSolutions is used. Specifically, assume that NetSolutions recorded the following four revenue transactions for March in its general journal:

| 2012 | | | | | |
|---|---|---|---|---|---|
| Mar. | 2 | Accounts Receivable—Accessories By Claire | 12/✓ | 2,200 | |
| | | Fees Earned | 41 | | 2,200 |
| | 6 | Accounts Receivable—RapZone | 12/✓ | 1,750 | |
| | | Fees Earned | 41 | | 1,750 |
| | 18 | Accounts Receivable—Web Cantina | 12/✓ | 2,650 | |
| | | Fees Earned | 41 | | 2,650 |
| | 27 | Accounts Receivable—Accessories By Claire | 12/✓ | 3,000 | |
| | | Fees Earned | 41 | | 3,000 |

For the above entries, NetSolutions recorded eight account titles and eight amounts. In addition, NetSolutions made 12 postings to the ledgers—four to Accounts Receivable in the general ledger, four to the accounts receivable subsidiary ledger (indicated by each check mark), and four to Fees Earned in the general ledger.

The preceding revenue transactions could be recorded more efficiently in a revenue journal, as shown in Exhibit 2. In each revenue transaction, the amount of the debit to Accounts Receivable is the same as the amount of the credit to Fees Earned. Thus, only a single amount column is necessary. The date, invoice number, customer name, and amount are entered separately for each transaction.

Revenues are normally recorded in the revenue journal when the company sends an invoice to the customer. An **invoice** is the bill that is sent to the customer by the company. Each invoice is normally numbered in sequence for future reference.

To illustrate, assume that on March 2 NetSolutions issued Invoice No. 615 to Accessories By Claire for fees earned of $2,200. This transaction is entered in the revenue journal, shown in Exhibit 2, by entering the following items:

1. Date column: *Mar. 2*
2. Invoice No. column: *615*

**EXHIBIT 2**   **Revenue Journal**

| | | | | | |
|---|---|---|---|---|---|
| | | | **Revenue Journal** | | *Page 35* |
| **Date** | | **Invoice No.** | **Account Debited** | **Post. Ref.** | **Accts. Rec. Dr. Fees Earned Cr.** |
| 2012 | | | | | |
| Mar. | 2 | 615 | Accessories By Claire | | 2,200 |
| | 6 | 616 | RapZone | | 1,750 |
| | 18 | 617 | Web Cantina | | 2,650 |
| | 27 | 618 | Accessories By Claire | | 3,000 |
| | 31 | | | | 9,600 |

3. Account Debited column: *Accessories By Claire*
4. Accts. Rec. Dr./Fees Earned Cr. column: *2,200*

The process of posting from a revenue journal, shown in Exhibit 3, is as follows:

1. Each transaction is posted individually to a customer account in the accounts receivable subsidiary ledger. Postings to customer accounts should be made on a regular basis. In this way, the customer's account will show a current balance. Since the balances in the customer accounts are usually debit balances, the three-column account form is shown in Exhibit 3.

   *To illustrate, Exhibit 3 shows the posting of the $2,200 debit to Accessories By Claire in the accounts receivable subsidiary ledger. After the posting, Accessories By Claire has a debit balance of $2,200.*

2. To provide a trail of the entries posted to the subsidiary and general ledger, the source of these entries is indicated in the Posting Reference column of each account by inserting the letter R (for revenue journal) and the page number of the revenue journal.

   *To illustrate, Exhibit 3 shows that after $2,200 is posted to Accessories By Claire's account, R35 is inserted into the Post. Ref. column of the account.*

3. To indicate that the transaction has been posted to the accounts receivable subsidiary ledger, a check mark (✓) is inserted in the Post. Ref. column of the revenue journal, as shown in Exhibit 3.

   *To illustrate, Exhibit 3 shows that a check mark (✓) has been inserted in the Post. Ref. column next to Accessories By Claire in the revenue journal to indicate that the $2,200 has been posted.*

4. A single monthly total is posted to Accounts Receivable and Fees Earned in the general ledger. This total is equal to the sum of the month's debits to the individual accounts in the subsidiary ledger. It is posted in the general ledger as a debit to Accounts Receivable and a credit to Fees Earned, as shown in Exhibit 3. The accounts receivable account number (12) and the fees earned account number (41) are then inserted below the total in the revenue journal to indicate that the posting is completed.

   *To illustrate, Exhibit 3 shows the monthly total of $9,600 was posted as a debit to Accounts Receivable (12) and as a credit to Fees Earned (41).*

Exhibit 3 illustrates the efficiency gained by using the revenue journal rather than the general journal. Specifically, all of the transactions for fees earned during the month are posted to the general ledger only once—at the end of the month.

**EXHIBIT 3**    **Revenue Journal and Postings**

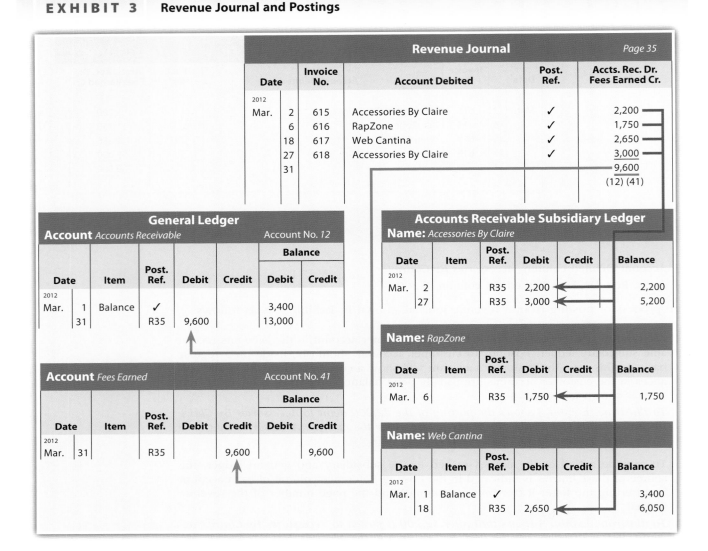

## Cash Receipts Journal

All transactions that involve the receipt of cash are recorded in a **cash receipts journal**. The cash receipts journal for NetSolutions is shown in Exhibit 4.

The cash receipts journal shown in Exhibit 4 has a Cash Dr. column. The kinds of transactions in which cash is received and how often they occur determine the titles of the other columns. For example, NetSolutions often receives cash from customers on account. Thus, the cash receipts journal in Exhibit 4 has an Accounts Receivable Cr. column.

To illustrate, on March 28 Accessories By Claire made a payment of $2,200 on its account. This transaction is recorded in the cash receipts journal, shown in Exhibit 4, by entering the following items:

1. Date column: *Mar. 28*
2. Account Credited column: *Accessories By Claire*
3. Accounts Receivable Cr. column: *2,200*
4. Cash Dr. column: *2,200*

The Other Accounts Cr. column in Exhibit 4 is used for recording credits to any account for which there is no special credit column. For example, NetSolutions received cash on March 1 for rent. Since no special column exists for Rent Revenue,

**EXHIBIT 4**    **Cash Receipts Journal and Postings**

### Cash Receipts Journal    *Page 14*

| Date | | Account Credited | Post. Ref. | Other Accounts Cr. | Accounts Receivable Cr. | Cash Dr. |
|---|---|---|---|---|---|---|
| 2012 | | | | | | |
| Mar. | 1 | Rent Revenue | 42 | 400 | | 400 |
| | 19 | Web Cantina | ✓ | | 3,400 | 3,400 |
| | 28 | Accessories By Claire | ✓ | | 2,200 | 2,200 |
| | 30 | RapZone | ✓ | | 1,750 | 1,750 |
| | 31 | | | 400 | 7,350 | 7,750 |
| | | | | (✓) | (12) | (11) |

### General Ledger

**Account** *Cash*                                    Account No. *11*

| Date | | Item | Post. Ref. | Debit | Credit | Balance Debit | Balance Credit |
|---|---|---|---|---|---|---|---|
| 2012 | | | | | | | |
| Mar. | 1 | Balance | ✓ | | | 6,200 | |
| | 31 | | CR14 | 7,750 | | 13,950 | |

**Account** *Accounts Receivable*                        Account No. *12*

| Date | | Item | Post. Ref. | Debit | Credit | Balance Debit | Balance Credit |
|---|---|---|---|---|---|---|---|
| 2012 | | | | | | | |
| Mar. | 1 | Balance | ✓ | | | 3,400 | |
| | 31 | | R35 | 9,600 | | 13,000 | |
| | 31 | | CR14 | | 7,350 | 5,650 | |

**Account** *Rent Revenue*                               Account No. *42*

| Date | | Item | Post. Ref. | Debit | Credit | Balance Debit | Balance Credit |
|---|---|---|---|---|---|---|---|
| 2012 | | | | | | | |
| Mar. | 1 | | CR14 | | 400 | | 400 |

### Accounts Receivable Subsidiary Ledger

**Name:** *Accessories By Claire*

| Date | | Item | Post. Ref. | Debit | Credit | Balance |
|---|---|---|---|---|---|---|
| 2012 | | | | | | |
| Mar. | 2 | | R35 | 2,200 | | 2,200 |
| | 27 | | R35 | 3,000 | | 5,200 |
| | 28 | | CR14 | | 2,200 | 3,000 |

**Name:** *RapZone*

| Date | | Item | Post. Ref. | Debit | Credit | Balance |
|---|---|---|---|---|---|---|
| 2012 | | | | | | |
| Mar. | 6 | | R35 | 1,750 | | 1,750 |
| | 30 | | CR14 | | 1,750 | — |

**Name:** *Web Cantina*

| Date | | Item | Post. Ref. | Debit | Credit | Balance |
|---|---|---|---|---|---|---|
| 2012 | | | | | | |
| Mar. | 1 | Balance | ✓ | | | 3,400 |
| | 18 | | R35 | 2,650 | | 6,050 |
| | 19 | | CR14 | | 3,400 | 2,650 |

Rent Revenue is entered in the Account Credited column. Thus, this transaction is recorded in the cash receipts journal, shown in Exhibit 4, by entering the following items:

1. Date column: *Mar. 1*
2. Account Credited column: *Rent Revenue*
3. Other Accounts Cr. column: *400*
4. Cash Dr. column: *400*

At the end of the month, all of the amount columns are totaled. The debits must equal the credits. If the debits do not equal the credits, an error has occurred. Before proceeding further, the error must be found and corrected.

The process of posting from the cash receipts journal, shown in Exhibit 4, is:

1. Each transaction involving the receipt of cash on account is posted individually to a customer account in the accounts receivable subsidiary ledger. Postings to customer accounts should be made on a regular basis. In this way, the customer's account will show a current balance.

   *To illustrate, Exhibit 4 shows on March 19 the receipt of $3,400 on account from Web Cantina. The posting of the $3,400 credit to Web Cantina in the accounts receivable subsidiary ledger is also shown in Exhibit 4. After the posting, Web Cantina has a debit balance of $2,650. If a posting results in a customer's account with a credit balance, the credit balance is indicated by an asterisk or parentheses in the Balance column. If an account's balance is zero, a line may be drawn in the Balance column.*

2. To provide a trail of the entries posted to the subsidiary ledger, the source of these entries is indicated in the Posting Reference column of each account by inserting the letter CR (for cash receipts journal) and the page number of the cash receipts journal.

   *To illustrate, Exhibit 4 shows that after $3,400 is posted to Web Cantina's account in the accounts receivable subsidiary ledger, CR14 is inserted into the Post. Ref. column of the account.*

3. To indicate that the transaction has been posted to the accounts receivable subsidiary ledger, a check mark (✓) is inserted in the Posting Reference column of the cash receipts journal.

   *To illustrate, Exhibit 4 shows that a check mark (✓) has been inserted in the Post. Ref. column next to Web Cantina to indicate that the $3,400 has been posted.*

4. A single monthly total of the Accounts Receivable Cr. column is posted to the accounts receivable general ledger account. This is the total cash received on account and is posted as a credit to Accounts Receivable. The accounts receivable account number (12) is then inserted below the Accounts Receivable Cr. column to indicate that the posting is complete.

   *To illustrate, Exhibit 4 shows the monthly total of $7,350 was posted as a credit to Accounts Receivable (12).*

5. A single monthly total of the Cash Dr. column is posted to the cash general ledger account. This is the total cash received during the month and is posted as a debit to Cash. The cash account number (11) is then inserted below the Cash Dr. column to indicate that the posting is complete.

   *To illustrate, Exhibit 4 shows the monthly total of $7,750 was posted as a debit to Cash (11).*

6. The accounts listed in the Other Accounts Cr. column are posted on a regular basis as a separate credit to each account. The account number is then inserted in the Post. Ref. column to indicate that the posting is complete. Because accounts in the Other Accounts Cr. column are posted individually, a check mark is placed below the column total at the end of the month to show that no further action is needed.

   *To illustrate, Exhibit 4 shows that $400 was posted as a credit to Rent Revenue in the general ledger, and the rent revenue account number (42) was entered in the Post. Ref. column of the cash receipts journal. Also, at the end of the month a check mark (✓) is entered below the Other Accounts Cr. column to indicate that no further action is needed.*

## Accounts Receivable Control Account and Subsidiary Ledger

After all posting has been completed for the month, the balances in the accounts receivable subsidiary ledger should be totaled. This total should then be compared with the balance of the accounts receivable controlling account in the general ledger. If the controlling account and the subsidiary ledger do not agree, an error has occurred. Before proceeding further, the error must be located and corrected.

The total of NetSolutions' accounts receivable subsidiary ledger is $5,650. This total agrees with the balance of its accounts receivable control account on March 31, 2012, as shown on the next page.

| Accounts Receivable (Control) | | NetSolutions Accounts Receivable Customer Balances March 31, 2012 | |
|---|---|---|---|
| Balance, March 1, 2012 | $ 3,400 | Accessories By Claire | $3,000 |
| Total debits (from revenue journal) | 9,600 | RapZone | 0 |
| Total credits (from cash receipts journal) | (7,350) | Web Cantina | 2,650 |
| Balance, March 31, 2012 | $ 5,650 | Total accounts receivable | $5,650 |

Equal debit balances

# Purchases Journal

All *purchases on account* are recorded in the **purchases journal**. *Cash purchases would be recorded in the cash payments journal.* The purchases journal for NetSolutions is shown in Exhibit 5.

The amounts purchased on account are recorded in the purchases journal in an Accounts Payable Cr. column. The items most often purchased on account determine the titles of the other columns. For example, NetSolutions often purchases supplies on account. Thus, the purchases journal in Exhibit 5 has a Supplies Dr. column.

To illustrate, on March 3 NetSolutions purchased $600 of supplies on account from Howard Supplies. This transaction is recorded in the purchases journal, shown in Exhibit 5, by entering the following items:

1. Date column: *Mar. 3*
2. Account Credited column: *Howard Supplies*
3. Accounts Payable Cr. column: *600*
4. Supplies Dr. column: *600*

The Other Accounts Dr. column in Exhibit 5 is used to record purchases on account of any item for which there is no special debit column. The title of the account to be debited is entered in the Other Accounts Dr. column, and the amount is entered in the Amount column.

To illustrate, on March 12 NetSolutions purchased office equipment on account from Jewett Business Systems for $2,800. This transaction is recorded in the purchases journal shown in Exhibit 5 by entering the following items:

1. Date column: *Mar. 12*
2. Account Credited column: *Jewett Business Systems*
3. Accounts Payable Cr. column: *2,800*
4. Other Accounts Dr. column: *Office Equipment*
5. Amount column: *2,800*

At the end of the month, all of the amount columns are totaled. The debits must equal the credits. If the debits do not equal the credits, an error has occurred. Before proceeding further, the error must be found and corrected.

The process of posting from the purchases journal shown in Exhibit 5 is as follows:

1. Each transaction involving a purchase on account is posted individually to a creditor's account in the accounts payable subsidiary ledger. Postings to creditor accounts should be made on a regular basis. In this way, the creditor's account will show a current balance.

   *To illustrate, Exhibit 5 shows on March 3 the purchase of supplies of $600 on account from Howard Supplies. The posting of the $600 credit to Howard Supplies accounts payable subsidiary ledger is also shown in Exhibit 5. After the posting, Howard Supplies has a credit balance of $600.*

2. To provide a trail of the entries posted to the subsidiary and general ledgers, the source of these entries is indicated in the Posting Reference column of each account by inserting the letter P (for purchases journal) and the page number of the purchases journal.

   *To illustrate, Exhibit 5 shows that after $600 is posted to Howard Supplies account, P11 is inserted into the Post. Ref. column of the account.*

**EXHIBIT 5**    **Purchases Journal and Postings**

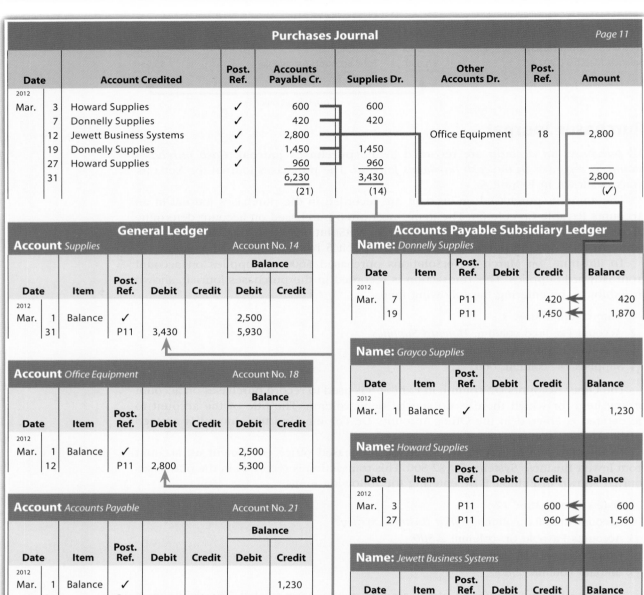

3. To indicate that the transaction has been posted to the accounts payable subsidiary ledger, a check mark (✓) is inserted in the Posting Reference column of the purchases journal, as shown in Exhibit 5.

   *To illustrate, Exhibit 5 shows that a check mark (✓) has been inserted in the Post. Ref. column next to Howard Supplies to indicate that the $600 has been posted.*

4. A single monthly total of the Accounts Payable Cr. column is posted to the accounts payable general ledger account. This is the total amount purchased on account and is posted as a credit to Accounts Payable. The accounts payable account number (21) is then inserted below the Accounts Payable Cr. column to indicate that the posting is complete.

   *To illustrate, Exhibit 5 shows the monthly total of $6,230 was posted as a credit to Accounts Payable (21).*

5. A single monthly total of the Supplies Dr. column is posted to the supplies general ledger account. This is the total supplies purchased on account during the month and is posted as a debit to Supplies. The supplies account number (14) is then inserted below the Supplies Dr. column to indicate that the posting is complete.

   *To illustrate, Exhibit 5 shows the monthly total of $3,430 was posted as a debit to Supplies (14).*

6. The accounts listed in the Other Accounts Dr. column are posted on a regular basis as a separate debit to each account. The account number is then inserted in the Post. Ref. column to indicate that the posting is complete. Because accounts in the Other Accounts Dr. column are posted individually, a check mark is placed below the column total at the end of the month to show that no further action is needed.

   *To illustrate, Exhibit 5 shows that $2,800 was posted as a debit to Office Equipment in the general ledger, and the office equipment account number (18) was entered in the Post. Ref. column of the purchases journal. Also, at end of month, a check mark (✓) is entered below the Amount column to indicate no further action is needed.*

## Cash Payments Journal

All transactions that involve the payment of cash are recorded in a **cash payments journal**. The cash payments journal for NetSolutions is shown in Exhibit 6.

The cash payments journal shown in Exhibit 6 has a Cash Cr. column. The kinds of transactions in which cash is paid and how often they occur determine the titles of the other columns. For example, NetSolutions often pays cash to creditors on account. Thus, the cash payments journal in Exhibit 6 has an Accounts Payable Dr. column. In addition, NetSolutions makes all payments by check. Thus, a check number is entered for each payment in the Ck. No. (Check Number) column to the right of the Date column. The check numbers are helpful in controlling cash payments and provide a useful cross-reference.

To illustrate, on March 15 NetSolutions issued Check No. 151 for $1,230 to Grayco Supplies for payment on its account. This transaction is recorded in the cash payments journal shown in Exhibit 6 by entering the following items:

1. Date column: *Mar. 15*
2. Ck. No. column: *151*
3. Account Debited column: *Grayco Supplies*
4. Accounts Payable Dr. column: *1,230*
5. Cash Cr. column: *1,230*

The Other Accounts Dr. column in Exhibit 6 is used for recording debits to any account for which there is no special debit column. For example, NetSolutions issued Check No. 150 on March 2 for $1,600 in payment of March rent. This transaction is recorded in the cash payments journal, shown in Exhibit 6, by entering these items:

1. Date column: *Mar. 2*
2. Ck. No. column: *150*
3. Account Debited column: *Rent Expense*
4. Other Accounts Dr. column: *1,600*
5. Cash Cr. column: *1,600*

At the end of the month, all of the amount columns are totaled. The debits must equal the credits. If the debits do not equal the credits, an error has occurred. Before proceeding further, the error must be found and corrected.

The process of posting from the cash payments journal, Exhibit 6, is as follows:

1. Each transaction involving the payment of cash on account is posted individually to a creditor account in the accounts payable subsidiary ledger. Postings to creditor accounts should be made on a regular basis. In this way, the creditor's account will show a current balance.

   *To illustrate, Exhibit 6 shows on March 22 the payment of $420 on account to Donnelly Supplies. The posting of the $420 debit to Donnelly Supplies in the accounts payable subsidiary ledger is also shown in Exhibit 6. After the posting, Donnelly Supplies has a credit balance of $1,450.*

**EXHIBIT 6**   Cash Payments Journal and Postings

### Cash Payments Journal

Page 7

| Date | | Ck. No. | Account Debited | Post. Ref. | Other Accounts Dr. | Accounts Payable Dr. | Cash Cr. |
|---|---|---|---|---|---|---|---|
| 2012 | | | | | | | |
| Mar. | 2 | 150 | Rent Expense | 52 | 1,600 | | 1,600 |
| | 15 | 151 | Grayco Supplies | ✓ | | 1,230 | 1,230 |
| | 21 | 152 | Jewett Business Systems | ✓ | | 2,800 | 2,800 |
| | 22 | 153 | Donnelly Supplies | ✓ | | 420 | 420 |
| | 30 | 154 | Utilities Expense | 54 | 1,050 | | 1,050 |
| | 31 | 155 | Howard Supplies | ✓ | | 600 | 600 |
| | 31 | | | | 2,650 | 5,050 | 7,700 |
| | | | | | (✓) | (21) | (11) |

### General Ledger

**Account** Cash                                          Account No. 11

| Date | | Item | Post. Ref. | Debit | Credit | Balance Debit | Balance Credit |
|---|---|---|---|---|---|---|---|
| 2012 | | | | | | | |
| Mar. | 1 | Balance | ✓ | | | 6,200 | |
| | 31 | | CR14 | 7,750 | | 13,950 | |
| | 31 | | CP7 | | 7,700 | 6,250 | |

**Account** Accounts Payable                              Account No. 21

| Date | | Item | Post. Ref. | Debit | Credit | Balance Debit | Balance Credit |
|---|---|---|---|---|---|---|---|
| 2012 | | | | | | | |
| Mar. | 1 | Balance | ✓ | | | | 1,230 |
| | 31 | | P11 | | 6,230 | | 7,460 |
| | 31 | | CP7 | 5,050 | | | 2,410 |

**Account** Rent Expense                                  Account No. 52

| Date | | Item | Post. Ref. | Debit | Credit | Balance Debit | Balance Credit |
|---|---|---|---|---|---|---|---|
| 2012 | | | | | | | |
| Mar. | 2 | | CP7 | 1,600 | | 1,600 | |

**Account** Utilities Expense                             Account No. 54

| Date | | Item | Post. Ref. | Debit | Credit | Balance Debit | Balance Credit |
|---|---|---|---|---|---|---|---|
| 2012 | | | | | | | |
| Mar. | 30 | | CP7 | 1,050 | | 1,050 | |

### Accounts Payable Subsidiary Ledger

**Name:** Donnelly Supplies

| Date | | Item | Post. Ref. | Debit | Credit | Balance |
|---|---|---|---|---|---|---|
| 2012 | | | | | | |
| Mar. | 7 | | P11 | | 420 | 420 |
| | 19 | | P11 | | 1,450 | 1,870 |
| | 22 | | CP7 | 420 | | 1,450 |

**Name:** Grayco Supplies

| Date | | Item | Post. Ref. | Debit | Credit | Balance |
|---|---|---|---|---|---|---|
| 2012 | | | | | | |
| Mar. | 1 | Balance | ✓ | | | 1,230 |
| | 15 | | CP7 | 1,230 | | — |

**Name:** Howard Supplies

| Date | | Item | Post. Ref. | Debit | Credit | Balance |
|---|---|---|---|---|---|---|
| 2012 | | | | | | |
| Mar. | 3 | | P11 | | 600 | 600 |
| | 27 | | P11 | | 960 | 1,560 |
| | 31 | | CP7 | 600 | | 960 |

**Name:** Jewett Business Systems

| Date | | Item | Post. Ref. | Debit | Credit | Balance |
|---|---|---|---|---|---|---|
| 2012 | | | | | | |
| Mar. | 12 | | P11 | | 2,800 | 2,800 |
| | 21 | | CP7 | 2,800 | | — |

2. To provide a trail of the entries posted to the subsidiary and general ledgers, the source of these entries is indicated in the Posting Reference column of each account by inserting the letter CP (for cash payments journal) and the page number of the cash payments journal.

*To illustrate, Exhibit 6 shows that after $420 is posted to Donnelly Supplies account, CP7 is inserted into the Post. Ref. column of the account.*

3. To indicate that the transaction has been posted to the accounts payable subsidiary ledger, a check mark (✓) is inserted in the Posting Reference column of the cash payments journal.

   *To illustrate, Exhibit 6 shows that a check mark (✓) has been inserted in the Post. Ref. column next to Donnelly Supplies to indicate that the $420 has been posted.*

4. A single monthly total of the Accounts Payable Dr. column is posted to the accounts payable general ledger account. This is the total cash paid on account and is posted as a debit to Accounts Payable. The accounts payable account number (21) is then inserted below the Accounts Payable Dr. column to indicate that the posting is complete.

   *To illustrate, Exhibit 6 shows the monthly total of $5,050 was posted as a debit to Accounts Payable (21).*

5. A single monthly total of the Cash Cr. column is posted to the cash general ledger account. This is the total cash payments during the month and is posted as a credit to Cash. The cash account number (11) is then inserted below the Cash Cr. column to indicate that the posting is complete.

   *To illustrate, Exhibit 6 shows the monthly total of $7,700 was posted as a credit to Cash (11).*

6. The accounts listed in the Other Accounts Dr. column are posted on a regular basis as a separate debit to each account. The account number is then inserted in the Post. Ref. column to indicate that the posting is complete. Because accounts in the Other Accounts Dr. column are posted individually, a check mark is placed below the column total at the end of the month to show that no further action is needed.

   *To illustrate, Exhibit 6 shows that $1,600 was posted as a debit to Rent Expense (52) and $1,050 was posted as a debit to Utilities Expense (54) in the general ledger. The account numbers (52 and 54, respectively) were entered in the Post. Ref. column of the cash payments journal. Also, at the end of the month, a check mark (✓) is entered below the Other Accounts Dr. column to indicate that no further action is needed.*

## Accounts Payable Control Account and Subsidiary Ledger

After all posting has been completed for the month, the balances in the accounts payable subsidiary ledger should be totaled. This total should then be compared with the balance of the accounts payable controlling account in the general ledger. If the controlling account and the subsidiary ledger do not agree, an error has occurred. Before proceeding, the error must be located and corrected.

The total of NetSolutions' accounts payable subsidiary ledger is $2,410. This total agrees with the balance of its accounts payable control account on March 31, 2012, as shown below.

| Accounts Payable (Control) | | NetSolutions Accounts Payable Creditor Balances March 31, 2012 | |
|---|---|---|---|
| Balance, March 1, 2012 | $1,230 | Donnelly Supplies | $1,450 |
| Total credits (from purchases journal) | 6,230 | Grayco Supplies | 0 |
| Total debits | | Howard Supplies | 960 |
| (from cash payments journal) | (5,050) | Jewett Business Systems | 0 |
| Balance, March 31, 2012 | $2,410 | Total | $2,410 |

Equal credit balances

## Exercises

### EX C-1   Identify postings from revenue journal

Using the following revenue journal for Gamma Services Inc., identify each of the posting references, indicated by a letter, as representing (1) posting to general ledger accounts or (2) posting to subsidiary ledger accounts.

**REVENUE JOURNAL**

| Date | Invoice No. | Account Debited | Post. Ref. | Accounts Rec. Dr. Fees Earned Cr. |
|---|---|---|---|---|
| 2012 | | | | |
| June   1 | 112 | Hazmat Safety Co. | (a) | $2,625 |
| 10 | 113 | Masco Co. | (b) | 980 |
| 18 | 114 | Eco-Systems | (c) | 1,600 |
| 27 | 115 | Nero Enterprises | (d) | 1,240 |
| 30 | | | | $6,445 |
| | | | | (e) |

### EX C-2   Identify journals

Assuming the use of a two-column (all-purpose) general journal, a revenue journal, and a cash receipts journal as illustrated in this chapter, indicate the journal in which each of the following transactions should be recorded:

a.  Sale of office supplies on account, at cost, to a neighboring business.

b.  Receipt of cash from sale of office equipment.

c.  Closing of drawing account at the end of the year.

d.  Providing services for cash.

e.  Receipt of cash refund from overpayment of taxes.

f.  Adjustment to record accrued salaries at the end of the year.

g.  Receipt of cash for rent.

h.  Receipt of cash on account from a customer.

i.  Providing services on account.

j.  Investment of additional cash in the business by the owner.

### EX C-3   Identify journals

Assuming the use of a two-column (all-purpose) general journal, a purchases journal, and a cash payments journal as illustrated in this chapter, indicate the journal in which each of the following transactions should be recorded:

a.  Purchase of an office computer on account.

b.  Purchase of services on account.

c.  Purchase of office supplies on account.

d.  Adjustment to prepaid rent at the end of the month.

e.  Adjustment to record accrued salaries at the end of the period.

f.  Purchase of office supplies for cash.

g.  Advance payment of a one-year fire insurance policy on the office.

h.  Purchase of office equipment for cash.

i.  Adjustment to prepaid insurance at the end of the month.

j.  Adjustment to record depreciation at the end of the month.

k.  Payment of six months' rent in advance.

### EX C-4 Identify transactions in accounts receivable ledger

The debits and credits from three related transactions are presented in the following customer's account taken from the accounts receivable subsidiary ledger.

**NAME** *Casey By Design*
**ADDRESS** *1319 Elm Street*

| Date | Item | Post. Ref. | Debit | Credit | Balance |
|------|------|-----------|-------|--------|---------|
| 2012 | | | | | |
| Feb. 3 | | R44 | 740 | | 740 |
| 6 | | J11 | | 80 | 660 |
| 16 | | CR81 | | 660 | — |

Describe each transaction, and identify the source of each posting.

### EX C-5 Identify postings from purchases journal

Using the following purchases journal, identify each of the posting references, indicated by a letter, as representing (1) a posting to a general ledger account, (2) a posting to a subsidiary ledger account, or (3) that no posting is required.

| | | | PURCHASES JOURNAL | | | | | Page 49 |
|---|---|---|---|---|---|---|---|---|
| Date | Account Credited | Post. Ref. | Accounts Payable Cr. | Store Supplies Dr. | Office Supplies Dr. | Other Accounts Dr. | Post. Ref. | Amount |
| 2012 | | | | | | | | |
| Mar. 4 | Arrow Supply Co. | (a) | 4,000 | | 4,000 | | | |
| 6 | Coastal Equipment Co. | (b) | 5,325 | | | Warehouse Equipment | (c) | 5,325 |
| 9 | Thorton Products | (d) | 1,875 | 1,600 | 275 | | | |
| 14 | Office Warehouse | (e) | 2,200 | | | Office Equipment | (f) | 2,200 |
| 20 | Office Warehouse | (g) | 6,000 | | | Store Equipment | (h) | 6,000 |
| 25 | Monroe Supply Co. | (i) | 2,740 | 2,740 | | | | |
| 30 | | | 22,140 | 4,340 | 4,275 | | | 13,525 |
| | | | (j) | (k) | (l) | | | (m) |

### EX C-6 Identify postings from cash payments journal

Using the following cash payments journal, identify each of the posting references, indicated by a letter, as representing (1) a posting to a general ledger account, (2) a posting to a subsidiary ledger account, or (3) that no posting is required.

| | | | CASH PAYMENTS JOURNAL | | | Page 46 |
|---|---|---|---|---|---|---|
| Date | Ck. No. | Account Debited | Post. Ref. | Other Accounts Dr. | Accounts Payable Dr. | Cash Cr. |
| 2012 | | | | | | |
| Aug. 3 | 611 | Energy Systems Co. | (a) | | 4,000 | 4,000 |
| 5 | 612 | Utilities Expense | (b) | 310 | | 310 |
| 10 | 613 | Prepaid Rent | (c) | 3,200 | | 3,200 |
| 16 | 614 | Flowers to Go, Inc. | (d) | | 1,250 | 1,250 |
| 19 | 615 | Advertising Expense | (e) | 640 | | 640 |
| 22 | 616 | Office Equipment | (f) | 3,600 | | 3,600 |
| 25 | 617 | Office Supplies | (g) | 250 | | 250 |
| 26 | 618 | Echo Co. | (h) | | 5,500 | 5,500 |
| 31 | 619 | Salaries Expense | (i) | 1,750 | | 1,750 |
| 31 | | | | 9,750 | 10,750 | 20,500 |
| | | | | (j) | (k) | (l) |

**EX C-7 Identify transactions in accounts payable ledger account**

The debits and credits from three related transactions are presented in the following creditor's account taken from the accounts payable ledger.

**NAME** *Apex Performance Co.*
**ADDRESS** *101 W. Stratford Ave.*

| Date | Item | Post. Ref. | Debit | Credit | Balance |
|------|------|-----------|-------|--------|---------|
| 2012 | | | | | |
| Mar. 6 | | P44 | | 12,000 | 12,000 |
| 11 | | J12 | 400 | | 11,600 |
| 16 | | CP23 | 11,600 | | — |

Describe each transaction, and identify the source of each posting.

## Problems

✔ 1. Revenue journal, total fees earned, $830

**PR C-1 Revenue journal; accounts receivable and general ledgers**

Newton Learning Centers was established on October 20, 2012, to provide educational services. The services provided during the remainder of the month are as follows:

Oct. 21. Issued Invoice No. 1 to J. Dunlop for $60 on account.

22. Issued Invoice No. 2 to K. Todd for $255 on account.

24. Issued Invoice No. 3 to T. Patrick for $55 on account.

25. Provided educational services, $100, to K. Todd in exchange for educational supplies.

27. Issued Invoice No. 4 to F. Mintz for $150 on account.

30. Issued Invoice No. 5 to D. Chase for $135 on account.

30. Issued Invoice No. 6 to K. Todd for $105 on account.

31. Issued Invoice No. 7 to T. Patrick for $70 on account.

**Instructions**

1. Journalize the transactions for October, using a single-column revenue journal and a two-column general journal. Post to the following customer accounts in the accounts receivable ledger, and insert the balance immediately after recording each entry: D. Chase; J. Dunlop; F. Mintz; T. Patrick; K. Todd.

2. Post the revenue journal and the general journal to the following accounts in the general ledger, inserting the account balances only after the last postings:

    12 Accounts Receivable
    13 Supplies
    41 Fees Earned

3. a. What is the sum of the balances of the accounts in the subsidiary ledger at October 31?

    b. What is the balance of the controlling account at October 31?

4. Assume Newton Learning Centers began using a computerized accounting system to record the sales transactions on November 1. What are some of the benefits of the computerized system over the manual system?

✔ 3. Total cash receipts, $32,870

**PR C-2 Revenue and cash receipts journals; accounts receivable and general ledgers**

Transactions related to revenue and cash receipts completed by Aspen Architects Co. during the period June 2–30, 2012, are as follows:

June 2. Issued Invoice No. 793 to Nickle Co., $4,900.

5. Received cash from Mendez Co. for the balance owed on its account.

6. Issued Invoice No. 794 to Preston Co., $1,760.

June 13. Issued Invoice No. 795 to Shilo Co., $2,630.

*Post revenue and collections to the accounts receivable subsidiary ledger.*

15. Received cash from Preston Co. for the balance owed on June 1.

16. Issued Invoice No. 796 to Preston Co., $5,500.

*Post revenue and collections to the accounts receivable subsidiary ledger.*

19. Received cash from Nickle Co. for the balance due on invoice of June 2.

20. Received cash from Preston Co. for invoice of June 6.

22. Issued Invoice No. 797 to Mendez Co., $7,240.

25. Received $2,000 note receivable in partial settlement of the balance due on the Shilo Co. account.

30. Recorded cash fees earned, $12,350.

*Post revenue and collections to the accounts receivable subsidiary ledger.*

**Instructions**

1. Insert the following balances in the general ledger as of June 1:

| 11 | Cash | $11,350 |
|----|------|---------|
| 12 | Accounts Receivable | 13,860 |
| 14 | Notes Receivable | 6,000 |
| 41 | Fees Earned | — |

2. Insert the following balances in the accounts receivable subsidiary ledger as of June 1:

| Mendez Co. | $7,970 |
|------------|--------|
| Nickle Co. | — |
| Preston Co. | 5,890 |
| Shilo Co. | — |

3. Prepare a single-column revenue journal (p. 40) and a cash receipts journal (p. 36). Use the following column headings for the cash receipts journal: Fees Earned Cr., Accounts Receivable Cr., and Cash Dr. The Fees Earned column is used to record cash fees. Insert a check mark (✓) in the Post. Ref. column when recording cash fees.

4. Using the two special journals and the two-column general journal (p. 1), journalize the transactions for June. Post to the accounts receivable subsidiary ledger, and insert the balances at the points indicated in the narrative of transactions. Determine the balance in the customer's account before recording a cash receipt.

5. Total each of the columns of the special journals, and post the individual entries and totals to the general ledger. Insert account balances after the last posting.

6. Determine that the subsidiary ledger agrees with the controlling account in the general ledger.

7. Why would an automated system omit postings to a control account as performed in step 5 for Accounts Receivable?

---

✔ **5b. Total accounts payable credit, $14,195**

**PR C-3   Purchases, accounts payable account, and accounts payable ledger**

English Garden Landscaping designs and installs landscaping. The landscape designers and office staff use office supplies, while field supplies (rock, bark, etc.) are used in the actual landscaping. Purchases on account completed by English Garden Landscaping during January 2012 are as follows:

Jan.  2. Purchased office supplies on account from Meade Co., $350.

5. Purchased office equipment on account from Peach Computers Co., $3,150.

9. Purchased office supplies on account from Executive Office Supply Co., $290.

13. Purchased field supplies on account from Yamura Co., $1,140.

14. Purchased field supplies on account from Naples Co., $2,680.

17. Purchased field supplies on account from Yamura Co., $1,050.

Jan. 24. Purchased field supplies on account from Naples Co., $3,240.

29. Purchased office supplies on account from Executive Office Supply Co., $260.

31. Purchased field supplies on account from Naples Co., $1,000.

**Instructions**

1. Insert the following balances in the general ledger as of January 1:

| | | |
|---|---|---|
| 14 | Field Supplies | $ 5,920 |
| 15 | Office Supplies | 750 |
| 18 | Office Equipment | 12,300 |
| 21 | Accounts Payable | 1,035 |

2. Insert the following balances in the accounts payable subsidiary ledger as of January 1:

| | |
|---|---|
| Executive Office Supply Co. | $340 |
| Meade Co. | 695 |
| Naples Co. | — |
| Peach Computers Co. | — |
| Yamura Co. | — |

3. Journalize the transactions for January, using a purchases journal (p. 30) similar to the one illustrated in this chapter. Prepare the purchases journal with columns for Accounts Payable, Field Supplies, Office Supplies, and Other Accounts. Post to the creditor accounts in the accounts payable subsidiary ledger immediately after each entry.

4. Post the purchases journal to the accounts in the general ledger.

5. a. What is the sum of the balances in the subsidiary ledger at January 31?

   b. What is the balance of the controlling account at January 31?

6. What type of e-commerce application would be used to plan and coordinate suppliers?

✔ 1. Total cash payments, $93,615

**PR C-4   Purchases and cash payments journals; accounts payable and general ledgers**

Green Mountain Water Testing Service was established on November 16, 2012. Green Mountain uses field equipment and field supplies (chemicals and other supplies) to analyze water for unsafe contaminants in streams, lakes, and ponds. Transactions related to purchases and cash payments during the remainder of November are as follows:

Nov. 16. Issued Check No. 1 in payment of rent for the remainder of November, $1,700.

16. Purchased field supplies on account from Hydro Supply Co., $4,380.

16. Purchased field equipment on account from Test-Rite Equipment Co., $16,900.

17. Purchased office supplies on account from Best Office Supply Co., $375.

19. Issued Check No. 2 in payment of field supplies, $2,560, and office supplies, $300.

   *Post the journals to the accounts payable subsidiary ledger.*

23. Purchased office supplies on account from Best Office Supply Co., $580.

23. Issued Check No. 3 to purchase land, $45,000.

24. Issued Check No. 4 to Hydro Supply Co. in payment of invoice, $4,380.

26. Issued Check No. 5 to Test-Rite Equipment Co. in payment of invoice, $16,900.

   *Post the journals to the accounts payable subsidiary ledger.*

30. Acquired land in exchange for field equipment having a cost of $8,000.

30. Purchased field supplies on account from Hydro Supply Co., $5,900.

30. Issued Check No. 6 to Best Office Supply Co. in payment of invoice, $375.

30. Purchased the following from Test-Rite Equipment Co. on account: field supplies, $900, and field equipment, $3,700.

30. Issued Check No. 7 in payment of salaries, $22,400.

   *Post the journals to the accounts payable subsidiary ledger.*

**Instructions**

1. Journalize the transactions for November. Use a purchases journal and a cash payments journal, similar to those illustrated in this chapter, and a two-column general journal. Use debit columns for Field Supplies, Office Supplies, and Other Accounts in the purchases journal. Refer to the following partial chart of accounts:

| | | | |
|---|---|---|---|
| 11 | Cash | 19 | Land |
| 14 | Field Supplies | 21 | Accounts Payable |
| 15 | Office Supplies | 61 | Salary Expense |
| 17 | Field Equipment | 71 | Rent Expense |

At the points indicated in the narrative of transactions, post to the following accounts in the accounts payable subsidiary ledger:

Best Office Supply Co.

Hydro Supply Co.

Test-Rite Equipment Co.

2. Post the individual entries (Other Accounts columns of the purchases journal and the cash payments journal and both columns of the general journal) to the appropriate general ledger accounts.

3. Total each of the columns of the purchases journal and the cash payments journal, and post the appropriate totals to the general ledger. (Because the problem does not include transactions related to cash receipts, the cash account in the ledger will have a credit balance.)

4. Sum the balances of the accounts payable subsidiary ledger.

5. Why might Green Mountain consider using a subsidiary ledger for the field equipment?

---

✔ 2. Total cash receipts, $58,160

**PR C-5    All journals and general ledger; trial balance**

The transactions completed by Sure N' Safe Courier Company during July 2012, the first month of the fiscal year, were as follows:

July    1.  Issued Check No. 610 for July rent, $7,500.

2.  Issued Invoice No. 940 to Capps Co., $2,680.

3.  Received check for $6,700 from Trimble Co. in payment of account.

5.  Purchased a vehicle on account from Browning Transportation, $34,600.

6.  Purchased office equipment on account from Austin Computer Co., $5,200.

6.  Issued Invoice No. 941 to Dawar Co., $5,970.

9.  Issued Check No. 611 for fuel expense, $900.

10.  Received check from Sing Co. in payment of $3,980 invoice.

10.  Issued Check No. 612 for $1,040 to Office To Go Inc. in payment of invoice.

10.  Issued Invoice No. 942 to Joy Co., $2,640.

11.  Issued Check No. 613 for $3,670 to Essential Supply Co. in payment of account.

11.  Issued Check No. 614 for $725 to Porter Co. in payment of account.

12.  Received check from Capps Co. in payment of $2,680 invoice.

13.  Issued Check No. 615 to Browning Transportation in payment of $34,600 balance.

16.  Issued Check No. 616 for $42,100 for cash purchase of a vehicle.

16.  Cash fees earned for July 1–16, $18,900.

17.  Issued Check No. 617 for miscellaneous administrative expense, $750.

18.  Purchased maintenance supplies on account from Essential Supply Co., $1,950.

19.  Purchased the following on account from McClain Co.: maintenance supplies, $1,900; office supplies, $470.

20.  Issued Check No. 618 in payment of advertising expense, $2,350.

20.  Used $4,000 maintenance supplies to repair delivery vehicles.

July 23. Purchased office supplies on account from Office To Go Inc., $600.

24. Issued Invoice No. 943 to Sing Co., $7,000.

24. Issued Check No. 619 to J. Bourne as a personal withdrawal, $3,000.

25. Issued Invoice No. 944 to Dawar Co., $6,450.

25. Received check for $4,500 from Trimble Co. in payment of balance.

26. Issued Check No. 620 to Austin Computer Co. in payment of $5,200 invoice of July 6.

30. Issued Check No. 621 for monthly salaries as follows: driver salaries, $18,900; office salaries, $8,300.

31. Cash fees earned for July 17–31, $21,400.

31. Issued Check No. 622 in payment for office supplies, $800.

## Instructions

1. Enter the following account balances in the general ledger as of July 1:

| | | | | | |
|---|---|---|---|---|---|
| 11 | Cash | $167,900 | 32 | J. Bourne, Drawing | — |
| 12 | Accounts Receivable | 15,180 | 41 | Fees Earned | — |
| 14 | Maintenance Supplies | 10,850 | 51 | Driver Salaries Expense | — |
| 15 | Office Supplies | 4,900 | 52 | Maintenance Supplies Exp. | — |
| 16 | Office Equipment | 28,500 | 53 | Fuel Expense | — |
| 17 | Accum. Depr.—Office Equip. | 6,900 | 61 | Office Salaries Expense | — |
| 18 | Vehicles | 95,900 | 62 | Rent Expense | — |
| 19 | Accum. Depr.—Vehicles | 14,700 | 63 | Advertising Expense | — |
| 21 | Accounts Payable | 5,435 | 64 | Miscellaneous Administrative Expense | — |
| 31 | J. Bourne, Capital | 296,195 | | | |

2. Journalize the transactions for July 2012, using the following journals similar to those illustrated in this chapter: cash receipts journal (p. 31), purchases journal (p. 37, with columns for Accounts Payable, Maintenance Supplies, Office Supplies, and Other Accounts), single-column revenue journal (p. 35), cash payments journal (p. 34), and two-column general journal (p. 1). Assume that the daily postings to the individual accounts in the accounts payable ledger and the accounts receivable ledger have been made.

3. Post the appropriate individual entries to the general ledger.

4. Total each of the columns of the special journals, and post the appropriate totals to the general ledger; insert the account balances.

5. Prepare a trial balance.

# NIKE INC ( NKE )

ONE BOWERMAN DR
BEAVERTON, OR, 97005–6453
503–671–3173
www.nikebiz.com

## 10–K

Annual report pursuant to section 13 and 15(d)
Filed on 7/20/2010
Filed Period 5/31/2010

**THOMSON REUTERS**

Westlaw. BUSINESS

An Internal Audit department reviews the results of its work with the Audit Committee of the Board of Directors, presently consisting of three outside directors. The Audit Committee is responsible for the appointment of the independent registered public accounting firm and reviews with the independent registered public accounting firm, management and the internal audit staff, the scope and the results of the annual examination, the effectiveness of the accounting control system and other matters relating to the financial affairs of NIKE as they deem appropriate. The independent registered public accounting firm and the internal auditors have full access to the Committee, with and without the presence of management, to discuss any appropriate matters.

**Management's Annual Report on Internal Control Over Financial Reporting**

Management is responsible for establishing and maintaining adequate internal control over financial reporting, as such term is defined in Rule 13a–15(f) and Rule 15d–15(f) of the Securities Exchange Act of 1934, as amended. Internal control over financial reporting is a process designed to provide reasonable assurance regarding the reliability of financial reporting and the preparation of the financial statements for external purposes in accordance with generally accepted accounting principles in the United States of America. Internal control over financial reporting includes those policies and procedures that: (i) pertain to the maintenance of records that, in reasonable detail, accurately and fairly reflect the transactions and dispositions of assets of the company; (ii) provide reasonable assurance that transactions are recorded as necessary to permit preparation of financial statements in accordance with generally accepted accounting principles, and that receipts and expenditures of the company are being made only in accordance with authorizations of our management and directors; and (iii) provide reasonable assurance regarding prevention or timely detection of unauthorized acquisition, use or disposition of assets of the company that could have a material effect on the financial statements.

While "reasonable assurance" is a high level of assurance, it does not mean absolute assurance. Because of its inherent limitations, internal control over financial reporting may not prevent or detect every misstatement and instance of fraud. Controls are susceptible to manipulation, especially in instances of fraud caused by the collusion of two or more people, including our senior management. Also, projections of any evaluation of effectiveness to future periods are subject to the risk that controls may become inadequate because of changes in conditions, or that the degree of compliance with the policies or procedures may deteriorate.

Under the supervision and with the participation of our Chief Executive Officer and Chief Financial Officer, our management conducted an evaluation of the effectiveness of our internal control over financial reporting based upon the framework in *Internal Control — Integrated Framework* issued by the Committee of Sponsoring Organizations of the Treadway Commission (COSO). Based on the results of our evaluation, our management concluded that our internal control over financial reporting was effective as of May 31, 2010.

PricewaterhouseCoopers LLP, an independent registered public accounting firm, has audited (1) the consolidated financial statements and (2) the effectiveness of our internal control over financial reporting as of May 31, 2010, as stated in their report herein.

Mark G. Parker
Chief Executive Officer and President

Donald W. Blair
Chief Financial Officer

### REPORT OF INDEPENDENT REGISTERED PUBLIC ACCOUNTING FIRM

To the Board of Directors and
Shareholders of NIKE, Inc.:

In our opinion, the consolidated financial statements listed in the index appearing under Item 15(a)(1) present fairly, in all material respects, the financial position of NIKE, Inc. and its subsidiaries at May 31, 2010 and 2009, and the results of their operations and their cash flows for each of the three years in the period ended May 31, 2010 in conformity with accounting principles generally accepted in the United States of America. In addition, in our opinion, the financial statement schedule listed in the appendix appearing under Item 15(a)(2) presents fairly, in all material respects, the information set forth therein when read in conjunction with the related consolidated financial statements. Also in our opinion, the Company maintained, in all material respects, effective internal control over financial reporting as of May 31, 2010, based on criteria established in *Internal Control — Integrated Framework* issued by the Committee of Sponsoring Organizations of the Treadway Commission (COSO). The Company's management is responsible for these financial statements and financial statement schedule, for maintaining effective internal control over financial reporting and for its assessment of the effectiveness of internal control over financial reporting, included in Management's Annual Report on Internal Control Over Financial Reporting appearing under Item 8. Our responsibility is to express opinions on these financial statements, on the financial statement schedule, and on the Company's internal control over financial reporting based on our integrated audits. We conducted our audits in accordance with the standards of the Public Company Accounting Oversight Board (United States). Those standards require that we plan and perform the audits to obtain reasonable assurance about whether the financial statements are free of material misstatement and whether effective internal control over financial reporting was maintained in all material respects. Our audits of the financial statements included examining, on a test basis, evidence supporting the amounts and disclosures in the financial statements, assessing the accounting principles used and significant estimates made by management, and evaluating the overall financial statement presentation. Our audit of internal control over financial reporting included obtaining an understanding of internal control over financial reporting, assessing the risk that a material weakness exists, and testing and evaluating the design and operating effectiveness of internal control based on the assessed risk. Our audits also included performing such other procedures as we considered necessary in the circumstances. We believe that our audits provide a reasonable basis for our opinions.

A company's internal control over financial reporting is a process designed to provide reasonable assurance regarding the reliability of financial reporting and the preparation of financial statements for external purposes in accordance with generally accepted accounting principles. A company's internal control over financial reporting includes those policies and procedures that (i) pertain to the maintenance of records that, in reasonable detail, accurately and fairly reflect the transactions and dispositions of the assets of the company; (ii) provide reasonable assurance that transactions are recorded as necessary to permit preparation of financial statements in accordance with generally accepted accounting principles, and that receipts and expenditures of the company are being made only in accordance with authorizations of management and directors of the company; and (iii) provide reasonable assurance regarding prevention or timely detection of unauthorized acquisition, use, or disposition of the company's assets that could have a material effect on the financial statements.

Because of its inherent limitations, internal control over financial reporting may not prevent or detect misstatements. Also, projections of any evaluation of effectiveness to future periods are subject to the risk that controls may become inadequate because of changes in conditions, or that the degree of compliance with the policies or procedures may deteriorate.

/s/   PRICEWATERHOUSECOOPERS LLP

Portland, Oregon
July 20, 2010

55

**NIKE, INC.**
**CONSOLIDATED STATEMENTS OF INCOME**

| | Year Ended May 31, | | |
| --- | --- | --- | --- |
| | 2010 | 2009 | 2008 |
| | (In millions, except per share data) | | |
| Revenues | $19,014.0 | $19,176.1 | $18,627.0 |
| Cost of sales | 10,213.6 | 10,571.7 | 10,239.6 |
| Gross margin | 8,800.4 | 8,604.4 | 8,387.4 |
| Selling and administrative expense | 6,326.4 | 6,149.6 | 5,953.7 |
| Restructuring charges (Note 16) | — | 195.0 | — |
| Goodwill impairment (Note 4) | — | 199.3 | — |
| Intangible and other asset impairment (Note 4) | — | 202.0 | — |
| Interest expense (income), net (Notes 6, 7 and 8) | 6.3 | (9.5) | (77.1) |
| Other (income) expense, net (Notes 17 and 18) | (49.2) | (88.5) | 7.9 |
| Income before income taxes | 2,516.9 | 1,956.5 | 2,502.9 |
| Income taxes (Note 9) | 610.2 | 469.8 | 619.5 |
| Net income | $ 1,906.7 | $ 1,486.7 | $ 1,883.4 |
| Basic earnings per common share (Notes 1 and 12) | $    3.93 | $    3.07 | $    3.80 |
| Diluted earnings per common share (Notes 1 and 12) | $    3.86 | $    3.03 | $    3.74 |
| Dividends declared per common share | $    1.06 | $    0.98 | $    0.875 |

The accompanying notes to consolidated financial statements are an integral part of this statement.

**NIKE, INC.**
**CONSOLIDATED BALANCE SHEETS**

| | May 31, | |
|---|---|---|
| | 2010 | 2009 |
| | (In millions) | |

### ASSETS

| | 2010 | 2009 |
|---|---|---|
| Current assets: | | |
| Cash and equivalents | $ 3,079.1 | $ 2,291.1 |
| Short−term investments (Note 6) | 2,066.8 | 1,164.0 |
| Accounts receivable, net (Note 1) | 2,649.8 | 2,883.9 |
| Inventories (Notes 1 and 2) | 2,040.8 | 2,357.0 |
| Deferred income taxes (Note 9) | 248.8 | 272.4 |
| Prepaid expenses and other current assets | 873.9 | 765.6 |
| Total current assets | 10,959.2 | 9,734.0 |
| Property, plant and equipment, net (Note 3) | 1,931.9 | 1,957.7 |
| Identifiable intangible assets, net (Note 4) | 467.0 | 467.4 |
| Goodwill (Note 4) | 187.6 | 193.5 |
| Deferred income taxes and other assets (Notes 9 and 18) | 873.6 | 897.0 |
| Total assets | $ 14,419.3 | $ 13,249.6 |

### LIABILITIES AND SHAREHOLDERS' EQUITY

| | 2010 | 2009 |
|---|---|---|
| Current liabilities: | | |
| Current portion of long−term debt (Note 8) | $ 7.4 | $ 32.0 |
| Notes payable (Note 7) | 138.6 | 342.9 |
| Accounts payable (Note 7) | 1,254.5 | 1,031.9 |
| Accrued liabilities (Notes 5 and 18) | 1,904.4 | 1,783.9 |
| Income taxes payable (Note 9) | 59.3 | 86.3 |
| Total current liabilities | 3,364.2 | 3,277.0 |
| Long−term debt (Note 8) | 445.8 | 437.2 |
| Deferred income taxes and other liabilities (Notes 9 and 18) | 855.3 | 842.0 |
| Commitments and contingencies (Note 15) | — | — |
| Redeemable Preferred Stock (Note 10) | 0.3 | 0.3 |
| Shareholders' equity: | | |
| Common stock at stated value (Note 11): | | |
| Class A convertible — 90.0 and 95.3 shares outstanding | 0.1 | 0.1 |
| Class B — 394.0 and 390.2 shares outstanding | 2.7 | 2.7 |
| Capital in excess of stated value | 3,440.6 | 2,871.4 |
| Accumulated other comprehensive income (Note 14) | 214.8 | 367.5 |
| Retained earnings | 6,095.5 | 5,451.4 |
| Total shareholders' equity | 9,753.7 | 8,693.1 |
| Total liabilities and shareholders' equity | $ 14,419.3 | $ 13,249.6 |

The accompanying notes to consolidated financial statements are an integral part of this statement.

57

**NIKE, INC.**
**CONSOLIDATED STATEMENTS OF CASH FLOWS**

| | Year Ended May 31, | | |
|---|---|---|---|
| | 2010 | 2009 | 2008 |
| | | (In millions) | |
| **Cash provided by operations:** | | | |
| Net income | $ 1,906.7 | $ 1,486.7 | $ 1,883.4 |
| Income charges (credits) not affecting cash: | | | |
| Depreciation | 323.7 | 335.0 | 303.6 |
| Deferred income taxes | 8.3 | (294.1) | (300.6) |
| Stock–based compensation (Note 11) | 159.0 | 170.6 | 141.0 |
| Impairment of goodwill, intangibles and other assets (Note 4) | — | 401.3 | — |
| Gain on divestitures (Note 17) | — | — | (60.6) |
| Amortization and other | 71.8 | 48.3 | 17.9 |
| Changes in certain working capital components and other assets and liabilities excluding the impact of acquisition and divestitures: | | | |
| Decrease (increase) in accounts receivable | 181.7 | (238.0) | (118.3) |
| Decrease (increase) in inventories | 284.6 | 32.2 | (249.8) |
| (Increase) decrease in prepaid expenses and other current assets | (69.6) | 14.1 | (11.2) |
| Increase (decrease) in accounts payable, accrued liabilities and income taxes payable | 298.0 | (220.0) | 330.9 |
| Cash provided by operations | 3,164.2 | 1,736.1 | 1,936.3 |
| **Cash used by investing activities:** | | | |
| Purchases of short–term investments | (3,724.4) | (2,908.7) | (1,865.6) |
| Maturities and sales of short–term investments | 2,787.6 | 2,390.0 | 2,246.0 |
| Additions to property, plant and equipment | (335.1) | (455.7) | (449.2) |
| Disposals of property, plant and equipment | 10.1 | 32.0 | 1.9 |
| Increase in other assets, net of other liabilities | (11.2) | (47.0) | (21.8) |
| Settlement of net investment hedges | 5.5 | 191.3 | (76.0) |
| Acquisition of subsidiary, net of cash acquired (Note 4) | — | — | (571.1) |
| Proceeds from divestitures (Note 17) | — | — | 246.0 |
| Cash used by investing activities | (1,267.5) | (798.1) | (489.8) |
| **Cash used by financing activities:** | | | |
| Reductions in long–term debt, including current portion | (32.2) | (6.8) | (35.2) |
| (Decrease) increase in notes payable | (205.4) | 177.1 | 63.7 |
| Proceeds from exercise of stock options and other stock issuances | 364.5 | 186.6 | 343.3 |
| Excess tax benefits from share–based payment arrangements | 58.5 | 25.1 | 63.0 |
| Repurchase of common stock | (741.2) | (649.2) | (1,248.0) |
| Dividends — common and preferred | (505.4) | (466.7) | (412.9) |
| Cash used by financing activities | (1,061.2) | (733.9) | (1,226.1) |
| Effect of exchange rate changes | (47.5) | (46.9) | 56.8 |
| Net increase in cash and equivalents | 788.0 | 157.2 | 277.2 |
| Cash and equivalents, beginning of year | 2,291.1 | 2,133.9 | 1,856.7 |
| Cash and equivalents, end of year | $ 3,079.1 | $ 2,291.1 | $ 2,133.9 |
| **Supplemental disclosure of cash flow information:** | | | |
| Cash paid during the year for: | | | |
| Interest, net of capitalized interest | $    48.4 | $    46.7 | $    44.1 |
| Income taxes | 537.2 | 765.2 | 717.5 |
| Dividends declared and not paid | 130.7 | 121.4 | 112.9 |

The accompanying notes to consolidated financial statements are an integral part of this statement.

## NIKE, INC.
## CONSOLIDATED STATEMENTS OF SHAREHOLDERS' EQUITY

| | Common Stock Class A Shares | Amount | Common Stock Class B Shares | Amount | Capital in Excess of Stated Value | Accumulated Other Comprehensive Income | Retained Earnings | Total |
|---|---|---|---|---|---|---|---|---|
| | | | | | (In millions, except per share data) | | | |
| **Balance at May 31, 2007** | 117.6 | $ 0.1 | 384.1 | $ 2.7 | $ 1,960.0 | $ 177.4 | $ 4,885.2 | $ 7,025.4 |
| Stock options exercised | | | 9.1 | | 372.2 | | | 372.2 |
| Conversion to Class B Common Stock | (20.8) | | 20.8 | | | | | |
| Repurchase of Class B Common Stock | | | (20.6) | | (12.3) | | (1,235.7) | (1,248.0) |
| Dividends on Common stock ($0.875 per share) | | | | | | | (432.8) | (432.8) |
| Issuance of shares to employees | | | 1.0 | | 39.2 | | | 39.2 |
| Stock−based compensation (Note 11): | | | | | 141.0 | | | 141.0 |
| Forfeiture of shares from employees | | | (0.1) | | (2.3) | | (1.1) | (3.4) |
| Comprehensive income (Note 14): | | | | | | | | |
| Net income | | | | | | | 1,883.4 | 1,883.4 |
| Other comprehensive income: | | | | | | | | |
| Foreign currency translation and other (net of tax expense of $101.6) | | | | | | 211.9 | | 211.9 |
| Realized foreign currency translation gain due to divestiture (Note 17) | | | | | | (46.3) | | (46.3) |
| Net loss on cash flow hedges (net of tax benefit of $67.7) | | | | | | (175.8) | | (175.8) |
| Net loss on net investment hedges (net of tax benefit of $25.1) | | | | | | (43.5) | | (43.5) |
| Reclassification to net income of previously deferred losses related to hedge derivatives (net of tax benefit of $49.6) | | | | | | 127.7 | | 127.7 |
| Total Comprehensive income | | | | | | 74.0 | 1,883.4 | 1,957.4 |
| Adoption of FIN 48 (Note 1 and 9) | | | | | | | (15.6) | (15.6) |
| Adoption of EITF 06−2 Sabbaticals (net of tax benefit of $6.2) | | | | | | | (10.1) | (10.1) |
| **Balance at May 31, 2008** | 96.8 | $ 0.1 | 394.3 | $ 2.7 | $ 2,497.8 | $ 251.4 | $ 5,073.3 | $ 7,825.3 |
| Stock options exercised | | | 4.0 | | 167.2 | | | 167.2 |
| Conversion to Class B Common Stock | (1.5) | | 1.5 | | | | | — |
| Repurchase of Class B Common Stock | | | (10.6) | | (6.3) | | (632.7) | (639.0) |
| Dividends on Common stock ($0.98 per share) | | | | | | | (475.2) | (475.2) |
| Issuance of shares to employees | | | 1.1 | | 45.4 | | | 45.4 |
| Stock−based compensation (Note 11): | | | | | 170.6 | | | 170.6 |
| Forfeiture of shares from employees | | | (0.1) | | (3.3) | | (0.7) | (4.0) |
| Comprehensive income (Note 14): | | | | | | | | |
| Net income | | | | | | | 1,486.7 | 1,486.7 |
| Other comprehensive income: | | | | | | | | |
| Foreign currency translation and other (net of tax benefit of $177.5) | | | | | | (335.3) | | (335.3) |
| Net gain on cash flow hedges (net of tax expense of $167.5) | | | | | | 453.6 | | 453.6 |
| Net gain on net investment hedges (net of tax expense of $55.4) | | | | | | 106.0 | | 106.0 |
| Reclassification to net income of previously deferred net gains related to hedge derivatives (net of tax expense of $39.6) | | | | | | (108.2) | | (108.2) |
| Total Comprehensive income | | | | | | 116.1 | 1,486.7 | 1,602.8 |
| **Balance at May 31, 2009** | 95.3 | $ 0.1 | 390.2 | $ 2.7 | $ 2,871.4 | $ 367.5 | $ 5,451.4 | $ 8,693.1 |
| Stock options exercised | | | 8.6 | | 379.6 | | | 379.6 |
| Conversion to Class B Common Stock | (5.3) | | 5.3 | | | | | — |
| Repurchase of Class B Common Stock | | | (11.3) | | (6.8) | | (747.5) | (754.3) |
| Dividends on Common stock ($1.06 per share) | | | | | | | (514.8) | (514.8) |
| Issuance of shares to employees | | | 1.3 | | 40.0 | | | 40.0 |
| Stock−based compensation (Note 11): | | | | | 159.0 | | | 159.0 |
| Forfeiture of shares from employees | | | (0.1) | | (2.6) | | (0.3) | (2.9) |
| Comprehensive income (Note 14): | | | | | | | | |
| Net income | | | | | | | 1,906.7 | 1,906.7 |
| Other comprehensive income: | | | | | | | | |
| Foreign currency translation and other (net of tax benefit of $71.8) | | | | | | (159.2) | | (159.2) |
| Net gain on cash flow hedges (net of tax expense of $27.8) | | | | | | 87.1 | | 87.1 |
| Net gain on net investment hedges (net of tax expense of $21.2) | | | | | | 44.8 | | 44.8 |
| Reclassification to net income of previously deferred net gains related to hedge derivatives (net of tax expense of $41.7) | | | | | | (121.6) | | (121.6) |
| Reclassification of ineffective hedge gains to net income (net of tax expense of $1.4) | | | | | | (3.8) | | (3.8) |
| Total Comprehensive income | | | | | | (152.7) | 1,906.7 | 1,754.0 |
| **Balance at May 31, 2010** | 90.0 | $ 0.1 | 394.0 | $ 2.7 | $ 3,440.6 | $ 214.8 | $ 6,095.5 | $ 9,753.7 |

The accompanying notes to consolidated financial statements are an integral part of this statement.

59

**NIKE, INC.**
**NOTES TO CONSOLIDATED FINANCIAL STATEMENTS**

### Note 1 — Summary of Significant Accounting Policies

#### Description of Business

NIKE, Inc. is a worldwide leader in the design, marketing and distribution of athletic and sports–inspired footwear, apparel, equipment and accessories. Wholly–owned NIKE subsidiaries include Cole Haan, which designs, markets and distributes dress and casual shoes, handbags, accessories and coats; Converse Inc., which designs, markets and distributes athletic and causal footwear, apparel and accessories; Hurley International LLC, which designs, markets and distributes action sports and youth lifestyle footwear, apparel and accessories; and Umbro Ltd., which designs, distributes and licenses athletic and casual footwear, apparel and equipment, primarily for the sport of soccer.

#### Basis of Consolidation

The consolidated financial statements include the accounts of NIKE, Inc. and its subsidiaries (the "Company"). All significant intercompany transactions and balances have been eliminated.

#### Recognition of Revenues

Wholesale revenues are recognized when title passes and the risks and rewards of ownership have passed to the customer, based on the terms of sale. This occurs upon shipment or upon receipt by the customer depending on the country of the sale and the agreement with the customer. Retail store revenues are recorded at the time of sale. Provisions for sales discounts, returns and miscellaneous claims from customers are made at the time of sale. As of May 31, 2010 and 2009, the Company's reserve balances for sales discounts, returns and miscellaneous claims were $370.6 million and $363.6 million, respectively.

#### Shipping and Handling Costs

Shipping and handling costs are expensed as incurred and included in cost of sales.

#### Advertising and Promotion

Advertising production costs are expensed the first time the advertisement is run. Media (TV and print) placement costs are expensed in the month the advertising appears.

A significant amount of the Company's promotional expenses result from payments under endorsement contracts. Accounting for endorsement payments is based upon specific contract provisions. Generally, endorsement payments are expensed on a straight–line basis over the term of the contract after giving recognition to periodic performance compliance provisions of the contracts. Prepayments made under contracts are included in prepaid expenses or other assets depending on the period to which the prepayment applies.

Through cooperative advertising programs, the Company reimburses retail customers for certain costs of advertising the Company's products. The Company records these costs in selling and administrative expense at the point in time when it is obligated to its customers for the costs, which is when the related revenues are recognized. This obligation may arise prior to the related advertisement being run.

Total advertising and promotion expenses were $2,356.4 million, $2,351.3 million, and $2,308.3 million for the years ended May 31, 2010, 2009 and 2008, respectively. Prepaid advertising and promotion expenses recorded in prepaid expenses and other assets totaled $260.7 million and $280.0 million at May 31, 2010 and 2009, respectively.

**NIKE, INC.**

**NOTES TO CONSOLIDATED FINANCIAL STATEMENTS — (Continued)**

### Cash and Equivalents

Cash and equivalents represent cash and short–term, highly liquid investments with maturities of three months or less at date of purchase. The carrying amounts reflected in the consolidated balance sheet for cash and equivalents approximate fair value.

### Short–term Investments

Short–term investments consist of highly liquid investments, primarily commercial paper, U.S. treasury, U.S. agency, and corporate debt securities, with maturities over three months from the date of purchase. Debt securities that the Company has the ability and positive intent to hold to maturity are carried at amortized cost. At May 31, 2010 and 2009, the Company did not hold any short–term investments that were classified as held–to–maturity.

At May 31, 2010 and 2009, short–term investments consisted of available–for–sale securities. Available–for–sale securities are recorded at fair value with unrealized gains and losses reported, net of tax, in other comprehensive income, unless unrealized losses are determined to be other than temporary. The Company considers all available–for–sale securities, including those with maturity dates beyond 12 months, as available to support current operational liquidity needs and therefore classifies all securities with maturity dates beyond three months as current assets within short–term investments on the consolidated balance sheet.

See Note 6 — Fair Value Measurements for more information on the Company's short term investments.

### Allowance for Uncollectible Accounts Receivable

Accounts receivable consists primarily of amounts receivable from customers. We make ongoing estimates relating to the collectability of our accounts receivable and maintain an allowance for estimated losses resulting from the inability of our customers to make required payments. In determining the amount of the allowance, we consider our historical level of credit losses and make judgments about the creditworthiness of significant customers based on ongoing credit evaluations. Accounts receivable with anticipated collection dates greater than 12 months from the balance sheet date and related allowances are considered non–current and recorded in other assets. The allowance for uncollectible accounts receivable was $116.7 million and $110.8 million at May 31, 2010 and 2009, respectively, of which $43.1 million and $36.9 million was classified as long–term and recorded in other assets.

### Inventory Valuation

Inventories are stated at lower of cost or market and valued on a first–in, first–out ("FIFO") or moving average cost basis.

### Property, Plant and Equipment and Depreciation

Property, plant and equipment are recorded at cost. Depreciation for financial reporting purposes is determined on a straight–line basis for buildings and leasehold improvements over 2 to 40 years and for machinery and equipment over 2 to 15 years. Computer software (including, in some cases, the cost of internal labor) is depreciated on a straight–line basis over 3 to 10 years.

### Impairment of Long–Lived Assets

The Company reviews the carrying value of long–lived assets or asset groups to be used in operations whenever events or changes in circumstances indicate that the carrying amount of the assets might not be

**NIKE, INC.**

**NOTES TO CONSOLIDATED FINANCIAL STATEMENTS — (Continued)**

recoverable. Factors that would necessitate an impairment assessment include a significant adverse change in the extent or manner in which an asset is used, a significant adverse change in legal factors or the business climate that could affect the value of the asset, or a significant decline in the observable market value of an asset, among others. If such facts indicate a potential impairment, the Company would assess the recoverability of an asset group by determining if the carrying value of the asset group exceeds the sum of the projected undiscounted cash flows expected to result from the use and eventual disposition of the assets over the remaining economic life of the primary asset in the asset group. If the recoverability test indicates that the carrying value of the asset group is not recoverable, the Company will estimate the fair value of the asset group using appropriate valuation methodologies which would typically include an estimate of discounted cash flows. Any impairment would be measured as the difference between the asset groups carrying amount and its estimated fair value.

*Identifiable Intangible Assets and Goodwill*

The Company performs annual impairment tests on goodwill and intangible assets with indefinite lives in the fourth quarter of each fiscal year, or when events occur or circumstances change that would, more likely than not, reduce the fair value of a reporting unit or an intangible asset with an indefinite life below its carrying value. Events or changes in circumstances that may trigger interim impairment reviews include significant changes in business climate, operating results, planned investments in the reporting unit, or an expectation that the carrying amount may not be recoverable, among other factors. The impairment test requires the Company to estimate the fair value of its reporting units. If the carrying value of a reporting unit exceeds its fair value, the goodwill of that reporting unit is potentially impaired and the Company proceeds to step two of the impairment analysis. In step two of the analysis, the Company measures and records an impairment loss equal to the excess of the carrying value of the reporting unit's goodwill over its implied fair value should such a circumstance arise.

The Company generally bases its measurement of fair value of a reporting unit on a blended analysis of the present value of future discounted cash flows and the market valuation approach. The discounted cash flows model indicates the fair value of the reporting unit based on the present value of the cash flows that the Company expects the reporting unit to generate in the future. The Company's significant estimates in the discounted cash flows model include: its weighted average cost of capital; long−term rate of growth and profitability of the reporting unit's business; and working capital effects. The market valuation approach indicates the fair value of the business based on a comparison of the reporting unit to comparable publicly traded companies in similar lines of business. Significant estimates in the market valuation approach model include identifying similar companies with comparable business factors such as size, growth, profitability, risk and return on investment, and assessing comparable revenue and operating income multiples in estimating the fair value of the reporting unit.

The Company believes the weighted use of discounted cash flows and the market valuation approach is the best method for determining the fair value of its reporting units because these are the most common valuation methodologies used within its industry; and the blended use of both models compensates for the inherent risks associated with either model if used on a stand−alone basis.

Indefinite−lived intangible assets primarily consist of acquired trade names and trademarks. In measuring the fair value for these intangible assets, the Company utilizes the relief−from−royalty method. This method assumes that trade names and trademarks have value to the extent that their owner is relieved of the obligation to pay royalties for the benefits received from them. This method requires the Company to estimate the future revenue for the related brands, the appropriate royalty rate and the weighted average cost of capital.

62

## NIKE, INC.
### NOTES TO CONSOLIDATED FINANCIAL STATEMENTS — (Continued)

*Foreign Currency Translation and Foreign Currency Transactions*

Adjustments resulting from translating foreign functional currency financial statements into U.S. dollars are included in the foreign currency translation adjustment, a component of accumulated other comprehensive income in shareholders' equity.

The Company's global subsidiaries have various assets and liabilities, primarily receivables and payables, that are denominated in currencies other than their functional currency. These balance sheet items are subject to remeasurement, the impact of which is recorded in other (income) expense, net, within our consolidated statement of income.

*Accounting for Derivatives and Hedging Activities*

The Company uses derivative financial instruments to limit exposure to changes in foreign currency exchange rates and interest rates. All derivatives are recorded at fair value on the balance sheet and changes in the fair value of derivative financial instruments are either recognized in other comprehensive income (a component of shareholders' equity), debt or net income depending on the nature of the underlying exposure, whether the derivative is formally designated as a hedge, and, if designated, the extent to which the hedge is effective. The Company classifies the cash flows at settlement from derivatives in the same category as the cash flows from the related hedged items. For undesignated hedges and designated cash flow hedges, this is within the cash provided by operations component of the consolidated statement of cash flows. For designated net investment hedges, this is generally within the cash used by investing activities component of the cash flow statement. As our fair value hedges are receive−fixed, pay−variable interest rate swaps, the cash flows associated with these derivative instruments are periodic interest payments while the swaps are outstanding, which are reflected in net income within the cash provided by operations component of the cash flow statement.

See Note 18 — Risk Management and Derivatives for more information on the Company's risk management program and derivatives.

*Stock−Based Compensation*

The Company estimates the fair value of options granted under the NIKE, Inc. 1990 Stock Incentive Plan (the "1990 Plan") and employees' purchase rights under the Employee Stock Purchase Plans ("ESPPs") using the Black−Scholes option pricing model. The Company recognizes this fair value, net of estimated forfeitures, as selling and administrative expense in the consolidated statements of income over the vesting period using the straight−line method.

See Note 11 — Common Stock and Stock−Based Compensation for more information on the Company's stock programs.

*Income Taxes*

The Company accounts for income taxes using the asset and liability method. This approach requires the recognition of deferred tax assets and liabilities for the expected future tax consequences of temporary differences between the carrying amounts and the tax basis of assets and liabilities. United States income taxes are provided currently on financial statement earnings of non−U.S. subsidiaries that are expected to be repatriated. The Company determines annually the amount of undistributed non−U.S. earnings to invest indefinitely in its non−U.S. operations. The Company recognizes interest and penalties related to income tax matters in income tax expense.

63

Table of Contents

**NIKE, INC.**

**NOTES TO CONSOLIDATED FINANCIAL STATEMENTS — (Continued)**

See Note 9 — Income Taxes for further discussion.

### Earnings Per Share

Basic earnings per common share is calculated by dividing net income by the weighted average number of common shares outstanding during the year. Diluted earnings per common share is calculated by adjusting weighted average outstanding shares, assuming conversion of all potentially dilutive stock options and awards.

See Note 12 — Earnings Per Share for further discussion.

### Management Estimates

The preparation of financial statements in conformity with generally accepted accounting principles requires management to make estimates, including estimates relating to assumptions that affect the reported amounts of assets and liabilities and disclosure of contingent assets and liabilities at the date of financial statements and the reported amounts of revenues and expenses during the reporting period. Actual results could differ from these estimates.

### Reclassifications

Certain prior year amounts have been reclassified to conform to fiscal year 2010 presentation, including a reclassification to investing activities for the settlement of net investment hedges in the consolidated statement of cash flows for the year ended May 31, 2008. These reclassifications had no impact on previously reported results of operations or shareholders' equity and do not affect previously reported cash flows from operations, financing activities or net change in cash and equivalents.

### Recently Adopted Accounting Standards:

In January 2010, the Financial Accounting Standards Board ("FASB") issued guidance to amend the disclosure requirements related to recurring and nonrecurring fair value measurements. The guidance requires additional disclosures about the different classes of assets and liabilities measured at fair value, the valuation techniques and inputs used, the activity in Level 3 fair value measurements, and the transfers between Levels 1, 2, and 3 of the fair value measurement hierarchy. This guidance became effective for the Company beginning March 1, 2010, except for disclosures relating to purchases, sales, issuances and settlements of Level 3 assets and liabilities, which will be effective for the Company beginning June 1, 2011. As this guidance only requires expanded disclosures, the adoption did not and will not impact the Company's consolidated financial position or results of operations. See Note 6 — Fair Value Measurements for disclosure required under this guidance.

In February 2010, the FASB issued amended guidance on subsequent events. Under this amended guidance, SEC filers are no longer required to disclose the date through which subsequent events have been evaluated in originally issued and revised financial statements. This guidance was effective immediately and the Company adopted these new requirements since the third quarter of fiscal 2010.

In June 2009, the FASB established the FASB Accounting Standards Codification (the "Codification") as the single source of authoritative U.S. GAAP for all non-governmental entities. The Codification, which launched July 1, 2009, changes the referencing and organization of accounting guidance. The Codification became effective for the Company beginning September 1, 2009. The issuance of the FASB Codification did not change GAAP and therefore the adoption has only affected how specific references to GAAP literature are disclosed in the notes to the Company's consolidated financial statements.

**NIKE, INC.**

**NOTES TO CONSOLIDATED FINANCIAL STATEMENTS — (Continued)**

In April 2009, the FASB updated guidance related to fair value measurements to clarify the guidance related to measuring fair value in inactive markets, to modify the recognition and measurement of other–than–temporary impairments of debt securities, and to require public companies to disclose the fair values of financial instruments in interim periods. This updated guidance became effective for the Company beginning June 1, 2009. The adoption of this guidance did not have an impact on the Company's consolidated financial position or results of operations. See Note 6 — Fair Value Measurements for disclosure required under the updated guidance.

In June 2008, the FASB issued new accounting guidance applicable when determining whether instruments granted in share–based payment transactions are participating securities. This guidance clarifies that share–based payment awards that entitle their holders to receive non–forfeitable dividends before vesting should be considered participating securities and included in the computation of earnings per share pursuant to the two–class method. This guidance became effective for the Company beginning June 1, 2009. The adoption of this guidance did not have a material impact on the Company's consolidated financial position or results of operations.

In April 2008, the FASB issued amended guidance regarding the determination of the useful life of intangible assets. This guidance amends the factors that should be considered in developing renewal or extension assumptions used to determine the useful life of a recognized intangible asset. The intent of the position is to improve the consistency between the useful life of a recognized intangible asset and the period of expected cash flows used to measure the fair value of the asset. This guidance became effective for the Company beginning June 1, 2009. The adoption of this guidance did not have a material impact on the Company's consolidated financial position or results of operations.

In December 2007, the FASB issued amended guidance regarding business combinations, establishing principles and requirements for how an acquirer recognizes and measures identifiable assets acquired, liabilities assumed, any resulting goodwill, and any non–controlling interest in an acquiree in its financial statements. This guidance also provides for disclosures to enable users of the financial statements to evaluate the nature and financial effects of a business combination. This amended guidance became effective for the Company beginning June 1, 2009. The adoption of this amended guidance did not have an impact on the Company's consolidated financial statements, but could impact the accounting for future business combinations.

In December 2007, the FASB issued new guidance regarding the accounting and reporting for non–controlling interests in subsidiaries. This guidance clarifies that non–controlling interests in subsidiaries should be accounted for as a component of equity separate from the parent's equity. This guidance became effective for the Company beginning June 1, 2009. The adoption of this guidance did not have an impact on the Company's consolidated financial position or results of operations.

*Recently Issued Accounting Standards:*

In October 2009, the FASB issued new standards that revised the guidance for revenue recognition with multiple deliverables. These new standards impact the determination of when the individual deliverables included in a multiple–element arrangement may be treated as separate units of accounting. Additionally, these new standards modify the manner in which the transaction consideration is allocated across the separately identified deliverables by no longer permitting the residual method of allocating arrangement consideration. These new standards are effective for the Company beginning June 1, 2011. The Company does not expect the adoption will have a material impact on its consolidated financial positions or results of operations.

In June 2009, the FASB issued a new accounting standard that revised the guidance for the consolidation of variable interest entities ("VIE"). This new guidance requires a qualitative approach to identifying a controlling financial interest in a VIE, and requires an ongoing assessment of whether an entity is a VIE and whether an

**NIKE, INC.**

**NOTES TO CONSOLIDATED FINANCIAL STATEMENTS — (Continued)**

interest in a VIE makes the holder the primary beneficiary of the VIE. This guidance is effective for the Company beginning June 1, 2010. The Company is currently evaluating the impact of the provisions of this new standard.

### Note 2 — Inventories

Inventory balances of $2,040.8 million and $2,357.0 million at May 31, 2010 and 2009, respectively, were substantially all finished goods.

### Note 3 — Property, Plant and Equipment

Property, plant and equipment included the following:

| | As of May 31, | |
| --- | --- | --- |
| | 2010 | 2009 |
| | (In millions) | |
| Land | $ 222.8 | $ 221.6 |
| Buildings | 951.9 | 974.0 |
| Machinery and equipment | 2,217.5 | 2,094.3 |
| Leasehold improvements | 820.6 | 802.0 |
| Construction in process | 177.0 | 163.8 |
| | 4,389.8 | 4,255.7 |
| Less accumulated depreciation | 2,457.9 | 2,298.0 |
| | $ 1,931.9 | $ 1,957.7 |

Capitalized interest was not material for the years ended May 31, 2010, 2009 and 2008.

### Note 4 — Acquisition, Identifiable Intangible Assets, Goodwill and Umbro Impairment

*Acquisition*

On March 3, 2008, the Company completed its acquisition of 100% of the outstanding shares of Umbro, a leading United Kingdom–based global soccer brand, for a purchase price of 290.5 million British Pounds Sterling in cash (approximately $576.4 million), inclusive of direct transaction costs. This acquisition is intended to strengthen the Company's market position in the United Kingdom and expand NIKE's global leadership in soccer, a key area of growth for the Company. This acquisition also provides positions in emerging soccer markets such as China, Russia and Brazil. The results of Umbro's operations have been included in the Company's consolidated financial statements since the date of acquisition as part of the Company's "Other" operating segment.

The acquisition of Umbro was accounted for as a purchase business combination. The purchase price was allocated to tangible and identifiable intangible assets acquired and liabilities assumed based on their respective estimated fair values on the date of acquisition, with the remaining purchase price recorded as goodwill.

Based on our preliminary purchase price allocation at May 31, 2008, identifiable intangible assets and goodwill relating to the purchase approximated $419.5 million and $319.2 million, respectively. Goodwill recognized in this transaction is deductible for tax purposes. Identifiable intangible assets include $378.4 million for trademarks that have an indefinite life, and $41.1 million for other intangible assets consisting of Umbro's

66

**NIKE, INC.**

**NOTES TO CONSOLIDATED FINANCIAL STATEMENTS — (Continued)**

sourcing network, established customer relationships, and the United Soccer League Franchise. These intangible assets are amortized on a straight–line basis over estimated lives of 12 to 20 years.

During fiscal 2009, the Company finalized the purchase–price accounting for Umbro and made revisions to preliminary estimates, including valuations of tangible and intangible assets and certain contingencies, as further evaluations were completed and information was received from third parties subsequent to the acquisition date. These revisions to preliminary estimates resulted in a $12.4 million decrease in the value of identified intangible assets, primarily Umbro's sourcing network, and an $11.2 million increase in non–current liabilities, primarily related to liabilities assumed for certain contingencies and adjustments made to deferred taxes related to the fair value of assets acquired. These changes in assets acquired and liabilities assumed affected the amount of goodwill recorded.

The following table summarizes the allocation of the purchase price, including transaction costs of the acquisition, to the assets acquired and liabilities assumed at the date of acquisition based on their estimated fair values, including final purchase accounting adjustments (in millions):

|  | May 31, 2008 Preliminary | Adjustments | May 31, 2009 Final |
|---|---|---|---|
| Current assets | $    87.2 | $    — | $    87.2 |
| Non–current assets | 90.2 | — | 90.2 |
| Identified intangible assets | 419.5 | (12.4) | 407.1 |
| Goodwill | 319.2 | 23.6 | 342.8 |
| Current liabilities | (60.3) | — | (60.3) |
| Non–current liabilities | (279.4) | (11.2) | (290.6) |
| Net assets acquired | $    576.4 | $    — | $    576.4 |

The pro forma effect of the acquisition on the combined results of operations for fiscal 2008 was not material.

*Umbro Impairment in Fiscal 2009*

The Company performs annual impairment tests on goodwill and intangible assets with indefinite lives in the fourth quarter of each fiscal year, or when events occur or circumstances change that would, more likely than not, reduce the fair value of a reporting unit or intangible assets with an indefinite life below its carrying value. As a result of a significant decline in global consumer demand and continued weakness in the macroeconomic environment, as well as decisions by Company management to adjust planned investment in the Umbro brand, the Company concluded sufficient indicators of impairment existed to require the performance of an interim assessment of Umbro's goodwill and indefinite lived intangible assets as of February 1, 2009. Accordingly, the Company performed the first step of the goodwill impairment assessment for Umbro by comparing the estimated fair value of Umbro to its carrying amount, and determined there was a potential impairment of goodwill as the carrying amount exceeded the estimated fair value. Therefore, the Company performed the second step of the assessment which compared the implied fair value of Umbro's goodwill to the book value of goodwill. The implied fair value of goodwill is determined by allocating the estimated fair value of Umbro to all of its assets and liabilities, including both recognized and unrecognized intangibles, in the same manner as goodwill was determined in the original business combination.

The Company measured the fair value of Umbro by using an equal weighting of the fair value implied by a discounted cash flow analysis and by comparisons with the market values of similar publicly traded companies. The Company believes the blended use of both models compensates for the inherent risk associated with either

67

## NIKE, INC.

### NOTES TO CONSOLIDATED FINANCIAL STATEMENTS — (Continued)

model if used on a stand–alone basis, and this combination is indicative of the factors a market participant would consider when performing a similar valuation. The fair value of Umbro's indefinite–lived trademark was estimated using the relief from royalty method, which assumes that the trademark has value to the extent that Umbro is relieved of the obligation to pay royalties for the benefits received from the trademark. The assessments of the Company resulted in the recognition of impairment charges of $199.3 million and $181.3 million related to Umbro's goodwill and trademark, respectively, for the year ended May 31, 2009. A tax benefit of $54.5 million was recognized as a result of the trademark impairment charge. In addition to the above impairment analysis, the Company determined an equity investment held by Umbro was impaired, and recognized a charge of $20.7 million related to the impairment of this investment. These charges are included in the Company's "Other" category for segment reporting purposes.

The discounted cash flow analysis calculated the fair value of Umbro using management's business plans and projections as the basis for expected cash flows for the next 12 years and a 3% residual growth rate thereafter. The Company used a weighted average discount rate of 14% in its analysis, which was derived primarily from published sources as well as our adjustment for increased market risk given current market conditions. Other significant estimates used in the discounted cash flow analysis include the rates of projected growth and profitability of Umbro's business and working capital effects. The market valuation approach indicates the fair value of Umbro based on a comparison of Umbro to publicly traded companies in similar lines of business. Significant estimates in the market valuation approach include identifying similar companies with comparable business factors such as size, growth, profitability, mix of revenue generated from licensed and direct distribution, and risk of return on investment.

Holding all other assumptions constant at the test date, a 100 basis point increase in the discount rate would reduce the adjusted carrying value of Umbro's net assets by an additional 12%.

### Identified Intangible Assets and Goodwill

All goodwill balances are included in the Company's "Other" category for segment reporting purposes. The following table summarizes the Company's goodwill balance as of May 31, 2010 and 2009 (in millions):

|  | Goodwill | Accumulated Impairment | Goodwill, net |
|---|---|---|---|
| May 31, 2008 | $ 448.8 | $ — | $ 448.8 |
| Purchase price adjustments | 23.6 | — | 23.6 |
| Impairment charge | — | (199.3) | (199.3) |
| Other | (79.6) | — | (79.6) |
| May 31, 2009 | 392.8 | (199.3) | 193.5 |
| Other | (5.9) | — | (5.9) |
| May 31, 2010 | $ 386.9 | $ (199.3) | $ 187.6 |

---

(1)     Other consists of foreign currency translation adjustments on Umbro goodwill.

Table of Contents

**NIKE, INC.**

**NOTES TO CONSOLIDATED FINANCIAL STATEMENTS — (Continued)**

The following table summarizes the Company's identifiable intangible asset balances as of May 31, 2010 and 2009.

| | May 31, 2010 | | | May 31, 2009 | | |
|---|---|---|---|---|---|---|
| | Gross Carrying Amount | Accumulated Amortization | Net Carrying Amount | Gross Carrying Amount | Accumulated Amortization | Net Carrying Amount |
| | | | (In millions) | | | |
| Amortized intangible assets: | | | | | | |
| Patents | $ 68.5 | $ (20.8) | $ 47.7 | $ 56.6 | $ (17.2) | $ 39.4 |
| Trademarks | 40.2 | (17.8) | 22.4 | 37.5 | (10.9) | 26.6 |
| Other | 32.7 | (18.8) | 13.9 | 40.0 | (19.6) | 20.4 |
| Total | $ 141.4 | $ (57.4) | $ 84.0 | $ 134.1 | $ (47.7) | $ 86.4 |
| Unamortized intangible assets — Trademarks | | | $ 383.0 | | | $ 381.0 |
| Identifiable intangible assets, net | | | $ 467.0 | | | $ 467.4 |

The effect of foreign exchange fluctuations for the year ended May 31, 2010 increased unamortized intangible assets by approximately $2 million.

Amortization expense, which is included in selling and administrative expense, was $13.5 million, $11.9 million and $9.2 million for the years ended May 31, 2010, 2009 and 2008, respectively. The estimated amortization expense for intangible assets subject to amortization for each of the years ending May 31, 2011 through May 31, 2015 are as follows: 2011: $13.4 million; 2012: $12.7 million; 2013: $10.8 million; 2014: $8.7 million; 2015: $5.1 million.

**Note 5 — Accrued Liabilities**

Accrued liabilities included the following:

| | May 31, | |
|---|---|---|
| | 2010 | 2009 |
| | (In millions) | |
| Compensation and benefits, excluding taxes | $ 598.8 | $ 491.9 |
| Endorser compensation | 266.9 | 237.1 |
| Fair value of derivatives | 163.6 | 68.9 |
| Taxes other than income taxes | 157.9 | 161.9 |
| Dividends payable | 130.7 | 121.4 |
| Advertising and marketing | 124.9 | 97.6 |
| Import and logistics costs | 80.0 | 59.4 |
| Restructuring charges[1] | 8.2 | 149.6 |
| Other[2] | 373.4 | 396.1 |
| | $ 1,904.4 | $ 1,783.9 |

[1] Accrued restructuring charges primarily consist of severance costs relating to the Company's restructuring activities that took place during the year ended May 31, 2009. See Note 16 — Restructuring Charges for more information.

[2] Other consists of various accrued expenses and no individual item accounted for more than 5% of the balance at May 31, 2010 and 2009.

69

**NIKE, INC.**

**NOTES TO CONSOLIDATED FINANCIAL STATEMENTS — (Continued)**

**Note 6 — Fair Value Measurements**

The Company measures certain financial assets and liabilities at fair value on a recurring basis, including derivatives and available–for–sale securities. Fair value is a market–based measurement that should be determined based on the assumptions that market participants would use in pricing an asset or liability. As a basis for considering such assumptions, the Company uses a three–level hierarchy established by the FASB which prioritizes fair value measurements based on the types of inputs used for the various valuation techniques (market approach, income approach, and cost approach).

The levels of hierarchy are described below:

- Level 1: Observable inputs such as quoted prices in active markets for identical assets or liabilities.

- Level 2: Inputs other than quoted prices that are observable for the asset or liability, either directly or indirectly; these include quoted prices for similar assets or liabilities in active markets and quoted prices for identical or similar assets or liabilities in markets that are not active.

- Level 3: Unobservable inputs in which there is little or no market data available, which require the reporting entity to develop its own assumptions.

The Company's assessment of the significance of a particular input to the fair value measurement in its entirety requires judgment and considers factors specific to the asset or liability. Financial assets and liabilities are classified in their entirety based on the most stringent level of input that is significant to the fair value measurement.

70

NIKE, INC.

**NOTES TO CONSOLIDATED FINANCIAL STATEMENTS — (Continued)**

The following table presents information about the Company's financial assets and liabilities measured at fair value on a recurring basis as of May 31, 2010 and 2009 and indicates the fair value hierarchy of the valuation techniques utilized by the Company to determine such fair value.

| | May 31, 2010 | | | | |
|---|---|---|---|---|---|
| | Fair Value Measurements Using | | | Assets / Liabilities at Fair Value | Balance Sheet Classification |
| | Level 1 | Level 2 | Level 3 | | |
| | | (In millions) | | | |
| **Assets** | | | | | |
| Derivatives: | | | | | |
| Foreign exchange forwards and options | $  — | $  420.2 | $  — | $  420.2 | Other current assets and other long−term assets |
| Interest rate swap contracts | — | 14.6 | | 14.6 | Other current assets and other long−term assets |
| Total derivatives | — | 434.8 | — | 434.8 | |
| Available−for−sale securities: | | | | | |
| U.S. Treasury securities | 1,231.7 | — | — | 1,231.7 | Cash and equivalents |
| Commercial paper and bonds | — | 461.9 | — | 461.9 | Cash and equivalents |
| Money market funds | — | 684.5 | — | 684.5 | Cash and equivalents |
| U.S. Treasury securities | 1,084.0 | — | — | 1,084.0 | Short−term investments |
| U.S. Agency securities | — | 298.5 | — | 298.5 | Short−term investments |
| Commercial paper and bonds | — | 684.3 | — | 684.3 | Short−term investments |
| Total available−for−sale securities | 2,315.7 | 2,129.2 | — | 4,444.9 | |
| **Total Assets** | $ 2,315.7 | $ 2,564.0 | $  — | $  4,879.7 | |
| **Liabilities** | | | | | |
| Derivatives: | | | | | |
| Foreign exchange forwards and options | $  — | $  165.1 | $  — | $  165.1 | Accrued liabilities and other long−term liabilities |
| **Total Liabilities** | $  — | $  165.1 | $  — | $  165.1 | |

71

**NIKE, INC.**
**NOTES TO CONSOLIDATED FINANCIAL STATEMENTS — (Continued)**

May 31, 2009

| | Fair Value Measurements Using | | | Assets / Liabilities at Fair Value | Balance Sheet Classification |
|---|---|---|---|---|---|
| | Level 1 | Level 2 | Level 3 | | |
| | | (In millions) | | | |
| **Assets** | | | | | |
| Derivatives: | | | | | |
| Foreign exchange forwards and options | $ — | $ 364.9 | $ — | $ 364.9 | Other current assets and other long–term assets |
| Interest rate swap contracts | — | 13.8 | — | 13.8 | Other current assets and other long–term assets |
| Total derivatives | — | 378.7 | — | 378.7 | |
| Available–for–sale securities: | | | | | |
| U.S. Treasury securities | 240.0 | — | — | 240.0 | Cash and equivalents |
| Commercial paper and bonds | — | 235.3 | — | 235.3 | Cash and equivalents |
| Money market funds | — | 1,079.5 | — | 1,079.5 | Cash and equivalents |
| U.S. Treasury securities | 467.9 | — | — | 467.9 | Short–term investments |
| U.S. Agency securities | — | 304.9 | — | 304.9 | Short–term investments |
| Commercial paper and bonds | — | 391.2 | — | 391.2 | Short–term investments |
| Total available–for–sale securities | 707.9 | 2,010.9 | — | 2,718.8 | |
| **Total Assets** | $ 707.9 | $ 2,389.6 | $ — | $ 3,097.5 | |
| **Liabilities** | | | | | |
| Derivatives: | | | | | |
| Foreign exchange forwards and options | $ — | $ 68.9 | $ — | $ 68.9 | Accrued liabilities and other long–term liabilities |
| **Total Liabilities** | $ — | $ 68.9 | $ — | $ 68.9 | |

Derivative financial instruments include foreign currency forwards, option contracts and interest rate swaps. The fair value of these derivatives contracts is determined using observable market inputs such as the forward pricing curve, currency volatilities, currency correlations and interest rates, and considers nonperformance risk of the Company and that of its counterparties. Adjustments relating to these risks were not material for the years ended May 31, 2010 and 2009.

Available–for–sale securities are primarily comprised of investments in U.S. Treasury and agency securities, commercial paper, bonds and money market funds. These securities are valued using market prices on both active markets (level 1) and less active markets (level 2). Level 1 instrument valuations are obtained from real–time quotes for transactions in active exchange markets involving identical assets. Level 2 instrument valuations are obtained from readily–available pricing sources for comparable instruments.

As of May 31, 2010 and 2009, the Company had no material Level 3 measurements and no assets or liabilities measured at fair value on a non–recurring basis.

72

## NIKE, INC.
## NOTES TO CONSOLIDATED FINANCIAL STATEMENTS — (Continued)

*Short–term Investments*

As of May 31, 2010 and 2009, short–term investments consisted of available–for–sale securities. As of May 31, 2010, the Company held $1,900.4 million of available–for–sale securities with maturity dates within one year and $166.4 million with maturity dates over one year and less than five years within short–term investments. As of May 31, 2009, the Company held $1,005.0 million of available–for–sale securities with maturity dates within one year and $159.0 million with maturity dates over one year and less than five years within short–term investments.

Short–term investments classified as available–for–sale consist of the following at fair value:

|  | As of May 31, | |
|---|---|---|
|  | 2010 | 2009 |
|  | (In millions) | |
| Available–for–sale investments: | | |
| U.S. treasury and agencies | $ 1,382.5 | $ 772.8 |
| Commercial paper and bonds | 684.3 | 391.2 |
| Total available–for–sale investments | $ 2,066.8 | $ 1,164.0 |

Included in interest expense (income), net for the years ended May 31, 2010, 2009 and 2008 was interest income of $30.1 million, $49.7 million, and $115.8 million, respectively, related to cash and equivalents and short–term investments.

For fair value information regarding notes payable and long–term debt, refer to Note 7 — Short–Term Borrowings and Credit Lines and Note 8 — Long–Term Debt.

## Note 7 — Short–Term Borrowings and Credit Lines

Notes payable to banks and interest–bearing accounts payable to Sojitz Corporation of America ("Sojitz America") as of May 31, 2010 and 2009, are summarized below:

|  | May 31, | | | |
|---|---|---|---|---|
|  | 2010 | | 2009 | |
|  | Borrowings | Interest Rate | Borrowings | Interest Rate |
|  | (In millions) | | | |
| Notes payable: | | | | |
| Commercial paper | $ — | — | $ 100.0 | 0.40% |
| U.S. operations | 18.0 | —[1] | 31.2 | 1.81%[1] |
| Non–U.S. operations | 120.6 | 6.35%[1] | 211.7 | 4.15%[1] |
|  | $ 138.6 | | $ 342.9 | |
| Sojitz America | $ 88.2 | 1.07% | $ 78.5 | 1.57% |

[1] Weighted average interest rate includes non–interest bearing overdrafts.

The carrying amounts reflected in the consolidated balance sheet for notes payable approximate fair value.

The Company purchases through Sojitz America certain athletic footwear, apparel and equipment it acquires from non–U.S. suppliers. These purchases are for the Company's operations outside of the United States, Europe and Japan. Accounts payable to Sojitz America are generally due up to 60 days after shipment of goods from the foreign port. The interest rate on such accounts payable is the 60–day London Interbank Offered Rate ("LIBOR") as of the beginning of the month of the invoice date, plus 0.75%.

**NIKE, INC.**

**NOTES TO CONSOLIDATED FINANCIAL STATEMENTS — (Continued)**

As of May 31, 2010, the Company had no amounts outstanding under its commercial paper program. As of May 31, 2009, the Company had $100.0 million outstanding at a weighted average interest rate of 0.40%.

In December 2006, the Company entered into a $1 billion revolving credit facility with a group of banks. The facility matures in December 2012. Based on the Company's current long–term senior unsecured debt ratings of A+ and A1 from Standard and Poor's Corporation and Moody's Investor Services, respectively, the interest rate charged on any outstanding borrowings would be the prevailing LIBOR plus 0.15%. The facility fee is 0.05% of the total commitment. Under this agreement, the Company must maintain, among other things, certain minimum specified financial ratios with which the Company was in compliance at May 31, 2010. No amounts were outstanding under this facility as of May 31, 2010 and 2009.

### Note 8 — Long–Term Debt

Long–term debt, net of unamortized premiums and discounts and swap fair value adjustments, is comprised of the following:

|  | May 31, | |
|---|---|---|
|  | **2010** | **2009** |
|  | (In millions) | |
| 5.375% Corporate bond, payable July 8, 2009 | $   — | $  25.1 |
| 5.66% Corporate bond, payable July 23, 2012 | 27.0 | 27.4 |
| 5.4% Corporate bond, payable August 7, 2012 | 16.1 | 16.2 |
| 4.7% Corporate bond, payable October 1, 2013 | 50.0 | 50.0 |
| 5.15% Corporate bond, payable October 15, 2015 | 112.4 | 111.1 |
| 4.3% Japanese Yen note, payable June 26, 2011 | 115.7 | 108.5 |
| 1.52125% Japanese Yen note, payable February 14, 2012 | 55.1 | 51.7 |
| 2.6% Japanese Yen note, maturing August 20, 2001 through November 20, 2020 | 53.1 | 54.7 |
| 2.0% Japanese Yen note, maturing August 20, 2001 through November 20, 2020 | 23.8 | 24.5 |
| Total | 453.2 | 469.2 |
| Less current maturities | 7.4 | 32.0 |
|  | $445.8 | $437.2 |

The scheduled maturity of long–term debt in each of the years ending May 31, 2011 through 2015 are $7.4 million, $178.1 million, $47.4 million, $57.4 million and $7.4 million, at face value, respectively.

The Company's long–term debt is recorded at adjusted cost, net of amortized premiums and discounts and interest rate swap fair value adjustments. The fair value of long–term debt is estimated based upon quoted prices for similar instruments. The fair value of the Company's long–term debt, including the current portion, was approximately $453 million at May 31, 2010 and $456 million at May 31, 2009.

In fiscal years 2003 and 2004, the Company issued a total of $240 million in medium–term notes of which $190 million, at face value, were outstanding at May 31, 2010. The outstanding notes have coupon rates that range from 4.70% to 5.66% and maturity dates ranging from July 2012 to October 2015. For each of these notes, except the $50 million note maturing in October 2013, the Company has entered into interest rate swap agreements whereby the Company receives fixed interest payments at the same rate as the notes and pays variable interest payments based on the six–month LIBOR plus a spread. Each swap has the same notional amount and maturity date as the corresponding note. At May 31, 2010, the interest rates payable on these swap agreements ranged from approximately 0.3% to 1.1%.

74

**NIKE, INC.**
**NOTES TO CONSOLIDATED FINANCIAL STATEMENTS — (Continued)**

In June 1996, one of the Company's Japanese subsidiaries, NIKE Logistics YK, borrowed ¥10.5 billion (approximately $115.7 million as of May 31, 2010) in a private placement with a maturity of June 26, 2011. Interest is paid semi–annually. The agreement provides for early retirement of the borrowing.

In July 1999, NIKE Logistics YK assumed a total of ¥13.0 billion in loans as part of its agreement to purchase a distribution center in Japan, which serves as collateral for the loans. These loans mature in equal quarterly installments during the period August 20, 2001 through November 20, 2020. Interest is also paid quarterly. As of May 31, 2010, ¥7.0 billion (approximately $76.9 million) in loans remain outstanding.

In February 2007, NIKE Logistics YK entered into a ¥5.0 billion (approximately $55.1 million as of May 31, 2010) term loan that replaced certain intercompany borrowings and matures on February 14, 2012. The interest rate on the loan is approximately 1.5% and interest is paid semi–annually.

**Note 9 — Income Taxes**

Income before income taxes is as follows:

| | Year Ended May 31, | | |
| --- | --- | --- | --- |
| | 2010 | 2009 (In millions) | 2008 |
| Income before income taxes: | | | |
| United States | $ 698.6 | $ 845.7 | $ 713.0 |
| Foreign | 1,818.3 | 1,110.8 | 1,789.9 |
| | $ 2,516.9 | $ 1,956.5 | $ 2,502.9 |

The provision for income taxes is as follows:

| | Year Ended May 31, | | |
| --- | --- | --- | --- |
| | 2010 | 2009 (In millions) | 2008 |
| Current: | | | |
| United States | | | |
| Federal | $200.2 | $ 410.1 | $ 469.9 |
| State | 50.0 | 46.1 | 58.4 |
| Foreign | 348.5 | 307.7 | 391.8 |
| | 598.7 | 763.9 | 920.1 |
| Deferred: | | | |
| United States | | | |
| Federal | 17.7 | (251.4) | (273.0) |
| State | (1.1) | (7.9) | (5.0) |
| Foreign | (5.1) | (34.8) | (22.6) |
| | 11.5 | (294.1) | (300.6) |
| | $610.2 | $ 469.8 | $ 619.5 |

75

**NIKE, INC.**

**NOTES TO CONSOLIDATED FINANCIAL STATEMENTS — (Continued)**

A reconciliation from the U.S. statutory federal income tax rate to the effective income tax rate follows:

| | Year Ended May 31, | | |
|---|---|---|---|
| | 2010 | 2009 | 2008 |
| Federal income tax rate | 35.0% | 35.0% | 35.0% |
| State taxes, net of federal benefit | 1.3% | 1.2% | 1.4% |
| Foreign earnings | −13.6% | −14.9% | −12.9% |
| Other, net | 1.5% | 2.7% | 1.3% |
| Effective income tax rate | 24.2% | 24.0% | 24.8% |

The effective tax rate for the year ended May 31, 2010 of 24.2% increased from the fiscal 2009 effective rate of 24.0%. The effective tax rate for the year ended May 31, 2009 was favorably impacted by a tax benefit associated with the impairment of goodwill, intangible, and other assets of Umbro (See Note 4 — Acquisition, Identifiable Intangible Assets, Goodwill and Umbro Impairment), and the retroactive reinstatement of the research and development tax credit. The Tax Extenders and Alternative Minimum Tax Relief Act of 2008, which was signed into law during the second quarter of fiscal 2009, reinstated the U.S. federal research and development tax credit retroactive to January 1, 2008. Also reflected in the effective tax rate for the years ended May 31, 2010, 2009 and 2008 is a reduction in our on-going effective tax rate resulting from our operations outside of the United States, as our tax rates on those operations are generally lower than the U.S. statutory rate.

Deferred tax assets and (liabilities) are comprised of the following:

| | May 31, | |
|---|---|---|
| | 2010 | 2009 |
| | (In millions) | |
| Deferred tax assets: | | |
| Allowance for doubtful accounts | $  16.7 | $  17.9 |
| Inventories | 47.3 | 52.8 |
| Sales return reserves | 52.0 | 52.8 |
| Deferred compensation | 143.7 | 127.3 |
| Stock–based compensation | 145.0 | 127.3 |
| Reserves and accrued liabilities | 85.8 | 66.7 |
| Foreign loss carry–forwards | 26.2 | 31.9 |
| Foreign tax credit carry–forwards | 148.3 | 32.7 |
| Hedges | 0.4 | 1.1 |
| Undistributed earnings of foreign subsidiaries | 128.4 | 272.9 |
| Other | 37.0 | 46.2 |
| Total deferred tax assets | 830.8 | 829.6 |
| Valuation allowance | (36.2) | (26.0) |
| Total deferred tax assets after valuation allowance | 794.6 | 803.6 |
| Deferred tax liabilities: | | |
| Property, plant and equipment | (99.3) | (92.2) |
| Intangibles | (98.6) | (100.7) |
| Hedges | (71.5) | (86.6) |
| Other | (8.1) | (4.2) |
| Total deferred tax liability | (277.5) | (283.7) |
| Net deferred tax asset | $ 517.1 | $ 519.9 |

76

**NIKE, INC.**

**NOTES TO CONSOLIDATED FINANCIAL STATEMENTS — (Continued)**

The following is a reconciliation of the changes in the gross balance of unrecognized tax benefits:

| | May 31, | | |
|---|---|---|---|
| | 2010 | 2009 | 2008 |
| | | (In millions) | |
| Unrecognized tax benefits, as of the beginning of the period | $ 273.9 | $251.1 | $122.5 |
| Gross increases related to prior period tax positions | 86.7 | 53.2 | 71.6 |
| Gross decreases related to prior period tax positions | (121.6) | (61.7) | (23.1) |
| Gross increases related to current period tax positions | 52.5 | 71.5 | 87.7 |
| Settlements | (3.3) | (29.3) | (13.4) |
| Lapse of statute of limitations | (9.3) | (4.1) | (0.7) |
| Changes due to currency translation | 3.2 | (6.8) | 6.5 |
| Unrecognized tax benefits, as of the end of the period | $ 282.1 | $273.9 | $251.1 |

As of May 31, 2010, the total gross unrecognized tax benefits, excluding related interest and penalties, were $282.1 million, $158.4 million of which would affect the Company's effective tax rate if recognized in future periods. Total gross unrecognized tax benefits, excluding interest and penalties, as of May 31, 2009 was $273.9 million, $110.6 million of which would affect the Company's effective tax rate if recognized in future periods.

The Company recognizes interest and penalties related to income tax matters in income tax expense. The liability for payment of interest and penalties increased $6.0 million, $2.2 million and $41.2 million during the years ended May 31, 2010, 2009 and 2008, respectively. As of May 31, 2010 and 2009, accrued interest and penalties related to uncertain tax positions was $81.4 million and $75.4 million, respectively (excluding federal benefit).

The Company is subject to taxation primarily in the U.S., China and the Netherlands as well as various state and other foreign jurisdictions. The Company has concluded substantially all U.S. federal income tax matters through fiscal year 2006. The Company is currently under audit by the Internal Revenue Service for the 2007, 2008, 2009 and 2010 tax years. The Company's major foreign jurisdictions, China and the Netherlands, have concluded substantially all income tax matters through calendar 1999 and fiscal 2003, respectively. It is reasonably possible that the Internal Revenue Service audits for the 2007, 2008 and 2009 tax years will be completed during the next 12 months, which could result in a decrease in our balance of unrecognized tax benefits. An estimate of the range cannot be made at this time; however, we do not anticipate that total gross unrecognized tax benefits will change significantly as a result of full or partial settlement of audits within the next 12 months.

The Company has indefinitely reinvested approximately $3.6 billion of the cumulative undistributed earnings of certain foreign subsidiaries. Such earnings would be subject to U.S. taxation if repatriated to the U.S. Determination of the amount of unrecognized deferred tax liability associated with the permanently reinvested cumulative undistributed earnings is not practicable.

During the year ended May 31, 2009, a portion of the Company's foreign operations was granted a tax holiday that will phase out in 2019. The decrease in income tax expense for the year ended May 31, 2010 as a result of this arrangement was approximately $30.1 million ($0.06 per diluted share). The effect on income tax expense for the year ended May 31, 2009 was not material.

Deferred tax assets at May 31, 2010 and 2009 were reduced by a valuation allowance relating to tax benefits of certain subsidiaries with operating losses where it is more likely than not that the deferred tax assets will not be realized. The net change in the valuation allowance was an increase of $10.2 million for the year ended May 31, 2010 and a decrease of $14.7 million and $1.6 million for the years ended May 31, 2009 and 2008, respectively.

77

## NIKE, INC.

### NOTES TO CONSOLIDATED FINANCIAL STATEMENTS — (Continued)

The Company does not anticipate that any foreign tax credit carry–forwards will expire. The Company has available domestic and foreign loss carry–forwards of $89.8 million at May 31, 2010. Such losses will expire as follows:

| | | | | Year Ending May 31, | | | | |
|---|---|---|---|---|---|---|---|---|
| | 2011 | 2012 | 2013 | 2014 | 2015 | 2016–2028 | Indefinite | Total |
| | | | | | (In millions) | | | |
| Net Operating Losses | $2.0 | $1.9 | $3.6 | $8.9 | $11.1 | $25.7 | $ 36.6 | $89.8 |

During the years ended May 31, 2010, 2009, and 2008, income tax benefits attributable to employee stock–based compensation transactions of $56.8 million, $25.4 million, and $68.9 million, respectively, were allocated to shareholders' equity.

### Note 10 — Redeemable Preferred Stock

Sojitz America is the sole owner of the Company's authorized Redeemable Preferred Stock, $1 par value, which is redeemable at the option of Sojitz America or the Company at par value aggregating $0.3 million. A cumulative dividend of $0.10 per share is payable annually on May 31 and no dividends may be declared or paid on the common stock of the Company unless dividends on the Redeemable Preferred Stock have been declared and paid in full. There have been no changes in the Redeemable Preferred Stock in the three years ended May 31, 2010, 2009 and 2008. As the holder of the Redeemable Preferred Stock, Sojitz America does not have general voting rights but does have the right to vote as a separate class on the sale of all or substantially all of the assets of the Company and its subsidiaries, on merger, consolidation, liquidation or dissolution of the Company or on the sale or assignment of the NIKE trademark for athletic footwear sold in the United States.

### Note 11 — Common Stock and Stock–Based Compensation

The authorized number of shares of Class A Common Stock, no par value, and Class B Common Stock, no par value, are 175 million and 750 million, respectively. Each share of Class A Common Stock is convertible into one share of Class B Common Stock. Voting rights of Class B Common Stock are limited in certain circumstances with respect to the election of directors.

In 1990, the Board of Directors adopted, and the shareholders approved, the NIKE, Inc. 1990 Stock Incentive Plan (the "1990 Plan"). The 1990 Plan provides for the issuance of up to 132 million previously unissued shares of Class B Common Stock in connection with stock options and other awards granted under the plan. The 1990 Plan authorizes the grant of non–statutory stock options, incentive stock options, stock appreciation rights, stock bonuses, and the issuance and sale of restricted stock. The exercise price for non–statutory stock options, stock appreciation rights and the grant price of restricted stock may not be less than 75% of the fair market value of the underlying shares on the date of grant. The exercise price for incentive stock options may not be less than the fair market value of the underlying shares on the date of grant. A committee of the Board of Directors administers the 1990 Plan. The committee has the authority to determine the employees to whom awards will be made, the amount of the awards, and the other terms and conditions of the awards. The committee has granted substantially all stock options at 100% of the market price on the date of grant. Substantially all stock option grants outstanding under the 1990 Plan were granted in the first quarter of each fiscal year, vest ratably over four years, and expire 10 years from the date of grant. In June 2010, the Board of Directors amended the 1990 Plan to require, among other things, that the exercise price for non–statutory stock options and stock appreciation rights may not be less than 100% of the fair market value of the underlying shares on the date of grant.

**Table of Contents**

## NIKE, INC.
### NOTES TO CONSOLIDATED FINANCIAL STATEMENTS — (Continued)

The following table summarizes the Company's total stock–based compensation expense recognized in selling and administrative expense:

| | Year Ended May 31, | | |
| --- | --- | --- | --- |
| | 2010 | 2009 | 2008 |
| | | (In millions) | |
| Stock options[1] | $134.6 | $128.8 | $127.0 |
| ESPPs | 13.7 | 14.4 | 7.2 |
| Restricted stock | 10.7 | 7.9 | 6.8 |
| Subtotal | 159.0 | 151.1 | 141.0 |
| Stock options and restricted stock expense — restructuring[2] | — | 19.5 | — |
| Total stock–based compensation expense | $159.0 | $170.6 | $141.0 |

[1] Accelerated stock option expense is recorded for employees eligible for accelerated stock option vesting upon retirement. Accelerated stock option expense reported during the years ended May 31, 2010, 2009 and 2008 was $74.4 million, $58.7 million and $40.7 million, respectively.

[2] In connection with the restructuring activities that took place during fiscal 2009, the Company recognized stock–based compensation expense relating to the modification of stock option agreements, allowing for an extended post–termination exercise period, and accelerated vesting of restricted stock as part of severance packages. See Note 16 — Restructuring Charges for further details.

As of May 31, 2010, the Company had $86.8 million of unrecognized compensation costs from stock options, net of estimated forfeitures, to be recognized as selling and administrative expense over a weighted average period of 2.2 years.

The weighted average fair value per share of the options granted during the years ended May 31, 2010, 2009 and 2008, as computed using the Black–Scholes pricing model, was $23.43, $17.13 and $13.87, respectively. The weighted average assumptions used to estimate these fair values are as follows:

| | Year Ended May 31, | | |
| --- | --- | --- | --- |
| | 2010 | 2009 | 2008 |
| Dividend yield | 1.9% | 1.5% | 1.4% |
| Expected volatility | 57.6% | 32.5% | 20.0% |
| Weighted average expected life (in years) | 5.0 | 5.0 | 5.0 |
| Risk–free interest rate | 2.5% | 3.4% | 4.8% |

The Company estimates the expected volatility based on the implied volatility in market traded options on the Company's common stock with a term greater than one year, along with other factors. The weighted average expected life of options is based on an analysis of historical and expected future exercise patterns. The interest rate is based on the U.S. Treasury (constant maturity) risk–free rate in effect at the date of grant for periods corresponding with the expected term of the options.

**NIKE, INC.**

**NOTES TO CONSOLIDATED FINANCIAL STATEMENTS — (Continued)**

The following summarizes the stock option transactions under the plan discussed above:

| | Shares (In millions) | Weighted Average Option Price |
|---|---|---|
| Options outstanding May 31, 2007 | 39.7 | $ 35.50 |
| Exercised | (9.1) | 33.45 |
| Forfeited | (0.9) | 44.44 |
| Granted | 6.9 | 58.50 |
| Options outstanding May 31, 2008 | 36.6 | $ 40.14 |
| Exercised | (4.0) | 35.70 |
| Forfeited | (1.3) | 51.19 |
| Granted | 7.5 | 58.17 |
| Options outstanding May 31, 2009 | 38.8 | $ 43.69 |
| Exercised | (8.6) | 37.64 |
| Forfeited | (0.6) | 51.92 |
| Granted | 6.4 | 52.79 |
| Options outstanding May 31, 2010 | 36.0 | $ 46.60 |
| Options exercisable at May 31, | | |
| 2008 | 16.2 | $ 32.35 |
| 2009 | 21.4 | 36.91 |
| 2010 | 20.4 | 41.16 |

The weighted average contractual life remaining for options outstanding and options exercisable at May 31, 2010 was 6.2 years and 4.8 years, respectively. The aggregate intrinsic value for options outstanding and exercisable at May 31, 2010 was $926.8 million and $636.0 million, respectively. The aggregate intrinsic value was the amount by which the market value of the underlying stock exceeded the exercise price of the options. The total intrinsic value of the options exercised during the years ended May 31, 2010, 2009 and 2008 was $239.3 million, $108.4 million and $259.4 million, respectively.

In addition to the 1990 Plan, the Company gives employees the right to purchase shares at a discount to the market price under employee stock purchase plans ("ESPPs"). Employees are eligible to participate through payroll deductions up to 10% of their compensation. At the end of each six−month offering period, shares are purchased by the participants at 85% of the lower of the fair market value at the beginning or the end of the offering period. Employees purchased 0.8 million shares, 1.0 million shares and 0.8 million shares during the years ended May 31, 2010, 2009 and 2008, respectively.

From time to time, the Company grants restricted stock and unrestricted stock to key employees under the 1990 Plan. The number of shares granted to employees during the years ended May 31, 2010, 2009 and 2008 were 499,000, 75,000 and 110,000 with weighted average values per share of $53.16, $56.97 and $59.50, respectively. Recipients of restricted shares are entitled to cash dividends and to vote their respective shares throughout the period of restriction. The value of all of the granted shares was established by the market price on the date of grant. During the years ended May 31, 2010, 2009 and 2008, the fair value of restricted shares vested was $8.0 million, $9.9 million and $9.0 million, respectively, determined as of the date of vesting.

**NIKE, INC.**

**NOTES TO CONSOLIDATED FINANCIAL STATEMENTS — (Continued)**

**Note 12 — Earnings Per Share**

The following is a reconciliation from basic earnings per share to diluted earnings per share. Options to purchase an additional 0.2 million, 13.2 million and 6.6 million shares of common stock were outstanding at May 31, 2010, 2009 and 2008, respectively, but were not included in the computation of diluted earnings per share because the options were anti–dilutive.

| | Year Ended May 31, | | |
| | 2010 | 2009 | 2008 |
|---|---|---|---|
| | (In millions, except per share data) | | |
| Determination of shares: | | | |
| Weighted average common shares outstanding | 485.5 | 484.9 | 495.6 |
| Assumed conversion of dilutive stock options and awards | 8.4 | 5.8 | 8.5 |
| Diluted weighted average common shares outstanding | 493.9 | 490.7 | 504.1 |
| Basic earnings per common share | $ 3.93 | $ 3.07 | $ 3.80 |
| Diluted earnings per common share | $ 3.86 | $ 3.03 | $ 3.74 |

**Note 13 — Benefit Plans**

The Company has a profit sharing plan available to most U.S.–based employees. The terms of the plan call for annual contributions by the Company as determined by the Board of Directors. A subsidiary of the Company also has a profit sharing plan available to its U.S.–based employees. The terms of the plan call for annual contributions as determined by the subsidiary's executive management. Contributions of $34.9 million, $27.6 million and $37.3 million were made to the plans and are included in selling and administrative expense for the years ended May 31, 2010, 2009 and 2008, respectively. The Company has various 401(k) employee savings plans available to U.S.–based employees. The Company matches a portion of employee contributions with common stock or cash. Company contributions to the savings plans were $34.2 million, $37.6 million and $33.9 million for the years ended May 31, 2010, 2009 and 2008, respectively, and are included in selling and administrative expense.

The Company also has a Long–Term Incentive Plan ("LTIP") that was adopted by the Board of Directors and approved by shareholders in September 1997 and later amended in fiscal 2007. The Company recognized $24.1 million, $17.6 million and $35.9 million of selling and administrative expense related to cash awards under the LTIP during the years ended May 31, 2010, 2009 and 2008, respectively.

The Company has pension plans in various countries worldwide. The pension plans are only available to local employees and are generally government mandated. The liability related to the unfunded pension liabilities of the plans was $113.0 million and $82.8 million at May 31, 2010 and 2009, respectively.

81

**NIKE, INC.**

**NOTES TO CONSOLIDATED FINANCIAL STATEMENTS — (Continued)**

**Note 14 — Accumulated Other Comprehensive Income**

The components of accumulated other comprehensive income, net of tax, are as follows:

| | May 31, | |
| --- | --- | --- |
| | 2010 | 2009 |
| | (In millions) | |
| Cumulative translation adjustment and other | $ (94.6) | $ 64.6 |
| Net deferred gain on net investment hedge derivatives | 107.3 | 62.5 |
| Net deferred gain on cash flow hedge derivatives | 202.1 | 240.4 |
| | $214.8 | $367.5 |

**Note 15 — Commitments and Contingencies**

The Company leases space for certain of its offices, warehouses and retail stores under leases expiring from 1 to 25 years after May 31, 2010. Rent expense was $416.1 million, $397.0 million and $344.2 million for the years ended May 31, 2010, 2009 and 2008, respectively. Amounts of minimum future annual rental commitments under non–cancelable operating leases in each of the five years ending May 31, 2011 through 2015 are $334.4 million, $264.0 million, $219.9 million, $177.2 million, $148.0 million, respectively, and $465.8 million in later years.

As of May 31, 2010 and 2009, the Company had letters of credit outstanding totaling $101.1 million and $154.8 million, respectively. These letters of credit were generally issued for the purchase of inventory.

In connection with various contracts and agreements, the Company provides routine indemnifications relating to the enforceability of intellectual property rights, coverage for legal issues that arise and other items where the Company is acting as the guarantor. Currently, the Company has several such agreements in place. However, based on the Company's historical experience and the estimated probability of future loss, the Company has determined that the fair value of such indemnifications is not material to the Company's financial position or results of operations.

In the ordinary course of its business, the Company is involved in various legal proceedings involving contractual and employment relationships, product liability claims, trademark rights, and a variety of other matters. The Company does not believe there are any pending legal proceedings that will have a material impact on the Company's financial position or results of operations.

**Note 16 — Restructuring Charges**

During fiscal 2009, the Company took necessary steps to streamline its management structure, enhance consumer focus, drive innovation more quickly to market and establish a more scalable, long–term cost structure. As a result, the Company reduced its global workforce by approximately 5% and incurred pre–tax restructuring charges of $195 million, primarily consisting of severance costs related to the workforce reduction. As nearly all of the restructuring activities were completed in fiscal 2009, the Company does not expect to recognize additional costs in future periods relating to these actions. The restructuring charge is reflected in the corporate expense line in the segment presentation of earnings before interest and taxes in Note 19 — Operating Segments and Related Information.

**NIKE, INC.**

**NOTES TO CONSOLIDATED FINANCIAL STATEMENTS — (Continued)**

The activity in the restructuring accrual for the years ended May 31, 2010 and 2009 is as follows (in millions):

| | |
|---|---:|
| Restructuring accrual — June 1, 2008 | $ — |
| Severance and related costs | 195.0 |
| Cash payments | (29.4) |
| Non-cash stock option and restricted stock expense | (19.5) |
| Foreign currency translation and other | 3.5 |
| Restructuring accrual — May 31, 2009 | 149.6 |
| Cash payments | (142.6) |
| Foreign currency translation and other | 1.2 |
| Restructuring accrual — May 31, 2010 | $ 8.2 |

The accrual balance as of May 31, 2010 will be relieved throughout the first half of fiscal year 2011, as final severance payments are completed. The restructuring accrual is included in Accrued liabilities in the Consolidated Balance Sheet.

**Note 17 — Divestitures**

On December 17, 2007, the Company completed the sale of the Starter brand business to Iconix Brand Group, Inc. for $60.0 million in cash. This transaction resulted in a gain of $28.6 million during the year ended May 31, 2008.

On April 17, 2008, the Company completed the sale of NIKE Bauer Hockey for $189.2 million in cash to a group of private investors ("the Buyer"). The sale resulted in a net gain of $32.0 million recorded in the fourth quarter of the year ended May 31, 2008. This gain included the recognition of a $46.3 million cumulative foreign currency translation adjustment previously included in accumulated other comprehensive income. As part of the terms of the sale agreement, the Company granted the Buyer a royalty free limited license for the use of certain NIKE trademarks for a transitional period of approximately two years. The Company deferred $41.0 million of the sale proceeds related to this license agreement, to be recognized over the license period.

The gains resulting from these divestitures are reflected in other (income) expense, net and in the corporate expense line in the segment presentation of earnings before interest and taxes in Note 19 — Operating Segments and Related Information.

**Note 18 — Risk Management and Derivatives**

The Company is exposed to global market risks, including the effect of changes in foreign currency exchange rates and interest rates, and uses derivatives to manage financial exposures that occur in the normal course of business. The Company does not hold or issue derivatives for speculative trading purposes.

The Company formally documents all relationships between hedging instruments and hedged items, as well as its risk management objective and strategy for undertaking hedge transactions. This process includes linking all derivatives to either specific firm commitments or forecasted transactions. The Company also enters into foreign exchange forwards to mitigate the change in fair value of specific assets and liabilities on the balance sheet, which are not designated as hedging instruments under the accounting standards for derivatives and hedging. Accordingly, changes in the fair value of hedges of recorded balance sheet positions are recognized

83

**NIKE, INC.**

**NOTES TO CONSOLIDATED FINANCIAL STATEMENTS — (Continued)**

immediately in other (income) expense, net, on the income statement together with the transaction gain or loss from the hedged balance sheet position. The Company classifies the cash flows at settlement from these undesignated hedges in the same category as the cash flows from the related hedged items, generally within the cash provided by operations component of the cash flow statement.

The majority of derivatives outstanding as of May 31, 2010 are designated as either cash flow, fair value or net investment hedges under the accounting standards for derivatives and hedging. All derivatives are recognized on the balance sheet at their fair value and classified based on the instrument's maturity date. The total notional amount of outstanding derivatives as of May 31, 2010 was $6.2 billion, which was primarily comprised of cash flow hedges denominated in Euros, Japanese Yen and British Pounds.

The following table presents the fair values of derivative instruments included within the consolidated balance sheet as of May 31, 2010 and 2009:

| | Asset Derivatives | | | Liability Derivatives | | |
|---|---|---|---|---|---|---|
| | **Balance Sheet Classification** | **May 31, 2010** | **May 31, 2009** | **Balance Sheet Classification** | **May 31, 2010** | **May 31, 2009** |
| | | (In millions) | | | | |
| Derivatives formally designated as hedging instruments: | | | | | | |
| Foreign exchange forwards and options | Prepaid expenses and other current assets | $ 315.9 | $ 270.4 | Accrued liabilities | $ 24.7 | $ 34.6 |
| Interest rate swap contracts | Prepaid expenses and other current assets | — | 0.1 | Accrued liabilities | — | — |
| Foreign exchange forwards and options | Deferred income taxes and other assets | 0.4 | 81.3 | Deferred income taxes and other liabilities | 0.1 | — |
| Interest rate swap contracts | Deferred income taxes and other assets | 14.6 | 13.7 | Deferred income taxes and other liabilities | — | — |
| Total derivatives formally designated as hedging instruments | | 330.9 | 365.5 | | 24.8 | 34.6 |
| Derivatives not designated as hedging instruments: | | | | | | |
| Foreign exchange forwards and options | Prepaid expenses and other current assets | $ 103.9 | $ 12.8 | Accrued liabilities | $ 138.9 | $ 34.3 |
| Foreign exchange forwards and options | Deferred income taxes and other assets | — | 0.4 | Deferred income taxes and other liabilities | 1.4 | — |
| Total derivatives not designated as hedging instruments | | 103.9 | 13.2 | | 140.3 | 34.3 |
| Total derivatives | | $ 434.8 | $ 378.7 | | $ 165.1 | $ 68.9 |

84

**NIKE, INC.**

**NOTES TO CONSOLIDATED FINANCIAL STATEMENTS — (Continued)**

The following tables present the amounts affecting the consolidated statements of income for years ended May 31, 2010 and 2009:

| Derivatives formally designated | Amount of Gain (Loss) Recognized in Other Comprehensive Income on Derivatives[1] | | Amount of Gain (Loss) Reclassified From Accumulated Other Comprehensive Income into Income[1] | | |
|---|---|---|---|---|---|
| | Year Ended May 31, 2010 | Year Ended May 31, 2009 | Location of Gain (Loss) Reclassified From Accumulated Other Comprehensive Income Into Income[1] | Year Ended May 31, 2010 | Year Ended May 31, 2009 |
| | (In millions) | | | | |
| Derivatives designated as cash flow hedges: | | | | | |
| Foreign exchange forwards and options | $ (29.9) | $ 106.3 | Revenue | $ 51.4 | $ 92.7 |
| Foreign exchange forwards and options | 89.0 | 350.1 | Cost of sales | 60.0 | (13.5) |
| Foreign exchange forwards and options | 4.7 | (0.4) | Selling and administrative expense | 1.0 | 0.8 |
| Foreign exchange forwards and options | 51.1 | 165.1 | Other (income) expense, net | 56.1 | 67.8 |
| Total designated cash flow hedges | $ 114.9 | $ 621.1 | | $ 168.5 | $ 147.8 |
| Derivatives designated as net investment hedges: | | | | | |
| Foreign exchange forwards and options | $ 66.0 | $ 161.4 | Other (income) expense, net | $ — | $ — |

[1] For the year ended May 31, 2010, $5.2 million of income was recorded to other (income) expense, net as a result of cash flow hedge ineffectiveness. For the year ended May 31, 2009, an immaterial amount of ineffectiveness from cash flow hedges was recorded in other (income) expense, net.

| | Amount of Gain (Loss) recognized in Income on Derivatives | | |
|---|---|---|---|
| | Year Ended May 31, 2010 | Year Ended May 31, 2009 | Location of Gain (Loss) Recognized in Income on Derivatives |
| | (In millions) | | |
| Derivatives designated as fair value hedges: | | | |
| Interest rate swaps[1] | $ 7.4 | $ 1.5 | Interest expense (income), net |
| Derivatives not designated as hedging instruments: | | | |
| Foreign exchange forwards and options | $ (91.1) | $ (83.0) | Other (income) expense, net |

[1] All interest rate swap agreements meet the shortcut method requirements under the accounting standards for derivatives and hedging. Accordingly, changes in the fair values of the interest rate swap agreements are exactly offset by changes in the fair value of the underlying long–term debt. Refer to section "Fair Value Hedges" for additional detail.

Refer to Note 5 — Accrued Liabilities for derivative instruments recorded in accrued liabilities, Note 6 —Fair Value Measurements for a description of how the above financial instruments are valued, Note 14 — Accumulated Other Comprehensive Income and the Consolidated Statement of Shareholders' Equity for additional information on changes in other comprehensive income for the years ended May 31, 2010 and 2009.

## NIKE, INC.
### NOTES TO CONSOLIDATED FINANCIAL STATEMENTS — (Continued)

*Cash Flow Hedges*

The purpose of the Company's foreign currency hedging activities is to protect the Company from the risk that the eventual cash flows resulting from transactions in foreign currencies, including revenues, product costs, selling and administrative expenses, investments in U.S. dollar–denominated available–for–sale debt securities and intercompany transactions, including intercompany borrowings, will be adversely affected by changes in exchange rates. It is the Company's policy to utilize derivatives to reduce foreign exchange risks where internal netting strategies cannot be effectively employed. Hedged transactions are denominated primarily in Euros, British Pounds and Japanese Yen. The Company hedges up to 100% of anticipated exposures typically 12 months in advance, but has hedged as much as 34 months in advance.

All changes in fair values of outstanding cash flow hedge derivatives, except the ineffective portion, are recorded in other comprehensive income until net income is affected by the variability of cash flows of the hedged transaction. In most cases, amounts recorded in other comprehensive income will be released to net income some time after the maturity of the related derivative. The consolidated statement of income classification of effective hedge results is the same as that of the underlying exposure. Results of hedges of revenue and product costs are recorded in revenue and cost of sales, respectively, when the underlying hedged transaction affects net income. Results of hedges of selling and administrative expense are recorded together with those costs when the related expense is recorded. Results of hedges of anticipated purchases and sales of U.S. dollar–denominated available–for–sale securities are recorded in other (income) expense, net when the securities are sold. Results of hedges of anticipated intercompany transactions are recorded in other (income) expense, net when the transaction occurs. The Company classifies the cash flows at settlement from these designated cash flow hedge derivatives in the same category as the cash flows from the related hedged items, generally within the cash provided by operations component of the cash flow statement.

Premiums paid on options are initially recorded as deferred charges. The Company assesses the effectiveness of options based on the total cash flows method and records total changes in the options' fair value to other comprehensive income to the degree they are effective.

As of May 31, 2010, $187.2 million of deferred net gains (net of tax) on both outstanding and matured derivatives accumulated in other comprehensive income are expected to be reclassified to net income during the next 12 months as a result of underlying hedged transactions also being recorded in net income. Actual amounts ultimately reclassified to net income are dependent on the exchange rates in effect when derivative contracts that are currently outstanding mature. As of May 31, 2010, the maximum term over which the Company is hedging exposures to the variability of cash flows for its forecasted and recorded transactions is 18 months.

The Company formally assesses both at a hedge's inception and on an ongoing basis, whether the derivatives that are used in the hedging transaction have been highly effective in offsetting changes in the cash flows of hedged items and whether those derivatives may be expected to remain highly effective in future periods. Effectiveness for cash flow hedges is assessed based on forward rates. When it is determined that a derivative is not, or has ceased to be, highly effective as a hedge, the Company discontinues hedge accounting prospectively.

The Company discontinues hedge accounting prospectively when (1) it determines that the derivative is no longer highly effective in offsetting changes in the cash flows of a hedged item (including hedged items such as firm commitments or forecasted transactions); (2) the derivative expires or is sold, terminated, or exercised; (3) it is no longer probable that the forecasted transaction will occur; or (4) management determines that designating the derivative as a hedging instrument is no longer appropriate.

**NIKE, INC.**
**NOTES TO CONSOLIDATED FINANCIAL STATEMENTS — (Continued)**

When the Company discontinues hedge accounting because it is no longer probable that the forecasted transaction will occur in the originally expected period, or within an additional two–month period of time thereafter, the gain or loss on the derivative remains in accumulated other comprehensive income and is reclassified to net income when the forecasted transaction affects net income. However, if it is probable that a forecasted transaction will not occur by the end of the originally specified time period or within an additional two–month period of time thereafter, the gains and losses that were accumulated in other comprehensive income will be recognized immediately in net income. In all situations in which hedge accounting is discontinued and the derivative remains outstanding, the Company will carry the derivative at its fair value on the balance sheet, recognizing future changes in the fair value in other (income) expense, net. For the year ended May 31, 2010, $5.2 million of income was recorded to other (income) expense, net as a result of cash flow hedge ineffectiveness. For the years ended 2009 and 2008, the Company recorded in other (income) expense an immaterial amount of ineffectiveness from cash flow hedges.

*Fair Value Hedges*

The Company is also exposed to the risk of changes in the fair value of certain fixed–rate debt attributable to changes in interest rates. Derivatives currently used by the Company to hedge this risk are receive–fixed, pay–variable interest rate swaps. As of May 31, 2010, all interest rate swap agreements are designated as fair value hedges of the related long–term debt and meet the shortcut method requirements under the accounting standards for derivatives and hedging. Accordingly, changes in the fair values of the interest rate swap agreements are exactly offset by changes in the fair value of the underlying long–term debt. The cash flows associated with the Company's fair value hedges are periodic interest payments while the swaps are outstanding, which are reflected in net income within the cash provided by operations component of the cash flow statement. No ineffectiveness has been recorded to net income related to interest rate swaps designated as fair value hedges for the years ended May 31, 2010, 2009 and 2008.

In fiscal 2003, the Company entered into a receive–floating, pay–fixed interest rate swap agreement related to a Japanese Yen denominated intercompany loan with one of the Company's Japanese subsidiaries. This interest rate swap was not designated as a hedge under the accounting standards for derivatives and hedging. Accordingly, changes in the fair value of the swap were recorded to net income each period through maturity as a component of interest expense (income), net. Both the intercompany loan and the related interest rate swap matured during the year ended May 31, 2009.

*Net Investment Hedges*

The Company also hedges the risk of variability in foreign–currency–denominated net investments in wholly–owned international operations. All changes in fair value of the derivatives designated as net investment hedges, except ineffective portions, are reported in the cumulative translation adjustment component of other comprehensive income along with the foreign currency translation adjustments on those investments. The Company classifies the cash flows at settlement of its net investment hedges within the cash used by investing component of the cash flow statement. The Company assesses hedge effectiveness based on changes in forward rates. The Company recorded no ineffectiveness from its net investment hedges for the years ended May 31, 2010, 2009, and 2008.

*Credit Risk*

The Company is exposed to credit–related losses in the event of non–performance by counterparties to hedging instruments. The counterparties to all derivative transactions are major financial institutions with investment grade credit ratings. However, this does not eliminate the Company's exposure to credit risk with

87

## NIKE, INC.
### NOTES TO CONSOLIDATED FINANCIAL STATEMENTS — (Continued)

these institutions. This credit risk is limited to the unrealized gains in such contracts should any of these counterparties fail to perform as contracted. To manage this risk, the Company has established strict counterparty credit guidelines that are continually monitored and reported to senior management according to prescribed guidelines. The Company utilizes a portfolio of financial institutions either headquartered or operating in the same countries the Company conducts its business. As a result of the above considerations, the Company considers the impact of the risk of counterparty default to be immaterial.

Certain of the Company's derivative instruments contain credit risk related contingent features. As of May 31, 2010, the Company was in compliance with all such credit risk related contingent features. The aggregate fair value of derivative instruments with credit risk related contingent features that are in a net liability position at May 31, 2010 was $18.3 million. The Company was not required to post any collateral as a result of these contingent features.

### Note 19 — Operating Segments and Related Information

*Operating Segments.*    The Company's operating segments are evidence of the structure of the Company's internal organization. The major segments are defined by geographic regions for operations participating in NIKE Brand sales activity excluding NIKE Golf. Each NIKE Brand geographic segment operates predominantly in one industry: the design, production, marketing and selling of sports and fitness footwear, apparel, and equipment. In fiscal 2009, the Company initiated a reorganization of the NIKE Brand into a new model consisting of six geographies. Effective June 1, 2009, the Company's new reportable operating segments for the NIKE Brand are: North America, Western Europe, Central and Eastern Europe, Greater China, Japan, and Emerging Markets. Previously, NIKE Brand operations were organized into the following four geographic regions: U.S., Europe, Middle East and Africa (collectively, "EMEA"), Asia Pacific, and Americas.

The Company's "Other" category is broken into two components for presentation purposes to align with the way management views the Company. The "Global Brand Divisions" category primarily represents NIKE Brand licensing businesses that are not part of a geographic operating segment, selling, general and administrative expenses that are centrally managed for the NIKE Brand and costs associated with product development and supply chain operations. The "Other Businesses" category primarily consists of the activities of Cole Haan, Converse Inc., Hurley International LLC, NIKE Golf and Umbro Ltd. Activities represented in the "Other" category are considered immaterial for individual disclosure. Prior period amounts have been reclassified to conform to the Company's new operating structure described above.

Revenues as shown below represent sales to external customers for each segment. Intercompany revenues have been eliminated and are immaterial for separate disclosure.

Corporate consists of unallocated general and administrative expenses, which includes expenses associated with centrally managed departments, depreciation and amortization related to the Company's headquarters, unallocated insurance and benefit programs, including stock−based compensation, certain foreign currency gains and losses, including hedge gains and losses, certain corporate eliminations and other items.

Effective June 1, 2009, the primary financial measure used by the Company to evaluate performance of individual operating segments is Earnings Before Interest and Taxes (commonly referred to as "EBIT") which represents net income before interest expense (income), net and income taxes in the Consolidated Statements of Income. Reconciling items for EBIT represent corporate expense items that are not allocated to the operating segments for management reporting. Previously, the Company evaluated performance of individual operating segments based on pre−tax income or income before income taxes.

88

**NIKE, INC.**

**NOTES TO CONSOLIDATED FINANCIAL STATEMENTS — (Continued)**

As part of the Company's centrally managed foreign exchange risk management program, standard foreign currency rates are assigned to each NIKE Brand entity in our geographic operating segments and are used to record any non–functional currency revenues or product purchases into the entity's functional currency. Geographic operating segment revenues and cost of sales reflect use of these standard rates. For all NIKE Brand operating segments, differences between assigned standard foreign currency rates and actual market rates are included in Corporate together with foreign currency hedge gains and losses generated from the centrally managed foreign exchange risk management program and other conversion gains and losses. For the years ended May 31, 2009 and 2008, foreign currency hedge results along with other conversion gains and losses generated by the Western Europe and Central and Eastern Europe geographies were recorded in their respective results.

Additions to long–lived assets as presented in the following table represent capital expenditures.

Accounts receivable, inventories and property, plant and equipment for operating segments are regularly reviewed by management and are therefore provided below.

Certain prior year amounts have been reclassified to conform to fiscal 2010 presentation.

89

**NIKE, INC.**
**NOTES TO CONSOLIDATED FINANCIAL STATEMENTS — (Continued)**

| | Year Ended May 31, | | |
|---|---|---|---|
| | 2010 | 2009 (In millions) | 2008 |
| Revenue | | | |
| North America | $ 6,696.0 | $ 6,778.3 | $ 6,660.5 |
| Western Europe | 3,892.0 | 4,139.1 | 4,320.0 |
| Central and Eastern Europe | 1,149.9 | 1,373.2 | 1,309.2 |
| Greater China | 1,741.8 | 1,743.3 | 1,353.6 |
| Japan | 882.0 | 925.9 | 822.4 |
| Emerging Markets | 2,041.6 | 1,702.0 | 1,630.3 |
| Global Brand Divisions | 105.3 | 95.3 | 117.9 |
| Total NIKE Brand | 16,508.6 | 16,757.1 | 16,213.9 |
| Other Businesses | 2,529.5 | 2,419.0 | 2,413.1 |
| Corporate | (24.1) | — | — |
| Total NIKE Consolidated Revenues | $19,014.0 | $19,176.1 | $18,627.0 |
| Earnings Before Interest and Taxes | | | |
| North America | $ 1,538.1 | $ 1,429.3 | $ 1,460.4 |
| Western Europe | 855.7 | 939.1 | 922.5 |
| Central and Eastern Europe | 281.2 | 415.1 | 358.4 |
| Greater China | 637.1 | 575.2 | 430.7 |
| Japan | 180.3 | 205.4 | 178.9 |
| Emerging Markets | 492.6 | 342.6 | 306.6 |
| Global Brand Divisions | (866.8) | (811.5) | (736.8) |
| Total NIKE Brand [1] | 3,118.2 | 3,095.2 | 2,920.7 |
| Other Businesses | 299.4 | (192.6) | 358.6 |
| Corporate | (894.4) | (955.6) | (853.5) |
| Total NIKE Consolidated Earnings Before Interest and Taxes | 2,523.2 | 1,947.0 | 2,425.8 |
| Interest expense (income), net | 6.3 | (9.5) | (77.1) |
| Total NIKE Consolidated Earnings Before Taxes | $ 2,516.9 | $ 1,956.5 | $ 2,502.9 |
| Additions to Long–lived Assets | | | |
| North America | $ 45.3 | $ 99.2 | $ 141.9 |
| Western Europe | 58.9 | 69.6 | 63.5 |
| Central and Eastern Europe | 4.3 | 8.1 | 5.5 |
| Greater China | 80.4 | 58.5 | 13.1 |
| Japan | 11.6 | 10.0 | 21.9 |
| Emerging Markets | 10.5 | 10.9 | 12.4 |
| Global Brand Divisions | 29.9 | 37.8 | 22.6 |
| Total NIKE Brand | 240.9 | 294.1 | 280.9 |
| Other Businesses | 52.1 | 89.6 | 61.5 |
| Corporate | 42.1 | 72.0 | 106.8 |
| Total Additions to Long–lived Assets | $ 335.1 | $ 455.7 | $ 449.2 |
| Depreciation | | | |
| North America | $ 64.7 | $ 64.3 | $ 52.4 |
| Western Europe | 57.1 | 51.4 | 61.1 |
| Central and Eastern Europe | 4.6 | 4.0 | 3.7 |
| Greater China | 11.0 | 7.2 | 3.8 |
| Japan | 26.2 | 29.9 | 20.4 |
| Emerging Markets | 11.0 | 10.2 | 10.8 |
| Global Brand Divisions | 33.8 | 42.3 | 34.3 |
| Total NIKE Brand | 208.4 | 209.3 | 186.5 |
| Other Businesses | 45.7 | 37.5 | 28.1 |
| Corporate | 69.6 | 88.2 | 89.0 |
| Total Depreciation | $ 323.7 | $ 335.0 | $ 303.6 |

## NIKE, INC.
### NOTES TO CONSOLIDATED FINANCIAL STATEMENTS — (Continued)

(1) During the year ended May 31, 2009, the Other category included a pre–tax charge of $401.3 million for the impairment of goodwill, intangible and other assets of Umbro, which was recorded in the third quarter of fiscal 2009. See Note 4 — Acquisition, Identifiable Intangible Assets, Goodwill and Umbro Impairment for more information.

(2) During the year ended May 31, 2009, Corporate expense included pre–tax charges of $195.0 million for the Company's restructuring activities, which were completed in the fourth quarter of fiscal 2009. See Note 16 — Restructuring Charges for more information.

| | Year Ended May 31, 2010 | 2009 |
|---|---|---|
| | (In millions) | |
| **Accounts Receivable, net** | | |
| North America | $ 848.0 | $ 897.7 |
| Western Europe | 401.8 | 508.8 |
| Central and Eastern Europe | 293.6 | 368.3 |
| Greater China | 128.9 | 122.3 |
| Japan | 166.8 | 207.2 |
| Emerging Markets | 327.2 | 268.2 |
| Global Brand Divisions | 22.8 | 53.3 |
| Total NIKE Brand | 2,189.1 | 2,425.8 |
| Other Businesses | 442.1 | 439.7 |
| Corporate | 18.6 | 18.4 |
| Total Accounts Receivable, net | $ 2,649.8 | $ 2,883.9 |
| **Inventories** | | |
| North America | $ 767.5 | $ 868.8 |
| Western Europe | 347.2 | 341.6 |
| Central and Eastern Europe | 124.8 | 278.1 |
| Greater China | 103.5 | 110.4 |
| Japan | 68.3 | 95.7 |
| Emerging Markets | 262.2 | 258.2 |
| Global Brand Divisions | 20.6 | 32.4 |
| Total NIKE Brand | 1,694.1 | 1,985.2 |
| Other Businesses | 346.7 | 371.8 |
| Corporate | — | — |
| Total Inventories | $ 2,040.8 | $ 2,357.0 |
| **Property, Plant and Equipment, net** | | |
| North America | $ 324.7 | $ 354.3 |
| Western Europe | 282.1 | 326.5 |
| Central and Eastern Europe | 12.3 | 15.0 |
| Greater China | 145.5 | 78.2 |
| Japan | 332.6 | 318.5 |
| Emerging Markets | 47.0 | 47.3 |
| Global Brand Divisions | 99.6 | 103.1 |
| Total NIKE Brand | 1,243.8 | 1,242.9 |
| Other Businesses | 167.4 | 163.7 |
| Corporate | 520.7 | 551.1 |
| Total Property, Plant and Equipment, net | $ 1,931.9 | $ 1,957.7 |

91

**NIKE, INC.**

**NOTES TO CONSOLIDATED FINANCIAL STATEMENTS — (Continued)**

*Revenues by Major Product Lines.*    Revenues to external customers for NIKE Brand products are attributable to sales of footwear, apparel and equipment. Other revenues to external customers primarily include external sales by Cole Haan, Converse, Exeter (whose primary business was the Starter brand business which was sold December 17, 2007), Hurley, NIKE Bauer Hockey (through April 16, 2008), NIKE Golf, and Umbro (beginning March 3, 2008).

|  | 2010 | Year Ended May 31, 2009 (In millions) | 2008 |
|---|---|---|---|
| Footwear | $ 10,333.1 | $ 10,306.7 | $  9,731.6 |
| Apparel | 5,036.6 | 5,244.7 | 5,234.0 |
| Equipment | 1,033.6 | 1,110.4 | 1,130.4 |
| Other | 2,610.7 | 2,514.3 | 2,531.0 |
|  | $ 19,014.0 | $ 19,176.1 | $ 18,627.0 |

*Revenues and Long-Lived Assets by Geographic Area.*    Geographical area information is similar to what was shown previously under operating segments with the exception of the Other activity, which has been allocated to the geographical areas based on the location where the sales originated. Revenues derived in the United States were $7,913.9 million, $8,019.8 million and $7,938.5 million, for the years ended May 31, 2010, 2009 and 2008, respectively. The Company's largest concentrations of long-lived assets primarily consist of the Company's world headquarters and distribution facilities in the United States and distribution facilities in Japan and Belgium. Long-lived assets attributable to operations in the United States, which are comprised of net property, plant & equipment, were $1,070.1 million, $1,142.6 million and $1,109.9 million at May 31, 2010, 2009 and 2008, respectively. Long-lived assets attributable to operations in Japan were $335.6 million, $322.3 million and $303.8 million at May 31, 2010, 2009 and 2008, respectively. Long-lived assets attributable to operations in Belgium were $163.7 million, $191.0 million and $219.1 million at May 31, 2010, 2009 and 2008, respectively.

*Major Customers.*    Revenues derived from Foot Locker, Inc. represented 8% of the Company's consolidated revenues for the year ended May 31, 2010 and 9% for the years ended May 31, 2009 and 2008. Sales to this customer are included in all segments of the Company.

92

# International Financial Reporting Standards (IFRS)

## The Need for Global Accounting Standards

As discussed in Chapter 1, the Financial Accounting Standards Board (FASB) establishes generally accepted accounting principles (GAAP) for public companies in the United States. Of course, there is a world beyond the borders of the United States. In recent years, the removal of trade barriers and the growth in cross-border equity and debt issuances have led to a dramatic increase in international commerce. As a result, companies are often reporting financial results to users outside of the United States.

Historically, accounting standards have varied considerably across countries. These variances have been driven by cultural, legal, and political differences, and resulted in financial statements that were not easily comparable and difficult to interpret. These differences caused problems for companies in Europe and Asia, where local economies have become increasingly tied to international commerce.

During the last decade, however, a common set of International Financial Reporting Standards (IFRS) has emerged to reduce cross-country differences in accounting standards, primarily in countries outside of North America. While much of the world has migrated to IFRS, the United States has not. Because of the size of the United States and its significant role in world commerce, however, U.S. GAAP still has a global impact. As a result, there are currently two major accounting standard-setting efforts in the world, U.S. GAAP and IFRS. These two sets of accounting standards add cost and complexity for companies doing business and obtaining financing internationally.

## Overview of IFRS

International Financial Reporting Standards (IFRS) have emerged during the last 10 years to meet the financial reporting needs of an increasingly global business environment.

**What Is IFRS?** International Financial Reporting Standards are a set of global accounting standards developed by an international standard-setting body called the International Accounting Standards Board (IASB). Like the Financial Accounting Standards Board (FASB), the IASB is an independent entity that establishes accounting rules. Unlike the FASB, the IASB does not establish accounting rules for any specific country. Rather, it develops accounting rules that can be used by a variety of countries, with the goal of developing a single set of global accounting standards.

**Who Uses IFRS?** IFRS applies to companies that issue publicly traded debt or equity securities, called **public companies**, in countries that have adopted IFRS as their accounting standards. Since 2005, all 27 countries in the European Union (EU) have been required to prepare financial statements using IFRS. In addition, over

100 other countries have adopted or are planning to adopt IFRS for public companies (see Exhibit 1). Canada will adopt IFRS by 2011, with Mexico following in 2012. Japan will consider mandatory use of IFRS in 2012. In addition, the G20 (Group of 20) leadership has called for uniform global accounting standards by June 2011.

**EXHIBIT 1**

**IFRS Adopters**

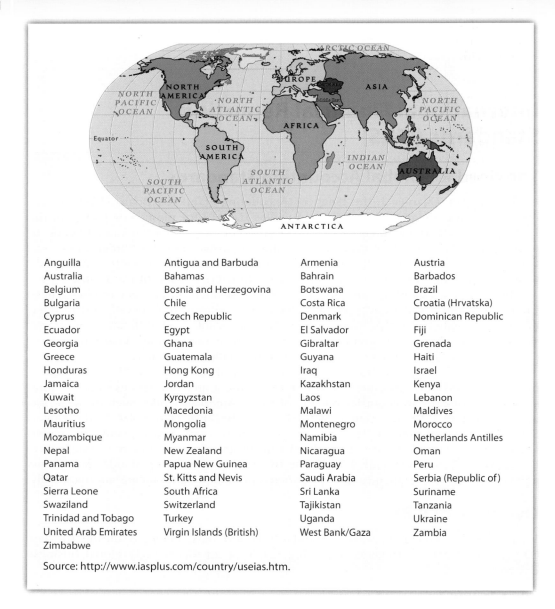

| | | | |
|---|---|---|---|
| Anguilla | Antigua and Barbuda | Armenia | Austria |
| Australia | Bahamas | Bahrain | Barbados |
| Belgium | Bosnia and Herzegovina | Botswana | Brazil |
| Bulgaria | Chile | Costa Rica | Croatia (Hrvatska) |
| Cyprus | Czech Republic | Denmark | Dominican Republic |
| Ecuador | Egypt | El Salvador | Fiji |
| Georgia | Ghana | Gibraltar | Grenada |
| Greece | Guatemala | Guyana | Haiti |
| Honduras | Hong Kong | Iraq | Israel |
| Jamaica | Jordan | Kazakhstan | Kenya |
| Kuwait | Kyrgyzstan | Laos | Lebanon |
| Lesotho | Macedonia | Malawi | Maldives |
| Mauritius | Mongolia | Montenegro | Morocco |
| Mozambique | Myanmar | Namibia | Netherlands Antilles |
| Nepal | New Zealand | Nicaragua | Oman |
| Panama | Papua New Guinea | Paraguay | Peru |
| Qatar | St. Kitts and Nevis | Saudi Arabia | Serbia (Republic of) |
| Sierra Leone | South Africa | Sri Lanka | Suriname |
| Swaziland | Switzerland | Tajikistan | Tanzania |
| Trinidad and Tobago | Turkey | Uganda | Ukraine |
| United Arab Emirates | Virgin Islands (British) | West Bank/Gaza | Zambia |
| Zimbabwe | | | |

Source: http://www.iasplus.com/country/useias.htm.

## U.S. GAAP and IFRS: The Road Forward

The United States has not formally adopted IFRS for U.S. companies. The wide acceptance being gained by IFRS around the world, however, has placed considerable pressure on the United States to align U.S. GAAP with IFRS. There are two possible paths that the United States could take to achieve this: (1) adoption of IFRS by the U.S. Securities and Exchange Commission and (2) convergence of U.S. GAAP and IFRS. These two options are briefly discussed below.

**Adoption of IFRS by the SEC** The U.S. Securities and Exchange Commission (SEC) is the U.S. governmental agency that has authority over the accounting and financial disclosures for U.S. public companies. Only the SEC has the authority to adopt IFRS for U.S. public companies. In 2008, the SEC presented a "roadmap" to adopting IFRS, which outlined a timetable along with a set of "milestones" that needed to be met before the SEC would be willing to adopt IFRS. In 2010, the SEC reiterated the milestones outlined in the roadmap. According to the work plan, the SEC plans on deciding whether to incorporate IFRS into U.S. GAAP for public companies by 2011. If adopted, companies could begin reporting under IFRS as early as 2015.

If the SEC adopts IFRS for U.S. GAAP, it has stated the FASB would retain a "critical and substantive role in achieving the goal of global accounting standards." This suggests that the FASB will not necessarily be eliminated. More likely, the FASB would provide input to the IASB so that U.S. accounting perspectives are considered.

**Convergence of U.S. GAAP and IFRS**  If the SEC does not adopt IFRS, an alternative approach would be for the FASB and IASB to converge U.S. GAAP and IFRS. This would involve aligning IFRS and U.S. GAAP one topic at a time, slowly merging IFRS and U.S. GAAP into two broadly uniform sets of accounting standards. To this end, the FASB and IASB have agreed to work together on a number of difficult and high-profile accounting issues. These issues frame a large portion of the disagreement between the two sets of standards and, if accomplished, will significantly reduce the differences between U.S. GAAP and IFRS. The projects selected for the convergence effort represent some of the more technical topics in accounting, and are covered in intermediate and advanced accounting courses. The FASB and IASB have set mid-2011 as the deadline for establishing final standards.

One of the major limitations of convergence is that both the FASB and IASB continue to operate as the accounting standard-setting bodies for their respective jurisdictions. As such, convergence would not result in a single set of global accounting standards. Only those standards that go through the joint FASB–IASB standard-setting process would be released as uniform. Standards that do not go through a joint standard-setting process may create inconsistencies between U.S. GAAP and IFRS. Thus, convergence does not guarantee complete uniformity between U.S. GAAP and IFRS. A brief summary of the major U.S. decisions related to IFRS are outlined in the table below.

|  | ***The Road to IFRS*** |
|---|---|
| 2002 | IASB and FASB jointly agree to work toward making IFRS and U.S. GAAP compatible. |
| 2005 | EU adopts IFRS for all companies engaged in international markets. |
|  | SEC and European Commission jointly agree to work toward a "Roadmap for Convergence." |
| 2007 | SEC allows foreign (non-U.S.) companies to use IFRS financial statements to meet U.S. filing requirements. |
| 2008 | SEC issues proposed "Roadmap" with timeline and key milestones for adopting IFRS. |
| 2010 | SEC reiterates milestones in the proposed "Roadmap." |
| 2011 | Target date for FASB and IASB convergence on major standard-setting projects. |
|  | Target date for SEC's tentative decision regarding IFRS adoption. |
| 2015 | Earliest date the SEC would require IFRS for U.S. public companies. |

# Differences Between U.S. GAAP and IFRS

U.S. GAAP and IFRS differ both in their approach to standard setting, as well as their financial statement presentation and recording of transactions.

**Rules-Based vs. Principles Approach to Standard Setting**  U.S. GAAP is considered to be a "rules-based" approach to accounting standard setting. The accounting standards provide detailed and specific rules on the accounting for business transactions. There are few exceptions or varying interpretations of the accounting for a business event. This structure is consistent with the U.S. legal and regulatory system, reflecting the social and economic values of the United States.

In contrast, IFRS is designed to meet the needs of many countries. Differences in legal, political, and economic systems create different needs for and uses of financial information in different countries. For example, Germany needs a financial reporting system that reflects the central role of banks in its financial system, while the Netherlands needs a financial reporting system that reflects the significant role of outside equity in its financial system.

To accommodate economic, legal, and social diversity, IFRS must be broad enough to capture these differences, while still presenting comparable financial statements. Under IFRS, there is greater opportunity for different interpretations of the accounting treatment of a business event across different business entities. To support this, IFRS often has more extensive disclosures that support alternative assumptions. Thus, IFRS provides more latitude for professional judgment than typically found in comparable U.S. GAAP. Many countries find this feature attractive in reducing regulatory costs associated with using and auditing financial reports. This "principles-based" approach presents one of the most significant challenges to adopting IFRS in the United States.

**Technical Differences Between IFRS and U.S. GAAP** Although U.S. GAAP is similar to IFRS, differences arise in the presentation format, balance sheet valuations, and technical accounting procedures. The Mornin' Joe International financial statements presented on pages 630–634 highlight the financial statement format, presentation, and recording differences between U.S. GAAP and IFRS. In addition, the International Connection boxes in Chapters 1, 4, 6, 9, 11, and 14 discuss some of the significant differences between U.S. GAAP and IFRS. A more comprehensive summary of the key differences between U.S. GAAP and IFRS that are relevant to an introductory accounting course is summarized in the table on the following pages.

## Discussion Questions

1. Briefly discuss why global accounting standards are needed in today's business environment.

2. What are International Financial Reporting Standards? Who uses these accounting standards?

3. What body is responsible for setting International Financial Reporting Standards?

4. Briefly discuss the differences between (a) convergence of U.S. GAAP with IFRS and (b) adoption of IFRS by the U.S. Securities and Exchange Commission.

5. Briefly discuss the difference between (a) a "rules-based" approach to accounting standard setting and (b) a "principles-based" approach to accounting standard setting.

6. How is property, plant, and equipment measured on the balance sheet under IFRS? How does this differ from the way property, plant, and equipment is measured on the balance sheet under U.S. GAAP?

7. What inventory costing methods are allowed under IFRS? How does this differ from the treatment under U.S. GAAP?

**Comparison of Accounting for Selected Items Under U.S. GAAP and IFRS**

| | U.S. GAAP | IFRS | Text Reference |
|---|---|---|---|
| **General:** | | | |
| Financial statement titles | Balance Sheet<br>Income Statement<br>Statement of Stockholders' Equity<br>Statement of Cash Flows | Statement of Financial Position<br>Statement of Comprehensive Income<br>Statement of Changes in Equity<br>Statement of Cash Flows | General |
| Financial periods presented | Public companies must present two years of comparative information for income statement, statement of stockholders' equity, and statement of cash flows | One year of comparative information must be presented | General |
| Conceptual basis for standard setting | "Rules-based" approach | "Principles-based" approach | General |
| Internal control requirements | Sarbanes-Oxley Act (SOX) Section 404 | | Ch 6; LO 1 |
| **Balance Sheet:** | **Balance Sheet** | **Statement of Financial Position** | |
| Terminology differences | "Payable"<br>"Stockholders' Equity"<br>"Net Income (Loss)" | "Provision"<br>"Capital and Reserves"<br>"Profit or (Loss)" | Ch 9<br>Ch 10<br>General |
| Inventory—LIFO | LIFO allowed | LIFO prohibited | Ch 5; LO 3, 4, 5 |
| Inventory—valuation | Market is defined as "replacement value"<br>Reversal of lower-of-cost-or-market write-downs not allowed | Market is defined as "fair value"<br>Reversal of write-downs allowed | Ch 5; LO 6<br>Ch 5; LO 6 |
| Long-lived assets | May NOT be revalued to fair value | May be revalued to fair value on a regular basis | Ch 8; LO 1 |

*(Continued)*

**Comparison of Accounting for Selected Items Under U.S. GAAP and IFRS** *(Continued)*

| | U.S. GAAP | IFRS | Text Reference |
|---|---|---|---|
| Land held for investment | Treated as held for use or sale, and recorded at historical cost | May be accounted for on a historical cost basis or on a fair value basis with changes in fair value recognized through profit and loss | Ch 8; LO 1 |
| Property, plant, & equipment—valuation | Historical cost | May select between historical cost or revalued amount (a form of fair value) | Ch 8; LO 1 |
| | If impaired, impairment loss may NOT be reversed in future periods | If impaired, impairment loss may be reversed in future periods | |
| Cost of major overhaul (Capital and revenue expenditures) | Different treatment for ordinary repairs and maintenance, asset improvement, extraordinary repairs | Typically included as part of the cost of the asset if future economic benefit is probable and can be reliably measured | Ch 8; LO 1 |
| Intangible assets—valuation | Acquisition cost, unless impaired | Fair value permitted if the intangible asset trades in an active market | Ch 8; LO 5 |
| Intangible assets—impairment loss reversal | Prohibited | Prohibited for goodwill, but allowed for other intangible assets | Ch 8; LO 5 |
| Deferred tax liability | The amount due within one year classified as current | Always noncurrent | Appendix E |
| **Income Statement:** | | **Statement of Comprehensive Income** | |
| Revenue recognition | Detailed guidance depending on the transaction | Broad guidance | Ch 3; LO 1 |
| Classification of expenses on income statement | Public companies must present expenses on the income statement by function (e.g., cost of goods sold, selling, administrative) | Expenses may be presented based either by function (e.g., cost of goods sold, selling) or by the nature of expense (e.g., wages expense, interest expense) | Ch 5; LO 1 |
| Research and development costs | Expensed as incurred | Research costs expensed | Ch 8; LO 5 |
| | | Development costs capitalized once technical and economic feasibility attained | |
| Extraordinary items | Allowed for items that are both unusual in nature and infrequent in occurrence | Prohibited | Ch 13; Appendix E |

*(Continued)*

**Comparison of Accounting for Selected Items Under U.S. GAAP and IFRS (*Concluded*)**

| | U.S. GAAP | IFRS | Text Reference |
|---|---|---|---|
| **Statement of Cash Flows:** | ***Statement of Cash Flows*** | ***Statement of Cash Flows*** | |
| Classification of interest paid or received | Treated as an operating activity | Interest paid may be treated as either an operating or a financing activity, interest received may be treated as an operating or investing activity | Ch 12; LO 3 |
| Classification of dividend paid or received | Dividend paid treated as a financing activity, Dividend received treated as an operating activity | Dividend paid may be treated as either an operating or a financing activity, dividend received may be treated as an operating or investing activity | Ch 12; LO 3 |

# Glossary

## A

**absorption costing** The reporting of the costs of manufactured products, normally direct materials, direct labor, and factory overhead, as product costs. (932)

**accelerated depreciation method** A depreciation method that provides for a higher depreciation amount in the first year of the asset's use, followed by a gradually declining amount of depreciation. (416)

**account** An accounting form that is used to record the increases and decreases in each financial statement item. (50)

**account form** The form of balance sheet that resembles the basic format of the accounting equation, with assets on the left side and Liabilities and Owner's Equity sections on the right side. (17, 222)

**account payable** The liability created by a purchase on account. (11)

**account receivable** A claim against the customer created by selling merchandise or services on credit. (12, 64, 362)

**accounting** An information system that provides reports to stakeholders about the economic activities and condition of a business. (3)

**accounting cycle** The process that begins with analyzing and journalizing transactions and ends with the post-closing trial balance. (164)

**accounting equation** Assets = Liabilities + Owner's Equity. (9)

**accounting period concept** The accounting concept that assumes that the economic life of the business can be divided into time periods. (104)

**accounts payable subsidiary ledger** The subsidiary ledger containing the individual accounts with suppliers (creditors). (225, C-1)

**accounts receivable analysis** A company's ability to collect its accounts receivable. (706)

**accounts receivable subsidiary ledger** The subsidiary ledger containing the individual accounts with customers. (225, C-1)

**accounts receivable turnover** The relationship between net sales and accounts receivable, computed by dividing the net sales by the average net accounts receivable; measures how frequently during the year the accounts receivable are being converted to cash. (378, 706)

**accrual basis of accounting** Under this basis of accounting, revenues and expenses are reported in the income statement in the period in which they are earned or incurred. (104)

**accrued expenses** Expenses that have been incurred but not recorded in the accounts. (108)

**accrued revenues** Revenues that have been earned but not recorded in the accounts. (107)

**accumulated depreciation** The contra asset account credited when recording the depreciation of a fixed asset. (117)

**accumulated other comprehensive income** The cumulative effects of other comprehensive income items reported separately in the Stockholders' Equity section of the balance sheet. (601)

**activities** The types of work, or actions, involved in a manufacturing process or service activity. (1209)

**activity analysis** The study of employee effort and other business records to determine the cost of activities. (1261)

**activity base (driver)** A measure of activity that is related to changes in cost. Used in analyzing and classifying cost behavior. Activity bases are also used in the denominator in calculating the predetermined factory overhead rate to assign overhead costs to cost objects. (798, 886, 1210)

**activity rate** The cost of an activity per unit of activity base, determined by dividing the activity cost pool by the activity base. (1210)

**activity-based costing (ABC) method** A cost allocation method that identifies activities causing the incurrence of costs and allocates these costs to products (or other cost objects), based on activity drivers (bases). (799, 1209)

**adjusted trial balance** The trial balance prepared after all the adjusting entries have been posted. (123)

**adjusting entries** The journal entries that bring the accounts up to date at the end of the accounting period. (105)

**adjusting process** An analysis and updating of the accounts when financial statements are prepared. (105)

**administrative expenses (general expenses)** Expenses incurred in the administration or general operations of the business. (221)

**aging the receivables** The process of analyzing the accounts receivable and classifying them according to various age groupings, with the due date being the base point for determining age. (369)

**Allowance for Doubtful Accounts** The contra asset account for accounts receivable. (365)

**allowance method** The method of accounting for uncollectible accounts that provides an expense for uncollectible receivables in advance of their write-off. (363)

**amortization** The periodic transfer of the cost of an intangible asset to expense. (422)

**annuity** A series of equal cash flows at fixed intervals. (1169)

**appraisal costs** Costs to detect, measure, evaluate, and audit products and process to ensure that they conform to customer requirements and performance standards. (1261)

**assets** The resources owned by a business. (9, 52)

**available-for-sale securities** Securities that management expects to sell in the future but which are not actively traded for profit. (593)

**average inventory cost flow method** The method of inventory costing that is based on the assumption that costs should be charged against revenue by using the weighted average unit cost of the items sold. (278)

**average rate of return** A method of evaluating capital investment proposals that focuses on the expected profitability of the investment. (1165)

# B

**backflush accounting** Simplification of the accounting system by eliminating accumulation and transfer of costs as products move through production. (1258)

**bad debt expense** The operating expense incurred because of the failure to collect receivables. (363)

**balance of the account** The amount of the difference between the debits and the credits that have been entered into an account. (51)

**balance sheet** A list of the assets, liabilities, and owner's equity as of a specific date, usually at the close of the last day of a month or a year. (15)

**balanced scorecard** A performance evaluation approach that incorporates multiple performance dimensions by combining financial and nonfinancial measures. (1089)

**bank reconciliation** The analysis that details the items responsible for the difference between the cash balance reported in the bank statement and the balance of the cash account in the ledger. (333)

**bank statement** A summary of all transactions mailed to the depositor or made available online by the bank each month. (330)

**bond** A form of an interest-bearing note used by corporations to borrow on a long-term basis. (542)

**bond indenture** The contract between a corporation issuing bonds and the bondholders. (544)

**book value** The cost of a fixed asset minus accumulated depreciation on the asset. (416)

**book value of the asset (or net book value)** The difference between the cost of a fixed asset and its accumulated depreciation. (118)

**boot** The amount a buyer owes a seller when a fixed asset is traded in on a similar asset. (428)

**break-even point** The level of business operations at which revenues and expired costs are equal. (895)

**budget** An accounting device used to plan and control resources of operational departments and divisions. (978)

**budget performance report** A report comparing actual results with budget figures. (1033)

**budgetary slack** Excess resources set within a budget to provide for uncertain events. (980)

**budgeted variable factory overhead** The standard variable overhead for the actual units produced. (1042)

**business** An organization in which basic resources (inputs), such as materials and labor, are assembled and processed to provide goods or services (outputs) to customers. (2)

**business combination** A business making an investment in another business by acquiring a controlling share, often greater than 50%, of the outstanding voting stock of another corporation by paying cash or exchanging stock. (590)

**business entity concept** A concept of accounting that limits the economic data in the accounting system to data related directly to the activities of the business. (7)

**business transaction** An economic event or condition that directly changes an entity's financial condition or directly affects its results of operations. (9)

# C

**capital expenditures** The costs of acquiring fixed assets, adding to a fixed asset, improving a fixed asset, or extending a fixed asset's useful life. (409)

**capital expenditures budget** The budget summarizing future plans for acquiring plant facilities and equipment. (997)

**capital investment analysis** The process by which management plans, evaluates, and controls long-term capital investments involving property, plant, and equipment. (1164)

**capital leases** Leases that include one or more provisions that result in treating the leased assets as purchased assets in the accounts. (410)

**capital rationing** The process by which management plans, evaluates, and controls long-term capital investments involving fixed assets. (1181)

**capital stock** The portion of a corporation's stockholders' equity contributed by investors (owners) in exchange for shares of stock. (10)

**carrying amount** The balance of the bonds payable account (face amount of the bonds) less any unamortized discount or plus any unamortized premium. (551)

**cash** Coins, currency (paper money), checks, money orders, and money on deposit that is available for unrestricted withdrawal from banks and other financial institutions. (327)

**cash basis of accounting** Under this basis of accounting, revenues and expenses are reported in the income statement in the period in which cash is received or paid. (104)

**cash budget** A budget of estimated cash receipts and payments. (994)

**cash dividend** A cash distribution of earnings by a corporation to its shareholders. (510)

**cash equivalents** Highly liquid investments that are usually reported with cash on the balance sheet. (338)

**cash flow per share** Normally computed as cash flow from operations per share. (643)

**cash flows from financing activities** The section of the statement of cash flows that reports cash flows from transactions affecting the equity and debt of the business. (641)

**cash flows from investing activities** The section of the statement of cash flows that reports cash flows from transactions affecting investments in noncurrent assets. (640)

**cash flows from operating activities** The section of the statement of cash flows that reports the cash transactions affecting the determination of net income. (640)

**cash payback period** The expected period of time that will elapse between the date of a capital expenditure and the complete recovery in cash (or equivalent) of the amount invested. (1166)

**cash short and over account** An account which has recorded errors in cash sales or errors in making change causing the amount of actual cash on hand to differ from the beginning amount of cash plus the cash sales for the day. (328)

**Certified Public Accountant (CPA)** Public accountants who have met a state's education, experience, and examination requirements. (6)

**chart of accounts** A list of the accounts in the ledger. (52)

**clearing account** Another name for the income summary account because it has the effect of clearing the revenue and expense accounts of their balances. (159)

**closing entries** The entries that transfer the balances of the revenue, expense, and drawing accounts to the owner's capital account. (159)

**closing process** The transfer process of converting temporary account balances to zero by transferring the revenue and expense account balances to Income Summary, transferring the income summary account balance to the owner's capital account, and transferring the owner's drawing account to the owner's capital account. (159)

**closing the books** The process of transferring temporary accounts balances to permanent accounts at the end of the accounting period. (159)

**common stock** The stock outstanding when a corporation has issued only one class of stock. (505)

**common-sized statement** A financial statement in which all items are expressed only in relative terms. (701)

**compensating balance** A requirement by some banks requiring depositors to maintain minimum cash balances in their bank accounts. (339)

**comprehensive income** All changes in stockholders' equity during a period, except those resulting from dividends and stockholders' investments. (601)

**consigned inventory** Merchandise that is shipped by manufacturers to retailers who act as the manufacturer's selling agent. (291)

**consignee** The name for the retailer in a consigned inventory arrangement. (291)

**consignor** The name for the manufacturer in a consigned inventory arrangement. (291)

**consolidated financial statements** Financial statements resulting from combining parent and subsidiary statements. (590)

**contingent liabilities** Liabilities that may arise from past transactions if certain events occur in the future. (469)

**continuous budgeting** A method of budgeting that provides for maintaining a 12-month projection into the future. (980)

**continuous process improvement** A management approach that is part of the overall total quality management philosophy. The approach requires all employees to constantly improve processes of which they are a part or for which they have managerial responsibility. (759)

**contra account (or contra asset account)** An account offset against another account. (117)

**contract rate** The periodic interest to be paid on the bonds that is identified in the bond indenture; expressed as a percentage of the face amount of the bond. (545)

**contribution margin** Sales less variable costs and variable selling and administrative expenses. (893, 933)

**contribution margin analysis** The systematic examination of the differences between planned and actual contribution margins. (947)

**contribution margin ratio** The percentage of each sales dollar that is available to cover the fixed costs and provide an operating income. (893)

**control environment** The overall attitude of management and employees about the importance of controls. (323)

**controllable costs** Costs that can be influenced (increased, decreased, or eliminated) by someone such as a manager or factory worker. (942)

**controllable expenses** Costs that can be influenced by the decisions of a manager. (1080)

**controllable revenues** Revenues earned by the profit center. (1080)

**controllable variance** The difference between the actual amount of variable factory overhead cost incurred and the amount of variable factory overhead budgeted for the standard product. (1041)

**controller** The chief management accountant of a division or other segment of a business. (758)

**controlling** A phase in the management process that consists of monitoring the operating results of implemented plans and comparing the actual results with the expected results. (759)

**controlling account** The account in the general ledger that summarizes the balances of the accounts in a subsidiary ledger. (225, C-1)

**conversion costs** The combination of direct labor and factory overhead costs. (764, 1257)

**copyright** An exclusive right to publish and sell a literary, artistic, or musical composition. (423)

**corporation** A business organized under state or federal statutes as a separate legal entity. (8)

**correcting journal entry** An entry that is prepared when an error has already been journalized and posted. (72)

**cost** A payment of cash (or a commitment to pay cash in the future) for the purpose of generating revenues. (761)

**cost accounting system** A branch of managerial accounting concerned with accumulating manufacturing costs for financial reporting and decision-making purposes. (792)

**cost allocation** The process of assigning indirect cost to a cost object, such as a job. (798)

**cost behavior** The manner in which a cost changes in relation to its activity base (driver). (886)

**cost center** A decentralized unit in which the department or division manager has responsibility for the control of costs incurred and the authority to make decisions that affect these costs. (1078)

**cost concept** A concept of accounting that determines the amount initially entered into the accounting records for purchases. (8)

**cost method** A method of accounting for equity investments representing less than 20% of the outstanding shares of the investee. The purchase is at original cost, and any gains or losses upon sale are recognized by the difference between the sale proceeds and the original cost. (587)

**cost object** The object or segment of operations to which costs are related for management's use, such as a product or department. (761)

**cost of finished goods available** The beginning finished goods inventory added to the cost of goods manufactured during the period. (768)

**cost of goods manufactured** The total cost of making and finishing a product. (768)

**cost of goods sold** The cost of finished goods available for sale minus the ending finished goods inventory. (768)

**cost of goods sold budget** A budget of the estimated direct materials, direct labor, and factory overhead consumed by sold products. (991)

**cost of merchandise sold** The cost that is reported as an expense when merchandise is sold. (218, 767)

**cost of production report** A report prepared periodically by a processing department, summarizing (1) the units for which the department is accountable and the disposition of those units and (2) the costs incurred by the department and the allocation of those costs between completed and incomplete production. (838)

**cost of quality report** A report summarizing the costs, percent of total, and percent of sales by appraisal, prevention, internal failure, and external failure cost of quality categories. (1263)

**cost per equivalent unit** The rate used to allocate costs between completed and partially completed production. (845)

**cost price approach** An approach to transfer pricing that uses cost as the basis for setting the transfer price. (1094)

**cost variance** The difference between actual cost and the flexible budget at actual volumes. (1033)

**costs of quality** The cost associated with controlling quality (prevention and appraisal) and failing to control quality (internal and external failure). (1261)

**cost-volume-profit analysis** The systematic examination of the relationships among selling prices, volume of sales and production, costs, expenses, and profits. (892)

**cost-volume-profit chart** A chart used to assist management in understanding the relationships among costs, expenses, sales, and operating profit or loss. (901)

**credit** Amount entered on the right side of an account. (51)

**credit memorandum (credit memo)** A form used by a seller to inform the buyer of the amount the seller proposes to credit to the account receivable due from the buyer. (227)

**credit period** The amount of time the buyer is allowed in which to pay the seller. (226)

**credit terms** Terms for payment on account by the buyer to the seller. (226)

**cumulative preferred stock** Stock that has a right to receive regular dividends that were not declared (paid) in prior years. (505)

**currency exchange rate** The rate at which currency in another country can be exchanged for local currency. (1180)

**current assets** Cash and other assets that are expected to be converted to cash or sold or used up, usually within one year or less, through the normal operations of the business. (157)

**current liabilities** Liabilities that will be due within a short time (usually one year or less) and that are to be paid out of current assets. (157)

**current position analysis** A company's ability to pay its current liabilities. (472, 703)

**current ratio** A financial ratio that is computed by dividing current assets by current liabilities. (180, 703)

**currently attainable standards** Standards that represent levels of operation that can be attained with reasonable effort. (1031)

# D

**debit** Amount entered on the left side of an account. (51)

**debit memorandum (debit memo)** A form used by a buyer to inform the seller of the amount the buyer proposes to debit to the account payable due the seller. (231)

**debt securities** Notes and bond investments that provide interest revenue over a fixed maturity.(583)

**decision making** A component inherent in the other management processes of planning, directing, controlling, and improving. (759)

**defined benefit plan** A pension plan that promises employees a fixed annual pension benefit at retirement, based on years of service and compensation levels. (467)

**defined contribution plan** A pension plan that requires a fixed amount of money to be invested on the employee's behalf during the employee's working years. (467)

**depletion** The process of transferring the cost of natural resources to an expense account. (421)

**depreciate** To lose usefulness as all fixed assets except land do. (117)

**depreciation** The systematic periodic transfer of the cost of a fixed asset to an expense account during its expected useful life. (117, 411)

**depreciation expense** The portion of the cost of a fixed asset that is recorded as an expense each year of its useful life. (117)

**differential analysis** The area of accounting concerned with the effect of alternative courses of action on revenues and costs. (1120)

**differential cost** The amount of increase or decrease in cost expected from a particular course of action compared with an alternative. (1120)

**differential income (or loss)** The difference between the differential revenue and the differential costs. (1120)

**differential revenue** The amount of increase or decrease in revenue expected from a particular course of action as compared with an alternative. (1120)

**direct costs** Costs that can be traced directly to a cost object. (761)

**direct labor cost** The wages of factory workers who are directly involved in converting materials into a finished product. (763)

**direct labor cost budget** Budget that estimates direct labor hours and related costs needed to support budgeted production. (990)

**direct labor rate variance** The cost associated with the difference between the standard rate and the actual rate paid for direct labor used in producing a commodity. (1038)

**direct labor time variance** The cost associated with the difference between the standard hours and the actual hours of direct labor spent producing a commodity. (1039)

**direct materials cost** The cost of materials that are an integral part of the finished product. (762)

**direct materials price variance** The cost associated with the difference between the standard price and the actual price of direct materials used in producing a commodity. (1036)

**direct materials purchases budget** A budget that uses the production budget as a starting point to budget materials purchases. (988)

**direct materials quantity variance** The cost associated with the difference between the standard quantity and the actual quantity of direct materials used in producing a commodity. (1036)

**direct method** A method of reporting the cash flows from operating activities as the difference between the operating cash receipts and the operating cash payments. (641)

**direct write-off method** The method of accounting for uncollectible accounts that recognizes the expense only when accounts are judged to be worthless. (363)

**directing** The process by which managers, given their assigned level of responsibilities, run day-to-day operations. (759)

**discount** The interest deducted from the maturity value of a note or the excess of the face amount of bonds over their issue price. (507, 545)

**dishonored note receivable** A note that the maker fails to pay on the due date. (375)

**dividend yield** A ratio, computed by dividing the annual dividends paid per share of common stock by the market price per share at a specific date, that indicates the rate of return to stockholders in terms of cash dividend distributions. (599, 718)

**dividends** Distribution of a corporation's earnings to stockholders. (13, 52)

**dividends per share** Measures the extent to which earnings are being distributed to common shareholders. (717)

**double-declining-balance method** A method of depreciation that provides periodic depreciation expense based on the declining book value of a fixed asset over its estimated life. (415)

**double-entry accounting system** A system of accounting for recording transactions, based on recording increases and decreases in accounts so that debits equal credits. (53)

**DuPont formula** An expanded expression of return on investment determined by multiplying the profit margin by the investment turnover. (1085)

# E

**earnings** The excess of the revenue over the expenses; also called *net income* or *profit*. (15)

**earnings per common share (EPS)** Net income per share of common stock outstanding during a period. (520)

**earnings per share (EPS) on common stock** The profitability ratio of net income available to common shareholders to the number of common shares outstanding. (543, 716)

**effective interest rate method** The method of amortizing discounts and premiums that provides for a constant rate of interest on the carrying amount of the bonds at the beginning of each period; often called simply the "interest method." (548)

**effective rate of interest** The market rate of interest at the time bonds are issued. (545)

**electronic data interchange (EDI)** An information technology that allows different business organizations to use computers to communicate orders, relay information, and make or receive payments. (1255)

**electronic funds transfer (EFT)** A system in which computers rather than paper (money, checks, etc.) are used to effect cash transactions. (329)

**elements of internal control** The control environment, risk assessment, control activities, information and communication, and monitoring. (322)

**employee fraud** The intentional act of deceiving an employer for personal gain. (322)

**employee involvement** A philosophy that grants employees the responsibility and authority to make their own decisions about their operations. (1254)

**employee's earnings record** A detailed record of each employee's earnings. (462)

**engineering change order (ECO)** The document that initiates changing a product or process. (1210)

**enterprise resource planning (ERP)** An integrated business and information system used by companies to plan and control both internal and supply chain operations. (1255)

**equity method** A method of accounting for an investment in common stock by which the investment account is adjusted for the investor's share of periodic net income and cash dividends of the investee. (588)

**equity securities** The common and preferred stock of a firm. (583)

**equivalent units of production** The number of production units that could have been completed within a given accounting period, given the resources consumed. (841)

**ethics** Moral principles that guide the conduct of individuals. (4)

**expenses** Assets used up or services consumed in the process of generating revenues. (12, 53)

**external failure costs** The costs incurred after defective units or services have been delivered to consumers. (1261)

**extraordinary item** An event or a transaction that is both unusual in nature and infrequent in occurrence. (724)

# F

**face amount** The principal of a bond or the amount that must be repaid on the dates the bonds mature. (545)

**factory burden** Another term for manufacturing overhead or factory overhead. (763)

**factory overhead cost** All of the costs of producing a product except for direct materials and direct labor. (763)

**factory overhead cost budget** Budget that estimates the cost for each item of factory overhead needed to support budgeted production. (991)

**factory overhead cost variance report** Reports budgeted and actual costs for variable and fixed factory overhead along with the related controllable and volume variances. (1045)

**fair value** The price that would be received for selling an asset or paying off a liability, often the market price for an equity or debt security. (591)

**favorable cost variance** A variance that occurs when the actual cost is less than standard cost. (1033)

**feedback** Measures provided to operational employees or managers on the performance of subunits of the organization. These measures are used by employees to adjust a process or a behavior to achieve goals. See management by exception. (759)

**fees earned** Revenue from providing services. (11)

**FICA tax** Federal Insurance Contributions Act tax used to finance federal programs for old-age and disability benefits (social security) and health insurance for the aged (Medicare). (456)

**financial accounting** The branch of accounting that is concerned with recording transactions using generally accepted accounting principles (GAAP) for a business or other economic unit and with a periodic preparation of various statements from such records. (3, 757)

**Financial Accounting Standards Board (FASB)** The authoritative body that has the primary responsibility for developing accounting principles. (7)

**financial statements** Financial reports that summarize the effects of events on a business. (15)

**finished goods inventory** The direct materials costs, direct labor costs, and factory overhead costs of finished products that have not been sold. (766)

**finished goods ledger** The subsidiary ledger that contains the individual accounts for each kind of commodity or product produced. (804)

**first-in, first-out (FIFO) inventory cost flow method** The method of inventory costing based on the assumption that the costs of merchandise sold should be charged against revenue in the order in which the costs were incurred. (278, 840)

**fiscal year** The annual accounting period adopted by a business. (178)

**fixed asset turnover ratio** The number of dollars of sales that are generated from each dollar of average fixed assets during the year, computed by dividing the net sales by the average net fixed assets. (427)

**fixed assets (or plant assets)** Long-term or relatively permanent tangible assets such as equipment, machinery, and buildings that are used in the normal business operations and that depreciate over time. (116, 157, 406)

**fixed costs** Costs that tend to remain the same in amount, regardless of variations in the level of activity. (888)

**flexible budget** A budget that adjusts for varying rates of activity. (982)

**FOB (free on board) destination** Freight terms in which the seller pays the transportation costs from the shipping point to the final destination. (233)

**FOB (free on board) shipping point** Freight terms in which the buyer pays the transportation costs from the shipping point to the final destination. (233)

**free cash flow** The amount of operating cash flow remaining after replacing current productive capacity and maintaining current dividends. (660)

**fringe benefits** Benefits provided to employees in addition to wages and salaries. (466)

# G

**general ledger** The primary ledger, when used in conjunction with subsidiary ledgers, that contains all of the balance sheet and income statement accounts. (225, C-1)

**general-purpose financial statements** A type of financial accounting report that is distributed to external users. The term "general purpose" refers to the wide range of decision-making needs that the reports are designed to serve. (4)

**generally accepted accounting principles (GAAP)** Generally accepted guidelines for the preparation of financial statements. (6)

**goal conflict** A condition that occurs when individual objectives conflict with organizational objectives. (980)

**goodwill** An intangible asset that is created from such favorable factors as location, product quality, reputation, and managerial skill. (424)

**gross pay** The total earnings of an employee for a payroll period. (454)

**gross profit** Sales minus the cost of merchandise sold. (218)

**gross profit method** A method of estimating inventory cost that is based on the relationship of gross profit to sales. (297)

# H

**held-to-maturity securities** Investments in bonds or other debt securities that management intends to hold to their maturity. (595)

**high-low method** A technique that uses the highest and lowest total costs as a basis for estimating the variable cost per unit and the fixed cost component of a mixed cost. (889)

**horizontal analysis** Financial analysis that compares an item in a current statement with the same item in prior statements. (73, 696)

# I

**ideal standards** Standards that can be achieved only under perfect operating conditions, such as no idle time, no machine breakdowns, and no materials spoilage; also called theoretical standards. (1031)

**in arrears** Cumulative preferred stock dividends that have not been paid in prior years are said to be in arrears. (505)

**income from operations (operating income)** Revenues less operating expenses and service department charges for a profit or an investment center. (221)

**income statement** A summary of the revenue and expenses for a specific period of time, such as a month or a year. (15)

**Income Summary** An account to which the revenue and expense account balances are transferred at the end of a period. (159)

**indirect costs** Costs that cannot be traced directly to a cost object. (761)

**indirect method** A method of reporting the cash flows from operating activities as the net income from operations adjusted for all deferrals of past cash receipts and payments and all accruals of expected future cash receipts and payments. (642)

**inflation** A period when prices in general are rising and the purchasing power of money is declining. (1180)

**installment note** A debt that requires the borrower to make equal periodic payments to the lender for the term of the note. (552)

**intangible assets** Long-term assets that are useful in the operations of a business, are not held for sale, and are without physical qualities. (422)

**interest revenue** Money received for interest. (11)

**internal controls** The policies and procedures used to safeguard assets, ensure accurate business information, and ensure compliance with laws and regulations. (320)

**internal failure costs** The costs associated with defects that are discovered by the organization before the product or service is delivered to the consumer. (1261)

**internal rate of return (IRR) method** A method of analysis of proposed capital investments that uses present value concepts to compute the rate of return from the net cash flows expected from the investment. (1173)

**International Accounting Standards Board (IASB)** An organization that issues International Financial Reporting Standards for many countries outside the United States. (7)

**inventory analysis** A company's ability to manage its inventory effectively. (707)

**inventory shrinkage (inventory shortage)** The amount by which the merchandise for sale, as indicated by the balance of the merchandise inventory account, is larger than the total amount of merchandise counted during the physical inventory. (238)

**inventory subsidiary ledger** A ledger containing individual accounts with a common characteristic. (225, 265)

**inventory turnover** The relationship between the volume of goods sold and inventory, computed by dividing the cost of goods sold by the average inventory. (294, 707)

**investee** The company whose stock is purchased by the investor. (586)

**investment center** A decentralized unit in which the manager has the responsibility and authority to make decisions that affect not only costs and revenues but also the fixed assets available to the center. (1084)

**investment turnover** A component of the rate of return on investment, computed as the ratio of sales to invested assets. (1085)

**investments** The balance sheet caption used to report long-term investments in stocks not intended as a source of cash in the normal operations of the business. (583)

**investor** The company investing in another company's stock. (586)

**invoice** The bill that the seller sends to the buyer. (226)

# J

**job cost sheet** An account in the work in process subsidiary ledger in which the costs charged to a particular job order are recorded. (795)

**job order cost system** A type of cost accounting system that provides for a separate record of the cost of each particular quantity of product that passes through the factory. (792)

**journal** The initial record in which the effects of a transaction are recorded. (55)

**journal entry** The form of recording a transaction in a journal. (56)

**journalizing** The process of recording a transaction in the journal. (56)

**just-in-time (JIT) processing** A processing approach that focuses on eliminating time, cost, and poor quality within manufacturing and nonmanufacturing processes. (855, 1248)

# L

**last-in, first-out (LIFO) inventory cost flow method** A method of inventory costing based on the assumption that the most recent merchandise inventory costs should be charged against revenue. (278)

**lead time** The elapsed time between starting a unit of product into the beginning of a process and its completion. (1249)

**ledger** A group of accounts for a business. (52)

**liabilities** The rights of creditors that represent debts of the business. (9, 52)

**limited liability company (LLC)** A business form consisting of one or more persons or entities filing an operating agreement with a state to conduct business with limited liability to the owners, yet treated as a partnership for tax purposes. (8)

**line department** A unit that is directly involved in the basic objectives of an organization. (758)

**liquidity** The ability to convert assets into cash. (179, 702)

**long-term liabilities** Liabilities that usually will not be due for more than one year. (157)

**lower-of-cost-or-market (LCM) method** A method of valuing inventory that reports the inventory at the lower of its cost or current market value (replacement cost). (288)

# M

**management (or managerial) accounting** The branch of accounting that uses both historical and estimated data in providing information that management uses in conducting daily operations, in planning future operations, and in developing overall business strategies. (3, 755)

**management by exception** The philosophy of managing which involves monitoring the operating results of implemented plans and comparing the expected results with the actual results. This feedback allows management to isolate significant variations for further investigation and possible remedial action. (759)

**management process** The five basic management functions of (1) planning, (2) directing, (3) controlling, (4) improving, and (5) decision making. (758)

**Management's Discussion and Analysis (MD&A)** An annual report disclosure that provides management's analysis of the results of operations and financial condition. (720)

**managerial accounting** The branch of accounting that uses both historical and estimated data in providing information that management uses in conducting daily operations, in planning future operations, and in developing overall business strategies. (757)

**manufacturing business** A type of business that changes basic inputs into products that are sold to individual customers. (2)

**manufacturing cells** A grouping of processes where employees are cross-trained to perform more than one function. (856)

**manufacturing margin** The variable cost of goods sold deducted from sales. (933)

**manufacturing overhead** Costs, other than direct materials and direct labor costs, that are incurred in the manufacturing process. (763)

**margin of safety** Indicates the possible decrease in sales that may occur before an operating loss results. (908)

**market price approach** An approach to transfer pricing that uses the price at which the product or service transferred could be sold to outside buyers as the transfer price. (1091)

**market rate of interest** The rate determined from sales and purchases of similar bonds. (545)

**market segment** A portion of business that can be assigned to a manager for profit responsibility. (942)

**master budget** The comprehensive budget plan linking all the individual budgets related to sales, cost of goods sold, operating expenses, projects, capital expenditures, and cash. (985)

**matching concept (or matching principle)** A concept of accounting in which expenses are matched with the revenue generated during a period by those expenses. (15, 104)

**materials inventory** The cost of materials that have not yet entered into the manufacturing process. (766)

**materials ledger** The subsidiary ledger containing the individual accounts for each type of material. (793)

**materials requisition** The form or electronic transmission used by a manufacturing department to authorize materials issuances from the storeroom. (795)

**maturity value** The amount that is due at the maturity or due date of a note. (374)

**merchandise available for sale** The cost of merchandise available for sale to customers calculated by adding the beginning merchandise inventory to net purchases. (767)

**merchandise inventory** Merchandise on hand (not sold) at the end of an accounting period. (218)

**merchandising business** A type of business that purchases products from other businesses and sells them to customers. (2)

**mixed cost** A cost with both variable and fixed characteristics, sometimes called a semivariable or semi-fixed cost. (889)

**mortgage notes** An installment note that may be secured by a pledge of the borrower's assets. (552)

**multiple production department factory overhead rate method** A method that allocated factory overhead to product by using factory overhead rates for each production department. (1205)

**multiple-step income statement** A form of income statement that contains several sections, subsections, and subtotals. (219)

# N

**natural business year** A fiscal year that ends when business activities have reached the lowest point in an annual operating cycle. (179)

**negotiated price approach** An approach to transfer pricing that allows managers of decentralized units to agree (negotiate) among themselves as to the transfer price. (1092)

**net income or net profit** The amount by which revenues exceed expenses. (15)

**net loss** The amount by which expenses exceed revenues. (15)

**net pay** Gross pay less payroll deductions; the amount the employer is obligated to pay the employee. (454)

**net present value method** A method of analysis of proposed capital investments that focuses on the present value of the cash flows expected from the investments. (1170)

**net realizable value** The estimated selling price of an item of inventory less any direct costs of disposal, such as sales commissions. (290, 365)

**net sales** Revenue received for merchandise sold to customers less any sales returns and allowances and sales discounts. (221)

**noncontrollable cost** Cost that cannot be influenced (increased, decreased, or eliminated) by someone such as a manager or factory worker. (942)

**nonfinancial measure** A performance measure that has not been stated in dollar terms. (1260)

**nonfinancial performance measure** A performance measure expressed in units rather than dollars. (1050)

**non-value-added activity** The cost of activities that are perceived as unnecessary from the customer's perspective and are thus candidates for elimination. (1264)

**non-value-added lead time** The time that units wait in inventories, move unnecessarily, and wait during machine breakdowns. (1249)

**normal balance of an account** The normal balance of an account can be either a debit or a credit depending on whether increases in the account are recorded as debits or credits. (54)

**notes receivable** A customer's written promise to pay an amount and possibly interest at an agreed-upon rate. (157, 362)

**number of days' sales in inventory** The relationship between the volume of sales and inventory, computed by dividing the average inventory by the average daily cost of goods sold. (295, 708)

**number of days' sales in receivables** The relationship between sales and accounts receivable, computed by dividing the net accounts receivable at the end of the year by the average daily sales. (378, 706)

**number of times interest charges are earned** A ratio that measures creditor margin of safety for interest payments, calculated as income before interest and taxes divided by interest expense. (556, 710)

## O

**objectives (goals)** Developed in the planning stage, these reflect the direction and desired outcomes of certain courses of action. (759)

**objectivity concept** A concept of accounting that requires accounting records and the data reported in financial statements to be based on objective evidence. (8)

**operating leases** Leases that do not meet the criteria for capital leases and thus are accounted for as operating expenses. (411)

**operating leverage** A measure of the relative mix of a business's variable costs and fixed costs, computed as contribution margin divided by operating income. (906)

**operational planning** The development of short-term plans to achieve goals identified in a business's strategic plan. Sometimes called tactical planning. (759)

**opportunity cost** The amount of income forgone from an alternative to a proposed use of cash or its equivalent. (1128)

**other expense** Expenses that cannot be traced directly to operations. (222)

**other comprehensive income** Income that includes unrealized gains and losses on available-for-sale securities as well as other items such as foreign currency and pension liability adjustments. (601)

**other income** Revenue from sources other than the primary operating activity of a business. (222)

**outstanding stock** The stock in the hands of stockholders. (504)

**overapplied factory overhead** The amount of factory overhead applied in excess of the actual factory overhead costs incurred for production during a period. (801)

**owner's equity** The owner's right to the assets of the business. (9)

## P

**paid-in capital** A main source of stockholders' equity; also known as contributed capital. (504)

**par** The monetary amount printed on a stock certificate. (504)

**parent company** The corporation owning all or a majority of the voting stock of the other corporation. (590)

**Pareto chart** A bar chart that shows the totals of a particular attribute for a number of categories, ranked left to right from the largest to smallest totals. (1263)

**partnership** An unincorporated business form consisting of two or more persons conducting business as co-owners for profit. (7)

**patents** Exclusive rights to produce and sell goods with one or more unique features. (423)

**payroll** The total amount paid to employees for a certain period. (453)

**payroll register** A multicolumn report used to assemble and summarize payroll data at the end of each payroll period. (460)

**pension** A cash payment to retired employees. (467)

**period costs** Those costs that are used up in generating revenue during the current period and that are not involved in manufacturing a product, such as selling, general, and administratvie expenses. (764)

**periodic inventory system** The inventory system in which the inventory records do not show the amount available for sale or sold during the period. (221)

**perpetual inventory system** The inventory system in which each purchase and sale of merchandise is recorded in an inventory account. (221)

**petty cash fund** A special cash fund to pay relatively small amounts. (337)

**physical inventory** A detailed listing of merchandise on hand. (277)

**planning** A phase of the management process whereby objectives are outlined and courses of action determined. (759)

**posting** The process of transferring the debits and credits from the journal entries to the accounts. (59)

**predetermined factory overhead rate** The rate used to apply factory overhead costs to the goods manufactured. The rate is determined by dividing the budgeted overhead cost by the estimated activity usage at the beginning of the fiscal period. (798)

**preferred stock** A class of stock with preferential rights over common stock. (505)

**premium** The excess of the issue price of a stock over its par value or the excess of the issue price of bonds over their face amount. (507, 545)

**prepaid expenses** Items such as supplies that will be used in the business in the future. (11, 105)

**present value** The estimated worth today of an amount of cash to be received (or paid) in the future (540)

**present value concept** Cash to be received (or paid) in the future is not the equivalent of the same amount of money received at an earlier date. (1168)

**present value index** An index computed by dividing the total present value of the net cash flow to be received from a proposed capital investment by the amount to be invested. (1171)

**present value of an annuity** The sum of the present values of a series of equal cash flows to be received at fixed intervals. (1169)

**prevention costs** Costs incurred to prevent defects from occuring during the design and delivery of products or services. (1261)

**price-earnings (P/E) ratio** The ratio of the market price per share of common stock, at a specific date, to the annual earnings per share. (716)

**prime costs** The combination of direct materials and direct labor costs. (764)

**prior period adjustments** Corrections of material errors related to a prior period or periods, excluded from the determination of net income. (517)

**private accounting** The field of accounting whereby accountants are employed by a business firm or a not-for-profit organization. (3)

**process** A sequence of activities linked together for performing a particular task. (1050, 1265)

**process cost system** A type of cost system that accumulates costs for each of the various departments within a manufacturing facility. (792, 834)

**process manufacturers** Manufacturers that use large machines to process a continuous flow of raw materials through various stages of completion into a finished state. (834)

**process-oriented layout** Organizing work in a plant or administrative function around processes (tasks). (1253)

**product cost concept** A concept used in applying the cost-plus approach to product pricing in which only the costs of manufacturing the product, termed the product cost, are included in the cost amount to which the markup is added. (1133)

**product costing** Determining the cost of a product. (1202)

**product costs** The three components of manufacturing cost: direct materials, direct labor, and factory overhead costs. (764)

**production bottleneck** A condition that occurs when product demand exceeds production capacity. (1135)

**production budget** A budget of estimated unit production. (987)

**production department factory overhead rates** Rates determined by dividing the budgeted production department factory overhead by the budgeted allocation base for each department. (1206)

**product-oriented layout** Organizing work in a plant or administrative function around products; sometimes referred to as product cells. (1253)

**profit** The difference between the amounts received from customers for goods or services provided and the amounts paid for the inputs used to provide the goods or services. (2)

**profit center** A decentralized unit in which the manager has the responsibility and the authority to make decisions that affect both costs and revenues (and thus profits). (1080)

**profit margin** A component of the rate of return on investment, computed as the ratio of income from operations to sales. (1085)

**profit-volume chart** A chart used to assist management in understanding the relationship between profit and volume. (902)

**profitability** The ability of a firm to earn income. (702)

**proprietorship** A business owned by one individual. (7)

**public accounting** The field of accounting where accountants and their staff provide services on a fee basis. (6)

**pull manufacturing** A just-in-time method wherein customer orders trigger the release of finished goods, which triggers production, which triggers release of materials from suppliers. (1254)

**purchase order** The purchase order authorizes the purchase of the inventory from an approved vendor. (276)

**purchases discounts** Discounts taken by the buyer for early payment of an invoice. (230)

**purchases returns and allowances** From the buyer's perspective, returned merchandise or an adjustment for defective merchandise. (231)

**push manufacturing** Materials are released into production and work in process is released into finished goods in anticipation of future sales. (1254)

# Q

**quantity factor** The effect of a difference in the number of units sold, assuming no change in unit sales price or unit cost. (947)

**quick assets** Cash and other current assets that can be quickly converted to cash, such as marketable securities and receivables. (472, 705)

**quick ratio** A financial ratio that measures the ability to pay current liabilities with quick assets (cash, marketable securities, accounts receivable). (472, 705)

# R

**radio frequency identification devices (RFID)** Electronic tags (chips) placed on or embedded within products that can be read by radio waves that allow instant monitoring or production location. (1255)

**rate earned on common stockholders' equity** A measure of profitability computed by dividing net income, reduced by preferred dividend requirements, by common stockholders' equity. (714)

**rate earned on stockholders' equity** A measure of profitability computed by dividing net income by total stockholders' equity. (713)

**rate earned on total assets** A measure of the profitability of assets, without regard to the equity of creditors and stockholders in the assets. (712)

**rate of return on investment (ROI)** A measure of managerial efficiency in the use of investments in assets, computed as income from operations divided by invested assets. (1085)

**ratio of cash to monthly cash expenses** Computed as cash as of year-end divided by monthly cash expenses; it assesses how long a company can continue to operate without additional financing or generating positive cash flow from operations. (340)

**ratio of fixed assets to long-term liabilities** A leverage ratio that measures the margin of safety of long-term creditors, calculated as the net fixed assets divided by the long-term liabilities. (709)

**ratio of liabilities to stockholders' equity** A comprehensive leverage ratio that measures the relationship of the claims of creditors to stockholders' equity. (22, 709)

**ratio of net sales to assets** Ratio that measures how effectively a company uses its assets, computed as net sales divided by average total assets. (240, 711)

**Raw and In Process (RIP) Inventory** The capitalized cost of direct materials purchases, labor, and overhead charged to the production cell. (1257)

**real (permanent) accounts** Term for balance sheet accounts because they are relatively permanent and carried forward from year to year. (158)

**receivables** All money claims against other entities, including people, business firms, and other organizations. (362)

**receiving report** The form or electronic transmission used by the receiving personnel to indicate that materials have been received and inspected. (276, 795)

**relevant range** The range of activity over which changes in cost are of interest to management. (886)

**rent revenue** Money received for rent. (11)

**report form** The form of balance sheet with the Liabilities and Owner's Equity sections presented below the Assets section. (223)

**residual income** The excess of divisional income from operations over a "minimum" acceptable income from operations. (1088)

**residual value** The estimated value of a fixed asset at the end of its useful life. (411)

**responsibility accounting** The process of measuring and reporting operating data by areas of responsibility. (1077)

**responsibility center** An organizational unit for which a manager is assigned responsibility over costs, revenues, or assets. (979)

**restrictions** Amounts of retained earnings that have been limited for use as dividends. (517)

**retail inventory method** A method of estimating inventory cost that is based on the relationship of gross profit to sales. (297)

**retained earnings** Net income retained in a corporation. (14)

**retained earnings statement** A summary of the changes in the retained earnings in a corporation for a specific period of time, such as a month or a year. (15)

**revenue** Increases in owner's equity as a result of selling services or products to customers. (11, 52)

**revenue expenditures** Costs that benefit only the current period or costs incurred for normal maintenance and repairs of fixed assets. (409)

**revenue recognition concept** The accounting concept that supports reporting revenues when the services are provided to customers. (104)

**rules of debit and credit** In the double-entry accounting system, specific rules for recording debits and credits based on the type of account. (53)

# S

**sales** The total amount charged customers for merchandise sold, including cash sales and sales on account. (11, 220)

**sales budget** One of the major elements of the income statement budget that indicates the quantity of estimated sales and the expected unit selling price. (986)

**sales discounts** From the seller's perspective, discounts that a seller may offer the buyer for early payment. (220)

**sales mix** The relative distribution of sales among the various products available for sale. (905, 944)

**sales returns and allowances** From the seller's perspective, returned merchandise or an adjustment for defective merchandise. (220)

**Sarbanes-Oxley Act of 2002** An act passed by Congress to restore public confidence and trust in the financial statements of companies. (320)

**Securities and Exchange Commission (SEC)** An agency of the U.S. government that has authority over the accounting and financial disclosures for companies whose shares of ownership (stock) are traded and sold to the public. (7)

**selling expenses** Expenses that are incurred directly in the selling of merchandise. (221)

**service business** A business providing services rather than products to customers. (2)

**service department charges** The costs of services provided by an internal service department and transferred to a responsibility center. (1080)

**setup** Changing the characteristics of a machine to produce a different product. (1209)

**single plantwide factory overhead rate method** A method that allocates all factory overhead to products by using a single factory overhead rate. (1203)

**single-step income statement** A form of income statement in which the total of all expenses is deducted from the total of all revenues. (222)

**Six Sigma** A quality improvement process developed by Motorola Corporation consisting of five steps: define, measure, analyze, improve, and control (DMAIC). (1254)

**slide** An error in which the entire number is moved one or more spaces to the right or the left, such as writing $542.00 as $54.20 or $5,420.00. (70)

**solvency** The ability of a firm to pay its debts as they come due. (179, 702)

**special-purpose fund** A cash fund used for a special business need. (338)

**specific identification inventory cost flow method** Inventory method in which the unit sold is identified with a specific purchase. (278)

**staff department** A unit that provides services, assistance, and advice to the departments with line or other staff responsibilities. (758)

**standard cost** A detailed estimate of what a product should cost. (1030)

**standard cost systems** Accounting systems that use standards for each element of manufacturing cost entering into the finished product. (1030)

**standards** Peformance goals, often relating to how much a product should cost. (1030)

**statement of cash flows** A summary of the cash receipts and cash payments for a specific period of time, such as a month or a year. (15, 640)

**statement of cost of goods manufactured** The income statement of manufacturing companies. (768)

**statement of stockholders' equity** A summary of the changes in the stockholders' equity in a corporation that have occurred during a specific period of time. (517)

**static budget** A budget that does not adjust to changes in activity levels. (981)

**stock** Shares of ownership of a corporation. (502)

**stock dividend** A distribution of shares of stock to its stockholders. (511)

**stock split** A reduction in the par or stated value of a common stock and the issuance of a proportionate number of additional shares. (519)

**stockholders** The owners of a corporation. (502)

**stockholders' equity** The owners' equity in a corporation. (10, 52)

**straight-line method** A method of depreciation that provides for equal periodic depreciation expense over the estimated life of a fixed asset. (413)

**strategic planning** The development of a long-range course of action to achieve business goals. (759)

**strategies** The means by which business goals and objectives will be achieved. (759)

**subsidiary company** The corporation that is controlled by a parent company. (590)

**subsidiary ledger** A ledger containing individual accounts with a common characteristic. (225, C-1)

**subsidiary inventory ledger** A ledger that records the amount of inventory available and helps to keep inventory at proper levels. (277)

**sunk cost** A cost that is not affected by subsequent decisions. (1123)

**supply chain management** The coordination and control of materials, services, information, and finances as they move in a process from supplier, through the manufacturer, wholesaler, and retailer to the consumer. (1255)

# T

**T account** The simplest form of an account. (50)

**target costing** The target cost is determined by subtracting a desired profit from a market method determined price. The resulting target cost is used to motivate cost improvements in design and manufacture. (1135)

**temporary (nominal) accounts** Accounts that report amounts for only one period. (159)

**theory of constraints (TOC)** A manufacturing strategy that attempts to remove the influence of bottlenecks (constraints) on a process. (1135)

**time tickets** The form on which the amount of time spent by each employee and the labor cost incurred for each individual job, or for factory overhead, are recorded. (796)

**time value of money concept** The concept that an amount of money invested today will earn income. (1164)

**total cost concept** A concept used in applying the cost-plus approach to product pricing in which all the costs of manufacturing the product plus the selling and administrative expenses are included in the cost amount to which the markup is added. (1138)

**total manufacturing cost variance** The difference between total standard costs and total actual costs for units produced. (1034)

**trade discounts** Discounts from the list prices in published catalogs or special discounts offered to certain classes of buyers. (236)

**trade-in allowance** The amount a seller allows a buyer for a fixed asset that is traded in for a similar asset. (428)

**trademark** A name, term, or symbol used to identify a business and its products. (423)

**trading securities** Securities that management intends to actively trade for profit. (591)

**transfer price** The price charged one decentralized unit by another for the goods or services provided. (1090)

**transposition** An error in which the order of the digits is changed, such as writing $542 as $452 or $524. (70)

**treasury stock** Stock that a corporation has once issued and then reacquires. (513)

**trial balance** A summary listing of the titles and balances of accounts in the ledger. (69)

# U

**unadjusted trial balance** A summary listing of the titles and balances of accounts in the ledger prior to the posting of adjusting entries. (70)

**underapplied factory overhead** The amount of actual factory overhead in excess of the factory overhead applied to production during a period. (801)

**unearned revenue** The liability created by receiving revenue in advance. (62, 106)

**unfavorable cost variance** A variance that occurs when the actual cost exceeds the standard cost. (1033)

**unit contribution margin** The dollars available from each unit of sales to cover fixed costs and provide operating profits. (894)

**unit of measure concept** A concept of accounting requiring that economic data be recorded in dollars. (8)

**unit price (cost) factor** The effect of a difference in unit sales price or unit cost on the number of units sold. (948)

**units-of-production method** A method of depreciation that provides for depreciation expense based on the expected productive capacity of a fixed asset. (414)

**unrealized gain or loss** Changes in the fair value of equity or debt securities for a period. (591)

# V

**value-added activity** The cost of activities that are needed to meet customer requirements. (1264)

**value-added lead time** The time required to manufacture a unit of product or other output. (1249)

**value-added ratio** The ratio of the value-added lead time to the total lead time. (1249)

**variable cost concept** A concept used in applying the cost-plus approach to product pricing in which only the variable costs are included in the cost amount to which the markup is added. (1140)

**variable cost of goods sold** Consists of direct materials, direct labor, and variable factory overhead for the units sold. (933)

**variable costing** The concept that considers the cost of products manufactured to be composed only of those manufacturing costs that increase or decrease as the volume of production rises or falls (direct materials, direct labor, and variable factory overhead). (892, 933)

**variable costs** Costs that vary in total dollar amount as the level of activity changes. (886)

**vertical analysis** An analysis that compares each item in a current statement with a total amount within the same statement. (127, 699)

**volume variance** The difference between the budgeted fixed overhead at 100% of normal capacity and the standard fixed overhead for the actual production achieved during the period. (1043)

**voucher** A special form for recording relevant data about a liability and the details of its payment. (330)

**voucher system** A set of procedures for authorizing and recording liabilities and cash payments. (330)

# W

**whole units** The number of units in production during a period, whether completed or not. (841)

**work in process inventory** The direct materials costs, the direct labor costs, and the applied factory overhead costs that have entered into the manufacturing process but are associated with products that have not been finished. (766)

**working capital** The excess of the current assets of a business over its current liabilities. (179, 703)

# Y

**yield** A measure of materials usage efficiency. (854)

# Z

**zero-based budgeting** A concept of budgeting that requires all levels of management to start from zero and estimate budget data as if there had been no previous activities in their units. (981)

# Subject Index

# Company Index

# Abbreviations and Acronyms Commonly Used in Business and Accounting

| | |
|---|---|
| AAA | American Accounting Association |
| ABC | Activity-based costing |
| AICPA | American Institute of Certified Public Accountants |
| CIA | Certified Internal Auditor |
| CIM | Computer-integrated manufacturing |
| CMA | Certified Management Accountant |
| CPA | Certified Public Accountant |
| Cr. | Credit |
| Dr. | Debit |
| EFT | Electronic funds transfer |
| EPS | Earnings per share |
| FAF | Financial Accounting Foundation |
| FASB | Financial Accounting Standards Board |
| FEI | Financial Executives International |
| FICA tax | Federal Insurance Contributions Act tax |
| FIFO | First-in, first-out |
| FOB | Free on board |
| GAAP | Generally accepted accounting principles |
| GASB | Governmental Accounting Standards Board |
| GNP | Gross National Product |
| IMA | Institute of Management Accountants |
| IRC | Internal Revenue Code |
| IRS | Internal Revenue Service |
| JIT | Just-in-time |
| LIFO | Last-in, first-out |
| Lower of C or M | Lower of cost or market |
| MACRS | Modified Accelerated Cost Recovery System |
| n/30 | Net 30 |
| n/eom | Net, end-of-month |
| P/E Ratio | Price-earnings ratio |
| POS | Point of sale |
| ROI | Return on investment |
| SEC | Securities and Exchange Commission |
| TQC | Total quality control |

# Classification of Accounts

| Account Title | Account Classification | Normal Balance | Financial Statement |
|---|---|---|---|
| Accounts Payable | Current liability | Credit | Balance sheet |
| Accounts Receivable | Current asset | Debit | Balance sheet |
| Accumulated Depletion | Contra fixed asset | Credit | Balance sheet |
| Accumulated Depreciation | Contra fixed asset | Credit | Balance sheet |
| Advertising Expense | Operating expense | Debit | Income statement |
| Allowance for Doubtful Accounts | Contra current asset | Credit | Balance sheet |
| Amortization Expense | Operating expense | Debit | Income statement |
| Bonds Payable | ZLong-term liability | Credit | Balance sheet |
| Building | Fixed asset | Debit | Balance sheet |
| Capital Stock | Stockholders' equity | Credit | Balance sheet |
| Cash | Current asset | Debit | Balance sheet |
| Cash Dividends | Stockholders' equity | Debit | Retained earnings statement |
| Cash Dividends Payable | Current liability | Credit | Balance sheet |
| Common Stock | Stockholders' equity | Credit | Balance sheet |
| Cost of Merchandise (Goods) Sold | Cost of merchandise (goods sold) | Debit | Income statement |
| Deferred Income Tax Payable | Current liability/Long-term liability | Credit | Balance sheet |
| Delivery Expense | Operating expense | Debit | Income Statement |
| Depletion Expense | Operating expense | Debit | Income statement |
| Discount on Bonds Payable | Long-term liability | Debit | Balance sheet |
| Dividend Revenue | Other income | Credit | Income statement |
| Dividends | Stockholders' equity | Debit | Retained earnings statement |
| Employees Federal Income Tax Payable | Current liability | Credit | Balance sheet |
| Equipment | Fixed asset | Debit | Balance sheet |
| Exchange Gain | Other income | Credit | Income statement |
| Exchange Loss | Other expense | Debit | Income statement |
| Factory Overhead (Overapplied) | Deferred credit | Credit | Balance sheet (interim) |
| Factory Overhead (Underapplied) | Deferred debit | Debit | Balance sheet (interim) |
| Federal Income Tax Payable | Current liability | Credit | Balance sheet |
| Federal Unemployment Tax Payable | Current liability | Credit | Balance sheet |
| Finished Goods | Current asset | Debit | Balance sheet |
| Freight In | Cost of merchandise sold | Debit | Income statement |
| Freight Out | Operating expense | Debit | Income statement |
| Gain on Disposal of Fixed Assets | Other income | Credit | Income statement |
| Gain on Redemption of Bonds | Other income | Credit | Income statement |
| Gain on Sale of Investments | Other income | Credit | Income statement |
| Goodwill | Intangible asset | Debit | Balance sheet |
| Income Tax Expense | Income tax | Debit | Income statement |
| Income Tax Payable | Current liability | Credit | Balance sheet |
| Insurance Expense | Operating expense | Debit | Income statement |
| Interest Expense | Other expense | Debit | Income statement |
| Interest Receivable | Current asset | Debit | Balance sheet |
| Interest Revenue | Other income | Credit | Income statement |
| Investment in Bonds | Investment | Debit | Balance sheet |
| Investment in Stocks | Investment | Debit | Balance sheet |
| Investment in Subsidiary | Investment | Debit | Balance sheet |
| Land | Fixed asset | Debit | Balance sheet |
| Loss on Disposal of Fixed Assets | Other expense | Debit | Income statement |
| Loss on Redemption of Bonds | Other expense | Debit | Income statement |